THAI-ENGLISH DICTIONARY

By

George Bradley McFarland, M.D.
(อำมาตย์เอก พระอาจวิทยาคม)

STANFORD UNIVERSITY PRESS
STANFORD, CALIFORNIA
LONDON: GEOFFREY CUMBERLEGE
OXFORD UNIVERSITY PRESS

CONTENTS

Copyright Reserved
สงวนลิขสิทธิ์

FOREWORD TO THE SECOND PRINTING

In 1944 the Stanford University Press issued a photolithic reprint of the McFarland *Thai-English Dictionary*, originally published in Bangkok in 1941. At the time of this first reprinting the Thai language was not a regularly listed course in the curriculum of any college or university in the United States. Its first appearance as such was in 1946 at the University of California, Berkeley, and at present the language is also taught at Cornell, Yale, and Georgetown universities. In spite of the expanding interest in Thai studies during the past decade, no new Thai-English dictionary of the size and scope of McFarland's has made its appearance in the interim. The work remains, then, an indispensable tool for all serious students of Thai. To meet this continuing need the Stanford University Press, now that its supply of the first reprinting is exhausted, has decided to issue a second reprinting. Since the second reprinting, like the first, has been produced by photolithography, the original text stands unchanged.

The excellence of the McFarland *Dictionary* resulted not only from the original contributions made by McFarland and his assistants but also from the fact that they wisely chose to use the official monolingual *Siamese Dictionary*, prepared by the Ministry of Education, as their principal source of reference and thus performed a very valuable service to English-speaking students of Thai by making the essential contents of this monolingual dictionary available with English definitions in place of Thai definitions.

In 1950 a new *Thai-Thai Dictionary*, again prepared by the Ministry of Education, made its appearance. It would be highly desirable if this work could also be made available with English in place of Thai definitions. But until this task is undertaken, we must continue to rely on the McFarland work as the principal Thai dictionary for English-speaking users.

Prospective users of the McFarland *Dictionary* will be well advised to have received some training in reading and writing the Thai language beforehand, since it is unquestionably not a book for the untrained beginner. But experience has shown that even reasonably advanced students need to be forewarned about the following more troublesome features:

1. Each main entry in the *Dictionary* includes a pronunciation aid in phonetic romanization. Deficient though the system is, its greatest weakness lies in its inconsistencies. The following instances are typical: (*a*) The high central unrounded vowel [y] is shown in three ways: *eu, ur,* and *u*. (*b*) The mid central unrounded vowel [ə] is written two ways: *ur* and *er*. (*c*) The digraph *ur* thus represents both [y] and [ə]. (*d*) The letter *u* is indiscriminately used for three different vowels, namely, [y], the high back rounded [u], and the low central unrounded [a].

2. Sometimes synonymous words are combined in a single entry. In this event the pronunciation aid applies only to the first of the synonyms, even though the aid actually follows not the first but the second of the synonyms. Examples:

Page	Column	Entry	Aid for First Word	Aid for Second Word (not given)
699	2	6	ra[6]-hai[2]	gkra[4]-hai[2]
712	1	1	rart[3]	rart[3]-sa[4]-daun

3. Most of the irregularities of the Thai writing system are properly taken care of by McFarland's pronunciation aids. The following exceptions require correction in tones:

Page	Column	Entry	Aid Given	Correction
504	1	2, 3	bpra[4]-yoke[3]	bpra[4]-yoke[4]
504	1	4	bpra[4]-yote[3]	bpra[4]-yote[4]
504	2	7	bpra[4]-wat[6]	bpra[4]-wat[4]

The inconsistencies and corrections discussed above will, it is hoped, help to point up some of the places where emendations in McFarland's work would have been made had a revised edition been feasible at this time. The reader who wishes information about recent works designed as pedagogical aids and recent researches into the phonetics and grammar of Thai is referred to the special section entitled "Addenda to the Bibliography" (see p. xxii).

MARY R. HAAS

University of California, Berkeley
September, 1953

INTRODUCTION

Four years ago the press commenced printing this dictionary. At the suggestion of friends, the first 144 pages were bound and thus made available to students who were interested in helping to make this volume as valuable as possible. As a result of the suggestions of these friends, many improvements were possible in the succeeding sections, many words were added, many definitions were enriched, many errors were eliminated from the manuscript. Also several friends very kindly offered to read proof. Special thanks are due Dr. R. L. Pendleton, Nai Boon Chuey Indrambarya, M. C. Chakrabandhubensiri Chakrabanbha, Mr. K. G. Gairdner, M. R. Chakrthong Thong Yai, and members of my own staff for this service. Owing to the great care taken to secure accuracy, it seems unnecessary to give an errata. That there are some mistakes is a foregone conclusion as 100% accuracy is rarely achieved. A much more serious matter is the absence of words which should be included, and more detailed definitions. For example, many of the descriptions of plants are inadequate giving information of their habitat and uses elsewhere. This was not of choice but of necessity as local uses and other information were not available to the author. Also it was impossible to incorporate all of the words in the Thai language because there is no place where they are all to be found, and gathering them from many sources means that many words were not included. This book does however contain a large number of words not found in the present Government dictionary. The new Government dictionary will doubtless remedy this but not being finished yet was not available for use in compiling this Thai-English Dictionary.

The author will be very happy to receive suggestions, corrections and additions from users of this volume and, if possible, would like to make such corrections and additions available to others.

As this book, which has occupied a central place in my thinking and a major part of my time during the past fifteen years, goes from my hand to other hands, I crave for it your forgiveness for all omissions and deficiencies, and hope that it may prove of service to many, and lead to a better knowledge and use of the Thai language.

June 1st, 1941

George B. McFarland

FOREWORD

The problems that confront one studying a foreign language are varied, perplexing and discouraging. Uppermost of all are those of pronounciation and definition of words. The need for a handy source of help towards meeting these two great necessities is apparent to all. My father was in the country only five years when he realized this great need and, new as he was, published his *English to Siamese Dictionary*. His sense of need and his willingness to work carried him through succeeding editions. The same spirit has led me into the preparation of this volume. To find the source of the idea and my inspiration, I must go back to the spirit that motivated my father, in whose footsteps I gladly tread.

The making of bilingual Siamese dictionaries is a process which has extended over a period exceeding a century. I have in my possession several of these dictionaries laboriously written by hand during the first half of the XIXth. Century. This was before the days of the commercial printing press in Siam. So far as I know, the first which went into print was the *Dictionarium Latinum Thai ad usum missionis Siamensis ex typographia Collegii, Assumptionis B. M. V.*, printed in 1850. As this is in Latin and romanized Siamese, it has had little use outside the circle for which it was prepared. The second was the *Siamese, French, English Dictionary* by Bishop D. J. B. Pallegoix printed in 1854, revised by J. L. Vey and again printed in 1896. This book is a huge tome and one of unquestioned value. The third was *McFarland's English-Siamese Dictionary* by my father, S. G. McFarland, printed in 1865 and now off the press in its tenth edition. Then followed a handy-sized volume, *Siamese-English Dictionary* by E. B. Michell, printed in 1892. The Rev. S. J. Smith, printed his huge five volume *Comprehensive Anglo-Siamese Dictionary* between the years 1899 and 1908. Next came *Essai de Dictionnaire Francais-Siamois* by M. J. Çuaz printed in 1903. This was followed by the *Siamese-English Dictionary* of B. O. Cartwright in 1906. In 1924, Luang Riem Virajbhakaya got out his *Dictionnaire Francais-Siamois*. On 4th July 1925, I purchased the rights to the E. B. Michell *Siamese-English Dictionary*, intending to reprint it as it was. Then I decided to revise it slightly since it was much out-of-date (owing to great and rapid changes in the Siamese language). On this task of revision I launched in 1926 expecting soon to have it ready for publication. Meanwhile two other dictionaries appeared, *viz.*, *The Scholars' Siamese-English Dictionary*, by the Staff of the Amnuey Silapa School in 1932, and *The Up-to-date Dictionary for Students, English-Siamese*, by "S. B." in 1934.

Of these, only the works of Pallegoix, Michell and Cartwright offered any help to the English-speaking student of Siamese and for many years even they were out of print. For this reason I felt a new work of this kind was urgently needed. What started as a reprint, developed into a revision, and finally into this *Siamese-English Dictionary*, for as I worked, my vision grew. When the *Siamese Government Dictionary* came out, I was granted permission by the Ministry of Public Instruction to use this work in any way I wished. I have, therefore, taken it as my major guide. I have also incorporated the Michell Dictionary and I have derived great additional help from Pallegoix and from the *Siamese Vernacular Dictionary* by Dr. Dan Bradley printed in 1874, which is very full of Siamese idioms. The *Dictionary of the Pali Language* by R C. Childars and the *Sanscrit-English Dictionary* by Sir Monier Monier-Williams have been veritable gold mines for me. These six dictionaries have greatly enriched mine, as numerous quotations testify.

Dictionary-making is monotonous though fascinating work. I have found it profitable and wise to do some original research. In no known volume have I been able to find the names of Siamese trees, plants, animals, birds, etc., giving the corresponding Siamese, scientific and common names. Many men and women have added greatly to our knowledge along these lines, but a work which identifies Siamese, scientific and common names is badly wanted. The result of my own research is incorporated in this dictionary and I feel is a valuable part of the work. I have gleaned from many sources but have found the *Journal of the Siam Society* and the *Supplement of the Natural History Society of Siam* especially helpful. An appended bibliography will guide other students to my sources of information, and will also serve as an acknowledgement of my own indebtedness.

Neither the words nor even the meanings of words in a dictionary can be proved by its compiler to belong exclusively to himself. It is not the mere aggregation of words and definitions, but rather the method of dealing with them and their arrangement, which constitutes the best right of any dictionary to be called an original production. I do not claim any superiority over my predecessors but I have endeavoured to compile a dictionary which, in my opinion, will be of the greatest assistance to students of the Siamese language. Obviously this dictionary is designed to meet the needs of two main groups of people, *viz.*, those to whom the Siamese language is their natural means of expression, and those to whom Siamese is a foreign language and English familiar. For the former group this book can do but one thing—it can suggest the English word, equivalent to his familiar Siamese word. For the help of this group, an effort has been made to include as many English words as possible having identical or similar meanings. The multiplicity of definitions does not necessarily elucidate the meaning but does offer the reader an increased English vocabulary. As for the other group, it will be proceeding from the unknown to the known. For this reason, idiomatic phrases have been included. The Siamese language has a simple grammatical construction, a great paucity of word forms, a vivid, picturesque way of forming cumulative nouns from other words which describe the object; it also has a wealth of idiomatic expressions. These unique characteristics make the Siamese language a very easy one to learn—except for the Westerner to whom its very simplicity makes it peculiarly difficult. A work giving the historical development of words and idiomatic expressions would be invaluable. This dictionary makes no attempt beyond the giving of literal translations of certain nouns which have derived their use from these literal meanings and which are therefore very suggestive and illuminating.

I am not unmindful of another difficulty of the average foreigner. Spelling is changing very rapidly these days. One runs across words in old books—not very old either, for the greater part of this change is still in the process of taking place—and unless the obsolete and obsolescent forms are given, the student is at a great loss. In many instances, there are several spellings for the same word and present day usage has not yet spoken with authority as to which is to prevail. I have therefore incorporated a great number of such words in this work. That there are many omissions I am painfully aware. That some of my spelling will be out-of-date by the time my book is through the press is inevitable. No dictionary of a vitally living language can avoid this, for new words and new spellings are coined continually.

I am also cognizant of the need of the foreigner to find some help toward the pronunciation of the Siamese word. The Siamese written language is phonetic with definite rules governing pronunciation. I have included a fairly comprehensive analysis of the construction of the Siamese written language, including rules governing tones. To the foreigner who reads the Siamese character readily and is familiar with the words themselves, such help to correct pronunciation is all that is necessary. But not all of my foreign readers are in this class. Some know the Siamese characters and can read very simple words but are utterly at a loss to apply tone rules or to find the correct pronunciation for words containing difficult vowel combinations. For this second group I want to offer some help.

The matter of romanization of Siamese words is a much and hotly debated one. Several forms are in vogue: none are wholly bad: none are wholly good. As a matter of fact, it is doubtful if any system of romanization will ever find universal acceptation. Perhaps this is well, for the method employed must be suited to the aim of the user. For certain purposes it is advantageous to indicate the derivation of the word. Some linguists tell us this is the *sine qua non* of all romanization; but not all agree that this is the main objective. There are times when a romanization or transliteration based wholly on pronunciation is essential. This is such a time. The average man only cares to learn how to express his thoughts in an understandable fashion. Therefore in this volume I will merely attempt a phonetic romanization which will be a guide to pronunciation. For the man who wishes to study derivations and development of words, I have indicated the immediate source language; the rest of the task is his, not mine. As many Siamese letters have no exact English equivalent, no romanization can be exact; the Siamese letters must themselves be the final criterion for pronunciation. If a person would learn to speak Siamese correctly he must learn to read the Siamese character and must learn the correct pronunciation of that character from one who speaks the language perfectly. It is with great reluctance that I incorporate any form of romanization into this dictionary. Perhaps it is even incorrect to call it a romanization for it is meant merely as an aid to pronunciation and not as a form for reproduction elsewhere than in this book which contains the key to its use. Romanization or transliteration are the customary words to use in this connection because it is a romanized form of the Siamese characters with which we are concerned. But since its purpose is so limited, I trust my scholarly friends will grant me their indulgence and realize I aspire to nothing so ambitious as romanization for general use. I leave that field to those far more competent than myself.

Romanization proper of the Siamese language is peculiarly difficult for several reasons. The major reason is fundamental, for it has its roots in the formation of the language. The Siamese language is by nature closely akin to the Chinese. But Siam is a melting pot. As she received the Thai peoples migrating southward, so she also received the Indian, Mon, Khmer, etc. Each influx of peoples brought a contribution which was accepted and made a part of the Siam of to-day—its blood, its culture, its religion, its language. As yet we know little of the early attempts at writing the Siamese language for the first record is that found on the Sukothai stone which attributes the Siamese alphabet to King Ram Kamheng in A. D. 1283. This was probably the culmination of a long-drawn-out attempt to reduce the spoken language to writing and the attempt was very crude and labored. Chinese could only suggest the elaborate ideograph,—the expression of the scholar and not too suitable to a simple, rural people. The natural alternative offered was the written language of India. Many Indian words had crept into the spoken Siamese language to express the religious and cultural ideas of the conquerors of Cambodia and Siam. These words, though Indian in origin, were pronounced with a strong Siamese brogue, as the Siamese language possessed fewer sounds than the Indian. Therefore when the Siamese accepted an alphabet based on the Indian alphabet, they found they had a number of letters representing identical sounds in their own tongue. These were really super-fluous and would doubtless have been eliminated at once, but for the fact that some of the words were Indian in source and were originally represented by different letters because pronounced differently by the Indian; so the early Siamese felt they too must have a multiplicity of letters. The sticklers for historicity in transliteration are to be found not only in the present generation. Thus it happens that the written Siamese language contains forty-four consonants with only twenty-one separate sounds. A tendency toward elimination of some of these similarly sounded letters has been manifest for some years and will doubtless evolve a simplicity which will greatly modify the Siamese language in the near future. It should also be mentioned that the Siamese found the Indian alphabet inadequate to fully represent their language and did add some original features which had no parallel in the Pali and Sanskrit.

This is not the place to go into any detailed analysis and comparison of the Pali, Sanskrit and Siamese languages, even if I were competent to attempt it, but one fact does have bearing on this matter of romanization of the Siamese language. The Sanskrit language has been very completely classified into gutturals, palatals, cerebrals, dentals and labials, and has been romanized scientifically. As the Siamese alphabet falls very naturally (with certain exceptions) into a similar classification, some scholars advocate taking over the Sanskrit romanization bodily for Siamese letters. This probably is the scientific and scholarly thing to do but I have not used this system for two reasons. First, the Siamese letter and the Sanskrit letter do not necessarily represent the same sound and my sole purpose is to guide to pronunciation. Secondly, to repre-sent the vowel sounds, a large number of special types are required which are not available in Siam. I have therefore blazed a new trail which seems to me better adapted to my needs.

Many criticisms of my system will be offered. With most of them I shall readily agree. My only hope is that those to whom the Siamese language is a foreign one but, who can claim some familiarity with the Siamese printed word, will here find help toward correct pronunciation. Certain it is that he who is best able to criticize my system is not the one requiring such help. It is not designed for him: all he will require is the Siamese character. Romanization (or trans-literation) is at best a very crude crutch.

I have mentioned certain sources of information which have been invaluable to me. To these I must add a long list of names of men and women to whom I am deeply indebted for assistance. H. H. Prince Dhani Nivat has been a sympathetic, helpful friend, to whom I have turned repeatedly for help and never in vain. H. E. Chao Phya Dharmasakti Montri has offered valuable suggestions incorporated in my Introduction. For several years, the late Phra Vibhajna Vidyasidhi devoted his whole time to assisting me in this work which he did not live to see com-pleted. I take this opportunity of honouring his memory and recording my indebtedness to him. I also wish to express my thanks for abundant help to the following,—Phya Jolamark Bhicharna, Director General of the Department of Agriculture and Fisheries; M. C. Laksanakara Kasemsanta, Acting Head of the Plant Industry Division; Luang Choola Cheep Bidyadhara, Officer-in-Charge,

Division of Fisheries; Dr. Hugh McCormick Smith, formerly also of this Ministry; Dr. A. F. G. Kerr, formerly Director of the Botanical Section of the Department of Commerce; Phya Winit Wanandorn, Assistant Director-General of the Royal Forest Department; Phya Vanpruk Picharn, formerly also of this Department; Luang Kira-ti-Vidyolar of the Technical Education Division of the Ministry of Public Instruction; Mr. Herbert G. Deignan, formerly of Prince Royal's College, and Mr. C. J. Aagaard, formerly of the Bangkok Waterworks. Special mention must be made of three members of the Department of Agriculture and Fisheries who are very kindly and most helpfully reading proofs with me, Dr. Robert L. Pendleton, Soil Scientist, Mom Chao Chakrabandhubensiri Chakrabanbhu and Nai Boon Chuay Indrambarya. Several members of my own staff have shared largely in this proof-reading and other phases of the work, especially my typist Nang Suvari, Nang Sao Wat Prasongsook and Nai Kim Heng Katesamanee. To The Bangkok Times Press Ltd., I owe more than a little thanks for patience and cooperation in what I am certain is the most difficult of their printing enterprises. It is a very great joy to me and benefit to my dictionary that my sister has come to join in the work as the manuscript passes through its final revision before it goes to the press. Many others have helped in one way or another, but the one who has been my constant inspiration and help is my wife, and to her I owe most for her encouragement, never failing help, sincere devotion and determination to see this task accomplished.

GEORGE BRADLEY McFARLAND

Holyrood, Bangkok
December, 1937

PREFACE TO THE AMERICAN EDITION

The first edition of the McFarland *Thai-English Dictionary* came from the press in Bangkok just five months before Pearl Harbor. A few copies reached the United States before communication ceased. Since then it has been impossible to secure additional copies for use outside of Thailand.

A very real need for this dictionary has been felt by those who have engaged in work involving the Thai language. All available volumes were pressed into service, but the demand could not thus be met. To supply this specific need the present edition has been printed. It is actually a photolithographic reprint of the first edition, with no attempt to carry out what was my late husband's plan for an addenda giving words omitted from the first edition. That must wait until the end of the war makes it possible to have access to Thai printing presses again.

The page-size of this edition is reduced somewhat, making a handier volume than the original. Otherwise there is no change.

BERTHA BLOUNT McFARLAND

San Francisco, California
August, 1944

INTRODUCTION

I. CONSONANTS

1. Consonant Forms.

There are 44 consonants in the Siamese language. These consonants represent, however, only 21 separate sounds. These consonants never vary in pronunciation except when placed at the end of a word. The following is a complete list and gives the romanization followed in this dictionary.

Consonants

		Initial	*Final*			*Initial*	*Final*			*Initial*	*Final*
ก	ไก่	gk	k	ฐ	ฐาน	t	t	ฟ	ไฟ	f	–
ข	ไข่	k	k	ฑ	มณโฑ	t	t	ภ	ภรรยา	p	p
ฃ	ขวด	k	–	ฒ	ผู้เฒ่า	t	t	ม	ม้า	m	m
ค	คิด	k	k	ณ	คุณ	n	n	ย	ยล	y	y
ฅ	คน	k	–	ด	เด็ก	d	t	ร	รักษา	r	n
ฆ	ระฆัง	k	–	ต	เต่า	dt	t	ล	วิลาส	l	n
ง	งู	ng	ng	ถ	ถวิล	t	t	ว	แหวน	w	o
จ	จาน	chj	t	ท	ท่าน	t	t	ศ	คอ	s	t
ฉ	ฉิ่ง	ch	–	ธ	เธอ	t	t	ษ	บอ	s	t
ช	ช่อ	ch	t	น	นิล	n	n	ส	ลอ	s	t
ซ	โซ่	s	t	บ	ใบไม้	b	p	ห	หีบ	h	–
ฌ	กะเฌอ	ch	t	ป	ปลา	bp	p	ฬ	บาฬี	l	n
ญ	หญิง, ใหญ่	y	n	ผ	ผึ้ง	p	–	อ	อ่าง	Mute——employed to support a vowel sound, as in เอา
ฎ	ชฎา	d	t	ฝ	ฝา	f	–				
ฏ	ปฏัก	dt	t	พ	พิมพ์	p	p	ฮ	นกฮูก	h	–

อ   is sometimes a consonant: at other times อ is a vowel.

ย   final does not exist as a consonant but as part of a combined vowel. Thus, ด้วย would be "doie."

ห   placed before another consonant is usually not pronounced but indicates the tone of the syllable. Thus, ใหม่ would be simply "mai." An exception to this rule is the word แหน. If the ห is not pronounced, the word means "duckweed": in the combination หวง แหน the ห is sounded; this work means "stingy."

Four words have อ in front, instead of ห, *viz.* อยู่, อยาก, อย่า, อย่าง. Otherwise they are quite regular.

Often a consonant placed in the middle of a polysyllabic word becomes the final letter of the syllable which precedes it, but is also the initial consonant of the following syllable which has its vowel understood though not written. This unwritten vowel is always short. Thus ราษฎร would be "rat-sa-dawn." This peculiarity of the Siamese language creates great difficulty for the foreigner.

A final consonant is always pronounced indistinctly as if the sound were being swallowed.

2. Double Consonants.

a. The Siamese language contains a certain number of double consonants, both of which are pronounced, *viz.*

กร	=	gkr		ตร	=	dtr
ขร	=	kr		ปร	=	bpr
คร	=	kr		พร	=	pr
กล	=	gkl		พล	=	pl
ขล	=	kl		กว	=	gkw
คล	=	kl		ขว	=	kw
ปล	=	bpl		คว	=	kw

b. Those double consonants which are represented by one consonant sound are

ทร   =   s

สร   =   s   When found as a monosyllabic word, สระ means "pond" or "to shampoo". When สระ is pronounced as a bisyllabic, it means "vowel".

จร }
สร }   ร is not sounded but the double consonant carries the
ศร }   sound of the initial one, *e. g.* จริง, สร้าง, ศรี, อธยา ศรัย. จรด and สรูป, are exceptions to this rule.

ตร   is sometimes erroneously placed in this group but when occurring at the beginning of a word, ตร is always pronounced with both sounds. (See above)

II. VOWELS

The Siamese vowels are very complicated. For the purpose of applying tone rules they fall into two groups, *viz.* long vowels and short vowels. But this simple classification is inadequate. They must also be grouped into three classes, *viz.* simple, combined and inherent.

1. Simple vowels are those represented by primary vowel forms which may be used with the various consonants. They are :—

ะ ◌ ̆ า ◌ ̀ ◌ ̂ ◌ ̃ ◌ ̌   ◌ ̦ ◌ ̩ โ ใ ไ ำ อ ว

(อ is sometimes a consonant.   ว is a vowel only when placed between two consonants.)

2. Combined vowels are those made up of the simple vowel forms in combination with certain consonants and with each other.
They are —

    a. *Compound vowels and Diphthongs.*

        เ—า (เอา), เ—ิ ̂ (เมิน), เ—ะ (เตะ), แ—ะ (แฉะ), แ— (แก),
        โ—ะ (โปะ), เ—าะ (เกาะ).
        Very rare forms เ—อย (เกอย), —ิ ̂ ย (ลิ ̂ย), เ—ยะ (เขยะ).

    b. *Combinations with อ.*

        เ—อ (เจอ), เ—อะ (เถอะ), เ—ือ (เรือ), เ—ือะ (เคือะ).

    c. *Combinations with ย.*

        เ—ย (เกย), เ—ีย (เสีย), เ—ียะ (เดียะ), —าย (นาย),
        —ุย (ขุย), —ูย (กูย), —ัย (ขัย), โ—ย (โรย).

    d. *Combinations with ว.*

        —ัว (กัว), —ัวะ (ผัวะ), —าว (ยาว), —ิว (สิว),
        —ูว (มูว), เ—ว (เลว), แ—ว (แมว).

    e. *Combinations with อ. ย. ว.*

        —อย (ลอย), —วย (มวย), เ—ียว (เขียว),
        เ—ือย (เนือย).

    f. *Compound vowels and consonants.*

        ฤ ฤๅ ฦ ฦๅ

3. Inherent vowels are those which are not written but are understood in certain consonant combinations. Thus, ฝน has a short "o" understood between the two consonants.

TABULATION OF VOWELS
For application of tone rules and romanization.

Short	romanization	illustration	Long	romanization	illustration
◌ะ, ◌ั	a or u (but)	สระ	า	a or ah	กา
			◌ี	e (he)	กี
◌ิ	i in (hit)	กิ	◌ื	u or ur (very inexact)	กื
◌ึ	u or ur (very inexact)	กึ	◌ู	oo (root)	กู
◌ุ	oo (root)	กุ	เ◌	a	เก
เ◌ะ	a	เกะ	แ◌	a or aa (rat)	แก
แ◌ะ	a or aa (rat)	แกะ	โ◌	o (go)	โก
โ◌ะ	o (go)	โกะ	◌อ	au or aw (haw)	กอ
เ◌าะ, ก็	au or aw	เกาะ	◌ัว	oo-ah	กัว
◌ัวะ	oo-ah	กัวะ	เ◌ีย	e-ah	เกีย
เ◌ียะ	e-ah	เกียะ	เ◌ือ	ur-ah	เกือ
เ◌ือะ	ur-ah	เกือะ	เ◌อ	ur or er	เกอ
เ◌อะ	ur or er	เกอะ	เ◌ิ	ur or er	เกิน
◌ัว	ue (hue)	กัว	ไ◌	ai	ไก
◌ุย	oo-ie	กุย	ใ◌	ai	ใส
เ◌า	a-oh or ay-oh	เกา	เ◌า	ow	เกา
◌ัย	ai	ลัย, กัย	◌ำ	am or um	กำ
◌ัม	um	ขัม, หัม	◌าย	ai	กาย, นาย
			◌อ	ur	กอ, มอ
			แ◌ว	aa-oh	แกว, แมว
			โ◌ย	oh-ie	โกย, โรย
			◌อย	au-ie, or aw-ie	กอย, ลอย
			◌วย	oo-ie	กวย, รวย
			เ◌ียว	ee-oh	เรียว, เกียว
			เ◌ือย	eu-ie	เกือย, เนือย
			เ◌ย	ur-ie	เกย, เอย
			◌าว	ow or auw	กาว, ยาว
			เ◌อก	eu-uk	เกอก, เลือก
			เ◌ียง	e-ung	เมียง, เสียง
			เ◌ียก	e-uk	เรียก, เบียก
			เ◌อย	ur-ie	เกอย, เขอย

III. TONES

The Siamese language is tonal with six primary tones. These have been given various names. I follow the terminalogy in the McFarland Handbook given by its author, William McFarland, except in the case of the sixth tone which I name. I place in parenthesis some other names in common use.

1. Common tone (Middle).
2. Question tone (Rising or Ascending).
3. Period tone (Falling or Dropped).
4. Depressed tone (Deep or Low).
5. Circumflex or Emphatic tone (Acute).
6. High Staccato tone (Short Slightly Emphatic).

Many attempts to express these tones by graphs have been made. No two are alike for the simple reason that no two people hear them exactly alike. Also no two voices are absolutely the same, and, while there is a similarity in trends of the lines, there is a great difference in the relative position of the lines representing tones.

So far as I know, the only attempt to record the Siamese tones mechanically was made by the Rev. Cornelius B. Bradley, Ph. D. of California University, Berkeley, California. As Dr. Bradley was born and raised in Siam, his pronunciation was as truly Siamese as that of one born a Siamese. I give the representation as he recorded it in the *University of California Publications in American Archeaeology and Ethnology, Vol. 12, No. 5, pp. 195–218, plates 1–5,* on October 11, 1916. The sixth tone does not appear on Dr. Bradley's graph but would normally be placed practically identical with the Circumflex tone but would be shorter since it only occurs where a short vowel is used.

Since Siamese is a tonal language and since no accurate pronunciation is possible which ignores this tonal element, I find it necessary to guide my foreign friends to the use of correct tones. There follows a list of tone rules and a tabulation of these rules for guidance of those familiar with the Siamese printed page. For those who must resort also to romanization, I use small numeral exponents after each syllable to indicate the tone. If no numeral is indicated, the tone is the Common tone; Question tone is [2]; Period tone is [3]; Depressed tone is [4]; Circumflex tone is [5]; High Staccato tone is [6]. Where two syllables are needed to represent one Siamese syllable, the accent is indicated after the second though it may really govern the first, *ex.* เกียว =gkee-oh[3].

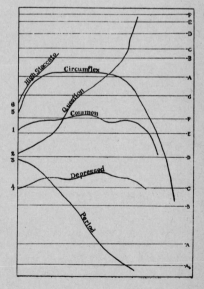

RULES FOR TONES

All tones in the Siamese language are governed by a few rules.

Each consonant of the alphabet falls into one of the three following classes, *viz.* High, Middle or Low.

High Class

ข ข ฉ ถ ฐ ผ ฝ ส ศ ษ ห

Middle Class

ก จ ฎ ด ฏ ต บ ป อ

Low Class

ค ต ฆ ง ช ฌ ซ ญ ย ท ธ ฑ ฒ น
ณ พ ฟ ภ ม ร ล ว ฬ ฮ

There are five tone marks, *viz.* ไม้เอก (') Mai-ek, ไม้โท (") Mai-to, ไม้ตรี (‴) Mai-tre or เลขเจ็ด Lekchet, ไม้จัตวา (+) Mai-chatawa or กากะบาด Kakabhat, and ไม้ ไต่คู้ (◌ั) Mai-taikoo or เลขแปด Lekbaat.

When pronouncing a word observe,

1. The class of the initial consonant.

2. The tone mark, if any.

3. Whether the word ends in the sound of k, p, or t.

4. Whether the vowel is long or short.

1. Rules governing the Common Tone.

(1) A syllable beginning with a Middle or Low Class consonant and ending in a long vowel requires the Common tone.

(2) A syllable beginning with a Middle or Low Class consonant, and ending in any consonant sound other than k, p, or t, requires the Common tone.

2. **Rules governing the Question Tone** (indicated by exponent figure "4").

(1) A syllable beginning with a High Class consonant, and ending in a long vowel, requires the Question tone.

(2) A syllable beginning with a High Class consonant, and ending in any consonant sound other than k, p, or t, requires the Question tone.

(3) A syllable beginning with a Middle Class consonant, and having a "+" (Mai-chatawa), requires the Question tone.

3. **Rules governing the Period Tone** (indicated be exponent figure "3").

(1) A syllable beginning with a Low Class consonant, and having a long vowel, and ending in the sound k, p, or t, requires the Period tone.

(2) A syllable beginning with a Low Class consonant, and having a "ı" (Mai-ek), requires a Period tone.

(3) A syllable beginning with a High or Middle Class consonant, and having the "ฯ" (Mai-to), requires the Period tone.

4. **Rules governing the Depressed Tone** (indicated by exponent figure "4")

(1) A syllable beginning with a High or Middle Class consonant, and ending in a short vowel, requires the Depressed tone.

(2) A syllable beginning with a High or Middle Class consonant, and having a short vowel, and ending in the sound k, p, or t, requires the Depressed tone.

(3) A syllable beginning with a High or Middle Class consonant, and having a long vowel, and ending in the sound k, p, or t, requires the Depressed tone.

(4) A syllable beginning with a High or Middle Class consonant, and having a "ı" (Mai-ek), requires the Depressed tone.

5. **Rule governing the Circumflex Tone** (indicated by exponent figure "5").

(1) A syllable beginning with a Low Class consonant, and having a "ฯ" (Mai-to), requires the Circumflex tone.

6. **Rules governing the High Staccato Tone** (indicated by exponent figure "6").

(1) A syllable beginning with a Low Class consonant, and ending in a short vowel, requires the High Staccato tone.

(2) A syllable beginning with a Low Class consonant, and having a short vowel, and ending in the sound k, p, or t, requires the High Staccato tone.

(3) A syllable beginning with a Middle Class consonant, and having the "ฅ" (Mai-tre),re quires the High Staccato tone. (The "ฅ" (Mai-tre) shortens the vowel, if long).

TABULATION OF TONE RULES

I. If no tone mark is used, syllables beginning with High Class Consonants and ending in long vowels require the Question tone.

II. If no tone mark is used, syllables beginning with Middle and Low Class Consonants and ending in long vowels require the Common tone. There are exceptions. See Rules XIII & XIV.

Tones to be used.

		High Class	Middle Class	Low Class
III.	Syllable ending in a Long Vowel	Question (2)	Common (1)	Common (1)
IV.	Syllable ending in any consonant sound other than k, p or t.	ขา, ถาม, ขิง	แก, ตาม กิน	ยา, งาม, ลิง
V.	Syllable ending in a Short Vowel	Depressed (4)	Depressed (4)	High Staccato (6)
VI.	Syllable having a Short Vowel and ending in k, p, or t.	ฉะ, ผัด	แตะ, จิบ	นะ, รัก
VII.	Syllable having a Long Vowel and ending in k, p, or t.	Depressed (4)	Depressed (4)	Period (3)
VIII.	Syllable with Mai-ek (`).	ถาก, ผ่า ข่ม	บาป, ด่า, บ่อน	ทาส, น่า, ร่ม
IX.	Syllable with Mai-to (้).	Period (3) ถ้า, ห้าง	Period (3) บ้า, กุ้น, จ้ะ	Circumflex (5) แท้, แม้น
X.	Syllable with Mai-chatawa (๊).	—	Question (2) ตั๋ว, จ๋า	—
XI.	Syllable with Mai-tre (๋).	—	High Staccato (6) บ๊ะ	—

XII. Syllable with Mai-taikoo (็). The syllable is shortened but the tone is unchanged.

XIII. When ห is placed before a Low Class Consonant, that syllable is governed by the rules for High Class Consonants.

XIV. When อ is placed before ย, it causes the syllable to be governed by the rules for Middle Class Consonants.

XV. Silent final consonants are indicated by the sign ทัณฑะฆาฏ (์) Tantakart.

IV. NUMBERICAL DESIGNATORY PARTICLES.

One peculiarity of the Siamese language is that there is no declension of nouns or abjectives. This being so, it is essential that some other way must be offered for indicating number. The Numerical Designatory Particle supplies this need. The noun is followed by a designatory particle and that in turn, by a number, e. g. one man = ผู้ชายคนหนึ่ง; two men= ผู้ชายสองคน; many men = ผู้ชายหลายคน. These designatory particles vary with the type of article indicated. A fairly complete list follows.

กระบอก	for	guns; cannon; cylinders; hypodermic needles; tubes; electric flash-lights.
กะบุง	„	fragments of piece goods.
กัณฑ์	„	sermons; discourses on religious subjects.
กลัก	„	pill boxes; ointment or match boxes.
กลุ่ม	„	balls of twine; spools of thread or cotton.
กอ	„	clumps of trees, grasses or shrubbery.
กอง	„	piles or heaps of stone; bricks; bodies of men or infantry.
ก้อน	„	lumps of sugar; stones; rocks; boulders; minerals in the crude state.
กิ่ง	„	branches of trees; electric-light brackets; sub-divisions of an organization; the tusks of elephants.
กุลี	„	bales of cloth goods or paper, hanks or skeins of yarn bound or strapped for transit.
เกล็ด	„	scales of fish; flakes of camphor gum; substances in crystal form.
ขด	„	rolls of wire, rattan or rope.
ขนัด	„	plots of garden land.
ขนาน	„	portions of prescribed medicines or bottles of drugs.
ขอน	„	logs (in the rough); objects which are not matched.
เข็ด	„	skeins of yarn, twine, string or silk.
โขลง	„	elephants (in a herd), either wild or a group of elephants used in logging.
คน	„	a single person; a child; persons (collectively).
คัน	„	umbrellas; carriages; motor-cars; motor-cycles; rickshas; waggons; bicycles; spoons.
คัมภีร์	„	the Bible; volumes of religious literature or magical treatises.
คำ	„	words (written or spoken); mouthfuls of food.
คู่	„	pairs of articles or animals (as earrings, shoes, gloves, horses, oxen).
แผนก	„	departments; sections or divisions of an organization or university.

งาน	for	celebrations; functions; festivities (as birthday parties, housewarmings, cremations, weddings).
จุก	,,	topknots; bulbs of onions, garlic, beet-root and turnips.
ฉบับ	,,	manuscripts; documents; letters.
ฉาก	,,	acts of plays; dramas; tableaux (where a curtain is used).
ชิ้น	,,	slices of meat; fragments of flat thin articles (as cloth, leather, hides).
ช่อ	,,	bunches of flowers; clusters of grapes or fruit.
เชือก	,,	an elephant.
ชุด	,,	dishes; games; plays (in sets).
ซอง	,,	envelopes; telescoping cigar holders; cone-shaped holders for ceri-leaves.
ซี่	,,	teeth; ribs; pailings or rungs of a balastrade.
ดวง	,,	stars; sun; lamps; individual lights; seals; postage stamps.
ดอก	,,	flowers; joss-sticks; fire-crackers; spots of eruptions on the skin (as measles).
ด้าม	,,	pens; pen-holders; fountain pens.
ดุ้น	,,	faggots; pieces or sticks of fire-wood.
ต้น	,,	trees; plants; posts; columns; pillars.
ตับ	,,	sections or divisions of infantry; strips of nipa palm fans sewed together.
ตลับ	,,	covered boxes for salve, ointment, face-powder or toilet-powder.
ตัว	,,	animals; insects; fishes; tables; chairs.
เถา	,,	vines; dishes; cups; trays (in sets of graded sizes).
ท่อน	,,	fragments; bits; pieces of cloth; odd ends of boards or posts.
นัด	,,	shots or discharges from a gun or cannon; charges of gun-powder or explosives.
แท่ง	,,	pencils; ingots of tin or lead; pieces or fragments of iron.
นาย	,,	civilians (used in preference to คน when it is desired to show more honour).
บท	,,	songs; hymns; tunes; chapters.
บาน	,,	windows; doors; mirrors; screens; hinges; panels.
ใบ	,,	buckets; oil-tins; tin-cans or any round hollow object.
ปาก	,,	fishing nets; witnesses giving a testimony; anyone giving a verbal account; cradles.
บั้น	,,	saws; hand-saws; circular-saws; belt-saws; gig-saws.
ผล	,,	fruits (as oranges or mangoes).

ผืน	for	sheets; strips of cloth; blankets; rugs; carpets.
ผูก	"	palm-leaf books; index cards strung together.
แผ่น	"	sheets of paper; bricks; tiles for roofing or paving; slabs of stone.
ฝัก	"	pods of fruit or lotus; fish-roe.
ฝา	"	lids; partitions; shells of oysters; mollusks or bivalves.
ฝูง	"	flocks; herds; droves; schools of fishes.
พวง	"	garlands; wreaths; strings of beads; pearls or diamonds.
พับ	"	bolts of cloth; silks, paper or cotton goods.
ม้วน	"	wrapping paper or toilet paper (if rolled); paper rolls for adding machines.
มวน	"	cigars; cigarettes; rolled ceri-leaves.
มัด	"	bundles of sticks; branches of trees; fire-wood; sheaves of rice stalks or corn stalks.
เม็ด	"	fruit pits; pills; gems.
ยก	"	printer's forms.
ราง	"	an abacus board; grooving planes; grooves in carpentering.
รูป	"	Buddhist monks.
เรือน	"	clocks; watches.
โรง	"	sheds; shanties; a theatrical troop.
ลูก	"	children; fruit; marbles; young of animals; birds or fowls (in compounds, as ลูกปืน, ลูกโดด, ลูกศร, ลูกธนู).
ลำ	"	stalks of standing or cut sugar cane; bamboo; boats.
เล่ม	"	spoons; knives; forks; candles; books; incense sticks (compare with คัน).
วง	"	rings; bands; a circle of players (as at cards or performers of an orchestra).
สาย	"	roads; rope; string or wire strung in the air (as a radio aerial or festoons of flags); bracelets; necklaces; belts; kite strings.
สำรับ	"	sets of dishes; suits of clothing.
เส้น	"	hairs of the head; strings; ropes; lines drawn in ink or underlinings.
หลัง	"	houses; mosquito-nets; rafts or logs or bamboo.
หวี	"	a bunch of bananas.
ห่อ	"	bundles; parcels; medicines (folded in paper).
ห่า	"	a shower of rain or hail.
องค์	"	holy personages; kings; princes or princesses; statues of the Buddha.
อัน	"	small objects; fragments; pieces of iron; things (in general).

V. WORD ARRANGEMENT.

1. The primary basis for word arrangement in this dictionary is the Siamese consonant, *viz* :—

ก ข ฃ ค ฅ ฆ ง จ ฉ ช ซ ฌ ญ ฎ ฏ ฐ ฑ ฒ ณ ด ต ถ ท ธ
น บ ป ผ ฝ พ ฟ ภ ม ย ร ล ว ศ ษ ส ห ฬ อ ฮ.

    a. Words which have double consonants in the first syllable take their place as if the first of these consonants were the only one. Thus, ทราย is placed under ท, เหมา is placed under ห.

    b. ฤ ฤๅ follow ร; ฦ ฦๅ follow ล.

2. The secondary basis for word arrangement lies with the vowels. I follow the Government Dictionary which offers a quite different arrangement from that of the มูลบทบรรพกิจ. Briefly, arrangement is as follows :—

     ะ ั า ี ึ ื ุ ู เ แ โ ใ ไ

with อ ว ย classified with the consonants. Owing to the large number of combined vowel forms the above arrangement is a simple key to the complete list and easy to remember. The complete list is as follows :—

ะ	ี	เ◌ะ (เกอะ)
—ั (กัน)	—ุย (กุย)	เ◌อก (เกือก)
—ัว (กัว)		เ◌ย (เกย)
—ัม (กัม)	ู	เ◌อย (เกอย)
—ัวะ (ผัวะ)	เ	แ
า	เ◌ะ (เกะ)	แ◌ะ (แพะ)
าว (ขาว)	เ◌า (เขา)	แ◌ว (แมว)
าย (นาย)	เ◌าะ (เจาะ)	โ
—ำ (กำ)	เ◌ิ (เกิน)	โ◌ะ (โปะ)
◌ิ	เ◌ี (เสีย)	โ◌ย (โอย)
◌ิว (กิว)	เ◌ียะ (เผียะ)	ใ
◌ี	เ◌ียก (เรียก)	ไ
◌ึ	เ◌ียง (เมียง)	วย (กวย)
◌ื	เ◌ียว (เสียว)	อย (กอย)
	เ◌ือ (เสือ)	

When no vowel is written but is inherent in the consonant arrangement, such a word precedes the words containing ะ. Thus, ขลา precedes ขะม่ำ; กน precedes กา.

3. **A tertiary basis** for word arrangement is found in the tone marks. Except in those cases where words with identical spellings occur, these tone marks are not considered in word arrangement.

Arrangement then follows the following order of tone marks :— (ˋ) ไม้เอก, (ˊ) ไม้โท, (˝) ไม้ตรี, (⁺) ไม้จัตวา, (˚) ไม้ไต่คู้.

4. **Special words.** There are certain classes of words which require special mention and a statement of the order followed.

    a. A large number of words begin with กะ or กระ. In some cases these two forms are used interchangeably and it is impossible to state which has the preference because both forms have the sanction of wide usage. In such case, the word will usually be found under กระ with the alternate spelling indicated.

    Words spelled only with กระ and never with กะ, of course, are to be found under กระ.

    b. Some of the words beginning with กะ are never spelled with กระ and will therefore be found where they belong under กะ.

    c. Also under กระ are those words which in their original form were spelled กุ. Thus, กุฏิ is found under กระฏิ and กุฏุมพี under กระฏุมพี. Also, words in which the original contained ข or ส. Thus, ขจาย is found under กระจาย and สะเทือน under กระเทือน.

    d. Those words in which กระ has been changed into กรร will be found under the form กรร. Thus, กระโชค is found under กรรโชค and กระชิง under กรรชิง.

    e. Other groups of words, in which the consonant ต or ป is followed by ะ, with or without ร, will be found under ตะ or ปะ, except only those words which are written only in the form ตระ or ประ.

    f. There is a group of words in which the initial consonant is repeated in combination with ะ as a prefix. Thus, มี่ becomes มะมี่; ริก becomes ระริก; ครืน becomes คะครืน or คระครืน; แย้ม becomes ยะแย้ม; วาบ becomes วะวาบ. Such words will be found under their simple forms.

    g. There are certain words in common use and sanctioned by usage, which are obviously erroneously spelled. Both forms are therefore to be found in their respective places. Thus, กระบถ should be กบฏ.

Note : Owing to these peculiarities of the Siamese written language and owing to the fact that several forms of the same word are in accepted use, it is impossible to know surely where to find such words. The user of this dictionary will therefore be obliged to look for such words where he thinks they should be. Then, if they are not to be found there, the above suggestions will indicate other places to search

VI. TYPOGRAPHICAL SIGNS

The following are the Siamese typographical signs. Many English signs are also in common use today.

ๆ   indicates preceding syllable or word is to be repeated.

ฯ   sign of abbreviation equivalent to *etc.* It is always used after the name of Bangkok.

ฯลฯ   equivalent to *etc.*

๏   indicates the beginning of a paragraph (obsolete).

ฯะ   indicates the end of a paragraph.

ฯ๛   equivalent to *finis* and used at the end of a book or chapter.

VII. ABBREVIATIONS

adj.	adjective.	*gram.*	grammatical.	*Port.*	Portuguese.
adv.	adverb.	*Hok.*	Hokkian.	pp.	pages.
ancient.	ancient form.	*i. e.*	that is.	*prep.*	preposition.
Anna.	Annamite.	*imper.*	imperative.	*pro.*	pronoun.
arch.	archaic.	*interj.*	interjection.	*prov.*	proverb.
Cam.	Cambodian.	*Jav.*	Javanese.	*provin.*	provincialism.
Chin.	Chinese.	*Laos.*	Laos.	*S.*	Sanscrit.
colloq.	colloquial.	*lit.*	literal meaning in the original language.	*sim.*	simile.
conj.	conjunction.			*slang*	slang.
e. g.	for illustration.	*n.*	noun.	*south.*	southern.
Eng.	English.	*obs.*	obsolete or obsolescent.	*sp.*	species.
ex.	example.	*onomat.*	onomatopoeia.	*syn.*	synonym or synonymous with.
exclam.	exclamation.	*P.*	Pali.		
figur.	figurative	*p.*	page.	*Teh.*	Teh Chiew.
f. or *ff.*	and following.	*Peg.*	Peguan.	*v.*	verb.
Fr.	French.	*poet.*	poetical.	*viz.*	namely.

Deig.	Herbert G. Deignan, sometime Teacher, Prince Royal's College, Chiengmai.
Gaird.	K. G. Gairdner, sometime Assistant Royal Survey Department.
Her.	E. G. Herbert, Assistant, Bombay Burmah Trading Corp. Ltd.
K.	A. F. G. Kerr, M. D., sometime Director of Botanical Section, Ministry of Commerce.
H. M. S.	Dr. Hugh McCormick Smith, sometime Adviser of Fisheries, Department of Agriculture and Fisheries.
M. S.	Malcolm Smith, M. D., Physician.
will.	Sir W. J. F. Williamson, Financial Adviser, Ministry of Finance.

VIII. BIBLIOGRAPHY

SYMBOLS

Aag. C. J. Aagaard: *The Common Birds of Bangkok.* Copenhagen, 1930.

Ala. Henry Alabaster: *The Wheel of the Law.* London, 1871.

A. S. S. S. Amnuay Silapa School Staff in collaboration with C. Dansuputra: *The Scholars' Siamese-English Dictionary.* Bangkok, 1st. ed. 1932; 2nd. ed. 1933.

Assumption Assumption College: *Dictionarium Latinum Thai ad usum missionis Siamensis.* Bangkok, 1850.

Antiq. of Ind. Lionel D. Barnett, M. A., Litt. D.: *Antiquities of India.* London, 1913.

C. B. B. Cornelius B. Bradley, Ph. D.: *On Plotting the Inflections of the Voice, in University of California Publications in American Archeology and Ethnology.* Vol. XII, NO. 5, pp. 195-218, plates 1-5. Berkeley, 1916.

D. B. B. Dan Beach Bradley, M. D.: *Siamese Vernacular Dictionary.* Bangkok, 1873.

Dan Beach Bradley, M. D.: *Bangkok Calendar 1859-1873.* Bangkok.

Burk. I. H. Burkill, M. A., F. G. S.: *A Dictionary of the Economic Products of the Malay Peninsula*, 2 Vols. London, 1933.

Car. (1) B. O. Cartwright, B. A.: *The Student's Manual of the Siamese Language.* Bangkok, 1915.

Car. (2) B. O. Cartwright, B. A.: *Siamese-English Dictionary.* Bangkok, 1907.

Chan. H. R. H. Prince Chantaburi: *Index to the Latin Names in " List of Common Trees, Shrubs, etc., in Siam" compiled by Phya Vanpruk Picharn, 1923.* Bangkok, 1928.

chd. Robert Caesar Childers: *A Dictionary of the Pali Language.* London, 1875.

Com. Dir. Commercial Directory, 3rd. ed. 1929.

A. C. Ananda Coomaraswamy, D. Sc.: *Buddha and The Gospel of Buddhism.* Bombay, 1928.

cb. W. G. Craib, M. A., E. L. S., F. B. S. E.: *Florae Siamensis Enumeratio*, Vol. I, Pt. 1-4. Bangkok, 1928, 1931.

H. B. S. Crowell's Handy Information Series: *Handy Book of Synonyms.* New York, 1907.

M. J. C. M. J. Cuaz: *Essai de Dictionnaire Français-Siamois.* Bangkok, 1903.

Damrong H. R. H. Prince Damrong Rajanubhab: *Siamese Musical Instruments.* Bangkok, 1931.

H. R. H. Prince Damrong Rajanubhab: *Thai History prior to the founding of Ayuthia.*

Dept. Agri. &
Fisheries Department of Agriculture and Fisheries: *Herbarium.*

Doeh. I. Charles Doehring: *Art and Art-Industry in Siam, Text* Vol. I. Bangkok, 1925.

Doeh. II. Charles Doehring: *Art and Art-Industry in Siam, Plate* Vol. II. Bangkok, 1925.

Med. Dict. W. A. Newman Dorland, A. M., M. D., F. A. C. S.: *American Illustrated Medical Dictionary*, 9th ed. Philadelphia & London, 1918.

H. C. D. John Dowson, M. R. A. S.: *Hindu Classical Dictionary of Hindu Mythology and Religion, Geography, History, and Literature.* London, 1928.

P. A. E. Rev. P. A. Eakin: *Manual for the Study of the Siamese Language.* Bangkok, 1926.

F. P. C. O. Frankfurter, P. Petithuguenin and J. Crosby: *Proposed System for the Transliteration of Siamese Words into Roman Characters.* Bangkok, 1928.

Frank.	O. Frankfurter, Ph. D.: *Elements of Siamese Grammar.* Leipzig, 1900.
web.	Funk and Wagnalls Co.: *A Standard Dictionary of the English Language.* New York & London, 1898.
Ger. (1)	G. E. Gerini: *Chulakantamangala or The Tonsure Ceremony as Performed in Siam.* Bangkok, 1895.
Ger. (2)	G. E. Gerini: *A Retrospective View and Account of the Origin of the Thet Maha Chat Ceremony.* Bangkok, 1892.
Pub. Instr.	Government Siamese Dictionary: *Prathanukrom.* Bangkok, B. E. 2470. *The Illustrated London News.* London.
N. H. J. S. S.	*Journal of the Natural History Society of Siam.* vols. I-XII. Bangkok, 1914-1939.
McM.	H. F. Macmillan, F. L. S.: *Tropical Gardening and Planting with special reference to Ceylon.* Colombo, 1925.
E. O. M.	E. Osborn Martin: *The Gods of India.* London, 1914.
S. G. M.	S. G. and G. B. McFarland: *McFarland's English-Siamese Dictionary.* Bangkok, 1st. ed. 1865, 10th. ed. 1937.
W. H. M.	W. H., E. H. and G. B. McFarland: *An English-Siamese Pronouncing Handbook.* Bangkok, 3rd. ed. 1929.
Michell	E. B. Michell: *Siamese-English Dictionary.* Bangkok, 1892.
Com. Rec.	Ministry of Agriculture and Commerce: *The Record, Journal of the Board of Commercial Department.* Bangkok, quarterly.
Palle.	D. J. B. Pallegoix: *Siamese, French, English Dictionary.* Bangkok, 1st, ed. 1854; Revised by J. L. Vey, 1896.
Cam. Glory	H. W. Ponder, F. R. G. S., F. R. S. A.: *Cambodian Glory.* London, 1936.
I. B. C.	John Murray, Publisher: *A Handbook for Travellers in India, Burma and Ceylon.* 11th ed. London, 1924.
Riem.	Luang Riem Virajbhakaya: *Dictionnaire Français-Siamois.* Bangkok, 1924.
	Peter Mark Roget, M. D., F. R. S.: *Thesaurus.* London, 1937.
S. J. S.	Samuel J. Smith, Litt. D.: *A Comprehensive Anglo-Siamese Dictionary,* 5 Vols. Bangkok, 1899–1908.
S. Y. B.	*Statistical Year book of the Kingdom of Siam,* B. E. 2474–75 (1931–33).
strong	Hilda Arthur Strong: *A Sketch of Chinese Arts and Crafts.*
J. S. S.	*The Journal of the Siam Society,* Vols. I—XXXIII: Bangkok, 1904–1941.
siam	The Ministry of Commerce and Communications: *Siam, Nature and Industry.* Bangkok, 1930.
S. B.	*The Up-to-Date Dictionary for Students, English-Siamese.* Bangkok, B. E. 2476 (1933).
Und.	M. M. Underhill B. Litt.: *The Hindu Religious Year.* Calcutta, 1921.
V. P.	Phya Vanpruk Picharn, F. L. S.: *List of Common Trees, Shrubs, etc. in Siam.* Bangkok, 1923.
wales	H. G. Quaritch Wales, M. A., Ph. D.: *Siamese State Ceremonies.* London, 1931.
Dict. E. P. I.	Sir George Watt, C. I. E., M. B., C. M., L. L. D., F. L. S.: *Dictionary of the Economic Products of India.* London, 1908.
watt.	Sir George Watt: *The Commercial Products of India.* London, 1908.
	Kenneth E. Wells, Ph. D.: *Thai Buddhism, it's Rites and Activities.* Bangkok, 1941.
S. E. D.	Sir Monier Monier-Williams, M. A., K. C. I. E.: *Sanskrit-English Dictionary.* Oxford, 1899.
W.	W. A. R. Wood, C. I. E.: *A History of Siam.* London, 1926.

ADDENDA TO THE BIBLIOGRAPHY

Supplied by MARY R. HAAS

The books and articles cited here were selected primarily on the basis of their usefulness to the student wishing to learn the Thai language. For the most part we list only items produced since 1941, the date when McFarland's *Dictionary* was published. The exceptions are a few dictionaries and textbooks not listed by McFarland. Readers wishing to consult a more extensive bibliography are referred to the Embree and Dotson work cited below.

DICTIONARIES

Except where otherwise noted, Thai words in Thai alphabetic writing only.

Bhaopichitr, Dr. Kamol. *Modern English-Siamese Dictionary.* Bangkok, B.E. 2492 (1949). 819 pp.

Haas, Mary R. *Phonetic Dictionary of the Thai Language.* University of California Press, Berkeley and Los Angeles, 1947. Part I : Thai-English, 387 pp.; Part II : English-Thai, 276 pp. Thai words in romanized phonetic writing only. (A reprinting of the *Special Dictionary of the Thai Language,* 1945.)

Jumsai, M. L. Manich. *Deutsch-Siamesisches Wörterbuch.* Bangkok, 1938. 494 pp.

———. *Dictionnaire français-siamois.* Bangkok, 1937. 1047 pp.

———. *English-Thai Dictionary.* 8th printing, Bangkok, B.E. 2490 (1947). 610 pp.

———. *Thai-English Dictionary.* 3d rev. ed., Bangkok, 1949. 692 pp.

Sreshthaputra, So, ed. *The New Model English-Thai Dictionary.* Bangkok, 1940. 3 vols., 4000 pp. Most entries include English illustrative sentences translated into Thai.

Thai-Thai Dictionary. Bangkok, B.E. 2493 (1950). 1057 pp. The most recent dictionary prepared by the Thai Ministry of Education. It supersedes the work referred to in McFarland's bibliography as the *Government Siamese Dictionary.*

TEXTBOOKS

Except where otherwise noted, Thai words in romanized phonetic writing only.

Haas, Mary R. *Beginning Thai.* Washington, 1942. 78 pp.

———. *Manual of Thai Conversations.* Berkeley, Calif., 1945. 77 pp.

———. *Thai Phrases.* Berkeley, Calif., 1945. 104 pp.

———. *Thai Reader (in Phonetic Writing).* Berkeley, Calif., 1945. 32 pp.

———. *The Thai System of Writing.* Washington, 1942. 101 pp. Most words in Thai alphabetic writing only.

Haas, Mary R., and Heng R. Subhanka. *First Thai Reader.* Berkeley, Calif., 1945. 46 pp. Thai alphabetic writing only.

———. *Spoken Thai.* Henry Holt and Company, Inc., New York, 1945–48, 2 vols., 701 pp.

Trittel, Walther. *Einführung in das Siamesische.* Berlin and Leipzig, 1930. 112 pp. Many Thai words in Thai alphabetic writing followed by a romanized phonetic writing.

PHONETICS AND GRAMMAR

Thai words in these items in romanized phonetic writing.

Fowler, Murray, and Tasniya Isarasena. *The Total Distribution of the Sounds of Siamese.* University of Wisconsin Press, Madison, 1952. 8 pp. + 4 microcards, containing 131 charts of sound distributions.

Gedney, William. *Indic Loanwords in Spoken Thai.* Unpublished dissertation, Yale University, 1947. 613 pp.

Haas, Mary R. *Outline of Thai Grammar.* Berkeley, Calif., 1950. 25 pp.

———. "Techniques of Intensifying in Thai," *Word,* II (1946), 125–30.

———. "Types of Reduplication in Thai," *Studies in Linguistics,* I (1942), No. 1, 1–6.

———. "The Use of Numeral Classifiers in Thai," *Language,* XVIII (1942), 201–5.

Henderson, Eugenie J. A. "Prosodies in Siamese : a Study in Synthesis," *Asia Major* n.s., I (1949), 189–215.

LITERATURE

Schweisguth, P. *Étude sur la littérature siamoise.* Paris, 1951. 409 pp.

BIBLIOGRAPHY

Embree, John F. and Lillian Ota Dotson. *Bibliography of the Peoples and Cultures of Mainland Southeast Asia.* Yale University Press, New Haven, 1950. 821 pp. See particularly "Thailand : Language and Writing," pp. 528–34 and "Literature and Folklore," pp. 534–39.

Mc FARLAND'S
SIAMESE – ENGLISH
DICTIONARY

To King Ram Kamheng is due the honour of giving to the Thai people the alphabet now in use. He altered the then existing Cambodian characters adapting them so as to make them suitable for Siamese script. He thus evolved an alphabet that was adopted in A. D. 1283 (w. p. 57) and used throughout Siam and the northern dominions. It consists of 44 consonants divided into 3 classes but with only 21 separate consonant sounds, 18 primary vowel forms and 5 tone marks.

ก The first consonant of the Thai alphabet. A middle or second class letter of which there are nine – ก, จ, ฎ, ฏ, ด, ต, บ, ป, อ. กอไก่ is the designating name. It occurs in words of Pali and Sanskrit origin. When thus used as a suffix to words meaning *number*, it implies *group* as, – เอกก group one or primary set: ทุก group two or secondary set. When used as a suffix to a verb, it conveys the idea of *person* and is equivalent to the Eng. *er* as,– จรก a traveller: ปาฐก a public speaker; ปฏิคาหก a receiver.

ก็ gkaw³ *adv. & conj.* then; also; consequently; quite; used as a sign of the present tense and to introduce a main clause, generally after a conditional idea expressed or understood. (It is always placed after the subject). ก็ช่าง, ช่างเถอะ never mind; leave it alone then: ก็ดี quite well; either: ก็ได้ *intensive* assuredly it may or can be: ก็ตาม accordingly: ก็ถูก quite correctly: ทั้งนั้นก็ดี nevertheless;

however; that is quite right; being granted: ท่านไปก็ได้ you may go if you so wish: นี่ก็ได้ นั้นก็ได้ either this or that; either one; แล้วก็ and then; afterwards.

กก gkok⁴ *v.* to clasp; to hug; to embrace; to hold in the arms against the breast; to coddle. *n.* a collective term for clumps, bunches of reeds, sedges, rushes, flag-like plants growing along the banks of canals, lagoons, ponds or sluggish waterways. When dressed and dried these are used for weaving into mats. กกขา a genus of flag-like rush with triangular stems which when dried are used for making rope or mats. กกไข่ to brood or sit on eggs till hatched: กกนอน to fondle, pet or caress while in a recumbent position: กกไม้ the root stocks, base, stump or ground-level of reeds or trees: กกลังกา a genus of flag-like rush having round stems. A name usually applied to *Cyperus digitatus*. A coarse sedge growing in marshy ground or along the edges of ditches (K): กกลังกา *Cy-*

perus alternifolius; "Umbrella plant" (N. H. J. S. S. IX, 3, p. 271). A native of Madagascar. This sedge usually of the smaller kind is occasionally seen cultivated in aquaria and other wet situations in this country. It is believed to have been introduced during the third reign of the present dynasty (1809-1851) probably from Ceylon as the Siamese name suggests: กกลูก to caress a baby; to brood over the young (as birds or hens): กกหู the base of the external ear: เสื่อกก reed mats or matting:

ก๊ก gkok[5] *v.* to mince; to slice: *Chin. n.* a group; a faction; a party; a family; a clique; a combination: *syn.* พวก, หมู่, นิกาย, คณะ, พรรค, สกุล: สามก๊ก three groups, tribes, factions or kingdoms. In the historical narrative known as "Sam Kok" the factional and racial wars between the Chinese and the Huen 763-823 B. E. (A. D. 220–280) are depicted. Scholars have discovered that these Huens are none other than ancestors of the Thai people who finally were welded into one political group. Under political pressure from the Chinese, these people migrated southward and south-west settling in the Mekong valley and Salwin valley. Those who settled in the Mekong valley established independent Thai states in the region now called "Sibsong Chu Thai," the twelve Thai rulers. (J. S. S. XIII, 2, p. 19 *f.* Damrong, Sam Kok 2471 B. E.).

กกุฏ gka[4]-gkoot[4] *n.* dove; pigeon.

กกุท gka[4]-gkoot[4] *S. n.* tip; pinnacle; leader; principal; main; royal regalia of kings: กกุทมาน a mountain; cattle having a hump on the shoulder; hump-shouldered bulls: กกุทมึนันยา *lit.* "a daughter of the mountain", *i. e.* a river: กกุทมี a mountain.

กกุธ, กกุท, กกุภ gka[4]-gkoot[4] *P. n.* insignia of kingship; the hump on an animal's back: เบญจราชกกุธภัณฑ์ the five insignia of kingship, viz: ฉลองพระบาท sandals, slippers, golden moccasins with points curved

upwards (Ger. (1) p. 130): ธารพระกร the royal staff or baton: พระขรรค์ชัยศรี the scepter; sword: พระมหาพิชัยมงกุฎ the state crown: แส้จามรี a chowry; a fly-flapper or whisk made of the tail-hairs of the Tibetan yak:

กกุภ see กกุธ

กกุสนธ์ gka[4]-gkoo[4]-son[2] *P. n.* the first Buddha in this era (of enlightenment).

กง, วง gkong *n.* a circle; an arch; an arc-shaped piece of wood or timber as bottom ribs for boats; the circumference of a circle or loop: กง (เกาะ) an island on the east coast of the gulf of Siam: กง (ขนม) a cake or sweet-meat: กง (เสลี่ยง) an armchair palanquin for the use of royalty carried in processions: กงกาง, โกงกาง a salt-water tree of the mangrove family, used principally for fire-wood; *Rhizophora candelaria (Rhizophoraceae)* (cb. p. 592): กงกางใบเล็ก (ต้น) *Rhizophora conjugata* (V. P. p. 23: K.): กงกางใบใหญ่ (ต้น) *Rhizophora mucronata* (V. P. p. 23: MCM. p. 444): กงกางหัวสุม (ต้น) *Bruguiera gymnorhiza* (V. P. p. 23); *Bruguiera sexangula (Rhizophoraceae)* (cb. p. 597): กงการ business; duty; job; task; work: กงเกวียน กำเกวียน a simile indicating the inevitable result of sin (as when one commits murder he will be murdered): กงโก้ stooped; arched; bent over as a position of the body (as while playing "leap frog"): กงค้าง, กงข้าง side ribs; short ribs of boats: These are attached perpendicularly along the inside, reaching part way to the center board: กงจักร์ the circle, circumference or arc of a wheel or of some mechanical appliance: กงรถ, กงเกวียน the rim or tire of wagon-wheels or ox-cart wheels: กงเรือ bottom rib; ribs of a boat: กงวาน bottom ribs placed alternately with the others: รูวาน a hole in the bottom ribs for the flow of bilge water.

ก่ง, ขน gkong[4] *v.* to bend (as a cane); to curve; to flex; to enhance the value of; to make bowed or arched (as in archery): ก่ง แร้ว to bend the rod serving as a spring for bird-traps: ก่งหน้าไม้ to arch the bow of a crossbow.

ก้ง gkong[3] *adj.* piebald, spotted or striped: ผ้าตาก้ง cloth with white and black dots or stripes. [grandfather.

ก๋ง gkong[2] *Hok. Teh. n.* one's maternal

กงฉาก gkong-chak[4] *n.* a carpenter's steel square; an instrument by which to measure or lay out right-angles; an angle.

กงฉ่าย, กงไฉ่ gkong-chai[4] *Hok. Teh. n.* fermented or pickled cabbage which forms a staple food among the Chinese.

กงเต๊ก gkong-dtek[6] *Chin. n.* Mahayana religious ceremonies for the dead, observed by the Chinese and Annamese.

กงพัด gkong-pat[6] *n.* lath, laths or slabs nailed to the base of a post or placed at the foundation of a column for additional support: กงพัดสีลม *n.* blades or arms of a windmill or wind-wheel.

กงสี gkong-see[2] *Chin. n.* a company; a combine; an organization carrying on business. This word is found in all Chinese dialects: ของกงสี belonging to the company or being for the common use of those in the combine.

กงสุล gkong-soon[2] *Eng. n.* consul.

กงสฎาร gkong-sa[4]-dan n. the bell of a Buddhist monastery.

กฎ, ข้อบังคับ, วินัย gkot[4] *n.* law; rule; precept; order; injunction; regulation: กฎกระทรวง ministerial order or regulation: กฎเกณฑ์ rule; standard; criterion; gauge: scale: กฎข้อบังคับ by-laws: กฎข้อบังคับกักขัง เพื่อตรวจ หรือเพื่อป้องกันโรค quarantine regulations: กฎธรรมชาติ national laws: กฎ ธรรมดา laws of nature: กฎบัตร กฎหมาย *idiomatic*: กฎมนเฑียรบาล royal family laws, first promulgated in 1450 A. D.: กฎ ยุทธวินัย code of military ethics: กฎ เสนาบดี replaced by กฎกระทรวง: กฎหมาย

laws; common laws; enactments; decrees: กฎหมายนา ๆ ประเทศ, กฎหมายระหว่างประเทศ International law: กฎหมายปิดปาก a law suppressing publicity: กฎหมายเหตุ, จดหมายเหตุ to make an entry of a transaction in a record book: กฎอัยยการศึก martial law: ตั้งกฎ, ออกกฎ to issue or promulgate a law, an order or a regulation: วิชชากฎหมาย jurisprudence.

กฎิ gka[4]-dti[4] *P. n.* the waist.

กฎูก, ตรึกฎูก gka[4]-dtook[4] *P. v.* to be jealous; to have incompatible dispositions; to be easily irritated: *adj.* hot; peppery; irritable; quick-tempered: กฎูกผล peppery, pungent fruit.

กฎูกโรหิณิ, ข่า (ต้น) gka[4]-dtook[4]-ro-hi[4]-ne *P. n.* a synonym for *Alpinia Galanga* (V. P. p. 38). *Alpinia siamensis* (V. P. p. 38). *Alpinia sanderiana (Scitamineae)* (MCM. p. 148-149, K.). A very handsome plant with leaves streaked and banded with white, used by the natives as an ingredient for curry powder.

กฐิน gka[4]-tin[2] *P. n.* a frame (similar to an embroidery frame), 2½ metres long (๖ ศอก) by 150 centimeters wide (๓ ศอก) by which robes for Buddhist monks are measured and cut; a set of robes for presentation to Buddhist monks: กฐินัตถการกรรม the process of measuring and cutting the cloth according to the standard size prior to sewing the pieces together in order to make the robes for Buddhist monks. กฐินเสฎะ presentation of robes to the Buddhist monks (after the prescribed time): ทอดกฐิน to observe the annual religious ceremony of presenting robes to the Buddhist monks at the various monasteries. The time for such visitations lasts a month, counting from the end of Lent.

กณิการ, กรณิการ์ กรรณิการ gka[4]-ni[6]-gkan *P. n.* the night-blooming tree of sadness; the night-blooming jasmine; *Nyctanthes arbor-tristis (Oleaceae)* (V. P. p. 28: K.: MCM. p. 441). A large shrub bearing fragrant yellow flowers. The leaves are harsh to the touch. The flowers yield a yellow dye, used as a cheap substitute for saffron in the dyeing of cotton cloth.

กนิฐนันต์   gka⁴-nit⁶-nan *adj.* delicate; intricate; fine; artful (descriptive of lines on porcelain or etchings).

กด   gkot⁴ *v.* to compress; to press or push down; to suppress: กด (ปลา) the cat-fish *Mystus micracanthus*; *Tachysurus argyropleuron* (Dept. Agri. & Fisheries): กดขาว (ปลา) *Tachysurus maculatus*: กดขี่ to oppress; to maltreat; to persecute: กดความ to forbid or prevent publicity; to suppress legal proceedings: กดคอ to compel (by manual force); to treat cruelly: กดจมน้ำ to immerse; to dip (in water): กดเพลิงแกลบ, คอคาน (นก) white-necked stork *Dissura episcopus* (Gaird. J. S. S. IX, I, p. 11): กดเพลิง, สายบัว (นก) black-necked stork *Xsnorhynchus asiaticus* (Gaird. J. S. S. IX, 1, p. 11): กดหัว to treat insultingly by pushing down the head: กดหัวหลาว (ปลา) *Tachysurus truncatus* (H. M. S.).

กต   gka⁴-dta⁴ *P. adj.* finished; completed; done; performed; accomplished: กตเวที a recipient who announces kindnesses received; one manifesting gratitude: กตัญชลี having the hands placed palm to palm in an attitude of reverence, respect or solicitation: กตัญญู appreciation for kindnesses bestowed; gratitude; gratefulness; faithfulness: กตัญ ญุตา a condition of gratefulness for favours or benefits received: กตาภินิหาร one having merit or superhuman power resulting from good deeds previously performed.

กติ   gka⁴-dti⁴ *S. n.* a hermit; an anchorite.

กติกา, กติกา   gka⁴-dti⁴-gka *P. n.* by-laws; articles of agreement; clause; item.

กติปยะ   gka⁴-dti⁴-bpa⁴-ya⁶ *P. adj.* two or three (articles); several.

กถา   gka⁴-ta² *S. n.* a discourse; words; sayings; a story; a tale; a fable; the magical rhymes of a magician: กถามัฐ the gist,

pith or essence of a story or discourse; the first volume of a book of stories or fables called กถาสริตสาคร, *lit.* "an ocean of stories," a collection of popular stories by Somadeva-bhatta of Kashmir, compiled about the beginning of the twelfth century A. D. (H. C. D. 303): กถาประพันธ์ fables; fiction; legends: กถาประสงค์ conversations; discourses; dissertations: กถามัย composed of fictitious, imaginary or false tales; groundless: กถามุข a preface; an introduction to a book; the second volume of a book of stories called กถาสริตสาคร: กถาโยค manners; gestures or equipment of a person conversing or delivering an address: กถามภ์ the beginning of a story, address or discourse: กถาราม a volume consisting of stories, fables or myths: กถาวเศษ, กถาเศษ *lit.* "one having only a biography", *i. e.* a dead person: กถาสงเคราะห์ place or volume where popular stories or fables are collected together: กถาอุทัย a foreword or introduction to a book or collection of stories.

กถิ, กถิก   gka⁴-ti⁴ *P. S. n.* a lecturer; a public speaker; a narrator; a relater of fables or stories; a story-teller by profession: กถิกาจารย์ a professor of elocution: ธรรม กถิก a speaker on religious subjects.

กถิก see กถิ

กถิกา see กติกา

กถี   gka⁴-te² *P. n.* a babbler; a prattler; a chatterer; a tattler.   [sires.

กทรรป   gka⁴-tap⁶ *v.* to have amorous de-

กทลิมฤค   gka⁴-ta⁴-li⁶-ma⁶-ruk⁶ *S. n.* a species of deer; the civet-cat; the musk-cat, the hides of which are tanned for various purposes.

กทลี   gka⁴-ta⁶-le *P. n.* a flag; an ensign; a certain variety of banana: กทลีกันท์ the roots of this variety of banana tree: กทลี ครรภ์ the stalk of this variety of banana tree.

กทาการ   gka⁴-ta-gkarn *S. adj.* ugly; unsightly (in appearance); loathsome.

กทาจาร   gka[4]-ta-chjarn *S. n.* unseemly manners; vile despicable behaviour.

กทาหาร   gka[4]-ta-harn[2] *S. n.* food that is harmful, improper or injurious.

กน   gkon *v.* to face (as duty); to intend; to plan; to determine or resolve to do; to set one's face to some line of action: *adj.* little; small; diminutive: กนแต่เศร้าโศรก to be occupied with an overwhelming sorrow; to devote one's self to the contemplation of a personal sorrow.

ก่น   gkon[4] *v. ancient usage* to intend; to plan to do; to be determined or to resolve to do; *modern usage* to dig up; to uproot; to clear or clean; to mow or level off (as a piece of land); to remove weeds; to fell and uproot (as trees); to turn up the soil: ก่น โค่น to dig around the roots (until the tree falls): ก่นเง่า to dig up bulbous roots (as potatoes or peanuts): ก่นที่ to clean up a plot of ground by cutting the undergrowth, digging up the roots and leveling off the surface: ก่นไร่ to reap a rice field: ก่น สร้าง to clean off a piece of land; to make a clearing (as for a road or canal).

ก้น   gkon[3] *n.* the seat; the buttocks; rump; base; bottom of (as of a hole or well): ก้น กบ, ก้นหย่อน (กระตุก) the coccyx: ก้นขบ a species of non-poisonous snake having black and white streaks alternating *Cylindrophus Rufus*: ก้นตะกรน sediment; dregs; lees: *adj.* worthless; refuse; waste: ก้นถุง the bottom of a bag: ก้นบิด (ต้น) *Stephania hernandifolia (Menispermaceœ)* (cb. p. 70), a a common herbaceous climbing plant with peltate leaves, *i. e.* the stalk of the leaf is attached under the blade and not at its edge, hence the Siamese name: ก้นบึ้ง the floor of a swamp or marsh: ก้นบึ้งบั้น the rear-most part or aperture of a gun: ก้นปล่อง (ยุง) a genus of mosquito of the family *Culi-cidae,* the *Anopheles* (Med. Dict.): ก้นปูด (นก) the larger or Hume's crow-pheasant (Lao), *Centropus Sinensis Intermedius* com-

mon in the brush bordering the rice fields (Deig. J. S. S. VIII, 3, p. 160): ก้นแมลงสาบ tapering to a roundish tip or end: ก้นข้อย the gluteal fold of the buttocks: ก้นหม้อ the bottom of a rice pot: ก้นหอย the extreme end or tapering spiral lines of a conch-shell, shell-fish or mud-snail: ติดก้น หม้อ to be stuck to the bottom of a rice pot.

กนก   gka[4]-nok[4] *P. S. n.* gold: กนก (ต้น) the palasa, thornapple or mountain ebony: กนกกทลี a variety of banana, *lit.* "golden banana": กนกการ a goldsmith: กนก ทัณฑ์ an umbrella with a long golden handle (for royalty): กนกบรรพต *lit.* "The Golden Mountain". According to Indian mythology, the central peak of the Himalayan range north of Manasa lake: กนกบัตร a flat circular gold earring worn by Indian women: กนกมัย plated with gold; washed with gold; golden: กนกรส gold in a liquid state: กนกศักดิ์ another name for the god of War (H. C. D. p. 150): กนกศีขริน tipped or flooded with golden sun-rays: the peak of the moun-tain Meru: กนกสถลี a gold mine; gold dust, sand or ore:- กนกสูตร, กนกาวลี neck-lace or chains of gold: กนกากร a gold mine: กนกาจล The Golden Mountain; the central mountain of an infinite number of solar systems called Meru (Ala. p. 13): ลาย กนก an artistic design.

กนิฏฐ see กนิษฐ

กนิษฐ, กนิฏฐ   gka[4]-nit[6] *P. S. adj.* small; little; young; lesser; least: *n.* the youngest member of a family; the antithesis of เชษฐ: กนา, กนี a girl; a maiden; a young maid; a little girl; a virgin; a daughter: กนิฏฐา, กนิษฐกา, กนิษฐา the youngest; the youngest born; the little finger; the antithesis of เชษฐ: กนิษฐประถม, กนิษฐมูล making or having the younger or youngest as the first: กนิษฐ ภคินี a younger sister: กนิษฐภาดา a younger brother: กันย the lesser one; the youngest (one of a family): กันยาคาร a boudoir: กันยาชาต illegitimate children: กันยกาบดี a son-in-law: กันยกุพช the modern form of the name is Kanaui, Kinnauj, Kannouj, or Kanoge, spelled in a variety of ways. An ancient city of Hindustan on the Kalinadi, an affluent of the Ganges and lying a little to the west of the. latter. It was once the capital of a powerful dynasty, known to the classical geographers as "Canogyza", which means "hump-backed damsel" and refers to a legend relating to the hundred daughters of King Kusa-nabha, who were all made crooked by Vayu for refusing to comply with his licentious desires. A great national division of the Brahman caste (H. C. D. p. 149): กันย กุมารึ, พระทุรคา, พระอุมา *lit.* "the virgin-damsel", names for Durga. Her worship extended to the southernmost extremity of India (H. C. D. p. 149).

กบ gkop[4] *n.* a frog; a carpenter's plane: *adj.* full; overflowing; overly full: กบ (ปลา) a species of salt-water fish; *Batrachus grunniens*: กบกระดี่, กบราง a grooving plane: กบกล้อ a plane for convex or rounded surfaces: กบแก้ม to hold in the cheek so that it bulges (as a monkey): กบ ขอด a short plane for rough work: กบจาน to fill a dish to overflowing (as with food): กบเจา the name of a district in Ayuthia: กบเจาะ the name of a district in Prachin province, north of Chantaboon: กบเต้น the name of a popular song sung during the Ayuthian period: กบทวาย a goldsmith's horn-shaped iron anvil with one end tapering to a flat horizontal point while on the other is a round ball: กบบรรทัด a plane for straight planing: กบบัว a small-sized frog; a plane for smoothing a convex surface; a plane used for convex surfaces or cornices: กบปากตะขาบ a concave plane for fluting or making friezes: กบรอก to pull the sailyard up tight against the pulley at the mast head: ขี้กบ shavings: ประกบ to place, attach or fasten two flat surfaces together: ไสกบ to plane.

กบฏ, ขบถ, กระบถ gka[4]-bot[4] *P. S. n.* crookedness; deceitfulness; treason; intrigue;

riot; revolt: กบฏประพันธ์ those associated with deceivers or engaging in intrigue: กบฏพจน์ deceitful words; treasonable language: กบฏเพศ feigned or disguised sex: กบฏเลขย์ false statements; forged documents.

กบดาน gkob[4]-dan *v.* to be completely embedded in (as in mud): กบเต้นกลางสระบัว a proverb expressing the disappointment felt at the estrangement of an intimate, trusted friend: กบเต้นต่อยหอย *proverb* to have thoughts of extreme indignation surpassing arrow thrusts that sadden the heart: a poetical verse: กบปาก to fill the mouth full or to overflowing: ยังกบอยู่ being still fully supplied.

[ridge pole.

กบทู gkob[4]-too *n.* the ridge of a roof; the

กบาล, กระบาล gka[4]-ban *P. S. n.* the crown of the head; the skull; the cranium; a dish; a plate; a tile; a water jar; fragments of a tile; a flat, smooth, concave vessel; a dish used by prisoners or convicts *vulgar*; articles or food given as offerings to spirits or used in sacrifices to them: กบาลเกตุ a comet: กบาลบ้าน an open space in the center of a village: กบาลมาลา a wreath of skulls; skulls strung together on a string: กบาลมลี *lit.* "one wearing a garland of skulls," *i. e.* the god Siva (H. C. D. p. 300): กบาลเมือง a public space or plaza in the middle of a city: กบาลเศียร *lit* "one who has a skull on the head", *i. e.* the god Siva: เสียกบาล to arrange a tray containing offerings to demons or spirits, along with which are placed several mud dolls all of which are thrown away into the brush. Prior to being thrown away the dolls are smashed to pieces.

กบินทร์, กเบนทร์, gka[4]-bin *n.* king of the monkey tribe, *lit.* "the valiant monkey warrior," *i. e.* the god Vishnu; Hanuman.

กบิล gka[4]-bin *P. S. n.* a monkey; a dark colour, shading toward red, yellow or brown; monkey-coloured; reddish-yellow; reddish-brown; a celebrated sage, the founder of the

Sankhya philosophy : กบิลทยุติ an appellation of the sun : กบิลธารา an appellation of
the Ganges.

กบิล gka⁴-bin *n.* pattern; order; system;
method; group; collection; class : กบิลความ
method or order of procedure : กบิลเมือง
groups or families of residents of a town or
city : กบิลไม้ a collection of various kinds
of timber or trees : กบิลว่าน various
species of plants with bulbous roots.

กบิลบูร see กบิลพัสดุ์

กบิลพัสดุ์, กบิลบูร gka⁴-bin-la⁶-pat⁶ *n.* a
city on the river Rohini, an affluent of the
Rapti, which was the capital of Suddhodana,
the father of Gotama Buddha (H. C. D. p. 150).
There Gotama Buddha lived while still an
ordinary man before becoming an ascetic
(Ala. p. 173).

กบิลา gka⁴-bi⁴-la *n.* a reddish-brown or
tawny-coloured mother cow.

กบิลาจารย์ gka⁴-bi⁴-la-chjan *n.* a celebrated Indian sage named Kapila, the founder
of the Sankhya philosophy and sometimes
identified with Vishnu or Agni. His one
glance is said to have destroyed the hundred
thousand sons of King Sagara (H. C. D. p. 150).

กบี gka⁴-be⁴ *P. S. n.* a monkey; an ape :
กบีธุช the flag representing Hanuman, king
of the monkey-warrior tribe, being one of a
pair which is borne before the king on official
occasions (the other is the Garuda); *lit.* " one
having the monkey flag as an ensign," *i. e.*
Phra Arjuna, the third of five Pandu princes.
He was a brave warrior, high-minded, generous, upright, handsome, more prominent, more
amiable and more interesting than his
brothers. He was taught the use of arms by
Drona (H. C. D. p. 21–22).

กเบนทร์ see กบินทร์

กบูร, กระบวร, กระบูร, ขบวร, ขบูร gka⁴-
boon *adj.* adorned; decorated; ornamented.

กโบร, กปปุร, กัปประ gka⁴-bone *P. S. n.*
the elbow joint; the elbow.

กโบล, กำโบล gka⁴-bone *P. S. n.* cheek;
the pouch of the cheek; the jowl of man or
elephant : กโบลบัตร lines or marks painted
on the cheek : กโบลบาลี one cheek : กโบล
ภิตติ the cheek bones : กโบลราค the colour
of the cheek or blood rushing to the cheek;
blushing.

กปณ, กปณก, กปณา, กฤปณ gka⁴-bpa⁴-
na⁶ *P. S. adj.* fatherless; poor; dejected;
pitiable; miserable; orphaned; friendless.

กปณก see กปณ

กปณา see กปณ

กปณี gka⁴-bpa⁴-ne *P. S. n.* an orphan; a
vagrant or friendless person.

กปปุร see กโบร

กบี gka⁴-bpi *P. S. n.* a monkey; an
elephant; the sun : กบีเกตน์, กบีธวัช one
who wears a sword or rapier as an insignia
of rank, as Phra Arjuna, the third Pandu
prince who was a brave warrior, highminded,
generous, upright, handsome. His skill in
the use of arms was marvellous and he was
given the most powerful weapons by Indra,
Varuna, Yama and Kuvera (H. C. D. p. 21–22):
กบีเกศ having reddish-brown hair : กบีบดี
the monkey chief or king, *i. e.* Hanuman :
กบีประภู master of the monkey, *i. e.* Phra Ram :
กบีรถ *lit.* " he who has a monkey for a
chariot ", *i. e.* Phra Ram : กบีโลหะ *lit.* " a
monkey-coloured mineral ", *i. e.* brass : กบี
เศียร, กบีสีสะ the bolt of a door; a wedge-
shaped wooden door-bolt : กบีสถล an abode
of the monkey.

กบิตถ (ต้นมะขวิด) gka⁴-bpit⁴-ta⁴ *P. S. n.*
Feronia elephantum (Rutaceae) (cb. p. 238);
wood-apple; elephant-apple, a small spiny tree,
30 to 40 feet high, with small, pinnate, glabrous, trifoliate leaves, native of Siam, India
and Ceylon. The globular or ovoid fruit is of

the size of a large cricket-ball, similar to the bael-fruit, but distinguished from it by the rough, woody, hard, white shell. It contains a mass of soft, bitter-sweet, mealy substance, which is used for making a pleasant cooling drink and a preserve and is also used in native medicine (MCM. p. 252).

กโปตะ, ปาราปตะ   gka⁴-bpo-dta⁴ *n.* a pigeon (ชาดก p. 196).

ก้ม   gkom⁵ *v.* to bend the body downward and forward; to bend or bow the head; to stoop down: ก้มเกล้า to bow the head (as in a condition of shame): ก้มหน้าก้มตา to attend earnestly to one's duties or business: ก้มหน้าทน to endure; to bear; to suffer patiently; to endure the inevitable with fortitude: ก้มหน้าทำมาหากิน to earn one's livelihood with patience and fortitude.

กมล, กระมล   gka⁴-mon *P. S. n.* lotus plant; lotus lily; "Sacred Bean" of Egypt; *Nelumbium speciosum (Nymphaeaceae),* a beautiful plant, with large handsome peltate, circular erect leaves. The flowers are large, bright pink or white and scented. Seeds and root-stock are edible (MCM. p. 174, 379). The petals are used as cigar wrappers; face; heart; a vesicle: *adj.* pale red or rose coloured, being like a lotus flower: กมล ขันธ์, กมลวัน a bundle or bouquet of lotus flowers: กมลครรภ์ *lit.* "he who burst forth from the lotus bud," *i. e.* the god Brahma, the impersonal and spiritual being pervading everything, so-called because he was born of a lotus flower: กมลนัยน์, กมลเนตร, กมลโลจน์, กมลากษ์ กมลเลกษณ์ lotus (like) eyes; *lit.* "having eyes as beautiful as a lotus blossom": กมลบัตร petals of the lotus lily: กมลพานธพ *lit.* "the friend of the lotus," *i. e.* the sun: กมลภพ, กมลโยนิ, กมลสมภพ *lit.* "he who was born from a lotus lily," *i. e.* the god Brahma: กมลภู "he who burst forth from the lotus flower," *i. e.* the god Brahma: กมลวัทน์ lotus (like) face; having a face as beautiful as a lotus flower: กมลากร a collection of

lotus plants; a lotus pond: กมลานนทน์ the joyfulness of Phra Lakshmi, the queen of the god Vishnu: กมลาสน์, กำมลาสน์ *lit.* "he who has the lotus flower as a seat," *i. e.* the god Brahma: กมลาหาส *lit.* "a smile like the unfolding of the lotus blossom": กมเลศ, กำมเลศ a large variety of lotus: ดวง กมล the heart.

กมลา   gka⁴-ma⁶-la *P. S. n. lit.* "a beautiful maiden," *i. e.* Phra Lakshmi or Sri wife of Vishnu and mother of Kama, the goddess of Fortune. She is said to have four arms, but is generally depicted as having only two, holding a lotus in one hand. She has no temples, but being the goddess of abundance and fortune, she continues to be assiduously courted and is not likely to fall into neglect (H. C. D. p. 176).

กมัณฑลุ   gka⁴-mun-ta⁶-lo⁶ *P. S. n.* an earthen or wooden receptacle for water; a gourd dipper.

กมุท   gka⁴-mot⁶ *n.* a lotus flower; the long-stemmed, white flowering lotus.

กย, กัย   gka⁴-ya⁶ *n.* the act or art of purchasing or buying.

กร   gkawn *P. S. n.* a hand; an arm; a workman; a labourer; an elephant's trunk; the claws of a crab; a craftsman; one who or that which does, makes or causes to be made: กรกช hands folded to suggest a lotus bud; the act of placing the hands in a position to resemble a lotus bud; to place the hands in a position suggesting a lotus bud (as when worshiping or showing adoration): กรกมล, กรบัทม์ *lit.* "hands handsome as a lotus blossom," the beautiful hands of a maiden being comparable to a lotus flower: กรกัณฏก, กรภู, กรศุก *lit.* "thorns of the hand," *i. e.* finger nails: กรโกษ hands held together in the shape of a cup (as for holding water): กรดล the palm of the hand: กรดาล cymbals; basso cymbals: กรทักษ์ handy; dexterous, skilful, expeditious, every-ready (hands): กรบัตร a saw: กรบัลลพ, กรศาขา *lit.* "offshoots of the hand," *i. e.* fingers; subdivisions of the hand: กรบาตร the act of splashing or throwing water while bathing: กรบาล *lit.* "weapon of protection for the hand," *i. e.* a sword: กรปฏ the act of placing the hands together palm to palm (in the attitude of respect): กรพาล, กรวาล a sword: กร มุกต์ *lit.* "a weapon thrown by hand," *i. e.* a dart or javelin: กรวีระ a sword; the thumb; a cemetery; a burial place: กรศึกร the water that an elephant expels from its trunk: กรศุทธิ the act of rubbing fragrant flowers in the hands: กรสวน, กรัสวัน the sound of clapping of the hands: กรสูตร a propitious thread or cord (as that slipped over the hands of the bride and groom at a wedding ceremony): กราฆาต the act of slapping, striking or hitting with the hand: กราลัมพัน anything used to assist the hand; tools; implements; apparatus; labour-saving devices: กโรทก water that is held in or poured into the hands: กางกร to reach out with or to stretch out the arms: ทองกร gold bracelets.

กร ๒ gkawn *P. S. n.* a ray of light; an halo; the rays of the sun or moon; customs fees or government income; government revenue; poll-tax: กรเคราะห์ a tax collector; the levying or collecting of a tax: กรชาล light rays; an halo; a bright globe or ball: กรบาล Director of a Customs Department or Station: กรสาท the veiling or fading away of glory or emanating rays: กรหาร the act of collecting taxes or duties: ทิวากร that which emits rays during the daytime: นิสา กร that which emits rays during the night-time.

กรก ๑ gka⁴-rok⁶ *P. S. n.* a hand; the shell of a coconut (dressed to serve as a vessel for holding water and used by Buddhist monks or ascetics).

กรก ๒ gka⁴-rok⁶ *P. S. n.* hail; tax; toll; duties; fees; the pomegranate tree.

กรกวรรษ, กรกา gka⁴-ra⁶-gka *n.* a rain of hailstones: กรกาภิฆาต, กรกาสาร a pestilential fall of hailstones: กรกามพุ a coconut tree.

กรกา see กรกวรรษ

กรกฎาคม gka⁴-ra⁶-gka⁴-da-kom *S. n.* the fourth month of the present official calendar, identical with July. The change from the old system of reckoning to a new one based on the Gregorian calendar was effected on April 1, 1889 which was made to correspond with Masayon 1st. of the 108th. year of the Bangkok Era (Ratanakosindr Sok). This change was necessary because of the inconvenience caused by the use of the Siamese lunar calendar along with the solar Gregorian calendar. The new system dates from the founding of Bangkok in 1782 A. D. by Chao Phya Chakkri, founder of the Chakkri dynasty. The only differences between this and the Gregorian calendar are 1st., the first month of the year is April not January and 2nd., the founding of Bangkok is taken as the starting point instead of the Birth of Christ. In 1913, another change was made and the Buddhist Era (Butta Sakarat) now takes the place of the Bangkok Era. The Buddhist Era ante-dates the Christian Era by 543 years. The present year (1938), dating from April 1st., is therefore Buddhist Era 2481.

กรกฎ ๑ gka-⁴ra⁶-gkot⁴ *n.* the cheek; the cheek pouch; the cheek, jaw or jowl of an elephant.

กรกฎ ๒ gka⁴-ra⁶-gkot⁴ *n.* a crab; the constellation of the Crab (Cancer): กรกฎศฤงค์ the pincers of the crab; the claws of the crab.

กรกศ see กรรกศ

กรกะ gka⁴-ra⁶-gka⁴ *P. S. n.* a receptacle for water; the husk of the coconut; the coconut shell made into a dipper or utensil; hail; taxes or duties; fees.

กรง gkrong *n.* an animal cage made with

wooden or iron slats; a cell for convicts; a cradle *poetical*: กรงนก a bird cage: กรงเลิบ a cage-like space formed by the closed talons of a bird: กรงเหลิก an iron cage: ลูกกรง a trellis; a railing; a baluster; one of a set of small pillars that support a hand-rail: ลูกกรงกรงนก the bars of a bird cage: ลูก กรงรัว the palings of a fence: ใส่กรง to confine in a cage or cell.

กรช, กรัช   gka⁴-ra⁶-cha⁶ *P. S. n. lit.* "one born from the hand," *i. e.* a finger-nail: *adj.* being formed from the dust of the earth: กรชกาย, กรัชกาย, ร่างกาย *lit.* "formed of the dust of the earth," *i. e.* the body; our bodies.

กรณ, กรณ์   gkawn or gka⁴-ra⁶-na⁶ *P. S. n.* the act of doing or of working; implements or instruments of various kinds; a helper; an assistant; a friend; a clerk or writer; organs for the production of vocal sounds (as vocal cords, lips and tongue): *adj.* clever; dexterous: กรณ *gram.* a prefix: กรณ, การก *gram.* the nominative case: กรณบุรพบท *gram.* the object of prepositions (always in the objective case): กรณประโยค the act or art of spelling or combining letters or words to form sentences; the use of enchantments by those claiming occult powers: กรณาธิการ a section or set of rules relating to methods of vocal production or expression: กรณาธิป the chief organ of life; a living soul: ฐาน กรณ์ the place of origin for the production of vocal sounds.

กรณ์ see กรณ

กรณิการ์ see กณิการ

กรณี   gka⁴-ra⁶-ne *n.* (1) *legal* a suit; an action; a case: (2) motive; reason; cause: (3) consequences; results; effects.

กรณฑ์, กรัณฑ์   gkron *n.* (1) a receptacle for water; a water jar; an ewer: (2) a basket or covered utensil made of woven bamboo strips: (3) the method of finding the square or cube root: หม้อกรณฑ์ a

bottle for water; an utensil for carrying water.

กรัณฑ์ see กรณฑ์

กรณีย์, กรณียะ   gka⁴-ra⁶-ne *P. n.* business; duty; obligation: *adj.* that which is obligatory or binding; that which ought or should be done; that which will probably be done: กรณีย์กิจ a responsibility likely to be discharged: ในกรณีย์ ที่จำเป็น in case of necessity.

กรณียะ see กรณีย์

กรด ๑   gkrot⁴ *n.* acid: *adj.* corrosive; sharply caustic; severe: กรด (ต้น) *Combretum trifoliatum (Combretaceae)*; *Combretum tetralophum* (cb. p. 621), a large-sized climber or shrub growing in low ground or near waterways: น้ำกรด a corroding liquid; an acid solution: ลมกรด a sharp, keen or biting wind.

กรด ๓   gkrot⁴ *n.* an ewer; a receptacle for lustral water; a ritual vase.

กรน   gkron *v.* to snore: กรนทา, กะลันทา, จี (ต้น) *Harrisonia perforata Simarubeae* (cb p. 244): กรนนเข้า, กระเข้า a flower basket: ครางกรน to groan while snoring.

กรบ   gkrop⁴ *n.* an harpoon; an instrument having three barbed prongs (used for spearing fish in shallow water): *v.* to use an harpoon.

กรบูร, การบูร   gka⁴-ra⁶-boon *S. n.* camphor: ต้นกรบูร camphor tree *Sphaeranthus indicus*: ยางกรบูร camphor gum.

การบูร see กรบูร

กรภ ๑   gka⁴-ra⁶-pa⁶ *P. S. n.* an elephant's trunk; an elephant calf; a young camel; a lid; a wall; the palm of the hand.

กรภ ๒ หัสต   gka⁴-ra⁶-pa⁶ *P. S. n.* a star; the thirteenth auspicious or lucky star.

กรภก   gka⁴-ra⁶-pok⁶ *S. n.* a camel.

กรภิน, กรภิ   gka⁴-ra⁶-pin *P. S. n. lit.* "one having a trunk," *i. e.* an elephant.

กรภิ see กรภิน

กรภิร์, กรภิระ   gka⁴-ra⁶-pe *S. n.* a lion.

กรภิระ see กรภิร์

กรม ๑ ตรม   gkrom *v.* to become melancholic; to become depressed; to be dejected or downcast; to be contused; to be bruised; to be confined by tough tissues (as an abscess):   กรมกรอม, กรมตรอม to be agitated in mind; to be perturbed: กรมเกรียม, กรมเตรียม to be sorrowful; to be sad; to be depressed; to be despondent by grief or affliction: กรมใจ to have the feelings hurt: อกกรม sorrowful; afflicted with a heavy burden: กรมหนอง a condition attendant to the formation of pus (as in an abscess).

กรม ๒   gkrom *n.* a cohort; a section; a division (as of troops); group; family; order; class; grade; series: เจ้ากรม the chief of a section or company; a title indicating the head of a family; the first of an order or series: ปลัดกรม a deputy or lieutenant of a section or company.

กรม ๓   gkrom *n.* a prefix to titles for princes of certain ranks: กรมขุน the title of a prince of the 4th rank: กรมท่า a former department of the government combining the duties of the Treasury and of the Foreign Office: กรมท่าขวา a former department of the government dealing with Indians: กรม ท่าซ้าย a former department of the government dealing with the Chinese: กรมท่าหลวง a former department of the government dealing with foreigners (other than Chinese and Indians):   กรมพระ the title of a prince of the 2nd. rank: กรมพระยา the title of a prince of the 1st. rank: กรมหมื่น the title of a prince of the 5th. rank: กรมหลวง the title of a prince of the 3rd. rank: สีกรมท่า navy blue colour.

กรม ๔ (ต้น)   gkrom *n. Aporosa villosa (Euphorbiaceae)* (V. P. p. 31: K.), a tree having short leaves which are pubescent underneath. The berries are densely velvety. The tree yields a red resin and the bark is used to make a red dye (Dict. E. P. I. p. 278).

กรมการ, กรรมการ   gkrom-gkarn *n.* a governmental official body; a governmental official committee: กรมเกษตร์และการประมง Department of Agriculture and Fisheries: กรมคลัง Finance Department: กรมเงินตรา Currency Department: กรมเจ้าท่า Harbour Department: กรมชลประทาน Irrigation Department: กรมช่างแสงทหารบก Military Arsenal: กรมชุมพลทหารเรือ Bangkok Naval Station: กรมตรวจกสิกรรม Agricultural Research Department (now abolished):   กรม ตรวจคนเข้าเมือง Immigration Department: กรม ตำรวจ Police Department: กรมตำรวจภูธร Gendarmerie Department: กรมทหารช่างที่ ๑ 1st. Guard Engineer Regiment: กรมทหารปืนใหญ่ ที่ ๑ 1st Guard Artillery Regiment: กรม ทหารม้าที่ ๑ 1st Cavalry Regiment: กรมทหาร รักษาวัง Royal Palace Guards Regiment: กรม ทหารอากาศ Royal Aeronautical Service: กรม ทะเบียน Statistical Department: กรมทะเบียน การค้า Department of Commercial Registration :   กรมทะเบียนที่ดิน Land Records Department: กรมทาง Department of Ways: กรมที่ดินและ โลหกิจ Land and Mines Department: กรม ที่ปรึกษา Office of the Adviser: กรมธรรมการ Ecclesiastical Department: กรมนคราทร Department of Municipal Affairs: กรม บัญชีกลาง Comptroller General's Department: กรมประกาสิต Protocol Department of the Ministry of Foreign Affairs: กรมปลัดทหารบก Adjutant General's Department: กรมปลัด ทัพเรือ Department of the Secretary of the Navy: กรมปลัดบัญชี Accountant Department (of any Ministry):   กรมป่าไม้ Royal Forest Department: กรมไปรษณีย์โทรเลข Post and Telegraph Department: กรมแผนที่ Royal Survey Department: กรมฝิ่นหลวง Opium Department: กรมพระคลังข้างที่ His Majesty's Privy Purse Department: กรม พระคลังมหาสมบัติ Treasury Department: กรม พระธรรมนูญทหารเรือ Naval Judicial Department: กรมพลศึกษา Physical Education Department:

กรมพลาธิการณ์ทหารบก Quarter Master General's Department: กรมพลำพัง General Administration Department: กรมพัศดุ Stores Department: กรมพัศดุทหารบก Military Stores Department: กรมพัศดุทหารเรือ Royal Naval Central Store: กรมยุทธโยธาทหารบก Military Works Department: กรมยุทธศึกษาทหารบก Military Education Section: กรมโยธาเทศบาล Public and Municipal Department: กรม รถไฟหลวงแห่งกรุงสยาม Royal State Railways of Siam: กรมรักษาที่หลวงและกัลปนา Department of State and Church Properties: กรมรักษา สัตว์น้ำ Department of Fisheries: กรมรังวัด ที่ดิน Cadastral Survey Department: กรมร่าง กฎหมาย Department of Legislative Redaction: กรมราชทัณฑ์ Prison Department: กรมราช โลหกิจและภูมิวิทยา Royal Department of Mines and Geology: กรมวิชชาธิการ Department of Technical Education: กรมวิทยาศาสตร์ Department of Science: กรมวิสามัญศึกษา Bureau of Technical Education: กรมศิลปากร Department of Fine Arts: กรมศึกษาธิการ Educational Department: กรมศุลกากร Department of Customs: กรมสถิติพยากรณ์ทั่วไป Department of General Statistics: กรม สรรพสามิตต์ Excise Department: กรมสรร- พากร Revenue Department: กรมสรรพาวุธ ทหารเรือ Royal Navy Ordnance Department: กรมสหกรณ์ Co-operative Department: กรม สัสดี Recruiting Department: กรมสามัญศึกษา Bureau of General Education: กรมสาธารณสุข Department of Public Health: กรมสารวัด ใหญ่ทหารเรือ Naval Police Department: กรม เสนาธิการทหารบก General Staff Department of the Army: กรมเสนาธิการทหารเรือ General Staff Department of the Navy: กรมสุรา Excise Department: กรมอัยยการ Department of Public Prosecution: กรมอากรค่าน้ำ Fishery Revenue Department: กรมอุทกศาสตร์ Hydrographic Department: กรมอู่ทหารเรือ Workshop and Dockyard Department of the Royal Navy:

กรมธรรม์, สารกรมธรรม์, สารกรม gkrom-tun *n.* an official receipt given in the purchase or sale of a slave; that document which binds a debtor to the service of his creditor; a document which must be legally registered (e.g. that for the sale of immovable property): กรมธรรม์ประกันชีวิต a life insurance policy.

กรมโยค gkrom-yok[3] *n.* accomplishment; achievement; the condition of completing or successfully concluding a duty, job or task.

กรมัฏฏ์ gka^4-ra^6-mat^6 *S.n.* the areca tree.

กรมาทิตย์, วิกรมาทิตย์, ท้าวสกันทคุปต์ gka^4-ra^6-mah-tit^6 *n.* a celebrated Hindu king วิกรมาทิตย์ of Ujjayini, India, who reigned about two thousand years ago and is said to have been the son of King Gardabhila. He belonged to the Samvat Era which commenced in 57 B.C. He was a man capable in warfare and in administrative affairs and was a great patron of learning, in-so-much that his court was made illustrious by the compilation of the "Nine Gems of Literature" or "Navaratna" by nine literary men. These were composed in poetry exalting the king's name and honour. One of the nine composers was Sivatas. Between the years 1719 and 1749 the king of Chaibura commanded that a translation of one of the Nine Gems of Literature, being a volume of 25 fables called เวตาล, be made into Braj-Bhasha (พรัชภาษา) the dialect of Braj, a form of the Hindu language spoken in the neighbourhood of Mathura and other of the northwestern provinces (H. C. D. p. 356–357).

กรมานุสาร gka^4-ra^6-ma-noo^6-$sarn^2$ *n.* proceedings that have been carried out according to rule; preparations suitable for an affair, occasion or celebration.

กรร gkan *v. arch.* to catch; to capture; to grasp: กงกรร, กรรกง a place or space enclosed (as by a fence or wall): กระ a prefix which is interchangeable with คะ.

กรรกฏักขี see กรรกฏักษ์

กรรกฏักษ์, กรรกฏักขี gkan-gka^4-tak^4-se^2 *n.* the cornea of the eye of a crab.

กรรกร, กรุกร   gkan-gkawn *n.* stone; lime-stone; a mirror; a hammer; salivary calculi; tartar.

กรรกศ, กรกศ   gkan-gkot[4] *P. S. n.* a sword; a dagger: *adj.* low; vulgar; fierce; coarse; cruel; unkind.

กรรไกร, กันไกร, ตะไกร   gkan-gkrai *n. lit.* "a two-bladed cutting implement," *i. e.* scissors.

กรรเจียก, ตรอเจียด   gkan-chje-uk[4] *Camb. n.* the ear; a bouquet worn over the ear: กรรเจียก, ใบกรรเจียก *obs.* the external ear; ear decorations attached to the headdress worn by actors: กรรเจียกจร floral decorations, ear loops, ear coverings or frontlets extending down on either side of the diadem or crown worn by lakhon actors (Ger. 1, p. 22).

กรรชิง, กระฉิง, กระชิง   gkan-ching *n.* a long-handled, tiered umbrella lined with red cloth and carried in processions as insignia or regalia of royalty: กรรชิงเกล็ด, กระฉิงเกล็ด an ancient, tiered umbrella lined with strips of white and blue cloth and used as the above: กนนเชอ, กรรเชอ, กระเชอ a small, close-meshed, bamboo, woven basket with crescent-shaped handle: กรรเช้า, กระเช้า a fine-meshed, woven, bamboo basket (used for washing rice).

กรรโชก, กระโชก, กันโชก gkan-chok[4] *v.* to pounce upon suddenly and secretly; to terrify; to startle by pouncing upon; to threaten, brow-beat or bully: *n.* a person guilty of threatening or brow-beating another (as for revenge): กรรโชกเอาทรัพย์ to extort money or jewelry by pouncing on one unawares.

กรรชั้นน, กระชั้น   gkan-san[5] *v.* to over-take; to come up with (as in a race or walk); to follow in quick succession.

กรรแชง   gkan-saang *adv.* alongside; near-by; cautiously; carefully.

กรรณ, กณณ, กรณ, กรรณา   gkan *P. S. n.* an ear; a rudder; the diameter of a circle; Karna, the king of Anga or Bengal and son of Pritha or Kunti by Surya, the Sun, before her marriage to Pandu. He was half-brother of the Pandavas but not known to them until after his death. Kunti, on one oc-casion, paid such attention to the sage Dur-vasas, that he gave her a charm by virtue of which she might have a child by any god she preferred to invoke. The Sun was chos-en and the result was Karna, who was born equipped with arms and armour. Being afraid of censure and disgrace, the child was exposed on the banks of the Yamuna, where he was found by Nandana or Adhiratha, the charioteer of Dhritarashtra. The charioteer and his wife, Radha, brought him up as their own child and when he grew up Indra disguised himself as a Brahman to cajole him out of his divine cuirass. In return In-dra gave him great strength and a javelin charged with certain death to whomsover it was hurled against (H. C. D. p. 151).

กรรณกษาย, กรรณคูถ, กรรณมล, กรรณวึษ gkan-gka[4]-sai[2] *n.* ear-wax; cerumen.

กรรณกุมาร   gkan-gkoo[4]-ma-re *P. S. n.* an appellation for the wife of Siva, Bhavani or Devi.

กรรณคูถ see กรรณกษาย

กรรณโคจร   gkan-ko-chjawn *n.* the hearing region of the ear; the range of hearing.

กรรณจาม   gkan-chjam *n.* shells strung to-gether and hung on the ears of elephants (as decorations).

กรรณชัป   gkan-chap[6] *n. lit.* "a whisperer in the ear," *i. e.* an informant; one who in-forms; one who purposely implicates another.

กรรณชิต   gkan-chit[6] *n.* he who has over-come Karna in a great war, *i. e.* Phra Arjuna, the third Pandu prince (H.C.D. p. 21).

กรรณดาล   gkan-dan *n.* the flapping of an elephant's ear.

กรรณธาร   gkan-tan *n.* a pilot; a sailor; a seaman; an helmsman.

กรรณธารีณี gkan-ta-ri[6]-ne *n.* a cow elephant.

กรรณบถ gkan-bot[4] *n.* the channel of hearing; the auditory canal.

กรรณบาลี, กรรณลดา, กรรณวัลลี gkan-ba-le *n.* the external ear.

กรรณบุฏ, กรรณวิวร gkan-boot[4] *n.* the external auditory meatus.

กรรณบุรี gkan-boo[4]-re *n.* the capital of Karna now call Bhagalpur, India, located in the province of Bihar and Orissa (I. B. C. p. 423).

กรรณบูร gkan-boon *n.* a floral decoration for the ear.

กรรณมล see กรรณกษาย

กรรณภูษณะ see กรรลังการ

กรรณภูษา see กรรณลังการ

กรรณมูล gkan-moon *n.* the base of the external ear.

กรรณยุคล gkan-yoo[6]-kon *n.* both ears.

กรรณลดา see กรรบาลี

กรรณวัลลี see กรรบาลี

กรรณวิวร see กรรณบุฏ

กรรณวิษ see กรรณกษาย

กรรณา see กรรณ

กรรณาการ์ see กณิการ

กรรณโยนิ gkan-yo-ne[6] *adj. n.* using the ear as a guide; proceeding or directed from the ear (as in archery the arrow leaves from near the ear).

กรรณโรค gkan-rok[3] *n.* diseases of the ear.

กรรณลังการ, กรรณาลงกรณ์, กรรณาภรณ์, กรรณภูษณะ, กรรณภูษา, กรรณโศภน gkan-lang-gkan *n.* an ornament for the ear.

กรรณวงศ์ gkan-wong *n.* a "crow's nest" built of leaves up in a tree (as for shooting purposes); a temporary, roofed platform of bamboo put up in the field for shelter while driving off birds.

กรรณวยาธ gkan-wa[6]-yat[3] *n.* the ceremony of piercing the ears.

กรรณวรรชิต gkan-wan-chit[6] *n.* *lit.* "one without ears," *i. e.* a snake.

กรรณวิษ gkan-wit[6] *adj. lit.* "poisonous, not amiable or agreeable"; displeasing or offensive to the ear (as slang or wrong proverbs).

กรรณศูล gkan-soon[2] *n.* earache from disease.

กรรณโศภน see กรรณลังการ

กรรณอัญชลี gkan-an-cha[6]-le *n.* an ill-formed ear or one tilted upwards.

กรรณา gkan-nah a prefix used in the preceding words; *poetical* the ear.

กรรณานุช, ยุธิษฐิร gkan-na-noot[6] n. the eldest of the five Pandu princes, represented in Indian mythology as the son of Dharma, the god of Justice. With the Hindus he is represented as a man of calm, passionless judgment, strict veracity, unswerving rectitude and rigid justice (H. C. P. p. 378–381).

กรรณารา gkan-na-ra *n.* tools or implements for piercing an elephant's ear.

กรรณาลงกรณ์ see กรรณลังการ

กรรณาภรณ์ see กรรลังการ

กรรณาวธาน gkan-na-wa[6]-tan *n.* the act of giving ear; the act of listening; listening attentively.

กรรณิกา gkan-ni[6]-gka *n.* an ornamental pinnacle for a pagoda or spire; earrings; an ornament for the ears; the pericarp of the lotus.

กรรดึก gkan-duk[4] *P. S. n. lit.* "stars of good omen", *i. e.* the Pleiades or ดาวลูกไก่ composed of six stars. According to Indian legends these represent the six nurses of the god of War, being daughters of a king in one legend but wives of Rishis according to another (H. C. D. p. 169).

กรรดึก, กตติก, การตติก　gkan-duk[4] n. the twelfth month according to the lunar calculations or the month in which the moon is full, near to the Pleiades, viz. October or November.

กรรติเกย, การติเกยะ　gkan-dti[4]-gkay-ya[6] n. the son of Siva; the deity of War (Mars) (H. C. D. p. 152).

กรรไตร see กรรไกร, กันไตร

กรรแทก　gkan-taak[3] v. poetical to hit; to bump against; to collide with.

กรรแทรก　gkan-saak[3] n. a protective division (of soldiers) intervening between the commander and the enemy.

กรรบาลิ see กรรปาลึก

กรรบิด, กัลบิด, กำบิด　gkan-bit[4] v. to cut; to knife; to shave: n. a cutting implement; a knife.

กรรปาสึก, กรรบาลิก　gkan-bpa-lik[6] n. cloth made of the fiber of Indian cotton.

กรรปุร, กโปร　gkan-poo[4]-ra[6] n. the elbow; the forearm; a linear measure; the elbow joint.

กรรพุม, กรรพุ่ม　gkan-poom n. a bunch, cluster or tuft; the position of the hands placed palm to palm and raised to the face or forehead in the attitude of adoration or worship: กรรพุมมาลย์ a cluster of flowers; a bush in bloom.

กรรพุ่ม see กรรพุม

กรรภิรมย์, กรรม์ภิรมย์, กันภิรมย์　gkan-pi[6]-rom n. a set of three, processional, white, five-tiered umbrellas, lined with silk and marked in gold with intricate cabalistic symbols, letters and numbers. These are carried in front of the royal equipage on occasions celebrating a victory. Sometimes these are carried encased in conical red bags.

กรรม์ภิรมย์ see กรรภิรมย์

กรรม, กรรม์　gkam S. (1) n. labour; toil; work; deeds; occupation; acts; office; business; performance: กรรม gram. objective case: กรรมกร an hireling; a labourer; a coolie; workmen: กรรมกรณ์ to inflict punishments by torture: n. instruments of torture or places incarceration for criminals: กรรมกรี female labourers or servants: กรรมกษัย the end or conclusion of a job or task: กรรมการ honorary committee members; committee men: กรรมการก gram. objective case: กรรมการบริษัท directors of a company: กรรมการผู้จัดการ managing directors: กรรมการิณี lady members of a committee; a committee formed of ladies: กรรมกาล the opportune time for a work or act: กรรมกุลก a launderer; a washerman: กรรมขวาต, กรรมมัชวาต an expulsive force originating from within (as pains in travail): กรรมขัย the conclusion of a job, task or undertaking; the duration of a job: กรรมคติ the manner of progress, advancement or skill in performance: กรรมจัณฑาล becoming a rascal or a degraded person (as a result of his actions): กรรมเจษฎา activity; diligence; determination in one's work: กรรมฐาน one of the modes of Buddhist meditation which may be called "analytical meditation". This meditation on the nature of elementary substances leads to a thorough appreciation of their impermanence and unsatisfactoriness (Ala. p. 154). He who exercises it, fixes his mind on any one element and reflects on it in all its conditions and changes until, so far as that element is concerned, he sees that it is only unstable, grievous and illusory (Ala. p. 204): กรรมโทษ actions that are wicked or punishable; sins: กรรมนิพันธ์ desirable results or the fruitage of a job or task: กรรมบถ rules governing the course of action or path of duty: กรรมพันธ์ the bonds of united action: กรรมพันธุ์, พันธุกรรม heredity; transmission of a tendency or trait; transmitted features: กรรม, พิธี rite; form; ritual; ceremony; ordinances (as prescribed by custom): กรรมมรรคา *lit.* "the way of deeds"; the means of salvation by disinterested activity (A. C. p. 353): กรรม ยุค, กลิยุค the fourth or last and most terrible era of the world: กรรมโยนิ the original cause of actions or events; the origin of sinful acts or lustful desires: กรรมวาจา *gram.* passive voice: กรรมวาจา an ecclesiastical edict, notice or proclamation made to an assembly of Buddhist monks (corresponds to a Papal Bull): กรรมวาจารย์ the proclaimer of the notice; one who shares in worship: กรรมวิธี rule of actions or observance; mode of conducting ceremonies: กรรมวิบาก calamity, disaster or perversity of actions; the consequences of human acts as experienced in a subsequent birth; future punishment (as a reward of deeds): กรรมวิเศษ various forms of special work: กรรมศาลา, กรรมสถาน a work-shop: กรรมศีล an assiduous labourer; one who perseveres in his duties regardless of the rewards: กรรมศูร a skilled or efficient workman: กรรมสักขี *lit.* "a witnesser of all (daytime) deeds", *i. e.* the sun: กรรมสัมปาทิก an executive of an association or business: กรรมสัมปาทิกสภา an executive committee or body: กรรมสาธก one who accomplishes his task or duty: กรรมสารถี an assistant; a co-worker; a partner in various acts or deeds: กรรมสิทธิ์ a monopoly; a just claim to ownership; right of ownership to: กรรมสิทธิ์เครื่องหมายและยี่ห้อค้าขาย trade-mark and patent rights: กรรมสิทธิ์ ผู้แต่งหนังสือ a copyright: กรรมหัสต์ efficient; dexterous (in the discharge of duty): ก่อกรรมทำเวร to increase one's future punishment by the continuance of evil deeds: กุศลกรรม meritorious deeds, good works and their rewards: กุศลกรรมบถ rules for the performance of meritorious deeds; rules defining meritorious deeds: คณะกรรมการ a committee: ตามบุญตามกรรม according to one's merit or demerit; " as the case may be ": ถึงแก่กรรม to have passed away: ทาสกรรมกร a slave; a worker without remuneration: วิธีสนากรรมฐาน meditation in quest of knowledge: สมถกรรมฐาน concentrated religious meditation: อกุศลกรรม unmeritorious deeds; evil actions.

(2) fruit, consequences or results of evil thoughts or words in a past existance or that which may follow in a future existance to bring the being into a state of punishment or torment; consequence; fate (Ala. p. 45): causality (A.C.); อกุศลกรรมบถ rules defining or designating non-meritorious deeds.

กรรม์ see **กรรม**

กรรมการ see **กรมการ**

กรรมา, กรรโม gkan-mah prefixes occurring in the following words.

กรรมาชีพ gkan-mah-cheep[3] *n.* ways or means of gaining a livelihood trade; profession.

กรรมาธิการ gkan-mah-ti[6]-gkan *n.* a committee vested with absolute authority to make final decisions; the right of action.

กรรมานุรูป gkan-mah-noo[6]-roop[3] *adj.* appropriate, befitting, suitable (actions, duty, behaviour or function).

กรรมาร gkan-man *n.* a goldsmith; a skilled workman or artizan in gold; a mechanic; a brazier.

กรรโม see **กรรมา**

กรรโมทาร gkan-mo-tan *n.* actions resulting in honour or glory; a display of bravery or magnanimity; prowess.

กรรโมปกรณ์ gkan-mo-bpa[4]-gkon *n.* one rendering assistance or supporting a cause by actual work.

กรรลึง, กระลึง, กระะลิง gkan-lung *v.* to catch; to grasp.

กรรษก, กสิก, กสิกร, กสิการ gkan-sok[4] *n.* a cultivator of the soil; one who lives by tillage of the soil; a farmer.

กรรสะ gkan-sa[4] *v.* to cough (used for royalty).

กรรแสง, กระแสง, กั้นแสง gkan-saang[2] *v. poetical* to project the voice; to cry; to weep.

กรรหาย, กระหาย gkan-hai[2] *v.* to thirst for; to desire; to lust after; to be thirsty or eager for.

กรรเหิม, กระเหิม, เหิม gkan-herm[2] *adj.* haughty; insolent; arrogant.

กรรโหย, โหย gkan-ho-ie[2] *v.* to lament; to wail; to bewail; to moan for.

กรรเอา, กระเอา, (กลมกล่อม) gkan-ow *adj.* complete in all respects; palatable; savoury; delicious (as curry).

กรรุณา, กรุณา gkra[4]-roo[6]-nah *n.* mercy; compassion; pity; the bestowing virtue (which is the leading passion in a Bodhisattva) (A. C. p. 353).

กรวด gkru-at[4] *n.* sea-side pebbles; coarse sand.

กรวด, จรวจ gkru-at[4] *v.* to pour water on (as a token of blessing or consecration); to cut; to slice : *n.* fire-works that shoot up into the air; sky rockets : กรวดน้ำ the ceremonial pouring on of water as a token of respect for the dead (this is the only case in which this combination of words occurs): น้ำตาลกรวด rock-sugar or candy : สูงกรวด rising higher and higher into the air.

กรวน gkru-an *n.* slices of the bulbous roots of *Dioscorea dacmona* or *Dioscorea hispida* (V. P. p. 35).

กรวบ gkru-ap[4] *interj.* an onomatopoeia (as when chewing on a grain of sand or walking on dry leaves).

กรวม (ครอบ) gkru-am *v.* to cover; to encase; to wrap around; to build over : กรวมความ to cover up; to hush up; to suppress a question or matter : กรวมตอ to build a house over the stump of a tree : กรวมทาง, ครอมทาง to bridge over; to build a house over a road or path:

กร้วม gkru-am[3] *interj.* an onomatopoeia (as when a dog grinds, crunches or chews a bone); the sound of the breaking of boards (as in a collision of boats).

กรวย gkru-ay *n.* a cone; a funnel : กรวย, ผีเสื้อหลวง (ต้น), a marsh-growing tree *Casearia kerrii (Samydaceae)* (V. P. p. 34: K.): กรวยเชิง a decorative, fluted, cone-shaped design for the edges of cloth or the tops of pillars and columns : กรวยเหลี่ยม a pyramid : กรวยอุบัชฌาย์ a vessel made of screw pine leaves stitched together. This contains flowers, candles and incense sticks, and is fitted with a conical cover. These are presented as gifts to the officiating Buddhist monk and his colleagues in the ceremony of initiation into the brotherhood : ผ้ากรวยเชิง cloth with conical designs along the edges.

กรวิก, การเวก (นก) P. gka[4]-ra[6]-wik[6] *n.* a bird of fairyland, whose sweet songs charm all the inhabitants of the forest (Ala. p. 309); the Indian cuckoo (S. E. D.).

กรสุทธิ gka[4]-ra[6]-soot[4] *n.* a Brahmanistic hand-cleansing ceremony, which is performed before engaging in any religious rite.

กรอ gkraw (1) *v.* to wind thread on to a spool or bobbin by the use of a machine; to twirl; to twist; to wind; to twine; to brandish a sword, stick or cane : (2) to approach close to (as in the attitude of flirting with or making love to a young lady): *adj.* poor; pitiable; poverty-stricken; moneyless; needy; wretched : กรอฟัน to file off the ends or grind down elongated or irregular teeth by means of a stone or file; to excavate by means of a dental burr.

กร้อ gkraw[3] *n.* a small shovel-like, woven, bamboo basket smeared with dammar and attached to the end of a long pole. This is used as a scoop for removing bilge water from large cargo-boats.

กรอก gkrauk[4] *v.* to pour (a liquid) into a

small aperture (as into the mouth of a bottle); to ingurgitate; to pour into the throat by means of a tube or funnel: กรอกนา to register the area of paddy fields; to enter the Title Deed numbers of fields into a register book: กรอกบัญชี to enter sums of money into an account book; to make a record of some monetary transaction: กรอกยา to pour medicine down the throat (as of horses): พูดกรอกหู to pour words into the ear (as by speaking incessantly).

กรอก gkrauk[4] *adj.* dried till the seeds or kernels can rattle (as peanuts); stunted; dried; lean; small; dwarfed: มะขาม กรอก tamarind pods, dried till the kernels rattle: ยางกรอก (นก) the chestnut bittern *Ardetta cinnamomea* (Gaird. J. S. S. IX, 1, p. 10): ลูกกรอก a still-born child; the child of wicked parents: ไส้กรอก sausages.

กรอกแกรก gkrauk[4]-gkraak[4] *interj.* an onomatopoeia (as when dry leaves are made to grate against each other): *n.* a gambling game.

กร็อกกร่อย gkrauk[4]-gkrau-ie[2] *adj.* impoverished; emaciated; thin; lean; scrawny.

กรอง gkraung (1) *v.* to string together (as beads); to sew or stitch together (as leaves): (2) *v.* to filter; to strain; to separate the liquid portion from the sediment,—the good from the bad: กรองทอง to weave cloth having interwoven threads of gold: กรอง มาลย์ to string flowers together into garlands or wreaths: กรองศอ necklaces: คากรอง the yang-lang grass, stitched or sewed together in strips for clothing or roofing: ปั๊ก กรอง to crochet; to embroider: (3) *Cam. n.* bracelets; anklets; armlets; ornaments: กรองเชิง anklets: กรองได bracelets; wristlets.

กรองกร่อย gkraung-gkrau-ie *adj.* slow; deliberate; tame; docile; gentle.

กรอด gkraut[4] *adj.* thin; emaciated; attenuated; wasted: *interj.* an onomatopoeia (as

when a rat is gnawing a board or as of the grinding of teeth).

กร่อน, ร่อยหรอ, สึกหรอ gkraun[4] *v.* to be worn away through friction; to produce a condition of attrition; to become sunken, smaller or shorter by friction.

กรอบ gkraup[4] *n.* border; frame; edge; margin; a curb or frieze along the top of a wall: *adj.* brittle; crisp; fragile; frail; poor; inferior: กรอบหน้า a coronet having extensions which frame the face.

กรอบแกรบ gkraup[4]-gkraap[4] *adj.* debilitated; exhausted; enervated; weakened (as after a sickness); dried by fire or heat: *interj.* an onomatopoeia (as the crackling of dry leaves): กรอบรูป a picture-frame: กรอบฝา the frame of a partition.

กรอม gkraum *adj.* overhanging in excess of what is necessary; being covered too loosely or too fully; excessive; over-abundant; super-abundant; superfluous: กรอมใจ, ระทมเกินส่วน to be over-burdened with grief, anguish or agony.

กร่อม gkraum[4] *adv.* slowly; deliberately; continuously (descriptive of walking, pumping of water or paddling a boat).

กร้อม (ต้น) gkraum[3] *Xylia kerrii (Leguminosae)*, a large tree yielding a valuable timber (K: cb. p. 546); (*Lythrarieae*).

กร๊อม (ต้น) gkraum[5] *n.* Crypteronia paniculata (*Crypteroniaceae*), a common forest tree. The wood is soft and the fruit poisonous (cb. p. 730: K.).

กร่อย gkrau-ie[4] *adj.* brackish (as water); uninteresting (as a play or some public entertainment); insipid (as fruit); briny.

กระ (เต่า) gkra[4] *n.* the tortoise; the shell of the hawk-bill turtle, the source of the commercial tortoise-shell, *Chelonia imbricata* (webster): *adj.* having or being covered with freckles or spots of discoloured skin: ตกกระ to have freckles; to be covered with variously coloured spots (appearing on the human skin or on the surface of over-ripe fruit).

กระ gkra⁴ (1) occurring as a prefix to words beginning with ก, กำ, กุ, ข, ค, ส, e. g. กทำ=กระทำ: (2) occurring in ancient literature, e.g. ตระกูล= กระกูล, ตระลาการ = กระลาการ: (3) added to some monosyllabic words, e. g. ซุ้ม =กระซุ้ม, โดด=กระโดด, พุ่ม =กระพุ่ม, ยาจก= กระยาจก: (4) used for the sake of euphony and in poetry, e. g. กระกรุ่น, กระเกริก, กระเกรียม, กระเกรียว, กระกลับกลอก, กระเกลือก.

กระกร gkra⁴-gkawn v. to emit rays of light or glory.

กระกรับกระเกรียบ gkra⁴-gkrap⁴-gkra⁴- gkre-ap⁴ adj. rough; tough; hard.

กระก, ตะเคียน gkra⁴-gke³ n. Hopea sp. Hopea odorata (Dipterocarpaceae) (Cb. p. 147: v. P. p. 119: MCM. p. 218): ตะเคียนทราย Shorea sp. (V. P. p. 120): ตะเคียนทอง Hopea odorata (V. P. p. 119): ตะเคียนเผือก Homalium damrongianum (Samydaceae) (Cb. p. 739: V. P. p. 120): ตะเคียนหนู Anogeisus acuminata var. lanceolata (Combretaceae) (Cb. p. 612: V. P. p. 119).

กระกรีด gkra⁴-gkreet⁵ interj. an onomatopoeia (as the screams of a frightened woman).

กระกรุ่น gkra⁴-gkroon⁴ adj. smoking; smouldering (as a smothered fire).

กระเกริก, กะเกริก gkra⁴-gkrerk⁴ interj. an onomatopoeia (as shouting or the sound of tumult caused by a great gathering of people).

กระเกริ่น, กะเกริ่น gkra⁴-gkrern⁴ adj. spreading far and wide (as some rumour).

กระเกรียม, ตระเตรียม gkra⁴-gkre-um v. to make ready; to get ready; to prepare; to equip; to provide in advance : n. preparation.

กระเกรียว gkra⁴-gkre-oh adj. boisterous; tempestuous; noisy; violent.

กระเกรียว gkra⁴-gkre-oh³ adj. ancient

poetic form grinding; grating; rubbing together (as teeth).

กระกลับกลอก gkra⁴-gklap⁴-gklauk⁴ v. to oscillate; to swing or move back and forth; to be unstable; to be inconstant.

กระกูล, ตระกูล gkra⁴-gkoon n. line; lineage; family; pedigree; ancestral line of consanguinity.

กระเกลือก, เกลือก gkra⁴-gklur-uk⁴ v. ancient poetic form to cause to roll, rotate or wallow (as over the floor or like buffaloes in a water-hole).

กระกวด gkra⁴-gkoo-at⁴ adj. high and steep; very tall and slender.

กระคาย, ระคาย gkra⁴-kai adj. rough; jagged; rasping to the fingers.

กระงกกระงั่น, กระงกกระเงิ่น gkra⁴- ngok⁴-gkra⁴-ngan adj. awkward; clumsy; uncouth; unskillful; bungling.

กระงกกระเงิ่น see กระงกกระงั่น

กระง่อนกระแง่น, กะง่อนกะแง่น, ง่อนแง่น gkra⁴-ngaun³-gkra⁴-ngaan³ adj. loose; infirm; liable to fall off; shaky.

กระเง้ากระงอด, กะเง้ากะงอด, เง้าๆงอดๆ gkra⁴-ngow⁵-gkra⁴-ngaut⁴ adj. angered; provoked; irritated; infuriated.

กระโงก, กะโงก Cam. gkra⁴-ngok⁴ n. poetical a peacock.

กระจก, กะจก gkra⁴-chjok⁴ n. glass; crystal; quartz used as an ornament: กระจกเงา a looking-glass; a mirror: กระจกตา the cornea: กระจกส่อง a hand-mirror.

กระจง, กระจร, กะจง, ขจร gkra⁴-chjong n. mouse-deer, a small deer, chevrotain, of the genus Tragulus inhabiting Java, Sumatra and the mainland of Asia. It is noted for its agility and cunning (Gaird. N. H. J. S. S. III, 2, p. 126: webster).

กระจร see กระจง

กระจอก ๎ *Cam.* gkra[4]-chjauk[4] *n. ancient* finger or toe nails; claws : กระจอก (นก) European tree sparrow *Passer montanus* (Gaird. J. S. S. IX, 1, p 3): กระจอกเทศ (นก) Indian house sparrow *Passer indicus (var flavicollis)* (Gaird. J. S. S. IX, 1, p. 3). This name is also applied to the ostrich : กระจอกบ้าน (นก) Malay tree-sparrow *Passer montanus malaccensis.* This is a very common bird in the city and villages but is rarely found in open country any distance from human dwellings (Deig. N. H. J. S. S. VIII, 3, p. 152): *Passer montanus* tree-sparrow (Will. N. H. J. S. S. II, 3, p. 195): กระจอกป่า (นก) the Pegu house-sparrow *Passer flaveolus* (Will. N. H. J. S. S. II, 3, p. 196). This bird is common in the rice-fields, and occasionally is seen or even found breeding close to houses on the outskirts of the city. After the breeding-season, they congregate in flocks of a hundred or more birds, which roost in favoured localities night after night and are very noisy (Deig. N. H. J. S. S. VIII, 3, p. 152): กระจอกพั้ง (นก) Malay weaver-bird *Ploceus atrigula infortunatus* (Deig. N. H. J. S. S. VIII, 3, p. 152): กระจอกหงอน (นก) the crested bunting *Melophus malanicterus* (Deig. N. H. J. S. S. VIII, 3, p. 153).

กระจอกงอกง่อย gkra[4]-chjauk[4]-ngauk[4]-ngau-ie[4] *adj.* limping; lame; hobbling; disabled; crippled : แมวกระจอก a species of large, black cat with yellow eyes.

กระจองอแง gkra[4]-chjaw-ngaw-ngaa *adj.* annoying (in manners, utterances and language); crying, bawling or screaming (as infants): ลูกกระจองอแง peevish, ill-natured babies.

กระจอนหู gkra[4]-chjaun-hoo[2] *n.* an earring.

กระจ้อน, กะจ้อน gkra[4]-chjaun[3] *n.* a species of rodent resembling a chipmunk : *adj.* small; dwarfish; diminutive.

กระจ้อย, กระจ้อยร่อย, กะจ้อยร่อย gkra[4]-chjoy[3] *adj.* small; tiny; diminutive.

กระจะ, กะจะ gkra[4]-chja[4] *adj.* clear; distinct; plain; obvious.

กระจั๊ก gkra[4]-chjak[4] *adj. poetical* serrated; notched like a saw.

กระจั๊ง, กะจั๊ง gkra[4]-chjang *n.* a decorative design used for edgings of shelves and along the base of pulpits. These are carved or chased in the shape of upright leaves : กะจั๊ง (ปลาตื๋น) mud gobies having the pectoral fins developed as feet, and commonly seen at low-tide moving along mud-flats bordering the canals, *Periophthalmodon schlosseri* (Dept. Agri. & Fisheries).

กระจัด gkra[4]-chjat[4] *v.* to drive out; to cause to separate from among; to be dispersed.

กระจัดกระจาย gkra[4]-chjat[4]-gkra[4]-chjai *adj.* scattered; dissipated; disseminated.

กระจัดพลัดพราย gkra[4]-chjat[4]-plat[6]-prai *v.* to be separated or lost from others.

กระจับ see กะจับ

กระจับบัง, กะจับบัง gkra[4]-chjap[4]-bping[3] *n. ancient spelling* a "fig leaf" worn by young girls.

กระจับบั, กะจับบั gkra[4]-chjap[4]-bpee[4] *n.* a four-stringed lute played by pinching, scraping or twanging the strings.

กระจ่า, กะจ่า, gkra[4]-chja[4] *n.* a large-sized ladle or spoon, made of a section of the coconut shell, fitted with a long, flat handle. The handle end is used for stirring, while the spoon end is used for dishing out rice or curry from a pot.

กระจ่าง, กะจ่าง gkra[4]-chjang[4] *adj.* clear; transparent; limpid; unclouded; unobscured : กระจ่าง *ancient spelling* : เห็นกระจ่าง to see clearly; to understand fully.

กระจาด, กะจาด gkra[4]-chjat[4] *n.* a basket for vegetables; a market basket; the gifts presented to Buddhist monks after the preaching of a sermon : กระจาดผ้าบ่า monks' robes and other gifts hung on a small tree placed in a huge, specially-woven basket, and carried in procession to some Buddhist temple or to present to some special priest. This ceremony is observed after Lent : งานกระจาดใหญ่ the gifts designed to be presented to a Crown Prince who has entered the Buddhist Priesthood as a novice. These are presented immediately after the sermon which follows the tonsorial ceremony : ทิ้งกระจาด to give alms according to Chinese custom by placing the gifts in woven baskets, which are thrown to the waiting crowd.

กระจาบ, กะจาบ (นก) gkra⁴-chjap⁴ *n.* the baya or weaver bird *Ploceus Baya*. The male in winter loses the yellow plumage on the head and is then known as the "paddy bird" (Gaird. J. S. S. IX, 1, p. 4); the eastern baya or weaver bird *Ploceus philippinus passerinus* (Herb. N. H. J. S. S. VI, 1, p. 115): กระจาบขี้หมู (นก) Hodgson's munia *Uroloncha acuticauda* (Herb. N. H. J. S. S. VI, 1, p. 121): the spotted munia *Uroloncha punctulata* (Will. N. H. J. S. S. II, 3, p. 194): กระจาบญี่ปุ่น (นก) the golden weaver-bird *Ploceella javanensis* (Herb. N. H. J. S. S. VI, 1, p. 119): กระจาบฝน (นก) the Formosan sky-lark *Alauda gulgula sala* (Will. N. H. J. S. S. II, 3, p. 205); the Bangkok white-tailed bush-lark *Mirafra cantillans williamsoni* (Will. N. H. J. S. S. II, 3. 207): กระจาบฝนเล็บยาว (นก) the Hainan sky-lark *Alauda gulgula sala* (Herb. N. H. J. S. S. VI, 2, p. 216): กระจาบฝนเล็บสั้น (นก) the Bangkok white-tailed bush-lark *Mirafra cantilans williamsoni* (Herb. N. H. J. S. S. VI, 2, p. 217): กระจาบฝนหางยาว (นก) the Malayan pipit *Anthus richardi malayensis* (Herb. N. H. J. S. S. VI, 2, p. 215): กระจาบหัวโต (นก) the brown shrike *Lanius cristatus* (Will. N. H. J. S. S. I, 2, p. 90): กระจาบหัวเหลือง (นก) the eastern baya or weaver-bird *Ploceus megarhynchus* (Will. N. H. J. S. S. II, 3, p. 191): กระจาบหัวเหลืองอกลาย (นก) the striated weaver-bird *Ploceus manyar* (Will. N. H. J. S. S. II, 3, p.

192): กระจาบอกฐานแดง หรือแดงครุ (นก) the chestnut-bellied munia, *Munia atricapilla rubronigra* (Herb· N. H. J. S. S. VI, 1, p. 121).

กระจาย gkra⁴-chjai *v.* to be dispersed ; to be scattered ; to be dispelled ; to be spread about or diffused : used in the combination กระจัดกระจาย for the sake of euphony but with no change in meaning : กระจายเสียง to broad-cast by means of a loud-speaker (either by radio or gramophone) : กระจายหางดอก a species of aquatic plant bearing flowers and pods similar to ผักบุ้ง *Ipomoea aquatica*. The seeds are ground and mixed with arrack and used as a cure for tiger, crocodile and mad-dog bites.

กระจิก an euphonic suffix for กระจุก.

กระจิง used with กระจุ่ง for euphony.

กระจิด gkra⁴-chjit⁴ *adj.* little ; small.

กระจิบ gkra⁴-chjip⁴ *n.* the smallest-sized cup for drinking or sipping.

กระจิบ, กะจิบ (นก) gkra⁴-chjip *n.* small warblers, titmice and wrens (Gaird. J. S. S. IX, 1, p. 1); the Malay tailor-bird *Orthotomus sutorius maculicollis* (Herb. N. H. J. S. S. VI, 1, p. 98): กระจิบกระไช (นก) the Indian tailorbird *Orthotomus sutorius* (Will. N. H. J. S. S. I, 2, p. 84): กระจิบกระไชคอดำ (นก) the blackthroated tailor-bird *Orthotomus atrigularis* (Will. N. H. J. S. S. I, 2, p. 85): กระจิบแกลบ (นก) the yellow-breasted sun-bird *Cinnyris flammaxillaris* (Gaird. J. S. S. IX, 1, p. 3): กระจิบคอดำ (นก) the black-necked tailor-bird *Orthotomus atrigularis* (Herb. N. H. J. S. S. VI, 1, p. 99): กระจิบสีถั่ว (นก) the common iora *Aegithina tiphia* (Will. N. H. J. S. S. I, 2, p. 78): กระจิบสวน (นก) the Siam scarlet-backed flowerpecker *Dicaeum cruentatum siamensis* (Herb. N. H. J. S. S. VI, 3, p, 294): กระจิบหางพัด (นก) the streaked fantail warbler *Cisticola juncidis cursitans* (Deig. N. H. J. S. S. VIII, 3, p. 149): กระจิบหางแพน (นก) the rufous fantail warbler *Cisticola cisticola cursitans* (Herb. N. H. J. S. S.

VI, 1, p. 100): กระจิบหางยาว (นก) the Siamese wren warbler *Prinia inornata herberti* (Herb. N. H. J. S. S. VI, 1, p. 105): กระจิบหางเรียว (นก) the Burmese wren warbler *Prinia blanfordi* (Will. N. H. J. S. S. 1, 2, p. 88).

กระจิบ   an euphonic suffix for กระจุบ.

กระจิม   used in euphonic combination with กระจุ่ม.

กระจิริด, กะจิริด   gkra⁴-chji⁴-rit⁶ *adj.* small; undeveloped (as infants or the young of animals); tiny; diminutive.

กระจี้, กะจี้, กะกลิ้ง, โกฐกะกลิ้ง   gkra⁴-chjee³ *n. Strychnos,* a genus of *loganiaceous* tropical trees (Med. Dict.). This plant is the source of strychnin, a white, bitter, poisonous crystalline alkaloid.

กระจี้   used in euphonic combination with กระจุ้.

กระจุก, กะจุก   gkra⁴-chjook⁴ *n.* a collection or mass of similar articles; a bunch (of grass); a tuft (of hair).

กระจุกกระจิก   gkra⁴-chjook⁴-gkra⁴-chjik⁴ *adj.* small; miscellaneous; trifling; insignificant (articles).

กระจุยกระจาย   gkra⁴-chjoo-ie-gkra⁴-chjai *adj.* scattered; dispersed; dissipated; disarranged; placed in a confused manner.

กระจุ่งกระจิ่ง, กะจุ่งกะจิ่ง   gkra⁴-chjoong²-gkra⁴-chjing² *adj.* slight; trifling but pleasing (descriptive of sounds).

กระจุบ, กะจุบ   gkra⁴-chjoop⁴ *n.* the chimney holder of a lamp; the burning point of a lamp; a cup, bottle or tin, used as a lamp.

กระจุบกระจิบ   gkra⁴-chjoop⁴-gkra⁴-chjip⁴ *adj.* small; trifling; unimportant (descriptive of household or family duties); a little at a time; nibbling (as at food).

กระจุ่มกระจิ่ม, กะจุ่มกะจิ่ม   gkra⁴-chjoom²-gkra⁴-chjim² *adj.* small, delicate but beautiful

(descriptive of jewelry, pottery etc.).

กระจุย, กะจุย, กระจุยกระจาย   gkra⁴-chjoo-ie *adj.* scattered; dissipated; diffused; dispersed.

กระจู้, กะจู้, อีจู้   gkra⁴-chjoo³ *n.* a bottle-shaped eel-trap made of woven bamboo strips.

กระจู้กระจี้, กะจู้กะจี้   gkra⁴-chjoo²-gkra⁴-chjee² *v.* to speak in whispers; to speak softly together (as on terms of intimacy).

กระจูด (ต้น)   gkra⁴-chjoot⁴ *n. Lepironia mucronata (Cyperaceae)* (K.), a sedge having round, hollow stems and growing in ponds or marshes. It is dried and used for weaving into cheap mats: เสื่อกระจูด mats woven with this kind of sedge.

กระเจอะกระเจิง see กระเจิดกระเจิง

กระเจา, กะเจา   gkra⁴-chjow *n. Corchorus capsularis, Corchorus olitorius (Tiliaceae)* (K.: cb. p. 192), two well-known jute plants. Both plants yield a fibre known as jute, used for the manufacture of gunny bags and cheap cordage. They are indigenous to tropical Asia and are seen in Siam as paddy-field weeds. They are the cheapest fibre and can be obtained in large quantities by cultivation. The former bears fruit about ½ inch long and the latter about two inches or longer: ปอกะเจา a valuable fibre obtained from the stems of several varieties of this annual plant with long, erect, thin stems and yellow flowers. The plant is indigenous to Siam, India and Malaya: ปอที่ฟอกแล้ว cleaned jute fibre. The fibre when spun is extensively used for making cordage, carpets, fishing nets and gunny-bags (MCM. p. 421): ปอที่ยังไม่ได้ฟอก uncleaned jute fibre.

กระเจาะ, กะเจาะ   gkra⁴-chjau⁴ *adj.* having an opacity, scar, ulcer or spots on the cornea: ตากระเจาะ an eye afflicted with an ulcer or opacity: เบี้ยกระเจาะ small cowry shells.

กระเจิง, กะเจิง   gkra⁴-chjerng *adj.* having

strayed; straying; having become separated from; separated; disconnected: กะเจิงอยู่ to be or remain in a separated condition or position: ตื่นกะเจิง to become scared and stampede: เที่ยวกะเจิง to wander about separately.

กระเจิดกระเจิง, กะเจิดกะเจิง, กระเจอะ กระเจิง, กะเจอะกะเจิง gkra[4]-chjert[4]-gkra[4]-chjerng *adj.* strayed off; separated from companions (descriptive of excited cattle on a ranch): เที่ยวกระเจิดกระเจิง to wander about in an excited manner (as one having lost the way).

กระเจียง, กะเจียง (ต้น) gkra[4]-chje-ung[3] *n. Dendrobium coelogyne (Ochidaceae)* (V. P. p. 15).

กระเจียบขาว, กระเจียบแดง, กระเจียบ เปรี้ยว gkra[4]-chjee-ap[5]-kow[2] *n. Hibiscus sabdariffa (Malvaceae)*, rozelle, an annual shrub, 6 to 8 feet high, native of the West Indies. It is cultivated in most warm countries (sometimes as an inter-crop), for the sake of its large, fleshy sepals, which remain after the flowers fall away and become enlarged and succulent (accrescent), enclosing the fruit capsule. These make excellent jelly. In an unripe state, the fruit is made into pickles, and a refreshing beverage called "sorrel-drink" is also prepared from it. The young, tender, acid leaves are sometimes used as a vegetable in curries (MCM. p. 264): กระเจียบมอญ *Hibiscus esculentus (Malvaceae) Okra* or *Ochro*, an erect annual of the "shoe-flower" family, 4 to 6 feet or more high, bearing large, roundish or palmate leaves and erect, horn-like pods, 5 to 8 inches long. When young, these are an agreeable mucilaginous vegetable, much relished when boiled and served either in salads or in soup. As the pods approach maturity they become fibrous and inedible (MCM. p. 304).

กระเจียบแดง see **กระเจียบขาว**

กระเจียบเปรี้ยว see **กระเจียบขาว**

กระเจียว, กะเจียว gkra[4]-chjee-oh *n. Curcuma domestica (Zingiberaceae)* (MCM. p. 342); turmeric *Curcuma*. This name is applied to several species of *Curcuma* belonging to the ginger family (K.). It is a perennial herb about 2 to 3 feet high, cultivated throughout tropical Asia. The tuberous rhizomes are of a bright orange-yellow colour, having a waxy, resinous consistency. They are ground into a fine powder which has an aromatic taste somewhat resembling ginger. It is commonly used as a condiment in cookery and is a prominent constituent of curry powders, and is also employed as a dye for cotton cloth and silks. Medicinal properties are ascribed to the rhizomes (MCM. p. 342).

กระแจะ, กะแจะ gkra[4]-chjaa[4] *n.* sachet powder; perfume powder; odorous pastes (Ger. (1) p. 71): กระแจะ, ข้างน้าว, ตาลกด, ตาล เหลือง *Limonia acidissima (Rutaceae)*. The leaves and bark are used as fomentations for rheumatic pains: กระแจะตะนาว sachet powder from Tenasserim, also used medicinally.

กระโจน, กะโจน, กระโดด, กะโดด, กระ- โตน gkra[4]-chjone *v.* to jump; to leap over; to move by bounds; to leap; to pounce upon.

กระโจม, กะโจม gkra[4]-chjome *v.* to surround; to reach over; to cross over (as with the arms): *n.* a tent; a pavillion; a temporary canopy for giving vapour baths: กระโจม กระจาม, กะโจมกะจาม to be rude or to use impolite manners; to be inconsiderate of others: กระโจมไฟ a light-house: กระโจมมอก to wear the loin cloth about the breast or chest: เข้ากระโจม to take vapour baths: ผ้ากระโจม a tent cloth: โรงหีบสามกระโจม a cane-mill having three canepresses.

กระฉอก, กะฉอก gkra[4]-chauk[4] *v.* to shake; to spill over by agitation: *adj.* fissured; having crevices or breaches; recessive or having a tendency to recede (as hair leaving a high forehead): กระฉอกกระแฉก to spill over by violent agitation: ละลอก กระฉอกไป to be shaken by small waves.

กระฉ่อน, กะฉ่อน gkra[4]-chaun[4] *adj.* shaking; tremulous; reverberating: เดินกระฉ่อน to walk agitatedly: ลือกระฉ่อน far-spreading news or rumours.

กระฉับกระเฉง, กะฉับกะเฉง gkra[4]-chap[4]-gkra[4]-cheng[2] *adv.* adroitly; efficiently; dexterously.

กระฉิ่ง, กรรชิง, กระชิง gkra[4]-ching[4] *n.* a ceremonial, fringed sunshade (carried in processions to designate rank).

กระฉีก, กะฉีก gkra[4]-cheek[4] *n.* a tasty sauce made of grated coconut and sugar, used as a filling for sweetmeats or frosting on glutinous rice, when eaten as dessert.

กระฉูด, กะฉูด, ฉูด gkra[4]-choot[4] *v.* to spring up; to burst forth from.

กระเฉง an euphonic suffix for กระฉับ.

กระเฉด, กะเฉด, ผักรู้นอน gkra[4]-chet[4] *n.* a watercress eaten as salad: กระเฉด (ผัก) *Neptunia oleracea (Leguminosae)* (V. P. p. 3 : K.), a floating aquatic plant, common in tanks throughout Siam and India. It is eaten as a pot-herb, and the pods sometimes as a vegetable. The plant is also used as a refrigerant and astringent in medicine (Dept. Agri. & Fisheries p. 348).

กระแฉก an euphonic suffix for กระฉอก.

กระโฉม, กะโฉม, โฉม gkra[4]-chome[2] *n.* a fragrant vegetable, used medicinally.

กระชดกระช้อย, กะชดกะช้อย gkra[4]-chot[6]-gkra[4]-chauy[5] *adj.* bashful; coy (as of girls); silly; adroit; affected; amorous or flirting (as mannerisms sometimes seen in actresses).

กระชวย an euphonic suffix for กระชุ่ม.

กระชอน, กะชอน gkra[4]-chaun *n.* a square-shaped sieve made of closely-woven, fine strands of bamboo, used for straining grated coconut; a colander: กระชอน (แมง) a beetle of the genus *Gryllotalpa*; mole cricket (Webster).

กระชอม gkra[4]-chaum *adj. ancient spelling* much; large; abundant (descriptive of a pile of vegetables or cabbage heads).

กระช้อย, ชดช้อย gkra[4]-chauy[5] *adj.* being curved upwards: ช้อยชด graceful (in form or action); easy in manner: ช้อยนางรำ a plant, the leaves of which are continually waving (as if they were dancing) *Desmodium gyrans* (K.).

กระช้อย an euphonic suffix for กระชด.

กระชัง, กะชัง gkra[4]-chang *n.* a hinged, weather-shield placed in front of market stalls; a bamboo container for keeping fish in water. It is either hung from the side, or let trail along from the stern of a boat.

กระชั้น see กรรชั้นน

กระชั้น, กะชั้น gkra[4]-chan[5] *adj.* being placed too close or too near together (as two dates); being pushed forward, hastened or accelerated: ถีกระชั้นกันนัก following in too close succession: วิ่งไล่กระชั้นเข้ามานัก pursuing very closely; the race or chase has been a very close one.

กระชั้น an euphonic suffix for กระโชก.

กระชับ, กะชับ gkra[4]-chap[6] *v.* to be fastened closely and firmly together; to make or place so as to fit closely together (as the edges of two boards): (ต้น) *n. Xanthium strumarium (Compositae)* (K.); cockle-burr (McM. p. 477: V. P. p. 3), an herb, the fruit of which is covered with small hooks or burrs. It has medicinal properties.

กระชาก, กะชาก gkra[4]-chak[3] *v.* to jerk with force; to jerk vigorously; to move with jerks: *n.* a short, sharp pull; a twitch.

กระชาย, กะชาย (ต้น) gkra[4]-chai *n.*

Kaempferia pandurata (Zingiberaceae) (V. P. p. 3 : K.), a rhizome of the ginger family, used in curry or as a remedy.

กระชิง see **กรรชิง, กระฉิ่ง**

กระชาเดิม gkra[4]-cha-derm *n.* a stall or floating-house store where perfumes, toilet powders or odorous pastes are sold.

กระชิด, ชิด gkra[4]-chit[6] *adj.* very near ; adjoining ; intimate.

กระชุ, กะชุ gkra[4]-choo[6] *n.* a crate made of loosely woven strips of bamboo, used for carrying coarse articles like cotton pods.

กระชุ่มกระชวย, กะชุ่มกะชวย gkra[4]-choom[3]-gkra[4]-choo-ey *adj.* strong ; healthy ; robust ; sturdy ; sound ; vigorous.

กระเชอ gkra[4]-chur *n.* a general name for small baskets made of inter-woven bamboo strips, and having a wide mouth and tapering to a square bottom. These are carried on the hip by women of the north, and used as market baskets : กระเชอก้นรั่ว *simile* wasteful ; lavish ; squandering.

กระเช้า gkra[4]-chow[5] *n.* a flower-basket ; a hanging orchid-basket ; a general name for fancy baskets of varying sizes, made of interwoven bamboo strips, and having a crescent-shaped handle : กระเช้า, กระเจา(ต้น) *Holoptelea integrifolia (Ulmaceae)* (V.P. p. 16), "fly-catching plants", a remarkable family of plants, mostly climbers, with variously shaped flowers which, in some species, are very large. Most of them have an offensive odour which attracts flies. In many species, the flowers are adapted to entrap these which, once inside, are unable to escape, owing chiefly to the numerous hairs in the tube, all pointing inward (MCM. p. 464) ; *Aristolochia indica, Aristolochia roxburghiana* (V. P. p. 3 : MCM. p. 55, 159).

กระเชียง, กรรเชียง gkra[4]-che-ung *n.* an oar ; the European oar, where the oarsman is seated facing backward while he pulls the oar

forward : กระเชียงปูทะเล the paddle-like legs or appendages of a crab : ตีกระเชียง to use the กระเชียง : หูกระเชียง an oar-lock ; the noose attaching the oar to the post which serves the purpose of an oar-lock.

กระแชง, กะแชง gkra[4]-chaang *n.* leaves of the various species of the *Pandanus furcatus, Pandanus leram,* the screw-pine, which are sewed together for portable roofing purposes (MCM. p. 102, 153).

กระโชก gkra[4]-chok[3] *v.* to frighten ; to startle ; to pounce upon ; to appear suddenly (as by leaping from a hiding place) : กระโชก กระชั้น, กระโชกกระชาก angrily ; boisterously ; intimidatingly : ขู่กระโชก to intimidate : พูดกระโชกกระชาก to speak angrily ; to intimidate by talking loudly.

กระซวย an euphonic suffix for กระซิก.

กระซ้อ an euphonic suffix for กระซี้.

กระซาบ an euphonic suffix for กระซิบ.

กระซิก, กะซิก gkra[4]-sik[6] *v.* to edge one's way gradually into : กระซิกๆ an onomatopoeia (as sobbing with quick respirations) : กระซิกกระซี้, กะซิกกะซี้ to jest ; to joke with or about ; to banter ; to speak or do in a joking manner : ร้องให้กระซิกๆ to sob ; to weep with quick inspirations.

กระซิบ, กระซิบกระซาบ, กระซุบกระซิบ, กะซุบกะซิบ gkra[4]-sip[6] *v.* to whisper ; to speak softly.

กระซุบกระซิบ see **กระซิบ**

กระซี้กระซ้อ gkra[4]-se[5]-gkra[4]-saw[5] *adv.* confidentially ; privately ; secretly (descriptive of conversations in order to allure or entice another).

กระซุ้ม, ซุ้ม gkra[4]-soom[5] *n.* an arbour ; a bower ; an archway covered with vines or decorated with leaves : ซุ้มประตู the lintel of a door.

กระชู่ gkra[4]-soo[3] n. the Asiatic two-horned rhinoceros *Rhinoceros sumatrensis* (Gaird. N. H. J. S. S. III, 2, p. 125).

กระเซ็น, กะเซ็น gkra[4]-sen v. to splash up (as spray); to dash against; to bespatter (as by rain).

กระเซอ, กะเซอ gkra[4]-sur *adj.* stupid; erratic; eccentric; absent-minded; untrained; uncouth.

กระเซอะกระเซอ, กะเซอะกะเซอ gkra[4]-sur[6]-gkra[4]-sue v. to manifest stupidity, ignorance or absent-mindedness.

กระเซ้า, กะเซ้า, กระเซ้ากระชี้ gkra[4]-sow[5] v. to talk teasingly or banteringly; to annoy by continual nagging.

กระเซ้ากระชี้ see กระเซ้า

กระเชิง, กะเชิง gkra[4]-serng v. to lift; to raise; to elevate; to praise: n. a thicket; a place grown up with weeds or covered with leaves; hair that is tousled: *adj.* untidy (as hair); dilapidated (as ruins); overgrown (as with weeds).

กระเชิง an euphonic suffix for กระเซอะ.

กระแซ, กะแซ gkra[4]-saa n. citizens of Manipur, a province of Assam.

กระแซง, กรรแทรก, บังแทรก gkra[4]-saang n. a circular, state sun-shade placed on a long staff and carried in processions as an insignia of rank. This particular sun-shade is of lesser size, has an embroidered body with serrated edges, and is placed perpendicularly on the end of the staff.

กระแซะ, กะแซะ gkra[4]-saa[6] v. to edge up close together gradually; to push gradually in closer; to edge one's way through a crowd.

กระโชกกระเช gkra[4]-so-gkra[4]-say *adj.* leaning; staggering; reeling.

กระฎี, กุฎี gkra[4]-de n. an abode for temple monks; a house of a single room; a dwelling; a shanty; a cottage; a hut; a hovel.

กระฎุมพี, กุฎุมพี gkra[4]-doom-pe n. an householder; a squire; the head of a family; a man of property; a wealthy person; the man of a house or home; an overseer of a village or plantation; a citizen.

กระดก, กะดก gkra[4]-dok[4] v. to teeter; to be higher on one side or corner than on the other: กระดานกระดก a see-saw.

กระดกกระดนโด่, กะดกกะดนโด่ gkra[4]-dok[4]-gkra[4]-don-do[4] v. to lie or rest unevenly: *adj.* uneven; not level; rocking; teetering.

กระดก, ตระหนก *ancient poetical form.*

กระด้ง, กะด้ง gkra[4]-dong[3] n. a wide, flat, shallow basket, used in winnowing rice; กระด้งมอญ a larger sized winnowing basket which was originally used by the Mons.

กระดวง, กะดวง, กราดวง gkra[4]-doo-ang *adj.* stunted, dwarfed, undeveloped (descriptive of coconuts when cut in half and used to scour the floor).

กระดวน, กะดวน gkra[4]-du-en v. to poke or prod (as a stick into a hole).

กระด้วมกระเดี้ยม, กะด้วมกะเดี้ยม gkra[4]-doo-am[3]-gkra[4]-dee-am[3] v. to walk slowly; to walk with difficulty (as of one just recovering from sickness): *adj.* toddling; waddling; clumsy.

กระดอ, กะดอ gkra[4]-dau n. the penis.

กระดอง, กะดอง gkra[4]-daung n. carapace; a hard shell or case; the covering of a crab or tortoise.

กระดองหาย, ดองหาย gkra[4]-daung-hai[2] n. an implement for spreading straw out on the threshing floor (as a pitchfork).

กระดอน, กะดอน gkra[4]-daun v. to rebound; to recoil; to be deflected; to glance from a surface: ลูกปืนกระดอน the bullet ricochetted.

กระดอม, กะดอม gkra[4]-daum n. a climbing plant with five-sided stems and four-sided, bitter fruit, which is used medicinally, *Gymnopetalum cochinchinense* (V. P. p. 7: cb. p. 755 : K.).

กระดักกระเดี้ย, กะดักกะเดี้ย gkra[4]-dak[4]-gkra[4]-dee-ah[3] *adj.* weak; feeble; infirm; debilitated.

กระดังงา, กะดังงา gkra[4]-dang-nga *n.* a tree or vine with scented flowers, growing in clusters: กระดังงาจีน *Artabotrys odoratissimus* (*Anonaceae*) (cb. p. 34: V. P. p. 35 : K.): กระดังงาแดง *Leea sp.* (V. P. p. 5), a species of small tree or shrub belonging to the natural order *Ampelideae*, which comprises about twenty-five species, most abundant in the tropics (Dept. Agri. & Fisheries p. 616): กระดังงาเถา *Artabotrys siamensis* (*Anonaceae*) (cb. p. 35), a woody climber found in mixed forests (K.): กระดังงาไทย *Canangium odoratum* (*Anonaceae*) (K.), ylang-ylang or ilang-ilang, a large quick-growing tree, 70 to 80 feet high, cultivated for the large greenish-yellow flowers which are strongly scented and yield, by distillation, the popular scent ylang-ylang or ilang-ilang (MCM. p. 458): กระดังงาป่า *Duabanga sonneratioides* (*Sonneratiacea*) (cb. p. 730), a lofty, deciduous tree with light-brown bark, peeling off in thin flakes. The wood is grey, often streaked with yellow, is soft and takes a good polish. It neither warps nor splits and is used for tea boxes (Dept. Agri. & Fisheries p. 196): กระดังงาสงขลา *Canangium fruticosum* (*Anonaceae*) (V. P. p. 5 : K.).

กระดาก, กะดาก gkra[4]-dak[4] *v.* to be abashed; to feel timid; to be easily frightened; to be too shy to proceed (as of girls in a public performance): *adj.* abashed; timid; shy; shrinking from danger or publicity; easily frightened.

กระดางลาง, กะดางลาง, หนุ่มกระดางลาง gkra[4]-dang-lang *adj.* shameless; clownish; rude.

กระด้าง, กะด้าง gkra[4]-dang[3] *v.* to become hardened or callous: *adj.* obstinate; indifferent (as to warning or instruction): กระด้างกระเดื่อง, กะด้างกะเดอง to be unyielding to entreaty or supplication; to become obstinate or contrary; to become disloyal.

กระดาด, กะดาด (ต้น) gkra[4]-dat[4] *n. Colocasia antiquorum, Alocasia (Xanthosoma) indica* (V. P. p. 6), two distinct forms of tuberous, herbaceous, perennial plants with large handsome leaves, long cultivated in tropical countries. The stems and rootstocks are edible when cooked (as in curries). The characteristic difference between the two is that the former has peltate leaves, *i. e.* the stalk is attached at or near the center of the lower surface of the leaf, while the latter has arrow-shaped leaves with the stalk joined at the leaf-base, as in ordinary leaves (MCM. p. 295).

กระดาน, กะดาน, ขะดาน gkra[4]-dan *n.* a plank; a board; a game (played on a board, as chess): กระดานชะนวน a slate for writing purposes: กระดานดำ a blackboard: กระดานถีบ a long, thin, narrow board curved and pointed at one end and used for sliding over mud banks. A mud-sled, on which the rider kneels on one knee, using the other foot to propel it: กระดานไฟ a bed or board on which a woman lies by the fire after parturition: กระดานลงหลุม a plank used by the Brahmins as a seat for those who swing in the annual Swinging Ceremony. After the ceremony is over this board is lowered, removed from the place of swinging, and buried at a Brahmin temple until needed again: กระดานสกา a board used in a game of Siamese backgammon which is played by two parties, the pieces being moved according to the numbers appearing on the dice thrown: กระดานหก a teeter-totter board; a balanced plank; a see-saw board: กระดานหมากรุก a chess board.

กระดาษ gkra[4]-dat[4] *n.* paper: กระดาษ ข่อย, กระดาษเพลา, กระดาษสา paper made from the fibre of *Streblus asper*: กระดาษเงิน,

กระดาษทอง silver and gold paper, scattered by the Chinese along the route of a funeral procession: กระดาษซับ blotting paper: กระดาษน้ำตะโก variously coloured papers, used for decorative purposes: กระดาษน้ำส้ม Chinese paper made from bamboo fibre: กระดาษฟาง Chinese straw-fibre paper: กระดาษว่าว Chinese, thin, tough paper, used in making kites.

กระดิก, กะดิก gkra[4]-dik[4] v. to move (as fingers or toes); to shake; to tremble (as leaves); to fidget; to move restlessly; to have the "fidgets": กระดิกหู to hear; to know what is being said: ไม่กระดิกหู inattentive.

กระดิ่ง, กะดิ่ง gkra[4]-ding[4] n. a hand-bell; a cow-bell.

กระดึง an euphonic suffix for กระตุ้ง.

กระดิบ, กะดิบ gkra[4]-dip[4] adj. slow; tardy.

กระดี่, กะดี่ (ปลา) gkra[4]-de[4] n. a species of fresh-water fish Trichopodus trichopterus (Dept. Agri. & Fisheries p. 5); Trichopodus maculatus (M. C. vipulya N. H. J. S. S. VI, 2, p. 225): กระดี่ชุง to raise a log by the use of a lever: กระดี่นาง (ปลา) Trichopodus leeri (Sunder Lal Hora, N. H. J. S. S. VI, 2, p. 182): Trichopodus microlepis (Dept. Agri. & Fisheries p. 5): กระดี่หม้อ (ปลา) Trichopodus trichopterus (Sunder Lal Hora, N. H. J. S. S. VI. 2, p. 182): Trichogaster trichopterus (H. M. S.).

กระดี้กระเดียม, กะดี้กะเดียม gkra[4]-de[3]-gkra[4]-de-um v. to be ticklish; to be easily excited by a touch: adj. ticklish; liable to be upset by a touch or tickle.

กระดึง, กะดึง gkra[4]-deung n. a small cylindrically-shaped bell, hung along the eaves of many Buddhist temples. Appended to the clapper is a metal leaf resembling the leaf of the bodhi: กระดึงช้าง Trichosanthes quinquangulata (Cucurbitaceae) (cb. p. 753), a climber growing over bushes along streams in evergreen forests. The flowers are white and the fruit

like scarlet globes: กระดิ่งพระราม Nepenthes distillatoria (Nepenthaceae) (MCM. p. 130, 141, 465), a species of fly-catcher or pitcher-plant. The leaf tips, by a prolongation of the midrib, are modified into curious pitcher-like structures, each with a lid at the top.

กระดุกกระดิก, กะดุกกะดิก gkra[4]-dook[4]-gkra[4]-dik[4] v. to move (as fingers or toes); to tremble (as leaves); to fidget; to move restlessly; to have the "fidgets".

กระดุ้งกระดิ้ง, กะดุ้งกะดิ้ง gkra[4]-doong[3]-gkra[4]-ding[3] adj. swaying; swaggering; strutting; bombastic in style (descriptive of a dude or flapper walking).

กระดุบ gkra[4]-doop[4] v. to move or to go slowly.

กระดุบกระดิบ, กะดุบกะดิบ, กระดุบกระดุบ gkra[4]-doop[4]-gkra[4]-dip[4] v. to wriggle; to squirm about; to wiggle; to creep imperfectly (as when an animal is injured).

กระดุม, กะดุม gkra[4]-doom n. a button.

กระดูก, กะดูก gkra[4]-dook[4] n. a bone: กระดูกไก่ (ต้น) Euonymus javanicus (V. P. p. 4: cb. p. 279): Chloranthus sp., a tree found in evergreen forests (K.): กระดูกเขียด (ต้น) Aglaia hoaensis (Meliaceae) (cb. p. 255): กระดูกงู (เรือ) the keel of a boat or ship: กระดูกช้าง (ต้น) Diospyros discolor, Diospyros sp. near Diospyros lucida, a medium-sized slow-growing tree of the ebony and persimmon family, native of Siam, south India and the Philippines. The beautiful, dull pink, velvety, round fruit is of the size of a large apple. The white, fragrant pulp, surrounding the large seeds, is considered edible though not very tempting (MCM. p. 260: V. P. p. 4): กระดูกแตก (ต้น) Hymenopyramis brachiata (Verbenaceae) (V. P. p. 4), a scandent shrub with small flowers and inflated fruit: กระดูกอึ่ง (ต้น) Desmodium biarticulatum (Leguminosae) (cb. p. 404: K.), a small, leguminous herb common in the moist, low country of Siam

and Ceylon, relished by cattle (MCM. p. 451):
Desmodium cephalotes, Desmodium lanceo-
latum (Leguminosae) (cb. p. 405, 411): *Desmo-*
dium gyrans, called "the telegraph plant"
from the rotary growth of the two lateral
leaflets which resemble semaphores. An erect,
leguminous perennial about 2 to 3 feet high,
common in most low localities. It is relished
by cattle. Other species of *Desmodium* are
also valued for fodder (MCM. p. 451).

กระเดก   an euphonic suffix for กระโดก.

กระเดก, กะเดก   gkra[4]-dake[4] *adj.* rocking;
rolling (as a boat); leaning from side to side.

กระเด้น, กะเด้น   gkra[4]-den *v.* to splash up
(as waves over the side of a boat); to rebound
(as a rubber ball); to bound up.

กระเด้า, กะเด้า   gkra[4]-dow[3] *v.* to make
indecent movements with the buttocks or
rump; to act lewdly.: *n.* lewdness: กระเด้า-
ดิ้น (นก) Java fantail *Rhipidura javanica*
(Gaird. J. S. S. IX, 1, p. 3): กระเด้าลม, กางเขน,
กั้งเขน (นก) Malay magpie robin *Copsychus
musicus* (Gaird. J. S. S. IX, 1, p. 1): กระเด้าลม,
นกแอ่นลม (นก) Formosan skylark *Alauda
wattersi* (Gaird. J. S. S. IX, 1, p. 4): กระเด้าลม,
อุ้มบาตร์ (นก) white-faced wagtail *Motacilla
leucopsis* (will. N. H. J. S. S. II, 3, p. 200: Deig. N.
H. J. S. S. VIII, 3, p. 153): กระเด้าลมหัวสีเทา (นก)
grey-headed wagtail *Motacilla flava thun-
bergi* (Deig. N. H. J. S. S. VIII, 3, p. 154): *Motacilla borealis* (will. N. H. J. S. S. II, 3, p. 201).

กระเดาะ, กะเดาะ   gkra[4]-daw[4] *v.* to toss
gently (as one tosses a stick in play): กระ-
เดาะปาก to make a clucking sound by removing
the tongue from the palate repeatedly.

กระเดิด, กะเดิด   gkra[4]-dert[4] *v.* to be raised
too high (as when attempting to match two
boards when one is a little high); to be
raised up off of a level; to be slanting upwards; to be tilted off the level.

กระเดีย   an euphonic suffix for กระดัก, กระดิก.

กระเดียด, กะเดียด   gkra[4]-dee-at[4] *v.* to

carry on the hip (as a woman carries a market basket); to be unevenly balanced: *adj.*
being disposed towards or for: กระเดียดข้าง
ระจิด tending to be rather weak and insipid:
กระเดียดขึ้น to elevate just a little: กระเดียด
หัวเรือ to move the bow of the boat to one
side by an extra effort: เรือกระเดียดขึ้น the
boat keeps a little ahead of the others: แล่น
กระเดียดเฉียดลม to sail up to the wind:

กระเดียม   an euphonic suffix for กระดี้.

กระเดียม   an euphonic suffix for กระค้วม.

กระเดือก, กะเดือก   gkra[4]-deu-ak[4] *v.* to
swallow with difficulty; to place in the mouth
and swallow little by little; to struggle in
order to get free (as one in danger of
drowning): กระดูกลูกกระเดือก the thyroid
cartilage; "Adam's apple".

กระเดื่อง, กะเดื่อง   gkra[4]-deu-ang[4] *n.* a
lever; a pestle attached to a horizontal bar,
resting on two supports, which act as a fulcrum. This is operated by a person alternatingly stepping on and off of the end of the
bar: *adj.* adamantine; firm; hard: กระ-
เดื่องราง a crude form of mortar and pestle used
by Siamese doctors of the old school. The
mortar is a grooved, crescent-shaped piece of
iron about 2 feet long, mounted on a base.
Into this groove, fits a sharp-edged, iron disc,
having a wooden core which extends about a
foot on either side. The operator stands on
these two wooden handles and dexterously
rocks the disc until the leaves, roots or bark
in the groove are pulverized: ครกกระเดื่อง
a mortar, with pestle attached to a bar as a
fulcrum, and raised by the weight of a person
stepping on and off: ลือกระเดื่อง being
spread abroad (as news).

กระแด็ก ๆ, กะแด็ก ๆ   gkra[4]-daak[4]-gkra[4]-
daak[4] *adj.* limping (as an injured bird);
hobbling about (as when one foot is injured).

กระแด่ว, กะแด่ว   gkra-[4]daa-oh[4] *adj.* restless (as an infant throwing legs and arms

about); squirming; wiggling; writhing; rolling from side to side.

กระโดก, กะโดก   gkra[4]-dok[4] v. to move up and down slowly (as when riding a see-saw): adj. rocking; rocking gently (as of a boat): กระโดกกระเดก rocking or pitching about (as of an empty boat when tossed by the waves).

กระโดง, กะโดง   gkra[4]-dong n. the mast of a ship; the spine of a fish; the large upright branches of a tree: adj. high: กระโดงคาง the prominence of the chin.

กระโดด see กระโจน

กระโดน, กะโดน (ต้น)   gkra[4]-don n. a small or medium-sized tree in northern Siam; Patana oak Careya arborea (Lecythidaceae). The bark is an astringent used for tanning as well as in native medicine (MCM. p. 443): กระโดนดิน (ต้น) Careya herbaceae (Lecythidaceae) (Cb. p. 674: Dept. Agri. & Fisheries p. 158).

กระใด, กะใด, กระไร   gkra[4]-dai adv. what; why.

กระได, กะได, บันได   gkra[4]-dai n. steps; stairway; ladder: กระไดแก้ว a wall-bracket or rack for holding palm-leaf books, swords or spears: กระไดลิง (ต้น) Bauhinia horsfieldii (Leguminosae), Bauhinia anguina, "snake-climber", a remarkable, wide-spreading climber with flattened, serpentine stems strongly curved in alternating directions between the nodes (MCM. p. 132).

กระตรกกระตรำ, กะตรกกะตรำ   gkra[4]-dtrok[4]-gkra[4]-dtrum adj. laborious; toilsome; tiresome; difficult.

กระตร้อ, กะตร้อ, ตะกร้อ   gkra[4]-dtrau[3] n. a ball made of woven strips of cane or leather with feathers attached (as badminton shuttlecocks); a half-egg-shaped basket made of small-sized rattan, fastened to a long pole and used to remove fruit from trees.

กระตรำ   an euphonic suffix for กระตรก.

กระตัวมกระเตี้ยม, กะตัวมกะเตียม   gkra[4]-dtoo-am[3]-gkra[4]-dtee-am[3] v. to walk with difficulty: adj. toddling; waddling clumsily.

กระต่องกระแต่ง, กะต่องกะแต่ง   gkra[4]-dtaung[4]-gkra[4]-dtaang[4] adj. irregularly attached; fluttering (as clothing); flopping; flapping.

กระต๊อบ, กะต๊อบ, กระท่อม   gkra[4]-dtaup[5] n. a hut; a shed for cattle; a field shack.

กระต้อยตีวิด, กะต้อยตีวิด   gkra[4]-dtau-ey[3]-dte-wit[4] n. a variety of small field bird; plover (carbuncled); the rain bird; any one of the numerous species of limicoline birds belonging to the family Charadricae, and other species of sandpipers (webster); the Burmese lapwing Lobivanellus atrounchalis (Gaird. J. S. S. IX, 1, p. 15).   [goad.

กระตัก, กะตัก, ประตัก   gkra[4]-dtak[4] n. a

กระตังกระตั้ว, กะตังกะตั้ว   gkra[4]-dtang-gkra[4]-dtiew[3] n. Echites sp. Echites rubro-venosa (Apocynaceae) (MCM. p. 129), "caout-chouc creeper", a name applied to several species of apocynaceous plants, all large, woody climbers yielding rubber (V. P. p. 7: K.).

กระตังใบ, กะตังใบ, ตั้งไก่   gkra[4]-dtang-bai n. Leea acuminata (Leeaceae) (Cb. p. 316); Leea expansa (Leeaceae) (Cb. p. 317: K.). These names are used for several species of leea, a genus of handsome, foliage shrubs having pinnate leaves with white or pinkish-grey midrib and nerves (K.: MCM. p. 121).

กระตังมูตร   gkra[4]-dtang-moot[3] n. urinary sediments: เกลือกระตัง sedimentary salts; deposits of the urine.

กระตรับ, กะตรับ, ตะกรับ, ปลาหมอช้าง เหยียบ   gkra[4]-dtrap[4] n. a fresh-water fish Pristolepis fasciata (M. C. vipulya N. H. J. S. S. VI, 2, p. 224: Dept. Agri. & Fisheries).

กระตั้ว, กะตั้ว   gkra[4]-dtoo-ah[3] n. cockatoo, a bird of the parrot family Cacatuinae, having a short, strong and much curved beak, and the head ornamented with a crest, which can be raised or depressed at will (webster).

กระตาก   an euphonic suffix for กระโตก.

กระต๊าก   gkra⁴-dtak⁵ *interj.* an onomatopoeia (as the cackle of a hen).

กระต่าย, กะต่าย   gkra⁴-dtai⁴ *n.* hare; rabbit: กระต่ายจีน a metal coconut-grater: กระต่ายชมจันทร์, กระต่ายต้องแร้ว names of folk solo dances: กระต่ายบ้าน tame rabbits: กระต่ายป่า wild hare.

กระติก   an euphonic suffix for กระตุก.

กระติก, กะติก   gkra⁴-dtik⁴ *n.* a canteen; a soldier's water flask: กระติกริก small; undeveloped.

กระตั๊ง   an euphonic suffix for กระตุ้ง.

กระตี๊ด (นก)   gkra⁴-dtit⁵ *n.* the Indian pipit *Anthus rufulus* (will. N. H. J. S. S. II, 3, p. 204).

กระติบ   gkra⁴-dtip⁴ *n.* a small, round, woven bamboo receptacle having a cover, and used for carrying cooked glutinous rice to be eaten on a journey (used by Laos tribes).

กระตอรอร้น, กะตอรอร้น   gkra⁴-dteureu-ron⁵ *v.* to be in haste about doing something; to be in earnest regarding a duty or task; to feel urgently impelled to accomplish a duty; to act energetically.

กระตุก, กะตุก   gkra⁴-dtook⁴ *v.* to jerk repeatedly; to pull sharply (as a jerking motion while flying a kite); to pull with jerks; to urge on for immediate action: กระตุกใจ to remind one's self.

กระตุกกระติก, กะตุกกะติก   gkra⁴-dtook⁴-gkra⁴-dtik⁴ *v.* to flap or flutter while hanging: *adj.* ossillating while hanging loosely or drooping downward.

กระตุ้งกระตัง, กะตุ้งกะตัง   gkra⁴-dtoong³-gkra4-dting3 *adj.* swaying; swinging; listless or abstracted (movements of the arms and body).

กระตุ่น   gkra⁴-dtoon⁴ *n.* a small, bamboo rat *Nyctocleptes badius* (Gaird. N. H. J. S. S. III, 2, p. 124): a mole *Parascaptor sp.* (Gaird. N. H. J. S. S. III, 2, 123).

กระตุ้น, กะตุ้น   gkra⁴-dtoon³ *v.* to thrust at with a sharp blow (as with a stick); to raise by an upward stroke or blow; to prop; to push up; to punch slightly (as with a finger); to remind; to exhort; to pulsate rhythmically (as the apex beat of the heart): ใช้มือกระตุ้นไม่ได้ it is impossible to push, punch, or elevate with the hand.

กระตรุม, ตะกรุม (นก)   gkra⁴-dtroom *n.* the adjutant bird *Leptoptilus argala* (Gaird. J. S. S. IX, 1, p. 10).

กระเตง, กะเตง   gkra⁴-dteng *n.* a fish trap used in Pitsanuloke: *adj.* hanging; swaying.

กระเต็น, กะเต็น (นก)   gkra⁴-dten *n.* kingfisher, an alcedinoid bird having a straight, deeply cleft bill with smooth edges, one of the numerous species of birds constituting the family *Alcedinidae.* Most of them feed upon fishes which are seized with the beak while the bird dives (webster): white-breasted kingfisher *Halcyon smyrnensis* (Gaird. N. H. J. S. S. IX, 1, p. 7): กระเต็นน้อย (นก) cómmon Indian kingfisher *Alcedo atthis bengalensis* (Deig. H. N. J. S. S. VIII, 3, p. 162): กระเต็นปักหลัก (นก) eastern pied kingfisher (Herb. N. H. J. S. S. VI, 3, p. 307): กระเต็นลาย (นก) pied kingfisher *Ceryle rudis leucomelanura* : กระเต็นใหญ่, กำกวม (นก) Burmese stork-billed kingfisher *Pelargopsis gurial burmanica* (will. N. H. J. S. S. II, 3, p. 334).

กระเตอะ, กะเตอะ   gkra⁴-dtur⁴ *adj.* becoming too hard or over-ripe (descriptive of the areca-nut or fruit).

กระเตาะ, กะเตาะ   gkra⁴-dtau⁴ *adj.* adolescent; approaching pubescence.

กระเตาะกระแตะ, กะเตาะกะแตะ   gkra⁴-dtau⁴-gkra⁴-dtaa⁴ *adj.* frail; insecure; waddling; not strong in the legs (as a child learning to walk).

กระเตี๊ยม   an euphonic suffix for กระต้วม.

กระเตื๊อง, กะเตื๊อง   gkra[4]-dteu-ang[3] v. to become movable; to improve in condition; to convalesce; to attain a higher standard of learning (as a student); to rise gradually; to become loosened (as in dislodging a stump or stone).

กระแต, กะแต   gkra[4]-dtaa n. a small gong or cymbal; (used by a watcher or guard, as a signal); a small squirrel or chipmunk; tree shrews (Gaird. N. H. J. S. S. III, 2, p. 123) *Tupaia sp* : กระแตไต่ไม้ (ต้น) *Drynaria quercifolia* (*Polypo diaceae*) (V. P. p. 7): น้องกระแต a small-sized gong or cymbal: หญิงกระแต a prattling and gossiping woman: หญิงตอแหล กระแตวับ a bold-faced and lying woman.

กระแตะ   an euphonic suffix for กระเตาะ.

กระแต่ง   an euphonic suffix for กระต่อง.

กระแตว   gkra[4]-dtaa-oh *adj.* annoying; vexatious (descriptive of making repeated requests).

กระแต่ว   gkra[4]-dtaa-oh[4] *adj.* importunate; pleading (as one desirous of receiving something): ร้องกระแต่วๆ whining.

กระโตกกระตาก, กะโตกกะตาก   gkra[4]-dtok[4]-gkra[4]-dtak[4] v. to raise a cry; to give an alarm; to sound a signal or appraise of danger: *adj.* frightened; startled.

กระโต๊ก   gkra[4]-dtok[5] *interj.* an onomatopoeia (as crowing).

กระโตงกระเตง, กะโตงกะเตง gkra[4]-dtong-gkra[4]-dteng *adj.* swaying; swinging; flapping (as threadbare ends of clothing in the wind or monkeys from the limbs of trees).

กระโต้งโห่ง   gkra[4]-dtong[3]-hong[4] *interj.* an onomatopoeia (as the call of the peacock).

กระโตน see กระโจน

กระถด, กะถด, กระเถิบ, กระเถิบ   gkra[4]-tot[4] v. to change or readjust a bit; to move back or out a little; to move in order to make more room for others.

กระถาง, กะถาง   gkra[4]-tang[2] n. a flowerpot; a receptacle for water; a pitcher.

กระถิน, กะถิน   gkra[4]-tin[2] n. *Leucaena glauca* (*Leguminosae*) (V. P. p. 7: Cb. p. 546), the wild or horse-tamarind, a small quick-growing leguminous tree, 15 to 20 feet or more high, with very fine bi-pinnate leaves. It is specially suited to dry districts. Sometimes it is used as shade for shrub crops. It furnishes good fuel and the foliage is relished by cattle. The seeds, which are abundant and hard, are used in making fancy bags, baskets and ornaments (Dept. Agri. & Fisheries p. 632 : MCM. p. 206): กระถินเทศ, กระถินหอม *Acacia farnesiana* (*Leguminosae*)(V. P. p. 8: Cb. p. 548), which are largely grown in southern France for the sake of the flowers, which are used in the preparation of perfumery (MCM. p. 457 : Dept. Agri. & Fisheries p. 49): cassia, a small tree common in the tropics. The bark is astringent; the pods contain a balsamic liquid used medicinally. The tender shoots and pods are used as a vegetable. Both of these plants are foreign but have been so long and so generally cultivated and are now found semi-wild, that the time of their introduction is unknown. Probably they came from Cambodia or direct from India before the middle of the XIV*th.* century A. D. (Phya winit, N. H. J. S. S. IX, 1, p. 98): กระถินพิมาน, กะถินวิมาน, หนาม ขาว *Acacia siamensis* (*Leguminosae*) (Cb. p. 551): *Acacia tomentosa, Dochrostachys cinerea* (*Leguminosae*) (Cb. p. 544): *Acacia sp.* (V. P. p. 8: K.: MCM. p. 457): "jungle nail", "elephant thorn", a shrub or small tree bearing thorns 3 to 4 inches long. This shrub is found in dry, stony, hill-side localities.

กระเถิบ see กระถด

กระโถน, กะโถน   gkra[4]-tone[2] *n.* a spittoon; a cuspidor; a commode: กระไถนท้อง พระโรง a scape-goat *idiomatic.*

กระทก, กะทก   gkra[4]-tok[6] *v.* to jerk with force; to pull vigorously with short jerks; to disentangle by pulling (as of a bow or slip-knot): กระทกข้าว, ผัดข้าว to separate white rice from the husks by using a flat basket. The basket is dipped on one side and by a toss and jerk, the rice is moved to the inner side and removed by hand.

กระทกรก, กะทกรก, กะทกลก   gkra[4]-tok[6]-rok[6] *n. Passiflora foetida (Passifloraceae)* (cb. p. 743 : K.): *Olax scandens* (cb. p. 271), *Passiflora edulis (Passifloraceae),* "passion vine," "sweet-cup," an herbaceous, ornamental, perennial vine (MCM. p. 279). Other names are เถางะ, เถาสิงห์โต, หญ้ารกช้าง.

กระทง, กะทง   gkra[4]-tong *n.* a count (as in an indictment); clauses or sectional divisions of a story or discourse; a room or section in a boat; baskets, trays or floats made of stitched, banana leaves or stalks on which tapers and incense sticks are placed. These are allowed to float along the canals or river as propitiatory offerings to spirits: *adj.* young (descriptive of fowls): กระทงความ the argument or sectional divisions of a story or discourse: กระทงเจิม a basket or vessel made of banana leaves, with a serrated decoration around the edge: กระทงแถลง synopsis or summary of a narrative, tale or history, submitted for special consideration: กระทงนา boundary ridges or low dikes surrounding paddy fields: กระทงผ้าจีวร one of the squares of cloth of which the robe is made for a Buddhist monk: กระทงเรือ planks placed across open boats and used by passengers as seats: กระทงลาย, กะทุงลาย *Celastrus paniculatus (Celastraceae)* (cb. p. 284 : MCM. p. 132, 378 : Dept. Agri. & Fisheries p. 238): ไก่รุ่น กระทง a young cock: เย็บกระทง to stitch folded leaves or paper together in making a basket, float or tray: ลอยกระทง an annual

ceremony of floating or launching these baskets. This is held in October or November.

กระทด   gkra[4]-tot[6] *v.* to bend (as a bow): *adj.* perverse; not straight-forward: กระทด กระทัน *ancient* bent; stooped; bowed.

กระทบ, กระทบกระทั่ง, กะทบ, กระทบกระ-แทก   gkra[4]-top[6] *v.* to strike against (as of two boats in collision); to collide; to impale (as a boat on hidden rocks); to clash with: กระทบกระเทียบ insulting (by use of odious comparisons); slurring (as remarks about people): กระทบกระเทือน to be moved; to be shaken by a violent contact; to hear or feel reverberations of: พูดกระทบกระเทียบ to attack with insults or veiled remarks; to use invidious remarks or comparisons.

กระทบกระทั่ง see **กระทบ**

กระทบกระแทก see **กระทบ**

กระทรวง   gkra[4]-su-ang *n.* (1) Ministry; group; company: (2) order; kind; family; species; class: (3) *ancient* scope; range; latitude: กระทรวงการต่างประเทศ Ministry of Foreign Affairs: กระทรวงกลาโหม Ministry of Defense: กระทรวงเกษตราธิการ Ministry of Agriculture: กระทรวงธรรมการ Ministry of Public Instruction & Religion: กระทรวง พาณิชย์-คมนาคม Ministry of Commerce & Communications. (This is now changed to กระทรวง เศรษฐการ Ministry of Economic Affairs): กระทรวงพระคลัง Ministry of Finance. (This is now changed to กระทรวงการคลัง): กระทรวง มหาดไทย Ministry of the Interior: กระทรวง ยุตติธรรม Ministry of Justice: ฟ้องผิดกระทรวง to sue in a wrong Court of Law: อำนาจ กระทรวงศาล the jurisdiction of the Courts of Justice.

กระทอ, กะทอ   gkra[4]-tau *n.* a close-meshed, telescopic, woven, bamboo container, lined with leaves and used by the northern mountain tribes for transporting clothing or food while travelling.

กระทอก, กะทอก   gkra⁴-tauk³ v. to stroke forcibly up and down; to rub up and down.

กระท่อนกระแท่น, กะท่อนกะแท่น   gkra⁴-taun³-gkra⁴-taan³ v. to be incomplete; to be disjointed or ragged (as pieces of boards); to be tattered; to be lacking here and there: adj. incomplete; insufficient.

กระท้อน, กะท้อน, สท้อน   gkra⁴-taun⁵ v. to rebound; to be reflected upwards: n. a variety of tree with edible fruit Sandoricum indicum (Meliaceae) (V. P. p. 9: MCM. p. 104, 270); a tall, erect, quick-growing tree with handsome pinnate leaves, native of Siam and Malaya. It produces large clusters of yellow, globular fruit in June and July. In appearance these are not unlike small oranges, at a distance. Like the rambutan, the soft, white aril covering the seeds (usually five) is edible and of a sweetish-acid taste. When fermented and mixed with rice, it makes an intoxicating drink. The wood is used for making carts and boats and is thought to be a particularly good and durable timber (Dept. Agri. & Fisheries p. 458).

กระท่อม, กะท่อม   gkra⁴-taum³ n. a hut; a hovel; a cottage: กระท่อม (ต้น) Mitragyna speciosa (Rubiaceae) (V. P. p. 9: K.), "negro peach", a robust semi-climbing or spreading shrub. The flowers, at first white and later changing to yellow, are strongly scented. The round, brownish, warty fruit is about the size of an apple. The leaves have long been used for chewing and people who form the habit find it as difficult to stop it, as do those who form the habit of taking opium. The leaves, when so taken, are reputed to act as a stimulant which enables one to endure fatigue, thus enabling him to go for a long time without food. The leaves yield an alkaloid known as Mitragynine (K.).

กระท้อมกระแท้ม, กะท้อมกะแท้ม   gkra⁴-

taum⁵-gkra⁴-taam⁵ adj. small; insignificant; unimportant; diminutive (as an undeveloped child); economical in the extreme (as a miser).

กระทะ, กะทะ   gkra⁴-ta⁶ n. a frying pan; a wide-mouth kettle or cauldron: ข้าวกระทะ rice cooked in a cauldron.

กระทั้งหัน, กะทั้งหน   gkra⁴-tang-han² n. Calophyllum inophyllum (Guttiferae), a medium-sized or large, handsome tree of Ceylon, India and local forests. The dried fruit or nuts, called "punnai nuts," yield abundant, dark green, thick and strongly scented oil, employed as a remedy for ulcers and hoof-diseases of cattle (MCM. p. 378, 395): Calophyllum tomentosum (MCM. p. 395).

กระทั่ง, กะทั่ง   gkra⁴-tang³ u. to clash with; to be up against; to herald (as with a bugle); to announce (as by a cough or any sound from the throat): prep. to; as far as: an euphonic suffix for กระทบ.

กระทัดรัด, กะทัดรัด   gkra⁴-tat⁶-rat⁶ adj. compact; neat; consolidated; small and handy.

กระทัน   an euphonic suffix for กระทด.

กระทั้น   an euphonic suffix for กระแทก.

กระทา, กะทา (นก)   gkra⁴-ta n. a quail; a partridge: Chinese francolin Francolinus chinensis (Gaird. J. S. S. IX, 1, p. 13): กระทา-ดง ferruginous wood partridge Caloperdix oculea: red-crested hill partridge Rollulus rouloul (Gaird. J. S. S. IX, 1, p. 13).

กระทาชาย, กระไทชาย   gkra⁴-ta-chai n. a man; a male.

กระทาส, ทาส   gkra⁴-ta-see² n. a slave; a man servant: ทาสกรรมกร a male servant or workman: ทาสทาน lit. "the meanest kind of alms," i. e. gifts that are thrown to a person or that which is given grudgingly: ทาสบัญญา lit. "knowledge that is slavish", i. e. knowledge that is base, evil or immoral: ทาสาทาสี slaves (in general): ทาสี a female slave or servant.

กระทาย, กะทาย gkra[4]-tai *v.* to separate kernels from husk (as in shelling peanuts): *n.* a small, cylindrical basket having a wide mouth.

กระทำ gkra[4]-tum *v.* to do; to make; to trim; to decorate; to originate; to build; to use necromancy in producing dire results on another: ผู้ถูกกระทำ the one so influenced or affected.

กระทิ, กะทิ (นก) gkra[4]-ti[6] *n.* the spotted munia (Aag. p. 78); Hodgson's munia *Uroloncha acuticauda* (will. N. H. J. S. S. II, 3, p. 194).

กระทิ, กะทิ gkra[4]-ti[6] *n.* coconut milk. The fresh coconut meat is grated and covered with water. The juice is then pressed out of the meat, producing a white milky fluid: มะพร้าวกะทิ a coconut in which the endocarpal meat has developed into a cheesy or milky substance but is still edible: หัวกะทิ milk pressed from the freshly grated coconut, without being mixed with water.

กระทิง, กะทิง (ต้น) gkra[4]-ting *n.* *Calophyllum inophyllum (Guttiferae)* (V. P. p. 8: cb. p. 120: MCM. p. 395), "punnai-nuts," a medium-sized or large, handsome tree. The dried fruit or "nuts" yield abundant, dark-green, thick and strongly scented oil, employed as a remedy for ulcers and hoof-diseases of cattle, the roots and bark as an application for rheumatic pains, the leaves, soaked in water, as an application to inflamed eyes. The bark is astringent and is used as a remedy for internal hemorrhages. The wood is of a reddish-brown colour, moderately hard and close-grained, and is used for masts, spars, railway sleepers, ship-building and cabinet work (MCM. p. 378, 395: Dept. Agri. & Fisheries p. 31): กระทิง, กะทิง (วัว) Indian bison, known in Malaya as the seladang *Bos Gaurus*: กระทิง (ปลา) "spiny eel" *Mastacembelus armatus* (H. M. S.).

กระทืบ, กะทืบ gkra[4]-teup[3] *v.* to stamp the foot angrily; to kill or tread upon with the heel (as a worm): กระทืบยอด, ไมยราบ (ต้น) *Biophytum sensitivum: Mimosa pudica (Leguminosae)* (cb. p. 546: V. P. 8: K: MCM. p. 476), "sensitive plant," a noxious creeper with thorny stems and small leaves. These leaves are bi-pinnate, very sensitive, and close immediately on being touched, or with the rain. The roots are used as an antidote for cobra bite and are used in a decoction as a remedy to relieve tendencies toward the formation of gravel or calculi in the bladder (Dept. Agri. & Fisheries p. 23): กระทืบธรณี *lit.* "to pound the earth forcefully with the heel," *i. e.* to tread heavily; to walk throwing the body weight down with force (considered offensive and indicative of anger).

กระทือ, กะทือ gkra[4]-teu *n.* *Zingiber zerumbet (Zingiberaceae)* (Dept. Agri. & Fisheries p. 366: K.). This plant is used by the Siamese on account of its rubefacient properties, and as an ingredient for curry powder. The rhizomes are used in making a dye which has a slightly aromatic odour. They possess similar properties to those of the officinal ginger, but are used as a counter-irritant remedy for coughs, asthma, leprosy and other special skin diseases.

กระทุง, กะทุง gkra[4]-toong *n.* a pelican; any large, web-footed bird of the genus *Pelecanus*, of which about a dozen species are known. They have an enormous bill, to the lower edge of which is attached a pouch in which captured fishes are temporarily stored (webster); spotted billed pelican *Pelecanidae Manillensis*; eastern white pelican *Pelecanidae Roseus* (Gaird. J. S. S. IX, 1, p. 10): กระทุงหมาบ้า (ต้น) *Tinospora thorelii (Menipermaceae)* (K.); *Dregea volubilis*: กระทุงเหว (ปลา) a fresh-water fish of the kneedle fish family *Tylosurus strongylurus* (Dept. Agri. & Fisheries): กระทุงเหวเมือง (ปลา) *Xenentodon cancila* (Dept. Agri. & Fisheries).

กระทุงลาย, กะทุงลาย   gkra[4]-toong-lai *n.*
Celastrus paniculatus (Celastraceae), a large
woody climber (K.) having bright yellow
fruit. The bark is used as a decoction by
native doctors to "strengthen the brain and
purify the blood". Oil from the seeds is used
to cure sores (MCM. p. 378); a scandant shrub
of the outer Himalayas (Dept. Agri. & Fisheries
p. 238).

กระทุ้ง, กะทุ้ง   gkra[4]-toong[5] *v.* to pound;
to tamp in tightly or firmly; to force down
tightly or solidly (as the wad in a gun); to
strike downwards with the tip end of a stick :
กระทุ้งช้อน to beat the shallows of a body of
water in the effort to catch fish :   กระทุ้งเส้า
to beat the cadence in a boat race; to tamp
in dirt or bricks around the base of a post or
pillar :   พูดกระทุ้ง a disguised, leading question or insinuation.

กระทุ่ม, กะทุ่ม ๑   gkra[4]-toom[3] *n. Excoecaria agalloch (Euphorbiaceae)* (Dept. Agri. &
Fisheries p. 307); *Mitragyna hirsuta*, a small,
evergreen tree of the coast and tidal forests.
The wood is white, very soft and spongy. It
exudes a poisonous sap that collects on the
surface in black, india-rubber-like lumps or
masses, considered by some to have medicinal
properties. The wood, when dried, is employed for general carpentry purposes, such as for
making toys, bedsteads and tables, but more
generally for fire-wood :   กระทุ่มกลอง *Polyalthia suberosa (Anonaceae)* (V. P. p. 9 : K.):
กระทุ่มก้านยาว, กระทุ่มบก *Anthocephalus cadamba* (V. P. p. 9), a flowering shrub, the leaves of
which are substituted for opium by those addicted to opium, when the drug is not available. The leaves have a strong drug-like taste :
กระทุ่มคลอง, กระทุ่มน้ำ *Sarcocephalus cordatus
(Rubiaceae)* (V. P. p. 9, 10 : K.: MCM. p. 218):
กระทุ่มนา, กระทุ่มหมู, กะทุ่มหมู *Mitragyna diversifolia (Rubiaceae)* (V. P. p. 10 : K.):   กระทุ่มหู
กวาง *Nauclea sessilifolia (Rubiaceae)* (V. P. p.
10 : K.):   กระทุ่มแบน the name of a district
west of Bangkok in the province of Samud
Sakon.

กระทุ่ม, กะทุ่ม ๒   gkra[4]-toom[3] *v.* to splash
water with the hands or feet while swimming ;
to strike, smite or beat the chest (as an expression of grief).

กระทู้, กะทู้   gkra[4]-too[5] *n.* heading, subject,
theme or text of a discourse or document :
กระทู้ความ summary ; text or principal points in
an address ; gist :   กระทู้ถาม questions prescribed by law, to be asked in judging a case :
เป็นกระทู้ fundamental ; basic ; principal :   เสา
กระทู้ main posts or pillars of an enclosure :
โครงกระทู้ a form of Siamese poetry.

กระเท่เร่, กะเท่เร่   gkra[4]-tay[3]-ray[3] *adj.* tilted ; sloping ; leaning ; inclined to one side :
เอียงกะเท่เร่ *idiomatic* slanting to one side.

กระเทย, กะเทย   gkra[4]-tur-ie *n.* a person
or animal in which the sex is indeterminable.

กระเทาะ, กะเทาะ   gkra[4]-tau[6] *v.* to scale
off ; to peal off in chips, layers or flakes ; to
shell (as peanuts) : *n.* the article or fruit that
has been so treated.

กระเทียบ   an euphonic suffix for กระทบ.

กระเทียม, กะเทียม   gkra[4]-tee-am *n.* garlic
Allium sativum (Liliaceae) (MCM. p. 346), a
bulbous-rooted perennial, much cultivated in
India and the East generally for its small,
white, onion-like bulbs which have a pungent
flavour and an overpowering odour. Each
root is composed of several lesser bulbs,
called "cloves of garlic," enclosed in a common membranous coat and easily separated.
As a medicinal remedy, it is much thought
of in the treatment of flatulent colic (Dept.
Agri. & Fisheries p. 173).

กระเทือน, กระเทือน, สะเทือน   gkra[4]-teu-
un *v.* to shake; to shatter; to sway; to
tremble; to waver (as in giving an opinion).

กระแท้, กะแท้   gkra[4]-taa[5] *n.* a small
insect (when crushed it emits an offensive
odour).

กระแทก, กะแทก   gkra[4]-taak[3] v. to dash violently against (as a ship against a rock); to hit or bump against; to collide with: กระแทกกระทั้น rude, rough, blunt or uncivil (as when elbowing one's way through a crowd); making invidious references concerning or to any one.

กระแทน, กะแทน (ต้น)   gkra[4]-taan n. Protium serratum (Burseraceae) (V. P. p. 7: K.), a tree about 10 m. high, growing in scrub jungle, and bearing green flowers.

กระแท่น   an euphonic suffix for กระท่อน.

กระแท้ม   an euphonic suffix for กระท้อม.

กระแทะ, ระแทะ   gkra[4]-taa[6] n. a small ox-cart (for rapid travel).

กระไทชาย see กระทาชาย

กระนก see กระหนก

กระนั้น, กะนั้น   gkra[4]-nan[5] adv. thus; in that way or manner.

กระนาล, กะนาน (ต้น)   gkra[4]-nan n. Pterospermum semisagittatum (Sterculiaceae) (cb. p. 177), a large, foliage tree of Siam and Burma with very large, oval, leathery leaves, snowy white or grey underneath, with prominent veins and long, fleshy, scented, yellow flowers (MCM. p. 103).

กระนี้, กะนี้   gkra[4]-nee[5] adv. in this manner; in this way: เป็นกระนี้ it is this way.

กระโน้น, กะโน้น   gkra[4]-non[5] adv. over there; as that is over there; as that is yonder.

กระไน, กะไน   gkra[4]-nai n. a small, wild bird similar to the wood-pecker.

กระบก, กะบก   gkra[4]-bok[4] n. the wild almond Irvingia malayana (Simarubaceae) (cb. p. 243), a tree with plum-like fruit. The kernel of the seed is edible (K.).

กระบถ see กบฏ

กระบวน, ขบวน   gkra[4]-bu-an n. a procession; a company; a group; deception; fraud; a trick to deceive: กระบวนกระบิด magic; strategy; sleight-of-hand; deceitful or underhanded methods: กระบวนเรื่อรบ a squadron of warships: กระบวนแห่ a section or division of a procession.

กระบวย, กะบวย   gkra[4]-boo-ay n. a dipper made of a small coconut-shell; a coconut-shell ladle.

กระบวร see กบูร

กระบอก, กะบอก ๑   gkra[4]-bauk[4] n. a cylinder; a section of bamboo (having the joint at one end and open at the other). This is used as a drinking vessel or to collect sap from the sugar palm: กระบอก (ปลา) sea mullet (Mugil tade); any one of numerous fishes of the genus Mugil, found on the coasts of both continents, and highly esteemed as food. They are salted and smoked in great quantities (webster): Mugil dussumieri (Dept. Agri. & Fisheries): กระบอกฉีด a syringe; an hypodermic syringe: กระบอก ดวด, กระบอกสะกา a dice box: กระบอกตา the bony socket which contains the eye; the ocular orbit: กระบอกปืน the barrel of a gun.

กระบอก, กะบอก ๒ (ต้น)   gkra[4]-bauk[4] n. Thevetia nereifolia (MCM. p. 117, 426), "lucky beans," "lucky seeds" produced by a small tree or large shrub of the West Indies. These seeds are hard, oblong and used as pendents or charms.

กระบอง, ตะบอง   gkra[4]-baung n. a club; a billy; a truncheon (as carried by policemen): กระบองเพ็ชร cactus Cereus sp. (V. P. p. 11).

กระบะ, กะบะ   gkra[4]-ba[4] n. a tray; a wooden tray; a serving tray: รถกระบะ a truck; a lorry.

กระบัด, ตระบัด ๑   gkra[4]-bat[4] adj. momentary; continuing only a moment: instantaneous.

กระบัด ๒   gkra⁴-bat⁴ *v.* to borrow (money) and then never pay it back.

กระบัวกระเบีย, กะบัวกะเบีย, กระบัวกระ-เบีย, กะปลกกะเปลี้ย   gkra⁴-boo-ah³-gkra⁴-bee-ah³ *adj.* weak; frail; infirm; unsteady on the feet (used of the aged): เดินกะปลก กะเปลี้ย to walk limpingly or lamely.

กระบาก, กะบาก   gkra⁴-bak⁴ *n. Anisoptera cochinchinensis; Anisoptera Curtisii (Dipterocarpaceae)*, a name applied to various species of *Anisoptera*, a genus of lofty, hardwood tree (V. P. p. 11: Cb. p. 139: K.).

กระบาย, กะบาย   gkra⁴-bai *n.* a variety of deep but small-sized basket.

กระบาล see กบาล

กระบิ, กะบิ   gkra⁴-bi⁴ *n.* a piece, portion, stub or remnant (as of glass or scantlings); a fragment: จมกระบิ to have a fragment still embedded (as in the trunk of a tree or in the flesh).

กระบิด, กะบิด   gkra⁴-bit⁴ *v.* to twist, in order to soften or to make pliable (as rattan or fresh bamboo strips); to tie or fasten with rattan, which has been softened by twisting; to tie; to fasten.

กระบิดกระบวน, กระเบ็ดกระบวน   gkra⁴-bit⁴-gkra⁴-bu-an *Cam. n.* magic; strategy; sleight-of-hand; deceitful methods; underhanded methods.

กระบิล see กบิล

กระบี่, กบี ๑   gkra⁴-bee⁴ *n.* a monkey.

กระบี่, กะบี ๒   gkra⁴-bee⁴ *n.* a sword and sheath worn with a uniform; a sword; the name of a district in southern Siam.

กระบือ   gkra⁴-beu *n.* a water buffalo; a carabao: กระบือเจ็ดตัว (ต้น) *Excaecaria bicolor (Euphorbiaceae)* (MCM. p. 120), a foliage

shrub with small, ovate leaves, green above and deep crimson beneath: บางกระบือ the name of a district in the northern part of Bangkok.

กระบุง, กะบุง   gkra⁴-boong *n.* a variety of basket having a square base, and used as a capacity measure for paddy.

กระบุ่มกระบ่าม, กะบุ่มกะบ่าม   gkra⁴-boom⁴-gkra⁴-bam⁴ *adj.* awkward; bungling; ungraceful; clumsy; rude; characterized by roughness.

กระบู้กระบี้, กะบู้กะบี้   gkra⁴-boo³-gkra⁴-bee³ *adj.* dinted; misshapen; illy-formed (as Sawankaloke pottery); out of proper shape; irregular in shape.

กระบูร see กบูร, กระบวร '

กระเบง, ตะเบ็ง, กระเบ็ญ   gkra⁴-beng *v.* to distend the abdomen while holding the breath (as in straining); to utter a loud cry while suspending or suppressing respiration.

กระเบ็ญ see กระเบง

กระเบน, กะเบน   gkra⁴-ben *n.* the rolled portion of the loin cloth, the end of which is fastened up behind: กระเบน (ปลา) the ray or skate; any of the numerous large, flat fishes of the genus *Raia*. These have a long, slender tail, terminated by small, caudal fins. The pectoral fins are large and broad and united to the sides of the body and head, giving a somewhat rhombic form to these fishes. The skin is more or less spinose. These fishes are found in salt water and some of the species are used as food (webster): กระเบนขาว (ปลา) white ray *Dasybatus bleekeri* (Dept. Agri. & Fisheries): กระเบนธง (ปลา) flag ray *Dasybatus sephen* (Dept. Agri. & Fisheries): กระเบนนก (ปลา) *Aetobatus narinari* (Dept. Agri. & Fisheries): กระเบนปากแหลม. กระเบนแมลงวัน sharp-snout ray *Dasybatus uarnak* (Dept. Agri. & Fisheries): กระเบนเผือก *Pteroplatea micrura* (Dept. Agri. & Fisheries): กระเบน

ไฟฟ้า *Astrape dipterygia* (H. M. S.): กระเบนหิน stone ray *Taeniura lymna* (Dept. Agri. & Fisheries): กระเบนเหน็บ the small of the back; the lumbar portion of the spine: โจง กระเบน to roll the edges of the panung together and fasten behind: ชายกระเบน the end of the rolled portion of the panung, which is tucked into the waist-band behind: หาง กระเบน the tail of the ray. These are used in two different ways. They may be hung up to dry, having a weight placed on the end to straighten them, and then be used as a whip. Or the tail may be cut into sections, the flesh removed and the skin wrapped around a joint of bamboo and allowed to dry. It is then used as a file for wood.

กระเบ็ดกระบวน see กระบิดกระบวน

กระเบา, กะเบา gkra[4]-bauw *n. Hydnocarpus anthelmintica* (*Flacourtiaceae*) (V. P. p. 10: cb. p. 96), a medium-sized tree of Siam, India, Burma, etc. An oil, similar to chaulmoogra oil, is obtained from the seed; sometimes this is used as a substitute for the true chaulmoogra oil (MCM. p. 386, 396, 463: V. P. p. 10). This name is also applied to other species of *Hydnocarpus* (K.).

กระเบียด, กะเบียด gkra[4]-bee-at[4] *n.* a quarter of an inch (according to the Siamese system of linear measurement).

กระเบียดกระเสียร, กะเบียดกะเสียร gkra[4]-bee-at[4]-gkra[4]-see-an[2] *adj.* frugal; sparing; saving; penurious; stingy; miserly; "tight-fisted".

กระเบียน, กะเบียน gkra[4]-bee-an *n. Gardenia turgida*, a small deciduous tree which yields a hard, yellow gum. A preparation from the root is employed as a remedy for indigestion in children; the root is regarded as a charm by the natives of Chota Nagpur, who wear it attached to the wrist by a cord (Dept. Agri. & Fisheries p. 483); *Xanthophyllum glaucum* (*Rubiaceae*) (V. P. p. 12: K.); also applied to *Hydnocarpus ilicifolia*, a tree

with globular, brown fruit, smaller than those of the กระเบา.

กระเบีย an euphonic suffix for กระบั่ว.

กระเบื่อง, กะเบื่อง gkra[4]-beu-ang[3] *n.* a roof-tile; pieces or fragments of broken earthenware.

กระแบ่, กะแบ่, กระบิ gkra[4]-baa[4] *n.* a piece, portion, stub or remnant.

กระแบก, กะแบก, กะแบกไข่, ตระแบก, ตราแบกปรั, ตะแบก, ตะแบกนา gkra[4]-baak[4] *n. Lagerstroemia flos-reginae* (*Lythraceae*) (cb. p. 723). This fine, flowering tree is found wild in Siam, India and Malaya. When in bloom, it is very showy. There is some variation in the colour of the flowers. Those usually seen are a mauve and purple, but there is a less common and more attractive pink variety (G. B. M. p. 153). The roots, bark, leaves and flowers are used medicinally. The roots especially, are prescribed as an intestinal astringent. The seeds are narcotic. The bark is purgative. The wood is used as house building material and the trunks for dugout boats: *Lagerstroemia calyculata* (cb. p. 719), a tree found in mixed, dry forests near streams. The flowers are pink (K.): *Lagerstroemia balansae* (cb. p. 718), a tree about 20 m. high, found in bamboo forests. The flowers are a pale mauve (K.): *Lagerstroemia floribunda* (cb. p. 722: V. P. p. 11), a tree about 10 m. high, common in evergreen forests and growing to a large size. The flowers are a pale mauve. It was once cultivated in H. H. Prince Bidyalongkarana's garden and is said to have come originally from Chantaboon (K.): *Lagerstroemia cuspidata* (cb. p. 721), a bush about 3 m. high, found in scrub jungle. The flowers are mauve (K.): ตะแบกเลือด *Terminalia mucronata* (cb. p. 605).

กระแบะ, กะแบะ gkra[4]-baa[4] *n.* a bag-net of about 100 feet in length; a piece, portion or fragment: กระแบะมื้อ small in size, equal to the palm of the hand: กระแบะแหละ even; smooth.

กระโบม, ตระโบม   gkra⁴-bom v. to embrace, caress or comfort; to encircle with the arms; to speak lovingly to.

กระปรี๊กระเปร่า, กะปรี๊กะเปร่า   gkra⁴-bpree³-gkra⁴-bprow⁴ adj. adroit; dexterous; expert; active; spry; nimble.

กระปลกกระเปลี้ย see กระบั๊วกระเบิย

กระปมกระปำ, กระปมกระเปา gkra⁴-bpom-gkra⁴-bpum adj. knotted; jointed: gnarled (as a portion of the trunk of a tree).

กระบ๊อกระแบ๊, กะบ๊อกกระแบ๊   gkra⁴-bpau³-gkra⁴-bpaa³ adj. feeble; weak; frail; easily broken.

กระบ๋อง, บ๋อง   gkra⁴-bpaung⁴ adj. bulging up or out; being rounded out from pressure within (as a balloon): แมลงบ๋อง a scorpion.

กระบ๋อง, กะบ๋อง   gkra⁴-bpaung² n. a tin pail; a tin dipper; tins for milk or preserves; an empty tin; a canister.

กระปอดกระแปด, กะปอดกะแปด gkra⁴-bpaut⁴-gkra⁴-bpaat⁴ adj. sickly; habitually indisposed.

กระบั๊วกระเบิย see กระบั๊วกระเบิย

กระปำ   an euphonic suffix for กระปม.

กระปำ ๑   gkra⁴-bpum⁴ n. a node, knot, knob or swelling (as at the joint of a stem): an euphonic suffix for กระปุ๋ม.

กระปำ, กะปำ ๒   gkra⁴-bpum⁴ adj. delicious to the taste; sweet to the palate; savoury: กระปำกระเป๋อ adj. forgetful.

กระปิ่ม   an euphonic suffix for กระปุ๋ม.

กระปุก, กะปุก   gkra⁴-bpook⁴ n. a small pot or jar; a jug; a small tin container: กะปุก

หมึก an inkwell; an inkstand.

กระปุกหลุก   gkra⁴-bpook⁴-look⁴ adj. chubby; adorable; lovable (as infants).

กระบุ๋มกระปำ, กระบุ๋มกระบุ๋ม   gkra⁴-bpoom⁴-gkra-bpum⁴ adj. rough; rocky.

กระบุ๊มกระบม see กระบุ๊มกระปำ

กระเปา   an euphonic suffix for กระปม.

กระเป๋า, กะเป๋า   gkra-bpow² n. a pocket; a purse; a hand-bag; a tobacco pouch or belt-pouch: กระเป๋าแห้ง out of cash; poor; penniless; destitute: กระเป๋าหนัก rich; wealthy; pockets full of cash.

กระเปาะ, กะเปาะ   gkra⁴-bpau⁴ n. a bulb; a root enlargement; a raised surface; a mound; an hillock: กะเปาะเหวน the bezel of a ring: กระเปาะเหลาะ rounded in shape and prominent or elevated: กระเปิ๋ย an euphonic suffix for กระบั๋ว: กระแบ๊ an euphonic suffix for กระบ๊อ: กระแปด an euphonic suffix for กระปอด.

กระโปก, กะโปก   gkra⁴-bpoke⁴ n. scrotum; testes: ลูกกระโปก testicles.

กระผม   gkra⁴-pom² pron. the first personal pronoun "I" used in speaking to persons of equal or superior rank (only used by men).

กระผลาม   an euphonic suffix for กระผลิ.

กระผลิกระผลาม, กะผลิกะผลาม   gkra⁴-plee²-gkra⁴-plam² adj. disordered; fearful; easily frightened; trembling with fear.

กระผาน   gkra-pan² n. the gluteal portion of the thigh; the buttocks.

กระผีก, กะผีก   gkra⁴-peek⁴ n. a capacity measure for rice (equal to ¼ of a กระเพาะ or about 2.55 liters): adj. little; small; trifling.

กระพริม   gkra⁴-prim⁵ adj. poetical flickering; twinkling; sparkling; scintillating.

กระเพลิศ, ตะเพิด   gkra⁴-plurt³ v. to frighten by loud shouting; to drive off by a loud noise (as when driving game); to eject or expel by creating a noise (as with gongs, fire-crackers etc.).

กระพอก, กะพอก ๑   gkra⁴-pauk³ n. a woven, bamboo container with lid (used by mountain travellers for carrying food):   ตั้ง กระพอกกินเหล้า to congregate for drinking purposes.

กระพอก ๒   gkra⁴-pauk³ v. to talk; to speak; to converse.

กระพอกวัว   gkra⁴-pauk³-woo-ah n. the striated marsh-warbler *Megalurus palustris* (Herb. N. H. J. S. S. VI, 1, p. 104).

กระพอง, กะพอง ๑   gkra⁴-paung n. the two humps on the sides of an elephant's head.

กระพอง, กะพอง ๒   gkra⁴-paung n. the top rails on the two sides of the freight space of an oxcart, to which perpendicular slats are attached.

กระพัก, กะพัก   gkra⁴-pak⁶ n. a series of over-hanging rocks, shelves or ledges, which can afford protection or shelter.

กระพัง, กะพัง   gkra⁴-pang n. a small depression in the ground or mountain side where water may be confined.

กระพังเหิร, กะพังเหิร   gkra⁴-pang-hern² n. a method the mahout has of using the iron driving goad or hook to make the elephant halt.

กระพังโหม, กะพังโหม   gkra⁴-pang-home² n. *Parderia linearis* applied to several species of *Paederia rubliaceue*, a genus of climbers with an offensive odour. It is used by the Siamese in medicine (K.). The juice abstracted from the leaves, mixed with flour, is used in the making of a sweet-meat.

กระพัด, กระพัตร   gkra⁴-pat⁶ v. to tie; to buckle on; to encircle (as with a belt):   n. a belly-band or strap for holding a howdah in place.

กระพัน, กะพัน   gkra⁴-pan adj. impenetrable by weapons (as when being attacked): คงกระพัน invulnerable.

กระพัตร see กระพัด

กระพาก, ตะพาก   gkra⁴-pak³ n. a species of fresh-water carp *Puntius darnphani* (H.M.S.).

กระพี้, กะพี้   gkra⁴-pee⁵ n. the inner lining of the bark; the sap-wood of trees: กระพี้ (ต้น) *Dalbergia lakhonensis* (*Leguminosae*) var. *appendiculata* (cb. p. 481), a valuable, deciduous timber tree: กระพี้เขาควาย *Millettia leucantha* (*Leguminosae*) (cb. p. 390); *Dalbergia Kurzii* (*Leguminosae*) (cb. p. 480); *Sindora sumatrana* (K.); *Dalbergia cultrata* (V. P. p. 12: Dept. Agri. & Fisheries p. 6), a moderate-sized tree growing in the forests of northern Siam. The wood is hard, heavy, black and fragrant, with curved lines resembling the shape of the buffalo's horns. The wood is employed for making agricultural implements, handles of spades, swords, and especially for furniture carvings. The tree is used for the propagation of lac and furnishes a useful oil.

กระพุ่ม   gkra⁴-poom³ n. the act of raising both hands placed palm to palm: กระพุ่มมือ to hold both hands placed palm to palm in the attitude of worship or adoration.

กระพุ้ง, กะพุ้ง   gkra⁴-poong⁵ n. a bulged-out or protuberant part or portion; the most convex part (as of a cask): กะพุ้งแก้มลิง a monkey's jowl: กระพุ้งเรือ the bulging portion of a boat.

กระพือ, กะพือ   gkra⁴-peu v. to wave; to flutter; to flap; to vibrate (as by a breeze): กระพือปีก to flap the wings.

กระเพิง, กะเพิง   gkra⁴-perng n. a projecting roof, forming a floorless protection from sun and rain; projecting eaves.

กระเพาะ, กะเพาะ gkra⁴-pau⁶ *n.* a bladder ; a sack ; an enlargement ; a capacity measure for rice (equal to about 10 liters): กะเพาะคูธ the lower intestines : กะเพาะน้ำ a pitcher : กะเพาะน้ำคร่ำ the amnion (the sac which encloses the foetus, forming the bag of waters): กะเพาะปีสสาวะ the urinary bladder : กะเพาะ อาหาร the stomach.

กระเพื่อม, กะเพื่อม gkra⁴-peu-am³ *v.* to be in ripples ; to be shaken irregularly ; to be ruffled : *adj.* bobbing (as of a floating object) ; rippling (as the surface of water): น้ำกระเพื่อม the water is agitated or shaken into waves.

กระแพง, กำแพง gkra⁴-paang *n. ancient poetical spelling* a wall of brick or stone.

กระพัดกระเพียด, กะพัดกะเพียด gkra⁴-fat⁶-gkra⁴-fee-at³ *adv.* angrily ; irritatedly ; excitedly (descriptive of manners).

กระฟาย an euphonic suffix for กระฟูม.

กระฟูมกระฟาย, กะฟูมกะฟาย gkra⁴-foom-gkra⁴-fai *n.* descriptive of being bathed with tears (as the face): *adv.* excessively ; abundantly ; extravagantly (as use of funds); improvidently.

กระเพียด an euphonic suffix for กระพัด.

กระมล see กมล

กระมวล gkra⁴-mu-an *n.* a place ; a locality.

กระมอบ gkra⁴-maup³ *n. Gardenia obtusifolia (Rubiaceae)* (V. P. 13), a small, deciduous tree which yields a fine, pellucid, yellow resin. The wood is white and moderately hard (Dept. Agri. & Fisheries p. 483).

กระมอมกระแมม, ขะมอมขะแมม gkra⁴-maum-gkra⁴-maam *adj.* dirty (of face or clothes); besmeared or bespattered (as with dirt).

กระม้า, หางกวาง (ต้น) gkra⁴-mah⁵ *n. Ancistrocladus extensus (Ancistrocladaceae)* (cb. p. 148), a scandent shrub. The leaves are used by villagers for thatching huts.

กระมัง, กะมัง ๑ gkra⁴-mang *adv.* perchance ; perhaps ; of doubtful condition.

กระมัง, กะมัง ๒ gkra⁴-mang *n.* a carp *Puntioplites proctozysron* (Dept. Agri. & Fisheries).

กระมิดกระเมี้ยน, กะมิดกะเมี้ยน gkra⁴-mit⁶-gkra⁴-mee-an⁵ *v.* to manifest an attitude of bashfulness, shyness or coyness.

กระมื่น, ตระมื่น, ทะมื่น gkra⁴-murn *adj. ancient spellings* high ; lofty ; towering ; outstanding ; sky-high.

กระมุท gkra⁴-moot⁶ *n.* the lotus flower ; the esculent white water-lily *Nymphaea esculenta* ; the red lotus *Nymphaea rubra*.

กระเมาะ, กะเมาะ (ปลา) gkra⁴-maw⁶ *n.* a mullet *Mugil speigerli* (Dept. Agri. & Fisheries).

กระเมี้ยน an euphonic suffix for กระมิด.

กระแมม an euphonic suffix for กระมอม.

กระย่อง an euphonic suffix for กระยิ้ม.

กระย่องกระแย่ง, กะย่องกะแย่ง gkra⁴-yaung³-gkra⁴-yaang³ *adj.* staggering ; tottering ; reeling : *adv.* imperfectly ; limpingly (as when walking with a lame leg).

กระย่อน, ขะย่อน gkra⁴-yaun³ *v.* to move in a vermicular manner ; to sway ; to churn ; to be agitated (as by rotating from side to side): *adj.* peristaltic : ความขะย่อนแห่งลำไส้ peristaltic motions of the intestines : กระย่อนกระแย่น, ขะย่อนแขะย้น *adj.* swaying ; movable ; loose.

กระย่อม, กะย่อม, ระย่อม gkra⁴-yaum³ *n. Rauwolfia serpentina (Apocynaceae)* (V. P. p. 13 : Dept. Agri. & Fisheries p. 398), a large climber. From ancient times the roots have been much valued as an antidote for the bites of poisonous reptiles and the stings of insects. They are also used as a febrifuge and as a remedy for dysentery and other painful affections of the intestinal tract (Dept. Agri. & Fisheries p. 398).

กระยา   gkra[4]-yah *n.* food; provisions; victuals; articles; implements; utensils: กระยาดอก, กระยาดอกเบี้ย property or commodities given in lieu of interest on a monetary loan (as fields, wife or children):   กระยาทาน food or articles given as alms: กระยาบวช food which does not contain fish, meat or fowl: กระยาเบี้ย *ancient legal term* interest on money loaned, or amount paid for slaves: กระยา-รงค์ paint; oil or water-colour for painting purposes: กระยาเรือนเบี้ย *ancient legal term* the primary amount of indebtedness: กระยาเลย various; mixed; sundry; diversified (descriptive of small articles or plants):   กระยา-สนาน propitiatory offerings made to spirits: กระยาสวย food (used for royalty):   กระยา-สังเวย propitiatory offerings made to ancestral or household spirits: กระยาสารท cakes or sweet-meats made of nuts, sesame-seeds and rice, for the "Sart" or 10th. month festival: กระยาหาร food (used for the nobility):   ไม้-กระยาเลย a conglomeration of timber (standing or sawn) other than teak or bamboo.

กระยาง, กะยาง   gkra[4]-yang *n.* a tripod; the pond heron, *Ardeola grayi* (Gaird. J. S. S. IX, 1, p. 10):   ยาง (นก) the black bittern, *Dupetor flavicollis* (Herb. N. H. J. S. S. VI, 4, p. 354):   ยางกรอก (นก) chestnut bittern, *Ardetta cinnamomea* (Gaird. J. S. S. IX, 1, p. 10); Indian pond heron *Ardeola grayii* (Herb. N. H. J. S. S. VI, 4, p. 352):   ยางขาว (นก) white cattle egret, *Bubalcus coromandus* (Deig. N. H. J. S. S. VIII, 3, p. 173). This bird is commonly seen on the backs of cattle in paddy fields: ยางแดง (นก) chestnut bittern, *Ixobrychus cinnamomeus* (Deig. N. H. J. S. S. VIII, 3, p. 173): ยางเสวย (นก) chestnut bittern, *Ixobrychus cinnamomeus* (Herb. N. H. J. S. S. VI, 4, p. 353): cattle egret, *Bubalous coromandus* (Gaird. J. S. S. IX, 1, p. 10):   ยางทอง (นก) little egret, *Egretta garzetta* (Herb. N. H. J. S. S. VI, 4, p. 351).

กระยาจก   gkra[4]-yah-chjok[4] *n.* a beggar.

กระยาด   an euphonic suffix for กระยืด.

กระยาหงัน, กะยาหงัน   *Cam.* gkra[4]-yah-ngan[2] *n.* the highest palace of the angels; a future place of bliss.

กระยิก, ขะยิก   gkra[4]-yik[6] *adj.* quick and often repeated; successive.

กระยิ้มกระย่อง, กะยิ้มกะย่อง   gkra[4]-yim[5]-gkra[4]-yaung[3] *v.* to manifest joy, delight, contentment or satisfaction.

กระยืดกระยาด, กะยืดกะยาด   gkra[4]-yeut[3]-gkra[4]-yat[3] *adj.* uncouth; inactive; slow; awkward; clumsy.

กระยูง, พยุง, ประดู่ลาย (ต้น)   gkra[4]-yoong *n.* *Dalbergia cochinchinensis* (*Leguminosae*) (cb. p. 475), a valuable, spreading, timber tree. The bark is yellowish brown (K.).

กระแย่ง   an euphonic suffix for กระย่อง.

กระรอก, กะรอก   gkra[4]-rauk[3] *n.* squirrel, *Sciurus sp.* (Gaird. N. H. J. S. S. III, 2, p. 124).

กระเรียน, กะเรียน (นก)   gkra[4]-ree-an *n.* *Grus antigone* sarus crane, a wading bird of the genus *Grus* and allied genera, of various species, having a long, straight bill, long legs and neck (Gaird. J. S. S. IX, 1, p. 14); *Grus sharpi*, a crane found in Siam.

กระไร   see กระใด

กระลบ, กลบ   gkra[4]-lop[6] *v.* to fill up with dirt (as a hole); to cover over with soil; to hide by burying in the ground; to cause to lap; to be folded; to be rolled over upon (as when reefing a sail).

กระลอก   gkra[4]-lauk[3] *adj. poetical* rolling; turning from side to side.

กระลัด   gkra[4]-lat[6] *adj.* brave; daring (as one in war).

กระลับ, กลับ   gkra[4]-lap[6] *v.* to return; to turn back; to change back to: กลับใจ to have a change of heart: กลับดีกัน to resume friendship.

กระลา   gkra⁴-lah *n.* members or people engaged in, or connected with a sacrifical ceremony : กระลาพิน, กระลาศรี women.

กระลาการ   gkra⁴-la-gkarn *n.* judge *ancient spelling* for ตระลาการ.

กระลายกระลอก   gkra⁴-lai-gkra⁴-lauk³ *v.* to be mixed ; to be mingled ; to be piled up in an irregular manner.

กระลาโหม, กะลาโหม   gkra⁴-la-hom² *n.* the meeting place of soldiers ; a place of assembly for soldiers : กระทรวงกลาโหม Ministry of Defense.

กระลำ, กระลำพร   gkra⁴-lum *n.* a severe punishment ; destruction ; ruin.

กระลำพัก, กะลำพัก   gkra⁴-lum-pak⁶ *n. Euphorbia Antiquorum (Euphorbiaceae)*, "milk-hedge," a spreading, leafless, quick-growing tree, 10 to 15 feet high, found in rocky places in the low-country. The branches are angled and very prickly. The acrid, milky juice is poisonous and sometimes causes blindness (MCM. p. 385). The juice, which flows from the branches, is used by the natives as a purgative. A plaster, prepared from the powdered roots and mixed with asafetida, is applied over the region of the stomach of children suffering from intestinal worms. The bark of the roots, in the form of a decoction, acts as a purgative (Dept. Agri. & Fisheries p. 295).

กระลำพุก, กะลำพุก, ตะลุมพุก   gkra⁴-lum-pook⁶ *n. Randia uliginosa (Rubiaceae)* (V. P. p. 14), a small, deciduous tree. The fruit is used as a dye. When eaten, it has an astringent action, so is used as a remedy in diarrhoea and dysentery. The leaves, when boiled, are relished as vegetables (Dept. Agri. & Fisheries p. 392).

กระลิง, กระลึง   gkra⁴-ling *v.* to catch ; to grasp ; to hold.

กระลี   gkra⁴-lee *n.* punishment ; dire calamity ; retribution : *adj.* cruel ; fierce ; brutal ; severe : กระลีชาติ a race of savages : กระลี-ยุค the last and most terrible of the four eras ; a time of calamity and misfortune.

กระลึง   see กรรลึง, กะลึง

กระลุมทาง   gkra⁴-loom-tang *n.* a drum having one head.

กระลุมพุก, ตะลุมพุก   gkra⁴-loom-pook⁶ *n.* a large shad, *Hilsa Alosa toli* (Dept. Agri. & Fisheries) : ไม้ตะลุมพุก a mallet with a long handle, used as a pestle for pounding paddy in a mortar.

กระลุมพู, กะลุมพู (นก)   gkra⁴-loom-poo *n.* a bird of the pigeon family : กระลุมพูไฟ (นก) the nutmeg pigeon *Carponago paenea* : กระลุมพูหม้อ (นก) the white, nutmeg pigeon *Myristicivora bicolar.*

กระลูน   gkra⁴-loon *n.* sorrow ; grief ; mournfulness : *adj.* being worthy of compassion, pity or sympathy.

กระเลียด, เกลียด   gkra⁴-lee-at³ *v. poetical* to detest ; to hate ; to abhor.

กระเลือก, เกลือก, เหลือก   gkra⁴-lur-uk³ *v.* to wallow ; to roll over on the back (as a horse) ; to rub against.

กระวน   gkra⁴-won *v.* to be disturbed ; to be uneasy ; to be anxious about ; to be distressed ; to be restless (as a delirious patient) : กระวนกระวาย to be perturbed ; to be agitated about ; to be disquiet.

กระวาด   an euphonic suffix for กระวีและกระวุด.

กระวาน, กะวาน   gkra⁴-wan *n. Amomum xanthioides (Zingiberaceae)* (V.P. p. 16), cardamoms, an herb found growing on the mountains of Siam at about 4,000 feet elevation. The seeds are exported to China for use as spices and medicine (K.). The seeds are stimulants and carminatives. Powdered seeds, mixed with butter, are administered in cases of dysentery. *Amomum krervanh* is a wild or bastard species (of Siam) ; *Elettaria cardam-*

omum (MCM. p. 331), " Mysore cardamon ", a perennial with large leafy shoots 8 to 12 feet long and strong, creeping root-stocks (rhizomes). Cardamons are a powerful aromatic and are used chiefly as an aphrodisiac in medicine, as an ingredient in curry powder, with masticatories for sweetening the breath, and in confectioneries (MCM. p. 332): กระวานหัวช้าง a medicinal herb.

กระวิน, กะวิน   gkra[4]-win *n.* the rings of a howdah band ; rings of the metal mouthpiece of a bridle ; a ring attached to a Buddhist monk's belt. These may be iron, ivory or bone.

กระวี   gkra[4]-wee *n.* a poet ; a rhymer.

กระวีกระวาด, กะวีกะวาด, กระวูดกระวาด, กะวูดกะวาด   gkra[4]-wee-gkra[4]-wat[3] *adv.* urgently ; speedily ; quickly.

กระวูดกระวาด see กระวีกระวาด

กระเวน, ตระเวน   gkra[4]-wane *v.* to keep watch around a place ; to keep guard : *adj.* exposing for ridicule or mockery (as criminals in chains) :   กระเวน (นก) a species of nightbird having two, long tail-feathers ; black racket-tailed magpie, *Crypsirhina varians* (will. N. H. J. S. S. I, 2, p. 76 : Herb. N. H. J. S. S. VI, 1, p. 91) : กระเวนกระวน to make circular trips back and forth (as a physician attending a patient).

กระแวน, กะแวน see กระเวน

กระศัย, กระษัย   gkra[4]-sai[2] *n.* a group of diseases of vague causation but producing general weakness and emaciation :   กระษัย กล่อน an enlargement of the scrotum, which may be an hydrocele, orchitis or epididymitis.

กระษัย see กระศัย

กระษาปณ์   gkra[4]-sap[4] *n.* specie ; a coin : โรงกระษาปณ์หลวง the Royal Mint.

กระเษียร   gkra[4]-see-an[2] *n. ancient poetical*   [milk.

กระสง, กะสง   gkra[4]-song[2] *n.* a species of fresh-water fish, *Ophicephalus lucius* (Dept. Agri. & Fisheries).

กระสน   an euphonic suffix for กระเสือก.

กระสม, กะสม, ไม้กระสม   gkra[4]-som[2] *n.* a revolving rod placed at the back of a loom to take up the woven cloth.

กระสรวล, กะสรวล   gkra[4]-soo-an[2] *v. poetical* to be happy ; to be pleased.

กระสร้อย, กะสร้อย (ปลา)   gkra[4]-saw-ie[3] *n.* a family of fresh-water fish, *Rasbora argyrotaenia* (H. M. S.) :   สร้อยบัว (ปลา) *Labeo dyocheilus* (Dept. Agri. & Fisheries) :   สร้อยลูกนุ่น (ปลา) *Dangila leptocheila* (Dept. Agri. & Fisheries).

กระสวน, กะสวน   gkra[4]-soo-an[2] *n.* a pattern ; a copy :   ถ่ายแบบ to copy from a pattern.

กระสวย, กะสวย   gkra[4]-soo-ay[2] *n.* the shuttle of a loom ; a weaver's shuttle.

กระสอบ, กะสอบ   gkra[4]-saup[4] *n.* a gunny bag (as for rice) ; a sack (as for flour) ; a bag made of split rushes (as for molasses or for an inferior grade of sugar).

กระสะ   gkra[4]-sa[4] *n.* mine tailings ; ore dirt ; mine washings ; mine refuse.

กระสัง, กะสัง   gkra[4]-sang[2] *n. Peperomia pellucida* (*Piperaceae*) (V. P. p. 14 : K.), a small fragrant plant eaten by the Siamese in salad or in a vegetable curry ; an herb growing on rocks or trunks of trees in evergreen forests. The flowers are white (K.).

กระสัน, กะสัน   gkra[4]-san[2] *v.* to desire ; to wish for ; to be desirous of :   *adj.* restive ; impatient :   กะสันปั่นป่วน perturbed by desires or emotions of love.

กระสับกระส่าย, กะสับกะส่าย   gkra[4]-sap[4]-gkra[4]-sai[4] *adj.* restless ; uneasy ; nervous.

กระสา, กะสา (นก)   gkra[4]-sah[2] *n.* a family

of fish-eating birds, having long, sharp bills and long legs and toes; the grey or common heron, *Ardea cinerea* (Gaird. J. S. S. IX, 1, p. 10).

กระสา, สา (ต้น) gkra[4]-sah[2] *n.* *Broussonetia papyrifera* (*Urticaceae*) (V. P. p. 254), paper mulberry, a medium-sized tree of the Pacific Islands, having large, ovate leaves. The inner bark furnishes a fine, fibrous material suitable for making paper. The famous "tapa" or "kapa" cloth of the Pacific Islands, made from this fibre, formed the only wearing attire of the indigenous inhabitants until comparatively recent years (MCM. p. 429).

กระสานต์ gkra[4]-san[2] *adj. poetical* quiet; calm; peaceful.

กระสาบ, กะสาบ gkra[4]-sap[4] *n.* a leather bag.

กระสาย, กะสาย gkra[4]-sai[2] *n.* a solvent (as alcohol); a diluent (as syrup or water): ยากระสายเหล้า medicinal ingredients (usually tied in a bag and steeped or soaked in arrack).

กระส่าย an euphonic suffix for กระสับ.

กระสินธุ gkra[4]-sin[2] *n. ancient poetical* a river.

กระสือ, กะสือ gkra[4]-seu[2] *n.* a group of female evil spirits or demons, reputed to feed on putrid meat and to inhabit women: กระหัง the corresponding group inhabiting men: โคมกระสือ a bull's-eye hand lantern: ผีกระสือ spirits or genii found in graveyards and reputed to devour the bodies of the dead: ไฟกระสือ a phantom light or spark; a will-o'-the-wisp; the ignis fatuus: หนอนกระสือ glowworms: อ่าวกระสือ a bay on the mainland east of Kohsichang.

กระสุน, กะสุน gkra[4]-soon[2] *n.* a bow with double strings, used for shooting dried mud-balls: กระสุนปืน ammunition; loaded shells: กระสุนวิถี the range of a missile or projectile: ลูกกระสุน dried mud-balls ready for shooting from a bow; a projectile: ลูกกระสุนดินดำ

bullets; cartridges; a charge of gunpowder: สายกระสุน the string of a bow.

กระสุทธิ gkra[4]-soot[4] *n.* the act of cleansing the hands before a Brahmin ceremony or rite.

กระสูบ, กะสูบ gkra[4]-soop[4] *n.* a species of fresh-water fish, *Hampala macrolepidota* (Dept. Agri. & Fisheries).

กระเสด, กะโสด gkra[4]-set[4] *n.* a sandbank standing above the level of the water.

กระเส็นกระสาย, กะเส็นกะสาย gkra[4]-sen[2]-gkra[4]-sai[2] *n.* chips; bits; remnants; scraps; fragments.

กระแสง see กรรแสง

กระเส่า, กะเส่า gkra[4]-sow[4] *adj.* soft and tremulous (descriptive of the voice or of musical notes).

กระเสาะกระแสะ, กะเสาะกะแสะ gkra[4]-sau[4]-gkra[4]-saa[4] *adj.* not being quite up to normal in health; having but little strength; rather unhealthy: เที่ยวกระเสาะกระแสะ to wander aimlessly hither and thither; to go snooking around seeing the sights: ป่วยกระเสาะกระแสะ sickly; suffering from ill-health.

กระเสียน gkra[4]-see-an[2] *adj.* appropriate; fitting (as of a gown or crown): กระเสียนอายุ proper age.

กระเสียร gkra[4]-see-an[2] *adv.* savingly; miserly; stingily; penuriously: a suffix for กระเบียด.

กระเสือกกระสน, กะเสือกกะสน gkra[4]-sur-uk[4]-gkra[4]-son[2] *adj.* striving; grasping; struggling; pushing (descriptive of one in dire necessity, leaving no stone unturned to get or accomplish).

กระแส gkra[4]-saa[2] *n.* current (as of flowing water); the course of water flowing in a river; a rope; a line; tape: เส้นกระแส a measuring tape, rope or line: กระแสความ

the course, progress or advancement of a matter in dispute : กระแสรับสั่ง a royal command, order or edict ; an order issued by royalty : กระแสลม, กระแสน้ำ currents of wind or water : กระแสเสียง the volume of a sound issuing forth : กระแสสลับ alternating electric current.

กระแสง, กะแสง   gkra⁴-sang² *n.* rays ; glory ; colour : *adj.* melodious ; agreeable (descriptive of the voice or of musical notes) : เสียงกระแสงไพเราะ sweet and musical notes or voices.

กระแสะ, กะแสะ   gkra⁴-saa⁴ *adj.* weak ; debilitated ; exhausted ; prostrated (as by protracted sickness).

กระโสง (ปลา)   gkra⁴-song² *n.* a species of fresh-water fish, *Ophicephalus lucius* (Dept. Agri. & Fisheries).

กระไส   gkra⁴-sai² *n. poetical* sand.

กระหน   gkra⁴-hon² *v.* to be excited ; to be restless ; to be greatly disturbed or perturbed ; *ancient form for* กระวนกระวาย.

กระหนก, กนก, กะหนก   gkra⁴-nok⁴ *n.* a lineal decorative design, of which there are three styles. In one, the surface is filled with rising tendrils, resembling leaping flames. In this design, decorative art has reached the culminating point of beauty. According to tradition, the " kanok " designs are not deduced from the flame but are the reproduction in art, of the blossoms of the rice plants (Doeh, I, p. 25) : *v. ancient* to be frightened ; to be startled : กระหนกครกเครื่อ one of these " kanok " designs representing garlands of flowers.

กระหนาบ, กะหนาบ, ขนาบ   gkra⁴-nap⁴ *v.* to bind the two sides together (as a hedge or the two edges of the mouth of a gunny bag) ; to tie together ; to compress ; to squeeze and bind tightly (as sheaves of rice stalks or corn shocks) ; to scold ; to reprimand ; to abuse (in a loud, angry manner) : กระหนาบคาบเกี่ยว

overlapping and hooked together (as old-fashioned roof tiles fitted with grooves).

กระหน่ำ   gkra⁴-nam⁴ *v.* to repeat (as strokes when pounding) ; to strike over and over again (as in flogging).

กระหมวด   gkra⁴-mu-at⁴ *v.* to twist and tie into a knot ; to cause to curl into ringlets, whorls or cowlicks (as hair) : *n.* a cerebral node or prominence on the skull of an elephant, the pale colouring of which is one of five diagnostic markings of a sacred white elephant. The others are hairs in the ears, on the tail, along the ridge of the back-bone and hairs in ringlets, whorls or cowlicks on the sides, just back of the front legs. This last one is considered of especial importance.

กระหมอบ   gkra⁴-maup⁴ *adj.* lessened in size ; diminished in capacity (as the abdomen in forced contraction of the muscles).

กระหม่อม   gkra⁴-maum⁴ *n.* the crown of the head : *adv.* yes ; as you say : *pro.* the first personal pronoun (used when speaking to a prince of the rank of Highness) : กระหม่อมฉัน, เกล้ากระหม่อม the first personal pronoun (used by a commoner to a prince or princess) : ทูลกระหม่อม a term of respectful address (used only for the children of a sovereign by a queen).

กระหมั่ง, กะหมั่ง   gkra⁴-mang⁴ *adv.* perhaps ; perchance ; *poetical term* for ดอกกระมัง, กระมัง.

กระหม่า   gkra⁴-mah⁴ *v.* to be abashed ; to be stage-struck ; *ancient spelling* for ประหม่า.

กระหมิด   an euphonic suffix for กระหมุด.

กระหมิบ, ขมิบ   gkra⁴-mip⁴ *v.* to cause to contract ; to close an aperture or opening by muscular action.

กระหมุดกระหมิด, ขมุดขมิด   gkra⁴-moot⁴-gkra⁴-mit⁴ *adj.* insufficiently tight ; inadequate to reach all the way (as a string around a package); almost enough; incapable of but almost able to attain.

กระหมุบ gkra[4]-moop[4] v. to pulsate; to throb; to beat or palpitate (as the heart or pulse): กระหมุบกระหมิบ, ขมุบขมิบ to twitch nervously (as the mouth); to pucker and slacken alternately (as the muscles of the mouth).

กระหย่ง, กระโหย่ง gkra[4]-yong[4] v. to increase the height by raising one's self on the toes: เดินกระหย่งเท้า to walk on the toes; to go on tip-toe: นั่งกระหย่ง to squat with the feet flat on the ground and touching each other.

กระหย่อม gkra[4]-yaum[4] n. a group; a cluster; a clump; a collection; a small pile (as of paving stones along the side of a road).

กระหยับ, ขยับ gkra[4]-yap[4] v. to move either way just a little (as people in a crowd to make way for one to pass).

กระหยิ่ม, ขยิ่ม gkra[4]-yim[4] v. to be glad; to manifest joy or satisfaction.

กระหริ่ง, กะริ่ง gkra[4]-ring[4] n. a snare or trap, fitted with a rattan, slip-knot loop or noose for large game (as deer).

กระหวน gkra[4]-hoo-an[2] v. to revert one's mind or thoughts back to; to reflect or meditate on the past: กระหวนกระโหยหา to have fond recollections regarding.

กระหวัด, ตวัด gkra[4]-wat[4] v. to encircle (as with a lasso); to surround (as with the arms); to bind or draw together; to strike or slash (as with a whip or lash): ช้างตวัดหญ้า the elephant slaps or slashes the grass that it holds in its trunk.

กระหัง, กระหาง, กะหัง gkra[4]-hung[2] n. a group of evil spirits or demons that feed on putrid meat and are reputed to inhabit men; the corresponding group of spirits, called กระสือ, inhabit women.

กระหาง see กระหัง

กระหึม, กะหึม gkra[4]-heum[2] adj. growling; gnarling; snarling; roaring: ฟ้ากระหึม the sky peals with thunder.

กระหืดกระหอบ, กะหืดกะหอบ gkra[4]-heut[4]-gkra[4]-haup[4] adj. breathless (as after running); laboured respiration (as in asthma).

กระเหนึ่จ gkra[4]-net[4] n. tactics; methods of procedure; strategy: กระเหนึ่จกระแหน่ strategy; artful or cunning devices; magical practices.

กระเหม็ดกระแหม่ gkra[4]-met[4]-gkra[4]-maa[4] v. to practice frugality; to economize; to be stingy or miserly; to save for future use (as funds).

กระเหม่น gkra[4]-mane[4] v. to vibrate from tenseness; to tremble; to quiver involuntarily (descriptive of muscular tremors and considered by ancient magicians as an omen of good or evil).

กระเหม่า, เขม่า gkra[4]-mauw[4] n. soot; a coating or furred condition of the tongue (a symptom of infantile throat diseases).

กระเหว่า, กาเหว่า, ดุเหว่า gkra[4]-wauw[4] n. Malayan coel, *Eudynamis malayana* (Gaird. J. S. S. IX, 1, p. 7).

กระเห่อ gkra[4]-hur[4] v. to become arrogant; to boast of one's standing or attainments.

กระเหิม gkra[4]-hurm[2] adj. bold; audacious; impudent; presumptuous.

กระแห, กะแห (ปลา) gkra[4]-haa[2] n. a family of edible fresh-water fish, *Puntius schwanefeldi* (Dept. Agri. & Fisheries).

กระแหน an euphonic suffix for กระแหนะ.

กระแหน่, กะแหน่ gkra[4]-naa[4] n. sleight-of-hand tricks; devices intended to deceive others: *syn.* แง่งอน, เล่ห์กล.

กระแหนะ, กะแหนะ gkra[4]-naa[4] n. ornamental mouldings overlaid with gold-leaf: v. to touch lightly or slightly; to cause to adhere or stick on in small pieces (as by a mere touch of the finger).

กระแหม่ว gkra⁴-maa-oh⁴ *adj.* being reduced in size or capacity (as the abdominal cavity, by forced contraction of the muscles): กระแหม่วท้อง to cause the abdomen to become less in size, by forcibly contracting the muscles.

กระแหร่ม gkra⁴-raam⁴ *v.* to make a forced cough or clearing of the throat (as when wishing to call one's attention).

กระโห้, กะโห้ gkra⁴-ho³ *n.* a species of large, herbivorous, fresh-water fish; the giant carp, *Cutlocarpio siamensis* (Dept Agri. & Fisheries).

กระโหนด, โตนด gkra⁴-note⁴ *n.* "Patana oak," *Careya arborea* (*Lecythidaceae*) (Cb. p. 674 : MCM. p. 443), a small or medium-sized tree. The bark yields a good fibre for coarse cordage and is used for tanning leather. Used medicinally, both locally and internally, it is an astringent. The round, green fruit, borne in great profusion, is in season in May and June. The fruit is sweet, when young. The flowers are white and coral pink (K.: Dept. Agri. & Fisheries).

กระโหย gkra⁴-hoh-ie² *v. poetical* to groan in grief or agony; to weep or cry.

กระโหย่ง see **กระหย่ง**

กระอ่วน an euphonic suffix for กระอั๋ก.

กระอวล gkra⁴-oo-an *adj.* having a pleasing, permeating fragrance.

กระอ้อกระแอ้, กะอ้อกะแอ้ gkra⁴-au³-gkra⁴-aa³ *interj.* an onomatopoeia (as of gutteral sounds): ทำกระอ้อกระแอ้ to act with hesitation, delay or awkwardness.

กระออดกระแอด, กะออดกะแอด gkra⁴-aut⁴-gkra⁴-aat⁴ *adj.* complaining incessantly in an undertone.

กระออม, กะออม, โคกกระออม gkra⁴-

aum *n. Cardiospermum halicacabum* (*Sapindaceae*) (Cb. p. 322), a perennial vine with medicinal properties (used as a native remedy). The roots and leaves are aperient (MCM. p. 378 : Dept. Agri. & Fisheries p. 156).

กระอ้อมกระแอ้ม, กะอ้อมกะแอ้ม gkra⁴-aum³-gkra⁴-aam³ *adj.* muttering; mumbling; speaking or uttering imperfectly pronounced words; making soft, gutteral, unintelligible sounds intended as words.

กระอัก gkra⁴-ak⁴ *v.* to bring up or be expelled with force (as from the lungs or stomach): กระอักกระอ่วน doubtful; uncertain; wavering; hesitating: กระอักกระไอ to manifest a hesitating, embarrassed, timid or scared manner while speaking and clearing the throat.

กระอิด gkra⁴-it⁴ *adj. poetical* weakened; depressed (in health or strength); debilitated; unnerved.

กระอึก gkra⁴-euk⁴ *v. poetical* to be noisy; to be boisterous.

กระอึด gkra⁴-eut⁴ *v.* to whine; to cry in a teasing manner.

กระเอบ gkra⁴-ape⁴ *adj. poetical* delicious; savoury; tasty; pleasing to the taste.

กระเอา gkra⁴-ow *adj.* well-rounded-out in all respects; perfect in all regards; complete with all the necessary ingredients (as well-seasoned or delicious curry).

กระเอิบ gkra⁴-erp⁴ *v.* to be completely satisfied (as with food); saturated (as a solution).

กระแอ้ an euphonic suffix for กระอ้อ.

กระแอก, กะแอก ๑ gkra⁴-aak⁴ *n.* a pair of back-straps or ropes for elephants. These follow along both sides of the spinal ridge from the collar to the crupper, and serve as hangers for ornamental trappings.

กระแอก, กะแอก (นก) ๒ gkra⁴-aak⁴ *Cum.*

the crow, *Corvus levaillanti andamanensis* (Deig. N. H. J. S. S. VIII, 3, p. 134).

กระแอด an euphonic suffix for กระออด.

กระแอบ gkra[4]-aap[4] *Cam. n.* the centipede.

กระแอม, กะแอม gkra[4]-aam *v.* to utter a forced cough; to pretend to clear the throat in order to attract attention: ทำกระแอม กระไอ, ทำกระไอกระแอม to give a signal by coughing; to act hesitatingly.

กระแอ้ม an euphonic suffix for กระอ้อม.

กระไอ, กะไอ, สะไอ gkra[4]-ai *v.* to cough: *n.* an offensive odour from the mouth or nose: เหม็นกระไอ odour of decaying, putrid or decomposing matter: an euphonic suffix for กระแอม, กระอัก.

กรัก gkrak[4] *n.* the core or heart-wood of the jack-fruit tree (used for dyeing the robes of Buddhist monks).

กรักขี gkrak[4]-kee[2] *n.* a species of *Cinnamoum* (*Leguminosae*). The bark is used in native medicine as a remedy for constipation (K.).

กรัง gkrang *v.* to be dried and matted together (as blood and hair); to be glued together; to be stuck tightly together.

กรัช see กรช

กรัชกาย gkrat[4]-gkai *n. lit.* "a form born from the dust of the earth", *i. e.* our bodies.

กรัญช gka[4]-ran-cha[6] *n. Crataeva Hygrophila* (V. P. p. 32).

กรัณฑ์ gkran *P. S. n.* a basket; a box; a small pill-box for lip-wax.

กรัณย์ gka[4]-ran *S. n.* duty; business; task.

กรัน, แกร็น gkran *adj.* small; undeveloped; dwarfed (as a plant or child): กล้วย กรัน a species of dwarfed banana: หม้อกรัน a small, earthen water-pot having a long spout.

กรับ gkrap[4] *v.* to be glued and dried together; to be gummed together as a mass: *n.* wooden clappers for beating time during theatrical performances: กรับพวง multiple castanets.

กรัม gkram *Eng. n.* gram, a fundamental unit of mass or weight.

กร่าเซก (ต้น) gkra[4]-sake[3] *n. Peltophorum dasyrachis* (*Leguminosae*) (cb. p. 498), a tree about 10 m. high, found in deciduous forests along foot-hills (K.).

กราก gkrak[4] *v.* to advance abruptly or rudely (as a tiger in an attack): *adj.* dry; parched; scorched; shriveled: *onomat.* from the sound of tearing cloth or dragged branches of trees: กรากกร่ำ in a hard or harsh manner (as convicts are made to work): กราก แกรก *onomat.* from a cracking sound.

กราฆาต see กร ๑

กราง gkrang *v.* to rub together; to reduce to fine particles or filings: กรางเกรี้ยง grating; rasping; scraping; scratching (as the leaves of the sugar palm when moved by the wind).

กร่าง (ต้น) gkrang[4] *n. Ficus benghalensis* (*Urticaceae*), the banyan, a large-spreading, smooth-barked tree with large, leathery, shiny leaves, very effective when bearing its crops of large, bright crimson berries (MCM.).
The milky juice is applied externally for pains and bruises and as an anodyne application in rheumatism and lumbago. The leaves, when, heated are applied as a poultice to abscesses (Dept. Agri. & Fisheries p. 345): *onomat.* from the clicking or clanging of wires when struck.

กราด gkrat[4] *n.* a long-handled broom; a curry-comb for dressing horses; a mechanical brace for clamping pieces of wood together (as after gluing): *adj.* scattered; splashed; sprinkled: กราด (ต้น) *Dipterocarpus intricatus* (*Dipterocarpaceae*) (cb. p. 136: V. P. p.

26), a tall, erect tree in the deciduous forests of the eastern provinces of Siam. The oil obtained from these trees is used for making torches (K.): กราดให้แน่น to drive down tightly (as a nail); to press or clamp together closely and firmly: ยิงกราด to be scattered (as bird-shot from a gun).

กราด an euphonic suffix for กรีด.

กราดเกรี้ยว gkrat⁴-gkreew³ *adj.* enraged; furious; raging; angry (as a wild animal when caged).

กราดวง see กระดวง

กราน gkran *v.* to be stretched upon; to be stiffened out against; to be propped up to; to prostrate one's self; to drop down into a bent over or crouching position: กรานกฐิน to measure by or stretch out beside a frame by which robes for Buddhist monks are measured in order to be cut to a standard size: เชิงกราน a portable, earthen fireplace: ยันกราน to place a prop against so as to prevent from leaning or falling: ยืนกราน to be insistent upon; to be unyielding in one's stand, purpose or opinion; to assume an attitude of stubbornness or willfulness: หมอบกราน, ก้มกราน to assume a bent over or crouching position of the body (as on the knees and elbows).

กร้าน gkran³ *adj.* hard; rough (as skin); horny (exterior); disfigured; unpolished (as a board or post in the rough).

กรานต์ see กันต์ ๓

กราบ gkrap⁴ *v.* to do obeisance; to prostrate one's self: *n.* bulwarks of a ship; narrow strips added to the upper edge of sideboards of small boats: กราบใต, ตราบใด to the final end; henceforth forever; whenever; from this time on: กราบทูล to inform; to present a petition to His Majesty or to a prince: กราบ พระ (ผ้า) a kneeling cloth or mat: กราบเรียน a title of address in letters (used to a superior or prince): กราบไหว้ to assume a position

of worship or profound respect by falling on the floor with hands clasped and bending the head on to the hands to the floor: หมอบ กราบ to sit sidewise on the floor raising the hands, placed palm to palm, to the face and bending over till the hands touch the floor (a respectful attitude when saluting or taking leave of royalty).

กราบัด (ต้น) gkra-bat⁴ *n. Cassia garrettiana* (*Leguminosae*) (cb. p. 510), a tree about 30 feet high, growing in deciduous forests. The flowers are yellow (K.).

กราม gkram *n.* molar teeth; the grinders: กรามช้าง (กล้วย) a species of banana: กราม-ช้าง (ผี) an abscessing molar or wisdom tooth: กรามช้าง (โรค) a cancerous condition developing in the region of the molar teeth.

กรามพลู, กานพลู gkram-ploo *n.* cloves *Eugenia caryophyllata* (V. P. p. 29: MCM. pp. 15,337), a small, conical tree 25 to 30 feet high, native of the Moluccas and introduced into most tropical countries. The cloves are dried, unexpanded flower buds, which are picked green by boys and spread in the sun for a few days to dry or until they become dark brown.

กราย gkrai *v.* to walk past another in close proximity; to walk in a swaggering manner: กราย (ปลา) *Notopterus chitala*, a species of feather-backs with 7 or 9 black spots along the sides of the body (Dept. Agri. & Fisheries): กรายแขน to swing the arms in an exaggerated manner: เดินกราย to swing the arms while walking (as one full of vanity): ทำกรีดกราย to assume a boastful, haughty attitude.

กราย an euphonic suffix for กรีด, กรุย.

กราล gkraw *Cam. v.* to spread down (as a carpet).

กราลัมพัน see กร ๑

กราว gkraw *adj.* in great numbers: *onomat.* from the pattering of rain or falling of pebbles on a roof or from the cheering of a crowd of people : กราวนอก, กราวใน. กราวรำ a group of working songs in march-time (such as the sailor's chantey).

กร้าว gkraw[3] *n.* hardness ; toughness : *adj.* hard ; tough.

กราสึก gkra[4]-ra-sik[4] *n.* cloth with cotton and silk threads interwoven.

กร่ำ gkram *adj.* bearing ; brooking ; undergoing ; suffering ; enduring (as trouble, persecution, misfortune or imprisonment).

กร่ำ gkram[4] *v.* to slash or cut stubble with a large field-knife : *n.* a sheltered place for trapping fish. Sticks, stakes or poles are planted along a water-course and the enclosed space is covered with branches of trees or fronds of coconut trees. When the fishes are to be caught, the whole is enclosed in a close-meshed net or screen made of bamboo, the leaves and some of the stakes are removed and the net drawn in on the catch ; stakes marking the channel for boats to follow (as along the sea indicating the mouth of a river) : เมากร่ำ being a habitual drunkard.

กร่ำกรุ่น gkram[4]-gkroon[4] *adj.* indistinct ; blurred (as regarding colour).

กริก gkrik[4] *onomat.* from the clicking of two glasses.

กริกกริว gkrik[4]-gkriw *adj.* vulgar ; rude ; menial : คนกริกกริว a low, inferior person.

กริกกรี, กรุงกรี gkrik[4]-gkree *adj.* southern *provincialism* dudish ; flirting ; coquettish.

กริงกริว gkring-gkriw *adj.* slight ; small ; puny ; diminutive in size or stature (as a pigmy).

กริง gkring[4] *v.* to be doubtful of another ; to mistrust another's veracity or motive : *n.* a tinkling sound (as of a bell) ; a clanging or a jingling sound : กริงใจ to suspect ; to doubt ; to distrust another.

กริ้งกริ้ว gkring[3]-gkriw[3] *adj.* scrawny ; small ; thin ; sordid.

กริณี, กริน, กริณี gka[4]-ri[6]-nee *S. n.* an animal with a proboscis (as the elephant or tapir) ; a female elephant : กริกุมภ์ a node or protuberance on the forehead of an elephant : กริกรรชิต the trumpeting of an elephant : the roaring of elephants : กริจรรม, กริจรมัน the hide of an elephant : กริทนต์ the tusks of an elephant : กริทารก a lion : กรินาสา the trunk of an elephant : กริโปต an elephant's calf : กริพันธ์ a tethering post for elephants : กริไพชยันดี the flag that a leading elephant carries : กริมาจล *lit.* " one that kills elephants," *i. e.* a tiger : กริมุข *lit.* " one that has an elephant's face," *i. e.* the god Ganesa (H. C. D.) : กริวร a valuable tusker ; a precious elephant : กริศาวก a baby elephant (aged up to about 5 years) : กริสกนธ์ a herd of wild elephants : กรินทร์ a strong elephant (one used in warfare).

กริน see กริณี

กริบ gkrip[4] *v.* to snip off ; to cut with short, quick strokes of scissors or shears (as hair or leaves of a hedge) : *adj.* completely : เงียบกริบ perfectly quiet.

กริม gkrim *n.* a species of small fish similar to the fighting fish *Ctenops vittatus* (Dept. Agri. & Fisheries).

กริ่ม gkrim[4] *v.* to be glad ; to be satisfied : กริ่มใจ gay ; joyful ; gleeful ; jovial.

กริยา gka[4]-ri[6]-yah *P. S. n.* a verb *gram* ; action (as the idea expressed by any verb) ; conduct ; manners ; manual labour ; business ; work ; used as a prefix, it helps form a noun indicating action : กริยากร one who performs ; one who acts : กริยาการ an agreement ; a rule ; an arrangement ; a beginner or novice ; one newly entering the Buddhist priesthood : กริยามิรเทศ evidence : กริยานุป conformable to the act ; according to the action : กริยานุเคราะห์ *gram.* an auxiliary verb : กริยาบถ the method or manner of rendering medical treatment ; the application of remedies : กริยาบท *lit.* " an action word," *i. e.* a verb : กริยาผล the results or consequences of acts : กริยาวิธิ a rule of action ; mode of performing any rite ; the conduct of affairs : กริยาวิเศษณ์ *lit.* " that which defines an action to make it more clear," *i. e. gram.* an adverb : กริยาวิเศษณ์วลี *gram.* an adverbial phrase : กริยาไม่มีรูป *gram.* impersonal verbs : กระทำกริยาตาย to feign or simulate death.

กริว ๑   gkri-oh *n.* a turtle ; a tortoise.

กริว ๒, กริวกราว   gkri-oh *adj.* tumultuous ; boisterous ; turbulent with anger ; riotous (as a mob yelling simultaneously).

กริ้ว   gkri-oh[3] *v.* to be angry ; to get angry ; to be out of patience (used only by or about royalty) : กริ้วโกรธ to get or be very angry.

กรี   gkree *n.* a sharp bone or spine on the head of a prawn.

กรีฑา   gkree-tah *S. n.* sport ; play ; amusements : *adj.* playing ; sporting ; frolicing ; sportive : กรีฑากร to perform in groups in sports : กรีฑาเกตน์, กรีฑาเคหะ a gymnasium ; a pleasure house : กรีฑาโกศล skill in sports or athletics ; the art of finding pleasure in sports : กรีฑานารี a courtezan ; a prostitute ; an harlot : กรีฑาบรรพต, กรีฑามหิธร a raised place or elevation where sports are held ; a stadium ; an artificial hillock or mound, built in a garden for pleasure : กรีฑาบุรา a town visited for amusement : กรีฑาประเทศ, กรีฑาสถาน a playground ; a sport arena ; athletic grounds : กรีฑาภิรมย์ affording or furnishing the greatest pleasure or entertainment in sports : กรีฑามยุร a peacock trained to perform or kept for sport : กรีฑามฤค animals trained or kept for sporting purposes ; tame deer : กรีฑามัย consisting of play or sport : กรีฑารถ a carriage used only for pleasure or sport ; a pleasure-chariot ; the antithesis of a war-chariot : กรีฑารมย์ enjoying sports or athletics : กรีฑารส a game afford-

ing great pleasure or excitement : กรีฑารัตน์ " the pinnacle or supreme degree of all pleasure ", *i. e.* the married state : กรีฑาวัน a park ; a reservation kept for sporting purposes ; a pleasure grove : กรีฑาวาปี hunting grounds or reservations where fish, animals and fowls are kept for sport ; game preserves : กรีฑาเวศม์ a gymnasium ; a house for pleasure : กรีฑาสกุนต์ birds kept for sport (as for exhibition or shooting) : กรีฑาสระ a pleasure pond.

กรีด   gkreet[4] *v.* to scratch or score ; to scrape lightly (as in vaccination) ; to cause to rush forth (as gas or water) : *n.* a shriek ; a scream ; a sound (as of a woman or child weeping) : กรีดกราด a cry or scream of terror or fright : กรีดกราย proudly ; vainly ; indifferently : กรีดนิ้ว to separate by stiffening the fingers apart.

กรีด, กรีดกร๊าด   gkreet[5] *onomat.* from a scream, a shrill cry or a shriek.

กรีธา   gkree-tah *v.* to remove from one place to another ; to transport military divisions ; to equip ; to review : กรีธาทัพ to change the position of a military body : กรีธาพล to mobilize an army ; to assemble an army ; to muster troops.

กรีษ   gka[4]-reet[4] *S. n.* excrement ; feces ; fecal matter ; cow-dung.

กรีส   gka[4]-reet[4] *S. n.* a linear unit for measuring land, equal to four อัมพณะ, approximately two acres or five rai.

กรึง   gkrunk *v.* to tie tightly ; to bind ; to fasten or nail to ; to cause to make tight or to hold firmly together.

กรุ   gkroo[4] *v.* to hide or secrete ; to shut up ; to cover over ; to over-lay with : *n.* an underground hiding place ; a cache ; a cell ; a place for storing one's belongings : กรุจาก to shut in with attap (as by sides or partitions) : กรุฝา to divide internally by a partition ; to cover with leaves ; to make a bamboo wall : กรุเรือ to spread out mats in the bottom of a

boat for the display of goods for sale : ติดกรุ
to put into a cell ; to incarcerate.

กรุก gkrook[4] v. to be engrossed with ; to be
consumed with interest in ; to be absorbed
mentally (as following a hobby, such as music
or play) : กรุกรัก out of order ; having
continued difficulty (as with some machinery
or project).

กรุกร see กรรกร

กรุง gkroong n. a capital city ; the chief
metropolis of a kingdom : กรุงเก่า, กรุงศรี-
อยุธยา ‘Ayuthia, a former capital of Siam :
กรุงไกร a very strongly fortified town : กรุง-
เทพฯ Bangkok, the present capital of Siam :
กรุงเทพมหานคร the great city of the angels :
กรุงพาลี the tutelary spirits of a place ; a place ;
a square dish made of banana leaves, used
to hold offerings made to spirits : กรุงสยาม
country or kingdom of Siam.

กรุงกรง see กริ๋กกริ๋

กรุงเขมา gkroong-kay[2]-mah n. a climbing
shrub. The roots have medicinal properties
(K.: Dept. Agri. & Fisheries p. 359).

กรุณา, กรุณ gka[4]-roo[6]-nah P.S. n. pity ; compassion ; mercy ; tenderness ; sympathy ; a
personal pronoun for the king : กราบบังคม
ทูลพระกรุณา a form of petition for royal clemency : กรุณาทฤคุณ humaneness : goodness
(combined with benevolence) : กรุณาบร with
compassion (as the sole purpose) : กรุณามัย
compassionate ; benevolent.

กรุ่น gkroon[4] adj. smouldering ; slight but
continuous burning ; enveloped in smoke or
odour of any kind : ไฟกรุ่นในครัว a fire kept
burning in the kitchen : หอมกรุ่น having
an enveloping fragrance.

กรุบ gkroop[4] n. the soft or undeveloped
coconut shell ; a kind of sweet-meat or cake :
onomat. from a crunching sound as when the
teeth hit against a grain of sand while chewing.

กรุ่ม gkroom[4] v. to coo often (as doves when
mating) : adj. continuous but slightly ; often ;
several times over.

กรุย gkroo-ay n. a fringe ; sticks, stakes or
posts used in marking out a road : กรุยกราย
shabbily or improperly dressed : กรุยที่ to
stake out a place by setting up landmarks :
ปักกรุย to mark by planting sticks or stakes
(as in marking out a road) ; to mark out ; to
stake out.

กรู gkroo v. to run in crowds ; to arrive in
crowds ; to run to : adj. gathered (in crowds
or in flocks) : กรูกันมา to run up in crowds :
กรูเกรียว, กรูกราว to run together tumultuously.

กรูด gkroot[4] onomat. from brush being
hauled, which scrapes or scratches objects it
touches.

กเรณุ gka-ray-noo[6] n. an elephant.

กเรณุกา gka[4]-ray-noo[6]-gkah n. a female
elephant.

กเรนทร์, กรินทร์ see กริณ

กโรทก see กร ๑

กฤช gkrit[4] n. a Malay or Javanese short,
two-edged knife or dagger.

กฤด, กฤต gkrit[4] P.S. n. an act ; an occupation ; a cause : adj. completed ; finished ;
satisfactorily accomplished : กฤตกร the god
Siva : กฤตกรรม an act or duty which has
been accomplished ; he who has accomplished
a deed or duty : กฤตกาม one who has
succeeded in his purpose or desire : กฤตทาร
a married man : กฤตธรรม one whose
conduct is as it should be ; one who has performed his duty well : กฤตนาม one who
has been given a name : กฤตบรรพ, กฤตยุค
the golden era of the world ; one of four eras
of the world, a period of 1,728,000 years
(H. C. D.) : กฤตประณาม one who makes or
does acts of obeisance : กฤตประโยชน์ one
who has accomplished his purpose or duty :
กฤตผล one who has fully attained results ;

one whose life is full of results of (good)
deeds : กฤตพุทธิ a wise man ; one who has
completed his studies : กฤตโภชน์, กฤตาหาร
one who has finished or completed eating :
กฤตมโนรถ one who has attained his desires
or purposes : กฤตมาล a species of deer
having stripes and dots : กฤตมุข dexterous ; efficient : กฤตมูลย์ having a fixed or
predetermined price : กฤตรุษ angered ; provoked : กฤตลักษณ์ precious ; having been
predetermined for a good purpose : กฤตวิทย์
one having finished his education ; one having
graduated in his scientific studies ; a philosopher ; a man of science : กฤตศิลป์ one
having graduated in the Arts ; one proficient
in arts : กฤตสัมพันธ์ one included in a pact
or agreement ; allies : กฤตหัสต์ one having
trained hands ; dexterous (skilled in the art
of shooting) : กฤตากรณ์ one who has completed dressing or decorating himself : กฤตา-
คม one in the lead (as a man in a race) ; the
winning one ; the champion : กฤตานน one
most experienced ; a very efficient one :
กฤตานุกร one imitating another ; an imitator ;
one incompetent in himself : กฤตานุกูลย์
one who favours another ; one who helps or
obliges another : กฤตานุสาร an established
precedence ; a well-founded custom ; customary proceedings : กฤตาปการ one doing
wrong ; one acting contrary to rule, instruction or custom : กฤตาภัย one who has
escaped misfortune or calamity : กฤตาภินิหาร
possessed with supernatural powers ; having
merit from previous good deeds : กฤตาลัย
one having attained an abiding place : กฤตา-
วธาน one who is attentive to duty ; one who
is cautious, careful and prudent : กฤตาวาส
a tenant ; one who lives in a house or dwelling
place belonging to another : กฤตาสบท one
who has secured an abode or a place to dwell
in : กฤโตปการ one having rendered assistance to another or who has been kind to
another.

กฤตยาเกียรณ gkrit⁴-yah-gkee-an adj.

having or being complete with honour and
distinction.

กฤตาอัญชลี gkrit⁴-dah-un-cha⁶-lee v. to
worship ; to show respect to by placing the
hands palm to palm ; to do obeisance to.

กฤติ, เกียรติ gkrit⁴-di⁴ n. ancient poetical
the act of preaching or proclaiming.

กฤดีกา, กฤตยฎีกา gkrit⁴-dee-gkah n. bye-
laws ; skill acquired from repeated performance ; agreement ; appointment.

กฤต see กฤด

กฤตติกา see กรรดึก ๑

กฤตย์ gkrit⁴ n. a task ; business ; a vocation ; a duty,

กฤตยฎีกา see กฤดีกา

กฤตยา gkrit⁴-dta⁴-yah n. ancient poetical
honour ; dignity ; distinction.

กฤติกา gkrit⁴-dti⁴-gka n. lit. "stars of good
omen," i. e. the Pleiades, composed of eight
stars which according to Indian legends represent the nurses of การดิเกยะ, the god of War,
being daughters of a king in one legend but
wives of Rishis according to another (H. C. D.).

กฤปณ see กปณ

กฤมิ gkri⁴-mi⁶ P. S. n. a worm ; maggots ;
ants ; silkworms ; insects ; spiders : กฤมิโกศ
a cocoon ; the chrysalis state of the silkworm :
กฤมิทนต์ toothache from dental caries : กฤมิ
บรรพต, กฤมิไศล an ant hill : กฤมิราค coloured
red from colouring matter produced by insects :
กฤมิศังข์ shell-inhabiting animals.

กฤศ gkrit⁴ P. S. adj. thin ; small ; emaciated ;
sparce ; needy ; low ; poor : กฤศชน a poor
man : กฤศนาศ, กฤศนาส lit. "one having
a small nose", i. e. the god Siva : กฤโศทร
one having a small waist.

กฤษก gkrit⁴-sa⁴-gka⁴ n. a farmer ; a plowman; an agriculturist; one who makes his living on the soil.

กฤษฎ์ gkrit[4]-sa[4]-dee *n.* the waist; the hips; comely in shape or form.

กฤษฎะ gkrit[4]-sa[4]-ta[4] *P. S. adj.* plowed; raked; harrowed: กฤษฎผล seedling rice, grain or cereals that have been sown or planted; rice stalks suitable to be reaped.

กฤษณะ gkrit[4]-sa[4]-na[6] *P. S. n. lit.* "black, dark, dark blue," *i. e.* the dark half of the lunar month, from full to new moon; name of the celebrated eighth incarnation of the god Vishnu or sometimes identified with Vishnu himself as distinct from his tenth incarnation. In the earlier incarnation, he appears as a great hero and teacher. In the latter incarnation, he is deified and is often represented as a young and amorous shepherd with flowing hair, and a lute in his hand. The following are a few particulars of his birth and history. Vasu-deva, who was a descendant of Yadu, son of king Yayati, the fifth king of of the Lunar race, had two wives, Rohini and Devaki; the latter had eight sons of whom the eighth was Krishna. Kansa, king of Mathura and cousin of Devaki, was informed by a prediction that one of these sons would kill him; he therefore kept Vasu-deva and his wife in confinement, and slew their first six children; the seventh was Balarama, who was saved by being abstracted from the womb of Devaki and transferred to that of Rohini; the eighth was Krishna, who was born with black skin and a peculiar mark on his breast. His father, Vasu-deva, managed to escape from Mathura with the child and, favoured by the gods, he found an herdsman named Nanda, whose wife Yase-da had just been delivered of a son, which Vasu-deva conveyed to Devaki, after substituting his own in its place. Nanda, with his wife Yaso-da, took the infant Krishna and settled first in Gokula or Vraja, and afterwards in Vrindavana, where Krishna and Balarama grew

up together, roaming in the woods and joining in the sports of the herdsmen's sons. Krishna, as a youth, contested the sovereignty of Indra, and was victorious over this god, who descended from heaven to praise Krishna, and made him lord over the cattle. Krishna is described as sporting constantly with the Gopis· or shepherdesses, of whom a thousand became his wives, though only eight are specified, Radha being the favourite. Krishna built and fortified a city called Dvaraka, in Gujarat, and thither transported the inhabitants of Mathura, after killing Kansa. Krishna had various wives besides the Gopis, and by Rukmini had a son, Pradyumna, who is usually identified with Kamadeva: *adj.* wicked; evil (S. E. D.): กฤษณกันท์ the red lotus: กฤษณเกศ having black hair: กฤษณโกหล a gamester; a gambler: กฤษณคดี, กฤษณยาม *lit.* "one whose way is black," *i. e.* fire: กฤษณครีพ having a black neck: กฤษณจุรณ rust or iron filings: กฤษณดาร *lit.* "black eyed," *i. e.* an antelope; the black of the eye: กฤษณทนต์ having black teeth: กฤษณไทวปายน a black islander, Vyasa, compiler of the Maha-bharata and of the Puranas, named so because of his dark complexion and because he was brought forth by Satyavati on an island in the Ganges: กฤษณเนตร black-faced; black-eyed; name of Siva: กฤษณปที a female with black feet: กฤษณปักษ์ the dark half of a month (fifteen days during which the moon is on the wane); time from full to new moon; *lit.* "standing on the side of Krishna," *i. e.* Arjuna: กฤษณภคินี Krishna's sister, Durga: กฤษณภักต์ a worshipper of Krishna: กฤษณภัสม์ sulphate of mercury: กฤษณมณฑล the black part of the eye: กฤษณมฤค the black antelope: กฤษณรักษ์ *lit.* "one beloved of Krishna," *i. e.* Vishnu: กฤษณโลหะ the lodestone; iron: กฤษณวรรณ of a black colour; being of a dark blue colour: กฤษณวาส *lit.* "one wearing black clothes," *i. e.* Siva: กฤษณศกุนิ *lit.* "a black bird," *i. e.* the crow: กฤษณสารถิ *lit.*

"having Krishna for a charioteer," *i. e.*
Arjuna : กฤษณามิษ iron ore (S. E. D.).

กฤษณา (ต้น) gkrit[4]-sa[4]-nah[2] *n.* egle-wood,
aloes-wood *Aquilaria agallocha* (*Thymelaeaceae*) (MCM. pp. 397, 412); *Photinia david-
soniae* (*Rosaceae*) (Cb. p. 578); *Eriobotrya
bengalensis* (*Rosaceae*) (cb. p. 580), a large tree
of Siam and Burma. The wood is rich in
fragrant resin from which a medicine is
obtained. It is also used for burning as
incense (as in temples).

กฤษณามิษ see กฤษณะ

กฤษาณ, กฤษิก gkrit[4]-san[2] *S. n.* a farmer ;
an agriculturist.

กฤษิ gkri[4]-si[4] *S. n.* farming ; plowing ;
agricultural work : กฤษิกรรม the act of
farming ; the planting of grain : กฤษิชีวิน
a farmer ; one who makes a living by farming or along agricultural lines.

กล ๑ gkon *S. n.* a cunning device or trick ;
sleight-of-hand ; artifice ; a device which will
deceive or delude ; chicanery : *adj.* dark or
shady ; dim ; misty ; mysterious ; deceitful :
กลไก a secret mechanism : กลฐต money ;
currency : กลไฟ (เรือ) an iron steamship ; a
steam launch : กลมารยา wily ; artful ; fraudulent (as secretly planning a plot) : กลเม็ด
a witticism ; an attempt at wit : กลยนต์
automatic ; self-acting (device or machinery) :
กลศึก military tactics or strategy : กลอุบาย
wiles ; ambuscade : กุญแจกล a mechanical
lock : คนเล่นกล a conjurer : จงกล a
stand for tapers, incense or joss sticks :
ชอบกล very well ; done with artfulness or
craft : แต่งหนังสือมีกลเม็ดดีจริง exceedingly
witty or clever in diction : พระเทศกัณฑ์นี้มี
กลเม็ดน่าฟัง this sermon preached by the monk
is most idiomatic and witty : เล่นกล to
exercise magical power or sleight-of-hand
tricks ; the art of juggling : เล่ห์กล craft ;
wile ; secret art ; the secret of an art.

กล ๒ gkon *adj.* similar ; resembling : *adv.*

as ; like : กลซ้อนกล stratagem (in the superlative degree) : กลลวง a trick to deceive
(sometimes used by judges to make a criminal
confess his guilt when finally the judge can
in no way help him).

กลด gklot[4] *n.* an umbrella with a long
handle (carried over kings or Buddhist monks
of high rank) : กลิ้งกลด a three-tiered umbrella : ทรงกลด luminous (as rays of light
encircling the sun or moon).

กล่น gklon[4] *adj.* scattered ; strewn about
plentifully.

กลบ gklop[4] *v.* to cover over ; to bury ; to
hide under ground : กลบเกลี่ย to bury and
then smooth over the earth : กลบบัตรสุมเพลิง
a Brahminic ceremony, consisting of burning
some paddy husk (performed to atone for
some sin or unpropitious deed) : กลบรอย
to cover up any trace or tracks : กลบลบ
to make up a deficit ; to pay instead of :
พูดกลบเกลื่อน to talk ambiguously so as to
cover up the meaning ; to talk with words
having a double meaning.

กลม gklom *adj.* round ; circular ; globular ;
spherical : กลมกลอก to make perfectly
round by rolling (as mud-balls between the
palms) : กลมกล่อม just right ; properly ;
sufficient in all respects : กลมกลิ้ง perfectly
round ; rounded with a lathe : กลมเกลียว
harmonious ; united in purpose or aim ; without dissatisfaction ; living peacefully (as a
family) ; unanimous : กลมเกลี้ยง perfectly
round and smooth.

กลละ gka[4]-la[6]-la[6] *P. S. n.* semen ; sperm.

กลวง gkloo-ang *adj.* hollow (all the way
through).

กลวม gkloo-am *adj.* scattered or strewn
about promiscuously.

กลวย (ต้น) gkloo-ay *n. Casearia grewiifolia, Casearia esculenta* (*Samydaceae*) (cb.
p. 737), an erect, unarmed shrub or small tree.

The wood and leaves are used medicinally and the fruit is edible (MCM. p. 548).

กล้วย   gkloo-ay[3] *n.* banana; plantain (of which there are twenty-eight varieties) (D. B. B.); *Musa sp.* (V. P. p. 34); *Musa paradisiaca*; *Musa sapientum* (K.: MCM. p. 245): กล้วยค่าง *Orophea fusca* (*Anonaceae*) (cb. p. 60); *Orophea enterocarpa* (K.): กล้วยไม้ orchids *Orchideae* (V. P. p. 34: MCM. p. 145): กล้วยไม้ต้นเต่า *Desmos dubius* (*Anonaceae*) (cb. p. 39): กล้วยลังกา *Revenala madagascariensis* traveller's tree (phya winit N. H. J. S. S. IX, 3, p. 280). Its palm-like stem, with a crown of banana-like leaves in fan-wise arrangement, renders the traveller's tree very singular and interesting in appearance. On this account the tree is now frequently grown in gardens. In olden days this tree was found only in the grounds of Buddhist monasteries. This is now true in northern Siam of *Musa glauca*, an indigenous plant of the same family. The traveller's tree is said to have been already well-known in the reign of King Phra Chaum Klao (1851–1868). From these facts, as well as from the Siamese name itself, the traveller's tree was evidently introduced from Ceylon by some religious body, probably during the reign of King Phra Nang Klao (1825–1851), in which period religious intercourse between Siam and that country was frequent. Early in the reign of King Vajiravudh, a Ceylonese priest brought this tree again to Bangkok and it was planted at Wat Lieb. The traveller's tree, as its botanical name implies, is a native of Madagascar: กล้วยสาสนา *Musa nepalensis*, a small quick-growing, very handsome tree, 10 to 20 ft. high, with an herbaceous stem composed of succulent leaf-stalks. It is naturally propagated by suckers and forms a cluster of stems. This plant has been observed at the Tap Tao cave, a religious sanctuary in the Muang Fang district of Chiengrai province. It is a native of Nepaul where Buddha ceased his earthly existance. Probably on account of this association, it has come to be looked upon as a sacred plant. A pilgrim is said to have brought the original plant to Tap Tao from Burma some years ago (Kerr N. H. J. S. S. VIII, 3, p. 208: MCM. p. 244): กล้วยเห็น *Mitrephora vandaeflora* (*Anonaceae*) (cb. p. 54): กล้วยหมูสัง *Uvaria purpurea* (*Anonaceae*) (cb. p. 31: V. P. p. 35): กล้วย (ปลา) a loach *Acanthopsis choirorhynchus* found mostly in sandy streams or watercourses.

กลศ, กลส, กลัส   gklot[4] *P. S. n.* a cup; a round vessel of earth, gold or silver (used for domestic purposes): หม้อกลศ a ceremonial vessel with a long spout (used for pouring consecrated, sacred or lustrous water).

กล้อ   gklau[3] *v.* to trim down or to make circular: *n.* a boat partly or imperfectly hewn out of a log or still in a rough condition: *adj.* rounded; circular; spherical; spheroidal: กล้อ (กบ) a plane for making convex or rounded surfaces: กล้อแกล้ to be loaded down to the water's edge (as a boat).

กลอก   gklauk[4] *adj.* vacillating; wavering; fluctuating; unstable; rolling back and forth: กลอกกลับ swaying back and forth; uncertain; unstable; variable; fickle: กลอกหน้ากลอกตา to turn the face or eyes from side to side; to make grimaces.

กลอง   gklaung *n.* a drum: กลองแขก a Javanese tom-tom: กลองชะนะ a kind of Javanese drum used in Court processions and in processional rites for the dead: กลองชาตรี a "chatri" drum: กลองไชยเภรี a victory drum: กลองทัด a "thut" drum: กลองเบ่งพรวด a kind of drum used in State funeral processions: กลองมอญ a kind of Peguan drum: กลองมะลายู a Malay tom-tom: กลองเบ่งมาง, กลองสองหน้า a two-headed drum: ตีกลองร้องฎีกา to beat the drum hung in former times in front of the Throne Hall to call the attention of the King to the applicant: หอกลอง a tower where three bells and three drums were hung in ancient times and beaten at 6 a. m. and 6 p. m., as signals or as an alarm in case of fire or on the approach of an enemy.

กล่อง   gklaung[4] *n.* a telescoping case for matches or cigars : กล่องเข็ม a needle case : กล่องดวงใจ the case or box in which the heart of Ravana was hidden prior to the final battle with Rama : กล่องดินสอ a pencil case or box : กล่องบุหรี่ a cigar case : กล่องหมาก a round telescoping box for the betel-nut outfit.

กล้อง   gklaung[3] *v.* to pound in a mortar ; to pound or thump with the fist ; to punch with the elbow : *n.* a telescoping tube ; an opera glass ; binoculars : กล้องจุลทัศน์ a microscope : กล้องถ่ายรูป a camera : กล้องโทรทัศน์ a telescope : กล้องบุหรี่ a cigar holder : กล้องเป่า a long tube for blowing mud-balls : กล้องยานัดถุ์ a snuff tube : ใช้กล้องส่อง to examine with a microscope or telescope : ส่องกล้อง *v.* to look through a telescope or microscope.

กล้องแกล้ง   gklaung[3]-gklaang[3] *adj.* weak ; feeble ; decrepit ; slender (as of a waist).

กลอน   gklaun *n.* poetry ; poems ; a bolt or catch for a door ; a latch : กลอนชอ notched rafters for holding battens : กลอนประตู a door bolt or pin : กลอนหน้าต่าง a window bolt : ภาพย์กลอน a rhyme or jingle : เชิงกลอน an eaves board : ยาลูกกลอน pills ; medicine in pill form.

กล่อน   gklaun[4] *n.* a condition characterized by infiltration of serum into the tissues of the scrotum : กล่อนน้ำ an hydrocele : กล่อนลงผัก an indefinite, indurated condition of the testicles.

กล้อน   gklaun[3] *adj.* sparse ; thinly diffused ; bare (as being denuded of hairs or feathers) : ถุงกล้อน an empty purse.

กล่อม   gklaum[4] *v.* to lull to sleep by singing ; to calm ; to pacify ; to make smooth and round ; to trim off the bark or branches (as of a tree) : *n.* a lullaby : กล่อม the fundamental unit of an ancient system of money and weights.

๑ กล่อม	=	1.17 decigrams (value ½ att)
๒ กล่อม	= ๑ กล่ำ	= 2.343 decigrams
๒ กล่ำ	= ๑ ไพ	= 4.687 decigrams
๔ ไพ	= ๑ เฟื้อง	= 1.875 grams
๒ เฟื้อง	= ๑ สลึง	= 3.75 grams
๔ สลึง	= ๑ บาท	= 15 grams
๔ บาท	= ๑ ตำลึง	= 6 decagrams
๒๐ ตำลึง	= ๑ ชั่ง	= 1.2 kilograms
๕๐ ชั่ง	= ๑ หาบ	= 60 kilograms

Other weights used are—

1 standard picul = 60 kilograms

1 standard catty (1/100 picul) = 600 grams

1 standard carat = 20 grams

(S. Y. B. 1931-33) : กล่อมเสาเรือน to trim or smooth off a house-post : กล่อมหอ to serenade a bride and groom on the wedding night.

กล้อมแกล้ม see กะล่อมกะแล่ม

กลอย   gkloo-ay *v.* to unite ; to support ; to follow casually : กลอยแก่ an old man dressed as a dude : กลอยใจ to be merged into one ; to associate intimately.

กลอย (ต้น)   gkloo-ay *Dioscorea doemona* (*Dioscoraceae*) (V. P. p. 35), a climber belonging to the yam family ; a poisonous plant with large, variegated leaves, the tubers of which are edible but which, even after proper boiling, are very nauseous. The liquid obtained by boiling the tubers is said to be used by the Javanese for making arrow-poison (MCM. p. 384).

กลัก   gklak[4] *n.* a small tube-shaped receptacle with a telescoping cover (as used for pins) ; a small circular pill-box ; a square paper or ivory pill-box : กลักไม้ขีดไฟ a match box.

กลัด   gklat[4] *v.* to cause to stop ; to suppress or be suppressed ; to repress ; to fasten together ; to pin together ; to fasten with a pin or sliver of bamboo : กลัดกลุ้ม to restrain or repress vexation or perplexity :

กลัดหนอง confined pus; pus under a tough skin or scab: กลัดอกกลัดใจ to suffer from oppression or depression of the spirits, feelings or passions: เข็มกลัด a pin; a brooch; a clasp: ไม้กลัด a pin made of wood.

กลั่น gklan[4] v. to select (as jewels); to distil; to eliminate the spurious: น้ำกลั่น distilled water: หม้อกลั่น a retort or pot for distilling purposes.

กลั้น gklan[3] v. to control by will power (as during hiccups); to refrain; to suppress: กลั้นพยาบาท to crush or quell the desire for revenge: กลั้นลมหายใจ to hold the breath: อดกลั้น to endure; to exert or manifest self-control.

กลันท์ gka[4]-lan P. S. n. a squirrel; a chipmunk.

กลับ gklap[4] v. to return; to turn back (as leaves of a book); to change back to: กลับ กลอก unstable; unreliable; changeable in character: กลับกลาย to change or alter an opinion, promise or conduct: กลับคืน to restore to the owner: กลับใจ to have a change of heart; to change one's mind: กลับดีกัน to resume friendship: กลับถ้อยคืนคำ, กลับคำ to revoke one's word or promise: กลับหลัง to turn backwards.

กัลป see กัปป

กลัมพก, กลัมพัก gka[4]-lam-pok[6] n. Ipomoea aquatica (Convolvulaceae) (V. P. p. 161), a small, semi-aquatic creeper with tender, arrow-shaped leaves, commonly cultivated in peasants' gardens. The leaves and young stems are used in vegetable curries (Dept. Agri. & Fisheries p. 476).

กลัว gkloo-wah v. to fear; to dread: adj. timid; fearful; afraid: กลัวเกรง to respect with fear: กลัวตาย fear of death: กลัว บาป to have a horror of committing sin; to be afraid of another's rough or vile words.

กลั้ว gkloo-ah[3] v. to mix; to blend; to wallow (as a buffalo in mud) to gargle or rinse; the mouth and throat (as with some remedy): กลั้วเกลี้ย v. to mix well together; to grate or scrape against something; to unite promiscuously into one mass: adj. almost finished; coming almost to an end (as a supply of food); down to the last bit: กลั้วเกษร to crawl or creep over the pollen of flowers (speaking of bees).

กลัส see กลส

กลา gka[4]-lah P. S. n. a fraction, quarter, or part of a circle, month or unit: กลากุศล dexterous (in performing tricks or sleight-of-hand performances); cunning: กลาธร n. lit. "one who sustains the quarters of the moon," i. e. the god Siva: adj. cunning or expert in tricks or sleight-of-hand performances: กลานาถ lit. "the king or god of the quarters," i. e. the moon: กลานิธิ lit. "a storehouse of the quarters," i. e. the moon: กลาป n. lit. "that which binds objects together," i. e. a cluster; a tuft; a clump; a rope or collar (for use around the neck of an elephant); a quiver (a length or internode of bamboo full of arrows); a bound tuft or bunch of feathers (as peacock tail-feathers): adv. completely: กลาปิน, กลาปี lit. "one having a cluster of feathers for a tail," i. e. the peacock: กลาภร one versed or proficient in arts or crafts: กลายน a professional or scientific dancer (as one who dances on sword points or blades): กลาวิกล a sparrow.

กล่า gklah[4] v. to cut or enlarge for the easy removal of the contents; to remove with skill or dexterity.

กล้า gklah[3] v. to be bold; to be fearless: n. young rice plants ready for transplanting: adj. hard; brave; fearless; daring; courageous: กล้าปาก to be bold in speech or fearless in expressing one's opinions: ตกกล้า to sow seedling rice: เหล็กกล้า hardened steel.

กลาก, ขี้กลาก gklak[4] n. a skin disease

appearing in patches and characterized by itching; a form of eczema.

กลากลาด　　gklah-gklat[4]　*adj.* abundant; plentiful; overmuch.

กลาง　　gklang　*n.* middle; midst; center; the point equally distant from the extremities or circumference: กลางเก่ากลางใหม่ neither old nor new; used; second-hand: กลางคน middle-aged: กลางคืน night; night-time: กลางแจ้ง an open space or clearing: กลางวัน day; day-time: กลางเวทา in mid-air: กลาง-หน, กลางทาง *idiomatic* half-way: กลางหาว in the middle of a clearing: คนกลาง a mediator; a referee; an arbitrator: ทิ้ง กลางคัน to give up or disband when the journey or task is half-finished.

กลาด　　gklat[4]　*adj.* promiscuous; scattered around.

กลาบาต　　gka[4]-lah-bat[4]　*n.* a sentinel or sentry keeping watch by a fire.

กลาป　　gka[4]-lap[4]　*P. S. n.* a group; a sheaf or shock of cut corn; a handful; a flock (of birds).

กลามแรด　　gka[4]-lam-raat[4]　*Aralia armata* (*Araliaceae*) (cb. p. 794), a tree or shrub, sometimes scandent when young and finally self-supporting. From this is made the rice paper of China (Dept. Agri. & Fisheries p. 239).

กล้าม　　gklam[3]　*n.* the meat or endocarpal lining of the coconut; hardened animal or vegetable fat: กล้ามเนื้อ hardened tissue; muscular tissue: กล้ามมะพร้าว meat of the coconut: น้ำมันเป็นกล้าม congealed oil.

กลาย　　gklai　*v.* to transform in shape or character; to change; to be changed: *n.* transformation: กลายกลับ a metamorphosis or change from one form into another: ปี-กลายนี้ last year.

กล้าย　　gklai[3]　*n.* a species of wild banana having edible fruit about 30 cm. long, *Musa sp.* (v. p. p. 32). This is a very coarse herbaceous plant usually with perennial root-stalks. The trunk is erect and soft, being formed of the thickened, closely imbricate leaf-sheets. The leaves are very large and strong and the fruit fleshy.

กล่าว　　gklow[4]　*v.* to speak; to say; to relate; to narrate; to lecture; to make an address of any kind; to conduct any ritual (as a marriage or funeral): กล่าวกัน to proclaim the banns of marriage: กล่าวขวัญ to talk about another; to speak of others in either laudatory or derogatory terms: กล่าวตาม to repeat after another (as in taking an oath): กล่าวถึง to speak about or of: กล่าวเถียง to contradict or refute: กล่าวโทษ to blame: การกล่าว civil marriage.

กล่ำ, มะกล่ำ (ต้น)　　gklam[4]　*n. Abrus precatorius* (*Leguminosae*), Indian liquorice, a slender, perennial climber, bearing small, scarlet seeds with black spots or "crabs' eyes." When soft, these are strung and worn as necklaces or are used as rosaries. The seeds furnish an acrid poison which is used for criminal purposes. They are powdered and formed into a paste with which arrows are dressed. This poisoned arrow wound is generally fatal within 24 hours. Boiling renders the seeds harmless. The roots and leaves are used in native medicine (MCM. pp. 383, 461).

กล้ำ　　gklam[3]　*v.* to fasten together; to bind together; to mix together: กล้ำกลาย to intrude; to pass or advance near another: *n.* obtrusiveness: กล้ำกลืน to swallow hastily; to put up with (as the inevitable): กล้ำชายผ้า to hem or make a binding along the edge of a strip of cloth: อักษรกล้ำ letters whose sound is produced in the throat; gutturals.

กลิ, กลี　　gka[4]-li[6]　*P. S. n.* spirits of evil named Kali, a group of evil spirits, inciting to evil or instilling evil in the human heart (corresponding to Satan). In playing dice, Kali is the one dot, and is the personification of ill-luck (S. E. D.): กลิกุญจิกา a younger sister or sisters of a husband: กลิปรีย์ quarrelsome (implying both anger and maliciousness): กลิยุค, กลิกาล the last age of the world, which commenced on 8th Feb. 3102 B. C. and is to endure for 432,000 human years. In this yuga, righteousness remains only to the extent of one-fourth, practices enjoined by the vedas, works of righteousness, and rites of sacrifice have ceased. Calamities, diseases, fatigue, faults (such as anger etc.), distresses, hunger and fear prevail. As the age revolves, righteousness declines and the people also degenerate. When they decay, their motives grow weak and the general decline frustrates their aims (H. C. D.): กลิการ to mix together: กลิเข็ญ misery (arising from misfortune): กลิเหตุ different calamities; trouble; sedition: เกิดกลิวุ่นวาย there arises some trouble and tumult.

กลิ้ง gkling[3] v. to roll; to roll along: กลิ้ง (ต้น) *Sindora fusca* (*Leguminosae*) (cb. p. 568): กลิ้งกลางดง a species of vine having a tuberous bulb above the ground. The stem grows creeping along the surface (hence the name): กลิ้งเกลือก to roll about on the grass or to wallow in mud or mire: กลิ้งขอน to roll a log along: ลูกกลิ้ง a roller.

กลิงค์, กลิ้งค์ gka[4]-ling *P. S. n.* the country along the Coromandel coast, north of Madras. (H. C. D.) Its inhabitants are called Kalinga: กลิงคราช the king of the Kalinga tribe: กลิงคราษฎร์ the territory of the Kalinga tribe.

กลิ่น gklin[4] *n.* scent; smell; odour: กลิ่นหอม fragrance.

กลี see กลิ

กลี gklee[4] *n.* a receptacle divided into several compartments for the areca-nut, tobacco, betel leaves, cigars etc.

กลีบ gkleep[4] *n.* petals of a flower; a segment (as of an orange): กลีบกระดาษ strips of paper folded or creased (as ancient Siamese accordian-like books): กลีบใบหู convolu-

tions of the external ear: กลีบเมฆ cumulus clouds.

กลึง gkleung v. to turn and trim (with a lathe); to polish or shape by means of a lathe; เครื่องกลึง a turning lathe.

กลึงกล่อม (ต้น) gkleung-gklaum[4] *n.* *Polyalthia suberosa*; *Polyalthia longifolia* (*Annonaceae*), a moderate-sized evergreen. The tree is symmetrical and upright with narrow, wavy leaves. This tree is much planted as a shade tree along avenues. It is drought-resisting and is suitable for rich or poor soil (MCM. p. 213). The bark is corky; the wood is hard, close-grained, tough and durable (Dept. Agri. & Fisheries p. 314: cb. p. 45).

กลึงค์ see กลิงค์

กลืน gkleun v. to swallow; to gulp down: กลมกลืน well-mixed; completely united or combined: กลืนคล่องคอ to swallow easily or freely: กลืนแค้น to swallow with difficulty: กลืนติดคอ to be or become lodged in the throat.

กลุ่ม gkloom[4] *n.* any globular or spherical body or object; a ball of thread or string; a packet or bundle of betel leaves; people or objects gathered into groups.

กลุ้ม gkloom[3] v. to be irritated; to be provoked; to be annoyed; to become confused: กลุ้มกลั้นใจ extremely irritated or provoked: กลุ้มพิษยา to be mentally confused by some poison: กลุ้มรุม to join in a fight.

กลู gkloo[4] v. to be scattered promiscuously around; to lie irregularly around.

กเลวระ, กเลพระ gka[4]-lay-wa[6]-ra[6] *P. S. n.* a body; a corpse; something that will decay: กเลวราก an undertaker.

กวกไหม gkoo-ak[4]-mai[2] *n.* *Garcinia speciosa* (*Guttiferae*) (cb. p. 118), an evergreen tree. The wood is used for posts of houses and bridges (Dept. Agri. & Fisheries p. 477).

กวด gkoo-at[4] v. to tighten forcibly; to twist

tightly together; to pursue with speed or follow up with the purpose of capture; to polish: กวดเก่ง to be the chief offender in a fight or in any act of violence: กวดขัน vigorously; energetically; strictly (as with a servant): กวดเชือก to tighten with a rope; to pull a rope tighter.

กวน gkoo-an v. to trouble; to annoy; to provoke; to stir (as with a spoon): กวนใจ v. to vex; to bother; to irritate the feelings; to tease; to provoke: adj. annoying; vexatious; irritating: กวนมุข a troop of Siamese clowns whose duty it is to perform during the intervals of a theatrical play: ความ กวนใจ worries; irritation of heart; harassment; annoyance; vexation: รบกวน to disturb; to pester; to annoy or irritate by continued harassing.

ก่วม (ต้น) gkoo-am⁴ n. Acer oblongum (Aceraceae) (cb. p. 338), a medium-sized tree the wood of which is used for agricultural implements and drinking cups (Dept. Agri. & Fisheries p. 70).

ก้วยเทศ, มะละกอ, แตง (ต้น) gkoo-ay³-tet³ n. Carica papaya (Caricaceae) (cb. p. 750), papaya, a tree-melon of the passion fruit family. It is a fast-growing, small, herbaceous, branchless and usually dioecious tree, about 15 to 20 feet high, cultivated throughout the humid tropics. It bears a crown of very large, handsome, palmate leaves, at the base of which the large, green fruit is produced. The fruit is very refreshing and agreeable to the taste and is esteemed as an acid table fruit. It is an aid to digestion (MCM. pp. 233, 234, 509, 517). The milk of the fruit is used medicinally (Dept. Agri. & Fisheries p. 159).

กวัก (นก) gkwak⁴ n. the Chinese white-breasted water-rail Amaurornis phoenicurus chinensis (Deig. N. H. J. S. S. VIII, 3, p. 169).

กวัก gkwak⁴ v. to summon by a gesture of the hand.

กวัดแกว่ง, กวัดไกว gkwat⁴-gkwaang⁴ v.

to swing (as a pendulum); to oscillate; to wave; to brandish.

กวา (แตง) gkwah n. a small cucumber.

กว่า gkwah⁴ adv. more; more than; sign of the comparative degree of an adjective or adverb: กว่าจะ until: กว่าอื่น overmuch; more than: กว่านี้ more than this: น้อย กว่า less than: มากกว่ามาก much too much; overly abundant: เล็กกว่า smaller than; of smaller size than; not so large as.

กวาง gkwang n. a stag; a deer; the Malay sambar Cervus unicolor equinus (Gaird. N. H. J. S. S. III, 2, p. 126).

กว้าง gkwang³ adj. wide; broad; expansive: กว้างขวาง spacious; affording ample room; capacious: ตามกว้าง according to the width: ใจกว้าง liberal-minded; generous: กว้างยาว length and breadth: คนกว้างขวาง a popular or widely-known person.

กวางตุ้ง gkwang-dtoong³ n. Cantonese: เมืองกวางตุ้ง Canton.

กวาด gkwat⁴ v. to sweep; to move people or animals en masse; to drive or chase by force or violence (as in hunting): กวาดครัว to remove the inhabitants of a country forcibly: กวาดต้อน to surround while driving the inhabitants out of their country: กวาดยา to swab the throat with a remedy: ไม้ขึงกวาด a broom; a duster: ยากวาด a remedy used for swabbing the throat: ลูกกวาด candy.

กว้าน ๑ gkwan³ n. a shed; a shack; a brick dwelling; a house; a place of abode.

กว้าน ๒ gkwan³ v. to haul in by means of a capstan; to drive in crowds (as prisoners of war); to corner the market: n. a capstan; an upright windlass (such as is used for hoisting anchors); an animal or game drive: กว้านสมอ to haul up an anchor by means of a capstan: เที่ยวกว้าน to search; to seek out; to seek for in all probable places:

พ่อค้ากว้านซื้อสินค้าไว้ขาย a merchant gets a corner on the market.

กวาวผู้ (ต้น) gkwow-poo^3 *n. Spatholobus parviflorus (Leguminosae)* (Cb. p. 447), a woody climber.

กว้าว, ค่าว (ต้น) gkwow^3 *n. Adina cordifolia (Rubiaceae)* (V. P. p. 33); *Nauclea cordifolia* (Com. Rec.), a large deciduous tree common in the western peninsula. The wood is yellow, moderately hard, durable, even-grained and takes a good polish. The small buds, ground with round pepper, are sniffed into the nose to relieve severe headache (Dept. Agri. & Fisheries p. 115).

กว้าวตุ้ม (ต้น) gkow^3-dtoom^3 *n. Mitragyna diversifolia (Rubiaceae)* (V. P. p. 33), a tree.

กว่าว, ทองกว่าว (ต้น) gkwow^4 *n. Butea frondosa (Leguminosae)* (Cb. p. 445 : V. P. p. 33), flame-of-the-forest, an erect tree with large, leathery, broad, trifoliate leaves, indigenous to the forests of the dry regions of Siam. It stands about 40 feet high and, in the dry months, bears a profusion of beautiful crimson or orange-scarlet flowers. The tree, especially sacred to the Brahmins in India, furnishes a resin, " kino," and a useful fibre is obtained from the bark, especially of the roots; a lac is produced on the young twigs; (this is considered one of the best trees for this purpose); the flowers yield yellow and orange dyes (McM. pp. 85, 206, 417, 440, 466). The gum is used medicinally as an astringent drug as well as in tanning and dyeing (Dept. Agri. & Fisheries p. 500).

กว่าวเคือ (ต้น) gkwow^2-keu-ah *n. Butea superba (Leguminosae)* (Cb. 446 : V. P. p. 33), an extensive climber yielding gum like that of *Butea frondosa*. The root yields a red dye and the young branches afford a strong and useful fibre; the leaves are regarded as a valuable fodder (Dept. Agri. & Fisheries p. 556); this climber is a food-plant for the lac insect.

กวิ, กวี, กระวี gka^4-wi^6 *P.S. n.* a thinker; a sage; a poet; an author; a composer; a professional singer: *adj.* wise; intelligent; gifted with insight. In Buddhistic literature, there are four classes of poets, viz. (1) จินตกวี the poet of imagination or fiction; (2) ปฏิภาณกวี the improviser or extemporaneous poet; (3) สุตกวี the poet of tradition; (4) อรรถกวี the poet of real life: กวิเชยษฐ์ *lit.* "oldest of poets," *i. e.* Valmiki, author of the great Indian epic poem, the Ramayana, which was supposed to have been composed about five centuries B. C.: กวินิพนธ์ rhetorical, poetical or rhythmical compositions by a poet or sage: กวีศึกษา instruction for poets: กวีชาติ, กวีวงศ์ a race or family of authors or sages: กวีราชา a king of poets: กวีประเสริฐ esteemed or praised by sages.

กษณะ gka^4-sa^4-na^6 *P. S. n.* a short period of time; a measure of time; a moment; an occasion; an opportunity.

กษมา gka^4-sa^4-mah *P. S. v.* to ask for pardon or forgiveness: *n.* suppression (of one's feelings); forgiveness; toleration; patience; forbearance: *adj.* enduring; bearing; suffering; submissive; unresisting (S. E. D.).

กษัตร gka^4-sat^4 *S. n.* the second, regal or warrior caste (H. C. D.); a king; power; authority; domain; kingdom; territory: กษัตร ธรรม the duty, office or responsibility of a king or ruler: กษัตรบดี an absolute ruler of a kingdom or territory; a king: กษัตร พันธุ์ of or in the lineage of a warrior; of kingly lineage: กษัตรรูป the methods of procedure or course of action of a king: กษัตรวิทยา a treatise on military strategy written by an absolutely experienced soldier: กษัตราธิราช a king; an absolute monarch.

กษัตริย gka^4-sat^4 *P. S. n. lit.* " one worthy of a domain," *i. e.* a ruler or one vested with kingly authority or power: กษัตริยชาติ of military lineage or caste: กษัตริยธรรม the office, duty or responsibility of one of military lineage : กษัตรียราช a chief or absolute monarch having tributary lords, vassals or kings paying homage to him.

กษัตรียา, กษัตรียาณี gka⁴-sat⁴-ri⁶-yah *n.* a ruling queen ; the wife of a skilled soldier or one in the military class or caste.

กษัตรี gka⁴-sat⁴-dtree *n.* a female of kingly or royal lineage.

กษัย ๑ gka⁴-sai² *S. n.* a house ; an abode ; a dwelling place ; a seat ; a bench ; a domicile.

กษัย ๒ gka⁴-sai² *S. n.* finality ; that which makes an end ; conclusion ; the conclusion of any work : กษัยกาล the end of all things ; the end of the world : กษัยกาส the cough of a tubercular person : กษัยปึกษ์ the waning period of the moon ; the latter half of the month : กษัยมาส a lunar month that is shortened so as to correspond exactly to the solar calendar : กษัยโรค pulmonary tuberculosis : กษัยสมบัท the final destruction of life or property ; annihilation ; dissolution or the breaking up of all things.

กษาย, กสาพ, กสาย, กสาว gka⁴-sai² *P.S.n.* that which has an astringent taste ; drugs that have been steeped in hot water and are sipped like tea ; a yellow colouring solution for dyeing Buddhist monks' robes. This must be made from the heart-wood of special trees as mineral dyes are forbidden to be used : *adj.* fragrant ; red ; light red ; reddish-yellow : กษายจิตร dyed with a yellow dye : กษายพัสตร์, กษายพัสน์, กษายพาส a complete set of Buddhist monks' robes consisting of three garments, viz. a loin cloth reaching to the knees and two other robes which can be worn interchangeably or one over the other (as in cold weather). A complete set is called ผ้าไตรจีวร.

กษิดินทร์, กษิดิศ, กษิตินทร์, กษิติศ gka⁴-si⁴-din *n.* an absolute monarch, king or ruler of a kingdom.

กษิต gka⁴-sit⁴ *S. n.* a citizen of a country ;

an inhabitant of the earth (opposed to celestial or cosmic beings) ; used as a suffix *e. g.* คิริกษิต one on a mountain or elevation ; ทิวิกษิต, โลกกษิต celestial beings.

กษิติ gka⁴-si⁴-dti⁴ *S. n.* an abode ; a dwelling ; a house ; the earth ; the world : กษิติ-กษิต *lit.* "a ruler of the world," *i. e.* a king or sovereign : กษิติกัมป์ an earthquake : กษิติ-ขัณฑ์ a clod of soil ; a lump of dirt : กษิติตนมัย, กษิตินนทน์, กษิติสุต *lit.* "the son of the earth," *i. e.* the planet Mars : กษิติตนัยทิน, กษิติตนัยวาร Tuesday : กษิติตล, กษิติบัฐ the surface of the earth : กษิติเทพ, กษิติเทวตา *lit.* "earth gods," *i. e.* a Brahmin : กษิติธร a mountain : กษิติ-นาถ, กษิติบดี, กษิติบาล *lit.* "lord of the earth," *i. e.* a king : กษิติประดิษฐ์ a dweller on the earth : กษิติภุช *lit.* "one who possesses the earth," *i. e.* a king : กษิติภุ *lit.* "daughter of the earth," *i. e.* Sita : กษิติมณฑล a realm, country or district : กษิติราช an absolute ruler or king : กษิติวรรธน์ *lit.* "an increaser of the soil," *i. e.* a dead body ; a corpse : กษิติศวร *lit.* "the most exalted one of a country or kingdom," *i. e.* the sovereign or king.

กษิตินทร์ see **กษิดินทร์**

กษิติศ see **กษิดินทร์**

กษิณ gka-seen² *P.S. adj.* final ; ultimate ; last ; pertaining to or coming to the end : กษิณ-โภค, กษิณธน one who has spent all his treasure or substance : กษิณชีวิต one who has reached the end of strength or life : กษิณบาป *lit.* "one who has come to the end of sin," *i. e.* one who is now purified : กษิณศักดิ์ one who has reached the end of his honour or title ; one who has lost his power.

กษิณายุส gka⁴-see²-nah-yoot⁶ *P. S. n.* one who has lived his quota of years.

กษิณาศรพ gka⁴-see²-nah-sop⁴ *P. S. n. lit.* "one who has been purged or purified of all sin," *i. e.* one having attained the highest degree of saintship according to the Buddhist religion.

กษียนะ gka[4]-see[2]-ya[6]-na[6] *P. n.* complaint; criticism.

กษีร gka[4]-see[2]-ra[6] *P. S. n.* water; fresh milk; thickened milk; liquid juice or sap of plants (chd.): กษีรกัณฐ์ *n. lit.* "one who still has milk in his mouth," *i. e.* a young child; an infant: กษีรกุณฑ์ an utensil or vessel for milk: กษีรตุมพี a bottle-shaped gourd, *Lagenaria Vularies*, boiled and eaten as a vegetable: กษีรทาตรี *lit.* "a supplier of milk," *i. e.* a fresh cow: กษีรธาตรี a wet nurse: กษีรธิ, กษีรมหรรณพ, กษีรรรณพ, กษีรวารี, กษีรสมุทร, กษีรสาคร, กษีรสินธุ์, กษีรารณพ, เกษียรสมุทร *lit.* "a sea of milk," *i. e.* a bountiful source of milk supply: กษีรนีร milk and water mixed (a figure of speech implying the act of embracing); union: กษีรบาน a drinker of milk: กษีรศรี milky; mixed with milk: กษีรสมภพ sour milk; milk curd: กษีรสาร essence of milk; cream; butter.

กสก gka[4]-sok[4] *P. S. n.* a farmer; a plowman; an agriculturist; an husbandman; a cultivator; the iron head of a plow (chd.).

กสสก see **กรรษก**

กสาพ see **กษาย**

กสาย see **กษาย**

กสาว see **กษาย**

กสิ, กสิกรรม, กสิกิจ gka[4]-si[4] *P. n.* husbandry; agriculture; cultivation of the soil: *adj.* plowing; tilling; agricultural (chd.).

กสิก see **กรรษก**

กสิกร see **กรรษก**

กสิกรรม see **กสิ**

กสิการ see **กรรษก**

กสิกิจ see **กสิ**

กสิณ gka[4]-sin[2] *P.S. n.* one of the ten objects for meditation and introspection as laid down by the Buddhist religion; one of the divisions of meditation, being a process by means of which mystic meditation may be induced. There are ten objects for meditation, *viz.* earth, water, fire, wind, blue, yellow, red, white, light and the sky seen through a narrow aperture (chd.): *adj.* full; entire; complete: *adv.* completely; wholly; entirely.

กเสียร, gka[4]-see-an[2] *n.* expiation; external acts performed to atone for sin, trouble and distress: *adj.* troublesome; painful; grievous; miserable (chd.).

กหังปายา gka[4]-hung[2]-bpah-yah *n.* the number 1181, used in calculating the year of the Chulasakaraj or lesser era, which began in 683 A. D., with relation to the Buddhist era. *ex.* If a year in the Chulasakaraj era is required, subtract 1181 from the current Buddhist year. If a year of the Buddhist era is required, add 1181 to the current Chulasakaraj year.

กหาปณะ, กระษาปณ์ gka[4]-hah[2]-bpa[4]-na[6] *n.* an early Indian coin which was also used as a weight and approximately equivalent to 2.50 baht. The coin is said to have four prongs or feet. This makes it roughly correspond to the Siamese "tamlung" or four baht coin (both weight and money value) with this difference, that while the ancient Indian coin กหาปณะ was equal to 2.50 bahts, the present "tamlung" is equal to 4.00 bahts; a certain weight; a certain coin (either of copper, silver or gold) (chd.).

กฬาร gka[4]-lan *P. S. n.* a servant; a messenger: *adj.* tawny coloured (brownish-yellow).

กอ gkau *n.* a tufted plant; a clump (as bamboo); a collection of stalks forming a bush; a group of people; a crowd: กอ (ต้น) *Pasania falconeri (Cupuliferae)* (v. p. p. 1); *Livistona Cochinchinensis*: กอกล้วย a clump of banana trees: กอข้าว stalks of rice plants: กอจาก a clump of nipa palms: กอต้นแขม a clump of pampas grass: คนกอแก a rogue; a knave: เหล่ากอ relatives; lineage.

ก่อ gkau[4] *v.* to start; to incite; to instigate; to begin; to commence; to originate; to build (as a wall): ก่อกรรม to increase one's demerit, future punishment or misfortune: ก่อการ, ก่อความ, ก่อเหตุ to originate or to instigate (as a fracas, fight, altercation or quarrel): ก่อไฟ to lay or build a fire; to start a fire: ก่อสร้าง to construct; to build: การก่อสร้าง construction work: ก่อขาว (ต้น) *Quercus thomsoni* (V. P. p. 1: Dept. Agri. & Fisheries p. 387); *Quercus polystachya* (K.): ก่อแบ้น (ต้น) *Castanoposis indica (Cupuliferae)* (V. P. p. 2: K.: Dept. Agri. & Fisheries p. 228), a medium-sized tree bearing edible fruit. The wood is grey, hard and suitable for making shingles: ก่อตาหมู (ต้น) *Quercus kerrii* (V. P. p. 2: K.); *Quercus helferiana* (Dept. Agri. & Fisheries p. 379: K.): ผู้ก่อการ prime movers; instituters; originators; starters: พวกก่อการ the prime movers in the political coup d'état of 1932.

ก้อ gkau[3] *adj.* vain; pompous; strutting (as of a peacock); acting as though full of vanity (descriptive of fowls): ก้อร่อ, ก้อร่อ ท้อติก full of conceit; swaggering: ทำก้อร่อ to act haughtily; to act with ostentation: ปดก้อ to lie unblushingly.

กอก gkauk[4] *v.* to suck by creating a vacuum; to use a cupping glass (as a remedy): กอก (ต้น) *Spondias mangifera* (V. P. p. 23) Otaheiti-apple or hog plum, a small tree with handsome bi-pinnate leaves. The round or ovoid fruit is of the size of a small mango, amber coloured when ripe; it has a large seed, surrounded by coarse fibre and a scanty acid pulp, having a flavour like that of an exceedingly bad mango, but it makes an excellent preserve (MCM. p. 270). The fruit is used in medicine for dyspepsia, the leaves and bark which are astringent and aromatic for dysentery and the juice of the leaves for earache. The Shans of north Siam use the sap or juice from the fruit as an antidote against the bites of poisonous insects or wounds of poisoned arrows. The timber is esteemed only for the sake of the oil which is used for illuminating purposes: กอกก่อ (ต้น) *Sindora siamensis (Leguminosae)* (cb. p. 539), a large, leguminous tree: กอกกั๋น (ต้น) *Canarium venosum (Burseraceae)* (cb. p. 248): *Odina wodier (Anacardiaceae)* (cb. p. 352), a large tree of Siam, India, Java, etc. A gum is obtained from the stems (MCM. p. 412). The gum when mixed with lime is used in white-washing. The bark is very astingent and is used in tanning and in remedies for ulcers. The leaves and young shoots afford fodder for cattle and elephants. The heartwood is not liable to be attacked by white ants and is used for making shafts, scabbards, yokes, etc.

ก๊อก gkauk[6] *n.* a tube or pipe; a faucet for water (as from a tank): ไม้ก๊อก a stopper; a cork.

กอง gkaung *v.* to pile up into a heap: *n.* a pile; a mass; a multitude; a crowd; a band, company or department; a bureau or sub-department: กองการกุศล a society organized for philanthropic purposes: กองช่าง a department of artisans: กองซุ่ม soldiers in ambush: กองดับเพลิง fire-brigade: กองตระเวน police on duty: กองตำรวจกุบาล Criminal Investigation Department: กองไต่สวน Investigation Department: กองทหาร a troop: กองทหารที่ถูกล้อม besieged forces: กองทหารที่ถูกล้อมในป้อม a besieged garrison: กองทหารที่ส่งไปนอกประเทศ an expeditionary force: กองทัพ an army corps: กองทัพทหารสมัคร volunteer battalions: กองทัพบก a regiment of infantry: กองทัพเรือ a regiment of marines: กองพลบินใหญ่ (น้อย) artillery brigades: กองพลใหญ่ an army division: กองพัน a battalion: กองพันทหารราบขี่ม้า a mounted infantry battalion: กองม้า a squadron of cavalry: กองแยกธาตุ Government Laboratory: กองร่างกฎหมาย Code Commission: กองเรือพี่เลี้ยง a convoy: กองลำเลียง supply columns: กองวิทยุโทรเลข Wireless Telegraph

Department: กองสัญญาณ Signal Service Corps: กองสุขาภิบาล Department of Public Health (in the provinces): กองหน้า a vanguard or advance band: กองหนุน reserves; persons or forces kept in reserve: กองอนุสาสนาจารย์ the Chaplain's Department: นายกอง a general: เป็นกอง abundantly: แม่กอง a leader of troops; the head of a band or gang.

กอง (ต้น) gkaung *n. Terminalia alata (Combretaceae)* (cb. p. 600); *T. densiflora (Combretaceae)* (cb. p. 604); *T. tomentosa* (K.), a large, deciduous tree yielding a red gum. The bark is used for dyeing, tanning and in medicine. The ashes of the bark are eaten with betel leaves as a substitute for lime. The wood is used for house building, furniture, etc. (Dept. Agri. & Fisheries).

ก้อง ๑ gkaung[4] *n.* an ornament for the breast or chest; a garment worn over the breast of a young girl: *adj.* bright; clear; beautiful.

ก้อง ๒ gkaung[4] *n.* a fishing apparatus, commonly used on the Mekong river. It is a net having one side fastened to a pole and is operated from a boat.

ก้อง gkaung[3] *v.* to reverberate (as thunder); to be resonant: *adj.* echoing; resounding: ก้องกังวาน, ก้องสนั่น to re-echo (as the sound of a large gong): ก้องแกบ (ต้น) *Ventilago calyculata (Rhamnaceae)* (cb. p. 294), a large, climbing shrub found in all tropical parts of Siam, India and Burma, yielding a good cordage fibre. Oil obtained from the seeds is used in cooking. The juice of the bark and young shoots is applied to the body surface as a remedy for pain. A ring made from the tendrils is worn as a charm against toothache (Dept. Agri. & Fisheries).

กองกอย gkaung-gkauy *n.* a group of spirits.

กอด gkaut[4] *v.* to embrace; to caress: กอดกัน to embrace each other: กอดคอ to

clasp affectionately around the neck: กอดอก to fold the arms over one's breast.

ก่อน gkaun[4] *adv.* previously; before; first: ก่อนเก่า having been made, used or known for a long time: ก่อนนมนาน in the dim distant past: คอยประเดี๋ยวก่อน just wait a moment (as a command to a servant): แต่ก่อน formerly; previously: ท่านแต่ก่อน ancestors: ประเดี๋ยวก่อน presently; soon: อย่าเพ่อก่อน not just yet; wait a while.

ก้อน gkaun[3] *n.* a lump; an ingot; mass; piece; morsel: ก้อนเส้า an iron tripod or bricks on edge, used for the support of a rice pot while boiling: ก้อนหิน rocks; broken stones: ก้อนอิฐ fragments of brick: ตำเป็นก้อน pounded to fragments or pieces.

กอบ gkaup[4] *v.* to gather up; to scoop up with the hands: กอบการ to work; to perform a deed or act: กอบกำ to gather together and hold in the fist: กอบด้วย, ประกอบด้วย to be composed of: กอบเดียว to gather and hold in one hand; a handful.

กอบโกย gkaup[4]-gko-ie *v.* to gather; to collect in handfuls; to accumulate by every possible means.

กอม (ต้น) gkaum *n. Grewia microcos (Tiliaceae)* (cb. p. 185: V. P. p. 32), a large shrub having stems which yield a strong fiber (MCM. p. 430). A decoction of the bark is used for treating bruised and swollen feet.

กอมขม, ดีงู (ต้น) gkaum-kom[2] *n. Picrasma javanica (Simarubaceae)* (cb. p. 240), a tree attaining the height of 60 ft. The bitter wood and bark are used as a substitute for quassia.

ก้อม gkaum[3] *n.* the end; the bottom; the farthest end or tip downward: *adj.* small; dwarfed; low; undeveloped (in height).

ก้อมก้อ gkaum[4]-gkau[3] *v.* to be small or undeveloped; to be dwarfed: เตี้ยก้อมก้อ to be low in stature; to be stooped or humpbacked.

ก้อย   gkauy[3] *adj.* last; least; little: นิ้ว
ก้อย the little finger: กิ่งก้อย terminal
branches.

ก้อย (นก)   gkauy[2] *n.* whimbrel *Numenius
phoeopus* (small bird), a small curlew having
a white rump; curlew *Numenius arquatus
lineatus* (larger bird), a scolopacoid shore-bird
having a very long, slender, curved bill with
the upper mandible terminally knobbed (web.).

ก้อร่อ, ก้อร่อก้อติก   gkau[3]-rau[3] *adj.* foppish; dudish.

กะ   gka[4] *v.* to estimate roughly; to suppose;
to surmise; to reckon; to guess the condition
of: *n.* the sign used to indicate a particular
meter, mode or style of Buddhist chants;
prep. with; also, *ex.* พูดกะน้อง: *adv.* as;
like; similar, *ex.* ราวกะ, เหมือนกะ: *provin.*
used as a prefix to the names of women
and of fruit, *ex.* กะนวม-นางนวม, กะเวียน-ทุเรียน,
กะม่วง-มะม่วง: used interchangeably with
"กระ" but in some cases for the sake of
emphasis or euphony "กะ" is used, *ex.* นก
ยาง-นกกะยาง, ลูกกะดุม: กะเกณฑ์ to impose or
compel obligatory service for the Crown;
to make serve as corvee labourer; to press
into service: กะที่ to fix or appoint a place
of meeting; to mark out (approximately)
the area of a plot of ground: กะราคา
to appraise (approximately) the price or value
of: กะวัน to estimate roughly the number of days for the completion of a job;
to appoint a day or date (as for a social
function, ceremony or time of departure):
หมายกะเกณฑ์ a notice served for corvee labour
or for enlistment in the army.

กะกร่อม, ตะกร่อม   gka[4]-gkraum[3] *n. south.
provin.* a trap for marine crabs, made by splitting the end of a bamboo pole and sharpening
the split ends, which are made to stay spread
by tying with wire or strips of rattan. The
bait is fastened in the crotch with a net underneath, and the trap stuck in the mud.

กะกร้าว   gka[4]-gkrow[5] *onomat.* from the

grinding of the teeth or from the sound of
bird-shot on a corrugated iron roof.

กะเกริก see กระเกริก

กะเกริ่น see กระเกริ่น

กะกลิง, พญามือเหล็ก, แสลงใจ (ต้น)   gka[4]-
gkling[3] *n. Strychnos nux-vomica (Loganiaceae)* (V. P. pp. 185, 260: MCM. p. 374), a moderate-
sized tree indigenous to Ceylon, India and Siam.
The flat, circular, ash-grey, poisonous seeds,
known as nux-vomica, are produced chiefly
from August to November. These are collected from wild trees and exported for the
purpose of extracting the alkaloid strychnine.
This is a powerful poison but valued in medicine as a tonic and stimulant.

กะก่อง   gka[4]-gkaung[4] *adj. poet.* beautiful;
graceful; ornamented; ornamental.

กะกิง   gka[4]-gkang *Cam. n.* an elder brother
or sister.

กะกี (ต้น)   gka[4]-gke[3] *n. Hopea odorata
(Dipterocarpaceae)* (CB. p. 147), a large evergreen tree common in the forests of Siam
and Burma. The wood is yellow or yellowish
brown, hard, close and even-grained (Dept.
Agri. & Fisheries p. 272). In Siam, the bark is
used in the fermentation of an intoxicating
drink and in tanning.

กะกีก, กีกๆ   gka[4]-gkeuk[4] *poet. onomat.*
from the sound of heels striking the floor in
walking or from a succession of thuds.

กะเกาะ   gka[4]-gkaw[4] *poet. onomat.* from the
sound produced by pounding or thumping the
chest.

กะง่อนกะแง่น see กระง่อนกระแง่น

กะง่อนกะแง่น   gka[4]-ngaun[5]-gka[4]-ngaan[5]
adj. crooked; tortuous; curved.

กะเง้ากะงอด see กระเง้ากระงอด

กะจก see กระจก

กะจง see กระจง

กะจ้อน see กระจ้อน

กะจ้อยร่อย see กระจ้อย

กะจะ see กระจัด, กระจะ

กะจัง see กระจัง

กะจับ, กระจับ (ต้น)　　gka⁴-chjap⁴ *n. Trapa bispinosa*; *Trapa bicornis (Onagraceae)*, water chestnut, a low, aquatic, floating plant common along the banks of streams or rivers of Siam, Ceylon and Malaya.　The nuts are commonly collected and eaten by the poorer classes. These nuts are hard, two-horned, dark-brown or black, resembling a minature bull's head. The interior is palatable when fried or peeled and eaten raw (Dept. Agri. & Fisheries p. 73 : MCM. p. 271).

กะจับบง see กระจับบง

กะจับบ see กระจับบ

กะจ่า see กระจ่า

กะจ่าง see กระจ่าง

กะจาด see กระจาด

กะจาบ see กระจาบ

กะจิริด see กระจิริด

กะจิ๊ see กระจิ๊

กะจุก see กระจุก

กระจุ๋งกะจิ๋ง see กระจุ๋งกระจิ๋ง

กะจุ๋มกะจิ๋ม see กระจุ๋มกระจิ๋ม

กะจุบ see กระจุบ

กะจุย see กระจุย

กะจู๋ see กระจู๋

กะจู๋กะจี๋ see กระจู๋กระจี๋

กะเจ (ต้น)·　　gka⁴-chjay *n. Pinanga kuhlii*; *Pinanga patula (Palmae)* (MCM. pp. 166, 518), various species of small, feather-leaved palms with several stems.

กะเจอะกะเจิง see กระเจิดกระเจิง

กะเจา see กระเจา

กะเจาะ see กระเจาะ

กะเจ้าะ (Laos), กะท้อน (Siam) gka⁴-chjau³ *n. Millettia latifolia (Leguminosae)* (cb. p. 391), a small tree found in dry, mixed forest or deciduous jungle.　The flowers are white (K.); *Millettia pubinervis* (cb. p. 393).

กะเจ๊าะ (ต้น)　　gka⁴-chjau⁵ *n. Millettia kangensis (Leguminosae)* (cb. p. 390), a tree or large climber.　Its roots are applied to sores or used to kill vermin on cattle.　It is also used to poison fish (Dept. Agri. & Fisheries p. 247).

กะเจิง see กระเจิง

กะเจิดกะเจิง see กระเจิดกระเจิง

กะเจี๊ยง see กระเจี๊ยง

กะเจียบ　　gka⁴-chjee-ap⁵ *n.* the roselle, okra or ochro, ladies' fingers *Hibiscus esculentus* (V. P. p. 2), an erect annual of the mallow family, bearing large, roundish or palmate leaves and erect, horn-like pods which are edible.

กะเจี๋ยว see กระเจี๋ยว

กะแจะ, กระแจะ　　gka⁴-chjaa⁴ *Ochna wallichii (Ochnaceae)* (cb. p. 245 : V. P. p. 15), a tree with hard, coarse-grained, reddish-brown wood (BURK. p. 1569); *Limonia acidissima (Rutaceae)* (K. : cb. p. 229 : V. P. p. 3), a small tree growing in rocky ground in evergreen forests of Siam.　An infusion of the bark is used in an embrocation as a remedy for stiffness.　An infusion of the roots has a purgative action and is employed in cases of colic.　An infusion of the dried fruit is employed as an intestinal tonic : กะแจะ an odorous paste, perfumed unguent or ointment composed of agallochum, camphor, musk and a species of fragrant *Crinum* bulb (โกฏฐ์ หัวบัว).　These are macerated on a grinding-stone with scented water and then mixed into a fragrant paste (GER. (1) p. 71).

กะโจน see กระโจน

กะโจม see กระโจม

กะฉอก see กระฉอก

กะฉอด, หญ้าลิเภา (ต้น)   gka⁴-chaut⁴ *n.* *Lygodium salicifolium (Schzaeaceae)*; *Lygodium scandens*, a species of creeping fern having hard and durable fibers. When dressed, they are used for weaving into baskets. It produces foliage (MCM. p. 160).

กะฉ่อน see กระฉ่อน

กะฉับกะเฉง see กระฉับกระเฉง

กะฉีก see กระฉีก

กะฉูด see กระฉูด

กะเฉด see กระเฉด

กะโฉม see กระโฉม

กะชดกะช้อย see กระชดกระช้อย

กะชอน see กระชอน

กะชะ   gka⁴-cha⁶ *n.* panniers; baskets used for the transportation of food, clothing or merchandise. These are fitted with loopholes for a rope to be run through and hung over the backs of beasts of burden : กะชะเครื่องมือ a basket so made and used for tools.

กะชัง see กระชัง

กะชั้น see กระชั้น

กะชับ see กระชับ

กะชามาศ   gka⁴-chah-mat³ *n.* hydraulically produced gold.

กะชาก see กระชาก

กะชาย see กระชาย

กะชาย see กะแอน

กะชิง   gka⁴-ching *n. Licuala elegans (Palm-*

ae), a small fan-palm having many stems ; *Licuala gracilis*, a bushy tree 5 to 7 feet high found in Java ; *Licuala grandis*, a common, potted fan-palm (MCM. p. 167): ร่มใบกะชิง a parasol made of the leaves of this kind of palm.

กะชุ see กระชุ

กะชุ่มกะชวย see กระชุ่มกระชวย

กะแช่   gka⁴-chaa³ palm toddy, a fermented drink made from the sap of the sugar or Palmyra palm *Borassus flabellifera* (MCM. p. 362). This tree produces commercial palm sugar.

กะแชง see กระแชง

กะซ้าหอย see กะส้าหอย

กะซิก see กระซิก

กะซิบกะซาบ see กระซิบ

กะซี่   gka⁴-see³ *n.* an abnormally developed areca-nut. The nut has no white lining under the green covering (MCM. p. 380).

กะซุบกะซิบ see กระซิบ

กะเซ็น see กระเซ็น

กะเซอ see กระเซอ

กะเซอะกะเซอ see กระเซอะกระเซอ

กะเซ้า see กระเซ้า

กะเซิง see กระเซิง

กะแซ see กระแซ

กะแซะ see กระแซะ

กะโซ้   gka⁴-so⁵ *n.* an hill tribe of Mon-Khmer origin. There are some living in เมืองกุศุมาลย์. The Gka So are a very dark-skinned race, their colour sometimes nearing black ; their speech much resembles that of the Khmer. They originally came from the left bank of the Mekong (district of Kammon),

The Gka So living in Siamese territory are mostly domiciled between the large, fresh-water lake of Nong Han Sakol and Nakon Panom; other groups live on the banks of Nam Songkram and on the northern slopes of the Pu Pan range. The Gka So dress like the Laos people, but their young women add to their costumes a gaudy, silk scarf wrapped round the head. They till the fields and keep cattle as the Laos do (siam p. 91).

กะโซ้, โซงโลง   gka⁴-so⁵ *n.* a basket used for irrigating purposes. This basket is smeared with dammar and attached to a long handle suspended from a tripod.

กะดกก see กระดก

กะดกกะดนโด่ see กระดกกระดนโด่

กะดั้ง see กระดั้ง

กะดวง see กระดวง

กะดวน see กระดวน

กะด้วมกะเดี้ยม see กระด้วมกระเดี้ยม

กะดอ see กระดอ

กะดอง see กระดอง

กะดอน see กระดอน

กะดอม (ต้น)   gka⁴-daum *n. Gymnopetalum cochinchinense (Cucurbitaceae)* (cb. p. 755), a climbing plant whose fruit is used in medicine (ᴋ.).

กะดอม see กระดอม

กะดักกะเดี้ย see กระดักกระเดี้ย

กะดังงา see กระดังงา

กะดัด (ต้น)   gka⁴-dat⁴ *n. Brucea sumatrana (Simarubaceae)* (ᴠ. ᴘ. p. 6), a slender shrub 4 to 5 feet high.   All parts of the plant have a bitter taste.   The seeds, known as Macassar kernels, are used as a remedy for colic and dysentery (ᴍᴄᴍ. p. 377 : ʙᴜʀᴋ. p. 372).

กะดาก see กระดาก

กะดางลาง see กระดางลาง

กะด่าง   an euphonic suffix for กะด่ำ.

กะด้าง   gka⁴-dang³ *v.* to become hardened; to become callous : *adj.* obstinate ; indifferent (to warnings or instruction) : กะด้าง (ต้น) *Lasianthus kurzii (Rubiaceae)* (ᴠ. ᴘ. p. 6): กะด้างกะเดื่อง to be unyielding (to entreaty or supplication) ; to be obstinate or contrary ; to become disloyal.

กะดาด see กระดาด

กะดาน see กระดาน

กะดำกะด่าง   gka⁴-dum-gka⁴-dang⁴ *adj.* irregular in colouring ; blackish-grey ; blurred.

กะดิก see กระดิก

กะดิ่ง see กระดิ่ง

กะดิบ see กระดิบ

กะดี   gka⁴-dee *n.* a Mohammedan temple for worship ; a mosque.

กะดี่ see กระดี่

กะดีกะเดียม see กระดีกระเดียม

กะดึง see กระดึง

กะดุกกะดิก see กระดุกกระดิก

กะดุ้ง, สะดุ้ง   gka⁴-doong³ *n.* a net for catching fish. This is strung, at the four corners, to rods attached to a pole, which can be lowered and raised by a lever.

กะดุ้งกะดิ้ง see กระดุ้งกระดิ้ง

กะดุบกะดิบ see กระดุบกระดิบ

กะดุบกะดุบ see กะดุบกะดิบ

กะดุม see กระดุม

กะดูก see กระดูก

กะเดก see กระเดก

กะเด็น see กระเด็น

กะเด้า see กระเด้า

กะเดาะ see กระเดาะ

กะเดิด see กระเดิด

กะเดียด see กระเดียด

กะเดียว, ประเดียว gka⁴-dee-oh² *colloq.*
just a moment; pretty soon; before long.

กะเดือก see กระเดือก

กะเดื้อง see กระเดื้อง

กะแด็กๆ see กระแด็กๆ

กะแด่ว see กระแด่ว

กะโดก see กระโดก

กะโดง see กระโดง

กะโดด see กระโจน, กระโดด

กะโดน see กระโดน

กะใด see กระใด

กะได see กระได

กะตรกกะตรำ see กระตรกกระตรำ

กะตร้อ see กระตร้อ

กะตรับ see กระตรับ

กะตรุม see กระตรุม

กะต้วมกะเตี้ยม see กระต้วมกระเตี้ยม

กะตอก gka⁴-dtauk⁴ *n. south. provin.* a
spittoon; a cuspidor.

กะต่องกะแต่ง see กระต่องกระแต่ง

กะต๊อบ see กระต๊อบ

กะต่อย gka⁴-dtau-ie⁴ *adj. south. provin.*
little; small; diminutive.

กะต้อยตีวิด see กระต้อยตีวิด

กะตัก see กระตัก

กะตังกะติ้ว see กระตังกระติ้ว

กะต้ม gka⁴-dtam³ *n.* a method used along
canals for catching fish. A space is walled
in on three sides with bamboo strips fastened
together, with a door on the fourth. The
whole space is covered with leaves.

กะตั้ว see กระตั้ว

กะตาก see กระตาก

กะต่าย see กระต่าย

กะติก see กระติก

กะติ๊กริ๊ก gka⁴-dtik⁵-rik⁶ *v.* to pass or come
away in driblets (as urine).

กะตีบ (ต้น) gka⁴-dteep⁴ *n. Protium ser-*
ratum (Burseraceae) (V. P. p. 7), a tree about
10 m. high, found in scrub jungle. The flowers are green (K.).

กะต่อรอร้น see กระต่อรอร้น

กะตุก see กระตุก

กะตุกกะติก see กระตุกกระติก

กะตุงกะตัง see กระตุงกระตัง

กะตุ้น see กระตุ้น

กะเตก gka⁴-dtek⁴ *v.* to prod, poke or goad
in order to make go faster (as cattle).

กะเตง an euphonic suffix for กะไตง.

กะเตง see กระเตง

กะเต็น see กระเต็น

กะเตอะ see กระเตอะ

กะเตาะ see กระเตาะ

กะเตาะกะแตะ see กระเตาะกระแตะ

กะเตื้อง see กระเตื้อง

กะแตง an euphonic suffix for กะติ้ง.

กะแต่ว gka⁴-dtaa-oh⁴ *adj.* importunate;
pleading (by word or manner): ร้องกะแต่วๆ
repeated pleadings (in case of need).

กะโตกกะตาก see กระโตกกระตาก

กะโตงกะเตง see กระโตงกระเตง

กะถด see กระถด

กะถาง see กระถาง

กะถิน see กระถิน

กะเถิบ see กระถด

กะโถน see กระโถน

กะทก see กระทก

กะทกรก see กระทกรก

กะทกลก see กระทกลก

กะทง see กระทง

กะทุงลาย see กระทุงลาย

กะทบ see กระทบ

กะทอ see กระทอ

กะทอก see กระทอก

กะท่อนกะแท่น see กระท่อนกระแท่น

กะท้อน see กะเจ้าะ

กะท้อน see กระท้อน

กะท่อม see กระท่อม

กะท้อมกะแท้ม see กระท้อมกระแท้ม

กะทะ see กระทะ

กะทั่ง see กระทั่ง

กะทั่งหัน see กระทังหัน

กะทัดรัด see กระทัดรัด

กะทันหัน gka⁴-tan-han² *adj.* urgent; pressing; imperative; immediate (without delay).

กะทา see กระทา

กะทาย see กระทาย

กะทิ see กระทิ

กะทิ่ง see กระทิ่ง

กะทึบ see กระทึบ

กะทือ see กระทือ

กะทื้อ see กะแอน

กะทุง see กระทุง

กะทุ้ง see กระทุ้ง

กะทุ่ม see กระทุ่ม

กะทู้ see กระทู้

กะทูด see กะหูด

กะเท่เร่ see กระเท่เร่

กะเทย see กระเทย

กะเทาะ see กระเทาะ

กะเทียม see กระเทียม

กะแท้ see กระแท้

กะแทก see กระแทก

กะแท่ง (ต้น) gka⁴-taang³ *n. Randia tomentosa (Rubiaceae)* (K.), a thorny shrub or small tree having apple-like fruit. The Annamese use its fruits for washing horses, and the Cambodians for washing their own hair. Its timber is excellent for carriage-building, etc. but small. The bush forms good hedges (Burk. p. 1865).

กะแทน see กระแทน

กะนวล (ต้น) gka⁴-nu-an *n. Garcinia merguensis (Guttiferae)* (cb. p. 116), a tree about 10 m. high, found in evergreen forests by streams. The flowers are crimson and fragrant. The tree yields a fragrant resin used for scenting hair-oil (K.). The Malays make a very pale varnish from this tree (Burk. p. 1865).

กะนั้น see กระนั้น

กะนาน see กระนาล

กะน๊ see กระน๊

กะโน้น see กระโน้น

กะไน see กระไน

กะบก see กระบก

กะบวย see กระบวย

กะบองเพ็ชร์ (ต้น)   gka⁴-bong-pet⁶ *n.*
Cereus hexagonus (Cactaceae) (cb. p. 783);
Cereus sp. cacti (V. P. p. 11).

กะบอก see กระบอก

กะบอนกะบิ๋ง see กะบิ๋งกะบอน

กะบ่อนกะแบ่น   gka⁴-baun⁴-gka⁴-baan⁴ *v.*
to be in rags; to be tattered or worn to fragments; to be in small remnants (as cloth).

กะบะ see กระบะ

กะบิ๋ง   gka⁴-bang *n.* flowers *Anna.*; a
means of protection or shelter; a guard; a
fish-trap made of bamboo slats placed in a
V-shape along water-courses : กะบังตา eye-
shields; blinders (for horses): กะบังลม the
diaphragm : กะบังหน้า a shield for the face;
a wire mask (as worn by a base-ball catcher):
กะบังหมวก the beak of a cap : กะบังหอก
the hilt of a sword or dagger.

กะบั๋วกะเบ๋ย see กระบั๋วกระเบ๋ย

กะบาก see กระบาก

กะบาย see กระบาย

กะบ่า (นก)   gka⁴-bah³ *n.* the common Indian night-jar, *Caprimulgus asiaticus* (Herb.
N. H. J. S. S. VI, 3, p. 302); Burmese long-tailed
night-jar, *Caprimulgus macrourus bimacu-*
latus (Deig. N. H. J. S. S. VIII, 3, p. 163).

กะบิ see กระบิ

กะบิ๋ง   gka⁴-bing³ *n.* a fragment; a piece; a
scrap; a bit; a small piece of land (less than ¼

of a rai); a designatory particle for piece-
goods; plots of garden land; flat objects.

กะบิ๋ด see กระบิ๋ด

กะบิ๋ล see กระบิ๋ล

กะบี่ see กระบี่, กบี่

กะบิ๋งกะบอน, กะบอนกะบิ๋ง   gka⁴-beung-
gka⁴-baun *v.* to murmur continually with
discontent : *adj.* grumbling; gloomy; morose;
melancholy.

กะบุง see กระบุง

กะบุ่มกะบ่าม see กระบุ่มกระบ่าม

กะบู้กะบิ๋ see กระบู้กระบิ๋

กะบูนขาว, ตะบูนขาว, ตะบูน (ต้น)   gka⁴-
boon-kow² *n. Xylocarpus obovatus (Meliaceae)*
(cb. p. 265) or *Carapa obovata* (V. P. p. 11),
a tree of moderate size growing along coasts
back of the mangrove belt. The timber
is durable and useful; the bark provides an
excellent dye for cloth. Both roots and bark
are medicinal (Burk. p. 453).

กะเบน see กระเบน

กะเบา see กระเบา

กะเบียด see กระเบียด

กะเบียดกะเสียร see กระเบียดกระเสียร

กะเบียน (ต้น)   gka⁴-bee-an *n. Gardenia*
turgida (Rubiaceae), a small, deciduous tree
yielding a hard, yellow gum. A preparation
from the root is employed as a remedy for
indigestion in children; the root is regarded
as a charm by the natives of Chutia Nagpur,
who wear it attached to the wrist by a cord
(Dept. Agri. & Fisheries).

กะเบียน see กระเบียน

กะเบ๋อง see กระเบ๋อง

กะแบ่ see กระแบ่

กะแบก see กระแบก

กะแบกไข่ see กระแบก

กะแบ่น an euphonic suffix for กะบ่อน.

กะแบะ see กระแบะ

กะปรอย an euphonic suffix for กะปริบ.

กะปรอย gka⁴-bprau-ie *adj.* dribbling; drizzling (as rain).

กะปรี้กะเปร่า see กระปรี้กระเปร่า

กะปลกกะเปลี้ย see กระบวกกระเบีย

กะปอ see กะพ้อ

กะป๊อกกะแป๊ see กระป๊อกกระแป๊

กะป๋อง see กระป๋อง

กะปอดกะแปด see กระปอดกระแปด

กะปะ (งู) gka⁴-bpa⁴ *n.* a species of poisonous snake. The head is arrow-shaped and dark brown in colour. The belly is yellow with black spots. The back is marked in dark brown diamond-shaped designs. This species is very commonly found throughout the southern districts of Siam; *Ancistrodon rhodostoma, A. bomhoffii* (M. S. N. H.J. S. S. VI, 1, p. 62).

กะบัวกะเบีย see กระบัวกระเบีย

กะป่ำ see กระป่ำ

กะปิ gka⁴-bpi⁴ *n.* shrimp paste; a condiment made of salted squills, prawns or shrimps. This is especially relished by the Siamese: กะปิกะปุด *colloq.* shrimp paste.

กะปุก see กระปุก

กะบุ่มกะป่ำ see กระบุ่มกระป่ำ

กะปู gka⁴-bpoo *n. south. provin.* nails.

กะเปะ gka⁴-bpay⁴ *n.* a dammared, basket-bucket, used for drawing water up from a well.

กะเป่า see กระเป่า

กะเปาะ see กระเปาะ

กะแบ้น (เรือ) gka⁴-bpaan³ *n.* a long, narrow, dug-out boat with long, scorpion-shaped tail-piece. This boat is used along the Maa Ping river.

กะแปะ, อีแปะ gka⁴-bpaa⁴ *n.* an ancient copper or lead coin.

กะโปก see กระโปก

กะโปรง gka⁴-bprong *n.* a cylindrical basket lined with leaves (used for overland transportation of goods); a garment hanging from or below the waist; a skirt; a petticoat.

กะผลึกกะผลาม see กระผลึกกระผลาม

กะเผลก, กะโผลก gka⁴-plake⁴ *adj.* limping (as in walking); lame; hobbling; disabled.

กะผีก see กระผีก

กะพง (ปลา) gka⁴-pong *n.* a common, edible fresh-water and sea-fish of the perch family: กะพง (หอย) a mollusk having a shell of two valves; *Modiola senhouseni*, an edible shell-fish found along the shores both of eastern and western Siam: กะพง (ต้น) *Tetrameles nudiflora (Datiscaceae)* (V. P. p. 12), a large, deciduous tree which attains an height of 100 to 150 feet. The wood is white, very soft and very light and well adapted for making tea boxes (Dept. Agri. & Fisheries p. 41): กะพงขี้เซา (ปลา) the triple-tail *Lobotes surinamensis* (Dept. Agri & Fisheries): กะพงดำ (ปลา) a black species of *Lobotes surinamensis*, an edible fish found in the warmer parts of all oceans and common along the southern and middle coasts of the United States. When living, it is silvery grey but becomes brown or blackish when dead. It's dorsal and anal fins are long and extend back on each side of the tail. It is also called black perch (web: Dept. Agri. & Fisheries): กะพงแดง (ปลา) the snapper or red perch *Lutjanus annularis* (H. M. S.); *Lutjanus fulviflamma* (Dept. Agri. & Fisheries): กะพงน้ำจืด (ปลา) bass, *Lates calcarifer*, an edible spiny, finny fish (Dept. Agri. & Fisheries): กะพงลาย, กะพงหิน (ปลา) striped perch; *Datnioides quadrifasciatus*, a common, freshwater, spiny, finny fish of the genus *Perca* (web: Dept. Agri & Fisheries): กะพงแสม (ปลา) *Pomadasys nageb* (H. M. S: Dept. Agri & Fisheries).

กะพรวดกะพราด　gka^4-proo-at^4-gka^4-prat^4 *adj.* careless; crude; unpolished; rough or violent in actions; thoughtless (as an untrained servant).

กะพร่องกะแพร่ง, กะพล่องกะแพล่ง gka^4-praung^3-gka^4-praang^3 *adj.* imperfect; incomplete; defective; impaired; faulty.

กะพริบ　gka^4-prip^6 *v.* to blink; to wink; to bat the eyes: ตากะพรุบกะพริบ blinking eyes.

กะพรุน, แมงกะพรุน　　gka^4-proon *n.* a jelly-fish.

กะเพรา, ลูกแมงลัก　gka^4-prow *n. Ocimum sp. (Labiatae)* (K.); *Ocimum basilicum* (MCM. p. 344: V. P. p. 221); *O. sanctum* (MCM. p. 379); "sweet basil," a fragrant and aromatic annual about two feet high. It is commonly cultivated for its yellowish-green essential oil obtained by distillation from the fresh shoots and leaves. It's highly fragrant and aromatic leaves are used for flavouring soups and curries. In decoctions, it is used for coughs and catarrh. Sometimes it is chewed as a substiute for the betel-nut. The plant is considered sacred and is commonly cultivated near Hindu temples.

กะแพร่ง　　an euphonic suffix for กะพร่อง.

กะพล้อ, กะพ้อ　gka^4-plau^5 *n.* a drinking cup or utensil having a kettle-like nozzle or spout.

กะพล่องกะแพล่ง see กะพร่องกะแพร่ง

กะพลอมกะแพลม　gka^4-plaum-gka^4-plaam *adv.* unevenly; roughly; jaggedly: *adj.* having a tendency to occur irregularly or intermittently.

กะพ้อ, กะปอ, กะพล้อ (ต้น)　gka^4-pau^5 *n. Licuala spinosa (Palmae)*, a variety of small, bushy fan-palm found in open dry places through out Malaysia. It grows up to 5 m. in height and bears many stems. At times these are used for roofing (BURK. p. 1342).

กะพอก see กระพอก

กะพอง see กระพอง

กะพองช้าง　gka^4-paung-chang^5 *n.* the two humps or nodes on the sides of an elephant's head.

กะพัก see กระพัก

กะพัง see กระพัง

กะพังเหิร see กระพังเหิร

กะพังโหม see กระพังโหม

กะพัน see กระพัน

กะพู see กระพู

กะพื่อ see กระพื่อ

กะพุ้ง see กระพุ้ง

กะเพาะ see กระเพาะ

กะเพิง see กระเพิง

กะเพื่อม see กระเพื่อม

กะพัดกะเพียด see กระพัดกระเพียด

กะฟูมกะฟาย see กระฟูมกระฟาย

กะมัง see กระมัง

กะมิดกะเมี้ยน see กระมิดกระเมี้ยน

กะมูติง (ต้น)　gka^4-moo-dting *n. Rhodomyrtus tomentosa (Myrtaceae)* (cb. p. 629), "hill-goose-berry," "hill-guava," a handsome shrub with small, thick, oval leaves, indigenous to the mountains. It produces a profusion of pale pink flowers, followed by small, round berries of a pale yellow colour. From these, a jelly is made, which somewhat resembles

apple-jelly in flavour.   An acclimatized variety, much admired as an ornamental shrub,
seldom bears fruit (MCM. pp. 116, 283).

กะเม็ง (ต้น)   gka⁴-meng *n. Ecipta erecta (Compositae)* (V. P. p. 12 : K.), a cosmopolitan weed
of the tropics. The leaves of this plant are
used as a dye. The roots are used medicinally
by native doctors in remedies for purifying the
blood (MCM. p. 378). They also are purgative
and emetic and are largely used in treating
constipation. The leaves are used in making
a decoction which is drunk (BURK. p. 890).

กะเมาะ see กระเมาะ

กะย่องกะแย่ง see กระย่องกระแย่ง

กะย่อม see กระย่อม

กะยาง see กระยาง

กะยาหงัน see กระยาหงัน

กะยิ้มกะย่อง see กระยิ้มกระย่อง

กะยืดกะยาด see กระยืดกระยาด

กะยุ   gka⁴-yoo⁶ *v.* to lift up; to be raised
higher on one side ; to be askew.

กะรอก see กระรอก

กะร่องกะแร่ง   gka⁴-raung³-gka⁴-raang³
adj. imperfect ; insufficient ; in small fragments, bits or pieces ; a little of this and a
little of that :   กร่องแกร่ง weak ; feeble.

กะร่อน   an euphonic suffix for กะเร่.

กะระตะ   gka⁴-ra⁶-dta⁴ *Cam. v.* to use means
for urging horses or cattle to go faster.

กะระหนะ   gka⁴-ra⁶-na⁴ *n.* an ancient tune
played on stringed instruments.

กะรัง (ปลา)   gka⁴-rang *n.* the grouper, a
salt-water fish, *Epinephelus boenack* (Dept.
Agri. & Fisheries).

กะรัต   gka⁴-rat⁴ *Eng. n.* a carat, a unit of
weight (for gems) equal to 3.0865 grains :
กะรัตหลวง a metric carat, according to the

standard established by the Siamese Government, equal to 20 centigrams (used in weighing precious stones).

กะร่า   an euphonic suffix for กะเร่อ.

กะราด   an euphonic suffix for กะเรี่ย.

กะริ่ง see กระหริ่ง

กะริ่งกะเรียด   gka⁴-ring-gka⁴-ree-at³ *adj.*
precocious ; adopting mannerisms beyond one's
age.

กะรุ่ง   an euphonic suffix for กะรุ่ง.

กะรุ่งกะริ่ง   gka⁴-roong³-gka⁴-ring³ *adj.*
ragged ; frayed.

กะเร (ต้น)   gka⁴-ray *n. Bryophyllum pin-
natum (Crassulaceae)* (cb. p. 586 : MCM. p.
40) ; *B. calycinum* (V. P. p. 13), a succulent plant
with thick, fleshy leaves, which, when slightly
toasted, are used as an application to wounds,
bruises, boils and bites of venomous insects
(Dept. Agri. & Fisheries p. 543) :   กะเรกะร่อน,
การการ่อน *Cymbidium finlaysonianum (Orchidaceae)*, a species of orchid (V. P. p. 18 : K.).

กะเร่กะร่อน   gka⁴-ray³-gka⁴-raun³ *v.* to
wander aimlessly about; to have no regular
place of abode (as gypsies).

กะเรียกะราด   gka⁴-ree-ah³-gka⁴-rat³ *adj.*
scattered ; lying about in a disorderly manner.

กะเรียด   an euphonic suffix for กะริ่ง.

กะเรียน see กระเรียน

กะไร see กระไร

กะลอเกลี้ยง (ต้น)   gka⁴-lau-gkle-ung³ *n.*
Macaranga denticulata (Euphorbiaceae) (V. P.
p. 13), a small evergreen tree, often gregarious, found from the Himalayas and southern
China to Java. A decoction of it is administered after child-birth, and is used for cleansing wounds (BURK. p. 1382). The wood is
much used for fencing and temporary huts
but is also adapted for cabinet work (Dept.
Agri. & Fisheries).

กะลอจี๋   gka⁴-lau-chjee² *n.* a sweet-meat of Chinese origin, sold along the streets by hawkers.

กะลอยายยทาย (ต้น)   gka⁴-lau-yai-tai *n.* *Mallotus barbatus* (*Euphorbiaceae*) (V. P. p. 14), a shrub. The Laos of parts of Indo-China extract a tallow from the seeds which they use for illumination (BURK p. 1395).

กะล่อน   gka⁴-laun³ *n.* a variety of small mango, very fragrant when ripe: *adj.* prevaricating; toying with speech (talking fluently but with little truth in what is said); crooked or deceiving (in character): คนพูด-กะล่อน one who is fluent in speech but whose words lack veracity.

กะล่อมกะแล่ม, กล้อมแกล้ม   gka⁴-laum³-gka⁴-laam³ *adj.* chewing imperfectly; speaking without distinctness or proper articulation; bolting down food without proper mastication.

กะล่อยกะหลิบ   gka⁴-lau-ay³-gka⁴-lip⁴ *adj.* active; dexterous; expeditious; quick (in the use of the hands): พูดกะล่อยกะหลิบ to speak fluently or rapidly; a flow of speech.

กะละบึงหา, กัลบึงหา   gka⁴-la⁶-bpang-ha² *n.* an alcyonarian coral; the branching or tree-shaped coral (in contradistinction to the stone-shaped coral or หินกะรัง).

กะละมัง   gka²-la⁶-mung *n.* enamelware.

กะละแม   gka⁴-la⁶-maa *n.* a taffy-like sweet-meat of glutinous rice, sugar and coconut milk, cut into squares: กะละแมเม็ด the aforementioned sweet-meat in lumps or balls.

กะละออม   gka⁴-la⁶-aum *n.* a waterpot; a water-goblet made of fine strips of bamboo woven into shape and dammared inside and out.

กะลังใบ see **กระตังใบ**

กะลัน, ลัน   gka⁴-lan *n.* an eel trap, made of a section of bamboo or of wicker work.

กะลันทา, กรนทา (ต้น)   gka⁴-lan-tah *n.* *Harrisonia perforata* (*Simarubaceae*) (cb. p. 244 : K.), an erect shrub found in evergreen forest. The plant is very bitter. The wood is medicinal (BURK. p. 1128).

กะลัยโกฏิ   gka⁴-lai-gkote⁴ *n.* an hermit having the face of a deer, and said to be the son of Rishya-sringa. According to the Ramayana and Maha-bharata, he was Rishya-sringa, the deer-horned hermit himself. He was the son of Vibhandaka, descended from Kasyapa, born of a doe, and had a small horn on the forehead. Until he was verging upon manhood, he saw no other human being except his father who brought him up in the forest. When a great drought fell on the country of Anga, King Lomapada was advised by his Brahman counsellors to send for the youth Rishya-sringa that he might marry the king's daughter Santa and be the means of obtaining rain. King Lomapada, therefore, sent a number of fair damsels to bring him; he accompanied them to the city; the desired rain fell; he then married Santa (H. C. D. pp. 268, 269).

กะลาโหม see **กระลาโหม**

กะลา   gka⁴-lah *n.* a half portion of the hard shell of the coconut: ถ้วยกะลา wide-rimmed cups and dishes similar in shape to a half coconut shell: ผมกะลา a hair-cut suggestive of the shape of a half coconut shell.

กะลา (ต้น)   gka⁴-lah *n.* *Costus speciosus* (*Zingiberaceae*), a flowering shrub with white, yellow-centerd tuberous roots. It is commonly used as food in Ceylon by poorer people but is not cultivated (MCM. pp. 109, 140, 311). The Malays use this plant in magic and in medicine. The juice of the fresh rhizome is purgative. They boil the plant, and bathe a patient with a high fever in the decoction; they bruise the leaves and poultice the head with them; they scrape the stems, and apply the scrapings to leprous skin; decoctions into which it enters may be used as lotions in small-pox and fever. (BURK. pp. 131-2, 671-2).

กะลาส์   gka[4]-lah-see[2] *n.* a sailor; a seaman; a mariner.

กะลาง, เจ๊กโกหก, อีเพาหัวหงอก (นก) gka[4]-lang *n.* the Siamese white-crested laughing thrush, *Garrulax diardi* (Gaird. J. S. S. IX, 1, p. 1).

กะลำพัก see กระลำพัก

กะลำพุก see กระลำพุก

กะลำเพาะ, โพตะโก๋ซ่า, อวดน้ำ, ใหลน้ำ (ต้น)   gka[4]-lum-pau[6] *n. Derris elliptica* (*Leguminosae*) (Cb. p. 489), a large, woody climber. The bark and flowers are commonly used as fish-poison and the juice as arrow-poison. When pounded up in water, the roots are used against termites, crickets, etc. It is cultivated for insecticidal purposes (MCM. pp. 385, 480).

กะลิอ่อง, กล้วยน้ำว้า   gka[4]-li[6]-aung[4] *n.* a common variety of banana.

กะลิง (นก)   gka[4]-ling *n.* the Malayan parrot *Psittinus incertus* (Gaird. J. S. S. IX, 1, p. 8): กะลิงปลิง, ตะลิงปลิง (ต้น) *Averrhoa bilimbi* (*Oxalidaceae*) (Cb. p. 207), "cucumber tree," a small, fine-foliaged tree commonly cultivated in the tropics (especially in the East) for its acid fruit, which is about 3 to 4 inches long, resembling a small green cucumber. It is esteemed as pickles and preserves, and is used for making jam and cooling drinks. It is also relished in curries (MCM. p. 255).

กะลิ่มกะเหลี่ย   gka[4]-lim[5]-gka[4]-lee-ah[3] *adj.* having a covetous disposition or grasping manners.

กะลุมพู see กระลุมพู

กะเล่อกะล่า   gka[4]-ler[3]-gka[4]-lah[3] *adj.* non-plussed; dazed; confused (in face of danger); scared; terrified; frightened (descriptive of both people and beasts).

กะเลิด   gka[4]-lert[3] *n.* a sled drawn by bullocks or buffalos (used by farmers for transporting bundles of rice-stalks or straw).

กะเลี่ยว   gka[4]-lee-oh *n.* a blue-black colour (as of horses); a breed of horse.

กะแล่ม   an euphonic suffix for กะล่อม.

กะโล่   gka[4]-loh[3] *n.* a broad, shallow, flat-bottomed basket, either plain or smeared over with dammar (used for dressing paraphernalia for infants, during the mother's lying-in period: หมวกกะโล่ sun helmet: ลูกกะโล่ a subordinate.

กะวอกกะแวก   gka[4]-wauk[3]-gka[4]-waak[3] *adj.* restless; fidgety (resembling the actions of a monkey).

กะวะ   gka[4]-wa[6] *n.* a close-meshed bag-net suspended from a hoop (used in catching shrimps or prawns along canals or on the seashore): กะวะรุนกุ้งรุนเคย to catch shrimps or prawns in the กะวะ.

กะวะ, กาหัง (นก)   gka[4]-wa[6] *n.* the great pied horn-bill *Dichoceros bicornis* (Gaird. J.S.S. IX, 1, p. 1).

กะวาน see กระวาน

กะวิน see กระวิน

กะวักกะวาด see กระวักกระวาด

กะวูดกะวาด see กระวูดกระวาด

กะแวก   an euphonic suffix for กะวอก.

กะแวน see กระแวน

กะสง see กระสง

กะสม see กระสม

กะส้มชื่น, ว่านน้ำ (ต้น)   gka[4]-som[3]-cheun[3] *n.* a marsh plant (*lit.* water tuber), having aromatic, creeping rhizomes, which run in the mud and give rise to tufts of narrow iris-like leaves, *Acorus calamus* (*Araceae*) (V. P. p. 14); "sweet-flag." The rhizomes or rootstocks are used in large doses as an emetic, but in smaller doses as a stomachic and carminative. It is a simple, useful remedy for flatulency, colic or dyspepsia and a pleasant adjunct to tonic or purgative medicines. It is also used in remittent fevers and ague and is held in high esteem as an insecticide, especially for fleas (Dept. Agri. & Fisheries). The rhizome is very fragrant, containing an aromatic, volatile oil, with which is associated a bitter principle and a trace of alkaloids (Burk. p. 34).

กะสร้อย see กระสร้อย

กะสวน see กระสวน

กะสวย see กระสวย

กะสอบ see กระสอบ

กะสัง see กระสัง

กะสัน see กระสัน

กะสับกะส่าย see กระสับกระส่าย

กะสา see กระสา

กะส้าหอย, กะซ้าหอย　　gka^4-sa^3-hoy^2 _n._ shells of clams or mollusks (such as are used in the making of shell-lime).

กะสาบ see กระสาบ

กะสาย see กระสาย

กะสือ see กระสือ

กะสุน see กระสุน

กะสูบ see กระสูบ

กะเสด see กระเสด

กะเส็นกะสาย see กระเส็นกระสาย

กะเส่า see กระเส่า

กะเสาะกะแสะ see กระเสาะกระแสะ

กะเสือกกะสน see กระเสือกกระสน

กะแส see กระแส

กะแสะ see กระแสะ

กะหนก see กระหนก

กะหน่องกะแหน่ง　gka^4-naung^2-gka^4-naang^2 _adj._ imperfect; faulty; defective (descriptive of speech).

กะหนะ　　　gka^4-na^4 _n._ fronds of the waterpalm or nipa palm, _Nipa fruticans_ (used largely as material for enclosing or roofing of huts or shacks of the poorer classes).

กะหนาบ see กระหนาบ

กะหนุงกะหนิง　gka^4-noong^2-gka^4-ning^2 _adj._ cooing; whispering; making love in low murmuring tones.

กะแหน　　　an euphonic suffix for กะหนอ.

กะแหนะ see กระแหนะ

กะหมั้ง see กระหมั้ง

กะแหยก (ต้น)　　gka^4-yaak^4 _n. Pedilanthus tithymaloides_ (_Euphorbiaceae_) (V. P. p. 13), an erect, half succulent shrub (commonly planted around paddy fields as fencing) (McM. pp. 74, 171). The juice from the roots is a powerful emetic. In Malaya it is applied for relief to scorpion and centipede bites (Burk. p. 1683).

กะหร่อง　　gka^4-raung^4 _adj._ pale; emaciated; thin (descriptive of one after an illness).

กะหร็อมกะแหร็ม　　gka^4-raum^2-gka^4-raam^2 _adj._ sparse; scattered here and there; few; incomplete.

กะหรี่　　gka^4-ree^4 _n._ an Indian curry, hot with pepper.

กะเหรี่ยง　　gka^4-ree-ang^4 _n._ the Karen, an ethnologically unclassified mountain tribe, inhabiting the western frontier of Siam. A great part of the Karen country lies outside Siam, in the southern Shan States and lower Burma, but it also extends over the border, chiefly along the hills of the western boundary, from the provinces of Me Hawng Sawn and Chiengrai in the north to the province of Petchaburi in the south. The Karens also extend eastward into the province of Lampun. There are the white Karens (ยางขาว) and the red Karens (ยางแดง) (siam p. 103).

กะแหร็ม   an euphonic suffiix for กะหร็อม.

กะหลับกะเหลือก   gka⁴-lap⁴-gka⁴-lur-uk⁴ *adj.* casting the eyes up and down alternately.

กะหลาป๋า   gka⁴-lah²-bpah² *n.* Batavia, the capital of Java; a variety of rose apple, green in colour but very sweet.

กะหล่ำปลี   gka⁴-lum⁴-bplee *n.* cabbage *Brassica oleracea* (*Cruciferae*) (MCM. p. 316). This useful vegetable is grown abundantly in up-country gardens. The green leaves are much prized by the peasants for vegetable curries. The seeds have a diuretic, laxative and stomachic effect. The leaves form a good application for gout and rheumatism (Dept. Agri. & Fisheries).

กะหลิบ   an euphonic suffix for กะล่อย.

กะโหลก   gka⁴-loke⁴ *n.* the skull; the cranium; the hard shell of a coconut, partly cut open and used as a dipper; descriptive of fruit that is developed larger than normal: กะโหลกหัวผี the cranium of a corpse: ลิ้นจี่กะโหลก an overly-large linchee (*Litchi*): หัวกะโหลก the head (a term sometimes used in contempt).

กะหลี่   gka⁴-lee⁴ *n.* a bunch or cluster of Indian hemp leaves or flowers: กะหลี่ข้าวโพชน์ corn-cobs.

กะหัง see กระหัง

กะหำ, ไข่หำ   gka⁴-hum² *n.* the testicles; the scrotum.

กะหิ่ม see กระหิ่ม

กะหึดกะหอบ see กระหึดกระหอบ

กะหูด, กะทูด   gka⁴-hoot⁴ *n.* a funnel-shaped fish-trap.

กะแห see กระแห

กะโห้ see กระโห้

กะอ้อกะแอ้ see กระอ้อกระแอ้

กะออดกะแอด see กระออดกระแอด

กะออม see กระออม

กะอ้อมกะแอ้ม see กระอ้อมกระแอ้ม

กะอิด (ต้น)   gka⁴-it⁴ *n. Capparis flavicans* (*Capparidaceae*) (V. P. p. 15), a spreading shrub about 3 m. high, found in open scrub forest (K.).

กะเอว, สะเอว   gka⁴-ay-oh *n.* the waist.

กะแอ   gka⁴-aa *n.* a sun-shade with a long handle, the base of which is sharpened to a point or fitted with an iron spike for sticking into the ground; beach or garden umbrella: *adj.* small; young; frisky (descriptive of calves).

กะแอก see กระแอก

กะแอน, กระชาย, กะชาย   gka⁴-aan *n. Kaempferia pandurata* (*Zingiberaceae*) (V. P. p. 3: K.), a medicinal herb growing in bamboo jungle. It is aromatic and stimulating like ginger. It is much used in decoctions in native medicine. The root stalks are edible (K.).

กะแอน, กะทือ (ต้น)   gka⁴-aan *n. Zingiber zerumbet* (*Zingiberaceae*) (V. P. p. 15), an herbaceous plant. The rhizomes are yellow inside and are used in making a dye. The plant has a slightly aromatic odour and possesses similar properties to those of officinal ginger but in a minor degree. It is employed locally as a hot remedy for coughs, asthma, "special diseases," leprosy and other skin diseases (Dept. Agri. & Fisheries).

กะแอม see กระแอม

กะไอ see กระไอ

กัก   gkak⁴ *v.* to prevent access or egress; to

detain; to hinder; to hold (as in quarantine):
กักกัน, กักขัง to confine or detain under custody: กักข้าว to withhold or defer the
sale of rice; to make a "corner" on rice:
กักด่าน to station sentinels or outposts in
order to prevent smuggling or unlawful immigration: กักเรือกักแพ to prevent the passage of boats, ships or rafts (as at provincial
Quarantine Stations or Customs Posts).

กั๊ก　　gkak[5] Chin. n. a waistcoat; an armless
garment; the intersection of two roads; cross
lines drawn on a surface for playing with
dice: กั๊กโป a dice-board: สี่กั๊กพระยาศรี
name of a district of Bangkok where a circle
is formed at the crossing of two streets.

กักขพะ　　gkak[4]-ka[4]-la[6] P.S. adj. hard; harsh;
rough; solid; cruel.

กักษา, กักษยา see กัจฉ

กั้ง　　gkang n. a species of monkey having
a short tail. They are trained by certain
tribes to help in collecting fruit; the pig-
tailed monkey Macaca nemestrin (Gard. N. H.
J. S. S. III, 2, p. 121): onomat. from the slam-
ming of a door.

กั้ง　　gkang[3] v. to enclose; to prevent access
or egress: n. a mantis-shrimp: ก้ามกั้ง claws
at the tips of the feet of small-sized shrimps,
by which they pick up food.

กั้ง (นก)　　gkang[3] n. Burmese barred-back
pheasant Syrmaticus humiae burmanicus
(Deig. N. H. J. S. S. VIII, 3, p. 168).

กั้งเกี่ยง　　gkang-gkee-ang v. to be ill-fitting; to be incapable of fitting together: adj.
badly fitting; loose; ill-shaped; lopsided.

กั้งขา　　gkang-kah[2] v. to suspect; to doubt
the sincerity of: n. doubt; doubt about the
past, the present and the future: adj.
suspicious; questionable; doubtful (S. E. D.).

กังวล　　gkang-won Cam. v. to worry; to
be anxious about; to be engrossed: ความ-
กังวล anxiety: เป็นกังวลด้วย to share in another's anxiety.

กังวาน　　gkang-wan n. echo; verberation:
adj. musical; melodious; sonorous.

กังส ๑　　gkang-sa[4] P.S. n. white-copper, bell-
metal or brass; queen's metal; any amalgam
of zinc and copper; a drinking vessel of
brass; a goblet; a gong or plate of bell-
metal, struck with a stick or rod; name
of a tyrannical king of Mathura, a cousin of Lady Devaki, the mother of the god
Vishnu, in one of his incarnations. It was
foretold that a son born of Devaki should kill
him, so he endeavoured to destroy all of her
children. Bala-rama, the seventh son was
smuggled away to Gokula and brought up by
Rohini. Krishna, the eighth child was taken
away by his parents after his birth. When
the fact was known to Kansa, an order for a
general massacre of all vigorous male infants
was enforced. By this act, Kansa became
the great presecutor of Krishna but was
eventually killed by him (H. C. D. p. 149)
กังสชิต name of Krishna, because he conquered Kansa: กังสวณิช a brazier or seller of
brass vessels: กังสวธ the act of killing
Kansa; the name of a drama, in seven acts,
upon the destruction of Kansa by Krishna.
The author is called Sesha-Krishna. The
play was probably written about two centuries ago (S. E. D. p. 149): กังสสถาล a vessel
made of metal; trays or utensils made of
brass.

กังส ๒　　gkang-sa[4] n. an ancient unit of
weight for gold or silver, equal to 16 mashas
or about 176 grains troy (S. E. D.).

กังสดาล　　gkang-sa[4]-dan P. n. metal;
bronze; a gong; a bowl to eat from (Chd.).

กังหัน　　gkang-han[2] n. the Siamese vowel-
mark " ั "; a weather-vane; a whirl-wheel;
a whirligig placed in trees by farmers:
แพ้วกังหัน a weather-cock in the shape of a flag.

กัจจานะ, กัจจายน์　　gkat[4]-chjah-na[6] P. n.
one of the Lord Buddha's disciples, whom he
praised as being the most capable of all his

disciples in explaining eptomized proverbs; a famous grammarian, author of a Pali grammar (chd.); Katyayana, an ancient writer of great celebrity, who came after Panini and who completed the correction of a grammar called Varttikas, containing supplementary rules and annotations. He was also the author of a Dharma-sastra (H. C. D. p. 154).

กัจฉ gkat⁴-cha⁴ S. n. (1) a forest of dead trees; dry woods; underbrush (often the lair of wild beasts); grass; dry grass; a spreading creeper or climbing plant: (2) a girdle; a zone; a belt; girth; hem; border: (3) the end of the nether garment (after the cloth is carried round the body, this end is brought up behind and tucked into the waist-band): (4) a surrounding wall; a wall; any place surrounded by walls: กัจฉบุฏ the axillary space; the arm-pit: กัจฉสาย lit. "a sleeper on dry grass," i. e. a dog: กัจโฉทก fog; mist; moisture in a thicket or in a dense forest: กัจฉโลม axillary hairs; the hair of the arm-pit.

กัจฉปะ gkat⁴-cha⁴-bpa⁴ P. S. n. a tortoise; a turtle; one keeping in or inhabiting a marsh.

กัจฉปาวตาร gkat⁴-cha⁴-bpah-wa⁶-dtan P. S. n. the tortoise incarnation of Vishnu.

กัจฉา gkat⁴-chah² n. a belly-band (used for an elephant) (S. E. D.).

กัญจนะ gkan-chja⁴-na⁶ n. gold; possessions in the form of gold.

กัญจุก gkan-chjook⁴ n. a garment fitting close to the upper part of the body; armour; mail; cuirass; corselet; bodice; jacket; the scarf-skin of a snake (S. E. D.).

กัญชา gkan-chah n. Cannabis sativa (Urticaceae), hemp, hashish or ganja, an annual, usually 4 to 5 feet high (sometimes 6 to 8 ft). In temperate zones, it is largely cultivated for its fibre and for the oil-seed. Resin exudes from the plant. It is a powerful narcotic but in small doses may be used as a stimulant (MCM. p. 384: V. P. p. 28). The seeds and flowers

are smoked and are also used as a seasoning for curry. When thus eaten, it produces a condition of violent excitement, simulating acute mania.

กัญญา gkan-yah n. a young woman; a girl; a virgin; a belle: a beautiful girl; long state-barges, propelled by some 50 or 60 men with paddles, and having an enclosed canopy over the center (S. E. D.).

กัฏฐ gkat⁴-ta⁴ n. a piece of wood or timber; fire-wood; chips; sticks; chunks or slabs of wood; wood or timber (in general).

กัณฏกะ, กัณฏกะ gkan-na⁶-dta⁴-gka⁴ P. S. n. a thorn; anything pointed; the point of a pin or needle; a prickle; a sting; a fish-bone; a finger-nail (S. E. D.).

กัณฐ gkan-ta⁴ P. S. n. neck; throat: กัณฐะ from the throat; distinct; guttural; staying or sticking in the throat; being in or upon the throat; the guttural group of consonants, viz. ก, ข, ค, ฆ, ง: กัณฐนาล the neck-stalk; the larynx; the throat; the neck; the throat (compared to a lotus-stalk): กัณฐปาศก a halter; an elephant's jowl: กัณฐพันธ์ a halter or neck-band for an elephant; a rope passing round an elephant's neck: กัณฐภังค์ lit. "a breaking of the voice," i. e. stammering; imperfect articulation: กัณฐภูษณ์, กัณฐภูษา, กัณฐลตา, กัณฐวิภูษณ์, กัณฐาภรณ์ an ornament for the neck; a necklace; a collar: กัณฐมณิ a jewel worn on the throat; a dear or beloved object; the thyroid cartilage: กัณฐมูล the deepest part of the throat: กัณฐา the plural form of กัณฐ: กัณฐาศเลษ the act of embracing or encircling the neck with the arms: กัณฐโศษ the condition of dryness of the throat; a dry throat.

กัณฐก gkan-tok⁴ n. a necklace; an ornament for the neck; the name of the horse used by Phra Sakaymuni.

กัณฐี gkan-tee² adj. suitable for the neck; appropriate to be worn as an ornament for the neck.

กัณฑ์　gkan *P. n.* a piece; a portion; a part; a chapter; a section (of a book); an arrow; a stalk: กัณฑ์เทศน์ the thirteen chapters of the Maha Chat: เครื่องกัณฑ์ gifts to Buddhist monks (as robes, lamps, mats, etc.).

กัณณ์, กรรณ　gkan *n.* ear; rudder; diameter; name of a child of the Sun (S. E. D.).

กัณณิกา see กรรณิกา

กัณหะ　gkan-ha[4] *adj.* black; dark: กัณห-บักขึ์ blackness; darkness; waning phase of the moon; the fifteen days during which the moon is on the wane: กัณหสัปปะ a black snake; a serpent; a serpent demon; the cobra. de-capello; the *Naja tripudians,* a highly venomous serpent (S. E. D.).

กัด　gkat[4] *v.* to bite; to cut or seize with the teeth; to corrode (as by an acid); to nibble (as fish at a bait): กัดกัน, ขบกัดกัน to bite while fighting: กัดขบ to crack with the teeth (as a nut): กัดพืด to worry (as a dog worries a rat or snake): กัดพื้น to grind or gnash the teeth: กัดลิ้น (ต้น) *Walsura trichostemon (Meliaceae)* (cb. p. 263), a small tree about 8 m. high, growing in open, deciduous jungle. The flowers are white (K.): ปลากัด the fighting-fish, *Betta splendens.*

กัตติกะ　gkat[4]-dti[4]-gka[4] *n.* the twelfth lunar month which falls about November; name of Phra Khanda Kumara.

กัตติกา　gkat[4]-dti[4]-gkah *n. lit.* "stars of good omen," *i. e.* the constellation Pleiades.

กัตติเกยา　gkat[4]-dti[4]-gkay-yah *n.* the son of Siva and Parvati, popularly regarded as god of War because he led the hosts of Siva against the demon hosts (S. E. D.).

กัทลี, กทลี　gkat[4]-ta[6]-lee *n.* flag; ensign; the plantain or banana tree (S. E. D.).

กัน ๑　gkan *v.* to prevent; to hinder; to keep out; to protect from (as sun or rain); to shave evenly (as around the top-knot); to shave or pluck hairs from around the edges:

pro. a collective personal pronoun: *conj.* with; together, *ex.* ไปด้วยกัน or ดีกัน: กันกง to surround; to encircle: กันชน bumper of a car: กันชิด a razor (used only for royalty): กันเจียก a head-dress or decoration (worn by Siamese actors): กันดา a virgin (used only for royalty): กันแดด, กันสาด a protection made of woven bamboo strips extending down from the eaves (against rain or sun): กันตัว to protect one's self from evil: to protect one's self: ซึ่งกันและกัน mutually; reciprocally: กันสนิม rust-preventing: ต่อกัน from one to another successively; to join together: ติดกัน to be assembled together; to stick fast together: ป้องกัน to protect against; to guard against: พบกัน to meet each other.

กัน ๒　gkan *Cam. v.* to catch with the hands; to hold in or with the hands: เกียดกัน, กันท่า to interrupt or hinder another person.

กั่น　gkan[4] *n.* the haft or hilt of a sword; the part of an instrument or weapon fixed into the handle: ก๋ากั่น bold; socially unconventional *slang.*

กั้น　gkan[3] *v.* to intercept; to intervene; to interpose; to prevent; to separate (as when two are fighting): กั้นกาง to hang up or put up something in between, in order to make a partition: กั้นขันหมาก to intercept the bridegroom on entering the home of the bride. This is a Siamese custom in which the wedding guests stand in pairs at the door to prevent the bridegroom and his friends from entering the bride's home, until after some forfeit is paid to each pair. After this is paid, he is permitted to pass along: กั้นม่าน to hang up a curtain: กั้นรั้ว, กั้นรั้ว to put up a fence: กั้นห้อง to put up a partition (as for a room).

กันเกรา　gkan-gkrauw *n. Fagraea fragrans (Loganiaceae)* (V. P. p. 28: MCM. p. 99: K.), a handsome, upright, evergreen, small-leaved

foliage tree of Siam, often planted along avenues for ornamental purposes. Planted trees
may attain a felling size after 30 years, but
certainly not sooner. Though of slow growth,
it retains its well-balanced habits. The pale
yellow wood, having a purplish tint, is heavy
and well-suited for building and flooring purposes (MCM. p. 212 : BURK. p. 994).

กันไกร see **กรรไตร**

กันโชก see **กรรโชก**

กันดาร gkan-dan *n.* a forest; a wilderness;
a waste place; a condition of famine; scarcity
of food; a calamity; a national calamity:
adj. needy; wretched; lonely; famine-strick-
en: กันดารบถ a difficult pathway through
the jungle; a forest path: กันดารภพ one
living in scarcity in the jungle; a dweller in
the woods: กันดารวาสินี *lit.* "wood-dweller,"
i. e. Durga (S. E. D.).

กันดาล gkan-dan *Cam. n.* middle; center.

กันต์ ๑ gkan *v.* to cut; to shave or trim off
(as the top-knot); to divide: *adj.* cutting;
cutting off; dividing off: เกสากันต์ to cut
the top-knot (for princes' children of the rank
of Serene Highness): โสกันต์ to cut and
shave the top-knot (for princes' children of
the rank of Royal Highness).

กันต์ ๒ gkan *v.* to cause to turn; to twist;
to spin; to twill with the hands (as thread);
to file off (as while revolving); to denude the
surface (by means of a file or stone) (S. E. D.
p. 304).

กันต์ ๓, กรานต์ gkan *v.* to advance into
(as the sun into a new zodiacal zone).

กันต์ ๔ gkan *n.* loveliness; beauty; splen-
dor; female beauty; personal decorations or
embellishments: *adj.* beautiful; pretty;
lovable; attractive (S. E. D.).

กันตัง gkan-dtang *n.* a sea-port town of
southern Siam, the amphur of Trang, in the
province of Bhuket.

กันไตร see **กรรไตร**

กันทร gkan-taun *S. P. n.* a great cliff; an
artificial or natural cave; a glen; a defile;
a valley: กันทรันดร the space, room or
cavity in a cave or cavern.

กันทรากร gkan-ta[6]-rah-gkaun *n.* a mountain.

กันโทรก (ต้น) gkan-trok[5] *n. Micromelum
minutum (Rutaceae)* (cb. p. 228), a small tree
about 5 m. high, growing by streams in evergreen forest. Leaf scars down the stems
are like those on the papaya. The flowers
are greenish white and very fragrant (K.).

กันภิรมย์ see **กรรภิรมย์**

กันยา, กันย์ gkan-yah *n.* a daughter; a virgin;
a young girl; Virgo, the sign of the zodiac:
กันยกุมารี "Virgin-damsel," a name for Durga
(ทุรคา): กันยากาล the age of puberty; maidenhood: กันยากุพชะ name of an ancient city
of great note, situated in the United Provinces
of northern India, on the Kali-nadi, a branch
of the Ganges. The popular spelling of the
name presents perhaps greater variations than
that of any other place in India (Kanauj, Kun-
noj, Kunnauj, Kinoge, Kinnoge, Kinnauj, Ka-
noj, Kannauj, Kunowj, Canowj, Canoje, Ca-
nauj). The modern official romanized spelling
is Kanauj. In antiquity, this city ranked next
to Ayodhya in Oude; it is known in classical
geography as Canogyza but the name applies
also to its dependencies and the surrounding
district. The current etymology is kanya,
"a girl," and kubja, "round-shouldered or
crooked," referring to a legend relating to the
hundred daughters of Kusanabha, the king of
this city, who were all rendered crooked by
Vayu for non-compliance with his licentious
desires. The ruins of the ancient city are said
to occupy a site larger than that of London,
though they are now very scanty and largely
destroyed (I. B. C.): กันยาครรภ์, กันยาชาต, กันยา-
บุตร an illegitimate child; the offspring of an
unmarried woman: กันยาทาดา a father who

gives a girl in marriage: กันยาทาน the giving of a daughter in marriage: กันยาทูษก the violator of a virgin; the calumniator of a girl: กันยาโทษ a blemish in a virgin (as disease or bad repute): กันยาธน a girl's property, portion or dowry: กันยาบดี, กันยาเวที a son-in-law: กันยาบาล the protector or father of a girl; a dealer in slave-girls; a dealer in spirituous liquors: กันยาประทาน the giving of a daughter in marriage: กันยาภาพ virginity; maidenhood: กันยายน the sixth solar month, September: กันยารัตน์ lit. "girl jewel," i. e. an excellent maiden; a lovely girl: กันยาราศี the sign of the zodiac, Virgo.

กันลง, กันลอง   gkan-long Cam. v. to jump; to cross over; to pass in front of: n. the carpenter beetle, a large solitary beetle that bores tunnels in wood or telephone cables for its nest, Xylocopa latipes. In Siam this beetle is commonly known as แมลงผู้ or แมงภู่; something that is left over or discarded; the act of trespassing; treason.

กันแสง see กรรแสง

กันหยั่น   gkan³-yan⁴ n. a two-edged sword (a weapon used by the Chinese).

กับ   gkap⁴ n. condiments eaten with rice; a spring-trap or snare for rats: conj. with; together; and: กับดักหนู a metal, spring rat-trap with serrated jaws: กับทั้ง all together.

กับๆ   gkap⁴-gkap⁴ onomat. from the galloping sound of hoofs or of a horse walking.

กับแก้   gkap⁴-gkaa³ n. a large wall-lizard; the gecko.

กัปตัน   gkap⁴-dtan Eng. n. a captain; a leader.

กัปป   gkap⁴-bpa⁴ P. n. time; a moment; precept; rule; ordinance; usage; mode: adj. proper; fit; competent; equal to; near to (chd.).

กัปปกะ, กัลบก   gkap⁴-bpa⁴-gka⁴ n. a barber; an hair-dresser; one who conforms to a settled rule or standard (as in a rite or ceremony) (chd.).

กัปประ ๑   gkap⁴-bpa⁴-ra⁶ n. the elbow joint; the knee.

กัปประ ๒   gkap⁴-bpa⁴-ra⁶ n. a cup; a pot; a bowl; bones of the head; skull; the cranium (chd.).

กัปปาสิก   gkap⁴-bpah-sik⁴ n. cotton cloth: adj. made of cotton (chd.).

กัปปิยะ, กัปปิย์   gkap⁴-bpi⁴-ya⁶ adj. right; proper; suitable; appropriate; acceptable; agreeable; as prescribed; settled or arranged for by ritual (chd.): กัปปิยการก one who waits on Buddhist monks; one who puts things in order for the Buddhist monks: กัปปิยภัณฑ์ suitable presents; the act of giving (to Buddhist monks) appropriate or proper articles as presents (chd.).

กัมบน, กัมป, กัมปนะ   gkam-bon P. S. n. a condition of tremor; trembling or shaking of the earth; an earthquake; unsteadiness: กัมปนาท the sounds produced during a general tremor or earthquake: adj. dreadful; fearful; calamitous.

กัมปนี, กำปนี   gkam-bpa⁴-nee Eng. n. a company (in business).

กัมประโด   gkam-bpra⁴-do Port. n. a compradore; a kind of steward or agent (China Coast).

กัมพล   gkam-pon n. hair-cloth (as camel's hair cloth); a blanket; a woolen garment (chd.); a woolen blanket or cloth; an upper garment: กัมพุ gold; bracelets; shells; a conch-shell (chd.).

กัมพุช, กัมโพช   gkam-poot⁶ n. a city of Cambodia; name of the country of Cambodia and its inhabitants (chd.): กัมพุชพากย์ language of the Cambodians.

ก้มมะ   gkam-ma[6] *n.* act; action; performance; business; any religious act or rite (as
sacrifice or oblation) originating in the hope
of future recompense; work; labour; activity; an objective (S. E. D.).

ก้มมาร   gkam-man *n.* an artificer; a goldsmith; a blacksmith; a mechanic; a brazier
(chd.).

ก้ย   gkai *P. S. n.* the act of buying; the
making of purchases; a purchase: ก้ยวิก้ย
trade; the act of trading in business; buying
and selling of goods or commodities; to barter; to trade in goods or produce.

ก้ล   gkan *n.* dawn; break-of-day; the
morning; a portion; a piece or fraction of
any article: *adj.* healthy; prepared; skilful
(chd.); free from sickness; hale; vigorous;
sound; strong; dexterous; auspicious (as
speech) (S. E. D.).

ก้ลบก, ก้ปปกะ   gkan-bok[4] *n.* a barber;
an hair-dresser; one who prepares or makes
ready (chd.).

ก้ลบิต   gkan-bit[4] *n.* an elephant armed or
caparisoned for war: *adj.* proper; complete;
caparisoned; made ready (chd.); fabricated;
composed; artificial; invented; well-arranged.

ก้ลป   gkan-la[6]-bpa[4] *n.*   (1) a vast period of
time; an age; a cycle of years or incomprehensible periods of time (chd.); a fabulous
period of time; a period of 4,320,000,000
solar years. A twenty-four hour period of
Brahma's time equals one thousand yugas:
(2) a sacred precept; law; rule; ordinance;
practice: *adj.* similar to; resembling; almost:
ก้ลปกษัย the time for the destruction of the
world; the end of a ก้ลป.   ก้ลปตรุ, ก้ลปดำรุ,
ก้ลบกดำรุ one of the five trees in Indra's paradise, fabled to fulfil all desires; the wishing-
tree; the tree-of-plenty: ก้ลปบาล *lit.* "an
order preserver," *i. e.* a king: ก้ลปพฤกษ์ a
fabulous, magic wishing-tree; limes in which
small silver coins are enclosed (to be distrib-

uted as alms to the poor in ceremonies such
as cremations):   ก้ลปพฤกษ์, ก้ลพฤกษ์ กาลพฤกษ์
(ต้น) *Cassia bakeriana (Leguminosae)* (cb. p.
508: V. P. p. 29)); *C. nodosa (L.)* (cb. p. 512:
MCM. pp. 86, 87, 459, 517: V. P. p. 29), pink
cassia. The beautiful, bright pink, rose-
scented flowers are used as temple offerings.
The tree is deciduous in dry weather: ก้ล-
ปมาตร a name for Siva: ก้ลป้าวสาน the
stage or state when life comes to an end; the
last period of existence (S. E. D.).

ก้ลปนา   gkan-la[6]-bpa[4]-nah *n.* preparedness;
forethought; accomplishment; a place, the
rent of which the owner dedicates to the up-
keep of a temple, as a memorial to the dead:
adj. preparing; making; forming; fashioning;
performing (S. E. D.).

ก้ลยะ, ก้ลล   gkan-ya[6] *n.* health; happiness;
dawn; morning: *adj.* strong; healthy; free
from sickness; hale; vigorous; sound in body;
dexterous: ก้ลยชัคธิ breakfast: ก้ลยบาล
a distiller; a seller of spirituous liquors:
ก้ลยวรรต a morning meal; any light meal;
any thing light; a trifle or trivial matter.

ก้ลยาณะ   gkan-la[6]-yah-na[6] *P.S. n.* name of
the uplands or plateau east of the ghats of
Bombay, India, now called Deccan or Dekkan:
adj. beautiful; agreeable; illustrious; noble;
generous; excellent; virtuous; auspicious;
fortunate; lucky: ก้ลยาณการก one causing
prosperity (to his fellow men), profit (in
business) or good fortune (to others):   ก้ล-
ยาณคุณ benefits, virtues or advantages of
a superlative degree: ก้ลยาณธรรม one of
virtuous character or of good conduct: ก้ล-
ยาณมนเทียร a temple; an abode for health
purposes; a place to increase one's prosperity
and happiness; a spirit-house: ก้ลยาณมิตร
a true friend; a good friend; one who wishes
you well; a good, true, loyal counsellor (the
antithesis of ปาปมิตร):   ก้ลยาณวัจน์, ก้ลยาณพจน์
loving words; friendly speech; good wishes:
ก้ลยาณวัตร conduct that is pleasing or praiseworthy: *adj.* praiseworthy (conduct).

กัลยาณี   gkan-la[6]-yah-nee *n.* a good lady; a beauty; a belle; one complete in all respects; happiness; prosperity; virtue : เบญจ-กัลยาณี five feminine charms, viz. fine hair, red lips, pearly white teeth, a blooming complexion and youth (chd.).

กัลยาบาล see **กัลยบาล**

กัลยาศ see **กัลยชัคธิ**

กัลเอา   gkan-ow *Cam. n.* melody; music (sounds pleasing to the ear).

กลบังหา see **กะละบังหา**

กัศมล   gkat[4]-sa[4]-mon *adj.* foul; dirty; impure; pusillanimous; sinful (s. e. d.).

กัศยป   gkat[4]-sa[4]-yop[6] *n.* one who has black teeth; a tortoise; name of an ancient sage, a descendant of Marici and author of several hymns of the Rigveda. He was the husband of Aditi and twelve other daughters of Daksha. He was the father of Vishnu in his tortoise incarnation. By his other twelve wives, he was the father of demons, reptiles, birds and all kinds of living beings : กัศยป-นนทน์ *lit.* "the offspring of กัศยป," *i. e.* the Krut, the bird of Vishnu (s. e. d.).

กัสสก   gkat[4]-sok[4] *n.* a plowman; a husbandman; a farmer; a plowshare; an ox.

กัสสป   gkat[4]-sop[4] *P. S. n.* one of the twenty-four Buddhas, the last before Gotama; name of a famous disciple of the Buddha.

กา ๑   gkah *S. adj.* wrong; bad; evil; worthless; useless; defective; imperfect; faulty (in composition), used to express deprecation : กากนก fragments of gold; gold filings (chd.) : กากษ a glance; a wink; the condition of frowning; looking scornfully or in displeasure : กาบถ a bad road; an evil way; bad conduct; heterodox doctrine; walking in a wrong road : กาบุรุษ a low or miserable person; a coward; a vagabond; off-scourings of society (s. e. d.).

กา ๒   gkah *n.* the sign or mark used in checking off items in a list or in a column of figures, *e. g.* +, ×, √ : กา (ปลา) a species of fresh-water fish *Morulius chrysophekadion* (Dept. Agri. & Fisheries) : กา (นก) a crow; an impudent or insolent fellow; a lame man; a cripple; the Andaman jungle crow *Corvus levaillanti andamanensis* (Deig. N. H. J. S. S. VIII, 3, p. 134); the Indian jungle crow *Corvus macrorhynchus*; the Burmese house crow *Corvus insolens* (Gaird. J. S. S. IX, 1, p. 5) : กา-จับหลัก a sharp-pointed piece of wood or iron attached to the trigger of a trap. This flies up when a bird or person sits down on it; a T-shaped stake stuck firmly in the ground, used for tying a prisoner prior to his being beheaded : กาจับหลัก (ต้น) *Vitex peduncularis* (*Verbenaceae*) (V. P. P. 17). The bark of this tree is used as a medicinal application for pain in the chest. The wood is purplish or reddish-grey, close-grained, hard and heavy, suitable for posts, beams and yokes (Dept. Agri. & Fisheries) : กาเทศ (นก) the ruby cheek *Chalcoparia singalensis* (Herb. N. H. J. S. S. VI, 3, p. 293) : กาน้ำ (ต้น) *Acalypha sp.* (K.), a group of ornamental foliage shrubs (MCM. p. 118) : กาน้ำ (นก) the little cormorant *Phalacrocorax pygmaeus*; the large cormorant *Phalacrocorax carbo* (Gaird. J. S. S. IX, 1, p. 10) : the water crow, the black diver, the sea raven. They devour fish voraciously and have become the emblem of gluttony : กาฝาก (ต้น) bird vine, *Loranthus sp.* (*Loranthaceae*) (V. P. p. 18), a group of semi-parasitic, evergreen plants growing on trees and shrubs of woody growth. This plant resembles mistletoe. Birds act as distributors carrying the seed and depositing it on the branches (MCM. p. 475) : การางหัวขวาน (นก) the Burmese hoopoe *Upupa epops longirostris* (will. N. H. J. S. S. II, 3, p. 338) : กาล่อน to tell a lie; a species of mango : กาลักน้ำ a siphon : กาวี the lower fore-top sail : กาเหว่า, กุเหว่า (นก) Malayan koel *Eudynamis malayana* (Gaird. J. S. S. IX, 1, p. 7) : กาเหว่าดำ, กาเหว่าลาย (นก)

the Indian koel *Eudinamis scolopaceus malayana* (Herb. N. H. J. S. S. VI, 3, p. 304): กาหัง, เงือก (นก) the great pied hornbill *Dichoceros bicornis* (Gaird. J. S. S. IX, 1 p. 7): สภากาชาด-สยาม National Red Cross Society of Siam.

กา ๓   gkah *n.* a kettle; baked, glazed, earthen-ware teapots or hot-water pots: กาเงิน a silver teapot: กาต้มน้ำ a kettle for boiling water: กาทองคำ a gold teapot: กาทองแดง a copper teapot: กาทองเหลือง a brass teapot: กาเพื่อง a teapot with fluted sides: กาไหล่ plated or washed with gold, silver, nickel or some other metal.

ก้า   gkah[5] *Chin. adj.* brave; bold; sportive; willing to take risks (as in gambling): ก้าก้า *onomat.* from the cawing of crows.

ก้า   gkah[2] *adj.* impudent; bold; audacious: อวดก้า to boast impudently.

กาก ๑   gkak *n.* chips; shells; chaff; refuse; dregs; lees: กากกะรุน carborundum or emery paper; a polishing powder: กากขยาก wooden shavings; scraps or chips left over in carpentering; sweepings (as from a lawn or garden): กากเพ็ชร์ carborundum; stone: กากร่าง an initial copy; a rough copy; a carbon copy: มีกากข้าว to have fragments of chaff or grains of unhulled rice mixed with the milled rice: หน้ากาก a mask.

กาก ๒   gkak[4] *P. S. n.* the crow: กากณึก name of a small coin of Indian currency; a small sum of money equal to twenty cowries or to a quarter of a pana; a seed of the มะก้ำ, *Abrus precatorius*, used as a weight (S.E.D.): กากตาลึย unknowingly; unexpectedly; suddenly: กากตาลึยกรรม an unintentional, accidental or incidental sin: กากบาท an accent mark like a crow's foot " + ," placed over middle class consonants to indicate a rising tone; marks or lines in the skin similar to a crow's foot; a sign marking an omission: กากปึกษ์ *lit.* "crow's wings," *i. e.* side-locks of hair on the temples of young men (there are five locks on each side left when the head is first shaved and allowed to remain there, especially in persons of the military caste): กากสูร *lit.* "one fearless as a crow," *i. e.* a person without shame; an audacious, impertinent or impudent person.

ก๊าก, ก๊าก   gkak[3] *onomat.* from laughter.

กากนาสูร   gkah-gka[4]-nah-soon[2] *n.* a female deity, a character in the Ramayana. She was the mother of Maricha, and was changed into a Rakshasi by Agastya. She lived in a forest called by her name, located on the Ganges, opposite the confluence of the Sarju, and ravaged all the country around (H. C. D.).

กากะทิง (ต้น)   gkah-gka[4]-ting *n. Calophyllum inophyllum (Guttiferae)* (K.: Dept. Agri. & Fisheries), a common tree growing along sandy sea-shores. It has white fragrant flowers and is sometimes cultivated in Bangkok. The oil obtained from the nut-kernel is highly esteemed as an external application in rheumatism; the bark of the tree, when wounded, exudes a small quantity of bright green gum, which is not collected, nor does it appear to be made use of in any way. The leaves, soaked in water, are employed as an application to inflamed eyes; the fixed oil obtained from the kernels of the seeds is said to cure scabies (McM. pp. 378, 395).

กากะเยีย   gkah-gka[4]-yee-ah *n.* a stand for palm-leaf or Pali books. This is made of eight small sticks fastened together crosswise, serving as a reading-desk.

ก้ากั้น   gkah[2]-gkan[4] *adj.* brave; audacious; fearless.

กากี, กาโก   gkah-gkee *n.* a female crow, personified as a daughter of พระกัศยป และนาง ตามรา and mother of crows and owls; a term of abuse used against low women of the street, as "dirty girl"; name of a woman in Siamese fables: *adj.* brownish-yellow; colour of iron rust; khaki cloth: อีกากี *simile* a bold impudent woman (S. E. D.).

กาง gkang *v.* to spread (as wings); to un-furl; to stretch out; to expand; to open (as an umbrella): *adj.* spreading (as of wings); separated (as two halves of the areca-nut when cut open); apart: กาง (ต้น) *Albizzia odoratissima* (*Leguminosae*) (V. P. p. 23), a large tree bearing pure white, sweet-scented flowers. The dark brown heart-wood is very hard (MCM. p. 206). This tree yields a dark brown gum in rounded tears, tasteless but soluble in water. The bark is used in dyeing and is applied externally in leprosy and to inveterate ulcers. The leaves, boiled in ghee, are used as a remedy for coughs. The wood is excellent timber, used for wheels, oil-mills, and furniture (Dept. Agri. & Fisheries): กางกร to spread out the the hands: กางกอ (ต้น) *Xanthophyllum flavescens* (*Polygalaceae*) (V. P. p. 24), a large tree with heavy, close-grained wood, useful for many purposes (Dept. Agri. & Fisheries): กางกั้น to divide (as by a partition); to separate (as by spreading out a curtain): กางขี้มอด(ต้น) *Dalbergia kerrii* (*Leguminosae*) (V. P. p. 24): *Derris robusta* (*Leguminosae*) (cb. p. 491): *Acrocarpus frax-inifolius* (*Leguminosae*) (cb. p. 507); " pink cedar," " shingle tree," a medium-sized or tall, quick-growing, upright, deciduous tree with handsome bipinnate leaves (crimson when young) and long, rather slender branches. The sap-wood is white, while the heart-wood is light red and moderately hard. It is used for shingles, furniture, building, tea-boxes, etc. (MCM. p. 178): กางแขน to extend the arms: กางมุ้ง to hang up a mosquito net: กางร่ม to raise an umbrella: กางหู to pay particular attention to; to listen attentively.

ก้าง gkang[3] *n.* a spicule, sliver or spine of bone; name of a species of serpent-head fish, *Ophicephalus gachua* (H. M. S.): ก้างปลา (ต้น) *Bridelia tomentosa* (*Euphorbiaceae*) (v. P. p. 24), a small evergreen tree. The wood is light olive-brown, hard and close-grained. The bark is used medicinally as an astringent: ก้างปลาขาว (ต้น) *Fluggea microcarpa* (*Euphor-*biaceae*) (V. P. p. 24 : K.), a shrub about 6 m. high. The fruit is white. It commonly grows in scant forests along river banks: ก้างปลาแดง (ต้น) *Phyllanthus reticulatus* (*Euphorbiaceae*) (v. P. p. 25), a large, often scandent shrub, common throughout tropical countries. It grows on low moist ground along river banks. The roots are used as a dye, producing a red colour. The leaves are used in the form of a decoction for diuretic purposes (Dept. Agri. & Fisheries): ก้างปลาทะเล (ต้น) *Breynia rhamoides* (*Euphorbiaceae*) (V. P. p. 24), a small tree of wide distribution: ก้างปลาเทศ (ต้น) *Chlorizandra orientalis* (V. P. p. 25).

กางเกง gkang-gkeng *n.* trousers; pantaloons.

กางเขน gkang-ken[2] *n.* the cross of Jesus Christ; a species of the magpie or robin family, *Copsychus saularis* (will. N. H. J. S. S. II, 3, p. 188).

ก้าง (ต้น) gkang[2] *n. Albizzia lebbekioides* (*Leguminosae*) (cb. p. 554), a tree about 30 m. high, found in scrub jungle (K.).

ก้างขี้มอด (ต้น) gkang[2]-kee[3]-maut[3] *n. Albizzia odoratissima* (*Leguminosae*) (cb. p. 556). This is the Laos name for กาง (ต้น).

ก้างหลวง (ต้น) gkang[2]-luang[2] *n. Albizzia stipulata* (*Leguminosae*) (cb. p. 557), a large tree with reddish stipules (MCM. pp. 214, 415) This tree yields a gum, which exudes copiously from the stem, and is used for sizing " Daphne " paper. The branches are lopped for cattle-fodder. The sap-wood is thick and white; the heart-wood is brown. The wood is soft and shining and generally not durable, but is used for charcoal (Dept. Agri. & Fisheries).

กาจ gkat[4] *adj.* fierce; ferocious (as a tiger); bold; savage; cruel; furious: มี กิริยาร้ายกาจ manifesting a vicious manner.

กาซองวาเซอะ (ต้น) gkah-chaung-wah-sur[4] *n. Hiptage candicans* (*Malpighiaceae*) (cb. p.

202), a small tree about 5 m. high, found on rocky ground in open evergreen forest (K.).

กาซ้อง (ต้น) gkah-saung[5] *n. Schleichera trijuga (Sapindaceae)* (CB. p. 329), a slow-growing tree, the foliage of which resembles that of the English oak. The wood is reddish, hard and durable (MCM. pp. 219, 317, 416, 417). The fruit contains a whitish pulp, which has a pleasant sub-acid taste and is often eaten during hot, dry weather. The seeds yield an oil which is used for culinary purposes and for illumination. The oil is valuable for cleaning the scalp and promotes the growth of the hair (Dept. Agri. & Fisheries).

กาซะลอง (ต้น) gkah-sa[4]-laung *n. Millingtonia hortensis (Bignoniaceae)* (V. P. p. 17), " Indian cork-tree," an erect tree reaching a height of 50 feet or more, bearing finely divided leaves. It bears a profusion of long, tubular, pure-white, fragrant flowers twice a year. It is often planted along avenues in India (MCM. p. 90). An inferior kind of cork is made from the bark (Dept. Agri. & Fisheries).

กาแซ (ต้น) gkah-saa *n. Albizzia lebbeck (Leguminosae)* (CB. p. 553), " women's tongue," a large tree with fine foliage, planted for shade. The excellent brown timber does not readily warp (MCM. pp. 206, 417, 446). It yields a gum, which is said not to be soluble in water but merely to form a jelly. ˙ The seeds, which are an astringent, are given in piles, diarrhoea, etc. The oil is useful in leprosy. The flowers are used for poulticing (BURK. pp. 86, 87 : Dept. Agri. & Fisheries).

กาแซะ (ต้น) gkah-saa[6] *n. Padbruggea atropurpurea (Leguminosae)* (CB. p. 396), a tree about 20 m. high. The flowers are dark purple with a yellow spot at the base of the standard. These are found in bamboo forest (K.).

กาโซ้ (ต้น) gkah-so[5] *n. Schima crenata (Ternstroemiaceae)* (CB. p. 130), an evergreen

tree 30 to 60 feet in height. The wood is not of much value but is said to be hard and durable, though liable to warp and split. It is used for house-posts and for rice mortars (Dept. Agri. & Fisheries).

กาญจนะ, กาญจนา gkan-chja[4]-na[6] *P. S. n.* gold ; riches ; possessions in the form of gold ; wealth ; property : กาญจนกันติ bright, shining or radiant ; resplendent (as gold) : กาญจน กันทร a gold mine : กาญจนคิรี, กาญจนาจล, กาญจนทรี *lit.* " golden-mountain," *i. e.* Meru : กาญจนจัย a pile of gold ; a heap of gold : กาญจนบุระ,กาญจนบุรี name of a city in a book called กถาสริตสาคร ; name of a city in the district of Rajaburi : กาญจนภู gold ore, sand, soil or dust : กาญจนภูษา yellow powder or earth, used in dyeing clothes to produce a golden or yellow colour ; ochre : กาญจนมาลา *lit.* " one having a golden garland," *i. e.* the daughter-in-law of Asoka : กาญจนรุจิ bright, shining and dazzling (as gold) : กาญจนาภา *lit.* " golden splendour," *i. e.* rays radiating with great brightness (S. E. D. p. 269).

กาญจนา see **กาญจนะ**

กาณ gkan *P. S. n.* a crow : *adj.* being blind in one eye ; monoculous ; one-eyed : อันธะ totally blind (S. E. D).

กาด (ผัก) gkat[4] *n.* a collective name for several varieties of vegetables ; cabbage : ผักกาดหอม lettuce *Lactuca sativa* (MCM. p. 220) : หัวผักกาด turnips *Brassica campestris var. rapa* (MCM. p. 326).

กาดูดู (ต้น) gkah-doo-doo[3] *n. Melastoma malabathricum (Melastomaceae)* (CB. p. 680), a spreading, ornamental shrub bearing pink, violet or mauve, fairly large flowers (MCM. p. 113). The fruit yields a purple dye used for dyeing cotton cloth. The ovoid, truncate fruit has an edible pulp, which is said closely to resemble the blackberry of temperate regions, both in taste and flavour (Dept. Agri. & Fisheries : Burk. pp. 1439–41).

กาตยายน์ see **กัจจานะ**

กาน   gkan v. to lop; to cut off branches; to trim or prune limbs of a tree.

ก่าน   gkan[4] adj. brave; fearless; bold (as a soldier).

ก้าน   gkan[5] n. twig; sprig; stem (of leaf or flower); stalk; mid-rib (of a leaf): ก้านกิ่ง twigs attached to a branch: ก้านขด name of a pattern used in surface-decorations where the lines make interlocking circles or loops: ก้านแข็ง name given to bracelets of a certain design: ก้านคอ the large tendons of the neck: ก้านตอง name given to rounded, curved strips of wood, nailed to the insides of small boats for extra protection (named thus because they resemble the mid-rib of the banana leaf): ก้านต่อดอก name given to a flower design in which the stem of one fits into the next flower; the name given to a meter or rhyme in Siamese poetry: ก้านกิ่ง (ต้น) Colubrina asiatica (Rhamnaceae), an erect shrub cultivated for medicinal purposes (K.); C. pubescens (cb. p. 301), an erect shrub with slender, flexnose branches and having yellowish flowers. It is cultivated for medicinal use (K.): ก้านมะพร้าว the mid-rib of coconut fronds when stripped for making into brooms: ก้านมะพร้าว (งู) a species of poisonous snake having V-shaped stripes (like the mid-rib of leaves of the coconut frond): ก้านพร้าว, โกฏฐก้านพร้าว one of an important group of medicinal herbs of the Artemisia genus: ก้านไม้, กิ่งไม้ a bough: ก้านยาว name of a species of durian: ก้านแบ่ง name of a pattern for mural decorations: ก้านเหลือง (ต้น) Sarcocephalus cordatus (Rubiaceae) (V. P. p. 30); Anthocephalus cadamba (Rubiaceae), a large, deciduous, fast-growing tree. The fruit is edible. The foliage is used as fodder for cattle. The bark is made into a decoction used as a tonic. The flowers are offered at Hindu shrines as they are sacred to Siva. The tree is often cultivated as an ornamental shade tree. The wood is used for beams and rafters on account of its cheapness and lightness but white ants attack it (Dept. Agri. & Fisheries: Burk pp. 172-4).

กานดา   gkan-dah S. n. a beloved or lovely woman; a wife; a mistress; a charming wife; a dutiful wife; a lady (S. E. D.).

กานต์   gkan P. S. n. any one beloved; a husband; a lover; the moon; iron; a stone: adj. desired; loved; dear; pleasing; agreeable: กานตปาษาณ, กานตโลหะ, กานตายส iron ore; lodestone; magnetic ore: กานตปักษี a lovely bird; a peacock (S. E. D.).

กานน   gkah-non P. S. n. a grove; a forest; a house or dwelling-place in a forest: กานโนก lit. "forest-dweller," i. e. a monkey.

กานน (ต้น)   gkah-non n. Vitex pubescens (V. P. p. 17), a large tree, having smooth grey wood with an olive-brown tinge (when old it becomes chocolate-coloured). This wood is very hard, close-grained, durable and is employed to make wooden bells and agricultural implements (Dept. Agri. & Fisheries: Burk. pp. 2239-40).

กานพลู see กรามพลู

กาน้ำ   gkah-nah[5] Chin. n. Chinese olives.

กาบ   gkap[4] n. the husk of a nut; a fibrous covering; the thin outer sheath found on some sea-shells; an envelope: กาบกอ the dried leaves attached to the base of clumps of tall grasses or citronella plants: กาบปูเล the fibrous sheath covering the flowers of the areca palm. These are used for sewing into baskets or trays: กาบไผ่ a leaf encircling the node of a bamboo joint: กาบพรหมศร a winding, surface decoration veneered on posts (as เสาบุษบก): กาบมะพร้าว the fibrous covering or pericarp of the coconut: กาบหยวก the outer layer of the banana tree: กาบหอย (ต้น) Cyanotis barbata (Commelinaceae) (MCM. p. 156): กาบกี้ a shell.

ก๊าบ ๆ   gkap[5]-gkap[5] onomat. from the quack, quack of ducks.

กาปาแย (ต้น)   gkah-bpah-yaa n. Hodgsonia capniocarpa (Cucurbitaceae) (cb. p. 751), an herbaceous vine of several metres in length, growing near the water. Tne fruit is about 6 inches in diameter; the seeds contain edible oil (Burk. p. 1178 : K.).

กาบิโตร๊ะ (ต้น)   gkah-bpee-dtro[5] *n. Eugenia limnaea (Myrtaceae)* (Cb. p. 650), a tree about 8 m. high. The flowers are white. It is found in evergreen scrub forests by streams (K.).

กาโบ๊ (ต้น)   gkah-bpo[3] *n. Polyalthia socia (Annonaceae)* (Cb. p. 44), a small tree about 5 m. high. The flowers are pale green. It is found in evergreen forest (K.).

กาพย์   gkap[4] *S. n.* a poem; a poetical composition with a coherent plot, written by a single author; a kind of drama in one act; one endowed with the qualities of a sage or poet; the planet Venus :   กาพย์กลอน writings of a poetical nature or character in contradistinction to ร้อยแก้ว : กาพยรส having a taste for poetical compositions : กาพยลักษณะ illustrative of poetry or rhetoric (S. E. D.).

กาพง (ต้น)   gkah-pong *n. Tetrameles nudiflora (Datiscaceae)* (Cb. p. 781), a large, deciduous tree, which attains the height of 100 to 150 feet. The wood is white, very light, soft, and useful for tea-boxes (Dept. Agri. & Fisheries : Burk. p. 2144).

กาพู้ (ต้น)   gkah-pee[5] *n. Dalbergia volubilis (Leguminosae)* (Cb. p. 485), a large climber. The wood is light-brown, hard and very tough. The plant has medicinal properties. It is applied to aphthae and is used as a gargle in sore-throat; the root-juice with cummin and sugar, is given in gonorrhoea. The leaves are eaten by cattle and goats (Dept. Agri. & Fisheries).

กาแฟ   gkah-faa *n.* coffee; the coffee plant *Coffea schmidtii (Rubiaceae)* (V. P. p. 17); *Coffea arabica*, a small tropical tree producing dark, cherry-like berries which are used for making a beverage called coffee. The plant was first known in Arabia in the thirteenth century. Many varieties are now grown elsewhere. Coffee-drinking spread to Venice in 1615 and to London in 1651. The first planting outside Arabia was in Java in 1696 (Kerr. N. H. J. S. S. VIII, 3, p. 202 : Burk. pp. 619-628).

กาม   gkam *S. n.* love; desire; lust; longing for; affection; sexual desire; love or sensuality : กามกรีฑา amorous sports : กามกวม (นก) the Burmese stock-billed kingfisher *Pelargopsis burmanica* (Gaird. J. S. S. IX, 1, p. 6) : กามกาม *lit.* "wishers' lustings," *i. e.* having various desires or wishes; following the dictates of passion : กามการ the condition of following one's own inclination; a spontaneous deed : a voluntary action; acting according to one's own free will : กามเกลี *lit.* "love sports," *i. e.* amorous sports; sexual intercourse; wanton indulgence : กามกูฏ the paramour of an harlot; harlotry; wanton caresses : กามคติ, กามคามี going or coming of one's own accord : กามคุณ *lit.* "quality of desire," *i. e.* affection; passion; satiety; prefect enjoyment; an object of sense; objects of the five senses as form, taste, odour, sound and touch; sensual enjoyment : กามจารี *lit.* "moving freely," *i. e.* one following his own pleasure; one who conducts himself as he wishes; a libertine : กามฉันท์ wishing for sexual enjoyment : กามชิต *lit.* "conquering desire," *i. e.* one who has conquered his desires : กามตัณหา sensuality; concupiscence in the extreme : กามทรรศนะ having the look of a charming person; looking lovely : กามเทพ the god of Love (represented as son of Dharma and husband of Rati); name of Vishnu (as the god who creates, preserves or destroys at will) : กามเทวี the Hindu Cupid; the god of Love; name of Vishnu : กามธรรม amorous behaviour; conduct characterized by sensuality : กามธาตุ the region of the wishes, lust or desire; a brothel; the place of those indulging in lustful pleasures : กามนีทา a brazier : กามพฤกษา a mythical tree supplying all desire :

กามพล the force of desire; sexual power: กามภพ sensual existence; existence in the world of sense: กามโภคี *lit.* "one to whom sexual pleasure is not denied," *i.e.* one outside the Buddhist priesthood: กามรส the taste or pleasure of sexual gratification; the enjoyment of sexual love: กามราค the passion for sexual indulgence: กามเรขา, กามเลขา a lovely woman; a voluptuous woman; a prostitute; an harlot; a courtezan: กามรูป a shape assumed at will; protean; a god; name of people and their country (east of Bengal and in the western part of Assam) (S. E. D.): กามลตา membrum virile; the penis: กามโลก the worlds of sense or sensual pleasures, of which there are eleven: กามวัลลภ *lit.* "love's favorite," *i.e.* spring; a species of mango tree: กามวัลลภา moonlight; the light of the moon: กามวาท words uttered according to one's desires; unrestricted utterances; speech at will: กามวาสี dwelling where one pleases; the choice or change of one's residence at will: กามวิตก meditations on lustful subjects or objects; thoughts about sensual matters: กามศัลย์ having love or lust for a shaft: กามศาสน์ *lit.* "the one wreaking vengeance or punishing the god of sensuality," *i.e.* Siva: กามสโมสรณ์ *lit.* "the consumation of sexual desire," *i.e.* the intermingling of sexual pleasures; the office of the one ruling the home; the husband: กามสุต otherwise called Aniruddha; son of the god of Love, known to the Siamese as อนิรุทธ์ or อุนรุท (H. C. D.): กามาตุร restive or restless with a desire for love; love-sick; affected by love or desire: กามาทีนพ the dire results of lustful deeds; the evils of sexual excess: กามาธิการ the influence of passion or desire: กามานล the fire of passion; lust; the fire of love: กามายุส a vulture; the Garuda: กามารมณ์ the mood, time or occasion for fulfilling sexual desire: กามาวจร, กามาพจร the worlds or spheres of desire, of which there are six: กามาศนะ the state or condition of eating unrestrictedly; the act

of eating that which one pleases: กามาศรม the hermitage of the god of Love: คนบ้ากาม a libertine; one carried away by his passions.

ก้าม   gkam[3] *n.* the claws of a crab; the nippers of a crab; ก้ามกราม (กุ้ง) a large-sized prawn, having spines along the claws: ก้ามกราม, ก้ามปู, จามจุรี (ต้น) "rain tree" *Enterolobium saman* (*Leguminosae*) (cb. p. 561); *Samanea saman*, a tall, erect tree with handsome, feathery foliage, bearing curious circular twisted pods in the dry weather (when it is deciduous) (MCM. p. 99: BURK. pp. 927-928: KERR, N. H. J. S. S. VIII, 3, p. 204). The rain tree is a native of tropical America but it is now widely cultivated in the tropics. It seems that it was first introduced into Siam from Burma by Mr. Slade, the first Conservator of Forests in Siam, about 1900: ก้ามกุ้ง (ต้น) *Begonia obovoidea* (*Begoniaceae*) (cb. p. 777), *Lantana camara*; *Lantana indica* (*Verbinaceae*) (V. P. p. 31: K.), a shrub growing to a height of about 15 m., found in open grassy forests. The flowers are pink (K.): ก้ามเกลี้ยง a large prawn, having small, smooth claws.

กามย์   gkam S. *adj.* lovable; desirable; attractive; amiable; agreeable: กามยเกียร speech or sounds that are attractive or facinating: กามยทาน a desirable gift; a voluntary gift: กามยพรต a bribe: กามยมรณ์ voluntary death; suicide.

กามัช   gkah-mat[6] P. S. *adj.* arising from, produced by, or begotten of lust or desire.

กามา   gkah-mah *lit.* "wish; desire," *i.e.* an object to be desired (S. E. D.).

กามิน   gkah-min S. *n.* a lover; a gallant, anxious husband; the red goose; a pigeon; a sparrow.

กามินี   gkah-mi[6]-nee P. *n.* a loving or affectionate woman; women (in general).

กาเมษฏ์   gkah-mate[4] *n. lit.* "desired by the god of Love," *i.e.* the mango (chd.).

กาเมสุมิจฉาจาร gkah-may-soo[4]-mit[6]-chah[2] chjarn *P. n.* adultery.

กาโมทย์ gkah-mote[4] *adj.* attractive; lovable; creative of amorous desires.

กาย, กายา gkai *n.* the body; the trunk of a tree; a violin (all except the wires); a house; an abode; an assemblage; a collection; multitude; an object to be attained; natural temperament: กายกรรม sports; calisthenics; physical drill: กายกำม์ carnal sins: กายขันธ์ organs of the body: กายคันถ์ lusts of the flesh: กายทวาร orifices or passages of exit of the body: กาบบริหาร acts, drills or exercises for the development of the body: กายพันธน์ a belt; a strait-jacket; a waist-band; a girdle (chd. p. 195): กายสิทธิ์ amulets; charms possessing magical power (S. E. D.).

ก่าย gkai[4] *v.* to cause to cross or pass over; to place one limb upon or over the other; to lean one article against another: ก่ายกอง to have in abundance; to heap up; to have an enormous amount: ก่ายกอม (ต้น) *Ehretia acuminata,* a medium-sized tree, yielding an insipidly sweet fruit which is eaten. The unripe fruit is pickled. The wood is light-brown with white specks. It is fairly even, compact, soft, not heavy and, being easily worked, is made into scabbards, sword-hilts, gun-stocks, agricultural implements and is used in building (Dept. Agri. & Fisheries); *Ehretia laevis (Boraginaceae)* (V. P. p. 32), a moderate-sized tree, common throughout India. The fruit is tasteless but is eaten, as also the inner bark, during famine. The leaves are used as cattle fodder. The greyish-white, hard, tough wood is durable, and is used for building purposes as well as for agricultural implements (Dept. Agri. & Fisheries): ก่ายกัน to embrace each other: กอดก่ายด้วยเท้า to trip slyly with the foot: เดินก่าย to walk or pass across in front of another: เอามือก่ายหน้า to place the hands across one's face or forehead: เอาไม้ก่ายขึ้น to make a lean-to with sticks or planks.

กายัสถ์ gkah-yat[6] *n. lit.* "an highly-prized creature," *i. e.* the supreme being, caste or tribe or one of that type; a class of half-breeds or persons of mixed blood, whose father is of the kingly caste and the mother of a lower caste.

กายา see กาย

กายาพยพ gkah-yah-pa[6]-yop[6] *P. n.* portions of the body (as hands or feet).

กายินทรีย์ gkah-yin-see *P. n.* the supremeness of the body; sensory organs of the body.

กาย (ต้น) gkah-yee[5]- *n. Dialium cochinchinense (Leguminosae)* (cb. p. 516), a tree about 10 to 15 m. high, found in mixed deciduous forest. The flowers are white and fragrant; the fruit is dark purple (K. : Burk. pp. 798–799).

กาเยาะบราเนาะ (ต้น) gkah-yau[6]-brah-nau[6] *n. Goniothalamus macrophyllus (Annonaceae)* (cb. p. 51), a shrub 1 to 5 m. high, found in evergreen forest. The plant is medicinal (Burk. pp. 1097–1099 : K.).

การ gkan *P. S. n.* a maker (of articles); a doer (of work); work; act; action; employment; task; business: *adj.* making; doing; working: การ is used to form many compound words. When placed as a suffix to a noun it indicates the one doing or performing the work, *e. g.* กุมภการ = a potter; สุวรรณการ = a goldsmith. When placed as a prefix to a noun it conveys the idea of office of place of transacting the specified work or business, *e. g.* การประปา = water works; การไฟฟ้า = electrical-works; การประมง = fisheries. When placed as a prefix to a verb it changes the verb into a noun, *e. g.* การทำบุญ = meritorious deeds; merit making; การนอน = sleeping; การเผาศพ = cremations; การวิวาทะมงคล = weddings, marriages; การเปรียญ = religious knowledge; the act of following a course of

Buddhist religious instruction : การเลี้ยง =
a banquet ; an entertainment : การสมโภช =
a celebration or festival : กิจการ action ;
work : ข้าราชการ a government employee
or official : คำให้การ facts, admissible as
testimony by a witness in legal court proceedings : ต้องการ to want ; to be in need
of : ติดการ to be busy ; to be engaged with
a task : เป็นการ successful ; it is a success ;
the affair is succeeding : พอการ as much
as is necessary ; sufficient : ราชการ government service : ให้การ to give evidence ;
to make a declaration ; to give testimony :
เอาการเอางาน painstaking (descriptive of the
character of a child or adult) (S. E. D. p. 274).

การก gkah-rok[6] *P.S. n.* one who produces or
creates ; one intending to act or do : *gram.*
the instrument bringing about the action
denoted by a verb ; denotes case (S.E.D. p. 274).

การณะ gkah-ra[6]-na[6] *P. S. n.* a cause ; motive ; reason ; means ; instrument or principal :
การณวาที *lit.* "cause-declarer," *i. e.* complainant ; a plaintiff (S. E. D. p. 274).

การณาภาพ gkah-ra[6]-nah-pap[3] *P. S. n.*
causelessness ; a condition of self-production ;
a condition of absence of cause (S. E. D. p. 274).

การนึก gkah-ra[6]-nik[6] *P. S. n. lit.* "investigating ; ascertaining the cause," *i. e.* a judge ; a
teacher ; a preceptor ; an investigator (S. E. D.
p. 274).

การด gkat[4] *Eng. n.* a guard ; carefulness ;
watchfulness ; vigilance ; alertness ; a caretaker ; a watchman.

การตึก see กรรดึก

การติเกยะ see กรรติเกย

การบูร gkah-ra[6]-boon *n.* camphor (either the
plant or the resinous exudation).

การย์, การิย gkan *P. S. n.* work ; business ;
duty ; responsibility ; office : *adj.* practicable ;
feasible ; proper to be done ; right ; fit ; appropriate (to do) ; imperative (to do) ; obligatory

(to be done) (chd. p. 188) : การยกาล time
for action ; appointed time ; season ; opportunity ; occasion ; working time ; time for
work : การยกุศล adroit ; proficient (in work) :
การยพัส the influence or power of a season in
rendering the work successful : การยพัสสุ
a task ; an imperative duty : การยวิบัติ a
task that has failed or has come to nought ;
a reversal in work or action : การยเศษ an
half-finished business or task ; incompleteness
of a work ; the remainder of a job or business :
การยสถาน an office ; a place of doing business :
การยสาธก an agent ; the director or manager
of a business ; one accomplishing an object :
การยสิทธิ์ success ; the accomplishment of a
task ; the successful attainment of an objective : การยาธิการ an official ; the director of
a department ; a superintendent of affairs ; a
manager (S. E. D. p. 276).

การเวก see กรวิก

การะเกด (ต้น) gkah-ra[6]-gkate[4] *n. Pandanus furcatus (Pandanaceae),* the screwpine, a large handsome tree growing 40 feet
high, characterized by long prickly leaves
which are arranged on the stem in the form
of a screw (McM. p. 102). It is used for matting (Burk. p. 1647).

การะบุหนิง (ดอก) gkah-ra[6]-boo[4]-ning[2]
Jav. n. the China box-tree flower. *Murraya
paniculata (Rutaceae)* (Cb. p. 230). In Lower
Siam, this tree is plentiful, and walking-sticks
are made from it and sent to Penang (Burk. p.
1506) ; *M. exotica* (V. P. p. 34). The Siamese
name is ดอกแก้ว.

การะบูน (ต้น) gkah-ra[6]-boon *n. Sphaeranthus indicus (Compositae)* (V. P. p. 18),
a low annual of the sub-tropical Himalayas.
The small, oblong seeds and the roots are
considered anthelmintic and are prescribed
in powder ; the latter is also given as a stomachic. The flowers are highly esteemed as
alteratives, depuratives and tonics. The bark,
when ground small and mixed with whey, is
said to be a valuable remedy for piles. An

oil is prepared by steeping the root in water and then boiling it in sesamum oil until the water is expelled. This said to be a valuable aphrodisiac (Dept. Agri. & Fisheries). This plant is also found in the Malay peninsula (Burk. p. 2062).

การะเวก (ต้น)   gkah-ra[6]-wake[3] *n. Artabotrys odoratissimus (Annonaceae)* (V. P. p. 18), a large, cultivated, climbing shrub. The odour of the strong-scented flowers is closely allied to that of the ilang-ilang (Dept. Agri. & Fisheries). The fruits are small and inedible (Burk. p. 243).

การัง (หิน)   gkah-rung *n.* coral formed in the shape of stones (in contradistinction to that formed as branches of trees).

การันต์   gkah-run *P. n.* the mark " ˘ " placed over the final consonant of a word to indicate that it is silent; also called ทัณฑฆาต.

การิณี   gkah-ri[6]-nee *n.* a woman worker; a woman who has a task to perform: การี masculine form of การิณี.

การิต   gkah-rit[6] *P. S. v.* to compel to do; to urge; to coerce; to cause to be made or done; to be constructed or performed (chd.).

การิน see การี

การิยะ see การย์

การี, การิน   gkah-ree *P. S. n.* a workman; a mechanic; a tradesman; an actor: *adj.* doing; making; effecting; producing (S. E. D. p. 274): กรรมการี a male labourer: กรรมการิณี a female labourer.

การุญ, การุณย์   gkah-roon *P. S. n.* compassion; loving-kindness; pity; mercy; tenderness (chd.): การุณิโก having pity; compassionate (S. E. D. p. 255).

กาล ๑   gkan *P. S. n.* darkness; blackness; the black part of the eye; a mountain; a poisonous serpent; the black cobra: *adj.* black; dark blue; dark purple (chd.): กาลกรรณิกา

misfortune; misery (predicted as the consequence of having black ears): กาลกรรณี, กาลกิณี misfortune; ill-luck; a catastrophy; adversity; the goddess of Adversity (chd.): กาลกัญชะ name of a fabulous race of Asuras, some of whom have ascended into heaven and there shine as stars: กาลกัญฎูก a bird of the eagle family; a gallinule: กาลกัณฐะ the peacock; the sparrow; the wagtail; a name for the god Siva: กาลกุญชร a name for the god Siva: กาลกูฏ a kind of black poison; poisons (in general); a poison produced at the churning of the ocean, and swallowed by Siva, causing the blueness of his neck: กาลขัญชน์, กาลขัณฑ์ the liver: กาลคุณ good or bad fortune (of an occasion): กาลเนตร, กาลโลจน์ one with black eyes: กาลปักษ์, ภาพปกฺษ the waning of the moon; the dark of the moon; the dark or moonless fortnight of the month (chd.): กาลพาหนะ, กาลวาหน a buffalo: กาลโภคี the black cobra: กาลมุข, กาลวัทน์ those with black faces; name of a fabulous race of people who sprang from men and Rakshasa females (H. C. D.): กาลเมฆ a dark or black cloud: กาลราตรี a night during the dark of the moon: กาลเวลา *lit.* "the time of Saturn," *i. e.* time or period of darkness; a particular time of the day at which any religious act is improper: กาลสาร having black eyes; having a black center or pupil; the black antelope: กาลสูตร *lit.* "a black thread," *i. e.* the thread of time or death; one of the twenty-one hells: กาลานุสาร gum benjamin, benzoin, *Styrax benzoides (Styracaceae)* (V. P. p. 22), a tree yielding a fragrant gum-resin which is soluble in water. Siam is one of the chief benzoin producing countries (Burk. p. 2105): กาลายส iron; being made of iron: กาลาโศก the title of a sovereign, probably the celebrated king พระจันทรคุปต์ Chandra-gupta, who founded the Mauryan dynasty, the third king of which was the great Asoka. Chandra-gupta died about 296 B. C. (Antiq. of Ind. p. 39): กาโลทายี, กาลุทายี name of one of the Buddha's pupils; a philosopher (S. E. D. p. 277): ผู้กาล a gangrenous abscess.

กาล ๒ *gkan P. S. n.* time (in general); a period or space of time; a fixed or right point of time; the proper time or season; time for action; occasion; circumstance; destiny; fate; time (as destroying all things): กาลกรรม *lit.* "time's act," *i. e.* death: กาลกริยา *lit.* "fixing of the times," *i. e.* death: กาลก่อน the past; in olden times: กาลกัลป์ deathly; death-like; fatal; deadly: กาลกุษฐ์ the god of Death; Yama: กาลคติ the passing of time: กาลจักร the wheel of time; time represented as a wheel which is always turning around; a given revolution of time; a cycle; the wheel of fortune (sometimes regarded as a weapon): กาลโจหิต summoned by death; acting under the influence of fate: กาลดุลย์ death-like; simulating death; deadly: กาลใด at what time; when: กาลตรัย the three periods of time, *viz.* past, present and future: กาลทัณฑ์ the rod of destruction; death: กาลทูต the angel of death; an omen pointing to death: กาลเทศะ difference in time and of locality: กาลธรรม the law, rule or operation of time; death; the line of conduct suitable to any time, occasion or season; seasonableness; the influence of time: กาลธารณา *lit.* "the extension of time," *i. e.* a pause: กาลนั้น at that time: กาลนาถ *lit.* "the lord of time," *i. e.* Siva; "Father Time": กาลนิธิ name for Siva: กาลนิโยค *lit.* "time's ordinance," *i. e.* fate; destiny: กาลนิรูปณ์ chronology: กาลนี้ at this time; during this present time: กาลเนมิ *lit.* "the felly (fierceness) of the wheel of time," *i. e.* name of a great Asura who was killed by Krishna: กาลบาศ *lit.* "the trap of Yama," "Yama's noose," *i. e.* death: กาลบัดนี้ now; this very moment: กาลบุรุษ, กาลมูรติ *lit.* "time personified," *i. e.* a servant of the god of Death: กาลประเพณี customs established by time: กาลภักษ์ *lit.* "he who devours time," *i. e.* a name for Siva: กาลเมื่อ when; at the time that: กาลฤกษ์ *lit.*

"the fifty-second year in a cycle of sixty years," *i. e.* the year of the planet Jupiter: กาลโชค the connections with or consequences of fate or destiny: กาลโยคี *lit.* "reigning over destiny," *i. e.* name of Siva: กาลราตรี *lit.* "the night of all-destroying time," *i. e.* the night of destruction at the end of the world; the night of darkness; the night of a person's death; a particular night in the life of a man, *viz.* the seventh day of the seventh month of the seventy-seventh year, after which period a man is exempt from attending to the usual ordinances: กาลรุทร, กาลาคนิรุทร Rudra, regarded as the fire that is to destroy the world: พระรุทร *lit.* "the howler or roarer," *i. e.* Rudra, the howling, terrible god, or the god of Storms, the father of the Rudras or Maruts. He is sometimes identified with the god of Fire. On the one hand, he is represented as a destructive deity who brings diseases upon men and cattle, and upon the other, he is a beneficent deity supposed to have a healing influence (H. C. D. p. 269): กาลวันนี้ now; today; at the present moment: กาลวันหน้า by and by; during some future day: กาลวิกรม *lit.* "the power of time," *i. e.* death; destruction: กาลวิทยา the science of calculating time or the making of calendars: กาลวิภาค a portion, section or part of time: กาลศักดิ์ the Saki or all-destroying time: กาลสกนธ์ (ต้น) *Diospyros embryopteris (Ebenaceae)*, a medium-sized, handsome tree of Ceylon, India, Malaya, etc., found at low and medium elevations. "Tunika-oil," used medicinally, is obtained in India from the seeds (MCM. pp. 206, 386). In Siam, it is used chiefly as a tan and dye (BURK. p. 830): กาลสังขยา the means or method of fixing or calculating time: กาลสิงคลี name of a disease characterized by blackness; plague: กาลสุรย์ the sun at the end of the world: กาลหาร the wastefulness of time; the loss of time; the uselessness of time: กาลาคนิรุทร the fire that is to destroy the world; the conflagration at the end of time: กาลาติบาต lateness; slowness of time; the delay of time: กาลาทิก the fifth month, according to the old Siamese reckoning; the month Caitra: กาลาธิจร name of a remedy correcting a periodically occurring disease: กาลานล conflagration at the end of the world; the fire that is to destroy the world: กาลานุกาล from time to time: นิจกาล eternity (S. E. D. p. 278).

กาล ๓ gkan *n.* a form of poetical meter; prosody.

กาลกิณี see กาลกรรณี in กาล ๑

กาลอัจนา gkah-la[6]-at[4]-chja[4]-nah *n.* Kalaka, a wife of the sage Kasyapa, who with her sister named Puloma, another wife of that sage, bore him 60,000 distinguished Danavas, called Paulomas and Kalakanjas, who were powerful, ferocious, and cruel (H. C. D. p. 140).

กาลัชญะ gkah-lat[6]-ya[6] *n.* an astrologer: one who forecasts coming events or knows the future; one knowing the fixed times or seasons.

กาลันดร gkah-lan-daun *n.* interval of time; intermediate time; another time; after some time; another opportunity.

กาลิก gkah-lik[6] *n.* relating to, connected with or depending on time; fit for any particular time or season; seasonable; lasting for a long time; belonging to time; the time, specified by rules, within which Buddhist monks are allowed to partake of food or medicine: สัตตาหกาลิก drinkables taken by Buddhist monks after mid-day (chd. p. 595): ยาวกาลิก eatables taken by Buddhist monks at prescribed times: ยามกาลิก prescribed times when Buddhist monks can partake of nourishment (S. E. D. p. 278).

กาลี gkah-lee *S. n.* (1) abuse; censure; defamation. (2) black; dark; a black colour; ink or blacking; night; a row or succession of black clouds; *lit.* "the black," *i. e.* a name for Krishna. (3) the goddess Kali. In Vedic days this name was associated with Agni

(fire) who had seven flickering tongues of flame for devouring oblations of butter. Of these seven, Kali was the black or terrific tongue. This idea has developed into the person of the goddess Kali, the fierce and bloody consort of Siva (H. C. D. p. 277): กาลีตนัย *lit.* "the offspring of the Ganges," *i. e.* the buffalo: กาลีวัลสี *lit.* "the husband of the goddess Kali," *i. e.* Siva, in one of his previous incarnations (S. E. D. p. 277).

กาลุทายี, กาโลทายี see กาล ๑

กาว gkow *n.* gum; glue; mucillage.

ก้าว gkow[3] *v.* to take a step; to walk; to advance: *n.* a step: ก้าว (ต้น) *Tristania rufescens (Myrtaceae)* (cb. p. 627), a small tree about 8 m. high, common in open ground (K.): ก้าวก่าย to overlap; to extend so as to rest partly on the next: ก้าวถอยไป to step back; to retreat step by step: ก้าวร้าว offensive (in word or action); rude: ย่างเท้าก้าวเดิน to march; to march slowly; to pace: แล่นก้าว to tack (as a boat when sailing).

กาววาว gkow-wow *adj.* bright; gay; striking; glaring (as to colour).

กาศยป gkah-sa[4]-yop[6] *P. S. n.* a Vedic sage to whom some hymns are attributed. All authorities agree in assigning to him a large part in the work of creation. According to the Ramayana, he was the son of Marichi, the son of Brahma, and the father of Vivaswat, the father of Manu, the progenitor of mankind (S. E. D.: H. C. D. p. 153): กาศยปนันทน์ *lit.* "the progeny of พระกัศยป," *i. e.* all the celestial beings or host (S. E. D. p. 281).

กาศยบ gkah-sa[4]-ya[6]-bpee *n.* a female descendant of กัศยป; the earth: กาศยบีภุช *lit.* "one enjoying the earth," *i. e.* a king; the royal ruler of a realm (S. E. D. p. 281).

กาศี gkah-si[4] *S. n. lit.* "shining one," *i.e.* the sun; the clenched hand; the first handful: กาศินคร, พาราณสี Benares (S. E. D. p. 280).

กาศิก, กาสิก gkah-sik⁴ *S. adj.* silky; interwoven with silk: กาศิกพัสตร์ a finely woven
cotton cloth from Benares (S. E. D. p. 280).

กาศ, กาสี gkah-see² *n.* Kasi, a celebrated
city and place of pilgrimage (the modern
Benares): กาสีนาถ *lit.* "the lord of Benares,"
i. e. Siva (S. E. D. p. 280).

กาษฐะ gkah-sa⁴-ta⁴ *n.* a piece of wood or
timber; wood or timber (in general); a stick;
an unit for measuring: กาษฐขัณฑ์ a stick;
a spar; a piece of wood; a cane: กาษฐจิตา
a pile of wood for cremation purposes:
กาษฐดักษ์ *lit.* "one cutting and framing timber," *i. e.* a carpenter: กาษฐภูต *lit.* "one
who has become wood or stands stock-still,"
i. e. a religious devotee or an ascetic: กาษ-
ฐวิวร the hollow of a tree; hollowness (of a
log) (S. E. D. p. 281).

กาษาย, กาสาย gkah-sah²-ya⁶ *v.* to dye a
reddish colour: *n.* dark brown; reddish-
brown: กาษายธารณ์, กาษายพัสน์, กาษายพาส the
condition of wearing reddish-brown garments:
กาษายพัสนา a woman wearing a brown garment;
a widow (S. E. D. p. 281).

ก๊าส gkat⁶ *Eng. n.* gas; gas fumes.

กาสร gkah-saun² *S. n.* a buffalo.

กาสัง (ต้น) gkah-sung² *n. Feronia lucida*
(*Rutaceae*) (cb. p. 239). In Siam, the sap,
mixed with orpiments, makes a yellow ink,
used for writing on palm leaves. The fruits
are used as a vegetable (BURK. pp. 998, 999).

กาสะ gkah-sa⁴ *P. S. n.* the act of coughing;
a cough (chd. p. 191): กาสกุณฐ์ *lit.* "one afflicted with a cough," *i. e.* Yama (S. E. D. p. 281).

กาสะท้อน (ต้น) gkah-sa⁴-taun⁵ *n. Pithe-*
cellobium clypearia (*Leguminosae*) (cb. p. 558),
a small tree about 4 m. high, growing abundantly in evergreen forest (K. : BURK. p. 1760).

กาสา gkah-sah² *n.* a bluish zinc-like ore.

กาสามปีก (ต้น) gkah-sam²-bpeek⁴ *n. Flem-*

ingia sootepensis (*Leguminosae*) (cb. p. 472);
Vitex peduncularis (*Verbenaceae*) (V. P. p. 19),
a tree, the bark of which is used in making
an external application for pains in the chest.
The wood is purplish or reddish-grey, heavy,
hard, close-grained and is a good timber. It
is used for posts and beams and also for
yokes (Dept. Agri. & Fisheries).

กาสาย see กาษาย

กาสาร gkah-san² *S. n.* a pond; a lake; a well
of water; a reservoir for water (S. E. D. p. 281).

กาสาวะ see กาษาย

กาสิก see กาศิก

กาสี see กาศี

กาเสดโคก (ต้น) gkah-set⁴-kok³ *n. Nep-*
tunia triquetra (*Leguminosae*) (cb. p. 545), an
herb.

กาเสา (ต้น) gkah-sow² *n. Lagerstroemia*
macrocarpa (*Lythraceae*) (cb. p. 725), a tree
about 6 m. high, having mauve flowers. It
is found in deciduous forests (BURK. p. 1299 : K.).

กาหล gkah-hon² *n.* a large-sized drum; the
sound of a trumpet or drum; a cat; a cock:
adj. speaking indistinctly or unbecomingly;
mischievous; excessive.

กาหลัง gkah-lang² *Jav. n.* the name of a
city in the story known as *Enow.*

กาหลา ๑ gkah-lah² *n.* a large-sized drum;
an ancient musical instrument (S. E. D. p. 281).

กาหลา ๒ gkah-lah² *Jav. adj.* flower-like;
gay.

กาหลี gkah-lee² *S. n.* a virgin; a young
girl or woman (S. E. D. p. 281).

กาไหล่ gkah-lai⁴ *v.* to nickel-plate; to
cover over with silver or gold: กาไหล่เงิน
to over-lay with silver: กาไหล่ทอง to gild.

กาเหว่า see กระเหว่า

กาฬ gkan *P. S. adj.* black; dark blue; of a

dark colour; wicked (chd. p. 176): กาพบักษ์ darkness; the waning of the moon; the dark or moonless fortnight of the month (chd. p. 176): กาพโรค bubonic plague (S. E. D. p. 277).

กำ gkam *v.* to clinch the fingers; to clinch the fist; to hold in the hollow of the hand: *n.* the fist; a handful; a bundle; a package; a measure of height or diameter, equal to about eight inches: กำเกรียก, กำตัด a betting game (played with seeds or shells). These are placed in a cup or held in the hands, and wagers are made as to the number that will remain after the banker counts out by fours. The banker pays equal to the stake laid. This game is similar to "fantan" of China: กำเกวียน the spokes of a wheel: กำถั่ว to gamble by betting on how many shells are held in both hands: กำปั้น the fist: กำมา a cubit (measured from the elbow to the knuckles): กำไว้ to hold in one's hand: กำหนึ่ง an handful: กำหมัด to clinch the fist tightly: ห้ากำ five times the length of the fist.

กำ gkam[4] *adj.* bright; vivid; striking (used describing rubies or pure gold): แดงกำ very red; blood-red: สุกกำ perfect ripeness.

กำกวม, กระเต็นใหญ่ (นก) gkam-gkoo-am *n.* the Burmese stork-billed king-fisher, *Pelargopsis gurial burmanica* (will. N.H.J.S.S. II, 3, p. 334): *adj.* doubtful; indistinct; undecided; wavering (in speech or manner).

กำกับ gkam-gkap[4] *v.* to superintend (as workmen); to control; to accompany (as a guide); to assist: ผู้กำกับ moderator; guardian: นั่งกำกับ to be seated while listening to or watching the proceedings of a meeting.

กำกรุ่น gkam[3]-gkroon[4] *adj.* reddish-white.

กำกิง gkam[3]-gkeung[4] *adj.* equidistant; equal chance of gain or loss; at almost equal distances from each other.

กำเกิน gkam[3]-gkern *adj.* intruding; beyond; not equidistant; at unequal distances from each other: *adv.* rudely.

กำเคือ (ต้น) gkam-keu-ah *n. Abrus precatorius* (*Leguminosae*) (V. P. p. 21), "Indian-liquorice," a slender perennial climber, the bright red and black seeds of which furnish an acrid poison and are often used criminally for killing cattle. The seeds are powdered and formed into a paste with which the darts or arrows are dressed. The poisonous property is believed to be in the red covering of the seed; boiling renders the seeds harmless. The juice of the green leaves is taken for purifying the blood; the root is taken for sore throat and rheumatism (MCM. pp. 377, 383, 461 : BURK. pp. 4-9).

กำจร gkam-chjaun *S. v.* to disseminate in the air (as smoke); to be rumoured about (as gossip or news); to move through space; to fly through the air (S. E. D. p. 334).

กำจัด gkam-chjat[4] *v.* to disperse; to expel; to ostracize or banish (as undesirable); to drive away: แดดกำจัดเมฆ the sun disperses the clouds.

กำจัด (ต้น) gkam-chjat[4] *n. Zanthoxylum budrunga* (*Rutaceae*) (CB. p. 219 : V. P. p. 21), a tree of the tropical Himalayas. The carpels are used medicinally. The wood is rather heavy, soft, yellowish-white and close-grained (Dept. Agri. & Fisheries : BURK. p. 2284).

กำจาย (ต้น) gkam-chjai *n. Caesalpinia digyna* (*Leguminosae*) (CB. p. 502 : V. P. p. 20 : MCM. p. 443 : BURK. p. 386 : Dept. Agri. & Fisheries), a prickly, climbing shrub of India and other tropical countries, rich in tannic acid (from 42 to 60 per cent). The root has marked astringent properties and is given medicinally in the form of a decoction. The oil expressed from the seeds is used for domestic purposes: งากระจาย, งากำจาย an elephant's tusk that has been broken.

กำชับ gkam-chap[6] *v.* to reiterate; to direct explicitly (as a command); to urge; to persist in demanding; to insist on obedience; to make two contiguous or adjoining surfaces or edges fit tightly or closely together.

กำซาบ gkam-sap³ *v.* to paint; to gloss or smear over; to wash over (as gilding or nickelling a frame).

กำด้น gkam-don³ *n.* the nape of the neck; the occipital portion of the head.

กำดัด gkam-dat⁴ *adj.* young; vigorous; flourishing; full of vigour: กำดัดร้อน heat (in the extreme degree).

กำเดา, ขะเดา gkam-dow *n.* heat epistaxis (blood flowing from the nostrils); nasal catarrh: ไข้กำเดา a nasal, catarrhal fever.

กำต้น (ต้น) gkam-dton³ *n. Adenanthera pavonina (Leguminosae)* (V. P. p. 21), a large deciduous tree. The gum obtained from this plant is known as "madatia." The wood is sometimes used as a dye, but chiefly as a substitute for the true red sandalwood. The powder made from the seeds is said to be a useful external application, hastening suppuration, a grateful application over boils, soothing the burning pain and hastening recovery. A decoction made from the leaves is given as a remedy for chronic rheumatism and gout; the wood affords a good timber, used for house-building and cabinet-making purposes (Dept. Agri. & Fisheries: Burk. p. 46).

กำตาก gkam-dtak⁴ *n.* the revenue given by the state, in ancient times, to those who performed the annual Ploughing or Swinging Ceremony: วันกำตาก the day on which the cultivation of the fields begins.

กำทอด (ต้น) gkam-taut³ *n. Phyllanthus emblica (Euphorbiaceae)* (V. P. p. 21), a small tree or shrub, commonly found wild in open land and grown in gardens for ornament, because of its graceful, feathery foliage. The round, green fruits, the size of marbles, have a comparatively large kernel and are made into a much-esteemed preserve and a cooling laxative, taken for dyspepsia. The timber is fair, close-grained and hard but warps and splits in seasoning. The bark and leaves are used for tanning, dyeing and in medicine (MCM. pp. 268, 379, 443: Burk. p. 920).

กำธร gkam-taun *adj.* shaky; vibrating; swaying; swinging; trembling (as in an earthquake).

กำนล gkam-non *Cam. n.* gifts or offerings made to spirits, in worship; a present given on paying a visit; a gift made for the purpose of getting a favour from the receiver.

กำนัน gkam-nan *v.* to protect; to ward off: *n.* an elder of a village; the village magistrate; the headman of a group or village; the headman of a commune; one who acts as a guardian of, or conciliator between members of his community.

กำนัล (นาง) gkam-nan *n.* a maid-in-waiting on the queen; the queen's attendant; a maid-of-honour; ladies of the palace: ของ กำนัล a gift or offering for friendship's sake.

กำเนิด gkam-nert⁴ *v.* to be born; to bring forth (as a plan or project): *n.* birth; origin; race: บาปแต่กำเนิด original sin: เอากำเนิด-เกิดมา to be born.

กำเนียจ, เกียจ gkam-nee-at³ *adj.* lazy; idle; indolent; inactive; dishonest; unfaithful.

กำบัง gkam-bang *v.* to veil; to cover; to make a shelter for: *Jav. n.* a flower: กำ-บังกาย to render one's self invisible; to hide one's self: กำบังไฟฟ้า a dielectric; a non-conductor; an insulator: ควันกำบัง a smoke-screen: ที่กำบัง a sheltered place.

กำบัด gkam-bat⁴ *v.* to sweep away with the hands; to brush away.

กำบิด see **กรรบิด**

กำโบล, กโปล gkam-bone *P. S. n.* the cheek; the cavity of the cheek; a jowl of man or elephant (S. E. D. p. 251).

กำเบ้อ (ต้น) gkam-bur[3] *n. Mussaenda sp.* (*Rubiaceae*) (V. P. p. 22), a handsome shrub or climber with yellow flowers and a large white calycine leaf, often cultivated in gardens (Dept. Agri· & Fisheries : Burk. p. 1518).

กำปนี see **กัมปนี**

กำบั่น gkam-bpan[4] *n.* a ship; a safe or strong-box; a species of durien : กำบั่นเหล็ก an iron chest; a safe : กำบั่นใบ a sailing ship : กำบั่นไฟ a steamship.

กำผลา gkam-pa[4]-lah *n.* an halberd; a long-handled knife with saw-teeth (used in ancient warfare).

กำพง gkam-pong *Jav. n.* a wharf; a landing-place; a district.

กำพร้า gkam-prah[3] *n.* epidermis : *adj.* abandoned; helpless; orphaned : กำพร้า (ต้น) *Canavalia obtusifolia* (*Leguminosae*); *C. maritima* (cb. p. 453 : V. P. p. 22 : MCM. p. 209), a creeping, leguminous, perennial plant with bright pink (sometimes white) flowers, which grows luxuriantly on sandy sea-shores (MCM. p. 209). It is a useful binder for loose sand (Dept. Agri. & Fisheries : Burk. p. 432) : ลูก กำพร้า an orphan : หนังกำพร้า outer cuticle.

กำพวด gkam-pu-at[3] *n.* the reed or tongue of metal or wood nearly closing the opening of a flute or organ pipe.

กำพอง gkam-paung *n.* the upper and lower strips of wood, on to which the side slats forming the body of an ox-cart are fastened.

กำพี้ (ต้น) gkam-pee[5] *n. Dalbergia cultrata* (*Leguminosae*) (cb. p. 476), a moderate-sized tree which exudes a red resin. The plant is used for the propagation of lac and furnishes a useful oil. The wood is employed for wheels, agricultural implements, handles of dahs and spears, but especially for carving (Dept. Agri. & Fisheries).

กำพืช gkam-purt[3] *n.* lineage; ancestors; pedigree; descendants.

กำพู gkam-poo *n.* the hub of an umbrella, on to which the ribs are fastened; the hub of a wheel.

กำเพลิง gkam-plerng *Cam. n.* a flint-lock gun; an ancient gun using flint instead of percussion caps.

กำแพ (ต้น) gkam-paa *n. Cosmos bipinnatus* (*Compositae*), an ornamental herb (Burk. p. 670).

กำแพง gkam-paang *n.* wall : กำแพงแก้ว the wall surrounding a pagoda : กำแพงเขย่ง votive tablets representing the Buddha in the act of walking : กำแพงเจ็ดชั้น *Salacia socia* (*Celastraceae*). These are shrubs or climbers. The wood is formed in layers up to seven. The flowers are small, greenish, with an unpleasant odour, and are used medicinally (K.) : กำแพงเพ็ชร์ the name of a district and city in northwestern Siam : กำแพงเคียร an hybrid species of fowl having a large serrated comb.

กำมลาสน์ gkam-ma[6]-lat[3] *P. S. n. lit.* " he who has a lotus as a seat," *i. e.* **Brahma** ; a lotus flower serving as a seat (S. E. D. p. 252).

กำมเลศ, กมเลศ gkam-ma[6]-let[3] *P. S. n.* a large variety of lotus (S. E. D. p. 252).

กำมะถัน gkam-ma[6]-tan[2] *n.* sulphur.

กำมะลอ gkam-ma[6]-lau *n.* anything prepared for the purpose of deceiving; a fake article; a make-shift article : ลายกำมะลอ designs made in imitation of black marble.

กำมะหยี่ gkam-ma[6]-yee[4] *n.* velvet : กำมะหยี่ (ต้น) *Tagetes erecta* (*Compositae*), a showy annual (K. : MCM. pp. 135, 199). There are orange, yellow and crimson varieties. The flowers yield a yellow dye. It is used as a remedy in eye diseases (Dept. Agri. & Fisheries); *Sinningia speciosa* (*Gesneraceae*), a Brazilian plant, first imported from England into Siam by Mr. Rivett Carnac about 30 years ago (Phya winit N. H. J. S. S. IX, 1, p. 104 : Burk. p. 2034).

กำมะหรีด   gkam-ma[6]-rit[4] *n.* worsted fabrics.

กำมังละการ   gkam-mang-la[6]-gkan *Jav. n.* a house or dwelling for royalty.

กำมังวิลิด   gkam-mang-wi[6]-lit[6] *n.* a royal summer-house or pavilion in an artificial lake.

กำยาน (ต้น)   gkam-yan *n.* benzoin; gum benjamin, *Styrax benzoides (Styracaceae)* (V. P. p. 22), a tree yielding a fragrant gum-resin which is soluble in water and is used medicinally (BURK. p. 2105).

กำยำ   gkam-yam *adj.* large; tall and strong; formidable; well-built (physically).

กำรอ   gkam-rau *Cam. adj.* poor; poverty-stricken; hard-up.

กำราบ, กราบ   gkam-rap[3] *v.* to threaten; to intimidate; to terrify; to make obeisance to, by raising the hands palm to palm to the face and bending the head down to the floor.

กำราล, กราล   gkam-ran *Cam. v.* to spread down (as a carpet): *n.* a carpet; a mat; a rug.

กำเริบ   gkam-rerp[3] *v.* to increase; to extend; to expand; to advance; to intensify; to get worse (as an ailment); to have one's head turned by praise; to become haughty or boastful: โรคกำเริบ the disease is increasing in intensity.

กำโรง (ต้น)   gkam-rong *n. Sterculia campanulata (Sterculiaceae)* (Cb. p. 166), a tree about 50 to 60 feet high, found in tropical forests. It yields a gum resembling African tragacanth. The wood is soft, white, coarsely fibrous and rather loose, but straight-grained (Dept. Agri. & Fisheries).

กำไร   gkam-rai *n.* profit; gain in trading; advantage; benefit: *adj.* profitable; increasing; accruing; remunerative: กำไรเท่าทุน gain equal to the capital; one hundred per cent profit: มีกำไร to get gain; to do better by trading: มีกำไรงาม to gain largely in trading: ไม่มีกำไร no financial gain.

กำลัง   gkam-lang *n.* strength; power; vigour; capacity; if placed as a prefix to a verb it signifies continuous action in the present tense, *ex.* กำลังไป: กำลังวังชา, กำลังกาย physical strength: กำลังกิน eating: กำลังเกิด nascent; beginning to exist or develop: กำลังงาน *n.* energy: *adj.* energetic; active; vigorous: กำลังดี suitable in every respect: กำลังเทียน candle-power: กำลังรบ in the midst of battle: กำลังเรือ capacity of a boat or ship: กำลังส่องสว่าง illuminating power.

กำลูน   gkam-loon *adj. P.* attractive; adorable (as an infant); lovable; interesting.

กำเลา   gkam-low *Cam. adj.* dull of intellect; stupid; slow of comprehension.

กำเลาะ   gkam-lau[6] *Cam. adj.* young; sprightly; adolescent.

กำไล   gkam-lai *n.* an inflexible bracelet; a heavy bracelet: กำไลข้อเท้า an anklet: กำไลมือ a bracelet resembling an anklet.

กำสรด   gkam-sot[4] *v.* to be sad; to mourn; to be sorrowful; to be melancholy.

กำสรวล   gkam-soo-an[2] *Cam. v.* to sob; to mourn over; to meditate mournfully over (as in the loss of money or a friend).

กำหนด   gkam-note[4] *v.* to decree; to appoint or to fix (as a time); to estimate (as the price or sum to be spent): *n.* act; decree; law; rule: กำหนดให้ to assign: กำหนดวันพิจารณา to set a date for trial.

กำหนัด   gkam-nat[4] *v.* to be pleased with; to be in love with; to be enamoured with: *n.* joy; pleasure; passion; love; voluptuousness.

กำแหง   gkam-haang[2] *adj.* brave; strong; adventuresome; daring; audacious; valiant.

กำแฮ (ต้น)   gkam-haa *n. Coreopsis grandiflora (Compositae).* The flowers are yellow with brown centres (MCM. p. 134).

กิก   gkik[4] *adj.* giggling; snickering: *onomat.* from the clicking of cups.

กิ่ง   gking[4] n. branch; the bough of a tree; a subdivision (as of a main clause): กิ่งก้าน, กิ่งไม้ branches, stems or stalks: กิ่งอำเภอ a branch office or sub-district of a commune: เรือกิ่ง a large, carved, gilt state-barge.

กิ่งหาย (ต้น)   gking[4]-hai[2] n. Crotalaria laburnifolia (Leguminosae) (V. P. p. 25), a shrub with pale yellow flowers, often seen in gardens on account of its flowering throughout the year (Dept. Agri. & Fisheries: Burk. p. 686).

กิ่งกร, กิ่งการ   gking-gkaun P. S. n. lit. "one who asks what is to be used or done and then does accordingly," i. e. a servant; an attendant; a slave; a waiter (Chd. p. 205); name of one of Siva's attendants: กิ่งกรี a female slave, attendant or waitress; the wife of a servant (S. E. D. p. 283).

กิ้งก่า   gking[3]-gkah[4] n. chameleon, a lizard-like reptile of the genus Chamaeleon. The skin is covered with fine granulations. Its colour changes more or less with the colour of objects about it (web.): กิ้งเขน, กางเขน (นก) the shama, Cittocincla macrura (Gaird. J.S.S. IX, 1, p. 1); the magpie-robin, Copsychus saularis saularis (Herb. N. H. J. S. S. VI, 1, p. 114): กิ้งเขนปากเรียว (นก) blue rock thrush, Monticola cyanus (Gaird. J. S. S. IX, 1, p. 1): กิ้งโครง (นก) the Chinese mynah, Sturnia sinensis (Gaird. J. S S. IX, I, p. 4); Siamese mynah, Aethiopsar grandis (H. M. S.): กิ้งโครงดำ (นก) the Burmese jungle-mynah, Aethiopsar fuscus grandis (Herb. N. H. J. S. S. VI, 1, p. 112).

กิ้งกือ   gking[3]-gkeu n. galley-worm (so called because the numerous legs along the sides move rhythmically like the oars of a galley); Achilognath myrapod of the genus Tulus, having numerous short legs along the sides; milleped; myriapod, having the body made up of numerous segments nearly all of which bear true jointed legs. When molested it curls itself up in a coil (web.).

กิ่งสุก, ทองกวาว (ต้น)   gking-sook[4] n. Butea frondosa (Leguminosae) (cb. p. 445: V. P. p. 142: Burk. p. 384: MCM. pp. 85; 206). In India, the flowers give a dye. The gum is medicinal. The bark tans. The seeds give oil and the leaves fodder: Spathodea campanulata (Bignoniaceae) (MCM. p. 95). The brilliant red flowers of this tree are very beautiful, hence often alluded to by poets (S. E. D. p. 282). The soft timber is thought to be good for paper pulp (Burk. p. 2060).

กิจ, กิจจ์   gkit[4] P. S. n. work; action; duty to be done or service to be rendered: business: adj. feasible; practicable; right; proper (to be done): กิจจานุกิจ work or duties of divers kinds; duties, great and small; all sorts of duties; the title of a book dealing with various subjects (Ala. p. 4): กิจลักษณะ characteristics; methods; style or methods in the discharge of a task or duty (S. E. D. p. 303): กิจวัตร daily programme or routine of work.

กิฏฐ์   gkit[4] P. S. n. seedling rice; seeds of all kinds (intended for planting or having been planted); cultivation of the soil; crops on the ground (Chd.): adj. ploughed, tilled, or cultivated (ground) (S. E. D. p. 306).

กิณณ์, กิณว์   gkin P. S. n. the yeast for starting fermentation of rice or sugar; a ferment; a yeast (Chd.); a ferment, drug or seed used to produce fermentation in the manufacture of spirits from sugar (S. E. D. p. 282).

กิตาการ, กิตยาการ   gki[4]-dah-gkan P. n. praise or news that is spread abroad; approbation; fame; renown; report; glory; speech, making mention of (S. E. D. p. 285).

กิดาหยัน   gki[4]-dah-yan[2] Jav. royal pages.

กิตก์   gkit[4] n. the name of a Pali grammar; a grammatical term (Chd. p. 205).

กิตต์, กิต   gkit[4] v. to make mention of; to recite; to repeat; to relate; to declare; to celebrate; to praise; to glorify (S. E. D. p. 285).

กิตติ　　gkit[4]-dti[4] *n. lit.* "the item of news or praise that is spread about", *i. e.* praise ; fame ; renown ; rumour ; report (S. E. D. p. 285).

กิตยาการ see กิดาการ

กิตาหรัง　　gkit[4]-dtah-rang[2] *n.* a crystal palace or a glass-enclosed apartment.

กิน　　gkin *v.* to eat ; to denude or to be eaten (as a post by barnacles) ; to be worn away (as the bank of a river) : กินกัน to eat together (as in a family) ; to fit together (as cog-wheels) : กินกำไร *lit.* "to eat the profit," *i. e.* to charge an excessive price ; to sell at a profit : กินขี้ (ต้น) *Capparis foetida (Capparidaceae) : C. micracantha* (cb. p. 83 : K.), a woody climber or spiny shrub, found on rocks or in evergreen forests. The flowers are white with yellow petals at the bases of the upper petals (Burk. p. 444) : กินงาน to eat the food supplied by a host during any function : กินเจ Chinese Lent, observed by abstaining from fresh food or fish : กินใจ to suspect ; to be doubtful regarding (the aim or purpose of another) : กินช้อน to use a spoon to eat with : กินดอก to collect interest on money lent : กินดิบ to obtain money or win easily without an effort or labour : กินตา to produce a blur by eye-strain ; to be difficult to see ; to be difficult to notice : กินเต็มบี้ขา a gambling term : กินตัว to be frayed (as a flag flapping in the wind) ; to ravel out or to loosen by ravelling : กินถอย to reduce gradually the regular amount eaten : กินแถว *lit.* "to take the whole row," *i. e.* to pick up the pool (as in a gambling game) ; to punish the whole crowd (as a gang of offenders) : กินนรเก็บบัว an ornate form of poetry : กินนรี, กินนรเรศร์ a group of mythological creatures, half-human and half-bird : กินปลี (นก) the Burmese yellow-breasted sun-bird, *Arachuechthra flammaxillaris* (will. N. H. J. S. S. II, 3, p. 208) : กินปลี-เล็ก (นก) the Burmese yellow-breasted sunbird, *Cyrtostomus flammaxillaris* (Herb. N. H. J. S. S.

VI, 2, p. 220) : กินปลีใหญ่ (นก) the brown-throated sunbird, *Anthrothreptes malaccensis* (Herb. N. H. J. S. S. VI, 2, p. 221) : กินเบี้ยว (นก) the white-collared kingfisher, *Sauropatis chloris* (will. N. H. J. S. S. II, 3, p. 337) : กินเปล่า to get something for nothing : กินเพรา meal-time ; breakfast time : กินเมือง to govern a city ; to control or master a city ; to capture a city : กินยืด to make provisions last a long time : กินรวย to be plentifully supplied with provisions : กินรูป appearing reduced in size (as a reflection in a concave mirror) : กินเรา *lit.* "eat us," *i. e.* to lose at a gambling game : กินแรง to profit by the strength or efforts of another (as a son repays his parent) : กินลม to take an outing for health or rest (as a stay at the sea-shore or a sea-trip) : กินสินจ้าง to live on wages only : กินสินบล to take a bribe : กินสินสอด to appropriate the money paid as a dowry : กินสี่ถ้วย a part of a ceremonial feast, comprising four dishes eaten with coconut milk or some similar sweet liquid, *viz.* sago, noodles, popcorn and glutinous rice : กินหน้า a term used in kite-flying to indicate that the kite is inclined at too great an angle towards the wind : กินหลัง indicates that the kite is inclined at too great an angle before the wind : กินหาง indicates that the kite has lost its balance and has gone into a tail-spin : กินหุ้ a gambling term : กินแหนง to suspect ; to doubt the purpose of : กินเหลือ foods that remain after eating : กินอยู่พูราย satiated with food : ทำมาหากิน to work for a living : รับกินรับใช้ *lit.* "to change defeat into victory," *i. e.* a player takes the pot in a game and promises to refund the amount whether he wins or loses.

กินนร　　gkin-naun *P. S. n.* a mythological bird ; "heavenly bird" ; a creature half-human, half-bird. According to Indian mythology they are mythical beings, celestial choristers and musicians, who dwell in the paradise of Kuvera on Kailasa. They are said to have sprung from the toe of Brahma with the

Yakshas and sons of Kasyapa (chd. p. 205).
A class of demigods in the service of Kuvera
(chd.). A mythical being with a human
figure and the head of a horse (or with a
horse's body and head of a man) (S. E. D. p. 283):
กินนรพ้อนโอ่, กินนรรำ, กินนรเลียบถ้ำ attitudes or
poses assumed in Siamese theatricals.

กินนร   gkin-na[6]-ree *P. S. n.* the female of a
mythological half-human, half-bird creature;
a nymph (chd.); a fabulous being, half-human,
half-bird (Ala. p. 300).

กิม   gkim *Chin. n.* gold.

กิมิ   gki[4]-mi[6] *P.S. n.* a worm; a grub; a maggot; an insect; a silk-worm; the lac insect
(S. E. D. p. 305): กิมิชาติ of the worm family;
worms (in general).

กิมิช   gki[4]-mit[6] *n.* threads produced by
worms; silk-fiber: *adj.* silken; made of or
like silk; being produced by a worm; silken
(S. E. D. p. 305).

กิระ   gki[4]-ra[6] *P. adj. lit.* "heard it said
that," *i. e.* rumoured; "they say"; it is said
(chd.).

กิรณ see กิรณี

กิริยา   gki[4]-ri[6]-yah *P. n.* action; a noun of
action; performance; manners; occupation;
business; an act; activity; work; exercises of
the limbs; conduct (S. E. D. p. 320).

กิเลน   gki[4]-lane *n.* a fabulous, Chinese, four-
footed, scaly creature with a dragon's head.

กิเลนห์   gki[4]-lane *Chin. n.* one of the four
fabulous creatures of China, said to have appeared at the birth of Confucius (Ger (1) p.
8, 178).

กิเลส   gki[4]-late[4] *P. S. n.* sin; impurity; sensuality; lustful desires; mental impulses
leading to sorrow or sin; one's lower nature;
depravity; corruption; human passion; moral
defilement; lust. The ten forms of evil
passions are desire, hate, ignorance, vanity,

heresy, doubt, sloth, arrogance, shamelessness,
hardness of heart (chd. p. 203); prejudice
(A. C.).

กิโลมก   gki[4]-loh-mok[6] *P. n.* a membrane;
a serous membrane (as the pleura or pericardium) (chd. p. 204).

กิษกินธ์   gkit[4]-sa[4]-gkin *n.* the name of a
mountain in the southern part of India (north
of Mysore); the country which was taken by
Rama from the monkey king, Bali, and given
back to Sugriva, the brother of the monkey
king and the friend and ally of Rama. The
capital city was Kishkindhya, situated in the
peninsula, thought to be in the Mysore
(H. C. D. p. 159).

กิโลกรัม   gki[4]-loh-gkram *n.* a kilogram,
a measure of weight, being a thousand
grams, equal to 2.2046 pounds avoirdupois
(15.432.34 grains).

กิโลเมตร   gki[4]-lo-met[3] *n.* kilometer, a
measure of length, being 1,000 meters, equal
to 3,280.8 feet or 0.62137 of a mile.

กิโลลิตร์   gki[4]-lo-lit[6] *n.* kiloliter, a capacity measure equal to 1000 liters or one
cubic meter. It is equivalent to 35.315 cubic
feet and to 220.04 imperial gallons or 264.17
American gallons of 231 cubic inches.

กี่   gkee[4] *n.* a frame for sewing the leaves
of a book together; a loom: *gram.* an interrogative numerical adverb: กี่ครั้ง how
many times? กี่นาฬิกา how many hours?
กี่หน, กี่ที how often? กี่มากน้อย how much?
กี่อัน how many small pieces? ไกลกี่มากน้อย
how far is it? ยาวกี่มากน้อย how long may
it be? what is the length of the article?
ราคากี่มากน้อย what may the price be? how
much is the price? สูงกี่มากน้อย how high
is it?

กี้   gkee[3] *n.* a previous occasion: *adj.* earlier; previous to; before: ก่อนกี้นี้ a little
while ago; just previously: เมื่อกี้ just a
minute ago; just now.

กี gkee[4] *Chin. n.* a stool or tripod for potted plants.

กีด gkeet[4] *v.* to prevent; to hinder (as by walking in front of another); to obstruct the passage of; to oppose; to retard: กีดหน้า ขวางตา *colloq.* to annoy by continually obstructing or intruding: ไม่มีเหตุกีดขวาง there is no obstructing cause or reason why.

กีบ gkeep[4] *n.* the hoof; the horny part of the foot; hooves of horses or cows: กีบแรด the name of a medicinal water-plant *Angiopteris evecta (Marattiaceae)*; a large stemless fern with rootstocks supposed to resemble the foot of a rhinoceros, hence the Siamese name (K.).

กีรติ gkee-ra[6]-dti[4] *P. S. n.* the act of speaking; the act of preaching or proclaiming; fame; renown; rumour; report: กีรติยุต famed; illustrious; famous: กีรติเศษ *lit.* "the leaving behind of nothing but fame," *i. e.* death; demise (S. E. D. p. 285).

กีละ gkee-la[6] *P. S. n.* a splinter; a sharp piece of wood; a gnomon; a stake; a pin; a peg; a bolt; a wedge; a brace; a post in a cow-house (for tethering cows); a position of the foetus pending delivery (S. E. D. p. 285): กีฏวิทยา entomology.

กีฬา, กรีฑา *P. S.* gkee-lah *n.* sports; plays; amusements; past-times; pleasures; the pleasure of playing or the enjoyment of amorous sports (S. E. D. p. 321).

กึก see กะกึก

กึกก้อง gkeuk[4]-gkaung[3] *adj.* echoing; resounding: *n.* a loud, far-reaching sound.

กึกกัก, กุกกัก gkeuk[4]-gkak[4] *v.* to produce abnormal or unsymmetrical sounds (as by loose parts in a moving machine): *onomat.* from clattering noises.

กึกกือ gkeuk[4]-gkur *adj.* marvellous; astonishing; portentous; miraculous.

กึ่ง gkeung[4] *adj.* half; midway; middle: กึ่งกัน just half (fifty-fifty): กึ่งเดือน half of a month: กึ่งทาง half-way: กึ่งปี half of a year: กึ่งอายุ half of one's age.

กือแยะบาตู (ต้น) gkur-yaa[6]-bah-dtoo *n. Eugenia operculata (Myrtaceae)* (cb. p. 654), a moderate-sized or even large evergreen tree. The fruit is eaten for rheumatism. The roots, when boiled down to a thick consistency, are rubbed on the joints. The leaves are much used as a dry fomentation. The bark is also employed medicinally. The wood is used for building purposes and agricultural implements (Dept. Agri. & Fisheries).

กุ ๑ gkoo[4] *v.* to tell a lie: *adj.* traceless; causeless; *colloq.* faked.

กุ ๒ gkoo[4] *P. adj.* bad; wicked; rowdy; ugly: a prefix implying inferiority or wickedness (chd.): กุกรรม wickedness; evil; wrong.

กุกู่กูด้อ, ปอลิง, ย่านชงโค (ต้น) gkoo[4]-gkoo[3]-gkoo-dau[3] *n. Bauhinia flammifera (Leguminosae)* (cb. p. 521), a large woody climber. The flowers are deep orange. The bark, which is very strong, is used for binding fences (Burk. p. 311). The origin is uncertain but probably Siam (K.): *Bauhinia variegata,* mountain ebony (S. E. D.).

กุก gkook[4] *onomat.* from cackling, clucking or clicking.

กุกกัก see กึกกัก

กุกกุฏ gkook[4]-gkoot[4] *P.S. n.* a jungle cock; a fowl; a cock (chd.); a firebrand; a spark of fire; a wisp of lighted straw or grass (S. E. D. p. 287).

กุกกุฏี gkook[4]-gkoot[4]-dtee *S. n.* a hen; a jungle hen; the small house lizard.

กุกกุระ gkook[4]-gkoo[4]-ra[6] *P. S. n.* a pup; a dog (chd.); a despicable man of mixed caste (S. E. D. p. 287).

กุกขหมู (ต้น) gkook[4]-kee[3]-moo[2] *n. Holi-*

garua kurzii (*Anacardiaceae*) (V. P. p. 22), a tree about 8 m. high, found in mixed, deciduous forest (K.).

กุกก่อง gkoo⁴-gkaung⁴ *adj.* clear; bright; brilliant; radiant.

กุง (ต้น) gkoong *n. Dipterocarpus tuberculatus* (*Dipterocarpaceae*) (Cb. p. 138), a large, deciduous, gregarious tree. The oleo-resin is used with asafoetida and coconut oil as an application for large ulcers. The wood is used for making canoes, but more generally for planking (Dept. Agri. & Fisheries).

กุ้ง gkoong³ *n.* prawns; a shrimp-like crustacean used as food: ก้ามกุ้ง the claws or pincers of the prawn: กุ้งก้ามกราม a large, blue-legged prawn which constitutes an acceptable substitute for lobster in both size and flavour (Com. Dir.): กุ้งเคย the smallest variety of shrimps, being only 1 to 2 centimeters long. These are very extensively gathered for making into a paste called "kapi": กุ้งเจ่า a fermented condiment made of prawns, which must be cooked before it is eaten with rice: กุ้งตะขาบ, กุ้งฝอย small shrimps found in ditches, canals or in flooded fields: กุ้งพืด, กุ้งแห้ง dried salted prawns (with the scales removed): กุ้งส้ม a pickle made of fresh prawns and vinegar.

กุ้งยิง gkoong³-ying *n.* a sty; inflamation of one or more of the sebaceous glands of the eyelids.

กุงอน (นก) gkoo⁴-ngawn *Cam. n.* the white ibis, *Ibis melanocephala* (Gaird. J. S. S. IX, 1, p. 11).

กุงาน gkoo⁴-ngan *Cam. n.* a goose; any one of the numerous species of large aquatic birds belonging to *Cygnus*. They have a large, strong beak and a long neck, and are noted for their graceful movements when swimming (web.).

กุโงก, กระโงก gkoo⁴-ngok³ *Cam. n.* a peacock; the male of any pheasant of the genus *Pavo*. The upper tail coverts, which are long and capable of erection, are each marked with a black spot bordered by concentric bands of brilliant blue, green and golden colours (web.).

กุจจี gkoot⁴-chjee *n.* Manthra (มนถรา), the ugly, hump-backed slave and nurse of Queen Kaikeyi (ไกเกยี). She stirred up the queen's jealousy against Ramachandra and influenced her to persuade King Dasaratha to banish Rama into exile. Satrughna, twin brother of Lakshmana, beat her and threatened to kill her, but she was saved by his brother Bharata (H. C. D. p. 199 : S. E. D. p. 787).

กุจฉิ gkoot⁴-chee⁴ *n.* gold.

กุจร gkoo⁴-chjaun *S. v.* to creep; to go slowly: *adj.* base; vile; wicked; menial; low; inferior; following evil practices (S. E. D. p. 787).

กุญจนาท, โกญจนาท gkoon-chja⁴-nat³ *P. S. v.* to trumpet: *n.* the roaring or trumpeting of an elephant (chd. p. 212): *adj.* resounding; far-reaching.

กุญแจ gkoon-chjaa *P. S. n.* a key: ไขกุญแจ to unlock: แม่กุญแจ a lock: ลั่นกุญแจ to lock (S. E. D. p. 287).

กุญชร gkoon-chaun *P. S. n.* an elephant that is well-trained or well-bred; the number "eight" (as there are eight elephants located at the eight cardinal points of the compass): *adj.* preeminent; honoured; valuable; precious; anything preeminent in its kind: กุญชรกร the trunk of an elephant: มุลีกุญชร eminent sages (S. E. D. p. 288): ราชากุญชร an eminent king.

กุญชราศน์ gkoon-cha⁶-rat³ *P. S. n. lit.* "food for the elephants," *i. e.* the holy fig tree; *Ficus carica* (*Urticaceae*) (MCM. p. 277), the cultivated fig, grown for its edible fruit (S. E. D. p. 288).

กุญชรี gkoon-cha⁶ree *P. S. n.* a female elephant (S. E. D. p. 288).

กุฏิ, กุฏิ see กระฏิ

กุฎุมพ   gkoo⁴-doom-pee *P. S. n.* a man of wealth; an householder; the head of a family; any one, including a servant belonging to a family (S. E. D. p. 288); an host; a farmer; a peasant.

กุฎุมพินี   gkoo⁴-doom-pee⁶-nee *P. n.* the wife of an householder; the mother of a family; a female servant of a house (S. E. D. p. 288).

กุฏ   gkoot⁴ *P. S. n.* a family; a house, cell or living-quarters; a fort; a stronghold; a water-pot; a pitcher; a jug; a hammer; an axe: กุฏธาริกา *lit.* "a woman who carries a water-jug on her hip," *i. e.* a female servant (S. E. D. p. 288).

กุฏาคาร, กูฏาคาร   gkoo⁴-dtah-kan *n.* a building with a peaked or pinnacled top; an upper room; a room off of a balcony; a roof-garden.

กุณฑ์, กุณฑ์   gkoon *P.S. n.* a water goblet; a bowl; a basin of water (especially consecrated to some holy purpose or person); a pitcher; a pool; a well; an illegitimate son; a bastard; an adulterine child: กุณฑโกล rice that is soured or fermented; a soup or sauce that is weak or watery; gruel: กุณฑเภที *lit.* "one who breaks water-pots," *i. e.* one who is neither skillful nor expert; one who is clumsy: กุณฑาพฤฒ adulterous; immoral: กุณฑโททร one having a bulging belly like a pitcher. (S. E. D. p. 289).

กุณฑล   gkoon-ton *P. S. n.* a ring; earrings (of gold); bracelets; ornamental chains; a fetter; a means of tying; a roll or coil of rope: กุณฑลธารณ์ the act of wearing or putting on earrings: กุณฑลาการ round or shaped like an earring; circular (S. E. D. p. 290).

กุณฑี   gkoon-tee *P.S. n.* a jug; a bowl; a pitcher; a pot; a clump; a particular appearance of the moon (as when surrounded by a circle) (S. E. D. p. 289).

กุณโฑ   gkoon-to *n.* a water goblet; a large; earthen basin; a large dish.

กุณป   gkoon-na⁶-bpa⁴ *P. S. n.* a corpse; a dead body (said contemptuously of the living body): กุณปคนธี having a putrid or foul odour (as of a corpse or carrion) (S. E. D. p. 289).

กุณาละ (นก)   gkoo⁴-nah-la⁶ *P. S. n.* a black bird, so named to resemble its call; the Malayan coel *Eudynamis malayana* (Gaird. J. S. S. IX, 1, p. 7) (S. E. D. p. 289).

กุณิ, กุณิ   gkoo⁴-ni⁶ *P. S. adj.* having a crooked or withered arm, or an arm without a hand or fingers; bent; shortened; crippled (S. E. D. p. 289).

กุด   gkoot⁴ *v.* to be cut off; to be shortened by amputation (as a stump of a leg): *n.* a large swamp: *adj.* shortened; cut off (as fingers); inverted (as eye-lashes): เขากุด shortened horns: ช่องกุด windows, doors, or peep-holes (built or pierced in a wall): มือกุด a maimed hand.

กุดั่น   gkoo⁴-dan⁴ *n.* filigree jewelry decorated with fake diamonds: ลายกุดั่น ornamentations representing gold filigree.

กุทัณฑ์, เกาทัณฑ์   gkoo⁴-tan *P.S. n.* a war-bow (used in ancient warfare); an eye-brow (as being shaped like a bow).

กุน   gkoon *n.* a pig; swine: ปีกุน the year of the pig or the 12*th.* year of the Siamese animal cycle.

กุนนที   gkoon-na⁶-tee *P. n.* a creek; a stream; a rivulet.

กุปะ   gkoo⁴-bpa⁴ *v.* to be increased, aggravated or augmented (as water whipped into waves by the wind).

กุเปรัน, กุเวร   gkoo⁴-bpey-ran *n.* Kuvera, the son of ทาวอัสเตียน, a character in the Ramakean, who became governor of Ceylon. He was a son of Pulastya, half-brother of Ravana, and the chief of the evil beings or spirits living in the realm of the shades. He once reigned over Lanka, and was expelled to Alaka in the Himalayas by Ravana. These two cities were both built by Viswakarma. Kuvera performed austerities for thousands of years and obtained the boon from Brahma that he should be immortal, one of the guardian deities of the world, and the god of Wealth. His region is the North. Brahma also gave him the great, self-moving aerial car, Pushpaka, which was stolen from him by Ravana. Kuvera is represented as a white man, deformed in body, having three legs but with only eight teeth, and waited upon by the Kinnaras, but receiving no worship (H.C.D. p. 173).

กุเพยะ (ต้น)   gkoo⁴-pa-ya⁶ *n. Cassia fistula* (*Leguminosae*) (cb. p. 510), " purging cassia "; " Indian laburnum "; " pudding-pipe," a small upright tree common in the forests of dry regions. It is a beautiful object when in blossom, bearing masses of yellow flowers in pendulous racemes, suggesting the laburnum. The flowers are used as temple offerings and the astringent bark for tanning and in native medicine. The black, cylindrical pods grow to a length of from 20 to 30 inches. The pulp of these pods is a well-known purgative (MCM. p. 85 : Burk. p. 475).

กุเพร   gkoo⁴-pane *P. S. n.* the name of a chief of the evil beings or spirits living in darkness ; Kuvera, the god of Wealth and regent of the North, son of Palastya and a half-brother of Ravana (H. C. D. p. 173): กุเพรคิรี *lit.* " mountain of the spirits of darkness ", *i. e.* the Himalayas : กุเพรพานธพ *lit.* " a relative of Kuvera," *i. e.* a name of Siva : กุเพราจร *lit.* " mountain of the spirits of darkness," *i. e.* the Kailasa mountain (S. E. D. p. 291).

กุม   gkoom *v.* to hold with the hand ; to lay hold of ; to cling to (a branch); to make an arrest ; to catch hold of : กุมกร to use the hands on another : กุมมือ to grasp with the hands.

กุ่ม (ต้น)   gkoom⁴ *n. Crataeva hygrophila* (*Capparidaceae*) (V. P. p. 32 : K.), a tree with edible leaves and flowers ; the bark is used medicinally : กุ่มดอง pickled leaves of these trees, used as a beverage : กุ่มน้ำ (ต้น) *C. nurvala* (Burk. p. 676); *C. roxburghii* (cb. p. 86 : V. P. p. 31), a tree about 4 to 5 m. high, very common along river banks. The leaves are eaten as a vegetable, either raw or preserved (K.): กุ่มบก (ต้น) *C. hygrophila*; *C. erythrocarpa* (cb. p. 85), a tree, the young leaves of which are eaten (K.).

กุมพล, กพนธ์   gkoom-pon *n.* Kabandha, a character in the Ramakean. This monstrous Rakshasa, slain by Rama, is described as " covered with hair, vast as a mountain, without head or neck, having a mouth armed with immense teeth in the middle of his belly, arms a league long, and one enormous eye in his breast." He is said to be originally a Gandharva, but his hideous deformity was due either to having been struck with Indra's thunderbolt which drove his head and thighs into the body or to the result of a curse of a sage. He asked to be cremated after his mortal wound. Rama in compliance with the request, burnt him and he came out of the fire in his real shape as a Gandharva, when he counselled Rama as to the conduct of the war against Ravana (H. C. D. p. 137).

กุมภ์   gkoom *P. S. n.* a jar; a pitcher; a waterpot; an ewer; a jar of unbaked clay; a golden ewer; an urn in which the bones of a dead person are collected; the sign of the zodiac, Aquarius, or " water carrier "; the frontal globe or prominence on the upper part of the forehead of an elephant, of which there are two, which emit an odour in the rutting season: กุมภกรรณ์ *lit.* " pot-eared," *i.e.* Kumbhakarna, a superhuman monster in the Ramayana, son of Visravas by his Rakshasa (goblin or evil spirit) wife Kesini. Under the curse of Brahma, he slept for six months at a time and remained awake for only a

single day. When Ravana was hard-pressed
by Rama, he sent to arouse Kumbha-karna.
This was effected with great difficulty.
After drinking 2000 jars of liquor, he went
to consult with his brother, and then
took the field against the monkey army.
He beat Su-griva, the monkey chief, with
a large stone and carried him a prisoner
into the city of Lanka. When he returned
to the battle, he encountered Rama, and after
a stout fight, he was defeated, and Rama cut
off his head (H. C. D. p. 171): กุมภการ a potter: กุมภทาสี a brothel keeper; a prostitute; an harlot; a bawd: กุมภลัคน์ the season in which Aquarius is above the horizon:
กุมภศาลา a pottery; a potter's kiln: กุมภัณฑ์
lit. "having testicles shaped like a pitcher or
water-pot," i. e. a class of demons, giants or
goblins: กุมภัณฑยักษ an ancient name for
a condition characterized by convulsions
(S. E. D. p. 293).

กุมภนิยา gkoom-pa⁶-ni⁶-yah n. a place
where oblations are offered; a grove at the
western gate of Lanka, for the performance
of sacrificial rites for the purpose of making
one invulnerable (S. E. D. p. 544).

กุมภาพันธ์ gkoom-pah-pan n. lit. "the
eleventh solar month," i. e. February; the
month of the crocodile.

กุมภีล์ gkoom-pee P. S. n. a crocodile of
the Ganges; the long-nosed alligator (S. E. D.
p. 293).

กุมม์, กุรมะ gkoom P. S. n. a turtle; a
tortoise.

กุมาร gkoo⁴-man P.S. n. lit. "dying easily,"
i. e. an infant; a youug lad; a child; a youth;
a son; a prince: กุมาราคาร lit. "a child's
room," i. e. a nursery; a play-room for children; a plant-house; a plant nursery (S. E. D.
p, 292).

กุมารี gkoo⁴-mah-ree P.S. n. a young girl of
about 10 to 12 years of age; a virgin; a
maiden; a daughter; any virgin (up to the

age of sixteen): กุมารีบุตร an illegitimate
daughter; one born out of wedlock; the child
of an unmarried woman (S. E. D. p. 292).

กุมุท gkoo⁴-moot⁶ P. S. n. the lotus flower;
the white, esculent water-lily: กุมุทนาถ,
กุมุทบดี, กุมุทินีนายก, กุมุทินีบดี, กุมุเทศ lit. "the
lord of the lotus," i. e. the moon: กุมุทพันธ์
lit. "the friend of the lotus" (the white
esculent lotus which expands its petals during
the night and closes them during the day
time), i. e. the moon: กุมุทวัน a place for
an assemblage of lotuses; a lotus pond.

กุมุทิน gkoo⁴-moo⁶-ti⁶-nee S. n. lit. "an assemblage of, or a place abounding in lotus
plants," i. e. a lotus pond (S. E. D. 292).

กุย gkoo-ay n. an animal of the deer family; a general name for animals with horns.

กุ๊ย gkoo-ay⁶ Chin. n. a group of ghosts or
shades of the departed (used concerning a
very low class of people); vagrants: adj.
vagrant; unsettled; roaming.

กุ๋ย gkoo-ay² n. a term of raillery, denoting a low-down ragged waif (as a poor
opium smoker, sleeping along the foot-paths
or on door-steps of shops).

กุยเฮง gkoo-ay-heng Chin. n. an outer
garment made according to a special Chinese
pattern, having buttons down the front.

กุรมะ see **กุมภ**

กุรร, กุรุร (นกเขา) gkoo⁴-ra⁶-ra⁶ P. S. n. a
dove; an osprey; a species of eagle (S. E. D. p.
293).

กุระ (ต้น) gkoo⁴-ra⁶ n. Sapium indicum
(Euphorbiaceae) (V. P. p. 19), a small tree
with smooth white bark and narrow willow-
like leaves. The acrid milky juice is very
poisonous (McM. pp. 378, 518). The wood is
used for fuel in the regions where the tree is
found; the seeds are employed as a fish intoxicant (Dept. Agri. & Fisheries). The chief
use is as a dye. The dyers of Lower Siam

and Kelantan dye their yarn a yellow-green colour with it, and obtain other colours by mixing it with other dyes (BURK. p. 1961).

กุรุ   gkoo⁴-roo⁶ *P. S. n.* name of a people of India and also of their country; name of a prince of the Lunar race, son of Samvarna by Tapati, a daughter of the Sun, who ruled over the Kurus, an Aryan people who lived on the plains of Kuru-Kshetra in the north-west of India, near Delhi. He was ancestor both of the Dhrita-rashtra and the Pandu people. The adventures of these princes form the theme of one of the great epic poems of India, entitled "Maha-Bharta," recording events which occurred between 3103 and 1194 B. C. Another epic is the Ramayana (H. C. D. p. 172): กุรุเกษตร *lit.* "the field of the Kuru's, the holy field," *i.e.* an extensive plain near Delhi, the scene of the great battles between the Kurus and Pandus and many battles in later days. In the centre of this field is an oblong sheet of water 3540 ft. in length, which is not only a place for pilgrims to congregate but is also the haunt of innumerable wild-fowl from the peliean to the snipe. It is surrounded by temples in every stage of decay, overshadowed by great trees and flights of dilapidated steps leading down to the water on all sides (I. B. C.). กุรุนนทน์ a family or descendant of the Kuru princes (as Phra Arjuna, one in the army of the god of Darkness): กุรุพิลวร์ a ruby; a blood-red stone: กุรุรัฐร์ the terri-tory, district or section of country situated near the country of the Pancalas (ปัญจาละ). It was probably a country beyond the most northern range of the Himalayas, often de-scribed as a country of everlasting happiness and considered by some to be the ancient home of the Aryan race (S. E. D. p. 294).

กุเรป่น   gkoo⁴-ra-bphan *Jav. n.* a king in the story "Enow".

กุล   gkoon *source-word of* "สกุล" *P. S. n.* a tribe; lineage; race; family; caste; com-pany; gang; herd; flock; troop; multitude; a number of quadrupeds, birds, insects or inanimate objects: กุลกันยา a well-born daughter or high-born ancestress: กุลกุฌี a woman of low caste; a prostitute; an harlot: กุลคุรุ the head of a family, tribe or group; a family preceptor: กุลชน a child of rank; a child born of honourable parents; a person belonging to a noble family: กุลชาต a high caste person; one having illustrious parentage; one born into a noble family: กุลติลก the glory of a family: กุลทูสก the enemy or foe of a family (meaning a Bud-dhist monk, who, against his ethics, makes advances towards a member of a family for wrong purposes): กุลเทวตา the angel or goddess of a family; the family deity: กุลธรรม manners, customs, practices or observ-ances peculiar to a tribe or family; duties peculiar to a caste or race: กุลนาค the king or chief of the snake or Naga tribe: กุลนารี a woman of good family: กุลนาศ *lit.* "an enemy or destroyer of his own tribe or family," *i.e.* a camel; a reprobate; an outcast: กุลบดี the head, leader or chief of a family: กุลบุตร a son or child of a well-to-do family; a respectable youth: กุลบุรุษ an adult member of a well-to-do family; a noble or respectable man: กุล-ประสูต born into or of a prominent family: กุลพธุ, กุลสตรี a woman of good family; a respectable or virtuous woman: กุลมิตร friend, ally or confederate of a family: กุลวาร *lit.* "a principal day," *i. e.* a day that is auspicious, *viz.* Tuesday or Friday: กุลศิริ chief; principal: กุลสันตติ the family circle; the propagation of a family; descendants: กุลเสวก an excellent attendant or servant: กุลางกูร the offspring of a family: กุลาจล a chief mountain range (any one of the seven principal ranges supposed to exist in each division of a continent): กุลาจาร the peculiar or proper duties of a family or caste: กุลา-จารย์ a family priest or teacher; a person well-versed in pedigrees and customs of different families and employed to contract marriages between them; a geneologist: กุโลปเทศ a family name; the surname of a family or tribe: โคกุล a herd of cows: พราหมณ์กุล a Brahman sect (S. E. D. p. 294).

กุลาวก gkoo⁴-lah-wok⁶ *P. n.* a nest; a bird's nest.

กุลิ ๑ gkoo⁴-lee *S. n.* the elder sister of a wife.

กุลิ ๒ gkoo⁴-lee *n.* a coolie; a labourer; a package of twenty pieces of cloth or panungs.

กุลิกุจอ gkoo⁴-lee-gkoo⁴-chjau *adj.* rolled in together; mixed up together (as foot-ball players).

กุเลา, กุเรา (ปลา) gkoo⁴-low *n.* a species of sea-fish; a thread fin fish, *Eleutheronema tetradactylum* (Dept. Agri. & Fisheries).

กุเวร see **กุเปรัน, กุเพร.**

กุศล gkoo⁴-son² *P. S. n.* virtue; merit; luck; fortune; happiness: *adj.* proper; correct; right; suitable; good; in good condition; prosperous; fit for; competent; skillful; clever; conversant with: กองกุศล accumulated merit; charity funds: การกุศล meritorious acts: กุศลกรรม merit and its rewards: กุศลกาม wishing to be happy; desirous of happiness; enjoying the rewards of virtue and merit: กุศลปริศนา the act of asking casually regarding another's health (corresponding to the salutation "Are you well today ?"); a friendly greeting or enquiry respecting a person's health or welfare; a salutation: บุญกุศล the reward of good deeds; merit: ฤทธิกุศล virtue: สร้างกุศล to accumulate merit by one's good deeds (S. E. D. p. 297).

กุษฐัง gkoot⁴-tang² *P. S. n.* leprosy (of which eighteen varieties are enumerated, seven are severe and eleven less so (S. E. D. p. 297): โรคเรื้อน a chronic, transmissible disease due to a specific microbe, *Bacillus leprae.*

กุส goot⁴-sa⁴ *P. S. n.* a grass; the sacred grass used at certain religious ceremonies; a species of wild grass, *Imperata arundinacea* (Gramineae) (V. P. pp. 59, 107: Burk. p. 1228: MCM. pp. 472, 474); *I. cylindrica,* lalang, used for making thatch and paper; a grass used in sacrificial offerings.

กุสล see **กุศล**

กุสา gkoo⁴-sah² *n.* a horse's bridle; a cord or rope for a horse's head (S. E. D. p. 297).

กุสาวด gkoo⁴-sah²-wa⁶-dee *P. n.* the capital city of southern Kosala, built upon the Vindhyas by Kusa, son of King Rama (H. C. D. p. [173).

กุสินารา see **โกสินารา**

กุสุม gkoo⁴-soom² *P. S. n.* a flower; flowers (in general); blossoms (S. E. D. p. 298): กุสุมเกตุ *lit.* "one using a flower as an insignia," *i.e.* the god of Love; a sign by which an object may be recognized; a banner: กุสุมโกมล pliable; flexible (as a flower); adjustable or tender (as flowers): กุสุมธนุ *lit.* "having flowers as his bow," *i.e.* Cupid with his decorated weapon: กุสุมนคร, กุสุมบุร, กุสุมวดี *lit.* "the city of flowers," *i.e.* Patali-putra or Patna (H. C. D. p. 173): กุสุมพาณ, กุสุมศร flower-arrowed; the god of Love's decorated missile: กุสุมวิจิตร flowery; using flowers for decorations; having various flowers: กุสุมากร a quantity of flowers; a place abounding with flowers; a nosegay; spring: กุสุมาธิป, กุสุมาธิราช *lit.* "the prince of flowers," *i.e.* the chumpa, *Michelia champaca (Magnoliaceae)* (cb. p. 26: V. P. p. 80: MCM. p. 216: Burk. p. 1465, a tree which yields serviceable building timber, good fuel and scented flowers: กุสุมายุธ *lit.* "flower-armed," *i.e.* Cupid's arrows which are tipped with flowers: กุสุมาสพ *lit.* "flower-liquor," *i.e.* honey; essences made from flowers (S. E. D. p. 298).

กุสุมภ์, กุสุมา gkoo⁴-soom² *P. S. n.* safflower, *Bixa orellana (Bixaceae)* (V. P. p. 64:

cb. p. 93 : BURK. p. 330 : MCM. p. 436), a large, quick-growing shrub or small tree with cordate leaves. It bears large clusters of brown or dark crimson, capsular, ovoid or round fruits covered with fleshy spines, at the ends of the branches. These contain a number of small seeds, the bright crimson covering of which affords the anatto dye of commerce (S. E. D. p. 298).

กุสุมาล　gkoo⁴-soo⁴-man *S. n.* a robber ; a thief (S. E. D. p. 298).

กุหก　gkoo⁴-hok⁴ *P. S. n.* the act of telling lies ; deceit ; untruthfulness ; a fraud ; an impostor ; an intriguer ; a cheat ; a rogue ; a juggler (S. E. D. p. 298) :　กุหกชีวี one who lives by sleight-of-hand tricks ; a juggler ; a cheat ; a conjurer ; one practicing magic or using charms (as a means of livelihood).

กุหนุง　gkoo⁴-noong² *Jav. n.* a mountain.

กุหลาบ　gkoo⁴-lap⁴ *n. Rosa sp.* (V. P. p. 19), a rose tree :　กุหลาบมอญ *Rosa damascena* (*Rosaceae*), damask rose (Phya Winit N.H.J.S.S. IX, 3, p. 281) ; the mon rose, which is the commonest and the hardiest of all the numerous varieties of roses now in cultivation in Siam. All others are known to have come into Siam only within the last sixty years or so. The kulab mon, however, is said to have been brought to Siam by the Mons (hence the Siamese name) from their country, the present Lower Burma, either during the reign of King Naresuan (1590-1605) or that of his father, King Maha Dhamaraja (1569-1590). Possibly it may have come to this country much earlier than the above periods. The Siamese have no generic name of their own for roses, the name kulab being borrowed from India :　กุหลาบเทียม *Pereskia bleo*, Barbados goose-berry (winit N. H. J. S. S. IX, 3, p. 278), a leafy cactus of Central and South America which is occasionally grown in gardens, sometimes as a plant for live-fences. It has been in Bangkok for about forty years. A dwarfed form, not over two or three feet in height, appeared a few years ago. The Siamese name, which is literally " bastard rose," has been given to the plant on account of its rose-like, pink flower :　น้ำกุหลาบ rose-water :　น้ำมันกุหลาบ attar of roses.

กู　gkoo *pro.* I ; me : the first personal pronoun (used in speaking to inferiors or used contemptuously in disdain or anger) (considered extremely vulgar) :　ว่ากูทำไม " why do you speak about me so ? "

กู่　gkoo⁴ *v.* to call or signal from afar : *n.* a rest-house ; a dwelling ; living-quarters : *onomat.* from the whistling sound of a rod or whip :　กู่กัน to call to another at a distance :　กู่รับ to answer one that calls from a distance :　กู่เพรียกไป to call or yell for help continually (as one lost in the forest) : ตะโกนกู่ to call loudly for a person.

กู้　gkoo³ *v.* to borrow (money) on interest ; to lend at usury ; to bail water out of a boat ; to recover one's self (as after a loss in gambling) :　กู้เงิน to borrow money with interest :　กู้ชื่อ to retrieve one's reputation : กู้เมือง, กู้บ้าน to save one's country ; to restore a ruined house or city :　กู้ยืม to contract debts ; to borrow money :　กู้เรือ to salvage a boat that has sunk :　กู้หน้า to correct one's mistakes ; to save one's face ; to take revenge ; to retrieve one's self :　เงินกู้ money lent on interest :　ดักลอบซอบหมั่นกู้ *prov.* " a laid trap needs constant care " :　ให้กู้ to lend on interest.

กู๊ก (นก)　gkook⁶ *n.* a night-bird of the owl family (so named in imitation of its call).

กูฏ　gkoot⁴ *P. S. n.* the bones of the forehead with their projections or prominences ; the horns of an animal ; the summit, peak, promontory or cliff of a mountain ; part of a plough ; the ploughshare (S. E. D. p. 299) : กูฏกรรม the act of deceiving ; trickery ; jugglery ; a fraudulent act :　กูฏการ false testimony ; a fraud ; a cheat :　กูฏดาบส a make-believe ascetic ; an hermit who plans fraud or deceit: กูฏธรรม a country where there is injustice in public affairs; a country where falsehood is considered a duty: กูฏบาศ, กูฏพันธ์ tricks to deceive; traps laid deceitfully; a trap: กูฏมาน a false measure or an incorrect weight: กูฏยนตร์ a steel trap or cage for trapping animals or birds; a trap; a snare.

กูฏาคาร gkoo-dtah-kan *P. S. n.* an upper room; a room off a balcony; a roof-garden; a pergola; an arbour; an apartment on the roof of a house; a pent-house (S. E. D. p. 299).

กูโฏบาย gkoo-dto-bai *P. S. n.* a trick; a sleight-of-hand performance; a puzzle; a sly procedure with dishonest intent; an illusion; fraud; deceit; stratagem (S. E. D. p. 299).

กูณฑ์ see กุณฑ์

กูด, โหรา (ผัก) gkoot[4] *n. Diplazium esculentum (Polypodiaceae)*, a common, somewhat tufted fern, generally about 3 ft. high (BURK. p. 835).

กูน gkoon *Cam. n.* a son or descendant; a child.

กูบ gkoop[4] *n.* an howdah; the hood of a victoria or phaeton: กูบช้าง a covered seat on an elephant; a saddle for elephants: รถกูบ *lit.* "a carriage with a hood," *i. e.* a phaeton: หลังกูบ curvature of the back; an hunchback.

กูมูย (ต้น) gkoo-moo-ay *n. Carallia brachiata (Legnotidaceae)* (cb. p. 599), a small spreading tree about 7 m. high, found in scrub jungle by streams and cultivated in temple grounds (K.). It is reported that this tree grows to a height of 80 ft. in Burma, with a girth of 6 or 7 ft. The wood is very handsome, having a silver grain (BURK. p. 448).

กูรบร see กโบร

กูรมะ gkoo-ra[6]-ma[6] *n. P. S.* a tortoise; a turtle; the earth (figuratively) considered as a tortoise swimming in the water (S. E. D. p.

300): กูรมปุราณะ a treatise descriptive of the tortoise incarnation of Vishnu, being the fifteenth volume of a set of eighteen: กูรมราช the king of the turtles (the mythological being that supports the world): กูรมาวตาร the tortoise incarnation of Vishnu, being his second incarnation when he descended in the form of a tortoise to support the mountain Mandara at the churning of the ocean (S. E. D. p. 300).

กูล gkoon *P. S. n.* a declivity; a slope; a shore; the bank of a river or shore of the sea; a heap; a mound; an hillock; a tope (S. E. D. p. 300).

กูลา (ต้น) gkoo-lah *n. Hydnocarpus castanea (Bixaceae)* (cb. p. 96: Burk. p. 1208), a tree about 20 m. high, found in evergreen forest on banks of streams. The flowers are white (K.).

กูวาชา (ต้น) gkoo-wah-sah *n. Rubus ellipticus (Rosaceae)* (cb. p. 570), a tall sub-erect bush. The fruit is yellow and has the flavour of raspberry. It is either eaten raw or made into a preserve. It is one of the best wild fruits of India. The wood is moderately hard, light brown and with very broad medullary rays (Dept. Agri. & Fisheries).

กูวิ (ต้น) gkoo-wi[6] *n. Dipterocarpus costatus (Dipterocarpaceae)* (cb. p. 134), a tree about 20 to 25 m. high, found in mixed oak jungle by streams. The flowers (picked up off the ground) are pink (K.). It contains a rather large amount of wood-oil and is a common source for this in Cambodia (BURK. p. 842).

เก gkay *adj.* distorted; twisted; crippled; lame; leaning; slanting: เกเรเกส valueless; worthless; being of a low class; being a vagabond; a scoundrel: โกเก impudent; saucy; insolent; disrespectful: ฟันเก irregular teeth: มือเก having a crippled, deformed hand.

เก่ gkay[4] *adj.* becoming; proper; fit; suitable (to a standard of duty, propriety or taste): ไม่เป็นเก่ unbecoming.

เก๊ gkay[6] *Chin. adj.* not genuine; false; fake: เงินเก๊ counterfeit money.

เก๋ gkay[2] *adj.* gay; smartly dressed; of fine appearance; showy (because of many colours).

เกก gkek[4] *adj.* bent abnormally; bent out of normal shape (as buffalo horns); curved; perverted; slanting: ควายเขาเกก a buffalo with bent or slanting horns: คนเกก, คนโกกเกก a rogue; a blackguard; a trifler; a deceitful, molesting person.

เก๊ก gkek[6] *Chin. v.* to discard; to throw away (as useless); to reject; to discharge with dishonour (as a servant or employé); to dismiss summarily.

เกกมะเหรก, เกเร gkek[4]-ma[6]-rek[4] *adj.* vain; proud; conceited; insolent or arrogant in manner; worthless; useless; good-for-nothing.

เก๋กัง gkey[3]-gkang *adj.* staggering; reeling; unsteady (as if drunk); having improper manners.

เกงเขง (ต้น) gkeng-keng[2] *n. Hibiscus sabdariffa (Malvaceae)* (V. P. p. 26), "Jamaica or red sorrel," the roselle, an annual shrub with reddish stems, leaves and fruits, cultivated in most warm countries for the sake of its large fleshy sepals which, remaining after the flowers fall away, become enlarged and succulent (accrescent), enclosing the fruit capsule. These make excellent jelly; unripe fruits are adapted for pickles and refreshing beverages. The leaves are used as a vegetable in curries (MCM. pp. 264, 311, 430). The stems yield a good, strong, silky fibre, known as the roselle hemp of commerce. The seeds of the roselle are used medicinally and have demulcent, diuretic and tonic properties (Dept. Apri. & Fisheries: Burk. p. 1170).

เก็ง gkeng *v.* to estimate (as to weight);

to approximate (as to price); to fix on as being a probable, proper amount or weight.

เก่ง gkeng[4] *adj.* bold; fearless; skillful; courageous; daring (used in a derogatory sense): เก่งกาจ ferocious; fierce: ขะโมยเก่ง given to stealing; being rather "light-fingered."

เก๋ง gkeng[2] *n.* the roof of the living quarters on a boat; the hood of a car or carriage; a small house (of Chinese pattern) built of boards on a boat or waggon: เก๋งพั้ง living-quarters; the upper deck; the state-room section of a ship: รถเก๋ง a gharry or covered carriage; a saloon, sedan or coupé car: เรือเก๋ง a boat with roof and sided living-quarters.

เก้งก้าง gkeng[3]-gkang[3] *adj.* awkward; ungainly; bungling; clumsy; uncouth (descriptive of manners).

เก็จ gket[4] *n.* coloured, ornamental glass; crystals (for decorations).

เกจิ gkey-chji[4] *P. adj.* belonging to one class or company; belonging to some troupe; homogeneous; some (people) (S. E. D.): เกจิอาจารย์ the teacher or instructor of a group of people, class or company.

เกณฑ์ gken *P. v.* to compel; to force; to command; to demand; to conscript for labour; to take for service (by lot): *n.* a levy; conscription for labour (without adequate pay); corvée; selected conscription: เกณฑ์ทัพ conscription for army service: เกณฑ์ฝน the rainy season recurring at definite periods or intervals of time: เกณฑ์เมืองรั้ง the rank of an acting governor of a district: เกณฑ์แห่ to conscript men or help for a procession: หมายเกณฑ์ a notice of conscription.

เกด (ต้น) gket[4] *n. Mimusops hexandra (Sapotaceae)* (V. P. p. 26), palu, a moderate-sized, hard-wooded, slow-growing timber, used for sleepers, etc. The bark is an astringent, and is recommended for tanning. It is commonly used for retarding fermentation in making toddy (MCM. pp. 219, 220, 443). This tree flowers in November and December and produces an olive-shaped, yellow berry, which is eaten. The wood is used for sugar-mills, beams, oil-presses, house-posts, etc. (Dept. Agri. & Fisheries).

เกิ๊ด (ต้น) gket[4] *n. Dalbergia ougeinensis* (*Leguminosae*) (V. P. p. 26), a moderate-sized, deciduous tree, yielding an astringent red gum. The bark, when incised, furnishes a kino-like exudation which is used in cases of dysentery and diarrhoea. A decoction of the bark is given among the hill-tribes, when the urine is highly coloured. The leaves are used as fodder for cattle. The wood is used for agricultural implements, carriage poles, wheels, furniture and building purposes (Dept. Agri. & Fisheries).

เกิ๊ดขาว (ต้น) gket[4]-kow[2] *n. Dalbergia kerrii* (*Leguminosae*) (V. P. p. 27), a tree about 12 m. high, found in scrub jungle. The flowers are purplish-green (K.).

เกิ๊ดดำ, กำพี้ (ต้น) gket[4]-dum *n. Dalbergia cultrata* (*Leguminosae*) (V. P. p. 27: cb. p. 476), a moderate-sized tree, exuding red resin. The plant is used for the propagation of lac. It yields a useful oil; the wood is employed for wheels, agricultural implements, handles of dahs and spears, but is especially suitable for carving (Dept. Agri. & Fisheries); *D. fusca* (*Leguminosae*) (cb. p. 479), a tree about 12 m. high, found in scrub jungle. The flowers are white (K.).

เกิ๊ดแดง (ต้น) gket[4]-dang *n. Dalbergia oliveri* (*Leguminosae*) (V. P. p. 27), a tree about 20 m. high, found in bamboo forest (K.); *D. dongnaiensis* (cb. p. 477), a small tree about 7 to 8 m. high, found in mixed deciduous jungle (K.).

เกิ๊ดซ่าน (ต้น) gket[4]-san[3] *n. Olea maritima* (*Oleaceae*) (V. P. p. 27), a genus of small, spreading trees with fragrant flowers (K.). This shrub or tree resembles the ilex. It seems to have no value (Burk. p. 1580).

เกิ๊ดลิ่น, เกล็ดปลาช่อน (ต้น) gket[4]-lin *n. Desmodium pulchellum* (*Leguminosae*) (cb. p. 415: V. P. 27), a shrub 3 to 6 feet high, met with in the eastern Himalayas and throughout India, Burma, Ceylon, etc. It has some medicinal value. Cattle eat it (Dept. Agri. & Fisheries: Burk. p. 794).

เกตกี่ (ต้น) gket[4] *P. S. n. Pandanus odoratissimus* (*Pandanaceae*), a forest tree bearing small, sweet fruit (S. E. D. p. 308).

เกตุ gket[4] *P.S. n.* brightness; clearness; rays of light; a lamp; a flame; a torch; daytime; an apparition; a form; a shape; a sign; an ensign; a mark; a flag; a banner; a leader; an eminent person; judgement; discernment; any unusual or striking heavenly phenomenon; a comet; a meteor; a falling star; the dragon's tail or the descending node (considered in astronomy as the ninth planet and in mythology as the body of a demon which was severed from the head of Rahu by Vishnu at the churning of the ocean, but was rendered immortal by having tasted of the elixir of life) (S. E. D. p. 309): เกตุเคราะห์ the descending node; the ninth planet or the dragon Rahu: เกตุดารา a comet: เกตุก a cloud: เกตุมาลา the radiancy, glory or brightness emanating from the head of the Buddha; one of the nine great divisions of the known world (the western portion of the Jambudvipa (ชมพูทวีป): เกตุรัตน์ *lit.* "the favorite gem of Rahu," *i. e.* the beryl stone (a hard green or reddish-green stone similar to the emerald, except in colour).

เกทาร gkay-tan *P. S. n.* a field; a meadow (especially one under water); a basin for water around the root of a tree; a bed in a garden or field (S. E. D. p. 309): เกทารขัณฑ์ a small dyke or ridge of earth raised between rice fields to keep the water either in or out: เกทารนาถ an appellation for Siva: เกทารเสตุ the earth placed or used to make a ridge or dike around a paddy field.

เกน gken *Jav. adj.* continuous (weeping); continued (sorrow); full (of grief).

เกนๆ gken-gken *v. adv.* repeatedy; continuously; often (used in reference to calling or talking).

เกนิบาต gkay-ni[6]-bat[4] *P. S. n.* the helm; the rudder of a boat; a large oar used as a rudder (as by the Chinese in their small boats) (S. E. D. p. 304).

เก็บ gkep[4] *v.* to keep; to collect; to preserve; to put away; to take care of; to pick up (as shells): เก็บกอง to collect into a pile: เก็บไว้ to keep safely: เก็บรวมไว้ to collect sundry articles into one place: เก็บเล็กประสมน้อย to pick up fragment by fragment; to save (money) little by little เก็บสระสมไว้ to collect and add to continually: เก็บหอมรอมริบไว้ *colloq.* to collect and keep sundry belongings carefully: เก็บเอาไป to pick up and carry away.

เกย gkur-ay *v.* to run aground (as a ship on a rock): *n.* a footstool; a stepladder; a platform for royalty to use in mounting a palanquin or elephant: เกยเกาะ to run aground on an island: เกยแก่ง to run aground on rocks in rapids: เกยชลา a portico; an interior gallery (speaking of a palace): เกยม้า a platform for mounting horses; a carriage block: เกยมาศ a raised platform which the king uses for mounting an elephant: เกยรถ a mounting platform from which to enter cars: เกยเรือ to draw a boat up on to the bank: เกยลา a small or low mounting platform: เกยเลย to pass beyond; to exceed beyond measure: เกยแห้ง to be raised high and dry out of the water: แม่เกย a table of final diphthongs.

เกยูร gkay-yoon *P. S. n.* a bracelet; a necklace; a bracelet worn on the upper arm; a delicately-made chain (S. E. D. p. 309).

เกรง gkreng *v.* to fear; to respect; to revere: *adj.* respectful; fitted to awaken esteem:

เกรงกลัว to reverence: เกรงขาม, ยำเกรง to respect with fear: เกรงใจ to fear to approach; to have respectful fear: ไม่เกรงใจ want of respect; impudent.

เกร็ง gkreng *adj.* hardened by contraction (as of muscles during cramps); strong; tense.

เกร็ด gkret[4] *n.* a detached portion; fragments; materials gathered at random; a narrow stretch of water between two large bodies of water; a channel: เกร็ดเกร่ to wander aimlessly about; to roam; to ramble; to straggle about: เกร็ดพงศาวดาร fragmentary historical materials: ตำรายาเกร็ด fragmentary medical prescriptions or treatises.

เกร้อ gkrur[4] *adj.* sufficient; ample; much; plenty.

เกรอะ gkrur[4] *v.* to filter; to strain; to evaporate the watery portions: *n.* refuse; trash; sediment: *adj.* dirty; foul; filthy: เกรอะกรัง sticking tightly to; united firmly with or to; matted into a lump.

เกราฏิยบักษ์ gkay-rah-dti[4]-ya[6]-bpak[4] *P.S. n.* a condition of duplicity of heart or speech; deceit; guile; deception: คนนกสองหัว a common simile expressing deceit, double-dealings or hypocrisy, *e. g.* one is compared to a "two-headed bird" or to a "double-faced person".

เกราะ gkrau[4] *n.* a cuirass; a metal breast-plate; a defensive covering for the body or for ships; armour; a bamboo, struck from time to time as a signal: *adj.* dry; brittle (as dry tamarind pods): เกราะกรอง to leave a sediment after filtering: เกราะแกระ the sound made when a signal is given by striking a slit bamboo: เกราะนาม a padded or cushioned cuirass: ตีเกราะ to strike a slit bamboo as a signal: เสื้อเกราะ a cuirass: แห้งเกราะ dry and crisp.

เกริก gkrerk[4] *adj.* loud; noisy; boisterous; having or making a loud sound (as firing of cannon).

เกริ่น   gkrern *n.* a lift; a mechanical means of raising a weight; an elevator operated by means of a windlass (as that used in raising or lowering an urn from a State funeral carriage during a royal cremation).

เกริ่น   gkern[4] *v.* to warn by a call; to make aware by a call (of probable danger or evil); to notify or signal by a call (as forest men signalling to each other): เกริ่นกราบ to call; to call from afar: เกริ่นกัน to call or warn one another from afar.

เกรียก   gkree-ak[4] *v.* to divide lengthwise; to separate into parts or pieces; to split up into thin strips (as bamboo or rattan for binding purposes): *n.* the distance between the tip of the thumb and forefinger, when spread out.

เกรียง   gkree-ang *n.* a mason's trowel, made of iron or wood: *adj.* large; abundant; plentiful: เกรียงไกร superior; excellent; powerful: ฤทธิเกรียงไกร very powerful.

เกรียน   gkree-an *adj.* worn by friction (as a table-knife); short (as grass on a lawn): เกรียนโกร๋น bare (as trees during the fall of the year); bald: เกรียนไป to become short; to be worn short: ขนเกรียน short feathers.

เกรียน (ต้น)   gkree-an *n. Melia toosendan* (*Meliaceae*) (V. P. p. 30), a tree about 10 m. high, found in mixed deciduous forest along the banks of the Meh Ping (K.).

เกรียบ   gkree-ap[4] *n.* a form of tin; tin in plates: *adj.* brittle; crisp: เกรียบกรอบ *onomat.* from walking on dry, crisp sand or leaves: เกรียบเกรียม dry (as when scorched or cooked too dry): ข้าวเกรียบ glutinous rice-batter made into round, thin, flat sheets. These are held over the fire until they become crisp: เข้าเกรียบปากหม้อ a sweetmeat.

เกรียม   gkree-am *adj.* parched; shrivelled with heat; dry (as the lips in fever); almost burnt (as in cooking meat or rice); scorched: ดำเกรียม carbonized: ไหม้เกรียม over-done; half-burnt.

เกรียมกรม, กรมเกรียม   gkree-am-gkrom *v.* to be sorrowful; to be depressed; to be despondent.

เกรียว, เกรียวกราว   gkre-oh *onomat.* from the noise, tumult or riotous anger of a crowd of people yelling simultaneously.

เกรียวกราด, กราดเกรียว   gkre-oh[3]-gkrat[4] *adj.* angered; shouting angrily; fierce; strict (in discipline): เกรียวโกรธ to be exceedingly angry.

เกเร   gkay-ray *adj.* worthless; useless; undeserving; good-for-nothing; behaving in a rough manner: เที่ยวเกเร wandering aimlessly about looking for, or causing trouble (as during a fair or festival).

เกล็ด   gklet[4] *v.* to strip or to peal off the covering (as a bird cleans off the husks from grains of paddy before eating the kernel): *n.* scales; scabs; pellicles: เกล็ดกระดี่ a form of blepheritis occurring commonly along the eyelids of children: เกล็ดนาค a decorative pattern for flat surfaces, in which circular lines resembling the scales of a fish, lie superimposed on one another: เกล็ดปลา fish scales: เกล็ดปลา (ต้น) *Desmodium triflorum* (*Leguminosae*) (Cb. p. 420), a very small, creeping, perennial herb, having small, trifoliate leaves and bright purple flowers. Sometimes it forms a close cover on dry rocky soil. It is common in turf as a drought-resistant and is an important constituent of pastures, but it yields very little fodder (MCM. pp. 26, 71, 209, 452: Burk. p. 795). The fresh leaves are applied to wounds and abscesses that do not heal well (Dept. Agri. & Fisheries): เกล็ดฝาเพี้ยม louver-boards; thin, fixed slats on the lower part of a window: ขอดเกล็ด, ขูดเกล็ด to remove the scales of a fish: ปากเกล็ด the openings of a short-cut canal across the bend of a river; the name of a town in the district of Nondaburi: หนูเกล็ดข้าว the rats have gnawed the rice.

เกลศ   see กิเลส

เกลอ   gklur *n.* a friend; a comrade; an intimate associate: ชาวเกลอ friends; comrades; associates: เป็นเกลอกัน being friends, associates or comrades to fraternize or hold fellowship together: สามเกลอ a timber fitted with two or more handles (used by Chinese as a mallet to drive down foundation piles or as a pile driver).

เกลา   gklow *v.* to trim roughly into shape (as a stalk of bamboo); to smooth off the roughness with a knife or plane; to smooth; to polish: *adj.* smooth; polished: เกลา-เกลี้ยง to trim till entirely smooth; to cut off all thorns, limbs or branches.

เกล้า   gklow[3] *v.* to twist; to gather the hair up into a knot: *n.* the head: ก้มเกล้า to bend the head; to salute: ก้มเกล้าแก่ to salute by bending the head: เกล้ากระผม, เกล้าผม the first personal pronoun, I (used in speaking to high officials): เกล้ากระหม่อม the first personal pronoun, I (used in speaking to princes): เกล้าจุก to twist or dress the topknot into shape: เกล้าผม to comb and arrange the hair: เกล้ามวย to dress a tuft of hair: กวดเกล้า to twist one's hair with force: โปรดเกล้า ฯ the form used to express the wish or intention of a prince, *lit.* "he has mercy or extends pardon"; part of a complimentary closing to a letter: รัดเกล้า a head-band; a decoration for the head; fillets or curved mouldings at the top of a column or around the lid of a box: เศียรเกล้า the head.

เกลาส see ไกลาส

เกลี่ย   gklee-ah[4] *v.* to level down; to spread out evenly; to flatten out; to make even; to equalize: เกลี่ยไกล่ to smooth out; to arrange for a settlement; to make peace; to reconcile in a quarrel; to come to an agreement or amicable settlement (as between two parties).

เกลี้ยกล่อม   gklee-ah[3]-gklaum[4] *v.* to persuade; to induce; to make an amicable set-tlement; to adjust differences or misunderstandings by persuasion; to allure; to give in (because of promises).

เกลียง   gklee-ang *n.* a kind of grass.

เกลี้ยง   gklee-ang[3] *adj.* smooth; level; not ruffled; having no remnants left: กล่อมเกลี้ยง to give good attention to; to nurture carefully (as bringing up and taking care of children): เกลี้ยงกลม round and well-polished; pleasing to the touch; soft: เกลี้ยงเกลา quite level; quite smooth; clean: เกลี้ยง (ส้ม) a species of smooth-skinned orange, *Citrus aurantium* (*Rutaceae*) (V. P. p. 263: BURK. p. 566); *C. sinensis*; *C. grandis* (MCM. p. 236).

เกลียด, กระเลียด   gklee-at[4] *v.* to detest; to hate; to abhor; to loathe; to dislike: เกลียดชัง to abominate: เกลียดน้ำหน้า to detest the conduct or manners of: น่าเกลียด distasteful; hateful; repulsive.

เกลียว   gklee-oh *v.* to entwine; to twist together: *n.* a thread (like a screw-thread); a spiral thread; the strands of a rope: เกลียวกลม, กลมเกลียว harmonious; without dissatisfaction; living peacefully (as a family): เกลียวข้าง the strong muscles along the sides of the body: เกลียวหลัง the strong prominent muscles of the back: เข้าเกลียว strands twisted into a cable: เชือกสามเกลียว a rope composed of three strands: ตีเกลียว to organize associates into a league; to twist strings or strands into a rope.

เกลียวดำ, เปลียวดำ   gklee-oh-dum *n.* an affection or illness due to extreme cold; chilblains.

เกลือ   gklur-ah *n.* a basic salt; sodium chloride or table salt: เกลือกะตัง uric acid salts: เกลือจืด a kind of salt for making face-powder: เกลือด่าง an alkaline salt: เกลือด่างคลี a salt used in Siamese medicine: เกลือทะเล sea-salts: เกลือฟอง an effervescing salt : เกลือสินเธาว์ a form of medicinal salt found in salt-licks : นาเกลือ salt-fields : ดีเกลือ magnesium sulphate (epsom salts).

เกลอ gklur-ah[3] *v.* to mix ; to blend together ; to mingle.

เกลอก gklur-uk[4] *v.* to roll over (as a horse) ; to wallow (as a buffalo) ; to rub against ; to roll back and forth (as an infant) : เกลือกกลั้วเกสร to roll on or crawl over the petals of flowers (as bees) : เกลือกกลิ้ง to tumble about ; to roll ; to be rolled ; to roll one's self back and forth : เกลือกว่า if perchance ; suppose that ; perhaps ; if by any chance ; lest by any hazard ; peradventure.

เกลื่อน gkleu-an[4] *v.* to dissipate (as an abscess) ; to spread ; to be scattered ; to cause to become diffused (as at a focus of local inflammation) : *adj.* dispersed ; dispelled ; scattered, crushed or subdued : เกลื่อนกลบ to placate ; to pacify ; to appease ; to allay : มีอยู่เกลื่อนไป to have plenty scattered about.

เกลื้อน gkleu-an[3] *n.* a form of skin disease producing white or yellowish brown spots or patches and attended with itching (chloasma).

เกวล, เกวัล gkay-wa[6]-la[6] *P. S. adv.* only ; merely ; solely ; entirely ; wholly ; absolutely : *adj.* not common to others ; excluding others ; unconnected with anything else ; entire ; isolated ; uncompounded ; unmingled (S. E. D. p. 309) : เกวลทรัพย์ the entire amount of one's wealth ; only or merely one's substance : เกวลาที eating by one's self ; one who eats alone.

เกวลัศะ gkay-wa[6]-lat[6]-sa[4] *adj.* entire ; every.

เกวลี, เกวลิน gkay-wa[6]-lee *P. S. n.* one who has completed or finished his education ; the whole of a philosophical system ; the doctrine of the absolute unity of the spirit ; the highest possible degree of knowledge (S. E. D. p. 310).

เกวัฏ, ไกวรรต gkay-wat[6] *P. n.* a fisherman.

เกวียน gkwee-an *n.* a bullock cart ; a cartload (of paddy) ; a coyan ; a capacity measure for paddy equal to 16 piculs, for cargo rice 22 piculs, for white rice 23 piculs. The rice miller's coyan is 82 buckets of 40 lbs. each : เกวียนหลวง a standard coyan equals 2 kilolitres ; a standard picul equals 60 kilograms (Department of Commercial Registration) : เกวียนระแทะ a small-sized cart.

เกศ, เกศา, เกศี, เกส, เกสา, เกสี gket[4] *P. S. n.* hair of the head ; a lock of hair on the crown of the head ; straggling hairs along the neck ; manes of horses or lions ; names for the god of Waters, *viz.* Neptune, Vishnu (S. E. D. p. 310) : เกศกรรม the act of dressing, arranging or decorating the hair : เกศกลาป a mass or quantity of hair ; a head of hair : เกศประสาร, เกศรานา a shampoo ; a washing or cleaning of the hair : เกศปักษ์ edge of the hair ; a tuft of hair : เกศภู *lit.* "a lawn or ground for the hair," *i. e.* the scalp ; the head : เกศมณฑล, เกศเวษ a tuft of hair ; a lock or tress of hair : เกศราช the act of dyeing or colouring the hair : เกศากันต์ the tonsorial ceremony ; the act or ceremony of cutting the topknot (used only for the rank of Mom Chao).

เกศา see เกศ

เกศี see เกศ

เกศพ see เกศว

เกศร see เกสร

เกศริน, เกศรี gkay-sa[4]-rin *P. S. n. lit.* "that having a necklace of hair," *i. e.* a horse ; a lion.

เกศว, เกศพ, เกสว gkay-sa[4]-wa[6] *S. n.* one having much long or beautiful hair ; names for Krishna or Vishnu (S. E. D. p. 310) : เกศวภักดี one loyal or devoted to Krishna : เกศวาวุธ *lit.* "Krishna's weapon," *i. e.* the mango tree : เกศวาลัย *lit.* "Krishna's abode," *i. e.* the holy fig tree.

เกศินี   gkay-si⁴-nee *n. lit.* "one with beautiful hair," *i.e.* wife of Visravas and mother of Ravana (H. C. D. p. 150).

เกษตร   gka⁴-set⁴ *S. n.* landed property; land; soil; a field; a place; a region; a country; a house; a town; a department or sphere of action; a sacred spot or district; a place of pilgrimage; "fertile soil," *i.e.* the fertile womb; a wife; the body (considered as the field of the indwelling soul (S. E. D. p. 332): เกษตรกร agriculture; farming pursuits; cultivating a field: เกษตรคณิต *lit.* "calculating planes for figures," *i.e.* geometry; a diagram: เกษตรบดี a farmer; the owner of farming land; a landowner; a landlord: เกษตรภูมิ land that has been ploughed and sown with seed; cultivated land: เกษตรลิปดา a minute or degree of the ecliptic: เกษตรสีมา a boundary; the limit or confines of a field, farm or of an holy place.

เกษม   gka⁴-sem² *n. P. S.* the state of being free from foes or enemies; happiness; bliss; completeness; prosperity; any secure, easy, comfortable state; the act of enjoying and acquiring (S. E. D. p. 332): *adj.* habitable; secure; affording rest and ease; being at ease; prosperous; peaceful; tranquil: เกษมกาม *lit.* "longing for rest," *i.e.* having a desire to be in a state of freedom from the worries of foes or plagues of enemies: เกษมโยค *lit.* "rest and exertion," *i.e.* the condition of being industrious and still being able to take rest: เกษมสันต์, เกษมสานต์ enjoying a state of felicity and bliss: เกษมสูร *lit.* "a hero in a safe place," *i.e.* a boaster; a braggart.

เกษียณ see กษีณ

เกษียน   gka⁴-see-an² *v.* to write or to inscribe (as by a stylus or any other instrument): *n.* additions made or additional matter inserted (as on palm-leaf books): *adj.* little; small; insignificant; trifling.

เกษียร   gka⁴-see-an² *P. S. n.* milk; thickened milk; the milky juice or sap of plants (S. E. D. p. 329).

เกษียรเนียร, กษีรนีร   gka⁴-see-an²-nee-an *P. S. n.* milk and water mixed; a condition of union (as milk and water mixed); a figure of speech implying the act of embracing.

เกส, เกสา, เกส์ see เกศ

เกสร, เกศร   gkay-saun² *n.* the eyebrow; fibres (as in the meat of a mango): manes (as of horses or lions); a necklace; the pollen of a lotus or of any vegetable; the tail of the yak, *Bos grunniens*, which furnishes the chowries or fly-flappers used in India (S. E. D. p. 310): เกสรวร saffron: เกสราธิคุณ the name of a Siamese blood-tonic.

เกสริน, เกสรี   gkay-sa⁴-rin *P. S. n. lit.* "one having a decoration for the neck," *i.e.* a lion or horse (as they have manes); name of the monkey Kesarin, husband of Anjana, the mother of Hanuman (H. C. D. p. 116): เกสรีสุต *lit.* "child of Kesarin," *i.e.* Hanuman, the great monkey warrior.

เกสว see เกศว

เกอ   gkur³ *adj.* abashed; bewildered; confused; over-awed; frustrated or disappointed in one's hopes.

เกะกะ   gke⁴-gka⁴ *adj.* being always in the way (as children); disorderly; rowdy (as roughs during any public occasion); seeking to annoy: คนเกะกะ a marplot; a meddler.

เกา   gkow *v.* to scratch; to drag along (as an anchor when it does not hold); to scrape with the nails or claws (as a cat or tiger): เกายุงกัด to scratch the bite of a mosquito: เกาหลัง to scratch the back: สมอเกา the anchor is dragging.

เก่า   gkow⁴ *adj.* old; ancient: เก่าคร่ำคร่า worn and defaced with usage and age: ของเก่า antique; antiquated: ของเก่าแก่ antiquities: ดังเก่า as formerly; as before.

เก้า gkow[3] *n.* the numeral nine : เก้าสิบ ninety : ที่เก้า ninth : ที่เก้าสิบ ninetieth : สิบเก้า nineteen.

เก้า (นก) gkow[3] *n.* the western Himalayan barred owlet, *Glaucidium cuculoides cuculoides* (Deig. N. H. J. S. S. VIII, 3, p. 164).

เกาณฑินย see โกณฑัญญะ

เกาตูหล see โกตูหล

เกาทัณฑ์, กุทัณฑ์, โกทัณฑ์ gkow-tan *P.S.* *n.* a bow ; a crossbow or war-bow (as used in ancient warfare) ; an eyebrow (from being shaped like a bow) (S. E. D. p. 313) : ลูก-เกาทัณฑ์ arrows for a crossbow.

เกาบิน gkow-bin *P. n.* pudenda ; a loin-cloth to cover the genitals.

เกรว see โกรพ

เกาลัด gkow-lat[6] *n. Castanea chinensis* (*Cupuliferae*), the Chinese chestnut (MCM. p. [275].

เกาศล see กุศล

เกาศัลย์ gkow-san[2] *S. n.* prosperity ; happiness ; welfare ; contentedness ; friendly inquiry ; a salutation : *adj.* dexterous ; adroit ; skillful ; experienced (S. E. D. p. 318).

เกาสามพี, โกสัม, โกสัมพี, วัสตบัต์ตนะ gkow-sam[2]-pee *S. n.* the name of an ancient capital of Vatsa, India, which is situated at the junction of the Ganges and the Jumna rivers. Kausambi is about thirty miles above Allahabad, and is said to be the scene of the drama Ratanavali (H. C. D. p. 155).

เกาไศย, โกไสย gkow-sai[2] *P. S. n.* cloth shot through with threads of silk ; silk cloth ; sheds, houses, articles or utensils made of lalang grass (*Imperata* spp.) or หญ้าคา (S. E. D. p. 317).

เกาสัลย์, โกสลุ gkow-san[2] *P. S. adj.* belonging to the inhabitants of Kosala (โกสล,) an ancient province of India (S. E. D. p. 318).

เกาสัลยา, เกาสุริยา gkow-san[2]-yah *S. n.* *lit.* "a daughter of the king of Kosala" (เจ้าโกสล). There are several women known by this name, *viz.* wife of Puru (ท้าวปุรุ) and mother of Janamejaya (ชนเมชัย) ; the mother of Dhrita-rashtra (ท้าวธฤตราราษฎร์) ; the wife of Dasa-ratha (ท้าวทศรถ) ; the mother of Rama-candra (พระรามจันทร์) *etc.* (S. E. D. p. 318).

เกาหลี gkow-lee[2] *Chin. n.* Korea.

เกาเหลา gkow-low[2] *Chin. n.* a Chinese soup or mild curry.

เกาเหลียง gkow-lee-ang[2] *Chin. n.* a strong liquor distilled from fermented sorghum grain.

เก้าอี้ gkow[3]-ee[3] *Chin. Teh. n.* a chair : เก้าอี้นวม an upholstered chair : เก้าอี้นอน a sofa : เก้าอี้โยก a rocking chair : เก้าอี้ ๔ คนหาม a sedan chair : เก้าอี้หมุน a revolving chair : เก้าอี้เอน a reclining chair ; an easy chair.

เกาะ gkau[4] *v.* to summon ; to subpoena ; to lay hold of (as of a runaway) ; to bring under arrest : *n.* an island : เกาะเกียน islands (in general) : เกาะลังกา the island of Ceylon or its capital city (H. C. D. p. 177) : เกาะหมาก an old name for the island of Penang : ปลิงเกาะ a leech is sticking there : มีนกเกาะ a bird is perching there : หัวเกาะ the out-jutting point or strategic point of an island.

เกาะสะเดียง (ต้น) gkau[4]-sa[4]-dtee-ang *n.* *Dipterocarpus obtusifolius* (*Dipterocarpaceae*) (cb. p. 137), a large, deciduous tree, commonly found forming small patches in the forests. It affords a clear, white or yellow resin, not an oil (Dept. Agri. & Fisheries : Burk. p. 838).

เกิด gkert[4] *v.* to be born ; to arise ; to originate (as trouble) ; to occur ; to be the cause of ; to have an origin : เกิดความ, เกิดเรื่อง, เกิดเหตุ to cause trouble ; to have some disturbance occur : เกิดผล to be productive ; to produce (as fruit) ; to bring forth :

เกิดหึงหวง to be jealous of; to arouse jealousy : วันเกิด, วันชาตะ, แซยิด *Chin.* a birthday : เกิด อดอาหาร to have a condition of famine arise.

เกิน gkern *v.* to give too much; to have some left over; to go beyond; to over-step or over-reach : *adv.* too much; too far; beyond; too far over; excessive : เกินการ more than is necessary; more than is proper : เกินกิน an over-abundance of eatables : เกิน-ขนาด an overdose (as of medicine) : เกินตัว over or beyond one's position, power, strength or ability; arrogant; overconfident; presumptuous; forward : เกินอำนาจ outside the scope of authority; beyond the jurisdiction of : เกินเลย beyond what is becoming or suitable (descriptive of conduct) : เหลือเกิน beyond what is seemly, befitting or appropriate (as a punishment).

เกียกกาย gkee-ak[4]-gkai *n.* the commissary department; the commissariat of an army : หัวหน้ากองสะเบียง the one in charge of the commissary department.

เกียง gkee-ang[4] *v.* to disagree; to be at variance with; to differ in opinion : เกียง-งอน to act unwillingly; to be unwilling; to act reluctantly : เกียงเลี่ยง, เอารัดเอาเปรียบ *colloq.* to dispute about something with the purpose of gaining more than is proper.

เกียง, มะเกียง (ต้น) gkee-ang[2] *n. Eugenia paniala (Myrtaceae)* (cb. p. 656), a large cultivated tree, having white flowers and black, edible fruit (K).

เกียจ, เกียจคร้าน gkee-at[4] *adj.* lazy; idle; indolent; inactive; unfaithful to duty : เกียจกล to deceive by a trick; to cheat by trickery; to be disloyal or unfaithful : เกียจกัน to hide from; to keep some back; to keep back the best; to outwit the opponent (as in a game).

เกียด gkee-at[4] *n.* the center pole of a threshing floor, to which the cattle are tied when treading rice grains off the rice stalks.

เกียรติ gkee-at[4]-dti[4] *P. S. n.* act of preaching or proclaiming; fame; renown; report; glory (S. E. D. p. 285): เกียรติยศ honour; dignity; fame; renown; esteem; veneration; respect; consideration : เกียรติสุกา a cousin of Sita and the wife of Sata-rutna (พระศัตรุฆน์) (H. C. D. p. 305): ถือเกียรติยศ to maintain one's rank; to uphold one's dignity : มี เกียรติยศ to be honoured; to be respected : เสียเกียรติยศ to lose dignity or respect (as by bad conduct, some misdeed or blunder):

เกียว gkee-oh[4] *v.* to hook up; to connect or couple up (as two cars); to cut; to reap (as rice); to gird; to enfold; to enclose : เกียวกระหวัด to hug : เกียวกอด to embrace : เกียวกัน in confusion; entangled; embarrassed : เกียวข้อง to be intimate with; to have business relations with or interest in : เกียวข้าว to harvest the rice : เกียวดอง associates; allies; partners; relationship; relatives (on either side of the family): เกียวเนื่อง to be related to : เกียวไว้ to hang on to; to attach to : เกียวหญ้า to cut grass with a sickle : ไม่เกียวข้อง to be a non-partizan.

เกียว ๑ gkee-oh[3] *Chin. n.* an enclosed carriage (used in the East); a Chinese palanquin.

เกียว ๒ gkee-oh[3] *v.* to bind around; to encircle; to entice; to allure; to court; to flirt with or try to seduce : *n.* an ornament of gold worn around the topknot : เกียวกัน to become entangled; to be embarrassed by advances from a man : เกียวคอไก่ to give the fastening knot of the loin-cloth an extra twist : เกียวผู้หญิง to seduce; to entice a girl or woman : เกียวพาราสี to tempt by offers; to entice or try to draw away from the path of virtue : เกียวเสียว a winding path; a crooked way; a liar : ผ้าเกียว a fine cloth decorated with flowers : ผ้าเกียวพุง an embroidered girdle : ผ้าเกียวลาย a panung of good quality.

เกียว gkee-oh[6] *Chin. n.* a Chinese soup made from wheat flour (the same as noodles but in thin sheets to enclose chopped pork).

เกิยะเปลือกบาง (ต้น) gkee-ah[6]-bpleu-ak[4]-bang *n. Pinus khasya (Coniferae)* (V. P. p. 35), a large tree 100 to 200 feet high. The wood is used for building purposes and for torches (Dept. Agri. & Fisheries).

เกิยะเปลือกหนา (ต้น) gkee-ah[6]-bpleu-ak[4]-nah[2] *n. Pinus merkusii (Coniferae)* (V. P. p. 35), a tree 50 to 60 feet high found in the Shan states, Martaban and Upper Tenasserim. Splinters are extensively employed as torches (Dept. Agri. & Fisheries).

เกือ gkeu-ah[3] *v.* to help; to assist; to succour: เกื้อกูล to render assistance: เกื้อหนุน to give monetary assistance; to lend one's influence; to uplift; to back up (as in some enterprise).

เกือก gkeu-ak[4] *n.* a shoe: เกือกสูง a top-boot: รองเท้า shoe (preferable to เกือก).

เกือบ gkeu-ap[4] *adv.* almost; nearly; approximately; soon: เกือบค่ำแล้ว nearly dark; dusk: เกือบจะตาย nearly dead; tired to death: เกือบจะถึง almost there; nearly to the end of the journey: เกือบจะมา will shortly arrive: เกือบตาย an exclamation equal to " how lucky to have escaped ".

แก gkaa *n.* a bird similar to the crow but smaller: *pron. of the 2nd. or 3rd. person* he, she, they or you: ทำกอแก to act cunningly.

แก (ต้น) gkaa *n. Combretum quadrangulare (Combretaceae)* (cb. p. 619), a tree 15 to 20 feet high found on flat land in scrub jungle. The flowers are pale yellow (K.).

แกคาง (ต้น) gkaa-kang *n. Glyptopetalum sclerocarpum (Celastraceae)* (cb. p. 280), a small spreading tree, about 5 m. high found on limestone rocks by streams. The seeds are red (K.).

แกดำ (ต้น) gkaa-dum *n. Combretum nanum (Combretaceae)* (cb. p. 617), a decumbent, low shrub used in native medicine (Dept. Agri. & Fisheries).

แก่ gkaa[4] *adj.* old; aged (if of a person); over-ripe (if of fruit); of long duration; strong; concentrated (as acid): *prep.* to (when followed by a noun or pronoun in the objective case): แก่กล้า strong; vigorous; robust: แก่ง, แก่เซอะชะ in one's dotage: แก่งอม to grow soft from ripeness: แก่จัด over-ripe: แก่เจียนตาย to be so old as about to die: แก่ชรา decrepit; broken with age: แก่เฒ่า an old man: แก่ดีกรี too concentrated; under the influence of liquor or drugs: แก่แดด to allow to ripen or to mature in the sun: แก่บ้าน a village head-man: แก่ไป to grow older; to be too concentrated: แก่ พอดี to be sufficiently old: แก่ล้ำ to be the oldest; to be the senior one: แก่วัด (คน) one being a long time in the Buddhist priesthood: แก่สุก ripe old age: แก่หง่อม to be feeble from old age; decrepit with age: แก่ออดแอด to be old and feeble: เก่าแก่ old; antiquated; worn out: คนแก่ an old man or person: เฒ่าแก่ one who arranges for a marriage; a go-between; a title of respect for ladies-in-waiting in the royal palace: ปัญญาแก่กล้า of a strong, sound mind: เป็นประโยชน์แก่เรา it is beneficial to us: ฝีแก่ an abscess on the point of bursting: ลูกไม้แก่ over-ripe fruit: ให้แก่ท่าน give to you: ให้ทานแก่คนยาก to give alms to the poor.

แก้ gkaa[3] *v.* to untie; to loosen; to solve; to correct; to alter; to repair; to mend; to answer or to unravel (as a riddle): *n.* a conch shell used for ironing the panung. The conch shell is attached to a perpendicular rod, weighted at the other end, and swung on a pivot: แก้กลอุบาย to thwart strategy: แก้เกี้ยว to ask another question or talk about something else so as to relieve embarrassment: แก้ขัด to make or use (as a makeshift); to temporize; to make trifling repairs (as to a leaky roof): *colloq.* to use for the time being; to get temporary relief from starvation or financial embarrassment by obtaining money or something as a substitute: แก้ไข to repair with trifling alterations; to better one's condition; to find means to alleviate one's immediate need: แก้ไข้ to reduce fever: แก้คาว to remove the odour of fish from the hands; to retrieve one's reputation: แก้คุย to check arrogancy: แก้แค้น to seek revenge: แก้เงิน to refine money or silver: แก้เงี่ยน to quench the desire (as for opium): แก้จน to manage to get out of a scrape; to avoid a checkmate (as in chess): แก้ใจ to reform one's mind (from evil to good): แก้ฉาว, แก้อึง to suppress (as exciting noises or disturbances): แก้เชือก to loosen or untie a cord: แก้ตก to be successful in solving a mystery or riddle: แก้ตัว to excuse one's self; to make a protest: แก้ต่าง to fight on behalf of (as an attorney acting for his clients): แก้ถุงเงิน to untie a bag of money: แก้ทอง to harden gold by making an alloy: แก้เนื้อ (ทอง) to purify gold: แก้บน to pay a vow or fulfil a promise: แก้บาป to do penance; to make restitution for sins: แก้เบี้ย to hide a cowry shell (as when the banker in a gambling game sees he is going to lose, and secretes a shell in his palm): แก้เผ็ด, แก้มือ to take vengence against; to seek an opportunity for retaliation: แก้ฝอย to correct mistakes in definitions or explanations: แก้ฝัน to interpret a dream: แก้โพย to open a bundle of lottery tickets: แก้พัน, แก้ถลุน to untwist the strands of a rope: แก้พับ, แก้แฟบ to raise; to restore to the proper shape (as a deformed, sunken or dinted nose is raised to a normal shape by plastic surgery): แก้มือ *lit.* "to untie one's hands," *i. e.* to repair one's loss (as a gambler tries to retrieve his losses by another play): แก้ยันหมาก to relieve nausea when chewing betelnut: แก้ยาพิศม์ to give remedies to counteract a poison: แก้รอด to have healed a sick person successfully: แก้ร้อน to find ways or means of relieving urgent distress or need: แก้รูต to keep on correcting repeatedly: แก้แรง to help support a weight by getting the assistance of another: แก้ลวง to repay one for his deception, by a trick:

แก้ว่า to answer; to deny: แก้หลุด to be successful in answering a charge; to be adroit in answering arguments: แก้อับจน to relieve dire need; to get help in time of distress: คำแก้ an excuse; an answer; a reply; an explanation: ยาแก้ a remedy for the relief of: ยาแก้อยากน้ำ a remedy for the relief of thirst.

แก๊ก gkaak[6] *onomat.* from the sound of a door-knocker or from a parrot-call or caw.

แกง gkaang *n.* a curry; stews, of which there are thirteen or more varieties: แกงบวด a sweetmeat made of fruit or yams, boiled in coconut-milk and sugar: แกงหมู pork curry.

แก่ง gkaang[4] *n.* rapids; falls of a river or stream; cascades: แก่งคอย name of a place along the Korat Royal Siamese Railway: เกาะแก่ง rocks or stones concealed in the water: ห้วยแก่ง a stream running down from the mountains over rocks.

แกงได gkaang-dai *n.* a mark or marks made instead of the signature (as lines or dots made by those who cannot write): แกงแนง stays or temporary supports to a post, used while it is being raised or set up, and before it is permanently fixed.

แก่งแย่ง gkaang[4]-yaang[4] *v.* to disagree; to differ in opinion; to be at variance; to fail to agree; to wrangle; to be given to altercation.

แกน gkaan *n.* the hardened inside (as of fruit); the axis: *adj.* hard; tasteless; unripe or undeveloped (as of fruit); hard-up; hardpressed; poor: แกนจักร the axle of a wheel: เป็นแกน hard and insipid (used regarding fruit): ส้มแกน an insipid and tasteless orange.

แกนมอ (ต้น) gkaan-mau *n. Rhus succedanea (Anacardiaceae)* (cb. p. 342), waxtree, a small tree that furnishes the "Japan vegetable-wax" of commerce. This is obtained from the waxy deposits on the berries, by boiling (MCM.). The milky juice of the tree is very acrid and is said to possess vesicant properties. The fruit is considered officinal in native medicine and is used in the treatment of phthisis. The wood is not used (Dept. AGRI. & Fisheries : BURK. p. 1905).

แก่น gkaan[4] *n.* the core; the centre; the heart-wood (as of a tree); a standby in time of trouble; a leader or adviser: *adj.* naughty; uncontrollable (as of children); firm; solid; strong-minded or stubborn: แก่นแก้ว to be extremely inferior; to be the lowest of the low: แก่นจันทร์ the heart-wood of the sandalwood tree: แก่นดง, ไกรทอง, หญ้าหุ่นไห้ (ต้น) *Erythroxylum cuneatum (Linaceae)*, a tree found from Burma to Java, usually near the coast. The tree is usually of small size but sometimes large. Its timber is pink, hard and very durable. The wood yields good house posts (K. : Cb. p. 200 : BURK. p. 950): แก่นสาร permanency; fixedness; durability; important; vital: คนพูดไม่เป็นแก่นสาร a talker of nonsense; a babbler: เป็นแก่น firm; constant: ไม้แก่น a tree with very hard wood.

แก๊บ gkaap[6] *Eng. n.* the percussion cap of a gun: หมวกแก๊บ an officer's cap.

แกม gkaam *adj.* adulterated; mixed; added to: ดีแกมชั่ว evil mingled with good (as in one's character).

แก้ม gkaam[3] *n.* the cheek: แก้มขวา the right cheek: แก้มช้ำ (ปลา) a beautiful, freshwater, cyprinoid fish with bright red cheeks (H. M. S.), *Puntius orphoides (Cyprinidae)* (Dept. Agri. & Fisheries: BURK. p. 1843): แก้ม ซ้าย the left cheek.

แกรก gkraak[4] *onomat.* from a crack, or the tearing of cloth.

แกร่ง gkraang[4] *adj.* hard; firm; solid.

แกร็น gkraan *n.* an animal or plant much below ordinary size: *adj.* small; undeveloped (as fruit); dwarfed; stunted.

แกร่ว gkraa-oh[4] *adj.* pitiful; sordid; destitute; lonesome; bearing hardships; having to bear oppression or affliction: เที่ยวแกร่ว อยู่คนเดียว wandering alone dejectedly.

แกล gklaa *v.* to be separated; to be led away by force: *n.* a window (used by royalty only).

แกล่ gklaa[4] *adv.* nearly; almost.

แกล้ง gklaang[3] *v.* to do spitefully; to do with intent to harass or annoy; to act or speak with design; to pretend; to speak or do with malice, spite or base intent: แกลัง-กลั่น. แกลังกลิ้ง to select something with a purpose in view: แกลังทำ to do with a purpose (as for revenge): แกลังป่วย, แสร้งป่วย to feign sickness; to make-believe being sick: แกลังว่า, ค่อนว่า to blame without cause; to revile or reproach intentionally: คนใจแกลัง a person having a spiteful or vindictive nature.

แกลน gklaan *v.* to be timid; to be afraid; to be seized with fear or apprehension.

แกลบ gklaap[4] *n.* chaff; the husk or shell of paddy or other grains: ม้าแกลบ a pony of small size: แมงแกลบ, ตั๊กแตน a jumping, paddy beetle found in piles of moist paddy husks (used as bait in fishing).

แกล้ม gklaam[3] *v.* to insert; to mix with; to unite or blend by stirring together: *n.* food eaten with a dose of medicine or strong liquor: กินกล้อมแกล้ม to gulp food without proper mastication.

แกล้ว gklaa-oh[3] *adj.* brave; bold; daring; active: แกล้วกล้า strong; courageous; audacious.

แกละ, ผมแกละ gklaa[4] *n.* tufts or tresses of hair left to grow on the sides of the head (as of children).

แกแล (ต้น) gkaa-laa *n.* the liver-coloured heart-wood or core of *Cudrania javanensis (Urticaceae)* (V. P. p. 20 : BURK. p. 700). This is used as a dye and medicinally : ย้อมแกแล to dye by means of this kind of wood.

แกส   gkaas *Eng.* gas.

แกว   gkaa-oh *n.* the Siamese who live on the border of Anam and gradually change their nationality : (ต้น) a species of yam eaten raw, *Pachyrrhizus erosus* (*Leguminosae*) (cb. p. 459), "the yam bean", "potato bean"; *P. tuberosus* (MCM. p. 288 : BURK. p. 1619): ญวนแกว a tribe of Anamites of Siamese origin : รู้แกว to have an inkling, hint or intimation of some secret : ลาวแกว a tribe of Anamites of Siamese origin.

แก้ว   gkaa-oh[3] *n.* glass; crystal; mica; the caterpillar before its transformation into a butterfly or moth : *adj.* brave; bold; daring : แก้ว (ต้น) the China box-tree, *Murraya paniculata* (*Rutaceae*) (cb. p. 230), a shrub or small tree 4 or 5 m. high, found in evergreen forest. The pale green flowers are fragrant and are used for making perfumery. The wood is used for making walking sticks (K. : BURK. p. 1505); *M. exotica* (V. P. p. 34), the "China box," a small tree with white, scented flowers, having small pinnate leaves (MCM. pp. 73, 113). The fragrant bark is more generally used as a cosmetic than is sandalwood. The wood is used for making handles of implements (Dept. Agri. & Fisheries); *Mimusops elengi* (*Sapotaceae*) (V. P. p. 33), a large tree, having a bitter bark which has a tonic effect. It is used in a distillation of arrack and also for snake bites (MCM. p. 379). The bark is used for dyeing shades of brown. The tree produces small fragrant flowers in abundance during the hot season. They fall in showers and are succeeded by small, oval berries which are yellowish when ripe, and have a small quantity of sweetish pulp. These are sometimes eaten by the poorer classes. The wood is used for house-building and is said to last for fifty years (Dept. Agri. & Fisheries : BURK. p. 1475): แก้ว (นก) the Burmese rose-headed paroquet, *Palaeornis cyanocephalus* (Gaird. J. S. S. IX, 1, p. 8): แก้วกุ้ง the fresh oil or brain of a prawn : แก้วแกลบ a white alkali; crystalline

sediment formed from a solution of paddy ash ; a form of soapstone used medicinally : แก้วตอไว (ต้น) *Pterolobium macropterum* (*Leguminosae*) (V. P. p. 34 : cb. p. 506): แก้วตา the image or reflection from the cornea or "apple of the eye": แก้วตาไว (นก) the black-headed shrike, *Lanius nigriceps* (will. N. H. J. S. S. I, 2, p. 89): แก้วมือไว (ต้น) *Pterolobium micranthum* (*Leguminosae*) (cb. p. 506), a straggling shrub, found in scrub jungle. It has an odd petal with yellow base (K.): แก้วรักนา, หญ้ารักนา, มะไฟนกคุ้ม (ต้น) *Ammannia baccifera* (*Lythraceae*) (cb. p. 715), a small, herbaceous plant, generally met with in wet places. It has a strong muriatic but not disagreeable odour. The leaves are exceedingly acrid, and are used universally to raise blisters in rheumatic pains, fevers, etc. (Dept. Agri. & Fisheries : BURK. p. 131): แก้ววิเชียร a form of follicular pharyngitis; an infantile disease : แก้วหิน rock crystal : แก้วหู the tympanic membrane : ถ้วยแก้ว a tumbler; a drinking glass : ที่รักดั่งแก้วตา "my love is as the apple of mine eye."

แกว่ง   gkwaang[4] *v.* to swing; to sway back and forth (as a pendulum); to brandish : แกว่งไปแกว่งมา to oscillate : คนใจแกว่ง one unstable in mind or purpose; a waverer : ใจแกว่ง an irregular, fluttering condition of the heart.

แกว่น   gkwaan[4] *n.* hardness; hardiness : *adj.* brave; quick (of action); hardy; bold; tough (in character).

แกะ   gkaa[4] *v.* to carve in wood or stone; to chisel out a statue; to pick out; to take out (as pits of fruit): *n.* sheep : แกะเกา to pick and scratch (as at a scab): แกะตัวผู้ a ram : แกะตัวเมีย an ewe : แกะรูป to carve out an image : แกะเมล็ดออก to take out the seeds (as of fruit): ช่างแกะ a sculptor : เนื้อแกะ mutton : ลูกแกะ a lamb; *figur.* a disciple.

โก้   gkoh[3] *Chin. v.* to be dressed gaily or

gaudily; to be flashy in dress: *adj.* gay; gaudy; striking; showy.

โก้ gkoh[2] *Chin. n.* a variety of Chinese pancake made of rice-flour.

โกก gkok[4] *n.* a yoke used on oxen or buffaloes while drawing a sled or plough. This yoke is double and is curved where it rests on the necks of the oxen. The แอก is also a double yoke but straight: *onomat.* from the sound when a joint or section of bamboo is struck.

โกกนท, โกกนุท gkoh-gka[4]-not[6] *P. S. n.* the flowers of the red water-lily: *adj.* being of the colour of the red lotus (S. E. D. p. 312).

โกกิล gkoh-gki[4]-la[6] *P.S. n.* the Malayan coel, *Eudynamis malayana* (Gaird. J. S. S. IX, 1, p. 7). The black or Indian cuckoo, frequently alluded to in Hindu poetry as its musical cry is supposed to inspire tender emotions (S. E. D. p. 312): โกกิลวาส *lit.* "the abode of the aforementioned bird," *i. e.* the mango tree.

โกง gkong *v.* to cheat; to swindle; to defraud grossly: *adj.* bent; curved; crooked; deceitful: คดโกง, ใจโกง to have a deceitful character; to be fraudulent in dealings: คิดโกง to meditate fraud: หลังโกง to be humpbacked.

โก่ง gkong[4] *v.* to arch; to be arched; to bend or draw (as a bow); to tighten; to enhance the value of; to raise (as a price): *adj.* bent over (as with age); arched: โก่ง คันแร้ว to bend down the spring rod of a snare or trap: โก่งนิ้ว to bend the fingers (or one finger) backwards: โก่งราคา to raise the price of: โก่งศร to aim an arrow on a drawn bow.

โกงกาง see กงกาง

โกงกอน, โกงเกง (ต้น) gkong-gkaun *n. Rhizophora mucronata (Rhizophoraceae)* (Cb. p. 593), mangrove, a moderate-sized, spreading tree found in saline coastal lagoons and along estuaries in the Eastern tropics. This wood is exceptionally fine as fire-wood since it burns with even heat. It also makes good charcoal. Its chief value is in tanning. An extract from the bark is used in tanning and dyeing (MCM. p. 444: Burk. p. 1897). The bark, mixed with dried ginger or long peppers and rose-water, is said to be a cure for diabetes. The fruits are sweet and edible; the juice is made into a light wine (Dept. Agri. & Fisheries).

โก้งเก้ง gkong[3]-gkeng[3] *adj.* top-heavy; too tall; too high; overpowering; awkward; clumsy; ungraceful.

โกงโก้ gkong-gkoh[3] *adj.* bent over forwards (as stooping when playing "leap frog").

โก้งโค้ง gkong[3]-kong[5] *v.* to bend the body forwards and downwards; to be inclined forwards; to stoop low.

โกเชาว์ gkoh-chow *P. n.* a woollen cloth; a blanket; a goat's hair coverlet of fine workmanship (S. E. D.).

โกญจะ gkon-chja[4] *P. n.* the sarus crane, *Grus antigone* (Gaird. J. S. S. IX, 1, p. 14); an osprey (S. E. D. p. 323): โกญจนาท penetrating; resounding; echoing (as the call of the wild sarus crane); loud; confused; indistinct (descriptive of sounds or noises).

โกฏ gkot[4] *P. S. v.* to strike; to cut; to break; to pound; to pulverize by pounding or beating (Chd. p. 210).

โกฏฐี gkot[4] *P. n.* any one of the viscera of the body (particularly of the stomach and abdomen); a granary; a store-room; a treasury; an inner apartment (S. E. D. p. 314); (ต้น) *Artemisia sp. (Compositae)*, a large, important genus of medicinal herbs found throughout the northern hemisphere. Many of them have a strong characteristic odour and are useful as flavourings or in medicine. It appears that the Egyptians made use of an *Artemisia*, and wormwood is mentioned in the Bible as a bitter substance. If these were not *Artemisia* *absinthium* itself, they were some very similar species. The physicians of the Levant, in and after the time of Christ, used *Artemisia* medicinally as a stomachic and to serve as an appetizer before meals (BURK. p. 243):

โกฏฐ์กะกลิ้ง see กะกลิ้ง

โกฏฐ์จุพะลำพา (ต้น)   *Artemisia vulgaris* (*Compositae*), wormwood, an herb which is cultivated in the Malay Peninsula by immigrants, both Chinese and Tamil. It is marketed by the Chinese in the important centres. The Chinese herbalists stock it freshly. The English name "wormwood" perhaps should have been "wormweed" or possibly "wormwot," *i. e.* worm protection. It also serves as an insecticide for its power of keeping vermin away (BURK. p. 246): โกฏฐ์ทั้งห้า, ทั้งเจ็ด, ทั้งเก้า household remedies composed of five, seven, or nine kinds of medicinal plants which are boiled and dosed out to the patient in the form of a decoction: โกฏฐ์น้ำเต้า *Rheum rhabarbarum* (*Polygonaceae*), rhubarb (MCM. p. 324: BURK. p. 1891): โกฏฐ์หัวบัว a species of fragrant crinum bulb, used in the preparation of an odorous paste or ointment called กะแจ (GER. (1) p. 41): โกฏฐาคาร a store-room; a store-house; any enclosed space or area (S. E. D. p. 314).

โกฏิ   gkot[4] *P. S. n.* the curved end of a bow or of claws; an edge or point (as of a sword); horns or cusps (of the moon); the highest point; an eminence; excellence; the end, tip, top or pinnacle of any spire, building or thing; the numeral "one" followed by seven ciphers (S. E. D. p. 312).

โกณ   gkoh-na[6] *n.* a corner; an angle; an intermediate point of the compass; an arch; a curve (S. E. D. p. 313): โกณทิศ dots denoting degrees on a compass: ตรีโกณ a triangle: ตรีโกณมิติ trigonometry.

โกณฑัญญะ   gkon-tan-ya[6] *P. S. n.* name of one of the twenty-four Buddhas (S. E. D. p. 315).

โกตูหพ, เกาตูหล   gkoh-dtoo-ha[4]-la[6] *P. S. n.* curiosity; excitement; agitation; interest in anything; anything causing curiosity; any unusual phenomenon (S. E. D. p. 316).

โกทัณฑ์ see เกาทัณฑ์

โกน ๑   gkon *Peg. n.* a child; a son or daughter.

โกน ๒   gkon *v.* to shave: โกนจุก to shave the topknot: โกนผม to shave the hair: ช่างโกน a barber: มีดโกน a razor: วันโกน days on which the Buddhist monks shave their heads, *viz.* the 7*th.* and 14*th.* of the waxing and the 22*nd.* and 29*th.* of the waning moon.

โกนาคมน์   gkoh-nah-kom *P. S. n.* the name of the second Buddha (CHD. p. 208).

โกมล   gkoh-mon *P. S. n.* water; silk: *adj.* tender; soft; bland; sweet; pleasing; charming; agreeable (S. E. D. p. 313): โกมลคีต music pleasing to the ear; a sweet song: โกมลทล *lit.* "without cushion-like leaves," "tender-leaved," *i. e.* the lotus plant.

โกมารภัจจ์   gkoh-mah-ra[6]-pat[6] *P. n.* a physician to King Pimpisarn (พระเจ้าพิมพิสาร), held in esteem to the present day as a preceptor of obstetrics and midwifery, the care of an infant and of a pregnant or a lying-in woman.

โกมุท, โกเมศ   gkoh-moot[6] *P. n.* the red lotus lily; the twelfth lunar month, viz. October or November (S. E. D. p. 316).

โกมุที   gkoh-moo[6]-tee *P. S. n.* moonlight; the period of the shining of the moon as it causes the water lily to blossom; moonlight, also personified as the wife of the moon (S. E. D. p. 316).

โกเมน   gkoh-men *n.* an almandine garnet; a dark red or blood-coloured garnet.

โกย   gkoh-ay *v.* to scoop up or gather together, using both hands (as gathering rice into a basket): โกยกอง to collect into piles; to accumulate: โกยแกลบ to gather together or rake up paddy husk: โกยทราย ขึ้นเป็นกอง to gather sand and pile up into a mound.

โกรก gkrok[4] *v.* to saw, using a large saw (as two men sawing a log); to pour; to cut: *n.* a deep cleft in a mountain; an abyss; a deep valley: *onomat.* from the sound produced by sawing or pouring: โกรกน้ำ to allow the gradual flowing or pouring of water: โกรกศีร์ษะ to pour water upon the head: ลงโกรก a profuse movement of the bowels: ลมโกรก a direct draught or strong current of air: ไหลโกรก excessive flowing or the sound made by liquids gushing from a spigot.

โกรกกราก gkrok[4]-gkrak[4] *n.* an auger or drill, the handle of which moves vertically up and down in a spiral groove; the name of a district in the province of Tachin (Smud Sakor).

โกร่ง gkrong[4] *n.* an apothecary's mortar; a species of cricket; the woven hilt of a sword.

โกรงเกรง gkrong-gkreng *adj.* ruinous (condition); dilapidated; partly destroyed or demolished: ศาลาโกรงเกรง a public rest-house in a ruinous condition.

โกร่งเกร่ง gkrong[2]-gkreng[2] *adj.* sparse (as a tree having only a few leaves); thinly scattered; thinly clad.

โกรต้น, โกสน gkroh-dton[2] *n.* the garden croton, *Codiaeum variegatum (Euphorbiaceae)* (V. P. p. 20: MCM. p. 119: BURK. p. 616). This highly ornamental foliage plant, with variously coloured and shaped leaves, is a native of the Moluccas and was introduced into Bangkok from India by Phya Bhasakarawongse about 1880 (winit N. H. J. S. S. IX, 1, p. 93).

โกรธ gkrot[4] *P. S. v.* to be or to get angry; to be provoked; to be displeased; to be incited to anger; to be peeved: *n.* anger; wrath; passion (S. E. D. p. 322): คนมักโกรธ an easily irritated person: ความโกรธ wrath; anger; indignation.

โกรธา gkroh-tah *S. n.* the name of one of the thirteen daughters of Daksha (พระทักษะ), the wife of Kasyapa (พระกัศยป). She was the mother of all sharp-toothed monsters that are devourers of flesh, whether on the earth, amongst the birds or in the waters (H. C. D. p. 169).

โกร๋น gkron[2] *v.* to be stripped or denuded of leaves, hair or feathers: *adj.* sparse; almost leafless; thinly covered with leaves; faded; jaded: ใบไม้โกร๋น ๆ เกร๋น ๆ the tree is stripped of its leaves: หัวโกร๋น a head or scalp thinly covered with hair owing to disease.

โกรพ, เการว gkoh-rop[6] *P. S. n. lit.* "related to or descended from or belonging to the Kurus" (S. E. D.), *i. e.* the direct descendants of Kuru (กุรุ); a patronymic, especially applied to the sons of Dhrita-rashtra (H. C. D. p. 154).

โกรม gkrom *Cam. adj.* low; menial; subordinate; inferior.

โกรย gkro-ay *Cam.* the back (of the body).

โกรศ gkoh-rot[6] or gkoh-rot[4] *S. n.* a cry; a yell; a shriek; a shout; the range of the voice in calling or hallooing; the sound of singing or crying; a chorus of voices (S. E. D. p. 322).

โกระอาน, โกหร่าน, โก้หร่าน gkoh-ra[6]-an *n.* the Koran, the Mohammedan sacred scriptures written in Arabic and professing to record the revelations of Allah to Mohammed.

โกโรโกเต gkoh-roh-gkoh-dtey *adj.* dilapidated; unsound (nearly falling); leaning (as a house).

โกโรโกโรค gkoh-roh-gkoh-rok[3] *adj.*
diseased; anaemic; pale; greatly emaciated.

โกโรโกโส gkoh-roh-gkoh-soh[2] *adj.* unfinished; ruinous (condition); leaning or
toppling over.

โกลน gklon *v.* to hew into shape roughly;
to be still unfinished; to be partly hewn out
of the rough: *n.* a stirrup: โกลนไม้ to
rough-hew wood: แจวโกลน a rough-hewn
oar: ชาติโกลน savages; rude tribes: ทอด
โกลน to put rollers under and draw: ยัง
โกลนอยู่ still unfinished; still in the rough:
เรือโกลน a dug-out boat; a log hollowed out
for a boat.

โกลมัน see กิโลมก

โกลาหล gkoh-lah-hon[2] *P. S. n.* an uproar;
a great tumult, excitement or disturbance;
agitation (as a riot); a loud and confused
noise (as of men or animals): *adj.* excited;
producing excitement; arousing action (S. E. D.
p. 313).

โกไล gkoh-lai *Cam. n.* prawn.

โกวิท gkoh-wit[6] *P. S. adj.* experienced;
well-versed in; skilled; well-advanced in any
branch of knowledge or skill (S. E. D. p. 314):
อัศวโกวิท one well-versed respecting horses.

โกวิทาร, โกวิพาร, ทองหลาง (ต้น) gkoh-
wi[6]-tan *P. n. lit.* "easily split," *i. e. Erythrina fusca (Leguminosae)*; *E. lithosperma*;
E. strica (Cb. pp. 400, 442: Burk. pp. 945, 946:
McM. pp. 27, 214), a tree cultivated in European
hot-houses for the sake of the brilliant red
flowers. In Siam, trees of this species are
most important as shade for fruit trees in
the Bangkok orchards. The timber is considered worthless but the leaves serve as fodder. The bark is used as elephant medicine
(S. E. D. p. 314): ทองหลางน้ำ (ต้น) *Erythrina
ovalifolia* (V. P. p. 143: Burk. p. 945), a prickly
tree of about 50 ft. growing near sea-fronts
or along rivers: ทองหลางใบมน (ต้น) *Erythrina arborescens*; *E. indica (Leguminosae)*

(V. P. p. 143: McM. p. 88), "tiger's claw," "Indian coral tree."

โกศ, โกส gkot[4] *P. S. n. lit.* "a vessel
for holding liquids," *i. e.* a cloud; a bucket;
an utensil for holding water; a cup; a
chalice; a cupboard; a scabbard; a sword;
a sheath; a treasury; a strong room; a
safe; a dictionary, a lexicon or vocabulary;
a spired funeral urn or repository for bones
(of the dead) (S. E. D. p. 314): โกศการ the
compiler of a dictionary; a lexicographer;
the silk worm (or the larva while in its
cocoon); a chrysalis or pupa; a maker of
boxes; a cabinetmaker: โกศการิกา females
of the bee family; a queen bee: โกศนายก,
โกศาธิบดี *lit.* "a chief over treasures," *i. e.* one
in charge of a godown, a store house or
treasury; a treasurer: โกศผล (ต้น) the
nutmeg, *Myristica fragrans (Myristicaceae)*
(V. P. pp. 87, 88: McM. p. 339: Burk. p. 1524).
The home of the nutmeg is somewhere in
eastern Malaysia. The seed of the fruit, as a
spice, was introduced into Europe about the
sixth century, presumably from India. It
would seem that India got its supplies from
Java, and Java from Malaysia: โกศเวศม์,
โกศาคาร a godown, shed or house; a storehouse; a treasury.

โกศล ses โกสล

โกศี gkoh-see[2] *S. n.* the mango tree (S. E. D.
p. 314).

โกส see โกศ

โกสน see โกรต้น

โกสล gkoh-son[2] *P. S. n.* the people of the
kingly caste belonging to the Kosala nation
(S. E. D. p. 314: smith p. 44).

โกสัช gkoh-sat[4] *P. n.* indolence; laziness;
slothfulness.

โกสัมพี see เกาสามพี

โกสัลล์ see เกาศัลย์

โกสินทร์, โกสีย์ ๑ gkoh-sin[2] *P. n.* names for Indra.

โกสินารา, กุสินารา gkoh-si[4]-nah-rah *n.* Kusinagara the name of the city where Buddha passed into Nirvana (smith p. 51).

โกสีย์ ๒ gkoh-see[2] *P. S. adj.* silken; made of silk; sheathed (as a sword) (S. E. D. p. 317).

โกสุม gkoh-soom[2] *P. S. adj. lit.* "coming from or belonging to flowers", *i. e.* flowery; made of flowers (S. E. D. p. 318).

โกสุมภ์ (ดอก) gkoh-soom[2] *P.S. n.* the flowers of *Mallotus philippinensis* (*Euphorbiaceae*), a widespread, small tree found from the Himalayas to eastern Australia (V. P. p. 65 : MCM. p. 440 : BURK. p. 1396); *Reinwardtia trigyna* (*Linaceae*) (cb. p. 199 MCM. pp. 116, 185): *adj.* decorated with a wreath made of the above flowers, or dyed with the above flowers, or dyed with the glandular tubescence of the fruit which yields a rich orange-red, permanent dye (S. E. D. p. 318).

โกไสย see **เกาไศย**

โกหก gkoh-hok[4] *P.S. v.* to tell a lie; to falsify; to forge; to violate the truth; to cheat; to defraud: *n.* a lie; a counterfeit article; falsehood; a fraud; a cheat; a rogue; prevarication; deception; trickery (S. E. D. p. 298).

โกหร่าน see **โกระอาน**

โก้หร่าน see **โกระอาน**

โกหัญ gkoh-han[2] *P. n.* the act of prevaricating; a falsehood; falsification; deceit; hypocrisy.

ใกล้ gklai[3] *adj.* near; close by; adjoining; neighbouring; adjacent: ใกล้กัน, ใกล้เคียง contiguous; neighbouring: คนใกล้ชิด an intimate friend: นั่งใกล้ to sit near: เรือนใกล้ a neighbouring house; an adjoining house: อยู่ใกล้ to be near.

ไก gkai *n.* a key; a lever; a latch for unlocking a piece of mechanism having a spring: กลไก delicate mechanisms; mechanical devices: ไกปืน the trigger of a gun.

ไก่ gkai[4] *n.* a fowl; fowls (in general); a prefix to which the particular designating species is added: ไก่กอม (ต้น) *Ehretia laevis (Boraginaceae)* (V. P. p. 20), a moderate-sized tree, common throughout Siam and India. The fruit is tasteless, but is eaten during times of famine, as is also the inner bark. The wood is used for building purposes and for agricultural implements (DEPT. Agri. & Fisheries): ไก่ขัน the crowing of a cock; cock-crow (in the morning): ไก่ไข่ a laying hen: ไก่งวง a turkey: ไก่จาว, ไก่สี, ไก่เผือก pure white fowls, supposed to be inhabited by spirits: ไก่เจี๊ยบ, ลูกไก่ chicks: ไก่แจ้ a bantam rooster: ไก่โจก the leader in a flock of chickens: ไก่ฉาบ the flying back and forth of fowls from fright or of cocks while fighting: ไก่ชน a fighting or game-cock: ไก่ต่อ a cock used as a decoy: ไก่ต๊อก the guinea fowl, *Numida meleagris*; *N. cristata*, an African gallinaceous bird. The common domesticated species has a coloured fleshy horn on each side of the head and is of a dark grey colour variegated with small spots (web.): ไก่ตอน a capon: ไก่ต้อย a small-sized chicken: ไก่ตะเภา *lit.* "fowls brought in junks from China," *i. e.* fowls of Chinese origin: ไก่ตั้งเกี้ย a mythical monster, the tonquin cock, having a traditional colour of light yellow: ไก่ตั้ง fighting cocks with very upright necks: ไก่ตัวผู้ a cock: ไก่ตัวเมีย a hen: ไก่เตี้ย, กำพร้า (ต้น) *Canavalia maritima* (*Leguminosae*) (cb. p. 453); *C. obtusifolia* (V. P. p. 22 : MCM. p. 209), a flowering, trailing, perennial that grows on sandy sea-shores; *C. rosea* (BURK. p. 434): ไก่เถื่อน a jungle fowl; wild fowl: ไก่นา a field bird: ไก่น้ำดำ the Indian moor-hen, *Gallinula chloropus in-*

dicus (Deig. N. H. J. S. S. VIII, 3, p. 169): ไก่-น้ำบิ๊กขาวหางยาว the pheasant-tailed jacana, *Hydrophasianus chirurgus* (Deig. N. H. J. S. S. VIII, 3, p. 170): ไก่น้ำหางสีดำแดง the bronze-winged jacana, *Metopidius indicus* (Deig. N. H. J. S. S. VIII, 3, p. 170): ไก่น้ำอกสีเทาแก้ the Indian blue-breasted banded rail, *Hypotaenidia striata* (Deig. N. H. J. S. S. VIII, 3, p. 169): ไก่บน *lit.* "upper cock" *i. e.* the winning one in a fight: ไก่บ้าน domesticated fowls: ไก่ป่า (พม่า) the Burmese jungle-fowl, *Gallus bankiva robinsoni* (Deig. N. H. J. S. S. 3, VIII, p. 167): ไก่ผู้เมีย a cock with feathers like a hen: ไก่ฟ้า (นก) the lineated silver pheasant, *Euplocamus lineatus* (Gaird. J. S. S. IX, 1, p. 12): ไก่ฟ้าพระยาลอ the Siam fireback pheasant, *Lophuar diardi* (Herb. N. H. J. S. S. VI, 4, p. 335): ไก่ฟ้าสีดาว Grant's silver pheasant, *Gennaeus lineatus sharpei* (Herb. N. H. J. S. S. VI, 4, p. 336): ไก่รอง the defeated cock; one kept as a substitute: ไก่รุ่นกระทง young fowls: ไก่เริง a fearless fowl; a tame fowl: ไก่ล่าง, ไก่ลง *lit.* "lower cock," *i. e.* the defeated one in a fight: ไก่เล็กฮอน a leghorn fowl: ไก่สาว a pullet: ไก่หยอง fowls with the feathers turned backwards: ไก่ฟุ่น, ไก่ลุ่น fowls with short tails: ไก่เพา, ไก่เลา fowls with both white and black feathers: ไก่อู cocks kept for fighting purposes: ไก่ฮกเกี้ยน a mythical monster, the Hokkien cock, with vermillion for its traditional colour.

ไก๊ (ต้น) gkai[6] *n. Bombax kerrii (Malvaceae)* (cb. p. 164), a tree common on hills throughout the rapids of the rivers of northern Siam (K.).

ไก๋ gkai[2] *adj.* appearing indifferent (as when at a distance).

ไก๋แดง (ต้น) gkai[2]-dang *n. Ternstroemia japonica (Ternstroemiaceae)* (cb. p. 124), a tree about 10 m. high, found in mixed deciduous forest. The flowers fall to the ground beneath (K.).

ไกเกย, ไกยเกษี์ gkai-gkay-yee *n.* a prin-cess of Kaikeya (ไกเกยะ), wife of King Dasaratha (ทศรถ), a king of the Sola race reigning at Ayodhya, and mother of Bharata (พระภรต) who was her third son. She carefully tended the king when he was wounded in battle, and in gratitude he promised to grant any two requests she might make. Urged by the malignant counsels of a female attendant, she made use of this promise to procure the exile of Rama, and to promote the advancement of her own son, his half-brother (H. C. D. p. 139).

ไกร gkrai *adj.* three; powerful; high; large; much; brave; valiant.

ไกรลาส see ไกลาส

ไกรว, ไกรพ gkai-ra[6]-wa[6] *S. n.* an inveterate gambler; a crook; a cheat; an enemy; the white lotus flower (blossoming at night) (S. E. D. p. 311): ไกรวพันธุ์ *lit.* "a friend of the lotus flower," *i. e.* the moon; ไกรวี the moon; moon-light.

ไกรศรี, ไกรศรี ๑, ไกรสร, ไกรสรี gkrai-saun[2] *n. lit.* "having a mane," *i. e.* a lion; lions (in general).

ไกรศรี ๒ gkrai-see[2] *n.* one enjoying prosperity, happiness or success in the highest degree.

ไกล gklai *adj.* far; distant; remote; greatly separated: ไกลกัน separated by a great distance: ไกลตา nearly out of sight: ทางไกล a long journey: ไปทางไกล to go far away: อยู่ไกล to be distant from: ห่างไกล distant; separated.

ไกล่ gklai[4] *v.* to paint or to coat over (as with white-wash); to varnish; to coat over with a layer (as with cement): ไกล่เกลี่ย to come to an agreement, amicable settlement or compromise (as between two parties); to make peace; to conciliate (in a misunderstanding).

ไกลาส, ไกรลาส, เกลาศ *S. n.* a mythological

mountain in the Himalayas, north of Manasa lake, said to be the paradise of Siva as well as the abode of Kuvera (H. C. D. p. 139): ไกลาสนาถ *lit.* " sovereign of the Kailasa mountain ", *i. e.* Kuvera (S. E. D.): ไกลาสบดี *lit.* " lord of the Kailasa ", *i. e.* Siva.

ไกว gkai *v.* to swing; to sway; to move backward and forward on a swing: ไกว ชิงช้า to swing one on a swing: ไกวลูก,

ไกวเปล to rock the baby in a cradle.

ไกวรรต *P. S. n.* a fisherman (S. E. D. p. 311).

ไกวัล see เกวล

ไก่ไห่ gkai^4-hai^4 *n. Capparis flavicans* (*Capparidaceae*) (cb. p. 80), a spreading shrub about 3 m. high, found in dry deciduous forests and usually on termite hills. The flowers are yellow (K.).

ข

ข The second consonant of the Thai alphabet, a high class letter pronounced as an aspirated gutteral with a rising inflection or intonation. The designating names are ขอข้อง, ขอไข่. It occurs in words of Pali and Sanskrit origin in which it is pronounced as " ขะ " and defined as air, sky. If it occurs as a prefix, *e. g.* " ขจร," it means floating about in space or atmosphere.

ขค kok^4 *P. S. n. lit.* " one or that which moves in the air," *i. e.* birds, bees, stars of omen; an arrow; a deity: ขคบดี, ขคราช, ขคาธิป *lit.* " chief of the bird tribe," *i. e.* the Krut or Garuda, Vishnu's vehicle, a mythical griffin on whose shoulders Vishnu rode. The Garuda is an enemy and destroyer of the Naga, or serpents (H. C. D. p. 110): ขควดี the earth; land; firmament: ขคสถาน *lit.* " nesting places of birds," " a bird's nest," *i. e.* a hollow place or cavity in a tree or stump: ขคาภิราม name of Siva: ขคาสนะ *lit.* " the seat of the sun," *i. e.* the name of the mountain Udaya (the eastern mountain over which the sun rises), also *lit.* " sitting on a bird " (on the Garuda), *i. e.* Vishnu.

ขคา ka^4-kah a prefix occurring in the aforementioned words.

ขเคนทร์, ขเคศวร ka^4-ken *P. S. n. lit.* " chief of birds," *i. e.* one of many names for the Garuda, a mythical bird or vulture, half-man, half-bird, on which Vishnu rode (H. C. D. p. 109).

ขงเขง (ต้น) kong^2-keng^2 *n. Hymenopyramis brachiata* (*Verbenaceae*) (V. P. p. 49).

ขงเขมา (ต้น) kong^2-ka^2-mah *n. Cissampelos pareira* (*Menispermaceae*) (cb. p. 70: MCM. p. 378), a lofty climber. The dried root occurs in the form of cylindrical, oval or compressed pieces, entire or split longitudinally. The greyish-brown bark has a taste which at first is sweetish and aromatic but afterwards intensely bitter. The dry roots and bark are used as mild tonics and diuretics in acute and advanced stages of chronic cystitis and catarrhal affections of the bladder. It apparently also exercises an astringent and sedative action on the mucous membranes of the genito-urinary organs. The leaves are applied to abscesses; the roots are used in fever and diarrhoea (Dept. Agri. & Fisheries: BURK. p. 559).

ขงจื๊อ, ขงจ๊อ kong^2-chjoo^6 *Chin. n.* Confucius, who was born in the year 551 B. C. in the city of Tasao, in what is the modern province of Shantung. His father was a man of strong personality and power and was a military officer in the ancient state of Lu, during the period when China was divided into small states ruled by vassal princes, who usurped the power of the real sovereign. His father had married two wives and had ten children, nine of whom were daughters, his only son being a cripple. Hoping for another son, he married again, and this time took as his wife the young daughter of a neighbouring family. A son was born, and it was he who became the Great Sage of China. When Confucius was three years old his father died, so that to the young mother, who removed to Ch'ufu, was left the entire care of this remarkable child, whose early years showed him to be sedate and fond of ceremony. He married at eighteen and took office as Comptroller of the Public Granaries. A group of young men soon gathered round him, and became his pupils for the study of morality and the teachings of the ancient sages, he already having earned an enviable reputation for his learning and reverence. He died in 479 B. C. He was buried in Ch'ufu in Shantung (strong p. 20).

ขจร   ka[4]-chjaun *P. S. v.* to move; to float about in the air; to be disseminated; to be diffused, or to circulate in the air: *n. lit.* "floating, moving or flying in the air," *i. e.* birds, clouds, moving stars, comets, or aerial spirits (S. E. D. p. 334): ขจร, สลิด (ต้น) *Telosma minor* (*Asclepiadaceae*) (V. P. p. 36: Burk. p. 2130: K.), the cowslip creeper, a species of small vine bearing clusters of yellow fragrant flowers and small pods 5 to 6 inches long. Both petals and pods are edible: ลือขจร the report spreads, or is widely circulated: เล่าขจร to spread by telling (as from mouth to mouth): หอมฟุ้งขจร a diffused, agreeable odour.

ขจอก   ka[4]-chjauk[4] *Cam. adj.* lame; hobbling; impaired; decrepit.

ขจัด   ka[4]-chjat[4] *Cam. v.* to expel; to drive out or away; to cause to be dissipated or dispelled: ขจัดขจร to disperse; to be scattered about in the air: ขจัดขจาย to be scattered about; to be spread about: ขจัด-พลัดพราย to be dispersed; to be separated; to be cast about irregularly: ขจัดเสียซึ่งโรค to dispel the illness; to cause the disease to disappear.

ขจาย, กระจาย, กำจาย   ka[4]-chjai *Cam. v.* to extend (as a boundary); to be scattered; to be diffused.

ขจิต   ka[4]-chjit[4] *P. S. adj.* studded; veneered or covered (as with gold-leaf); being set (as jewels in a ring); having been inlaid with jewels; having been adorned with precious stones (S. E. D. p. 335).

ขจิตร   ka[4]-chjit[4] *P. S. n. lit.* "a picture in the sky", *i. e.* anything impossible or not existing; a delusion; a deception; delusiveness; a phantom, apparition or mental image; an impossibility; an improbability (S. E. D. p. 334).

ขจิ   ka[4]-chjee *Cam. adj.* soft; cushion-like; tender; young; new; light green.

ขชล   ka[4]-chon *S. n. lit.* "air-water," "moisture in the atmosphere", *i. e.* mist, dew, rain, fog, frost, hoar-frost (S. E. D. p. 334).

ขณะ   ka[4]-na[4] *n.* any immeasurably short period of time; an instant; a moment; a twinkling of an eye (S. E. D.): ขณะก่อน the previous moment: ขณะทำการตามหน้าที่ at the instant one was executing his duty: ขณะนั้น at that time; then: ขณะเมื่อ when; whereas.

ขด   kot[4] *v.* to roll into a coil; to coil or wind into rings; to be rolled in a spiral form: *n.* a circle; a coil; rings formed by winding: ขดชักนำ (ไฟฟ้า) an induction coil.

ขตอย   ka[4]-dtaw-ie *Cam. n.* a scorpion.

ขน ๑   kon[2] *P. S. v.* to wriggle in (as an eel into mud); to delve into; to worm into a hole; to root up or into (S. E. D. p. 336).

ขน ๒   kon[2] *v.* to transport; to haul away; to carry off; to remove belongings; to take away in quantity: *n.* hair; feathers: ขนแกะ wool; fleece: ขนของ to remove personal effects: ขนคิ้ว the eyebrows: ขนตา eyelashes: ขนนก bird feathers: ขนระบัด pin-feathers; new feathers growing out after the moulting season: ขนลุก, ขนชัน hair

standing perpendicularly from fright or fear :
ขนหยึ่ง the hair stands on end from fear (as
of cats); fear ; alarm ; terror ; dread :   ขนอ่อน
soft, delicate or tender hairs :   ปากกาขนท่าน
a quill pen.

ข้น   kon³ *adj.* thick (as liquids); dense ;
viscid ; compact ; semi-fluid :   ข้นแค้น, ข้นจน
to be in want ; to need ; to be reduced to
poverty.

ขนก   ka⁴-nok⁴ *P. S. n.* a digger ; a miner ;
destroyers of houses (as robbers or rats); an
excavator (S. E. D. p. 336).

ขนง   ʹka⁴-nong² *Cam. n.* the eyebrows.

ขนงเนื้อ   ka⁴-nong²-nur-ah⁵ *n.* the roasted
hide of an animal, that has been boiled until
suitable for food.

ขนด   ka⁴-not⁴ *n.* crookedness ; tortuous-
ness ; a condition of being curled or twisted
crooked (as the coils of a snake); the twisted
portion of a Buddhist monk's robe, which is
rolled and worn around the arm.

ขนน   ka⁴-non² *Cam. n.* a three-cornered
pillow.

ขนบ   ka⁴-nop⁴ *n.* a system ; a pattern ; a
manner or method ; usual practice ; order of
procedure :   ขนบธรรมเนียม manners ; customs ; practices ; habits.

ขนม   ka⁴-nom² *n.* bread ; sweetmeats ;
cakes ; cereal foods :   ขนมกง a sweetmeat
made of peanut flour mixed with sugar.
These are rolled out, shaped into circles and
sprinkled with spices (as wheels or doughnuts,
etc., with a total of about 32 kinds) :   ขนม
กะละแม a sweetmeat like toffee, made of
cooked glutinous rice-flour, sugar and coconut
milk :   ขนมโก้ a sweetmeat of Chinese
origin made of cooked, pulverized, sun-dried
rice mixed with sugar :   ขนมจีน vermicelli
eaten with a pepper sauce :   ขนมปัง bread
(made of wheat flour).

ขนอง   ka⁴-naung² *Cam. n.* the back ; the
rear portion.

ขนอน   ka⁴-naun² *n.* a custom-house ; a
provincial tax station ; a place of waiting :
หนังสือเบิกด่านขนอน a paper releasing goods
held by customs officials.

ขนอบ ๑   ka⁴-naup⁴ *v.* to be composed of ; to
be put together ; to be made of ; to be mixed
together :   *n.* a pattern ; a model ; attitudes ;
appearances ; manner of procedure :   *adv.*
around (so as to encircle on all sides).

ขนอบ ๒   ka⁴-naup⁴ *Peg. n.* to be quiet ;
to be silent ; to be still.

ขนัด   ka⁴-nat⁴ *v.* to impede ; to interrupt ;
to obstruct ; to hinder the passage of ; to force
delay :   *n.* a line of (as people) ; a queue ; a
row (as of soldiers) ; a series (as of dishes) ; a
small piece (as of land) :   ขนัดดาบ a row
or line of swordsmen (as in a procession) :
สวนขนัดหนึ่ง a plot of garden land.

ขนั้น   ka⁴-nun² *v.* to prevent ; to obstruct ;
to oppose ; to surround ; to encircle ; to bind
up ; to bandage (tightly) :   *n.* a tree of the
jack-fruit tree family (ขนุน) :   *adj.* amusing ;
laughable :   ขนั้นศพเด็ก to wrap up ; to
envelop the corpse of a child in cloth.

ขนาก   ka⁴-nak⁴ *n.* a kind of sedge plant.

ขนาง   ka⁴-nang² *v.* to doubt ; to suspect ;
to be estranged ; to be at variance with ; to
be abashed :   อย่าได้ขนางใจกัน be not at
variance with each other ; be not of a doubting heart.

ขนาด   ka⁴-nat⁴ *n.* a long-handled basket
(used by the Chinese for watering plants) ; an
estimation of magnitude, shape, size, form or
model ; a scoop made of wicker-work, water-
proofed with damar and fitted with a handle
across the opening (used for bailing water
from a boat) :   เกินขนาด, นอกขนาด in excess ;
too much ; oversized :   ขนาดกลาง medium
in size :   ขนาดเล็ก of the smaller size :
ขนาดหลวง in size or capacity as designated by
the Government :   เต็มขนาด full measure :
ถึงขนาด as best suits ; sufficient.

ขนาน   ka^4-nan^2 v. to be or lie parallel (as two lines); to give or settle upon (as a name); to call by a name: n. a kind of boat; a group; a portion of a prescribed remedy: ขนานนาม to give a name to; to name: เดิน-ขนานกัน to march in parallel lines: ผูกเรือ-ขนานกัน to lash boats side by side: ยาหลาย-ขนาน many different varieties or several portions of medicines.

ขนาบ, กระนาบ   ka^4-nap^4 v. to bind; to tie together (as two sides of a hedge or the mouth of a basket); to compress; to squeeze and bind together (as sheaves of rice stalks); to hold or confine by compression or pressure.

ขนาย   ka^4-nai^2 Cam. n. the tusks of a female elephant.

ขนิษฐ, ขนิษฐา   ka^4-nit^6-ta^4 (obs. see กนิษฐ) n. the younger members of a family; the little finger; a lesser wife: adj. small; little; young; lesser; least.

ขนุน (ต้น)   ka^4-noon^2 n. the jack-fruit, Artocarpus integrifolia (Urticaceae) (V. P. p. 36: MCM. p. 216: Dept. Agri. & Fisheries: Burk. pp. 247, 258), a large tree, native of South India and Malaya. The enormous fruits, one of which may weigh up to 100 lbs. or more, are borne on the trunk and older branches. The fruit forms a very important article of food with the poorer people in the Eastern tropics. The large albuminous white seeds, when cooked and served in curries, are especially relished (MCM. p. 254). The heart-wood is the source of a common yellow dye used in dyeing mats and the robes of Buddhist monks: ขนุน (ปลา) Caranx carangus (Carangidae) (Dept. Agri. & Fisheries: Burk. p. 449), the yellow-tail or horse-mackerel: ขนุนทอง (ต้น) Ananas comosus (A. sativus) (Bromeliaceae) (V. P. p. 37), the pineapple, a perennial stemless plant, with long, narrow, fibrous and usually spiny leaves, cultivated on commercial lines. The fruit is borne on an erect, stout stalk issuing from the centre of the plant, which dies after maturing the fruit, and is usually repro-

duced by suckers (ratoons) from the base (MCM. p. 231). The fruit is generally regarded as one of the most delicious fruits in tropical regions. The fresh juice of the leaves is regarded as a powerful anthelmintic (Dept. Agri. & Fisheries: Burk. p. 148): ขนุนป่าน (ต้น) Artocarpus sp. (Urticaceae), a genus of about forty evergreen trees having a milky sap. The timber is generally good and durable (Dept. Agri. & Fisheries: V. P. p. 37: Burk. p. 247): ขนุนละมุด a species of jack-fruit with a tender rind: ขนุนสำมะลอ a species of jack-fruit: ขนุน-หนัง a species of jack-fruit with a tough rind.

ขบ   kop^4 v. to crack with the teeth; to bite; to hold between the teeth; to solve (as a riddle); to be painful (as the burrowing stage of pus formation in an abscess): ขบ-เผาะ applied to young, half-developed or brittle mangoes because when bitten into, a cracking sound is produced: ขบพื้น to grind the teeth: ขบสะเก็ด being bound down or confined by a scab (as over an ulcer).

ขบขัน   kop^4-kan^2 adj. amusing; laughable; ridiculous; funny.

ขบถ see กบฏ

ขบวร see กบูร

ขบุกเพลี่ยง   ka-^{4}book^4-plee-ang Cam. v. to call back (as by incantations or propitiatory offerings); to receive the protecting genii.

ขบูร see กบูร

ขม   kom^2 n. a variety of rattan: adj. bitter (in taste): ขมฝาด, ขมเฝื่อน bitter and astringent or puckery: ขม (หอย) a genus of shell-fish resembling, in shape, the fresh water or pond snail; the vivipara: ขมหวานจ้อ (ต้น) Evodia viticina (Rutaceae) (Cb. p. 218), a somewhat aromatic shrub found in scrub jungle or evergreen forest (K.: Burk. p. 987).

ข่ม   kom^4 v. to press downwards; to depress; to compress; to squeeze; to bear down;

to exert pressure upon: ข่มขี่ oppression; tyranny; subjection to unjust hardships: ข่มขืน to coerce; to constrain by force or fear; to compel: *n.* coercion; cruel oppression; persecution: ข่มขืนชำเรา to rape: ข่มท้อง to exert pressure on the abdomen to expel the foetus: ข่มนาม to insult an enemy in effigy before engaging in war: ข่มเหง to tease; to vex; to harass in a petty way; to annoy; to irritate; to abuse one's authority; to overtax; to persecute; to maltreat; to treat severely.

ขมม　　　ka[4]-mom[2] *v.* to praise; to eulogize; to applaud; to show appreciation.

ขมวด, กระหมวด　　　ka[4]-moo-at[4] *v.* to twist into a knot (as when tying a rope); to tie a knot; to encircle with a string or band: ขมวดจุก to twist or dress the topknot into shape: ขมวดผม to wind one's hair up into a knot: ขมวดยา (เรือ) a style of boat with tapering, upturned bow and stern, propelled by paddles: ผมขมวด hair that has been knotted or done up.

ขมวน　　　ka[4]-moo-an[2] *n.* maggots found in putrid flesh; odour (as of something burning) (Palle. p. 312): *adj.* softened; disintegrated (as having been eaten by insects or moths); rotten.

ขมัว　　　ka[4]-moo-ah[2] *adj.* dark; indistinct; hazy; misty; smoky: เมฆขมัว darkened by clouds or smoke.

ขมอง　　　ka[4]-maung[2] *n.* the skull; the head; the cranium.

ขม่อม　　　ka[4]-maum[4] *n.* the top of the head; the crown of the head.

ขมั้ง　　　ka[4]-mang[2] *Cam. n.* an archer; a bow-sportsman; a hunter with bow and arrow.

ขมับ　　　ka[4]-map[4] *n.* the temporal fossa.

ขมา see กษมา

ขม้ำ, ขย้ำ　　　ka[4]-mam[3] *v.* to chew in a slob-

bering, indecent or ravenous manner: *adv.* greedily; ravenously; voraciously; eagerly.

ขมิ้น　　　ka[4]-min[3] *n. Curcuma domestica,* (*Zingiberaceae*); *C. longa,* an East Indian plant, the rhizomes and roots of which are used as a condiment, dye or face powder called turmeric (V. P. p. 37: MCM. p. 342: Dept. Agri. & Fisheries: Burk. p. 704): ขมิ้น (นก) Gyldenstolpe's babbler, *Mixornis rubricapilla minor* (Herb. N. H. J. S. S. VI, 1, p. 92): ขมิ้น-เครือ, มันแดง (ต้น) *Combretum extensum* (*Combretaceae*) (cb. p. 615: K.): ขมิ้นเครือ (ต้น) *Cissampelos pareira* (*Menispermaceae*), a lofty climber (see ขงเขมา): ขมิ้นชัน (ต้น) *Curcuma zedoaria* (*Zingiberaceae*), a plant resembling the ginger (K.: Burk. p. 714): ขมิ้นป่า (ต้น) *Curcuma parviflora* (*Zingiberaceae*) (V. P. p. 37), an erect herb with aromatic, fleshy rootstocks. The leaves are distichous, oblong to oblong-elliptic or obovate, usually tufted: ขมิ้นมัททรี (ต้น) *Flemingia lineata* (*Leguminosae*) (cb. p. 470: K.), a shrub found in scrub jungle (Burk. p. 1025): ขมิ้นหลังคอดำ (นก) the Burmese black-naped oriole, *Oriolus chinensis tennirostris* (Deig. N. H. J. S. S. VIII, 3, p. 150): ขมิ้นเหลืองอ่อน (นก) the common iora, *Aegithina tiphia tiphia* (Herb. N. H. J. S. S. VI, 1, p. 93); the black-naped oriole, *Oriolus indicus;* the Indian black-headed oriole, *Oriolus melanocephalus* (will. N. H. J. S. S. I. 3, pp. 201, 202): ขมิ้นหอม (ต้น) *Curcuma aromatica* (*Zingiberaceae*) (V. P. p. 37), an herb flowering in the hot season. Its principal use is as a dyeing agent. The rhizomes are used medicinally, being regarded as tonic and carminative (Dept. Agri. & Fisheries: Burk. p. 705): ขมิ้นอ้อย (ต้น) the rhizome of *Curcuma zedoaria* (*Zingiberaceae*), a plant resembling ginger (Burk. p. 714).

ขมิบ, กระหมิบ　　　ka[4]-mip[4] *v.* to compress; to contract; to close an orifice by muscular action (as by the sphincter muscles); to confine or to restrict by muscular action.

ขมีขมัน　　　ka[4]-me[2]-ka[4]-man[2] *Cam. adj.* active; quick; speedy; immediate (action).

ขมึ่ง   ka⁴-murng² $v.$ to stare at; to fix the eyes upon in a steady gaze:

ขมึ่งทึ่ง   ka⁴-murng²-teung $adv.$ horrible; dreadful; terrifying or shocking in appearance.

ขมุ   ka⁴-moo⁴ $n.$ a mountain tribe from across the Menam Khong, inhabiting the Shan states and northern Siam and being descendants of the original Khmer stock (w. p. 42).

ขมุกขมัว   ka⁴-mook⁴-ka⁴-moo-ah² $n.$ eventide; early evening time; twilight; a period of time just before dark; dusk.

ขมุดขมิด see กระหมุดกระหมิด

ขมุบ, กระหมุบ   ka⁴-moop⁴ $v.$ to throb; to pulsate; to beat (as the heart or pulse).

ขมุบขมิบ see กระหมุบกระหมิบ

ขมุม   ka⁴-moom² $Cam.$ $n.$ the honey bee: ตึกขมุม honey.

เขม่า see กระเหม่า

ขย   ka⁴-ya⁶ $P.$ $n.$ diminution; finality; destruction; end (s. e. d. p. 328).

ขยด   ka⁴-yot⁴ $v.$ to shift a little from one position to another; to move on slightly or to leave one's place; to retire slightly.

ขยม   ka⁴-yom² $Cam.$ $n.$ a servant; a slave: $pron.$ I; me.

ขยล   ka⁴-yon² $Cam.$ $n.$ wind; air.

ขยอก   ka⁴-yawk⁴ $v.$ to swallow quickly; to bolt (food); to gulp down without sufficient mastication: $n.$ a worm pest of young rice stalks.

ขย้อน see กระย่อน

ขยะ   ka⁴-ya⁴ $n.$ rubbish; sweepings; trash; waste; refuse; shavings.

ขยะแขยง   ka⁴-ya⁴-ka-yaang² $v.$ to detest the sight of; to have a feeling of abhorrence; to revolt at the sight of; to have a feeling of repulsion, alienation or estrangement, arising from anger, hate or disgust.

ขยัก   ka⁴-yak⁴ $v.$ to keep back some; to reserve part of; to withhold some portion (as of salary): $adj.$ wavering; fluctuating: ขยักขย่อน to move or pull in and out; to move in a vermicular manner; to waver; to fluctuate; to be unstable.

ขยัน   ka⁴-yan² $adj.$ diligent; industrious; persistent; persevering.

ขยั้น   ka⁴-yan⁵ $v.$ to intimidate; to put in fear of; to be afraid of; to reverence with fear.

ขยับ   ka⁴-yap⁴ $v.$ to move a little into place (as roof tiles); to adjust or cause to fit by a slight adjustment; to be "on the marks" ready for a race; to be ready to begin: $adj.$ slight; trifling; little; insignificant: ขยับ กรับ the striking of castanets (as an accompaniment to song or dance): ขยับขยด to approach or to retire slowly: ขยับขยาย to change or readjust a little (as a fence); to expand or enlarge slightly: ขยับเขยื้อน to be moved from one place to another: ขยับ เข้ามา to approach; to come nearer; to bring closer together: ขยับตัว to change one's place (as when sitting or standing): ขยับท่า it looks as if, or as though: ขยับเท้า to draw back or move the foot a trifle: ขยับมือ to withdraw the hand: ขยับหู to give ear to some one; to adjust the head in order to hear more distinctly; to turn the ear towards (as when trying to hear better): ขยับออก to retire; to go away; to remove a little at a time.

ขยาด   ka⁴-yat⁴ $v.$ to be fearful or afraid; to be timid; to be intimidated or baffled by danger; to be horrified; to fear (as to the consequences): เกรงขยาด to abandon an undertaking from fear: ขยั้นขยาด to fear; to reverence with respect.

ขยาบ   ka⁴-yap⁴ $n.$ an adjustable roof or sun-shade for the bow or stern of some kinds of Siamese boats.

ขยาย (ตัว)   ka⁴-yai² $v.$ to expand; to cause to swell; to cause to be dilated:

ขยายขนาด to amplify; to magnify: ขยาย-
ส่วน to enlarge; to extend; to augment:
ขยายความ to explain; to elucidate: ขยาย-
เรื่อง to unfold a secret: ขยายใบเรือ to unfurl (as a sail): ขยายรูป to magnify; to
enlarge a picture: ขยายที่ to extend the
boundaries or limits of a place.

ขย่ำ ka⁴-yum² *v.* to mix, mingle or make
homogeneous or uniform by using the finger-
tips or hands with alternate relaxations; to
use the fingers or hands in mingling, blending, compounding or amalgamating (as when
mixing curry with the rice): ขย่ำขยี้ to
knead: บีบขย่ำ to squeeze; to macerate
with the fingers or hands.

ขย้ำ see ขม้ำ

ขยิก ka⁴-yik⁴ *also* ka⁴-yik² *adv.* quickly
and often repeated; consecutively; successively: *n.* following in rapid, uninterrupted
succession.

ขยิบ ka⁴-yip⁴ *v.* to wink; to blink or bat
the eyes; to make signs with the eyes:
ขยิบตา to indicate with the eyes: ขยุบขยิบ
to move restlessly.

ขยุ่ม see กระหยุ่ม

ขยี้ ka⁴-yee³ *v.* to apply pressure with a
slight rotary motion; to rub hard with the
hands (as in washing clothes); to iron out
with the finger (as a bruise); to press down
firmly with a rotary movement; to squash
(as in killing an insect).

ขยุกขยิก ka⁴-yook⁴-ka⁴-yik⁴ *v.* to be
fidgety; to move restlessly; to shake; to
tremble; to manifest a condition of unrest.

ขยุกขยุย ka⁴-yook⁴-ka⁴-yoo-ie² *adj.* ragged; frayed; rough; broken.

ขยุบ ka⁴-yoop⁴ *adj.* wriggling; wiggling;
worming; creeping (as worms); being slow
or imperfect in motion (descriptive of the
actions of insects, worms or animals).

ขยุม ๑ ka⁴-yoom² *Cam. n.* a servant; a
slave: *pron.* I; me: ขยุมแต่ I; me.

ขยุม ๒ ka⁴-yoom² *adj.* performed in a
short, rapid, uninterrupted succession of
strokes, blows or knocks (as paddling a boat
or chewing food): พายเรือขยุมไปบ้าน to
paddle a boat home with short, rapid, consecutive strokes.

ขยุ้ม ka⁴yoom³ *v.* to pick up or to gather
up with the five fingers; to grasp with the
five fingers: ขยุ้มมือหนึ่ง that which, or as
much as can be held with the five fingers; a
pinch: หยิบเอาขยุ้มหนึ่ง to take up what the
fingers can hold.

ขยุย ka⁴-yoo-ie² *adj.* scattered; dissipated;
diffused.

ขร kon² *S. P. n.* pebbles; the name of a
man-eating Rakshasa, a goblin or evil spirit,
the younger brother of Ravana. He was
killed by Rama-chandra (H. C. D. p. 156): *adj.*
hard; harsh; rough; sharp; pungent; acid;
dense (as clouds); hurtful; cutting (as speech
or words); sharp-edged; cruel (S. E. D. p. 337).

ขรม krom² *adj.* noisy; boisterous.

ขรรค์ kan² *n.* a rhinoceros; the horn of a
rhinoceros; a large sacrificial knife; a double-
edged weapon (similar to a bayonet) (S. E. D.
p. 335).

ขรัว kroo-ah² *n.* a patriarch; an abbot of
advanced years; an aged Buddhist monk:
ขรัวเจ้าวัด the superior abbot of a monastery:
ขรัวเจ้าใหญ่ the superior one who has the chief
authority; a general overseer: ขรัวยาย
a title of rank accorded the grandmother of
a prince or princess having the rank of
Royal Highness: เจ้าน้ำเจ้าขรัว *idiom.* com-
manders; superiors.

ขรึม kreum² *n.* reserve (as of a person);
a state of meditation; reflection in private.

ขรุขระ kroo⁴-kra⁴ *adj.* rough; untrimmed;
nodular.

ขลวน kloo-an² *Cam. n.* a physical object;
a person.

ขลัก (ต้น)   kluk[4] *n. Bruguiera sexangula* (*Rhizophoraceae*) (CB. p. 597), a tree about 15 m. high growing along rivers of the mangrove forest (K.). *Bruguiera* is a small genus (BURK. p. 375).

ขลัง   klang[2] *adj.* strong; zealous; enthusiastic; having miraculous power: วิชาขลัง expert knowledge or skill, capable of producing results through alchemy: คนขลังวิชา one enthusiastic in educational pursuits.

ขลับ   klap[4] *adj.* glistening; bright; shining; burnished; lustrous: ดำขลับ shiny black; dark and lustrous.

ขลา   kla[2] *Cam. n.* a tiger.

ขลาด   klat[4] *adj.* timid; fearful; bashful; timorous; shy; easily frightened.

ขลิบ   klip[4] *v.* to clip the edges together; to attach to the edge; to put on a border or band (as on a hat); to face a garment with silk or other cloth: *n.* fringe; lace-edging: ขลิบทอง to fasten a gold fringe along the edge; to supply with a lace-of-gold border: ขลิบริม to trim or bind the edges.

ขลุก   klook[4] *adj.* frequent; repeated; continuous; absorbed or wholly occupied (as by music or a play); concentrated (attention): *onomat.* from the sound of small stones or bullets rolled around in a vessel: ขลุกขลัก an out-of-order noise; having continued difficulty (as in some machinery or with a project); without continuity; lacking in order or regularity: ขลุกขลิก the game of betting or gambling where stakes are placed on the spots on dice, which have been shaken in a covered receptacle: ขลุกขลุ่ย continuous; absorbed mentally (as in following a hobby).

ขลุบ   kloop[4] *n.* a ball used in competitive games (as golf, cricket or tennis balls).

ขลุม   kloom[2] *n.* a muzzle used on dogs; a nose piece or mouth guard for vicious animals.

ขลุ่ย   kloo-ay[4] *n.* a flute; a musical windinstrument made from a joint of a reed; a reed pipe.

ขลู่   kloo[4] *n. Pluchea indica* (*Compositae*) (V. P. p. 44: Dept. Agri. Fisheries: BURK. p. 1773), a small bush used by the natives, for its medicinal properties. The leaves are eaten as a flavouring.

ขวง (ผัก)   koo-ang[2] *n. Mollugo* (*Glinus*) *oppositifolius* (*Ficoidaceae*) (CB. p. 785), a plant eaten as a vegetable; a spirit; a ghost; genii: เสี้ยงขวง to worship the household spirits; to make propitiatory offerings of food to the spirits.

ขวด   koo-at[4] *n.* a bottle; used as a prefix to other nouns in order to form the name of different varieties of bottles: ขวดเจียรไน a cut-glass bottle: ขวดดิน an earthen bottle or jug-like vessel: ขวดโหล a glass jar with a large glass stopper.

ขวน, ขวนขวาย   koo-an[2] *v.* to seek for; to look for; to search for by making inquiries; to endeavour to find; to investigate with diligence.

ขว่น   koo-an[4] *v.* to scratch with finger-nails or claws: หยิกขว่น to pinch and scratch with the finger-nails (as one who is in a rage).

ขวบ   koo-ap[4] *n.* the revolution of a period of time; a year.

ขวย   koo-ay[2] *v.* to be bashful; to be shy or timid; to be ashamed to meet other people; to shrink from public notice: ขวยเขินสะเทิน อาย to be bashful; to be timorous from fear or shame.

ขวักไขว่   kwak[4]-kwai[4] *adj.* oscillating; swinging; swaying; being or lying crossed or massed together; entangled; mixed.

ขวัญ   kwan[2] *n.* an old Thai word (probably of Chinese derivation) meaning fortune, luck, auspiciousness, beauty, charm, grace or prosperity: กล่าวนินทาขวัญ to slander; to speak evil of some one by referring invidiously to the protecting genii : ขนขวัญ a lucky or auspicious feather or tail hair (as of a white elephant): ขวัญเกี้ยง being an omen of ill-luck; having disaster as a result: ขวัญข้าว a thank offering made to a teacher or by a patient to his doctor : ขวัญดิน richness of the soil: ขวัญบ่า to cause to lose one's charm; to offend the protecting genii : ขวัญผม the circle of hair forming the crown : ขวัญหาย, ขวัญบิน the protecting genius or charm has departed from one : ไข่ขวัญ the egg or food for the propitiation of the "Khuan" or "Manito" or good fortune of the tonsured. This surmounts the conical structures in the confirmation tonsorial ceremony and no doubt symbolizes the vital principle and represents the idea of rebirth. As the candidate eats this, it is evident the act signifies that the Khuan is reborn in his body and that he has entered upon a new life of prosperity, happiness and composure. This forms a part of the ceremonies attending topknot cuttings, initiations of Buddhist monks, and also ceremonies for new-born babes: ของขวัญ a mascot; a gift: ค่าทำขวัญ a compensation made for injury done: จอมขวัญ the upper extremity of the circle or tuft of hair on the head; name of the wife's or husband's daughter or of a lovable girl (a term of affection): ตลาดขวัญ an attractive or prosperous market: ทำขวัญ to make a compensation or to atone for an injury (whether moral or material) to a person or thing; to make an offering to fairies, spirits or genii by proper invocations and conjurations: เป็นขวัญเมือง a monument which is the glory and pride of a city: เป็นขวัญนัยนา, ขวัญตา a lovely sight; one charming to the eyes; *colloq.* sweetheart: ผูก ขวัญ to place threads or cords strung with charms around the neck, wrists or ankles of infants or of the sick; to ward off the power of evil spirits or to insure protection to the individual through propitiatory incantations or magical formulas and offerings: รับขวัญ to call back the protecting spirit by proper invocations and conjurations: หมอขวัญ a spirit-doctor or specialist in the matter, who must be engaged to perform invocations to propitiate the genii (he is one who possesses a thorough knowledge of the Khuan's habits and speaks with a soft flowing melodious voice, two elements indispensable to success) (Ger. (1) pp. 157–8): ขวัญกล้า courageous.

ขวัดแคว้ง kwat[4]-kwaang[5] *v.* to run to and fro; to be restive.

ขวับ, ขวับเขวี่ยว kwap[4] *onomat.* from the whistling sound of a whip swishing rapidly through the air.

ขวา kwah[2] *adj.* right (hand): ขวา (นก) the silver pheasant (Laos), *Gennaeus* (Deig. N. H. J. S. S. VIII, 3, p. 168): ขวาซ้าย right and left: ข้างขวา towards the right hand; on the starboard side.

ขวาก kwak[4] *n.* spikes or barbed points of wood or iron used in traps or placed in snares as protection against thieves (as around fruit trees): ขวาก, แขวก (นก) the Chinese white-breasted water-hen, *Amaurornis phoenicura chinensis* (Herb. N. H. J. S. S. VI, 4, p. 341): ขวากกะจับ a four-pronged, sharp-pointed wooden or iron trap, so made that it rests on three prongs with the others projecting upright: ขวากตน (นก) the eastern grey heron, *Ardea cinerea rectirostris* (Deig. N. H. J. S. S. VIII, 3, p. 173): ขวากหนาม to place or hide thorns (as traps laid for thieves).

ขวาง kwang[2] *v.* to lie athwart; to put or be across the line of advance; to obstruct; to oppose: *adj.* lying athwart; intersecting; transverse; crosswise: กว้างขวาง wide; spacious; large; ample; vast: ขวางเรือ to allow a boat to lie crosswise in a canal or river: ขวางหน้า, ขวางทาง to obstruct another while advancing; to block the passage.

ขว้าง kwang[3] *v.* to hurl; to throw; to cast; to fling: ขว้างกา a wooden weapon sharpened at both ends and hurled or flung as a weapon of defense : ขว้างค้อน (งู) a species of short snake that can hurl or propel its body in jumps when travelling in haste (as one would throw a hammer).

ขวาด (ต้น) kwaat[4] n. Garcinia speciosa (Guttiferae) (cb. p. 118), an evergreen tree yielding inferior gamboge. The wood is uniformly yellow or reddish-brown, close-grained, very heavy and used for house and bridge posts and for yokes (Dept. Agri. & Fisheries : Burk. p. 1050).

ขวาน kwan[2] n. an axe ; a hatchet : ขวาน ปูล, ขวานปูเท้า an ancient, long-handled battle-axe with a spear fitted to the metal head : ขวานโยน an axe having a metal cutting-edge, attached to a wooden body through which a long, curved handle passes : ขวานเหงาะ an adze ; a carpenter's tool formed with a thin arching blade set at right angles to the handle (used for chipping a flat or concave surface) : ขวานหมู an ordinary small hatchet : หัวขวาน (นก) the Malay scaly-bellied green wood-pecker, Picus vittatus vittatus (Herb. N. J. S. S. VI, 3, p. 298).

ขวนขวาย see ขวน

ขว้าว (ต้น) kwow[3] n. Adina cordifolia (Rubiaceae) (V. P. p. 56), a large deciduous tree. The small buds, ground with round pepper, are sniffed into the nose in cases of severe headaches. The yellow, moderately hard, even-grained wood is used in construction of furniture, agricultural implements, opium boxes, writing-tablets, gun-stocks, combs, and occasionally for dug-out canoes (Dept. Agri. & Fisheries : Burk. p. 51).

ขวิด kwit[4] v. to attack with the horns or antlers ; to horn.

ขอ kaw[2] v. to beg for ; to plead with ; to ask for : n. a hook of wood or iron ; a hook on a long handle : ขอเกี่ยว a grapnel ; a hook used to unite or join two bodies : ของ้อ to plead for reinstatement (as after being in

disfavour) : ของ้าว a war scythe ; an ancient weapon of warfare, used while riding on an elephant : ขอฉาย a bamboo stick 4 to 6 feet long having a pointed, curved end (used for removing straw from the threshing floor) : ขอช้าง a curved hook or blade mounted on a long handle (used by mahouts in controlling or guiding elephants) : ขอ เดชะ "may it please" (Your Majesty), the stereotyped form used to address a Siamese monarch : ขอทาน to beg ; to ask for alms : ขอประทาน "be pleased to grant" (a form of address from an inferior to a superior) : ขอเฝ้า the chief of the pages in attendance at the palace of a Siamese prince, whose duty it is to conduct visitors into the royal presence : ขอพระราชทาน "be pleased to grant" (a form of address or request used to His Siamese Majesty or to princes of high rank) : ขอยืม to borrow ; to receive on trust with the intention of repaying or returning : ขอร้อง to pray or plead for help or succour ; to beseech ; to solicit ; to supplicate : ขอรับ a word of assent as "yes, sir," used by an inferior to his superior or between equals in rank ; also used for politeness at the end of a sentence, as the word, "sir." This word is used only by men and boys, never by women : ขอรับกระผม, ขอรับผม "yes, sir" (a form of consent or affirmation used by an inferior to noblemen of high rank) : ขอรับกระหม่อม "yes, sir" (a form of assent used to a Mom Chao) : ขอรับใส่เกล้าใส่กระหม่อม "yes, Your Royal Highness" (a form of assent used to a prince of the Somdet Chao Phya rank) : ขอแรง, วาน to ask the help of ; to ask the assistance of : ขอษมา to apologize : ขออภัย, ขอษมา, ขอโทษ to beg pardon ; to ask for clemency : สู่ขอ to ask for in marriage : ห่วงรับขอสับ hook and eye fasteners (as for garments) : เหลือขอ incorrigible ; incapable of being corrected or amended.

ข่อ (นก) kaw[4] n. the brown-breasted hill-partridge, Arborophila brunneopectus (Deig. N. J. S. S. VIII, 3. p. 168).

ข้อ kaw[3] *n.* a joint; a movable articulation of bones; a bamboo joint; a verse; a paragraph or section; a knot or joining of a cord: ข้อแก้ตัว *legal* defence: ข้อขอด, ข้อสำคัญ important problems: ข้อขัดขวาง hindrances; obstructions; delays; interruptions: ข้อความ counts or charges; *legal* clause or point: ข้อความซึ่งเถียงไม่ได้ an irrefutable fact: ข้อแทรก *legal* a rider: ข้อแทรกในพินัยกรรม *legal* a codicil: ข้อต่อ an articulation: ข้อเท้า ankle: ข้อบังคับ *legal* regulation: ข้อประเด็น *legal* point at issue: ข้อมั่นคง an irrevocable promise: ข้อมือ wrist: ข้อยกเว้น exceptions: ข้อลับ a mystery; a secret: ข้อสัญญา *legal* stipulations: ข้อเสือ an universal joint; the rod connecting the piston with the crank-shaft: ข้อหารือ problems or matters to be considered.

ขอก kauk[4] *n.* locality; a place; inhabitants of a place: ขอกนคร citizens of a capitol city: ขอกนา a farmer: คนบ้านนอกขอกนา rural people or citizens of the country; rustic folk.

ของ ๑ kaung[2] *n.* things; belongings; goods; chattels; movable property: ของกลาง stolen articles that have been found or returned to the owner; articles on exhibition; articles in dispute deposited in the court awaiting the decision of the judge; articles proving criminality in a suit at law: ของกำนัล a present; a gift: ของขวัญโดยพินัยกรรม *legal* legacy: ของแข็ง solids: ของคาว fish or meat eaten with the rice: ของชำ things or subjects that must be kept secret (as stolen property): ของชำร่วย, ของช่วย a souvenir or keepsake given to a person in return for help; presents given to the participants in any function, in return for gifts made by them: ของชะเลย booty of war: ของใช้สรอย utensils of various kinds: ของเถื่อน contraband or illicit goods: ของแถมพก a gift made in return for services rendered at a function; a complimentary present: ของที่ใช้บ้างแล้ว second-hand goods or articles:

ของที่ต้องมอบให้ตามพินัยกรรม a bequest made according to a will: ของผสม mixtures: ของฝาก articles given over into the custody of another: ของเย็น unsuspected or unstolen articles: ของร้อน, ของโจร an article secured by fraud (as something stolen which must be hidden); suspected articles; stolen property: ของลับ private organs or secret possessions: ของเล่น toys; playthings: ของว่าง food or refreshments eaten between meals: ของหลวง property of the Crown: ของเหลว liquids: ของไหล fluids: ของหวาน candies or sweets eaten after a meal: ข้าวของ personal effects; that which belongs to a person; possessions; property: เจ้าของ an owner; a proprietor.

ของ ๒ kaung[2] *gram.* sign of the possessive case, *ex.* เรือนของผม = my house.

ข้อง kaung[3] *v.* to be associated with; to be mixed up in an affair: *n.* a large wicker basket for confining fish: ข้องเกี่ยว to be mixed up with; to be implicated in: ข้องขัด to be in want; to be impoverished; to be in difficulty; to raise objections to (as opposing a project); to put hindrances in the way of: ข้องแวะ to be associated with (as in evil practices); to be in danger of being led astray; to be connected with: ข้องอยู่ to remain entangled or stationary while floating (as carrion).

ขอด kaut[4] *v.* to scrape off (as barnacles from the bottom of a boat); to take from or off; to pare off; to evaporate; to lessen by degrees: *n.* a knot; a protuberance or swelling; the hard, gnarled portion of the trunk of a tree: *adj.* almost dry (as water in a canal); nearly empty (as a rice pot); nearly exhausted (as a supply): ขอดเกล็ดปลา to remove fish scales: ขอดข้าวในหม้อ to scrape the remaining rice from the bottom of the pot: ขอดค่อน to make slurring or disparaging remarks to, or about; to malign or speak evil of: ขอดหม้อ to remove nearly

all the contents from a rice pot : ข้าวขอด-
หม้อ a pot almost empty of rice : เงินขอด-
กระเป๋า a purse containing very little money :
น้ำขอดคลอง a canal left almost dry by the
tide : น้ำขอดโอ่ง to remove nearly all the
water from a water jar.

ขอน   kaun[2] *n.* a log ; a round bulky section
of the trunk of a tree ; one of a pair : *adj.*
single ; sole ; solitary : กำไลขอนหนึ่ง one of
a pair of bracelets : ขอนดอก (ต้น) *Asclepias
gigantia* (chd. p. 25), a plant used medicinally :
ขอนสัก a teak log.

ข้อน   kaun[4] *adj.* turbulent ; disturbed ;
agitated ; being inclined ; having a tendency
to ; being disposed to.

ข้อน   kaun[3] *v.* to hammer ; to pound down ;
to forge with a hammer ; to strike with a
mallet : *n.* a hammer.

ขอบ   kaup[4] *v.* to be grateful ; to acknowledge or repay benefits : *n.* an edge ; rim ;
brim ; border ; margin ; verge ; boundary ;
circumference : ขอบขัณฑเสมา a rampart
over which is built a superstructure in the
shape of leaves ; the circumferential boundaries
of a kingdom : ขอบเขตร boundary limits ;
the outermost limits of a territory : ขอบ-
คุณ to be grateful for ; to give thanks for ;
to be in a condition of gratitude towards ; to
please by satisfying some wish : ขอบใจ to
express gratitude for a favour or kindness
bestowed : ขอบตา the periphery of the
eye ; the white of the eyeball : ขอบพระทัย
to thank ; to express gratitude for a favour or
kindness bestowed (used only to royalty) :
ขอบฟ้า the horizon : ขอบไร completeness ;
complement ; the quantity required to make
a situation complete.

ขอบนาง (ต้น)   kaup[4]-nang *n. Salacia
flavescens* (*Celastraceae*) (cb. p. 289), a climbing
jungle shrub found from Tenasserim and
Siam to Singapore. The leaves are opposite,
exstipulate, entire or somewhat toothed. The
flowers are greenish-white. The fruits are
sweetish and may be eaten (burk. p. 1942 : k.).

ขอม   kaum[2] *n.* the Cambodian nation ; the
alphabet of the ancient Cambodians in which
the sacred books of the Siamese are written,
being in part the source of the modern Siamese
characters (Ala. p. 291).

ข่อย   kau-ay[4] *n. Streblus asper* (*Urticaceae*)
(V. P. p. 57 : McM. p. 74 : Dept. Agri. & Fisheries :
Ger. (3) p. 264 : Burk. p. 2084). The bark of this
shrub or small tree is used for making paper.

ข้อย   kau-ay[3] *pron.* myself ; I ; me.

ขะแข่น, ขะแข้น   ka[4]-kaan[4] *adj.* dry ;
parched ; evaporated ; feverish ; hot.

ขะจาว (ต้น)   ka[4]-chjow *n. Holoptelea integrifolia* (*Urticaceae*) (V. P. p. 36), the Indian
elm, a tree 50 to 162 ft. high, with handsome
drooping branches (McM. p. 206). Oil is expressed from the seed. The wood is light,
yellowish-grey, and moderately hard. There
is no heart-wood. It is used for building
purposes (Dept. Agri. & Fisheries : Burk. p.
[1181].

ขะจิริด see กะจิริด

ขะจุย see กะจุย

ขะเจ๊าะ (ต้น)   ka[4]-chjaw[6] *n. Millettia pen-
dula* (*Leguminosae*) (V. P. p. 36), a tree or
shrub, sometimes climbing. The leaves are
odd-pinnate and the flowers showy. The
wood has a beautiful grain, making it suitable
for ornamental work (Burk. p. 1471).

ขะแจะ (ต้น)   ka[4]-chjaa[4] *n. Limonia acidissima* (*Rutaceae*) (V. P. p. 36), a spinous glabrous shrub or small tree, with very acid,
round, berry fruits which are edible, or can
be used instead of soap. The wood is yellow
and hard and is used for axles of oil-presses,
rice-pounders, etc. The leaves are supposed
to be a remedy for epilepsy ; the root is purgative and sudorific and is employed as a cure
for colic and cardialgia ; the dried fruit is
tonic and gives the one who eats it power to
resist the contagion of small-pox and of
malignant and pestilent fevers. It is also an

excellent antidote to various poisons (Dept. Agri. & Fisheries).

ขะเดา see กำเดา

ขะโดง see กระโดง

ขะแถก see กระแทก

ขะดาน see กระดาน

ขะเน็ด ka[4]-net[6] *n.* any tough, flexible materials that can be twisted together for binding purposes (as rice-straw for binding sheaves of rice-stalks or vines for tying bundles of fire-wood).

ขะบวน see กระบวน

ขะบวร see กระบวน

ขะบูร see กระบูร

ขะมอมขะแมม see กระมอมกระแมม

ขะมักเขม้น ka[4]-mak[6]-ka[4]-men[3] *v.* to perform a task with determination or alacrity; to show briskness, quickness or sprightliness in the performance of duties.

ขะมุกขะมอม ka[4]-mook[6]-ka[4]-maum *v.* to be spattered with mud or dirt: *adj.* unclean, dirty; foul; filthy; squalid.

ขะเมา (ต้น) ka[4]-mow *n. Eugenia grandis* (*Myrtaceae*) (cb. p. 644), a large evergreen tree, growing on the seashores around the Malay Peninsula, Siam and Borneo. It does not burn and has been found valuable as a fire-resister. The wood is of a dull red, or light brown colour, moderately hard, coarse in grain and fairly durable (Dept. Agri. & Fisheries: Burk. p. 968).

ขะโมย ka[4]-mo-ay *v.* to commit a burglary; to steal; to purloin: *n.* a thief; a robber; a burglar; a brigand.

ขะยม (ต้น) ka[4]-yom *n. Aglaia odorata* (*Meliaceae*) (cb. p. 257: V. P. p. 38), an elegant shrub or small tree, often cultivated in gardens on account of the sweet-scented flowers. The young shoots are covered with stellate hairs, rapidly becoming glabrous (Dept. Agri. & Fisheries: Burk. p. 74).

ขะยอม (ต้น) ka[4]-yaum *n. Shorea floribunda* (*Dipterocarpaceae*) (cb. p. 142: V. P. p. 38), a valuable timber tree (Dept. Agri. & Fisheries.

ขะยาง (ต้น) ka[4]-yang *n. Dipterocarpus alatus (Dipterocarpaceae)* (cb. p. 133), a large tree found in Burma and down into northern Malaya. This tree yields a wood-oil in great quantity and exudes a dirty-brown resin; the sap-wood is white; the heart-wood is reddish-grey, moderately hard, smooth, mottled, takes a fine polish and is used for house-building and canoes, but is not durable (Dept. Agri. & Fisheries: Burk. p. 841).

ขะยิก ka[4]-yik[6] *v.* to draw nearer to another gradually by slight motions (as of moving a chair while in a crowd of people); to move towards another by short steps or slight motions of the body: ขะยิกเข้าไปใกล้ ๆ to edge closer a little at a time; to make advances by degrees.

ขะยูก ka[4]-yook[6] *v.* to use force in pushing one's way gradually through a crowd (as by using the elbows).

ขะแยะ ka[4]-yaa[6] *v.* to pound or macerate gently; to pulverize or pound, combined with a scraping of the ingredients down under the pestle or rollers; to use the shoulder in forcing a passage through a crowd.

ขัง kang[2] *v.* to confine; to shut up (as in a prison); to imprison; to restrict the movements of; to incarcerate: ขังข้อ leaving or having the joint remain (as in a section of bamboo, for the purpose of using it to carry water, or for holding sap of the sugar palm).

ขัช, ขัชช์ kat[4] *P. n. lit.* "that which may be masticated", *i.e.* food; victuals; eatables.

ขัญช kan[2]-cha[6] *P. S. adi.* limping; disabled; lacking the natural use of the limbs.

ขัณฑ์, ขัณฑ kan² or kan²-ta⁶ *n.* a lump; a clod; a piece, part, portion or fragment (as of broken crockery); a section, chapter, part or portion of a work : ขัณฑธารา a pair of scissors; shears : ขัณฑบาล a vender of sweetmeats, confections or preserves; a confectioner : ขัณฑมณฑล an incomplete sphere; a segment or portion cut out of a circle; part of a circle or sphere : *adj.* not full or round : ขัณฑศรรกรา, ขัณฑสกร rock-sugar; rock-candy; thick molasses; syrup, used as a medicine : ขัณฑศีลา *lit.* "one who is unstable or impermanent in conduct," *i. e.* an unchaste wife : ขัณฑสีมา, ขัณฑเสมา, ขันธสีมา, ขันธเสมา boundary; outer limit; a part or portion of a boundary.

ขัด kat⁴ *v.* to polish; to scrub off (as rust); to brighten (as silver or brassware); to clog; to choke; to embarrass; to oppose; to enclose or to put into a case (as a belt-knife) : ขัด, ขัดใบยาว (หญ้า) *Sida acuta (Malvaceae)* (V. P. p. 52 : Burk. p. 2024 : K.), a small, medicinal shrub, up to 3 ft. in height, found widely in the tropics : ขัดขวาง to hinder; to obstruct; to oppose; to block the passage or progress of; to hamper; to impede : ขัดข้อง to obstruct; to be obstructed; to resist; to prevent; to object; to hinder : ขัดขืน to fail to perform a deed according to the command; to act in opposition, or to disobey instructions; to resist with force or violence : ขัดคอ to provoke; to arouse to anger or passion : ขัดเคือง to be angered; to provoke to anger : ขัดใจ to be angry against another; to be annoyed; to be indignant over ill-treatment or provocative language; to be irritated; to get impatient with : ขัดเงิน to be in need of money or funds; to be hard-pressed for funds : ขัดดอก to place a person or child to work out interest on a debt : ขัดตา unsightly; ugly; offensive to the eye : ขัดตาทัพ to be on guard against an enemy; to be on the defensive (as of an army) : ขัดแตะ to weave strips of bamboo perpendicularly into fences or partitions : ขัดเบา to suffer

from an obstruction to the flow of urine; to be unable to pass urine : ขัดมอน (ต้น) *Sida rhombifolia (Malvaceae)* (Cb. p. 151), a species of small erect shrub, used medicinally. The stems afford a good fibre. The roots are held in great repute in the treatment of rheumatism. The stems abound in mucilage and are employed by the natives as demulcents and emollients for external uses (Dept. Agri. & Fisheries : Burk. p. 2025) : ขัดมอนหลวง (ต้น) *Sida cordifolia (Malvaceae)*, a small, slightly woody plant found throughout the tropics (Cb. p. 150 : Burk. p. 2024 : K.) : ขัดรับสั่ง to disobey a command : ขัดสน poor; in want; needy; worthy of pity or sympathy : ขัดสมาธิ sitting in a cross-legged, tailor-like attitude : ขัดสมาธิ์เพ็ชร a tailor-like or Turkish style of sitting with the soles of the feet turned up : ขัดหนัก to suffer from bowel obstruction; to suffer from constipation : พูดขัดคอ to use irritating or offensive language; to speak opposing another's wishes or plans.

ขัตติย see กษัตริย์

ขัน kan² *v.* to twist or turn a mechanical nut up or down (as with a screw-driver or wrench); to crow; to coo (as a dove) : *n.* a copper or brass basin; an utensil of brass for dipping water; the crowing of a cock : *adj.* ludicrous; droll; ridiculous; funny; queer : ขันกว้าน to wind by turning a capstan; the act of winding a rope around a stake to hold what is pulled or hauled in : ขันชะเนาะ to twist a band of wire or rattan up tight by means of a stick : ขันเชิง a large brass bowl with base permanently attached : ขันทอง (ต้น) *Swintonia schwenkii (S. floribunda)* *(Anacardiaceae)* (Cb. p. 353), a forest tree somewhat resembling the mango in appearance (Burk. p. 2111) : ขันน้ำพานรอง a middle-sized brass or silver covered bowl with a supporting stand, used for drinking water : ขันล้างหน้า a wash-basin : ขันสาคร a large-sized basin with handles : · ขันสู้

to be an opponent in a race or competition;
to challenge: ขันหมาก a tray containing
prepared areca nut and betel leaf together with
other articles (carried during a wedding ceremony as a gift to the bride's mother or
guardian): ขันหู a large brass bowl having
handles.

ขันข้อ (ต้น) kan^2-kau^3 *n. Cissus (Vitis)
quadrangularis (Ampelidaceae)* (cb. p. 308), a
climber in dry evergreen forest near the sea
(K.). This is an Indian species, with a square
fleshy stem. The young shoots are eaten in
curries; they are acid, the acidity increasing
with age (BURK. p. 2247).

ขั้น kan^3 *v.* to place between (as a piece of
paper between two leaves of a book): *n.*
grade; steps; gradations; degrees; tiers.

ขันติ kan^2-dtee *v.* to bear patiently; to
endure; to put up with; to suppress anger:
n. long-suffering; endurance, forbearance or
patience under opposition, being one of the
ten transcendent virtues, *viz.* ขันตี patience
under opposition, ทาน alms-giving, เนกขะ
(เนกขัม) relinquishment of the world and
worldly possessions, ปัญญา wisdom, เมตตา
charity, วิริยะ energy or fortitude, ศีล morality, สัจจะ truth, อธิษฐาน firm purpose or
determination, อุเบกขา poise or equanimity
(Ala. p. 184).

ขันท kan^2-ta^6 *P. n.* one of many titles for
the god of War or " The Commander-in-chief
of the Divine Army " (H. C. D. p. 152).

ขันทองพยาบาท (ต้น) kan^2-taung-pa^6-yah-
bat^4 *n. Gelonium multiflorum (Euphorbiaceae)* (V. P. p. 52 : BURK. p. 1064), a small tree
found in Bengal, Burma, Siam and down the
peninsula as far as Malacca. It is ornamental
in foliage; *Hippocratea cambodiana (Celastraceae)* (cb. p. 287).

ขันที kan^2-tee *n.* an eunuch; an oriental
palace official (male).

ขันธ ๑ kan^2 *P. n.* one of the five elements

of being; one of the bodily senses (Ala. p. 23);
a group of physical organs; a living being,
group or company of persons; the shoulder
or nape of the neck; the throat; the stem or
trunk of a tree (where the branches begin);
the five constituent elements of being, *viz.*
รูป bodily form, เวทนา sensation (of pleasure,
pain etc.), สัญญา perception (enabling one to
distinguish things), สังขาร predisposition or
active tendency to arrangement, วิญญาณ intelligence, consciousness or thought-faculty (Ala.
p. 172).

ขันธ ๒ kan^2 *P. n.* a name for Karttikeya,
the second son of Indra, otherwise known as
the god of War (H. C. D. p. 152); the military
deity of the Hindus.

ขันธาวาร kan^2-tah-wan *P. n.* a military
stockade; an army; a body of soldiers; the
king's camp or headquarters; a royal residence.

ขับ kap^4 *v.* to drive (as horses in harness);
to drive out; to expel; to eject; to sing or
lead the singing (as for dancers); to recite:
ขับกล่อม to sing with pleasing or absorbing
melody; to utter sweet melodious sounds:
ขับขัน, คับขัน a difficult or perplexing position
(as one requiring victory or surrender):
ขับเคี่ยว having patiently endured to the end (as
bearing pain or distress without shrinking):
ขับผี to exorcize; to cast out evil spirits from
those being demon-possessed: ขับไม้ to perform on musical instruments: ขับรถ to
drive a motor car or carriage: ขับร้อง to
sing or dance with instrumental accompani-
ments: ขับไล่ to eject with force; to turn
out or expel (as from the possession of land):
ขับเสภา to sing songs of an amatory nature
delivered a-solo by an actor who accompanies
the melody with the clapping of castanets;
the attendant band playing an intermezzo at
intervals (GER. (1) p. 54).

ขัย see ขย

ขัว koo-ah^2 *n.* a bridge.

ขั้ว   koo-ah[3] *n.* core; stem (as of fruit); stalks (as of rice plants):   ขั้วโลก the poles of the earth: ขั้วโลกใต้ South Pole: ขั้วโลกเหนือ North Pole.

ขา   kah[2] *n.* the legs; the limbs; the lower extremities; one of a company or faction; a leg of a pair of compasses, a tripod, table or chair: *adj.* "yes" (used only by women to their superiors as a reply in response to a call):   ขากบ (ว่าว) the lower prongs or projections of a star-kite; frog's legs: ขากรรไตร the jaw; the lower maxillary bone; the blades of a pair of scissors: ขากลับ, ขามา the return trip: ขากอม bow-legged: ขากาง to stand with the legs spread apart: ขาไก่ a kind of mushroom: ขาขอด a leg deformed by a concavity or biconcavity of the tissues: ขาเขียด a kind of vegetable: ขาคีม the handles of a pair of pincers or pliers: ขาฉ a deformed leg in an abducted position: ขาด้วน an amputated leg: ขาตาย (ต้น) *Solanum verbascifolium* (Solanaceae) (V. P. p. 39), a large shrub, covered with a dense yellowish-grey tomentum. The fruit is poisonous (MCM. p. 387); though it may be eaten when cooked, the chief value seems to be medicinal (Burk. p. 2049):   ขาทราย a prop composed of two poles tied at one end, used for hoisting or bracing a long post (as in raising a telegraph pole):   ขานกยาง name of a kind of gun; name of a kind of ankle chain: ขานักเลง a member of a rowdyish or rough crowd: ขานาง (ต้น) *Tristania merguensis* (Myrtaceae) (cb. p. 627: Burk. p. 2186), a tree with hard wood, growing in the mountains of western and southern Siam; *Tomalium tomentosum* (Samydaceae) (cb. p. 742), a large deciduous tree. The bark is fine-grained and is of a pale greyish-green colour, which marks the tree very distinctly and unmistakably. The wood is brown with dark-coloured, very hard, heavy and durable heart-wood, and is used for furniture-making (Dept. Agri. & Fisheries):   ขาบาป to be on the side of some sinful act: ขาบุญ to be

partners in some meritorious deed: ขาเบี้ย (ต้น) *Symphorema involucratum* (Verbenaceae); *Hymenopyramis brachiata* (V. P. p. 39), a large, deciduous, scandant, shrub. The wood is heavy and is used for fuel (Dept. Agri. & Fisheries):   ขาไพ่ one of a party in a game of chance or in a card game; card partners: ขามควะ (ต้น) *Pterospermum semisagittatum* (Sterculiaceae) (cb. p. 177), a tree about 8 m. high found in scrub jungle. The flowers are white (K.). The bark is a masticatory in French Indo-China (Burk. p. 1834): ขาล้า weary-footed: ขาหยั่ง a tripod (as for a camera or some other mechanical apparatus); a scaffold for executions: ขาออก, ขาไป the out-going trip or turn: ขาอ่อน the posterior portion of the thigh: อยู่ขาเรา to be on our side: เอาคนร้ายไปขึ้นขาหยั่ง to put a criminal in a pillory.

ข่า   kah[4] *n.* a tribe of people occupying the Shan States, being direct descendants of the Khmers, as are also the Mons or Talaings of Pegu and the Kamuks of French Laos, all scions of the same original stock (W. p. 42). ข่า (ต้น) *Alpinia galanga* (Zingiberaceae); *A. siamensis* (V. P. p. 38); *A. sanderiana* (MCM. p. 149: K.), used as an ingredient in curry powder as well as in medicine. The genus *Alpinia* is wrongly applied to these plants which are really of an allied family, *Languas* (Burk. p. 1302):   ข่ากะลา (ต้น) *Rhizoma galangae* (Scitaminaceae).

ข้า   kah[3] *n.* an attendant or servant; one under the authority of, or devoted to the service of another: *pro.* I or me: ข้าเก่า a venerable, trusted servant; a former attendant: ข้าเก่าเต่าเลี้ยง a venerable, trusted servant of the family from youth up: ข้าเจ้า I; myself (used by a person speaking to one he respects or reveres):   ข้าต้นเรือน a trusted servant of the head of the house: ข้าน้อย I; myself (used in speaking to a person of higher rank or social position):   ข้าผูกดอก a slave pays interest rather than work for his debt:

ข้าแผ่นดิน citizens of a country or realm:
ข้าเผ้า royal pages or personal attendants in
the service of a sovereign: ข้าไท the
attendant of one of rank or authority:
ข้าพเจ้า I (used in formal discourse or when
speaking to a superior or to an equal in
rank, and also in official documents): ข้า-
พระ one who has been dedicated by some
one to serve the Buddhist monks in the
temples; temple servants: ข้าพระเจ้า, ข้า-
พระองค์ I (used in the presence of a former
sovereign or when addressing the Buddha):
ข้าพระพุทธเจ้า I (used when addressing His
Majesty the King or Her Majesty the
Queen or any of the higher princes):
ข้าราชการ a government official or one in the
service of the Crown: ข้าราชการพลเรือน an
official in the Civil Service: ข้าศึก enemies;
foes; adversaries: ข้าหลวง an official of
the Crown; an official sent by the Crown to
a provincial post or to a foreign country; a
member of the diplomatic or consular body;
female servants in the Royal Palace: ข้า
หลวงเดิม a former personal attendant in a
prince's family or one in the service of a
sovereign and registered as his valet or page
before accession to the throne: ข้าหลวงต่าง
พระองค์ an envoy appointed by the Crown:
ข้าหลวงน้อย a personal attendant of princes or
nobles: ข้าหลวงพิเศษ a special temporary
commissioner of the Crown to the provinces;
a special envoy abroad representing the
Crown: ข้าหลวงใหญ่ a High Commissioner.

ขาก kak[4] v. to bring up and spit mucus or
phlegm from the throat; to remove mucus
from the pharynx: ขากน้ำลาย to expectorate.

ขาง kang[2] Cam. n. an egg: ขางขาว (ต้น)
Xanthophyllum siamense (Xanthophyllaceae); Xanthophyllum virens (Xanthophyllaceae) (Cb. p. 107), a tree in evergreen forest.
The flowers are white, having two yellow
upper petals (K.): ขางคั่ง (ต้น) Dunbaria
longeracemosa (Leguminosae) (Cb. p. 463), a
climber (K.): ขางคันนา (ต้น) Desmodium sili-
quosum (Leguminosae) (Cb. p. 418), a spread-

ing shrub having purple or blue flowers (K.):
ขางแดง, ขางน้ำครั่ง (ต้น) Pithecolobium bigemi-
num (Leguminosae) (V. P. p. 50), a large tree
with poisonous seeds, but the Burmese and
Karens eat them as a condiment with preserved fish. The wood, sometimes called
iron-wood, is dark-coloured and heavy. A
decoction of the leaves is applied as a remedy
for leprosy and as a stimulant to promote
the growth of hair (Dept. Agri. & Fisheries):
Connarus griffithii (Connaraceae) (Cb. p. 364),
a woody climber found in evergreen forest
by rivers. The flowers are white (K.: Burk.
p. 650): ขางปอย (ต้น) Alchornea rugosa
(Euphorbiaceae) (V. P. p. 50), a shrub extending from Burma to the Philippines and New
Guinea. In Malacca, the roots and leaves are
boiled and used in fever and ague (Burk. p.
89): ขางปากปุด (ต้น) Melochia corchorifolia
(Sterculiaceae) (Cb. p. 179), an erect branching
herb or under-shrub. The stems are used as
a vegetable (Dept. Agri. & Fisheries: Burk. p.
1448): ขางแมงโบ้ง (ต้น) Uraria lagopoides
(Leguminosae) (Cb. p. 426), a medicinal plant,
given with milk to women in the seventh
month of their pregnancy to produce abortion.
In Vedic times, the plant was invoked as a
goddess (Dept. Agri. & Fisheries: Burk. p. 2207):
ขางหัวหมู (ต้น) Miliusa velutina (Annonaceae)
(Cb. p. 60: V. P. p. 50), a large, deciduous tree,
flowering in March and April, and producing
berries much like black cherries, in June and
July. The berries are used as food; the
heart-wood and sap-wood which are not distinct, are sulphur-yellow when fresh but light
brown when old. It is moderately hard and
is used for small beams, cart-poles, yokes,
agricultural implements, spare-shafts and bars
(Dept. Agri. & Fisheries: Burk. p. 1470): ไข่ขาง
eggs laid by flies (Siamese usage).

ข่าง kang[4] n. a spinning top; a toy top:
ดาวข่าง a cluster of four stars in the shape of
a top.

ข้าง kang[3] n. side; the lateral part of a

surface or object; boundary: *adj.* facing partners (as in a game); edges of: *prep.* towards: ข้างขวา towards the right hand: ข้าง ๆ along the side of; obliquely: ข้างขึ้น the waxing period of the moon (from the 1st. to the 15th. of the lunar month): ข้างควาย the two laths placed parallel to the ridge-pole on Siamese houses, and fastened together by barbed bamboo pins holding down the attap: ข้างเคียง adjoining; by the side of; neighbouring: ข้างต้น towards the first or from the beginning: ข้างใต้ towards the south or lower side: ข้างท้าย towards the stern (of a boat); at the rear (of a house): ข้างใน inside: ข้างแพ้ the defeated side: ข้างลาย (ปลา) a species of salt-water fish, *Therapon pula (Serranidae)*; *T. jarbua*; *T. sexlineatus*; a species of carp, having 5 vertical black patches on the side, *Puntius sumatranus*; a species of carp, *Osteochilus vittatus*, having a black line running from the eye to the base of the tail (Dept. Agri. & Fisheries: Burk. pp. 1843, 2152, 1611): ข้างหน้า in front of: ข้างหลัง in the rear of; behind; towards the back: ข้างไหน where; which side; which direction: เขาไปข้างไหน in which direction has she or he gone: ไปข้าง ๆ to go along the side of; to go beside: เรือข้างกระดาน a covered boat (ประทุน) built of boards: ลากข้าง the vowel า (สระอา).

ขาณุ, ขานุ   kah²-nu⁶ *P. S. n.* a stump; a stem; trunk; stake; post; pillar; a name for Siva (who is supposed to remain as motionless as the trunk of a tree during his austerities): *adj.* standing firmly; stationary; fixed; immovable; motionless (S. E. D. p. 1262).

ขาด   kat⁴ *v.* to be torn; to be in want; to fail; to be separated from; to be defective; to be incomplete; to be lacking in measurement, capacity or weight: *adv.* entirely; absolutely: ขาดกลาง to be broken or cut off in the middle (as of a story): ขาดแคลน to be impoverished (as without food or funds): ขาดความ unintelligible; lacking meaning: ขาดคราว, ขาดตลาด to have none in the market;

being out of stock: ขาดคอช้าง to be mortally wounded or killed while on the neck of an elephant in combat: ขาดค่า the minimum price; the price reduced to the lowest limit: ขาดจากกัน to be disjointed; to be completely separated from: ขาดใจ *lit.* "to have the heart torn or broken," *i. e.* to die: ขาดตัว the net price; an unalterable price; not less than: ขาดทุน to suffer loss in a transaction; the capital is cut into: ขาดนัดศาล non-appearance in court: ขาดมือ none in hand (as money): ขาดลอย to break away from the moorings (as a boat); to float away (as a kite); to be unrecoverable (as stolen goods or escaped convicts): ขายขาด to dispose of without reservation: โดยเด็ดขาด, เป็นอันขาด absolutely; irrevocably; unconditionally: ผัวเมียขาดกัน a condition of divorce: ยังไม่ขาดคำ to stop before the speaker has finished speaking: สั่งขาด to command absolutely.

ขาต   kah²-dta⁴ *P. n.* a well; a pond of water; an open mine; an excavation; a cavern: *adj.* having been dug up or excavated; having been dug up or into (S. E. D.): ขาตมูล having had the roots cut into or dug up.

ขาทะนียะ   kah²-ta⁶-nee-ya⁶ *P. S. n. lit.* "foods or provisions which should be masticated", *i. e.* various foods that are hard or tough (S. E. D. p. 339).

ขาน ๑   kan² *S. n.* food-stuffs; nourishment; nutriment: *adj.* eating; edible: ขาในทก the coconut tree (S. E. D. p. 339).

ขาน ๒, ข่าน   kan² *S. n.* a Mogul emperor.

ขาน ๓   kan² *v.* to answer (as when called): *n.* the act of calling one by name (as in a roll-call); *S.* perception; knowledge (S. E. D. p. 341): ขานไข to explain; to enlarge upon; to elucidate: ขานนาค the answering of questions by a novice when entering the Buddhist monkhood: ขานยาม the reply of a night-watchman; the call of the watches of the night: ขานรับ, ขานตอบ to answer in the affirmative.

ข่าน see ขาน ๒

ขานุ see ขาณุ

ขาบ   kab[4] *adj.* dark blue; navy blue (colour): เข้มขาบ a gold-embroidered, navy blue coat worn by magistrates or nobles.

ขาม   kam[2] *v.* to fear; to be afraid of; to reverence; to respect: คร้ามขาม to . dread; to be terrified of, or about.

ข้าม   kam[3] *v.* to cross over; to pass over; to over-step: ข้ามฟาก to cross from one side of a river to the other: ข้ามหน้า to pass in front of; to be situated in front of, or over against; to be opposite: ข้ามหน้าข้ามตา to affront; to offend by word or act; to show insufficient respect to; to over-step in propriety: เสื่อข้ามห้วย playing leap-frog over the prostrate body of one of the players, the purpose being to see who jumps farthest. The one who fails pays a forfeit.

ขาย   kai[2] *v.* to sell; to discard; to reject: การค้าขาย trades; business affairs: ขายเชื่อ to sell on credit: ขายตามคำพรรณา to sell by description of the goods or by catalogue: ขายตามตัวอย่าง to sell by sample: ขายทอดตลาด to sell by public auction: ขายปลีก to sell at retail: ขายฝาก to sell with a proviso of future redemption: ขายผ่าเท้า to be disgraced by a son, relative or servant: ขายล้างร้าน a clearance sale: ขายหน้า to be put to shame; to be abashed before others: ขายเหมา to sell at wholesale: ขายหู, ไขหู to feign ignorance to a call; to pretend not to hear: ผู้ขาย a vendor; a seller of goods; a dealer: เอาชื่อไปขาย to bring dishonour on one's name; to barter or trade on another's name or reputation.

ข่าย   kai[4] *n.* stake-nets, used for trapping animals (as rabbits); a stockade: ข่ายดักนก a net-trap (for birds): ข่ายแห่งพระมหากรุณา the range of His Majesty's graciousness: ตาข่าย meshes of a net: ตาข่ายกรอง network or squares of decorative flowers.

ขาร   kan[2] *P. n.* a corrosive, acrid or saline substance; an alkali (as soda or potash): *adj.* caustic; biting; corrosive; acrid; pungent; saline; capable of being converted to an alkali or ashes by distillation; sharp; keen (as the wind) (S. E. D. p. 327).

ขาล   kan[2] *Cam. n.* a tiger: ปีขาล year of the tiger, being the third year in the Siamese animal cycle of twelve years.

ขาว   kow[2] *adj.* white; clear; lucid; fresh; pure; free from blame; pale: ขาว (ปลา) carp, *Puntius binotatus* (Dept. Agri. & Fisheries): ขาวซีด to become blanched, pale or bleached: ตาขาว *lit.* "to show the white of the eyes," *i. e.* a coward; to be afraid, timid, stupified or astonished.

ข่าว   kow[4] *n.* news; report; rumour: ข่าวสาร news or report (as conveyed by letter, by newspaper or by a person): บอกข่าว to announce news or to make a report.

ข้าว   kow[3] *n.* rice; cereals; grain; a common noun used as a prefix to which the particular designating name for kind, condition or species is added: ข้าวเกรียบ crisp rice-cakes. These are made with batter flavoured with sesame-seeds and spread out in thin pancake-like sheets. When toasted they become crisp and are considered quite a delicacy: ข้าวกล้อง milled rice imperfectly cleaned of husks and bran: ข้าวกล้า tender rice plants intended for transplanting: ข้าวแขก small rice cakes with a frosting of seasoned coconut milk: ข้าวแช่ boiled rice, which after being soaked in water, is eaten cold with various condiments: ข้าวต้ม soft boiled rice; congy or rice soup with chopped fish, meat or chicken: ข้าวต้มผัด a cake made of partly cooked glutinous rice, coconut milk and banana, wrapped in a banana leaf and boiled: ข้าวต้ม (ต้น) *Wissadula periplocifolia* (*Malvaceae*), one of a small genus of shrubs found throughout the tropics. Its bark is fibrous and has been suggested as a substitute for jute (V. P. p. 46 : cb. p. 152 : BURK. p. 2262) : ข้าวตอก popped rice, mixed with coconut milk or sprinkled with sugar and rolled up into balls : ข้าวตอก (ต้น) *Viburnum sp.* (*Caprifoliaceae*) (V. P. p. 46 : BURK. p. 2230) ; *Callicarpa longifolia* (*Verbenaceae*), a genus of shrubs found in the warmer parts of Asia. Its use is largely medicinal (Dept. Agri. & Fisheries : BURK pp. 402–3) : ข้าวตอกแตก (ต้น) *Calycopteris florifunda* (*Combretaceae*), a sprawling shrub common in hot and rather dry places from India, through Burma and Siam to Penang and Keddah. The plant yields water for drinking purposes and is also used medicinally (V. P. p. 46 : cb. p. 611 : Dept. Agri. & Fisheries : BURK. p. 416) : ข้าวตัง crisp, scorched rice, being the layer adhering to the bottom of the cauldron or pot left to become dried and eaten like toast : ข้าวตาก sun-dried cooked rice, commonly used as food on a journey : ข้าวตู pulverized sun-dried rice mixed with sugar and eaten as a sweetmeat : ข้าวทิพย์ "angelic rice", a sweetmeat consisting of rice and various palatable ingredients : ข้าวบัตร cooked glutinous rice wrapped up in leaves of trees or leaves of the screw-pine (ใบเตย). Usually these are prepared for presentation to Buddhist monks during the ceremonies in connection with the close of Buddhist Lent : ข้าวบิณฑ์ rice balls put up in a cone-shaped receptacle : ข้าวเบา, ข้าวไว a variety of rice plants which mature rapidly and are reaped during November : ข้าวเบือ pulverized, uncooked rice, mixed with curry (used by northern mountain tribes) : ข้าวปลูก paddy reserved for planting : ข้าวเปลือก paddy ; unmilled rice ; rice still in the husks : ข้าวเปียก rice paste ; rice seasoned with salt and boiled with coconut milk till dry (relished as a food for invalids) ; rice pudding : ข้าวผอก uncooked rice wrapped up as provision for a noon-day meal : ข้าวผัด cooked rice fried with the necessary condiments : ข้าวพอง a fried rice cake made of popped rice placed

in layers. The rice is first roasted or popped, mixed with sugar, and then made into the proper cake-size and placed in layers : ข้าวฟ่าง (ฝ่าง) *Phalaris sp.* (*Gramineae*) (V. P. p. 47) ; *Phalaris arundinacea*, "ribbon grass," "Gardner's garter," a small grass with variegated leaves that head like wheat and is commonly used as a bird-food (MCM. pp. 172, 154, 74) : ข้าวโภชน์ Indian corn ; maize ; *Zea-mays* (*Gramineae*) (V. P. p. 47 : MCM. p. 307 : Dept. Agri. & Fisheries : PALLE. p. 321 : BURK. p. 2285), a monoecious annual grass 5 to 8 feet high, cultivated from very early times. When properly cooked, the unripe, tender heads are a nutritious and delicious vegetable. The ripe grains are made into flour which, in some countries, form the staple food of the inhabitants : ข้าวมัน rice boiled with coconut milk : ข้าวเม่า roasted or popped rice cleaned of the husks and then pounded flat : ข้าวเม่า (ปลา) sea-perch, *Ambassis baculis* (*Ambassidae*) ; *Ambassis thomassi* ; a species of fresh water fish, *Laubuca caeruleostigmata* (H. M. S.) : ข้าวยาคู a sweetmeat made of immaturely developed rice kernels which have been pounded flat and boiled with sugar : ข้าวเย็นเหนือ, ข้าวเย็นใต้ a species of bulbous plant. The bulbs are commonly used as ingredients in native medicine : ข้าวละมาน darnel ; tares, an unidentified weed that grows among wheat or other kinds of grain (Web.) : ข้าวสวย cooked rice ; rice from which the water has been poured off and the kernels allowed to become fluffed ; rice somewhat dried by letting the rice pot remain over the coals : ข้าวสาร milled rice ; white rice ; rice which has been hulled and cleaned : ข้าวสาร (ต้น) *Myriopteron extensum* (*Asclepiadaceae*) ; *Maesapermollis* (*Myrsinaceae*) ; *Phyllanthus columnaris* (*Euphorbiaceae*) ; *Raphistemma pulchellum* (V. P. pp. 48, 49 : MCM. p. 129 : K.) : ข้าวสารน้อย (ต้น) *Maesa indica* (*Myrsinaceae*), a shrub or small tree found from India to Java. Its fruit is eaten in the Himalayas but not in Malaya. The leaves are said to be capable of poisoning fish (V. P. p. 49: Dept. Agri. & Fisheries: BURK. p. 1391): ข้าวสารหลวง (ต้น) *Maesa ramentaceae* (*Myrsinaceae*), a tree about 30 feet in height. Its use is medicinal (V. P. p. 49: BURK. p. 1391): ข้าว-สาลี wheat: ข้าวนึ่ง cooked rice not having had the water poured off but allowed to evaporate by gentle heat: ข้าวหนัก a variety of slowly maturing rice plants. These take about six months to mature and are reaped during January: ข้าวเหนียวแก้ว a glutinous rice sweetmeat: ข้าวเหนียวแดง a glutinous rice sweetmeat made by using palm sugar (thus the name): ข้าวเหนียวเปียก a mushy, glutinous rice sweetmeat eaten with various condiments: ข้าวหมาก, ข้าวหมัก fermented glutinous rice; a sweetmeat hawked about the streets, made of steamed glutinous rice which is allowed to ferment by the addition of a yeast: ข้าวหลาม glutinous rice with coconut milk put into bamboo joints and roasted: ข้าวห่อ boiled rice and condiments, wrapped in a banana, or lotus leaf and steamed. This is distributed by the host at a Krathin (กระฐิน) ceremony.

ข้าศึก　　kah[3]-seuk[4] *n.* an enemy; an adversary; a foe: *adj.* belligerent; warlike.

ขำ　　kum[2] *adj.* secret; concealed (from general notice); sharp; clever; amusing; witty; funny: งามขำ masked or concealed beauty (as a picture, article or person, which, the longer it is looked at, the more attractive it becomes): ความขำ an amusing, witty or cunning incident, matter or story.

ขำเขียว　　kum[4]-kee-oh[2] *adj.* urgent; pressing; hurried; hasty.

ขิกๆ　　kik[4]-kik[4] *n.* a silly laugh; a nonsensical giggle: *onomat.* from a giggle of joy or laughter.

ขิง　　king[2] *n. Zingiber officinale* (*Zingiberaceae*), ginger, a well-known spice, stimulant and aromatic taken for indigestion, fever, etc. Its use is known from the earliest times in India and China (V. P. p. 50: MCM. p. 337: BURK. p. 2296f.): ขิงแครง a species of ginger used medicinally: ขิงแง่ง young rhizomes of ginger: ขิงดอง ginger steeped in alcohol or liquor: ขิงแห้ง sun-dried ginger used medicinally: ขนมขิง a sweetmeat made of young ginger rhizomes: น้ำขิง a drink flavoured with ginger.

ขิม　　kim[2] *Chin. n.* a Chinese cymbalo; a stringed musical instrument of Chinese origin, somewhat like a zither. The strings are struck with a pointed felt mallet attached to a flexible handle.

ขี่　　kee[4] *v.* to ride upon; to straddle; to mount: ขี่ช้าง to ride on an elephant: ขี่ม้า to ride on horseback.

ขี้　　kee[3] *v.* to have an evacuation of the bowels: *n.* an odd number; shavings; feces; dregs; sweepings; fecal matter; refuse: *adj.* disposed; likely to be; addicted to (some vice, implying an established habit); being in odd numbers: ขี้กบ wood shavings: ขี้กา (ต้น) *Adenia nicobarica* (*Passifloraceae*) (cb. p. 747: V. P. p. 40: K.), a species of vine with medicinal properties: ขี้กวาง (ต้น) *Eugenia leptalea* (*Myrtaceae*) (cp. p. 649), a small tree about 7 m. high, found in open evergreen forest on sandy ground. The fruits are purple-red (K.): ขี้กาดิน (ต้น) *Trichosanthes wawraei* (*Cucurbitaceae*), a climbing herb found from south-eastern Asia to Australia (cb. p. 754: K.: BURK. p. 2179): ขี้กาแดง (ต้น) *Trichosanthes integrifolia* (*Cucurbitaceae*) (cb. p. 752: K.), an herb. The flowers are white and open at night. A decoction of the berry is a poison to bedbugs: ขี้กาน้อย (ต้น) *Trichosantes integrifolia* (*Cucurbitaceae*) (cb. p. 751), an herb having white flowers which open at night (K.); *Gymnopetalum quinquelobum* (*Cucurbitaceae*) (cb. p. 557), an herb found in evergreen forest (K.): ขี้กาลาย (ต้น) *Bryonopsis laciniosa* (*Cucurbitaceae*) (cb. p. 762), a climber having pale green flowers and green fruit growing on white stalks (K.):   ขี้กาใหญ่ (ต้น) *Trichosanthes bracteata* (*Cucurbitaceae*) (cb. p. 752), a climber found in south-eastern Asia (K.); *T. tricuspidata* (cb. p. 754 : burk. p. 2179), a climber found throughout western Malaysia. The plant has medicinal properties. The flowers are white (K.): ขี้เกียจ with a tendency toward laziness: ขี้ไก่, กระจาบฝน (นก) the Formosan skylark, *Alauda gulgula sala*; the Bangkok white-tailed bush-lark, *Mirafra cantillans williamsoni* (will. N. H. J. S. S. II, 3, pp. 205, 207), a species of bird of the tree-pipit family, found in the furrows of dried ploughed ground: ขี้ขม (ปลา) a carp, *Osteochilus hasselti* (Dept. Agri. & Fisheries): ขี้ขลาด inclined to be a coward: ขี้ข้า a slave; a menial person; a person of inelegant or unrefined taste: ขขย (ปลา) a species of salt water fish, *Polycaulus uranoscopus* (*Synancejidae*) (Dept. Agri. & Fisheries): ขี้ครอก (ต้น) *Urena lobata* (*Malvaceae*) (cb. p. 154 : V. P. p. 40), a large, erect shrub, common in the tropics. The stems yield a jute-like fibre, used for cordage, etc. It is cultivated in Madagascar and Cuba, and also in Brazil, where it is known as "Aramina" fibre (MCM. p. 432). The root is employed as an external remedy for rheumatism (Dept. Agri. & Fisheries). It is said that paper can be made from it (burk. p. 2209): ขี้ครั่ง sealing wax; rosin: ขี้ควาย (ปลา) a species of salt water fish, damsel fish, *Pomacentrus tripunctatus* (*Pomacentridae*) (Dept. Agri. & Fisheries): ขี้คาด (ต้น) *Cassia alata* (*Leguminosae*) .(V. P. p. 40), a coarse, slightly woody herb, reaching 6 feet in height, native of America but now its distribution in the Old World is doubtless due to its medicinal properties. The leaves are held in high esteem as a local application for skin diseases; the roots, mixed with borax and made into a paste, are used as a specific for ringworm. The bark is used in tanning. The flowers are yellow and orange (Dept. Agri. & Fisheries : burk. p. 473 : MCM. p. 109): ขี้ฉ้อ being inclined to cheat, to swindle or to defraud: ขี้ช้าง (ต้น) *Acacia microcephala* (*Leguminosae*)

(V. P. p. 40), a woody climber, found in evergreen forest (K.): ขี้เซา *lit.* "a sleepy head," *i. e.* sleepy; drowsy: ขี้ดั่ง (ต้น) *Flemingia kerrii* (*Leguminosae*) (cb. p. 470), a shrub found in open spaces along the river bank. The flowers are greenish white; the berries are purple (K.): ขี้ตะกวัน, ขี้ตะกอน dregs; lees; sediment; precipitate; dross; slack: ขี้ตะกั่ว oxide of lead: ขี้ตระหนี่ penurious; avaricious; miserly; stingy: ขี้ติ้ว (ต้น) *Cratoxylon pruniflorum* (*Hypericaceae*) (cb. p. 113 : V. P. p. 41 : K.), a tree about 1.6 m. high, found in open deciduous forest. The flowers are pink: ขี้ติ้วใบเลื่อม (ต้น) *C. polyanthum* (*Hypericaceae*) (cb. p. 113 : K.), a shrub about 1.4 m. high found in evergreen forest. The flowers are red: ขี้ตุ่น (ต้น) *Helicteres obtusa* (*Sterculiaceae*) (cb. p. 174 : K.), a shrub growing in deciduous jungle. The flowers are pale mauve: ขี้เต่า dried secretions lodged in the arm-pits: ขี้ใต้ burnt refuse of a torch: ขี้ใต้ (ต้น) *Eurya acuminata* (*Ternstroemiaceae*) (cb. p. 126 : Dept. Agri. & Fisheries), a small evergreen tree or shrub grown on the hills: *Decaspermum fruticosum* (*Myrtaceae*) (cb. p. 613 : burk. p. 773 : K.), a tree about 8 m. high, growing in evergreen forest by streams. The flowers are white; *D. paniculatum*, *Rhodamnia trinervia* (*Myrtaceae*), a small tree found from Tenassarim to Australia. The hard, heavy timber is used in many ways for it is tough and durable. If it could be obtained in large pieces, it would be very valuable. The leaves and roots are used medicinally (V. P. p. 41 : burk. p. 1902): ขี้เท่า ashes: ขี้นก, ขี้หนู (พริก) a pepper of small size: ขี้บ่น having a tendency to grumble or complain: ขี้ปด being inclined to falsify: given to lying: ขี้ปลาวาฬ amber: ขี้ปาก words, utterances, stories or gossip; a low fellow whom others jeer or ridicule: ขี้ผึ้ง bees-wax: (ต้น) *Micromelum hirsutum* (*Rutaceae*) (cb. p. 228 : V. P. p. 42 : burk. p. 1468), a small tree found from Siam to the Malay

Islands. The flowers are white (K.). The leaves are used medicinally. Pounded with tamarind and salt, they are applied to the skin to draw out the pain and irritation which stinging caterpillars produce: ขี้แมลงวัน freckles; a small black mole; small black spots on the skin; the excrement of the fly: ขี้มอด (ต้น) *Dalbergia maymyensis* (*Leguminosae*) (cb. p. 481), a small tree about 5 m. high, found in deciduous jungle (K.); *Derris robusta* (*Leguminosae*) (cb. p. 491: Dept. Agri. & Fisheries), a deciduous tree about 30 to 40 feet high, yielding timber of a dark brown colour which is used for tea-boxes: ขี้มูก mucus from the nose; nasal discharges; rheum from the nose: ขี้ยอก (ปลา) a small carp, *Mystacoleucus marginatus* (Dept. Agri. & Fisheries): ขี้รังแค, ขี้ลม dandruff; scurf of the head: ขี้ริ้ว rags; tattered or shabby clothing; ragged; wearing frayed or shabby garments; unkempt; unbecoming; low; vulgar; vile or base: ขี้เรื้อน leprosy: ขี้แรด (ต้น) *Caesalpinia digyna* (*Leguminosae*), Tari pods (MCM. p. 443: BURK. p. 387), a woody climber found in India and extending into the Malay Peninsula. The pods contain tannin and tan excellently. The roots are astringent and are used medicinally: *Acacia pennata* (*Leguminosae*) (V. P. p. 42: cb. p. 550: BURK. p. 22), a stout, prickly climber, of the moister parts of India, tropical Africa and rather open country throughout Malaysia. Its use is medicinal. It is also an ingredient of ipoh poison; *Taxotrophis ilicifolia* (*Urticaceae*) (REC. p. 238: BURK. p. 2126: Dept. Agri. & Fisheries), a prickly, climbing shrub, rich in tannic acid of which high hopes have been formed as a tanning material. It is found in jungle or open mixed forest of Siam: ขี้แรดใหญ่ (ต้น) *Mezoneurum phyllum* (*Leguminosae*) (cb. p. 500), a woody climber, found in scrub jungle. The flowers are yellow (K.): ขี้ไร้ poor; needy; distressed by lack of means for gaining a living: ขี้ล้อ (ต้น) *Walsura villosa* (*Meliaceae*) (V. P. p. 2),

a tree about 8 m. high, found in deciduous forest. The flowers are white (K); *Harpullia confusa* (*Sapindaceae*) is also referred to in this connection (BURK. p. 1128): ขี้ลิง (ปลา) a sea cat fish, *Arius sagor* (Dept. Agri. & Fisheries): ขี้สนิม rust: ขี้หนอน (ต้น) *Zollingeria dongnaiensis* (*Sapindaceae*) (cb. p. 327: V. P. p. 41), a tree about 12 m. high found in scrub jungle. The flowers are white (K): *Schoepfia fragrans* (*Olacaceae*) (cb. p. 272); *Crypteronia paniculata* (*Lythraceae*) (cb. p. 730: BURK. p. 693), a rather tall tree from Burma and Siam to Java and the Philippine Islands. The timber is very hard and durable and is used for house-building wherever it occurs. The new wood is white; the heart-wood is red-brown. The leaves are bitter. The young shoots are eaten as a flavouring with rice in the Dutch Indies; *Choepfia acuminata* (*Olacaceae*) (cb. p. 272), a kind of tree used for medicinal purposes (MED. DICT.): ขี้หนาง (ต้น) *Wallichia caryotoided* (*Palmai*) (V. P. p. 41: MCM. p. 167), a fan-leaved palm of the Himalayan region: ขี้หนู the excrement of the rat; name of a certain kind of sweetmeat: ขี้หู ear-wax; cerumen: ขี้เห็น (ต้น) *Cordia sp.* (*Borangenaceae*) (V. P. p. 44: BURK. p. 660: Dept. Agri. & Fisheries), a deciduous tree found throughout the warmer parts of the world. The wood is hard and has a fragrant scent: ขี้หมากแห้ง (ต้น) *Colona auriculato* (*Tiliaceae*) (cb. p. 188: K.), a shrub about 4 to 5 feet high, found in open deciduous forest along rocky banks of streams. The sepals are reddish inside, spreading with 1 to 4 stamens, lying flat on each bright yellow petal which is spotted red: ขี้หมุด (ต้น) *Shorea sp.* (*Dipterocarpaceae*) (V. P. p. 44: Dept. Agri. & Fisheries: BURK. p. 2001), a considerable genus of trees found from India to the Philippine Islands. They are valuable trees by virtue of their very abundance though the timber is not, in itself, the most valuable: ขี้หมู (ต้น) *Padbruggea pubescens* (*Leguminosae*) (cb. p.

397 : K.), a tree, bearing dark reddish-purple flowers with a yellow patch, found in ever-green forest : the excrement of pigs : ขี้เหร่ unbecoming; unsuitable; unattractive; un-pleasing (as in dress) : ขี้หึง inclined to be jealous : ขี้เหล็ก (ต้น) *Cassia siamea (Leguminosae)* (cb. p. 513 : MCM. p. 220 : Dept. Agri. & Fisheries : Burk. p. 480), a tree of moderate height found from India through most of Malaysia. The timbers are reasonably immune from termites. The tree has smooth bark, whitish sap-wood, dark brown nearly black heart-wood, which is very hard and durable, and in Ceylon, is considered one of the best kinds of fuel for locomotives : ขี้เหล็กคันชั่ง, ขี้เหล็กบิ่นชั่ง (ต้น) *C. timoriensis* (V. P. p. 43 : cb. p. 514 : Burk. p. 481 : Dept. Agri. & Fisheries), a handsome small evergreen tree, found from Tenasserim to Timor. In Java the timber is greatly prized as uprights for houses. The dark brown, nearly black wood is also used for furniture. In Siam, the tree is medicinal : ขี้เหล็กโคก, ขี้เหล็กบ่า, ขี้เหล็กแพะ (ต้น) *C. garrettiana* (cb. p. 510 : K.), a tree about 30 ft. high, found in deciduous forest. The flowers are yellow : ขี้เหล็กเทศ, ขี้เหล็กผี (ต้น) *C. occidentalis* (cb. p. 513 : V. P. p. 43 : MCM. p. 311 : Dept. Agri. & Fisheries : Burk. p. 478), a partly woody plant, probably of American origin, but now found throughout the tropics. The seeds are sometimes used as a substitute for coffee. The young leaves and pods may be cooked and eaten with rice. If not cooked, the seeds are purgative. The flowers are bright orange yellow : ขี้เหล็ก-บ้าน (ต้น) *C. glauca* (cb. p. 511 : V. P. p. 43 : Dept. Agri. & Fisheries), a small tree. The bark, mixed with sugar and water, is given in diabetes and a preparation of the bark and leaves, mixed with cummin seed, sugar and milk is given in virulent gonorrhoea : ขี้เหล็กเลือด (ต้น) see ขี้เหล็กคันชั่ง (ต้น) : ข้อน (ต้น) *Helicteres hirsuta (Sterculiaceae)* (cb. p. 172 : V. P. p. 44 : Burk. p. 1134), a shrub found in south-eastern Asia and Malaysia. It has a

fibrous bark which is used for making a rough cordage in Indo-China, Java and the Philippine Islands. The ropes appear durable during the rainy season. The flowers are dark purplish-red (K.); *H. lanata* (cb. p. 173), a shrub, found in open scrub. The flowers are pale mauve (K.); *H. obtusa* (cb. p. 174), a shrub, growing in deciduous jungle. The flowers are pale mauve (K.) : ข้อวด having a tendency to boast or to brag : ข้ออ้น being easily moved to tears; given to crying : ข้อาย having a tendency to be shy or to be bashful : ข้อ้าย (ต้น) *Terminalia triptera (Combretaceae)* (cb. p. 609 : K.), a tree about 8 m. high, found in deciduous jungle. The flowers are white : ขี้แฮด (ต้น) *Polyalthia viridis (Annonaceae)* (cb. p. 45), a tree about 15 m. high, found in mixed forest by a stream (K.); *Capparis winitii (Capparidaceae)* (V. P. p. 44) : เล่นคู่ขี่ to play a game where stakes are placed on the odd or even number turned up in a throw of dice.

ขีณะ kee²-na⁶ *S. P. adj.* wasted; worn away; diminished; weakened; emaciated; feeble; waning (as of the moon) (S. E. D. p. 328).

ขีณาสพ, กษีรนาศรพ kee²-nah-sop⁴ *S. n. lit.* "with sin gone," "one who has been purged or purified of sin," *i. e.* one having attained the highest degree of saintship in the Buddhist religion (S. E. D. p. 328).

ขีด keet⁴ *v.* to scratch; to draw; to trace; to make lines : *n.* limitation; boundary; a dividing line or mark : ขีดเขียน to write or make marks on paper or parchment : ไม้ขีดไฟ *lit.* "a stick that scratches fire," *i. e.* a match.

ขีดขินธ์ keet⁴-kin² *n.* a country in the Indian Peninsula (thought to be in the Mysore) which was taken by Rama from the monkey king Bali, and given back to his brother Su-griva, the friend and ally of Rama. The capital city was Kishkindya (H. C. D. 159).

ขีร kee²-ra⁶ *P. S. n.* water; fresh milk;

thickened milk; liquid juice or sap of plants (S. E. D. p. 329).

ขิง keung[2] *v.* to stretch; to draw taut; to fix the eyes in a steady gaze; to stare; to look at with a stare: ขิงขิง healthy; strong; vigorous; broad-chested; ขิงจอ to stretch taut and fasten (as the curtain for a picture show): ขิงอุด to lie or sleep on the back with the body stretched out and completely covered with a cloth drawn over tightly: ขิงตา to fasten the eye on in a steady stare.

ขิง keung[3] *v.* to be angry or provoked; to excite anger or resentment: ขิงเดือด to manifest an attitude of anger purposely (as when jealous); to be indignant; "to boil with rage".

ขึ้น keun[3] *v.* to rise; to get up; to inflate; to ascend; to mount; to climb or rise: *n.* the act of rising; ascent; an ascending course; the act of beginning to appear: may be added to certain verbs, expressing the idea of ascension or augmentation, *e. g.* ลุกขึ้น: ขึ้นครู to show esteem or respect for a teacher; to pay one's respects at the home of a teacher: ขึ้นใจ capable of remembering well: ขึ้นชื่อลือนาม illustrious; famous: ขึ้นต้น to begin; to commence: ขึ้นต้นไม้ to climb a tree: ขึ้นทะเบียน to enroll: ขึ้นที่ to ascend a throne or pulpit: ขึ้นบรรทัดใหม่ to begin on a new line: ขึ้นบัญชี to place or enter on account: ขึ้นปาก to have a memory so that words come spontaneously to the lips: ขึ้นพลับพลา name of a Siamese song: ขึ้นระวาง to enroll horses or elephants in their proper department or section: ขึ้นราคา to raise the price: ขึ้นเรือน an housewarming: ขึ้นหม้อ notorious; fluffy; soft (as when rice is boiled or steamed till it becomes soft and fluffy): ข้างขึ้น the period of the waxing of the moon: ท่องขึ้นใจ to memorize: ท้องขึ้น to have the abdomen distended with gas: น้ำขึ้น flood-tide: ศพขึ้น a gas-distended corpse.

ขืน keun[2] *v.* to do or go contrary to orders;

to coerce; to compel; to resist; to oppose: *n.* a topmost point; the highest point: ขืนขืน to talk teasingly in order to accomplish one's purpose; to talk in a harassing or annoying manner to accomplish an object: ขืนขว้าจำหงาย to compel one to do something against his will: ขืนใจทำ to force one's self into doing: ขืนตัว to exercise self-control; to force one's self into doing or resisting: ขืนทำ to insist on doing: ขืนรู้ผู้ใหญ่ to over-estimate one's knowledge; to consider one's self better than one's superiors: ขืนเรือ to trim a boat evenly; to put weights or ballast in the side of a boat to make it ride evenly: ขืนให้ทำ to compel to do; to insist on being done.

ขืน keun[4] *adj.* bitter; acrid; biting (taste): ฝาดขืน puckery and bitter.

ขื่อ keu[4] *n.* a beam; a horizontal piece of wood supporting parts of a roof or building; a joist; a shackle or fetters for the feet; stocks: กำไลขื่อผี an expanding bracelet: ขื่อกะละบึงหา the four end-rafters to which are attached the gable ends and decorations (like bird's wings) of a Siamese house: ขื่อคอ a pillory: ขื่อคัด the supplementary rafters of the roof of a Siamese house: ขื่อจมูก the bones composing the nasal septum: ขื่อเชิงกราน the pubic bones of the pelvis: ขื่อตีน stocks for the feet: ขื่อผี a natural arch formed by a forking of two limbs of a tree, or any other plant, which again unite. This is also used of any other abnormal arrangement (as of stones, etc. forming a natural arch): ขื่อมือ handcuffs: ขื่อมุกต์ the joint connecting the two shells of a pearl oyster.

ขุ (ต้น) koo[4] *n. Mangifera indica Anacardiaceœ* (cb. p. 344: BURK. p. 1402), the mango, a medium or large-sized, spreading and quick-growing tree, indigenous to tropical Asia. It bears large panicles of greenish-white, scented flowers, usually in January to March, followed about 2½ to 3 months later by the fruit. A second crop is sometimes obtained in August to September. The round or ovoid fruit is somewhat flattened, generally with a more or less pronounced beak near the apex. It has a tough, thin, skin and when ripe, is yellow, reddish or green. The flesh is usually of a reddish tint with a distinct, pleasant, aromatic flavour; in inferior varieties it is turpentiney, somewhat resinous and fibrous. In the centre is the large fibrous, ovoid, flat seed. It is considered an article of food as well as dessert, whilst it also enters largely into the preparation of chutneys and preserves (McM. pp. 243, 518).

ขุก   kook[4] *adj.* impulsively or unexpectedly irritated or peeved : *onomat.* from the hack, hack of a dry cough : ขุกขัก *onomat.* from the sound of walking, or from children playing overhead : ขุกเข็ญ troublous; difficult; something perplexing arising unexpectedly : ขุกค่ำขุกคืน an urgent incident or affair occurring at night : ขุกใจ immediately; quickly; suddenly.

ขุขัน   koo[4]-kan[2] *n.* a hiding place; a cave; a cavern : (1) a name of the god of War (see Karttikeya): (2) a king of the Nishadas or Bhils, who was a friend of Rama : (3) a people in the south of India near Kalinga, who possibly got their name from him (S. E. D.).

ขุขันธ์   a town in north-eastern Siam.

ขุด   koot[4] *v.* to dig; to hollow out; to turn the ground up (as with a hoe or mattock).

ขุน   koon[2] *v.* to feed; to nourish (used only for animals): *n.* a leader; a ruler or herdman; the lowest title of conferred nobility : *adj.* grand; imposing; noble; great : ขุนเขา a large, lofty mountain peak : ขุนทอง (นก) the Malay talking mynah, *Gracula javanensis* (Gaird. J. S. S. IX, 1, p. 5): ขุนนาง a nobleman; one with a conferred title : ขุนบาล a holder (from the government) of the exclusive right to revenues from lottery or

gambling : ขุนพัฒน์ the holder of a gambling farm (from the government): ขุนเมือง a petty officer of a provincial town : ขุนศาล a judge : ขุนหมากรุก the king (in chess): ขุนหมื่น the lowest title for one appointed locally (inferior to Khun, a Crown appointment): ลูกขุน a judge appointed by the Crown; a jury.

ขุ่น   koon[4] *v.* to be in distress; to be vexed or irritated; to manifest an uncheerful attitude: *adj.* cloudy (as a liquid); impure; tarnished (as in character); melancholy; gloomy; sullen : ขุ่นข้น a thick, cloudy liquid : ขุ่นแค้น irritated to the extent of being revengeful.

ขุม   koom[2] *n.* a walled-in well; a ditch; an abyss : ขุมถ่านเพลิง, ถ่านหิน a coal-mine : ขุมทอง a gold-mine : ขุมนรก the abyss of hell : สุขุม deep in meaning; difficult to understand.

ขุย   koo-ay[2] *n.* fine particles of dirt or burrowings (as seen at the mouth of ant or cricket holes): ขุยไผ่, ลูกไผ่ the seeds of the bamboo : ไผ่ตายขุย dying after bearing fruit.

ขุร   koo[4]-ra[6] *P. S. n.* a razor; a sharp blade; a horse's hoof : ขุรกิจ *lit.* "to perform with a razor," *i. e.* the act of shaving : ขุรนัศ *lit.* "having a nose similar to a horse's hoof," *i. e.* a blunt nose; a flat nose; flat-nosed (S. E. D. p. 340).

ขู, โข   koo[2] *adj.* much; plenty; abundant.

ขู่   koo[4] *v.* to scold harshly; to reprimand sharply; to threaten; to brow beat: ขู่กรรโชก to intimidate by threatening; to blackmail.

ขูด   koot[4] *v.* to grate; to scratch; to scrape.

เข, เหล่   kay[2] *n.* a condition in which one eye is deviated from its proper direction; a squint; strabismus.

เขก   kake[4] *v.* to strike, rap or knock with the knuckles.

เข่ง   keng[4] *n.* an open-work bamboo basket ; (ขนม) a kind of Chinese sweetmeat steamed in small basket trays.

เขจร   kay[2]-chjaun *P. S. n. lit.* " one moving or flying in the air," *i. e.* a bird ; a messenger or envoy of celestial beings : *adj.* moving in the air or being able to fly ; aerial (S. E. D. p. 334).

เข็ญ   ken[2] *Cam. n.* trouble ; difficulty ; adversity ; want ; misfortune ; a calamity : เข็ญใจ poor ; unfortunate.

เขดา   ka[4]-dow *Cam. adj.* hot ; heated.

เข็ด   ket[4] *v.* to be afraid of offending again after a correction ; to have profited by reproof or punishment ; to be reformed through fear or punishment : *n.* a skein (as of twine or silk) : เข็ดขาม to submit through fear : เข็ดปาก to be surfeited with a person's remarks : เข็ดฟัน the teeth are set on edge ; the teeth are sensitive : เข็ดมือ to be afraid of another's hand or methods : ผมเข็ดแล้ว I will not do so again ; I have learned my lesson.

เข็ดคาว (ต้น)   ket[4]-kow *n. Randia siamensis (Rubiaceae)* (V. P. p. 52), a climber having white flowers (K.).

เขตต์, เขตร see เกษตร

เขท   ket[4] *S. n.* lassitude ; depression ; exhaustion ; affliction ; distress ; pain (S. E. D. p. 340).

เขน ๑   ken[2] *n.* a shield attached to the forearm.

เขน ๒ see เขล

เข็น   ken[2] *v.* to push with force (as logs pushed by elephants) ; to transport by pushing ; to pull ; to draw (as a boat upon the shore).

เข่น   ken[4] *v.* to attenuate or fashion by pounding (as silver-smiths in making a bowl) ; to forge and shape metal into knives, etc. : เข่นเขี้ยว to grind the teeth in extreme anger.

เขนง   ka[4]-neng[2] *Cam. n.* the horns of an animal : เขนงดินปืน a powder-horn or box.

เขนทะ (ต้น)   ken[2]-ta[6] *n. Glycosmis pentaphlla (Rutaceae)* (V. P. p. 53), a common evergreen shrub, found in south-eastern Asia and Malaysia. The fruits are edible ; the twigs are used for tooth picks ; the wood is white, hard and close-grained ; the roots, pounded and mixed with sugar, ar egiven in cases of low fever. The wood, bruised with water, is administered internally as an antidote for snake-bite (Dept. Agri. & Fisheries).

เขนย   ka[4]-ner-ay[2] *Cam. n.* a pillow ; a cushion ; a head-rest.

เขบ็จ   ka[4]-bet[4] *Cam. adj.* sharp-pointed.

เขบ็จขบวร   ka[4]-bet[4]-ka[4]-boo-an *v.* to arrange ; to decorate ; to beautify : *n.* attitude ; manner ; program ; deception ; deceit ; stratagem.

เขป   kep[4] *v.* to dash, throw, pelt or shower with (as with rice at weddings).

เขม see เกษม

เข็ม   kem[2] *n.* a needle ; (ดอก) the ixora flower ; (ปลา) the wrestling or needle fish (H. M. S.) : เข็มกลัด a pin ; a clasp (as worn by Siamese officials) ; a brooch : เข็มขัด a belt : เข็มทิศ the needle of a compass : เข็มนาฬิกา the hands of a clock or watch : เข็มรากตึก piles used in the foundations of a building.

เข็ม (ต้น)   kem[2] *n. Rauwolfia serpentina (Apocynaceae)* (V. P. p. 54), a large climbing or twining shrub found from India to Ceylon and Siam, and in Java. The root is extensively medicinal. It is much valued as an antidote for the bites of poisonous reptiles and the stings of insects, and also as a febrifuge (Dept. Agri. & Fisheries : Burk. p. 1885) : *Desmodium cephalotoides (Leguminosae)* (V.P. p. 54), a shrub about 1 m. high, found in mixed forest. The flowers are creamy white

(K.) : เข็มขาว (ต้น) *Chasalia curviflora* (*Rubiaceae*) (V. P. p. 54), a shrub found in evergreen forest, bearing white flowers (K.) : เข็มเจ้าพระยา (ต้น) *Ixora macrothyrsa* (*Rubiaceae*); *I. coccinea* (Burk. pp. 1259, 1260), a shrub found in India, Ceylon and Siam, cultivated chiefly for its flowers. It has some value medicinally, especially in dysentery : เข็มดอย (ต้น) *I. pavettaefolia* (V. P. p. 55), a thin shrub about 2 m. high, found in evergreen forest. Tne flowers are white (K.) : เข็มแดง (ต้น) *I. spectabilis* (V. P. p. 55), a slender tree about 4 m. high, found in evergreen forest (K.) : เข็มป่า (ต้น) *I. cibdela* (V. P. p. 55), a flowering shrub (MCM. p. 208) : เข็มฝรั่ง (ต้น) *I. coccinnea* (V. P. p. 55), a shrub with very showy scarlet flowers. The flowers and bark are used for bloodshot eyes, and the leaves for sores, ulcers, etc. (MCM. pp. 112, 141, 379 : Burk. p. 1260) : เข็มพญาอินทร์ (ต้น) *Euphorbia splendens* (*Euphorbiaceae*) (V. P. p. 56) : เข็มแพะ (ต้น) *Pavetta indica* (*Rubiaceae*) (V. P. p. 56), a shrub found from the north-western Himalayas and southern China to Australia. It bears long white clusters of flowers in profusion (MCM. pp. 115, 141, 208). An infusion of the leaves is used externally as a local application in certain complaints. The flowers and fruits are edible (DEPT. AGRI. & Fisheries : BURK. p. 1678) : เข็มเล็ก (ต้น) *I. subsessilis* (V. P. p. 56), a flowering shrub (MCM. p. 208) : เข็มเศรษฐี (ต้น) *I. macrothyrsa* (winit N. H. J. S. S. IX, 1, p. 97), an East Indian shrub. This red-flowered ixora is said to have been introduced by Phya Pradibhat Bhubal about 30 years ago, probably from Singapore : เข็มอร่าม (ต้น) *Yucca gloriosa* (*Liliaceae*) (wipat : MCM. p. 117), Adam's needle : เข็มใหญ่ (ต้น) *I. multibracteata* (V. P. p. 55), a shrub about 4 m. high, found in bamboo forest. The flowers are white (K.).

เข้ม kem[3] *adj.* vehement; very ardent; impetuous; concentrated; strong (as acids or coffee) : เข้มงวด austere; harsh; stern.

เข้มขาบ kem[3]-kap[4] *n.* a kind of cloth woven with the design running lengthwise.

เขม็ง ka[4]-meng[2] *adj.* austere; strict; severe; tight; twisted hard and tight (as in making rope) : ถือเคร่งเขม็ง to lead a rigid, strict life; to lead the life of an ascetic : ป่านเขม็ง string with tightly twisted strands : พื้นด้าย ให้เขม็ง to twist the strands of thread tightly.

เขมัง kay[2]-mang *n.* the condition of being safe, free from punishment (as in a lawsuit), danger, catastrophe or calamity (BRAD. p. 70).

เขม็ดแขม่ see กระเหม็ดกระแหม่

เขม่น see กระเหม่น

เขม่น ka[4]-men[3] *v.* to gaze at; to stare at; to look intently : เขม่นตาดู to fix the eyes intently upon.

เขม่นขมัก see ขะมักเขม้น

เขมร ka[4]-men[2] *n.* Cambodians; Khmers. The Khmers were the ruling race of Cambodia which built Angkor Wat in the XIIth. century. The origin of this people has been the subject of careful study for years. There are several blended strains. Most certainly one element, probably Mon, brought to it the Hindu culture, religion and literature; another element, Malay or Indonesian, brought to it the remnants of their ancient civilization; a third element was the local population of that area who mixed with their conquerors. These latter were Melanesians and their influence is noted in the physical characteristics of their statues at Angkor, which are distinctive because of the bulging foreheads, broad noses, thick lips and short chins. These characteristics are common among the present Cambodians who are descendents of the Khmers of the Angkor period.

เขมา ka[4]-mow[2] *Cam. adj.* black.

เขม่า ka[4]-mow[4] *n.* soot; carbon (as in a smoke-stack); lampblack.

เขม็อบ ka[4]-meu-ap[4] *v.* to gulp down; to swallow ravenously.

เขย ker-ay[2] *n.* a male relative by marriage: เขยตาย (ต้น) *Glycosmis cochinchinensis* (*Rutaceae*) (cb. p. 223: BURK. p. 1086: K.), a tree found in south-eastern Asia and Malaysia. It bears small thorns along the edges of the leaves. In the Dutch East Indies the roots are used for swollen spleen: น้องเขย a younger sister's husband: น้าเขย the mother's younger sister's husband: พี่เขย an elder sister's husband: ลุงเขย the father's or mother's older sister's husband: ลูกเขย a son-in-law: หลานเขย a nephew by marriage; a grandson by marriage (on the husband's side): อาเขย the father's younger sister's husband.

เขยก ka[4]-yek[4] *adj.* walking with a stiff leg; limping; hobbling.

เขย่ง ka[4]-yeng[4] *v.* to tip-toe; to stand or walk on tip-toes; to hop along on one foot.

เขย้อแขย่ง ka[4]-yur[3]-ka[4]-yaang[4] *adj.* striving; struggling; trying with constant effort; assiduous; persevering.

เขยอะขยะ ka[4]-yur[4]-ka[4]-ya[4] *adj.* having fragments attached in an untidy, unsightly or disorderly manner (as ribbons on a dress, rags on a beggar, or branches on a felled tree): *adv.* unsightly (from having fragments attached in a disorderly manner).

เขย่า ka[4]-yow[4] *v.* to shake; to agitate; to cause to sway; to swing; to oscillate or vibrate repeatedly.

เขยิน ka[4]-yern *adj.* projecting; bulging; prominent; being out of line or conspicuous in position: ฟันเขยิน a protuberant tooth.

เขยิบ ka[4]-yerp[4] *v.* to move forward or backward a little (as when a post is to be moved into a straight line); to move or to be moved slightly from one position to another.

เขยียวขยอน ka[4]-yee-ow[2]-ka[4]-yaun[2] *Cam.* *adj.* tottering; shaky; unsteady; tremulous.

เขยื้อน ka[4]-yeu-an[3] *v.* to be slightly movable; to be able to have the position changed or modified.

เขล ken[2] *S. v.* to shake; to shudder or quiver; to move to and fro; to whirl; to move in circles: *n.* games; plays; amusements; entertainments: *adj.* playful; sportive; jovial; frolicsome (S. E. D. p. 340).

เขลง kleng[2] *v.* to lie; to recline; to prostrate one's self: เขลง (ต้น) *Dialium cochinchinense* (*Leguminosae*) (cb. p. 516: BURK. p. 799), a tree resembling the tamarind. It is therefore called the black tamarind in Africa and the tamarind plum in Asia. In Indo-China the bark of some species is used as a substitute for areca nut; *D. ovoideum* (V. P. p. 50), velvet tamarind, a tall tree indigenous to the semi-dry region of Ceylon. The dark brown, small, velvety fruits are produced in large clusters. The thin, brittle shell, enclosing one or two seeds, is surrounded by a sweet-acid pulp, which is edible and is used in the preparation of chutney (MCM. p. 259).

เขลา klow[2] *adj.* stupid; foolish; ignorant: บัญญาเขลา dull of intellect; unintelligent: โฉดเขลา extremely ignorant; mentally inactive; dull of perception.

เขลาะ klau[4] *Cam.* *adj.* young; sprightly; vivacious; lively.

เขว kwey[2] *adv.* diagonally across; awry; distortedly; obliquely: เข้าใจเขวไป to misunderstand; to mistake the meaning: แล่นเรือเขวทางไป the boat is being run in a wrong course or direction.

เขษม, เกษม ka[4]-sem[2] *P. n.* the state of being free from one's foes or enemies; bliss; completeness.

เขฬะ key[2]-la[6] *P. S. n.* saliva; spittle; phlegm (S. E. D.).

เขะขะ key[4]-ka[4] *adj.* obstructive; hindering; preventing; opposing.

เขา kow[2] *n.* horn; antler: *pro.* third personal pronoun, *viz.* he; she; they: เขา (นก) Malay spotted dove, *Turtur tigrinus* (Gaird. J. S. S. IX, 1, p. 12): เขา (ภู) a mountain; a hill: เขากวาง the antlers of a deer; a stag's horns: เขากวาง (ต้น) *Homalium griffithianum (Samydaceae)* (Burk. p. 1183); *H. dasyanthum* (V. P. p. 45: cb. p. 740): เขา แกะ, เขาควาย (ต้น) *Rhynchostylis coelestic (Orchidaceae)* (V. P. p. 45): *Saccolabium curvifolium* (MCM. p. 146), an orchid with small salmon-red flowers: เขาเขิน a lofty mountain: เขาเขียว (นก) the thick-billed green pigeon, *Treron nipalensis* (*Treronidae*) (Gaird. J. S. S. IX, 1, p. 12): เขาควาย a buffalo's horns: เขาชวา (นก) the barred ground dove, *Geopelia striata* (Gaird. J. S. S. IX, 1, p. 12: Burk. p. 855): เขาตำแย immature, undeveloped antlers (as those with hair, fuzz or soft down still growing on them): เขาทอง (นก) the emerald dove, *Chalcophaps indica* (Gaird. J. S. S. IX, 1, p. 16: Burk. p. 855), a showy little bird caught on the ground, decoyed by means of another bird: เขาทั้งหลาย the others; they; them: เขาเปล้า, ลำภู (นก) the imperial green pigeon, *Carpophaga aenea,* an excellent table bird (Burk. p. 856): the purple wood pigeon, *Alsocumus puniceus* (Gaird. J. S. S. IX, 1, p. 12): เขาไฟ (นก) the eastern ruddy ring dove, *Turtur humilis* (Gaird. J.S.S. IX, 1, p. 12): the Burmese red turtle-dove, *Streptopelia chinensis tigrina* (Gaird. J. S. S. VI, 4, p. 334): เขาว่า it is said; they say that: เขาใหญ่ (นก) the Burmese spotted dove, *Streptopelia chinensis tigrina* (Herb. N. H. J. S. S. VI, 4, p. 334); ช่างเขาเถิด take no heed of him; just be indifferent to them; pay no attention to him; never mind them: เนินเขาเขิน the base of a high, steep mountain: ขนยอดเขา to ascend to the top of a mountain.

เข่า kow[4] *n.* the knee: ข้อเข่า the knee joint: เข่าตุ้น knee-deep (as in water or mud): คุกเข่าลง to kneel down.

เข้า kow[3] *v.* to enter; to penetrate; to invade; to be affiliated with: เข้ากัน to participate with; to share in; to show preference for another: เข้ากันได้ to be capable of being blended; to be mixable into a body or mass: เข้าข้อ syphilitic arthritis: เข้า ๆ ออก ๆ to visit frequently; to frequent a place: เข้าคอ to make advances with flattering words or fawning manners so as to become friendly or familiar: เข้าค้า appropriate, fitting or suitable to the fashion, place or occasion: เข้าใคล used to characterize a mango when it is so ripe that the seed becomes hard: เข้าใจ to understand; to make intelligible; to comprehend: เข้าใจผิด to misunderstand: เข้าฌาน to be in a hypnotic state of contemplation or meditation: เข้าด้วย to join with or in: เข้าด้าย เข้าเข็ม to be in a condition of extreme distress or need; to be in a dilemma or in a position of extreme embarrassment; to be at one's wits end: เข้าได้เข้าไฟ eventide; early night-time: เข้าท่าเข้าที่ appropriate; fitting; proper: เข้านอน to retire; to go to bed or to sleep: เข้าเนื้อ to take out, or to chip into the principal (as of funds): เข้าไป to enter in: เข้าเฝ้า to appear before royalty; to have an audience with the king or a prince: เข้าไม้ to splice two timbers; to trim two boards so as to fit snugly; to dovetail pieces of wood together: เข้ารอยเข้ารูป to be satisfactory in every detail: เข้ารีต to embrace another religion: เข้าสนับ to be circumcised: เข้าสมาธิ to be in a state where the mind is fixed on some one object: เข้าหุ้นเข้าส่วนกัน to enter into partnership with; to be engaged in the same pursuits; to be involved in the same practices as the others: เข้าออกได้ง่าย easily accessible; รุกเข้าไป to invade; to trespass.

เขิน kern[2] *n.* a people found chiefly in the state of Keng Tung but extending into Chiengrai province. They seem to be only a branch of the Lu tribe (siam p. 99): เขิน เตินเต่อ gradually rising or sloping upward (as the ground approaching a hill); *colloq.*

becoming more shallow (as the bed of a canal) : คลองเขิน a shallow canal ; a canal gradually getting more shallow : เครื่องเขิน lacquer-ware (as made and used by the northern tribes of Siam) : นาเขิน paddy fields on high ground.

เขี่ย kee-ah[4] v. to dislodge ; to scratch ; to scatter about (as with the fingers or a stick) : เขี่ยได้ to scrape off the ashes or charred portion from the burning end of a torch ; to snuff a torch : เขี่ยผงในตา to dislodge a foreign body in the eye : คุ้ยเขี่ย to dig by poking at or into (as with a stick).

เขียง kee-ang[2] n. a chopping block ; a temporary sun-shade ; a platform built in the fields for shelter while driving off the rice birds : เขียงเท้า a clog ; a wooden-soled shoe : สะไบเขียง to wear a scarf across the shoulder, following the former fashion of Siamese women.

เขียงพร้า (ต้น) kee-ang[2]-pra[5] n. Carallia brachiata (Legnotidaceae) (cb. p. 599 : Burk. p. 448), a tree of moderate size found in India, southern China and throughout Malaysia to Australia. The timber is very handsome, having a silver grain. It is hard, and the sap-wood is yellowish rose, but sometimes is red, brown or orange-brown. It is moderately heavy and not subject to insect-attack. The wood is used for house-building, rice-pounders (in Burma), agricultural implements, etc. The fruit is edible. The leaves and bark are medicinal. The seed contains some oil. It is cultivated in temple grounds (K.).

เขียด kee-at[4] n. a small green frog.

เขียน kee-an[2] v. to write ; to sketch ; to inscribe ; to draw ; to put down in writing : เขียนจดหมาย to compose or write a letter : เขียนรูป to paint or sketch a portrait : ช่าง-เขียน a painter ; a good penman ; a draughts-man : เครื่องเขียน writing implements.

เขียม kee-am[2] Chin. adj. miserly ; saving ; sparing ; economical ; frugal.

เขียว ๑ kee-oh[2] adj. swift ; rapid ; urgent ; speedy ; fast : ข่าวเขียว an urgent message ; a message requiring prompt delivery.

เขียว ๒ kee-oh[2] adj. green : เขียวแก่ dark green : เขียวคราม indigo blue : เขียว-ครามแก่ dark blue ; deep blue : เขียวฟ้า sky blue ; azure : เขียวหวาน (ส้ม) lit. "green-sweet," i. e. a sweet orange having a green skin ; (แกง) a kind of hot curry made with green peppers : เขียวหางไหม้ (ง) the common green pit viper, Trimeresurus gramineus (M. S., N. H. J. S. S. VI, 1, p. 63) : เขียว-อ่อน light green ; pale green : ตาเขียว eyes that are inflamed with anger : ฟัก-เขียว Benincasa hispida (Cucurbitaceae) (cb. p. 757) ; B. cerifera, the white gourd or ash-pumpkin, a thick, cylindrical, smooth fruit, 10 to 15 inches long and about 3 to 4 inches in diameter, usually brownish-yellow when fullgrown and ripe. It is probably a native of Malaysia but is now spread throughout the tropics. The fruit is either cooked and used as a vegetable or peeled and sliced in salads, being a good substitute for the cucumber proper, of which it is but a variety. The seeds contain a bland oil, and are eaten fried by the Chinese, who regard them as medicinal. The juice of the leaves is cooling and is rubbed on bruises. There are various other medicinal uses (MCM. p. 291 : V. P. p. 196 : Burk. p. 317).

เขี้ยว kee-oh[3] n. the canine teeth ; an eye tooth of either human or animal : เขี้ยวการ the face of an imaginary spirit represented with huge canine teeth (painted on the gable ends or doors of houses) : เขี้ยวแก้ว a tooth of the Buddha ; the poison fangs of a snake : เขี้ยวเนื้อ (ต้น) Barleria prionitis (Acanthaceae) (V. P. p. 57 : Burk. p. 303), a small, spiny bush with plentiful, buff-coloured flowers, found throughout tropical Africa and Asia. The juice of the leaves is used medicinally in catarrhal affections of children which are accompanied with fever and much phlegm. In Siam a febrifuge is prepared from the roots. The juice of the leaves is applied externally to the feet to prevent cracking (Dept. Agri. & Fisheries): เขี้ยวมังกร (ต้น) *Lagerstroemia undulata* variety *subangulatā* (*Lythraceae*) (cb. p. 728), a secondary shrub found in mixed decidous forest: แยกเขี้ยวยิงฟัน to show the teeth by drawing the lips back, indicating anger.

เขี้ยวขยอน　kee-oh²-ka⁴-yaun² *adj.* tremulous; turbulent; riotous; agitated; convulsed.

เขือ　kur-ah² *n.* a friend; a partner: *pro.* you; thou; him: เขือ (ปลา) a fish of the goby family, *Apocryptes serperaster* (Sunder Lal Hora N. H. J. S. S. VI, 2, p. 179).

เขื่อง (ต้น)　keu-ang² *n. Leea sp.* (*Ampelidaceae*) (V. P. p. 51: Burk. p. 1326), a genus of shrubs, herbs and small trees found in the topics of the Old World: เขื่องเข้าไหม้ (ต้น) *Desmodium thorelii* (*Leguminosae*) (cb. p. 419), an under-shrub about 1.5 m. high, found in bamboo jungle and common in teak forest. The flowers are white (K.): เขื่องแข้งม้า (ต้น) *L. pallida* (V. P. p. 51); *L. acuminata* (cb. p. 316): เขื่องหมู่ (ต้น) *Caryota mitis* (*Palmae*) (V. P. p. 51: Burk. p. 471), a small, tufted palm, attaining 25 or even 40 ft. in height, found from Burma and Indo-China southwards through Malaysia. The wood is scanty but strong. In the Dutch Indies it is used for spinning-wheels. A little sago is to be got from the stems. The fruits have an edible seed inside a poisonous fruit-wall: เขื่อง หลวง (ต้น) *C. urens* (V. P. p. 52), the Kitul or toddy palm, which grows in moist low country up to 300 ft. It is a sub-tropical palm, indigenous to Siam, Ceylon, Malay, etc. The tree attains a height of 40 to 50 ft. The leaves are bipinnate, very handsome with drooping spadices 8 to 10 feet long. From the young spadix, a copious flow of sweet sap is obtained, which upon boiling yields a quantity of brown sugar or jaggery. When fresh, this is known as "sweet toddy," and on becoming sour as "fermented toddy," which is intoxicating. The palm is fit to tap when about 15 to 20 years old, when it commences to flower. The Kitul palm yields excellent sago from the stem, also a commercial bristle-fibre from the base of the leaf-stalks (MCM. pp. 162, 164, 169, 361, 512, 517). The wood is hard and durable, useful for building purposes (Dept. Agri. & Fisheries): เขื่องหูช้าง (ต้น) *Caryota macrophylia* (V. P. p. 52): เขื่อง หมม้า (ต้น) *L. parallela var. puberula* (cb. p. 319), a genus of small trees, found in deciduous jungle of Siam.

เขื่อง　keu-ang⁴ *adj.* rather too big; too large: เขื่องไปหน่อย a little too large; a little larger than is necessary.

เขื่อน　keu-an⁴ a dike or embankment to protect low land from inundation; a protecting or retaining wall for water fronts.

แข　kaa² *Cam. n.* the moon; the orbit of the moon.

แข้, จระเข้　kaa³ *n.* an alligator; a crocodile.

แขก　kaak⁴ *n.* a stranger; a visitor; a caller; a foreigner; Asiatics, other than Chinese or Japanese; a collective name for natives of India: แขกเต้า (นก) a species of parrot: แขกเต้า (ต้น) *Protium serratum Burseraceae* (V. P. p. 49), a tree about 10 m. high, found in scrub jungle. The flowers are green (K.): แขกบรเทศ, แขกมอญ names of tunes played by Siamese musicians: แขก บ้านแขกเมือง strangers or visitors to the city: แขกมะลายู Malays: คนรับแขก an host; one who receives the guests: รับแขก to receive; to entertain one's friends, visitors or acquaintances: เลี้ยงแขก to entertain one's friends by giving a feast or dinner.

แข็ง　kaang² *n.* hardness; firmness; energy; strength; degree of intensity; perverseness; *adj.* hard; solid; compact; dense; obstinate; headstrong; perverse: แข็งข้อแข็งมือ to devote one's self unflaggingly to a task; to be unflinching in the facing of an ordeal: แข็งใจ to suffer patiently; to be courageous in facing danger; to endure with fortitude: แข็งต่อศึก to strengthen the defenses against the advances of the enemy: แข็งตัว to nerve one's self (as when about to face an operation); to make one's self stiff or motionless: แข็งมือ to be more strict; to be more exacting, more severe or stern; to exert one's self more energetically: แข็งเมือง to be able to regain independence or autonomy; to restore self-government: แข็งแรง strong; robust; muscular (descriptive of the body); durable; firm; strong; solid (as a building or bridge); industrious (as a good working man); being habitually occupied: แข็งฤทธิ์ to increase; to enhance; to intensify the potency, inherent ability, strength or power: ใจแข็ง to be unyielding; to be immovable (against entreaties or supplications): ปากแข็ง to be harsh, uncivil, abusive or bitter (in words or speech); to be hard; to be stiff in the mouth (as a horse).

แข่ง, แข่งขัน kaang⁴ v. to race; to compete with; to contend with; to contest for; to vie or to strive for (as victory or a prize): แข่งบุญแข่งวาสนา to emulate; to compete with others for official standing or degree of merit: แข่งม้า horse-racing: แข่งเรือ boat-racing: วิ่งแข่งกัน a foot-race; sport racing.

แข้ง kaang³ n. the distal portion of the leg: กระดูกแข้ง, หน้าแข้ง the ridge of the tibia; the shin; the shin bone: ขาแข้ง idiom. for แข้ง.

แข้งกวาง (ต้น) kaang³-gkwang n. Wendlandia tinctoria (Rubiaceae); W. ligustrina (V. P. p. 51), a small elegant tree, with large crowded panicles of small, white, sweet-scented flowers. The bark is largely employed as a mordant in dyeing and as an external application to the body to relieve the cramps of cholera (Dept. Agri. & Fisheries).

แขน kaan² n. the arm: แขนกุด, แขนด้วน a handless arm; an arm partly amputated: แขนคอก a stiffness of the elbow; a deformity of the elbow: แขนหนึ่ง an arm's length.

แข่น, แข้น kaan⁴ v. to dry by heat; to evaporate to dryness; to be heated till dry: adj. hard; dry.

แขนง ka⁴-naang² n. a twig; small branches of a tree or bush: แตกแขนง to put forth shoots, sprouts or twigs.

แขนะ ka⁴-naa⁴ v. to puncture; to pierce; to make forms or figures by chiselling; to carve (as wood or stone).

แขม ๑ kaam² n. a division or sub-classification of the Cambodians or Khmers.

แขม ๒ (ต้น) kaam² n. Sorghum halapense (Gramineae) (V. P. p. 56: MCM. p. 477: Burk. p. 2056: Dept. Agri. & Fisheries), a tall, perennial grass, native of Turkey. It is often called Johnson grass from the name of the man who carried it from Turkey to the U. S. A. In places it proves a valuable fodder-grass but is coarse and in Malaya produces little foliage.

แขม่บ ka⁴-maap⁴ adj. short; shallow; gentle (descriptive of respirations): ท้อง แขม่บขึ้นแขม่บลง the abdomen rises and falls with short breathing.

แขม่ว ka⁴-maa-oh⁴ adj. reduced in size (as can be done with the abdominal muscles); having the abdominal cavity reduced in size by muscular contraction; reduced in size by degrees: แขม่วท้องลง to lessen the size of the abdomen.

แขย็กๆ ka⁴-yaak⁴-ka⁴yaak⁴ adj. moving up or down in short steps or degrees (descriptive of a fowl swallowing a large morsel of food or a person climbing a limbless tree with difficulty).

แขยง ka⁴-yaang² v. to loathe; to abhor; to feel a repugnance towards; to regard with disgust; to be repulsive to: แขยงแข็งขน

to feel a loathing for; to have a nauseated feeling at the sight of, causing goose-flesh.

แขยง (ปลา)　ka⁴-yaang² *n.* a species of fresh water fish, *Macrones nemurus* (*Bagridae*); *M. nigriceps*; *M. wolffi* (Dept. Agri. & Fisheries: Burk, p. 1386), cat-fish found in tropical fresh water: แขยงทอง (ปลา) *Heterobagrus bocourti* (Dept. Agri. & Fisheries): แขยงน้ำเงิน (ปลา) *Cosmochilus harmandi Sauvage* (Dept. Agri. & Fisheries): แขยงหิน (ปลา) *Leiocassis siamensis* (Dept. Agri. & Fisheries).

แขย่ง see แขย็ก ๆ

แขวก (นก)　　kwaak⁴ *n.* the night-heron, *Nycticorax nycticoras* (Herb. N. H. J. S. S. VI, 4, p. 353).

แขวง　　kwaang² *n.* district; section; a division of a province; the region round about: แขวงจังหวัด within the provincial limits: ขุนแขวง the chief of a village, section or region.

แขวน　　kwaan² *v.* to hang; to suspend; to be suspended; to dangle; to be unsuccessful; to fail in accomplishing; to remain in the original state or condition (as a project or enterprise): แขวนคอตาย death by hanging: แขวนอยู่ to remain in a suspended condition.

แขวะ　　kwaa⁴ *v.* to scoop out the inside of; to hollow out; to empty; to incite; to instigate a quarrel by using insulting, disparaging or abusive language.

แขสร　　ka²-saa² *Cam. n.* a piece of rope.

โข　　koh² *adj.* much; plenty; abundant.

โขก　　kok⁴ *v.* to knock with the knuckles; to give a fillip: โขกหัว to strike a blow with a knuckle or the knuckles (as on the head). In Siam this is a common way of inflicting minor punishment on children.

โขง (แม่น้ำ)　　kong² *n.* the Mekong river.

โข่ง (หอย)　　kong⁴ *n.* a species of invertebrate animal whose shell consists of a number of spiral whorls; mud snails; fresh-water snails; apple snails.

โขด　　kot⁴ *n.* a mound; a knoll; an hillock; a slight elevation or eminence of land; a ford or shallow passage across a body of water: โขดเขิน *idiom.* for โขด.

โขน　　kon² *n.* plays, dramas or comedies enacting scenes from the Ramayana (performed by male, masked actors): โขนเรือ a dragon-like bow-piece for boats; a long main piece of carved timber added to the bow and stern of some kinds of boats: โขนหนัง shadow-plays or comedies in which the actors wear masks: เล่นโขน plays or pantomimes by mute, masked, male characters: หัวโขน a mask fitting down over the face.

โขม　　kom² *P. n.* a linen cloth; a cloth woven from leaf fibers (as pina cloth) (chd. p. 201): โขม (ผัก) *Amaranthus viridis* (*Amarantaceae*) (V. P. p. 53: Burk. p. 125: Dept. Agri. & Fisheries), spinach, a quick-growing annual, widely found in all tropical and many temperate regions. The young leaves are used as a vegetable: โขมสวน (ผัก) *Amaranthus gangeticus* (*Amarantaceae*) (V. P. p. 53: MCM. p. 311: Burk. p. 126: Dept. Agri. & Fisheries), a spinach with tender stems and leaves. It is an edible herb used as food in Siam and Ceylon by the poorer classes, but is not cultivated. It is used in India in the form of an emollient poultice: โขมหนาม (ผัก) *A. spinosus* (V. P. p. 53: MCM. pp. 311, 473, 476: Burk. p. 127), a weed, native of tropical America and now throughout the whole tropics. It is a cattle and pig food in Indo-China. It is used as food in Siam and Ceylon by the poorer classes, but is not cultivated. The ashes of this plant are used in dyeing; the whole plant is used as an antidote for snake poison; and the root as a specific for colic. The root has been found useful in the treatment of gonorrhoea as it is said to arrest the discharge (Dept. Agri. & Fisheries): โขมหิน (ผัก) *Boerhaavia diffusa* (*Nyctaginaceae*) (V.

P. p. 54 : Burk. p. 343. McM. p. 311), an edible, herb, very common in India, spreading southwards into the Malay Peninsula. It is commonly used as food by the poorer classes in Siam and Ceylon, but is not cultivated. The root is used in an infusion or given in powder, which acts as a laxative, diuretic anthelmintic and cooling medicine (Dept. Agri. & Fisheries).

โขมง   ka-[4]mong[2] v. to be filled with smoke or noxious vapours : adj. smoky ; murky ; crabbed ; quarrelsome ; fretful : บ่นโขมง to complain or grumble in a fretful manner.

โขมด   ka[4]-mote[4] n. a ghost ; a phantom ; a " will o' the wisp " ; the phosphorescent light produced by the oxidation of marsh gas, sometimes seen in swamps ; the two humps or nodes on the sides of an elephant's head.

โขมดขมัง   ka[4]-mote[4]-ka[4]-mang[2] Cam. n. a corpse.

โขยก   ka[4]-yoke[4] adj. crippled or disabled in the leg ; lame ; limping ; footsore.

โขยง   ka[4]-yong[2] n. a family ; relations ; relationship ; consanguinity ; a company, crowd or mob (of people) ; a flock (of birds) : adj. all ; entire ; complete ; in a collective manner : โคตรโขยง the entire family, lineage or race (used as a malediction).

โขย่ง   see กระโหย่ง

โขลก   kloke[4] v. to pound ; to pulverize in a mortar : คนโขลกเขลก a base, vile person ; a blackguard.

โขลง   klong[2] n. a herd ; a drove ; a stench ; a very bad odour : โขลงช้าง a herd of (tame) elephants.

โขลน   klone[2] n. an order or organization of women palace-guards.

โขลนทวาร   klone[2]-ta[6]-wan n. an opening or way of entrance into a forest or jungle ; women guards or door-keepers for the royal palace.

โขนม see โขม

ไข   kai[2] v. to open ; to unfold ; to explain ; to unlock : n. tallow ; hard, animal fats ; stearin : แก้ไข to do or to arrange so as to overcome difficulties : ข้นเป็นไข a congealed or coagulated condition : ไขกุญแจ to unlock ; to open a lock : ไขนาฬิกา to wind a watch or clock : ไขน้ำ to open a sluice-gate, floodgate or faucet : ไขเสนียด (น้ำคร่ำ) polluted water ; a slushy condition under native kitchens, resulting from waste water having been poured down apertures without provision for drainage : ไขสันหลัง the spinal cord : เทียนไข tallow candles : แปรไข, ไขความ to explain ; to elucidate ; to expound ; to interpret ; to reveal the meaning.

ไข่   kai[4] v. to lay eggs : n. an egg : ไข่ไก่ hens' eggs : ไข่ขาง fly-blow (eggs laid by flies in meat) : ไข่ขาว the white of an egg : ไข่เคี่ยว (ต้น) Shorea sp. (Dtpterocarpaceae) (Dept. Agri. & Fisheries : Burk. p. 2001), a genus of valuable timber tree found from India to the Philippines : ไข่เค็ม salted eggs : ไข่จระเข้, ไข่จิ้งหรีด the names of certain kinds of Siamese confections : ไข่เจ่า, ไข่ลม an unfertilized egg : ไข่เจียว omelet : ไข่ดาว a condiment composed of fried eggs : ไข่แดง the yolk of an egg : ไข่เต่า, ไข่นกกระสา names of certain kinds of confections : ไข่เน่า (ต้น) Vitex glabrata (Verbenaceae) (V. P. p. 45 : Dept. Agri. & Fisheries : Burk. p. 2238), a large tree found from north-eastern India to northern Australia. The timber is moderately hard, tough, close-grained and grey. It is used for cart-wheels and deserves attention for furniture, etc. The fruit is eaten in Siam : ไข่ปลา the eggs of fishes ; fish roe ; mildew ; spots on paper : ไข่ปู (ต้น) Rubus ellipticus (Rosaceae) (Cb. p. 570 : McM. p. 189 : Dept. Agri. & Fisheries), a bramble : ไข่เป็ด duck eggs : ไข่มุก pearls : ไข่หวาน a kind of sweet cake, made of boiled eggs and sugar : ไข่ห้ำ the scrotum : ไข่เหา the name of an ancient system or table of measurements : ไข่เหี้ย a kind of cake ; a sweetmeat : รูปไข่ oval ; elliptical in shape.

ไข้ kai[3] v. to be ill with a fever ; to have a rise of temperature : n. a fever ; a rise of temperature : ไข้คอตีบ diphtheria : ไข้จับ an intermittent fever ; chills and fever ; ague ; malaria : ไข้จับสั่น malarial fever : ไข้ดำแดง scarlet fever ; scarletina : ไข้ทรพิษ small-pox : ไข้ปอดอักเสบ pneumonia : ไข้มารยา a feigned sickness or ailment : ไข้รากสาด เทียม para-typhoid fever : ไข้รากสาดใหญ่ typhus fever : ไข้สุกใส chicken-pox ; vari-cella : ไข้เหนือ, ไข้ป่า a form of malaria occurring in northern Siam ; jungle-fever : ไข้หวัด nasal-catarrh accompanied by a cold : ไข้หวัดใหญ่ influenza : ไข้หัด measles ; mor-billi : คนไข้ a sick person ; a patient : ความไข้ illnesses (in general) : เป็นไข้ to suffer with fever.

ไข่ดัน kai[4]-dan n. the inguinal region : ต่อมไข่ดัน inguinal glands.

ไขว่ kwai[4] v. to place or be placed crosswise or across each other ; to walk across in front of another (as on a road) ; to over-lap ; to interlace ; to be intermingled : adj. crisscross ; promiscuous : ไขว่คว้า to grab or hold with the hands promiscuously or at random : ไขว่ห้าง the manner of lying or sitting with one leg over the other knee, while it is in an upright position : เดินไขว่กัน to cross over in front of another person who is walking in the same direction.

ไขว้ kwai[3] v. to place crosswise ; to place together crisscross ; to alternate ; to ex-change : ไขว้เขว to interweave ; to mix indiscriminately ; to be disarranged : เข้า-ใจไขว้เขวกัน to be misunderstood : นั่งไขว้ขา to sit cross-legged.

ไขสอ kai[2]-seu[2] v. to dissemble.

ไขเสนียด see ไข

ไขหู kai[2]-hoo[2] v. to pretend not to hear ; to turn a deaf ear.

ข

ข The third consonant of the Thai alphabet, a high or first class letter of which there are eleven, viz. ข, ฃ, ฉ, ถ, ฐ, ผ, ฝ, ส, ศ, ษ, ห. ขอขวด is the desig-nating name. This letter is now obsolete ; ข (ขอไข่) is used in its place.

ค

ค The fourth consonant of the Thai alphabet, a low or third class letter of which there are 24, viz. ค, ค, ฆ ง, ช, ฌ, ซ, ญ, ฑ, ฑ, ธ, ฒ, ณ, น, ณ, พ, ฟ, ภ, ม, ร, ล, ว, ฬ, ฮ. คอคิด and คอควาย are the designating names. ค is a soft guttural, used extensively in Pali, Sanskrit and Siamese. In Pali and Sanskrit it means " to go," ex. วิหค = one who goes or flies through the air (as birds).

คก kok[6] adj. swift ; rapid ; fast (descriptive of flowing water).

คคน ka[6]-ka[6]-na[6] P. S. n. sky ; the expanse of the heavens ; the atmosphere ; firma-ment : คคนกุสุม lit. " musing about the sky," " flowers in the sky," i. e. a delusion ; an absurdity ; an impossibility ; any un-real or fanciful thing : คคนจร lit. " one moving in the air," i. e. a bird : คคนจาร

one or something coming out of the sky or air (as sounds or voices): คคนวิหารี *lit.* "one that moves, sports or glides in the sky or atmosphere," *i. e.* the sun, moon or celestial beings: คคนัมพร the great expanse of the sky or firmament: คคนางค์ a segment or portion of the sky: คคนานต์ the sky-line or limit of the sky; the horizon: คคนามพุ *lit.* "water from the sky," *i. e.* rain; rainwater: คคเนจร *lit.* "one moving in the air, atmosphere or sky," *i. e.* a bird; a star of omen (good or evil); a lucky star, a heavenly spirit or agent (S. E. D. p. 341).

คง kong *adj.* sure; firm; solid; permanent; durable; enduring; constant: คงกะพัน, คง- แก่พัน invulnerable; proof against weapons or firearms; impenetrable: คงจะดีขึ้น sure to improve: คงได้ certain to obtain: คงที่ to be stable; to be immovable, unchanged or unalterable: คงไป sure to go: คงอยู่ that which is stable or firm: เป็นอันมั่นคง certain; solid; everlasting; permanent: มั่น- คง certain; solid; firm: ยังคงอยู่บ้าง there is still more remaining: อยู่คง the art of making one's self invulnerable.

คงคา kong-kah *S. n. lit.* "flowing swiftly," *i. e.* the river Ganges, personified as a goddess and considered as the eldest daughter of Himavat and Mena. She became the wife of king Santanu (ท้าวศานตนุ) and mother of Bhishma (S. E. D.): คงคาเกษตร the Ganges and holy places on its banks. These places are considered sacred and hallowed. Any one dying in the water or along the bank is sure of entrance to a celestial abode (whatever his crimes may have been): คงคา- ชล the water of the Ganges, which is considered sacred for bathing and for use in various ceremonies (S. E. D. p. 341): คงคาเดือด (ต้น) *Arfeuillea arborescens (Sapindaceae)* (cb. p. 336), a medicinal tree about 10 m. to 15 m. high, found in scrub jungle. The flower is whitish or brown (K.: BURK. p. 237): คงคา- ทวาร *lit.* "the door of the Ganges," *i. e.* the

opening in the Himalaya mountains through which the river descends into the plains, now known as Hardwar (หริทวาร) (H. C. D. p. 109): คงคาธร *lit.* "the ocean or the one who receives the waters of the Ganges; one who supports the Ganges," *i. e.* the god Siva, thus named because Ganga was angry at being brought down from heaven, and Siva, to save the earth from the shock of her fall, caught the river on his brow and checked its course with his matted locks. From this action he is called Ganga-dhara, "upholder of the Ganges" (H. C. D. p. 108): คงคาบุตร *lit.* "one born of low or mixed lineage," *i. e.* Bhishma, son of the Ganges, otherwise known as the god of War and the planet Mars (H. C. D. p. 152). He was son of the holy river goddess Ganga and King Santanu. Bhishma, being desirous of marrying a young and beautiful wife had to make a vow to the girl's parents, who were not of royal lineage, that he would never accept the throne nor would he marry another wife nor become the father of children. Throughout his life, Bhishma exhibited a self-denial, devotion, and fidelity which remained unsullied to the last (H. C. D. pp. 53, 54): คงคายาตรา the act of making a pilgrimage to, or worshipping along the banks of the Ganges or conveying the sick there to be bathed or to die (S. E. D.): คงคาสนาน bathing in the Ganges: คงคา- สัปตมี the seventh day of the waxing moon of the sixth Siamese lunation. This corresponds to the Wisakha festival, held in honour of the birth, inspiration and death of the Buddha (1909, BANGKOK DIRECTORY p. 29): คงคาสาคร the estuary or mouth of the Ganges; a holy bathing-place sacred to Vishnu (H.C.D. p. 109): คงคาสุต a name for พระการติเกย otherwise known as the god of War; the planet Mars, also called Skanda (H. C. D. p. 152): สรงคงคา to bathe in the river Ganges.

คงไคย kong-kai *P. S. n. lit.* "being in or on the Ganges; coming from, belonging or related to the Ganges," *i. e.* the name of an illustrious rank of elephants which have yellow hides, like cummin (S. E. D. p. 353).

คช   kot⁶ *P. S. n.* an elephant (S. E. D. p. 342): คชกันยา, คช๎ a female elephant: คชกุรมาศี *lit.* "devouring an elephant and a tortoise," *i. e.* a name for the Garuda (an allusion to his swallowing both these animals while they are engaged in contest with one another (S. E. D.): คชตา a herd of elephants: คชทนต๎ the ivory tusks of the elephant; a pin; wall pegs or brackets on which to hang articles; a name of Ganesa (who is represented with an elephant's head): คชทาน secretions exuding from the temple glands of the elephant (as in time of must): คชนักร *lit.* "elephant-crocodile," *i. e.* the rhinoceros: คชนาสา the trunk of an elephant: คชบาล a mahout; an elephant keeper: กรมคชบาล Department for the Care of Royal Elephants: คชพันธน๎ the post to which an elephant is tied: คชมัณฑนะ elephant trappings; the ornaments with which an elephant is decorated (especially the coloured lines on his head): คชมาตร as tall as an elephant: คชมุข, คชวัทน๎, คชานน *lit.* "elephant-faced," *i. e.* Ganesa, the god of Wisdom and remover of obstacles (H. C. D.): คชโยธี *lit.* "fighting on an elephant," *i. e.* soldiers: คชราช, คชินทร๎, คเชนทร๎ *lit.* "king of elephants," *i. e.* a noble elephant; a war or state elephant: คชสถาน an elephant stockade; an enclosure, stall or pen made for elephants: คชสาร well-bred or well-trained elephants; an excellent elephant; the leader of a herd: คชสีห๎ a mythical animal representing a lion with an elephant's trunk; the figure on the seal of the Ministry of Defence: คชาชีพ a mahout; one who gains his livelihood by tending elephants: คชาธาร a royal elephant used by His Siamese Majesty: คชาภรณ๎ elephant trappings: decorative paraphernalia for elephants: คชายุรเวท a medical treatise dealing with elephants' diseases and their treatment: คชารี *lit.* "the enemy of elephants," *i. e.* a lion.

คชสาน   kot⁶-cha⁶-san⁴ *n.* a species of yellow watermelon which is very sweet.

คณ, คณะ   ka⁶-na⁶ *P. S. n.* an assembly; a party, group or category; a chapter (as of priests); a community; an organization; a flock; troop; multitude; number; tribe; series; class (of animals or inanimate beings): คณเทวตา troops of deities; deities who generally appear or are spoken of in classes. There are nine such classes, viz. (1) Adityas (อาทิตย๎), (2) Visawas or Visvas-devas (วิศวะ), (3) Vasus (วส), (4) Tushitas (ดุษิต), (5) Abhasvaras (อาภาสวระ), (6) Anilas (อนิล), (7) Maharajikas (มหาราชิก), (8) Sadhyas (สาธยะ), (9) Rudras (รุทระ). These inferior deities are attendant upon Siva, under the command of Ganesa. They dwell on Ganga-parvata, *i. e.* Kailasa (H. C. D.): คณนาถ *lit.* "lord of the various classes of subordinate gods," *i. e.* Siva: คณนายก *lit.* "the principal or leader of the groups of Siva's hosts or attendants," *i. e.* Ganesa, under whose command are the Gana-devatas (H. C. D. p. 104); the head of an assemblage or corporation: คณบดี *lit.* "leader of a class, a troop or assemblage," *i. e.* Siva; Ganesa; Department of the Dean of a University: คณบรรพต, คณาจล the mountain called เขาไกลาส, where the celestial forces of Siva congregate or live; also, precincts of ท๎าวกุเวร, the chief of the evil spirits living in the shades (H. C. D. p. 173): คณประมุข, คณมุขย๎ the head of an organization or corporation: คณโภชน๎ the act of eating in common: คณศรี those who are associated or combined for a common purpose: คณาจารย๎ a leader or teacher of a group or sect of people; a preceptor: คณาธิป the leader of a sect, community or troop; name of Siva and Ganesa: คเณศ name of Ganesa, the god of Wisdom, and of Obstacles. He is the son of Siva and Pravati. Though he causes obstacles, he also removes them; hence he is invoked at the commencement of all undertakings and at the opening of all compositions.

He is represented as a short fat man with a
protuberant belly, frequently riding on a rat,
or attended by one, and to denote his sagacity,
has the head of an elephant, which however
has only one tusk. The appellation Ganesa
alludes to his office as chief of the various
classes of subordinate gods who are regarded
as Siva's attendants (S. E. D. p. 343): คเณศ-
จาตุรถี fourth day of the waxing moon of the
Bhadra (ภาทฺร) month occurring between
August and September, reputed to be the
birthday of Ganesa.

คณนะ, คณนา ka[6]-na[6]-na[6] *P. S. v.* to count,
calculate, reckon or compute: *n.* the act of
counting, calculating or reckoning; computation (S. E. D. p. 343): คณนามหามาตร the
Minister of Finance คณนาวิทยา mathematics (as arithmetic or algebra).

คณา ka[6]-nah used as a prefix denoting an
assemblage, group, company, order or class:
คณานก a family or species of birds: คณานาง
a group or rank of women in the royal household: คณาญาติ groups of relatives.

คณิกา ka[6]-ni[6]-gkah *P. S. n.* a female
elephant; an harlot; a courtezan; a woman of
ill-repute (S. E. D. p. 343).

คณิต ka[6]-nit[6] *P. S. n.* the science of
computation, comprising arithmetic, algebra
and geometry: *adj.* counting; being reckoned, numbered or calculated (S. E. D. p. 343):
ปาฏิคณิต arithmetic: พีชคณิต algebra: เรขา-
คณิต geometry: คณิตศาสตร์ mathematics;
the science of computation.

คณิติน ka[6]-ni[6]-dtin *S. n.* an expert accountant; a "shark" on figuring; one who has
calculated or is capable of doing so (S. E. D.
p. 344).

คณิน, คณี ka[6]-nin, *S. n. lit.* " one who has
attendants or is surrounded by them; one
having a class of pupils," *i. e.* a teacher
(S. E. D. p. 344).

คด kot[6] *v.* to bend; to dip out; to be

crooked: *n.* a stone lodged in an animal's
head or in a tree (considered to be an effective
charm); a bend; a turn; a curve; crookedness:
adj. bent; perverse; not straight-forward:
คดโกง crooked (in business dealings); dishonest; perfidious: คดกฤช a decorative
design where the long lines wave back and
forth in the form of a Malay dagger: คดข้าว
to dip rice out of a boiling pot: คดเคี้ยว
winding: คดนกกูด (ต้น) *Aralidium pin-
natifidum (Cornaceae)* (cb. p. 795), a shrub
about 4 m. high, growing along streams in
evergreen forest. The fruit is white and the
flowers green. It is used medicinally and the
smoke of burning leaves is said to be useful
in driving insect pests from rice-fields (K.:
BURK. p. 212): คดในข้องอในกระดูก untruthful; deceitful; dishonest; unfaithful.

คดี ka[6]-dee *P. S. n.* state; condition; mode;
existence; way; path; course; procedure;
progress, manner or power of going; methods
or principles of living; story; an account of
any transaction; a case in court; a lawsuit:
คดีโลก worldly methods or deportment: คดี-
ธรรม the observance of ethics, principles or
precepts, as means of success (S. E. D. p. 347):
ข้อคดี statements in any litigation.

คต ka[6]-dta[4] or kot[6] *P. S. adj.* ended; gone
by; past; dead and gone; forsaken: คตชีพ,
คตชีวิต dead; lifeless; deceased; departed
from the world: คตทิน yesterday; a day
that is past and gone (S. E. D. p. 347).

คติ ka[6]-dti[4] *P. S. n.* rebirth; a method or
manner of going; the act of departing;
progress; advancement towards a better state
or existence (S. E. D. p. 347).

คท ka[6]-ta[6] or kot[6] *P. S. n.* sickness;
disease; a sentence; poison (S. E. D. p. 344).

คทา ka[6]-tah *P. S. n.* a mace; a club; a
bludgeon; a policeman's club: คทาธร *lit.*
" one holding a club," *i. e.* Krishna, the most
celebrated hero of Indian mythology and the
most popular of all deities (H. C. D. p. 160):

คทายุทธ์ a fight or combat with clubs : คทา-
ยุธ, คทาวุธ *lit.* "having a weapon," *i. e.* being
armed with a club : คทาหัสต์ being armed
with a mace (S. E. D. p. 344).

คน   kon *v.* to stir (with the hand or spoon);
to mix (by hand or ladle).

คน   kon *n.* a person of either sex; a
single person or child; the numerical particle for persons collectively ;   คนกลาง an
arbitrator ; an intermediate agent ; a person
who arbitrates : คนเกียจคร้าน a lazy person : คนขยัน an industrious person : คน-
คุม a warden or guard of prisoners : คนใช้
domestic servants : คนดี a good person :
คนทรง a sorceress ; a witch ; a spirit-charmer :
คนไทย a Siamese person ; the Thai race : คน-
ปอบ, คนชะมบ a keeper of evil spirits which
may be sent by him to do harm to others (as
feared by the Laos people): คนพวง a prisoner
with an iron collar or chains (term of contempt); a worthless fellow : คนละ different ;
dissimilar : คนละสิ่ง each with a different
article : คนละอย่าง each differing from the
other : คนโหด an hard-hearted person :
ช่วยผู้ช่วยคน a general benefactor : บางคน,
ลางคน some one ; some people : ผู้คน men ;
servants ; slaves.

ค้น   kon[5] *v.* to look for ; to scrutinize with
care ; to search for : ค้นของ to examine the
luggage : ค้นคว้า to search with the idea
of confiscating (as contraband goods); to look
through carefully ; to scrutinize (as for illicit
goods): ค้นด้าย to spin ; to explore ; to
investigate : ค้นหุก to sort fibres of cotton
or silk into suitable sizes preparatory to
weaving : ค้นหา to examine into everything
(as by Customs Officials).

คนทา (ต้น)   kon-tah *n. Harrisonia perforata* (*Simarubaceae*) (cb. p. 244), a wild,
thorny tree of bitter taste, used medicinally
by the Siamese (BURK. p. 1128): คนทาน้ำ (ต้น)
Rosa clynophylla (*Rosaceae*) (cb. p. 575), a
shrub, found forming a thick growth 2 to 3 m.

high on low lying ground near the Mekong.
The petals are white (K). The wood is
scented : คนทารส, คนทาเรส perfumery made
from this scented wood.

คนทิสอ (ต้น) kon-ti[6]-sau[2] *n. Vitex trifolia*
(*Verbenaceae*) (V. P. p. 68 : BURK. p. 2240 : Dept.
Agri. & Fisheries), a shrub or small tree, found
scattered throughout India, Siam, Malaya and
Java in the tropical and sub-tropical regions.
A clear, sweet oil of a greenish colour is
extracted from the root. The flowers are
blue ; the root is considered a tonic, febrifuge and expectorant. The aromatic leaves
are a tonic and vermifuge. A decoction of
the leaves with the addition of long peppers
is given in catarrhal fever with heaviness
of the head and dullness of hearing. The
juice of the leaves is said to remove foetid
discharges from ulcers. Oil prepared with
the juice of the leaves is applied to sinuses
and scrofulous sores.

คนที see กุณฑี

คนทีเขมา   kon-tee-kay[2]-mah *n.* a small,
medicinal plant like the คนทิสอ, only not
having down-covered leaves.

คนทีดน (ต้น)   kon-tee-don *n. Desmodium
ovalifolium* (*Leguminosae*) (cb. p. 414 : BURK.
p. 792), a branchless, prostrate shrub common
along paths in open, waste ground or evergreen forest (K.).

คนโท see กุณโฑ, กุณฑ์

คนธ์   kon *n.* an odour ; a perfume ; a
fragrant substance ; when used as a prefix it
signifies *fragrance* : *adj.* scented.

คนธรรพ์   kon-tan *P. S. n.* Gandharvas,
"the heavenly Gandharvas" of the Vesa.
He was a deity who knew and revealed the
secrets of heaven and divine truths in general
(H. C. D. p. 105). His habitation is the sky ;
his especial duty is to guard the Soma. He
is supposed to be a good physician because

the Soma is considered the best medicine. He is also regarded as one of the genii who regulate the course of the sun's horses. He follows after women and is desirous of intercourse with them (S. E. D. p. 346).

คบ kop[6] v. to associate with; to conspire; to join in company or partnership, ex. คบ-คนพาลๆ พาไปหาผิด, คบบัณฑิตๆ พาไปหาผล: n. a torch made of dry grass or wood (for fighting bees); lanterns; the main branch or fork of a tree: คบ (ต้น) Crypteronia paniculata (Lythraceae) (V. P. p. 69), a lofty tree found in Burma, Siam, Java and the Philippine Islands. The timber is very hard and durable and is used for house-building. The new wood is white; the heart-wood is red-brown (K.: Burk. p. 693). The fruit is poisonous (K.): คบค้า to be associated in business relations; to be greatly loved and respected: คบคิด to unite in a plot or scheme; to intrigue with others: คบพาล associating with a trouble-maker or an evil companion: คบ-เพลิง a kind of torch; a lantern: จุดคบ to light a torch.

คม ๑ kom P. S. n. a journey; the act of travelling to or from a place; a march; a course; a decampment (S. E. D. p. 348).

คม ๒ kom Cam. v. to bend over; to make a bow; to raise clasped hands to the forehead in the attitude of adoration.

คม ๓ kom n. the thin cutting edge of a blade; a sharp terminating border or point; adj. sharp; edged; keen: คมขวาน (ต้น) Hydnocarpus ilicifolia (cb. p. 97), a bushy tree about 8 m. high, found from Indo-China through Siam to northern Malaya. The oil is very similar to that of H. anthelmintica and is useful for treating leprosy (Burk. p. 1208): คมคาย, คมสัน shrewd; sagacious; sharp; witty; sarcastic: คมบาง (ต้น) a grass with sharp-edged blades: คมมีด the sharp edge of a knife: มีดคม a sharp knife: ลับให้คม to sharpen, whet or hone.

คมน ka[6]-ma[6]-na[6] P. S. n. the act of transporting or going; the act of arriving at one's destination: adj. going; moving (S. E. D. p. 348).

คมนาการ ka[6]-ma[6]-nah-gkan P. S. n. departure; decampment; the setting out (for war or for an attack): adj. going to; approaching; undergoing; attaining (S. E. D. p. 348).

คมนาคม ka[6]-ma[6]-nah-kom P.S. n. communication; intercourse; commerce.

คมนีย ka[6]-ma[6]-nee-ya[6] P. adj. obligated to go or arrive at; accessible; approachable; able to be reached; departing (S. E. D. p. 348).

คมาคม ka[6]-mah-kom S. n. traffic; intercommunications; commerce.

คมิก ka[6]-mik[6] P. n. a traveller; a pilgrim; one preparing for a journey; a sojourner: adj. travelling; going (chd. p. 141).

ครก krok[6] n. a mortar: ครกกระเบื้อ (the correct term is ครกข้าวเบื้อ), the pestle used in a mortar: ครกตำข้าว a large mortar used for pounding rice: ครกตำหมาก a small metal mortar used by old women for macerating the areca nut and betel leaf: ครกหิน a stone mortar: ขนมครก cakes made of coconut milk and flour, baked in cup-shaped depressions in an earthenware tray: ปืนครก a mortar; a piece of ordnance for firing heavy shells at great angles of elevation.

ครบ krop[6] adj. entire; complete; total; whole; perfect; full measure: ครบครัน full; complete: ครบถ้วน free from any deficiency (as a cook rendering a marketing account): ครบบริบูรณ์ full measure: รู้ครบ to know all; to know the whole story perfectly.

ครับ krap[6] adv. yes. This is a corrupted form of ขอรับ.

ครรชนะ kan-cha[6]-na[6] P. S. n. boisterousness; a noise indicative of violence (as the growl of a lion or the howl of a dog or wolf):

adj. roaring; thundering; rumbling; growling; excessive indignation (chd. p. 140).

ครรชิต kan-chit[6] *adj.* roaring; growling; bellowing; uttering a threatening sound (S. E. D. p. 349).

ครรทภ kan-top[6] *S. n. lit.* "a crier; a brayer," *i. e.* an ass; a donkey (S. E. D. p. 349).

ครรภ kan-pa[6] or kap[6] *S. n.* a room; the womb; the matrix; a foetus; an embryo; a child; a brood or offspring (of birds); a woman's courses: ครรภทาส a slave from birth; the condition of being born in bondage: ครรภธรา the state of nurturing a foetus; the condition of being pregnant: ครรภธาน, ครรภาธาน the condition of fecundation, impregnation or fertilization of the ovum; ครรภบาต an abortion; a miscarriage: ครรภบาตน์ the act of producing an abortion: ครรภมณฑป, ครรภเวศม์, ครรภาคาร a bed-chamber; an inner room or apartment: ครรภมาส the month when pregnancy began: ครรภร desirous of pregnancy; desiring children: ครรภรักษา prenatal care or attention: ครรภรูป *lit.* "foetus-like," *i. e.* a young child; a youth: ครรภาวดี pregnant; being with child: ครรภวิบัติ the condition of being still-born: ครรภศัยยา, ครรภสถาน, ครรภาศัย, ครรโภทร womb; uterus; a cradle for the foetus: ครรภไสยกะ *lit.* "born from the womb," *i. e.* a babe; an infant; a child; a mammal: มีครรภ์ pregnancy; being with child (S. E. D. p. 349).

ครรเภศวรี kan-pay-sa[4]-wa[6]-ree *n. lit.* "a sovereign by birth," *i. e.* a princess.

ครรโลง kan-long *n.* a form of rhyme or poetry.

ครรไล, ไคล kan-lai *v.* to go: *n.* perspiration that dries on the skin or can be removed by hard friction.

ครรหิต ๑ kan-hit[4] *S. adj.* blamed; censured; despised; contemptible; forbidden; worse than (S. E. D. p. 350).

ครรหิต ๒ kan-hit[4] *P. adj.* grasped; seized; caught; held; laid hold of (S. E. D. p. 362).

ครวญ kroo-an *v.* to groan; to sigh for; to utter a continued distressed sound: ครวญ-คราง, ครวญคร่ำ to groan or moan constantly (as in pain or sorrow): ครวญถึง to speak of, or about with affection; to sigh in love for.

ครว ka[6]-ra[6]-wee *n.* air: atmosphere; a gaseous medium.

ครหณะ, คหณะ ka[6]-ra[6]-ha[4]-na[6] *S. n.* the act of holding, receiving, grasping, mastering or clinging to the world (chd. p. 139).

ครหณ, เคราะหณ ka[6]-ra[6]-ha[4]-nee *S. n.* an imaginary organ supposed to lie between the stomach and the intestines (the small intestines or that part of the alimentary canal where the bile assists digestion and from which vital warmth is said to be diffused) (S. E. D. p. 372).

ครหะ ka[6]-ra[6]-ha[4] *n.* luck; fortune: *P. S.* the act of seizing, laying hold of, obtaining or receiving (S. E. D. p. 372).

ครหา ka[6]-ra[6]-hah[2] *P. S. v.* to calumniate; to slander; to defame; to censure; to abuse: *n.* defamation; a false tale or report, uttered with intent to injure the reputation of another; disgust exhibited in speech (S. E. D, p. 350): ครหานินทา slander.

ครอก krauk[3] *n.* a brood; a litter; slaves: ขี้ครอก (ต้น) *Urena lobata (Malvaceae)* (MCM. p. 432), a large, erect shrub common in the tropics. The stems yield a jute-like fibre used for cordage. The length of the cordage is small, but properly prepared, it is a trifle stronger than jute. It is also used to make a tough paper (Burk. p. 2211): ครอกหนึ่ง a brood; a covey: ลูกครอก, ขี้ครอก son of a slave.

ครอง kraung *v.* to rule; to govern; to regulate by authority; to direct; to exercise dominion: ครองกะฐิน to receive and care for the robes given to Buddhist monks at the time of the Krathin: ครองใจ to govern one's heart and desires: ครองตัว to exert self-control; to remain unmarried: ครองผ้า to put on robes (as Buddhist monks).

คร่อง   kraung³ *adj.* limping; lacking strength; enfeebled; weak.

ครองแครง   kraung-kraang *n.* a small season cake made of flour boiled in coconut milk and shaped like cockle shells.

ครอบ   kraup³ *v.* to cover with a lid; to shelter; to impart (as knowledge to a pupil, *ex.* ครูครอบศิษย์): *n.* a glass cover or lid; a lid, fitting well down over the edges; ครอบครอง to oversee; to govern; to rule over; to reign over; to manage or direct; to manage the affairs of; to take possession of: ครอบครัว a family: ครอบงำ to shelter; to defend; to shield; to cover; to over-shadow: ครอบ จักรวาล (ต้น) *Abutilon indicum (Malvaceae)* (cb. p. 153 : Burk. p. 10), a small shrub common throughout the hotter parts of India. The stems contain a good fibre suitable for cordage; the leaves yield a mucilaginous extract, used as a demulcent; an infusion prepared from the roots is given in fevers as a cooling remedy; it is said also to be useful in the treatment of leprosy; the seeds are considered laxative and demulcent, and are given in the treatment of coughs (Dept. Agri. & Fisheries): ครอบไว้ to cover: ตัณหาครอบงำ to be under the domination of passion: ยกครอบครัวไป to move one's family elsewhere.

คร่อม   kraum³ *v.* to super-impose (as a bridge over a klong); to bestride; to straddle (as when on horseback): คร่อมกัน one over the other (as when sitting cross-legged): คร่อมหลัง to sit astride (as a mahout): ไม้-คร่อมคอวัว a yoke.

กระใคร   kra⁶-krai *pro.* who.

กระยิก see กระยิก, ขยิก

กระแลง   kra⁶-laang *v.* to list to one side

(as a boat): กระแลงจัด a heavy list: กระ-แลงไป กระแลงมา to roll; to pitch; to rock back and forth.

กระไล   kra⁶-lai *v.* to retire; to go away.

กระวัก, กระวี่, กระแวง   kra⁶-wak⁶ *Cam.* *v.* to wave; to brandish; to shake; to beckon.

กระหน, กระหน   kra⁶-hon² *v.* to be excited; to be disturbed mentally; to be perturbed.

กระหวน see ครวญ

กระหาย, กระหาย   kra⁶-hai² *v.* to be in want of (as of knowledge); to need; to crave; to thirst after: *adj.* thirsty.

กระหิว   kra⁶-hew² *n.* want; need; desirability.

กระโหย   kra⁶-hoh-ie² *adj.* tired; fatigued; weary; irksome.

ครั้ง (ต้น)   krong⁵ *n. Anplectrum barbatum (Melastomaceae)* (cb. p. 698), a woody climber found at the edge of evergreen forest. The flowers are pink (K.).

ครั่ง   krang³ *n.* sealing wax: ครั่ง (กล้วย) the red-skinned banana: ครั่ง (กอฮอ) shellac varnish: ครั่ง (จากกิ่งไม้) stick-lac; lac: ครั่ง (ตัว) an East Indian scale-insect, *Coccus* or *Carteria lacca* (web.); *Tachardia lacca* (Dept. Agri. & Fisheries), is the producer of the lac from which shellac is made. These insects affix themselves to the twigs of certain trees. They suck the sap from the bark, giving it out again as an excretion which solidifies on contact with the air and gradually forms a scale about their bodies, called lac. This scale protects them from their enemies. Their span of life is about six months. Twice a year the young swarm. Each female produces a family of 1,000, 5% of which are males. In June and November the encrusted twigs are broken from the trees. These are called stick-lac. They are crushed; the lac cleaned, melted and made into lac-varnish, shellac, etc.

ครั้ง   krang[5] *n.* time; occasion; opportunity: กาลครั้งหนึ่ง once upon a time; กี่ครั้ง how many times? ครั้งก่อน previously: ครั้งนี้ this occasion; this time: ครั้งนั้น that time; then: ครั้งเมื่อ when; whereas; while: ครั้งหลัง past occasions.

ครัดเคร่ง, เคร่ง   krat[6]-kreng[3] *adj.* strict; stern; austere; severe.

ครัน   kran *adj.* much; sufficient; the superlative degree: ครบครัน complete; perfect: พอครัน it is enough; sufficient: มากครัน overly much.

ครั่น   kran[3] *v.* to feel feverish; to have a feeling of chilliness; to feel timid about making an attempt; to fear; to dread the consequences: ครั่นกาย to tremble with fear; to suffer with numbness; to shiver; ครั่นคร้าม to be agitated; to have trepidations: ครั่นตัว to feel chilly; to feel hot, then cold; to feel a sickly stiffness.

ครั้น   kran[5] *adv.* when; since; at the time of: ครั้นเป็นอย่างนั้น if it were so; since that was so: ครั้นมาถึง on arriving at: ครั้นเมื่อ when; at the time that: ครั้นว่า but if; for if; but at the time that.

ครัว   kroo-ah *n.* hearth or home; family; kitchen: กวาดครัว to carry off by families (as captives or hostages of war): ครัวไฟ kitchen: ครัวอพยบ families which have migrated: เทครัว to attempt to take possession of; to conquer the whole family: พวกครัว a crowd of captives; cooks: พ่อครัว a male cook: แม่ครัว a female cook.

ครา, ครั้ง   krah *n.* occasion; time; times: ครานี้ at this time: ครานั้น at that time: หลายครั้งหลายครา a repetition of, or several times already.

คร่า   krah[3] *v.* to pull; to haul; to drag along laboriously; to carry off by force; to abduct: คร่าไปคร่ามา to drag back and forth (as when polishing a floor).

คราก   krak[3] *v.* to be separated from; to be turned off from; to increase a small rent or crack: โครกคราก *onomat.* from something breaking or tearing: แตกแยกคราก to be separated; to break off.

คราง   krang *v.* to groan; to moan (as if in pain or sorrow): *n.* a species of sea-shell similar to the ark-shell or cockle shell, *Arca ectocomata*: กรนคราง to snore and groan in sleep (as persons who are ill): ครางครวญ to sigh; to groan; to sigh with sorrow or pity.

คราญ   kran *adj.* attractive; beautiful; lovely: นงคราญ a handsome or lovely girl.

คราด   krat[3] *v.* to scrape together; to draw; to pull; to haul; to harrow: *n.* rake; an harrow; a curry-comb: คราดนา to harrow a field; to rake hay or weeds in a field: คราด, คราดหัวแหวน (ผัก) *Spilanthes acmella (Compositae)*, a small herb with yellow flowers, found all around the world. The leaves and flowers are used for toothache and sore throat; it is also given to women in childbirth (MCM. p. 380: Dept. Agri. & Fisheries: Burk. p. 2065).

คร้าด (ต้น)   krat[5] *n. Dipterocarpus obtusifolius (Dipterocarpaceae)* (cb. p. 137), a large deciduous tree, said to afford a clear white or yellow resin, not an oil. This is reported to burn readily, but is not used for any purpose. The wood is reddish-brown, rough and moderately hard. Because of the resin it contains, the timber is a little difficult to saw. Otherwise it is easily worked (Dept. Agri. & Fisheries).

คราธ see คราส

คร้าน   kran[5] *adj.* lazy; indolent; slothful: เกียจคร้าน lazy; idle; averse to exertion: ขี้คร้าน given to laziness: อย่าเกียจคร้าน don't be idle.

คราบ   krap[3] *n.* scarf-skin: คราบงู the cast-off skin of a snake: คราบน้ำ slime formed on the bottom of boats: คราบปู the cast-off covering of a crab: ลอกคราบ to cast off the scarf-skin.

คราม ๑, ครามกะ, ครามโภชก, ครามวาสิน,
คาม kram *S. n.* a house; a village; a hamlet (S. E. D. p. 373): คราม (เกาะ) an island off the east coast of the Gulf of Siam. It is noted as spawning grounds for green turtles and hawkbill turtles.

คราม ๒ kram *n.* indigo: คราม (ต้น) *Indigofera tinctoria (Leguminosae)* (CB. p. 382: V. P. p. 69: BURK. p. 1239), indigo, a blue dye obtained from this species and from *I. arrecta*, *I. sumatrana*, *I. anil* and *I. guatamalensis*. All are shrubby, annual or perennial plants 3 to 6 ft. high. The use of this dye is of great antiquity, the original home being Gujarat, India. *I. arrecta* is especially recommended both on account of its heavier yield of crop and also its higher indigotin content (MCM. pp. 26, 438: Burk p. 1232 *f.*): เขียวคราม dark blue: ครามอ่อน light blue: สงคราม warfare.

คร้าม kram[5] *v.* to be rather timid or afraid of; to keep back something; to do wrong, and then to be in fear of being found out; to fear or dread the consequences of an act or deed: คร้ามกัน to be timid before another: คร้าม-เกรงฤทธิ์เดช to dread the power of another: คร้ามใจ to be mentally afraid of; to dread: คร้ามมือ to be fearful of the opponent (as a boxer): ครั่นคร้าม to dread; to fear; to have respectful fear.

ครามขน (ต้น) kram-kon[2] *n. Indigofera hirsuta (Leguminosae)* (CB. p. 378), a shrub about 1 m. high. The flowers are pink (K.).

ครามคร้น kram-kran *adj.* much; abundant; ample.

ครามณ ๑ krah-ma[6]-nee *S. n.* the head of the house or family; the leader or chief of a village or community; lord of the manor (S. E. D. p. 373).

ครามณี ๒ krah-ma[6]-nee *S. n.* the indigo plant (S. E. D. p. 373).

ครามณิย์ krah-ma[6]-nee *S. n.* a trainer of horses or elephants; a mahout; a carriage driver.

ครามานตระ krah-man-dta[4]-ra[6] *S. n.* another village; the space between villages or houses.

ครามิณี krah-mi[6]-nee *S. n.* a woman of the street; a prostitute.

คราโมปจาร krah-moh-bpa[4]-chjan *S. n.* the outskirts of, or the entrance to a village; the religious instructor of a village (chd. p. 141).

คราว krow *n.* occasion; time; opportunity: คราวก่อน a previous occasion: คราวนี้ this time: คราวนั้น, คราวโน้น that time: คราว-หน้า a future occasion: ข่าวคราว news of some occasion or event: แมวคราว a large-sized cat.

คร่าว krow[3] *n.* scantling; a small-sized timber for studs or rails: *adj.* indistinct; illegible; irregular; dim; blurred.

คราส, คราธ krat[3] *S. v.* to seize with the mouth; to swallow; to devour; to eat; to consume; to cause an eclipse; to slur over words pronounced indistinctly (S. E. D. p. 371).

คร่าห์ krah[3] *S. n.* the act of seizing, holding, grasping or devouring greedily (as the hippopotamus or alligator does) (H. C. D. p. 114).

คร่าหยุม (ต้น) krah[3]-yoom[2] *n. Dalbergia floribunda (Leguminosae)* (CB. p. 478), blackwood, a small spreading tree or woody climber about 15 to 20 m. high. The flowers are yellowish white. Some species of *Dalbergia* grow to 70 feet or more in height and some give important heavy, hard timber of great value (K.: Burk. p. 753).

คร่ำ kram *n.* foul or filthy water: น้ำคร่ำ dirty water; sewer water.

คร่ำ kram[3] *v.* to inlay with gold or silver: *adj.* blackened; antique; much used: คร่ำคร่า

very old (as much-used porcelain); old; ancient; rickety (as a house); deteriorated; weakened: คร่ำครื้น noise of thunder; a resounding or reverberating sound: คร่ำเครอ worn-out; feeble: คร่ำเครอะ filthy; dirty; besmeared with grime: คร่ำเงิน silver inlay: คร่ำทอง gold inlay: น้ำคร่ำ the amniotic fluid, or liquor amnii: มีดคร่ำ a knife inlaid with gold.

คร่ำครวญ kram³-kroo-an v. to cry or moan continuously; to grumble or mutter almost uninterruptedly.

คริร 'ka⁶-ri⁶-ra⁶ n. a plant shoot; a bamboo shoot or sprout.

คริสต krit⁶ Eng. n. Christ, one who frees or saves from suffering and sorrow: คริสต-มัส Christmas Day: คริสตศักราช the Christian era: คริสตสาสนิกชน Christians; followers or disciples of Jesus Christ.

ครีบ kreep³ n. fins (dorsal and ventral); serrations of leaves (as of the palm leaf).

ครีพ kreep³ S. n. the neck; the throat; the back part of the neck; nape of the neck; the neck of a bottle (S. E. D. p. 374).

ครีษมะ kreet³-sa⁴-ma⁶ S. n. the summer season; the hot season (chd. p. 147).

ครุ krur⁶ adj. wearing shabby, soiled garments; having a shabby appearance; rough, broken or jagged (in outline).

ครุก krurk⁶ v. to do; to perform; to make.

ครุกครื้น krurk⁶-krurn⁵ adj. gay; merry; jolly; exciting; entertaining.

ครุกโครม krurk⁶-krom adj. noisy; boisterous; turbulent; excited.

ครึ่ง kreung³ adj. half; partial: ครึ่ง ๆ กลาง ๆ partially: ครึ่งทาง, กึ่งทาง half-way: ครึ่งท่อน one half of a piece.

ครึน kreun n. a slip-noose snare for birds or fowls.

ครึ้ม, ครึ้มครุ kreum n. the denseness of a jungle; a jungle full of thick undergrowth: ครึ้มคร่ำ meditatively; silently; quietly; reservedly.

ครุ้ม krurm⁵ v. to become overcast or shaded: adj. cloudy; overcast (as the sky); cool and shady; sheltered, veiled or protected from the sun: ครุ้มเครี้ยว to reproach severely in ambiguous words: บ้านนี้ครุ้มนัก this jungle is densely dark.

ครืด kreut³ onomat. from the sound of scratching or dragging.

ครืดคราด (ปลา) kreut³-krat³ n. a salt water fish, a grunt, Pomadasys hasta; Therapon jarbua (Dept. Agri. & Fisheries).

ครืน ๑ krurn onomat. from the sound of thunder.

ครืน ๒, ครื้น, ครื้นครั่น, ครื้นครั้น krurn adj. being very noisy; boisterous; chattering; babbling (as a crowd of people).

ครื้นเครก krurn⁵-kreuk⁶ adj. gay; merry; jolly; exciting; entertaining.

ครื้นเครง krurn⁵-kreng adj. gay; merry and boisterous.

ครือ kreu adj. fitting snugly, neither too large nor too small; well-fitting; the right size to move freely (as a bolt).

ครุ ๑ ka⁶-roo⁶ P. S. n. a parent; a teacher; a religious preceptor; an instructor: adj. heavy; loud; accentuated (as a long vowel or syllable in poetry); vehement; violent; excessive; hard; difficult; grievous; important (S. E. D. p. 359).

ครุ ๒ ka⁶-roo⁶ n. a water-basket or bucket made of woven bamboo strips, smeared over with dammar.

ครุกะ ka⁶-roo⁶-gka⁴ P. adj. heavy; weighty; severe; grievous; important (chd. p. 144): ครุภัณฑ์ heavy, immovable household articles,

ครุคระ   kroo[6]-kra[6] *adj.* jagged; rough to the touch; having inequalities or notches on the surface; ragged.

ครุฑ, ครุฑ   kroot[6] *P. S. n. lit.* "devourer," *i. e.* Garuda, a mythical bird (chief of the feathered race), descended from Kasyapa (พระกัศยป) and Vinata (นางวินตา), one of the daughters of Daksha. He is the enemy of the serpent race, and vehicle of Vishnu. He is represented as having the head, wings, talons, and beak of an eagle, the body and limbs of a man, a white face, red wings, and golden body (chd. p. 109: s. e. d. p. 348): ครุฑเกตุ *lit.* "one having the Garuda as his symbol," *i. e.* Vishnu: ครุฑธวัช *lit.* "one using the Garuda as a banner," *i. e.* the chariot of Krishna: ครุฑปุราณ name of the 17th. volume of the series of books (ปุราณะ) that Vishnu recited in the Garuda Kalpa, relating chiefly to the birth of Garuda from Vinata. In it there are 19,000 stanzas (H. C. D. p. 110): ครุฑพ่าห์ *lit.* "one using the Garuda as a chariot or means of transportation," *i. e.* Phra Narayana (พระนารายณ์).

ครุฑโยธี   kroot[6]-ta[6]-yoh-tee *S. n. lit.* "one that fights with its wings," *i. e.* a partridge; a quail (s. e. d. p. 349).

ครุ่น, ครุ่นคริว   kroon[3] *v.* to be vexed or annoyed; to be disturbed by repeated acts; to be worried or harrassed.

ครุมเครือ   kroom-kreu-ah *adj.* obscure; smoky; murky; cloudy; feeling hot and cold alternately (as from ague).

ครุ่ม   kroom[3] *anomat.* from the sound of a victory drum.

ครุย   kroo-ay *n.* lace; fringe; edging (as of pendant cords): ครุยผม long curly hair: ชายครุย lace edging: ถักครุย to make fringes or lace edging; to embroider: เสื้อครุย a long, thin, embroidered robe worn over other garments to denote rank.

ครุฬ ๑   ka[6]-roon *P. n.* the Garuda, a gigantic race of birds, ever at war with the Nagas (chd. p. 144).

ครุฬ ๒   ka[6]-roon *S. n.* the Krut or Garuda.

ครุวนา   ka[6]-roo[6]-wa[6]-nah *n.* a parable; a simile.

ครุฬ see **ครุฑ**

ครู   kroo *P.S. n.* a teacher; a tutor; a preceptor or one to whom respect is due: พระครู the title for a Buddhist monk who serves in the capacity of a teacher or counsellor (chd. p. 151).

ครู่   kroo[3] *v.* to be dragged along; to be scratched, scraped or rubbed against: *n.* a short period of time (say ten or twenty minutes): ครู่หนึ่ง a moment; a few minutes: สักครู่เขาจะมา he will be coming in a short time; they will be along shortly.

ครูด   kroot[3] *v.* to scratch, scrape or rub against (as a moving boat against overhanging limbs): ครูดคราด *anomat.* from the sound of scratching or scraping: ครูดผม to disentangle hair; to comb hair that is in disorder.

ครึโมษ   kreu[6]-kot[3] *v.* to appear enraged; to growl (as a tiger): *adj.* gay; festive.

ครึธร   kreut[5] or kreu[6]-tra[6] *S. n.* a vulture: *adj.* covetous; avaricious; desirous (s. e. d. p. 361): ครึธรกูฏ, คิชฌกูฏ *lit.* "vulture-peak," *i. e.* a mountain near Raja-griha (ราชคฤห์) the capital of Magadha. Its site is still traceable in the hills between Patna and Gaya (s. e. d. p. 361: H. C. D. p. 253): ครึธรจักร the vulture and the cakravaka (s.e.d. p. 361): ครึธรบดี, ครึธรราช the lord of vultures, called Jatayu (ชฎายุ, สดายุ), said to be the son of the Garuda. He was an ally of Rama, who fought furiously against Ravana, to prevent the carrying away of Sita. He was overpowered, left mortally wounded, and was found by Rama just in time to hear his dying words and to learn what had become of Sita (H. C. D. pp. 134, 135),

คฤห kreu[6]-ha[4] *S. n.* a house; an abode; a dwelling-place; an habitation; a home; a servant; a temple; a sign of the zodiac (S. E. D. p. 361): คฤหการย์ household duties or occupations: คฤหชน the family; an household; members of an household: คฤหชาต *lit.* "those born in an household," *i. e.* slaves born in their master's home: คฤหทาร the posts of a house: คฤหทาส the slave of an household; a slave of a family; a domestic slave: คฤหทาสี a female domestic slave: คฤหเทวดา the joss, spirit or deity of a home: คฤหนาศน์ *lit.* "one that destroys or mutilates the partitions of a house," *i. e.* pigeons: คฤหบดี the head of an household; an householder of peculiar merit (as one giving alms and performing all the prescribed ceremonies); a headman or judge of a village: คฤหบดินี the mistress of a house or home; an householder's wife: คฤหบาล *lit.* "one who watches a house," *i. e.* a dog belonging to a house: คฤหพยาบาร household or family duties; acts of beautifying the house to the highest degree: คฤหพลี *lit.* "a domestic oblation," *i. e.* giving the remnants of food to domestic animals: คฤหมณี *lit.* "jewels of the house," *i. e.* lamps: คฤหมฤค *lit.* "domesticated deer," *i. e.* a dog: คฤหเมฆ a village or collection of houses: คฤหราช *lit.* "lord of the house," *i. e.* fire: คฤหศายี *lit.* "dwellers in a house," *i. e.* pigeons: คฤหศุทธิ ceremonies for the purification of a house: คฤหสาร property: คฤหาจาร *lit.* "house-customs," *i. e.* the duties of the head of the household or the housewife towards a caller or visitor: คฤหารมก์ the act of building a house: คฤหาราม a garden or grove near or around the house: คฤหาศยา the areca nut palm; the betel tree: คฤหาสน์ a castle; a house; a dwelling-place; an abode; a domicile: เทวดาคฤห a joss-house.

คฤหัสถ์ kreu[6]-hat[4] *S. n.* heads of the household or residents of the house; one who is not in the priesthood; one living or staying in one's home; an householder; a Brahman in the second period of his religious life, having finished his studies and having been invested with the sacred thread, performing the duties of a father and master of his house (S. E. D. p. 361).

คฤหา kreu[6]-hah[2] a prefix meaning *house, home, domicile.*

คล ๑ kon *S. n. lit.* "that which percolates or oozes out easily," *i. e.* gum; gum-resin; turpentine (S. E. D. p. 350).

คล ๒ kon *P. S. n. lit.* "swallower," *i. e.* the organ of deglutition; the throat; the pharynx: คลทวาร *lit.* "the door to the throat," *i. e.* the mouth: คลภูษณ์ decorations or adornments for the neck: คลเมขลา a necklace: คลศุณฑิกา the uvula.

คลวง kloo-ang *n.* a house; the abode of a prince or princess; a resting or sitting-place.

คลอ klau *v.* to be moistened (as eyelids with tears, *ex.* น้ำตาคลอตา); to be full of; to be moist with tears: คลอเคลี่ย to go in confusion; to accompany another side by side: คลอตา to let the eyes be bathed in tears: คลอเสียง a stringed instrument, played as an accompaniment to a singer.

คลอก klauk[3] *v.* to scald; to burn; to singe or heat while holding over a flame: คลอกทุ่ง to burn a prairie: คลอกป่า to burn a jungle: คลอกปลา to roast fish on a spit: คลอกไฟ to singe, scorch or burn by a flame (an ancient form of torture where the prisoner was confined in a cage and burned to death).

คลอง klaung *n.* a canal; a watercourse: คลองช้างเผือก the Milky Way: คลองเลื่อย the passage made by a saw: ปากคลอง the mouth of a canal: ลำคลอง a canal.

คล่อง klaung[3] *adj.* fluently; aptly; easily; conveniently; freely: คล่องคอ to be free from obstructions in the throat: คล่องแคล่ว adroit; expert; dextrous; deft; without hindrance or obstruction: คล่องใจ to be free

from impediments to action or mind : คล่อง
อก to be free in all respects : เดินคล่องสะดวก
to travel without hindrances, accidents or
adversity : อ่านหนังสือคล่อง to read fluently.

คล้อง klaung[5] *v.* to make words rhyme
(as in poetry); to catch or snare with a slip-
noose; to be caught in a loop : คล้องคอ to
encircle the neck with a scarf : คล้องจอง
an euphonious combination of words in phrases
or sentences, producing a pleasing effect :
คล้องช้าง to snare elephants by the use of a
loop : คล้องเชือก to lasso with a rope; to
put a rope around.

คลอด klaut[3] *v.* to give birth; to be born.

คลอน klaun *adj.* infirm; shaky; swaying;
loose (in a socket); loose or rattling about (as
the contents of a package) : คลอนแคลน
swaying from side to side; about to drop out
(as a loose tooth) : คลอนขลุก ๆ *onomat.*
from an unstable condition (as a loose stanchion moving back and forth) : คลอนมะพร้าว
to shake a coconut to find out whether
it contains water or not : คลอนโยก to be
shaky; to be able to be shaken : เคลื่อนคลอน
to vacillate; to move; to swing : ฟันคลอน
the tooth is quite loose.

คล้อย klau-ey[5] *v.* to look around (as while
walking); to play out a line or rope (as in
fishing); to lower (as a bucket); to pass a
person in motion : คล้อยกัน to pass one
another on a road (after meeting); to cross
each other on the way : คล้อยตาม to repeat
words spoken by another (as in taking an
oath) : คล้อยไปประเดี๋ยว he has just passed
by : เคลื่อนคล้อย to change one's place
continually : ยานคล้อย pendant; hanging
loosely : เห็นคล้อยด้วย to be of the same
opinion; to coincide with the views of another.

คละ kla[6] *adj.* mixed together; composed
of many elements or persons : *adv.* unitedly;
in concert; in the same place; at the same
time : คละคล่ำ intimately mixed.

คลัก klak[6] *v.* to be close together; to be
crowded together (as steerage passengers);
to be tightly packed together; to be spattered
with mud : ตกคลัก to get to the point
where further action can be taken only with
difficulty : ลูกคลัก (ลูกขัด) a wood toggle
or fastening pin.

คลัง klang *n.* bamboo joints strung on a
rope or chain (used for tethering animals to
posts or fastening boats); a treasure house;
a treasury : การคลัง finance : คลังมหา-
สมบัติ a royal treasury : คลังศุภรัต a section
of the Palace Department whose duty it is to
prepare the articles used by His Majesty in
merit-making : คลังสรรพาวุธ the royal arsenal.

คลั่ง klang[3] *v.* to be delirious; to be restless : *adj.* delirious; suffering from strong
excitement or mental aberration.

คลับคล้ายคลับคลา klap[6]-klai[5]-klap[6]-klah
adj. uncertain : *adv.* indistinctly; obscurely;
confusedly.

คลา klah *v.* to go; to walk; to advance :
คลาคล่ำ to go together in flocks or droves :
คลาไคล to go away; to pass on; to pass forward (as one walking past another); to withdraw from.

คล้า (ต้น) klah[5] *n. Maranta dichotoma*
(*Marantaceae*) (V. P. p. 59), a smooth, tough
palm resembling the rattan. When dressed,
it is used for making mats.

คลางแคลง klang-klaang *v.* to be in doubt;
to be uncertain; to waver (as to which way
to go); to suspect another's motive.

คลาด klat[3] *v.* to be disjoined; to be separated from others; to slip from the proper
place; to miss meeting another : คลาดเคลื่อน
to be displaced or out of proper position :
คลาดนัด to fail to keep an appointment :
คลาดเวลา to mistake the time of an appointment.

คลาน ๑ klan *v.* to crawl; to creep; to go

on hands and knees; to prostrate one's self; to steal up to on hands and knees; to advance stealthily.

คลาน ๒   klan *S. n.* weakness; prostration; weariness; exhaustion; sickness: *adj.* wearied; languid; emaciated; torpid (S.E.D. p. 350).

คลาย   klai *v.* to untwist; to unroll by degrees; to become insipid; to disentangle; to diminish gradually and disappear: คลาย กลิ่น to lessen in fragrance: คลายเกลียว to unscrew: คลายเกลียวเชือก to untwist the strands of a rope: คลายคลี่ to unfurl or unfold: คลายเคล่ง to extend in order to make straight; to walk straight along: คลายทุกข์ to lessen sorrow, pain or trouble.

คล้าย, คล้ายคลึง   klai[5] *adj.* nearly like; almost alike; very similar to.

คล่าว   klaw[3] *v.* to cause to flow; to pour (as lustrous water).

คลำ   klam *v.* to fumble; to feel for: คลำ เคล้น to touch caressingly; to caress: คลำ ไคล่ to manipulate with the fingers (as in massage): คลำดู to examine by touching: คลำหาทาง to grope about trying to find the way: ลูบคลำ to stroke; to caress fondly.

คล่ำ   klam[3] *n.* a group; a company: *adj.* mixed together: *adv.* abundantly.

คล้ำ   klam[5] *adj.* being rather dark, swarthy, or dusky (of skin); blurred: เขียวคล้ำ dull green: คลุ้มคล้ำ half-mad; frantic: คล้ำ-มัว darkened or misty; foggy: สีคล้ำ of a dull colour.

คลิ้งโคลง (นก)   kling[5]-klong *n.* the black necked mynah, *Gracupica nigricollis*; Burmese pied mynah, *Sturnopastor super ciliaris* (Gaird. J. S. S. IX, 1, p. 4).

คลิด (เคลิด)   klit[6] *v.* to sprain (as a joint); to have a minor dislocation; to wrench, twist or strain a tendon, joint or muscle; to have a twinge of pain in the joints.

คลิบ   klip[6] *v.* to face a garment with silk or other material.

คลี   klee *n.* polo; a ball (as used in various games): เตาะคลี to strike a ball; to bounce a ball; to bowl: ตีคลี to play polo: ผงคลี fine dust; particles flying in the air.

คลี่   klee[3] *v.* to unfold; to unfurl; to unroll or open out; to expand: คลี่กลีบ to bloom or open out (as petals of a flower): คลี่คลาย to unwind or untangle a string: คลี่ใบ to unfurl a sail: คลี่ผ้า to unroll a bolt of cloth.

คลี (ต้น)   klee[5] *n. Terminalia alata (Combretaceae)* (cb. p. 600), a tree about 8 m. high, found in deciduous forest and cultivated in temple grounds (K.). This is the best species of the genus and is used for beams inside houses and for other purposes. It is well spoken of for tool-handles (Burk. p. 2134).

คลึง   kleung *v.* to spin with the fingers (as a top); to roll into a ball by hand (as a pill or as rolling out a wax taper); to soften by rolling (as a lemon on the table): คลึงเคล้น to grasp and rotate with the hand; a form of massage: คลึงไคล้, คลึงเคล้น to caress; to fondle; to move over upon (as bees over the pollen of flowers).

คลื่น   kleun[3] *v.* to be nauseated: *n.* waves; billows; a swell; a surge: คลื่นลม wind and wave: คลื่นละลอก ripples: คลื่นชาย ทะเล surf: คลื่นไส้, คลื่นเหียน to feel squeamish; to feel nauseated: เมาคลื่น seasickness.

คลุก   klook[6] *v.* to mix together (as rice and curry); to knead (as dough): คลุกเคล้า, คลุกคลี to be mixed up together (as players at foot-ball); to associate intimately with: คลุกคลีตีโมง complicity in some evil deed.

คลุ้ง   kloong[5] *adj.* having a musty, rancid, rotten, unpleasant odour: คลุ้ง (ต้น) *Dipterocarpus tuberculatus (Dipterocarpaceae)* (cb. p. 138: Dept. Agri. & Fisheries), a large, deciduous, gregarious tree. The oleoresin of this tree is used with asafoetida and coconut oil as an application for large ulcers; the wood is sometimes used for canoes, but more generally for planking (Dept. Agri. & Fisheries): คลุ้งเน่า odour of tainted or decaying fish or meat.

คลุม kloom v. to cover (as with a shawl); to envelop; to hide: adj. covered over; sheltered; protected; concealed: คลุมจีวร to dress or envelop themselves (as do the Buddhist monks with their robes): คลุมโปง to be over-spread with a cloth; to cover the body completely: คลุมหัว to cover the head with a cloth or turban.

คลุ่ม kloom³ adj. convex (in shape); having an oblique or slanting side or shape (as a rice-pot cover); being bent down over (as an umbrella when raised).

คลุ้ม kloom⁵ adj. dark; cloudy; dim; murky: คลุ้มคลั่ง to be morbidly gloomy; to be dejected, mad, delirious, restless: คลุ้มฝน overcast by rain clouds: คลุ้มมืด, คลุ้มมัว murky; dusky; overcast by clouds or smoke: คลุ้มหมอก misty; foggy.

ควง koo-ang v. to screw (as in playing billiards); to spin; to twist; to twirl; to curve a ball (as a pitcher in baseball): n. a screw; shade of a tree; a palm leaf press; brackets used to enclose any part of a text: ควงแขน arm in arm: ควงจาน to twirl a plate on the end of a stick: ควงตะบอง to twirl a club or long sparring pole: ควงตีหนังสือ a screw-press, used for flattening out palm leaves prior to gilding the edges: ควงถอนจุกขวด a cork-screw.

ควน koo-an n. a mound; a small-sized hill; a slight elevation of ground; an hillock.

ควบ koo-ap³ v. to twist into one strand; to plait the hair; to gallop: ควบเกลียว to twist string or thread into one strand: ควบขับ to urge a horse with spurs: ควบคุม to supervise or superintend in person (as of workmen): ควบด้าย to twist or spin threads

together: ควบม้า, ควบห้อ to ride horseback at a gallop.

ควย koo-ay n. the penis; gentitalia viri.

ควร koo-an ought to: ควรกัน well-matched (as shoes): ควรแก่การ befitting; appropriate; justly; suitable for the circumstance or place: ควรแล้ว agreeing with (as of opinions); quite correct: ควรอยู่ to coincide with; as it should be: พอควร sufficient; quite enough: สมควร worthy; suitable; proper; fitting; deserving.

ควัก kwak⁶ v. to extract; to pick out (as wax from 'the ears); to pick out with the hands (as from a bag); to dip out (as cooked rice from a pot): ควักกระเป๋า to take out from the pocket: ควักตา to enucleate the eye: ควักล้วง to insert the hand or an instrument in order to extract: ควักลูกไม้ชายผ้า to crochet an edging on a garment: ควักไหมพรม to knit or crochet with yarn.

ควักค้อน kwak⁶-kaun⁵ v. to look intently at a person from a corner of the eye (expressing anger).

ควั่งคว้าง kwang³-kwang⁵ adj. swinging to and fro; whirling (as in an eddy); moving in a circle.

ควัน kwan n. smoke: ควันคลุ้ม enveloped in smoke: ควันสงคราม the after-effects or results of war: ควันหลง something occurring later involving the previous incident; an after-clap, ex. "ควันความ บ่ควรความ ฤๅจักบิดจักป้องคง."

ควั่น kwan³ v. to girdle (as of trees for felling); to cut across the grain (as of a log or sugar-cane stalk): n. the act of twirling or twisting several strands of thread or cord together; the place of union of the ends of rope made by intertwining the strands: ควั่นอ้อย to cut sugar cane into disks.

คว้า kwah⁵ v. to grasp at; to reach for

with the hand ; to swoop down and seize (as a hawk) ; to snatch at : คว้าว่าว to turn the head of a kite down (as when manipulating the star kites) : คว้าหา to grope around in search of, and grab : ค้นคว้า to search for, and seize ; to investigate.

ควาก　　kwak[3] *adj.* enlarged ; increased in size or diameter : *onomat.* from the sound of tearing cloth.

คว้าง　　kwang[5] *adj.* revolving slowly (as a wind-wheel in a soft breeze) ; lying athwart or transversely (as a loose boat in a canal) ; having nothing to hold to : แกว่งคว้าง to oscillate while revolving : คว้างหัน playing freely in the wind or tide (as a boat at an-chor) : ตาคว้างเคว้ง wild, unsteady eyes : หลอมคว้าง, เหลวคว้าง to melt metals thorough-ly ; to fuse into a liquid state.

ควาญ　　kwan *n.* an elephant-driver ; a mahout : ควาญท้าย one sitting on the rump of an ele-phant (as the second mahout) : ควาญเท้า a mahout who guards the foot of an elephant in battle. There are four of these for each fighting elephant.

ควาน　　kwan *v.* to fumble about ; to feel for something : ควานหา to search for anything by groping.

คว้าน　　kwan[5] *v.* to extract the seed, core or kernel (as of fruit) ; to scoop out (as a cyst in surgery) ; to make or enlarge an opening or cavity.

ความ　　kwam *n.* a lawsuit ; a subject ; a topic ; an affair ; a prefix used to change a common noun into an abstract noun ; sign of the sub-stantive : กระบวนความ procedure in court : ความกดขี่ tyranny : ความขัดสี friction : ความ-ขำ a clever or amusing story ; a matter or story which should not be divulged : ความเข้ม intensity : ความเข็ญใจ trouble ; poverty ; hardship : ความคลาด aberration ; irregu-larity ; abnormality : ความคิดที่มาก่อน pre-meditation : ความโค้ง curvature : ความ-

จริง truth ; fact : ความจำนน insolvency : ความจำเป็น necessity : ความจุ capacity : ความเฉื่อย inertia : ความชื้น humidity ; mois-ture : ความซึมได้ permeability : ความต้น pressure : ความตึ่ง, ความตึง tension : ความ-ต้านทาน resistance : ความตาย death : ความ-ถ่วง, ความดูด gravity : ความน้อยเนื้อต่ำใจ in-feriority complex : ความนำ conductivity : ความแน่น density : ความปลอดภัย safety : ความประมาท negligence : ความเบิดเผย dis-closure : ความเป็นกลาง neutrality : ความผิด ที่เป็นลหุโทษ petty offense : ความฝัน a dream or vision : ความพยาบาท malice : ความ-มุ่งมาด aspirations : ความมุ่งหมาย object or purpose : ความมุ่งหวัง motive : ความยืด elasticity : ความเร็ว speed : ความระงับ-สิ้นไป extinction : ความระมัดระวัง precaution : ความรู้ทุจริต connivance : ความละเมิดอำนาจศาล contempt of court : ความสัตย์ซื่อต่อพระเจ้าแผ่น-ดิน allegiance : ความสุข happiness ; joyous-ness : ความเสียหายไกลกับเหตุ remoteness of damage : ความหนักแน่น fortitude : ความ-หนืด viscosity : ความหมายสองทาง ambiguous : ความเห็นของมหาชน public opinion : ความอนุบาล guardianship : ความอิสสระทางทะเล freedom of the sea : ความอิสสระทางสาสนา religious liberty : ชำระความ to settle or decide a suit or dispute : เดินความ to be engaged in a lawsuit ; to undertake a matter ; to proceed with a matter or subject : ได้ความว่า I have found out that ; I have got at the root of a matter : ถ้อยความ lawsuit ; litigation : เป็นความ to be engaged in a lawsuit : ไม่ได้-ความ that which cannot be understood ; un-intelligible : ลูกความ parties in a lawsuit : สืบได้ความว่า after investigation the matter is as follows : หมอความ, ทนายความ a lawyer.

ควาย　　kwai *n.* buffalo : ควายเถื่อน, ควาย เปรียว wild buffaloes : ควายหม่อ a buffalo calf.

คว้าย (ต้น)　　kwai[5] *n. Xylia kerrii (Legu-minosae)* (cb. p. 546), a tree about 25 m. high, common in bamboo forest. The wood is not durable (K. : BURK. p. 2274).

คว่ำ kwam[3] *v.* to turn up-side down; to overturn or capsize (as a boat): คว่ำกะลา, คว่ำขนน *colloq.* to be ostracized from friends or relatives: คว่ำบาตร *lit.* "to turn the alms bowl upside down," *i. e.* implying punishment of a priest by the clergy pending investigation of his wrong-doing; excommunication by the Supreme Counsellors' Association of Buddhist monks: คว่ำมือ *colloq.* to refuse a gift; to turn down a favour: คว่ำลง to turn face or top down; to turn a bucket upside down: นอนคว่ำ to sleep on one's face.

ควินิน (ต้น) kwi[6]-nin *n. Azadirachta indica (Meliaceae)* (cb. p. 251: burk. p. 1443), a small, medium-sized or tall, straight, evergreen tree of India, Ceylon, etc. The strong-smelling, aromatic oil obtained from the fruit, is much valued in native medicine, being a universal external application for rheumatism, etc., and is taken internally by women during pregnancy. It is also antiseptic and is commonly used for animals, both internally and externally. It is a most valuable tree to the peasants, all parts of it being used for medicine or for domestic purposes. The leaves and fruit are vermifugal; the fruit is purgative. The Hindustanis prize twigs of this tree for use instead of tooth brushes. The oil cake made from the fruit is an excellent fertilizer which also keeps termites away. The white flowers are sweet-scented. This tree stands drought well and is much planted along avenues in India. The leaves are used as mulch in tobacco cultivation at Jaffna, etc. (McM. pp. 27, 206, 212, 377, 394, 518).

ควิปอก kwi[6]-bpauk[4] *v.* to say farewell; to bid adieu; to express a wish for prosperity when leaving or parting.

ควิว ๆ kwiew-kwiew *adj.* light-headed; giddy; dizzy.

ควิวควัง, ควิวคว่าง kwiew-kwang, *adj.* large; spacious.

คห, คหบดี, คหปตานี ka[6]-ha[4] *n.* the head of a household; the mistress of a house.

คหณะ, ครหณะ ka[6]-ha[4]-na[6] *P. n.* the act of catching, grasping, seizing, acquiring or holding (chd. p. 139).

คหณี ka[6]-ha[4]-nee *n.* an organ situated between the stomach and small intestines (probably the uterus).

คหนะ ka[6]-ha[4]-na[6] *P. S. n.* a jungle; a forest; a thicket: *adj.* dense; confused; tangled; impervious (chd. p. 139).

คหัฏฐ์ see **คฤหัสถ์**

คอ kau *n.* neck; throat; the slender part of a vessel or fruit; a long, narrow strip of land between two bodies of water; an isthmus; an enthusiastic partner in a game or task: แขวนคอตาย to die by hanging: คอแข็ง stubborn; headstrong; indisputable; incontestible; *lit.* hard-necked," *i. e.* one on whom alcoholic drinks have no effect: คอ-ซอง, คอเรือ the neck or constriction at the bow of ancient boats: คอเดียว a species of long-necked bird: คอแดง (๑) *Tropidonotus sub-miniatus* M. S. N. H. J. S. S. I, 1, p. 15): คอ-ต่อ, ต้นคอ the nape of the neck: คอพอก goitre: คอไฟ the burning end of the wick: คอระฆัง the neck of a pagoda spire; the narrowed portion of the spire; name of the sixth consonant of the Thai alphabet: คอหอย glottis: คอหอยกลวง a great eater: คอเหล้า an inveterate drinker of alcoholic liquors: ติดคอ to be lodged in the throat: บางคอ-แหลม Bangkolem, a district in the southern part of Bangkok, *lit.* "district with a sharp pointed neck": ลำคอ the cavity of the throat.

คอแร้ว (ต้น) kau-raa-oh[5] *n. Hymenopyramis brachiata (Verbenaceae)* (V. P p. 58), a species of woody climber (K.).

คอแลน (ต้น) kau-lan *n. Nephelium hypoleucum (Sapindaceae)* (cb. p. 330: V. P. p.

58), a large tree about 25 m. high, found in evergreen forest. The fruits are said to be edible (K.).

คอเหนียว (ต้น) kau-nee-oh[2] *n. Duabanga sonneratioides (Lythraceae)* (V. P. p. 58), a lofty, deciduous tree, found from north-eastern India to the Malay Peninsula. The bark is light-brown, peeling off in thin flakes. The wood is grey, often streaked with yellow. It is soft, seasons well, takes a good polish and neither warps nor splits. Canoes are made of it and it is used for tea-boxes (Dept. Agri. & Fisheries : Burk. p. 869).

คอแห้ง (ต้น) kau-hang[3] *n. Carallia brachiata (Legnotidaceae)* (cb. p. 599 : Burk. p. 448), a tree of moderate size found in India, southern China, and throughout Malaysia. The timber is very handsome, especially when cut to show the beautiful silver grain. It is hard and the sap-wood is yellowish rose, which turns greyish rose. The wood is used for house-building, rice-pounders, agricultural implements and ornamental work ; *C. lucida* ; *C. lanceaefolia* (V. P. p. 58).

คอแห้ม (ต้น) kau-ham[3] *n. Grewia lacei (Tiliaceae)* (cb. p. 185 : V. P. p. 58), a small tree growing to a height of about 1 to 5 m., found in deciduous, evergreen forest (K.).

คอไหมด้อ (ต้น) kau-mai[2]-dau[3] *n. Calophyllum polyanthum (Guttiferae)* (cb. p. 121), an evergreen tree of northern and eastern Bengal. The wood is largely used for making masts, spars, rafters and sometimes for building small boats and canoes (Dept. Agri. & Fisheries).

คอเฮ้ย (ต้น) kau-he-ah[5] *n. Xerospermum intermedium (Sapindaceae)* (cb. p. 329), a fair-sized tree found from Burma to Singapore. The timber is hard, very durable and is used for building. The flowers are white ; the fruits have scanty, sweet and pleasant pulp (K. : Burk. p. 2272).

ค้อ (ต้น) kau[5] *n. Schleichera trijuga (Sapindaceae)* (cb. p. 329), " Ceylon oak," a large tree of Siam, Ceylon, India, Burma, etc. The seeds, which are edible, are rich in oil, said to be the original " Macassar oil " (MCM. pp. 219, 397, 416, 417). This tree exudes a yellowish resin. The lac produced upon this tree is known as Kusum lac and is the most highly prized quality. A dye is said to be obtained from the flowers. The oil is a valuable stimulating and cleansing application to the scalp, promoting the growth of hair. It is also used for the cure of itch and acne. The wood is used for making pestles, axles of wheels, the teeth of harrows and for the helical geared rollers of sugar mills, and of cotton and oil presses (Dept. Agri. & Fisheries : Burk. p. 1978).

คอก kauk[3] *n.* a pen ; an enclosure ; a palisade : *adj.* deformed ; bent stiff; out of shape : แขนคอก a deformed elbow-joint : คอกไก่ a chicken coop : คอกควาย a stable or enclosure for buffaloes : คอกวั้ว a pen or stable for oxen : คอกหมู a pig sty.

ค่องอ้อย kaung[3]-au-ay[3] *n.* a betting game played with sugar-cane stalks. A player slashes the stalk with a knife and then both guess how much longer one end is than the other ; the winner gets the sugar-cane ; if both guess correctly the stalk is divided between them.

คอด kaut[3] *adj.* narrowed ; small in places ; worn away (as bridge posts eaten by borers) ; to have inequalities in size or to be constricted in places (as a tree being small at the base and large farther up) : คอดกิ่ว narrowed in the middle : คอคอด the narrowest portion of land lying between two bodies of water : รัดจนคอด to constrict by an encircling force : เสานี้คอดไป this post is too small or narrowed in certain parts.

คอน kaun *n.* a perch for birds (as in a cage) : *adj.* lop-sided ; heavier on one side (as while carrying two baskets of unequal weight suspended from a pole across the shoulder); a single person paddling a boat; a single load carried on a pole across the shoulder: คอนเรือ to row with one oar only: เรือคอน a row boat: หาบคอน to balance unequal weights on a pole across the shoulder.

ค่อน kaun[3] v. to revile; to use provocative language; to use degrading or vulgar comparisons: adj. more than half; almost full ($\frac{2}{3}$ or $\frac{3}{4}$ full): ค่อนขอด to use degrading or vulgar comparisons intentionally; to revile purposely: ค่อนข้าง inclined to one side: ค่อนทาง more than half the journey: ค่อน-ไปข้างซ้าย a little too much to the left; inclined towards the left: ค่อนว่า, แกล้งว่า to revile or reproach intentionally.

ค้อน kaun[5] v. to glance sidewise (with intent of flirting or in anger): n. a hammer: ค้อนติง to speak jealously; to manifest envy in conversation; to disagree (as in an argument: ค้อนทอง (นก) a species of bird of the wood-pecker family which makes the sound "pook pook" as it pecks at trees; the crimson-breasted barbet, Xantholaema haematocephala (will. N. H. J. S. S. II, 3, p. 325): ค้อนหอย, ช้อนหอย (นก) a fish-eating bird of the heron family; pelican ibis, Tantalus leucocephalus (Gaird. J. S. S. IX, 1, p. 11): ตีด้วยค้อน to beat out with a hammer or to pound with a mallet: ไม้ค้อน a wooden mallet.

ค้อนก้อง (ต้น) kaun[5]-gkaung[3] n. Capparis mekongensis (Capparidaceae) (cb. p. 82), a deciduous plant, found in Lampoon (K.).

ค้อนก้องเคือ (ต้น) kaun[5]-gkaung[3]-kur-ah n. Capparis latifolia (Capparidaceae) (cb. p. 81), a woody climber found in deciduous forest, on the edge of swampy ground (K).

ค้อนก้อม (ต้น) kaun[5]-gkaum[3] n. Moringa oleifera (Moringaceae) (cb. p. 87: Burk. p. 1495); M. pterygosperma (V. P. p. 68), horse-radish tree, a slender tree, about 25 ft. high, with small tripinnate leaves, cultivated in gardens throughout Ceylon, India, etc. The roots are used as a substitute for horse-radish, to which, however, it is much inferior in flavour. The leaves are used for vegetable curries as well as for seasoning and in pickles, and the long unripe pods (drumsticks) as a curry vegetable, the latter being boiled and sliced like beans. The flowers and bark are used in native medicine. A valuable oil (ben oil) obtained in India from the seeds, is used by watchmakers and in cosmetics. The bark, leaves and roots are acrid and pungent, and are taken to promote digestion. They are also used externally as a rubefacient (MCM. p. 305, 436, 378, 396).

ค้อนก้อมผีแป้ลง (ต้น) kaun[5]-gkaum[3]-pee[2]-bplaang n. Parkia leiophylla (Leguminosae) (cb. p. 541 : V. P. p. 69), a tree about 15 m. high growing along the edge of streams (K.)

ค้อนหมาแดง, คันทรง (ต้น) kaun[5]-mah[2]-daang n. Ancistrocladus extensus (Ancistrocladaceae) (cb. p. 148), a woody climber, found in scrub jungle near the sea. The leaves are used in villages for thatching huts. The young leaves are used as a flavouring (K.: Burk. p. 155).

คอบ kaup[3] v. to turn over; to turn back; to protect; to defend; to govern: โดยรอบ-คอบ in all respects; perfectly; well-rounded-out.

คอม kaum n. a yoke used on buffaloes, when hauling.

ค่อม kaum[3] adj. dwarfed; stunted; deformed; low (descriptive of human beings or of plants): ค่อมทอง (แมลงทับเล็ก) Hypomeces squamosus, an insect of the family Curculionidae. It is widely distributed in southern Asia and is considered a great pest as it feeds on various cultivated crops (Dept. Agri. & Fisheries): นางค่อม a dwarfish woman.

ค้อม kaum[5] v. to bend down; to crouch; to be bent over: adj. curved; arched; deflected : คอค้อม curved ; bent or twisted downward : หลังค้อม an hunchback.

คอย, รอ kauy *v.* to linger ; to wait : คอยดู to guard (as a watchman) : คอยท่า to wait for : คอยฟัง to listen (as for instruction) : คอยระวัง to watch carefully : คอยอยู่ to remain for a while : หอคอย a watch-tower ; a light-house.

ค่อย kauy[3] *adv.* by degrees ; slowly ; gradually ; without haste ; gently : ค่อยดีขึ้น convalescing : ค่อยทำค่อยไป to get along as best one can ; to proceed as usual : ค่อยยัง-ชั่ว improving (but still not entirely well) ; ค่อยอยู่ค่อยไป to loiter or to be dilatory : ค่อย-ล่า to retreat little by little : จึงค่อย then, *ex.* เมื่อเขาถามจึงค่อยพูด = when they ask, then reply : ไม่ค่อยมี not abundantly : ค่อย-ผ่อนใช้ to pay on account.

ค้อย kauy[5] to linger ; to wait for : *adv.* gently ; often ; frequently ; softly.

คะ ka[6] *adv.* yes ; a prefix added to the following words without changing the meaning, in order to supply an additional syllable (as needed in composing poetry), *viz.* คะคก, คะคร่อง, คะคร้าม, คะคริน, คะคล้อย, คะคลา, คะคลาน, คะคล่ำ, คะคล, คะคว้าง, คะควิกคว้าง, คะค้อย, คะคัก, คะคิก, คะคึก, คะเครง, คะแคล้ว, คะแคว้ง, คะใคร, คะใคร้ : เคอะคะ inexperienced ; awkward ; unskilled : เจ้าคะ, เจ้าค่ะ yes (used by a woman to an equal or superior).

คะโก (ต้น) ka[6]-gkoh *n.* *Albizzia lebbek* (*Leguminosae*) (V. P. p. 59 : Burk. p. 86), East Indian walnut, a large tree with fine foliage, native of tropical Asia and Africa, often planted for shade. It has excellent brown timber which does not readily warp (MCM. pp. 206, 417, 446). It yields a gum, which is said not to be soluble in water, but merely to form a jelly. The bark is said to be used in tanning. The seeds are officinal, forming part of a remedy used for ophthalmic diseases. They are astingent and are given- in piles, diarrhoea, gonorrhoea, etc. Oil extracted

from them is considered useful in leprosy ; the bark is applied to injuries to the eye (Dept. Agri. & Fisheries).

คะไขว่ ka[6]-kwai[4] *adj.* confused ; disarranged ; mixed.

คะค้อย ka[6]-kauy[5] *v.* to walk in close formation ; to proceed without separation from others.

คะคึง ka[6]-keung *adv.* reverberating loudly.

คะนน ka[6]-non *n.* a large-sized rice or curry pot (used in transporting palm sugar).

คะนอง ka[6]-naung *v.* to be wild with joy ; to be exuberant over one's success ; to manifest a cheerful spirit : คะนองศักดิ์ to rejoice in one's conferred rank : คะนองเด็ก joyful, childish pranks, antics or capers : ใจคะนอง high spirits ; gaiety.

คะนาง (ต้น) ka[6]-nang *n.* *Homalium tomentosum* (*Samydaceae*) (cb. p. 742 : Burk. p. 1183), a large deciduous tree, growing to a height of 80 to 90 feet. The wood is used for making the teeth of harrows and for furniture (Dept. Agri. & Fisheries).

คะนึง ka[6]-neung *Cam.* to think of ; to have pleasant memories ; to be mindful of kindnesses ; to meditate.

คะเน ka[6]-nay *n.* to guess ; to conjecture ; to judge at random ; to surmise : คะเนเอา คะเนไว้ to approximate ; to guess at : คะน้ำ-คะเน to conjecture ; to imagine ; to estimate approximately.

คะเนจร ka[6]-nay-chjaun *v.* to wander about without fixed habitation ; to roam.

คะเนี่ยง (ต้น) ka[6]-ne-ang *n.* *Pithecellobium jiringa* (*Leguminosae*) ; *P. lobatum*, a large, unarmed tree, even up to 80 feet in height, found from Tenasserim and Siam throughout western Malaysia. The wood exudes a blackish resin. Tender shoots are eaten and the seeds serve as a seasoning.

The curious odour of these seeds makes them objectionable to Europeans but they are much appreciated by the Malayan population. The seeds are covered with a quantity of edible, fleshy pulp (Cb. p. 600: BURK. pp. 1758–1761: Dept. Agri. & Fisheries: K.).

คะแนน ka[6]-naan *n.* an average; the mean; credit marks (as given in an exercise or examination); counters in a game, or for bags of rice; a vote: ลงคะแนน to vote: หัก-คะแนน to deduct credit marks for errors: ให้คะแนน to grade or give credit marks (as in grading examination papers).

คะใน ka[6]-nai *prep.* in.

คะมำ ka[6]-mum *v.* to fall face downwards.

คะมึก ka[6]-meuk[6] *adj.* strong; vigorous physically; well-built.

คะยั้นคะยอ ka[6]-yan[5]-ka[6]-yau *adj.* urged to do; teased or harassed in a petty way into doing.

คะยอม (ต้น) ka[6]-yaum *n. Shorea floribunda (Dipterocarpaceae)* (V.P. p. 59), a flowering tree found in deciduous forest (K.).

คะเยอ ka[6]-yur *adj.* being very itchy.

คะยำ (ต้น) ka[6]-yum *n. Acacia tomentosa (Leguminosae)* (Cb. p. 552: MCM. p. 556: BURK. p. 12), elephant thorn, "jungle nail". The wood is used for fuel.

คัก, คั่ก kak[6], kak[3] *onomat.* from the sound of laughter or heavy rainfall.

คัคนะ,คัคนัมพร,คัคนางค์,คัคนานต์ kak[6]-ka[6]-na[6] *P. S. n.* sky; the expanse of the heavens; a segment or portion of the sky; the sky-line; the horizon (S. E. D. p. 341).

คั่ง kang[3] *adj.* obstructive; causing impediment; congested; jammed (as of traffic); stalled or stopped by any obstruction; impeded by a jam of people or cattle: เขายังคั่งกันอยู่ there is still variance or discord

between them: คั่งกัน to be jammed together or congested: คั่งคาม plenteous; sufficient for every purpose; well-provided for: คั่งคับ to be inconvenienced by a dense crowd: คั่งแค้น to suppress anger; to restrain one's temper: เรือคั่งกัน the boats impede each other by being jammed.

คัณฐิ kan-ti[6] *P. n.* the knot of a cord; a knot tied in the end of a garment (for keeping money); the joint of a reed or cone; a joint of the body; difficulty; doubt (S. E. D. p. 371).

คัณฐี kan-tee *P. n.* a treatise explaining Pali words.

คัณฑ kan-ta[6] *P. S. n.* a cheek; the whole side of the face (used for a cow, horse or elephant); side; edge; border; froth; abscess; pimple; gland; bone; joint: *adj.* best; most precious; highly esteemed (S. E. D. p 344): คัณฑคราม a village of great size: คัณฑเทศ, คัณฑประเทศ, คัณฑเลขา the region or area of the cheek: คัณฑมาลา name given to abscessing glands of the neck; abscesses occurring along either side of the neck: คัณฑศิลา, คัณฑไทบล a boulder; a stone of great size (S. E. D. p. 344).

คัด kat[6] *v.* to pick out; to cull from among; to choose by preference; to copy; to trace from a pattern; to force open (as a box); to pry open with a lever; to be obstructed (as the nose when one is suffering from a cold): คัดขึ้น to raise with a lever: คัดเข้าคัดออก to direct a boat (either towards starboard or port); to select (as men for the army): คัดค้าน to oppose; to contradict; to resist; to hinder; to offer opposition: คัดง้าง to hinder; to pry open and then pull out; to influence a person to alter his acts; to oppose (as proceedings in court): คัดจังกูด, คัดฉาก, คัดหางเสือ to guide a boat by holding the rudder; to steer a boat: คัดชง to raise a beam or log with a lever: คัดท้าย to turn the rudder so the boat will turn to the left: คัดเลือด to arrest an haemorrhage; to stop the flow of blood : คัดไว้ to select and put aside : คัดไว้ต่างหาก to put those selected or examined aside : คัดสำเนา to copy or transcribe : นมคัด milk stagnation ; mastitis ; local engorgement of the breast, occurring during early lactation.

คัดเค้า (ต้น) kat[6]-kow[5] n. *Randia siamensis* (*Rubiaceae*) (V. P. p. 67), a climber. The flowers are white (K.).

คัดชุน kat[6]-choon n. an instrument to bend saw-teeth in order either to lessen or increase the kerf or channel made by the saw.

คัดมอน (ต้น) kat[6]-maun n. *Sida rhombifolia* (*Malvaceae*), an erect shrub, common in most tropical countries. The stems afford a good fibre (BURK. p. 2025); *S. tiliaefolia*, cultivated in China for the excellent fibre obtained from the stems ; *S. retusa*, " paddy's lucerne " (MCM. pp. 431, 477).

คัตวร kat[6]-dta[4]-waun S. *adj.* transient ; fleeting ; perishable (S. E. D. p. 347).

คัทรภะ kat[6]-tra[6]-pa[6] *P. n. lit.* a " crier ; a brayer," *i. e.* an ass (S. E. D. p. 349).

คัน kan v. to itch ; to itch for ; to manifest a restless desire for : n. the earthen dyke around a paddy field for impounding water ; a long handle (as of a frying pan); a wand ; a rod ; the numerical designatory particle for carriages, umbrellas, spoons, etc. : คนคันขา, คนสำรอง an alternate, substitute or reserve person or player : คัน (ต้น) *Paranephelium macrophyllum* (*Sappindaceae*) (cb. p. 335), a small tree about 7 m. high, found in scrub jungle by the river. The flowers are pink (K.) : คันกะสุน the flexible wooden part of a bow : คันคาย rough to the touch and irritating : คันฉ่อง a toilet powder-set ; a mirror ; a table-mirror : คันฉาย a looking-glass : คันชัก a violin bow ; a plough handle ; the tongue of a waggon or cart : คันชั่ง the beam of a pair of scales : คันชีพ a shoulder-strap worn by soldiers, as mark of rank : คันซอ a violin

bridge : คันดอกเทียน small limber rods, into the ends of which roman candles are stuck and adjusted around a pole. When lighted by a fuse, the candles wave to and fro : คันตัว the body itches : คันไถ the handle of a plough : คันนา the low dyke of earth around rice fields : คันเบ็ด a fishing rod : คันโพง the long spout of a gardener's watering-pot : คันร่ม an umbrella handle : คันแร้ว a bent stick or spring rod of a bird-trap.

คั่น kan[3] v. to separate from ; to divide into (as with a partition) ; to place in between : คั่นกลาง to divide in the middle (as by a partition) : คั่นกะได stairs or steps ; rungs of a ladder : คั่น ๆ in steps : คั่นตะไกร marks of scissors or shears on the hair : ตัดเป็น คั่นตะไกร to cut the hair unevenly, leaving marks of the scissors : คั่นหนังสือ to put a marker in a book : คั่นหน้าผ้า to encircle the forehead with a thread or band.

คั้น kan[5] v. to squeeze out with pressure ; to macerate and squeeze out (as milk from the grated coconut) : คั้นคอ to strangle.

คันถ kan-ta[4] *P. n.* a literary composition ; a book in prose or verse ; a composition ; a treatise : *adj.* tied, bound, knotted or strung together (S. E. D. p. 371) : คันถธุระ the burden of study ; the burden of contemplation : คันถรจนาจารย์ a sage who compiles a treatise ; the author of a literary work.

คันคาก (ต้น) kan-kak[3] *n. Raphiolepis fragrans* (*Rosaceae*) (cb. p. 579), a slender tree about 8 to 10 m. high, common in evergreen forest. The flowers are white and fragrant (K.).

คันซุง, คันทรง (ต้น) kan-soong *n. Colubrina pubescens* (*Rhamnaceae*) (cb. p. 301), an erect shrub with slender branches, cultivated for medicinal use. The flowers are yellowish (K.); *Ancistrocladus extensus* (*Ancistrocladaceae*) (cb. p. 148 : BURK. p. 155), a woody climber, found in scrub jungle on sandy land near the sea. The leaves are used in villages for thatching huts (K.).

ค้นหามเสือ (ต้น) kan-ham²-sur-ah² *n.* *Aralia armata* (*Umbelliferae*) (cb. p. 792), a slender shrub about 3 m. high, having a leaf over a metre long; *Trevesia valida* (*Araliaceae*) (cb. p. 796), a shrub or small tree about 5 m. high, found on rocks by the stream in evergreen forest (K.).

ค้นธ kan-ta⁶ *P. S. n.* an odour; a perfume; a fragrant substance; fragrance; scent; perfume (S. E. D. p. 345): ค้นธกุฎี a kind of perfume; anything used to impart fragrance; a perfumed room; one of the abodes of the Buddha: ค้นธชล, ค้นโธทก perfumery; fragrant water: ค้นธทรัพย์ scented powder; scents of various kinds; a fragrant substance: ค้นธนาที, ค้นธนาลี *lit.* "the organ of smell," *i. e.* the nose: ค้นธปาษาณ sulphur: ค้นธพันธุ์ the mango tree: ค้นธมฤค, ค้นธเศขร, ค้นธสุขี musk: ค้นธมาท a general of Rama's monkey allies. He was killed by Ravana's son Indrajit (อินทรชิต) but was restored to life by the medicinal herbs brought by Hanuman from Mount Kailasa (H. C. D. p. 105): ค้นธมาทน์ *lit.* "intoxicating with fragrance," *i. e.* name of a mountain renowned for its fragrant forests: ค้นธรส odour and flavour; perfumes and spices: ค้นธวณิช, ค้นธาชีพ *lit.* "living by perfumes," *i. e.* a vender of perfumery or scented powders; a dealer in toilet waters: ค้นธวาหะ *lit.* "a bearer of fragrances," *i. e.* the wind: ค้นธสาร sandalwood: ค้นธาลี a wasp (S. E. D. p. 345).

ค้นธา, ค้นโธทก kan-tah a prefix occurring in the above words, meaning *fragrant*.

ค้นธาร kan-tan *P. S. n.* a country and city on the west bank of the Indus above Attock. Mahommedan geographers call it Kandahar (ก้นทหาร), but it must not be confounded with the modern town of that name. It is the Gandaritis of the ancients, famous for its breed of horses (H. C. D. p. 105): ค้นธารราษฎร์

name of a chapter of the พระปฏิมากร, used in the religious ceremony of praying for rain.

ค้บ kap⁵ *adj.* fitting closely; tight: คับกัน to inconvenience each other; to embarrass one another: คับขัน imperative; not to be avoided or evaded; obligatory; binding; to be hedged in or wedged in: คับคั่ง to be crowded; to be squeezed in together: คับคั่น to be heaped up; to be dried up: คับแค้น distressing; troublesome; needy: คับแคบ narrow; crowded: คับใจ to be distressed; to be nonplussed; to be embarrassed; to be discontented or disconcerted: คับที่อยู่ได้คับใจ อยู่ยาก it is better to be crowded in a room than to be harrassed in heart: คับไป too tight; too large to fit easily.

คับคา (นก) kap⁶-kah *n.* the blue-tailed bee-eater, *Merops philippinus* (will. N. H. J. S. S. II, 3, p. 328).

คับแค (นก) kap⁶-kaa *n.* the cotton teal goose, *Nettapus coromandelianus* (Gaird. J. S. S. IX, 1, p. 11).

คัพภ์ see ครรภ

คัพภระ kap⁶-pa⁶-ra⁶ *P. n.* a cave; a cavern; a grotto; an arbour; a bower: *adj.* impervious; impenetrable (S. E. D. p. 352).

คัพโภทร see ครรโภทร

คัพยุต kap⁶-pa⁶-yoot⁶ *S. n.* a linear measure equal to 12,000 feet (S. E. D. p. 351).

คัพยุติ kap⁶-pa⁶-yoo⁶-dti⁴ *S. n.* a region or district having green pasture land (S. E. D. p. 351).

คัมภีร์ kam-pee *P. S. adj.* deep; profound; hollow-toned; the depth of a man's navel, voice, and character are praised together: คัมภีร นาท a deep or hollow sound; thundering; roaring: คัมภีรภาพ depth; profoundity; abstruseness (S. E. D. p. 346).

คัล kan *Cam. v.* to interview; to call upon, or to visit (used only for princes).

คั่ว   kua[3] *v.* to roast (as coffee); to pop (as corn, rice, etc.):   (ไพ่) to wait for the third of three identical cards to be turned up from a pack of playing cards: คั่วช่อง see คั่วไพ่: คั่วสองช่อง to wait for two pairs of identical cards to be turned up (terms used in playing ไพ่ตอง):   คั่วแห้ง to work servants or slaves mercilessly; to over-work one's self or others without gaining the expected results.

คา   kah *v.* to be lodged in (as a broken off screw); to remain in (as a broken needle in the flesh); to dangle (as a bird that is shot hangs from the limb of a tree):   *n.* a form of stock or iron ring for the necks of prisoners: คา (หญ้า) *Imperata arundinacea* (*Gramineae*) (V. P. p. 59); *I. cylindrica* (Burk. p. 1228), "illuk," "lalang," a thatch grass of Siam and Malaya. The grass grows 3 to 4 feet high, and is often a pest in the moist low-country, generally in badly drained, sour, or neglected land. Sometimes it is a very troublesome plant. The strong, rigid leaves make excellent thatch. The plant, when dried, is used in Siam for the production of paper (MCM. pp. 472, 475, 477). The fibre is used to prepare the sacrificial thread of the Hindus. The leaves are employed for thatching (Dept. Agri. & Fisheries): คากรอง an hermit's dress: คาขื่อ to be confined in stocks or neck fetters: คาคอ to be lodged fast in the throat: คา- ราคาท่า, คาราคาซัง unfinished; incomplete (either a sentence or a task): คาหลังคาเขา caught with plunder or stolen goods still in hand (as a bullock thief who is caught red-handed in possession of the carcass): จับได้คามือ to be caught red-handed in the act of crime: ชายคา eaves: สากคาครก the pestle remains in the mortar: หลังคา roof.

คาลิ้น (ต้น)   kah-lin[5] *n. Walsura trichostemon* (*Meliaceae*) (cb. p. 262), a small tree about 8 m. high, found in open ground in open deciduous jungle. The flowers are white (K).

คาหลวง (ต้น)   kah-luang[2] *n. Saccharum spontaneum* (*Gramineae*) (V. P. p. 59: Burk. p. 1923), a coarse, perennial grass, abundant throughout India. The grass is largely used as a thatching material; the leaves are manufactured into ropes, mats, etc. The young coarse grass is a favourite fodder of buffaloes, and is also given to elephants. This beautiful and superb grass is highly celebrated in the Puranas, the Indian god of War having been born in a plain covered with it, which burst into a flame. It is often described with praise by the Hindu poets for the whiteness of its blossoms, which, at some distance, give a large plain the appearance of a broad river (Dept. Agri. & Fisheries).

ค่า   kah[3] *n.* price; value: ค่าขี้หมู (ต้น) *Padbruggea pubescens* (*Leguminosae*) (cb. p. 398), a tree about 20 m. high, found in scrub jungle or evergreen forest. The flowers are dark reddish-purple with a yellow spot at the base of the standard (K.):   ค่าจ้าง wages; salary; compensation: ค่าเช่า rent: ค่า- เชิงเดิน reward for services rendered: ค่า- ใช้สรอย expenses: ค่าโดยสาร passage money; fare on a boat or ship: ค่าตัว debt (as when sold into slavery); ransom money: ค่าไถ่ ransom; the paid debt: ค่าทาส the money or price paid for a slave: ค่าธรรม- เนียม fee; impost; customs dues: ค่านา a tax on fields: ค่าเสียหาย compensation for damages done; indemnity: ค่าอยู่ค่ากิน the price of board and lodging: มีค่ามาก that which has a great value; it has a high price: หาค่ามิได้ worthless; valueless.

ค่าสามซีก   kah[3]-sam[2]-seek[3] *n. Polyalthia cerasoides* (*Annonaceae*) (cb. p. 42), a large evergreen tree, found in dry forests on eastern exposures. The wood is much used in carpentery and for making masts and small spars for boats (Dept. Agri. & Fisheries: Burk. p. 1786).

คากี   kah-gkee Eng. *adj.* yellowish-brown; rust colour.

ค้า, ค้าขาย kah[5], kah[5]-kai[2] *v.* to buy and sell; to trade; to barter; to vend: การค้าขาย commerce: คบค้า to associate with; to frequent the company of: เที่ยวค้า to carry merchandise around for sale; to peddle: บีดประตูค้า to have the monopoly in buying or selling; to close the door of trade in certain commodities: พ่อค้า a merchant: แม่ค้า a shop-keeper (woman): ลูกค้า a small merchant; clients of a merchant or store: สินค้า merchandise: สินค้าเข้า imports: สินค้าออก exports.

ค้าคบ kah[3]-kop[6] *n.* a large fork of a tree.

ค่ามัน (ต้น) kah[3]-man *n. Sindora fusca* (*Leguminosae*) (cb. p. 538), a lofty tree about 30 m. or more in height, common in evergreen forest (K.).

ค้าค้า kah[5]-kah[5] *v.* to be bold, brave or audacious.

คาง kang *n.* chin: คาง (ต้น) *Albizzia lebbekoides* (*Leguminosae*) (V. P. p. 67: cb. p. 554: Burk. p. 86), a large, deciduous, spreading tree of wide distribution. It yields a gum which is said not to be soluble in water but merely to form a jelly; the bark is said to be used in tanning leather; oil extracted from the seed is considered useful in leprosy; the seeds are officinal, forming part of a remedy used for ophthalmic diseases. They are astringent and given in piles, diarrhoea, gonorrhea, etc.; the bark is applied to injuries to the eye (Dept. Agri. & Fisheries); *A. odoratissima* (V. P. p. 67: Cb. p. 556: Burk. p. 88), a large tree with pure white, sweet-scented flowers (MCM. p. 206). This tree yields a dark-brown gum in rounded tears, tasteless but soluble in water; the bark applied externally, is considered efficacious in leprosy and inveterate ulcers; the boiled leaves are used as a remedy for coughs; the wood is used for wheels, oil-mills, and furniture. The timber is excellent for all purposes requiring strength and durability (Dept. Agri. & Fisheries):

คางเคือง, คางข้อง with difficulty; unwillingly; reluctantly: คางทูม mumps; parotitis: คางโทน (ต้น) a medicinal tree: คางเบือน (ปลา) a fresh-water cat fish, *Belodontichthys dinema* (*Siluridae*), similar to the star-fish (Dept. Agri. & Fisheries): คางหมู a triangular plot of land, resembling a pig's snout (large at one side and gradually tapering to a narrow point).

คางคาว(ต้น) kang-kow *n. Aglaia pirifera* (*Meliaceae*) (cb. p. 258), a tree about 10 m. high, found in evergreen forest. The fruits are edible. The wood is used for boat-oars and carrying-sticks (K).

ค่าง kang[3] *n.* langur or long-tailed monkey (Gaird. N. H. J. S. S. III, 2, p. 121).

ค่างเต่น (ต้น) kang[3]-dten[4] *n. Derris dalbergioides* (*Leguminosae*) (cb. p. 488: BURK. p 789), a tree about 25 m. high, found in evergreen forest. The tree is found from Tenasserim and Cochin-China to Java. The flowers are pale purple (K).

ค้าง kang[5] *v.* to be interrupted (as during a meal); to dangle; to remain over; to remain unfinished: *n.* a pergola; a prop for vines: *adj.* incomplete; unfinished: การยังค้างอยู่ the work remains unfinished: ค้างคราว a missed opportunity: ค้างคืน to stay over night: ค้างเติง left undone or incomplete; an unfinished game of chance played with dice; *colloq.* any uncompleted or unaccomplished task: ค้างน้ำ to be delayed from one tide till the next: ค้างพริกไทย a prop for pepper bushes: ค้างพลู a prop for the betel plant: ค้างมรสุม to be delayed past one season into the next (as from one monsoon into the following): ค้างแห้ง left dry by the receding tide: เงินค้าง an unpaid debt: น้ำค้าง dew.

คางคก kang-kok[6] *n.* a toad (the species with a coarse skin). The common species in Bangkok is *Bufo melanostictus.*

ค้างคาว (ต้น)   kang[5]-kow *n. Aglaia piri-fera (Meliaceae)*, a species of vine (Cb. p. 258): ค้างคาว (นก) fruit-bats or flying foxes (Gaird. N. H. J. S. S. III, 2, p. 123): ค้างคาวแม่ไก่, ค้างคาว ลูกหนู a species of bat.

คาด   kat[3] *v.* to gird; to encircle; to surround; to guess; to suppose; to conjecture; to hold in abeyance or in a state of suspension: คาดการ to estimate or foretell regarding the future of any job or task (as to how long it might take to finish it): คาดเข็มขัด to buckle on a belt: คาดคะเน to conjecture; to guess at: คาดคั้น to purpose; to have a fixed design or determination; to resolve: คาดใจ to estimate; to assign a value: คาดเตี่ยว to cover the private parts: คาดโทษ to approximate the punishment; to reserve or hold punishment in abeyance until some future time: คาดบั้นเอว to gird one's loins: คาดปูน to cover with lime: คาดผี to cover a corpse: คาดพุง to put a girdle around the waist: คาดราคา to appraise; to estimate the price: คาดเวร to determine on a revenge: คาดหมัด, คาดเชือก to wrap rope around the hands in lieu of boxing gloves: คาดหมาย to approximate.

คาถา   kah-tah[2] *P. S. n.* a song; a verse; a religious verse (one not taken from the Vedas but from the epic poetry of legends); any metre not enumerated in the regular treatises on prosody (S. E. D. p. 352): เทศน์คาถาพัน the act of delivering the complete series of 1000 chapters of the มหาเวสสันดรชาดก which is written in Pali. If preached according to the Siamese version, it comprises thirteen sermons.

คาธ see คราส

คาน   kan *v.* to block; to clog; to choke; to impede; to support: *n.* a pole or stick used for carrying loads on the shoulder; a prop, pillar or beam for support; the timbers on which a ship is placed for repair work; a shaft: คานเรือ to put a boat on rollers: คานหาบ a shoulder pole with which one carries

any weight: คานหาม a stretcher or palanquin: เอาเรือขึ้นคาน to raise a boat on the ways and firmly prop it in place.

ค้าน   kan[5] *v.* to oppose; to obstruct; to reject; to hinder; to offer an objection; to refuse any proposition: ค้านพยาน to challenge a witness.

คาบ   kap[3] *v.* to hold in the mouth (as a dog does a bone) or in the beak (as a crow holds food): *n.* time; periods of time: คาบ-ชุด (ปืน) a gun or cannon having a fuse or match for ignition: คาบศิลา (ปืน) a flint-lock gun: คาบกัน interlocking; dove-tailing; hinged; resting or bearing on another.

คาบสมุทร   kap[3]-sa[4]-moot[4] *n.* a peninsula.

คาพยุต see คัพยุติ

คาม   kam *P. n.* an inhabited place; a hamlet; a village; the collective inhabitants of a place, community or race (S. E. D. p. 373): คามจรรยา *lit.* "village custom," *i. e.* customs of the village governing the mingling of the sexes; sexual intercourse; sensual love: คามชาล a collection of villages; a district: คามชิต a conqueror (of his group); a conqueror (of troops): คามณี *lit.* "leader; chief," *i. e.* the leader or chief of a village or lord of the manor; a squire; a female peasant or villager; an harlot: คามธรรม the observance of ceremonies, customs or rites of a village: คามบุรุษ a chief of a community or village: คามพาลชน a young peasant; an adult of 20 to 30 years of age (one eligible for the army): คามโภชก a chieftain or village leader; a village headman: คามมฤค *lit.* "a village animal," *i. e.* a dog: คามมุข a market place: คาม-ยุทธ์ a factional fight in a village; an uprising, riot or tumult in a community: คาม-รัถยา a street; a lane; an alley (in a village): คามวาสี those who are living in villages; village-folk; Buddhist monks located near a village: คามสิงห์ *lit.* "a domesticated lion," *i. e.* a dog: คามสีมา the boundary of a compound or village; a plaza adjoining a village:

คามหาสก an older, or younger brother-in-law (on the husband's side): คามันตร another village; the space between villages (S. E. D. p. 373).

คามเคือ (ต้น) kam-kur-ah *n. Indigofera hendecaphylia (Leguminosae)* (cb. p. 378), a shrub, found climbing over a river bank. The flowers are deep pink (K.).

คามเถือน (ต้น) kam-tur-an[4] *n. Indigofera suffruticosa (Leguminosae)* (cb. p. 382: BURK. p. 1239), a shrub about 2.5 m. high. This is an American indigo which the Dutch brought into Malaysia where it now grows in some places as a weed. It is cultivated in Siam (K.).

คามกะ kam-ma[6]-gka[4] *P. n.* a small group of houses.

คามณีย์ kam-ma[6]-nee *S. n.* a mahout.

คามน see คามณี

คามภีรย์ kam-pee *S. n.* depth (of water); deepness (of the voice); depth or profundity of character; earnestness; depth of meaning; dignity; generosity (S. E. D. p. 354).

คามิก kah-mi[6]-gka[4] or kah-mik[6] *P. S. n.* a traveller; a sojourner: *adj.* going; leading to (as a way); travelling (chd. p. 141).

คามี kah-mee *P. S. adj.* a suffix used to convey the idea of arrival at a destination or attainment of Nirvana, *ex.* นิพพานคามี (chd. p. 141).

คามูปจาร kah-moo-bpa[4]-chjan *P. n.* outskirts or entrance to a village; the religious instructor of a village (chd. p. 141).

คาย ๑ kai *v.* to spit out; to expel or eject from the mouth (as bitter medicine): *adj.* rough; irritating to the touch; rasping (as sandpaper): คายแกงบวนออกมา to reject the curry by spitting or vomiting it out: คายบวน to eject from the stomach (as in vomiting): หยาบคาย rude; vulgar; impolite: คายคม

sharp; keen-edged; witty; fanciful; cute (as speech).

คาย ๒ kai *S. n.* a folklore love-song or ode; a song or hymn.

ค่าย kai[3] *n.* a stockade; an encampment; an enclosure made with sharpened posts planted in the ground: ค่ายคู a moat around a fort, camp or city: ตั้งค่าย to encamp; to protect by entrenchments.

คายก kah-yok[6] *P. S. n.* a singer of songs or hymns; a chorister (S. E. D. p. 352): คายก คณะ a choir; assistant singers; chorus girls; a band of singers.

ค่ายคัง, คล้ายคลึง kai[3]-keung *adj.* similar; resembling; somewhat alike.

คายน kah-yon or kah-ya[6]-na[6] *P. S. n.* the act of singing (chd. p. 145).

คายันต์ kah-yan *P. v.* to sing (chd. p. 145).

คารบ, ครบ kah-rop[6] *adj.* entire; complete; total.

คารพ, คารวะ kah-rop[6] *P. n.* respect; veneration; reverence; authority; importance (chd. p. 143).

คารม kah-rom *n.* eloquence; speech; oratory.

คารัยห์ kah-rai *P. adj.* culpable; blameworthy; contemptible; low; base; absurd (chd. p. 143).

คาว kow *n.* an odour or scent (as of fresh fish or meat): คนนั้นมีคาว that person deserves censure, or is faulty: คาวปลา a raw, fishy odour.

ค้าว, เค้า (ปลา) kow[5] *n. Wallago attu,* a species of fresh-water fish; catfish (Dept. Agri. & Fisheries).

คาวะ kah-wa[6] *n.* an ox; a bull; a bullock (chd. p. 145).

คาวี kah-wee *P. n.* a cow.

คาวุต see คาพยุต

คาหก   kah-hok[4] *P. S. n.* one who holds, catches or receives: *adj.* holding; taking; receiving (chd. p. 138).

คาหะ see คร่าห์

คำ ๑   kam *n.* gold.

คำ ๒   kam *n.* the spoken word; speech; eloquence; doctrine; a mouthful: คำ (ต้น) *Bixa orellana (Bixaceae)* (V. P. p. 64: burk. p. 330), annatto or arnatto, a large quick-growing shrub or small tree with cordate leaves, native of tropical America, naturalized in parts of west tropical Africa. It prefers a deep, loamy soil. At the ends of the branches it bears large clusters of brown or dark-crimson seeds, the covering of which affords the annatto dye of commerce. The fruits are collected when nearly ripe, and as the shells dry they burst open and disperse the seeds, which are then either pressed and made into annatto paste, or merely dried with their covering, when they are marketed as annatto seed (MCM. p. 436). The bark yields a good cordage, and is also used as an astringent and is slightly purgative. It is considered a good remedy for dysentery and kidney diseases (Dept. Agri. & Fisheries):   คำกลาง the decision of a middleman or umpire: คำกล่าว speech; conversation: คำขาว (ต้น) *Vitis discolor (Ampeledaceae)* (V. P. p. 64: burk. p. 2244), a moderately large vine, with prettily variegated leaves; *Cissus discolor* (see *Vitis discolor*) (burk. p. 559: MCM. p. 129): คำครุ a word with either short or long vowel (used in poetry):   คำจำเลย defence: คำแดง (ต้น) *Mallotus philippinensis (Euphorbiaceae)* (V. P. p. 64: burk. p. 1396), a moderate-sized tree of Ceylon, India, Malaya, Siam, etc. The glandular pubescence of the fruit yields a rich, orange-red, permanent dye, known as kamela dye (MCM. p. 440). The bark is used in tanning. The plant is used as an external application in medicine (Dept.

Agri. & Fisheries); *Cissus discolor (Ampelidaceae)* (cb. p. 306):   คำต้น (ต้น) *Entada scandens (Leguminosae)* (V. P. p. 65: burk. p. 925), a big climber, found throughout tropical Asia and out into the Pacific Islands. The stems, often twisted like a cork-screw, bear enormous flat pods, 3½ to 5 feet long by 3 to 4 inches broad. The large, hard, brown, polished, flat seeds are sometimes made into ornaments, snuff-boxes, etc. (MCM. pp. 132, 461, 462). A preparation from the seeds is used in pains of the loins and also in debility. The bark of this plant is used for cordage and ropes (Dept. Agri. & Fisheries): คำตอบ answer; reply: คำตาย a final sound not represented by a letter: คำต่ำ low or vulgar words: คำใต้ (ต้น) *Acacia farnesiana (Leguminosae)* (cb. p. 548: V. P. p. 64: burk. p. 20), cassia or acacia, a small tree, common in the tropics, largely grown for the sake of the pleasant scent of the flowers. An industry in perfume from this tree took its origin at Cannes in southern France. *A. farnesiana* is a host for the lac insect (MCM. p. 457):   คำนับ the act of saluting: คำบอก a notice; a preface; dictation: คำป่า (ต้น) *Mallotus philippinensis (Euphorbiaceae)* (V. P. p. 65), a moderate-sized tree of Ceylon, India, Malaya, Siam, etc. The glandular pubescence of the fruit yields a rich, orange-red, permanent dye, known as kamela dye (MCM. p. 440). The bark is used in tanning; the plant is used as an external application in medicine (Dept. Agri. & Fisheries); *Reinwardtia trigyna (Linaceae)* (cb. p. 199), a tufted, glabrous under-shrub 2 to 3 feet high, met with in the hilly regions. The flowers are yellow and grow in small clusters. The plant is said to be used as a remedy for founder in cattle (Dept. Agri. & Fisheries): คำเปรียบ a parable; an allegory: คำผีแปง (ต้น) *Caesalpinia minax var. burmanica (Leguminosae)* (cb. p. 503), a species of shrub, found in scrub jungle: คำฝอย (ต้น) *Carthamus tinctorius (Compositae)* (V. P. p. 65: burk. p.

465), safflower or false saffron, a prickly, shrubby annual, 2 to 4 ft. high, supposed to be indigenous to India but cultivated in Egypt, China, India, Persia, Spain, Siam, etc. for the seeds, which yield safflower-oil by pressure, and for the orange-yellow florets of the aster-like flower, which are used as a dye. These are collected fresh in the morning, dried in the shade, on muslin trays, and afterwards stored in tins. The oil is used in India for culinary purposes, and also in the manufacture of paint and soap, and in the preservation of leather and ropes (MCM. pp. 395, 439). This plant is the kusumbhu of Sanskrit writers who describe the seeds as purgative, and mention a medicinal oil which is prepared from the plant for external application in rheumatism and paralysis (Dept. Agri. & Fisheries): คำพอง (ต้น) *Blumea balsamifera (Compositae)* (V. P. p. 66), a sub-bushy plant having a tall stem, corymbosely branched above, leaves 4 to 8 inches long, coriaceous, elliptic or oblanceolate in shape, usually silky above, and serrate. The whole plant smells strongly of camphor, which may, indeed, be prepared from it. A warm infusion acts as a pleasant sudorific and is a useful expectorant in decoctions (Dept. Agri. & Fisheries: Burk. p. 334): คำพราง a lie; a falsehood: คำพยาน evidence: คำรวม a compound word: คำรอก (ต้น) *Ellipanthus tomentosus (Connaraceae)* (cb. p. 366), a shrub about 2 m. high, found in deciduous forest about ½ mile from Sriracha. The brown fruits are distributed singly on the branch (K.): คำล้วน plain, familiar style without high-sounding words: คำลหุ a short word or syllable used in poetry to complete the metre: คำสอน doctrine; teaching; advice: คำสัตย์ truth; truthful words: คำหนึ่ง a mouthful (as of betel-nut): คำเอื้อง (ต้น) *Dendrobium chrysotoxum (Orchidaceae)* (V. P. p. 67), a plant which grows on trees in open evergreen forest. The flowers are yellow (K.): คำฮ่อ (ต้น) *Lagerstroemia indica (Lythraceae)* (cb. p. 724: Burk. p. 1299),

Indian lilac, bonnet-flower, crepe myrtle, a native of China but long cultivated in southeastern Asia and India. The beautiful purple-lilac flowers, in large panicles, are very showy. There are also white and pink varieties (MCM. pp. 113, 206: Dept. Agri. & Fisheries): คำเฮ (ต้น) *Coreopsis tinctoria (Compositae)* (V. P. p. 67), a showy annual and perennial, having crimson flowers (MCM. p. 134): ถ้อยคำ advice; counsel: ลูกประคำ a rosary.

คํ่า kam[3] *n.* night. According to the old Siamese calendar, dates were reckoned by nights (ค่ำ), as ขึ้น ๕ ค่ำ, เดือน ๖, or the fifth day of the waxing moon of the sixth month: ค่ำมืด the dead of night: ค่ำสนทยา evening time; dusk: ยังค่ำ at all times; all day until dark: เย็นค่ำ evening; twilight: วันยังค่ำ all day: เวลาค่ำ the evening: หัวค่ำ night-fall.

คํ้ำ kam[5] *v.* to prop up; to uphold: *n.* the act of supporting; a side that is braced: ค้ำจุน to provide for by personal aid or finances; to prop up or keep from falling; to support by means of a prop: ค้ำชู to support; to keep from fainting; to stimulate; to uphold; to defend: ผู้ค้ำประกัน one who guarantees the borrower: ยาค้ำชูหัวใจ a cardiac stimulant.

คำแคง kam-kaang *v.* to lull to sleep; to sing lovingly: *adj.* loud; boisterous.

คำนวณ kam-noo-an *v.* to calculate; to compute; to estimate by figuring.

คำนวร see ควร

คำนับ kam-nap[6] *v.* to salute; to pay respect or reverence to: คำคำนับ an address of salutation; a salutatory speech.

คำนัล see คัล

คำนึง see คะนึง

คำนูณ see คูณ

คำโบล   kam-bone *v.* to anoint with oil or perfume ; to stroke or caress fondly ; to pat, rub on, or apply gently.

คำเพลิง   kam-plurng *Cam. n.* a gun ; fire-arms.

คำฝอย see **คำ**

คำรน   kam-ron *v.* to groan (as in pain) ; to cry out or make a noise ; to growl or snore : เรือเสือคำรนสินธุ์ name of one of the torpedo boats in the Royal Navy.

คำรบ see **ครบ**

คำราม   kam-ram *v.* to use threats or to make threatening sounds (as a tiger) ; to snore ; to growl or roar : ขู่คำราม to threaten or intimidate with violent speech or actions.

คำแหง, กำแหง   kam-haang[2] *adj.* brave ; strong ; adventuresome ; daring.

คำโอง ๑   kam-ong *Cam. n.* a boaster ; a braggart ; boastfulness.

คำโอง ๒   kam-ong *n.* a stag.

คิก   kik[6] *adj.* playful ; sportive ; joking ; jesting : *onomat.* from the sound of suppressed laughter : คิกๆ a giggling or tittering sound.

คิชฌะ   kit[6]-cha[6] *P. n.* a vulture (S. E. D. p. 361) : คิชฌกูฏ *lit.* "the vulture's peak," *i.e.* a mountain peak of the capital of Magadha, a site still traceable in the hills between Patna and Gaya (H. C. D. p. 253).

คิด   kit[6] *v.* to think ; to contemplate ; to imagine ; to meditate on ; to study ; to ponder or plan ; to make a charge (as in selling goods or in rendering service) : คิดกัน to consult with or about : คิดคด to betray ; to be dishonest ; to be treacherous : คิดตุ to ponder or weigh in the mind with deliberation : คิดตรึกตรอง to ponder over : คิด-ถึง to think of an absent person, thing or country ; to call to mind pleasantly : คิด-ในใจ to suppose ; to imagine : คิดเป็น to estimate ; to charge (as a price) : คิดไปคิดมา to reflect waveringly upon : คิดรัก to feel affection for : คิดร้าย to contemplate cruel, harsh or fierce deeds : คิดว่า to think independently (often given as an excuse by an underling) : คิดให้ to estimate remuneration (as a wage or salary) : คิดออก to solve a problem : คิดอดสู, คิดอาย to feel a sense of mortification ; to be ashamed : คิดอ่าน to form a plan ; to devise : คิดอ่านให้ to give advice on plans devised : ลูกคิด an abacus.

คินิ   ki[6]-ni[6] *P. n.* fire (chd. p. 148).

คิมหะ, คิมหันต์, คิมหานะ   kim-ha[4] *P. n.* summer ; the hot season (chd. p. 147).

คิริ, คิริ, คิรี   ki[6]-ri[6] *P. S. n.* an elevation ; a mountain ; a knoll ; a mound ; a low hill ; a small hill ; a cloud ; rising ground ; a mouse (S. E. D. p. 355) : คิริกรรณิกา the earth : คิริกัจฉป *lit.* "a mountain tortoise," *i.e.* a foot-hill (shaped as a tortoise or turtle) : คิริ-กานน a mountain grove : คิริคุหา a cave, cavern or cleft in a mountain : คิริจักรพรรดิ *lit.* "king of mountains," *i.e.* the Himalayas : คิริชาล a mountain range : คิริทวาร a road or path over a mountain ; a mountain pass : คิริธาตุ red chalk : คิรินคร *lit.* "a mountain city," *i.e.* the modern Girnar : คิรินทร์ *lit.* "a prince among mountains," *i.e.* a lofty mountain : คิริพรช *lit.* "mountain fenced," *i.e.* capital of Magadha, situated between Patna and Gaya : คิริสาร tin ; iron or galvanized iron.

คิริเมขล์   ki[6]-ri[6]-mek[4] *n.* name of the elephant of พระยามาร.

คิลานะ   ki[6]-lah-na[6] *P. n.* a patient ; one that is sick or ailing (chd. p 147) : คิลานบัจจัย medical requisites or drugs ; food adapted to sickness : คิลานเภสัช compounded remedies for a patient's use.

คิว kew *Eng. n.* a cue for playing billiards.

คิว kew[5] *n.* the bony process forming the eye-brow; a sculptured edging or border for decorating purposes: ขนคิ้ว the eye-brow: คิ้วนาง (ต้น) a species of bean-pod, curved in the shape of an actress's eye-brow, hence the name: *Bauhinia winitii (Leguminosae)* (ch. p. 530), a giant, woody climber, found in evergreen forest on a limestone hill. The flowers are white (K.): ยักคิ้ว to raise one's eye-brows playfully.

คี่ kee[3] *adj.* unequal; being an odd number; leaving one as a remainder.

คีต, คีตกะ keet[3] *P. S. n.* a song; a hymn; the act of singing and playing on a musical instrument; melody: *adj.* chanted; intoned; sung; praised (in songs) (S. E. D. p. 356): คีตศาสตร์ the science or art of singing and playing on any musical instrument: คีตาจารย์ an instructor in music (either vocal or instrumental); a singing master.

คีต, คีตกา kee-dti[4] *P. S. n.* the act of singing or playing musical instruments; a song: คีติสูตร a Sutra composed in the Giti metre (S. E. D. p. 356).

คีบ keep[3] *v.* to catch or squeeze by means of forceps, tongs, pincers or nippers; to nip (as a crab).

คีบอง (ต้น) kee-baung *n. Shorea sp. (Dipterocarpaceae)* (V. P. p. 60), a valuable timber tree with wood like teak. This is largely grown in India.

คีม keem *n.* pliers; forceps; tongs; pincers: คีมจับหลอดโลหิต artery forceps: คีมถอนฟัน dental forceps.

คีว kee-wa[6] *P. n.* neck; throat (chd. p. 148).

คีวัฏฐิ kee-wat[6]-ti[4] *P. n.* bones of the neck; the collar-bone (chd. p. 148).

คีไวย, คีไวยกะ kee-wai, kee-wai-ya[6]-gka[4] *P. n.* ornaments for the neck; necklaces; bangles; a neck-scarf (chd. p. 148); a chain worn round the neck of an elephant (S. E. D. p. 374).

คึก keuk[6] *adj.* exciting; excitable; impetuous; noisy; clamorous: คึกคื้อ pomp; gay preparations: ไฟลุกคึก ๆ the fire burns violently: วิ่งคึก ๆ to run noisily.

คึกคัก keuk[6]-kak[6] *adj.* gay; vivacious; vigorous; pompous; boastful.

คืน kurn *v.* to restore; to return; to retract; to give back: *n.* night; night-time: กลางคืน during the night: คืนขึ้นมา to rise again; to reappear: คืนคำ to recant or recall one's words: คืนนี้ this night; to-night: คืนดีกัน reconciliation; atonement: คืนตัว to revert to the original position, condition, size or form: คืนไปคืนมา to borrow and return repeatedly: คืนยังรุ่ง during the whole night: คืนวานนี้ night before last: คืนหนึ่ง for one night: คืนให้, ส่งคืน to return; to restore; to give back: คืนอำนาจเดิม retrocession: คืนเอามา to bring back; to give back: เที่ยงคืน midnight.

คืบ kurp[3] *v.* to crawl by extending the head and drawing the body up step by step (as leeches do): *n.* a unit of linear measure (from the end of the thumb to the tip of the middle finger when the hand is spread flat, about 9 or 10 inches or ½ a cubit); ¼ of a metre.

คือ kur *v.* to be or to become equal; to make even: *adv.* namely; such as; for example; that is: คือว่า as for instance.

คุ koo[6] *v.* to burn or char in an oven (as charcoal).

คุก kook[6] *v.* to kneel; to bend the knee to the floor: *n.* jail; prison; gaol: คุกข้าว a rice bin: คุกคลาน to crawl along on the hands and knees, or on the knees only: จำคุก to be sentenced to imprisonment: ติดคุก *colloq.* to be imprisoned.

คุกคาม   kook[6]-kam *adj.* threatening (as in anger); growling.

คุกพาทย์   kook[6]-pat[3] *n.* a tune played by the Siamese on their musical instruments.

คุคะ (ต้น)   koo[6]-ka[6] *n.* a medicinal vine (thus named because it is rough and twisted): *adj.* distorted; twisted; rasping; rough to the touch.

คุง   koong *adj.* final; entire; total; complete; completive: คุงเท่าวันตาย "till death us do part."

คุ้ง   koong[5] *n.* the bend of a river on the side where the current cuts away the bank: *adj.* circuitous; far; distant; winding: คุ้งน้ำ the current side of a bend in a river or canal: คุ้งนี้ this bend of a river or canal: (อี) คุ้ง (นก) the Indian purple coot, *Porphyrio policephalus policephalus* (Herb. N. H. J. S. S. VI, 4, p. 343).

คุด, คุฬ   koot[6] *S. n.* sugar; molasses; a ball; a globe; a mouthful of food (chd p. 150).

คุณ   koon *P. S. n.* a single thread or strand of cord or twine; a string; thread; rope; a garland; a bow-string; a sinew; the string of a musical instrument; a chord; (also คุณ) with numerals it signifies *fold* or *times* or a *multiplier*; as an epithet it means virtue, merit, excellence, good qualities, grace, benefits, advantages (S. E. D. p. 357). When placed before a noun or used as a title, คุณ shows additional respect or honour, *ex.* คุณพ่อคุณแม่ = respected father and mother; คุณท่าน = respected sir; พ่อคุณ = benefactor: กระทำคุณ a method of doing evil to one's acquaintances or to strangers by casting a spell over them; witchcraft; enchantment: ขอบคุณ to express thanks: คุณตรัย *lit.* "the three normal constituent properties or qualities (of a person)," *viz.* (1.) สัตตวะ = goodness; (2.) รชัส = passion; (3.) ตมัส = ignorance; darkness: คุณธรรม virtue; kindness; the duty incident to the possession of certain qualities (as clemency is the virtue and duty of royalty):   คุณนิธิ *lit.* "a treasury of good qualities," *i. e.* an excellent man: คุณพจน์, คุณวจนะ *lit.* "word denoting a quality," *i. e.* an attributive adjective: คุณพระเจ้า the Lord; the great benefactor: คุณราศรี *lit.* "having a great number of qualities," *i. e.* Siva; a name of a Buddha: คุณลักษณะ outer manifestations of inner goodness: คุณวิเศษ different property: คุณวิฑฒะ prosperous through merit, or virtue: คุณวฑฒิ prosperity attendant on goodness, or merit: คุณศัพท์ an adjective; the twang of a bow-string: คุณสดุดี praise; enconium: คุณสมบัติ great merit; perfection: คุณากร a multitude of merits; one endowed with, or possessing all virtue: คุณาลัย rich in virtue or moral excellence: คุณาธิป *lit.* "the load of graciousness," *i. e.* His Majesty the King: คุณาภาส semblance or similarity of qualities: คุณาลัย *lit.* "the abode of good qualities," *i. e.* one endowed with all virtue: แทนคุณ to be grateful for a benefit; to return a kindness: บุญคุณ benefits; favours bestowed: เป็นคุณ useful; beneficial; lucrative: ผู้ถูกคุณ the one on whom the spell of witchcraft is cast; the enchanted: พระคุณ loving-kindness: รู้คุณ to show gratitude to one's benefactor; to be grateful: ลบหลู่คุณ to be ungrateful: สนองคุณ to return thanks for a kindness: สรรพคุณยา different virtues or actions attached to remedies; therapeutic effects: มีคุณ useful; advantageous; beneficial.

คุณา   koo[6]-nah a prefix occurring in the above words.

คุณูปการ, คุโณปการ   koo[6]-noo-bpa[4]-gkan *n.* the act of assisting in the performance of philanthropic acts; the furtherance of benefits to others.

คุด   koot[6] *n.* a quick plunge under water; a sudden downward movement (as of the head): *adj.* curvate; curved inwards, or downwards; ingrown (as eye-lashes or toe nails); ingrowing; crooked; twisted; contorted; shortened: คุดคู้ twisted; distorted; rolled.

คุดทะราด koot[6]-ta[6]-rat[4] *n.* yaws; a specific tropical skin-disease, characterized by small red spots that develop into tubercles.

คุตต์, คุปต์ koot[6] *P. v.* to care for, or have the control of; to guard or protect; a dynasty of kings who reigned in Magadha (H. C. D. p. 115): *adj.* protected; guarded; preserved; concealed; secreted; kept secret (Chd. p. 151).

คุตติ, คุปติ koot[6]-dti[4] *P. n.* the act of guarding, governing or caring for: *adj.* preserving; protecting; restraining (of body, mind and speech); concealing; hiding (S. E. D. p. 359).

คุ้น koon[5] *adj.* intimate; familiar; well-known; tame; accustomed to: คนคุ้นเคยกัน a friend of long acquaintance.

คุป koop[6] *P. S. v.* to govern; to guard; to protect; to be concealed or guarded (S. E. D. p. 359).

คุม koom *v.* to stand watch over; to accompany; to care for; to guard diligently (as a gaoler); to gather or collect together: ควบคุม to be in charge of personally: คุมแค้น to hold or harbour anger, rage or spite against another: คุมเชิง vigilance; watchfulness of an enemy's or opponent's tactics: คุมตัว to guard or protect another; to chaperon or escort: คุมท้อง vigilant watchfulness of a maternity case: ผู้คุม a gaoler; a guard over prisoners; a guardian.

คุ่ม (นก) koom[3] *n.* a small bird of the quail family: *adj.* arched; rounded; bent over (as by age).

คุ้ม koom[5] *v.* to guard or protect; to cover all expenses (as in trading); to accompany for purposes of protection: *n.* the house or abode of a provincial governor; a palace: คุ้ม (นก) Blanford's button quail, *Turnix maculosa* (Gaird. J. S. S. IX, 1, p. 13): คุ้มเกรง

to govern or exert authority over others in order to command respect: คุ้มไก่นา (นก) the blue-throated quail, *Exalfactoria chinensis chinensis* (Herb. N. H. J. S. S. VI, 4, p. 336): คุ้มครอง to exert authority over; to govern, defend or shield from harm: คุ้มเจ้าพนักงาน to fulfil exactly the requirements of local officials: คุ้มเท่า up to; until: คุ้มหม้อ (นก) the Burmese bustard-quail, *Turnix javanica plumbipes* (Herb. N. H. J. S. S. VI, 4, p. 337): ทำพอคุ้มตัว to work or earn sufficient to cover personal expenses, or just what is necessary: ไม่คุ้มค่าโสห้ย not sufficient to cover expenses: หนังสือคุ้มตัว exemption papers: หนังสือคุ้มห้าม a writ of exemption from certain charges or obligations.

คุ้มดีคุ้มร้าย koom[5]-dee-koom[5]-rai[5] *n.* mental instability; alternating spells of sanity and insanity: *adj.* being unstable or fickle.

คุมพ์ koom *S. n.* a cluster or clump of trees; a thicket; a bush; a shrub; a company of troops; a troop or guard of soldiers; the spleen (S. E. D. p. 360).

คุย koo-ay *v.* to converse; to chat; to talk familiarly together: *n.* (ต้น) a creeper used as a red dye, and as a medicine.

คุ้ย koo-ay[5] *v.* to dig; to scratch or claw in the ground (as a hen): ขุดคุ้ย to dig and scrape away the refuse earth: คุ้ยขึ้น to excavate; to dig up out of the ground: คุ้ยเขี่ย to dig and scrape around (as in looking for some hidden object).

คุยห koo-ay-ha[4] *P. n.* the private organs; a secret; secretiveness (ch. p. 151): คุยหรหัสย์ a private matter that should be kept [secret.

คุรี koo[6]-ree *adj.* far; distant.

คุรุ koo[6]-roo *P. S. n.* a teacher; a preceptor; a tutor (S. E. D. p. 359): คุรุกรรม the duties of a spiritual adviser: คุรุกัณฐ์ a peacock: คุรุรัตน์ a topaz: คุรุวาร *lit.* "the auspicious day of the week," *i. e.* Thursday: คุรุศิขร

lit. a venerable mountain," *i. e.* the Himalayas : คุรุโศกานล *lit.* "the fire of heavy sorrow," *i. e.* affliction ; grief ; sadness ; misery : คุรุเสถียร *lit.* "very firm," *i. e.* stable ; constant ; enduring ; staunch.

คุลา   koo[6]-lah *P. n.* a gland ; pimples ; a pock (chd. p. 150).

คุลิกา   koo[6]-li[6]-gkah *S. n.* a ball (as a missile) ; a small ball or globule ; a ball used in playing games ; a pill ; a pearl ; head (of cattle) (S. E. D. p. 360).

คุลิก่า   koo[6]-li[6]-gkah[4] *n.* an ancient remedy made from enlarged glands of monkeys or baboons.

คุลี   koo[6]-lee *S. n.* a ball ; a round body ; any small globular substance ; a pill ; smallpox (S. E. D. p. 360) : คุลีกรีฑา any game played with balls ; polo ; golf : คุลีการ to make round (as a ball or sphere) ; to make or roll into a ball ; to mix together and make into pills or pellets.

คุห   koo[6]-ha[4] *S. n. lit.* "reared in a secret place," *i. e.* Karttikeya, the god of War ; name of Siva or Vishnu ; a king of the Nishadas who was a friend of Rama (S. E. D. p. 360) : คุหพาหนะ *lit.* "Skanda's (Karttikeya) vehicle," *i. e.* his peacock.

คุหา, คูหา   koo[6]-hah[2] *P. S. n.* the heart ; a cave ; a large cave ; a cavity ; a cavern ; a grotto ; a hiding place ; hollowness ; a vaulted or arched space in a mountain or in the earth ; an archway ; a gable end : คูหาจร *lit.* "moving in secret," *i. e.* in the heart : คูหามุข a wide cavernous mouth, opening, orifice, or aperture ; open-mouthed ; wide-mouthed (S.E.D. p. 360).

คุหาศัย   hoo[6]-hah[2]-sai[2] *n.* a cave-dweller ; a dweller in privacy, secrecy or retirement ; that which abides in the heart (as affections).

คุพ, คุฑ   koon or koo[6]-la[6] *P. n.* sugar ; molasses ; a ball ; a glove ; a mouthful of food (chd. p. 150).

คู   koo *v.* to coo or mourn (as doves or pigeons) : *n.* a ditch ; a moat ; a canal for irrigating : คูบ้าน a small, shallow ditch dug around a house : คูค่าย a ditch surrounding a military camp.

คู่   koo[3] *n.* a couple ; a pair : คู่กัน in pairs ; a pair : คู่ขอน a bunch of three or five fruits : คู่แข่งขัน a rival ; a competitor : คู่ครอง life mates ; friends for life ; partners through life : คู่ชีวิตร husband and wife living together : คู่ความ parties in a lawsuit : วัวคู่หนึ่ง a yoke of oxen : เล่นคู่คี่ to play games where the remaining pieces come out odd or even, as in jack-straws : คู่เคียง a partner ; an associate ; an equal : คู่โค paddy fields on which the tax is estimated according to the Title Deed and paid yearly (different from those on which the tax is paid only when and where the land is cultivated) : คู่มือ handy or near by : คู่รัก a mate ; a lover.

คู้   koo[5] *v.* to bend ; to curve ; to bow : คู้-เข้ามา to arch over towards or near another object (as a tree).

คูณ   koon *v.* to multiply ; to double ; to increase by multiplication : ทวีคูณ twice as much ; double : ตรีคูณ three times as much ; treble.

คูถ   koot[3] *P. S. n.* ordure ; dung ; excrement ; feces (chd. p. 151) : คูถนรก a hell composed of ordure.

คูน (ต้น)   koon *n.* an edible plant similar to plants of the calladium family, bearing clusters of yellow flowers ; *Cassia fistula* (*Leguminosae*) (cb. p. 510 : V. P. p. 68), "purging cassia" ; Indian laburnum ; pudding pipe, a small upright tree, common in the forests of the dry regions of Siam, Ceylon and India. It is a beautiful object when in blossom, bearing masses of yellow flowers in pendulous racemes, suggesting the laburnum. The flowers are used as temple offerings. The

astringent bark is used for tanning and with
other medicines for rheumatism. The black
cylindrical pods grow to a length of from
20 to 30 inches. The pulp of these is a well-
known purgative (MCM. pp. 85, 206, 369, 378, 462).
The wood is used for making posts and is
good for carts, agricultural implements, rice-
pounders, etc. (Dept. Agri. & Fisheries: BURK.
p. 475).

คูหา see คูหา

เก้, เก้เก้, ลัม   kay[5] v. to be felled.

เก็จฉ์   ket[6] v. to go; to go to; to proceed;
to depart (Chd. p. 138).

เจร, คะเนจร   kay-chjaun v. to wander
about without settled destination; to roam;
to rove about.

เคณฑะ   ken-ta[6] P. n. a toy top.

เค้น   ken[5] v. to squeeze; to crush; to tight-
en; to press; to hold down.

เค็ม   kem adj. salty; salted; audacious,
clever, cunning (when describing a person).

เคย, เคอย   kur-ay n. small-sized shrimps
or prawns used in making kapi (shrimp-
paste): adj. accustomed to; familiar; in the
habit of: เคยกุ้ง pickled prawns: เคยกิน
accustomed to eat: เคยตัว to be emboldened
by familiarity; to become habituated: เคยไป
accustomed to go: เคยอยู่ familiar with;
accustomed to stay in a certain place: น้ำเคย
a sauce made of pickled prawns: เยื่อเคย
shrimp-paste.

เครง   kreng adj. noisy; boisterous: เครง-
ครืน jolly; sociable and lively.

เคร่ง, เคร่งครัด   kreng[3] adj. severe; austere; strictly observing exacting rules;
rigorous.

เครา   krow n. side-whiskers; side-burns;
beard.

เคร่า   krow[3] v. to wait for; to linger; to
loiter.

เคราะห์   kraw[6] P. S. n. luck; chance; fate;
calamity; fortune; omen; act of holding,
catching or receiving; lit. "one who clutch-
es," "the seizer," "the eclipser," i. e. Rahu,
the mythological creature supposed to be
ready to swallow the moon or sun at the time
of an eclipse; a group of nine auspicious
objects of the sky typifying Deva angels,
which are supposed to hold the omens of good
or evil for all people. These nine auspicious
objects of the sky are, viz. Sun (อาทิตย์),
Moon (จันทร์), Mars (อังคาร), Mercury (พุธ),
Jupiter (เสาร์), Venus, Saturn, Earth, Shooting or Falling stars; name of particular evil
demons or spirits who seize, or exercise a bad
influence on the body and mind of man
(as those causing insanity) (S. E. D. p. 372):
เคราะหนายก, เคราะหบดี lit. "the chief of the
stars of omen," i. e. the Sun: เคราะหเนมี
the Moon: เคราะหบีฑา lit. "pain by Rahu,"
i. e. the act of being harassed or held in the
mouth of the dragon Rahu: เคราะหโภชน์ี a
horse: เคราะหยุทธ์ the conjunction of planets:
เคราะหราช the Sun; the Moon; the planet
Jupiter: เคราะหวิจารี one knowing the course
of the planets; astrologers; astronomers:
เคราะห์ดี good fortune; a happy result: เคราะห์-
ร้าย calamity; misfortune; mischance; mishap:
เคราะห์ หาม ยาม ร้าย an unexpected calamity:
เคราหาธาร lit. "the support of the planet,"
i. e. the polar star, Polaris: ดาวพระเคราะห์
the star of good luck or fortune in a person's
horoscope: สะเดาะเคราะห์, เสียเคราะห์ to avert
the effects of a bad omen.

เคราะหณ see ครหณ

เครียด   kree-at[3] adj. tense; stern; severe;
rigid; tight.

เครียว   kree-oh v. to arrive; to reach: n.
time; occasion; a short space of time.

เครือ   kreu-ah v. to be indistinct; to become
blurred or smeared; to be vague: n. a vine;
a creeper; lineage; pedigree; a bunch of
bananas: เครือกล้วย a bunch of bananas:

เครือเขา a vine : เครือญาติ lineage ; a family line ; scion ; descendants ; kindred : เครือวัลล์พันไม้ a posture assumed by Siamese actors : คร่ำเครือ that which has been used ; worn-out : ตกเครือ to put forth fruit in bunches (used only for bananas) : เสียงเครือ an indistinct voice ; a dry, hoarse voice or cough.

เครื่อง   kreu-ang[3] n. utensils ; food for the king or royalty ; machinery ; implements ; equipment ; building materials : เครื่องกระยาบวช cakes made of flour or vegetables but which have not involved the taking of animal life (used in religious ceremonies) : เครื่องกลั่น a condensing or distilling apparatus : เครื่องแกง spices for making curry : เครื่องเขียน stationery : เครื่องจักร์ machinery : เครื่องชั่ง a weighing machine ; scales : เครื่องชา a tea set : เครื่องใช้ในการรบ implements of warfare : เครื่องเดินทาง baggage ; luggage : เครื่องต้น table utensils or provisions for the use of the king : เครื่องตวง utensils for measuring liquids : เครื่องถม niello ware : เครื่องทรง clothing, ornaments or uniforms worn by the king : เครื่องใน the entrails of animals : เครื่องบน roof timbers of a house : เครื่องบิน aeroplanes ; hydroplanes : เครื่องบูชา offerings ; sacrifices : เครื่องแบบ uniforms : เครื่องประจำกองทหาร a soldier's kit : เครื่องผูก a house composed of parts tied together with rattan : เครื่องมือ instruments ; tools ; hand implements : เครื่องยศ insignia of rank ; court uniforms : เครื่องราง charms, amulets and talismans : เครื่องเรือน household furnishings : เครื่องลับ a house, the parts of which are joined and held together by splicing ; intricate, hidden machinery : เครื่องวัด instruments for ascertaining linear measure : เครื่องว่าง food eaten between meals by princes or nobles ; light refreshments (eaten between meals) ; syn. ของว่าง : เครื่องสด decorations of fresh flowers, leaves or banana stalks (used during the tonsure or cremation ceremonies) : เครื่องสาย stringed or wind musical instruments : เครื่องสูง paraphernalia indicating rank : เครื่องหมาย sign ; symbol : เครื่องหอ the first household articles belonging to the bride and groom ; wedding presents given by the bride's parents : เครื่องอาวุธ weapons of various kinds : ทรงเครื่องใหญ่ to be dressed in royal robes denoting the highest rank.

เคล่ง   kleng[3] adj. suspended ; hanging loosely ; drooping downward.

เคล็ด   klet[6] v. to sprain ; to dislocate a bone slightly : n. ceremonies ; observances ; customs ; finesse ; artifice ; stratagem ; tactics ; snares ; secret mechanisms : ผู้รู้เคล็ดอาจจะตีกองทัพนี้แตก one who knows the secret key or tactics may be able to win this battle.

เคล้น   klen[5] v. to massage by slight motion and pressure ; to squeeze or press with a finger or palm of the hand : เคล้นใคล, เคล้นคลึง to compress with a rotary motion.

เคล้า   klow[5] v. to cause to mingle together ; to mix together thoroughly ; to knead (as materials for bread-making) : เคล้าคลุก to intermingle (as members of a faction) : ตำให้เคล้ากัน to mix by pounding or macerating.

เคล้าคลึง   klow[5]-kleung v. to fondle ; to caress ; to embrace ; to flatter.

เคลิบเคลิ้ม   klerp[3]-klerm[5] v. to be forgetful ; to be absent-minded ; to be mistaken in an identification : n. a condition of mental distraction or lack of concentration.

เคลิ้ม   klerm[5] adj. sleepy ; drowsy ; semi-conscious ; absent-minded : เคลิ้มตื่น, เคลิ้มม่อย, เคลิ้มหลับ half-asleep ; half-awake : เคลิ้มสติ to be in an unconscious state or condition ; being in a coma or stupor.

เคลียคลิง   klee-ah[5]-kling v. to soothe ; to pacify ; to calm or quiet ; to flatter.

เคลื่อน   kleu-an[3] v. to remove to another place ; to be changed from its proper place ; to vary ; to be incorrect : เคลื่อนคลาดจากที่

to be mislaid from the appointed place:
เคลื่อนคลาย to improve gradually (as one recovering from an illness: เคลื่อนลง to recede
(as a tide); to lessen in severity; to subside:
เคลื่อนคลา to change the place or position (as
of troops): เคลื่อนที่ to change the position.

เคลือบ kleu-ap[3] v. to cover over; to varnish;
to enamel; to plate or cover (as gold or nickle
plating); to veneer: กระเบื้องเคลือบ glazed
tiles: แก้วเคลือบ frosted glass: เคลือบ-
แคลง doubtful; ambiguous; dubious; uncertain: เคลือบคลุม indistinct; undefined;
confused: เคลือบดีบุก to plate with tin:
เคลือบทอง to gild: เคลือบแฝง vague; hidden
(as regards meaning); suspicious; given to
distrust: เคลือบสี to varnish or paint in
various colours.

เคว้ง kweng[5] adj. revolving slowly (as a
wind-wheel in a soft breeze); lying athwart
or transversely (as a loose boat in a canal).

เคห, เคหา key-ha[4] P. S. n. a house; a
dwelling; a place of abode (S. E. D. p. 363):
เคหนกุล the muskrat: เคหบดี the head of
an household; the owner of a house; the
husband.

เคโหปวัน key-hoh[2]-bpa[4]-wan P. S. n. a
thicket or small jungle near a house (S. E. D.
p. 363).

เคอะ kur[6] adj. awkward; clumsy; uncouth.

เค้า kow[5] n. cause; beginning or root of a
matter; origin; source; primary cause: adj.
old: เค้า (ปลา) Wallago attu (Siluridae), a
large, fresh water catfish (Dept. Agri. & Fisheries): เค้าคู่, กินผี (นก) Horsfield's scops
owl, Scops lempiji (Gaird. J. S. S. IX, 1, p. 8):
เค้าเงื่อน, เค้ามูล a primary cause; a fore-ordain-
ed motive: เค้าดำ (ปลา) Wallago miostoma
(Siluridae) (Dept. Agri. & Fisheries): เค้าแมว
(นก) collared pygmy owlet, Glaucidium bro-
diei (Gaird. J. S. S. IX, 1, p. 9).

เคารพ see คารวะ

เค้าสนามหลวง kow[5]-sa[4]-nam[2]-loo-ang[2] n.
ruling officials; provincial governors (used
only for the Province of Chiengmai).

เคาะ kaw[6] v. to tap; to knock; to rap;
to hint; to allude to; to imply: adj.
implicative; implying; involving (as in
referring to something said): เคาะ, เคาะเคราะ
(ต้น) Dipterocarpus alatus (Dipterocarpaceae)
(cb. p. 133), a large tree met with in Burma and
distributed to Siam and British Malaya. It
yields a wood-oil in great quantity and exudes a dirty-brown resin. The wood is used
for making canoes, railway sleepers, etc. but
is said to last only three to four years because it deteriorates when exposed to the
weather (Dept. Agri. & Fisheries: Burk. p. 841);
Tristania rufescens (Myrtaceae) (cb. p. 627:
V. P. p. 71), a tree about 7 m. high, found in
open evergreen forest (K.): เคาะขมิ้น (ต้น)
Adina polycephala (Rubiaceae) (V. P. p. 71),
a large, deciduous tree growing from north-
eastern India to Indo-China (Dept. Agri. & Fisheries: Burk. p. 52): เคาะประตู to knock at
the door: เคาะผง to shake off the dust.

เคาะแคะ (พูด) kau[6]-kaa[6] v. to talk entic-
ingly; to speak in a familiar way; to converse
alluringly; to court or flatter: เคาะจิ๊ก (ต้น)
Schleichera trijuga (Sapindaceae) (V. P. p.
71), "Ceylon oak", a large tree of Siam, Ceylon, India, Burma etc. The seeds, which are
edible, are rich in oil, said to be the original
" Macassar oil". It is not so called at present
(McM. pp. 219, 397, 416, 417: Burk. p. 1978). A dye
is said to be obtained from the flowers; the oil
is a valuable stimulating and cleansing application to the scalp, promoting the growth of the
hair. The fruit contains a whitish pulp,
which has a pleasant sub-acid taste and is
often eaten during hot dry weather. The
wood is much used for the manufacture of
articles where strength in small space is required (Dept. Agri. & Fisheries).

เคิม (ต้น) kerm n. Lophopetalum wallichii (Celastraceae) (V. P. p. 70), a large, glabrous

tree growing in Burma and Siam. The bark, roots and fruit are used as a febrifuge; the wood is used for making writing boards, etc. The genus is interesting because of its poisonous properties. The Igorots of Luzon use the bark for arrow-poisons (Dept. Agri. & Fisheries: Burk. p. 1365),

เคียกุ๋ย (ต้น) ke-ah-gkoo-ie[4] *n. Ampelocissus martinii (Ampelidaceae)* (CB. p. 304: BURK. p. 2245), a climber with a tuberous root, found from Indo-China southwards through Siam to Kedah, and also in the Philippines. It bears a grape-like fruit. Attempts to make wine from these fruits have not been very successful (K.).

เคียเนีย (ต้น) ke-ah-ne-ah[5] *n. Lagerstroemia villosa (Lythraceae)* (CB. p. 728), a tree about 20 m. high, found in mixed deciduous forest. The flowers are pale mauve; the bark is rough (K.).

เคียะ (ต้น) ke-ah[6] *n. Opuntia dillenii (Cactaceae)* (V. P. p. 70), the prickly pear, a branching, leafless shrub, with large circular or oval tubercles, covered with tufts of sharp spines 3 to 4 in. long. Some forms are almost spineless. About the middle of the eighteenth century it was introduced into the East. It has no uses except for fencing and is a pest in some places (BURK. p. 1586). The fruits are edible, but tufts of small spines covering them are an objection. They are sometimes turned into useful food in periods of drought or famine. It is probable the plant was first introduced into the East because the sailors found its use as a vegetable prevented scurvy. It is best when boiled, crushed and flavoured with salt. Mixed with ensilage or other fodder it is said to have a fattening effect. A spineless form raised by the late Mr. Burbank in California, is well spoken of as stock feed (MCM. pp. 74, 171, 267). A coarse kind of fibre obtained from this plant can be used as a paper material; the leaves mashed up and applied as a poultice are said

to allay heat and inflammation (Dept. Agri. & Fisheries): เคียะไก่ให้ (ต้น) *Pedilanthus tithymaloides (Euphorbiaceae)* (V. P. p. 70: BURK. p. 1683), a half succulent plant, native of tropical America and cultivated throughout the tropics. It is commonly used for hedges (MCM. pp. 74, 171: K.): เคียะเทียน (ต้น) *Sarcostemma brevistigma (Asclepiadaceae)* (V. P. p. 71), a trailing, leafless, jointed shrub, often brought from a distance by farmers to extirpate termites from the sugar-cane fields (Dept. Agri. & Fisheries).

เคียง kee-ang *adj.* adjoining; contiguous: *adv.* near by: ของเคียง hot delicacies served in small separate dishes placed close together (being an ancient custom observed at important functions): เคียงกัน near together: เคียงข้าง close beside: เคียงคู่ partners: วางเคียงเรียง laid in order close together.

เคียด kee-at[3] *v.* to be angered; to arouse anger or passion; to irritate; to inflame: เคียด (ต้น) *Cinnamomum iners (Lauraceae)* (V. P. p. 68), a tree of moderate size, which is found from western India and Tenasserim to Sumatra and Java and eastwards to the southern parts of the Philippines. It supplies the markets with a bark which is sold as cinnamon. The seeds, bruised and mixed with honey or sugar, are given to children in dysentery and coughs; combined with other ingredients, they are given in fevers. The bark and roots are used for curries (Dept. Agri. & Fisheries: BURK. p. 551): เคียดกัน to excite ill-temper towards others: เคียดขึ้ง, ขึ้งเคียด being offended or irritated with.

เคียน kee-an *v.* to tie up; to wrap up; to bandage; to wind around; to encircle the head with a cloth: เคียนกาย to clothe one's self: เคียนพุง, เคียนเอว to tie a scarf around the waist.

เคียม kee-am *Cam. v.* to bend the body over; to crouch on knees and elbows; to prostrate oneself in an attitude of adoration : เคี่ยมคั้ล to prostrate oneself before princes.

เคี่ยม (ต้น) kee-am[3] *n. Cotylelobium lanceolatum (Dipterocarpaceae)* (cb. p. 142 : Burk. p. 672 : v. p. p. 70), a tree in evergreen forest, much used for timber, especially for railway sleepers (K.)

เคี่ยร kee-an *P. n.* voice; speech; words; utterances (chd. p. 148).

เคียว kee-ow *n.* a sickle; a scythe : เคียว-สับ๊ะใล่ a bill-hook; an halberd.

เคี่ยว kee-ow[3] *v.* to boil down; to reduce the liquid portion by evaporation : เคี่ยวขัน to oppose with various obstacles; to compete amid various hindrances : เคี่ยวขับ, เคี่ยวเข็ญ to treat cruelly or severely; to use oppression or force in order to get one to accomplish a task; to nag or urge continually : เคี่ยว-ให้แห้ง to boil dry : เคี่ยวให้งวด to let solutions simmer till they are almost dry.

เคี้ยว kee-ow[5] *v.* to chew; to masticate : คดเคี้ยว tortuous; winding : เคี้ยวฟัน to grind the teeth : เคี้ยวเอื้อง to chew the cud.

เคือกำ (ต้น) kur-ah-gkum *n. Abrus precatorius (Leguminosae)* (cb. p. 435 : Burk. p. 4), Indian liquorice, a slender, perennial, climbing shrub occurring throughout the tropics. The juice of the green leaves is taken for "purifying the blood"; the roots are taken for sore throat and rheumatism. The bright red and black seeds furnish an acrid poison, which is often used criminally in India for killing cattle. The seeds are powdered and formed into paste with which darts or arrows are dressed. An arrow-wound is thus generally fatal within 24 hours. The poisonous property is believed to be in the red covering of the seed. Boiling renders the seeds harmless. The seeds are used for rosaries, necklaces, goldsmiths' weights, etc. (MCM. pp. 377, 383, 461).

เคือเขาแกบ (ต้น) kur-ah-kow[2]-gkaap[4] *n. Desmos chinensis (Anonaceae)* (cb. p. 37), a woody climber with fragrant flowers, found in mixed, deciduous forest in southern China and southwards throughout Malaysia (K. : BURK. p. 796); *Ventilago ochrocarpa (Rhamnaceae)* (cb. p. 296), a woody climber found in evergreen forest of the Old World (K.).

เคือเขาน้า (ต้น) kur-ah-kow[2]-nam[5] *n. Cissus repanda (Ampelidaceae)* (cb. p. 308), a large, woody climber found in deciduous forest. The flowers are a reddish-brown (K.); *Tetrastigma lanceolarium (Ampelidaceae)* (BURK. p. 2243 : cb. p. 313), a woody climber with flattened stem, found in mixed jungle by a stream (K.).

เคือเขาปุ่น (ต้น) kur-ah-kow[2]-bpoon[2] *n. Cissus modeccoides var. kerrii (Ampelidaceae)* (cb. p. 308), a climber having black fruits (K.).

เคือเขาปู่ (ต้น) kur-ah-kow[2]-bpoo[4] *n. Pueraria candollei (Leguminosae)* (cb. p. 449), a woody climber found on a limestone hill. The standard was pale pink (K.).

เคือเขาผู้ (ต้น) kur-ah-kow[2]-poo[3] *n. Spatholobus parviflorus (Leguminosae)* (cb. p. 447), a large woody climber bearing white flowers, found in deciduous forest (K.).

เคือเขาหนัง (ต้น) kur-ah-kow[2]-nang[2] *n. Bauhinia detergens (Leguminosae)*, a climber allied to *Bauhinia bassacensis*, but differing in the longer, narrower leaves, the lobes of which are obtuse or obtusely acuminate at the apex (cb. p. 520).

เคือคางควาย (ต้น) kur-ah-kang-kwai *n. Dalbergia abbreviata (Leguminosae)* (cb. p. 473), a woody climber found in open deciduous forest (K.).

เคืองเท่า (ต้น) kur-ah-ngu-how[4] *n. Toddalia asiatica (Rutaceae)* (cb. p. 220), a rambling shrub. The leaves yield a pale yellowish-green limpid oil, having the odour of citron peel, and a bitter and aromatic taste. The unripe fruit and root are rubbed down with oil to make a stimulant liniment for rheumatism. The fresh leaves are eaten raw; the ripe berries are pickled; both have a strong pungent taste. *syn. Toddalia aculeata* (*Rutaceae*) (Dept. Agri. & Fisheries). The flowers of the plant are yellow and slightly scented (K.).

เคือจางน้อย (ต้น)　　kur-ah-chjang-noi[5] *n. Clematis subpeltata* (*Ranunculaceae*) (cb. p. 15), a climber found by the stream in bamboo forest at the foot of Doi Sudeb, Chiengmai (K.).

เคือจ่ายแดง (ต้น)　　kur-ah-chjai[2]-dang *n. Pterolobium macropterum* (*Leguminosae*) (cb. p. 505), a species of climber found growing at Doi Sudeb, Chiengmai (K.).

เคือตับปลา (ต้น)　　kur-ah-dtap[4]-bplah *n Derris thorelii* (*Leguminosae*) (cb. p. 493), a woody climber, found in scrub jungle. The flowers are creamy white (K.).

เคือตาป่า (ต้น)　　kur-ah-dtah-bpah *n. Derris scandens* (*Leguminosae*) (cb. p. 493), a strong, woody climber with smooth bark, found throughout Asia to Australia. The flowers are pure white in large masses and quite ornamental (MCM. p. 132). The bark affords a coarse rope fibre (Dept. Agri. & Fisheries: Burk. p. 791).

เคือตาลาน (ต้น) see เคือเขาปู่ (ต้น)

เคือติดต่อ (ต้น)　　kur-ah-dtit[4]-dtau[4] *n. Oxymitra desmoides* (*Anonaceae*) (cb. p. 49), a woody climber, found in evergreen forest (K.).

เคือนมงัว (ต้น)　　kur-ah-nom-ngoo-ah *n. Anomianthus heterocarpus* (*Anonaceae*) (cb. p. 55), a woody climber, found in dry mixed forest. The fruit is edible (K.).

เคือบ (ต้น)　　kur-ah-bpee[3] *n. Dalbergia foliacea* (*Leguminosae*) (cb. p. 478), a large straggling shrub. The wood is white, porous and with a small, dark heart-wood, in structure resembling that of *Dalbergia stipulacea* (Dept. Agri. & Fisheries).

เคือมะถั่วเน่า (ต้น)　　kur-ah-ma[6]-too-ah[4]-now[3] *n. Combretum winitii* (*Combretaceae*) (cb. p. 622: K.), a climber having large leaves, found growing near a stream in deciduous forest.

เคือแมด (ต้น)　　kur-ah-maat[3] *n. Dalbergia volubilis* (*Leguminosae*) (cb. p. 485), a large climber. The wood is light-brown, hard and very tough. The leaves are eaten by cattle and goats. The root-juice is given with cummin and sugar in gonorrhoea. A gargle beneficial to sore-throat is made (Dept. Agri. & Fisheries).

เคือไส้ไก่ (ต้น)　　kur-ah-sai[3]-gkai[4] *n. Diploclisia glaucescens* (*Menispermaceae*) (cb. p. 68), a woody climber found in evergreen forest (K.).

เคือไหล (ต้น)　　kur-ah-lai[2] *n. Derris thorelii* (*Leguminosae*) (cb. p. 493), a woody climber, found in scrub jungle. The flowers are creamy white (K.).

เคือ　　keu-ah[5] *adj.* pretty; beautiful.

เคือง　　keu-ang *v.* to irritate or be irritated; to offend; to annoy; to make angry; to be offended with: เคืองกัน to be angry against another: เคืองขุ่น indignant or offended; เคืองตา to be an eye-sore (as a rong-tao); to be irritating to the eye; to feel "sand in the eyes": ผีดเคือง to be hampered, or embarrassed financially; to be impeded in motions or actions (as by rust on pieces of machinery).

แค (ต้น)　　kaa *n. Stereospermum fimbriatum* (*Bignoniaceae*) (Red. p. 243), a tall deciduous tree found from Burma to Malaya. The heart-wood is small and dark brown and the sap-wood is light brown. It is used for beams and posts but is not durable in the soil (BURK. p. 2082 : Dept. Agri. & Fisheries); *Sesbania grandiflora (Leguminosae)* (cb. p. 399); *Sesbania (Agati) grandiflora (Leguminosae)*, a small, erect, quick-growing, sparsely branched, soft-wooded tree, about 15 to 20 feet high, bearing large pendulous flowers. The fleshy petals, as well as the tender leaves, are relished in curries and soups, or fried with butter. The long pendulous pods do not appear to be eaten. The bark, leaves and flowers are used medicinally. It is propagated by seed and is commonly cultivated in Siam and Ceylon (MCM. pp. 305, 311 : Burk. p. 1997): แคขาว (ต้น) *Dolichandrone rheedii (Bignoniaceae)* (V. P. p. 60), a small tree yielding a fibre. The wood is white and soft (Dept. Agri. & Fisheries).

แค่   kaa[3] *adv.* nearly equal to ; as far, or as long as ; approximately ; almost : แค่กัน equal to ; even to ; up to : แค่นั้น, แค่โน้น that far ; to that point, distance or size : แค่นี้ this far ; up to this spot.

แคงโค (ต้น)   kaang-koh *n. Bauhinia malabarica (Leguminosae)* (cb. p. 524), a moderate-sized, bushy, deciduous tree. The leaves are very acrid and edible ; the young shoots are eaten as a vegetable. When cooked they are slightly bitter but very palatable (Dept. Agri. & Fisheries).

แคน   kaan *n.* a Laosian reed mouth-organ. The usual compass of this organ is fourteen reeds, each of which contains a small metal tongue by the vibrations of which the notes are produced ; Pandean pipes.

แค้น   kaan[3] *v.* to do intentionally ; to do on purpose ; to do with an intention of offending or insulting : แค่นแคะ, แค่นได้ to talk teasingly in order to accomplish one's purposes ; to draw forth by artful means so as to accomplish an object ; to worm a request out of another : แค่นทำ to insist on doing : แค่นว่า to persist in speaking : แค่นให้ to give

unwillingly a thing which has once been refused.

แค้น   kaan[5] *v.* to be indignant at ; to be angry ; to be provoked : แก้แค้น to revenge ; to retaliate ; to inflict vengeance : แค้นคอ to be irritating to the throat, or lodged in it : ความแค้นใจ rancour ; bitter and vindictive enmity ; indignation.

แคบ   kaap[3] *adj.* narrow : แคบนัก too small ; too cramped ; too restricted : แคบไปหน่อย slightly too small : ใจคับแคบ narrow-minded ; avaricious ; void of affection ; selfish : ที่คับแคบ the place is too narrow : ผ้าแคบ ไม่พอตัดเสื้อ there is not sufficient material to make a coat or jacket.

แคม   kam *n.* edge ; margin ; brink : แคมเรือ the edge or edges of a boat.

แคร   kraa *v.* to tie ; to bind.

แคร่   kraa[3] *n.* a stretcher ; a litter ; a small bed or bench made of bamboo : แคร่เรือ bamboo slats sewed together with rattan strips (used as flooring for Siamese boats) : แคร่หาม a stretcher borne by carrying poles ; a palanquin.

แคร่ครั้ง   kraa[3]-krang[3] *v.* to be over-crowded ; to be greatly congested or cramped for space.

แคริง   kraang *n.* a species of edible sea-shell, *Arca*, ark shell or cockle ; a basket made of plaited bamboo, dammared over and having a long handle (used for scooping, splashing or dipping water from large boats).

แคระ   kraa[6] *adj.* diminutive ; small ; stunted ; under-sized (as a child who is stunted or dwarfed).

แคลง   klaang *v.* to doubt ; to suspect ; to lean or turn to one side (as a witness) ; to lean to one side (as a boat) ; to turn or twist sideways (as a foot) : คลางแคลง to suspect ; to have a suspicion about ; to doubt : แคลงใจ to suspect another as untruthful or disloyal : แคลงระแวง, ระแวง-แคลง dubious; doubtful; hesitating in one's suspicion; uncertain : เคลือบแคลง to dissemble one's feelings; to conceal one's suspicion : ผัวเมียแคลงกัน the husband and wife suspect each other : ยุให้แคลงใจ to incite jealousy : เรือแคลงโคลง the boat rocks or rolls.

แคลน   klaan *adj.* needy; needful; insufficient; being too near the edge (as while walking along a cliff) : แคลนขัด, ขัดแคลน to be in want of : แคลนใจ miserable ; poor : คลอนแคลน movable; shaky; wabbly.

แคล้ว   klaa-ow⁵ *v.* to pass unseen while travelling in opposite directions; to fail of hitting or meeting; to pass by without seeing (as one in a crowd); to escape (as from an accident); to escape from, or to be able to avoid (as danger) : แคล้วกัน to pass one another in opposite directions.

แคล่วคล่อง   klaa-ow³-klaung³ *adj.* adroit; expert; clever : *adv.* easily; quickly; actively; expeditiously.

แคว   kwaa *n.* a branch of a river; crossroads; the fork of a road; a by-path; a district bordering on a branch of a river : แควน้อย name of a tributary of the Chow Phya river : แควใหญ่ a large tributary stream.

แควก   kwaak³ *onomat.* from a sound of tearing cloth.

แคว้ง   kwaang⁵ *v.* to whirl around in a circle; to eddy; to move in an eddy; to circle around; to be curved or bent : แคว้งคว้าง, เคว้ง to wander aimlessly about; to circle or revolve round and round; to drift about without definite purpose.

แคว้น   kwaan⁵ *n.* country; district; border; boundary or limit of a section of territory.

แคะ   kaa⁶ *v.* to pick out, or pry out (as seeds from fruit); to extract; to extricate : *n.* Hak Kah, a dialect or tribe of Chinese

from a province between Canton and Shanghai : แคะได้ to question very minutely; to use crafty persistence to gain information : แคะปม to pick loose or untie a knot.

โค   koh *P. S. n.* an ox; a bull; a cow; kine; a herd of oxen; a star; rays of light or glory; sun; earth; sky; name for Saraswati (พระ-สรัสวดี), the goddess of Speech (H. C. D. p. 284); anything coming from or belonging to an ox or cow (as milk, flesh, hide, leather, bowstring, sinew, etc.) (S. E. D. p. 363) : โคกุล a herd of oxen or cattle; a pen for cattle; a pastoral district on the Yumana, about Mathura, where Krishna passed his boyhood with the cowherds (H. C. D. p. 113) : โคคลาน a medicinal plant : โคฆาต a butcher : โคฆาส grass or fodder for cattle : โคงาน draught cattle : โคจร a pasture ground for cattle; a clearing or field where work is done; the range of the organs of sense : โคจรคาม a place which a priest is allowed to frequent in quest of alms (as the houses of pious laymen) : โค-จรภูมิ a pasture; a field for grazing cattle; a place with plenty of fodder or pasturage : โคจรรยา *lit.* " animal-like manners," *i. e.* coarse, vulgar behaviour : โคชล, โคทรัพ, โคมูตร the urine of cows : โคชีพ one living on, or trading in cattle; a cattle herder or cattle raiser : โคดม, โคตมะ Gotama Buddha, the founder of the Nyaya school of philosophy; in the lineage of Buddha; a name of the sage Saradwat, a son of Gotama; a name common to many men (H. C. D. pp. 111–113) : โคตร a barn; a cattle shed or pen; a protection or shelter for cows; a stable for cattle; an umbrella or parasol; a cloud; a road : โคตรเทวดา the celestial beings or guardian spirits of a family; deities; household gods : โคตรนาม a surname; the family name : โคตรภู Buddhist monks whose customs are different from orthodox priests but who still consider themselves Buddhists; one who adheres to the sacred doctrines of Buddhism; one who is in a fit state to receive sanctification :

โคตรภูญาณ the wisdom necessary for the reception of the Paths: โคตรภูสงฆ์ Buddhist monks who are not very zealous in their religious life but who still consider themselves priests: โคเถลิง name of a plant: โคทม *lit.* "a conqueror," *i. e.* one attaining heaven and earth: โคทาวรี, โคธาวารี *lit.* "granting water or kine," *i. e.* name of a river in the Dekkan in the southern part of India, on the bank of which is situated Panchavati, a temporary abode of Rama during his exile (H. C. D. p. 258): โคโทห *lit.* "the milking of cows," *i. e.* fresh cows: โคธน, โคยูถ possession of cows; a herd of cows; live-stock (considered as property): โคธรรม *lit.* "rule of cattle," *i. e.* promiscuity: โคธิ *lit.* "hair receptacle," *i. e.* the brow; the forehead: โคธูม *lit.* "vapour or smoke of the earth," *i. e.* waving stalks of wheat: โคนม milch cows: โคนาค an excellent ox: โคนาถ an herdsman; a cow-boy; a keeper of cattle; a bull; a cow-herd: โคนาย a master of cattle; an herdsman; a cow-herd: โคนิหาร, โควิษ cow-dung: โคเนื้อ a cow slaughtered for beef: โคบดี the lord of cow-herds; a leader; a chief; a name often applied to Indra; a bull; *lit.* "lord of rays," *i. e.* the sun; *lit.* "lord of stars," *i. e.* the moon; *lit.* "earth-lord," *i. e.* a king; *lit.* "the chief of herdsmen," *i. e.* Krishna or Vishnu; *lit.* "lord of water," *i. e.* Varuna; Indra: โคบท the marks or impressions of a cow's hoof in the soil: โคบาล, โคปาล, โควินท์ a cow-herd; *lit.* "earth protector," *i. e.* a king: โคบุตร a young bull; *lit.* "son of the sun," *i. e.* Karna; a kind of gallinule: โคป, โคปก an herdsman; a guardian; a keeper of cows: โคปนะ the act of governing; the act of caring for, treating or guarding: โคแพทย์ a veterinary surgeon: โคภุช *lit.* "one enjoying the earth," *i. e.* a king: โคมณฑล a herd of cows; *lit.* "earth orb," *i. e.* the globe: โคมัย defiled with cow-dung: โคมิคุน a bull; a cow: โคมุข *lit.* "having a face like a cow," *i. e.* an alligator: โคมุตร cow's urine; a mark in-

dicating the end of a chapter or story (as used in old Siamese literature): โคเมท *lit.* "cow fat," *i. e.* a gem brought from the Himalaya mountains and the Indus, being of four sorts, *viz.* white, pale-yellow, red and dark-blue: โคยาน *lit.* "transportation by means of oxen," *i. e.* an oxcart; a bullock-cart; a vehicle drawn by oxen: โคยุค a yoke or pair of cattle; a pair of animals (in general): โครส *lit.* "a bovine flavour," *i. e.* milk, of which there are five forms, *viz.* fresh milk, sour milk, white butter, cheese and cream: โครักษ์ a species of orange tree; an animal tender, or breeder; the business of an herdsman: โคราช Nagor Rajasima, a populous city in north-eastern Siam; the head herdsman; a chief cow-boy: โคราสย์ *lit.* "one who makes play-mates of cattle," *i. e.* Phra Krishna: โคโรค a disease of cattle similar to glanders: โควัธ the act of killing cattle: โควาส a cattle-pen: โควินท์ *lit.* "a cow-keeper," *i. e.* a name for Krishna (H. C. D. p. 114): โควิษาณ cow-horns: โคศาล a cow-pen; *lit.* "one born in a cow-pen," *i. e.* name of an influential disciple of พระมหาวีระ who founded the นิกายอาชีวิก sect of Buddhistic monkhood: โคษฐ์ a cow-pen; a cattle shed; a meeting place; a fold for sheep; an utensil for holding water; a place where cows are kept: นมโค cow's milk: หนังโค cow hides.

โคก kok[3] *n.* a knoll; a hill or mound: โคกขาม name of a place near Tacheen: โคกนา a mound or hillock in a rice field: โคกวัด mounds found in ruined temple grounds: โคก (ปลา) *Dorosoma chacunda (Clupeidae)* and *D. nasus,* two species of shad of considerable economic value (BURK. p. 854); *Anodontostoma chacunda (Dorosomidae)* and *A. nasus* (Dept. Agri. & Fisheries).

โคกกระสุน (ต้น) kok[3]-gka[4]-soon[2] *n. Tribulus terrestris (Zygophyllaceae)* (cb. p. 205), a common, low trailing annual plant. The fruit is used medicinally; the young leaves and stems are eaten as a pot-herb; the prickly fruit is also gathered and used as food in times of scarcity, being ground to a powder and eaten in the form of bread (Dept. Agri. & Fisheries).

โคกกะออม (ต้น) kok³-gka⁴-aum *n.* *Cardiospermum halicacabum (Sapindaceae)* (Burk. p. 457 : Cb. p. 322), a pan-tropic weed used medicinally from ancient times. The roots and leaves are aperient; they are also used as a hair-wash (MCM. p. 378). The root is used in medicine as an emetic, laxative, stomachic, and rubefacient; it also possesses diaphoretic, diuretic and tonic properties. The leaves are cooked as a vegetable; the shoots are eaten as greens (Dept. Agri. & Fisheries).

โคกม้า kok³-mah⁵ *n.* an expert veterinarian.

โคกแล้ (ต้น) kok³-laa⁵ *n.* *Mangifera indica (Anacardiaceae)* (cb. p. 344 : Burk. p. 1402), the mango, a medium or large-sized, spreading and quick-growing tree, indigenous to tropical Asia. It bears large panicles of greenish-white scented flowers. The round or ovoid fruit is somewhat flattened, generally with a more or less pronounced beak near the apex. It has a tough, thin skin and when ripe is yellow, reddish or green. The flesh is usually of a reddish tint, with a distinct, pleasant, aromatic flavour. In inferior varieties it has a pronounced flavour of turpentine, and is somewhat resinous and fibrous. In the centre is the large, fibrous, ovoid, flat seed. The mango is the fruit par excellence of Siam and India, where it has been cultivated from time immemorial. Here it may be considered an article of food as well as dessert, whilst it also enters largely into the preparation of chutneys and preserves (MCM. pp. 242, 243, 518).

โค่ง kong³ *adj.* great; high; large; big; overgrown : โก่งเก่ง too high; top-heavy : เบี้ยโค้ง a mollusk of the genus *Cypraea moneta* which supplies the much esteemed cowry shells.

โค้ง kong⁵ *v.* to bend over; to be arched over; to be curved downward : *adj.* curved; bent over; crooked : โก้งโค้ง to stoop : โค้งโก่ง to bend over.

โคจร, โคดม, โคตมะ, โคตร, โคตรภู see **โค**

โคธา, จะกวด, ตะกวด koh-tah *P. S. n.* the monitor or water lizard, *Varanus salvator*, an aquatic animal of the same family (*Varanidae*) as the iguana, but with a long tail and spots along the body, found in the Old World tropics (BURK. p. 2221).

โคน kon *n.* base; pedestal; bottom; the bishop (in chess) : โคนต้นไม้ the base of a tree : เห็ดโคน a kind of mushroom.

โค่น kon³ *v.* to cut down; to fell; *colloq.* to cause ruin or destruction.

โคนก koh-nok⁶ *P. n.* a woolen coverlet with very long fleece (chd. p. 149); a carpet with a heavy nap.

โคปผกะ kop³-pa⁴-gka⁴ *P. n.* the ankle; ankle-bones; the prominences of the ankle (chd. p. 149).

โคเพลาะ koh-plaw⁶ *n.* the wild ox.

โคม kom *n.* lamp; lantern; an ancient dish or basin : โคมแขวน a hanging lamp : โคมตั้ง a table lamp : โคมลอย a balloon; a groundless rumour; information without foundation, reason or cause : โคมเวียน a revolving light; name of a Siamese song : โคมหวด a censer-shaped glass lamp suspended from the ceiling in Buddhist sanctuaries.

โครก, โครกครอก krok³ *onomat.* from the sound of gas in the intestines, or from snoring : โครกเครก being unfit for; being too large.

โครง krong *n.* a skeleton (as of a boat); a scheme, plan or model (made in miniature); a replica : โครงการ a programme, plan or policy : โครงจมูก the bridge or ridge of the nose : โครงสร้าง a structure : ซี่โครง an individual rib.

โคร่ง krong[3] *n.* a huge tiger: *adj.* large; tall; over-sized; immense; enormous; of abnormal size: โคร่งคร่าง large.

โครพ see คารวะ

โครม, โครมคราม krom *onomat.* from the sound of something falling or being crushed.

โคร่ำ, กูรัม, เลียงผา koh-ram *n.* goat antelope, *Capriconis sumatrensis* (K.).

โคโรค see โค

โคลง klong *v.* to lean or roll from side to side: *n.* verses in rhyme; rhymes or jingles: *adj.* wabbly; unsteady: โคลงเคลง (ต้น) *Melastoma polyanthum (Melastomaceae)* (cb. p. 683: Burk. p. 1441), a shrub about 1 to 5 m. high. The flowers are bright purple (K.): โคลงเคลงตัวผู้ (ต้น) *Melastoma orientale (Melastomaceae)* (cb. p. 682), a shrub about 1 to 5 m. high, found in low scrub jungle. The flowers are purple (K.). It is too small to be useful as a timber tree but its medicinal properties are esteemed. It is used in elephant medicine: โคลงเรือ to cause a boat to tilt, rock or roll.

โคลน klon *n.* mud; mire: โคลนตม mud and mire: ลุยโคลน to walk or wade in the mud: จมโคลน to sink in the mud.

ใคร krai *pron.* who; whoever; who is that? ใครทำ who did that? who made that? ใครมา who has come? ใครว่า who said so?

ใคร่ krai[3] *v.* to wish; to want; to like; to desire; to covet.

ใคร่ครวญ krai[3]-kroo-an *v.* to investigate; to examine into; to think over; to weigh the evidence.

ใค see ไคล

ไค้ kai[5] *v.* to pick out (as serumin from the ear); to scoop out (as seeds from fruit): ไค้น้ำ (ต้น) *Homonoia riparia (Euphorbiaceae)* (V. P. p. 62). a small, rigid, evergreen shrub, found on rocky and stony river-beds. The wood is grey or greyish brown, moderately hard and close-grained (Dept. Agri. & Fisheries: Burk. p. 1186).

ไคร้เครือ krai[5]-kreu-ah *n.* a medicinal vine.

ไคล klai *v.* to go; to advance: *n.* skin-scurf removed by hard rubbing; slime that collects on the bottom of boats; dried excretions of the skin: ขี้ไคล loose skin-scurf thrown off in minute scales: ไคลคลา to advance; to walk along; to creep along: ไคลงอกบนหิน lichens growing on rocks: ไคลน้ำ vegetation that grows as a scum on water.

ไคล้ klai[5] *n.* charms; magic; sorcery: ใส่ไคล้ to produce dire results on a person by means of witchcraft or sorcery.

ฅ

ฅ The fifth consonant of the Thai alphabet, a low class letter of which there are twenty-four, *viz.* ค, ฅ, ฆ, ง, ช, ฌ, ฎ, ญ, ฑ, ฒ, ณ, ท, ธ, ฑ, ฒ, น, ฌ, ณ, พ, ฟ, ภ, ม, ร, ล, ว, ฬ, ฮ. ฅอฅน is the designating name. This letter is now obsolete and replaced by ค.

ฆ

ฆ The sixth consonant of the Thai alphabet, a low class or third group letter of which there are twenty-four, *viz.* ค, ฅ, ฆ, ง, ช, ฌ, ฌ, ญ, ฎ, ฑ, ฒ, ฑ, ฒ, น, ฌ, ณ, พ, ฟ, ภ, ม, ร, ล, ว, ฬ, ฮ. ฆอระฆัง is the designating name.

ฆฏ ka[6]-dta[4] *P. S. n.* a water pot; a water jar; a basin with handles; the uppermost portion; the head; a boundary; the zodiac sign Aquarius (S. E. D. p. 375): ฆฏการ a potter: ฆฏทาสี a procuress; a pander: ฆฏราช a large earthen jar; a water jar: ฆฏโศรศร Kumbha-karna, a superhuman character in the Ramayana (กุมภกรรณ). He was the son of Visravas by his Rakshasa wife, Kesini, and full brother of Ravana. He was a monster who, under the curse of Brahma (or as a boon, according to some), slept for six months at a time and remained awake for only a single day. When Ravana was hard-pressed by Rama, he sent to arouse Kumbha-karna. This was effected with great difficulty. After drinking 2,000 jars of liquor he went to consult his brother, and then took the field against the monkey army. He beat down Su-griva, the monkey chief, with a large stone, and carried him as a prisoner into the city of Lanka. When he returned to the battle he encountered Rama. After a stout fight, he was defeated, and Rama cut off his head (H. C. D. pp. 170, 171): ฆโฏทร, ฆัณโฏทร *lit.* "pendant bellied or pot-bellied," *i. e.* Ganesa, son of the god Siva.

ฆฏี ka[6]-dtee *P. S. n.* the feminine form for ฆฏ: ฆฏีกร a female potter: ฆฏียนตร์ a bucket attached to a long pole or rope, used for drawing water from wells; the buckets of a well or any contrivance for raising water (S. E. D. p. 375).

ฆต ka[6]-dta[4] *P. S. n.* oil; butter; ghee or clarified butter; butter which has been boiled gently and allowed to cool (it is used for culinary and religious purposes and is highly esteemed by the Hindus); fat (as an emblem of fertility); fluid grease (S. E. D. p. 378).

ฆน ka[6]-na[6] *P. S. n.* a cloud; a striker; a killer; a destroyer; a murderer; an iron club; a mace; a weapon shaped like a hammer; any compact mass or substance: *adj.* compact; solid; hard; firm; dense; coarse;

viscid; thick (S. E. D. p. 376): ฆนกาล, ฆนสมัย *lit.* "time or season for clouds," *i. e.* the rainy season: ฆนจัย a cloud; a fleck or cloud drift; a mass of clouds: ฆนชวาล, ฆนชิวาล lightning; a beam of light radiating through a cloud: ฆนธาตุ *lit.* "the inspissated element of the body," *i. e.* lymph: ฆนบท the cube root: ฆนบทวี, ฆนวิถี *lit.* "the pathway for clouds," *i. e.* the sky; the firmament: ฆนรส *lit.* "thick juice," *i. e.* camphor; medicinal extracts; decoctions: ฆนวารี *lit.* "water from the clouds," *i. e.* rain: ฆนวาหนะ *lit.* "one riding on clouds," *i. e.* the god Siva: ฆนศยาม *lit.* "being black like a storm-cloud," *i. e.* Phra Krishna; Rama: ฆนศัพท์ *lit.* "sounds; a loud noise from a cloud," *i. e.* thunder: ฆนสาร *lit.* "being dense and hard," *i. e.* camphor gum: ฆนากร *lit.* "a multitude of clouds," *i. e.* the rainy season: ฆนาคม *lit.* "the approach of clouds," *i. e.* the rainy season: ฆนามัย the date tree: ฆนารุณ a deep, bright red; the condition of being crimson, scarlet or bright red: ฆนาศัย *lit.* "the abode of the clouds," *i. e.* the atmosphere: ฆนคร *lit.* "opposed to solid," *i. e.* liquid; fluid; watery: ฆโนทัย *lit.* "the season for the gathering together of the clouds," *i. e.* the beginning of the rainy season: ฆโนบล *lit.* "cloud stones," *i. e.* hail.

ฆนา, ฆเน, ฆโน ka[6]-nah *P. S.* used as a prefix in the above words meaning *cloud.*

ฆร ka[6]-ra[6] *P. n.* a house; a home; an habitation; an abode (chd. p. 146).

ฆรณี ka[6]-ra[6]-nee *P. n.* the lady of the house; a matron; a wife (chd. p. 146).

ฆราณ, ฆาน ka[6]-ran *P. S. n.* the nose; the organ of smell; the perception of odour, smell, scent (S. E. D. p. 379).

ฆราวาส ka[6]-rah-wat[3] *P. n.* a person other than a member of the clergy; the laity; one vested with authority in a house; life in the world; a layman's life as opposed to the life of an ascetic (chd. p. 146).

ฆฤต, ฆต kreut[6] *S. n. lit.* "ghee," *i. e.* clarified butter or butter which has been boiled gently and allowed to cool; cheese; butter; ghee: ฆฤตเกศ *lit.* "one whose hair is dripping with butter," *i. e.* พระอัคนิ, Agni. He is one of the most ancient and most sacred objects of Hindu worship. He is represented as having seven tongues for licking up the butter used in the sacrifices. Each of these tongues has a distinct name. He is guardian of the south-east quarter, being one of the eight loka-palas; his region is called Pura-jyotis (H. C. D. pp. 6, 7): ฆฤตพรต one existing on ghee only: ฆฤตาหุตี the act of giving ghee as alms; the ghee oblation (S. E. D. p. 378).

ฆ้อง kaung[5] *n.* a gong: ฆ้องกะแต a small gong or cymbal, used by a troop inspector as insignia of rank: ฆ้องชัย the victory gong: ฆ้องวง a musical instrument composed of gongs or cymbals strung in a semicircle on a frame: ฆ้องสามย่าน (ต้น) *Kelanchoe laciniata (Crassulaceae)*; *K. spathulata* (Cb. pp. 587, 588: Dept. Agri. & Fisheries): ฆ้องเหม่ง a small brass gong with a circular convex center: ฆ้องโหม่ง a large gong used during tonsorial ceremonies or to mark time for the marching of troops: ย่ำฆ้อง to beat gongs during the night, as a signal for changing guards.

ฆัญ, ฆัญญ์ kan *P. n.* the act of taking life or killing; the act of doing harm or destroying; destruction (chd. p. 146).

ฆัฏ, ฆัฏฏ์ kat[6] *P. S. v.* to slip; to slide; to touch; to harass; to irritate; to rub over (with the hands); to shake; to stir up; to incite; to have a bad effect or influence on (S. E. D. p. 375).

ฆัณฏา kan-dtah *P. S. n.* a bell; a gong; a cymbal; a plate of iron or mixed metal struck as a clock (S. E. D. p. 375): ฆัณฏาตาฬ a bell-striker: ฆัณฏานาท the sound of a bell: ฆัณฏาบถ *lit.* "a bell road," *i. e.* a main thoroughfare; a principal street; an avenue: ฆัณฏาวาทย์ the sound of a clock striking.

ฆัณโฏทร, ฆโฏทร kan-dtoh-taun *n. lit.* "pendant bellied, or a lambodara," *i. e.* Ganesa, a son of the god Siva.

ฆัส kat[6] *P. S. v.* to eat; to devour; to consume; to capture (as in chess): *n.* food; fodder; meadow-grass: *adj.* eating; pasturing (chd. p. 146).

ฆ่า kah[3] *v.* to kill; to destroy; to take life: ฆ่าคนโดยความประมาท to cause death by carelessness or negligence: ฆ่าคนโดยความอาฆาต to commit murder with malice or revenge: ฆ่าคนโดยเจตนา to commit murder with intent: ฆ่าคนโดยบังเอิญ homicide by accident: ฆ่าคนโดยไม่เจตนา murder without malice: ฆ่าคนในการป้องกันตน to cause death in self-defense: ฆ่าคนเพื่อสินจ้าง to commit murder for a bribe.

ฆาต kat[3] *P. S. n.* the act of taking life, killing or destroying; devastation; destruction: *adj.* slaying; injuring; hurting (S. E. D. p. 377): ฆาตกรรม the act of killing; murder; homicide: ฆาตกรรมโดยชอบธรรม justifiable homicide: ฆาต กรรมเด็กน้อย infanticide: บิตุฆาต parricide; the murder of a parent or of an ancestor: เพ็ชรฆาต an executioner: มาตุฆาต matricide, the killing of one's mother; one who kills his mother.

ฆาตก kah-dta[4]-gka[4] *P. n.* one who kills or destroys; a murderer (S. E. D. p. 377).

ฆาน see ฆวาณ

ฆาส kat[3] *P. S. v.* to eat: *n.* food; bait; meadow; pasture grass (S. E. D. p. 377).

ฆายนะ kah-ya[6]-na[6] *P. n.* the act of inhaling an odour; odours: *adj.* odorous (chd. p. 147).

ฆายนีย์ kah-ya[6]-nee *P. adj.* fragrant; odorous; suitable to be inhaled (chd. p. 174).

เฆี่ยน kee-an[3] *v.* to whip; to flog; to scourge with a rattan: เฆี่ยนขับ to scourge and then drive away: เฆี่ยนหลัง to flog on the back.

โฆร koh-ra[6] *P.S. adj.* frightful; terrible; shocking; awful; terrific; dreadful; vehement (as pains or disease): โฆรวาศน์ *lit.* "one with blood-curdling bark or howl," *i.e.* the fox or jackal: โฆรวิส a poisonous snake; a viper: *adj.* very poisonous; venomous: โฆรสังกาศ having a horrible form; having a terrifying figure or frightful appearance; hideous (S. E. D. p. 379).

โฆษ, โฆส kot[3] *S. n.* a proclamation; a sound; the sound of words spoken at a distance; indistinct noises; the confused cries of a multitude; a battle-cry; cries of victory; cries of woe or distress; the sound of a drum, a conch shell, or a carriage; the roaring of a storm, or the thunder of water (S. E. D. p. 378).

โฆษก, โฆสก koh-sok[4] *S. n.* one who advertises; one who proclaims or makes a thing known; a crier; a proclaimer (S. E. D. p. 378).

โฆษณา, โฆสนา kot[3]-sa[4]-nah *S. v.* to sound abroad; to proclaim; to advertise; to make known to all: *n.* the act of advertising or making known; the act of proclaiming aloud; public announcements: โฆษณาการ an advertisement; a public notice in a newspaper or periodical; a notification (S. E. D. p. 378).

โฆษิต, โฆสิต koh-sit[4] *S. adj.* sounded; declared; proclaimed (S. E. D. p. 378).

โฆษวันต์, โฆสวันต์ kot[3]-sa[4]-wan *P. n.* a group of sonant letters, or those uttered with a short articulation as ย, ร, ล, ว, ห, ฬ: *adj.* sonant; resonant; sounding (S. E. D. p. 378).

ง

ง The seventh consonant of the Thai alphabet, a low class letter of which there are twenty-four, *viz.* ค, ฅ, ฆ, ง, ช, ฌ, ซ, ญ, ย, ท, ธ, ฑ, ฒ, น, ณ, พ, ฟ, ภ, ม, ร, ล, ว, ฬ, ฮ. งอฺ is the designating name. ง is used either as an initial letter, as งู, งก, งง, งด or as a final consonant, as ลิง, ตั้ง, คาง.

งก ngok[6] *adj.* overly greedy; gluttonous: งกงัน, งกเงิ่น, งะงกงะงัน shaky; clumsy; tremulous; excited; agitated; shivering: งกเงิน grasping for money; avaricious.

งง ngong *v.* to be perplexed, astonished, stupefied or dazed: งงงวย to be confused; to be astonished; to be stupefied; to be in a mystified state; to be half asleep; to be forgetful.

งด ngot[6] *v.* to stop work; to stay any proceedings; to halt; to interrupt; to suspend action: งดก่อน, งดการ a command to desist from further action: งดไว้ to waive or postpone, pending further action or consideration: งดให้ to drop or defer action in behalf of another.

งดงาม ngot[6]-ngam *adj.* beautiful; pretty; attractive.

งบ ngop[6] *v.* to collect or assemble together; to gather together; to close (as an account): *n.* a lump; a round, flat cake or condiment made of fish or prawns, wrapped in leaves, baked and eaten with rice: งบดุลย์ a balance sheet: งบน้ำตาล a flat, round cake of palm sugar: งบประมาณ a budget; estimated expenses and receipts for a year or for any fixed period.

งม ngom *v.* to grope for something hidden; to grope for something sunk in the water or embedded in the mud; to fumble about in the dark: งมกุ้ง, งมปลา to feel around in the water or mud for water-snails, crawfish, or prawns: งมงาย to search for, or feel around uncertainly; to grabble for blindly: งมเงอะ stupid; clumsy: งมหอย to dive for shell-fish.

งวง ngoo-ang *n.* a trunk; a snout; a spout; a proboscis; a curved handle; a flowering stalk (as of the sugar-palm): งวงกา, พวยกา the curved outlet of an ewer: งวงครุ the curved handle on a water-tight bamboo bucket used for carrying water: งวงคชสีห์ the trunk of the elephant appearing on the Royal Siamese seal: งวงช้าง (งู) the elephant's trunk snake, *Acrochordus javanicus* (M. S. N. H. J. S. S. I, 1, p. 13): งวงช้าง an elephant's trunk: งวงช้าง (หญ้า) *Heliotropium indicum (Boraginaceae)* (V. P. p. 73: Dept. Agri. & Fisheries), an herb or shrubby plant found in all the warmer parts of the world. It is widely used as a poultice for herpes and rheumatism (Burk. p. 1136): งวงสุ่ม (ต้น) *Calycopteris floribunda (Combretaceae)* (Cb. p. 611: Dept. Agri. & Fisheries: Burk. p. 416), a sprawling shrub found in hot and rather dry parts of India, Burma, Siam, Penang and Kedah. Tribes near Bombay cut the stems to get water for drinking. The flowers are used in Penang to make a poultice for headache. In Cambodia, flowers and leaves are used as a tonic: ไก่งวง a turkey.

ง่วง, ง่วงงุน ngoo-ang[3] *v.* to be sleepy; to feel like sleeping; to become drowsy: ง่วงงง to be dazed or stupefied while still drowsy: ง่วงงุย to be benumbed by fever or by cold; to be semi-conscious; to be inactive or torpid; to be sluggish in action: ความง่วงเหงา drowsiness; sleepiness.

งวด ngoo-at[3] *v.* to be diminished by heat; to evaporate to dryness: *n.* a recurring period (usually every 3 months); a period of time; an occasion; seasonal flowering or fruitage: ส่งเงินงวดหนึ่ง to make a partial payment.

ง้วน ngoo-an[3] *adj.* absorbed in or about; engrossed completely, continuously or unceasingly; diligent; untiring.

ง้วน ngoo-an[5] *n.* savour; taste; relish; a specific flavour or quality: ง้วนดิน that element of fertility in the soil which produces sweetness in vegetation or fruit: ง้วนผึ้ง the yellow, sweet and fragrant pollen of flowers which bees gather into their hives.

งวย, งวยงง ngoo-ay *v.* to forget; to lose presence of mind; to be stunned or bewildered from surprise.

งอ ngaw *v.* to bend; to curve; to bow; *adj.* curved; hooked; bent; twisted: งอก่อ the state or condition of being curled up from cold or starvation: งอขด coiled up together (as snakes in a heap): งอเข่า to bend the knee: งอช้อน bent or curved upwards: งอแง incapable; clumsy; awkward: งอหงิก curly; waving.

ง้อ, ง้องอน ngaw[5] *v.* to try to conciliate; to endeavour to regain favour; to reconcile: ง้อเขา, ง้องอน to humble oneself or yield to another's wishes for the sake of reconciliation or to regain favour.

งอก, งอกเงย ngauk[3] *v.* to sprout; to bud forth; to grow; to send up shoots: งอกเงื่อม a river bank gradually being extended (as by the deposit of alluvium); a projecting or overhanging rocky promontory: ดินงอก new land formed by the deposit of alluvium: ถั่วงอก sprouted beans.

งอกแงก ngauk[3]-ngaak[3] *adj.* tottering; unstable; infirm; shaky.

ง่อง ngaung[3] *n.* a martingale.

ง่องแง่ง see กะย่องกะแย่ง

งอด (งู) ngaut[3] *n. Simotes cyclurus* (M. S. N. H. J. S. S. I, 2, p. 98): งอดแงด angry.

งอน ngaun *n.* the curved handle of a plough; a curved, bullock-cart tongue with an ornamented end: *adj.* bent; curved; gracefully curved forward (as an elephant's tusks); shy; pretending to be angry; cheeky; knavish:

งอนช้อย, งอนชด curved backwards (as the fingers of Siamese actresses): พูดงอน cunning or coquettish in speech.

ง่อนแง่น ngaun[3]-ngaan[3] *adj.* uncertain; infirm; threatening to fall out, or come out.

งอนหง่อ ngaun-ngau[4] *adj.* bent over; curled up (as when one is trying to keep warm).

งอบ ngaup[3] *n.* farmers' hats made of palm leaves, shaped like an inverted basin, with a close-fitting, inside crown made of thin bamboo strips plaited together.

งอม ngaum *v.* to be over-ripe; to be very tired; to be very old; to be greatly bruised: งอมแงม (indicating the superlative degree); very old; very troubled; very tired; as bad as can be; utterly bad (never used to indicate good fortune).

งอย ngau-ay *v.* to be located near the border; to be placed near the edge; to hang or be hanging (as from an edge or ledge).

ง่อย ngau-ay[3] *adj.* withered; motionless; palsied.

งะ nga[6] formerly used as a prefix consonant, *e. g.* งะงกงะงัน=งกงัน shaky; shivering; clumsy; stupid.

งักๆ ngak[6]-ngak[6] *adj.* the condition of shivering or shaking (as from cold or ague).

งั่งๆ ngang-ngang *adj.* a manner characterized by speed or urgency (as in sewing, writing, or running).

งั่ง ngang[3] *n.* an ore cast into various ancient and superstitious images. This ore was used by alchemists in their manipulations of base metals to produce precious metals: *adj.* stupid; unlearned.

งัด ngat[6] *v.* to pry open or up; to raise by putting power underneath; to force up; to raise by using a lever: งัดฝาเรือนเข้าไป to open the side of a house with levers and enter.

งัน ngan *v.* to fail to germinate (as stalks of rice or bulbs); to be compelled to stop or desist; to be silent from fright and nervousness; to fail to explode (as a fire-cracker).

งันงก ngan-ngok[6] *adj.* shaking; quivering (as from fear); shivering; trembling.

งับ ngap[6] *v.* to seize with the teeth; to close partly; to half-shut: งับกิน to seize food when thrown (as a dog snaps at food): งับงาบ to open the mouth repeatedly (as in yawning): งับประตู to close a door partly: งุบงับ secluded; secreted; concealed; underhanded.

งัว (วัว) ngoo-ah *n.* (irregular spelling) a bullock; an ox; a cow; a bull: งัว (ปลา) *Monacanthus curtorhynchus* (Dept. Agri. & Fisheries).

งั่ว ngoo-ah[3] *n.* a species of bird.

งั่วซัง (ต้น) ngoo-ah-sung *n. Capparis thorelii (Capparidaceae)* (cb. p. 84)·

งัวเงีย ngoo-ah-ngee-ah *v.* to be drowsy; to be stupefied; to be sleepy: เมางัวเงีย sleepy or torpid from drunkenness.

งั่วเลีย (ต้น) ngoo-ah-le-ah *n. Capparis flavicans (Capparidaceae)* (cb. p. 80).

งา ๑ ngah *n.* sesame, an East Indian herb containing oily seeds: งา (ปลา) *Engraulis setirostris (Engraulidae)* (Dept. Agri. & Fisheries): งาขาว (ต้น) *Sessamum indicum (Pedaliaceae)* (v. p. p. 73: Burk. p. 1994): งาตัด a sweetmeat made of sesame seeds boiled with rice-flour and sugar and cut into squares: งาไทร (ต้น) *Sideroxylon ferrugineum (Sapotaceae)* (Rec. p. 244: K.): งาลั่ว a sweetmeat made of sesame seeds and sugar boiled together and spread out into thin sheets: เต้าลั่ว the same when peanuts are used instead of sesame seeds: เมล็ดงา sesame seeds.

งา ๒ ngah *n.* ivory; the movable barbs in the opening of a fish-trap: งาช้าง an elephant's tusks; a species of banana or gourd growing in the shape of an elephant's tusk : งาแซง movable or flexible barbs or spikes placed in the necks of baskets, or openings of fish-traps : คำถามเป็นเงี่ยงงา a catch question.

ง่า ngah[3] v. to raise the arm (as when about to strike); to raise (as a sunshade); to force open (as the mouth of a dog): ง่าก้าม to pry open or separate the jaws of a crab : ง่ามีด to raise a knife in the attitude of striking.

ง้าง ngang[5] v. to haul up; to lift up; to open (as the blade of a penknife); to pull back (as the hammer of a gun); to pull away : ง้างกัน to be at variance; to offer an opposing opinion : ง้างงัด to pry apart with force : พูดง้าง to contradict.

ง่าเงย ngah[3]-ngur-ie adj. imposing; grand; magnificent; regal; royal.

งาน ngan n. work; function; duty; business; a surface measure equal to one fourth of a rai, or 100 square metres : งานบ่าวสาว nuptials : งานบี้ an annual festivity; งาน-เมือง a celebration by the inhabitants of a city (as the Ploughing or Swinging Ceremonies): งานราษฎร์ a celebration by citizens : งาน-สมโภช a dedicatory service, or celebration : งานหลวง a state function : นายงาน a manager; an overseer; a foreman.

ง่าน ngan[3] v. to be anxious to obtain; to have a lustful desire; to be inflamed with passion; to be agitated by anger or lust : ง่านใจ a disposition characterized by easy irritation or anger.

งาบ ๆ ngap[3]-ngap[3] v. to open the mouth repeatedly, closing it gradually : adj. gaping; yawning.

งาม, งามแงะ ngam, ngam-ngaa[6] adj. pretty; beautiful; graceful; charming : งาม-ขำ unattractive at first sight, but the more one looks, the more beautiful the object becomes : งามงอน pretty but coquettish : งามจริง very pretty; truly beautiful : งาม-ผาด attractive at first sight, but the more one

looks, the less beautiful the object seems : งามพิศ beautiful, yet not attractive at first sight, but the more one looks the more attractive the object seems : งามหน้า honoured by the good reputation, or notoriety of wife, children or servants.

ง่าม ngam[3] n. a prong; a fork of a tree or vine; something that has diverging parts; a bifurcation : ง่ามต่อ the forked iron end of a punting-pole for pushing boats : งุ่มง่าม dilatorily; slowly : ถ่อง่าม a punting-pole with a forked end : พูดสองง่าม ambiguous language : มดง่าม name of a species of ant.

งาย ngai n. morning; daylight : งายแก่ late in the day : เพลางาย south. provin. from sunrise until about 9 a.m.

ง่าย ngai[3] adj. easy : adv. easily : คน ใจง่าย an easily satisfied person; a complaisant person : มักง่าย heedless; careless; inconsiderate; reckless; negligent.

ง้าย (ต้น) ngai[5] n. Caesalpinia sappan (Leguminosae) (cb. p. 504), sappanwood (MCM. pp. 73, 440 : Dept. Agri. & Fisheries : Burk. p. 390), a small prickly tree. Its sap-wood is white; its heart-wood hard, becoming dark red. It is chiefly known as a dye-wood but is also used for cabinet-work.

ง้าว ngow[5] n. a long-handled, curved sword or halberd of Chinese origin : ง้าว (ต้น) the smooth silk cotton tree (Bombax) : ง้าว-ป่า (ต้น) Bombax kerrii (Malvaceae) (cb. p. 164 : V. P. p. 75).

งำ ngam v. to shelter; to enclose; to guard, govern, protect or provide for : ครอบงำ to keep under one's control : งำเมือง a provincial magistrate; a governor : พูดงุงำ to speak or talk indistinctly.

ง่ำ ngam[3] onomat. from a dog growling while eating.

ง้ำ ngam[5] adj. projecting; jutting out; protruding : หน้าง้ำ leaning forwards in excess of the normal position (as of a kite); a facial expression, indicating unwillingness or anger.

งว ngiew[5] *n.* a Chinese comedy: งิ้ว (ต้น) *Bombax malabaricum* (*Malvaceae*) (cb. p. 164: V. P. p. 75: Burk. p. 345), the red cotton tree (MCM. pp. 83, 218: Dept. Agri. & Fisheries); *Bombax heptaphyllum* (Chd. p. 477): งิ้วน้อย (ต้น) *Ceiba pentandra* (*Malvaceae*), (*Eriodendron anfractuosum*), kapok or tree-cotton (cb. p. 164: MCM. p. 423: Burk. p. 501): งิ้วป่า, งิ้วผา (ต้น) *Bombax kerrii* (*Malvaceae*) (cb. p. 164: V. P. p. 75); *Bombax insigne* (Dept. Agri. & Fisheries): งิ้วสาย, นุ่นทะเล (ต้น) *Ceiba pentandra* (*Malvaceae*) (V. P. p. 75: MCM. p. 423: Dept. Agri. & Fisheries: Burk. p. 501).

งีบ ngeep[3] *v.* to be half asleep; to be drowsy: หลับงีบหนึ่ง to take a short nap.

งึก ๆ ngeuk[6]-ngeuk[6] *adj.* indicating approval by nodding.

งืน see เงิน

งึม (ซึม) ngeum *adj.* dull; inactive; inattentive; listless; languid; heedless: งึมงำ *onomat.* from the sound of murmuring: งึมหงอย dull; lazy; benumbed; sleepy; drowsy.

งุนงง see งง

งุ่นง่าน ngoon[3]-ngan[3] *v.* to be irritated by anger; to manifest passion or rage; to become infuriated.

งุ่น (ต้น) ngoon[5] *n. Tetrameles nudiflora* (*Datiscaceae*) (cb. p. 781: V. P. p. 73: Dept. Agri. & Fisheries: Burk. p. 2144), a lofty tree found from India to Malaya. It stands leafless once a year. The timber is not durable and is used for making packing-cases and temporary structures: งุ่นผึ้งขาว (ต้น) *Claoxylon indicum* (*Euphorbiaceae*) (V. P. p. 74: K.: Burk p. 516): งุ่นสะบานงา (ต้น) *Canangium latifolium* (*Anonaceae*) (cb. p. 36: Burk. p. 421: K.), a deciduous tree of Burma, Indo-China, Siam and Malaya. The tree

reaches a height of 70 feet; the flowers are fragrant; the wood is white, soft and very perishable.

งุบ ngoop[6] *v.* to nod; to sit dozing; to nod sleepily; to bite; to seize with avidity (as fish taking a bait): งุบง่ว to nod; to fall asleep; to nod sleepily; to nod drowsily.

งุบงิบ ngoop[6]-ngip[6] *v.* to whisper; to speak indistinctly; to do in secrecy: *n.* privacy; concealment; retirement.

งุ้ม ngoom[5] *adj.* slightly bent downwards; curved downwards (as the beak of a parrot); crooked; hooked; inverted.

งุ่มง่าม ngoom[3]-ngam[3] *adj.* rude; ill-bred; awkward; slow; tottering.

งุย ngoo-ay *adj.* giddy; drowsy; listless; heedless.

งู ngoo *n.* a snake; a serpent; an adder; the naga. This is a general term used for all members of the snake family. Different kinds of snakes have their individual names to which งู is added as a prefix. These various names will therefore be found in their proper places with (งู) to indicate their classification and complete name. Thus งูคอแดง will be found as คอแดง (งู).

งูบ ngoop[3] *v.* to bow the head sleepily.

เง ngey[5] *v.* to raise the arm and hand as high as possible and strike with full strength.

เงก ngek[3] *adj.* being of the worst degree; being in the worst condition possible; being at the utmost point of endurance.

เงิน see เงิน

เงย (แหงน) ngur-ie *v.* to look up; to raise; to turn upwards: เงยคาง to raise the chin: เงยหน้า to raise the head or face: เงยเศียร to raise the head (used for royalty).

เงอะ, เงอะงะ nger[6] *adj.* silly; imbecile; awkward; clumsy; incapable; impertinent.

เงา　ngow　*n.* lustre; gleam; reflection; shadow; shade: เงาตัวในกระจก the image of one's self in the mirror: เงาไม้ in the shade or shadow of a tree: เงารูป a shadow or reflection of a figure or scene.

เง่า　ngow[3] *n.* the root of a tree; a bulb; a stump; origin: เง่าไง่ being stupid, dull, stolid or ignorant.

เง้า　ngow[5] *adj.* curved; crooked; distorted: โกรธเง้า having features distorted by anger: หน้าเง้า a face distorted by anger.

เง้างอด see กะเง้ากะงอด

เงาะ (พวก)　ngaw[6] *n.* Negrito, an aboriginal jungle race allied to negroid pygmies found in the Philippines, New Guinea and parts of Africa. They were probably among the first inhabitants of the Malay Peninsula, having once had a far more extended range, but now few in number and rapidly approaching extinction. They are to be found in Kedah and several other Malay States as well as in the mountains of Patani and Nakon Sri Tamarat, as far north as the province of Chaiya. The Negritos are small in stature, very dark, with flat, fleshy features, protuberant stomachs and fuzzy, closely-curled hair, hence the Siamese name, "hair resembling the rambutan". They are not combative nor given to intermarriage with other tribes, but live in small groups, in shelters made of leafy branches, "a simple, kindly folk, fond of laughter and flowers, song and dance." By nature hunters and fruit-gatherers, these people practice agriculture to some extent but still prefer the roving life of the forest and the more primitive method of food-getting, subsisting on what the jungle offers in the way of roots, fruit and wild animals: เงาะ (ต้น) the rambutan, a fruit tree found in the tropics, *Nephelium lappaceum (Sapindaceae)*. The fruit is yellow or crimson and edible (cb. p. 330: BURK. p. 1545: V. P. p. 76): *adj.* curly; curled; woolly-haired.

เงิน　ngern　*n.* silver; money; specie; currency: เงิน (ปลา) silver fish; a small carp of silver colour: เงินค้าง arrears: เงินเดือน salary; wages: เงินแดง, เงินปลอม a false coin; a counterfeit coin: เงินตรา minted currency; a silver coin: เงินทอง wealth: เงินที่ต้องเสียสำหรับผ่านทาง toll: เงินที่ลงทุน an investment: เงินที่ส่งให้ a remittance: เงินที่สามีต้องให้แก่ภรรยาตามซึ่งศาลจะกำหนดให้ alimony: เงินทุน capital: เงินน้ำห้ามน้ำหก indicating percentage or quantity of silver in a coin: เงินบาท a tical (a weight of 15 grams): เงินปลีก coins of small denomination; change; small money: เงินแผ่น a silver coin; silver leaf: เงินภาคหลวง royalties: เงินมัดจำ earnest money; a deposit made to clinch the bargain: เงินลดเมื่อใช้เงินสด discount for cash: เงินลิ่ม an ingot of silver: เงินส่วนแบ่ง dividends: เงินสิบลดชักหนึ่งสำหรับถวายพระตามสาสนา tithing: เงินเสียค่าประกันชีวิตรประกันภัย premium: เงินเอื้อง (ต้น) *Dendrobium draconis (Orchidaceae)* (V. P. p. 74: K.): เงินเหรียญ a flat coin; a dollar: นายเงิน an employer; a money-lender; a creditor: ยืมเงิน to borrow money.

เงย　ngee-ah[3] *v.* to lean to one side; to incline; to let down or lower: เงยลง to bend down; to lean towards: เงยหู to incline the ear; to give ear to; to listen solicitously; to listen; *syn.* เงยฟัง, เงยโสตร์.

เงี่ยง　ngee-ang[3] *n.* a barb; a backward projecting point on a sharp weapon: เงี่ยงชะนัก the barbs on a spear: เงี่ยงเบ็ด the barb on a fish-hook: เงี่ยงปลา the smooth, or serrated spine of the fins of fish: เงี่ยงปลากะเบน the spine on the tail of the ray: เงี่ยงลูกศร the barbs of an arrow: เงี่ยงสมอ the flukes of an anchor: มีเงี่ยง armed or provided with barbs, hooks or sharp points, slanting backward.

เงี่ยน　ngee-an[3] *v.* to desire; to thirst or long for (as for opium); to crave sexual pleasure.

เงียบ, เงียบเชียบ　ngee-ap³ *adj.* silent; oblivious; mute; secret; inactive : เงียบเหงา lonely; secluded : นอนเงียบ to sleep profoundly.

เงียว　ngee-ow⁵ *n.* serpents (in general); the Shans, a tribe living in northern Siam.

เงอ　ngur-ah⁵ *v.* to raise the hand in the attitude of striking.

เงือก　ngeu-ak³ *n.* a fabulous siren which inhabits the rivers or seas : เงือกปลา a mermaid; a fabulous siren, the upper part of whose body resembles a woman, and the lower part a fish : เงือก (นก) small pied hornbill, *Anthracoceros albirostris*; Malayan wreathed hornbill, *Rhytidoceros undulatus* (Gaird. N. H. J. S. S. IX, 1, p. 7).

เงื่อง, เงื่องหงอย　ngeu-ang³ *adj.* slow; sluggish; inactive; slothful.

เงื่อดงด　ngeu-at³-ngot⁶ *v.* to repress; to suppress; to stifle; to tarry; to stay behind; to abide : เงื่อดหยุด to refrain from (as when about to strike).

เงื่อดเงื้อ see เงื้อ

เงือน see เงิน

เงือน　ngeu-an³ *n.* the ends of a rope or string, when tied; the knotted extremities or ends : เงื่อนกะทก a slip-knot; a knot easy to loosen : เงื่อนเกิดขึ้นภายหลัง a condition resulting subsequently : เงื่อนไข an explanatory paragraph, verse or sentence : เงื่อนไขในสัญญา *legal* a conditional clause in the agreement : เงื่อนงำ *lit.* "concealed ends," *i. e.* secret or concealed from view or knowledge; an unseen knot, plot or scheme : เงื่อนที่เกิดเป็นตัวอย่าง a condition resulting in a precedent : เงื่อนที่เวลาบังคับไว้ a time-limit clause : เงื่อนตาย a hard or fast knot; *fig.* any problem difficult to solve; trickery; chicanery; stratagem : ซ่อนเงื่อน to hide the ends; to conceal one's aim, game or purpose : หัวเงื่อน the end of a thread or cord when rolled up into a ball.

เงื้อม　ngeu-am⁵ *n.* a projection; a lean-to; a rock or mass of earth that juts outward : เงื้อมเขา, เงื้อมดอย, เงื้อมผา high and overhanging rock : เงื้อมง่อน the projecting forward of rocks; the jutting outward of an overhanging rock : เงื้อมมือ within reach of the hand; within grasp of the hand; within arm's reach; the capacity of the hand; power : ตกเงื้อมมือสัตรู to fall into the hands, or power of the enemy.

แง ๆ　ngaa-ngaa *onomat.* from the sound of children crying fretfully.

แง่　ngaa³ *n.* scheme; policy; a sharp point or prominence; an angle; a corner; a cusp; stratagem; any artifice, craftiness, or cunning scheme : แง่งอน arrogancy; presumption; deception; strategy : แง่ทราย the name of an ancient gunboat with pointed prow : แง่หิน the sharp point or edge of a stone or rock : ทั้งแง่ทั้งงอน being deceptive, misleading, crafty or shrewd : หัวแง่ a point (as of projecting land); a corner.

แง่ง　ngaang³ *n.* the young sprouts of bulbous plants (as ginger): *onomat.* from the growling or snarling of dogs.

แง่น　ngaan³ *v.* to gnaw; to bite : ง่อนแง่น to totter; to vacillate; to be very loose and shaky.

แง้ม　ngaam⁵ *v.* to be ajar (as a door); to be slightly opened (as a half-blown flower): *n.* edge; margin; lip; rim; a corner : แง้มข้างบน slightly broadened or expanded above : แง้มข้างล่าง slightly spread out below.

แงะ　ngaa⁶ *v.* to pry open; to pick out; to extract : แงะ (ต้น) *Shorea obtusa* (*Dipterocarpaceae*) (Cb. p. 143 : V. P. p. 75 : Dept. Agri. & Fisheries : Burk. p. 2205), a much used timber tree, rather more durable than other species of *Shorea*.

แงะงาม (งาม)   ngaa[6]-ngam *adj.* pretty; beautiful; graceful; charming, *ex.* "อย่าเยาะ ว่า เงาะไม่งามแงะ."

โง   ngoh *v.* to turn up (as the face); to tilt; to lift up: *adj.* sloping; inclining; bending over: โงเง unsteady or dizzy, with swaying of the body.

โง่, โง่เง่า   ngoh[3] *adj.* stupid; ignorant; unlearned.

โงก   ngok[3] *v.* to nod; to be so sleepy that one nods.

โงกเงก   ngok[3]-ngek[3] *v.* to be very loose; to be able to be shaken: *adj.* vacillating; swinging; swaying.

โงง, โงงเงง   ngong *v.* to be giddy or to stagger (as when rising quickly); to reel; to feel dizzy; to be unstable.

โง่งๆ   ngong[3]-ngong[3] *adj.* too high; too heavy on one side; top-heavy.

โง้ง   ngong[5] *adj.* curved upwards; bent upwards; arched.

โงน, โงนเงน   ngon *adj.* swaying back and forth because of improper balance; tottering.

ไง้   ngai[5] *v.* to pry open; to raise with a lever; to wrench.

ไงซาน (ต้น)   ngai-san *n. Cassia garrettiana (Leguminosae)* (cb. p. 510: K.).

จ

จ   The eighth consonant of the Thai alphabet, a middle or second class letter of which there are nine, *viz.* ก, จ, ฎ, ด, ฏ, ต, บ, ป, อ. จ จาน or จ เจริญ is the designating name. จ is used extensively in Pali and Sanskrit words. จ has no English equivalent except where it is used as a final; then the sound is that of " t." In the romanization here given จ is transliterated " chj " to remind the reader that this letter has no English equivalent and that correct pronunciation contains the sounds of " ch " and " j."

จก   chjok[4] *v.* to snatch up (as a hawk); to dig with the hands (as in sand); to run the hand into a pocket or bag; to blaze or cut (as a tree or log); to mince (as meat): จก (ต้น) *Arenga saccharifera (Palmae)*, the sugar-palm, a native of Malaya but also found in Java. This palm is a very large, handsome tree, bearing pinnate leaves 25 to 30 feet long, glaucous beneath. The sap or toddy is rich in sugar which is extracted and collected in a manner similar to that practised with the coconut, etc. The fiber obtained from the leaf-sheaths is used in making brushes, etc.

In the Philippines this fiber is extensively used in making durable ropes and for thatch. (MCM. pp. 163, 361, 429, 516: BURK. p. 230).

จ๊ก   chjok[6] *onomat.* from the sound of clucking made by a hen, or night-bird.

จง   chjong *v.* (an auxilliary verb used to create the imperative mood of the verb) may it be; make it so; must; should: จงกระทำ to do (imperative form): จงใจ set (your) mind on a task: จงดี (you) must be good or well; (it) should be in order: จงได้ be sure to accomplish (as commanded): จง-ผลาญ to devastate, or to demolish with determination *imperative form:* จงรัก *imperative mood* to fix one's heart with determination on love and loyalty: จงรัก-ภักดี to be loyal; to be sincere in service: จงล้าง, จงผลาญ to destroy; to cause ruin; to annihilate with intention.

จงกรม   chjong-gkrom *S. v.* to walk or change one's position (as after a long time): *n.* a walk; a place for walking about; a covered walk; a portico; a cloister (S. E. D. p. 382).

จงกรมณ์ chjong-gkrom *S. n.* the act of
walking back and forth (for relief, or as a
change of position); walking up and down;
rotation (as of a wheel); the condition of
walking slowly or along a zigzag course
(S. E. D. p. 382).

จงกล chjong-gkon *n.* the name of one of
the lotus family; an iron stand in the shape
of a lotus flower (used for receiving wax
tapers in front of a Buddhist pulpit).

จงกลนี chjong-gkon-la[6]-nee *n.* the name of
one of the lotus family, the stem of which
bears multiple white flowers.

จงอร chjong-aun *Cam. v.* to point out; to
point to; to elucidate; to make intellectually
clear.

จงอาง (งู) chjong-ang *n.* the king cobra or
hamadryad, *Naja hannah* (H. S. N. H. J. S. S.
VI, 1, p. 59).

จด chjot[4] *v.* to make note of; to jot down;
to mark; to touch; to reach out to; to place
in juxtaposition: จดกัน to join, or make
continuous (as placing of floor tiles adjoining
each other): จดจ้อง, จด ๆ จ้อง ๆ to waver
mentally; to be uncertain whether to perform
a deed or not; to approach stealthily or with
caution: จดจำ to remember; to heed; to
memorize; to pay particular attention to:
จดชื่อ to sign one's name: จดทะเบียน to
register: จดบัญชี to place on a debit account: จดไว้ to record or inscribe; to make
a note of: จดหมาย a note, or letter; a
document: จดสำมะโนครัว to take a census:
จดหมายบันทึก a memorandum: จดหมายเหตุ
a newspaper.

จตุรงค์ see จตุร ๑

จตุ chja[4]-dtoo[4] *P. adj. prefix* four (chd.
p. 100): จตุกาลธาตุ a black remedy composed
of four ingredients, *viz.* ว่านน้ำ *Acorus
calamus (Araceae)* (MCM. pp. 173, 377: Burk.
p. 33), เจตมูล *Erythroxylum cuneatum*

(V. P. p. 85: Burk. p. 950), แคแกร, and พะนม-
สวรรค์: จตุทิพยคันธา a fragrance of superlative strength such as is characterized by the
fragrance of the four following flowers, *viz.*
ดอกพิกุล, ชะเอมเทศ, มะกล่ำเครือ, ขิงแครง: จตุปริสา
a nation; an organization or sect composed
of four divisions, *viz.* the governing body,
the judge, the clergy and the Brahmans or
astrologers. The four assemblies or classes
of Buddhist disciples, *viz.* ภิกษุ monks, ภิกษุณี
nuns, อุบาสก lay disciples, and อุบาสิกา female
devotees: จตุปัจจัย the four requisites or
necessities of a Buddhist priest, *viz.* raiment,
food, bedding, and medicine: จตุปาริสุทธิสีล
the four precepts of purity, *viz.* (1) restraint
according to the precepts; (2) restraint or
subjugation of the senses (as the eyes, ears,
the nose, the tongue, and the sense of touch);
(3) purity or propriety of conduct; and (4)
discernment in the proper use of the four
necessities of a Buddhist priest (which are
clothing, food, bedding and medicine) (chd. p.
100): จตุภูมิ, จตุรภูมิ the four future domains,
viz. (1) กามาวจร being for those who sojourn
in the realms of lustful desire; (2) รูปาวจร
for those who have become engrossed in
(beauty of) shape and form; (3) อรูปาวจร for
those who find delight in etherial or formless
substances (as sounds and odours); (4) โลกุตตร
for those who have passed beyond the allurements of the world: จตุลังคบาท *lit.* "the
four feet of an elephant," *i. e.* the four aides-
de-camp or body-guards attending a royal
elephant in time of war: จตุโลกบาล, จตุรม-
หาราช *lit.* "the four guardians of the world,"
i. e. four angels who rule respectively over
the East, South, West and North divisions
of the universe.

จตุร ๑, จตุรงค์ chja[4]-dtoo[4]-ra[6] *S. adj.* four
(S. E. D. p. 384): จตุรคุณ four-fold; four
times; being tied with four strings (as the
upper garment of a Buddhist priest): จตุรงค์
lit. "having four limbs or extremities," *i. e.*
an army composed of four division, *viz.* war

elephants, war chariots, cavalry, and infantry: จตุรงคกรีฑา playing at chess; a kind of chess played by four persons: จตุรงคพลาธิบัตย์ a supreme military commander: จตุรงคล a unit of measurement equal to four fingers of the hand (not including the thumb); four fingers broad; four inches (wide or long): จตุรทนต์ *lit.* "having four tusks," *i.e.* Indra's elephant, ช้างไอราพต. An elephant produced at the churning of the ocean and appropriated by the god Indra (H. C. D. p. 9): จตุรนต์ *lit.* "being bordered on all four sides," *i. e.* the earth; the world: จตุรพร, จตุรภัทร, จตุร-วรรค any four of the following auspicious objects of human desire, *viz.* longevity, know-ledge, nobility, virtue, wealth and Nirvana: จตุรพรรณ, จตุรวรรณ the four principal colours; a collection of four articles or things; the four castes, *viz.* (1) the sacerdotal and learned class, the members of which may be, but are not necessarily, priests; (2) the regal and warrior caste; (3) the trading and agricultural caste; and (4) the servile caste, whose duty it is to serve the other three (H. C. D. pp. 71, 336): จตุรพักตร์, จตุรานน *lit.* "four-faced", *i.e.* Brahma, the first member of the Hindu triad; the Supreme Spirit, manifested as the active creator of the universe (H. C. D. p. 56): จตุรพิธ, จตุรวิธ four-fold; of four sorts or kinds; in four ways: จตุรภาค the fourth part; one quarter: จตุรภุช, จตุรพาหุ *lit.* "four-armed," *i. e.* names for Vishnu and Ganesa; a quad-rangular figure: จตุรมหาราช the four great kings or guardians of the lowest of the six sensuous heavens: จตุรเมธ one who knows the incantations necessary, and has offered the four sacrifices, *viz.* (1) อัศวเมธ the horse sacrifice; (2) บุรุษเมธ the human sacrifice; (3) สรวเมธ the inanimate object sacrifice; and (4) ปิตฤเมธ the sacrifice of a father: จตุรยุค the four ages, or eras of the world; a long mundane period of years. The four eras or ages of the world comprise an aggregate of 4,320,000 years and constitute a maha-yuga: จตุรเลข having four lines on the forehead:

จตุรวิทย์, จตุรเวที being familiar with the four Vedas: จตุรวิธาหาร made up of four kinds of food, *viz.* (1) those which are to be eaten (masticated); (2) those which are to be en-joyed, eaten slowly, sucked or sipped; (3) those which are to be licked; and (4) those which are to be drunk or quaffed: จตุรัศร, จตุรัสส์ a square, four-cornered, quadrangular, or regular object.

จตุร ๒ chja^4-dtoo^4-ra^6 *P. S. adj.* swift; quick; dextrous; clever; ingenious; shrewd; charming; visible: จตุรค one going quickly (S. E. D. p. 386).

จตุสดมภ์ chja^4-dtoo^4-sa^4-dom *n. lit.* "the four pillars," *i. e.* four officials, ministers or departments of the government of Somdetch Pra Rama Tibaudee I, the first king of the Ayuthian dynasty founded in 1350 A. D. (w. pp. 59, 69), *viz.* (1) ขุนเมือง local governors and magistrates whose duty it was to further the welfare of the people, reduce crime and inflict punishment, when necessary, on the offenders; (2) ขุนวัง the official in charge of the royal household and palace; (3) ขุนคลัง the official in charge of the treasury, revenues and in-come of the kingdom; and (4) ขุนนา the official in charge of agriculture and providing of food for the capitol, commonly called เวียง, วัง, คลัง, นา.

จน chjon *v.* to be defeated; to be check-mated (as in chess); to be stalled: *adj.* poor; embarrassed; destitute; distressed: *conj.* until; till: คราวจนกันดาร a time of want or famine: จนกระทั่ง, จนถึง to such time as; until; till; up to the time when; up to the last: จนใจ at one's wits end; at the end of one's resources; baffled: จนชั้น even that; at least: จนได้ until accom-plished: จนแต้ม to have no opportunity to compete or surpass; to be balked; to be frustrated: จนมุม to be cornered; to be checkmated: จนสิ้น, จนที่สุด until the last; entirely.

จบ chjop⁴ v. to raise an article to the forehead as a sign of blessing on receipt of, or while bestowing alms; to end; to finish; to salute (as an elephant when raising his trunk in salutation): n. finality; a finale; termination; the end: จบกัน the end has come; "better stop": จบพระหัตถ์ to place the hands together palm to palm denoting sanction and blessings when giving alms (used only by royalty).

จปล chja⁴-bpa⁴-la⁶ P. S. adj. shaking; trembling; unsteady; wavering; fickle; inconstant; moving to and fro (S. E. D. p. 388).

จม chjom v. to sink; to be imbedded; to be buried (as a thorn in the flesh): จมกั้น to stab clear to the hilt: จมเงี่ยง to be imbedded deeper than the barbs (as a fish hook): จมดิน to be buried in earth or mud: จมน้ำตาย to kill by immersion; to drown.

จมร chja⁴-maun P. S. n. the yak, having a bushy tail which is employed as a chowry, or long brush for whisking off insects, mosquitoes, or flies. It is also employed as streamers for lances and halberds. and as decorations hanging from the prows of state barges, and from the heads of state horses and elephants. It is one of the insignia of royalty (S. E. D. p. 388): จามจุรี, จามรี, จมรี a female yak.

จมู chja⁴-moo P. S. n. an army, or a division of an army (S. E. D. p. 388): จมูบดี commander-in-chief.

จมูก, จระมูก chja⁴-mook⁴ n. the nose; a nozzle; a spout: จมูกวัว a pipe, or nozzle by which air or gas carries the flame into the crucible (as a blowpipe): รูจมูก the nostrils.

จร ๑ chjaun Cam. n. a look; a glance of the eye; a cast of countenance.

จร ๒ chjaun P. S. v. to go; to move; to wander about; to behave; to act (used as a suffix, as วนจร); to wander about in the forest; เขจร to move in an orbit (as the moon or earth): adj. movable; going; walking; wandering; unsteady; practising (S. E. D. p. 389): จรกลู่ to float, scattered promiscuously around: จรจรัล to roam over or through; to traverse at random; to roam hither and thither: จรจัด vagrant; having a wandering course; having no settled home or abode: จรคล to wander or roam over the land (as pilgrims in strange lands); to journey aimlessly: จรบน to diffuse (as dust); to disseminate in the air; to fly or float in the air: จรบาท, บทจร to use the feet in travelling; to go on foot: จรมัน to make stable or solid; to strengthen: จรลวง, จรล่วง to pass on; to pass out of sight; to go on beyond; to go too far: จรลาย to be dissolved (as in water); to disappear; to evaporate; to be dissipated: จรลี́ to walk spreading the arms and throwing the body listlessly about; to walk languidly, heedless of what is passing: จรลู่ to ramble along a path leisurely: จรหลีก to wander away; to pass or escape from others; to walk so as to evade others: จราจร the aggregate of all created things whether movable or immovable, locomotive or stationary, moving or fixed (as animals and plants) (S. E. D. p. 389).

จรก chja⁴-rok⁴ P. S. n. a wanderer; a wandering religious student; a spy; a kind of ascetic; name of a Muni physician. The serpent king, Sesha, who was the recipient of the Ayur-veda, once visited the earth, and finding it full of sickness, determined to become incarnate as the son of a Muni for alleviating disease. He was called Caraka because he had visited the earth as a kind of spy. He then composed a new book on medicine, based on older works of Agnivesa, and other pupils of Atreya; name of a lexicographer; name of a branch of the black Yajur-veda (S. E. D. p. 389).

จรณะ chja⁴-ra⁶-na⁶ P. S. n. a foot; a pillar; a support; the root (of a tree); a line of a stanza; a section; a subdivision; a school or branch of the Veda; motion; course; performance; observance; behaviour; conduct of life (S. E. D. p. 389): จรณกมล, จรณบัทม์, จรณาร-พินท์ *lit.* "lotus-foot," *i. e.* a beautiful foot: จรณครันถิ *lit.* "foot-joint," *i. e.* the ankle: จรณประสาร stretching the legs: จรณยุค both feet; two lines of a stanza: จรณโยธิน *lit.* "a foot fighter," *i. e.* a cock: จรโณปธาน a footrest; a footstool.

จรณาภรณ์ chja[4]-ra[6]-nah-paun *S. n.* ornaments for the feet.

จรณิ chja[4]-ra[6]-ni[6] *S. n.* a person; a man; a human being.

จรด chja[4]-rot[4] *v.* to be touching or joining at the edge or boundary; to be down on their marks (as contestants in a race); to place against a mark or line: จรดพระกรรไตรกรรบิด to prepare the scissors and razor for the tonsorial ceremony of a prince's children: จรด-พระนังคัล the ceremony of the first ploughing of the year.

จรทก, จรเทิญ chja[4]-ra[6]-tok[6] *v.* to be reduced to extreme misery and want.

จรรจก chjan-chjok[4] *S. n.* a speaker; a lecturer; one who repeats or emphasizes important points in his discourse (S. E. D. p. 389).

จรรจวน, จรรจา chjan-chjoo-an *S. v. lit.* "repeating over in thought," *i. e.* consideration; conversation; deliberation; discussion; the alternate recitation of a poem by two persons (S. E. D. p. 390).

จรรม chjam *P. S. n.* hide; skin; bark; parchment; shield (S. E. D. p. 390): จรรมกรณ์ working in skins or leather: จรรมการ a worker in leather; a shoemaker (offspring of a Condala woman by a fisherman, or of a Vaïdeha female by a Nishada, or of a Nishada woman): จรรมการก, จรรมศิลบ์ a shoemaker: จรรมการิณี a woman on the second day of her courses: จรรมการี a shoemaker's wife: จรรมกูป a leathern bottle: จรรมขัณฑ์ a piece of skin or leather: จรรม-จิตร a white form of leprosy: จรรมทณฑ์

lit. "a leather stick," *i. e.* a whip: จรรม-นาสิกา a rope or whip made of leather or hide; a leather thong: จรรมบาทุกา shoes, slippers or other footwear made of leather or untanned hides: จรรมพันธ์ a leather band or strap: จรรมพันธน์ pepper: จรรมมัย made of skin; leathern: จรรมรัตน์ a leathern lucky-bag: จรรมวาทย์ *lit.* "skin-instrument," *i. e.* a drum; a tabor: จรรมสาร *lit.* "skin-essence," *i. e.* lymph; serum.

จรรยา chjan-yah *P. S. n.* behaviour; conduct; due observance of all rites and customs; a religious mendicant's life; occupation; deportment; usage: *adj.* practicing; performing; engaging in (S. E. D. p. 390): มีจรรยาวาจาดี elegant in manner and fluent in speech.

จรรโลง chjan-long *v.* to prop up; to prevent from falling; to support; to keep from leaning; to sustain; to lead: จรรโลงโลกา to preserve or nourish mankind.

จรลํ่า chja[4]-ra[6]-lam[3] *v.* to loiter; to walk slowly; to be absent a long time.

จรลิ่ว chja[4]-ra[6]-liew[3] *v.* to float away (as clouds); to go to a great distance.

จรวจ chja[4]-roo-at[4] *v.* to examine; to inspect: *Cam. v.* to pour (as liquids); to splash water (against one another); to shoot up into the air (as a rocket).

จรวจไจร chja[4]-roo-at[4]-chja[4]-rai *v.* to inspect or oversee (as of workmen).

จรวดจรี chja[4]-roo-at[4]-chja[4]-ree *n.* the tip of a high spire.

จรอก chja[4]-rauk[4] *Cam.* a narrow passageway; a lane.

จระเข้ chjau-ra[6]-kay[3] *n.* a crocodile, *Crocodilus siamensis* (fresh water) and *C. porosus* (brackish water): ลายจระเข้ขบฟัน a zigzag or saw-tooth pattern of needlework resembling the arrangement of an alligator's teeth.

จระคลับ, จระคลุ้ม chja[4]-ra[6]-klap[6] *adj.* cloudy; dark; overcast; murky.

จระคล้าย   chja⁴-ra⁶-klai⁵ v. to approach in a very close manner; to pass by closely; to come in contact with, or to meet intimately.

จระจุ่ม   chja⁴-ra⁶-chjoom⁴ v. to cast off; to throw away; to burn.

จระทก, จระเทิน   chja⁴-ra⁶-tok⁶ v. to shudder; to tremble; to be dazed.

จระนำ   chja⁴-ra⁶-nam n. an archway, facade, or carved front, decorated by ช่อฟ้า and ใบระกา, the characteristic naga heads and serrated decorations found on Siamese Buddhist temples and on some royal palaces.

จระบาน   chja⁴-ra⁶-ban v. to attack; to fight.

จระมูก, จมูก   chja⁴-ra⁶-mook³ n. the nose.

จระลาด   chja⁴-ra⁶-lat³ n. a market; a bazaar.

จรัล   chja⁴-ran v. to walk; to advance; to move.

จรัส   chja⁴-rat⁴ adj. clear; bright; lustrous; shining.

จราญ   chja⁴-ran v. to extinguish (as a flame); to push down; to scatter; to destroy.

จราว   chja⁴-rao n. the sea-turtle, highly esteemed and eaten by the Siamese: adj. plenteous; abundant.

จริ   chja⁴-ri⁶ S. n. animal (S. E. D. p. 389).

จริก   chja⁴-rik⁶ v. to peck at; to tear into small pieces (as do birds).

จริง   chjing adj. genuine; true; not false; sincere: ความจริง truth; veracity: จริงจัง not playfully; sincere: แท้จริง truly; certainly; verily; surely.

จริต   chja⁴-rit⁴ P. S. n. course; motion (as of asterisms); adventures; acts; deeds; practices; behaviour: adj. gone; gone to; attained; going; moving; acting; doing (S. E. D.

p. 389): ดัดจริต to reform; to convert: ศาลาพยาบาลคนเสียจิตต an insane asylum: เสียจริต to become insane.

จริตร   chja⁴-rit⁴ S. n. custom; a law (as based on custom); habit; nature; disposition; adventure.

จริย, จริยา see จรรยา

จรี   chja⁴-ree n. a sword; a spear; a knife: จรีกาง to raise a sword or knife menacingly: จรีรำ to brandish a sword or spear; to dance the sword or spear dance.

จรุก   chja⁴-rook⁶ Cam. n. a pig; a hog; swine.

จรุง, จรูง   chja⁴-roong v. to entice or lure; to lead: จรุงกลิ่น odours that incite the desire to continue smelling: จรุงใจ to stir one's affections; to increase one's desires.

จรูญ   chja⁴-roon adj. prosperous; beautiful; gay; shining.

จรูส   chja⁴-root³ adj. high; tall.

จเร   chja⁴-ray P. n. a spy; an inspector; an investigator: adj. going; moving; roaming; walking around (chd. p. 100): จเรทัพ an army inspector: จเรแพทย์ a medical inspector: จเรการคมนาคม Inspector General of Communications.

จล   chjon P. S. adj. moving; trembling; shaking; unsteady; loose; fluctuating; disturbed (S. E. D. p. 391): จลกรรณ astron. the changeable hypothenuse (the true distance of a planet from the earth): จลจิตต์ fickleminded; capricious: จลทนต์ a loose tooth: จลนิเกต having a perishable abode: จลไจล to be in confusion; to oscillate actively; to vibrate gently: จลาจล being both movable and immovable; having means of locomotion and being stationary.

จลน   chja⁴-la⁶-na⁶ P. S. n. a foot; a deer; an antelope: adj. moving; movable; tremulous; shaking; moving about (on the feet);

wandering; roaming; turning off from (S. E. D. p. 391).

จลน์   chja⁴-la⁶-nee *P. S. n.* a swift antelope (chd. p. 98).

จลา   chja⁴-lah *n.* an offering (as of flowers or incense); a name for Indrani, wife of Indra, and mother of Jayanta and Jayanti, the goddess of Luck or Fortune, because she is said to be the most fortunate of females, "for her husband shall never die of old age". She has never been held in very high esteem as an Indian goddess (H. C. D. pp. 127, 128).

จวก   chjoo-ak⁴ *v.* to cut with a sword, knife or axe.

จิ๊วก   chjoo-ak⁶ *adj.* indicating the superlative degree for whiteness, *ex.* ขาวจิ๊วก pure white.

จวง (ต้น)   chjoo-ang *n.* a tree found in eastern and southern Asia, belonging to the genus *Cinna-momum sp.* (*Lauraceae*) (V. P. p. 85): จวงจันทน์ an incense containing sandalwood; sandalwood perfumes: จวงเจิม to anoint with scents or perfumes mixed with sandalwood oil.

จิ๊วง   chjoo-ang³ *v.* to reach down forcefully and extend the arms up after each motion (as boatmen paddling the royal barges); to reach down and dip up (with force): จิ๊วงจาบ insulting by use of offensive words; impudent; insolent: จิ๊วงพาย to paddle at full speed: จิ๊วงน้ำ to dip up water at arm's length: จิ๊วงมือ to grope with the hands under water.

จวด (ปลา)   chjoo-at⁴ *n.* salt water fish, *Johnius belengeri* (*Sciaenidae*) (Dept. Agri. & Fisheries): จวดหัวแหลม (ปลา) *Otolithes argenteus* (*Otolithidae*) (Dept. Agri. & Fisheries: Burk. p. 1613). This genus is most abundant in shallow coastal waters and estuaries wherever there is mud or muddy ground. These fish are insipid and watery, and without oil. For this reason they are usually salted or dried.

จวน ๑   chjoo-an *n.* the house and grounds of a governor or high official in the provinces: *adv.* very near; almost to hand; close by: จวนเข้ามา approaching near to the appointed time: จวนค่ำ nearing dusk: จวนเจียน, จวนแจ not far distant; drawing nigh; very nearly: จวนโจม to rush upon; to make an attack upon: จวนได้, เจียนได้ almost accomplished; nearly succeeding: จวนตัว cornered: จวนตาย, เจียนตาย almost dead: จวนเวลาอยู่แล้ว the time is near at hand; not far distant: รำจวน to think lovingly of some one; to desire.

จวน ๒   chjoo-an *P. S. n.* death; the act of passing away; dissolution; demise; disintegration (S. E. D. p. 403): จวนธรรม destined to sink in the series of re-births; destined to fall from any divine existence (so as to be re-born as a man).

จวบ   chjoo-ap⁴ *v.* to meet; to come together; to reach, or attain: จวบจวน almost meeting; coming nearly together: จวบพบ nearly finding, or almost meeting.

จอ   chjau *n.* the year of the dog, *viz.* the 11th. year of the cycle of the twelve beasts; the curtain for a magic lantern or cinema picture: จอหนัง the curtain for a shadow performance; a movie screen.

จ่อ   chjau⁴ *v.* to touch; to make continuous; to make almost touching: จ่อกันเข้า to adjust so as nearly to touch; to be arranged close together: จ่อเข้ามา to come near to: จ่อปาก to hold close to the mouth: จ่อไฟ to hold near to a fire: จ่อรอ to rivet one's attention on an object and await results: จ่อรู to put something (as a trap) at the mouth of a hole to catch the animal as it emerges: ใจจดใจจ่อ with concentration; with eager expectation.

จ้อ   chjau³ *adj.* continuous; continual; uninterrupted (used only in connection with speech or music): คนพูดจ้อ a babbler; a great talker; a chatter-box : จ้อแจ้ to be loquacious; to talk much; to babble; to warble.

จ้อ chjau² *Chin.* *v.* to sit; to be seated; *Siam.* a monkey; a word used to call a monkey : นั่งจ้อ to sit and imitate a monkey.

จอก (ต้น) chjauk⁴ *n.* *Pistia stratiotes* (*Araceae*) (V. P. p. 82), water-lettuce, a floating plant found throughout the tropics. Its growth is encouraged by the pig-farmers as they desire it for pig food. The Chinese eat the young leaves cooked (BURK. p. 1756 : MCM. p. 175); a cup; a chalice : จอกแก้ว a glass tumbler : จอกถม a niello cup : จอกบ้าน (นก) the Malay tree-sparrow, *Passer montanus malaccensis* (Deig. N. H. J. S. S. VIII, 3, p. 152) : จอกป่า (นก) the Pegu house-sparrow, *Passer flaveolus* (Deig. N. H. J. S. S. VIII, 3, p. 152) : จอกพ้า (นก) the Malay weaver-bird, *Ploceus atrigula infortunatus* (Deig. N. H. J. S. S. VIII, 3, p. 152) : จอกรอก brassy; audacious : จอกแหน *Lemna minor* duckweed.

จ้อกแจ้ก chjauk³-chjaak³ *adj.* speaking noisily.

จ้อก chjauk⁶ *v.* to be defeated (used only in connection with cock-fighting) : *onomat.* from the sound of clucking made by a hen, or that of gurgling water.

จอง chjaung *v.* to pre-empt land; to select and lay claim to; to indicate ownership; to indicate a desire for; to tie up; to bind (as by a loop of wire or string) : จองกฐิน to select a temple and indicate the intention of making Kathin offerings at that place : จองกรรม to devise evil against some one : จองคช a squad of fighting elephants placed between sections of the army in time of war : จองจำ to incarcerate; to put in irons or stocks; to fetter and imprison : จองถนน to expropriate land for a road; to pre-empt land for a road : จองเวร to meditate revenge; to keep hatred against another in one's heart : จองง่อง to wait despondently (as prisoners) : จับจอง

to stake a claim for a piece of land : นั่งจอง คร่อม sitting in a state of dejection : ใบจอง the initial legal title deed of any property : ปักไม้จองที่ไว้ to place stakes as a sign of intended ownership of a piece of ground.

จ้อง chjaung³ *v.* to look intently at; to crouch and aim (as with a gun); to wait and watch; to be in a condition of watchful waiting : *n.* a shade; an umbrella; a shady place : จ้อง (ต้น) *Hibiscus macrophyllus* (*Malvaceae*), a tall tree found from north-eastern India to Java. The bark gives rough ropes, like those given by *H. floccosus*, used by Burmese, Siamese and Malays (BURK. p. 1167 : cb. p. 158) : จดจ้อง to go with measured step : จ้องคอย to crouch in ambush (as a tiger); to hide in ambuscade : จ้องดู to peep intently (as through a hole).

จ่อง chjaung² *adj.* lonely; lonesome; despondent; uninteresting (as a fair or festival).

จองเปรียง chjaung-bpree-ang *n.* a Brahman lantern procession observed in the middle of the twelfth month as part of a religious ceremony.

จองหง่อง chjaung-ngaung⁴ *adj.* sitting despondently brooding over trouble.

จ้องหน่อง chjaung³-naung⁴ *n.* a spinet; a jew's-harp; a Javanese bamboo, musical instrument held between the lips, the tongue of which is made to vibrate by jerking a short string.

จองหอง chjaung-haung² *v.* to be conceited; to be vain; to be overproud or arrogant : *adj.* cheeky; impertinent; exhibiting a haughty behaviour.

จอแจ chjau-chjaa *adj.* confused; noisy; clamorous.

จ้อแจ้ chjau²-chjaa² *onomat.* from the sound of many voices.

จอด chjaut⁴ *v.* to stop; to remain for a time; to arrive; to land or moor a boat; to tie a boat to a buoy, or wharf; *colloq.* to be finished for; to come to the end of things: จอดเรือ to make a boat come up to a landing place: ที่จอด, ทุ่นจอด a berth, or mooring buoy for a ship or boat.

จ้อน chjaun[3] *n.* a squirrel: *adj.* small; slender; undeveloped (as of an infant, or a plant): จ้อนไป to grow thinner: เด็กที่ จ้อนนม a child which does not thrive for want of suitable milk: นุ่งผ้าจ้อน to wear the loin-cloth drawn up too high.

จอนจ่อ chjaun-chjau[4] *adj.* sad; silent; noiseless; in a meditative mood (as one in trouble).

จอนหู chjaun-hoo[2] *n.* a decoration resembling leaping flames (กะหนก), worn over the ears of actors; part of a fancy head-dress extending down in front of the ears.

จอบ chjaup[4] *v.* to be in hiding, or ambush: *n.* a hoe; a mattock: จอบจีน a heavy Chinese hoe or mattock: จอบมือ a small spade: จอบหงอน a pickaxe: จอบหัวหงอน a mattock with a long, curved head.

จอม chjaum *n.* the highest; the topmost; a title given to the concubines of the Second King: จอมกษัตริย์, จอมราช the first in a line of kings: จอมเขา the peak of a mountain: จอมไตร the supreme ruler of the three worlds, *viz.* heaven, earth and hell (referring either to the Buddha, or to Siva): จอม- ปราสาท the summit, tip or pinnacle of a spire or castle: จอมพล a field-marshal: เจ้าจอม ladies-in-waiting, who are taken by the King as concubines: เจ้าจอมมารดา one of the King's concubines who has given birth to a son or daughter.

จ่อม chjaum[4] *v.* to come to a landing place (as a boat); to come to a fatal, unexpected ending (as death or defeat); to expel by pressure; to kneel or crouch (used only in connection with elephants); to submerge; to sink; to dip (as an article of food in a sauce); to press down: *n.* a pickle or preserve made of small edible fishes.

จ่อมจ่าย chjaum[4]-chjai[4] *v.* to dispense or distribute a little at a time (as market-money or medicines).

จอมทอง (ต้น) chjaum-taung *n. Butea superba* (*Leguminosae*) (Burk. p. 384: V. P. p. 89); *B. frondosa* (Cb. p. 445), the flame-of-the-forest, a host plant for producing a high-grade lac, rich in colouring matter. The flowers are used in India to produce a yellow or orange-red dye.

จอมปลวก chjaum-bploo-ak[4] *n.* a mound formed by termites.

จอมปลอม chjaum-bplaum *adj.* inferior; imitated; spurious; resembling something genuine with intent to deceive or defraud.

จ้อมป้อม, จอมเป๊าะ chjaum[3]-bpaum[3] *adj.* having rounded, convex sides; with flanging sides.

จ้อย chjau-ay[3] *adj.* small; diminutive; tiny; little: กะจ้อยร่อย under-sized and under-weight.

จ๋อย chjau-ay[2] *adj.* dull; uninteresting; sad; lonely; despondent.

จะ chja[4] *v.* (an auxillary verb, denoting the future tense, or signifying intention) shall; will: *adj.* clear; distinct: จะใคร่ wanting; wishing; longing for: จะไป shall or will go: จะมา shall or will come: จะละทิ้ง will abandon or forsake; will omit; will reject.

จ้ะ chja[3] *adj.* an affirmative response (used to an inferior or among equals); yes; yes sir.

จ๊ะ chja[6] *adj.* unexpected; unforeseen; accidental; unpremeditated; casual; coincident.

จ๋ะ chja[2] used as a response to a call, meaning, "What have you to say, please?"

จะกรุน chja[4]-gkroon *adj.* black.

จะกลละ, จะกลาม, ตะกลาม chja[4]-gkla[4] *n.*
persons supposed to be possessed with evil
spirits and therefore able to eat ravenously
or indiscriminately.

จะกวด, ตะกวด chja[4]-gkoo-at[4] *n.* a common brown lizard found in gardens at all
elevations; a monitor, *Varanus nebulosus*
(Gaird. J. S. S. 1, 1, p. 40).

จะขาบ chja[4]-kap[4] *n.* the millipede, or
centipede; a lace flag having a centipede
design; a large clapper made of bamboo, hung
in fruit trees, with a rope attached so that it
may be pulled to drive off birds or bats.

จะเข้ chja[4]-key[3] *n.* a stringed musical instrument with a hollow body, larger, but
similar to a guitar. The performer sits on
the floor beside the instrument and vibrates
the strings with a pick.

จะเข็บ chja[4]-kep[4] *n.* a worm having feet
similar to those of the centipede.

จะไค (ต้น) chja[4]-kai *n. Cymbopogon citratus (Gramineae)* (V. P. p. 77: Burk. p. 724),
lemon grass, a grass of the Old World tropics,
formerly thought to be of the large genus
Andropogon. This grass has long been used
as flavouring for food. It is also used medicinally. As a flavouring, it is used with fish
and in sauces, and added to other aromatic
substances in spicing liquor. It is sometimes
taken as a substitute for tea by those whose
digestions are weak. This plant resembles
Citronella grass in general appearance, but is
distinct by the odour of the leaves and less
robust habit of growth. It gives a smaller
yield of oil, known as lemon-grass oil, which
however commands a higher price than *Citronella* oil. Lemon-grass oil is grown to a
small extent in Ceylon, but the chief supply
of the oil is obtained from southern India
(MCM. pp. 347, 399, 400, 401).

จะงอย chja[4]-ngaw-ie *n.* the extreme tip.

จะจะ chja[4]-chja[4] *adj.* not crowded together;

separated or arranged so as to be easily seen
or read; legible; lucid; distinct.

จะจ้า chja[4]-chjah[3] *onomat.* from the sound
of crying.

จะแจ้ง chja[4]-chjaang[3] *adj.* clear; lucid;
manifest; easily understood or read; obvious.

จะแจ่ม chja[4]-chjaam[4] *adj.* clear; bright;
distinct; free from opacity.

จะไจ้ chja[4]-chjai[3] *adv.* repeatedly; often;
continuously.

จะบิง, จับบิง chja[4]-bping[3] *n.* an ornamental gold or silver shield suspended from a
cord or chain fastened around the waist of a
small girl.

จะมั่ง (ต้น) chja[4]-mang[3] *n. Quisqualis
indica (Combretaceae)* (V. P. p. 77: Burk. p.
1860), "Rangoon creeper," a big woody climber
found throughout south-eastern Asia and
Malaysia. The flowers are pale pink to deep
crimson, growing in drooping clusters. They
are pleasantly scented (MCM. pp. 127, 130, 208).

จะละเม็ด (ปลา) chja[4]-la[6]-met[6] *n.* a kind
of sea fish, butter fish. There are three
species of this genus *Stromateus, viz. S.
cinereus, S. niger,* and *S. sinensis:* ไข่จะ-
ละเม็ด the eggs of the green turtle.

จะละหวั่น chja[4]-la[6]-wan[4] *v.* to be confused;
to be disconcerted; to be in disorder (as of a
retreating army); to be agitated and turbulent.

จัก chjak[4] *v.* to cleave; to split; to divide
lengthwise; to be serrated or notched: *adj.*
having serrations like those of the saw; a
part of the verb denoting the immediate
future tense, *ex.* ทำดีจักได้ดี: จักตอก to split
fresh bamboo into thin, pliable strips (as for
tying purposes): จักหยัก to be notched; to
produce serrations; to become toothed: รู้จัก
to become acquainted; to know.

จักก์ see จักร

จักขุ chjak[4]-koo[4] *P. n.* the eye; insight; perception; supernatural insight or knowledge (chd. p. 98): จักขุทวาร the passage for light to pass into the eye; the orbital opening: จักขุบอด blindness: จักขุประสาท the optic nerve; the retina: จักขุวิญญาณ knowledge which comes through vision: จักขุสัมผัส the consciousness of light coming into contact with the retina.

จักจั่น chjak[4]-chjan[4] *n.* insects commonly known as cicadas, belonging to the family *Cicadidae* of the order *Homoptera*.

จักจี้ chjak[4]-gka[4]-chjee[3] *v.* to tickle.

จักร, จักร์ chjak[4] *S. n.* the wheel (of a carriage, of the sun's chariot, or of Time); a potter's wheel; a discus, or sharp circular missile weapon (especially that of Vishnu); an oil-mill; a circle; an astronomical circle; a mystical circle or diagram; a cycle of years, or of seasons (S. E. D. p. 380): จักรกฤษณ์ Phra Narai, or Krishna riding or holding the "Chakra," a quoit-like weapon with sharp serrations which, in India, is the emblem of power of the king of angels: จักรจารี *lit.* "flying in a circle," *i. e.* a bird: จักรชีวิน *lit.* "living by his wheel," *i. e.* a potter: จักรธาร จักรธร, "a wheel-bearer"; a sovereign; an emperor; the governor of a province: จักรนาภิ the nave of a wheel: จักรนายก the leader of a troop: จักรบาท *lit.* "wheel-footed," *i. e.* a carriage; *lit.* "circular-footed," *i. e.* an elephant: จักรบาล the superintendent of a province; one who carries a discus; a circle; the horizon: จักรปาณิ, จักรปาณี, จักรหัสดิ์ *lit.* "discus-handed," "the one having the Chakra in his hand," *i. e.* Vishnu: จักรพรรติ, จักรเรศ *lit.* "rolling everywhere without obstruction," *i. e.* a ruler, the wheels of whose chariot roll everywhere without obstruction; emperor; sovereign of the world; ruler of a Cakra (a country described as extending from sea to sea); supreme; one holding the highest rank: จักรพราก, จักรวาก a mytho-logical bird or vulture said to make a wailing sound at night if one of the couple is separated from the other: จักรพานธพ *lit.* "friend of these mythical birds," which are supposed to couple only during the day time, *i. e.* the sun: จักรพาล, จักรวาล, จักรวาฬ a circle; a mass; a multitude; number; an assemblage; the name of a mythical range of mountains (encircling the orb of the earth and being the limit of light and darkness): จักรเภทินี, จักรเมทินี *lit.* "the separator of these mythical birds," *i. e.* night-time; darkness: จักรมุข *lit.* "having curved tusks," *i. e.* a hog: จักรยาน any wheeled vehicle; a bicycle; a tricycle: จักรราศี the orbits in which planets move around the sun: จักรวาท a mountain range; a circular mountainous boundary; a fabulous belt of mountains bounding the outermost regions of the seven seas and dividing the visible world from the regions of darkness (S. E. D. p. 380: H. C. D. p. 180): จักรวาต a whirlwind: จักรวาลธิ *lit.* "one having a curled tail," *i. e.* a dog: จักระจี้ see จักจี้: จักระจี้จักระเดียม see กระด๊กกระเดียม.

จักราการ chjak[4]-gkrah-gkan *n. lit.* "disc-shaped," *i. e.* the earth; a globe; a sphere.

จักราธิวาส chjak[4]-gkrah-ti[6]-wah-see[2] *n. lit.* "the abode of mythical birds," *i. e.* the orange tree.

จักรายุธ, จักราวุธ chjak[4]-gkrah-yoot[6] *n. lit.* "one whose weapon is the discus," *i. e.* Vishnu (S. E. D. p. 380).

จักรารธจักรวาล chjak[4]-gkrat[4]-ta[6]-chjak[4]-gkra[4]-wan *S. n.* a semi-circle; an arc of 180 degrees (S. E. D. p. 380).

จักรี chjak[4]-gkree *P. S. n. lit.* "one bearing a discus," *i. e.* Krishna; a sovereign of the world; a king; *lit.* "one driving in a carriage," *i. e.* Siva (S. E. D. p. 381).

จักเรศวร chjak[4]-gka[4]-ray-soo-an[2] *n. lit.* "lord of the discus," *i. e.* Vishnu; *lit.* "lord of the troops," *i. e.* Bhairava; Siva (H. C. D. p. 45).

จักษุ chjak[4]-soo[4] *P. S. n.* the eye (S. E. D.

p. 382): จักษุโคจร Coming within the range
of the eye: จักษุนิมิต fixed by (a measure
taken by) the eye: จักษุนิมิตต์ the eyes
as means, causes or organs of sight: จักษุ
นิโรธ an obstruction to the eyesight: จักษุ
บถ the range of sight: จักษุมุษ lit.
"robbing the sight," i. e. blinding the eyes:
จักษุวิษัย the range of sight; a visible object:
จักษุประสาท the optic nerve: ฝอยจักษุประสาท
the retina.

จักแหล่น chjak[4]-gka[4]-laan[4] adj. close (as
passing near something): adv. very near to;
nearly touching; narrowly escaping; almost:
จักแหล่นจะชนกัน a narrow escape from collision.

จัง chjang adv. (denoting the superlative
degree) most; very greatly; very surely;
truly; in the extreme slang: จังออน a
capacity measure equaling one fourth of a
tanan: หนาวจัง excessively cold.

จังกวด, จะกวด chjang-gkoo-at[4] n. an animal similar to the monitor but with a long
tail and spots along the body.

จังกอบ chjang-gkaup[4] v. to tie; to bind:
n. a tax; the port dues for an incoming ship;
provincial property tax: เก็บจังกอบ to collect provincial property tax.

จังกา chjang-gkah n. sheer-legs; a tripod:
ปืนจังกา a gun set on a tripod.

จังก้า chang-gkah[3] v. to be in position
ready for action; to interfere.

จังกูด chjang-gkoot[4] n. the long-handled
rudder used on boats of northern Siam.

จังโกฏก์ chjang-gkot[4] n. a casket (chd. p.
99).

จังงัง chjang-ngang adj. stupefied; dazed;
incapable of action from fright.

จังจรด chjang[3]-chjot[4] v. to stop; to remain;
to tarry; to lodge.

จังทาน see จัณฑาล

จังมัง chjang-mang n. the four main pieces
of wood used in strengthening the bottom of
baskets: adj. strong; durable.

จังหรีด chjang-reet[4] n. a cricket; the other
spelling จิ้งหรีด is preferable.

จังหวะ chjang-wa[4] n. a bar; an interval or
division in music; rhythm; final words of
lines that rhyme.

จังหวัด chjang-wat[4] n. a district; a parish;
a boundary: จ่าจังหวัด, ผู้ว่าราชการจังหวัด the
governor of a commune or district.

จังหัน chjang-han[2] n. rice or food (used for
Buddhist monks only); a wind-wheel; a
weathercock.

จัจจร, จัตวร, จัตวาร chjat[4]-chjaun P. n.
a place where two streets cross; a junction
of two or more roads or lines of traffic (S. E. D.
p. 386).

จัญไร chjan-rai adj. low; mean; accursed;
unlucky.

จัณฑ chjan-ta[6] P. S. adj. wrathful; passionate; harsh; cruel; fierce; savage; violent
(chd. p. 99); impetuous; hot; ardent with
passion; angry (S. E. D. p. 383): จัณฑประโทยต
name of the king of อุชเชนี in the third Veda
(H. C. D. p. 275): จัณฑเวค having an impetuous course or current (said of the sea, of
a battle, and of time): น้ำจัณฑ์ alcoholic
liquors (used by royalty).

จัณฑาล chjan-tan P. S. n. an outcast; a
man of the lowest and most despised of the
mixed tribes (having a Sudra father and a
Brahman mother) (S. E. D. p. 383).

จัด chjat[4] v. to prepare; to adjust: to arrange for: adj. severe; vehement; strong
(as of wind or sunlight); intense: จัดการ
to manage a business: จัดจ้าน fluent; bold;
skillful: จัดแจง to get ready; to fit up; to
prepare for (high officials do not approve of
this word): จัดสรร to provide; to select a

place for, or to make ready for : จัดใหม่ to revise ; to alter ; to make a new arrangement of : จัดหา to search for ; to provide for : ปากจัด sharp-tongued : ผู้จัดการ a business manager : จัดให้ to supply, equip, make ready, or arrange.

จัดจอง chjat⁴-chjaung *n.* a small boat.

จัตตาฬีส chjat⁴-dtah-lee-sa⁴ *P. adj.* forty (chd. p. 100).

จัตวร, จัตวาร chjat⁴-dta⁴-waun *P. S. n.* a quadrangular place ; a place in which many ways meet ; a cross-way ; a levelled spot of ground prepared for a sacrifice (S. E. D. p. 386).

จัตวา chjat⁴-dta⁴-wah *P. adj.* four ; fourth (chd. p. 100) : จัตวาศก the fourth year in the cycle of ten years of the lesser era : ไม้จัตวา the tone mark " ˆ " (as in จ๋า).

จัตุ chjat⁴-dtoo⁴ *P. adj. prefix* four or four-fold (chd. p. 100) : จัตุบาท four-footed animals ; quadrupeds.

จัตุร chjat⁴-dtoo⁴-ra⁶ *P. adj.* four (S. E. D. p. 384) : จตุราริยสัจจ์ the four certainties of life, *viz.* birth, old age, illness and death : จตุราบาย *lit.* "birth attended by the four plagues," *i. e.* hells, ghosts, evil beings, and four-footed beasts : จตุรมุขข์ having four fronts, sides or porticoes ; a tetrahedron.

จั่น chjan⁴ *n.* the blossom of the coconut or betel palm ; a snare or trap for birds ; a gold bracelet set with precious stones : จั่นดักปลา a kind of fish-trap : จั่นดักหนู a kind of rat-trap : จั่นมะพร้าว the covering sheath of the coconut flower : จั่นหมาก the covering sheath of the betel flower : เบี้ยจั่น a yellow cowry shell : เสาบันจั่น a mechanical crane.

จันกะพ้อ (ต้น) chjan-gka⁴-pau⁵ *n. Gynocardia odorata (Bixaceae)* (V. P. p. 88 : Burk. p. 1120), a large tree of north-eastern India which grows in dense rain-forests. In times past, its seeds produced part of the chaulmu-

gra oil used. Latterly the *Hydnocarpus kurzii* has replaced it for good reasons.

จันท์ see จันทร์

จันทบุรี chan-ta⁶-bu⁴-ree *n.* the most important district and town in the south-eastern coastal provinces : จันทิมา being shaped like the moon.

จันทน์ (ต้น) chjan *P. S. n. Sirium myrtifolium*, sandal, either the tree, wood or the unctuous preparation of the wood held in high estimation as perfume (S. E. D. p. 386) ; sandalwood ; *Pterocarpus santalinus (Leguminosae)*, red sandalwood, red sanders wood, caliatur wood, a tree found in the tropics of the Old and New Worlds. The wood has long furnished the Hindus with a coloured powder for caste-marks. It has medicinal properties and is also used for house-posts as termites do not attack it (MCM. p. 441 : Burk. p. 1832) : จันทน์คิรี, จันทนาจล a mountain covered with sandalwood trees, *i. e.* the Himalayas : จันทน์บุษบก cloves : จันทน์รส, จันทน์วารี, จันทน์สาร, จันทโนทก sandalwood oil : จันทน์เทศ (ต้น) *Myristica fragrans (Myristicaceae)* (V. P. p. 87 : Burk. p. 1524), the nutmeg tree, a moderate-sized or large tree, usually 40 to 50 feet high (sometimes 70 to 80 feet), native of the Moluccas, introduced into Ceylon about 1804. The nutmeg of shops is the hard, brown, ovoid kernel of the fruit. It is enclosed in the thin brittle shell, immediately surrounding which is the scarlet aril or mace in the form of a nut ; next to this is the large, thick, fleshy and juicy husk. The pale-amber fruit resembles a large apricot. When ripe, about 6 to 7 months from flowering, the husk splits open and discloses the glossy, dark-brown nut (seed) covered with the mace, as already stated. The fruit is then picked or the nuts are allowed to drop to the ground, when they are collected ; they are then separated from the mace, and both dried separately in the shade. Oil obtained from the seed is used in perfumery (MCM. pp. 339, 518).

จันทน์ chjan-ta[6]-nee *P. n. lit.* " one anointed with sandalwood oil," *i. e.* Siva (S. E. D. p. 386).

จันทโนทก chjan-ta[6]-noh-tok[6] *P. S. n.* sandalwood oil.

จันทร์, จันทร chjan *P. S. n.* the moon, either as a planet or a deity. The second day of the week, Monday. The eyes or circles of colour in the tail of a peacock; camphor; water: *adj.* glittering; shining (as gold); having the brilliancy or hue of light (said of gods and of water) (S. E. D. p. 386): จันทร์ (ต้น) *Ipomoea bona-nox (Convolvulaceae)*, the moon flower, a perennial climber with very large pure white flowers which open late in the evening and close early the next morning. The fleshy calyces are often used as a vegetable for curries, soups, etc. (MCM. p. 304: Burk. p. 1245): จันทรกษัย *lit.* " waning of the moon," *i. e.* a new moon: จันทรเกตุ name of a son of Lakshmana: จันทรคราส an eclipse of the moon: จันทรคุปต์ *lit.* " moon-protected," *i. e.* Chandra-gupta or Sandracottus, a famous emperor of India. He founded the Maurya dynasty of Magadha about the end of 321 B. C. His father was a prince of the royal house, his mother of low birth, and he was banished by the Nanda king. In the troubles following on Alexander's death, he collected troops, with which he fought successfully against the Macedonian garrison and became dominant in the north-west. He then turned upon Magadha, slew the last Nanda king, and became ruler of Magadha, Anga, Benares, and Kosala (Onah), ultimately extending his authority from the Arabian sea to the bay of Bengal (Antiq. of India p. 39). He established himself at Patali-putra (กรุงปาฏลิบุตร), the capital of the Nandas. He began to reign in 315 B. C. and reigned twenty-four years (H. C. D. p. 67): จันทรเคราะห์ an eclipse of the moon: จันทรโคลิกา the rays of the moon; moonlight:

จันทรชนก *lit.* " moon progenitor," *i. e.* the sea: จันทรทักษิณ offering anything bright (as gold) in sacrifice: จันทรทาร *lit.* " moon-wives," *i. e.* the twenty-seven lunar mansions (S. E. D. p. 386): จันทรนิภ *lit.* " moon-like," *i. e.* bright; handsome: จันทรบาท a moonbeam: จันทรบุตร *lit.* " moon-born," *i. e.* the planet Mercury: จันทรประภาพ splendid as the moon: จันทรประมาณ *lit.* " moon-measured," *i. e.* lunar; approximating the size of the moon: จันทรปราสาท, จันทรศาลา *lit.* " a moon palace," *i. e.* an apartment, a chamber or open area on the house-top: จันทรพิมพ์, จันทรมณฑล the moon-disc; the flattened appearance of the moon; the halo around the moon: จันทรภาคา the name of a river in the Punjab, now called the Chenab: จันทรภาส *lit.* " moon-brilliant," *i. e.* a sword: จันทรภูติ silver: จันทรมนัส one of the ten horses of the moon: จันทรมัส the moon; the Moon, considered as a Danava or giant who warred against the gods (H. C. D. p. 80): จันทรมาส a lunar month: จันทรมกุฏ, จันทรโมลี, จันทรเศขร *lit.* " moon-crested," *i. e.* Siva: จันทรเมาะห์ a dog: จันทรโยค a conjunction of the moon with any asterism: จันทรรัตน์ a pearl: จันทรวงศ์ the lunar race of kings, the second great line of royal dynasties, the progenitor of which was Soma (พระโสม) the Moon, child of the Rishi Atri (พระฤษีอัตริ), and father of Budha (Mercury). The latter married Ila (อิฬา), daughter of the solar king Ikshvaku (ท้าวอิกษวากุ), and by her had a son, Aila or Pururavas (ปุรูรพ); this last had a son by Urvasi (อุรวศี), named Ayus (อายุส), from whom came Nahusha (นหุษ), father of Yayati (ยยาติ); the latter had two sons, Puru (ปุรุ) and Yadu (ยทุ), from whom proceeded the two branches of the lunar line. In that of Yadu were born Krishna (กฤษณะ) and Bala-rama (พระพลราม); in that of Puru came Dushyanta (พระทุษยันต์), hero of the Sakuntala (ศกุนตลา) and father of the great Bharata (ภรต); ninth from Bharata came Kuru (กุรุ), and fourteenth from him Santanu (ศานตนุ), who had a son Vicitravirya (วิจิตรวีรยะ) and a step-son Vyasu (วยาสุ); the latter married the two widows of his half-brother, and by them had Dhritarashtra (ธฤตราษฎร์) and Pandu (ปาณฑุ), the wars of whose sons form the subject of the Maha-bharata (S. E. D. p. 386): จันทร-วรรณ of brilliant colour: จันทรสมภพ, จันทร-สุต, จันทรบุตร *lit.* "a son of the moon," *i. e.* the planet Mercury: จันทรานน *lit.* "moon-faced," *i. e.* Skanda, the god of War, or Karttikeya (H. C. D. p. 152): จันทราภา the rays of the moon; the glorious light of the moon: จันทรภาส an appearance in the sky like the moon; a false moon: จันทรารถ a half-moon; one who has adorned his forehead with a crescent mark: จันทราริ *lit.* "moon enemy," *i. e.* Rahu: จันทราโลก the name of a work on rhetoric by Jaya-deva: จันทรุปราคา, จันทโรปราค an eclipse of the moon: จันทโรทัย *lit.* "moon-rise," *i. e.* an open hall; name of a Pandava warrior.

จันทรา, จันทโร chjan-trah *prefix* moon, moon-like or moon deity.

จันทัน chjan-tan *n.* a rafter; the side beams of a roof: จันทันใหญ่ the principal rafters: จันทันพราง common or intermediate rafters.

จันทิร chjan-ti[6]-ra[6] *S. n.* the moon; an elephant (S. E. D. p. 386).

จันทิล chjan-tin *S. n.* a barber (S. E. D. p. 386).

จันลอง chjan-laung *Cam. n.* a stream; a creek.

จันเลา, จันเลาะ chjan-low *Cam. n.* a rivulet; a small watercourse.

จั่นหับ chjan[4]-hap[4] *n.* an animal snare which has a trap-door.

จั่นห้าว chjan[4]-how[3] *n.* a trap for large animals, so built that a hair-trigger fires a gun, or releases a spear which kills the victim.

จันอับ chjan-ap[4] *n.* a kind of Chinese cake made of many ingredients.

จับ chjap[4] *v.* to catch; to overtake; to take hold of; to adhere; to arrest: จับเขม่า to dress the hair or stray locks with a pomade of soot and oil: จับไข้ to suffer from malarial fever; to have chills and fever: จับกุม to arrest: จับกุมด้วยความพยาบาท a malicious arrest: จับจด half-hearted; insincere; of a "rolling stone" disposition: จับจอง to claim initial ownership of land; to settle on new land without a title; to acquire by taking (as a squatter): จับจองถือและปก-ครองโดยปรปักษ์ to usurp the control of land: จับจองที่ดิน to pre-empt land: จับจิตต์, จับใจ pleasing to the mind, or that which is captivating (as music, an address, or any experiment): จับเจ่า to stand still; to be miserable; to be dejected; to remain quietly: จับได้-คาที่ to catch in the very act; to arrest "red-handed": จับตา beautiful; attractive; fascinating: จับพลัดจับผลุ to occur or happen unintentionally; to grab at random (as from a grab-bag); to occur inadvertently: จับถือ to seize; to grip: จับทำ to begin a job: จับปลา to catch fish: จับมือถือแขน to be able to seize a thief in the act of crime: จับยาม to divine; to prognosticate by augury: จับระบำ an attitude assumed by Siamese actors; to dance alone with gestures or movements: จับไว้ to occupy; to hold: จับหลัก stationary; fixed; *fig.* exhibiting no change in position, or condition: จับหืด to suffer with an attack of asthma: ใบจับจองถือ a possessory title: ผู้จับจอง a squatter.

จับ ๆ chjap[6]-chjap[6] *onomat.* from the sound of masticating food, or smacking the lips.

จับกัง chjap[4]-gkang *Chin. n.* coolies; workmen; labourers (of the Chinese class).

จับจ่าย chjap[4]-chjai[4] *v.* to distribute; to dispense; to scatter; to purchase for distribution.

จับเจียว chjap[4]-chjee-oh[2] *Chin. n.* a small earthenware kettle.

จับฉ่าย chjap[4]-chjai[4] *Chin. n. lit.* "ten

different articles or pieces," *i. e.* an heterogenous collection of articles; things not arranged in sets or kinds (as dishes); a mixture of vegetables; a curry composed of ten varieties of vegetables.

จับเดิม　chjap[4]-derm *adv.* from the beginning; originally.

จับบิ่ง　chjap[4]-bping[3] *n.* a "fig-leaf" or medallion made of gold or silver worn by little girls; see จะบัง.

จับโป่ง　chjap[4]-bpong *n.* a disease characterized by pain in the joints; articular rheumatism.

จับหวย　chjap[4]-hoo-ay[2] *Chin. lit.* "mixed bits soup," *i. e.* a dish composed of many ingredients. This is probably the origin of the name chop-suey, a popular dish served at Chinese restaurants in Europe and America, consisting of a stew made of chicken or pork, noodles, vegetables, sesame seeds, etc.

จัมบก, จัมปก, จัมปา　chjam-bok[4] *n. Michelia champaca (Magnoliaceae)* (cb. p. 26 : v. p. p. 80 : burk. p. 1465), a tree of the moist forests of India; elsewhere it is commonly cultivated for its fragrant flowers. It is frequently planted in temple grounds. In Siam they are called จำปี, and when infused, supply a cosmetic used after bathing. They are put away with clothes, sprinkled on bridal beds, and used to scent hair-oils. The timber is very durable and is used in India for planking, furniture, house-building, etc. It yields serviceable building timber and good fuel. The heart-wood is dark purple when freshly cut, turning to brown (mcm. pp. 216, 518).

จัมป　chjam-bpa[4] *S. n.* Champa, the name of the founder of the city of Champa, a son of Prithu-laksha, a descendant of Yayati through his fourth son, Anu (h. c. d. p. 65).

จัมปา　chjam-bpah *S. n.* name of an ancient city in India, near Bhagalpur; the capital city of the country of Ange. It is also called

Malini, Champa-malini, or Champa-puri, from its being surrounded with champaka trees as with a garland, or wreath (h. c. d. p. 65 : s. e. d. p. 388): จัมปา (ต้น) see จัมบก.

จัมม, จรรม　chjam-ma[6] *P. n.* the hide of an animal; the bark of a tree; a shield. (s. e. d. p. 390).

จิ๋ว　chjoo-ah[4] *Chin.* a word of Chinese origin meaning to draw out, turn up or open (used in reference to cards in playing a card game): *n.* the triangular end of the roof; the gable end; a younger brother of a Buddhist monk.

จ่า　chjah[4] *v.* to tell; to address; to be fined (as while playing โยนหลุม): *n.* a protector; a leader; a dignitary among the king's pages; จ่ากลอง the chief drummer: จ่าโขลน a position of rank among the queen's ladies-in-waiting: จ่าจังหวัด, จ่าเมือง the Lieutenant Governor of a district: จ่าตรี Third Petty Officer (Navy): จ่าแตรยาว Trumpet Major: จ่าแตรสั้น Bugle Major: จ่าโท Second Petty Officer (Navy): จ่านายสิบ Sergeant Major: จ่านายสิบประจำกรมทหาร Regimental Sergeant Major: จ่านายสิบพลรบ (ประจำกองทัพ) Troop Sergeant Major: จ่านำทาง Pioneer Major: จ่าปี่ the chief flute, fife or oboe: จ่าฝูง the leader in a flock or herd of animals: จ่าศาล the Seal Keeper or Chancellor of a Court of Justice: จ่าหน้า to write a heading, title or caption; to address (as a letter): จ่าอศวบาท Farrier Major: จ่าเอก First Petty Officer (Navy): พันจ่า Warrant Officer (Navy): พันจ่าตรี Third Warrant Officer (Navy): พันจ่าโท Second Warrant Officer (Navy): พันจ่าเอก First Warrant Officer (Navy).

จ้า　chjah[3] *n.* crescendo (in music): *adj.* strong; vehement; increasing in volume; bright or deep (as of a colour): *onomat.* from the sound of crying with increasing vehemence: จ้า, จาน (ต้น) *Butea frondosa (Leguminosae)* see จอมทอง (ต้น): จ้าขาม (ต้น) *Albizzia lebbeck (Leguminosae)* (cb. p. 553 :

Burk. p. 86), "woman's tongue" of the West Indies; a large tree with fine foliage, native of tropical Asia and Africa, often planted for shade. The timber is good and there is a growing demand for it as a substitute for walnut: แดงจ้า bright red: แดดจ้า a very hot sun: เสียงจ้า a confusion of loud voices.

จ๋า   chjah[2] adj. used as a reply when one is called, as "yes, sir"; used after a name to indicate respect, or as a mark of politeness: จ๋ะจ๋า used as a salutation for, or by children.

จาก   chjak[4] v. to to be separated from: จาก (ต้น) Nipa fruticans (Palmae), the nipa palm, "water palm," a palm with a short prostrate, blanched trunk, on the ends of which arise pinnate leaves, 20 ft. and more in length. It grows in tidal mud from the mouths of the Ganges to Australia. In the Malay Peninsula it grows chiefly about estuaries around the coasts, for fresh water is necessary to its growth. Toddy sugar and spirit is obtained from the spadix. The leaves are employed for thatching houses (v. P. p. 81: MCM. pp. 165, 170, 175: Burk. p. 1557): จากกัน to be lost or separated from: จากกันไป to take leave of: จากข้อความมีความเห็นว่า to infer that: จากตับหนึ่ง a strip of attap: จากบ้าน away from home: พ้นจาก to escape; to be delivered from: พ้นจากอันตราย to be able to evade misfortune: มงจาก to cover with attap strips: ออกจากที่ to abdicate; to vacate an office.

จากพราก see จักรวาก, จักรพราก

จาค   chjak[4] P. n. liberality; benevolence; charity; self-sacrifice (Chd. p. 97): จาคศีล forsaking; resigning; abandoning; sacrificing; relinquishing; generous.

จาคี   chjah-kee P. n. one who has resigned (as an ascetic who abandons worldly objects); one who is liberal or enjoys giving alms (S. E. D. p. 456).

จาง   chjang adj. tasteless; insipid; pinched; pale (as the face of one in suffering); too diluted: จางจิตต์ not ingenious; rather stupid: จางหลวง (ต้น) Clematis subpeltata (Ranunculaceae) (Cb. p. 16); C. smilacifolia (V. P. p. 83), a climber having small white flowers. The leaves are ovate with seven nerves (Burk. p. 580: MCM. p. 140): จืดจาง to become uninteresting (as a game); to become tasteless or unsavoury (as food): สีจาง, ซีดจาง faded: ใสจาง greatly diluted; very clear: หมึกจาง ink that is colourless or faded.

จ้าง ๑   chjang[3] Chin. n. the name of a kind of cake made of glutinous rice, rolled in bamboo leaves and boiled.

จ้าง ๒   chjang[3] v. to hire: ค่าจ้าง wages; salary: จ้างทำของ to hire some one to make an article: จ้างแรงงาน to hire the services of some one: นายจ้าง an employer: รับจ้าง to work under employment: เรือจ้าง a boat for hire; a ferry-boat: ลูกจ้าง an hireling; a workman; an employé: สินจ้าง wages; a bribe.

จางวาง   chjang-wang n. a deputy; the head official of a palace, or one in charge of some governmental work; an officer of the Royal Pages' Department.

จามฺพจน์   chjah-doo[4]-pot[6] S. n. words of commendation, approbation, or praise; flattery (S. E. D. p. 392).

จาณักย์   chjah-nak[6] S. n. Chanakya, a celebrated Brahman minister of state who took the leading part in the destruction of the Nandas, or the Magadha dynasty of kings who reigned at Patali-putre (ปาฏ-ลิบุตร์), and in the elevation of king Chandra-gupta (พระเจ้าจันทรคุปต์) to the throne about 315 B. C. He was a great master of finesse and artifice, and has been called the Machiavelli of India. A work upon morals and policy called Chanakya Sutra is ascribed to him (H. C. D. p. 66 : S. E. D. p. 392).

จาด   chjat[4] *n.* a white foundation material used in mixing paint :   จาดตะกั่ว white lead.

จาตุ   chjah-dtoo[4] *P.* a word derived from จตุ : *adj.* four ; fourfold (chd. p. 100) :   จาตุกรณีย์ the four governmental duties, *viz.* (1) to give judgement in the courts ; (2) to forward the interests of the citizens ; (3) to increase internal revenues ; and (4) to protect or take charge of defensive measures for the capital or country : จาตุทฺทสี the fourteenth day of the waxing or waning moon ; belonging to the fourteenth day :   จาตุทิศ the four points of the compass ; the four cardinal points.

จาตุมมหาราช see จตุโลกบาล

จาตุร ๑   chjah-dtoo[4]-ra[6] *P. S.* a word derived from จตุ : *n.* four ; fourfold (S. E. D. p. 392) : จาตุรงค์ composed of four parts or having four chiefs or guardians ; consisting of four divisions : จาตุรงคสันนิบาต the occasion on which the members of the Buddhist brotherhood met for the first time to recite the "Patimokah" (ปาติโมกข์). This meeting was distinguished in the following four ways, *viz.* (1) the day was that of the full-moon of Magha (มาฆ), the month of the zodiacal sign of Capricornus, corresponding to January and February (S. E. D. p. 805) ; (2) the 1,250 monks who were assembled all came together voluntarily without having received any previous notice ; (3) all these monks were from the rank of those whom the Buddha had admitted into the brotherhood by pronouncing the formula (invitation) "Come here, Oh ye Bikkhus" ; and (4) the monks were those who were freed from the bondage of the flesh, *i. e.* birth, old age, sickness, and death.

จาตุร ๒   chjah-dtoo[4]-ra[6] *P. S. adj.* clever ; cunning ; witty ; shrewd ; flattering (S. E. D. p. 392).

จาตุรนต์, จาตุรันต์   chjah-dtoo[4]-ron *P. n.*

lord of the earth, or of the four points (of the compass) :   จาตุรนตรัศมี *lit.* "one shedding light or glory to the four corners of the earth," *i. e.* the sun (chd. p. 101).

จาน   chjan *v.* to mix with water ; to adulterate with water : *n.* a dish ; a plate : ข้าวจานน้ำ rice mixed with water :   จานเชิง a dish or tray placed on a raised standard : จานรอง a saucer.

จานเจือ   chjan-chjur-ah *v.* to render assistance (as by sharing financial resources) ; to support a cause (as by a union of effort) ; to help ; to support ; to uphold ; to prop or sustain (as in time of dire distress).

จ้าน   chjan[3] *adv.* (used to indicate the superlative degree) very ; exceedingly ; excessively : ขันจ้าน most amusing :   พูดจัดจ้าน very fluent or impressive (as a speaker).

จาบ   chjap[4] *v.* to plunder ; to rob ; to steal : จาบจ้วง to offend by improper speech ; to overstep by word or deed ; to snatch stealthily.

จาบัล, จาบัลย์, จาปล   chjah-ban *S. n.* agitation ; unsteadiness ; fickleness ; swiftness ; mobility ; flurry (S. E. D. p. 393).

จาป ๑   chjah-bpa[4] *P. S. n.* a bow ; an arc ; a rainbow ; a quiver (for arrows) ; a crossbow : จาปคุณ bow strings :   จาปธร one holding a bow ; one being bow-armed :   จาปลตา the flexible portion of a bow ; the body of a bow :   จาปเวท the science of archery : จาปาจารย์ an instrument used in archery (S. E. D. p. 393).

จาป ๒   chjah-bpa[4] or chjap[4] *n.* the cub of wild animals (as of tigers or bears).

จาม   chjam *v.* to slash with a large knife ; to sneeze : *n.* the Chams, an ancient people of Anam. They were of Hindu civilization and in early times spread over most of Anam. Many monuments testify to their greatness and to their wide distribution. Encroachments by the Anamese drove them southward into southern Anam and eastern Cochin-China. Their capitol was Champa, the "Cyambo" of Marco Polo who visited it in 1280. According to early Chinese records they were a rich and prosperous people and rivalled Angkor in splendour.

จามร   chjah-maun *P. S. n.* a whip or tuft of horse hairs fastened at one end to a handle (used as a mosquito switch); a chowrie; a plume; tufts of horses' tail hairs, fastened to each side of elephants' or horses' heads (S. E. D. p. 393); a state-processional, leaf-shaped sun-protector, of an intermediate size, with embroidered body placed perpendicularly on a long staff, and carried as an insignia of rank.

จามร ๑   chjah-ma[6]-ree *n.* chamari or chowries made of the tail of the (จมร) chamara (yak *Bos grunniens*), used as fly-flaps and reckoned as one of the insignia of royalty. They are also employed as a sort of streamer for lances and halberds, and are tied to both sides of the head of state horses and elephants. Since they are considered such beautiful objects and are so greatly esteemed, a legend has been fabricated in India to the effect that the yak cow is so proud of her tail that if it gets entangled in anything, she would rather await death than injure it (Ger. p. 119). These chowries are frequently hung over temples or other holy places to keep away evil spirits and are used for the same purpose at funerals. They are also used to brush flies away. The yak is docile enough with its owner, but sometimes takes a violent dislike to a European and will assume the offensive. It has the head of a cow, the tail of a horse, and the grunt of a pig. Its meat and milk are food and drink and its dung a fuel. It is a beast of burden, a sometimes spirited charger, and a household companion.

จามร ๒, ก้าม กราม, จามจุรี (ต้น)   chjah-ma[6]-ree *n. Enterolobium saman (Leguminosae)* (Cb. p. 561 : Burk. p. 927), the rain tree, a shade tree native of northern South America, but widely dispersed throughout the tropics

since the middle of the last century. In central and northern Siam this tree is frequently used as a host for the lac insect; *Albizzia lebbeck* (Cb. p. 553 : V. P. p. 89 : Burk. p. 86), East Indian walnut, a large tree with fine foliage, a native of tropical Asia and Africa, often planted for shade. It has excellent brown timber which does not readily warp (McM. pp. 206, 417, 446).

จามีกร   chjah-mee-gkaun *P. S. n.* gold; utensils of gold; vessels of gold (S. E. D. p. 293).

จามีกราจล   chjah-mee-gka[4]-rah-chjon *P. S. n. lit.* "the golden mountain," *i. e.* Meru, a fabulous mountain in the navel or centre of the earth, on which is situated Swarga, the heaven of Indra, containing the cities of the gods and the habitations of celestial spirits. It is also called Su-meru (H. C. D. p. 208).

จ่าย   chjai[4] *v.* to distribute; to disperse (as money for supplies before making a journey); to scatter; to divide; to make purchases: จ่ายเกิน to overdraw an account: จ่ายของ to give out goods from a godown: จ่ายคน to send people out (to labour on some task): จ่ายเงินเดือน to pay salaries or wages: จ่าย-เงินทดรอง, จ่ายเงินล่วงหน้า to make an advance payment of money: จ่ายตลาด to do daily marketing: จ่ายสินค้า to sell or dispose of merchandise: วันจ่าย the day before a fete (as New Year) set apart for buying needful supplies.

จาร ๑   chjan *P. S. n.* a spy; a bond; a fetter; a prison; a course (as of asterisms); an official of a secret police corps (S. E. D. p. 393): จารบถ a cross-way; an intersecting roadway or path: จารบุรุษ a spy: จารภัฏ a (valorous) soldier: จารวายุ a summer wind; a hot weather breeze: จาราธิการ a spy's office, or duty.

จาร ๒   chjan *Cam. v.* to write with an iron stylus (as on palm leaves): เหล็กจาร an iron point, or stylus for writing purposes,

จ่ารง   chjah[4]-rong *n.* a cannon mounted on an iron fork (used in ancient times).

จารณ   chjah-ra[6]-na[6] *S. n.* a wandering actor or singer; a celestial singer (S. E. D. p. 393); panegyrists of the gods (H. C. D. p. 71); a troop of wandering theatricals or musicians: จารณทาร an actress; a cabaret dancer; the wives of members of a troop of travelling theatricals (dancers).

จาระไน   chjah-ra[6]-nai *v.* to explain thoroughly or completely; to elucidate.

จาริก, จาริก ๑   chjah-rik[6] *P. S. n.* one who goes from place to place; a wayfaring man; a pilgrim (chd. p. 99).

จาริตร, จารีตร   chjah-rit[6] *S. n.* conduct; condition; ceremony; customs; practices; usages; manners: *adj.* good conduct, character, or reputation (S. E. D. p. 393): จาริตรประเพณี ท้องถิ่น local customs.

จารี   chjah-ree *S. n.* a trap; a snare: a net (for catching birds): *adj.* walking or wandering about; moving; roaming; acting; proceeding; practising (S. E. D. p. 393).

จารึก   chjah-reuk[6] *v.* to engrave; to inscribe; to impress deeply; to infix: จารึก- ไว้ที่แผ่นศิลา to inscribe; to carve on a tablet of stone.

จารุ   chjah-roo[6] *P. S. n.* gold: *adj.* attractive; pretty; esteemed; beloved; elegant; agreeable (S. E. D. p. 393): จารุกรรณ having handsome or well-formed ears: จารุจุณ gold-dust: จารุทรรศน์ good-looking: จารุ ทรรศนา a comely woman: จารุเนตร having pretty eyes: จารุพักตร์, จารุมุข having a beautiful face: จารุรพ having a sweet, melodious voice: จารุโลจน์ an antelope; "beautiful-eyed": จารุโลจนา a fine-eyed woman: จารุวาที one with a melodious voice: จารุเวศ a well-dressed person (in the latest style): จารุศิลา *lit.* "a beautiful stone," *i. e.* a jewel: จารุสาร *lit.* "essence of that which is lovely," *i. e.* gold.

จ้าละหวั่น   chjah[3]-la[6]-wan[4] *n.* an agitation; a public commotion or disturbance: *adj.* conglomerate; heterogeneous (as people in a mob).

จาว   chjow *n.* pulp or pith found in fruit: *adj.* far separated; distant; remote: จาว- มะพร้าว a soft, spongy, pithy, growth about the size of an orange, sometimes found in coconuts. This growth is the normally expanding, germinating embryo of the coconut, and is the absorbent and digester of the stored food in the nut for the use of the growing palm.

จำ   chjam *v.* to remember; to recollect; to be able to identify; to imprison; to tie; to bind; to observe a fast-day, or Lent; to compel; to force: จำกว่า to give in increasing quantities: จำคุก to imprison: จำจอง to incarcerate; to bind with chains or rope: จำใจ to do against the will, or inclination; to do of necessity: จำใช่ to chain; to fetter: จำทำ, จำต้องทำ to compel; to force: จำทวย to be stationed in a crowd or company: จำได้ดี having a good memory; able to memorize well: จำตาย sentenced to death; doomed: จำนำ to pawn; to mortgage: จำลอง to make a copy; to duplicate: จำทูล to carry a verbal message for delivery to another; to bear a royal message verbally: จำบ่ม unripe fruit which must be ripened under cover of leaves: จำเป็น it cannot be avoided or evaded; it is imperative: จำไป must go: จำปุน a bush found in the southern parts of Siam, bearing white fragrant flowers: จำพรรษา, จำวรรษา to remain in a Buddhist temple during the rainy season: จำห้าประการ to fasten with five chains, *viz.* one around the neck, and one around each wrist and each ankle: จำแล่น to sail a boat: จำวัด to sleep in a Buddhist temple enclosure (used only for Buddhist monks): จำไว้ to remember; to memorize: จำศีล to remain in Buddhist temples and observe the commandments or precepts: จำศีลกินทาน

to observe religious rites after receiving alms on sacred days: จำหน้าได้ to be able to recognize another: มัดจำ to mortgage; to pawn.

จ้ำ chjam[3] v. to pierce; to puncture; to act repeatedly and quickly; to paddle or row with quick short strokes: พูดจ้ำ to converse rapidly or freely.

จำกัด chjam-gkat[4] v. to circumscribe; to limit or be limited; to confine; to restrict; to have none to spare: พูดจำกัดจำเขี่ย to speak with prudence, circumspection, or discretion.

จำงาย chjam-ngai n. late in the day; afternoon: Cam. adj. distant; far separated.

จ้ำจี้ chjam[3]-chjee[3] n. a game played to the accompaniment of a nursery rhyme: adv. repeatedly; teasingly.

จำเจ chjam-chjay adv. often; repeatedly.

จำเดิม chjam-derm adv. from the beginning; from the start.

จำทับ chjam-tap[6] v. to make fall on top of with force (as bricks or stones hurled from an elevation); to cause to fall; to pounce down upon (as a tiger).

จำเทิด chjam-tert[3] v. to grow up tall; to spring up high; to make a high jump; to vault over.

จำแทง chjam-taang v. to make stand up; to prop up; to sprout, grow, or germinate (as from a bulbous root).

จำนง chjam-nong v. to desire; to determine; to will, or hope to do.

จำนน chjam-non v. to be beaten in a fight; to be vanquished; to be cornered (as in chess).

จำนรรจา chjam-nan-chjah S. v. to converse with a repetition of words; to discourse; to make conversation; to chat (S. E. D. p. 394); to speak; to say.

จำนวน chjam-noo-an n. the number or quantity of anything; the total amount.

จำนอง chjam-naung v. to mortgage; to clinch an agreement by the payment of money: จำนองที่ดิน to mortgage land.

จำนับ chjam-nap[6] v. to catch; to overtake; to take hold of; to stick to; to arrest.

จำนำ ๑ chjam-nam v. to pawn; to pledge; to give as security; to mortgage: จำนำหลุด to forfeit the ownership of a pawned article by default of payment: เจ้าจำนำ a good customer.

จำนำ ๒ chjam-nam Cam. v. to guarantee; to give as security.

จำเนียม chjam-nee-am v. to be on one's guard; to be ready for the future; to be circumspect.

จำเนียร chjam-nee-an adj. long ago; formerly (as in olden times): จำเนียรมาช้านาน after a very long time; a long time ago: จำเนียรภาค a period of time or years long past.

จำแนก chjam-naak[3] v. to distribute; to divide; to separate into portions; to segregate.

จำโนทย์ chjam-not[3] v. to accuse; to prosecute; to admonish.

จำบัง chjam-bang v. to hide; to secrete one's self; to be under shelter.

จำแบ chjam-baa v. to be spread out: n. dressed, salted, and sun-dried fish.

จำปาดะ chjam-bpah-da[4] n. a kind of jackfruit with thick, sweet, yellowish-red meat.

จำบี (ต้น) chjam-bpee n. Michelia champaca (Magnoliaceae) (V. P. p. 81: BURK. p. 1465), champaka or champa, a large, quick-growing tree found in eastern and south-eastern Asia. It has long leaves and scented, creamy-white flowers. It yields serviceable building timber and good fuel. The heart-wood is dark purple when freshly cut, turning to brown (MCM. pp.

216, 518); *M. longifolia* (cb. p. 27); *M. manipurensis* (cb. p. 27).

จำบู้, คำไทย, คำแสด (ต้น)　chjam-bpoo³ *n.* *Bixa orellana (Bixaceae)* (cb. p. 93), anatto, a large, quick-growing shrub or small tree with cordate leaves, native of tropical America and brought to southern Asia in early times. It thrives from sea-level to about 3000 ft. in a moist climate, and prefers a deep, loamy soil. At the end of the branches it bears large clusters of brown or dark-crimson, capsular, ovoid, or round fruits, covered with fleshy spines. These contain a number of small seeds, the bright crimson covering of which affords the anatto dye of commerce. The fruits are collected when nearly ripe, and as the shells dry they burst open and disperse the seeds, which are then either pressed and made into "anatto paste," or merely dried with their covering, when they are marketed as "anatto seed" (McM. p. 436). The leaves are medicinal. The wood is useless. It is said the bark produces a fairly good fibre (Burk. p. 330).

จำปูน　chjam-bpoon *n.* the name of a flowering tree.

จำพวก　chjam-poo-ak³ *n.* a congregation; an assembly; a company; a group; a society; a species; a genus.

จำเพาะ　chjam-pau⁶ *adv.* especially for; barely enough; only; just enough; confidentially (as of a private communication); solely for; specifically; precisely: จัดไว้จำเพาะ reserved for: จำเพาะแต่ที่ต้องการ only that which is absolutely necessary.

จ้ามํ่า　chjam³-mam³ *adj.* corpulent: อ้วนจ้ามํ่า very fat; excessively fleshy.

จำรัส see จรัส

จำราญ see จราญ

จำรูญ see จรูญ

จำเริญ see เจริญ

จำเรียง see เจรียง

จำลอง ๑　chjam-laung *Cam. n.* a horse-saddle; the howdah of an elephant.

จำลอง ๒　chjam-laung *v.* to make a print or copy; to transcribe; to reprint; to reproduce (as by a duplicating process).

จำเลย　chjam-lur-ie *n.* the culprit; the defendant in a litigation; the accused: จำเลย รวมกันกับผู้อื่น the defendant and his confederates.

จำแลง　chjam-laang *v.* to assume another form (as when Satan took the form of a serpent); to change one's bodily form; to undergo a process of metamorphosis; to be transfigured (in form).

จำหนับ　chjam-nap⁴ *v.* to catch; to overtake; to grasp; to stick; to arrest.

จำหน่าย　chjam-nai⁴ *v.* to distribute; to give out (as souvenirs); to dispose of; to sell; to offer for sale; to discard: จำหน่ายเงินตรา to put currency into circulation.

จำหระ　chjam-ra⁴ *n.* a slice; a part; a piece.

จำหล่อ　chjam-lau⁴ *n.* chevaux de frise; obstacles or obstructions made of projecting spikes (used to hinder the progress of cavalry).

จำหลัก see ฉลัก

จำหัน, จำหาย　chjam-han² *n.* a hat; a decoration for the head.

จำอวด　chjam-oo-at⁴ *n.* a clown; a conjurer; a performer of sleight-of-hand tricks, or one performing to afford amusement: *adj.* for purposes of show or ostentation; for amusement.

จิก　chjik⁴ *v.* to peck at; to tear into small pieces (with the beak): จิก (ต้น) *Barringtonia spicata (Myrtaceae)* (V. P. p. 82: Burk. p. 306), a tree or shrub growing in Siam, and south to Java. The bark, leaves and roots are medicinal. In Java the very young leaves are eaten. The timber is used for house-building; *B. acutangula* (cb. p. 668 : v. p. p. 82); *B. edaphocarpa* (cb. p. 669 : burk. p. 306); *B. macrostachya*; *B. marcanii* (*Lecythidaceae*) (cb. p. 671); *B. racemosa* (cb. p. 672 : burk. p. 306); *Shorea obtusa* (*Dipterocarpaceae*) (cb. p. 144) : คนจุกจิก a quarrelsome person; a person particular about trifles; a meticulous person : จิกกิน the picking up of food : จิกผม, จิกหัว to pinch the hair and pull : จุกจิก meticulous; finical.

จิ้งจก   chjing³-chjok⁴   *n.* the small house lizard.

จิ้งจ้อ (ต้น)   chjing-chjau³ *n. Ipomoea tur-pethum* (*Convolvulaceae*) (v. p. p. 83), false jalap, a twining creeper with three or four winged stems. The tuberous roots are used as a purgative and are considered a good substitute for jalap. It is cultivated in peas-ants' gardens (mcm. p. 379); *Ipomoea vitifo-lia* (v. p. p. 83), an ornamental climber. The flowers are bright yellow (mcm. p. 208).

จิ้งจอก   chjing³-chjauk⁴   *n.* the fox.

จิ้งจัง   chjing-chjang   *n.* a pickle made of small edible fish and parched rice, in the same manner as ปลาจ่อม.

จิ้งโจ้   chjing-chjoh³   *n.* the kangaroo.

จิ้งหรีด   chjing³-reet⁴   *n.* all insects belong-ing to the family *Gryllidae* commonly known as crickets : จิ้งหรีดตะเภา the largest cricket in Siam. They are found in holes and are used by the natives for food : จิ้งหรีด ทองแดง, ทองดำ a species of large cricket, *Liogryllus bimaculatus* (*Gryllidae*). The na-tives use them for fighting, similar to cock-fights : จิ้งหรีดแอ็ด a small species of the cricket family *Gryllidae*, used by the natives for fighting : จิ้งหรีดโกร่ง *Gryllus testaceus* (*Gryllidae*), a cricket feeding on all vegetable crops, and sometimes proving a serious pest.

จิ้งเหลน   chjing³-len² *n. Scincus officinalis*, the skink; a scincoid lizard.

จิต   chjit⁴ *P. S. v.* to have been piled up; to be placed in a line : *adj.* collected; gained; forming a mass (as hair); covered; inlaid with (s. e. d. p. 394).

จิตก   chjit⁴-dta⁴-gka⁴ *P. S. n.* a heap; a pile; a funeral pyre (chd. p. 106).

จิตกา, จิตกาธาน   chjit⁴-dta⁴-gkah *P. S. n.* an iron-grating platform on which the urn or coffin is placed at cremations, the fire passing up through the interstices consuming the body; a funeral pyre (chd. p. 106).

จิตต์   chjit⁴ *P. S. n.* the heart; the mind; the memory; intelligence; reason; intention; aim; wish; thought; the thinking mind (s. e. d. p. 395) : จิตตเจตสิก thought; con-ceptions of the mind; mental impulses : จิตต โจร *lit.* "a heart-thief," *i. e.* a lover; an usurp-er of another's affections : จิตตนาถ *lit.* "the lord of the heart and affections," *i. e.* a lover; a husband : จิตตประสาท *lit.* "a glad heart or mind," *i. e.* cheerfulness; joyfulness; bliss : จิตตบีฑา a state of unconsciousness : จิตตภู *lit.* "originating from, or born of the heart," *i. e.* love; affections; the god of Love : จิตตวิการ a disturbed, altered, or abnormal mental condition : จิตตเวทนา sorrow, pain, or distress of mind; mental trouble, or wor-ries : จิตตาโภค a state of full consciousness; concentration of thought : จิตตารมย์ *lit.* "a reviver, or stimulant to the heart," *i. e.* a medicine which acts as a heart stimulant : จิตตวิทยา psychology.

จิตติ   chjit⁴-dti⁴ *S. n.* thought; idea; reflec-tion; wisdom; determination; devotion (s.e.d. p. 396).

จิตร ๑   chjit⁴ *S. n.* name of the fifth lunar month (Chaitra) corresponding to April (s.e.d. p. 397).

จิตร ๒, จิตรา   chjit⁴ *P. S. n.* the art or act of drawing, painting, portraying or delineating in different ways, or with a variety of colours: *adj.* conspicuous; variegated; distinguished; clear; bright coloured; spotted; speckled (S. E. D. p. 396): จิตรกร a painter; an artist; a draughtsman; one whose father is an architect and whose mother is a woman of the Sudra (servile) caste: จิตรกรรม a painting; a portrait; pictures portraying various occupations; any extraordinary act or wonderful deed: จิตรกษัตร *lit.* " one whose domain is brilliant," *i. e.* Agni, the god of Fire: จิตรกัณฐ์ *lit.* " one having a speckled neck," *i. e.* a pigeon: จิตรกัมพล a carpet or cloth with variegated designs: จิตรกาย *lit.* " one having a striped body," *i. e.* a tiger; a panther: จิตรการ a marvel; a wonderful deed; any extraordinary act; a miracle; a supernatural phenomenon; astonishment: จิตรกูฏ *lit.* "bright-peak," *i. e.* a mountain peak, the seat of Valmiki's hermitage in which Rama and Sita found refuge at different times. It is the modern Chitrakote on the river Pisuni about 50 miles south-east of Banda in Bundelkhand. It is a very holy place, and abounds with temples and shrines to which thousands resort annually (H. C. D. p. 72): จิตรคุปต์ name of an attendant of Yama (พระยม), the god of the Dead. He is Yama's recorder of every man's deeds, either good or evil: จิตรตุลิกา the brush or brushes of artists or painters: จิตรบาทา *lit.* " one having stripes over the feet or claws " (as though painted), *i. e.* the common mynah bird: จิตรพยัคฆ์ a leopard: จิตรพัสตร์ a kind of cloth of the best weave: จิตรภาษย์ an orator; an eloquent speaker: จิตรภุฏ having been painted, decorated or coloured in designs: จิตรมนัส name of a horse of the Moon: จิตรมฤค the spotted antelope: จิตรเมฃละ *lit.* " one having variegated feathers," *i. e.* a peacock: จิตรยาม *lit.* " one having a brilliant path," *i. e.* the god of Fire: จิตรโยธิ *lit.* " one fighting in various ways," *i. e.* Arjuna (อรชุน), the third Pandu prince. He was a brave warrior, high-minded, generous,

upright and handsome (H. C. D. p. 21): จิตรรถ *lit.* " one having a bright chariot," *i. e.* the god of Fire; the sun; stars of the four points of the compass; name for the king of the Gandharvas (คนธรรพ) or singers and musicians of Indra's heaven (H. C. D. p. 107): จิตรลดา *lit.* " garden with a profusion of celestial vines," *i. e.* the name of a garden where Indra once stayed: จิตรลิขิต having been painted or decorated with colours: จิตรเลขา a portrait; a picture; name of a nymph who was skilled in painting and in the use of magic art (H. C. D. p. 73): จิตรวัน *lit.* " of a variegated appearance," *i. e.* name of a wood near Gandaki (คัณฑกี) on the river Gandak, in the province of Oudh (H. C. D. p. 104): จิตรวิจิตร being variously coloured; having a diversity of colour; multiform in appearance: จิตรวิทยา the art of painting: จิตรเวษ *lit.* " one having a variegated dress," *i. e.* Siva: จิตรศาลา a painted room, or one ornamented with mural paintings: จิตรเสน one having a bright spear; name of a son of Viswavasu (วิสวาวสุ), a chief of the Gandharvas in Indra's heaven (H. C. D. p. 368): จิตรหัสต์ being ambidextrous; having particular movements of the hands in fighting: จิตราคาร an opera-house; a theatre; a beautiful house or cottage: จิตรายส well-tempered steel: จิตราวุธ having a diversity of weapons: จิตรามภ์ the prominent or conspicuous part in a picture or painting: จิตรารจิส the sun.

จิตรจุล　　chjit⁴-dtra⁴-chjoon *n.* a turtle (used by royalty).

จิตรา　　chji⁴-dtra a prefix occurring in words under จิตร ๒.

จิทัมพรัม　　chji⁴-tam-pram *n.* name of a city in the central region of the world (India).

จินเจา　　chjin-chjow *Chin. n.* name for a kind of Chinese silk.

จินดา　　chjin-dah *P. S. n.* consideration; meditation; deliberation; reflection: *adj.* thinking of; reflecting upon; anxious concerning

(S. E. D. p. 398): จินดามณี *lit.* "thought gem," "wish gem," *i. e.* a jewel supposed to have the power to supply all desires; the "philosophers' stone," the supreme object of alchemy, being a substance supposed to change other metals into gold or silver (H. C. D. p. 72): จินดามัย *lit.* "consisting of mere ideas," *i. e.* imagination.

จินดาหนา see จันทน์ (ต้น)

จินดาหรา chjin-dah-rah[2] *Jav. adj.* clever.

จินต์ chjin *P. S. v.* to have a thought or an idea; to reflect; to consider; to meditate; to contemplate: จินตกวี a poet; a gifted or clever author of rhymes; one who thinks or reflects (S. E. D. p. 398): จินต์จล to be agitated in mind; to be timorous or fearful of danger.

จินตน chjin-dta[4]-na[6] *P. S. n.* meditation; reflection; thought; contemplation; deliberation (S. E. D. p. 398).

จินตนาการ chjin-dta[4]-nah-gkan *P. v.* to think; to be in a state or condition of meditation.

จินตา chjin-dtah *P. S. n.* thought; care; anxiety (S. E. D. p. 398): จินตามัยปัญญาณ, จินตามัยปัญญา knowledge gained during meditation or contemplation.

จิบ chjip[4] *v.* to sip; to suck and swallow a little at a time: จิบดักปลา a bag-net fishing apparatus used in the rivers and watercourses of north-east Siam. It has a triangular mouth, and is operated from a fixed, elevated platform called ห้างจิบ against the current of the water: จิบดู, ลิ้มดู to taste a little at a time: รับประทานจิบๆ to sip (as tea).

จิปาถะ, ติปาถะ chji[4]-bpah-ta[4] *adj.* indiscriminate (no one thing in particular); promiscuous; unrestricted.

จิ่ม, จวน, ใกล้ chjim[4] *v.* to touch or join at the edge, line or boundary; to place against a mark or line; to be adjacent or adjoining: จิ่มจะตาย to be nigh unto death.

จิ้ม, จุ้ม chjim[3] *v.* to dip into; to immerse; to pick or poke into; to moisten (as by dipping into): จิ้มน้ำพริก to dip food into chilli sauce: จิ้มน้ำหมึก to dip in ink: จิ้มฟัน to pick one's teeth: ไม้จิ้มฟัน a toothpick.

จิยอบ (หญ้า) chji[4]-yop[3] *n. Mimosa pudica* (*Leguminosae*) (V. P. p. 79), sensitive plant, an American slightly woody plant that has been carried to, and become a weed in many parts of the tropics where the climate is warm and moist. The stems are thorny; the leaves are small, bipinnate and sensitive to the slightest touch, closing immediately. It has been used successfully as pasturage but if the cattle swallow the pods, intestinal inflamation ensues. It is therefore more of a curse than blessing (MCM. pp. 209, 472, 476: Burk. p. 1474).

จิ้มลิ้ม chjim[3]-lim[5] *adj.* attractive; graceful (used only of girls); smartly dressed; having attractive manners.

จิร chji[4]-ra[6] *P. S. adj.* lasting a long time; existing from ancient times; long; protracted; lengthy (S. E. D. p. 398): จิรการ the condition of working slowly; a task that may be performed leisurely: จิรกาล belonging to a remote period; existing for a long time: จิรชีวี one who attains a great age; long-lived (said of Vishnu, Parsasu-Rama and Hanuman): จิรประวาส, จิรัปปวาส to be separated from others for a lengthy period: จิรประวาสี the one or ones who have been separated from others for a long time: จิรมิตร a friend of long standing: จิรราตร a long time: จิรโรค a chronic disease: จิรเสวก an old servant: จิรัฏฐิติกาล durability; permanency; stability: จิรันดร the interval of time between two long periods; a time long past: จิรายุส *lit.* "longlived," *i. e.* a deity; a crow.

จิโรจ chji[4]-rot[3] *v.* to be prosperous; to be enlightened or civilized.

จิ๋ว chjiw[6] *Chin. n.* a Chinese intoxicating

drink made from fermented rice; samshu; a general term for wines and liquors.

จิว chjiw[2] *adj.* smallest; least; most diminutive.

จี่ chjee[4] *v.* to roast; to scorch; to broil on a spit over a fire: *n. Anna.* an elder sister: ลิ้นจี่ the lichee.

จี้ chjee[3] *v.* to tickle; to point or poke a finger at: *n.* an ornament worn suspended about the neck; a kind of sweetmeat: จี้-กุตั่น a pendant set with rubies, suspended from the neck by a chain.

จี๋ chjee[2] *adv.* very; exceedingly; intense; a sign of the superlative degree, *ex.* ร้อนจี๋ to be piping hot; วิ่งจี๋ to run very fast.

จิงามัช (ต้น) see เจงกั๋ล

จิแจ็บ (นก) chjee-chjap[4] *n.* Indian magpie robin, *Copsychus saularis saularis* (Deig. N. H. J. S. S. VIII, 3, p. 142 : Burk p. 654).

จิด chjeet[6] *adj.* most diminutive; smallest; least.

จิด (ปลา) chjeet[4] *n.* a catfish, *Saccobranchus fossilis clariidae* (Dept. Agri. & Fisheries).

จีน chjeen *n.* the Chinese: *P. S.* a kind of deer; a banner; a bandage for the corners of the eyes; lead (S. E. D. p. 399): ลูกจีน the son of a Chinese man by a Siamese mother; a Simo-Chinese: จีนบิษฐ์ minium; a vivid red, opaque lead-oxide used chiefly as a pigment; cinnabar: จีนแส, ขิ้นแส doctor; fortune-teller; teacher.

จีบ chjeep[4] *v.* to plait; to double over in narrow folds; to pucker; to gather (in sewing): จีบปาก to pucker the lips; จีบพลู to roll the betel leaf: ขนมจีบ a sweetmeat enclosed in a thin sheet of dough, the edges of which are pinched together making a small bag; a kind of Chinese food made of minced pork and other condiments covered with pastry and steamed: จีบผ้า to gather or frill cloth:

จีบเพื่อย a long-tailed coat or garment: ผ้าจีบ cloth which is accordian-plaited.

จีม chjeem *v.* to plug up cracks or holes (as in the bottom of a boat); to tighten by forcing in a wedge.

จีร chjee-ra[6] *P. S. n.* a long narrow strip of cloth of bark; clothes; rags; ragged clothing; tatters; a stroke; a line; a strip of cloth (as in a flag) (S. E. D. p. 399): จีรขัณฑ์ a piece of cloth; scraps of cloth: จีรภวันดี an elder sister of a wife: จีรวาส clothed in rags or strips of bark.

จีวร chjee-waun *P. S. n.* iron filings; the dress, robes or tattered garments of a religious monk (especially of the Buddhist or Jain sects): ไตรจีวร the three pieces comprising the garb of the Buddhist priest, *viz.* ผ้าทาบ a broad strip worn on the shoulder, ผ้าห่ม a skirt cloth or waist piece, ผ้านุ่ง an outer robe that is twisted into a roll, and thrown over the shoulder with the end wrapped about the arm: จีวรกรรม the act of a Buddhist monk in preparation of his robes prior to making a journey (as washing or re-dyeing them): จีวรการสมัย the time for Buddhist monks to cut and sew their robes: จีวรกาลสมัย the two seasons of year suitable for presenting robes to Buddhist monks, *viz.* from the first of the waning moon of the 11th. month, to the full moon of the 12th. month, and from that time on to the end of the cold season: จีวรทาน-สมัย the time, season or occasion for making presentation of robes to Buddhist monks: จีวรภาชก *lit.* "one who distributes the robes," *i. e.* one of the monks of a temple elected to be the authorized person to make presentation of robes to other monks.

จึง, จึ่ง chjeung *conj.* then; therefore.

จืด chjurt[4] *adj.* fresh (as of water); tasteless; insipid; uninteresting (as of a fair or cinema): จืดจาง to show an unfriendly attitude; to be indifferent; to manifest a decrease in affection: จืดชืด very tasteless; most insipid.

จุ chjoo⁴ *v.* to contain; to hold: *adj.* full; sufficient: *adv.* enough: *onomat.* from the sound produced by the mouth when bidding silence; hush: จุ๋ปาก to impose silence or correction by this sound; to take a mouthful; to be suitable or just enough for the capacity of the mouth.

จุก chjook⁴ *v.* to cork; to tie together into a bundle (as of onions or garlic); to suffer from a colicky pain: *n.* a topknot; a cork; a bunch or bundle tied by a cord.

จุกจิก chjook⁴-chjik⁴ *adj.* easily dissatisfied; particular about trifles; continually grumbling; fussy; fretful; fidgety; meticulous; hard to please.

จุกช, ชุกช chjook⁴-gka⁴-chee *n.* a wooden or cement base for an image of the Buddha.

จุกผาม chjook⁴-gka⁴-pam² *n.* an obstructive ulcer of the stomach.

จุกผามม้ามย้อย chjook⁴-gka⁴-pam²-mam⁵-yauy⁵ *n.* a condition resulting from an enlarged spleen.

จุกโรหินี (ต้น) chjook⁴-gka⁴-roh-hi⁴-nee *n.* a medicinal tree, *Radix valeriane.*

จุง see จรุง

จุ่ง chjoong⁴ a word indicating a command or an entreaty, as จุ่งไปให้ได้: จุ่งจะลิงตัวแม่ (ต้น) *Tinospora cordifolia (Menispermaceae)* (V. P. p. 84 : MCM. p. 380 : BURK. p. 2163), a woody climber, found in the tropics of the Old world but chiefly in Asia and Malaysia. The plant carries a glucoside which makes it beneficial medicinally.

จุทา chjoo⁴-tah *S. n.* a single lock or tuft of hair left on the crown of the head (especially as worn by most Hindus); topknot; the hair on the crown of the head; the crest of a cock or peacock; any crest, plume or diadem; the top room (of a house)

(S. E. D. p. 401): จุฑากรณ์, จุฑากรรม *lit.* "forming the crest or topknot," *i. e.* the ceremony of tonsure; one of twelve purificatory rites performed on a child in the first or third year: จุฑาธิปไตย the condition of being the highest or greatest (in rank); a king; a supreme ruler: จุฑาบาศ a mass or tuft of hair on the top of the head: จุฑามณี a jewel worn on the top of the head by men or women. In Siamese, a pin to hold the topknot in place, being one of the ornaments employed in tonsure ceremonies by the nobility and people (GER. (1) p. 4); an eclipse of the sun on Sunday or an eclipse of the moon on Monday: จุฑามาศ a jeweled, gold crinal pin: จุฑารัตน์ a jewel worn on the head: จุฑาลักษณ์ the tonsure (S. E. D. p. 401).

จุณณ์, จุรณ, จูรณ chjoon *P. S. n.* powder; dust; flour; minute particles; aromatic powders; chalk; lime (S. E. D. p. 401): จุณณเกศ a small lock or tuft of hair: จุณณ์แก่นจันทน์ finely powdered sandalwood: จุณณ์เจิม to anoint with perfume or place scented powder on the forehead: จุณณโยค a fragrant compound; perfumed powders: จุณณ์วิจุณณ์ exceedingly fine dust.

จุณณิยบท chjoon-nee-ya⁶-bot⁴ *P. n.* a form of short, easy, Pali prose to be read or chanted before the main discourse is delivered (S. E. D. p. 401).

จุด chjoot⁴ *v.* to light a fire; to mark; to indicate by a stroke of a pen or pencil; to place scented powder on the forehead: *n.* a mark; a spot; a dot; a period: จุดจุด spotted; pox-marked: จุดไต้ to light a torch: จุดไต้ตำตอ *proverb* unexpectedly to find a stranger who was being sought: จุดทุ่ง to set a field of dry grass or rice stubble on fire: จุดเทียน to light wax tapers: จุดไฟ to set on fire; to start a blaze: จุดยา to apply a caustic, or remedy to an ulcer or wound.

จุติ chjoot⁴-dti⁴ *P. v.* to fall from a state of divine existence so as to be reborn a man (used in regard to angels); to leave one world and to be born into another; to die: *n.* disappearance; death (chd. p. 108).

จุตูปปาตญาณ chjoo⁴-dtoo-bpa⁴-bpah-dta⁴-yan *P. n.* knowledge concerning the death and birth of human beings or animals; the super-natural power of seeing beings leaving one world and being reborn in another (chd. p. 108).

จุททส chjoot⁴-ta⁶-sa⁴ *P. n.* the fourteenth (chd. p. 108).

จุน chjoon *v.* to prop; to add strength; to support; to relieve distress (in reference to finances): จุนค้ำ to support or strengthen by a prop: จุนเจือ to give a helping hand; to succour: สั้นจุนจู๋ being very short.

จุ๋น chjoon⁴ *n.* a variety of monkey: สะ-ดือจุ๋น having a protruding navel.

จุนจ้าน chjoon³-chjan³ *v.* to perform a deed openly: *adj.* undisguised; unreserved; ingenuous; frank.

จุนทการ chjoon-ta⁶-gkan *P. n.* a person who uses a turning-lathe (chd. p. 108).

จุนสี chjoon-na⁶-see² *n.* sulphate of copper crystals.

จุบ chjoop⁴ *v.* to suck gently; to suckle (as of infants); to draw in or hold by suction with the mouth (as of an eel): จุบหอย to suck shell-fish or snail meat from the shells.

จุ๊บ ๑ chjoop⁶ *onomat.* from the sound of a kiss or the smack of the lips.

จุ๊บ ๒ chjoop⁶. *Eng. n.* a tube or pipe.

จุบจิบ chjoop⁴-chjip⁴ *adv.* intermittently; irregularly (as eating between meals); period-ically (as of medicine taken at stated times).

จุ๊บแจง chjoop⁶-chjaang *n.* a salt water gastropod, *Cerithidea obtusa* (s.).

จุ่ม chjoom⁴ *v.* to immerse; to dip food in a sauce: (ปลา) *Alectis indica* (*Carangidae*)

(suvatti p. 115): จุ่มตัว to douse the body in water (as while bathing): จุ่มน้ำ to sub-merge oneself in water: จุ่มมือ to dip the hand into: ศีลจุ่ม immersion; the sacrament of immersion.

จุ๋ม see จุ๊ม

จุมพก ๑ chjoom-pok⁶ *P. S. n.* a magnet; a load-stone (chd. p. 108).

จุมพก ๒ chjoom-pok⁶ *P. S. n.* one who kisses much (S. E. D. p. 400).

จุมพฏ chjoom-pot⁶ *P. n.* a circular roll of cloth used as a support for a vessel carried on the head; a coil; a circlet; a hoop (chd. p. 108).

จุมพรวด (ปลา) chjoom-pru-at³ *n.* a goby which lives on mud flats in estuaries or along the coast, *Boleopthalmus boddaerti* (*Perio-phthalmidae*) (H. M. S.).

จุมพล, จุ่มพล chjoom-pon *P. n.* a command-er-in-chief; an officer highest in command; a field-marshal.

จุมพิต chjoom-pit⁶ *v. P. S.* to kiss; to fondle (as a parent does a child).

จุ๋ยเชียน (ต้น) chjuey⁶-see-an *n. Polyan-thus narcissus; Narcissus tazetta* (winit N. H. J. S. S. IX, 1, p. 99), the narcissus, a native of Europe, the Canary Islands, China and Japan. It has been known in Siam for at least a century. The variety *orientalis*, Chinese Sacred Lily, having a wholly yellow flower, is rare in Siam.

จุรณ, จุรณ see จุณณ์

จุร see จร

จุไร chjoo⁴-rai *n.* the line of depilation around the topknot or forehead: ถอนไร the operation of pulling out the hair bulbs (an ancient custom performed on girls about the age of puberty).

จุล, จุฬะ chjoon *P. S. adj.* small; little; minute; inferior; microscopic (chd. p. 108):

จุลจักรพรรดิ a sovereign : จุลบิดา the father's younger brother ; an uncle : จุลพน *lit.* "small jungle," *i. e.* name of the sixth chapter in the Vessantara (เวสสันดรชาดก) story : จุลภาค a small part or fragment ; a short sentence : จุลมารดา, น้าสาว a mother's younger sister ; an aunt : จุลวรรค a short sentence or paragraph ; a section, division or subdivision of a unit of persons or things ; name of a portion of the Vinaya or Buddhist Scriptures (chd. p. 575) : จุลศักราช the Siamese lesser era which began on the 21st. March, 638 A. D. The Mahasakaraj or the greater era commenced in the year 78 A. D. (F. P. C. p. 136).

จุฬา chjoo[4]-lah *n.* the star-shaped kite ; the male kite in distinction to the female (ปักเป้า), or the one with a long single tail : จุฬามณี name of the pagoda where the hair of Buddha is buried ; see จุฑามณี : จุฬาลัมพา see โกฏฐ-จุฬาลำพา : จุหล่า, จุฬา a title conferred on an Indian Phya.

จู (หมา) chjoo *n.* a small pug-nosed dog with long hair ; a Pekinese dog.

จู่ chjoo[4] *v.* to rush in suddenly ; to enter unannounced : *adv.* directly ; by a direct course ; unhesitatingly : จู่จับ to attack suddenly and place under arrest : จู่มา to come upon unexpectedly : จู่จู่ to rush in upon and interrupt the conversation or intercept the way or passage : *adj.* petulant ; rude ; saucy ; insolent ; pert ; brazen-faced : จู่โจม to make a charge (as in battle) ; to pounce upon.

จูง chjoong *v.* to lead by the hand ; to induce or allure : จูงควาย to lead a buffalo by a rope : จูงนางเข้าห้อง name of a game similar to parchisi : จูงนางลีลา an attitude assumed by the mahouts while taking part in a ceremonial dance in front of the war elephants on the occasion of their first trial in combat, or contest during the period of training : เดินจูงมือ to walk hand in hand.

จู๊จี๊ chjoo[3]-chjee[3] *adj.* fussy ; fretful ; peevish ; finical ; capricious : จุ๊บจุ๊บัต *slang* to talk slurringly in an indirect way.

จุ๊จี๊ chjoo[2]-chjee[2] *onomat.* from the sound of whispering, or the squeaking of rats.

จูบ chjoop[4] *v.* to kiss ; to smell (as the Siamese kiss).

จุฬะ see จุล

เจ๊ chjey[6] *Chin. n.* an elder sister.

เจ๊ก chjek[6] *Chin. n.* a Chinese man ; the Chinese ; a younger brother of a father ; an uncle.

เจง (ต้น) chjeng *n. Holoptelea integrifolia* (*Urticaceae*) (V. P. p. 84), Indian elm, a tree with handsome drooping branches, 50 to 162 ft. high, found widely in India, China and Siam. The timber is good, light yellow to grey in colour, moderately hard and easily worked. It has been suggested as a substitute for ash or walnut and is good for turnery (Burk. p. 1181 : MCM. p. 206).

เจ้ง chjeng[4] *n.* an elephant.

เจ๊ง chjeng[3] *n.* pleasing tones of music ; melodious sounds of singing ; the sweet chirping of birds : ซอเจ้ง a kind of stringed musical instrument.

เจ๊ง chjeng[6] *Chin. v.* to be defeated or routed ; to be vanquished ; to be surpassed ; to yield after a contest.

เจงกัล, บนัก (ต้น) chjeng-gkan *n. Balanocarpus maximus* (*Dipterocarpeae*) (V. P. p. 79 : MCM. p. 218 : Burk. p. 287), a large or fairly large tree found in the Malay Peninsula. It is not considered valuable ; *B. heimii* (V. P. p. 84).

เจฏ chjet[4] *P. S. n.* a servant ; a messenger ; a slave (S. E. D. p. 401).

เจ็ด chjet[4] *Chin. n.* the numeral seven : เจ็ดสิบ seventy.

เจดีย์, เจติย chjey-dee *P. S. n.* a pagoda ; a monument erected in memory of the dead ; a funeral monument, mound, or stupa ; a pyramidal column containing the ashes of deceased persons ; a place of reverence or worship (S. E. D. p. 402) ; a sacred tower or edifice, usually pyramidal in form, tapering to a plain or decorated tip, supported either on a round or square base, and profusely adorned. In the earliest days of Buddhism, these sacred tumuli were raised upon shrines wherein relics of the Buddha had been deposited. With the passage of years, these places have become the sacred depositories of the Buddhist scriptures, or of the relics of distinguished religious persons who acquired eminence by their scientific and moral attainments. In many instances a pagoda has been built up, not for the sake of sheltering relics of the Buddha, but for the pious purpose of reminding the people of the holy relics, and to kindle in their souls a tender feeling of affectionate reverence for the person of the Buddha and his religion (Bigandet I, pp. 32, 227) : เจดีย์ฐาน, เจดีย์สถาน a place made sacred by a monument or sanctuary (S. E. D. p. 402).

เจต chjet[4] *P. S. n.* the mind ; the intellect ; the faculty of reasoning, or understanding ; the heart ; thoughts (Chd. p. 102) : เจตรมาศ the fifth lunar month or the first month of the Siamese calendar.

เจ็ตคลี่ chjet[4]-dta[4]-klee *n.* a fabric having stripes and flowery designs in colours ; chintz.

เจตนา chjet[4]-dta[4]-nah *P. S. n.* design ; intention ; inclination ; purpose ; determination ; end or aim in any plan, measure or exertion (Chd. p. 102) : เจตนาจะฉ้อโกง an intent to defraud : เจตนาจะทำร้าย a criminal intent.

เจตพังคี (ต้น) chjet[4]-dta[4]-pang-kee *n.* a Siamese medicinal plant.

เจตภูต chjet[4]-dta[4]-poot[3] *n.* person ; body ; self ; individuality ; life ; mind ; soul ; a creature ; a being (Chd. pp. 65, 171).

เจตมูลเพลิง (ต้น) chjet[4]-dta[4]-moon-plerng *n.* a Siamese medicinal plant of which there are three varieties, viz. (1) เจตมูลเพลิงขาว (ต้น) *Plumbago zeylanica* (*Plumbaginaceae*) (V. P. p. 85 : BURK. p. 1775), " Ela-Nitul," a small, perennial herb or small shrub with white flowers and long succulent roots, which are acrid and poisonous and sometimes used for illegal purposes (MCM. pp. 116, 142, 386, 387) ; (2) เจตมูลเพลิงแดง (ต้น) *Plumbago rosea* (V. P. p. 86), " Rat-Nitul," rose scarlet, (MCM. p. 116) ; (3) เจตมูลเพลิงฝรั่ง (ต้น) *Plumbago capensis*, a flowering shrub 3 to 5 ft. high with beautiful delicate blue flowers, which has long been cultivated in Bangkok gardens. It is not known by whom it was introduced but the white-flowered variety was first grown in Bangkok a few years ago (Sakol, N. H. J. S. S. VIII, 3, p. 209 : MCM. p. 135).

เจตสิก chjet[4]-dta[4]-sik[4] *P. S. n.* conceptions of the mind (Palle. p. 94) ; modes of mental expression (Ala. p. 237) : *adj.* mental (chd. p. 102).

เจติย see เจดีย์

เจน chjen *adj.* being accustomed to ; able to do efficiently ; expert ; proficient ; familiar with ; habituated ; experienced : เจนจบ skilled ; well-versed : เจนใจ well-acquainted or familiar with (as the result of study or practice) : เจนตา to become familiar to the sight ; to cease being offensive to the eye : เจนทั้งสองมือ ambidextrous : สิบรู้ไม่เท่าเจน *prov.* experience is ten times better than theory.

เจ็บ chjep[4] *v.* to be sick or ill ; to have a distemper ; to be in pain ; to be hurt : เจ็บจำ to bear a grudge (as for something borrowed and not returned) : เจ็บใจ to be indignant ; to be provoked ; to be distressed in mind ; to have wounded feelings ; to be heart-sick : เจ็บช้ำน้ำใจ to have one's feelings hurt : เจ็บท้อง to be in labour ; to be in travail ; to suffer from a pain in the abdomen : เจ็บปวด painful ; sore to the touch.

เจรจา   chjen-ra[6]-chjah *S. v.* to discuss ; to converse ; to negotiate : *n. lit.* "repeating what is in one's thoughts," *i. e.* discussion ; deliberation ; consideration (S. E. D. p. 390) : เจรจาความเมือง to hold political intercourse or negotiations : เจรจาปราศรัย to speak with in a friendly manner ; to converse amicably : เจรจาสนธิสัญญาทางพระราชไมตรี to negotiate a treaty.

เจริญ   chja[4]-rern *v.* to increase ; to expand ; to grow greater, or larger ; to prosper ; to improve in character ; to recite or chant ; to offer sacrifices ; to practice ; to observe (as a rite) : *Cam. adj.* much : เจริญงาช้าง to cut the tusks of an elephant : เจริญธรรม to practice the laws of truth and living as laid down by the Buddhist religion : เจริญพร a blessing signifying a wish for one's increased prosperity, but generally it means yes ; yes, sir (a form of assent used only by Buddhist monks) : เจริญมนตร์ to recite portions from the "Laws and Truths" or Dharm, or portions from a list of the thirty-two elements : เจริญยา to throw away the medicine ; to abandon a remedy : เจริญรอย to observe the precepts ; to follow the example or conduct of some one.

เจริด see เจิด

เจรียง   chja[4]-ree-ang *v.* to sing ; to chant or recite stanzas ; to lull to sleep by singing ; to sing a lullaby : ขับลำจำเรียง to dance and sing.

เจล   chjen *P. n.* cloth ; clothing ; a garment (chd. p. 102).

เจลียง   chja[4]-lee-ang *n.* an intermittent fever ; the tertian form of malarial fever.

เจษฎา ๑   chjet[4]-sa[4]-dah *P. S. n.* the chief ; the first in rank or authority ; the most prosperous one ; the eldest (chd. p. 168).

เจษฎา ๒   chjet[4]-sa[4]-dah *S. v.* to move the arms and feet ; to change the position of the body (as in dancing) ; to strive after ; to struggle for ; to gape (S. E. D. p. 424) : *n.* conduct ; an attitude in Siamese dancing.

เจ๊สัว   chjey[6]-soo-ah[2] *Chin. n.* a rich Chinese man ; a Chinese millionaire.

เจอ, เจอะ   chjur *v.* to meet ; to come together ; to see each other again ; to find : จนเราเจอกันอีก "till we meet again" : เจอตัว to meet another after a separation ; to locate another after a search.

เจ่อ   chjur[4] *v.* to protrude ; to be enlarged or swollen (used only for the lips) ; to bulge.

เจ๋อ, เจ๋อเจ๊อะ   chjur[2] *v.* to come before another without being invited or summoned ; to intrude one's self ; to push one's self in, or forward.

เจ่า   chjow[4] *v.* to sit silently or dejectedly ; to rest quietly (as a bird or monkey on the limb of a tree) : *n.* a stew containing prawns or small fish : เจ่าจุก squatting sulkily, sleepily, or meditatively.

เจ้า   chjow[3] *n.* a term indicating one of royal rank or kingly lineage ; a lord ; a master ; a king ; used as a prefix denoting one of high rank, *ex.* เจ้ากรม the director of a department : เจ้ากรรม unfortunate ; unhappy ; one guilty of gross sins : เจ้ากระทรวง the executive of a Ministry : เจ้าการ the proprietor of a business : เจ้ากู the second and third personal pronoun (used only to Buddhist monks of standing) : เจ้าขรัว an honorary title for the maternal grandfather of a royal prince : เจ้าของ owner : เจ้าของที่ดินสำหรับเช่า landlord : เจ้าขา, เจ้าข้า, เจ้าค่ะ yes (a form of assent used only by Siamese women to superiors) ; an exclamation : เจ้าเข้า one possessed by evil spirits ; a seller or peddler of rice : เจ้าคณะ the Lord Abbot of a Buddhist monastery : เจ้าครอก a personal pronoun (used in ancient times for royal princes or princesses) :

เจ้าคุณ a personal pronoun used for both the 2nd. and 3rd. person, referring to a Phya, or to a Lord Abbot of a monastery : เจ้าคุณจอม a personal pronoun (used in ancient times for the king's chief concubine) : เจ้าเงิน an employer ; the banker in a game of chance ; a creditor ; a slave's master : เจ้าจอม a personal pronoun (used in ancient times for a lesser concubine of a Siamese king) : เจ้าจอม มารดา a personal pronoun for the mother of a royal prince or princess : เจ้าจำนวน an official in the Ministry of Finance ; the Comptroller General of the Finance Department : เจ้าจำนำ a good customer ; a constant trader, or purchaser : เจ้าชีวิตร, เจ้าแผ่นดิน *lit.* "one having power over the lives of his subjects," *i. e.* a king : เจ้าชู้ a lover ; a beau ; an enticer of young girls ; a paramour : เจ้าเฌร a division of the Buddhist monks which adheres only to the ten commandments : เจ้า-แดง, เจ้าหนู a term of endearment (used as a personal pronoun for children) : เจ้าตัว the person spoken of ; the one referred to in conversation : เจ้าทรัพย์ a property owner ; a proprietor : เจ้าที่ the spiritual landlord of a place ; the genii or joss of an establishment : เจ้าทุกข์ a complainant : เจ้าไทย Buddhist monks ; bonzes : เจ้านาย those having royal blood ; members of the royal family : เจ้าบท, เจ้ากลอน a skilled writer of poetry or rhymes : เจ้าบ่าว a bridegroom : เจ้าเบญจานายเงิน an owner or holder of slaves : เจ้าปัญญา one proficient in knowledge ; an expert in matters of learning : เจ้าประคุณ a personal pronoun of respect (used for persons without official rank) : เจ้าแผ่นดิน the ruler of a realm ; the king : เจ้าพนักงาน a governmental official ; officials, or persons in charge of special matters : เจ้า-พนักงานกองหมาย a bailiff : เจ้าพนักงานตรวจคน เข้าเมือง an immigration officer : เจ้าพนักงาน ผู้จัดการไต่สวนพลิกศพ a coroner : เจ้าพนักงาน ผู้จัดการสำมะโนครัว an enumerator : เจ้าพนัก-งานผู้รับอำนาจจัดการและตรวจตรากิจการกุศล a charity commissioner : เจ้าพนักงานฝ่ายธุรการ an administration officer : เจ้าพนักงานศุลากร

a customs officer : เจ้าพนักงานสรรพสามิตต์ an excise officer : เจ้าพระยา Chao Phya, the fifth or highest rank of conferred Siamese civil nobility. These ranks are, *viz.* (a) ขุน, (b) หลวง, (c) พระ, (d) พระยา, (e) เจ้าพระยา : เจ้าฟ้า the child of a king and his queen, or his concubine whose rank is Serene Highness or higher : เจ้าภาพ a host : เจ้ามือ the banker in a gambling game ; the one holding the purse in any game of chance : เจ้าเมือง a governor : เจ้าเล่ห์ a cunning, scheming, perfidious, or tricky person : เจ้าวัด one who builds a temple or monastery for the use of Buddhist monks ; the abbot of a monastery : เจ้าสาว a bride : เจ้าสำนวน one who speaks with perfect idiom : เจ้าสำ-นักโรงแรม an innkeeper : เจ้าหน้า an agent ; a runner for any concern ; a business manager : เจ้าหน้าเข้าตา a supplanter ; a competitor using questionable means for his own advancement while in the employ of another : เจ้าหน้าที่, เจ้าพนักงาน officials in charge of an office, or in a department ; authorities : เจ้าหนี้ creditors : เจ้าหนี้ตามคำพิพากษา a judgement creditor : เจ้า-หนี้บุริมสิทธิ a preferential creditor : เจ้าหนี้ผู้ซึ่ง รับการะในการจัดการมรดก a creditor executor : เจ้าหนี้รวมกันกับผู้อื่น a joint creditor ; เจ้าหมู่ a corporal : เจ้าหัว, เจ้าอยู่หัว, พระเจ้าอยู่หัว *lit.* "ruler higher than the head," *i. e.* H. M. the King (used as a personal pronoun) : เจ้า-เหนือหัว lord, sovereign or ruler over all : เจ้าอาราม, เจ้าอาวาส the chief head of the Buddhist monks in any one of the monasteries : ปู่เจ้า the spirit, angel, or genii of a place : แม่เจ้าเอ๋ย an exclamation of surprise, as "gracious me !"

เจ้า chjow[6] *Chin. v.* to discontinue ; to be forced to stop (as in a gambling game, or a fight).

เจาะ chjau[4] *v.* to use an auger ; to bore a hole ; to puncture ; to pierce ; to perforate : เจาะกัน to touch each other gently (as two billiard balls) ; to touch each other (as two pennies when thrown) : เจาะจง to be explicit; to be precise: เจาะชื่อ, ระบุชื่อ to designate by name: เจาะหุ to pierce a hole in the lobe of the ear.

เจ้าะซ๊อก, มะม่วง (ต้น)   chjau[4]-sauk[6] *n.* *Mangifera indica* (*Anacardiaceae*) (cb. p. 344: Burk. p. 1402), the mango, a medium or large-sized, spreading and quick-growing tree, indigenous to tropical Asia. It bears large panicles of greenish-white, unpleasantly scented flowers, usually in January to March, followed by the fruit about $2\frac{1}{2}$ to 3 months later. A second crop is sometimes obtained in August or September. The round or ovoid fruit is somewhat flattened, generally with a more or less pronounced beak near the apex. It has a tough, thin skin and when ripe is yellow, reddish, or green. The flesh is usually of a reddish tint, with a distinct, pleasant, aromatic flavour; in inferior varieties it is turpentiney, somewhat resinous, and fibrous. In the centre is the large fibrous, ovoid, flat seed (MCM. pp. 242, 243).

เจิ่ง   churng[4] *v.* to be high or in flood (used in reference to a river or canal); to be inundated.

เจิด   chjert[4] *adj.* beautiful; worthy of being flaunted as a beauty.

เจิ่น   chjurn[4] *v.* to reach beyond (as a cannon ball that over-reaches the target); to be estranged; to wander or stray from others of a company: หลงเจิ่น to be misdirected, misled, or to have lost the way: เดินเจิ่นไป to go past or further from; to go far beyond the point of destination.

เจิม   chjerm *v.* to anoint; to consecrate (as by the sprinkling of lustral water, or applying consecrated unguents to the forehead); to bless by anointing; to wish increased prosperity: *n.* the eyebrows: เจิมกระแจะ, เจิมแป้ง to anoint with moistened, scented powders: เจิมขวัญ to tie the protective thread or cord around the wrists, as a means of warding off evil influences.

เจียก   chjee-ak[6] *onomat.* from the sound made by little chicks, or the chatter of monkeys.

เจียด   chjee-at[4] *v.* to divide and take but a little; to buy in small quantities (as of medicine), *ex.* ไปเจียดยาขาว to go and buy doses of quinine: *n.* a tray raised on a pedestal, made of lacquer and mother-of-pearl inlay (used in ancient times as insignia of Siamese official rank): เจียดเงิน, เจียดทอง (พาน) a silver or golden tray used by royalty to indicate their rank: เจียดกัน to distribute; to share; to deal out amongst others.

เจียน   chjee-an *v.* to trim, cut, or lop off; *adv.* near by; almost; very nearly; at the point of: เจียนจะตาย almost dead; near death's door: เจียนพลู to prepare the betel leaf by cutting it into strips prior to chewing: เจียนมา soon to come; imminent: เจียนหมาก the process of preparing the betel nut prior to chewing. The thin green outer layer is first peeled off in narrow strips by a sharp knife, the hard fibrous sub-layer is then pared away and separated from the kernel: จวนเจียน before long; presently; shortly; promptly.

เจียน   chjee-an[2] *n.* a condiment to give relish to rice (as fish fried and seasoned), *ex.* เจียนปลาทู, เจียนปลาสลิด.

เจียบ   chjee-ap[6] *onomat.* from the sound made by little chicks.

เจียม   chjee-am *v.* to be moderate (as in expenses); to conserve; to be thrifty; to save one's strength or money: *n.* a kind of carpet having a long nap: *adj.* temperate; prudent; moderate; frugal; economical: เจียมกาย to act with moderation; to act circumspectly: เจียมใจ to be meek, lowly or humble: เจียมวาจา to be guarded in speech; to speak with moderation.

เจียร   see   จิร

เจียรณ์   chjee-an *S. n.* conduct; behaviour; deportment; demeanour; observance; performance (as the fulfilment of a vow) (S. E. D. p. 399).

เจียรไน   chjee-ah-ra[6]-nai *v.* to cut; to burnish diamonds or precious stones: ผู้เจียรไน เพ็ชร์ a lapidary.

เจียระบาด   chjee-ah-ra[6]-bat[4] *n.* a belt or girdle adorned with tinsel or embroidery, worn so that the ends reach to the knees.

เจียว   chjee-ow *v.* to fry; to try out the fat or lard (as from pork): *adv.* surely; certainly; positively; unfailingly: ไข่เจียว an omelet: เจียวน้ำมัน to fry out the fat or lard.

เจียวจ๊าว   chjee-ow[6]-chjow[6] *onomat.* from the noise made by several persons talking.

เจียวตากวน   chjee-ow-dtah-gku-an *n.* Tchou Ta-Kuan, a Chinese official who accompanied the ambassador sent to the Khmer Court in 1295 by the Yuan Emperor Tch'eng-Tsing (successor to Kublai Khan, who died in 1294). They arrived at Angkor in 1296 and left in 1297. Tchou Ta-Kuan was of a good family from Yong-Kia in the province of Tcho-Kiang and bore the title of Ts'ao-t'ing. On his return to China, he submitted his book on Cambodia to the famous poet Won K'ieon Yen who wrote several poems in its praise. It seems probable that the ambassador with whom Tchou Ta-Kuan travelled was sent to Cambodia as a gentle reminder that the matter of tribute due to the Chinese Emperor had not been attended to for the last couple of centuries (camb. glory pp. 130, 132). It might be inferred from this, that Cambodia was tributary to China at that time.

เจือ   chjeu-ah *v.* to mix; to compound; to add to; to dilute: เจือจันทน์ to mix scents: เจือจาน to divide convertible wealth and add to, or make up a common fund; to put finances into a joint fund; to support with funds from a general source: เจือด้วย to be mixed

with (as an ingredient): เจือเติม to mix while adding to; to add more, and mix in together with the original amount: เอาน้ำ-เจือเหล้า to dilute wine or spirits with water.

เจือก   chjeu-ak[6] *onomat.* from the sound made when sticking a knife into a banana tree.

เจือน   chjeu-an[4] *v.* to be abashed, embarrassed, or confused.

เจือย   chjeu-ay[3] *adv.* freely; smoothly; softly; continually; excessively; *may be used to express the superlative degree, ex.* ยาวเจือย very long; much too long.

แจ ๑   chjaa *adv.* close up to; in a close manner; near by: แจจน, แจจัน crowded together; standing too close; pressed tightly together.

แจ ๒   chjaa *Chin. n.* Chinese Lent: กินแจ to observe Chinese Lent (when no meat is eaten).

แจ้   chjaa[3] *n.* a bantam rooster, or hen: *adj.* small; low; little: บานแจ้ to be expanded to the utmost limit (as of flowers).

แจ๋   chjaa[2] *adj.* vivid; bright red; very red; strong or bright (sun rays); a word indicating the superlative degree for colour or rays of light.

แจก   chjaak[4] *v.* to distribute; to apportion; to allot; to divide into parts and give a portion to each: แจกกัน, แจกของ to distribute gifts (as at Christmas): แจกคนละอัน to give one to each: แจกให้ to distribute.

แจ๊ก   chjaak[6] *onomat.* from the sound of the warbling of birds.

แจกัน   chjaa-gkan *n.* a vase; a flower-stand; a vase-shaped stand for incense sticks.

แจง   chjaang *v.* to distribute; to arrange in order; to explain or elucidate; to make an explanation of facts and conditions in order

to allay doubts: แจง (ต้น) *Niebuhria dec-*
andra (*Capparidaceae*) (cb. p. 78); *N. siam-*
ensis (cb. p. 79: v. p. p. 85): แจงเบี้ย to
count and arrange cowrie shells in piles to
discover the remaining number (a betting
game).

แจ้ง　chjaang[3] *v.* to make manifest; to make
clear; to make known; to inform: *adj.*
plain; distinct; intelligible: กลางแจ้ง in
the open; in plain sight of; in broad daylight: แจ้งความ to inform; to notify; to
give notice: แจ้งความเท็จ to make a false
statement: แจ้งความมายัง a common form
used in addressing letters or envelopes to
equals or inferiors in rank: แจ้งประจักษ์
clearly; undimmed: แจ้งให้รู้ to make
known; to inform: ที่แจ้ง a clearing; an
open space or place.

แจด　chjaat[4] a word denoting the superlative degree of intensity of colour or heat;
very; vivid; excessive.

แจ๊ด　chjaat[6] *onomat.* from the sound of a
bird calling insistently to its mate: *adv.*
very; most (intensive).

แจ๊ดๆ　chjaat[3]-chjaat[3] *onomat.* from the
sound of birds chirping.

แจ่ม　chjaam[4] *adj.* clear; bright; distinct;
free from cloudiness or obscurity: หน้าแจ่ม
of a cheerful countenance; having a serene
facial expression.

แจรก, แจก　chjraak[4] *v.* to distribute, scatter, separate, or disperse.

แจรง, แจง　chjraang *v.* to arrange in
order of sequence; to distribute; to classify.

แจว　chjaa-ow *v.* to row using an oar; to
run away after being defeated in a fight, or
after having done some evil deed: *n.* a long
oar (as used by Siamese boatmen): แจวท้าย
the steering oar: แจวเรือ to row a boat
with one oar: แจวหัว the head oarsman:
ใบแจว the blade or broad portion of an oar:

หมวกแจว the cross-piece of an oar handle:
หูแจว the thread loop, or hinge holding the
oar in place on the upright standard: หลัก-
แจว the upright stanchion to which the long
oar is hinged.

แจ้ว　chjaa-ow[4] *n.* a condiment composed
of chilli sauce and pickled fish (eaten with
vegetables).

แจ้ว　chjaa-ow[3] *adj.* talkative; lusty (as
the crowing of a cock); warbling (as a bird);
chattering (as a monkey); pleasing to the
ear: แจ้วจับใจ captivating melodies: แจ้ว
เจ้อย, แจ้วเสียง a clear, pleasing voice.

แจ๋ว　chjaa-ow[2] *adj.* clear-eyed; bright:
ลืมตาแจ๋ว to open bright eyes (used in connection with new-born babes).

แจะ　chjaa[4] *v.* to touch another lightly; to
come close enough to touch: *onomat.* from
the sound of chewing.

โจก　chjok[4] *n.* a leader; the principal one
in a line, or community; the chief of a band;
a ringleader: ควายโจกฝูง the leader of a
herd of buffaloes: หัวโจกในบ้าน an instigator;
the ringleader of a community or village;
the chief of a band or gang.

โจ๊ก　chjok[6] *v.* to be defeated: *onomat.*
from the sound of water flowing freely from
a faucet.

โจง　chjong *v.* to twist the edges of a cloth
together (as in making the end of the panung);
to draw or pull the loin-cloth up tightly
around the waist: โจงกะเบนตีเหล็ก an attitude assumed by Siamese actors.

โจ้ง　chjong[4] *adj.* opened; exposed to view;
unconcealed; public.

โจ้ง　chjong[2] *onomat.* from the sound produced by a Malay drum: โจ้งครึ่ม to interrupt senselessly: โจ้งเจ้ง clear; lacking
solid ingredients (as curry or soup).

โจ่งครุ่ม   chjong[4]-kroom[3] *adj.* prominent; conspicuous; public; taking the leading part in any affair: *onomat.* from the sound of a Malay drum.

โจจ   chjot[4] *P. n.* bark; skin; hide; the coconut shell; a banana tree (S. E. D. p. 402).

โจทก์   chjot[4] *P. S. n.* he who objects, rebukes or exhorts; he who questions (chd. p. 107); the accuser; the prosecutor (chd. p. 107): โจทก์รวมกันกับผู้อื่น a joint plaintiff; a joint prosecutor: ผู้เป็นโจทก์ one who prosecutes.

โจทนา   chjot[4]-ta[6]-nah *P. S. n.* accusation; incrimination; rebuke; reproof; prosecution (chd. p. 107).

โจทย์, โจท   chjot[4] *P. S. v.* to bring charges; to accuse; to criticize, or to be criticized; to be impelled; to be incited; to be rebuked (S. E. D. p. 400): โจทย์เจ้า the act of leaving one royal master to join another: โจทย์นาย the act of leaving one's leader to join his or her master or mistress.

โจน, กะโดด   chjon *v.* to pounce upon; to jump forwards, or down upon; to leap upon: โจนจากเรือน to leap from a house: โจนน้ำ to jump or leap into the water: โจนร่ม name of an ancient play or game: หลุมโจน a kind of fish-trap.

โจม, กระโจม   chjom *v.* to pounce forwards, or down upon; to burst in upon suddenly: *n.* a canopy; a tent; a cloth protection against the weather: โจมจับ to swoop down upon and seize: โจมตี to make an attack; to advance troops suddenly: โจมทัพ a group or company of military elephants: โจมพัน to attack suddenly and slash with knives or swords: โจมรบ to fight without warning.

โจร   chjon *P. S. n.* a thief; robbers; burglars; a plagiarist (S. E. D. p. 400): โจรกรณ์ the act of inciting another to become a burglar; the act of calling one a robber: โจรกรรม the act of thieving, plundering or robbing; a theft; larceny: โจรกัณฑก, หญ้าเจ้าชู้ a species of grass, *Chrysopogon aciculatus*; "love-grass" (MCM. pp. 71, 452): โจรผู้ร้าย thieves; robbers; dacoits: โจรรูป a clever burglar, or thief: โจรสลัด a pirate; piracy.

โจล ๑   chjon *P. S. n.* a jacket; a bodice; a garment; a corset (S. E. D. p. 402).

โจล ๒   chjon *S. n.* a country and kingdom of southern India about Tanjore, once called Chola-mandala (โคโรมณฑล), hence the name Coromandel (H. C. D. p. 73); name of a people in southern India on the Coromandel coast (S. E. D. p. 402).

โจษ   chjot[4] *v.* to communicate; to publish abroad; to blazon; to advertise abroad; to circulate (as a report): *n.* a rumour or unverified report: โจษกัน to be spread by report; to discuss rumours: โจษจน, โจษจัน, โจษแจ to spread from mouth to mouth; to gossip (as in the market places): โจษว่า according to gossip; from market talk; by rumour.

โจ๊ะ (ต้น)   chjo[6] *n. Schleichera trijuga* (*Sapindaceae*) (V. P. p. 80: Burk. p. 1978), "Ceylon oak," "Kusumb," a large tree of India, Java and eastern Malaysia. The seeds, which are edible, are rich in oil, said to be the original "Macassar oil" (MCM. pp. 219, 397 416, 417).

ใจ (ดวงใจ)   chjai *n.* mind; disposition; the middle or central part or portion: กลับใจ to repent: กลุ้มใจ vexed; worried; perplexed: กินใจ doubtful of; suspicious of: เกรงใจ having respect; having respectful fear: ขอบใจ, ขอบคุณ to thank; to be grateful: ขัดใจ to be angry: เข้าใจ to understand: แข็งใจ brave; courageous: แข็งใจทน to be brave; to endure manfully: ความขุ่นใจ indignation: คับใจ being dissatisfied or discontented: จนใจ to be at one's wits' end; to be reduced to the last extremity: จับใจ attractive; fascinating; pleasing: จิตต์ใจ, น้ำใจ disposition: เจ็บใจ to be annoyed:

ใจกระด้าง, ใจแข็ง to be hard-hearted, callous, obdurate, unfeeling, or unyielding; to be self-willed, stubborn, or head-strong: ใจ-กลาง the centre; the core; the bull's eye of a target: ใจกว้าง liberal-minded; generous; magnanimous; unselfish: ใจขุ่น to be displeased; to be irritated, piqued, vexed or angered: ใจความ the gist or substance of a matter; the meaning; a summary: ใจคอ disposition: ใจแค้น of a revengeful nature: ใจแคบ selfish; unaffectionate; narrow-minded; illiberal; bigoted: ใจง่าย easily influenced: ใจจดใจจ่อ with concentration; with eagerness; with determination: ใจจืด unsympathetic: ใจเฉื่อย uninterested; inattentive; unmindful: ใจชื้น rejoicing; jubilant: ใจดำ the central black spot or point; selfish; unsympathetic: ใจดี kind; affectionate; benevolent; loving: ใจเด็ด undaunted: ใจเดียวกัน friendly; congenial; being of the same mind: ใจโต, ใจ-ใหญ่ magnanimous; generous; unselfish: ใจเท้า the instep: ใจน้อย easily displeased, offended, or irritated; touchy; peevish; sensitive; inclined to feel slights, or to be faint-hearted: ใจบาน free from anxiety; glad; happy: ใจเบา to be easily moved, led, induced, or controlled: ใจป้ำ fearless; brave: ใจฝ่าใจขม hostile; unfriendly in attitude: ใจมืดใจดำ to be harsh, severe, austere, uncivil, cruel, or brutal: ใจมือ the palm of the hand: ใจไม้ไส้ระกำ to be lacking in mercy, compassion, and helpfulness: ใจเย็น being cool and calm in disposition; having presence of mind: ใจร้อน quick-tempered; impetuous; irascible; easily provoked: ใจรวนเร being of an unstable disposition: ใจร้าย cruel; merciless; pitiless: ใจลอย to be absent-minded: ใจสูง reserved; haughty in manner: ใจสัตย์ซื่อ loyal; faithful: ใจหาย feeling stunned or nonplussed: ใจเหี่ยว, ใจแห้ง saddened by sorrow: ใจอ่อน meek; humble; submissive: ใจอิดโรย to be heartsick; to be weary at heart: ใจอุ่น free from anxiety: ชอบใจ pleased with; attracted to: เชื่อใจ to trust; to have confidence in: ชื่นใจ joyous; cheerful; gladsome; being in good spirits: ดีใจ glad: ตั้งใจ to intend; to mean; to purpose: เต็มใจ to be willing; to give consent to: ตกใจ to be frightened; to be struck with fear, or astonishment: ตรอมใจ, โทมนัส being sorrowful in the extreme: ถอนใจ to sigh heavily: ท้อใจ to be discouraged; to be disheartened: ท่องขึ้นใจ to memorize: นอนใจ, ทอดใจ to take no heed of; to be neglectful of one's responsibility: น้อยใจ peeved; disappointed; dejected; indignant: น้ำใจ intention; purpose; design: แน่นใจ a feeling of shortness of breath; a feeling of oppression in the chest: ปลื้มใจ having mental satisfaction: พอใจ to be satisfied with: เย็นใจ not manifesting temper; having presence of mind: รำพึงใจ to think over; to meditate: ร้อนใจ to be fearful about; to be troubled in mind respecting some uncertain matter or situation; to apprehend danger: เรียนขึ้นใจ to memorize: ร่วมใจ unitedly; conjointly: ไว้ใจ to hope: สิ้นใจ to die: ใส่ใจ, สนใจ to take notice of; to pay attention to; to heed; to listen to; to be in earnest: สบายใจ happy; comfortable: เสียใจ to despair of; to be desperate; to be disheartened; to be sorry: แสดงน้ำใจดี to manifest good will or feelings: สุดใจ whole-heartedly; willingly; favourably inclined (to the utmost degree): หนักใจ to be worried, anxious, or heavy-hearted: แหนงใจ a feeling of incompatibility, or irritation: หายใจ to breathe: หวานใจ to feel pleased with gratifying commendation: หัวใจ the heart; the organ of circulation: อ่อนใจ exhausted; discouraged: อิ่มใจ satisfied; contented.

ไจ chjai n. a skein of thread, or yarn.

ไจ้ๆ, จะไจ้ chjai³-chjai³ adv. often; repeatedly.

ฉ

ฉ The ninth consonant in the Thai alphabet, a high class letter, of which there are eleven, *viz.* ข, ฃ, ฉ ฐ, ฐ, ผ, ฝ, ศ, ษ, ส, ห. ฉอฉิ่ง is the name of this letter. ฉ is used extensively in Pali and Sanskrit where it is pronounced cha⁴.

ฉ ๒ chau² *P. adj. prefix* six; sixth: ฉกามาพจร-วจร (กามาพจร) *lit.* "belonging to, or within the domain of sensual pleasure," *i.e.* the six heavens of the inferior or sensual angels, *viz.* (1) จาตุมมหาราชิก which is level with the summit of Yukunthun (ยุคนธร), the circular range next to Mount Meru, in which dwell the four guardians of the world; (2) ดาวดึงส์ which is level with the summit of Mount Meru, in which is the palace of Indra where flourish the kamapkruk (กามพฤกษ) trees, whose branches furnish everything that the angels can desire; (3) ยามะ which rests entirely on air; (4) ดุสิต the joyful heaven, wherein Buddha and others passed their last existence before being born on earth; (5) นิมมานรดี a heaven in which the mere will of the angels dwelling in it creates for them all they desire; (6) ปรนิมมิตวสวัตดี a heaven in which angels have all they desire, without having to create it by their own will, subsidiary angels gratifying their desires. In this highest of the luxurious sensual heavens, dwells Mara (มาร) the angel who takes the place of Satan, being the tempter of the Buddha (chd. p. 117: Ala. p. 308): ฉกษัตริย์ six kings; name of the twelfth chapter of the Thet Maha Chat: ฉทวาร six physical apertures, as eyes, nose, ears, etc.: ฉทาน ศาลา, ศาลาฉทาน six houses, places or localities where gifts, donations or alms are given (chd. p. 111); six centres of charity: ฉศก the sixth year in the cycle of ten years, according to the Chulasakarat or lesser era.

ฉก chok⁴ *v.* to snatch and run; to jerk away; to strike (as a cobra); to seize with talons (as a hawk); to pull or force away by violence: ฉกฉวย, ฉกลัก to grab; to clutch; to rob or plunder.

ฉกจวัก chok⁴-chja⁴-wak⁴ *v.* to raise the head with hood spread, ready to attack (as a cobra).

ฉกรรจ์ cha⁴-gkan *adj.* dangerous; serious; severe (as a wound); ferocious; barbarous; fatal; brave: ใจฉกรรจ์ brave-hearted; savage; fierce; brutal: ชายฉกรรจ์ a man physically eligible for the army (20 to 30 years of age).

ฉกาจ cha⁴-gkat⁴ *adj.* fierce; savage; brutal; cruel; pitiless; murderous.

ฉงน cha⁴-ngon² *v.* to be in doubt; to waver or to be unsettled in one's opinion; to vacillate: ฉงนไป to mistake one person for another; to be uncertain in identification.

ฉงาย ๑ cha⁴-ngai² *v.* to doubt; to mistrust; to regard with jealousy; to be suspicious.

ฉงาย ๒ cha⁴-ngai² *Cam. adj.* far; distant; separated; remote.

ฉณ cha⁴-na⁶ *P. n.* a festival (chd. p. 104); an occasion of joy, or a musical entertainment.

ฉนวน ๑ cha⁴-noo-an² *Cam. v.* to cover; to veil; to shelter; to separate (as by a partition); to insulate: ฉนวน (ต้น) *Dalbergia nigrescens (Leguminosae)* (V. P. p. 91: cb. p. 482).

ฉนวน ๒ cha⁴-noo-an² *n.* a temporary passageway enclosed by boards or curtains, to provide ladies of the palace a private passage or walk (as to a boat-landing).

ฉนัง cha⁴-nang² *Cam. n.* an earthen pot.

ฉนาก (ปลา) cha⁴-nak⁴ *n.* a species of sea fish, the saw-fish, *Pristis perotteti* (Dept. Agri. & Fisheries).

ฉนำ cha⁴-nam² *Cam. n.* a year.

ฉพ see ฉวะ

ฉม chom² *Cam. n.* fragrance; perfume; various scents or fragrant powders.

ฉมวก cha⁴-moo-ak⁴ *n.* a two- or three-pronged harpoon for spearing fish.

ฉมวย ๑ cha⁴-moo-ey² *v.* to catch; to seize; to arrest; to snatch.

ฉมวย ๒, ฉมัง, ฉม่ำ cha⁴-moo-ey² *adj.* accurate; sure; correct; protected by charms; invulnerable.

ฉมัน cha⁴-man² *n.* a stag; a deer.

ฉมา cha⁴-mah² *P. n.* the earth (chd. p. 104): ฉมาดนัย *lit.* "a son of the earth," *i. e.* the planet Mars: ฉมาดล the earth's surface; ground: ฉมาบดี *lit.* "a lord of the earth," *i. e.* a king: ฉมามณฑล the orb; the whole earth.

ฉม่ำ see ฉมวย ๒

ฉล cha⁴-la⁶ *P. S. v.* to defraud; to cheat; to deceive: *n.* fraud; deceit; sham; disguise; a pretence; a delusion; fiction; a trick; fallacy; stratagem (S. E. D. p. 405).

ฉลวย cha⁴-loo-ey² *adj.* beautiful and gradually tapering to a point (as a pagoda).

ฉลอเฉลา cha⁴-lau²-cha⁴-low² *adj.* elegant (Michell).

ฉลอง cha⁴-laung² *v.* to cross over; to make a facsimile of; to support; to substitute; to celebrate; to dedicate with a grand ceremony: ฉลองได a back scratcher (used for royalty): ฉลองพระ the ceremony of dedicating, or celebrating a statue of Buddha: ฉลองพระเนตร a pair of spectacles (used for royalty): ฉลองพระบาท sandals; shoes (used for royalty): ฉลองพระหัตถ์ a spoon; a fork; chopsticks; gloves; anything to be worn on the hand (used for royalty): ฉลองพระองค์, ฉลององค์ wearing apparel (used for royalty): ฉลองพระโอษฐ์ a cuspidore; a spittoon (used for royalty): ฉลองวัด to perform the dedicatory ceremony of a temple or church: วันฉลอง a day of celebration or dedication.

ฉลอม cha⁴-laum² *n.* a small sea-going sailboat: ฉลอมท้ายญวน a kind of sea-going sailboat having a pointless or cut-off stern (used in the district of Rayong).

ฉลัก, จำหลัก cha⁴-lak⁴ *v.* to carve; to chisel decorative designs (in wood or stone); to shape by cutting.

ฉลาก cha⁴-lak⁴ *n.* a raffle or lottery ticket: a label: ฉลากกินแบ่ง a lottery: ฉลากกินรวม a raffle: จับฉลาก to cast lots; to draw a ticket in a raffle: ทิ้งฉลาก to throw lottery tickets to a crowd of people: ลูกฉลาก limes enclosing a ticket drawing a prize (as given out at cremations).

ฉลากบาง cha⁴-lak⁴-bang *n.* a kind of boat.

ฉลาด cha⁴-lat⁴ *adj.* smart; marked by acuteness or shrewdness; cunning; clever; skillful; crafty: ฉลาด (ปลา) *Notopterus notopterus*, featherback fish (Dept. Agri. & Fisheries: H. M. S. N. H. J. S. S. XI, 2, p. 256): เฉลียวฉลาด *an euphonic form* very clever; shrewd, tricky or adroit.

ฉลาม (ปลา) cha⁴-lam² *n.* a shark: ฉลามปลาวาฬ (ปลา) *Rhineodon typus* (*Rhineodontidae*), whale shark: (H. M. S.); *Scoliodon intermedius* (Dept. Agri. & Fisheries): ฉลามกบ, ฉลามหิน (ปลา) *Chiloscyllium indicum* (*Orectolobidae*), a small shark of no particular importance. The flesh is eaten fresh or salted (Burk. p. 525: Dept. Agri. & Fisheries): ฉลามลาย, ฉลามเสื้อ (ปลา) *C. plagiosum* (Dept. Agri. & Fisheries): ฉลามหนู (ปลา) *Scoliodon palasorrah* (Dept. Agri. & Fisheries): ฉลามหัวข้อน (ปลา) *Sphyrna blochi* (*Sphyrnidae*), hammer-head shark: ปากฉลาม an anteroposterior flap used as a covering for an amputation of arm or leg.

ฉลาย cha⁴-lai² *adj.* injured; broken; cracked; fissured (as a precious stone); impaired; damaged (as having a flaw).

ฉลัก see ฉัก

ฉลาน (ที่) cha⁴-lan² *v.* to mow; to clear a piece of ground; to level (Michell).

ฉลุ cha⁴-loo⁴ *v.* to carve; to chase; to engrave; to shape by means of a scroll-saw; to perforate, making some design.

ฉลุกฉลวย cha⁴-look⁴-cha⁴-loo-ey² *adj.* quick; active; sprightly; lively; urgent; speedy.

ฉลู cha⁴-loo² *Cam. n.* the ox; the second year of the Siamese animal cycle of twelve years.

ฉ่วงฟ้า (ต้น) choo-ang⁴-fah⁵ *n. Lagerstroemia tomentosa (Lythraceae)* (cb. p. 727); "leza," a moderate-sized, handsome tree, native of hot and moist parts of Burma. It blossoms twice a year, in April and October, bearing large erect panicles of white flowers, produced from the ends of the branches (MCM. pp. 89, 90 : BURK. p. 1298).

ฉ่วงมู (ต้น) choo-ang⁴-moo *n. Lagerstroemia flos-reginae (Lythraceae)* (cb. p. 723), queen's flower, pride of India, a mediumsized spreading tree, native of Siam, Ceylon, India and Malaya. This is undoubtedly one of the most strikingly showy of flowering trees, and from April to July or later bears, from the ends of the branches, erect panicles of large, beautiful, mauve or pink flowers. The older trees are deciduous for a short period during the dry weather. There are two or more varieties which are very attractive (MCM. pp. 89, 210, 213, 518).

ฉวย choo-ey² *v.* to seize; to snatch; to grab at, or catch : ฉวยฉาบ to carry away suddenly and swiftly by hand, or in the beak; to steal; to pilfer; to filch : ฉวยฉุด to snatch away with force; to seize and drag away :

ฉวยได้ to have been seized or grabbed; to have been able to seize : ฉวยตัว, คว้าตัวได้ to have been able to capture a person by force : ฉวยผิด, คว้าผิด to have seized wrongly or by mistake : ฉวยมีด to snatch or grab a knife : ฉวยมือ to grasp or clutch the hand rudely : ฉวยไม้ to grip a stick : ฉวยยื้อ, ยื้อแย่ง, ฉวยแย่ง, ฉกชิง to grab and snatch away violently : ฉวยลาก, ฉุดลาก to seize suddenly and drag : ฉวยว่า if perchance; peradventure; if; perhaps; in order that : ฉวยไว้, จับไว้, คว้าไว้ to catch and fasten (as the rope of a run-away horse or cow).

ฉวะ, ฉพ cha⁴-wa⁶ *P. n.* a corpse; a cadaver; carrion (S. E. D. p. 1059).

ฉวัดเฉวียน, เฉวียน cha⁴-wat⁴-cha⁴-wee-an² *v.* to move rapidly in a circle; to whirl round rapidly; to circumrotate : *adj.* rotatory.

ฉวาง cha⁴-wang² *v.* to obstruct by placing something crosswise; to be placed in a crisscross position : *n.* an advanced arithmetic (Siamese) : *adj.* wide; spacious.

ฉวี cha⁴-wee² *P. S. n.* skin; hide; cuticle; colour of the skin; complexion; beauty; splendour; a ray of light (s. E. D. p. 405).

ฉ้อ chau³ *v.* to defraud; to cheat; to injure by embezzlement : ฉ้อกระบัด, ฉ้อฉล to cheat; to swindle or defraud : ฉ้อได้ able to swindle or cheat another : ฉ้อราษฎร์บังหลวง to pecculate from the people and also from the Crown.

ฉอก chauk⁴ *adj.* receding; slanting or sloping backwards : ผมฉอก frontal baldness; a high forehead.

ฉอด chaut⁴ *adj.* ready in the use of words; voluble; fluent or gifted in speech.

ฉอเลาะ chau²-lau⁶ *adj.* flattering, fawning, beseeching, or pleading words.

ฉะ cha⁴ *v.* to cut or bark with a few strokes of a knife (as a tree); to slash at random; to chip; to notch; to cut deeply and quickly.

ฉะ, ฉา ๆ cha[3] an exclamation indicating surprise, doubt or contradiction.

ฉะฉ่ำ cha[4]-chah[4] *onomat.* from the sound of falling water at a water-fall; an antiphonal chorus sung intermittently during burlesques, comic plays or dancing.

ฉะฉาด cha[4]-chat[4] *onomat.* from the sound of ringing metal, produced by striking cymbals.

ฉะฉาน cha[4]-chan[2] *adj.* lucid; clear; easily understood; perspicuous (used in reference to a sermon or discourse).

ฉะฉ่ำ cha[4]-cham[4] *adj.* fascinating; attractive; gladsome; joyful; pleasing.

ฉะฉี่ see ฉี่

ฉะเฉื่อย cha[4]-cheu-ay[4] *adj.* slow; sluggish; gentle but constant (as a blowing wind); soft (as a breeze).

ฉะเชิงเทรา cha[4]-cherng-sow *n.* Patriew (a town, and a province east of Bangkok).

ฉะนั้น cha[4]-nan[5] *adv.* in that way; on that wise; therefore; thus: เหตุฉะนั้น on that account; consequently; therefore; for that reason.

ฉะนี้ cha[4]-nee[5] *adv.* in this way or manner; on this wise; so.

ฉะบัง, ฉะบำ cha[4]-bang *n.* an ancient form of rhyme or poetry, each line having sixteen syllables.

ฉะบัด cha[4]-bat[4] *adj.* clear; definite; concise.

ฉะบับ, ฉะบบ cha[4]-bap[4] *n.* pattern; volume; book; letter; manuscript; used as a numerical classifier of papers or books, *ex.* จดหมาย ๒ ฉะบับ two letters; จดหมายเหตุรายวัน ๓ ฉะบับ three daily newspapers: ฉะบับเดิม the original copy of any document or book.

ฉะบำ see ฉะบัง

ฉะเพาะ cha[4]-pau[6] *v.* to reserve; to withhold; to keep especially: *adj.* exclusively for; only for; solely for (this person); being limited: จัดไว้ฉะเพาะ reserved for: ฉะเพาะหน้า in the presence of: ฉะเพาะตัว private and confidential (as a letter).

ฉะมบ cha[4]-mop[6] *n.* a group of evil spirits; a spear or harpoon (as a sharpened bamboo pole).

ฉะอ้อน cha[4]-aun[3] *v.* to implore; to beseech or entreat: *adj.* slender, delicate and charming (in shape or figure).

ฉักกะ chak[4]-gka[4] *P. adj.* consisting of six; grouped in sets of six; occurring for the sixth time (S. E. D. p. 1180).

ฉัฏ, ฉัฏฐม chat[4] *P. S. adj.* sixtieth; consisting of sixty (S. E. D. p. 1109).

ฉัตร chat[4] *P. S. n.* an umbrella; a parasol; an ensign of royal or delegated power; a particular constellation; *lit.* "a shelter of pupils," *i. e.* a teacher (S. E. D. p. 404): ฉัตรกระดาษ paper umbrellas made in tiers (used as decorations): ฉัตรทอง golden or gilded umbrellas in tiers (used as decorations): ฉัตรธาร a parasol bearer; a royal parasol (Ala. p. 147); the royal parasol or state canopy; one of the insignia of royalty or sovereignty (chd. p. 104): ฉัตรบรรณ, สัตตบรรณ, ต้นตีนเป็ด *Cerbera odollam; Alstonia scholaris (Apocynaceae)*, a tall tree found from Ceylon to Australia. This tree has been cultivated in India from rather remote times, being an ornamental tree with medicinal uses. Its bark is made into a vermifuge, and is also considered a tonic and febrifuge. The timber is soft, light, and perishable, and seasons badly, lasting not more than six months in the soil. It has a peculiar use, however, for it has long been used to make slates. These wooden slates are cleaned by erasing the writing with *Delima* leaves. This use has given the tree its name *scholaris*. The wood has been tried for matches and found suitable (BURK. pp. 114–115): ฉัตรเบญจรงค์ an umbrella of five colours and in five tiers: ฉัตรพระอินทร์ (ต้น) *Leonotis nepetifolia* (*Labiatae*), a tall herb, which grows in Africa and India, approaching the Malay Peninsula and northern Siam. In India, the ash of the flower buds is applied to scalds and burns, and to ringworm and itch (BURK. p. 1329: V. P. p. 92). In Ceylon, it is an ornamental herb. The orange-scarlet flowers are handsome (MCM. p. 141): ฉัตรภังค์ *lit.* "destruction of the royal parasol," *i.e.* loss of the domain; anarchy; widowhood: เศวตรฉัตร a white umbrella. When hung or placed over the King's throne it has nine tiers, as an insignia of highest rank. When hung or placed over a throne for the Queen or Crown Prince it has seven tiers.

ฉัททันต์　　chat[4]-tan *P. n.* name of a mythical elephant; name of one of the great lakes. The lake is probably named for this mythical elephant who lives in a golden palace on the shores of the Himalayan lake, attended by eighty thousand ordinary elephants (CHD. p. 103); king of elephants (Ala. p. 295).

ฉัทม　　chat[4]-ta[6]-ma[6] *P. n.* a roof (Chd. p. 103); an external covering; a deceptive dress; a disguise; a pretext; a pretence; deceit; fraud (S. E. D. p. 404): ฉัทมเพศ *lit.* "one whose sex is disguised," *i. e.* one able to assume various forms, or appearances; a deceptive person; one having a dual personality.

ฉัทวร　　chat[4]-ta[6]-waun *S. n.* a tooth (S. E. D. p. 404).

ฉัน　　chan[2] *v.* to eat (used only for Buddhist monks): *adv.* however; wherefore; as; thus: *pron.* I; myself: ฉันจังหัน to partake of food or rice (used only for Buddhist monks): ฉันใด however; wherefore: ฉันนั้น thus; that way; therefore: ฉันเพล to partake of food before noon (as required of Buddhist monks): ฉันเอง, ข้าเอง the pronoun I (used

by country people): ดีฉัน I (used only by women): หม่อมฉัน I (used only to a prince).

ฉันท์　　chan[2] *P. S. n.* approval; consent; satisfaction; a metrical composition (S. E. D. p. 404): ฉันทศาสตร์ metrical science (S. E. D. p. 404); name of the oldest known work on "Chhandas," or "Prosody of the Vedas," ascribed to the great author Pingala. He is supposed to have written it about two centuries B. C. (H. C. D. pp. 71, 234).

ฉับ　　chap[4] *adj.* urgent; pressing; instant; important; requiring haste: *onomat.* from the sound made by striking brass cymbals: ฉับเฉียว, ฉับไว smart; lively; quick; nimble; agile: ฉับพลัน immediately; instantly; at once.

ฉัพพัณณรังษี　　chap[4]-pan-na[6]-rang-see[2] *n.* six rays of light or glory; one possessing six characteristics.

ฉ่า　　chah[4] *onomat.* from the sizzling sound of frying: ฉ่า, ฉะฉ่าฉะ an antiphonal chorus sung during the comic or burlesque dancing of the peasantry.

ฉาก　　chak[4] *n.* stage scenery; a curtain; a movable screen; a carpenter's square: *adj.* straight: ฉากน้อย, ฉากใหญ่ attitudes assumed by Siamese actors: มุมฉาก a right-angle; an angle of 90 degrees.

ฉาง　　chang[2] *n.* a granary: ฉางเกลือ a salt bin: ฉางข้าว a rice bin.

ฉ่าง　　chang[4] *v.* to draw cuts; to throw dice; to throw a coin in order to see who, or which side, starts off first: *onomat.* from the sound of Chinese cymbals or gongs.

ฉ่าฉาว　　chah[4]-chow[2] *adj.* a tumultuous noise.

ฉาด　　chat[4] *onomat.* from the sound of slapping or striking.

ฉาดฉาน　　chat[4]-chan[2] *adj.* adroit; dextrous; expert; deft; distinct, clear or obvious (as in the use of words): *onomat.* from the sound of clapping the hands, or water lapping the bank, or waves dashing.

ฉาต, ฉาตก chah²-dta⁴ *P. S. v.* to be hungry; to be famished; to be starving (chd. p. 104): ฉาตกภัย the pestilence of famine.

ฉาทนะ chah²-ta⁶-na⁶ *P. S. n.* a covering; a sheath; a wing; raiment; a place of concealment (S. E. D. p. 404).

ฉาน chan² *v.* to be broken; to be scattered; to be opened; to be skillful or experienced; to be proficient: *n.* an open space; a verandah, or platform in front of a seat: ดีฉาน *ancient.* I: แตกฉาน clearly; distinctly; definitely; plainly; explicitly.

ฉาบ chap⁴ *v.* to smear over; to paint; to varnish; to glaze; to spread over (as with frosting): *n.* a cymbal struck for keeping time in Siamese music: ฉาบปูน to white-wash: ฉาบหน้า to apply externally (as paint, oil, or lotions): เดินฉาบกันไป to pass close to others: นกบินฉาบกันลงมา the bird swoops down.

ฉาบฉวย chap⁴-choo-ey² *adj.* speedily; quickly; expeditiously; suddenly; taken quickly away (as a hawk seizes a chick): ทำงานฉาบฉวย to perform a task quickly and efficiently: บินลงมาฉาบฉวย to dart down and seize with the beak or claws.

ฉาป, จาป chap⁴ *P. S. n.* a cub or young of any animal; a child (chd. p. 104); *syn.* จาป.

ฉาย ๑ chai² *S. n.* a shade; a shelter; a shadow; a reflection (S. E. D. p. 406): พระฉาย a looking-glass (used only for royalty); a photograph of royalty.

ฉาย ๒ chai² *v.* to reflect light (as a mirror); to emit rays (as the sun): คันฉาย a pitch-fork: ฉายเฉิด beautiful; handsome; having a clear, fresh complexion; striking; attractive: ฉายดิน to level off the ground smoothly (as a garden plot).

ฉายา chah²-yah *P. S. n.* a picture; a photograph; a reflection; a shade; a shadow; a shelter; a protection; wife of the Sun god and mother of the planet Saturn (S. E. D. p. 406): ฉายาดนัย *lit.* "son of the Sun god," *i.e.* the planet Saturn: ฉายาบถ, ทางช้างเผือก the Milky Way; the Path of Light: ฉายากัษัตตา *lit.* "the husband of พระนางฉายา," *i.e.* the Sun: ฉายามาน an instrument for measuring shadows: ฉายามิตร *lit.* "a shade-friend," *i.e.* a parasol: ฉายายนตร์ *lit.* "a shadow instrument," *i.e.* a sun-dial.

ฉาว, เอิกเกริก chow² *adj.* tumultuous; widespread; producing excitement; rumoured, *ex.* อย่างคนบิดบังความชั่วไว้ภายหลังมีคนรู้โจษกันออกฉาวไป: แก้ฉาว to suppress a report.

ฉ่ำ cham⁴ *adj.* pleasing; pleasant; agreeable; delightful; delicious: เย็นฉ่ำ agreeably cool: ลมพัดเฉื่อยฉ่ำ a refreshing breeze: หวานฉ่ำ luscious; delicious; agreeably sweet.

ฉำฉา (ต้น) cham²-chah² *Chin. n. Kleinhovia hospita (Sterculiaceae)* (V. P. p. 91), a large, spreading Malayan tree with heart-shaped leaves. It bears large, terminal panicles of rose-coloured flowers, chiefly during July to August. It thrives in the moist, low country (MCM. p. 89: BURK. p. 1281); *Enterolobium saman (Leguminosae)* (cb. p. 561: BURK. p. 927), rain-tree, a tree of the northern parts of South America which has been dispersed throughout the tropics since the middle of the last century. It is valued as a quick-growing, luxurious shade tree; the crown may be 60 or 70 feet across: ฉำฉาญี่ปุ่น (ต้น) Japanese pine, *Podocarpus macrophylla, var. Maki, Podocarpus japonica,* a shrub, native of China and Japan, with long, linear, ornamental leaves. It is said to have been first brought to Bangkok by the Japanese for decorating the rockeries of the Dusit Palace gardens, about 1900 (KERR. N. H. J. S. S. VIII, 3, p. 210: MCM. p. 188).

ฉำแนะ see แนะ

ฉิ, ฉิ chi⁴ an exclamation of surprise, unbelief, or aversion (Michell).

ฉิ่ง   ching[4] *n.* a timbrel; alto-cymbals; a Siamese musical instrument.

ฉิ่ง   ching[3] *v.* maimed, stiff, or broken (descriptive of an arm, leg, or joint) (Michell).

ฉิน   chin[2] *v.* to slander; to defame, or blame; to find fault: *adj.* similar; somewhat alike; corresponding to: ติฉินนินทา to malign; to calumniate.

ฉินท์   chin[2] *P. S. v.* to cut; to sever; to cut down; to interrupt; to stop; to remove; to destroy: ฉินทภาคย์ a piece or portion cut off or separated from the main part.

ฉิบ   chip[4] *adj.* hasty; swift; animated; nimble; prompt; an exclamation of surprise and disgust (as when an article is lost); *syn.* หายฉิบ; ขะโมยลักเอาไปฉิบ;   ฉิบหาย to be utterly destroyed or ruined; to put an end to; to annihilate; to perish; to exterminate (a word indicating contempt).

ฉิมพลี (ต้น)   chim[2]-pa[6]-lee *n. Bombax malabaricum (Malvaceae)*, silk-cotton tree. This tree is found from the Himalayas and Ceylon, through Siam and Malaya to Australia.   As the floss is inferior to kapok, it would not be likely to find a place in international trade, though it is used locally (BURK. p. 345).

ฉิว   chiew[2] *v.* to get angry; to be in a rage: *adj.* speedy; quick; rapid: ลมพัดฉิว ๆ a gentle steady breeze; a zephyr: หมุนฉิว to make rapid revolutions.

ฉี่, ฉะฉี่   chee[4] *onomat.* from the sizzling or hissing sound produced while frying, or as water is poured on live coals.

ฉี่ (ต้น)   chee[3] *n. Micromelum minutum (Rutaceae)* (CB. p. 228 : BURK. p. 1468), a small tree found from Indo-China to the Pacific. The timber is light but durable and is used for houses.   In Sumatra, the bitter roots are chewed with betel for coughs.   In Malaya, a poultice of the boiled roots is applied for ague.

ฉีก, ฉลีก   cheek[4] *v.* to tear; to rend; to pull apart with violence: แผลฉีก a lacerated wound.

ฉีด   cheet[4] *v.* to inject; to squirt: กระบอก-ฉีด a rubber syringe; a bamboo squirt-gun: เข็มฉีด an hypodermic needle: ฉีดยา to inject a remedy (into the tissues).

ฉุ   choo[4] *adj.* fluffy; bloated; flabby: เนื้อ-บวมฉุ ๆ oedematous tissue.

ฉุก   chook[4] *v.* to occur unexpectedly; to be sick at heart; to be suddenly in anguish (as on the occurrence of any calamity):   ฉุกใจ to be troubled at heart; to be distressed in spirit; to have doubtful forebodings; to have anguish of mind: ฉุกเฉิน immediately; speedily; hastily; swiftly: ฉุกละหุก to be in great confusion; to be perplexed; to be distraught (as in time of a fire).

ฉุงฉิง   choong[2]-ching[2] *adj.* peevish; fretful; tiresome: *onomat.* from the clanging of chains, or swords, or the sound of chains dragging on the pavement while the wearer is walking.

ฉุด   choot[4] *v.* to pull; to haul; to drag with violence: ฉุดคร่า, ฉุดลาก to drag off forcibly; to abduct for an immoral purpose.

ฉุน   choon[2] *v.* to be vexed with; to be angry; to be indignant; to be out of patience: *adj.* pungent; stimulating; strongly acrid; biting (used in reference to taste and odour): กลิ่นฉุน an odour, or gas that causes smarting in the nostrils (as ammonia, or sulphur fumes): ใจฉุนเฉียว to be easily provoked; given to being incensed, vexed, or exasperated: ฉุนเฉียว, โกรธจัด to be wrathful; to be very much vexed; to be enraged: พูดฉุนเฉียว to speak in an irritating manner; to use impetuous language: ยาสูบฉุน strong tobacco.

ฉุบ   choop[4] *onomat.* from the sound of a post let forcibly down into a muddy hole.

ฉุยฉาย choo-ey[2]-chai[2] *v.* to be elegantly dressed; to be affected in dress or manner: *n.* an attitude assumed by Siamese actors: ฉุยกลิ่น, ฉุยแฉก to scatter; to squander; to be disseminated, or dissipated: ฉุยฉายเข้าวัง an attitude assumed by Siamese dancers.

ฉู, พุง choo[4] *adj.* diffusible (as smoke or odours): *onomat.* from the sound made by a swarm of bees, or mosquitoes.

ฉู่ฉี่ choo-[4]chee[4] *n.* fried fish or pork served with a sauce (so named from the sizzling sound produced while cooking).

ฉูด choot[4] *adj.* rapid; moving with celerity; advancing with speed; very swift or quick (used in connection with football players when making a run with the ball): ฉูดฉีด to squirt, or spout out with force.

ฉูดฉาด choot[4]-chat[4] *adj.* striking; flashy; gaudy; dazzling; showy (in reference to colours or dress).

เฉ chey[2] *adj.* leaning to one side, slanting; deviating; oblique.

เฉก ๑ chek[4] *adj.* like; similar; resembling: ขาวเฉกผ้าย white like cotton.

เฉก ๒ chek[4] *P. S. adj.* sharp; clever; cunning; shrewd; expert (S. E. D. p. 407).

เฉโก chey[2]-gkoh *adj.* villainous; artful; deceitful; trickish; fraudulent; perfidious.

เฉ่ง cheng[4] *Chin. v.* to pay off; to pay the balance due; to meet all liabilities: เฉ่ง-เงินเดือน to pay the salary due: วันเฉ่งเงินเดือน monthly pay-day.

เฉด chet[4] *v.* to chase; to drive off (used as a command to dogs).

เฉท chet[4] *P. S. n.* the act of cutting, tearing, picking, plucking, or dividing (Chd. p. 105).

เฉนียน cha[4]-nee-an[2] *n.* the edge of a pond; the bank, or brink of a river or stream.

เฉย cher-ey[2] *v.* to be indifferent; to be disinterested; to be impartial; to sit aimlessly; to keep silent; to be negligent or careless: เฉยเมย to manifest unconcern; to be apathetic.

เฉลย cha[4]-lur-ey[2] *v.* to refute a charge; to reply to an accusation: เฉลยไข to enlarge upon; to give an answer in explanation.

เฉลว cha[4]-lee-oh[2] *n.* a device made by folding and crossing thin bamboo strips to the shape of two equilateral triangles, so interlaced as to form a six-pointed figure, having open spaces between the slats. This chaleo design is ancient and well-known. It serves many purposes, *viz.* as a " For Sale " advertisement, as a charm to keep off evil spirits (a small chaleo being stuck upright on the covering of the pot in which medicines are boiled), and as a boundary mark. In connection with its use in ancient times, it is of interest to relate how the chaleo was used as a mark of public contempt on an unfaithful wife. The woman, having been adorned with garlands of red hibiscus and wearing a chaleo in front of her face, was paraded through the streets for three days by officials beating gongs. The chaleo, in this case, probably denoted a certain kind of " For Sale " advertisement. A chaleo was one of the distinguishing marks stamped on bullet, silver coins, now very rare, minted during the reign of Somdet Phra Nang Klao (1824–1851) (Le May J. S. S. XVIII, 3, p. 171).

เฉลา, สวย, งาม cha[4]-low[2] *adj.* beautiful; elegant; handsome; bewitching, *ex.* โฉมเฉลาเยาวยอดเสน่หา.

เฉลิม cha[4]-lerm[2] *v.* to build additions; to anoint on the forehead; to celebrate by having illuminations and festivities: *adj.* excellent; worthy; choice; surpassing; transcendent: เฉลิมพระเกียรติ to increase the honour, glory, fame or prestige of royalty.

เฉลี่ย cha[4]-lee-ah[4] *v.* to divide expenses or loss equally; to strike an average (as of a student's grades).

เฉลียง cha⁴-lee-ang² *n.* a gallery; a verandah; a covered balcony: *adj.* oblique; inclined from the perpendicular; slanting; aslant: ตัดเฉลียง to cut in a slanting or biased direction.

เฉลียง, เสลียง cha⁴-lee-ang⁴ *n.* a palanquin.

เฉลียว cha⁴-lee-ow² *v.* to be quick to understand; to be keen, astute, or bright intellectually: *adj* mentally active: เฉลียวใจ to have an afterthought; to recollect (as after some incident has passed); to suspect.

เฉวียง cha⁴-wee-ang² *adj.* diagonal; leaning, or veering to one side: *adv.* crosswise: *Cam. adj.* turning to the left.

เฉวียน see ฉวัดเฉวียน

เฉา chow² *v.* to wither; to droop; to fade; to lose freshness; to shrivel: *adj.* ignorant; unlettered; unlearned; withered; faded: เฉาโฉด, ไฉ่ very stupid and ignorant: ทำเฉา to act in a silly, stupid manner.

เฉาก๊วย chow²-gkoo-ey⁶ *Chin. n.* an imported Chinese jelly, prepared by boiling portions of a certain vine with sugar.

เฉาะ chaw⁴ *v.* to cut; to trim; to slice off the outer covering (as when preparing to open a soft coconut); to split open.

เฉิด chert⁴ *adj.* showy; gaudy; gay; beautiful; magnificent: เฉิดฉัน, เฉิดฉิน attractive or pleasing because of finery: เฉิดฉาย attractive because of neatness and beauty of dress; enticing by virtue of a clear, fresh complexion: เฉิดโฉม having a graceful, elegant carriage, or bearing.

เฉิบ cherp⁴ *adj.* slow; sluggish; dilatory; deliberate; wearisome.

เฉียง chee-ang² *adj.* deviating; swerving; deflected; turning: เฉียงใต้ veering toward the south; going or coming southward: เฉียงบ่า crosswise on the shoulder: เฉียงพร้าดำ (ต้น) *Justicia ventricosa (Acanthaceae)*,

a tropical herb (V. P. p. 91): เฉียงพร้านางแอ (ต้น) *Carallia brachiata (Rhizophoraceae)*; *C. integerrima* (Cb. p. 598: Burk. p. 448: V. P. p. 92), a small or medium-sized, low-growing, symmetrical tree with a spreading head and rather small, dark green leaves. It is specially suited to the seacoast. This tree is entirely evergreen with an excellent, handsome timber. It is hard and the young sapwood is yellowish rose which turns a greyish rose (MCM. pp. 206, 212): เฉียงพร้ามอญ (ต้น) *Justicia gendarussa* (V. P. p. 92), a small bushy shrub 3 to 4 ft. high (MCM. p. 73).

เฉียด chee-at⁴ *adj.* near; neighbouring; not far distant; almost touching (as when two moving boats are passing each other): แล่นเฉียดลม to tack close to the wind.

เฉียบ chee-ap⁴ *adj.* very sharp; pointed; piercing: เฉียบขาด, เด็ดขาด decisiveness: เฉียบแหลม direct; characterized by distinctness of meaning and pithy expression; smart; brilliant; clever: เย็นเฉียบ exceedingly cold.

เฉียว chee-ew² *adj.* strong; vigorous; rapid; hasty; adroit; skillful; adept; expert (as in the acquiring of knowledge or skill): เฉียว ฉุน wrathy; full of rage; incensed; angry.

เฉียว, โฉบ chee-ew⁴ *v.* to swoop; to descend rapidly from a height and seize some prey (used in reference to birds): เฉียวฉาบ, เฉียว โฉบ to swoop down upon and seize.

เฉือน cheu-an² *v.* to carve; to cut; to cut up meat; to cut into slices; to shave off (as when trimming horses' hoofs).

เฉื่อย cheu-ay⁴ *adj.* gentle; soft (as wind); slow; heedless; sluggish; regardless; indifferent: เฉื่อยฉ่ำ to be peaceful in mind; to be free from worry: เฉื่อยชา, เฉื่อยแฉะ dilatory; inactive; loitering; lingering; procrastinating: เฉื่อยเฉย inconsiderate; lethargic; inattentive: ลมเย็นพัดเฉื่อยๆ a gentle, cool breeze.

แฉ chaa[2] *Chin.* *v.* to spread out in full view; to cause to be separated; to scatter; to examine or count by separating each article or portion so it can be seen clearly; to march in procession in loose formation: *n.* cymbals (as used by the Chinese in this procession): แฉโพย to expose a secret.

แฉ่ chaa[4] *onomat.* from the gentle falling of rain, or the hissing sound of a piece of hot metal dipped into water.

แฉก chaak[4] *adj* indented; serrated; notched; toothed (like certain leaves); bifurcated: พัดแฉก a long-handled, leaf-shaped fan, embroidered and having serrated edges. These are conferred upon Buddhist monks of high rank.

แฉ่ง chaang[4] *adj.* smiling; cheerful or amused (expression of the face): ยิ้มแฉ่ง the only word in which this combination occurs, being a combination used for euphony.

แฉลบ cha[4]-laap[4] *v.* to turn or avert the head to one side suddenly (as a kite when flying); to avoid; to turn away from; to go in a crooked or zigzag manner: บินแฉลบ to fly in a zigzag course: พูดแฉลบ to speak in an indirect manner; to use insinuations: แฉลบขาว (ต้น) *Delaportea armata* (*Leguminosae*) (V. P. p. 91): แฉลบแดง (ต้น) *Acacia leucophloea* (*Leguminosae*) (cb. p. 549: V. P. p. 91: Burk. p. 22), a moderate-sized or large tree, found in the drier parts of India, in the dry zone of Burma, in Siam and Java. It can not grow in evergreen forest as its seedlings must have light. The branches are wide-spreading; the flowers a bright, pale yellow. The heartwood is hard and durable. In India the timber is little used but in Java it is held in estimation for houses, bridges and furniture. In Java the bark is used in tanning: แฉลบ (หอย) a salt-water bivalve, *Perna ephippium.*

แฉล้ม, แชล่ม cha[4]-laam[3] *adj.* handsome; admirable.

แฉละ, ชำแหละ cha[4]-laa[4] *v.* to cut; to carve; to slice.

แฉว cha[4]-waa[2] *adj.* concave, hollowed, and rounded out (as the current side of a bend of a river).

แฉะ, ฉ่ำแฉะ chaa[4] *v.* to be wet or damp; to be muddy: *adj.* wet; moist; humid; sluggish; slow; inactive: เฉอะแฉะ muddy; dirty; slushy: ตาแฉะ watery eyes; bleareyed: นั่งแฉะแบะ to mope; to sit lazily; to sit inactively for a long time: ปากแฉะ garrulous; loquacious.

โฉ choh[2] *v.* to be disseminated; to be diffused (as gases or odours): คนโฉเก a vagabond: โฉเก to cheat; to swindle.

โฉ่ choh[4] *adj.* being evil or vile in odour (as decaying fish); stinking.

โฉ่งฉ่าง chong[4]-chang[4] *onomat.* from the sound of clanging chains, clicking cymbals, or of ringing metal.

โฉงเฉง chong[2]-cheng[2] *adj.* to act in a disorderly, rowdy or riotous manner.

โฉด chot[4] *adj.* ignorant; stupid; silly: โฉดเฉา stupid; very dull; wanting in understanding, or alertness; foolish.

โฉนด cha[4]-note[4] *n.* a title deed for a piece of land: ฟ้องแย่งกรรมสิทธิ์โฉนด to contest the ownership of a title deed in a law court.

โฉบ chop[4] *v.* to swoop down; to descend; to pounce upon: โฉบฉวย, โฉบเฉี่ยว to descend upon and clutch the prey (like a hawk or falcon): โฉบบิน to swoop down upon and fly off.

โฉม chom[2] *n.* comeliness; grace; elegance (of figure): โฉมงาม elegant; dainty: โฉม ฉาย shapely; having regular features; being graceful and elegant in manner: โฉมเฉลา well-formed; well-shaped: โฉมเฉิด beautiful; choice, *ex.* โฉมเอยโฉมเฉิด เป็นเมียพี่เถิดอย่า

กล้วยยาก: โฉมตรู lovely in shape or form: โฉมนาง an attractive or amiable virgin, *ex.* โฉมนางแน่งน้อยช้อยชด: โฉมยง well-proportioned; handsome in figure: โฉมศรี graceful; elegant; displaying grace and beauty in form or action.

โฉลก, โชค cha[4]-loke[4] *n.* chance; fortune; luck; fate; a treatise on methods of fortune-telling: โฉลกดี a favourable issue.

ไฉน cha[4]-nai[2] *n.* an oboe; a wooden, flute-like, wind instrument of soprano compass: *adv.* why; how; by what means; for what reason, *ex.* ไฉนเราท่านจะพ้นวิญญาณ.

ไฉไล chai[2]-lai *adj.* pretty; glossy; smooth and shining (as a snake, or the scales of a fish); glistening; gleaming.

ช

ช The tenth consonant of the Thai alphabet, a low class letter of which there are twenty-four, viz. ค, ค, ฆ, ง, ช, ฌ, ซ, ญ, ฑ, ฒ, ท, ธ, ฑ, น, ณ, พ, ฟ, ภ, ม, ร, ล, ว, ฬ, ฮ. ชอช้อ and ชอช้าง are the designating names. It occurs in words of Sanskrit and Pali origin. In these languages this letter means *to originate, to be born,* and is used as a suffix, as สโรช *lit.* "originating in a pond," *i. e.* the lotus; วาริช *lit.* "born in the water," *i. e.* fishes.

ชก chok[6] *v.* to fight; to strike; to hit with the fists; to box.

ชค cha[6]-ka[6] *P. S. n.* the world; the earth; people; mankind; animals: *adj.* moving; movable; locomotive; living; that which moves or is alive (S. E. D. p. 408): ชคตรัย the three worlds, *viz.* heaven, earth and the lower world: ชคสัตว์ animals of the earth: ชคัตยาพดงส์ the supreme one or lord over the three worlds.

ชคดี, ชคตี cha[6]-ka[6]-dee *P. S. n.* a female animal; a cow; the world; the universe; mankind (S. E. D. p. 408): ชคดีจร *lit.* "earth-walker," *i. e.* man: ชคดีชานิ *lit.* "one whose wife is the earth," *i. e.* a sovereign; a king: ชคดีดล *lit.* "the earth's surface," *i. e.* ground; soil; sand: ชคดีธร *lit.* "an earth-supporter," *i. e.* a mountain: ชคดีบดี *lit.* "an earth-lord," *i. e.* a king: ชคดีบาล *lit.* "an earth-pro-

tector," *i. e.* a king: ชคดีภุช *lit.* "an earth-enjoyer," *i. e.* a king.

ชคท chok[6]-ta[6] *n.* people; mankind; humanity; men and animals (S. E. D. p. 408): ชคทัณฑ์ the universe; the mundane egg: ชคทันดก *lit.* "world-destroyer," *i. e.* death: ชคทันต์ the end of the world: ชคทาธาร *lit.* "a supporter of the universe," *i. e.* the wind; air; Rama: ชคทานนท์ "one rejoicing the world": ชคทาตุ *lit.* "life-spring or life-giver of the world," *i. e.* the air; wind: ชคทิศ *lit.* "world-lords," *i. e.* Brahma; Vishnu: ชคทีศวร *lit.* "a world-lord," *i. e.* Siva; a king.

ชคล cha[6]-kon *S. n.* a kind of spirituous liquor; a fluid suitable for distillation; an intoxicating drink (S. E. D. p. 408).

ชคัต, ชคัจ, ชคัช, ชคัท, ชคัน cha[6]-kat[6] *n.* air; atmosphere; wind; people; mankind; beings that are able to move or are alive; men and animals (S. E. D. p. 408): ชคัจจักษุ *lit.* "the eye of the universe," *i. e.* the sun: ชคัจจิตร *lit.* "a wonder of the universe," *i. e.* the universe viewed as a picture: ชคัชชีพ the living beings of this world: ชคัตกษัย, ชคัทวินาศ the destruction of the world: ชคัตตรัย the three worlds, *viz.* heaven, earth and the lower world: ชคัตบดี *lit.* "the lords of the world," *i. e.* Vishnu or Krishna; the sun; a king; Agni: ชคัตบิดา

lit. "the world's father," *i. e.* Siva: ชคัต-
ประกาศ the light of the world: ชคัตประธาน
lit. "a chief or chieftain of the world," *i. e.* the
god Siva: ชคัตประภู *lit.* "lords of the
world," *i. e.* Brahma; Siva; Vishnu: ชคัต-
ประสิทธิ known throughout the world: ชคัต-
ปราณ *lit.* "world-breath," *i. e.* the atmosphere;
air; Rama: ชคัตปรายณะ *lit.* "chief of the
universe," *i. e.* Vishnu: ชคัตปรีติ *lit.* "one
who is the world's joy," *i. e.* Siva: ชคัตสรรพ์
the universe: ชคัตสวามี *lit.* "the lord of
the world," *i. e.* Vishnu: ชคัตสักขี *lit.* "the
world's witness," *i. e.* the sun: ชคัทคุรุ *lit.*
"teachers of the world," *i. e.* Brahma; Vishnu;
Siva; Rama (as Vishnu's incarnation): ชคัท-
ธาดา *lit.* "the creator of the world," *i. e.*
Vishnu: ชคัทธาตรี *lit.* "world-nurse," *i. e.*
the Saraswati (สรัสวดี) which is primarily a
river, but is celebrated both as a river and a
deity. As a river goddess, she is lauded for the
fertilizing and purifying powers of her waters,
and as the bestower of fertility, fatness and
wealth (H. C. D. p. 284): ชคัทพล *lit.* "world-
strength," *i. e.* the wind: ชคัทพิมพ์ see ชค-
ทัณฑ์: ชคัทพช *lit.* "the seed, grain, or origin of
the world," *i. e.* Siva: ชคัทโยนิ *lit.* "the
world's womb," *i. e.* Brahma; Vishnu; Krishna: ชคัทวันทย *lit.* "one to be adored by
all mankind," *i. e.* Krishna.

ชคันนาถ cha[6]-kan-nat[3] Jagan-natha *lit.* "lord
of the world," *i. e.* Vishnu, or rather Krishna.
He is worshipped in Bengal and other parts
of India, but Puri, near the town Cuttack, in
Orissa, is the great seat of his worship, and
multitudes of pilgrims resort thither from
all parts, especially at the two great festivals
of the Snana-yatra and Ratha-yatra, in the
months of Jyaishtha (June) and Ashadha
(July). The first of these is when the image
is bathed with 108 pitchers of water drawn
on that day from a special well, and the
second, or car festival, when the image is
brought out upon a car with images of his
brother Bala-rama and his sister Su-bhadru,

and is drawn through the streets by devotees.
It is believed that anyone catching a glimpse
of Jagan-natha on the way will be saved
from rebirths (H. C. D. p. 129: Und. p. 81):
ชคันนิธิ *lit.* "world-receptacle," *i. e.* Vishnu:
ชคันนิวาส *lit.* "world-abode," *i. e.* Vishnu, Krishna, or Siva: ชคันเนตร *lit.* "world-eye,"
i. e. the moon (but if used in a plural sense,
it means both the sun and moon): ชคัน
มารดา *lit.* "world-mothers," *i. e.* Durga (พระ-
ทุรคา) and Lakshmi (พระลักษมี).

ชคัท, ชคัน see ชคัต

ชง chong *v.* to steep; to soak in a liquid; to
macerate; to soak and pour off the liquid; to
infuse: ชงใบชา to steep tea leaves; to
make an infusion of tea.

ชงโค (ต้น) chong-koh *n. Bauhinia integrifolia* (*Leguminosae*); *B. decipiens* (cb. p.
520 V. P. p. 96); *B. monandra*; *B. polysper-
ma* (cb. p. 525); *B. saccocalyx* (cb. p. 527); *B.
subsessilis*; *B. sulphurea* (cb. p. 530); *B. tomentosa* (cb. p. 531: BURK. pp. 309, 312), a
small tree or large shrub, with slender
branches and yellow flowers. The heart-wood
is hard, dark-red and very tough (MCM. pp. 83,
206): ชงโคขี้ไก่ (ต้น) *B. malabarica*; *B.
harmsiana* (cb. p. 522: V. P. p. 96): ชงโค-
นา, ชงโคใบเล็ก (ต้น) *B. racemosa* (cb. p. 527:
V. P. p. 96), a small tree of Ceylon, India,
Malaya and Siam. The fibre from the inner
bark is used for making ropes and cordage
(MCM. p. 429).

ชงฆ์, ชงฆา see ชังฆา

ชงโลง, โชงโลง chong-long *n.* an oblong
scoop attached to a long handle, suspended
from a tripod, and used for irrigating purposes.

ชฎา, ชฏา cha[6]-dah *P. S. n.* the hair twisted
together (as worn by ascetics, by Siva and
by persons in mourning): *adj.* wearing the
hair in twisted locks (S. E. D. p. 409); a crown
or pointed head-decoration worn by Siamese

actors : ชฎากลาป, ชฎาชาล, ชฎาพันธ์, ชฎามณฑล a knot of braided hair : ชฎาเจียร Siva : ชฎาชวาล *lit.* "flame-tufted," *i. e.* a lamp : ชฎาดินหน, ชฎาเบี่ยง an actor's crown made with decorations in the shape of leaves, or petals of flowers : ชฎาธร a sect of ascetics ; Siva ; the name of a people in southern India : ชฎาธารี those wearing matted hair : ชฎามังศี (โกฏฐี) *Nardostachys* (*Valerianaceae*), a small genus of Himalayan perennial herbs, allied to the common valerian. An oil made from the roots of the principal species, *N. jatamansi* (ชฎามังศี), highly prized in India as a perfume for the hair, is thought to be the spikenard of St. Mark's Gospel (see 14 : 3) (web.) : ชฎาสุร Jatasura, a Rakshasa (a goblin or evil spirit) who disguised himself as a Brahman and carried off Yudhi-shthira, Saha-deva, Nakula and Draupadi. He was overtaken and killed by Bhima (H. C. D. p. 134) ; name of a people in north-eastern Madhya-desa ; the middle country, described by Manu as "the tract situated between the Himavat and the Vindhya ranges to the west of Prayaga" (Allahabad) (H. C. D. p. 182).

ชฎายุ cha⁶-dah-yoo⁶ *S. n.* name of the king of vultures (S. E. D. p. 409). According to the Ramayana, he was a bird who was the son of Vishnu's bird, the Garuda. He became an ally of Rama and fought furiously against Ravana to prevent the carrying away of Sita. Ravana overpowered him and left him mortally wounded (H. C. D. p. 134).

ชฎิน, ชฎิน, ชฎี, ชฎี, ชฎิน, ชฎิน cha⁶-din *S. n.* an ascetic ; matted, knotted, or twisted hair (as worn by Siva and by all ascetics) ; an elephant attaining an age of 60 years (S. E. D. p. 409).

ชฎิล, ชฎิล cha⁶-din *S. n.* one wearing, or having clotted or tangled hair ; an ascetic ; a hermit ; a recluse.

ชด chot⁶ *v.* to moisten ; to adulterate ; to mix ; to add to : *adj.* curved ; flexible ; pliable ; bending upwards and tapering to a point : ชดช้อย flexible ; readily bent upwards, or into a circle ; graceful (as arms of a dancer) : ชดเชย to make additions ; to increase the original amount by a gift ; to add a thinning medium ; to adulterate : ชดใช้ to compensate ; to remunerate ; to reimburse.

ชตา see ชาตา

ชตุ cha⁶-dtoo⁴ *S. n.* lac ; gum ; rosin (S. E. D. p. 409) : ชตุการ red lac : ชตุเคหะ *lit.* "a place of torture," *i. e.* a house plastered with lac and other combustible substances. Such a house was built for the reception of the Pandavas princes by Purochana, the emissary of Dur-yodhana (ทุรโยธน์), who attempted to burn the princes in their house, but was burnt in his own house by Bhima (see Maha-bharata H. C. D. p. 247) : ชตุมณี *lit.* "lac-jewel," *i. e.* a mole : ชตุรส *lit.* "lac-juice," *i. e.* lac.

ชตุกา cha⁶-dtoo⁴-gkah *P. S. n.* a bat (S. E. D. p. 409).

ชน ๑ chon *Chin. v.* to bump against (as boats) ; to butt (as goats) ; to collide (as motor cars) ; to hit against with force ; to strike, or to knock with the head and fight with the horns : ชน (นก) the white ibis, *Threskiornis melanocephalus melanocephalus* (Herb. N. H. J. S. S. VI, 4, p. 349) : ชนกระบือ to pit buffaloes against each other : ชนไก่ to fight cocks : ชนขวบ to complete one year (as of age) : ชนโค to have bulls fight : ชนช้าง to have elephants fight : ชนปลา to have fish fight : น้ำชน a point where two currents, flowing in opposite directions, meet.

ชน ๒ chon *P. S. n.* man ; people ; persons ; a race ; living beings ; creatures (S. E. D. p. 410) : ชนกรี, ชนการี stick-lac ; red lac : ชนจักษุ *lit.* "the eye of all creatures," *i. e.* the sun : ชนเทพ *lit.* "man-god," *i. e.* a sovereign ; a king : ชนนาถ, ชนบดี, ชนราช, ชนาธินาถ, ชนาธิป, ชเนศ, ชเนศวร, ชนิศ, ชนิศวร *lit.* "man-lord," "a protector of the race," *i. e.* a king : ชนบท an empire ;

a community ; a nation ; people (in contrast to the sovereign) ; inhabitants of a country or realm : ชนบทมณฑล a district ; a province ; a circle or region formed in a country : ชนบาน beverages suitable for human beings : ชนปทาธิป, ชนปเทศวร *lit.* "a ruler of a realm, kingdom or domain," *i. e.* a king or monarch : ชนปทายุต composed of citizens or peasants : ชนปทิน a ruler or sovereign of a country : ชนประวาท, ชนวาท, ชนเวาท *lit.* "words spoken by people," *i. e.* rumours ; gossip ; prattle : ชนมาร *lit.* "men-killer," *i. e.* an epidemic : ชนเมชัย *lit.* "one who causes man to tremble," *i. e.* Janamejaya, a celebrated king, son of Parikshit (ท้าวปริกษิต), and great-grandson of Arjuna. It was this king to whom the Maha-bharata was recited by Vaisampayana (พราหมณ์ไวศัมปายนะ). The king listened to it in expiation for the sin of killing a Brahman (H. C. D. p. 133) : ชนวาที a talker ; a speaker ; a newsmonger : ชนสถาน *lit.* "a resort of men," *i. e.* name of a forest of Dandaka (ทัณฑก) in the Deccan, lying between Godavari and Narmada. This forest is the scene of many of Rama's and Sita's adventures and is described as "a wilderness over which separate hermitages are scattered, while wild beasts and Rakshasas everywhere abound" (H. C. D. p. 80) : ชนสมพาธ a throng of people ; human beings densely massed : ชนาเกียรณ์ crowded with people : ชนาจาร popular customs and usages : ชนาปวาท evil reports or rumours : ชนายน *lit.* "that which leads the populace," *i. e.* a road ; a path ; a highway : ชนรณพ *lit.* "man-ocean," *i. e.* a caravan of traders : ชนาศน์ *lit.* "man-eater," *i. e.* a wolf : ชนาศัย *lit.* "man-shelter," *i. e.* an inn ; a hotel ; a caravansary ; a temporary hall or asylum : ชเนนทร์ *lit.* "man-lord," *i. e.* a king : ชโนทาหรณ์ *lit.* "man-laudation," *i. e.* eulogy ; praise ; fame ; encomium.

ชนก cha[6]-nok[6] *P. S. n.* a father ; a progenitor ; name of a king, sovereign of Mithila (มิถิลา) ; name of Janaka, the father of Sita : *adj.* generating ; begetting ; producing ; caus-

ing (S. E. D. p. 410) : ชนกนันทินี, ชนกสุดา names of the daughter of Janaka (ท้าวชนก), *i. e.* the lady Sita (นางสีดา).

ชนกาธิบดี cha[6]-na[6]-gkah-ti[6]-bau-dee *n.* the father of a king.

ชนน, ชนน cha[6]-na[6]-na[6] *P. S. n.* a progenitor ; a creator ; life ; birth ; race ; lineage (S. E. D. p. 410) : ชนนานดร another world ; a previous existence ; a former life.

ชนนี chon-na[6]-nee *n.* a mother ; a queen-mother ; a bat.

ชนม์ chon *S. n.* birth ; production ; origin ; existence ; life (S. E. D. p. 411) : ชนม์พรรษา, ชันษา the year of birth ; age.

ชนยิดา, ชนิดา cha[6]-na[6]-yi[6]-dah *S. n.* one who generates, begets or brings into existence ; a father ; a parent (S. E. D. p. 411).

ชนยิตรี cha[6]-na[6]-yi[6]-dtree *S. n.* a mother.

ชนา see ชน ๒

ชนิ cha[6]-ni[6] *S. n.* a woman ; a wife ; a mother (S. E. D. p. 411) : ชนิกรรดา one coming into existence : ชนิกาม one desiring a wife.

ชนิก cha[6]-ni[6]-gka[4] *P. S. n.* a father (S. E. D. p. 410).

ชนิกา cha[6]-ni[6]-gkah *P. S. n.* a mother (S. E. D. p. 410).

ชนิต cha[6]-nit[6] *P. adj.* born ; brought forth or into being ; engendered ; produced ; occasioned (S. E. D. p. 411).

ชนิตร cha[6]-nit[6] *S. n.* a birthplace ; a place of origin ; a home ; parents ; relatives ; generative or procreative matter (S. E. D. p. 411).

ชนินทร์ see ชเนนทร์

ชนี cha[6]-nee *S. n.* a mother (S. E. D. p. 411).

ชเนตตี cha[6]-net[4]-dtee *P. n.* a mother (S. E. D. p. 411).

ชปน cha⁶-bpa⁴-na⁶ *P. S. n.* the act of whispering or muttering (S. E. D. p. 412): ชปนมนตร์ a muttered chant.

ชป่า cha⁶-bpah *P. S. n.* a rose; the China rose (S. E. D. p. 412).

ชม, ชมชั่ว chom *v.* to admire; to praise; to regard with approbation; to approve: ชมเชย to praise; to eulogize; to extol; to laud; to glorify: ชมดู to delight in; to appreciate the beauties of: ชมตลาด, ชมดง-นอก, ชมดงใน names of Siamese songs: ชม-โฉม to admire the comeliness of: ชมเล่น to manifest pleasure in admiring an article, flowers or plants.

ชมด (ต้น) cha⁶-mot⁶ *n. Hibiscus abelmoschus (Malvaceae)* (cb. p. 157: BURK. p. 1163), musk mallow, "ambrette" of the French, an annual shrub with large, mallow-like flowers. The seeds yield an oil of a musk-like odour, used in inferior perfumes. Mucilage from the roots is used in China for sizing paper. The Malays use the roots and leaves for poulticing (MCM. p. 457).

ชมพู ๑ chom-poo *P. S. n.* name of a fabulous river flowing from the mountain Meru (formed by the juice of the fruits of the immense jambu tree on that mountain) (S. E. D. p. 412): ชมพูทวีป (a) *lit.* "the land of the rose-apple tree," *i. e.* ancient name of India; (b) one of the seven islands or continents of which the world is made up; the great mountain Meru stands in its centre, and India is its best part (H. C. D. p. 132); (c) one of the four great continents of the universe, representing the inhabited world, as fancied by the Buddhists, and so-called because it resembles in shape the leaves of the jambu tree (chd. p. 165): ชมพูธวัช the central one of the seven continents surrounding the mountain Meru, India (named so, either from the jambu trees abounding in it, or from an enormous jambu tree on Mount Meru visible like a standard to the whole continent) (S. E. D. p. 412): ชมพูนท,

ชมพูนท *lit.* "coming from the Jambu river," *i. e.* a form of gold found in the Jambu river: ชมพูบรรพต name of a mountain in the Jambudwipa (ชมพูทวีป): ชมพูสร a city called Jambooseer (ชมพูเสียร), situated between Cambay and Baroch.

ชมพู (ส) ๒ chom-poo *adj.* pink or rose-coloured.

ชมพู่, ชมพู่น้ำดอกไม้ (ต้น) chom-poo³ *Hindi n. Eugenia jambos (Myrtaceae)* (cb. p. 647: V. P. p. 100: Burk. p. 969), the rose-apple, a medium-sized, handsome, dense, evergreen tree, native of Siam, India and Malaya, and introduced into Ceylon probably in the time of the Portuguese. The fragrant, pinkish-white fruit, about the size of a hen's egg, has a sweetish rose-water flavour, and is said to be used sometimes in preserves. As a fruit, however, it has little to recommend it, being usually woolly and almost juiceless; but it varies somewhat with different trees and different localities. This tree thrives best in moist districts, at medium elevations up to about 4,000 feet, preferring a deep, rich soil (MCM. pp. 216, 217, 260, 470, 488): ชมพู่ขาว, ชมพู่เขียว (ต้น) *Eugenia javanica (Myrtaceae)* (cb. p. 647: Burk. p. 969: V. P. p. 100), wax jambu, a small, ornamental, Malayan tree, producing clusters of pretty, glossy, rose-pink or pinkish-white, waxy-looking fruits. Each fruit is about the size of a large strawberry, with the base laterally compressed; it is sweetish-acid, but usually too fragrant and pithy to be agreeable. The tree is propagated by seed and thrives at low and medium elevations (MCM. p. 261): ชมพู่แดง, ชมพู่สาแหรก (ต้น) *Eugenia malaccensis (Myrtaceae)* (cb. p. 652: V. P. p. 100: Burk. p. 970), the Malay apple, jambu, peria jambu, a handsome tree, indigenous to Malaya. It grows 30 to 50 ft. high having large, leathery, oval leaves. It produces a great profusion of beautiful crimson flowers, the bright crimson stamens of which make a thick carpet under the tree as they drop. The pear-shaped, waxy-white or red fruits are in season chiefly during May and June. The snowy-white, woolly pulp is edible, but not of much account. This tree thrives at low and medium elevations (MCM. pp. 261, 482, 517): ชมพู่นก, ชมพู่ป่า (ต้น) *Eugenia aquea* (BURK. p. 960); *E. formosa* (V. P. p. 100 : cb. p. 641); *E. megacarpa*; *E. siamensis* (cb. pp. 652, 662): ชมพู่น้ำ (ต้น) *E. diospyrifolia* (cb. p. 639).

ชมพูพาดบ่า chom-poo-pat^3-bah^4 *n.* a gesture or posture assumed by the mahouts, while dancing in a propitiatory ceremony before the elephants, after their first trial in combat or contest, during their period of training.

ชมพูพาน, ชามภูวราช chom-poo-pan *n.* name of a monkey king, a character in the Ramayana who was an ally of Rama in his invasion of Lanka.

ชมเลาะ, ทะเลาะ chom-law^6 *v.* to quarrel; to have a dispute.

ชย, ชัย cha^6-ya^6 *P. S. Hindi n.* conquest; victory; triumph: *adj.* winning; victorious (as in a battle, or when playing with dice, or in a law-suit) (S. E. D. p. 412): ชยกุญชร a victorious elephant (as over rival elephants): ชยโฆษ shouts of victory: ชยธวัช a flag of victory: ชยบาน the drink of a victorious warrior: ชยบาล *lit.* "victory-leaper," *i. e.* a king; Brahma; Vishnu: ชยพฤกษ์ (ต้น) *Cassia renigera (Leguminosae)* (BURK. p. 479); *C. fistula* (cb. p. 510: BURK. p. 475: MCM. p. 85), Indian laburnum; pudding-pipe: ชยภูมิ a field of triumph (chd. p. 90): ชยเภรี *lit.* "drum of victory": ชยมงคล the glory or good fortune secured in achieving a victory; a royal elephant: ชยลักษมี, ชยศรี the goddess of Victory: ชยเลข *lit.* "victory-records," *i. e.* papers or documents recording a victory: ชยวาทย์ any instrument sounded to proclaim a victory: ชยสังข์ a conch shell sounded to proclaim a victory: ชยศัพท์ cheers proclaim-

ing a victory; repeated exclamations of "Chai yo": ชยสดมภ์ a column, flag-staff or trophy indicating the place or fact of a victory: ชยสวามี *lit.* "the lord of victory," *i. e.* a name for Siva: ชยารพ a shout of victory: ชยาศิร, ชยาศีส a prayer for victory.

ชยัมบดี cha^6-yam-bau-dee *P. S. n.* a husband and wife (chd. p. 168).

ชยา, ชยาบาศ cha^6-yah *S. n.* a bowstring; the chord of an arc: ชยาการ a bowstring maker.

ชยุติ cha^6-yoo^6-dti^4 *S. n.* splendour; brightness; lustre; majesty; dignity (S. E. D. p. 427).

ชยุติมันต์, ชยุติมา see ชุติมันต์, ชุติมา

ชโย cha^6-yoh *P. S. n.* victory; triumph; conquest: *onomat.* from an exclamatory shout of applause or encouragement (chd. p. [168].

ชร see ชวร

ชรอกชรัง chrauk^3-chrang *adj.* seclusive; secretive; concealed from general notice or knowledge; hidden.

ชรงมไพร chra^6-ngom-prai *n.* a forest of huge dimensions.

ชระดัด chra^6-dat^4 *v.* to bend the fingers backwards; to crack the knuckles.

ชระเดียด chra^6-dee-at^4 *adj.* scattered; strewed; plentiful; abundant.

ชระเดียดชระดัด chra^6-dee-at^4-chra^6-dat^4 *adv.* lying around loosely or carelessly.

ชระทึง chra^6-teu-ang *n.* a river.

ชระบอบ chra^6-baup^4 *v.* to feel a condition of contusion, lassitude or languor.

ชระบาบ chra^6-bap^4 *adj.* smooth; even; level; flat.

ชระมัว chra^6-moo-ah *n.* dawn; early dawn; the break of day; the first appearance of light.

ชระมุ่น chra^6-moon^3 *v.* to be in a condition

of mental perturbation, agitation or discomposure.

ชระเมี่ยง   chra[6]-mee-ang *v.* to turn the head sideways and look out of the corner of the eyes.

ชระเมี่ยน   chra[6]-mee-an *adj.* near; nigh; adjacent; contiguous; close; near by; close at hand.

ชระไม   see   ชะไม

ชระลอ   see   ชะลอ

ชระลอง, ชระล่อง   chra[6]-laung *Cam. n.* a stream; a channel (as of a river); a fissure, crevice or gorge (in the mountains).

ชระลัด   chra[6]-lat[6] *n.* a short-cut; a direct or shorter passage, route, way or path.

ชระลุ   chra[6]-loo[6] *v.* to be porous; to pierce full of holes; to perforate; to carve or chisel designs; to chase or ornament by indenting.

ชระแลง   see   ชะแลง

ชระโลง   see   ชะโล, ชะโลง

ชระอับ, ชระอ่ำ, ชระอื้อ, ชระอุ่ม   chra[6]-ap[4] *adj.* dark; overcast; darkened by mist or clouds; obscured; murky; clouded.

ชระเอม   chra[6]-em *adj.* shady; sheltered; cool and shaded.

ชรัด   chrat[6] *v.* to sip; to drink; to suck up; to quaff (as wine); *ancient* for ชด.

ชรัว   chroo-ah *n.* a mountain gorge, crevice or canyon; a valley.

ชรา   cha[6]-rah *P. S. n. lit.* "becoming old," *i. e.* debility consequent upon old age; decrepitude; old age; senility (S. E. D. p. 414): ชราภาส a cough developing in old age; a senile cough: ชราคุร infirm from age: ชราธรรม the laws of old age; old age or decay as an inevitable result; senility: ชราภิภูต decrepit from age: ชราภีรุ *lit.* "being afraid of, or opposed to old age," *i. e.* the god of Love: ชรามฤตยุ dying from age; old age and death:

ชราลักษณ์ *lit.* "old age signs," *i. e.* grey hairs: ชราสันธ์ *lit.* "born in halves but united by the Rakshasi Jara-sandha," *i. e.* a son of Brihad-ratha (ท้าวพฤหัทรถ), and king of Magdha. Brihad-ratha had two wives, who after being long barren, each brought forth a half of a boy. These aborted portions were regarded with horror and so were thrown away. A female, man-eating demon, named Jara, picked them up and put them together to carry them off. On their coming into contact, a boy was formed, who cried so lustily that he brought out the king and his two queens. The demon explained what had happened, resigned the child and retired. The name Jarasandha was given to the child because he had been formed of two halves by Jara. Future greatness was prophesied for the boy, who became an ardent worshipper of Siva, by whose favour he was able to prevail over many kings (H. C. D. p. 133).

ชราบ   chrap[3] *v.* to know; *ancient* for ทราบ.

ชราบชรับ   chrap[3]-chrap[6] *v.* to be moistened with; to absorb, or percolate into; to be over-laid or washed.

ชราย (ชะรายุ), ชลาพุ   cha[6]-rah-yoo[6] *S. n.* the scarf or cast-off skin of a serpent; a perish-able covering; the outer skin (covering) of the embryo; the after-birth; the uterus (S. E. D. p. 414).

ชรูก   chrook[6] *v.* to hide; to secrete; to keep, or put out of sight; *ancient* for ซุก.

ชรูบ   chroop[3] *v.* to waste away; to get thinner; to grow paler; *ancient* for ซูบ.

ชล   chon *P. S. n.* water: *adj.* stupid; dull; drowsy; torpid (S. E. D. p. 414): ชลกร tax or revenue derived from water (as from fisheries): *adj.* making or pouring forth water: ชลกรงค์ a conch-shell; a coconut; a lotus flower; a cloud; a wave: ชลกันดาร, ชลบดี, ชลาธิบดี, ชลาธิป *lit.* "one whose path is water, a water-lord," *i. e.* Varuna (พระวรุณ),

" the universal encompasser, the all-embracer "
(H. C. D. p. 336); one of the oldest of the Vedic
deities, a personification of all-investing sky,
the maker and upholder of heaven and earth.
As such, he is king of the universe, king of
gods and men, possessor of illimitable knowledge, the supreme deity to whom especial
honour is due. In later times he was chief
among the lower celestial deities called Adityas, and later still he became a sort of
Neptune, a god of the seas and rivers, who
rides upon the Makara (มังกร), a huge sea
animal, which has been taken to be the
crocodile, the shark, or the dolphin, but is
probably a fabulous animal. It is the vehicle
of Varuna, the god of the Ocean (H. C. D. p.
195): ชลกานต์ lit. " water-love (lover)," i. e.
the wind : ชลกิราฏ a shark : ชลกุมภ์ a
water-jar ; an ewer : ชลคุลม์ lit. " a pond of
circling water," i. e. a whirlpool ; a turtle :
ชลจร lit. " a water-goer (goers)," i. e. aquatic
animals ; fishes : ชลจราชีพ, ชลชาชีพ lit.
" living by fish (fishes)," i. e. fishermen :
ชลช lit. " those that are born in, produced in,
living or growing in water," " things coming
from, or which are peculiar to water," i. e.
aquatic animals, fish, sea-salt, conch-shells,
water flowers, lotus, etc.: ชลชันตุกา a leech :
ชลชันม lit. " being born in the water," i. e.
lotus plants : ชลชาสน์ lit. " lotus-seated,"
i. e. Brahma : ชลชินี lit. " lotus-friend," i. e.
the sun : ชลชีวี lit. " those living in or
near water," i. e. fishermen : ชลตรงค์ a
wave : ชลท, ชลัท lit. " water-giver," i. e. a
rain-cloud ; the ocean : ชลทกาล, ชลทสมัย lit.
" cloud-season," i. e. the rainy season : ชล-
ทักษัย lit. " the time when clouds disappear,"
i. e autumn ; the cold season : ชลทาคม lit.
" the season for the approach of clouds," i. e.
the rainy season : ชลเทพ lit. " having water
as its deity," i. e. the constellation Ashadha
(Cancer) : ชลธร lit. " holding or having
water," i. e. a rain-cloud ; the ocean : ชลธาร
a river ; a stream of water ; a water-course or
channel ; a lake : ชลธารณ์ lit. " holding

water," i. e. a ditch ; a well ; a pond : ชลธารา
a stream of water ; the current or flow of
water : ชลธิ, ชลธี, ชลธิศ lit. " water receptacle," i. e. a lake ; the ocean : ชลธิรศน์ lit.
" one that is encompassed by the ocean," i. e.
the earth : ชลธิชา lit. " daughter of the
ocean," i. e. Lakshmi (พระลักษมี). According
to the Ramayana, she sprang from the froth
of the ocean, when it was churned by the
gods, in full beauty, with a lotus flower in
her hand (H. C. D. p. 176) : ชลนกุล, ชลนร,
ชลพิฑาล, ชลาขุ lit. " water-man," " water-cats,"
" water-rats " : ชลนัยน์ ชลมา, ชนเนตร tears :
ชลนาฑี a water-course : ชลนิธิ lit. " a water
reservoir," i. e. the sea ; the ocean : ชลนิรคม,
ชลหารณี a water-course ; a drain, channel or
passage for water : ชลบาตร, ชลภาชน์ a vessel
for water ; a water-pot : ชลบาน the drinking of water : ชลบิตต์ lit. " the bane of
water," i. e. fire : ชลบุษบ์ flowers of aquatic
plants : ชลประลัย lit. " destruction by
water," i. e. a deluge ; a flood ; an inundation :
ชลปักษิน an aquatic bird : ชลพฤศจิก lit.
" water scorpion," i. e. sea prawns ; shrimps :
ชลพันธุ์ lit. " friends of water," i. e. fishes :
ชลพินทุ drops of water ; fine particles of water ;
spray ; mist : ชลภู clouds : ชลภูษณ์ lit.
" that which decorates water," i. e. a wind ; a
breeze : ชลมนเทียร a bath-room with drains
for carrying off the water : ชลมนุษ lit. " a
water-man," i. e. a mythical water-being :
ชลมารค a water-course ; a drain ; an ocean
track or route : ชลยนตร์ a water pump ; a
machine for raising water ; motor pumps :
ชลยาตรา a sea voyage : ชลยาน lit. " water-
vehicles," i. e. boats ; ships : ชลรณฑ์ a
whirlpool ; fine spray or sprinkling of water ;
a drizzle ; a snake : ชลรส sea-salt : ชล-
รากษส name of a female demon (mother of
the Nagas), who tried to prevent Hanuman
from crossing the straits between the continent and Ceylon by attempting to swallow
him. He escaped by reducing himself to the
size of a thumb, darting through her huge
body, and coming out at her right ear :

ชลราศิ *lit.* " water quantity," *i. e.* any running or flowing water; the ocean: ชลเรขา, ชลเลขา a line or streak appearing on the surface of a large body of water: ชลลดา *lit.* " water-creeper," *i. e.* a wave; surf dashing upon the shore: ชลวาสิน, ชลวาสี *lit.* " those living in the water," *i. e.* divers: ชลโศษ *lit.* " the drying up of water," *i. e.* drought; lack of rain: ชลสถาน, ชลาธาร a reservoir; a dam; a pool or pond: ชลสนาน the act of bathing: ชลสมุทร a lake of fresh water: ชลสรรบิณ์ *lit.* " a glider in water," *i. e.* a leech: ชลสุกร *lit.* " a water-hog," *i. e.* a crocodile: ชลเสก, ชลาภิเษก the act of sprinkling with water: ชลหาร a carrier of water: ชลหารี a woman water-carrier: ชลากร *lit.* " a water-source," *i. e.* a spring: ชลาคม *lit.* " the approaching of water," *i. e.* the coming of rain; the setting in of the rainy season: ชลานุสาร one going or moving like water: ชลามัตร a water-bucket; a tin-dipper; a pail: ชลายุกา a leech: ชลารณพ the rainy season: ชลาลัย a reservoir for water; a lake; the ocean; a river: ชลาวดาร a landing place; a berth or wharf along a river's bank: ชลาศรัย a pond; a well; a wolf; a floating-house: ชลาศัย a reservoir; a pond; the ocean; a fish: *adj. lit.* " lying in water," *i. e.* stupid; foolish; torpid; ignorant: ชลเศ, ชลเศวร the ocean: ชโลทร *lit.* " water-belly," *i. e.* dropsy; an abnormal collection of water in the abdomen: ชโลบล *lit.* " water-gravel," *i. e.* hailstones.

ชลาพุ, ชรายุ   cha[6]-lah-poo[6] *P. S. n.* the uterus; the womb (chd. p. 164).

ชลาพุช, ชลามพุช   cha[6]-lah-poot[6] *P. S. adj.* viviparous; born from the womb (as mammals) (chd. p. 164).

ชลูกา, ชัลลกา, ชัลลุก   cha[6]-loo-gkah *P. S. n.* the leech (chd. p. 164).

ชเล   cha[6]-lay *S. n.* water (S. E. D. p. 215): ชเลจร *lit.* " living in water," *i. e.* an aquatic animal; a fish; any kind of water-fowl: ชเลชาต *lit.* " water-born," *i. e.* the lotus:

ชเลพ่าห์ a diver: ชเลศัย *lit.* " resting in, or abiding in water," *i. e.* fishes.

ชเลศ, ชเลศวร, ชโลทร, ชโลธร, ชโลบล
see ชล

ชว, ชัพ   cha[6]-wa[6] *P. S. n.* swiftness; speed; velocity; impulses (of the mind) (S. E. D. p. 416): *adj.* quick; fast; rapid; swift; expeditious: ชวกรรม, ชวการ, ชวกิจ *lit.* " urgent business," *i. e.* the telegraph: ชวยุกต์ characterized by speed; capable of fleetness: ชวเลข shorthand: ชวธึก the quickest; the most speedy: ชวานิล *lit.* " a swift wind," *i. e.* a gale; a hurricane.

ช่วง   choo-ang[3] *n.* (1) part; portion; section (2) reach; extent; length; stretch: *adj.* (1) shining; bright; luminous; (2) following; subsequent; subordinate; succeeding: ช่วง (ต้น) *Lagerstroemia villosa* (*Lythraceae*) (cb. p. 729): ช่วงชัย a ball game played by two opposing sides, using a ball made of a rolled and knotted scarf. The object is to gain a player by hitting some one on the opposite side: ช่วงบาท *lit.* " the length of a step," *i. e.* an implication that one is only a step distant; a messenger; a servant: ช่วงยาว a great distance; a major expanse: ช่วงสั้น a short distance, or stretch: เช่าช่วง to sub-rent; to sub-lease; to sub-hire.

ช่วงชิง   choo-ang[3]-ching *v.* to snatch; to grab; to try to capture on succeeding occasions.

ช่วงใช้   choo-ang[3]-chai[5] *v.* to force payment; to make payment; to use for personal profit (as boats or cars); to remunerate; to retaliate.

ชวด   choo-at[3] *v.* to starve; to fast; to go without; to have no more left: *n.* the rat: ปีชวด name of the first year of the animal cycle of twelve.

ชวน ๑   choo-an *v.* to exhort; to persuade; to entice; to induce; to influence: ชวนหัว to act or speak so as to induce laughter.

ชวน ๒, เชาวน์   cha[6]-wa[6]-na[6] *P. S. n.* a fast horse; a courser; a fleet horse: *adj.* quick; swift; active; spirited (S. E. D. p. 416).

ชวย see **โชย**

ช่วย   choo-ie[3] *v.* to help; to assist; to furnish aid in time of trouble or sickness; to support a cause; to contribute financial aid: ช่วยดู แล to help in supervising; to help in the care of; to watch over a person or child: ช่วยทาษ to pay a debt, or free a slave: ช่วยให้รอด to rescue; to save.

ชวร, ชร   choo-an *S. v.* to be sick; to be diseased; to be feverish: *n.* fever; affliction; grief; illness (S. E. D. p. 428): ทรงประชวร to be sick (used only for royalty).

ชวลิต   cha[6]-wa[6]-lit[6] *S. adj.* lighted; blazing; flaming; shining (S. E. D. p. 428): ชวลิต จักษุ, ชวลิตนัยน์, ชวลิตเนตร fiery-eyed; gazing angrily or fiercely.

ชวาล, ชาลา   cha[6]-wan *S. n.* a light; a lamp; a flame; a torch; an illumination: *adj.* burning; blazing; glittering; brilliant; causing a flame to blaze (S. E. D. p. 428).

ชวาลา   cha[6]-wah-lah *S. n.* a lamp; a flame; a torch; a vessel in which oil is burnt through wicks in one or more projecting jets (S. E. D. p. 428): ชวาลาธวัช *lit.* " flame-marked," *i. e.* fire.

ช่อ   chau[3] *v.* to cheat; to defraud; to trick; *n.* a bunch; a tuft; a cluster; a bouquet of flowers: ช่อฟ้า *lit.* " sky tassels," " sky bunches," *i. e.* the characteristic architectural decorations for the roofs of Siamese Buddhist sacred buildings (as bote, viharn, mondop). These consist of a block of hard wood, carved to represent multiple, pointed heads of the Naga in an open fan-shaped position, with a piece like a gracefully curved finger pointing upwards, rising above the whole; thus the building represents a group of glittering spires. Each block is raised and placed into position with appropriate ceremonies, as a final finish to the ends of the main roof and at the corners of the triple-storied roofs: ช่อม่วง a kind of fire-works.

ช้อ (ต้น)   chau[5] *n. Helicteres isora (Ster-culiaceae)*, a shrub found from India to Java. The fruit is conspicuously twisted. The stems contain a good fibre. This plant is medicinal. In India, the roots and bark are said to be substituted for the fruits in certain preparations (Cb. p. 173: MCM. pp. 111, 430: Burk. p. 1135).

ช้อก, มะม่วง (ต้น)   chauk[5] *n. Mangifera indica (Anacardiaceae)* (cb. p. 344), mango, a medium or large-sized, spreading and quick-growing tree, indigenous to tropical Asia. It bears large panicles of greenish-white, scented flowers. The round or ovoid fruit is somewhat flattened, generally with a more or less pronounced beak near the apex. It has a tough, thin skin and, when ripe, is yellow, reddish or green. The flesh is usually yellow or having an orange tint, with a distinct, pleasant, aromatic flavour; in inferior varieties it is turpentiney, somewhat resinous and fibrous. In the centre is the large fibrous, ovoid, flat seed. The mango is the fruit par excellence of Siam and India, where it has been cultivated from time immemorial. Here it may be considered an article of food as well as dessert, whilst it also enters largely into the preparation of chutneys and preserves (MCM. pp. 242, 243, 518: BURK. p. 1402).

ช้อกช้ำ see **ช้ำ**

ชอง   chaung *n.* a race of people living in the district of Chandaburi.

ช่อง, ชะช่อง   chaung[3] *n.* an opportunity; an orifice; a hole; an aperture; a gap: ช่องข้ามเขา a mountain pass: ช่องดาล a finger hole for lifting a bolt: ช่องปืนตามกำแพง an embrasure in a wall (as for a cannon): ได้ช่องดี an auspicious opportunity or occasion; an opportune time: ไม่มีช่องที่จะทำมาหากินได้ having no chance for gaining a livelihood.

ช้อง   chaung[5] *n.* a switch or tress of hair added to the natural hair to increase its size; a wig; a transformation : ช้องนางคลี่ (ต้น) *Lycopodium sp. (Lycopodiaceae)*, often called club-mosses, found throughout the world (K. : Burk. p. 1377) : ช้องแมว (ต้น) *Gmelina villosa (Verbenaceae)*, a shrub or tree with yellow flowers. The medicinal properties of this plant were well-known and prized by the early Portuguese when they held Malacca. The fruit cannot be used for food, but is used medicinally in the same way as the leaves. Both are used for headaches, skin eruptions and rheumatism (K.: Burk. p. 1089) : ช้องนางรำ, ช้อยนางรำ (ต้น) *Desmodium gyrans (Leguminosae)*, the telegraph plant, whose small leaflets make curious jerky movements (K).

ช้องระอา (ต้น)   chaung-ra[6]-ah *n. Barleria lupulina (Acanthaceae)*, a small shrub with yellow flowers. This is used for snake-bites and toothache (K.: Burk. p. 302).

ชอน   chaun *v.* to drill or auger in a bent, devious track; to make a serpentine, or curved underground passage : *adj.* crooked; winding; sinuous; devious; indirect : ชอน (ปลา) *Lepidocephalus hasselti (Cobitidae)*, a loach (Dept. Agri. & Fisheries).

ช่อน (ปลา)   chaun[3] *n.* a common, delicious, fresh water fish, *Ophicephalus striatus (Ophicephalidae)*, a serpent-headed fish or murrel (Dept. Agri. & Fisheries : Burk. p. 1582) : ช่อนงูเห่า (ปลา) *Ophiocephalus marulius*, a serpent-headed fish (Dept. Agri. & Fisheries) : ช่อนน้ำเค็ม (ปลา) *Ophiocara porocephala*, a goby (Dept. Agri. & Fisheries) : ช่อนทะเล (ปลา) *Rachycentron nigrum (Rachycentridae)*, a sea fish called the sergeant fish (Dept. Agri. & Fisheries).

ช้อน   chaun[5] *v.* to dip up; to scoop up : *n.* a spoon; a triangular, spoon-shaped net for catching fish : ช้อน (นก) the white ibis, *Threskiornis melanocephalus melanocephalus* (Herb. N. H. J. S. S. VI, 4, p. 349) : ช้อนปลา to

capture fish by using a hand-net : ช้อน (หอย) a shell used as a spoon : ช้อนหอย (นก) the pelican ibis, *Tantalus leucocephalus* (Gaird. J. S. S. IX, 1, p. 11).

ชอนตะวัน, ทานตะวัน (ต้น)   chaun-dta[4]-wan *n. Helianthus annuus (Compositae)*, the sunflower, a tall, quick-growing annual, reaching to a height of 6 to 8 ft. (sometimes much more), a native of Peru, and extensively cultivated in parts of India, China, Russia, South America, Siam, etc., for the seed, which is rich in oil. The plant thrives in ordinarily good soil, in a warm and moderately moist climate. It flourishes in Ceylon at medium or high elevations (MCM. p. 393 : Burk. p. 1132).

ชอบ   chaup[3] *v.* to like; to be pleased with; to be satisfied with : ชอบกล seeming or appearing all right; suited to an object or purpose; reasonable; appropriate : ชอบกัน to have a friendly attitude : ชอบใจ see ใจ : ชอบธรรม righteousness; uprightness; rectitude; justice : เห็นชอบด้วย to agree; to comply with; to conform to; to see fit or suitable (as proposed by another) : ความรับผิดชอบ responsibility.

ชอม   chaum *v.* to sink; to press down; to penetrate below the surface.

ช้อย   choy[5] *adj.* curved gracefully upwards : ช้อยชด graceful in form or action; easy in manner.

ช่ออินทนิน (ต้น)   chau[3]-in-ta[6]-nin *n. Thunbergia laurifolia (Acanthaceae)* a big, rather soft, but woody climber, which grows to the tops of considerable trees, and falls over their branches in dense masses covered with beautiful, dark lilac flowers. It kills the trees which it smothers. The Malays use it medicinally (MCM. pp. 127, 130 : Burk. p. 2158).

ชะ   cha[6] *v.* to cleanse or rinse; to wash; to purify : *exclam.* sometimes denoting anger, but generally pleasure in, or approbation of what is seen : ชะแผล to cleanse and dress a wound.

ชะคราม, ช้าคราม (ต้น) cha⁶-kram *n.* an edible plant growing in salt marshes, *Suaeda maritima (Chenopodiaceae)* (V. P. p. 93 : Burk. p. 2108 : K.).

ชะง่อน cha⁶-ngaun³ *n.* projecting or over-hanging rocks ; stalactites.

ชะงัก cha⁶-ngak⁶ *v.* to stop abruptly (as from fright or surprise).

ชะงัด, ช้างัด cha⁶-ngat⁶ *adj.* sure ; confident beyond a doubt ; accurate ; exact ; precise ; correct ; effective.

ชะงาก cha⁶-ngak³ *adj.* opening and closing the mouth mechanically (as during spasms or convulsions).

ชะง้า cha-⁶ngam⁵ *adj.* tall and overhanging ; high and projecting outwards and arched downwards.

ชะงุ้ม cha⁶-ngoom⁵ *adj.* projecting out and extending down low (like a lean-to roof).

ชะเง้อ cha⁶-ngur⁵ *v.* to crane or stretch the neck (as when observing something up high).

ชะเง้อม cha⁶-ngeu-am⁵ *adj.* projecting from a height ; overhanging ; over-reaching.

ชะแง้ cha⁶-ngaa⁵ *v.* to look upward ; to turn the face while looking up.

ชะโงก cha⁶-ngok³ *v.* to peer out or over ; to project, protrude or lean out (as from a window) : ชะโงกผา a rocky promontory or cliff projecting from the side of a mountain.

ชะฉ่า cha⁶-chah⁴ *exclam.* a response or chorus in some Siamese songs.

ชะช่อง see ช่อง

ชะชิด see ชิด

ชะโด (ปลา) cha⁶-doh *n.* a common, fresh water, serpent-headed fish, *Ophicephalus micropeltes (Ophicephalidae)*. This fish is com-mon in canals and ponds but rare in rivers (Dept. Agri. & Fisheries).

ชะนวน cha⁶-noo-an *n.* a slate ; a tablet, or slab for writing purposes ; a fuse : ชะนวน-ดอกเห็ด a primer : รูชะนวน a fuse hole in a cannon or musket.

ชะนะ, ชำนะ cha⁶-na⁶ *v.* to gain a victory ; to win ; to surmount ; to excel : กลองชะนะ a drum used to denote victory ; the victory drum : ชะนะแก่ to vanquish ; to prevail against ; to succeed ; to surpass : วิ่งชะนะ to out-run.

ชะนัก cha⁶-nak⁶ *v.* to tie ; to clasp ; to fasten with a clasp, or circle of rattan : *n.* an harpoon, with rope attached, used for spearing crocodiles, and large predaceous fish.

ชะนาง cha⁶-nang *n.* a fish-trap made of bamboo strips sewed together with rattan. These may be triangular or basket-like. If in triangular form, they are used like the ช้อน to scoop up the fish.

ชะนิด cha⁶-nit⁶ *n.* kind ; class ; category ; nature ; race ; character.

ชะนี cha⁶-nee *n.* the white-handed gibbon. The common Siamese species is *Hylobates lar*, of which there are several coloured varieties. It is easily domesticated and often seen in captivity (Gaird. J. S. S. III, 2, p. 121) : ชะนีร่ายไม้ an attitude assumed by Siamese actors.

ชะนุง cha⁶-noong *n.* a pair of sticks fastened crosswise, used for stretching or holding skeins of yarn or any spun fibre.

ชะเนียง (ต้น) cha⁶-nee-ang *n. Pithecolobium jiringa (Leguminosae)*, a tree of fair size, even up to 80 feet in height, found from Tenasserim and Siam throughout western Malaysia. The seeds may be eaten after two or three boilings on successive days. They are mostly used as a flavouring for food. Immature seeds are used as well as ripe ones. In

lower Siam, seeds from wild trees are preferred to those of the cultivated tree. Jiring
pods give a purple dye on silk. In Borneo,
the bark is used for dyeing matting black. In
another method of dyeing, the leaves are used
instead of the bark. The black colour is said
to be very fast. The leaves have medicinal
qualities. The timber is soft, reddish or white,
shining, with little or no heart-wood. It is
of little value but is used for coffins and
firewood (cb. p. 560 : Burk. p. 1761).

ชะเนาะ cha⁶-nau⁶ *n.* a stick used as a
lever for twisting or tightening rope, rattan
or wire wound around bundles of bamboos,
or floats of logs (as while rafting).

ชะบา (ต้น) cha⁶-bah *n. Hibiscus rosasinensis (Malvaceae)*, shoe flower, a bush
with large flowers, long cultivated in China,
Japan, and the Pacific. When Europeans
first reached the Far East, they found
many races of this plant in cultivation, some
having flowers of various shades from pink to
white. In China, they met with a yellow-
flowered race. In older Japanese books on
flowers, rose, white and yellow races are
represented. Europeans crossed it, obtaining
races with very beautiful flowers, some being
double. Decoctions from the roots and leaves
are used medicinally. Among the Malays
these flowers have occult usage (cb. p. 159 :
MCM. pp. 111, 112, 184 : Burk. p. 1168 : V. P. p. 93) :
ชะบาจีน (ต้น) *Hibiscus syriacus*, a Chinese
shrub which got its name from the erroneous
belief that its home was Syria. Hedges are
made of this plant ; the leaves have medicinal
uses (Burk. p. 1172). There are two varieties
of this ornamental erect shrub of fastigiate
habit cultivated in this country, one with a
purple, the other with a white flower which,
in both, is double. The latter variety, however, is less common. This plant grows best
in northern Siam. It was probably introduced from China as the name suggests
(winit, N. H. J. S. S. IX, 1, p. 96) ; *Achania mal-*

vaviscus (V. P. p. 93). This plant is the same
as *Malvaviscus pilosus* : ชะบาหนุ (ต้น)
Malvaviscus pilosus ; *(M. arboreus)* (winit,
N. H. J. S. S. IX, 3, p. 277).

ชะพลู, ช้าพลู (ต้น) cha⁶-ploo *n.* the wild
betel leaf bush, the leaves of which are used
to roll the (เมี่ยง) meang (as used among the
northern tribes), *Piper* sp. (V. P. p. 93).

ชะมวง (ต้น) cha⁶-moo-ang *n. Garcinia
cowa (Guttiferae)*, a tree of Bengal, Assam
and Siam. The timber is hard but not first
class. The leaves and fruit are eaten (cb. p.
114 : V. P. p. 94 : Burk. p. 1048).

ชะมด (ต้น) cha⁶-mot⁶ *n. Hibiscus abelmoschus (Malvaceae)*, musk mallow, a shrub
with mallow-like flowers, the seeds of which
yield an oil used in inferior perfumes. Its
odour is like musk (Burk. p. 1163) : ชะมด
(ตัว) the Burmese civet, *Civerra zibetha
pruinosa* : ชะมดเชียง the secretions of the
civet, imported from China.

ชะมบ cha⁶-mop⁶ *n.* a group of evil spirits ;
signal stakes to mark a proposed road or
boundary.

ชะม้อย cha-⁶mau-ey⁵ *v.* to close the eyes
and hide the face in shame.

ชะมา cha⁶-mah *Cam. n.* a cat.

ชะม้าย cha⁶-mai⁵ *v.* to glance sideways or
upwards.

ชะแม่ cha⁶-maa³ *n.* a royal concubine.

ชะไม, ชระไม cha⁶-mai *Cam. adj.* both ;
two together ; including both ; two of a kind ;
a pair.

ชะรอย cha⁶-rau-ey *adv.* perhaps ; probably ;
peradventure ; perchance ; possibly ; sometime ;
if by chance.

ชะลอ, ชระลอ cha⁶-law *v.* to cherish ; to
foster ; to support carefully while being
carried ; to carry cautiously (as a piece of
frail furniture) ; to move or transport with
caution.

ชะลอม   cha[6]-laum *n.* a coarse, open-meshed bamboo basket tied at the neck, commonly used for carrying market produce.

ชะล่า   cha[6]-lah[3] *n.* a boat, made principally of a hollowed-out log (used in northern Siam): *adj.* officious; impertinent; obtrusive.

ชะลูด   cha[6]-loot[3] *v.* to suffer with diarrhoea (used only in reference to elephants): *adj.* tapering to a tall point: ชะลูด (ต้น) *Alyxia lucida* (*Apocynaceae*) (K.), a climber with fragrant white flowers and fragrant bark.

ชะเลง   cha[6]-leng *n.* a kind of fish-trap.

ชะเลย   cha[6]-ler-ie *n.* hostages of war; a prisoner; captives: ชะเลยใจ, ชะล่าใจ to be careless, indifferent or inattentive: ชะเลยศักดิ์ pertaining to quackery; being outside that which is customary or authorized: หมอชะเลยศักดิ์ medical impostors; charletans; quack doctors.

ชะเลี่ยง   cha[6]-lee-ang *n.* an ancient tribe of people.

ชะแลง, ชระแลง   cha[6]-laang *n.* a crowbar; an iron rod used as a lever.

ชะโล, ชะโลง, ชระโลง   cha[6]-loh *v.* to lead by a rope (as cattle); to tether or tie to a stake; to give support (while being carried).

ชะโลม   cha[6]-lom *v.* to anoint; to consecrate by unction; to smear or daub; to apply paint or oil.

ชะวัด   cha[6]-wat[6] *v.* to pull; to haul; to draw.

ชะวา   cha[6]-wah *n.* Java; Javanese: ปี่ชะวา a kind of flute or fife used by the Javanese.

ชะวาก   cha[6]-wak[3] *n.* an enclosure approached by a tortuous entrance.

ชะอม (ต้น)   cha[6]-om *n. Acacia insuavis* (*Leguminosae*) (cb. p. 549); *A. pennata* (V. P. p. 94).

ชะอ้อน, ฉะอ้อน   cha[6]-aun[3] *v.* to implore; to beseech; to entreat.

ชะอ่ำ, ชะอื้อ, ชะอุ่ม   cha[6]-am[4] *adj.* dark; murky; cloudy; hazy; shady.

ชะเอม (ต้น)   cha[6]-em *n. Myriopteron paniculatum* (V. P. p. 94), cinnamon, used as a spice: ชะเอมป่า (ต้น) *Albizzia myriophylla* (*Leguminosae*), a woody climber in Peninsular Siam; the roots are used medicinally (cb. p. 555: V. P. p. 94: Burk. p. 87): เปลือกชะเอม cinnamon bark.

ชะแอง (ต้น)   cha[6]-aang *n. Rhodamnia trinervia* (*Myrtaceae*), a small tree of secondary forest; the wood is hard and useful (cb. p. 630: Burk. p. 1901).

ชะโอน (ปลา)   cha[6]-on *n.* a species of catfish, *Cryptopterus apogon* (H. M. S.); *Callichrous bimaculatus* (*Siluridae*) (Dept. Agri. & Fisheries): ชะโอนหิน (ปลา) *Silurichthys phaiosoma* (*Siluridae*), an edible sheat-fish (Suvatti p. 72: Burk. p. 2031).

ชัก   chak[6] *v.* to pull; to draw; to attract; to haul; to have a spasm or convulsion: *n.* convulsions: คนชักหัวเบี้ย a banker who gathers up the cowrie shells in a gambling den; the croupier: ชักกะบี่สี่ท่า, ชักซอสามสาย, ชักแบ้งผัดหน้า attitudes assumed by Siamese actors: ชักโครก a flush toilet: ชักจุง, ชักนำ to entice; to allure; to inveigle; to direct; to persuade; to advise: ชักชวน, ชักจูง to tempt by offers; to allure or induce; to incite; to persuade; to become prejudiced; to instigate: ชักจูงให้ทุนสาบาน to suborn: ชักนำให้รู้จักกัน to introduce; to make acquainted; to acquaint: ชักเย่อ, ชักกะเย่อ the game, tug-of-war; to pull; to drag against an opposing side: ชักหน้าบึ้ง to show anger, rage or impatience by wrinkling the face or brows: ชักหน้าไม่ถึงหลัง *proverb* impossible to make ends meet financially: ชักว่าว to fly a kite, or pull at a kite string: ชักศพ to convey a corpse to the place of cremation; a funeral cortège.

ชัค see ชค

ชัง chang *v.* to hate; to dislike; to abhor; to detest; to abominate.

ชั่ง chang[3] *Chin. v.* to weigh; to deliberate; to value; to examine the merits of: *n.* a unit of weight equal to a catty or $1\frac{1}{3}$ lbs. or 604.53 grams; 50 catties equals one hap (หาบ) which is a pikul or $133\frac{1}{3}$ lbs.; a balance; a scale for weighing purposes; steelyards: ชั่งกลอง (ต้น) *Polyalthia suberosa* (V. P. p. 96): ชั่งใจ to weigh, consider or deliberate; to try to come to a decision: ชั่งใจดู to weigh mentally or consider: ชั่งเถิด never mind, let it alone; need not care for, nor do it: ชั่งเป็นไร never mind: ชั่งหลวง a Siamese government unit of weight equal to 600 grams: คันชั่ง the beam of a balance.

ชังฆ chang-ka[6] *P. S. n.* the leg; the lower part of the leg from the knee to the ankle (chd. p. 166).

ชังฆา, ชงฆ์, ชงฆา chang-kah *P. S. n.* the shank; from the ankle to the knee (S. E. D. p. 409): ชังฆากร *lit.* "active with the shanks," *i. e.* a runner; a courier; one running quickly; fleetness: ชังฆาตราณ *lit.* "armour for the shank," *i. e.* puttees: ชังฆาบิณฑี the calf of the leg: ชังฆาพล *lit.* "strength of the shanks," *i. e.* flight; swiftness; the act of absconding, escaping or running off: ชังฆา-มาตร *lit.* "measuring or counting by a shank," *i. e.* 2.5 feet: ชังฆาวิหาร a walk; the act of walking for exercise, pleasure or recreation.

ชัจจันธ์ chat[6]-chjan *P. adv.* congenitally blind (chd. p. 163).

ชัชวาล chat[6]-cha[6]-wan *S. n.* a light; a torch; a flame: *adj.* blazing; burning; shining; luminous; brilliant (S. E. D. p. 428).

ชัฏ chat[6] *P. n.* a forest that is dense; a forest choked with undergrowth; a dense thicket; the tangled branches of bamboos and other trees (chd. p. 166).

ชัด, ชัดเจน chat[6] *adj.* being clearly visible; unobliterated; legible; distinct; correct: พูดชัด to talk very clearly or succinctly: รูป ชัด a clearly defined picture or photograph.

ชัน chan *n.* dammar; pitch; a preparation of rosin used in caulking seams, and covering the bottom of Siamese boats: *adj.* steep; abrupt; precipitous; rising or reaching straight up: ชันขน, พองขน to cause the hair to stand (as a cat): ชันคอ to be able to stiffen the neck and hold up the head (used in reference to infants about three months old): ชันตะเคียน hardened sap or gum of the ตะเคียน tree: ชันน้ำ dammar mixed with water: ชันพอน thin dammar used as an outer layer: ชันยอด (ต้น) *Gardenia coronaria (Rubiaceae)* (V. P. p. 99): ชันหอย (ต้น) *Shorea macroptera (Dipterocarpaceae)*, a large tree from 100 to 150 feet in height, found in Sumatra, the Malay Peninsula, and Borneo. The timber is of rather poor quality being not at all durable. The resin is dull yellow, opaque, of little value and seems not to be used (Cb. p. 143: Burk. p. 2016).

ชั้น chan[5] *n.* series; order; layer; a storey; a grade (as in school); rank or degree (as of conferred title); a shelf; a tier of shelves: ชั้นเชิง chicanery; deception; artifice; trickery; fraudulency; stratagem: ชั้นต้น initial or primary stage or state: ชั้นหลัง a successor; a later generation: ผ้าชั้นใน inner lining: เสื้อชั้นใน underclothing.

ชันตาฆร chan-dtah-ka[6]-ra[6] *P. n.* a room in which a fire is kept burning; a superheated room for medicinal, diaphoretic purposes; a fireplace.

ชันตุ chan-dtoo[4] *P. S. n.* a child; an offspring; a living creature; a man; a person; any animal of the lowest organism (as worms or insects) (S. E. D. p. 411): ชันตุมารี *lit.* "worm-killer," *i. e.* the citron; lemons; limes: ชันตุรส *lit.* "insect-essence," *i. e.* the red-lac; sealing wax.

ชันนะตุ   chan-na[6]-dtoo[4] *n.* a disease of the scalp characterized by the formation of pustules or pimples.

ชันนุ see ชานุ

ชันโรง   chan-na[6]-rong *n.* the honey-ant, commonly found making nests or tunnels of adhesive material in cracks or crevices about houses.

ชันษา   chan-na[6]-sah[2] *n.* age; an abbreviation of ชนมั่พรรษา.

ชันสูตร   chan-na[6]-soot[4] *v.* to verify by an experiment; to test; to prove; to examine by analysis: ชันสูตรดูเงินตรา to assay silver coins: ข้อชันสูตร test questions.

ชัปน see ชปน

ชัพ see ชวะ

ชัมพูนท see ชมพูนท, ชมพูนุท

ชัย see ชย

ชัยยาวรมาน   chai-yah-wa[6]-ra[6]-man *n.* Jayavarman II (802-869 A. D.), a king of the Angkorean Period, which extended from the 9th to the 14th century. He came from Sumatra and descended from the family of Srivijaya of Solar lineage. He named his capital Indrapura, claiming to be the grand nephew of Pushkaraksha, Rajah of Kambupura (Cambodia). During his long reign he united the Khmer Empire into one state and constructed several temples dedicated to Devaraja, a new cult which he inaugurated with the help of Hiranyadana, a Brahman deeply versed in magic, whose symbol was the linga or phallic emblem. Among the numerous edifices constructed during this reign, the Prah Khan of the Angkor group was the most important (Tourists' Guide).

ชัลลุก see ชลูกา

ชั่ว   choo-ah[3] *n.* wickedness; iniquity; a period of time; a cycle; a series of years, months or days; a revolution of time or years: *adj.* bad; wicked; perverse: *prep.* until; unto; throughout; all through: ชั่วกัปป์, ชั่วกัลป์ eternity; endless time: ชั่วโคตร์ all through the family line or lineage: ชั่วช้า very wicked; atrocious; villainous; nefarious; iniquitous: ชั่วนาฬิกาหนึ่ง in an hour's time; an hour: ชั่วใน in the course of; within the time of: ชั่วปีนี้ during the current year: ชั่ววันหน้า during the days to come: ชั่วพ่อชั่วแม่ handed down from the father and mother; heritage: ชั่วแล่น time occupied in passing over a section of a nautical course: ชั่วเวลา during the time or course of: ชั่ว-อายุคน during one's age; during a generation.

ชั้ว   choo-ah[5] *n.* a set of shelves for knick-knacks. supported from the floor by upright pieces; a cupboard; a buffet or sideboard.

ชั้วชม   choo-ah-chom *v.* to praise; to commend; to eulogize.

ชา   chah *v.* to feel numb; to be deprived of the power of sensation: *adj.* sluggish; inactive; torpid; lethargic; benumbed: ชา (ต้น) *Chin.* the tea plant, *Camellia thea (Ternstroemiaceae)* (Burk. p. 417: MCM. p. 349): ชาจีน China tea: ชาเลว inferior tea: ต้นชา-ญวน tea plant in Cochin-China: น้ำชา an infusion of tea leaves: ใบชา tea leaves.

ช้า   chah[5] *n.* a song or solo composing part of a Siamese theatrical performance called เพลงช้า: *adj.* slow; dilatory; deliberate; long; lingering; tardy: ต่ำช้า low; vile; rude; indecent: ช้าการ slow in accomplishing: ช้าครวญ name of a plaintive solo or song, sung during a Siamese theatrical performance: ช้านางนอน an attitude assumed by Siamese actors.

ช้ากะเดา (ต้น)   chah[5]-gka[4]-dow *n. Chukrasia velutina (Meliaceae)* (cb. p. 267).

ชาคร   chah-ka[6]-ra[6] *P. S. n.* wakefulness; a vision in a waking state; perseverance; (S. E. D. p. 417).

ชาครรยา, ชาครีย์   chah-kan-yah *S. n.* alertness; carefulness; wakefulness; vigil; perseverance: *adj.* awake; waking; keeping watch (S. E. D. p. 417).

ชาครีต   chah-ka^6-rit^6 *P. n.* one who has long been awake or is exhausted with sleeplessness (S. E. D. p. 417).

ชาครียานุโยค   chah-ka^6-ri^6-yah-noo^6-yoke^3 *P. n.* perseverance in self-purification by not indulging in sleep or indolency.

ช่าง   chang^3 *v.* to take no heed of; to be indifferent; to be disinterested; to feel apathetic regarding: *n.* a mechanic; an artificer; an artisan; a machinist; a workman of skill: ช่างกระไร blamable; culpable; reprehensible (a word indicating contempt, blame or censure): ช่างกลึง an expert with a turning lathe: ช่างก่อ one skilled in masonry: ช่างแกะ a sculptor; a professional carver: ช่างเขียน one who draws or paints; an artist; a draughtsman: ช่างคิด thoughtful; meditative: ช่างเงิน a silversmith; an expert in making silverware: ช่างชุน (ปลา) *Cynoglossus puncticeps* (*Cynoglossidae*), a marine, flat fish; a sole (Dept. Agri. & Fisheries): ช่างเถอะ, ช่างมัน *vulgar* oh, don't bother about it! ช่างทอง a goldsmith: ช่างปั้น a potter: ช่างพูด talkative: ช่างไม้ a carpenter: ช่างเย็บ a seamstress or tailor: ช่างเรือ an expert regarding boats: ช่างเล่น playful: ช่างหล่อ an expert in smelting: ช่างเหล็ก a blacksmith; a species of bird, the Indian crimson-breasted barbet, *Xantholaema haemacephala indica* (Herb. N. H. J. S. S. VI, 3, p. 299).

ช้าง   chang^5 *n.* an elephant: โขลงช้าง a herd of elephants: ช้างค่อม a dwarf elephant: ช้างงาเดียว (ต้น) *Paramignya scandens* (*Rutaceae*) (cb. p. 235): ช้างชำนิ an elephant used by royalty: ช้างดำ (กล้วยไม้) an orchid: ช้างแดง (กล้วยไม้) an orchid: ช้างต่อ an elephant used as a decoy: ช้างเถื่อน wild elephants: ช้างทำลายโรง an attitude assumed by Siamese actors: ช้างนรกาย male

elephants with short tusks: ช้างน้าว (ต้น) a wild plant used medicinally; *Ellipanthus tomentosus* (*Connaraceae*), a small tree or shrub (v. P. p. 97); *Ochna wallichii* (*Ochnaceae*) (cb. p. 245); *Ouratea thorelii* (cb. p. 246): ช้างน้าวเอื้อง (ต้น) *Dendrobium dalhousieanum* (*Orchidaceae*); *D. pulchellum* (V. P. p. 97): ช้างเนียม an elephant whose tusks are just appearing: ช้างนำ a leading elephant, or leader of a herd: ช้างน้ำ a mythological animal with an elephant's head and a fish's tail: ช้างประสานงา an attitude assumed by Siamese actors; the name of a Siamese song: ช้างผะชด tame elephants used as decoys: ช้างเผือก the "white elephant," a sacred elephant having certain distinctive marks: ช้างเผือก (กล้วยไม้) an orchid: ช้างเผือก (ต้น) *Arfeuillea arborescens* (*Sapindaceae*), a tree of Cambodia and central and northern Siam, which attains a height of 45 feet, with a broad, round crown. It grows well in Singapore and has been recommended as a roadside tree (Burk. p. 237: V. P. p. 97): ช้างเผือกหลวง (ต้น) *Homalium tomentosum* (*Samydaceae*) (cb. p. 742: Burk. p. 1183), a tree distributed throughout the tropics. It gives the excellent Maulmein lancewood of Burma, but as produced in Java, its dark brown heart-wood is found of small value, as it splits badly and is not durable. It is not known in British Malaya: ช้างพลาย a male elephant: ช้างพัง a female elephant: ช้างร้อง a kind of fire-works causing a roar like elephants trumpeting: ช้างสบัดหญ้า an attitude assumed by Siamese actors: ช้างสาร a well-built, male elephant; a nail-puller made of a square piece of iron about 15 inches long tapering to a point, fitted with a loop which engages the head of a nail: ช้างสีดอ a tuskless elephant, known for its great courage, sagacity and strength. It is therefore much used in elephant hunts: ช้างสีปลาด the colour variant or extraordinary elephant: ช้างสำคัญ a type of noble or distinguished elephant: ช้างหน้ายักษ์ an ogre or large-headed elephant (a rare type):

ช้างหน้าหนู a mouse-headed elephant, having a small head (a much more common type): ช้างแหก (ต้น) *Spatholobus ferrugineus* (*Leguminosae*) (cb. p. 446: V. P. p. 98: Burk. p. 2061), a very big climber found throughout western Malaysia. The strong stems make rough cordage for binding hedges. In Java the plant is medicinal: ช้างเหยียบ (ปลา) *Pristolepis fasciata* (*Pristolepidae*), a freshwater, perch-like fish. It does not occur in any quantity, but wherever caught is considered good eating (Dept. Agri. & Fisheries: Burk. p. 1809): งวงช้าง the trunk of an elephant: อย่าแบกงาช้าง *prov.* keep from courting danger and destruction.

ชาจุ้มมุ่น (ต้น)　　　chah-chjoom³-moon³ *n.* *Calophyllum polyanthum* (*Guttiferae*) (cb. p. 121).

ช้าช้อน　　　chah⁵-chaun³ *adj.* beautiful; handsome; pretty.

ชาญ, ชำนาญ　　　chan *P. adj.* wise; conscious; proficient; skilled; well-versed in; understanding (chd. p. 165): เชี่ยวชาญ having had experience in; very skillful; proficient; learned.

ชาด　　　chat³ *n.* vermilion: *adj.* bright-red tending toward orange: ชาด (ต้น) *Bixa orellana* (*Bixaceae*), annato or arnatto, a large, quick-growing shrub or small tree with cordate leaves, native of tropical Africa. It thrives from sea-level to about 3,000 feet in moist climate, and prefers a deep, loamy soil. At the ends of the branches, it bears large clusters of brown or dark-crimson, capsular, ovoid or round fruits covered with fleshy spines. These contain a number of small seeds, the bright crimson covering of which affords the annatto dye of commerce. The fruits are collected when nearly ripe, and as the shells dry they burst open and disperse the seeds, which are then either pressed and made into "annatto paste," or merely dried with their covering, when they are marketed as "annatto seed" (MCM. p. 436: V. P. p. 99: Burk. p. 330); *Dipterocarpus obtusifolius* (*Dipterocarpaceae*) (cb. p. 137): ชาดก้อน vermilion in the natural state.

ชาดก, ชาตก　　　chah-dok⁴ *P. S. n.* birth; nativity; a birth or existence in the Buddhist sense; a narrative or tale of the former births of Buddha. These 550 birth-stories which are placed in the mouth of Buddha, all contain a moral, a warning or an example (chd. p. 166).

ชาต　　　chat³ *P. S. adj.* born; brought into existence by; engendered by; grown; produced; arisen; caused; appeared; appearing on or in; destined for; apparent; manifest (S. E. D. p. 417): ชาตกรรม a birth-ceremony (consisting of touching a newly-born child's tongue thrice with ghee, after appropriate prayers): ชาตกลาป *lit.* "one with a gorgeous tail," *i. e.* a peacock: ชาตทนต์ *lit.* "one having teeth growing," *i. e.* a child: ชาตบุตร one having had a son; one who has brought forth a son: ชาตพล one having great physical strength: ชาตพุทธิ one attaining wisdom; a sage; a wise man: ชาตมฤต being still-born; dying at birth: ชาตมาตร just or newly born; just or merely arisen or appeared: ชาตรูป beautiful; brilliant; shimmering; golden; gold: ชาตโรม a hairy man: ชาตวิทยา science of embryology; science of biology; knowledge of what exists: ชาตเวท fire: ชาตศิลา a real or massive stone: ชาตสระ a natural receptacle or reservoir for water.

ชาตก see ชาดก

ชาตบุษย์　　　chat³-dta⁴-boot⁴ *n.* a species of lotus plant.

ชาตยันธ์ see ชัจจันธ์

ชาตรี ๑　　　chah-dtree *n.* name of a theatrical performance, as played according to southern Siamese style.

ชาตรี ๒   chah-dtree *n.* a member of the military or reigning order (which in modern times constitutes the second caste of India) (S. E. D. p. 325).

ชาตา, ชตา   chah-dtah *P. S. adj.* born; produced; caused; arisen (Chd. p. 167).

ชาติ   chat[3] *P. S. n.* class; tribe; race; birth; production; the form of existence (as man, or animals); position assigned by birth, rank, caste, family, race or lineage; mace; the nutmeg (S. E. D. p. 418): ชาติโกศ, ชาติผล, ชาติสัสย์, ชาติสาร, จันทน์เทศ (ต้น) *Myristica fragrans* (*Myristicaceae*) (V. P. p. 87: BURK. p. 1524), the nutmeg tree, a moderate-sized or large tree, usually 40 to 50 feet high (sometimes 70 to 80 feet), native of the Moluccas, introduced into Ceylon about 1804, and now often met with in low-country gardens or compounds. The nutmeg of shops is the hard, brown, ovoid kernel of the fruit. It is enclosed in the thin brittle shell, immediately surrounding which is the scarlet aril or mace in the form of a nut; next to this is the large, thick, fleshy and juicy husk. The pale-amber fruit resembles a large apricot. When ripe, about 6 to 7 months from flowering, the husk splits open and discloses the glossy, dark-brown nut (seed) covered with the mace, as already stated. The fruit is then picked or the nuts are allowed to drop to the ground, when they are collected; they are then separated from the mace and both are dried separately in the shade, or on shelves in heated sheds. Oil obtained from the seed is used in perfumery (MCM. pp. 339, 518): ชาติธรรม a caste; a scion; lineage; duties of those belonging to a family line; generic or specific property: ชาติพราหมณ์ a Brahman by birth; the sacerdotal and learned class, being the first of four castes, as found established in the code of Manu; these may be, but are not necessarily, priests: ชาติมาลา subdivisions of, or shoots from an ancestral family line or race; ancestral tree or line;

name of a work on the caste system: ชาติรส a natural juice (as of the grape or sugar-cane): ชาติวานร of the monkey race (a curse): ชาติสัมบันน์ belonging to a noble family; possessing eminence regarding pedigree: ชาตินี้ the present generation: ชาติหน้า the future or coming generation or existence.

ชาน   chan *n.* the refuse fibre (as of sugar-cane); waste matter; trash; dregs; residuum: ชานสถานี, ชานชาลา the platform of a railroad station: ชานหมาก the tasteless quid of betel: นอกชาน a balcony; an open-floored area, or an uncovered verandah.

ชานกี   chah-na[6]-gkee *S. n.* a patronymic of Sita (นางสีดา), daughter of Janaka, king of Mithila (กรุงมิถิลา) of the Solar race (H. C. D. pp. 132, 133: S. E. D. p. 418): ชานกีนาถ *lit.* "Sita's lord," *i. e.* Rama: ชานกีวัลลภ *lit.* "Sita's lover," *i. e.* Rama (H. C. D. p. 261).

ชานบท   chah-na[6]-bot[4] *P. S. n.* residents or inhabitants of the country; those living in rural districts; belonging to, or suited for country life; one who belongs to the country; a rustic (S. E. D. p. 418).

ชานปทิก   chah-na[6]-bpa[4]-ti[6]-gka[4] *P. S. adj.* relating to a country or to its subjects (S. E. D. p. 418); involving communal interests, manners or customs.

ชานราชย์   chah-na[6]-rat[3] *S. n.* sovereignty (S. E. D. p. 418).

ชานวาทิก   chah-na[6]-wah-tik[6] *S. n.* one knowing how to converse pleasingly, entertainingly or agreeably; one knowing popular reports (S. E. D. p. 418).

ชานุ, ชานุกะ, ชันนุ   chah-noo[6] *P. S. n.* the knee (S. E. D. p. 418): ชานุมณฑล the patella; the kneepan: ชานุสนธิ the knee-joint.

ชาบัตตาเว๋ย (ต้น)   chah-bpat[4]-dtah-we-ah *n. Malpighia coccigera* (*Malpighia*), a small tree or bush. It has been adopted for pot-culture and is often trained on wire frames into bizarre shapes. It flowers freely, fruits occasionally, and is used for hedges in the uplands of Java. It is common in Bangkok gardens, usually grown as a hedge plant. It is said to have been first imported by one Nai Soot, a late Bangkok plant dealer, about fifteen years ago, probably from Batavia, as one (the earliest) of the local names indicates (winit, N. H. J. S. S. XI, 1, p. 99: Burk. p. 1398: MCM. p. 74).

ช้าบ chah[5]-bpee[4] *n.* a Siamese song.

ช้าแบ้น chah[5]-bpaan[3] *n.* a bush of the มะเขือพวง family, *Solanum torvum* (*Solanaceae*), bearing poisonous berries (V. P. p. 203). The statement that these berries are poisonous is denied by Burkhill who says they are used in curries. The roots are medicinal (Burk. pp. 2046-7).

ช้าพลู (ต้น) see ชะพลู (ต้น)

ชาม cham *n.* a plate; a dish; a bowl; a platter: ชามกะลา an inferior dish or one made of burnt clay: ชามแกง a curry dish: ชามแก้ว a glass dish: ชามข้าว a rice dish: ชามโคม a large bowl: ชามเทพนม, ชามเบ็ญจรงค์ Siamese porcelain decorated with figures of angels: ชามฝา a covered dish: ชามลายนรสิงห์ Siamese porcelain decorated with half-human, half-lion figures: ชามอ่าง a basin; a wide, open dish.

ชามพูนท cham-poo-not[6] *S. n. lit.* "a mineral from the Jambu river (แม่น้ำชมพู)," *i. e.* gold (S.E.D.) p. 419).

ชามภูวราช see ชมพูพาน

ชามา chah-mah *S. n.* a daughter (S. E. D. p. 419).

ชามาดร, ชามาดา, ชามาตุ chah-mah-daun *n.* a son-in-law (S. E. D. p. 419).

ชาย ๑ chai *n.* a male; a man; mankind: ชายชู้ an adulterer: หญิงมีชู้ a woman who has a paramour.

ชาย ๒ chai *v.* to turn or alter the course of; to have passed the highest point of (as the sun passes the meridian): *n.* edge; border; shore; verge; brim: ชายกะเบน the end of the rolled portion of the loin-cloth, which is fastened to the belt behind: ชายเกาะ the beach or outer extremity of an island: ชายเขา the foot of a mountain: ชายคา the eaves: ชายแคร่ง a scarf so worn that the ends hang down over both knees: ชายจาก the projecting edge or eaves of an attap roof: ชายแดน land bordering on a boundary line: ชายทะเล the seaside; the seashore; a beach: ชายทุ่ง the edge or boundary of a clearing or stretch of paddy fields: ชายธง the tapering end (as of a pennant or pennon): ชายป่า the edge of a forest or jungle: ชายผ้า the edges of a strip of cloth; the selvage: ชายผ้าสีดา (ต้น) a species of orchid; *Platycerium coronarium* (*Polypodiaceae*), an epiphytic fern found from Burma and Siam throughout Malaysia. In the Peninsula it is very frequent. The Malays rub the ashes of it over the body for enlargement of the spleen (v. P. p. 102: Burk. p. 1769): ชายพก the two ends of the loin-cloth after having been twisted together in front: ชายเฟือย grass or reeds growing beyond the accustomed limit along the water's edge: ชายเลน mud forming a bank along the edge of a river or sea: ชายหางตา the distal corners of the eye: ชายไหว a decorative flap worn in front suspended from the belt (suggestive of the Scotch sporran): เนื้อชายธง a flap of tissue to cover an amputated limb: ลอยชาย to wear the loin-cloth with the ends flying loosely.

ชาย ๓ chai *v.* to blow gently: ชายตา to glance sidewise: ตะวันชาย to decline or set: ลมชาย a softly blowing wind.

ชาย ๔ chai *adv.* about; perhaps; possibly, *ex.* ชายจะเบากว่าพ่อชาลี (มหาชาติ).

ชายา chah-yah *P. S. n. lit.* "one bringing forth," *i. e.* a wife; a consort (S. E. D. p. 419):

ชายาชีพ *lit.* "earning a living by his wife," *i.e.* a man whose wife is a danseuse or actress: ชายานุชีพ *lit.* "one living off his wife," *i.e.* a man supported by a prostitute: ชายาบดี a man and his wife: ชายิกา a wife: ชาเยนทร์ the wife recognized by the laws of the land; a legal wife: ชาเยศวรี the head-wife.

ชาร chan *P. S. n.* a paramour; a lover; the paramour of a married woman; a confidential friend (S. E. D. p. 419): ชารครรภ์, ชารชาต a child by a paramour; a bastard; an illegitimate child.

ชารี chah-ree *P. S. n.* an adulteress (Chd. p. 166).

ชาล chan *P. S. n.* a net (for catching birds or fishes); a hair net; a snare; a cobweb; any reticulated or woven textile; a wire net or sieve; a coat of mail; a wire helmet; a lattice window; the web or membrane on the feet of water-birds; a web (S. E. D. p. 419): ชาลกรรม *lit.* a net occupation," *i.e.* fishing: ชาลการ *lit.* "a web maker," *i.e.* a spider: ชาลทัณฑ์ net poles; trap supports: ชาลบท, ชาลบาท *lit.* "web-footed," *i.e.* ducks; geese; water-fowl: ชาลพันธ์ a net-trap; a snare: *adj.* being caught in a snare or trap (as birds): ชาลมาลา a net used by casting: ชาลามุข a lattice window.

ชาลา ๑, ชวาล chah-lah *n.* a flame; a light (of sun or fire); brightness; lustre; distinction: *adj.* sparkling; lustrous; brilliant; glittering; scintillating.

ชาลา ๒ chah-lah *n.* an uncovered verandah; a floor projecting in front of Siamese houses.

ชาลิก chah-lik *P. S. n. lit.* "one living by his net," *i.e.* a fowler; a bird catcher; fishermen (S. E. D. p. 420).

ชาลินี chah-li-nee *P. S. n. lit.* "having a net," *i.e.* snared; *figur.* a condition abounding in traps, meshes, pitfalls and allurements

which inveigle one into lustful temptations and sinful practices (S. E. D. p. 420: Chd. p. 164).

ช้าเลือด (ต้น) chah-leu-at *n. Premna integrifolia* (*Verbenaceae*), a large shrub found along the sea coasts of southern Siam, the northern parts of British Malaya and Malacca (BURK. p. 1806); *Caesalpinia mimosoides* (*Leguminosae*) (Cb. p. 503).

ชาว chow *Chin. n.* citizens or inhabitants of; a prefix used to denote "belonging to" a company, country, house or clan: ชาวนอก male attendants in the outer precincts of a palace: ชาวนา farmers; agriculturists; husbandmen: ชาวใน ladies or attendants in the inner precincts of a palace: ชาวบ้าน people of a village; laymen; neighbours: ชาวประโมง fishermen: ชาวป่า foresters: ชาวเมือง inhabitants or citizens of a city or town: ชาววัง people belonging to a palace: ชาวสวน gardeners: ชาวเหนือ northern tribes or people: คนชาวบ้านนอก a countryman; a peasant: ชาวบ้านนอก rustic; rural; uncultivated: ชาวเรา we; all of us.

ช้าหมอง (ต้น) chah-maung *n.* a medicinal tree.

ช่ำ chum *v.* to soak or plant a cutting or slip temporarily: ร้านช่ำ a grocery; a grocer's store or shop; a restaurant.

ช้ำ chum *adj.* joyful; manifesting joy; delightful; rejoicing; gratifying: ช่ำใจ pleasing; satisfactory or satisfying to the mind.

ช้ำ, ช้ำชอก, ชอกช้ำ, ฟกช้ำ chum *adj.* contused; bruised: ช้ำรั่ว a condition characterized by incontinence of urine or frequent micturition: ช้ำเลือดช้ำหนอง an hematoma; a contused wound where effused blood is confined: ช้ำอกช้ำใจ to feel annoyed or grieved by a loss or betrayal of some kind: แผลช้ำชอก a bruised wound.

ช้างัด see ชะงัด

ชำงาย see จำงาย

ชำงือ chum-ngeu *v.* to meditate over; to think about; to cogitate; to contemplate; to ruminate or muse upon : *n.* mind; heart.

ชำช่อง chum[3]-chaung *v.* to have experience; to be an expert or specialist.

ชำช่า, จืด chum[3]-chah[3] *adj.* insipid; unsavoury; without flavour or taste; vapid.

ชำนน chum-non *v.* to collide; to hit or strike against.

ชำนรร chum-nan *Cam. v.* to tread upon; to step upon; to crush with the foot.

ชำนะ see ชะนะ

ชำนัญ chum-nan *P. v.* to know; to gain knowledge; to comprehend; to perceive; to ascertain; to be intelligent (chd. p. 165).

ชำนาญ see ชาญ

ชำนิ ๑ chum-ni[6] *Cam. v.* to ride (as on horses or cattle).

ชำนิ ๒ chum-ni[6] *v.* to be skilful in; to be an expert : ชำนิชำนาญ experienced, accustomed to; skilful; ingenious.

ชำมะนาด, ชำมะนาดกลาง (ต้น) chum-ma[6]-nat[3] *n. Vallaris pergulana* (*Apocynaceae*), a woody climber or tree found in tropical Asia and Malaysia. The flowers have a strong odour (V. P. p. 95 : Burk. p. 2217 : winit, N. H. J. S. S. IX, 3, p. 284) : ชำมะนาดเล็ก (ต้น) *Vallaris heynei* (winit, N. H. J. S. S. IX, 3, p. 284).

ชำมะเลียง, พุมเรียง (ต้น) chum-ma[6]-lee-ang *n. Otophora fruticosa* (*Sapindaceae*), a tree or shrub found in south-eastern Asia and Malaysia. The fruits are eaten; when roasted they taste like chestnuts (V. P. p. 96 : Burk. p. 1613) : ชำมะเลียงบ้าน (ต้น) *O. cambodiana*, a shrub which is cultivated (cb. p. 328 : Burk. p. 1613).

ชำร่วย chum-roo-ey[3] *v.* to help; to reward;

to recompense; to do or give something in return.

ชำระ chum-ra[6] *v.* to cleanse; to wash; to purify; to clear up an affair by an investigation; to pay off; to clear off all responsibilities or liabilities : ชำระความ to judge a legal case : ชำระเงินแก่ศาล to pay money into the court : ชำระใจ to purge the heart; to confess or repent : ชำระตัว to cleanse or purify oneself : ชำระหนี้ to discharge an obligation.

ชำราบ chum-rap[3] *v.* to have knowledge concerning; to be aware of as true or actual.

ชำรุด chum-root[6] *v.* to be damaged; to have a defect; to have a blot on one's character; to be in a dilapidated or ruinous condition : ชำรุดทรุดโทรม in a semi-demolished condition; ruined; dilapidated.

ชำเรา ๑ chum-row *Cam. v.* to do or perform in secret; to do secretly; to be kept hidden.

ชำเรา ๒ chum-row *n.* rape; carnal knowledge : ข่มขี่ทำชำเรา to violate; to ravish; to deflower : ชำเราผิดธรรมดามนุษย์ sodomy.

ชำเราะ chum-raw[6] *n.* a recess; a crevice; a cleft or rocky fissure with gradations upwards or inwards.

ชำแรก chum-raak[3] *v.* to mix in or with; to penetrate down into; to permeate or become diffused through; to force a passage through; to penetrate by force.

ชำลา chum-lah *adj.* partly sun-dried; still semi-fresh; sun-cured in some degree (referring to fish or meat).

ชำเลือง chum-leu-ang *v.* to look or glance askance; to look sidewise.

ชำแหละ, แฉละ cham-laa[4] *v.* to cut or carve; to slice roughly (as a butcher) : ชำแหละศพ to dissect a cadaver.

ชิ ! ช์ ! chi[6], chee[5] *onomat.* from the word used when giving a command, or emphasizing obedience, or indicating anger.

ชิง ching v. to snatch; to wrest away from; to take by force; to pluck; to pull; to grasp without permission; to be the first to get or do: ชิงช่วง a game played in the water when some article that floats is thrown in among the players and all try to seize it: ชิงชัง to dislike on first acquaintance; to have a preconceived dislike for a person: ชิงชัย to gain the victory in a contest; to become victorious in a competition: ชิงเชิง the end of the threads that are to be cut off a cloth while still in the process of being woven; to take advantage by trickery or chicanery: ชิงดวง a floral decoration where the designs are connected as links in a chain.

ชิง ching[3] adj. bent; crooked; bowed; curved; mutilated; crippled; ex. ชาชิง

ชิงชัน (ต้น) ching-chan n. Dalbergia bariensis (Leguminosae), a woody climber found in the tropics of both Worlds (cb. p. 474).

ชิงช้า ching-chah[5] n. a swing: ชิงช้าชาลี (ต้น) Tinospora cordifolia (Menispermaceae), a woody climber with medicinal properties. It is used in fevers and as a diuretic and tonic medicine (burk. p. 2164: mcm. p. 380): ถีบชิงช้า to swing.

ชิงชี่ (ต้น) ching-chee[3] n. Capparis micracantha (Capparidaceae), a thorny bush found from Burma to the northern part of British Malaya, on sea-shores and in sandy places, occurring again in Java and the Philippine Islands. The round, purple fruit has a pulp with a sweet, aromatic flavour; it is eaten in the Philippine Islands. It is unsafe to eat unless ripe. The plant is said to be good for asthma and pains of the heart. The leaves and fruit are used to poultice swellings (burk. p. 444); C. siamensis (cb. p. 85: v. p. p. 99).

ชิชะ, ชิชู้ chi[6]-cha[6] onomat. from a word used when giving a command or emphasizing obedience.

ชิณณ chin P. adj. old; ancient; not being new or fresh; antique.

ชิด, ชะชิด chit[6] n. a fruit, the meat of which is similar to that of the nipa palm: adj. close; near; adjoining; intimate: ลูก-ชิดเชื่อม preserved nipa palm fruit.

ชิต chit[6] P. S. v. to have conquered; to have vanquished a foe; to have acquired by force.

ชิตินทรีย์, ชิเตนทรีย์ chi[6]-dtin-tree P. n. one invested with power to achieve or to become victorious.

ชิน ๑ chin n. lead or black lead; an ore.

ชิน ๒ chin v. to establish a tolerance for; to become familiar with; to be accustomed to; to be tolerant; to be habituated; to be in the habit of doing or taking (as a drug); to overlay or to cover (as with copper sheets): ชินชิด habitual intimacy: ให้ชินอากาศ to become acclimatized; to become acclimated: ให้ชินหู to become familiar with by repetitions; to learn by rote.

ชิน ๓ chin P. S. n. a victor; the victorious one; a Buddha; one who has overcome mental or moral conflicts (S. E. D. p. 421): ชินธรรม the doctrine of Jina (พระชินะ) who at the age of thirty adopted a spiritual career. He later acquired the title Maha-vira (มหาวีระ) or Great Hero and was acknowledged to be a Jain (spiritual conqueror). He lived 599 to 527 B. C. and became the founder of the Jain religion of India (I. B. C. pp. LXXVI, LXXVII): ชินราช (1) Jain-Suri (1591–1643), a noted Indian philosopher and teacher of the Jain religion; (2) a bronze image of Buddha in sitting posture in Wat Boromatat, Pitsanuloke, once known as โอฆบุรี. This image is 3.95 m. high and 2.85 m. wide. After three vain attempts, it was successfully cast in 1500 B. E. (957 A. D.) by the king of Siam, Somdet Phra Tama Tripidok. Previously this king had his capital at Sukhothai, but in 1463 proceeded to เชียงแสน where the capital remained for about twenty-five years. He there built Wat Mahatat and in the bote placed พระชินราช and another image subsequently cast. A facsimile of พระชินราช was cast by King Chulalongkorn at Pitsanuloke and later installed in Wat Benchamabopitr, Bangkok : ชินวร the most illustrious of the victors, an appellation for the Buddha; the most renowned thinker or sage : ชินศรี the title of a king, later applied to the Buddha by his followers : ชินาลัย the abode of the Buddha : ชิเนนทร์ a name for the Buddha : ชิโนรส, ชิโนสร, พระโพธิสัตว์ Gautama before attaining enlightenment; any individual, self-dedicated to the salvation of others, and destined to the attainment of Buddhahood (Gos. of Bud.); a being that will be a Buddha (Alab.); a Bodhisatta.

ชิน (สิ้น) chin[3] v. to come to an end; to close up; to be exhausted or finished.

ชิน chin[5] n. a piece (as of porcelain); a part; a portion; a slice; a bit; a fragment หั่นเป็นชิ้น ๆ to cut into slices.

ชิม chim v. to taste; to try; to attempt; to make a trial : ชิมลองดู to sample by tasting : ชิมลาง to have a vision or dream prognosticating future good or evil; augury; divination.

ชิยา see ชยา

ชิร see ชร

ชิรณ see ชิรณ

ชิรณัคคิ see ชิรณ

ชิวหา chew-hah[2] P. S. n. the tongue (S. E. D. p. 422); name of a dragon appearing as a character in the Ramayana : ชิวหาสดมภ์ a disease characterized by stiffness of the tongue and jaw.

ชี chee S. n. "Sir," "Master," " Mr.," titles indicating respect or reverence for a bonze (S. E. D. p. 422) : ชีต้น a bonze of long standing who acts as a teacher or preceptor : ชีปะขาว, ชีผ้าขาว, ชีผะขาว, นางชี, ยายชี an order of

Buddhist nuns who wear white robes and shave their hair and eyebrows; a species of white moth : ชีเปลือย a sect of Indian ascetics who wear no clothing (nudists): ชีพ่อพราหมณ์ an honorary title for a Brahman priest.

ชี (ผัก) ๒ chee n. parsley : ผักชีลา, ผักชีล้อม Apium graveolens (Umbelliferae), celery, a biennial herb of Europe and northern Asia, yielding edible leaf-stalks (web. : Burk. p. 192).

ชี ๓ chee v. to disentangle or separate balls of fibres (as of cotton or finely cut tobacco).

ชี chee[3] n. a black tooth-paste made of the exudation or sweat from burning wood or burnt coconut shell (used to blacken the teeth).

ชี chee[5] v. to show; to point; to point out; to direct the finger for designating an object : ชีขาด to give an ultimatum; to make a final proposition or decision : ชีแจง to make plain; to interpret; to elucidate; to expound clearly : ชีฟ้า (พริก) a species of very strong pepper, the pods of which point upward : ชีโพรงให้กะรอก prov. to show a defrauder an opportunity to defraud : ชีตัว, ชีหน้า to identify a person (used contemptuously): ชีด่า to point the finger while cursing a person : ชีนิ้ว to direct work without giving a helping hand : ชีบอก to indicate or direct the way by pointing : นิ้วชี the index [finger.

ชีพ see ชีวะ

ชีพจร cheep[3]-pa[6]-chjaun n. the pulse; pulsations; beating or throbbing of the blood- [vessels.

ชีพิต see ชีวิต

ชีพิตักขย, ชีพิตักษัย see ชีวิตักษัย

ชีร chee-ra[6] P. S. adj. quick; agile; nimble; lively; brisk; swift; rapid (S. E. D. p. 422).

ชีรณ, ชิรณ, ชิรณัคคิ, เชียรณ์ chee-ra[6]-na[6] P. S. adj. old; ancient; withered; wasted;

decayed; antiquated (S. E. D. p. 422), *ex.* ชีรณ-
กถา an ancient fable or legend: ชีรณพัสตร์
a fragment of old cloth; a worn or tattered
garment; one wearing old clothes: ชีรณัคคิ
a digestive ferment; an enzym: ชีรโณทยาน
a garden left neglected, desolate, barren or
waste.

ชีว, ชีวะ, ชีวา, ชีโว chee-wa[6] *P. S. n.* life;
existence; the principle of life; the vital
breath; vitality; the living or personal soul
(S. E. D. p. 422): ชีวโกศ, ชีวมนเทียร, ชีวาคาร
a case (or sheath) enveloping the personal
soul: ชีวงคต *lit.* "to depart from life," *i. e.*
death: ชีวธน animate possessions (as cattle, buffaloes, *etc.*); wealth in flocks and herds:
ชีวธานี *lit.* "the receptacle of living beings,"
i. e. the earth: ชีวนิกาย a being endowed
with life: ชีวบดี a living husband: ชีว-
บัตนี a woman whose husband is alive:
ชีวโภชน์ giving or affording enjoyment to the
living soul; the pleasures of living beings:
ชีวรักต์, โชตรัต the menstrual blood: ชีวโลก
humanity; the world of living beings; mankind: ชีววิมัย the duration of life: ชีววิษาณ
the horn of a live animal: ชีวสาธนี์ *lit.*
"means for sustenance of life," *i. e.* rice;
grain; cereals; paddy: ชีวหิงสา oppression
or cruelty to living beings: ชีวันตราย a
danger to life; death: ชีวาตมํ the living,
personal, or individual soul: ชีวาทาน *lit.*
"the letting go or taking away of all sense
or consciousness," *i. e.* a faint; a swoon; an
anaesthetic: ชีโวบาย the means, power or
energy for subsistence.

ชีวน chee-wan *S. n.* a living being; wind;
a son; life; means of living; water; milk;
fresh butter; marrow: *adj.* vivifying; giving
life; enlivening (said of the wind); the sun
(S. E. D. p. 423).

ชีวนต์ chee-wan *S. n.* life; a drug; name
of a medicinal and edible plant: *adj.* long-
lived; attaining a great age (S. E. D. p. 423).

ชีวา chee-wah *prefix* as in ชีวาวาย death.

ชีวิต, ชีพิต chee-wit[6] *P. S. n.* life; age;
livelihood: *adj.* having lived through a
period of time; enlivened; animated; living;
alive (S. E. D. p. 423): เจ้าชีวิต *lit.* "lord of
life," *i. e.* His Majesty, the King: ชีวิตกาล
the duration of life: ชีวิตนาถ *lit.* "the lord
of one's heart," *i. e.* a husband: ชีวิตภูต
lit. "one having lived (in the past)," *i. e.* the
deceased: ชีวิตสงสัย dangers to life; risk or
perils of life.

ชีวิตักษัย, ชีพิตักขย, ชีพิตักษัย chee-
we[6]-dtak[4]-sai[2] *S. n. lit.* "the termination of
life," *i. e.* death: ชีพิตักษัย death (used only
for those of the Mom Chao rank).

ชีวิน, ชีว chee-win *P. S. n.* life; the state
of being alive (S. E. D. p. 423).

ชีโว see ชีว

ชืด churt[3] *adj.* tasteless; insipid.

ชื่น churn[3] *v.* to rejoice; to be glad; to
exult; to gladden; to be buoyant; to be
rapturous: *adj.* jubilant; rejoicing; shouting
with joy; glad; animated: ชื่นใจบานตา to
give cause for rejoicing or exultation.

ชื้น churn[5] *adj.* moist; damp; humid;
moderately wet.

ชื่อ chur[3] *n.* name; title; appellation:
ชื่อปลอม alias; pseudonym; nom de plume:
ชื่อตั้ง a given title: ชื่อตัว a given name
or title: ชื่อเสียง reputation; fame; public
esteem; renown: ได้ชื่อว่า to merit the
name of: ตั้งชื่อ to give a name to: ผู้มีชื่อ
the undersigned: มีชื่อฦๅนาม noted or famed:
เสียชื่อ to defame one's name; to bring reproach
on one's good name: ออกชื่อ to nominate;
to call by name.

ชื้อ chur[5] *adj.* cold and damp; humid; too
cold.

ชุก chook[6] *adj.* abundant; ample; sufficient.

ชุกชี, จุกชี chook[6]-gka[4]-chee *n.* a base,

platform, altar, or pedestal made of wood or masonry, for images of the Buddha or those held in veneration.

ชุ้ง　　　choong[3] *conj.* therefore; in consequence of; in that case.

ชุ้ง　　　choong[5] *n.* a bend or crook: *adj.* crooked; curved upward; of, or pertaining to a curve.

ชุณห, ชุณหา　　　choon-ha[4] *P. n.* the moon's rays; moonlight (Chd. p. 172): ชุณหบักขํ the moonlit half of the month; the period of the waxing of the moon.

ชุด　　　choot[6] *n.* a fish-trap; a paper smudge; paper rolled or twisted and used as a smudge or wick; tinder; articles in a series or sequence; a suit (of clothes); a set, collection or group (as of dishes); a suite (of rooms).

ชุตสนะ　　　choot[6]-sa[4]-na[6] *P. S. n.* a moonlight night; moonlight; splendour (S. E. D. p. 427): ชุตสนปักษ์ *lit.* "light-winged," *i. e.* the moonlit half of the month; the period of the waxing of the moon.

ชุติ, โชตินี์　　　choo[6]-dti[4] *P. n.* brilliancy; brightness; sparkling brightness or lustre (S. E. D. p. 500).

ชุติมันต์, ชุติมา, ชยุติมันต์, ชยุติมา　　　choo[6]-dti[4]-man *P. n.* one endowed with splendour or brightness: *adj.* resplendent; brilliant; majestic; dignified (S. E. D. p. 500).

ชุน　　　choon *v.* to darn; to mend; to make embroidery: ชุนแห to mend a net by darning.

ชุบ　　　choop[6] *v.* to produce life in an inanimate object, by supernatural power; to dip; to soak; to plate; to overlay (as with nickel); to gild; to harden iron by a process of immersion; to temper steel; to support; to keep up: ชุบตัว to change one's form or character: ชุบมือเปิบ *prov.* to receive or enjoy the results of another's completed efforts: ชุบข้อม to provide for; to afford the best support possible: ชุบเลี้ยง to provide means for the main-

tenance or support of; to nourish with care: ชุบสรง a bath robe or bathing cloth used by the nobility or by Buddhist monks: ชุบศร to dip arrow heads (as into some poison): ชุบหนังสือ to illuminate books or documents: ชุบเหล็ก to temper or harden iron (as knife blades): ชุบอาบ a bath robe or bathing cloth: ชุบอักษร to retouch dim letters or writing.

ชุบชู　　　choop[6]-choo *n.* a kind of sweetmeat.

ชุม　　　choom *v.* to come together; to congregate; to assemble: *adj.* plentiful; abundant; ample; fully sufficient to meet all needs: ชุมค่าย to camp; to set up a camp; to build a stockade: ชุมชี a sect, gathering or assembly of Buddhist monks; a community of nuns: ชุมทาง a railroad junction; a meeting of roads or paths: ชุมพล to mobilize infantry; to assemble an army: ชุมรุม to assemble a great force and work together unitedly: มีการประชุม to congregate; to hold or call a meeting or an assembly: มีชุม in abundance (as birds or fishes).

ชุ่ม　　　choom[3] *v.* to make humid or moist; to moisten; to dampen: ชุ่มชื่น, ชุ่มชื้น to be happy; to be joyous; to rejoice; to be glad.

ชุมนุม, ชุนุ้ม　　　choom-noom *n.* a gathering; a congregation; an assembly; a sect or party.

ชุมพา　　　choom-pah *n.* the llama, a quadruped with long fleece (similar to the sheep).

ชุมเพ็ด (ว่าน)　　　choom-pet[6] *n.* a species of sedge used medicinally.

ชุมสาย　　　choom-sai[2] *n.* insignia of royal rank, being three- or five-tiered umbrellas made of variously coloured cloth, silk or velvet, with designs in tinsel or small pieces of isinglass, and decorated with diagonally placed coloured silk threads. These are carried at cremations, in processions, or in court functions, such as coronations: พลับพลาชุมสาย a temporary pavilion such as is used at cremations and other public functions (these have a raised floor, a white cloth ceiling and tinsel decorations).

ชุมแสง (ต้น)　choom-saang[2] *n.* a plant used medicinally, *Xanthophyllum glaucum* (*Xanthophyllaceae*) (cb. p. 106 : V. P. p. 101 : burk. p. 2268).

ชุมเห็ด (ต้น)　choom-het[4] *n. Cassia spp.* (*Leguminosae*) (V. P. p. 101) : ชุมเห็ดเขาควาย, ชุมเห็ดไทย, ชุมเห็ดนา, ชุมเห็ดเล็ก (ต้น) *Cassia tora* (*Leguminosae*), a fetid herb, often slightly woody at the base, found throughout tropical Asia. In Ceylon the leaves and flowers are commonly used by the poorer people as food (cb. p. 515 : V. P. p. 102 : MCM. pp. 182, 311 : Burk. p. 481) : ชุมเห็ดเทศ, ชุมเห็ดใหญ่ (ต้น) *Cassia alata*, a coarse, slightly woody herb, reaching 6 ft. in height, native of America but now distributed throughout the tropics. It is used chiefly for skin complaints and as a purgative (Burk. p. 473) ; *C. occidentalis* (*Leguminosae*), a partly woody plant the young leaves and pods of which are eaten partly, if not usually, as a medicine. The seeds are sometimes used as a substitute for coffee. The flowers are bright yellow (cb. p. 513 : V. P. p. 102 : MCM. pp. 140, 311 : Burk. p. 478).

ชุ่ย　choo-ey[3] *v.* to pierce ; to prick or puncture ; to perform imperfectly or carelessly ; to manifest intentional neglect ; to do in a slighting manner.

ชุลมุน　choon-la[6]-moon *adj.* heterogeneous ; tumultuous ; disorderly : คนชุลมุนกัน a miscellaneous, disorderly crowd.

ชุลี, อัญชลี, ชุลีกร　choo[6]-lee *n.* the act of placing the hands palm to palm and raising them to the face or forehead in the attitude of adoration or worship.

ชู　choo *v.* to raise up high ; to improve ; to elevate ; to cause to rise ; to uphold ; to support ; to sustain ; to enhance (as a price) : ชูกลิ่น to cause an odour or fragrance to continue or endure : ชูชีพ a life-preserver ; a

drug used to sustain or prolong life : ชูรส to cause the flavour to permeate : ชูรูป to place a picture in a place of honour or prominence ; to enlarge a figure or picture : ชูศรี to glorify ; to enhance honour or fame : ชูหน้า, ได้หน้า to make oneself conspicuous or prominent : ชูหัว, ยกหัว to raise the head (as a cobra).

ชู้　choo[5] *n.* a lover ; an adulterer ; a seducer : การไปกับชู้ an elopement : การรู้ชู้ adultery : ชายชู้ a man with adulterous intentions : ชู้สาว a girl enamoured with a man : ทำเจ้าชู้ to flirt : ลูกชู้ one born in adultery : หญิงมีชู้ see ชาย ๑.

ชูชก　choo-chok[6] *P. S.* a Brahman character in the เวสสันดรชาดก.

เช็ก　chek[6] *Eng. n.* a cheque : เช็กขีดตรง โดยฉะเพาะ a cheque specially crossed.

เช้ง (งาม)　cheng[5] *adj.* beautiful ; pretty ; handsome.

เชฏฐ, เชษฏ์, เชษฐู้　chet[3]-ta[4] *P. S. n.* the eldest brother ; one pre-eminent ; one most or more excellent ; a preferred wife : *adj.* first ; chief ; best ; greatest (S. E. D. p. 426) : เชฏฐ-พฺฌนทฺ *lit.* "one highest in rank among the infantry," *i. e.* a field-marshal ; a general : เชฏฐมูล the seventh month according to the lunar calculations.

เช็ด　chet[6] *v.* to wipe ; to clean by wiping or rubbing ; to cleanse ; to erase : เช็ดหม้อ to pour off the remaining water after the rice has been sufficiently boiled : ผ้าเช็ดตัว a towel : ผ้าเช็ดหน้า a handkerchief : ผ้าเช็ดมือ a napkin.

เช็ดหน้า (ไม้)　chet[6]-nah[3] *n.* the timbers forming the frame for a door or window.

เชตวัน, เชตุพน　chet[4]-dta[4]-wan *P. n.* name of a famous monastery in the forest of Jeta-vana near the city of Sravasti (สาวัตถี) in the kingdom of Kosala, long the residence of Buddha, where he preached and taught his doctrines. This monastery was erected by

Anatha-pindika, a wealthy householder of the agricultural caste (Chd. p. 168).

เชตุดร   chet[4]-dtoo[4]-daun *P. n.* a city mentioned in เวสสันดรชาดก, the story of the last human existence of Gautama Buddha previous to that in which he attained the Buddhahood (Ala. p. 184).

เช่น   chen[3] *n.* manner; pattern; specimen; sample; mode; instance: *adj.* similar to; virtually equivalent to; equal or nearly equal; like; thus; as if; as for example; *ex.* เช่นนี้, เช่นนั้น, เช่นใด.

เชย   chur-ie *v.* to squeeze, compress or extract; to fondle; to handle lovingly; to caress; to make familiar by frequent touching: ฝนเชย to be moistened by a few drops of rain: เชยชม to fondle or caress; to admire; to elevate by praise; to extol the beauty or virtues of: เชยน้ำมันงา to express teel or sesame oil.

เชรา   cha[6]-row *n.* a ravine; a deep gorge; a mountain stream.

เชราะ   cha[6]-raw[6] *v.* to cut a course down deeply through forests, rocks or gravel: *n.* a gorge cut by the current of a river; a canyon.

เชริด   cha[6]-rert[4] *n. ancient* for เทริด.

เชลง   cha[6]-leng *Cam. v.* to prepare; to compile; to arrange; to put in place; to compose metric compositions, as lyric poetry, songs or hymns: เชลงพจน์ to compile verbal material into a literary production; to compose: เชลงอรรถ to prepare and arrange foot-notes or sundry explanatory remarks.

เชวง   cha[6]-weng *v.* to be famed, illustrious, [or prosperous.

เชษฐ์, เชษฏ์ see เชฏฐ

เชอรี่ (ต้น)   chur-ree[3] *n. Malpighia glabra* (*Malpighiaceae*), the Barbados cherry, a native of tropical America and the West Indies, which is occasionally grown in this country by some, under the impression that it is the true cherry tree, *Prunus Cerasus.* The tree has been known in Bangkok for about sixty or seventy years. It is a frequent food-plant in the West Indies and is regarded as one of the best hedge plants of the islands. Also known among some Bangkok people as a cherry tree, is a plant, apparently a *Ficus,* whose young lenticellated stem and branches in a way resemble those of the true cherry tree (winit, N. H. J. S. S. IX, 3, p. 276: Burk. p. 1379).

เช่า   chow[3] *v.* to rent; to lease; to hire; to let: ค่าเช่า rent; rental: เช่าควาย, จ้างควาย to hire cows or bullocks: เช่าซื้อ hire-purchase: เช่าทรัพย์ the hire of property: ให้เช่า to let; for rent.

เช้า   chow[5] *n.* morning; ante meridian: เช้าตรู่ early sunrise: เช้ามืด daylight; early dawn: รุ่งเช้า early morning.

เชาวน์ see ชวน ๒

เชิง   cherng *Cam. n.* a stand; a foot; a base; a pedestal (as for a statue); basis; support: เชิงกราน an earthenware, portable fireplace (used for cooking purposes while travelling in boats): เชิงกลอน the skirting of eaves: เชิงโกรย the hind feet: เชิงชั้น to employ tricks, artifice or deceitful methods: เชิงชาย eaves: เชิงตะกอน a pedestal supporting the coffin during a cremation: เชิงเทิน earth thrown up for a pedestal or base; earthworks thrown up for a fortification or means of defense: เชิงซ้อน complex; intricate; involved; complicated: เชิงเดี่ยว simple; uninvolved; uncombined: เชิงประกอบ compounded; amalgamated; intermingled: เชิงผะสม mixed; mingled; a mixture: เชิง-หลอม fused; melted; smelted: เชิงเทียน the base of a candlestick: เชิงมาตร the base of a pedestal or supporting structure: เชิง-อรรถ a foot-note.

เชิญ   chern *v.* to invite; to bid courteously

to come ; to entreat ; to induce to come or go ;
to carry or transport (as an urn or coffin) :
คำเชิญ an invitation : เชิญเครื่อง to bring in
or place food before a person of rank :
เชิญเข้ามา please come in : รับเชิญ to accept
an invitation.

เชิด chert[3] v. to elevate, advance or increase
one in honour or esteem ; to lift to a higher
place ; to exalt : n. an attitude assumed by
the actors in a masked play ; a tune played
during the acts of a play : เชิดฉิ่ง a song
accompanying a masked play performance,
with the addition of cymbals in the orchestra :
เชิดชู to lift to a higher plane ; to exalt ; to
praise ; to eulogize : เชิดเพลงรำ, เชิดหุ่น to
make marionette figures act or dance : เชิด-
หนัง to display shadow pictures.

เชิ้ด chert[5] Eng. n. a shirt.

เชีย chee-ah Chin. v. to invite to depart ;
to induce to leave.

เชียง chee-ang Laos n. a city ; a chief northern provincial town of a province : เชียง
ใหม่, เชียงราย, เชียงตุง, เชียงเงิน, เชียงแสน names
of northern cities : ชะมดเชียง a species
of musk-cat.

เชียน (หมาก) chee-an[3] n. a tray for the
betel-nut and all accessories.

เชียร see ชร

เชียรณ์ see ชรณ

เชียว chee-oh[3] adj. proficient ; skilled ;
swift ; rapid ; strong (as the current of a river):
เชียวชาญ expert ; proficient ; trained ; talented :
clever ; skilled ; thoroughly versed ; vigorous.

เชียว (ต้น) chee-oh[3] n. Shorea floribunda
(Dipterocarpaceae) (cb. p. 142).

เชื่อ cheu-ah[3] v. to believe ; to credit ; to
trust ; to rely on the integrity of : ความเชื่อ
faith : เชื่อใจ to place confidence in ; to
trust ; to depend on ; to rely upon as a true
friend : เชื่อดี to be confident that what

one has is the best : เชื่อถือ to believe ; to
respect ; to reverence : เชื่อบาป listening to
or following after some sin : เชื่อบุญ to
trust in the results of good deeds or merit :
เชื่อฟัง to obey ; to submit to the government :
ซื้อเชื่อ to purchase on credit ; to have goods
charged.

เชื้อ ๑ chur-ah[5] n. race ; origin ; line (family) ; progeny ; tribe ; clan ; nation : เชื้อกษัตริย์
of royal lineage or family : เชื้อสาย posterity ; lineage ; pedigree ; family.

เชื้อ ๒ chur-ah[5] n. a germ ; a microbe ; bacillus ; a ferment ; a yeast ; an enzym : ขนม
ไม่มีเชื้อ unleavened bread : เชื้อโรค the germ
of a disease.

เชือก cheu-ak[3] n. a rope ; a numerical designatory particle used for elephants : เชือก-
เขา any tough mountain vine used instead of
twine or string : เชือกบ่วง a rope with a
running loop (as used for snaring animals):
เชือกป่าน a string ; a cord ; twine : เชือกลวด
a wire rope : เชือกหนัง a thong : ใช้เชือก-
พัน to tie or wrap with a rope : พันเชือก to
twist strands of material into a rope.

เชื่อง cheu-ang[3] adj. tame ; gentle ; docile ;
teachable.

เชื้อเชิญ chur-ah[5]-chern v. to invite to
come ; to urge to attend ; to extend a warm
invitation.

เชือด cheu-at[3] v. to cut ; to carve ; to slice
roughly : เชือดหนัง to flay ; to skin.

เชือน cheu-an adj. indirect ; not following
the shortest way ; circuitous ; slow ; late ;
tardy : เชือนแช dilatory ; slow ; neglectful.

เชื่อม cheu-am[3] v. to join by soldering ; to
unite surfaces of two metals by metallic
cement : n. syrup : adj. comatose ; abnormally sleepy ; stuporous ; giddy ; having a
whirling or swimming sensation in the head ;
heedless ; languid ; listless : เชื่อมซึม to be
in a semi-comatose condition characterized by

syncope and giddiness: เชื่อมมิ่น a condition: เชื่อมเหล็ก to solder pieces of iron
together.

แช chaa *adj.* dilatory; late; tardy; deviating from a direct course: ทำแช to loiter.

แช่ chaa[3] *v.* to soak; to saturate·; to steep;
to imbrue: แช่เบ้า unfinished; incomplete:
แช่ยา, ดองยา to digest a drug in a medium:
แช่เหล้า, ดองเหล้า to steep a drug or drugs in a
spirituous medium: แช่อิ่ม fruit preserved
in sugar; fruit preserves.

แช่ง chaang[3] *v.* to curse; to revile; to vil-
lify; to abuse; to imprecate.

แช่ม chaam[3] *adj.* gay; merry; amiable;
pleasing; kind-hearted; attractive; winning:
แช่มชื่น joyous; joyful; cheery; satisfied:
แช่มช้อย amiable; winsome; lovable.

แชร์ chaa *Eng. n.* a share in a company or
corporation.

แชรง chraang *v. ancient* of แชง to be on
guard; to be careful.

แชล่ม cha[6]-laam[3] *adj.* pretty; attractive;
winning; amiable; handsome; lovely.

โชก choke[3] *adj.* soaking wet.

โชค choke[3] *n.* fortune; luck (may be good
or ill); lot: โชคดี favorable.

โชงโลง chong-long *n.* a basket smeared
with dammer, attached to a long handle suspended from a tripod, and used for irrigating
purposes.

โชด (ต้น) chote[3] *n. Celastrus paniculata*
(*Celastraceae*), a sprawling shrub, found from
the Himalayas to Ceylon and to the Malay
archipelago. The fruits are bright yellow.
In Java the leaves are used for dysentery.
In the Philippines the sap is used as an
antidote for opium-poisoning. In India the
oil extracted from the seeds is medicinal. The
bark is said "to strengthen the brain and
purify the blood" (v. P. p. 99: BURK. p. 505:
MCM. pp. 132, 378).

โชต chote[3] *P. v.* to shine upon; to illuminate: *adj.* bright; shining; sparkling; brilliant; illustrious (chd. p. 172).

โชตก, โชดก choh-dta[4]-gka[4] *P. n.* one
who illuminates; one who gives lustre to; one
who illustrates or explains: *adj.* illucidat-
ing; explaining (chd. p. 172).

โชตน์ see ชุติ

โชติ chote[3] *P. S. n.* light (as of the sun, dawn,
fire or lightning); brightness (as of the sky)
(S. E. D. p. 427): โชติบาล a former existence
of Buddha (Ala. p. 78): โชติรส a brilliant
precious gem (as the finest diamond).

โชติก, โชดึก choh-dti[4]-gka[4] *P. n.* one
who is illuminating; one giving light; one
who illustrates (chd. p. 172).

โชติวิทยา chote[3]-wit[6]-ta[6]-yah *S. n.* astronomy.

โชตรัต chote[3]-dta[4]-rat[6] *n.* a medical
treatise elaborating on the menses.

โชน chone *adj.* shining; shimmering;
radiant with light; strong; swift.

โชมโรม chom-rom *n.* a meeting place; a
rest-house.

โชย, โชยชาย choh-ie *v.* to blow gently
but steadily; to blow softly and regularly:
ลมพัดโชยๆ a soft, gentle wind; a zephyr.

โชรม, โชม chrome *v. ancient* to bathe; to
pour on; to rub on; to anoint.

ใช่ chai[3] *adv.* it is so; indeed; yes; quite
correct; let it be that way; very well; used
also in the negative, as ใช่ว่า, ไม่ใช่ no; not so:
ใช่กิจ, ไม่ใช่การ it is none of your business:
ใช่คนนั้น not that person: ใช่นั้น not that
one: ใช่ว่าอันนั้น that is not the one: ใช่-
หรือ is this the correct one? ใช่เหตุใช่ผล
ของเขา it is no concern of theirs; better
leave them alone: ใช่อื่นใช่ไกล it is nothing
else but———: มิใช่, ไม่ใช่ no; not; not that

one: มีใช่มีแต่เท่านั้น, มีไม่ใช่แต่เท่านั้น to have not only that much, but more.

ใช้ chai[5] v. to use; to send (as on an errand); to pay back (as money borrowed); to occupy a house or boat (as a tenant); to employ (as a servant): คนรับใช้ a servant; an attendant: เครื่องใช้สอย utensils; implements; vessels; tools; instruments (as necessary in one's profession): ใช้การได้ fit or suitable to be used, though not meeting the requirements exactly (as some spare parts): ใช้การไม่ได้ impossible to be used: ใช้การยุยง to incite; to instigate; to rouse to action: ใช้ทุน to use the capital (available for investment): ใช้โทษแทน to expiate; to atone: ใช้วิธีหมุนทุน to make reinvestments for quick returns: ใช้สอย to use in an exclusive manner; to consume on one's lusts; to use in a selfish way: ใช้หนี้ใช้สิน to make payment on one's debt: ใช้อำนาจและตำแหน่งในทางทุจจริต malfeasance in office: ใช้อำนาจแห่งตน to exercise one's authority or right: ใช้อุบายหลอกลวงเพื่อได้เงินหรือสิ่งของ to obtain money or goods by false pretences: รับใช้ to be sent on an errand; to minister to; to wait on or attend: สาวใช้ an handmaid.

ไช chai v. to bore a hole, with auger or gimlet; to worm in, or into (as eels in the mud); to drill; to pierce; to penetrate: เหล็กไช an auger; a gimlet; a steel-cutting, pointed bit.

ไชย chai P. adj. better; preferable; surpassing; superior in excellence, amount or value; conquered (chd. p. 169): ไชยเภท lit. "endowed with power of growth and development," i. e. an infant: ไชยนาท name of a provincial town in northern Siam.

ไชยพฤกษ์ (ต้น) chai-pruk[6] n. Cassia renigera, a small tree of northern Burma, introduced into gardens. It is exceedingly beautiful when its pink flowers are open, and is sure of extended cultivation (Burk. p. 479); Cassia fistula (Leguminosae), Indian laburnum, pudding-pipe, a small upright tree, common in the forests of the dry regions of Siam, Ceylon and India. It is a beautiful object when in blossom, bearing masses of yellow flowers in pendulous racemes, suggesting the laburnum. The flowers are used as temple offerings, and the astringent bark for tanning and in native medicine. The black cylindrical pods grow to a length of from 20 to 30 inches; the pulp of these is a well-known purgative. It is also used with other medicines for rheumatism (cb. p. 510: MCM. pp. 85, 206, 369, 378, 462, 517: Burk. p. 475).

ซ

ซ The eleventh consonant of the Thai alphabet, a low class letter of which there are twenty-four, viz. ค, ค, ฆ, ง, ช, ฌ, ซ, ญ, ฑ, ฒ, ณ, น, ณ, พ, ฟ, ภ, ม, ร, ล, ว, ฬ, ฮ. ซอโซ่ is the name of this letter. It is used only in purely Siamese words. It is pronounced like the English "s."

ซก sok[6] adj. damp; moist; wet.

ซงแดง (ต้น) song-dang n. Ventilago calyculata (Rhamnaceae), a woody climber (V. P. p. 104).

ซ่งอู (ต้น) song[3]-oo n. pomelo, shaddock, Citrus maxima (Rutaceae) (cb. p. 238).

ซด sot[6] v. to sip (as hot tea); to suck; to draw in or imbibe by any process which resembles sucking.

ซน, ซุกซน son v. to be mischievous; to make mischief: adj. naughty; inclined to do harm; destructive; injurious: ซนไฟ to poke or push pieces of wood into the fire.

ซ้น son[5] v. to be dislocated backwards; to

over-ride; to be forced backwards or upwards : กระดูกขึ้น *n.* a dislocated bone riding upwards.

ซ่นเท้า son[3]-tow[5] *n.* a heel : ซ่นปืน the butt of a gun.

ซบ sop[6] *v.* to hang the head (as in grief); to bend down (as in the attitude of prayer) : ซบเซา hanging the head while being sad; grave; dull; affected with grief or unhappiness; serious.

ซม som *v.* to be semi-conscious; to be in a semi-comatose condition; to be in a stupor : ซมซาน weak; tottering; infirm (as from age); having dimmed eyes (as in old age) : ซม-ทราม imbecility; senility : หลับซม to be half-asleep; to be overcome with drowsiness.

ซมพอ (ต้น) som-paw *n. Caesalpinia pulcherrima (Leguminosae)*, peacock's crest, a large bush of uncertain origin, perhaps South America, but now found all through the tropics, chiefly in cultivation. There is a race with golden-yellow flowers, and one with red and yellow flowers. The Chinese have preferred the yellow race for ceremonial use, owing to the sanctity of its colour. The plant has medicinal properties (cb. p. 504 : McM. pp. 108, 109, 207 : Burk. p. 390).

ซวดเซ soo-at[3]-say *v.* to stagger, or to be inclined to one side; to sway or lean from side to side; to roll; to be dashed against the side.

ซวดทรง soo-at[3]-song *n.* form; image; shape; model; external appearance; configuration.

ซวน soo-an *v.* to lean or turn to one side; to tilt to one side; to lop over sidewise; to stagger : เซซวน leaning; nearly falling; bending or bent over.

ซวย soo-ay *Chin. adj.* in a bad condition; unlucky; "down and out"; in a run-down condition.

ซอ saw *n.* a stump or clump of bamboo; a two-stringed Chinese fiddle or violin : ซออู้, ซอด้วง Siamese fiddles : สีซอ to play on such a fiddle.

ซ้อ (ต้น) saw[3] *n. Gmelina arborea (Verbenaceae)*, a tree of moderate size, or sometimes large, with brilliant orange flowers, found from the Himalayas southward to Ceylon and northern Siam. It grows fast and is not uncommonly planted in India in gardens and in avenues. It coppices well. The timber is good, durable under water, and has many uses. It supplies mine-timbers in Upper Burma. The root has a great medicinal reputation in India, being given in the form of a decoction for gonorrhoea and catarrh of the bladder. It is a bitter tonic, stomachic and laxative. Young leaves may be used instead of the root. The fruit is sweet and bitter at the same time; it is used in medicinal decoctions (V. P. p. 103: Burk. p. 1088).

ซอก sauk[3] *v.* to be hidden in a recess or corner; to be lodged in a crevice : *n.* a fissure; a blind alley; the narrow space between two houses : ซอกซอน to make one's way in and out; to escape; to hide oneself in a crevice or secret place; to dodge; to hide : ซอกซัง to hide; to conceal; to keep oneself out of view : ซอกแซก to edge one's way in or through (as in a crowd of people); to devise ways and means (as in the raising of funds); to use devious or indirect means : *adj.* crooked; winding; devious.

ซอง saung *n.* an envelope; a sheath; a case; a flat receptacle for holding the rolled betel leaf; a " v " shaped trap or stall where horses or elephants are driven and captured : ซองบุหรี่ a cigar-case : ซองมือ the concavity or palm of the hand.

ซ้อง, ซะซ้อง saung[3] *v.* to sing in unison; to sing in harmony : *adj.* going leisurely; slow; deliberate; dilatory; tardy : ซ้องแซ่ shaky; staggering; not smart in appearance.

ซ้อง   saung[5] *v.* to sing in unison; to praise in song or chorus.

ซองแมว, ซ้องแมว (ต้น)   saung-maa-ow *n.* *Gmelina villosa* (*Verbenaceae*), a shrub or small tree found throughout most of Malaysia. It makes good hedges. It is much used medicinally, chiefly in poultices. The leaves are cathartic. When the Portuguese held Malacca they considered it a very valuable medicine and called it "rais Madre de Deos" or "root of the Mother of God" (K.: Burk. p. 1089).

ซอแซ   saw-saa *onomat.* from the sound of the chattering of many birds.

ซอน   saun *v.* to conceal; to hide in secret places (as money or keys).

ซ่อน   saun[3] *v.* to put out of sight; to hide; to secrete; to conceal; to keep secret: ซ่อน-กลิ่น, ซ่อนชู้ (ต้น) *Polianthes tuberosa* (*Amaryllideae*), tuberose, a tuberous herbaceous plant having very fragrant, creamy white flowers. It is much cultivated in southern France for the perfume obtained by enfleurage from the strongly scented flowers. The plant grows and flowers freely at medium and high elevations in the tropics. In Siam it flowers well at sea-level (MCM. pp. 139, 458: Burk. p. 1784): ซ่อนทราย (ปลา) *Acanthopsis choirorhynchus* (*Cobitidae*) (Dept. Agri & Fisheries).

ซ้อน   saun[5] *v.* to increase or grow to twice the size (as a double flower); to place one upon another; to pile up layer on layer; to pile in sets (as cups, plates, etc.): ซ้อนชับ to place in multiple layers; to pile up in many layers: ซ้อนดอก to have two wives, or two husbands.

ซอม (ต้น)   saum *n.* *Crypteronia paniculata* (*Lythraceae*), a rather tall tree found from Burma and Siam to Java and the Philippine Islands. The timber is very hard and durable and is used for house-building wherever it occurs. The new wood is white; the heart-wood is red-brown. The leaves are bitter. The young shoots are eaten as a flavouring for rice in the Dutch Indies (Cb. p. 730: V. P. p. 106: Burk. p. 693).

ซ่อม   saum[3] *v.* to renovate; to repair; to sharpen to a point: *n.* a fork: ซ่อม (นก) the eastern golden plover, *Charadrius fulvus* (Gaird. J.S.S. IX, 1, p. 14); the woodcock, *Scolopax rusticula*; the common snipe, *Gallinago coelestis* (Gaird. J. S. S. IX, 1, p. 15): ซ่อมเสียง a tuning fork: ซ่อมแซม to renew to a good condition; to mend; to repair, or adorn: ซ่อมแปลง to change, alter, or restore to a sound or good state after decay or injury.

ซ้อม   saum[5] *v.* to pound, to husk, or to shell in a mortar (as paddy); to rehearse (as for an entertainment); to exercise; to train; to drill (as soldiers); to repeat (what has already been said); to recount: ซ้อม (นก) pintail snipe, *Capella stenura* (Deig. N. H. J. S. S. VIII, 3, p. 172): ซ้อมข้าว to hull rice by pounding in a mortar; to whiten rice by pounding with a pestle: ซ้อมค้าง to repeat or narrate stories or gossip as though they were true; to talk about what belongs to another as though it belonged to oneself: ซ้อมซัก to ask repeatedly; to catechize minutely or severely; to cross-question; to cross-examine (as a witness): ซ้อมน้ำ (นก) the painted snipe, *Rostratula benghalensis benghalensis* (Deig. N. H. J. S. S. VIII, 3, p. 170): ซ้อมพวน to mill sugarcane a second time: ซ้อมพยาน to have a witness recapitulate evidence prior to giving testimony: ซ้อมเหยี่ยน (นก) the wood-sandpiper, *Tringa glareola* (Deig. N. H. J. S. S. VIII, 3, p. 172).

ซอมซ่อ   saum-saw[3] *adj.* hollow-chested; narrow-chested; diminutive; of small size; little; shabby.

ซอลาเปล (ต้น)   saw-lah-bplay *n.* *Melastoma normale* (*Melastomaceae*), a shrub of northern Siam, China and India (Cb. p. 681).

ซอย   sau-ay *v.* to divide into thin strips;

to cut into small pieces; to strike or cut with quick strokes; to mince : คลองซอย small canals leading from a larger one; intersecting canals : ซอยเท้า to take short steps; to move the feet up and down; to mark time with the feet (as soldiers keeping step without advancing) : สับซอย to chop small; to hash meat or vegetables.

ซะซร้าว   sa[6]-sow[5] *omonat.* from the sound made by an excited crowd.

ซะซ่อง   see   ซ่อง

ซะซอเซีย   sa[6]-saw-see-ah *onomat.* from the sound made by birds chattering.

ซะซิกซะแซ   sa[6]-sik[6]-sa[6]-saa *onomat.* from the sound of crying and sobbing.

ซะซิบ   sa[6]-sip[6] *onomat.* from the chirping of small birds.

ซะซุย (ต้น)   sa[6]-soo-ie *n. Citrus ichangensis (Rutaceae)* (cb. p. 237).

ซะเซาะ   see   เซาะ

ซะเซียบ   sa[6]-see-ap[3] *adj.* silent; still; quiet.

ซัก   suk[6] *v.* to wash; to question; to catechize; to inquire minutely : ซักซ้อม to cross-question; to question repeatedly; to interrogate several times; to catechize minutely or severely.

ซักไซ้   suk[6]-sai[5] *v.* to interrogate minutely; to get the truth by adroit questioning; to examine by interrogation.

ซัง   sung *n.* rice stubble; a corn-cob; the white fibre covering the meat of the jackfruit; the corner spaces in a chess-board : คนเซอะซัง a vagabond; one who wanders about aimlessly; a tramp : เที่ยวเซอะซัง to wander about at will; to stroll according to one's fancy.

ซังกะตาย, ซังตาย   sung-gka[4]-dtai *v.* to do or perform against one's will; to do grudgingly.

ซังแก (ต้น)   sung-gkaa *n. Combretum quadrangulare (Combretaceae)*, a host tree for lac in Indo-China (cb. p. 619).

ซังแซว   see   แซงแซว

ซัด   sat[6] *v.* to entangle another; to involve; to implicate (as an accomplice); to splash water or waves against; to scatter; to throw or dash; to wash against (as waves) : *n.* a fruit used as a dye giving fragrance to the cloth : คลื่นซัดเรือ the waves are dashing against the boat : ซัดกัน to shift on to others responsibility for some deed performed : ซัดเซ to wander about with no regular abiding place; to roam aimlessly : ซัดทอด to blame; to refer to (implying blame or censure); to pass the blame on to another : ถูกซัดไป to be driven (by wind or wave) : ผู้ร้ายซัดเขา the culprit makes him (them) a participator in the deed : หอกซัด a missile weapon; a javelin.

ซั้น   san[5] *adj.* urgent; requiring quickness; in rapid succession.

ซับ   sap[5] *v.* to diffuse, or permeate; to be absorbed; to dry (as in blotting); to use a blotter; to mop up (as water with a cloth) : กระดาษซับ blotting-paper : ซับซ้อน indiscriminately piled up in tiers, or in a pile.

ซับซี้   sap[6]-see[3] *v.* to whisper; to speak softly; to converse in a suspicious manner.

ซั้ว   soo-ah[5] *onomat.* from the sound "shoo" used in driving chickens.

ซา   sah *v.* to diminish; to appease; to moderate; to grow less violent or virulent; to become relaxed or quiet; to abate; to lessen : *n.* an ancient kind of boat : ไฟซาลง the fire is subsiding : ลมซาลง the wind is abating.

ซ่า   sah[3] *n.* goose-flesh; a kind of orange : *onomat.* from the sound of falling water : ซ่า (ปลา) *Dangila siamensis (Cyprinidae)* ; *D. lineata,* a carp; *Osteochilus hasselti (Cypri-*

nidae), a carp of considerable economic value in Malaya. They are generally taken during the wet season when they crowd together, presumably for spawning (Dept. Agri. & Fisheries : Burk. p. 1611).

ซาก sak[3] *n.* a corpse; a dead body; a carcass; carrion: ซาก (ต้น) *Serianthes grandiflora; Erythrophloeum succirubrum* (*Leguminosae*), a kind of wood used to make charcoal (cb. p. 540).

ซาง (ไม้) sang *n.* the long, jointless, straight stem of the pampas grass : โรคซาง a follicular pharyngitis, or laryngitis common to Siamese children.

ซ่าง (ต้น) sang[3] *n. Terminalia myriocarpa* (*Combretaceae*), a large tree of northern Burma and Siam (cb. p. 606).

ซาน san *v.* to lean to one side; to deviate from a perpendicular position.

ซ่าน san[3] *Chin. v.* to be scattered; to be strewn around; to diffuse quickly; to feel a sensation of flushness (as the blood courses through the vessels when a constriction on a limb is released): ซ่านเซ็น to be scattered ; to be routed (as an army); to be diffused; to be dispersed.

ซาบ sap[3] *v.* to infiltrate quickly; to be absorbed rapidly : ซาบซ่าน to be permeated throughout quickly ; to be diffused completely; to pass through the whole body rapidly; to be wet through.

ซาโปะ sah-bo[4] *Jav. n.* a blanket, shawl or scarf.

ซ้าย sai[5] *adj.* towards the left: ข้างซ้าย, เบื้องซ้าย on the left side : มือซ้าย the left hand : ถนัดมือซ้าย to be left-handed.

ซาร์ sah *n.* czar, the emperor of Russia (of the former régime).

ซารินา sah-ri[6]-nah *n.* czarina, the empress of Russia (of the former régime).

ซาว sow *v.* to wash thoroughly with water ; to use the hand in cleaning the rice prior to boiling : *adj.* the numeral twenty (used by the northern Thai): ซาวน้ำ a peppery, sour sauce made of dried prawns, garlic and spices, eaten with vermicelli.

ซ่าหริ่ม sah[3]-rim[4] *Jav. n.* a sweetmeat similar in shape to noodles.

ซำพอ, หางนกยูงฝรั่ง (ต้น) sum-paw *n. Delonix regia* (*Leguminosae*) (cb. p. 507); *Poinciana regia* (*Leguminosae*) (cb. p. 507: v. p. p. 103: Burk. p. 777), the flame tree, flamboyant, gold-mohur, a gorgeous tree when in full blossom, bearing immense panicles or long sprays of scarlet or orange flowers. It is a native of Madagascar but after its discovery by Boyer, apparently in 1824, the seeds went to England. It is not known when it reached the East but certainly before 1840. The tree grows to 40 or 50 feet in height. It is suited to moist as well as dry regions, especially near the sea, being a rapid grower and liable to develop surface and buttressed roots. There are three distinct varieties, that with flowers of a bright orange shade being especially attractive (MCM. pp. 91, 93, 103, 207, 213, 461).

ซ้ำ sam[5] *v.* to repeat; to reiterate; to occur in succession or consecutively: *adv.* often; repeatedly; again; anew; afresh; once more: ซ้ำซี้, ซ้ำซาก *colloq.* a tiresome or unpleasant repetition of words : ซ้ำซาก to say or repeat many times; to reiterate in a tiresome manner: ทำซ้ำ to do repeatedly; to do over and over.

ซิ si[6] *v.* the suffix which transforms a verb into the imperative mood, expressing command, entreaty or urgency of action, *ex.* มาซิ, ไปซิ, ทำซิ.

ซิก sik[6] *n.* Sikhs: *adj.* being drenched with perspiration.

ซิกซี้ sik[6]-see[5] *v.* to chuckle or laugh at in

ridicule, or contempt; to make fun of arrogantly; to mock; to satirize; to express amused contempt by laughter.

ชิชะโพ้ะ, กาดุดู้ (ต้น)　si[6]-sa[6]-poh[6] *n. Melastoma malabathricum (Melastomaceae)*, a small shrub found very plentifully, from the Mascerene Islands to Australia, and in segregate species or subspecies, extending to the remote islands of the Pacific. It is an aid to reafforestation. The fairly large flowers are violet, mauve or pink. The seeds are coated with a little red flesh, which stains the mouth when they are eaten. The flesh is sweet and slightly astringent. When quite young, the sour leaves are eaten with food in Java. The leaves, roots and vegetable parts of the plant are used in medicine. A pink dye is made from the bark and roots. The timber is rather hard, reddish-yellow and variegated, but is too small to be cut for use (cb. p. 680 : BURK. p. 1439 : McM. pp. 113, 141).

ชินแส　　sin-saa[2] *Chin. n.* a teacher; a doctor; a physician; a fortune-teller; one highly respected.

ชิบ　　sip[6] *adj.* oozy; weeping; slowly leaking; gently dripping (as perspiration or blood).

ชิบซับ　　sip[6]-sap[6] *v.* to whisper; to converse in a soft, suspicious manner.

ชิว (ปลา)　　si-ew *n.* a small edible fish, *Rasbora argyrotaenia (Cyprinidae)*; *R. retrodorsalis*, a carp (Dept. Agri. & Fisheries): ชิวควาย (ปลา) *R. lateristriata* (Dept. Agri. & Fisheries: BURK. p. 1869): ชิวใบไผ่ (ปลา) *Danio malabarica* (Dept. Agri. & Fisheries).

ชี　　see *v.* a suffix which transforms a verb into the imperative mood expressing command, entreaty, or urgency of action.

ชี่　　see[3] *adj.* a designatory particle: ซี่โครง a rib: พื้นซี่หนึ่ง a tooth: ลูกกรงซี่หนึ่ง a fence paling.

ซีก　　seek[3] *n.* a section; a half; a piece or part; a portion.

ซีกเดียว (ปลา)　seek[3]-dee-oh *n. Cynoglossus lingua (Cynoglossidae)*, a marine flat fish (Dept. Agri. & Fisheries).

ซีซอน　　see[5]-sawn *adj.* secret; covert; furtive; private; secluded.

ซีด　　seet[3] *adj.* pale; wan; pallid; whitish; sallow; dim; faint; faded.

ซีบาย　　see-bpai[4] *n.* sepoy.

ซึก　　seuk[6] *adj.* deeply worn by friction; ground down by rubbing: ซึก (ต้น) see จามจุรี (ต้น).

ซึ่ง　　seung[3] *pro.* who; which; that: *prep.* as: ซึ่งว่า as has been mentioned; that is; being so: ซึ่งเป็นไปไม่ได้ that is an impossibility.

ซึ้ง　　seung[5] *adj.* deep; distant (as the perspective): ลึกซึ้ง profound; mysterious.

ซึม　　seum *v.* to permeate or percolate through; to ooze or weep through the pores (as of the skin); to absorb: *adj.* drowsy; half-asleep; semi-conscious: ไข้ซึม a condition characterized by a continued fever, causing the patient to lie stupefied: ง่วงซึม drowsy; overcome with sleep: ซึมซาบ to permeate thoroughly; to ooze through.

ซื่อ　　sur[3] *adj.* truthful; honest; straightforward; upright; faithful; loyal: ใจซื่อ trustworthy: ซื่อตรง reliable and faithful; just; artless: ซื่อสัตย์ to be upright, true or loyal; to be honest; to be faithful to duty; to have integrity, faithfulness and veracity.

ซื้อ　　sur[5] *v.* to buy; to purchase; to acquire or procure by payment: ซื้อรู้ to lose money by trickery; to be defrauded; to be cheated; to be injured by embezzlement; to learn by some sad experience: ซื้อขาย to traffic; to barter; to buy and sell: ซื้อเชื่อ to purchase on credit: นายหน้าซื้อ a purchasing agent: ผู้ซื้อ the purchaser; a buyer.

ซุก, ซรุก   sook[6] v. to hide; to secrete; to conceal from knowledge; to be concealed or secreted: ซุกเข้าไป to crawl into a hiding place: ซุกซน naughty; mischievous; inclined to do harm; hurtful; injurious; destructive: ซุกซิก devious; serpentine; indirect; leading from, or into narrow passages or rooms: ซุกซ่อน hidden; secreted; concealed; pushed into a place of concealment: พูดซุกซิกซุ้ซิกัน to whisper in a suspicious manner.

ซุง   soong n. logs, intended for a saw-mill: (ต้น) Rhus javanica (Anacardiaceae), a tree or shrub (cb. p. 342): แพซุง a raft of logs: สายซุงว่าว the two strings that balance the kite.

ซุน   soon v. to bend down; to crouch; to hide: adj. leaning; deviating from a perpendicular line.

ซุบ   soop[6] Eng. n. soup; strong, meat broth.

ซุบซิบ   soop[6]-sip[6] adj. whispering in a low soft voice, or in a mysterious manner.

ซุ่ม   soom[3] to hide; to lie in ambush: ซุ่มคม lit. "to secrete the sharp edge," i.e. to conceal strategy; to hide an artful practice, or contrivance.

ซุ้ม   soom[5] n. an arbour; a bower; an archway covered with vines or decorated with leaves: ซุ้มกระต่าย (ต้น) Blinkworthia lycioides (v. p. p. 165): ซุ้มประตู the façade of a window or door (either carved or plain); the lintel of a door or window.

ซุ่มซ่าม   soom[3]-sam[3] adj. awkward; bungling; ungraceful; clumsy; rude; ill-bred; rowdy.

ซุมแซว   soom-saa-ow adj. boisterous; noisy; tumultuous; clamorous; impetuous (descriptive of the sounds of a mob or crowd of people).

ซุย   soo-ie n. a Laos clasp-knife: adj. crumbly; brittle; pliable; crisp: ซุยซุย easily crushed or worked with the fingers (descriptive of fertilized soil).

ซู่   soo[3] n. a condition characterized by having goose-flesh: ซู่ซ่า onomat. from the sound of dashing rain, or waves blown by a strong wind.

ซู้ (ต้น)   soo[5] Karen n. Melanorrhoea usitata (Anacardiaceae), (M. usitatissima), the "varnish tree" of Burma. It is a large tree having broad, oval leaves. A resinous juice is obtained from the stem (cb. p. 351: MCM. p. 412).

ซูดซาด   soot[3]-sat[3] onomat. from the sound made by inhaling and exhaling air after eating peppery food.

ซูบ, ซรูบ   soop[3] adj. pale; anaemic; emaciated: ซูบผอมลงมาก to become greatly emaciated, thinner or leaner.

เซ   say adj. sagging; reeling; staggering; leaning; tottering; wavering in mind: เซซัง awkward; ungraceful; swaying from side to side (as while walking): เซซุด to escape sinking, or being sunk: เที่ยวเซซัง to wander about in a dejected, disheartened manner (as a low vicious fellow).

เซ็ง   seng adj. tasteless; insipid; unsavoury: เซ็งแซ่ noisy; tumultuous; excited; boisterous: จืดเซ็งไป to become vapid, flat, dull or insipid.

เซงคง (ต้น)   seng-kong n. Eriobotrya bengalensis (Rosaceae) (cb. p. 580: BURK. p. 937), an evergreen tree found in subtropical Asia. It attains considerable size, and has good hard timber. It is rare in Malaya.

เซ่ง (ต้น)   seng[3] n. Triumfetta bartramia (Tiliaceae), a slightly woody herb found throughout the tropics of the Old World; in the Peninsula it is common on waste ground generally. It is usually a weed and nothing else. The leaves are said to serve as a famine-food. It is reported that cattle eat them (cb. p. 190: BURK. p. 2189); T. rhomboidea, a common, shrubby perennial or annual, 5 to 6 feet high having burr-like fruits (V. P. p. 105: MCM. p. 432).

เซ้ง seng[5] *Chin. v.* to dispose of a going concern by sale; to sell the good-will of a stall, or place of business; to change hands (in business).

เส้น ๑ sen *n.* the horizontal cross-pieces of wood over which bamboo strips are woven, or leaves are attached, in making the walls of Siamese houses (of the poorer classes).

เส้น ๒ sen *Eng. v.* to sign one's name: เจ้าเซ็น a sect of Indian fire-worshippers and fire-walkers: ลายเซ็น a signature.

เซ่น, สังเวย sen[3] *v.* to make offerings of food to the spirits.

เซ็นต์ sen *Eng. n.* a cent: *adj.* one hundredth; of, or pertaining to a hundred.

เซ็นติกรัม sen-dti[4]-gkram *Eng. n.* a centigram, or 0.15432 of a grain.

เซ็นติเมตร sen-dti[4]-mate[6] *Eng. n.* a centimetre, or 0.3937 of an inch.

เซ็นติลิตร sen-dti[4]-lit[6] *Eng. n.* a centilitre, or 0.338 of a fluid ounce.

เซ่อ, เซอะ sur[3], sur[6] *adj.* stupid; erratic; eccentric; absent-minded; untrained; uncouth; silly; besotted.

เซอรเว sur-way *Eng. v.* to survey a place; to make a survey.

เซา sow *v.* to stop: *adj.* being half-asleep; torpid; sluggish; moping.

เซ้าซี้ sow[5]-see[5] *v.* to ask repeatedly; to nag; to urge continually: *adj.* troublesome; murmuring; peevish; easily vexed.

เซาะ, ชะเซาะ saw[6] *v.* to scrape off; to erode; to be worn away by action of water or waves; to cut or chisel into gradually: *n.* a narrow ravine formed by the force of a mountain stream: ซึมเซาะ to percolate, filter, or ooze through gradually (as water making a passage in a dike).

เซิง serng *v.* to lift; to raise; to elevate; to praise: *n.* hair that is tousled; an uncultivated tract of land overgrown with grass, bushes, shrubs, etc., and covered with leaves: ผมเซิง hair that is disarranged or untidy; tousled hair.

เซียก, เซือก (ต้น) see-ak[3] *n. Terminalia alata (Combretaceae)*, a tree, the best species of the genus. It is used for beams inside of houses and for other purposes, and is well spoken of for tool handles. It reaches northern Siam, but not the Malay Peninsula (cb. p. 600: BURK. p. 2134).

เซียน see-an *Chin. n.* an angel; genii.

เซียบ see-ap[3] *adj.* quiet; sheltered; secluded: เงียบเชียบ extremely quiet; silent; unfrequented.

เซียว see-oh *adj.* small; slender; withered; shriveled; wrinkled; hardened (used in reference to the meat of yams or potatoes); sickly; having a withered expression.

เซี้ยว see-oh[5] *Chin. adj.* mad; insane.

เซือง seu-ang[3] *adj.* slow; drowsy; dilatory.

แซ saa *n.* an ancient Siamese gunboat used in the annual procession of the Kathin ceremonies.

แซ่ saa[3] *Chin. n.* a clan; a tribe; a clique; a sect; lineage; progeny: *adj.* noisy; clamorous.

แซ่ซ้อง saa[3]-saung[5] *v.* to cry out, or call very loudly; to clamour for.

แซง saang *v.* to be careful; to take care of: *n.* a kind of boat used in state ceremonies on the river: *adj.* interposed; inserted; intervening; interfering; interrupting.

แซงแซว, ซังแซว (นก) saang-saa-ow *n.* the black drongo or king-crow, *Buchanga atra*, a common bird whose plumage is deep black, glossed with steel blue, and having two long tail feathers: แซงแซวหางบ่วง (นก) the black drongo, *Dicrurusater* (will. N. H. J. S. S. I, 2, p. 82): แซงแซวสีเทา (นก) the white-cheeked drongo, *Dicrurus leucogenys* (will. N. H. J. S. S. I, 2, p. 81): แซงแซวหางบ่วง (นก) the great racket-tailed drongo, *Dissemurus paradiseus* (Gaird. J. S. S. IX, 1, p. 3).

แซด　saat[3] *onomat.* from the sound of many mosquitoes flying.

แซบ　saap[3] *adj.* savoury; well-flavoured; delicious.

แซม　saam *v.* to splice; to mend by replacing old materials with new; to patch; to insert or weave new strips (as in a basket); to introduce among; to thrust in: ซ่อมแซมกะบุง to weave in new strips (as while mending a basket).

แซว (นก)　saa-ow *n.* the Chinese black drongo, *Dicrurus macrocercus cathoecus* (Deig. N. H. J. S. S. VIII, 3, p. 147).

แซ่ว　saa-ow[3] *adj.* destitute; dejected; crushed; disheartened; needy; poor.

แซะ　saa[6] *v.* to enlarge with a chisel or knife; to spade or loosen up the soil (as around the roots of a plant); to dig the turf (so as to be able to lift it up in large pieces or sheets): แซะ (ต้น) *Adinobotrys atropurpureus* (V. P. p. 106); *Whitfordiodendron atropurpureum* (*Leguminosae*), a tree (Burk. p. 2256); *Padbruggea atropurpurea* (*Leguminosae*) (cb. p. 396); *P. pubescens* (cb. p. 397): แซะศาลา, ยี่โถฝรั่ง (ต้น) *Thevetia peruviana* (*Apocynaceae*), the yellow oleander, a yellow-flowered shrub found from Mexico and the West Indies to Brazil. It was brought into cultivation in Europe in 1735, and from Europe distributed to the tropics in general, as a showy plant. It was brought to Siam from Ceylon in 1843 or 1844, and was named รำเพย after a royal princess. All parts of the plant are poisonous. It is used as a fish-poison. The plant is used medicinally. In Java it is said that Indian immigrants sometimes dry and smoke the leaves. As there is

no Malay name for this shrub it is probably not found there (V. P. p. 106: MCM. pp. 117, 462: Burk. p. 2154): แซะเอื้อง (ต้น) *Vanda caerulea* (*Orchidaceae*), a showy orchid having stems 1 to 3 feet in length, bearing large sprays of beautiful, light blue flowers (V. P. p. 106: MCM. p. 146).

โซ　soh *adj.* beggarly; poor; destitute; needy; in want; famished; penniless.

โซเก (ต้น)　soh-gkay *n. Hopea odorata* (*Dipterocarpaceae*) (cb. p. 147).

โซ่　soh[3] *n.* a tribe of Karens; a chain: โซ่ตรวน fetters: ติดโซ่ chained: ลูกโซ่ the links of a chain.

โซก　sok[3] *adj.* soaked in moisture; very damp; wet; full of moisture.

โซ่ง　song[3] *n.* a tribe of the Laos people, the women wearing the hair high on top of the head.

โซเซ　soh-say *adj.* leaning; staggering; reeling.

โซดา　soh-dah *Eng. n.* soda.

โซเดียม　soh-dee-am *Eng. n.* sodium.

โซม　som *v.* to anoint; to bathe; to apply with a cloth or brush: *onomat.* from a command when making an elephant kneel.

โซรม　som *v.* to gather together in a crowd; to combine with others: โซรมประเทียด to unite in cursing by use of comparisons.

ไซ　sai *n.* a fish-trap made of bamboo strips.

ไซ ๑　sai[5] *v.* to dig for food with the snout, beak or bill (as pigs, birds or ducks).

ไซ้ ๒　sai[5] *adj.* what; whatsoever; which.

ไซร้　sai[5] a word used instead of the apodosis, meaning then, certainly, positively, or confidently, *ex.* ถ้าเป็นเช่นนั้นไซร้, ถ้าเป็นดังนั้นไซร้, ถ้าเป็นสัตย์จริงไซร้.

ฌ

ฌ The twelfth consonant in the Thai alphabet, a low class letter of which there are twenty-four, *viz.* ค, ฅ, ฆ, ง, ช, ฌ, ซ, ญ, ฑ, ฒ, ท, ธ, ณ, น, ฌ, พ, ฟ, ภ, ม, ร, ล, ว, ฬ, ฮ. ฌอเฌอ or ฌอฌาน are the names of this letter. It is pronounced like the English "ch"; it is very rarely used except in words of Pali and Sanskrit origin.

ฌลา cha⁶-lah *S. n.* a girl; a daughter; sunshine; the sun's rays; a cricket (S. E. D.

ฌลิ cha⁶-li6 *S. n.* the betel-nut. [p. 428).

ฌษ, ฌส, ฌัษ, ฌัส chot⁶ *P. S. n.* a fish; the constellation of the fish, Pisces (S. E. D. p. 429).

ฌัลล์ chan *S. n.* a pugilist; an expert boxer; a prize-fighter (S. E. D. p. 428).

ณัลลกัณฐู chan-la⁶-gkan *S. n.* a domestic pigeon (S. E. D. p. 429).

ฌาน chan *P. n.* jhana; meditative absorption; contemplation (Ala.); a series of four grades or states of abstract meditation or ecstatic trances, the attainment of which is the highest accomplishment of a Buddhist saint (Ger.); meditation (the mental exercise, so-called; in particular, the four ecstasies of the Buddha); a state of trance; the conditions of ecstasy enjoyed by the inhabitants of the Brahma-lok heavens; a religious exercise productive of the highest spiritual advantage, leading after death to re-birth in one of the Brahma heavens, and forming the principal means of entrance into the four Paths. The four jhanas are four stages of mystic meditation, whereby the believer's mind is purged from all earthly emotions and detached, as it were, from the body, which remains plunged in a profound trance. The priest desirous of practising jhana retires to some secluded spot, seats himself cross-legged, and shutting out the world, concentrates his mind upon a single thought. Gradually his soul becomes filled with a supernatural ecstasy and serenity, while his mind still reasons upon and investigates the subject chosen for contemplation; this is the first jhana. Still fixing his thoughts upon the same subject, he then frees his mind from reasoning and investigation, while the ecstasy and serenity remain, and this is the second jhana. Next, his thoughts still fixed as before, he divests himself of ecstasy, and attains the third jhana, which is a state of tranquil serenity. Lastly, he passes to the fourth jhana, in which the mind, exalted and purified, is indifferent to all emotions, alike of pleasure and of pain (chd. p. 169): ฌานมรรคา the intellectual way; means of salvation by knowledge (Gos. of Buddha).

ฌาปน, ฌาปนกิจ chah-bpa⁴-na⁶ *P. n.* conflagration; consumption by fire; the act of cremating the bodies of the dead (chd. p. 170).

ฌูก chook³ *Cam. n.* the lotus flower or [plant.

เฌอ chur *Cam. n.* a tree.

เฌาลิก chow-lik⁶ *S. n.* a holder, or telescoping case for cigars, rolled betel leaf and betel-nut; a small bag (S. E. D. p. 429).

โฌฑา choh-ta⁶ *S. n.* the betel-nut palm (S. E. D. p. 429).

ญ

ญ The thirteenth consonant in the Thai alphabet, a low class letter of which there are twenty-four, *viz.* ค, ฅ, ฆ, ง, ช, ฌ, ซ, ญ, ฑ, ฒ, ท, ธ, ณ, น, ฌ, พ, ฟ, ภ, ม, ร, ล, ว, ฬ, ฮ. ญอหญิง and ญอฌาติ are the names of this letter. It is pronounced like the English " y " except when used as a final consonant; then it is pronounced like "·n ".

ญวน   yoo-an *n.* Annamese.

ญัตติ   yat[6]-dti[4] *P. n.* the announcement of a subject, problem, proposition or motion put before a meeting for consideration; a resolution; an announcement; a declaration (Chd. p. 262).

ญาณ   yan *P. n.* supernatural power; miraculous knowledge; transcendent faculty (Ala.); knowledge; the higher degree of knowledge (derived from meditation on the one Universal Spirit (S. E. D. p. 426): ญาณกีรติ one attaining honour by supernatural knowledge or power; name of a teacher of Buddhism: ญาณทัสสนะ supreme knowledge: ญาณประภาส *lit.* "brilliant with knowledge," *i. e.* a name for a Bodhisatta: ญาณปรีชา advanced in knowledge: ญาณศาสตร์ the science of fortune-telling; a treatise on prophecy, prognostication and prediction; divination; augury: ญาณสมภาร a repository for a great amount of knowledge; a library: ญาณารณพ *lit.* "an ocean of knowledge," *i. e.* a sage; a philosopher; one with great intellectual power.

ญาณี   yah-nee *P. n.* one endowed with knowledge, or intelligence; one having the higher knowledge, or knowledge concerning the spirit; an astrologer: *adj.* wise; intelligent; knowing (S. E. D. p. 426).

ญาดา, ญาตา   yah-dah *P. n.* one who knows; a philosopher (Chd. p. 262).

ญาตก   yah-dta[4]-gka[4] *P. n.* a relative; a kinsman (Chd. p. 262).

ญาติ   yart[3] *n.* a kinsman; a near relation; kindred; relatives (S. E. D. p. 425): ญาติกรรม the act or duty of a kinsman: ญาติดี to be true kinsmen or kinsfolk; to agree not to penalize each other; to refrain from taking advantage of one another; to gain or lose unitedly: ญาติทาสี a female house-slave: ญาติบุตร the son of a relative: ญาติภาพ relationship; kindred: ญาติเภท a condition of dissension, discord, or want of harmony in families: ญาติฝ่ายบิดา agnate: ญาติฝ่ายมารดา cognate: อา the younger brother or sister of the father: น้า the younger brother or sister of the mother: ป้า the elder sister of a father or mother: ลุง the elder brother of the father or mother: หลาน a grandchild, nephew or niece.

ญาปก   yah-bpok[4] *P. S. n.* one causing others to know; a teacher; a preceptor; the act of teaching, informing, or suggesting (S. E. D. p. [426).

ญิบ   yip[6] *adj.* two: ญิบพัน two thousand.

ญี่ปุ่น   yee[3]-bpoon[4] *n.* Japan: *adj.* Japanese.

เญยย   yur-ie-ya[6] *P. S. adj.* known; learned; should be understood, ascertained, investigated, inquired into or perceived (S. E. D. p. 426): เญยยธรรม, ไญยธรรม the principles, precepts or doctrines of the Buddhist religion that should be known.

ฎ

The fourteenth consonant in the Thai alphabet, a middle class letter of which there are nine, *viz.* ก, จ, ฎ, ฏ, ด, ต, บ, ป, อ. ฎอชฎา is the name of this letter, which is used in words of Pali and Sanskrit origin as a substitute for "ฏ" but does not occur in Siamese words. It is pronounced like the English " d ".

ฎีกา   dee-gkah *P. S. n.* a petition for clemency from the Crown; a subscription for Buddhist temple funds; an invitation to a Buddhist monk; bills or statements presented for payment (as to the Royal Treasury); a scholium; a book of Pali explanatory notes on the อัฏฐกถา treatise (chd. p. 505): ถวาย-ฏีกา to present a petition to the king or to a prince: ศาลฏีกา the Supreme Court of Appeal.

ฏ

The fifteenth consonant in the Thai alphabet, a middle class letter of which there are nine, *viz.* ก, จ, ฎ, ฏ, ด, ต, บ, ป, อ. ฏอประฏัก or ฏอรกชัฏ are the names of this letter which is pronounced like a combination of the English "d" and "t" unless it occurs as a final consonant; then it is pronounced "t." It sometimes, though rarely, occurs as an initial consonant. It is used only in words of Pali and Sanscrit origin.

ฏกระ   dta[4]-ka[6]-ra[6] *S. n.* wanton sports; licentious amusements; a state of wandering of the mind: *adj.* squint-eyed (S. E. D. p. 429).

ฏังกนะ   dtang-gka[4]-na[6] *S. n.* the act of tying, binding, enclosing or surrounding (S. E. D. p. 429).

ฏังกะ   dtang-gka[4] *P. S. n.* a spade; a hoe; a hatchet; a stone cutter's chisel; a scabbard; a leg; a peak or crag shaped like the edge of a hatchet; the slope or declivity of a hill; a weight of four มาษะ (S. E. D. p. 429): ฏังกบดี the master or superintendent of a mint: ฏังกศาลา a mint.

ฏังการ   dtang-gkan *S. n.* a howl; a growl; a roar; a clang; a twang (as of a stringed instrument) (S. E. D. p. 429).

ฏังกิกา   dtang-gki[4]-gkah *S. n.* an ax; a chisel (S. E. D. p. 429).

ฏังคณะ   dtang-ka[6]-na[6] *S. n.* borax (S. E. D. p. 429).

ฏังคะ   dtang-ka[6] *S. n.* a spade; a hoe; a mattock; a kind of sword; a weight of four มาษะ (S. E. D. p. 429).

ฏังคา   dtang-kah *S. n.* the leg (S. E. D. p. 429).

ฏิฏฏุนิ   dtat[4]-dta[4]-nee *S. n.* the small house-lizard (S. E. D. p. 429).

ฏางกร   dtang-gkaun *S. n.* a manufacturer of matches.

ฏางการ   dtang-gkan *S. n.* a libertine; a law-breaker; a blackguard; an ill-conducted fellow (S. E. D. p. 429).

ฏาร   dtah-rah[6] *S. n.* a horse; one discovered guilty of sodomy; a good-looking boy kept for unnatural purposes (S. E. D. p. 429).

เฏระ, เฏรกะ   dtay-ra[6] *S. adj.* squinting; having strabismus; cross-eyed (S. E. D. p. 430).

โฏฏฏะ   dtoh-dta[4] *S. adj.* small; little; diminutive; younger; junior.

ฐ

The sixteenth consonant in the Thai alphabet, a high class letter of which there are eleven, *viz.* ข, ฃ, ฉ, ถ, ฐ, ผ, ฝ, ศ, ษ, ส, ห. ฐอฐาน and ฐอสัณฐาน are the names of this letter. It is pronounced as an aspirated English "t." It is used in Pali words and means "to be established," *ex.* คหัฏฐะ.

ฐปนะ see ฐาปนะ

ฐักกุร, ฐากุร   tak[4]-gkoo[4]-ra[6] *Beng. n.* a deity; an idol; an object of worship or reverence; a chief; used as a suffix to names of men of rank, as โควินทฐากูร Tagor (S. E. D. p. 430).

ฐาน tah²-na⁶ or tan² *P. n.* a place; a spot; a station; a base; a platform; a state or condition; a post; an office; an appointment with rank, dignity and honour; a proposition; the source; the origin; a cause; a reason (chd. p. 502): ฐานทัพ a military base: ฐานพระพุทธรูป the pedestal on which an image of the Buddha is placed: ฐานันดร a particular post or office; an appointment with title and designation of duties: ฐานานุกรม the making of appointments by an abbot (such as determining office, or conferring ecclesiastical orders on junior members of the brotherhood): ฐานานุรูป those who are deemed worthy of receiving appointment or advancement, as defined in the above.

ฐานบัทม์ tan²-na⁶-bat⁴ *P. n.* a base or pedestal representing lotus petals in tiers, on which images of the Buddha are placed.

ฐานิก tah²-nik⁶ *P. adj.* holding the place of: ครุฐานิก holding the position of a teacher (chd. p. 503).

ฐานีย ta²-nee-ya⁶ *P. n.* a city; a capitol:

adj. suitable or fit for a position of rank; based upon (chd. p. 503).

ฐานะ tah²-na⁶ *n.* condition; position; standing; status; state, cause or origin; special office.

ฐาปนะ, ฐาปนา, ฐปนะ tah²-bpa⁴-na⁶ *P. v.* to construct; to establish or found; *n.* the act of constructing (as of a city); the act of establishing, placing, erecting, repairing or renovating (chd. p. 503).

ฐายี tah²-yee *P. v.* to be established; to establish; to endure: *adj.* lasting; firm; steady; enduring; continuing; living (chd. p. 504); *suffix, ex.* กัปปัฏฐายี lasting for an aeon, or eternity.

ฐิต, ฐิตก ti⁶-dta⁴ *P. adj.* standing upon; stayed; stopped; immovable (chd. p. 504).

ฐิติ ti⁶-dti⁴ *P. n.* durability; stability; endurance; perpetuity; state or condition of permanence (chd. p. 504).

ฐิติก ti⁶-dti⁴-gka⁴ *P. n.* one who continues, or that which endures; one who is permanent, immovable, and enduring forever: *adj.* lasting; continuing; existing; living on (chd. p. 504).

ฑ

ฑ The seventeenth consonant in the Thai alphabet, a low class letter of which there are twenty-four, *viz.* ค, ฅ, ฆ, ง, ช, ฌ, ซ, ญ, ฑ, ฒ, ฐ, ฑ, ณ, ท, ธ, น, ฑ, พ, ฟ, ภ, ม, ร, ล, ว, ฬ, ฮ. ทอไพทูรย์ and ทอมณโฑ are the names of this letter. It is pronounced either as " ท " in ไพทูรย์ or as " ด " in มณฑป or like the English " t ", or " d." It occurs in words of Pali and Sanskrit origin, usually as a final consonant, rarely as the initial letter. As a final consonant it always has the sound of " t."

ฑังส dang-sa⁴ *P. n.* a horse-fly; a horse-tick; a gad-fly (chd. p. 111).

ฑาก tak³ *P. n.* a vegetable; a pot-herb (chd. p. 110); pickled vegetables; the leaves of the wild tea, steamed and left to ferment, then done up in bundles with a pinch of salt and chewed much as a quid of tobacco; see เมี่ยง.

ฑาห tah-ha⁴ *P. n.* heat; fire (chd. p. 109).

ฑาหก tah-hok⁴ *P. n.* one sitting on fire;

fire (chd. p. 109).

ฑิกกรี tik[6]-gkree *S. n.* a daughter; an unmarried girl; a maiden; a young woman.

ฑิมภ์ tim *S. n.* a new-born child; a young animal; a young shoot; an infant; an egg; a cub; a whelp (S. E. D. p. 430).

ฒ

ฒ The eighteenth consonant in the Thai alphabet, a low class letter of which there are twenty-four, *viz.* ค, ฅ, ฆ, ง, ช, ฌ, ซ, ญ, ย, ท, ฑ, ฒ, น, ณ, พ, ฟ, ภ, ม, ร, ล, ว, ฬ, ฮ. ฒอผู้เฒ่า and ฒอเจริญ are the names of this letter which is used in two Siamese words only; other usage is in words of Pali origin where it is a final letter. It is pronounced like the English "t."

เฒ่า tow[3] *n.* a person of age and standing; a chief; an older or aged person: *adj.* old; aged: เฒ่าแก่ women palace-guards; one who arranges marriages; a procuress; a Chinese head-man or contractor; an elder (a Christian Church official).

ณ

ณ The nineteenth consonant in the Thai alphabet, a low class letter of which there are twenty-four, *viz.* ค, ฅ, ฆ, ง, ช. ฌ, ซ, ญ, ย, ท, ธ, ฑ, ฒ, น. ณ, พ, ฟ, ภ, ม, ร, ล, ว, ฬ, ฮ. ณอเณร and ณอคุณ are the names of this letter. It is pronounced like the English "n." It is used in words of Pali and Sanskrit origin.

ณ na[6] *prep.* at; by; near; in; on; upon; within: ณวัน on the day of.

ณัฐ, ณัฏฐ์ nat[6] *P. n.* a sage; one endowed with a high degree of knowledge; a person of experience, prudence and foresight.

เณร nen *n.* novices in the Buddhist priesthood; an ascetic; a Buddhist monk; a Buddhist priest (chd. p. 427).

ด

ด The twentieth consonant in the Thai alphabet, a middle class letter of which there are nine, *viz.* ก, จ, ฎ, ฏ, ด, ต, บ, ป, อ. ดอเด็ก is the name of this letter. It is pronounced like the English "d."

ดก dok[4] *adj.* fertile; productive (as a fruit tree); abundant (as fruit or flowers); teeming: ดอกดก flowers in great plenty: ลูกดก, ผลดก abounding in fruit.

ดง dong *v.* to dry cooked rice by placing the pot over hot coals: *n.* a thick forest of tall grass or trees: ชาวดง the inhabitants of a forest: ดงดอน forest or jungle on high ground or low hills: ดงดาน a dense, extensive forest (as where the foliage is so thick the sun does not shine through): ดงดึก a forest that is dense and impenetrable.

ดงวาย, ถวาย dong-wai *v.* to give; to present; to hand (used only for princes or Buddhist monks).

ด้น don[3] *v.* to stoop low; to crawl or move in a crouching posture (as when going through a fence); to run a seam by hand (generally taking a series of stitches on the needle at one time): กลอนต้น extemporaneous verse: ต้นกลอน to speak or sing in extemporaneous verse: ต้นถอยหลัง to backstitch: ต้นลอด to pass, by crouching or stooping through some difficult or almost impassable place: ลัดต้น to crawl on hands and knees along roadless places, or through an obstructed passage; to penetrate by main force.

ดนตรี, ต้นตระ don *P. S. n.* a loom; the warp, or threads that run the long way of a fabric; the leading, principal, or essential part; the characteristic feature; a system; framework; doctrine; rule; theory; a scientific work or any chapter of such a work; a class of works teaching magical and mystical formulae; an army; a row; a number; a series (of troops); wealth; a house; happiness; the wire or string of a lute; the strings of the heart (S. E. D. p. 436): ดนตรการ the author of any scientific treatise: ดนตรวาย a weaver; a spider.

ดนตรี don-dtree *S. n.* an instrument having strings, threads, or cords; stringed, musical instruments; articles spun, woven or corded (S. E. D. p. 436).

ดนย, ดนัย da⁴-na⁶-ya⁶ *P. S. n.* a son (S. E. D. p. 435): ดนัยสร a mother.

ดนยา, ดนัยา da⁴-na⁶-yah *P. S. n.* a daughter (S. E. D. p. 435).

ดนุ, ดนู, ด้านู da⁴-noo⁶ *P. S. n.* the body; a person; an individual: *pron.* I; me; oneself: *adj.* thin; slender; attenuated; emaciated; small; little; minute; delicate; fine (S. E. D. p. 435): ดนุจฉัท feathers; clothing; raiment; garments; *lit.* "a guard for the body," *i. e.* armour (S. E. D. p. 435): ดนุช, ดนุภพ a son: ดนุชา, ดนุภวา a daughter: ดนุตล a measure of length equal to the arms outstretched; two yards; one wah; one fathom: ดนุตร *lit* "body-guards," *i. e.* ar-

mour; means of self-defence: ดนุทร a small slender waist: ดนุทาน a scanty gift; a meagre present; the offering of the body (for sexual intercourse): ดนุธี little-minded; narrow-minded; stingy; miserly; sordid: ดนุนุช the youngest of a family: ดนุพล strength; physical power: ดนุภัสตรา *lit.* the "body-bellows," *i. e.* the nose: ดนุมัธย์ *lit.* "middle portion of the body," *i. e.* the waist: ดนุรส *lit.* "body fluid," *i. e.* sweat; perspiration: ดนุลดา a slight, slim, slender, or frail body.

ดบัน da⁴-ban *P. S. n.* the sun; heat; the hot season; a division or degree of hell: *adj.* shining; burning; warming; causing pain or distress (S. E. D. p. 437).

ดบัสวิน, ดบัสวี da⁴-bat⁴-sa⁴-win *P. S. n.* one practising austerities; an ascetic; a hermit; a mendicant; a pauper: *adj.* distressed; wretched; poor; miserable (S. E. D. p. 437): ดบัสวินี a female devotee; a poor, wretched woman (S. E. D. p. 437).

ดม dom *v.* to smell; to inhale (as an anesthetic): ดมกลิ่น to inhale odours or perfumes: ยาดม drugs used by inhalation.

ดมไร dom-rai *Cam. n.* the elephant.

ดมัน da⁴-man *S. n. lit.* "becoming breathless," *i. e.* suffocation; death by intentional suppression of breathing (S. E. D. p. 438).

ดยูก (often written ดยุ๊ก) da⁴-yook³ *n.* a duke: ดัสเชส a duchess; the consort of a duke.

ดร daun *P. S. n.* a raft or float; the act of being towed (as boats) (chd. p. 497): แพ (เรือน) a floating house; a house built on pontoons.

ดรงค์ da⁴-rong *P. S. n.* waves; billows; ripples along the shore; a chapter (S. E. D. p. 438): ดรงคมาลี *lit.* "wave-garlanded," *i. e.* the sea: ดรงควดี *lit.* "having waves," *i. e.* a river.

ดรณิ da⁴-ra⁶-ni⁶ *S. n.* the sun: *adj.* moving forward (as the sun); passing over quickly; untiring; energetic; carrying over (S. E. D. p. 438): ดรณีรัตน์ *lit.* "a jewel of the sun," *i. e.* a ruby.

ดรณี da⁴-ra⁶-nee *P. S. n. lit.* "something that glides along," *i. e.* a boat or sailing vessel.

ดรธาน, อันตรธาน dau-ra⁶-tan *v.* to disappear; to melt away; to vanish from sight or vision.

ดรรชน, ดัชชน dat⁴-cha⁶-nee *S. n.* the index finger; the forefinger: พระดรรชนี the index finger (used only for kings or princes).

ดรล ๑, ดรลา da⁴-ron *P. S. n.* intoxicants; fermented drinks; the bee; soft-boiled rice; rice gruel (S. E. D. p. 439).

ดรล ๒ da⁴-ron *P. S. n.* the central gem of a necklace; a ruby; iron; a level surface; the deepest part or portion (S. E. D. p. 439).

ดรี, ดรี da⁴-ri⁶ *P. S. n.* a boat (S. E. D. p. 439).

ดรุ da⁴-roo⁶ *P. S. n.* a tree; bushes (S. E. D. p. 439): ดรุขัณฑ์, ดรุบัณฑ์ a group, or clump of trees: ดรุช *lit.* "what a tree produces," *i. e.* roots, leaves, flowers, etc.: ดรุชีวัน the root of a tree or bush: ดรุดล the level ground around the trunk of a tree: ดรุนัข *lit.* "tree-nails," *i. e.* thorns: ดรุมณฑป a bower: ดรุมฤค *lit.* "tree animals," *i. e.* apes; monkeys: ดรุมูล the root of a tree: ดรุราค *lit.* "tree-charm," *i. e.* a bud; *lit.* "the progenitor of a bush or tree," *i. e.* the flower: ดรุวัลลิ, เถาวัลลิ a common vine growing on trees or bushes; a creeper: ดรุศายี *lit.* "sleeping on trees," *i. e.* birds: ดรุสาร *lit.* "tree-essence," *i. e.* camphor.

ดรุณ, ดรุณี da⁴-roon *P. S. n.* one approaching adolescence; a young man or woman; a girl: *adj.* young; tender; juvenile; new; fresh: ดรุณาณัติ a teacher of children in a class room.

ดรู, ตรู da⁴-roo *Cam. adj.* handsome; beautiful; pretty.

ดฤถิ see ดิถิ

ดล ๑, บันดล don *P. S. n.* base; bottom; the lower part; depth; the basement (S. E. D. p. 440): ดลดาล the act of clapping the hands: ดลประหาร a slap with the palm or paw: ดลภาค a level or smooth surface; the unit of square measure; a square metre: ดลมุข a particular position of the hands while dancing: ดลยุทธ์ *lit.* "palm-fight," *i. e.* clapping: ดลโลก *lit.* "the lower-world"; ดลศัพท์ the clapping of the hands.

ดล ๒ don *Cam. v.* to arrive; to reach a destination.

ดล ๓ don *v.* to inspire; to influence; to animate; to move (as by some supernatural power); to set up (as a new course of conduct); to awaken or kindle (as a correct sense of right and wrong): ดลใจ to produce a conviction of the conscience (as by a spiritual power); to correct evil in the heart (as by divine power).

ดวง doo-ang *n.* a numerical designatory particle signifying round in shape; an orb; a sphere; a disc; a circle: ดวงจันทร์ the moon: ดวงใจ the heart: ดวงชาตา the zodiac; the astrologers' circle: ดวงดาว stars (in general); the orb of the stars: ดวงตา the eye: ดวงตรา a seal: ดวงพักตร์ a face; a round, handsome face: ดวงไฟ a light or lamp: ดวงสมร a term of endearment (as "you are the flower of my heart," or "the light of my life"): ดวงอาทิตย์ the orb of the sun; the sun: เป็นดวง ๆ blotchy; soiled; spotted with dirt or mildew.

ด้วง doo-ang³ *n.* a large worm that attacks trees; a grub: ขนมด้วง a kind of sweetmeat made in the shape of vermicelli (macaroni): ซอด้วง a two-stringed violin, the body of which is made of a bamboo joint with a bow attached: ด้วงกุหลาบ a worm which attacks

roses, particularly *Adoretus comprevus* : ด้วง-
ขี้หนู larvae found in dunghills : ด้วงงวง
weevils : ด้วงดักหนู a mouse-trap made of
a bamboo joint, fitted with a flexible bamboo
rod for a spring, and a noose carefully hidden
in the mouth of the joint : ด้วงมะพร้าว the
coconut rhinocerus beetle, grub, or larva,
Oryctes rhinocerus : ด้วงโสน the grub of
a beetle feeding on the stem of *Sesbania rox-*
burghii (*Leguminosae*) (cb. p. 400). During
certain seasons, when these grubs are plentiful, the natives collect them for food, considering them rather a delicacy : เป็นด้วงเป็น-
แมง used in reference to worm-eaten timber.

ดวจ see ดุจ

ดวด   doo-at[4] *v. colloq.* to drink liquor : *n.*
a game played with dice and cowries (similar
to backgammon) : *adj.* single ; high ; lofty :
ควงน้ำ *slang* to drink : เทดวด to throw cowries in the same manner as dice.

ด่วน   doo-an[4] *adj.* urgent ; pressing ; requiring haste ; hasty ; precipitant : การด่วน
urgent business : ด่วนไป urgently needing
to go : โดยด่วน urgently ; hurriedly ; speedily : รถไฟด่วน an express railway train.

ด้วน   doo-an[3] *v.* to be cut off ; to be amputated or shortened ; to be abbreviated or
curtailed : คลองด้วน a blind canal : มือ-
ด้วน an amputated hand ; a maimed hand :
หางด้วน a docked tail.

ด้วมเดี้ยม see กะด้วมกะเดี้ยม

ด้วย   doo-ie[3] *adv.* with ; at the same time ;
when followed by a noun it means "with,"
or "together" ; when used at the end of a
sentence it means "also," or "too" : *prep.* by,
ex. ลบด้วย, คุณด้วย, หารด้วย : *conj.* that ; nevertheless : กินด้วยกัน to partake in company
with : เข้าด้วย to agree with ; to participate
in ; to associate with : ด้วยกัน together :
ด้วยความพยาบาท maliciously ; spitefully : ด้วย-
ความพร้อมใจกัน harmoniously ; peaceably ; una-

nimously : ด้วยมือ using the hands : ด้วยว่า-
on account of ; whereas ; because : ด้วยอันใด
why ; how is it ? นอนด้วย to sleep with ; to
lie beside : บอกด้วย to tell me also ; to
inform me likewise.

ดวล   doo-an *Eng. n.* a duel.

ดอก   dauk[1] *v.* to accrue ; to increase ; to be
added to : *n.* interest ; usury ; figures or
prints on cloth ; flowers ; blossoms ; used as
the generic name for all flowers, to which the
name of the specific flower is added, *ex.* ดอก
พิกุล ; names of some trees also contain this
word ดอก as a part of the specific name, *ex.*
ต้นดอกสร้อย : *adv.* certainly ; surely (this
word gives emphasis when used at the end of
a sentence, *ex.* ทำไม่ได้ดอก) : ขัดดอก to fail
to pay interest and be forced to place a child
in servitude in lieu of interest : ดอกกระมัง
probably ; still doubtful ; perhaps ; not certain :
ดอกจอก the flower of the water plant, *Pistia*
stratiotes ; the stomach of animals (as of the
cow or buffalo because it is in folds or
wrinkles as the leaf of the water lettuce) :
ดอกจันทน์ an asterisk ; the flower of the nutmeg tree : ดอกชนต้นเงิน the interest equals
the principal : ดอกตั้ว the mammae ; the
human breast : ดอกดิน the flower of *Aegi-*
netia pedunculata : ดอกเบี้ย interest on
money ; usury : ดอกเบี้ยค้าง interest in
arrears : ดอกเบี้ยทบต้น compound interest :
ดอกไม้เงินทอง gold and silver trees given as
tribute by vassal princes : ดอกไม้ตาด a kind
of variously coloured fireworks : ดอกไม้-
เทียน a kind of fireworks ; roman candles :
ดอกไม้พุ่ม fireworks made in the shape of a
bush burning with coloured lights : ดอกไม้-
เพลิง, ดอกไม้ไฟ fireworks ; a pyrotechnic display : ดอกไม้ร่วง a design for cloth or
decorations in the shape of suspended bunches
of flowers : ดอกไม้รุ่ง a slow, all-night burning fuse hung in a sala to give light instead
of a lamp : ดอกไม้ไหว a bouquet of gold
or silver artificial flowers on spring wires
(used for decorations) : ดอกเล็บ white spots

on the fingernail : ทั้งต้นทั้งดอก both the principal and the interest : ผ้าดอก calico ; a fabric figured in weaving, or by printing : ผูกดอก to borrow money with interest.

ดอกคั้ง, ขางคั้ง (ต้น) dauk[4]-kang[3] *Laos n. Dunbaria longeracemosa (Leguminosae)*, a tree found in Chiengmai, etc. This species resembles *D. bella* but has much longer racemes (cb. p. 463).

ดอกผึ้ง (ต้น) dauk[4]-peung[3] *n. Vanda teres*, an orchid (MCM. p. 146).

ดอกทอง dauk[4]-taung *n.* a courtesan ; a prostitute ; an harlot ; an obscene term of abuse ; a curse.

ดอกไม้หนัง (ต้น) dauk[4]-mai[5]-nang[2] *n. Alphonsea pallida (Anonaceae)*, a small tree or shrub found in Nakorn Sritamarat (cb. p. 63).

ดอกสมัด (ต้น) dauk[4]-smat[4] *Laos n. Micromelum hirsutum (Rutaceae)*, a small tree, widely distributed in Siam and Malaya. The leaves have magical and medicinal uses (cb. p. 228 : Burk. p. 1468). See ขี้ผึ้ง, also known as มองคอง, จุ๊มุกตัวผู้ *Laos.*

ดอกสาก (ปลา) dauk[4]-sak[4] *n. Sphyraena obtusata (Sphyraenidae)*, a baracuda of northern Siam (suvatti p. 108).

ดอกสร้อย (ต้น) dauk[4]-soi[3] *n. Combretum apetalum (Combretaceae)*, a tree or shrub of northern Siam (cb. p. 615 : V. P. p. 113).

ดอกหมาก (ปลา) dauk[4]-mak[4] *n. Gerres punctatus*, a small carnivorous marine fish ; *Xystaema abbreviatus ; Xystaema lucidum (Gerridae)* (suvatti pp. 134, 135).

ดอง daung *v.* to pickle ; to preserve in vinegar, or by acid fermentation ; to preserve by soaking in a solution (as pathological specimens) : *n.* the method of wearing a Buddhist monk's robe, the rolled ends lying across the shoulder : เกี่ยวดอง to be allied to ; to be of the same kindred or family : ดองแช่ to steep macerated drugs in rice water till fermentation takes place, when they are taken as a remedy : น้ำดอง fresh nipa palm juice (not yet having been boiled down) : ปรองดอง to consult together ; to take counsel with ; to act in accordance with others : ยาดอง macerated drugs tied in a bag and soaked in brandy, wine, or arrack.

ด่อง ๆ daung[4]-daung[4] *adj.* slow ; dilatory ; deliberate : เดินด่อง ๆ to walk at a slow, deliberate pace ; to walk slowly ; to loiter.

ด้อง daung[3] *n.* a catfish, found in rivers and streams but seldom in ponds. This name is usually applied to young catfish of the family *Pangasiidae* : ด้องแด้ง to sway ; to swing ; to oscillate while in a hanging position (used in regard to birds which, after having been shot, are lodged in the branches of trees) : เดินด้องแด้ง to swing or sway the body while walking.

ดองดึง (ต้น) daung-durng *n. Gloriosa superba (Liliaceae)*, a bulbous climber found in south Ceylon, tropical Asia and Africa and cultivated for its beautiful scarlet and yellow flowers. It has whorled leaves, whose tips end in a spiral tendril. The large, fleshy tubers are poisonous and not infrequently are eaten by the poorer classes in mistake for edible yams, often with fatal results. The poisonous property is colchicium which is a drug used for gout (V. P. p. 113 : MCM. pp. 124, 138, 141, 385, 386 : Burk. p. 1078).

ดองหาย daung-hai[2] *n.* an implement for spreading out straw on the threshing floor (as a pitchfork).

ดอด daut[4] *v.* to steal upon, or to approach stealthily ; to steal up unnoticed ; to approach unannounced ; to look by stealth ; to peek or spy slyly : ดอดไปดอดมา to move to and fro stealthily in order to spy : ดอดมอง to look slyly through a hole or crevice.

ดอน daun *n.* an elevated place, or high rising ground not exposed to inundations :

นาดอน paddy field on high ground : ลุ่ม ๆ-ดอน ๆ undulating ground ; an uneven surface ; rough ground.

ด่อน   dawn[4] *n.* a container ; a holder (as a socket for sky-rockets or fireworks) : *adj.* dirty white ; dull ; dusty ; pinkish white ; albino (used in reference to the colour of certain animals, as elephants or buffaloes) : ด่อนนกบิน a socket for holding fireworks that sail up as a bird.

ดอม ๑   daum *Cam.* n. a row or line (as of trees) ; a stick, or line for hanging clothes ; a hand-rail : ดอมไพร a boundary, edge, line, or skirt of a forest.

ดอม ๒   daum *v.* to imbibe ; to inhale ; to smell the odour of : *n.* perfumery ; scents of various kinds : *prep.* with ; together.

ด้อม   daum[3] *v.* to peep at through a crevice ; to peek at secretly ; to creep up to slyly or noiselessly : เดินด้อม ๆ to approach craftily (as on tiptoes or when hunting wild game) : นอนด้อม to lie in wait secretly.

ดอย   daw-ie *v.* to tie ; to bind with a band or cord ; to pound or forge with a hammer ; to pull ; to pitch (as quoits) ; to box ; to strike : *n.* used as a general term for hills or mountains in northern Siam.

ด้อย   daw-ie[3] *v.* to sink ; to subside ; to settle (as an approach to a bridge) ; to become lower than normal.

ดะ   da[4] *adv.* roughly ; imperfectly ; crudely, *ex.* ถางป่าดะ ๆ ไปก่อน.

ดะด่อน   da[4]-daun[4] *adj.* dirty white, or pinkish white (as an albino) ; dun-coloured.

ดะดัก   da[4]-dak[4] *adj.* beset with difficulties ; hard to do or make ; troublesome ; annoying ; vexatious ; irksome ; laborious ; perplexing.

ดะโดลิเต๊าะ, โศกน้ำ (ต้น)   da[4]-doh-lee-dtaw[6] *Malay* n. *Saraca bijuga (Leguminosae),* a small tree found in the peninsular part of Siam and in Malaya. The Siamese eat the flowers and young leaves (cb. p. 534 : BURK. p. 1964).

ดะหมั้ง   da[4]-mang[2] *Jav.* n. an army ; a body of armed men ; a company of soldiers.

ดัก   dak[4] *v.* to catch in a net ; to lay snares or traps for ; to lie in wait for ; to intercept ; to watch for in order to capture : ดักข่าววิทยุ to intercept radio messages : ดักคอ antecedent (in words or opinions) ; to anticipate others in expressing one's opinions : ดักนก to trap birds ; to set snares ; ดัก (ปลา) *Amblyceps mangois (Amblycipitidae)* (suvatti p. 79) : ดักปลาไหล to lay traps for eels ; to catch eels in a trap.

ดักดน, ดักดาน   dak[4]-don, dak[4]-dan *adj.* miserable for a long time ; wretched ; grievously unhappy ; unfortunate.

ดักเดีย   dak[4]-dee-ah[3] *v.* to be in want ; to be miserable ; to wander about in destitution.

ดักแด้, แด็กแด้   dak[4]-daa[3] *v.* to be wretched and oppressed by extreme want ; to be profoundly dejected : *n.* a chrysalis.

ดักษก, ดัจฉก   dak[4]-sok[4] *S.* n. *lit.* "a cutter," *i. e.* a carpenter (S. E. D. p. 431) : ดักษณ a cutter ; an abrader (as knives, files, etc.) ; a divisor employed to reduce a quantity : *adj.* cutting ; paring ; peeling ; abrading (S. E. D. p. 431).

ดักษณี, ดัจฉนี   dak[4]-sa[4]-nee *S.* n. an ax ; an adze (S. E. D. p. 492).

ดักษัน   dak[4]-san[2] *S.* n. a wood-cutter ; a carpenter (S. E. D. p. 431).

ดั้ง (ดั้ง) ๑   dang n. the nose ; nostrils.

ดั้ง ๒   dang *adj.* loud : *adv.* just as ; similar to ; somewhat alike : ความนี้ดั้งมาก this affair causes a great consternation, uproar or much publicity : ดั้งเก่า as before ; as formerly : ดั้งจริง quite true to facts ; genuine ; real : ดั้งเช่น such as ; as much as: ดังนั้น in that way: ดังนี้ in this way; thus; so: ดังหรือ, ดังๆ whereby; how; why; for what cause or reason: ดังหนึ่ง as; just as; in the same manner as: ดังนั้น tumultuously or with a resounding noise: พูดตัง to speak loudly: พูดให้ตัง talk or speak louder (a command): เสียงตัง boisterous; noisy (cries or crashings).

ดัง dang[4] *adj.* as; just as; similar to; like; after the same manner: ดังคิด as - one thinks: ดังจะแกล้ง as if intentionally done: ดังใจ as it is wished: ดังเดิม as in, or from the beginning: ดังได้ยินว่า as is heard said or rumoured.

ดั้ง, ด้าง dang[3] *v.* to advance in the lead; to go forward first: *n.* a shield; a flotilla of vessels which follows the king in a procession; elephants arrayed as an auxiliary in an army: ดั้งแขน a buckler or long, narrow shield for the arm: ดั้งจมูก the ridge of the nose: ดั้งแขวน a king-post; a king-rod (hanging): ดั้งโล่ห์ a large shield: เสาดั้ง king-posts (which support the ridge-pole).

ดั้งเดิม dung[3]-derm *adj.* beginning; first; ancient; as from the first: แต่ดั้งเดิมมา from the very beginning.

ดัจฉก see ดักษก

ดัจฉนี see ดักษณี

ดัชชนี see ดรรชนี

ดัชเชส see ดยูก (also spelled ดยุ๊ก)

ดัด ๑ dat[4] *v.* to awaken from slumber; to bend by force; to straighten; to coerce; to constrain: ดัดกาย manual training or drilling: ดัดคดี to alter or change the course of a lawsuit, making it according to the truth: ดัดจริต to reform one's conduct; to correct from evil to good; to feign or pretend in manner: ดัดแปลง to change or correct; to alter; to make, or set right: ดัดผทม, ดัดบรรทม to arouse from slumber (used only for royalty): ดัดให้ตรง to straighten.

ดัด ๒ dat[4] *v.* to partition off; to divide into distinct parts by walls: ดัดพิดาน to furnish with a ceiling; to line the roof; to separate into rooms (as from the ceiling down).

ดัดปลัก dat[4]-bplak[4] *n.* a month.

ดัน dan *v.* to push; to shove; to press by physical force: ไข่ดัน the glands of the groin: ดันเข้า to exert more energy in pushing or shoving (as while urging labourers in effort to move a heavy weight): ดันทุรัง being stubborn; unreasonable; obstinate: ดันไปจนได้ finally to break through; eventually to accomplish after arduous efforts: ดันไปจนตลอด to push or break clear through: ดื้อดัน to be stubborn, headstrong, or unyielding; to act contrary to the wishes of others (used especially regarding wilful children): ดันป่า to force one's way through a jungle (as by cutting, crouching or crawling) (BRAD.).

ดั้น dan[3] *v.* to make one's way by hazard; to duck the head and go along an obstructed passage: *n.* a kind of poetry or metre.

ดั้นเหิม, ดั้นเหิม dan-herm[2] *v.* to be glad, joyful or gay.

ดับ dap[4] *v.* to quench; to extinguish or exterminate; to subdue or conquer (as one's passions): ดับความ to hush up a quarrel: ดับใจ to die: เดือนดับ the dark of the moon: ระดับน้ำ a water-level: ลำดับ a series; an order; a file or row: ลำดับไว้ to arrange in the proper place, in series, or according to serial number: ให้เป็นลำดับ to place in order, series, files or rows: ดับโทโม to allay anger.

ดัมพ์ see ดามพ์

ดัวเดีย doo-ah[3]-dee-ah[3] *adj.* slow; sluggish; inactive; deliberate.

ดัสกร dat[4]-sa[4]-gkaun *S. n.* an enemy; a robber; burglars; plunderers (S. E. D. p. 441).

ดัสกรี dat[4]-sa[4]-gkree *S. n.* an exceedingly

evil-minded woman; one with an harlot's inclinations (S. E. D. p. 441).

ดา   dah v. to make a combined attack; to advance in a body: adj. abundant; ample; plentiful: ดา (แมลง) Lethocerus indicus, the giant water-bug or the giant electric-light bug, an insect of blue and green colouring, found in the fields during the rainy season: ดาดาษ abundant; enough to be scattered everywhere; profuse; lavish; prodigal; exuberent: ดาดำ black; entirely black: สระ-ตาดาษด้วยดอกบัว a pond profusely covered with lotus blossoms.

ดา (ต้น)   dah n. Garcinia xanthochymus (Guttiferae), a tree of India and southwards through Burma into Siam. It is called egg-tree (from its ovoid or conical shape). It is a symmetrical, bushy tree, growing to 25 or 30 feet high, having large leathery leaves, 10 to 15 inches long and 2½ to 3½ inches broad. The handsome, yellow, smooth fruit, produced in great abundance, usually in December to February, is of the form and size of a small orange, with a pointed (stigmatic) projection at the end or on one side. The yellow, juicy pulp has an acid but refreshing taste. The tree is propagated from the large seeds, and thrives best at medium elevations. Yellow dye obtained from the bark is extensively employed in Assam for dyeing cloth, etc. In Malaya it is chiefly cultivated for its fruit. In India it is used in making sherbets, and mendicaments (v. P. p. 110: MCM. pp. 263, 440, 518: BURK. p. 1056).

ด่า   dah⁴ v. to swear at; to imprecate ill upon; to curse; to load with abuses: คนขี้ด่า one given to profanity; an insolent person: ด่ากัน to curse each other: ด่าแช่ง to revile another wishing him evil: ด่าทอ to swear fiercely; to scold another sharply; to answer another's swearing with curses; to vilify: ด่าทอว่าอะไร what is this you are cursing about? คำด่า injurious, slanderous words.

ดาก   dak⁴ n. protruding tissues forced out

from the anus; a prolapsing of the rectum: ดากครก a false bottom or removable plug for the bottom of a rice mortar: ดากตะบัน the removable plug for the bottom of a cylindrical mortar in which areca nut and betel leaf is macerated by old women: ดากออก, ดากไหล to be in a prolapsed or protruding condition (referring only to the anus) (BRAD.).

ด่าง   dang⁴ n. an alkaline salt; potash: adj. spotted, speckled or covered with white spots: เกลือด่าง a salt of potash: ด่างทับทิม potassium permanganate: ด่างพร้อย not clean; still stained; covered with spots: น้ำด่าง lye; a solution of caustic potash: เป็นด่างๆ, สีด่าง covered with spots; speckled; piebald; mottled.

ด้าง see ดิ้ง

ดาด   dat⁴ v. to spread out over; to spread down (as carpet); to stretch tensely (as cloth for a ceiling); to pave: adj. not steep; not precipitous; slightly inclined: ดินดาด plentiful: ดาดปูน to whitewash; to overlay with mortar (as for a floor or foundation): ดาดเพดาน to stretch cloth or paper up, as a ceiling: ดาดฟ้า the upper deck of a vessel: เรือมีดาดฟ้า a vessel having an upper deck.

ดาน   dan n. a removable wedge-shaped bolt for a door or window; a shoal of mud or sand, or projecting rocks in a river; a sand bank; a rapid: adj. lumpish; hard; immovable: ดักดาน permanent; stable; unchangeable; consistent: ดานเลือด, ดานเสมหะ, ดานลม a mass in the abdomen, due to an accumulation of blood, gas, phlegm, or mucus: ดานในท้อง a non-inflammatory lump, or mass in the abdomen: ดินดาน hard pan: เป็นดาน suffering from a hard, immovable, abdominal lump or mass: หัวดาน a point or extremity of a shoal (BRAD.).

ด่าน   dan⁴ n. a customs house; an out-lying office for inspection of contraband goods, or for collection of duty: ชาวด่าน customs officials: ด่านขนอน a look-out, or observation station for inspection officials: ด่านตรวจโรคหรือป้องกันผู้ มีโรค a quarantine station: ด่านภาษ a customs post: นายด่าน the chief officer of a customs house: เสียค่าด่าน to pay the duty levied by the customs officials.

ด่านราชสีห์ (ต้น)　　dan⁴-rat³-cha⁶-see² *n.* *Tephrosia repentina (Leguminosae),* an herb or shrub of central and southern Siam (cb. p. 385).

ด้าน　　dan³ *n.* direction; side; region; quarter (as north side, south side); exterior; front surface; the flat surface of a part, or of the whole edifice: *adj.* unfinished or undecorated (surface); hard; callous; obstinate; unex-ploded (as a cartridge, bomb or fire-cracker): ด้านกิน to eat in a headstrong manner, that which has been forbidden: ด้านขวา the right side or quarter: ด้านเข้ามา, เข้าไป persistently to enter; doggedly to enter even though requested not to do so: ด้านซ้าย the left side: ด้านตวันออก towards the east: ด้าน-หนึ่ง only one, or any one side: ด้านหลัง towards the back or rear: ดื้อด้าน stubborn; refractory; obstinate; obdurate: แบ่งคนละ-ด้าน to apportion to each his task or sphere of action: สี่ด้าน a quadrilateral figure; a square: หนังด้าน callousness of the skin: หน้าด้าน shameless; brazen-faced; impudent; immodest: หัวด้าน a block-head; a stubborn fellow (used with contempt): ห้าด้าน a pentagon.

ดาบ　　dap⁴ *n.* a sword; a sabre: แกว่งดาบ to brandish a sword: ถือดาบ to hold a sword: ฝักดาบ a scabbard: สายดาบ a sword belt; a shoulder belt.

ดาบเงิน (ปลา)　　dap⁴-ngern *n. Trichiurus savala (Trichiuridae),* a widely distributed marine fish usually not longer than 4 feet. This fish is usually sold fresh; otherwise it is dried. Salt is not necessary for drying. It is not highly esteemed (Dept. Agri. & Fisheries: Burk. p. 2176).

ดาบลาว (ปลา)　　dap⁴-lao *n. Chirocentrus dorab (Chirocentridae),* an extremely valuable sea-fish reaching a length of 12 feet or more. It inhabits the Indian ocean and seas of China and Japan. It is usually sold fresh (Burk. p. 526); *Macrocheirichthys macrochirus,* a carp (Dept. Agri. & Fisheries.).

ดาบส　　dah-bot⁴ *P. S. n.* an hermit; an anchorite; a recluse; a practiser of religious austerities; an ascetic (S. E. D. p. 442); one practicing self-mortification; one observing moral practices, virtue, piety, and devotion (Chd. p. 497): ดาบสินี a woman practising religious austerities.

ดาป　　dap⁴ *P. n.* heat; warmth (S. E. D. p. 442).

ดาม　　dam *v.* to splice; to strengthen by splicing; to mend; to unite; to solder to-gether; to repair a broken part by splicing: ดามกันเข้า to splice fragments or ends together: มีผือกดาม having splints applied.

ด้าม　　dam³ *n.* a handle.

ด้ามจิ้ว　　dam³-chjiw³ *n.* a folding fan from China.

ดามพ์, ดามร, ดัมพ์　　dam *P. S. n.* copper; copper ore; articles made of copper, or having a coppery-red colour (S. E. D. p. 443): ดามพ-การ a workman in copper: ดามพกรรภ์ copper sulphate; blue stone: ดามพทวีป *lit.* "copper island," *i. e.* Ceylon: ดามพธาตุ red chalk: ดามพเนตร having reddish eyes: ดามพมัย made of, or finished in copper; coppery: ดามพมฤค a species of copper-coloured deer; the red deer: ดามพวรรณ copper-coloured; dark-red: ดามพศิขี *lit.* "red-crested," *i. e.* a cock.

ดามาลาเมาะบาบี (ต้น)　　dah-mah-lah-mau⁶-bah-bee *Malay Pattani n. Dipterocarpus kerrii (Dipterocarpaceae),* a big tree found in Burma, Sumatra and the Malay Peninsula. The Siamese and Burmese extract oleo-resin from it. It is one of the most frequently tapped of the Malay trees (cb. p. 136 : BURK. p. 844).

ดาย dai *v.* to cut; to trim the surface free of grass; to cut grass close to the ground; to cut or make a clearing free from grass : *adj.* being free (from grass or rubbish); abandoned; vacant; alone : ดายสวน to rid a garden of grass or weeds by mowing or cutting : ดูดาย to appear indifferent; to be diffident : เที่ยว-ดาย to walk apart from others : เสียดาย to express regret, or remorse (as when something is lost or broken); alas! what a pity : อยู่-เดียวดาย *colloq.* to live singly, alone or in solitude, far from human society.

ด้าย dai³ *n.* cotton thread : ด้ายกลุ่ม a ball of thread : ด้ายเข็ด a skein of thread : ด้ายดิบ unbleached cotton thread : ด้ายมอ white thread dyed a light blue with indigo : ด้ายไหม silk thread : ผ้าด้าย cotton fabric.

ดาร dan *S. n.* a high, shrill, loud note in music; a high tone (S. E. D. p. 443) : ดารนาท a loud or shrill sound : ดารากร camphor gum.

ดารก, ดารา dah-rok⁶ *P.S.* a star; a constella-tion; the pupil of the eye; the eye (S. E. D. p. 444) : ดารากร, ดาราคณะ a multitude of stars; decorative trappings for a horse or elephant; stars as ornaments, or ornamented with stars : ดาราบดี *lit.* "the husband of Tara (นางดารา)," *i. e.* Siva; the monkey Bali (พาลี) : ดาราบถ *lit.* "star-path," *i. e.* the sky; the pathway of the heavenly bodies : ดาราพร the firmament; the sky and stars : ดารากษา *lit.* "star-dec-orated," *i. e.* night : ดารามณฑล *lit.* "star-circle," *i. e.* the zodiac; *lit.* "eye-circle," *i. e.* the pupil of the eye : ? ดารามฤค *lit.* "star-antelope," *i. e.* a lunar asterism called Mriga-siras (มฤคศิรษะ), being composed of three stars, the chief one of which is Orionis (HINDU Relig. year p. 18) : ดาราวรรษ *lit.* "star-rain," *i. e.* falling stars : ดาราวลี a cluster, collection, or multitude of stars : ดาราศาสตร์ astronomy.

ดารณี dah-ra⁶-nee *P. S. n. lit.* "a means of

transportation over water," *i. e.* a boat or vessel (S. E. D. p. 444).

ดาร์ลิ่ง dah-ling *Eng. n.* darling.

ดาล ๑ dan *P. S. n.* the palmyra tree or fan-palm; a dance; a cymbal; a trochee; the hilt of a sword; a gold-smith; a span measured by the thumb and middle finger (S. E. D. p. 444) : ดาลเกตุ *lit.* "palm-bannered," *i. e.* a name for Bishma (ภีษม์); Bala-Rama (พระพล-ราม) : ดาลครรภ palm juice; toddy; arrack : ดาลธวัช *lit.* "palm-bannered," *i. e.* Bala-Rama (พระพลราม) : ดาลธารก *lit.* "one keeping or observing rhythmic measures," *i. e.* a dancer : ดาลนวมี the 9th. day of the waxing moon of the 10th. month, according to lunar calcula-tions : ดาลผล the fruit of the sugar-palm or fan-palm : ดาลพฤนต์ a palm-leaf used as a fan; fans (in general) : ดาลลมัย being made of palm leaves : ดาลมาตร as big or as high as a palm tree : ดาลยนตร์ a lock; a lock and key; a pair of small pincers or forceps (a surgical instrument) : ดาลวัน a grove of palmyra palms : ดาลวาทย์ applause; the act of clapping the hands (as in approba-tion) : ดาลศัพท์ the sound caused by the falling of a palm-fruit.

ดาล ๒ dan *v.* to make or cause to be made, produced, effected, created or originat-ed; to become hardened, dense, or compact : ดาลเดือด to have anger develop, grow or in-crease; to arouse, excite, or provoke anger.

ดาลัด dah-lat⁶ *Jav. n.* glass; crystal.

ดาลุ dah-loo⁶ *P. S. n.* the palate (S. E. D. p. 445) : ดาลุช palatal (as some vowels and consonants, as อิ, อี, จ, ฉ.) : ดาลุชิวห์ *lit.* "one having the palate in place of a tongue," *i. e.* an alligator : ดาลุนาศ *lit.* "one having the palate destroyed by thorny food," *i. e.* the camel : ดาลุมูล *lit.* "the root of the palate," *i. e.* the uvula : ดาลุสถาน palatal letters.

ดาว dow *n.* a star : ดาวกระจาย (ต้น) *Coreopsis grandiflora (Compositae)*, a garden plant, native of North America, having yellow flowers with brown or crimson centres (MCM. pp. 134, 198): ดาวจักรราศี the zodiac: ดาวแกะตัวผู้ (ราศีเมษ) *Aries*, the Ram, a constellation; the first sign of the zodiac: ดาวโคตัวผู้ (ราศีพฤษภ) *Taurus*, the Bull, a constellation; the second sign of the zodiac: ดาวคนคู่ (ราศีมิถุน) *Gemini*, the Twins, Castor and Pollux, a constellation; the third sign of the zodiac: ดาวปู (ราศีกรกฎ) *Cancer*, the Crab, a constellation; the fourth sign of the zodiac: ดาวสิงห์โต (ราศีสิงห์) *Leo*, the Lion, a constellation; the fifth sign of the zodiac: ดาวนางสาว (ราศีกันย์) *Virgo*, the Virgin, a constellation; the sixth sign of the zodiac: ดาวคันชั่ง (ราศีตุล) *Libra*, the Balance, the Scales, a constellation; the seventh sign of the zodiac: ดาวแมลงป่อง (ราศีพฤศจิก) *Scorpio*, the Scorpion, a constellation; the eighth sign of the zodiac: ดาวธนู (ราศีธนู) *Sagittarius*, the Archer, a constellation; the ninth sign of the zodiac: ดาวแพะ (ราศีมังกร) *Capricornus*, the Goat, the Horn Goat, a constellation; the tenth sign of the zodiac: ดาวหม้อน้ำ (ราศีกุมภ์) *Aquarius*, the Water-Carrier, a constellation; the eleventh sign of the zodiac: ดาวปลา (ราศีมีน) *Pisces*, the Fish, a constellation; the twelfth sign of the zodiac: ดาวนพเคราะห์ a planet: พระพุธ Mercury: พระศุกร์ Venus: พระพิภพ Earth: พระอังคาร Mars: พระพฤหัสบดี Jupiter: พระเสาร์ Saturn: มฤตยู Uranus: เทพเจ้าแห่งสมุทร Neptune: ดาวประจำรุ่ง Venus, as a morning star: ดาวประจำเมือง Venus, as an evening star: ดาวบริวาร a satellite: ดาวเหนือ the North Star: ทางช้างเผือก, ฉายาบถ, สวรรค์มรรค the Milky Way: ดาวนักษัตร an asterism; certain small stellar groups marking the divisions of the lunar track (chd. p. 256); mansions of the moon. At first they were twenty-seven in number, but were increased to twenty-eight. Mythologically, they are said to be the daughters of Daksha (a son of Brahma) who were married to the Moon (H. C. D. .p. 214). They have

symbolic figures representing them, of which the following are a few :— อัศวินี a horse's head: ภรณี the pudendum mulibre: โรหิณี a carriage on wheels; a temple: อารทรา a gem: ปุนรวสุ a horse: ปุษย an arrow; a crescent: อศเลษา a potter's wheel: มาฆ a house: วิศาข a garland: อนุราธา a row of offerings: เชยษฐ a ring or earring: อุตตรภาทรปทา a two-faced figure or a couch: เรวตี a tabor: ธนิษฐา a drum (Antiq. of India): ดาวหมู่, ดาวกลุ่ม a constellation: ดาวหมีใหญ่ *Ursa Major*, the Great Bear; The Dipper, a large northern constellation containing seven conspicuous stars two of which point to the North Star: ดาวหมีเล็ก *Ursa Minor*, the Little Bear: ดาวม้าบิน *Pegasus*, The Winged Horse: ดาวสุนัขใหญ่ *Canis Major*: ดาวสุนัขเล็ก *Canis Minor*: ดาวพิณ *Lyra*: ดาวนายพราน *Orion*, a hunter of gigantic size and great beauty; a southern constellation: but visible in middle, northern latitudes: ดาวลูกไก่ the *Pleiades*, a group of stars in the constellation *Taurus*: ดาวเรือง (ต้น) *Calendula pluvialis*, cape marigold; *Tagetes patula* (*Compositæ*), french marigold, a native of Mexico (MCM. pp. 197, 199): ดาวเลื่อนที่, ดาวตก meteors; falling or shooting stars: ดาวหาง a comet.

ด่าว dow[4] *adj.* characterized by writhing, wriggling or contortions.

ด้าว dow[3] *n.* limit; boundary; area; district: คนต่างด้าว an alien; a foreigner: ด้าวท้าย the aft part of a ship or boat; the stern.

ดาวดึงส์ dow-wa[6]-durng *n.* the second tier of heaven above the earth, in which Indra dwells. Buddha is supposed to have ascended to this heaven, seven years after his attainment of Buddhahood, to preach to the angels, and particularly to his mother (Ala. p. 201).

ดาษ, ดาษดา dat[4] *adj.* abundant; plentiful; widely distributed: ดาษดื่น to be lavishly spread out in abundance: ผีดาษ smallpox,

ดาหงัน dah-ngan[2] *Jav. v.* to make war; to carry on hostilities.

ดาฬ dan *P. n.* a wedge-shaped bolt used to fasten doors or windows (as in Buddhist buildings); a strong pin or peg (for fastening purposes); a key; a lock; a bolt (chd. p. 445): ลูกดาฬ a key for moving a wedge-shaped bolt.

ดำ dum *v.* to dive; to plunge into the water; to transplant seedling rice in a flooded field that has been ploughed: *adj.* black: ใจดำ villainous; hard-hearted; ungrateful: ดำดึง capable of being extended, submerged, sunk, or excavated: ดำแดง brown; reddish-black; dark red: ดำนา to transplant young rice plants: ดำลึง delicious; voluptuous: ดำแห to dive after a net that has been caught by a snag.

ดำ dum[4] *v.* to sink down deeply; to extend down to a great depth; to be drawn downwards (as by the current).

ดำกล dum-gkon *v.* to set up; to raise; to build up; to establish.

ดำเกิง dum-gkerng *v.* to go up; to arise; to ascend; to spring up: *adj.* tall; high; magnificent; flourishing.

ดำแคง dum-kaang *v.* to spread from mouth to mouth (as fame); to disseminate; to circulate or be diffused.

ดำดง (ต้น) dum-dong *n. Diospyros ebenum* (*Ebenaceae*), ebony. There are many species of this genus but the *D. ebenum* of southern India and Ceylon is the best, for it is the only one giving black wood without any streaks, or markings. The heart-wood is very hard, closely and evenly grained; the sap-wood is grey, often streaked with black. The wood is used for turnery, cabinet work, keys of pianos, rulers, backs of brushes, stands for ornaments, etc. (MCM. p. 218: V. P. p. 112: BURK. p. 829).

ดำนาณ dum-nan *P. S. n.* protection; de-fence; shelter; a protection for the body; armour; a helmet (S. E. D. p. 457); a statement of the defendant in a lawsuit; a place of refuge from injury or harm; the knowledge of self-protection and self-preservation: *adj.* preserved; protected; guarded.

ดำนาน, ตำนาน dum-nan *n.* a history; records of important events; a narrative.

ดำนู see ดนู

ดำเนิน see เดิน

ดำเนียน, ติเตียน dum-nee-an *v.* to slander; to criticize.

ดำบล, ตำบล dum-bon *n.* a commune; a locality; a district; a group of villages.

ดำโพง dum-pong *n.* the skull of an elephant.

ดำรง dum-rong *v.* to stand; to endure; to last; to continue; to sustain; to uphold: *adj.* permanent; durable; straight.

ดำรวจ, ตรวจ dum-roo-at[4] *v.* to examine (as evidence); to reflect; to consider; to weigh in the mind.

ดำรัส, ตรัส dum-rat[4] *v.* to say; to speak, talk or command (used for royalty): *n.* words, sayings or speech of royalty.

ดำริ, ตริ dum-ri[4] *v.* to think; to consider; to resolve or plan: *n.* thought, purposes, plans (used for royalty).

ดำรี, ดำไร dum-ree *Cam. n.* an elephant.

ดำรู, ตรู dum-roo *adj.* beautiful; lovable; attractive.

ดำฤษณา, ตัณหา dum-rit[2]-sa[4]-nah[2] *P. S. n.* lust; desire; carnal appetite (chd. p. 495).

ดำเลิง, เถลิง dum-lerng *Cam. v.* to rise; to hold; to disseminate; to cause to circulate.

ดำแลง, แถลง dum-laang *adj.* alterable; explanatory; interpreting; defining; unfolding.

ดำหนิ, ติ dum-ni[4] *v.* to have a defect or fault; to criticize.

ดำอวด see จำอวด

ดิกๆ dik⁴-dik⁴ *n.* palpitations; pulsations: *adj.* shaky; fluttering; quivering; tremulous: ไหวดิกๆ consisting of vibrations.

ดิง, ดึง ding *v.* to cause vibrations which make a tone (as a piano wire); to strike or pick in order to make a sound (as on a banjo string).

ดิ่ง (ลูก) ding⁴ *n.* a plummet; a sounding line: *adj.* perpendicular; exactly upright.

ดิฏฐี dit⁴ *P. v.* to stand; to stand aside; to be excepted or omitted; to remain behind; to stay, stop or remain; to abide; to last; to endure, live or exist (chd. p. 509).

ดิตถ์, ดิษฐ dit⁴ *P. S. n.* a passage; a way; a road; a ford; stairs for descent to a river's edge; a place of pilgrimage on the banks of sacred streams; a body of water; a bathing place (S. E. D. p. 449): ดิตถกร one creating a passage (through life), *i. e.* Siva; the head of a sect: ดิตถการ any kind of work connected with or carried on at a landing place: ดิตถจรรยา a visit to any shrine; a pilgrimage to a place of peculiar sanctity: ดิตถบดี name of the chief or head of an ocean-worshipping sect: ดิตถวาก the hair of the head: ดิตถวิธี the rites observed at a shrine: ดิตถศิลา stone steps leading to a bathing place.

ดิถิ, ดฤถิ di⁴-tee² *P. S. n.* a lunar day (chd. p. 508): ดิถิกษัย the last day of the waning moon, according to lunar calculations: ดิถีเท่าไร what day of the month is this?

ดิน din *n.* earth; ground; soil of any kind: ดิน (งู) a term applied indiscriminately to many of the earth snakes among which is *Typhlops braminus* (*Typhlopidae*), (M. S. N. H. J. S. S. I, 1, p. 18): ดินดอน, ดินดล high land; elevated ground; a plateau: ดินดาน hard sub-soil; dry, hard clay along a river bed: ดินดำ, ดินปืน powder used for fire-works; gunpowder; explosive ammunition: ดินแดง red iron oxide (used for painting): ดินถนำ (ต้น) *Lycopodium fernallies* (*Lycopodiaceae*), an herb suited to low or medium elevations (MCM. p. 160); a golden coloured clay (used medicinally). It is reported to fall from heaven or to be of meteoric origin and is believed to endow all who partake of it with miraculous virtues: ดินนวล a finely prepared white clay used for making, or glazing pottery or roof tiles: ดินประสิว saltpetre; nitre (so called colloquially and commercially): ดินประสิวขาว nitre; nitrate of potassium; a white crystalline salt: ดินโป่ง earth impregnated with salt; clay around a salt-lick (to which animals resort): ดินเผา burnt earth (used to fertilize fields and plants): ดินสำลี, ดินระเบิด a highly explosive gunpowder: ดินลุ่ม low ground; swamps: ดินสอดำ a lead pencil: ดินสอแดง a red pencil: ดินสอพอง a soft, prepared chalk used as face powder: ดินหู an active priming ammunition for ancient flint-lock guns: แผ่นดิน the period of a sovereign's reign, *ex.* แผ่นดินพระบาทสมเด็จพระนั่งเกล้าฯ the reign of King Phra Nang Klao.

ดิ้น din³ *v.* to squirm or struggle (as a child when being vaccinated); to move or toss about restlessly; to throb: *n.* tinsel: ดิ้นแด่วๆ to wriggle (as a lizard when injured): ดิ้นรน to manifest speed or haste; to toss restlessly; to be discontented with one's lot.

ดิบ dip⁴ *adj.* raw; unripe; half-cooked: คนดิบ one not having spent any time in the Buddhist priesthood: ด้ายดิบ unbleached cotton thread: ผ้าดิบ unbleached cloth: ผีดิบ a corpse buried, or kept, but not yet cremated.

ดิบดี dip⁴-dee *adj.* in good condition or order; well-arranged, suitably fixed or furnished (as an apartment).

ดิรัจฉาน, เดียรัจฉาน di⁴-rat⁶-chan² *P. n.* domestic quadrupeds; quadrupeds (in general); an animal; a beast (chd. p. 508).

ดิลก, ติลก   di⁴-lok⁴ *P. S. n.* freckles (compared to sesame seeds); a mark on the forehead made with coloured earths, sandal-wood or unguents, either as an ornament or as a sign of sectarial distinction (S. E. D. p. 448): (ต้น) the sesame plant, *Sesamum indicum* (*Pedaliaceae*) (Burk. p. 1994):   ดิลกาศัย *lit.* "the place of, or suitable for, the sectarial distinctive mark," *i. e.* the forehead.

ดิ้ว   diw³ *n.* strips of rattan or bamboo bent in a circle, to which ribs of a cage are fastened; a lath (about ½ an inch wide) placed horizontally, to which bamboo strips are fastened with rattan, in making a wall or partition for a Siamese house.

ดิ้วเดี้ยว   diw³-dee-oh³ *v.* to be weak or overcome with hunger.

ดิษฐ see ดิตถ์

ดี   dee *n.* gall; bile: *adj.* good; pleasing; satisfactory; well: กะเพาะน้ำดี the gall-bladder: เข้าไปดีกัน to approach for purposes of reconciliation: ดีกว่า better than: ดีเกลือ epsom salts; magnesium sulphate: ดีขึ้น to improve a little; to continue getting better by degrees: ดึงเหลื่อม the boa's gall; ดีใจ to be happy, glad or gratified; to be joyful: ดีเดือด intermittent insanity; a mania or frenzy of short duration: ดีจริง, ดีที่สุด, ดีนักหนา best; excellent: ดีนาคราช (ต้น) a medicinal vine: ดีเนื้อดีใจ, ค๊อกดีใจ to be overjoyed; to be exceedingly happy or glad: ดีปลี (ต้น) *Piper sylvaticum*; *P. chaba* (v. P. p. 110: Burk. p. 1742); *P. longum* (Phra Montri), long pepper. The home of this species is India, at the foot of the Himalayas and in the hills of southern India. In the fourth century B. C. Theophrastus knew two kinds of pepper, one of which was undoubtedly *P. longum*. In the time of Pliny, long pepper was worth twice as much, in Rome, as black pepper. The oil distilled from it contains piperine and cadinine. It has an odour suggesting ginger and a taste milder than pepper oil. The roots and dried flower-spikes are used for coughs, dyspepsia, etc. (MCM. pp. 341, 379: Burk. p. 1744); *P. nigrum*, black pepper, white pepper (พริกไทย). The original home is not known but it early spread all over Burma, Siam, Malaysia, etc., where it was found by Marco Polo in 1280. The trade in pepper was a very considerable one, and was one of the causes of trade controversy during the period of Portuguese activity (Burk. p. 1746):   ดีผา a black, glistening, medicinal stone resembling coal (when pulverised it is used to combat fever):   ดีมาก, ดีนัก, ดีที่สุด very good; superior; excellent: ดียา, ดีหิน black lines found in marble and similar rocks: ดีร้าย perhaps; by chance: ดีหมี (ต้น) a term applied to various plants, as *Gonocaryum lobbianum* (*Icacinaceae*) (cb. p. 274); *G. subrostratum* (cb. p. 275); *Cleidion spiciflorum* (*Euphorbiaceae*) bear's gall, a poisonous plant found from India to New Guinea (v. P. p. 111: Burk. p. 579):   ผู้ดี a nobleman: one in the lineage of an illustrious family: พอดีพอร้าย passably; middling; tolerably; very closely; nearly; escaping by a hair's breadth: มิดี unbecoming; dishonoured; bad; unfortunate.

ดีคน, กะดัด, ราชดัด (ต้น)   dee-kon *n.* *Brucea amarissima* (*Simarubaceae*), a small shrub reaching 6 feet in height, found from India to northern Australia; in the Malay Peninsula it is common in open country, but is not able to spread into forests, and therefore is more or less dependent on man for its place. It has rather wide medicinal uses among the Malays. The whole plant is bitter. The seeds, known as "Macassar kernels," are much used in Java as a cure for dysentery; *B. sumatrana* (v. P. p. 110: cb. p. 241: Burk. p. 370: MCM. p. 377).

ดีควาย (ต้น)   dee-kwai *n.* Laos (*Lampang*) *Gonocaryum subrostratum* (*Icacinaceae*) (cb. p. 275).

ดึงู (ต้น)   dee-ngu *n. Picrasma javanica* (*Simarubaceae*), a tree occurring in many parts of Indo-Malaysia (cb. p. 240).

ดิฉัน   dee-chan[2] *pron.* a personal pronoun, I, me (used by women, or a superior person to an inferior).

ดีด   deet[4] *v.* to pry or raise with a lever; to use a jack-screw; to fillip (as while calculating on the abacus); to pick or play on a stringed instrument with a pointed piece of ivory or quill; to push or elbow one's way through a crowd; to kick (as crickets or insects): ดีดดื้น to be boastful; to be impudent, seeking or asking no favours: ดีดปอ to shred jute into fibres: ดีดผ้าย to gin cotton: ดีดสี to pick or bow (as on a violin): ดีดเสาเรือน to raise a sunken post by means of a jack-screw or lever: ดีดออกไป to steal away; to avoid: ผู้ดีดสีเป่า the personnel of an orchestra of stringed or wind instruments.

ดีดขัน   deet[4]-kan[2] *n.* a beetle that fillips itself making a slight sound (as cracking the knuckles). When it does so in a brass basin, the vessel makes a distinct noise.

ดีดัก   dee-dak[4] *adv.* indicating past time, *ex.* หลายปีดีดัก many years ago; a long time past.

ดีบุก   dee-book[4] *P. S. n.* tin; lead (chd. p. 508): เหมืองดีบุก a tin mine.

ดีหลี   dee-lee[2] *adv.* sure; certain; in truth; precisely right.

ดึก   deuk[4] *n.* late at night; the night, far advanced: *adj.* deep; extensive (as a forest or jungle): ดึกๆ very late: ดึกดื้น far into the night: ดึกดำบรรพ์ very old; antique; exeedingly ancient; antiquated: ดึกสองยาม midnight; the second watch.

ดึง   deung *v.* to pull; to stretch out; to pluck (as hair): ดึงขึง tightly stretched; to remain motionless: ดึงดัน, ดื้อดึง to be obstinate, stubborn or resisting: ดึงดือ, ดื้อดึง

to resist obstinately; to be headstrong or stubborn; to resist correction or restraint.

ดึงสะ   deung-sa[4] *P. S. adj.* the numeral thirty (chd. p. 506).

ดื้น   durn[4] *adj.* many; plenty; bountiful; numerous: ดื้นดาษ full; plentiful; abundant: ดื้นไป having plenty scattered about.

ดื่ม   durm[4] *v.* to drink; to swallow: ดูดดื่ม to suck and swallow; to absorb, or cause to permeate (as through the pores of the skin).

ดื้อ   dur[3] *adj.* stubborn; headstrong; contumacious; mulish; dogged; intractable; obdurate: ดื้อด้าน shamelessly stubborn or obstinate: ดื้อทื่อ dull; blunt (as a knife).

ดุ   doo[4] *v.* to display anger; to be irritable; to be cross or angry: *adj.* angry; severe; cross; fierce; ferocious; wild (as of animals): ดุดัน undisciplined; disobedient; unruly; irritable; implacable: ดุร้าย angry; fierce or severe in the extreme; savage; ferocious.

ดุก, ดุกด้าน (ปลา)   dook[4] *n.* the fresh-water catfish, *Clarias batrachus* (*Clariidae*) (Dept. Agri. & Fisheries): ดุกทะเล (ปลา) *Plotosus anguillaris* (*Plotosidae*), a marine catfish noted all over Malaya for causing a very painful wound with either dorsal or pectoral spines. The flesh is excellent food; *Plotosus canius* (*Plotosidae*) (Dept. Agri. & Fisheries: Burk. p. 1733): ดุกอุย (ปลา) *Clarias macrocephalus* (*Clariidae*), a fresh-water catfish (Dept. Agri. & Fisheries).

ดุกดิ๊ก   dook[4]-dik[4] *v.* to fidget; to move about restlessly.

ดุ้ง   doo-ng[3] *adj.* bent (outwards or upwards); convexed or bulging on the side; arched or curving upwards: กลางดุ้งขึ้น to bulge out or up in the middle: ดุ้งขึ้นข้างหนึ่ง one side raised in excess of the other: ดุ้งขึ้นดุ้งลง undulating; waving; bobbing up and down: ดุ้งเด้ง to oscillate up and down; to teeter or tilt at one end or side.

ดุ้งดิ้ง   doong[3]-ding[3] *adj.* boastful; bragging; impetuous; vaunting; seeking or asking no favours: ดุ้งดิ้งสูงสิง affected; feigning; professing sham; simulating; pretending.

ดุจ, ดวจ   doot[4] *adv.* like; just as; similar; as if: ดุจดัง, ดุจหนึ่ง such as; likewise; like unto; for example: ดุจดังอกจะทะลาย as though the heart or feelings were crushed: ดุจเหมือน as if; exactly like: ดุจอันเดียวกัน in like manner; analogous to.

ดุด   doot[4] *v.* to dig or root with the snout (used in reference to swine): ดุดดุน to push up or grub with the snout for food.

ดุน   doon *v.* to push, punch or poke (as with the elbow); to emboss; to decorate with figures (as in repoussé work or in bas-relief): มีลายดุน ลายนูน embellished with bas-relief figures or designs.

ดุ้น   doon[3] *n.* a numerical designatory particle for pieces or sticks of cut wood (as fire-wood): ดุ้นไฟ a burning piece of fire-wood; a firebrand: ทอนเป็นดุ้น to cut into short lengths or sections: พื้นดุ้นหนึ่ง a stick of fire-wood.

ดุบ ๆ   doop[4]-doop[4] *adj.* pulsating (an of an artery); a crawling sensation: ไต่ดุบ ๆ to crawl along in a trembling manner.

ดุม   doom *n.* a button: ดุมเกวียน, ดุมล้อ the hub of a wheel; the nave of an ox-cart; the axle-nut of a wheel; the nave box: รังดุม, เรือนดุม a buttonhole: ลูกดุมเสื้อ a coat button.

ดุ่ม ๆ   doom[4]-doom[4] *adv.* intently; fixedly; abstractedly (descriptive of walking and being oblivious to the surroundings): เดินดุ่ม ๆ to walk in a preoccupied manner.

ดุมซี่ (ปลา)   doom-see *n. Nandus nebulosus* (*Nandidae*) (Dept. Agri. & Fisheries).

ดุรค, ดุรค์   doo[4]-rok[6] *P. S. n. lit.* "the animal that travels rapidly," *i. e.* a horse; a courser (Chd. p. 513).

ดุรงค์, ดุรงคม   doo[4]-rong *S. n. lit.* "going quickly," *i. e.* a horse; one riding on horseback (S. E. D. p. 450): ดุรงค์, ดุรงคมี a mare (S. E. D. p. 451).

ดุรงคี   doo[4]-rong-kee *n.* a mare; a horseman; a groom; a troop of horses (S. E. D. p. 451): ดุรงคิณีเสนา a mounted woman serving as a soldier.

ดุริย, ดุริยางค์   doo[4]-ri[6]-ya[6] *S. n.* stringed or wind musical instruments; musical instruments (in general) (Chd. p. 513).

ดุล   doon *P. S. n.* a balance; a pair of scales; a beam or rafter; a unit of weight equal to twenty catties (Chd. p. 512); Libra, the Balance; the Scales, a constellation; the seventh sign of the zodiac.

ดุลย์   doon *P. S. n.* equality: *adj.* equal to; of the same kind, class, number, or value; similar; comparable; like (S. E. D. p. 451): ดุลยกุลย์ *lit.* "of the same family," *i. e.* a relative: ดุลยเดช equal in splendour: ดุลยบุลย์ having equal value; being equal in price: ดุลยพล equal in strength or power: ดุลยภาพ a combination of like sets; a uniformity in all respects: ดุลยาธิกรณะ words or phrases conveying similar meaning; the quality of being synonymous.

ดุลิยา   doo[4]-li[6]-yah *P. n.* a flying fox (Chd. p. 512).

ดุษฎี   doot[4]-sa[4]-dee *S. v.* to be satisfied; to be pleased; to be joyful (Chd. p. 513): *n.* happiness; joy; bliss.

ดุษณ   doot[4]-sa[4]-nee *n.* quietness; serenity; silence: *adv.* silently; quietly (S. E. D. p. 453): ดุษณีภาพ the condition of being silent; stillness.

ดุษิต, ดุสิต   doo[4]-sit[4] *S. n.* the joyful heaven, wherein Buddha and others pass their last existence before being born on earth (Ala. p. 308); name of the angels inhabiting the fourth devaloke (Chd. p. 513).

ดุส   doot[4] *P. n.* substance; wealth; riches (chd. p. 513).

ดุเหว่า, กาเหว่า (นก)   doo[4]-wow[4] *n.* the Malayan koel, *Eudynamis malayana,* a bird of the crow family which derives its Siamese name from its cry (Gaird. J. S. S. IX, 1, p. 7).

ดู   doo *v.* to look; to observe; to stare; to consider; to judge; to estimate (as to value), *ex.* ดูช้างให้ดูหาง ดูนางให้ดูแม่ : คิดดู to reflect; to think over; to contemplate; to meditate : ชิมดู to taste; to make a trial : ดูกร, ดูก่อน, ดูแน่, ดูแน่ะ, ดูรา ho !; verily; hi, there !; moreover; wherefore : ดูการ, ดูแล to oversee or look after; to care for; to provide for : ดูแคลน to offer an indignity; to insult; to treat with insolence or contempt (by words or actions) : ดูดาย to look at but take no heed; to be indifferent; to be disinterested : ดูดู๋ manifesting disapproval : ดูถูก *lit.* "to consider of little value," *i. e.* to offer insults or abuses; to treat with abuse : ดูเบา to treat as though of little value or importance; to belittle; to disparage : ดูหมิ่น, ดูถูก to insult; to despise; to disdain : ดูเหมือน as if; as though; as in the manner of; probably; perhaps : ดูอย่าง to emulate the example of : น่าดู attractive; good-looking; worth seeing : ลองดู to try; to test out; to try as by an experiment : หมอดู a fortune-teller; a soothsayer; a clairvoyant.

ดู่, ประดู่ (ต้น)   doo[4] *n. Pterocarpus macrocarpus (Leguminosae),* a large, beautiful timber tree (cb. p. 486 : V. P. p. 111).

ดูด   doot[4] *v.* to suck; to draw in; to attract (as a magnet); to cause to adhere; to allure; to absorb (as through a membrane).

ดู่เคือ (ต้น)   doo[4]-keu-ah *Laos n. Millettia racemosa (Leguminosae)* (cb. p. 394 : V. P. p. 111).

ดู่ด้อง, ดู่แดง (ต้น)   doo[4]-daung[3] *Laos (Prae and Nan) n. Dalbergia floribunda (Leguminosae)* (cb. p. 478).

ดู่ลาย (ต้น)   doo[4]-lai *Laos (Lampang) n. Dalbergia bariensis (Leguminosae)* (cb. p. 474).

ดูรค์ see ดุรค

เด, ดั้น   dey *adj.* plentiful; abundant; ample; [copious.

เด่ see โด่

เด็ก   dek[4] *n.* a child; an infant : เด็กชาย a boy; a son : เด็กซึ่งเกิดภายหลังบิดาตาย a posthumous child : เด็กซึ่งไม่มีรูปร่างสมประกอบ a monstrosity : เด็กซึ่งอยู่ในความปกครองของ ผู้อื่น a ward : เหมือนเด็ก ๆ childish.

เด็กชา   dek[4]-chah *n.* a messenger or errand boy in the Royal Pages' Department.

เดคากรัม   day-kah-gkram *n.* a decagram, equivalent to 0.353 ounce avoir dupois.

เดคาเมตร   day-kah-met[3] *n.* a decametre, equivalent to 393.7 inches.

เดคาลิตร   day-kah-lit[6] *n.* a decalitre, equivalent to 9.08 quarts, dry measure.

เดิ้ง   deng[2] *v.* to be arched, curved or convexed horizontally; to be distended or bulged out in the middle.

เด็จ   det[4] *Cam. v.* to be explicit; to be irrevocable; to be unalterable.

เดช, เดชะ   det[4] *P. S. n.* a flame; heat; fire; light; splendour; majesty; dignity; prestige; glory; fame; influence; power (chd. p. 501): ขอเดชะ the customary introductory formula used in petitions to His Majesty, the King : เดชะบุญรอดได้ to escape by good fortune; to be freed by the help of previously acquired merit.

เดชน   day-cha[6]-na[6] *P. S. n.* the shaft of an arrow; a grenade; a cannon ball; a bullet (S. E. D. p. 454).

เดโช   day-choh *P. S. n.* fire; light; the rays, glow or glare of a flame (S. E. D. p. 454): เดโชชัย a conquest or victory by might and power : เดโชพล the power of might or authority.

เดชิกรัม   day-si⁶-gkram *n.* a decigram; a weight of one tenth of a gram, equal to approximately 1,543 grains Troy.

เดชิเมตร   day-si⁶-met⁶ *n.* a decimetre, a measure equal to 1/10 of a metre, or 3.937 inches.

เดชิลิตร   day-si⁶-lit⁶ *n.* a decilitre, a measure of capacity equal to 1/10 of a litre, or 0.845 of a gill, or 6.1022 cubic inches.

เด็ด   det⁴ *v.* to pick; to pluck, or pinch off with the finger-nails: *adj.* brave; bold; fearless; daring; heroic: เด็ดขาด irrevocably; surely; indisputably; infallibly: เด็ด-เดี่ยว being cut off sharply; being removed by a keen edge.

เดน   den *n.* fragments; remnants (as of cloth); left-overs; leavings.

เด่น   den⁴ *adj.* prominent; conspicuous; apparent; manifest.

เดนมารก   den-mark⁴ *Eng. n.* Denmark.

เดอง   derng *n.* a town; a city.

เดา   dow *v.* to guess; to conjecture; to express an opinion without accurate knowledge: เดาสวด to repeat Buddhist chants without exactness: ทำเดา ๆ to perform a job in a careless, uncertain, or ignorant manner.

เด่า, เด่า ๆ   dow⁴ *adj.* writhing; wriggling; squirming; wrenching; struggling (descriptive of contortive movements of the limbs, as when a child is being whipped, or a person is enduring pain).

เดาะ   dau⁴ *v.* to bat with the hand; to toss or throw a ball or article up and strike it with the palm of the hand (as in playing games): *adj.* cracked; splintered; partly broken: กระดูกเดาะ *surgical* a greenstick fracture in which one side of the bone is broken, the other being bent; an infraction.

เดิน, เดิร, ดำเนิน   dern *v.* to walk; to travel; to go or move by mechanical means: การเดิน-เรือ navigation: คนเดินทาง a traveller: เดิน-ความ to proceed with or carry on (as a case in court): เดินโต๊ะ to serve at the table (for meals): เดินทาง to travel; to tour through; to journey over: เดินธุระ to transact business for another: เดินไป to go on foot: เดินเรือ to travel by boat: เดินสาน, โดยสาน to take passage on a conveyance belonging to another person: เดินหน, เดินบก to travel by land: เดินหน้า to precede another: เดิน-หลัง to follow; to go behind: เดินหนังสือ to deliver a letter or document: อุจจาระเดิน to suffer from diarrhoea.

เดิม   derm *n.* beginning; origin; the first cause; commencement; foremost: แต่เดิม, เดิมที from the first: บิดามารดาเดิม our first parents (Adam and Eve).

เดีย   dee-ah³ *adj.* low; short; small; stunted.

เดียง ๑   dee-ang *Cam. v.* to know; to perceive; to apprehend clearly: เดียงษา to be of age; to have complete mental cognition (contracted from เดียงภาษา): ไร้เดียงษา, อะเดียงษา lacking knowledge or age; childish; irresponsible; infantile.

เดียง ๒   dee-ang *v.* to pound down; to strike or beat down.

เดียด   dee-at⁴ *v.* to abhor; to detest or dislike; to oppress: เดียดฉันท์ to be dissatisfied with on account of dislike, doubt, jealousy, enmity, or suspicion.

เดียร   dee-an *P. S. n.* a shore; a bank; a coast; land adjacent to a body of water (S. E. D. p. 449).

เดียรดาษ   dee-ah-ra⁶-dat⁴ *adj.* spread out in great abundance; strewn promiscuously and profusely around (as leaves under a tree).

เดียรถ์   dee-an *P. S. n.* stairs of a landing place for descent into a river, or at a bathing place (S. E. D. p. 449).

เดียรถีย์   dee-ah-ra⁶-tee² *P. S. n.* non-Buddhistic sects of ascetics (S. E. D. p. 449).

เดียรัจฉาน see **ดิรัจฉาน**

เดียว   dee-oh *adj.* one; single; only; alone: มีใจอันหนึ่งอันเดียวกัน to be united in mind and purpose: อย่างเดียวกัน of the same kind; identical.

เดียว   dee-oh[4] *n.* the elevation of a house or of a storey (measured from the floor to the ceiling): เดียวชั้นกลาง the altitude of the middle floor: เดียวชั้นล่าง the height of the ground floor: เดียวหลังคา the height measured from the joist to the ridge pole.

เดียว   dee-oh[2] *adj.* momentary: เดียวนี้ now; at once; immediately; ephemeral: ในประเดียวใจ instantly; summarily: ประเดียว in a moment; directly; shortly: ประเดียวก่อน wait another moment; after a while; presently.

เดียะ   dee-ah[4] *adj.* dextrous; expert; quick; prompt; nimble.

เดือ, มะเดื่อ (ต้น)   deu-ah[4] *n.* the wild fig, *Ficus roxburghii* (*Urticaceae*), a small tree of the eastern Himalayas and Burma, which produces large figs at the base of the trunk. They can be made into very good jam (V. P. p. 114: Burk. p. 1014): เดื่อเกี้ยง (ต้น) *F. glomerata*, a medium-sized tree, much used as shade for coffee in South India; it is also popular as an avenue tree. It can be propagated by cuttings (V. P. p. 114), (MCM. pp. 215, 417): เดื่อป้อง, มะเดื่อปล้อง (ต้น) *F. hispida* (V. P. p. 115: Burk. p. 1010), a coarse tree, of rather small size, found throughout southeastern Asia, Malaysia, and to Australia; in the Malay Peninsula it is common in lowland woods, and on stream sides, chiefly in the northern parts. It is used medicinally by Malays and Javanese. The fruits are edible. The leaves are a cattle-food in India, where the bark is used to make a rough twine. This tree is used as permanent shade for coffee in South India (MCM. p. 353).

เดือด   deu-at[4] *v.* to boil by heat; to be irritated; to be provoked: เดือดดาล to be annoyed, piqued or vexed in the extreme; to be exasperated: เดือดร้อน troubled; agitated; worried; full of affliction or anxiety.

เดือน   deu-an *n.* a month; a moon: เดือนขึ้น the crescent moon: เดือนดับ the last period of the moon: เดือนเต็ม the full moon: เดือนเพ็ญ the day of full moon: เดือนเย็น the winter months: เดือนร้อน the summer months: เดือนแรม the waning period of the moon: เดือนหงาย moon-light; the period when the moon is shining: ไส้เดือน a long burrowing earth-worm (commonly used as fishing bait); an intestinal parasite.

เดือย   deu-ay *n.* a tenon; a projection on the end of a timber for inserting in a socket or mortised cavity; the spurs of a cock: เข้าเดือย to join by a mortise and tenon: เดือย (ต้น) *Coix lachryma-jobi* (*Gramineae*), Job's tears, a robust grass with broad leaves, 4 to 6 feet high, found wild in Africa and Asia, introduced into America, and probably also into Africa. In south-eastern Asia there are cultivated races as well as wild. These cultivated races have been selected for easy husking, the seed being protected by a thin shell, whereas in the wild races the shell is hard. In the cultivated races the fruit is usually brown; in the wild they are grey, bluish-grey, brown or black. It has long been known as a cereal of some importance and, in countries suited to hill-rice, it often forms a staple when the rice crop fails. When polished, the seeds are used for rosaries, bead-work, etc., and are sometimes made into bead curtains (V. P. p. 116: Burk. p. 629: MCM. pp. 171, 308, 310, 448, 461): เดือยไก่ (ต้น) bird pepper, *Capsicum frutescens* (*Solanaceae*), a somewhat woody plant about three or four feet high which, escaping from cultivation, is established wild up and down the East. Cayenne pepper should be a powder of the fruits of bird pepper, but it is easily adulterated (BURK. p. 447):

เดือยประตู the staple for a door : รูเดือย a mortised cavity.

แด   daa *Cam. n.* mind ; heart : แดดาล to originate ; to be created, formed, or produced from the mind ; to reach, affect or influence the mind : แดดิ้น to have a condition of mental uneasiness or unrest : แดขั้น to have a condition of bewilderment or embarrassment.

แด่   daa[4] *prep.* to, or for (a sign of the dative) ; it is used in place of " to," in addressing the King, or any high personage.

แดก (พูด)   daak[4] *v.* to use repulsive, insolent language purposely ; to make invidious comparisons :   แดก (กิน) to eat ravenously ; to devour voraciously, or rapaciously :   แดก (ปลา) pickled salted fish :   แดกขึ้น to suffer from a colicky, epigastric pain :   แดกดัน, แดกให้ to use irritating, repulsive or insulting language :   แดกท่า to devour or gorge greedily ; to eat as though possessed with an insatiable demon.

แด็ก ๆ   daak[4]-daak[4] *n.* contortive ; writhing ; moving from side to side ; wriggling (descriptive of an injured lizard, insect, or bird).

แดกงา   daak[4]-ngah *n.* a sweetmeat made of flour mixed with sesame seeds.

แด็กแด้, ดักแด้   daak[4]-daa[3] *v.* to be miserably oppressed by extreme want ; to be desperately poor :   *n.* the pupa of a moth or butterfly.

แดง   daang *n.* red ; one of the primary colours :   แดง (ต้น) *Xylia xylocarpa (Leguminosae)* (cb. p. 547) ; *X. kerrii*, a timber tree found in Burma and Siam. The timber is very valuable, and is exported from both countries. The wood is dark reddish-brown, very hard, difficult to saw, and somewhat liable to crack in seasoning. It is used for sleepers, for which it is admirable ; also for house-posts, bridges, buffers, ship-building,

road pavements, etc. (BURK. p. 2274 : cb. p. 546) ; *Eugenia cymosa* (*Myrtaceae*), a small, or medium-sized tree found from north-eastern India southwards and throughout western Malaysia ; in the Malay Peninsula it occurs all down the west side. There is doubt regarding the value of the timber : it has been mentioned as useful for houses, and also for rafters and fuel. The bark was formerly used as a dye in Sumatra (BURK. p. 967 : cb. p. 637) ; *E. oleina*, a tree found in Peninsular Siam (cb. p. 653) ; *E. spissa*, a tree of Burma and Peninsular Siam (cb. p. 663) :   แดงก่ำ, แดง ๆ blood red ; bright red :   แดงเข่า (ต้น) *E. circumscissa*, a tree of south-eastern Siam and Cochin China (cb. p. 635) ; *E. rhamphiphylla*, a tree of Southern Burma and Peninsular Siam (cb. p. 659) :   แดงแขแหย (ต้น) (*Eastern Laos*) *Schoutenia hypoleuca* (*Tiliaceae*) (cb. p. 193) :   แดงครู (นก) the chestnut-bellied munia, *Munia atricapilla rubronigra* (Herb. N. H. J. S. S. VI, 1, p. 121) :   แดงจ๋า crimson ; carmine : แดงจีน (ต้น) *Dalbergia cochinchinensis* (*Leguminosae*) (cb. p. 475) :   แดงดำ brown ; dark red : แดงนา (ต้น) *Eugenia polyantha* (cb. p. 656 : BURK. p. 973), a tall tree found in Burma and southwards throughout western Malaysia ; in the Peninsula it is found from the Siamese border to Singapore. The wood is fairly hard, but splits on drying. It is used for house-building and is durable. The bark is considerably used in the Dutch Indies for tanning fishing-nets, and for colouring mats. The bark, roots and leaves have medicinal properties. In the Dutch Indies the young leaves are commonly used with food. The fruit may be eaten :   แดงเล็กแดงใหญ่ a species of the jack-fruit ; a species of the ลำไย, *Nephelium longana* :   แดงสองเปลือก (ต้น) *Eugenia longiflora* (cb. p. 651 : BURK. p. 970), a tree of fairly large size found in the Malay Peninsula from Kedah southwards, becoming common towards Singapore and in the moister parts of Java. The timber is white to yellowish white, strong and durable, but with a tendency to split. The bark can be used for tanning fishing-nets: แดงแสม (ต้น) *Schoutenia hypoleuca* (*Tiliaceae*) (cb. p. 193).

แดง (ปลา)   dang *n. Cryptopterus bleekeri*, a fresh-water catfish which is especially good smoked (suvatti p. 70); *Lutjanus annularis* (*Lutianidae*) a red snapper (Dept. Agri. & Fisheries: suvatti p. 127).

แดด   daat[4] *n.* the sun; the sunlight; the sun's rays.

แดน   daan *n.* boundary; border; frontier; limit; confines: แดนต่อแดน contiguous; adjoining (boundaries): แดนไตร the three boundaries; the boundary of the three worlds of future existence, *i. e.* กามภพ, รูปภพ, อรูปภพ: แดนทุ่ง the limit, confines or verge of an open field or clearing: แดนผลุ a road-side; the edges, borders, or margins of a road, path or highway: พรมแดน the frontier.

แด่น   daan[4] *adj.* white or brown markings on the face or nose of animals.

แดะ   daa[4] *adj.* moving from side to side; oscillating.

โด่   doh[4] *adj.* extending vertically to a great height: โด่เร๊ movable stanchions about a metre long for supporting the ends of sliding sunshades either in front of, or behind the living quarters of Siamese boats.

โดกเดก   dok[4]-dek[4] *adj.* tottering; swaying from side to side.

โด่ง   dong[4] *adj.* proceeding or ascending higher; elevated; lofty: โด่งดัง illustrious; renowned; distinguished; eminent.

โด้ง, มะปราง, มะปริง (ต้น)   dong[3] *n. Bouea burmanica* (*Anacardiaceae*), a Burmese tree found in Siam. Its fruits are edible and the timber is good. It sometimes yields a gum (cb. p. 346: Burk. p. 355).

โดด   dote[4] *v.* to jump; to leap; to spring; to bound: *adj.* single; solitary; separate; alone: ลูกโดด a rifle ball.

โดน   don *v.* to collide; to hit, strike, knock, or bump against: โดน, กะโดน, กระโดน (ต้น) *Careya arborea* (*Myrtaceae*), patana oak, a small or medium-sized tree of Ceylon, India, etc. The astringent bark is used for tanning as well as in medicine. The round green fruits, borne in great profusion, are in season in May to June. The heart-wood is dull red, or claret-coloured, even-grained, beautiful, moderately hard, and very durable. It is described as useful for building, furniture, mouldings, turnery, and, as lasting well under water, when used as piles. The fibrous bark is made into cord in India and Indo-China. The tussar silk-worm is fed on the leaves in India. The seeds are poisonous; the bark tans (Burk. p. 458: McM. p, 443: Cb. p. 674): โดน-ทะเล (ต้น) *Barringtonia asiatica* (*Myrtaceae*), a tree of moderate size found from India to Malaysia, along sandy shores; in the Peninsula it is scarcely common, apparently because suitable sandy shores are not common. The fruits are used in many places to intoxicate fish, for which purpose they are pulped and thrown into the rivers, etc. Though poisonous, the pods are eaten in Indo-China, after cooking, which destroys the saponin. The timber is of little value (cb. p. 668: Burk p. 304): โดน-ทุ่ง (ต้น) *Erythroxylum cambodianum* (*Erythroxylaceae*), a tree found widely distributed in Siam and French Indo-China (cb. p. 199).

โดม ๑   dom *Eng. n.* a dome; a cupola.

โดม ๒   dom *Cam. n.* the line, direction or course of a stream or waterway.

โดม ๓, สูง   dom *adj.* high; elevated; raised; lofty.

โดมไพร   dom-prai *Cam. n.* the outline, fringe or border of a forest or jungle.

โดมร   doh-maun *P. S. n.* a lance; a javelin (S. E. D. p. 455): โดมรธร a lance-bearer; fire.

โดย ๑   doh-ie *P. S. n.* water (S. E. D. p. 456):

โดยกฌ drops of water; spray; mist: โดย-กรรม *lit.* "the water ceremony," *i. e.* ablution of the body; the bathing ceremony for the dead: โดยจร moving in water, (as aquatic animals); an aquatic animal: โดยธร *lit.* "containing water," *i. e.* a rain cloud: โดย-ธาร current; continuous onward movement of water in a stream: โดยธิ, โดยนิธิ, โดยาลัย *lit.* "water-receptacle," *i. e.* the ocean: โดย-บาต *lit.* "the falling of water," *i. e.* rain: โดยมล sea foam: โดยมุจ *lit.* "water-yielder," *i. e.* a cloud: โดยยนตร์ *lit.* "a water-clock," *i. e.* an hydrometer: โดยราช *lit.* "water-king," *i. e.* the ocean: โดยราศี *lit.* "a heap of water," *i. e.* a pond; a lake: โดยาธาร, โดยาศัย *lit.* "a water reservoir," *i. e.* a lake; a river.

โดย ๒   doh-ie *v.* to follow; to pursue; to attend: *adv.* in accordance with; according to; accordingly; in conformity to; by reason of; on account of; because, *ex.* โดยเขาบอก because he was told: *prep.* by; through; with; by means of, *ex.* รอดโดยเพื่อนช่วย saved by the help of friends: *prefix* when used as a prefix to an adjective it forms an adverb, *ex.* โดยจริง truly; surely: โดยเจ้าพนักงานยังไม่ได้อนุญาต unlicensed; not permitted by law: โดยชอบด้วยกฎหมาย lawfully; legally: โดยด่วน urgently; hastily; precipitately: โดยดี friendly; amicably: โดยได้มีก่อนแล้ว priority: โดยทุจจริต in bad faith: โดยน้ำใสใจจริง in true faith; sincerely: โดยปริยาย evidently; tacitly; implicitly: โดยผิดหลง by mistake: โดยไม่ทันรู้ไม่ทันเห็น inadvertently: โดยไม่รู้เท่าถึงการ having inadequate knowledge: โดยไม่สงสัย beyond any doubt: โดยเร็ว quickly: โดยละเอียด in detail: โดยวาจา verbally; by word of mouth: โดยสมควร suitably; fitly: โดยสุจริต in good faith; bona-fide.

โดร   doh-ra[6] *v.* to bloom; to blossom.

โดรณ   doh-ron *P. S. n.* an arch; an arched doorway; decorations or festoons over doorways (as of boughs of trees or garlands) (S. E. D. p. 456).

ใด   dai *pron.* who; whoever; whichsoever; whatever: *adj.* any; a; an: *adv.* what: ใด ๆ whosoever; anyone: ผู้ใด someone; anyone; who? มาด้วยประการใด what is your purpose in coming? Why do you come? สิ่งใด anything; something; what thing? อันใด which?

ได   dai *Cam. n.* a hand.

ได้   dai[3] *v.* (1) can; may; might; to be able to; to have the right to; to be permitted to, *ex.* ออกไปก็ได้; (2) to get; to gain; to obtain; to acquire; to procure; to receive; to possess, *ex.* ได้แก่, ได้มรดก, ได้กำไร; (3) to have an issue, *ex.* ได้ลูกผู้ชาย; (4) an auxiliary verb and sign of the past tense, *ex.* ได้ไป: ได้กัน to be well-matched (as a pair of horses); to agree or settle (as in matrimony); to become man and wife: ได้การ usable; satisfactory; suitable; used as an expression indicating approval, satisfaction, praise or approbation: ได้แก่ as for instance; by way of illustration: ได้ความ to have ascertained the facts regarding: ได้ใจ to have become haughty, conceited, elated, or boastful: ได้ที่ to have reached a suitable or appropriate place; to have attained or procured one's objective: ตามแต่จะได้ according to one's ability; as one may: ถามให้ได้ความ to enquire until in possession of the facts: ก็ได้ permission is given; yes.

ต

ต   The twenty-first consonant of the Thai alphabet, a middle class letter of which there are nine, *viz.* ก, จ, ฎ, ฏ, ด, ต, บ, ป, อ. ตอเต่า or ตอตรา are the names of this letter. It is pronounced as a combination of the English "d" and "t". Because this letter has no English equivalent, it is romanized in this dictionary by using "dt".

ตก   dtok[4] *v.* to be deficient; to be insufficient; to fall; to drop: *adj.* complete; ended; finished: ช้างตกมัน to be in rut. a state both physical and mental, in which all tuskers become highly dangerous: ตกกระ to have freckles, or any small or large discolouration of the skin: ตกกล้า to transplant seedling rice: ตกข้าว to make a money deposit on an expected delivery of rice; to make advance payments on paddy: ตกเงิน to make an advance deposit of money on goods expected to be delivered: ตกใจ to become frightened; to be excited or scared; to be startled: ตกตะลึง to be dazed from fear; to be embarrassed by apprehension: ตกแต่ง to decorate; to adorn; to embellish: ตกไถง the west: ตกท้องช้าง the sagging of a kite-string caused by overweight: ตกนรก to be re-born in hell; to go to perdition: ตกเนื้อตกใจ *idiomatic* to be frightened: ตกเบ็ด, ตกปลา to fish with a baited hook and line: ตกประหม่า to be fearful or timid; to dread; to feel a painful apprehension: ตกปลอก to cover with a band (as the tip of a walking stick); to tether the legs with a halter or loop (as for elephants): ตกพระโลหิต to have an abnormal issue of blood; to have an abortion or miscarriage (used for royalty): ตกฟาก *lit.* "to roll on to the carpet," *i. e.* to be born: ตกมูก to pass bloody mucus: ตกยาก to be very poor; to be indigent or impoverished in the extreme: ตกลงกัน to reach an agreement, or to come to amicable terms; to concur: ตกลงไป to fall into: ตกลงเรื่องหนี้ to come to an agreement regarding the debt: ตกลูก to bring forth the young (used only for animals): ตกเลือด, ตกโลหิต to have a miscarriage; to have an abnormal issue of blood: ตกฤดูหนาว to approach the cold season: ตกว่า as; for instance; like; similar to; for example; finally; lastly: ตกแสก to wear the hair parted

in the middle: ตกหนัก to suffer or endure ill-fortune, accident or calamity for another; to bear a misfortune for another (as in case of a guarantor): ตกอับ to reach the extreme of bad luck: ตกอยู่ในความบังคับค่าภาระติดพัน *legal* to continue to be subject to charges: ตกอยู่ในระหว่างความ *legal* to continue to be involved during the process of litigation: ถนนตก the end of a road: สอบไล่ตก to fail in an examination: สีตก to become faded.

ตง   dtong *n.* a joist; one of several parallel timbers stretched on edge, from wall to wall, for the support of ceiling laths or floor boards: ไม้ไผ่ตง (ต้น) *Dendrocalamus giganteus (Gramineae)*, a giant bamboo of Burma, Siam, and southwards. In the Botanic Gardens at Peradiniya, Ceylon, this bamboo grows in clumps with 300 to 400 haulms, and exceeds 100 feet in height. The diameter of a haulm reaches ten inches. They make the most capacious water buckets which some jungle tribes know, and so are greatly valued (MCM. p. 172: Burk. p. 781).

ตัง   dtong[2] *Chin. v.* to make fast the rope which has been hauled in: ค่าตัง the fee that the banker or croupier collects from a winner in a gambling game.

ตงกั๊ก   dtong-gkok[6] *Chin. n.* the country of China.

ตงฉิน   dtong-chin[2] *Chin. adj.* loyal; faithful; trusty; sincere.

ตงิดๆ   dta[4]-ngit[4]-dta[4]-ngit[4] *adj.* slight; gentle; weak; not decidedly marked (used regarding odours), *ex.* หอมตงิด ๆ.

ตงุ่น   dta[4]-ngoon[4] *adj.* having a gummy or sticky consistency (as sugar boiled down).

ตจะ   dta[4]-chja[4] *P. n.* the skin (of men or serpents); the hide (of cattle); bark; rind; peel; the surface (of the earth) (S. E. D. p. 463): ตจชล *lit.* "skin-water," *i. e.* perspiration; sweat: ตจโทษ diseases of the skin; leprosy:

ตจพึล having a convexity on the back side; a spoon; a ladle: ตจปัญจกกัมมัฏฐาน the use of the skin of the body as the subject of one's analytical meditation, being the fifth of the group of five elements of the corporal being. The others are the hair of the body and head, the teeth, and the nails: ตจสาร a bamboo haulm (S. E. D. p. 463).

ตด   dtot⁴ *v.* crepitus; the discharge of flatus from the bowels; a fart (indecent).

ตติย   dta⁴-dti⁴-ya⁶ *P. S. adj.* third: *adv.* thirdly (S. E. D. p. 453): ตติยทิวัส *lit.* "the third day," *i. e.* the day after tomorrow: ตติยปกติ *lit.* "the third nature," *i. e.* an eunuch; the neuter gender; the third sex: ตติยวาร for the third time.

ตถาคต   dta⁴-tah²-kot⁶ *P. S. n.* a sentient being; a name for the Buddha.

ตน   dton *n.* self; body; a person; a man: แก่ตน to oneself: ตนเอง oneself: แห่งตน of oneself.

ต้น   dton³ *n.* the trunk (of a tree); a base or supporting part; a chief, a leader or head; a numerical designatory particle for trees, plants, posts, etc.: *adj.* first; chief; foremost; cardinal; fundamental; principal: คนต้น-บาญชี a chief accountant: คนต้นเรือน the head of a family: คนต้นเสียง a precentor: ต้นขั้ว a counterfoil: ต้นคอ the nape of the neck: ต้นเงิน capital; the principal in business: ต้นดีปลายร้าย *colloq.* a project or career which started auspiciously but whose end is disaster: ต้นทุน assets: ต้นไม้ trees (in general): ต้นหน the steersman; the captain of a ship (used for a native): ต้นเหตุ the original or primary cause: แต่ต้น-จนปลาย from the beginning to the end: เป็นต้นไป, เป็นต้นว่า that is to say; for example.

ตนัย see ดนัย

ตนุ ๑ see ดนุ, ดนู ตนุมัธยา, ตนุมัธยมา poetry composed of four lines, each containing six feet.

ตนุ ๒   dta⁴-noo⁴ *n.* a sea-turtle.

ตบ   dtop⁴ *v.* to slap; to bat; to hit with the hand; to hit with the paw: ตบ (ผัก) *Monochoria hastata (Pontederiaceae)*, or *M. hastaefolia*, a marsh herb, found in tropical Asia and Malaysia; in the Peninsula its chief habitat being ditches, it is most abundant in the well-inhabited parts. The flowers are a brilliant purple. The leaves are not a little eaten as a vegetable, and the inflorescence with them. They are used both raw and steamed. In Celebes the rhizomes are cooked for cattle-food, and pounded with charcoal, they are used for scurf (BURK. p. 1489: V. P. p. 179: MCM. pp. 174, 312): ตบ-ชวา (ผัก) *Eichhornia speciosa (Pontederiaceae)*, water-hyacinth, a floating plant forming dense masses and rapidly covering still, warm water, in climates which suit it. Its blue flowers are of great beauty, and for their sake the plant, a native of Brazil, has been cultivated in Europe for a century and a half and latterly has been introduced to the eastern tropics where it has now become a costly pest, owing to its vigour and rapid spread in sluggish streams. It was introduced first into Java in 1894. The leaves and bladder-like leaf-stalks are rich in potash and are used for manure; they are employed in Malaya for feeding pigs, and in the West Indies as feed for donkeys. Spraying with white arsenic (arsenious oxide) and soda (sodium carbonate) is used in Florida for controlling the pest. Its cultivation in Ceylon, where it was introduced in 1905 as an ornamental plant by Lady Blake, wife of the Governor at that time, is now prohibited by law (BURK. p. 891: MCM. pp. 174, 476, 477: V. P. p. 179): ตบตา *colloq.* to cheat or deceive; to trick; to impose on with some counterfeit article: ตบมือ to clap the hands; to applaud: ตบหัวลูบหลัง *colloq.* to insult; to treat severely or cruelly and then make flattering overtures.

ตบะ   dta⁴-ba⁴ *P. n.* heat; warmth; pain;

suffering; bodily mortification; penance; religious austerity; devout meditation (S. E. D. [p. 437).

ตปน see **ตบัน**

ตปนียะ dta⁴-bpa⁴-nee-ya⁶ *P. S. n.* gold purified with fire (S. E. D. p. 437).

ตม ๑, ตโม dta⁴-ma⁶ *S. n.* darkness; gloom; the darkness of hell; mental darkness; ignorance; stupidity; illusion; error (S. E. D. p. 438): ตโมนุท *lit.* "the one who dispels darkness," *i. e.* the sun; the moon: ตโมไพรี *lit.* "the enemy of darkness," *i. e.* fire: ตโมหร *lit.* one who removes darkness," *i. e.* the moon.

ตม ๒ dtom *n.* mud; mire.

ต้ม dtom³ *v.* to. boil; to cook in water; to be the victim of a confidence trick; to be filched; to be duped: ขนมต้ม a sweetmeat made by enclosing sugar in a dough batter rolled into a ball: ต้มกลั่น to distil: ต้มกะทิ a curry made of sliced salted meat or fish, boiled in coconut milk, with tamarind and onions added: ต้มกะปิ a curry made with onions, pepper and essence of prawns, or shrimp paste: ต้มข่า a food made by boiling the flesh of ducks or fowls with sliced tender shoots of *Languas siamensis* (*Alpinia*) and coconut milk. This is served with pepper sauce: ต้มเค็ม meat or fish that is boiled with salt and slightly sweetened with sugar: ต้มโคล้ง, ต้มปลาร้า, ต้มเปรต, ต้มยำ, ต้มยำกะทิ, ต้มส้ม names of different kinds of curries: ถูกต้ม to be the victim of a trick.

ตมน, ตมัน see **ดมัน**

ตโม see **ตม**

ตยาค, ตยาคี see **จาค, จาคี**

ตยุติ see **จุติ**

ตรง dtrong *adj.* true; faithful; straight; explicit: *adv.* straightly; punctually; strictly; truly; candidly; specifically: *prep.* at: [in.

ตรณ see **ดรณ**

ตรม see **ตรอม**

ตรรก dtak⁴ *S. n.* conjecture; speculation; doubt; reasoning; a system or doctrine founded on speculation or reasoning (S. E. D. p. 439): ตรรกวิท *lit.* "one knowing logic," *i. e.* a philosopher: ตรรกวิทยา, ตรรกศาสตร์ *lit.* "the science of reasoning," *i. e.* logic; a manual of logic; a philosophical treatise.

ตรละ ๑ dta⁴-ra⁶-la⁶ *P. S. n.* rice-gruel (S. E. D. p. 439).

ตรละ ๒ dta⁴-ra⁶-la⁶ *P. S. n.* the central gem of a necklace; a necklace; a ruby: *adj.* moving to and fro; trembling; quavering; glittering; unsteady; vain; hollow (S. E. D. p. 439).

ตรลา dta⁴-ra⁶-lah *S. n.* spirituous liquors; wines; rice-gruel; a bee (S. E. D. p. 439).

ตรวจ dtroo-at⁴ *v.* to examine; to verify; to confirm; to authenticate: ตรวจตรา to make inspection trips: ตรวจน้ำ to anoint one with water, thereby imparting merit, or a blessing: ตรวจสอบบัญชี to audit the accounts: เรือตรวจการ a boat used in surveying or policing.

ตรวน dtroo-an *n.* fetters; chains; manacles.

ตรอก dtrauk⁴ *n.* a lane; an alley; a narrow passage.

ตรอง dtraung *v.* to meditate; to reflect; to think over.

ตรอม, ตรอมตรม, ตรม dtraum *v.* to be sorrowful, disconsolate, or sad; to grieve.

ตระ dtra⁴ *n.* a Siamese tune or song; a piece, stretch or portion (used in reference to land).

ตระ (ต้น) dtra³ so-called by the ส่วย (*N. E. Siam*) *n. Erythrophloeum succirubrum* (*Leguminosae*) (cb. p. 540).

ตระกล dtra⁴-gkon *adj.* abundant; plentiful.

ตระกวน *Cam.* ผักบุ้ง (ต้น) dtra⁴-gkoo-an *n. Ipomoea aquatica* (*Convolvulaceae*), a small semi-aquatic creeper with tender arrow-shaped leaves, often cultivated in peasants' gardens. The leaves and young stems are commonly used for vegetable curries. It thrives best in a shallow trench where moisture can be retained (MCM. p. 304 : BURK. p. 1245).

ตระกอง dtra[4]-gkaung *Cam. v.* to embrace; to hug; to encircle with the arms.

ตระการ dtra[4]-gkan *adj.* beautiful; wonderful; various; diverse; different.

ตระกูล dtra[4]-gkoon *n.* line; lineage; family; pedigree; ancestral line of consanguinity.

ตระคัร, กฤษณา (ต้น) dtra[4]-kan *P. S. n.* *Aquilaria agallocha (Thymelaeaceae)*, eagle-wood, aloes wood, a large tree of Siam, rich in fragrant resin from which is obtained an essential oil valued in perfumery and medicine. It is also used for burning in temples as an incense. The most valuable finds of this tree are pathological. This has led to much superstitious use of taboos and magic, both in the gathering of the timber and in its subsequent use (MCM. p. 397 : BURK. pp. 197-204).

ตระง่อง dtra[4]-ngaung[3] *v.* to crouch and peek; to look intently; to peep slyly from concealment; see ง้อง.

ตระจัก, ตระชัก dtra[4]-chjak[4] *Cam. adj.* cool; shady.

ตระดก, ตระหนก dtra[4]-dok[4] *v.* to be startled, frightened or alarmed; to be taken by surprise.

ตระดาษ dtra[4]-dat[4] *adj.* whitish; tinged with white; like an albino; blonde.

ตระเตรียม dtra-[4]dtree-am *v.* to make ready; to get ready; to prepare for; to equip; to provide : *n.* preparation.

ตระนาว see ตะนาว

ตระไน, กระไน, กะไน (นก) dtra[4]-nai *n.* a small, wild bird of the woodpecker family.

ตระบอก (กลีบ) dtra[4]-bauk[4] *Cam. n.* petals (of a flower); sections (of an orange).

ตระบัด ๑ dtra[4]-bat[4] *Cam. adj.* momentary; continuing but an instant; instantaneous.

ตระบัด ๒ dtra[4]-bat[4] *Cam. v.* to borrow money and make a default in payment.

ตระบัน dtra[4]-ban *Cam. n.* double petals.

ตระเบิ่ง see ตะเบิ่ง

ตระแบก (ต้น) see กระแบก (ต้น)

ตระแบง dtra[4]-baang *v.* to wear or place across the shoulder (as a cloth or strap).

ตระแบน, ตระแบ่น dtra[4]-baan *v.* to throw down; to fall or spread down, *ex.* ตระแบ่นไว้กลางดิน.

ตระโบม dtra[4]-bom *v.* to embrace; to hug; to caress or comfort; to encircle with the arms : ตระโบมโลมเล้า to caress; to console; to flatter.

ตระพัง see ตะพัง

ตระมวล, กระมวล dtra[4]-moo-an *n.* a place; a locality; a district.

ตระมั่น, ทะมั่น dtra[4]-meun[3] *adj.* large and high; tall and prominent.

ตระโมจ dtra[4]-mote[4] *Cam. adv.* lonely.

ตระลบ, ตลบ dtra[4]-lob[4] *v.* to cover or to spread over by throwing from behind (as a net over a bird or chicken); to spread by tossing from the reverse side; to be diffused (as smoke or odours): *adj.* turned, tossed or tilted (up and forward from the back): ตระลบฉม to have a fragrant odour diffused in the air : ตระลบไล้ to pursue by a circuitous route.

ตระลอด see ตลอด

ตระลาการ dtra[4]-lah-gkan *n. lit.* "one acting as a balance," *i. e.* a judge.

ตระลาด see ตลาด

ตระเลิด see เตลิด

ตระวัน see ตะวัน

ตระเวน see ตะเวน ตระเวนเวทา an attitude assumed by Siamese actors.

ตระสัก dtra⁴-sak⁴ *adj.* fine; elegant; showy; beautiful; pleasing to the eye.

ตระหง่าน dtra⁴-ngan⁴ *adj.* high; tall; prominent.

ตระหนก see ตระดก

ตระหนัก dtra⁴-nak⁴ *adj.* confident; sure; positive; able to perceive clearly; manifest; [plain; distinct.

ตระหน่ำ see กระหน่ำ

ตระหนี่ dtra⁴-nee⁴ *adj.* miserly; stingy; avaricious; sparing: คนตระหนี่ a niggardly man; an avaricious person; a miser: ความตระหนี่ greediness; stinginess; cupidity; miserliness; parsimony.

ตระเหว็ด, เตว็ด dtra⁴-wet⁴ *n.* the figure of an image or angel traced on paper, or carved on wood, and placed in spirit shrines before which offerings are made.

ตระอาล dtra⁴-an *adj.* shaking; tremulous; quivering.

ตระโอม dtra⁴-om *Cam. v.* to embrace; to [hug.

ตรังค์ see ดรงค์

ตรังคิณี dta⁴-rang-ki⁶-nee *S. n.* a river (S. E. D. p. 438): ตรังคิณีนาถ *lit.* "lord of the rivers," *i. e.* the sea.

ตรับ, ตรับฟัง dtrap⁴ *v.* to hear; to give ear to; to listen; to attend: ตรับเหตุ to listen to the cause or origin of a matter.

ตรัยตรึงศ์ dtrai-dtreung *P. S. n.* thirty-three, the number of devas in the retinue of the "lord of the gods," Indra (S. E. D. p. 457); see ดาวดึงส์.

ตรัส, ดำรัส dtrat⁴ *Cam. v.* to speak; to command; to utter (used in reference to royalty): ตรัสรู้ to know; to perceive; to discern clearly.

ตรัสสา dtrat⁴-sa² *n.* an honorary title for princesses of royal blood (เจ้าฟ้าฝ่ายใน).

ตรา dtrah *n.* a seal; a stamp: ตราจอง a certificate of land ownership issued by the Umphur prior to the title deed (โฉนด) issued by the land office of the local district: ตราชู a balance; a pair of scales: ตราแดง a certificate of land ownership issued by the Nai Umphurs of Ayuthia, Angtong, Lopburi, and Supanburi and good for two years: ตราภูมิ a license issued exempting a person from paying revenue taxes or from serving the Crown; an official paper granting immunity from taxes and corvée: ตราแผ่นดิน the seal of the kingdom or of the reigning king: ตราสัง (ศพ) to wrap, bind and seal a corpse: ตราสิน to register or make declaration of a complaint (as before the police when an article is stolen, or as a permanent registration with the postal officials): ตอกตรา to imprint a seal, tradename, or initials of the owner (as on silverware or on logs): ตีตรา to set or affix a seal; to mark with a stamp; to fasten with a seal or seals: ท้องตรา an official letter or order from a ministry to a district officer: วางท้องตรา to present the officially signed letter to the addressee: ใบเหยียบย่ำ a certificate of land ownership issued by the Nai Umphur: เสียตราจอง to pay the land tax.

ตรากตรำ dtrak⁴-dtram *adj.* menial; servile; enduring hardship and oppression.

ตราบ dtrap⁴ *n.* side; edge; border; gunwale: *adv.* when; whenever: *prep.* whensoever; till; to the time of; until; up to that time; till then: *conj.* by then; until that time: ตราบใด thenceforth; whenever; from that time on; so long as: ตราบเท่า, กราบเท่า ending; concluding; throughout all time; final: ตราบนั้น then; at that time.

ตรำ   dtrŭm *adj.* enduring; suffering; undergoing privations, dangers, or persecutions: ตรำแดดตรำฝน obliged to endure all kinds of weather.

ตรํ่า   dtrŭm[4] *v.* to cut, *ex.* ตรํ่าหญ้า.

ตริ ๑, ดำริ   dtri[4] *v.* to think; to consider; to reflect on; to weigh in the mind.

ตริ ๒ see ตรี

ตริว   dtriew *n.* a large, fresh-water turtle found in northern Siam.

ตรี (ปลา)   dtree *Cam. n.* a fish.

ตรี   dtree *P. S. n.* three; third (S. E. D. p. 457); a trio: ตรีกฏุก the three pungent spices, *viz.* black pepper, *Piper nigrum (Piperaceae)*; long pepper, *P. chaba*; and dry ginger, *Zingiber officinale* (Burk. pp. 1742, 1746, 2296: MCM. pp. 337, 338, 380): ตรีกาล the three times or tenses, *viz.* past, present, and future, or the three periods of the day, *viz.* morning, noon, and evening (S. E. D. p. 457): ตรีกูฏ, ตรีมุกูฏ *lit.* "having three peaks, humps or elevations," *i. e.* the name of a mountain in Ceylon on the top of which the city of Lanka was situated: ตรีโกณ a triangle: *adj.* triangular: ตรีโกณมิติ *Eng.* trigonometry: ตรีคณะ a triad of duties, *viz.* justice, love and purpose: ตรีคัมภีร์ three volumes of profound or sacred teachings: ตรีคุณ the process of using three as a multiplier; three-fold; three times three, etc.; the three groups of qualities or characteristics (of a person), *viz.* (1) purity; goodness; good sense; courage; energy (S. E. D. p. 1135); (2) passion; emotion; affection (S. E. D. p. 863); (3) mental darkness; ignorance; illusion; error (S. E. D. p. 438): ตรีจีวร the three vestments of a Buddhist monk; the three robes or garments of a Buddhist priest; the tattered dress of a mendicant: ตรีชฏา the name of a Rakshasa (goblin), a character mentioned in the Ramayana, who was friendly to Sita: ตรีชาต three spices, *viz.* mace, cardamom, and

cinnamon: ตรีทศ, ไตรทศ "three multiplied by ten," thirty-three (in round numbers); the thirty-three celestial deities attendant upon Indra, which are as follows, twelve Adityas (อาทิตย์), eight Vasus (วส), eleven Rudras (รุทร), and two Aswins (อัศวิน) (H. C. D. pp. 4, 342, 370, 29). The abode of these deities is the Devadungsa heaven (ดาวดึงส์) (Ala. p. 201): ตรีทศบดี *lit.* "lord of the deities," *i. e.* Indra: ตรีทศาจารย์ *lit.* "the thirty-god-preceptor," *i. e.* Brishaspati, the name of a deity in whom the action of the worshipper of the gods is personified. He is also regent of the planet Jupiter (H. C. D. pp. 63, 64): ตรีทศาธิบดี a name for Siva: ตรีทศายุธ *lit.* "the divine weapon," *i. e.* the rainbow: ตรีทศาลัย *lit.* "the abode of the gods," *i. e.* the Devadungsa heaven: ตรีทศาหาร *lit.* "divine food," *i. e.* nectar; the elixir of life: ตรีทเสนทร์, ตรีทเศส, ตรีทเศศวร์ *lit.* "god-chief," *i. e.* Indra: ตรีทิพ, ไตรทิพ the third or most sacred heaven: ตรีทิพินทร์, ตรีทิเพนทร์ names for Indra: ตรีทิเพศ *lit.* "the owners of heaven," *i. e.* celestial beings in general: ตรีทิเพศวร์ *lit.* "lord of heaven," *i. e.* Indra: ตรีโทษ disorder of the three humours of the body; vitiation of the blood, bile, and phlegm: ตรีธาร *lit.* "three-streamed," *i. e.* the Ganges: ตรีเนตร, ตรีโลจน์ *lit.* "three-eyed"; tri-ocular, the three-eyed Hindu god, *i. e.* Siva. This third eye burst from Siva's forehead with a great flame when his wife playfully placed her hands over his eyes after he had been engaged in austerities in the Himalayas (H. C. D. p. 320): ตรีบถ a place where three roads meet; reached by three roads, ways, or paths: ตรีบท *lit.* "three-footed," *i. e.* Yama (พระยม). the god of the dead: ตรีปริวรรต *lit.* "turning thrice," *i. e.* the wheel of the law: ตรีปิฎก the three baskets, canons or collections of Buddhist sacred writings, which are, *viz.* (1) พระวินัย "discipline" consisting of a series of instructions for the monks, (2) พระสูตร "things strung together," or sermons and addresses to all,

(3) พระอภิธรรม " superior truths or metaphysics " (Ala. pp. 166, 167) : ตรีปุระ " the triple
city," i.e. the three strong, aerial cities of triple
fortifications (built of gold, silver and iron
by Maya, a Daitya from the race of demons
and giants, who was architect and builder for
the Asuras). These cities were afterwards
burned by Siva : ตรีปุรุษ three generations :
ตรีพรหม, the " triple form," i.e. the Hindu
triad consisting of the gods Brahma, Siva
and Vishnu, representatives of the creative,
destructive and preservative principles (H. C. D.
p. 320) : ตรีภพ, ตรีภูมิ, ไตรโลกย์, ไตรภพ, ไตรภูมิ
lit. " the three forms of existence," i. e. sensual,
corporal and formless ; lit. " the three worlds,"
i. e. heaven, earth, and hell ; according to the
Buddhist sense, there are also worlds of gain,
increase and welfare : ตรีกูช triangular ; a
triangle : ตรีมธุร lit. " the three sweet substances," i. e. sugar, honey and ghee or clarified butter : ตรีมูรติ see ตรีพรหม : ตรีรัตน์
lit. " the three gems," i. e. the Buddha, the
law, and the brotherhood of monks : ตรี-
โลกนาถ a name for Indra and Siva : ตรี-
โลเกศ Vishnu ; Siva ; the sun : ตรีโลห the
three metals, viz. copper, brass, and bell-metal :
ตรีโลหก the three metals, viz. gold, silver and
copper : ตรีศัลย์ lit. " three-pointed," i. e.
an arrow : ตรีศูล a trident ; the weapon of
Siva ; a three-pointed pike or spear with a
short handle : ตรีศูลิน lit. " one bearing the
trident," i. e. Siva : ตรีศูลินี name of Siva's
consort, queen Uma (พระอุมา) : ตรีสัตย์ lit.
" the condition of being trebly truthful," i. e.
in thought, word and deed : ตรีสุคนธ์ lit.
" the three spices," i. e. mace, cardamom, and
cinnamon.

ตรึก dtreuk[4] P. S. v. to reflect, upon ; to
think about ; to have in one's mind ; to intend ;
to try to discover or ascertain by reasoning
or speculation ; to conjecture ; to guess (S. E. D.
p. 439).

ตรึกถอง dtreuk[4]-taung[2] adj. abundant ;
ample ; fully sufficient ; plentiful.

ตรึง dtreung v. to tie tightly ; to bind ; to
transfix with a nail or nails ; to make tight
or to hold firmly together.

ตรึงศ dtreung-sa[4] adj. thirty (chd. p. 506).

ตรุ ๑ dtroo[4] n. a prison ; a jail.

ตรุ ๒ see ดรุ

ตรุณ see ดรุณ

ตรุณี see ดรุณี

ตรุศจีน, เฟื่องฟ้า (ต้น) dtroot[4]-cheen n.
Buginvillaea spectabilis (Nyctagineae), a
small genus of shrubby climber, native of
tropical America. The insignificent flowers
are surrounded by conspicuous bracts, which
make these climbers very striking. There
are several varieties, purple, rose, brick-red,
etc. It is free-flowering, showy and ornamental (MCM. pp. 73, 188 : BURK. p. 382).

ตรุษ dtroot[4] n. a Siamese, national, religious
ceremony held at the close of each year, or a
New Year's celebration observed as a holiday.
This invariably falls on the 14th and 15th of
the waning of the fourth, and the first of the
waxing of the fifth Siamese lunar month,
which marks the beginning of the Siamese
luni-solar year (1909 Bangkok Directory p.
27) ; a very minute space of time ; destruction ;
loss (S. E. D. p. 462).

ตรู, ดรู, ดำรู dtroo adj. beautiful ; handsome ; pretty.

ตรู่ dtroo[4] n. dawn ; the break of day ; the
first appearance of light.

ตฤณ dtrin P. S. n. grass, herbs ; a blade of
grass, or straw (often used as a symbol of
minuteness and worthlessness) (S.E.D. p. 453):
ตฤณเกตุ, ตฤณธวัช the bamboo : ตฤณโคธา a
house-lizard ; a chameleon : ตฤณชาติ different kinds of grass ; the vegetable kingdom :
ตฤณพฤกษ์ the fan palm ; the sugar palm ; the
coconut tree : ตฤณมัย made of grass ; grassy ;

covered with grass: ตฤณราช *lit.* "the king of grasses," *i. e.* the coconut tree; sugar-cane: ตฤณสิงห์ *lit.* "reed-lion," *i. e.* an ax.

ตฤตีย dtri[4]-dtee-ya[6] *S. adj.* third (S. E. D. p. 453): ตฤตียบุรุษ third personal pronoun, he; she.

ตฤท dtrit[4] *S. v.* to pierce; to cleave; to split open; to let out; to set free; to destroy (S. E. D. p. 453).

ตฤป dtrip[4] *S. v.* to satisfy oneself; to become satiated; to be pleased with (S. E. D. p. 453): ตฤปตฤณ to pasture.

ตฤปต์ dtrip[4] *S. v.* to be surfeited; to be contented or satisfied (S. E. D. p. 454).

ตฤษ dtrit[4] *S. n.* hunger; thirst; an eager desire or longing for (S. E. D. p. 454).

ตฤษณา see **ตัณหา**

ตฤา, ตรี dtree *Cam. n.* fish (the equivalent of the Siamese ปลา).

ตล dta[4]-la[6] *P. n.* surface; plane; base; the lower part (chd. p. 494).

ตลก dta[4]-lok[4] *n.* a clown; a buffoon; a low jester.

ตลบ see **ตระลบ** ตลบตะแลง deceitful; trickish; unstable; fickle; changeful.

ตลอด dta[4]-laut[4] *adv.* from the beginning to the end: *prep.* from end to end: through-out the entire length of; all through to the end.

ตละ dta[4]-la[6] *adj.* such as; just as; of a like kind: *adv.* as; iike; similar to: ตละ-ยักษ์ like a dragon or demon.

ตลับ dta[4]-lap[4] *n.* a small, round, smooth, flat box fitted with a lid (such as is used by Siamese ladies for lip-salve); a chrismatory cup: ตลับนาก a species of the mango.

ตลาด, ตระลาด dta[4]-lat[4] *n.* a market-place: ขายทอดตลาด to auction off goods; to hold an auction: เจ้าตลาด a tax collector for market stalls: ชาวตลาด market people; venders of goods in a market: ตลาดเงินตรา a money market: ตลาดนัด a day appointed for marketing or bartering edibles or garden produce; market day: ออกตลาด to market goods.

ตลิ่ง, ตาผั่ง dta[4]-ling[4] *n.* a bank, side, border, or shore (as of a river or canal).

ตลึง, *Jav.* อัญชัญน์, *Siam.,* อังชัน *Laos* (ต้น) dta[4]-leung *n. Clitoria ternatea (Leguminosae),* a climber with conspicuous blue flowers, prob-ably South American, but now found through-out the tropics. It must have been carried to India very early, and from India was sent to the gardens of Europe about the end of the seventeenth century. It probably reached Malaysia from India. For years the flowers have been used to colour rice boiled with them blue. In the Dutch Indies the juice is sometimes used to colour food green. The flowers have been used in some places to give a fleeting colour to white cloth. It is used on matting in the Rhio Archipelago. The colour can be used, in the same way as litmus, as a reagent for detecting acid and alkaline liquids. Sheep and goats will eat the foliage. The seeds are aperient, and contain a toxic alkaloid; the roots are cathartic. There are other medicinal uses (cb. p. 436: MCM. p. 124: BURK. pp. 588, 589).

ตวง dtoo-ang *v.* to pour into a capacity or liquid measure (as rice into a bucket meas-ure); to measure (as by quantity).

ต่วน (แพร) dtoo-an[4] *n.* a kind of glazed, glossy silk; satin.

ต้วมเตี้ยม see **กระต้วมกระเตี้ยม**

ตวัด dta[4]-wat[4] *v.* to entwine with the arms (as when the contestants close up in boxing).

ตวาด dta[4]-wat[4] *v.* to scold harshly; to use loud, truculent language in anger.

ตอ　dtau *n.* a stump; a snag; a fixed or rooted remnant of anything: ตอหม้อ intermediate posts to support a floor, or dwarf intermediate posts, as are used in a rice godown, the main posts piercing the floor and supporting the roof, while intermediate posts placed about five feet apart, support the floor.

ต่อ ๑ (ตัว)　dtau[4] *n.* a wasp.

ต่อ ๒　dtau[4] *v.* to use a decoy; to make additions on; to add to; to increase; to join on to; to add the sides to a boat: *n.* a decoy: ไก่ต่อ a chicken used as a decoy: ช้างต่อ a tame elephant acting as a decoy: ต่อตั้ง to build up or make up; to build up a form: ต่อแต้ม dominoes; an exaggeration, or something added to a story: ต่อนัด-ต่อแนง to haggle or quibble over the price; to argue about trifling things: ต่อนั้น-ไป from now on; henceforth; henceforward: ต่อไป, ต่อไปนี้ more in advance; further; additional; moreover; in addition to what has been said: ต่อมา afterwards; subsequently; in succeeding time: ต่อรอง to give a handicap: ต่อราคา to bargain for; to beat down in price: ต่อเรือ to build a boat: ต่อล้อต่อเถียง disputative; argumentative; inclined to be contentious: ต่อโลง to make a coffin: ต่อว่า to protest; to remonstrate; to object: ต่อสัญญาประกันภัย to renew the insurance: ต่อไส้ (ต้น) (*Laos*) *Allophylus fulvinerirs (Sapindaceae),* a small tree found from Tenasserim to Java, down the west coast in the Peninsula and in the south. The wood is used for rafters but is not durable; it furnishes firewood. A poultice is made from the boile droots, which is used for stomach-ache (V. P. p. 117: Burk. p. 104); (*Peninsula*) *A. sootepensis* (cb. p. 324): ต่อหัวต่อหาง to make ends join: ติดต่อ to be contiguous; to connect with; to join onto; to be in juxtaposition: สามต่อหนึ่ง three to one (as offers made in betting).

ต่อ ๓　dtau[4] *prep.* against; before; opposite; abreast; towards: ต่อกร to strike with the arms (as in a fight, or while boxing); to fight: ต่อต้าน to resist, withstand or hinder; to strive against: ต่อตี to make a forward attack: ต่อแย้ง to protest, oppose or hinder; to prevent by force: ต่อสู้ to withstand, antagonize, or fight against; to resist (as when being arrested): ต่อหน้า in front of; before the face; in the presence of; opposite to: ผู้เป็นต่อ the winner: ผู้เป็นรอง the runner-up in a game: เอามาต่อปีหน้า to be added to a new year.

ต้อ (ตา)　dtau[3] *n.* a corneal opacity; a corneal ulcer.

ตอก　dtauk[4] *v.* to pound or hammer down; to drive in or down by force: *n.* thin strips of fresh bamboo (for tying purposes or for weaving baskets).

ต๊อก　dtauk[6] *n.* a small drum used for beating time in Siamese music: ไก่ต๊อก see ไก่.

ตอง (ไพ่)　dtaung *n.* a Chinese game of cards, usually played by six persons, the object being to get a sequence of three cards which is called ตองหนึ่ง: ตอง (ใบ) banana leaves stripped from the midrib: ไพ่ตอง a Siamese card game of Chinese origin.

ต้อง　dtaung[3] *v.* to touch; to hit; a sign of the imperative, "must," *ex.* ต้องไป, ต้องนอน: ความต้องการ destitution: ต้องการ to be in want or in need; to be destitute; to want; to require; to desire: ต้องคดี to be sued; to be prosecuted; to be tried at law: ต้องใจ to like; to be pleased with: ต้องตา to be attractive; to be pleasing to the eyes: ต้อง-โทษ to require punishment as a penalty; punishable: ต้องหา to be charged with a crime; to be the defendant in a suit; to be blamed with: ต้องอาบัติ to be against the Vinaya, the discipline of the Buddha: เห็น-ต้องด้วย to coincide; to concur with, in opinion.

ตองตอย　dtaung-dtoi *adj.* shabby; paltry;

improperly fitting (as a garment).

ตองเต้า (ต้น) dtaung-dtow[3] *Laos,* ปอหู *Siam (Saraburi) n. Hibiscus macrophyllus (Malvaceae),* a tall tree found from northeastern India to Java. The bark gives tough ropes, like those given by *H. floccosus*; they are used by the Malays, Siamese and Burmese. The wood is very light but may be used for house-building (CB. p. 158 : BURK. p. 1167).

ต้องเต dtaung[3]-dtey *n.* a children's game, similar to quoits.

ตองแตก (ต้น) dtaung-dtaak[4] *n. Baliospermum axillare (Euphorbiaceae),* a stout, subherbaceous shrub, up to 6 feet in height, found in waste places through northern India and Siam to Java. Its leaves are purgative. In Siam the root is the part usually administered, while in the Malay States it is the leaves. In India, on the other hand, it is the seeds that are used; they administer one bruised seed in water for every evacuation they wish the patient to have. The leaves are also used for poulticing wounds (S. S. M. P. p. 4 : V. P. p. 128 : BURK. p. 289).

ต้องแต่ง, ต้องแต้ง dtaung[4]-dtaang[4] *adj.* oscillating; swaying.

ตองม่อม (ต้น) dtaung-maum[3] *Shan, Me Hong Son n. Pterospermum grande (Sterculiaceae),* a tree of the open evergreen forest at about 1500 m. elevation, found in northwestern Siam (CB. p. 176).

ต้องสู้, ต้องซู้ dtaung[3]-soo[3] *n.* a northern Siamese trader tribe, closely related to the Shans, and well-known all over Siam and Cambodia as far as the lower reaches of the Mekong. They are found over the whole of the western part of the southern Shan states. They do not spread northwards, nor are they found east of the Salween except in Siamese territory. In the Shan states they are cultivators, but when they go abroad are most commonly elephant and horse dealers. They

are nominally Buddhists but make offerings to spirits (Gazetteer of upper BURMA and the Shan states I, p. 554).

ตองแห้ง (ต้น) dtaung-haang[3] *n. Hedyotis auricularia (Rubiaceae),* a soft herb, found from the Himalayas to Australia and the Pacific. After boiling, the leaves may be used for rubbing on aching places. The Cinghalese eat the leaves with rice (BURK. p. 1130); *H. capitellata,* a sprawling herb, found from southern China and Tenasserim to western Malaysia; in the Peninsula it occurs everywhere. It is much used medicinally, being one of the chief plants with which the Malays make poultices, using it for snake-bites, broken bones, bruises, rheumatism, lumbago, ague, and after child-birth. It is given for constipation, indigestion, heart-burn, gastric vertigo, dysentery, and as a tonic in mixtures. The leaves are eaten with rice as a salad (MCM. p. 441 : BURK. p. 1130).

ตอด dtaut[4] *v.* to bite; to nibble (as fish); to experience a throbbing sensation (as when pus is confined in an abscess).

ตอน dtaun *v.* to castrate; to use the gootee method of layering or marcottage to make a branch root. To do this, one half inch of the bark is removed all around a limb under a leaf-bud. Around this a ball of adhesive soil is applied, wrapped with coir fibre. All is then bound firmly around the branch and kept moist by hanging over it a dripping earthen pot so as to keep the gootee continually moist (MCM. p. 39); when sprouted, the limb is cut off and planted : *n.* part; region; district; quarters; a paragraph : ตอนหัว forepart of a ship or boat; the bow : ตัดเป็นตอนๆ to cut into short lengths; dinted; dimpled; compressed at the side.

ต้อน dtaun[3] *v.* to drive into a trap or enclosure by encircling the animals (as is done with rabbits); to chase towards a destination by an advancing surrounding movement (as victims, prisoners or elephants); to prevent, to oppose by encompassing : *n.* a fish-trap placed across a water-way : ต้อนรับ to receive a guest with gladness; to welcome.

ตอบ dtaup[4] *v.* to reply; to answer; to respond; to retort : *adj.* dinted; dimpled : ตอบแทนคุณ to reply to a kindness; to reimburse; to remunerate; to make return for a kindness : ตอบสาร to reply by mail or messenger; to make a written reply.

ตอปิโด, ตอรปิโด dtau-bpi[4]-doh *Eng. n.* a torpedo.

ตอม dtaum *v.* to pester or beset in an irritating way; to fly around constantly, causing annoyance (as flies or insects); to swarm around (as ants).

ต่อม dtaum[4] *n.* a gland; a secreting organ : ต่อมโลหิต the ovaries; the menses.

ต๋อม dtaum[2] *onomat.* from the sound of a stone dropping into water.

ต่อย dtoi[4] *v.* to strike or attack with the fist; to box; to be stung (as by a scorpion).

ต้อย dtoi[3] *adj.* small; diminutive; low.

ต้อยๆ dtoi[3]-dtoi[3] *adj.* following with a slow jogging motion (as a dog trots along after a person) : ติดต้อยห้อยตาม to follow along behind another.

ต้อยติ่ง (ต้น) dtoi[3]-dting[4] *n. Ruellia tuberosa (Acanthaceae)*, a plant about a foot high, with beautiful violet flowers. It is emetic, and is said to be a substitute for ipecacuanha (MCM. p. 135 : BURK. p. 1920).

ต้อยตีวิด (นก) dtoi[3]-dti[4]-wit[6] *n.* a species of small bird of the plover family; Burmese lapwing, *Lobivanellus atronuchalis* (GAIRD. J. S. S. IX, 1, p. 15).

ตอแย dtau-yaa *v.* to trouble or irritate; to annoy or tease.

ตอแหล dtau-laa[2] *v.* to lie or prevaricate; to equivocate.

ต่อหิ (ต้น) dtau[4]-hi[4] *Karen (Kanburi) n. Millettia ovalifolia (Leguminosae)* (CB. p. 393).

ตะ dta[4] *v.* to encrust; to cover or wash over with silver, gold or nickel (as electroplating) : ตะทองลาย to electroplate in designs with gold.

ตะกับทะเล (ปลา) dta[4]-gkap[4]-ta[6]-lay *n. Lobotes surinamensis (Lobotidaè)*, a sea-perch which attains a large size but is not sufficiently common to be of any commercial value. The flesh is considered good (suvatti p. 126 : BURK. p. 1359).

ตะกรน dta[4]-gkron *n.* a shuttle made of bamboo, enclosing a spool of thread (used in cloth weaving).

ตะกรม dta[4]-gkrom *n.* a large sea-shell of the oyster family, found attached to stakes in the sea.

ตะกร้อ dta[4]-gkrau[3] *n.* a Siamese football, a ball made of woven cane strips or of leather, sometimes with feathers attached; an oblong basket made of small-sized bamboo or rattan strips fastened to a long pole (for removing fruit from trees).

ตะกรัน dta[4]-gkran *n.* refuse; sediment; precipitate; a deposit.

ตะกรับ dta[4]-gkrap[4] *n.* a perforated, circular baked clay grating for portable braziers or chetties (อั้งโล่) : ตะกรับ (ปลา) *Pristolepis fasciata (Pristolepidae)*, a fresh water perch-like fish. It does not occur in any quantity, but whenever caught is considered good eating. It is caught in traps, casting-nets, or by hook and line (BURK. p. 1809); *Scatophagus argus (Scatophagidae)* (suvatti pp. 139, 143).

ตะกร้า dta[4]-gkrah[3] *n.* an openwork basket made with plaited strips of bamboo or rattan.

ตะกรุด dta[4]-gkroot[4] *n.* "magic jewellery,"

charms or amulets. These consist of hollow brass, lead or silver cylinders containing small tightly rolled pieces of cloth, marked with cabalistic designs, symbols and letterings. These are strung on a small cord and worn around the waist, or as necklaces or armlets. They are believed to protect the wearer against injury from all forms of weapons.

ตะกรุม (นก)　　　dta⁴-gkroom *n.* a bird of the stork family; adjutant bird, *Leptoptilos argala* (Gaird. J. S. S. IX, 1, p. 10).

ตะกรุมตะกราม　　　dta⁴-gkroom-dta⁴-gkram *adj.* clumsy; awkward; uncouth.

ตะกลอง (ปลา)　　dta⁴-gklaung *n. Gnathanodon speciosus* (*Carangidae*) (Dept. Agri. & Fisheries); *Caranx speciosus*, horse-mackerel, or yellow-tails, which are very important food-fishes in several parts of the world (BURK. pp. 449, 450).

ตะกละ, ตะกลาม　　　dta⁴-gkla⁴ *adj.* greedy; gluttonous; pertaining to a glutton.

ตะกวด see จะกวด

ตะกอ　　　dta⁴-gkau *n.* an implement to separate the warp from the weft in weaving: *adj.* adolescent; adult; young; youthful; vigorous; in the flower of youth (M.).

ตะกอน　　　dta⁴-gkaun *n.* deposit; precipitate; sediment.

ตะกั่ว　　　dta⁴-gkoo-ah⁴ *n.* lead; type-metal; pewter: ตะกั่วเกรียบ tin foil: ตะกั่วนม lead foil: ขี้ตะกั่ว oxide of lead.

ตะกาง　　　dta⁴-gkang *n.* a crocodile trap.

ตะกาด　　　dta⁴-gkat⁴ *n.* low land near the seashore where salt water can be let in to evaporate (as salt fields or " salt pans ").

ตะกาย　　　dta⁴-gkai *v.* to claw or bite (as a caged wild animal trying to escape); to climb or creep by aid of the hands (as up a steep mountain).

ตะกาว　　　dta⁴-gkow *n.* a hook at the end of a pole or rope (often used by ferry boatmen along the river).

ตะกุกตะกัก　　　dta⁴-gkook⁴-dta⁴-gkuk⁴ *adj.* jagged; having notches; rough.

ตะกุย, ตะกุยตะกาย　　　dta⁴-gkoo-ey *v.* to scratch, scrape or dig with the fingers, paws or claws.

ตะกูด, จังกูด　　　dta⁴-gkoot⁴ *n.* the rudder of a boat; the helm.

ตะเกียกตะกาย　　　dta⁴-gkee-ak⁴-dta⁴-gkai *n.* assiduity; diligence; persistence.

ตะเกียง　　　dta⁴-gkee-ang *n.* a lamp: ไส้ตะเกียง a wick.

ตะเกียบ　　　dta⁴-gkee-ap⁴ *n.* chopsticks: (เสา) ตะเกียบ a pair of coupling posts connected by two horizontal bars, on one of which a third post or pole operates as on a pivot. The lower horizontal bar holds the upright center post or pole firmly in position after it has been raised (as can be seen in Buddhist temple grounds).

ตะแกรง　　　dta⁴-gkraang *n.* a sieve; a flat shallow basket with close meshes (used for dipping up shrimps or fishes).

ตะโก (ต้น)　　　dta⁴-gkoh *n. Diospyros spp.* (*Ebenaceae*), ebony; *D. rhodocalyx* (V. P. p. 117): ตะโกสวน, พลับ (ต้น) *Diospyros embryopteris*, a moderate-sized, evergreen, symmetrical, handsome tree of Ceylon, India, Siam, Malaya, etc., found at low and medium elevations. The foliage is handsome and the branches spreading. " Tunika oil," used medicinally in India, is obtained from the seeds. The bark and unripe fruits are very astringent, the latter are commonly used in Siam for colouring and toughening fishing nets, etc. In the unripe fruit there is much gum, which is used in India for painting the bottoms of boats as a preservative, and for caulking seams. The timber is useful, and is employed in India (MCM. pp. 206, 396, 443, 517: BURK. p. 830).

ตะโก้   dta[4]-gkoh[3] *n.* a sweetmeat; a wind blowing during the rainy season; a monsoon.

ตะโกก (ปลา)   dta[4]-gkok[4] *n.* an edible fresh-water fish, *Cyclocheilichthys enoplos* (*Cypri-nidae*); *Albulichthys albuloides*; *Ambly-rhynchichthys truncatus*, a species of carp (Burk. p. 130); *Cosmochilus harmandi* (Suvatti pp. 42, 45, 46, 53).

ตะโกน   dta[4]-gkon *v.* to call loudly, or to signal from afar.

ตะโกรง   dta[4]-gkrong *v.* to exert every effort to acquire; to desire exceedingly; to crave: ตะโกรงขาว (ปลา) *Atropus atropus* (*Carangidae*) (suvatti p. 115).

ตะไกร see กรรไกร (p. 13) เหยี่ยวตะไกร (นก) a black-legged falconet, *Microhierax fringilla-rius*.

ตะขบ (ต้น)   dta[4]-kop[4] n. a genus of trees: ตะขบไทย (ต้น) *Flacourtia cataphracta* (*Fla-courtiaceae*), a small thorny tree, native of India and Malaya, producing round berries of the size of large cherries, purplish or deep-red in colour and of a rather pleasant tart flavour (cb. p. 94: V.P. p. 117: MCM. p. 262); *F. inermis*, an ornamental, thorn-less tree, found in cultivation throughout the Dutch Indies and also in Malaya. It grows to about 25 or 30 feet high, bearing a great profusion of bright red, cherry-like berries, which are attractive-looking but deceptive, being exceedingly sour; they make good jelly or preserves, but require much sugar. They are always propagated by seed and thrive in any moderately good soil at low elevations (V. P. p. 117: MCM. pp. 262, 471, 518: Burk. p. 1022): ตะขบฝรั่ง (ต้น) *Muntingia calabura* (*Tiliaceae*), Japanese cherry, a Mexican tree, which was introduced into the Philippine Islands for the sake of its edible

berry, at a comparatively recent date, and then into Siam, whence it extended to the Malay Peninsula. As a shade-tree it is good. The round orange or red berry is very sweet and pleasant to eat. The fibrous bark is used in the West Indies for rough cordage. The wood is soft and of no value. An infusion of the leaves is used as tea in Caraccas (MCM. p. 266: cb. p. 193: V. P. p. 117: Burk. p. 1504).

ตะขาบ, see จะขาบ (p. 236): ตะขาบ (นก) the Burmese roller, *Coracias affinis* (will. N.H. J. S. S. II, 3, p. 326); *C. benghalensis affinis* (Herb. N. H. J. S. S. VI, 3, p. 301): ตะขาบปาก-แดง (นก) the Indian broad-billed roller, *Eury-stomus orientalis orientalis* (Herb. N. H. J. S. S. VI, 3, p. 301).

ตะขิดตะขวง   dta[4]-kit[4]-dta[4]-koo-ang[2] *adj.* ashamed; abashed; bashful; shy.

ตะเข้ขบฟัน   dta[4]-kay[3]-kop[4]-fun *n.* crossing or double joints found in some kinds of bam-boo, considered valuable, and used for making walking sticks.

ตะเข็บ   dta[4]-kep[4] *n.* a twice-sewed seam: กุ้งตะเข็บ small prawns.

ตะโขง   dta[4]-kong[2] *n.* a large horned croc-odile.

ตะคร้อ (ต้น)   dta[4]-krau[5], มะโจ๊ก *Chieng-mai,* มะเคาะ *Lampang,* ค้อ, ตะค้อ *Eastern Laos,* กาซ้อง *Karen, Kanburi n.* a genus of wild, tall trees bearing very sour fruit. The timber is very hard and heavy and is excellent for charcoal: ตะคร้อไข่ (ต้น) *Schleichera trijuga* (*Sapindaceae*), Ceylon oak, a large tree of Ceylon, India, Burma, Java, etc. The foliage resembles that of the English oak. The wood is reddish, hard, tough, strong and durable and is used for handles of implements and wheels of oxcarts. The fruit is sour and the seeds, which are edible, are rich in oil, said to be the original "Macassar oil," but is not the oil so called at the present time. This tree forms the best host plant for lac (MCM. pp. 219, 397, 416, 417: CB. p. 329): ตะคร้อหนาม (ต้น) *Delpya muricata*, a small or medium-sized tree with spiney fruit, the seeds of which yield an oil used for illumination (V. P. p. 119).

ตะครอง (ต้น) dta⁴-kraung *n.* a species of wild tree with thorns along the branches, *Zizyphus cambodiana* (*Rhamnaceae*). It bears an astringent fruit which is chewed with betel-nut (CB. p. 297).

ตะครั่นตะครอ dta⁴-krun³-dta⁴-krau *v.* to chill; to feel alternate sensations of cold and heat.

ตะคริว dta⁴-krew *n.* cramps; a painful spasmodic muscular contraction.

ตะครบ dta⁴-kroop⁶ *v.* to pounce upon and seize (as a cat does a rat).

ตะคร้า (ต้น) dta⁴-krum⁵, **หวีด** *Chiengmai*, **ค้า** *Lampang n. Garuga pinnata* (*Burseraceae*), a tree found from the foot of the Himalayas to Siam. The wood is of fair value, of a handsome reddish-brown colour. The bark tans, and the gum and juice are medicinal in India (CB. p. 247: BURK. p. 1061).

ตะคอก see **ตวาด**

ตะคัน dta⁴-kan *n.* an ancient dish-shaped clay receptacle used as a lamp, or for burning gum spices and incense, or for fumigating; a censer.

ตะค้า (ต้น) dta⁴-kah⁵ *n.* a genus of tough rattan.

ตะคาก dta⁴-kak³ *n.* the haunch-bone; the ilium.

ตะคุ่ม dta⁴-koom³ *adv.* indistinctly; obscurely; confusedly; undefinedly.

ตะเครียว dta⁴-kree-oh *n.* a silk crocheted hand-bag.

ตะเคียน, ตะเคียนทอง (ต้น) dta⁴-kee-an

n. Hopea sp.; *Hopea odorata* (*Dipterocarpaceae*), a large tree that is used for sawing planks, and also for boats. The largest dugouts in the world are the Siamese royal barges made of this wood. The wood stands exposure and is not attacked by termites. An oleo-resin, or dammar runs from the wood but is not first grade dammar; this dammar has medicinal properties. A brew of the leaves is said to be useful in preventing leather, tanned by means of mangrove, from becoming too hard. (CB. p. 147: V. P. p. 119: BURK. p. 1192): ตะเคียนเผือก (ต้น) (*N. Siam*) *Homalium damrongianum* (*Samydaceae*) (CB. p. 739: V. P. p. 120): ตะเคียนหนู (ต้น) *Anogeissus acuminata var. lanceolata* (*Combretaceae*), a handsome deciduous tree of the central parts of India, Chittagong, Burma, Tonkin, and southwards into Siam, rather characteristic of stream sides. The timber is moderately hard; it warps and cracks in seasoning, and is not durable. It is suitable for mouldings, planking, and general purposes. It is considerably stronger than teak, and much heavier (CB. p. 612: V. P. p. 119: BURK. p. 170).

ตะเคียว dta⁴-kee-oh *v.* to lie propped up on one side (as dice when not lying flat).

ตะแคง dta⁴-kaang *v.* to tilt on one side; to list; to lean or be inclined to one side.

ตะไคร่ dta⁴-krai³ *n.* moss (on rocks); lichens or alga (on trees); mould (on damp walls): ตะไคร่น้ำ (ต้น) forms of aquatic vegetation found adhering as a slimy pest on the bottoms of boats or as a scum on stagnant water. This is skimmed off and fed to pigs.

ตะไคร้, จะไค้ (ต้น) dta⁴-krai⁵ *n. Cymbopogon citratus* (*Gramineae*), lemon grass, a grass of the Old World tropics, formerly thought to be of the large genus *Andropogon*. This grass has long been used as an aromatic flavouring for food, being used with fish and in sauces, and added to other aromatic substances in spicing liquor. It is also used medicinally as a local counter-irritant. It is sometimes taken as a substitute for tea by those whose digestions are weak. This plant resembles *Citronella* grass in general appearance, but is distinct by the odour of the leaves and less robust habit of growth. It gives a smaller yield of oil, known as lemongrass oil, which however commands a higher price than *Citronella* oil. Lemon-grass oil is grown to a small extent in Ceylon, but the chief supply of the oil is obtained from southern India (Burk. p. 724, v. p. p. 77: McM. pp. 347, 399, 400, 401); *C. nardus* (*Gramineae*), citronella grass, large grass, 4 to 5 feet high, cultivated in Ceylon and Java for the essential oil obtained from the leaves by distillation. India or Ceylon is probably the country of origin as it grows wild in both. The grass grows in ordinary soil and thrives best in a hot and moist climate. It flourishes up to about 2,000 feet elevation in Ceylon, but its commercial cultivation is confined to the sea-coast in the south-west part of the island, where it is estimated some 30,000 acres are under production. The grass is readily propagated by root division (fertile seed being rarely produced), and is planted about 2 feet by 3 feet apart in rows (McM. p. 400 : Burk. p. 727).

ตะไคร้น้ำ   dta[4]-krai[5]-nam[5] *Homonoia riparia* (*Euphorbiaceae*), a shrub found from the Himalayas to the Philippines. In Siam it is found along mountain streams and rocky banks of rivers. The Malays use the leaves and fruit medicinally. The charcoal is also used medicinally. The wood is grey, or greyish-brown, moderately hard and close-grained. The juice is used in Java for blackening teeth, and is said to make them firm, if loose (Burk. p. 1186); *Cephalanthus occidentalis* (V. P. p. 118).

ตะไคร้บก, สนุ่น (ต้น)   dta[4]-krai[5]-bok[4] *n.* *Salix tetrasperma* (*Salicaceae*), willow, a

small tree of sub-tropical India and China, which has been brought southward—the male sex only—into the Malay Peninsula. It is found along mountain streams and river beds all over Siam and in every village in some of the northern parts of the Peninsula. It rarely flowers and as a result the finding of a flower is considered a propitious sign. Propagation is by cuttings. It is usually planted in the garden boundary fence. The Chinese are particularly fond of planting it on embankments of tanks and mines. It is said to be used for fever. A decoction is used cold for ulceration of the nose (Burk. p. 1943).

ตะเม้   dta[4]-key[3] *n.* a two- or four-wheeled truck for hauling logs; a lorry.

ตะดิน   dta[4]-dtin *adj.* leisurely; deliberately; slowly (as a boat sailing).

ตะแตร้น, ตระแตร้น   dta[4]-dtraan[3] *onomat.* from the sound of elephants trumpeting.

ตะนอย   dta[4]-noi *n.* a species of black ant inflicting a painful sting.

ตะนาว, ตระนาว   dta[4]-now *n.* incense; perfumes; gum-spices.

ตะนาวศรี   dta[4]-now-see[2] *n.* Tenasserim province, a narrow strip of land extending along the east side of the gulf of Martaban. The productions are rice, cotton, and indigo; teak is largely exported. Moulmein, near the mouth of the Salween is the capital. At the present time this province forms a part of Burma, but formerly it belonged to Siam and was the western end of the overland route so commercially important during the reign of King Narai of the Ayuthia dynasty.

ตะบม   dta[4]-bom *adv.* constantly; persistently; perpetually.

ตะบอง   dta[4]-baung *n.* a club; a short bludgeon; a policeman's billy: ตะบองเพ็ชร์ (ต้น) a plant of the cactus family.

ตะบอย   dta⁴-boi *adv.* slowly; leisurely; deliberately; constantly; clumsily.

ตะบัน   dta⁴-ban *v.* to pierce or poke repeatedly, penetrating or perforating entirely through: ตะบันหมาก *n.* a metal tube about six inches long with a removable bottom (used by old women for macerating a quid of betel by the aid of a chisel-shaped pestle fitted to a handle): *adj.* persistent: *adv.* perseveringly: ตะบัน (ต้น) *Xylocarpus moluccensis* (*Meliaceae*) (Cb. p. 264); *Xylocarpus moluccensis var. gangeticus* (Cb. p. 265); *Carapa moluccensis* (identical with *X. moluccensis* but some botanists prefer to give the Malayan species the special designation *Xylocarpus*), a low tree found from the Mascarene Islands to the islands of the Pacific. The sap-wood is white; the heartwood is brown and very hard. Owing to the low-branching habit of the tree, and to the tendency of the trunk to grow crooked, it is difficult to find large straight timbers. It is used for small objects, and for native house-posts, and is employed all through the coasts of the East. Penang draws supplies from Siam. The Malays value it for ribs of boats. In Indo-China it is used for spokes of cart-wheels. Elsewhere it is used for boat-building, furniture and tree-nails. The bark is used as a tan in Indo-China and Perak. The bark and roots are medicinal (V. P. p. 121: Burk. p. 455): ตะบันไฟ a fire-syringe; a short cylinder made of buffalo horn, enclosing some ignitable substance which is set on fire by air compressed by a blow on the piston.

ตะบิดตะบอย   dta⁴-bit⁴-dta⁴-boi *adj.* deliberate: *adv.* deliberately; leisurely; constantly.

ตะบิ้ง, ตะพัด   dta⁴-beung *adv.* directly; persistently; unswervingly.

ตะบูน (ต้น)   dta⁴-boon *n.* a species of salt-water tree, *Xylocarpus obovatus* (*Meliaceae*) (Cb. p. 265): ตะบูนขาว (ต้น), ตะบูนดำ (ต้น)

Xylocarpus (*Carapa*) *sp.* (V. P. p. 120).

ตะเบ็ง, ตระเบ็ง   dta⁴-beng *v.* to distend the abdomen while holding the breath (as in straining); to utter a loud cry while suspending or suppressing respiration.

ตะแบก (ต้น) see กระแบก (ต้น)

ตะแบง   dta⁴-baang *adv. adj.* awry; turned toward one side; asquint: ตะแบง (ต้น) (*Ubol to Udorn, Krabin*) *Dipterocarpus intricatus* (*Dipterocarpaceae*); *D. obtusifolius* (Cb. pp. 136, 137): ตะแบงมาน a manner of wearing the scarf-cloth (started from behind, passed under the arm pits, across the chest and with the ends tied behind the neck).

ตะโบม   dta⁴-bom *v.* to comfort; to solace; to cheer.

ตะไบ   dta⁴-bai *v.* to file: *n.* a file.

ตะบัดตะป่อง   dta⁴-bpat⁴-dta⁴-bpaung⁴ *adj.* wavering; faltering; swaying; vacillating (in mind, purpose or manner).

ตะปุ่มตะป่าม, ตะปุ่มตะป่ำ   dta⁴-bpoom⁴-dta⁴-bpam⁴ *adj.* jagged; rough; uneven; notched.

ตะปู incorrect, see ตาปู

ตะพด (ไม้)   dta⁴-pot⁶ *n.* a bamboo spiked stick about a metre long, having a cord attached to the end; a goad (used by farmers): สายตะพด the whip portion of this stick.

ตะพอง see กระบอง

ตะพัง, ตระพัง   dta⁴-pang *n.* a well; an excavation made for water: ตะพังศิลา an artesian well, with gushing water.

ตะพัด (ปลา)   dta⁴-pat⁶ *n. Scleropages formosus* (*Osteoglossidae*), a rare fresh-water fish, which, at present, is only known from Krat (Dept. Agri. & Fisheries).

ตะพั้น   dta⁴-pan⁵ *n.* a disease of infancy characterized by spasms of the hands and feet.

ตะพาก (ปลา)   dta⁴-pak³ *n. Puntius daru-phani (Cyprinidae)*, a small fish which is eaten and liked (Dept. Agri. & Fisheries).

ตะพาน, สะพาน (preferable)   dta⁴-pan *n.* a bridge; a structure spanning two pillars; a passage-way leading from a landing to a floating platform or pontoon: เชิงตะพาน the approach to a bridge: ตะพานช้าง a bridge built of masonry: ตะพานทุ่น a floating, or pontoon bridge: ตะพาน (มี) ล้อ a traversing bridge, *i. e.* one capable of being rolled horizontally backward and forward: ตะพานหก a bascule or draw-bridge: ตะพานห้อย a suspension bridge: ตะพานหัน a swing bridge, one operating on a turn-table: ทอดตะพาน to span; to construct or lay a bridge.

ตะพาบ, ตะพาบน้ำ   dta⁴-pap³ *n.* the snapping turtle; the soft-shelled turtle, *Trionyx cartilagineus*: พระตะพาบ a water-goblet (used by royalty).

ตะพาย   dta⁴-pai *v.* to wear suspended from the shoulder: ตะพายแล่ง to wear suspended from one shoulder down across the breast (as a quiver or canteen strap): สายตะพาย a sash worn over one shoulder and hung diagonally across the breast, the ends meeting at the other side; a rope passed through the septum of the nose of a bullock or buffalo.

ตะพืด, ตะพืดตะพือ   dta⁴-peut⁶ *adj.* continuous; without interruption: *adv.* perseveringly; always; perpetually; continually; regularly: ไล่ตะพืดไป to pursue unremittingly.

ตะพุ่น   dta⁴-poon³ *n.* a class of government conscripts whose duty it is to cut grass for the royal stables: สีตะพุ่น a shade of blue lighter than navy-blue; a bright dark blue.

ตะเพิง   dta⁴-perng *n.* an over-hanging rock, or projecting portion of a mountain.

ตะเพิด   dta⁴-pert³ *v.* to frighten by a loud disturbance; to drive off by loud shouting; to scare by a noise (as when driving game); to eject or expel by creating a commotion (as with gongs, fire-crackers, etc.).

ตะเพ่น   dta⁴-pern³ *adj.* straying; rambling; wandering; roaming.

ตะเพียน (ปลา)   dta⁴-pee-an *n.* a family of common, edible, fresh-water fish, *Puntius javanicus (Cyprinidae)*, a carp: ตะเพียนขาว (ปลา) *P. bramoides*: ตะเพียนทราย (ปลา) *P. brevis*, a carp which attains a length of about ten inches. The flesh is considered good: ตะเพียนหางแดง, ตะเพียนทอง (ปลา) *P. schwanefeldi*: ตะเพียนน้ำเค็ม, ตะโคก (ปลา) *Anodontostoma chacunda (Dorosomidae)*, gizzard shad (Dept. Agri. & Fisheries).

ตะโพก   dta⁴-pok³ *n.* the gluteal portion of the thigh; the buttock.

ตะโพง   dta⁴-pong *v.* to run limpingly (as an injured dog).

ตะโพน   dta⁴-pon *n.* a drum capable of producing eight tones.

ตะเภา   dta⁴-pow *n.* a Chinese junk: ตะเภา (ปลา) *Plectorhinchus pictus (Pomadasidae)* (Suvatti p. 129): ลมตะเภา "junk wind," the southwest monsoon prevailing from April to June, so termed because favourable to junks sailing up to China, also called "kite wind": หนูตะเภา a guinea pig.

ตะม่อ see ตอหม้อ

ตะมอย   dta⁴-moi *n.* a felon; a whitlow; *Paronychia* (Medical Dict.); a species of rattan used medicinally.

ตะรังกะนู   dta⁴-rang-gka⁴-nu *n.* Trengganu, one of the five Unfederated Malay States, bounded on the north by the Gulf of Siam and the China Sea, on the east by the China Sea, on the south by Pahang and on the west by Pahang and Kelantan. In 1785 Burmese troops invaded the Peninsula with partial success. The Siamese then drove out the

Burmese, regaining their control over Kedah and Patani and extending their control to include Kelantan and Trengganu (wood p. 273). Sir Hugh Clifford, the first European to explore the state, described it in 1895 as "a land of streams." No fewer than twelve distinct river basins are to be found in the confines of the territory. The main stream is the Trengganu, which is little else but a succession of formidable falls, the interior being peculiarly inaccessible. Rice, maize, tapioca, yams, gambier (สีเสียด) *Uncaria gambir* (Burk. p. 2198), cutch (Gerini p. 190), sugar-cane and rubber are its chief agricultural interests. The majority of the people devote themselves to fishing. There are extensive tin mines, and gold and wolfram are found in paying quantities. In 1909 Siam signed a treaty whereby this state was turned over to Great Britain: *adj.* used to denote the source.

ตะรังตังช้าง (ต้น)　　dta[4]-rang-dtang-chang[5] *n.* a species of wild tree with poisonous leaves.

ตะราง　　dta[4]-rang *n.* a jail; a penitentiary; a prison.

ตะล่อม　　dta[4]-laum[3] *v.* to garner; to gather together; to assemble together in a heap or pile: ตะล่อมข้าว a rice-bin; a granary.

ตะละ　　dta[4]-la[6] *adv.* as; like; similar to; thus; one by one: ตะละคน one person at a time: ตะละอัน one thing at a time: ตะละว่า exactly as was said.

ตะลาน　　dta[4]-lan *n.* a species of harmless red ant.

ตะลิงปลิง, กะลิงปริง *Siam.* **(ต้น)**　　dta[4]-ling-bpling *n. Averrhoa bilimbi* (*Geraniaceae*), cucumber tree, a small fine-foliage tree, native of tropical America, now widely distributed throughout the tropics. It is cultivated for its acid fruit, which is about three to four inches long, resembling a small green cucumber, which are produced in clusters on the

trunk and oldest branches. It is esteemed in pickles and preserves, being sometimes used for making jam and cooling drinks. It is also much relished in curry. The juice of the fruit takes stains out of linen, and the fruit is sometimes used on the hands as soap, when they are very dirty. There are various medicinal uses of the fruit and leaves. The wood is white, tough, soft, and even-grained (MCM. p. 254: Cb. p. 207: Burk. p. 270).

ตะลีตะลาน　　dta[4]-lee-dta[4]-lan *adj.* speedy; quick; urgent; requiring haste; with precipitation.

ตะลึง, ตกตะลึง　　dta[4]-leung *v.* to be suddenly alarmed, surprised, frightened or terrified.

ตะลุง　　dta[4]-loong *n.* stakes or posts for tethering elephants: หนังตะลุง perforated hides used for making shadow pictures.

ตะลุ่ม　　dta[4]-loom[3] *n.* a tray popularly used by the Siamese for serving priests on ceremonial occasions. It is made of woven rattan, covered with black lacquer and inlaid with mother of pearl. The tray rests on a pedestal.

ตะลุมบอน　　dta[4]-loom-baun *v.* to fight hand to hand with short weapons; to fight at close quarters: ไล่ตะลุมบอน to pursue with ardour and engage in close combat.

ตะลุมพุก　　dta[4]-loom-pook[6] *n.* a wooden mallet fitted with a handle, used for pounding paddy in a mortar: ตะลุมพุก (ปลา) *Hilsa toli* (*Clupeidae*), shad.

ตะลูบ *Korat,* มะขาม *Siam.,* ม่องโคล้ง *Karen,* อำเบียล *Khmer, Surin* **(ต้น)**　　dta[4]-loop[3] *n. Tamarindus indica* (*Leguminosae*), tamarind, a moderate-sized or large, handsome, evergreen, slow-growing tree, with straight, erect stem and small pinnate leaves. It is a long-lived tree, well adapted for avenues. It is noted for its hard and beautifully marked timber. Several varieties are recognized in India. It is readily propagated from seed. The chief use in Siam is as a relish which is made from the pulp of the inner portion of the pods. A sweet-pod form, growing about Nong khai, N. E. Siam, is eaten raw, as one would eat peanuts, and is highly esteemed. The flowers are eaten in curries, and as a vegetable. The leaves and tender seedlings may also be eaten. The boiled or fried seeds are eaten in India. In Java, and elsewhere, medicinal preparations of the pulp and other parts are used as laxatives; on the other hand the seed-coat and bark are astringent. The heart-wood is very hard, but there is little of it. It is used locally for tool-handles, agricultural implements, and other objects kept under cover (MCM. pp. 27, 207, 213, 376, 380, 519: Cb. p. 534: BURK. p. 2121).

ตะลุย　dta[4]-loo-ie　*adv.* unhesitatingly.

ตะเลง　dta[4]-leng, มอญ (more commonly used), รามัญ (their own name for themselves) *n.* the Mons (Kalinga or Talings of Pegu or Martaban) represent one of the oldest civilizations of Indo-China, large numbers of them forming part of the population of Siam today. Early records regarding them date back to the reign of King Asoka of Magadha, India. According to a rock inscription, he invaded the country of the Kalinga in southern India and over a hundred thousand natives were made prisoners, while large numbers were slain. It is probable that, dating from this invasion, these people fled eastward forming Indian colonies along the coasts of the countries now known as Pegu, Siam, Cochin-China and Cambodia. Some time after this conquest King Asoka became a Buddhist and in a literature handed down to them, the Mons claim to have been visited by Buddhist missionaries. In the early centuries of the Christian era, learned men, well-versed in the Tripitaka and in Vedic lore, were at Thaton, the capital of the Mon kingdom. It is certain that, in the

eleventh century, Anawratha, King of Pagan, then rising to power, looked to the learning of the Mon capital to help him in his efforts to purify the religion of his own people. Mon priests going to Pagan were well received by the king, and changed their nationality. From them the Burmese monarch apparently learned all about the resources of the Mon king, and subsequently took steps to acquire the treasures of Thaton. After a protracted seige, the city fell and he carried off to Pagan not only rich treasure but also the king, men of learning, and all upon which he could lay his hands.

For some reason, whether oppression or otherwise, the Mons repeatedly sought refuge in Siam and at different times during the Siam-Burma wars were brought over as prisoners of war. There were at least three great immigrations of Mons to Siam, perhaps four, as Siamese history records. They settled chiefly in settlements of their own which are to be found on the Meklong, Petchaburi and Tachin rivers, at Paklat, above Lopburi, along the early trade routes between Burma and Siam, etc. In the main they are agriculturists (Halliday: Wood), but have extensive kilns for the burning of red pottery, bricks, floor and roof tiles,—an industry which was once in their hands.

ตะแลงแกง　dta[4]-laang-gkaang　*n.* a place for the execution of criminals.

ตะไล　dta[4]-lai　*n.* small porcelain cups, used for steaming custard, or dispensing ointment; a kind of fireworks which, when lighted, go sailing in the air by means of small palm-leaf blades or wings: ขนมถ้วยตะไล a custard sweetmeat steamed in a porcelain cup.

ตะวัน, ตระวัน　dta[4]-wan　*n.* the sun: ตะวันขึ้น sunrise: ตะวันตก sunset; the west: ตะวันบ่าย afternoon: ตะวันเที่ยง noonday: ตะวันออก the east: ตะวันสาย late in the day; nearing noon,

ตะเวน, ตระเวน dta⁴-wen *v.* to police ; to patrol ; to be on watch or guard ; to act as a sentinel : ตะเวนคนโทษ to keep watch over criminals ; to conduct criminals ignominiously around the town (Pale.) : กองตะเวน a detachment of police.

ตะหนึ่งรัด dta⁴-neung⁴-rat⁶ *Cam. adj.* main ; mighty ; highest ; chief ; foremost.

ตะหลุง dta⁴-loong² *n.* the four axle supports of an ox-cart.

ตะแหมะแขะ dta⁴-maa⁴-kaa⁴ used as a suffix indicating the superlative degree of low, *ex.* เตี้ยตะแหมะแขะ.

ตัก dtuk⁴ *v.* to dip up or out : *n.* the lap : การตัก the act of dipping out with a spoon or any utensil : ตัก (ปลา) *Hemirhamphus unifasciatus (Hemiramphidae)*, half-beak (suvatti p. 92) : ตักบาตร์ to give alms to a Buddhist monk.

ตักก dtuk⁴-gka⁴ *n.* buttermilk mixed with water (chd. p. 494).

ตักกสิลา dtuk⁴-gka⁴-si⁴-lah *P. n.* the city of Takshasila in the Punjab. It was a renowned university town (chd. p. 494). It was the residence of Taksha, son of Bharata, and nephew of Rama-chandra, and perhaps took its name from him (H. C. D. p. 316). Alexander the Great called this city Taxila, by which name the ruins are generally known. There is no city there now.

ตักเตือน see เตือน

ตักแตน, ตั๊กกะแตน dtuk⁴-gka⁴-dtaan *n.* a grasshopper.

ตักร dtuk⁴ *S. n.* buttermilk mixed with a third part of water (chd. p. 431) : ตักรบิณฑ์ curd : ตักรสาร fresh butter.

ตักษก, ตัจฉก see ดักษก

ตักษณ dtuk⁴-sa⁴-na⁶ *S. n. lit.* "instruments for cutting or filing," *i. e.* a knife ; a file ; an ax.

ตักษณี, ตักฉนี dtuk⁴-sa⁴-nee *P. S. n.* an ax ; an adze.

ตั้ง dtang *n.* a gluey, viscous substance composed of gum and bullock's hair, used for ensnaring birds or insects ; fly paste : *onomat.* from the sound of something heavy falling.

ตั้ง, บิฐ dtang⁴ *n.* a chair ; a seat ; a stool ; a footstool ; a square seat raised on feet, fitted with, or without a back.

ตั้ง dtung³ *v.* to appoint ; to establish ; to decree ; to ordain ; to assign ; to set or place in a position : *n.* a pile (as dishes or saucers) ; square cuts of sweetmeat ; layers, cakes, or plugs of tobacco : ตั้งไข่ to train an infant to stand (generally accompanied by a nursery song) : ตั้งครรภ์ to be impregnated ; to become pregnant : ตั้งใจ to fix the mind upon ; to intend ; to purpose ; to contemplate accomplishing : ตั้งชื่อ, ให้ชื่อ, ขนานนาม to name : ตั้งเดือน about a month in time : ตั้งต้น, เริ่มทำ, ขึ้นต้น to begin ; to commence : ตั้งแต่ from ; since the...... : ตั้งแต่ง to install in a position of rank ; to raise to a position of honour : ตั้งแต่นั้นมา from that time to this : ตั้งแต่นี้จนถึง from this time to that : ตั้งแต่นี้ไป from this time forward ; henceforth : ตงโต๊ะ to lay the table (as for a meal) : ตั้งปี about a year in time : ตั้งกฎหมาย, ออกกฎหมาย to legislate : ตั้งประเด็น *legal* to fix the issue : ตั้งราคา to assess : ตั้งหน้า to set the face towards ; to determine ; to intend.

ตั้งเกีย dtung-gkee-ah² *n.* Tonkin.

ตั้งเม dtung-may *n.* toffy.

ตั้งวาย, ถวาย dtung-wai *Cam. v.* to give ; to present (as to a prince).

ตั้งโอ๋ (ผัก) dtung³-oh² *Chin. n. Apium graveolens (Umbelliferae)*, celery, a vegetable used for food, and as a flavouring (cb. p. 788 : V. P. p. 125 : Burk. p. 192).

ตัณฑุล   dtan-doon *P. S. n.* rice husked, winnowed, and ready for boiling (chd. p. 495); grain after threshing and winnowing.

ตัณหา, ตฤษณา, ดำฤษณา   dtan-hah[2] *P. n.* lust; longing for; desire; carnal appetite; concupiscence; human passion; craving (chd. p. 495): ตัณหาตาบอด *prov.* love is blind.

ตัด   dtat[4] *v.* to cut off; to sever; to cut loose from; to hew (as wood): ตัดใจ to manifest bravery; to be firm in confronting danger or pain; to cease from solicitude and anxiety for oneself: ตัดกัน to sever the bond of friendship; *geometry* to meet or to cross (as lines): ตัดทาง to obstruct the passage of; to hinder from passing; to bar; to stop; to clog or impede; to close a way or passage: ตัดพ่อ to manifest lack of respect for parents or relatives, by word or deed: ตัดสิน to decide; to give a final judgement or opinion: ตัดสิทธิ์ to deprive one of personal rights; to infringe on a right: ตัดหัว to behead; to decapitate.

ตถิย์   dtat[4] *S. n.* truth; veracity: *adv.* verily; in truth; in fact; really; truly; with great confidence (s. e. d. p. 434).

ตัน ๑   dtan *Eng. n.* one ton; a weight equal to 1680 catties or 2,240 pounds.

ตัน ๒   dtan *adj.* not hollow all the way through; clogged; choked: กระบอกปืนนั้นตัน that gun is choked: ตันปัญญา to be unable to decide, think, say or do; to be irresolute; to waver: ตันอกตันใจ to be puzzled, bewildered, or perplexed; to be in an awkward position.

ตันตระ   see ดนตร์

ตันติ   dtan-dti[4] *P. S. n.* a string; a line; a cord; the string of a lute; a sacred text; a passage from a sacred text (chd. p. 496); pattern; method; plan; system: ตันติภาษา a systematized language.

ตันหยง, กุน *Jav.*, พิกุล *Siam.* (ต้น)   dtan-yong[2] *n. Mimusops elengi (Sapotaceae)*, a large tree, found widely distributed in the southern parts of India, in Burma and Ceylon. The leaves are green, shining, elliptic and glabrous; the flowers are axillary, solitary, in pairs, or fascicled and fragrant; the corolla is white. The fruit is ovoid, about an inch or less long, one or rarely two-seeded. It yields a gum known as Madras gum, while the fruits are used medicinally in diseases of the gums and teeth. By distillation, a sweet-scented water may be obtained which is used as a stimulant in south India. The chief uses of the tree are medicinal. A volatile oil is distilled from the flowers, while a fixed oil, which is used for culinary purposes, and is also burned in lamps, is obtained from the seeds by compression. It is supposed to be sacred to the Mohammedans of southern India. In Siam an infusion is used as a cosmetic after bathing (The Ornamental Trees of Hawaii p. 172: V. P. pp. 30, 185: MCM. p. 379: Burk. p. 1475).

ตันเหิม, ดันเหิม   dtan-herm[2] *v.* to have an enjoyable time; to be happy; to have freedom from care.

ตับ   dtap[4] *n.* the liver; a split bamboo for spitting fish; a forked stick for roasting or broiling meat or fish; a numerical designatory particle for sewed strips of nipa palm used for roofing purposes, or rows of guns in a rack, or cartridges in a case, *ex.* ปืนห้าตับ, ลูก-ปืนสองตับ, จาก ๕ ตับ: ตับขนุน (ปลา) *Polynemus heptadactylus (Polynemidae)*, thread-fins (suvatti p. 109): ตับแข็ง (โรค) cirrhosis of the liver, a disease characterized by a thickening of the elements of the stroma, which contract and produce a degeneration of the organ: ตับคา (นก) blue tailed bee-eater, *Merops philippinus* (Gaird. J. S. S. IX, 1, p. 6): ตับเต่า (ปลา) *Hemirhamphus var. (Hemiramphidae)*, half-beaks (suvatti p. 91): ตับเต่า (ต้น) a species of water plant and mushroom: ตับเต่าน้อย *n. Laos*, กล้วยไม้ตับเต่า *Siam.* (ต้น)

Desmos dubius (*Anonaceae*) (cb. p. 39): ตับเป็ด (หิน) a black rock, which, when pulverized, is used as a colouring matter for potter's clay : ตับเป็ด (สี) a dark red colour (as that of a duck's liver): ตับเหล็ก the entrails of swine : ตับอ่อน the pancreas (human): ไม้ตับจาก the rods or strips of bamboo to which nipa palm leaves are sewed.

ตัว   dtoo-ah *n.* a body; a person; oneself; a numerical designatory particle for animals, cigars, or actors: ตัวกลั่น a chosen one: ตัวการ, ตัวเอ้ the principal one, a ringleader, or the agent in an act of violence or crime: ตัวเก็ง the most desperate in an association of out-laws; the star in a troupe of actors: ตัวคูณ the multiplier: ตัวตั้ง the one responsible for; the dividend; the multiplicand: ตัวแทนฐานประกัน a creditor's agent: ตัวผู้ the male (of animals): ตัวเมีย the female (of animals): ตัวไม้ a prepared piece of timber (as for a house or building): ตัวหาร the divisor: แก้ตัว to make excuses; to exculpate oneself: ถือตัว to be proud, vain, or haughty: ถือไพ่ตัวเก็ง to hold a trump card; to be sure to win: เป็นตัวอย่าง for example; as an example to others: ไม่เป็นตัว incorporeal: เลี้ยงตัวเอ็ง self-supporting: สิ้นตัว poverty-stricken; indigent: เสียตัวเสียคน to dishonour oneself: ออกตัว to free oneself; to evade blame.

ตั๋ว   dtoo-ah[2] *Chin.* a ticket: ตั๋วจับฉลาก a lottery ticket: ตั๋วชานชาลา a railroad platform ticket: ตั๋วดุลคร a theatre ticket: ตั๋วโดยสารเรือ a boat ticket: ตั๋วไปมา a return ticket: ตั๋วรถไฟ a railroad ticket: ตั๋วแลกเงิน a bill of exchange.

ตั๋วโผ   dtoo-ah[3]-poh[2] *Chin. n.* the driller, or leader of the actors of a theatrical troupe, or of a Chinese comedy play; the owner of an orchestra.

ตั๋วโฮ่งจี๊ *Chin.* (for the seeds), กระเบา, กะ-เบา, กระเบาน้ำ *Siam.,* กาหลง *Siam.* (for flowers only), กะเบา *Laos,* กราเบาตึ๊ก *Khmer* (ต้น)   dtoo-ah[3]-hong[3]-chee[6] *n. Hydnocarpus anthelminthica* (*Bixaceae*), a tree of Indo-China and Siam. It grows to a considerable size, trees being known with a girth of over 15 feet at 6 feet from the ground. Its seeds are brought to Bangkok where they are used as a vermifuge, and the oil as a remedy for leprosy and skin complaints. This tree is chief of those called กระเบา by the Siamese and is similar to the *H. kurzii.* In Cambodia the oil is used for illumination. The timber is light in colour, and is sometimes cut into planks (Burk. p. 1207); *H. wightiana,* a medium-sized tree of the ghats of south-western India. An oil similar to chaulmoogra oil is obtained from the seed, which is sometimes used as a substitute for the true chaulmoogra oil (MCM. pp. 386, 396, 463 : Cb. p. 96 : BURK. p. 1209).

ตา ๑   dtah *n.* maternal grandfather; used as an honorary title for any old man : ตาทวด a maternal great grandfather: พ่อตา a father-in-law.

ตา ๒   dtah *n.* the eye; the organ of sight; the node or joint of a stem; the meshes of a net, or the squares in a chess-board; interstices: แก้วตา the crystalline lens : ขนตา eyelashes: ต่อมตา the lacrymal gland : ตาสั้น myopia; near-sightedness : น้ำตา tears: ม่านตา the iris : ลูกตา the eyeball : หนังตา the eyelids: หัวตา the inner or nasal canthus of the eye: หางตา the outer or temporal canthus of the eye.

ตา ๓   dtah *n.* time, turn, or round to play (as in a card game); opportunity : ตากบตาเขียด *lit.* "frog's eyes," *i. e.* parboiled (an idiomatic expression to indicate parboiled rice): ตากุ้ง *lit.* "shrimp's eye" *i. e.* dark-purple (as the colour of a shrimp's eyes): ตาไก้ง (ผ้า) cloth woven with large designs: ตาไก่ *lit.* "a hen's eye," *i. e.* the character (๏) sometimes used to indicate the beginning of a paragraph; eyelets:

ตาข่าย the interspaces, or meshes of a net (as fish-nets or rabbit-snares): ตาขาว the sclerotic coat of the eye; the white portion of the eye: *adj.* fearful; easily frightened; cowardly; faint-hearted; timid; afraid: ตาแข็ง to be sleepless; to have insomnia; to be wakeful; to have lost the normal sensitiveness of the eye: ตาค้าง to remain with the eyes open (as a dead person); to be unable to close the eyelids: ตาจน a check-mate; a complete check; a time of defeat or overthrow: ตาชง a balance; scales for weighing purposes; dots or marks indicating fractions in a weigh-scale: ตาช้าง, มะกล่ำตาช้าง (ต้น) a species of *Adenanthera pavonina* (*Leguminosae*), bead-tree, a moderate-sized, quickgrowing, upright tree, with small pinnate leaves and light, open foliage. The characteristic bright-red, hard seeds are used for necklaces, etc. and also for jewellers' and apothecaries' weights. The red dye from the wood makes it a substitute for red sanders, but it is little used in dyeing. The leaves are medicinal (McM. pp. 206, 214, 461, 512, 516: Burk. p. 46): ตาช้างตาม้า, ตาม้าตาเรือ an idiomatic expression to indicate a condition of uncertainty or vacillation between right and wrong, or what should or should not be done: ตาเดียว, ลิ้นหมา (ปลา) *Cynoglossus microlepis* (*Cynoglossidae*), a sole having both eyes on the same side of the head (Dept. Agri. & Fisheries): ตาแดง, ตะเพียนทราย (ปลา) *Dangila sumatrana* (*Cyprinidae*), a carp; *Cyclocheilichthys apogon*, a carp about 10 inches long (Burk. p. 722: Dept. Agri. & Fisheries): ตาตั๊กแตน (ต้น) *Impatiens balsamina* (*Balsaminaceae*), the garden balsam plant, used medicinally. It is widely known in Asia that the flowers may be used instead of henna for dyeing the finger-nails (Burk. p. 1227): ตาตุ่ม bone prominences at the ankle; a tuberosity or prominence of a bone (as tibia or fibula); a tree, the gum of which, when eaten, causes diarrhoea: ตาตุ่ม see ตาเหลือก(ปลา): ตาตุ่มใน inner malleolus of the tibia: ตาตุ่มนอก outer malleolus of the fibula: ตาเต็ง Chinese weighing scales: ตาถั่ว one having an opaque spot or area on the cornea (a term of contempt): ตาโถง a large-meshed cloth: ตาทัพ the route that an army is going to take, compared to the squares or moves in a chess game: ตานกแก้ว a prominence of bone at the wrist: ตานิน (ปลา) *Amblyrhynchichthys truncatus* (*Cyprinidae*) (Suvatti p. 46): ตาน้ำ a spring; a subterranian course or vein of water: ตาบอด blindness; blind: ตาปลา corns (on the toes): ตาปี yearly; annually; lasting a year; coming every year: ตาปี-ตาชาติ always; evermore; during eternity; for an indefinite future period: ตาปู *lit.* "crab's eyes," *i.e.* a kind of nail (ตะปู is the usual spelling for "nail"): ตาปูควง a screw: ตาโป้ง the space crossed by moving a chessman diagonally: ตาโพลง open-eyed amazement: ตาพอง open-eyed surprise: ตาพอง (ปลา) *Stromateus sinensis* (*Stromateidae*), butter-fish, the most highly esteemed fish in Siamese waters (Suvatti p. 113): ตามด a minute hole; the hole of an ant's nest; a small leak (as in the bottom of a rice pot or any utensil): ตาราง the interspaces or meshes between lines drawn, in lattice-work, or in gratings: ตารางวา a square wah or four square metres: ตารางเหล็ก an iron grating placed under the body in cremations: ตารางเหลี่ยม a quadrangle: ตาร้าย an ill-omen according to one's horoscope; a time of calamity, misfortune, disaster, or adversity: ตาริ้ว the arrangement of infantry or people in two or more parallel lines, or in single files: ตาเรือ the eyes on a boat or junk: ตาลาน (งูเห่า) a species of cobra: ตาลีตาลาน to hasten: ตาเมล็ดงา a minute hole (the size of a sesame seed): ตาสมุคร cloth with small, square, checked designs: ตาหมากรุก the squares on a chess board: ตาเหล่ crosseyed: ตาเหลือก, ตาตุ่ม (ปลา) *Megalops cyprinoides* (*Elopidae*), a giant herring (Burk. p. 1430); *Pellona dussumieri* (*Clupeidae*), a bony, insipid fish which salts well (Dept. Agri.

& Fisheries: BURK. p. 1685): ไม่ดูตามม้าตาเรือ *idiom.* to move carelessly or blindly into a dangerous zone.

ตาก　　dtak[4] *v.* to expose or be exposed to the air, sun or rain; to air or dry; to be sun-dried: *adj.* separated; unconnected; distinct: ควายเขาตาก a buffalo whose horns are spreading or pointing divergently: เดินตากฝน, เดินตรำฝน to travel or walk exposed to the rain: ตากตน to expose oneself to sun or breeze.

ตากล่ำ, มะกล่ำตาหนู *Siam.,* เคือกำ, กำ่ตาไก่, มะกำ่แดง *Laos,* เกมกรอม *Khmer, Surin* (ต้น)　dtah-gklum[4] *n. Abrus precatorius* (*Leguminosae*), Indian liquorice (cb. p. 435: MCM. pp. 377, 383, 461: BURK. p. 4): see กล่ำ (ต้น).

ต่าง ๑　dtang[4] *n.* a pack-saddle: ม้าต่าง a pack-horse.

ต่าง ๒　dtang[4] *adj.* various; diverse; different: *pron.* a collective pronoun, *ex.* ต่างตึกัน: *adv.* instead of; in place of: ต่าง ๆ promiscuous; miscellaneous; mixed; mingled; dissimilar; diverse: ต่างตาต่างใจ substitution; a substitute; one who, or that which is substituted in place of another; to differ in opinion: ต่างท้อง (คน) a half-brother or sister: ต่างประเทศ a foreigner; an alien: ต่างว่า for instance; to wit; thus; as if; used to introduce a result: ต่างหน้า (คน) a stranger: ต่างหาก separate; disconnected; detached; distinct: ต่างหูต่างตา one empowered to act for another; a representative: หน้าต่าง a window: ต่างคนต่างมีความเห็น each differing in opinion: ต่างคนต่างไป each going independently.

ต่างน้อย, มันสำปะหลัง (ต้น)　dtang[4]-noi[5] *n. Manihot utilissima* (*Euphorbiaceae*), tapioca, the cassava, a shrubby perennial 6 to 7 ft. high. Two distinct kinds are recognised, *viz.* "bitter" and "sweet" (*M. utilissima* and *M. aipi* respectively), and of these there are many varieties. All are characterized by the presence of hydrocyanic or prussic acid, which not infrequently results fatally to persons eating the roots carelessly prepared. The large tuberous roots being cooked, are used as a vegetable, or made into cassava meal and bread. The roots are grown on a large scale in south Siam where starch is made from them. The wet starch is rolled into small balls, cooked and dried to make the commercial "sago" or "tapioca." (MCM. p. 299: BURK. p. 1411: V. P. p. 125): มันสำปะหลัง is the name commonly used in Siam.

ตาด (ผ้า)　dtat[4] *n.* a linen cloth interwoven with silver or copper threads; (ที่) a waterfall.

ตาตุ่มทะเล (ต้น)　dtah-dtoom[4]-ta[6]-lay *n. Excoecaria agallocha* (*Euphorbiaceae*), a small tree with milky, acrid juice which blisters the skin. The tree is held in fear by the natives of Fiji, where the juice is used as a cure for leprosy (MCM. p. 384: BURK. p. 990: V. P. p. 122).

ตาน (โรค)　dtan *n.* a disease common to Siamese childhood: ตานขะโมย a common chronic ailment of Siamese children characterized by thin arms and legs but enlarged abdomen (usually due to intestinal worms): ตานครบ *Siam.,* โดนทุ่ง *Siam. Peninsula,* มะโหกต้น *Laos* (ต้น) *Erythroxylum cambodianum* (*Erythroxylaceae*) (cb. p. 199: V. P. p. 129): ตานควาย (*Laos*) (ต้น) *Nauclea sessilifolia* (*Rubiaceae*) (V. P. p. 129): ตานจอมทอง *Siam. Chumpawn,* ทองเครือ *Siam.,* กว่าวเคือ, จานเคือ *Laos,* โพ้ตะกุ *Karen, Kanburi* (ต้น) *Butea superba* (*Leguminosae*), a host-plant for the lac insect. It also yields gum. In Cambodia it is used as a lotion and in poultices (cb. p. 445: BURK. p. 384): ตานดำ *Siam. Peninsula* (ต้น) *Diospyros montana* (*Ebenaceae*), a small tree very widely distributed through much of India and forward to Australia. The timber is strong and is used in India for small objects (**v.** P. p. 129 : Burk. p. 833) ; *D. ebenum*, ebony (MCM. p. 218 : Burk. p. 829) : ตานเสี้ยน (ต้น) a medicinal plant : ตานทราย, *Siam. Peninsula* (ต้น) *Waltheria indica (Stercubiaceae)*, an herb found in China, India and throughout Malaysia. In the Philippine Islands the plant is regarded as a febrifuge and anti-syphilitic (V. P. p. 130 : Burk. p. 2253) : ตานหม่อน (ต้น) *Vernonia elaeugnifolia (Compositae)*, an herb or shrub. The smoke of the burning wood is used in Cambodia for treating ulceration of the nose (V. P. p. 130 : Burk. p. 2226).

ต้าน   dtan[4] *adj.* outer ; external ; towards or going to the extreme side ; a word of command used by the ploughman to indicate to the buffalo his desire to plough close to the outermost boundary.

ต้าน   dtan[3] *v.* to resist ; to oppose ; to hinder ; to thwart : ต้านทาน to withstand : to impede, *ex.* ต้านทานไม่ไหว being impossible to withstand ; indomitable ; irresistable.

ตาน   dtah-nee *n.* the Malays of Pattani (ปัตตานี) ; a species of banana, the meat of which is full of seeds ; thick oil used as hair-oil.

ตาบ   dtap[4] *n.* a decorated or embroidered collar or neck-piece worn by Siamese actors : ตาบทิศ two bands ornamented with gold and silver tinsel or studded with precious stones, worn from each shoulder, crossing in the front and in the back. They are secured in place with elaborate brooches and form part of an actress' stage costume.

ตาบัง   *Pang-nga, Satul,* หูกวาง *Siam.* (ต้น) dtah-bpang *n. Terminalia catappa (Combretaceae)*, Singapore almond, a tall tree, native only upon the Pacific, but in cultivation far beyond its natural area. It has the disadvantage of shedding its leaves twice a year, usually during February and September, causing a considerable litter on the ground.

Before dropping the leaves, however, it is a striking object, the mature leaves becoming bright yellowish-red. The bark contains tannin, which is used as an astringent in dysentery, etc. The oil extracted from the fruit is medicinal, equally with almond oil (MCM. p. 105 : Cb. pp. 601, 602 : Burk. p. 2137) : หูกวาง is the usual Siamese name.

ตาผึ้ง see ตลิ่ง

ตาฟาง (นก)   dtah-fang *n.* the Burmese long-tailed night-jar, *Caprimulgus macrurus bimaculatus* (Herb. N. H. J. S. S. VI, 3, p. 303).

ตาม   dtam *v.* to follow ; to accompany : to fetch ; to go or come for : *adj.* following ; succeeding ; ensuing : ตามความจริง ipso facto ; according to the facts : ตามใจ to yield to the wish of another ; to acquiesce ; to concur : ตามตอบแทนกัน mutually ; reciprocally : ตามแต่จะทำได้ all that one can do : ตามแต่จะให้ whatever is seen fit to give : ตามแต่จะได้ whatever is possible to get : ตามที่ as it may be ; as is wished : ตามรูปลูกบาศก์ cubical ; cuboidal : ตามไป to follow after ; to pursue : ตามผิว superficially : ตามมี according to the means available ; in conformity to the circumstances ; suitable to what one has : ตามมีตามเกิด according to one's possessions and inheritance : ตามเรื่อง according to the inevitable ; let the matter drop : ตามว่า as is said or reported to be : ตามสมควร as is fitting or proper : ทำตาม to imitate ; to follow the example of : ตามเส้น linear ; lineal : ทำตามตำแหน่ง done in an official capacity ; authoritative : ไปตามมา to go and bring ; to fetch ; to go and get.

ตามพะ see ตามพ์ p. 325.

ตาย   dtai *v.* to die ; to expire ; to perish ; to terminate (as a license) ; to reach the time limit : *adj.* lifeless ; immovable ; apathetic ; terminated ; insensible (as a paralysed limb) ; unexploded (as a bomb) : ตายขุย to bear fruit once and then die (as the bamboo) :

ตายคาที่ immediate death: ตายโคม unfruit-ful; unproductive; unfertile (as some eggs): ตายใจ to trust implicitly; to confide in completely; to repose absolute confidence in: ตายซาก to die, leaving the body exposed to the air until it becomes desiccated (as frogs or spiders): ตายด้าน to fail to ignite or to explode (as fireworks): ตายตัว impossible to move; unchangeable; checkmated; defeated; cornered (as in chess): ตายทั้งกรม dying during pregnancy (including the foetus): ตายฝอย dying from drought (as seedling rice): ตายพราย to die before the fruit is formed (as some species of bananas): ตายห่า to die from some form of contagious disease: ตาย-โหง to die an unnatural death: แทบตาย *colloq.* meaning "near to death," *as,* "I almost died running": เป็นตายเท่ากัน a condition of uncertainty as to whether the result will be life or death: เป็นหรือตาย are you, or is it alive or dead? น้ำตาย a neap tide: ไม่รู้ตาย incorruptible; everlasting; eternal.

ต้าย dtai[3] *n.* the pillars or posts of a stock-ade, fence, dike, bund, or break-water.

ตาราไต dtah-rah-dtai *Jav. n.* a water-lily; the lotus flower.

ตาล dtan *n.* (1) (ต้น) *Borassus flabelliformis* (*Palmae*), the palmyra tree or fan-palm. It is considered as a measure of height. To pierce seven fan-palms with one shot is held to be a great feat: (2) a measure, the short span: (3) a musical instrument of metal struck with the hand or a stick; a gong; a cymbal (chd. p. 495): ตาลตะโหนด (ต้น) *Borassus flabel-lifera* (*Palmae*), an erect dioecious palm, 60 to 70 ft. high, with a stout, erect trunk and a crown of short, rigid, fan-shaped leaves. Like the coconut palm, the palmyra supplies food and drink and serves numerous uses; no part of it is wasted; the fruit and leaves are the most important. The large black fruits, "nots," produced in a cluster at the base of the leaves, contain a refreshing sap, much relished as a cooling drink; the soft kernels

of the young fruits are much used as an article of food. The leaves have long been used as a writing material, probably long before the great Chinese traveller Huien Tsiang recorded this use between 629 and 646 A.D. They are also plaited to make hats, bags, buckets, etc. and are used for priests' fans, the petiole making the handle and the blade trimmed to shape. In Siam, sugar is one of the major products (mcm. p. 362: burk. p. 347): ตาลบัตร a palm leaf with a long handle furnished to Buddhist monks, and used as a fan or face-screen (chd. p. 495). It is probable that the word "talapoin" used to designate Buddhist priests, is a corruption of this word: ตาลบัตรฤๅษี *Siam.,* ตองต้วม *N. Laos* (ต้น) *Leea macrophylla* (*Leea-ceae*), (cb. p. 319); *Opuntia dillenii* (*Cacta-ceae*); *O. ficus-indica*. These as well as other species of *Opuntia*, which have become a serious pest in certain countries, are some-times turned into a useful food for stock in periods of drought or scarcity of food. It is best when boiled or crushed and flavoured with salt, or mixed with ensilage or other fodder, and in this way is said to have a fat-tening effect. The pear-shaped fruit is edible. A spineless form, raised by the late Mr. Bur-bank in California, is well spoken of as stock feed (mcm. pp. 74, 171, 267, 454, 475, 477): *Lim-nocharis flava* (*Alismaceae*), an herb (the hermit's water-lily) spreading along ditches and rice-fields. In Pattani it is called บอนจีน. Vanpruk records นางกวัก as a Siamese name for it. This would indicate a confusion of classification (v. p. p. 121: burk. p. 1347): น้ำตาล sugar: น้ำตาลกรวด rock-sugar or candy: น้ำตาลทราย granulated sugar.

ตาลุ dtah-loo[6] *P.S. n.* the palate; the ceiling (s. e. d. p. 445).

ตาลุช dtah-loo[6]-cha[6] *P. n.* a palatal sound (chd. p. 496); see ตาลุช.

ตาว dtow *n.* a sword; a long knife: a tree similar to เต่าร้าง (ต้น).

ตาพ   dtan *P. n.* a key; a bolt; a door-latch (chd. p. 495).

ตาเสือ *Siam.,* มะหางก่าน *N. Laos,* ตาบู *Laos, Krabin,* โทะกาช่า *Karen, Nakawn Sawan* (ต้น)   dtah-seu-ah[2] *n. Amoora polystachya* (*Meliaceae*), a moderate-sized tree. Oil from the seed is used for lighting, etc. (MCM. p. 394 : Cb. p. 261 : V. P. p. 122).

ตำ   dtum *v.* to pierce; to puncture; to be pricked (as by a thorn); to pound (as paddy in a mortar); to pulverize (by means of a mortar and pestle); to triturate (as crude medicinal plants).

ต่ำ   dtum[4] *adj.* low; depressed; dwarfed: ต่ำใจ to be peeved; to be vexed; to be disheartened; to be piqued: ต่ำช้า depraved; bad; corrupted; contaminated; unworthy; degraded: ต่ำตน to abase or humiliate oneself: ที่ต่ำ a place that has sunken or become low: ไม่ต่ำกว่า not less than: ราคาเงินตกต่ำไป a fall in the exchange of money; a devaluation of the currency: ราคาตกต่ำไป to be depreciated in price.

ตำนาน   dtum-nan *n.* history; a record or story of the past; a series of accounts: ผู้แต่งตำนาน an historian; a chronicler or recorder of events, past or present.

ตำเนิน (ห่ามมาก)   dtum-nern *adj.* being still unripe or green (as fruit); nearly ripe.

ตำบล   dtum-bon *n.* a place; locality; district; commune; a group of houses.

ตำปุก   dtum[3]-bpook[4] *onomat.* from the sound of a heavy article falling from a height.

ตำผาง   dtum[3]-pang[2] *onomat.* from the sound as when two articles clash in falling.

ตำพรวด   dtum[3]-proo-at[3] *onomot.* from the sound as when an article drops into a bush, or into tall grass.

ตำแย (ต้น)   dtam-yaa *n. Laportea crenulata* (*Urticaceae*), fever-nettle, devil-nettle, a large shrub with large oval leaves. The whole plant is clothed with minute, irritant hairs, which sting severely, the distressing effects often remaining for many days (V. P. p. 123 : MCM. p. 385): ตำแยช้าง (ต้น) *Girardinia heterophylla* (*Urticaceae*), elephant or nilgiri-nettle, a tall herb, covered with stinging, poisonous hairs (V. P. p. 123 : MCM. p. 385): ตำแยตัวผู้, ตำแยแมว (ต้น) *Acalypha indica* (*Euphorbiaceae*), an herb found in fields and waste places throughout the hotter parts of the world. It is vermifugal and carminative, and is also applied to sores. The leaves are edible (MCM. pp. 311, 377 : V. P. p. 123 : Burk. p. 25): ตำแยตัวเมีย (ต้น) *Fleurya interrupta* (*Urticaceae*), an herb found throughout the tropics of the Old World, in some places occurring as a garden weed (V. P. p. 123 : Burk. p. 1026): ตำแยใหญ่ *Nakorn Rachasima* (ต้น), *Mucuna monosperma* (*Leguminosae*) (Cb. p. 444): หมอตำแย a midwife; an accoucheur of the Old School.

ตำรวจ   dtam-roo-at[4] *n.* the police: ตำรวจนครบาล local police force; city police: ตำรวจภูธร provincial gendermerie: ตำรวจลับ police in mufti; police in civilian clothes; detectives: ตำรวจสภา Assembly Guard: ตำรวจหลวง palace police; palace guard.

ตำรับ   dtam-rap[4] *n.* a formula; a recipe; a prescription; a book of formulas: ตำรับยา a medical prescription.

ตำรา   dtam-rah *n.* technical books; a collection of recipes or formulas; a text-book.

ตำฤษ see ตฤษ

ตำลึง   dtam-leung *n.* a value, or weight of four ticals: ตำลึง, ผักตำลึง *Siam.,* ผักแคบ *Laos, Chiengmai* (ต้น) *Coccinia indica* (*Cucurbitaceae*), a gourd with a small fruit, cultivated in the Straits by Javanese immigrants, but wild throughout most of Malaysia. The inhabitants of Indo-China and Java eat the young shoots and the fruit when cooked with rice ; sometimes the fruits are candied. In Siam it serves as a vegetable ; in India the fruits are eaten. In India and the Dutch Indies the whole plant is medicinal (Burk. p. 593) ; *C. cordifolia* (Cb. p. 761 : V. P. p. 124) : ตำลึงตัวผู้ *Siam., Prachuap,* บังกา-เริ่น *Siam., Kanburi* (ต้น) *Melothria heterophylla (Cucurbitaceae),* a sprawling or climbing plant found from Afghanistan to Malaysia. Its fruits can be eaten unripe as a green vegetable. The root is considered to be a purgative (Burk. p. 1450) ; *M. leucocarpa* (Cb. pp. 763, 764) : ตำลึงทอง (ต้น) *Heterostemma sp.* (V. P. p. 124).

ตำเสา *Siam. Peninsula* (ต้น) dtam-sow[2] *n. Fagraea fragrans (Loganiaceae),* a handsome, upright, evergreen, small-leaved tree of Malaya. Though of rather slow growth, this has excellent qualities for an avenue tree, retaining its upright, well-balanced habit (MCM. pp. 99, 212 : V.P. p. 124) : ตำเสาหนู *Siam. Peninsula,* ฝาดแดง (ต้น) *Lumnitzera coccinea (Combretaceae),* a tree of tidal swamps, found from the east coast of Africa to the Pacific. In the Malay Peninsula it is common. It is often seen as a small tree but may grow to more than 100 feet in height. The timber is hard and very durable. The wood is dark grey, becoming lighter after exposure to the air. It is fine-grained and keeps its shape remarkably well. When first cut, it has the odour of roses. In consequence of the demand for the timber, the tree is usually cut before it has attained a large size. The timber is suitable for bridges, wharf-building, axles of carts, flooring, tool-handles, etc. (V. P. p. 125 : Burk. p. 1372).

ตำหนัก dtam-nak[4] *n.* a house, home or residence of royalty : พระตำหนัก the abode of a prince or princess.

ตำหนิ dtam-ni[4] *n.* a fault ; a defect ; a blemish or scar ; an imperfection ; a failing :

คนมีตำหนิ one tainted with a trace or germ of disease ; one with a tarnished character ; one with a dishonoured history (as by corruption and vice) : ขี้ตำหนิ to point out the vices or imperfections of.

ตำหยาว, ส้มม่วงชูหน่วย *Siam. Peninsula,* มะม่วงหิมพานต์ *Siam.,* ยาร่วง *Siam. Pattani,* มะม่วงเล็ดล่อ, มะม่วงสิงหพ, มะม่วงกุลา, มะม่วงหยอด *Laos,* มะม่วงกาสอ *Laos, Lapla* (ต้น) dtam-yow[2] *n. Anacardium occidentale (Anacardiaceae),* cashew-nut, a shrub or small tree, found rather widely in tropical America, and probably carried by the Portuguese to Malaysia. The fruit consists of two distinct parts, *viz.* (a) the large swollen pear-shaped stalk (cashew apple), 2 to 4 inches long, which is juicy, astringently acid, and sometimes used in preserves ; (b) the small kidney-shaped, grey or brown nut (about 1 inch long) at the extremity. The latter has an edible kernel (seed), which when roasted has a very agreeable nutty taste and is much relished for dessert (MCM. pp. 210, 218, 249, 252 : Cb. pp. 62, 345 : Burk. p. 144) ; *Alphonsea elliptica (Anonaceae),* a small tree of 70 feet in height. It occurs from the Siamese Malay States southwards through the Peninsula. It is unlikely that the fruit is edible (Burk. p. 110).

ตำหระ dtam-ra[4] *n.* a piece ; a portion ; a plot (as of land) ; a division ; a section or quarter (as of the body).

ตำแหน่ง dtam-naang[4] *n.* position ; place ; rank : ไม่รู้ตำแหน่งแห่งหนที่อยู่ being unacquainted with one's domicile.

ติ, ติเตียน dti[4] *v.* to censure ; to find fault with ; to reprimand ; to reproach : ติฉิน to defame another's character ; to back-bite : ติโทษ to incriminate ; to charge with a crime.

ติกกะ dtik[4]-gka[4] *P. n.* a triad ; three (chd p. 505).

ติกาหลัง dti⁴-gkah-lang² *Jav. n.* a glass house; a crystal palace.

ตั้ง dting⁴ *n.* an excrescence; an unnatural or disfiguring outgrowth (as a double thumb, etc.).

ตั้งๆ dting²-dting² *onomat.* from the sound of dropping water; a word used to call dogs.

ตั้งส dting-sa⁴ *P. adj.* thirty (chd. p. 506).

ตั้งหาย, หิงหาย (ต้น) dting⁴-hai² *n. Crotalaria laburnifolia (Leguminosae)*, a more or less woody plant of seashores in southeastern Asia. It grows two to four feet high and bears pale yellow flowers: It has been tried as a green manure but soon went woody, did not stand cutting well, and is subject to pests (v. p. p. 126: MCM. p. 109: BURK. p. 686: cb. p. 372).

ติณ dtin *P. n.* grass; herbs; weeds (chd. p. 506).

ติด dtit⁴ *v.* to adhere; to be attached to; to link up with; to join by adhesion; to be addicted to (as to the use of opium); to light or kindle (as fire): ติดกัน to be agglutinated or stuck together (as sheets of postage stamps): ติดกับ (ดักหนู) to be caught in a spring-trap: ติดการ, ติดธุระ to be engaged; to be busy; to be preoccupied: ติดเงิน to owe money: ติดใจ to become fascinated by; to become enamoured with: ติดฉลาก to stick on a label: ติดด้วยกาว to stick together with glue: ติดดวงตรา (ไปรษณีย์) to stamp; to affix a postage stamp: ติดตรา (ยศศักดิ์) to pin medals or conferred decorations on uniforms: ติดตราง to be imprisoned; to be jailed: ติดตาม to follow after: ติดธง to fasten or string up flags: ติดบ่อน (ไก่) to have betting cock-fights: ติดบ่อน (ปลา) to have betting fish-contests: ติดบ่อน (ไพ่) to arrange for **card** gambling games: ติดเบ็ด (ปลา) to be caught on a fish-hook: ติดป้าย to set up a name plate, sign, or bill-board: ติดพัน devoted to;

partial to: ติดโรค to contract a contagious disease: ติดลูกกระดุม to fasten on buttons: ติดสันดอน to be aground on the bar: ติดสินบน to offer a bribe: ติดหนี้สิน to be involved in debt: ติดอ่าง to develop stammering.

ติตติก dtit⁴-dti⁴-gka⁴ *P. n.* a bitter taste (chd. p. 508).

ติตติร dtit⁴-dti⁴-ra⁶ *P. S. n.* the francolin partridge (chd. p. 511).

ติตถ์ see ดิตถ์

ติถิ see ดิถิ

ติปา dti⁴-bpah *Jav. v.* to fall; to drop.

ติปาถะ see จิปาถะ

ติมิ, ติมิงคิละ dti⁴-mi⁶ *P. S. n.* a kind of whale or fabulous fish of an enormous size; a fish (S. E. D. p. 447).

ติร, ตีระ dti⁴-ra⁶ *P. n.* the bank or brink of a river or canal; the shore: *adj.* beyond; across; over; on the other side (chd. p. 508).

ติรัจฉาน see ดิรัจฉาน

ติล dti⁴-la⁶ *P. S. n.* (1) (ต้น) teel seed, sesame seed of the *Sesamum indicum* (much used in cookery). It is supposed to have originated from Vishnu's sweat-drops. The blossom is compared to the nose; (2) a mole; a small particle; (3) the right lung (S. E. D. p. 448): ติลรส sesame oil.

ติลก dti⁴-lok⁴ *P. S. n.* a mole or freckle; a sectarial mark on the forehead; a mark or marks made with coloured clay or unguents, placed upon the forehead between the eyebrows (chd. p. 505).

ตั้ว dtiew³ *n.* short, flat, bamboo sticks used by the Chinese in fortune-telling; chips; tally sticks (used when counting baskets of paddy, etc.); counters (used in games): *adj.* fast; rapid; swift; hurried (descriptive of an exceedingly quick circular motion, or of running): ตั๋ว, ขี้ตั๋ว N. Laos, ราแง้ง Khmer, Surin, เน็กเครแย่ Lawa, Chiengmai, แต้ว Siam. (ต้น) Cratoxylon pruniflorum (Hypericaceae) (cb. p. 113 : V. P. pp. 133, 134): ตั๋วเกี๋ยง, ขี้ตั๋ว-ใบเลื่อม Laos, Chiengmai (ต้น) Cratoxylon polyanthum (Hypericaceae); C. polyanthum var. ligustrinum, a tree of moderate size, found from northern India and southern China to the Philippine Islands. The timber is durable. It is pale brown, or reddish, with fine hard grain, not splitting in drying. It is used for inside fittings and cabinet work. In Sumatra, a decoction of the bark and leaves is used for fever. The Malays take a decoction of the root after child-birth as a protective medicine (cb. p. 113 : V. P. p. 133 : burk. p. 679): วิ่งตั๋ว to run with great speed : หมุนตั๋ว to revolve rapidly.

ตี dtee v. to strike; to beat; to thrash; to flog; to wage a combat against: ตีกระเชียง to row with oars (in European style): ตีกรับ to strike strips of bamboo together for marking time in Siamese music (an alternative for the use of castanets or clapping of the hands): ตีเกลียวเชือก to' join or splice together; to entwine threads or fibre into rope: ตีกลอง to beat a drum: ตีกะบี่ a form of sport at festivals where the two contestants spar with decorated staves: ตีกัน to be in combat; to be fighting: ตีไก่ to have a cock-fight; to let cocks fight: ตีเข่า to sit so close to another that the knees touch, thus indicating disrespect: ตีข้าวบิณฑ์ a manner of preparing rice as gifts for Buddhist monks during the new-year celebrations, by enclosing it in cone-shaped receptacles made of banana leaves: ตีเขื่อน to drive in posts or piles as supports for a bunding: ตีเข็ม to drive piles for a foundation: ตีไข่ to whip eggs; to beat eggs into froth: ตีคลี an ancient form of military horsemen's sport similar to polo: ตีคลุม to appropriate for oneself articles of any kind belonging to another

person (as a forgotten umbrella): ตีความ to make the meaning clear; to explain; to elucidate; to translate; to interpret (as a dream): ตีคอ to cajole; to flatter for a favour: ตีค่าย to attack an enemy's fortifications: ตีแคม to adjust one's seat in a boat in order to make it ride evenly; to trim the boat: ตั๋งให้ก๋ากิ๋น to harm another without profit to oneself: ตีชิง to rob or snatch the property of another: ตีตนก่อนไข้ to manifest fear before the cause arrives; to be apprehensive; to expect with anxious foreboding: ตีตนตายก่อนไข้ prov. do not cross the bridge before you reach it; do not regret without just cause: ตีตรา to affix a seal: ตีตั๋ว to book tickets; to purchase tickets: ตีตัวออกห่าง to become estranged by what is said or done; to break with friends: ตีต่าง for example: ตีแตะ to make a wall or fence by weaving strips of split bamboo: ตีถัว, เฉลี่ย to strike an average; to apportion pro rata; to apportion to each equally: ตีทอง to beat gold into sheets: ตีทัพ to attack an armed force: ตีท้ายครัว colloq. to cajole the wife of one from whom a favour is desired; to have dealings on the sly, or at the back door; to make friends with the wife or family of a party for purposes of personal gain; to intrigue: ตีโทรเลข to send a telegram or cablegram: ตีบรรทัด. ตีเส้น to draw a line; to draw a line using a ruler: ตีบังกั้น to belittle another (as from jealousy): ตีบาตร์ to hammer or beat out a Buddhist alms-bowl into the proper shape: ตีบ้านตีเมือง to wage war on a city or country: ตีประจบ to flatter in order to capture the affections: ตีประเมิน to make a rough estimate (as to price or dimensions): ตีปัญหา to interpret the meaning (as of a hidden saying or proverb): ตีป่า to blame or punish every one regardless of right or wrong; to make indiscriminate accusations: ตีปีก to manifest joy, glee or happiness by moving the elbows up and down (as imaginary wings): ตีผี skittles, a game played with pins which are bowled down : ตีผึ้ง to drive or smoke bees from a nest : ตีแผ่ to substantiate one's veracity by every means possible (verbally or by showing private papers): ตีพิมพ์ to print ; to make an impression from type or blocks : ตีไพ่ to lay down cards while playing : ตีโพยตีพาย to evade the issue by blaming others ; to elude by creating a counteraction or excitement : ตีภาษี to estimate the amount of duty to be paid : ตีม้าล่อ to keep on striking a gong (as in a Chinese dragon procession, or as a signal in case of danger, fire or flood) : ตีไม้นวม to muffle the time-beaters on Siamese musical instruments : ตีรั้ง similar ; equal to ; like, but not completely identical : ตีรัน to attack with weapons : ตีรันฟันแทง to use various kinds of weapons in making an attack : ตีรั้ว to put up a fence (as around a compound): ตีราคา to make an estimate (as to price): ตีลังกา to turn a somersault backwards (as from a spring-board into the water): ตีวง to form or enlarge a circle (as while playing a game): ตีวัวกระทบคราด to defame another maliciously : ตีว่าว to jerk a kite string in order to make it turn in the direction desired : ตีสนิท to appear friendly or confidential with others (for personal gain); to court favour by assuming friendliness : ตีสาย to send a telegram, cable or telephone message : ตีเสมอ to assume an arrogant, or haughty attitude even in the presence of superiors : ตีเสียว่า to guess at ; to approximate (as to price or distance): ตีหนังสือใบลาน to press or iron out palm leaves smoothly for the purpose of binding them into books : ตีหน้า to conceal displeasure by appearing loving and sweet : ตีหม้อ to pat half-dried pots or earthern utensils into the proper shapes : ตีห่าง to act estranged ; to act indifferent or distant : ตีหลังกองทัพ to attack the rear of an army : ตีเหล็ก to hammer heated pieces of iron into shape : ตีอวน to cast a fishing net and drag it along the bottom of the water : ตีอ้อตีอิ่

to be stubborn ; to be obstinate ; to keep silent and indifferent : เข้าตีลูกสาว to make amorous advances towards the daughter of some person, with an ulterior motive : ปราณี-ตีเรือ to turn against a benefactor (as after the separation of two who are quarrelling, they manifest a dislike towards the one who separates them).

ตี dtee[4] *n.* a meaningless sound used in a game played by Siamese boys where sides are chosen and a line drawn dividing the sides. A player running out from one side and crossing the line crying "dtee," tries to get back to the goal before his breath gives out. The opposing side tries in every way to delay or trip the player to prevent his reaching his goal. If the player succeeds in sounding "dtee" all the time till his return, the opposing side loses a player. If the player stops sounding "dtee" by a fall or laugh before reaching his goal, he sits down or joins the opposing side. This keeps up until there are no players left on one side.

ตีทอง (นก) dtee-taung *n.* the crimson-breasted barbet, or coppersmith, *Xantholaema haematocephala* (will. N. H. J. S. S. II, 3, p. 325).

ตีน dteen *n.* a foot ; a stand ; a pedestal ; a paw : ชั่งมีสองตีน bi-pedal ; having two feet : ตีน (ปลา) *Periophthalmodon schlosseri* (*Periophthalmidae*) (suvattti p. 158): ตีนกา (หญ้า) *Eleusine indica*, goose grass or yard grass, a coarse tufted annual (V. P. p. 130): ตีนเต่า small half-formed bananas at the end of the bunch : ตีนตุ๊ดตู่ a stencil or paper punch of decorative design resembling the fleur-de-lis (paper so cut is used on coffins or for fancy flags): ตีนเทียน a candle-stand ; a candle-stick : ตีนท่า the lower steps of a pier or ladder leading down from a landing place to the water in front of Siamese houses ; a bathing place with steps leading down : ตีนนก *Laos,* กานน, สมอตีนเป็ด, สมอหิน (ต้น) *Vitex limonifolia (Verbenaceae);* V.

pubescens, a large evergreen tree with quadrangular branches, found throughout southeastern Asia and Malaysia. It often persists in lalang, and will grow in rather poor soil if it has full light. It has been mentioned as possibly useful for re-clothing old tin workings. The leaves consist of five leaflets which are sessile and during the inflorescence, are densely clothed with a soft, tawny pubescence. The inflorescence is dense, pyramidal, three to five inches across. The wood is smooth, gray, hard and close-grained (V. P. p. 131 : Burk. p. 2239) : ตีนบันได the foot of the steps or ladder : ตีนเป็ด (ต้น) *Cerbera odollam* (*Apocynaceae*), a small tree found along the seashores of south-eastern Asia, Malaysia, tropical Australia, and Polynesia. It has acrid, milky juice and white, scented flowers. The seeds are an irritant poison. The wood is soft, grey or white, and gives a fine charcoal. It is reported that in 1778 the Siamese were using this charcoal for gunpowder. The seeds contain oil used in illumination, but they are poisonous, while no other part of the tree is so. The poison is cerberin, or cerberid, which acts powerfully on the heart. With it is adollin, another poison. The bark affords an excellent purgative (BURK. p. 514 : MCM. p. 385); *Laos, Alstonia scholaris* (*Apocynaceae*), a tall, glabrous tree reaching a height of over sixty feet, producing an abundance of milky sap. The branches are whorled, the leaves verticilate, leathery, about eight inches long, oblong-obovate, rounded at the apex and pointed at the base. The flowers are arranged in terminal cymes, which are umbellately branched. The small white flowers are numerous and crowded. The follicles are pendulous, slender, cylindrical and eight to sixteen inches long (V. P. p. 131) : ตีนหน้า the front feet; the foot of a page : ตีนหลัง the hind feet : สองตีน a biped.

ตีบ   dteep[4] *n*. a species of dwarfed banana (used medicinally); a stricture; an abnormal narrowing of a canal, duct or passage; a lessening in the lumen of a tube (as for the passage of excretions or secretions): *adj*. narrowed; contracted.

ตีรถะ see ดิตถ์ p. 329.

ตีระ see ตีระ p. 367.

ตื, ตุ   dteu[4] *adj*. putrid; spoiled; rotten; decayed; descriptive of the odour of tainted meat or fish : เหม็นตื ๆ a bad odour emitted from spoiled meat.

ตืก   dteuk[4] *n*. a brick building; a handsome mansion.

ตืก ๆ   dteuk[4]-dteuk[4] *onomat*. from the sound of the throbbing of the heart.

ตื่ง   dteung *adj*. stretched or drawn tight; taut; hard-drawn; tense : *onomat*. from the sound as when a weight falls on a wooden floor : หูตื่ง to be hard of hearing; to pay no attention; to be deaf to : ตื่งเกินไป drawn too tightly; cramped; constricted.

ตื่งตั้ง   dteung-dtang *onomat*. from the sound made when people are walking or playing overhead.

ตืด   dteut[4] *n*. tapeworms; intestinal pinworms : *adj*. having an evil odour; not being free, easy or smooth in motion (as bearings in machinery).

ตื่น   dteun[4] *v*. to be awake; to be frightened (as cattle); to be excited or manifest alarm; to have just awaked from sleep : ตื่นข่าว to be surprised or excited over some news : ตื่นเต้น to manifest an excited behaviour; to act astonished; to be greatly alarmed : ตื่นแตก to be scattered in a panic; to be in a commotion; to be generally alarmed (as wild animals); to be panic stricken : ตื่นฟ้า to be frightened at the abnormal condition of the sky.

ตื้น   dteun[3] *adj*. shallow; superficial : ความคิดตื้น lacking in discernment, forethought, discretion, or insight: คำตื้น ๆ words, sayings or proverbs that are easily defined, understood or solved: ที่ตื้น a shoal; a hidden sand-bank; a place with shallow water.

ต่อ dteu[3] *adj.* slowly; laboriously; tediously; descriptive of the motion of heavily loaded boats: คนต่อ ๆ an inactive, sluggish, or indolent person.

ต่อ dteu[5] *adj.* speedy; quick; swift; hasty; [nimble.

ตุ see ตื p. 370.

ตุ้, ตุ้ตื้ะ dtoo[6] *adj.* fat; corpulent; pursy; obese; puffy.

ตุ้กแก dtook[6]-gkaa *n.* the gecko; the large sluggish house-lizard six to nine inches long of the *gecknoidae* family. They are mostly nocturnal with large and vertical pupils and eyes having a curiously fixed stare owing to the absence of movable eyelids. They are marked with red and green spots and tubercles. The toes and soles of the feet are covered with horned plates, adhesive disks or "lamelle" by means of which they can cling to perfectly smooth surfaces. They feed on moths, winged ants and small crustaceans, and derive their name from the call which they make: ตุ้กแก (ปลา) *Bagarius bagarius* (*Sisoridae*), lizard-fish, a coarse feeder having oily flesh. It it not much esteemed and has low economic value (BURK. p. 283); *Saurida gracilis* (*Synodontidae*), lizard-fish (suvatti pp. 80, 88).

ตุ้กตา, ตุ้กกะตา dtook[6]-gka[4]-dtah *n.* dolls.

ตุ้กติ้ก dtook[4]-dtik[4] *adj.* oscillating; swinging to and fro; swaying.

ตุ้ง dtoong *v.* to be latterly distended; to be bulging or overly prominent; to be abnormally dilated or puffed out.

ตุ้งก่า dtoong[3]-gkah[4] *n.* a water pipe for smoking Indian hemp or the prepared leaves of *Cannabis indica.*

ตุ้งตึ้ง dtoong[3]-dting[3] *n.* a pendant for the ear; an ear-ring.

ตุ้ดตู้ dtoot[6]-dtoo[4] *n.* an imaginary ogre whose name is invoked to frighten children into obedience.

ตุ้ตื้ะ see ตุ้ p. 371.

ตุน dtoon *Chin. v.* to keep on hand; to store away (as surplus stock).

ตุ้น dtoon[4] *n.* the bamboo-rat, a rodent resembling in form an over-fed or bloated guinea-pig; sometimes called rodent moles, having cylindrical bodies, short stout limbs, small eyes and ears, large claws and a short tail. They are clean feeders but burrow for roots more extensively than porcupines. The smaller species, *Rhyzomys badius*, having a length of 7 to 9 inches is found in well-drained jungle or garden land; the large species, *Rhyzomys sumatrensis*, is found chiefly in bamboo jungle and measures, head and body, 15 to 19 inches; the mole, *Talpa leucura*, an insectivorous burrowing mammal found on the higher mountains in Siam. The name ตุ้น was applied by early translators to the rock-rabbit, tree hyrax or cony, a small animal outwardly resembling the rabbits (*Rodentia*) but which is included with the order *Ungulata.*

ตุ๋น dtoon[2] *Chin. v.* to steam; to cook by steaming: หม้อตุ๋น a fireless cooker; a pot for steaming rice.

ตุนาหงัน dtoo[4]-nah-ngan[2] *Jav. v.* to become engaged to be married.

ตุบ ๆ, ตุบตับ dtoop[4]-dtoop[4] *adj.* throbbing; pulsating; palpitating (as an abscess): *onomat.* from the sound as when pounding something solid with the fist.

ตุ้บัดตุ้บ่อง dtoo[4]-bpat[4]-dtoo[4]-bpaung[4] *adj.* leisurely; deliberately; slowly.

ตุ่ม dtoom[4] *n.* a water-jar; a small unnatural

swelling or enlargement (as pimples or rash);
a small protuberance of the skin: ตุ่ม (ปลา)
Puntius bulu (Cyprinidae), a small fish,
ranging from about 8 to 25 cm.; they prefer
clean water. They are eaten and liked, and
are salted for local use (Dept. Agri. & Fisheries:
Burk. p. 1843).

ตุ้ม dtoom[3] *adj.* round, flat and tapering
(at the ends): ตุ้มหมุ่ย a ball-shaped
weapon with a handle: ลูกตุ้ม a plummet;
a sound; a surgical probe; scale-weights or
clock-weights.

ตุ้ม dtoom[2] *onomat.* from the sound as
when a stone drops into the water.

ตุ้มกา dtoom-gkah *n.* two varieties of
medicinal plants, *viz.* ตุมกาขาว, ตุมกาแดง.

ตุ้มต้อม dtoom[2]-dtaum[2] *onamat.* from the
sound as when children are trying to swim,
or dogs are pawing the water.

ตุ้มบี dtoom[3]-bpee[4] *n.* a hat or ornamental
cap terminating in a rounded peak, resembling
an inverted pomegranate flower or a mitre;
Eng. a topee, an Indian sun-helmet of pith;
a sola-hat.

ตุ้มพ dtoom-pa[6] *P. S. n.* a water-vessel
with a spout or slender nozzle; an ancient
measure of capacity for grain (chd. p. 512).

ตุ้มพรวด (ปลา) see จุมพรวด (ปลา) p. 254.

ตุ้มหู dtoom[3]-hoo[2] *n.* an ear-ring.

ตุ้ย dtoo-ey[4] *adj.* protuberant; swelled;
enlarged; bulging (as the lips); puffed; inflated; distended.

ตุ้ย dtoo-ey[6] *Chin v.* to hit or poke with
the fist.

ตุ้ยตุ้ย dtoo-ey[2]-dtoo-ey[4] *n.* a kite with
numerous long tails which, when flying, makes
a noise as its name indicates.

ตุรค see ดุรค p. 332.

ตุรงค์ see ดุรงค์ p. 332.

ตุริยางค์ see ดุริยางค์ p. 332.

ตุลลิ see กะเพรา (ต้น) p. 77.

ตุลา dtoo[4]-lah *P. S. n.* a balance; a pair of
scales; a certain weight or measure (S. E. D.
p. 451): ตุลาการ see ตระลาการ.

ตุหรัดตุเหร่ dtoo[4]-rat[4]-dtoo[4]-ray[4] *adj.*
vagrant; roaming around as a vagrant; having a wandering course; roaming; roving;
nomadic.

ตู dtoo *pron.* I; me; myself; we (used in
ancient stone inscriptions): ตูข้า I; myself.

ตู้ dtoo[4] *v.* to claim another's wealth, or
possessions falsely. This is divided into three
phases, *viz.* (1) to assert ownership, (2) to assume or feign ownership, (3) to acquire possession by force or fraud: ตู่ตัว incorrectly;
inaccurately (used in regard to pronunciations
while reading): ตู่แปลกทรัพย์ท่าน undue
enrichment: พูดตู่ to speak incorrectly.

ตู้ dtoo[3] *n.* a chest of drawers: ตู้ถ้วยชาม
a cupboard: ตู้เสื้อผ้า an almirah; a wardrobe: ตู้หนังสือ a bookcase.

ตูก dtook[4] *Cam. n.* a boat; a vessel.

ตูด dtoot[4] *n.* the anus; the seat; the
buttock; the rump: *adj.* inflated; bulging;
enlarged; distended: ตูดหมูตูดหมา (ต้น) see
กระพังโหม (ต้น) p. 41.

ตูบ dtoop[4] *n.* a hut; a small crude dwelling;
a shanty; a hovel; a shed: *adj.* drooping:
หูตูบ pendant ears.

ตูม dtoom *adj.* being in bud; budding; undeveloped (as a flower): ตูมตาม *onomat.*
from the sound as booming of cannon or
bursting of gunpowder: มะตูม (ต้น) *Aegle
marmelos (Rutaceae)*, the bael-fruit, a very
important fruit-tree of India. From India
its cultivation has spread south-eastwards.

The bael-tree is mentioned in sanskrit literature and had two uses, medicinal and sacred :
มะขิ่น *N. Laos* (V. P. p. 208 : cb. p. 239 : MCM.
pp. 251, 377 : Burk. p. 55).

ตูวัด (นก)   dtoo-wit[6] *n.* the Burmese red-
wattled lapwing, *Lobivanellus indicus atron-*
uchalis (Herb. N. H. J. S. S. VI, 4, p. 347).

เต็ง ๑ เต็งรัง *Siamese*, แพะ, แงะ, จิก *Laos,*
ประเจอ *Khmer, Surin,* ล่าไน้, เหล่าไน้ *Ka-*
ren, เจือ *Lawa* (ต้น)   dteng *n.* a large
forest tree, *Shorea obtusa (Dipterocarpaceae).*
This is one of the most important hard
woods of Siam. The resin is used for torches
(cb. p. 143 : Burk. p. 2005).

เต็ง ๒   dteng *n.* a Chinese form of scales
(used by jewellers) with a marked horizontal
bar having a sliding counter-weight suspended
by a thread or string ; a steelyard.

เต่ง   dteng[4] *adj.* elevated and firm ; distended
and tense ; unwithered or shriveled ; firm (as
a virgin's breast).

เต๊ง   dteng[6] *Chin. n.* an upper floor ; a garret.

เตช, เตโช see เดช p. 333.

เต้น   dten[3] *v.* to jump ; to throb ; to palpitate : เต้นรำ to dance.

เต็นต์   dten *Eng. n.* a tent.

เต็ม   dtem *adj.* full ; filled up ; sufficient ;
ample ; complete ; perfect : เต็มคราบ abundantly furnished or provided for ; filled to
the utmost capacity (used in reference to the
stomach, as อิ่มเต็มคราบ) : เต็มใจ see ใจ :
เต็มที่ much ; great in quantity or amount ;
many in number ; an expletive used indicating
objection ; horrible ; terrible ; awful ; เต็มที่
utmost ; of the highest degree or the largest
amount : เต็มเปี่ยม brimfull : เดินเต็มที่
to go at full speed.

เตย (ต้น)   dtur-ie *n. Pandanus ordoratis-*

simus (Pandanaceae), a woody plant, the
long leaves of which are sewed together and
used for a temporary sunshade or shelter
against rain, or are stripped and woven into
matting ; ลำเจียก (V. P. p. 239).

เตร็ดเตร่, เตร่   dtret[4]-dtrey[4] *v.* to wander
or stroll aimlessly about.

เตรียจ see เกี่ยงงอน under เกี่ยง p. 126.

เตรียบ   dtree-ap[4] *Cam. adj.* near ; contiguous ; nigh.

เตรียม   dtree-am *v.* to prepare ; to get
ready ; to make ready ; to equip : *adj.* prepared : เตรียมพะยานเท็จ to fabricate false
evidence : เตรียมเริ่มบริษัท to float a company.

เตละ   dtay-la[6] *P. S. n.* oil ; sesamum oil
(S. E. D. p. 455) : เตลการ a maker or ex-
tractor of oil ; an oil-miller : เตลกุณฑ์,เตลบาตร
an oil-pitcher ; an oil-pot or can : เตลบรรณ
camphor, sandal, turpentine, olibanum : เตล-
ประทีป an oil-lamp : เตลผล *lit.* "that which
produces oil," *i. e.* the sesamum plant : เตล-
ยนตร์ an oil-mill ; a place for extracting oils.

เตลิด see กระเจิดกระเจิง p. 23.

เตะ   dte[4] *v.* to kick ; to attack with the
foot, or hind feet.

เตา   dtow *n.* a stove : เตาไฟ a fire-place
for cooking ; a stove ; a fire-place : เตา-
ไฟฟ้ารีดผ้า an electric iron : เตารีด a flat-iron
for pressing clothes : เตาสูบ a forge :
เตาอบ an oven ; a sterilizer : เตาอิฐ a brick
kiln.

เต่า ๑   dtow[4] *n.* a small breast-garment
fastened on by strings tied behind (worn by
children).

เต่า ๒   dtow[4] *n.* a tortoise ; a timber supporting the stanchion for an oar (as used by
the Siamese) : เต่ากระ see กระ (เต่า) : เต่า-
ทอง lady-bug : เต่าทะเล a sea turtle : เต่านา
a small tortoise found in rice fields : เต่า-

เลื่อน an amulet or charm shaped like a turtle; any one of the numerous species of small beetles of the genus *Coccinella* and allied genera (web.).

เต้า ๑   dtow[3] *v.* to go; to come: *n.* a form of water-goblet (shaped like a lotus flower); a short cross-beam fastened to the king-post for supporting roof-timbers: เต้านม the mammae; a breast; an udder: ลูกเต้าเหล่ากอ *colloq.* family descendents; children's children.

เต้า ๒ *Chin.,* ถั่ว *Siam.* dtow[3] *n.* peanuts; peas; beans: เต้าเจี้ยว soya bean sauce (used as a condiment):   เต้าหู้ soya beans made into square cakes which are used as food: เต้าหู้ทอด fried soya bean cake, which is widely eaten by the Chinese.

เต๋า   dtow[2] *Chin. n.* dice.

เต่าเกียด (ต้น)   dtow[4]-gkee-at[4] *n.* a tree resembling the หมาก (ต้น), *Areca catechu* (*Palmae*), an elegant palm, often rather tall, undoubtedly of Malaysian origin but it is impossible to point to any restricted part of Malaysia as its home. Undoubtedly this palm has been widely grown for a long time, as the extremely great variety of its names throughout the Archipelago shows. The seeds, miscalled "nuts," are chewed in both a ripe and unripe state. At the present time only a very few peculiarly backward tribes do not prefer to chew betel when they can get it. The roots, leaves and nuts are all used medicinally (V. P. p. 220: BURK. p. 223).

เต่าร้าง, เขืองหมู่ *Laos* (ต้น)   dtow[4]-rang[5] *n.* *Caryota mitis* (*Palmae*), a small, tufted palm, attaining 25 or even 40 feet in height, found in Burma, and Indo-China southwards through Malaysia. The wood is scanty but strong and in the Dutch Indies is used for spinning-wheels. Whole fruits may be poisonous owing to a poisonous fruit-wall inside of which are edible seeds. The fibre at the base of the leaves is used by wild tribes for making the wad behind the dart in their blowpipes. Among the Malays this would seem to be the chief use of the plant, judging from its vernacular names (V. P. p. 123: Burk. p. 471).

เตาะแตะ   dtaw[4]-dtaa[4] *adj.* toddling; walking unsteadily (as a little child); having small capital in a gambling game and trusting to luck for more.

เต็ง   dterng[4] *v.* to stick or remain clogged half-way through: *n.* the board on which dice games are played.

เติ่นเต่อ   dtern-dter[4] *adv.* high; elevated; in a lofty manner; higher or loftier than necessary.

เติบ   dterp[4] *adj.* large; big: เติบโต to increase in size (as a growing child).

เติม   dterm *v.* to add more to; to increase; to augment.

เตี่ย   dtee-ah[4] *Chin. n.* a father.

เตี้ย   dtee-ah[3] *adj.* low; dwarfed; below a recognized level.

เตียง   dtee-ang *n.* a bedstead: เตียงเหล็ก an iron bedstead.

เตียน   dtee-an *adj.* cleared of underbrush; cleaned; free from trees, obstructions or hindrances; flat and even; level: ติเตียน to blame; to censure; to accuse: ท่าเตียน a river-market and landing-place in Bangkok.

เตียบ   dtee-ap[4] *n.* a tray from 15 to 18 inches in diameter, having a base about 15 in. high, used for carrying food. A cloth, generally red, is placed over the food and the tray (not the base) is enveloped in another cloth which is tied or sealed at the top. The whole tray and covering is called a เตียบ.

เตียรถ์ see เดียรถ์ p. 334.

เตี่ยว   dtee-oh[4] *n.* underdrawers; shorts; a narrow loin cloth twisted and fastened behind; long strips of banana leaf used as binders for packages of sweetmeats; a piece of cloth used between the boiler and the steaming part of a Siamese cooking utensil.

เตี้ยหลิว   dtee-ah³-liew² *Chin. n.* a long-handled, iron, scoop-shaped kitchen utensil for removing food from a frying pan.

เตื้อ   dtur-ah³ *Laos. n.* time; trip: *adj.* occasional: *adv.* timely; when; occasionally.

เตือน   dtur-an *v.* to advise, counsel or warn; to remind; to call to mind or attention; to notify or request a person to perform some deed: ตักเตือน to offer counsel and encouragement; to rally; to embolden; to inspire obedience; to stimulate activity: เตือนหนัง *lit.* "to urge the hide," *i. e.* to use the stirrups in urging a horse to quicken his pace.

แต (นก)   dtaa *Laos. n.* Burmese red-wattled lap-wing, *Lobivanellus indicus atronuchalis* (Deig. N. H. J. S. S. VIII, 3, p. 171).

แต่   dtaa⁴ *adj.* only; sole; single; solitary: *prep.* from; out of; beginning with; starting at; with; since; ever after; a sign of the ablative, a case of Latin and Sanskrit nouns denoting from, within or by: *onomat.* from the sound used to induce children to dance: ตั้งแต่ since; from the time that: แต่ก่อน ๆ before; aforetime: แต่ต้นจนปลาย from the beginning to the end: แต่เท่านี้ only this much: แต่นั้นมา from that time on till now: แต่นี้ไป from henceforth: แต่บุแต่ชาติ from time immemorial: แต่ว่า but; however: แต่ไหน whence: มาแต่ from; to come from; to originate at: แล้วแต่, สุดแต่ as you wish: เว้นแต่ except; unless: สุดแท้แต่ as you wish; be it according to your command: สุดแท้แต่ใจ whatever you wish: อย่าว่าแต่เท่านี้ not only this much but—.

แต่ ๑   dtaa³ *adv.* very (a sign of the superlative degree): ยิ้มแต้ cheerfully; happily; animatedly; smilingly: วิ่งแต้ quickly; rapidly; swiftly; nimbly; fleetly.

แต้ ๒, มะค่าหนาม *Laos,* มะค่าแต้, มะค่าลิง *Siamese,* กอเก๊าะ *Khmer, Surin,* กอกก้อ *Korat* (ต้น)   dtaa³ *n. Sindora siamensis* (*Leguminosae*), a large tree found in the peninsular part of Siam, and in Singapore. The wood is used for planking. The sapwood is at first white, but soon darkens and a black resin exudes in rings. The heartwood is at first dark red, then dark and light brown (cb. p. 539: burk. p. 2033).

แตก   dtaak⁴ *v.* to be shattered (as a vase fallen on the floor); to be broken off (as bonds of friendship); to be severed into pieces; to be wrecked or ruined (as a stranded ship): ใจแตก to be estranged; to be alienated; to have differences of opinion: ตีหัวแตก to inflict a blow on the head causing a wound: แตกกัน to have differences or disagreements: แตกฉาน dextrous; characterized by ingenuity; skillful or adroit; artful; clever: แตกตื่น to be separated by fright; to get scared and run in a confused manner (as wild animals); to run or flee in a bewildered manner (as a routed army): แตกใบ to send forth fresh leaves: แตกพวกแตกคณะ to be separated from one's class or community: แตกระแหง to be cracked from excessive drought: แตกร้าว to be split or cracked; to have a falling out due to difference in opinion: แตกหัก irrevocable; unalterable: แตกแหลก to be broken into bits; to be completely demolished (as buildings after an earthquake): ทัพแตก a routed or overpowered army: บ้านแตกสาแหรกขาด *colloq.* to have a complete disruption in domestic felicity: ปืนแตก the bursting of a gun when fired: หน้าแตก dismayed; appalled; daunted; scared; disheartened: เหงื่อแตก to exude, ooze or trickle down (as perspiration).

แตง   dtaang *n.* a collective name for a group of climbing plants, many of which produce excellent vegetables, as cucumbers, pumpkins, squashes, melons, etc.: แตงกรม *Siam., Surat* (ต้น) *Melothria perpusilia var. subtruncata* (*Cucurbitaceae*) (cb. p. 765): แตงกวา, แตงร้าน *Siam., Bangkok,* แตงช้าง *Laos, Chiengmai* (ต้น) *Cucumis sativus* (*Cucurbitaceae*), cucumber, a thick, cylindrical, smooth fruit, 10 to 15 inches long and about 3 to 4 inches in transverse diameter, usually brownish-yellow when full-grown and ripe. The yellow flowers are about 2 in. across. The fruit is either cooked and used as a vegetable, or, peeled and sliced, in salads, being a good substitute for the cucumber proper, of which it is but a variety (McM. pp. 291, 292: cb. p. 760: Burk. p. 697): แตงกะลา *Siam., Kampangpet* (ต้น) *Passiflora quadrangularis* (*Passifloraceae*), grenadilla, a strong, quick-growing climber, with large oval leaves and square stems, native of tropical America. The large, oblong, green or greenish-yellow fruit is not unlike a watermelon, and contains in its hollow centre a mass of purplish sweet-acid pulp mixed with the flat seeds. In the unripe state the succulent shell may be boiled and used as a vegetable. The root is usually swollen and fleshy, and is sometimes cooked and eaten like a yam (McM. pp. 267, 268: cb. p. 744: Burk. p. 1676): แตงต้น *Siam., Satul,* มะละกอ *Siam., Bangkok,* ลอกอ *Siam., Pangnga,* ก้วยเทศ *Laos, Chiengmai* (ต้น) *Carica papaya* (*Cucurbitaceae*), papaw, papaya, papeta, or tree-melon. This fruit-tree comes from tropical America. The Spaniards took the plant to Manila, together with its name. The fruit is usually eaten ripe, but it may be boiled when young and used as a vegetable, or may be pickled in vinegar. Right through the plant latex is formed. This latex contains pepsin in quantity, a ferment with a digestive action on albuminous matter, powerful in an alkaline medium (Burk. p. 459: Craib p. 750); *Passiflora laurifolia* (*Passifloraceae*), passion-fruit, a climbing perennial vine of moderately vigorous growth, a native of the West Indies, but cultivated throughout the tropics. The

fruit is roundish oblong, about 5 cm. or more in length, yellowish, smooth, and of an agreeable, acid flavour. The foliage produces hydrocyanic acid, and is therefore poisonous (Burk. p. 1677): แตงไทย (ต้น) *Cucumis melo* (*Cucurbitaceae*), musk melon, a round or ovoid fruit, about 4 to 5 in. in diameter, with "netted" or smooth skin, red or greenish-white flesh, produced by a creeping annual gourd with large angular leaves. The fruit has a strong pleasant odour, the interior being of a somewhat floury consistency. The best varieties are highly prized on account of their luscious flavour (McM. p. 240: cb. p. 760: Burk. p. 696): แตงนก *Siam., Kanburi,* แตงหนูขน *Siam., Prachuap,* แตงหนู *N. & E. Laos* (ต้น) *Melothria maderaspatana* (*Cucurbitaceae*) (cb. p. 764): แตงโม *Siam., Laos* (ต้น) *Citrullus vulgaris* (*Cucurbitaceae*), water-melon, a smooth, ovoid gourd, usually about 8 to 10 inches long, sometimes round, produced by a quick-growing, creeping vine, cultivated in warm countries generally. The fruit is dark-green, often streaked with white, with a reddish juicy flesh, which is cool and refreshing, though rather insipid. Some species are found growing to 3 to 4 ft. in length and from 5 to 20 inches in diameter. The smaller-sized varieties are, however, the best. It is easily propagated from seed (McM. pp. 236, 292: cb. p. 761: Burk. p. 561): แตงหนู *Siam., Chumpawn* (ต้น) *Melothria affinis* (*Cucurbitaceae*), a sprawling or climbing plant found in the peninsular part of Siam, Malaya, and Borneo. Its fruits are eaten (cb. p. 762: Burk. p. 1449).

แต่ง dtaang[4] *v.* to arrange, decorate or adorn; to garnish: แต่งกว้าน to inspect officially and adjust matters (as in the provinces): แต่งคน, แต่งม้าใช้ to assign and equip a commissioner: แต่งคำฟ้อง to draw up an indictment or entry of claim in court: แต่งงาน to wed; to marry: แต่งตั้ง to elect; to promote or appoint to an office; to confer

a title : แต่งตัว to dress oneself : แต่ง
ทนายว่าความ to appoint a lawyer to represent
one in a legal matter : แต่งทูต to appoint and
give credentials to an ambassador or agent :
แต่งผู้แทนไป to send a substitute : แต่งเมือง
to govern or rule a city : แต่งไม้ to trim or
shape timbers prior to using them (as for
building purposes) : แต่งหนังสือ to compose ;
to compile ; to write or pen (as in literary
work) : ตบแต่ง to embellish ; to beautify :
มีการแต่งงาน to have a marriage, or wedding
party going on.

แต้จิ๋ว dtaa³-chjiew² *n.* a dialect of Chinese
from near Canton.

แตด dtaat⁴ *n.* clitoris (สตรีลึงค์, เพศหญิง) :
แตดลิง *Siam., Prachuap* (ต้น) *Arytera littoralis* (*Sapindaceae*), a tree attaining 70 feet,
but generally much less, found in the Andaman Islands, Tenasserim, and Indo-China,
southwards through Malaysia. Its timber is
sometimes used for rafters ; it is reddish,
hard, heavy and durable. The orange fruit
is produced at any season of the year and is
rather sour. The embryo has an aromatic
flavour (cb. p. 333 : Burk. p. 260) ; *Guioa pleu-
ropteris* (*Sapindaceae*), a small tree found
from Indo-China to Sumatra, Borneo and the
Philippine Islands. The timber is scanty,
but is said to be durable and elastic. In
north-eastern Pahang the root is used medicinally in the form of a decoction for fever and
stomach-ache (cb. p. 333 : Burk. p. 1116).

แตน (แมลง) dtaan *n.* a wasp.

แต้ม dtaam³ *v.* to make a finger-mark
with scented oil, chalk or colouring matter
(on the face or forehead) ; to anoint (by so
placing a mark) ; to daub or smear with something sticky : *n.* a score, count or trick (as
in games) ; a sign or mark made by a finger-
print : จะเดินแต้มไร what change, move or
procedure would better be adopted : เดินแต้ม
to change the position of a piece (as in games) :

เดินแต้มสูง to move or act with great ingenuity
or subtlety : แต้มคู strategy ; artifice ; craftiness ; wile ; cunning deception : แต้มแผล
to apply caustics to an ulcer : แต้มลึก knowledge combined with skill : แต้มสี to retouch or remove imperfections by painting ;
to paint rudely or roughly : ต่อแต้ม to
give a handicap ; the game of dominoes :
รูปแต้มสี a blotched or roughly painted picture.

แตร dtraa *n.* a bugle ; a clarion, or trumpet :
แตรวง a brass band : เป่าแตร, ประโคมแตร to
blow trumpets in unison.

แตระ dtraa⁴ *n.* flowers.

แต้ว (ต้น) dtaa-oh³ *Peninsula n. Cratoxylon prunifolium* (*Hypericaceae*), a group
of plants with gummy sap ; *C. neriifolium* ;
C. formosum (v. p. p. 135).

แต้ฮวย (ต้น) dtaa³-hoie *n. Camellia
japonica* (*Ternstroemiaceae*), the camellia,
which has had a long period of cultivation
in the far East for the sake of its beautiful
flowers. The Japanese are said to use the
leaves as a substitute for tea. There is oil
in the seed to the extent of 40%. This native
of China and Japan is said to have been
introduced into Siam by the late Luang
Rajakit Kenikorn about 40 years ago (winit,
N. H. J. S. S. IX, 1, p. 92 : Burk. p. 417).

แตะ dtaa⁴ *v.* to hit or strike lightly ; to
touch with the tips of the fingers (as in
playing tag) : เดินแตะ ๆ the toddling walk
of a child : ตีแตะ, ขัดแตะ to weave split
bamboo into a fence or partition : ฝาแตะ
a partition of woven split bamboo.

โต dtoh *adj.* large ; big ; broad ; vast ; huge ;
superior : ใหญ่โต immense ; monstrous.

โต้ dtoh³ *v.* to contest ; to dispute ; to
oppose ; to refute : โต้ความที่ศาล to argue
or plead a case in court : โต้ตอบ to make
reply ; to answer : โต้เถียง to argue ; to
debate ; to controvert : โต้แข้ง to con-

tradict : โต้ลม to go, sail or force one's way contrary to the wind : หนังสือโต้ตอบ correspondence.

โตก   dtok⁴ *n.* to equalize two metals by weight (as gold and silver): *n.* a large raised metal tray or stand with turned up, serrated or decorated edge.

โต่ง   dtong⁴ *n.* the end; the conclusion : *adv.* finally; after all others in time or order : ท้ายโต่ง bringing up the rear or being the last one.

โต้ง   dtong³ *adj.* tall; high; towering; lofty.

โตงเตง   dtong-dteng *n.* the two suspended bars of a loom, on which the thread is wound : *adj.* swaying back and forth while suspended ; oscillatory.

โตฎก   dtoh-dok⁴ *P. S. n.* name of a form of Siamese rhyme; a measure of verse; a stanza, each line containing twelve syllables.

โตนด (ต้น) see ตาล (ต้น) p. 364.

โตมร   dtoh-maun *P. S. n.* a lance; a javelin (S. E. D. p. 455): โตมรธร a lance-bearer; fire.

โตย see โดย p. 338.

โตรัก (ต้น) see ช้อก (ต้น) p. 283.

โตรกไตร   dtrok⁴-dtrai *adj.* precipitous ; very steep and deep.

โต้หลง   dtoh³-long² *Chin. v.* please to help ; kindly do a favour; kindly render aid.

โต๊ะ   dto⁶ *n.* a table; a stand for offerings ; a raised silver or brass tray : ตั้งโต๊ะ to set a table or lay places on a table : โต๊ะ the Malay name for grandmother : โต๊ะกลม a round table : โต๊ะอิมั่ม, โต๊ะอิหม่ำ an Islamic priest : โต๊ะเท้าคู่ a table or stand resting on horses : โต๊ะสี่เหลี่ยม a square table.

ใต้   dtai³ *adj.* low : *adv.* below; in a low way; in a low position : *prep.* under; be-

neath in point of place : ใต้ถุน the space beneath a Siamese house or floor : ใต้เท้า you (used to nobility of high rank): ใต้เท้า- กรุณา you (used to nobility of the rank of Chao Phya): ใต้เท้ากรุณาเจ้า you (used to a nobleman of the rank of Somdet Chao Phya): ใต้ฝ่าพระบาท you (used to royalty): ใต้ฝ่าละอองพระบาท you (used to high princes or those next in rank to His Majesty, the King): ใต้ฝ่าละอองธุลีพระบาท you (used to His Majesty, the King): ใต้ลม, บังลม to be on the lee, or sheltered side : ทางทิศใต้ southern : ทิศใต้ the south, a point of the compass.

ไต   dtai *n.* the kidney; the glandular organ that excretes urine; hard, superficial, or deep masses of extraneous inorganic matter col- lected in the tissues, or in a cavity.

ไต่   dtai⁴ *v.* to climb or crawl by means of the hands and feet (as up a coconut tree); to walk carefully or gingerly (as over a pre- carious bridge); to creep along (as worms); to scamper along the limb of a tree (as squirrels); to grow clinging to the limb of a tree or a support (as vines); to move by adhering to a smooth surface (as lizards): ไต่คู้ (ไม้) an accent mark shaped like a Siamese figure eight, placed over words to indicate a short sound, as ก๊ : ไต่ลวด to walk or dance on a tight rope : ไต่สวน to investigate; to interrogate.

ไต้   dtai³ *n.* a torch.

ไตร ๑   dtrai *v.* to examine; to estimate; to approximate; to fix (as a rate): ไตรตรา to weigh or consider mentally; to examine and mentally make note of what is seen and heard.

ไตร ๒   dtrai *S. adj.* three; used as a prefix *ex.*, ไตรรัตน์, ไตรทวาร, ผ้าไตรจีวร, หอไตรปิฎก see ตรี : ไตรจักร์, ไตรภพ, ไตรภูมิ, ไตรโลกย์ see ตรีภพ: ไตรจีวร see ตรีจีวร: ไตรตรึงส์ see ตรัยตรึงส์: ไตรทวาร *lit.* "the three doors," *i. e.* (กาย) body,

(วาจา) speech, and (ใจ) mind : ไตรทิศ, ไตรทิพ, ไตรทิพย์ see ตรีทิพ : ไตรบิฎก see ตรีปิฎก : ไตรเพท the three Vedas, which are the foundation of the Hindu religion (H. C. D. p. 344): ไตรยางค์ three shares; having three parts; one third : ไตรรงค์ tri-colour : ไตรรัตน์ see ตรีรัตน์ : ไตรลักษณ์ *lit.* "the three characteristics of existence," *i. e.* (อนิจจตา) perishableness, (ทุกขตา) pain, and (อนัตตา) that which has no self (Ala. p. 227): ไตรสรณะ *lit.* "the three-fold refuge," *i. e.* the three-refuge formula of the Buddha.

ไตรกิศยา dtrai-gkit⁴-sa⁴-yah *P. n.* the practice of medicine; the act of healing or curing (chd. p. 505).

ไตร่ตรอง dtrai⁴-dtraung *v.* to meditate; to weigh carefully mentally; see ตรี p. 344.

ถ

ถ The twenty-second consonant in the Thai alphabet, a high class letter of which there are eleven, *viz.* ข, ฃ, ฉ, ฐ, ฑ, ผ, ฝ, ศ, ษ, ส, ห. ถอถวิล, and ถอถุง are the designating names. It is pronounced as the English aspirated " t."

ถก, ถลก tok⁴ *v.* to flay; to skin; to denude; to strip off; to expose the underlying tissues by pulling the skin backwards (as in an amputation); to peel off (as the skin of a rabbit, or the rind of an orange); to uncover; to lay bare by rolling up (as the sleeve or trousers): ถกเขมร a method of wearing the loin-cloth or bathing scarf. The garment is passed round the waist, and fastened in front, the edges are then rolled, the ends are fastened behind, thus exposing most of the body (a mode of dress adopted by the Khmers and Laos mountain tribes).

ถงัน ta⁴-ngan² *v.* to jump or leap forwards.

ถงาด ta⁴-ngat⁴ *v.* to assume an attitude as though ready to make a leap; to crane the neck (as though looking over a wall, or out of a car window).

ถด tot⁴ *v.* to retreat; to move backwards; to withdraw.
[p. 503].

ถน ta⁴-na⁶ *P. n.* the female breast (chd.

ถนน ta⁴-non² *n.* a street; a road : ถนนหลวง a public highway; a thoroughfare.

ถนป ta⁴-nop⁴ *P. n.* a suckling; an infant (chd. p. 503).

ถนอม ta⁴-naum² *v.* to cherish; to nurture kindly (as a delicate child); to conserve; to save; to be frugal (as when dealing with funds); to handle carefully (as when admiring delicate pieces of ceramic ware); to hold dear and precious (as an heirloom); to treat tenderly and affectionately (as an invalid): ถนอมกำลัง to conserve one's energy; to husband one's strength : ถนอมกาย to be solicitous regarding one's physical condition : ถนอมใจ to be temperate; to be moderate and reasonable in one's desires.

ถนัด ta⁴-nat⁴ *adv.* clearly; distinctly : *adj.* handy; apt; clever: ถนัดมือซ้าย dextrous with the left hand : ฟังไม่ถนัด to hear indistinctly.

ถนำ (ดิน) ta⁴-nam² *Cam. n.* a yellowish clay reputed by the Siamese to be efficacious as a remedy : ถนำทึก a remedy incorporating the above clay as an ingredient.

ถนิม ta⁴-nim² *n.* decorative ornaments; jewelry.

ถนิมสร้อย ta⁴-nim²-soi³ *adj.* delicate, tender; frail (descriptive of children).

ถบ (เป็ด) top⁴ *n.* a marvellous, mythical duck possessing supernatural powers.

ถบดี ta⁴-bau-dee *P. n.* a carpenter (chd. p. [503]).

ถบวง see กระทรวง p. 33.

ถม ๑ tom² *v.* to protect the person or dwelling place by the employment of charms, amulets, or sorcery.

ถม ๒ tom² *v.* to fill up (as a hole with earth); to raise with earth filled in (as the embankment for a road, or foundation of a building); to cover with soil or earth : เครื่อง- ถม niello ware : ถมด้วยเถ้าแกลบ to use the ash of paddy husk as filling material : ถม ถี่ค, ถมเถ, ถมไป *adj.* abundant; fully sufficient; ample; much; plenty : ถมปรักมาศ pieces of niello worked in gold or silver designs : ถมปีทมิ์ niello made on a copper base : ถม- น้ำยา niello enamel ware.

ถ่ม (น้ำลาย) tom⁴ *v.* to spit; to eject saliva from the mouth (an inelegant word as it manifests disrespect or contempt and is considered equal to a curse, especially if the saliva falls on a person) : บ้วนน้ำลาย a more refined expression than ถ่มน้ำลาย : ถ่มเสมหะ to expectorate mucus.

ถมอ ta⁴-mau² *Cam. n.* a rock; a stone.

ถมึงทึง ta⁴-meung²-teung *adj.* fierce; savage; vicious; violent; sulky; ill-humoured (descriptive of the attitude assumed, or of disposition).

ถล ton² *P. n.* soil; land; dry ground; terra firma; high ground (chd. p. 502).

ถลก see ถก p. 379.

ถลกบาตร ta⁴-lok⁴-bat⁴ *n.* a removable alms-bowl pouch or sack with shoulder-strap attached : ถลกบาตร์ *Siam., Chantaburi* (ต้น) *Tetrastigma campylocarpum (Ampelidaceae)* (cb. p. 312).

ถลน ta⁴-lon² *v.* to protrude or be forced out from an orifice; to bulge or project (as mucus membrane from the anus).

ถลม ta⁴-lom² *adj.* consisting of holes, pits, or depressions.

ถล่ม ta⁴-lom⁴ *v.* to sink into (as in mud); to subside or settle (as the bank of a river); to drop or fall (as earth and rocks in a landslide).

ถลอก ta⁴-lauk⁴ *v.* to have the skin excoriated, abraded, stripped or scratched off : แผลถลอก a wound thus produced.

ถลัน ta⁴-lan² *v.* to force one's way in stubbornly; to enter or intrude regardless of consequences.

ถลา ta⁴-lah² *v.* to go sideways; to lean to one side : บินถลา to fly in a zigzag course.

ถลาก ta⁴-lak⁴ *adj.* skidding; sliding; slipping; gliding : ถลากถลำ heedless; thoughtless; careless; continually making mistakes : ถลากไถล dallying; loitering; not going or coming directly; inclined to saunter; dawdling; dilatory.

ถลาย ta⁴-lai² *v.* to destroy; to pull down; to break into pieces; to bring to naught; to annihilate.

ถลำ, พลั้ง, พลาด ta⁴-lam² *v.* to act or move recklessly; to be unappreciative of danger; to be trapped or tripped in a hole (as cattle in pitfalls); to make an error in judgement (as following advice that appears good but turns out to be bad); to make an error inadvertently by not foreseeing the results (as in making an investment); to lose money in a game of chance; to infringe or transgress (as over another's boundary line) : ถลำปาก to make a slip of the tongue : จ่าย-เงินถลำไป to over-pay; to make an error in payment : ถลำร่อง to stumble or make a misstep into a hole or crack in the floor : ถลำถลาก habitually heedless; thoughtless; careless.

ถลีถลำ ta⁴-lee²-ta⁴-lam² *v.* to rush heedlessly into, or carelessly along; to go at random into or through; not to discern what is right or wrong.

ถลึง ta[4]-leung[2] v. to fix the eyes in an angry, fierce stare; to gaze at in an ill-humoured or haughty manner, see ขึ้งตา p. 161.

ถลุง ta[4]-loong[2] v. to smelt ore; to liquefy by heat (in order to separate the metal from the dross).

ถลุน ta[4]-loon[2] v. to twist (as jute fibre into a rope); to unite by twisting into a strand.

ถ่วง too-ang[4] v. to weight (as a fish-hook or casting net); to impede; to hinder the speed or progress of (as by trailing the foot in the water, over the edge of a boat); to cause to be submerged (by attaching a weight): ลูกถ่วง counter-weights: ถ่วงให้ชักช้า to cause unnecessary delay; to obstruct (as by making trifling objections): ถ่วงเรือ to place ballast in a boat or ship.

ถ้วน too-an[3] adj. complete; entire; total as agreed upon; without deficiency: ถ้วนถี่ exact; precise; marked by nicety or exactness: คนถ้วนถี่ a person particular in all the details: นับเงินดูว่าถ้วนหรือไม่ count the money to see that the proper amount is there: นับไม่ถ้วน countless; unbounded; limitless; innumerable.

ถ้วย too-ey[3] n. a cup: ถ้วยแก้ว a tumbler; a drinking glass: ถ้วยชา a tea-cup: ถ้วย-ชาม pottery; crockery: ถ้วยสามารถ a prize cup awarded for some athletic event: ถ้วย-กระบอก a tube-shaped drinking glass: ถ้วย-ปากไป่ a trumpet-shaped drinking glass.

ถ้วยโถง too-ey[3]-tong[2] v. to arrange or form into groups or companies (as troops on a field).

ถวัด, ถวัน ta[4]-wat[4] adj. quick; active; expeditious; adroit; dextrous.

ถวัล ta[4]-wan[2] P.S. adj. large; thick; coarse; clumsy; stupid (chd. p. 505).

ถวัลย์ ta[4]-wan[2] v. to reign; to govern;

to regulate by authority; to exercise the right to command: adj. big; large; mighty.

ถวาย, ดงวาย, ตั้งวาย ta[4]-wai[2] v. to give; to present (used for the act of presentation to a Buddhist priest, or royal personage): ถวายเพลง to sing a hymn in holy reverence: เครื่องถวาย presents; offerings; gifts to royalty or Buddhist monks: ถวายตัว to give one-self in complete allegiance: ถวายบูชาแก่ to offer in sacrifice to: ถวายบังคม to pay homage to H. M. the King, to some high personage, or to a sacred relic.

ถวิน ta[4]-win[2] n. loops, or a buckle through which a girdle or sash is passed, binding the clothing.

ถวิล ta[4]-win[2] v. to think of; to yearn for; to think longingly about.

ถ่อ tau[4] v. to push forward by the use of poles; to pole a boat: n. a long slender bamboo pole used for pushing or punting boats: ถ่อกาย, ผันกาย to subdue the physical nature; to overcome physical desire by dis-cipline: ถ่องง่าม a pushing or punting pole with an iron prong at the end.

ถอก tauk[4] v. to expose an underlying surface, tissues, or organ by pushing or forc-ing the superficial layer back; to uncover by drawing back the foreskin (as of the mem-brum virile).

ถ้อง taung[2] v. to punch; to inflict a blow by use of the elbow.

ถ่อง taung[4] adj. bright; shining; brilliant; clear; distinct; positive; confident: ถ่องแถว a straight, definite line, rank or file (as soldiers marching abreast); a series of persons or things lined up in distinct rows: ถ่องแท้ manifest; plain; distinct; clear; certain: ได้ยินโดยถ่องแท้ to be heard distinctly; to be able to perceive clearly.

ถอด taut[4] v. to remove; to take off (as a garment); to dismiss; to discharge (as from an office or from being an employé); to remove (as a hat): ถอดเครื่องจำจอง to un-shackle; to unfetter: ถอดรองเท้า to remove the shoes: ถอดเปลี่ยนใหม่ to replace with a new one (as some spare part): ถอดแบบ to take a copy of; to make a facsimile of: ถอดจากตำแหน่ง to be removed from an official position: ถอดฟ้อง to delete a case from the court's agenda: ใหม่ถอดด้าม absolutely new; fresh from the factory.

ถ้อถ้อย see ท่อถ้อย

ถอน taun[2] v. to pull up; to pull out; to root out (as weeds); to extract (as teeth); to pluck (as hairs); to raise or hoist (as an anchor); to revoke; to annul; to retract; to rescind; to cancel (as a promise or contract): ถอนคดี to withdraw a case: ถอนใจใหญ่ to heave a sigh; to take a deep breath: ถอนพินัยกรรม์ to abrogate a will: ถอนฟ้อง to withdraw a charge in court: ถอนพิศม์ to apply remedies to counteract a poison, or relieve inflammation; to use an antidote for poison.

ถ่อน Siam., N. Laos, เชะบ้อง Karen, Kan-buri (ต้น) taun[4] n. Albizzia procera (Leguminosae), a moderate-sized tree, native of India, Burma and Siam, but not found in Peninsular Malaya. It is useful in various ways,—tan bark, edible leaves, etc. (cb. p. 556: v. p. 136: Burk. pp. 82, 83): Sapindus tri-foliatus (Sapindaceae), soap-nut tree of India. It is said that, in very early days, its fruits were an article of trade from India to Egypt. These fruits are extensively used in southern India for soap, and must have been so used from very early times. Both Hindus and Mohammedans use this tree and its fruit extensively in their pharmacopoeia (v. p. p. 136: Burk. p. 1959).

ถอบแถบ Siam. (ต้น) taup[4]-tap[4] n. Con-narus cochinchinensis (Connaraceae); ขางแตง, ขางน้ำครั่ง Laos, Lampang, C. griffithii (cb. pp. 363, 364); C. semidecandrus, a sprawling shrub, found from Tenasserim and Siam to Sumatra. The Malays use this plant medici-nally (v. p. p. 137: Burk. p. 650): ถอบแถบน้ำ Siam. (ต้น) Derris trifoliata (Leguminosae), a plant of wide distribution about the muddy shores of the Indian and Pacific oceans. It is a fish-poison of Australia, the Pacific Islands, and parts of eastern Malaysia. It has been claimed useful as an insecticide, though a weak poison. The plant is medicinal in India as a stimulant, anti-spasmodic, and counter-irritant. Rough cordage can be made from the stems which are very tough (cb. p. 494: Burk. p. 792).

ถ่อม taum[4] v. to be humble; to be humiliated; to become submissive; to yield to authority or power; to be meek; to be defer-ential; to express a sense of inferiority; to be docile and obsequious: ถ่อมกาย, ถ่อมความ courtesy; humility; submissiveness; unob-trusiveness; lowliness, ex. ถ่อมกายวาจาใจ to be unostentatious in acts, unboastful in speech, and humble in spirit: ถ่อมตัว self-abase-ment; self-humiliation; a spirit of abnegation: ถ่อมถ้อย to be unassuming; to be modest and unpresumptuous.

ถอย toi[2] v. to move; to abandon; to with-draw (as from a military position); to recede (as the tide); to retire (as taking a position in the rear); to abate (as anger, or the symp-toms of a disease): ถอยกำลัง to become weakened: ถอยความเพียร to become less industrious or persevering: ถอยจากที่ to remove from a place: ถอยทรัพย์, ถอยสิน to become impoverished: ถอยทัพ to retreat (as an army): ถอยยศ to be degraded or demoted: ถอยหลัง to move backwards: ถอยหน้าถอยหลัง to vacillate or fluctuate in mind, purpose or action; a condition of in-decision or uncertainty: ถอยถด to become discouraged: ท้อถอย to be disinclined to continue.

ถ่อย toi[4] n. wickedness: adj. bad; low;

vile; base; mean; despicable (used contempt-uously).

ถ้อย   toi[3] *n.* speech; utterance; vocal expressions: เชื่อถ้อยฟังความ to believe the opinion of one side in a controversy or dis-cussion; to obey; to side with: ถ้อยความ an indictment pleading particulars, or a formal charge of crime presented to a court: เป็น-ถ้อยเป็นความ a disagreement; a controversy: ถ้อยคำ words; sayings; talk; expressions; terms (as legal or technical pronouncements): ถ้อยคำเท็จ a lie; a fabrication: ถ้อยที่ถ้อยคำ to give "tit for tat," or retaliation in kind; to answer word for word (as when two are quarrelling): ถ้อยที่ถ้อยผลัดกัน alternating: เป็นถ้อยเป็นความ litigation: มีถ้อยมีความกัน disagreements; discord; dissensions: วาสนา-น้อยกล่าวถ้อยบ่อยิน *prov.* the words of the low in rank can not be heard.

ถะกล   ta[4]-gkon *v.* to set up; to build; to erect; to do, or make.

ถะเกิ่ง   ta[4]-gkerng *Cam. adj.* elevated; prominent (as in rank); resounding in name or fame; illustrious; renowned.

ถะเกิน   ta[4]-gkern *adj.* high; propped up; held up.

ถะถั่น, ถั่น ๆ   ta[4]-tan[4] *adj.* rapid; fast; speedy; nimble; swift; hasty.

ถะถับ   ta[4]-tap[4] *onomat.* from the sound of flipping or snapping the fingers.

ถะถุนถะถั่น   ta[4]-toon[2]-ta[4]-tan[2] *adj.* in-decent; immodest; bad; vicious (used in reference to language).

ถะเมิน   ta[4]-mern *Cam. n.* an ancient form of ถะเมินไพร, a hunter.

ถัก   tak[4] *v.* to plait; to braid (as hair or the queue): ถักปลอก to weave strips of rattan or bamboo into rings, bands or loops (for harnessing cattle or encircling the feet of elephants): ถักลูกไม้ to do crochet work:

ถักลวดทองลวดเงิน to entwine gold or silver wire into articles of adornment: ถักลวด-ทองเหลือง to weave brass wire into screening, or into a sieve: ถักไหม to do crochet work with silk thread.

ถัง   tang[2] *n.* a bucket; a pail; a tank; a capacity measure equal to 20 litres.

ถั่ง   tang[4] *v.* to flow swiftly and in great volume (as when a river is in flood); to go; to reach: ถั่งถ้อย to give evidence; to testify in court.

ถัญ, ถัญญ์   tan[2] *P. n.* mother's milk (chd. p. 503).

ถัณฑิล   tan[2]-di[4]-la[6] *P. n.* the earth; dry land; the ground: ถัณฑิลสายี sleeping on the bare ground (chd. p. 503).

ถัด ๑   tat[4] *v.* to move forward, or over a little (as in crowds); the adjoining one in a series: *adj.* next; nearest in place: *adv.* at a later time: *prep.* nearest to: ถัด-ขึ้นไป ๓ ปี over three years: ถัดแต่นั้นมาจน-บัดนี้ from that time on till the present: ถัดไปอีกวันหนึ่ง on the following day: ถัดลงมา ๓ ปี within the next three years: นั่งถัดกัน sitting next; the next one in a row; adjoining.

ถัด ๒   tat[4] *adj.* furthermost; to the side or edge; nearest to the outer edge (used when directing cattle while ploughing a field).

ถัทธ   tat[4]-ta[6] *P. adj.* firm; hard; solid; dense; obstinate; stolid; stubborn (chd. p. 502): ถัทธกรรณ *lit.* "stiff-eared," *i. e.* an antelope; a lion: ถัทธโรม *lit.* "stiff-haired," *i. e.* a boar; a hog (S. E. D. p. 1258).

ถัน   see ถน p. 379.

ถั่น   tan[4] *v.* to flow.

ถั่น ๆ   see ถะถั่น p. 383.

ถับ, ถับ ๆ   tap[4] *adv.* immediately; rapidly; speedily; hastily; nimbly.

ถัมภ์   tam[2] *P. n.* a post; a stake; a pillar; a column; the post to which an elephant is tied (chd. p. 502).

ถั่ว, เฉลี่ย   too-ah[2] *v.* to obtain the share of each by calculating the mean of several; to divide pro rata : ถั่วค่าเสียหาย to average the amount of the loss arising by damage to a ship or cargo.

ถั่ว   too-ah[4] *n.* beans; peas; a gambling game played with cowries : ถั่วขาว *Siam., Ranawng, Krabi,* ถั่วแดง *Siam., Satul,* ปรุ๊ย *Malay, Satul,* ประสักขาว *Siam., Chantaburi* รุ๊ย *Siam., Tachin* (ต้น) *Bruguiera cylindrica* (*Rhizophoraceae*), a tree upwards of 70 feet high, or very rarely taller, found from India throughout Malaysia. It occupies the highest parts of the mangrove forest, where submergence is occasional, *i. e.* at spring tide; it often forms extensive pure stands. It is used for firewood and timber. The timber is usually both lighter in weight and lighter in colour than *Rhizophora* wood, but it is not separated in commerce. The wood is reddish, hard, heavy, close-grained, with a pretty silver grain. The young radicles are occasionally eaten, after boiling, as a vegetable or preserve (cb. pp. 595, 596: burk. p. 374); ถั่วขาว (only) *Bruguiera sp.* (V. P. p. 137), found only in the Peninsula; *B. parviflora,* a tree found from India throughout Malaysia, but not in Siam north of Ranong. It reaches 70 feet in height but is generally much less. Where it grows mixed with *Rhizophora conjugata,* it is evidently under conditions which suit it, as then it attains its largest size. As firewood it is somewhat inferior, but this is its principal use. The bark is deficient in tannin which makes it poor as a tanning agent. Burkhill mentions ลังกะได (*Malay*), ถั่วทะเล (*Siam., Ranawng*) and ถั่วดำ (*Siam., Krabi*) as other names for this tree (cb. p. 596 : burk. p, 374) : ถั่วเขียว *Siam.* and *Laos,* ถั่วทอง (kind with yellow seeds) *Siam.* (ต้น) *Phaseolus radiatus* (*Leguminosae*) (cb. p. 456); see ถั่วทอง;

(*P. mungo ?*), green-gram, a small, erect, hairy annual, about 16 in. high, with narrow, cylindrical, straight, radiating pods, about 3 in. long, and trifoliate leaves. It is a native of India, where it has been cultivated as a food crop from time immemorial. The young pods may be used as a vegetable, but it is the ripe seed (pulse) that is chiefly valued, this being cooked and used in various forms. The straw is useful as fodder (mcm. pp. 289, 310 : V. P. p. 137 : burk. p. 1710) : ถั่วแขก, ถั่วฮอลันเต้า peas in pod : ถั่วคร้า *Siam., Bangkok,* ถั่วพร้า *Siam.* (ต้น) *Canavalia microcarpa* (*Leguminosae*), sword-bean, jack-bean, or horse-bean, a climber, usually found near the sea, from the Mascarene Islands to the Pacific; in the Malay Peninsula it apparently occurs down both coasts, and also here and there inland. It is said to prove a valuable green manure for flat land (cb. p. 453 : burk. p. 434); *C. ensiformis,* a robust, woody, perennial, climbing bean, bearing large coarse, rather flat, sword-shaped pods, 10 to 12 in. long or more, by about $1\frac{1}{4}$ to $1\frac{1}{2}$ in. broad, containing large, white seeds. In the young and tender state the pods may be sliced, and used as a vegetable. The tender seeds may be peeled and used as broad-beans. The plant requires strong and durable supports, such as a fence or a low spreading tree. It is successful as a green manure (mcm. pp. 26, 209, 285, 286, 310 : burk. p. 432) : ถั่วงอก sprouted peas or beans : ถั่วดิน, ถั่วลิสง, ถั่วยิสง *Siam.,* มะถั่วดิน *N. Laos* (ต้น) *Arachis hypogaea* (*Leguminosae*), groundnut, monkey-nut, peanut, a cultigen which was already very widely cultivated and of much importance in America when Columbus crossed the Atlantic, and is still of increasing importance to man. In the East the plant is now grown from the southern half of Japan southwards down the whole seaboard of China and up its river valleys, in sufficient quantity to supply the home markets and to leave a surplus which is exported southwards. It is grown through India, Indo-China, and the

more civilized parts of Malaysia to Australia.
Groundnuts are used extensively, everywhere
they are grown, for domestic oil-extraction.
The European mill-industry began to use
them rather more than a century ago, when
the supplies of olive-oil were deficient, and
when spinners in France were ready to take
an alternative. The oil is also used in
soap-making. Better grade oil is largely
used in making margarine. Not a little of it
is chemically built up into harder oils. The
oil has been admitted into some pharmacopoeias as a substitute for olive-oil. The peanut is also used for human food (cb. p. 402 :
Burk. p. 205 : McM. pp. 302, 310, 394, 396 : V. P. p.
139): ถั่วดำ (ต้น) *Bruguiera caryophylloides*
(*Leguminosae*) (V. P. p. 138); see ถั่วขาว (ต้น):
ถั่วแตง (a dwarf cultivated form), *Siam.,*
Bangkok, ถั่วผี (wild form), *Siam., Bangkok,*
มะแป๋, ถั่วแป๋ *Laos, Chiengmai* (ต้น) *Phaseolus*
calcaratus (*Leguminosae*) (cb. p. 454); see ถั่วผี
(ต้น): ถั่วทอง *Siam.,* ถั่วเขียว *Siam., Laos,*
(ต้น) *Phaseolus radiatus* (*Leguminosae*),
black-gram. This variety differs from green-
gram in having longer stems and a more
trailing habit, also in the plant being more
hairy, and the seeds fewer, larger, and
usually dark-brown in colour (cb. p. 456 : McM.
p. 289): ถั่วนก *Siam., Bangkok,* ถั่วไฟ *Laos,*
Chiengmai (ต้น) *Phaseolus adenanthus* (*Le-*
guminosae) (cb. p. 454): ถั่วผักยาว, ถั่วนา, ถั่วดำ
Siam., ถั่วสายเสื้อ, ถั่วใส้หมู, ถั่วปี้ *Laos, Chieng-*
mai (ต้น) *Vigna sinensis* (*Leguminosae*), a
plant of such ancient cultivation that its
country of origin is uncertain ; but it is
originally either Asiatic or African, and was
spread to Europe early enough for the Greeks
and Latins to grow it : it was known in
India in sanskritic times. As a fodder-crop
it is especially valuable, owing to the ease of
growing, and particularly to the fact that it
smothers any weeds. As a green manure it
returns a very valuable amount of material
to the soil. There are limited medicinal uses.
In Assam the leaves are used in dyeing to

obtain a green dye (cb. p. 458 : Burk. p. 2231):
ถั่วบ้ง *Laos, Chiengmai,* มันแกว *Siam.,* หมากบ้ง
Laos, Lomsak (ต้น) *Pachyrrhizus erosus*
(*Leguminosae*), yam bean, potato bean, an
herbaceous climber, native of tropical America.
It was brought to the Philippine Islands by
the Spaniards. The tuberous root is sweetish,
and is eaten raw or cooked. Apparently, in
Indo-China and in Siam the plant runs wild,
and occasionally also in the Malay Peninsula.
The tubers can be dug after four months when
they are ready for eating, or may be left for
7 to 8 months. About this time, starch begins to accumulate, and if left to do so, a kind
of arrowroot can be prepared. The Chinese of
San Francisco import old tubers from Canton
for making starch. The young pods can be
eaten as a substitute for French beans. The
leaves are poisonous as are also the seeds.
The seeds have medicinal properties. The
plant can be used as a green manure (cb. p.
459 : Burk. p. 1619); *P. tuberosus,* a strong-
growing climbing bean, native of tropical
America, naturalized and cultivated in the
Philippines. There are blue and white-
flowered varieties. It produces an edible
tuber as well as pods, the latter being about
6 to 8 in. long, and used when young. It
takes two years for the tubers to reach full
size (McM. pp. 288, 289 : Burk. p. 1620): ถั่วปู,
N. Laos, ถั่วพู *Siam.* (ต้น) *Psophocarpus tetra-*
gonolobus (*Leguminosae*), winged bean, princess bean, a strong-growing, climbing bean
with large, pale blue (sometimes white)
flowers, bearing peculiar four-angled pods.
The latter are 6 to 8 inches long, and have
a leafy fringe running along the length of
each of their four ridges. In the tender
state they are sliced, cooked, and usually
much relished. The young leaves can be
eaten as a vegetable. The oil in the seeds is
similar to that of the soya bean. Its tuberous roots are used as an article of food. The
leaves and roots have medicinal uses (McM.
p. 290 : cb. p. 459 : Burk. p. 1819): ถั่วแปบ,

ถั่วหนัง *Siam.*, *Laos* (ต้น) *Dolichos lablab* (*Leguminosae*), bonavista bean, a strong-growing, climbing bean, producing flat, broad pods with warted or wavy margins 4 to 5 inches long, which when young and tender are boiled and eaten, as are also the imma-ture seeds. It occurs in several varieties with white, pink, or purplish flowers and white or reddish seeds. The plant is used for fodder throughout the East. It may also be converted into green manure. The Malays find many medicinal uses for the leaves (McM. pp. 26, 286, 310 : Cb. p. 460 : V. P. p. 138 : Burk. p. 851) : ถั่วผี, ถั่วแดง, ถั่วแป๋ (ต้น) *Phaseolus calcaratus* (*Leguminosae*), rice bean, a twining annual, native of south-eastern Asia, found wild and also in cultivation from the Himalayas and central China through Malaysia. It is good for green manuring. In northern India, the seeds are used as food and the whole plant as fodder, but it is of small importance there. It is more important in Burma. The pods shatter when ripe and are likely to scatter much grain before they can be harvested. The grain has a high feeding-value and produces no hydrocyanic acid. In Perak the leaves are used medicinal-ly ; *Vigna luteola* (Cb. pp. 454, 457) : ถั่วผักยาว (ต้น) see ถั่วนา (ต้น)   ถั่วบิสง, ลิสง (ต้น) see ถั่วดิน (ต้น) :   ถั่วราชมาด *Siam.*, *Bangkok*, บ่า-บอย *Laos*, *Chiengmai* (ต้น) *Phaseolus luna-tus* (*Leguminosae*), lima bean, duffin bean, a climber of south American origin, first met with by Europeans in the vicinity of Lima, Peru. There are several varieties. They bear racemes of small white or pink flowers and rather dense foliage. The short, flattish, and rather curved pods are not generally eaten but the large, flat seeds, when boiled, make an excellent dish and have an agreeable flavour. The food value is high. The plant has been used as a cover crop of short duration, and as green manure. The vines can be used as fodder (Cb. p. 455) : ถั่วแระ *Siam.*, มะแฮะ *Laos* (ต้น) *Cajanus in-*

dicus (*Leguminosae*), pigeon pea, congo-bean, red-gram, a perennial shrub, 6 to 8 feet high, with thin, wiry branches and narrow trifoliate leaves. It is widely distributed in Siam and is commonly cultivated in most tropical coun-tries, where the dark grey or yellow seeds, of the size of small peas, are almost a universal article of food. When dried and split they are used in curries, vegetable soups, etc. The young pods are eaten raw with nam prick. The plant resists drought well, being recom-mended as a restorative crop in rotations, and has been widely cultivated in Siam as host plant for the lac insect. The leaves are used as fodder. It is customary to cut off the twigs when the pods have been harvested and give them to animals. The plant is used as green manure, but on the whole is not well suited for the purpose. It is sometimes grown for special reasons, for instance as a prop for vanilla. The Malays use the leaves medicinally (McM. pp. 25, 285, 310, 417, 517 : Cb. p. 461 : V. P. p. 139 : Burk. p. 394) : ถั่วเหลือง, ถั่วพระเหลือง *Siam.*, ถั่วเน่า *Laos*, *Chiengmai* (ต้น) *Glycine max* (*Leguminosae*), soya bean, an erect annual, varying in height, according to variety and soil, usually from about $1\frac{1}{2}$ to 2 feet, though sometimes reaching 4 to 5 feet or more. It is a native of China and Japan, where it has been cultivated for food from time immemorial. The short, hairy pods contain 2 to 4 seeds each ; the latter are a nutritious food and a standard article of diet in the home of the plant. The smooth pea-like seeds (beans) vary from white to yellow and black, and are cooked and prepared for food in numerous ways, being boiled, roasted, or ground into flour. The famous soya-sauce is made from the seeds. A useful paint, domestic and commercial oil are obtained from them. The refuse after the extraction of the oil is an article of commerce in Siam for fertilizer. Milk made from the soya bean has high nutritive value and is used in parts of the East as a substitute for cows' milk ;

a soft cheese is also commonly made, forming an important item of diet in China. The bean is also used in modern automobile factories in the manufacture of accessories (MCM. p. 287 : BURK. p. 1080 : cb. p. 438).

ถา   tah[2] *v.* to go, or to lean to one side ; to sharpen ; to whet ; to hone : ถาขวาน to rub an ax against a grindstone ; ถาเข้าไป to enter abruptly, suddenly or unceremoniously (as one lacking etiquette or respect) ; to have effrontery : ถาโจม to pounce down upon (as a tiger) : ถาโถม (บิน) to swoop down upon (as a hawk).

ถ้า ๑   tah[3] *conj.* if : ถ้าชีวิตรหาไม่แล้ว if already dead : ถ้าเช่นนั้น if that is so : ถ้าดังว่านั้น if it is as has been said : ถ้าเป็นเช่นนั้น if such is the case : ถ้ามิได้แล้วจะทำประการใด if not, then what is to be done ? ถ้ามิยอม if not permitted : ถ้าแม้นว่า therefore ; however : ถ้าเรา if we : ถ้าเห็นด้วย if you are agreeable ; if you concur in my opinion : ถ้าเหมือนว่า if it is as has been said : ถ้าอยู่ if present.

ถ้า ๒   tah[3] *adv.* perchance ; perhaps ; peradventure ; possibly : ถ้าจะได้ will probably get ; will be granted or paid (as a request for money or bill due) : ถ้าจะแพ้ probable defeat : ถ้าจะไม่ดี perhaps ; this article is spurious : ถ้าจะไม่ได้ของคืนเสียแล้ว probably the article will never be returned (as when stolen) : ถ้าจะ ไม่รอดฝั่งเสียแล้ว perchance (we) will never reach the shore (as in a shipwreck) : ถ้าจะ ไม่รอดเสียแล้ว the recovery is problematic : ถ้ายังสงสัยอยู่ก็ให้งด provided there is still some doubt, then better wait : ถ้ารู้ว่ามีอันตราย ถ้าจะไม่ไป if I had foreseen danger, perhaps I would not have gone : ถ้าว่า, หากว่า supposing that.

ถ้า ๓   tah[3] *adv.* as ; since ; because ; when : ถ้าจะต้องการจะผ่อนใช้ให้ when it is needed, part payments will be made : ถ้าท่านจะต้องการผม จะยอม since you desire it, permission will be granted : ถ้าและ, ท่านจะเอาต้นเงินเมื่อใด since

such is the case, when do you want the principal paid ?

ถาก   tak[4] *v.* to denude the surface by using an ax ; to chip off in pieces (as with an ax or adze) : ถากถาง (พูด) to use satire ; to use sarcasm, or to speak ironically : ถากไม้ to trim a timber roughly into the proper size and shape : ถากเสา to trim the bark off, or smooth the sides of a post : ไม้ที่ยังไม่ได้ถาก unhewn, unwrought, unfashioned timber.

ถาง   tang[2] *v.* to use a knife forcefully in clearing or freeing from obstructions or hindrances : ถางทาง to prepare a way (as through tropical forests) : ถางที่ to make a clearing (as in a jungle) : ถางไร่ to remove weeds from a field : ถางหญ้า to remove grass by using a large knife.

ถ่าง   tang[4] *v.* to separate ; to draw away from each other ; to widen an aperture by holding apart the sides ; to make divergent : *n.* abduction ; the withdrawal of a part from the axis of the body : กล้ามถ่างขา an abductor muscle of the leg.

ถาด   tat[4] *n.* a tray ; a metal serving-dish ; a waiter or salver.

ถาน   tan[2] *n.* a water-closet or privy in the precincts of a Buddhist monastery.

ถ่าน   tan[4] *n.* charcoal : ถ่านหิน coal.

ถาม   tam[2] *v.* to ask ; to question ; to interrogate ; to quiz : คนมักถาม an inquisitive person : คำถาม a question : ถามข่าว to inquire regarding the news of ; ถามเขา to ask them or him : ถามโดยละเอียดถึงเรื่อง to catechize regarding a matter or subject : ถามเรื่องความที่ศาล to make inquiries regarding the progress or outcome of a case in court.

ถามะ   tah[2]-ma[6] *P. n.* strength ; power (chd. p. 502).

ถ่าย   tai[4] *v.* (1) to decant ; to pour out or from : ถ่ายน้ำ to remove water from one vessel to another ; to replace with fresh water (as in a boiler or aquarium): (2) to evacuate; to void: ถ่ายท้อง to purge (as resulting from a disease): ถ่ายปัสสาวะ to void urine: ถ่ายยา to purge (as with a drug): ถ่ายอาจม to pass fecal matter: (3) to transfer (as troops); to remove from one person or place to another: ถ่ายชาม to change from one dish into another: ถ่ายแบบ to convey from one surface to another (as a drawing): ถ่ายรถ to change from one car to another: ถ่ายรูป to take or make a photograph: ถ่ายเท merciful; lenient; forgiving; forbearing: มีใจถ่ายเท to be considerate of others; to manifest a spirit of conciliation.

ถ่าว tow[4] *adj.* young; youthful; not yet having reached adolescence, maturity or age; just approaching womanhood.

ถาวร tah[2]-waun *n.* endurance; fortitude: *adj.* permanent; stable; constant; enduring; abiding; strong: ถาวรวัตถุ an article or building which is permanent, durable and indestructible.

ถ้ำ tam[3] *n.* a cave; a cavern; a grotto: เข้าถ้ำลงเหว to enter a cave and descend into the chasm: ถ้ำชา a tea caddy: ถ้ำมอง a kaleidoscope; a picture peep-show: ถ้ำเหว a cave containing a pit or subterranean passage.

ถิ่น tin[4] *n.* a house; a dwelling-place; an abode; a habitation: กลับสู่ถิ่นเดิม to re-enter or return to one's former habitat: ถิ่นของเขา his or their region, district, province or territory: ถิ่นของตน one's own country or birth-place: ถิ่นฐานบ้านเมือง natal, natural or mother country: ล้ำเข้าถิ่นเขา to invade another's property or domain.

ถิร ti[4]-ra[6] *P. adj.* (1) firm; hard: (2) solid; compact; strong: (3) fixed; immovable; motionless; steady; unfluctuating; durable: (4) lasting; permanent; changeless: (5) stern; relentless; hard-hearted (S. E. D. p. 1264):

ถิรพุทธิ steady-minded; resolute; stable; determined; steadfast: ถิรมติ firm; fixed; unwavering (as in opinion): ถิรมนัส loyal; faithful; true (as to a friend or cause): ถิรโลจน์ *lit.* "steady-eyed," *i. e.* one whose gaze or stare is fixed intently: ถิรานุราค constant in affection or love: ถิรายุ long-lived.

ถี tee[2] *P. n.* a woman (chd. p. 504).

ถี tee[4] *adj.* (1) in quick succession (as strokes of a hammer, or whip): (2) close together (as a line of stakes or posts): (3) dense, closely placed, or choked (as trees in a forest): ถี่เกินไป too solid or compact (as typewritten words or lines): ถี่ถ้วน particular; exact; minute; precise; thorough; not superficial; marked by careful attention throughout: ถี่เท้า a speedy, swift or rapid walker.

ถีน tee[2]-na[6] *P. n.* idleness; slothfulness; dullness (chd. p. 504): ถีนมิทธะ drowsiness; apathy.

ถีบ teep[4] *v.* to push or shove with the sole of the foot: ถีบระหัด to tread a water-wheel to raise water for irrigating purposes.

ถึก teuk[4] *adj.* young; wild; vicious; refractory (referring to stags, buffaloes or cattle on a ranch).

ถึง teung[2] *v.* to reach; to arrive at a destination; to accomplish, attain, succeed or obtain (as the result of perseverance or determination): *prep.* to; till; as far as; so far; until; towards: ถึงกระนั้น although; be it so; suppose that; notwithstanding: ถึงกัน to be contiguous, adjoining, or in contact with; to cohabit; to have intercourse (sexually): ถึงกำหนดเวลา, ขนาด, ที่ to reach the allotted time, place or size: ถึงแก่กรรม to die (used for all in ordinary standing and for well-to-do persons): ถึงแก่พิราลัย to die (used for those of the highest rank of conferred nobility as สมเด็จเจ้าพระยา): ถึงแก่มรณภาพ

to die (used for those of the Buddhist priest-hood) : ถึงแก่อนิจกรรม to die (used for those of the rank of conferred nobility up to the พระยา) : ถึงแก่อสัญญกรรม to die (used for those of conferred nobility of เจ้าพระยา rank) : ถึงขนาด the greatest amount ; abundantly furnished or provided ; ample ; not wanting in any respect ; perfect ; having within it all that it can contain : ถึงจอม, ถึงยอด to gain the highest place, or to reach the top (as in a position of rank, or the pinnacle of a spire or summit of a mountain) : ถึงใจ satisfactory ; entirely or completely content : ถึงดิน down to the ground : ถึงตาย, สิ้นชีวิตร to the final end ; till death ensues : มาถึงแล้ว to have arrived : ถึงที่ to have reached the inevi-table ; to be at the end of one's resources : ถึงผ้า menstrual ; the monthly flow ; pertaining to a menstruum : ถึงเผ็ดถึงร้อน, ถึงพริกถึงขิง caustic ; taunting ; severely sarcastic ; satirical : ถึงเพียงนี้ to this amount, place or point : ถึง-ว่า even though ; notwithstanding ; granting that.

ถือ teu[2] *v.* to believe in ; to hold ; to carry ; to bear (as a soldier carrying a gun, or as a flag-bearer) ; to abide by (as a promise) ; to retain or be in possession of (as one caught with stolen property) ; to respect or observe (as doctrines of a religion) ; to celebrate the occasion (as the observance of a religious rite) ; to hold in high esteem, respect or honour (as a deity, or god, or the king) : คนไทยถือ the Siamese people honour or respect (a person), or hold inviolable (a custom or tradition) : ถือ (ของ) to hold in the hand : ถือคำสอน to abide by the teachings of : ถือใจ to be positive or certain ; to be firm ; to be confident beyond doubt : ถือดี to be con-ceited or proud of one's abilty : ถือเดา to stick to the uncertain ; to cleave to in a haphazard manner : ถือตัว to be conceited ; to become haughty : ถือท้าย to steer the boat ; to take the helm : ถือโทษ to hold a grudge against ; to be of an unforgiving

spirit : ถือน้ำพระพิพัฒน์สัตยา to drink the water of allegiance ; to take the oath of loyalty to a government : ถือฝัน to be a believer in dreams : ถือยศ to be puffed up by rank or office ; to esteem personal rank ; to attach undue importance to personal rank or office : นับถือ to respect ; to show reverence for : ถือศีล to observe a religious rite : ถือศาสนา to adhere to a religion : ถือสวน to lease or work a plot of garden land : ผู้ถือศาสนา an adherent of a religion.

ถุง toong[2] *n.* a bag ; a sock ; a wallet ; a pouch : ถุงเงิน a purse ; a pocket-book : ถุงตะเครียว a bag which is closed by means of a cord run through loops. It is used to hold together the alms-bowl, cover and base, but its use is limited to one occasion during the priesthood ordination : ถุงเท้า socks ; hose : ถุงเท้ายาว stockings : ถุงมือ gloves : ถุงย่าม a bag, such as is carried by Buddhist monks and rural people : ถุงนก a game-bag : ถุงยา a medicine bag : ถุงเครื่องมือ a bag or satchel for instruments or tools : ถุงหนัง a leather bag.

ถุน toon[2] *v.* to drink a solution of a drug instead of smoking it : ถุนขี้ยา to drink opium dross or dregs dissolved in water : ถุนฝิ่น to dissolve opium in water and drink it rather than smoking the drug : ใต้ถุน the ground or space under the floor of a house built on posts.

ถุย too-ey[2] *v.* to spit ; to expectorate : *onomat.* from the sound made when spitting.

ถูก, ถูล see ถูล p. 390.

ถุลลัจจัย the third of seven offenses against the Vinaya of the Buddha. It is an อาบัติ or misdemeanor and may be got rid of by confession.

ถู too[2] *v.* to rub ; to polish ; to scour (as the floor) ; to wipe (as furniture with a cloth) : ถูกัน a condition of friction, grating or rub-bing : ถูขัด to burnish ; to brighten ; to clean (as silverware).

ถูก ๑　　　took[4] _v._ (1) to hit; to knock, touch, or strike against: ถูกต้อง to be in accordance with; to be fitting, becoming or suitable: ถูกต้องกับความประสงค์ befitting to the desires of: เรือถูกหิน the boat strikes a rock: (2) to be the victim of: ถูกทำ, ถูกต้ม to be the victim of chicanery; to be the victim of fraud; to be duped by deliberate deception: ถูกขะโมย to be robbed: ถูกจำ to be jailed: ถูกต่อย to be hit with the fist: ถูกตี to be struck with a stick: ถูกถอด to be degraded or expelled (as from an office): ถูกแผลฉกรรจ์ mortally wounded: ถูกปรับ to be fined; to be penalized: ถูกวางยาเบื่อ to be poisoned.

ถูก ๒　　　took[4] _adj._ (1) right; correct; accurate; proper; faultless; conforming to truth, rectitude, and propriety: (2) cheap; of little value; of small cost; inexpensive: ของถูก cheap, shoddy goods: ข้าวถูก rice at a cheap price: ซื้อถูกขายแพง to buy cheaply and sell at an enhanced price: ถูกกัน, ชอบกัน friendly; amicable; peaceable: ถูกต้องกับแบบ corresponding exactly with the pattern; an exact duplicate: ถูกทำนอง according to rule, custom, authority or tune: ถูกล็อตเตอรี่ to win a prize in a lottery: ถูกอกถูกใจ to be well-pleasing in every respect: ทำไม่ถูกทำนอง acting contrary to the custom: ร้อง- ไม่ถูกทำนอง singing out of tune, or off the key.

ถูป　　　too[2]-bpa[4] _P. n._ a knot or tuft of hair; the upper part of the head; the crest, or summit; a heap or pile of earth or bricks; a Buddhist monument; a pagoda (generally of a pyramidal or dome-like form, erected over sacred relics of the great Buddha, or on spots consecrated as the scenes of his acts); any relic-shrine or relic-casket made of various materials, such as terra cotta, clay, elaborately formed brick, or carved stone, often very small and portable, and enclosing a fragment of bone or a hair (S. E. D. p. 1266): ถูปารหบุคคล he who is worthy of having his bones enshrined.

ถูล　　　too[2]-la[6] _P. adj._ large; thick; stout; massive; bulky; big; huge; corpulent; doltish; stupid; ignorant (S. E. D. p. 1266): ถูลกาย large-bodied; corpulent: ถูลครีพ thick-necked: ถูลนาส _lit._ "large-nosed or thick-nosed," _i. e._ a boar: ถูลบัฏ, ถูลสาฎก cotton cloth; coarse, thick cloth: ถูลบาท "large-footed, having swelled legs," _i. e._ an elephant; ถูลลักษ์ _lit._ "having large aims or attributes," _i. e._ munificent; liberal; generous; wise; learned; mindful of both benefits and injuries; taking a broad view; having wide interests: ถูลหัสต์ the thick trunk (of an elephant); a large or coarse hand: ถูลันดร the large intestine; the descending colon.

ถูลู่ถูกัง　　　too[2]-loo[3]-too[2]-gkang _adv._ ruthlessly; unmercifully: ทำโดยถูลู่ถูกัง to do grudgingly; to show reluctance: ลากถูลู่ถูกัง to drag or haul roughly, scraping and scratching along (as a dead animal by a rope).

เถน　　　ten[2] _P. n._ a thief; a robber (S. E. D. p. 1260): เถนนิเคราะห์ the restraining or punishing of thieves; the suppression of thefts.

เถมิล　　　ta[4]-mern[2] _adj._ grouped.

เถยยะ　　　tey[2]-ya[6] _P. n._ the act of becoming, or condition of being a thief, or a pilferer (chd. p. 504): เถยยจิตต one purposing to become a thief: เถยยเจตนา one who becomes a thief with deliberate intention.

เถระ　　　tey[2]-ra[6] _P. n._ a Buddhist monk who has been in the priesthood for ten or more years; a venerable priest; a virtuous old man (chd. p. 504): เถรภูมิ a grade, rating or class of Buddhist priests who have served ten or more years in the priesthood: เถรานุเถระ high priests, or all classes of monks who have attained at least ten years in the priesthood.

เถรี　　　tey[2]-ree _P. n._ women who have taken Buddhist vows and have served ten or more years as nuns.

เถลไถล　　　ta[4]-ley[2]-ta[4]-lai[2] _adj._ truant; dilatory.

เถลิก, เถิก   ta⁴-lerk⁴ *adj.* uncovered (as
when clothing is blown back by the wind);
inverted (as when an umbrella is blown inside
out by the wind): เถลิกเปิดเปิง exposed
(as when an awning is torn loose by the
wind).

เถลิง, ดำเลิง   ta⁴-lerng² *v.* to rise; to rise
up high; to mount; to ascend (as a kite); to
achieve, win or attain a high degree of
honour, rank or prestige: เถลิงกุญชร to
ride, or mount an elephant: เถลิงเกยโถง
to ascend an unroofed or unprotected elephant
mount: เถลิงถวัลยราชย์ to assume the rule
over a realm; to ascend the throne: เถลิงศก
to begin a new era, or reign.

เถลือกถลน   ta⁴-lur-uk⁴-ta⁴-lon² *adj.* aggressive; tending to encroachment.

เถ่อ see เท่อ

เถอะ, เถิด   tur⁴ *v.* to stop; to close (as an
interview); sufficient for the present; a word
which, when added to a verb, makes it an
entreaty or a mild form of the imperative:
เถอะนา a word of entreaty (as, pray do this
for me): เถอะเอย an euphonic ending for
a line of poetry, or for a request: ไปเถอะ
kindly go; please leave my presence.

เถะ ๆ   te⁴-te⁴ *adj.* genuine; natural; not
spurious, false or adulterated: เนื้อเถะ ๆ
real; pure.

เถา   tow² *n.* (1) a vine; a climbing or
creeping plant: (2) a set, or an assortment
of dishes of graded sizes: เถาขี้หนอน *Siam.,*
Chonburi (ต้น) *Atylosia scarabaeoides* (*Le-*
guminosae), a small herbaceous climber, found
from Madagascar to New Guinea and North
Australia; and also in West Africa and the
Malay Peninsula. It has been tried as a
green manure (cb. p. 464 : Burk. p. 267): เถา-
เข้าหมู *Siam., Chantaburi* (ต้น) *Spatholobus*
compar (*Leguminosae*), a woody, climbing
vine (cb. p. 446): เถาคัน *Siam., Bangkok*

(ต้น) *Columella trifolia* (*Ampelidaceae*), a
vine of rather small size, found in north-
eastern Asia and to the Pacific. It is not
common in Malaya, except in the more inhabited parts. The leaves are used medicinally (cb. p. 311 : Burk. p. 2247): เถาคันเหล็ก
Laos, Korat (ต้น) *Ventilago cristata* (*Rham-*
naceae) (cb. p. 294): เถาเงาะ, เถาสิงห์โต *Siam.,*
Chinat, กระทกรก *Siam., Bangkok,* หญ้ารกช้าง
Siam., Pangnga (ต้น) *Passiflora foetida*
(*Passifloraceae*), an herbaceous climber which
belongs to tropical America but was taken to
Europe in 1731. A hundred years ago it was
taken to India and within a short time was
running wild there, in Ceylon, and also
in China. The fruit can be eaten, but is
little used. Animals will not eat the plant.
Hydrocyanic acid is present in the foliage.
The plant is used to cure itch (cb. p. 743 :
Burk. p. 1676): เถาตาปา *Laos, Korat* (ต้น)
Derris alborubra (*Leguminosae*), found in
Hainan, Hong Kong, Tongkin, Laos, Ubon,
Pakchong and Bangkok (cb. p. 487): เถา-
ทองเลื้อย *Siam., Ratburi,* กวาวผู้, เครือเขาผู้ *N.*
Laos (ต้น) *Spatholobus parviflorus* (*Legumi-*
nosae), found in India, Indo-China and China
(cb. p. 447): เถานั่งฮุ่ง *Laos, Chiengmai* (ต้น)
Osbeckia pulchra (*Melastomaceae*) (cb. p. 677):
เถาวัลย์ขน *Siam., Ratburi,* ส้มกุ่ย *Siam., Sara-*
buri, เคียกุ่ย *Laos, Ubon* (ต้น) *Ampelocissus*
martini (*Ampelidaceae*), a vine with a tuberous root, found from Hong Kong, Indo-China,
southwards through Siam to Kedah, and also
in the Philippines. It produces small black
grapes, or, in the Philippines, greenish-salmon
grapes. Attempts at wine-making have
proved disappointing as the result is poor acid
wine or vinegar (cb. p. 303 : Burk. p. 2245):
เถาวัลย์เปรียง *Siam.,* เครือตาปา *Laos, Korat* (ต้น)
Derris scandens (*Leguminosae*), a strong,
woody climber with smooth bark, found
throughout south-eastern Asia and to Australia. The sap is said to be fish-poison in the
Kangean Islands. The flowers are pure white,
in large masses and ornamental (McM. p. 132 :

Burk. p. 791 : cb: pp. 492, 493 : V. P. p. 136) : เถาวัลย์เหล็ก, รางแดง, แสงอาทิตย์ *Siam.*, ก้องแกบ *Laos* (ต้น) *Ventilago calyculata (Rhamnaceae)*, found in India, Burma, Indo-China and Malaya (cb. p. 294) : เถาหญ้านาง *Siam.*, จอยนาง *Laos, Chiengmai* (ต้น) *Tiliacora triandra (Menispermaceae)*, a slender, woody climber, found in Indo-China, Tenassarim and southwards to the northern parts of the Malay Peninsula (Cb. p. 65 : Burk. p. 2161) : เถาอรคน *Siam.* (ต้น) *Tetracera indica (T. assa) (Dilleniaceae)*, a small, woody climber found in Cochin-China, Siam, and western Malaysia. The rough leaves are used instead of sandpaper. The stems are tough and are used for cordage. Both the roots and leaves are medicinal (cb. p. 19 : Burk. p. 2143) : รสสุคนธ์, เสาวรส *Siam., Bangkok,* เถาอรคน *Siam.,* ยานป้อด, ปด *Siam., Peninsula* (ต้น) *Tetracera loureiri (Dilleniaceae)*, a vine cultivated in Bangkok under the name of "Greengrocer Creeper" from its odour recalling the mixture of scents from a fruiterer's shop. Schomburgk remarks that the white flowers of this vine have an exquisite odour (cb. p. 20 : V. P. pp. 136, 231) : ต้นเถา the largest of the set : ปลายเถา the smallest of the set.

เถ้า tow[3] *n.* ashes ; cinders : ขี้เถ้า see ขี้เท่า p. 158 : เถ้ารึ้ง dead coals which are still warm.

เถ้าเก, เถ้าเก๋ tow[3]-gkay *Chin. n.* a Chinese contractor ; a headman among Chinese workmen.

เถาะ taw[4] *n.* a rabbit ; a hare : ปีเถาะ the fourth year of the Siamese animal cycle.

เถิก see เถลิก p. 391.

เถิง, ถึง terng[2] *v.* to get to ; to reach ; to attain ; to arrive.

เถิด see เถอะ p. 391.

เถิดเทิง tert[4]-terng *n.* a long drum.

เถิน tern[2] *adj.* elevated ; high ; lofty in situation.

เถียง tee-ang[2] *v.* to dispute ; to debate ; to controvert ; to strive or contend for an opposite opinion : เถียงกัน to argue in an angry, boisterous manner ; to wrangle : เถียงดื้อ ๆ to defend one's opinion stubbornly in an argument : เถียงไม่ได้เรื่อง to dispute without reason ; to be disputatious ; to be argumentative : เถียงยืดไป a long-drawn-out contention : เถียงว่า to plead or contend for a client (as in court).

เถียร see ถิร p. 388.

เถือ, เชือด teu-ah[2] *v.* to cut ; to carve ; to slice roughly.

เถือก teu-ak[4] *adj.* sole ; solitary ; standing or shining alone by reason of superior brilliancy or excellency (used in regard to colour, *ex.* แดงเถือก) : เถือกถ่อง sparkling or glowing with lustre or light ; brilliant ; radiant ; possessing conspicuous beauty of itself : เถือกทินกร brilliant red (as the sun's rays).

เถื่อน teu-an[4] *n.* a forest ; a jungle ; a wood ; a wilderness : ไก่เถื่อน, ไก่ป่า jungle fowl : ฝิ่นเถื่อน smuggled or unlawful opium : เหล้าเถื่อน jungle liquor ; illicit liquor.

แถก taak[4] *v.* to push, shove or thrust forward (as pieces on a shuffle board) ; to dilate or separate the edges (as an aperture by forceps) : แถกเหงือก to pry open the gills of a fish (as for passing a string through).

แถง ta[4]-ngaa[2] *n.* the moon ; a month.

แถน taan[2] *n.* supernatural beings ; spirits ; demons ; elves.

แถบ taap[4] *n.* (1) tape ; braid ; plaited threads of gold or silver ; a flat narrow strip for binding or ornamenting uniforms or fabrics (as gold braid) ; a coin used in the north : เงินแถบ the rupee : (2) section ; district ; quarter ; region ; side : คุมละแถบ one on a side : แถบขวาเรือ along the right side of the boat : แถบบน the upper region or quarter :

แถบเหนือ the northern region : นาแถบ paddy
fields in the district of—: อยู่แถบนั้น living
or staying somewhere there : (3) length
or width of—: ครึ่งแถบ half the width
of—: ผ้าแถบหนึ่ง a strip of cloth : แพร-
แถบนี้ this piece of silk.

แถม taam² v. to give in addition to what
was bargained for; to give an extra amount,
gratis : แถมพก to give with the compliments of ; to give for the sake of goodwill :
แถมให้ something thrown in to manifest the
unselfishness of the seller ; a gratuity.

แถลง, ดำแถลง ta⁴-laang² v. to tell ; to
recount ; to describe ; to narrate ; to give an
account of ; to rehearse or recite (as a story) :
แถลงไข to expound ; to interpret ; to clear of
obscurity ; *legal* to answer (as a charge or
indictment).

แถลบ ta⁴-laap⁴ *adj.* veering or swerving
to one side, *ex.* นกบินแถลบ.

แถว taa-oh² *n.* (1) a series ; a column or
order : แถวหน้า front or first in line (as by
rank or rating) : เรือนเป็นแถว ๆ houses placed
in a row, or side by side : เลขสามแถว
three columns of figures : (2) a row, line or
range (as trees or mountains) : เขาอยู่แถวไหน
whereabouts does he live ? เดินเป็นแถว ๆ
walking in single file : แถวน้ำ bordering
along the edge of a water-way : แถวป่า
along the range or edge of a forest : แถว-
หนึ่ง a row or stretch (as posts or pillars) :
นาแถวหนึ่ง a strip of paddy land : อยู่แถว-
กลาง situated in the middle.

แถวจะราศ taa-oh²-chja⁴-rat³ *n.* clarity of
line or design.

โถ toh² *n.* a water goblet with a lid : โถ-
หู a vase or goblet with handles.

โถง tong² *adj.* spacious ; vast in extent ;
roomy ; ample ; capacious : คนโอ่โถง a
pompous person ; one given to ostentation :
ผ้าตาโถง cloth woven with wide interstices :

ห้องโถง a large, spacious room : โอ่โถง lofty
and large (as an assembly hall).

โถงเถง tong²-teng² *adj.* high and isolated ;
lofty and beautiful in architecture.

โถบถา top⁴-tah² *v.* to swoop down (as a
hawk) ; to come down suddenly and violently ;
to be precipitated (as a fall of rocks or a
land-slide).

โถม tom² *v.* to jump in on, or pounce
down upon : โถมกระโจมจับ to descend with
a leap or a spring, and capture (as one would
do from an elevation) : โถมเข้าไป to appear,
or approach suddenly (as winged ants or
moths to a light) : โถมลงน้ำ to jump into
the water.

โถมน toh²-ma⁶-na⁶ *P. n.* praise ; commendation ; approval ; approbation : applause
(chd. p. 505) : โถมนาการ the act of praising,
commending and approving (as when observing a marvellous deed) : โถมนพ่าห์ the act
of praising with a loud voice, or by acclama-
tion ; a shout of assent, or approbation.

ไถ tai² *v.* to plough ; to till the ground :
n. a plough : คันไถ a plough-handle :
แถกไถ to push with great effort (while ploughing) : ไถคู่ to plough with a pair of horses
or oxen : ไถดะ to plough in irregular
furrows : ไถแปร the second ploughing or
that which is done in regular furrows.

ไถ่ tai⁴ *v.* to redeem ; to recover by payment
of a fine ; to purchase back ; to ransom or
rescue from captivity or bondage : ไถ่ถอน
to re-purchase pledged goods (as getting them
out of pawn) : ไถ่ทาส to pay the ransom
for a slave : ไถ่โทษ to atone for ; to redeem
(from sin or punishment) : ค่าไถ่ see p. 196.

ไถ้ tai³ *n.* a long bag usually worn around
the waist, used for carrying rice, or currency
while travelling overland. The contents of
the bag are particularly for personal use.

ไถง   ta⁴-ngai² *Cam. n.* day; day-time; the [sun.

ไถย see เถยยะ p. 390.

ไถล   ta⁴-lai² *v.* to skid; to slide instead of revolving; to slide; to slip (as falling); to slip off (as a machine belt): เถลไถล truant; loitering; shirking duty; wandering from business: พูดไถล evading the point by circumlocution.

ท

ท   The twenty-third consonant in the Thai alphabet, a low class letter of which there are twenty-four, *viz.* ค, ค, ม, ง, ช, ฌ, ช, ญ, ฬ, ท, ธ, ฑ, ฒ, น, ณ, พ, ฟ, ภ, ม, ร, ล, ว, ฬ, ฮ. ทอทหาร or ทอท่าน are the names of this letter. It is pronounced as the English "t" and the Sanskrit and Pali equivalent of "ดะ". When ท and ร occur together they are pronounced together as "ซ", *ex.* ทราบ is pronounced ซาบ. When used as a prefix to a noun "ท" means "a person," *ex.* ทะนาย, ทะแกล้ว; if as a suffix, it means "to give", *ex.* อายุท, วัณณท.

ทก ๑, ทุก   tok⁶ *adj.* each; every, *ex.* ทก-พวก, ทกพาย.

ทก ๒   tok⁶ *n.* water (S. E. D. p. 465): ทก-รากษส a mermaid; a water butterfly (Ger. (1) p. 107); a female water dragon or sea nymph; a water ogre: ทโกทร a disease characterized by accumulation of fluid in the abdominal cavity; abdominal ascites.

ทกล้า, ทแกล้ว   ta⁶-gklah³ *n.* a soldier; a man of courage, or bravery.

ท่ง, ทุ่ง   tong³ *n.* a plain; a level place; a place which has been cleared off: ทุ่งนา paddy fields.

ทด   tot⁶ *v.* to intercept; to hinder from passing; to impede (as placing obstructions in the way of advancing troops); to bar; to obstruct or to dam up; to dike (as a waterway or river); to increase by adding to: กรมชลประทาน the Irrigation Department: ถอยทด, ช่อท้อ to be afraid to go forward or advance: ทดถอย see ถอยทด: ทดแทน to reward; to recompense: ทดแทนบุญคุณ to show gratitude by making a remuneration: ทดน้ำ to put up a weir; to raise water to a higher level by placing a dam or gate; to use a treading water-wheel (as when irrigating fields): ทดรอง to advance money: ทดลอง to experiment; to test; to try out; to test by trial: ทดเลข to carry forward the tens in arithmetic.

ทท   tot⁶ *P. S. v.* to relinquish; to yield; to give: *n.* a giver; a bestower; a grantor (Chd. p. 109): กามทท an imparter of sexual pleasure.

ทธิ   ta⁶-ti⁶ *P. S. n.* milk curds (chd. p. 109).

ทน ๑   ton *v.* to endure; to bear; to submit; to suffer patiently: ทนกรรม to bear the inevitable results of sin: ทนเฆี่ยน to suffer a flogging: ทนด่า to tolerate being cursed: ทนแดดทนฝน to brook inclement weather: ทนทุกข์ to endure suffering, trouble or adversity: ทนสาบาน perjury: ทนเยาะเย้ย to endure ridicule.

ทน ๒   ton *v.* to continue; to last; to hold out till the end: คนเหนียวทน an indefatigable person: ตึกนี้ไม่ทนนาน this building will not last long: ทนทาน enduring; permanent; stedfast; firm; strong: สีนี้ไม่ทน this is not a lasting or fast colour: เหนียวทน flexible and leathery; tough and durable (as a rope or wire).

ท้น   ton⁵ *v.* to be reflected or pulled backwards and upwards; to move up against a head wind or swim against the current of a stream (as fish).

ทนด๋   ton-dee *P. n.* an elephant (chd. p. 111).

ทนด๋   ton *P. S. n.* a tooth; an elephant's tusk; ivory; a pin used in playing a lute (S. E. D. p. 468):   ทนตกรรยณ์ *lit.* "that which injures teeth," *i. e.* lime: ทนตการ an expert in ivory carving: ทินตกาษรู้ a small piece of wood used for cleaning the teeth (made by fraying the fibres at one end):   ทนตฆาต the act of biting; chewing; a bite: ทนตจาล looseness of the teeth; separation of the teeth: ทนตทรรศน์ the act of showing the teeth (as a dog):   ทนตบาลิ an ivory hilt of a sword: ทนตบาล๋ the gums: ทนตปุร the city of the Buddha's tooth; the capital of Kalinga, the country along the Coromandel coast, north of Madras (H. C. D. p. 144):   ทนตพยาบาร working in, or carving ivory: ทนตพัสตร์ *lit.* "coverings for the teeth," *i. e.* the lips: ทนตพืช see ทับทิม: ทนตมล impurities of the teeth: ทนตมัย adorned with or made of ivory: ทนตมูล the root of a tooth: ทนตรจนา the act of cleaning the teeth: ทนตโรค a disease of the tooth; toothache: ทนตวรรณ *lit.* "tooth-coloured," *i. e.* glistening; brilliant: ทนตศัฐ *lit.* "bad for the teeth," *i. e.* acids; acidity of the food: ทนตศาณุ a tooth powder; a dentifrice: ทนตายุธ *lit.* "tusk-weaponed," *i. e.* a hog; the walrus; a boar: ทนตาลัย *lit.* "teeth-abode," *i. e.* the mouth: ทนตาวล๋ a row of teeth: ทนตาวัล *lit.* "tusked," *i. e.* an elephant: ทนตะแพทย์ a dentist.

ทนโท่   ton-toh[3] *adj.* clear; distinct to the vision; obvious; discernible; manifest.

ทนม, ทม   ta[6]-nom *n.* a house; a home.

ทนาย   ta[6]-nai *n.* a lawyer; an attorney; barristers; solicitors; counsellors: ทนาย-ความ, หมอความ a lawyer; one who pleads for a client in court: ทนายเลือก a committee to supervise and act as umpire in sports or games (as boxing or wrestling matches).

ทบ   top[6] *v.* to fold one layer over another (as cloth when making a hem); to bend or flex (as the arm or leg); to double (as two strings or rope):   *adj.* winding; tortuous; having bends or lateral turns; folded, gathered, collected, or united: ช่องขาทบ the space behind the knee; the popliteal space: ดอก-ทบทุน to add the interest to the principal: เดินทบไปทบมา to walk back and forth (as for exercise on a small ship's deck):   ตรวจทบทวน to re-investigate; to re-examine; to re-count (as money):   ทบกลับ to bend reversely: ทบกลาง to fold double in the middle: ทบ-เข้าสองเส้น to make two strands into one: ทบเข้าสามชั้น to fold, making three layers: ทบไปทบมา to bend or fold back and forth several times: ทบหลังกลับ to flex the body backwards (as turning a sumersault backwards):   ทางทบ the junction of two roads: สมทบ to be added to; to be united with or reinforced (as by the union of two armies): หักทบ to re-break (as a badly set bone of long standing):   ไส้ทบ the small intestine.

ทม   ta[6]-ma[6]. *P. S. n.* (1) a house; a home: (2) self-command; self-control; self-restraint; subduing the senses; self-denial (S. E. D. p. 469):   *Cam. adj.* large; big.

ทมกะ   ta[6]-ma[6]-gka[4] *P. S. n.* one who practices self-mortification by living on the remnants of proffered food (chd. p. 110).

ทมนะ   ta[6]-ma[6]-na[6] *P. S. n.* subjugation of the senses; suppression of the desires; overpowering the natural propensities; rendering oneself passionless (S. E. D. p. 469).

ทมิฬ   ta[6]-min *n.* a district on the southeastern coast of India; Tamil, the name of the inhabitants of south-eastern India: *adj.* vicious; dangerous; base; depraved; unruly.

ทมิ่น   ta[6]-meun[3] *adj.* black; jet black.

ทยา   ta[6]-yah *P. S. n.* mercy; compassion; sympathy (S. E. D. p. 469):   ทยากร one who manifests mercy; one showing compassion, leniency or benevolence: ทยานิธิ *lit.* "a treasury of mercy, *i. e.* a very humane person: ทยาศีล charitable; benignant; merciful; tender.

ทยาลุ, ทยาลุก ta[6]-yah-loo[6] *P. S. adj.* compassionate; pitying; merciful; sympathetic; commiserative; tender-hearted (S. E. D. p. 470).

ทร taw-ra[6] *adj.* a prefix to nouns equal to "un" or "dis," *ex.* unmerciful; disloyal; implying evil; bad; difficult; troublesome; lacking: คนทรยศ an ungrateful, rebellious or unthankful person: ทรกรรม hardship; oppression; severity; calamity: ทรชน an out-law; a criminal, culprit or rascal: ทรชาติ, ทุรชาติ an evil race: ทรธึก unlucky; unauspicious; unpropitious; unfavourable (as day or occasion): ทรพล, ทุรพล weak; feeble; exhausted; sickly; lacking strength; physically frail: ทรพิษ virulent; dangerous; noxious: ไข้ทรพิษ small-pox; variola: ทรภาค, ทรภิกษ์, ทุรภิกษ์, ทรภาค a condition of deficiency or scarcity of food; a time of famine: ทรยศ, ทุรยศ rebellious; ungrateful; unthankful: ทรยุค, ทรลักษณ, ทุรลักษณ having evil characteristics: ทรหน a pathway full of hardships, perils or difficulties: ทรหู to hear with difficulty: วันทรธึก unfavourable days for any function.

ทรง ๑ song a word used only in speaking of deity or royalty. (1) a prefix for verbs, applied to the actions of the king and princes: In religious literature it refers to the actions, attributes and conditions of divinity. In both cases it expresses reverence, deference, honour and respect: (2) *v.* to have; to be in, or to be supplied with, *ex.* ทรงกลด to have or be invested with an umbrella of rank; descriptive of the sun or moon when surrounded by a halo (as though with an umbrella): ทรงครรภ์ to be with child: ทรงประชวร to be ill: ทรงพระนาม to be called; to be named: ทรงพระพิโรธ to be angry; to become enraged: ทรงพระเยาว์ to be in the period of adolescence:

ทรงพระวิตก to be in a state of anxiety: ทรงพระสุคนธ์ to be perfumed; to be anointed with scents: ทรงพระสุบิน to have a dream: ทรงวอ to be borne in a palanquin: ทรงพระยอด to suffer from a condition where pimples or rash (as measles) is formed (for royalty only): ทรงยอด to come to a head (as an abscess); to form a pustule (as in small-pox): (3) to do; to perform, *ex.* ทรงเครื่อง to cut or dress the hair (for princes only): ทรงเครื่องใหญ่, ทรงเครื่องพระสำอาง to be barbered; to comb or dress the hair: ทรงช้าง to mount an elephant: ทรงนั่ง to sit: ทรงบรรทม to sleep: ทรงผนวช to enter the Buddhist brotherhood: ทรงพรต to enter upon the life of an ascetic: ทรงพระกรรแสง to cry; to weep: ทรงพระดำเนิน to walk: ทรงรับสั่ง to reply: ทรงอาเจียน to vomit: (4) to maintain; to sustain; to preserve, *ex.* ทรงชัย (ผู้) one who continues victorious; one whose victory is lasting; a king: ทรงดำรงค์อยู่เป็นนิจ to be endued with everlasting life; to be immortal: ทรงธรรม one who upholds virtue, morality and duty: ทรงพรหมจารีย์ to maintain a state of chastity: ทรงราชย์ to rule or reign; to govern a city: ทรงไว้ซึ่งความยุติธรรม to uphold or vindicate the cause of justice: ทรงไว้ซึ่งความสัตย์จริง to uphold truthfulness and integrity: ทรงอำนาจ to be vested with power or authority: (5) to manifest; to show, *ex.* ทรงพระกรุณา to manifest a spirit of compassion or mercy: พระเจ้าทรงรักมนุษย์โลก God so loved the world.

ทรง ๒ song *n.* form; shape; figure: คนทรง a spirit-possessed person: ทรงกลม a round body; a sphere; a globe: ทรงกะทาย a type of porcelain or pottery with a flaring mouth: ทรงเครื่อง (ปลา) *Labeo bicolor (Cyprinidae)*, a carp (suvatti p. 23): ทรงภพ (ผู้) the ruler of a realm or kingdom: ทำเป็นทรงพระอุโบสถสามัญ made in the shape, or following the ordinary style of the sanctuary in a Buddhist monastery: พระรูปทรงม้า the equestrian statue of His Majesty the King: รูปทรง an erect figure.

ทรงกะเทียม (หญ้า)   song-gka⁴-tee-am   *n.* a grass with an edible bulbous root.

ทรงบาดาล (ต้น)   song-bah-dan   *n.* a yellow flower from Java, used medicinally.

ทรพ ๑   tau-ra⁶-pee   *P. S. n.* a spoon made from a section of coconut shell, fitted to a long handle, the broad end of which serves to stir rice or curry; a ladle (S. E. D. p. 470).

ทรพ ๒   tau-ra⁶-pee   *n.* a buffalo that killed its father (referred to in the Ramayana); used as a simile for any one wicked or ungrateful towards his parents.

ทรมาทรกรรม see **ทรกรรม** p. 396.

ทรมาน   tau-ra⁶-man   *P. S. v.* to subdue by punishing, torturing, tormenting or oppressing; to tame, repress or pacify by self-control (as the passions): ทรมานร่างกาย to mortify the flesh (as by fasting) (S. E. D. p. 409): ทรมานสัตว์ cruelty to animals: ผู้ทรมานม้า a tamer of horses.

ทรรทึง ๑   tan-teung *Cam. v.* to wait.

ทรรทึง ๒ see **ทระทึง** p. 397.

ทรรป, ทัปป์   tap⁶ *S. n.* pride; arrogance; conceit; haughtiness; boastfulness (S. E. D. p. 470): ทรรปหร one, or that, which is pride-destroying.

ทรรปณ์, ทัปปนะ   tap⁶ *S. n.* a mirror; a looking-glass (chd. p. 112).

ทรรศนะ, ทัศน์, ทัสสน   tat⁶-sa⁴-na⁶ *S. n.* vision; eye-sight; inspection; examination; perception: *adj.* seeing; looking; observing; noticing (S. E. D. p. 470): ทรรศนโคจร, ทรรศนบถ the range or radius of vision: ทรรศนภูมิ the range of perception: ทรรศนวิษัย the line or extent of any one's range of vision.

ทรรศนีย์, ทัศนีย, ทัศไนย์   tat⁶-sa⁴-nee *S. adj.* visible; worthy of being seen; good-looking; beautiful (S. E. D. p. 471).

ทรวง   soo-ang *n.* breast; bosom; chest;

heart: นั่งพิงทรวงอก to sit leaning against the bosom of another: พระมหากษัตริย์ทรงทราบเหตุผลเต็มพระทรวง the king fully comprehends the causes and the results of—.

ทระทึง, ทรรทึง ๒   tau-ra⁶-teung *v.* to grumble; to complain; to urge continually; [to nag.

ทระนง see **ทะนง**

ทระสองทระสุม   tau-ra⁶-saung²-tau-ra⁶-soom² *v.* to assemble; to meet together; to congregate.

ทระสุม   tau-ra⁶-soom² *adj.* bunched; clustered.

ทระหด   tau-ra⁶-hot⁴ *adj.* enduring; resisting without yielding or flinching.

ทระหวล   tau-ra⁶-hoo-an² *adj.* being carried away (as by a wind).

ทระอง   tau-ra⁶-eung *v.* to be conceited or proud.

ทระอุ้ม   tau-ra⁶-oom³ *v.* to be in darkness or overcast.

ทรัพย์, สมบัติ   sap² *n.* wealth; goods; property; possessions; treasures; riches; substance; a thing (S. E. D. p. 501): ทรัพย์คณะ a class or group of similar substances: ทรัพย์ครรพิต proud or arrogant from possessing wealth: ทรัพย์ชาต possessions of all kinds: ทรัพย์เทวดา the god of Wealth: ทรัพย์ประโยชน์ benefits accruing from the employment of wealth: ทรัพย์พฤทธิ the growth or increase of riches: ทรัพย์ลักษณ์ the characteristics of an article or a person: ทรัพย์ศุทธิ the cleansing of household articles (as furniture, etc.): ทรัพย์สัญจัย the accumulation of property or wealth: ทรัพย์สิทธิ the acquirement of wealth; affluence; opulence; success gained by riches: ทรัพย์ซึ่งมีอยู่เพื่อสาธารณประโยชน์ public property: ทรัพย์ซึ่งตกทอดติดเนื่องกับที่ดิน heirlooms: ทรัพย์หรือรายได้ซึ่งสามีกำหนดไว้ให้แก่แม่หม้าย jointure: ธนทรัพย์ wealth in respect to assets: ผลาญทรัพย์

needless extravagance : โภคทรัพย์ wealth in respect to (1) grain, food or provisions that may be eaten at some future time (บริโภค) : (2) an abundance of sundry articles for personal use or pleasure (as clothing or garments) (อุปโภค) : วิญญาณกทรัพย์ animate possessions : อวิญญาณกทรัพย์ inanimate possessions.

ทรัสต์   trat[6]-sa[4]-dtee *Eng. n.* a trustee; a custodian of property.

ทราบ   sap[3] *v.* to know; to perceive; to comprehend clearly : ทราบเกล้าทราบกระหม่อม to know (used only when speaking to royalty); ทราบเกล้า ๆ the abbreviated form.

ทราม   sam *adj.* (1) low; mean; menial; servile; inferior; degraded : (2) tender; smooth; delicate (as the skin); young; adolescent; juvenile : ทรามชม young and admirable : ทรามเชย soft and lovable : ทรามวัย youthful : ทรามสงวน tender and cherishable : ทรามสวาท lovable; marriageable.

ทราย   sai *n.* sand : กระดาษทราย sandpaper : ซ่อนทราย (ปลา) *Acanthopsis choirorhynchus*; *Lepidocephalus hasselti* (*Cobitidae*) (Dept. Agri. & Fisheries) : ทราย (เนื้อ) the hog-deer, *Cervus porcinus* (Gaird. N. H. J. S. S. V, 3, p. 126) : น้ำตาลทราย granulated sugar : หาดทราย a sand-bank.

ทริทร, ทลิททร์, ทลิททก   ta[6]-rit[6] *S. adj.* poor; needy; destitute; deprived of (S. E. D. p. 470 : chd. p. 110).

ทรุด   soot[6] *v.* to shrink; to grow less in size; to subside : ทรุดโทรม dilapidated; neglected; exhibiting neglect; badly decayed; being in a tumbled down or ruined condition : ทรุดลง to get worse (as a patient); to be depressed below the normal level (as ground); to settle (as a foundation or a house).

ทรุม   troom *S. n.* a tree; trees in general; a plant (S. E. D. p. 502) : ทรุมขัณฑ์, ทรุมมัณฑ์ a group, cluster or clump of trees : ทรุมมัย

made of wood; wooden : ทรุมวาสี *lit.* "tree-dwellers," *i. e.* monkeys; apes : ทรุมเศรษฐ์ *lit.* "the best of all trees," *i. e.* the toddy palm, *Borassus flabellifer*, see ตาล (ต้น) p. 364 : ทรุมารี *lit.* "an enemy or foe of trees," *i. e.* the elephant : ทรุมาลัย a place of shelter or a dwelling in trees.

ทรู้   soo[3] *v.* to cause to rub against (as by hauling or dragging).

ทฤฆ, ทฤฆชาติ, ทฤฆายุ   ta[6]-ri[6]-kha[6] *adj.* long; protracted; extended (in time); extensive; far reaching; see ที่ฆ.

ทฤษฎิ, ทฤษฎี   trit[6]-sa[4]-di[4] *S. n.* sight; vision; the faculty of seeing with the mind's eye; intelligence (S. E. D. p. 492); theory; hypothesis; supposition : ทฤษฎิคุณ a mark, or object to look at, or to aim for; a target for archers : ทฤษฎิคุรุ *lit.* "the lord of sight," *i. e.* Siva : ทฤษฎิโคจร, ทฤษฎิบถ the range of sight; the radius of vision; visible objects : ทฤษฎิทาน *lit.* "aspect-giving," *i. e.* the appearance of objects : ทฤษฎิโทษ an evil look of the human eye : ทฤษฎิบท a theorem : ทฤษฎิบาต *lit.* "falling of the sight," *i. e.* a squint; a side glance; a glimpse : ทฤษฎิประสาท the favour of a look; objects that are interesting or fascinating to the eyes : ทฤษฎิพันธุ์ *lit.* "a night-time friend of the eyes," *i. e.* a fire-fly : ทฤษฎิพาณ *lit.* "eye's arrow," *i. e.* a winking of an eye; a leer; a malicious, or amorous glance : ทฤษฎิพิษ *lit.* "having poison in the eyes," "being poisoned by the mere look," *i. e.* a snake; a viper : ทฤษฎิมณฑล the pupil of the eye; the circle or range of sight : ทฤษฎิโรค diseases of the eye : ทฤษฎิวิทยา the science of vision; optics.

ทฤษัท   tri[6]-sat[4] *S. n.* a rock; boulders; a millstone (S. E. D. p. 492) : ทฤษทุบล a grindstone for condiments; the upper and lower millstones.

ทล   ton *P. S. v.* to explode; to destroy; to

divide; to split up into pieces: *n.* a fragment; a piece torn or split off; a small shoot, blade, petal, or leaf: ทลโกมล the lotus: ทลมาลิณ์ cabbage leaves: ทลโมทก the nectar of flowers: ทลสูจิ *lit.* "leaf-needle," *i. e.* a thorn.

ทลบม ton-la⁶-bom *v.* to sprinkle; to spray; to apply with a brush; to rub gently with the hand.

ทลอึง ton-la⁶-eung *v.* to be firmly established; to be permanently installed; to be substantially placed or fixed.

ทลิทท์, ทลิททก see ทริทร p. 398.

ทวง too-ang *v.* to dun; to demand or importune for payment (as from a debtor); to solicit urgently for the return of a borrowed article: ทวงของ to remind another for the return of an article: ทวงค้าง to urge for payment of money due: ทวง (ของ) กิน to beg for something to eat: ทวง (ดอก) เบี้ย to urge for the payment of interest (as on a loan) (Bradley): ทวงทองหยอง to ask for the return of borrowed jewelry: ทวงหนี้ to request urgently for the payment of a debt.

ท้วง too-ang⁵ *v.* to protest against a thing, or with a person (as by advising a different line of action); to offer or submit a counter opinion (as in a debate or argument): ท้วงติง to counsel or advise against (as an older person opposes the action of a junior): ทักท้วง to remonstrate with; to warn or reprimand in an appealing manner.

ท่วงที too-ang³-tee *n.* stratagem; a maneuver or scheme for deceiving an opponent or enemy.

ทวด too-at³ *n.* great-grandfather or mother: ตาทวด maternal great-grandfather: ปู่ทวด paternal great-grandfather: ย่าทวด paternal great-grandmother: ยายทวด maternal great-grandmother.

ทวน too-an *v.* to go or act against the wishes of others; to act contrary to the customs of the land or against one's religious principles; to beat with a leather whip: *n.* a goldsmith's clamping device; a tasselled lance: *adj.* reversed; turned backwards: ใช้แจวทวนน้ำ to back water with the oar: ทวนขึ้นไป to re-ascend: ทวนทบ to travel in the reverse direction; to retrace one's steps: ทวนธง a lance with a standard attached (as used in state processions): ทวนทอง a lance with a gold or enamelled handle: ทวนน้ำ to travel contrary to the tide: ทวนลม to sail against a head wind.

ท่วม too-am³ *v.* to be submerged; to be overwhelmed (as with business or sorrow); to be overrun (as a city with visitors): *adj.* flooded; excessive; super-abundant (in the amount of water): น้ำท่วมทุ่ง the fields are completely flooded: *prov.* น้ำท่วมทุ่งผักบุ้งโหรง-เหรง: *prov.* เมื่อน้ำท่วมตักน้ำมาก ๆ.

ทวย too-ey *n.* a group; an assemblage of persons or things: *adj.* modest; bashful; shy; coy: ทวยหาญ a group of brave people, or soldiers.

ท้วย too-ay⁵ *adj.* charming; appropriate; graceful; elegant in curvature or design (as mouldings, cornices or projecting decorations).

ทวยะ see ทวัย p. 399.

ทวะ ta⁶-wa⁶ *P. S. n.* a forest; a jungle; heat; fever (S. E. D. p. 471): ทวทาน setting fire to a forest: ทวานล a forest fire.

ทวัตดึงส์, ทวดึงส์ ta⁶-wat⁶-deung *adj.* the thirty-second; consisting of thirty-two: ทวัตดึงสาการ the thirty-two constituent parts that compose the human body.

ทวัย, ทวยะ ta⁶-wai *P. S. n.* a pair; a couple; both together; two things (S. E. D. p. 503): ทวัยวาที *lit.* "double-tongued," *i. e.* one who is insincere; one whose word cannot be relied upon.

ทวา   ta⁶-wah *P.S. adj.* two; twain (S. E. D. p. 503): ทวาช a child of two fathers: ทวาทศ twelve; twelfth: ทวาทศกร *lit.* "the twelve-handed," *i.e.* the god of War (H. C. D. p. 52): ทวาทศมาส consisting of twelve months; a year: ทวาทศมูล *lit.* "one descended from twelve roots or ancestral lines," *i.e.* Vishnu: ทวาทศายุส *lit.* "one whose span of life is twelve years," *i.e.* a dog: ทวาบร that dice, or side of a dice, which is marked with two spots; the two-spot dice.

ทวาร, ทรวาร   ta⁶-wan *P.S. n.* entrance; gate; door; opening; orifice; meatus; foramen; aperture; a way, means or medium of entrance (S. E. D. p. 504): ทวารกัณฏก *lit.* "door-thorn," *i.e.* the bolt of a door or gate: ทวารนายก, ทวารบดี, ทวารบาล, ทวารรักษี a watchman; a door-keeper; a porter; a warden: ทวารพาหุ, ทวารศาขา, ทวารสดมภ์ a door-post: ทวารมุข *lit.* "door-mouth," *i.e.* a door-way; an entrance way; an opening: ทวารยนตร์ a door-bolt: ทวารเบา the urinary passage or meatus: ทวารหนัก the anus.

ทวิ   ta⁶-wi⁶ *P.S. adj.* two (S. E. D. p. 504): ทวิคุณ twice; double; two times or two-fold: ทวิชาติ *lit.* "twice-born," *i.e.* an Aryan, especially a Brahmin; one marked by wearing the twice-born thread: ทวิชานี one who has two wives: ทวิทนต์ *lit.* "one having only two teeth (as a mark of age)," *i.e.* an elephant: ทวิชาภิเษก one doubling the length of reign of any previous sovereign: ทวิบถ a cross-roads; a junction of two roads: ทวิบท, ทวิบาท bipeds; bipedal: ทวิบุรุษ one whose height is equal to that of two persons: ทวิป *lit.* "one capable of double drinking," *i.e.* an elephant (by the mouth and through the trunk): ทวิประดิษฐ์ two-legged: ทวิพินทุ *lit.* "double dots," *i.e.* the Siamese character, วิสรรชนีย์, composed of two dots, *ex.* กะ: ทวิภาค a double portion or share: ทวิมุข *lit.* "double-mouthed," "double-faced," *i.e.* a leech; certain kinds of worms or snakes; a

waterjar or vessel having two openings: ทวิยาม two night-watches; a period of six hours: ทวิรท *lit.* "double-tusked," *i.e.* an elephant: ทวิรสนี *lit.* "double-tongued," *i.e.* a snake: ทวิวรรษ, ทวิหายน having attained the age of two years: ทวิศรีระ *lit.* "double-bodied," *i.e.* one of many names for Ganesa, lord of the Ganas or troops of inferior deities, especially those attendant upon Siva (H. C. D. p. 106): ทวิศาล a house with two rooms: ทวิศิข forked; double-pointed: ทวิสม consisting of two equal portions; having two equal sides: ทวิหัน *lit.* "one capable of striking twice," *i.e.* an elephant (with the trunk and with the tusks): ทวิหัสต์ being equal to two hands in length: ทวิหายน being two years old.

ทวิช, ทิช   ta⁶-wit⁶ *S. n. lit.* "twice-born, oviparous," *i.e.* birds, fowls, etc. (the first appearance is as an egg); teeth (temporary and permanent sets): ทวิชากร a flock of [birds.

ทวิตีย, ทวิตียา see ทุติย, ทุติยา

ทวิร   ta⁶-wi⁶-ra⁶ *S. adj.* two; second; twice (S. E. D. p. 506): ทวิรพจน์ repetition; reiteration; recapitulation: ทวิรภาพ (1) a reduplication (as photographs or mimeographed copies); a facsimile; a reprint; a counterpart; a reproduction; an exact copy: (2) counterfeit; duplicity; double-dealing; insincerity; deceit: ทวิราป *lit.* "a double-drinker," *i.e.* an elephant (by mouth and by trunk).

ทวิษ   ta⁶-wit⁶ *S. n.* an enemy; a foe; hostility; an antagonist; an adversary (S. E. D. p. 506).

ทวิษฏ์, ทิฏฐ ๒   ta⁶-wit⁶ *S. adj.* odious; disliked; hostile; hated; abhorred; repulsive (S. E. D. p. 507).

ทวี   ta⁶-wee *adj.* two; twain: ทวีคุณ two-fold; double; twice over: ปรับไหมทวีคุณ to be fined double the amount.

ทวีป   ta⁶-weep³ *S. n.* a continent, generally given as seven in number (H. C. D. p. 102);

any large body of land surrounded by water (S. E. D. p. 507).

ทวีป ta[6]-wee-bpee *S. n. lit.* "one having spots as islands," *i. e.* a tiger; a panther or leopard (S. E. D. p. 507).

ทศ ๑ tot[6] *n.* the selvage edge of a strip of cloth.

ทศ ๒ tot[6] *S. adj.* ten (S. E. D. pp. 471, 472): ทศกัณฐ์, ทศกันธร, ทศครีพ *lit.* "ten-necked," *i. e.* Ravana (Dosa-kantha), the demon king of Lanka or Ceylon, from which he expelled his half-brother Kuvera (H. C. D. p. 264): ทศกัณฐชิต *lit.* "the enemy of Ravana," *i. e.* Rama; the seventh incarnation of Vishnu: ทศคุณ ten-fold; ten times ten; ten times larger or more; in powers of ten: ทศ- ชาติ the last ten re-births in the transmigrations of the Buddha: ทศทิศ *lit.* "the ten points, regions or directions," *i. e.* the four points of the compass, plus the four intermediate points, plus the heavens and the earth beneath: ทศนาลี the length in time of ten minutes multiplied by twenty-four: ทศพนธ์, ทศวางค์ a tenth part; one tenth: ทศพร "the Ten Blessings," being Canto the 1st. of the "Thet Maha Chat," so called because it recounts Gotama Buddha's last re-birth but one on earth in the form of a virtuous prince named Wetsandon (เวสสันดร). In these "Ten Blessings," Indra invites a Deva's daughter, named Phussati (ผุสสตี), to take a re-birth in the material world as a queen, and to become the mother of the Bodhisatta. She consents on the condition that ten boons are bestowed upon her which will render her the most privileged and happy amongst women. Indra grants her request and calls upon her the ten blessings wished for, *viz.* 1st. to be born in the Kshatriyas (กษัตริย์) caste and to become queen to the king of Sivi; 2nd. to be endowed with eyes as beautiful and brilliant as the gazelle's, and with graceful, velvety brows; 3rd. to continue to bear on earth the name

of Phussati (blossoming) as she was called in the Devaloka (เทวโลก); 4th. to become the mother of an illustrious son, and to be delivered without pain; 5th. to keep her slender form whilst with child; 6th. to keep her breasts even, after having become a mother, as fair as blooming lotus buds; 7th. to preserve her youthful, maiden features and her black hair free from hoariness and decay; 8th. to be graced with a complexion of a delicate hue, and a soft, brilliant skin; 9th. to be allowed, on becoming a queen, to release all prisoners from jail; 10th. to obtain anything on earth she might wish for (GER. (2) p. 20): ทศพล *lit.* "one possessing ten powers," *i. e.* the Buddha: ทศพักตร์, ทศมุข *lit.* "one having ten faces," *i. e.* Tot-sa-kan: ทศพาหุ *lit.* "ten-armed," *i. e.* Siva: ทศมาสย์ *lit.* "one aged ten months," *i. e.* a child nearing birth: ทศมาศ ten months: ทศรถ *lit.* "having ten chariots," *i. e.* name of Rama's father: ทศวักตร์ a magical formula pronounced over weapons to make them effective in warfare: ทศเศียร, ทศานน, ทศาสยะ *lit.* "ten-headed," *i. e.* Ravana: ทศศีล the ten commandments: ทศหรา *lit.* "a taker-away of the ten sins," *i. e.* the Ganges; Dasahara, or Ganga Puja, a festival in worship of the Ganges, held on the tenth day of June. It is one of the greatest bathing days of the Hindu calendar. Durga Puja, popularly miscalled Dasahara, is a festival held in October in honour of Durga: ทศางค์ one tenth part; a decimal figure: ทศางคุลี a length of ten fingers: ทศาธิบดี a corporal: ทศาสยชิต *lit.* "the conqueror of Ravana," *i. e.* Rama.

ทศา ta[6]-sah[2] *S. n.* (1) the fringe of a garment; loose ends of any garment, skirt or hem; the selvage edge: (2) a state or period of life (as youth, manhood etc.): (3) the fate of men as depending on, or indicated by the position of planets: (4) a wick (S. E. D. p. 473): ทศากรรษ *lit.* "a wick-drawer," *i. e.* a lamp: ทศานต์ the end of a wick ; the end of life : ทศาบดี the planet governing a person's life : ทศาผล the results of varying conditions of life ; the future fate of a person : ทศามัย a title for Siva : ทศาวิเศษ any particular state in life.

ทหระ ta[6]-ha[4]-ra[6] *P. S. n.* a child ; a younger brother : *adj.* small ; fine ; young (child or animal) (S. E. D. p. 473).

ทหาร ta[6]-harn[2] *n.* a soldier ; a person employed in military service : กองทหาร a regiment : ทหารแตร a bugler ; a trumpeter : ทหารประจำการ the regulars : ทหารปืนใหญ่ artillery men : ทหารม้า the cavalry : ทหารยามรักษาการ a sentry : ทหารราบ, ทหารบก infantry : ทหารเรือ marines : ทหารเวรขี่ม้า a mounted orderly : ทหารสื่อสาร a signalling corps : ทหารอาสาสมัคร militia : ที่พักทหาร barracks : นายทหาร an officer.

ทอ tau *v.* (1) to weave, *ex.* ทอผ้า to weave threads into cloth : ทอแพร to weave silk fabrics : ทอเสื่อ to weave reeds into mats or matting : ช่างทอ a weaver : (2) to gore (as with the horns or antlers) : (3) to butt (as a goat) : (4) to answer back in an angry manner, *ex.* ด่าทอ to slander ; to lampoon ; to curse : (5) to emit rays or reflect light, *ex.* ทอแสง.

ท่อ tau[3] *n.* (1) a metal tube or pipe, *ex.* ท่อไอน้ำ a steam pipe : ท่อถ้อย to defame ; to refute ; to answer : ท่อไอเสีย an exhaust pipe : (2) a flume ; a chute ; a conduit for water, *ex.* ท่อธาร a public drinking fountain : ท่อน้ำ a water pipe : ท่อน้ำประปา a water main : ท่อยาง a rubber tube : ท่ออิฐท่อหิน an aqueduct : (3) an enclosed smoke passage ; a chimney, *ex.* ท่อเพลิง a flue for fire and smoke : ฝังท่อ to lay a water main, or drain underground.

ท้อ tau[5] *v.* to be disinclined to proceed with (as a project or aim) ; to demur or hesitate ; to be daunted : ท้อใจ depressed ; melancholy ; discouraged ; cast down ; de-

jected : ท้อถอย inclined to abandon ; disheartened ; fearful of consequences : ท้อถ้อย, ถ้อถ้อย see ท่อถ้อย : ท้อแท้ weakened ; exhausted ; enfeebled ; tottering.

ทอก (นกยางทอก) tauk[3] *n.* an ancient name for the black-winged egret.

ทอง taung *n.* gold : ทอง (ขนม) a kind of sweetmeat : ทอง, ทองกวาว *Siam.,* จอมทอง *Siam., Peninsula,* ก้าว, กว๋าว *N. Laos,* จาน *E. Laos,* จ้า *Khmer, Surin* (ต้น) *Butea frondosa* (*Leguminosae*), the flame of the forest, a widespreading tree growing in the plains subject to flood. It reaches a height of about 40 feet and bears a profusion of beautiful, crimson or orange-scarlet flowers in the dry months. The tree furnishes a resin (kino), and a useful fibre from the bark ; a lac is produced on the young twigs, and in India the flowers yield yellow and orange dyes. In northern Siam these trees were protected and leased out for growing sticklac (Cb. p. 445) ; *B. monosperma,* a tree of Java, India and Siam. In India it gives a dye which is impermanent on cotton but better on silk, but which can never be useful in international trade. Its gum is medicinal, and is also used by dyers. The bark tans, and can be made into cordage· The seeds give oil. The leaves serve as fodder. The wood is used for various objects connected with wells, as it stands soaking. The lac insect feeds on the tree, which, in Java, has no use beyond supplying fuel (BURK. p. 384) ; *Erythrina suberosa* (*Leguminosae*), an erect tree with large, leathery, broad, trifoliate leaves, indigenous to the forest of dry regions of India, Ceylon, Burma, Siam and Malaya. The timber is soft, but sufficiently light and durable for many purposes. It is used for sieve-frames, packing-cases, water-troughs, planking, boxes intended to be lacquered, and scabbards of native swords. It is suitable for matches and match-boxes (MCM. pp. 85, 206, 417, 440, 466 : BURK. p. 946 : V. P. p. 141) : ทอง (ปลา) *Parasilurus* (Dept. Agri. &

Fisheries) : ทองกร bracelets ; armlets (used only for royalty) : ทองขาว aluminium : ทองเครือ *Siam.*, ตานจอมทอง *Siam.*, *Chumpawn*, กว่าวเคือ *N. Laos*, จานเคือ *E. Laos*, โพ้ตะกุ *Karen, Kanburi* (ต้น) *Butea superba* (*Leguminosae*), a tree found as far south as the Siamese Malay States (cb. p. 445 : Burk. p. 384) : ทอง-คำ pure gold : ทองคำขาว platinum : ทอง-คำเปลว gold in tissue ; gold-leaf : ทองเคลือบ, กาไหล่, อาบ gold plated ; gold washed : ทอง-ดำ, ทองปลายแขน (ต้น) a species of the mango : ทองเดือนห้า *N. Laos*, ทองบ่า *Laos*, ทองหลาง *Laos, Lampang* (ต้น) *Erythrina stricta* (*Legumi-nosae*), a tree of south and south-west India. The light wood is used by Malabar fishermen for floats (cb. p. 441 : Burk. p. 946) : ทองแดง copper : ทองทราย gold-dust ; gold-sand : ทองแท่ง ingots of gold : ทองธรรมชาติ gold in the natural state : ทองนพคุณ the purest quality of gold : ทองเนื้อต่ำ an inferior grade of gold : ทองบ้าน *N. Laos* (ต้น) *Ery-thrina variegata, var. orientalis* (*Legumino-sae*), coral-tree, a moderately tall tree, native of the coastal forests from Bombay to the Pacific Islands, and much planted inland, so that it can be found in most places south of the Himalayas and southward from southern China. The tree is used for supporting pep-per, shading coffee, etc, and for making fences. It is easily grown from cuttings. The timber is white and is of little use, but can be made into packing-cases. The bark is used in the Malay Peninsula for curing tooth-ache. In the Peninsula the leaves are used for poulticing sores, while in the Nether-lands East Indies they are eaten as a vegetable. The seeds are poisonous when raw, but are eaten when boiled or roasted. Hypophorine is found in the seeds and erythrinine in the leaves and bark—both poisonous alkaloids. Saponin is also present in leaves and bark (cb. p. 442 : Burk. p. 948) : ทองใบ gold-leaf : ทองปราย an ancient fire-arm : ทองแปรธาตุ alchemy : ทองเผือก (ต้น) *Erythrina indica*

(*Leguminosae*), thorny dadad, a medium-sized, quick-growing tree with large trifoliate leaves ; it is deciduous in the dry season, un-less coppiced. The bright red flowers are borne in tufts at the tips of the branches when the latter are bare of leaves, in the dry season (MCM. p. 88 : V. P. p. 142) : ทองพันชั่ง (ต้น) *Rhinacanthus communis* (*Acanthaceae*) (Kerr), a bush growing about three feet high. A tincture of the macerated roots is a specific for many skin diseases : ทองพันดุลย์ *Siam.* (ต้น) *Decaschistia parviflora* (*Malvaceae*) (cb. p. 155) : ทองพลุ a sweetmeat made of rice-flour and fried in lard : ทองม้วน a sweet-meat : ทองย่อน name of a Siamese song : ทองย้อย, ทองสุก a sort of durian : ทองลิ่น, มะลิเลื่อย, สร้อยนกเขา (ปลา) *Dangila kuhli* (*Cy-prinidae*), a carp (Dept. Agri. & Fisheries) : ทองแล่ง a pattern of gold-tinsel embroidery : ทองรูปพรรณ *lit.* "gold in irregular shapes," *i. e.* ornaments, trinkets, fragments of gold (lumped together to be sold or melted) : ทองหยอด a kind of sweetmeat : ทองหยิบ a kind of sweetmeat ; a species of jack-fruit : ทองหลาง, ทองโหลง *Siam., Laos* (ต้น) *Erythrina fusca* (*Leguminosae*), a prickly tree of about 50 feet, and even up to 100 feet in height, found in the Mascarene Islands, and from north-eastern India, to Ceylon, Java and Polynesia, near the seashore, on riversides, and places where the soil conditions prevent truly high evergreen forest. The wood is capable of the same uses as other *Erythrinas* (cb. p. 439 : Burk. p. 945) ; ทองมืดขุด *Laos, E. lithosperna* ; *E. stricta* see ทองเดือนห้า *N. Laos* ; *E. variegata, var. orientalis* see ทองบ้าน (cb. pp. 440, 441, 442) ; *Erythrina spp.* (V. P. p. 143), dadad, a moderate-sized, spineless tree of very rapid growth, with trifoliate leaves which afford a quantity of foliage valued for mulching or green manuring. There are scarlet and orange-flowered varieties ; they are rather showy (MCM. pp. 27, 37, 214, 356, 446, 517) : ทองหลางใบมน (ต้น) *Erythrina arborescens* (*Le-guminosae*), tiger's claw, Indian coral tree.

It is found in northern India, northern Siam and French Indo-China: also in Bangkok orchards. It reaches a height of forty-five feet. The branches and branchlets are stout, and armed with many sharp prickles; the leaflets, of which there are three in a leaf, have a broad base and are nearly triangular in outline; the racemes are terminal and bear numerous large red flowers before the appearance of any foliage. The pods are four to eight inches long containing several dark carmine coloured seeds the size of a bean (J. F. ROCK: The orn. Trees of Hawaii p. 119: V. P. p. 143: MCM. p. 88): ทองเหลือง brass: ทองอังกฤษ copper-tinsel (imported from China).

ท่อง taung[3] v. to walk back and forth: ท่องเที่ยว to go sightseeing: ท่องน้ำ to wade through the water: ท่องบ่น to memorize by rote.

ท้อง taung[5] n. (1) the visceral cavity; a hollow space, place or organ (as the stomach): (2) a region, area or surface (as land or water): (3) a depression; a concavity; a hollowed-out reach of ground (as a canal): ท้อง (ช่องนาภี) the abdominal cavity; ท้องแก่ great with child; the last months of pregnancy: ท้องขึ้น flatulency: ท้องคลอง a canal; the canal-bed: ท้องคุ้ง the concave bank in the bend of a river or canal; the current side of a river's bend: ท้องฉนวน a curtained passage (for ladies of a palace to pass in private): ท้องเดิน, ท้องร่วง diarrhoea: ท้องตรา an official order bearing the seal of a minister of state: ท้องที่ a district, section or sphere of authority (as in a commune), ex. เกิดฆ่ากันตายในท้องที่ของเรา a murder was perpetrated in the region under our supervision: ท้องทุ่ง, ท้องนา a paddy field, region or quarter, ex. ท้องทุ่งแขวงกรุงเก่า in the rice-field tract skirting Ayuthia: ท้องน่อง the calf of the leg: ท้องน้อย the supra-pubic region; the hypo-gastrium; the bladder: ท้องปลิง (ตะไบ) a file with concave and convex surfaces: ท้องผูก constipated; constipation: ท้องพล

แปบ, แปบขาว, แปบควาย, ดาบลาว, ผักพร้า(ปลา) Chela oxygastroides (Cyprinidae), a river fish of the Peninsula. It is highly esteemed by the Malays who salt and dry all they do not consume locally. These salted fish are sent to Siam and Indo-China (BURK. p. 522); Culter siamensis; Macrocheirichthys macrochirus (Cyprinidae) (Dept. Agri. & Fisheries): ท้องพลุ้ย, พุงโร, ท้องโป่ง pot-bellied; a protrubing abdomen: ท้องพอง a gas-distended abdomen: ท้องฟ้า the arch, vault or canopy of the heavens: ท้องเฟ้อ flatulency with eructation of gas: ท้องมาน abdominal dropsy; ascites: ท้องมือ, ฝ่ามือ the palm of the hand: ท้องร่อง irrigating ditches; garden water-ways: ท้องเรื่อง the main points, gist, important parts or high lights of a story or history: ท้องลาน concaved; rounded along the upper surface (as the petiole of a palm leaf): ท้องสาว a primipara: ท้องเสีย a disordered condition of the digestive tract: ท้องไม้ the belly of a timber: ท้องพระโรง a throne-hall: ท้องร้อง, ท้องลั่น a rumbling sound due to gas passing along the intestines: ท้องเรือ the hold of a ship; the freight space of a boat; the bottom of a boat (inside and outside): มีท้อง, มีครรภ์, ตั้งท้อง to be with child; to become pregnant: ท้องสนาม a lawn; an open arena for sports; a plaza (as in front of provincial government offices): ท้องเสียด, เสียดท้อง lancinating pain in the abdominal cavity: ท้องแห้ง to be in a starved condition: ตลาดท้องน้ำ a water-market.

ทอด ๑ taut[3] v. to fry; to prostrate oneself; to lay down; to throw; to drop or cast; to dismiss (as from the mind); to cast off or set aside (as responsibilities): ทอดกฐิน see กฐิน p. 3: ทอดโกลน to lay down rollers or runners (as under a boat or log to facilitate transportation): ทอดแขน, ทอดขา to extend the arms and legs in a relaxed position: (ขาย) ทอดตลาด to sell at random; to sell by auction: ทอดตาดู to settle the eyes on a distant object; to look with a steady gaze: ทอดทฤษฎี to look intently at; to gaze fixedly at: ทอดทั้ง

to discard ownership; to ignore all responsibility for: ทอดน่อง to walk leisurely or deliberately along: ทอดผ้าป่า to lay or spread clothing as if found in the forest; a method of presenting robes to Buddhist monks at a monastery. These, along with numerous other gifts, are hung on, or laid at the base of a decorated tree placed in a huge ornamented basket, which is carried in procession to the monastery where the priests help themselves: ทอดพระที่ to lay, spread, or hang the necessary paraphernalia for a royal boudoir or bedchamber: ทอดพระเนตร to look at; to turn the face towards (used only for royalty): ทอดมัน fish or prawns rolled in chilli sauce and fried: ทอดยอด to extend fresh shoots (descriptive of growing vines): ทอดรวง to head out (as rice heads, wheat heads, etc.): ทอดสะพาน to bridge; *colloq.* to employ an emissary to carry on negotiations: ทอดเสียง to prolong the voice (as in singing): ทอดหญ้า to spread out grass (as fodder for cattle or elephants): ทอดหุ่ย to lie sprawled out (as from exhaustion): ทอดเหตุ to drop, dismiss or discard issues, or questions of disagreement (as in controversial matters): ทอดขนม to fry cakes: ทอดโขลง (ช้าง) to free a herd of elephants: ทอดตัว to become submissive to the authority of another: ทอดทุ่น to lay buoys or floats; to cast overboard cork floats attached to fishing tackle: ทอดธุระ to relinquish all obligation or liability for: ทอดปลา to fry fish: ทอดอาลัย to renounce all responsibilities and entanglements; to be resigned to the inevitable.

ทอด ๒   taut[3] *n.* a part, section or stretch of a course to be run or travelled: ทอดตรง the straight portion (as of a racecourse): ทอดที่มีอันตราย the dangerous section of the journey, the course or route: ไปทอดนี้แล้ว-เราพ้นภัย after passing this part we are out of the zone of danger.

ทอด ๓   taut[3] *n.* regarding time, as duration, portion, period, span, or spell: เดิน-ทอดเดียวก็ถึง the whole distance can be walked without stopping: ทอดเดียว at one time; without intermission or interruption; from start to finish without stopping: นอนทอด-เดียว to sleep for only a spell: ว่าให้แล้วใน ทอดเดียว all is to be said at one time.

ทอน   taun *v.* (1) to cut (as forest timber into the required lengths): (2) to make change (as large bills into a variety of small coins): (3) to break up or divide into smaller pieces or shorter lengths (as making firewood): เงินทอน the amount returned: ทอนเงิน to return the change (as after a purchase): ทอนทุน see ขาดทุน p. 154: ทอนอายุ to shorten one's life (as by nefarious practices).

ท่อน   taun[3] *n.* a piece or remnant (as cloth); a bit, part, portion, section, segment or fraction (as of a stalk of sugar-cane): ตัดเป็นท่อนๆ to cut into sections or lengths: ท่อนตัว, ท่อนองค์ the trunk or middle portion of the body: ท่อนหัว the head section (as of fish): หินท่อนใหญ่ a chunk or lump of rock or stone.

ทอย   toy *v.* to pitch or project from the hand by swinging the arm like a pendulum: to throw underhand (as quoits or stangs): เดินทอยๆ กันไป to walk in consecutive order or in single file: ทอยกอง a game where pennies, cowries or rounded pieces of roof tiles are pitched in a pile: ทอยเรียด to throw (so as to make the thing thrown follow the surface of the ground): ลูกทอย wooden pegs driven into the trunk of a tree, serving as steps or as a ladder.

ทะทัด   ta[6]-tat[6] *v.* to shake (as a garment); to make tremble, or to cause to vibrate rapidly; to jolt.

ทะทา see กระทา (นก) p. 34.

ทะทาย   ta[6]-tai *v.* to catch; to take hold of.

ทะท้าว   ta[6]-tow[5] *adj.* quaking; quivering; shivering; trembling.

ทะนง, ทระนง ta⁶-nong v. to be self-confident; to be arrogant, haughty or overbearing: ทะนงศักดิ์ to glory in, or to be exultant in one's rank or official position.

ทะนน ta⁶-non n. a large-sized earthen pot for holding water or palm-sugar.

ทะนนไชย, ลังไทร Laos, Krabin, แพงพวย– บ้า Siam., ลันไชย Siam., Ratburi, รวงไทร Laos, Ubon, ศรีทนนไชย Laos, Korat (ต้น) ta⁶-non-chai n. Buchanania siamensis (Anacardiaceae), a tree with indifferent timber (cb. p. 350).

ทะนะ, เทอญนะ, เถิดนะ ta⁶-na⁶ a form of polite request implying immediate response on the part of the one spoken to, ex. ขอให้ทำเทอญนะเพื่อเห็นแก่คนป่วย will you not kindly do it for the sake of the sick person: ขอให้ไปทะนะ will you kindly go (for me).

ทะนาน ta⁶-nan n. a coconut shell capacity measure for milled rice. The shell is dressed, polished thin, with a hole in the bottom, about 5 cm. in diameter. Owing to the irregularities in size, this method proved most unsatisfactory as no two shells contain the same quantity. In ordinary dealings, twenty of these measures is assumed to equal a bucket of rice. This measure has now been superseded by the ทะนานหลวง, one litre, the standard capacity measure adopted by the government.

ทะนุ, ทะนุก ta⁶-noo⁶ v. to provide sustenance for (as physical, moral and financial); to act in the capacity of a guardian: ทะนุถนอม, ทะนุกถนอม to foster or cherish with tender, loving, motherly care; to lavish affectionate care upon: ทะนุบำรุง to care for by supplying the necessaries (as food, shelter and education, for a ward), or for repairs and up-keep (as for buildings).

ทะบุ ta⁶-boo n. a fort; a fortress; a fortification; a castle; a citadel.

ทะเบียน ta⁶-bee-an n. a record; a roll; a register; a catalogue; an inventory.

ทะมุน ta⁶-meun³ adj. extremely high, as though touching the sky.

ทะโมน ta⁶-mon adj. high and large; standing alone and tall (as a mountain peak).

ทะยอย ta⁶-yoi n. a Siamese song: adj. following gradually or straggling along (as members of a caravan).

ทะยาทะแยแส ta⁶-yah-ta⁶-yaa-saa² v. to be solicitous; to be interested in; to care for.

ทะยาน ta⁶-yan adj. ambitious; aspiring; desirous (as in striving to attain some difficult objective): ทะยานใจ, เหิมใจ to be possessed with a self-exalted spirit.

ทะเยอทะยาน ta⁶-yur-ta⁶-yan v. to be grasping; to be greedy of gain; to be avaricious.

ทะแยง ta⁶-yaang adv. diagonally.

ทะลวง ta⁶-loo-ang v. to hollow out or bore a hole through the central portion (as a worm in the trunk of a tree); to make a hole or passage through (as by digging underground); to excavate (as a tunnel): ทะลวงพื้น to force a passage into or through by cutting with a knife (as in underbrush).

ทะลัก ta⁶-lak⁶ v. to protrude (as brain matter through a fracture of the skull); to gush forth in an uncontrolled manner (as water from an artesian well); to be ejected from the mouth (as vomited matter).

ทะลักทะแลง ta⁶-lak⁶-ta⁶-laang adj. irregular; uncontrolled; not conforming to rule or order.

ทะลาย ta⁶-lai v. to be utterly destroyed (as buildings from an earthquake); to fall or tumble down (as a wall in a ruinous condition): n. a bunch or cluster of fruit (as coconuts or areca nuts).

ทะลึ่ง　　ta⁶-leung³ v. to act boisterously; to intrude by word or action; to force oneself in without invitation.

ทะลุ　　ta⁶-loo⁶ adj. perforated (as type impressions through a paper); pierced through; penetrating; extending the entire distance through (as a bullet penetrating the chest or thorax into the lung): ทะลุกลางปล้อง lit. "perforated midway," i. e. interrupted during a conversation.

ทะลุดทะลาด　　ta⁶-loot⁶-ta⁶-lat³ adj. heedless; thoughtless; careless: ทำโดยทะลุดทะลาด quickly and imperfectly done.

ทะเล　　ta⁶-lay n. a sea: ทะเล (งู) the sea snake, Enhydrina valakadien (M. S., N. H. J. S. S. I, 3, p. 177): ทะเลทราย a desert: ทะเล- บ้า a turbulent sea: ทะเลสาป a lake: ทะเลหลวง the high seas; the ocean.

ทะเล้น, ทะลัก　　ta⁶-len⁵ v. to bulge; to protrude; to extend beyond the surface (as intestines from an abdominal perforation).

ทะเลาะ　　ta⁶-lau⁶ v. to quarrel; to dispute: การทะเลาะวิวาท an altercation; a controversy; a contention.

ทวาย　　ta⁶-wai n. (1) Tavoy, a city on the Tavoy river about 30 miles from its mouth, and the headquarters of the district of that name on the Tenasserim coast of southern Burma; to the east and west, ranges of hills run nearly north and south. Tavoy is almost directly west of Bangkok. The surrounding land is under rice cultivation. Wolfram and tin are the valuable mineral products (Murray's Handbook India p. 647); other spellings, Tavil, Tawoy (Anderson p. 32): (2) fruit ripening out of season.

ทะเวน　　ta⁶-wen v. to expose prisoners to public view for derision.

ทัก　　tak⁶ v. to accost; to speak to; to address a friend in passing: ทักท้วง to oppose or object to; to contradict: ทักทาย to chat

with; to converse with in a familiar manner: วันทักทิน an inauspicious day (used in fortunetelling).

ทักข์, ทักษ　　tak⁶ n. the right hand, or side; efficient; competent (H. C. D. p. 76); ability; power; strength; intelligence; skill.

ทักขิญญ์, ทากษิณย์　　tak⁶-kin² P. n. dexterity; skill; gallantry; kindness; consideration; piety; belonging to, or worthy of a sacrificial fee (S. E. D. p. 475).

ทักขิณ　see ทักษิณ p. 407.

ทักขิณา　see ทักษิณา p. 408.

ทักขิณาบถ　　tak⁶-ki⁴-nah-bot⁴ P. n. the southern country (chd. p. 110).

ทักขิณาวัฏ　　tak⁶-ki⁴-nah-wat⁶ adj. turning to the right (chd. p. 110); moving or turning towards the right hand (observed as a token of respect when leaving sacred objects).

ทักขิโณทก, ทักษิโณทก　　tak⁶-ki⁴-noh-tok⁶ P. n. water poured into the right hand of a priest as a ratification of an offering of value that either has been made, or is about to be made; "water of donation" (chd. p. 110): น้ำกรวด consecrated water poured as a blessing on donated objects which are too large to handle (as a sala, or battle-ship.)

ทักษ　　tak⁶-sa⁴ P. S. n. right; towards the right hand or side; ability; fitness; talent; strength of will; energy (S. E. D. p. 465): ทักษกันยา, ทักษชา a daughter of Daksha (พระ- ทักษา), who was a son of Brahma, and a lawgiver (H. C. D. p. 76): ทักษบดี lord of the faculties.

ทักษิณ, ทักขิณ　　tak⁶-sin² S. n. the right hand or side when facing the east, thus south; an appellation of Siva (S. E. D. p. 465): ทักษิณนิกาย a southern religious group or sect in contradistinction to อุตตรนิกาย a northern religious sect: ทักษิณบัญจาล belonging or relating to the Panchala (sometimes identified with the Punjab) (H.C.D. p. 226): ทักษิณบี้ศจิม, ทักษิณาบร south-west; south-western: ทักษิณ-ภาค the southern hemisphere: ทักษิณาจล *lit.* "mountains to the south," *i. e.* the Himalayas: ทักษิณาจาร one whose conduct is correct or upright: ทักษิณาจารี followers of the right-hand form of Sakta ritual (H. C. D. p. 79): ทักษิณาธิบดี the lord of the Deccan, a part of India south-west of the Nerbudda river or as far as the Kistna river: ทัก-ษิณายน *lit.* "the southward way," *i. e.* the way to Yama's quarters, or in the direction of the god of Death: ทักษิณาวรรต circling (in procession) towards the right or clockwise: .ทักษิณาศา the southern quarter: ทักษิณาศาบดี *lit.* "lord of the south," *i. e.* Phra Yama or the god of Death.

ทักษิณา, ทักขิณา   tak[6]-si[4]-nah *S. n.* a gift; alms given to Buddhist monks; towards the right when facing the east; the southern quarter (chd. p. 109); the circumambulatory ceremony: ทักษิณาเทศน์ a thanksgiving gift or offering: ทักษิณาบถ the southern region, *i. e.* the Deccan.

ทัคธี์   tak[6] *S. adj.* burnt; scorched; consumed by fire; tormented; distressed; hungry; dry; insipid (S. E. D. p. 466).

ทั่ง   tang[3] *n.* an anvil.

ทั้ง   tang[5] *adj.* entire; complete; whole; undivided: *adv.* wholly; entirely; also; likewise; besides: *prep.* with; in the time of; in addition to: กับทั้ง together with: ทั้งนั้น all that; all those: ทั้ง all of these: ทั้งบ้าน the whole village: ทั้งพวก an un-divided company, group or gang: ทั้งเพ the complete number; the whole crowd: ทั้งมวญ entirely: ทั้งเมือง the entire city: ทั้งแม่ทั้งลูก both mother and child: ทั้งวัง the complete number of those in the palace: ทั้งสอง both together: ทั้งสิ้น altogether: ทั้งหมด, ทั้งหลาย, ทั้งปวง all.

ทั้งวล, ทั้งวํทั้งวล   tang-won *v.* to be anx-ious for or about: *n.* anxiety; solicitude.

ทัณฑ์   tan *P. S. n.* (1) a stick; a staff; a rod; a pole; a club or cudgel; the stalk, branch or stem (of a tree); the handle (of a ladle, saucepan, fly-flap or parasol): (2) in reference to power, the rod as a symbol of judicial power, authority and punishment; control; restraint; violence (S. E. D. p. 466): ทัณฑกรรม punishment: ทัณฑฆาต the inflic-tion of capital punishment; the name of a mark " ๎ " which, when placed over a letter, indicates that it is to be silent; a dead letter mark: ทัณฑธร *lit.* "a rod-bearer," *i. e.* a punisher; a judge; a king; Yama: ทัณฑ-นายก *lit.* "rod-applier," *i. e.* a judge; a mag-istrate; an officer of the law: ทัณฑนีติ an application of the rod; the administration of justice; laws: ทัณฑ์บน a verbal or written promise of good behaviour or deport-ment, otherwise of being willing to stand the punishment: ทัณฑปาศก *lit.* "one holding a noose to catch offenders," *i. e.* a policeman: ทัณฑภัย the dread of punish-ment: ทัณฑมุข *lit.* "the leader of a column or army," *i. e.* a captain; a general: ทัณฑ-ยาตรา a procession; a military expedition; a bridal procession: ทัณฑยาม a day: ทัณฑ-วาลธิ *lit.* "stick-tailed," *i. e.* an elephant: ทัณฑสถาน a division of an army: ทัณฑหัสดี์ *lit.* "staff-handed," *i. e.* a door-keeper; a watchman: ทัณฑาธิบดี a chief judge.

ทัณฑี   tan-tee *n. lit.* "one who carries a cane," *i. e.* an old man; a gate-guard; a policeman.

ทัด   tat[6] *adj.* equal; equivalent; tantamount: ทัดกัน to equal another in skill (as in needle-work): ทัดดอกไม้ to wear a flower behind the ear: ทัดบุหรี่ to carry a cigar behind the ear: ทัดหู to wear tucked in the ear (as coins), or behind the ear (as a pencil).

ทัดทาน   tat[6]-tan *v.* to make objection or opposition in a controversy; to oppose; to resist.

ทัน   tan *v.* to be equal to another (as in a race):   เทือบทันกัน to be a good runner-up; to be almost able to overtake another; almost to equal another (as in grades during an examination):   ทันกัน to be able to overtake; to be able to come up to another: ทันการทันงาน to be prompt at work: ทันกิน in time to be eaten: ทันควัน prompt; alert; quick: ทันใด, ทันที instantly; at the same moment; at once: ทันตา during one's lifetime; having the privilege of seeing: ทันน้ำ to be in time for the tide: ทันอกทันใจ immediately; without delay; quick as the mind demands: บ่าทัน see พุดซา: ไล่ทัน to catch up with (as in a race or a competition):   ไม่ทันรู้ตัว to be taken unawares.

ทันต ๑   tan-dta[4] *P. S. n.* a tooth; an elephant's tooth; ivory (S. E. D. p. 468):   ทันตกัฏฐะ a small piece of wood (of a particular tree) used as a toothpick: ทันตโปณ *lit.* " teeth-cleaner," *i. e.* a small piece of wood; tooth-brushes.

ทันต ๒   tan-dta[4] *P. v.* to be tamed; to be subdued; to be trained; to exert self-control; to be temperate (chd. p. 111).

ทันติน, ทันตี   tan-dtin *P. n. lit.* " an animal with tusks," *i. e.* an elephant (chd. p. 111).

ทันธ   tan-ta[6] *P. adj.* idle; slothful; slow; heavy; foolish (chd. p. 111).

ทับ   tap[6] *v.* to lay one article on top of another (as boards into a pile); to fall on top of (as bricks from a building); to be held in place (as paper by a weight); to be oppressed or weighed down (as by sorrow or adversity): *n.* a hut; a shack; a hovel: กลั่นสามทับ three times over (as re-distillation):   ทับกัน to be super-imposed: ทับควาย a shed for buffaloes: ทับทรวง to press upon the chest or breast (as with ornaments, jewelry, decorations or a breastplate):   ทับทาง (งู) a poisonous snake, deriving its name from the fact that the victim dies on the road where he is bitten.

ทับทิม (พลอย)   tap[6]-tim *n.* (1) a ruby: (2) ทับทิม, ทนตพืช (ต้น) *Punica granatum* (*Punicaceae*), pomegranate, a small ornamental tree, with large scarlet flowers, native of Persia. The fruit is the size of a large apple, with a tough rind, of a bright red or orange-yellow colour when ripe, and crowned with persistent calyx lobes. The succulent, juicy coating of the numerous seeds is of a sweet acid taste, though sometimes very tart and astringent. Superior varieties are described as " almost seedless, very sweet, deliciously perfumed, and as large as an infant's head." The fruit ferments easily and yields a wine, with the flavour of raspberries, which was used in ancient Egypt. In ancient Egypt, Greece and India, the pomegranate was used medicinally, the uses being varied. In Java, ink is sometimes made from the leaves infused with native vinegar. The Syrians and Phoenicians used the rind for tanning, and it is still so used in some continental countries. The wood is hard and can be used for small objects (MCM. p. 269 : Burk. p. 1839):   *adj.* red.

ทับสมิงคลา (งู)   tap[6]-sa[4]-ming[2]-klah *n.* a poisonous snake with black and white rings along the body.

ทัพ   tap[6] *n.* army; fighting forces; flight; motion; sport; retreat: กองทัพ, กองพลรบ troops; soldiers: ขัดตาทัพ to out-wit, or cut off the lines of an enemy: กองทัพผี a squad of ambushed forces or spies (as in guerilla warfare):   ทัพหน้า the front line or vanguard of an army: ทัพหนุน reserve forces: ทัพหลัง the rear-guard: แม่ทัพ a general: ยกกองทัพ to advance an army.

ทัพพะ   tap[6]-pa[6] *P. n.* wealth; property; goods; money; substance; a thing; an object (as personal belongings) (S. E. D. p. 501): ทัพพสัมภาร sundry wooden materials necessary for the building of a house, boat or carriage.

ทัพพี   see ทรพี ๑ p. 397.

ทัย see ทยา p. 395.

ทั่ว   too-ah[3] *adj.* entire; whole; total; complete in all parts; containing all; every: *adv.* all over: แจกให้ทั่ว ๆ กัน to distribute to each one: ดูให้ทั่ว ๆ to search every place carefully: ทั่วทุกคน everybody: ทั่วทุกแห่ง every place; everywhere: ทั่วไป including all: ทั่วหน้า without exception: ทาสีให้ทั่ว ๆ to paint the whole surface or structure: เที่ยวเสียทั่วเมือง to have travelled the whole city over.

ทัศ   tat[6] *adj.* ten; a suffix to numerals indicating completeness: ยี่สิบทัศ twenty articles: สิบทัศ a total of ten articles.

ทัศน์, ทัสสน see ทรรศนะ p. 397.

ทัศนาการ   tat[6]-sa[4]-nah-gkan *n.* sight; a look.

ทัศนีย, ทัศไนย์ see ทรรศนีย์ p. 397.

ทัพพ   tan-ha[4] *P. n.* bonds; fetters; chains: *adj.* fixed; firm; solid; strong; massive; tight; close; firmly fastened (S. E. D. p. 490): ทัพพกาณฑ์ *lit.* "strong-stemmed," *i. e.* a bamboo: ทัพพการี *lit.* "one acting firmly," *i. e.* a resolute, persevering person: ทัพพนีร *lit.* "strong-juiced," *i. e.* the coconut tree: ทัพพบาท *lit.* "firm-footed," *i. e.* a name for Brahma: ทัพพประหาร a hard or violent stroke: ทัพพผล *lit.* "having hard fruit," *i. e.* the coconut tree: ทัพพมูล *lit.* "having strong hard roots," *i. e.* a coconut tree: ทัพพโลม *lit.* "one having coarse hair or bristles," *i. e.* a hog.

ทัพพหิกรณ์   tan-hi[4]-gkaun *n. P.S.* corroboration; confirmation; ratification (S. E. D. p. 490).

ทัพพหิกรรม   tan-hi[4]-gkum *P. n.* the process of making stronger, firmer or more permanent (as by the repetition of strokes) (chd. p. 110).

ทา   tah *v.* to rub or apply with the hands (as face powder); to smear or daub on with the finger-tips or a pledget of cotton (as an ointment or a remedy); to apply with a brush (as paint or varnish): เครื่องทา sundry materials to be applied (as coloured oils or colour washes): ทาเครื่องปรุง to anoint with, or to rub on a compound of scents, or a mixture of perfumes: ทาโล้ *N. Laos,* หมูบี้ *Shan* (ต้น) *Schima wallichii (Ternstroemiaceae),* a tree of fair size (cb. p. 130): ยาทา sundry remedies to be applied (as embrocations or liniments).

ท่า   tah[3] *n.* (1) an attitude; a posture; a gesture; a position or manner (as while dancing, walking or performing acrobatic stunts): คอยท่าอยู่ waiting for; waiting; lingering; delaying; tarrying: ดูท่าทางไม่ดี apprehensive of evil: ได้ท่าได้ทาง to have secured a favourable chance for—; the occasion provides a good opportunity to—: ท่าทาง air; manner; mien; bearing; carriage; style (as of a person whose appearance arouses suspicion): ทำท่า to assume a position in preparation: ทำท่าจะต่อย to take an attitude in preparation for a fight: ทำท่าจะไป to pretend to go: ทำท่าทาง to assume positions or make various gestures: (2) a place for boats or ships to approach the land; a berth for ships to dock; a wharf; a landing place along a river's bank: ตีนท่า the foot of the ladder or steps at a landing stage: ท่าข้าม a fording place for carts or cattle: ท่าช้าง a fording or bathing place for elephants: ท่าซุง a landing or loading place for logs: ท่าตะพาน a pier: ท่าน้ำ a landing platform provided with steps: ท่าเรือ, เมืองท่า a harbour; a port: ท่าเรือจ้าง a ferry-boat landing: ท่าลอก *Siam., Pitsanulok, Korat and Krat,* มะพอก *Siam., Rachaburi,* มะมื่อ, หมักมื่อ *N. Laos,* พอก *E. Laos,* ตะโลก *Khmer, Surin,* เหลอะ *Sui, Surin* (ต้น) *Parinarium annamense (Rosaceae),* a tree whose flowers are infused into a cosmetic used after bathing. A substance like tinder lies in the fruit cavity between the fruit-wall and the seed (cb. p. 563 : Burk. p. 1666): ท่าวัง a landing pavilion in front of a palace: ท่าวัด

a landing stage in front of a Buddhist temple : ท่าสบ the mouth of a river ; an estuary.

ท้า, ท้าทาย tah[5] v. to dare ; to defy ; to challenge to a combat : คำท้าทาย to provoke or excite by defiant words or actions (such as will induce a fight).

ทาก tak[3] n. a land leech (ปลิง water leech) ; [a slug.

ทากษิณย์ see ทักขิญญ์ p. 407.

ทาง tang n. (1) the midrib of broad leaves (as bananas, palms and coconut fronds) : ทางมะพร้าว (ง) *Coluber radiatus*, a snake commonly distributed in plains, gardens and low elevations. Is is nonpoisonous but it strikes fiercely in defence and at the same time expands the neck vertically to intimidate enemies (in contradistinction to the cobras which expand the neck horizontally) (M. S., N. H. J. S. S. I, 2, p. 95) : (2) a way ; a route ; a course : เดิน-ทางบก to use land conveyances or transports : ทางกันดาร a road through a famine-stricken district : ทางช้างเผือก the Milky Way : ทางเดิน a pathway ; a foot-path : ทางตาย a path to destruction or death : ทางน้ำ a route by water : ทางแปด (๘) or มรรค ๘ the holy eightfold path ; the doctrines of the Buddha : ทางผิด a wrong course : ทางไมตรี for the sake of union, friendship or treaty alliance : ทางลัด a cross-cut (as across a river's bend) ; the shorter course : ทางหลวง a public highway : ทางอ้อม a detour : ไปปทางน้ำ to travel by means of water-transports : ไม่รู้จะไปทางไหน to be in doubt which way or course to pursue : (3) n. scheme ; plan ; method ; means : ทางความ the method or plan of procedure of a case in court : ทางทุจจริต methods or means that are deceitful, beguiling or fraudulent : ฟ้องทางอาชญา to institute criminal proceedings against : หาทางให้ดี-กว่านี้ to devise a better expedient than this.

ท้าง tang[5] an ancient form of ทั้ง.

ทาฐะ, ทาฒะ tah-ta[4] n. a tusk ; a fang ; a canine tooth (chd. p. 113).

ทาฐิกะ, ทาฒิกะ tah-ti[4]-gka[4] n. a beard ; whiskers (S. E. D. p. 475)

ทาตา tah-dtah *P. S. n.* a giver ; a donator ; a donor (chd. p. 113).

ทาน ๑ tan *P. S. n.* a donation ; a gift ; alms-giving ; the act of giving, imparting, or teaching (S. E. D. p. 474) : ทานกาม one fond of giving ; a magnanimous person : ทานธรรม one observing liberality as a duty ; generosity : ทานบดี, ทานาธิบดี *lit.* "liberality-lord," *i. e.* a munificent person ; an extraordinarily generous person . ทานบารมี the height of liberality : ทานมัย beneficence ; munificence : ทานโยคย์ worthy of a gift, alms or donations : ทานวัตถุ causes for, or objects worthy of gifts, presents or donations : ทานศาลา a hall or place for alms-giving : ทานศีล liberally disposed ; generous : ทำทาน, ให้ทาน to give alms ; to make a donation.

ทาน ๒ tan v. to serve as a support or prop, ex. ทานกำลัง to keep up the strength : น้ำทานเรือไว้ the water supports the boat.

ทาน ๓ tan v. to be able to stop, oppose or resist, ex. ไม้นี้ทานน้ำหนักไม่ไหว this timber is unable to support the super-imposed weight : เรือทานลมไม่ไหว the boat is unable to withstand the wind.

ทาน ๔ tan v. to re-read ; to re-examine ; to re-tell, ex. ทานบัญชี to re-examine the accounts : ทานหนังสือ, อ่านทาน to re-read (as while comparing with the original) : สอบ-ทาน to corroborate by telling (as the details).

ทาน ๕ tan v. to turn toward : ทานตะวัน (เครื่องสูง) an embroidered sunshade with serrated edge, mounted on a long handle and carried in royal processions : ทนตะวัน (ต้น) *Helianthus annuus (Compositae)*, sun-flower, a native of America, whence it was brought to Spain in the middle of the sixteenth century. It was first grown as a crop in Batavia in 1725. It produces a good edible oil. The disk of the flower-head can be eaten like that of the Jerusalem artichoke. The pith is inferior to sola pith for helmets, nor does it seem suitable to the other purposes for which pith is used. There is a little fibre in the outer part of the stem—too little to be useful—but when freed from pith it can be made into good paper (BURK. p. 1132); *Tithonia diversifolia*, the sun-flower, a very large yellow flower, with a dark-brown centre. The dwarf bushy sorts, 3 to 4 feet high, with small yellow flowers having black centres, are showy and useful as cut flowers.

ท่าน tan[3] *pron.* the second and third personal pronoun, you (as among equals); he; him: ท่านเจ้าคุณ, ท่านเท้า, ท่านพระครู forms of address; honourable sir: ท่านนอบตนจงนอบแทน to reciprocate respect: ท่านรักตนจงรักตอบ to reciprocate or mutually exchange affection.

ทานต์ ๑ tan *S. adj.* tamed; restrained; subdued; broken in; mild (S. E. D. p. 475).

ทานต์ ๒ tan *S. adj.* made of ivory (S. E. D. p. 475).

ทานพ, ทานว tah-nop[6] *P. S. n.* Titans; a class of demons held to be implacable enemies of the gods, sometimes reckoned to number forty, or as many as a hundred (S.E.D. p. 474): ทานพครู a preceptor of the Titans, regent of the planet Venus: ทานพบดี king of the Titans; a name for Rahu (the dragon causing eclipses).

ทาบ tap[3] *v.* see ทับ: to lay one piece upon another as a medium of union, contact or support, as cloth (for a patch), as paper (for tracing over carbon), as metal (for soldering), as a strip of wood (on a cracked carrying pole), as a splint (over a fractured bone): ทาบตัว to place against the body (as while fitting a garment): ทาบทาม to act as an intermediary.

ทาม tam *P. n.* a string; a cord; a rope; a fetter; a girdle; a chaplet; a wreath; a garland for the forehead (S. E. D. p. 475).

ท่ามกลาง tam[3]-gklang *n.* the centre; the central area; the middle: *adv.* in the middle: *prep.* amidst.

ทามริก tam-ma[6]-rik[6] *n.* a traitor; a betrayer: ทามริกภาพ the condition of being guilty of treason, or of betraying one's country.

ทาโมทร tah-moh-taun *S. n. lit.* "having a rope around the waist," *i. e.* an appellation for Krishna. He one day broke the vessels of milk and curds and ate the butter, which made Yasoda (wife of the cowherd Nanda, and foster-mother of Krishna) angry. She fastened a rope round his body, and tied him to a large bowl, but he dragged the bowl away till it caught between two trees and up-rooted them—thus the name (H.C.D. p. 165).

ทาย ๑, ทำนาย tai *v.* to prophesy; to conjecture what the future will be; to foretell by divination; to prognosticate; to predict: หมอทาย, ผู้ทำนายเคราะห์ a fortune-teller; a soothsayer; a sorcerer.

ทาย ๒ tai *v.* a gift; the separate property of a wife (chd. p. 114).

ทาย ๓ tai *P. n.* a forest; a wood; a grove; a clump of trees or bushes (chd. p. 114).

ทาย ๔ tai *P.S. n.* a share; a portion; a part; an inheritance (S. E. D. p. 474): ทายพันธุ์ *lit.* a partner in the inheritance; a brother: ทายภาค a partitioning of the inheritance: ทายวิภาค a division of the property amongst the different heirs: ทายาท a receiver of the inheritance; an heir; a son; a daughter; a kinsman (near or remote): ทายาทโดยพินัย-กรรม์ legatees: ทายาทโดยธรรม a statutory heir: ทายาทย์ the amount of the inheritance: รัชชทายาท a Crown Prince.

ท้าย tai[5] *n.* the rear; the end; the last of a series or file (as of a procession): กระดูก-ท้ายทอย the occipital bone: ท้ายโด่ง the extreme rear; the hindmost part or portion: ท้ายทอย the occipital portion of the skull:

ท้ายเรือ the stern of a boat or vessel: นาย-
ท้าย see นาย: ผลสุดท้าย final results; finally:
สุดท้าย the posterior part; the extreme rear
end: ท้ายบ้าน in the rear of a village or at
the back door of a house: ท้ายน้ำ the last
or lowest stages of a tide; the lower reaches
of a river (in contradistinction to the source
of a river).

ทายก   tah-yok[6] *P. S. n.* a giver; a teller;
a granter; a bestower; a donor: ทายิกา
the feminine form of ทายก (S. E. D. p. 474).

ทายาท   tah-yat[3] *adj.* brave; bold; stubborn;
enduring (as pain or hardship).

ทาร   tan *P. S. n.* a wife (S. E. D. p. 475):
ทารกรรม, ทารกริยา, ทารปริเคราะห์, ทารสงเคราะห์ marriage; the taking of a wife: ทารสัมพันธ์
union with a wife; marriage: ทารสุต wife
and child: ทาราธีน one dependent on a wife.

ทารก   tah-rok[6] *P. S. n.* an infant; a boy;
a son; a child (S. E. D. p. 476): ทาริกา the
feminine form of ทารก, a daughter.

ทารุ   tah-roo[6] *P. S. n.* wood; timber; a
piece of wood; firewood (S. E. D. p. 476):
ทารุกรรม the cutting of wood; wood carving:
ทารุคุรรภ, ทารุบุตรี a wooden puppet; a doll:
ทารุช wooden; made of wood: ทารุบาตร
wooden vessels; a wooden alms-bowl: ทารุ-
ยนตร์ an automatic wooden puppet, doll, or
toy; a marionette: ทารุสตรี a wooden doll.

ทารุกา   tah-roo[6]-gkah *P. S. n.* a wooden
doll or puppet (S. E. D. p. 476).

ทารุณ   tah-roon *P. S. adj.* severe; cruel;
hard; harsh; rough; pitiless; intense; violent
(S. E. D. p. 476): ทารุณกรรม tyranny; oppression; violent treatment.

ทาว   tow *S. n.* fire; heat; distress; a conflagration (S. E. D. p. 476).

ท้าว   tow[5] *n.* an honorary prefix for names
of senior Buddhist monks and aged men
held in respect; a title of rank for lady

attendants in the Royal Household: ท้าวเพี้ย
an ancient title conferred on nobility in the
Laos Royal Court.

ทาส   tat[3] *n.* a male slave; a servant:
ทาสาทาสี slaves in general: ทาสี a female
slave, or a woman servant.

ทำ ๑   tum see กระทำ p. 35: *v.* to do, to
perform, to work, *ex.* แกล้งทำ to do intentionally or wilfully: ทำการทำงาน to perform
manual labour: ทำการผิด to commit offenses;
to give displeasure: ทำการสมรส to marry:
ทำกีดขวาง to obstruct; to hinder: ทำแขวน
to work under great difficulties or handicaps:
ทำคุณ to perform deeds of kindness: ทำเงิน
to work as a silversmith: ทำจ้าง to work
as an hireling: ทำตามคำสั่ง to follow instructions: ทำโทษ to inflict a punishment:
ทำน้ำ, ทำหนอง to work in rivers and swamps
(as catching and marketing fish): ทำนา to
cultivate the land: ทำบุญ to perform
meritorious deeds: ทำป่า to work a forest
(for timber): ทำผิดๆถูกๆ to do in a
haphazard manner: ทำร้าย to assault:
ทำเวร to work in shifts (เข้าเวร on shift, ออกเวร
off shift): ทำเวรทำกรรม to be guilty of
unmeritorious or punishable deeds.

ทำ ๒   tum *v.* to make, *ex.* ค่อยทำค่อยไป to
work along gradually; to refrain from haste
but manifest perseverance: ทำเงินปลอม to
make counterfeit coins or money: ทำตาม-
แบบ to imitate the pattern: ทำโทษอย่างสูง-
สุด to impose capital punishment: ทำบริคณ-
สัญญา to enter into an agreement or contract:
ทำปลอม to falsify: ทำเป็นป่า to make resemble a forest: ทำพินัยกรรมมอบมรดกให้ to
bequeath: ทำมาหากิน to earn a livelihood:
ทำรายงาน to make a report: ทำร้ายร่างกาย
to cause bodily harm: ทำสงคราม to wage
a war: ทำสัญญา to make a contract:
ทำหนังสือปลอม to make a forged document:
ทำเหลว to make a failure or fail to carry out
a project to completion: ทำให้เป็นกลาง to
neutralize: ทำให้เป็นไปตามกฎหมาย to make

conform to law; to legalize: ทำให้ไร้ความ-
สามารถ to render incapable; to incapacitate.

ทำ ๓, ทำให้ tum *v.* to cause; to arouse;
to incite, *ex.* ทำให้เกิดผล to cause to become
fruitful; to stimulate productivity: ทำให้-
เกิดความลำเอียง to incite prejudice: ทำให้-
เกิดความวิวาท to stir up a quarrel: ทำให้-
เกิดความสงสัย to excite discredit or doubt:
ทำให้โกรธกัน to arouse animosity: ทำให้-
ขาดความภักดี to instill enmity; to cause dis-
loyalty: ทำให้คนตาย to cause the death of
a person or persons: ทำให้แตกความเกี่ยวข้อง-
ทางทูต to provoke a severance of diplomatic
relations: ทำให้เป็นของชาติ to insist on becoming nationalized: ทำให้มีเหตุเกิดขึ้น to be
the means of creating trouble or disagreement.

ทำ ๔ tum *v.* to act as; to play the part
of, *ex.* ทำจริง ๆ to act in earnest or sincerely:
ทำเป็นเด็ก ๆ to act childishly: ทำเป็นลิง to act
like a monkey; to act ludicrously: ทำเล่น ๆ
to act in a playful manner; to manifest
insincerity.

ทำนบ tum-nop[6] *n.* a dam; a weir, a dike
or embankment.

ทำนอง tum-naung *n.* way; manner; method;
usual practices; a tune; a mode of chanting
rhymes or poetry.

ทำนาย tum-nai *v.* to prophesy; to predict;
to foretell: ผู้ทำนาย a prophet.

ทำนุ tum-noo[6] *v.* to nurture; to nourish;
to foster; to care for tenderly; to nurse (as a
sickly child or aged invalid): ทำนุบำรุง to
preserve the original condition of some important building or religious edifice by providing means for its restoration and main-
[tenance.
ทำนูน see ทูล p. 421.

ทำเนา tum-now *v.* to reduce vigilance; to
slacken; to ease up on (as the care of something of minor importance): *adv.* never
mind; let it be so.

ทำเนียบ tum-nee-ap[3] *v.* to compare; to
liken: *n.* a directory of government officials;
a government provincial rest-house; a parable; a proverb; a comparison.

ทำไม tum-mai *adv.* why; wherefore; for
what cause, purpose or reason.

ทำลาย tum-lai *v.* to destroy; to abolish;
to overthrow; to dissolve; to pull down;
to break down: ทำลายสมรส to dissolve a
marriage: ทำลายหุ้นส่วน to dissolve partnership.

ทำเล tum-lay *n.* a place; a domicile; a
location; a locality.
[a biped.
ทิ ti[6] *P. adj.* two (S. E. D. p. 504): ทิปท

ทิคัมพร ti[6]-kum-paun *P. S. n. lit.* "sky-
clothed," "those whose only garment is the
atmosphere," *i. e.* nudists; a nude mendicant
(S. E. D. p. 480).

ทิ้ง ting[5] *v.* to throw away (as worn out
garments); to discard; to reject (as something
not meeting the requirements); to give up; to
abandon (as a bad proposition); to separate
from (as man from wife); to seek a divorce:
ทิ้งการ to give up a job or employment:
ทิ้งขว้าง to cast off; to pay no attention to; to
be unsolicitous for: ทิ้งขว้างกลางคัน to abandon midway; to leave half-finished: ทิ้ง-
ทอด to dismiss from the mind forever; to
throw away for good (as being of no more
service): ทิ้งน้ำ to dump into the water:
ทิ้งพ่อ, ทิ้งแม่, ทิ้งเมีย to forsake, or renounce
father, mother and wife: ทิ้งให้ร้าง to
allow to become run down and dilapidated;
to be left deserted and neglected.

ทิช see ทวิช p. 400.

ทิฏฐ ๑ tit[6]-ta[4] *P. S. adj.* seen; beheld;
perceived; noticed; apparent; visible (S. E. D.
p. 491): ทิฏฐธรรม this world; the present
time; mundane existence: ทิฏฐธรรมิก belonging to this world; temporal: ทิฏฐานุคติ
a pattern to follow; an example to emulate.

ทิฏฐ ๒ see ทวิษฏ์ p. 400.

ทิฏฐิ   tit[6]-ti[4]   *P. n.* sight; perception; the faculty of seeing and apprehending by mental activities (S. E. D. p. 492).

ทิฏฐุชุกรรม   tit[6]-too[4]-choo[6]-gkum   *n.* the ability to form correct opinions regarding what has been seen.

ทิตต์, ทิปต์   tit[6]   *P. adj.* blazing; shining; bright; brilliant; glorious; splendid; luminous (S. E. D. p. 481).

ทิน, ทินา   tin   *P. S. n.* a day (S. E. D. p. 478): ทินกร *lit.* "a maker of day or light," *i. e.* the sun: ทินกษัย *lit.* "day-decline," *i. e.* evening: ทินเกศพ, ทินเกสร *lit.* "day-hair," *i. e.* darkness: ทินจรรยา daily acts; duties incident to each day: ทินนาถ, ทินราช, ทินบดี *lit.* "day-lord," "day-king," *i. e.* the sun: ทินนิศ a day and a night: ทินประภา daylight; sunshine: ทินพันธุ์ *lit.* "a friend of the day," *i. e.* the sun: ทินมณี, ทินรัตน์ *lit.* "the day-jewel," *i. e.* the sun: ทินมุข, ทินารมภ์ *lit.* "day-face," *i. e.* day-break; dawn: ทินาคม, ทินารมภ์ dawn; day-break: ทินาวสาน *lit.* "day-close," *i. e.* evening; twilight.

ทินน   tin-na[6]   *P. v.* given; granted; presented; placed; extended (S. E. D. p. 467).

ทินนาทายี   tin-nah-tah-yee   *P. n. lit.* "one taking only what is given," *i. e.* honesty (chd. p. 124).

ทิบท, ทิปท   ti[6]-bot[4]   *P. n.* two-footed; a biped; a person (chd. p. 124).

ทิพ   tip[6]   *P. S. n.* the heavens; sky; day (S. E. D. p. 478).

ทิพย์   tip[6]   *S. adj.* superhuman; supernatural; spiritual; divine; heavenly; celestial (S. E. D. p. 479): ทิพยกานน a celestial grove: ทิพยคายน celestial singers, carolers or musicians: ทิพยจักษุ, ทิพยเนตร supernatural vision; an all-seeing eye: ทิพยญาณ superhuman or divine insight: ทิพยนารี a celestial female; an Apsaras. The Apsarases are the celebrated nymphs of Indra's heaven. They are fairy-like beings, beautiful and voluptuous (H. C. D. p. 19): ทิพยประภาพ one possessing celestial or superhuman power: ทิพยมนตร์ the mystical syllable, "OM", or "A. U. M." a word of solemn invocation, affirmation, benediction and consent, used at the commencement of prayers and religious ceremonies. Originally it was typical of the three Vedas, for in Vedic times there were three principal objects in nature, earth, water, and fire (sun); and three worlds, earth, air and sky; and three forms of matter, solid, liquid and gaseous; and the three Vedic gods, Fire, Wind and Sun—Agni, Indra-Vayu, and Surya. In later times the monosyllable represents the Hindu triad or the union of Vishnu, Siva and Brahma (H. C. D. p. 224): ทิพยมานุษ a demigod; one heavenly born: ทิพยรส *lit.* "a magical liquid," *i. e.* quicksilver; mercury: ทิพยรูป *lit.* "heavenly form," *i. e.* beautiful; pretty; handsome: ทิพยโสตร *lit.* "superhuman ears," *i. e.* an all-hearing ear: ทิพยอาหาร immortal food; spiritual bread; "living bread" (st. john's Gospel 6: 42–51).

ทิพโยทก   tip[6]-pa[6]-yoh-tok[6]   *S. n. lit.* "superhuman water," *i. e.* rain-water.

ทิพา   ti[6]-pah   *P. S. n.* day (S. D. E. p. 478): ทิพากร *lit.* "day-maker," *i. e.* the sun: ทิพาจร a wanderer by day: ทิพานิทรา a sleeper during the day: ทิพาประทีป *lit.* "a day-lamp," *i. e.* an obscure, suspicious, or questionable person: ทิพาภีติ *lit.* "one fearing the day," *i. e.* an owl: ทิพามณี *lit.* "a day-jewel," *i. e.* the sun: ทิพามัธย์ midday; noon: ทิพาวิหาร a rest during the day: ทิพาศัยยา sleeping during the day.

ทิ่ม   tim   *n.* a row of rooms for resting, living, or for storage purposes.

ทิ่ม, แทง   tim[3]   *v.* to prick or be pricked (as by a needle or goad); to be pierced or stabbed (as with a pointed weapon); to poke with a stick; to be gored: ทิ่มแยง, แหย่ to thrust a rod in and out (as when probing a cricket hole).

ทิรัตต์   ti⁶-rat⁶ *P. n.* a period of two days or two nights; a festival lasting that long (S. E. D. p. 505).

ทิว ๑   ti⁶-wa⁶ *adj.* in a row, series, order, file or line: ทิวภูเขาสูง a range of high mountains: ทิวธง a line or festoon of flags.

ทิว ๒   ti⁶-wa⁶ *P.S. n.* the sky; the heavens; day (S. E. D. p. 478): ทิวกาล day-time.

ทิวงคต   ti⁶-wong-kot⁶ *S. v. lit.* "to enter the domain of heaven," *i. e.* to die (for those of high royal rank).

ทิวสะ, ทิวา   ti⁶-wa⁶-sa⁴ *P.S. n.* a day (S. E. D. p. 478): ทิวสภาค a part or portion of a day; day-time.

ทิวากร   ti⁶-wah-gkaun *n. lit.* "day-maker," *i. e.* the sun.

ทิศ, ทิศา   tit⁶ *n.* direction; points of the compass; a region; a quarter, side or section of the horizon: ทิศตะวันออก, ทิศบุรพา the east: ทิศตะวันตก, ทิศประจิม the west: ทิศ-ใต้, ทิศทักษิณ the south: ทิศเหนือ, ทิศอุดร the north: ทิศานุทิศ the four cardinal points including the sub-divisions; in all directions: ทิศบดี, ทิศัมบดี a king; a ruler (chd. p. 125): ทิศาปาโมกข์ famed far and wide; eminent: ทิศาภาค a quarter; a region of the horizon.

ทิส   ti⁶-sa⁴ *n.* an enemy (chd. p. 125).

ที่   tee *n.* time; a favourable or fit occasion; the repeated occurrence of an action or event; the temporal relation of a verb, *ex.* ขอที please desist from doing (as a request when separating parties in a fight): ขอไปที kindly allow me to pass (as when edging one's way through a crowd): จริงที่เดียว absolutely correct: ได้ที having found an opportune

time (as for wreaking vengence): ที่นี้ที่เดียว this once only; no more (under any consideration): ที่แรก the first time; before anything else: ที่ละเล็กที่ละน้อย repeated a little at a time: ที่หน้าที่หลัง at any future time: ที่หลัง subsequently; afterwards: บางที, ลางที sometimes: มาที่เดียว come at once: เห็นที it appears as though; it probably will be so: เห็นที่เขาจะมา probably he will come at—.

ที่ ๑   tee³ *n.* place; locality; district, *ex.* ที่กักขัง a place of confinement: ที่เกิด a birth-place: ที่ใด, ที่ไหน where? ที่นั่ง a place to sit; a chair; a seat: ที่นั้น, ที่นั่น there; at that place: ที่นี่ here: ที่โน่น, ที่โน้น yonder: ที่บ้าน at home: ที่พึ่ง a place of refuge; one who affords help in distress or difficulty: ที่รอด a place of salvation: ที่ร้าง a dilapidated place: ที่ไว้ศพ a morgue: ที่สาธารณ-สถาน a public place: ที่หลังบ้าน behind the house: ที่หลับที่นอน a bed; a mattress: ที่อื่น elsewhere: ที่อยู่ a home; a dwelling.

ที่ ๒   tee³ *adj.* that; such as, *ex.* ที่ยังไม่มา those who have not arrived: ที่รัก such as are worthy of love, amiable, attractive or beloved: ที่เห็นได้ that which can be seen; the visible: มีที่ทาง wealthy or affluent.

ที่ ๓   tee³ *pron.* whose; who; which, *ex.* เจ้าที่ spirits or genii who preside over a place: ที่ชัง those who are detestable: ที่ชั่ว those who are wicked: ที่ดี those who are good.

ที่ ๔   tee³ *adv.* explicitly; affirmatively: ที่จริง of a truth; certainly; honestly; verily: ที่สอง secondly: ที่หนึ่ง firstly: ที่ห้า fifthly.

ทีม, ทีรฆ   tee-ka⁶ *P. S. adj.* long (applied either to time or distance); lofty; high; deep(s. E. D. p. 481): ทีมกาย *lit.* "long-bodied," *i. e.* tall: ทีมเกศ *lit.* "long-haired," *i. e.* a bear: ทีมชงฆ์ *lit.* "long-legged," *i. e.* a camel: ทีมนิกาย *lit.* "a long series or collection," *i. e.* the first division or canto of the Buddhist scriptures which contains thirty-four sutras: ทีมบาท *lit.* "long-legged," *i. e.* the heron: ทีมปฤษฐ์

lit. "long-backed," *i. e.* the snake : ที้นรท
lit. "long-tusked," *i. e.* the hog : ทีนรสน์ *lit.*
"long-tongued," *i. e.* the serpent : ทีนวักตร์,
ทีนพักตร์ *lit.* "long-faced," *i. e.* the elephant :
ทีนายุ long-lived : ทีนายุธ a long weapon ;
a spear ; a javelin.

ทีนาร tee-nan *n. P. S.* a gold coin (used as
a weight) ; a gold ornament (S. E. D.p. 481).

ทีป, ทีปก tee-bpa⁴ *P. S. n.* a lamp ; a light ;
a lantern ; a blaze (S. E. D. p. 481) : ทีปธวัช
lit. "lamp-sign," *i. e.* soot : ทีปภาษน์ *lit.*
"light-receptacle," *i. e.* a lamp : ทีปมาลา a
row or festoon of lamps ; an illumination :
ทีปศัตรู *lit.* "a lamp-foe," *i. e.* moths : ทีปศิขา
the point of a shining body ; the flame of a
lamp.

ทีบังกร tee-bpang-gkaun *P. S. n.* the name of
one of the twenty-four Buddhas (Chd. p. 124).

ทีก see ตู่ p. 372.

ทีกทัก see ตีกๆ p. 370.

ทึก teuk⁶ *Cam. n.* water : ทึกกะลา clear
water : ทึกขะมุม honey : ทึกตระชัก cold
water.

ทึง teung⁵ *v.* to pull ; to draw or pluck out
forcibly ; to tug at ; to tear off ; see ดึง p. 331.

ทึดทือ (นก) turt⁶-tur *n. Bubo orientalis,*
horned owl ; forest horned owl (Gaird. J. S. S.
IX, 1, p. 8).

ทึนทึก turn-turk⁶ *adj.* crotchety ; eccentric ;
having notions or ways of a spinster.

ทึบ turp⁶ *adj.* dense ; compact ; opaque :
บัญญาทึบ slow to understand ; dull ; lacking
sharpness of perception ; stupid ; obtuse.

ทึม turm *n.* a morgue ; a building in which
corpses are kept before cremation.

ทื่อ, ทู่ tur³ *adj.* blunt (as a knife) ; dull ;
stupid (as of understanding) ; torpid ; inactive
(as motions of the bowels) ; simple ; foolish ;
doltish (as one lacking intelligence).

ทุ ๑ too⁶ *P. S. adj.* a prefix implying
wickedness, badness or difficulty (Chd. p. 127) :
ทุจริต evil or false in conduct : ทุปบัญญา
obtuse or stupid.

ทุ ๒ too⁶ *adj.* two (Chd. p. 131) : ทุวิธ
of two kinds.

ทุก ๑ took⁶ *adj.* every ; each ; complete ;
entire ; all : ทุกคน everybody : ทุกเมื่อ
always ; ceaselessly ; perpetually ; at all times :
ทุกแห่ง every place ; everywhere.

ทุก ๒ took⁶ *P. S. n.* second section, division,
clause or group ; a pair (Chd. p. 128) : ทุก,
เค้าตำ, อีทุบ (ปลา) *Wallago moistoma (Siluridae),* sheat fish (suvatti p. 69).

ทุกกฏ took⁶-gkot⁴ *P. S. n.* a sinful act ; an
offence ; a sin ; wickedness (Chd. p 128).

ทุกกร took⁶-gkaun *P. adj.* difficult (Chd.
p. 128) : ทุกกรกิริยา *n.* deeds that are difficult to perform (Chd. p. 128).

ทุกข์ took⁶ *P. n.* trouble ; pain ; affliction ;
sorrow ; distress ; unhappiness (Chd. p. 128) :
ทนทุกข์ to bear or suffer sorrow or distress :
ทุกขฐาน the foundation causes of pain or
grief : ทุกขนิโรธ the state where pain and
sorrow are blotted out, Nirvana : ทุกขเวทนา
a consciousness of trouble, grief or pain :
พ้นทุกข์ to have escaped from a calamity :
ไว้ทุกข์ to wear mourning.

ทุกขักษัย took⁶-kak⁴-sai² *P. S. n.* the
state of cessation of suffering (Chd. p. 128).

ทุกัง, ทุกัง (ปลา) too⁶-gkung *n. Tachysurus leiotetocephalus (Tachysuridae),* a species
of salt water cat-fish having no scales (suvatti
p. 62).

ทุกูล too⁶-gkoon *P. S. n.* a quality of fine
cloth ; woven silk (Chd. p. 128).

ทุคคตะ took⁶-ka⁶-dta⁴ *P. adj.* distressed ;
poor ; indigent ; wretched (Chd. p. 127).

ทุคคติ took⁶-ka⁶-di⁴ *P. n.* the state of
punishment ; hell (Chd. p. 127).

ทุ่ง   tung³ *v.* to pass fecal matter : *n.* (1) feces ; excrement : (2) a plain ; an expanse of level land : ทุ่งนา a paddy field : ทุ่งพระเมรุ the name of the site where royal cremations [are held.

ทุ่ง see ตุง p. 371.

ทุงงา (ปลา)   tung-ngah *n.* a fish, *Lissochilus dukai (Cyprinidae)* (suvatti p. 55).

ทุงแม่หม้าย (ปลา)   tung-maa³-mai³ *n. Hemirhamphus var. (Hemiramphidae),* a kind of fish closely allied to the family of the gar-fish and the flying fish (suvatti p. 91).

ทุจจริต   toot⁶-chja⁴-rit⁴ *P. S. n.* evil or crooked in disposition : *adj.* deceitful ; false ; tricky ; fraudulent ; misbehaving ; bad (chd. p. 127).

ทุฏฐ   toot⁶-ta⁴ *P. S. adj.* corrupt ; depraved ; wicked ; impotent ; low ; vile ; bearing ill-will (chd. p. 130).

ทุฏฐูลล   toot⁶-toon²-la⁶ *P. adj.* lewd ; vulgar ; inelegant ; unrefined (chd. p. 130) : ทุฏฐูลล-วาจา one using unrefined or immodest language.

ทุด   toot⁶ *onomat.* from the sound of spitting in contempt.

ทุติย, ทวีติย   too⁶-dti⁴-ya⁶ *P. S. n.* a son ; a successor ; a companion ; a fellow (friend or foe) : *adj.* for the second time ; doubled ; accompanied by, or furnished with (S. E. D. p. 506).

ทุติยา, ทุติยิกา, ทวิติยา   too⁶-dti⁴-yah *P. S. n.* a female companion or friend ; a wife (S. E. D. p. 506).

ทุน   toon *n.* capital ; resources or wealth available for investments : ขาดทุน to lose in an investment or financial transaction : ทุนเดิม the original amount invested : ทุน-ทรัพย์ money invested ; collateral or funds used as capital : ทุนนอน frozen capital : ทุนรอน capital reserve ; money available for

unexpected investment : ลงทุน to make an investment : ทุนน้อย a small amount of capital.

ทุ่น ๑   toon³ *v.* to act in a subsidiary capacity ; to be supplementary (as aid or support), *ex.* ทุ่นกำลัง one who, or that which strengthens and sustains.

ทุ่น ๒   toon³ *n.* wooden or cork floaters ; a pontoon (as for a landing stage) : ทุ่นเบ็ด a float for a fishing line : ทุ่นสมอ an anchored buoy : ทุ่นอวน floats attached to bag nets.

ทุนนิมิตต์   toon-ni⁶-mit⁶ *n.* omens indicating future disaster or evil.

ทุบ   toop⁶ *v.* to pound into pieces (as breaking bricks) ; to hammer down (as nails) ; to inflict a blow with the fist : ทุบถอง to hit with the fist and nudge or poke with the elbow : ทุบตี to pound with repeated blows (as when killing a snake) : ทุบให้ละเอียด to pulverize by pounding.

ทุบทู้, ทุบทู, ทุบทู   toop⁶-too³ *n.* armour ; a protecting shield ; a large buckler.

ทุพพรรณ   toop⁶-pun *P. adj.* ugly ; unpleasing to the sight ; repulsive (chd. p. 127).

ทุพพล see ทุรพล under ทุร p. 419.

ทุพภาสิต   toop⁶-pah-sit⁴ *P. n.* ill-spoken words, or evil language ; name of the seventh อาบัติ (chd. p. 127).

ทุพภิกข   toop⁶-pik⁶-ka⁴ *P. S. n.* a condition of famine or dearth of food ; a scarcity of food (chd. p. 127) : ทุพภิกขภัย the calamity of a famine, or shortage of food.

ทุพภิกขันดรกัปป์   toop⁶-pik⁶-kun²-da⁴-ra⁶-gkap⁴ *n.* the period of famine.

ทุม   too⁶-ma⁶ *P. n.* trees (in general) (chd. p. 129) : ทุมราชา, โพธิ์ *lit.* "the chief among trees," *i. e.* the boh tree.

ทุ่ม   toom³ see ทิ้ง *v.* to throw down into a

hole (as dirt or garbage): *n.* hour (used to designate the time, from 6 p.m. to 6 a.m., *ex.* ทุ่มหนึ่ง 7 : 00 p. m. : เจ็ดทุ่ม 1 : 00 a. m. : สามทุ่ม 9 : 00 p. m.): ทุ่มเถียง to argue; to contradict each other violently (as in a quarrel): ทุ่มทรวง to beat the chest (as in a fit of anger): ทุ่มเท to pitch in, cast into, or toss down in great quantities (as earth for filling purposes).

ทุ่ม   toom[5] *n.* bass; the lowest tones of the male voice, or of an instrument : ระนาดทุ่ม basso xylophone.

ทุย   similar to แกร็น p. 129.

ทุ้ย   (in common usage ทุ่ย) tuey[5] *v.* to utter carelessly; to conjecture, or to speak unthinkingly, *ex.* พูดทุ้ย ๆ ไป.

ทุร   too[6]-ra[6] *P. S. adj.* a prefix denoting bad, difficult or impoverished (S. E. D. p. 484): ทุรค difficult of access or approach; impossible; unattainable; a narrow passage; a place difficult of access (as a citadel); a stronghold; a fortress : ทุรคม to be traversed with difficulty; to be inaccessible : ทุรคา the river Ganges; the name of Siva's consort, also called Uma : ทุรโฆษ *lit.* "harsh-sounding (roar)," *i. e.* a bear : ทุรชน a villain; a scoundrel; a bad, malicious man or person : ทุรชล water that is impure, polluted or infected with germs : ทุรชัย to be conquered or won with difficulty; invincible : ทุรชาติ a race of people who are miserably oppressed and wretched : ทุรทิน a rainy or clouded day; bad weather : ทุรเทศ an uninhabitable place : ทุรธร difficult to be carried, borne or suffered; irrepressible : ทุรธี weakminded; stupid; silly; having evil intentions : ทุรนิมิต incorrectly measured; irregular : ทุรนิมิตต์ an ill-omen : ทุรพล weak; feeble; thin; slender; emaciated; scanty; lean : ทุรภาษิต words, spoken or uttered not in accordance with good standards of taste : ทุรภิกษ์ a scarcity or dearth of provisions; famine; want; distress : ทุรภูต harm; calamity;

disaster; adversity; misfortune : ทุรมนัส sad; distressed; melancholy; morbid; gloomy; low-spirited : ทุรยศ disgrace; ignominy : ทุรลักษณ์ badly marked : ทุรวรรณ of a bad colour, species or class; impure; inferior : ทุรวาท defamatory words; slander; abuse; reproach : ทุรวาสนา evil inclinations or disposition : ทุราคม difficult or impossible to be traversed; impassable; unattainable; inaccessible : ทุราจาร evil conduct; bad behaviour; immoral habits; immodesty : ทุรานม difficult to bend (as a bow) : ทุราศัย evilminded; malicious : ทุราสิต an impolite manner of sitting : ทุรุปจาร difficult of approach : ทุรุปเทศ injudicious; wanting in judgement.

ทุรนทุราย   see กระวนกระวาย p. 44, กระสับ กระส่าย p. 45.

ทุรัศ   too[6]-rat[6] *P. S. adj.* far; remote; distant (S. E. D. p. 489).

ทุราธุวา   too[6]-rah-too[6]-wah *n.* a long difficult road, or journey; one beset with hardships and perils.

ทุเรศ   too[6]-ret[3] *adj.* piteous; pitiable; wretched; miserable; immodest, obscene or shameless : ทำหน้าทุเรศ to inflict; to impose grievous torments.

ทุเรียน (ต้น)   too[6]-ri-an *n. Durio zibethinus (Malvaceae)*, durian, "civet fruit," a very large, handsome, upright tree, probably native of Borneo, but cultivated for the sake of its celebrated fruit. It grows wild in the Philippine Islands. The fruit varies somewhat in shape from round to ovoid, and is greenish yellow when ripe. It is covered with thickly set, sharp-pointed prickles about ½ inch long, and when mature, possesses a very strong odour, offensive to many people. The creamy white, custard-like pulp surrounding the seed is generally highly prized. The large seeds may be roasted and eaten like chestnuts. The tree grows to a height of 80 to 90 feet.

The timber is white, tending to be tinted red or brown towards the centre. It is coarse in structure and not durable, but can be used for various purposes. The high esteem in which the fruit is held prevents its extensive use as a timber tree. The Malays look upon the root as medicinal. Ashes of the fruit-wall are used by dyers in Pekan and Pattani for making silk white (MCM. p. 240: BURK. p. 873): ทุเรียนเทศ (ต้น) *Annona muricata* (*Annonaceae*), a small evergreen tree, native of tropical America, which was early taken from the West Indies to other parts of the tropics. It derives its name in Siam from its appearance which resembles that of the durian. The fruit is pleasantly acid and is used as flavouring for ices, etc. A fermented drink, like cider, is made from it in the West Indies. The lac insect will feed on this tree (CB. p. 55: V. P. p. 140: MCM. p. 252: BURK. p. 166): มะม่วงทุเรียน a species of mango.

ทุลักทุเล   too[6]-luk[6]-too[6]-lay *adj.* mixed; tangled; jumbled together: ทุลักทุลี to be dashed or smashed into minute particles (BRADLEY. p. 285).

ทุเลา   too[6]-lao *v.* to alleviate, mitigate, relieve, or remove (as the untoward symptoms of a virulent disease); to cause an improvement in a dire condition (as financial distress): ขอทุเลา to ask for a postponement, extension or delay of action, or for leniency.

ทุวิชาน   too[6]-wi[6]-chan *P. S. n.* one who understands with difficulty (S. E. D. p. 487).

ทุวิธ   too[6]-wit[6] *P. S. adj.* two-fold; of two sorts (CHD. p. 130).

ทุศศีล, ทุสสีล   toot[6]-sin[2] *adj.* immoral; impious; unchaste; licentious (CHD. p. 129).

ทุสส์   toot[6] *n.* cloth (CHD. p. 129).

ทู (ปลา)   too *n. Rastrelliger chrysozonus* (*Scombridae*) (suvatti p. 111): ทูน้ำจืด (ปลา) *Chanos chanos* (*Chanidae*), milk fish, salmon

herring, white mullet, a fish of considerable importance in the Philippine Islands and elsewhere. Along the gulf of Siam extensive fishing is carried on for these fish appear in large shoals and are easily trapped. It is a vegetable feeder and fattens rapidly. A year-old fish should measure approximately 20 in. and it is estimated that 33 per cent should attain a marketable size within that period (suvatti p. 8).

ทู   see ท้อ p. 417.

ทูต   toot[3] *P. S. n.* an envoy; a messenger; a representative; a negotiator (S. E. D. p. 489): ทูตทหาร a militiary attaché: ทูตี a female messenger; a procuress; a go-between: ราช-ทูต an ambassador; the representative of a sovereign or state in a foreign country: อัครราชทูต a minister plenipotentiary: อุปทูต a vice-ambassador: สถานทูต an embassy.

ทูตานุทูต   too-dtah-noo[6]-toot[3] *n.* all ranks of ambassadors, envoys or ministers.

ทูน ๑   toon *v.* to lift up or hold over the head; to support a weight by the head: ทูนกระหม่อม placed on the head; elevated over the head (as to indicate the highest honour or esteem for the article so held): แม่ทูนหัว, พ่อทูนหัว terms of endearment for infants (as while being held over the head).

ทูน ๒   toon *adj.* toward the near side; close to the boundary of a paddy field (used by buffalo drivers while ploughing).

ทูม   toom *adj.* distended; enlarged; bulging: คางทูม *lit.* "a swollen chin," *i. e.* mumps; contagious parotiditis.

ทูร   toon *P. S. adj.* far off; far away; distant; remote (S. E. D. p. 489): ทูรคาการ making difficult or impossible; hazardous of approach: ทูรทรรศน์ *lit.* "one that is far-seeing," *i. e.* a vulture; one with foresight; far-sightedness: ทูรทรรศี one with long sight; a far-sighted person; a prophet; a seer; a vulture: ทุรทฤศ a learned man: ทุรบถ a long way; a great distance: ทุรภาพ remoteness; distance: ทุรยายี one travelling far and wide: ทุรวาสี one residing in a distant land.

ทูล　toon *Cam. v.* to tell; to relate; to inform; to report; a word used in court language: ข้าทูลละออง those in the government service: ทูลกระหม่อม a personal pronoun for a prince or princess of the highest rank: ทูลความ to narrate; to tell; to relate: ทูลถาม to ask: ทูลทัด, ทูลขัด to remonstrate against an action, or to contradict what has been said: ทูลลา to take leave of with due ceremony.

ทูษก, ทสก　too-sok[4] *P. S. n.* a seducer; an offender; a disparager; a trangressor; a low, contemptible person (S. E. D. p. 488).

เท　tay *v.* to pour off or out; to decant; to tilt or lean to one side (as a house, tower, or building): *n.* a liquid measure for locally distilled spirits or arrack, equal to twenty litres. Standard jars of this capacity are used and filled at one pouring, thus called เทหนึ่ง: *adj.* slanting; tilting: เทกันไป to go in crowds, flocks or herds (as excited people, or wild animals): เทขวด to pour the contents from a bottle: เทครัว to drive, move or carry into captivity by families; to transport people, bag and baggage, into another place: เทดวด to throw dice.

เท่　tay[3] *adj.* leaning; slanting; sloping.

เทง　teng *v.* to knock; to beat or pound upon: เทงทวาร to knock at an entrance.

เท้ง, ทึ้ง　teng[5] *v.* to throw away; to discard: *n.* a boat or boats tied side-by-side, serving as floats or pontoons for a floating house.

เท้งเต้ง　teng[5]-dteng[3] *adj.* floating to and fro independently (as a free kite or boat).

เท็จ　tet[6] *adj.* false; untrue; dishonest; de-

ceptive; spurious; *compare* โกหก p. 135: คำเท็จ a lie: สาบาลเท็จ perjury.

เทพ　tep[3] *P. S. n.* a deity; a god on earth or among men; a king or prince; *poetical* "your majesty," "your honour": *adj.* divine; godlike; descriptive of superior terrestrial beings (S. E. D. p. 492): เทพกรรม the worshipping of the gods: เทพกษัตร domain or realm of the gods: เทพกันยา celestial nymphs of Indra's heaven; "wives of the god"; "daughters of pleasure" (H. C. D. p. 19): เทพกาม one loving the gods; a pious person: เทพกณฑ์ *lit.* "a divine well," *i. e.* a natural spring: เทพกุล a deity's house; a temple; a joss-house; "a high place": เทพกุสุม *lit.* "flowers fit for a deity," *i. e.* cloves: เทพเกษตร the realm or domain of the gods: เทพขาต *lit.* "dug by the gods," *i. e.* natural ponds or reservoirs; a cave, cavern or mountain fissure: เทพคณิกา *lit.* "celestial courtezans," "daughters of pleasure," *i. e.* the Apsarases: บิตฤเทพ having a deity for a father: มาตฤเทพ having a goddess for a mother: เทพดา see เทวดา: เทพด้ำรู the old or sacred trees of a village; celestial trees of paradise: เทพทัตต์ given by a deity: เทพธิดา a female deva; a goddess or angel: เทพนม a picture or design representing goddesses with hands placed palm to palm in the attitude of adoration: เทพนารี a goddess; a queen; a princess: เทพนิรมิต *lit.* "god-made," *i. e.* created; natural; the established or regular course of nature; the existing system of the world: เทพบดี *lit.* "lord of the celestial hosts," *i. e.* Indra, god of the firmament, the personified atmosphere, or "ruler of the atmosphere" (H. C. D. pp. 122, 127): เทพบถ *lit.* "god's path," *i. e.* the heavens; the Milky Way: เทพบริษัท a group or an assembly of deities: เทพบุตร the son of a god: เทพบุปป์ see เทพกุสุม: เทพประติมา the image of a deity; an idol: เทพยาตรา a procession of a deity or idol; a festival when sacred images are carried in procession : เทพาดิเทพ *lit.* " a god surpassing all other gods," *i. e.* a name applied to Siva, Vishnu and the Buddha : เทพาธิบดี *lit.* " lord over the celestials," *i. e.* Siva : เทพาธิป *lit.* " king of the gods," *i. e.* Indra.

เทพพทารู, เทพพทาโร (ต้น)　　tep³-tah-ru *n.* a species of pine, the leaves of which smell like peppermint, and are used in Siamese medicine ; *Cinnamomum parthenoxylon* (*Lauraceae*), a big tree, with whitish bark, found from Tenasserim and Siam throughout western Malaysia. A very similar tree of southern China and Tonkin has been called *C. parthenoxylon.* The bark is aromatic, and is used for flavouring food. The timber is a good ordinary building wood, rather soft, brownish in colour. In Java it is much appreciated, but should not be exposed to rain. It smells like fennel and aniseed, and retains this odour for some years. Oil from this wood is greatly valued by the Malays but its market value in Europe is low, because it has a competitor in camphor oil. The roots are used medicinally like those of other cinnamons (V. P. p. 145 : BURK. p. 554).

เทพย　　tep³ *S. n.* divine power (S. E. D. p. 496).

เทพา, สวายหนู (ปลา)　　tay-pah *n. Pangasius sanitwongsei* (*Pangasiidae*), a fresh water cat fish. It is rare, and noted for its size, but is not comparable to its ally, ปลาบึก, of the Mekong river (suvatti p. 87).

เทพิน　　tay-pin *S. n.* a female deity ; a goddess ; a queen ; a princess ; a lady (the consecrated wife or daughter of a king, also any woman of high rank) (S. E. D. p. 496).

เทพบักษ์　　tay-pee-bpak⁴-see² *n.* a form of disease common to children, characterized by disordered digestion, cold hands and feet and feverish head.

เทเพนทร์ see เทเวนทร์ in เทว ๑

เทโพ (ปลา)　　tay-poh *n. Pangasius lar-*

naudii (*Pangasiidae*), a cat fish found in rivers. It is esteemed by the Siamese (suvatti p. 85).

เทริด see จำหัน p. 248.

เทว ๑　　tay-wa⁶ *P. S. n.* a deity ; a god (S. E. D. p. 492) : เทวทัณฑ์ the rod of punishment of the gods (possibly lightning) : เทวทัตต์ name of a cousin (or younger brother) and opponent of Gotama Buddha : เทวทูต a divine messenger : เทวเทพ *lit.* " the god of gods," *i. e.* Brahma ; the supreme spirit which, according to Hindu mythology, is represented as the active creator of the universe, so is lord and father of all creatures (H. C. D. p. 56) : เทวธรรม religious rites or duties : เทวธานี *lit.* " divine abode," *i. e.* name of Indra's city : เทวธิดา *lit.* " daughters of the gods," *i. e.* goddesses : เทวนาครี *lit.* " the divine city's writing," *i. e.* the characters in which Sanskrit is usually written : เทวนาถ *lit.* " lord of the celestial hosts," *i. e.* an appellation for Siva : เทวนิกาย a sect, host or assembly of gods ; heaven ; paradise : เทวนินทา doctrines contrary to an orthodox religion ; heresy : เทวบาท *lit.* " the feet of a god or king," *i. e.* the royal presence or person ; a personal pronoun equivalent to ใต้ฝ่าละอองธุลีพระบาท : เทวพราหมณ์ a Brahmin esteemed by the gods : เทวาคาร, เทวายตนะ, เทวสถาน, เทวธานี *lit.* " a dwelling place for the gods," *i. e.* a shrine ; a temple ; a joss-house : เทวายธ *lit.* " a weapon of celestial beings," *i. e.* an appellation for Indra, for he sends the lightning and hurls the thunder bolt, and the rainbow is his sign (H. C. D. p. 125) : เทวายุษ the lifetime of a god : เทวารัณย์ a divine grove : เทวาลัย, เทวาวาส *lit.* " a residence of the gods, *i. e.* a temple ; heaven ; a general name for all Brahminical temples : เทวาหาร *lit.* " food for celestials," *i. e.* ambrosia : เทเวช offering sacrifices to the gods : เทเวชย์ *lit.* " a teacher of the gods," a name for the planet Jupiter : เทเวทธ์ *lit.* " kindled by the god," *i. e.* fire : เทเวนทร์, เทวินทร์, เทพินทร์, เทเพนทร์ *lit.* "chief of the gods," *i. e.* Indra; Siva : เทเวศวร์ *lit.* "sovereign of the gods," *i. e.* Siva : เทโวทยาน *lit.* "a grove of the gods," *i. e.* a sacred grove.

เทว ๒　　　tay-wa[6] *P. S. adj.* two (S.E.D. p. 504) : เทวภาวะ dual state ; double nature : เทวสุคนธ์ a compound of dual fragrance ; the roots of บุนนาค *Mesua ferrea (Guttiferae)* and บุนนาค or พังตาน *Schima crenata (Ternstroemiaceae).*

เทวดา, เทวัญ, เทพดา　　　tay-wa[6]-dah *P. S. n.* an image of a deity ; an idol (S. E. D. p. 495) ; these are an order of beings according to an ancient Brahminical system, occupying six seats or abodes of happiness, placed in rising succession above the abode of man. They are benign spirits endowed with a body so subtle and ethereal as to be able to move with the utmost rapidity from their seat to that of man, and vice versa. They play a conspicuous part in the affairs of this world, and are supposed to exercise a considerable degree of influence over man and other creatures. Fear, superstition, and ignorance have peopled all places with their shrines. Every tree, forest, fountain, village, and town has its protector. Their power is supposed to be very great. (Legend of the Burmese Buddha I, pp. 17, 18) : เทวดาคาร, เทวดามนเทียร, เทวดาลัย, เทวดาเวศม์ houses for the abode of the spirits of the departed ; shrines ; joss-houses ; temples ; chapels : เทวดาสหาย *lit.* "accompanied (only) by the gods," *i. e.* alone ; unaccompanied by others ; single.

เทวนะ　　　tay-wa[6]-na[6] *P. S. n.* sport ; play ; pastime ; throwing dice for gambling (S. E. D. p. 495).

เทวระ　　　tay-wa[6]-ra[6] *P. S. n.* a husband's younger brother ; the husband of a woman previously married (S. E. D. p. 495).

เทวษ, เทวศ　　　ta[6]-wet[3] *n.* hatred ; dislike ; repugnance ; enmity (S. E. D. p. 507).

เทวษิน, เทสสี　　　tay-wa[6]-sin[2] *n.* an enemy ; a foe ; a hater ; a disliker ; one hostile or malignant (S. E. D. p. 507).

เทวอ　　　ta[6]-wer *Cam. v.* to do ; to make or [perform.

เทวัญ see เทวดา

เทวัน　　　tay-wan *n.* the husband of an elder or younger sister ; a brother-in-law (S. E. D. p. 495).

เทวิน　　　tay-win *P. S. n.* a gambler (S. E. D. p. 496).

เทวินทร์ see เทเวนทร์ in เทว ๑

เทวี, เทพี　　　tay-wee *P. S. n.* a female deity ; a goddess ; a queen ; a princess (S. E. D. p. 496) : เทวีภาพ the dignity of a queen.

เทศ　　　tet[3] *P. S. n.* a region ; a spot ; a place ; a part ; portion ; country ; province ; kingdom ; institute ; ordinance : *adj.* foreign ; remote (S. E. D. p. 496) : เทศกาล time and place where annual religious or civil functions are observed : เทศกาลเข้าพรรษา religious functions at the beginning of Lent : เทศบาล a municipality : เทศัช *lit.* "country born," *i. e.* native ; born or produced in the place ; genuine : เทศาจาร local usage or custom : เทศานดร one of another country ; one from abroad ; an alien : ผ้าเทศ imported cloth : ม้าเทศ horses from abroad : สมุหเทศาภิบาล the lord lieutenant of a province.

เทศก　　　tay-sok[4] *P. S. n.* one who shows ; one who points out ; an indicator ; an instructor ; a guide (S. E. D. p. 496).

เทศน์, เทศนา　　　tet[3] *v.* to preach ; to teach ; to explain : *n.* an exhortation ; instruction ; a sermon ; a discourse on doctrinal subjects (S. E. D. p. 496) : ผู้เทศนา, นักเทศน์ a preacher.

เทสสี see เทวษิน

เทห, เท่ห์　　　tay-ha[4] *n.* the body (S. E. D. p. 496) : เทหกร *lit.* "a body-former," *i. e.* a father : เทหกษัย *lit.* "body-decay," *i. e.* sickness ; disease : เทหโกศ *lit.* "body-coverings," *i. e.* skin ; feathers ; wings : เทห-

จรรยา the care of one's body; personal hygiene : เทหทาห์ *lit.* "body-heat," *i. e.* fever : เทหทีป *lit.* "body-lamps," *i. e.* the eyes : เทหธารก *lit.* "body-supporters," *i. e.* bones : เทหธารี *lit.* "having a body," *i. e.* one living or still alive : เทหบาด *lit.* "dissolution of the body," *i. e.* death : เทหกฤช *lit.* "possessing a body," *i. e.* name of Siva : เทหเภท *lit.* "destruction of the body," *i. e.* death : เทหมัธย์ *lit.* "the mid section of the body," *i. e.* the waist; hips : เทหยาตรา *lit.* "means of supporting the body or of prolonging life," *i. e.* food; nourishment : เทหลักษณ์ *lit.* "a body-mark," *i. e.* a mole; a scar : เทหวรมัน *lit.* "body-armour," *i. e.* the skin : เทหวฤนต์ *lit.* "body-stalk," *i. e.* the navel; the umbilicus : เทหวายุ *lit.* "body-wind," *i. e.* vital air : เทหสัญจาริณี *lit.* "issued from or passing through (her father's body)," *i. e.* a daughter : เทหสาร *lit.* "body-essence," *i. e.* marrow : เทหัช *lit.* "body-born," *i. e.* a son; a child : เทหาวรณ์ *lit.* "body-screens," *i. e.* dress; clothes; armour; shields : เทหาวสาน *lit.* "end of the body," *i. e.* death.

เท่อ   tur[3] *adj.* inactive; stationary; descriptive of a kite that while flying, does not move laterally.

เท้อ   tur[5] *adj.* quiescent; rising or falling slightly (as the tide) : เวลาน้ำเท้อ the slack period between the rise and fall of the tide.

เทอญ, เถิด   tern *adv.* an expletive added for emphasis to any word, address or treatise, *ex.* ไปเทอญ, ไปเถิด better go.

เทอม   term *Eng. n.* a fixed period or definite limit of time for study (as a term in school).

เทา   tow *Cam. v.* to go; to proceed : *adj.* เทา (สี) gray.

เท่า, เถ้า p. 392. tow[3] *n.* ashes; cinders : *adj.* equal to; level with; equable; equivalent; commensurate : เขาไปไกลเท่าไร how far did he go; how far has he gone : เท่าๆ กัน equally; all alike : เท่าใด, เท่าไร how much;

how many, *ex.* มีเท่าไร, มีเท่าใด, ไกลเท่าไร, สูงเท่าไร, ราคาเท่าไร : เท่านั้น so much; that much; as much as that : เท่าเส้น a hair's breadth; equal to the size of a hair : ได้กำไรเท่าตัว a colloquial form of speech meaning "equal to the capital," or 100% profit : สองเท่า twice as much.

เท้า   tow[5] *v.* to lean against (as on a cane); to supply with a prop (as an extending timber supporting a weather shield) : *n.* a foot; feet : กราบเท้า to address or salute with respect; to make obeisance : ใช้ศอกเท้า to use the elbow as a support (as while sitting at a table) : เท้าแขน, ไม้เท้าแขน a prop to support a sun shield, or awning struts, or supports for roof timbers : เท้าสิงห์ a scroll or carved design representing lion's feet : ฝ่าเท้า the sole of the foot : ไม้เท้า a cane; a walking-stick.

เท้ายายม่อม (ต้น)   tow[5]-yai-maum[3] *n.* *Clerodendron indicum (Verbenaceae)*, a tall herb common in India, Indo-China, and southwards into the Malay Peninsula and Java. In Java it is used as a substitute for Indian hemp. The leaves are smoked to cure asthma. In India the pounded root is given with ginger for asthma, and it is used for other pulmonary complaints. The juice is used for skin diseases. Necklaces made of bits of the stem are used as charms (BURK. p. 584); *Tacca pinnatifida (Taccaceae)*, an herb of tropical Asia and Polynesia. It has large tubers which are very bitter when raw, but by suitable preparation can be made edible. Sometimes, they reach a weight of two pounds. Tahiti arrowroot is prepared from them. The stems make good braiding material, marketable in Europe for the manufacture of hats (K. : V. P. p. 146 : BURK. p. 2118).

เท้าสาน (ต้น)   tow[5]-sarn[2] *n. Rhapis humilis*, cane palm. This low fan-palm with cane-like groupy stems is now very common in gardens, often kept dwarfed as a pot plant. It was introduced about thirty-five years ago, probably from China, its native country (winit, N. H. J. S. S. IX, 3, p. 281).

เทิ่ง   terng[3] *adj.* large; bulky :   เรือเทิ่ง a large houseboat used by the Chinese and fitted as a shop to sell imperishable supplies like kerosene, matches, etc., often seen anchored along small water-ways.

เทิ่งบอง   terng-baung *n.* a long drum.

เทิด   tert[3] *v.* to support; to hold up; to make or lay contiguously; to raise or hold over the head;   เทิดทาย to wave or brand-
[ish overhead.

เทิน   see ทูน p. 420.

เทิบ   terp[3] *adv.* slowly; deliberately; drowsily; sluggishly; tardily :   เทิบทาบ slack; loose; relaxed; slow; tardy.

[wall.
เทียง   tee-ang *n.* a wall :   เทียงผา a stone

เที่ยง   tee-ang[3] *n.* noon; midday :   *adj.* true; correct; sure; straight; impartial : เที่ยงคืน midnight :   เที่ยงธรรม upright : honest; just; righteous; moral.

เทียน   tee-an *n.* a candle; a wax taper; the balsam plant :   เทียนกิ่ง, เทียนขาว, เทียนแดง *Siam.* (ต้น) *Lawsonia inermis (Lythraceae)*, the henna-tree, a bush, thorny or not thorny, apparently native of Asia from the western edge of India westwards, very fragrant when in flower, and much cultivated within, and far from, its home. In Siam there are races with different coloured flowers. The leaves are oblong-elliptical, pointed, and about an inch or more long; the flowering panicle is ten to twelve inches long, and usually straw-coloured; the fruit is a depressed globose capsule. Henna leaves are used as a dye for hands and feet and have a ceremonial use at Malayan marriages. The colouring matter can also be extracted as orange-yellow crystals, and used as a dye for wool and silk.

Henna leaves and roots are used medicinally. The wood is grey, hard, close-grained, and suitable for tool-handles and other small objects.   In the Dutch Indies tooth-cleaners are made from the twigs (J. F. ROCK, The ornamental Trees of Hawaii p. 160 : BURK. p. 1323 : cb. p. 718); *Lawsonia alba (Lythraceae)*, henna, tree-mignonette, a deciduous, much-branched shrub, 6 to 8 feet high, indigenous to Western India, Persia, etc. It is cultivated for its small oval leaves, which yield the henna dye; it is also often grown as a hedge plant.   The leaves are imported into France for the extraction of a dye used in the preparation of hair dye, etc. (MCM. pp. 74, 141, 459 : cb. p. 718 : V. P. p. 144) :   เทียนดำ *Siam. and Laos* (ต้น) *Abroma augusta (Sterculiaceae)*, devil's cotton, a tall, half-woody, quick-growing shrub of India and Java.   The bark yields a fibre; the vegetable parts are used medicinally. Considerable tests have been made with the fibre which when dry is tougher then jute.   However, the quantities obtained are inadequate, as the plant can not be got to yield enough in a close stand, and to collect the wild plants would be too slow for commercial use. The scanty wood is light brown and soft. The root-bark is medicinal in India (MCM. p. 428 : cb. p. 180 : V. P. p. 144 : BURK. p. 1) : เทียนแดง *Siam.* (ต้น) *Asclepias curassavica (Asclepiadaceae)*, milk weed, an erect, perennial, herbaceous American shrub, now found throughout the tropics.   Probably it was taken to Europe and forwarded to India as an ornamental plant. The roots and flowers are used medicinally. The active substance is asclepiadin, which in large doses will cause death.   That the plant is a cattle-poison, may be considered as all but proved. There is fibre in the stem that can be spun; and the silky hairs on the seeds are used, in some places, for stuffing pillows; but they can not be spun on account of their elasticity, unless chemically altered, whereafter they may be mixed with cotton. Bee-honey from this plant is bitterish, dark and thick (MCM. pp. 108, 377, 429 : BURK. p. 261) : เทียนนา, *Siam.* (ต้น) *Jussieua linifolia (Onagraceae)*, a slightly woody herb found in grass-covered swamps, open wet places, old rice fields, etc. throughout tropical Asia. As it is by no means uncommon in rice-fields, it makes part of the herbage which is ploughed in as green manure. The plant has medicinal uses and is one of the plants most generally stocked by Chinese herbalists (BURK. p. 1273 : cb. p. 733) : เทียนน้ำ, หรือ เทียนนา *Hydrocera triflora (Balsaminaceae)*, an herb of marshes found throughout south-eastern Asia and Malaysia. The flowers may be used in the same way as henna, for dyeing the finger-nails. The fruits are fleshy, and apparently water-birds eat them and distribute the seeds (BURK. p. 1210 : cb. p. 214 : V. P. p. 145) : เทียนน้ำ *Siam., Trang,* หญ้ารักนา, หญ้าลักนา *N. Laos* (ต้น) *Jussieua suffruticosa (Onagraceae)*, a slightly woody herb, of wide distribution in the world, found in wet places. The mucilaginous leaves are used for poulticing in a variety of complaints —possibly in all. There are several other medicinal uses. A kind of tea is made from the leaves (cb. p. 734 : BURK. p. 1274) : เทียน-บ้าน *Siam., and Laos* (ต้น) *Impatiens balsamina (Balsaminaceae)*, garden balsam which has long been in cultivation. In Malaysia it is cultivated, and here and there has run wild from cultivation. It is used as a substitute for henna in dyeing the finger-nails. The leaves are used for poulticing. The Balinese eat the leaves (cb. p. 208 : BURK. p. 1227) : เทียนบ้า *Siam.* (ต้น) *Impatiens calcicola (Balsaminaceae)* or any wild species of *Impatiens. I. calcicola* is an annual plant growing in crevices in limestone rocks in central Siam (cb. p. 209).

เทียบ๑   tee-ap[3] *v.* to compare; to liken (as a parable) : ชิมเทียบ to compare by tasting (as wines) : เทียบท่า to come along side a wharf (as a ship); to approach a land-

ing (as a small boat for passengers) : เทียบ-พระโอสถ to prepare or compound a remedy for a royal patient : พูดเป็นคำเปรียบเทียบ to make injurious comparisons or allusions (as is often done without mentioning any name).

เทียบ๒   tee-ap[3] *v.* to act as an escort; to accompany; to conduct : เทียบพยุ่ห์ to superintend or supervise a procession.

เทียม๑   tee-am *v.* to be untrue; to feign; to pretend; to falsify, *ex.* ของเทียม imitated goods or articles : เงินเทียม false, spurious or counterfeited coins : ทำเทียม hypocrisy : เทียมว่าเจ็บ to feign sickness : เป็นการเทียบ-เทียม an unjust comparison : คนทำเทียม a hypocrite.

เทียม๒   tee-am *v.* to make equal or uniform with others, in standing or rank : เทียมเสมอผู้ดี to simulate being equal to a man of rank : ให้เทียมเท่าผู้อื่น to be made uniform (in standing) with others.

เทียม๓   tee-am *v.* to harness up : เทียมคู่ to put in double harness : เทียมเดี่ยว to put in single harness : เทียมม้า to harness a horse : เทียมวัว to yoke cattle.

เทียร, เที้ยร   tee-an *v.* to be small or diminutive; to be dwarfed or stunted in growth.

เทียรฆ   tee-an *P. S. adj.* long (in space or time); lofty; high; tall; deep (S. E. D. p. 481) : เทียรฆราตร for a long time or period.

เที่ยว   tee-oh *v.* to retrace one's steps repeatedly; to walk back and forth stopping to examine articles or to make a purchase (as is done at a fair or bazaar) : *adv.* surely; immediately; at once (indicating the imperative mood), *ex.* ไปเที่ยว.

เที่ยว   tee-oh[3] *v.* to wander about; to promenade : *n.* trip; time or times, *ex.* กี่เที่ยว how many trips : เที่ยวแรก the first trip : เที่ยวหลัง succeeding trips : ไปเที่ยวเล่น to stroll about for pleasure or sightseeing.

เทอ   tur-ah⁵ *adj.* bulky; heavy; cumbersome; impeding progress, *ex.* หนักเนื้อและเทื้อองค์; *also* synonym for ทื่นทึก.

เทือก   tur-uk³ (1) *n.* line; pedigree; family; lineage; seed; offspring: เทือกเถา a direct line of ancestors as far back as a great grandfather or mother: เทือกเถาเหล่ากอ ancestors: (2) mud; mire.

แท้   taa⁵ *adj.* true; sure; genuine; real: แท้จริง, แท้ที่จริง, ที่จริง truly; certainly; definitely; surely; verily; positively; explicitly.

แทง   tang *v.* to stab; to prick; to pierce; to puncture (as in a surgical operation): ถูกแทงตายคาที่ instant death resulting from a stab: แทงใจ to read another's mind; to guess, or mentally to discern another's motive: แทงบัญชี to enter a remark or make a note of (as in a roll book or account book): แทงม้าแข่ง to place a stake, lay a wager, or make a bet on a horse in a race: แผลถูกแทง a stab or punctured wound.

แท่ง   tang³ *n.* a numerical designatory particle, used to describe a small chunk or piece: ดินสอหนึ่งแท่ง a pencil: หมึกจีนหนึ่งแท่ง a cake of Chinese ink: เหล็กแท่ง pig iron; an ingot; a piece, bar or chunk of iron.

แท้ง   tang⁵ *v.* to miscarry; to have or produce an abortion.

แทงทวย   similar to กระทุ่ม (ต้น) p. 36.

แทงวิสัย   tang-wi⁶-sai² *n.* a form of sport in which the players, attired in fancy costumes, attack each other with lances or long spears.

แทตย์   tat³ *S. n.* a son of queen Diti (พระนางทิติ); a demon (s.e.d. p. 497): แทตยคุรุ, แทตยปุโรหิต *lit.* "preceptor of the Daityas," *i. e.* a name for the planet Venus: แทตยเทพ *lit.* "god of the Daityas," *i. e.* Varuna (พระวรุณ), one of the oldest of the Vedic deities, a personification of the all-investing sky, the maker and upholder of heaven and earth

(h. c. d. p. 336): แทตยนาศน์ *lit.* "Daityas-destroyer," *i. e.* Vishnu: แทตยนิษูทน์ *lit.* "Daityas-destroyer," *i. e.* Indra: แทตยยุค the age of the Daityas, equal to four ages of man.

แทน   tan *v.* to substitute (one person or thing for another); to replace; to exchange (as a good article for a defective one): ตอบแทน to recompense: แทนที่จะ instead of; in place of (indicating a contradiction): แทนที่จะนอนเขากลับนั่ง he sits instead of lying down: แทนที่จะยาวไป, กลับสั้นไป instead of being too long, it is too short: ทำแทน to serve in place of another: พูดแทนผู้อื่น to be a mouth-piece for another: รับดูแลแทน to replace another as a supervisor: รับโทษแทน to bear punishment for sins in place of another: ให้ทดแทน to offer in place of; to offer in compensation for.

แท่น   tan³ *n.* a dais; an altar; a throne.

แทบ   tap³ *adv.* almost; nearly; closely; narrowly; in close relation to, or on the point of (as disaster): *prep.* close by: แทบจะว่า just on the point of saying.

แทรก   sak³ *v.* to squeeze in (as into a crowd of people); to adulterate (as water in kerosene); to mix; to add (as an ingredient in a remedy or spice in a pudding); to insert (as a splice between two existing pieces of board): เข้าไปแทรก to intervene or interfere with (as in a fight): แทรกแซง, แทรกซอน to pass in (as a wedge); to occur in, or at the time of: โรคแทรกแซง a complicating condition in the course of a disease.

แทะ   taa⁶ *v.* to gnaw; to browse; to nibble (as cattle on short grass).

โท   toh *P. S. adj.* two; second (s.e.d. p. 504): *n.* the second accent mark of the Siamese language, called ไม้โท (ˊ).

โท่   toh³ *adv.* clearly; distinctly.

โทง   tong *adj.* very tall or too high; top-heavy: โทงทาง, กระทุงทาง (ปลา) *Istiopho-*

rus sp. (Istiophoridae), spear fishes (suvatti p. 112).

โทณะ   toh-na^6 *P. S. n.* a wooden bucket ; a trough ; a vessel for the soma juice (S. E. D. p. 502) :   โทณมุข the officer in charge of 400 villages.

โทน   tone *n.* a drum enclosed at one end : *adj.* single ; alone ; solitary :   ยางโทน (นก) the little egret, *Egretta garzetta garzetta* (Herb. N. H. J. S. S. VI, 4, p. 351).

โทมนัสส์, โทรมนัสย์   tom-ma^6-nat^6 *P. S. n.* grief ; vexation ; dejection ; melancholia ; gloom (Chd. p. 126).

โทร   toh-ra^6 *adj.* far ; distant ; remote ; reaching a long distance (S. E. D. p. 489) : โทรทัศน์ a spy glass or binocular :   โทรภาพ television :   โทรเลข *lit.* "letters to a great distance," *i. e.* a telegram ; a cablegram : โทรศัพท์ *lit.* "voices reaching a great distance," *i. e.* the telephone :   วิทยุโทรเลข a radiogram : ส่งโทรเลข to telegraph ; to send a telegram.

โทรม   som *v.* to be in a ruined state or in a dilapidated condition ; to abet, incite, instigate, or seduce :   โทรมศัสตราวุธ to unite together ; to force an entrance with weapons : โทรมหญิง to join in, or abet for rape.

โทรลี   tro-lee *Eng. n.* trolley.

โทลา   toh-lah *P. S. n.* a swing ; a hammock ; a litter ; a palanquin (S. E. D. p. 498).

โทวจัสสตา   toh-wa^6-chjat^4-sa^4-dtah *n.* unruliness ; stubbornness ; abusiveness (Chd. p. 127).

โทษ   tot^3 *n.* offenses worthy of punishment ; a misdeed ; a fault ; vice ; defect ; blemish ; guilt ; crime ; wickedness ; sinfulness :   กล่าวโทษ to accuse of a fault or offense :   ขอโทษ, ขออภัยโทษ to beg one's pardon :   คนโทษ a prisoner ; a convict :   ต้องโทษ punishable ; guilty ; culpable :   ทำโทษ to punish :   โทษคุณ with bad and good qualities :   โทษตรัย vitiation of the three humours ; any combina-

tion of three offenses or defects :   โทษานุโทษ punishments of major or minor degrees.

โทษา ๑   toh-sa^2 *S. n.* night ; darkness (S. E. D. p. 498) :   โทษากร *lit.* "night-workers," "night-makers," *i. e.* the moon ; stars :   โทษาดิลก *lit.* "a night-ornament," *i. e.* a lamp : โทษารมณ์ *lit.* "night's lover," *i. e.* the moon.

โทษา ๒   toh-sa^2 *S. n.* the arm (S.E.D. p. 498).

โทโษ, โทส, โทโส   toh-soh^2 *n.* anger ; wrath ; rage ; fury ; ire ; indignation.

โทหฬะ   toh-ha^4-la^6 *P. S. n.* the longing of a pregnant woman for the "happy event" ; any morbid desire or wish (S. E. D. p. 499).

โทหฬินี   toh-ha^4-li^6-nee *P. S. n.* a pregnant woman (Chd. p. 126).

ไทย ๑   tai *n.* the Siamese nation. The Tai race probably originated in south-western China where there are still many Tai speaking people. In addition, numbers of the Tai race are found as far east as Tonkin and Hainan and as far west as Assam. It is really a far-flung race but in current Siamese parlance, Tai is understood to mean the people living between the towns of Utaradit in the north and Petchaburi in the south and from Kanburi in the west to Saraburi in the east, *i. e.* the so called seven Inner Circles. Father south the people, being mixed with Laos prisoners from Lampoon as well as with Malays and Chinese, speak a peculiar dialect : *adj.* independent ; free :   ไทยนับสาม,-ห้า a secret ancient Siamese code in which only the third and fifth letters of the message are read : ไทยบ้านนอก Siamese peasants of the rural class :   ไทยใหญ่ the Greater Thai race ; the Shans, a race of ancient Siamese, inhabiting the north and north-western parts of Siam.

ไทย ๒   tai *adj.* fit or proper for a gift ; fit to be given in matrimony ; fit to be granted or shown :   ไทยทาน articles that are suitable for alms :   ไทยธรรม *lit.* "the duty of giving," *i. e.* charity.

ไทร (ต้น) sai *n. Ficus bengalensis (Moraceae)*, the banyan tree, a wide spreading but not lofty tree of India, well known for its descending aerial roots which may form a forest of supporting trunks under horizontal limbs. Like other species of *Ficus* it begins life as an epiphyte, the fruits being carried by birds into the branches of other trees and there the seeds germinate later on, dealing death to the host, by strangling. The fruits are edible and serve as a famine-food in India. The leaves are fed to elephants (V. P. p. 140 : J. F. ROCK, The Ornamental Trees of Hawaii, p. 63 : Burk. p. 1004) : ไทรกร่าง

(ต้น) *F. gibbosa*, a tree found from the eastern Himalayas and southern China to Malaysia. The bark is said to be rich in tannin (V. P. p. 141 : Burk. p. 1009) : ไทรย้อย (ต้น) *F. retusa*, a large tree found from India to New Caledonia. The latex is full of resin. The tree is medicinal in India where roots and leaves are used for applications to wounds and bruises; the bark and leaves for head-ache; the juice of the leaves, externally for colic, and the juice of the bark internally for liver disease (V. P. p. 141 : Burk. p. 1014).

ไทวะ tai-wa[6] *n.* fate; fortune; luck; an angel; the sky; the air.

ธ

ธ The twenty-fourth consonant of the Thai alphabet, a low class letter of which there are twenty-four, *viz.* ค, ค, ฆ, ง, ช, ฌ, ซ, ญ, ฑ, ฏ, ธ, ฑ, ฒ, น, ณ, พ, ฟ, ภ, ม, ร, ล, ว, ฬ, ฮ. ธอเธอ and ธอธง are the designating names of this letter, which is found only in words of Pali or Sanskrit origin. To this rule there are two or three exceptions, *viz.* ธง and เธอ. ธ is represented by the English "t".

ธ ta[6] *pron.* you; he (used only for persons of high rank, as His Majesty the King).

ธง tong *n.* a flag; a banner; an ensign; a standard : ธงลม a weathercock : วันธงชัย, วันอธิบดี auspicious days, as calculated by the royal astrologers.

ธงก์ tong *P. n.* a crow; a hawk; a beggar; one with an insatiable appetite (as crows); a discontented person; a house (S. E. D. p. 522): ธงกราว having a voice like a crow.

ธช, ธุช ta[6]-cha[6] *P. n.* a flag; a signal; a characteristic sign; an emblem (S. E. D. p. 522).

ธชี ta[6]-chee *P. n.* one having or bearing a banner or sign (as a vendor of spirituous

liquors); a chariot; a snake; a peacock (S. E. D. p. 522).

ธตรฐ, ธตรัฐ,-รฏฐี-รัฏฐี, ธฤตราษฏร์ tot[6]-dta[4]-rot[6] *P. S. n.* one whose empire is firm; a powerful king; a name for the elephant of Indra (S. E. D. p. 519).

ธน ton *P. S. n.* wealth; treasures; money; riches; possessions; capital : ธนกษัย loss of money or property : ธนกาม one desirous of wealth : ธนเกลี one sporting with wealth : ธนทรัพย์ wealth in respect to cash, silver, gold, securities, or bonds (S. E. D. p. 508).

ธนครรพ์ ton-kun *n. lit.* "purse-proud," *i. e.* one conceited by wealth.

ธนชาต ta[6]-na[6]-chart[3] *n.* arising from wealth; produced by money : ธนชิต, ธนญชัย one winning a prize, or one who is victorious in a contest; a wealth-acquiring person.

ธนตัณหา ta[6]-na[6]-dtun-hah[2] *n.* a passion for money; covetousness.

ธนทรรป ta[6]-na[6]-tup[6] *n.* the state of being conceited because of wealth : ธนทัณท์ a fine or penalty levied as a punishment.

ธนธานี   ta⁶-na⁶-tah-nee *n.* a receptacle for valuable articles; a storehouse for merchandise.

ธนบดี   ta⁶-na⁶-bau-dee *n.* lord of wealth; a rich man; a king: ธนบัตร bank notes; paper currency: ธนบาล a treasurer; a guardian of money.

ธนปิศาจ   ta⁶-na⁶-bpi⁴-sart⁴ *n.* one thirsting for wealth; an avaricious person.

ธนภักษ์   ta⁶-na⁶-pak⁶ *n.* riches (as a means of enjoyment).

ธนมัท   ta⁶-na⁶-mat⁶ *n.* one proud of his money; one intoxicated by his wealth: ธนมิตร *lit.* "wealth considered as friends," *i. e.* a merchant: ธนมูล assets; capital; principal; that which proceeds from, or is founded on wealth.

ธนรรฆ   ta⁶-nuk⁶ *n.* one worthy of, or deserving a reward or prize.

ธนโลภ   ta⁶-na⁶-lop³ *n.* an inordinate longing for riches; cupidity; avarice.

ธนวิภาค   ta⁶-na⁶-wi⁶-pak³ *n.* the distribution or division of one's wealth or fortune.

ธนสญจัย   ta⁶-na⁶-son²-chjai *n.* the collecting or accumulating of large possessions: ธนสมบัติ opulence; the accumulation of riches.

ธนหร   ta⁶-na⁶-horn² *n.* one who steals money; a thief; an heir: ธนหีน one who is destitute; a poor person.

ธนักกีตา   ta⁶-nuk⁶-gkee-dtah *n.* a woman bought with money.

ธนากร   ta⁶-nah-gkaun *n.* the fountain of wealth; the origin of riches.

ธนาคม   ta⁶-nah-kom *n.* the accession of wealth, gain; profit; interest on, or benefits from investments: ธนาคาร a bank; a banking house.

ธนาฒย์   ta⁶-nart³ *n.* one who is opulent; the rich.

ธนาณัติ   ta⁶-nah-nut⁶ *n.* a money order; a postal money order; a sight draft.

ธนาธิการ   ta⁶-nah-ti⁶-gkarn *n.* the title or right to property: ธนาธิการี a treasurer; the receiver of an inheritance; an heir: ธนาธิการิณี the feminine form, an heiress: ธนาธิบดี, ธนาธิป "the lord of treasure," "god of wealth," *i. e.* Kubera (ท้าวกุเวร): ธนาธิบัตย์ the dominion or authority over treasures.

ธนาปหาร   ta⁶-nah-bpa⁴-harn² *n.* the taking away of property; fines; amercement; plunder.

ธนาสา   ta⁶-nah-sah² *n.* longing after wealth; the desire for riches; the hope of gaining money; avarice.

ธนญชัยบาศ   ta⁶-non-chai-bart⁴ *n.* a Brahmin ceremony observed in the dedication of an elephant.

ธนิต   ta⁶-nit⁶ *P. v.* to send forth a loud sound: *n.* thunder; sound: *adj.* loud; heavy; reverberating (S. E. D. p. 522).

ธนุส, ธนุ, ธนู, ธนุร, ธนุรา   ta⁶-noot6 *S. n.* a bow; a fiddlestick; Sagittarius, the ninth sign of the zodiac; an arc or segment of a circle (S. E. D. p. 509): ธนุกัณฑ์ a bow and arrow: ธนุขัณฑ์ a portion of the bow (as the cord or arrow-head): ธนุคคหะ an archer: ธนุคุณ a bow-string: ธนุรทรุม *lit.* "the bow-tree," *i. e.* the bamboo (as it is used for making bows): ธนุรธร an archer; one armed with a bow: ธนุรมารค *lit.* "bow-line," *i. e.* a curve: ธนุรวิทยา, ธนุรเวท the science or art of archery: ธนุรหัสต์ having or holding a bow: ธนุราการ *lit.* "bow-shaped," *i. e.* bent; curved; arched: ธนุศิลป, ธนุศิลป skill in shooting with a bow; the practice of handling a bow and arrow.

ธเนศ, ธเนศวร   ta⁶-net³ *S. n. lit.* "wealth-lord," *i. e.* a rich man; a millionaire; the god of Opulence (S. E. D. p. 508).

ธโนปจัย   ta[6]-noh-bpa[4]-chjai *S. n.* the accumulating of riches.

ธไนศวรรย์   ta[6]-nai-sa[4]-wan[2] *S. n.* the legitimate right over wealth.

ธม ๑   tom *Cam. adj.* large; massive; royal; regal.

ธม ๒   tom *S. n.* one who blows a fire or sounds a trumpet; a name for Yama (S. E. D. p. 509).

ธมกรก   ta[6]-ma[6]-gka[4]-rok[4] *P. n.* a filter used by Buddhist monks, being a bamboo joint, or a galvanized iron or brass cylinder, with a cloth tied tightly over one end.

ธร   taun *P. S. n.* the condition of holding, supporting, bearing, carrying, wearing, possessing, or sustaining (S. E. D. p. 510).

ธรณะ   tau-ra[6]-na[6] *P. S. n.* the state of holding, supporting, or upholding; the female breast; rice; corn; the bank of a river; a dike or retaining wall (S. E. D. p. 510).

ธรณินทร์, ธรณิศร์, ธรณิศวร์   tau-ra[6]-nin *n. lit.* " earth-lord," *i. e.* a king.

ธรณี   tau-ra[6]-nee *P. S. n.* the angel of the earth; the earth; the soil or ground; a beam or rafter of a roof; a vein or tubular vessel of the body (S. E. D. p. 510): ธรณีดล the earth's surface: ธรณีธร *lit.* " one bearing or sustaining the earth," *i. e.* a king; a tortoise; Vishnu; Siva: ธรณีบดี a king; the sovereign of a realm: ธรณีบูร *lit.* " flooding the earth," *i. e.* the ocean: ธรณีประตู door sill: ธรณีมณฑล *lit.* " the earth's sphere," *i. e.* the globe: ธรณีสาร objects considered unlucky or evil: ธรณีสุดา *lit.* " daughter of the earth's presiding angel," *i. e.* name of Sita, Rama's wife.

ธรมาธิกรณ์   tau-ra[6]-mah-ti[6]-gkaun *S. n.* a centre for the administration of justice; a law court; a judge.

ธรรม, ธรรม์   tum *n.* the Law; justice; the eternal principles followed by nature; the law of nature (Ala pp. 170, 288); nature; condition; quality; property; duty; doctrine; law; virtue; piety; the Law or Truth of the Buddha; the Buddhist scriptures; religion (chd. p. 118: S. E. D. p. 510): ค่าธรรมเนียม fines, fees or penalties: ธรรมกถา a religious discourse; a discourse upon the Law: ธรรมกถึก one who expounds the Law; one who has the gift of preaching (chd. p. 117); a preacher; one lecturing on doctrinal subjects, or ecclesiastical matters: ธรรมกรรม works of duty; pious actions: ธรรมกาม one who delights in justice, piety, virtue and truth: ธรรมกาย *lit.* " law-body," *i. e.* the name of one of the three bodies of Buddha (รูปกาย, นามกาย, ธรรมกาย): ธรรมการ a doer of the Law; a religious adherent; one whose duties pertain to the Buddhistic religion; a bureau of Buddhistic monastery affairs; the Ecclesiastical Department: ธรรมการย์ the cause of virtue: ธรรมการย์ acts of kindness; deeds done, or duties fulfilled respecting one's religious obligations; meritorious acts: ธรรมกิตติ์, ธรรมกีรติ,-เกียรติ *lit.* " glory of the Law," *i. e.* name of a philosopher and poet: ธรรมเกต having justice for a banner; the standard of the Law (chd. p. 117): ธรรมเกษตร *lit.* " law-field," *i. e.* a man of piety and virtue; a plain in north-western India near Delhi: ธรรมโกศ, ธรรมโกษ a treasury or collective body of the Laws and Duties.

ธรรมคุตต์, ธรรมคุปต์   tum *lit.* " law-protected, or law-directed," *i. e.* one who adheres to the commandments as laid down by the Law, ordinances or creeds.

ธรรมจร   tum-chjaun *n. lit.* " law-observer," *i. e.* one whose conduct is governed by the doctrines of the Law (chd. p. 117); virtuous: ธรรมจรณะ, ธรรมจรรยา an observance of the Law; the performance of duty: ธรรมจริยา religious life; piety (chd. p. 117): ธรรมจักร the

Wheel of the Law; the domain of the Law (chd. p. 116): ธรรมจักษุ the eye of the Law; having eyes on the Law, or for what is right: ธรรมจาคะ abandonment of one's religion; apostacy: ธรรมจารี observing the Law; fulfilling one's obligations or duties; virtuous; dutiful; moral: ธรรมจินดา consideration of the Law, or duty; virtuous reflection.

ธรรมชาติ tum-ma[6]-chart[3] *n.* things which are derived from, or are produced by nature, and which are governed by natural laws: ธรรมชีวัน one living by the fulfilment of duties.

ธรรมญาณ tum-yarn *n.* knowledge of the Law or of one's duties.

ธรรมดา tum-ma[6]-dah *n.* power of the universe with all things that it contains, including their phenomena and laws; custom; habit; nature (Chd. p. 118).

ธรรมทวาร tum-ta[6]-warn *n.* the virtues or duties, as a means of acquiring the highest wisdom: ธรรมทักษิณา a fee for instruction in law: ธรรมทาน the gift of the Law: ธรรมทาร a lawful or legal wife: ธรรมทาส *lit.* "duty slave," *i.e.* the endeavour to make adherence to justice and duty the supreme effort in life: ธรรมเทพ the god of Justice; a name of Yama, the judge of the Dead (H. C. D. p. 88): ธรรมเทศนา religious teaching; a sermon; a discourse on religion (chd. p. 117).

ธรรมธร tum-taun *n.* a Law-supporter: ธรรมธาตรี a female Law-supporter: ธรรมธาต having the element of the Law, or of existence; an appellation for the Buddha (whose essence is Law): ธรรมธารัย maintaining the Law.

ธรรมนาถ tum-ma[6]-nart[3] *n.* a law protector; one who enforces the laws: ธรรมนาศ law-ruin; the revoking of laws: ธรรมนิตย์ one constant in duty: ธรรมนิยม, ธรรมนิยาม the certainty of nature and of nature's laws: ธรรมนิเวศ religious devotion: ธรรมนูญ a

code of laws: ธรรมเนตร *lit.* "law-eyed," *i.e.* discernment; insight; the faculty of penetration: ธรรมเนียม custom; common or recognized usage; habits established by practice.

ธรรมบดี tum-ma[6]-bau-dee *n.* the lord or guardian of law and order: ธรรมบถ the path of duty and probity: ธรรมบร *lit.* "one intent on virtue," *i.e.* one who is pious, exemplary and righteous: ธรรมบรรยาย the preaching of the Law by quoting examples: ธรรมบัตนี a lawful or legal wife: ธรรมบาล *lit.* "law-guardian," *i.e.* punishments; penalties; fines or sword: ธรรมบาส *lit.* "bonds of law or duty," *i.e.* a restraining or controlling power like a "loop" which enforces obedience: ธรรมบิฐ *lit.* "a law-seat," *i.e.* a judge's seat; a place where judgements or verdicts are pronounced: ธรรมบีฑา a transgression or violation of law or duty: ธรรมบุตร a legitimate child; a rightful heir: ธรรมบุรัสการ one who places duty above all other obligations.

ธรรมประจาร tum-bpra[4]-chjarn *n. lit.* "the course of law or right," *i.e.* a sword: ธรรมประศิรูป a counterfeit of moral rectitude: ธรรมประทีป *lit.* "the light of the Law," "the lamp of virtue," *i.e.* the radiance of virtue, truth and righteousness: ธรรมประธาน one eminent in piety: ธรรมประภาส an illuminator of the Law: ธรรมปริศนา inquiry into the Law: ธรรมปรึกษา having an eye for what is right; investigations into the law as a means of serving the cause of justice.

ธรรมพินทุ tum-pin-too[6] *n. lit.* drops or particles of the Law," *i.e.* the gradual explaining or elucidation of the Law.

ธรรมภคินี tum-pa[6]-ki[6]-nee *n.* a female who has the rights of a sister; a sister in respect of religion: ธรรมภาคี one who has acquired merit; a virtuous person.

ธรรมมิตร tum-ma[6]-mit[6] *n. lit.* "having

justice as a companion," "being a friend of law," *i.e.* one fair, honest, and honourable in all dealings : ธรรมมูล the foundation of law and religion.

ธรรมยุกต์   tum-ma[6]-yook[6] *n.* one whose conduct is in accordance with the Law; a righteous person : ธรรมยุตต์ a sect of Buddhist monks : ธรรมยุทธ์ an honest fight (over religious matters).

ธรรมรติ, ธรรมรดี, ธรรมรัต   tum-ma[6]-ra[6]-dti[4] *lit.* "delighting in virtue," *i.e.* virtuous : ธรรมรส the taste or sweetness of the Law (chd. p. 118) : ธรรมราช king of Justice; the god of Death : ธรรมรุจี delighting in, or devoted to virtue : ธรรมโรธ opposed to law; illegal; immoral; unethical.

ธรรมลักษณ์   tum-ma[6]-luck[6] *n.* essential marks of law or ethics (as courts of justice, or places and times when justice is meted out) : ธรรมโลป violations of law; neglect of duty; the forsaking of one's religion.

ธรรมวยาธ   tum-wa[6]-yart[3] *n. lit.* "hunters endued with a sense of justice," *i.e.* those who know it is a sin to kill animals but who from poverty are compelled to do so; a Brahmin who, as a result of a curse, turns to hunting : ธรรมวาท discussions or arguments about law or duty : ธรรมวาสร *lit.* "the day of religious duties," *i.e.* the day of full moon : ธรรมวิจาร investigations or research on the subjects of law and duty : ธรรมวิชัย the victory of justice or virtue : ธรรมวิท one who knows the Law or path of duty; one who is pious and virtuous : ธรรมวิทยา knowledge of law or of what is just; jurisprudence : ธรรมวิธี the cause of law; a legal preceptor, or an injunction : ธรรมวิวรณ์ explanations of the Law : ธรรมวิเวก a dissertation on the Law.

ธรรมศรพณ์   tum-ma[6]-sop[4] *n.* the hearing of a sermon : ธรรมศรีระ a body or collection of virtues or sacred relics : ธรรมศาลา a

tribunal; a court of justice : ธรรมศาสตร์ the science of morals and ethics : ธรรมศาสตรโกวิท one versed in jurisprudence : ธรรมศาสน์ a volume of codified laws : ธรรมศีล one of a virtuous disposition; a just or pious person : ธรรมศทธิ a correct knowledge of the Law.

ธรรมสกนธ์   tum-sa[4]-gkon *n. lit.* "branches of doctrines," *i.e.* divisions of the Buddhist scriptures which are made into 84,000 articles or sections of the Law : ธรรมสงเคราะห์ a collection of Buddhistic technical terms : ธรรมสถล *lit.* "a place of justice," *i.e.* the law courts; halls of justice : ธรรมสภา a tribunal; a court of justice : ธรรมสมัย a legal obligation : ธรรมสหาย a companion in religious duties : ธรรมสังคีติ a discussion about the Law; a meeting of a Buddhist council : ธรรมสากัจฉา a conversation regarding religious matters : ธรรมสาคร, ธรรมสินธุ *lit.* "an ocean of justice," *i.e.* a code of laws, or volume of legal doctrines or religious truths : ธรรม-สาธนะ the fulfillment of one's duties; any act or virtue essential to a system of duties : ธรรมสามี *lit.* "lord of law and right," *i.e.* a Buddha : ธรรมสาร the essentials or essence of the Law : ธรรมสิงห์ *lit.* "a lion of virtue," *i.e.* one fearless in the observances of justice : ธรรมสูตร *lit.* "words strung together," *i.e.* a treatise on law and custom : ธรรมเสตุ having law and justice serving one as a barrier against the advance of evil.

ธรรมหาน   tum-ma[6]-hah[2]-nee *n.* the state of neglect of duty.

ธรรมอักษร, ธรรมักษร   tum-ma[6]-ack[4]-sorn[2] *n. lit.* "letters of the Law," *i.e.* formulas or confessions of faith : ธรรมอาคม, ธรรมาคม *lit.* "law-tradition," *i.e.* a law-book.

ธรรมากร   tum-mah-gkaun *n.* a mine of virtue or law.

ธรรมาจารย์   tum-mah-chjarn *n.* a preceptor or teacher of law or customs.

ธรรมาทิตย์   tum-mah-tit[6] *n. lit.* "the sun of justice," *i.e.* a Buddha.

ธรรมาธรรม tum-mah-tum *n.* antitheses, as right and wrong, justice and injustice, moral and immoral: ธรรมาธิกรณ์, ธรรมาธิการ *lit.* "civil administration, or courts of justice," *i.e.* nai umphurs; magistrates; judges; censors: ธรรมาธิปไตย the upholding of justice (as the supreme object to be attained): ธรรมาธิษฐาน *lit.* "founded upon equity," *i.e.* a court of justice; the administration of justice.

ธรรมานล tum-mah-non *n. lit.* "letting justice serve as a fire," *i.e.* in the destruction of iniquity: ธรรมานุสาร conforming to law or to a standard of virtue, a course or practice of duty.

ธรรมาภิมุข tum-mah-pi[6]-mook[6] *n.* turning to, or advancing towards virtue.

ธรรมายน tum-mah-yon *n. lit.* "the course of law or justice," *i.e.* a lawsuit; prosecutions in the law-courts.

ธรรมารัณย tum-mah-run *n. lit.* "a grove of religion," *i.e.* a sacred forest or grove dedicated to the cause of furthering the knowledge of religion.

ธรรมาโลก tum-mah-loke[3] *n.* the light of the law.

ธรรมาโศก tum-mah-soke[4] *n. lit.* "the Asoke of justice," *i.e.* king Asoka, a follower of the Buddhistic religion, who ruled the kingdom of Magadha during the third century before Christ, and, desiring to extend the Buddhist religion, had edicts cut in stone in various parts of his domain (Ala. p. 34): ธรรมาสน์ *lit.* "the throne of justice," *i.e.* a judgement seat; the seat of a judge; the bench.

ธรรมิก tum-mik[6] *n.* righteous; virtuous; pious; just; abiding in the right; conformable to justice.

ธรา ta[6]-rah *P. S. n. lit.* "the all-supporter," *i.e.* the earth (S. E. D. p. 510): ธราดล the surface of the earth: ธราธร *lit.* "earth bearer," *i.e.* Vishnu: ธราธิพ *lit.* "an earthly lord," *i.e.* a king: ธราธารา the earth: ธราธิบดี, ธราธิป names for Vishnu: ธราภาค a part, parts or portion of the earth: ธราภุช *lit.* "one who lives off the earth," *i.e.* a king; a chief or sovereign: ธรามร *lit.* "an earthly god," *i.e.* a Brahmin: ธราศัย a sleeper on the earth; one sleeping on the ground: ธเรศวร์ *lit.* "a great personage of the earth," *i.e.* a king.

ธวชิน, ธวชี see ธช: ธวชินี *lit.* "a multitude led by an ensign," *i.e.* an army: ธวชินีบดี, ธวชินีบาล a leader of an army; the commander-in-chief of troops.

ธวัช, ธช ta[6]-wat[6] *S. n.* a banner; a flag; a standard (S. E. D. p. 522): ธวัชคฤห์ a hall in which banners are kept; a place from which standards wave: ธวัชทรุม the palm tree (used for making flag-staffs); having banners as numerous as trees: ธวัชบัฏ *lit.* "banner-cloth," *i.e.* a flag or ensign: ธวัชประหรณ์ *lit.* "a banner striker or waver," *i.e.* the air, wind, or breeze: ธวัชภังค์ the fracture of a flag-staff or the falling of a banner; the falling of the male organ; impotence: ธวัชยนตร์ *lit.* "banner-instrument," *i.e.* any means or contrivance for keeping a flag-staff upright: ธวัชยัษฎิ the staff of a flag.

ธังก see ธงก์ p. 429.

ธช tut[6] *n.* a flag; a sign, mark or symbol (chd. p. 116).

ธัญญ ๑ tan-ya[6] *P. adj.* fortunate; lucky; rich; good; pleasing (chd. p. 120): ธัญญลักษณ์ an omen or mark of future good fortune.

ธัญญ ๒ tan-ya[6] *P. n.* grain; corn; cereal; consisting or made of grain (S. E. D. p. 514): ธัญญกูฏ a granary: ธัญญโกศ a store of grain or cereals in quantity: ธัญญเขตต์ a rice field; an area of corn fields: ธัญญจารี *lit.* "such as eat grains," *i.e.* birds: ธัญญชาติ cereals in the natural state (unmilled): ธัญญชีว *lit.* "such as subsist on grains," *i.e.* birds: ธัญญตัจ the husks of corn or paddy: ธัญญธน

wealth; landed property: ธัญญูเธนุ a heap of rice-stalks made into the shape of a cow, to be presented to a Brahmin as an offering: ธัญญูบาตร a vessel for holding corn or cereals: ธัญญูบูล a bundle or sheaf of corn-stalks: ธัญญูเบญจก five sorts of cereals, *viz.* (1) ข้าวสาลิ, ข้าวโพด *Zea mays (Gramineae)*, Indian corn (V. P. p. 48: Burk. p. 2285); (2) ข้าวเปลือก grains of *Oryza sativa*, rice (V. P. p. 46: Burk. p. 1593); *Myriopteron extensum, Maesa permollis (Myrsinaceae)* (V. P. p. 48) and *Phyllanthus columnaris (Euphorbiaceae)* (V. P. p. 49); (3) ลูกเดือย the fruit of *Coix lachryma (Gramineae)* (V. P. p. 116); *C. lachryma-jobi*, Job's tears (Burk. p. 629); (4) ถั่ว peas; beans; (5) ข้าวกษุทร rice: ธัญญูพืช (ผักชี) coriander, *Coriandrum sativum* (Burk. p. 663): ธัญญูมาส a particular capacity measure for grain: ธัญญูราช *lit.* "the king of all cereals," *i. e.* barley, *coix lachryma* (V. P. p. 116): ธัญญูสาร the essence of grain; shelled corn (removed from the cob): ธัญญูาหาร cereals or rice used as food.

ธันยา tan-yah *S. n.* a nurse (S. E. D. p. 509).

ธันยาวาท tan-yah-wart[3] *S. n.* praise; applause; thanksgiving (S. E. D. p. 509).

ธันวาคม tan-wah-kom *n.* the ninth month (according to the Gregorian calendar, December); *Sagittarius* (the Archer): ธันวาจารย์ a professor in the science of archery.

ธาดา tah-dah *P. n.* a founder; an establisher; a creator; a supporter; one who arranges or orders (S. E. D. p. 514).

ธาตรี, ธาติ, ธาษตรี tah-dtree *P. S. n.* a female supporter; a nurse; a midwife; a mother; the earth (S. E. D. p. 514): ธาตรีธร *lit.* "earth-bearers," *i. e.* mountains.

ธาตุ tat[3] *P. S. n.* an element; an ingredient; a constituent part; an essential ingredient of the body; the three humours of the body, *viz.* phlegm, air and bile; the seven fluids or secretions of the body, *viz.* chyle,

blood, flesh, fat, bone, marrow and semen; the primary elements of the earth, *viz.* metals, and mineral ore; the five physical organs of sense and the properties of the elements perceived by them; a grammatical root, radical or base of a word; the ashes of the body; relics (S. E. D. p. 513): ธาตุกษัย, ธาตุวิการ the wasting away or extinction of the humours, *i. e.* consumption: ธาตุโกศล one skilled in metals or minerals; an alchemist; a metallurgist: ธาตุโขภ a condition in which the four elementary constituents of the body,—earth, water, air and fire—are abnormally active: ธาตุจุรณ a mineral powder: ธาตุบล *lit.* "a stone-like mineral," *i. e.* chalk: ธาตุแท้ an element: ธาตุผสม a chemical compound: ธาตุไพรี *lit.* "a metal-enemy," *i. e.* sulphur: ธาตุมล impure excretion from the fluids of the body, *i. e.* feces; the most impure of metals, *i. e.* lead: ธาตุมัย *lit.* "a place containing elements or sacred relics," *i. e.* a phrachadee: ธาตุมารี *lit.* "a dissolver of metals," *i. e.* sulphur: ธาตุวัลลภ *lit.* "a friend of metals," *i. e.* borax: ธาตุวาท a treatise on metallurgy or alchemy: ธาตุโศธนะ, ธาตุสมภพ lead: ธาตุสตุป a receptacle for relics; a phrachadee: ธาตุหัน *lit.* "a destroyer of metals," *i. e.* sulphur: แปรธาตุ alchemy: พระธาตุ the sacred relics of the Buddha: ไฟธาตุ the agents, enzymes or gastric acids that produce digestion of food.

ธาน, ธานิศ tah-nee *P. n.* the site of habitation; a city; a capital city; a town (S. E. D. p. 514): ธานินทร์ a large city; a place of great importance: ราชธานิ a royal city.

ธาร ๑ tan *P. S. n.* a supporter; a maintainer; an upholder; a prop; a stay (S. E. D. p. 515): ธารพระกร *lit.* "supporting the hand," *i. e.* a staff; a cane; a walking-stick (used only for royalty): ธารยักษ์ a violent storm; a hurricane: พระธาร the king's baton or staff of sovereignty.

ธาร ๒ tan *n.* a stream; a current of water;

a flood; a jet or gush of water; a drop (of any liquid); rain; a shower (s. e. d. p. 515).

ธารคำนัล   tah-ra[6]-kum-nan *n.* an audience hall; a parlour; a room for the reception of visitors; an assembly room.

ธารณ   tah-ra[6]-na[6] *S. adj.* (1) preserving; protecting; retaining; maintaining; possessing: (2) enduring; suffering: ธารณบาตร a circular stand or pedestal for a Buddhist monk's alms-bowl (s. e. d. p. 515).

ธารณา   tah-ra[6]-nah *S. n.* memory; intellect; understanding; mental concentration; the retention of knowledge within the grasp of the mind: ธารณามัย consisting of abstraction of the mind: ธารณาโยค loyalty; allegiance; fidelity; true devotion (s. e. d. p. 515).

ธารา ๑   tah-rah *P. S. n.* a natural water course; a stream; rain; drops (of any liquid) (s. e. d. p. 515): ธาราคม *lit.* "the season for the appearing of clouds," *i. e.* the rainy season: ธาราเคห a shower-bath; a bathroom with flowing water: ธารางกูร raindrops; hail: ธาราธร *lit.* "water-bearer," *i. e.* clouds: ธารานิบาต, ธาราบาต, ธาราวรรษ a torrential rain; a heavy shower: ธารายนตร์ *lit.* "an automatic water-machine," *i. e.* a spring; a fountain: ธาราวนี wind.

ธารา ๒   tah-rah *S. n.* the margin; the rim; the sharp edge of a blade (as of a knife or sword); the rim of a wheel; the tip of the ear; the highest point or summit (as of a mountain) (s. e. d. p. 515): ธาราชล blood dripping from the edge of a sword: ธาราธร, ธาราสลิล *lit.* that which must maintain a sharp edge," *i. e.* a sword: ธาราบถ *lit.* "rim-path," *i. e.* the rut made by a wheel: ธาราพิษ *lit.* "having a poisoned edge," *i. e.* a sword; a scimitar.

ธำมรงค์   tum-ma[6]-rong *n.* a finger-ring (used only for royalty).

ธำรง   tum-rong *v.* to sustain; to uphold; to support.

ธิดา   ti[6]-dah *n.* a daughter (chd. p. 122).

ธิติ   ti[6]-dti[4] *P. n.* firmness; constancy; permanency; satisfaction; contentment; joyfulness (s. e. d. p. 519): ธิติมุษ *lit.* "fortitude-stealer," *i. e.* discouragement; despondency; hopelessness; despair; perplexity.

ธีร ๑   tee-ra[6] *P. S. n.* a philosopher: *adj.* wise; intelligent; learned; skilful; clever; adroit (s. e. d. p. 517).

ธีร ๒   tee-ra[6] *S. adj.* (1) firm; resolute; constant; brave; composed; calm; self-possessed; courageous: (2) deep; low; dull; gentle; soft (descriptive of sounds or of the voice): ธีรประศานต์ a deep, calm, pleasing voice: ธีรภาพ constancy; firmness; solidity: ธีรศานต์ brave and calm: ธีรสกนธ์ *lit.* "strong-shouldered," *i. e.* a buffalo.

ธุช see ธุช p. 429.

ธุดงค์   too[6]-dong *P. S. n.* a group of thirteen ascetic practices, the observance of which is meritorious for a Buddhist priest. It is not intended that all should be kept at the same time, but of course the more that are kept the greater is the merit (chd. p. 123).

ธุตต   toot[6]-dta[4] *P. S. n.* games of chance; gambling (especially with dice, but also with any inanimate object); a battle, a fight or contest; the prize or booty won in a game or battle (s. e. d. p. 500): ธุตตกชน, ธุตตกร, ธุตตการ those given to practicing gambling; inveterate gamblers: ธุตตกีฬา gambling with dice: ธุตตธรรม the laws concerning gambling: ธุตตพีช a cowrie or cowries (small shells used as coins in games): ธุตตภูมิ a gambling place or den: ธุตตมณฑล a circle or party of gamblers: ธุตตศาลา, ธุตตสภา, ธุตตสมาช a gaming house; an assembly of gamblers.

ธุม   toom *P. n.* smoke; vapour; mist (s. e. d. p. 518): ธุมเกตุ fire; a column of smoke.

mist or clouds occurring abnormally : ธุม-ชาล a bank of clouds ; smoke belching or curling out (as from a volcano) : ธุมธวัช *lit.* " smoke-marked," *i. e.* fire : ธุมนิรคมน์ *lit.* " smoke-outlet," *i. e.* a chimney : ธุมบาน the inhalation of smoke or vapours (as from cigars, or cigarettes) : ธุมมหิษี *lit.* smoke's-wife," *i. e.* fog ; mist : ธุมโยนิ *lit.* " smoke-engendered," " vapour-born," *i. e.* a cloud : ธุมสิขา a fee ; a salary ; a reward ; gifts ; a prize or present : ธุมาการ having the form of smoke ; smoky : ธุมางค์ a cloud of dust : ธุมาวลี a ring, circle or mass of smoke.

ธุระ   too⁶-ra⁶ *P. S. n.* duty ; business ; a burden ; a load ; a yoke ; anything grievous, oppressive or difficult to bear (S. E. D. p. 517) : ธุรการ executive administration : ธุระส่วนตัว one's private affairs : เอาเป็นธุระ to assume the responsibility for.

ธุลี   too⁶-lee *P. n.* dust ; powder ; pollen (S. E. D. p. 518) : ธุลีธงษ์ the crow : ธุลีธวัช *lit.* " dust-bannered," *i. e.* air ; wind : ธุลีบดล clouds of dust : ธุลีมัย covered with dust.

ธุว   too⁶-wa⁶ *P. .adj.* firm ; fixed ; constant ; lasting ; immovable ; enduring ; eternal (as

the earth, a mountain, a pillar) (S. E. D. p. 521) : ธุวเกษตร having a firm position or abode : ธุวเกษม firmly fixed ; immutable ; unchangeable ; immovable : ธุวคติ a firm position : ธุวดารา the North Star : ธุวภาค the constant longitude of fixed stars : ธุวมณฑล the polar regions : ธุวยัษฏิ the axis of the poles : ธุวโยนิ having a firm resting place : ธุวศีล having a permanent abode : ธุวอักษร *lit.* " the eternal syllable," *i. e.* OM (โอม), a name of Vishnu.

ธูป   toop³ *P. S. n.* incense ; aromatic vapours or smoke proceeding from gum or resin (S. E. D. p. 517) : ธูปเนตร a pipe for smoking : ธูปบาตร a perfume box ; a vessel for incense ; a censer.

เธียร   tee-an *n.* a sage ; a philosopher : *adj.* wise ; intelligent ; clever ; skilful ; brave ; firm ; steady ; constant (S. E. D. p. 517).

เธอ   tur *pro.* you ; he : น้องยาเธอ the younger brother of the king. พี่ยาเธอ the elder brother of the king :

โธวน   toh-wa⁶-na⁶ *P. adj.* washing ; cleansing ; purifying (chd. p. 122) : โธวนกิจ the process of washing, bathing, or of purifying.

น

น   The twenty-fifth consonant of the Thai alphabet, a low class letter of which there are twenty-four, *viz.* ค, ฅ, ฆ, ง, ช, ฌ, ซ, ญ, ท, ธ, ฑ, ฒ, ฐ, น, ณ, พ, ฟ, ภ, ม, ร, ล, ว, ฬ, ฮ. นอนิล or นอหนู are the names of this letter. It is used extensively in words of Pali and Sanskrit origin. น is a palatal, represented by the English " n ".

นก   nok⁶ *n.* a bird ; birds (in general) ; a prefix to which the particular designating species is added. These various names will be found in their proper places with (นก) to indicate their classification and complete name. Thus นกพิลาป will be found as พิลาป (นก) :

นก (ต้น) a family of small wild tuber : ดักนก to trap birds : นกกระจอก (ปลา) *Cypselurus oligolepis* (*Exocoetidae*), a flying fish, a fish which is able to leap from the water, and fly a considerable distance by means of its large and long pectoral fins. It may be found in the warmer parts of all the oceans (suvatti p. 93 : web.) : นกขุนทอง (ปลา) *Cheilinus fasciatus* (*Coridae*) (suvatti p. 148) ; *Cheilinus fasciatus* (*Labridae*), a species of highly coloured fish of little or no food-value (burk. p. 522) : นกยูงไทย, หางนกยูงไทย (ต้น) *Caesalpinia pulcherrima* (*Leguminosae*), peacock-flower, peacock's crest, a large bush of uncertain origin, perhaps South America, but now found throughout the tropics, chiefly in cultivation. It was in the gardens of India in 1680 and apparently was taken from there to Malaysia. There are two races, one with golden-yellow flowers and one with red and yellow flowers. The yellow race was more common and favoured, and to it the Anglo-Indians gave the name of gold-mohur flower; that name now has been transferred to *Poinciana regia*. The Chinese preferred this yellow race for ceremonial use owing to the sanctity of the colour (orn. Trees of Hawaii, J.F. Rock, p. 109: V. P. p. 148: MCM. pp. 108, 109: Burk. p. 390): นกยูงฝรั่ง (ต้น) *Poinciana regia* (*Leguminosae*), (*Delonix regia*), flamboyant, flametree, goldmohur, a gorgeous tree when in full blossom, bearing immense panicles or long sprays of scarlet or orange flowers. It is a native of Madagascar. It grows from 40 to 50 feet in height, with a spreading habit, and has very handsome, fine, feathery, long, bipinnate leaves (MCM. p. 91: V. P. p. 149: Burk. p. 777): นก (ปืน) the hammer of a gun: คนนกสองหัว one who prevaricates; one who practices deception, duplicity or craftiness.

นกุล   na[6]-gkoon *P. S. n. lit.* "an enemy of mice and serpents," *i. e.* the Bengal mongoose; name of the fourth Pandu prince. He was the twin son of Madri (มาทรี), the second wife of Pandu, sister of the King of the Madras. He was learned in the science of astronomy which he studied under Drona, and was also well acquainted with the management of cattle (H. C. D. pp. 184, 214, 272: S. E. D. p. 523).

นข, นัข   na[6]-ka[4] *P. S. n.* finger-nails; toenails; claws; talons; the spur of the domestic cock (S. E. D. p. 524): นขกฏฏิ์ *lit.* "a cutter of nails," *i. e.* a barber; a manicurist: นขทารณ์ *lit.* "that which tears with the claws," *i. e.* a hawk; a falcon: นขบท *lit.* "nailmark," *i. e.* a scratch: นขลิขิต a parenthesis: นขเลขา a scratch with the nail; nailtinting: นขวาทย์ *lit.* "nail music," *i. e.*

musical sounds produced on instruments by thrumming with fingers or finger-nails: นขเลขา finger-nail marks, tracks or scratches: นขาอุธ *lit.* "claw-armed," *i. e.* a cock; a tiger; a lion: นขาศี *lit.* "eating with claws," *i. e.* an owl.

นค, นัค   na[6]-ka[6] *S. n. lit.* "that which is immovable," *i. e.* a mountain; a hill; the sun (S. E. D. p. 525): นคช *lit.* "mountain-born," *i. e.* elephants; mountaineers; hill-tribes: นคนันทินี *lit.* "a daughter of the mountain," *i. e.* name of Durga, the great goddess, wife of Siva and daughter of the Himalaya mountains (H. C. D. pp. 86, 99): นคบดี, นคาธิราช *lit.* "the chief of mountains," *i. e.* the Himalayas: นคภิท *lit.* "a rock-splitter," *i. e.* an axe; a crow; Indra: นควาหน *lit.* "mountain-borne," *i. e.* name of Siva: นคอัคร, นคาคร mountaintop: นคาวาส *lit.* "tree-dweller," *i. e.* a peacock: นคาศรัย one who lives in mountains: นคเนทร์ *lit.* "mountain-lord," *i. e.* the Himalayas: นโคทร *lit.* "mountainrift," *i. e.* a cavern; a ravine.

นคร   na[6]-kawn *n.* a town; a city (S. E. D. p. 525): นครกาก *lit.* "a town-crow," *i. e.* an undesirable person; a term of contempt: นครคามี a road leading to a town: นครฆาต *lit.* "town-destroyer," *i. e.* an elephant: นครจตุบถ an intersection of four roads in a town: นครบดี a town-chief: นครมัฌฑนา *lit.* "townbeauties or ornaments," *i. e.* courtesans: นครรักษี a town-watchman: นครวาสี *lit.* "towndweller," *i. e.* a citizen: นครโสภินี harlots; prostitutes: นครหลวง a capital city; a metropolis: นคราทร a municipality: นครินทร์ the lord of a town; a governor: นคเรศ a town; a city; a district.

นครปฐม   na[6]-kawn-bpa[4]-tom[2] *n.* Nagor Pathom, site of the much revered sanctuary and stupa, Phra Pathom Chedi. Nagor Pathom is situated in latitude 13°-50 North and longitude 100°-04 East. During the many centuries of its existence, dating back as far as 500 B. C., it has encountered many vicissitudes and alterations in form. When first built it had the form of an Indian stupa possibly surmounted by a spire, for it was the work of the Indianized Mon people. During Khmer domination, this Buddhist sanctuary became Brahmin. The stupa which had fallen into disrepair was restored, but instead of having the spire of a Chedi, it was crowned with a prang 40 metres high. After the lapse of about 800 years King Mongkut (1851-68) repaired the sanctuary and rebuilt the Phra Chedi. King Chulalongkorn (1868-1910) brought the work to a happy end, which is the present and imposing enormous bell-shaped structure. The colossal stupa stands on a large square brick mount rising in two terraces and reaching 115 metres above the ground. Inside this, and under this stupa are hidden the former buildings of the old stupa and prang.

นง   nong *n.* a woman; a girl; a lady: นง-คราญ a beautiful woman: นงนุช a younger sister; a little girl: นงพาล, นงเยาว์ a virgin; a young woman: นงลักษณ์ a woman or girl of charm.

นงคุฐ   nong-koot[6] *P. n.* the tail of an animal (chd. p. 260).

นท   note[6] *P. S. n.* a roarer; a bellower; a crier; a brayer; an emitter of sound; a cloud (as a thunder-cloud); a raging river (S. E. D. p. 526).

นที, นที   na[6]-tee *P. S. n.* a river; flowing water (S. E. D. p. 526): นทีกานต์ *lit.* "a lover of rivers," *i. e.* the ocean: , นทีกาศยป name of a contemporary of Sakya-Muni: นทีกุล, นทีเดียร the bank or brink of a river: นทีตร the crossing of a river (as by swimming): นทีธร *lit.* "bearer of the river (Ganges)," *i. e.* a name for Siva (H. C. D. p. 300): นทีนาถ *lit.* "lord of rivers," *i. e.* the ocean: นทีบงก์ *lit.* "river-mud," *i. e.* the marshy, muddy bank of a river: นทีบดี *lit.* "lord of flowing waters," *i. e.* the sea; the ocean: นทีบุร *lit.*

"river-flood," *i. e.* a river in spate; a tidal river at full tide: นทีมุข the mouth of a river; an estuary: นทีรัย, นทีเวค the current of a river: นทีวักร, นทีวงก์, นทีวังก์ the bends or curves in the course of a river; นทีวาส standing in a river (a form of penance).

นน, กานน (p. 93) *Siam., Peninsula,* สมอตืน-เปิ็ด, สมอหิน, ตืนนก (p. 369) *Laos* (ต้น) non *n. Vitex pubescens (Verbenaceae)*, a large evergreen tree with quadrangular branches, found throughout Asia and Malaysia. The leaves consist of five leaflets which are sessile, and densely clothed with a soft, tawny pubescence. The inflorescence is dense, pyramidal, and three to five inches across. The bracts are persistent. The drupe is small, globose and bluish-black. The timber seems to be commercial in the Philippine Islands. The wood is hard, heavy, fine-grained, with no distinction between sap-wood and heart-wood, yellow, greyish, or olive-coloured, very durable in contact with the ground. It is the most in demand of any, for the manufacture of Malay ploughs and other agricultural implements. The leaves and bark are medicinal (V. P. p. 152: BURK. p. 2239).

นนตรา *Jav.* for กระถิน (ต้น) p. 32.

นนท์, นันท non *P. S. n.* (1) delight; happiness; pleasure; bliss; felicity; prosperity: (2) a small earthen water-jar (S. E. D. p. 526).

นนทก non-tok[6] *adj.* delighting in; rejoicing; gladdening; making happy; joyful; joyous: *n.* a name for Krishna's sword (S. E. D. p. 526).

นนทรี *Siam.,* ร้าง *E. Laos,* ราง *Sui, Surin,* กร้าเซก *Khmer, Surin,* อะราง *Chaobon, Korat* (ต้น) non-see *n. Peltophorum dasyrachis (Leguminosae)*; also *P. pterocarpum, (P. ferrugineum, P. inerme)* two sorts of rather similar, large, quick-growing, symmetrical trees, with a spreading top and fine, graceful feathery foliage, indigenous to Ceylon and Malaya. They blossom twice a year at irregular seasons, some specimens being in blossom while others by their side are in ripe fruit. The flowers are rusty-yellow, sweet-scented, and borne in large erect panicles. The trees are a magnificent sight when in full blossom. They are excellent shade trees and can be used to eradicate lalang, and also as a shade for coffee. They are wind-firm and are not attacked by boring beetles. The young leaves and shoots are covered with a brown velvety tomentum. The bark of one variety is used for colouring cotton a yellow-brown, and considerable quantities are consumed in the batik industry in Java: the other is not so good a dye. The astringent bark has medicinal use. Cattle eat the leaves (MCM. pp. 90, 92, 206, 213, 518: Cb. p. 499: BURK. p. 1686).

นนทลี̃   non-ta[6]-lee *n.* a mother.

นนทิ, นนทิการ, นันทิ   non-ti[6] *n. lit.* " the happy one," *i. e.* Vishnu; name of an attendant of Siva; felicity; welfare (S. E. D. p. 527): นนทิกร causing joy or happiness: นนทิ-ตุริยางค์ a musical instrument played on occasions of merry-making: นนทิรุทร name of Siva in a joyful or serene form: นนทิ-วรรธน์ that which increases pleasure and promotes cheer or rejoicing, *viz.* a son, children, or friends: นนทิศวร name of the chief of Siva's attendants.

นบ   nop[6] *v.* to bow or bend the head; to salute by joining the two hands together resembling a lotus bud, and bending the head: นบนอบ to submit or be subject to; to obey: มีใจนบนอบ to be submissive.

นปุงสก, นปุงสกลิงค์,–ลึงค์   na[6]-bpoong-sok[4] *P. S. n.* the neuter gender; an eunuch (chd. p. 260).

นพ   nop[6] *adj.* the numeral nine (chd. p. 262): นพศก the ninth year of a decade, according

to the Siamese enumeration: นพคุณ, นวคุณ nine attributes: นพคุณ (ทอง) a term applied to gold of the maximum, or ninth degree of purity: นพเคราะห์, นวเคราะห์, นวครหะ a planet (see ดาวนพเคราะห์ p. 327): นพปฎล, นวปฎล being of nine layers or tiers (as the royal umbrella): นพรัตน์ the nine gems, *viz.* diamond (เพ็ชร์), ruby (ทับทิม), emerald (มรกต), topaz (บุษยราคัม), garnet (โกเมน), sapphire (นิล), moon-stone (มุกดา), hyacinth, zircon (เพทาย), cats-eye (ไพฑูรย์) (Ger. (1) p. 150); name of a state decoration royally conferred: แหวนนพรัตน์, นพแก้ว the nine gemmed ring which symbolizes the nine planets and is most auspicious if worn during the days ruled over by the latter. It is most efficient in averting the malignant influences likely to proceed at any time from any of them, and is capable of ensuring success in all undertakings, prosperity and a long life (Gerini (1) p. 150).

นพนิต see นวนิต ใน นว ๑ p. 444.

นภ   na[6]-pa[6] *P. n.* the sky; the firmament; air; atmosphere (S. E. D. p. 527): นภกานต์ *lit.* " a sky-walker," *i. e.* a lion (from the lion-like shape of certain clouds): นภเกตน์ *lit.* " sky-banner", *i. e.* the sun: นภคช *lit.* " a sky-elephant," *i. e.* a cloud: นภคติ *lit.* " sky-going," *i. e.* flying, soaring, artificial, or supernatural passing through the air: นภ-จร *lit.* " sky-goers," *i. e.* celestials; a god; birds; clouds; wind: นภจักษุ *lit.* " eye of the sky," *i. e.* the sun: นภตล *lit.* " sky-surface," *i. e.* the firmament; atmosphere: นภทวีป *lit.* " islands of the sky," *i. e.* clouds: นภปราณ, นภวาส *lit.* " breath of the sky," *i. e.* air; wind; atmosphere: นภมณฑล *lit.* " sky-circle," *i. e.* the horizon: นภมณี *lit.* " jewel of the sky," *i. e.* the sun: นภมัย foggy; misty; hazy; vaporous: นภรุป *lit.* " cloud-coloured," *i. e.* dark; gloomy; murky; overcast: นภเรณุ *lit.* " sky-dust," *i. e.* fog; mist: นภลัย *lit.* " sky-dissolved," *i. e.* smoke: นภวิถี *lit.* " sky-road," *i. e.* the sun's path; นภสถล *lit.* " sky-resider," *i: e.*

Siva: นภสระ *lit.* "sky-lakes," *i. e.* the clouds: นภสินธุ์ *lit.* "sky-river," *i. e.* the Milky Way.

นม ๑ na⁶-ma⁶ *P. S. n.* an obeisance; a reverential salutation; a bow indicating veneration or adoration; food (S. E. D. p. 528): นมครู *lit.* "a spiritual teacher," *i. e.* a Brahmin: นมวาก *lit.* "reverential obeisance," *i. e.* placing the hands palm to palm, and raising them to the face: นมัการ, นมัสการ worshipful adoration; bowing the head in reverence, humility and fealty.

นม ๒ nom *n.* the breasts; the mammae; a pap; an udder: นมควาย *Siam.* and *Laos,* นมฝาย *Laos, Chiengmai* (ต้น) *Uvaria rufa* (*Annonaceae*), a woody climber which is used medicinally in Java (cb. p. 31: v. p. p. 153: burk. p. 2215): นมช้าง *Laos, Chiengmai* (ต้น) *Uvaria macrophylla* (*Annonaceae*), a woody climber of considerable size, found from Ceylon to Java. The fruits are eaten in Ceylon (cb. p. 30: v. p. p. 153: burk. p. 2215): นมตำเลีย (ต้น) *Hoya parasitica* (*Asclepiadaceae*), a climber with milky juice, often epiphytic (K.): นมนาง the vowel mark " ะ ": นมผา stalagmites of white lime resembling a virgin's breasts: นมพิจิตร *Siam., Krat,* หมากน้อย *Siam., Saraburi,* บวบงู *Siam.* (ต้น) *Trichosanthes anguina* (*Cucurbitaceae*), snake-gourd, club-gourd, a quick-growing, annual gourd, native of China and Malaya, bearing long, cylindrical, green or greenish-white fruits, 4 to 5 feet or more in length. In an unripe state these are sliced and cooked, being commonly used and much relished as a curry-vegetable. Seeds are sown at the beginning of the rains, against a trellis-work of bamboo or other supports. A crop should be obtained in 3 months from planting. It is customary to fasten a small stone to the end of each fruit whilst growing, so as to weight the latter down and induce it to grow straighter, and perhaps longer, than it would otherwise do (cb. p.

751: McM. pp. 294, 292, 380: Burk. p. 2178): นมแมว *Siam.* (ต้น) *Rauwenhoffia siamensis* (*Annonaceae*), an ornamental climber sometimes cultivated for its pale yellow flowers (burk. p. 1885: cb. pp. 45, 46); *Uvaria curtisii; Ellipeia cherrevensis* (v. p. p. 154): นมไม้ a breast-shaped block of wood, used for exerting localized pressure while one is in a recumbent position: นมวัว *Laos* (ต้น) *Uvaria ridleyi* (*Annonaceae*), a sprawler found in the Malay Peninsula, in the north-western part and in the southern half. As it grows in open country it usually has nothing to climb over, but sprawls over itself. The fruits are small but sweet, and are eaten (burk. p. 2216); *Artabotrys siamensis; Anomianthus heterocarpus; Rauwenhoffia siamensis* (see นมแมว) (v. p. p. 154): นมสวรรค์ *Siam., Peninsula* (ต้น) *Clerodendron paniculatum* (*Verbenaceae*), pagoda-flower, a shrub 5 to 6 feet high, found from Burma and southern China to Java and Ternate and apparently throughout the Malay Peninsula. It has occult and also medicinal uses. It is supposed to be excellent elephant-medicine, making them brave. The leaves are large, angular and very showy; the flowers are large, erect, scarlet panicles (McM. p. 109: v. p. p. 155: burk. p. 585): นมหวา *Siam., Surat,* กาสะท้อน *N. Laos* (ต้น) *Pithecolobium clypearia* (*Leguminosae*), a small tree found from the eastern Himalayas to the Philippine Islands; in the Malay Peninsula it is common in open country and woods. Its wood is soft, light, and is used for sheaths of weapons. The leaves are used for poulticing, and are said to poison cattle. The bark is used to tan fishing-nets (cb. p. 557: v. p. p. 154: burk. p. 1759).

นมนาน nom-narn *adj.* very slow; a long time ago: ทำมานมนานแล้ว I have been at this for a long time already: นมนานมาแล้ว a very long time ago.

นย, นัย na⁶-ya⁶ *P. S. n.* sense; meaning (as in the interpretation of a word or phrase);

conduct; behaviour; the condition of leading (as of an army); conducting or directing; a policy in civil and military government; plan; purport; design; system; method (S. E. D. p. 528): นยโกวิท one skilled in administrative policies; one who is sagacious: นยจักษุ *lit.* "the eye of prudence," *i. e.* wisdom; knowledge: *adj.* smart; clever: นยเนตฺตุ, นยเนตา a master in policies or politics: นยศาสตร์ the doctrines of political wisdom: นยสิทธิ์ political successes: นโยบาย policies.

นยนะ, นยนา, นัยน์ na⁶-ya⁶-na⁶ *P.S. n. lit.* "the leading organ," *i. e.* the eye; the leader; the director; the conductor; the pupil of the eye (S. E. D. p. 528): นยนโคจร within the range of sight; visible: นยนจริต *lit.* "the playing with the eye," *i. e.* ogling: นยนชล, นยนสลิล *lit.* "eye-water", *i. e.* tears: นยนบถ the range or field of vision: นยนบุฏ the eyelids: นยนปรีติ *lit.* "eye-delight." *i. e.* lovely sights; the friendly look: นยนวิษัย the limit of sight; the horizon: นยนศาณ medicines or lotions for the eyes; a collyrium: นยนาวุธ *lit.* "one having eyes as weapons," *i. e.* the god of Death.

นยักษ์ na⁶-yak⁶ *S. adj.* low; inferior (descriptive of conduct) (S. E. D. p. 571).

นร na⁶-ra⁶ *P.S. n.* a person; a man; a male; a husband; a hero (S. E. D. p. 528): นรกบาล the human skull: นรเกสรี, นฤเกสรี *lit.* "the man-lion," *i. e.* Vishnu in his fourth incarnation. He assumed this form to deliver the world from the tyranny of a demon, who by the favour of Brahma, had become invulnerable and was secure from gods, men and animals (H. C. D. p. 37): นรเทพ, นรนาถ, นรนายก, นรบดี, นรบาล *lit.* "man-god," *i. e.* a king; an emperor; a sovereign: นรมาลา a string or girdle of human skulls: นรยนตร์ *lit.* "a gnomon-instrument," *i. e.* a sundial: นรยาน a carriage drawn by a man or men: นรราช *lit.* "king of men," *i. e.* a king: นรรูป the human form: นรโลก

lit. "men's world," *i. e.* the earth; mortals; men; populace: นรวร an excellent man: นรวาหน *lit.* "one borne (as on a palanquin) or drawn by man," *i. e.* Kuvera (ท้าวกุเวร), the regent of the north, the keeper of gold and silver, jewels and pearls, and all the treasures of the earth (H. C. D. p. 174): นรวีร a hero; one brave or fearless: นรวยามร์, นรพยัคฆ์ *lit.* "a tiger-man," *i. e.* an eminent or illustrious man: นรศฤงค์ *lit.* "man's-horns," *i. e.* any thing preposterous, improbable or non-existent, *ex.* หนวดเต่าเขากระต่าย: นรเศรษฐ the best of men: นรสกนธ์ an assembly or multitude of men: นรสิงห์, นรเกสรี, นฤเกสรี, นฤหรี *lit.* "lion-man," *i. e.* Vishnu in his fourth incarnation (when he was half man, half lion): นราธม a wretch; a low, vile man.

นรก, นิรย na⁶-rok⁶ *P. S. n.* hell; a place of torment; the infernal regions (S. E. D. p. 529): นรกบาต the falling into hell: นรกภูมิ a division of hell: นรกวาส the remaining in hell: นรกามัย the soul after death; a ghost: นรกาวาส an inhabitant of hell: นรกุณฑ์ a pit in hell for tormenting the wicked. Eighty-six of these are said to exist.

นรการ nau-ra⁶-gkan *n.* a tuskless elephant.

นรี na⁶-ree *S. n.* a woman; a female; a wife (chd. p. 260): นรีเวชชวิทยา gynecology.

นเรศวร na⁶-ray-suan² *n.* Naresuan, the eldest son of King Maha Tamma-racha-tirat and of a daughter of Queen Suriyotai, was born in Pitsanuloke in A. D. 1555, and died at Muang Hang Luang on 16th May, 1605, aged 50. The grandmother, Queen Suriyotai, is a heroine of the Siamese nation, for, wearing men's armour, she mounted an elephant, fought bravely side by side with the men, sacrificing her own life in saving her royal husband, in deadly combat with a Burmese prince. To keep her memory fresh, a monument still stands in Ayuthia. Her grandson, King Naresuan the Great, was the most celebrated hero and warrior who ever played a part upon the stage of Siamese history. He was strong, sturdy, brave and active, born a great leader of men, having every quality of a great general, quick conception of situation, courage in time of danger, kindness and firmness in dealing with his subordinates, good judgement, a strong will, and decision in his resolutions. He was a king whose memory all Siamese may well hold in honour (wood p. 156).

นฤ na[6]-rur[6] *S. n.* a person; a man; a hero; mankind; the pin or gnomon of a sun-dial (S. E. D. p. 567): นฤกเลวระ a human body; a corpse: นฤการ *lit.* "manly-deed," *i. e.* heroism; bravery: นฤเกสรี see นรเกสรี p. 442. นฤจักษุ the condition of seeing with human eyes: นฤชล *lit.* "man-water," *i. e.* human urine: นฤชิต one who conquers men: นฤตม most manly, strongest or most vigorous: นฤเทพ *lit.* "man-god," *i. e.* a king: นฤธรรม *lit.* "acting as a man," *i. e.* Kuvera (see กุเปรัน; กุเวร p 111): นฤดี *lit.* "lord of men," *i. e.* a king, ruler, monarch or sovereign: นฤบัตนี a king's wife; a queen: นฤบาณ giving drink to men: นฤบาล *lit.* "men-protector," *i. e.* a king: นฤประชา the children of men: นฤพาหุ a man's arm: นฤมฬัส one mindful of, or considerate of men: นฤมร murder; homicide: นฤเมฆ *lit.* "a man compared to a cloud," *i. e.* one bestowing favours or yielding rain: นฤโลก the world of men: นฤวร the best or chief of men; a king: นฤวราห *lit.* "the boar-man," *i. e.* Vishnu in his third incarnation when he raised the earth from the waters after a demon had dragged it to the bottom of the sea. To recover it, Vishnu assumed the form of a boar and after a contest of a thousand years, he slew the demon and raised the earth (H. C. D. p. 37): นฤวาหณ carrying or conveying men: นฤศัสตร praised by men: นฤสิงห์ see นรสิงห์ p. 442: นฤเสน, นฤเสนา an army of men: นฤโสม *lit.* "moon-man," *i. e.* a great or illustrious man.

นฤโฆษ see นิรโฆษ p. 459.

นฤตย์ na[6]-rit[6] *S. adj.* dancing; gesticulating; acting; active (S. E. D. p. 568): นฤตยคีต the act of singing and dancing: นฤตยคีตวาทย์ the act of dancing and singing with instrumental accompaniment: นฤตยปรีย์ *lit.* "one fond of dancing," *i. e.* a peacock; an appellation for Siva: นฤตยศาลา, นฤตยสถาน a dance-hall or ball-room: นฤตยศาสตร์ the art of dancing.

นฤป na[6]-reu[6]-bpa[4] *P.S. n. lit.* "a protector of men," *i. e.* a king; a sovereign: (S. E. D. p. 568): นฤปกริยา *lit.* "a king's business," *i. e.* government: นฤปการย์ the affairs or business of a king: นฤปทวิษ the state of dislike or hatred towards a king or monarch: นฤปทีป a king or monarch compared to a lamp (lighting his people to prosperity): นฤปนีติ royal methods or policies of administration; king-craft: นฤปพฤกษ์,ราชพฤกษ์(see คูน p. 206): นฤปมนเทียร *lit.* "a king's house," *i. e.* a palace: นฤปลักษม์ *lit.* "the insignia of a king," *i. e.* the royal, white, nine-tiered umbrella: นฤปเวศม์ a royal court; a law-court: นฤปสภ an assembly of princes; a royal palace: นฤปสุต a king's son; a prince: นฤปานุจร a king's attendant; a minister of state: นฤปามัย *lit.* "king's disease," *i. e.* tuberculosis: นฤปาลัย, นฤปาสบท a king's residence; a palace.

นฤมิต see นิรมิต p. 459.

นฤพาน see นิพพาน p. 458.

นฤมาณ see นิรมาณ p. 459.

นลาฎ na[6]-lat[3] *P.S. n.* the forehead (chd. p. 256).

นลิน na[6]-lin *P.S. n.* a lotus flower; a water-lily (S. E. D. p. 530): นลินทล lotus petals: นลินอาสน์, นลินาสน์ *lit.* "lotus-throned," *i. e.* names of Brahma.

นลินี na[6]-li[6]-nee *S. n.* a collection of lotus flowers; a lotus pond (S. E. D. p. 530): นลินีขัณฑ์ an assemblage of lotus flowers: นลินีนันทน์ a garden of Kuvera (see กุเวร p. 111): นลินีรุหะ *lit.* "lotus born," *i. e.* name of Brahma.

นว ๑   na[6]-wa[6] *P. S. adj.* new; fresh; recent; young; modern (S. E. D. p. 530): นวกรรม, นวการ, นวกิจ new work or enterprise (as the erection of a building): นวกรรมิก the superintendent of work under construction: นวขาส new or fresh food: นวชาต new; fresh; recent: นวตร newer; fresher; younger: นวทวีป *lit.* "the new island," *i. e.* a place now called Nuddea or Nadiya, situated on the west bank of the Bhagirathi river 55 miles north of Calcutta. The Nadiya or Hugli river is the most westerly and, commercially, the most important of the mouths of the Ganges. It is formed by the confluence of three streams from the main stream of the Ganges, *viz.* the Bhagirathi, the Jalangi and the Churni, a branch of the Matabhange (Longman's Gazetteer of the World): นวนิต, นพนิต ghee, clarified butter: นวพธู a daughter-in-law: นวพัสตร์ new cloth: นวชาส a bride: นวเยาวน์ the bloom of youth; adolescence: นวสถาน *lit.* "one always having a new place," *i. e.* the wind: นวาหะ *lit.* "a new day," *i. e.* the first day of a fortnight: นวีภาพ a condition of becoming new; renovation.

นว ๒   *P. n.* nine; of nine kinds (S. E. D. p. 531): นวค118หะ, นวเคราะห์ see นพเคราะห์: นวคุณ see นพคุณ: นวทวาร, นวมุข the nine physical doors or apertures, *viz.* 2 eyes, 2 ears, 2 nostrils, the mouth, anus, and meatus urinarius: นวปฎล see นพปฎล: นวรถ the father of Dasa-ratha (ทศรถ), a character in the Ramayana (H. C. D. p. 256): นวรัตน์, เนาวรัตน์ the nine gems (see นพรัตน์). The nine men of letters at the court of Vikra-maditya (วิกรมาทิตย์), a celebrated Hindu king who reigned at Ujjayini, now known as Ujjain. His name has been given to the Samvat era, commencing 57 B.C. He was a great patron of learning and his Court was made illustrious by these nine philosophers who flourished there (H. C. D. p. 356): นววิธ ninefold; consisting of nine parts.

นวก ๑   na[6]-wa[6]-gka[4] *P. S. n.* one who is young, new or recently admitted; a newcomer (S. E. D. p. 531).

นวก ๒   *P. S. n.* a group, series or set consisting of nine; the aggregate of nine (S. E. D. p. 531).

นวด   nuat[3] *v.* to apply a systematic friction, stroking and kneading of the body; to massage: นวดข้าว to thresh rice-stalks by the treading of bullocks: นวดพั้น to massage or knead a portion of the body thoroughly for the relief of over-strained muscles.

นวม   nuam *n.* padding; stuffing; excelsior or crinkled paper (as for packing bottles): ถุงมือนวม padded boxing-gloves: ผ้านวม a quilt or padded comforter: ห้องนวม a padded cell or room.

น่วม   nuam[3] *adj.* soft; pliable; impression- [able; velvety.

นวยนาด see กรีด p. 53.

นวล   nuan *adj.* creamy white: นวลจันทร์, นางเกล็ด (ปลา) *Cirrhinus microlepis* (*Cyprinidae*); *Thynnichthys thynnoides* (suvatti pp. 24, 46): นวลจันทร์ทะเล (ปลา) see ทูน้ำจืด (ปลา) p. 420.

นวาระ   na[6]-wah-ra[6] *Jav. n. lit.* "queen of flowers," *i. e.* the rose.

นหาดก   na[6]-hah[2]-dok[4] *P. n. lit.* "one who is bathed, or has been purified," *i. e.* one whose spiritual instruction is complete. This is a Brahminical term. It is applied to the young Brahmin who has returned from the house of his preceptor, his studies being completed. He is so called because previous to leaving his preceptor, he goes through the ceremony of bathing which implies that he has nothing more to learn (chd. p. 256).

นหาน   na[6]-harn[2] *P. n.* the act of bathing (chd. p. 255).

นหาร na⁶-harn² *P. n.* a tendon; a muscle (chd. p. 256).

นหุต na⁶-hoot⁴ *P. n.* a vast number; a digit followed by twenty-eight ciphers (chd. p. 256).

นพ, นัท, ไม้อ้อ (ต้น) na⁶-la⁶ *P. n.* a kind of reed, cane or rush (chd. p. 257); *Arundo donax (Gramineae)*, a very widely distributed grass, sometimes as tall as 20 feet, but usually 4 to 5 feet high, found across Europe and Asia; south of the Himalayas it appears wild only in the mountains of India; elsewhere it is in cultivation. The well-grown reeds have many uses, such as for baskets, mats, trays, wind-breaks, etc. In ancient times they furnished arrow-shafts; the Romans used them as pens. The grass makes good paper. In Taiping it is used to fix embankments. As it reproduces very readily from the root, it serves this purpose well, rapidly taking hold of the bare surface (V. P. p. 274: BURK. p. 260): นพการ one who plaits rushes; a weaver of rushes, or a basket-maker (chd. p. 257).

นพป see ช่อน (ปลา) p. 284.

นพาคิริ na⁶-lah-ki⁶-ri⁶ *S. n.* the name of an elephant belonging to a king of Kasi or Mathura who reigned in the time of the Buddha (H. C. D. p. 10: S. E. D. p. 525).

นอ, หน่อ naw *n.* a horny protuberance on the head (as young horns of the rhinoceros, deer or bison): นอแรด rhinoceros horn, greatly prized in Chinese medicine and valued at Baht 400.00 per chang of 1.33 lbs. The "horn" is composed of agglutinated hairs.

นอก nauk³ *n.* outside; external; exterior; *adj.* excepted; extraneous; alien; foreign; *prep.* from; without; beyond: ข้างนอก externally; outside; unrelated: คนนอกบ้าน strangers; an outsider: นอกคอก opposed to, or contrary to custom; eccentric; unconventional: นอกความ irrelevant to the matter or point in question: นอกใจ unfaithful; disloyal; deceitful: นอกจำนวน superfluous; in excess of the number fixed or required; supernumerary: นอกใจผัว infidelity (on the part of the wife): นอกชาน an uncovered veranda; a balcony; a platform (added to old-style houses): นอกแต่ excepting; all but; save what has been said or given: นอกทาง, นอกรีต apostasy; desertion of one's faith, party, religion or principles: นอกที่-นอกทาง contrary to the accepted rule, law or custom: นอกทุ่ง an open field, plain or clearing (as outside of a village): นอกนั้น, นอกกว่านั้น besides that; also: นอกประเด็น, เหนือประเด็น irrelevancy: บ้านนอก an out-of-town place; a suburban section; a rural village; a country place: เมืองนอก abroad; a foreign country: นอกจาก provided; except; on the condition that.

นอง naung *v.* to be flooded; to be so submerged that the water overflows; to be soaking wet (as a lawn by rain); to be in a condition of inundation (as when a river is in spate): นองแนว overflowing water running off in a channel or course: นองเนือง น้ำนอง a flood or spate (an expression commonly used by boatmen, river people and timber workers); overflowing repeatedly: นานองน้ำ a field saturated with water.

น้อง naung³ *n.* the calf of the leg.

น้อง naung⁵ *n.* the younger members of a family: น้องเขย a younger sister's husband: น้องชาย a younger brother: น้องผัว the younger sister or brother of the husband: น้องเมีย the younger sister or brother of the wife: น้องยาเธอ the king's younger brother: น้องร่วมท้อง a full younger sister or brother: น้องสะใภ้ the wife of a younger brother; a sister-in-law: น้องสาว, น้องหญิง a younger sister: พี่น้องกัน relations; relatives; kindred: ลูกพี่ลูกน้อง cousins.

น้องแน่ง naung³-naang³ *adj.* muddled up together; being twisted or tangled with others (as many entangled pieces of rope or string): ติดกันน่องแน่ง to be held together by threads or fragments hanging loosely.

นอน nawn v. to lie down; to recline: ที่หลับที่นอน a place to lie and rest (an euphonic combination): ทำด้วยนอนใจ to do in a leisurely manner but confident of success: นอนคว่ำ to lie flat on the face: นอนใจ to be overly sanguine; to be at rest in mind; to be without worry; to be improvident: นอนวัน to spin or revolve accurately (as a top or spindle): นอนหงาย to lie flat on the back: ไปนอน to go to bed; to retire: พระนอน the reclining image of the Buddha: หัวนอน the head of the bed: หาวนอน to be heavy with sleep; to be drowsy.

นอบ naup[3] v. to do obeisance to; to manifest obedience; to bow or salute with a bending of the body: นอบนบ, นอบน้อม to show respect by obeisance; to bow or curtsy; to show submission, respect, or obedience, by joining the hands together resembling a lotus bud, and bending the body forwards.

น้อม naum[5] v. to bend over, face downward: ใจอ่อนน้อม submission; obedience; surrender: น้อมกาย to kneel; to make obeisance; to lower the body by bending down or crouching; to bend over in a low posture: น้อมนำ to lead off; to entice away: อ่อนน้อมตามผู้ใหญ่ to acquiesce to the wishes of superiors.

น้อย ๑ noie[5] adj. little (in size); small; tiny; diminutive: น้อยช้อย wee; puny: น้องน้อย the younger brother or sister.

น้อย ๒ adj. few (in number); small (in number); scarce; scant; rarified: น้อยคน a few people: น้อยตัว few and far between (as game or birds): มีกระบือออยู่น้อยตัว having a limited number of cattle.

น้อย ๓ adj. dearth (in quantity); want: น้อยนัก too little; not enough: น้อยไป to be decreased (in number, quality or quantity);

not to give the full credit (as praise or commendation).

น้อย ๔ adj. little (in disposition, spirit or temperament): น้อยใจ, ใจน้อย to be easily offended, irritated, or inclined to feel slights; to be faint-hearted: น้อยหน้า, น้อยแง่ to have a feeling of inferiority, or of being lower in rank, importance or standing than others: น้อยเนื้อต่ำใจ to be disappointed (as in the non-fulfilment of one's hopes); to be disgruntled at a trick of fortune: น้อยหรือ onomat., indicating displeasure or anger (see ชิ p. 295): น้อยแนะ an exclamation indicating gentle surprise or polite dissent, etc.

น้อยหน่า Siam., มะออจ้า Shan, น้อยแหน่ N. Laos (ต้น) noie[5]-nah[4] n. Annona squamosa (Annonaceae), sugar-apple; sweet-sop, a small tree, native of tropical America, commonly cultivated throughout the tropics for its fruit. These are of the size of a large apple, and have a peculiar rind, which appears to be formed of scales; when ripe, these break away separately, exposing the white, granular, sweet, custard-like pulp (MCM. pp. 232, 233, 516: cb. p. 55: V. P. p. 158: BURK. p. 168). It is probable that the Siamese name น้อยหน่า derives from the scientific name annona.

น้อยโหน่ง Siam., มะเหนี่ยงแฮ้ง Laos, Chiengmai (ต้น) noie[5]-nong[4] n. Annona reticulata (Annonaceae), custard-apple, oxheart, bullock's heart, a small, bushy tree commonly grown in gardens throughout the tropics. The large heart-shaped or round fruit, brownish-red in colour, contains darkbrown seeds interspersed among the sweet custard-like, granular, edible pulp (MCM. pp. 252, 253, 428: Cb. p. 55: V. P. p. 158: BURK. p. 167). In common usage in Siam, น้อยหน่า is the custard apple and the น้อยโหน่ง is the bullock's heart or ox-heart.

นะ na[6] a final syllable or sound used as sign of the vocative, equal to "please," ex.

ยังนะ not for a while yet, please : อยู่นะ kindly remain.

นะแน่ง na⁶-naang³ *adj.* cunning ; adorable ; lovable (used in reference to children).

นะโมตะสะ na⁶-moh-dta⁴-sa⁴ *n.* an expression used by all Buddhist monks to preface religious discourses. It may be translated as follows, " I adore, or adoration to the Blessed, Perfect and most Intelligent." Or it may be considered as a short confession of faith meaning, " I take refuge in the Buddha (พระพุทธ), the Law (พระธรรม), and the Assembly (พระสงฆ์)" (Legend of the Burmese Buddha I, p. 1).

นัก ๑ nuk⁶ *Cam. n.* a person ; a man ; one skilled in, or one talented or experienced in ; an expert ; a devotee ; one ardent in some line of work or pursuit : นักการ a messenger : นักการเมือง a politician : นักกีฬา a sportman ; a sports-fan ; an athlete : นักโกง one given to swindling ; a trickster ; a cheat : นักเทศน์ an eloquent preacher ; นักโทษ prisoners ; criminals ; convicts : นักธรรม one versed in the various precepts or doctrines of a religion : นักบวช a member of a priesthood : นักบิน an aviator ; one experienced in flying : นักบุญ one zealous in merit-making ; a very meritorious person, or a saint : นักปราชญ์ a poet, a sage, or a literary expert : นักประพันธ์ a skilled writer ; an author : นักพรต an hermit ; a recluse ; an ascetic : นักพะนัน a gambler ; one who enjoys gambling : นักมวย a professional boxer ; a pugilist : นักรบ a warrior ; a soldier ; one who is trained in methods or science of warfare : นักร้อง a cultured or superior singer : นักเรียน students ; pupils ; scholars : นักเลง a rogue ; a rascal ; a ruffian ; a dishonest and unprincipled person ; a knave ; a scamp ; a true sport ; a specialist : นักเลงสุรา an habitual drinker, or a hard drinker ; an intoxicated carouser : นักสนม female servants in a royal palace : นักสวด one excelling, or proficient in the repetition of ritual : นัก-

สิทธิ์ an hermit ; a recluse : นักสืบ a detective ; a spy ; a scout ; an informer.

นัก ๒ nuk⁶ *adj.* a sign of the superlative : แก่นัก too old : นักหนา too ; very ; excessive ; intense : มากนัก too much ; too many : ร้อนนัก very hot ; extremely hot.

นักต nuk⁶-dta⁴ *S. n.* night (S. E. D. p. 524).

นักร nuk⁶-gka⁴-ra⁶ *P. S. n.* a crocodile ; an alligator (S. E. D. p. 524) : นักรเกตน์ *lit.* " one using a crocodile flag as an emblem," *i. e.* the god of Love ; Cupid (H. C. D. p. 145) : นักรจักร many crocodiles : นักรราช *lit.* " the king of crocodiles," *i. e.* the shark, a large sea animal belonging to the genera *Carcharhinus Carchardon.* They have several rows of large sharp teeth with serrated edges (web.).

นักษัตร, นักขัตต์ see ดาว p. 327 : นักษัตร-โกศ *lit.* " a list of stars," *i. e.* the title of a book on astronomy (S.E.D. p. 256) : นักษัตรจักร a diagram of the fixed stars ; a planetary map : นักษัตรทรรศ *lit.* " a star-gazer," *i. e.* an astronomer : นักษัตรนาถ, นักษัตรราช *lit.* " the lord or king of the stars," *i. e.* the moon : นักษัตร-เนมี the North Star ; the polar star ; Polaris : นักษัตรบดี Mercury (the planet) : นักษัตรบถ *lit.* " star-path," *i. e.* the starry-sky : นักษัตร-บูชิต *lit.* " star-honoured," *i. e.* auspicious ; propitious ; lucky : นักษัตรปาฐก *lit.* " a star-reader," *i. e.* an astrologer : นักษัตรมณฑล *lit.* " star-cluster," *i. e.* a constellation : นักษัตรมาลา *lit.* " star-circle," *i. e.* a necklace of stars, as of twenty-seven pearls : นักษัตรโยค the conjunction of the moon with a stellar group : นักษัตรโลก *lit.* " the world of the stars," *i. e.* the starry firmament : นักษัตร-วิทยา *lit.* " star-knowledge," *i. e.* astronomy ; astrology.

นัคค, นัคน nuk⁶-ka⁶ *P. S. adj.* naked ; nude ; bare ; desolate (S. E. D. p. 525).

นัคราภิบาล nuk⁶-ka⁶-rah-pi⁶-barn *n.* a municipal corporation.

นั่ง nung[3] *v.* to sit: ที่นั่ง a seat; a bench: นั่งขัดสมาส to sit cross-legged, tailor or Turkish style: นั่งโงก to sit nodding the head: นั่งขัง to be in a position or corner, free from capture by the opponent (used in games): นั่งทาง to wait in ambush along a pathway or road, for evil purposes (as highway robbers): นั่งปรก to sit with concentrated mind, with four other Buddhist monks, during the recitation of the ritual on religious occasions: นั่งโป่ง to wait for game at a salt-lick, in a concealed position: นั่งพัก to take a rest or period of relaxation (as in the shade): นั่งพับเพียบ a polite sideways sitting posture in which the lower limbs are flexed backwards, and the soles of the feet are everted behind (turned away from the guest). The arm on the opposite side usually supports the weight of the body and bends to form the shape of a bow. The arms of young girls are trained from infancy to assume this supple attitude which is considered very graceful: นั่งเมือง to rule, reign or govern a city or town: นั่งยองๆ to sit on the heels: นั่งร้าน scaffolding: นั่งห้าง to sit on a raised platform or machan awaiting game, this platform built in a tree or bamboo clump 12 to 20 feet above the ground: นั่งสมาธิ a posture of meditation assumed by Buddhist monks, *i. e.* cross-legged, the soles of the feet turned up and the hands flat, one over the other on the lap: พระที่นั่ง a throne; the royal palace: หน้าพระ-ที่นั่ง before the royal presence or throne.

นั่งคัล nung-kun *P. S. n.* a plough (chd. p. 260).

นัจ nut[6] *P. n.* a dance; a nautch; an acrobatic performance (chd. p. 254).

นัฏ, นัฏก nut[6] *P. S. n.* a dancer; a mime; a pantomimist; an acrobat (chd. p. 261).

นัด ๑ nut[6] *v.* to fix a time or make an appointment; to pre-arrange a time for meeting: ดินบื่นนัดหนึ่ง a charge, or load of gun-powder: นัดแนะ to make an appointment with full explanations: นัดหมาย to issue notices for a meeting: ผัดนัด to postpone an appointment: ผิดนัด to fail or miss an engagement: เวลานัด a fixed time; an occasion agreed upon: ตลาดนัด an open air market held at regular intervals.

นัด ๒ a numerical designatory particle for shots or discharges from a gun or cannon, and for charges of gunpowder or explosives.

นัดดา nut[6]-dah *P.S. n.* a grandson; a descendant (chd. p. 261).

นัตถุ nut[6]-too[4] *P. S. n.* the nose (chd. p. 262): *v. Siam.* to inhale, squirt, atomize or spray the nose (with a remedy): ยานัตถุ snuff.

นั่น nun[3] *prep.* that (while pointing); ที่นั่น there: ที่นั่นที่นี่ here and there; being here and there; being all around; everywhere: นั่นแหละ that's it! นั่นหรือ is that it? นั่น-อะไร what is that there?

นั้น nan[5] *adj.* that; the: เท่านั้น only that much: เมื่อนั้น at which time; when; then.

นันท see นนท์ p. 439.

นันทวัน, นันทอุทยาน names for Indra's gardens.

นันทิ see นนทิ p. 440.

นับ nup[6] *v.* to count; to enumerate; to reckon: คำนับมายัง respectfully addressed to: นับโคตร to enumerate the ancestors: นับตรวจดู to count over carefully: นับตั้งแต่ to estimate or calculate from (such a date, place or amount): นับถือ to have respect for; to hold in esteem or confidence; to honour (as parents): นับหน้า to have confidence in; to trust: นับหน้าถือตา to be held in respectful esteem: นับใหม่ to re-count (as money): นับไม่ถ้วน incalculable; beyond calculation; too many to count.

นัย see นย p. 441.

นัยน์ see นยนะ p. 442.

นา   nah *n.* rice fields; paddy fields; in idiomatic expressions often added to a verb implying *entreaty*:   ชาวนา peasantry or peasants; farmers or farm-labourers: ทำนา to cultivate rice plots or fields: ทุ่งนา an expanse, or open field space: นาเกลือ salt-fields; salt-pans; salt-pond: นาโคก, นาดอน paddy fields situated on high or rising land: นาโคกคู่ tracts of cultivated paddy land on which the tax is collected according to the area specified on the title deed: นาน้ำฝน fields relying on the rainfall for water: นาป่า cultivable rural land: นาบัก, นาดำ fields where seedling rice is transplanted: นาปรัง fields worked outside the ordinary season; mid-year crops: นาฟางลอย areas of stubble; rural paddy fields on which the tax is paid according to the area from which the grain is harvested: นาร้าง waste or neglected paddy land: นาหว่าน arable land where paddy is sown broadcast: ปูนา small field crabs: ไร่นา farming or arable land.

น่า   nah[3] *v.* a prefix for verbs or nouns to intensify their meanings: น่ากิน, น่ารับประทาน appetizing; tempting: น่ากลัว frightful; terrifying: น่าเกลียดน่าชัง most detestable; disgusting: น่านับถือ most worthy of respect: น่ารัก very lovable; adorable; attractive.

น้า   nah[5] *n.* aunt or uncle; the mother's younger brother or sister: น้าชาย the mother's younger brother: น้าสาว the mother's younger sister.

นาก   nak[3] *n.* an alloy of gold and copper; gold bronze; red gold; the *Otter* (*Lutra* species) (Gaird. N. H. J. S. S. III, 2, p. 123).

นากบุด *Siam., Peninsula,* บุนนาค *Siam.* (ต้น)   nak[3]-boot[4] *n. Mesua ferrea* (*Guttiferae*), a moderate-sized, broad, conical, slow-growing, handsome tree, growing from the Himalayas to the southern part of the Malay Peninsula. It is cultivated throughout Java, and has sometimes run wild there; it is cultivated elsewhere. In cultivation, it re-tains its branches to the ground and is very attractive, but in the forest, as it grows upwards, it loses its lower branches. It is a sacred tree in India, where it possesses names derived from the Sanskrit "Naga kesara." It blossoms profusely in the month of April or May, the large white flowers, each with its yellow centre of numerous stamens, being delicately scented. The young leaves, which appear twice a year, are of deep crimson, rendering the tree a striking object. The timber is good, and is profitably exploited in north-eastern India, where the tree grows to a large size and is plentiful enough even to supply sleepers, as well as to be used for buildings, bridges, piers, etc. Its durability in the soil is great. It has a slight tendency to crack and to warp, so that it is not favoured for planking. It is as hard as ebony, and its strength is great (MCM. pp. 15, 57, 90, 91, 101, 213, 216, 518: Cb. p. 123: BURK. p. 1458: V. P. p. 149).

นาค   nak[3] *P. S. n.* (1) a snake, the Naga or serpent-demon. This mythical race, supposed to have a human face with serpent-like lower extremities, and sprung from Kadru, a wife of Kasyapa, inhabits the regions under the earth (S. E. D. p. 532). Kadru was a daughter of Daksha and one of the thirteen married to Kasyapa (H. C. D. p. 138); a fabulous race of serpents (Ala.); a cobra or hooded snake (Chd. p. 255); (2) an elephant; (3) tin; lead; (4) the best or most excellent of anything: นาคทนต์ elephant tusks; ivory; a peg placed in the wall for hanging purposes: นาคนาสา *lit.* "the elephant's nose," *i. e.* the trunk of an elephant: นาคบาศ a magical noose (used in battles); a weapon of Varuna, the sovereign of Water (H. C. D. p. 338); name of an arrow used by Indrajit (อินทรชิต), a character in the Ramayana; "the conqueror of Indra," who was mysteriously changed into a snake (H. C. D. p. 127):   นาคบุร another name for Hastinapura (หัสดินาปุระ), the capital city of the Kauravas, for which the great war of the Maha-bharata was waged. It was founded by Hastin, son of the first Bharata, and called by some the "elephant city" (H. C. D. p. 120): นาคปรก name of an image of the Buddha during one transmigration, seated under a canopy of Naga heads: นาคภูษณ์ *lit.* "one decorated with serpents," *i. e.* a name of Siva: นาคมลล์ (ช้างไอราพต) *lit.* "an athlete among elephants," *i. e.* name of Indra's elephant: นาครงค์ an orange tree: นาคราช, พระยานาค the serpent-king: นาคเรณุ red lead: นาคลดา *lit.* "snake vine," *i. e.* the Piper betle (V. P. p. 186); the betel-vine, an evergreen climber with heart-shaped leaves which are used for chewing: นาควิถี *lit.* "serpent's path," *i. e.* the moon's path through certain asterisms: นาคาญจนา an elephant's trunk: นาคานตก *lit.* "the destroyer of serpents," *i. e.* the Garuda (H. C. D. p. 110): นาคาสน์ *lit.* "a snake-eater," *i. e.* a peacock: นาคินทร์, นาคนทร์, นาคศ, นาคศวร names for serpent-chiefs; a large or noble elephant.

นาคร nah-korn *P. S. n.* town-born; town-bred; relating or belonging to a town or city (S. E. D. p. 533).

นาคินี, นาคี nah-ki[6]-nee *n.* feminine of the Naga, snake or serpent (chd. p. 255).

นาง nang *n.* a lady; a dame; a married woman; a title for all ladies without rank or title, corresponding to นาย for men. In former times "อี" and "อำแดง" were used but "นาง" is preferable: ขุนนาง nobles; government officials is general: นางกราย a dancing attitude assumed by mahouts or elephant keepers, on the occasion of the first decoration of the elephant's tusks: นางเกล็ด, นวลจันทร์ (ปลา) *Thynnichthys thynnoides* (*Cyprinidae*), a carp (suvatti p. 46): นางชี nuns. Siamese nuns wear white robes, shaving the head and eyebrows, and observing the eight Buddhist commandments: นางท้าว ladies having conferred titles, who hold positions of responsibility in the royal palace: นางพรหมจารี

a virgin: นางฟ้า female celestial beings: นางไม้ female spirits inhabiting trees: นางรม (หอย) the oyster: นางระบำ dancing girls: นางลม (นก) the swift: นางล้อม a species of sedge: นางสาว a title used for all unmarried women: นางสาวแก่ a spinster: นางห้าม royal concubines: นางอ้าว (ปลา) *Barilius guttatus* (*Cyprinidae*) (suvatti p. 32): นางแอ่น (นก) the swallow.

นางจรัล nang-chja[4]-run *n.* the main posts of a veranda.

นางนวล (นก) nang-nuan *n.* the sea-gull; the sea-mew; the river terns, *Sterna sp.*

นางนาค nang-nak[3] *n.* the name of a Siamese tune.

นางนูน *Siam.,* อีนูน *Siam., Kanburi,* ผักสาบ *N. Laos* (เถา) nang-noon *n. Adenia pierrei* (*Passifloraceae*) (cb. p. 748); *A. viridiflora* (cb. p. 749): V. P. p. 150).

นางแย้ม (ต้น) nang-yam[5] *n. Clerodendron fragrans* (*Verbenaceae*), a shrub of China, Sumatra and Java, having fragrant flowers. The species must have been in Siam many centuries, as it was already well known in the reign of the Ayuthian King Trilokanart (1448-1488), its name being familiarly mentioned in the Siamese literature of that period. The local people naturally regard the plant as native, and those who have seen much of its occurrence in this country will perhaps not feel inclined to do otherwise (winit, N. H. J. S. S. IX, 3, p. 271: McM. p. 110: Burk. p. 584: V. P. [p. 150].

นางรำ (ต้น) see ช้องนางรำ p. 284.

นางหงส์ nang-hong[2] *n.* an orchestral instrument used by the Mons.

นาฏ nat[3] *P. S. adj.* dancing; acting; playing (S. E. D. p. 534): นาฏนารี a dancing girl.

นาฏก see นัฏ, นัฏก p. 448.

นาฏย nah-dta[4]-ya[6] *S. n.* dramatic art; mimical representations (S. E. D. p. 534):

นาฏยเวที a dancing stage or platform : นาฏย-
ศาลา a ball-room ; a dance hall ; a theatre :
นาฏยศาสตร์ the art of producing musical performances and dances.

นาฏี, นาฑี nah-tee *S. n.* a minute of time ;
sixty seconds.

นาถ nat[3] *P. S. n.* one who affords protection, aid or refuge (S. E. D. p. 534).

นาท nat[3] *P.S. n.* any sound or tone ; a
loud sound ; a roar ; a bellow ; a cry (S. E. D.
p. 534).

นาน narn *adj.* long (duration) ; durable
lasting : ช้านาน, นานกาล protracted ; delayed
prolonged, *ex.* เจ็บมาช้านาน suffering with a
lingering illness : นานเกินกำหนด far beyond
the appointed time : นานไป henceforth :
นานไปก็อาจจะรู้ some time in the future, one
will know : นานไปเบื้องหน้า a long time in
the future ; later on ; indefinitely : นานมาแล้ว
long ago ; many a long day past : นาน-
เหลือเกิน entirely too long (as an address or
sermon) : เนิ่นนาน, นานนมนม, นมนาน, นานล้ำ
long past the proper time ; late in arriving
(as a tardy employé) ; long delayed : มิช้า-
มินานก็จะกลับ the return will not be long
delayed.

น่าน, น่านน้ำ nan[3] *n.* a watercourse :
เมืองน่าน a city in north-eastern Siam.

นานา nah-nah *P.S. adj.* diversified ; different ; divers ; various (S. E. D. p. 535) :
นานัปปการ, นานาประการ manifold ; varied ; dissimilar ; motley : นานาคติ *lit.* "one moving
in, or having different paths," *i.e.* the wind :
นานาประเทศ internationalism : *adj.* pertaining
to or affecting other nations or countries :
นานาพรรณ differing in colour or hue ; variegated : *n.* variegation.

นาบ narp[3] *v.* to apply heat and pressure ;
to press down snugly and firmly : นาบข้าว
to press down the standing crop so that it is
"laid" all in one direction, to facilitate reap-

ing, and to avoid "lodging" by wind : นาบ-
พลู to iron out heated betel leaves with a hot
sand-bag.

นาภิ, นาภี nah-pi[6] *P. S. n.* the abdomen ;
the navel ; a navel-like cavity ; the central
point or portion (as of a wheel) (S. E. D. p. 535) :
นาภิช *lit.* "navel-born," *i. e.* name of Brahma
(said to have first appeared on the lotus,
sprung from the navel of Vishnu) : นาภิมาตร
in height equal to the level of the navel.

นาม narm *P.S. n.* name ; appellation ;
epithet ; form ; nature ; kind ; a characteristic mark or sign (S. E. D. p. 536) : *gram.*
a noun : ทรงพระนามว่า bearing the royal
name of — : นามกร the fixing upon
a name : นามกรณ์ the ceremony of giving
a name to an infant ; the calling of a
person by some name : นามกรรม name-giv-
ing : นามโคตร an individual's surname, also
that of his family and ancestors ; a cognomen :
นามโจร *lit.* "a robber of names," *i. e.* a forger
or counterfeiter of a name : นามทวาทสี a
ceremony performed in the worship of Durga
(พระทุรคา), the great goddess, wife of Siva,
when any one of her twelve names is
recited (H. C. D. pp. 86, 99) : นามธรรม a
group of four attributes of corporal being, *viz.*,
intellect, happiness, sensation of pleasure,
pain (Ala. p. 172) ; an abstract noun : นาม-
ทา the giver of a name : นามธาตุ a verb
derived from a noun : นามไธย a name ; a
title ; an appellation : นามนิธาน a dictionary ;
a vocabulary, or phrase book : นามบท a
name ; an appellation : นามบัตร a calling
card : นามมุทรา a seal-ring ; a ring engraved
with a name or monogram ; an intaglio (ring) :
นามวรรชิต one without a name ; a useless,
stupid person : นามวาจก a proper noun :
นามเศษ *lit.* "one with only a name or
reputation left," *i. e.* one deceased : นาม-
สงเคราะห์ a collection of nouns : นามมักษร
the syllables forming a name ; name-writing :
an autograph : นามานุศาสน์ name of a dictionary of nouns : นามาภิไธย a conferred

name or title : นามารูป name and form, which alone constitutes an aggregate into a seeming personality or unit. Psychologically, "an embodiment" without the idea of any thing embodied ; mind and body, or mind and matter (A. C. p. 354) ; distinction, and the expression of distinction, which must exist simultaneously, are the result of intelligence (Ala. p. 236).

นาย nai *n.* master ; owner ; chief ; a title of address preceding the name for boys and men, as Mister : จ่านายสิบ sergeant major : นายกอง, นายก๊ก, นายหมู่ leader ; headman of a party, group, gang or set of workmen : นายคลังสินค้า a warehouse or godown superintendent : นายงาน, นายการ a foreman : นายเงิน creditors : นายจ้าง an employer : นายช่าง a master craftsman : นายช้าง a head mahout : นายด่าน a provincial customhouse officer : นายตรวจ an inspector : นายทหาร an army officer : นายทะเบียน a registrar : นายท้าย (การ) a boss, manager or foreman of a job, or project : นายท้าย (เรือ) a steersman : นายน้ำ the holder of a fishery monopoly : นายประกัน a guarantor : นายประมง a chief fisherman : นายพลตรี a major-general : นายพลโท a lieutenant-general : นายพลเอก a general : นายพันตรี a major : นายพันโท a lieutenant-colonel : นายพันเอก a colonel : นายร้อย a captain : นายร้อยตรี a sub-lieutenant : นายร้อยโท a lieutenant : นายร้อยเอก a captain of a company of troops : นายเรือ, ต้นหน the captain (of a boat) : นายสถานี a railway station-master : นายสิบตรี a lance-corporal : นายสิบโท a corporal : นายสิบเอก a sergeant : นายหน้า an agent ; a broker ; one entrusted with authority to act for another : นายห้าง the proprietor of a store : นายอากร the holder of a government monopoly : นายอำเภอ a district chief officer : นายพราน a chief hunter : พวกนายร้อย officers.

น่าย nai[3] (see ยุ่ย) *v.* to make or render friable, fragile, frangible, or pulverized : ต้ม-

จนน่าย to boil until soft and tender : หมักให้-น่าย to make into a pulpy consistency by fermentation.

นายก nah-yok[6] *P. S. n.* a guide ; a leader ; a chief ; a lord ; the principal one, or president of an assemblage or board ; a name of Gotama Buddha (S. E. D. p. 536) : นายกรัฐมนตรี a Premier.

นายกาธิป nah-ya[6]-gkah-tip[6] *S. n.* the chief one among a group of leaders ; a sovereign ; a king (S. E. D. p. 536).

นายิกา nah-yi[6]-gkah *P. S. n.* a woman president of a society or board ; a woman leader ; a noble lady (S. E. D. p. 536).

นารา, นิภา nah-rah *n.* glory ; rays of emitted light ; lustre ; the condition of being luminous or radiant.

นารายณ์ nah-rai *P. S. n.* Narayana, the son of Nara, the original man (with whom he is generally associated or coupled). He is identified with Brahma, who, according to Manu, was so called because the waters were his first place of motion (S. E. D. p. 536), with Vishnu or Krishna, the deity who was before all worlds (H. C. D. p. 220) : นารายณหัตถ์ a back-scratcher (used only for royalty) : นารายณเทพ the god Narayana.

นารี nah-ree *P. S. n.* a girl ; a woman ; a wife ; a female (S. E. D. p. 537) : นารีทุษณ์ a woman's misdemeanors, usually described as six in number, *viz.* (1) use of intoxicants ; (2) keeping bad company ; (3) deserting her husband ; (4) rambling abroad ; (5–6) sleeping and dwelling in a strange house : นารีนาถ *lit.* "having a woman for a possessor or owner," *i. e.* a household, home or abode : นารีบุร a gynaeceum ; an emperor's seraglio ; *botanical* the embryonal vesicle : นารีแพทย์ a woman physician ; a woman gynecologist : นารีรัตน์ *lit.* "a jewel of a woman," *i. e.* one worthy, excellent, honourable or respected.

นาลิ nah-lee *P. S. n.* a tube; a pipe; the tubular stalk of any plant; a hollow cylindrical organ or vessel of the body, *ex.* นาลิ-รัตตะโลหิต an artery: นาลิกาพะโลหิต a vein; a hollow bamboo, used as bellows for fanning a fire (S. E. D. p. 534).

นาลิวัน nah-li⁶-wan *P. n.* an ulcer; a fistula (chd. p. 257).

น้าว now⁵ *v.* to draw; to bend (as a bow); to make bend over by pulling (as in felling a tree): น้าวกระสุน to curve a bow (as when projecting an arrow or mud ball): น้าวธนู to arch the bow of a crossbow.

นาวา nah-wah *P. S. n.* boats; ships; vessels (in general) (chd. p. 262): นาวี the singular form of นาวา.

นาวิก nah-wik⁶ *P. S. n.* a pilot; a helmsman; a sailor; a navigator (S. E. D. p. 538): นาวิกนายก, นาวิกบดี *lit.* "sailor-chief," *i. e.* the captain of a boat, ship or vessel.

นาศ nat³ *P. S. n.* destruction; ruin; annihilation; disappearance; a total loss; death (S. E. D. p. 538).

นาสนะ nah-sa⁴-na⁶ *P. n.* the causing of ruin, destruction, or slaughter (chd. p. 260): นาสนังคะ sins involving expulsion from the Buddhist priesthood, *viz.* destruction of life, theft, impurity, lying, drinking strong drink, speaking evil of the Buddha, propagation of false doctrines, and sexual intercourse with a nun.

นาสา, นาสิกา, นาสิก nah-sah² *P. S. n.* the nose (S. E. D. p. 538): นาสาฉิทร the nasal orifice or aperture; a nostril: นาสามูล the base of the nose.

นาฟาคิรี see นภาคิรี p. 445

นาฬิกา nah-li⁶-gkah *P. n.* a tube; a pipe; an hollow cylinder (chd. p. 256); a clock; a timepiece: ชั่วหนึ่งนาฬิกา one hour: นาฬิกาแดด a sun-dial: นาฬิกาน้ำ a water glass, water-clock or clepsydra; a meter for measuring water: นาฬิกาพก a pocket watch: นาฬิกาปลุก an alarm clock: นาฬิกาข้อมือ a wrist watch.

นาฬิเกร์ nah-li⁶-gkay *n.* the coconut tree (chd. p. 256).

นาฟี see นาฏี p. 451

นำ num *v.* to guide; to lead; to conduct: นำทาง to lead or show the way: นำพา to take an interest in; to supply means for relief; to be solicitous (as a mother over her child): นำร่อง to pilot a ship; to guide or direct the way: นำหน้า to go in advance of: นำให้รู้จักกัน to introduce; to make acquainted with: แนะนำ to direct or suggest (as to ways or means out of some difficulty): ผู้นำ a guide or leader.

น้ำ, อุทก, นิร, นร num⁵ *n.* water; liquids; fluids; aqua, used to designate the colour, brilliancy or clearness of precious stones: ข้าน้ำเงิน slaves: ค่าน้ำเงิน taxes: ชั่งน้ำหนัก to weigh: ดำน้ำ to dive (as when sporting in the water): ตาน้ำ a natural opening from which water oozes or flows (as from the side of a mountain or through the sand at the bottom of a well): ท่องน้ำ to wade around in the water: ท่าน้ำ a landing stage, jetty, wharf or pier for boats or ships: น้ำกรด *lit.* "sharp, biting water," *i. e.* acids in liquid form (Ger. (1) p. 39): น้ำกลั่น distilled water: น้ำกาม semen; sperm: น้ำเกิด flood or full tide; high water: น้ำแข็ง ice: น้ำคร่ำ filthy refuse water found under some Siamese houses: น้ำคร่ำ the liquor amnii; the amniotic fluid: น้ำค้าง dew: น้ำคาวปลา the lochia or lochial discharge: น้ำคำ speech; sayings (as idiomatic expressions): น้ำเค็ม salt water: น้ำเคย shrimp sauce (used as a condiment): น้ำเงิน (กรด) nitrate of silver: น้ำเงิน (สี) navy blue: น้ำจัณฑ์ liquors; intoxicating drinks (only used for royalty): น้ำใจ will; purpose: น้ำชา tea: น้ำชุบ the immersing fluid for plating gold, silver or nickel; a solution into which heated iron is immersed for purposes of hardening; the solution used for tempering steel: น้ำดอกไม้ *Eugenia jambos (Myrtaceae)*, a kind of rose-apple (MCM. p. 260: BURK. p. 969), see ชมพู่ (ต้น) p. 278: น้ำดอกไม้ (ปลา) *Sphyraena jello (Sphyraenidae)*; *S. obtusata barracudas*, a carnivorous, pike-like, marine fish. There are four species recorded as inhabiting Malayan waters. Some attain a length of 5 feet. The flesh is consumed locally (suvatti p. 108: BURK. p. 2064): น้ำด่าง an alkaline solution: น้ำดูด a sucking or drawing down condition of water (as an undercurrent or whirlpool): น้ำเดือด boiling water: น้ำตก a waterfall, cascade or cataract: น้ำตะโก a kind of paper having one side overlaid with English gold-leaf: น้ำตับ sausages made of entrails of cows or buffaloes, hung up to dry, and then sliced, boiled or fried, before eating: น้ำตา tears: น้ำตาเทียน *lit.* "candle tears," *i.e.* melted wax drops or tallow droppings: น้ำตาย a tideless period: น้ำตาล sugar: น้ำตาลจีน (มะม่วง) a sort or variety of mango: น้ำตาลปึก palm sugar in cakes: น้ำตาลหม้อ palm sugar in varying sized pots: น้ำเต้า the bottle gourd: น้ำเต้า *Siam.*, มะน้ำเต้า *n. Laos* (ต้น) *Lagenaria vulgaris (Cucurbitaceae)*, calabash cucumber or bottle gourd, an annual, herbaceous climber, with white flowers about 2½ inches across. There are many races differing in the shape of the fruit, and in its palatability. It is found in both Old and New Worlds, but Africa is probably its original home. This gourd, peculiar for the hardness of the outer layer of the fruit, which is durable enough to be used as a water vessel, is one of the most popular of vegetables, and is largely cultivated. The unripe fruits, when boiled, are an insipid though wholesome vegetable. It is not uncommonly used in curries. In Siam the gourd is often used for collecting palm-toddy, etc. In Borneo the dried gourd sometimes furnishes a sound-box for musical instruments. The pulp around the seeds is purga-tive; the leaves too have purgative action, and are so used in India. They were a medicine in the East at a remote time, but their place has now been largely taken by the American pumpkin, the seeds of which are oily. The Malays still use it medicinally, and in magic. The leaves are said to be valuable when carried as a protective charm when elephant-hunting (MCM. pp. 292, 293, 463: cb. pp. 756, 762: V. P. p. 148: BURK. p. 1296): น้ำเต้าผี (ต้น) *Macrozanonia macrocarpa (Cucurbitaceae)* (cb. pp. 769, 770): น้ำเต้าแล้ง (ต้น) *Polyalthia erecta (Annonaceae)*, a tree or shrub found in the Old World tropics: น้ำนม milk: น้ำนมราชสีห์ (ต้น) *Euphorbia hirta (Euphorbiaceae)*; *E. pilulifera*, a small, annual, semi-creeping weed, common in cultivated ground, especially in dry, sandy soil. The whole plant is considered medicinal. In Malaya, the latex is dropped into the eye for conjunctivitis and ulcerated cornea. It is used in poulticing sores on the legs, and for bruises and wounds due to the marine worm *Chloeia*. The Filipinos also poultice with it. In the Dutch Indies the plant has many uses. It is preeminently a children's medicine in Java and Sumatra. In Brazil it is used in a decoction for gonorrhoea. The tender shoots are said to be edible and are used in India as a famine food (MCM. p. 378: V. P. p. 148: BURK. p. 979): น้ำวล bright; charming; attractive (used in reference to children): น้ำนอง a flood or spate of rivers: น้ำนอง (ตัว) the black army ant: น้ำบ่า a tidal wave: น้ำประสานทอง a flux; a soldering fluid or medium (as for gold); borax: น้ำประสานดีบุก salammoniac or ammonium chloride: น้ำประปา city hydrant water: น้ำปลา fish sauce; essence of fish: น้ำผลึก water of crystallization: น้ำผึ้ง honey: น้ำผึ้ง, รวงผึ้ง *Siam.* (ต้น) *Shoutenia peregrina (Tiliaceae)* (cb. p. 193): น้ำฝน rain water: น้ำพักน้ำแรง strength, power, ability (voluntarily given), used in reference to one person helping another: น้ำพระไทย,-ทัย will and pleasure; discretion;

intent; purpose: น้ำพระพิพัฒน์สัตยา consecrated water used in the ceremony of taking
the oath of allegiance to His Majesty the
King: น้ำพริก pepper sauce, made of shrimp
paste, garlic, onions, etc., pounded together:
น้ำพุ a fountain; a spring: น้ำไฟ (ปลา)
Xenocheilichthys gudgeri (*Cyprinidae*), a carp
(suvatti p. 57): น้ำมนตร์ holy water; water
consecrated by a priest: น้ำมัน oil: น้ำมัน-
กำมะถัน oil of vitriol (กรดกำมะถันอย่างแรง): น้ำ-
มันกานพลู oil of cloves, an aromatic and stimulating volatile oil from cloves: น้ำมันก๊าส
kerosene; illuminating oil distilled from crude
petroleum: น้ำมันเขียว oil of cajeput, a
volatile oil from *Melaleuca leucadendron*
(Burk. pp. 1431, 1433): น้ำมันงา oil of benné;
sesame oil; a fixed oil from the seeds of
Sesamum orientale (Burk. p. 1994): น้ำมัน-
จันทน์ sandalwood oil, a fragrant, volatile oil
distilled from sandalwood, *Santalum album*
(Burk. p. 1952): น้ำมันชัก (สี) แห้ง linseed oil,
the fixed drying oil of flax; *Linum usitatis-
simum* (Burk. p. 1352): น้ำมันดิน tar; coal
tar: น้ำมันตะไคร้ oil of citronella grass,
Cymbopogon citratus (V.P. p. 118: Burk. p. 724):
น้ำมันตับปลา cod-liver oil, a fixed oil from the
liver of the cod-fish, *Gadus morrhua*: น้ำมัน-
ถั่วยี่สง (ลิสง) peanut oil, the fixed oil expressed
from the seed of the common peanut, *Arachis
hypogaea* (Burk. p. 205): น้ำมันเปลือกส้ม oil
of orange-peel, a volatile oil made from the
rind of the orange: น้ำมันมะนาว oil of lemon,
the volatile oil made from the rind of the lemon,
Citrus macroptera (Burk. p. 569): น้ำมัน-
มะพร้าว coconut oil, a fixed oil extracted from
copra. Chemists report that the oils contained in the different races, types and varieties of coconuts do not vary to any appre-
ciable degree (Burk. p. 602): น้ำมันเมล็ดฝ้าย
cotton-seed oil, a fixed oil derived from the
seed of various species of *Gossypium*, and
much used in pharmacy (Burk. p. 1102): น้ำมัน-
ยาง (ชนิดยา) balsam of copaiva, a resinous
juice of various leguminous trees of tropical
America, especially *Copaifera officinalis* and

C. langsdorffii (Burk. p. 652): น้ำมันยาง
(ชนิดสินค้า) an aleo-resin obtained from all of
the species *Dipterocarpus*. The best known
producer in Siam is *D. alatus*. To procure
the oil, the tapper hacks a big triangular hole
near the base of the tree and lets the oleo-
resin collect in its apex. He then fires the
surface to make it run anew, thus burning
off the varnish coating which the drying
oleo-resin had formed during the time of
exposure to the air. Then the flow begins
again. This oleo-resin is used and exported
chiefly as a varnish for boats. Mixed with
dammar it is used to caulk boats (Burk.
p. 840, 757): น้ำมันยี่หร่า a volatile oil extracted from the fruits or seeds of caraway,
the umbelliferous plant *Carum carui* (Burk.
p. 468): น้ำมันระกำ oil of wintergreen, a
fragrant volatile oil derived from *Gaultheria
procumbens*: น้ำมันละหุ่ง castor-oil, a thick,
purgative, fixed oil derived from the seeds of
Ricinus communis: น้ำมันสน oil of turpentine, a volatile oil derived from the
resinous sap of various pine trees: น้ำมัน-
สลัด sweet-oil, olive oil, a fixed oil derived
from the fruit of *Olea europaea var. oleaster*
(Burk. p. 1580): น้ำมันสะระแหน่ oil of peppermint, the volatile oil of *Mentha piperita*:
น้ำมันสระลอด croton oil, a thick, fixed oil extracted from the seeds of *Croton tiglium*:
น้ำมันหมู lard: น้ำมันอบเชย a fragrant, volatile
oil derived from *Cinnamomum iners* (Burk.
p. 551): น้ำมันอำพัน oil of amber, prepared
by the destructive distillation of amber.
Considerable heat is required for the complete
decomposition of amber, a fossil resin of
several coniferous tree: น้ำมือ workmanship; craftsmanship: *adj.* skilful or cunning
with the hands: น้ำมูก nasal secretions:
น้ำมูตร์ urine: น้ำยา paint or colouring
material (for portrait painting); a developing
solution (for photographs); a chilli sauce
eaten with vermicelli or noodles: น้ำแร่
medicinal mineral water: น้ำลาย saliva;
spittle: น้ำลูกไม้ fruit juices: น้ำวน a

whirlpool; an eddy: น้ำส้ม vinegar: น้ำ-
เสียง tone; the voice; utterances; speech;
enunciation: น้ำใสใจจริง unfeigned; undisguised; unperjured; as good as one's word:
น้ำส้มสายชู vinegar made from arrack: น้ำ-
หนวก abnormal secretions from the ear: น้ำ-
หนัก weight; importance; potentiality: น้ำ-
หนักของปรมาณู atomic weight: น้ำหน้า facial
appearance or characteristics: น้ำหมึก ink:
น้ำหมาก betel saliva: น้ำหอม a scented or perfumed oil made of the oil squeezed from the
seeds of the *Samrong* berry (ลูกสำโรง), *Sterculia
foetida*. In this are steeped fragrant blossoms
of 108 varieties, and this is hallowed with
mystic formulae. Its invention is ascribed
to Uma, Siva's consort. The local Hindu-
Buddhist legend tells how beautiful Uma was.
In a preceding existence, she spit upon a
monk named Jekapotta. As a consequence
of the misdeed, she was reborn with a body
exhaling malodorous effluvia, comparable to
the ichor exuding from the temples of the
male elephants during the rutting period.
She thus found it necessary to compose the
above scented oil, which, combining the
essences of many flowers, diffuses a fragrance
so powerful as to overcome the disagreeable-
ness of her person. There are 108 varieties of
flowers required, a mystic number frequently
resorted to in magical combinations, and supposed to bring good luck (Ger. (1) p. 72):
น้ำเหงื่อ sweat; perspiration: น้ำเหลือง secretions from an ulcer, or corpse; normal lymph:
น้ำไหล flowing water: น้ำอบ perfumery;
scented water; perfumes: น้ำอ้อย molasses:
น้ำอ่อ tide on the point of rising; slack water:
บ่อน้ำ a well: ปลายน้ำ, หัวน้ำ the head,
source or origin of a stream or river: ปลาย-
น้ำลงหัวน้ำขึ้น at the turn of the tide: มีน้ำ-
หนักมาก of great importance or potency:
แม่น้ำ a river: ลูกน้ำ mosquito larvae:
ว่ายน้ำ to swim: สมน้ำหน้า "it serves you
right"; "you get what you deserve": สรงน้ำ,
อาบน้ำ to bathe (used for royalty): สระน้ำ
a pond; a pool: ให้ด้วยน้ำใจ given with

good will.

นิกขะ nik[6]-ka[4] *P. S. n.* a golden necklace,
or ornament for the neck, or breast (chd. p. 283).

นิกขันต์ nik[6]-kan[2] *P.S. adj.* gone out;
passed beyond; departed (chd. p. 283).

นิกร (กอน) ni[6]-gkaun *P. S. n.* a group;
a company; a multitude; a crowd of people,
or flock of birds (chd. p. 282).

นิกาย ni[6]-gkai *P. S. n.* an association; a
class, order, group, congregation, sect, denomination, or fraternity; an assemblage, or
collection of persons performing like duties
(chd. p. 282): ทักษิณนิกาย, อุตตรนิกาย see
ทักษิณ p. 407.

นิคคหะ, นิเคราะห์ nik[6]-ka[6]-ha[4] *P. n.* subjugation; suppression; coercion; rebuke;
punishment (chd. p. 280): นิคคหกรรม a
punishment inflicted on novices by superior
monks in the Buddhist brotherhood to prevent
recurrence of an offence.

นิคคหิต, นฤคหิต nik[6]-ka[6]-hit[4] *P.S. adj.*
restrained; held back; rebuked; punished
(chd. p. 280): *Siam. lit.* "a dew-drop," *i.e.*
name of a small circular accent mark placed
over vowels. It occurs only twice, *viz.* " ำ ",
" ็ ". In Pali words it indicates a nasal sound
like " ง "; in Sanskrit words it indicates a
" ม " sound.

นิคม ni[6]-kom *P.S. n.* a town; a country,
region, place or district; a market town (chd.
p. 280).

นิครนถ์ ni[6]-kron *P.S. n.* one free from
all ties or hindrances; one without possessions;
a saint who has withdrawn from the world
and lives either as a hermit, or as a religious
mendicant wandering about naked; a naked
ascetic (S. E. D. p. 541).

นิโครธ ni[6]-krote[3] *P.S. n.* the banyan, or
Indian fig-tree (chd. p. 280); see ไทร p. 429.

นิ่ง ning[3] *v.* to be hushed; to be speechless;

to be quiet; to be still or silent: *n.* quietness; stillness: นิ่งความ to keep a matter secret; to suppress information; to conceal by silence: นิ่งเงียบ complete silence: นิ่งเฉย silent indifference: นิ่งเดือด suppressed anger: นิ่งตรึกตรอง to think, ponder or reflect inaudibly: นิ่งเถิด, นิ่งเสีย hold your tongue and keep silent; cry no more; do not speak again: นิ่งบึ้ง to keep silent with a scowling face; to frown in silence: นิ่งอดนิ่งทน to bear mutely, with fortitude, resignation and submission: นิ่งอาย to be speechless from shame: ไปโดยนิ่ง ๆ to go silently: เมื่อถามก็นิ่งอยู่ to refrain from making reply.

นิจ, นิจจ์ nit[6] *adj.* constant; continued; durable; unswerving: นิจภัตตาหาร a constant supply of food.

นิด nit[6] *adj.* small; diminutive; little: เด็กนิด ๆ an infant; a very small child: นิดหน่อย a tiny bit; a very small portion.

นิตย์ nit[6] *P. S. adj.* perpetual; eternal; continuing; constantly dwelling on, or engaged in; intent upon (S. E. D. p. 547): นิตยคติ *lit.* "that which is continually on the move," *i. e.* air; wind: นิตยทาน daily alms-giving: นิตยพรต perpetual practices or observance of (as for life): เนื่องนิตย์ eternal (an euphonic combination): นิตยภาพ eternity; perpetuity: นิตยยุช one having his mind constantly fixed upon one object: นิตยศรี one possessing permanent beauty: นิตยเสวก one continually serving others (as a waiter, servant, or messenger): นิตยาจาร conduct that is invariably good.

นิติ see นิติ p. 461.

นิติกรรม ni[6]-dti[4]-gkum *n.* a juristic act: นิติบุคคล a juristic entity.

นิติวิษัย ni[6]-dti[4]-wi[6]-sai[2] *n.* within the power, limitations or confines of laws, customs, or established practices.

นิทเทส nit[6]-tet[3] *P. S. v.* to explain; to disclose; to elucidate; to expound; to exhibit; to point out or show (as the sense, meaning or import) (chd. p. 279).

นิทรา, นิททา nit[6]-trah *P. S. v.* to fall asleep: *n.* sleep; slumber; drowsiness(S. E. D. p. 548): นิทรากร that which, or one who produces sleep or drowsiness: นิทราคม approaching the time of sleep; bedtime: นิทราดุร sleepy; faint; languid: นิทรารมณ์ the state of being asleep.

นิทัศน์ ni[6]-tat[6] *P. S. n.* something that fully shows or indicates the original (as a facsimile); sample; specimen; example or illustration; a view or sight of the object (chd. p. 278).

นิทาฆ ni[6]-tah-ka[6] *P. S. n.* heat; warmth; the hot season; sweat; perspiration (S. E. D. p. 548): นิทาฆกร *lit.* "heat-cause," "hot-rayed," *i. e.* the sun: นิทาฆกาล, นิทาฆสมัย *lit.* "the time of heat," *i. e.* the hot season.

นิทาน ni[6]-tan *P. S. n.* the first or primary cause; a tale; a story (S. E. D. p. 548): นิทานวจนะ the narration of a story of beginnings; a chronicle of early events.

นิธาน ni[6]-tan *P. S n.* a place for keeping, laying down, or depositing; a receptacle (as for a corpse); a place of cessation, or rest; a cemetery (S. E. D. p. 548), a catafalque.

นิธิ ni[6]-ti[6] *P. S. n.* a treasure; a hoard; a store; a place or receptacle for storing accumulated wealth (S. E. D. p. 548).

นินทา nin-tah *P. S. v.* to blame; to censure; to defame; to revile; to slander; to reproach; to backbite; to calumniate (S. E. D. p. 549): นินทาลับหลัง to speak ill of behind one's back.

นินนะ nin-na[6] *P. S. n.* a depression; low ground; a natural cavity: *adj.* profound; abstruse; deep (S. E. D. 551).

นินนคา nin-na[6]-kah *P. S. n.* a river; a mountain stream (S. E. D. p. 551).

นินนหุต   nin-na[6]-hoot[4] *P. n.* an arithmetical notation in which the digit is followed by thirty-five ciphers (chd. p. 286).

นินาท, นินนาท, นฤนาท   ni[6]-nat[3] *P. n.* a noise; a sound; an echo; reverberations (chd. p. 286).

นิบาต   ni[6]-bat[4] *P. S. v.* to fall; to descend; to alight; to fall from, or to rush in upon (s. e. d. p. 549).

นิพนธ์   ni[6]-pon *P. S. v.* to compose; to draw up (as an account or history); to write down; to bind on; to tie, fasten, or unite together (as fragments of information): *n.* a composition; a literary compilation; an essay (s. e. d. p. 550).

นิพพาน, นฤพาน   nip[6]-pan *P. S. n.* Nibbana, Niruphan, Nirwana, Nipphan, Nirvana, ethically, the dying out of lust, resentment and illusion; psychologically, release from individuality. It is a state of salvation to be realized here and now; those who attain, are released from becoming, and after death return no more. Nibbana does not imply the "annihilation of the soul" for Buddhism teaches that no such entity as a soul has ever existed (gos. of buddha). Nibbana is the release from existence; a creed which begins by saying that existence is suffering, must end by saying that release from existence is the highest good. Accordingly we find that annihilation is the goal of Buddhism, the supreme reward held out to those faithful to its precepts (chd. p. 265).

นิพพิทา   nip[6]-pi[6]-tah *P. n.* disgust, aversion for, or weariness with the vanities of the world (chd. p. 276).

นิพัทธ์   ni[6]-pat[6] *P. adv.* constantly; continually; always; unendingly (chd. p. 265): นิพัทธกุศล merit or good deeds done constantly.

นิภา see นารา p. 452.

นิ่ม, นิ่มนวล   nim[3] *adj.* soft; plump; delicate (as the flesh of a child); supple; pliant; flexible (as tin or gold foil); fuzzy; downy; fluffy (as the fur of a cat): นิ่ม (สัตว์) the pangolin, scaly-ant-eater, *Manis javanica* (Gaird. j. s. s. III, 2, p. 126). The name pangolin is of Malay origin, meaning "roller" from the fact that these animals roll themselves up so as to cover the vulnerable parts of the body and thus present, on all sides, one entire coat of mail: The under parts of the body being destitute of scales, the pangolin, for purposes of self-defence, places its head between the hind legs, while the broad and massy tail is brought over the head and muzzle to render security doubly sure. In this attitude it sleeps the whole day with a soundness which neither fear nor pain can interrupt. This animal is the only one in Siam which wages war on the terrible termites: นิ่มนวล, ลำใย *Siam.* and *Laos* (ต้น) *Nephelium longana* (*Sapindaceae*), a tree of relatively small size, cultivated in southern China, in some parts of India, throughout Malaysia and Siam to the southern limits of Malaya. It is grown from the seed and can be grafted on the rambutan. Like the litchi it is exacting in the conditions which it requires for fruiting. The fruit is eaten, and is like an acid litchi. Like the litchi, the Chinese dry it, but only the flesh, which is then used for making tea. This tea is regarded as a tonic. Its use in Java was reported long ago. The Chinese also use the dried flowers medicinally. The seeds contain saponin, and are used in China for washing the hair. The timber is red, hard, good for furniture and buildings, but even where the tree is at home is rarely available (mcm. p. 267: burk. p. 1547). The name ลำใย is more commonly used than นวล.

นิมนต์, นิมนตร์   ni[6]-mon *P. S. v.* to invite to enter, or to do something: *n.* an invitation (chd. p. 284): นิมนต์เทศน์ to be invited to preach a sermon (used only to Buddhist monks).

นิมิต see นิรมิต p. 460.

นิมิตต์ ni⁶-mit⁶ *n.* a cause; a motive; a sign mark; a token; an omen; pudendum (chd. p. 284): นิมิตต์สุบิน a dream taken as a sign or omen: ลูกนิมิตต์ a stone or tablet marking a Buddhist sanctuary under which some treasure is buried.

นิยต ni⁶-yot⁶ *P. S. adj.* fixed; certain; definite; permanent (chd. p. 295).

นิยม ni⁶-yom *P. S. n.* a self-imposed religious observance; a voluntary performance of a meritorious act (chd. p. 295): *adj.* popular; recognized or approved by the people: กรรมนิยม a popular (carnal) pleasure.

นิยยาน ni⁶-yah-na⁶ *P. S. n.* an exit; a departure; the state of being led or guided forth (chd. p. 296).

นิยยานิก ni⁶-yah-ni⁶-gka⁴ *P. adj.* a going out, marching forth, or leading to salvation (chd. p. 296).

นิยาม ni⁶-yarm *P. S. n.* way; mode; manner; method; standard or pattern (chd. p. 295).

นิยาย ni⁶-yai *n.* fables, folklore or traditional tales.

นิยุต ni⁶-yoot⁶ *P. S. v.* to put together firmly; to be fixed or fastened (s. e. d. p. 552).

นิร ๑ ni⁶-ra⁶ *P. S. n.* water; liquids; fluids (chd. p. 287).

นิร ๒ ni⁶-ra⁶ a prefix denoting the negative, or absence of, no more, none; equivalent to the Latin *non* and the reversal of the action of a verb as signified by *un* or *less*.

นิรคุณ ni⁶-ra⁶-koon *adj.* lacking all good qualities or virtues; ungrateful; bad; worthless; vicious.

นิรโฆษ, นฤโฆษ ni⁶-ra⁶-kote³ *S. adj.* quiet; noiseless; silent; secret.

นิรชร ni⁶-ra⁶-chorn *S. n.* a deity; a god: *adj.* not becoming old; unfading; young;

fresh; imperishable (s. e. d. p. 541): นิรชรา an apsaras; water-nymphs; the celebrated nymphs of Indra's heaven (h. c. d. p. 19).

นิรทุกข์, เนียรทุกข์ ni⁶-ra⁶-took⁶ *P. adj.* free from suffering, agony or pain; unscathed (chd. p. 279).

นิรโทษ ni⁶-ra⁶-tote³ *P. adj.* faultless; guiltless; free from punishment, or penalty (chd. p. 279).

นิรโทษกรรม ni⁶-ra⁶-tote³-gkum *n.* an act unworthy of punishment; a justifiable act.

นิรมล ni⁶-ra⁶-mon *S. adj.* untainted; pure; freed from blame or stigma.

นิรมาณ, นฤมาณ ni⁶-ra⁶-marn *S. n.* work; production; creation; erection; measurement (s. e. d. p. 556).

นิรมิต, นฤมิต, นิมิต ni⁶-ra⁶-mit⁶ *P. S. v.* created; built; formed; constructed; manufactured (s. e. d. p. 556): การนิรมิต an invention: นิรมิต (เครื่องจักร์) an invented mechanical appliance.

นิรย, นรก ni⁶-ra⁶-ya⁶ *P. S. n.* hell (chd. p. 288); Manu enumerates twenty-one hells (h. c. d. p. 219): นิรยบาล a keeper of hell, or the guardian of one of the hells.

นิรันดร, นิรันตร ni⁶-run-dorn *P. S. adj.* continuous; uninterrupted; perpetual; eternal (chd. p. 287).

นิรัพพุท ni⁶-rup⁶-poot⁶ *P. S. n.* an arithmetical notation in which the digit is followed by sixty-three cyphers, or $10,000,000^9$ (chd. p. 287).

นิรา ni⁶-rah *v.* to drive away; to turn off or keep away; to remove; to reject; to refuse; to repudiate; to spurn, or oppose: *adv.* none; without (s. e. d. p. 553).

นิรามัย ni⁶-rah-mai *P. S. adj.* well; whole; hearty; sound in body and mind; free from sickness, sorrow or care (chd. p. 287).

นิรามิษ ni⁶-rah-mit⁶ *S. adj.* free from

worldly taint (as bribery): free from induce-ments, allurements, or temptations; pure or orthodox (doctrine) (chd. p. 287).

นิราลัย ni[6]-rah-lai *P. adj.* free from attach-ment, desire or entanglement; homeless (chd. p. 287).

นิราศ ni[6]-rat[3] *S. adj.* free from desire; utterly indifferent to anxiety or surrounding conditions; hopeless; apathetic (chd. p. 288).

นิราศรัย ni[6]-rah-sai[2] *S. adj.* not living, nor located permanently in any one place; nomadic.

นิราส ni[6]-rat[3] *S. n.* separation; dispersion; banishment. This word is used in prose and poetry, expressing a state of passive dejection or melancholy abandon on leaving one's home to lead a rambling or roaming life. It occurs in the title of poems, as นิราศลอนดอน "The Voyage to London," by Mom Rajot'ay, the in-terpreter of the Siamese Embassy to England 1857–58. The first line of this poem runs thus, นิราศเรื่องเมืองลอนดอนอาวรณ์ถวิล จำจากมิตต์-ขนิษฐายุพาพิน. It is well written and is an official report in which the author gives an exact idea of such novelties as the railway, the telegraph, and even the circus. These were absolutely unknown in Siam and had never before been seen by the author (Siamese Embassies to Europe, by H. R. H. Prince Damrong).

นิรุตติ ni[6]-root[6]-dti[4] *P. n.* language; speech; the explanation of words; a logical exegesis of the words or text of the Buddhist scrip-tures; a glossary (chd. p. 289): นิรุตติ-ปฏิสัมภิทา a compound derived from the above root, containing the idea of analysis, discrimi-nation, or breaking up in detail of words or expressions of a language; philology.

นิรุทก ni[6]-roo[6]-ta[6]-gka[4] *P. S. adj.* free from water; waterless; dry; parched (chd. p. 289).

นิรุทธ์ ni[6]-root[6] *P. adj.* destroyed; extin-

guished; annihilated; brought to an end; dead (chd. p. 289).

นิโรช ni[6]-rote[3] *P. adj* insipid; tasteless; unsavoury (chd. p. 289).

นิโรธ ni[6]-rote[3] *P. S. n.* cessation; annihila-tion; Nirvana (chd. p. 288): นิโรธสมาบัติ *lit.* "attainment of cessation," *i. e.* catalepsy, or the mesmeric sleep which constitutes the highest degree of mystic meditation.

นิล, นิล nin *n.* sapphire; a hard, trans-parent, semi-precious stone: *adj.* dark blue; dark green or black (S. E. D. p. 566): นิลตะโก bloodstone; a green jasper containing red spots (often cut as a gem).

นิลนนท์, นิลพัทธ์ nin-la[6]-non *n.* soldiers of Rama, appearing as characters in the Ramayana.

นิ่ว ๑ new[3] *n.* calculus, an abnormal con-cretion occurring within the animal body and usually composed of mineral salts: นิ่ว-กระเพาะปัสสาวะ urinary or vesical calculus; stone; gravel found in the urinary bladder.

นิ่ว ๒ new[3] *adj.* wrinkled; puckered; con-tracted into furrows, folds and ridges (de-scriptive of the face): นิ่วหน้า, ทำหน้านิ่ว to pucker the face (as in pain or anger).

นิ้ว new[5] *n.* a finger; a unit of linear measure; a Siamese inch: นิ้วมือ the fingers: นิ้วเท้า the toes: นิ้วชี้ the index finger: นิ้วกลาง the middle finger: นิ้วนาง the ring finger: นิ้วก้อย the little finger: นิ้ว-หัวแม่มือ the thumb: ข้อนิ้วมือ the knuckles: นิ้วมือหนึ่งนิ้ว one of the digits of the hand (excluding the thumb).

นิ้วมือพระนารายณ์, มือเทวดา *Laos, Chieng-mai,* มือพระฤาษี *Laos, Nakawn Panom* (ต้น) new[5]-meu-pra[6]-nah-rai *n. Schefflera clarkeana (Araliaceae),* one of a genus of shrubs and trees found throughout the tropics. They are aromatic (cb. p. 797: BURK. p. 1972).

นิวรณ์　ni[6]-worn　*P. n.* obstacle ; hindrance. There are five obstructions to one leading a religious life, *viz.* lust ; malice ; sloth ; pride ; doubt (chd. p. 293).

นิวัตต์　ni[6]-wat[6]　*P. adj.* returned ; turned back ; recoiling ; stopped (chd. p. 294).

นิวาต　ni[6]-wat[3]　*P. n.* lowliness ; humility (chd. p. 294).

นิวาส　ni[6]-wat[3]　*P. n.* a residence ; an abode ; a dwelling ; a station ; night quarters ; a rest house (chd. p. 294).

นิวาสน์　ni[6]-wat[3]　*P. S. n.* clothing ; raiment ; an under-garment (chd. p. 293).

นิเวศน์, นิเวศ　ni[6]-wet[3]　*P. S. n.* a palace ; an habitation ; a house ; a residence ; a city ; a town (chd. p. 294).

นิศา　ni[6]-sah[2]　*S. n.* night (S. E. D. p. 560) : นิศากร　*lit.* "a night-maker," *i. e.* the moon : นิศากาล night-time : โพล้เพล้ twilight ; the beginning of night : นิศาจร *lit.* night-prowlers," *i. e.* an owl ; a snake ; a jackal : นิศาจรี a female night-prowler ; an harlot : นิศาชล *lit.* "night-water," *i. e.* dew : นิศาทิ *lit.* "the approach of night," *i. e.* late twilight ; nightfall : นิศานาถ, นิศาบดี *lit.* "the sovereign of the night," *i. e.* the moon : นิศามณิ, นิศารัตน์ *lit.* "night-jewel," *i. e.* the moon : นิศาเวที *lit.* "a night-time knower," *i. e.* a cock.

นิษาท, เนษาท　ni[6]-sart[4]　*P. S. n.* name of a tribe of aborigines in India, who lived by fishing, hunting and stealing (chd. p. 264).

นิสสัย　nit[6]-sai[2]　*P. n.* protection ; a place of refuge ; shelter ; help ; habit ; disposition (chd. p. 291).

นิสัชช์　ni[6]-sat[4]　*P. n.* the act of sitting (chd. p. 289) ; session : นิสัชชาการ a manner, or the condition of being seated.

นิสีทนะ　ni[6]-see[2]-ta[6]-na[6]　*P. n.* a mat or cloth for Buddhist monks to sit on (chd. p. 290).

นี่　nee[3]　*adv.* here ; hither : ที่นี่ at this place ; right here : นี่แนะ see ; behold ; lo : นี่ ๆ นั่น ๆ this and that : นี่โน่น here and there : นี่และ this is it ; look ; here it is : มานี่ซิ better come here : มานี่นะ come here (imperative).

นี้　nee[5]　*adj.* this ; these ; a demonstrative, pointing out something near or present : นี้นั้น this and that : นี้โน้น these and those : นี้และ this is it ; this is the right thing or place ; so it is.

นีติ, เนติ, นิติ　nee-dti[4]　*P. S. n.* guidance ; direction ; management ; polity ; practice ; propriety ; prudence ; moral philosophy or precept ; correct standards of conduct or behaviour ; statesmanship (S. E. D. p. 565 : chd. p. 292) : นีติกถา, นีติศาสตร์ any work or treatise on moral or political science : นีติกุศล, นีติวิที one conversant with political science : นีติโทษ error of conduct ; mistake in policy : นีติธรรม ethical principles : นีติวิทยา moral or political science : นีติวิษัย the sphere of morality or prudence in conduct.

นีนั่น, อึกทึก　nee[3]-nun　*adj.* noisy ; boisterous.

นีร　nee-ra[6]　*P. S. n.* water (S. E. D. p. 566) : นีรจร *lit.* "moving in water," *i. e.* a fish or any aquatic animal : นีรชาต *lit.* "water-born," *i. e.* produced from water ; aquatic : นีรตรังค์ water waves ; billows : นีรนิธิ *lit.* "reservoir for water," *i. e.* the ocean ; the sea : นีรราศี *lit.* "a mass of water," *i. e.* the ocean : นีราขุ *lit.* "water-rat," *i. e.* the otter.

นีล, นิล　neen　*P. S. adj.* blue ; dark blue ; dark green or black ; dyed with indigo (S.E.D. p. 566) : นีลกมล, นีลบัทม์, นีลุบล, นีโลตบล the blue lotus or water-lily : นีลกัณฐ์ *lit.* "blue-necked," *i. e.* a peacock ; a gallinule or waterhen ; a rail-like bird ; a sparrow ; an epithet for Siva (as having a black throat from swallowing the poison produced at the churning of the ocean): นิลเกศี see คราม (ต้น) p. 181: นิลดำรู, มะพร้าว (ต้น) *Cocos nucifera* (*Palmae*), coconut palm (MCM. p. 389: V. P. p. 211: BURK. p. 598): นิลบัฏ a black garment: นิลปฤษฐี *lit.* "black-backed," *i. e.* name for Agni the god of Fire, one of the most ancient and most sacred objects of Hindu worship (H.C.D. p. 6): นิลรัตน์ the sapphire: นิลามพร *lit.* "one dressed in a blue garment," *i. e.* the planet Saturn: นิลารุณ dark red; the first dawn of day: นิโลบล a blue stone; a sapphire.

นึก neuk[6] (see คิด p. 220) *v.* to have an intuition, feeling or sense of, as นึกกลัว, นึกเกลียด, นึกอยาก, นึกรัก. นึกหัวเราะ, นึกสงสัย, นึกอาย, นึกเกรง: นึกเอา to suppose that; to surmise that: นึกได้, นึกขึ้นมา, นึกออก to call to mind; to recollect; to think a problem out.

นึ่ง nung[3] *v.* to cook by steam; to harden under steam pressure; to vulcanize (as rubber): นึ่งไก่, นึ่งปลา, นึ่งขนม, นึ่งข้าวเหนียว to cook articles by means of steam: นึ่งเครื่อง-มือ to sterilize instruments by means of steam (under pressure): หวดนึ่ง a baked clay steamer for rice, consisting of a steaming pot with perforations in the bottom, fitted snugly over a pot in which water boils.

นุง nung *adj.* confused; disordered; tangled: นุงถุง hopelessly intertwined: นุงนัง frayed, or ravelled along the edge; torn into tatters; ragged: นุงกัน a condition of disagreement, wrangling or quarrelling (as among students or members of a clique): ยุ่งนุงถุง to be badly tangled or snarled.

นุ่ง nung[3] *v.* to wear a cloth or garment by fastening it around the waist: เครื่อง-นุ่งห่ม clothing (in general): นุ่งจีบ to wear the loin-cloth plaited, and hanging from the belt: นุ่งโจงกะเบน to wear a loin-cloth or the panung with the edges rolled together, and ends fastened to the belt behind: นุ่งม่วง to wear a blue silk panung: นุ่งลอยชาย to

wear the above without twisting and fastening the ends (considered an uncouth method).

นุช noot[6] *P. adj.* younger; junior (chd. p. 42): นุชนาฏ a young girl; a younger sister.

นุต noot[6] *P. S. adj.* praised; extolled; eulogized (chd. p. 297).

นุ่น noon[3] *n.* kapok: นุ่น, นุ่นทะเล *Siamese,* งิ้วน้อย *Laos, Chiengmai* (ต้น) *Ceiba pentandra* or *Eriodendron anfractuosum* (*Malvaceae*), kapok or silk-cotton, a small or moderate-sized, quick-growing, upright, thornless tree, branching horizontally, in whorls, at right-angles to the stem. Until recently it was thought to be of American origin, but it develops that the American and Asiatic trees differ in many points and should be considered as separate species. The tree is deciduous in the dry season, usually February to April, the greenish-white flowers being produced in clusters shortly after the leaves have dropped. The fruit pods, which ripen about two months after flowering, contain a quantity of silky, creamy-white floss (kapok), consisting of lustrous, unicellular hairs about $\frac{1}{2}$ to 1.2 in. long, closely packed around the black, round seeds. The floss has been used for centuries for stuffing cushions and pillows, but does not spin well because of its springiness and slippery surface. It is especially esteemed for life-belts at sea, and for mattresses on board ship—mattresses which could be used as floats in an emergency. The seeds contain 20–25 per cent of oil, which is almost identical with cotton-seed-oil, and is capable of the same uses (MCM. pp. 422, 517: cb. p. 164: V. P. p. 153: BURK. p. 501).

นุ่ม, นุ่มนิ่ม noom[3] *adj.* soft; flabby; springy; yielding to the touch (as skin or flesh): นุ่มเนื้อ plump; fat; chubby; fleshy (as the limbs of children or infants).

นุ้ย nuey[5] *adj.* small; tiny; insignificant.

นูน noon *adj.* convexed; raised; elevated: ลายนูน carved bas-relief.

เนกขะ see นิกขะ p. 456.

เนกขัมม์ nek³-kum² *P. n.* renunciation of the world; the giving up of the world, and devoting oneself to ascetic life; the entering into the Buddhist priesthood (chd. p. 263).

เนตร net³ *P. S. n.* the eye (as the guiding organ); a leader; a guide (S. E D. 568): เนตร-โคจร *lit.* "within the range of the eyes," *i. e.* visibility: เนตรชล, เนตรวารี *lit.* "eye-water," *i. e.* tears: เนตรนารี a woman guide; a girl guide: เนตรบิณฑ์ the eyeball: เนตรมล excretions of the eye: เนตรโยนิ *lit.* "the thousand-eyed," *i. e.* an appellation for Indra, whose body, after his adultery with นางอหัลยา, the wife of the sage Gautama, was covered with marks which resembled the female organ. These were afterwards changed to eyes. (H. C. D. p. 125): เนตรโรม eyelashes.

เนติ see นีติ p. 461.

เนติบัณฑิต nay-dti⁴-bun-dit⁴ *P. n.* guidance; prudent counsel; right conduct; polity; policy (chd. p. 292); a barrister-at-law; a lawyer; an attorney; a counsellor.

เน้น nen⁵ *v.* to reiterate; to stress; to speak with forcefulness: เน้นข้อความตามกล่าว to emphasize (by repetition) the poignant points of what has been said: เน้น (หัว) ตะปู, ตะปูควง to counter-sink a nail or screw.

เนมิ nay-mi⁶ (see กง p. 2: กรอบ p. 18) *P.S. n.* the felly or rim of a wheel; any circumference or edge (S. E. D. p. 569): เนมิโฆษ, เนมิศัพท์ the noise of a wheel; the din of carriage wheels: เนมิจักร a prince descended from Pari-Kahit (ท้าวปรีกษิต), said to have removed the capital city of India to Kousambi (เกาสามพี see p. 125) to replace Hastina-pura (hastin=elephant), which, according to tradition, was washed away by the Ganges. The ruins are traceable near an old bed of the Ganges, about fifty-seven miles north-east of Delhi (H. C. D. p. 120).

เนมิตตกะ nay-mit⁶-dta⁴-gka⁴ *P. n.* a fortuneteller; a necromancer; one who predicts the future from bodily signs or omens (chd. p. 264).

เนย nur-ie *n.* butter: เนยแข็ง cheese.

เนรคุณ see นิรคุณ p. 459.

เนรเทศ nay-ra⁶-tet³ *v.* to deport; to banish; to exile; to proscribe; to expel; to [ostracize.

เนรมิต see นิรมิต p. 460.

เนระพูสี, เนระภูสี (ต้น) nay-ra⁶-poo-see² *n.* a Siamese medicinal plant, *Dryopteris syrmatica* (V. P. p. 147).

เนรัญชร, เนรัญชรา nay-run-chaun *P. n.* the name of a river flowing through Magadha, the modern Nilajan (chd. p. 264).

เนษาท see นิษาท p. 461.

เนา ๑ now (see ตรึง p. 345) *v.* to tie or sew temporarily; to baste (as in sewing).

เนา ๒ now *S. n.* a ship, boat or vessel (S. E. D. p. 571): เนากรรณ the helm of a ship: เนาจร *lit.* "one permanently in a ship," *i. e.* a sailor: เนาทัณฑ์ *lit.* "boat-pole," *i. e.* an oar; a paddle: เนายาน *lit.* "going in a ship," *i. e.* navigation.

เน่า now³ *adj.* rotten; decayed; putrified.

เนาวนิต see นวนิต in นว ๑ p. 444.

เนิน nern *n.* rising ground; a gradual rising incline; a mound; a knoll.

เนิ่น nern³ (see ช้า p. 289) *adj.* slow; tardy; dilatory; late; delayed: การเนิ่นไป-มาก the work has been considerably retarded (as by floods): ความเนิ่นไปนาน the proceedings (in court) have been protracted: ใจ-เนิ่น of a procrastinating disposition: เนิ่นช้า delinquent: เนิ่นนัก very tardy; extremely late: เนิ่นมานานแล้ว a long time past: มาเนิ่น to come after the time appointed: เนิ่นวัน, เนิ่นปี prolonged for days and years.

เนิบ, เนิบนาบ nerp[3] *adj.* sluggish; dilly dallying; loitering; lazy; slothful; indolent.

เนียง nee-ang *n.* a lady; a woman; a mother.

เนียน nee-an *n.* a polisher or burnisher for gold, silver ornaments or other articles (as brush-wheels, buff or felt wheels, disks of cloth or chamois leather, cones of soft wood or cork): สนิทแนบเนียน close; fitting tightly or snugly (as a joint in carpentering).

เนียม (ต้น) nee-am *n. Leucopogon sp.,* a small bush of the tea family, having fragrant leaves which, when smeared with lime, are chewed with betel nut. The Malays dry the leaves for medicinal use: ช้างเนียม an elephant with short tusks.

เนียรทุกข์ see นิรทุกข์ p. 459.

เนียรเทศ see เนรเทศ p. 463.

เนื้อ neu-ah[5] *n.* tissue; flesh; meat; a collective name for deer: เนื้อกล้าม muscle; muscular tissue: เนื้อแกะ mutton: เนื้อความ the gist or summary of a story, incident or matter: เนื้อดี fine in texture (as cloth); pure in quality (as gold): เนอทราย *Cervus porcinus,* hog deer (J. S. S. III, 2, p. 126): เนื้อแท้ genuine: เนื้ออย่าง, smoked meat: เนื้อร้าย vicious wild animals (as bears, lions, tigers); *surgery* proud flesh; sloughing tissues: เนื้อลูกแกะ veal: เนื้อวัว beef: เนื้อสด fresh meat or flesh: เนื้อหนัง skin and underlying tissues: เนื้อแห้ง dried beef, or other meat: ผ้ายเนื้อหนัง carnal.

เนื่อง neu-ang[3] (see ติด p. 367) *v.* to be connected with; to be allied to; to be an incident of: เนื่องจาก arising from.

เนื่องๆ neu-ang-neu-ang *adv.* continually; constantly; perpetually: เนื่องนิตย์ ceaseless; perpetual; unvarying; incessant.

เนื่องนอง see นองเนื่อง p. 445.

เนื้อที่ neu-ah[5]-tee[3] *n.* area; extent of any surface, or space of land: เนื้อที่ดินที่ได้จากทะเล alluvium deposited by the sea.

เนื้อไม้ neu-ah[5]-mai[5] *n.* the grain of wood; the heart of fragrant wood.

เนือย neu-ie *adj.* weak; infirm; apathetic; unconcerned.

เนื้อหา neu-ah[5]-hah[2] *n.* charges in a law case; a person or an article sought for.

เนื้ออ่อน (ปลา) neu-ah[5]-on[4] *n. Callichrous bimaculatus (Siluridae); Cryptopterus apogon (Siluridae); C. micronema* (suvatti pp. 69, 71).

แน่ naa[3] *v.* to be in a state of relaxation or unconsciousness; to be completely under an anaesthetic: *adj.* sure; certain; truthful; without doubt: ใจแน่นอน firmness; constancy: แน่แก่ใจ to be convinced: แน่แท้สุจริต bona fide; in good faith: แน่นอน steadfastly; surely; assuredly: แน่นิ่ง to be motionless: แน่แน่ว, แน่วแน่ being steadfast in mind or purpose.

แน่ง naang[3] (see งาม p. 223) *adj.* beautiful; pretty: แน่งน้อย small, slender and graceful.

แน่น naan[3] *v.* to suffer from a feeling of tightness or fullness (as in the chest or abdomen): *adj.* dense; compressed; crowded (as a room, house or hall); solidified (as cement when set): เนื้อแน่น imporous; close-grained (as wood): แน่นแฟ้นหนา substantial; solid; compact; durable; firm (as building projects): อัดให้แน่น to tighten (as the nut on a bolt); to cork up firmly (as a bottle); to caulk a boat.

แนบ naap[3] (see ทาบ p. 412) *v.* to be close to; to come adjacent to (as a boat or ship to a landing): แนบกาย to make fit close to the body (as clothes or trowser legs): แนบเคียง to place at close quarters or side by side (as paddlers in a boat): แนบเนียน closely fitting; joined snugly or well together (descriptive of couplings or attachments in a building or in artistic carpentry) : แนบเนื้อ to apply directly to the skin (as a poultice or plaster).

แนว naa-oh (see ทิว p. 416) *n.* file; line as infantry); crease; crack; gap; row or streak : ชันยาแนว resin or pitch used for caulking spaces between boards (of a boat) : ได้แนวแถว in straight lines or files; in symmetrical rows.

แน่ว naa-oh[3] (see ตรง p. 341) *adj.* straight; direct; unswerving.

แนะ naa[6] *v.* to direct, indicate, or advise; to draw another's attention to : แนะนัด to propose an appointment; to notify or designate (a person or place) : แนะนำ to explain; to admonish; to direct or point out (as the way to a destination); to recommend or advise (as to the best method to pursue) : แนะนำให้รู้จักกัน to introduce another to a friend : แนะทาง to suggest or to intimate the route (as when one is planning an itinerary).

แน่ะ naa[4] *onomat.* from a sound indicating to look out, to be careful, or to be on the alert (as pointing to some danger) : นั่นแน่ะ there! look there! นี่แน่! look here! here it is! this is it!

โน nooh *v.* to bulge up or out; to protrude or swell up : *n.* a swelling; a protuberance; a protruding lump (as on the skin) : ตีหัวโน to cause a lump on the head by a heavy blow.

โนน non (see โคก p. 215) *n.* an elevation, hill or highland.

โน่น non[3] *adv.* there; that; in, or at that place; thither : โน่นอะไร what is that over there? ว่าน่ว่าโน่น to talk about unrestrictedly, or to blame indiscriminately.

โน้น non[5] *adv.* yonder; there; being at a place indicated : ข้างโน้น on that other side : ฟากน้ำโน้น on the other side of that water.

โน้ม nom[5] *v.* to bend down or over; to cause to curve.

ใน nai *n.* the members of a family : *prep.* in; admist; into : เครื่องใน edible entrails of an animal; tripe : ในประเด็น relevant; ในระหว่าง in between : ภายใน, ข้างใน inside; within : เมล็ดใน kernel; stone or pip (of fruit) : เหล็กใน a sharp offensive of defensive organ of bees or wasps, capable of inflicting a painful wound; the sting.

ไน nai *n.* a spinning-wheel.

บ

บ The twenty-sixth consonant in the Thai alphabet, a middle class letter of which there are nine, *viz.* ก, จ, ฎ, ฏ, ด, ต, บ, ป, อ. บอใบไม้ is the name of this letter. In Siamese words it is pronounced like the English labial "b" while in words of Pali and Sanskrit origin it is used interchangeably with "ป."

บ, บ่, บมิ, บ่มิ bɔɔu *Laos adj.* no; not; never; sign of the negative : บราง, บ่ราง to be impossible : บมิแรง to be without

strength; to be impossible of doing or accomplishing : บแรงภักษ์ to lack enough strength to eat : บเอ, บ่เอ *lit.* "not individually or singly," *i. e.* many; plentiful; abundant.

บก bok[4] *n.* land above water-level; high ground; dry land : ขึ้นบก to disembark : ลากขึ้นบก to drag up on to high ground (as a fishing net or a ship).

บกพร่อง bok[4]-prong[3] *v.* to be deficient; to

be inefficient (as in the carrying out of instructions or duty); to be still lacking in some
respects (as in conduct or previous high
standard of study): *adj.* remiss; negligent;
careless; ineffective; incomplete.

บง (ไม้)　　　*Laos* bong　*n. Bambusa tulda,*
a species of long-jointed bamboo (V. P. p. 160).

บ่ง　　　bong[4] *v.* to liberate (as pus by an
incision); to extricate by picking with a pin
(as a thorn or splinter in the flesh):　บ่งถึง,
บ่งตัว to make special reference or allusion to
some paragraph or person:　หนามยอกเอา-
หนามบ่ง if pricked by a thorn, use a thorn in
dislodging it; *prov.* "like cures like."

บงก์　　　bong *P. S. n.* mud; mire; dirt; clay
(S. E. D. p. 576):　บงกช, บงกชาต *lit.* "mud-
born," *i. e.* lotus (in general); a species of lotus
the flower of which closes in the evening,
Nelumbium speciosum (Nymphaeaceae) (V. P.
p. 164):　บงกชนาภ *lit.* "having a lotus
springing from his navel," *i. e.* one of many
names of Vishnu:　บงกชมาลี *lit.* "one wearing a lotus-crown," *i. e.* Vishnu:　บงกทนต์
lit. "having mud or clay between the teeth":
บงกภาช being buried or sunk in mud or mire:
บงกวาส *lit.* "mud-dweller," *i. e.* a crab; eels.

บงการ ๑　　　bong-gkan *v.* to issue a direct
command; to give explicit instruction regarding (as in some vocation or undertaking).

บงการ ๒　　　bong-gkan *n.* a dike, dam, bund
or embankment; a raised path through inundated fields; steps; stairs; see เขื่อน p. 168.

บงสุ์, บงสุ, บางสุ, บังส์　　　bong *P. S. n.*
crumbling soil; dust; sand; dung; manure
(S. E. D. p. 613):　บงสุกูลี *lit.* "quantity of
dust," *i. e.* a public road or thoroughfare:
บงสุกุล, บังสุกุล, บั้งสุกุล *lit.* "a dust heap," *i. e.* a
collection of rags from a dust heap, which in
former days, Buddhist monks would wash,
dye, and use as robes. The present day meaning refers to sets of robes which are laid on
a coffin during the religious services, and are

taken off by the monks prior to the cremation:
บงสุกูลิก one who wears clothes made of rags
taken from a dust heap. The theory of the
dress of a Buddhist monk was that it should
be pieced together from dirty rags taken from
a dust or refuse heap or from a cemetery.
Numerous exceptions were allowed (being
mentioned in the ordination service) and at
the present day the rule is never enforced:
บงสุขัล a pile of sand:　บงสุจันทน์ an appellation for Siva:　บงสุจามร a heap of dust;
a tent; a bank which is overgrown with lalang grass, *Imperata arundinacea,* or *I.
cylindrica (Gramineae)* (MCM. p. 475):　บงสุช,
บงสุภพ *lit.* "earth-born," *i. e.* rocks; fossil-
salt:　บงสุฐาน a heap of sand or dust:
บงสุนิบาต, บงสุวรรษ a dust storm; a cloud of
dust:　บงสุหร *lit.* "a sweeper or raiser
of dust" (said of the wind).

บฏ, บัฏ, บั๊ฏ　　　bot[4] *n.* cloth; woven fabric;
a blanket; a garment; a veil; a screen (S. E. D.
p. 579):　บฏการ a weaver; a painter; an
artist:　บฏมณฑป, บฏเวศม์ *lit.* "a canvas
house," *i. e.* a tent:　บฏวาส a corset; per-
fumed powder.

บด　　　bot[4] *v.* to crush (as stone); to grind; **to
pulverize** (as crude drugs or coffee); to **roll**
(**as** rubble on a road by means of a roller):
กระดานบดผ้า an ironing board:　บดข้าว to
separate the husk (by rolling) when sampling
paddy:　บดเสื้อผ้า to iron clothes:　บดอาหาร
to chew or masticate food:　บดเอื้อง to
chew the cud (as ruminants).

บดินทร์　　　bau-din *n.* a sovereign or monarch.

บดี, บดิ　　　bau-dee *P.S. n.* a master; an owner;
a ruler; a sovereign; a husband (S.E.D. p. 582):
บดีกามา one desirous of a husband:　บดีเทวา
one who regards her husband as a divinity;
one honouring a husband above all others:
บดีธรรม the rightful duties towards a husband:
บดีพรต, บดิวรดา loyalty or fidelity to a husband:
บดีมดี a married woman; one having a lord
or master:　บดีโลก *lit.* "a husband's world,"

i. e. the sphere of a husband in a future life : บดีวงศ์ those belonging to a husband's family.

บถ bot[4] *P. S. n.* a way ; a path ; a road ; a course (S. E. D. p. 582).

บท bot[4] *n.* a step ; a pace ; a stride ; a foot-step ; a trace ; a vestige, mark or print of a foot ; the foot itself ; a chapter, section, clause or article (in a composition) (S. E. D. p. 583) : บทกลอน a poem ; verses in rhyme : บทจร to walk, tramp or travel by foot : บทนี้ one following in the steps of another : บท-บงกช a lotus-like foot : บทบงสุ์, บทรัช dust of the feet : บทบูรณ์ a word added to a sentence for euphony, *ex.* พี่ผ์เสียดายที่จะไม่ได้-เห็นกันอีก ; to complete a poetic measure or strophe : บทพันธ์ a footstep ; a pace : บท-เพลง a hymn : บทภาชนีย์ a composition ; a chapter or clause needing some explanation or alteration : บทวี a leader ; a guide ; a fore-runner ; a road ; a path ; a way ; a track ; a reach ; a range : บทเรียน a lesson to be learned : บทศัพท์ footfalls ; the noise of footsteps : บทสถาน footprints ; foot-marks.

บน bon (1) *prep.* in or on an elevation or eminence : บนโต๊ะ on the table : บนภูเขา on a mountain : บนเรือน up in the house : (2) in a position vertically overhead : ข้าง-บน above ; overhead ; aloft : เครื่องบน super-structures (for a roof) : ชั้นบน upper layer or stories (as in a building) : บนเวหา among the clouds or in the higher regions of the atmosphere : บนสวรรค์ in heaven.

บ่น bon[4] *v.* to complain ; to murmur ; to mutter, lament or deplore : บ่นหา, บ่นถึง to enquire after solicitously.

บนบาน bon-ban *v.* to vow promising a thank-offering if the request is granted.

บพิตร, ประวิตร, ปวิตร bau-pit[6] *P. S. n.* one worthy of respect : *adj.* pure ; clean ; holy ; sacred ; sinless ; purified (S. E. D. p. 611).

บ่ม bom[4] *v.* to cure (as tobacco leaves) ; to ripen fruit (by placing in a warm, moist place).

บร, ปร bau-ra[6] *P. S n.* a foreigner ; an enemy ; a foe ; an adversary (S. E. D. p. 586) : *adj.* far ; distant ; remote ; beyond ; extreme ; further than : บรกถา speaking of or in regard to others : บรกรรม the serving of another ; the being of service to another : บรจักร the army of an enemy or foe : บรจินดา thinking of or caring for another : บรชน another person ; a stranger ; a foreigner : บรชนม์, บรโลก a future birth ; another exis-tence : บรชิต conquered by another : บรทาร another's wife or wives : บรทารกรรม the violation of another's wife : บรทารี one who takes, approaches or enjoys another's wife ; an adulterer : บรเทวดา the highest deity : บรเทศ another or a foreign country ; a hostile country : บรโทษ the proclaiming of another's faults ; censoriousness : บรธรรม another's duty, office or business ; the duties of those of another caste : บรนิรวาณ (see นิพพาน p. 458) Nirvana (according to the Buddhists) : บรปาก another's food or meal : บรปิณฑ์ *lit.* "those nourished by another's food," *i. e.* servants : บรบุรุษ the husband of another woman : บรประโยชน์ useful or beneficial to others : บรปักษ์ the opposing side ; the hostile party ; the enemy : บรพรหม *lit.* "the Supreme Spirit of the universe," *i. e.* Brahma (H. C. D. p. 56) : บรพล the foe's power or army : บรเพ็ชร์ (ต้น) *Tinospora cordi-folia (Menispermaceae)*, an Asiatic species of woody climber. There are about twenty-five species of this genus but most of them have not been adequately studied (V. P. p. 159 : BURK. p. 2163) ; *T. crispa* ; *T. nudiflora* (V. P. p. 159) ; *T. rumphii*, a climber well-known for its bitter principles due to a glucoside. The stems of *T. rumphii* are used as a tonic and in the treatment of fever (BURK. p. 2163) : บรภาค superior power or merit ; supremacy ; good fortune ; prosperity : บรภาพ one manifesting love towards others : บรภาษา a foreign language : บรภูมิ a foreign or hostile country : บรมัต differing in opinion or doctrine ; heterodoxy : บรมัท the highest degree of intoxication: บรรษฎร์ the country of an enemy: บรวาณิ a judge; a year: บรวาท the words or utterances of others: บรวาที an opponent; a controversialist: บรสัมพันธ์ the relation or connection with another: บรศาสน์ another's order: บรหิต befriending; benevolent.

บรม, ปรม   bau-rom   *P. S. adj.* highest; chief; most prominent or conspicuous; most excellent; supreme (S. E. D. p. 588): บรมเจต *lit.* "all the heart," *i. e.* whole-heartedness; willingness; voluntariness: บรมทารุณ most cruel; harsh; violent; dreadfully severe, intense or pitiless: บรมธาตุ most precious of relics: บรมบท the highest state or position; a condition of pre-eminence: บรม-พรหม the Supreme Spirit: บรมรส *lit.* "the most delicious of beverages," *i. e.* butter-milk mixed with water: บรมวงศ์ of royal race or lineage: บรมวิหาร most beautiful of sanctuaries: บรมศุข supreme happiness.

บรมัตถ์   bau-ra⁶-mat⁶   *P. n.* the best or highest moral sense; truthfulness; perfection; completeness (Chd. p. 334).

บรรจง, บรรยง, บันจอย, ประจง   bun-chjong *v.* to manifest accuracy, precision or carefulness (as while writing, etching or in handicraft work): *adv.* nicely; elegantly; delicately; exactly; neatly; realistically: เขียนบรรจง to write in a painstaking manner.

บรรจถรณ์, บัจจถรณ์, บัจจัตถรณ์   bun-chja⁴-taun² *P. S. n.* a cushion, mat or carpet to sit on; the mattress of a bed or couch (chd. p. 309).

บรรจบ, ประจบ   bun-chjop⁴ *v.* to place in close contact, or to make fit (as edges of boards or the occlusion of artificial teeth): นับบรรจบ to include additional articles, or a sum of money not mentioned in the original list, or amount: บรรจบรอบ to complete (as a cycle of years or a lap or circuit of a race course).

บรรจวบ see ประจวบ p. 497.

บรรจุ, ประจุ   bun-chjoo⁴ *v.* to put into; to fill up with; to insert: บรรจุซอง enclosed in an envelope: บรรจุด้วย filled with: บรรจุที่ to install in a position: บรรจุปืน to load a gun: บรรจุสินค้าลงเรือ to load freight into a boat: บรรจุหีบ to pack or put into a box (as a typewriter prior to shipment): เรือบรรจุสินค้า a freighter.

บรรเจิด, ประเจิด   bun-chjert⁴ *v.* to make or cause to become pretty; to beautify: *adj.* handsome; see งาม p. 223.

บรรณ, บัณณ   bun *P. S. n.* a wing; a pinion; a leaf (regarded as the plumage of a tree); feathers (as of an arrow) (S. E. D. p. 606): บรรณกุฎี a hut made of leaves: บรรณขัณฑ์ a tree without apparent flowers: บรรณนร, บรรณบุรุษ *lit.* "a man of leaves," *i. e.* an effigy or scarecrow stuffed with leaves or made of leaves (and finally burnt as leaves): บรรณนาล a leaf-stalk; a petiole: บรรณวาทย์ *lit.* "leaf-music," *i. e.* sounds produced by blowing into a folded leaf or one stretched between the fingers: บรรณศัพท์ the sound of the rustling of leaves: บรรณศัยยา a mattress or couch of leaves: บรรณศาลา *lit.* "a leaf-hut," *i. e.* a hut of leaves and grass; an arbour; an hermitage: บรรณาการ a gift; a present; offerings: บรรณาคม a room for books: บรรณาธิการ an editor of books or papers (masculine); บรรณาธิการิณี (feminine): บรรณารักษ์ a librarian: บรรณาศน์ the feeding on leaves, or vegetables.

บรรดา   bun-dah   *n.* whole; entire; total: *adj.* all; everyone; every.

บรรดาก   bun-dak⁴   *P. S. n.* a flag; a pennon; a banner; a sign or emblem (S. E. D. p. 581).

บรรดาศักดิ์   bun-dah-sak⁴   *P. S. n.* an official title or rank.

บรรตานึก see บัตตานึกะ p. 520.

บรรถร, บัตถร   bun-taun²   *P. n. lit.* "a flat

surface," *i. e.* a bed, a sleeping mat or mattress (chd. p. 372).

บรรทม, ผทม, ประทม　　bun-tom　*v.* to lie down; to sleep (used only for royalty).

บรรทัด　　bun-tat[6] *n.* a line, stroke or streak; a rule or injunction laid down : บรรทัดฐาน an accepted rule or standard of procedure or practice : ไม้บรรทัด a straight-edged guide or ruler for drawing purposes.

บรรทาน see ประทาน p. 501.

บรรทึก, บันทึก　　bun-teuk[6] *v.* to note; to seal or put on record.

บรรทุก, ประทุก　　bun-took[6] *v.* to load up with; to put into; to fill up with (as with freight).

บรรเทา　　bun-tow *v.* to give relief or amelioration in case of sickness or distress; to improve the condition of.

บรรเทือง see ประเทือง p. 501.

บรรพ๑, บัพพ, บั๊พพะ　　bup[4] *P. S. n.* a knot, node, or joint (of trees); a limb or member (of the body); a break, pause, division or section (in literature); the steps or gradation of elevation in a staircase; a fixed period (as time) (S. E. D. p. 609) : บรรพทักษิณา the teacher's fee for instruction : บรรพภาค the wrist; บรรพเภท violent pain in the joints : บรรพมูล the time of new moon and full moon : บรรพวิบ้ท the moon.

บรรพ ๒　　bun-pa[6] *P. S. adj.* former; prior; preceding; previous to; earlier than; being before; first; original; eastern (S. E. D. p. 643) : บรรพบุรุษ a forefather; an ancestor; see บุพพบุรุษ p. 485 : บรรพสัตรี the first woman of a line, family or lineage.

บรรพชา, บัพพัชชา, บั๊พพัชชา　　bun-pa[6]-chah *P. S. n.* the state of becoming a Buddhist monk or priest; the leaving of the world and adopting the life of an ascetic; the taking of the robe (chd. p. 305) : อุปสมบทบรรพชา the

ordination ceremonies of a Buddhist monk into the brotherhood.

บรรพชิต, บัพพชิต, บั๊พพชิต　　bun-pa[6]-chit[6] *P. S. n.* one who has given up the world; one having become an ascetic, mendicant or a Buddhist monk; one having taken the robe or one who has been ordained (chd. p. 305).

บรรพต, บัพพตะ, บั๊พพต　　bun-pot[6] *P. S. n.* a mountain; a mountain range; a hill; a rock : *adj.* knobby; ragged; jagged (said of mountains) (S. E. D. p. 609) : บรรพตศีลา the earth : บรรพตชาล, บรรพตมาลา a range or chain of mountains : บรรพตธาตุ *lit.* "mountain-metal," *i. e.* ore; mineral : บรรพตราช the Himalayas : บรรพตวาสี those living in the mountains; a mountaineer; mountain people or tribes : บรรพตศิขร the summit, top or peak of a mountain : บรรพตาศัย *lit.* "resting on mountains," *i. e.* a cloud.

บรรยงก์, บัลลังก์, บั๊ลลังก์　　bun-yong *n. P. S.* a bed; a couch; a sofa; a litter or palanquin (S. E. D. p. 607).

บรรยเวกษก์　　bun-ya[6]-wek[3] *n.* a superintendent.

บรรยากาศ　　bun-yah-gkart[4] *n.* the atmos-
[phere.

บรรยาย, บริยาย see ปริยาย p. 509.

บรรลัย see ประลัย p. 504.

บรรลาย see ปลาย p. 512.

บรรลุ, ประลุ see ถึง p. 388.

บรรเลง　　bun-leng *v.* to sing; to give forth or produce music, melody or harmony pleasing to the ear : เครื่องบรรเลง instruments producing music; a band or orchestra.

บรรษัท see บริษัท p. 471.

บรรสพ see ประสพ p. 505.

บรรสม see ประสม p. 505.

บรรสาน see ประสาน p. 505.

บรรสาร see ประสาร p. 505.

บรรหาร see บริหาร p. 471.

บรัด, ปรัต brat[4] v. to decorate; to dress or adorn oneself: n. decoration; embellish-[ment.

บรัศ see แก้ว p. 130.

บรากรม, ปรักกมะ, ปรากรม brah-gkrom P. S. n. courage; heroism; power; strength; energy; exertion; enterprise (S. E. D. p. 589).

บราง, บ่ร่าง, บร้าง, บ่ร้าง see ป p. 465.

บราทุกรา see บาทุกา p. 480.

บริกขาร, บริษการ, ปรักขาร, ปริษการ bau-rik[6]-karn[2] P. n. the eight requisites, or outfit of a Buddhist priest, viz. an alms-bowl, a loincloth, a mantle or outer garment, a shoulder scarf, a girdle, a razor, a needle and a water strainer (chd. p. 342).

บริกขารโจฬ bau-rik[6]-karn[2]-chjone n. pieces of cloth for various uses (as handkerchiefs, towels, or rags, being accessories to the above outfit).

บริกรม bau-ri[6]-gkrom S. v. to step or walk about; to go past; to escape; to roam around; to circumambulate (S. E. D. p. 592).

บริกรรม, ปริกรรม bau-ri[6]-gkum P. S. v. to adorn, decorate, paint or perfume the body (as after bathing): n. purification; preparation; a servant; an attendant; an assistant (S. E. D. p. 591).

บริกัปป bau-ri[6]-gkap[4] P. S. v. to perform; to execute; to make, contrive, arrange or accomplish; to fix, settle or determine (S. E. D. p. 592).

บริการ bau-ri[6]-gkan v. to help or assist; to aid: n. one who, or that which helps or assists; see ช่วย p. 283.

บริคณ, ปริคณ bau-ri[6]-kon P. S. v. to count over; to reckon completely; to ascertain by calculation: n. a house (S.E.D. p. 592).

บริคณสนธิ, บริคณสัญญา bau-ri[6]-kon-son[2]-ti[6] n. an agreement; a covenant or convention (as made between a company and the shareholders).

บริคณห์ bau-ri[6]-kon P. v. to take hold of; to grasp; to carry along with one; to include, surround or to take possession of; to embrace (chd. p. 340).

บริจาค, ปริจจาค, ปริตยาค bau-rit[6]-chjak[4] P. S. n. the act of giving up, leaving, deserting, abandoning, neglecting or renouncing; the making of a personal sacrifice (S. E. D. p. 595).

บริจเฉท, ปริเฉท bau-rit[6]-chet[4] P. S. n. the act of cutting, severing, separating or dividing; exact discrimination (as between the false and true, the right and wrong); decision; judgement; determination; a section or chapter of a book (S. E. D. p. 594): บริจเฉทกาล a predetermined or specified period of time.

บริจารก bau-ri[6]-chjah-rok[6] P. S. n. an assistant or attendant; a servant (S.E.D. p. 593).

บริจาริกา, ปริจาริกา bau-ri[6]-chjah-ri[6]-gkah P. S. n. a female attendant; a maid-in-waiting (S. E. D. p. 593).

บริชน bau-ri[6]-chon P. S. n. a surrounding company of people; entourage; attendants; servants; followers; suite; train; retinue (S. E. D. p. 594).

บริณายก bau-ri[6]-nah-yok[6] S. n. a leader; a guide (S. E. D. p. 595).

บริบาล bau-ri[6]-ban P. S. v. to take care of one's own or another's property; to act as a guardian, keeper, or maintainer (S.E.D. p. 597).

บริบูรณ์, บริบวรณ์ bau-ri[6]-boon P. S. v. to be perfect, entire, complete, full: adj. plentiful; abundant; fully satisfied; contented S. E. D. p. 597): จบบริบูรณ์ to come to a successful, complete finish or ending (as a story or novel).

บริพนธ์ see ปริพนธ์ p. 509.

บริพพาชก see ปริพพาชก p. 509.

บริพพาชิกา see ปริพพาชิกา p. 509.

บริพัตร see ปริวรรต p. 509.

บริพันธ์ see ปริพนธ์ p. 509.

บริพาร see บริวาร p. 471.

บริภัณฑ์, ปริภัณฑ์ bau-ri[6]-pun *P. S. n.* a girdle, zone, belt or ring (chd. p. 337).

บริภาษ, ปริภาษ bau-ri[6]-pat[3] *P. S. v.* to speak to; to admonish, teach, explain or define; to accuse, censure, blame or charge with (s. e. d. p. 598).

บริภาษณ์, ปริภาษณ์ bau-ri[6]-pat[3] *P. S. n.* admonition; reproof; a reprimand (S.E.D.p. 598).

บริโภค, ปริโภค bau-ri[6]-poke[3] *v.* to partake of (food); to use: *n.* possession; enjoyment (chd. p. 338).

บริมาส bau-ri[6]-mart[3] *n.* the period of full moon.

บริยัต์ see ปริยัต์ p. 509.

บริรม bau-ri[6]-rom *S. v.* to take pleasure in; to be delighted with (s. e. d. p. 599).

บริรักษ์ bau-ri[6]-ruk[6] *v.* to guard well or completely; to rescue or defend from; to protect, rule or govern (s. e. d. p. 599).

บริราช bau-ri[6]-rat[3] *S. v.* to shine on all sides; to spread radiance everywhere (s. e. d. p. 600).

บริวัตร see ปริวรรต p. 509.

บริวาร, บริพาร, ปริชน, ปริวาร, บริสชน bau-ri[6]-wan *P. S. v.* to attend; to linger around in order to serve: *n.* retainers; train; retinue; satellites; followers; servants or attendants (s. e. d. p. 601).

บริวาส see ปริวาส p. 510.

บริเวณ, ปริเวณ bau-ri[6]-wane *n.* vicinity; precinct; neighbourhood; environment; surroundings.

บริศาจ see ปิศาจ p. 527.

บริษการ see บริกขาร p. 470.

บริษัท, บรรษัท, ปริษัท bau-ri[6]-sat[4] *P. S. n.* an assembly; a group; a circle; a council; a congregation; a company (in business); a meeting; an audience (S. E. D. p. 602): บริษัท-จำกัด a limited liability company: บริษัท-เดินรถราง a tramway company: บริษัทรับประกันภัย an accident insurance company: บริษัทรับส่ง a transport company.

บริสุทธ์, บริสุทธิ์, ปริสุทธ, ปริสุทธิ bau-ri[6]-soot[4] *P. S. n.* pureness; purity; virtue: *adj.* pure; clean; chaste; flawless; blameless; having no weak spot, crack or fissure; genuine; acquitted; discharged (S. E. D. p. 602): ขาวบริสุทธ์ absolutely flawless: ความบริสุทธ์ holiness; purity.

บริหาร, บรรหาร, ปริหาร bau-ri[6]-harn[2] *P. S. v.* to answer or refute (as a charge or indictment); to give attention or care; to guard, keep or preserve (chd. p. 341).

บริหาส, ปริหาส bau-ri[6]-hart[4] *P. S. v.* to laugh at; to jest, joke, ridicule or make merriment (S. E. D. p. 604).

บวก bu-ak[4] *v.* to add together (as figures); to join or unite (so as to increase the quantity or number); to sum up (as the total in a column of figures): *n.* addition; the plus sign (+): เครื่องบวกเลข an adding machine.

บวง, บวงสรวง see บนบาน p. 467.

บ่วง boo-ang[4] *n.* a loop: บ่วงแร้ว traps; snares; wiles; pitfalls; gins; places of allurement.

บวช boo-at[4] *v.* to be ordained as member of a holy brotherhood; to be invested with ministerial rank; to perpetrate a swindle, fraud or deception: พิธีบวช an ordination ceremony : เขาบวชฉันเสียแล้ว *slang* to be the victim of a deception.

บวชชี boo-at[4]-chee *v.* to take vows as a nun : *n.* a sweetmeat made by boiling bananas in coconut milk with sugar and a little salt.

บวน (แกง) boo-an *n.* a curry made of pork and the entrails of the pig, together with salt, pepper and other necessary condiments.

บ้วน see ถ่ม p. 380 : บ้วนน้ำลาย to eject saliva : บ้วนน้ำหมาก to spit betel saliva : บ้วนปาก to rinse the mouth (as with water, or a medicinal solution).

บวบ, บวบขม, บวบหอม *Siam.*, มะนอยขม

Laos, Chiengmai (ต้น) buap[4] *n. Luffa cylindrica (Cucurbitaceae)*, loufah, dish-rag gourd, cultivated all over the world but a native of the Old World tropics. It gives the loufah sponge known in Egypt for centuries and now largely cultivated in Japan. These sponges are used as a substitute for cork-soles for placing inside boots. The fruits are slightly purgative but not sufficiently so to prevent their being good food. Later, they are distinctly purgative and they are so used medicinally. The juice and seeds also have medicinal uses (Burk. p. 1371 : cb. p. 757); *Trichosanthes cucumerina (Cucurbitaceae)*, a climber found from India to Australia. The fruit is very bitter and aperient. It is used medicinally in India (V. P. p. 162 : Burk. p. 2179); *Luffa acutangula* see บวบเหลี่ยม : บวบงู *Siam.*, หมากนอย *Siam.*, *Saraburi*, นมพิจิตร์ *Siam.*, *Krat* (ต้น) *Trichosanthes anguina (Cucurbitaceae)*, snake-gourd, club-gourd, a quick-growing, annual gourd, native of China and Malaya, bearing long, cylindrical, green or greenish-white fruits, 4 to 5 feet or more in length. In an unripe state these are sliced and cooked, being commonly used and much relished as a curry-vegetable. It is customary to fasten a small

stone to the end of each fruit whilst growing, so as to weight the latter down and induce it to grow straighter, and perhaps longer, than it would otherwise do (MCM. pp. 292, 294, 380 : cb. p. 751 : V. P. p. 162 : Burk. p. 2178) : บวบเหลี่ยม *Siam.*, มะนอย, หมักน้อย *Laos, Chiengmai* (ต้น) *Luffa acutangula (Cucurbitaceae)*, a distinct gourd, 8 to 10 inches long, with several sharp longitudinal ridges, commonly used in a tender state as a curry-vegetable, the outer part being peeled off before cooking. The plant is an annual and is commonly grown in India, Ceylon and throughout the world. All parts of the plant and the ripe fruits give a bitter purgative juice, which is used medicinally. It is said that the root is used as a purge in Russia. In Java and India there are numerous medicinal uses of the plant. The seeds contain about 50% oil which can be used as food.

บวม buam *v.* to swell or be swollen (as a result of inflammation) : *n.* tumefaction ; a swelling ; puffiness : *adj.* swelled ; swollen.

บวร bau-worn *P.S. adj.* chief ; best ; noble ; excellent (chd. p. 374) ; used as a prefix, as บวรนิเวศ.

บอ bau *adj.* inclined towards lunacy ; bordering on insanity, *ex.* บ้า ๆ บอ ๆ.

บ่อ bau[4] *n.* a well ; a pond : บ่อเกิด the place of origin or place of first cause : บ่อแร่ an ore mine : บ่อเลี้ยงปลา a pond for rearing fishes.

บอก bauk[4] *v.* to tell ; to say ; to inform ; to explain ; to relate or narrate : *n.* see กระบอก p. 37 : *adj.* a numerical designatory particle for guns : บอกกล่าว to announce, report or testify regarding a crime or felony : บอกข่าว to tell the news ; to make an announcement : บอกแขก to solicit the help of neighbours (as in a harvesting bee) : บอกบท to line out poetry or music (as by a precentor) : บอกราคา to quote a price : บอกเลิก to give notice that some agreement is to be cancelled :

บอกเล่า to describe : บอกให้รู้ตัว to fore-warn ; to advise beforehand : ผู้บอกบท a precentor or prompter.

บ้อง baung[3] *n.* a cylindrical piece of wood with a hole in the centre (like a section of bamboo), or with a hole, chamber or slot (as a file, chisel or sword handle) : บ้องตื้น a metaphor to indicate an imbecile or an ignoramus : บ้องสูบกัญชา a bamboo water-pipe for smoking kancha, hashish, or the hemp-plant (Burk. p. 437) : สูบกัญชาบ้องหนึ่ง one portion or a series of inhalations while smoking kancha.

บ้องไฟ bong[3]-fai *n.* a name for Laos sky rockets.

บ้องแบ๊ว bong[3]-baa-oh[6] *adj.* deformed ; twisted out of normal shape ; malformed (descriptive of the face and eyes).

บอด baut[4] *adj.* darkened ; blinded : ตาบอด blind ; sightless.

บอน (ต้น) born *n. Caladium (Araceae)*, a family of small tuberous plants with large, ornamental, hastate-peltate leaves. It is mostly of South American origin, including many beautiful hybrids or varieties. They require rich soil, well-decomposed manure, and an abundance of moisture. They thrive best in moderate shade, though many of the hardier varieties are also adapted for growing in open borders or beds. They are propagated by suckers or by division of the roots or tubers (corms). The leaves die down once a year in the dry season, after which the tubers should be kept in a fairly dry state. They may be left undisturbed in the ground, or taken up and stored in earth or sand in a shed, until the next season for planting (MCM. p. 136 : Burk. p. 396) : *adj.* ceaseless ; indecent ; indiscreet ; unreserved, used in reference to actions of the hand, as mischievous (มือบอน) ; of speech, as gossipy (ปากบอน) : บอนจีน see ตาลปัตรฤๅษี p. 364 : บอนฝรั่ง (ต้น) *Caladium bicolor (Araceae)*, of Brazil. Locally named กระนกกระทา and ถมยาประแบ้ง, it first made its appearance in Bangkok, and is said to have been sent from Europe by some European. Since then more varieties and forms have been introduced, together with those of a few other species. Not a few interesting ones have sprung up in local cultivation as the result of bud variation. There are at present over two hundred varieties and forms of *Caladiums* as named locally. Phya Prabha Karavongs is responsible for the introduction of a great number of them. The *Caladiums* have long been favourites among the Siamese. In 1906-1907 when collecting and displaying of the aroids was for the first time in vogue in this country, prices paid by local enthusiastic collectors for certain rare and unique kinds are known to have run up to as much as four figures in ticals (winit, N. H. J. S. S. IX, 1, pp. 91, 92 : Burk. p. 396) : บอนลายกนก, กนกนารี, กนกนฤมิตร์ (ต้น) *Nephthytis picturata*, a native of Congo. This aroid is occasionally seen cultivated in Bangkok greenhouses on account of its variegated leaves whose white markings form an artistic pattern much resembling the Siamese design known as ลายกนก. The aroid was first seen about forty years ago with Prince Sanpasart who had a rich collection of exotic foliage plants (winit, N. H. J. S. S. IX, 3, p. 277) : บอนส้ม *Siam., Pattani* (ต้น) *Begonia prolixa (Begoniaceae)* (Cb. p. 777).

บ่อน baun[4] *v.* to nibble, gnaw, bite or bore into (referring to worms or insects into fruit, stems or roots) ; to litter any place ; to scatter things carelessly : *n.* a gaming-house ; a bed (of straw or leaves) : บ่อนเบี้ย a gambling place where cowries are used.

บอบ baup[4] *adj.* weakened or worn out by ill-usage (as cattle or horses) ; frail (as after a sickness) ; weakened and exhausted (as after buffeting) : บอบบาง, บอบแบบ frail ; breakable ; thin (as china, dishes or crockery).

บ้อม baum[3] *v.* to beat, pound, strike or slap ; see ตี p. 368 and ทุบ p. 418.

บ่อย, บ่อยๆ   boy[4] *adv.* repeatedly , often ; frequently ; see เนื่องๆ p. 464.

บ่อย   boy[2] *Eng. n.* a male servant ; a domestic attendant ; a Chinese table boy or cabin boy.

บอระเพ็ด, บรเพ็ชร์ (ต้น)   bau-ra[6]-pet[6] *n.* *Tinospora cordifolia (Menispermaceae)*, one of a genus of about twenty-five woody climbers found in the tropics of the Old World, chiefly in Asia and Malaysia. The stems are used for fevers, skin diseases, jaundice and syphilis (MCM. p. 380 : BURK. p. 2163 : V. P. p. 159) ; *T. crispa* ; *T. nudiflora.*

บอระมาน   bau-ra[6]-marn *n.* paste.

บ๊ะ   ba[6] *onomat.* an expletive indicating surprise or amazement.

บะฉ่อ (แกง)   ba[4]-chau[4] *Chin. n.* a curry made of minced pork.

บะหมี่   ba[4]-mee[4] *Chin. n.* yellow macaroni in strips, cooked with pork sauce, and served as a soup.

บะเหย่อง *Laos, Chiengmai,* หมามุ่ย *Siam.,* โพล่ยู *Karen, Kanburi* (ต้น) *n. Mucuna pruriens (Leguminosae)*, malabar bean, horse-eye bean, cowage or cowitch, a climber found in south-eastern Asia and Malaysia. The large ovoid seed is considered to resemble the eye of a horse. The boiled seeds have been used in India from sanskritic times as an aphrodisiac, and its roots as a tonic. It is said to be medicinal in Indo-China. The pods are covered with brown irritant hairs, commonly used as a vermifuge, but strong doses of the hairs cause diseases of the bowels, and may bring about death. Mixed with the slime of a slug, they are used criminally (MCM. pp. 379, 461 : BURK. p. 1503 : Cb. p. 445).

บัก   buk[4] *n.* the male generative organ.

บัง   bung (see กำบัง p. 103) *v.* to screen ; to conceal ; to hide ; to veil ; to protect from view :

บังโคลน mudguards ; fenders : บังแดด a sun-shield : บังตา an eye-shade, shield or veil ; blinders ; a screen or half curtain for a door or window : บังใบ a method of joining boards (for a partition) by bevelling opposite edges : บังเพลิง a light reflector ; a fire screen : บังพื้น to use secret means, sorcery, witchery, or witchcraft to do harm, or to kill others : บังมืด to intercept the light ; to produce darkness by means of cutting off the light : บังลม a wind-shield : เบียดบัง to filch.

บั้ง   bung[3] *v.* to blaze ; to mark (a tree) by chipping or peeling : *n.* a mark on a tree to trace a path so indicated ; a strip of tape on uniforms, as insignia of rank ; streaks or welts on the skin resulting from flogging.

บังกัด   bung-gkut[4] *v.* to hide ; to secrete ; to conceal ; *syn.* ปิดบัง p. 526.

บังเกิด   bung-gkert[4] *v.* to come into existence ; to be born ; see เกิด p. 125.

บังคน   bung-kon *n.* urine or fecal matter (used only for royalty) : ทรงบังคนเบา to urinate : ทรงบังคนหนัก to pass fecal matter.

บังคม   bung-kom *Cam. v.* to perform an act of obeisance, homage or reverence before a monarch (used only for the king) : บังคมทูล to address His Majesty after making due obeisance.

บังควร   bung-kuan *adj.* becoming ; opportune ; acceptable ; suitable ; proper or advisable in the utmost degree.

บังคับ   bung-kup[6] *v.* to control ; to order ; to insist on obedience : *n.* authority ; rule ; power to enforce obedience : ข้อบังคับ a regulation ; a rule ; an order : คำบังคับบัญชา an order or mandate : บังคับให้มา to compel one to come : ผู้บังคับการที่กล้าหาญ an intrepid commander : ใต้บังคับ subject to rule or authority.

บังคั้ล   bung-kun *Cam. v.* to enter the presence of a king or monarch.

บังแทรก bung-saak[3] *n.* a small embroidered sunshade having serrated edges, carried in processions or during state ceremonies, as an insignia of royal rank.

บังสูรย์ bung-soon[2] *n.* an embroidered sunshade shaped like a boh leaf on a long handle, carried in processions or during state ceremonies, as an insignia of royal rank.

บังหวน bung-huan[2] *v.* to cause smoke to rise in an enveloping or protecting screen or cloud; to make a smoke-screen.

บังเหียน bung-hien[2] *n.* a bit or bridle: สายบังเหียน a bridle rein.

บังอร bung-on *n.* a woman, girl or virgin; a handsome girl; see นาง p. 450.

บังอวจ bung-oo-at[4] *Cam. n.* a window.

บังอาจ bung-art[4] *v.* to be very bold, daring or fearless; to overstep the bounds of propriety.

บังอิง bung-ing *Cam. v.* to lean against or upon: *n.* a back supporter.

บังเอิญ bung-urn *adv.* accidentally; unexpectedly; *syn.* เผอิญ.

บัญจก bun-chjok[4] *P. n.* consisting of five (as a set of rules or commandments) (chd. p. 327).

บัญชร bun-chorn *P. S. n.* a cage; a net; a latticed window; an aviary; a dove-cote (s. E. D. p. 575).

บัญชา, สั่ง bun-chah *v.* to order, command or make a declaration: *n.* an order or enjoinment: บัญชาการ to order, or direct a work, undertaking or function.

บัญชี, บาญชี bun-chee *S. n.* a list; a register; a role; a catalogue; an index; an almanac (S. E. D. p. 578): บัญชีกระแสรายวัน a current account: บัญชีกำไรและขาดทุน a profit and loss account: บัญชีงบดุลย์ a balance sheet: บัญชี (เงิน) a financial account: บัญชีราคาขายของ a price list: บัญชี-

สินค้าในเรือ a manifest: สมุหบัญชี a secretary; an account clerk.

บัญญัติ, บัญญัตติ bun-yat[4] *P. S. v.* to prescribe; to settle; to publish (as laws or ordinances): *n.* information; instruction; agreement; engagement (S. E. D. p. 659): บัญ-ญัติว่า to enact or promulgate (as rules).

บัญหา bun-hah[2] *P. S. n.* a question; a query; an interrogation; a demand (S. E. D. [p. 695].

บัฏ, บัฏฏ see บฏ p. 466.

บัณฑร bun-da[4]-ra[6] *P. S. adj.* white; pale; whitish-yellow (S. E. D. p. 616): บัณฑรทนต์ *lit.* "one having white teeth or tusks," *i. e.* the elephant: บัณฑรภิกษุ *lit.* "a white-robed mendicant," *i. e.* name of a particular religious sect.

บัณฑิต bun-dit[4] *P. S. n.* cleverness; scholarship; erudition; skill (S. E. D. p. 616).

บัณฑิตย์ bun-dit[4] *P. S. n.* a sage; a man of learning; a wise person (chd. p. 328).

บัณฑุ bun-doo[4] *P. S. adj.* white; yellowish-white: *n.* a sacred elephant: บัณฑุกัมพล a white woollen covering or blanket; a warm upper garment; the housings of a royal elephant: บัณฑุนาค a white elephant: บัณฑุบัตร a pale leaf: บัณฑุมุข pale-faced: บัณฑุราค whiteness; paleness; pallor: บัณฑุโรค a disease characterized by yellowness; jaundice: บัณฑุโลหะ *lit.* "a white metal," *i. e.* silver: บัณฑุวรรณ white; whiteness (S. E. D. p. 616).

บัณฑูร bun-toon *n.* a command, order or instructions (used in ancient court language).

บัณเฑาะก์ bun-daw[4] *P. S. n. lit.* "of the neuter gender," *i. e.* an eunuch (chd. p. 328).

บัณเฑาะว์ bun-daw[4] *n.* a small two-faced drum, mounted on a handle. From the side of the drum is suspended a small ball which acts as a clapper when the handle is rotated in the fingers. This is used by Brahmins in various functions.

บัณณรส   bun-na[6]-rot[6] *P.S. adj.* fifteen (chd. p. 330).

บัณณรสี   bun-na[6]-ra[6]-see[2] *P.S. adj.* fifteenth; the fifteenth day of the half month (chd. p. 330).

บัณฑาส   bun-nat[3] *P.S. adj.* fifty (chd. p. 330).

บัด   but[4] *n.* time; occasion; period; season; epoch: บัดดล near the time of arrival: บัดเดี๋ยว, ประเดี๋ยว shortly; presently; directly: บัดนั้น then; therefore: บัดน now; at this moment: บัดแบ่ง half-time: บัดแมล่ง afternoon; evening.

บัดกรี   but[4]-gkree *v.* to solder; to fuse together (by means of heat and a flux).

บัดซบ   but[4]-sop[6] *adj.* ignorant or stupid in the extreme; silly.

บัดบง   but[4]-bong *v.* to vanish or disappear completely.

บัดสี   but[4]-see[2] *adj.* shameful; disgraceful; indecent or infamous; see ขายหน้า p. 155.

บัตร, บัตต   but[4] *P.S. n.* the wing of a bird; a pinion; a feather; the feathers of an arrow: (2) the leaves of a book; paper; a letter; a document; a leaf for writing upon: (3) a car; a horse; a chariot; any vehicle or means of conveyance (S. E. D. p. 581): บัตรทารก *lit.* "a leaf-divider," *i.e.* a saw: บัตรธารา the edge or border of a leaf: บัตรบดี *lit.* "the chief of birds," *i.e.* the Garuda: บัตรบาฐ the examination or perusal of a writing: บัตรบาล, บัตรลดา a kris; a long knife; a dagger: บัตรพลี an oracle; charms; auguries; offerings (used when invoking the power of genii or spirits): บัตรพาล an oar: บัตรพาหะ, บัตรรถ *lit.* "using wings as a vehicle," *i.e.* a bird: บัตรเรขา a decoration consisting of lines or streaks drawn on the face and body with musk and other fragrant substances: บัตรสนเท่ห์ an anonymous letter: บัตรสูจิ *lit.* "leaf-needles," "tree-needles," *i.e.* thorns:

บัตรหมาย an official notice, order or call for corvée: สัญญาบัตร a diploma, or letter of patent conferring a title.

บัน   bun *n.* the gable end of a roof or building: บันแถลง a small gable placed in front of the main one; see จั่ว p. 242.

บั่น, ตัด, ทอน   bun[4] *v.* to cut into short lengths (as firewood); see ตัด p. 359.

บั้น   bun[3] *n.* a half; a part; a portion; a piece; a measure of capacity for paddy or salt equaling 1000 litres. One บั้น equals 50 ถัง of 20 litres each. This is half of the เกวียน or coyan: บั้นพระองค์ the mid-portion of the body; the waist (used only for royalty): บั้นหลวง the standard measure of capacity, equal to one thousand litres: บั้นเอว the hips; the waist; the loins.

บันจวบ   bun-chjuap[4] *v.* to decorate; see แต่ง p. 376.

บันจอย   see บรรจง p. 468.

บันดล   see ดล p. 319.

บันดาล   bun-darn *v.* to cause to occur, originate, germinate or produce (implying by superhuman power).

บันเดิน, เดิน (p. 334)   bun-dern *v.* to walk.

บันโดย   bun-doie *v.* to show, behave, manifest or exhibit (as joyousness or cheerfulness).

บันได   bun-dai *n.* a ladder; stairs; a staircase: ขั้นบันได the rung of a ladder; the tread of a staircase.

บันทึก   bun-turk[6] *v.* to make a short summary or brief (for filing); to make a note or record for placing on file (as of incidents that have occurred, or correspondence): *n.* a brief; an abstract or summary; see บรรทึก p. 469.

บันทึ่ง   bun-turng *Jav. v.* to wait for; to expect the arrival of; to remonstrate regarding another's absence while longing for his return; see คอย p. 192.

บันเทิง, บำเทิง, ตันเหิม (see p. 359) bun-terng *v.* to be joyful; to rejoice; to be full of glee or cheerfulness.

บันลือ bun-lur *v.* to utter a loud and far-reaching call.

บันเหิน เหาะ bun-hern[2] *v.* to fly; to ascend into the air (by mechanical means or by supernatural power).

บัปผาสะ see บั๊ปผาสะ p 521.

บัพพ see บรรพ ๑ p. 469.

บัพพชิต see บรรพชิต p. 469.

บัพพตะ see บรรพต p. 469.

บัพพัชชา see บรรพชา p. 469.

บัพพชน์ see บั๊พพาชนะ p. 521.

บัพพาชนียกรรม bup[4]-pah[3]-cha[6]-nee-ya[6]-gkum *n.* a ceremony of purification, performed by Buddhist monks, for sins committed.

บัล see ปละ p. 511.

บัลลวะ, บัลลพ, บั๊ลลพ bun-la[6]-wa[6] *S. n.* a sprout; a shoot; a twig; a spray; a bud or blossom (metaphorically, fingers, toes, lips); a strip of cloth or a scarf (S. E. D. p. 610).

บัลลังก์ see บรรยงก์ p. 469.

บัว bu-ah *n.* a collective name for the lotus or water-lily; a cornice or moulding; a frieze or fillets (resembling the lotus flower) at the head of a column or pillar; used metaphorically to indicate the mammae: บัว (ปลา) *Labeo dyocheilus* (*Cyprinidae*), a carp; *Osteochilus vittatus* (*Cyprinidae*), a carp (suvatti pp. 24, 25): บัวกลุ่ม decorations around a pagoda or about the base of an image of the Buddha, made in the shape of tiers of lotus petals: บัวกินสาย, บัวขม, บัวแดง, บัวจงกลนี *Siam.*, ป้านแดง *Laos, Chiengmai*, บัวขี้แปะ *Laos, Korat*, ประลัก *Khmer* (ต้น) *Nymphaea lotus, var. pubescens* (*Nymphaeaceae*), a rose-flowered or white

water-lily. It is a native of Africa, and owes its place in Asia to cultivation, probably from ancient times; it is now widespread. In India the seeds are eaten as famine food, and sometimes in normal times, by the poorest. In Siam it quite highly esteemed. They are also eaten in the Philippine Islands. In India they are pounded and made into a kind of bread. The rhizomes are also cooked and eaten in India and China; sometimes the young fruits are eaten as a salad (BURK. p. 1566: MCM. p. 175: V. P. p. 165: cb. p. 73): บัวตุม a wild-growing vine with large flowers resembling the lotus flower, and used medicinally: บัวทอง *Helianthus annuus* (*Compositae*), the sunflower of which there are several varieties. It is a native of America, whence it was brought to Spain in the middle of the sixteenth century. It was first grown as an oil crop in Batavia in 1725, and then in France in 1787. At the present time countries in central and eastern Europe grow it as an oil crop; but the seed has no well-established place in the markets. The Russians habitually eat the seeds; and races in which these are large have been selected. The oil is a good edible oil (MCM. p. 134: BURK. p. 1132: V. P. p. 163): บัวบก *Siam.*, ผักหนอก *Laos, Chiengmai* (ต้น) *Centella asiatica* (*Umbelliferae*), a small herb found growing in moist places. The leaves are taken as a tonic and blood-purifier, and also for indigestion, nervousness and dysentery. The stalks and leaves are eaten as a vegetable in salad, both cooked and raw (MCM. pp. 321, 379); *Hydrocotyle asiatica* (*Umbelliferae*), a creeping herb, widely distributed throughout the tropics; in the Malay Peninsula it is very common and general. It has been used in Java on plantations to prevent soil erosion. Everywhere in the East it is medicinal. In Sanskrit works it is recommended as an alternative and tonic in diseases of the skin, the nervous system, and the blood. It is still extensively used in India. Because the plant acts as a diuretic, it relieves complaints of the urinary organs. Perhaps it is as a diuretic that it purifies the blood (cb. p. 786 : Burk. p. 1211) :　บัวบาท *lit.* " feet with circular decorations as of lotus flowers," *i. e.* feet of a meritorious person, as the Buddha.　According to the legend, lotus flowers grew up to support his feet :　บัวผัน *Nymphaea cyanea* (V. P. p. 164) :　บัวเผื่อน *Nymphaea stellata* (*Nymphaeaceae*), the little blue water-lily, found in ditches in some parts of the Malay Peninsula.　The species is found wild throughout the whole of south-eastern Asia and Malaysia.　It is very easily distinguished from other blue water-lilies, as its leaves are freely toothed all around but those of the Egyptian *N. coerulea* are not; its flowers are smaller in size than those of the *N. capensis*.　In India roots and seeds are famine-food.　Root-tubercles are marketed in Tonkin.　The juice of the leaves is applied to the skin for fever (MCM. pp. 175, 312, 476 : cb. p. 74 : Burk. p. 1566 : V. P. p. 164) :　บัวฝรั่ง *Zephyranthes rosae* (*Amaryllidaceae*), a bulbous herb from the West Indies, which has been in European conservatories since 1828. It was brought to Singapore in 1893.　The flowers are rose-coloured (V. P. p. 164 : Burk. p. 2292) :　บัววิกโตเรีย *Victoria regia* (*Nymphaeaceae*), the giant water-lily of the Amazon, which was detected in 1801, and brought into cultivation in 1838.　It was brought to Singapore in 1874, or perhaps earlier.　It can be grown successfully if given plenty of manure.　The seeds can be used as food. The leaves are very striking, being flat, five to seven feet in diameter, with a raised margin two to three inches high.　The large flowers are cream or pink and open at dusk.　The scent is heavy (MCM. p. 175 : Burk. p. 2230 : V. P. p. 165) :　บัวสา *Laos, Pre,* เมือง *Laos, Nakon Panom, Crotalaria juncea* (*Leguminosae*), sunn-hemp, an erect annual, 6 to 10 feet high, with bright yellow flowers, cultivated for the sake of the strong and useful fibre obtained from the stem by retting.

When young the plant may also serve as fodder for cattle, or for green-manuring (MCM. pp. 26, 424 : Burk. p. 685 : cb. p. 371) : บัวใส the breasts of a virgin ; breasts beautifully formed :　บัวหลวง *Siam.*, and *Laos* (ต้น) *Nelumbo nucifera* (*Nymphaeaceae*) (cb. p. 75) ; *Nelumbium nelumbo*, the sacred lotus, a member of a genus which has its home in south-eastern Asia.　We know it was grown in ancient Egypt.　The supposition is, it reached the Nile from Persia about the time of the Persian conquest (708 B. C.).　It has many uses.　In some countries the rhizomes are eaten all the year round, but it is grown less for food than for beauty.　Its association with Buddhism is intense.　From religion, it entered art, and a multitude of designs depend on representing its flowers or leaves.　The lotus is much planted near palaces and temples.　The seeds are highly esteemed and have been exported from Siam to Singapore.　In Siam the petals are used as wrappers for cigarettes (BURK. p. 1539) ; *Nelumbium speciosum*, a lotus lily with large handsome, peltate, circular, erect leaves, and large bright pink or white scented flowers.　The leaves are incapable of being made wet, owing apparently to the waxy surface, but really to closely set minute hairs. It is a beautiful plant ; the seeds and root-stock are edible (MCM. pp. 36, 174, 312, 379, 466, 516).

บะราลี, ปะราลี　　ba⁴-rah-lee *n.* miniature spires or serrated decorations placed along the roof edges of palaces or other important buildings.

บา　　bah *n.* a teacher, professor or preceptor ; a young man :　บาธรรม a preceptor or one versed in the law, doctrines or tenets of a religion ; see ครู p. 183.

บ่า　　bah⁴ *v.* to overflow or flow out of in a great quantity (as flood-water from a river): *n.* the shoulder :　บ่านี้ why ? for what cause, purpose or reason ? what ? why is this ? บ่าอ้าย (นก) the Indian scarlet minivet, *Pericrocotus flammeus* (Deig. N. H. J. S. S. VIII, p. 146).

บ้า bah[3] *n.* madness; idiocy; lunacy: *adj.* idiotic; crazy; insane: บ้า (ปลา) *Leptobarbus hoeveni (Cyprinidae)* (suvatti p. 45): บ้าจี้ to be ticklish: บ้าน้ำลาย a condition characterized by incoherent or disconnected speech: บ้าบิ่น a condition characterized by rashness, recklessness or mental instability; a kind of sweetmeat: บ้าเลือด a condition characterized by extreme anger or provocation to the extent of not fearing death even though blood should flow: บ้าบ๋า a person whose father is a Chinese and mother a Malay: บ้ายศ to be infatuated with honour, rank or position: บ้ายอ crazy after flattery; covetous of praise: ลมบ้าหมู (โรค) epilepsy: คนบ้ากาม one affected with nymphomania.

บาก bark[4] *v.* to cut or chip off the sides (as when squaring a log); to open a passage or widen a way (as by chopping the brush in a jungle); to chisel out the sides of a mortised timber so as to fit the tenon: บากท่าให้ to give another person a clew, intimation or inkling that leads to the solution of some problem or mystery: บากบั่น to be untiring in efforts to succeed; to be exceedingly industrious: บากหน้าเข้าหา to turn towards another for help; see ตั้งหน้า p. 358.

บาง bang *n.* a place; a locality; a village: *adj.* thin; sparce; scarce; rare; limited; fine (in billiards): คนบาง, บางตา few; scarce; not many people: บาง, ใบไผ่ (ปลา) *Opisthopterus macrognathus (Clupeidae)*, herring (suvatti p. 11): บางที sometimes; occasionally: บางเบา decreasing; lessening (used in reference to an epidemic or some serious symptoms): บางสิ่ง something: บางฮอก (นก) the large Malay green-billed malkoha, *Phopodytes tristis longicasedatus* (N. H. J. S. S. VIII, p. 160).

บ่าง bang[4] *n.* the flying lemur, *Galeopterus volans*, a peculiar mammal, at present included with the insectivora (Gaird. N. H. J. S S. III, 2 p. 123): บ่างใน the flying squirrel, including the genera *Petaurista Pteromys* and *Sciuropterus (Rodentia)* (Gaird. N. H. J. S. S. III, 2 p. 123).

บ้าง bang[3] *adj.* some: *adv.* somewhat; in some degree; about: อย่างนั้นบ้าง, อย่างนี้บ้าง sometimes like this, sometimes like that; some of this, and some of that.

บางสุ see บงสุ์ p. 466.

บาจก bah-chjok[4] *P. S. n.* a cook: บาจิกา a female cook (S. E. D. p. 614).

บาจรีย์ see ปาจรีย์ p. 523.

บาญช see บัญช p. 475.

บาด bat[4] *v.* to cause or make a cut, wound or mark; to feel rough, rasping or sharp to the fingers: มีบาดเจ็บ to be suffering from a cut: ให้บาดใจ to feel aggrieved at, or by: ให้บาดตา to be obnoxious or offensive to the eye: บาดทะจิตต์ a disease of lunatics characterized by a condition of fear or fright: บาดทะยัก tetanus: บาดแผล cuts or wounds; scars or scratches: บาดพิษ blood-poisoning: บาดเสี้ยนบาดหนาม a thorn wound complicated with inflammation: ให้บาดหมาง to be at variance; to be irritated; to be in a condition of dissension or disagreement with others.

บาดหลวง bat[4]-luang[2] *n.* Roman Catholic priests.

บาดาล bah-darn *P. S. n.* one of the seven regions under the earth, and the abode of the Nagas or serpents and demons; an excavation; a hole in the earth (S. E. D. p. 616).

บาต bat[4] *v.* to fall; to drop: บิณฑบาต *lit.* "the falling of masses of rice," *i. e.* that which drops into a priest's alms-bowl: อสนิบาต *lit.* "the falling of a line or streak from the skies," *i. e.* lightning.

บาตร bat[4] *S. n.* an open-mouthed pot of a truncated, spheroidical form, made of earth, iron, or brass, without ornaments, used by the Buddhist monks when going abroad, in their morning excursion, to receive the alms bestowed on them by the admirers of their holy mode of life (Legend of the Burmese Buddha I, p. 33); a drinking vessel; a goblet; a bowl; a cup; a dish; a plate; a pot; a meal (as placed on a dish) (S. E. D. p. 612): ตักบาตร to place alms or food in an alms-bowl: ไป ตักบาตร to go forth for alms.

บาท, ปาท bat[4] *P. S. n.* the foot (of men or animals); the foot or leg of an inanimate object, as a column or pillar; the foot or root of a tree; a foot or measure in poetry (S. E. D. p. 617): รองพระบาท shoes; slippers (used only for royalty): รอยพระบาท royal foot-prints: บาทนิเกต a footstool or foot-rest: บาทมงสุ์ dust of the feet: บาทบริจาริกา *lit.* "the feet of a maid who tries to please," *i. e.* a wife (chd. p. 314): บาทบูรณ์ a word or syllable added to fill out a line or to complete the poetical measure of a verse: บาทภัฏ infantry; foot-soldiers: บาทภาค one fourth part; a quarter: บาทมุทรา the impression of a foot-step; any mark or sign: บาทมูล *lit.* "foot-root," *i. e.* the sole or heel (also a polite designation for a person): บาทมูลิกากร *lit.* "the group nearest to the sole or heel of a king," *i. e.* government officials: บาทยุคล both feet (used for the king): บาทรช, บาท-รัช the dust of the feet: บาทรถี *lit.* "foot-vehicle," *i. e.* a shoe: บาทศาขา *lit.* "foot-branch," *i. e.* a toe: บาทศรรม numbness of the foot.

บาทุกา, บราทุกรา bah-too[6]-gkah *P. n.* a slipper; shoes; foot-wear (chd. p. 315).

บาน ๑, ป่าน ๑ barn *P.S. n.* a drink; a draught; the drinking of spirituous liquors especially; the drinking of saliva (as kissing); a drinking cup or vessel (S. E. D. p. 613): บาน-บาตร a drinking-vessel; a cup; a goblet: บานโภชน์ the act of eating and drinking: บานมงคล a drinking party; a drinking-bout; a tavern; a bar; a saloon: สุราบาน fermented liquors; whisky; intoxicants.

บาน ๒, คลี่ barn *v.* to unfold; to be in bloom (as flowers); to be opened or expanded:

n. panes (as glass); the hinged or sliding panels that close a door or window: *adj.* excessive; much as: เสียบาน, เสียมาก used to express great losses in games of chance: ใจเบิกบาน joyfulness; happiness: บาน ๆ ตูม ๆ part in bud and part in bloom (as an assortment of flowers): บานชื่น (ต้น) *Zinnia elegans (Compositae)*, a showy annual plant found from the south-western parts of the United States to Chili. They have been imported into Malaya and Siam. They seed themselves but the process tends to eliminate the finer flowers so that cultivation from imported seed is best (V. P. p. 160: MCM. p. 202: BURK. p. 2304): บานทะโรค piles; haemorrhoids: บาน!เที่ยง, ผักเบี้ยเล็ก (ดอก) *Portulaca quadrifida (Portutacacae)*, a small succulent herb, found as a weed in all the warmer parts of the world. It may serve as a vegetable but it is difficult to collect sufficient of such a small plant. The Malays use it to poultice boils and abscesses but in Sumatra it is used as a poultice for abdominal diseases; in Java it is used as cooling in fever (cb. p. 110: BURK. p. 1802): บานบุรี (ดอก) *Allamanda cathartica (Apocynaceae)*, willow-leaved *Allamanda*, a native of Brazil. This ornamental, quick-growing and free-flowering climber, with bright yellow flowers, received its name from its early use as a cathartic. The bush may be planted to form an ornamental hedge, but needs much trimming, which rather spoils its flowering. It makes a good stock on which to graft the less vigorous species of the genus (MCM. p. 122: V. P. p. 160: BURK. p. 98): บาน-บุรีม่วง (ดอก) *Allamanda violacea*, this purple-flowered *Allamanda*, native of Brazil, is said to have come to Bangkok about thirty years ago. It is not known when or by whom it was introduced. Also known by the above Siamese name, are two other purple-flowered garden climbers, *Cryptostegia grandiflora* and a *Bignonia*, neither of which, however, has the hairy branches and leaves of the *Allamanda* (winit, N. H. J. S. S. IX, 3, p. 266: BURK. p. 694); *Cryptos-*

tegia floribunda (winit, N.H.J.S.S. IX, 3, p. 271):
บานบุรีแสด (ดอก) *Odontadenia speciosa* (*Apo-cynaceae*), a woody climber cultivated in Malaya and Siam, but which originated in America. The flowers are beautiful: there is a little rubber in the stems (MCM. p. 127); Burk. p. 1577): บานบุรีหอม (ดอก) *Odontade-nia grandiflora*, an *Allamanda*-like fragrant flowering climber, native of tropical South America and usually known under the horti-cultural name of *Dipladenia harrissii*. It is not known when the plant first came to this country; but it appears that it was first introduced to Bangkok by Mom Rajotai about twenty-five years ago, probably from the Malay Peninsula (winit, N. H. J. S. S. IX, 1, p. 99): บานบุรีเหลือง (ดอก) *Allamanda, cathartica*, a handsome climber now very common in Siam, having been cultivated here for at least 35 years. The species is a native of tropical South America (V. P. p. 160: MCM. p. 122: winit, N. H. J. S. S. IX, 1, p. 89): บาน-ประตู the panel of a door: บานแผนก an index; an introduction to a story or book: บาน-พับ hinges: บานไม่รู้โรย (ดอก) *Gomphrena globosa* (*Amarantaceae*), globe amaranth, an annual, probably of American origin. It is free-flowering and is cultivated for its purple flowers in round heads. In the Moluccas it is a vegetable but elsewhere it seems culti-vated only for its flowers (V. P. p. 161: MCM. 134: Burk. p. 1097): บานเย็น (ดอก) *Mirabi-lis jalapa* (*Nyctaginaceae*), marvel-of-Peru; four o'clock flower, an annual herb coming from America but now common in all the tropics. It grows about two feet high and has white or pink flowers. The big tubers were formerly mistaken in Europe for jalap, and used as a purgative, but their action is very feeble. In western India the dried root is given in milk as a strengthening medicine. Bruised leaves are used in India and Java for poulticing boils and abscesses. Several parts of the plant are considered useful for the complexion (MCM. pp. 200, 386:

V. P. p. 161): บานหน้าต่าง the panel of a window.

บ้าน, บ้านช่อง ban[3] *n.* a house; a dwelling-place; a compound; a village: คนบ้านนอก peasantry; country people: บ้านนอก a country village: บ้านเมือง native land: เพื่อนบ้าน neighbours: ลูกบ้าน members of a village or family.

บานยะ see ปานิย p. 524.

บาบ bah-bee *P. S. n.* a sinner; a criminal; a reprobate; a scoundrel (S. E. D. p. 619).

บาป, ปาปะ bap[4] *P. S. n.* sin; wickedness; vice: *adj.* bad; vicious; wretched; villainous; depraved (S. E. D. p. 618): ดาวบาปเคราะห์ an inauspicious planet, as Mars, Saturn, Rahu, Ketu: บาปกำเหนิด original sin: บาปทฤษฎี an evil-eyed person: บาปมิตร a friend of sin: บาปวาท an inauspicious cry (as of the crow); rasping sounds which are obnoxious: ศีลแก้บาป the sacrament of penance.

บาพก see ป่าวก p. 525.

บาย bai *Cam. n.* rice; boiled rice: บายศรี *lit.* "propitious or auspicious rice," *i. e.* rice offered to the mysterious psyche hoping to bring good fortune (Ger. (1) p. 156).

บ่าย bai[4] *v.* to step to one side, *ex.* บ่ายพระ-ยาทเบี่ยง to deviate from a prescribed course or channel: บ่ายหน้า to turn the face from: บ่ายหัวเรือ to turn the bow of a boat (as when trying to avoid a rock while shooting the rapids): บ่ายเบี่ยง to swerve to one side (as a cunning argument to escape defeat): เวลาบ่าย afternoon.

บ้าย, ป้าย bai[3] *v.* to smear, daub or rub on roughly or carelessly; to throw the blame on, or incriminate another (as in a fault or offense); see ทา p. 410.

บายสุหรี่ bai-soo[4]-ree[2] *Jav. n.* a pond.

บารนี, ดั้งนี้ bah-ra[6]-nee *adj.* thus.

บารมี, ปารมี   bah-ra⁶-mee *P.S.* *n.* the transcendent virtues, of which there are ten, *viz.* (1) almsgiving; (2) morality; (3) relinquishing of the world and worldly possessions; (4) wisdom; (5) energy or fortitude; (6) patience under opposition; (7) truth; (8) firm purpose or determination; (9) charity; (10) indifference or equanimity (Ala. p. 184); completeness; perfection; the highest state (chd. p. 334).

บ้าระห่ำ   bah³-ra⁶-hum⁴ *adj.* audacious; impudent; turbulent; noisy.

บาเรียน   bah-rien *n.* a highly qualified student; one versed in the ethics, truths or tenets of a religion; a learned man.

บาล, ปาล   barn *P.S.* *v.* to guard; to preserve, protect, defend, rule or govern; to keep; to maintain; to observe (S. E. D. p. 622): *n.* a guardian or keeper: บาลเมือง the governor of a city.

บาลี, ปาลี   bah-lee *P.S.* *n.* Pali, (1) the language of the books of the southern Buddhists (Ala. p. 246); language of the sacred text; a secret text; a passage in a text: (2) a line; a row; a range; a ridge; a bank; a causeway; a series (Chd. p. 321); see มคธ.

บ่าว   bow⁴ *n.* a servant; an attendant; a slave; a young man: เจ้าบ่าว a bridegroom: เจ้าสาว a bride: งานบ่าวสาว a wedding: บ่าวสาว the bride and groom.

บาศ, ปาส   bat⁴ *P.S.* *n.* a snare; a trap; a noose; a band; a cord; a chain; a fetter (S. E. D. p. 623).

บาศก์   bat⁴ *P.S.* *n.* a dice (S. E. D. p. 623): รูปลูกบาศก์ a cube.

บ้าหมู (โรค)   bah³-moo² *n.* epilepsy: บ้าหมู (ลม) a whirlwind.

บาหลี   bah-lee² *n.* a small cabin at the stern of a junk: เกาะบาหลี the Island **Bali**.

บ๋ำ   bum² *adj.* dinted; dented; depressed (as if made by a blow).

บำเทิง see บันเทิง p. 477.

บำนาญ   bum-narn *n.* a reward; remuneration; a prize: เบี้ยบำนาญ a pension.

บำบัด   bum-bat⁴ *v.* to counteract; to check; to hinder; to afford means of relief (as in case of sickness); to act in opposition: บำบัดอันตราย to avert; to prevent (as danger or misfortune).

บำเพ็ญ   bum-pen *v.* to do; to observe or perform (as religious functions); to execute (as a religious duty); to fulfil to completeness: บำเพ็ญทาน to observe the duty of alms-giving: บำเพ็ญศีล to observe religious precepts.

บำราบ   bum-rap³ *v.* to subjugate; to subdue or overcome; to intimidate; to repress.

บำราศ   bum-rat³ *v.* to cause to disappear; to disperse or repel; to be free from (as enemies).

บำรุง   bum-roong *v.* to repair; to keep up in good condition; to support; to care for; to maintain: บำรุงเลี้ยง to nourish; see ตบแต่ง.

บำรู   bum-roo *v.* to decorate, adorn or ornament.

บำเรอ, เปรอ   bum-rur *v.* to wait on, serve or try to please; to help maintain the honour of: บำเรอเชอภักดิ์ to serve with loyalty and devotion: ผู้บำเรอชู้ one who lives on the earnings of a prostitute.

บำเหน็จ, รางวัล   bum-net⁴ *n.* a reward; remuneration; compensation; a bonus; a special return for services rendered

บิ   bi⁴ *v.* to pinch off or pick into small pieces (as when counting the petals of a flower); to separate into small shreds or fine pieces.

บิฐ, ตั่ง   bit⁴ *P.S.* *n.* a chair; a stool; a bench; the counter of a shop (chd. p. 385); see ตั่ง p. 358.

บิณฑ, บิณฑะ bin-da[4] *P.S. n.* a ball; a globe; a knob; a button; a clod; a lump; a piece; a roundish lump of food; a bite; a morsel; a mouthful; a ball of rice or flour; daily bread; livelihood (S. E. D. p. 625): บิณฑบาต a ladle full of rice which falls into an alms-bowl; the giving of alms to Buddhist monks: บิณฑบาตร an alms-dish or food-bowl: บิณฑ-บาท *lit.* "thick-footed; clod-like feet," *i. e.* an elephant.

บิด bit[4] *v.* to twist or twirl (as a lock of hair); to pervert, distort or misrepresent (as falsifying a statement); to play truant (as evading school duties); to feign or falsify by actions (as pretending to be sick): บิดกาย to twist, writhe, wrench or distort the body: บิดขี้เกียจ to seek to evade some duty through sheer laziness; to stretch or twist the body for the relief from malaise caused by laziness: บิดควง to screw in a bolt or screw: บิดละกูด *lit.* "to turn the rudder," *i. e.* to cause to sway or go crooked in course or conduct (implying vagrancy): บิดไปบิดมา to wriggle, squirm or writhe: บิดพลิ้ว to shirk; to avoid or evade the issue; to feign another occupation or errand; to use a false excuse: *n.* a subterfuge: บิด (โรค) dysentery.

บิดร, บิดา, บิตุ bi[4]-daun *P. n.* a father (chd. p. 385).

บิดหล่า bit[4]-lah[4] *n.* an auger; a gimlet.

บิตุฆาต bi[4]-dtoo[4]-kat[3] *P. n.* the murdering of a father; parricide (chd. p. 385).

บิตุจฉา see ปิตุจฉา p. 526.

บิตุรงค์, บิตุเรศ bi[4]-dtoo[4]-rong *n.* a father.

บิตุล, บิตุลา bi[4]-dtoon *n.* a father's older or younger brother; บิตุลานี a father's older or younger sister.

บิน bin *v.* to fly (by natural or artificial means): บินร่อน to fly hovering overhead.

บิ่น bin[4] *v.* to make a nick or notch in a sharp edge or blade; to nick (the edge of porcelain): *adj.* nicked; notched; blunted.

บิศาจ see ปิศาจ p. 527.

บี bee[3] *v.* to crush or mash out of shape; to cause a dint or depression (as in a silver bowl).

บีฑา, บีฑ, ปีฑา bee-tah *P.S. n.* pain; suffering; harm; injury; violation; damage; devastation (S. E. D. p. 629).

บีบ beep[4] *v.* to squeeze; to press; to compress; to express (as fruit juice): บีบคอ to strangle; to choke by a constricting force: บีบคั้น to oppress cruelly; to compress and extract the juice: บีบน้ำตา to cause tears [to flow.

บีเยศ see ปีย p. 527.

บุก (ปลา) buk[4] *n. Pangasianodon gigas* (*Pangasiidae*), a species of large scaleless fish found in the Mekong river (suvatti p. 88).

บุกบั่น burk[4]-burn *v.* to be stubbornly insistent or persistent; see ดื้อ p. 331.

บุง, บุ้ง burng *n.* an extensive swamp or marsh; low, flooded land.

บุ้ง burng[3] *adj.* sulky; sullen; cross; ill-humoured (used regarding facial expression): นั่งบุ้งตึง to sit scowling with ill-temper: บุ้ง (ตัว) *Melopaeus albostriatus*, mygale, an insect nesting in holes underground, which is eaten roasted in the fire, its eggs being also relished. This is the largest variety of mygale found in Indo-China. It is known that mygales are eaten boiled or stewed in Siam, Laos and Kamboja, while their eggs are considered a delicacy (J. S. S. II, 2, p. 158).

บุ boo[4] *v.* to supply with an internal lining (as a coat, dress or the pleura); to beat sheet metal into a required shape (as silver bowls or copper vessels).

บุก book[4] *v.* to press forward under adversity; to make headway through difficulties of jungle or underbrush (by cutting away the undergrowth): *n.* an edible species of large tuber similar to the calladium, having a gum that produces itching: บุกบั่น to be intrepid or unshaken in the presence of danger; to have undaunted courage: บุกรอ a species of large tuberous plant similar to the calladium, used medicinally by the Siamese: บุกรุก to trespass; to invade or penetrate by force: บุกรุกเข้าไปโดยกำลัง to enter by violence: บุกรุกลอบเข้าไป to enter secretly: ผู้บุกรุก a trespasser; an aggressor.

บุคคล, บุทคล, ปุคคล   book[4]-kon *P. n.* a creature; a being; a man; an individual or person as opposed to a multitude or class (chd. p. 390): บุคคลผู้ที่ he who; one who: บุคคลนิติสมมต a juristic person; a business firm, organization or any material possession having established rights and responsibilities in the eyes of the law. These are held culpable in case of infringement of law (as a boat, car, building or company): บุคคล-ผู้มีประโยชน์อันจะได้จะเสีย an interested person: บุคคลภายนอก a third party; a stranger to the consideration.

บุคคลิก   book[4]-ka[6]-lik[6] *P. adv.* individually; personally; specifically; concerned with an individual: บุคคลิกทาน alms given to a specified purpose or person (chd. p. 390): บุค-คลิกลักษณะ personality.

บุ่ง see บิ้ง p. 483.

บุ้ง (สัตว์)   boong[3] *n.* a caterpillar: บุ้ง (ตะไบ) a large coarse-toothed file for use on wood: บุ้ง (ผัก) *Ipomoea aquatica (Convolvulaceae)*, a small semi-aquatic creeper, with tender arrow-shaped leaves, often cultivated in peasants' gardens. The leaves and young stems are commonly used for vegetable curries. It thrives best in a shallow trench where moisture can be retained (MCM. p. 304: V. P. p. 161: Burk. p. 1245).

บุญ, บุญญ์, ปุญญ์   boon *P. S. n.* assets in the future life's balance sheet, resulting from good deeds; the antithesis of กรรม; merit; happiness or reward (as laid up for the future state or condition): *adj.* meritorious; pure; holy; sacred; good; auspicious; propitious; virtuous (S. E. D. p. 632): ใจบุญ of a meritorious disposition; kind-hearted; benevolent: ตามบุญตามกรรม according to one's merit or demerit: บุญญานุภาพ a supernatural power attained as a result of accumulated merit: บุญญาภิสังขาร *lit.* "merit plus complete adornment," *i. e.* the superior status or supernatural condition that results from merit: รู้บุญรู้คุณ grateful: ลูกบุญธรรม an adopted child: หาบุญไม่ dead.

บุณฑริก, ปุณฑริก   boon-da[4]-rik[6] *P. S. n.* the white lotus; an arithmetical notation in which the digit is followed by 112 cyphers (S. E. D. p. 631).

บุตร, ปุตตะ   boot[4] *P. S. n.* a son; a child (S. E. D. p. 632): บุตรกาม one desirous of sons or children: บุตรชาต one to whom a son is born: บุตรทาร a son and his wife: บุตรธรรม to observe the parental duty to a son; to perform the usual ceremony on the birth of a son: บุตรบุตร sons and grandsons: บุตรลับ, ลูกชู้ a bastard: บุตรหรือ ธิดาผู้สืบสายโลหิต an heir of the body: บุตรา-จารย์ (a father) having his son for his teacher.

บุตรี   boot[4]-dtree *P. S. n.* a daughter (S. E. D. p. 632).

บุถุชน, ปุถุชน   boo[4]-too[4]-chon *P. n.* a man of the lower classes or of low character; a common or ordinary man; one who is yet unconverted, as opposed to one who has entered the Eight-fold Path; a worldly, natural or unsanctified man; a sinner (chd. p. 396).

บุทคล, ปุทคล   boot[4]-kon *P.S. n.* the soul; the personal entity; man; the body (S.E.D. p. 633).

บุนนาค *Siam.*, นากบุค *Siam.*, *Peninsula* (ต้น)   boon-nak[3] *n. Mesua ferrea (Ternstroemiaceae)*, ironwood; Indian rose chestnut;

a moderate-sized, broad, conical, slow-growing, handsome tree, found from the Himalayas to the south of the Malay Peninsula. It blossoms profusely in the month of April or May, the large white flowers, each with its yellow centre of numerous stamens, being delicately scented. The young leaves, which appear twice a year, are of deep crimson, rendering the tree a striking object. It is a sacred tree in India. The timber is very good, and is profitably exploited in northern India, where the tree grows to a large size, and is plentiful enough even to supply sleepers, as well as to be used for buildings. Its durability in the soil is great. Oil is present in the seeds in sufficient quantity to suggest a trade in the seeds. The cake contains a bitter resin. Resin oozes from the base of the fruits while they are young and, diluted with turpentine, it can be used as a varnish; but it is not commercial. Pounded kernels are used medicinally after child-birth. The leaves enter largely into magic in Malaya (MCM. pp. 90, 91, 101, 213 : cb. p. 123 : BURK. p. 1458); *Schima crenata* (cb. p. 130); see กาไข้ p. 92.

บุบ   boop^4 *v.* to be dented, distorted or battered out of shape; to pound or knock lightly : *adj.* bent or pounded out of normal shape : บุบสลาย despoiled; cracked; broken or ruined.

บุปผ, ปุปผะ   boop^4-pa^4*P. n.* a flower; a blossom; the menses (chd. p. 393).

บุพพ ๑, บุรพ, ปุพพ, ปุรพ   boop^4-pa^6 adj. being before or in front; first; former; prior; preceding; previous to; earlier than; eastern; towards the east (S. E. D. p. 643): บุพพกรรม evil, wilful deeds or demerit of a previous existence; deeds done in a former existence : บุพพกาย the front part of the body (of men): บุพพการี *lit.* " previous benefactor," *lit.* father or mother : บุพพช *lit.* " one born first," *i. e.* the first-born; the eldest son; an ancestor; forefathers : บุพพชา the older sister or daughter : บุพพชาติ

a former birth; a previous state of existence or life : บุพพทักษิณ south-eastern : บุพพนิมิตต์ *lit.* " a forecasting dream or omen," *i. e.* a prognostic sign : บุพพนิวาส *lit.* "a former habitation," *i. e.* a former existence : บุพพบท, บุรพบท a preposition; the first member of a company : บุพพบุรุษ a forefather; an ancestor : บุพพประโยค what has formerly happened, or been fixed : บุพพเปตพลี merit made for those of the family who have previously died : บุพพภาค the fore part; the upper portion : บุพพัณหสมัย *lit.* " the beginning period of a day," *i. e.* the morning : บุพพาจารย์ *lit.* "the first teacher," *i. e.* a father and mother : บุพพาสา the east : บุพเพนิวาสานุสสติญาณ knowledge derived from the recollection of former existences (chd. p. 389) : บุพเพสันนิวาส the state of living in company with others in previous existences : บุพพาภาคชน the prior or preceding party.

บุพพ ๒, บุพโพ, ปุพโพ   boop^4-pa^6 *P. S. n.* ichor; pus; purulent matter; the discharge from an ulcer or wound (S. E. D. p. 641).

บุพพวิเทห์   boop^4-pa^6-wi^6-tay *P. n.* one of four large continents towards the east of India (chd. p. 389).

บุ่ม   boom^5 *adj.* dented; distorted (in shape).

บุ่มบ่าม   boom^4-bam^4 *adj.* awkward; uncouth; bungling; ungraceful; clumsy; rude; characterized by roughness.

บุ้ย   boo-ie^3 *v.* to pout : บุ้ยปาก to protrude or thrust out the lips in ill-humour.

บุร ๑, บุร, ปุระ   boo^4-ra^6 *P.S. adj.* in front; in advance; before (of place or time); in the presence of (S. E. D. p. 634).

บุร ๒   boo^4-ra^6 *P. S. n.* a fortress; a castle; a city; a town (S. E. D. p. 635): บุรชน, บุรโลก citizens of a city or town; townsfolk : บุรเทวดา the tutelary deity of a town : บุรนารี *lit.* " a town-woman," *i. e.* a courtezan.

บุรณะ, ปุณณ, ปุรณะ, ปูระ, ปูรณะ　　boo⁴-
ra⁶-na⁶ *P. S. adj.* full; fulfilled; complete;
entire (chd. p. 392).

บุรพ see บุพพ p. 485.

บุรัตถิมทิศ, ปุรัตถิมทิศ　　boo⁴-rat⁶-tim²-tit⁶
P. n. lit. "the front direction of the compass,"
i. e. east; eastern quarter (chd. p. 394).

บุราณ, เบาราณ, โปราณะ, ปุราณ　　boo⁴ran
P.S. adj. old; ancient; antique; belonging
to ancient or olden times (S. E. D. p. 635).

บุรินทท, ปุรินทท　　boo⁴-rin *P. n.* a name for
Indra (chd. p. 394).

บุรินทร์, บุ๋รินทร์　　boo⁴-rin *S. n.* a governor.

บุริมทิศ, ปุริมทิศ　　boo⁴-rim-tit⁶*P. n. lit.* "the
forward point of the compass," *i. e.* the east
(chd. p. 394): บุริมสิทธิ์ preferential rights.

บุรี, ปุรี　　boo⁴-ree *P.S. n.* a city; a town
(S. E. D. p. 636).

บุรุษ, ปุริส, ปุรุษ, โปส　　boo⁴-root⁴*P. S. n.*
man; a person; a male; people; mankind (S. E.
D. p. 637): บุรุษกาม sensual desire: บุรุษการ
human efforts; manly acts; heroism; virility;
pride: บุรุษชน men; people; citizens; populace: บุรุษธรรม personal rules or precepts:
บุรุษดี *lit.* "lord of men," *i. e.* Rama: บุรุษ-
มฤค a deer; a male antelope: บุรุษวร the
best men: บุรุษศารทูล *lit.* "a tiger-man,"
i. e. an eminent man: บุรุษสังสการ a ceremony performed over a dead person; a ceremony or religious service held in honour of
the dead (as the seventh-day rites).

บุษกร, ปุษกร　　boot⁴-sa⁴-gkaun *P.S. n.* a blue
lotus-flower; a lotus; the tip of an elephant's
trunk; an arrow; the hide head of a drum;
the sky (S. E. D. p. 638).

บุษบ, บุษป, ปุษป　　boot⁴-sa⁴-ba⁴ *P. S. n.* a
flower; a blossom (S. E. D. p. 639): บุษบกาล,
สมัยบุษบ *lit.* "flower-time," *i. e.* the spring; the
period of the menses: บุษบเกตน์, บุษบธวัช *lit.*

"characterized by flowers," *i. e.* the god of Love:
บุษบทาม, บุษบมาลา, บุษบเศขร a garland of flowers:
บุษบธนุ, บุษบพาณ *lit.* "armed with a bow of
flowers," *i. e.* name of the god of Love: บุษบ-
พลี an oblation of flowers: บุษบภาชน์ a
flower basket: บุษบรถ *lit.* "flower-chariot,"
i. e. a car for travelling or for pleasure:
บุษบรส *lit.* "flower-juice," *i. e.* the nectar or
honey of flowers: บุษบราค, บุษบราคัม *lit.*
"flower-hued," *i. e.* a topaz: บุษบวรรษ *lit.*
"flower-rain," *i. e.* flowers showered upon a
hero on any great occasion: บุษบหาส *lit.*
"smiling with flowers," *i. e.* a flower garden:
บุษบากร rich in flowers; flowery: บุษบาคม
lit. "flower-advent," *i. e.* the spring: บุษบา-
ปัณ a flower market: บุษบายุธ *lit.* "flower-
armed," *i. e.* the god of Love: บุษบาราม a
a flower garden.

บุษบามินตรา, พุทธรักษา (ต้น)　　boot⁴-sa⁴-
bah-min-dtrah *Jav. n. Canna spp.* (V. P. p. 194).

บุษย, ปุษย　　boot⁴-sa⁴-ya⁶ *S. n.* nourishment;
food; provisions (S. E. D. p. 640).

บุหงัน　　boo⁴-ngan² *Jav. n.* a flower: *adj.*
strong; physically powerful; robust; see แข็ง-
แรง p. 169.

บุหงา　　boo⁴-ngah² *Jav. n.* favours given at
weddings, composed of heavily scented flower-
petals enclosed in small fancy lace bags:
บุหงาปะหงัน, พุทธชาต (ดอก) *Jasminum auriculatum* (V. P. p. 193): บุหงามลาซอ, มะลิลา
(ดอก) *Jasminum sambac (Oleaceae)* (MCM.
pp. 112, 125: BURK. p. 1265), Arabian jasmine,
pichcha a shrub of Asia, cultivated from remote
times, but its earlier history is lost. There
are races with double flowers which have
been raised by man: บุหงาเบ๋า (ดอก) *Oxymitra
maclellandi (Annonaceae)* (V.P. p. 159): บุหงา
ใหญ่ (ดอก) *Uvaria rufa (Annonaceae)*, a
woody climber which is used medicinally in
Java. The bark, and in small measure the
leaves also, hold an alkaloid. This species

has been cultivated in Singapore (V. P. p. 159 : BURK. p. 2215).

บุหรง　　　boo⁴-rong² *Jav. n.* a bird; the peacock or peahen.

บุหรี่　　　boo⁴-ree⁴ *n.* cigars.

บุหลัน　　　boo⁴-lun² *Jav. n.* the moon.

บู่, บู่จาก, บู่ทราย, บู่ทอง, บู่หิน (ปลา) boo⁴ *n. Oxyeleotris marmorata (Eleotridae)*, sleeper (suvatti p. 151); *Glossogobius giuris (Gobiidae)*, gobies (suvatti p. 153): บู่เกล็ด แข็ง (ปลา) *Butis butis (Eleotridae)* (suvatti p. 150): บู่ขาว, บู่ทะเล (ปลา) *Acentrogobius caninus (Gobiidae)* (suvatti p. 155): บู่ดำ, บู่เอื้อย (ปลา) *Oxyeleotris siamensis (Eleotridae)* (suvatti p. 151): บู่ตะกั่ว (ปลา) *Drombus viridipunctatus (Gobiidae)* (suvatti p. 156): บู่เสือ (ปลา) *Thaigobiella sua (Gobiidae)* (suwatti p. 157): บู่หัวโต (ปลา) *Ctenogobius criniger* (Suvatti pp. 152, 153): บู่หัวมัน (ปลา) *Ophiocara porocephala (Eleotridae)* (suvatti p. 150).

บู้　　　boo³ *adj.* dented; damaged; flattened; distorted in shape: บู้บี้ disfigured; deformed.

บูชนีย　　　boo-cha⁶-nee *P. adj.* worthy of being revered or worshipped; venerable; honourable (S. E. D. p. 641).

บูชา, ปูชา　boo-chah *P. S. v.* to pay homage to superiors, or adoration of the gods. Such offerings are principally flowers, wax tapers and incense-sticks, which are offered before idols and in other holy places, also before the remains of deceased persons and to the tutelary deities of trees (Ala. p. 201): *n.* veneration; reverence; honour; worship; respect (S. E. D. p. 641): บูชายัญ a Brahmin sacrificial ceremony; burnt-offerings.

บูชิต, ปูชิต　　boo-chit⁶ *P. adj.* honoured; revered (chd. p. 391).

บูด　　　boot⁴ *P. adj.* rancid; sour; putrid; stinking : foul; corrupted (as in character); wry or distorted by pain (as the face) (chd. [p. 396).

บูรพ see บุพพ p. 485.

บูรพา　　　boo-ra⁶-pah *S. n. lit.* "the front direction of the compass," *i. e.* east (S. E. D. p. 643).

เบ้　　　bay³ *adj.* wry; bulging; twisted or distorted (as the lips protruding after a blow or as the result of inflammation): เบ้ *Karen*, สีเสียด *Siam.* (ต้น) *Pentace burmanica (Tiliaceae)*, a very large tree of rapid growth, with a valued timber which is exported to Europe, and is used locally. It is used in Burma for making boats, boxes, etc. where lightness is of value. In appearance it resembles mahogany and is sold as Burma mahogany (cb. p. 182 : BURK. p. 1688): หน้าเบ้ wry-faced (as a child about to cry).

เบ่ง　　　beng⁴ *v.* to strain or exert force in trying to expel (as fecal matter); to cause to swell, expand or be inflated by forcing air into; to be puffed up or protruding (as by gas or the result of inflammation).

เบ็ญกานี (ต้น)　ben-ya⁶-gkah-nee *n. Ponax cochleatum*, used as a remedy.

เบ็ญกาย　ben-ya⁶-gkai *n.* the wife of Hanuman the monkey-king, a character in the Ramayana.

เบ็ญจ, บัญจ　ben-chja⁴ *P. adj.* five (chd. p. 326): เบ็ญจกัลยาณี five feminine charms, *viz.* fine hair, red lips, pearly teeth, a blooming complexion, and youth: เบ็ญจกามคุณ five objects of desire or pleasure; objects of evil desire that are connected with the five senses: เบ็ญจกูล five spices, *viz.* ขิง *Zingiber officinale* (v. P. p. 50); ดีปลี *Unona latifolia* (v. P. p. 111); ช้าพลู, ชะพลู *Piper sp.* (V. P. p. 93); สะค้าน *Piper* (V. P. p. 249); เจตมูลเพลิงขาว *Plumbago zeylanica* (v. P. p. 85): เบ็ญจขันธ์ the five elements or attributes of corporeal being, *viz.* (1) form or matter; (2)

sensation of pleasure and pain ; (3) perception, enabling us to recognize or distinguish
things ; (4) consciousness ; (5) discrimination
(Ala. p. 172) : เบ็ญจครรภ an ewer for water
consecrated by means of Brahmanical mantras
in which are placed five gold plates as talismen, used in state ceremonies and the tonsure ceremony (Ger. (1) p. 39) : เบ็ญจคุปต์ *lit.*
" covered or protected in a five-fold manner,"
i. e. a tortoise (because it draws in its four feet
and head) (S. E. D. p. 575) : เบ็ญจตบะ " the five
fires" to which an ascetic who practices self-
mortification exposes himself, *viz.* one fire
towards each of the four quarters and the
sun overhead, thus sitting between the five
fires (S. E. D. p. 576) : เบ็ญจบรรพต the five
peaks (of the Himalayas) (S. E. D. p. 576) :
เบ็ญจพรรณ, เบ็ญจวรรณ *lit.* " five coloured," *i. e.*
five-fold ; of five kinds (S.E.D. p. 577) : เบ็ญจ-
พล *lit.* " the five physical forces, *viz.* (1) ศรัทธา
energy, firm purpose, determination (Ala. p.
184), faith, trust, devoutness ; (2) วิริย diligence, bravery ; (3) สติ attention, attentiveness, consciousness (Chd. p. 466) ; (4) สมาธิ
calmness, tranquility in mind (Chd. p. 435) ;
contemplation (Ala. p. 195) ; self-concentration ;
(5) ปัญญา reason, wisdom, wit, knowledge
(S. E. D. p. 576) : เบ็ญจพรรณ *lit.* " one having
five arrows," *i. e.* the god óf Love ; Eros ;
Cupid (H. C. D. p. 145) : เบ็ญจเพส twenty-five
years of age (Chd. p. 328) : มีอายุถึงเบ็ญจเพส
the attaining of the age of twenty-five years.
This, according to tradition, is considered a
very important period in that person's life,
because he generally has big ideas and pro-
digious schemes which the ancients believed
foretell his future actions : เบ็ญจภุช *lit.*
" five-armed," *i. e.* a name for Ganesa ; a pentagon ; pentagonal (S. E. D. p. 576) : เบ็ญจภูต
the five elements, *viz.* earth, air, fire, water,
atmosphere : เบ็ญจมาศ(ดอก) *Chrysanthemum
spp.*, an annual and perennial. There are
numerous varieties bearing flowers of various
colours. The plant grows 1½ to 3 feet high
(McM. p. 134 : V. P. p. 162) : เบ็ญจมุตร the

urine of five female animals, *viz.* the cow,
goat, sheep, buffalo and ass : เบ็ญจยุค a
cycle of five years ; a lustrum : เบ็ญจรงค์
containing five elementary colours : เบ็ญจ-
โลหะ a metallic alloy containing five metals,
viz. copper, brass, tin, lead and iron : เบ็ญจ-
โลหกะ the five metals, *viz.* gold, silver, copper,
tin and lead : เบ็ญจวรรค a class, group or
series of five, *viz.* (1) the five constituent
elements of the body ; (2) the five classes of
spies, *viz.* a pilgrim or rogue, an ascetic who
has violated his vows, a distressed agriculturist, a decayed merchant, a fictitious dévo-
tee ; (3) the five organs of sense ; (4) the five
devotional acts : เบ็ญจวรรณ see เบ็ญจพรรณ
p. 488 : เบ็ญจวัคคีย์ *lit.* " belonging to a group of
five," *i. e.* the five Brahmins who accompanied
Gotama Buddha when he embraced asceticism
(Chd. p. 328) : เบ็ญจศก the fifth year of
a decade according to Thai enumeration :
เบ็ญจศีล the five precepts or branches of moral
practice, *viz.* (1) abstinence from taking
life ; (2) from theft ; (3) from fornication ;
(4) from lying ; (5) from intoxication (Ala.
p. 174) : เบ็ญจางค์ (1) the five members or
parts of the body ; (2) the five parts of a
tree, *viz.* root, bark, leaf, flower, fruit ; (3)
the five modes of devotion, *viz.* silent prayer,
oblations, libations, bathing idols and feeding
Brahmins : เบ็ญจามฤต the five kinds of ambrosial food, *viz.* milk, coagulated or sour
milk, butter, honey and sugar.

เบ็ญจก, ปัญจก ben-chjok[4] *P. S. adj.* consisting of five ; relating to five ; made of five
(S. E. D. p. 578).

เบ็ญจม, เบ็ญจม ben-chja[4]-ma[6] *P. S. adj.*
the fifth ; forming a fifth part (S. E. D. p. 578) :

เบ็ญจา ben-chjah *n.* a dais under a temporary white canopy, erected during state ceremonies, or for the bath after the tonsorial
ceremony (Ger. (1) p. 41).

เบ็ด bet[4] *n.* a barbed hook : ตกเบ็ด to
angle for fish : เบ็ดตกปลา a fish-hook :

เบ็ดเตล็ด various; incidental; trifling; miscellaneous: เบ็ดเสร็จ altogether; entirely; collectively: สายเบ็ด a fishing-line and hook: เชือกเบ็ด a fishing-line: คันเบ็ด a fishing-rod.

เบน ben v. to turn the bow (as a boat to avoid a collision); to incline or turn to one side; to swerve to one side.

เบ๊อ, เบอะ, เหวอะ bur[3] adj. severe (descriptive of a deep gaping wound).

เบ๊อ เร่อ bur[3]-rur[3] adj. large; huge; gigantic.

เบะ, เบ้ be[4] adj. wry; twisted or contorted (as the face of a child about to cry).

เบา bow v. to pass urine: adv. lightly; gently; softly: ใจเบา wavering or unstable in mind; easily influenced: ดูเบา to show disdain or scorn: น้ำเบา urine: เบาความ forgetful, careless or not sufficiently attentive to particulars in matters of importance; inconsiderate; imprudent: เบาใจ being happy, free or light-hearted; care-free: เบาบาง few; sparse; alleviated; relieved: เบามือ gentle; having a light touch; having need to work but little: เบาหวาน diabetes: ไปเบาๆ to go slowly or cautiously (as a boat or car).

เบ้า bow[3] n. a crucible; a melting-pot for metals: เบ้าขลุบ a covered crucible; one having a lid.

เบาราณ see บุราณ p. 486.

เบาะ bau[4] n. a cushion: adj. having been struck or cut slightly or lightly: เบาะแส a clue; an intimation or inkling: เบาะแส สำนักงานใหญ่น้อยทั้งปวง all principal business offices; a permanent place of doing business (as an office).

เบิก burk[4] v. to open (as a blossom); to expose, disclose or dilate; to request payment by submitting authority for payment: เบิกของ to make a requisition for goods (as from a godown): เบิกเงิน to cash an order from a bank or treasury: เบิกทูต to present an envoy or minister to His Majesty the King or to other royal persons: เบิกบาน to be hilarious, joyful, happy or delighted: เบิกพระเนตร lit. "to open the eyes," i.e. to pencil in the pupil in newly made images of the Buddha by the use of a fine-pointed stylus. The image is not considered complete unless this is done by an expert, who is entitled to a small fee: เบิกเรือ to spread the sides of a canoe made from a hollowed log, by means of heat: เบิกล่อง (ใบ) a license for a boat or vessel to pass a port; port clearance papers: เบิกความ to give evidence in court; to make a statement of facts seen or heard.

เบิ่ง berng[4] v. to look; to stare; to turn or raise the head while looking (descriptive of the attitude assumed by surprised or enraged cattle).

เบี้ย beer[3] n. cowrie shells; money: ดอกเบี้ย interest; usury: บ่อนเบี้ย(โรง) a gaming house: เบี้ยทำขวัญ money or a fine paid by one party to another, in lieu of damages done; amount paid as a compensation: เบี้ยบำเหน็จ, เบี้ยบำนาญ a pension: เบี้ยโบก a gambling game where cowries are dashed into a bamboo joint and money staked on the number thrown in: เบี้ยประกันภัย insurance premium: เบี้ยปรับ the fine or fee paid into the court by the losing party in a lawsuit: เบี้ยเลี้ยง daily allowance for food: เบี้ยหวัด annual salary: เบี้ย (หอย) cowries; a variety of small ornamental shells used as money in ancient times. During the Ayuthian period the legal value was 800 to a fuang. In A. D. 1862 they ceased to be used for such purposes (Le May, J. S. S. XVIII, 3, p. 194): เล่นเบี้ย to use cowries in gambling games.

เบียก bee-ak[4] v. to divide; to distribute: เบียกย้าย, เบียกแว้ง to make a proportionate division of funds; to distribute pro rata.

เบี่ยง bee-ang[4] v. to turn aside (in order to

avoid): เบี่ยงบ่าย to evade meeting (by turning away); to put aside funds (for a time of want): พูดเบี่ยงบ่าย to speak in an ambiguous manner or in a way to avoid the issue or conceal the truth; to equivocate.

เบียด bee-at[4] *v.* to squeeze or press closely between other bodies (as in a crowd): เบียด-กัน to be closely or compactly placed together (as passengers in a tram car); see ชิด p. 296.

เบียดกรอ bee-at[4]-gkraw *adv.* miserly; selfishly; penuriously: *adj.* living from hand to mouth; impecunious.

เบียดบัง bee-at[4]-bung *v.* to misappropriate; to cheat, steal or filch.

เบียดเบียฬ bee-at[4]-bien *v.* to oppress unjustly; to persecute unduly; to worry, annoy or molest others.

เบี้ยว biew[3] to be pressed, pulled, twisted or distorted from a nomal shape: เบี้ยว (ปลา) *Belodonichthys dinema (Siluridae)* (suvatti p. 69): ปากเบี้ยว a disfigured mouth (as from paralysis).

เบียฬ bien *v.* to ill-treat; to persecute unjustly or unduly; to cause pain, worry or hardship; to oppress, squeeze or pinch (as when inflicting a punishment).

เบือ bua *v.* to be surfeited with; to have too much.

เบื่อ bua[4] *v.* to cause death by poisoning; to have a feeling of revulsion, dislike or disgust: เบื่อปลา to catch fish by poisoning: ยาเบื่อ a narcotic; a poisonous or toxic drug: *adj.* having power to produce toxic symptoms.

เบื้อ bua[3] *n.* a mythological animal resembling a human being.

เบื้อง, ข้าง buang[3] *n.* side; direction: *prep.* towards: *adj.* facing; situated at, or on one side: เบื้องขวา on the right side: เบื้องน่า in the future; in front of: เบื้องปลาย the end; the extremity: เบื้องว่า if; provided that: เบื้องหลัง behind; that which is past.

เบือน bur-an *v.* to turn (the face away from); to twist or distort: เบือนหนี to wheel and flee: เบือนหลัง to turn the back towards.

แบ baa *v.* to spread out; to unfold, reveal or open out for inspection: แบมือ to open the palm of the hand.

แบ้ baa[3] *adj.* twisted or turned backward (as horns of cattle); crooked.

แบก bak[4] *v.* to carry on the shoulder; to support (as a scheme or proposition): แบกไป to carry off on the shoulder or back: เเบก ไว้แทน to assume responsibility for another (as in trouble); to be a coworker with others.

แบ่ง, บั่น bang[4] *v.* to divide, separate or share with; to apportion; to allot; to assign: แบ่งเงินปันผล to pay a dividend: แบ่งภาค to assume a human form; to be embodied in the flesh: *n.* incarnation: แบ่งไม่ได้ indivisible: แบ่งแยก to separate; to partition off (as a piece of land).

แบน ban *adj.* flat: level; even.

แบบ bap[4] *n.* a pattern; a plan; a copy; a a model; a system or scheme to follow: *adj.* weak, exhausted or worn out (as a result of disease or hardship): แบบเคร้งการ a schedule or program of proceedings: แบบที่หวงแหน reserved rights on a plan: แบบบาง frail; thin; delicate; fragile; easily damaged: แบบ แผน established customs; treaties; text-books; rules; patterns: แบบเรียน text books: แบบ อย่าง an example (as laid down by common usage).

แบรก, แปรก brak[4] *n.* a square wooden frame through which the axle of a bullock cart passes, and to which the shafts are fastened.

แบหลา baa-lah[2] *Jav. v.* to die: *adj.* lying supinely as though dead.

แบะ baa[4] *v.* to be spread wide open, or to gape (as a large incised wound): to break open or split apart: *adj.* being spread out;

lying flattened out (as a book) : แบะแฉะ lazy; neglecting duties; indolent.

โบ้, โบ๋   boh[4] *adj.* perforated; containing holes (as a deep, gaping wound).

โบก   bok[4] *v.* to swing or wave back and forth (as a fan or flag); to flap; to apply plaster or cement over a surface : โบกธง to signal by waving a flag : โบกมือ to beckon with the hand.

โบกขร, โบษขร, โปกขร   bok[4]-kaun[2] *P. S.* *n.* a lotus; a lotus leaf, *Nelumbium speciosum* (*Nymphaeaceae*); *Nymphaea nelumbo* (chd. p. 387); *Nelumbium nelumbo*, the sacred lotus (Burk. p. 1538 : see บัวหลวง) : โบกขรพรรษ, โปกขรพรรษ a shower of rain, the drops of which collect on the lotus leaves.

โบกขรณี, โปกขรณี   bok[4]-ka[4]-ra[6]-nee *P.* *n.* a lotus pond; a tank; a reservoir (chd. p. 387).

โบดก, โปดก (p. 537)   bote[4]-gka[4] *P. S.* *n.* the young of an animal (chd. p. 388).

โบตัน *Chinese, Bangkok* (ต้น)   boh-dtun *n.* *Epiphyllum oxypetalum* (*Ficoideae*) (cb. p. 783); *E.* (*Cactaceae*), night blooming cereus, a leafless plant, bearing very showy, bright pink or crimson flowers. Its home is tropical America. Numerous species and varieties exist and have an unmerited reputation for producing longevity. This is doubtless due to their slow growth for the plant seems to have no medicinal value (MCM. pp. 171, 202 : BURK. p. 930).

โบย, เฆี่ยน   boie *v.* to whip, thrash, strike, beat or flog (chd. p. 388); see เฆี่ยน p. 220.

โบราณ   boh-rarn *P. adj.* ancient; primeval; former (chd. p. 387) : โบราณคดี ancient stories, fables, legends or histories.

โบสถ   boh-sot[4] *P. n.* the sanctuary in a Buddhist monastery; the hall or chapel where the ปาติโมกข์ is read (chd. p. 535); see p. 524.

ใบ   bai *n.* a designatory particle for thin, round, flat objects, as leaves, sails, fruit, buckets, marbles : ใบกำกับของ a way-bill : ใบขนุน (ปลา) *Pseudorhombus arsius* (*Paralichthyidae*), bustard halibuts (suvatti p. 94) : ใบเงินใบทอง *Graptophyllum hortense* (*Acanthaceae*), the caricature plant, a garden herb with leaves blotched with red. It grows 4 to 5 feet high. It is used medicinally as an application to cuts, and the juice is squeezed into the ear for ear-ache. It is recommended for application in certain skin complaints, and in an infusion to be drunk for constipation (MCM. p. 120 : BURK. p. 1110) : ใบจักร the blades of a propeller : ใบแจ้งความ *legal* a circular : ใบเชื่อ a credit note : ใบฎีกา a subscription issued by Buddhist monks soliciting donations for meritorious objects ; an invitation : ใบตราสิน an affidavit : ใบตอง banana leaves or that portion stripped from the midrib : ใบตาล (ปลา) *Helostoma temmincki* (*Helostomidae*) (suvatti p. 103) : ใบถือหุ้น share-warrant; share-certificate : ใบบอก an official notice or letter (as from a suburban official to a superior) : ใบบุญ *lit.* "merit as a protecting leaf," *i. e.* a condition of peacefulness and joy under the power of merit : ใบเบิก an order for goods or money : ใบปก the binding or cover of a book : ใบประกัน, ใบประทวน a warrant : ใบประกาศ notifications : ใบปลิว leaflets (for distribution) : ใบพัด wind wheel blades : ใบโพธิ์ (ปลา) *Drepane punctatus* (*Drepanidae*) (suvatti p. 141) : ใบไม้ the leaves of a tree : ใบยกเว้น an exemption ticket or certificate : ใบรับดอกเบี้ย a coupon : ใบรับสินค้า a bill of lading : ใบเรือ the sails of a boat : ใบรูปพรรณสัตว์ a registration paper for animals : ใบลาน prepared palm leaves (intended for writing purposes) : ใบสั่งจ่าย a cheque; an order for the delivery of goods; a draft : ใบสำคัญที่ว่าได้จดทะเบียนแล้ว a certificate of registration : ใบสำคัญหุ้นส่วน a share certificate : ใบสุทธิ a certificate of honourable dismissal : ใบเสร็จ, ใบรับเงิน a receipt : ใบเสร็จที่บริษัทให้เมื่อกู้เงิน a debit-warrant : ใบหน้า a facial expression or characteristic : ใบหนังสือ a sheet or page of a book : ใบหู the external ear : ใบเหยี่ยบย่ำ see ตราจอง p. 343 : ใบอนุญาต a license : ใบอนุญาตขับรถยนตร์ a license to drive a motor car : ใบอนุญาตนำสินค้าเข้าประเทศ

an import license : ใบอนุญาตมีอาวุธปืน a firearm license : ใบอนุญาตส่งสินค้าออกจากประเทศ an export license.

ใบ้   bai³   *adj.* dumb ; mute.

ป

ป The twenty-seventh consonant in the Thai alphabet, a middle class letter of which there are nine, *viz.* ก, จ, ฎ, ฏ, ด, ต, บ, ป, อ. ปอปลา is the name of this letter. It is nearly equal to the English "p," a labial pronounced like "ปอ." In Sanskrit and Pali it is pronounced like "ป" It is used interchangeably, in Siamese, with "บ" in combination with verbs and their derivatives.

ป   bpaw   *P. adj.* front ; foremost ; first leading ; previous ; mostly used in connection with a verb, especially with a verb of motion which is often to be supplied, though sometimes it precedes the verb ; rarely is it used as a separate word (S. E. D. p. 652).

ปก   bpok⁴   *v.* to cover, hide or veil ; to put upon ; to over-spread : *n.* that which is spread or fitted over, or which encloses anything ; a cover : ปก (นก) Burmese crimson-crested barbet, *Xantholaema haemacephala indica* (Deig. N. H. J. S. S. VIII, 3, p. 159) : ปก, ปกส้ม (ปลา) *Puntius orphoides (Cyprinidae)* (suvatti p. 29) : ปกเกล้าปกกระหม่อม a form of address used when speaking to His Majesty and royalty : ปกครอง to govern ; to look after ; to take care of ; to keep under control ; to rule over : ปกคลุม to spread over or upon : ปกป้อง, ปกปักรักษา to protect or shelter (from harm) ; to keep safely : ปกปิด to hide, conceal or secrete : ใบปก a cover or back (as for a book) : ผู้ปกครอง a guardian ; a possessor : ผู้ปกครองที่ดินตามข้อและตามเวลากำหนดในหนังสือเช่า a tenant by lease.

ปกติ, ปรกติ   bpa⁴-gka⁴-dti⁴   *P. n.* original or natural form ; conventional, traditional, natural or unaltered state ; normal (chd. p. 319).

ปกรณ์   bpa⁴-gkaun   *P. S. n.* a dissertation ; an exposition ; a literary composition ; a treatise ; a book (chd. p. 318).

ปกิณณกะ   bpa⁴-gkin-na⁶-gka⁴   *P. adj.* miscellaneous ; scattered (chd. p. 319).

ปกิต, ประกิต   bpa⁴-gkit⁴   *P. S. adj.* announced ; proclaimed ; revealed ; said ; stated ; mentioned (chd. p. 319).

ปโกฏิ   bpa⁴-gkote⁴   *P. n.* a numeral in which the digit is followed by fourteen ciphers, *ex.* 100,000,000,000,000 (chd. p. 321).

ปคุณ   bpa⁴-koon   *P. S. adj.* straight ; plain ; familiar ; known by heart (chd. p. 316).

ปชา, ปชากร   see **ประชา, ประชากร** p. 498.

ปชุณหะ   bpa⁴-choon-ha⁴   *P. n.* a cloud (chd. p. 318).

ปฏล   bpa⁴-dta⁴-la⁶   *P. S. n.* a covering ; a coating ; a membrane or film ; a roof (chd. p. 356).

ปฏิการ   bpa⁴-dti⁴-gkarn   *P. n.* atonement ; a remedy ; amends ; reparation (chd. p. 361).

ปฏิกูล   bpa⁴-dti-gkoon   *P. adj.* contrary ; disagreeable ; offensive ; loathsome (chd. p. 362).

ปฏิคม   bpa⁴-dti⁴-kom   *P. n.* an host ; an hostess.

ปฏิคคหิต   bpa⁴-dti⁴-ka⁶-hit⁴   *P. adj.* received; admitted; assented to; approved (chd. p. 361).

ปฏิคคาหก bpa⁴-dtik⁴-kah-hok⁴ *P. n.* a recipient of alms (chd. p. 361).

ปฏิฆะ bpa⁴-dti⁴-ka⁶ *P. n.* wrath; rage; anger; hatred (chd. p. 361).

ปฏิญญา, ปฏิญาณ, ปะฏิชญา, ประฏิญาณ, ประดิชญา bpa⁴-dtin-yah *P. n.* an agreement, promise or vow; a solemn declaration (chd. p. 364).

ปฏิทิน, ประดิทิน, ประติทิน bpa⁴-dti⁴-tin *n.* an almanac; a calendar.

ปฏิบถ bpa⁴-dti⁴-bot⁴ *P. n.* a confronting road (chd. p. 365).

ปฏิบัต, ปฏิบัตติ์, ปรนนิบัต bpa⁴-dti⁴-bat⁴ *P. v.* to serve or minister to; to perform; to practise (as religious rites); to observe (as ceremonial functions); to keep or obey (as precepts): *n.* conduct; practice; occupation; acquisition (chd. p. 365).

ปฏิปทา bpa⁴-dti⁴-bpa⁴-tah *P. n.* ingress; access; way; step; course; progress; practice; conduct (chd. 364).

ปฏิบักขี์ bpa⁴-dti-bpak *P. n.* an opponent or enemy; hostility (chd. p. 365).

ปฏิพัทธ์ bpa⁴-dti⁴-pat⁶ *P. v.* to be joined together or associated with: *adj.* being bound to, or dependent upon (chd. p. 358).

ปฏิภาค bpa⁴-dti⁴-pak³ *P. n.* proportion; comparison; resemblance: *adj.* equal to; resembling; similar (chd. p. 358).

ปฏิภาน bpa⁴-dti⁴-pan *P. n.* understanding; intelligence; wisdom; readiness or confidence of speech (chd. p. 358): ปฏิภานปฏิสัมภิทา discrimination; analysis (chd. p. 366).

ปฏิมา, ปฏิมากร bpa⁴-dti⁴-mah *P. n.* a counterpart; a representation; a figure; an image; a picture (chd. p. 362): ปฏิมาฆร a hall in a Buddhist temple in which a counter-

part, image, figure, or picture is placed (as a statue of the Buddha).

ปฏิรพ bpa⁴-dti⁴-rob⁶ *P.* an echo (chd. p. 365).

ปฏิรูป bpa⁴-dti⁴-roop³ *P. n.* a figure or image used as a pattern or for the sake of comparison: *adj.* suitable; fit; proper (chd. p. 366).

ปฏิโลม bpa⁴-dti⁴-lom *P. adj.* contrary; reverse: *adv.* in inverse order; backwards (as of a Sudra father and Brahmin mother) (chd. p. 362).

ปฏิวาต bpa⁴-dti⁴-wart³ *P. adv.* against the wind (chd. p. 370).

ปฏิวาท bpa⁴-dti⁴-wart³ *P. n.* a retort; a recrimination (chd. p. 370).

ปฏิเวธ bpa⁴-dti⁴-wet³ *P. n.* penetration; comprehension; attainment (chd. p. 370).

ปฏิสนธิ์ bpa⁴-dti⁴-son² *P. n.* entering the womb in a new existence; conception; rebirth (chd. p. 368); transmigration.

ปฏิสสวะ, ประติศรัพ bpa⁴-dtit⁴-sa⁴-wa⁶ *P. n.* the breaking off or non-fulfillment of a promise (chd. p. 369).

ปฏิสังขรณ์ bpa⁴-dti⁴-sung²-kaun² *P. n.* restoration; repairs (chd. p. 368).

ปฏิสันถาร bpa⁴-dti⁴-sun²-tarn² *P. n.* a welcome; a friendly greeting; a salutation expressing kindliness, affection or friendliness (chd. p. 368).

ปฏิสัมภิทา bpa⁴-dti⁴-sum²-pi⁶-tah *P. n.* analytical science; discrimination (chd. p. 366).

ปฏิเสธ bpa⁴-dti⁴-set⁴ *P. v.* to deny; to abjure, renounce or disavow; to prohibit: *n.* prohibition (chd. p. 368): ปฏิเสธข้อหา to refute the allegation.

ปฐพี, ปฐวี, ปถพี, ปถวี bpa⁴-ta⁴-pee *P. n.* the earth (chd. p. 357).

ปฐม, ประถม bpa⁴-tom² *P. adj.* first;

initial; primary; foremost; earliest; previous; principal; chief; best (chd. p. 357): ปฐม-กรรม *lit.* "the first duty," *i. e.* an obligation discharged (as after some great achievement); name of the ceremony observed in celebration of a signal victory. In ancient times it is said that, as part of this ceremony, the feet of the victorious king were sprinkled with the blood of the vanquished. However in succeeding years this ceremony has taken on a more lenient aspect in the form of a religious service after a successful victory achieved. During the period of King Naresuan this ceremony was observed after a victory over the Cambodians. On December 3rd, 1918, with unforgettable impressiveness, this ceremony, the พระราชพิธีปฐมกรรม, was observed in the open air on the Pramane Ground by His Majesty King Rama VI as a service of Thanksgiving for the victorious termination of the Great World War (The Bangkok Times, 3rd December, 1938): ปฐมฌาน the initial stage of a series of states of mystic or abstract meditation. Of this state there are six spiritual faculties, *viz.* วิตก consideration, which, like the wings of a bird, raises the mind to contemplation; วิจาร reflection, which is contemplation itself; ปีติ which is the satisfaction which fills the body; สุข which is the thorough happiness following on the satisfaction; เอกัคคตา which is fixedness of the mind on a single object; อุเบกขา which is perfect indifference to everything (Ala. p. 195: Chd. p. 139); see ญาณ p. 314: ปฐมบุรุษ a personal pronoun. According to the Pali grammar it is the third person or the one spoken of as "he," "she." According to Siamese grammar it is the first personal pronoun as "I," "we": ปฐมยาม the first watch. Formerly the night was divided into three watches of four hours each, the first ปฐมยาม, the second มัชฌิมยาม, the third ปัจฉิมยาม (chd. p. 595): ปฐมวัย *lit.* "in the prime of youth," *i. e.* from the first to the twentieth years: ปฐมสมโพธิ a biography of the life of the Buddha, or the

first (festival of) omniscience (Ala. p. 75).

ปณต, ปณม, ปณาม see ประณต p. 499.

ปณิธาน, ปณิธิ, ประณิธาน, ประณิธิ bpa⁴-ni⁶-tarn *n.* the formulation of a purpose, determination or scheme to be carried out in the future (especially used in regard to some huge undertaking).

ปณีต see ประณีต p. 499.

ปด, ปดโป้ bpot⁴ *v.* to lie; to prevaricate, evade or conceal the truth: *n.* a falsehood or untruth.

ปติวรัดา bpa⁴-dew-rat⁶-dah *S. n.* the faithfulness of a wife to her husband; a virtuous wife.

ปติ bpa⁴-dti⁴ *P. S. n.* master; owner; lord; chief; ruler; husband (chd. p. 358): ปติวัตร fidelity; love; conduct or faithfulness of a wife towards her husband.

ปติยัตต์ bpa⁴-dti⁴-yat⁶ *P. S. v.* to prepare; to make ready; to provide; to arrange; to adorn (chd. p. 371).

ปถพี, ปถวี see ปฐพี p. 493.

ปทัสถาน bpa⁴-tat⁶-tarn² *S. n.* the approximate cause (chd. p. 314).

ปทาน see ประทาน p. 501.

ปทานุกรม bpa⁴-tah-noo⁶-gkrom *n.* a dictionary; a lexicon; a word-book.

ปทีป see ประทีป p. 501.

ปธาน see ประธาน p. 501.

ปน, ปะปน bpon *v.* to mix; to combine; to impregnate or mingle with; to adulterate: ปนเป intermixed; miscellaneous; mixed indiscriminately together.

ป่น bpon⁴ *v.* to pound or crush: *n.* a sauce used as a condiment: *adj.* powdered; pounded; broken (as rice): ป่นปี้ totally defeated or routed (as an army); completely ruined (financially).

ปนุท see ประณุท p. 499.

ปบ bpop[4] *v.* to chase after and catch with both hands (as crickets or grasshoppers).

ปบาต see ประบาต p. 502.

ปบัญจะ bpa[4]-bpun-chja[4] *P. n.* slowness; sluggishness; tardiness (chd. p. 331): ปบัญจธรรม *lit.* "desires or practices inducing sluggishness," *i. e.* ตัณหา carnal lust; มานะ pride; arrogance; vanity (chd. p. 238); ทิฏฐิ false doctrine; heresy (chd. p. 126).

ปพาพ see ประพาล p. 502.

ปภพ see ประภพ p. 503.

ปภัสสร, ประภัสสร bpa[4]-pat[6]-saun[2] *P. n.* brightness; illumination: *adj.* shining (as the moon's rays) (chd. p. 306).

ปภา see ประภา p. 503.

ปภาพ see ประภาพ p. 503.

ปเภท see ประเภท p. 503.

ปม, บุ่ม bpom *n.* a knot; a knob; a node; [a protuberance.

ปมุข see ประมุข p. 503.

ปโย bpa[4]-yoh *P. S. n.* water; milk; rain; any fluid or juice (S. E. D. p. 586): ปโยชนม์ *lit.* "water-birth-place," *i. e.* a cloud: ปโยธร *lit.* "containing water or milk," *i. e.* a cloud: ปโยธรา a woman's breasts; an udder: ปโยนิธิ *lit.* "a receptacle for water," *i. e.* the sea: ปโยราศิ *lit.* "a collection of water," *i. e.* the ocean.

ปรก, ปิด bprok[4] *v.* to cover, shelter, hide or veil: *n.* a place where Buddhist monks live apart or are kept under restraint, being one of the ecclesiastical punishments (chd. [p. 348).

ปรกติ see ปกติ p. 492.

ปรคนธรรพ์ (พระนารท) bpa[4]-ra[6]-kon-tun *S. n.* chief of the heavenly musicians and the inventor of the lute (H. C. D. p. 218).

ปรง *Siam., Chantaburi,* ปรงแดง *Siam., Tachin,* โปลง *Siam., Chumpawn,* แหม่ *Siam.,*

west coast of the Peninsula, from Pangnga southwards (ต้น) bprong *n. Cycas circinalis (Cycadeae)*, a palm-like plant, 8 to 15 feet high or more, with very handsome, long, feathery leaves. The large farinaceous seeds are ground and made into a useful sago by the low-country peasants of Ceylon (MCM. p. 366); *Ceriops tagal (Rhizophoraceae)* (cb. p. 594): ปรงขาว *Siam., Tachin,* แหม่ *Siam., Puket,* แสม่มาเนาะ *Siam., Satul* (ต้น) *Ceriops roxburghiana (Rhizophoraceae)* (cb. p. 593 : V. P. p. 175): ปรงญี่ปุ่น, ปรงจีน (ต้น) *Cycas revoluta,* an ornamental foliage shrub. This cycad, a native of China and Japan, has been in cultivation in Bangkok for about 50 years. It is not known who first brought it into the country. Its leaves are in much demand for the making of wreaths (N. H. J. S. S. VIII, 3, p. 202 : MCM. pp. 119, 151 : BURK. p. 719).

ปรตยักษ์ see ประจักษ์ p. 497.

ปรตยาค see ประจาค p. 498.

ปรตเยก see ปัจเจก p. 519.

ปรน, ปรนปรือ bpron *v.* to feed, care for, shelter or protect; see บำรุง p. 482.

ปรนนิบัติ see ปฏิบัติ p. 493.

ปรบ bprop[4] *v.* to strike against; to clap; to beat time (according to the rhythm of music): ปรบไก่ (เพลง) a Siamese folklore song sung antiphonally by men and women, the hands being clapped in unison with the rhythm of the music: ปรบปีก to flap the wings: ปรบหัตถ์ to clap the hands; to applaud: ปรบหู to flap the ears (as an elephant); see ตบ p. 340 and ขยับ p. 142.

ปรม bprom *P. adj.* highest; first; best; greatest; chief; exceeding; extreme (chd. p. 335): ปรมัตถ์ usefulness in the highest degree; the best or highest sense or state; completeness; perfection (chd. p. 334): ปรมาณู *lit.* "the finest of dust," *i. e.* a particle; an atom (chd. p. 334): ปรมาภิไธย *lit.* "the most exalted one," *i. e.* a title for His Majesty the King : ปรมินทร์, ปรเมนทร์ he who is the chief or greatest : ปรเมศวร์ *lit.* "he who is lord of all," *i. e.* a name for Siva : ปรเมษฐ์ *lit.* "he who is excellent," *i. e.* the Hindu Brahma or any supreme deity (chd. p. 93).

ปรเมหะ bpa⁴-ra⁶-may-ha⁴ *n.* the title of a medical treatise relating to the diseases originating from disorders of the kidneys and urine.

ปรวด bpa⁴-ruat⁴ *n.* a cyst ; a name for an elephant doctor.

ปรวนแปร bpruan-bpraa *v.* to cause to alter, change, differ or be transformed.

ปรศุ bpa⁴-ra⁶-soo⁴ *S. n.* an axe ; a hatchet (chd. p. 381) : ปรศุราม *lit.* "Rama with the axe," *i. e.* an incarnation of Vishnu (H. C. D. p. 37).

ปร๋อ bpraw² *adj.* fast ; quick ; speedy.

ปรองดอง bpraung-daung *adi.* being amiable or agreeing with others ; manifesting harmony ; conciliatory ; see ตกลงกัน p. 339.

ปรอด (นก) bpa⁴-raut³ *n.* Blanfords or the ashy-fronted bulbul, *Pycnonotus blanfordi* (Gaird. J. S. S. IX, 1, p. 2) : ปรอดหัวโขน (นก) the Bengal red-whiskered bulbul, *Otocompsa emeria* (will. N. H. J. S. S. I, 2, p. 79) : ปรอด-หน้านวล (นก) the yellow-vented bulbul, *Pycnonotus analis* (will. N. H. J. S. S. J, 2, p. 79) : ปรอดสวน (นก) Blanford's bulbul, *Pycnonotus blanfordi* (will. N. H. J. S. S. I, 2, p. 80).

ปรอท bpa⁴-raut³ *P. n.* mercury ; quick-silver (chd. p. 333).

ปรอย, โรย bproy *adj.* drooping (as eyelids) ; continuous but gentle (as rain).

ประ bpra⁴ *v.* to sprinkle ; to spray ; to cause to hit : ประไก่ to make trial of strength (as in a combat between two cocks) : ประแป้ง to apply face-powder in spots : ประวิสรรชนีย์ to write the vowel as double dots (ะ) : ประพรม an euphonic combination.

ประกบ, ประกับ bpra⁴-gkop⁴ *v.* to mend, unite or join together by splicing (as by overlapping or bevelling the ends of timbers) ; to fit surface to surface (as lengthwise boards or timbers) : ประกบกัน the condition where two flat surfaces are made to come together (as the position of two kites when flying).

ประกฤต bpra⁴-gkrit⁴ *P. S. v.* to do ; to make in great quantities (chd. p. 319).

ประกฤติ bpra⁴-gkrit⁴ *S. n.* root ; origin : *adj.* ordinary ; in its natural or original state ; sound and healthy (chd. p. 319).

ประกวด, ประกวดประขัน bpra⁴-gkuat⁴ *v.* to contest for ; to compete or contend for : *n.* a contest ; a competition ; a conflict ; a rivalry ; see แข่งขัน p. 169.

ประกอบ bpra⁴-gkaup⁴ *v.* to be endowed with (as supernatural power) ; to be added, fitted, or joined together to form a design (as colours in a painting or sections in inlaid work) : ประกอบกัน supporting ; acting as an auxiliary or accessory : ประกอบด้วย mixed, compounded or composed of (as ingredients in a remedy) : สมประกอบ to substantiate or corroborate (as secondary evidence by witnesses) : ส่วนประกอบ ingredients ; component parts.

ประกัน bpra⁴-gkun *v.* to go security for ; to bail out ; to guarantee : *n.* bond ; bail ; security ; guaranty : ประกันชีวิตร life insurance : ประกันภัยค้ำจุน guarantee insurance : ประกันภัยทะเล marine insurance : ประกันไฟ fire insurance.

ประกาย bpra⁴-gkai *n.* a flash or rays of radiating light ; a spark : ประกายพฤกษ์ Venus as a morning star ; see ดาวประจำรุ่ง p. 327.

ประการ bpra⁴-gkarn *P. S. n.* sort ; kind ; species ; manner ; items ; count (as separate charges in an inditement) : จะทำประการใด what would better be done ? ทุกประการ in every respect (chd. p. 318).

ประกาศ   bpra⁴-gkart⁴ *S. v.* to make manifest or known; to proclaim or announce publicly: *n.* a notification; a proclamation (chd. p. 319): ประกาศโฆษณา to issue a public notification: ประกาศสงคราม a declaration of war: ประกาศให้ใช้กฎอัยยการศึก to proclaim martial law: ป่าวประกาศ to give public notice.

ประกาศก   bpra⁴-gkah-sok⁴ *S. n.* an announcer; a proclaimer; one who explains, illustrates or makes known (chd. p. 318).

ประกาศนียบัตร   bpra⁴-gkah-sa⁴-nee-ya⁶-bat⁴ *n.* a diploma; a testimonial or certificate.

ประกาศิต   bpra⁴-gkah-sit⁴ *S. n.* an exposition; a publication; an order or command; a notification (chd. p. 318).

ประกิจ see **ประกอบ** p. 496.

ประกิต see **ปกิต** p. 492.

ประคด   bpra⁴-kot⁶ *n.* a cloth used as a girdle, sash or breast covering.

ประคบ   bpra⁴-kop⁶ *v.* to apply heated salt, sand or medicinal herbs tied in a cloth as a compress (used with a gentle circular pressure in case of bruises): ลูกประคบ name of the small bag so made and used.

ประคบประหงม   bpra⁴-kop⁶-bpra⁴-ngom² *v.* to care for with solicitude.

ประคอง   bpra⁴-kaung *v.* to carry or handle cautiously (as when moving a piece of furniture); to hold or support carefully (as with both hands to prevent toppling over); to watch over assiduously (as an infant or a sickly child).

ประคับประคอง   bpra⁴-kup⁶-bpra⁴-kaung *v.* to watch and guard with meticulous care.

ประคำ   bpra⁴-kum *n.* a rosary; a chaplet or garland (as of roses): ประคำร้อย (ฝี) abscessing glands along the side of the neck:

ประคำน้ำเงิน (นก) fairy bluebird, *Irena puella* (Gaird. J. s. s. IX, 1, p. 2.)

ประเคน   bpra⁴-ken *v.* to present an offering or gift to a Buddhist monk. This is done by approaching him in a respectful manner. The gift, being held with both hands, is raised and lowered directly into his hand.

ประโคน (เสา)   bpra⁴-kon *n.* a large boundary post or stake.

ประโคม   bpra⁴-kom *v.* to play on various instruments as a prelude or overture.

ประจง see **บรรจง** p. 468.

ประจบ, ประเหลาะ   bpra⁴-chjop⁴ *v.* to make two ends join or meet closely (as boards): ประจบประแจง to flatter, fawn over, cajole or play up to for selfish purposes; to make use of sycophancy, fulsome compliments, undue praise, or attention, in order to ingratiate oneself.

ประจวบ, บรรจวบ   bpra⁴-chjuap⁴ *v.* to meet; to find or come together accidentally.

ประจ๋อประแจ๋   bpra⁴-chjaw²-bpra⁴-chjaa² *adj.* flattering; honey-mouthed; smooth-tongued; blandiloquent (used in regard to speech).

ประจักษ์, ปรตยักษ์, ปรัตยักษ์   bpra⁴-chjuk⁴ *P. adj.* clear; plain; perceptible (to the senses); visible; evident (chd. p. 308): ประจักษ์แจ้ง manifest; striking; prominent; apparent; glaring; conspicuous: ประจักษ์ความ direct evidence: ประจักษ์พะยาน an eye-witness.

ประจัญ, ประจญ   bpra⁴-chjun *v.* to meet in combat; to fight against or oppose: ประจัญบาน a forward attack; a charge of military forces armed with short weapons: ประจัญภัย to face disaster or calamity: ประจัญหน้ากัน to come face to face with another.

ประจัน   bpra⁴-chjun *v.* to partition off (as a room or living quarters); to separate or divide off by means of a partition or barricade; see กั้น p. 85.

ประจาค, ปรตยาค, ประยาค bpra⁴-chjak⁴ *P. v.* to give; to abandon; to be separated from: *n.* abandonment; renunciation; sacrifice; liberality (chd. p. 338).

ประจาร bpra⁴-chjarn *S. v.* to insult, expose, or abuse publicly; to humiliate, disgrace or dishonour openly.

ประจำ bpra⁴-chjum *v.* to be placed permanently; to be regular, constant, steady or continual; to be retained (as a lawyer or physician): ประจำการ being or serving constantly on duty: ประจำครั้ง to seal or fasten up enduringly: ประจำตัว habitual: ประจำปี annually: ประจำยาม the name for a pattern of decorative art: นักเรียนประจำ boarding-pupils: โรคประจำ a disease that is firmly established from long continuance: โรคประจำเดือน the menses; menstration.

ประจุ see บรรจุ p. 468.

ประจุคมน์ bpra⁴-chjoo⁴-kom *v.* to rise from one's seat in token of respect to a visitor.

ประเจก see บัจเจก p. 519.

ประเจิด see บรรเจิด p. 468.

ประเจิดประเจ้อ bpra⁴-chjert⁴-bpra⁴-chjur³ *adj.* unduly exposed or uncovered (as portions of the body); unconcealed; unclothed.

ประเจียด (ผ้า) bpra⁴-chjee-at⁴ *n.* magic handkerchiefs or napkins. These are marked with intricate cabalistic designs, symbols, lettering and numbers believed to make the wearer proof against bullets, bayonets and bombs.

ประแจ see กุญแจ p. 110

ประชด, ประทยด, ประเทียด bpra⁴-chot⁶ *v.* to damn with faint praise; to use sarcastic, derisive or disrespectful comparisons; to indulge in personalities; to ridicule in indirect ironical language: คำประชด ridicule; derision; disrespect; disparagement.

ประชวร, บัชชร bpra⁴-chuan *v.* to be sick, indisposed or ill (used for royalty).

ประชัน, ประชน bpra⁴-chun *v.* to compete; to meet in competition or combat.

ประชา, ปชา, ปชากร bpra⁴-chah *P. S. n.* a creature; an animal; man; mankind; people; subjects (of a prince); offspring; children; race; descendants (S. E. D. p. 658): ประชากร, ประชาชน, ประชาราษฎร์ populace; citizens; inhabitants; residents; villagers: ประชากัลป์ the time or era of creation: ประชาคมวิทยา sociology: ประชาทาน *lit.* "people's gift," *i. e.* silver; money: ประชาธิปไตย a republic: ประชาบดี *lit.* "lord of creatures," *i. e.* a divinity presiding over procreation; a protector of life; a creator: ประชาบาล *lit.* "protector of creatures," *i. e.* a name of Krishna; a ruler; a governor; a municipality: ประชาภิบาล the office of a protector of the people; a royal office.

ประชายินี bpra⁴-chah-yi⁶-nee *S. n.* one bearing, bringing forth or about to bring forth; a mother.

ประชิด bpra⁴-chit⁶ *v.* to come nearer; to approach closer to; to be contiguous: *adj.* neighbouring; adjoining; adjacent; *geom.* adjacent (angles).

ประชุม, ประชวม, ผะชุม bpra⁴-choom *v.* to assemble; to meet; to congregate: การประชุมใหญ่ a general meeting: การประชุมใหญ่สามัญ an ordinary general meeting: การประชุมวิสามัญ an extraordinary general meeting: การประชุมสามัญ an ordinary meeting: การประชุมโดยเบิดเผย a public meeting: การประชุมโดยไม่เปิดเผย a meeting *in camera*: การประชุมตั้งบริษัท a statutory meeting: ที่ประชุม a meeting-place.

ประเชิญ bpra⁴-chern *v.* to collide; to hit; to strike; to bump; to encounter (as friends); to join the edges of cloth together.

ประฏาก bpra⁴-dak⁴ *P. S. n.* a flag, banner or ensign (S. E. D. p. 581).

ประณต, ประณม, ประณาม, ปณต, ปณม,
ปณาม bpra[4]-not[6] *n.* a salutation rever-
ently made (as by placing the palms of the
hands together and bending forwards, or
bowing the head) (S. E. D. p. 659).

ประณีต, ปณีต bpra[4]-neet[3] *S. adj.* exact;
careful; accurate; precise; correct; scrupulous; particular; delicate; fine; executed with
mathematical precision (as craftsmanship)
(S. E. D. p. 660).

ประณุท, ปนุท bpra[4]-noot[6] *P. v.* to check;
to relieve, or cause the condition to improve;
to remove, drive or scare away (chd. p. 331).

ประดง bpra[4]-dong *n.* a rash or skin
disease characterized by excessive itching and
burning; a form of eczema.

ประดน ๑ bpra[4]-don *S. adj.* old; ancient
(S. E. D. p. 661): ประดนธรรม ancient truths,
practices or doctrines; see เก่า p. 124.

ประดน ๒ bpra[4]-don *v.* to add more; to
give in addition to what has already been
given; to make up what is still lacking; see
ประดวน see กระดวน p. 26. [แถม p. 393.

ประดอน bpra[4]-daun *v.* to cork, plug or
stop up a hole.

ประดักประเดิด bpra[4]-duk[4]-bpra[4]-dert[4] *adj.*
troublesome or inconvenient, or accomplished
with great difficulty.

ประดัง bpra[4]-dung *adj.* pressing; squeezing; crowded together (as animals in a stampede): งานประดัง urgent work requiring
the simultaneous efforts of many: เสียง
ประดัง the shouting in unison of a vast crowd.

ประดับ, ประดับประดา bpra[4]-dup[4] *v.* to
decorate, ornament, adorn or beautify: เครื่อง
ประดับ ornaments; decorations: ประดับกาย
to adorn oneself.

ประดา ๑ bpra[4]-dah *v.* to advance in rows,
or side by side; to march abreast: *adj.* all;
entire; complete: ประดาทัพ to place or
arrange troops in lines standing abreast:
ประดาพล to advance troops in lines moving
abreast: ประดาเสีย inferior, low, wicked,
completely disgraced or dishonoured.

ประดา ๒ bpra[4]-dah *adj.* strong; able to
endure or bear; tolerant; see ทน p. 394:
คนประดาน้ำ an expert diver.

ประดาป, ประตาปะ bpra[4]-dap[4] *S. n.* dignity; power; strength; energy; glowing
heat; warmth; splendour; brilliance (S. E. D.
[p. 661).

ประดิชญา see ปฏิญญา p. 493.

ประดิทิน see ปฏิทิน p. 493.

ประดิษฐ์ bpra[4]-dit[4] *P. S. v.* to originate,
invent, devise, make, or set up: *n.* fixity;
strength (chd. p. 369); steadfastness; firmness
(S. E. D. p. 671): ประดิษฐ์ประดอย to be decorated profusely, delicately and gracefully
(an euphonic combination).

ประดิษฐาน bpra[4]-dit[4]-sa[4]-tarn[2] *P. S. v.* to
lay, place or enshrine permanently (as sacred
relics): *n.* establishment; standing; permanency; a firm resting place, ground or
foundation; a pedestal (S. E. D. p. 671).

ประดุจ bpra[4]-doot[4] *adv.* as; as if; like
unto; such as; for example; see ดัง ๒ p. 323.

ประดู่ *Siam.,* ดู่ *N. Laos* (ต้น) bpra[4]-doo[4]
*n. Pterocarpus cambodianus (Leguminosae);
P. indicus,* a large tree, native of Malaysia,
but so extensively planted that it is not easy
to ascertain its natural distribution. The
tree likes a rainfall of more than 60 inches,
and deep well-drained soil. Young plants
seem to need more light than is allowed in a
forest. Therefore it grows best along the
road-side or in fairly isolated plantings. The
durability of the wood is good (BURK. p. 1829);
P. macrocarpus (cb. pp. 485; 486: V. P. p. 174),
a handsome, very large tree of Burma, having a spreading round head, long drooping
branches, and rather small pinnate leaves. It

bears a profusion of yellowish, sweet-scented flowers in March or April, followed by small, circular, winged pods (MCM. pp. 103, 213, 219, 518). The leaves are three to six inches long, and have seven to eleven ovate leaflets which are bluntly pointed. The seed pod is circular in outline, short-beaked, flat, and of a papery texture. The sap-wood is small, while the heart-wood is dark red, close-grained, moderately hard, quite durable and is not attacked by white ants (The Orn. Trees of Hawaii, p. 115): ประดู่ขาว *Laos, Surin,* สะตือ *Thai.* (ต้น) *Crudia chrysantha (Leguminosae)* (cb. p. 537): ประดู่ทะเล *Thai., Bangkok* (ต้น) *Afzelia retusa (Leguminosae),* a timber tree (cb. p. 533): ประดู่ลาย *Thai., Chonburi,* ประดู่เสน *Thai., Krat,* กระยุง *Khmer, Surin,* หัวสีเมาะ *Chinese* (ต้น) *Dalbergia cochinchinensis (Leguminosae)* (cb. p. 475); *Pterocarpus gracilis var. Nitidus (Leguminosae),* a beautiful tree (cb. p. 486).

ประเด, ผะเด   bpra[4]-day *v.* to give over the whole to another; to pour out lavishly (as funds); see ทุ่มเท p. 419.

ประเด็น, ผะเด็น   bpra[4]-den *n.* an important question, point or matter at issue.

ประเดิม, ผะเดิม   bpra[4]-derm *v.* to begin, start, or commence; to be the first to initiate (as a scheme or plot); see ตั้งต้น p. 358.

ประเดี๋ยว   bpra[4]-diew[2] *adv.* shortly; presently; immediately: คอยประเดี๋ยว just wait a moment.

ประแดง, บาแดง, ผะแดง   bpra[4]-dang *n.* a carrier or conveyor of notices, orders or messages; an envoy; a low official rank in the Civil Service.

ประแดะ   bpra[4]-daa[4] *n.* a goldsmith's hammer; a horn, chisel-shaped implement used by silversmiths.

ประโดย see โดย p. 338.

ประตง (โจร)   bpra[4]-dtong *Jav. n.* a robber; a burglar; a plunderer.

ประตยาค see ประจาค p. 498.

ประตัก see กระตัก p. 30.

ประตาปะ see ประดาป p. 499.

ประติชญา, ประติญาณ see ปฏิญญา p. 493.

ประติทิน see ปฏิทิน p. 493.

ประติรพ, ประติรพ   bpra[4]-dti[4]-rop[6] *v.* to scream, yell or squawk loudly.

ประติศรัพ see ปฏิสสวะ p. 493.

ประตู   bpra[4]-dtoo *n.* a gate; a door; an entrance; an exit; the goal (in football): ประตูป่า a gateway or archway decorated with branches of trees, erected as part of the funeral ceremonies before removing a corpse from the house, or in celebration of bringing an elephant into the city, or when troops march out of a city: ประตูลม the space between the base of adjacent fingers or toes. From a surgical standpoint the Siamese consider these spaces vital localities as the air (blood) might unduly escape as a result of a puncture or wound: ประตูน้ำ a watergate [or lock.

ประถม see ปฐม p. 493.

ประทม see บรรทม p. 469.

ประทวน   bpra[4]-tuan *n.* a ministerial warrant, diploma or certificate appointing an official to a post or office.

ประทักษ์   bpra[4]-tuk[6] *adj.* industrious; diligent; efficient; smart.

ประทักษิณ, ปทักขิณ   bpra[4]-tuk[6]-sin[2] *S. v.* to turn towards persons or things so as to place them on one's right; moving to the right; standing or placed on the right (S. E. D. p. 679).

ประทัง   bpra[4]-tung *v.* to temporize; to prolong; to use palliative means to mitigate some exigency (as the endeavour to prolong life); a transitory policy.

ประทัด   bpra⁴-tut⁶ *n.* firecrackers: ประ-ทัดลม a small toy torpedo exploded by being thrown with force: ประทัด, ประทัดจีน *Thai., Bangkok* (ต้น) *Quassia amara (Simarubaceae)*, a flowering shrub which is a native of tropical America and not of China as the local name might imply. It was known to the American Indians before the Spanish discovery of America, and was made known in Europe in 1696. The tree furnishes the quassia wood of commerce. Extract of quassia is used as an insecticide in order to impart to leaves, etc., a flavour which prevents injurious insects from eating them. It was first brought to Bangkok by Mom Rajotai some 20 years ago (winit, N. H. J. S. S. IX, 1, p. 103: MCM. p. 116: Cb. p. 239: BURK. p. 1849): ประทัดฝรั่ง (ต้น) *Russelia juncea, Zucc*, coral plant. A grass-like leafless flowering plant, native of tropical America. It was first introduced to Bangkok, 29th June, 1933 (winit, N. H. J. S. S. IX, 1, p. 103: BURK. p. 1921).

ประทับ   bpra⁴-tup⁶ *v.* to stop, stand, sit or be in residence (used only for royalty): ประทับตรา to affix a seal or stamp: บ่าประทับบ่า to shoulder a gun: เรือพระที่นั่งประทับท่า to come alongside a landing stage and stop (as a royal barge).

ประทุม, หนอน   bpra⁴-tum *Cam. n.* a worm; a maggot.

ประท่า   bpra⁴-tah³ *n.* the opposite bank of a river.

ประทากล้อง, ประทาราศ   bpra⁴-tah-gklaung³ *n.* gold-leaf of the best and thickest quality.

ประทาน, บรรทาน, ปทาน   bpra⁴-tarn *S. v.* to give; to grant; to bestow (used only for royalty) (S. E. D. p. 679): ของประทาน a gift; a donation; a present; a bequest; a gratuity; a peace-offering.

ประทีป, ปทีป   bpra⁴-teep³ *S. n.* a lamp; a light; a torch (S. E. D. p. 680); a lantern; an [enlightener.

ประทุก see บรรทุก p. 469.

ประทุน   bpra⁴-toon *n.* a half-moon shaped cover for Thai boats, which is made of two layers of woven bamboo strips, between which are strips of sewn nepa palm leaves or other waterproof material. These are stitched together with rattan.

ประทุษ   bpra⁴-toot⁶ *P. S. v.* to manifest or exhibit a desire to harm or oppress; to commit an offence against; to become faithless, depraved, corrupt, or defiled (S. E. D. p. 680): ประทุษร้าย to conceive, manifest, perform, or be guilty of harm, damage, injury or oppression; to inflict want or injury: ประทุษร้าย-ส่วนแพ่ง to do civil injury or tort.

ประทุษฏี   bpra⁴-toot⁶ *P. S. adj.* corrupt; wicked; bad; sinful; wanton; licentious: ประทุษฏจิตต์ evil-mindedness; anger; revenge.

ประเทศ, ผะเทศ   bpra⁴-tet³ *P. S. n.* place; region; district; country; territory; nation (S.E.D. p. 680): ต่างประเทศ foreign: ประเทศ-ซึ่งมีสงครามกัน belligerent nations: ประเทศที่-เปนกลางในเวลาสงคราม a neutral country in time of war: ศาลต่างประเทศ Court of Foreign Causes; the International Court.

ประเทา   bpra⁴-tow *v.* to cause to improve or to be relieved in condition or state; to convalesce; to ameliorate or mitigate; to make [milder.

ประเทียด see ประชด p. 498.

ประเทียบ   bpra⁴-tiep³ *n.* a royal concubine: รถพระประเทียบ a carriage for the use of royal concubines: เรือพระประเทียบ boats or barges for the use of royal concubines.

ประเทือง, บรรเทือง   bpra⁴-tuang *v.* to exert means for the improvement of position or condition; to bolster, prop or support by any means; to alleviate the condition.

ประธาน, ปธาน   bpra⁴-tarn *S. adj.* principal; chief; pre-eminent; excellent (chd. p. 314): *n.* a chief thing or person; the most important or essential part of anything; the principal or first: ผู้เป็นประธานในที่ประชุม a chairman.

ประธานาธิบดี bpra⁴-tah-nah-ti⁶-bau-dee *n.* a president (one chosen by the people): ผู้รองประธานาธิบดี a vice-president.

ประนอ, ประนอม .bpra⁴-naw *v.* to humour; to concede to another's wishes; to agree with or consent to (in order to pacify in a strained condition); see ถนอมใจ p. 379.

ประนัปดา bpra⁴-nup⁶-dah *S. n.* a great-grandson (s. e. d. p. 681).

ประนี้, อย่างนี้ bpra⁴-nee⁵ *adv.* thus; like this; in this way or manner.

ประบาต, ปบาต bpra⁴-bat⁴ *S. v.* to fall down from, out or into; to precipitate oneself from a rock: *n.* a chasm; an abyss; a cliff; a precipice; a cascade; a waterfall (s. e. d. p. 682).

ประปราน bpra⁴-bpran *n.* the ˙ sound of crying, shouting or yelling.

ประปราม bpra⁴-bpram *v.* to beat or pound one's chest (in manifestation of sorrow or despair).

ประปราย bpra⁴-bprai *adj.* slightly; trifling; scattered; sparse; thinly diffused (as rain or spray).

ประปา bpra⁴-bpah *S. n.* a place for supplying water; a supply of water; a place for watering cattle, or a shed on the roadside containing a reservoir of water for travellers; a fountain; a cistern; a well (s. e. d. p. 682); city water supply. The scheme for the Bangkok waterworks was sanctioned by King Chulalongkorn on February 23rd, 1908. The first appropriation towards the cost appeared in the Budget estinates of 1909.

ประเปรี้ยง bpra⁴-bprieg³ *adj.* a loud ear-splitting sound (as a peal of thunder).

ประเปรียว bpra⁴-bpriew *adj.* adroit; clever; dextrous; active; nimble; see คล่อง p. 184.

ประพจน์, ปาพจน์, ปาวจนะ bpra⁴-pot⁶ *S. n.* the discourse or word of the Buddha; the Buddhist holy scriptures (chd. p. 374); a recitation; oral instruction; an exposition; an interpretation or announcement; excellent speech or language.

ประพนธ์, ประพันธ์ bpra⁴-pon *P. S. v.* to compose or compile a literary work in flowery words, or in serial story.form: *n.* any literary production; a composition; a continuous literary series; a narrative; fiction (chd. p. 305).

ประพฤติ bpra⁴-prut⁶ *S. v.* to behave, act, or perform: *n.* (1) practice; observance; performance (as of religious duties) (chd. p. 365); (2) manner; deportment; conduct; behaviour.

ประพฤทธ์ bpra⁴-prut⁴ *S. adj.* growing; increasing; developing; advancing (chd. p. 374).

ประพัทธ์ bpra⁴-pat⁶ *v.* to join or be joined together; to be connected, bound, tied or united in an uninterrupted manner (as in verse or rhyme); see เนื่อง p. 464.

ประพาต see ประวาต p. 504.

ประพาล, ปพาฬ, ปวาฬ bpra⁴-parn *S. n.* coral; a hard calcareous substance of various colours and shapes secreted by marine polyps for support and habitation (s. e. d. p. 691).

ประพาส, ประวาส, ปวาส bpra⁴-pat³ *S. v.* to dwell or go abroad; to be absent from home; to be addicted to living away from home; to travel or sojourn abroad (used for royalty) (s. e. d. p. 691).

ประพิณ see ปวีณ p. 513.

ประพุทธ์ bpra⁴-poot⁶ *P. v.* to be awakened; to be aroused from sleep; to know, understand or be enlightened; to be clear-sighted, clever and wise (s. e. d. p. 683).

ประเพณี, ประเวณี, ปเวณี bpra⁴-pay-nee *P. S. n.* tradition; custom; rule; usage; succession; line; the condition of being handed down from generation to generation in accordance with custom or tradition (chd. p. 376).

ประแพร่งประแพรว bpra⁴-praang³-bpra⁴-praa-oh *adj.* beautiful because sparkling, twinkling or radiant.

ประโพธ bpra⁴-pote³ *P. n.* one becoming conscious after waking from sleep; an awakening; enlightenment; intelligence (chd. p. 307: S. E. D. p. 683).

ประไพ, ประไพร, งาม bpra⁴-pai *adi.* beautiful; pretty; handsome.

ประภพ, ปภพ bpra⁴-pop⁶ *S. n.* birth-place; source; origin; production (S. E. D. p. 684); the place where an object is first perceived (chd. p. 306).

ประภา, ปภา bpra⁴-pah *S. n.* light; radiance; splendour; light variously personified (S. E. D. p. 683).

ประภากร bpra⁴-pah-gkaun *S. n. lit.* "making light," *i. e.* the sun; the moon; fire; *lit.* "light-giving," *i. e.* an epithet of the sun (chd. p. 306): ประภาคาร, กระโจมไฟ a light-house.

ประภาพ, ปภาพ bpra⁴-pap³ *S. n.* power; might; majesty; dignity (chd. p. 307).

ประภาษ bpra⁴-pat³ *P. S. v.* to speak; to tell; to declare, disclose or explain; to call or name (S. E. D. p. 684).

ประภาส bpra⁴-pat³ *P. S. v.* to shine; to illumine; to glitter; to enlighten (S. E. D. p. 684): *n.* illumination; light.

ประเภท, ปเภท bpra⁴-pet³ *S. n.* variety; species; kind; sort; subdivision (S. E. D. p. 684); distinction; difference (chd. p. 307).

ประมง see **ประโมง** p. 503.

ประมวญ, ประมวล bpra⁴-moo-an *v.* to collect or gather together; to codify; to systematize (as laws); to collect together: ประมวญกฎหมายแพ่ง และ พาณิชย์ a criminal and

commercial code: ประมวญกฎหมายอาชญา the Penal Code: ประมวญแพ่ง the Civil Code.

ประมัตตะ bpra⁴-mut⁶-dta⁴ *P. S. adj.* inattentive; careless; heedless; negligent; forgetful; indulging in mental inactivity (S. E. D. p. 685).

ประมาณ, ปริมาณ bpra⁴-marn *P. S. v.* to estimate; to approximate (as to weight, dimensions or cost): *n.* an approximation (S. E. D. p. 685): พอประมาณ approximately enough.

ประมาท bpra⁴-mart⁴ *S. v.* to be careless or negligent; to be indifferent or heedless about; to idle away time; to neglect duty; to underrate or deprecate others (S. E. D. p. 685): พูดสพประมาท, พูดหมิ่นประมาท to libel; to use contemptuous language to a person: สพประมาท to insult the dignity of.

ประมุข, ปมุข bpra⁴-mook⁶ *S. n.* a chief; a chieftain; a leader; a principal; a patron (S. E. D. p. 686).

ประมุท bpra⁴-moot⁶ *S. v.* to become joyful; to rejoice greatly; to be delighted or pleased with: *n.* pleasure; gladness; happiness (S. E. D. p. 686).

ประมูล bpra⁴-moon *v.* to overbid (as for a contract); to offer more or to increase the price (in competition); to compete (in price): การรับประมูล to receive tenders: การเรียกประมูล to call for tenders.

ประเมิน bpra⁴-mern *v.* to conjecture; to surmise; to guess at or make a casual estimate of; to express a random opinion about.

ประโมง, ประมง bpra⁴-mong *n.* a fisherman.

ประยงคุ์ *Siam., Bangkok,* **หอมไกล** *Siam., Peninsula,* **พยง, ยะยม** *Laos, Chiengmai* **(ต้น)** bpra⁴-yong *n. Aglaia odorata* (*Meliaceae*), a drug used to cause vomiting; panick seed, a medicinal plant (chd. p. 386); a bush which is wild in Indo-China and southern China, whence it has spread in cultivation. The wild plant has most of its leaves in threes, and they are relatively small. The cultivated plant has its leaves mostly in fives. The flowers are used by the Chinese for scenting tea. In Java they are used to perfume clothes, and, also, they are one of the ingredients of a param, or powder, applied to the body after child-birth. The wood is hard, and excellent for small objects. Its weight is 76 lbs. per cubic foot (cb. p. 257: V. P. p. 172: MCM. p. 308); *Panicum miliaceum*, Indian millet (Burk. p. 74).

ประยุทธ์   bpra[4]-yoot[6] *S. v.* to fight; to attack; to meet an enemy or foe: *n.* a fight; a battle (S. E. D. p. 688).

ประโยค   bpra[4]-yoke[3] *P. S. n. gram.* a sentence; an occasion; object; motive; purpose; design; aim (chd. p. 377).

ประโยคสัมปทา   bpra[4]-yoke[3]-sum[2]-bpa[4]-tah *n.* success through perseverence.

ประโยชน์   bpra[4]-yote[3] *S. n.* advantage; profit; use; object; aim; benefit; utility: ประโยชน์อันคอยมุ่งแต่จะได้ภายหน้า expected profit or interest: เป็นประโยชน์ useful for; requisite or suitable for: ผลประโยชน์ proceeds from; income accruing from (as interest or rentals): ผู้รับผลประโยชน์ a beneficiary: หมดประโยชน์ useless (S. E. D. p. 688).

ประโรหิต   bpra[4]-roh-hit[4] *P. S. n.* a Brahmin who is a king's domestic chaplain (chd. p. 395).

ประลมพ์   bpra[4]-lom *S. v.* to hang down, dangle from or be pendulous (as flowers or branches): *n.* a drooping branch, a garland or bouquet of flowers: *adj.* slow; dilatory (S. E. D. p. 689).

ประลอง   bpra[4]-laung *v.* to practice; to drill (as infantry): ประลองยุทธ์ a sham battle; a battle drill; manoeuvers.

ประลัย, บรรลัย   bpra[4]-lai *S. n.* destruc-

tion; dissolution; annihilation; death; the destruction of the world at the end of Kalpa (S. E. D. p. 689).

ประลาต see ปลาต p. 512.

ประลาย see ปลาย p. 512.

ประลึง   bpra[4]-leung *v.* to touch or handle; to stroke or fondle.

ประลุ see บรรลุ p. 469; see ถึง 388.

ประเล้าประโลม   bpra[4]-low[5]-bpra[4]-lom *v.* to comfort, soothe, console, solace or give cheer.

ประวรรตน์, ปวัตน์   bpra[4]-wat[6] *S. n.* procedure; existence: *adj.* starting; setting out; going on; proceeding; existing (chd. p. 376).

ประวัติ, ปวัติ   bpra[4]-wat[6] *P. S. n.* a biography; a report; a record; an account; news; tidings: ประวัติการ ancient history: ประวัติกาล modern history (chd. p. 375).

ประวาต, ปวาต, ประพาต   bpra[4]-wat[3] *S. v.* to flow forth; to blow (S. E. D. p. 691).

ประวาล, ปวาล   bpra[4]-warn *S. n.* a young shoot, sprout or branch (S. E. D. p. 691).

ประวาลบัทม์   bpra[4]-wah-la[6]-bpat[4] *n.* the red lotus flower: ประวาลผล the red sandalwood: ประวาลวรรณ red coral (S.E.D. p. 691).

ประวาส see ประพาส p. 502.

ประวิง   bpra[4]-wing *v.* to obstruct, impede or cause delay; to retard or encumber (in order to prevent advance); to cause procrastination: ประวิงการใช้เงิน to defer or postpone a payment: ประวิงความ *legal* to delay a case or stay proceedings.

ประวิช, ปวิช, แหวน   bpra[4]-wit[6] *n.* a ring.

ประวีณ   bpra[4]-ween *S. adj.* clever; skilful; conversant with or versed in (S. E. D. p. 693).

ประเวณี see ประเพณี p. 502.

ประเวศ, ปเวศ   bpra[4]-wet[3] *S. n.* an entrance; the act of entering; the penetration or intrusion into (S. E. D. p. 692).

ประสม bpra⁴-som² *S. v.* to become calm; to be pacified or soothed; to be allayed or eased (S.E.D. p. 695); *n.* tranquility; quietness.

ประศาสน์, ปสาสน์ bpra⁴-sart⁴ *S. n.* admonition; instruction; government; guidance (S. E. D. p. 695).

ประสก bpra⁴-sok⁴ *n.* a pious Buddhist, not in orders; a devout or faithful layman; a lay devotee (chd. p. 531).

ประสงค์ bpra⁴-song² *S. n.* desire; want; attachment; inclination or devotion to; fondness for; indulgence in (S. E. D. p. 696): ตาม-แต่ใจจะประสงค์ according to the heart's desire.

ประสพ, บรรสพ bpra⁴-sop⁴ *n.* the condition of meeting (as friends), of getting (as physical desires), of being united (as in wedlock), of gaining (as wealth, luck or fortune), of begetting, procreating (as offspring, posterity) (S. E. D. p. 698).

ประสม, บรรสม, ผะสม bpra⁴-som² *v.* to add together (as various ingredients); to collect into a whole (as fragments of wood into a pile); to cross-fertilize (as of flowers); to amalgamate; to impregnate; to fructify: เก็บประสม to amass by picking here a little and there a little: ประสมประสาน, เก็บเล็ก-ประสมน้อย to accumulate a little at a time (as coins in a savings box or small amounts in a banking account).

ประสะ bpra⁴-sa⁴ *v.* to cleanse; to wash; to shampoo (as the hair); see ชำระ p. 295.

ประสัก (ลูก) bpra⁴-sak⁴ *n.* wooden pegs or pins, used as bolts in fastening together the boards or planks of a boat or vessel.

ประสังสา bpra⁴-sung²-sah² *S. n.* praise; applause; flattery; commendation.

ประสา, ประสีประสา bpra⁴-sah² *n.* language; customs; propriety; etiquette; good manners: คนไม่รู้จักประสีประสา one ignorant of any or all of the foregoing; an impolite person: ประสาเด็ก ๆ childish manners, pranks or conduct.

ประสาท, ปสาท, ประสาทรูป bpra⁴-sart⁴ *S. n.* clearness; brightness; tranquility; calmness; serenity of disposition (S. E. D. p. 696): ประสาทวิถี nerve.

ประสาธน์ bpra⁴-sart⁴ *S. n.* decorations; ornaments (chd. p. 352).

ประสาน, บรรสาน, ผะสาน bpra⁴-sarn² *v.* to solder together; to weld by means of heat and a flux; to cause to unite; to join together.

ประสาร, บรรสาร bpra⁴-sarn² *S. v.* to stretch or spread out; to expand or unfold; to exhibit; to expose (chd. p. 353).

ประสิทธิ์ bpra⁴-sit⁴ *P. n.* accomplishment; success; attainment (S. E. D. p. 697): ประสิทธิ์ภาพ efficiency.

ประสูต, ปสูต bpra⁴-soot⁴ *S. adj.* delivered; born; engendered (chd. p. 356).

ประสูติ, ปสูติ bpra⁴-soot⁴ *S. v.* to bring forth; to give birth to; to procreate or beget: *n.* birth; child-birth; delivery; bringing forth; a flowing out (chd. p. 356).

ประสูติกรรม bpra⁴-soo²-dti⁴-gkum *n.* the act of giving birth; child-birth.

ประเสริฐ bpra⁴-sert⁴ *P.S. adj.* praised; precious; best; excellent; esteemed; superb (chd. p. 353).

ประหนึ่ง bpra⁴-neung⁴ *adj.* such as; like; similar to; see เช่น p. 301.

ประหม่า bpra⁴-mah⁴ *v.* to tremble in fear or dread; to feel a painful apprehension of; to be bashful or timid (as when appearing in public).

ประหยัด bpra⁴-yat⁴ *v.* to be frugal, sparing, saving or cautious in the use of money; to exercise economy.

ประหรณ์ bpra⁴-horn² *P. S. n.* the act of striking, cutting, attacking, killing, removing or dispelling (S. E. D. p. 701).

ประหลาด   bpra⁴-lart⁴ *adj.* strange; odd; queer; wonderful; astonishing; extraordinary; singular; marvellous: ประหลาดใจ astonished.

ประหลาท   bpra⁴-lart⁴ *S. n.* delight; joy; excitement; happiness; gladness (S.E.D. p. 701).

ประหล่ำ, ปะวะหล่ำ   bpra⁴-lum⁴ *n.* a bracelet; a wristlet (made of round beads or balls similar to a rosary).

ประหวั่น   bpra⁴-wan⁴ *v.* to fear or apprehend; to have a feeling of dread.

ประหาร, ประหัตประหาร, ปหาร   bpra⁴-harn² *P. S. n.* a strike; a blow; a stroke; a thump; a knock (S. E. D. p. 701): *adj.* striking; wounding; killing; destroying: ประหารชีวิต to render lifeless by a stroke; to execute; to behead; see ฆ่า p. 219.

ประหาส, ปหาส   bpra⁴-hart⁴ *P. S. v.* to burst into laughter; to laugh with or at; to mock; to deride or ridicule (S. E. D. p. 700).

ประเหล, ประเล่ห์   bpra⁴-hen² *adj.* such as; like; as though.

ประอบ, ผอบ   bpra⁴-op⁴ (see ตลับ p. 346): *n.* a vessel mounted on a low base and fitted with a cover which is decorated with a fancy tapering tip (used for scented oil or ointment).

ปรักปรำ   bpruk⁴-bprum *v.* to declare positively; to insist emphatically; to speak with absolute assurance.

ปรักหักพัง   bpruk⁴-hak⁴-pung *v.* to be damaged, dilapidated, ruined or disfigured.

ปรัง (นา)   bprung *n.* paddy fields which have been worked out of the regular season; the secondary planting of fields: *adj.* beyond the specified time: ข้าวปรัง paddy planted in the dry season: จมปรัง delayed overtime.

ปรัชญา   bprat⁴-yah *n.* philosophy.

ปรัด   bprut⁴ *v.* to decorate, adorn or beautify.

ปรัตถจริยา   bpa⁴-rut⁶-ta⁴-chja⁴-ri⁶-yah *n.* conduct manifesting a spirit of philanthropy.

ปรัตยักษ์ see ประจักษ์ p. 497.

ปรัตยุตบัน, ปรัตยุบัน see ปัจจุปบัน p. 519.

ปรัตยุษ see ปัจจุส p. 519.

ปรัน   bprun *v.* to press or force in or through; to shove or push with force repeatedly; to elbow rudely; to 'butt or shove one's way through (as in a crowd).

ปรับ ๑   bprup⁴ *Cam. v.* to tell; to inform; to relate: ปรับทุกข์ to relate or complain about one's troubles, misfortunes, or hardships.

ปรับ ๒   bprup⁴ *v.* to fine; to punish by inflicting a pecuniary penalty; to make even or level (as two boards); to make fit evenly (as joints in woodwork); to overhaul and make as new; to confiscate in lieu of payment of a fine: ปรับเป็นพินัย *legal* fines paid to the Government.

ปรัมปรา   bpa⁴-rum-bpa⁴-rah *P. adj.* being handed down in series, successions or sequences (as lineage or race) (chd. p. 336).

ปรัศนา see ปัญหา p. 519.

ปรัศนี   bprut⁴-sa⁴-nee *S. n.* an inquiry; a question; an interrogator; the interrogation mark " ? " (S. E. D. p. 696).

ปรัศว์   bprut⁴ *P. S. n.* side; flank (chd. p. 355).

ปร่า   bpra⁴ *adj.* abnormal; unnatural; perverted (descriptive of taste): ปร่าปาก a bad taste in the mouth (as during a digestive disorder), indicated by a coated tongue.

ปรากฏ   bprah-gkot⁴ *P.S v.* to be or become apparent; to be plainly visible; to be known publicly: *n.* clear; evident; manifest (chd. p. 319): ปรากฏการณ์ a phenomenon; see [แจ้ง, แจ่ม p. 261.

ปรากรม see บรากรม p. 470.

ปรากฤต   bprah-gkrit⁴ *S. n.* low; vulgar; unrefined or illiterate words or speech (S. E. D.

p. 703); colloquialisms used by people of various districts.

ปราการ bprah-gkarn *S. n.* a wall; a fence; a rampart; an enclosure elevated on a mound of earth (S. E. D. p. 703); a couch surrounded by a curtain or screen (chd. p. 318): สมุทร-ปราการ a fortified town; the name of a district at the mouth of the Menam Chao Phya, commonly called Paknam.

ปราคภาร bprak[4]-parn *P. S. n.* a mountain (chd. p. 306).

ปราคาร bprah-karn *S. n.* the top or peak of a mountain (chd. p. 306); a principal building (S. E. D. p. 703).

ปราง bprang *n.* the cheek; see แก้ม p. 129.

ปรางค์ bprang *n.* a stupa; a dome-like structure erected as a monument or memorial, to commemorate some event, or to mark a spot revered by the followers of the Buddha.

ปรางคณะ bprang-ka[6]-na[6] *S. n.* a courtyard; a lawn (S. E. D. p. 703).

ปราจีน bprah-chjeen *S. adj.* eastward; eastern (S. E. D. p. 704).

ปราชญ์ bprat[4] *S. n.* a wise or learned man: *adj.* intelligent; wise; clever (S. E. D. p. 702).

ปราชัย bpa[4]-rah-chai *P. S. n.* defeat; losing at play or in a lawsuit (chd. p. 333).

ปราชาบัตยวิวาหะ bprah-chah-bpat[4]-dta[4]-ya[6]-wi[6]-wah-ha[4] *S. n.* a form of marriage consummated without any monetary transaction (S. E. D. p. 703).

ปราณ, ปาณ bpran *S. n.* inspiration; air; breath; life; vitality; a living being; a creature; energy; vigour (chd. p. 331).

ปราณี, ปาณี bprah-nee *v.* to show compassion or pity for: *P. S. n.* a living being; a creature; an animal; man (S. E. D. p. 706): ความปราณี mercy; compassion; favour: ปราณี-ประนอม to effect a reconciliation by a compromise; to be indulgent; to agree to settle

amicably; to accomplish by a conciliatory policy.

ปราด bprat[4] *adj.* speedy: *adv.* speedily; [quickly.

ปราทุกรา see **ปาทุกา** p. 524.

ปราบ bprap[4] *v.* to subdue, subjugate or conquer; to level; to tame: ปราบปราม to intimidate or subdue; to quell; to put down (as an epidemic); to subjugate; to pacify.

ปราปต์ bprap[4] *P. S. adj.* attained to; arrived at; reached; met with; found; incurred; acquired; gained (S. E. D. p: 707).

ปราปดาภิเษก bprap[4]-dah-pi[6]-sek[4] *S. v.* to attain, achieve or acquire (as a crown) (S. E. D. p. 707) (used in reference to a victorious king being anointed, crowned and proclaimed king in honour of his victory).

ปราภพ bprah-pop[6] *n.* destruction; decay; ruin; discomfiture; humiliation; contempt (chd. p. 333).

ปราม (ห้าม) bpram *v.* to forbid; to hinder; to stop; to obstruct or prevent; to suppress.

ปรามาส bpa[4]-rah-mart[3] *P. n.* the act of touching, stroking, or coming into contact with (in an insulting or impolite manner) (chd. p. 334); careless; heedless; negligent; forgetful of due respect (S. E. D. p. 685).

ปราโมทย์, ประโมทย์, ปาโมชช์ bprah-mote[3] *P. S. n.* to become joyful or exultant (S. E. D. p. 686); joy; bliss; delight; happiness (chd. p. 325).

ปราย (โปรย) bprai *v.* to sow; to scatter; to strew broadcast (as seed rice); to dash or throw (as sand or powder in the face): ลูกปราย small shot, bullets or pellets of lead (as fired from a shotgun in shooting birds); bird-shot.

ปรารถนา bprat[4]-ta[4]-nah[2] *S. v.* to desire, wish, want, or need; to pray for: *n.* aspiration; hope; request; desire; resolve (chd. p. 371).

ปรารภ bprah-rop[6] *S. v.* to think of or ask about with solicitude; to be anxious for, or apprehensive concerning; to resolve, plan or consider (as regarding some undertaking or project).

ปราศ bprat[4] *v.* to be free from; to have no lien or claim upon; to be without (any flaw or imperfection): ปราศจากความลำเอียง fair; impartial: ปราศจากสินจ้าง given, or done without recompense; gratuitous.

ปราศรัย, ปรศัย, ปราไส bprah-sai[2] *P. S. v.* to confer or converse amicably: *n.* respectful demeanour; modesty; humility; deferential affection; manifested courtesy (S. E. D. p. 696).

ปราสาท, ปาสาท bprah-sart[4] *S. n.* a building erected on high foundations and approached by means of steps; a terrace; a turreted palace; a mansion (chd. p. 352); a palace; a temple; a building inhabited by a prince or a king (Ala. p. 290): พระเจ้าปรา-สาททอง an important king of the Ayuthian period, known in history as "King of the Golden Palace," born about 1600 A. D., died August 8th 1656 A. D. (wood pp. 174, 187).

ปริ bpri[4] *v.* to open or expand slightly (as flowers just about to bloom); to push up or swell forth from the earth (as sprouting seeds); to issue forth (as tender sprouts from nodes on the branches of trees or bushes): ยิ้มปริ to burst forth into a smile.

ปริก bprik[4] *n.* the fancy tapering tip on the cover of a golden powder-box: ปริก (นก) the bronze-winged jacana, *Metopidius indicus* (Herb. N. H. J. S. S. VI, 4, p. 345).

ปริกขาร see บริกขาร p. 470.

ปริกรรม see บริกรรม p. 470.

ปริกัลป, ปริกัปปี bpa[4]-ri[6]-gkun-bpa[4] *P.S. n.* determination; resolution: ปริกัลปมาลา *gram.* a mode; a manner of being or doing; a method.

ปริขา, บริขา bpa[4]-ri[6]-kah[2] *P.S. n.* a trench, ditch or moat surrounding a fortified position (chd. p. 342).

ปริคณ see บริคณ p. 470.

ปริง *Siam., Peninsula* (ต้น) bpring *n. Pterospermum acerifolium* (Sterculiaceae), a large tree with very large, oval, leathery leaves, snowy white or grey underneath, with prominent veins. The scented flowers are long, fleshy and of a yellowish colour. In northern India the flowers are used as an insecticide, and may be eaten. Half of their dry weight is formed of carbohydrates. They are mucilaginous and with a little tannin (McM. p. 103 : V. P. p. 174 : Burk. p. 1834).

ปริจจาค see บริจจาค p. 470.

ปริจเฉท see บริจเฉท p. 470.

ปริจาริกา see บริจาริกา p. 470.

ปริชน see บริวาร p. 471.

ปริญญา bpa[4]-rin-yah *P. n.* exact knowledge; ascertainment; thorough education; a degree (chd. p. 345): ปริญญาทางนิติศาสตร์ Doctor of Laws: ปริญญาธรรมศาสตร์บัณฑิต Doctor of Civil Law: ปริญญาทางวิทยาศาสตร์ Master of Science: ปริญญาทางวิทยาศาสตร์-บัณฑิต Doctor of Science: ปริญญาทางแพทย์-ศาสตร์นิสสิต Bachelor of Medicine: ปริญญา-ทางแพทย์ศาสตร์บัณฑิต Doctor of Medicine: ปริญญาทางอักษรศาสตร์ Bachelor of Arts: ปริญ-ญาทางวิชชาสามัญ Master of Arts: ปริญญา-ทางศาสนา Doctor of Divinity.

ปริณาม bpa[4]-ri[6]-nam *S. n.* change; alteration of form or state; an issue or event (chd. p. 343).

ปริณามัคคิ bpa[4]-ri[6]-nah-muk[6]-ki[6] *P. n.* a digestive fluid, or enzyme.

ปริณายก, บริณายก (see p. 470) bpa[4]-ri[6]-nah-yok[6] *S. n.* a governor; a chief; a prince; an aged eminent priest (chd. p. 344).

ปรัตโตทก   bpa^4-rit^6-dtoh-tok^6 *P. n.* lustral water consecrated by a Buddhist priest.

ปริตร, บริตร   bpa^4-rit^6 *S. n.* protection; self-defence; the warding off of a blow (chd. p. 347): *adj.* few in number; little; trifling; brief; limited; see น้อย p. 446.

ปริทัยหัคคี   bpa^4-ri^6-tai-huk^4-ki^6 *P. n.* a toxic enzyme or ferment causing a condition of uneasiness of the body.

ปริเทพ, ปริเทพน์, ปริเทว, ปริเทวน   bpa^4-ri^6-tep^3 *P. n.* grief; lamentation; wailings; mourning; complaints.

ปริบ   bprip^4 *adj.* winking; blinking (as the eyelids); dripping; trickling; dropping (as water or rain); twinkling.

ปริบันถ์   bpa^4-ri^6-bpun *P. n.* danger; misfortune; hindrance; an obstacle; that which stands in the way (chd. p. 345).

ปริพนธ์, บริพนธ์, บริพันธ์, ปริพันธ์   bpa^4-ri^6-pon *P. v.* to compose or write (as a literary work); to be bound together (chd. p. 337).

ปริพพาชก, บริพพาชก   bpa^4-rip^6-pah-chok^6 *P. n.* a wandering religious mendicant; a pilgrim; a Buddhist priest (chd. p. 337).

ปริพพาชิกา, ปริพพาชี, บริพพาชิกา   bpa^4-rip^6-pah-chi^6-gkah *P. n.* a female ascetic or pilgrim; a Buddhist nun (chd. p. 337).

ปริพัตร see ปริวรรต p 509.

ปริภัณฑ์ see บริภัณฑ์ p. 471.

ปริภาษ see บริภาษ p. 471.

ปริภาษณ์ see บริภาษณ์ p. 471.

ปริภุญช์   bpa^4-ri^6-poon *P. S. v.* to eat; to be eaten or enjoyed; to wear or to be worn [chd. p. 338).

ปริโภค see บริโภค p. 471.

ปริม   bprim^4 *adj.* almost full; nearly brimful or brimming; almost sinking; well down to the water's edge (as a fully loaded boat).

ปริมณฑล   bpa^4-ri^6-mon-ton *P. S. adj.* circular; round; spreading over; covering entirely (chd. p. 343).

ปริมัท   bpa^4-ri^6-mut^6 *P. v.* to touch; to knead; to stroke; to squeeze or massage (chd. p. 343).

ปริมิตตาญาสิทธิราช   bpa^4-ri^6-mit^6-dtah-yah-sit^4-ti^6-rat^3 *n.* a limited monarchy.

ปริมาณ see ประมาณ p. 503.

ปริย, ปริยา, ปรียา, ปรีย   bpa^4-ri^6-ya^6 *P. S. n.* a lover; a friend; a husband: *adj.* affectionate; beloved; dear; liked; fond of, attached or devoted to (S. E. D. p. 710): ปริยกษัตร one who rules benevolently: ปริยชาต *lit.* "one dear when born," *i.e.* the god of Fire, the most ancient and most sacred of Hindu gods: ปริยชานิ a person given to compassion, helpfulness or mercy: ปริยทรรศน์ one pleasing and graceful to the sight; a parrot: ปริยเทวัน one fond of games, plays or gambling: ปริยมธุ the "wine-loving" Bala-rama, the elder brother of Krishna, who was as much addicted to wine as his brother Krishna was devoted to the fair sex (H. C. D. p. 41): ปริยรณ one delighting in war: ปริยวาท agreeable speech: ปริยวาที a flatterer; one speaking kindly or agreeably: ปริยานุช a beloved younger brother or sister.

ปริยัต, บริยัต   bpa^4-ri^6-yat^6 *P. n.* that which is learned by heart; the text of the Buddha's word (chd. p. 350): ปริยัตธรรม the Buddhist scripture with its nine divisions (chd. p. 350).

ปริยาย, บรรยาย, บริยาย   bpa^4-ri^6-yai *P. n.* (1) way; manner; order; turn: (2) teaching; exposition; narration (chd. p. 550).

ปริโยสาน   bpa^4-ri^6-yoh-sarn^2 *P. n.* termination; end; conclusion (chd. p. 350).

ปริวรรต, บริวัตร, ปริวัฏ, ปริวัตร, บริพัตร   bpa^4-ri^6-wat^6 *P. S. v.* to turn round or to roll over; to revolve or be whirled round (as a potter's wheel); to exchange or return (as a dress or robe with another priest or priestess) (S. E. D. p. 349); to circumambulate.

ปริวาร see บริวาร p. 471.

ปริวาส, บริวาส　　bpa⁴-ri⁶-wart³ *P. n.* the condition of living apart; being put under restraint; one of the ecclesiastical punishments (chd. p. 348).

ปริวิตก　　bpa⁴-ri⁶-wi⁶-dtok⁴ *P.S. n.* thought; reflection (chd. p. 349).

ปริเวณ see บริเวณ p. 471.

ปริศนา　　bprit⁴-sa⁴-nah² *P.S. n.* a question; an inquiry; an interrogation (chd. p. 328); an allegory; a riddle; a parable.

ปริษการ see บริขขาร p. 470.

ปริษัท see บริษัท p. 471.

ปริสัญญ　　bpa⁴-ri⁶-sun²-yoo *P. n.* one acquainted with modes of procedure and parliamentary rules of assembly (chd. p. 346).

ปริสุทธ, ปริสุทธิ see บริสุทธิ์ p. 471.

ปริหาน　　bpa⁴-ri⁶-harn² *P. n.* decrease; decay; diminution; loss; a condition of falling off (chd. p. 340).

ปริหาร see บริหาร p. 471.

ปริหาส see บริหาส p. 471.

ปรี́　　bpree⁴ *adj.* too much; too full; in excess of (allotted space or capacity); overflowing; filled nearly to overflowing (as a cup of liquid).

ปรีชา　　bpree-chah *P.S. n.* perception; intuition; apperception; the state of having grasped, understood or known; self-consciousness (chd. p. 338)：　ปรีชาญาณ comprehensive wisdom; comprehension; sagacity.

ปรี́ด　　bpreet⁵ *adj.* rapid; swift (descriptive of a forward motion of water); fast; speedy; fleet; nimble; agile (descriptive of motion).

ปรี́ดา, ปรี́ตะ　　bpree-dah *S. v.* to be glad, joyful or happy：　*n.* joy; pleasure; mirth; happiness; delight (S. E. D. p. 711).

ปรี́ดี, ปีติ　　bpree-dee *P.S. n.* any pleasurable sensation; affection; love; delight (S. E. D. p. 711)：　ปรี́ดิเปรม joy coupled with affection.

ปรีย, ปรียา see ปรีย p. 509.

ปรึก　　bpreuk⁴ *n.* siccative oil used as an ingredient in paint or varnish.

ปรึกษา　　bpreuk⁴-sah² *S. v.* to consult with; to ask advice or take counsel of：　*n.* advice; counsel; recommendation; a trial or experiment (S. E. D. p. 712).

ปรือ, ปรู้　　bpruh² *adj.* very fast; swift; darting; swooping down (descriptive of birds flying downwards).

ปรุ　　bproo⁴ *v.* to produce holes or pores：　*adj.* full of holes; porous：　ปรุไปทั้งนั้น thoroughly perforated with small holes：　รู้ปรุ thoroughly conversant with, or expert in.

ปรุง　　bprung *v.* to mix or compound (as a remedy); to put together or construct (as different parts of a house); to make up (as a fictitious story or excuse)：　ปรับปรุง an euphonic combination.

ปรู　　*Siam.,* ปู้ *N.* and *E. Laos* (ต้น)　　*n.* *Alangium salviifolium; Hexapetalum (Alangiaceae),* a tree with scented heart-wood, used medicinally by the Siamese (cb. p. 807: V. P. p. 172).

ปรูด　　bproot⁴ *adj.* gliding, sliding or moving rapidly (as a rocket, rat or shooting star).

ปฤงคพ see ปุงคพ p. 529.

ปฤจฉา, ปุจฉา　　bprit⁴-chah² *S. n.* an inquiry; a question; an interrogation (chd. p. 389)：　ปฤจฉาคุณศัพท์ *gram.* an interrogative adjective：　ปฤจฉาสรรพนาม an interrogative pronoun.

ปฤษฎางค์　　bprit⁴-sa⁴-dang *n.* an organ situated towards the back of the body.

ปฤษฐ, ปฤษฏ์ bprit⁴-sa⁴-ta⁴ S. n. the back, the rear, the hind part of anything; the posterior surface; superficies (chd. p. 385).

ปลกเปลี้ย see กะปลกกะเปลี้ย p. 38.

ปลง bplong v. (1) to make an irrevocable resolve, ex., ปลงใจ to make an unalterable decision; to take an unchangeable stand: ปลงใจเชื่อ to have a steadfast faith, belief or confidence in: ปลงใจรัก to have an undying love for: (2) to lay down or surrender, ex., ปลงชีวิต to give up or sacrifice one's life; to be killed; to die voluntarily: (3) to repudiate or disavow responsibility for, ex., ปลงธุระ to disclaim or refuse obligation for: (4) to remove or extract hair, ex., ปลงผม to shave the head: (5) to commit or consign to the earth or to the flames, ex., ปลงศพ to bury a body or cremate a corpse: (6) to purge or cleanse, ex., ปลงอาบัติ to expiate misdemeanors, sin or guilt: (7) to relinquish or give up all hope, ex., ปลงอาลัย to abandon all hope of life (as resulting from an incurable disease or some adversity): (8) to ponder, consider or reflect, ex., ปลงสังขาร to speculate about the body (as to its transitoriness and its inevitable end).

ปลง, ปลอด bplong⁴ adj. saved from or clear of (as danger or calamity); affording a harmless passage through; safe; free from trouble or disaster (as while making a journey).

ปลด bplot⁴ v. to unloose; to unhitch; to unshackle; to unchain; to unhook; to untangle; to unlace; to untie; to undo: ปลดจากตำแหน่ง to remove from office; to cause to retire: ปลดจากหนี้ to release from debt.

ปล้น bplon³ v. a dacoity; a gang robbery.

ปลวก bpluak⁴ n. termites; white ants.

ปลอก bplauk⁴ n. a ring, hoop, or loop; an encasement: ปลอกมือ a thimble; boxing-gloves: ปลอกหมอน a pillow-slip or pillow-cover.

ปล่อง bplaung⁴ n. a tube; a spout; a hole or passage out from a cave: ปล่องควัน a chimney; a flue; see ช่อง p. 283.

ปล้อง bplaung³ n. the length or space between two joints or knots (as of bamboo); a species of reed: ปล้องฉนวน (ง) a species of snake: ปล้องไฉน the space above the frieze or decorative moulding of a column, or the spire of a pagoda: ปล้องอ้อย (ปลา) Acanthopthalmus kuhli (Cobitidae) (suvatti p. 58).

ปลอด see ปล่ง p. 511: ปลอดภัยไว้ก่อน, รู้รักษาตัวรอดเป็นยอดดี safety first.

ปล้อน bplaun³ v. to be able to extricate oneself from a predicament; to pick out or extract the pip or seeds (as out of fruit); to be resourceful in ideas; to be able to achieve by evading difficulties; see ออกตัว p. 360.

ปลอบ, ปลอบโยน bplaup⁴ v. to pacify; to subdue; to assuage the anger, or calm the feelings; to soothe or appease; to mitigate or soften.

ปลอม bplaum v. to imitate, copy or disguise: n. hypocrisy: adj. spurious; counterfeit; fraudulent; false; hypocritical: ปลอมตัวเปนผู้อื่น to impersonate another: ปลอมหนังสือ to forge a document; see เทียม๑ p. 426.

ปล่อย bploy⁴ v. to let go, release, relinquish or discharge: ปล่อยปละละเลย to abandon utterly; to forsake or renounce; to quit completely; to leave; to resign: ปล่อยเสีย to be released (as prisoners).

ปละ, บัล bpla⁴ adj. separated; parted; abandoned; sundered; severed; loosed or freed: ควายปละ a buffalo which the owner allows to roam about at will.

ปลัก bpluk⁴ n. a piece or stretch of land having mud-holes or miry patches (as is often seen in paddy fields).

ปลั่ง bplung⁴ adj. shining; bright; sparkling; clear; lustrous; plump; sleek; smooth; healthy-looking (as the face of a healthy child).

ปลัด bpa⁴-lat⁴ *n.* a deputy; a deputy official; a lieutenant: ปลัดกรม a deputy director: ปลัดกิ่งอำเภอ the assistant to the officer of a sub-district: ปลัดทหารบก an adjutant general: ปลัดอำเภอ the assistant to a district officer: พระปลัด the Deputy Governor; the Lieutenant Governor.

ปลา bplah *n.* fish; a generic name followed by the specific designating name: ปลา (งู) the freshwater snake, *Homalopsinae* (M. S., N. H. J. S. S. I, 2, p. 99): ปลากริ่ม a sweet-meat made with vermicelli, coconut milk and sugar: ปลาจ่อม, ปลาเจ่า, ปลาแดก, ปลาแนม, ปลาม้ำ, ปลาส้ม names of fish condiments, either pickled or salted (resembling caviar): ปลาย่าง smoked fish: ปลาร้า fish steeped in brine: ปลาวาฬ whales, *Cetacea* (*sp.*) N. H. J. S. S. III, p. 126): ปลาแห้ง dried fish: ปลาไหลเผือก *Siam.*, เพียก *Siam.*, *Peninsula*, แฮบันซัน *Laos*, *Lampang* (ต้น) *Erycoma longifolia* (*Simarubaceae*) (cb. p. 242): น้ำปลา essence of salted fish or prawns: ปลาโลมา-หัวบาต porpoises, *Orcoella sp.* (N. H. J. S. S. III, p. 126).

ปลาก bplark⁴ *n.* place; locality; district.

ปลาต, ประลาต bpa⁴-lart³ *P. v.* to run away; to flee; to escape; to retreat (chd. p. 321).

ปลาบ, แปลบ bplap⁴ *adj.* lancinating; acute; darting; piercing; shooting or intermittent (as pain): ปลาบปลิ้มใจ to be glad, joyful, happy or pleased with (as though the sentiment of pleasure pierced the heart).

ปลาย, บรรลาย, ประลาย bplai *n.* the end; the top; the point; the tip; a final condition: ต้นปลายไม่ตรงกัน discrepancies between the beginning and ending (as a discordant testimony): ปลายทาง the destination: ปลายน้ำ the source of a river or stream: ปลายมือ the climax of all things.

ปล้ำ, ปล้ำปลุก bplum³ *v.* to wrestle; to contend or grapple with an opponent, each striving to throw the other to the ground; to strive vehemently for some end.

ปลิง bpling *n.* a leech: *adj.* adhesive; sticky: ปลิงทะเล an edible sea-slug, a Chinese dainty; bêche de mer: ปลิงเหล็ก a mechanical clasp or clamp; a temporary rivet: ผ้าปลิง adhesive plaster.

ปลิด see เด็ด p. 334: ปลิดเกลี้ยง to pick clean or bare: ปลิดเปลื้องไปเกลี้ยง to be stripped clean or robbed of all: ปลิดเปลื้อง-ให้หมด to peal, pick or clean all off smoothly (as a stalk of bamboo cleared of all branches).

ปลิ้น bplin³ *v.* to turn inside out (as a glove); to peal or skin; to extricate with adroitness; to manoeuvre through: คนปลิ้น-ปล้อน one using adroit or artful moves or means: ปลิ้นปลอก, ปลิ้นปล้อน to use or acquire by deceptive means.

ปลิโพธ bpa⁴-li⁶-pote³ *P. n.* entanglements; impediments; hindrance; obstacles (in the effort to lead a religious life) (chd. p. 322).

ปลิว bpliew *v.* to be blown, wafted, or carried off by the wind: ใบปลิว a handbill; a dodger (as small sheets for advertising purposes).

ปลี bplee *n.* the blossom of the banana tree: ปลีน่อง the fleshy mass at the back of the leg below the knee; the calf (of the leg).

ปลีก bpleek⁴ *v.* to divide into small pieces: ปลีกตัว to separate oneself from a company; to evade the presence of others: ขายปลีก to sell by retail: เงินปลีก small change [(money).

ปลื้ม see ชื่น p. 298.

ปลุก bplook⁴ *v.* to awaken or arouse (as out of sleep); to warn, caution or apprise of (as by spiritual exhortation); to endue with a spirit of bravery or loyalty (as by words or example): นาฬิกาปลุก an alarum-clock.

ปลูก bplook⁴ *v.* to plant (as trees or plants); to instil or inculcate (as knowledge); to institute or establish (as principles of right living in the minds of the young): ปลูกบ้าน, ปลูกเรือน to build a house: ปลูกผึ้ง to inscribe upon; to imprint; to impress; to instil into permanently: ปลูกฝี to vaccinate; to innoculate with virus as a protection against smallpox.

ปวง, ทั้งปวง bpoo-ang *adj.* all; entire; every; complete; whole; see ทั้ง p. 408.

ป่วง (โรค) bpoo-ang⁴ *n.* diseases incident to indigestion; cholera.

ปวด bpoo-at⁴ *v.* to be in pain; to suffer from pain: *n.* a pain; an ache: ปวดท้อง ขี้, ปวดท้องทุ่ง to be impelled to evacuate the bowels: ปวดท้องเบา, ปวดท้องเขี่ยว to be impelled to urinate: ปวดบาดเจ็บ to suffer pain from an injury or wound: ปวดผี pain resulting from an abscess: ปวดฟัน toothache: ปวดเจ็บ to be sore and painful: ปวดตุบ ๆ throbbing pain: ปวดแสบปวดร้อน a smarting burning pain (as after a burn or scald): ปวดหัว headache.

ป่วน bpoo-an⁴ *v.* to be confused, disconcerted, troubled, anxious or uneasy about: ป่วนปั่น to be turbulent or in great confusion; to be greatly disconcerted.

ป้วน bpoo-an³ *adj.* absorbed; busied with; being engaged, engrossed or mixed up with: ป้วนเปี้ยน to be perplexed or bewildered; to be encircled, entwined or twisted together; see ง่วน p. 221.

ป่วย bpoo-ie⁴ *v.* to be sick, ill or ailing; to be of no use; to waste (as time): ค่าป่วยการ compensation; indemnity: ป่วยการกล่าว to waste time in discussion: ป่วยการ to do in vain; to make useless or fruitless efforts: ลาป่วย to be on sick leave; see เจ็บ p. 256.

ปวัตน์ see ประวรรตน์ p. 504.

ปวัติ see ประวัติ p. 504.

ปวาต see ประวาต p. 504.

ปวาล see ประวาล p. 504.

ปวาส see ประพาส p. 502.

ปวาฬ see ประพาล, ปพาฬ p. 502.

ปวิช see ประวิช p. 504.

ปวิตร see บพิตร p. 467.

ปวิเวก bpa⁴-wi⁶-wek³ *P. n.* a place of retirement; solitude; seclusion; a hermitage fitted for solitude (chd. p. 377).

ปวีณ, ประพิณ bpa⁴-wee-na⁶ *P. adj.* clever; skilful; conversant or acquainted with by study (chd. p. 376).

ปเวณี see ประเพณี, ประเวณี p. 502.

ปเวส see ประเวศ p. 504.

ปศุ, ประศุ, ปสุ bpa⁴-soo⁴ *P.S. n.* domesticated animals (as goats or sheep) (chd. p. 355)..

ปสัยห, ประสัยห์ bpa⁴-sai²-ha⁴ *P. n.* force; violence; oppression (chd. p. 353): ปสัยหาหาร, ประสัยหาหาร the condition of plundering with violence.

ปสาท see ประสาท, ประสาทรูป p. 505.

ปสาสน์ see ประศาสน์ p. 505.

ปสุ see ปศุ p. 513.

ปสุต see ประสูติ p. 505.

ปสูติ see ประสูต p. 505.

ปหาร, ประหาณ bpa⁴-harn² *P. n.* rejection of evil; abandonment; getting rid of (chd. p. 316).

ปหาร see ประหาร, ประหัตประหาร p. 506.

ปหาส see ประหาส p. 506.

ปอ bpaw *n.* a common Asiatic annual

herb of the linden family. The fiber obtained from the inner bark is used for bags and ropes: ปอ (แมลง) the dragon-fly.

ปอกะเจา *Thai.,* เส้ง *Laos, Chiengmai* (ต้น) bpaw-gka[4]-chjow *n. Corchorus capsularis (Tiliaceae)*, an herb found all around the world, which yields the greatest part of the jute of commerce (BURK. p. 658); *C. olitorius*, jute or gunny-fibre plant. This valuable fibre is obtained from the stem of cultivated varieties of *Corchorus capsularis* and *C. olitorius,*-annual plants with long, erect, thin stems and yellow flowers, attaining a height of 8 to 12 feet. Of the numerous varieties, those of *C. capsularis* are generally preferred, as they yield better fibre and come to maturity earlier than those of *C. olitorius* (MCM. pp. 421, 422: cb. p. 192: V. P. p. 166: BURK. p. 659): ปอมุ้ง *Laos, Chiengmai,* ปอเกี๋ยน *Laos, Nan,* แสลงพัน-แดง *Laos, Loi* (ต้น) *Bauhinia kerrii (Leguminosae)* (cb. p. 523): ปอแก้ว *Siam., Petchabun,* ปอผ้าย *Laos, Chiengmai* (ต้น) *Hibiscus pungens (Malvaceae)* (cb. p. 159): ปอ-ขนุน *Siam.,* ปอฟาน *Laos, Chiengmai* (ต้ม) *Sterculia guttata (Sterculiaceae)* (cb. p. 166: V. P. p. 166): ปอขี้ไก่ *Siam., Nakawn Tai,* ปอเอี๋เก้ง *Siam., Nakawn Sawan,* ปอขี้ลิ้น *Laos, Nawngkai* ปอขี้แตก *Laos, Korat,* and *Saraburi,* กำโรง *Khmer, Krabin* (ต้น) *Sterculia campanulata (Sterculiaceae)* (cb. p. 165): ปอขี้ต่น *Laos, Lapla,* ขี้หมากแห้ง *Laos, Sawankalok,* ปอปาน *Laos, Korat,* ปอพราน *Siam., Chantabun* (ต้น) *Colona auriculata (Tiliaceae)* (cb. p. 188): ปอคาว *Laos, Chiengmai,* ปอแจ, ปอแบ้, ปอม้าให้ *Laos* (ต้น) *Sterculia colorata (Sterculiaceae)*, a moderate-sized tree 40 to 50 feet high. The brilliant orange-scarlet flowers, appearing in great profusion when the tree is leafless, render the tree a conspicuous and handsome object. The Veddas (aboriginals of Ceylon) sang odes to it (MCM. p. 94: cb. p. 166: V. P. pp. 166, 169): ปอเจี๋ยน *Laos, Chiengmai,* แสลงพัน *Siam., Chonburi* (ต้น) *Bauhinia bracteata (Leguminosae)* (cb.

p. 517); *B. rufa* (V. P. p. 166): ปอด่อน *Laos, Nakawn Tai* (ต้น) *Helicteres vinosa (Sterculiaceae)* (cb. p. 175): ปอด้าย *Laos* (ต้น) *Hibiscus cannabinus (Malvaceae)*, Bombay-hemp, bimlipatam-jute, a shrub 10 to 15 feet high, with prickly stems. It is cultivated for the fibre obtained from the inner bark. In cultivation, the plants are grown close together, so as to produce straight clean stems. The fibre is superior to jute, but it can only demand the same price as jute and even then is often not bought willingly. The fibre is shorter and less flexible than jute, but stronger, more lustrous and durable, and the ultimate fibres are longer. The oil is used in Africa for burning, and for rubbing on the body. The cake and young leaves are edible, and the old leaves act as an aperient. The juice of the flowers is a popular remedy for biliousness in India (MCM. p. 430: V. P. p. 167: BURK. p. 1164): ปอแดง *Siam., Pitsanulok* and *Saraburi,* ปอตบ, ปอหูช้าง *N. Laos,* เสี่ยวกาช้างนา *Karen* (ต้น) *Sterculia ornata (Sterculiaceae)* (cb. p. 168): ปอแดงดง *Laos, Loi,* มักลิ้นอง *Laos, Chiengmai* (ต้น) *Sterculia augustifolia (Sterculiaceae)* (cb. p. 165): ปอต๊อก *N. Laos* (ต้น) *Sterculia thorelii (Sterculiaceae)* (cb. p. 169): ปอตบ-หูช้าง *Laos* (ต้น) *Sterculia villosa; S. fulgens* (V. P. p. 168): ปอเต๊า *Laos, Chiengmai,* ปอ-เลี้ยงผ้าย *Laos* (ต้น) *Kydia calycina (Malvaceae)*, a small tree found in the drier parts of India, Burma and northern Siam. In India its fibrous bark is made into coarse ropes; its mucilaginous properties are used for clarifying sugar; and the wood is occasionally converted into small articles for domestic use. A lac-insect feeds on it (cb. p. 151: BURK. p. 1288): ปอเต๊า *Laos* (ต้น) *Mallotus barbatus*, a shrub, found from southern China to Java; and again on the Malabar coast of India; in the Malay Peninsula it is known to occur down the west side. It is recorded that in Kedah a poultice for colic is made by pounding it with pepper, ginger and rice. The Laos of parts of Indo-China extract a tallow from the seeds which they use for illumination, and it can be made into candles (V. P. p. 167: BURK. p. 1394): ปอเต่าไห้ *Laos, Lampoon* (ต้น) *Grewia vestita (Tiliaceae)*; *Grewia asiatica; Linostoma scandens* (cb. p. 187: V. P. p. 167): ปอเตียง *Laos* (ต้น) *Mitrephora tomentosa* (V.P. p. 167): ปอแตง *Laos* (ต้น) *Trema amboinensis* (V. P. p. 167): ปอแต่ง *Laos, Lomsak* (ต้น) *Colona elobata (Tiliaceae)* (cb. p. 189): ปอเถื่อน *Laos* (ต้น) *Calotropis gigantea (Asclepiadeae)*, akund-fibre, madar-fibre, an erect shrub found throughout India, reaching Ceylon, extending into China, and southwards to Singapore, Borneo, Java and the lesser Sunda Islands and Moluccas. It is wild in Java but cultivated elsewhere. In sanskritic India it was used in magic but does not enter into the magic of Malaya. Immigrants from India like to have it at hand for medicinal purposes, and the Malays have adopted its use too. The leaf is applied for poulticing sores; it is burned, and the smoke inhaled for ulceration of the nose. The latex is dropped into wounds and into hollow aching teeth. The Malays believe that it kills the worms which cause toothache; and by an extension of the idea, in Perak, leaves are placed in the runnels by which water enters rice-fields, that the worms and other pests, carried along by the water, may be killed before they enter. The leaves and roots are an elephant medicine, used externally and internally. The stems yield a fine hemp-like fibre, used for fishing lines, etc. The silky floss from the fruit is used for stuffing pillows, etc. The green leaves are applied to dispel swellings. The root is a tonic; the milk (latex) from stems is used for leprosy (V. P. p. 168: MCM. pp. 378, 429: BURK. p. 415): ปอทะเล *Siam.*, ปอนา (ต้น) *Hibiscus tiliaceus (Malvaceae)*, a large shrub or small tree, common at low to medium elevations in most parts of the tropics, chiefly near the seacoast and rivers. It yields a strong fibre used for cordage and mats. The fibre

is also used for tow and is used extensively in Malaya for caulking boats. In Singapore it is also used as lint. The timber is used in the Pacific for planking and for building light boats; in Malaysia for floats and rough household implements, and, in the eastern part, for the framework of boats. It is said to last well in contact with moisture. It is used generally as fire-wood. The roots and leaves are medicinal. The leaves may be fed to cattle, and are sometimes used in Java instead of teak leaves in conveying the ferment to soy-bean pulp in the manufacture of sauce (cb. p. 161: MCM. pp. 45, 430: V. P. p. 168: BURK. p. 1172): ปอทับ *Laos, Chiengmai*, ปอ-ปีด *Siam.*, *Ratburi*, ช้อ *Karen* (ต้น) *Helicteres isora (Sterculiaceae)*, a shrub or small tree with hazel-like leaves, found from India to Java. The fruit is conspicuously twisted with a rope-like appearance. It is dried, and sold abundantly for medicinal purposes throughout the Malay Peninsula. Apparently it is a harmless, very mild demulcent and astringent with little medicinal effect. The stems contain good strong fibre, to be obtained by retting, in which process some care is necessary. In southern India it is used as cordage for sewing gunny-bags, and for making bullock nose-ropes (MCM. p. 430: cb. p. 173: V. P. p. 169: BURK. p. 1135): ปอผ่าสาม *Laos, Nawngkai* (ต้น) *Sterculia lanceolata (Sterculiaceae)*, a small or medium-sized tree of Java, South China, etc., with rather small lanceolate leaves. It is very handsome when bearing its profusion of bright orange-scarlet fruit, consisting of a cluster of 5 follicles (usually in April to May). These spread out horizontally, opening on the under side, and display the large, shiny, blacks seeds which remain adhering to the margin of each follicle (MCM. p. 95: cb. p. 165): ปอหมัน (ต้น) *Cordia myxa (Borraginaceae)*, a small-sized tree fifteen to thirty feet in height, and nearly glabrous. The leaves are ovate or elliptical-ovate, entire and have a somewhat wavy margin. The inflorescence is corymbose and axillary, bearing very small, sessile, white or yellowish-white flowers. The drupe is fleshy, ovoide, yellowish-white and somewhat enclosed by the persistent and enlarged calyx. The fruit, which is very mucilaginous, is used medicinally, the mucilage being given in diseases of the chest and also as an astringent gargle. It is also employed as a laxative in bilious affections, and the kernels are considered a remedy for ring-worm. The wood is grey, moderately hard, but readily attacked by insects (The Orn. Trees of Hawaii, J. F. Rock p. 183).

ป้อ   bpaw[3] *adj.* strutting; pompous (as a cock).

ป้อ   bpaw[2] *adj.* dudish; foppish; affected.

ปอก   bpauk[4] *v.* to pare (as fruit); to peel (as an orange or banana); to skin or flay (as a rabbit): *adj.* skinned, pared or stripped off: ปอกเปลือก to remove the bark: ปอกลอก to swindle or defraud; to delude or beguile; to practice fraud.

ปอง (มุ่ง)   bpaung *v.* to purpose, propose or determine to do: ปองร้าย to plot or conspire to injure: ปองเอา to hope to get or accomplish (by craft or guile): ปองหมาย to will or wish to do.

ป้อง   bpaung[4] *n.* a scorpion: *adj.* bulging up or out; being rounded out or protruding by pressure from within (as a balloon).

ป้องๆ   bpaung[4]-bpaung[4] *adj.* restless; agitated; impatient; boisterous; violent (descriptive of one extremely angry); see งุ่นง่าน p. 224.

ป้อง   bpaung[3] see กัน p. 85: การยิงป้อง a protecting fire (military): ป้องกัน to use preventative means (as against some contagious disease); to afford a shelter (as against intrusion or for defensive purposes); to insure safety (as against injury or damage).

ปอด   bpaut[4] *n.* the lung. *adj.* withered;

shrunken; collapsed; dinted or caved in: ปอดน้ำ *N. Laos*, แพงพวย, พังพวย *Siam.* (ผัก) *Jussieua repens (Onagraceae)*, a plant floating in shallow swamps and rooting in mud, found throughout the tropics. It is used by the Malays in Perak for poulticing in skin complaints and may be seen stocked in Chinese herbalists' shops in the northern part of the Peninsula (cb. p. 733: Burk. p. 1273): ปอดแปด pliable; soft; easily dinted or distorted (out of normal shape).

ปอน   bpaun *adj.* inferior; dirty; old; dilapidated; worn out; see ขะมุกขะมอม p. 149.

ป้อน   bpraun[3] *v.* to place in the mouth (as food given to a child or medicine to an invalid); to hand to, or feed bit by bit.

ป้อแป้   bpaw[3]-bpaa[3] *adj.* weak; frail; sickly; cowardly; see ท้อแท้ p. 402.

ป้อม   bpaum[3] *n.* a fort; a citadel: *adj.* rounded; spherical: ป้อมล้อมวัง forts surrounding a palace; the fortified walls of a [palace.

ป้อม   bpaum[2] see ตุ่ม p. 372.

ปอย   bpoie *n.* a hank or skein (of thread or yarn): ปอยผม a tuft (of combed out hair).

ป้อย   bpoie[3] *v.* to curse, swear, scold or defame; see แช่ง p. 303.

ป้อยอ   bpaw[3]-yaw *v.* to praise, flatter or fawn over; to make use of fulsome compliments or undue praise.

ปะ   bpa[4] *v.* to meet with, find, or see; to patch; to mend or repair (by patching); to meet; to come together (in a casual way as when out on pleasure bent); to succeed in finding (as some strayed animal or lost article).

ปะกาปะกัง   bpa[4]-gkah-bpa[4]-gkang see งัก p. 222.

ปะการัง   bpa[4]-gkah-rang *n.* a form of tree coral.

ปะขาว   bpa[4]-kao[2] *n.* a sect of white-robed, ascetics (male or female).

ปะคำน้ำเงิน (นก)   bpa[4]-kum-num[5]-ngern *n.* the fairy bluebird, *Irena puella* (Gaird. J. S. S. IX, 1, p. 2).

ปะงับปะง่อน, ปะหงับปะง่อน   bpa[4]-ngup[6]- bpa[4]-ngaun[3] *adj.* weak; unstable; inclined [to topple over.

ปะเตะ see **เตะ** p. 373.

ปะทะ   bpa[4]-ta[6] *v.* to collide or come into contact with; to meet face to face.

ปะทะปะทัง   bpa[4]-ta[6]-bpa[4]-tung *v.* to use temporary means for relief; to use emergency measures to tide over a crisis.

ปะทุ   bpa[4]-too[6] *v.* to explode; to burst by force from within; to flash up noisily.

ปะบุก   bpa[4]-book[4] *n.* a venomous snake of the viper family.

ปะปน see **ปน** p. 494.

ปะมง see **ประโมง** p. 503.

ปะราลี see **บะราลี** p. 478.

ปะรำ   bpa[4]-rum *n.* a pavilion or temporary shelter roofed with cloth, canvas, thatch or leaves.

ปะลอม   bpa[4]-laum *v.* to eat ravenously or gluttonously; to gorge; to glut; see **กิน** p. 107.

ปะแล่ม   bpa[4]-laam[3] *adj.* slightly sweet in taste; sweetish.

ปะวะหล่ำ see **ประหล่ำ** p. 506.

ปะสัก *Thailand,* **พังกาหัวสุม** *Siam., Peninsula* (ต้น)   bpa[4]-suk[4] *n. Bruguiera conjugata* (*Rhizophoraceae*), a tree reaching 120 feet in height, found from eastern Africa to Polynesia. It marks the last stage of the mangrove forest, where ordinary land forest is intruding. It is probably the longest lived of the mangroves. The timber is brownish, or yellowish brown, heavy, fine-grained, with distinct sapwood and heart-wood. It seasons badly unless protected from the weather, and large trees are likely to have rot. For charcoal the tree ranks with *Rhizophora*. The bark has moderate tanning-value. The phlobaphene colouring-matter associated with the tan is sometimes used as a dye in Malaya and is preferred for black colours to *Nelastoma*. The Chinese use it as a black dye on cotton. It is not known that the Malays obtain any other colours with it, but appropriate treatment will obtain from it orange-reds, brown and violet shades. The fruits are sometimes used as an astringent in the betel-quid. They are eaten, but not when anything better is available. The bark is used as an astringent medicine for diarrhoea and sometimes in malaria (cb. p. 595 : V. P. p. 171 : Burk. p. 373).

ปะหงับปะง่อน see **ปะงับปะง่อน** p. 517.

ปะสักแดง see **กงกางหัวสุม** p. 2.

ปะหูด *E. Laos,* **ปราโฮด** *Khmer, Surin, Thailand, Bangkok* (ต้น)   bpa[4]-hoot[4] *n. Garcinia vilersiana* (*Guttiferae*) (cb. p. 118).

ปะเหลาะ see **ประจบ** p. 497.

ปะแฮ้ (นก)   bpa[4]-haa[5] *n.* the Siamese pied wood-pecker, *Dryobates analis longipeunus* (Deig. N. H. J. S. S. VIII, 3, p. 157).

บัก   bpuk[4] *v.* to force or ram into the mud (as fishing stakes); to pound into (as tent stakes into the ground): **บักกล้า** to imbed seedling rice plants : **บักเกษ** to insert in the hair (as flowers or fancy hairpins): **บักกรอง** to make embroidery : **บักชน** see **ชน** p. 299 : **บักมีด** to transfix with a knife or scalpel (as in opening an abscess) : **นาบัก** fields where the rice plants have been transplanted.

บักข์ see **บักษ์** p. 518.

บักเบ๊า (ปลา)   bpuk[4]-bpow[3] *n.* the globe fish, *Tetraodon etoile* (*Tetraodontidae*); *T. fluviatilis*; *T. leopardus*; *T. lunaris*; *T. oblongus* (Suvatti pp. 165, 166): **บักเบ๊า (ว่าว)**

the long-tailed kite; the lady kite: บัก-
เบ้าเขียว, บักเบ้าน้ำจืด (ปลา) *Tetraodon palem-
bangensis (Tetraodontidae)* (suvatti p. 166):
บักเบ้าดำ (ปลา) *Tetraodon leiurus (Tetraodontidae)* (suvatti p. 165): นักเบ้าทะเล (ปลา)
Tetraodon etoile (Tetraodontidae) (suvatti p.
165): บักเบ้าทอง (ปลา) *Chonerhinos modestus
(Tetraodontidae)* (suvatti p. 167): บักเบ้า-
ทุเรียน (ปลา) *Diodon novemmaculatus (Diodontidae),* a poisonous marine fish. Darwin, in
his *Voyage of a Naturalist,* gives an account
of this fish. He states that it is frequently
found floating and alive in the stomach of a
shark and occasionally eats its way out and
escapes (suvatti p. 167: burk. p. 811): บักเบ้า-
หนามทุเรียน (ปลา) *Diodon hystrix (Diodontidae)*
(suvatti p. 167).

บักคหะ   bpak^4-ka^6-ha^4 *n.* supreme perseverance.

บักษ, บักข   bpuk^4 *S. n.* a wing; a pinion;
a side, party or faction; a half of a lunar
month; a fortnight (S. E. D. p. 573): บักษกษัย
the end of a half moon: บักษคณนา, บักขคณนา
the half of a lunar month: บักษคม *lit.*
"moving with wings," *i. e.* birds: บักษจร
one straying from the herd (as an elephant);
a maverick: บักษชนม์ *lit.* "one born during the middle of a month," *i. e.* the moon:
บักษทวัย *lit.* "including the two phases of the
moon," *i. e.* a month: บักษธร *lit.* "those
having wings," *i. e.* birds; an appellation for
the moon: บักษนาที a quill (pen): บักษบาต
lit. "the descending of wings," *i. e.* the flying
or mounting up of birds: บักษบาลี a wing;
บักษพินทุ *lit.* "spotted winged," *i. e.* the heron:
บักษภาค the side or flank of an elephant:
บักษเภท the difference or disagreement between two sides in an argument; the variance
between the two halves of a lunar month:
บักษวาหน *lit.* "those whose vehicles are wings,"
i. e. birds: บักษานคร, บักขันตร the other
party or parties: บักษาวสาน the last day of
each half-moon; the day of new or full-moon.

บักษิน, บักษี   bpuk^4-sin^2 *P. S. n. lit.* "any

winged animal," *i. e.* a bird (S. E. D. p. 574):
บักษิบดี *lit.* "a king of birds," *i. e.* the son of
the Garuda: บักษิมารค *lit.* "the path for
birds," *i. e.* the air or atmosphere: บักษิราช
lit. "the king of birds," *i. e.* the Garuda:
บักษิศาลา birds' nests; a bird-house: บักษิ-
สิงห์ *lit.* "a lion among birds," *i. e.* the Garuda.

บัง ๑   see ขนม p. 139.

บัง ๒   bpung *onomat.* from the sound of a
blow or bang; the explosion of a firecracker
or the slam of a door: *adj.* having hit the
object aimed at.

บงส์   see บงสุ์ p. 466.

บังสุกุล   see บังสุกุล p. 466.

บัจจถรณ์, บัจจัตถรณ์   see บรรจถรณ์ p. 468.

บัจจนึก, บัจจามิตร   bpat^4-chja^4-nuk^4 *P. n.*
an enemy; a foe; an adversary: *adj.* adverse; hostile (chd. p. 308).

บัจจยาการ   bpat^4-chja^4-yah-gkarn *P. n.*
originating as a necessary result from a cause;
a chain of causation and effect (chd. p. 359).

บัจจเวกขณ์   bpat^4-chja^4-wek^3 *P. n.* looking at; consideration; contemplation; self-
examination (chd. p. 309).

บัจจันต์, ปรัตยันต์, ปรัตยนต์   bpat^4-chjun
P. adj. skirting; bordering on; adjacent to
(chd. p. 308); contiguous: บัจจันตคาม a
frontier village; a town on the border:
บัจจันตประเทศ an adjoining territory.

บัจจัย, บัตยัย   bpat^4-chjai *P. n.* cause;
motive; ground; faith; conviction; four requisites for comfort, or for a Buddhist monk,
viz. clothing, provisions, place of residence or
shelter and remedies (chd. p. 309).

บัจจามิตร   bpat^4-chjah-mit^6 *P. n.* an enemy;
an adversary (chd. p. 308).

บัจจุคมนะ   bpat^4-chjoo^4-ka^6-ma^6-na^6 *P. n.*
the going forth to meet a guest (as a sign of

respect); the rising from a seat to meet or welcome a guest (chd. p. 311).

บัจจุปบัน, บัจจุบัน, ปรัตยุตบัน, ปรัตยุบัน bpat[4]-chjoop[4]-bun *P. n.* that which is existing now; the present time; the immediate present (chd. p. 312): บัจจุปบันพยาบาล to render first aid.

บัจจุส, บัจจุส, ปรัตยุต bpat[4]-chjoot[4] *P. n.* morning; dawn; the morning (chd. p. 312): บัจจุสกาล, บัจโจสกาล, บัจจุสสมัย day-break; early dawn; a short time before sunrise.

บัจจุหะ bpat[4]-chjoo-ha[4] *n.* danger; or obstruction.

บัจเจก, ประเดยก, ประเจก, ปรตเยก, ปรัต- เยก bpat[4]-chjeck *P. S. adj.* singly; individually; personally; one by one; one at a time (chd. p. 309): บัจเจกพุทธะ one who has attained, like a Buddha, by his unaided powers, the knowledge necessary to attain Nirvana, but who does not preach it to men (chd. p. 309); Pacheka Buddhas, an inferior class of Buddhas. They are beings who attain to the same personal wisdom and perfection as true Buddhas, but have none of that compassion which leads true Buddhas to be teachers of mankind. They only appear in the world when there is no true Buddha living (Ala. p. 187): บัจเจกโพธิ the condition of being a Pacheka Buddha.

บัจฉา bpat[4]-chah[2] *P. adj.* behind; after; afterwards; back; backwards; westward (chd. p. 310): บัจฉาภัตต์ the time following the partaking of food, *viz.* the afternoon, during which time the Buddhist clergy are forbidden to eat: บัจฉาสมณะ a junior priest who accompanies a senior priest when he leaves the monastery to beg alms or to make a journey, and walks a short distance behind him (chd. p. 311).

บัจฉิม, บัศจิม, ประจิม bpat[4]-chim[2] *P. n.* west: *adj.* behind; after; hindmost; last; western (chd. p. 311): บัจฉิมชน a people,

tribe or citizens living towards the west; those born later: บัจฉิมภาค the latter end, time or season: บัจฉิมยาม see ปฐมยาม p. 494: บัจฉิมลิขิต *lit.* " written or added later," *i. e.* a postscript: บัจฉิมวัย the closing years of life; old age.

บัชชธร see **ประชวร** p. 498.

บัญจ see **เบ็ญจ** p. 487.

บัญจก see **เบ็ญจก** p. 488.

บัญจม see **เบ็ญจม** p. 488.

บัญญัตติ see **บัญญัติ** p. 475.

บัญญา bpun-yah *P. n.* wisdom; intellect; reason; intelligence; talent; genius; sense (Ala. p. 184: chd. p. 329): บัญญาไว of quick intelligence.

บัญญาส bpun-yart[3] *P.S. n.* fifty (chd. p. 33): บัญญาสชาดก name of a volume of the Buddha's birth stories.

บัญหา, ปรัศนา bpun-hah[2] *P. n.* a question; a problem (chd. p. 328); a riddle: บัญหากฎหมาย a point of law: บัญหาเท็จจริง *legal* a point of fact.

บัฎ see **บฎ, บัฏ** p. 475.

บัฎนะ bpat[4]-dta[4]-na[6] *P. S. n.* a port; a seaport town or village (chd. p. 371).

บัณณ see **บรรณ** p. 468.

บัณณรส, บัณณรส์ bpun-na[6]-ra[6]-sa[4] *P. n.* the fifteenth; the fifteenth day of the month; the day of the full, or of the new moon (chd. p. 330).

บัณหิ bpun-hi[4] *P. n.* the heel (chd. p. 328).

บัด bput[4] *v.* to brush, wipe, mop or clean (as furniture of dust); to disregard; to turn one's attention away (as though assuming no responsibility for); to fan or cause to be wafted away (as smoke); to swing or wave the hands (so as to drive off insects): บัดเกล้า

an attitude assumed by a mahout while performing a propitiatory dance on the occasion of trying the strength of his animal : บัดขวา-บัดซ้าย a right carriage return ; a left carriage return (descriptive of typewriters) : บัดตลอด marked with white or black lines from head to tail (used in regard to cats) : บัดที่นอน to air and make the bed : บัดเป่า to make sweeps, passes and repasses with the hands, coupled with blowing from the head down towards the feet (as a means of exorcizing evil spirits possessing the person); to disentangle oneself by the above means : บัดยุง to brush off mosquitoes : บัดใยแมลงมุม to sweep down cobwebs : บัดรังควาน to excorcize evil spirits from a house or out of a person : ไม้บัด a dust brush or duster : ลูกบัด beads.

บัตตานีกะ, บัตตานึก, บรรตานึก, บัตติก bpat⁴-dtah-nee-gka⁴ *P. n.* a pedestrian ; infantry ; a foot-soldier ; a footman (chd. p. 372).

บัตตาเวีย (ดอก) bpat⁴-dtah-weah *n. Jatropha pandurifolia (Euphorbiaceae)* (mcm. p. 113 : Burk. p. 1267).

บัตนิ, บัตนี bpat⁴-dta⁴-ni⁴ *S. n.* a wife ; a mistress ; a female possessor (S. E. D. p. 582).

บัตยัย see บัจจัย p. 518.

บัถพี see ปถพี p. 493.

บัถพีวิทยา bpat⁴-ta-pee-wit⁶-ta⁶-yah *n.* the science of the soil ; the name of a section in the Ministry of Agriculture.

บัทม, บัทม์, ปทุม bpat⁴-ma⁶ *P. S. n.* a lotus ; the lotus flower, *Nelubrium speciosum* ; one of the high numerals, ten millions raised to the 15th power, or a digit followed by 119 cyphers (chd. p. 315) : บัทม-กร a lotus-like hand (S. E. D. p. 584). บัทม-เกตุ name of an offspring of the Garuda : บัทมคนธ์ a lotus-like odour : บัทมครรภ *lit.* "lotus born," *i. e.* Brahma : บัทมนาภ Vishnu, from whose navel sprang the lotus which

contained Brahma, the future creator (S. E. D. p. 584) : บัทมนาล lotus stalks or stems : บัทมปาณิ "lotus-handed ;" one holding a lotus, *i. e.* Brahma ; Vishnu : บัทมพันธุ์ *lit.* "progeny of the lotus," *i. e.* the bee : บัทมพืช the lotus seed : บัทมภาส *lit.* "one brilliant with, or like a lotus," *i. e.* descriptive of Vishnu : บัทมมูล the lotus bulb or root : บัทมราค, ปทุมราค *lit.* "lotus-hued," *i. e.* a ruby ; a red or semi-precious stone : บัทมเรขา a line ; a line in the palm of the hand indicating the acquisition of great wealth : บัทมวาสา *lit.* "one whose abode is the lotus," *i. e.* Lakshmi, goddess of Beauty and Fortune, wife of Vishnu and mother of Karma (H. C. D. p. 176) : บัทมสังกาศ resembling the lotus : บัทมหาส *lit.* "smiling like a budding lotus flower," *i. e.* Vishnu : บัทมากร a lotus pond or an assemblage of lotus blossoms or plants : บัทมาการ shaped like a lotus : บัทมาลัย *lit.* "one dwelling in a lotus," *i. e.* Brahma : บัทมาสน์ a seat or pedestal decorated to represent upright or inverted lotus petals (as can often be seen under images of the Buddha) ; a posture in religious meditation.

บัน see แบ่ง p. 490 : บันกัน, แบ่งสันปันครึ่ง to divide fifty-fifty : บันการ to subdivide or sectionalize work : บันข้าวของ to divide one's personal effects for distribution.

บั่น bpun⁴ *v.* to cause to revolve, spin or turn on an axis : ท้องปั่นป่วน a feeling of uneasiness or uncertainty as regards the action of the bowels : ปั่นป่วน to feel perturbed, confused, uncertain, wavering or uneasy as regards emotions or actions : ปั่นฝ้าย to spin cotton thread (not kapok).

บั้น, บ้าน bpun³ *v.* to feign or make believe ; to mould wax, mud or soft clay into shape : *n.* a clod or lump ; a terracotta teapot : บันน้ำเป็นตัว *lit.* "to make water appear as a physical form," *i. e.* to represent the incredible as credible ; to make fiction appear as truth ; to make the improbable appear as probable : บั๋นเป็นรูป to form an image or statue out of mud or wax : บั๋นยศ to display undue arrogance or pride : บั๋น-สีหน้า to mask a falsehood ; to equivocate.

บั๋นจั๋น bpun³-chjun⁴ *n.* a crane for hoisting purposes.

บั๋นจุเหร็จ bpun-chjoo⁴-ret⁴ *n.* a chaplet, coronet or fancy headband.

บั๋นปิ่ง bpun³-bpung⁴ *adj.* feigning displeasure by appearing sullen.

บั๋นลม bpun³-lom *n.* an ornamental gable end for Thai houses.

บั๋นล่ำ bpun³-lum³ *v.* to be proud, arrogant, puffed up, or boastful.

บั๋นหยา bpun³-yah² *n.* a pattern of Thai architectural design for common houses, without ornamental gable ends.

บั๋นเหน่ง bpun³-neng⁴ *n.* a belt ; a girdle.

บับ bpup⁴ *onomat.* from the sound of a thud or thump (as when struck while boxing).

บั๋ปผาสะ, บั๊ปผาสะ bpup⁴-pah²-sa⁴ *P. n.* the lung (chd. p. 332).

บั๊พพชิต see บรรพชิต p. 469.

บั๊พพต see บรรพต p. 469.

บั๊พพะ see บรรพ ๑ p. 469.

บั๊พพัชชา see บรรพชา p. 469.

บพพาชนะ, บั๊พพาชน์ bpup⁴-pah-cha⁶-na⁶ *P. n.* the act of driving out, off, away, or of separating oneself from the world (as by becoming a Buddhist monk) ; banishment ; ordination (chd. p. 305).

บั๊พภาระ bpup⁴-pah-ra⁶ *P. n.* a cave in a mountain (chd. p. 306) ; an over-hanging rock or projection with a cave-like space underneath.

บั๋ยยกะ, บั๋ยยกา bpai-ya⁶-gka⁴ *P. n.* a paternal great-grandfather (chd. p. 378).

บั๋ยยิกา bpai-yi⁶-gkah *P. n.* a paternal great-grandmother.

บั๋ลลพ, บั๋ลลวะ see บัลลวะ p. 477.

บั๋ลลังก์ see บรรยงก์ p. 469.

บั๋วเปี๋ย bpoo-ah-bpee-ah *v.* to be mixed up or associated with (used in a derogatory sense).

บั๋วเปี๋ย bpoo-ah³-bpee-ah³ *adj.* wabbling ; frail ; weak ; infirm.

บัสสาวะ bpat⁴-sah²-wa⁶ *P. n.* urine (chd. p. 355) : ถ่ายบั๋สสาวะ to pass urine : บั๋ส-สาวะจืด (โรค) diabetes insipidus ; a chronic disease marked by the passage of a large amount of urine with no excess of sugar, attended with great thirst, voracious appetite, loss of strength and emaciation : บั๋สสาวะ-หวาน (โรค) diabetes mellitus ; glycosuria ; a disease marked by the passage of an excessive amount of urine containing an excess of sugar.

บั๋สสาสะ bpat⁴-sah²-sa⁴ *P. n.* exhaled breath ; an exhalation (chd. p. 354).

ปา see ขว้าง p. 145 : ทิ้ง p. 414.

ป่า bpah⁴ (see ดง p. 317) *adj.* wild ; uninhabited ; unproductive : ชาวป่า savage people or tribes ; barbarians : ป่าจาก a thicket of nepa palms : ป่าช้า a cemetery : ป่าดง a jungle ; a forest choked with undergrowth : ป่าดงพงทึบ (combined for euphony) a jungle : ป่าบึ่ง, ป่าโป่ง a forest of tall trees : ป่าไผ่ clumps of bamboo : ป่าไม้ a forest ; woods ; forest land : ป่าละเมาะ groves of small trees in clumps : อย่างคนป่า unrefined ; ill-bred ; ill-mannered ; uncouth.

ป้า bpah³ *n.* an elder sister of the father or mother ; an aunt : ป้าสะใภ้ an aunt by marriage.

ปาก, โอฐ, มุกขะทวาร bpark⁴ (see ทวาร p. 400) *n.* an orifice ; a mouth ; a designatory particle for fishing-nets : คึ่มปากคืบ claw-shaped forceps : ปากกบ a beveled or mitred joint ; the junction of two ends or edges at an angle of 45° (as in a picture-frame) : ปากกระจับ a serrated rim or edge (as of a tray or cuspidor) : กระจับ a tray thus made : ปากกริว a square-edged joint, formed by two edges meeting in a corner (a carpenter's term) : ปากกล้า bold and insolent in speech, with an argumentative tendency : ปากกว้าง (นก) the Burmese eared nightjar, *Lyncornis cervini-ceps* (Gaird. J. S. S. IX, 1, p. 6) : ปากกะปะ (งู) a species of poisonous snake, *Ancistrodon rhodostoma* (M. S., N. H. J. S. S. VI, 1, p. 62) : ปากกา, ปากไก่ a pen ; a pen nib : ปากกา *Thailand., Krabi,* หมากหมก *Thailand, Chumpawn* and *Surat* (ต้น) *Adenia angustisepala* (*Passifloraceae*) (cb. p. 745) : ปากกา *mechanical* calipers ; compasses : ปากกาหมึกซึม a fountain pen : คนปากกว้าง *lit.* "bottle-mouthed," *i. e.* one with a very small mouth : ปากขาด, ปากแหว่ง congenital hare-lip : ปากแข็ง given to stubborn contradicting or arguing ; a hard bit or mouth-piece of a bridle : ปากคม sharp-tongued : ปากคีบ forceps ; pliers ; tweezers ; pincers : ปากจะขาบ, ปากตะขาบ converging ends (as the nippers of a centipede) : ปากจัด contradictory ; given to sarcasm or tongue lashing : ปากจิ้งจก (งู) a species of small green snake, having a mouth similar in shape to that of the house lizard : ปากโจทย์ the testimony or attestation of an accuser : ปากช้าง, ปากฉลาม an opening or aperture shaped like an elephant's mouth (as a two-sided surgical flap) : ปากตรอก the entrance to a lane : ปากแตร a trumpet-shaped opening : ปากใต้, ผึ้ง, มูด, ยาลู, รากกล้วย, ลูกผึ้ง (ปลา) *Gyrinocheilus kaznakovi* (*Cyprinidae*) (suvatti p. 54) : ปากน้ำ the mouth of a river ; an estuary : ปากบอน gossiping ; tattling ; blabbing or back-biting conversation : ปากเบา given to crying, complaining or grumbling : ปากเปิด (ต้น) *Vanda parishii* (*Orchidaceae*), an orchid of south-eastern Asia and Malaysia (V. P. p. 174) : ปากเปราะ loquacious ; talka-tive ; given to groundless, harsh, angry or faultfinding words. If used in reference to a dog, the word means barking readily at everything ; a ready-barker : ปากเปราะเราะร้าย, ปากคอเราะร้าย the use of quarrelsome or irritating language without provocation : ปากปลา (เรือ) a form of ancient boat whose prow is shaped like the mouth of a fish : ปากไปล่ a type of dish having a large brim but small base (resembling an inverted palm leaf hat) : ปากภาชนะ the edge, brim, rim, side, mouth, flange or margin of any utensil (as cups, buckets, etc.) : ปากมาก, ลิ้นยาว loquacious ; chattering ; given to extravagant or exaggerating market-talk : *slang* long-tongued : ปากไม้ the aperture or opening mortised in a timber, into which a tenon is fitted : ปากร้าย the use of angry, vulgar or contemptuous language : ปากปลิง the point of a stem or stalk of a fruit when attached to the tree-trunk (as jack-fruit) : ปากลาก (นก) the black-capped kingfisher, *Halcyon pileata* (Gaird. J. S. S. IX, 1, p. 7) : ปากสว่าง given to exposing, revealing or divulging secrets easily : ปากหนัก *lit.* "close-mouthed," *i. e.* not given to much talking ; secretive : ปากหมด prevaricating ; equivocating : ปากหวาน polite, polished or pleasing talk (sarcastic in meaning) ; mouth-honouring ; double-tongued ; caustic ; spiteful : ปากหอย, ปากปู given to slanderous, defaming, blaming or calumniating talk : ปากห่าง (นก) the open-bill ibis, *Anastomus oscitans* (Herb. N. H. J. S. S. VI, 4, p. 350) : ปากอ่าว the sea or gulf entrance to a river or port : มีปาก to have something to say or speak : มีปากมีคอ contentious ; quarrelsome : ริมฝีปาก the lips.

ปาง bpang (see ครั้ง p. 180 : คราว p. 181) epoch : *adv.* almost ; nearly ; wellnigh ; all but ; close upon : ปางก่อน previously ; prior to ; antecedent to : ปางตาย nearly at death's door : ปางเมื่อพระมหากระษัตริย์เสด็จไปนั้น at the time of the king's passing : อวตารปางที่ ๓ the third incarnation (as of Vishnu).

ป้าง bpang³ *n.* a hypertrophy of the spleen due to chronic malarial poisoning; the so called ague-cake.

ปาจนะ bpah-chja⁴-na⁶ *P. n.* a goad (chd. p. 307).

ปาจรีย์, บาจรีย์ bpah-chja⁴-ree *P. n.* a pupil (chd. p. 307).

ปาจิตตีย์ bpah-chjit⁴-dtee *P. n.* offences of the Buddhist clergy requiring expiation (chd. p. 312).

ปาจีน bpah-chjeen *P. adj.* eastern; eastward (chd. 312).

ปาฏลิ (ต้น) bpah-dta⁴-li⁶ *P. S. n.* the trumpet flower, *Bignonia suaveolens* (*Bignoniaceae*) (chd. p. 356); see แค (ต้น) p. 212.

ปาฏลิบุตร bpah-dta⁴-li⁶-boot⁴ *S. n.* Pataliputra, "The City of Flowers," the Palibothra of the Greek writers and described by them as being situated at the confluence of the Sone and Ganges rivers. It was the capital of the Nandas and of the Maurya dynasties, founded by Chandragupta who succeeded them as ruler of Magadha. The city has been identified with the modern Patna (H.C.D. p. 233); name of the capital of Magadha near the confluence of the Sone and the Ganges (S. E. D. p. 615).

ปาฏิบท bpah-dti⁴-bot⁴ *P. S. n.* the first day of either the waxing or waning of the moon: *adj.* belonging to the first day of the lunar fortnight (chd. p. 364).

ปาฏิบุคคลิก bpah-dti⁴-book⁴-ka⁶-lik⁶ *n.* an individual or person: *adj.* individual; single; existing as an entity.

ปาฏิโภค bpah-dti⁴-poke³ *P. n.* a surety; a guarantor; security; a sponsor (chd. p. 359).

ปาฏิหาริย์, ปราติหารย์ bpah-dti⁴-harn² *P. n.* a miracle; a portent (chd. p. 361).

ปาฐ bpah-ta⁴ *P. S. n.* a recitation; a reading; text; a passage of a text (chd. p. 358).

ปาฐก bpah-tok⁴ *P. S. n.* a reader; a reciter; a lecturer; one who reads or studies the lineaments of the body; a fortune-teller (chd. p. 357).

ปาฐกถา bpah-ta⁴-gka⁴-tah² *n.* a lecture; a discourse read or spoken (as for instruction).

ปาณ bpah-na⁶ *P. n.* breath; life; vitality; a living creature; energy; vigour; strength (chd. p. 331): ปาณทัณฑ์ capital punishment: ปาณนาถ *lit.* "the lord of life," *i. e.* a husband; the god of Death, Yama: ปาณนาศ, ปาณวินาศ *lit.* "a vanishing of life," *i. e.* death: ปาณบดี *lit.* "the sovereign of life," *i. e.* the soul: ปาณภูต living creatures: ปาณสาร dexterity: ปาณาติบาต the act of killing or destroying life.

ปาณก, ปาณกชาติ bpah-na⁶-gka⁴ *P. n.* a small creature; a worm; an insect (chd. p. 326).

ปาณิ ๑ bpah-ni⁶ *P.S. n.* the hand; a wooden hand or trowel; an instrument; a tool (chd. p. 328): ปาณิเคราะห์ *lit.* "the clasping of a bride," *i. e.* a wedding; a marriage: ปาณิดล the palm of the hand: ปาณิธรรม a marriage ceremony: ปาณิมุกต์ a missile weapon; a javelin; a lance: ปาณิมูล *lit.* "the base of the hand," *i. e.* the wrist.

ปาณิ ๒ bpah-ni⁶ *P. n.* a sentient living being; a creature; an animal; a man: *adj.* alive; living (chd. p. 329).

ปาด bpart⁴ (see เฉือ p. 392; เชือด p. 302) *v.* to slice, shave, pare or prune diagonally; to excise (as removing a defect from fruit): *n.* a species of tree frog: ปาด *Thailand, Pangnga* and *Puket,* ลำพู *Thailand* (ต้น) *Sonneratia caseolaris* (*Sonneratiaceae*) (cb. p. 731); *S. caseolaris* (*Lythraceae*), a tree up to 70 feet in height and 5 feet in girth, found on, or near the banks of tidal rivers, from India throughout Malaysia; in the Peninsula it is abundant. The young fruit is sour and is esteemed for flavouring chutnies and curries.

When ripe, the fruits have a cheese-like taste and are eaten raw or cooked. The fruit has medicinal uses. The timber is of very little use except as firewood. The bark contains tannin, but less than several other trees of the mangrove forest (BURK. p. 2052).

ปาติโมกข์   bpah-dti[4]-moke[3] *P. n.* the Buddhist sacred books of precepts (Ala. p. 190): The name is given to a collection of various precepts contained in the Vinai. These are solemnly read twice a month in every monastery, and individual priests are invited to make confession if they have broken any of the precepts read out. It may be described as the criminal code of the Buddhist priests [chd. p. 363).

ปาท see บาท p. 480.

ปาทป   bpah-top[6] *P. S. n.* a tree (chd. p. 314).

ปาทุกา, บาทุกา, บราทุกรา, ปราทุกรา bpah-too[6]-gkah *P. S. n.* a shoe; a slipper; footwear (chd. p. 315).

ปาน ๑ see บาน ๑ p. 480.

ปาน ๒   bpan *n. lit.* "a mother's mark," *i. e.* nevus; a mole; a pigmented spot on the skin, either congenital or acquired; a reddish patch on the skin formed by dilated blood-vessels: *adj.* like; equal to: ปานฉะนี้, ปานนี้, ปานนี้ such time as this; up to such time as this.

บาน (ต้น)   bpan[4] *n. Boehmeria nivea (Urticaceae)*, ramie grass, rhea grass, Chinese grass, a shrub found from Japan down the eastern side of China to Malaysia, in two varieties. Within these two varieties are races, some of which give a little more fibre than others. From the inner bark of the stems is obtained the rhea-fibre of commerce, which is pure white, of a silky lustre, and is used in the manufacture of fine linen, incandescent gas mantles, etc. (MCM. p. 426: BURK. [p. 341).

บ้าน see บน p. 520.

บ้านดำ *Laos, Chiengmai* (ต้น)   bpan[3]-dum *n. Nymphaea cyanea (Nymphaeaceae)*, a water-lily (cb. p. 73): บ้านแดง *Laos, Chiengmai*, บัวแดง, บัวจงกลนี *Siam.*, บัวขี้แปะ *Laos, Korat*, ประลีก *Khmer* (ต้น) *Nymphaea lotus, var. pubescens (Nymphaeaceae)*, a rose-flowered or white water-lily, a native of Africa, but long cultivated in Asia and now widespread. The seeds are a delicacy in Thailand. In India they are pounded and made into a kind of bread (MCM. pp. 175, 312: BURK. p. 1566).

ปานิยะ, บานิยะ   bpah-nee-ya[6] *P. S. n.* an appetizing or tempting drink; a beverage: *adj.* drinkable (chd. p. 329): ปานีโยทก drinking water.

ป้าบ   bparp[6] *onomat.* from the sound of a slap or spank with a flat ruler.

ปาปะ see บาป p. 481.

ปาพจน์ see ประพจน์ p. 502.

ปามขวด (ต้น)   bparm-kuat[4] *n. Roystonea regia (Palmae)* (BURK. p. 1917); *Oreodoxa regia*, the royal palm or bottle palm, a native of the West Indies, which is commonly planted in Bangkok gardens and big compounds, usually as an avenue tree. It is said to have been introduced from Singapore by Phya Pradibhat Bhubal some 38 years ago (winit, N. H. J. S. S. IX, 1, p. 100): ปามโคลัมโบ (ต้น) *Stevensonia grandifolia (Phoenicophorium sechellarum) (Palmae)*, a native of the Seychelle Islands. It was brought under cultivation in 1855, and seeds were sent to Singapore in 1875 and at subsequent dates. It was first obtained for Thailand from Ceylon. It has leaves of a reddish tint (winit, N. H. J. S. S. IX, 1, p. 105: BURK. p. 2083): ปามจีน, ปามเชี่ยงไฮ้ (ต้น) *Livistona chinensis (Palmae)*, a palm used for making hats in the Philippine Islands (BURK. p. 1358); *Latania borbonica (Palmae)* (winit, N. H. J. S. S. IX, 3, p. 276: MCM. p. 167): ปามน้ำมัน (ต้น) *Elaeis guineensis (Palmae)*, an oil-palm which has supplied the negroes of many

parts of Africa with oil for cooking from remote times. The oil first reached Europe in
the sixteenth century; but it was only at the
beginning of the nineteenth century that its
commercial possibilities were realized. There
are two oils in the fruit; one is in the fruit-
wall; the other is in the kernel. That in the
fruit-wall is the more fluid, and was the first
to enter into international commerce, under
the name Palm Oil. The thicker and more
valuable fat from the kernel came into international commerce rather later (winit, N. H.
J. S. S. IX, 3, p. 273 : MCM. p. 164 : BURK. p. 893):
ปามบึงมา to burst in excitedly, noisily or
abruptly : ปามพัด, ปามหางปลา (ต้น) *Pritchar-
dia pacifica* (winit, N. H. J. S. S. IX, 3, p. 280):
ปามข่าวา (ต้น) *Livistona rotundifolia (Palmae)*,
a palm, the leaves of which are used as
packing-paper in some parts of the Dutch
Indies. It is said to have been first brought
from Java by King Chulalongkorn in 1901,
the year in which the memorable Java weed
was also introduced into Siam (winit, N.H.J.S.S.
IX, 1, p. 98 : Burk. p. 1358).

ปาโมกข์ bpah-moke[3] *P. n.* one being
first, in front of, principal or excellent; a
chief; one eminent (chd. p. 325).

ปาโมชช์ see ปราโมทย์ p. 507.

ป่าย (ปีน) bpai[4] *v.* to climb or clamber
(as up a tree); to work ones way up (as over
a mountain side); to aspire to a higher plane
(as in social position).

ป้าย bpai[3] (see บ้าย p. 481.) *n.* a name or
bulletin board; a placard.

ปายาส bpah-yart[3] *P. n.* rice with milk;
rice porridge; a porridge made of boiled rice
and sugar (chd. p. 377).

ปาร bpah-ra[6] *P. S. n.* the further or opposite shore of a sea, or bank of a river. Nirvana, as being the goal reached by the pilgrim
crossing the ocean of existence (chd. p. 334).

ปารคู bpah-ra[6]-koo *P. n.* one who has
crossed to the other side; one who has passed
beyond or escaped from (the state of suffering) (chd. p. 333).

ปารษณิ, ปราษณิ bpart[4]-sa[4]-nee *P. S. n.*
the heel (chd. p. 328).

ปาราชิก bpah-rah-chik[6] *P. n.* one meriting
expulsion. Sins involving expulsion from
the priesthood are the most heinous of the
priestly offences enumerated in the Vinaya
and are placed at the head of the list. There
are four, *viz.* (1) fornication; (2) theft; (3)
taking of life; (4) falsely laying claim to the
possession of Arhatship or any of the other
supernatural gifts (chd. p. 333): *adj.* defeated;
guilty of any of the above mentioned.

ปาริฉัตต์, ปาริฉัตตก์, ปาริชาต bpah-ri[6]-
chart[4] *n.* a tree of paradise; a tree in Indra's
heaven; the coral tree, *Erythrina indica
(Leguminosae)* (MCM. p. 88 : chd. p. 342).

ปารุปนะ bpah-roo[6]-bpa[4]-na[6] *P. n.* mantle,
cloak, blanket, upper garment or robe (chd.
p. 351).

ปาลิ bpah-lee *P. n.* a guardian; a keeper
(chd. p. 323); see บาลิ p. 482.

ป่าว bpow[4] *v.* to publish abroad; to proclaim, or cause to be broadcast: ป่าวร้อง
to announce aloud or in a public manner; to
proclaim.

ป๊าว bpow[6] *onomat.* from the sound of
the mewing of a cat.

ป๊าว ๆ bpow-bpow *onomat.* from the sound
of loud and repeated shouting.

ปาวก, บาพก bpah-wok[6] *P. S. n.* fire
(chd. p. 374).

ปาวามัลละ bpah-wah-mun-la[6] *P. S. n.* a
city of the Mallas, (มัลละ), near Raja-griha
the capital of Magadha. The site is still
traceable in the hills between Patna and Gaya
(H. C. D. p. 253).

ปาวาร bpah-warn *P. n.* woollen cloth; a cloak or mantle (chd. p. 374).

ปาษาณ, ปาสาณ, ปราษาณ bpah-sarn^2 *S. n.* a stone; a small stone used as a weight (S. E. D. p. 624).

ปาสาทิกะ bpah-sah^2-ti^6-gka^4 *P. adj.* pleasing; amiable; gracious; engaging (chd. p. 352).

ปาหุณ bpah-hoo^4-na^6 *P. S. n.* a guest; a visitor (chd. p. 317); see แขก p. 168.

ปาหุไณย์ bpah-hoo^4-nai *P. adj.* worthy of being guests; worthy of hospitality (chd. p. 317): ปาหุไณยบุทคล those worthy of hospitality.

ป้ำ, พ้ำ bpum *v.* to fall face downwards; to tumble, slip, fall or trip headlong; to fall prostrate; to drop point downwards (as an arrow into the ground); see คว่ำลง p. 189.

ป้ำ bpum^3 *adj.* sporting; daring; plucky; nervy: ใจป้ำ venturesome; ready to risk, tackle or jump in on any proposition.

ป้ำเป้อ bpum^3-bpur^3 *adj.* fat, bulky or clumsy in stature; huge or gigantic physically.

ป้ำๆ เป้อๆ bpum^3-bpum^3-bpur^2-bpur^2 *adj.* heavy; inactive; lethargic; forgetful.

ปิ้ง bping^3 *v.* to bake (as bread); to roast (as corn or meat); to toast (as bread); to broil on a spit (as fish over a fire).

ปิงคละ bping-ka^6-la^6 *P. S. n.* the brown elephant: *adj.* brown; tawny; brownish-yellow or reddish-brown (chd. p. 384).

ปิฎก bpi^4-dok^4 *P. S. n.* a basket; a box; a granary; a collection of writings; an ornament on Indra's banner; a boil; a blister (S. E. D. p. 625); see ตะกร้า p. 349.

ปิฏฐิ bpit^4-ti4 *P. n.* the back; the hinderpart; the top; the upper surface (chd. p. 385).

ปิด ๑ bpit^4 *v.* to shut; to close (as an opening); to hide; to conceal; to put out of sight:

การปิดปาก *legal* estoppel; prohibition: การ-ปิดปากโดยสำนวน *legal* estoppel by the record: เงินปิดปาก hush-money: ปิดความ to conceal, hide, keep silent about, hush up or suppress a matter: ปิดทางเดิน to occlude, obstruct or block a passage: ปิดน้ำ to dam or block a water-passage: ปิดเบา to suffer from retention of urine: ปิดบัง to screen, cloak, mask or disguise (as valuable information): ปิดบังผู้กระทำผิด to harbour an offender: ปิด-บัญชี to close an account: ปิดป้อง, ปิดกั้น to protect by some superimposed means; to ward off (as a calamity by some superior power): ปิดประชุม to prorogue, close or terminate a meeting or session: ปิดประตู to shut the door; to prevent entrance or exit: ปิดประตูค้า to monopolize the marketing of a commodity: ปิดยา to spread on, or cover over with a remedy (as ointment over an ulcer): ปิดรู to cork or tamp a hole: ปิดหน้า to shade, cover, muffle or conceal the face: ปิดหนัก to suffer with constipation or obstruction of the bowels: ๒ ปิด and ติด (see p. 367) are often used synonymously, *ex.* ปิดหรือติดดวงตราไปรษณีย์ to stick on a postage stamp: ปิดหรือติดทอง to cover or over-lay with gold (leaf) (as some sacred object): ปิดหรือติดฉลาก (ขวด) to glue or paste a label (as on a bottle).

ปิตต bpit^4-dta^4 *P. S. n.* bile; the bilious humour (chd. p. 385).

ปิตา, บิดา p. 483 bpi^4-dtah *n.* father (chd. p. 385).

ปิตุ bpi^4-dtoo^4 *P. n.* father (chd. p. 385): ปิตุมาต patricide: ปิตุภูมิ fatherland.

ปิตุจฉา, บิตุจฉา bpi^4-dtoot^4-chah^2 *P. n.* a father's sister; an aunt (chd. p. 386).

ปิ่น bpin^4 *n.* a plain, or ornamented pin, usually of gold, around which the topknot hair of children is twisted and to which flowers are sometimes attached; summit; pinnacle: ปิ่นพิภพ summit of the world.

ปิ่นโต　bpin⁴-dtoh　*n.* a tiffin-carrier.

ปิปผลิ, ดีปลี (see p. 330) bpip⁴-pah⁴-lee *P. S. n. Capsicum minimum* (*Solanaceae*), red pepper; *Piper chaba*, the long pepper. There are several medicinal uses, but it is also used with dart poison and more especially does it have occult value (MCM. p. 334 : V. P. p. 110 : chd. p. 385 : BURK. p. 1742).

ปิ้ม　bpim³ (see เกือบ p. 127, แทบ p. 427): ปิ้มจะตาย at the point of death; dying: ปิ้ม-ปาน as; as if; almost.

ปิย, ปิเยศ　bpi⁴-ya⁶ *P. adj.* dear; beloved; agreeable; pleasant; kind; loving (chd. p. 386): ปิยวาจา pleasing speech.

ปิยังคุ see ประยงคุ์ p. 503.

ปิลันธน์　bpi⁴-lun *P. adj.* wearing or putting on an ornament or personal adornments.

ปิว　bpew² *adj.* small; diminutive; tiny; minute.

ปิศาจ, บริศาจ (p. 471), บิศาจ　bpi⁴-sart⁴ *P. S. n.* Satan; the devil; a class of demons; a sprite (chd. p. 385); an ogre; a demon; a malevolent or devilish being (S E. D. p. 628). According to Indian mythology these evil spirits may be grouped under three classes, each class having a distinct origin :—

(a) the spirit emanating from one who has died a violent death, either by accident, suicide, or capital punishment, and has not had his proper funeral ceremonies performed afterwards;

(b) the spirit of a deformed or crippled person, or of one defective in some limb or organ, or of a child that was born prematurely. This class is not necessarily evilly-disposed to men;

(c) a demon created by men's vices. It is the ghost of a murderer, drunkard, liar, adulterer, or criminal of any kind, or of one who died insane.

ปิศาจคนอง goblins : ปิศาจน้อย imps : ปิศาจบดี

lit. "chief or master of demons," *i. e.* Siva : ปิศาจร้าย fiends : ปิศาจวิทยา voodooism.

ปิหก　bpi⁴-hok⁴ *P. n.* the spleen (chd. p. 383).

ปิฬก　bpi⁴-la⁶-gka⁴ *P. n.* a boil; a pustule; a pimple (chd. p. 383).

ปี　bpee *n.* year. As in other countries of the Far East, the method of naming years in cycles of twelve after the names of animals is in common use in Thailand. The order is as follows, ชวด rat; ฉลู ox; ขาล tiger; เถาะ hare, rabbit; มะโรง dragon or Great Snake; มะเส็ง small snake; มะเมีย horse; มะแม goat; วอก monkey; ระกา cock; จอ dog; กุณ swine: ชั่วปีหนึ่ง the whole year : ลูกหัวปี the eldest child.

ปี่　bpee⁴ *n.* a class of wind instruments, *viz.*, ขลุ่ย flute; ปี่ชะวา the Javanese oboe (a flute-like instrument of soprano compass); ปี่อ้อ, ปี่ไฉน (see p. 274), ปี่นอก, ปี่ใน, ปี่ซอ, ปี่แก้ว: ปี่-พาทย์ an orchestra with pieces from five groups of instruments, *viz.* oboes (flutes), castanets, xylophones (percussion); kyeewain (gongs strung on circular frames), and drums.

ปี้　bpee³ *v.* to serve, cover or copulate (used for birds or fowls): *n.* counters (used in gambling) made of glass (green, white and yellow), porcelain and brass or bronze. During the period when gambling was a recognized institution, the small fuang and salung bullet-shaped coins were found inconvenient to handle. To overcome this the owners of gambling establishments introduced these special counters, on which were inscribed, in Chinese characters, the name of the establishment, the value, and a classical quotation, and in Thai characters the value which the counter was supposed to represent. These were issued, not by, but with the authority of the Government and, though originally intended only as gambling counters, rapidly became a favourite medium of exchange, for they were found to fill so well a long felt want for small money, so that the circulation went much beyond its legal sphere. The control by the Government became naturally more and more difficult, and at last in 1871 (three years after King Mongkut's death) it became necessary to prohibit and stop completely all circulation of these counters (le May, J. S. S. XVIII, 3, p. 395).

ปี̃ bpee[2] n. a game played with dice (in which the gain or loss is paid at the end of each round): adj. full; plenty; abundant; much: เต็มปี̃ full to overflowing; see เต็ม p. 373.

ปีก bpeek[4] n. wing; side; party: ปีกกา (กองทัพ) the flanking forces of an army: ปีกนก (เรือน) a narrow roof projecting from a gable end (on Thai houses): ปีกไม้ a slab (the outside cut when squaring a log).

ปี̃, ปี̃ฎก bpee-ta[4] P. S. n. a stool; a chair; a seat; a bench; the seat of a religious student (S. E. D. p. 629).

ปีด bpit[6] onomat. from the sound of a [whistle.
ปีดิ see ปรีดิ p. 510.

ปีน see ป้าย p. 525, ตะกาย p. 350.

ปีนัง bee-nung n. Penang; Pulo Pinang; The Island of the Betel Palm, Areca Catecha. It gets this name from this palm which is still grown in profusion all over the island (see เกาะหมาก p. 125). The first mention of Penang which can be traced among English writers is in 1591 when Captain Lancaster, afterwards Sir James Lancaster, in command of an expedition of three ships on behalf of the East India Company, set out from England. In June 1592 he found himself with his crews suffering from scurvy and, in urgent need of rest and refreshment, he anchored off Penang where no fewer than twenty-six of the small complement of the fleet died. Captain Francis Light was in that company's service and was first heard of in 1771 when he wrote to

Warren Hastings, then Governor-General of India. As the builder of Penang, his achievement is comparable to those of Albuquerque in Malacca and Stamford Raffles in Singapore. They are the three most brilliant stars in the history of the British East Indian Colony. Light was born on December 15th, 1740 at Dallinghoo near the town of Melton in Suffolk. He died in Penang of malarial fever on October 21st, 1794. Penang was the first British colony in the Straits. On July 15, 1786 the formal occupation of the island was made when the Union Jack was hoisted on the flag staff; a salute from the ships Eliza, Prince Henry and Speedwell was fired. A proclamation was made that the island in the future would be known as Prince of Wales Island in honour of the Heir Apparent (afterwards George IV), whose birthday fell on the following day; the capital would be known as Georgetown out of compliment to the Sovereign, George III. Situated 5°, 25′ N. latitude 100°, 15′ W. longitude off the west coast of the Malay Peninsula at the northern extremity or entrance to the straits of Malacca, it is about 15 miles long and 9 miles broad, and contains an area of 108 sq. miles. In shape it is an irregular parallelogram and, with the exception of a couple of plains on its eastern and western sides respectively, is entirely hilly (The Malay Peninsula p. 22: official Guide East India p. 324: Twentieth century Impressions of British Malaya p. 51: seaports of the East pp. 276, 277, 278).

ปีบ (ต้น) bpeep[4] Millingtonia hortensis (Bignoniaceae), Indian cork-tree, an erect tree with finely divided leaves, reaching a height of 50 feet or more. It is a native of Burma but is now cultivated in many places for its beauty. It bears twice a year, chiefly in November to June, a profusion of long, tubular, pure-white fragrant flowers. It is a favourite tree in Indian gardens. The wood is soft, yellowish-white, and can be used for furniture. The bark supplies an inferior cork (McM. p. 90: V. P. p. 176: Burk. p. 1472): ปับฝรั่ง (ต้น) *Isotoma longiflora* (*Campanulaceae*), a small annual plant 1 to 2 feet high, with white flowers. This weedy-looking campanulaceous herb, native of the West Indies, is said to have been in Thailand for about ten years. It is not known when or from which country it came. Its introduction was probably accidental. The plant is locally so named because of the passing resemblance its individual flower bears to that of the so called Indian cork-tree which is indigenous to Thailand. Its chief use is to furnish bark for tanning the thread used in making fishing-nets. The timber is used in house-building, though it is said not to be very durable. The leaves are used for poulticing. Both roots and leaves are medicinal (winit, N. H. J. S. S. IX, 1, p. 97: McM. pp. 135, 386: Burk. p. 1258).

ปับ bpeep[6] *onomat.* from the sound of the peeping of little chickens, or the cry, screech, or wail of the tiger.

ปับพ, ปับพา see บิทา p. 483.

ปัก bpurk[4] *n.* a clod; a lump of clay: *adj.* firm; solid; massive: น้ำตาลปัก palm sugar in dish-shaped cakes: ปักแผ่น firmness; stability; durability; see ก้อน p. 68.

ปัง bpung *onomat.* from the sound caused by an explosion, or the sound of a cannon.

ปัง bpung[4] *adj.* displaying ostentatious or proud manners: ปังชา feigning anger by assuming indifference.

ปัง bpung[2] *onomat.* from the sound caused by the vibrations of a harp or piano wire, or of a string pulled to breaking.

ปัด bpurt[6] *adj.* stupid; dull; ignorant; see ไง่ p. 227.

ปัน bpurn *n.* a gun; fire-arms; a piece of ordnance: กระบอกปืน a gun-barrel: ด้ามปืน

gun-stock: บรรจุปืน to load a fire-arm or gun: ปืนกระบอกเกลียว a screw-bore gun: ปืนกล a machine gun; an automatic-firing gun: ปืนโก้ a revolver: ปืนคาบศิลา a flint-lock gun: ปืนแฝด a double-barrelled gun: ปืนพกชนิดบรรจุลูกทางปากกระบอก a muzzle-loading pistol: ปืนยาพิษ a cross-bow with which poisoned arrows were used; "a poisoned gun": ปืนสั้น a carbine; a musket; a horseman's rifle: ปืนหลัก a gun mounted on a support or tripod: ปืนใหญ่ a cannon: ปืนใหญ่สนาม field howitzers: แผลลูกปืน a gunshot wound: รถบรรทุกปืน a gun-carriage: ลูกปืน shot; bullets; cannon-balls; projectiles.

ปืน bpurn[3] *n.* a blade (as of a saw).

ปือ bpur[3] *adj.* jet black; very dark (in the superlative degree).

ปือ bpur[2] *adj.* livid; jet (the superlative degree for colour); see จัด p. 238.

ปุ bpoo[4] (see ปะ p. 516): *onomat.* from the sound produced when slapping the abdomen which is distended by gas.

ปุ bpoo[6] *onomat.* from the sound produced when throwing a stone or brick into mud or against a soft substance.

ปุก bpook[4] *onomat.* from the sound produced when pounding rice in a mortar: เท้าปุก a form of talipes or club-foot in which the foot is shaped like a fist.

ปุกปุย bpook[4]-bpoo-ie *adj.* shaggy; fuzzy; scrubby (as covered with rough tousled feathers or hair).

ปุงกี bpoong[3]-gkee[2] *Chin. n.* a clam shell shaped basket with side-handles through which a rope is fastened. It is carried on a pole for transporting bricks or dirt.

ปุงคพ, ปุงควะ, บุงคพ bpoong-kop[6] *P.S. n. lit.* "a bull," *i.e.* a chief; a leader; the superior or excellent one (chd. p. 392).

ปุงลิงค์, ปุงลึงค์, ปุลลิงค์ bpoong-ling *P.S.* *n.* manhood; male sex; *gram.* masculine gender (chd. p. 391).

ปุญฺญ์ see บุญ p. 484.

ปุฏ bpoot[4] *P. n.* a bottle; a cup; a water-jar; a vessel; a basket (chd. p. 396).

ปุด bpoot[4] *n.* a stitch (in sewing): *adj.* bubbling gently (as the beginning of ebullition): *onomat.* from the sound produced when picking a harp string, or snapping a [wire.

ปุตตะ see บุตร p. 484.

ปุถุชน see บุถุชน p. 484.

ปุบ bpoop[4] *adv.* hastily; quickly; nimbly; adroitly (as in snatching or grabbing).

ปุบบับ bpoop[4]-bpup[4] *onomat.* from the sound produced when acting in a hurry, rudely or roughly.

ปุม, ปุมา bpoo[4]-ma[6] *P. S. n.* manhood; the male sex (chd. p. 391).

ปุ่ม bpoom[4] *n.* a node; a knot; a knob, or swelling (as at the joint of a stem).

ปุ้ม bpoom[3] *adj.* blunted or rounded (as the point of a sword); see ที่อ, ทู่ 417.

ปุ๊ม bpoom[2] *onomat.* from the sound produced when something small falls into the water or fishes jump.

ปุมเบ้า, ต้นตายใบเป็น (ต้น) bpoom-bpow[3] *n.* a succulent *Bryophyllum* which may be propagated from leaves, if placed on a damp surface of light sandy soil, and kept in position by being partly buried or held down with small wooden pegs. It will produce buds at the margins which will develop into plants (MCM. p. 40).

ปุย bpoo-ie *n.* vegetable fibres; filaments (as cotton).

ปุ๋ย bpoo-ie[2] *n.* manure; a fertilizer.

ปุเรจาริก bpoo[4]-ray-chjah-rik[6] *P. S. adj.* led or guided by thoughts of faith (chd. p. 394).

ปุโรหิต, โปโรหิต bpoo[4]-roh-hit[4] *P.S. n.* a Brahmin who is a king's domestic chaplain (chd. p. 395).

ปุลลิงค์ see ปุงลิงค์ p. 530.

ปุพว bpoo[4]-la[6]-wa[6] *P. n.* a worm; maggots (chd. p. 391).

ปู, ลาด bpoo *v.* to spread out; to lay or stretch out (as a carpet): *n.* a crab; a common noun followed by the specific designating name for kinds of crabs: ปูจ๋า a steamed Thai condiment composed of lobster meat and eggs, with seasoning: ปูทะเล a marine ten-footed crustacean; a sea-crab: ปูนา field-crabs.

ปู่ bpoo[4] *n.* paternal grandfather: ปู่เจ้า a title for a respected aged person: ปู่เจ้าที่ the tutelary genius of a place: ปู่เจ้าไม้ the tutelary king-tree of a forest: ปู่ทวด a great grandfather: ปู่ย่าตายาย ancestors.

ปูชก bpoo-cha[6]-gka[4] *P.S. n.* a worshipper; one paying homage to; one offering sacrifice to (chd. p. 391).

ปูชนียะ bpoo-cha[6]-nee-ya[6] *P. adj.* honoured; venerable; worthy of respect, homage or worship (chd. p. 391).

ปูด, กะปูด (นก) bpoot[4] *n.* the Burmese concal or crow pheasant, *Centrococcyx intermedius* (Gaird. J. S. S. IX, 1, p. 8).

ปูติ bpoo-dti[4] *P. S. adj.* putrid; stinking; foul (chd. p. 396): ปูติกาย a foul body; a mass of corrupted flesh; a Buddhist epithet for the body: ปูติมัจฉา putrid fish: ปูติลตา the shrub, *Cocculus cordifolius* (*Menispermaceae*) (Burk. p. 594).

ปูน ๑ bpoon *n.* lime; calcium oxide; hydroxid; the time or period of blooming or fruitage: *adj.* comparing; rivaling; equaling; relative: ปูนก่อน the first period of fruitage:

ปูนกัด corroded or irritated by the action of lime : ปูนกัดปาก to suffer from the deleterious action of lime on the mouth : ปูนสอ slacked lime : ปูนหลัง the last or final period of fruitage : ปูนหอย shell-lime : ปูนหิน stone-lime : เตาปูน a lime kiln.

ปูน ๒ bpoon *Chin. v.* to give, share, or divide among ; to add to, over and above what is due : ปูนบำเหน็จ to reward with a gift, for services rendered ; see แจก p. 260.

ปูม bpoom *n.* a pattern of dotted silk ; a note book or sheets of paper with lines drawn for recording purposes ; a memorandum book or calendar.

ปู๊ยี่ปู๊ย่ำ bpoo³-yee³-bpoo³-yam (see ช้ำชอก p. 294) : *adj.* bruised ; damaged ; ruined.

ปูลู bpoo-loo *n.* a large, heavy, long-handled ax (used in felling or trimming logs).

ปูวะ bpoo-wa⁶ *P. n.* a cake ; a sweetmeat (chd. p. 397) ; see ขนม p. 139.

เป๋ bpey³ (see ตะแคง p. 352) *adj.* being out of the perpendicular ; leaning ; sloping ; tilted.

เป้ bpey² *adj.* twisted ; distorted ; veering from a straight line.

เปก bpek₄ *onomat.* from the sound of slapping or striking two sticks together.

เปกข์ bpek⁴ *P. n.* expectation ; wish ; desire (chd. p. 378) : อุปสัมปทาเปกข์ one wishing for, or expecting ordination.

เป่ง bpeng⁴ *adj.* distended ; swollen ; puffed up or out ; enlarged ; tumid.

เป้ง bpeng³ *n.* a species of tree similar to the areca-nut with thorny stems or branches : *adj.* large ; big : *onomat.* from the sound of blows made heavily with a stick.

เป๋ง bpeng² *adj.* direct ; straight (as one walking) ; drawn or pulled taut and fastened (as the hoop around a box or barrel) : *onomat.* from the sound of hammering sheet iron.

เป็ด bpet⁴ *n.* a duck ; a kind of native boat with flattened prow and stern ; a species of medicinal water plant : เป็ด (นกหิ่) the Java fantail flycatcher, *Rhipidura javanica* (Herb. N. H. J. S. S. VI, 1, p. 112) : เป็ดไก่ poultry : เป็ดเทศ Muscovy or Barbary ducks : เป็ดน้ำ (นก) the lesser whistling teal, *Dendrocygna javanica* (Gaird. J. S. S. IX, 1, p. 11) : เป็ดผี (นก) the little grebe, *Tachybaptes fluviatilis* (Gaird. J. S. S. IX, 1, p. 16).

เปต bpey-dta⁴ *P. n.* the dead ; the departed ; the manes or spirits of dead persons ; a deceased relative (chd. p. 378) : เปตพลี offerings made to the spirit of a deceased relative or person.

เป็น bpen (1) *substantive verb* to exist ; to occur ; to live ; to continue : กินปลาทั้งเป็น to eat fish which are still alive : จัดเป็นลำดับ to be arranged in serial order ; to cause to occur in rotation : จะเป็นก็ให้เป็นไป if it is going to occur, then let it be so : ทั้งผู้เป็น และผู้ตาย to be both of the living and of the dead : เป็นตายเท่ากัน to have equal chance of life and death : ยังเป็นอยู่, ทั้งเป็น to be living or still alive.

เป็น (2) *copulative verb* used with nouns, adjectives or adjective phrases : เขาเป็นเจ้าของ he is the owner : เขาเป็นแต่เด็ก he is only a child : เขาเป็นที่รักของบิดา he is the beloved of his father : เขาเป็นไข้ he is suffering from fever : (ข้าว) เป็นตัว to be unbroken (as kernels of rice) : (ไข่) เป็นตัว (see ไข่ p. 171) to become fecund ; to be formed in the shell : จะเป็นคุณ it will be, or is going to be useful : จะเป็นพยาน he is going to give evidence : จะเป็นมา it is going to happen : เป็นการ (I) am successful in an undertaking : เป็นของ ๆ เขา it is his property ; it belongs to him : เป็นความจริง the truth is ; truly : เป็นใจ to be an accomplice, promoter or participant : เป็นดังว่า to be as has been said : เป็นเด็กดี to be a good child : เป็นต้นว่า as if ; as for example : เป็นตัวการ

see ตัว p. 360 : เป็นตัว (หนอน) to be infested with worms or maggots : เป็นแต่เรื่องเล็กน้อย it is only a trifling matter : เป็นโทษ to be worthy of punishment : เป็นธรรม to be just or impartial : เป็นนักเป็นหนา to be exceedingly common or prevalent : เป็นนิตย์ continually ; perpetually ; eternally ; unceasingly : ปี๊นปากเป็นเสียง they are quarreling : เป็นนาย he is the master : เป็นพ่อ he is the father : เป็นพะยานเท็จ to be a false witness : เป็นมาอย่างนี้ it came about in this way : เป็นโรค to be suffering from a malady : เป็นสุข to be happy : เป็นห่วง to be anxious about : เป็นหนี้ to be in debt : เป็นเหตุให้ is the cause of : เป็นอันขาด absolutely ; irrevocably ; under no circumstance : เป็น-อันมาก abundantly ; copiously : เป็นอย่างนี้ thus ; in this way : เป็นเอิ้ง to be an act of God ; to be from natural causes ; to be the result of certain preceding causes ; *lit.* " it happened of itself " : ไม่เป็นธรรม (see ธรรม p. 431) such (an act) is unjust, or contrary to duty or piety : ไม่เป็นอะไร it is going to make no difference ; it is a matter of no importance : ยังไม่เป็นตัวเป็นตนขึ้น to be not yet consummated.

เป็น (3) to be able : เป็นได้ to be possible ; to be permissible : ถ้าเป็นได้ if it is permitted to be : ทำเป็น see ทำ p. 414 : ทำ-ไม่เป็น to be unable to do (from lack of knowledge) : ทำไม่ไหว to be unable to do (from lack of strength) : เป็นไปไม่ได้ it is incredible that such a thing should happen : ไม่เป็นไปได้ to be contrary to all reasonable expectation : สูบบุหรี่เป็น to be able (to know how) to smoke a cigar or cigarette.

เปรต, เปต bpret[4] *S. n.* the spirit of a dead person ; a ghost ; a departed spirit in a state of punishment and suffering on account of sins committed in a former existence. He is doomed to live in the solitary recesses of uninhabited mountains, smarting under the pangs of never-satiated hunger (S. E. D. p. 711).

This is one of the most miserable forms of being. Some are condemned to a weary life in regions beyond the walls of the world, where no light ever penetrates. Others rove about on earth, incessantly in motion. They suffer particularly from hunger and thirst, being extremely voracious (Ala. p. 189) : เปรตวิษัย, เปตวิสัย regions of, or places for the spirits of the departed.

เปรม ๑, เปม bprem *v.* to be happy, gay, or merry.

เปรม ๒ bprem *S. n.* love ; affection ; kindness ; joys ; pleasures (chd. p. 378).

เปรย bpru-ie *adv.* indirectly ; unconnectedly ; at random ; inferentially : เปรยปราย indiscriminate ; promiscuous ; hetrogeneous : ฝนตกเปรยปราย a desultory rainfall : พูด-เปรยปราย to speak incoherently, allusively, or insinuatingly.

เปรษณีย์ see ไปรษณีย์ p. 538.

เปรอะ bprur[4] *adj.* dirty, muddy, soiled, stained or tarnished.

เปราะ (ต้น) bpraw[4] *n.* a sedge or flag-like herb with fragrant leaves and used medicinally by the Thai : *adj.* fragile ; brittle ; frail ; breakable.

เปราะแประ bpraw[4]-bpraa[4] *adj.* sprinkling or raining in small scattered drops.

เปรี้ยง see ตักร p. 358.

เปรี้ยง bpre-eng[3] *onomat.* from the sound of thunder and lightning occurring together ; a clap of thunder.

เปรียญ bpa[4]-ri-en *n.* a graduate of some university or school of Buddhist religious instruction ; one with a literary degree ; a philosopher.

เปรียบ bpree-ap (see เทียบ p. 426) : *v.* to contrast, placing side by-side so as to perceive the similarity or dissimilarity ; to institute a comparison; to draw a parallel: คำเปรียบ an allegory; a simile; as for example: เปรียบปราย, เปรียบเปรย making invidious comparisons: เปรียบเทียบ (ความ) to arbitrate for settlement in a case: เปรียบเหมือน analogous to; having a similarity to.

เปรี้ยว bpree-oh *adj.* wild; untamed; active.

เปรี้ยว bpree-oh³ *v.* to become sour, fermented or spoiled (as food): *adj.* sour; acid (in taste): เปรี้ยวปราด extremely or bitingly sour: เปรี้ยวปาก a disagreeable taste in the mouth (resulting from hyperacidity of the stomach).

เปรี้ยะ, เปรี้ยะ bpree-oh⁴ *adj.* broken; demolished; destroyed: *onomat.* from the sound of the splintering of glass.

เปรื่อง bpreu-ang⁴ *adj.* smart; clever; bold: *onomat.* from the sound of the clicking of glasses or dishes.

เปรื่อย bpru-ie³ *adj.* free; unobstructed; moving freely: พูดเปรื่อย being fluent or ready in speech; see คล่อง p. 184.

เปล bplay *n.* a cradle; a litter: เปลตาข่าย a net-cradle, one in which the aperture is formed of light smoothly trimmed wood with perforations about one inch apart, to which the hanging ropes are attached. Through these, unbleached cords are run and knotted together in meshes (as a net) extending about two feet down and attached to the edges of a bottom board: เปลญวน a a hammock: เปลหาม a hammock suspended from a pole and borne on the shoulders of men.

เปล่ง bpleng⁴ *v.* to cause to issue forth or be diffused; to shoot out beams: *n.* the condition or act of sending forth; see ฉาย p. 269: *adj.* shining; lustrous; beamy; radiant; reflected; plump; rounded; full; distended (as cheeks or tissues of an infant or child): เปล่งเสียง to project the voice.

เปลว bpla-oh *adj.* flaccid; flabby; fragile; flimsy (descriptive of articles in soft thin sheets): ทองเปลว gold-foil: เปลวไฟ flames; a blaze: เปลวมัน layers or shreds of fatty tissue: เปลวหมู lard.

เปลา bplow *adj.* tall, straight and limbless (descriptive of trees).

เปล่า bplow⁴ *adj.* empty; vacant; void (when used as a negation); no; nothing; in vain: ที่เปลี่ยวเปล่า wild, uncultivated, deserted land: เปล่าเปลี่ยวใจ lonely; dreary; friendless; forlorn; forgotten by the world: ไปมือเปล่า to go empty-handed: เสียเปล่า in vain; useless; of no value: หาเปล่า ๆ to accuse unjustly; to search or hunt for vainly: อยู่เปล่า ๆ to be at leisure, idle or unoccupied.

เปล้า (ต้น) bplow³ *n. Grewia paniculata* (*Tiliaceae*), a tree found from Thailand and Cambodia throughout Malaysia. The Malays use it medicinally, making a decoction from the roots for fever; and an infusion for abdominal trouble; and a poultice of the leaves for itch, and a lotion of leaves and bark for broken bones. In Indo-China the root is used for coughs. The wood burns brightly and is considered suitable for use in the fire lit near a woman after child-birth. It makes good charcoal (BURK. p. 1113); *Croton griffithii* (*Euphorbiaceae*), a shrub or small tree found commonly throughout the Malay Peninsula. The wood is light, brittle and close grained, but of little use (BURK. p. 689); *Croton argyratum* (*Euphorbiaceae*), a small tree found from Burma throughout Malaysia. Its timber is of little use but may be used for houses. The leaves and stems have medicinal uses (V. P. p. 173: BURK. p. 688): เปล้า (นก) the Burmese green pigeon, *Crocopus phoenicopterus viridifrons* (Deig. N. H. J. S. S. VIII, 3, p. 166); the red turtle dove, *Aenopopelia tranquebarica humelis* (Aagaard p. 185).

เปลาะ bplaw⁴ *n.* the distance or section

between knots (of a rope or cord): ผูกไว้ เป็นเปลาะ to tie in separated knots.

เปลี้ย bplee-ah[3] (see ง่อย p. 222) *adj.* feeble; weak; tired; lacking physical strength (as when suffering from over-exertion or when paralyzed): เปลี้ยน้ำ just above the surface of the water (as the gunwale of a boat when tilted in the extreme).

เปลี่ยน bple-an[4] *v.* to exchange (as an old for a new article): เปลี่ยนแทน to replace one for another: เปลี่ยนโทษ to commute punishment: เปลี่ยนแปลง to make renovations or alterations: เปลี่ยนแผ่นดิน to replace one ruling sovereign by another; to change kings: เปลี่ยนศาลที่พิจารณา to make a change of venue: ผลัดเปลี่ยนกัน to alternate with [another.

เปลี่ยม see เปี่ยม p. 535.

เปลี่ยว bpliew[4] *n.* the condition of maturity in cattle: *adj.* having attained adult age or maturity (used in regard to cattle); wild; not tamed; solitary; deserted; abandoned.

เปลี่ยวดำ bpliew[4]-dum *n.* a disease or condition resulting from excessive cold; frostbite.

เปลือก bpleu-ak[4] *n.* rind; husk; bark; shell: งามแต่เปลือก beauty only skin deep.

เปลือง bpleu-ang *v.* to be consumed rapidly or lavishly (as money or funds); to use or burn excessively (as electric light or benzine); to be overly reduced, squandered, or dissipated: *adj.* wasteful; extravagant; improvident; prodigal.

เปลื้อง bpleu-ang[3] *v.* to take off; to strip off: เปลื้องเสื้อผ้า to remove the clothing.

เปลือย bpleu-ie *adj.* naked; undressed; uncovered: เปลือยกาย nude; unclad.

เปศ bpay-sa[4] *S. n.* an architect; a carpenter (S. E. D. p. 648).

เปศล bpay-sa[4]-la[6] *S. adj.* artificially form- ed; decorated; beautiful; delicate; charming; graceful; lovely (S. E. D. p. 648): เปศลมัธย์ supple or slender-waisted.

เปศัส bpay-sut[4] *S. n.* form; shape; colour; ornaments (S. E. D. p. 648): เปศัสการิน a wasp; see แตน p. 377: เปศัสการี a female embroiderer.

เปสการ bpet[4]-sa[4]-gkarn *P. n.* a weaver (chd. p. 378).

เปสล bpay-sa[4]-la[6] *P. adj.* beautiful; delightful; amiable (chd. p. 378).

เปสุญญ์, เปสุไณย bpay-soon[2] *P. n.* slander; backbiting; defamation (chd. p. 378): เปสุญญวาท the act of using slanderous or irritating language.

เป้อเย้อ bpur[3]-yur[5] *adj.* boastful; proud; vain.

เป้อเหลอ bpur[2]-ler-ie[2] (see เซ่อ p. 311) blank or stupid (descriptive of facial expressions).

เปะ bpa[4] *v.* to add to, paint, daub, plaster on, or slap on roughly (as paint or whitewash).

เปะปะ bpey[4]-bpa[4] *adj.* disordered, irregular; confused; see เกะกะ p. 124.

เป่า bpow[4] *v.* to blow; to perform on wind instruments: เป่าขลุ่ย to play on a flute: เป่าแล่น to solder, weld or fuse together (as with a blowpipe).

เป้า bpow[3] *n.* a target; a mark; a shooting butt: เป้าเสื้อ, เป้ากางเกง an inside pocket of a coat or trowsers.

เปาะ bpaw[4] *adv.* continually; constantly; an *onomat.* derived from the beating of bamboo sticks or the sound of blows: ชมเปาะ to praise uninterruptedly.

เปาะเหลาะ bpaw[4]-law[4] (see กระทัดรัด p. 34: กลมกล่อม p. 57).

เปิก bperk[4] (see ถก p. 379) *adj.* opened

up or out; swelled or blown (as a garment lifted by a gust of wind).

เปิง   bperng (see ทะลาย p. 406) *adj.* ruined; tumbled down; frayed (as the edges); damaged; full of holes (as a sail): วิ่งเตลิดเปิดเปิง to run at full speed with garments flying in the air: หลังคาเปิดเปิง a roof blown into holes (by the wind).

เปิงๆ   bperng⁴-bperng⁴ *adv.* loudly; boisterously (as a call, yell or cry).

เปิงมาง   bperng-mang *n.* a two-faced drum, used as a part of a Thai orchestra.

เปิด   bpert⁴ (see กาง -p. 91) *v.* to open; to spread out to view; to reveal (as a secret): เปิดความลับ to betray a secret: เปิดบัญชี-ฝากเงิน to open a banking account: เปิดเผย to disclose; to declare openly: เปิดไฟฟ้า to turn on electric light or power: เปิดน้ำ to turn on the water.

เปิน   bpern⁴ (see เซ่อ p. 311) *adj.* stupid; silly; simple; bewildered; overawed; confused; awkward.

เปิบ   bperp⁴ *v.* to use the five fingers in raising rice to the mouth (in place of a spoon).

เปิ๊บ   bperp⁶ *onomat.* from a sound as of the call of the doe or antelope.

เปีย (ผม)   bpee-ah *n.* hair braided and hanging down the back; a queue; the pendant part or tassels of a garland: ขนมเปีย a Chinese cake or sweetmeat with stuffing placed in layers.

เปียก   bpee-ak⁴ *v.* to boil rice without removing the water: *adj.* wet; moist; soaking wet; damp: ข้าวเปียก rice soup: แป้ง-เปียก flour paste.

เปี่ยม, เปลี่ยม   bpee-am⁴ *v.* to be completely filled; to be brim-full or full to overflowing: เปี่ยมแคร่ิม filled to the edge.

เปี๋ยว   bpee-oh³ *n.* a small stick or post supporting the seri leaf vine.

เปือก see ตม ๒ p. 341.

เปื้อน, แปดเปื้อน   bpeurn³ *v.* to become dirty, tarnished, stained, soiled or filthy: เปื้อนโคลน bespattered with mud.

เปื่อย   bpeu-ie⁴ *v.* to become softened by disintegration (as a fallen tree): ต้มจนเปื่อย to boil till tender: เปื่อยเน่า to be rotten by decomposition; to be in a state of putrifaction.

แป   bpaa *n.* a purlin (one of several horizontal timbers resting on posts supporting the rafters of a roof): *adj.* flat: แปลาน intermediate purlins: มือแป a hand with ankylosed fingers.

แป้ง   bpaang³ *n.* meal; flour; face-powder: แป้งข้าวหมาก, แป้งเหล้า yeast for making fermented rice which is to be distilled into arrack: แป้งจี่ a sweetmeat made of glutinous rice and coconut, seasoned with salt and sugar, and fried in small discs: แป้งนวล toilet-powder: แป้งหอม perfumed powder: ผัดแป้ง to apply face-powder; to powder oneself (as after a bath).

แป๋ง   bpaang² *onomat.* from the sound of a clock striking, or the hitting a brass vessel.

แปด   bpaat⁴ *n.* the numeral eight: ที่แปด eighth: แปดสิบ eighty: แปดสามหรก *lit.* "eight dignitaries," *i. e.* the four ancestors on both sides in high class families.

แป๋ด   bpaat⁶ *onomat.* from the sound of the honking of a small motor car horn.

แปดปน   bpaat⁴-bpon *v.* to be mixed with other ingredients.

แป้น   bpaan³ *n.* a washer (for bolts); a potter's wheel; a round board surmounting a post or pillar: *adj.* thin, round and flat (as cover glasses for microscopical slides): แป้น (ปลา) *Leiognathus dussumieri* (*Leiognathidae*); *L. splendens* (suvatti p. 119): แป้น-ชักลวด a wire drawplate with graduated holes: แป้นใหญ่ (ปลา) *Leiognathus equulus* (*Leiog-*

nathidae) (suvatti p. 119): ยิ้มแป้น a pleasing or broad smile (used in reference to children): ส้มแป้น a small flat orange.

แปบ bpaap[4] *adj.* small; slender; thin: flattened; pressed thin (as bananas prior to being roasted): แปบ (ปลา) *Paralaubuca typus (Cyprinidae)* (suvatti p. 49): แปบขาว (ปลา) see ชิ้วควาย (ปลา) p. 309: แปบควาย (ปลา) see ท้องพลุ (ปลา) pp. 404–5: แปบทะเล (ปลา) *Gazza minuta (Leiognathidae)* (suvatti p. 120); see แบน p. 490.

แปม bpaam (see กลั้ว p. 60) *v.* to be mixed: แปมปน to become mixed up with, mingled, combined, or associated with.

แปร bpraa *v.* to change or be transformed; to turn; to separate into component parts or kinds: การแปรธาตุ alchemy: แปรธาตุ to assay ore; to separate compound ores: แปรปรวน fluctuation; transformation; transposition: ไม่มีความแปรปรวน unchangeable; permanent.

แปร๋, แปร๋แปร้น bpraa[2] *onomat.* from the sound made by the trumpeting of elephants.

แปรก, แบรก (p. 490) bpraak[4] *n.* a square wooden frame through which the axle of a bullock cart passes, and upon which the shafts of the cart are supported.

แปรง bpraang *v.* to brush; to clean by brushing: *n.* brush; mane; bristles.

แปร่ง bpraang[4] *adj.* dialectal; provincial (as speech or pronunciation): พูดแปร่ง to speak with a brogue: เสียงแปร่ง changed; altered; incorrect (as judged by the standards of the country); harsh; shrill; discordant; squeaking; discrepant (as a false tone).

แปร๊ด bpraat[6] a word indicating the superlative degree of acidity or saltness: *adv.* exceedingly acid or salty; see จัด p. 238.

แปร้น bpraan[3] *onomat.* from the sound of tumultuous, discordant or confused noises or voices: แปร้นแปร๋ (เสียง) words, shrill voices or sounds uttered in extreme anger or while quarrelling.

แประ bpraa[4] (see เต็มที่ p. 373) *adj.* fully loaded or filled to the brim (as a small boat).

แปล bplaa *v.* to translate, explain or interpret (as a proverb or letter in a foreign language); to reveal the meaning.

แปล้, ไปล่ bplaa[3] *adj.* (1) lowered; bowed; flattened down smooth (as wings of a bird at rest): (2) brim-full; filled to the utmost capacity (as a loaded boat); see เต็ม p. 373.

แปลก bplaak[4] *adj.* changed; strange; different; unlike (the original) or unrecognizable; unnatural: คนแปลกหน้า a stranger: แปลกปลอมมา to come in disguise; to come in as a stranger, or as a spy.

แปลง bplaang (see จำแลง p. 248) *n.* a numerical designatory particle for garden lots, blocks, fields or pieces of land: แปลงชาติ to become naturalized: แปลงกฎหมาย to alter or recode the laws.

แปลน ๑ bplaan *v.* to appear, bob up or jump up (as fishes from the surface of the water).

แปลน ๒ bplaan *adj.* empty; hollow; vacant; desolate; see เปล่า p. 533.

แปลบ see ปลาบ p. 512: เจ็บแปลบ ๆ lancinating, stabbing pain (as in pleurisy).

แป้ว bpaa-oh[3] *adj.* deflated (as a motor car tire); flat; not symmetrically round; contorted; nicked or notched.

แป๊ว bpaa-oh[6] *onomat.* from the sound of the mewing of a cat.

แปะ bpaa[4] *v.* to slap gently (with the hand); to make or cause to fit up close to another surface: *onomat.* from the sound of slapping.

แป๊ะซะ bpaa[6]-sa[6] *Chin. n. lit.* "plain

boiled," *i. e.* a method of boiling fish which is eaten with vinegar sauce and vegetables.

โป bpoh *n.* a protuberance; a Chinese gambling game using a telescoping quadrilateral brass body enclosing dice. The brass body is shaken and opened; the betting is on the number of dots on the dice: *adj.* protuberant; bulging; projecting: โปก๊ำ a game in which cowries are gathered in the hands and then laid on the table. The betting is on the even or odd number of cowries.

โป้ bpoh³ *v.* to falsify, fib or lie: ปดโป้ an euphonic combination.

โป๊ bpoh⁶ *v.* to mend or repair (as chipped corners in masonry); to caulk cracks between boards (as by plugging in putty); to seal up nail-holes in a wall (by inserting plaster or cement); to renovate by making minor repairs.

โปก bpok⁴ *onomat.* from the sound caused when knocking a board or rivetting iron bolts.

โปกขรณี see โบกขรณี p. 491.

โปง (ผ้า) bpong *n.* a cloth, robe or blanket covering the whole body.

โป่ง, ป่ง bpong⁴ *n.* a condition of inflation with gas or air; salty earth (found in forests); a group of evil spirits; a bag inflated with air or gas; a forest of tall trees: *adj.* distended with gas or air: ลูกโป่ง toy balloons.

โป้ง bpong³ *adj.* boastful; loquacious: *onomat.* from the sound of a blow or of beating some hard substance: คนปากโป้ง a boaster; a braggart: โป้งโล้ง ill-shaped; too big and clumsy; out of proper or normal proportion.

โป้งโหยง bpong³-yong² *adj.* proud; conceited; vain: คนโป้งโหยง a puffed up or vain-glorious person.

โปดก, โบดก (p. 491) bpoh-dok⁴ *P.S. n.* the young of any animal (chd. p. 388): โปดิกา the feminine gender of โปดก.

โปตถกะ bpote⁴-ta⁴-gka⁴ *P. n.* a manuscrip; a book (chd. p. 388).

โปน bpon *adj.* swollen; bulging up, elevated or enlarged (out of proper proportion or shape); see นูน p. 462.

โปร่ง, ปรุ (p. 510) bprong⁴ *adj.* full of holes or passages (as mosquito netting): โปร่งตา transparent: โปร่งแสง translucent.

โปร่งฟ้า *Laos, Krabin,* หัดสะคุนดง *Thai., Korat* (ต้น) bprong⁴-fah⁵ *n. Murraya siamensis (Rutaceae)*, a small tree of the orange family with pungent aromatic leaves. The Thai use it as a constant ingredient in curries (cb. p. 231).

โปรด bprote⁴ *v.* please to do, or grant a favour; kindly do or render aid: ขอโปรด please be so kind as to: คนโปรด a favourite of: โปรดปราน to show kindnesses to; to manifest love towards, devotion to, or love for: โปรดสัตว์ to show mercy or clemency towards creatures; the Buddhist monk goes out for morning alms.

โปรย, โรย bpro-ie *v.* to scatter; to sow; to strew: โปรยปราย being disseminated; being cast about irregularly or thoroughly: พูดหว่านล้อม using ensnaring or entangling words or forms of speech.

โปราณะ see บุราณ p. 486.

โปรีสภา (ศาล) bpoh-ree-sa⁴-pah *P. n.* the police court, a primary or low court in Bangkok; a congregating place of the city's people [or citizens.

โปโรหิต see ปุโรหิต p. 530.

โปส see บุรุษ p. 486.

โปสก bpoh-sok⁴ *P.S. n.* a supporter; a benefactor; a patron; a friendly helper; one who renders nourishment (chd. p. 387).

โปสาวนิกมูล bpoh-sah²-wa⁶-ni⁶-gka⁴-moon

P. n. expenses incident to rendering help or nourishment (chd. p. 387).

โป๊ะ   bpoh[6] *n.* a pontoon (for a landing); a lamp-shade, globe or reflector; a sea-fishing trap made of stakes stuck into the mud, with wings or leaders extending some distance out.

โป๊ะจ้าย (เรือ)   bpoh[6]-chjai[3] *n. Chin.* lighters; large cargo boats (as seen transporting freight to or from ships).

ไป   bpai *v.* to go, depart, proceed or move forward; a sign of the imperative: เป็นบ้าไป to become or go mad: เป็นไป to become: ไปถึง to arrive at; to reach a destination: ไปๆมาๆ to go to and fro; to frequent a place: ไปตราด to go on an inspection or surveying trip or tour: ไปไหน where are you going: ไปไหนมา where have you been: สุกเกินไป it has become too ripe.

ไป่   bpai[4] *Laos adj.* no; not; it is incorrect.

ไปย   bpai-ya[6] *P. n.* beverages; liquids that may be swallowed; water; milk (chd. p. 377).

ไปยาล   bpai-yarn *P. n.* the dotted line used when words are intentionally omitted; abbreviation marks; et cetera, *ex.* ๆ ลๆ, ๆ เปๆ.

ไปรษณีย, เปรษณีย์   bpai-sa[4]-nee *S. v.* to be sent or dispatched (chd. p. 712): *n.* articles posted; things sent by post; delivery or posting of messages or articles; post, an established system for transporting mails: ไปรษณีย์บัตร a postcard: ไปรษณียบุรุษ, บุรุษ-ไปรษณีย์ (ordinary usage) a postman: ไปรษณีย-ภัณฑ์ an article sent by post; parcel post: ไปรษณีย์อากาศยาน a mail-airship.

ไปล่ see **แปล้** p. 536.

ไปศาจ   bpai-sart[4] *S. n.* a class or group of demons, spirits or goblins; a fiend: *adj.* pertaining to or connected with devils, demons or spirits: ไปศาจวิวาทะ *lit.* "marriage after the manner of ghosts or fantoms," *i. e.* an elopement; see ปิศาจ p. 527.

ไปศาจี   bpai-sah[2]-chjee *S. n. lit.* "the language of ghosts, demons, or devils," *i. e.* the language of a tribe of people in India.

ผ

ผ   The twenty-eighth consonant in the Thai alphabet, one of the high class letters of which there are eleven, *viz.* ข, ฃ, ฉ, ถ, ฐ, ผ, ฝ, ส, ศ, ษ, ห. ผอผึ้ and ผอผึ้ง are the names of this letter. In Pali and Sanskrit it is pronounced "ผะ"; it is used exclusively as an initial consonant.

ผก, ผะผก   pok[4] *v.* to turn the face (as in looking backwards); to roll or veer to the side (as a boat about to capsize); to turn upside-down: ผกผงก to raise the head in order to look back or around: ผกผัน, หกกลับ to elevate the head in order to look backwards (as an injured snake).

ผกเรือก see **ไทร (ต้น)** p. 429.

ผกา   pa[4]-gkah *Cam. n.* a flower.

ผกากรอง (ต้น)   pa[4]-gkah-gkraung *n. Lantana camara (Verbenaceae)*; *L. nivea,* an American species of shrub which reached the East at an early date, or, in the opinion of Lam, a group of species in process, in the East, of consolidation by hybridization into one species. In some places it has become a pest and there is legislation against it. It is thought that the plant has antiseptic properties; and so pounded leaves are applied to cuts and ulcers. In Java a fomentation is made for rheumatism (BURK. p. 1316); *L. nivas* (V. P. p. 178: McM. p. 113).

ผกาย, ประกาย   pa[4]-gkai *Cam. n.* a star;

a flash or rays of light; sparks.

ผง pong[2] *n.* dust; powder: กลายเปนผง-
คลีดิน to revert to the dust of the earth:
ทำเป็นผง to reduce to a powder: ผงคลี่ the
finest of dust or particles.

ผงก pa[4]-ngok[4] *v.* to raise; to elevate (as
the face); to support in an upright position;
to raise partially (as by a lever under one
[side].

ผงม see ประคบประหงม p. 497.

ผงอน pa[4]-ngaun *v.* to turn or twist (as
the body): *n.* the earth's surface.

ผงอบ pa[4]-ngaup[3] *adj.* very weak; tired
or near dying.

ผงะ pa[4]-nga see ชะงัก p. 285: *v.* to stop
or draw back from terror or excitement.

ผงาด pa[4]-ngart[4] *adj.* splendid; flashing;
dashing; gay (as dress or decorations); prominent; conspicuous.

ผจง pa[4]-chjong *Cam. v.* to do or perform
with one's best endeavour: *n.* determination;
concentration (of mind); see ฅ่อย p. 192.

ผจัญ pa[4]-chjun *Cam. v.* to meet in combat;
to fight against; to attack; to oppose or try
to stop an assault; *Thai* ผจญ, ประจัญ.

ผจาน pa[4]-chjarn *Cam. v.* to insult, expose or abuse (a person) publicly; to humiliate
or disgrace publicly; *Thai* ประจาร see p. 498.

ผณ pa[4]-na[6] *P. S. n.* a nostril; the ala-nasi
(the cartilaginous flap or outer side of each
nostril); the expanded hood or neck of a
cobra; a stick shaped like a serpent's hood
(S. E. D. p. 716): ผณกร a snake; a serpent:
ผณธร a name for Siva: ผณมณี *lit.* "the
hood-gem," *i. e.* the markings or spots on the
hood of a cobra.

ผณา pa[4]-nah feminine form of ผณ: ผณากร,
ผณาธร a snake (feminine gender).

ผณิน, ผณี pa[4]-nin *S. n.* a snake (in com-

pound words the final consonant is omitted)
(S. E. D. p. 716): ผณิเขล a quail; see กระทา
p. 34 (usual form): ผณินายก the king of
the Nagas or serpents who lived in Patala.
He was used by the gods and Asuras for a
coil around the mountain Mandara at the
churning of the ocean (H. C. D. pp. 343, 291):
ผณิบดี a snake of enormous size: ผณิปรีย์
lit. "a companion of snakes," *i. e.* the wind;
air: ผณิเผณ *lit.* "the saliva of snakes," *i. e.*
opium: ผณิภุช *lit.* "an eater of snakes,"
i. e. the peacock: ผณิลดา, ผณิวัลลี (พลู) the
leaf of the *Piper betle*; betel-leaf: ผณินทร์,
ผณีศวร the king of the serpent race or Nagas,
and of the infernal region called Patala. He
is a serpent with a thousand heads, which
was the couch and canopy of Vishnu whilst
sleeping during the intervals of creation
(H. C. D. p. 291): ผณิทรสมพัตสร, ปีมะโรง the
year of the great snake in the animal cycle
of twelve years.

ผด pote[4] *n.* rash; spots (as prickly heat).

ผดุง the correct spelling is ผะดุง. see p. 541.

ผทม pa[4]-tom *Cam. v.* to sleep; to lie down
(used only for royalty); *Thai* บรรทม see p. 469.

ผนวก pa[4]-nu-ak[4] *v.* to add to; to mix
with; to compound.

ผนวช pa[4]-nu-at[4] *v.* to ordain a member
into the Buddhist priesthood; to be in, or to
enter the Buddhist priesthood; see บวช p. 471.

ผนัง pa[4]-nung[2] *n.* a wall or brick partition:
ก่อฝาผนัง to build a solid wall.

ผนึก pa[4]-neuk[4] *v.* to seal (as an envelope);
to close up securely; to make adhere firmly
together: ผนึกตรา to affix a seal; to attach
a stamp.

ผม pom[2] *n.* hair: *pron.* I; me (a respectful term used only by males): ผมนาง (ปลา)
see จุ่ม (ปลา) p. 254: ผมปลอม a wig: ผม-
หงอก grey hairs: ผมหยิก curly hair: ผม-
มหาดไทย *n.* a circular brush-shaped topknot,

an ancient style of wearing the hair. The head is shaved all but a patch about four inches in diameter on the fore part of the head. In this the hair about one inch long stands erect : ผมออกดอก (โรค) *n. Tinea Nodosa*, a disease of the hair, characterized by nodular masses around the hairs. These black nodules are of varying sizes, smaller than nits, are attached to and tend to encircle the hairs, usually eccentrically ; a nodule may be 1/8 inch (0.3 cm) long but is usually much smaller. The larger nodules are usually found along the distal portions of the longer hairs and are discrete. The shafts of the hairs are never involved nor do the hairs break easily. The scalp itself is unaffected. The disease appears to be much more common in children in south Thailand (W. H. Kneedler, M. D.).

ผยอง   pa[4]-yaung[2] *v.* to jump or struggle for freedom (as a caged animal) ; to rear on the hind legs and pounce upon (as a tiger).

ผรณ   pa[4]-ra[6]-na[6] *P. n.* pervasion ; permeation ; penetration (chd. p. 381).

ผรณาปีติ   pa[4]-ra[6]-nah-bpi[4]-dti[4] *P. n.* a condition of pervading or thrilling joy (chd. p. 381).

ผรสุ   pa[4]-ra[6]-soo[4] *P. n.* an hatchet (chd. p. 381) ; an ax ; see ขวาน p. 146.

ผริต   pa[4]-ri[6]-dta[4] *P. v.* to flash ; to shine forth ; to pervade, diffuse, emit or send forth (chd. p. 381).

ผรุพก   pa[4]-roo[6]-pok[6] *S. n.* a betel-box or a spittoon (S. E. D. p. 716) ; see กระโถน p. 33.

ผรุส   pa[4]-roo[6]-sa[4] *P. adj.* harsh ; abusive ; insulting ; unkind ; fierce ; savage ; rough ; severe ; cruel (chd. p. 381) : คำผรุสวาท abusive language.

ผล   pon[2] *P.S. n.* (1) fruit ; a numerical designatory particle for fruits in general, as ส้มสามผล three oranges : (2) the product, answer or result of a calculation, as ผลที่-

ได้เมื่อลบเลข the remainder in a problem of subtraction : ผลที่ได้เมื่อหาร the quotient : (3) the consequences, rewards, effects or retribution of deeds, good or evil, as ผลของ-กรรม results or penalties due to sin or impiety : (4) the issue or end of a condition or action, as ได้ผลดี to be successful ; to get favourable results : ไม่เป็นผล unsuccessful ; unfruitful ; there are no results : (5) compensation ; advantage ; benefits, as ผลประโยชน์ salary ; stipend ; emoluments ; rentals ; interest on investments ; rewards (S. E. D. p. 716) : ผลแห่งความชอบ remuneration for services rendered : ผลกาม desirous of rewards, profits or gain : ผลกาล season or period of fruitage, profits or gain : ผลเกสร *lit.* "that which has hairy fruit," *i. e.* the coconut tree, because the fruit is covered with a fibrous coat resembling hairs : ผลขัณฑพ the pomegranate tree (see ทับทิม (ต้น) p. 409) : ผลทาตรี yielding or giving results, or emoluments : ผลประทาน *lit.* "a condition producing results," *i. e.* a marriage ceremony : ผลปริฌาม a fruitful harvest : ผลพฤกษ์ fruit-producing trees : ผลภุช *lit.* "those enjoying fruit," *i. e.* monkeys : ผลมูล shoots, bulbs, fruits or roots of trees or shrubs : ผลราช *lit.* "the chief or king of fruits," *i. e.* the watermelon : ผลวากย์ the promise of a reward or bounty : ผลเศรษฐ์ *lit.* "the best of all fruits," *i. e.* the mango : ผลสมบัท the abundance of fruit ; prosperity ; success : ผลสิทธิ์ the realization of a purpose or object ; a prosperous issue : ผลาทนี์, ผลาศนี์ *lit.* "eaters of fruit or berries," *i. e.* parrots ; see แก้ว p. 130 : ผลานต์ *lit.* "that which ends life with fruit," *i. e.* the bamboo : ผลาผล fruits of varying sizes : ผลาราม a fruit orchard ; a fruit garden : ผลาหาร *lit.* "using fruit as food," *i. e.* one eating fruit in place of solid food ; a vegetarian : ผโลทัย the appearance, consequences or results of gain (as in trading or business) ; recompense ; reward.

ผลคุ   pon[2]-la[6]-koo[6] *S. n.* a red powder

(made from the rhizomes of the wild ginger) used to sprinkle on, or throw at each other during a seasonal Hindu festival called Holi or Holika, held on the full moon of Phalguna (March). This is a very popular festival and has its roots in the worship of the sun, now well on its northward course, and bringing the welcome burning heat (The Religious Life of India, p. 44).

ผลคุน, ผัคคุณ, ผาลคุน pon[2]-la[6]-koon *P. S. n.* the month Phalguna, corresponding to the solar month Pisces (March) (The Religious Life of India, p. 18: chd. p. 380): *adj.* red; light red; being born under the constellation Pisces (S. E. D. p. 718).

ผลคุน, ผลคุน pon[2]-la[6]-koo[6]-nee *S. n.* name of a double lunar mansion (S.E.D. p. 718): ผลคุนีบุรพมาส the full moon in the month Phalguna (March).

ผลอ plau[2] *adj.* flattering; cajoling: พูดผลอ, ปากผลอ to use fulsome compliments or undue praise; see ประจบประแจง p. 497.

ผล็อง plaung[2] *onomat.* from the sound of a stone falling into a water jar.

ผล็อย plau-ie[2] *adv.* quickly; speedily; vigorously (used in combination with กระโดด).

ผละ pla[4] *v.* to be separated from; to part with or cause to move away from; to push away from, push back or repel.

ผลัก plak[4] *v.* to push; to expel; to shove with the hand.

ผลัด plat[4] *v.* to change places with; to take turns with; to change by alternation; to take the place of another: ผลัดกัน alternately: ผลัดวันประกันพรุ่ง procrastination.

ผลับ plup[4] *adj.* quick (as a door slammed shut by the wind): *onomat.* from the sound of a dog lapping water.

ผลั่วะ ploo-ah[4] *onomat.* from the sound of

a stone thrown into a bush, or a bird flying out from a thicket.

ผลา plah[2] *Cam. n.* a long-handled sword: *Mohn* a rock; a stone: *adj.* sharp-pointed; keen-edged.

ผลาญ plarn[2] *v.* to destroy; to disperse or spend lavishly (as did the prodigal son); to use or spend wastefully or ruthlessly: ถูกไฟผลาญ to be utterly destroyed by fire: ผลาญชีวิตร to kill relentlessly: ผู้ผลาญทรัพย์ a spendthrift.

ผลิ, เผล็ด pli[4] *v.* to bud; to open out (as a flower or leaves): ฤดูใบไม้ผลิ springtime.

ผลิต, ผลิตผล pa[4]-lit[6] *P. S. v.* to produce fruit; to bear fruit or have a crop (chd. p. 381): *adj.* fruitful; successful; accomplished; bearing; yielding; producing fruit or results (S. E. D. p. 717).

ผลิน, ผลี pa[2]-lin *S. adj.* fruit-bearing (chd. p. 381).

ผลีผลาม plee[2]-plarm[2] *adj.* being too fast, rapid or hasty; being ill-mannered or ill-bred.

ผลึก, ผลิกะ pa[4]-leuk[4] *n.* crystal quartz: ผลึกศิขรี, ผลึกาจล *lit.* "the crystal mountain," *i. e.* a mountain in the Himalayas north of Manasa lake. Siva's and Kuvera's abodes are said to be there (H. C. D. p. 139): ผลึกศิลา rock crystal.

ผลึง pleung[4] *v.* to swell up; to be swollen; to be inflated.

ผลือ plur[2] *n.* a knot; see ปม p. 495.

ผลุ ploo[4] *onomat.* from the sound of dough, putty or pieces of other pliable material falling against a hard surface.

ผลุง ploong[2] *adv.* swiftly; speedily (indicative of articles thrown or pitched, as a base-ball or cricket-ball): *onomat.* from the sound of a rock, stone or nail dropping into the water.

ผลุด   ploot[4] *v.* to slip out or in quickly (as in or out of a motor car); to crawl in or out quickly through a hole (as a dog through a hedge): *Cam. n.* an elephant's tusk.

ผลุน   ploon[2] *v.* to go suddenly or quickly (as without notice): ผลุนผลัน with a sudden start; hastily; urgently; unceremoniously; urgently; quickly: ผลุนผลันไป to escape suddenly; to make off.

ผลุบ   ploop[4] *v.* to dive down; to jump down into; to duck the head down under (so as to hide from pursuers): *adv.* hurriedly; urgently; indicating the manner of a bird darting into a thicket, or one ducking down under the water: ผลุบผลับ rudely; suddenly: ผลุบผลับไป to disappear unexpectedly: ผลุบ-โผล่ to dive down under the water and occasionally bob up again; to duck and raise the head alternately (while in the water).

ผลุย   ploo-ie[2] *adj.* the sudden slipping of a knot tied in a string or rope, when it is pulled.

ผลู   ploo[2] *Cam. n.* a path; a way; a route or road: ผลูก a winding or curving road or path: ผลูแบก the forks of a road or path.

ผวน   poo-an[2] *v.* to turn back; to retrace one's steps over the same path; see ทวน p. 399.

ผวย   poo-ie[2] *n.* a thick blanket or steamer rug.

ผวา   pa[4]-wah[2] *v.* to be frightened, scared, surprised or startled; to swoop down, or pounce upon suddenly (as a hawk on prey): บินผวา to fly off in a scared manner: ผวา-กอด to be seized suddenly in the arms: ผวา-ตื่น to be awakened by fright, or suddenly aroused from slumber (by some alarm): วิ่ง-ผวา to run off suddenly (as from fright).

ผอก   pauk[4] *n.* rice or food carried for a noonday lunch (as to work, or on a journey).

ผอง   paung[2] *adj.* all; complete; total (amount or number); see ทั้งสิ้น p. 408.

ผ่อง, ผะผ่อง   paung[4] *adj.* pure; clean; free from blemish or tarnish; bright; white: ผ่องแผ้ว clean, pure (implying the heart or affections): ผ่องใส joyous; smiling (descriptive of facial expressions): ผิวผ่อง skin that is clear, clean, and free from blotches or blemishes.

ผอด   paut[4] *v.* to breathe or inhale (as respiration).

ผ่อน   paun[4] *v.* to slacken or play out a little at a time (as a rope or kite string); to reduce or lessen (as a sentence or judgement): ผ่อนใช้, ผ่อนจ่าย to make part-payments; to pay by instalment: ผ่อนปรน to show clemency; to reduce the punishment for an offence: ผ่อนผัน to allow or accept postponement (in the settlement of financial matters); to make the terms of settlement as easy as possible.

ผอม   paum[2] (see ซูบ p. 310) *adj.* thin; lean; shrunken: ซูบผอม emaciated from sickness or starvation.

ผ็อย   poy[2] *adv.* suddenly; at once; immediately (as falling asleep quickly, or having eyelids drooping easily).

ผอูน, โผอูน   *Cam.* pa[4]-oon *n.* a younger brother or sister.

ผะคม   pa[4]-kom *v.* to place the hands palm to palm and raised to the face in an attitude of worship or reverence (sometimes written บังคม p. 474).

ผะแคง   pa[4]-kaang *adj.* jammed; crowded; crushed together or squeezed; see ประดัง [p. 499.

ผะชุม   see ประชุม p. 498.

ผะดา   pa[4]-dah (see ค้ำชู p. 201: ช่วย p. 283) *v.* to prop; to support; to uphold or render assistance.

ผะดุง, ผดุง   pa[4]-doong *v.* to care for, nourish, support, sustain, aid or administer the necessary nursing or treatment: นาง-

ผดุงครรภ์ an obstetrical nurse : แพทย์ผดุงครรภ์ an obstetrician.

ผะเด see ประเด p. 500.

ผะเด็น see ประเด็น p. 500.

ผะเดิน, บันเดิน pa⁴-dern *v.* to walk.

ผะเดิม see ประเดิม p. 500.

ผะแดง see ประแดง p. 500.

ผะเทศ see ประเทศ p. 501.

ผะผก see ผก p. 538.

ผะผ่อง see ผ่อง p. 542.

ผะผ้าย pa⁴-pai³ *v.* to get up; to return; to go back : *adv.* speedily; hastily; hurriedly; urgently.

ผะผ้ำ pa⁴-pum³ *v.* to walk quickly or rapidly (as infantry on double-quick march).

ผะษา see ภาษา

ผะสม see ประสม p. 505.

ผะสาน see ประสาน p. 505.

ผะอบ, ประอบ (p. 506) pa⁴-op⁴ *n.* a chrismatory cup with base and tapering lip (sometimes used as an urn).

ผะโอน pa⁴-on *v.* to bend or be inclined forward or backwards (as a tree or branch in a storm).

ผัก pak⁴ *n.* a vegetable; a common noun which is followed by the specific designating name, *ex.* ผักกะเฉด, ผักหนอง see กระเฉด (ผัก) p. 24 : ผักกระเฉดบก *Thailand, Chantaburi,* มะขามเบี้ย *N. Laos* (ผัก) *Cassia mimosoides* (*Leguminosae*), a slightly woody plant found through-out south-eastern Asia and to Australia; in the Malay Peninsula it is found in the most occupied parts. It has been tried as a green manure and, though first trials seemed favourable, it is now considered of little value as such. It is said to be medicinal, in Java,

and the roots are used for cramps in the stomach. The Japanese are said to make tea from the leaves, and to cultivate it, apparently for this purpose (MCM. p. 474 : cb. p. 512 : BURK. p. 477) : ผักกาดนก *Thailand and Laos* (ผัก) *Nasturtium montanum* (*Cruciferae*) (cb. p. 76) : ผักกาดหอม see กาด p. 92 : ผักก้านถิน see กระถิน p. 32 : ผักขม see ขม p. 140 : ผักขวง, ผักขี้ขวง, สะเดาดิน see ขวง p. 144 : ผักโขมหนาม, ผักโขมหิน see โขม p. 170 : ผักคราดหัวแหวน see คราด p. 180 : ผักเค็ด *Thailand, Bangkok* (ผัก) *Cassia sophera* (*Leguminosae*) (cb. p. 514) : ผักจ้ำ *Laos* (ผัก) *Ardisia humilis* (*Myrsinaceae*), a shrub six to ten feet in height, with thick, fleshy glabrous branches. The leaves are obovate oblong, acute at the base and rounded at the apex, thick, fleshy and smooth on both sides, and are on very short leaf-stalks. The inflorescence is glabrous, drooping and shorter than the leaves. The flowers are pinkish-purple with small black dots dispersed over the surface of the petals and sepals; the berry is subglobose and dark purple (V. P. p. 179 : The Orn. Tree of Hawaii, J. F. ROCK p. 171) : ผักตื่นแตน *Thailand, Chonburi,* มะบ้าวอก *N. Laos* (ผัก) *Entada glandulosa* (*Leguminosae*), a woody climber (cb. p. 542) : ผักเบี้ยเขียว *Thailand, Kanburi* (ผัก) *Glinus lotoides* (*Ficoideae*) (cb. p. 785) : ผักเบี้ยเล็ก, บานเที่ยง *Thailand, Bangkok* (ผัก) *Portulaca quadrifida* (*Portulacaceae*), a small succulent herb, found as a weed in all the warmer parts of the world. It may serve as a vegetable. The Malays use it to poultice boils and abscesses. In Sumatra it is also used for poulticing, but in this case for abdominal diseases; and in Java, as cooling in fever (cb. p. 110 : BURK. p. 1802) : ผักเบี้ยใหญ่ *Thailand, Bangkok* (ผัก) *Portulaca oleracea* (*Portulacaceae*), a succulent herb, found as a weed throughout the warmer parts of the world. It is a common pot-herb, obtained from plants that come up in cultivated and waste ground. The garden races of Europe, of which there are several, are not found in Malaya, nor is there any indication that they have been tried (MCM. pp. 135, 201, 312, 476: BURK. p. 1801): ผักปรังขาว *Basella cordifolia*, a stomachic (V. P. p. 180): ผักปรังแดง *Basella rubra* (*Chenopodiaceae*), Ceylon spinach, Malabar nightshade, an herb of the Old World tropics, widely cultivated, wild in both Africa and Asia in such a way as to suggest that it is a native of both. In cultivation there are several races, which have been taken for species. The species is cultivated throughout Malaya for use as spinach, in better races than occur wild. It is gently laxative and is said to be rich in vitamins. It is slightly medicinal, the pulped or bruised leaves being used to poultice sores. There are other medicinal uses (MCM. p. 303: BURK. p. 307: V.P. p. 108): ผักไผ่ต้น *Laos, Chiengmai* (ผัก) *Pittosporum nepaulense* (*Pittosporaceae*) (cb. p. 98): ผักปลาบ a grass used medicinally by the Thai: ผักแมะ *Thailand, Trang* (ผัก) *Momordica subangulata* (*Cucurbitaceae*) (cb. p. 759): ผักเขี่ยววัว *Thailand, Nakawn Sawan* (ผัก) *Millettia caerulea* (*Leguminosae*) (cb. p. 388): ผักรด *Thailand, Korat*, ผักฮาก *Laos, Lampang* (ผัก) *Erythropalum scandens* (*Olacaceae*), a big climber with red, evil-smelling fruit, containing an indigo-coloured seed. It is common but of no known use (cb. p. 271: BURK. p. 949): ผักแว่นเขา *Thailand, Krat*, ผักหนอก *Thailand, Chumpawn*, ผักหนอกข้าง *Laos, Nan* (ผัก) *Hydrocotyle javanica* (*Umbelliferae*), an herb found throughout south-eastern Asia, and to Australia. Its leaves, mixed with those of *Piper aduncum*, are used in the Sunda Islands to stupefy small fish. The Dyaks of Borneo and the Tamils of Ceylon use them similarly (cb. p. 787: BURK. p. 1212): ผักเสี้ยน *Thailand*, ส้มเสี้ยน *Laos, Chiengmai* (ผัก) *Gynandropsis pentaphylla* (*Capparidaceae*), a tropical herb having strongly aromatic leaves, reputed as a cure for cobra-bite (MCM. pp. 312, 378: cb. p. 78: V. P. p. 181): ผักเสี้ยนป่า *Thailand, Ratburi* (ผัก) *Polanisia*

chelidonii (*Capparidaceae*) (cb. p. 77); *Cleome chelidonii*, a weedy herb found in India, south of the Gangetic plains, and here and there on the coasts of Malaysia. The natives of French Indo-China use an infusion for skin complaints. The Madoerese drop warm juice from its leaves into the ear. The roots are said to possess a vermifuge action (BURK. p. 580): ผักเสี้ยนผี *Thailand*, (ผัก) *Polanisia viscosa* (*Capparidaceae*) (cb. p. 77: V. P. p. 181); *Cleome viscosa* (*Capparidaceae*), a sticky herb of waste places, found widely throughout the tropics. Malays, Tamils and Chinese all use it medicinally. A little is taken with food, as mustard or horse-radish may be in Europe. It stimulates the appetite. The Malays administer a decoction for intestinal complaints such as colic, and even in advanced dysentery. It is used as a poultice for headaches, and in an embrocation for rheumatism. In Guam the seeds serve alone as a vermifuge. In the Dutch Indies it is used as a narcotic, being mixed with tobacco or smoked as opium (BURK. p. 581): ผักหนาม *Lasia heterophylla* (*Araceae*) (V. P. p. 179): ผักหวานบ้าน *Sauropus albicans* (*Euphorbiaceae*) (V. P. p. 181): *S. androgynus*, a small shrub, found in India and throughout Malaysia, cultivated and not uncommonly wild; in the Malay Peninsula it is grown generally and occurs wild near villages. It is a popular spinach, the leaves, when cooked, being rather firm and slightly acid. A sweetmeat is made in Java from the fruits. In the Dutch Indies food is often coloured by means of it. The roots, and to a lesser extent the leaves, are medicinal. A decoction of the roots is given for fever and for stricture of the bladder (BURK. p. 1967): ผักหวานป่า *Meliantha sauvis* (V. P. p. 181): ผักให *Thailand, Nakawn Sritamarat*, มะระ *Thailand, Bangkok*, หมักห่อบ *Laos, Chiengmai* (ผัก), *Momordica charantia* (*Cucurbitaceae*), carilla fruit, a rather slender vine, bearing an ovoid, warty gourd, 6 to 8 inches long, bright orange-yellow when ripe. This climber which is cultivated throughout the tropics, occurs as if wild and plentifully in the neighbourhood of cultivation. Its original home is not known, but clearly it was the Old World; and was taken to the New World by slave-traders or their slaves. It is commonly cultivated in the tropics as a vegetable, and sometimes for ornament. The fruit is very bitter, and is adapted for pickling, being one of the most common ingredients in Indian pickles. There are several varieties, one of which has white fruits (MCM. p. 29ε: Burk. p. 1485: cb. p. 758): ผักอี๊ด *Derris elliptica* (*Leguminosae*), a large, woody climber from Chittagong, found throughout Indo-China and Malaysia to New Guinea. It is abundantly wild in Thailand. The bark and flowers are commonly used as fish-poison, and the juice as arrow-poison. The roots, pounded up in water, are used against termites, crickets, etc. Cattle are said to have died from eating it (MCM. p. 385: cb. p. 488: Burk. p. 789).

ผัคคุณ see **ผลคุน** p. 541.

ผัคคุณ see **ผลคุน** p. 541.

ผัง   pung[2] *v.* to go; to run or move under sail (as a boat): *n.* a stick with sharp, forked ends stuck into the edges of cloth, serving to stretch cloth that is being woven; the pegs or strings attached to the pegs outlining the shape and showing where the posts of a house are to be planted: ผังตราชู the balance beam of a weigh scale.

ผัด   pat[4] *v.* to fry; to move promiscuously here and there, back and forth; to incite an animal to give chase (as in bull-fights); to postpone or ask for a postponement or a delay (as in legal cases): *n.* fried food (as meat and vegetables fried in lard): ผัดผัน to move in a circle and then reverse; to move in one direction and then return: ผัดเพี้ยน to make a subsequent postponement, *ex.* a postponement is allowed and a second postpone-

ment is made: ผัดหน้า to powder the face: ไม้ผัด the vowel mark "ˇ".

ผัน   pun[2] *v.* to deviate; to depart from; to swerve (as from a principal or purpose): *n.* the red lotus (similar to บัวเผื่อน): ผันแปร to turn, change, alter or be transformed (see แปร p. 536): ผันผยอง to walk bravely, boldly or fearlessly: ผันผวน to go or move back and forth: ผันผ่อน, ผ่อนปรน to show leniency or clemency; to allow more time (as in payment of a debt): ผันผาด to run back and forth wildly, or with gestures: ผันผาย to walk forwards; to return or retrace one's steps: to wander about: ผันอักษร to modulate the tone in pronouncing letters of the alphabet or words, either high or low, as indicated by the accent marks.

ผับ, เร็ว   pup[4] *adv.* quickly; hastily (indicative of the manner of walking); adroitly (manner of performing a deed).

ผัว   poo-ah[2] *n.* a husband.

ผัวะ   poo-ah[4] *onomat.* from the sound of a stick breaking; a cracking or snapping sound.

ผัสสะ   pat[4]-sa[4] *P. n.* the condition or act of touching or coming into contact (chd. p. 382): ผัสสคุณ *lit.* "a beneficial contact," *i. e.* the wind: ผัสสลัชชา *lit.* "one that is ashamed of being touched," *i. e.* the sensative plant (see กระทืบยอบ (ต้น) p. 35): ผัสสนาน the act of bathing or coming into contact with water on the day of an eclipse: ผัสสานันทา *lit.* "those whose touch produces pleasure or joy," *i. e.* the celebrated nymphs of Indra's heaven (H. C. D. p. 19).

ผา   pah[2] *n.* stones; rocks; mountains: ผาคำสามเข่า, เขาตรีกูฏ *lit.* "three peaks," *i. e.* the mountain on which the city of Lanka was built (H. C. D. p. 320): ผาเผือก, เขาไกลาส a mountain in the Himalayas, north of Manasa lake. Siva's paradise is said to be on this mountain (H. C. D. p. 139): ผาหอมหวาน, เขา-คันธมาทน์ a mountain and forest in Ilavrita, the central region of the world, which contains the mountain Meru (H. C. D. p. 104): หน้าผา a precipice.

ผ่า   pah[4] *v.* to slit, split, or cleave lengthwise (as bamboos); to rend, open or separate by force: บุกป่าผ่าหนาม to scramble through jungle and bush by cutting a way: ผ่าเข้าไป to rush in or intrude roughly, rudely or offensively: ผ่าฝี to lance an abscess: ผ่าเหล่า to have a division, or separation among the members of a family or clan.

ผ้า   pah[3] *n.* cloth; a general name for woven fabrics: ผ้ากราบ a cloth on which Buddhist monks kneel when making confessions, or worshipping before the image of the Buddha. Meanwhile they assume the most humble attitude, when knees, head and hands touch the floor: ผ้าขี้ริ้ว rags: ผ้าเช็ดตัว towels: ผ้าเช็ดมือ napkins: ผ้าเช็ดปาก, ผ้าเช็ดหน้า handkerchiefs: ผ้าถูตัว wash cloth: ผ้าทิพย์ the cloth (or the reproduction of it in a permanent form) hanging from the lap of an image of the Buddha: ผ้านุ่ง the loincloth; a langouti: ผ้าป่า robes presented to Buddhist monks on occasions other than at the Kathin ceremony, and classed as robes presented at cremations: ผ้าม่าน curtains (for doors or windows): ผ้าลาย chintz; figured cloth: ผ้าสักหลาด flannel; woollen goods: ผ้าห่ม scarfs; blankets: ผ้าไหว้ cloth or clothing presented by the groom to the parents of the bride on the occasion of a marriage (as a token of respect): ผ้าอ้อม diapers; an infant's breech-cloth.

ผาก, หน้าผาก   pak[4] *n.* the brow; the forehead; a species of bamboo having long, intermediate spaces between the joints: *adj.* dry; parched; pale; withered: แห้งผาก, ผากแผ้ง to become dry, parched, crisp or brittle by heat; to be arid.

ผาง   pang[2] *onomat.* from the sound of waves dashing, or of slapping with the hand.

ผาณิต   pah[2]-nit[6] *P. S. n.* the inspissated juice of the sugar-cane and other plants (S. E. D. p. 718); molasses (Chd. p. 381).

ผาด   part[4] *v.* to pass or flit by quickly: *adj.* indistinct: ผาดผัง to go or move swiftly or rapidly (as a boat): ผาดโผน to jump and spring upon: *adj.* strong; durable; flashing; dashing; gay (in dress or decorations): ผาดเพ่ง to glance or look at casually: ผาดเสียง to shout out loudly and roughly.

ผาติ   pah[2]-dti[4] *P. S. adj.* growing; improving; increasing (Chd. p. 382): ผาติกรรม the act of improving, renovating or making as good as new (implying the act of replacing new Buddhist robes for the old ones); repairing or exchanging new articles for old ones.

ผ่าน   pan[4] *v.* to walk past in front of (as troops in a review); to cross-cut across; to rule over, manage or direct: ผ่านเผ้า being over, higher or covering the head: ผ่านพิภพ to rule over or govern a country or territory; to administer or manage monetary possessions; *n.* a ruler, monarch or sovereign: ผ่านฟ้า a king: ผ่านราคา to over-charge: ม้าผ่าน a piebald or dappled horse.

ผาย, ผ้าย   pai[2] *v.* to go; to come; to open, reveal, extend or expand; to spread out or bend over on all sides (as a flower in bloom): ผายผัง, ไผ่ผัง to go, run or walk quickly (away from): ผายผัน to walk; to sojourn: ผายะยัน to replace in a vertical position; to re-assume an upright position: ผายลม to expel gas from the anus: ผายลมมาน to to expel the air through the nose, or to exhale with force producing a sound (as made by horses): ยาทำให้ผายลม a medicine that produces the expulsion of gas from the anus.

ผาล   parn[2] *P. S. n.* a ploughshare (Chd. p. 381); a kind of hoe or shovel (S. E. D. p. 717): ผาลเขลา name for the quail; see กระทา (นก) p. 34.

ผ่าว   pow[4] *adj.* issuing or radiating (used in regard to intensity of heat).

ผาสุก   pah[2]-sook[4] *P. n.* peace; joy; happiness; comfort; agreeableness (chd. p. 382).

ผ้า ๆ   pum[3]-pum[3] *adv.* indicative of haste; speedily; hurriedly; lively.

ผิ, ผิว, ผิว้, ผิว่า   pi[4] *conj.* if; if so; provided that; supposing that.

ผิง   ping[2] *v.* to place or hold close to a fire or heat; to hold over a flame; to smoke over a fire: *n.* a Thai sweetmeat composed of flour, eggs and sugar, which is then placed by a gentle heat to harden into small roe-like globules: ผิงแดด to expose oneself to the sun: ผิงไฟ to warm oneself by a fire.

ผิด   pit[4] *adj.* wrong; erroneous; mistaken; false; incorrect: ความผิด an error; sin: ทำผิด to commit an error or fault: ผิดกัน to differ; to be unlike: ผิดต่อกฎหมาย illegal; unlawful: ผิดต่อศีลสักสิทธิ์ sacrilegious: ผิดนัด to fail to meet an appointment: ผิดไป to err or blunder: ผิดเมีย to commit adultery: ผิดหลง to make a mistake; to be in error: ผู้ผิด a transgressor: ผู้รู้ผิดชอบ one responsible for: ไม่มีผิด innocent; having no guilt.

ผิน   pin[2] *v.* to turn towards: ผินหน้าเข้าหากัน to turn the face towards a partner: ผินหน้าให้ to face towards: ผินหลังให้ to turn one's back towards another.

ผิว   piew[2] *n.* the outer covering; the cuticle or epidermis; the rind; the surface: ผิวน้ำ the surface of the water: ผิวปาก to whistle (with the lips): ผิวพรรณ complexion; outward appearance: ผิวหนัง skin.

ผี   pee[2] *n.* a corpse; an evil spirit; a general term to which is added the name of any particular spirit alluded to; a ghost; a beneficent guardian spirit; the tutelary deity of a place. These may be either male or female.

If the offerings take a phallic form, it indicates that the deity is of the female sex; if stones are piled up in a heap with offerings, it indicates that the deity is of the male sex: เครื่องกันผี amulets to protect oneself against the evil spirits: ใช้ผี to send a demon to harm another person: ผีกระสือ see กระสือ p. 46: ผีกะหาง see กระหัง p. 46: ผีกุมาร the spirit of an infant who dies in the womb or shortly after birth. If precautions are not taken to bury such a child in a proper manner, the spirit may return and, entering the mother, may cause her death: ผีเข้า to be possessed by evil spirits or demons: ผีเข้า, เจ้าเข้า when the lord of spirits enters a person, he is known as "คนทรง" or one possessed by spirits. It is thought that by the words or acts of such an one the wishes or abode of the spirit can be traced: ผีตากผ้าอ้อม rays of the sun reflected on evening or late twilight clouds: ผีตายโหง, ผีตายห่า the malevolent ghosts of those who have died suddenly or by violent deaths, as by weapons falling from a great height, or in childbirth. Knowledge regarding this class of spirits is most useful to sorcerers and witches: ผีนางไม้ female tree spirits or genii inhabiting certain big forest trees. They are goodhearted fairies and it is reported that sometimes when monks are on pilgrimages and leave their alms-bowls at the foot of such trees, these fairies will fill them with food: ผีบุญ persons who pretend to be possessed with occult or mystical powers of spirits or tutelary deities, in order to make people believe in their power: ผีปอบ a class of malevolent genii or demons held in great respect among the Laos and mountain tribes. These may be sent by the sorcerers to devour the entrails of one on whom harm is desired: ผีป่า genii or spirits of the jungle: ผีปีศาจ, ผีดิศาจ the devil; demons; malevolent genii: ผีเปรต see เปรต p. 532: ผีโป่ง, ผีไพร, ผีโป่งค่าง genii or spirits of the jungle. These have the appearance of a black monkey. They frequent heavy jungle trees and are reported to come and suck the blood from the big toe of a casual sleeper in the jungle. Such sleepers are recommended to sleep with their feet touching in order to guard against these demons: ผีพราย demons which the sorcerers entertain in their houses: ผีเรือน a guardian angel or spirit of the house, whose abode is a little wooden house or shrine on the top of a pole. These are to be found near almost every Thai house: ผีเสื้อ a generic name for butterflies: ผีเสื้อ *Thailand* (ต้น) *Desmodium obcordatum* (*Leguminosae*) (cb. p. 413): ผีเสื้อ (ปลา) *Monodactylus argenteus* (*Monodactylidae*) (suvatti p. 140): ผีเสื้อน้ำ *Laos, Lampang* (ต้น) *Desmodium retroflexum* (*Leguminosae*) (cb. p. 416): ผีเสื้อน้ำ malevolent spirits, genii or fierce-looking giants who carry iron clubs; they reside in the water and are often blamed in cases of drowning: ผีเสื้อยักษ์ *Attacus atlas*, the giant saturnid moth commonly known as *Attacus* moth; the huge atlas moth, a most conspicuous member of this group. It has reddish brown wings in which are noticed transparent sections like windows. The caterpillars of this moth are voracious feeders and can do a lot of damage to trees, particularly citrus and guava, in a very short time (Siam-Nature and Industries p. 46): ผีเสื้อหลวง, สีเสื้อหลวง *Laos*, กล้วย *Thailand, Chonburi, Ratburi* (ต้น) *Casearia grewiifolia* (*Samydaceae*), a tree or shrub found in the tropics. The roots are used in Cambodia for diarrhoea, and the bark as a tonic (burk. p. 472); *C. kerrii* (cb. p. 737): ผีหลอก phantoms; spectres; ghosts; spirits of dead persons which haunt a locality and may appear in certain houses, chiefly old and abandoned ones, or in ancient ruins: เรือผีหลอก, เรือกัตรา a a kind of boat used for catching fish, being a long narrow shallow boat having a white wing-like board on one side, projecting into the water, with a net on the opposite side. A light in the bow attracts the fish which leap into the net or boat as it is paddled along the canals at night: ผีหลอก (ปลา) see กบ (ปลา) p. 6: ผีอำ the spirit causing nightmare. It is reported to sit on the chest, or tread on a person just as he or she is dropping off to sleep in a strange place, and that person can only groan or emit inarticulate sounds while the spirit is there: เสียผี, เสียเคราะห์, เส้นผี to sacrifice or make offerings to the demons or evil spirits: หมอผี a sorcerer.

ผีต, ผิต   pee[2]-dta[4] *P. adj.* prosperous; flourishing (in worldly goods) (chd. p. 392).

ผีว์   see ผิ p. 547.

ผึง   purng[2] *onomat.* from the sound made when a rope or string breaks or snaps because pulled too tightly: *adv.* completely; entirely; perfectly (used in combinations as แห้งผึง = แห้งสนิท): เชือกขาดดังผึง the ropes break with a snap.

ผึง   peung[4] *v.* to spread out; to expose or hang in the sun or wind (as clothes to dry): *n.* an adze: *adj.* being spread out; broadened out or hung up (to get the effects of the sun or wind): ผึงผาย fully expanded; amply broad or enlarged (as the chest); not being stoop-shouldered or narrow-chested.

ผึ้ง   peung[3] *n.* a general name for bees: ขี้ผึ้ง wax: น้ำผึ้ง honey: ผึ้ง (ปลา) *Gyrinocheilus kaznakovi* (Dept. Agri. & Fisheries): รังผึ้ง, รวงผึ้ง a beehive or honeycomb.

ผืน   purn[2] *n.* a numerical particle for strips of cloth, mats, dried hides, leather or carpets, *ex.* เสื่อสองผืน.

ผื่น   purn[4] *n.* spots; general eruption or rash on the skin (as measles).

ผุ, ยุ่ย   poo[4] *adj.* rotten; decayed; brittle; friable; crumbling; see เปื่อย p. 535.

ผุด poot[4] *v.* to rise, jump or spring up above the surface of the water (as fish); to appear as an eruption (as elevated pimples or rash on the skin): ผุดผาย, ผุดผ้าย to get up and go.

ผุดผ่อง poot[4]-paung[4] *adj.* fair; clear (of complexion); bright; sparkling; flawless (as a jewel or diamond).

ผุดผาด poot[4]-part[4] *adj.* pretty; gay; flashing; lovable; beautiful; attractive (used in regard to children or dress).

ผุยผง poo-ie[2]-pong[2] *n.* powder or dust of the finest grade.

ผุสสราคา see บุษบราค p. 486.

ผู้ poo[3] *n.* a designatory particle for a person or for sex: *adj.* one who; one that; when combined with a verb it denotes the noun of the agent: ผู้กระทำผิด an offender; a malefactor; a criminal; see กระทำ p. 35: ผู้กระทำผิดชั้นลหุโทษ a petty offender: ผู้กระทำผิดอันเกี่ยวด้วยรัฐประศาสน์ a political offender: ผู้กล่าว the speaker; see กล่าว p. 61: ผู้กล่าวเท็จ, ผู้โกหก a liar; a prevaricator; a quibbler: ผู้ก่อการวุ่นวาย an instigator of a disturbance; a rioter: ผู้กู้เรือที่แตกทิ้งอยู่ในทะเล the salvager of a wrecked ship; see กู้ p. 116: ผู้แกล้งป่วยเพื่อหลีกเลี่ยงหน้าที่ one feigning sickness to evade duty; see แกล้ง p. 129: ผู้ข่มเหง an oppressor; a tyrant; see ข่ม p. 140: ผู้ขอยื่นคำร้อง a petitioner; see ขอ p. 146: ผู้ขอยืม a borrower: ผู้ขาย a vendor; a seller; see ขาย p. 155: ผู้ขู่กระโชกเรียกเงินจากผู้อื่นโดยหาว่าเป็นผู้กระทำผิดต่าง ๆ a blackmailer; see ขู่ p. 162: ผู้จำนำ a pawner; a pledger; see จำนำ p. 247: ผู้ช่วย an assistant, helper, deputy or subordinate; see ช่วย p. 283: ผู้ช่วยปลัดทหารบก an assistant adjutant general: ผู้ชาย a man or male person; see ชาย p. 293: ผู้ซื้อ a purchaser; see ซื้อ p. 309: ผู้เฒ่า an aged person; a patriarch; see เฒ่า p. 317: ผู้ดี a respected person; **a gentleman; see** ดี p. 330: ผู้เดิน a walker; see เดิน p. 334: ผู้ใด ๆ whosoever; whoever; see ใด p. 338: ผู้ใดซึ่งไม่เชื่อในข้อสาสนาที่คนหมู่มากในสาสนานั้นเชื่อว่าเป็นความจริง an heretic: ผู้ได้รับอนุญาต a licensee; see ได้ p. 338: ผู้ตรวจการทั่วไป a general inspector; see ตรวจ p. 341: ผู้แต่งงานกับหญิงคนอื่นในระหว่างที่ภรรยาของตนยังมีชีวิตอยู่ a bigamist; see แต่ง p. 376: ผู้น้อย a junior; one younger or inferior (in office or responsibility); one subject to: ผู้นำ a leader or guide: ผู้ไม่เข็ดหลาบ a confirmed criminal; a recidivist; see เข็ด p. 163: ผู้รั้ง one acting for, or a deputy in a position of responsibility (as governor of a province): ผู้ร้าย one committing a crime; a malefactor: ผู้ร้องขัดทรัพย์ *legal* an intervenor; see ขัด p. 150: ผู้รับของขวัญ a donee: ผู้รับของขวัญโดยพินัยกรรม a legatee: ผู้รับจำนอง a mortgagee; see จำนอง p. 247: ผู้รับจ้างต่อ, ผู้รับจ้างช่วง a subcontractor: ผู้รับจ้างหรือรับเหมา a contractor; see จ้าง ๒ p. 243: ผู้สมคบคิด, สมรู้ a conspirator; an accomplice: ผู้สมัครเข้าสอบ a candidate for an examination: ผู้สืบสันดาน a descendant: ผู้หนีการทหาร a military deserter: ผู้หญิง a woman: ผู้ใหญ่ an adult: ผู้ใหญ่บ้าน a chief or head man.

ผูก pook[4] *v.* to tie or fasten with string or rope; to determine or purpose to do: *n.* a looseleaf book: ผูกดอก to borrow or lend money in lieu of service or interest: ผูกบทกลอน to compose in rhyme or poetry: ผูกพัน to be in love with or interested in; to be friendly towards: ผูกภาษีอากร to be the farmer of one of the government's monopolies: ผูกไมตรี to form a bond of friendship or an alliance: ผูกรถ to harness (as horses) to a carriage: ผูกเวร to be revengeful; to harbour revenge.

เผง peng[2] *onomat.* an exclamation used when the right place aimed at is hit (as in target practice or archery when a bull's-eye is made).

เผชิญ pa[4]-chern *Cam. v.* to meet; to be confronted or challenged: เผชิญภัย to be confronted with, to meet or to face some danger, calamity, disaster or misfortune.

เผ็ด   pet[4] *adj.* pungent; peppery: แกงเผ็ด a curry, highly seasoned with pepper: เผ็ด-ร้อน irritating, strong or revengeful; heated, hot or bitter (words or language).

เผดิม   pa[4]-derm a corruption of ผะเดิม, ประ-เดิม see p. 500.

เผดียง, *Cam.*, ประเดียง *Thai* see นิมนต์ p. 458.

เผน   pa[2]-na[6] *S. n.* foam; froth; scum; moisture of the lips; saliva (S. E. D. p. 718): เผนคิ้ว a mountain near the mouth of the river Indus (chd. p. 293): เผนธรรม *lit.* "having the nature of froth or foam", *i. e.* temporary; transient; of short duration.

เผ่น see กระโดด, กระโจน p. 23.

เผนิก see เบิก p. 489.

เผย, เบิด, ขยาย   pur-ie[2] *v.* to open, enlarge or spread out slightly; to reveal or disclose.

เผยอ   pa[4]-yur[2] *v.* to raise or lift up just a little (as a box when wanting to pass a rope under it); to open partially; to be partly opened (as a blossom or bud): *adj.* assuming a proud or arrogant attitude.

เผยิบ   pa[4]-yerp[4] *adv.* flapping the wings slowly (indicative of the manner of big birds when flying).

เผรุ   pay[2]-roo[6] *S. n.* a fox; a jackal (S. E. D. p. 719).

เผล, เผล้   play[2] *adj.* leaning; sloping; deviating from the perpendicular; see เฉ p. 271.

เผล่   play[4] *adv.* broadly; expansively (as when one grins from ear to ear).

เผล็ด, เพล็ด   plet[4] *v.* to sprout up or out; to bud or be just opening out (as flowers or leaves in springtime).

เผลอ   plur[2] *v.* to be reckless, incautious, rash, absent-minded or forgetful.

เผละ, เผะ   ple[4] *onomat.* from the sound as a thud when throwing mud, or when mud falls on a surface.

เผาะ   plaw[4] *onomat.* from the sound as "pop" when pulling out a cork or stopper from a bottle.

เผาะแผละ, เผาะแผะ   plaw[4]-plaa[4] *n.* a small, round, flat-bottomed, thin glass, toy bottle with a mouthpiece which makes the above sound when the air is sucked or forced in.

เผลียง   plee-ang[2] *Cam. n.* rain.

เผอเรอ   pur[2]-rur *adj.* careless; untidy; slovenly; extravagant; needlessly lavish.

เผออิญ   pa[4]-urn *Cam. adv.* accidentally; unexpectedly (to meet another); corresponding in the Thai language to เพออิญ, พรรเออิญ.

เผา   pow[2] *v.* to burn or be consumed (as by fire or passion); to set fire to; to heat (as for annealing purposes): เผาถ่าน to burn charcoal: เผาศพ to cremate a corpse: เผาอกเผาใจ to be consumed with profound grief, or "the fire of passion."

เผ่า   pow[4] *n.* family, lineage, kinsfolk, stock, relationship or race: *adj.* feeling a radiating heat or warmth.

เผ้า   pow[3] *n.* hair.

เผาะ   paw[4] *n.* a species of mushroom (similar to เห็ดยาง): *adj.* brittle; friable: *onomat.* from the sound of the cracking of the knuckles or joints, or a bursting or breaking.

เผิน   pern[2] *adv.* superficially; carelessly; inattentively; see ตื้น p. 370.

เผยน   pee-an[2] *v.* to cause to revolve, twirl or whirl.

เผอ   pur-ah[2] *pron.* I; me; a comrade or friend.

เผื่อ   pur-ah[4] *adj.* reserved for (as in case of need); in case of; provided that: *conj.* if:

prep. for : เผื่อแผ่ magnanimous ; broad-minded ; philanthropic : เผื่อว่า if ; suppose that ; perhaps ; peradventure.

เผือก (ต้น)   peu-uk[4] *n. Colocasia antiquorum Aroideae,* coco-yam, tannia, tanier, addo, taro, etc., a tuberous herbaceous perennial, with large handsome leaves, long cultivated in tropical countries and occurring under various names in different localities. There are two distinct varieties, one of which is characterized by peltate leaves. The other form is sometimes placed under the genus *Xanthosoma* (MCM. 4″ Edition p. 288). In Thailand and Indo-China taro grows wild along streams and in any places where it can find sufficient moisture. Owing to its prevalence all over northern Thailand, taro tubers are a very common article of diet of peasants. The theory has been formulated that taro-eating peoples are more subject to leprosy than those who do not eat it. It is not thought that eating taro produces leprosy, but that its use results in certain bodily deficiencies which prevent the eaters from combating leprosy successfully. The theory has not yet been fully proven : *adj.* albino (as a buffalo or an elephant).

เผือด   peu-at[4] *adj.* pale ; faded ; dim ; gloomy ; dejected.

เผือน (ป่า)   pur-an[2] *n.* a forest.

เผือน   pur-an[4] *n.* a species of water-lily with blue flowers, a counterpart to the lotus which has red flowers.

แผ่   paa[4] *v.* to expand (as the hood of a cobra) ; to spread out, lay down or flatten out ; to stretch out or beat out into thin sheets (as gold or silver) ; to attenuate : ใจเผื่อแผ่ benevolent ; generous : แผ่ตน to be boastful, or ostentatious ; to assume a "spread eagle" attitude in manners and dress : สำ-แดงความแผ่เผื่อ to manifest a spirit of brotherly love : แผ่อาณาเขตต์ to extend or expand the boundary of : แผ่อำนาจ to increase or enlarge one's power or influence.

แผก   paak[4] *v.* to be separated, divided or broken up into parts or sections : *Cam. adj.* differing ; various ; dissimilar ; strange.

แผง   paang[2] *n.* a woven bamboo mat, shelter or partition : เรือแผง an ancient kind of boat used by ladies of rank : สาน-แผง to weave bamboo strips into mats.

แผด   paat[4] *v.* to utter a loud penetrating call or cry ; to reflect strong or intense rays of light.

แผน   paan[2] *n.* a plan ; a pattern ; a scheme ; a model ; a Brahmin treatise, formula or representation : แผนผัง a plan, pattern or sketch (as for a house or building) : แผนที่ a map or chart.

แผ่น   paan[4] *n.* the surface : *adj.* a designatory particle for flat, thin objects (as sheets of paper, planks, tiles, etc.) : แผ่นดิน *lit.* "surface of the earth," *i.e.* ground, territory, tract or region ; the period of reign of a king : แผ่นผงอน, แผ่นพก, แผ่นภพ the ground, land or earth's surface.

แผนก   pa[4]-naak[3] *n.* class ; division ; section ; sub-department : *adj.* differing ; various ; dissimilar ; strange : บานแผนก the preface together with the table of contents.

แผล   plaa[2] *n.* a wound ; a break in the skin or flesh caused by disease or violence : บาดแผล a cut, gash or wound as caused by a sharp implement ; a punctured wound : แผล-เป็น a scar ; a cicatrice : แผลถูกแทง a punctured wound.

แผลง   plaang[2] *v.* to manifest or evince (as anger or power, see จำแลง p. 248) ; to change, alter or transform the shape of (as the devil in the form of a serpent) : แผลงผลาญ to kill or destroy with violence : แผลงฤทธิ์ to reveal or exert one's full power or strength : แผลงศร to shoot an arrow with one's full strength.

แผลิบ   plaap[4] *adj.* rapidly in succession (as protruding the tongue and withdrawing it repeatedly, or as flashes of lightning).

แผล็ว   plaa-oh[2] *adv.* quickly; sprightly; lively (used in combination with กระโดด, as กระโดดแผล็วๆ).

แผละ   plaa[4] *adv.* limply; limberly (descriptive of manner of sitting, as นั่งแผละลง): *onomat.* from the sound produced when mud is thrown, or of a splashing thud.

แผ่ว   paa-oh[4] *adv.* gently; lightly; slightly; shallowly; superficially: มือแผ่ว gentle in touch: เสียงแผ่ว soft in voice.

แผ้ว   paa-oh[3] *v.* to sweep; to clean the surface free of grass or weeds; to level down high ground (as termite hills or knolls): *adj.* clean; level; flat.

โผ   poh[2] *v.* to spring or jump away; to leap or bound away (as a tiger); to swoop down upon; see โจม p. 262.

โผเผ   poh[2]-pay[2] *adj.* weak; feeble; tired; exhausted.

โผง   pong[2] *adj.* loud; boisterous; boastful: *onomat.* from the sound of the pounding of waves, or the breaking or snapping of branches of trees.

โผฏฐัพพะ   pote[4]-tup[4]-pa[6] *P. v.* to be touched by a sense of joy or sorrow; to have feelings resulting from heat or cold touching the body; to touch; to reach (chd. p. 382).

โผน   pon[2] *v.* to leap or bound away; to spring or jump away; see โจน p. 262.

โผย   po-ie[2] *v.* to produce or yield (as fruit-trees or grain): โผยผล to yield fruit; to produce results.

โผล่   ploh[4] *v.* to appear, bob up or rise up from (as from a hiding-place, or as fish from the water).

โผลกเผลก   ploke[4]-plek[4] *adj.* uneven; irregular (as ground); limping (as a horse with a lame foot); descriptive of the manner of walking.

โผละ   ploo[4] *onomat.* from the sound caused when breaking, chopping or pounding open a coconut shell.

โผอน   see ผอุน p. 542.

โผะ   po[4] *onomat.* from the sound of a yell or cry used by mahouts in their training of elephants (indicative of derision or displeasure at the animal's actions).

ไผ่ (ต้น)   pai[4] *n. Bambusa arundinacea* (*Gramineae*), a name by which the Indian bamboo was long known: it is now called *B. bambos*; *B. vulgaris*, yellow or golden-bamboo, which grows to fair size, with rather open tufts, and drooping at the tips, and perhaps more widely distributed in the world in cultivation than any other. It is of unknown origin, but is found now very commonly in India and Malaysia, and here and there in tropical Africa and America. The haulms grow fast. They attain 12 feet in a fortnight, and 30 feet in three months. They are very useful for scaffolding and building, for they have strength and durability (MCM. p. 173: V. P. p. 178: BURK. p. 300): ไผ่กะ (ต้น) *Alpinia siamensis* (*Zingiberaceae*) (COM. REC.): ไผ่ข้าวหลาม (ต้น) *Cephalostachyum pergracile* (COM. REC.): ไผ่คาย, ไผ่ไล่ *Oxytenanthera albociliata* (*Gramineae*), a bamboo (COM. REC.): ไผ่ซาง, ไผ่นวน *Dendrocalamus membranaceus* (*Gramineae*) (COM. REC.): ไผ่ดง (ต้น) *Thyrsostachys oliveri* (V. P. p. 178): ไผ่บง, ไผ่หก (ต้น) *Dendrocalamus hamiltonii* (*Gramineae*), a bamboo of the moister parts of the Himalayas and eastward to Burma. It is big but thin-walled, and inferior to some of the other bamboos. It is too weak for uprights, but is used for walls and baskets (COM. REC.: MCM. p. 173: BURK. p. 781): ไผ่-หางช้าง (ต้น) *Bambusa tulda* (COM. REC.).

ไผท   pa[4]-tai *n.* the earth; ground: ไผทโกรม *lit.* "the underlying ground or earth," *i. e.* the surface of the ground on which we walk.

ไผ่ผัง   see ผายผัง in ผาย p. 546.

ฝ

The twenty-ninth consonant of the Thai alphabet, a high class letter of which there are eleven, *viz.* ข, ข, ฉ, ถ, ฐ, ผ, ฝ, ศ, ษ, ส, ห. ฝอฝน and ฝอฝา are the names of this letter, which is used exclusively as an initial consonant. It is equivalent to the English " ph " or " f ".

ฝน   fon[2] *v.* to rub, whet, or sharpen (as a knife): *n.* rain: น้ำฝน rain-water: ฝน-ชะลาน harvest time or the January rains, sometimes called the mango showers: ฝนตก to rain: ฝนทอง the small stroke placed over the vowel " ิ " to change it to the " ี ": ฝนฝอย mist; rain in fine drops: ฝนแสนห่า a method of using figures in place of letters or words (as in a code); a kind of fireworks where the sparks come down like " a hundred thousand " drops of rain; a species of tree: หน้าฝน the rainy season: หินฝนทอง a touch-stone (for testing the purity of gold by rubbing).

ฝรั่ง   fa[4]-rang[4] *n.* the white race of people; Europeans: ฝรั่ง *Thailand, Bangkok* มะปูน *Thailand, Nakawn Tai,* ยามู *Thailand, Surat,* มะถ้วย *Laos, Chiengmai,* มะมั้น *Laos, Lampang,* สีดา *Laos, Nakawn Panom,* ยะริง *Lawa, Chiengmai* (ต้น) *Psisium guajava* (*Myrtaceae*), guava, a large spreading shrub or small tree, 10 to 15 feet high, native of tropical America. The best cultivated varieties have large juicy fruits, round or ovoid in shape, becoming lemon-yellow when ripe, with a reddish or yellow pulp mixed with numerous small seeds, and are usually of a sharp tart flavour. The chief use of the fruit is for making the well-known guava jelly (MCM. pp. 268, 471: cb. p. 628: V. P. p. 183).

ฝรั่งเศส   fa[4]-rang[4]-set[4] *n.* Frenchmen or French people: ประเทศฝรั่งเศส France.

ฝรั่น   fa[4]-run[4] *n. Crocus sativus* (*Iridaceae*), saffron crocus, a plant giving saffron. It has been known from remotest times, classic Greek and Latin writings often mentioning it. In those times it was grown in various Mediterranean countries. The Phœnicians dyed the marriage vests of women with it; the priests used it in their ceremonies. It was formerly grown in Mesopotamia, and has been cultivated in Kashmir for many centuries. It is a highly prized dye for weddings in India. Saffron is really the stigmas of flowers and nothing more. As the yield of each plant is so small, saffron is always costly. Second grade saffron has the anthers mixed with the stigmas (BURK. p. 683).

ฝ่อ   fau[4] *v.* to be withered, wilted, attenuated, lessened or compressed: ใจฝ่อ to be afraid or scared.

ฝอย   foy[2] *n.* fibers; minute drops or particles; spray; introductory explanations for the use of drugs, charms or amulets: ทำ-ให้เป็นฝอย to spray or produce as a spray: ฝอยทอง a sweetmeat made of the yolk of eggs, well-mixed, and run through the opening in a small cone. It is then dropped into hot syrup, producing fine vermicelli-like lengths.

ผัก   fuk[4] *n.* a scabbard, sheath or case (as for knives or swords); pods, or the seed capsules of plants or trees; the testicle: ผักแค the paper covering for fuses; the long pendulous pods of *Sesbania gradiflora* or *agata*, a small, erect, quick-growing, soft-wooded tree, bearing large, edible, pendulous flowers (MCM. p. 305: V. P. p. 60): ผักดาบ *Thailand, Chantaburi,* เสี้ยดกา *Thailand, Krabin,* วารา-โย่ง *Khmer, Krabin* (ต้น) *Chukrasia tabularis* (*Meliaceae*) (cb. p. 266): ฝักบัว (นก) the painted stork, *Pseudotantalus leucocephalus leucocephalus* (Herb. N. H. J. S. S. VI, 4, p. 349):

ผักพร้า the sword-bean, an edible sword-shaped bean, *Canavalia gladiata* (*Leguminosae*), doubtless of Asiatic origin. The flat pods, when young, can be sliced, cooked and eaten with impunity, or even eaten raw. In Java the ripe seeds are eaten also, but only after adequate boiling with salt; and both the flowers and young leaves are steamed and used as flavouring. Any inferior race must be used with great caution. These are pink-flowered, and the seeds are usually of a curious bright pink. There are also one or more races with brown seeds. These are as much to be avoided as the pink-seeded plants (BURK. p. 433: MCM. p. 285): ผักเพกา an ornamental tip for pagodas, composed of from 9 to 10 imitation knife blades placed in circular tiers: ผักมะขาม a club, cudgel or billy about two feet long (shaped similar to the tamarind pod), used by ruffians as a weapon: ผักเห็ด *Thailand, Peninsula* (ต้น) *Cassia occidentalis*, a partly woody plant, probably of American origin, but now found throughout the tropics. The seeds are sometimes used as a substitute for coffee. West Africa sends seeds to Europe for this purpose. Without roasting, the seeds are purgative. The leaves are used in the Dutch Indies for poulticing the cheek for toothache. Apparently the plant has many other medicinal uses elsewhere (MCM. pp. 140, 311: V. P. p. 183: BURK. p. 478).

ผักผ่าย fuk⁴-fai⁴ *n.* side; company, group or party; see ข้าง p. 153.

ผักใผ่ fuk⁴-fai⁴ *v.* to pay attention to; to take an interest in, or be connected with.

ผัง fung² *v.* to be imbedded in (as in mud or dirt); to bury; to inter: ผังเพ็ชร์ to set a diamond (as in a ring): ผังลาย to adorn jewelry by imbedding gold or silver wires (as in niello work): ผังศพ to bury a corpse.

ผัง fung⁴ *n.* the bank; a shore; a side; a seashore; a coastline: เกยผัง see เกย p. 120:

ขึ้นผัง to go ashore (as passengers from a boat): ผังฝา firmness; stability; durability: *adj.* well-to-do; rich (as used in reference to persons of means).

ผัด fut⁴ *v.* to winnow (rice), sift or separate the grains from the chaff (by using a fan or a winnowing basket): กระด้งผัดข้าว a large round shallow winnowing basket.

ผัน fun² *v.* to dream: *n.* a dream: แก้ผัน to interpret dreams.

ฝา fah² *n.* a cover; a lid; a partition; a crust; cream; shells (of bivalves or shell-fish): ฝาผนัง an external wall or internal partition of brick.

ฝ่า fah⁴ *v.* to act in opposition to orders; to undergo hardships or dangers: *n.* the palm (of the hand) or sole (of the foot): ฝ่าฝืน to disobey, resist, go or act contrary to instructions: ฝ่าพระบาท the sole of the foot (of royalty): *pron.* you; him (used only in reference to royalty): ฝ่ามือ the palm of the hand.

ฝ้า fah³ *n.* skum; ceiling; film or membrane (covering ulcers): *adj.* dim; indistinct; misty; hazy; lacking luster; tarnished: กระจกฝ้า opaque glass: มองฝ้าไป seeing indistinctly.

ฝาก fak⁴ *v.* to put in, or place under the care of; to entrust to another: *prep.* for; for the sake of: ผู้ฝากเงิน a depositor (of money): ฝากเงิน to make deposit of money (in a bank): ฝากเงินประจำ to make a fixed deposit: ฝากบำเรอ to ask help towards, or to provide support for: ฝากผัง to give over or put into the care of: ฝากหนังสือ to send a letter by post or messenger: หนังสือฝาก a letter by post or messenger; see กาฝาก p. 89.

ฝาง *Thailand, N. Laos,* ง้าย *Karen, Kanburi* (ต้น) fang² *n. Caesalpinia sappan* (*Leguminosae*), sappan-wood, a small, straggling, prickly tree indigenous to India and

Malaya. The dark-red heartwood yields a red dye. This dye is used in India for colouring starch, which is scattered and used as face-marks at the Holi Festival. The timber has the hardness of ebony; the grain is rather coarse, but dense and even; it takes a lustrous polish. When freshly cut it is yellow to deep orange, and then oxidizes to an olive-brown. The deepest colour is near the root where the stem is knotted; the best billets come from the oldest trees, thus with the temptation great, it easily happens that over-working is allowed to destroy a profitable crop. It is used for cabinet-work, inlaying, etc., to a small extent. The bark contains tannin. There is tannin also in the pods, which are used in India with iron to get a black dye. There are also medicinal uses (cb. p. 504: mcm. pp. 73, 441, 517: v. p. p. 183: burk. p. 390).

ฝาชี fah[2]-chee *n.* a large cone-shaped, woven bamboo covering for trays of food (usually covered with red cloth).

ฝาด fart[4] *adj.* puckering (in taste); astringent; erroneous; mistaken (in regard to objects seen): ฝาดขาว *Thailand* (ต้น) *Lumnitzera racemosa (Combretaceæ)*, a small tree found from the Mascarene Islands to the Pacific. The timber is like *L. coccina*, but the lesser growth of the tree makes it consequently less useful. The bark can be used for tanning (cb. p. 613: v. p. p. 184: burk. p. 1373): ฝาดแดง *Thailand, northern coasts of Gulf*, ทำเสาล *Thailand, Pang-nga, Krabi and Trang* (ต้น) *Lumnitzera littorea (Combretaceæ)* (cb. p. 613).

ฝาน farn[2] *v.* to slice or cut into thin pieces (slantingly); see เชือด p. 302; เฉือน p. 272.

ฝาแฝด fah[2]-faat[4] *adj.* twins; double (for child-birth).

ฝาย fai[2] *n.* a dam; a dike or weir.

ผ่าย fai[4] *n.* side; party; group; community or those on the side of; see ข้าง p. 153: ผ่าย-กรม departmental: ผ่ายราชการ governmental: ผ่ายว่า concerning; regarding; as for: ผ่ายศาล judicial.

ฝ้าย (ต้น) fai[3] *n. Gossypium herbaceum (Malvaceæ)*, a cotton shrub, a short-staple type, yielding the Indian or Tinnevelly cotton (mcm. p. 420: v.p. p. 184): ฝ้ายเคือ *Laos, Chiengmai* (ต้น) *Hibiscus scandens (Malvaceæ)* (cb. p. 160): ฝ้ายแดง *Thailand, Bangkok* (ต้น) *Gossypium arboreum (Malvaceæ)*, a cotton tree which attains a height of 15 to 20 feet. It is considered a native of Africa, but is not cultivated for fibre (cb. p. 162: mcm. p. 420): ฝ้ายเทศ *E. Laos*, สำลี *Thailand, Bangkok*, ฝ้าย-หลวง *N. Laos* (ต้น) *Gossypium brasiliense (Malvaceae)*, the best of all cottons which was found in Brazil, both in a wild state and in cultivation, by the early European voyagers. The floss began to be known in European commerce about the middle of the seventeenth century; but probably the Portuguese, in the sixteenth century, had carried its seeds overseas to various countries. Piso brought it to Holland in 1648. The silky fibre is 1 5/8 to 2 1/4 inches long. Owing to its wide distribution this species is one of the most used medicinally. The Arabs use the juice of the leaves for colic. In India they are used for dysentery. In Cambodia cotton-plants are used for fevers. The root is more active than the leaves, being a diuretic. Sometimes cotton leaves are eaten as an esculent vegetable. Also the fruit is sweetish and much eaten (cb. p. 163: v. p. p. 184: mcm. p. 420: burk. p. 1106).

ฝาละมี fah[2]-la[6]-mee *n.* the lid of a rice or curry pot.

ผิน *Thailand, Laos* (ต้น) fin[4] *n. Papaver somniferum (Papaveraceae)*, the opium poppy. The ancient Greeks were accustomed to sprinkle its seeds over cakes, using them as almonds are used. They well knew the narcotic properties of the rest of the plant, for they had a preparation, an extract of the vegetable parts called neconion, which was used as a soporific drug and entered into a soothing drink. Leaves, stems, and capsules were used in making it; and the capsules seem to have become commercial. Then it was discovered that the narcotic properties resided in the latex, which could be collected by scratching the capsules, allowing it to dry along the capsules, and then scraping it off. The early trade passed into Arab hands. Arabs, and Persian sailors employed by them, took it eastwards, and established it in other countries. It is said the Chinese learned how to smoke opium in the time of Kublai Khan (1279-94). The Portuguese and later the Dutch strove to secure a monopoly of the opium trade, finding it extremely lucrative. The medicinal value of opium in its various forms is well-known. Poppy seed oil derived from the seed is used chiefly as a salad oil and also in artists' paints (MCM. pp. 201, 375, 397: Cb. p. 75: Burk. p. 1658): ฝิ่นดิบ crude opium: ฝิ่นเถื่อน illicit opium: สูบฝิ่น to smoke opium: ห้องสูบฝิ่น an opium divan or den: โรงยาฝิ่น an opium house.

ผ fee[2] *n.* an abscess, boil or pustule; used as a prefix descriptive of manner or mode of action: คนมฝีมือ a craftsman: ผีจักร power or speed in the revolutions of an engine: ผีดาษ small-pox; variola: ผีเท้า speed, gait or action of the feet (in walking or running): ฝีประคำร้อย inflamed glands of the neck: ฝีปาก skill, proficiency or eloquence of language: ฝีพระโอษฐ์ the same, only used for royalty: ฝีกบัว a carbuncle: ฝีพาย power, strength, ability or dexterity of oarsmen or paddlers (in boats): ฝีมือ skill, dexterity, cleverness, ability, or handicraft (in working with the hands): *n.* craftsmanship; workmanship: ฝีแมน power, cleverness, skill or dexterity of celestial beings; supernatural or celestial power.

ผ fee[4] *n.* a mountain crevice or ravine with gradations of trees, bushes or articles placed in tiers so that each one partly conceals the one above it.

ผก, ผกปรือ, ผกหัด furk[4] *v.* to drill, train, practice, exercise or teach (by repetition): ผู้ผึกหัดหรือผู้เรียนวิชาอาชีพ an apprentice.

ผด furt[4] *adj.* moving with difficulty (as machinery); laborious; obstructed (in movements); see ขัด p. 150: ผัดเคือง hard-pressed (for funds); poor: หายใจผัด obstructed or difficult respiration (as in attacks of asthma).

ผืน furn[2] *v.* to resist, disobey or act contrary to instructions: ฝืนใจ to exert self-control; to restrain or control the desires: ฝืนท้อง to exert rotary pressure on the uterus after child-birth.

ผืน foon[4] *n.* dust; powder: ฝุ่นขาว face-powder; prepared chalk: ฝุ่นฝอย refuse; sweepings; garbage: ฝุ่นเมือง *lit.* "dregs of the city or country," *i. e.* natives; the masses, rabble or populace.

ฝูง, หมู่ foong[2] *n.* a drove; a flock; a herd; a crowd; a squadron; a group (of people); a pack (of dogs); a bevy (of birds); a swarm (of bees); a school or shoal (of fish): เพื่อนฝูง acquaintances; comrades; friends; associates.

เผา fow[3] *v.* to watch; to attend or be on guard: ข้าเฝ้า government officials or courtiers: เข้าเฝ้า to enter the presence of the king or members of the royal family: เฝ้ายาม to be on guard or stand as sentry: เฝ้าระวัง to guard carefully; to observe or take care of: เฝ้าล้อเฝ้าเลียน to joke, jest or provoke by mimicking.

เผื่อ feu-ah[2] *n.* a surface measure equal to twenty-five square wahs or one hundred square meters: *adj.* disordered; infested, or covered with weeds: เหลือเผื่อ superabundant.

เผือก feu-ak⁴ *n. surgical* splints ; a movable framework of bamboo strips wattled together for use as fish traps (placed across shallow waterways) ; a bier or framework for carrying a corpse to the grave : เข้าเผือก to apply splints : ล้อมเผือก to surround with, or to place movable bamboo frames for trapping fish.

เผือน fur-an⁴ *adj.* changed from the normal in taste : รสเผือนขม bitter-tasting : รสเผือนฝาด changed to an ill-flavoured, puckering, insipid or unpalatable taste (used in regard to over-ripe fruit or long-kept food).

แฝก (หญ้า) faak⁴ *n. Typha elephantina*, elephant grass, a long grass used for roofing purposes ; *Typha angusilfoia (Typhaceae)*, bulrush, an erect ribbon-like grass (MCM. p. 175) : แฝกหอม a species used medicinally.

แฝง faang² *v.* to hide, secrete, conceal or evade : *adj.* ambiguous ; doubtful ; indistinct (as words or expressions) : แอบแฝงอยู่ to be in hiding or seeking shelter ; to be concealed (as robbers).

แฝด faat⁴ *n.* twins ; couplets ; doubles : ปืนแฝด a double-barreled gun : ลูกแฝด twins : ยาแฝด love potions (given by a man) ; philters.

ใฝ่ fai⁴ *v.* to determine, intend or hope for ; to think of : ใฝ่ใจ to be engaged with, enamoured by, desirous of, or entangled with : ใฝ่ฝัน to be constantly thinking about, interested in, or paying attention to ; to be desirous of.

ไฝ fai² *n.* a mole, pimple, black-head or small protuberance (on the skin).

พ

พ The thirtieth consonant of the Thai alphabet, a low class letter of which there are twenty-four, viz. ค, ค, ฆ, ง, ช, ฌ, ซ, ญ, ฑ, ท, ฒ, ฑ, ฒ, น, ณ, พ, ฟ, ภ, ม, ร, ล, ว, ฬ, ฮ. พอพินธุ์, พอพาน are the names of this letter. It is pronounced like the English "p," labial but short. When used as a prefix the meaning is *father, chief, leader, ex.* พนักงาน, พนาย, พ่อนาย father or leader of workmen. In words of Sanskrit or Pali origin "พ" may be used instead of "ว" *ex.* วิจิตร, พิจิตร ; บริวาร, บริพาร.

พก ๑ pok⁶ *v.* to hide or secrete on the person (as a dagger or clasp knife) ; to put into the pouch pocket of the panung : *n.* firmament ; earth ; ground ; a pocket formed by tucking the end of the front fastening twist of the panung into the belt or waistband : *adj.* contused ; fatigued ; tired : นาฬิกาพก a pocket-watch : พกนาฬิกา to carry a pocket-watch : พกไฟ contused ; fatigued ;

weary ; listless : พกนุ่น *lit.* "holding cotton," *i. e.* easily influenced ; unstable in disposition ; silly : พกลม *lit.* "holding air," "a gas bag," *i.e.* deceptive ; falsifying ; lying ; untrustworthy ; unreliable : พกหิน *lit.* "holding stone," *i. e.* stable in disposition ; strong-minded ; brave. The above three are used as similes or in proverbial expressions.

พก ๒, นกยาง pa⁶-gka⁴ *S. n.* the pond heron, *Ardeola grayi* (Gaird. J. S. S. IX, 1, p. 10) ; a kind of heron or crane (S. E. D. p. 719) : พกจร *lit.* "one behaving as a pond heron," *i.e.* a crook ; a double-faced person : พกชิต *lit.* "one who conquered an Asura (a demon or enemy of the gods) named Vaka (พกาสุร)," *i. e.* Bhima, Bhimasena, mythically son of Vayu, the god of the Wind, whom he seized by the legs and tore asunder (H. C. D. p. 50).

พกุระ pa⁶-gkoo⁴-ra⁶ *S. n.* a horn trumpet ; a bullock's or ram's horn used as a bugle or wind instrument (S. E. D. p. 719).

พกุล, พิกุล pa[6]-gkoon *S. n.* (a corrupted form of พิกุล) *Mimusops elengi* (*Sapotaceae*), a large tree reaching a height of forty-five feet. This tree is widely found in India, Burma, Ceylon and Thailand. The flowers are popular and children string them into necklaces. The leaves are green, shining, elliptic and glabrous; the flowers are axillary, solitary, in pairs or facicled, and fragrant; the corolla is white. The fruit is ovoid, about an inch or less long, one- or rarely two-seeded. It yields a gum known as Madras gum. The fruits are used medicinally in diseases of gums and teeth. A volatile oil is distilled from the flowers; a fixed oil which is used for culinary purposes and is also burned in lamps is obtained from the seeds by compression. The chief uses are medicinal, all parts of the tree having such uses. It is supposed to be sacred to the Mohammedans of southern India (The ornamental Trees of Hawaii, J. F. Rock, p. 172: chd. p. 546: Burk. p. 1475).

พง pong *n.* a dense stretch of tall wild grass; clumps or clusters of wild bamboos, trees or rushes: พง, กาพง *Thai, Peninsula,* จุ้น *N. Laos,* สะพง *E. Laos,* ปัง *Shan, Me Hawng Sawn* (ต้น) *Tetrameles nudiflora* (*Datiscaceae*), a lofty tree of India, extending to the northern parts of the Malay Peninsula, and from Java to Timor; it stands leafless once a year. The timber is not durable, but is marketed where the tree is plentiful, for making packing-boxes and temporary structures. It serves also for match-sticks. Among the Cambodians the tree is medicinal. The bark is laxative and diuretic, and enters into decoctions taken for rheumatism, oedema, ascites and icterus (cb. p. 781: Burk. p. 2144): พง (หญ้า) *Saccharum spontaneum* (*Gremineae*) (V. P. p. 188: Burk. p. 1923): พงพี an extensive or vast jungle of tall trees or wild grasses.

พงวิด (นก) pong-wit[6] *n.* the painted snipe, *Rostratula benghalensis* (Herb. N. H. J. S. S. VI, 4, p. 348).

พงศ์ pong *S. n.* a stalk of bamboo, or stalk of any long reed-like grass (as pampas grass); a floor beam; a reed-pipe; joist; a joint; lineage; race; family; stock; descendants; relations (S. E. D. p. 910): พงศกฐิน a clump or thicket of bamboo (grouped together): พงศกร the founder of a family; the progenitor or perpetuator of a race or ancestoral line; a son: พงศกรรม a manufacturer of baskets; one doing bamboo work or weaving bamboo into various utensils: พงศจรัต a genealogy; the detailed history of a family, race or dynasty: พงศธร the maintaining or supporting of a family; the continuer of a family: พงศนรรคี *lit.* "a dancer or actor in a family," *i.e.* a clown; a buffoon: พงศนาที a bamboo pipe or tube for conducting water: พงศพราหมณ์ a treatise called Brahmana; *lit.* "belonging to Brahmins," *i.e.* works composed by and for Brahmins, being that part of the Veda which was intended for the guidance of Brahmins in the use of the hymns of the Mantra. The Vedas are the holy books which are the foundation of the Hindu religion (H. C. D. pp. 60, 344): พงศพันธุ์ descendants of a family, line or lineage: พงศมูล the root of the sugar-cane: พงศาวดาร history or annals of members of a line, dynasty or kingdom: พงศาวลี a genealogical diagram; a list or record of ancestors and pedigree of a family or line.

พจน์ pot[6] *P. S. n.* words; sayings; speech; declarations; utterances; expressions; text (chd. p. 541): พจนา reading; reciting; teaching; declaring (chd. p. 541): พจนานุกรม a dictionary; a vocabulary: พจนารถ the meaning of words or proverbial sayings: พหุพจน์ *gram.* the plural number: เอกพจน์ the singular number.

พจนีย์ pot[6]-chja[4]-nee *S. adj.* licensed (as to words of correction, reproaches, censure) (S. E. D. p. 912).

พจมาน   pot[6]-chja[4]-marn   *P. n.* utterances ; expressions ; passages ; sentences ; sayings, or text (Chd. p. 541).

พจร   pa[6]-chjorn   *n.* a cock ; a low person (S. E. D. p. 912).

พจี   pa[6]-chjee   *n.* ' words ; speech ; advice ; injunction ; order (Chd. p. 542).

พชระ   pot[6]-cha[6]-ra[6]   *S. n.* a diamond ; something adamant ; a stone that cuts gems ; the thunderbolt of Indra (Chd. p. 546).

พญา   pa[6]-yah   *n.* an ace ; a chief ; a leader ; a king ; the supreme one :   พญาโจร a leader of ruffians or robbers :   พญาชิงแดน an unrivalled invader :   พญาเดิน a Thai marching tune :   พยานาค see นาค p. 449 :   พญาพยาตต์ the foremost among sages or philosophers : พญามาร, พระยามาร *lit.* "king of demons," *i.e.* Mara, the angel of evil desire, love, death. Though King Mara plays the part of the Christian's Satan, the tempter, he and his host formerly were great givers of alms, which led to their being born in the highest of the Dewa heavens, there to live, surrounded by all the luxuries of sensuality. From this heaven the filthy one (as the Thai describe him) descended to the earth to tempt and excite to evil (Ala. p. 213). This tempter, the evil principle, the archangel Mara, the ruler of the highest of the six Kamadevalokas, has three daughters, Tanha (ตัณหา), concupiscence, Raka (ราคะ), love, Arati (อรดี) anger, who tempt men to sin (Chd. p. 240) :   พญามือเหล็ก (ต้น) *Strychnos sp.*, a considerable genus of the family *Loganiaceae* found throughout the tropics, renowned for its poisonousness (Burk. p. 2091 : V. P. p. 185) : พญามุตตี (ต้น) *Streptocaulon sp.* (*Asclepiadaceae*), a small genus of woody climbers found in south-eastern Asia and Malaysia. The *S. wallichii* is found in the northern parts of British Malaysia, about the edges of forest. No use is recorded (Burk. p. 2086) :   พญา-มุนิน _Thailand, Saraburi_ (ต้น) *Crotalaria calycina* (*Leguminosae*) (Cb. p. 368) :   พญาไร้ใบ

(ต้น) *Sarcostemma brevistigma* (V. P. p. 185) : พญาลอ (ไก่) the grey peacock-pheasant of the genus *Polyplectron thibetanum*, found in western Thailand (Gaird. J. S. S. IX, 1, p. 12) : พญาสัตบรรณ (ต้น) *Alstonia scholaris* (*Apocynaceae*), a tall, glabrous tree reaching a height of over sixty feet, producing an abundance of milky sap. It is found from Ceylon to Australia and to the Solomon Islands, and also in the Malay Peninsula, from Penang to Malacca and in Pahang, but is not general in low country. It is both wild and seems to have been grown there from rather remote times, partly as an ornamental tree and partly being medicinal. The branches are whorled, the leaves verticillate, leathery, about eight inches long, oblong-obovate, rounded at the apex and pointed at the base. The flowers are arranged in terminal cymes, which are umbellately branched. The small white flowers are numerous and crowded. The follicles are pendulous, slender, cylindrical and eight to sixteen inches long. The bark is an astringent and is given as a tonic. The milky juice is applied to ulcers and is also used to restore the tone of the stomach in debility. The timber is soft, light, and perishable, and seasons badly. It has been found to last less than six months in the soil. It has a peculiar use in schools, being used instead of slates. The slate is cleaned by sand-papering off the writing by using *Delima* leaves. The wood has been found satisfactory for making matches (The Orn. Trees of Hawaii, J. F. Rock p. 178 : McM. p. 218 : Burk. p. 113).

พณหัว, พณหัวเจ้า, พระณหัว   pa[6]-na[6]-hoo-ah[2] *n. lit.* "father over-head," *i. e.* a form of respectful address for superiors :   พณหัวเจ้า-ท่าน a form of address or title (in petitions) for Departmental Ministers, equal to "Lord Minister of my heart" : abbreviated form, ๆ พณ ๆ.

พณิช   pa[6]-nit[6]   *S. n.* a trader (Chd. p. 549) ; a merchant ; a trafficker (S. E. D. p. 915).

พณิชยา   pa[6]-nit[6]-cha[6]-yah   *n.* trade; commerce (chd. 549).

พด see งอ p. 221:   พดด้วง *lit.* "coiled as a grub," *i.e.* the round or bullet tical (an ancient name).

พธู   pa[6]-too   *n.* a bride; a young wife; a girl; a daughter-in-law (chd. p. 544); any young female relative; the female of any animal (S. E. D. p. 917):   พธูกาล the time during which a woman is held to be a bride: พธูชน a wife; a woman: พธูธน the personal property of a wife: พธูประเวศ the ceremony or function of conducting the bride to her new home: พธูวร a newly wedded couple; the bride and bridegroom.

พน   pon *P. S. n.* a forest; a wood; a grove; a thicket; a quantity of lotus or other plants growing in a thick cluster: *adj.* wooded; plenty; abundant: พนขัณฑ์, พนษัณฑ์, พนสัณฑ์ the limits, edge, or skirt of a forest (chd. p. 548):   พนโคจร people dwelling or wandering in a forest; denizens or inhabitants of a forest; a forester; a hunter (S. E. D. p. 917): พนจร, พนจรก, พนเจร one roaming or living in the woods; a woodman; a forester; wild animals: พนจรรยา one roaming about or dwelling in a forest: พนช ·a woodman; a forester; an elephant: *adj.* sylvan; wild; rustic; rural; forest-like: พนชีวิกา forest life (living by gathering leaves and fruits): พนชีว์, ชายชาวป่า a forester: พนทาห์ a forest fire: พนธารา an avenue of trees: พนมานุษ *lit.* "the wild man," *i. e.* the orangoutang: พนมุต clouds: พนราช *lit.* "the king of the forest," *i. e.* the lion: พนวาสน์ *lit.* "one living in the forests," *i. e.* the Burmese civet, *Viverra zibetha pruinosa*:   พนวาสี an hermit; an anchorite; a forest-dweller: *adj.* living in the forest (the antithesis of คามวาสี living in a village):   พนโศภน *lit.* "that which adorns the water," *i. e.* lotus flowers: พนาขุ *lit.* "a forest rat," *i. e.* a rabbit; the Thai hare, *Lepus siamensis*:   พนานคร the interior of a forest; the depth of a forest: พนานต์ *lit.* "forest region," *i. e.* an extensive dense forest; bounded by a forest: พนาบต a forest stream: พนารจก *lit.* "forest-worshipper," *i. e.* a florist; a maker of garlands: พนาลกต์ *lit.* "wild lac," *i. e.* red earth or soil; ruddle: พนาลัย forest-habitation; living in the forest: พนาลี *lit.* "the embellishing or beautifying of a forest," *i. e.* rows of trees; roads or paths in a forest; a long handsome track of trees: พนาวาส a dwelling or residence in a forest: พนาเวศ trips or excursions into the forest: พนาศ *lit.* "living on the water (in a forest)," *i. e.* a kind of wild barley: พนาศรม *lit.* "one taking up an abode in the forest," *i. e.* an anchorite; a Brahmin dwelling in a forest: พนาศรัย *lit.* "a forest dweller," *i. e.* a sort of crow or raven: พโนบล *lit.* "forest stones," *i. e.* shaped and dried cow-dung.

พ่น   pon[3] *v.* to blow, squirt, spray or eject (with force) from the mouth: พ่นควันบุหรี่ to exhale tobacco smoke: พ่นน้ำมนต์ to blow out a spray of consecrated water: พ่นน้ำยา to blow a medicinal solution out in a spray (as on a sick person):   พ่นน้ำลาย to spit; to expectorate (violently):   พ่นพิษ to eject venom (as a viper); *figuratively* to pour forth vile, slanderous language.

พ้น   pon[5] *v.* to pass beyond; to cross over safely; to escape (as from a calamity or accident); to be exempt from (as corvée):   ไปให้พ้น to be off; to go away: พ้นทุกข์พ้นร้อน to be delivered from misery or hardship: ล่วงพ้นไปแล้ว passed for the present.

พนม   pa[6]-nom *Cam. n.* a mountain; a hillock: พนมเปิญ Pnom-penh, the capital city of Cambodia situated on the right bank of the Mekong river at its confluence with the Tonle-Sap, 280 metres distant from the sea. It has been the capital since 1434 but the seat of Government has on various occasions been transferred to different places until finally in 1867 it was re-established here again during the reign of King Norodom.

The site has been called Pnom Don Penh or Hill of the Lady Penh from the hill 27 metres high in the center of the city.

The origin of the name is a legendary chronicle in which it is stated that in the year 1372, at a time when the country around was inundated, a Cambodian lady named Penh, whose abode had been built on the side of a hillock, perceived one evening in the waters at her feet, the trunk and branches of a huge tree. She and her neighbours having dragged it ashore so that, when dry, its wood might be made use of, discovered within a hollow of the trunk, much to her amazement, four bronze effigies of the Buddha and another of Vishnu. The fact of the images of the Buddha having been conveyed by the tree-trunk to the place where she resided was convincing proof to her that this spot must have been chosen by the deities for their new home in place of the devastated and ransacked Angkor. It was decided to build a sanctuary at the summit of the hill with the wood of the tree, to receive the four images of the Buddha, and another at a point lower down for the image of Vishnu (From Tourist's Guide to Saigon, Pnom-Penh and Angkor).

พนักงาน   pa[6]-nuk[6]-ngarn *n. lit.* "father of workmen," *i. e.* an overseer; an official; an employer; the principal or chief (over workmen); a functionary: ให้เป็นพนักงานดูแล to assume the responsibility for.

พนังนั่ง *Laos, Chiengmai* (ต้น)   pa[6]-nung-nung[3] *n. Stephania glabra (Menispermaceae)* (cb. p. 69).

พนัส   pa[6]-nut[6] *S. n.* loveliness; longing; desire; lust (S. E. D. p. 918); *Thai* wood; forest.

พนาย   pa[6]-nai *n. lit.* "master father," *i. e.* an ancient form of address used by a superior to those of rank under his control.

พนิดา, พนิตา   pa[6]-ni[6]-dah *S. n.* a woman;

women in general; a betrothed girl; a loved wife; a mistress (S. E. D. p. 918).

พนิต   pa[6]-nit[6] *S. adj.* solicited; asked for; desired; loved (S. E. D. p. 918).

พนียก   pa[6]-nee-ya[6]-gka[4] *S. n. lit.* "one worthy of respect," *i. e.* a mendicant; a beggar; a pauper; a Buddhist monk (chd. p. 549).

พบ   see เจอะ p. 257 :   พบพาน to meet or come across another person by chance.

พบู   pa[6]-boo *n.* the physical body (chd. p. 550): see ตัว p. 360.

พมพี   *Laos, Udawn* (ต้น)   pom-pee *n. Aglaia meliosmoides (Meliaceae)* (cb. p. 256).

พยง, ขะยม *Laos, Chiengmai,* ประยง *Thailand, Bangkok,* หอมไกล *Thailand, Peninsula* (ต้น)   pa[6]-yong *n. Aglaia odorata (Meliaceae)*, a bush which is wild in Indo-China and southern China, whence it has spread in cultivation. The wild plant has most of its leaves in threes, and they are relatively small; the cultivated plant has the leaves mostly in fives. The Chinese use the flowers to scent tea. In Java they are used to perfume clothes, and also they are one of the ingredients of a powder which is applied to the body after child-birth. The wood is hard, and excellent for small objects. The weight is 76 lb. per cubic foot. This heaviness is connected with slow growth. The shrub makes nice hedges, but only after a long time (cb. p. 257: burk. p. 74).

พยช   pa[6]-yot[6]-cha[6] *S. n.* to ride or drive (as horses): see ขับ p. 151.

พยชน์, พยัชน์   pa[6]-yot[6] *S. n.* a fan.

พยติบาต   pa[6]-ya[6]-dti[4]-bart[4] *S. n.* a term in astronomy meaning the time at which the sun and moon are situated directly opposite to each other.

พยติเรก   pa[6]-ya[6]-dti[4]-rake[4] *n. lit.* "the

more lengthy, the more divergent," *i. e.* a long complex sentence, where the meaning in the first portion differs from that in the last portion; a group of words in Pali grammar.

พยนต์, พยันต์ pa⁶-yon *adj.* scattered; unfolded; expounded; elucidated (as to the meaning); see กระจาย p. 21; จารไน p. 246.

พยบาย pa⁶-ya⁶-bai *n.* the end, ending, or finish; see จบ p. 230.

พยศ pa⁶-yot⁶ *S. v.* to acquire, get or attain; to reach; to get a share in.

พยส pa⁶-yot⁶ *S. v.* to abandon or throw away; to scatter or chase away; to go after; to cause harm or injury (as a horse or elephant to the rider or keeper).

พยสน์ pa⁶-yot⁶ *S. n.* trouble; hardship: misfortune; calamity; fate.

พยอม *Thailand,* ขะยอม *N.* and *E. Laos,* เชียว *Karen, Chiengmai* (ต้น) pa⁶-yawm *n. Shorea floribuda (Dipterocarpaceae)* (cb. p. 142: V. P. p. 185).

พยัคฆ์, พยาฆร์ pa⁶-yak⁶ *P. n.* the tiger, *Felis tigris:* พยัคฆนายก, พยัคฆเสวก *lit.* "the tiger's guide or attendant," *i. e.* the Malay wild dog, *Guon rutilans* or *javanicus:* พยัคฆินทร์, พยัคเมนทร์ an especially fierce or big tiger; an ace of tigers: พยัคฆี, พยัคฆิน a tigress.

พยังค์ pa⁶-yung *S. adj.* deformed; lame; bodiless; crippled; motionless.

พยัญชนะ, วยญฺชะ pa⁶-yun-cha⁶-na⁶ *P. n.* a consonant; an organ of the body; the character or condition of the body.

พยัตต์, พยาตต์ pa⁶-yat⁶ *P. n.* a student; a scholar, or one versed in literature: *adj.* learned; quick (mentally): พยัตตคณิต the science of figures; arithmetic: พยัตตคนธา the long pepper; see ดีปลี p. 330.

พยากร pa⁶-yah-gkorn *P. S. v.* to predict, prophesy or prognosticate; see ทำนาย p. 414.

พยากรณ์ pa⁶-yah-gkorn *P. S. n.* predictions of the sages; oracles; a treatise on predictions based on astronomical observations.

พยางค์ pa⁶-yang *n.* a syllable.

พยาช pa⁶-yart³ *S. n.* deception; crookedness; the act of counterfeiting, changing, disguising or faking.

พยาท; พยาล pa⁶-yart³ *S. n.* any carnivorous animal; snakes; vipers: *adj.* dangerous; intent on harm or injury.

พยาธ pa⁶-yart³ *S. n. lit.* "one who pierces or punctures," *i. e.* a hunter; one who stalks game for a living: พยาธคีดี the mimicking cry or call (as a decoy) of a hunter: พยาธภีต *lit.* "those who are afraid of the hunter," *i. e.* the deer.

พยาธิ pa⁶-yart³ *P. n.* a sickness; a malady; a disease; a parasitic worm located either in the intestines or on the skin: พยาธิปากขอ the hookworm, *Uncinaria,* a genus of nematode worms occurring in the human intestines (Med. Dic.): พยาธิแบนมีเป็นปล้อง ๆ a tapeworm; a parasitic intestinal cestode, worm or species of flattened tape-like form, and composed of separate joints: พยาธิวิทยา pathology: แพทย์พยาธิวิทยา a pathologist.

พยาน pa⁶-yarn *S. n.* the act of breathing; one of the vital airs which is diffused throughout the body (S. E. D. p. 920).

พยาบาท pa⁶-yah-bart⁴ *P. n.* revenge; resentment; hatred; malice; see ปองร้าย p. 516.

พยาบาร pa⁶-yah-barn *S. n.* business; occupation; duty; service.

พยาบาล pa⁶-yah-barn *v.* to nurse or care for the sick: นางพยาบาล a nurse: พยาบาลคนไข้ to minister to a sick person: รักษาพยาบาล to render care and treatment to the sick: สถานที่พยาบาล a hospital; an asylum.

พยาม pa⁶-yarm *P. S. n.* a wah (in length), equal to two metres; a fathom.

พยายา *Thailand, Korat, Bangkok* and *Kanburi*, แจะ, กะแจะ *N. Laos*, ตุมตั้ง *E. Laos*, พินิยา *Khmer, Surin* (ต้น) pa⁶-yah-yah *n. Limonia acidissima (Rutaceae)* (CB. p. 229).

พยายาม pa⁶-yah-yarm *P. n.* patience; perseverance; a continual effort or exertion; an earnest striving for.

พยายุธ pa⁶-yah-yoot⁶ *S. adj.* defenseless; without defensive means.

พยาล, พยาฑ pa⁶-yarn *n.* any carnivorous animal; a beast of prey; a snake (CHD. p. 547); lions; tigers: พยาลมฤค any vicious, wild animal.

พยุง *Thailand* and *E. Laos*, พยุงใหม่ *Thailand, Saraburi*, แดงจีน *Thailand, Krabin*, ประดู่ลาย *Thailand, Chonburi*, ประดู่เสน *Thailand, Krat*, กระยูง *Khmer, Surin*, หัวลีเมาะ *Chinese* (ต้น) pa⁶-yoong *n. Dalbergia cochinchinensis (Leguminosae); D. latifolia*, Indian rose-wood or Bombay blackwood, a tree attaining 70 feet in height, found from the foot of the Himalayas southward in India, with very close allies beyond the southern limits of its distribution. The timber is a valuable furniture wood which is exported to Europe from southern India. It is used for making agricultural implements (CB. p. 475: V. P. p. 185: McM. pp. 218, 219: BURK. p. 754): พยุงแกลบ *Thailand, Saraburi*, ชิงชัน *Thailand, Korat*, พยุงแดง *Thailand, Nakawn Tai*, คู่ลาย *Laos, Lampang* (ต้น) *Dalbergia bariensis (Leguminosae)* (CB. p. 474).

พยุห, พยุ่ห์ pa⁶-yoo⁶-ha⁴ *P. n.* army; troops; host; multitude: พยุหบาตร infantry: หยุหชาตรา to march in formation or by regiments: พยุหโยธา companies or regiments of soldiers: พยุหเสนา, พยุหแสนยา companies or regiments of troops.

พยุหร pa⁶-yoo⁶-horn² *n.* a term used in ancient military treatises dealing with conscripting soldiers, whereby the total required of those conscripted was figured out by a special method.

พยูณ pa⁶-yoon *S. n.* way; path; course; line (S. E. D. p. 920).

พร porn *P. S. n.* a boon; a blessing; a benediction; a favour; a choice; one who, or that which is chosen; one who makes his own choice: พรา the feminine form, *ex.* บดิมพรา a woman who chooses her husband: ขอพร to ask a blessing: ขอให้ได้สมพร may the blessing, as requested, be fully granted: อวยพร to bless (as for success in some achievement, or on an auspicious occasion); to bestow compliments.

พรณ prone *S. n.* a wound; a sore; a boil; an abscess (CHD. p. 548).

พรต prot⁶ *S. n.* observance; habit; practice; religious rites, duty or acts (CHD. p. 556); customs; laws; one observing the ritual of a religion, *ex.* นักพรต an ascetic; an anchorite or saint; see ปฏิบัติ p. 493.

พรม prome *v.* to sprinkle or spray (as perfumery); to be spotted: *n.* carpet; rugs; floor coverings: พรม, พรมหัวเหมื่น, สร้อยนกเขา, นกเขา (ปลา) *Osteocheilus melanopleura (Cyprindae); O. hasselti*, a fresh water fish of the carp family (suvatti pp. 50, 51): พรม, พลอง *Thailand* (ต้น) *Memecylon coeruleum (Melastomaceae)*, a shrub found plentifully near the coasts of the Malay Peninsula, and, rarely, inland. It is also in the Andaman Islands. The wood is hard and heavy, useful for house-construction, and a good fuel. The fruit is edible and so are the leaves (BURK. p. 1451): หนเมพรม (ต้น) *Carissa carandas (Apocynaceae)*, a spiny shrub, native of India, where it is extensively cultivated for its fruit. It occurs wild—run wild—in Java, and again in Timor. The pinky white fruits are very acid, but stewed with an abundance of sugar make a very pleasant conserve. They are used also as a seasoning with curry and, just before ripeness, for pickles. A good jelly can be made from them. The wood is white, hard and smooth-grained; but there is very little of it (cb. p. 704: P. V. p. 195: MCM. p. 257: BURK. p. 464): พรมมะคด *Thailand*, *Chantaburi* (ต้น) *Kurrimia robusta* (*Celastraceae*), a tree of fair height, found from north-eastern India to Singapore and in Borneo. The wood is dark in colour, and not durable. It is considered excellent for cabinet-work (cb. p. 286: BURK. p. 1288): พรมมิแดง *Thailand, Prachuap* (ต้น) *Trianthema triquetra* (*Ficoideae*) (cb. p. 784).

พรมแดน   prom-daan *n.* frontier; the boundary line of adjoining territory, or between two states.

พรรค, พรรค์   pak[6] *S. n.* a class; a set; a group; a troop; a multitude (of similar articles); company; family; tribe; party (chd. p. 545): พรรคกลิ่น marine engineers: พรรค-นาวิกโยธิน marines: พรรคนาวิน officers and the crew trained for service on a battle-ship: พรรคบท, พรรคมล the corners of a square surface: พรรคพวก followers; accomplices; members of a gang.

พรรคานต์   pak[6]-karn *n.* a class of final consonants such as ง, ญ, ณ, น, ม.

พรรณ, พัณณ์   pun *P. S. n.* form; figure; shape; colour; complexion; tint; dye; pigment; species; kind; sort; gender (S. E. D. p. 924); appearance; beauty; praise; fame; a vowel; a syllable (chd. p. 549): พรรณจารก a painter: พรรณเชษฐ์, พรรณเศรษฐ์ *lit.* "the highest in caste (among the Hindus)," *i. e.* a Brahmin; one belonging to the best of tribes: พรรณดูลี *lit.* "letter brushes," *i. e.* pens; pencils; Chinese brush-pens; paint-brushes: พรรณ-ทาตรี *lit.* "that which imparts colour," *i. e.* turmeric, a perennial herb. The tuberous rhizomes are of a bright orange-yellow colour and are ground into a fine powder. This is

commonly used as a condiment in cookery; see ขมิ้น p. 141: พรรณทูต *lit.* "letters as messengers," *i. e.* an epistle; correspondence; letters: พรรณบารฐ *lit.* "letter-register," *i. e.* the alphabet; consonants: พรรณประสาทน์ see กฤษณา (ต้น) p. 57: พรรณผักกาด kinds or species of cabbages: พรรณเรขา chalk; a white mineral often confounded with chalk: พรรณวาที a panegyrist; an eulogizer; a speaker of praise: พรรณวิลาสินี powdered turmeric (used as a face-powder); see ขมิ้น p. 141: พรรณสมโยค *lit.* "the union of tribes, races or castes," *i. e.* matrimonial connection or inter-marriages between members of different tribes, races or castes: พรรณสังกร the mixing or blending of colours; the interbreeding between castes, tribes or races; the inter-mixture of plant pollen.

พรรณนา   pun-na[6]-nah *S. v.* to depict; to comment upon; to explain; to inform; to describe or relate: *n.* description; narration; explanation or comment (chd. p. 549).

พรรดึก   pun-ra[6]-deuk[4] *n.* a lump; a ball; a pill (chd. p. 560); *Thailand* hard lumps of fecal matter.

พรรษ   pat[6] *S. n.* rain; a year (chd. p. 554): พรรษโกศ a month; an astrologer: พรรษธร *lit.* "an upholder of rain," *i. e.* the clouds: พรรษธรรษ an eunuch: พรรษบท a calendar: พรรษบาต the season of having rain: พรรษ-ประเวศ the commencing of a new year: เถลิง-ศก see เถลิง p. 391: พรรษฤดู the rainy season: พรรษวร an eunuch; a woman's messenger or chamberlain: พรรษวุฒดิ a birth-day; the gradual increase, passing or growth of a year: พรรษายุต a period of ten thousand years: พรรโษทก rain-water: พรรโษบล hail-stones.

พรรษา   pun-sah[2] *S. n.* rain; the rainy season of a year: เข้าพรรษา the beginning of Buddhist Lent: พรรษากาล the rainy season: พรรษาพืช hail-stones: พรรษากุ *lit.* "those born during the rainy season," *i. e.* frogs; toads: พรรษามัท *lit.* "those taking pleasure in the rain," *i. e.* the peacock.

พรรเหา pun-how[2] *P. S. adj.* much; many; large; ample (chd. p. 77).

พรรเอิญ see เผอิญ p. 550.

พรวงเพรียง pru-ang-pree-ang *v.* to praise; to flatter.

พรวด pru-at[3] *adv.* quickly; hastily (as objects passing): พรวดพราด hastily and rudely, or angrily and excitely (as one leaving the presence of another): พรวด *Thailand, Krat,* กาๆ *Thailand, Chumpawn,* โทะ *Thailand, Surat and provinces to the south of it,* ปุ๊ย *Khmer,* กะมุคิง *Malay, Song-kla* (ต้น) *Rhadomyrtus tomentosa (Myrtaceae),* hill guava; hill-gooseberry, a shrub found in south-eastern Asia and throughout Malaysia; in the Peninsula it occurs in all the more open parts. The fruit is edible, and is used wherever the shrub grows. It produces a profusion of pale pink flowers, followed by small round berries of pale yellow colour; from these a jelly is made, which, in flavour, somewhat resembles apple-jelly. A decoction is made from the root, and sometimes from the leaf, which is drunk for diarrhoea, stomach-ache, and as a protective medicine after child-birth. In the Dutch East Indies the leaves are used for wounds. The leaves are used in magic ceremonies during epidemics when evil spirits are being exorcized. The red wood has a fine grain, and can be used for very small objects (MCM. pp. 116, 283: cb. p. 629: BURK. p. 1903).

พรวน pru-an *n.* a species of mango; a string of neck-bells (for domestic animals): พรวนดิน to loosen the soil (as by spading around the roots of plants): ลูกพรวน one or more neck-bells on a string.

พรหม prom *P.S. n.* (neuter) (1) a Brahma angel; the Hindu Brahma (chd. p. 93): (2)

a class of superior angels whose pleasures are simply intellectual or meditative but who are yet mundane, in that they have bodies or forms (Ala. p. 13): (3) the supreme soul of the universe, self-existent, absolute, and eternal, from which all things emanate, and to which all return (H. C. D. p. 56); the one self-existent spirit; the absolute (S. E. D p. 738): พรหมกาย name of a particular class of deities (S. E. D. p. 738): พรหมโดล หรือ จักรวาล a world or heaven of Brahma angels. This is divided into the "world of corporal Brahmas" and the "world of formless Brahmas." The Brahma angels are a higher order of angels than the devas of the Devaloka, being free from sexual passion and insensible to heat and cold (chd. p. 94): พรหมจรรย์ the state of an unmarried religious student; the state of continued chastity; one leading the life of an unmarried religious student: พรหมจักร Brahma's wheel; the symbol of sovereignty; the circle of the universe: พรหมจารี a religious student; a holy celibate; one observing chastity (chd. p. 94): พรหมจาริณี (feminine form of พรหมจารี) a woman who observes the vow of chastity; a virgin: พรหมชายา the wife of a Brahmin: พรหมทัณฑ์ Brahma's staff; the name of a mythical weapon; the curse of a Brahmin: พรหมทาดา one imparting religious knowledge: พรหมนนที *lit.* "Brahma's river," *i. e.* a name for the Saraswati (สรัสวดี). In the Vedas it is primarily a river but is celebrated in the hymns both as a river and deity. As a river, it was one boundary of Brahmavartta, the home of the early Aryans, and was to them, in all likelihood, a sacred river, as the Ganges has long been to their descendants. As a river goddess, Saraswati is lauded for the fertilising and purifying powers of her waters and as the bestower of fertility, fatness and wealth (H. C. D. p. 284): พรหมบถ the way leading to a knowledge of Brahma, whereby the greatest good may be attained: พรหม-บท the place, station or rank of Brahma or of a Brahmin : พรหมบริษัท an assembly of Brahmins : พรหมบิดา *lit.* " Brahma's father," *i. e.* Vishnu, because Brahma is represented as proceeding from a lotus which grew from Vishnu's·navel while he was sleeping afloat upon the waters (H. C. D. p. 360): พรหมบุตร the son of Brahma : พรหมบุตรี *lit.* " Brahma's daughter," *i. e.* a name for the river Saraswati (สร้สวดี): พรหมปุโรหิต the high priests of Brahma ; name of a class of Brahmin divinities ; name of an ancient medical treatise dealing with the origin of man : พรหมพันธุ์ *lit.* " sprung from Brahma," *i. e.* Brahmins (chd. p. 94): พรหมฤติ *lit.* " the beginning of night," *i. e.* dusk ; twilight ; evening time : พรหมรัตน์ any valuable present made to Brahmins : พรหมรูป a name for Vishnu : พรหมเรขา, พรหมลิขิต *lit.* " Brahma's lines," *i. e.* the lines of a man's destiny, supposed to be written by Brahma on the forehead of a child on the sixth day after its·birth : พรหมโลก the realm of Brahma ; the world or heaven of Brahma angels (chd. p. 94): พรหมวิหาร the excellent or perfect state ; life or abode in the Brahma world (chd. p. 95); the four perfect states ; the four virtuous inclinations *viz.*, (1) เมตตา desiring for all living things the same happiness which one seeks for oneself ; (2) กรุณา compassionate interest in the welfare of all beings ; (3) มุทิตา love for, and pleasure in all beings ; (4) อุเบกขา impartiality ; preventing preference or prejudice (Ala. p. 198): พรหมสูตร the sacrificial or sacred thread worn by the Brahmins (from the shoulder across the breast to the opposite side of the waist): พรหมัญญตา the condition of belonging to the suite of Mahabrahma (Chd. p. 94): พรหมันตราย forceful assault or abuse ; rape : พรหมาคาร the residence of the chief Brahmin or priest : พรหมาณฑ์ *lit.* " Brahma's egg," *i. e.* the world ; the globe ; the universe : พรหมาวรรต the holy land ; the name of the country north-west of Delhi, lying between the rivers Saraswati and Drishadwati (ทฤษัท-

วดี), which the sages have named Brahmavartta because it was frequented by the gods (H. C. D. p. 63): พรหมาสตร์ *lit.* " Brahma's missile," *i. e.* the bow, a mythical weapon (H. C. D. p. 57): พรหมาสน์ the seat or pulpit of the chief priest ; a particular posture suited to devout religious meditation.

พรอก prauk[3] *v.* to speak, prattle or talk : พรางพรอก to use deceiving or lying language.

พร่อง praung[3] *adj.* not full ; partly used, or nearly empty ; being gradually lessened by use or removal : น้ำมันพร่องขวด the bottle is only partially full of oil.

พร้อง praung[5] *v.* to converse, speak or declare ; to call or cry ; to harangue (see กล่าว p. 61): พร้องเพรียก to call.

พรอด praut[3] *onomat.* from the sound made when water and air are bubbling out from an opening or from the mouth of a bottle.

พร้อม praum[5] *adj.* ready ; altogether ; at the same time ; completed ; finished : ทำการ-พร้อมกัน all working in unison : พร้อมกัน all at the same time or instant : พร้อมใจกัน unanimous ; with common consent : พร้อม-พรัก, พร้อมพรั่ง, พร้อมเพรียง conjoined ; united ; in unison ; all ready ; all united in purpose and aim ; with one accord : พร้อมมูล complete ; lacking nothing ; having all that is required ; perfect ; entire : มีพร้อม everything is in readiness.

พร้อมพร้อ prom[3]-praw[5] *adv.* ungracefully ; awkwardly ; inelegantly ; crudely.

พร่อย see คร่ำคร่า p. 181 ; แก่ p. 127.

พร้อย proy[5] *adj.* piebald ; spotted ; covered with spots, blotches or specks.

พระ pra[6] *n.* a title given to a priest, a clergyman, a padre, a minister, a monk or a talapoin ; a term indicating the highest respect ; a conferred Civil Service title just below " Phya"; a prefix denoting royalty, holiness, honour or perfection: *adj.* precious; excellent; best; noble (Chd. p. 551); great; holy; the best (Ala. p. 164); sacred: พระกร the hand of the king: พระกรน้อย an undergarment of the king: พระกันแสง see กันแสง p. 17: พระขนง *Cam.* พระภมุ, ภมุกะ *P.* a king's eyebrow (see ขนง p. 139): พระ-ขรรค์ชัย the Sword of State: พระขันทอง a royal golden bowl: พระคลัง *obsolete* the Minister of Foreign Affairs: พระคลังมหา-สมบัติ the Royal Treasury: พระเจ้า the Christian's God; a prefix for all of the king's various names, and for those of royal lineage: พระเจ้าทรงศีล the great king or god of Goodness: พระเจ้าแผ่นดิน, พระเจ้าอยู่หัว titles of respect for the king: พระองค์ a pronoun for God, the king or royalty: พระชนม์ age (of royalty); see ชนม์ p. 277: พระณหัว, พณหัว *lit.* "father overhead," *i. e.* a form of respectful address for superiors: พระเดช-พระคุณ *lit.* "power and goodness," *i. e.* you, a form of address for superiors in rank, equal to Your Royal Highness or Your Excellency: พระดัชนี the king's forefinger: พระเต้า a water jar, goblet, mug of gold, silver or earthenware (for royal use): พระทอง a tune played by Thai bands: พระที่ a royal bed: พระที่นั่ง a throne; a royal palace or vehicle (as a boat): พระที่ใหญ่ the royal bed of state: พระนม a wet-nurse for the children of a princess: พระนาง a princess: พระ-นางเจ้า the queen or empress (one superior in rank to a พระมเหสี): พระนาย a title or form of address for the chiefs in the Royal Pages' Department: พระบรมราชโองการ a royal mandate or command: พระบรมราชา-นุญาต a royal permission: พระบาท the foot of a king or of royalty; a foot-print of the Buddha: พระประธาน the largest image of the Buddha in a Buddhist sanctuary: พระ-เป็นเจ้า, พระผู้เป็นเจ้า a deity or celestial being, as Siva; a greatly respected monarch or ruler; a title for the Christian's God: พระพร a blessing: พระพุทธเจ้า the Buddha; a form of address for a monarch or king (now obsolete): พระพุทธเจ้าข้า a form of reply or assent equivalent to "yes, Sir" (used to royalties): พระพุทธเจ้าข้าขอรับ a form of assent or answer for high princes as "yes, Your Royal Highness": พระพุทธเจ้าข้าขอรับใส่เกล้าใส่กระหม่อม a form of assent or answer to His Majesty the King: พระพุทธเจ้าอยู่หัว an ancient title for His Majesty the King: พระยอด a boil or an abscess (used in referring to royalty): พระยา the fourth rank of conferred title for government Civil Service officials (sometimes considered equal to marquis, but in reality very different in prerogatives): พระราชกำ-หนด an act royally promulgated: พระราชทาน to give (used in reference to royalty): พระ-ราชทานเบี้ยบำนาญ a pension granted by royal decree: พระราชเสาวฌี an edict of H. M. the Queen: พระราชวินิจฉัย royal consideration or decision: พระราชหัตถ์เลขา royal writings or manual: พระราชอำนาจ the royal prerogative: พระราชโองการ a royal edict or command: พระวงศ์ a king's family or relations: พระเสียรพระเจ้าแผ่นดิน the king's head: พระสงฆ์ a Buddhist monk: พระหนุ the king's chin.

พระยาช้างเผือก *Thailand, Kanburi,* กำลัง-ช้างเผือก *Laos, Chiengmai,* กาชองวาเซอะ *Karen, Kanburi* (ต้น) pra[6]-yah-chang[5]-peu-ak[4] *n. Hiptage candicans (Malpighia-ceae),* a small tree (Cb. p. 202); see กาชองวาเซอะ p. 91.

พระหา pra[6]-hah[2] *P. S. v.* to increase; to expand; to promote; to be thick, grow great or strong; to make big, fat or strong (S. E. D. p. 735): *adj.* large; great (Chd. p. 93): พระ-หารฌย์, พระหารัฌย์ a forest of extensive dimensions: พระหาวัน a forest of dense growth: พระหาสุข a condition of great permanent happiness.

พระหาม, พระยาม pra[6]-harm[2] *n.* dawn; daylight.

พรักพร้อม   prak[6]-praum[5] *adj.* prepared; assembled, ready for use or action; convenient; available; handy.

พรั่ง, พะพรั่ง   prung[3] *adv.* excessively; furiously; violently (as overflowing tears); densely packed or crowded together; several: พรั่งพร้อม congregated or arranged in readiness; all assembled; ready: พรั่งพรู crowded; conglomerate; massed; multitudinous.

พรัด   prut[6] *v.* to be separated from; to be estranged from a group or sect, or strayed from companions (as while out on a shooting expedition).

พรั่น, พะพรั่น   see กลัว p. 60; see คร้าม p. 181: ไม่พรั่นใคร to be fearful of no one.

พรับ   see ขยิบ p. 143.

พร่า   prah[3] *v.* to abandon; to destroy or scatter: *adj.* indistinct; blurred.

พร้า   prah[5] *n.* a knife with a big long blade: พร้าได้ a large knife with curved blade: พร้าหวด a long heavy knife with the handle placed at right angles to the blade (used by farmers for clearing weeds off the rice-fields).

พราก   (see จาก p. 243) *adj.* falling fast; abundant (as tears): ความพรัดพราก bereavement; separation: ผัวพรากเมีย the husband is separated from his wife: พรัดพรากจากกัน, พรากจากกัน to be separated from others.

พราง   prang *v.* to hide or secrete; to deceive or delude; to make dim or indistinct; to keep quiet about (for the purpose of deceiving): พรางพรอก to speak deceivingly; to tell a lie.

พร่าง   prang[3] *adj.* indistinct; in a confused manner; clouded or blurred.

พราด, พรูด   prat[3] *onomat.* from the sound of struggling or flapping wings (as when fowls are trying to free themselves).

พราน   pran *n.* a hunter: a trapper of game.

พราย   prai *n.* scattered bubbles of air rising to the surface (of water); a teraph or small image consulted as an oracle; *adj.* brilliant; bright; sparkling: ผีพราย an evil spirit or ghost: พรายตา dazzling to the eyes: พรายแพรว gorgeous; brilliant; dazzling (as luminious showers of fireworks): แพรวพราย radiant; resplendent.

พราว   prow *adj.* sparkling; brilliant; glistening: พราวแพรว bright; glowing.

พราหมณ์   pram *P. S. n.* a Brahmin (masculine): พราหมณี (feminine) the first of the four castes; the sacerdotal class, the members of which may be, but are not necessarily, priests. A Brahmin is the chief of all created beings; his person is inviolate; he is entitled to all honour, and enjoys many rights and privileges. He is a human god. His chief duty is the study and teaching of the Vedas, and the performance of sacrifices and religious ceremonies (H. C. D. p. 59): พราหมณการก inducing or making a person to become a Brahmin (S. E. D. p. 741): พราหมณกุล a Brahmin's house or abode; one of Brahminical lineage, race or caste: พราหมณโภชน์ the feeding or presenting of food to Brahmin priests (similar to the ceremony of feeding Buddhist priests): พราหมณมหาศาล a wealthy Brahmin: พราหมณมานพ an adult Brahmin.

พรำ, พะพรำ   prum *adj.* falling or drizzling gently or constantly (as rain): น้ำค้างลงพรำ ๆ the dew is falling gently: ฝนตกพรำ ๆ sprinkling rain.

พร่ำ, พะพร่ำ   prum[3] *adv.* constantly; continually; unceasingly: บ่นพร่ำ to murmur or complain continually: สอนพร่ำเพรื่อไป to generalize in one's constant instruction.

พร้ำ   prum[5] *adj.* ready.

พริก   prick[6] *n.* peppers; chillies (a general name): พริก (นก) the watercock, *Gallicrex cinereus*; the bronze-winged jacana, *Metopidius indicus*; the pheasant tailed jacana, *Hydrophasianus chirurgus* (GAIRD, J. S. S. IX, 1, pp. 13, 14) : a small bird found in marshes or in flooded rice-fields : พริกกับเกลือ a condiment or relish eaten with rice, composed of chillies, roasted coconut and salt, pounded together : พริกขิง peppers and garlic used for seasoning a hot curry : พริกขี้หนู (ต้น) *Capsicum minimum* (*Solanaceae*), bird-chillie or guinea-pepper, a small annual or biennial, herbaceous, shrubby plant, cultivated throughout the tropics for the sake of the pungent fruits, usually an indispensable constituent in the food of people in tropical countries (V. P. p. 187 : MCM. p. 334) : พริกชี้ฟ้า (ต้น) *Capsicum frutescens* (*Solanaceae*), goat or spur-pepper; bird pepper, a somewhat woody plant about three or four feet high, which, escaping from cultivation, is established wild up and down the East. The uses are in the main those of *C. annum*, but when much pungency is required *C. frutescens* is preferred. Cayenne pepper should be a powder of the fruits of bird pepper, but is very easily adulterated (V. P. p. 188 : MCM. p. 334 : BURK. p. 447) : พริกไทย (ต้น) *Piper nigrum* (*Piperaceae*), pepper, a creeping perennial vine. Both black and white pepper are obtained from the same plant. The berries (pepper-corns) are picked when of a reddish colour and spread in the sun, when they become black and shrivelled. When ground with the outer covering left on, "black pepper" is found. Deprived of the black covering (first by soaking in water for 7 or 8 days, then rubbed or macerated with the feet or otherwise), "white pepper" is obtained (V. P. p. 188 : MCM. p. 340 : BURK. p. 1764) : พริกฝรั่ง (ต้น) *Rivina humilis* (*Phytolaccaceae*), rouge plant; blood berry; coral-berry, a small plant with bright red berries. The root is said, but not proved, to be poisonous. Cattle eat the herbage in Australia; it imparts an unpleasant odour to the milk (MCM. p. 135 : BURK. p. 1913) : พริกหยวก (ต้น) *Capsicum grossum*

(*Solanaceae*), chillies or bell-pepper, a small, annual, bushy plant, of which numerous varieties are cultivated. Though related to the smaller pungent kinds of pepper-chillies, they are distinguished from them by the large, quite pungentless, hollow fruits. These are round or oblong, much wrinkled, 3 to 5 inches in diameter, varying from deep green to orange, bright red, amber, etc., and are much relished when boiled and used as a vegetable, or served raw in salads. The plants thrive best in loose, rich soil, under light shade, and are suited to low and medium elevations, provided the rainfall is not excessive (V.P. p. 188 : MCM. p. 303) : ตำน้ำพริก to pound up pepper seasoning : น้ำพริก a semi-liquid seasoning of pounded peppers.

พริ้ง   pring[5] *adj.* pretty; attractive; graceful; beautiful (used in regard to girls or women) : พริ้งเพริศ graceful or agreeable in every manner.

พริบ   see ขยิบ p. 143 : ในพริบตาเดียว in the twinkling of an eye.

พริบไหว   prip[6]-wai[2] *n.* cleverness; adroitness; agility; nimbleness (used of mental activity when evading trouble or calamity).

พริ้ม   see แช่ม p. 303 : พริ้มพร้อม beautiful in all respects : พริ้มพราย, พริ้มเพรา prim; gay; joyous; smiling : พริ้มเพริศ endowed with an open, pleasing countenance.

พรึง   preung *n.* thin horizontal strips of wood enclosing the ends of weather boards of Thai wooden houses; binding planks; side planks : พรึงสะกัด connecting strips running across the partition boards of a wooden Thai house.

พรึบ   preup[6] *adj.* quick; instantaneous (as the shutter in a camera) : *onomat.* from the sound of marching troops or of steps taken in unison.

พรุ   proo[6] *v.* to crumble; to rot away; to be disintegrated.

พรุก   prook[6] *n.* tomorrow.

พรุ่ง, พรุ่งนี้   proong[3] *n.* the day following; tomorrow.

พรุณ, วรุณ see แทตยเทพ p. 427.

พรุน, ปรุ   proon *adj.* full of holes; holed: ขาดพรุน torn to tatters and in holes: พรุน-กลวง full of small holes leading to an inside cavity or space.

พรู, พะพรู, พะพรู   proo *adj.* going in crowds, swarms or flocks; many going together: พรำพรู talking incessantly or volubly: วิ่งพรูกันไป the entire company flees or runs; see กรู p. 54.

พรูด see พราด p. 568.

พฤ, วิ   prur[6] prefixes used interchangeably when euphonic combinations are desired in rhymes or poetical compilations.

พฤกษ์, พฤกษก   pruk[6] *S. n.* a tree; trees; consisting of, relating to, or belonging to trees (S. E. D. p. 945): พฤกษเกศ *lit.* "having trees resembling hair," *i. e.* mountains: พฤกษจร *lit.* "sojourners among the trees," *i. e.* monkeys: พฤกษชาติ the vegetable kingdom; trees or bushes of various kinds: พฤกษทล leaves: พฤกษเทวดา tree-spirits: พฤกษภพน์ holes or hollow spaces in trees: พฤกษภิท *lit.* "destroyers of trees," *i. e.* axes or hatchets: พฤกษราช, มะเดื่อ the fig tree: พฤกษศายิกา *lit.* "living on trees or among branches," *i. e.* squirrels: พฤกษศาสตร botany: พฤกษาหน์ a chisel; an adze.

พฤฒ see พฤฒ์ p. 570.

พฤฒิ see พฤฒ์ p. 570: พฤฒิบาศ a group or sect of Brahmins whose duty it is to sprinkle consecrated water at royal ceremonies.

พฤตต์   preut[6] *v.* to revolve, whirl or move in a circle: *n.* see ประพันธ์ p. 502: *adj.* round; spherical: พฤตตผล the pomegranate fruit; see ทับทิม p. 409: พฤตตศัสตร์ one proficient

in, or having graduated in the science of fighting or the use of weapons of war.

พฤตตี   preut[6] *S. n.* conduct; profession; livelihood; behaviour; see ประพฤติ p. 502; poetic metre or rhythm (chd. p. 591): พฤตติการ an author of books explaining grammatical rules and construction of sentences: พฤตติ-การณ์ the cause and course of human events.

พฤฒ์, พฤฒ, พุฑฒม์, พุฑฒ   preut[6] *S. n.* one full-grown; an old man; senility; the infirmity or imbecility of old age (S. E. D. p. 945): *adj.* increasing; growing; prospering; advantageous; large; old; clever; skilful: พฤฒโกศ a millionaire; a very rich person; one having a lucrative occupation: พฤฒ-ประธาน a paternal great grandfather: พฤฒ-พาล both the aged and young: พฤฒวาคินี the Malay wild-dog, *Cuon rutilans* or *javanicus.*

พฤฒิ, พฤฒิ, พุฑฒิ, พุฑฒิ   preut[6] *P. n.* growth; increase; prosperity; advantage (chd. p. 590); gain; interest: พฤฒิชีวัน a money lender's charging of exorbitant interest (S. E. D. p. 945).

พฤณต์   preun *S. n.* leaf-stems; fruit-cores; prickles or thorns.

พฤนท์   preun *S. n.* a group, bunch, or cluster (of fruit or flowers); a choir or band (of musicians); a high numerical notation where the digit is followed by 49 cyphers (chd. p. 92).

พฤนทา   preun-tah *S. n.* otherwise called Radha (นางราธา), the first and favourite wife of Krishna (H. C. D. pp. 251, 166): พฤนทารัณย์, พฤนทาวัน the famous forest of Lady Radha in the province of Mathura, on the left bank of the Jumna. There Krishna lived among the cowherds (H. C. D. p. 251); see กฤษณะ p. 56.

พฤนทาร see เทวดา p. 423.

พฤฎษณ, วิภูษณะ   prur[6]-poo-sa[4]-na[6] *P. n.* adornments (chd. p. 566).

พฤภูษิต, วิภูษิต　　　prur[6]-poo-sit[4]　P. adj.
adorned (chd. p. 566).

พฤศจิก　　　preut[6]-sa[4]-chjik[4]　S. n. a scorpion;
the zodiacal sign Scorpio (chd. p. 566):
พฤศจิกายน November, the eighth month according to the Thai solar calculation: พฤศจิ-
กาลี the constellations forming the zodiacal
sign Scorpio.

พฤษ　　　preut[6]　S. n. an ox; a bull; a rat:
พฤษเกตน์, พฤษธวัช lit. "the one having a bull
as his personal attendant," i. e. Siva (H. C. D.
p. 217): พฤษภาสา, อมราวดี lit. "sun-splendour,"
"city of the gods," i. e. the capital of Indra's
heaven, renowned for its splendour and greatness. It is situated somewhere in the vicinity
of Meru (H. C. D. p. 11): พฤษโลจน์ lit. "those
with the eyes a bull," i. e. rats: พฤษวาหน
lit. "he who rides a bull," i. e. Siva: พฤษ-
มาหาร lit. "those that feed on rats," i. e. cats.

พฤษภ　　　preu[6]-sop[4]　S. n. a bull; an eminent
person; the constellation Taurus (chd. p. 537):
พฤษภาคม May (the month of the bull); the
second month according to the Thai solar
calculation.

พฤหัต　　　preu[6]-hat[4]　S. adj. large; great
(chd. p. 93); lofty; high; strong; solid; mighty; wide; vast (S. E. D. p. 735): พฤหัตกถา
name of an extensive compilation of fables.

พฤหัสบดี　　　preu[6]-hat[4]-sa[4]-bau-dee　S. n.
Brihas-pati, son of Angiras, พระอังคีรส (H. C. D.
p. 16). He is one of the seven great Rishis
(an inspired poet or sage) to whom many of
the hymns of the Rig-Veda are attributed.
In mythology Brihas-pati is a deity in whom
the action of the worshipper upon the gods
is personified. He is the suppliant, the sacrificer, the priest who intercedes with gods on
behalf of men and protects mankind against
the wicked. He is called "the priest of the
gods," "the lord of sacrifice." As an astronomical personification, he is regent of the
planet Jupiter, or the planet itself (H. C. D.

p. 63): The fifth day of the week, Thursday:
พฤหัสบดีจักร lit. "the cycle of Brihas-pati,"
i. e. the period of the planet Jupiter's travel
in its orbit; sixty years: พฤหัสบดีวาร
"Jupiter's day"; Thursday.

พล　　　pon P. S. n. strength; power; force;
forces; an army; troops (chd. p. 78); force
considered as a sixth organ of action; military
force (S. E. D. p. 722): พลกาย lit. "armed
body," i. e. an army: พลการ inspiring
strength; strengthening: พลความ points,
matters, or issues that are unimportant:
พลตระเวน obsolete, พลตำรวจ policemen of lowest
rank: พลเทพ air; atmosphere; Bala-tep,
name of the elder brother of Krishna: พล-
ราม Bala-rama see กฤษณะ p. 56: พลไพร่
commoners; peasants; "countryfolk": พล-
เมือง citizens of a city or town; "townsfolk":
พลรบ combatants: พลเรือน government
Civil Service officials; civilians: พลแตรเดี่ยว
trumpeters; see แตร p. 377: พลากร an
army; troops: พลาดิศัย the impossible;
beyond human power or strength: พลานึก
soldiers; warriors.

พลบ, พระลบ　　　plop[6]　n. twilight; dusk;
late in the evening: จนพลบ till evening,
or till darkness sets in: พลบค่ำ approaching
darkness.

พลว　　　pa[6]-la[6]-wa[6]　P. adj. strong; intense;
intensive (chd. p. 79); used as a prefix, ex.
พลวเหตุ a violent cause, or agent of a great
calamity (as flood or earthquake).

พลวก　　　plu-ak[3]　v. to collapse, subside or
give way from under (as props or posts under
a house); see ถล่ม p. 380.

พลวง Thailand, Korat, Kampengpet, ควง
Thailand, Pitsanulok, กุง Laos, N. Ubon,
Krabin, ติง N. Laos, คลุ้ง Chaobon, Korat,
โคล้ง Khmer, Surin, พลอง Sui, Surin,
หล่าเทอะ, ตะหล่าอออาขว่า Karen, Chiengmai, เกาะสะแต้ว, สะเติง Lawa, Chiengmai

(ต้น)　　plu-ang *n. Dipterocarpus tuberculatus* (*Dipterocarpaceae*), a large tree found extensively in Burma and elsewhere. The timber is used in the Indian railway workshops for rolling-stock, the supplies coming chiefly from Rangoon (cb. p. 139 : V. P. p. 191 : BURK. p. 839) :　พลวงหิน (ปลา) *Labeobarbus soro* (*Cyprinidae*), a carp (suvatti p. 35).

พลวด (ปลา)　　pluat[3] *n. Trypauchen vagina* (*Trypauchenidae*) (suvatti p. 159).

พลอง *Thailand* (ต้น) plaung *n. Memecylon ovatum* (*Melastomaceae*) (cb. p. 711 : V. P. p. 192); see พลวง (ต้น):　พลองแก้มอ้น *Thailand, Langsuan,* เม้จ่าง *Thailand, Surat* (ต้น) *Pternandra coerulescens* (*Melastomaceae*), a small tree found from Tenasserim, or the Andamans, Thailand and Cambodia to the Moluccas; common in lowland forests throughout the Malay Peninsula. The timber is rather light in weight, pale brown in colour with obscure rings. The fruits and seeds have medicinal and magical uses in Malaya (BURK. p. 1825 : cb. p. 702); พลอง แก้ม อ้น *Thailand, Chumpawn,* กำซำ *Thailand, Peninsula* (ต้น) *Memecelon mysinoides* (*Melastomaceae*) (cb. p. 710); พลองขาว *Thailand, Songkla* (ต้น) *Memecylon oleifolium* (*Melastomaceae*) (cb. p. 710):　พลองขี้ควาย *Thailand, Langsuan,* ขี้ใต้ *Thailand, Songkla* and *Satul* (ต้น) *Descapermum fruticosum* (*Myrtaceae*), a shrub; or more rarely a slender tree, reaching 50 feet in height, found from upper Burma and southern China to tropical Australia; very common in the Malay Peninsula, chiefly on the edges of forests. The wood is never large. It has a fine grain and a dirty colour. It can be used for making small objects but it is said to split and warp in drying. Fences, toolhandles and rice-pounders are made from it. In Malacca it is used for houses. Firewood is obtained from the tree (cb. p. 631 : BURK. p. 173):　พลองขี้ใต้, พลอง ลำบิด *Thailand, Prachuap,* พลอง เสม็ด *Thailand, Chumpawn* (ต้น) *Rhodamia siamensis* (*Myrtaceae*) (cb. p. 629); *R. trinervia,* a

small tree found from Tenasserim and the Andaman Islands to Australia, but not in the Philippine Islands; in the Malay Peninsula it is very common throughout. It is a tree of secondary forest, and appears quite early upon the bared surfaces of landslides. The wood is very hard, and is used for the smaller parts of houses and for small objects. Charcoal is made from it in west Sumatra. Wood-tar may be made from it for blackening the teeth. The leaves and the roots are used medicinally. The fruit can be eaten. The bark is said to be useful in dyeing black, and also for toughening nets (BURK. p. 1902); *Memecylon pauciflorum* (*Melastomacese*) (cb. p. 712):　พลองขั้นก *Thailand, Prachinburi* and *Prachuap,* เหมื่อดฟอง, เหมื่อดจี้ *N. Laos* (ต้น) *Memecylon scutellatum* (*Melastomaceae*) (cb. p. 714):　พลองดำ *Thailand, Prachuap,* พลองใหญ่ *Thailand, Korat,* เหมี่อด *Laos, Surin* (ต้น) *Memecylon edule var. brevipes* (*Melastomaceae*) (cb. p. 706):　พลองแดง *Thailand, Prachuap,* พลองใหญ่ *Thailand, Krabin* (ต้น) *Memecylon floribundum* (*Melastomaceae*) (cb. p. 708):　พลองใบเล็ก *Thailand, Krat,* พลองแล้ง *Sui, Surin* (ต้น) *Memecylon geddesianum* (*Melastomaceae*) (cb. p. 708):　พลอง (ไม้) a club; a weighted stick used as a weapon; พลองอิน *Thailand, Trang* (ต้น) *Anplectrum glaucum* (*Melastomaceae*), a sprawling shrub, found all through the western parts of Malaysia; in the Peninsula throughout. The Malays boil the roots and give the decoction for fever and ague. This use seems to be not infrequent. In Upper Perak, the decoction used for malaria is not simple, but *Phyllanthus pulcher, Polychroa repens,* and *Cnestis palala* enter into it (cb. p. 698 : BURK. p. 171).

พลัอ see พ้อ p. 577.

พลอน　　plaun *v.* to peel (the rind); to rob, steal or filch (as in a confidence trick or gambling): *adj.* ruined; full of holes; porous (as a sponge); *surgical* crooked or deviating (track or sinus); see ซอน p. 284.

พลอมแพลม   plaum-plaam *adj.* uneven; irregular; alternating (as the flash-light of a lighthouse); diving and rising (as divers or fishes); see ประปราย p. 502.

พลอย   ploy *n.* gems or precious stones: *adj.* following or joining in with others; emulating the example of others: พลอยดี-พลอยชั่ว to imitate the good or evil example of others: พลอยเป็นไปด้วย to participate in, or follow the example of another: พลอย-พูด to mix or join in conversation with others: พลอยรับประทานกับเขา to partake with others: พลอยหุง spurious or fake gems.

พล่อย   ploie[3] *adv.* easily; fluently; readily; thoughtlessly: พูดพล่อย ๆ to talk without reflection; to babble regardless of results.

พลั่ก   pluk[3] *adj.* excessive; in great quantities; immoderate; extreme (as blood issuing from a wound, or water leaking into a boat): *onomat.* from the sound of boiling.

พลั่ง   plung[3] *adj.* flowing with a gurgling sound (as liquid from a bottle); fluent; impetuous; voluminous (in speech).

พลั้ง   plung[5] *v.* to be deceived or mistaken in; to err, miss, or fail: ผิดพลั้ง to fall (into sin); to err (in conduct): พลั้งเผลอ to slip or err through thoughtlessness: ไม่-ผิดพลั้ง infallible: สี่ตีนยังรู้พลาดนักปราชญ์ยังรู้-พลั้ง *prov.* a quadruped may stumble, thus a sage may blunder.

พลัด   plat[6] *v.* to trip and fall; to be lost, or strayed away (from the fold, or a company): พลัดคู่ separated from the mate or companion: พลัดตก accidentally to let fall from the hand, or drop into a hole or pit: พลัดที่ dislocated; removed from the natural place of abode: พลัดพ่อพลัดแม่ to be deprived of, or separated from parents; orphans: พลัดพรากจากกัน to be separated from one another.

พลัน   plun *adv.* quickly; smartly; urgently; immediately; see ด่วน p. 320.

พลับ, มะพลับ (ต้น)   plup[6] *n. Diospyros embryopteris* (*Ebenaceae*), a moderate-sized, evergreen, symmetrical tree with handsome foliage and spreading branches, native of India and eastwards to Thailand. It occurs again in Java and Celebes, not uncommonly planted. It is chiefly used as a dye and tan. In Thailand its extremely astringent young roots are used to colour and toughen fishing-nets. In India the young fruits are medicinal in many ways. There is oil in the seeds which is used in Indian medicine. The timber is useful and is employed in India (MCM. pp. 206, 396, 443: V. P. p. 194: Burk. p. 830): พลับจีน (ต้น) *Diospyros kaki* (*Ebenaceae*), persimmon, kaki or date-plum, a small tree, native of north-eastern India and from there extending to Japan. Its cultivation dates from long before Europeans first visited the East. It is perhaps the most commonly grown staple fruit of the Far East. Until ripe, the fruits are astringent; but immediately they become ripe the best of them are excellent. Owing to this characteristic of the fruit, various methods of curing the persimmon are in use. The Japanese who have many superior races, most of which have red fruit, but some with yellow, pack the unripe fruit in wooden casks made of *Crypteronia* wood, which have held their saki beer: the casks are closed for a few days to allow the fruit to ripen: the tannin disappears, and the flesh remains firmer than without this treatment, so that the fruit stands transport better. The calyces and peduncles of the fruit are dried for medicinal use and are considered a specific for coughs and dyspnoea. The tannin of unripe fruits is used for dyeing and preserving wood (MCM. p. 277: V. P. p. 194: Burk. p. 831): ย้อมยางพลับ to use the juice, bark or unripe fruit of the persimmon for tanning or dyeing (as for fishing nets.)

พลับพลา   plup[6]-plah *n.* a rest pavillion or temporary shelter for His Majesty, princes or high officials: ปลุกพลับพลา to erect a pavillion, tent or temporary abode.

พลับพลึง (ต้น) plup[6]-pleung *n. Crinum asiaticum* (*Amaryllidaceae*), a tuberous herb, with leaves up to 6 feet long, found in southeastern Asia, Malaysia, and Polynesia, naturally on the coast, and in the interior in gardens. It has white scented flowers. The herb is used medicinally. Taken internally it acts as an emetic but is not used much in this way. In India it is used to produce vomiting. Dutch soldiers, wounded by poisoned arrows, are reported to have chewed its roots, and swallowed the juice, that their vomiting might break the power of the poison, and then they poulticed the wound with it. The Malays also use the pounded leaves as a poultice in treating fevers, lumbago, head-aches, and swellings. By boiling the plant a lotion may be made, which is used anywhere on the body (MCM. pp. 138, 191: V. P. p. 195: BURK. p. 681).

พลั่ว ploo-ah[3] *n.* a farmer's curved spade and shovel combined.

พล่า plah[3] *n.* a condiment, or relish made with seasoned raw meat: ยำพล่า a salad containing raw meat or fish duly seasoned: พล่ากุ้ง the same only using prawns or shrimps.

พลากร, พลาดิศัย, พลานึก see พล p. 571.

พลาง plang *adv.* in the meantime; whilst; during the interval; at intervals of: กิน-พลางพูดพลาง to converse while eating: เดิน-พลางร้องไห้พลาง to cry whilst walking: หัวเราะ-พลางร้องไห้ไปพลาง mingled crying and laughing.

พลาด plat[3] *v.* to slip; to stumble; to fall; to err; to slide off from: พลาดตก to slip or slide from a height: พลาดล้ม to stumble and fall.

พล่าน plan[3] *adj.* turbulent; agitated; having a tendency to disturb neighbours; see ป่วนปั่น p. 513.

พลาม plam *adj.* greedy; ravenous; gluttonous; eating with open mouth.

พล่าม plam[3] *adj.* talkative; babbling or prattling uselessly; talking endlessly to no purpose.

พลาย, ช้างพลาย plai *adj.* male (used for [elephants).

พลายม้า see พายม้า p. 583.

พลาหก pa[6]-lah-hok[4] *P. S. n.* a cloud (chd. p. 546); rain- or thunder-clouds; any one of the seven clouds appearing at the time of the destruction of the world (S. E. D. p. 723).

พลำพัง (กรม) pa[6]-lum-pang *n.* a department in the Ministry of the Interior.

พลิ see พลี ๑ p. 574.

พลิก plik[6] *v.* to turn over (as pages of a book); to roll over or change the position (of the body): พลิกคว่ำ to roll over on to the face: พลิกคำ to revoke or retract one's word or promise: พลิกซ้ายพลิกขวา to turn or roll from left to right and then reverse the action; to be on the alert: พลิกไปพลิก-มา to roll back and forth restlessly: พลิก-แพลง to retract artfully; to change the position of, or act in a contrary manner: พลิก-ศพ to examine a corpse to ascertain the cause of death (a procedure in jurisprudence), การพลิกศพ a coroner's inquest: พลิกหงาย; พลิกท้อง to turn over and lie on the back: พูดพลิกแพลง to equivocate.

พลิพัทท์ pa[6]-li[6]-pat[6] *P. n.* an ox (chd. p. 79).

พลิ้ว pliew[6] *v.* to twist, alter or bend; to shuffle or scuffle (as in hiding some stolen article); to act wrongly or misconduct oneself: บิดพลิ้ว to play truant or falsify one's actions; see บิด p. 483.

พลี ๑, พลิ pa[6]-lee *P. S. n.* tribute; tax; a grant; a gift; an offering or sacrifice; royal revenue; an oblation or a religious offering; a propitiatory sacrifice (S. E. D. p. 723): ญาติ-

พลิ the rendering of aid or succor to relatives: เทวดาพลิ the making of propitiatory offerings to a deity, idol or spirit. This may be either ธรรมพลิ merit for the departed, or อามิสพลิ gifts to the living: พลิตน to make personal sacrifices for others (as to time and efforts): เปตพลิ the making of merit on behalf of the dead: พลิกาก the crow (chd. p. 79); see กา (นก) p. 89: ราชพลิ the making of a contribution or subscription to the Crown (as tribute or tax): ศึกษาพลิ an educational tax or assessment: อติถิพลิ the ministering to, or befriending of strangers.

พลิ ๒　　pa[6]-lee *P. adj.* strong (chd. p. 79).

พลิ ๓　　pa[6]-lee *v.* to be got, taken or received after propitiatory offerings have been made to the spirits or genii inhabiting trees or mountains (as is done by Thai doctors when they would cut down or take parts from trees of the forest for important remedies).

พลิมุข　　pa[6]-lee-mook[6] *n.* monkey.

พลุ　　ploo[6] *n.* a kind of fireworks (exploding with a sound like cannons): *adj.* puffy; fluffy; spongy.

พลุก　　plook[6] *n.* an elephant's tusks.

พลุกพล่าน　　plook[6]-plarn[3] *v.* to be scattered about in confusion or disorder; to wander as though spying when trespassing on another's ground.

พลุ่ง　　ploong *v.* to spout forth or gush out (as water or oil from a well); to issue forth (as smoke); to burst out (as water or steam): ใจพลุ่งพล่าน to "boil," or be inflamed with rage: เดือดพลุ่ง to boil violently.

พลุ้น　　ploon[5] *adj.* undeveloped; unripe; soft (used regarding coconuts before they are fully ripe).

พลุ่มพล่าม　　ploom[3]-plarm[3] *adv.* rudely; roughly; uncouthly; carelessly (used in regard to untrained servants): see ตะกรุมตะกราม p. 350.

พลุ่ย　　pluie[3] (see ง่าย p. 223) *adj.* coming out easily (as seeds); running smoothly (as machinery).

พลุ้ย　　pluie[5] *adj.* pouched; distended; obese: ท้องพลุ้ย pot-bellied; corpulent: อ้วนพลุ้ย overly fat; very corpulent.

พลู (ต้น)　　ploo *n. Piper betle (Piperaceae)*, betel-vine, a perennial, evergreen climber or creeper with large heart-shaped leaves, cultivated throughout tropical Asia for the sake of the leaves. They are universally used in the Eastern Tropics for chewing in a green state, forming the masticatory commonly known as "betel," the other ingredients being lime, areca-nut, etc. The leaves have a sharp pungent taste and sustaining properties (MCM. p. 381: V. P. p. 186: Burk p. 1737) พลูสะบาด *Khmer*, ส้านน้อย *Thailand and Laos, E. Thailand* (ต้น) *Dillenia hookeri (Dilleniaceae)* (cb. p. 22).

พลูแก　　ploo-gkaa *n.* a climber of the betel-vine family; *Piper sp.* (used medicinally by the Thai).

พวก　　poo-ak[3] *n.* company; community; association; party; a sect or society; a crowd; a flock; troops: พวกเดียวกัน of the same company or sect: พวกทั้งงาน strikers: พวกผู้ร้าย a gang (as of robbers): พวกพ้อง friends; relatives; companions: พวกราษฎรที่ชุมนุมกันเป็นหมู่มาก a mob: สมัครเข้าพวก to join or be affiliated willingly with a party or society.

พวง　　poo-ang *n.* a garland; a bunch or cluster of flowers: พวงคอ a neck-chain for criminals: พวงทอง *Thailand,* ระคนทอง *Laos, Chiengmai* (ต้น) *Tristellateia australasiae (Malpighiaceae),* golden-rod, a plant of the neighbourhood of the sea, from China and Indo-China to the Pacific; in the Peninsula it occurs round the coast. It makes a pretty garden climber, and is in cultivation. The flowers are erect, yellow racemes. It is a free bloomer (MCM. pp. 127, 208 : cb. p. 201 : BURK. p. 2187) : พวงบุหรี่ *Thailand, Supan* and *Korat*, บุหรี่ผี, ปิ้งแป้ *Laos, Chiengmai* (ต้น) *Alsomitra sarcophylla* (*Cucurbitaceae*) (cb. p. 769) : พวงม่วง (ต้น) *Duranta repens* (*Verbenaceae*), golden dewdrop, commonly known as *Duranta plumieri*, an unarmed, glabrous, erect shrub six to ten feet high with the branches often drooping. The leaves are obovate-elliptical, the base is wedge-shaped and the margins toothed above the middle. The axillary racemes form terminal panicles, which are slender and spreading, with the flowers mostly on one side of the rachis; the former are blue or white; the fruit is fleshy, ovoid, and yellow. It is not known certainly who introduced this tropical American plant, now commonly cultivated, into Thailand. Possibly it was Mrs. D. McGilvary, as the species has long been known in Chiengmai (The orn. Trees of Hawaii, J. F. Rock. p. 187 : MCM. pp. 73, 74, 111, 183, 517 : Kerr. N. H. J. S. S. III, 3, p. 203 : Burk. p. 871) : พวงมาลัย a jasmine wreath or garland of flowers; *nautical* a steering wheel; the steering wheel for guiding motor cars : พวงมาลัยชูชีพ a life-preserver; พวงมาลัย (กล้วยไม้) *Rhyncostylis retusa*, the foxtail orchid. The flowers are white and spotted with amethyst-purple. They are very showy (MCM. p. 146); *R. retusa* (*Saccolabium guttatum*), the white flowers are in brush-like, pendulous racemes, dotted with violet-pink. They are very handsome (MCM. p. 148 : V. P. p. 191) : พวงมาลัยเปีย a garland with multiple tassels : พวงมาลา wreaths (used at funerals) : พวงหยก (กล้วยไม้) *Dendrobium findlayanum* (*Orchidaceae*) (V. P. p. 191).

พ่วง   poo-ang[3] *v.* to tow (as boats on a rope); to attach boats by a tow-line : *n.* a raft, pontoon or float : *adj.* enlarged; swollen; augmented; having a tendency to grow bigger or obese : พ่วงแพ to tow a raft of bamboos or posts; to raft the same ready for towing : พ่วงพี fat; chubby; plump (as the cheeks).

พวน   poo-an   *n.* a large rope; a cable or hawser; rice stalks threshed the second time; remilled sugar-cane.

พวย   poo-ie   *n.* a spout; the nozzle of an ewer or tea-pot; a beak-shaped point; see งวง p. 221.

พวยพุ่ง   poo-ie-poong[3] *adj.* bright; luminous; radiant (as the brightness of a star).

พศค   pa[6]-sok[4] *P. S. n.* one being in the power of another; one obedient, subject to or dependent on others (S. E. D. p. 929 : chd. p. 55).

พศก   pa[6]-sok *P. S. n. lit.* "those abiding in or inhabiting," *i. e.* citizens; inhabitants; population; dwellers; denizens (S. E. D. p.947).

พสนะ, วสนะ   pa[6]-sa[4]-na[6] *P. n.* clothing; clothes; cloth (chd. p. 551).

พสมเส็ด   pa[6]-som[2]-set[4] *n.* the Malay tapir, *Tapirus indicus* (Gaird. J. S. S. III, 2, p. 126).

พสุ ๑   pa[6]-soo[4] *n.* an ox; a bull; see โค p. 214.

พสุ ๒   pa[6]-soo[4] *P. S. n.* a class of Hindu demi-gods; wealth (chd. p. 555) : *adj.* good; excellent; beneficent (S. E. D. p. 930) : พสุทา *lit.* "one granting wealth," *i. e.* the soil of the earth : พสุเทพ the Hindu god, Krishna : พสุธา *lit.* "one producing wealth," *i.e.* the earth; ground; soil; a country or kingdom : พสุธาดล the earth's surface : พสุธาธร *lit.* "one bearing or supporting the earth," *i.e.* a king; a prince; a mountain : พสุธารณี *lit.* "treasure-holder," *i.e.* the earth : พสุธาวิลาสี the king, ruler or sovereign (of a country) : พสุนธรา the earth; a kingdom : พสุประภา *lit.* "seven-tongued," *i.e.* an epithet for Agni, the god of Fire. Each tongue for licking up the butter used in sacrifices has a distinct name : พสุปัตนี *lit.* "a mistress of wealth," *i.e.* a cow : พสุมดี the earth; a country; a kingdom.

พหุล   pa[6]-hon[2] *P. S. n.* thick; dense; compact; firm; solid (S. E. D. p. 724).

พหุ, พหู pa⁶-hoo⁴ *P. S. n gram.* a plural
form: *adj.* much; many; ample; large (Chd.
p. 77): พหุกร one with many interests; a
a busy person; one useful in many ways:
พหุกรณีย์ an industrious person: พหุกรี *lit.*
"that which does a great deal of work," *i. e.*
a broom: พหุคุณ *lit.* "many threaded (as
a rope)," *i. e.* having many good qualities or
virtues; multifarious: พหุนาท *lit.* "loud
sounding," *i. e. a conch-shall; a bugle:* พหุ-
พจน์, พหุพจน์, พหุศัพท์ many; much; the plural
number; the case-endings and personal terminations in the plural number: พหุภาษี
a talkative person; a loquacious person; garrulous people: พหุพล *lit.* "one of great
strength," *i. e.* the lion: พหุมล *lit.* "that
which has much dross," *i. e.* lead: พหุมุข
lit. "one with many mouths," *i. e.* a ventriloquist; one capable of speaking variously; a
polyhedron: พหุโรม *lit.* "having much hair
or wool," *i. e.* sheep: พหุสรุต, พหุสสุต, พหุ-
สสุต one who has studied much; one very
learned; one versed in the Vedas: พหุสุต
one having many children.

พหุล pa⁶-hoon² *P. S. adj.* thick; dense;
broad; wide; spacious; ample; large; numerous; many; much (S. E. D. p. 726).

พอ paw *v.* to have sufficient, enough or
adequate for any need or demand: *adv., conj.*
as soon as: พอกับการ amply supplied; abundant for all needs: พอเขาไป whenever he
leaves: พอใจ to be satisfied, contented or
pleased with; to agree with; to be willing
to do: *adv.* suitably: *adj.* appropriate;
suitable or expedient: พอใช้ passably
good: *adj.* fair; not too inferior (as grades
in an examination); still fit for use or service:
พอดี middling; just sufficient: พอดีพอร้าย
not too inferior but still not the best: พอได้
to just get or receive: พอได้เห็น as soon
as was seen: พอตัว not too inferior; just
suitable for or suited to; just capable to do:
พอทำได้ just what can be comfortably done:
พอแรง just sufficient or ample for one's power;

not over-taxing the strength; in an excessive amount or degree (as bleeding from a
wound): พอแล้ว quite sufficient: พอว่า
whenever: มีพอกินพออยู่ just having enough
to satisfy life's needs.

พ่อ, ชนก, บิดา paw³ *n.* father; male; a
title of honour: คุณพ่อ, พ่อคุณ a benefactor:
พ่อเกลอ the father's closest or most intimate
friend: พ่อครัว a cook: พ่อค้า a merchant: พ่อค้าของจำนวนใหญ่, พ่อค้าขายส่ง a
whole-sale dealer: พ่อค้าขายปลีก a retail
dealer: พ่อคุณพ่อหัว, พ่อทูลหัว forms of respectful request (used by supplicants): พ่อเฒ่า
a respectful form when addressing men of
age and standing; see เฒ่า p. 317: พ่อตา a
father-in-law (of the wife): พ่อบ้าน, พ่อเจ้า-
เรือน the head of a family; head of a community; the father of the home; the steward of
the home: พ่อผัว a father-in-law (of the
husband): พ่อม่าย a widower: พ่อแม่
the father and mother: พ่อเลี้ยง a step-
father; a foster-father; a putative father.

พ้อ, พล้อ paw⁵ *v.* to utter contemptious,
insulting or outrageous words or language:
คำตัดพ้อ injurious, slanderous or insulting words
that sever friendship: ตัดพ้อ to break off
friendship by use of insulting language:
พ้อเอา to use angry or insulting language.

พอก pauk³ *v.* to cover in layers; to apply
by laying on layers; to increase by accretion:
ไข่พอก pickled eggs covered with a paste of
cinders and salt: คอพอก (โรค) goitre:
พอกพูน to support, feed or care for; to add
favours one by one: พอกพูนบำเหน็จ to
shower blessings or kindnesses upon one:
พอกยา to apply a poultice or plaster: ยา-
พอก a poultice.

พอง paung *v.* to swell or rise in blisters or
pustules: *adj.* swelling; puffed up; inflated:
ขนลุกขนพอง having the hair standing on end
or bristling from fear or fright: ดินสอพอง
chalk; carbonate of lime: พองตัว self-
inflation; self-agrandizement.

พ้อง pawng[5] *adj.* synonymous; coincident; simultaneous; allied; kindred; identical: ผิดพ้องหมองป้าก to have differences of opinion or dissensions; to sever relations by disrespectful words: พวกพ้อง relatives; comrades; friends; those of the same clan or society: พ้องพาน to meet face to face; to be connected with or interested in; to be associated with or confederates (in some lawless deed).

พ้อม paum[5] *n.* a large woven bamboo receptacle with a small orifice (used for storing or transporting rice in the husk).

พอหะแย่ *Malay, Pattani* (ต้น) paw-ha[4]-yaa[3] *n. Elaeocarpus parvifolius* (*Elaeocarpaceae*) (cb. p. 197); *E. parvifolius* (*Tiliaceae*), a tall tree in Thailand, the Malay Peninsula, and Borneo; in the Peninsula it is common generally. The timber is light, and not durable when exposed (burk. p. 903).

พะ pa[6] *v.* to meet with or find; to come against; see ปะ p. 516: *n.* an attap roofed lean-to or roof over a veranda, on houses of the poorer class: พบพะ to meet or find another: พะกันเข้า to collide, or come into contact violently: พะพาน to accuse another falsely on meeting.

พ่ะ see จ้ะ p. 235; ขอรับ p. 146.

พะงา (เพาพะงา) pa[6]-ngah *n.* handsomeness; loveliness; beauty; *adj.* attractive; pretty; beautiful: พะงางาม one who is beautiful or attractive (used in respect to women or girls).

พะเจ้าหามก๋าย *N. Laos,* ปู่เจ้า *Laos, Nan* (ต้น) pa[6]-chjow[3]-harm[2]-gkai[2] *n. Terminalia tripteroides* (*Combretaceae*) (cb. p. 610): พะเจ้าห้องค์ *Laos, Chiengmai* (ต้น) *Dracontomelum mangiferum* (*Anacardiaceae*), a tree of considerable size, found from India to Malaysia; in the Peninsula it probably grows throughout in the low country. The edible fruit is eaten as a sour relish with fish by the Malays. The flowers and leaves also have a sour taste, and seem to enter into food as flavourings in the Moluccas. Possibly the bark is medicinal. At any rate it enters into a decoction given by the Malays for dysentery. The timber lacks strength and durability (cb. p. 357: burk. p. 859).

พะทา (นก) pa[6]-tah *n.* Phayre's Burmese francolin, *Francolinus pintadeanus phayrei* (Deig. N. H. J. S. S. VIII, 3, p. 168).

พะทำมะรง pa[6]-tum-ma[6]-rong *n.* a prison jailer or warden.

พะนมสวรรค์, นมสวรรค์ (p. 441) *Thailand, Peninsula* (ต้น) pa[6]-nom-sa[4]-wan[2] *n. Clerodendron paniculatum* (*Verbenaceae*), the pagoda flower, a shrub found from Burma and southern China, to Java and Ternate; in the Peninsula it is apparently throughout. In north-central Sumatra this plant is used as a 'summoner of spirits' and it is apparently so used by the Malays. It is one of the plants used in composing the leafy brush for sprinkling consecrated rice-gruel in the wedding ceremony, in the blessing of fishing-stakes, and in the taking of the rice-soul (V. P. p. 155: mcm. p. 109: burk. p. 585).

พะนอ see ถนอม p. 379.

พะนอง pa[6]-naung *n.* a forest; see ป่า p. 521.

พะนอม, พระนอม, พระน้อม pa[6]-naum *n.* a mountain peak, mountain or place covered with bushy trees or shrubbery.

พะนัก pa[6]-nuk[6] *n.* a back-rest or support: พะนักเรือ the back of a seat in a boat: พะนักอิง the back of a chair or seat.

พะนัง pa[6]-nung *n.* the leather or flannel side-flaps of a saddle.

พะนัน pa[6]-nun *v.* to bet, stake, wager money, or gamble: พะนันกัน to wager, bet, or gamble together: เล่นพะนันกัน to try one's luck in gambling games: เล่นพะนัน-ขันต่อ to risk a wager, offering handicaps.

พะนาด, พระนาด see เบาะ p. 489.

พะเน้าพะนึง pa⁶-now⁵-pa⁶-neung *v.* to manifest an angry unwillingness.

พะเนิน pa⁶-nern *n.* a large hammer (for forging iron); a mound, artificial hill, or rising foot-hill; a pile or heap.

พะเนียง pa⁶-nee-ang *n.* a Roman candle; a bamboo joint or tube filled with powder for fireworks; a tree bearing edible flat seeds in pods, *Pithecolobium jiringa*: ไหพะเนียง a glazed earthen container, water-pot or jug.

พะเนียด pa⁶-nee-at³ *n.* a trap for catching doves; an enclosure or kraal for elephants; provincial government rest-houses.

พะแนง pa⁶-naang *n.* a thick curry containing large pieces of roast meat or chicken: ไก่พะแนง roast fowl.

พะแนงเชิง pa⁶-naang-cherng *n.* a sitting posture with the legs crossing each other, the soles turned upwards (as seen in images of the Buddha).

พะบู pa⁶-boo *Cam. n.* the face: *adj.* fair; white; see ด่อน p. 322.

พะพรอง, พะพรั้ง see งาม p. 223.

พะพรั่ง see พรั่ง p. 568.

พะพรั่น see พรั่น p. 568.

พะพราย pa⁶-prai *adj.* sparkling; twinkling; [luminous.

พะพรำ see พรำ p. 568.

พะพร่ำ see พร่ำ p. 568.

พะพรึก see พรฤ p. 570.

พะพาน see พบ p. 561; ปะ p. 516; เจอะ p. 257.

พะพิง, อิง pa⁶-ping *v.* to depend on, or rely upon (for help); to lean upon, or against.

พะเพรียม pa⁶-pree-am⁵ *adj.* diligent; industrious; studious.

พะเพิง see เพิง p. 598.

พะแพรว, พะแพร้ว pa⁶-praa-oh *adj.* scintillating; emitting flashes of light; sparkling; twinkling.

พะม่า, พุกาม, พู่กาม pa⁶-mah³ *n.* Burmese: ประเทศพะม่า Burma.

พะยอม, ขะยอม (see p. 149) *N.* and *E. Laos*, เชียว *Karen, Chiengmai* (ต้น) pa⁶-yaum *n. Shorea floribunda* (*Dipterocarpaceae*) (cb. p. 142: V. P. p. 38).

พะยัก pa⁶-yak⁶ *v.* to indicate by a sign or signal: พะยักพะเขิด to have complete knowledge without making or giving any outward sign or indication of the same; to make vague but continuous signs (to another); พะยักหน้า to warn or signal by facial expression: พะยักหัว to indicate by a nod.

พะยับ pa⁶-yup⁶ *n.* dull, overcast or cloudy weather; see ครึ้ม p. 182: พะยับแดด a condition of figured shadows, mist or optical delusions seen now and then when the sun is hot and bright; a mirage: พะยับฝน a clouded sky (as prior to rain).

พะยาน pa⁶-yarn *n.* a deponent; a witness; evidence (in court); proof: คำพะยาน the testimony or evidence of a witness: ค้าน-พะยาน to object to, or to refute a witness: ตายด้วยพะยาน to be convicted by the testimony of witnesses: พะยานเท็จ a false witness or perjurer: พะยานนำ a witness brought by either one of the litigants themselves without a subpena: พะยานบอกเล่า hearsay evidence: พะยานบุคคล oral evidence: พะยานประกอบ corroborating evidence: พะยานประพฤติเหตุ-ห้อมล้อมกรณีย์ circumstantial evidence: พะ-ยานวัตถุ real evidence; articles produced as evidence: พะยานหักหลัง rebutting evidence: พะยานเอกสาร documentary evidence: สืบ-

พะยาน to examine a witness : อ้างพะยาน to produce witnesses : อ้างหลักถานเป็นพะยาน to file documents as proof.

พะยุง see ช่วย p. 283 : พะยุงขึ้น to lift; to support; to raise (as the injured on to a stretcher or bed); to help sustain a burden.

พะยูน, หมูน้ำ, วัวทะเล pa⁶-yoon *n. Halicore sp.*, the sea-cow; an aquatic mammal of the East Indies and Australia (suvatti).

พะเยิบ, เผยิบ see กระพือ p. 41.

พะเยย pa⁶-yee-ah *n.* a cluster; a bunch (as of grapes); the pollen of flowers; see เกสร p. 124.

พะรุงพะรัง, รุงรัง pa⁶-roong-pa⁶-rung *adj.* disordered; ill-fitting or tattered (as clothing); encumbered (as by many small pieces of baggage); unsightly (as superabundant clothing).

พะไล, พาไล pa⁶-lai *n.* a veranda; a porch (attached to Thai houses); a gallery.

พะวง, พะวักพะวน pa⁶-wong *v.* to be anxious for, or uneasy about; to be on the alert, ready for action; see กังวล p. 83.

พะว้าพะวัง pa⁶-wah⁵-pa⁶-wang *v.* to be on the look out for on all sides; to be on the watch under all conditions.

พะอง pa⁶-aung *n.* a pole or post having cross-pieces attached, serving as a ladder for gardeners or fruit-pickers : พะอง *Laos, Loi,* คอไหมต้อ *Karen, Kampengpet,* ชาจุ้มมุ่น *Karen, Chiengmai* (ต้น) *Calophyllum polyanthum (Guttiferæ)* (cb. p. 121); see ชาจุ้มมุ่น p. 291.

พะอากพะอำ pa⁶-ark⁴-pa⁶-um *v.* to suffer from a sense of mental uneasiness, trouble or depression; see คับใจ p. 195.

พัก puk⁶ *v.* to tarry, stop or stay temporarily : เขาพักอยู่ที่นั่น he is stopping there : เวลาพัก a recess; an interval of time for rest.

พักตา puk⁶-dtah *P. n.* a speaker; one who tells; one who speaks sensibly (chd. p. 558).

พักตร์ puk⁶ *P. S. n.* the mouth; the face; the muzzle; a snout; a proboscis, jaws or beak (S. E. D. p. 912) : พักตรคุณฑ์ *lit.* "elephant-faced, having a proboscis on the face," *i. e.* Ganesa, lord of the ganas or troops of inferior deities, especially those attendant upon Siva (H. C. D. p. 107) : พักตรทล *lit.* "a part of the mouth," *i. e.* the palate.

พัคค์, พรรค puk⁶ *P. n.* class; company; tribe; party; troops; multitude (chd. p. 545).

พัง pang *v.* to tumble down, fall or break down; to be in a ruinous condition : ช้างพัง a female elephant.

พังคา pung-kah *n.* a troop or regiment of military elephants.

พังงา pung-ngah *n.* a handsome maid; a tiller (a lever fitted to the rudder for steering).

พังผืด pung-purt⁴ *n.* fascia; membrane : พังผืดหุ้มกระดูก periosteum : พังผืดหุ้มปอด pleura : พังผืดหุ้มหัวใจ pericardium : พังผืด-บุห้องหัวใจ endo-cardium.

พังพอน pung-paun *n.* the mongoose, *Mongos siamensis* (N. H. J. S. S. III, p. 122).

พังพาน pung-parn *n.* the hood of a cobra.

พังพาบ pung-parp³ *v.* to lie with the face down flat on the floor.

พังเพย pung-pur-ie *n.* an interposed word or phrase added by way of explanation, or to fill out a line or metre.

พัช see วัช

พัชนี, เพียชนี, วิชนี pat⁶-cha⁶-nee *P. n.* a Buddhist monk's fan (Ala. p. 170 : chd. p. 570).

พัญจก pun-chjok⁴ *P. S. n.* a deceiver; a deluder or beguiler.

พัททฒกี, วัททฒกี pat⁶-ta⁶-gkee *n.* a carpenter, artisan or mason (chd. p. 543).

พัทฒ์, พัฒ pat⁶-ta⁶ *P. adj.* prospering; thriving; increasing (chd. p. 543).

พัทฒนะ, พัฒน   pat[6]-ta[6]-na[6] *P. n.* prosperity; enlargement; increase (chd. p. 543).

พัณณ์ see พรรณ p. 564.

พัด   pat[6] *v.* to fan; to blow (as wind): *n.* a fan: พัดโบก a long-handled ceremonial palm-leaf fan (Ala. p. 170): พัดแขวน a punkah: พัดลม *lit.* "air fan," *i. e.* an electric fan; พัดมณี a jewelled fan.

พัดชา   pat[6]-chah *n.* a Thai tune or air.

พัดดึงส์   pat[6]-deung *n.* a gold coin of eight bahts (thirty-two salungs) value, of the 4th. reign.

พัดติงสะ   put[6]-dting-sa[4] *P. adj.* thirty-two (chd. p. 80).

พัตร see พัสตร์ p. 582.

พัทธยา   put[6]-ta[6]-yah *n.* wealth that is due the Crown: พัทธยากร taxes; Crown dues; revenue.

พัทร see พุทรา (ต้น) p. 594.

พัน   pun *v.* to wind, bind, encircle, wrap or tie together: *n.* an official rank under the Ministries of Defense and Interior: *adj.* thousand: กองพัน a battalion: คงกะพัน invulnerable; proof against weapons or fire-arms; impenetrable: พันตา, พันเนตร *lit.* "the thousand-eyed," *i. e.* a name for Indra (H. C. D. p. 125): พันปี a form of address for a sovereign's mother; a thousand years: พันพัว blended; joined; related; combined; mixed; mingled: พันวรรษา an ancient form of address for the king or sovereign: พันแสง *lit.* "the thousand rayed," *i. e.* a name for the sun.

พันจ่า   pun-chjah[4] *n.* a title of rank in the Royal Marine Service.

พันจำ   *Peninsula* (ต้น)   pun-chjum *n. Varica sp.* near *V. Grandifloran* (V. P. p. 194).

พันจุล   *Laos, Korat,* เนื้อเหนียว *N. Laos,* เบื่อนทะลาย *Khmer, Surin* (ต้น)   pun-

chjoo[4]-lee *n. Lophopetalum wallichii (Celastraceae)* (Cb. p. 283).

พันตู   pun-dtoo *Jav. v.* to fight against; to be in combat with.

พันทาง   pun-tang *n.* mixed breeds; mongrels (as of chickens).

พันธ์   pun *P. v.* to tie; to bind; to unite or bandage (chd. p. 79); to fasten or encircle by means of strings, rope or wire.

พันธนะ   pun-ta[6]-na[6] *P. n.* fetters; bonds; chains; a ligature; a snare or trap (chd. p. 79): พันธนาการ imprisonment; incarceration: พันธนาคาร a prison (chd. p. 79).

พันธุ์, พันธุ   pun *P. n.* a kinsman; relationship (chd. p. 79).

พันลอก, ผลิ see งอก p. 221.

พันลาย   pun-lai *adj.* differing; varying; promiscuous (in design or pattern).

พันลึก, พันลึกพันลื่อ   pun-leuk[6] *adj.* strange; odd; remarkable; different; dreadful; awful (as forms of ghosts); see แปลก p. 536.

พันเลิด   pun-lert[3] *adj.* supreme; excellent; best (a form indicating the superlative degree).

พับ   pup[6] (see ทบ p. 395) *v.* to fold; to double up: *n.* a bolt (of cloth): บานพับ a hinge: เป็นพับไป forfeited; penalized; confiscated (as loss incurred through fault or omission): พับพะแนงเชิง see นั่งขัดสมาส p. 448: พับเพียบ see นั่ง p. 448: รอยพับ a crease mark.

พัลลภ   pun-lop[6] *P. n.* a favourite (chd. p. 547; a preferred friend.

พัลวัน see เกี่ยว, เกี่ยวกัน p. 126; ติด, ติดกัน p. 367.

พัว   poo-ah *adj.* clustered; collected together; joined; bunched; grouped: พัวพัน complicated; interwoven; intermixed; entangled.

พัสดี   pat[6]-sa[4]-dee *n.* a jail superintendent;

the chief warden or governor over convicts (probably derived from วสวัตติ, วศวรดี, พัศวดี *lit.* "one who holds creatures under his control").

พัสดุ   pat[6]-sa[4]-doo[4] *P. n.* goods (personal or household); articles; riches; possessions; wares; substance; cause; plot or subject of a story or narrative; belongings (in general) (chd. p. 558).

พัสตรึ, พัตร   pat[6] *P. S. n.* cloth; clothes; raiment (chd. p. 558): พัสตรเปดึ a fringe; margin; border (as of a garment): พัสตร-เกทึ *lit.* "a cutter of cloth," *i. e.* a tailor: พัสตรเวช a (canvas) •tent: พัสตราคาร a tailoring shop or establishment.

พัสถาน   pat[6]-sa[4]-tarn[2] has no meaning in itself and occurs as a suffix only, as in สมบัติ-พัสถาน meaning riches or property in general.

พัสส   pat[6]-sa[4] *P. n.* a year; rain (chd. p. [554].

พา see นำ p. 453.

พาก   pak[3] *n.* an epidemic disease occurring among cattle.

พากพูม, ภาคภูมิ   pak[3]-poom *adj.* proud; pompous; imposing; magnificent.

พากเพียร   pak[3]-pee-an *v.* to be diligent; to be industrious; to be assiduous; to be unremitting (in efforts to succeed); to be indefatigable.

พากย์   pak[3] *P. n.* speech; language; a sentence (chd. p. 546); the speaking of a part during a theatrical performance (as by an actor or precentor): หนังพากย์ a sound cinema film in which the songs and talking are not produced mechanically but by persons behind the scenes: พากย์โขน an intonation during a masked theatrical performance: พากย์หนัง intonations during shadow shows, marionette or Punch and Judy exhibitions.

พากษ์   park[3] (see กล่าว p. 61) *v.* to deliver or read a judgement: พิพากษา see ตัดสิน p. 359.

พาเก *Thailand, Surat*, ตุ๊เจ้ารอยทา *Thailand, Pitsanulok*, อ้อยช้าง *Laos*, ชะระด่องอาย่อ *Karen, Kanburi* (ต้น)   pah-gkey *n.* Heteropanax fragrans (Araliaceae) (cb. p. 802).

พาง, พ่าง, ปาง (p. 522)   pang *adv.* such as; as if; as though; like as.

พ่างเพียง, แทบ   pang[3]-pee-ang *adv.* almost; nearly on to; on the point of.

พาช, วาช   pah-chee *S. n.* a horse; strength; vigour; energy; speed (especially of a horse) (S. E. D. p. 938): พาชินี a mare.

พาณ ๑   parn *P. n.* an arrow; a bullet or cannon ball (S. E. D. p. 727): พาณโยชน์ *lit.* "arrow-union," *i. e.* a quiver: พาณวาร *lit.* "a protector from a multitude of arrows," *i.e.* a shield; a breastplate; armour: พาณาสน์ *lit.* "an arrow-discharger," *i. e.* a bow; a bowstring.

พาณ ๒   parn *P. S. n.* a sound; a noise (S. E. D. p. 939).

พาณารสึ, พาราณสึ   pah-nah-ra[6]-see[2] *n.* Benares or Kasi, originally called Varanasi by the Hindus. Benares is situated on the banks of the Ganges, 25° 20′ N. latitude, 83° 0′ E. longitude. It has been the religious capital of India from beyond historical times. The past history of this ancient city is involved in obscurity. The Chinese travellers Fa-Hian and Hiuen Tsang visited it in 399 A. D. and in 629–645 A. D. respectively. The latter mentions about 100 temples sacred to Siva with 10,000 votaries. In past ages it has been a city of sanctity and learning, the home of philosophers and grammarians. It is however certain that it was a most flourishing and important place six centuries before the Christian era, for Sakyamuni (the Buddha) who was born in 622 B. C. and died in 543 B. C. came to it from Gaya to establish his religion, which he would not have done had it not been then a great centre (I. B. C. pp. 63, 64 : chd. p. 96).

พาณิช   pah-nit[6] *S. n.* a trader; a merchant (chd. p. 549) : การปิดท่าเรือเพื่อพาณิชการ a commercial blockade : พาณิชกรรม commerce.

พาณิชย์   pah-nit[6] *P. S. n.* traffic; trade; commerce; merchandise (chd. p. 549 : S. E. D. p. 939).

พาณินี   pah-ni[6]-nee *S. n.* a danseuse; an actress; a clever or intriguing woman; an intoxicated woman (S. E. D. p. 939).

พาณี ๑   pah-nee *P. n.* sound; words; diction; speech; language; used in reference to Saraswati, wife of Brahma, the goddess of Speech and Learning, inventress of the Sanskrit language and patroness of the Arts and Sciences (H. C. D. p. 284).

พาณี ๒   pah-nee *P. S. n.* a speaker (S. E. D. p. 939).

พาด   pat[3] (see ก่าย p. 96) *v.* to place or lean something against another (as a ladder propped against a house) : พาดบ่า to place or wear upon the shoulder : พาดพะอง to place a ladder or stepping pole (against a tree); see พะอง p. 580 : พาดพิง to be connected with, attached to or leaning on another (as servants relying on the protection of their masters); to refer to, or cite another's testimony, evidence or statements.

พาต, ลม   pat[3] *P. S. n.* air; wind; wind emitted from the body; name of the god of Wind (S. E. D. p. 934).

พาท   pat[3] *P. S. n.* words; speech; talk utterances; a discourse (S. E. D. p. 939).

พาทย์   pat[3] *S. n.* instrumental music (S.E.D. p. 940).

พาธ, พาธา   pat[3] *P.S. n.* an annoyance; affliction; distress (chd. p. 76); a tormentor; a harasser; pain; trouble; injury; damage; danger (S. E. D. p. 728).

พาน ๑   parn (see พบ p. 561; ปะ p. 516; ปะทะ p. 517) *n.* a metal or gilded tray supported on a pedestal.

พาน ๒, ปื้น   parn *P. n.* a gun; an arrow (chd. p. 80).

พานร   pah-norn *P. n.* a monkey; an ape (chd. p. 548).

พานรินทร์, พานเรศ   pah-na[6]-rin *n.* the king or chief of monkeys.

พาม, วาม   parm *adj.* left; reverse; inverted; opposite (chd. p. 548).

พาย ๑   pai *v.* to paddle (a boat): *n.* a paddle; a spatula.

พาย ๒   pai *P. S. n.* a thread; a strap; a leader; a guide (S. E. D. p. 943).

พาย ๓   pai *P. n.* the wind; air (chd. p. 561); พระพาย angels of the wind and tempest (Ala. pp. 90, 185); the god of the Wind; Eolus (H. C. D. p. 343).

พ่าย (แพ้)   pai[3] *v.* to be defeated or vanquished; to flee; to lose (in a contest).

พายม้า, พลายม้า, ไพม้า   pai-mah[5] *n.* a kind of two-oared dug-out boat with curved, tapering stem and stern, with sideboards added (used in rivers and canals).

พายัพ   pah-yup[6] *P. S. n. lit.* "the quarter of the wind," *i. e.* the north-west (S.E.D. p. 943).

พายุ   pah-yoo[6] *P. S. n.* (violent) air; wind; storm; tempest (chd. p. 561): พายุเกตุ *lit.* "wind sign," *i. e.* dust: พายุโกณ *lit.* "wind corner," *i. e.* the north-west quarter: พายุโคจร the track or range of the wind: พายุชาต *lit.* "one born of the wind," *i. e.* Hanuman, a celebrated monkey chief. He was son of Pavana, "the Wind," by Anjana, wife of a monkey named Kesari. He was able to fly, and is a conspicuous figure in the Ramayana (H.C.D. p. 116): พายุทาร clouds: พายุเทพ the fifteenth lunar asterism, or the star

Arcturus, the principal star in the constellation Bootes : พายุบุตร *lit.* "son of the wind," *i. e.* Hanuman : พายุผล *lit.* "wind fruit," *i. e.* hail-stones ; the rainbow : พายุพ่าห์ *lit.* "having the wind as a means of transportation," *i. e.* smoke : พายุสขี *lit.* "having the wind for a friend," *i. e.* fire (S. E. D. p. 942).

พารณะ   pah-ra⁶-na⁶ *P. n.* an elephant (chd. [p. 550].

พารณานน see พักตรดุณฑ์ p. 580.

พารา   pah-rah *n,* a city.

พาราณส์ see พาณารส p. 582.

พาล ๑   parn *P. S. n.* hair of the head ; hair of animals ; the hairy tail of an animal (chd. p. 547) ; see ขน ๒ p. 138.

พาล ๒   parn *P. S. n.* a child ; used in reference to children it is divided into two periods, *viz.* ; พาลกุมาร from birth to five years of age ; พาลศิศุ from five to eight years of age : *adj.* young ; ignorant ; foolish (chd. p. 79) ; mischievous ; bad : พาลมฤค a fawn ; a doe in its first year.

พาลี   pah-lee *n.* the monkey king appearing in the Ramayana ; creases or convolutions of bone at the base of the horns of cattle or buffaloes.

พาลุก, วาลิกา, วาลุกา   pah-look⁶ *P. n.* sand (chd. p. 547).

พาโล   pah-loh *v.* to charge falsely ; to calumniate or defame another's character ; *colloquial form* พาโลโสเก.

พาไล see พะไล p. 580.

พาส see วาส

พาสน์ see วาสน

พาสนา see วาสนา

พาสุกรี, พาสุกี, วาสุกรี   pah-soo⁴-gkree *P. S. n.* three kings of the Nagas or serpents, who lived in Patala. The first is Vasuki

who was used by the gods and Asuras for a coil around the mountain Mandara at the churning of the sea. The second is Sesha king of the serpent race or Nagas, and of the infernal regions called Patala. He is a serpent with a thousand heads and was the couch and canopy of Vishnu whilst sleeping during the intervals of creation. The third is Takshaka, a chief of snakes and son of Kadru, a daughter of Daksha. She was mother of "a thousand powerful many-headed serpents, the chief amongst whom were Sesha, Vasuki and many other fierce and venomous serpents" (H. C. D. pp. 343, 291, 316, 138).

พาห, พาหุ   pah-ha⁴ *P. S. n.* the arm ; a horse ; a bearer ; a porter ; a vehicle or cart (chd. p. 545).

พาหนะ   pah-ha⁴-na⁶ *v.* to carry ; to bear along ; to carry off ; to experience (chd. p. 545) : *n.* any vehicle or conveyance ; the act of drawing, bearing or carrying : สัตว์พาหนะ a draught animal ; elephants ; horses ; bullocks (used as means of locomotion or transportation) : ยานพาหนะ mechanical means of locomotion or transportation (as boats or cars).

พาหา, พาห   pah-hah² *P. S. n.* the arm ; the forearm (chd. p. 76).

พาหิร, พาหิรกะ   pah-hi⁴-ra⁶ *P. adj.* external ; outside ; foreign ; heretical ; non-Buddhist ; external to the individual ; objective (chd. p. 77) : พาหิรุทยาน a garden or park in the out-lying districts of a city, country or territory ; a game preserve.

พาหุ, พาห   pah-hoo⁴ *P. S. n.* the arm ; the forearm (between the elbow and wrist) (chd. p. 77 : S. E. D. p. 730) : พาหุนฑ์ wings : พาหุทัณฑ์ *lit.* "arm-staff," *i. e.* a long arm ; a blow or punishment inflicted with the arm or fist ; a blow, punch or pound : พาหุมูล *lit.* "the arm-root," *i. e.* the axillary space or arm-pit : พาหุทธ์ *lit.* "arm-fight," *i. e.* a close fight (as boxing, wrestling) ; a wrestler, or

.boxer : พาหุรัด ornaments of gold, or any adjunct for the arms (as bracelets or shields): พาหุศิขร the upper part of the arm; the shoulder : พาหุสมภพ *lit.* "one born from the arm of Brahma," *i. e.* a king or royal ruler.

พาฬ pah-la[6] *P. n.* a beast of prey (as lions, tigers); a snake (chd. p. 547): พาฬี the feminine form of พาฬ.

พาฬหะ pah-la[6]-ha[4] *P. adj.* severe; heavy; hard; excessive (chd. p. 79).

พ่ำ see ป่ำ p. 526.

พ่ำลา (ช้าง) pum-lah *n.* a wild, vicious elephant; a rogue elephant; an elephant unsuitable for service.

พิกล, วิกล pi[6]-gkon *P. adj.* mutilated; maimed; impaired; imperfect; abnormal; defective; wanting in, or deprived of normal function (chd. p. 571): พิกลพิการ to be disabled by a deformity: ไม่มีตำแหน่งโดยพิกลการ to be incapable of holding an office owing to some imperfection.

พิกเลนทรีย์ pi[6]-gka[4]-len-see *P. S. n.* a monstrosity; a freak of creation; one having impaired or defective organs of sense (S. E. D. p. 593).

พิกัด pi[6]-gkut[4] *n.* tax, dues or duty; estimated duty to be paid; standard or limit of imposed dues; a term used in fixing the value of logs so as to calculate the rate of duty: ของต้องพิกัด taxable or dutiable goods or merchandise: พิกัดภาษี tariff.

พิกัติ pi[6]-gkut[4] *P. n.* a condition of change; an altered form or product; diversified pursuits, sorts or kinds (chd. p. 572).

พิการ, วิการ pi[6]-gkarn *P. S. adj.* changed; altered; lame; deformed; defective; imperfect; incomplete (chd. p. 572); a change in the form or nature; an alteration or deviation from any natural state; a transformation, modification or change of body or mental condition;

disease; hurt; injury; perturbation (S. E. D. p. 954).

พิกุล, พิกัน (ต้น) pi[6]-gkoon *n. Mimusops elengi (Sapotaceae)*, a tree found widely in the southern parts of India, in Burma, and Ceylon; and cultivated in various parts of the tropics. Children string the flowers into necklaces; women make an infusion of them for use as a cosmetic after bathing. The chief uses of the tree are medicinal. The leaves are commonly used in applications; they may be boiled and applied to the head as a cold compress for headache; pounded with *Nigella* seed, they may be applied inside the nose for ulceration; an alternative treatment is to burn the leaves and inhale the smoke. Their juice may be squeezed into the eye for sore eyes. The bark may be boiled along with tamarind bark in the decoction used as a lotion for skin complaints. The bark and flower may be made to yield an astringent tonic and febrifuge used in fever and for diarrhoea. The root is more often used internally. The young fruits are employed in a gargle for treating sprue, and in India they serve as a masticatory to fix loose teeth. The flowers are used in Java for diarrhoea. Unripe fruit, if eaten, causes costiveness. The ripe fruit can be eaten but is worth little. The timber is hard and heavy, and is used for oil-mills, piles, shafts, axles, naves of wheels, boats, cabinet-work, and walking-sticks. The sap-wood is pale red; the heart-wood is dark red, very fine-grained and with a bitter taste (V. P. p. 185 : MCM. p. 784 : Burk. p. 1475): พิกุลทอง (ต้น) *Erythroxylon burmanicum (Linaceae)* (V. P. p. 186).

พิเคราะห์, วิเคราะห์ pi[6]-kraw[6] *P. S. v.* to consider, examine, determine or reflect (mentally) (chd. p. 569); to analyze or examine critically.

พิฆน์ pik[6] *S. n.* a deterrent; trouble; misfortune; danger (chd. p. 531); an obstacle;

an obstruction; a barrier; rocks or stones in a river; rapids.

พิมเนศ, พิมเนศวร pik[6]-net[3] *S. n.* Ganesa, son of Siva and Parvati, and worshipped at the beginning of every enterprise as the remover of obstacles. He is always represented, as a round-bellied figure with an elephant's head and one tusk, and usually as holding a rosary, noose and elephant-goad, with a rat in attendance (Antiquities of India p. 21). According to mythology, Ganesa was conceived during Siva's interrupted yoga. The gods visited Siva, taking along with them the great elephant of Indra. Parvati was so terrified by the beast that the child she bore had the head of an elephant (B. de Zoete and W. Spies, Dance and Drama in Bali, p. 323).

พิฆาต pi[6]-kart[3] *n.* to kill; to destroy; to expel; see ฆ่า p. 219.

พิง ping *v.* to lean on or against; to depend [upon another.

พิจล see วิจล

พิจย, พิจัย pi[6]-chja[4]-ya[6] *P. S. n.* research; investigation (Chd. p. 566).

พิจาร, พิจารณ์, พิจารณา pi[6]-chjarn *P. n.* examination; investigation (Chd. p. 566).

พิจิต pi[6]-chjit[4] *P. S. v.* to seek, search, investigate, or examine; to gather together or collect (for careful consideration) (Chd. p. 567).

พิจิตร pi[6]-chjit[4] *P. S. adj.* variegated; painted; adorned; embroidered (Chd. p. 567); many-coloured; motley; various; diverse; strange; wonderful (S. E. D. p. 959).

พิชญ์ pit[6] *S. n.* a sage; a person of learning, experience, prudence, and foresight; see นัก- ปราชญ์ p. 447.

พิชย, พิชัย pi[6]-cha[6]-ya[6] *P. n.* victory; the condition of being victorious; triumph (Chd. p. 531); a contest for victory; a conquest (S. E. D. p. 960): พิชัยสงคราม a treatise describing strategic methods of gaining a victory in warfare.

พิชลิวบ้าน (นก) pit[6]-cha[6]-liew-barn[3] *n.* Burmese red-whiskered bulbul, *Elathea jocosa erythrotis* (Deig. N. H. J. S. S. VIII, 3, p. 140).

พิชิต, วิชิต pi[6]-chit[6] *P. v.* to gain a victory; to conquer: *n.* a master; one who has triumphed over; one who has gained or won a conquest (Chd. p. 571): พิชิตมาร *lit.* "one who conquered Mara," *i. e.* the Buddha.

พิเชียร, วัชระ pi[6]-chee-an *P. n.* a precious stone, gem or diamond; adamant; the thunderbolt of Indra; a stone which bores gems (Chd. p. 546).

พิฑูรย์, ไพฑูรย์ (preferred spelling), ไพรฑูรย์ pi[6]-toon *n.* lapis lazuli; the cat's eye.

พิณ pin *P. S. n.* the Indian lute, invented by Narada (พระนารท), chief of the heavenly musicians (H. C. D. p. 219). It is an instrument of the guitar class, usually having seven wires or strings, raised upon nineteen frets or supports, fixed on a long rounded board, to the end of which is fastened two large gourds. The compass is said to be two octaves, but there are many varieties, according to the number of strings (S. E. D. p. 1005): พิณน้ำเต้า gourd lute: พิณพาทย์, preferably ปี่พาทย์, a Thai orchestra, consisting of five or more pieces, *viz.,* ตะโพน a small two-faced drum, held on the lap and struck with both hands; an oboe; a kyeewain (gongs strung on a circular rack); basso xylophone; and drums of varying sizes: พิณพาทย์, ข้างตะเภา, มะโหรี, ระนาด (ปลา) *Therapon theraps* (*Theraponidae*) (Suvatti p. 132).

พิตรก, วิตก pi[6]-drok[4] *P. n.* reflection; thought; argument; reasoning (Chd. p. 586).

พิดาน see เพดาน p. 596.

พิโดร, ไพโดร pi[6]-don *v.* to be spread, disseminated or dissipated, scattered or diffused (as an odour or smoke).

พิถี pi[6]-tee[2] *P. n.* a row; a line; a road, a street or highway (Chd. p. 587).

พิถีพิถัน pi[6]-tee[2]-pi[6]-tun[2] *adj.* fussy ; punctilious regarding details ; over-particular about trifling things ; strict in religious observances ; see จู้จี้ p. 255.

พิทย์ pit[6] *S. n.* attainment ; achievement ; accomplishment : *adj.* acquiring ; gaining (S. E. D. p. 965).

พิทยา pit[6]-ta[6]-yah *S. n.* knowledge ; wisdom ; learning ; comprehension ; perception ; science ; philosophy ; scholarship (S. E. D. p. 963) : พิทยาคม the studying of the sciences : พิทยาคาร, พิทยามนเทียร, พิทยาลัย a school : พิทยาทาดา an imparter of knowledge ; a teacher ; a preceptor ; a tutor : พิทยาธร one possessed of the science of spells ; a group of supernatural beings dwelling in the Himalayas, attending upon Siva and possessed with magical power : พิทยาธรี the feminine form of พิทยาธร : พิทยาพล the power of magic : พิทยารัตน์ valuable knowledge ; the jewel of learning.

พิทักษ์ pi[6]-tak[6] *v.* to care for ; to watch over, keep carefully or protect ; see ดูแล p. 333.

พิทูร, วิทูร pi[6]-toon *P. S. adj.* knowing ; skilled ; wise (chd. p. 568).

พิเทศ pi[6]-tet[3] *P. n.* foreign ; another country (S. E. D. p. 966).

พิธาน, วิธาน pi[6]-tarn *P. S. v.* to allot ; to assign ; to appoint ; to fix, order or prescribe ; to provide (chd. p. 567).

พิธี, วิธี pi[6]-tee *P. n.* any prescribed act rite or ceremony ; a rule ; a formula ; an injunction ; a precept, law or ordinance (S. E. D. p. 968) : พระราชพิธี a royal ceremony ; a State function.

พิธุ pi[6]-too[6] *P. n.* the moon (chd. p. 568).

พิธุร pi[6]-too[6]-ra[6] *adj.* troublous ; troublesome ; vexatious ; separated ; departed.

พินทุ pin-too[6] *P. S. n.* a drop or globule (of water) ; a dot or spot (as a period) ; a symbol placed over the vowel " ◌ " (as " ◌ ") ; a high arithmetical notation equal to 10,000,000[7], or the initial figure followed by 49 cyphers (chd. p. 92) : พินทุกัปปี the act of placing an identification dot, circle or mark upon a corner of the robes worn by Buddhist monks in accordance with their code of ethics : พินทุผล, ไข่มุก a pearl.

พินพัง, พิ่นพั่ง pin-pung *adj.* abundant ; plenty ; multitudinous.

พินอบพิเทา pi[6]-naup[3]-pi[6]-tow *v.* to show reverence to ; to make obeisance ; to regard with respect or veneration ; see เคารพ p. 199.

พินัย pi[6]-nai *P. S. n.* a code of ethics ; law ; a regulation ; a rule of morals ; a legal fine or money charged by the Court ; name of a portion of the Buddhist scriptures ; discipline ; training (chd. p. 575) : พินัยกรรม์ a will or testament ; a schedule of legacies (made at time of death) : ทำพินัยกรรม์ to make a will.

พินาศ pi[6]-nart[3] *P. S. n.* ruin ; destruction ; loss ; perdition (chd. p. 575) ; utter loss ; annihilation ; decay ; death (S. E. D. p. 969).

พินิจ pi[6]-nit[6] *v.* to examine, consider or investigate ; to weigh the evidence of a problem or matter in dispute.

พินิต, พิเนต pi[6]-nit[6] *v.* to lead ; to advise ; to teach ; to rule over or control ; see แนะ p. 465.

พินิศจัย, วินิจฉัย pi[6]-nit[6]-chjai *P. S. v.* to give an ultimation ; to decide, judge or pronounce a verdict : *n.* a decision ; an opinion ; a firm resolve regarding (S. E. D. p. 971).

พิบัติ pi[6]-but[4] *P. n.* calamity ; adversity ; misfortune ; failure (chd. p. 580).

พิบัสสี, วิบัสสี pi[6]-but[4]-see[2] *P. adj.* wise ; seeing clearly (mentally) (chd. p. 580).

พิบาก pi[6]-bark[4] *P. n.* result ; product ; consequence ; fruits ; reward ; good or evil results ; retribution (chd. p. 579).

พิบุล, พิบูล   pi⁶-boon *P. S. v.* to be perfect, complete, full; to have ample or sufficient: *adj.* large; extensive; wide; great; abundant; numerous (S. E. D. p. 974); see เต็ม p. 373.

พิปริต   pi⁶-bpa⁴-rit⁴ *P. S. v.* to be reversed; to be opposite or contrary; to differ; to be wrong or false (Chd. p. 580); to be abnormal: *adj.* reversed; acting in a contrary manner; various; wrong; adverse; inauspicious; false; untrue (S. E. D. p. 974).

พิปลาส   pi⁶-bpa⁴-lat³ *P. S. v.* to be changed or reversed (from normal) (Chd. p. 580): *n.* reversal; change.

พิพักพิพ่วน see กังวล p. 83.

พิพากษ์, พิพากษา   pi⁶-park³ *v.* to judge or decide; to determine (after hearing the evidence): ผู้พิพากษา a judge.

พิพาท   pi⁶-part³ *P. S. v.* to quarrel, dispute or accuse (others) (Chd. p. 588); see เกี่ยง p. 126; ทะเลาะ p. 407.

พิพิธ   pi⁶-pit⁶ *P. S. adj.* various; manifold (chd. p. 589).

พิภพ, วิภวะ   pi⁶-pop⁶ *n.* world; universe; birth-place or origin; power; property; wealth; majesty; splendour; prosperity (chd. p. 566).

พิภัช   pi⁶-put⁶ *P. S. v.* to apportion; to divide; to distribute or share with; see แจก p. 260.

พิภาค   pi⁶-park³ *P. S. n.* division (chd. p. 665).

พิภัษณ์, พิเภก   pi⁶-peet³ *S. n.* a king of the giants appearing as a character in the Ramayana.

พิภูษณ์, วิภูษณ์   pi⁶-poot³ *P. n.* adornments (personal) (chd. p. 566).

พิเภกก์, พิเภก, พิเภทก์, สมอพิเภก   pi⁶-pet³ *P. n.* the Palmyra palm, *Terminalia belerica* (burk. p. 2136).

พิมพ์   pim *P. v.* to print; to cast in a form or mould; to type: *n.* mould; figure; image; pattern; print; imprint of: ตัวพิมพ์ printing type; type: ตีพิมพ์ to print; to strike off from a pattern: พระพิมพ์ศิลาจำหลัก votive tablets: พิมพ์แท่นหิน a lithograph printing machine: พิมพ์ดีด a typewriter: พิมพ์แท่น a type-printing machine: เรียงตัวพิมพ์ to set type: สำนักพิมพ์ a printing office or place: หนังสือพิมพ์รายวัน a daily news-paper.

พิมพา   pim-pah *P. n.* Nang Phimpha, otherwise called Yasodhara, wife of Prince Sidharta, her cousin, before he became a Buddha. She was a daughter of Suddhodana's sister Amita, married to Prince Supprabuddha (Ala. p. 211: chd. p. 92).

พิมพิสาร   pim-pi⁶-sarn² *P. n.* a king reigning over Magadha (the country of South Bihar, where the Pali language was spoken) (H. C. D. p. 183). He reigned during the time of the Buddha and was a convert of the Buddha (chd. p. 92).

พิมโพหนะ   pim-poh-ha⁴-na⁶ *P. n.* a pillow (chd. p. 92).

พิมล   pi⁶-mon *P. S. adj.* spotless; pure; clear (chd. p. 573).

พิมเสน (ต้น)   pim-sen² *n. Pogostemon patchouli* (*Labiatae*); *P. cablin*, an herbaceous shrub 3 to 4 feet high, cultivated for the sake of the oil obtained from the leaves and shoots. This is used in perfumes, scented soaps, etc. The young shoots are cut about 6 months from planting and dried in the sun preparatory to the extraction of the oil by distillation. The production and distillation of the oil has been pushed somewhat in the Peninsula, dried leaves even being imported to cope with the demand. The camphor-like crystals are pulverized and inhaled, serving the same purpose as smelling-salts. Leaves are sometimes placed in books to keep insects away. The plant flowers rarely, so rarely that such flowering is an event to be recorded (MCM. p. 399 : BURK. p. 1782) : พิมเสนมัน a species of juicy mango.

พิมาน   pi⁶-marn *P. S. n.* a celestial mansion, abode or residence; a pagoda or palace of seven stories, the abode of devas (chd. p. 574); heaven, a dwelling-place of angels; the palace of an emperor or supreme monarch; any mythical, self-moving, aerial car.

พิมุข   pi⁶-mook⁶ *P. S. adj.* averted (chd. p. 574); having the face averted, turned backwards or turned away from; disappointed; downcast; averse or opposed to (S. E. D. p. 980).

พิโมกข์, พิโมกษ์   pi⁶-moke³ *P. v.* to be freed, escaped or delivered from : *n.* release (from human passions); escape; deliverance; salvation; Niravana; annihilation (chd. p. 574).

พิโยกพิเกน   pi⁶-yoke³-pi⁶-gken *v.* to be uncertain (in actions); to waver, falter or be irresolute (in one's purposes).

พิโยค   pi⁶-yoke³ *P. v.* to be separated from; to be left destitute, deprived of or absent from (chd. p. 589) : *n.* separation; deprivation; loss; death; see จาก p. 243.

พิร, พีร   pi⁶-ra⁶ *P. S. n.* a hero; a strong or mighty person : *adj.* strong; mighty; heroic (chd. p. 582) : พิเรนทร์, วิเรนทร์ a hero; one mighty or formidable to the enemy; a great or valiant warrior; a king or sovereign; see กล้า p. 60.

พิรากล   pi⁶-rah-gkon *adj.* sly; tricky; cunning; deceptive.

พิราพ   pi⁶-rap³ *n.* a cry (of pain or sorrow); a condition of mourning; a demon or giant appearing as a character in the Ramayana.

พิราม   pi⁶-ram *S. v.* to stop; to pause; to cease; to come to an end; to abandon, abstain or desist from (S. E. D. p. 982) : *n.* a name for Vishnu.

พิราลัย   pi⁶-rah-lai *n.* death (used for

officials with rank of สมเด็จเจ้าพระยา); the place of abode of Indra and warriors; heaven.

พิริยะ   pi⁶-ri⁶-ya⁶ *n.* strength; vigour; fortitude; energy; exertion; influence (Ala. p. 184 : chd. p. 582); patience; diligence; bravery; a warrior : พิริยพฤนท์ a group, company or band of warriors; soldiers : พิริยโยธา fearless soldiers; brave and experienced militia.

พิรุณ, วรุณ, พรุณ   pi⁶-roon *n.* rain; water; the ocean : พระพิรุณ the god or guardian spirit of the sea, water or rain; see พระวรุณ p. 427.

พิรุธ, วิรุธ   pi⁶-root⁶ *P. S. v.* to hinder, obstruct or beseige; to encounter opposition from; to be impeded or checked (S.E.D. p. 983) : *n.* fault; vice; defect : คนพิรุธ a culprit : จับพิรุธได้ to detect falseness, wrong actions, or irregularities in conduct or in respect to a trust.

พิรุฬห์   pi⁶-roon *P. S. n.* a guardian deity presiding over the south point of the compass : *adj.* blossoming; growing; blooming (chd. p. 582).

พิเราะ   pi⁶-raw⁶ *Cam. adj.* agreeable to the ear; musical; harmonious; melodious; *Thailand* ไพเราะ.

พิโรธ   pi⁶-rote³ *P. v.* to be angry, hostile or adverse towards : *n.* an enemy or opponent : *adj.* opposing; obstructing (chd. p. 582).

พิโรธนะ   pi⁶-rote³-na⁶ *P. n.* anger; wrath; ire; opposition; contradiction (chd. p. 582).

พิไร   pi⁶-rai *adv.* pitifully; mournfully (as grumbling or murmuring).

พิลังกาสา   pi⁶-lung-gkah-sah² *n.* a species of medicinal tree with dark green leaves and purplish small edible fruit, *Ardisia littoralis* (*Myrsinaceae*) (Burk. p. 220).

พิลาป   pi⁶-lap³ *P. S. v.* to moan; to bewail; to lament; to wail; to deplore; to utter moaning sounds; to complain irrationally (from

excessive grief) : *n.* lamentation (chd. p. 573) :
พิลาป (นก) a pigeon (*Columbidae*).

พิลาลส, ลาลส pi[6]-lah-lot[6] *P. n.* thirst
for ; avidity ; passion ; ardent desire (chd.
p. 218).

พิลาส pi[6]-lart[3] *S. v.* to assume a haughty
or pompous attitude ; see กรีดกราย p. 53 : *n.*
sport ; play ; pastime ; pleasure : *adj.* light ;
bright ; clear ; shining forth ; manifested
(S. E. D. p. 985).

พิลึก pi[6]-leuk[6] *adj.* strange ; terrible ;
funny ; curious ; astonishing : พิลึกจริง this
is very strange.

พิโลน, สุกใส pi[6]-lone *adj.* lustrous ; shining.

พิโลล pi[6]-lone *S. adj.* moving to and fro,
or from side to side ; rolling ; waving ; tremulous (S. E. D. p. 986).

พิไล, งาม pi[6]-lai *adj.* pretty ; beautiful ;
attractive.

พิศ pit[6] *v.* to gaze or stare at ; to look at.

พิศวกรรม, วิศวกรรม, เวสสุกรรม pit[6]-
sa[4]-wa[6]-gkum *P. n.* name of the celestial architect who acts as an expert artist and architect
to the devas (gods) (chd. p. 585) ; Civil Engineering Department of the University.

พิศวง pit[6]-sa[4]-wong[2] *v.* to be in doubt
about ; to be amazed or puzzled about ; to be
suspicious of or uncertain about ; see เคลือบ-
แคลง p. 209.

พิศวาส, วิศวาส pit[6]-sa[4]-wat[4] *P. S. n.* intimacy ; familiarity with ; confidence ; trust
(chd. p. 585) ; faith ; reliance (S. E. D. p. 995).

พิศาล, ไพศาล, วิศาล pi[6]-sarn[2] *S. adj.*
broad ; wide ; extensive ; great ; spacious ; important ; powerful (chd. p. 583).

พิสุทธ์, วิสุทธ์, วิสุทธิ์ pi[6]-soot[4] *P. n.*
purity ; holiness ; rectitude ; correctness (chd.
p. 586) : *adj.* pure ; clean ; immaculate ; white ;
innocent ; without blemish.

พิเศษ, ไพเศษ pi[6]-set[4] *P. S. n.* distinction ;
discrimination ; specification ; kind ; superiority ; peculiar merit or advantage : *Thailand*
adj. special ; specific ; distinguishing ; particular (S. E. D. p. 990).

พิษ pit[6] *P. n.* poison ; venom ; anything
actively injurious ; harmful alkaloids (chd.
p. 583) : พิษกัณฐี *lit.* "one having poison at
the neck," *i. e.* a descriptive epithet for Siva
(from having swallowed the poison produced
at the churning of the ocean which stained
his neck blue and gained for him the name
"Nila-Kantha," "blue neck") : พิษกุมภ์ a
jar of poison : พิษดุลย์ dangerous (as a
poison) ; fatal ; deadly : พิษนาศน์ *Mimosa*
sirissa, used as an antidote against poisoning :
พิษคฤงคี *lit.* "one having a poisonous sting,"
i. e. a wasp ; a hornet : พิษสมโยค a cake or
lump of colouring matter or dye ; vermilion :
พิษานน *lit.* "one with a poisonous mouth (or
fangs)," *i. e.* a snake ; serpents : พิษาร poisonous or venomous snakes.

พิษณุ, วิษณุ pit[6]-sa[4]-noo[6] *S. n.* Vishnu ; *lit.*
"to pervade," *i. e.* the second god of the Hindu
triad. As preserver and restorer, Vishnu is a
very popular deity, and the worship paid to
him is of a joyous character. His wife is
Lakshmi or Sri, the goddess of Fortune. His
vehicle is the bird, Garuda. He is represented
as a comely youth of a dark-blue colour and
dressed like an ancient king. He has four
hands, one holding the conch-shell ; the second
a chakra or quoit weapon ; the third a club ;
the fourth a lotus. He is sometimes represented seated on a lotus with Lakshmi beside
him or reclining on a leaf of that plant (H. C. D.
p. 360).

พิษณุโลก pit[6]-sa[4]-noo[6]-loke[3] *n.* Bhisanulok. Ancient names are Bisnuloke, Visnu-
loke, เมืองสองแคว. The town of Bhisanulok is
located on the Nan river about 389 kms.
north of Bangkok and is the seat of government for a province occupying an area of

about 6000 sq. kms. The greater part of the area is mountainous, abounding in teak forests. The Sak (ส้ก) and Yom (ยม) rivers also flow through this province. Being well watered, the region raises much rice. Paddy, fish, teak and other timbers are exported. Small quantities of copper are found in some of the umphurs.

Bhisanulok was once one of the ancient capitals of Thailand. The site of the original Bhisanulok was a small town on the Nan river some 9 kms. to the south of the present city. This dated from the time of Cambodian supremacy over Thailand. When the Thai regained their independence, this town was removed to the present site and was called เมืองสองแคว. About the year B. E. 1900 (1357 A. D.) King Lu Tai (ลิไทย), a ruler of Muang Chieng San, also called Sri Dumma Traipataka from his thorough knowledge of the Buddhist scriptures, built walls and forts around the city to insure its peace against attacking enemies.

Some time during the Ayuthian period (1350–1767 A. D.) the name was changed to Bhisanulok in honour of the god Vishnu (วิษณุ). During the reign of the king Barom-Trai-Loka-nat (สมเด็จพระบรมไตรโลกนารถ) (1463 A. D.), Bhisanulok became a capital city for 25 years. During this time many royal palaces and magnificient temples were built. Two famous images of the Buddha were cast in Bhisanulok in B. E. 1907 (1364 A. D.) by order of King Lu Tai. One is พระพุทธชินราช now in Wat Su-tat; the other, พระพุทธชินศรี, was brought to Bangkok during the reign of King Phra Nang Klao and placed in วัดบวรนิเวศน์.

พิษัย, พิสัย, วิสัย, วิสย pi-sai[2] *P. S. n.* district; region; country; realm; domain; range; sphere; scope (of authority or work) (chd. p. 584).

พิสดาร pit[6]-sa[4]-darn *P. S. n.* extension; expansion; wideness; amplification; diffuseness (S.E.D. p. 1001): *Thailand adv.* minutely; intricately; particularly; exactly.

พิสมร pit[6]-sa[4]-morn[2] *n.* a small square talisman, charm or amulet worn around the neck or waist.

พิสมัย, วิสมัย pit[6]-sa[4]-mai *P. S. n.* love; joy; gladness: *adj.* worthy of praise, wonder, surprise, amazement, perplexity or bewilderment (S. E. D. p. 1002).

พิสัช pi[6]-sat[4] *S. v.* to send forth; to emit; to throw off or shoot; to let go or dismiss; to leave or forsake (chd. p. 585); see ทิ้ง p. 414.

พิสัญญู, วิสัญญู pi[6]-san[2]-yee *adj.* unconscious; having lost feeling: *n.* a state of anesthesia.

พิสัฏฐ์ pi[6]-sit[4] *P. S. adj.* precious; excellent; noble; superior (chd. p. 584).

พิสุทธ์ pi[6]-soot[4] *adj.* pure; clear; clean; sparkling; see บริสุทธ์ p. 471.

พิสูจน์ pi[6]-soot[4] *v.* to show or prove by experiment; to convince by proof; to weigh the evidence of; see ชี้ p. 297: พิสูจน์ลุยไฟ to prove innocency by the ordeal of fire (àn ancient practice).

พิหค pi[6]-hok[4] *P. n. lit.* "one going in the air," *i. e.* a bird: พิหคเนทร์ the king or chief of birds.

พิหาร, ไพหาร, วิหาร, อุโบสถ pi[6]-harn[2] *P. n.* dwelling; monastery; temple; a Buddhist monastery or convent; a state or condition of life (chd. p. 569); the present time meaning is, the sanctuary where an image of the Buddha is placed (as is seen in all temple enclosures).

พิฬาร pi[6]-larn *P. n.* a cat (chd. p. 92).

พี pee *adj.* large; big; fat; stout: พงพี an extensive thicket.

พี่ pee[3] *n.* elder brothers or sisters; a prefix to the name of one older than the speaker though unrelated: พี่เขย an elder sister's husband: พี่ชาย an elder brother: พี่น้อง kinsfolk; relatives; brethren: พี่น้องชาย male relatives: พี่เลี้ยง a nurse; a benefactor : พี่สาว an elder sister : พี่สะใภ้ an elder brother's wife.

พี, นี้ pee[5] *adj.* this ; see นี้ p. 461.

พืชะ, พืช, พืชคาม pee-cha[6] *P. n.* seed ; a germ ; cause ; origin ; source ; germination (chd. p. 92) : พืชคณิต algebra : พืชคาม transplanted seedlings, plants, shoots or sprouts (in contradistinction to ภูตคาม permanently planted plants or sprouts) : พืชดิน climate : พืชพรรณ species ; family (of various grains or vegetables) : หว่านพืช to sow grain or seeds.

พีไพ้ see กันดาร p. 86.

พีร see พีร p. 589.

พึง purng *v.* (a sign of the imperative) ; ought ; should ; must ; to be required by necessity : พึงเข้าใจว่า you must understand that : พึงใจ agreeable to ; satisfied with ; suitable for ; see ชอบ p. 284 : พึงชัง ought to be hated : พึงไป should or ought to go.

พึ่ง purng[3] *v.* to ask or seek the protection or help of (as in time of distress) : *adj.* first : *adv.* just ; but now ; a moment ago ; this moment : พึ่งถึง just having arrived : พึ่งทำ beginning to do it just now.

พับ, เร็ว purp[3] *adv.* quickly ; suddenly ; unexpectedly : *onomat.* from the sound made when a bird suddenly darts up and flaps its wings in flight.

พืม, พืมพื purm *onomat.* from the sound of muttering, or grumbling softly or half-audibly.

พืด purt[3] *n.* row ; line ; file or stretch (as infantry, hedges or trees) : เหล็กพืด a sheet of iron (as the blade of a saw, or hoops for a bucket).

พืน purn *n.* floor ; foundation ; pavement ; base ; a flat extensive surface or stretch of land. ผ้าพื้น a plain woven loin-cloth : พื้นดิน the surface of the ground : พื้นเพ a condition, state, class or social grade (of people or families) : พื้นเสีย *colloquial* to get angry or have the feelings rumpled ; see โกรธ p. 133 : พื้นที่ area of land.

พุ poo[6] *v.* to gush up ; to be forced out (as gas or steam) : น้ำพุ a fountain or spring : พุพอง a skin disease characterized by small pustules in the first stages, which, owing to the severe itching and burning, become ulcers of varying sizes by scratching.

พุก pook[6] *n.* field rats (with white bellies) ; porcelain electric wire insulators (nailed to the wall) ; a cleat of wood nailed to a post for additional support.

พุกาม, พูกาม, พะม่า (p. 579) poo[6]-gkarm *n.* Burma : ชาวพุกาม, ชาวพะม่า Burmese.

พุง poong *n.* belly ; abdomen : พุงพวง, พุงพ่วง corpulent ; obese ; portly ; plethoric ; pursy (especially in respect to the abdominal region) : ไส้พุง entrails ; see ท้อง p. 404.

พุ่ง poong[3] *v.* to throw ; to thrust ; to project (as a javelin) ; to spout or gush out ; to send forth or break out by some internal force (as an oil or gas well) ; to dart or shoot in or out suddenly (as forces into a citadel) : ผีพุ่งได้ a falling star.

พุงแก, พุงขี้ (ต้น) poong-gkaa *n.* *Capparis siamensis (Capparidaceæ)*, the caper-bush (V. P. p. 190 : BURK. p. 443 : cb. p. 84).

พุงดอ (ต้น) poong-daw *n.* *Azima sarmentosa (Salvadoraceæ)*, a thorny creeper whose black-headed thorns about 3/4 inch long, produced from every joint, cause severe pain in a wound even when pulled out. The plant is found in Thailand but not in the too-moist Malay Peninsula (V. P. p. 190 : BURK. p. 276).

พุงทะลาย *Thailand* (for seeds only), สำรอง *Thailand, Krat* and *Chantabun* (ต้น) poong-ta[6]-lai *n.* *Sterculia acerifolia (Sterculiaceae)*

(MCM. p. 178); *S. sp.*, a moderate-sized tree with large, glossy, angular, palmate leaves, which produces large masses of brilliant red blossoms. The fruit, when soaked in water, swells out and, when sugar is added, is used as a refreshing drink (CB. p. 170); *S. scaphigera* (V. P. p. 190).

พุงปลา (ต้น)   poong-bplah   *n.* *Dischidia rafflesiana* (*Asclepideae*), an ephiphyte with leaves of two kinds—(1) flat and fleshy, (2) deeply saccate, affording nesting-places for ants of the genus *Iridomyrmex*, into whose nests in turn the plant thrusts its roots. It is found from Tenasserim to Borneo and Java; in the Peninsula it is found where the air is laden with moisture, near the sea and on the mountains (MCM. p. 464: BURK. p. 847).

พุทฒ์, พุฒ see พฤทธ์ p. 570.

พุทฒิ, พุฒิ see พฤทธ์ p. 570.

พุด (ต้น)   poot[6] *n.* *Ervatamia coronaria* (*Apocynaceae*), a species of bush bearing white fragrant flowers. It probably came from northern India. It is often double-flowered, and has curious differences in the length of the style. The pulp on the seeds is used in the Himalayas as a red dye, and the wood is used medicinally as a refrigerant, burned for incense, and used in perfumery. The Malays use it medicinally in various ways. The leaves are pounded with sugar-candy and water, exposed for a night to the dew, then the infusion is administered for coughs. In the Dutch Indies an extract of the roots is given to stop diarrhoea; and in the Moluccas is used for various abdominal complaints. The pounded roots are applied to sore eyes. In Kedah the leaf is applied to the heads of infants as a fetish (V. P. p. 192: BURK. p. 941): พุด, พุดจีน, พุดใหญ่ *Gardenia augusta* (*Rubiaceae*), the gardenia, a native of China and perhaps Japan. The Chinese, at some remote time, selected and fixed the double-flowered bush, which is more familiar outside China than the single-flowered one. Its double flowers have two, or three or, rarely, four tiers of petals. The leaves and roots have medicinal uses (BURK. p. 1057): พุดนา (ต้น) *Gardenia obtusifolia* (*Rubiaceae*), used medicinally by the Thai (V. P. p. 193).

พุดตาล (ต้น)   poot[6]-dtarn   *n.* *Hibiscus mutabilis* (*Malvaceae*), a Chinese plant which has been cultivated in that country from remote times. The three familiar races are, (1) rose-pink flowered and double, (2) white flowered and double, (3) changing from white to pink, and also double. The single-flowered rose-pink parent is wild in China, and also cultivated, but perhaps not in Malaya. The Chinese use the flowers for pulmonary complaints and import them into the Malay Peninsula in a dried state. Also, they apply the leaves to swellings. There is some fibre of inadequate strength in the bark. *H. mutabilis rosea*, 5 to 6 feet high and having large pink flowers (V. P. p. 193: MCM. p. 111: BURK. p. 1167).

พุทธ   poot[6]   *P. n.* a Buddha; a supreme Buddha; Gotama Buddha or Sakyamuni. A Buddha is a man possessed of infinite and infallible knowledge. He spends his life in preaching this knowledge to men under the name of the Truth. He thus becomes the Saviour of mankind, for, by knowing the Truth, and living a life in accordance with its precepts, men are redeemed from the misery of existence, and attain Nirvana or the annihilation of being. The supernatural knowledge of a Buddha is earned by a long course of probation in countless existences, during which he practices in the most perfect manner such virtues as charity, self-sacrifice and truth, and, in so doing, voluntarily and repeatedly undergoes the severest sufferings and privations. At his death the Buddha ceases to exist. Innumerable Buddhas have already appeared and, of some of the last, the names and a few other details are preserved.

The present dispensation is that of Gotama
Buddha, who was born as a royal prince
in the year 622 B.C. at Kapila Vastu, a
city on the river Rohini, an affluent of the
Rapti, which was the capital of Suddhodana,
the father of Gotama Buddha (H. C. D. p. 150;
see กบิลพัสดุ p. 7). He attained Buddhahood
in 588 and died in 543 B.C. at Kusinagari not
far from the place of his birth (chd. p. 96).
Gotama Buddha was the founder of Buddhism. Vishnu's ninth incarnation is that of
Gotama Buddha (H. C. D. p. 64). "The Wise"
is the principal title of every Buddha (Ala. p.
163). พุทธ is not a proper name but an appellation given to one who has attained enlightenment in the same way as Gotama Buddha:
พุทธกาล, พุทธสมัย the period of a Buddha; during the dispensation of the Buddha (chd. p.
96): พุทธจักร the sphere of influence or
power of Buddhism; the extent of the Buddha's power or wisdom; see จักร p. 237:
พุทธภูมิ the degree or condition of a Buddha;
Buddhaship (chd. p. 95): พุทธศักราช the
Buddhist Era, dating from the death of the
Buddha, 543 B.C. To convert the Christian
Era into the Buddhist Era, add 543 to the year
A. D. to be converted: พุทธศาสนา the commandments, precepts or religion of the Buddha
(chd. p. 96): พุทธังกูร, พุทธางกูร an embryo
Buddha; one destined to become a Buddha
(chd. p. 95): พุทธันดร the period between
the death of one Buddha and the appearance
of another (chd. p. 95): พุทธุปบาทกาล the
appearance or birth of a Buddha in the world
(chd. p. 96).

พุทธชาต (ต้น) poot[6]-ta[6]-chart[3] *n.* a species
of white flowering bush of the *Gardenia*
family; *Jasminum auriculatum* (V. P. p. 193).

พุทธรักษา (ต้น) poot[6]-ta[6]-ruk[6]-sah[2] *n.*
Canna sp. (Cannaceae), a handsome herbaceous perennial 3 to 5 feet in height with
tumeric-like tubers and with variously coloured flowers (V. P. p. 194; Burk. p. 435).

พุทธิ poot[6]-ti[6] *P. n.* understanding; knowledge; intelligence (chd. p. 96).

พุทรา, พุดซา *Thailand*, **มะตัน, มะตันหลวง**
N. Laos, **มะท้อง** *Karen, Kanburi* **(ต้น)**
poot[6]-sah *n.* *Zizyphus jujuba (Rhamnaceae)*, Indian jujube or Chinese date, a small
thorny, spreading tree found chiefly in dry
districts of India, China and Malaya. There
are many varieties but China seems to
have the greatest number. It has been
estimated that there are 300 to 400 races
there, where the fruits are candied in sugar
syrup and known as "honey date" or "zour."
In Java it grows wild throughout the low
country. In India, coming down from sanskritic times, the fruit has been held to purify
the blood, and to aid weak digestion. At
the present time, the bark and seeds are given
as a remedy for diarrhoea, and the root in the
form of a decoction for fever. The powdered
root and a poultice of the leaves are used on
wounds. The bark will tan. The lac-insect
feeds on the tree. The fruit is the size of a
large cherry, yellowish in colour, with a hard
kernel (MCM. p. 272; Cb. p. 298; Burk. p. 2305).

พุธ, ดาวพระพุธ poot[6] *P. S. n.* the planet
Mercury; one who is awake; one who is
intelligent, wise or learned: พุธชน a person
who knows; a wise man: พุธตาต *lit.* "the
father of the planet Mercury," *i. e.* the moon:
พุธทิน, พุธวาร Wednesday: พุธรัตน์ *lit.* "the
gem of the planet Mercury," *i. e.* emeralds.

พุ่ม poom[3] *n.* a bush; a shrub; a grove;
a floral piece made in the shape of a lotus
bud. This may be made of fresh or artificial
flowers or their imitation in wax. This is
then placed on a raised tray and given as a
lental offering to Buddhist monks; a fireworks
display where Roman candles are attached to
flexible bamboo strips fastened in tiers around
a pole. When lighted the whole resembles a
huge burning bush: พุ่มพวง fat, chubby
and beautiful; comely (used in regard to
girls); see งาม p. 223.

พุมเรียง (ต้น) see ชำมะเลียง (ต้น) p. 295.

พุ้ย (น้ำ) poo-ie[5] *v.* to paddle with short swift strokes (as in a boatrace); to splash water with the hands or dip out with a long-handled watering basket (as from the bottom of a brick- or sand-boat).

พู poo *n.* the sectional divisions or segmental partitions of fruit (as of the durian); a fold; a wrinkle; a ridge or crease; see กลีบ p. 62: ถั่วพู see ถั่ว p. 385.

พู่ poo[3] *n.* a tassel; a tuft; a pendant ornament (as a tuft of threads, or of horse or yak hairs, often seen hanging from behind the ears of war horses or elephants or from the bows of royal barges): พู่เรือหงส์, พู่ระหง, ภู่ระหงษ์ *Thailand,* หางหงษ์ *Laos* (ต้น) *Hibiscus schizopetalus (Malvaceæ),* bearing long drooping orange red or variegated flowers, having petals fringed, and reversed on slender arching branches (MCM. p. 112: cb. p. 160: V. P. p. 186).

พู่กัน poo[3]-gkun *n.* a brush-pen or painting brush (commonly used by the Chinese for writing): พู่กันรัศมี pencils of rays (as may be seen at the time of sunset).

พูกาม see พะม่า p. 579.

พูด poot[3] *v.* to speak; to discourse; to talk or say; see กล่าว p. 61: คนช่างพูด a loquacious person: คนพูดมาก a great chatterer; a chatter-box: พูดจา to carry on a conversation: พูดเพ่งเล็งถึง to indicate explicitly; to refer by implication to what has been said about some incident (either past, present or future): พูดโลนลามกในสาธารณสถาน to use obscene language in public places.

พูน poon *v.* to heap up to overflowing; to add more to or upon what is already full: *adj.* elevated; heaped; piled (up full).

พู้น poon[5] *pron.* that one: *adv.* yonder; there; thither; beyond; see โน้น p. 465.

พูม poom *adj.* gay; haughty; pompous;

bold; lofty (in demeanour): *adv.* smartly dressed; fully attired.

เพกา (ต้น) pay-gkah *n. Oroxylum indicum (Begoniaceae),* a tree with immense, slightly curved pods, almost the size of a cricket bat. The bark is a bitter tonic; the seeds have a thin, white, membranous, flat, circular wing (MCM. pp. 379, 461: V. P. p. 186).

เพ็ง incorrect spelling for เพ็ญ (p. 596).

เพ่ง peng[3] *v.* to stare at, or gaze intently at; see จ้อง p. 234.

เพ็จ pet[6] *adj.* dwarfed; under-sized; scrubby; diminutive; stunted; small (descriptive of shrubs, trees or plants): เพ็จไม้ bamboos which are of the smallest size though the toughest, and generally selected for canes.

เพ็ชฌฆาต pet[6]-cha[6]-kart[3] *n.* an executioner.

เพ็ชร pet[6] *n. lit.* "a hard or mighty one," *i. e.* a diamond; a thunderbolt (of Indra); adamant (S. E. D. p. 913): เพ็ชรกำมะลอ, เพ็ชรเทียม imitation diamonds (see กำมะลอ p. 104): เพ็ชรฆาต death by a thunderstroke (lightning): เพ็ชร-จรรม *lit.* "one with a hard (tough) hide," *i. e.* a one-horned rhinoceros, *Rhinoceros sondaicus:* เพ็ชรดา hardness; impenetrability; imperviousness: เพ็ชรคุณฑ์ *lit.* "one with a hard (strong) beak," *i. e.* a vulture; a mosquito: เพ็ชรทนต์ *lit.* "hard-tusked," *i. e.* a hog; a boar; a rat: เพ็ชรนาภ *lit.* "having a hard nave (as the hub of a wheel)," *i. e.* the fiery discus of Krishna: เพ็ชรปาณี *lit.* "thunderbolt-handed," *i. e.* one wielding a thunderbolt; a name for Indra; the state of being a wielder of a thunderbolt: เพ็ชร-ฤกษ์ a hard or clearly manifested omen (considered as a prophetic sign): เพ็ชรสังฆาต *Thailand* (ต้น) *Hylocereus undatus (Cactaceæ),* a climber with square-shaped stems, used medicinally by the Thai (cb. p. 783): เพ็ชรหึ่ง (ต้น) a species of giant orchid, *Grammatophyllum speciosum,* found from Tenasserim throughout Malaysia to the Solomon Isles. It has large ochre-yellow flowers blotched with brown. It is not recorded as medicinal among the Malays (V. P. p. 245 : BURK. p. 1109 : MCM. p. 145) : a tempest, tornado, typhoon or violent wind-storm : เพ็ชราวุธ *lit.* "one having a thunderbolt as a weapon," *i.e.* Indra (chd. p. 546).

เพ็ญ pen *Cam. adj.* full ; whole : พระจันทร์ ทรงเพ็ญ full moon.

เพทูรย์ see ไพทูรย์ p. 603.

เพณี, เวณี pay-nee *P. n.* hair ; a woman's hair simply plaited without ornament (chd. p. 563).

เพ็ดทูล pet⁶-toon *v.* to address, speak with, relate or report to princes of high rank.

เพดาน, พิดาน pay-darn *P. S. n.* ceiling ; wainscot ; the mouth ; speech ; utterance (chd. p. 542) : เพดานปาก the palate.

เพตร pet³ *S. n.* a cane ; a walking-stick ; the rod or mace of an officer ; the staff of a door-keeper (S. E. D. p. 1015).

เพท, เวท pet³ *P. n.* knowledge ; pleasure ; emotion ; excitement ; the (Hindu) Veda (chd. p. 562) ; the Veda or "divine knowledge." The Vedas are the holy books which are the foundation of the Hindu religion. They consist of hymns written in an old form of Sanskrit and were composed between 1500 and 1000 B. C. The Vedas are four in number, (1) Reg Veda ; (2) Yajur Veda ; (3) Sama Veda ; (4) Atharva Veda. The last is of comparatively modern origin. The other three are spoken of by Manu as the "three Vedas" and are said by him to have been "milked out as it were" from fire, air and the sun (H. C. D. p. 345).

เพทนา, เวทนา pet³-ta⁶-nah *S. n.* consciousness ; realization of pleasure, pain and indifference, being one of the five elements of corporal being (Ala. p. 172) ; feeling ; sensation ; perception ; pain ; suffering (chd. p. 561) : *Thai v.* to show mercy, pity or affection.

เพทาย pay-tai *n.* a zircon.

เพทุบาย, เพโทบาย pay-too⁶-bai *v.* to play a trick ; to use stratagem, craftiness or cunning means or methods.

เพ่นพ่าน see เกะกะ p. 124 ; กระจัดกระจาย p. 20.

เพไนย, เวไนย์ pay-nai *P. n.* a tractable, teachable or impressionable person ; one who can be converted to Buddhism (chd. p. 563).

เพ้ย pur-ie⁵ *v.* to remonstrate with ; to scold, or threaten angrily ; see ขู่ p. 162 ; ต่อว่า p. 347.

เพรง preng *adj.* former ; see ก่อน p. 68 ; เก่า p. 124.

เพรา prow *n.* morning : *adj.* beautiful ; see งาม p. 223 : เพรางาย late morning ; early noon : เพราพริ้ง beautiful ; bright.

เพราะ praw⁶ *adj.* melodious ; sweet-sounding ; agreeable to the ear ; tuneful : *adv.* by reason of : เพราะฉะนั้น therefore ; consequently ; for that reason : เพราะฉะนี้ thus ; in this case ; under these circumstances or conditions ; for this reason : เพราะว่า because ; since : เพราะเหตุอะไร why ; for what cause, purpose or reason.

เพริด prurt³ *adj.* lost ; wandering ; strayed (from a herd or company) ; at large ; at liberty (as buffaloes or elephants) ; see กระเจิดกระเจิง p. 23.

เพริศ (งาม) prurt³ *adj.* beautiful ; showy ; handsome : เพริศพราย, เพริศแพร้ว shining (implying the superlative degree of brilliance) ; glistening ; gleaming ; lustrous : sparkling (as diamonds).

เพรียก pree-ak³ *v.* to call : เพรียกพร้อง to call or shout for ; to cry ; to bewail or lament loudly for.

เพรียง pree-ang *n.* barnacles ; any of the numerous marine crustacea of the order

Cirripedia which, though free-swimming in the larva state, are permanently fixed in the adult state and are protected by a calcified shell of several pieces. From the opening of the shell the animal throws out a bundle of curved cirri looking like delicate curls. They adhere to rocks, flotsam, floating timbers and along the bottoms of boats or ships: พร้อม- เพรียง ready: หน้าเพรียง a pox-marked face.

เพรียม, พรีม, พรีมพราย pree-am[5] *adj.* prim; pretty; smiling; graceful; agreeable; เพรียมพราย gay; coquettish.

เพรียว pree-oh *adj.* tapering to a point; growing smaller by degrees; see ฉลวย p. 265: เรือเพรียว a long slender boat with tapering ends (used for racing purposes).

เพรื่อ preu-ah[3] *adj.* dispersed; irregular; going from place to place; disconnected: กินเพรื่อไป to eat promiscuously or a little, frequently: พูดเพรื่อไป to talk incoherently or disconnectedly.

เพรื่อง preu-ang *n.* a small bell; cattle bells; see กระดิ่ง p. 28.

เพล pen *S. n.* time; the hour for Buddhist monks to partake of the midday meal (S. E. D. p. 1018); see กาล ๒ p. 99: ฉันเพล to partake of the midday meal (this must end before twelve o'clock noon): เวลาเพล eleven a. m.

เพลง pleng *n.* song; harmony; melody; music: บทเพลง a hymn: เพลงปรบไก่, เพลงฉ่อย folklore songs sung by the peasants, especially during bright moonlight nights: ร้องเพลง to sing: เสียงเพลง the sound of singing or instrumental music.

เพลิด see เผลิด p. 550.

เพล้โพล้, พี้โพ้ play[5]-ploh[5] *adj.* desolate; waste; barren; vacant.

เพลา ๑ plow *n.* an axle; a shaft; a thill; a sail-yard; a stake or handle: *adj.* decreasing (in severity); improved (in condition); be-

coming less dangerous or virulent: กระดาษ- เพลา ancient paper made from the bark of *strebleus asper*; see ข่อย p. 148.

เพลา ๒ plow *Cam. n.* the thighs; the lap, or legs: พระเพลา same for royalty.

เพลา ๓ plow *P. n.* time of day; hour; period; occasion; limit of time (chd. p. 563); see คราว p. 181; กาล ๒ p. 99.

เพลาะ plow[6] *v.* to splice together (as rope or boards): *n.* a wild ox having distorted horns: เพลาะผ้า to sew the edges of cloth together: สนามเพลาะ a trench prepared for protection of soldiers.

เพลิง plerng *Cam. n.* flame; a blaze; fire: ถวายพระเพลิง to light the fire in a cremation ceremony for royalty: ลูกเพลิง sparks.

เพลิดเพลิน, เพลิน plert[3]-plern *adj.* interested; absorbed; amused; entertained (till forgetful of all other duties).

เพลีย plee-ah *v.* to be exhausted, tired, weak, or deprived of strength or energy; see ถอยกำลัง p. 382.

เพลี้ย, เพี้ย plee-ah[5] *n.* an insect that attacks rice-stalks (causing the death of the plants); the aphis, a plant-louse.

เพลี่ยง, พลาด plee-ang[3] *v.* to slip (as in falling); to turn aside (from the points in an argument or discussion); to miss the bull's eye (as in shooting): เพลี่ยงพล้ำ to err or make a mistake.

เพศ pet[3] *P. S. n.* form; body; kind or sort; dress; apparel; equipment; disguise (chd. p. 564); *grammar* gender, equivalent to ลิงค์.

เพส pet[3] *P. n.* the numeral twenty (chd. p. 583): เบญจเพส twenty-five.

เพ่อ pur[3] *v.* to cease; to discontinue; to desist; to stay; to stop: *adv.* this moment; just now; but only a moment ago; a sign of the present tense :   อย่าเพ่อก่อน wait for a moment :   อย่าเพ่อทำ to stop ; to cease now from doing :   อย่าเพ่อโกรธ do not get angry just now :   อย่าเพ่อไป to desist from going ; to wait a bit.

เพ้อ   pur[5] *v.* to be delirious :   พูดเพ้อเจ้อ to talk or speak nonsense, at random or thoughtlessly (as during delirium) :   พูดเพ้อ to talk incoherently ; to talk confusedly or without reflection (as during a high fever).

เพอิญ see เผอิญ p. 550.

เพะ   pa[6] *v.* to throw down carelessly ; to daub on roughly and abundantly (used in reference to paint, dammar, dirt from an excavation, or hair-oil).

เพา, พะงา   pow *adj.* beautiful ; see งาม p. 223 : เพาพะงา a beautiful, charming, attractive girl or lady.

เพาะ   paw[6] *v.* to plant, sow, propagate or make grow (as seeds, plants or ideas).

เพิกเฉย   perk[3]-chur-ie[2] *v.* to be inattentive, listless or negligent ; to be heedless or careless (as regards duty or instructions).

เพิง, พะเพิง   perng *n.* a low, projecting roof (from one side of Thai houses, forming a floorless protection from sun and rain or over a veranda) ; a lean-to.

เพิดเพ้ย   pert[3]-pur-ie[5] *v.* to shout at mockingly ; to laugh at in derision or ridicule.

เพิ่ม, เพิ่มพูน, เพิ่มเติม   perm[3] *v.* to add to or increase the amount of ; to enrich or exceed (what has already been given or promised) ; to amend by adding to : เพิ่มโทษ to augment a sentence or punishment.

เพีย (ปลา)   pee-ah *n. Ambassis ranga* (*Ambassidae*) (suvatti p. 122).

เพีย ๑   pee-ah[5] *n.* a conferred rank among the northern Thai or Laos officials, equivalent to Phya or First Grand Councillor.

เพีย ๒, เพลีย   pee-ah[5] *n.* a bamboo musical instrument held between the lips, the tongue of which is made to vibrate by striking the free end with a finger. It is similar to the จ้องหน่อง p. 234.

เพีย ๓ (ปลา) see กา (ปลา) p. 89.

เพียก *Thailand, Peninsula,* ตุงสอปลาไหล, เผือก *Thailand,* แฮบีนซ้น *Laos, Lampang* (ต้น)   pee-ak[3] *n. Eurycoma longifolia* (*Simarubaceae*), a small tree found from Tonkin to the Malay Peninsula, Borneo and Sumatra ; in the Peninsula it is probably throughout. The roots, and particularly the bark of the roots, are used as a febrifuge. The bark is intensely bitter, and is traded in sparingly, so that it is imported into Singapore from Borneo, though it is plentifully available in the Peninsula. The Malays give a decoction when a tonic is useful, as after child-birth. It is pounded and applied externally as a poultice for headache, on wounds, ulcers, and syphilitic sores. It is said that the fruits are used for dysentery (cb. p. 242 : V. P. p. 188 : Burk. p. 984).

เพียง, เพี้ยง   pee-ang *adv.* until ; about ; as ; as much as ; as far as ; equal to : ไกลเพียงใด about how far is it : แต่พอเพียง just sufficient for : เพียงดัง like ; as ; as aforesaid : เพียงใด until when ; how (far) ; how much more : เพียงนั้น that much ; that far, or equal to that (in distance, quantity, or price) : เพียงนี้ this much ; this far ; as much as ; equal to this : เพียงพอ, แต่เพียงพอ just sufficient ; middling ; not too much.

เพียงออ   pee-ang-au *n.* a bass flute, played as a companion to a soprano flute ; see ทุ้ม p. [419.

เพียชน์, วิชนี see พัชนี p. 580.

เพียน, เพี้ยน   pee-an *adj.* dissimilar or differing just a little ; not exactly alike, or correct : เขียนเพียนตัว to make a slight error in writing : เพียนผัด to put off ; to defer, delay or postpone ; to ask for a delay or postponement : เสียงเพี้ยน a discordant sound ; one a trifle out of tune.

เพี้ยน (ปลา) pee-an *n. Puntius stigmatosomus (Cyprinidae)*; *P. schwanefeldi* (suvatti pp. 30, 31).

เพียบ, เพรียบ pee-ap[3] *v.* to be loaded to the water's edge ; to be loaded to full capacity, or over-loaded : เจ็บเพียบ to be in a collapsed or moribund condition (from sickness or as the result of an accident) : เต็มเพียบ quite full, or too full.

เพียร pee-an *P. v.* to be diligent, industrious, persevering or brave (in trying to accomplish a task) : *n.* strength ; vigour ; energy ; fortitude ; exertion ; dignity (chd. p. 582) ; diligence ; patience ; see บากบั่น p. 479.

เพื่อ pur-ah[3] *prep.* in order that ; for the purpose of : เพื่อจะดู in order to see or observe : เพื่อว่า so that.

เพื่อน pur-an[3] *n.* companion ; friend ; comrade ; associates ; see เกลอ p. 122 : เพื่อนบ้าน neighbours.

แพ paa *n.* a raft : แพ *Thailand, Surat, Nakawn Sritamarat and Pattani,* หว้าขี้มด *Thailand, Krat,* แดงนา *Thailand, Chumpawn,* มัก *Thailand, Ranawng and Langsuan* (ต้น) *Eugenia polyantha (Myrtaceae),* a tall tree found in Burma and southwards throughout western Malaysia ; in the Peninsula it is found from the Thai border to Singapore. The wood is fairly hard, but splits on drying. It is used for house-building and is durable. The bark is considerably used in the Dutch Indies for tanning fishing-nets, and for colouring mats. For this purpose, it is pounded in water ; after straining, the split bamboos used for the matting are repeatedly dipped in the infusion, over two days. Then they are immersed in mud to blacken. An extract of the bark is given in Java for diarrhoea ; as, also, alternatively is an infusion of the leaves. The bark, root, and leaves are used by the Malays for poulticing for itch. In the Dutch Indies the young leaves are commonly eaten with food. The fruit may be eaten (cb. p. 656 : Burk. p. 973) : แพขาว *Thailand, Nakawn Sritamarat,* เม่าน้ำ *Thailand, Pattani,* หว้าน้ำ *Thailand, Krat,* กะปิโตร๊ะ *Khmer, Krat,* (ต้น) *Eugenia limnaea (Myrtaceae)* (cb. p. 650) : แพซุง a raft of logs or timber : เรือนแพ a house on bamboo floats.

แพ้ paa[5] to be defeated, beaten, overcome or conquered ; to have an idiosyncrasy or susceptibility to being poisoned (by some drug) ; to have an allergia to some food or remedy : แพ้แก่พิสูตร to be disproved by evidence or ordeal : แพ้เขา to be surpassed by another (as in a game, combat, or race) : แพ้ท้อง morning sickness ; a condition of early pregnancy : แพ้เปรียบ unequalled ; handicapped ; disadvantageous : แพ้ผม grey-haired while not yet old ; becoming grey unduly soon or early : แพ้ฟัน losing one's teeth unduly soon or early in life : แพ้เมีย losing one's wife unduely soon (either by death or by divorce) : แพ้ยา to feel the poisonous effects of a drug : แพ้รู้ to be foiled, balked, tricked, deceived or frustrated by another ; to fall into another's trap.

แพง pang *v.* to be considered precious ; to be worth conserving : *adj.* dear ; expensive ; costing much : ข้าวยากหมากแพง a condition of famine exists.

แพ่ง pang[3] *v.* to examine, investigate or look at intently or carefully : *n.* strength ; power ; force : *adj.* pretty ; beautiful : ศาลแพ่ง the Civil Court ; a lower tribunal.

แพงพวย, พังพวย *Thailand,* ผักปอดน้ำ *N. Laos* (ต้น) pang-puie *n. Jussiae repens (Onagraceae),* water-cress, an edible aquatic plant used as a vegetable in curries (cb. p. 733 : Burk. p. 1273 : V. P. p. 190) : แพงพวยป่า see ทะนนไชย p. 406 : แพงพวยฝรั่ง (ต้น) *Vinca rosea (Apocynaceae),* Madagascar periwinkle (mcm. pp. 136, 208) ; *Lochnera rosea (Apocyna-*

ceae), a slightly woody plant, with pretty white, or pink flowers, for the sake of which it was brought into cultivation in Europe in 1757. It is said that its seeds came from Madagascar, but it remains unexplained how this American plant came to be in Madagascar. It is injurious to cattle, but is reputed to be a remedy for diabetes. It has been found to contain a compound which has some of the properties of digitalin; it is thought that this is a useful substance.

แพทย์ pat[3] *n.* a physician; a doctor of medicine (Chd. p. 563): แพทย์ศาสตร์ the science of medicine.

แพน paan *v.* to spread, dilate, or expand (as the hood of a cobra); to assume a fan-shape (as the tail feathers of a bird): *n.* a flat, thin, fan-shaped article or object; a shield: รำ-แพน to strut with the tail feathers spread (as a peacock).

แพ่น paan[3] *v.* to strike with a heavy blow; to intrude rudely or violently.

แพร (ผ้าไหม) praa *n.* silk cloth.

แพร่ praa[3] *v.* to scatter or cause to diffuse, disperse, spread out or propagate; to disseminate or broadcast: แพร่หลาย to cause to disseminate; to be broadcasted or scattered in all directions; see กระจัดกระจาย p. 21.

แพรก praak[3] *v.* to branch off; to lead in diverging directions (as roads): (ต้น) *n. Cynodon dactylon (Gramineae)*, Bermuda grass, dub-grass, a creeping grass of all parts of the tropics, but not at home in the climates of Singapore and Kuala Lumpur. Vast amounts of hay are made from it in Bengal. It is very important in Java. It is also a perfect lawn grass. Towards its northern limits the value goes, as there it produces too little foliage, while freely spreading into places where it is not wanted. When it grows well its herbage attains a depth of 12-18 inches, and a single plant may cover

several square yards (MCM. pp. 71, 448: Burk. p. 729). It is one of the five auspicious articles used in religious offerings, and in the tonsure ceremony (Ger. (1) pp. 40, 64).

แพร่ง prang[3] to be separated or diverging; to branch off; to break off: *n.* cross-roads, or the point where roads or paths diverge: แพร่งพราย to disclose, make known, or publish abroad (as a rumour, gossip or secret).

แพรว, แพร้ว, แพรวพราย, พรายแพรว praa-oh *adj.* bright; sparkling; shining; luminous; twinkling; flashing.

แพลง plaang *v.* to be twisted, sprained or slightly dislocated; to be wrenched or diverted from a normal position (as a bone); see ตะแคง p. 352; บิด p. 483.

แพลม plaam *v.* to project or extend slightly from an orifice, edge or surface (as an erupting tooth).

แพละโลม plaa[6]-lome *v.* to make amorous advances; to flirt with or express ardent affection for.

แพ้ว paa-oh[5] *v.* to set up scarecrows (on trees or in fields): แพ้วจังหัน a whirling scarecrow; a whirligig: แพ้วธง a notice flag, or paper notices hung up in fruit gardens or fields: แพ้วนกแพ้วกา to scare birds or crows away by means of scarecrows.

แพศย์, เวศย์ paat[3] *P. S. n.* a member of the Varna (วรรณ) class or caste, being the third of the four castes established in the code of Manu, *viz.* merchants; traders; farmers; agriculturists (H. C. D. pp. 332, 336).

แพศยา, เวศยา paat[3]-sa[4]-yah[2] *P. S. n.* an harlot; a prostitute; a courtesan or "free lover" (S. E. D. p. 1019).

แพะ paa[6] ¯ *n.* the goat, a ruminant of the genus *Capra*. There are several species and varieties. The domestic goat is raised for its milk, flesh and skin: แพะ (ปลา) *Upeneus suphereus (Mullidae)*, red mullets; *U. tragu-*

la; *Puntioplites proctozsyron* (*Cyprinidae*)
(suvatti pp. 56, 135, 136).

โพ, โพธิ์ (ต้น). poh *n.* bodh-tree, pipal
tree, *Ficus religiosa* (*Urticaceae*), the most
sacred tree of India and Ceylon. This considerable tree begins its life epiphytically
and then strangles its host, or, on buildings,
its far-growing roots extend to the ground
and it establishes itself as an independent
tree. It is a native of the sub-Himalayan
tract, Bengal, and central India, whence it
has been extensively distributed by cultivation. It is a sacred tree among the Hindus.
It is also sacred among the Buddhists, as the
Buddha received enlightenment while sitting
under a bodh-tree. The clappers of the bells
of Thai and Burmese Buddhist temples are
often shaped like a leaf of this fig, and being
flat are easily moved by the wind so that the
least breeze produces a tinkle, tinkle of these
temple bells. The lac-insect feeds on this
tree (S. E. D. p. 734: Burk. p. 1013: MCM. p. 466):
โพขนุน (ต้น) *Ficus nervosa* (V. P. p. 187): โพ-
ทะเล *Thailand*, บากู *Malay*, *Pattani* (ต้น)
Thespesia populnea (*Malvaceae*), tulip tree,
Portia-tree, Pacific rose-wood, a small tree of
the coast, in appearance not unlike *Hibiscus
tiliaceus*, and like it in giving fibre, in consequence they share vernacular names. It is
found in all tropical Asia, in Africa, and in
the West Indies. It is common all round
the shores of the Malay Peninsula. The sea-
faring Malays, in the past, evidently relied
on the fibrous bark for caulking their boats
and for cordage. There is tannin in both bark
and wood. The timber is hard. The heart-
wood is dark red, smooth and durable. In the
Philippine Islands it is highly prized for musical instruments. In Malaysia and India it is
used for cart-wheels and other parts of carts,
gun-stocks, furniture, etc. Throughout much
of the Pacific the tree is sacred; it is planted
about temples. The wood gives an orange
yellow solution which dyes wool a deep brown;

it seems useless on silk. The capsules and
flowers also dye. The leaves and fruit are
medicinal with various uses. In Africa a thick
oil is sometimes extracted from the seeds (MCM.
p. 207: Cb. p. 162: V. P. p. 187: Burk. p. 2153):
โพบ้า *Thailand* (ต้น) *Thespesia lampas* (*Malvaceae*), a stiff, small shrub with a pretty
flower. It occurs wild in tropical east Africa,
Asia, and Malaysia, but not in the Malay
Peninsula, though it is found in Thailand.
In Java, where the plant finds the climate of
the teak forests favourable, so that it is
plentiful, its fibre is used, the stems being
retted that it may be extracted. The flowers
contain a dye (Burk. p. 2153); *T. macrophylla*,
a shrub. The flowers are bright yellow, with
a dark crimson centre (MCM. p. 142: Cb. p. 161:
V. P. p. 187): โพฝรั่ง *Thailand, Bangkok*,
หัสคุนเทศ *Thailand* (ต้น) *Kleinhovia hospita*
(*Sterculiaceae*), a small tree found from the
Mascarene Islands to Polynesia; in the Peninsula it is rather local, probably because its
seedlings can only grow if they obtain sunlight, and so it is restricted to sandy river-
banks and artifically opened places, being
found in Perak, Malacca, the islands off the
coast, and Singapore. The trunk is sometimes
knotty, and then the twisted wood is valued
for knife- and kris-handles. In eastern
Malaysia the juice of the leaves is regarded
as a good eye-wash. The bark and leaves are
poisonous, and the leaves are used as a hair-
wash to help to destroy lice. The bark is
fibrous, and where the tree is plentiful it is
used for rough cordage, but it does not last
(MCM. p. 89: Cb. p. 171: Burk. p. 1281).

โพก poke[3] *v.* to cover (by means of a cloth,
band or shawl): โพกหัว to cover or wrap
cloth around the head.

โพง pong *v.* to dip up or bail water out;
see ตัก p. 358: *n.* an irrigating apparatus
composed of a tripod with a long-handled
basket-dipper suspended (used by farmers).

โพงพาง pong-pang *n.* a form of deep-water fish or prawn trap, having long bag-nets attached to stakes placed in a line across water-ways. The nets are to be lowered or raised according to the condition of the tide.

โพชฌงค์ pote[3]-chong *n.* the seven requi-sites for attaining the supreme knowledge of a Buddha, *viz.* recollection; investigation; en-ergy; joy; calm; contemplation and equanim-ity (Chd. p. 93); the seven constituents of the highest wisdom, *viz.* memory; confidence; energy; joy; self-collection or quietude; re-search into law; and indifference (Ala. p. 196); a sutra (พระสูตร) or sermon recited by the talapoins for the benefit of those who are nearing death. In the Buddhist scriptures, a sutra is composed of words of the Buddha "strung together," as a sermon or dialogue. In Hindu scriptures, a sutra is a connected series of aphorisms (Gospel of Bud. p. 356).

โพธ ๑ pote[3] *P. S. n.* knowledge; wisdom; intelligence; astuteness; supreme knowledge (Chd. p. 93).

โพธ ๒ pote[3] *adj.* clever; beautiful; see ฉลาด p. 265: นางโพธ a beautiful maiden.

โพธิ poh-ti[6] *P. S. n.* the knowledge pos-sessed by a Buddha; supreme or infinite knowledge; omniscience; the Truth; Buddha-hood; the supernatural knowledge of an Arhat (Chd. p. 93); the illuminated or enlightened intellect; the sacred fig-tree (S.E.D. p. 734); the tree under which the Buddha sat during the meditation which raised him to omniscience. These are to be found in the grounds of almost every temple in Thailand (Ala. p. 163): โพธิญาณ the omniscience of a Buddha (Ala. p. 164); one who has attained to the state of saving truth; the state of one who has at-tained Nirvana. One who has walked in the "Four Paths" then enters Nirvana (Gos. of Buddha): โพธิสัตว์ a being who is passing come a Buddha (Ala. p. 163); a being destined through transmigrations on the way to be-to attain Buddhaship. This term is applied

to a Buddha in his various states of existence previous to attaining Buddhahood (Chd. p. 93); name of Gotama before he entered on his spiritual mission (Crawford's Embassy to Siam Vol. 2, p. 91); Gotama before attaining en-lightenment; any individual self-dedicated to the salvation of others and destined to the attainment of Buddhahood (Gospel of Bud. p. 352).

โพน pone *v.* to catch, capture, trap, decoy or snare (used regarding elephants); see จับ p. 241.

โพ้น pone[5] *adv.* in that place; there; yon-der; beyond; far off; see โน้น p. 465.

โพนทะนา pone-ta[6]-nah *v.* to speak evil of, or about; to defame another's character.

โพยเพน pone-pen *v.* to sway, swing or wobble (back and forth); to lean to one side; to be top-heavy or unstable; see โงนเงน p. 227.

โพย po-ie *v.* to thrash, flog or whip; see ตี p. 368: *n.* danger; calamity; peril.

โพยม, โพยมัน, โพยมาน pay-yome *S. n.* air; atmosphere; sky; the upper strata of the air (S. E. D. p. 1041): โพยมเกศี *lit.* "sky-haired," *i.e.* one of the many epithets of Siva: โพยมคุณ *lit.* "a quality of the air," *i.e.* sound; noise: โพยมจร a planet: โพยมธารณ์ the planet Mercury; see ดาวพระพุธ p. 327: โพยม-ธูม *lit.* "sky-smoke," *i.e.* smoke; a cloud: โพยมบุษบ์ *lit.* "a flower in the air," *i.e.* any impossibility or absurdity; "castles in the air": โพยมยาน *lit.* "sky-vehicles," *i.e.* a celestial car; a chariot of the gods; *Thai* airships; airplanes: โพยมรัตน์ *lit.* "sky-jewel," *i.e.* the sun.

โพรก proke[3] *adj.* deficient; incomplete; unfilled; porous; without pulp or flesh.

โพรง prong *n.* a hole; a cavity or hollow place or space (as caries of bone or tooth structure); see ช่อง p. 283.

โพระดก, โพระโดก (นก) poh-ra[6]-dok[4] *n.*

the lineated barbet, *Cyanops hodgsoni* (Gaird. J. S. S. IX, 1, p. 8).

โพล่ ploh[3] *n.* a woven bamboo basket or vessel for storing rice, or, when dammered, for holding water.

โพลง plong *adj.* bright; clear; colourless: ขาวโพลง perfectly white; spotless.

โพล่ง plong[3] *adj.* thoughtless; foolish; heedless; used in combination with พูด as พูดโพล่ง ๆ senseless speech: *onomat.* from the sound of an article of some size falling into the water.

โพลั้ง plong[5] *n.* a species of large shell used for polishing a starched loin-cloth.

โพล้เพล้ ploh[5]-play[5] *n.* evening; dusk.

โพละ plo[6] *onomat.* from the sound of breaking or shattered glass, or the falling and breaking to pieces of an earthen vessel, pot or water-jar.

โพสพ, ไพสพ (p. 605) poh-sop[4] *n.* rice; paddy; the tutelary deity or goddess of rice and grain.

ไพ pai *n.* a copper coin minted during the reign of King Somdet Phra Nang Klao (1824–1851), in value equal to 1/32 of a baht or to about three stangs of the present currency: ไพ *Thailand, Surat,* มะกั่ำต้น *Laos, Chiengmai* (ต้น) *Adenanthera microsperma (Leguminosae); A. pavonina,* a tree distributed through India, into south-east China, and to the Moluccas, growing, where truly wild, in deciduous forest, and itself standing bare for a short time. It has been distributed by man all round the tropics, Malaya included. The high rain-forest is not its natural home. It is probably indigenous in both Java and India. The timber is of some value, being hard, close-grained, having red heart-wood weighing 56 lb. per cubic foot. It is used in south India for house-building, and for cabinet work. There is dye in the wood and saponin in the bark. A gum exudes from the stem. The seeds, roasted and shelled, are eaten with rice in Java. The raw seeds are considered intoxicant. Powdered and made into plasters, they serve in India to hasten the ripening of boils, and for headache, rheumatism, etc. Goldsmiths use these seeds in soldering, equally with the seeds of *Abrus precatorius.* Bead necklaces are made of them through the Malay Islands (Cb. p. 543: V. P. p. 186: Burk. p. 46).

ไพ่ pai[3] *n.* a playing or gambling card: ไพ่นกกระจอก mah-jongg, a Chinese game for four players, with 144 pieces called tiles.

ไพจิตร, ไพรจิตร pai-chiit[4] *P. S. adj.* variegated; painted; ornamented; embroidered (Chd. p. 567).

ไพชน, ไพรชน pai-chone *P. n.* a quiet, deserted, secluded place; a place free from people or annoyance (Chd. p. 570).

ไพชยนต์, ไพรยนต์ pai-cha[6]-yone *P. S. n.* a banner; a flag; an ensign; the palace of Indra; an auspicious omen indicating a victory; the necklace of Vishnu (S.E.D. p. 1021).

ไพฑูรย์, เพฑูรย์, พิฑูรย์, ไพรฑูรย์ pai-toon *P. S. n.* a light green, precious gem, *Lapis lazuli;* a cat's eye (S. E. D. p. 1021).

ไพโดร see พิโดร p. 586.

ไพที, ไพรที pai-tee *P. n.* an altar; a bench; a ledge; a cornice; eaves; an ornamental cornice or moulding around the base of a pagoda (Chd. p. 562).

ไพบูลย์, ไพรบูลย์ pai-boon *S. n.* development (Chd. p. 563); largeness; spaciousness; breadth; thickness (S. E. D. p. 1023).

ไพพรรณ pai-pan *n.* the condition of differing in sex, kind or colour.

ไพเพิด (see ตะเพิด p. 355) pai-pert[3] *v.* to scare away by a shout or noise.

ไพมอก   pai-mauk[3] *v.* to groan, moan, or murmur pitifully or mournfully ; see คร่ำครวญ

[p. 182.]

ไพม้า see พายม้า p. 583.

ไพร   prai *n.* forest; wood; margin; edge; rim; brim; border; see ขอบ p. 148 : ตอก-ไพร to attach a strip of bamboo or rattan around the brim or rim of a basket (as a finishing binder) : ไพรปาก the circumference or margin of the lips : ไพรระหง a forest of tall trees : ไพรวัน an extensive or vast stretch of forest or woods : ไพรสณฑ์, ไพร-สัณฑ์, ไพรสาณฑ์ the border or margin of a forest, open space or wide tract of land : ไพรสามกอ, กะอวม see กระออม p. 49.

ไพร่   prai[3] *n.* a citizen; a commoner; the rabble : บ่าวไพร่ servants and slaves; followers : ไพร่พล troops; attendants; a multitude : ไพร่ฟ้า *lit.* "slaves of heaven," *i. e.* citizens : ไพร่สม fresh recruits for the Crown, between the ages of 18 and 20 years; able-bodied males of between 18 and 20 years of age who have just been enrolled or registered at the provincial offices, and who will be required to serve the Crown : ไพร่ส่วย those who should render obligatory service to the Crown but pay an exemption tax instead : ไพร่หลวง those who are physically fit, or may be called to render obligatory service to the Crown (composed of purely national subjects; slaves, hostages of war or aliens are exempted) : ไพร่ทำโทษแก่กันเอ็ง to lynch another as a means of revenge.

ไพรจิตร see ไพจิตร p. 603.

ไพรชน see ไพชน p. 603.

ไพรชยนต์ see ไพชยนต์ p. 603.

ไพรทูรย์ see ไพฑูรย์ p. 603.

ไพรบูลย์ see ไพบูลย์ p. 603.

ไพรเราะ see ไพเราะ p. 604.

ไพรศรพณ์ see ไพศรพณ์ p. 604.

ไพรัชช์   pai-rat[6] *n.* a foreigner; an alien : *adj.* foreign to the country.

ไพริน, ไพรี   pai-rin *P. S. n.* an enemy; a revengeful person (chd. p. 363); a hostile person or party (S. E. D. p. 1025) : ไพรินทร์ a hostile king; a king who is an enemy.

ไพรู (งาม)   pai-roo *adj.* beautiful; shining; glowing; luminous.

ไพเราะ, ไพรเราะ   pai-raw[6] *adj.* sweet; melodious; musical; harmonious; worth listening to.

ไพโรจน์   pai-rote[3] *a[l]j.* beautiful; shinning; glowing; luminous (chd. p. 582), referring to Indra whose "robes are of changing dyes," of course referring to the clouds (gods of India p. 51); coming from or belonging to the sun; solar; a son of Surya (the sun or its deity) (S. E. D. p. 1025).

ไพล (ต้น)   plai *n. Zingiber casumunar (Zingiberaceae)*, an herb with stems 1 to 6 feet high, rising from a thick rhizome which is pale yellow inside, and which, when fresh, possesses a strong camphoraceous odour, and a warm, spicy, bitteris[l] taste. It is found in various parts of India and throughout Malaysia (burk. p. 2293). It is a household remedy among the Thai people as an embrocation for bruises, swellings and painful conditions.

ไพล่   plai[3] *v.* to swerve or turn aside; to avoid another by making a quick detour; to cross or be crossed (as one knee over the other); to deviate to one side; to go in different directions; see ไขว้ p. 172 : ไพล่หลัง to cross the arms behind, while another is holding on to one arm (as one being handcuffed and under arrest).

ไพศรพณ์, ไพรศรพณ์   pai-sop[4] *S. n.* a name of Kuvera (ท้าวกุเวร), the god of Wealth; see กุเปรัน p. 111 (chd. p. 564).

ไพศาข   pai-sark[4] *n.* one of the twelve months constituting the Hindu lunar year, answering to April and May, being the month in which the moon is full, nearest the southern scale or the constellation Visakha (S. E. D. p. 1026): ไพศาขบูรณมี day of full moon of this month, during which festivals are held

[(chd. p. 564).

ไพศาล see พิศาล p. 590.

ไพศาลี, เวสาลี　　pai-sah[2]-lee　*n.* Vesali has been identified with a locality in the Muzaffarpur, a district of the province of Bihar, India, now called Basarh. At one time it was the capital of the king of the Vajjis, a contemporary of the Buddha (also known as Licchavis), who ruled over the principalities of Videha, Kosala and a part of Magadha.

The ruling class of the Vajjis formed an oligarchy of which each member had his own territory over which he had absolute power. Therefore each of them was referred to as king though his sovereignty as regards their country as a whole was only collective. We learn from the *Sutta-nipata*, that later on Vesali was annexed by the king of Magadha.

ไพศุภราช　　pai-sup[4]-pa[6]-rat[3] *n.* draft-animals (as cattle) that are important in agricultural

[lines of work.

ไพเศษ see พิเศษ p. 590.

ไพสพ, โพสพ (แม่เจ้า)　　pai-sop[4]　*n.* the goddess or tutelary deity of rice and cereals.

ไพหาร see พิหาร p. 591.

ฟ

ฟ　The thirty-first consonant in the Thai alphabet, a low class letter of which there are twenty-four, *viz.* ค, ค, ฆ, ง, ช, ฌ, ซ, ญ, ฑ, ฒ, ฑ, ฑ, ฒ, ณ, ฑ, พ, ฟ, ภ, ม, ร, ล, ว, ฬ, ฮ. ฟอไฟ and ฟอฟัน are the names of this letter, which is often used as an initial letter, equivalent to the English " f."

ฟก　　fok[6] *adj.* contused; swelling; swollen; tumid: ฟกช้ำ bruised; livid; see ช้ำ p. 294.

ฟัง see พุง p. 609.

ฟอ　　faw[3] *onomat.* from the hissing of a cobra.

ฟอ　　faw[5] *adj.* fine; beautiful; flourishing; healthy; merry; see พรัง p. 569: *onomat.* from the hissing of a cobra.

ฟอก　　fauk[3] *v.* to cleanse; to purify or wash; to scald by fire or heat: ช้างฟอกเสื้อผ้า a washerman or laundress: ช่างฟอกหนัง a tanner: ฟอกซัก to cleanse thoroughly; to investigate thoroughly by cross-questioning (as a witness): ฟอกน้ำตาล to clarify sugar: ฟอกหนัง to tan leather: ที่ฟอกหนัง a tannery.

ฟอง　　fong *v.* to increase in a desire for; see กำเริบ p. 105: *n.* a numerical designatory particle for eggs; the roe or spawn of fishes; foam; bubbles; see ไข่ p. 171: เป็นฟอง foamy: ฟองกาม to have an intensified lustful or sexual desire: ฟองไข่ eggs: ฟองน้ำ sponges: หินฟองน้ำ corals; see ปะการัง p. 516.

ฟอง　　fong[3] *v.* to float (used in combination with ลอย as ลอยฟ่อง to float attractively, freely or projecting up high).

ฟ้อง　　fong[5] *v.* to accuse; to denounce; to sue; to make accusation or charge against; to bring a legal action: คำฟ้อง a charge; a complaint; an accusation; an indictment or writ: ถอนฟ้อง to withdraw an action or charge: ฟ้องความเท็จ to bring a false action: ฟ้องความเท็จด้วยความพยาบาท to make a malicious prosecution: ฟ้องแย้ง to make a counter claim or cross action: ฟ้องร้อง to appeal to a superior, or to a higher court for judgement: ฟ้องเรียกค่าเสียหาย to sue for damages: ฟ้องอนาถา to sue in forma pauperis: ฟ้องอย่า to enter suit for divorce: ฟ้องอุทธรณ์ to appeal: ยกฟ้อง to dismiss a case or action.

ฟองมัน, ตาไก่ fong-mun *n.* a character represented by a double circle "๏" placed at the beginning of a paragraph or chapter (now practically obsolete); see ตาไก่ p. 360.

ฟอด faut[3] *adj.* frothy; decaying; fermenting; mushy; turning sour (as fruit): *onomat.* from the sound of kissing (according to the national manner).

ฟอน fawn *v.* to bite out or gnaw away the inside of (as termites or vermin do): *adj.* fragmentary; incomplete; minced: พื้นฟอน to cut into fragments or pieces; to be thoroughly minced; see ป่อน p. 473.

ฟ่อน fawn[3] *n.* a sheaf; a bundle; a handful (as of grass or rice stalks): มัดเป็นฟ่อนๆ to bind into bundles; see กำ p. 102.

ฟ้อน fawn[5] *v.* to dance (solo); to gesture or make movements (as in dancing); see กราย p. 51; to act in pantomime: ฟ้อนหาง to strut about with the tail spread (as turkeys or peacocks).

ฟอร์ม form *v.* to decorate; to build; to make; to arrange or prepare; see แต่ง p. 376: *Eng. n.* form; shape; example (contracted from uniform).

ฟะพัด fa[6]-fut[6] *v.* to fan or winnow (as paddy or grain); to flap violently (as sails or awnings of a boat or launch).

ฟะพั้น fa[6]-fun[3] *adj.* disordered; miscellaneous; see เผื่อ p. 556.

ฟะพ้าย, เพ้อย fa[6]-fai[3] *adj.* long; slender; tapering to a point (as a spire); centering in, or extending to a point (as rows of trees).

พัก fuk[6] *v.* to incubate; to hatch out; to brood (over eggs); see กกไข่ p. 1: *n.* a family of cucurbitaceous or gourd-like plants: พักข้าว *Thailand* (ต้น) *Momordica cochinchinensis (Cucurbitaceae)*, a gourd-like plant. This vigorous climber is found from India and Japan to New Guinea. The fruit is eaten by the jungle tribes of Pahang, and sometimes in India and the Philippines. The very young leaves are eaten in Bali, and the Philippines. The Chinese use the seeds to treat tumours, malignant ulcers, obstructions of the liver and spleen, etc. The people of Indo-China apply a paste of them to warts, abscesses, and buboes. In French Indo-China they come to market as oil-seeds. The oil makes 47 percent of the weight of the kernel. It is solid at ordinary temperatures, and pale green in colour when fresh, but loses this colour after a short exposure to atmosphere and light, and, at the same time, is changed by oxidization. Heating has a similar result; after which its behaves as a semi-drying oil. This oil is used as an illuminant in Indo-China. The root froths in water, and can be used as soap for washing (cb. p. 758: V. P. p. 197: Burk. p. 1488): พักเขียว *Thailand, Bangkok,* พักหม่น *Laos, Chiengmai* (ต้น) *Benincasa hispida (Cucurbitaceae)* (cb. p. 757); *B. cerifera,* ash-pumpkin or white gourd, a large, handsome, ovoid gourd, grown throughout the tropics, as well as in sub-tropical countries. It grows wild in Java; but Malaya is too humid for it to be native; in cultivation it is more frequent in the drier northern states than in the south. There are two races, one with a somewhat hairy fruit, and the other with a smooth fruit. The fruit is covered with a whitish waxen bloom (hence its popular names), and is used as a vegetable, sometimes candied as a sweetmeat. The plant is an annual, with large angular leaves, and may often be seen growing over the roofs of peasants' houses (MCM. p. 291: V. P. p. 196: Burk. p. 317): พักทอง, พักเหลือง *Thailand, Bangkok,* น้ำเต้า *Thailand, Patalung,* พักแก้ว *Laos, Chiengmai,* หมักอึ *Laos, Krubin,* เหลืองเคข้า *Karen, Kanburi* (ต้น) *Cucurbita moschata (Cucurbitaceae),* the musk melon, an American cultigen, distributed widely throughout the world. It is the commonest of its genus in the American tropics, and perhaps the best fitted for the eastern tropics. In appearance it is very like the *C. maxima*. The fruits are eaten boiled, or in curries. They can be kept for quite a long while and transportation is easy. The leaves are eaten in the Dutch Indies; *C. maxima*, the squash, a cultigen which originated in America. It was taken to the Old World shortly after the discovery of America. It does not flourish in a very damp climate. The oil in the seeds is apparently like that of other *Cucurbita*, bland, and semidrying. Saponin has been found in the seeds, and perhaps the presence of this body accounts for the occasional use of the fresh seeds as an anthelmintic (MCM. p. 292 : cb. p. 762 : V. P. p. 196 : Burk. p. 698).

พักพุน fuk[6]-foon[5] *adj.* soft; smooth and delicate to the touch (as skin); see นุ่ม p. 462.

พักฟูม fuk[6]-foom *v.* to nurse; to take care of or bring up (with assiduous care).

พึง fung *v.* to listen to; to hear; to obey, heed or trust the words of; see เชื่อ p. 302 : ไม่เชื่อฟัง to be disobedient or unheeding (to the words or instruction of another).

พึงกา *Laos, Buriram,* หนามหัดหนามหัน *Thailand, Rachaburi* (ต้น) fung-gkah[2] *n. Caesalpinia godefroyana* (*Leguminosae*) (cb. p. 502).

พัด fut[6] *v.* to shake, knock about, or swing from side to side (as a dog with a snake or a cat with a rat), *ex.* สุนัขกัดพัดงูตัวใหญ่; to rhyme; to jingle rhythmically; see คล้อง p. 185 : กลอนพัดกัน alternating verses which rhyme : กุ้งพัดๆ shelled, boiled or sun-dried shrimps.

พัน fun *v.* to cut; to chop or slash with a knife or sword; see ตัด p. 359 : *n.* a tooth : พันกราม a molar tooth; grinders : พันดาบ a contest or combat with swords; a duel; fencing : พันปลา *lit.* " fish teeth," *i. e.* serrations; saw-teeth (decorations) : พันเฟือง cogs

in cog-wheels : พันเลื่อย saw-teeth marks : พันสี, ครอบจักรกระวาฬ *Thailand, Bangkok,* มะ-ก่องข้าว *N. Laos,* โผงผาง *Thai* (ต้น) *Abutilon indicum* (*Malvaceae*), the country mallow, the moon-flower (cb. p. 153); see ครอบจักระ-วาฬ p. 179 : พันหนู the two strokes placed over " ◌ั " as " ◌ี " : ยาสีพัน a dentifrice; a tooth-powder : แรงกินพัน decayed teeth.

พัน ๑ fun[3] *v.* to twist or twirl fibers or strands together (as into string or rope) : เกรียงพันเทียน a board on which wax is rolled into tapers : พันเทียน to roll wax into tapers (or candles).

พัน ๒ fun[3] *v.* to be mixed together; to be tangled up, or generally out of order : พัน-เผื่อ to be indistinct, clouded, mixed up or tangled together : พันเพื่อน to become clouded or deranged mentally; to be forgetful or absent-minded; to be distorted (in intellect).

ฟ้า fah[5] *n.* sky; heaven : ขอบฟ้า horizon : ดาดฟ้า the upper deck of a ship : ฟ้าผ่า *lit.* " a condition of rending of the heavens," *i. e.* streaked lightning : ฟ้ามุ่ย *Laos* (ต้น) *Vanda coerulea* (*Orchidaceae*), an orchid having light blue flowers in large sprays on stems one to three feet long. It is a beautiful species (V. P. p. 196 : MCM. p. 146) : ฟ้าร้อง, ฟ้าลั่น thunder : ฟ้าแลบ a flash of lightning : ฟ้า-แลบ *Thailand, Nakawn Sritamarat* (ต้น) *Rubus alceifolius* (*Rosaceae*), a bramble found throughout western Malaysia and northwards to Tonkin. Neither Malays nor Thai distinguish it from *R. moluccanus*. The following medicinal uses belong to either species. The Malays drink a decoction of the roots for dysentery and urinary trouble, and apply the leaves externally for fever. Also, they steam a woman, over a period of seven days after child-birth, by means of boiling water into which the leaves have been placed (BURK. p. 1918 : cb. p. 569); ฟ้าแลบ *Thailand, Surat and Ranawng,* ส้มกุ้ง *Thailand, Chantaburi* (ต้น) *R. moluccanus*, a bramble like *R. alceifolius*, found in western Malaysia. In Java the young leaves are chewed for sprue and coughs, and in eastern Malaysia to prevent miscarriage; they are also applied to boils. The fruit is edible but not worth eating (cb. p. 573 : Burk. p. 1918): พ้าหิน, กำพรวด (ปลา) *Cyclocheilichthys tapiensis* (*Cyprinidae*), a carp (Suvatti p. 23).

ฟาก fark[3] *n.* shore; bank; side (of a water-way); strips of split bamboo, or wooden slats sewed together with rattan and used for flooring in houses or boats: ฟากข้างนี้ this shore or bank: ฟากข้างโน้น yonder bank or side: เหล็กฟาก iron grating.

ฟาง fang *n.* straw: *adj.* dim; indistinct; blurred; cloudy (descriptive of a condition of the eyes): ฟางข้าว rice straw or thrashed rice stalks: ฟางลอย see นาฟางลอย p. 449.

ฟ้าง (ข้าว) fang[3] *n. Sorgum vulgare* (*Gramineae*), great millet, sorghum, an annual grain crop. Sorghum was unknown to the Greeks. After the time of Christ, Persia received it. It has no Sanscrit name, and India can only have received it during the Christian era: but it has become a crop of such importance, that probably many of the very numerous races in India have been selected within the country, and are definitely of Indian origin. In the Peninsula this grain crop is not much grown on account of the difficulties of securing the harvest and keeping the grain. *S. vulgare* is used for fodder exclusively, and may so serve in countries where grain-production is not the object (McM. p. 306 : Burk. p. 2056).

ฟาด fat[3] *v.* to strike; to slash; to whip, or beat: ฟาดด้วยไม้เรียว to strike with a whip: ฟาดผ้า to pound clothes on a board or stone in washing: ฟาดเนื้อฟาดตัว to brush the body with a bundle of twigs dipped in consecrated water (as a means of dispelling evil spirits): เรือฟาดตอ the boat strikes a [snag.

ฟาน see เนื้อทราย p. 464.

พ้าผอ fah[5]-faw[4] *Karen n.* a term of respectful salutation to superiors or governors, as พระพ่อ honoured father.

พาม, น่วม (p. 444) farm[3] *adj.* soft; fluffy; pulpy.

ฟาย fai *v.* to be liberal; to have ample, or a superabundance; to overflow: ฟายมือ a measure of capacity equal to a handful, or what the hollow of the hand will hold: ฟายน้ำตา to shed tears in a great quantity.

พืด fit[6] *onomat.* from the sound of wheezing, or sneezing.

พืบ, แฟบ fip[6] *adj.* depressed; flattened (used in regard to the condition of the nose): จมูกพื่บ snub-nosed; see ฟุบ p. 609.

ฟ, พี fee[3] *onomat.* from the sound of air escaping or leaking from a punctured tyre or a rubber balloon, or from wheezing asthmatic respiration.

พืน furn *n.* firewood; wood fuel: พื้นฝอย small chips or chunks of kindling wood.

พื้น furn[5] *v.* to regain consciousness or to recover partially from either sickness or an anesthetic: พื้นจากความตาย to regain life after (apparent) death: พื้นจากหลับ to awaken from sleep: พื้นดิน to loosen up, or turn over the soil (as around plants): พื้นฝอย to rekindle, or bring to life trifling, quarrelsome, or irritating subjects or matters (once forgotten): รื้อพื้น, พื้นจากไข้ to recover from an illness.

พืม furm *n.* "the reed" or comb-like part of a loom, being a narrow frame with transverse wires or metal reeds between which two or more threads of warp pass. It hangs from the frame called batten and is to drive the threads, after each intersection, up close to the portion already woven.

ฟุ, ฟุฟะ, ฟอด foo[6] *adj.* not firm; decaying; rotting; soft; yielding to pressure; see ฉุ p. 270; น่วม p. 444.

พุ้ง, พั้ง foong[5] *v.* to be wafted about, or floating in the air (as smoke); to be noised or spread abroad (as rumours or gossip): พุ้งเผ่อ puffed up (as with pride); conceited; boastful; see คะนอง p. 192: พุ้งเพ่อง to be spread far and wide (as fame or reputation); see กระจาย p. 21: *adj.* proficient; expert; wise; see ชาญ p. 291: พุ้งส้าน to be incoherent; to be irrational (in speech or actions); to be unsettled in purpose; see พล่าน p. 574.

ฟุบ foop[6] *v.* to crouch or stoop down low; to collapse; to be caved in: นอนฟุบ to lie in a collapsed condition or a crouching position (as when over-tired).

พุบ foop[3] *onomat.* from the sound of a puff of ignited gun-powder, or of a burning fuse.

พุมเพ่อย foom[3]-fur-ie *adj.* overabundant; amply sufficient; very rich; being on the road to wealth: มีใช้พุมเพ่อย to be able to use lavishly (as funds, motor cars or servants); to be well heeled.

ฟู foo *v.* to become fluffy; to rise or swell (as by the power of yeast or fermentation): ฟูฟ่อง to improve gradually, or make progress upwards (as to fame or prosperity); see ดึขึ้น p. 330: ขนมถ้วยฟู a fluffy rice flour cake.

ฟู foo[3] *onomat.* from the sound of blowing on smoldering coals or embers which will burst into flame.

ฟูก fook[3] *n.* a mattress.

ฟูด food[3] *v.* to swell up from confined gas; to bubble, froth, or overflow (from some internal force): *onomat.* from the sound of air escaping, or of the deflating of a rubber balloon or tyre: ฟูดฟาด *onomat.* from the sound of the harsh respiration of a horse or elephant.

ฟูม foom *adj.* abundant; excessive; bathed (as with tears); soaking wet; overflowing: ฟูมไปด้วยโลหิต covered with blood: ฟูมฟัก to caress, nurse, care for or treat with kind-ness and affection: ฟูมฟาย to lather or play with froth or foam (as blowing soap-bubbles): *adv.* excessively; abundantly; extravagantly; improvidently (as use of funds): หน้าฟูมฟายไปด้วยน้ำตา a tear-bathed face.

เฟ้น fen[5] *v.* to select; to choose; see คัด p. 193; บีบนวด to massage, using compression.

เฝอ fur[5] *v.* to be distended or oppressed with gas (as in disordered digestion).

เฟอะ, เฟอะฟะ, เฟะ, แฟะ fur[6] *adj.* softened by decay; rotten into a pasty condition (as carrion); soggy; mushy; muddy.

เฟิน (ต้น) fern *Eng. n. Pleopeltis sinuosa (Polypodiaceae)*, a tropical fern: เฟินขนนก (ต้น) *Adiantum farleyense (Polypodiaceae)*, a fern which is a native of Farley Hill, Barbados, and is botanically considered a variety of *Adiantum tenerum*, which is about the commonest of maidenhairs in Bangkok. It is said to have been introduced from Europe by Prince Sanpasart about 1900 (winit, N. H. J. S. S. IX, 1, p. 89): เฟินขนนกก้านแข็ง (ต้น) apparently a dwarf variety of *Adiantum tenerum*, differing from *Adiantum farleyense* in its rigid and soriferous habit. It is found cultivated in Bangkok (winit, N. H. J. S. S. IX, 1, p. 89): เฟินทอง (ต้น) gold fern, *Ceropteris calomelanos, var. chrysophylla (Gymnogramma)*, the most beautiful of gold ferns, which has been in cultivation in Thailand for about 30 years. It is indigenous to tropical America and tropical West Africa (winit, N. H. J. S. S. IX, 1, p. 92: BURK. p. 517).

เฟี้ยม fee-am[5] *v.* to conceal oneself or evade the presence of others in a becoming manner; see แฝง p. 557: *n.* boards nailed with overlapping edges: ฝาเฟี้ยม a partition made with boards nailed with overlapping edges: เฟี้ยมเฝ้า to enter the presence of a king or royalty with decorum or politeness.

เฟือ fur-ah *v.* to have some left over; to be well-filled, satisfied and yet have some remaining.

เพอ   fur-ah[5] *v.* to be anxious for, or worried about.

เพอง   feu-ang *n.* the cogs of a wheel or gear-wheel; the flutings of a pillar or column; the sectional divisions or partitions of fruit (as of the durian).

เพอง, พุ้ง   feu-ang[3] *v.* to be noised abroad or scattered about (as news or gossip): *n.* festoons; decorations hanging in loops, tassels, semicircles, streamers or pennants.

เพอง   feu-ang[5] *n.* a silver (flat or bullet) coin of the Bangkok dynasty (1782-1924) equal to 8 atts, ⅛ of a baht or 12½ stangs.

เพอย see พะพ่าย p. 606.

แพ   faa[3] *adj.* gay; flashy; striking (used in regard to dress): *onomat.* from the sound made when igniting a match.

แฟง (ต้น)   faang *n. Cucurbita pepo (Cucurbitaceae)*, pumpkin, vegetable-marrow, a culigen of American origin but not at all fitted to stand the wet climate of the Malay Peninsula. It is cultivated in a few races, chiefly in the northern parts, and success may be attained if the growth is timed for fruiting in a dry spell. It grows rapidly and trails over the surface of the ground producing large oblong gourds. It is eaten as a vegetable; fresh seeds are used as a vermifuge. The plant may be used as fodder. There are medicinal uses (MCM. pp. 292, 327: BURK. p. 699).

แฟบ   faap[3] *adj.* flattened; depressed; deflated (as a motor car tyre); see แบน p. 490.

แฟ้ม   faam[5] *n.* a correspondence folder, file or binder.

ไฟ   fai *n.* fire: ก่อไฟ to kindle a fire: ทิ้งไฟ, วางเพลิง arson: ไฟกัลป์ the fire that destroys the world at the termination of each Kalpa. In Hindu mythology, Brahma's life is said to consist of a hundred of his own years, and a year consists of days each of which is equal to 4,320,000 of our years, followed by a night of equal duration. At the close of each Kalpa, the universe is destroyed and has to be recreated after Brahma has rested through his prolonged night (H. C. D. p. 382): ไฟธาตุ the body heat of human beings or animals; the action of digestive fluids or enzymes: ไฟพะเนียง a form of fire-works: ไฟฟ้า electricity: ไฟไหม้ *v.* to burn: *n.* a conflagration: ลูกไฟ sparks; firebrands: ไม้ขีดไฟ matches.

ภ

ภ   The thirty-second consonant in the Thai alphabet, a low class letter of which there are twenty-four, *viz.* ค, ฅ, ฆ, ง, ช, ฌ, ซ, ญ, ฑ, ฒ, ธ, ฑ, ฒ, ณ, น, พ, ฟ, ภ, ม, ร, ล, ว, ฬ, ฮ. ภอสำเภา and ภอภรรยา are the names of this letter. ภ is used either as an initial letter, or as a final letter of a word. It has the sound of the English "p." ภ occurs extensively in words derived from Pali and Sanskrit.

ภค, ภัค   pa[6]-ka[6] *P. S. n.* power; majesty; good fortune; fame; glory; merit; virtue (chd. p. 80); distinction; dignity; prosperity; beauty; loveliness (S. E. D. p. 743).

ภควดี   pa[6]-ka[6]-wa[6]-dee *P. S. n.* the divine or adorable one (a title for the consort of Siva); Lakshmi the goddess of Fortune, wife of Vishnu and mother of Kama (S. E. D. p. 743: H. C. D. pp. 176, 325).

ภควัต, ภควันต์, ภควาน, ภควา   pa[6]-ka[6]-wat[6] *S. n.* one possessing fortune; one who is illustrious, divine, venerable or holy; a title of Siva, or of the Buddha (S. E. D. p. 743):

ภควัทคีตา Krishna's song; the name of a celebrated mystical poem.

ภคันทลา pa[6]-kun-ta[6]-lah *P. n.* a fistula in
the anus (chd. p. 80).

ภคินิ pa[6]-ki[6]-nee *P. S. n.* a sister (chd. p.
81); any woman, or wife: ภคินีภรรดา a
sister's husband.

ภณ pa[6]-na[6] *P. S. v.* to speak; to say; to
tell; to recite; to preach (chd. p. 82).

ภณิดา pa[6]-ni[6]-dah *S. n.* one who says,
speaks, preaches or tells: *adj.* uttered;
spoken; said; related (S. E. D. p. 745).

ภพ see ภว p. 612.

ภมการ pa[6]-ma[6]-gkarn *P. S. n.* one who
works a turning-lathe; a turner (chd. p. 81).

ภมร, ภระมร, ภุมระ pa[6]-maun *P. S. n.* a
bee; a carpenter-bee; a lathe: ภมรินทร์,
ภุมรินทร์ a very large bee; a queen bee.

ภมรี, ภุมรี, ภระมรี pa[6]-ma[6]-ree *P. n.* female bees (chd. p. 81).

ภมุ, ภมุกะ pa[6]-moo[6] *P. n.* an eyebrow
[chd. p. 81].

ภย, ภัย pa[6]-ya[6] *P. S. n.* fear; danger;
dread; misfortune; calamity (chd. p. 87):
ภยันตราย a catastrophy; peril; extreme danger;
ภยาคติ fear; dread: ภัยอุบาทว์ an unfortunate accident: ราชภัย calamities or punishments inflicted by law, or by royal command:
โรคภัย maladies, scourges, or epidemics of
diseases: อัคคีภัย misfortune or calamity
caused by fire; อุทกภัย calamity caused
by flood.

ภร pa[6]-ra[6] *P. v.* to support, feed or care
for (chd. p. 83); see ค้ำจุน p. 201.

ภรต pa[6]-rot[6] *P. S. n.* Bharata, the younger
brother of Rama (S. E. D. p. 747): นักภรต
an expert dancer; an actor: ภรตวรรษ the
country of Bharata, otherwise called India.

ภรรดา, ภรรดร, ภัสดา, ภรัสดาษ pun-dah
n. a husband (chd. p. 84).

ภรรยา, ภริยา, ภารยา pun-ra-yah *n.* a
wife (chd. p. 83); a spouse: บุตรภรรยา a
family: รับเป็นภรรยา to take as a wife:
สามีภรรยา husband and wife.

ภรัทวาช pa[6]-rat[6]-ta[6]-wart[3] *n.* one of the
seven Rishis; an inspired poet or sage (H. C. D.
p. 268: chd. p. 83).

ภรัษฏ์ prut[6] *S. adj.* fallen; dropped; fallen
down from, or off of (S. E. D. p. 769).

ภราดร, ภราดา, ภาดา, ภาตร, ภราตร ๑ pa[6]-
rah-daun *n.* a brother (chd. p. 84): ภราดร-
ภาพ, ภราตรภาพ, ภราตฤภาพ, ภราตร ๒ a brotherhood; a fraternity (S. E. D. p. 770).

ภรานต์, ภันต์ pran *P. S. n.* a potter's
wheel, or a turner's lathe: *adj.* revolving;
whirling; turning around (S. E. D. p. 770); see
กลึง p. 62.

ภรู proo *S. n.* an eyebrow; the brow (chd.
p. 90): ภรูมณฑล the arch of the eyebrow,
or the space between the eyebrows.

ภฤงคาร, ภิงคาร, ภิงการ pring-karn *P. S.
n.* a golden pitcher, ewer or vase; a water-
jug used at the coronation of a king (S. E. D.
p. 765).

ภฤดก prur[6]-dok[4] *S. n.* an hireling; a servant
[(chd. p. 84).

ภฤดี prur[6]-dee *S. n.* hire; wages for service;
maintenance; support (chd. p. 84).

ภฤตย์, ภัจจ์ prurt[6] *P. S. v.* to be nourished
or maintained (chd. p. 80): *n.* a dependant;
a servant; an hireling or attendant; see
คนใช้ p. 176.

ภฤศ prut[6] *S. adj.* vehement; mighty;
powerful; abundant; harsh; vigorous; severe
(S. E. D. p. 765); see จัด p. 238.

ภฤษฏ์ ๑ prut[6] *S. adj.* fallen; dislodged
(as fruit from a tree) (S. E. D. p. 766).

ภฤษฏ์ ๒ prut[6] *S. adj.* parched; fried;
roasted or boiled down dry (chd. p. 84).

ภว, ภพ pa⁶-wa⁶ *P. S. n.* origin; birth; production; existence; the state of being; life (S. E. D. p. 748); general formal existence (Ala. p. 239): ภวกษัย the end of existence; Nirvana; cessation of birth or existence (chd. p. 84): ภวเศขร *lit.* "the one who is Siva's crest," *i. e.* the moon: ภวาภพ the antitheses, existence and non-existence, prosperity and adversity.

ภวนะ pa⁶-wa⁶-na⁶ *P.S. n.* a place of abode; a mansion; a house, home, dwelling or palace (S. E. D. p. 749).

ภวปาระ pa⁶-wa⁶-bpah-ra⁶ *P. n. lit.* "the shore of future existence," *i. e.* Nirvana.

ภวังค์ pa⁶-wang *P. n.* the subconscious state or condition.

ภวันดร pa⁶-wan-daun *P. n.* another birth or existence, *viz.* either a previous or a subsequent one (chd. p. 85).

ภักขะ see ภักษ์ p. 612.

ภักดี, ภักติ puk⁶-dee *S. v.* to have a fondness for; to be attentive to; to do homage; to worship; to show piety; to have faith in, or love for (S. E. D. p. 743): *n.* attachment or devotion: ใจภักดี of a charitable, loyal or benevolent disposition.

ภักตะ, ภัตต์, ภัตร puk⁶-dta⁴ *S. n.* food; a meal; boiled rice; edible grains or cereals boiled with water; one loyal, or faithful to, or honouring his superior (S. E. D. p. 743): ภักตกฤตย์ the preparation of food for a meal: ภักตการ a food-preparer; a cook.

ภักษ์, ภักขะ, ภัษย์ puk⁶ *v.* to eat: *n.* food; diet; prey (S. E. D. p. 742): ใช้เนื้อเป็นภักษา to use meat as a food: ภักษาการ *lit.* "a food-maker," *i. e.* a baker; a cook: ภักษาหาร various forms of food, diet or nourishment.

ภัค see ภค p. 610.

ภัคน์ puk⁶ *S. adj.* broken; torn; split; defeated; frustrated; disturbed (S. E. D. p. 744); see แตก p. 375.

ภังค pung-ka⁶ *P. S. n.* humiliation; abatement; downfall; decay; ruin (S. E. D. p. 744).

ภัญชะ pun-cha⁶ *P. S. v.* to cause to break; to crush; to destroy (chd. p. 82); to make a breach in; to rout; to put to flight; to split; to shatter (S. E. D. p. 744).

ภัฏ put⁶ *P. S. n.* a mercenary; a hired soldier, a warrior, or combatant; a servant; a slave (S. E. D. p. 745).

ภัณฑ์ pun *P. n.* utensils; implements; goods; wares; property; the stock-in-trade of a tradesman (chd. p. 82): ครุภัณฑ์ heavy articles: ภัณฑครรภ a store-room: ภัณฑบดี a merchant or trader: ภัณฑบฏ a barber; a shaver of the hair: ภัณฑศาลา a warehouse: ภัณฑาคาร a godown or storehouse: ภัณฑาคาริก, ภัณฑาคารักษ์ a storehouse keeper or one responsible for a warehouse.

ภัณฑนะ pun-da⁴-na⁶ *P. n.* a quarrel or strife (chd. p. 82); a division between parties; see ทะเลาะ p. 407.

ภัณฑุ pun-doo *P. adj.* close-shaven; bald (chd. p. 82).

ภัทร pat⁶-tra⁶ *P. S. adj.* good; excellent; noble; worthy; pious; fortunate; auspicious; happy; blest (chd. p. 80); propitious; beautiful (S. E. D. p. 745): ภัทรกุมภ์ an auspicious jar; a golden jar filled with water from a holy place, as from the Ganges: ภัทรปิฐ a splendid seat; a throne: ภัทรมนัส name of the mother of the elephant Airavata (the one that Indra rides) (H. C. D. p. 9).

ภัพพ์, ภาพย์ pup⁶ *P. adj.* right; proper; well-conducted; good (chd. p. 80); see สมควร [p. 187.

ภัย see ภย p. 611.

ภัสตรา pat⁶-sa⁴-dtrah *S. n.* a leather bottle or vessel; a skin pouch; a leather bag; a bellows; a large hide with valves and a clay nozzle (used as a bellows) (S. E. D. p. 750).

ภัสมะ pat⁶-sa⁴-ma⁶ *P. S. v.* to chew; to

pulverize; to be consumed, or devoured; to be calcined by fire; to be reduced to ashes (S. E. D. p. 750): ภัสมกูฏ a pile of ashes: ภัสมกูล snow; frost; a dust-storm: ภัสมภูต *lit.* "to become dust or ashes," *i. e.* death.

ภัสสร pat⁶-sorn₁² *P. n.* light; glory, or rays (of sunshine): *adj.* shining; brilliant (chd. p. 83).

ภา pah *P. S. n.* light; ray; splendour (chd. p. 80); brightness: ภากร *lit.* "one producing light," *i. e.* the sun (chd. p. 81): ภาโกศ *lit.* "light repository," *i. e.* the sun.

ภาค, ภค park³ *P. n.* a portion; a share; a part; a side; a region; a quarter; a time; lot; destiny (chd. p. 81): ภัยภาคหน้า a future calamity or distress: ภาคทัณฑ์ *lit.* "to share the penalty," *i. e.* to remit punishment on promise of good behaviour; to reprimand for a first offense; see ติเตียน p. 366.

ภาคย์ park³ *P. S. n.* fortune; lot; destiny, merit and demerit acquired in former existences (chd. p. 81); luck; fate; good fortune; happiness; welfare; reward (S. E. D. p. 752).

ภาคิไนย์ pah-ki⁶-nai *P. S. n.* an older or younger sister's son; a nephew (chd. p. 81); the anthithesis of ภาติยะ, the son of an older or younger brother.

ภาคี, ภาคิน pah-kee *P. S. n.* a partner; a member; one partaking in; a possessor; a fortunate person; the whole, as consisting of parts (S. E. D. p. 751).

ภาคิยะ pah-kee-ya⁶ *P. S. v.* to be divided: *adj.* connected with; partaking in; belonging to (chd. p. 81).

ภาชนะ part³-cha⁶-na⁶ *P. n.* a vessel; a bowl; a jar; a dish (chd. p. 81): เครื่องภาชนะใช้สอย various household utensils.

ภาชนีย pah-cha⁶-nee-ya⁶ *P. v.* to be divided or distributed: *n.* articles which should be shared or divided among others (as presents, gifts or alms).

ภาชี pah-chee *P. S. n.* one who shares or divides with others: ภาชินี the feminine form of ภาชี.

ภาณ pah-na⁶ *P. adj.* saying; reciting; telling; proclaiming (chd. p. 82): ภาณวาร a recitation; a portion for recital; a complete period of discourse, prayer or devotion; see กล่าว p. 61.

ภาณก pah-na⁶-gka⁴ *P. n.* a discourser; a lecturer, preacher, or one who informs others (chd. p. 82).

ภาณฑี parn-dee *S. n.* a razor case.

ภาณี pah-nee *P. n.* a preacher; a discourser or informer: *adj.* speaking; talking (chd. p. 82): ภาณินี the feminine form of ภาณี.

ภาดร, ภาดา, ภาตร, ภาตา, ภาต, ภาติกะ, ภาติยะ pah-dorn *n.* a brother.

ภานุ pah-noo⁶ *P. S. n.* brightness; light, or rays of light; lustre; splendour; the sun; a king, prince or master (S. E. D. p. 751): ภานุวงษ์ the race or lineage of the sun: ภานุรังษี *lit.* "city of the sun's rays," *i. e.* Benares, a celebrated city in India: ภานุมาต *lit.* "that which possesses, or is an emitter of light," *i. e.* the sun; fire.

ภาพ parp³ *n.* property; nature; state; condition; meaning; intention; gesture; amorous dalliance; substance; a thing, form or image (chd. p. 87); used as a suffix, as เขียนภาพ to draw pictures or forms: ภาพยนตร์ *lit.* "moving or automatic pictures," *i.e.* the cinematograph: ภาพหมู่ a group photograph or picture: รูปภาพ pictures or drawings: ภาพถ่าย a photograph: ถ่ายภาพ, ถ่ายรูป to take a photograph: มรณภาพ the condition or state of death: ภาพสีน้ำมัน an oil painting.

ภาย pai *n.* a side; a part; a state; a time; see ข้าง p. 153: ภายค่ำ, เวลาค่ำ night-time: ภายนอก exterior; external; outside: ภายใน

interior; inside; concealed; within: ภายหน้า
future; a time to come; the foreside; in the
future: ภายหลัง afterward; subsequently;
after; past and gone.

ภาร, ภาระ parn *P. n.* a weight; a load; a
burden; a charge; a duty; business; an important affair (chd. p. 83); a serious undertaking: *adj.* heavy; burdensome: ภารโรง
a janitor; a care-taker: ไม่เป็นภารธุระ, ไม่ใช่-
ธุระ it is none of my business.

ภารดี, ภารติ pah-ra[6]-dee *n.* speech; voice;
words; eloquence; literature; the dramatic art
of recitation; the Sanskrit speech of an actor
(S. E. D. p. 753); Saraswati (พระสรัสวดี), wife of
Brahma, and the goddess of Speech and
Learning, the inventress of the Sanskrit
language and patroness of the Arts and
Sciences (H. C. D. p. 284).

ภารต pah-ra[6]-dta[4] *S. n.* the Mahabharata
(chd. p. 83); the descendants of Bharata, a
prince of the Puru branch of the Lunar race,
son of Dushyanta and Sakuntala; the Indian
race (H. C. D. p. 47).

ภารยา see ภรรยา p. 611.

ภารัทวาช pah-rat[6]-ta[6]-wart[3] *P. n.* name
of one of the ten Rishis (chd. p. 83).

ภารา pah-rah *P. n.* a unit of weight, equal
to twenty tulas (ตุล); a load (chd. p. 83).

ภาวนา pah-wa[6]-nah *P. n.* earnest consideration; meditation: *adj.* producing; increasing; developing; being devoted to;
realizing; attaining (chd. p. 85); concentrating
the mind upon the attainment of the state of
goodness: เจริญเมตตาภาวนา to persevere in
mercy and meditation (Ala. p. 168): คำภาวนา
prayers.

ภาวะ pah-wa[6] *P. S. n.* the state or condition of being; origin; birth; existence; appearance (S. E. D. p. 754): ภาวบุษบ์ *lit.* "the
heart compared to a flower," *i. e.* attractive;
beautiful; alluring or charming (in character):

ภาวพันธ์ fettering, gripping, holding, or joining
the hearts (as by love or affection): ภาวรูป
real; actual; really existing in conformity to
one's position or condition in life; distinction
of sex (Ala. p. 237): ภาวศุทธิ the state of
mental purity: ภาวะพระสงฆ์ the Buddhistic
ecclesiastical state: ภาวะนิ่ง the state or
condition of being silent: ภิกขุภาวะ the
person, or state of being a talapoin.

ภาษ, สัมภาษ part[3] *S. v.* to speak, talk,
say or tell; to announce, declare, describe,
name or call (S. E. D. p. 755): ภาษก a
speaker: ภาษณ์, ภาสน์ the act of talking,
speaking or declaring.

ภาษา, ภาสา pah-sah[2] *S. n.* language;
speech; idiom: คนละภาษา persons speaking
different languages: พูดไม่รู้จักภาษากัน to
talk an unfamiliar language: ภาษาเด็ก
childish prattle, or speech after the manner
of children's talk: ภาษาไทย the Thai
language: ส่งภาษา to act in the capacity
of an interpreter.

ภาษิต pah-sit[4] *S. n.* speech; words; utterances (chd. p. 83); proverbs; wise sayings;
pithy utterances.

ภาษี pah-see[2] *n.* taxes; duties; profits;
gains: เก็บภาษี to collect taxes or dues:
เจ้าภาษี the head of a tax collecting station:
ตามภาษีภาษาของเขา according to their wishes, or
in their own way: ผูกภาษี to purchase the
sole right of collecting taxes: ภาษีที่ดิน land
tax: ภาษีรายได้ income tax: ภาษีสินค้า
ขาเข้า import duties: ภาษีสินค้าขาออก export
duties: ภาษีอากร customs duties: โรง-
ภาษี, กรมศุลกากร a Custom House: เสีย ภาษี
to pay duties or taxes.

ภาส part[3] *P. S. n.* light or rays of light;
lustre; brightness; glory; splendour; majesty
(S. E. D. p. 756): ภาสกร *lit.* "one producing
light," *i. e.* the sun: *adj.* shining; glittering;
bright: ภาสกรี the planet Saturn; Sugriva,
the monkey king who was dethroned by his

brother Balin, but, after the latter had been killed, Sugriva was reinstated by Rama as king of Kishkindhya. He, with his adviser Hanuman and their army of monkeys, were the allies of Rama in his war against Ravana, in which war he was wounded (H. C. D. p. 306).

ภาสวร, ภาสุ part³-sa⁴-wa⁶-ra⁶ *S. n.* the sun (S. E. D. p. 756).

ภาสุร pah-soo⁴-ra⁶ *S. adj.* shining; radiant; brilliant (as a crystal) (chd. p. 84).

ภิกขา pik⁶-kah² *P. n.* the soliciting of alms; begging food or boiled rice (chd. p. 88); food: ภิกขาจาร going the rounds for alms (chd. p. 88): ภิกขาหาร the food received as alms.

ภิกษ์ pik⁶ *S. v.* to beg or solicit; to wish for, or desire; to beg anything from another (S. E. D. p. 756): ภิกษา the act of begging or asking; food given as alms; anything obtained by begging: ภิกษาจรรยา the going about for alms; going the rounds (chd. p. 88); mendicancy: ภิกษาจาร one going the rounds for food or alms; a mendicant: ภิกษาสี a man who eats begged food: ภิกษาหาร food obtained by begging: ภิกษุ, ภิกขุ a Buddhist mendicant or monk; a beggar: ภิกษุณี, ภิกขุณี a Buddhist female mendicant or nun.

ภิงการ, ภิงคาร see ภฤงคาร p. 611.

ภิงส see ภิส p. 615.

ภิงสนะ ping-sa⁴-na⁶ *P. S. adj.* cruel; dreadful; horrible (chd. p. 88).

ภิตติ, ภิกติ pit⁶-dti⁴ *P. S. n.* a wall of earth or masonry (chd. p. 89); a wall; a partition; a panel; a wall-like surface (S. E. D. p. 757): ภิตติขาตนี *lit.* "a wall digger," *i. e.* rats; mice.

ภิท, ภินท pit⁶ *P. S. v.* to split, cleave, break, cut or rend asunder; to pierce or destroy; to transgress; to violate (S. E. D. p. 756).

ภินทน pin-ta⁶-na⁶ *P. S. n.* the act of breaking or destroying (chd. p. 88).

ภินทิบาร, ภินทิวาล pin-ti⁶-barn *P. n.* a kind of spear or lance; a spear-like weapon (chd. p. 89).

ภินทุ pin-too⁶ *S. n.* a breaker; a destroyer; bubbles on liquids; a woman who brings forth a still-born child (S. E. D. p. 757).

ภินโนทร pin-noh-taun *S. n. lit.* "born from different mothers," *i. e.* half-brothers or sisters (S. E. D. p. 757).

ภิยโย, ภิโย, ภิญโญ pi⁶-ya⁶-yoh *P. adv.* again; further; besides; separately; frequently; much (chd. p. 89): *adj.* excellent; supreme; best; elevated.

ภิษัช see ภิสัก p. 615.

ภิส, ภิงส pit⁶ *P. n.* the film or fibres of the stalk of the water-lily (chd. p. 89).

ภิสสา pit⁶-sah² *S. n.* boiled rice; food (chd. p. 88).

ภิสัก, ภิษัช pi⁶-sak⁴ *n.* a physician (chd. p. 89).

ภี pee *S. n.* fear; fright (chd. 88); apprehension; alarm; dread.

ภีตะ, ภีต pee-dta⁴ *P. S. adj.* frightened; afraid (chd. p. 89); fearful.

ภีติ pee-dti⁴ *S. n.* fear (chd. p. 89); danger.

ภีม pee-ma⁶ *P. S. n.* dreadfulness; horribleness; cruelty (chd. p. 88).

ภีรุ, ภีรุก pee-roo⁶ *P. S. adj.* timid; afraid (chd. p. 89): ภีรุกชาติ timid; afraid; fearful; cowardly (as a race).

ภุกก pook⁶ *P. v.* to bark (as dogs).

ภุกต, ภุตต pook⁶ *S. adj.* eaten; possessed; used (chd. p. 92): ภุกตเศษ *lit.* "what is left after eating," *i. e.* remnants of a meal; leavings; fragments from a meal (S.E.D. p. 759).

ภุช ๑ poo⁶-cha⁶ *P. S. n.* the arm; the trunk of an elephant; a branch; a bough; a bend,

curve or coil (of a snake) (S. E. D. p. 759):
ภุชค, ภุชงค์, ภุชงคม *lit.* "one going in curves,"
i. e. a snake : ภุชคทารณ์ *lit.* "a serpent destroyer," *i. e.* the Garuda : ภุชคโภชoctี, ภุชคกภุช
lit. "serpent eater," *i. e.* a peacock : ภุชคลดา
the betel vine : ภุชงคประยาต *lit.* "a serpent-
like course," *i. e.* the meter of a hymn addressed to Siva : ภุชทณฑ์ *lit.* "arm-staff,"
i. e. a long arm : ภุชทล *lit.* "arm-leaf," *i. e.*
the hand : ภุชพันธน์, ภุชสมโภค clasping in the
arms ; an embrace : ภุชมัธย์ *lit.* "the space
between the arms," *i. e.* the chest ; the breast ;
the thorax : ภุชมูล *lit.* "the root of the
arm," *i. e.* the shoulder.

ภุช ๒   poo⁶-cha⁶ *S. v.* to bend ; to be curved
or bowed down ; to be disheartened : *adj.*
curved ; arched ; bent (S. E. D. p. 759).

ภุช ๓   poo⁶-cha⁶ *P. S. v.* to enjoy ; to possess ;
to use ; to eat and drink (S. E. D. p. 759).

ภุชา   poo⁶-chah *S. n.* the arm ; the hand :
ภุชามัธย์ *lit.* "the mid-portion of the arm," *i. e.*
the elbow (S. E. D. p. 759).

ภุญช   poon-cha⁶ *P. v.* to eat ; to be eaten or
partaken of (chd. p. 91).

ภุม   poom *Cam. adj.* no ; not : ภุมนาน
none : ภุมบาน cannot ; impossible.

ภุมม์   poom *P. n.* terrestrial (chd. p. 91) ;
the planet Mars ; see พระอังคาร p. 327 : ภุมม-
รัตน์ coral : ภุมมวาร, ภุมมสาร Tuesday.

ภุว, ภุว   poo⁶-wa⁶ *n.* earth.

ภุวัส   poo⁶-wat⁶ *S. n.* the air ; atmosphere ;
the sky ; the heavens (S. E. D. p. 760).

ภุวิส   poo⁶-wit⁶ *S. n.* the sea ; the ocean
(S. E. D. p. 760).

ภุส   poo⁶-sa⁴ *P. n.* poorly developed rice ;
the husk or hull of paddy ; chaff of wheat :
adj. much ; excessive ; severe (chd. p. 91).

ภู ๑   poo *P. S. n.* the earth ; ground ; soil ;
land ; property ; a place, spot or piece of ground

(S. E. D. p. 760):   ภูกษิต, ภูทาร *lit.* "one that
destroys the earth," *i. e.* the wild boar ; a hog :
ภูเกศ *lit.* "earth-hair," *i. e.* the Indian fig tree :
ภูโคล the terrestial globe ; the earth : ภูจักร
lit. "the earth-circle," *i. e.* the equator ; the
equinoctial line : ภูฉาย, ภูฉายา *lit.* "earth's
shadow," *i. e.* darkness : ภูดล the surface
of the earth or ground : ภูเทพ, ภูสุร a divinity upon the earth ; an earth god ; a Brahmin ;
a name for Siva : ภูธน *lit.* "one whose
property is the earth," *i. e.* a king : ภูธร *lit.*
"earth-bearing," *i. e.* a mountain ; a king :
ภูธเรศวร์ *lit.* "the lord of mountains," *i. e.* the
Himalayas : ภูนาถ *lit.* "guardian of the
earth," *i. e.* a king (chd. p. 91) : ภูนายก a
king ; a prince : ภูบดี a king ; a ruler ; a
sovereign : ภูบท *lit.* "earth-fixed," "earth-
rooted," *i. e.* a tree : ภูบาล *lit.* "one who
rules a realm," *i. e.* a king : ภูบุตร, ภูสุต
lit. "son of the earth," *i. e.* the planet Mars
(considered as a diety) : ภูบุตรี, ภูสุตา *lit.* "a
daughter of the earth," *i. e.* Sita, Rama's
consort : ภูรมณ์ a king ; a prince : ภูลดา
an earthworm : ภูวัลลภ *lit.* "a favourite
of the earth," *i. e.* a king ; a prince : ภูสวรรค์
lit. "the earthly paradise," *i. e.* the sacred
Sumern mountain.

ภู ๒   poo *n.* a mound, pile or hill of rocks
or stones : ภูเขา a mountain : ภูเขาไฟ
a volcano : ภูผา a cliff ; a precipice ; a projecting or overhanging rock.

ภู่ (แมลง)   poo³ *n.* the carpenter beetle or
bee, *Xylocopa tenuiscapa* (MCM. p. 479).

ภูชิชย์   poo-chit⁶ *S. n.* a person who has
regained his liberty by redeeming his pledge
(S. E. D. p. 759) : *adj.* free ; independent.

ภูดาด (เสมียน)   poo-dart⁴ *n.* a clerk or
writer ; an amanuensis.

ภูต   poo-dta⁴ *P. S. n.* the ghost of a deceased person ; a demon ; genii : *adj.* existent ;
actual ; achieved ; past ; former ; finished ;
occurred (S. E. D. p. 761) : ภูตกรรตา *lit.* "the

maker of creatures," *i. e.* Brahma : ภูตกาล the past ; the past tense : ภูตคราม, ภูตคาม vegetation (as grass, plants, shrubs, trees) (chd. p. 91) ; a multitude of plants ; any aggregate or elementary matter ; the body : ภูตธรา retaining or remembering the past ; the supporter of beings ; the earth : ภูตธาตรี *lit.* "the restorer of beings," *i. e.* sleep : ภูตบดี, ภูตป, ภูตป the king of ghosts ; the chief of animals or creatures ; a giant chief or king (chd. p. 91) : ภูตภรรดา, ภูตราช *lit.* "the lord of beings or spirits," *i. e.* Siva : ภูเตศวร *lit.* "lord of (evil) beings," *i. e.* Siva.

ภูติ, ภูตี, ภูดี poo-dti[4] *P. S. n.* being ; existence ; welfare, personified in Lady Lakshami, goddess of Abundance and Beauty (H. C. D. p. 176) ; prosperity (Chd. p. 91 : S. E. D. p. 762).

ภูม poom *S. n.* a step ; a degree ; a stage ; the floor of a house ; an area ; a storey ; the base of a geometrical figure (S. E. D. p. 763).

ภูมิ poom *P. S. n.* a district ; a place ; a site ; a situation ; a position ; the earth ; soil ; ground ; a country or territory (S. E. D. p. 763) : ไชยภูมิ the place of victory : ไตรยภูมิ the three districts, heaven, earth, and hell : พระ-ภูมิ earthly angels : พระภูมิเจ้าที่ a guardian angel of the place : ภูมิกันทร fungus ; fungi or mushrooms ; toadstools : ภูมิกัมบน, ภูมิจล an earthquake ; a shock or trembling of the earth : ภูมิคุหา subterranean cavities or holes in the earth : ภูมิโคจร an inhabitant of the earth ; mankind : ภูมิช *lit.* "produced from the earth," *i. e.* sprung from the ground ; a man ; a kind of snail ; vegetables : ภูมิชีวี *lit.* "those living by the soil," *i. e.* farmers ; gardeners ; merchants ; traders : ภูมิดนัย, ภูมิบุตร the planet Mars : ภูมิเทพ *lit.* "earthly gods," *i.e.* Brahmins : ภูมินทร์ a king (chd. p. 91) ; an earth lord (the title of a king) : ภูมิบริมาณ a table for calculating square measure : ภูมิรู้ education ; knowledge : ภูมิ-ลำเนา an habitat : ภูมิลำเนาโดยการเลือก a domicile by choice : ภูมิลำเนาโดยความจำเป็น

a domicile by necessity : ภูมิลำเนาโดยการบังเกิด a domicile by birth : ภูมิลาภ *lit.* "the state of gaining the earth," *i. e.* death ; dying : ภูมิวิทยา, เกษตรศาสตร์ geology : ภูมิศาสตร์ geography : ภูมิสี see จตุรภูมิ p. 228 : ศาล-พระภูมิ a shrine dedicated to gods of the place : สมรภูมิ a field of battle : สุวรรณภูมิ *lit.* "earth of gold," *i. e.* name of a province.

ภูมิ poo-mee *S. n.* the earth ; ground [(p. 763). (s. E. D.

ภูรโลก poo-ra[6]-loke[3] *S. n.* the terrestrial globe ; the world ; the earth ; the region south of the equator (S. E. D. p. 763).

ภูริ ๑ poo-ri[6] *P. S. adj.* much ; many ; abundant (chd. p. 91) ; frequent ; numerous ; great ; important ; strong ; mighty (S. E. D. p. 764) : ภูริกรรม doing much ; having many obligations ; very busy : ภูริจักษุ *lit.* "a much see-er," *i. e.* one affording mainfold appearances (said of the sun) : ภูริรส *lit.* "that which has much juice," *i. e.* the sugar cane.

ภูริ ๒ poo-ri[6] *P. n.* the earth (chd. p. 91).

ภูริ ๓, ภูรี poo-ri[6] *P. n.* wisdom ; astuteness (chd. p. 91).

ภูวน poo-wa[6]-na[6] *S. n.* a being ; a living creature ; man ; mankind ; the world ; the earth (S. E. D. p. 760) : ภูวนตรัย *lit.* "the three worlds," *i.e.* earth, heaven and hell ; see ตรีภพ p. 345).

ภูษณ poo-sa[4]-na[6] *S. n.* ornaments ; decorations ; adornments (chd. p. 91) : ภูษณพาส clothes ; garments ; personal adornments or ornaments.

ภูษา poo-sah[2] *P. S. n.* an ornament ; a decoration (S. E. D. p. 764).

ภูษิต poo-sit[4] *P. S. v.* to be adorned or decorated (S. E. D. p. 764).

เภกะ, เภคะ pay-gka[4] *P. S. n.* a frog : เภกภุช *lit.* "eaters of frogs," *i. e.* snakes.

เภตรา pay-dtrah *n.* a ship ; a junk,

เภท pay-ta[6] *P. S. adj.* breaking; splitting; rending; tearing; piercing; disclosing; betraying; gaping; blossoming; sprouting or shooting forth (S. E. D. p. 766): เภทภัย misfortune; calamity; disasters (of various forms): เภทุบาย various tricks to lure or deceive; craft; fraud; guile; wile; artifice; cunning procedure.

เภรว, ไภรพ pay-ra[6]-wa[6] *P. n.* terror; fear; timidity: *adj.* fearful; terrible (chd. p. 88).

เภราคาร pay-rah-karn *n.* a drum tower; a tocsin or alarm-bell tower.

เภริ, เภรี, ไภรี, ไภริน, เภริน pay-ri[6] *P. n.* a big drum; a kettle-drum: ภัยเภรี a drum or tocsin for announcing a calamity or approaching danger: เภริจรณ์ to proclaim by beating a drum.

เภสัชช์, เภสัช, ไภษัชย์ pay-sut[4] *P. S. n.* a remedy; medicine; drugs; (chd. p. 88): เภสัชวิทยา pharmacology: เภสัชห้า five domestic remedies, *viz* butter (เนยใส), ghee (เนยข้น), milk (น้ำนม), honey (น้ำผึ้ง), molasses (น้ำอ้อย).

โภค poh-ka[6] *P. S. v.* to eat, use or enjoy; to curl, bend or coil: *n.* a snake's body; a snake's expanded hood; a fold; property; fortune; goods; riches; wealth (chd. p. 89): โภคบดี *lit.* "a revenue lord," *i.e.* a viceroy; the governor of a town or district: โภควัต

riches; wealth; a wealthy person: โภควดี feminine form of โภควัต.

โภคิน poh-kin *S. n.* a serpent, or serpent demon: *adj.* curved; ringed; furnished with windings, curves, or rings (S. E. D. p. 767): โภคินี a female naga or snake.

โภไคย poh-kai *P. n.* assets; wealth (chd. p. 89).

โภไคศวรรย์ poh-kai-sa[4]-wan[2] *n.* the rightful ownership of wealth or property.

โภชก poh-cha[6]-gka[4] *P. n.* a village headman (chd. p. 89); one who partakes of food: คามโภชก a Nai Umphur or Kumnan.

โภชช์, โภชย์ pote[3] *P. S. n.* eatables; food: *adj.* edible (chd. p. 90): โภชนาคาร a restaurant.

โภชน poh-cha[6]-na[6] *P. S. n.* the act of eating; a meal; food; offering or affording anything as food: *adj.* feeding; voracious (S. E. D. p. 768): โภชนะห้า five groups of foods or nourishment, *viz.* (1) boiled, cooked or prepared rice; (2) freshly prepared sweetmeats (which may soon become putrid); (3) dried or preserved cakes (as biscuits, cheese, toast); (4) fish (including shell-fish); (5) meats (as beef, mutton, chicken or ducks): โภชนะสาลี wheat foods: เสวยโภชนา to partake of food (used in regard to royalty).

ม

ม The thirty-third consonant of the Thai alphabet, a low class letter of which there are twenty-four, *viz.* ค, ค, ฆ, ง, ช, ฌ, ซ, ญ, ฑ, ฑ, ฒ, ณ, ฑ, น, ณ, พ, ฟ, ภ, ม, ร, ล, ว, ฬ, ฮ. มอม้า is the name of this letter. It occurs extensively in Thai, Pali and Sanskrit words, and also as a prefix.

มก *Anam,* หมาก *Thailand* (ต้น) mok[6] *n. Areca catechu (Palmae),* areca-nut or betel-

nut, a tall, slender, erect palm, 30 to 40 (sometimes up to 50) feet high, with a straight stem, native of Malaya, extensively cultivated in Ceylon and elsewhere throughout tropical Asia for its nuts (seeds), which in the husk are each about the size of a hen's egg, and usually yellow or orange-yellow when ripe. The brown, conical nuts are commonly used throughout the eastern tropics as a masticatory. In preparing the latter, in Thailand a few thin slices of the nut are taken into the mouth; to which is added a dash of lime-paste spread on a betel leaf, a portion of fine cut tobacco, and a few cardamoms or cloves. The nut, ground into powder, is commonly used as a vermifuge for dogs and other animals; also it is used in the preparation of denti-fices. In addition to local consumption, about 6,000 to 7,000 tons of areca-nuts are exported annually from Ceylon, chiefly to India (MCM. p. 380: V. P. p. 220: BURK. p. 223).

มกร　　ma⁶-gkawn　P. S. n. a dragon; name of a mythical fish or sea monster (CHD. p. 233); name of the tenth sign of the zodiac; see ราศีมังกร p. 327 (S. E. D. p. 771): มกรกุณฑล a dragon-shaped earring: มกรเกตน์, มกรธวัช lit. "one who bears a banner displaying this mythical monster," i. e. the god of Love or Cupid (H. C. D. p. 146): มกรพาหน lit. "one having the dragon for his vehicle," i. e. Varu-na, lord of the Waters (พระพรุณ): มกรากร, มกราลัย, มกราวาส lit. "the birth-place or recep-tacle of monsters," i. e. the sea.

มกราคม　　ma⁶-gka⁴-rah-kom n. the tenth solar month; January; the zodiacal sign Cap-ricornus.　　　　　[มกร.

มกรี　　ma⁶-gka⁴-ree n. the feminine form of

มกส　　ma⁶-gka⁴-sa⁴ P. n. a gnat; a mos-quito (CHD. p. 233): มกสกุฏี a mosquito whisk.

มกุฏ, มงกุฏ　　ma⁶-gkoot⁴ P. S. n. a crown; a crest; a diadem (CHD. p. 233): มงกุฏราช-กุมาร the heir-apparent to a Crown.

มกุล　　ma⁶-gkoo⁴-la⁶ P. S. n. an opening bud; a bush or ball (CHD. p. 233): adj. bud-ding; see ตูม p. 372.

มค see มฤค p. 624.

มคธ　　ma⁶-kot⁶ P. S. n. Makhot, commonly known as Pali (see p. 482) the Aryan vernacular language of Magadha, the "holy land of Bud-dhism," which is the modern country of South

Bihar (พิหารใต้). It was spoken in the sixth century before Christ, and was the language in which Gotama Buddha preached, and was that in which the sacred books were first written, being the legends of Buddha's life which pro-bably reproduced the oral traditions accepted by the members of the Third Buddhist Council in 246 B. C. It is reasonable to believe that the sacred books were first written in Pali, for otherwise we can not account for the Pali lan-guage being used at all. Sanskrit, the orna-mental classical language of India, would have been used as it was by the Northern Buddhists, had not tradition been on the side of Pali (Ala. p. 246): มคธพากย์ the vernacular which was the language of Magadha: มคธภาษา lit. "language of the Magadha people" or "Magadhese language." It is the only name used in the old Southern Buddhist texts for the sacred language of Buddhism. Magadhi language is equivalent to Palibhasa which means "language of the texts" (CHD. p. 225).

มฆ　　ma⁶-ka⁶ P. S. n. gift; bounty; a re-ward or prize; name of the tenth lunar as-terism containing five stars (H. C. D. p. 214): มฆไทย the giving of a prize, or an awarding of rewards: มฆวา, มฆวาน, มฆวัน lit. "a giver of prizes, or a distributer of wealth," i. e. Indra (CHD. p. 226).

มง see มุง p. 653.

มงโกรย, แมว (ปลา)　　mong-gkro-ie n. En-granlis mystax (Engraulidae), a herring found both in salt and fresh water, more especially in the north-eastern parts of Thai-land (suvatti p. 15).

มงคล　　mong-kon P. S. n. auspiciousness; happiness; luck; joy; that belonging to state occasions or festivals (CHD. p. 237); glory; fortune: งานวิวาหมงคล nuptials: เป็น-มงคล to express happiness and blessings, or to afford glory and prestige to the contracting parties: มงคลพิธี celebrations on propitious occasions: มงคลวาท the bestowing of blessings, expressing happiness or wishing prosperity: มงคลวาร Tuesday: มหามงคล glory or happiness in the highest degree.

มงคลาวาส　　　mong-ka[6]-lah-wat[3] *S. n. lit.* "a place where festivals are held," *i. e.* a Buddhist sanctuary or monastery; an auspicious dwelling (S. E. D. p. 773).

มณฑ์, มัณฑ　　　mon *P. S. n.* the scum of boiled rice; the thick part of milk; cream; scented oils; perfumes; ornaments; personal decorations (S. E. D. p. 775): มณฑป, มรฑาป a tent; a canopy; a dome; a spire (Ala. p. 290); a decorated building topped by an artistic spire (over a revered object).

มณฑก, มัณฑุก, มณฑุก　　　mon-tok[6] *P. S. n.* a frog (chd. 236): ปืนมณฑก an ancient Thai cannon or mortar.

มณฑนะ　　　mon-da[4]-na[6] *P. S. n.* an adornment; an ornament; a decoration; jewels; dress (chd. 236).

มณฑล　　　mon-ton *P. n.* a circle; a globe; an orb; a disk; a ring; a ball; a wheel; the circumference; a district comprising a number of provinces or villages; a civic division of a state, territory or country and its inhabitants; a group; a band; a company or collection of people or society; the path or orbit of a heavenly body (S. E. D. p. 775): มณฑลี *lit.* "one radiating rays," *i. e.* the sun.

มณฑิร, มณเฑียร, มนทิร, มนเทียร, มันทิร, มันทิราลัย　　　mon-ti[6]-ra[6] *P. S. n.* a house; an edifice; a town (chd. p. 236) (the first two are preferred spellings): มณเฑียรบาล the guardians of a palace: กฎมณเฑียรบาล royal family law, first promulgated in 1450 A. D: ราชมณเฑียร a palace.

มณโฑ see มนโททรี p. 622.

มณิกะ　　　ma[6]-ni[6]-gka[4] *P. n.* a water-pot; a water-jar or pitcher (chd. p. 237).

มณี, มณิ　　　ma[6]-nee *P. S. n.* a gem; a jewel; crystal; a water-pot; any ornament or amulet (chd. p. 237): มณีกานน *lit.* "a garden of jewels," *i. e. metaphorically* the neck (as being the place where diamond or pearl necklaces are hung): มณีการ a gem expert; a jeweller; a lapidary: มณีธนุ *lit.* "a jewelled bow," *i. e.* a rainbow: มณีพืช, มธุพืช see ทับทิม (ต้น) p. 409: มณีมาลา a string or necklace of jewels or pearls: มณีรัตน์ a jewel; a gem: มณีราค see ชาด p. 291: มณีศิลา a jewelled stone slab.

มด　　　mot[6] *n.* ants (in general): มด, มอด (ปลา) *Clarias teysmanni* (*Clariidae*) (suvatti p. 84): มดแดง large red ants: มดไฟ red ants whose sting burns like fire: มดหมอ *colloq.* physicians (in general): แม่มด a woman spirit-charmer; a sorceress; a witch: รังมด ants' nests.

มดยอบ (ต้น)　　　mot[6]-yaup[3] *n. Commiphora sp.* (*Burseraceae*), myrrh, a genus of shrubs and trees, often thorny, found for the most part in very dry climates in eastern Africa and western Asia. The resins of the various members of the genus have been traded in from extremely remote times. It is known that myrrh was imported into Egypt in 1700 B.C. and perhaps the trade was then already old. The date at which myrrh reached Malaysia is unknown, and it can never have been an import which was purchased in more than extremely small quantities. It may be assumed that the Hindu colonists took a knowledge of it to Java bringing with it, its Sanskrit name "gandha rasha" which nowadays is given everywhere in Malaysia to the inodorous *Gendarussa*. It seems probable that myrrh did not come into Malaya direct from India but by way of Java. Since the name "mur" is the present Malay word for myrrh, a name derived from Arabic, it would seem that myrrh had been difficult to obtain and something else was substituted for it. Probably it was essential to their magic (BURK. p. 647).

มดลูก   mot[6]-look[3] *n.* the uterus; the womb.

มดาย   ma[6]-dai *Cam. n.* a mother.

มต see มฤต p. 624.

มตก, มฤตก   ma[6]-dta[4]-gka[4] *P. n.* a ghost; a corpse: *adj.* dead; belonging to the dead (chd. p. 242): มตกภัตต์ food offered to obtain merit on behalf of the dead.

มติ (มะติ)   ma[6]-dti[4] *P. S. n.* mind; understanding; intelligence; thought; imagination; knowledge; wisdom; wish; opinion; advice (chd. p. 242); decision; resolution.

มท   ma[6]-ta[6] *P. S. n.* hilarity; rapture; excitement; intoxication; sexual desire or enjoyment; wantonness; lust; ruttishness; rut (especially of an elephant); the fluid or oil that exudes from a rutting elephant's temples (S. E. D. p. 777): มทกล one who sings softly or incoherently while under the influence of an intoxicant; one ruttish, furious or mad (as an elephant): มทชล the temple juice (of a ruttish elephant): มทราค *lit.* "one affected by passion or by intoxication," *i. e.* the god of Love; a drunken man: มทวารณะ a furious elephant; one while in rut: มทามพร the elephant that Indra rides.

มทนะ, มัทน   ma[6]-ta[6]-na[6] *P. n.* lust; love; the god of Love; the plant *Vanguiera spinosa* (chd. p. 224); oil for anointing the lips.

มทนิยะ, มัทนิยะ   ma[6]-ta[6]-nee-ya[6] *P.S. adj.* intoxicating (chd. p. 224); love-inducing or exciting.

มธุ, มฤธุ   ma[6]-too[6] *P.S. n.* honey; the Soma juice; milk; sugar; fruit juices; sweet wines; the nectar of flowers: *adj.* sweet; delicious; pleasant; delightful (S. E. D. p. 779): มธุกร, มธุลีห์ *lit.* "makers of honey," "lickers of honey," *i. e.* bees (chd. p. 224): มธุรี a queen bee: มธุการี a bee: มธุโกศ, มธุปฎูล *lit.* "honey receptacle," *i. e.* a beehive; a honeycomb: มธุชา obtained from honey;

sugar made from honey; candy; fruit preserves: มธุตฤณ sugar-cane: มธุทูต *lit.* "a messenger of spring," *i. e.* the mango tree: มธุป *lit.* "honey drinkers," *i. e.* bees (chd. p. 224); "a drinker of the Soma juice," *i. e.* a drunkard: มธุพรต a large black bee: มธุพืช see ทับทิม (ต้น) p. 409: มธุมิศร์ mixed with honey or sweet milk: มธุรส the juice of honey; sweetness; sugar-cane; a bunch of grapes: มธุศรรกรา congealed honey; honey-sugar: มธุเศษ wax.

มธุร, มาธุร, มาธูร   ma[6]-too[6]-ra[6] *P. n.* the red sugar-cane; sweetness (as treacle or syrup); melodious; pleasing to the ear; mellifluous (chd. p. 224): มธุรตรัย three delicious or savoury things, *viz.* sugar; honey; butter: มธุรพจน์ one using musical, sweet, or harmonious words or language.

มน ๑   mon *v.* to be stable, permanent, unchanging, constant (used in regard to planets or stars of good omen): *adj.* round; circular; having a curved contour or surface.

มน ๒   mon *n.* the mind; the intellect; the heart (chd. p. 238); purpose (Ala. p. 216); see มนัส p. 622.

มั่น see ชุก p. 310; แทรก p. 427.

มนต์, มนตร์   mon *P. S. n.* speech; an instrument of thought; a sacred text or formula; a prayer or song of praise; a vedic hymn or sacrificial formula; a mystic verse; a magic spell (S. E. D. p. 785): น้ำมนตร์ consecrated or hallowed water: มนตร์เสก to repeat exorcisms: มนตร์ดน to be influenced by charms or incantations: สวดมนตร์ to chant prayers.

มนตรี   mon-dtree *S. n.* a counsellor; a statesman; a wise man; the office or vocation of a Minister of State; ministry (S. E. D. p. 786): มนตรีสภา an assembly of State Ministers.

มนท์   mon *P.S. n.* Saturn: *adj.* slow; tardy; loitering; idle; lazy; sluggish; apathetic;

indifferent; dull-witted; silly; stupid (S. E. D. p. 787): มนทกานติ *lit.* "one having a soft lustre," *i. e.* the moon: มนทาทร having little respect for; careless about: มนโททรี, นาง-มณโฑ Ravana's favourite consort, a character appearing in the Ramayana.

มนทิร, มันทิร, มันทิราลัย mon-ti⁶-ra⁶ *P. S. n.* a house; a palace; a temple, camp, or town (chd. p. 236).

มนสิการ ma⁶-na⁶-si⁴-gkarn *P. S. n.* attention (chd. p. 235); the taking to heart (of something).

มนัส ma⁶-nut⁶ *S. n.* the mind; intellect; understanding; perception; intention; the breath or living soul which escapes from the body at death; the spirit or spiritual principle (S. E. D. p. 783): มนัสตาป mental pain; anguish; repentance; the burning of the mind: มนัสวี one who is smart, astute, wise, clever.

มนุ, มนู ma⁶-noo⁶ *S. n.* the man *par excellence*, or the representative man and father of the human race; Manu (S. E. D. p. 784).

มนุษย์ ma⁶-noot⁶ *S. n.* a human being; a man; mankind (chd. p. 240); people: มนุษย-การ the deeds of a man; human exertion: มนุษยชาติ mankind; the human race: มนุษย-เทพ *lit.* "a man-god," *i. e.* a Brahmin: มนุษย-ธรรม the law, duty, state or character of man: มนุษยโบต infants; children; a little boy: มนุษยยาน *lit.* "human means of transporation," *i. e.* a palanquin; a litter: มนุษยโลก humanity (in general); the people of 'this world': มนุษย์วิทยา anthropology.

มนุสาร, มนุสาร, มโนสาร ma⁶-noo⁶-sarn² *n.* Manu-Sanhita, the code of Manu or Institutes of Manu. It is attributed to the first Manu and is supposed to have been composed in about the fifth century B. C. It is the earliest of all the post-Vedic writings and is chief of the works classified as Smriti (*i. e.* "remembered" or "traditional"). It is said to have consisted originally of 100,000 verses,

arranged in twenty-four chapters; Narada shortened the work to 12,000 verses and Sumati made a second abridgement reducing it to 4,000, but only 2685 are extant. It is the foundation of Hindu Law, a collection or digest of current laws and creeds rather than a planned systematic code. It is frequently quoted today in law courts, and by Hindus in all cases where the customs of Hindu society and the observances of caste are under question (The Gods of India p. 16: H. C. D. p. 201).

มนู ma⁶-noo *S. n.* the Manus (rulers over long periods of time) (Gods of India p. 19). The name is especially applied to fourteen successive mythical progenitors and sovereigns of the earth, described as creating and supporting this world through successive long periods of time (S. E. D. p. 784). The Manu of the present age is the seventh, named Vaivaswata. He was son of Surya, and father of Ikshwaku, the founder of the solar race of kings (H. C. D. p. 332). With the seventh Manu is connected the following very curious and interesting legend of the deluge, the first account of which is found in the Satapatha Brahmana (H. C. D. p. 200: Gods of India p. 109). One morning Manu caught a small fish in the water which had been brought to him for washing his hands. He caught the fish which immediately pleaded for protection until it should be grown, promising in return salvation from the great flood which should destroy mankind. Manu kept the fish, which grew rapidly, until nothing except the ocean was large enough to contain it. Then he let it go, but at that time the fish foretold the time of the coming flood and instructed Manu to make a big boat in which he was to save his life. Manu did as directed, and when the flood did come, the fish returned, and Manu fastened the cable of his ship to the fish's horn. Thus he passed over the northern mountain (the Himalayas, as a commentator explains) where he was instructed to fasten his ship to a tree until the waters should subside.

มโน   ma⁶-noh *S. n.* the mind; the intellect; thought; desire; mood; temper; spirit (S. E. D. p. 785): มโนคติ *lit.* "the heart's course," *i. e.* wish; desire: มโนช *lit.* "born of the mind," *i. e.* love: มโนชญ์, มาโนชญ์, มนุญญ์, มนุญ *lit.* "agreeable to one's mind," *i. e.* pleasing; beautiful; charming: มโนธรรม an inherent sense of justice, virtue and rightness: มโนนุกูล stimulating or uplifting the mind or mood: มโนภพ *lit.* "mind born," *i. e.* imaginary; visionary; arising or being in the mind only: มโนคินิเวศ close application of the mind; tenacity or firmness of purpose: มโนภิปราย, มโนภิลาษ the longing for; desire; wish of the heart or mind: มโนมัย springing from the mind; caused by the mind (chd. p. 239); consisting of spirit or mind; mental; spiritual: มโนรถ *lit.* "the heart's joy," *i. e.* a wish; a desire; a wish expressed in an indirect manner: มโนรม *lit.* "gratifying the mind," *i. e.* attractive; charming; beautiful: มโนรา a fabulous nymph of the forest (a character occurring in Thai folklore stories and songs): มโนลัย a condition of unconsciousness: มโนหร fascinating; beautiful; charming; captivating to the mind (chd. p. 239).

มยุระ, มยุร, มยุรี   ma⁶-yoo⁶-ra⁶ *P. n.* a peacock (chd. p. 245): มยุระคนธรรพ์ a mythical monster; the fairy-peacock: มยุระเวรไตย์ a mythical monster, half garuda, half peacock.

มยุข   ma⁶-yoo-ka⁴ *P. n.* a ray or rays of light (chd. p. 245).

มร   ma⁶-ra⁶ *P. S. n.* death (chd. p. 240).

มรกฏ, มรรกฏ   maw-ra⁶-gkot⁴ *S. n.* a monkey; an ape (S. E. D. p. 791).

มรกต   maw-ra⁶-gkot⁴ *n.* an emerald (S. E. D. [p. 789).

มรฑาป see มณฑาป p. 620.

มรณ์, มรณะ   morn *P. S. n.* the act of dying; death; passing away; cessation (S. E. D. p. 789): มรณธรรม death; the law of nature: มรณ-

นิสสัย one determined to die: มรณภัย the fear of death: มรณภาพ death (used only for the bonzes): มรณานต์ ending in death.

มรรค, มรรคา, มารค   muk⁶ *P. S. n.* "The Path," "The Way," Cattaro Magga (the Four Paths). Nirvana is reached by four paths, stages or degrees leading to saintship, each of which is subdivided and these are sometimes referred to as "the Four Paths and the Four Fruits" or otherwise "the Eight Paths." The Four Paths leading to the highest degrees of saintship are as follows,—(1) โสดาบัตติมรรค "The First Path" or degree, described as "the state of entering into the stream of wisdom," thus becoming a converted man. The saint who has attained this can not have more than seven births among men and angels before he enters Nirvana (Ala. p. 171: chd. p. 225): (2) สกิทาคามิมรรค "The Second Path" or degree. One who enters this path is called "he who must come back once," because after attaining this degree there will be only one more birth among men or angels before reaching Nirvana (Ala. p. 171): (3) อนาคามิมรรค "The Third Path" or degree. One who enters this path is called "he who will not come back," because there will be another birth but not in the world of sensuality. From the heavens of the Brahmas, Nirvana will be attained (Ala. p. 171: chd. p. 30): (4) อรหัตตมรรค "The Fourth Path" or last degree. One who enters this path is called "the Venerable," "the state of being an Araha or attaining Arhatship," final sanctification. This is the perfect saint who will pass to Nirvana without further birth (Ala. p. 171: chd. p. 54): ปัสสาวมรรค the urethra: เว็จจมรรค the anus; the rectum.

มรรตย, มรรตัย   mun-dta⁴-ya⁶ *S. n.* he who, or that which must die; the world of mortals; a mortal (S. E. D. p. 791).

มรรทน   mut-ta⁶-na⁶ *S. n.* the act or condition of rubbing, grinding, crushing, tramping (chd. p. 224), destroying, tormenting or ruining (S. E. D. p. 791).

มรรยาท, มริยาท mun-yart[3] *P.S. n.* a boundary ; a limit ; rectitude ; conduct or behaviour
(Chd. p. 240) ; a covenant ; an agreement ; a bond
or contract ; a rule or custom (S. E. D. p. 791).

มรสุม maw-ra[6]-soom[2] *n.* the season of wind,
storm or monsoon : พิศม์มรสุม violence or
severity of the monsoon.

มรักษณ์ ma[6]-ruk[6] *S. n.* a medicinal oil for
smearing or applying ; the act of rubbing the
body (with fragrant oils) (S. E. D. p. 792).

มรัมเทศ ma[6]-rum-ma[6]-tet[3] *n.* Burma.

มริจ ma[6]-rit[6] *P. n.* pepper (Chd. p. 240) ;
the pepper shrub ; black pepper (S. E. D. p. 790).

มริยาท see **มรรยาท** p. 624.

มรีจิ ma[6]-ree-chji[4] *P. n.* a ray of light ; a
mirage (Chd. p. 240) : *adj.* radiant ; having
rays (S. E. D. p. 790).

มรุ ma[6]-roo[6] *P.S. n.* a wilderness ; a sandy
waste or desert ; a mountain ; a rock.

มรุต ma[6]-root[6] *P.S. n.* the storm god ; the
god of the Wind ; wind ; air ; breath (S. E. D.
p. 790).

มฤค, มค ma[6]-rurk[6] *P.S. n.* a forest animal ; a wild beast ; a deer ; a gazelle ; an
antelope ; a stag ; a musk-deer : มฤคี a hind
(feminine form) : มฤคทาย the deer park ;
the place where Gotama Buddha preached
his first sermon : มฤคพยาธ a hunter :
มฤคราช, มฤคินทร์, มฤคเนนทร์ *lit.* " king of beasts,"
i. e. the lion : มฤควัน a wild animal park
or preserve ; a forest abounding in wild animals : มฤคสาวก a doe ; a fawn ; a young
deer : มฤคางกะ *lit.* " deer-marked," *i. e.* the
moon : มฤคาทน์ *lit.* " an animal devourer,"
i. e. a hunting leopard ; a hyena (S. E. D. p. 828).

มฤคย์ ma[6]-rurk[6] *S. adj.* questionable ; uncertain ; shadowy (S. E. D. p. 829).

มฤคยา ma[6]-rurk[6]-ka[6]-yah *S. n.* the chase
or hunt (of wild animals or deer) (S. E. D. p. 829).

มฤจฉา, มิจฉา ma[6]-rit[6]-chah[2] *P. S. adv.*
falsely ; wrongly (Chd. 246) : มฤจฉาชีพ, มิจ-
ฉาชีพ wrong or improper means of gaining
a livelihood : มฤจฉาทิฏฐิ, มิจฉาทิฏฐิ wrong
views ; false doctrine ; scepticism ; heresy ; unbelief (Chd. p. 247).

มฤดก, มฤตก, มรดก ma-ra[6]-dok[4] *S. n.*
" the deceased," understood by the Thai as
inheritance ; patrimony : เจ้ามฤดก, ผู้รับมฤดก
heir ; executor : ได้มฤดก to receive an inheritance or heritage : ตัดมฤดก to disin-
herit : แบ่งมฤดก to divide the legacy :
ผู้จัดการมฤดกฝ่ายชาย an executor of a will :
ผู้จัดการมฤดกฝ่ายหญิง an executrix (S. E. D. p. 827).

มฤต, มต ma[6]-rit[6] *S. v.* to die (Chd. p. 243) :
adj. dead ; deathlike ; torpid ; rigid ; departed
(S. E. D. p. 827).

มฤตก, มตก ma[6]-rur[6]-dta[4]-gka[4] *S. n.* the
dead ; a corpse (S. E. D. p. 827).

มฤตยุ ma[6]-rurt[6]-dta[4]-yoo *S. n.* death ; the
god of Death ; Yama (S. E. D. p. 827) ; Uranus.

มฤทวีกา ma[6]-rurt[6]-ta[6]-wee-gkah *S. n.* a
vine ; a bunch of grapes (S. E. D. p. 830).

มฤทุ, มฤทุกะ ma[6]-rur[6]-too[6] *S. adj.* soft ;
delicate : tender ; mild ; gentle ; feeble ; moderate (S. E. D. p. 830) : มฤทุกิริยา the act of
softening or mollifying : มฤทุปาณิ one with
soft, delicate hands : มฤทุภาพ softness ;
mildness : มฤทุหฤทัย tender-hearted.

มฤธุ see **มธุ** p. 621.

มฤษา ma[6]-rur[6]-sah[2] *S. adv.* falsely ; wrongly ;
feignedly ; uselessly ; in vain ; to no purpose
(S. E. D. p. 831) : มฤษาญาณ ignorance ; stupidity ; the state of holding to a wrong notion
or opinion : มฤษาภาษิน, มฤษาวาทิน one speaking falsely ; a liar : มฤษาวาจ, มฤษาวาท untrue
speech ; irony ; sarcasm : มฤษาสากษี a false
witness ; a perjurer.

มล mon *P. n.* impurity ; sin ; vice ; fault ;
stain ; dirt ; filth ; excrement ; defect ; taint
(Chd. p. 234).

มลทิน, มุทิน   mon-tin *n.* stain; flaw; fault; blot; vice; defect: เป็นมลทิน polluted; vitiated; tainted; stained: หมดมลทิน purified; clean; flawless; stainless: หามลทิน-มิได้ innocent; without fault or flaw; untainted.

มลวก see ลวก

มล่อน see มอญ p. 629.

มล่อย see ม่อย p. 630.

มลังเมลือง   ma[6]-lung-ma[6]-leu-ang *adj.* bright; lustrous; shining.

มล้า see ล้า

มลาก   ma[6]-lark[3] *v.* to draw, drag, tow, or haul: *adj.* much; many; abundant.

มลาน ๑   ma[6]-larn *S. adj.* faded; withered; exhausted; languid; weak; feeble; dejected; relaxed (S. E. D. p. 838).

มลาน ๒ see ตะลึตะลาน p. 356.

มล่าน   ma[6]-larn[3] *v.* to run hurridly or excitely (as one fleeing for his life).

มลาย   ma[6]-lai *v.* to be broken into pieces; to be destroyed; to die; to come to naught; see แตก p. 475.

มลาว   ma[6]-lao *n.* Laos *corrupted form.*

มล่าวเมลา   ma[6]-lao[3]-may[6]-lao *adj.* beautiful; gay; attractive; see งดงาม p. 220.

มลิน   ma[6]-lin *P. S. adj.* dirty; black; brown; impure; tainted (chd. p. 234).

มลื่น   ma[6]-lurn[3] *v.* to be slippery, smooth, sliding or gliding easily.

มลื้น   ma[6]-lurn[5] *v.* to have the feelings hurt; to be ashamed; to be sorry or sad; see เจ็บใจ p. 256.

มวก (ต้น)   mu-ak[3] *n. Urceola esculenta* (*Apocynaceae*), a woody climber of Burma, producing an edible fruit, and also a blue dye (McM. p. 271): มวกผา chaste: มวกเหล็ก, มวกใหญ่ medicinal trees.

ม่วง   mu-ang[3] *adj.* purple; violet: ม่วง (นก) the emerald cuckoo, *Chrysococcyx maculatus* (Gaird. J. S. S. IX, 1, p. 7): ผ้าม่วง silk loin-cloths (in general): สีม่วง purple in colour.

มวน   mu-an *v.* to roll (cigars or cigarettes): มวนเขียว (แมลง) the orange bug, *Rhynchocoris humeralis* (*Pentatomidae*) (Dept. Agri. and Fisheries): มวนท้อง colic; an uncertain feeling in the intestinal tract, attended with acute pain.

ม้วน   mu-an[5] *v.* to roll into a ball (as thread or string); to wind or coil (as rope): *n.* a coil (of rope); a bolt (of cloth): ด้ายหนึ่งม้วน a ball or spool of thread: ม้วนด้าย to wind thread into a ball; to reel thread on to a bobbin.

มวย ๑   mu-ie *n.* the act of boxing; hair done up in a knot (behind); a topknot or forelock of hair: ชกมวย to strike with the fists; see ชก p. 274: ตั้งมวย to assume the attitude of boxing: มวยปล้ำ to wrestle while boxing: หัดมวย to practice boxing.

มวย ๒   mu-ie *Cam. adj.* one; single.

ม้วย   mu-ie[5] *v.* to come to the end, or to be finished; to die; to be destroyed or ruined: ม้วยชีวา to end one's life: ม้วยบัลลัย to be completely consumed or destroyed: ม้วย-มรณา to die.

มวล, มูล   mu-an *n.* root; origin; stump; base; see เง่า p. 225: *adj.* all; entire: คน-ทั้งมวล everybody; the whole crowd or mass of people: ทั้งมวล all together *used collectively.*

มสาร, มสารก ๑   ma[6]-sarn[2] *S. n.* the emerald or sapphire (S. E. D. p. 793).

มสารก ๒   ma[6]-sah[2]-ra[6]-gka[4] *P. n.* a sort of bed (chd. p. 242); a bed fitted with carrying poles at the corners.

มสารคัลล์   ma^6-sah^2-ra^6-kun $P.$ $n.$ a precious stone; a sort of cat's eye, also called the variegated or clouded gem (chd. p. 241).

มสิ   ma^6-si^4 $P.$ $n.$ soot; ink (chd. p. 242).

มห ๑   ma^6-ha^4 $P.$ $v.$ to magnify; to esteem highly; to worship, honour or revere (S. E. D. p. 794).

มห ๒   ma^6-ha^4 $P.S.$ $adj.$ great; mighty; strong; abundant (S. E. D. p. 794); much used in the formation of compound nouns and adjectives (chd. p. 226).

มหรณพ, มหรรณพ, มหารณพ, มหัณณพ   ma^6-haw^2-ra^6-nop^6 $P.$ $n.$ the ocean (chd. p. 229); a large body of water.

มหรรฆ, มหัคฆ   ma^6-huk^4-ka^6 $P.$ $adj.$ of great value; costly; valuable (chd. p. 228).

มหรสพ, มโหรสพ   ma^6-haw^2-ra^6-sop^4 $P.$ $n.$ a great festival (chd. p. 232); an occasion of merry-making; various amusements, games and ceremonies in honour of the opening or dedication of a monastery.

มหัจฉริย   ma^6-hut^4-cha^4-ri^6-ya^6 $P.S.$ $adj.$ most wonderful; exceedingly strange or miraculous.

มหัต, มหันต์, มหันต   ma^6-hut^4 $P.$ $adj.$ great; large; big; eminent; much; excessive; excellent (chd. p. 229).

มหัทธนะ   ma^6-hut^4-ta^6-na^6 $P.$ $n.$ a millionaire: $adj.$ wealthy; rich (chd. p. 229).

มหันตโทษ   ma^6-hun^2-dta^4-tote^3 $n.$ punishments of the greatest severity or intensity (as in a penitentiary, a house of correction or a penal settlement); the antithesis of ลหุโทษ light sentence: มหันตราช a great and powerful ruler.

มหัลล, มหัลลกะ   ma^6-hun^2-la^6 $P.$ $n.$ an old man: $adj.$ old; aged (chd. p. 229).

มหัศจรรย์   ma^6-hut^4-sa^4-chjun $adj.$ most strange; curious; marvellous; extraordinary; miraculous.

มหา ๑   ma^6-hah^2 $n.$ an honorary degree conferred on members of the Buddhist clergy who have graduated from some school of Buddhist religious instruction; this is used as a prefix to his name; see เปรียญ p. 532.

มหา ๒   ma^6-hah^2 $adj.$ supreme; maximal; maximum; utmost; paramount; preeminent; inimitable: มหากษัตริย์ the greatest of kings: มหากาย the highest or largest (in stature): มหาทาน a paramount gift: มหานุภาพ one with great power, excellency or goodness; a philanthropist: $adj.$ powerful; mighty (chd. p. 229): มหาบท an unequalled road or highway: มหาบุรุษ an unparalleled person: มหาพน an unsurpassed forest: มหาภัย a matchless calamity or peril: มหาหพ a great war (chd. p. 228); a conflict or battle.

มหากาฬ   ma^6-hah^2-gkarn $n.$ name of a household remedy used to cure ulcers of the mouth and tongue.

มหาชน   ma^6-hah^2-chon $P.$ $n.$ the generality of men; mankind; people; the populace; the the public; a multitude (chd. p. 228).

มหาชาติ   ma^6-hah^2-chart^3 $n.$ $lit.$ "The Great Birth" story. Gotama Buddha attained enlightenment only after having passed through a succession of earthly forms. The most interesting and honoured of his incarnations are the last ten before the one in which he reached full enlightenment and ended his earthly career. These ten are called Thotsachat (ทศชาติ). In each of these some perfection of virtue was attained, patience, energy, determination, self-sacrifice, wisdom, morality, truth, love, kindness, indifference, all culminating in the tenth incarnation, which is called the Maha Chat (มหาชาติ). The Maha Chat is the story of Vessantara who gathered unto himself all the virtues of the heroes of the previous incarnations with an individual characteristic virtue of charity. Vessantara was married to the beautiful Princess Maddi; a son and daughter were born to them. In the capital city was a pure white elephant which had supernatural powers and in time of drouth brought rain to his country. The neighbouring country of Kalinga was threatened with drouth and the king sent asking Prince Vessantara for this priceless white elephant, which the prince gladly gave him. Having been already prominent in his charitable inclinations, this brought down on him the wrath of the people who demanded his exile. His father realizing the justice of the popular clamours, sent his son away into the forest. There he continued his abundant giving, not sparing his two children from slavery, nor his wife who was asked for by an old Brahmin, who turned out to be Indra in disguise. Indra eventually returned his wife to him. The children were redeemed from slavery by their grandfather, who then besought his son to return from exile. This story, the Maha Chat, is said to have been narrated by the Buddha to a large assembly including his father. It is now annually recited in the assemblies of Buddhists. The story has been written by many various writers. It is recorded that as early as 1482 A. D. King Trailokanath composed the Maha Chat Kham Luang (the King's version) fragments of which still remain. King Song Tham (1602-1628) is also reputed to have composed a version, which has not been definitely identified, although it has been suggested by Prince Damrong that this might have been identical with what is now known as the Kab Maha Chat (กาพยมหาชาติ).

The version now in general use was composed by various authors of a century ago. From a literary point of view it is one of the best works ever produced in the Thai language, and is still looked upon as a gem of Thai classic literature : เทศน์มหาชาติ the reading and expounding in public of the "Great Birth" poem. This has become a regular practice and has formed the object of yearly assemblies of Buddhists, ever since the time that their great Teacher disappeared from the scene of this world. The poem, written mostly in Chanda verse (ฉันท์), was a very bulky work, and to be delivered in a single day became very tedious, soon tiring the auditors. Thus listening attentively to the rehearsal of the whole thirteen Cantos, came to be looked upon as a great feat. So as to render their audition less tiresome, without sensibly altering the original sense, a new version, having a more varied rhythmical arrangement of verses, was later compiled.

มหาดไทย ma^6-hart^4-tai *n. lit.* "The Great Thai" : กระทรวงมหาดไทย Ministry of Interior. Prior to 1892 there was no centralized system of Civil Provincial administration of the kingdom. Besides the metropolitan area, which was under the Ministry of Local Government, the country was divided into a number of provinces. These provinces were under three different Ministries, *viz.* those of the Interior, of War, and of Foreign Affairs, while the head of each province was practically independent in matters of administration. Thus there was lack of uniformity in the policies pursued by the four Ministries concerned. King Chulalongkorn adopted a system aiming at consolidation and centralization, whereby all the provinces came under the control of the Ministry of the Interior, including such provinces as Chiengmai, which were hither-to practically autonomous, and the Metropolition area which had been under the Ministry of Local Government : hence the Ministry of Local Government was in time merged in the Ministry of the Interior (Siam, General and Medical Features pp. 9, 10).

มหาดเล็ก ma^6-hart^4-lek^6 *n.* the personal attendant, messenger, or chamberlain of a great personage ; a page.

มหาเทพ ma^6-hah^2-tep^3 *n. lit.* "the great deity," *i. e.* Siva.

มหาเทพี, มหาเทวี ma^6-hah^2-tay-pee *n.* epithets for Lady Uma, Siva's consort.

มหานสะ ma^6-hah^2-na^6-sa^4 *P. n.* a kitchen (chd. p. 229).

มหานิกาย ma^6-hah^2-ni^6-gkai *n.* a great sect; a big denomination; see นิกาย p. 456.

มหานิล ma^6-hah^2-nin *n. P. S.* a sapphire; a variety of bdellium: *adj.* dark blue; deep black (S. E. D. p. 797).

มหาภิเนษกรมณ์ ma^6-hah^2-pi^6-net^3-sa^4-krom *n.* the Great Retirement. By this is meant Gotama's retirement from the world and adoption of the ascetic life preparatory to the attainment of Buddhaship (chd. p. 227).

มหาภูต ma^6-hah^2-poot^3 *P. n.* the four principal elements, *viz.* earth, fire, water, air (chd. p. 227).

มหาเมฆ ma^6-hah^2-mek^3 *n.* a species of sedge; a very great cloud.

มหายาน ma^6-hah^2-yarn *P. n.* "Northern Buddhism," "The Great Vehicle," "The Great Way," "The Broad Way of Salvation," "The Large Waggon," epithets for a sect of Buddhism. About the end of the first century A. D., King Kaniska, under whom rose the Mahayana sect of Buddhism in the Punjab, sent missionaries to China, Tibet, and southern India. From the latter point, Mahayanism spread to the powerful kingdom of Srivijaya in Sumatra, which extended its sway over the Malay Peninsula up to about the twelfth century A. D. Thus Mahayana Buddhism found its way to southern and central Thailand and Cambodia (siamese state ceremonies p. 13). According to tradition there are as many as eighteen sects already recognized as orthodox by a general council summoned by King Asoka, the "Constantine of Buddhism," whose reign began in 270 B. C. Mahayana Buddhism split itself into numerous sects which prevail in China, Korea and Japan and, in a corrupted form, in Thibet.

In Japan at the present day there are twelve recognized Buddhist sects and forty-nine subsects, all of the Mahayana School (The Buddha and christ by streeter p. 77).

มหาวงศ์ ma^6-hah^2-wong *n.* "The Great Dynasty." This is the name of a famous history of Buddhism in Ceylon written in Pali by a priest named Mahanama (พระมหานาม), in the fifth century A. D. (chd. p. 231).

มหาวิทยาลัย ma^6-hah^2-wit^6-ta-yah-lai *n.* a university.

มหาสดมภ์ ma^6-hah^2-sa^4-dom *n.* a disease characterized by stiffening of the jaw; lockjaw.

มหาสมุทร ma^6-hah^2-sa^4-moot^4 *S. n.* an ocean; the great sea (S. E. D. p. 801).

มหาสันนิบาต ma^6-hah^2-sun^2-ni^6-bart^4 *n.* a great assembly, gathering, or conference: มหาสันนิบาตชาติ The League of Nations.

มหาสาวก ma^6-hah^2-sah^2-wok^6 *P. S. n.* a great disciple (chd. p. 231).

มหาเสวก ma^6-hah^2-say^2-wok^6 *n.* a title conferred on members of high standing in the Royal Household.

มหาหิงคุ์ ma^6-hah^2-hing^2 *n.* assafoeteda; *Ferula* (Burk. p. 999).

มหาอำมาตย์ ma^6-hah^2-um-mart^4 *n.* Grand Councillor; a title formerly conferred on Civil Service officials of the Government.

มหิ ma^6-hi^4 *P. S. n.* the Great World; the earth; the ground; place; land (chd. p. 231: S. E. D. p. 803): มหิดล the surface of the ground, earth or world: มหิธร a mountain (chd. p. 232); one supporting the earth; an appellation for Vishnu, and for a king or sovereign: มหิบดี *lit.* "an earth-lord," *i. e.* a king; a sovereign: มหิบาล, มหิป *lit.* "an earth-protector," *i. e.* a king.

มหิทธิ ma^6-hit^4-ti^6 *P. adj.* possessing supernatural power; miraculous; magical (chd. p. 232).

มหิมา, มหึมา ma⁶-hi⁴-mah *P. S. adj.* immense; very great; gigantic; vast (S. E. D. p. 803).

มหิษ ma⁶-hit⁴ *S. n.* a buffalo (chd. p. 232).

มหิษี ma⁶-hi⁴-see² *P. S. n.* a king's wife; a queen (chd. p. 231).

มหึรุหะ ma⁶-hee²-roo⁶-ha⁴ *P. n.* a tree; the vegetable kingdom (chd. p. 232).

มหุรดี ma⁶-hoo⁴-ra⁶-dee *n.* an hour; a moment: a space of time; see ขณะ p. 138.

มหู ma⁶-hoo² *Jav. n.* want; need; desire; *Thai* omen; fortune; fate; luck; presage: มหูดี a lucky augury or prediction: มหูดี-ฤกษ์ a favourable hour.

มเหนทร, มหินท์ ma⁶-hen²-ta⁶-ra⁶ *P. n.* Mahendra, a great Buddhist missionary, son of the Indian king Dhammasoka. He converted. Ceylon to the Buddhist faith about three hundred years B. C., and translated the Pali commentaries on the Buddhist scriptures into Singhalese (chd. p. 232).

มเหศวร ma⁶-hay²-su-an² *S. n.* an appellation for Siva; a king or great lord of the world (S. E. D. p. 802).

มเหสักข์ ma⁶-hay²-suk⁴ *P. adj.* possessing great authority or influence; powerful; eminent (chd. p. 231): มเหสักข์เทวราช a powerful deva king.

มเหสิ, มเหสี ๑ ma⁶-hay²-si² *P. n.* a great sage; a great saint; the great "Rishi," a common epithet of the Buddha, or of any Buddha (chd. p. 231).

มเหสี ๒ ma⁶-hay²-see² *P. n.* a king's wife; a queen (chd. p. 231).

มเหาฬาร, มโหฬาร ma⁶-how²-larn *adj.* greatest; most powerful; most excellent; having very great pomp; splendid; magnificient.

มเหาษธ, มโหษธ ma⁶-how²-sot⁴ *S. n.* name of a certain class of very strong or pungent plants (such as dried ginger, garlic, long pepper) (S. E. D. p. 802).

มโหฆ ma⁶-hoh²-ka⁶ *P. n.* a torrent; a flood (chd. p. 232).

มโหรสพ see มหรสพ p. 626.

มไหศวรรย์ ma⁶-hai²-sa⁴-wan² *S. n.* condition of being the greatest, most powerful, or having the highest rank in a realm or kingdom (S. E. D. p. 802).

มอ (สี) maw *adj.* grey; ash coloured; dun; drab; livid; ashen: เขามอ a small hill; an hillock: แต่งกายมอซอ to be slovenly dressed or untidy; to be tattered in dress: มอ (เรือ) a kind of large cargo boat propelled by oars: *onomat.* from the sound of the mooing of a cow or bellowing of a bull: มีหน้ามอซอ to have a dull, stupid, or listless facial expression.

มอง maung *v.* to look; to peer or pry into every hole or corner; to inquire: ด้อมมอง to stoop or bend over, while observing what is going on; see ด้อม p. 191: มองดู to look at; to look on; to glance around; to turn the eyes on; see ดู p. 333: มองเสี้ยว an attitude assumed by Thai masked actors: มองหา-ท่าทาง to search for a method (in order to accomplish an object or evade an issue): สอดมอง, ลักมอง to peek; to peep; to peer or pry; to spy upon: มองหา to seek or search for.

มองคร่อ maung-kraw³ *n.* a disease of cattle and horses characterized by mucus or phlegm lodged in the bronchial tubes; the heaves.

มอญ mawn *n.* the Peguans; see ตะเลง p. 357: มอญรำ a Peguan dance.

มอด mort³ *v.* to die out gradually (as live coals); to become cold or extinguished (as a fire): *n.* the weevil: มอดม้วย to wane; to decline; to fall away; to languish, decay or crumble; to die.

ม่อต้อ maw³-dtaw³ *adj.* fat, but short in stature.

มอบ maup³ *v.* to deliver into the hands of; to put under the care of; to make over to; to turn over to: มอบตัว to submit; to resign or surrender oneself (as to the inevitable): มอบไว้, มอบให้ to relinquish the care of, or authority over, to another: มอบ-สมบัติ to convey or assign one's wealth or possessions to another: มอบหมาย to assign, consign, or turn over to the care or control of another.

มอม maum *v.* to be disfigured or rendered hideous by dirt, powder, or paint: *adj.* dirty; hideous; nasty: เปื้อนมอมแมม dirty from head to foot; polluted: มอมแมม foul; dirty; bespattered (as with mud): มอมเหล้า to be drunk to the limit; to be disgracefully drunk: หน้ามอมแมม a face that is dirty or blackened (as when representing a negro or clown).

ม่อย moy³ *v.* to be half asleep; to doze or be drowsy: *adj.* sleepy; drowsy; dozing; see เคลิ้ม p. 208.

ม่อลอกม่อแลก maw³-lauk³-maw³-laak³ *adj.* dirty; muddy; see เปื้อน p. 535.

มะ ๑ ma⁶ a contracted form for หมาก which, in ancient literature, could be rendered as ลูก or ผล the fruit of a tree. Thus, in modern usage, it forms a common prefix to the names of fruits of various kinds.

มะ ๒ ma⁶ *Mohn n.* a prefix to proper nouns, equivalent to Nai, Mister, Master.

มะกรูด (ส้ม) ma⁶-gkroot⁴ *n. Citrus hystrix (Rutaceae)*, kaffir lime, a tree, rather outstanding in character, in the genus. Being so distinct, some have tried to exclude it from *Citrus*, calling it *Papeda hystrix*, but there is insufficient reason for placing it in a separate genus. It is a small tree, with a pear-shaped fruit, the skin intensely green, or ultimately yellowish and wrinkled. The Malays use it for washing the hair and other parts of the body. It also enters into their universal tonic medicines; apparently its function is the driving away of evil spirits. The juice is very acid; but it is sometimes used as a flavouring in sauces, but only in small quantities as much of it upsets the digestion. Before the fruit is ripe the juice is gummy, but with ripeness becomes thin and watery, though never abundant. The timber is a favourite material for tool-handles in some parts of the Dutch Indies (V. P. p. 200: MCM. p. 236: Burk. [p. 567].

มะกล่ำ see กล่ำ p. 61.

มะกอก *Thailand* and *Laos*, ไพ้ย *Karen*, *Kanburi* (ต้น) ma⁶-gkawk⁴ *n. Spondias pinnata (Anacardiaceae)* (cb. p. 356), *S. mangifera*, otaheite-apple, hog plum, a small tree with handsome pinnate leaves. It is a native of the Pacific Islands, etc., and is commonly grown in the tropics. The round or ovoid fruit is the size of a small mango, amber-coloured when ripe, having a large stone (seed) surrounded by coarse fibre, and a scanty acid pulp with the flavour of "an exceedingly bad mango." It makes an excellent conserve, for which some varieties are better than others (MCM. p. 270: V. P. p. 198): มะกอกน้ำ *Thailand* (ต้น) *Elaeocarpus madopetalus (Elaeocarpaceae)* (cb. p. 196): มะกอกฝรั่ง *Thailand, Bangkok* (ต้น) *Spondias cytherea (Anacardiaceae)*, a fruit-tree of the eastern Pacific, now widely distributed in the tropics. The fruits which may be as large as a hen's egg, are pleasant to eat when stewed, and make good jam. When cooked they have a suggestion of the flavour of pine-apple. The tree may fruit at the age of four years. The young leaves are eaten in Java, after steaming them. They are also cooked with tough meat to make it tender. The wood is very brittle, so much so that the wind is apt to break the boughs. A gum runs from the bark (BURK. p. 2067: cb. p. 355: V. P. p. 199).

มะกัน   ma⁶-gkun *Jav. v.* to eat; see กิน p. 107.

มะกา (ต้น)   ma⁶-gkah *n. Bridelia burmanica (Euphorbiaceae); B. siamensis,* the leaves of which are used as a purgative (V. P. [p. 198).

มะก่าแดง see เคอก่ำ p. 211.

มะเกี๋ยง (ต้น)   ma⁶-gkee-ang³ *n. Citrus aurantium (Rutaceae),* sour orange, Seville orange. This orange reached the Mediterranean in the ninth or tenth century, and was well known in Europe long before the tardy arrival of the sweet orange. Then early European voyagers brought it back to the East and established it in the Philippine Islands. It is the best orange for marmalade but has no place as a dessert fruit. The peel is sometimes candied (BURK. p. 566); *C. sinensis,* sweet orange, coolie orange. This is the most important species of the genus *Citrus.* It is of Asiatic origin, and only found its way to Europe in the fourteenth century but has given rise, particularly outside of China, to many, familiar races, such as St. Michael or Blood, Jaffa, Joppa, Valencia, and Washington Navel. The sweet orange usually has leaves with very narrowly winged petioles, jointed to the blade, white flower buds, flowers rather smaller than *C. aurantium,* fruits usually globular, but sometimes ellipsoid, or pearshaped, with a smooth skin, in colour orange or yellowish-orange, surrounding a sweet juicy pulp. Oil of Sweet Orange is obtained by expression of the peel, in southern Italy and Sicily; also in the West Indies. It contains d-limonene. Oil of the leaves can be made by distillation. Dried rind, the outer part only, is sometimes substituted in European medicine for the dried rind of the bitter orange, *C. aurantium* (MCM. pp. 236, 399 : BURK. p. 574).

มะเกลือ (ต้น)   ma⁶-gklu-ah *n. Diospyros mollis (Ebenaceae),* a very well-known tree of moderate size, of rather dry forest, found from the Shan Hills to the latitude of Bangkok.

It is sometimes cultivated. Its fruits and leaves are much used to give a black dye (V. P. p. 201 : BURK. p. 833); *D. ebenum,* a large tree of southern India and Ceylon. It is the best Indian ebony-tree, the only one giving black wood without any streaks, or markings, and a very valuable asset to Ceylon, where it is plentiful. The heart-wood is very hard, very closely and evenly grained; the sap-wood is grey, often streaked with black. The wood is used for turnery, cabinet work, piano keys, rulers, backs of brushes, stands for ornaments, etc. The fruit is used as a black dye. The medicinal properties of the fruits are well known. They are commonly used as a cathartic in the treatment of tape worm and other intestinal parasites (MCM. p. 218 : BURK. p. 829).

มะขวิด *Thailand,* มะฟีด *Laos, Chiengmai* (ต้น)   ma⁶-kwit⁴ *n. Feronia elephantum (Rutaceae), F. limonia,* wood-apple, elephant-apple, a small spiny tree, 30 to 40 feet high, with small, pinnate, glabrous, trifoliate leaves. The globular or ovoid fruit is of the size of a large cricket ball, similar to the bael-fruit, but distinguished from it by the rough woody, hard, white shell. It contains a mass of soft, bitter-sweet, mealy substance which is used for making a pleasant cooling drink and a preserve; also in native medicine. Its cultivation extends eastwards to the China Sea; and through Thailand it passes into the northernmost parts of British Malaya. It is cultivated in the dry parts of India, chiefly for its fruit, but having several other uses. It can be propagated by root-cuttings, seeds, and budding. The timber is yellowish, hard, and is used in India for house-building, naves of carts, oil-crushing rollers, and agricultural implements. In Java it is used as firewood. Gum is extensively collected from the trunk. It forms a tasteless mucilage with water. In India it has a medicinal reputation, and is used in the place of gum arabic. The sap, mixed with orpiment, makes a yellow ink, with which the Thai write on palm leaves (MCM. pp. 251, 262, 378, 511 : Cb. p. 238 : V. P. p. 201 : Burk. p. 998).

มะขาม see ตะคุบ p. 356.

มะขามเครือ *Thailand, Korat,* มะขามเคือ *Laos, Lampang* (ต้น) ma[6]-kam[2]-kru-ah *n. Roureopsis stenopetala (Connaraceae)* (Cb. p. 362).

มะขามเทศ *Thailand* (ต้น) ma[6]-kam[2]-tet[3] *n. Pithecellobium dulce (Leguminosae),* Manila tamarind, a spiny tree of tropical America, now widely cultivated around the world. It was brought into cultivation in the earlier days of transatlantic voyages, and grows as if wild in southern India. As it has a name in the Philippine Islands derived from a Mexican source, it is evident that the Spaniards brought it eastward across the Pacific, but probably it travelled westwards also via Europe. This tree makes excellent hedges. The leaves are small, in two pairs, and the branches prickly. This tree yields a transparent gum of a polished appearance and a deep reddish brown colour. This gum is soluble in water and forms a brownish mucilage. The bark contains about 25% of tannin (The Orn. Tree of Hawaii, J. F. Rock, p. 79 : MCM. pp. 73, 74, 207, 213, 518 : Cb. p. 559 : V. P. p. 202 : Burk. p. 1760) : มะขามป้อม (ต้น) *Phyllanthus emblica* or *Emblica officinalis (Euphorbiaceae),* a tree of small or moderate size found in tropical south-eastern Asia, and through Malaysia to Timor. It has graceful, feathery foliage. The round green fruits, of the size of marbles, have a comparatively large kernel and are made into a much-esteemed preserve. The fruit is collected from plants in the wild state when in season, chiefly from November to February. The fruits are a cooling laxative, and are taken for dyspepsia. The Malays use the fruits as a seasoning in food and as a pickle. They are similarly used in India and the Dutch Indies, and are made into a sweetmeat with sugar. The Malays only use them thus and in medicine, but in India and Thailand the tree supplies tanning material to an important degree, the fruit, leaves, and bark alike being used as a dye on silk. Pretty brown tints are obtained by the use of the leaves, and the colour is turned black with iron-mordants. The Chinese of Hong Kong so use it. The timber is fair. It is red, hard, close-grained, but warps and splits in seasoning (MCM. pp. 268, 379 : V. P. p. 202 : Burk. p. 920).

มะเขือขาว (ต้น) ma[6]-ku-ah[2]-kow[2] *n. Solanum melongena (Solanaceae),* egg-plant, brinjal, aubergine, a low bushy annual, usually with sharp prickles along the stems and leaf-stalks, a native of south-eastern Asia, but now cultivated throughout the warmer parts of the world. A wild, very prickly variety of it, known as var. *insanum* occurs in India, particularly in the dry hills to the west of Bengal. Sometimes the plant runs wild in Malaya, and is yellow-fruited. The Persians seem to have carried it from India to Africa. The Arabs took it to Spain. In cultivation there are many races, varying in shape and colour of the fruit, also somewhat in earliness, prickliness, number and size of the fruits in a bunch, etc. The fruit makes an excellent vegetable. These fruits may be round, ovoid, or cucumber-shaped, and white, grey, or purple, the latter colour being usually characteristic of the best varieties. There are various medicinal uses. The Malays use the ashes of the fruit in a dry, hot poultice on haemorrhoids. They also pound the root and apply inside the nostrils for ulceration. There is an Arabian superstition that the fruit is exceedingly heating and breeds melancholia and madness. The people of the Bera River place the prickly stem on the threshold of a house in which the first-fruits of the rice harvest, *i.e.* soul of the rice, have been lodged ;

evidently the prickles are held to act protectively (MCM. p. 305 : V. P. p. 202 : BURK. p. 2044) : มะเขือขื่น (ต้น) *S. xanthocarpum*. This plant is used for catarrhal fever, asthma, etc. The yellow fruits are used as a vegetable (MCM. pp. 312, 380) : มะเขือพวง (ต้น) *S. torvum*, a small shrub found widely in the tropics ; in the Peninsula it is common more or less throughout. The yellow fruits are eaten in curries, both by the Malays and in many parts of Malaysia. They are preferred unripe. The root is medicinal for poulticing cracks in the feet (V. P. p. 203 : BURK. p. 2046).

มะค่า (ต้น)　　　ma⁶-kah³ *n. Ormosia sp.* near *O. nitida* ; *Intsia bijuga* (*Leguminosae*), a tree of medium size found on sea coasts, particularly in such places as where, just behind mangroves, the ground rises a little ; it occurs from the Mascarene Islands to Polynesia ; in the Malay Peninsula it is uncommon. The timber is like *I. bakeri*, yellowish or reddish in colour ; and is rather coarse-grained, but takes a good polish. In some parts of the Pacific it is the most sought after of the available timbers ; and in eastern Malaysia it is much valued. White ants scarcely touch it, not only on account of its hardness, but from the yellow powder which occurs in it here and there. It has an odour like peanuts. It is short in the grain, and therefore not well adapted for carrying heavy weights, but it makes good flooring and satisfactory furniture. Its durability in contact with water is questioned. The colouring-matter in the wood is so soluble that it comes out of the timber and makes unsightly brown stains ; consequently all wood should be soaked in water for several days before use, or be left exposed to the rain, and the paint used on it must be watertight. The bark is used to stop diarrhoea ; it contains tannin. The fruit appears to be a laxative (V. P. p. 203　BURK. p. 1244).

มะคำดีควาย (ต้น)　　　ma⁶-kum-dee-kwai *n. Sapindus rarak* (*Sapindaceae*), soap-nut, a

tree of considerable size, found from Burma to Malaysia. It is commonly planted in Java for its fruits which are used as soap (MCM. p. 397 : BURK. p. 1958).

มะงั่ว (ต้น)　　　ma⁶-ngua³ *n. Citrus medica* (*Rutaceae*), citron, a small tree, much cultivated in southern Europe and the Mediterranean region for its large, spherical fruit, which is usually about 4 to 6 inches in diameter (sometimes nearly double that size), being round or ovoid in shape, according to variety. *C. medica* had reached Persia before the time of the Achaemenides (Cyrus, Darius, and their successors), and Alexander the Great's invasion of Persia brought an accurate knowledge of it to the Greeks. Its juice was regarded as medicinal, and given with wine to expel bile and poison ; its fruits were used to flavour meat and to perfume the breath, and, deductively, were considered to preserve clothes and to purify the place where a man had died. It was brought to Italy about the time of Christ, and gradually became established ; but the use of the fruit by the Jews at the Feast of Tabernacles is certainly not, by many centuries, as old as the the feast itself. It was the " Apple of Media and Persia " of Theophrastus and subsequent writers. Though early traders brought the species to Malaysia, it did not become common, probably because the pomelo, which is so similar in many respects, was already in cultivation. The flowers are medicinal among the Chinese. Citron oil is made from three different races in southern Italy and Sicily, by expression from the rind (MCM. p. 276 : V. P. p. 205 : BURK. p. 571).

มะซาง (ต้น)　　　ma⁶-sang *n. Bassia pierrei* (*Sapotaceae*) (also known as *Madhuca pierrei*), a large forest tree with milky latex. The astringent fruits are cool, sweet, green, of the size of betel-nut and turn yellow on ripening (Kerr.).

มะดัน *Thailand, Bangkok* (ต้น) ma[6]-dun *n.* *Garcinia schomburgkiana (Guttiferae)* (cb. p. 117).

มะดูก *Thailand and Laos,* บักโค้ก *Khmer, Surin* (ต้น)   ma[6]-dook[4] *n. Siphonodon celastrineus (Celastraceae)* (cb. p. 293).

มะเดหวี   ma[6]-day-wee[2] *Jav. n.* a title of the second queen of a Javanese king.

มะเดื่อปล้อง (ต้น)   ma[6]-du-ah[4]-bplaung[3] *n. Ficus hispida (Urticaceae),* a coarse tree, of rather small size, found throughout south-eastern Asia, Malaysia, and to Australia; in the Malay Peninsula it is general in lowland woods, and on stream-sides, chiefly in the northern parts. It is used medicinally both by the Malays and Javanese. There is no record of the use of the fruits by the Malays. However the fruits are edible and Chinese women make a sweetmeat of them in Java. In India the leaves are a cattle-food. The bark is used for making a rough twine in India and in the Andaman Islands. The tree is used as permanent shade for coffee in South India (V. P. p. 206: MCM. p. 353: BURK. p. 1010): มะเดื่ออุทุมพร (ต้น) *Ficus glomerata (Urticaceae),* guler, a medium-sized tree, much used as shade for coffee in South India; also popular as an avenue tree (MCM. 2 5: V. P. p. 206).

มะต้อง *E. Laos,* กะท้อน *Thailand* มะตืน, สะโต *Malay, Pattani* (ต้น)   ma[6]-dtong[3] *n. Sandoricum indicum (Meliaceae),* a rather tall fruit-tree, found throughout Malaysia, rare in a wild state, but commonly cultivated, and extended in cultivation northwards into Thailand, Cochin-China, and to Rangoon; and in the last century taken to Mauritius and the West Indies, etc. It is met with all through the Malay Peninsula, and the village elders point out that when it flowers the time for rice-planting has come. The fruit is a poor one. Within the capsule wall, and coating the three or four big seeds, is an edible, fleshy aril of sour taste, which is vinous when ripe. It is said that an excellent jelly can be made from the fruit. The timber is red, moderately hard, close-grained and takes a beautiful polish. It is used for carts and boats in Burma; for house-building in Java; for clogs in Malaya; and for light framing, cabinet-work, house-posts, etc. in the Philippine Islands. The pounded bark may be applied for ringworm. The water in which the leaves have been pounded may be drunk for remittent fever, or the leaves may be boiled and the decoction taken. Another treatment, involving magic, is to chew the leaves and bespatter the face of the patient (cb. p. 253: Burk. p. 1946); see กระท้อน p. 34.

มะตาด *Thailand,* ส้านบ้าว *Laos, Chiengmai* (ต้น)   ma[6]-dtart[4] *n. Dillenia indica (Dilleniaceae),* a handsome, moderate-sized round-headed, symmetrical tree, characterized by large, oblong, glabrous, serrate leaves, which are 10 to 12 inches long. These trees are found from India to western Malaysia; in the Peninsula they are general, both wild and planted. The flowers are very large, pure white, 6 to 7 inches in diameter. The fruits, which are produced in abundance, are enclosed in fleshy sepals of an acid flavour, similar to that of an unripe apple. They are eaten as a flavouring with curries, and may be made into jam. In the Thai Malay States the pulp of the fruit is used to wash the hair. The timber is red with white specks, close-grained and moderately hard. It is not much used anywhere. It has been tried in India for gun-stocks and helves, and in house-and ship-building; and in Java for telegraph poles. It is said to turn jet black under water. Experimental sleepers made from treated timber lasted in India only about three years. It is often difficult to turn to good use because the trunks are so crooked (MCM. pp. 98, 260: cb. p. 23: V. P. p. 207: Burk. p. 809).

มะตาหะรี   ma⁶-dtah-ha⁴-ree *Jav. n.* the sun.

มะตี   ma⁶-dtee *Jav. v.* to die: *adj.* dead.

มะตูม (ต้น)   ma⁶-dtoom *n. Aegle marmelos* (*Rutaceae*), the bael-fruit, a very important fruit-tree of India, occurring either wild or in cultivation almost throughout the country, where it has a long fruiting season and is generally available. From India its cultivation has spread south-eastwards. There is but little difficulty in growing it in northern Philippines and none in the drier parts of Java, where it is also cultivated, though less easily, in the moister parts. In the Malay Peninsula there is a very restricted area over which it will fruit. In Sanskrit literature the bael-tree had two names, one religious, meaning "holy fruit," and one medicinal. Both are retained in India today. Its presence in Java probably dates from the establishment of the Hindu kingdom there about the beginning of the Christian Era, but this is not proved. When direct intercourse between Europe and India commenced, the valuable qualities of the fruit were at once appreciated by the Europeans, who took it into their system of medicine in the place of the quince. In India two races are recognized; one is a smaller-fruited wild tree, and the other a large-fruited cultivated tree. The medicinal properties are more powerful in the wild fruit, and so it is preferred for medicinal use. The fruit is best just as it is turning ripe. It is common to make a kind of sherbet with its pulp; it is still commoner to slice it and dry the slices. They are sold in every bazaar. Half-ripe fruit is used in the form of a pickle, or a powder, or a marmalade. In Java the fruits are generally used half-ripe for chronic dysentery, atonic diarrhoea, and constipation. The ripe fruit is used as a laxative. The bark is used for intermittent fevers in Indo-China. The timber is yellowish white or greyish white, hard, and with a strong aromatic scent when fresh. It serves well for making turnery but not for larger objects, as it warps and twists in seasoning, and cracks. In Thailand the fruit-rind is used for scenting hair-oil. The young leaves are used in Java for seasoning. In India they are medicinal and the juice is used for catarrh and fever. The root is used for palpitation of the heart in both India and Java (Burk. p. 55).

มะนาว   ma⁶-now, ส้มมะนาว *Thai* and *Laos*, ส้มมะงั่ว *Thai*, มะนาวรีปน *Laos*, *Chiengmai* (ต้น) *n. Citrus medica* (*Rutaceae*), citron. The plants which form the species *C. medica* culminate in the true citron; that is to say, there are many races, the best of which pass as citrons. Formerly this word included also the lemon and perhaps the lime, and in French is still applied to the lemon. *C. medica* reached Persia before the time of the Achaemenides (Cyrus, Darius, and their successors), and Alexander the Great's invasion of Persia brought an accurate knowledge of it to the Greeks. Its juice is regarded as medicinal, and is given with wine to expel bile and poison; its fruits were used to flavour meat and to perfume the breath, and deductively, were considered to preserve clothes and to purify the place where a man had died. Of all the varieties and races of *C. medica* none is more valued in the East than the fixed abnormality, *C. medica*, var. *sarcodactylis*. In it the carpels fail to unite to form the rounded fruit, remaining detached as fingers, which causes the Chinese to give it a name meaning Buddha's hand. Fruits, flowers, fresh shoots and leaves are all medicinal. Citron oil is made from three different races in Italy and Sicily, by expression from the rind (Burk. p. 571); *C. acida* (*Aurantifolia*), a lemon; a lime. A small, spiny tree, cultivated in all tropical countries for its acid juicy fruit. The latter varies in size, acidity, juiciness, oil content, etc.; also in shape, from almost round to ovoid.

It is used by all races for flavouring and other culinary purposes, and the juice is largely employed for making lime-juice cordial and other cooling drinks. It also enters much into native medicine. Applied externally, it is sometimes considered a cure for snake-bite (MCM. p. 238: cb. p. 238): มะนาวเทศ *Thai* (ต้น) *Triphasia trifolia* (*Rutaceae*), a shrub, sometimes said to be of Chinese origin, widely cultivated in the East and introduced during the last centuries to other parts of the tropics. It must have been in Malay a long time, and the Malays grow it. They conserve the fruits as a sweetmeat by boiling them in syrup. In the Dutch Indies the natives apply the leaves to the body for various complaints, such as diarrhoea, colic and skin diseases; they use them also in cosmetics. The shrub makes a shapely hedge; few shrubs are as good. The wood is useful for small objects, such as tool-handles; it makes satisfactory charcoal. It is used for both purposes in Guam. A gum runs from the stem (cb. p. 229: Burk. p. 2185): มะนาวผี *Thai* (ต้น) *Atalantia monophylla* (*Rutaceae*), a plant of wide distribution in India, Burma and Thailand, which reaches the coast of the northern parts of the Malay Peninsula. It is one of a small genus of woody sprawlers or shrubs very closely allied to *Citrus*, the fruits appearing like small green oranges (cb. p. 236: Burk. p. 265).

มะนาวไม่รู้โห่   ma[6]-now-mai[3]-ru[5]-hoh[4] กาล-วัลย์ *Bangkok*, หนามแกว *Sriracha*, หนามพรม (ต้น) *Carissa carandas* (*Apocynaceae*), (or *arduina?*) a small tree, or large shrub, with sharp, rigid, forked thorns and small oval leaves, native of the dry region of Ceylon, also of India and Thailand. The pinky white fruits are very acid, dark purple when ripe, and contain a number of small seeds. The fruits when stewed with an abundance of sugar make excellent tarts and puddings, resembling goose-berries in flavour. When ripe, they make a good jelly. The plant is commonly employed for barrier hedges and is propagated from seed (MCM. p. 257: Burk. p. 464).

มะนิมนา   ma[6]-nim-nah *adv.* quickly; hastily; speedily; urgently.

มะปราง   ma[6]-bprang (cultivated) and มะปริง (wild) *Thai*, โด้ง *Khmer, Surin* (ต้น) *n. Bouea burmanica* (*Anacardiaceae*), a fruit-tree from Burma which approaches British Malaya as far as Bangkok. It is a tree very like the *B. microphylla* and has been confused with it in literature. The fruits are edible and the timber good. It sometimes yields a gum (cb. p. 346: V. P. p. 210: Burk. p. 355).

มะผ่อ (ต้น)   ma[6]-faw[4] *n. Trewia nudiflora* (V. P. p. 211).

มะพร้าว (ต้น)   ma[6]-prow[5] *n. Cocos nucifera* (*Palmae*), coconut palm, one of the most important trees of the vegetable kingdom. Though extensively grown in most tropical regions, the native habitat of the palm is uncertain, for it is known only in a cultivated state. The dried inner portion (endocarp) of the nut, known as copra, yields a valuable oil used in cookery, soap-making, and in the making of margarine, cosmetics, etc. The same part used in the fresh state, is made into desiccated coconut, which is esteemed in confectionery and cooking. The husk (pericap), when retted for about a month in water, yields coir fibre, which is made into rugs, brushes, etc., or into coarse string or ropes. The palm supplies food, coconut milk used largely in cookery in Thailand, palm-wine (toddy), sugar, the terminal bud which is a great delicacy, spirituous liquor, and many requisites (MCM. p. 389: V. P. p. 211: Burk. p. 598): มะพร้าวเต่า (ต้น) *Cycas siamensis* (*Cycadaceae*), a palm-like or fern-like perennial plant with dark green, shining leaves much used in funeral wreaths. It has the habitat of *C. circinalis*, but is easily distinguished by its narrow leaf-segments. It is found in Burma, Indo-China, Thailand and just into the northern parts of British Malaya. It is very close to *C. pectinata*; and perhaps only a geographical form of it. It has been introduced into cultivation rather extensively as an ornamental plant. *C. pectinata* furnishes food in the eastern Himalayas, and so may this species, but nothing is known of its use in Malaya (MCM. p. 119: V. P. p. 211: BURK. p. 721): มะพร้าวสามเหลี่ยม, หมากสามเหลี่ยม (ต้น) Mauritius palm, *Hyophorbe verschaffeltii* (*Palmae*) (BURK. p. 1216); *Areca verschaffeltii*. This palm was first introduced to Thailand from Singapore by Luang Tanat Pojanamaht in 1919. It has derived one of its names from its resemblance to the coconut palm and to its three-cornered stem (winit, N. H. J. S. S. IX, 1, p. 97).

มะพลับ (ต้น) see พลับ (ต้น) p. 573.

มะพูด　　ma[6]-poot[3] *Thai*, ปะหุด *E. Laos*, ปราโฮด *Khmer, Surin* (ต้น) *n. Garcinia vilersiana* (*Guttiferae*); *G. xanthochymus*, eggtree (from its ovoid or conical shape), a symmetrical, bushy tree, growing to 25 or 30 feet high, with large leathery leaves, 10 to 15 inches long and 2½ to 3½ inches broad. The handsome, yellow, smooth fruit, produced in great abundance, usually in December to February, is of the form and size of a small orange, with a pointed (stigmatic) projection at the end or on one side. The yellow juicy pulp has an acid but refreshing taste. This tree is found in India and southwards through Burma into Thailand. It is cultivated in the Malay Peninsula for the sake of the acid fruits. From immature fruit, an inferior gamboge paint may be made. The bark dyes cotton black (MCM. pp. 263, 440, 518: V. P. p. 211: BURK. p. 1056).

มะเฟือง　　ma[6]-fu-ang *Thai* and *Laos* (ต้น) *n. Averrhoa carambola* (*Geraniaceae*), belimbing, or cucumber tree, cultivated for its fruit,

which is about 3 to 4 inches long, resembling a small green cucumber, produced in clusters on the trunk and oldest branches. It is esteemed in pickles and preserves, being sometimes used for making jam and cooling drinks. This shrub, or small tree, is found wild in Java and to the eastward, and is cultivated widely. It likes a climate which has dry seasons, and it associates with teak in Java. The wood is white, turning reddish, moderately hard and close-grained. There are medicinal uses and the flowers are used as a vermifuge (MCM. p. 255: cb. p. 208: V. P. p. 212: BURK. p. 271): มะเฟืองช้าง *Thai, Ratburi*, มะเฟืองป่า *Laos* (ต้น) *Lepisanthes siamensis* (*Sapindaceae*) (cb. p. 327).

มะไฟ (ต้น)　　ma[6]-fai *n. Baccaurea sapida* (*Euphorbiaceae*), a tree found both wild and cultivated in India; from there it extends into Thailand. Formerly, it was regarded as wild also in Malaya, but the specimens so named have been transferred to *B. wrayi*. Flowers and leaves are eaten in Bangkok. The timber is soft and splits (BURK. p. 281); *B.* (*Pierardia*) *motleyana*, the rambeh or rambai of Malaya, a handsome tree of Sumatra, with large oval leaves, bearing long pendulous clusters of large smooth berries (yellow when ripe) along the older branches. The sweet-acid, juicy fruit is relished by some people. The season of fruitage is August-September. The timber is of a poor quality. The bark is useful for dyeing. It is used medicinally for eyes, and after child-birth (MCM. p. 255: BURK. p. 280).

มะม่วง see ช้อก p. 283.

มะม่วงหิมพาน see ตำหยาว p. 366.

มะมาก　　ma[6]-mark[3] *Cam. n.* a gnat.

มะม่าว　　ma[6]-mow[3] *v.* to be weakened, tired [or exhausted.

มะมี่ see มี่ p. 652.

มะมุง　　ma[6]-moong *Cam. n.* the cockroach.

มะเมอ   ma[6]-mur v. to speak or act while asleep; to cry out unconsciously (similar to a nightmare); see สะเมอ.

มะเมีย   ma[6]-me-ah n. a horse: ปีมะเมีย the seventh year of the animal cycle; the year of the horse; see ปี p. 527.

มะแม   ma[6]-maa n. a goat: ปีมะแม the eighth year of the animal cycle; the year of the goat; see ปี p. 527.

มะยง (ต้น)   ma[6]-yong n. Bouea burmanica (Anacardiaceae), a tree similar to the yellow plum and often confused in literature with B. microphylla. The fruits are edible and the timber good. Its home is Burma but it is found as far south as Bangkok (V. P. p. 214: Burk. p. 355).

มะยม (ต้น)   ma[6]-yom n. Phyllanthus distichus (Euphorbiaceae), otaheite-gooseberry; star gooseberry, a shrub or small tree, with long graceful branches and feathery foliage. The pale green, round, faintly ribbed, acid fruit, has a hard kernel, and is commonly used for pickling but makes a delicious preserve. A crop is procured twice a year, in April and August (MCM. p. 268: V. P. p. 214); Cicca acida (Euphorbiaceae), country gooseberry, a tree of small or moderate size, of uncertain origin, cultivated throughout Malaysia, and in other parts of the tropics for its fruits. The root is medicinal. It is poisonous, but the degree of poisonousness has been exaggerated. The Malays boil it, or heat it, and inhale the steam for coughs. The leaves are medicinal in Java and Borneo (Burk. p. 536).

มะระ   ma[6]-ra[6] Thai, Bangkok, ผักไห Nakawn Sritamarat, หมักห่อย Laos, Chiengmai (ต้น) n. Momordica charantia (Cucurbitaceae), carilla fruit, a rather slender climber which is cultivated throughout the tropics, occurring as if wild in the neighborhood of cultivation. Its original home is unknown, but clearly it was in the Old World and was taken to the New World by slave-traders or their slaves. It is chiefly cultivated on account of its bitter fruits which are eaten, usually when they are just unripe and after soaking in salt water, with subsequent cooking. They are, in particular, an ingredient of curries. They are considered to be tonic and to purify the blood. They preserve a bitter but wholesome taste. The young fruits may be pickled. In appearance the fruits are an ovoid, warty gourd, six to eight inches long, bright orange-yellow when ripe. There are several varieties, one of which has white fruits. The seeds contain an edible oil. As a medicine, the vegetable parts are chiefly used. It is common to pound the leaves and apply them to the body for skin diseases in India, Malaya, and elsewhere. They are applied for burns, scalds and to the abdomens of children for stomach-ache, and in a mixture for diarrhoea. The leaf-juice is taken in India for bilious complaints. It is emetic and purgative. There is a record of a child's death produced by overdose (Cb. p. 758: MCM. p. 293: Burk. p. 1485).

มะริต, มฤต, รามัญ   ma[6]-rit[6] n. Mergui, a seaport of Burma on an island in the Tenasserim river, two miles from its mouth at 12° 27' north latitude and 89° 35' east longitude. The district of which it is the chief seaport is bounded on the west by the bay of Bengal and on the east by Thailand; the area is 9789 square miles. Two principal ranges cross the district from north to south, running almost parallel to each other for a considerable distance with the Tenasserim river winding between them till it turns south and flows through a narrow rocky gorge in the westernmost range to the sea. It has acquired importance from the discovery of valuable pearl-beds in its vicinity. During the sixteenth and seventeenth centuries Tenasserim was a tributary state of Thailand and a commercial emporium of not a little importance. At Mergui, merchandise from foreign countries, especially those of high value and small bulk, such as silks, porcelain, scented woods, calico and dyes, were unloaded from sea-vessels and loaded into small boats propelled partly by sail and partly by oar. These proceeded up the little Tenasserim river, then across a dangerous section a distance of 40 miles, by bullock carts to the river Praan via Kui and bound for Ayuthia, which was reached in twelve to fifteen days. Passengers were carried by sedan chairs across the portage. Importers preferred this route to the all-sea route which was exceedingly hazardous owing to piracy. During the period of Thai rule it appears that Mergui was a rich and densely populated country. On its occupation by the British in 1824-25 it was found to be almost depopulated, the result of border warfare and the cruelties exercised by the Burmese conquerors.

มะรืน ma[6]-rurn *n.* the day after tomorrow : พรุ่งนี้มะรืนนี้ in two or three days.

มะรุม ma[6]-room · *Thai,* ทิตา *Laos, Chiengmai* (ต้น) *n. Moringa oleifera (Moringaceae),* horse-radish tree, drum sticks, a small tree found wild in northern India and now spread by cultivation throughout the tropics. Its early history is difficult to trace; but its cultivation in India is certainly ancient. The vegetable parts of the plant contain a glucoside, with a biting taste similar to the allyl compounds of mustard and horse-radish. On this account, Europeans in the tropics sometimes use its root as a seasoning with food in the place of horse-radish, and named it the horse-radish tree. Pods, flowers, twigs, and leaves may also serve as milder seasonings; they are always cooked before use. The leaves are tripinnate. The flowers and bark are used in native medicine and a valuable oil (Oil of Ben) is obtained from the seeds. The pods are used as a vegetable in curries and the leaves may be similarly used. The fried seeds taste like peanuts. Cattle eat the

leaves readily. The root acts like a mustard plaster; the leaves are used for poulticing, and internally as an aid to digestion. The leaves are diuretic and are recommended for gonorrhoea; the juice of the leaves mixed with lime is prescribed in India for dropsy. A gum which issues from the bark is regarded as medicinal in India and Java. The bark contains a coarse fibre. The wood is soft, white, spongy, and perishable. It is said to contain a blue dye (MCM. pp. 305, 346, 379, 396 : V. P. p. 215 : Cb. p. 86 : Burk. p. 1495).

มะรุมมะตุ้ม ma[6]-room-ma[6]-dtoom[3] *adj.* ragged; entangled; tattered.

มะเริ่ง ma[6]-reng *n.* cancer; malignant growths or tumours.

มะเรื่อง ma[6]-reu-ang[3] *n.* the fourth day hence; three days ahead.

มะโรง ma[6]-rong *n.* the great dragon : ปีมะโรง the fifth year of the animal cycle; the year of the dragon; see ปี p. 527.

มะละกอ see แตงต้น p. 376.

มะละแหม่ง ma[6]-la[6]-maang[4] *n.* Moulmein.

มะลายู ma[6]-lah-yoo *n.* Malays of Thailand, an Austronesian race of people. The modern Malay is of a very mixed race, but it seems fairly certain that his main derivation is from the Jakuns or Proto-Malays, a primitive jungle tribe scattered through the peninsula. The Jakuns are an aboriginal community who inhabit the plains and lower hill-country of the interior of Pahang. Malays living in Thailand are found mostly in the southern provinces. The Pattani Malays are strongly mixed with Semang, the original inhabitants of that part of the country (Siam, Nature and Industry p. 86).

มะลำ, มาลำ ma[6]-lum *Jav. n.* night-time; night; darkness.

มะลิ ma[6]-li[6], มัลลิกา (ต้น) *n. Jasminum*

sambac (*Oleaceae*) and other species, Arabian jasmine, pichcha, a shrub of Asia cultivated from remote times and its earliest history lost, but undoubtedly its earliest home was western India. There are races with double flowers, which have been raised by man. The flowers are pure white and very strongly scented; the leaves are glabrous. Owing to the heavy perfume, the flowers are much used by women to give fragrance to the hair and person. In China they are used to give an aroma to tea. The flowers are medicinal but the leaves are more so. The root is given for fever in the Dutch Indies (v. p. p. 215: mcm. pp. 112, 125: burk. p. 1265): มะลิป่า (ต้น) *Jasminum pubescens* (*Oleaceae*) (mcm. p. 125: [v. p. p. 215).

มะลิน see กระบก p. 37.

มะลิม ma[6]-lim *n.* a name for a group of Thai songs.

มะวาร, มาวาร *Jav.* see กุหลาบ p. 116.

มะแว้ง (ต้น) ma[6]-waang[5] *n. Solanum indicum* (*Solanaceae*), Sparrow's Brinjal, a shrub growing on waste land; a native medicinal plant. The root is much used for bronchitis and asthma. The fruit is sometimes eaten as a vegetable and half ripe in curries (burk p. 2043: mcm. pp. 380, 312): มะแว้งเครือ (ต้น) *Solanum trilobatum*, a small, thorny shrub, native of south-eastern Asia, found in gardens, and sometimes on waste ground in the Malay Peninsula. It is much used by the Tamils as a medicine, the bitter roots and young shoots being given as an electuary, a decoction, or a powder for consumption. The Tamils seem to have introduced it into Malaya where Chinese herbalists sometimes stock it (burk. p. 2047).

มะสัง see กาสัง p. 101.

มะเส็ง ma[6]-seng[2] *n.* the small snake or dragon: ปีมะเส็ง the sixth year of the animal cycle; the year of the small dragon; see ปี p. 527.

มะหวด ma[6]-hu-at[4] *Thai* and *Laos*, กำซำ, กะซ่ำ *Thai, Peninsula* (ต้น) *n. Erioglossum rubiginosum* (*Sapindaceae*), a big tree found from Asia to Australia; in the Peninsula it occurs throughout. The small red-to-black astringent fruits are produced in big bunches. Their aril is edible, but not worth eating, though Malay children commonly eat it. In Java the shoots, newly produced, are used as a vegetable. They are said to arrest insomnia. The wood is hard and heavy, reddish and does not split in drying. It is not a strong wood, but, being hard, it is used for rice-pounders and tool-handles in Java. The roots are medicinal. An astringent decoction made from them is given in fever. The fruits enter into a mixture drunk after childbirth. The seeds are used in a decoction given for whooping-cough. Roots and leaves are used by the Malays for poulticing both the head, during fever, and the body for skin complaints. In the Dutch Indies the leaves may be used for poulticing (cb. p. 325: v. p. p. 219: burk. p. 938).

มะหอกะนี *Thai* (ต้น) ma[6]-hock[4]-gka[4]-nee *n. Swietenia mahagoni* (*Meliaceae*) mahogany, one of a genus of five species of tree found in tropical America. This gives the true mahogany. In the early days of sailing across the Atlantic the timber of *S. Mahogani* became known in the West Indies as valuable for repairing ships. Raleigh used it; and then as early as the reign of Queen Elizabeth it was recognized as a cabinet wood. The seed reached India in 1795, where it can be grown so well that very fine timber has been produced in Calcutta. A larger braver sort from Honduras, now much planted as a street tree in Bangkok, is *S. macrophylla*. From India, the tree was taken to the Malay Peninsula and Java. The timber holds the premier position in its class in European markets. The bark contains tannin, and may serve as an antipyretic, tonic, and astringent. A gum runs from the tree (BURK. p. 2109 : MCM. p. 104 : cb. p. 266 : V. P. p. 219).

มะหะหมัด ma⁶-ha⁴-mut⁴ *Arabic n.* Mohammed ; Mahomet, an Arabian religious and military leader, founder of Islam, and author of the Koran. The Arabian is Maham-mad (whence the followers are called Mohammedans). He was born at Mecca on 29th August, 570 A.D. in the Koreish (*Kuriash*) ruling tribe. His father, Abdulla, was a merchant, son of Abdul Muttalib, the Patriarch of the House of Hasbim ; his mother's name was Amina. His father died before his birth, his mother when he was barely five years old. He remained three years in the charge of his grandfather and on the latter's death passed to the care of his uncle. At the age of forty, Mohammed claimed to have received his first divine communication in the solitude of the mountain Hira, near Mecca, where the call came to him, and the Angel Gabriel commanded him to preach the new religion. He and his followers were persecuted for his preaching and threatened with death. He fled from Mecca to Medina on 16th July, 622 A. D. From this flight, called the Hegira, dates the Moslem Era. He died on 8th June, 632 and was buried at Medina ("MOSLEM world," zwemer p. 3).

มะหาด ma⁶-hart⁴, หาด (ต้น) *n. Artocarpus lakoocha,* a large deciduous tree of India, Ceylon, Malaya (Tampang-manis), etc. It has tomentose branchlets, and oblong leaves, 8 to 12 inches long. The flat, broad seeds are edible and considerably esteemed by the natives of the East, but are not in favour with Europeans. The timber is good ; it is used for house-posts, beams, and for boats, but is considered inferior to that of some of the other species of the genus. It seasons well, and takes a good polish. It is marketed in India. It is useful for cabinet-making, brushbacks, turnery, inlaying, and fancy-work generally. A yellow dye can be obtained

from the wood. The bark contains 8.5 per cent of tan. It is chewed, in Assam, as a substitute for betel-nut. A fibre can be extracted from it, and is used for cordage in India (MCM. p. 254 : V. P. p. 218 : BURK. p. 257).

มะโหระทึก ma⁶-hoh²-ra⁶-tuk⁶ *n.* a large one-faced bronze drum, being one of the musical instruments used in state processions.

มะโหรี ma⁶-hoh²-ree *n.* a band consisting of stringed, wind, and percussion instruments, somewhat resembling an orchestra (GER. (1) p. 45).

มะอึก (ต้น) ma⁶-euk⁴ *n. Solanum ferox* (*Solanaceae*), a small plant with spiny stem and furry fruit and leaves, found throughout south-eastern Asia and Malaysia. The fruit is about the size of that of the jujube tree, and is used for vegetable curries. Proverbially they typify a soured old man, as they get more acid toward ripeness. The seeds are used for treating toothache by means of burning them and inhaling the smoke. A cigar is made by rolling the seeds in a dried banana leaf ; after smoking, the mouth is treated with a hot gargle. The root enters into a decoction swallowed to give relief when there are violent pains all over the body ; and discomfort after meals. The roots are extensively used externally in a bath for fever at nights, and in a poultice for itch. The roots enter into a medicine applied to elephants' bodies in a more or less magic way, for chills and to make elephants fat (BURK. p. 2043).

มัก muk⁶ (1) *v.* to want ; to like ; to wish or fancy ; see ชอบ p. 284 : มักคุ้น to be desirous or wishful for friendly intimacy ; see คุ้น p. 205 : มักน้อย to manifest a willingness to be satisfied with the little one has : มักมาก to be grasping, craving or manifesting a mania for gain or plenty : มักใหญ่ to be an aspirant or solicitant of rank, position or prestige.

มัก (2) *adv.* generally ; commonly ; repeatedly ;

ขะโมยมักมากลางคืน thieves for the most part come during the night.

มัก   (3) *adj.* prone to; given to; liable: มักโกรธ addicted to anger: มักง่าย careless; inattentive: มักชอบมักชัง liable to having periods of friendship and enmity; see ชัง p. 288: มักได้ desirous of; covetous: มักพูด tending towards being a babbler, or a chatter-box: มักมี given to having (as periods of fits or spasms): มักหลง tending to forgetfulness; erring: มักหลับ drowsy; inclined to sleep.

มักกฏกะ   muk⁶-gka⁴-dta⁴-gka⁴ *P. n.* a spider (chd. p. 233).

มักกฏะ   muk⁶-gka⁴-dta⁴ *P. n.* a monkey [(chd. p. 233).

มักข   muk⁶-ka⁴ *P. n.* concealing one's vices; hypocrisy (chd. p. 233); the act of showing no gratitude to one's benefactor; one of the six-teen depravities or sins (chd. p. 528); the act of dishonouring kindnesses offered.

มักขัก   muk³-kuk³ *adj.* fat and overgrown (descriptive of a man).

มักขิกา   muk⁶-ki⁴-gkah *P. n.* a fly (chd. [p. 233).

มัคค, มรรค   muk⁶-ka⁶ *P. n.* a trace; a track; a road; a path; a course; a passage; the urethra (chd. p. 225: Ala. p. 170): มัคค-นายก *lit.* "a leader or guide," *i. e.* one who leads or tells others when or how to perform meritorious acts; a deacon (in the christian church): มัคคนายิกา a deaconess: มัคคผล the eight paths to sanctity.

มัคคุทเทศก์   muk⁶-koot⁶-tet³ *P. n.* a guide; a conductor (as for sightseers).

มัฆวา, มัฆวาน, มฆวา, มฆวาน   muk⁶-ka⁶-wah *n.* names for Indra (chd. p. 226).

มั่ง   mung³ *v.* to have much or plenty; to be rich; to have an abundance or superfluity: *adj.* partly, half dried or semi-hardened by sunlight (as clay pots): มั่งคั่ง powerful; firm; very bulky: มั่งมี very rich; opulent; wealthy.

มังกง   mung-gkong *n.* a small, scaleless, edible, salt-water fish about the size of one's thumb, frequenting salt-water canals. It has a spine on each side of the head while a third one stands nearly erect on its neck.

มังกร   mung-gkawn *P. n.* a mythical fish or sea monster (chd. p. 233); a fabulous sea-dragon; name of the tenth zodiacal sign; Capricorn: มังกร, หลด (ปลา) *Muraenesox cinereus (Muraenesocidae)*; *Mystus guilio (Bagridae)*; *Pterois russellii (Scorpaenidae)*, scorpion fish; rock cod (suvatti pp. 22, 72, 144).

มังกุ ๑   mung-gkoo⁴ *n.* a boat with a large or weighted keel; a long barge rowed by oars.

มังกุ ๒   mung-gkoo⁴ *P. adj.* troubled; rest-less; disturbed; put out; irritable; annoyed (chd. p. 237); see กระดาก p. 27.

มังคละ see มงคล p. 619.

มังคุด (ต้น)   mung-koot⁶ *n. Garcinia mang-ostana (Guttiferae)*, mangosteen, a small or moderate-sized, conical tree, with large, leathery leaves, indigenous to Malaya, intro-duced into Ceylon about 1800. Its globular, purplish-brown, smooth fruit, about the size of an apple, is famed as one of the most deli-cious fruits of the tropics, and is considered by some to "partake of the flavour of the strawberry and the grape." The delicate, white, melting, juicy pulp, surrounding and adhering to the seed, is the part eaten. In striking contrast to this is the dense, thick, reddish-purple rind, which contains tannic acid and a dye. The fruit is in season in Bangkok in March. It grows best in the peninsula at Sritamarat. The tree is of very slow growth, and does not usually come into bearing till at least nine or ten years old, but takes several more years to attain full size. The essential conditions are a hot, moist climate, deep, rich, and well-drained soil, and a sheltered locality. Light shade is beneficial; in the young state it is essential. The tree responds to manuring, and thrives up to about 2,000 feet elevation in the moist region. Propagation is usually by seed, but may with difficulty be effected also by "gootee" or layering. Seeds should be sown in pots or boxes under cover. The plants are of very slow growth, taking two years or more to become large enough for planting out, being then only about 12 inches high (MCM. pp. 241, 242 : BURK. p. 1052).

มังสะ, มางสะ   mung-sa[4] *P. n.* flesh; muscle (human) (chd. p. 234); see เนื้อ p. 464.

มังส์   mung-see[2] *n.* a pair of scissors used for cutting and slicing areca-nuts, commonly made of iron, but sometimes of brass.

มังหงัน   mung-ngun[2] *Jav. n.* the inflorescence of the coconut palm.

มัจจุ   see มฤตยู p. 624.

มัจฉ, มัจฉา   mut[6]-cha[4]   *P. n.* a fish (chd. p. 223).

มัจฉาชาติ, มัจฉชาติ   mut[6]-chah[2]-chart[3] *n.* a school or shoal of fishes; fishes (in general).

มัจฉระ, มัตสร   mut[6]-cha[4]-ra[6]   *P. adj.* niggardly; envious; grudging (chd. p. 223); see ตระหนี่ p. 343.

มัจฉริยะ   mut[6]-cha[4]-ri[6]-ya[6]   *P. n.* avarice; niggardliness; selfishness; envy (chd. p. 223 : Ala. p. 206).

มัจฉรี, มัตสรีน   mut[6]-cha[4]-ree   *P. n.* a stingy, penurious or tight-fisted person (chd. p. 223).

มัชช   mut[6]-cha[6]   *P. n.* strong drink; spirituous liquor; wine; spirits (chd. 232),

มัชชาร   mut[6]-chah-ra[6]   *P. n.* a cat (chd. p. 232).

มัชฌ   mut[6]-cha[6]   *P. n.* middle; centre; interior (chd. p. 233).

มัชฌันติก   mut[6]-chun-dti[4]-gka[4] *P. n.* mid-

day; noon (Chd. p. 233) :   วิมัชฌันติก midnight :   มัชฌันติกสมัย noontime.

มัชฌิม   mut[6]-chi[6]-ma[6] *P. adj.* middle; central; mean; moderate; of medium size (chd. p. 233) :   มัชฌิมบุรุษ a man of mean or medium size :   มัชฌิมประเทศ the Central Region; Central India : This region bore a sacred character in the eyes of Buddhists, embracing as it did places such as Rajagaha and Savatthi hallowed by the residence or frequent visits of the Buddha. It is said to be nine hundred yojanas in circuit (chd. p. 233). One yojana is equivalent to about twelve miles (chd. p. 604) :   มัชฌิมยาม the middle watch of the night; midnight.

มัญจ, มัญจก   mun-chja[4] *P. S. n.* a bed; a raised seat; a dais; a throne; a stage or platform in a palace, or one supported on columns (S. E. D. p. 773).

มัญชีร   mun-chee-ra[6] *S. n.* a foot ornament; an anklet (S. E. D. p. 774).

มัญชุ   mun-choo[6] *P. S. adj.* beautiful; charming; pleasing (S. E. D. p. 774); see งาม p. 223.

มัญชิษฐ, มัญเชฏฐะ   mun-chit[6]-ta[4] *S. adj.* bright red; very bright (S. E. D. p. 774).

มัญชุสา, มัญชูสา   mun-choo[6]-sah[2] *P. n.* a basket; a box; a bag; a casket (chd. p. 237).

มัฏฐ, มัฏฐ   mut[6]-dta[4]   *P. adj.* polished; cleansed; pure (chd. p. 244).

[p. 236).

มัณฑุก   mun-doo[4]-gka[4] *P. n.* a frog (chd.

มัด   mut[6] *v.* to tie, bind, strap, bundle up or fasten together (as by a string or wire); see ผูก p. 549 : *n.* a pack, a parcel, package or bundle : กิ่งไม้ (ใช้เป็นฟืน) มัดหนึ่ง a faggot : ข้าวมัดหนึ่ง a sheaf of grain or rice-stalks : เทียนมัดหนึ่ง a bundle of incense tapers : มัดจำ a pledge; a security; a monetary deposit (made to clinch a bargain).

มัตต   mut[6]-dta[4] *P. S. adj.* overjoyed; delighted; excited by sexual passion or desire; drunk; intoxicated (S. E. D. p. 777).

มัตตัญญู   mut⁶-dtun-yoo *P. n.* moderation; temperance; one capable of acting with sobriety and discretion as to when and how much money to spend (Chd. p. 244).

มัตติกา   mut⁶-dti⁴-gkah *P. n.* earth; loam; clay; mud; soil (Chd. p. 245).

มัตถก, มัสดก   mut⁶-ta⁴-gka⁴ *P. n.* the crown of the head; the top; the summit; excellence; eminence (Chd. p. 244).

มัตถลุงค์   mut⁶-ta⁴-loong *P. n.* the brain (Chd. p. 245).

มัตสยะ, มัตสยา   mut⁶-sa⁴-ya⁶ *P. n.* a fish [(Chd. p. 223).

มัตสร see **มัจฉระ** p. 643.

มัทนน   mut⁶-ta⁶-na⁶ *P. n.* the act of grinding, crushing or trampling (Chd. p. 224).

มัทน see **มทนะ** p. 621.

มัทนียะ see **มทนียะ** p. 621.

มัธยม   mut⁶-ta⁶-yome *adj.* being, or placed in the middle; middlemost; intermediate; middling; moderate; impartial; mean; medial (S. E. D. p. 782): ความอุดมชั้นมัธยม a medium state, condition, or amount of abundance or proficiency: มัธยมศึกษา a middle term of schooling; a secondary or intermediate course or standard of education.

มัธยันห์   mut⁶-ta⁶-yun *S. n.* midday; noon (S. E. D. p. 782).

มัธยัสถ์   mut⁶-ta⁶-yut⁶ *S. adj.* standing impartially, or taking a medium course (S. E. D. p. 782). *For the Thai meaning see* ประหยัด p. 505: กินอยู่มัธยัสถ์ cutting out all luxuries in life.

มัธวาธาร   mut⁶-wah-tarn *S. n.* wax (S. E. D. p. 781).

มัน (ต้น)   mun *n.* (1) a generic name for many species of upright and creeping plants. *Dioscorea alata* (*Dioscoraceae*), cultivated for their edible bulbous roots, as yams, and

potatoes (Burk. p. 814); see กลอย p. 59; แกว p. 130: มันแกว *Pachyrhizua erosus* (*Leguminosae*), yam-bean, a herbaceous climber, native of tropical America, where the early European voyagers found large crops of it. It reached the Philippine Islands by Spanish agency. It is cultivated now widely in India and eastern Africa. It is not perfectly suited to a very wet climate. The tuberous root is sweetish, and is eaten raw or cooked. It should be dug before the seeds ripen, as it is then relatively tender. In Indo-China and Thailand the plant runs wild, and occasionally, also, in the Malay Peninsula. Starch begins to accumulate at the end of seven or eight months and, if left to do so, a kind of arrowroot can be prepared. The Chinese in San Francisco import old tubers for making starch. The young pods can be eaten as a substitute for French beans. The leaves contain a poison, from the effect of which horses are exempt. The seeds are poisonous and, if pounded and dropped into water, stupify fish. The powdered seeds are used in Java for applying to skin affections of the nature of prickly heat. In Fiji the stems are said to yield a fibre used for fishing-nets. The plant can be used as a green manure (Burk. p. 1619); see ถั่วบัง p. 385: มันเชือก *Dioscorea esculenta* (*Dioscoraceae*), the lesser yam, a prickly climber, apparently a native of Indo-China, and undoubtedly of ancient cultivation throughout the East. The tubers are produced in bunches underground, and peculiar thorny roots are produced above them as a protection in the wild and less highly cultivated races. The races which are most highly cultivated do not produce these thorns. Many of the races are slightly sweet. The tubers usually measure only a few inches in length, and as they bruise easily are unsuited for transport to distant markets. Raw tubers may be grated and used for an application on swellings (Burk. p. 818): มันแดง *Thai, Nakawn Sritamarat,* ขมิ้นเคือ *N. Laos,* แหนเคือ *E. Laos* (ต้น) *Combretum extensum (Combretaceae)* (Cb. p. 615: BURK. p. 644): มันเทศ *Ipomoea batatas (Convolvulaceae)*, sweet potato, a creeping or trailing perennial producing succulent tuberous roots, which are a tasty and nutritious article of food. The sweet potato is a native of America from whence Columbus took it to Europe, but it is now cultivated in the tropics generally. It is cultivated in all warm countries, and may be grown successfully in sheltered valleys up to about 3,000 to 4,000 feet in the tropics, but does not usually thrive in the hills when exposed to heavy rains. The sweet potato, in the East, is gradually ousting the yam, because it is a crop which is so much quicker in giving a return. The sweet potato has the disadvantage of keeping badly. Various devices are resorted to in order to store it. Some races with firm tubers can be stored for a year but the tubers of most races decay after two months. A rotation of races offers a close succession of these tubers for the market. Alcohol can be made from the tubers but is not profitable as the food value is too high. The tops can be eaten as a vegetable. The tops are also used for poulticing. The Chinese slice the tubers, scald and dry the slices, and make from them a tea to allay thirst (BURK. p. 1247: MCM. p. 298): มันนก, มันขมิ้น *D. bulbifera (Dioscoraceae)*, a climber which rarely reaches a greater height than 20 feet from the ground. It is found throughout the moist tropics of the Old World. In past times it must have been of greater importance as a food plant for man than it is now. As a result, there has been much improvement of the races. The big bulbils of the best races of this variety are good to eat when properly cooked, and have been put to considerable use in certain places. Tubers of wild varieties are eaten by the Pagan races of the Peninsula (BURK. p. 816): มันสำปะหรัง, มันสำโรง *Manihot utilissima (Euphorbiaceae)*, cassava, a shrubby perennial, 6 to 7 feet high, native of tropical America, but now cultivated in all tropical countries. It is supposed to have been first introduced into India and Ceylon by the Portuguese in the seventeenth century. Two distinct kinds are recognized, *viz.* bitter and sweet, and of these there are many varieties. The group called sweet is characterized by a relative freedom from poisonous properties; but these properties any one of them may perhaps at times possess. It is by smell rather than by any bitter taste that, in the East, those who eat them classify them broadly into the two groups. The cassava is one of the great gifts of the New World to the Old World. The sweet potato is of quicker growth than the cassava and it spread more rapidly in the Far East than did the cassava, but in Africa the cassava early became established and new races have been developed there. Just when and how the cassava came to the Far East is uncertain but industrialization began in about 1850. The Chinese in Malacca and elsewhere raised the cassava and, by following a process similar to that of making sago, they produced tapioca, a product able to hold its own against the tapioca of Brazil. In southern Thailand it is much grown for this purpose. Because this plant is so hard on the soil there is a prohibition against raising much of it in Malaya. Therefore the Chinese are coming farther north and raise it in Thailand. The tubers contain about 26 per cent of starch, but as the proteid element is not more than 2 per cent, the tubers should not make a very large part of any dietary, but in the home of the plant they do make a very large part, and their importance tends to grow in the East. The preparations of these tubers for eating are varied; they may be rasped or peeled, steamed, pounded into a paste, shaped into cakes, dried in the sun, and then roasted and eaten; or they may be pounded into paste which is then kneaded in water until the milky juice is washed out, then steamed and made into cakes, dried in the sun and baked for eating; again, the paste may be made up with sugar and coconut, etc. in various ways. The juice squeezed from the tubers can be boiled down to the consistency of molasses and used in the making of a sauce. The tubers make good pig and fowl food. The leaves are widely used as food (MCM. p. 299: BURK. p. 1411): มันหั้ง *D. pentaphylla* (*Dioscoraceae*), a wide-spread yam found throughout the warmer moist parts of Asia and to the remotest islands of the Pacific; in the Peninsula, though not common, it is general in the low country and up to about 2,000 feet. Like the *D. bulbifera* it has been of sufficient importance to man in the past for cultivated varieties to be selected; and perhaps its occurrence in some parts of the Pacific is the result of transport by canoes as a food plant. The Sakai in the Peninsula encourage its growth and plant it on the edge of such small patches of cultivation as they may have (BURK. p. 823).

มัน   mun *n.* (2) fat; grease; oil: *adj.* lardy; oily; greasy; nutty (as the taste of coconut milk, น้ำกะทิ); sheeny; bright; shining; glossy; clean (as polished brass or silverware): *pron.* he; she; it; her; him; *used contemptuously in place of the name* (as of children, fowls, cattle, or low characters): มันปู the colour resulting from mingling black, red and yellow together: มันมากเกินไป entirely too much fat or oil intermixed.

มั่น   mun[3] *v.* to be affianced; to be betrothed; to be engaged to in marriage; to be espoused: *adj.* firm; durable; strong; constant; certain; sturdy; stable; reliable: ของมั่น, ทองมั่น golden ornaments or valuable articles presented as pledge of engagement (in marriage): ถือมั่น, เชื่อมั่น to adhere to strictly; to be obedient to the doctrines, or to the rule: มั่นคง strong and durable; unchangeable; not fluctuating; reliable: มั่นใจ to be sure of; to be certain in mind; to believe undoubtingly or implicitly: มั่นแม่น, แม่นมั่น truly; really; certainly.

มันตา   mun-dtah *P. n.* wisdom; knowledge (chd. p. 239).

มันทิร, มันทิราลัย see มนทิร p. 622.

มับ   mup[6] *adj.* full; overloaded; descriptive of the manner of grasping or snatching excitedly: บันทุกเรือเต็มมับ loaded to the water's edge.

มัย   mai *P. adj.* made of; consisting of (chd. p. 245); finished off with: ตฤณมัย consisting of grass.

มัลล   mun-la[6] *P. n.* a professional wrestler; a boxer; name of a people. The Mallas were a tribe of Hindustan; one of their towns was Pava (chd. p. 234): *adj.* boxing; wrestling; pugilistic.

มัลลก   mun-la[6]-gka[4] *P. n.* a tumbler or cup (chd. p. 234).

มัลลิกา   mun-li[6]-gkah *P. n.* a garland; the double jasmine (chd. p. 234); see มะลิ p. 639.

มัว   moo-ah *adj.* dull; indistinct; dim; cloudy: *adv.* attentively engaged in; absentmindedly: ตามัว dim or blurred eye-sight: มัวเมา to be held in the power of (passions); to be addicted to; to have the habit of: มัวหมอง guilty; tainted; dishonoured: มืดมัว dark; cloudy or overcast.

มั่ว   moo-ah[3] *v.* to congregate; to assemble; to be clumped or bunched together (as a gang of outlaws): มั่วมูล to be assembled in great numbers: มั่วสุม to congregate secretly in great numbers (as accomplices or associates).

มัศยา preferably มัตสยา p. 644.

มัสตุ, มัสตุ   mut[6]-sa[4]-doo[4] *S. n.* whey; fat (chd. p. 245).

มัสมั่น (แกง)   mut[6]-sa[4]-mun[4] *n.* a kind of peppery Indian curry.

มัสรู้   mut[6]-sa[4]-roo[3] *n.* a pattern of striped silk cloth, imported from India; name of an Indian curry.

มัสสุ mut[6]-soo[4] *P. n.* the beard or whiskers (chd. p. 242): พระมัสสุ royal term for the same.

มา ๑ mah *P. n.* the moon (chd. p. 223).

มา ๒ mah *v.* to come; to approach: กลับมา to return or come back: แขกมาหา some guest comes to visit; a visitor drops in: ไปมาหาสู่กัน to visit back and forth frequently: มาเป็นแขก to come as a guest; to come unexpectedly: มาโดนหรือชนกัน to collide with: มาถึง, มายัง to arrive; to reach: เอามา to to fetch or bring: อยู่มา after that; it happened that: อยู่มาวันหนึ่ง one day it occurred that.

ม้า mah[5] *Mandarin n.* a horse or mare; a bench or stool; the knight (in chess): ม้า-ก่าน a horse with black or white patches over the back: ม้าใช้ a mounted messenger (used in ancient times): ม้าน้ำ hippocampus or sea-horse, a kind of lophobranchiate in which the head and neck have some resemblance to those of a horse. They swim slowly in an erect position and often cling to seaweeds by means of the incurved prehensile tail. The male has a ventral pouch, in which it carries the eggs till hatched: ม้าแพน a lance-soldier's mount: ม้าย่อง a Thai orchestral tune: ม้าโยงยาน draught horses: ม้าเร็ว an army scout's or errand man's mount: ม้าลาย a zebra.

มาก mark[3] *adj.* much; many; abundant; ample: กี่มากน้อย how much; how many; เป็นอันมาก in great numbers; very much: มากนัก too much; super-abundant: มาก-มาย too much; too many; more than is enough; over-abundant; amply; in great numbers or quantity: รู้มาก wise; sly; cunning: สักกี่มากน้อย about how much or how many?

มาคธ mah-kot[6] *P. n.* name of the people and country of south Bihar (chd. p. 225): *adj.* belonging to the country of south Bihar where the Pali language was spoken (H. C. D. p. 183).

มาฆ mah-ka[6] *P. S. n.* the month of the zodiacal sign Capricornus, corresponding to January and February (S. E. D. p. 805): มาฆ-บูชา the Buddhist festival of All Saints held during the middle of the third lunar month: มาฆมาศ the third lunar month.

ม้าง mang[5] *v.* to destroy or demolish.

มางสะ mang-sa[4] *n.* flesh; meat (S. E. D. p. 805).

มาณพ mah-nop[6] *P. S. n.* a young man; a youth, especially a young Brahmin (chd. p. 236); a lad; a youngster (S. E. D. p. 806).

มาณวิกา mah-na[6]-wi[6]-gkah *P. n.* a young woman; a girl; a Brahmin girl (chd. p. 236).

มาด mart[3] *v.* to intend, resolve, or purpose; to determine; to fix one's mind upon: มาด (เรือ) a dug-out made from a single log with the middle part expanded into shape by heat, having pointed stem and stern. These are used only in canals and are propelled by paddling.

มาดา mah-dah *P. n.* a mother (chd. p. 242).

มาตงค์, มาตังค mah-dtong *P. n.* an elephant; a man of the lowest caste (chd. p. 242).

มาตร mart[3] *S. n.* a measure; a quantity (S. E. D. p. 804); calculation: *conj.* if; provided that: มาตรว่า, มาตรแม้น even if; provided that; although: มาตรฐาน standard: มาตร-ส่วน a metal scale marked off into inches and fractions thereof: มาตรหมาย to decree, determine, or resolve upon.

มาตรา mart[3]-dtrah *S. n.* a table for making calculations (as measurements, exchange, quantities, time and angles); a syllabic foot; a unit of measurement; a unit of time or degree (S. E. D. p. 804): *Thai* a section, clause, chapter or paragraph *legal.*

มาตฤ mah-dtri[4] *S. n.* a mother; parents (S. E. D. p. 807).

มาตฤกะ   mah-dtri[4]-gka[4] *S. adj.* maternal ; pertaining to a mother ; coming from, or belonging to a mother (S. E. D. p. 807).

มาตฤกา   mah-dtri[4]-gkah *S. n. lit.* "the source or birthplace," *i. e.* a mother (S. E. D. p. 807).

มาตฤช   mah-dtri[4]-cha[6] *S. n. lit.* "one born from a mother," *i. e.* a child.

มาตฤยะ   mah-dtri[4]-ya[6] *S. n.* maternal relatives.

มาตลิ   mah-dta[4]-lee *P. n.* the charioteer of Sakka or Indra (chd. p. 242).

มาตสรรย์, มัตสรรย์   mart[3]-sun[2] *S. n.* envy; jealousy ; displeasure ; dissatisfaction (S. E. D. p. 808) ; selfishness (chd. p. 223).

มาตังค see มาตงค์ p. 647.

มาตา   mah-dtah *P. n.* a mother (chd. p. 242).

มาตามหะ   mah-dtah-ma[6]-ha[4] *P. n.* a maternal grandfather (chd. p. 242).

มาตามห้ยยก   mah-dtah-ma[6]-hai[2]-ya[6]-gka[4] *n.* a maternal great-grandfather.

มาตามห้ยยิกา   mah-dtah-ma[6]-hai[2]-yi[6]-gkah *n.* a maternal great-grandmother.

มาตามหา   mah-dtah-ma[6]-hah[2] *P. n.* a maternal grandmother (chd. p. 242).

มาติกา   mart[3]-dti[4]-gkah *P. n.* a conduit ; a water-course ; a canal for irrigation ; a heading ; a head ; an outline ; a sketch ; a text ; a list ; a table of contents (chd. p. 242).

มาติ   mah-dtee *P. n.* a conduit or canal (chd. p. 242).

มาตุ   mah-dtoo[4] *P. n.* a mother (chd. p. 242): มาตุการ maternity : มาตุฆาต matricide : มาตุบักขี a maternal relative : มาตุราช, มาตุเรศ a royal mother.

มาตุคาม   mah-dtoo[4]-karm *P. n.* womankind ; a woman ; a female (chd. p. 245) ; the mother of a family.

มาตุจฉา   mah-dtoot[4]-chah[2] *P. n.* a mother's sister ; an aunt (chd. p. 245).

มาตุภาดา   mah-dtoo[4]-pah-dah *P. n.* a mother's elder brother ; an uncle.

มาตุรงค์, มาตุเรศ   mah-dtoo[4]-rong *n.* a mother.

มาตุละ, มาตุลา   mah-dtoo[4]-la[6] *P. n.* a mother's brother ; an uncle (chd. p. 245).

มาตุลานิ   mah-dtoo[4]-lah-nee *P. n.* a mother's brother's wife ; an aunt (chd. p. 245).

มาตุลุงค์   mah-dtoo[4]-loong *P. n.* a citron tree (chd. p. 245) ; see มะนาว p. 635.

มาท, มาทน   mart[3] *S. n.* intoxication ; pride (chd. p. 225) : คันธมาทน์ intoxicated with pleasing odours ; name of a mountain mentioned in the Vesantara Jataka.

มาน ๑ (โรค)   marn *n.* dropsy : ท้องมาน dropsy affecting the abdominal cavity : มาน-เลือด a collection of extravasated blood.

มาน ๒   mah-na[6] *P. S. n.* the act of measuring or counting (chd. p. 235).

มาน ๓   mah-na[6] *P. S. n.* pride ; arrogance ; vanity (chd. p. 238).

ม่าน   marn[3] *n.* a screen ; a veil ; a curtain ; a blind : กั้นม่าน to draw the curtain ; มีม่านกั้น to be separated by a screen or curtain.

ม้าน   marn[5] *v.* to fade ; to wither : *adj.* faded ; sad-looking ; pale from shame (used regarding the facial expression) ; dry ; nearly dry.

มานพ   mah-nop[6] *P. n.* mankind ; man ; a young man (chd. p. 236).

ม่านลาย   marn[3]-lai *n.* the soft-shell turtle, an aquatic creature of the tortoise family, having a big spotted body and pointed snout, of the genus *Trionyx*; a large long-necked river turtle.

มานะ   mah-na⁶ *n.* determination ; diligence ; application ; perseverance ; persistence.

มานิต   mah-nit⁶ *P. adj.* revered ; honoured ; respected (Chd. p. 237).

มานุษ   mah-noot⁶ *S. n.* mankind ; human beings : *adj.* belonging to mankind ; favourable or propitious to man ; humane (Chd. p. 240).

มาบ   marp³ *n.* a lagoon ; a marsh ; a swamp or low ground ; a water-pocket.

มาปก   mah-bpa⁴-gka⁴ *P. n.* one who causes something to appear by super-natural power (Chd. p. 240).

ม้าม   marm⁵ *n.* the spleen : ม้ามย้อย (โรค) an enlarged spleen.

มาย   mai *P. n.* a measure (of capacity) ; measurement ; calculation ; counting (Chd. p. 245).

ม่าย   mai³ *v.* to turn away (as from a person or object) ; to turn aside bashfully (as with girls) : *n.* a widow ; widowhood.

มายา   mah-yah *P. S. n.* an illusion ; a phantom ; a deceptive appearance ; deceit ; jugglery ; magic (Chd. p. 245 : Ala. p. 79) : พระสิริมหามายา Maya, name of the mother of the Buddha : มายากร an illusion-maker ; a conjurer ; a juggler ; an artificer : มายาโยค the application or employment of illusion ; the use of magical arts : มายาวาจนะ deceptive or hypocritical speech : มายาวาทนะ the doctrine affirming the world to be an illusion.

มายาวี   mah-yah-wee *P. S. n.* one who is deceitful, hypocritical, subject to illusion, or deluded (Chd. p. 245).

มายุ   mah-yoo⁶ *P. n.* bile ; gall (Chd. p. 245).

มายุริกะ   mah-yoo-ri⁶-gka⁴ *P. n.* a peacock hunter (Chd. p. 245).

มาร   mah-ra⁶ *P.S. n.* Mara, the evil one ; the tempter ; the destroyer of goodness ; an obstacle ; hindrance ; destruction ; a slayer (S.E.D.

p. 811) ; a demon ; a wicked angel (Ala. p. 149) ; see พญามาร p. 559 ; ปีศาจ p. 527 : นางมาร a female demon or temptress : มารชิ *lit.* " the conqueror of Mara," *i. e.* an epithet of the Buddha : มารวิชัย, มารวิชิต *lit.* " one who conquered Mara," *i. e.* the Buddha. Name for a posture of the Buddha sitting with the legs crossed on which lies his right hand, representing the attitude assumed by the Buddha when he was attacked by the host of Mara, whom he conquered.

มารก   mah-rok⁶ *P. n.* a slayer of animals ; a hunter (Chd. p. 240) ; a killer ; a murderer ; any deadly disease ; plague ; pestilence (S. E. D. [p. 811).

มารค   see มรรค, มรรคา p. 623.

มารชาร   mah-ra⁶-charn *S. n.* a wild cat ; a civet (S. E. D. p. 813).

มารดร, มารดา   marn-dorn *P. n.* a mother : สมนาคุณมารดา to return a mother's love by acts of kindness.

มารยา   marn-yah *n.* fraud ; coquetry ; artifice ; crookedness ; pretence ; a trick ; a delusion ; deceit : หญิงมารยา a woman who seduces by her wiles, snares or artifices.

มารยาท   mah-ra⁶-yart³ *n.* morals ; manners ; rectitude ; good conduct (Chd. p. 240) ; see มรรยาท p. 624 : มีกิริยามารยาทดี having good manners, morals and conduct ; well-behaved.

มารษา   marn-sah² *n.* a lie ; falsehood ; misleading words.

มาริ   mah-ri⁶ *Jav. v.* to come or approach.

มาริต   mah-rit⁶ *P. adj.* killed ; destroyed ; murdered (Chd. p. 240).

มาริษ   mah-rit⁶ *S. n.* an honoured person ; a worthy or respectable person (used as an honourable or polite form of address to one's superior) (S. E. D. p. 811).

มารุดี   mah-roo⁶-dee *S. n. lit.* " a descendant of the wind," *i. e.* Hanuman, the monkey king.

มารุต mah-root[6] *S. n.* wind : *adj.* pertaining to the wind ; relating to, or derived from the wind ; aerial (S. E. D. p. 812).

มาล marn *P. n.* a pavilion ; a pagoda (chd. p. 234).

มาลก mah-lok[6] *P. n.* a circular enclosure ; a yard ; a terrace ; a consecrated enclosure where religious functions or ceremonies are held (as around the sacred Boh tree) (chd. p. 234).

มาลย์, มาลัย marn *P.S. n.* a flower ; a garland or tassel of flowers (chd. p. 234) ; a wreath ; a chaplet (S. E. D. p. 814).

ม้าล่อ mah[5]-law[3] *n.* a brass, tray-shaped Chinese cymbal used in processions ; it plays an important part in Chinese bands (similar to Thai drums).

มาลา mah-lah *P. S. n.* a wreath ; a garland ; a necklace ; a crown ; a string of beads ; a rosary (S. E. D. p. 813) : มาลากรรม the handicraft of sewing flowers together ; a garland-maker : มาลาการ a garland-maker ; a florist ; a gardener : มาลาธร crowned ; wearing a garland ; honoured with a wreath of flowers : สุวรรณมาลา gold flowers sent as a token of homage.

มาลิ mah-li[6] *P. S. n.* a florist ; a gardener [(chd. p. 234).

มาลินี mah-li[6]-nee *P. S. n.* the wife of a garland-maker or gardener ; a female florist (S. E. D. p. 813).

มาลี mah-lee *P. n.* flowers in general (used in poetical language) : *adj.* garlanded (chd. p. 234).

มารุต mah-loot[6] *P. n.* wind ; air (chd. p. 234).

มาศ mart[3] *n.* gold ; precious elements or articles ; sulphur. [p. 242].

มาส mart[3] *P. S. n.* a month ; moon (chd.

มาสก mah-sok[4] *P. n.* an ancient coin of low value, five of which equals one baht (chd. p. 241).

มาหิส mah-hi[4]-sa[4] *P. n.* buffalo or carabao meat : *adj.* belonging to buffaloes (chd. p. 232).

มิ mi[6] *adv.* no ; not ; a form of negation : มิจริง false : มิช้ามินาน soon ; shortly ; presently : มิใช่ not so ; no ; not that at all : มิได้ no ; do not ; impossible ; that is not right ; no, sir *polite negative* : มิเป็นเช่นนั้น that is not so : มิให้ so as to prevent ; for fear that : มิอย่ารา restlessly ; ceaselessly : มิอย่าเลย not to be discontinued ; unchangeable ; in a continual or continuous manner : หาจริงมิได้ finding. no truth in what is said : หามิได้ not at all.

มิค see มฤค p. 624.

มิคลุทธ์ mik[6]-ka[6]-loot[6] *n.* a hunter ; one living on game.

มิครอน mi[6]-krawn *n.* a micron, a measure of length ; the thousandth part of one millimeter or 1/1,000,000 of a meter.

มิคี mi[6]-kee *P. n.* a doe (chd. p. 247).

มิโครกรัม mi[6]-kro-gkrum *n.* a microgram, equal to 1/1,000 of a milligram or 1/1,000,000 of a gram.

มิโครลิตร mi[6]-kro-lit[6] *n.* microliter, equal to 1/1,000 of a milliliter or 1/1,000,000 of a liter.

มิ่ง ming[3] *n.* the Manito or tutelary deity of Good Fortune ; a good omen ; good luck ; glory ; happiness : มิ่งขวัญ the tutelary genii of children ; anything bringing good luck, glory or happiness : มิ่งเหมี่ a queen : ยอดมิ่ง very beautiful, powerful or most auspicious : เรียกมิ่งขวัญ the ceremony of calling back the tutelary genii (supposed to have taken flight).

มิ่งโค ming-koh *Jav. n.* a week.

มิจฉา mit[6]-chah[2] *P. adj.* false ; wrong ; mistaken; wrong views or false doctrines (chd. p. 274); impious; irreligious: มิจฉาจริยา *lit.* "erring in morals," *i. e.* deceit; crookedness: มิจฉาจาร wrong conduct or living (chd. p. 246); adultery: มิจฉาชีพ the earning of one's livelihood by wrong or deceitful methods: มิจฉาทิฏฐิ see มฤจฉาทิฏฐิ p. 624: มิจฉาบถ a way, method or system leading to bad results: มิจฉามติ wrong judgements: มิจฉาวาจา *lit.* "wrong sayings or language," *i. e.* the use of deceptive words: มิจฉาสติ wrong reflections or meditations.

มิญช min-cha⁶ *P. n.* marrow; pith; the kernel of a fruit or vegetable; vegetable membrane (chd. p. 247).

มิด mit⁶ *adj.* covered; shut in or hid completely; entirely enclosed (as from sight or the sun): ปิดจุกให้มิด to cork (as a bottle); to cover tightly: ปิดฝาหีบให้มิด to fasten the lid (of a box) snugly: ปิดตาให้มิด to cover the eyes entirely: มิดชิด, มิดเม้น, มิด-เมี้ยน completely covered or hidden; hermetically sealed; bound up air-tight.

มิดมิร้าย mi⁶-dee-mi⁶-rai⁵ *adj.* middling; not too good.

มิต mi⁶-dta⁴ *P. adj.* measured; reckoned; moderate (chd. p. 248): *adv.* approximately enough: มิตภาณี a moderate talker; one speaking in moderation (chd. p. 248).

มิตร mit⁶ *S. n.* a friend; a companion; an associate (S. E. D. p. 816): เป็นมิตรกัน to be united in friendship; to be friendly: มิตร-กรณ์ the making of friends: มิตรการย์ the business of a friend; a friendly office: มิตร-จิตต์ love; compassion on the basis or bond of friendship; equality: มิตรภาพ the state of friendship; a friendly disposition; friendliness: มิตรลาภ the acquisition of friends or of friendship: มิตรอันแท้ true friends.

มิถยา mi⁶-ta⁴-yah *S. adv.* incorrectly; untruly; wrongly; improperly; contrarily (S.E.D. p. 817).

มิถุน mi⁶-toon² *P. S. n.* a couple (chd. p. 248); a pair; twins; copulation; the third sign of the zodiac, Gemini.

มิถุนายน mi⁶-too⁴-nah-yon *P. n.* the third solar month, June.

มิทธิ mit⁶-tee *P. adj.* sleepy; drowsy; torpid; sluggish (chd. p. 247).

มินตรา see กระถิน p. 32.

มิ้ม ๑ see เม้ม p. 656.

มิม ๒ mim⁵ *n.* a hornet; a species of bee.

มิใย mi⁶-yai *conj.* even; even if; in spite of; notwithstanding: มิใยจะว่า will say in spite of (being blamed).

มิลลิกรัม min-li⁶-gkrum *n.* milligram; a standard of weight in the metric system, being the thousandth part of a gram or 0.0154 grains Troy.

มิลลิเมตร min-li⁶-met⁶ *n.* a millimetre or 1/1000 of a meter, a lineal measure in the metric system, equal to 0.03937 of an English inch.

มิลลิลิตร min-li⁶-lit⁶ *n.* a millilitre; a measure of capacity containing the thousandth part of a liter, or 0.061028 English cubic inches, dry measure.

มิลักข, มิลักขู mi⁶-luck⁶-ka⁴ *P. n.* a barbarian; a foreigner; an outcaste; a hillman; one of the aborigines (chd. p. 247).

มิลาต mi⁶-lah-dta⁴ *P. adj.* withered; faded; languid; faint (chd. p. 247).

มิศร, มิสส mit⁶-sa⁴-ra⁶ *S. P. adj.* mined; mixed (chd. p. 248); mingled; blended; combined (S. E. D. p. 817).

มิสสกวัน mit⁶-sa⁴-gka⁴-wan *n.* Indra's park, grove, or garden of paradise.

มี mee *v.* to have (as ownership); to consist of (as ingredients); to exist (as life or vitality); to appear (see ปรากฏ p. 506); to endure (see

คงอยู่ p. 173); to be affected with (as an ailment or disease): มีกำไรเกินสมควร profiteering: มีแก่ใจ to have the heart of a benefactor; to be benevolent: มีเงินเพื่อนหลาย, หมดเงินเพื่อน- หาย affluence brings friends, poverty drives them away; the rich have friends, the poor have none: มีสติพันเพื่อนแต่กำเนิด congenital idiocy: มีหน้ามีตา *lit.* "having face and appearance," *i. e.* well-known; renowned; honourable; respected; popular; well-liked: มีอันจะกิน *lit.* "having enough to eat," *i. e.* well-to-do; a middle class person; one bordering on affluence.

มี่, มะมี่ me[3] *adj.* noisy; boisterous; tumultuous; uproarious: ความนั้นมี่ฉาวแล้ว the matter has been spread abroad or talked about already; see แซ่ p. 311.

มีด meet[3] *n.* a knife; a dagger: มีดโกน a razor: มีดตอก a short-bladed but long, curved-handled knife for splitting and trimming bamboo. When being used, it is held braced against the knee: มีดโต๊ะ a table-knife: มีดผ่าผี a surgeon's scalpel: มีดพร้า a long-handled knife; knives (in general) มีดพับ a clasp, pocket or pen knife: มีดเหน็บ a poniard, dagger, belt knife or stiletto.

มีน meen *P. S. n.* a fish; the twelfth sign of the zodiac; Pisces (chd. p. 248).

มีนาคม mee-nah-kom *P. n.* the twelfth solar month, March.

มีล mee-la[6] *P. S. v.* to wink; to blink; to close the eyes (S. E. D. p, 819).

มีฬห meen-ha[4] *P. n.* excrement; feces (chd. p. 247).

มึง, เจ้า meung *pron.* you; thou *impolite.*

มึน murn *v.* to be slightly dizzy or giddy; to be stunned: ทำมึนตึง to assume a state of sulking, pouting or dislike for: มึนตึง to sulk; to pout; to have the bond of friendship broken: มึนเมา to be drugged.

มืด, มืดมน murt[3] *adj.* dark; obscure: เข้ามืด daylight: มืดฟ้ามัวฝน to be over-cast by rain-clouds: มืดหน้า to faint; to be nauseated into a fit; to swoon: หน้ามืด vertigo bordering on a fainting fit.

มืน murn[3] *v.* to open: มืนตา to open the eyes; see เปิด p. 535.

มือ meu *n.* the hand; tendrils (of creepers); a handle; a lever for a portable paddy-mill: เข้ามือด้วย to be participants in: มือกาว *lit.* "gummed fingers," *i. e.* given to stealing; being light-fingered: มือขวา the right hand: มือผี *lit.* "a ghost or phantom hand," *i. e.* a person joining in card games just to provide a partner (not being responsible for any loss or gain): มือลิง short supplementary strips of timber or ribs for Thai boats, attaching additional side-boards to the gunwale: มือไว *lit.* "light-fingered," *i. e.* given to petty stealing or pocket-picking: มือเสือ a species of large edible yam: ลงมือ to begin doing or working; to set to work: ลูกมือ assistant workmen: ลายมือ handwriting.

มื้อ meu[5] *n.* time (occasion); see ครั้ง p. 180: รับประทานวันละสามมื้อ to eat three times a day.

มุ, มุทะลุ moo[6] *adj.* prone to anger; irascible; irritable; violent in speech; abusive; foul mouthed; rude; rash; violent: มุทะลุขึ้น to become furious, violent or impetuous.

มุก mook[6] *n.* the pearl oyster, *Meleagrina margaritifera.*

มุกดา, มุกดาหาร mook[6]-dah *P. n.* a pearl (chd. p. 252); a semi-precious stone resembling the pearl, having a grey dull colour.

มุกุร moo[6]-gkoo[4]-ra[6] *P. S. n.* a mirror (chd. p. 251).

[p. 251].

มุกุล moo[6]-gkoo[4]-la[6] *P. S. n.* a bud (chd.

มุข mook[6] *P. n.* the mouth; the face; the visage; a front entrance; the commencement; a means; a cause (chd. p. 250); the snout or muzzle of an animal; the beak of a bird; direction; quarter (S. E. D. p. 819): มุขเด็จ, มุขกระสัน a second small portico projecting from the main one: มุขลด a portico on a lower level than that of the main floor or main portico: หน้ามุข the front portico of a building; see ปาก p. 521.

มุขย moo[6]-ka[4]-ya[6] *P. S. n.* the first; a chief; one principal or superior one; that which is in, coming from, or belonging to the mouth or face; that being at the head, or at the beginning (S. E. D. p. 820): มุขยประโยค *grammar* a main clause: มุขยมนตรี a Prime Minister; the chief of the ministers; the chief of the mandarins.

มุคค, มุทค mook[6]-ka[6] *P. n.* a kind of kidney bean (chd. p. 250); see ถั่วเขียว p. 384.

มุคคร, มุทคร mook[6]-ka[6]-ra[6] *P. n.* a hammer; a mallet; a club; a mace (chd. p. 250).

มุคธ์ mook[6] *S. adj.* stupid; foolish; simple (chd. p. 249); gone astray; perplexed; bewildered; ignorant; inexperienced; artless (S. E. D. p. 825).

มุง moong *v.* to put on a roof; to congregate; see ประชุม p. 498: มุงหลังคาจาก to roof with attap: หลังคามุงกระเบื้อง a tile-roof.

มุ่ง, มุ่ง moong[3] *v.* to aspire to; to pay earnest attention; to regard attentively; to intend to do; to devote oneself entirely to: ความมุ่งมาด aspirations: ความมุ่งหมาย intention; purpose; aim: มุ่งมาด to hope, expect or purpose to do: มุ่งร้าย to intend to do harm: มุ่งหมาย to fix one's attention on; to apply oneself to the performance of a deed; see เจาะจง p. 258.

มุ้ง moong[5] *n.* a mosquito net.

มุจจน moot[6]-chja[4]-na[6] *P. n.* the condition of being released; freedom; liberty (chd. p. 249).

มุจฉา moot[6]-chah[2] *P. n.* a faint; a swoon or faintness (chd. p. 249).

มุญช moon-cha[6] *P. S. n.* a coarse grass, *Saccharum munja*, from the fibre of which the Brahminical sacred string is made (chd. p. 252).

มุฏฐิ moot[6]-ti[4] *P. n.* the fist; a handful; a smith's hammer (chd. p. 253).

มุณฑ, มุณฑกะ moon-da[4] *P. adj.* shaved; bald; bare (chd. p. 252).

มุด moot[6] *v.* to crawl underneath; to slip in or hide beneath; to dive (as fishes); to get down under, behind or into (as boys hiding in an empty box); to burrow into the mud (like fishes).

มุตต ๑ moot[6]-dta[4] *P. adj.* released; delivered; free from; discharged (chd. p. 253).

มุตต ๒ moot[6]-dta[4] *P. n.* urine (chd. p. 253): มุตตกิด fluor albus; leucorrhoea; *whites*: มุตตฆาต a disease characterized by pus or blood in the urine; hematuria.

มุตตนิ moot[6]-dta[4]-ni[6] *P. n.* one having the menstrual period.

มุตตา moot[6]-dtah *P. n.* a pearl; a pearl-like gem (chd. p. 252).

มุตติ moot[6]-dti[4] *P. n.* release; deliverance; freedom; Nirvana (chd. p. 253).

มุติ, มติ moo[6]-dti[4] *P. n.* understanding; intelligence (chd. p. 252); familiarity; wisdom; opinion.

มุติงค์, มุทิงค์ moo[6]-dting *P. n.* a small drum; a tabor (chd. p. 252); see ตะโพน p. 355.

มุททา, มุทรา, มุทริกา moot[6]-tah *P. n.* a seal; a signet; a seal-ring; a stamp; an impression (chd. p. 248).

มุทธาภิเสก see มูรธาภิเษก p. 655.

มุทา moo[6]-tah *P. n.* joy; pleasure; happiness (chd. p. 249).

มุทิตา moo[6]-ti[6]-dtah *P. n.* a feeling of benignity or kindliness; rejoicing with others in their happiness or prosperity ; the opposite of envy or malice. It is the complement of Karuna (Chd. p. 250) ; joy, being one of four virtuous inclinations (Ala. p. 38).

มุทิน see มลทิน p. 625.

มุทุ moo[6]-too[6] *P. adj.* soft; mild; weak; blunt; slow (Chd. p. 250); flabby; tender: มุทุตา softness; impressibility; mildness; kindliness; tenderness.

มุ่น moon[3] *v.* to twist up in a knot; to bind together in the form of a corolla (as hair); to be anxious or worried; to be agitated; see กระหมวด p. 47; กังวล p. 83 : มุ่นจุก to do up or arrange the topknot : มุ่นใจ to be unhappy or troubled; to be heavy-hearted, anxious, uneasy or indignant : มุ่นหมก to be agitated about, or absorbed in (as loveaffairs); see ขุ่น p. 162.

มุนิ, มุนี moo[6]-ni[6] *P. S. n.* a philosopher; a sage; an inspired man; an ascetic; a saint (Chd. p. 252); a hermit; a teacher; a monk; a devotee : มุนิกุญชร an epithet of the Buddha : มุนินทร์ the chief of sages; a great sage or ascetic; an epithet of the Buddha (Chd. p. 252).

มุม moom *n.* angularity; a cusp; an angle; a corner; a nook; a niche : เป็นมุม angular : มุมฉาก an acute or right angle; an angle of 90 degrees : มุม (นก) the grey-headed Imperial pigeon, *Carpophaga griseicapilla* (Gaird. J.S.S. IX, 1, p. 16) : มุมเอียง an angle of inclination : สี่มุม, สี่เหลี่ยม quadrangular : หกมุม, หกเหลี่ยม hexagonal.

มุ้ม moom[5] *v.* to pucker, compress or pinch together : มุ้มปาก to pucker the lips.

มุ่ย moo-ie[3] *adj.* frowning; pouting; see บึ้ง p. 483 : กินมุ่ยๆ to eat ravenously : หน้ามุ่ย a frowning face.

มุสล moot[6]-sa[4]-la[6] *P. n.* a club; a pestle (Chd. p. 252).

มุสา moo[6]-sah[2] *P. v.* to fabricate; to falsify; to lie; to utter a falsehood (Chd. p. 252): คนมุสา a liar : คำมุสา a lie : มุสาวาท a lie; a falsehood (Chd. p. 252); see ผิด p. 547.

มุหุตต์ moo[6]-hoot[4] *P. n.* a moment; a little while; a period of forty-eight minutes (Chd. p. 250).

มูก ๑, มูค moo-gka[4] *S. adj.* mute; dumb; taciturn; silent; speechless or reserved (S. E. D. p. 825).

มูก ๒ mook[3] *n.* mucus (as from the nose); glutinous liquor : มูกเลือด bloody flux; dysentery : สั่งน้ำมูก, สั่งขี้มูก to blow one's nose free of mucus.

มูกมัน see โมกมัน p. 660.

มูเซอ moo-sir *n.* the Musso or Lahu, a Tibeto-Burman race of people inhabiting many of the high mountains of northern Thailand, reaching as far south as latitude 17° 30′, on the hills to the west of the Meh Ping in Chiengmai province. There are two tribes recognized, the Musso La or Musso Dam (the black Musso) and the Musso Deng (the red Musso). They use large, round silver clasps for the coat. The silver neck-ring, without a plaque, seems to be worn by the women only (Siam, Nature and Industry p. 95).

มูตร moot[3] *P. n.* urine (Chd. p. 253).

มูทู moo[3]-too[3] *adj.* blunt; rounded; see บ้าน p. 520.

มูน moon *v.* to add more to; to add oil or coconut milk to rice or glutinous rice in order to loosen the grains and enrich the flavour : *n.* a pile; a mound; an hillock or heap : *adj.* much; abundant; ample; see พอกพูน p. 577 : มูนมอง very much; numerous; abundant; ample; see มากมาย p. 647.

มูมมาม moom-marm *adj.* dirty; filthy; foul; ill-behaved; see เปื้อน p. 535 : กินมูมมาม to eat greedily or in a filthy manner : ตามูมมาม bleared or foul eyes.

มูรดี, มูรติ moo-ra[6]-dee *n.* a manikin; the body; a form, figure or mould shaped like the body.

มูรธ, มูรธา, มูรธา moo-ra[6]-ta[6] *S. n.* the forehead; the head (in general); the skull; the highest or first part of anything; the top; the summit; a point; a pinnacle; the front or chief (S. E. D. p. 826): มูรธาธร the Department of the Keeper of the Royal Seal (now abolished): มูรธาภิเษก, มุทธาภิเษก *lit.* "a- nointment of the head" *i. e.* the Royal ceremo- nial bath of purification; "head-sprinkling"; royal consecration; inauguration.

มูล ๑ moon *P. n.* a root; the lowest part; base; foundation; origin; source; commence- ment: front; foremost; first cause; nearness; sum; mass; price; money; capital; the prin- cipal; fundamentals (chd. p. 251): ได้บังอาจ- มีผินมีมูลผิน dared to have opium or traces of opium in his possession: เป็นมูลเป็นเค้า to get an inkling of something (as the basis for an investigation): มูลคดี cause of a lawsuit: มูลนิธิ foundation, capital or funds bequeathed to any philantropic organization: มูลวิวาท the origin of a controversy: มูลเหตุ origin or cause of an affair or event.

มูล ๒ moon *n.* excrement of animals; ref- use; rubbish; waste matter; useless frag- ments or pieces: มูลของ ordinary articles; things of moderate quality; common things: มูลโค cow dung: มูลไถ (นก) the forest wagtail, *Limonidromus indicus* (Gaird. J. S. S. IX, 1, p. 2): มูลฝอย rubbish; waste matter; sweepings from off the street.

มูลย moon-la[6]-ya[6] *S. n.* wages; payments; price; value; salary (S. E. D. p. 827).

มูลิก moo-lik[6] *P. n.* a servant; an atten- dant; one subject to another: มูลิกากร a group or company of attendants or servants.

มูลี moo[3]-lee[3] *n.* blinds; a drop curtain used on the outside of a house to exclude or admit light (lined or unlined, made of small

bamboo strips sewed together horizontally and hoisted or rolled up by means of ropes).

มูษา, มูษ์ moo-sah[2] *S. n.* a crucible (chd. p. 252).

มูสิก moo-sik[4] *P. n.* a mouse; a rat (chd. p. 252): มูสิกทันต์ *lit.* "rat's teeth," *i. e.* the two parallel marks placed over อ to change to into อ้.

มูฬห moon-ha[4] *P. adj.* foolish; ignorant; deceived; erring; straying; misguided; per- plexed; confused (chd. p. 251).

เม may *Cam. n.* a mother.

เมขล may-ka[4]-la[6] *S. n.* a girdle; a belt; a band (S. E. D. p. 831).

เมขลา ๑ may-ka[4]-lah *P. S. n.* a zone; a belt; a girdle; a sash (chd. p. 246); the girth strap of a saddle; a sword belt (S. E. D. p. 831).

เมขลา ๒ mek[3]-ka[4]-lah[2] *n.* the guardian goddess of the sea.

เมฆ mek[3] *P. S. n. lit.* "sprinkler," *i. e.* a cloud; storm-clouds; rain-clouds (S.E.D. p. 831): เมฆนาท *lit.* "cloud-noise," *i. e.* thunder; rum- bling, or sounds like thunder: เมฆมณฑล *lit.* "cloud-sphere," *i. e.* the atmosphere; region of the air: เมฆวรรณ having the hue of a cloud.

เมจก may-chjok[4] *P. S. adj.* black; dark- blue (chd. p. 246).

เมณฑ men-da[4] *P. n.* a ram; a groom; an herdsman (chd. p. 246).

เม็ด, เมล็ด met[6] *n.* a general designatory particle for seeds, pits, stones or kernels (of fruit); a pustule (as in smallpox); a small inflamed elevation on the skin (as a pimple); a chess-man placed on the right of the king: กลเม็ด deceit; artifice; craft: หัวเม็ด an ornamental knob forming the top of a pillar or post.

เมตตา met[3]-dtah *P. n.* goodwill towards

all; friendliness; a friendly feeling; good-will; kindness; love; charity; compassion; benevolence; indulgence (chd. p. 246): เมตตา-กรุณา, เมตตาปรานี compassion; pity; long-suf-[fering.

เมตตี้ see **ไมตรี** p. 661.

เมตไตรย met[3]-dtrai *n.* a Bodhisatta now in the Tusita heaven, who is to be the next Buddha (chd. p. 246); an incipient Buddha; one coming five thousand years after Phra Kodom. The expected Messiah of the Buddhists, sometimes called พระศรีอารีย์.

เมตร met[6] *n.* a metre or 39.37 inches; one half of a wah.

เมตริกควินตัล met[6]-dtrik[4]-kwin-dtun *n.* a mass of 100 kilograms weight; metriquintel (a measured hundred weight).

เมตริกตัน met[6]-dtrik[4]-dtun *n.* a ton; a mass of 1000 kilograms weight; a ton measured by cubic metres.

เมถุน may-toon[2] *P. n.* the condition of being a couple; sexual intercourse, union (chd. p. 246); carnality: เมถุนธรรม the natural law of love: เสพเมถุน to indulge in illicit sexual intercourse.

เมท, เมโท may-ta[6] *P. n.* a serous secretion that flows throughout the fibres or tissues; fat; sweat; perspiration (chd. p. 246).

เมทนี, เมทินี may-ta[6]-nee *P. n.* the earth (chd. p. 246): เมทนีดล the earth's surface.

เมธ may-ta[6] *P. S. n.* a sacrifice (chd. p. 246); meat broths; strengthening drinks (S. E. D. p. 832).

เมธค may-tok[6] *P. S. n.* a quarrel; strife (chd. p. 246); see ทะเลาะ p. 407.

เมธา may-tah *P. S. n.* intelligence (chd. p. 246); mental vigour or power; prudence; wisdom (S. E. D. p. 833).

เมธาวี, เมธี may-tah-wee *P. n.* an intelligent person; a sage; a philosopher (chd. p. 246).

เม่น men[3] *n.* the short-tailed porcupine; the *Hystrix*; *Acanthion brachyurus bengalensis* (N. H. J. S. S. III, 2, p. 124).

เม้น, มิม, เม้ม men[5] *v.* to hem; to fold down the raw edge of a fabric twice and sew: เม้มปาก to fold or turn one's lips in as if to bite them.

เมรย, เมรัย may-ra[6]-ya[6] *P. n.* intoxicating liquor, spirits, rum, arrack (chd. p. 246): สุราเมรัย various intoxicating drinks.

เมรุ mane *P. n.* a mythical fabulous Indian mountain in the middle of the world, variously called "The Golden Mountain," "The Jewelled Peak," "The Lotus Mountain," "The Mountain of the Gods," hence a pagoda, symbolizing the mountain; an elaborate many-storied pagoda; a cremation tower: เมรุมาศ *lit.* "a golden funeral pyre," *i. e.* a funeral pyre for a king (S. E. D. p. 833).

เมลก may-lok[6] *P. n.* an assemblage; a congregation (chd. p. 246).

เมล็ด see **เม็ด** p. 655.

เมษ met[3] *P. n.* a ram: เมษราศี the zodiacal sign of Aries (chd. p. 246): เมษวิถี the course of the sun through Aries.

เมษายน may-sah[2]-yon *n.* the first solar month, April; month of Aries.

เมห, เมห์ may-ha[4] *P. S. n.* urine (chd. p. 246); an excessive flow of urine; diabetes (S. E. D. p. 834).

[(chd. p. 246).

เมหน may-hon[2] *P. S. n.* membrum virile

เมา mow *v.* to be drunk; to be intoxicated: *adj.* intoxicated: คนขี้เมา a drunkard: มัว-เมา addicted to; devoted to: เมาคลื่น to be nauseated by the motion of the waves; sea sick: เมาต่อสู้เจ้าพนักงานผู้จับกุม drunk and resisting arrest: เมาผู้หญิง to be led astray by women: เมามาย to be greatly intoxicated: เมาอาละวาด to be drunk and disorderly.

เมารํ   mow-ree *n.* a pea-hen.

เมาลิ   maw-lee, เมาฬิ,โมฬิ *S. n.* the head;
a topknot; a tuft or lock of hair left on the
crown of the head; a diadem; a crown; a
crest; the chignon; hair ornamented and
braided round the head (S. E. D. p. 837).

เมาะ   maw[6] *n.* a pillow used for a nursing
baby; a loosely stuffed bed for children.

เมิน   mern *v.* to turn the face away from;
to look away from a person or thing; to turn
the face aside shamefully, proudly or heedlessly: เมินเฉย to take no interest in; to
be heedless of; to be careless; to pay no attention to: เมินเสียเถิด will not heed you
or give you any favour: เมินหน้า to turn
the face away in indifference or contempt.

เมีย   me-ah *n.* a wife; a spouse; a consort:
ตัวเมีย female (animal): แกะตัวเมีย an ewe:
ม้าตัวเมีย a mare: สุนักข์ตัวเมีย a bitch:
เสือตัวเมีย a tigress: หมาจิ้งจอกตัวเมีย a vixen:
เมียน้อย,อนุภรรยา a lesser wife: เมียช่วย a
wife redeemed from slavery; a bondsmaid
wife: เมียลับ a concubine: เมียหลวง a
legal or legitimate wife: ยกให้เป็นเมีย to
give a maid in marriage.

เมียง   mee-ang *v.* to approach and look
at stealthily; to look at from the corner of
the eye; see ชำเลือง p. 295: เมียงม่าย to
glance at furtively (as a girl flirting).

เมี่ยง   mee-ang[3] *n.* The Thai wild tea-plant,
the fermented leaves of which are chewed or
sucked, with salt, by the northern tribes in
place of betel leaves; tea-leaves used for
masticatory purposes. This plant grows high
up in the mountains of Thailand: เมี่ยงคำ,
เมี่ยงลาว,เมี่ยงส้ม different sorts of relishes rolled
in the leaves of the wild tea-plant and chewed.

เมียน   me-an[5] *adj.* hidden; covered; concealed; see มิด p. 651: เก็บไว้มิดเมี้ยน carefully gathered up and hidden.

เมอ, เมื่อ   mur-ah *v.* to go and then to
return (as going on a round trip).

เมื่อ   mur-ah[3] *n.* time; period; see ครั้ง
p. 180: *prep.* when; as soon as; by the time
that: เมื่อจำเลยถูกลงโทษสองกะทงต้องรับโทษ-
นั้นในคราวเดียวกัน concurrent sentences *legal*:
เมื่อโจทย์จำเลยทั้งสองฝ่ายต่างก็ได้เปรียบบ้างจากคำพิพากษ-
ษา distributive findings of the issue *legal*:
เมื่อตะกี้นี้ just a moment ago: เมื่อนั้น then;
at about that time: เมื่อไร when: เมื่อหน้า
hence; henceforth.

เมือก   mur-ak[3] *n.* a thick, greasy, glutinous
liquid; mucus: *adj.* sticky.

เมือง   mur-ang *n.* a kingdom; a city; a
country; a province; a town: เมืองขึ้น a
colony: เมืองท่า a sea port: เมืองหลวง
a principal or capital city: หัวเมือง a country district.

เมือบ   mur-ap[3] *adj.* much; full; many.

เมื่อย   mur-ie[3] *v.* to be suffering from a
physical indisposition; to feel fatigued and
worn out: เมื่อยเนื้อเมื่อยตัว a general feeling of malaise or weariness (as after an attack
of fever): เมื่อยระบม a general contused
feeling of the muscles: หน้าเมื่อย to have
a rye face from shame.

แม่   maa[3] *n.* mother: แม่ปะ (เรือ) a long,
shallow-draft boat having a low canopied
freight space in the middle, covered living
quarters in the stern, and a scorpion-tail-
shaped tail-piece. These were used by the
northern people as transports along the rivers
and down to Bangkok before the railroad
was laid: แม่รํแม่แรด proud; pompous;
boastful; pretentious: แม่หม้าย, แม่ร้าง a
widow: แม่หม้ายไม่ได้หมายให้ไหมใหม่ไหม้ แต่
หม้ายหมายให้ไม้ใหม่ ๆ ไหม้ the widow did not
propose to let the new silk be burnt, but she
intended to burn the new wood instead.

แม่   (1) *a prefix to names of women of the
middle class,* as, แม่แดง, แม่แปลก.

แม่   (2) *for vocational women*, as, แม่ครัว a female cook : แม่ครู a teacher : แม่ค้า female hucksters; tradeswomen; women hawkers : แม่คู่ a precentor or starter of music or chanting : แม่นม a wet-nurse : แม่แปรก a chaperon : แม่มด a witch; a sorceress : แม่ยั้วเมือง, แม่หยั้วเมือง chief of the ladies-in-waiting in a royal palace; one, or those ranking next to the king as attendants; a chief maid : แม่เย้า, แม่เรือน a wife; the mistress of a home : แม่สื่อ a marriage negotiator; a procuress; a go-between; an intermediary : แม่หมอ a female physician.

แม่   (3) *for the chief of a unit*, as, แม่กอง a petty officer; the leader of a company : แม่กองคนงาน the person in charge of a gang of workmen; a superintendent : แม่กองนางพยาบาล the chief of a unit of nurses : แม่ทัพ a commander-in-chief : แม่เท้า the chief of the foot; the big toe : แม่น้ำ a principal water-way; a river : แม่มือ the chief of the hand; the thumb.

แม่   (4) *for mechanical appliances*, as, แม่กระได a string board; a string piece; a stair horse; a string course for stairs; the upright of a ladder : แม่กุญแจ a lock : แม่แคร่ the frame of a stretcher; the carriage frame of a typewriter : แม่เตาไฟ frames for portable fire-places : แม่ประตู door-posts : แม่แรง a vice; a jack used for lifting heavy weights; a crane or derrick : แม่สะดึง an embroidery frame : แม่เหล็ก a magnet : แม่เหล็กสนาม a field magnet.

แม่   (5) *referring to relationships*, as, แม่ผัว the husband's mother; a mother-in-law : แม่เลี้ยง a step-mother; an adopted mother : แม่ยาย a wife's mother.

แม่   (6) *terms of endearment*, as คุณแม่, แม่จ๋า mother, dear : แม่ทูนหัว my darling; see ทูน ๑ p. 420 : แม่อยู่หัว my queen.

แม่   (7) *grammatical and numerical tables* : (a) syllables according to endings, as แม่กก, แม่กน, แม่กบ, แม่กด, แม่กอกา :   (b) แม่สูตรเลข multiplication tables.

แม่   (8) *for spirits*, as แม่ซื้อ the guardian goddess of infants : แม่ย่านาง the guardian goddess of boats.

แม่   (9) *exclamations of surprise or delight*, as แม่เจ้าโวย Oh my gracious! แม่โวย Oh my!

แม่   (10) *for species of fish*, as แม่กระแชง (ปลาสลิด) the *Trichopodus pectoralis* (*Osphronemidae*) (suvatti p. 103).

แม่   (11) *referring to snakes*, as แม่เบี้ย (งูเห่า) the hood of a cobra : แม่ตะงาว, งูแมวเซา a provincial term used in the Ayuthia and Lopburi districts for the Russel's viper, *Vipera russelli*, (standard name แม่แมวเซา).

แม้   maa[5] *conj.* if; provided that; even; although; though : แม้กระนั้น even so : แม้ว่า [even if.

แมก see **แฝง** p. 557.

แมง   maang *n.* a prefix to the names of some animals belonging to the *Arthropods* that are not true insects. Often used interchangeably, though incorrectly, with แมลง or true insects : แมงกะพรุน a jelly-fish : แมงคาเรือง a luminous milliped; the luminous wood-louse : แมงดานา a water bug, also known as electric-light bug, *Belostoma indica*. They have long fringed legs that act like oars. They come out of the water and fly about at night. Natives pickle them in fish sauce for flavouring : แมงดาทะเล a horseshoe crab : แมงป่อง a scorpion : แมงป่องช้าง a giant scorpion : แมงมุม a spider : แมงวัน the house fly, *Musca domestica* : แมงเหนี่ยง a water bug of the family *Gyrinidae*, commonly known as whirligigs.

แมงลัก (ลูก)   maang-luck[6] *n. Ocimum basilicum* (*Labiatae*), sacred or sweet basil, a strong-scented herb, 2 to 3 feet high, found thoughout the Old World tropics. From the leaves, an essential oil which is used in scented soaps, and perfumes, is distilled. This oil of *O. basilicum* is a yellow liquid with an aromatic pleasant odour, containing about 55 per cent of methyl-clavicol and, in addition, linalol. The oil is used to give the scent of mignonette. Camphor is found in oil from Reunion, one of the Mascarene islands. In Malaya and elsewhere the oil, or a decoction of the leaves, has various medicinal uses. For treating coughs in children the flowers are used (MCM. pp. 344, 397: V. P. p. 221: Burk. p. 1571).

แม่น man[3] *adj.* exact; accurate; precise (as a marksman hitting the object aimed at); see เที่ยง p. 425: จำแม่น to have a retentive memory: ยิงแม่น to be skillful in shooting.

แม้น man[5] *adj.* like; similar to; resembling: *conj.* even if; but: มาทแม้น nevertheless: แม้น ๆ กัน almost alike: แม้นว่า, ถึงแม้นว่า if; even if; although.

แมลง ma-laang *n.* a collective name for true insects or those having a distinct head, thorax, abdomen, three pairs of legs and a pair of antennae or feelers: แมลงกะชอน mole cricket: แมลงแกลบ a small insect of the cockroach group: แมลงช้าง the ant-lion or larvae of *Neuropteroid* insects that make sand pits for trapping ants and other crawling insects: แมลงทับ a *Buprestid* beetle, specifically *Sternocera aequisignata*, but can also mean any beetle that has a green colour: แมลงปอ the dragon-fly, *libellula*: แมลงภู่ the carpenter bee of the genus *Xylocopa*: แมลงภู่ (หอย) a species of mollusk having ovid bivalve shells of a dark green colour, resembling the irridescent green colour of the wings of *Xylocopa*: แมลงหวี่ fruit flies of the genus *Drosophila*.

แมว maa-oh *n.* a cat; a prefix to which the particular designating name for the species is added: *onomat.* the mewing of a cat: แมว (ปลา) *Setipinna melanochir* (*Engraulidae*); *Lycothrissa crocodilus* (Suvatti pp. 16, 17): แมวเซา, แมวมอง a sentinel; a scout; a spy; an ancient name for scouts: แมวน้ำ a seal; a sea-cat: แมวป่า the leopard; the jungle-cat, *Felis bengalensis* (Gaird. N. H. J. S. S. II, 1, p. 22).

แม้ว ๑ maa[5]-wa[6] *conj.* if; see ถ้า p. 387.

แม้ว ๒ maa-oh[5] *n.* an (unclassified) tribe of northern Thailand hill-people called by the Chinese " Miao—tza " and by themselves " Mong"; " Meo " is the name they go by in Thailand. They are to be found here and there on the mountains of northern Thailand, coming as far south as about Lat. 17° on the range to the north-east of Petchabun. They are also widely spread through south-western China. " The original home of the White Meo or Meo Puak was not in Thailand but in the Ho country (Yunnan) in China " (Seidenfaden S. S. XVIII, 3, p. 153). Some authorities have grouped the Meo with the Mon; others consider the Meo as pure Mongols pointing out that their language shows a striking similarity to the Kwan Hua or Mandarin language of China. The Meo are divided into several tribes, chiefly distinguished from each other by the dress of the women. The two tribes most often met with in Thailand are called the Meo Kao or White Meo and the Meo Lai or Striped Meo (Siam, Nature and Industry p. 100).

แมะ maa[6] *v.* to meet; see ปะ p. 516.

โม *Thai* and *Laos* (แตง) moh *n.* *Citrullus vulgaris* (*Cuburbitaceae*), a water-melon (cb. p. 761: Burk. p. 560); see แตงโม p. 376.

โม่ moh[3] *v.* to operate or grind with a mill: *n.* a hand rice-mill: โม่แป้ง to mill flour: โม่หิน to crush stone: หินโม่ millstones; grindstones.

โม้ moh[5] *interj.* a call for dogs.

โมก (ต้น) mok[3] *n.* *Wrightia religiosa* (*Apocynaceae*), an ornamental shrub found planted in rows in the grounds of some Buddhist monasteries (V. P. p. 222: Burk. p. 2266):

โมกมัน (ต้น) *Wrightia tomentosa*, a tree the white smooth fine-grained wood of which is used for carving, cabinet-work, and also for paddles, pencils, etc. (V. P. p. 222 : BURK. p. 2266).

โมกข์ ๑   moke[3] *P. adj.* principal; pre-eminent; outstanding; important (chd. p. 249).

โมกข์ ๒, โมกษ์   moke[3] *P. n.* a condition of liberation; freedom; independence; Arhat-ship; Niravana (chd. p. 249); final emancipa-tion; exemption from further transmigration.

โมฆ   moh-ka[6] *P. adj.* vain; vacant; useless; foolish; stupid (chd. p. 248) :   โมฆสัญญา *lit.* "void or useless promises," *i.e.* an illegal license, lease, document or agreement.

โมฆิย   moh-ki[6]-ya[6] *P. S. adj.* becoming vain, useless or insignificant (S. E. D. p. 835) : โมฆิยสัญญา a disannulled promise when the disannulment takes place after a void prom-ise *legal.*

โมง   mong *n.* an hour; a numerical means of counting hours of the day; see นาฬิกา p. 453 : ชั่วโมงหนึ่ง the duration of an hour.

โม่ง   mong[3] *adj.* very big; huge; gigantic : *n.* a person clad in a gown from head to feet; a phantom or ghost : โม่งโค่ง ill-shaped; too big to correspond to the proper size : เล่นอ้ายโม่ง to play blind-man's-buff.

โมงโกรย (ปลา)   mong-gkro-ie *n.* herring, a fish found both in salt and fresh water, found especially in the north-eastern part of Thailand; *Alosa kanagurta* (Dept. Agri. & Fisheries).

โมงครุ่ม   mong-kroom[3] *n.* music performed during comedies; a musical performance dur-ing royal festivals.

โมจน   moh-chja[4]-na[6] *P. n.* release; change (chd. p. 248); the condition of granting free-dom; a releasing, freeing or delivering from (S. E. D. p. 835).

โมทนา   moh-ta[6]-nah *P. n.* the act of rejoic-ing; felicitations (chd. p. 248); giving thanks or congratulations : โมทนาคุณ to express gratitude (for services rendered) : อนุโมทนา the offering of felicitations or congratulations.

โมน   moh-na[6] *P. n.* silence (chd. p. 249).

โมไนย   moh-nai *P. n.* the state of being a sage; the practice or culture of a philosopher : โมไนยปฏิบัติ the act of practicing the principles of a philosopher.

โมมุทธ, โมมูฬห, โมมูห์   moh-moot[6]-ta[6] *P. adj.* silly; mad; demented (chd. p. 249); see เขลา p. 165.

โมร   moh-ra[6] *P. S. n.* a peacock (S. E. D. p. 835): เมารี, โมรี *feminine forms* : โมรกลาป the expanded tail of a peacock.

โมรา   moh-rah *n.* a form of precious marble or quartz; a precious stone.

โมษ, โมษก   moh-sa[4] *S. n.* a robber; a thief; a plunderer (S. E. D. p. 836).

โมห, เมาห์, โม่ห์   moh-ha[4] *P. S. n.* faint-ing; loss of conciousness; ignorance; delusion; error; folly; illusion or infatuation (through passion) (chd. p. 248); bewilderment; per-plexity; distraction (S. E. D. p. 836) : โมหาคติ injustice through ignorance.

โมโห, โมโหโทโส   moh-hoh[2] *v.* to be angry or irritated : *n.* anger (chd. p. 248); see โกรธ p. 135 : มักโมโห easily angered; very irascible; touchy.

โมฬี, โมลี see เมาลี p. 657.

ไม่   mai[3] *adv.* no; not; do not (an express-ion of denial or negation) : ใช่หรือไม่ is it that or not? ถูกหรือไม่ is that correct or not? ไม่ชอบด้วยกฎหมาย illegal; unlawful : ไม่ใช่ not so : ไม่ได้ it cannot be; it is im-possible : ไม่ถูกต้องตามกฎหมาย irregular : ไม่ทราบ, ไม่รู้ได้ being ignorant of : ไม่น่าสมจริง improbable; impossible : ไม่เป็นหนี้ solvent : ไม่มีพินัยกรรม์ intestate; see พินัย p. 587 : ไม่ให้-ถือเอาเปรียบ without prejudice : ไม่ไหว un-

able to; being too heavy : ไม่เอาถ่าน reject-
ing training and instruction (said regarding
minors in a reformatory school) : รู้ไม่ได้
it is impossible to know : ไม่รู้ไม่ชี้ to have
absolutely no knowledge of; it is none of your
business; a sarcastic reply : ไม่รู้สิ้นสุด to
know no end; everlasting : ไม่รู้จักหน้าที่ to
be ignorant of one's duties, or obligations :
ไม่รู้จักทำ to be unacquainted, or inexperienced
(with the job in hand) : ไม่รู้จัก uninform-
ed; untaught; uninitiated; unversed.

ไม้　　mai[5] n. wood; timber; the vegetable
kingdom; verdure : ดอกไม้ a flower : ต้น-
ไม้ a tree; a plant : ผลไม้ see ผล p. 540 :
ไม้กงพัด see กงพัด p. 3 : ไม้กวาด a broom :
ไม้กากบาท the fourth accent mark " ๋ " indicating a rising tone : ไม้กางเขน, ไม้กางแขน
an ancient instrument of torture consisting
of two crossed timbers on which the condemned were fastened and exposed until they
died. As the instrument of Christ's death,
it has become an emblem of Christianity :
ไม้คัดท้ายปืน a steering-rod or lever for turning
military field-pieces : ไม้คาบชุด handles for
fuse-lighters : ไม้คาบดอกเทียน handles for
highly inflammable torches : ไม้จริง lit.
"genuine wood," i. e. hardwood; heart-wood :
ไม้จัตวา the fourth accent mark " ๋ " : ไม้ซุง
logs of felled timber : ไม้ตรี the third accent mark " ๊ " : ไม้ตะบอง a club; a billy;
a cudgel : ไม้ตาย a death-blow that ends
the fight; a knock-out blow : ไม้เถา a vine;
a creeper : ไม้เท้า a walking-stick; a cane
or prelate's staff : ไม้โท the second accent
mark " ้ " : ไม้ปลายแหลม สำหรับหัดฟันดาบ

dummy swords used in fencing practices :
ไม้ผัด a vowel mark " ั " : ไม้พลอง a tough
species of wood made into canes or clubs and
used as weapons; see พลอง p. 572 : ไม้พุ่ม
a bush; a shrub : ไม้มลาย the vowel " ไ " :
ไม้ม้วน same as ไม้มลาย but written in the form
" ใ " : ไม้ยัดปืน a ramrod : ไม้ยัดปืนปลาย-
มีพู่ a ramrod with brush : ไม้เรียว a whip;
a tapering rod for flogging children : ไม้ไล่
a thornless bamboo; trees (in general) colloq. :
ไม้วา a measuring rod of the length of 2 metres
or 1 wah : ไม้สอย a pole used for gathering
or dislodging fruit from the topmost branches :
ไม้หน้า the two Thai vowels " เ " and " แ " :
ไม้หนึ่ง a yard-stick; a yard in length; a bolt
of silk or cloth; hunks of meat, smoked or
dried fishes strung together on sticks (for
easy handling when being transported or
offered for sale) : ไม้หนึ่ง (เมื่อรำกะบี่) a series
of attacks and defenses while fencing; an
attitude assumed by a fencer; a time limit
(as with foil or sword) : ไม้หันอากาศ the
vowel mark " ั " : ไม้เอก the first accent
mark " ่ " : ไม้โอ the vowel " โ ".

ไมตรี, เมตติ　　mai-dtree S. n. friendship;
good will; love; charity; concord; benevolence personified (S. E. D. p. 834) : ทางไมตรี
friendly relations : ผูกไมตรี to contract a
friendly alliance : มิตรไมตรีแท้ true friends;
real friendship : หนังสือพระราชไมตรี a treaty
of alliance or friendship (as between two
nations).

ไมยราบ (ต้น) see กระทืบยอด (ต้น) p. 35.

ไมล์　　mai Eng. n. a mile, or about 40 sen.

ย

ย　　The thirty-fourth letter of the Thai
alphabet, a low class letter of which
there are twenty-four, viz. ค, ต, ฆ, ง, ช,
ซ, ฌ, ญ, ฑ, ฒ, ท, ธ, ฒ, น, ณ, พ, ฟ, ภ, ม, ร, ล, ว, ฬ,
ฮ. ยอยักษ์, ยอยินยล are the names for this
letter, which is in general use both as a prefix
and suffix.

ยก ๑　　yok[6] (ก) v. to lift; to raise; to erect;
to hoist; to heave : ยกตนข่มท่าน self-exaltation
with scornful contempt of others : ยกธง

to hold up a flag with out-stretched arm
(ชักธง to hoist a flag; see ชัก p. 287; โบกธง
see โบก p. 491): ยกใบ (เรือ) to hoist a sail:
ยกประทุนรถ,-เรือ to raise the hood of a car, or
canopy of a boat: ยกเรือน, ปลูกเรือน to erect
a house: ยกสมอ to weigh anchor; see
ถอน p. 382.

(ข) ยก to desist; to discontinue; to relinquish;
to abstain from doing: ยกความผิดบาป to
grant remission of sins: ยกคำร้อง to disregard, or reject a petition: ยกโทษ to
forgive; to remit punishment: ยกผิด to
grant pardon; to exonerate: ยกฟ้อง *legal*
to abrogate, revoke, or nullify; see ฟ้อง p.
605: ยกเลิก to cancel (a contract); to rescind (an action in court): ยกเสีย to ab-
solve; to acquit; to exculpate.

(ค) ยกขึ้น to draw up; to exalt; to elevate:
ถ้าเราถูกยกขึ้นจากแผ่นดินแล้ว "I, if I be lifted up
from the earth" (Gos. st. John 12:32): พระ-
ยะโฮวาทรงประคองผู้ที่มีใจถ่อมลง "The Lord lifteth
up the meek" (Psalms 147:6): พระองค์ได้ทรง
ชูข้าพเจ้าขึ้น "Thou hast lifted me up" (Psalms
31:1).

(ฆ) ยกขึ้น (กล่าว) อ้างว่า to institute; to allege;
to quote; to cite (in support of): ยกขึ้นเป็น-
ตัวอย่าง to cite as an example: ยกขึ้นเป็น-
เหตุให้ to allege; to constitute as a cause for:
ยกขึ้นมารับรอง to support by quoting (so as to
substantiate the point): ยกขึ้นให้เป็นผู้แทน
to institute (as a proxy).

(ง) ยกไป to transfer; to be displaced, or
shifted: ถูกยกไปเป็นชะเลย to be carried
away as prisoners of war: ยกเก้าอี้ไป to
remove a chair (as when it is in the way):
ยกจำนวนสิบไปบวกจำนวนร้อย *arithmetic* to carry
forward the tens, and add to the hundreds:
ยกทัพ to move, transfer, convey, transport, or
shift troops: ยกทัพไป to advance an army
(as into action); *ex.* แล้วให้พระรามเมศวรราชบุตร-
ยกทัพไปตีกรุงกัมพุชาธิบดี: ยกไปไว้ที่อื่น to shift
to another place: ยกไปไว้บนตึก,-เรือน to
take it upstairs: ยกลูกยกเมียไป to abscond,
decamp, or bolt with the family: ยกย้ายไป
to change the place of; to remove from one

place, office, or station to another (as an
official).

(จ) ยกมา to bring; to fetch; to be transported;
ex. พระยาละแวกยกมาตีพระนครเป็นหลายครั้งพ่ายแพ้-
กลับไปเมือง: ยกเก้าอี้มา to move, or shift
the chair here (เอาเก้าอี้มา to fetch a chair):
ยกเข้ามา to be brought closer; to bring into
relation with; *ex.* ขณะนั้นพระยากัมพุชายกเข้ามาตี-
เมืองจันทบุรี: ยกผลไม้มา to bring the fruit:
ยกมาตั้งที่นี่ to give a lift, placing it here.

(ช) ยกยอ to ascribe glory to; to eulogize; to
flatter: ยกยอสรรเสริญ to commend; to
praise; to encourage (so that the future
efforts may be better): ยกย่อง to extol;
to glorify the greatness or goodness of; to
admire (as after the achievement of some
great success): ยกย่องตนเอง, ยกเนื้อยกตัว
self-commendation; self-glorification.

(ฉ) ยกยอ to raise a square dip net; see ยอ
p. 666.

(ช) ยกไว้, ยกเว้น to desist from; to exempt; to
omit; to excuse: ยกไว้ก่อน to stop; to
defer action; see งด p. 220: ยกเลิกการทะ-
เลาะไว้ก่อน to desist from quarrelling for the
present.

(ฌ) ยกให้ to give; to grant; to bestow; *ex.*
ยกวังให้ทำเป็นวัดพระศรีสรรเพ็ชร์: ยกเงินให้ to
donate funds (as for a cause): ยกที่ดินให้เป็น-
ถนนหลวง to dedicate land for a public highway: ยกบุตรีให้ to give one's daughter (as
in marriage, or for adoption).

ยก ๒　　(ก) *n.* (a) a printer's term for counting pages in sets, or series of four, eight,
sixteen, or thirty-two; a form: (b) a saw-
miller's, or carpenter's term for measuring
timber amounting to one *sok* wide, one *new*
thick and sixteen *wah* long. In English
measurements this is the equivalent of 9/10
inches thick, 20 inches wide, 16 times 80
inches long (siam Directory for 1892, p. 59).

(ข) ยก the issue, or events occurring in succession at varying periods of time: เฆี่ยน-
สามยก ๆ ละสิบที scourged on three occasions,
each time ten strokes; see ครั้ง p. 180: ยามา-
แล้วหลายยก having been patched already many

times: ทวงเงินหลายยกแล้ว to have been dunned already on many occasions.

(ค) ยก, ผ้ายก an ancient Thai gold thread fabric.

ยกกระบัตร, ยุกกระบัตร yok[6]-gkra[4]-but[4] *n.* a rank in the provincial Public Prosecutors' Department.

[595].

ยกน ya[6]-gka[4]-na[6] *P. n.* the liver (chd. p.

ยง yong *adj.* pretty; see งาม p. 223; strong; durable: ยงยุทธ to fight bravely; to make a hard-fought fight: ยิ่งยง surpassing all others in strength or beauty.

ยงโย่, โยงโย่ yong-yoh[3] *v.* to touch the floor with the hands while bending over; to stand on all fours.

ยติ ๑ ya[6]-dti[4] *P. S. n.* a devotee; an ascetic; a Buddhist monk (chd. p. 598); a hermit; a recluse; one who has restrained his passions and abandoned the world (S. E. D. p. 841).

ยติ ๒ ya[6]-dti[4] *P. S. n.* restraint; control; ceasing; stopping; a religious mendicant whose passions are completely under control (S. E. D. p. 845).

ยถา ya[6]-tah[2] *P. S. adv.* in which manner or way; in accordance to, or conformity with; as; like; how; when (S. E. D. p. 841): ยถากรรม according to one's actions; according to circumstances: ยถากาล the proper time; the suitable moment: ยถาภูตญาณ real, right, true or correct knowledge.

ย่น yon[3] *v.* to shorten; to abbreviate: *adj.* rumpled; crumpled; wrinkled; creased; roughened or folded: ย่นความ to abridge or epitomize (as evidence): ย่นย่อ to retire; to withdraw; to give up; to be discouraged (in the pursuit of, or in the effort to acquire): หน้าย่น an angry looking, puckered face.

ยนต์, ยนตร์ yon *P. S. n.* any mechanical implement, instrument, contrivance, or engine; a prop; a support; a barrier; a fetter; a band; a tie or thong (S. E. D. p. 845).

ยม ๑ yom *v.* to weep or cry.

ยม ๒ yom *P. S. n.* a rein, curb or bridle; the act of checking, curbing, restraining or suppressing; self-control (S. E. D. p. 846); the name of the sovereign of the infernal regions (chd. p. 595); the Aryan god of the Dead; the regent of the south. According to Brahministic mythology his abode is hell, a place built of brass and iron. He has a sister who controls all the female culprits, as he exclusively deals with the male sex: ยมขันธ์ the forces or troops of hell; see กอง p. 67: ยมทูต those whose duty it is to bring the souls of the newly dead to the god of Death's palace for judgement: ยมบาล guardians of hell whose duty it is to inflict punishment according to the god of Death's judgement: ยมราช the ruler of the infernal regions: ยมโลก the domain of the god of Death; hell (S. E. D. p. 846).

[(chd. p. 595).

ยม ๓ ya[6]-ma[6] *P. S. n.* a pair; a couple

ยมก ya[6]-mok[6] *P. S. n.* a pair; the mark "ๆ" used in Thai literature where the reader has to repeat the preceding phrase or word; a repetition mark: *adj.* doubled; paired (chd. p. 595).

ยมขาว yom-kow[2] *N. Laos,* โค้โข้ง *Karen, Chiengmai,* สะเดาหิน *Thai,* สะเดาช้าง *Thai, Korat,* ช้ากะเดา *Thai, Peninsula,* ยมหิน *N. Laos* (ต้น) *n. Chukrasia velutina (Meliaceae)* (cb. p. 267).

ยมนา, ยมุนา ya[6]-ma[6]-nah *P. n.* the Jumna river (chd. p. 595), which flows into the Ganges at Allahabad.

ยมล ya[6]-mon *P. S. n.* a pair; a brace (chd. p. 595); a singer in a duet (S. E. D. p. 846).

ยมหอม yom-haum[2] *N. Laos,* เล้บ *Karen, Kanburi,* สีเสียดต้อม *Thai,* สีเสียดหอม *Thai, Pitsanuloke,* สะเดาดง *Thai, Kanburi* (ต้น) *n. Cedrela toona (Meliaceae),* the toona tree, Indian mahogany, a very handsome, lofty tree found in the Himalaya up to 4,000 feet, and southwards in the hills of the peninsula of India, through parts of Burma to the northern circles of Thailand. South of this, in a wild state, it disappears, to reappear in the extreme east of Malaysia and extend to the warmer parts of Australia. Into the lands between these two areas of distribution it has been introduced rather freely by man. The pinnate leaves are long and graceful and, when young, are of a crimson tint. The tree grows to a height of 50-60 feet or more and yields excellent timber which is exported from India to Europe. The wood is red and prettily marked; it is easily worked. In India the timber is universally used for all kinds of furniture, being one of the best timbers procurable for the purpose. It is used for planks and tea-boxes in Assam; cigar-boxes in Madras; for oil-casks in Travancore; for dugouts and sampans in Chittagong; and for carving and musical instruments. It is without doubt the most valuable timber produced in some parts of Australia, and is in general use there. It is equal to mahogany, to which it bears a good deal of resemblance, except that it is much lighter in weight. When kept dry it is very durable. There is considerable shrinkage in seasoning, and the process lasts for some time. The flowers are used for dyeing, in India, giving yellows and reds. They contain nyctanthin—a colouring-matter present in the flowers of *Nyctanthes*—quercetin, and a flavone-dye. The seeds are said to dye. The bark is astringent, and is used in India for dysentery, poultices to wounds, etc. (CB. p. 267: MCM. p. 178: V. P. p. 232: BURK. p. 500).

ยรรยง   yun-yong *adj.* pretty; see งาม p. 223.

ยล (มองดู)   yon *v.* to look; to glance at.

ยว, ยวา   ya[6]-wa[6] *P. S. n.* barley; barley-corn: any seed or grain (S. E. D. p. 847).

ยวกสา   ya[6]-wa[6]-gka[4]-sah[2] *n.* a welding fluid or flux for tin.

ยวง   yu-ang *n.* the pulp, aril or meat attached to fruit-pits (as in the durian and jack-fruit):   เงินยวง pure or refined silver.

ยวด   yu-at[3] *adv.* extremely; utterly; finally; supremely: งามยวดยิ่ง superbly handsome: ยวดยง, ยวดยิ่ง skillful; clever; brave; best; excellent.

ยวดยาน   yu-at[3]-yarn various means of transportation (as vehicles, palanquins).

ยวน ๑   yu-an *S. n.* Annamese; Greeks; people in the Payap Circle of Thailand; Cochin-Chinese: ยวนแกว the Tonkinese.

ยวน ๒   ya[6]-wa[6]-na[6] *v.* to lure; to love voluptuously; to arouse lust or sexual desire: ยวนยี to induce lust, or sexual pleasure; to caress or fondle.

ยวน ๓   yu-an *Thai, Pattani* (ต้น) *n. Koompassia parvifolia (Leguminosae); K. excelsa,* a lofty tree found in the Malay Peninsula, Sumatra, Borneo, and the Island of Palawan in the Philippines. In the Peninsula it is found as far north as Kedah and Kelantan. It is most found in stream valleys, or on the lower slopes of ridges, or foot-hills; not as a very abundant tree, and strangely absent from large sections of the country. It grows to a very great size, with a wide-spreading crown and large buttresses. One tree, as much as 265 feet tall, has been measured. Three hundred and fifty trees of commercial size were measured and found to have an average diameter of 40 inches, the largest being 107 inches. The timber is excessively hard, very heavy, red or reddish-brown, splitting badly, and not durable. The sap-wood is white or pale yellow, 3 or 4 inches thick; the grain is very crooked and irregular. The wood burns very readily and is more often used for making charcoal than for any other purpose. The tree is often left when the jungle is felled, because it is so hard to cut. It is possible to burn the tree down, and this is sometimes done in clearing land for a plantation. There is, in some quarters, a superstitious objection to cutting the tree down. The tree is completely desiduous, and may remain bare of leaves for some weeks. Fruit has rarely been collected. Natural regeneration is rather scanty, although germination occurs readily and quickly, and the young seedlings seem to be fairly hardy. The large branches often bear masses of honeycomb containing honey made by wild bees. In the Malay Peninsula it is considered that these trees are haunted. The bark is used in a medicinal bath for fever. The sap is poisonous, causing an inflammation on the skin suggesting erysipelas (BURK. p. 1284); *Antiaris toxicaria* (*Urticaceae*), sack-tree, upas-tree, a giant tree found in southern India, Ceylon, and from Burma and southern China to the eastern limits of Malaysia; in the Peninsula it is sporadic northwards from Malacca and probably also in Johore. The tree is the largest tree of the forests of the western Ghats of India, and one of the largest trees of Ceylon. Over the wide area of its habitat it is sometimes the chief poison, but not always. The latex is sometimes used pure; but it is more commonly mixed with other poisons, with the idea of making it more effective. Evidently some of these irritant substances make the victim feel wounded more quickly, as *Antiaris* shows no immediate irritant effect, and a fatally wounded animal may for a short time almost exhibit unconcern. As soon as Europeans reached Malaysia they were bound to become acquainted with poisoned arrows and darts; but it was a long time before the poisons were traced to the plants which produced them. *Antiaris* poison consists of two glucosides which both act alike. They act on the heart much more powerfully than digitalin, arresting its action. Antidotes are scarcely effective. The bark gives bark-cloth which is prepared in Malaya and Borneo as an alternative to *Artocarpus* bark. It must be prepared with care in order that the latex may not get into any wound in the operator's skin; and also the latex must be all removed or the cloth is apt to set up an irritation of the skin in the wearer. Elsewhere, the bark furnishes material for sacks and bags. It also seems possible to make a very good paper from it; also cordage. In the Andaman Islands the leaves are given as fodder to elephants (cb. p. 515: MCM. pp. 383, 428, 429: BURK. p. 174).

ยวบ yu-ap[3] *adj.* waving; flapping; shaking; bending; vacillating: เรือเอียงยวบ ๆ the boat is suddenly leaning to one side.

ยวส ya[6]-wa[6]-sa[4] *P. n.* grass; pasture; fodder; a bundle of grass (chd. p. 600).

ยวาคุ see ยาคุ p. 671.

ยศ yot[6] *S. n.* fame; renown; reputation; honour (chd. p. 596); a person of respectablity; a celebrity; an object of honour (S. E. D. p. 848): เครื่องยศ insignia of rank: แต่งเต็มยศ being attired in full-dress: ปริวารยศ being attended with a numerous retinue and with great pomp: ยศศักดิ์ conferred honour, prestige or splendour.

ยโส ya[6]-soh[2] *adj.* respected; honoured; venerated; worthy (of praise) (S. E. D. p. 848): คนบ้ายโส one mad for rank; one possessed with a desire for prestige or honour: ยโส-ธรา *lit.* "an honoured person," *i.e.* the wife of Siddhartha (Gotama) before he became the Buddha (chd. p. 596); see พิมพา p. 588.

ยอ yaw *v.* to praise (unreasonably); to flatter; to extol: *onomat.* from the call used to stop buffaloes, horses and cattle: *n. Morinda citrifolia* (*Rubiaceae*), a small fruit tree cultivated in villages throughout southeastern Asia and Malaysia, or at least encouraged to grow. It is in the Pacific Islands, and, by unconfirmed report, is said to be in east Africa. It grows to 20 feet in height, with a short trunk and a head ovoid in outline; it bears ellipsoid fruits of a greyish transparent white, in appearance anything but appetizing, and in flavour as soap and sugar mixed, with a smell like decaying cheese. In Indo-China it is eaten with salt. For the Javanese dyeing industry, this *Morinda* is cultivated on well-drained soil, in rows, sometimes on a considerable scale, occupying the ground for upwards of two years. At harvest the roots are dug, washed, and, by beating, the bark is removed from the larger of them, while the smaller are preserved whole. The quality of the product varies with the proportion of these two, and with the age of the old roots, while apparently some localities produce a better dye-stuff than others. However, the Malay Peninsula does not grow the plant for dyeing but for medicinal use. The over-ripe fruit is stated to be used as an emmenagogue both in Malaya and in Cochin-China. The fruit and the juice are also used for a variety of other complaints. The very young leaves serve as a vegetable in Java, and the old leaves may be wrapped round food which is being cooked. *M. citrifolia* is sometimes planted to serve as a support for pepper. It has been named as a shade-tree for coffee but the coffee would seem likely to outgrow it. The dry wood is yellowish-brown, or dull olive, but of a rather bright yellow when fresh. It is soft and splits excessively in drying, so that it is useless, unless for posts (BURK. p. 1493: V. P. p. 225); a crab net; a square-shaped dip-net with a long handle attached to a prop or fulcrum (used for dipping up fishes in canals): ยอบ้า (ต้น) *Morinda tinctoria*, a shrub of which the roots are used as a red dye (V. P. p. 225); *M. elliptica*, a bush, very common in a wild state in the Malay Peninsula and northwards to Tavoy. It has leaves smaller and more narrowed towards the base than those of *M.*

citrifolia, and with a much smaller, drier head of fruit. In Malacca it is used as a dye and fishing-nets and sails are treated with it. Because it is very common and almost always available, it is the *Morinda* most used medicinally by the Malays. Its leaves may be added to rice for loss of appetite and taken for headache, cholera, diarrhoea, and particularly in fever. They are applied externally to the spleen, etc.; smeared with oil and heated for fever; applied in a pounded condition upon the spleen and wounds; a lotion of them is used for haemorrhoids and upon the body after childbirth. They are also used for convulsions (BURK p. 1493): ยอแสง to lessen the rays of (as of the evening sun): ตวันยอแสง twilight: ยอ a square dip net. The four corners are attached to the four ends of two cross-pieces which are joined at right angles to a center piece. This is all suspended from the end of a long pole which works on a pivot. By depressing or raising the land-end of the pole the net is raised or submerged in the water. After a catch, the net is swung to land: เรือยอ a boat with a square net placed in the bow: นักยอ a flatterer.

ย่อ yaw[3] *v.* to be discouraged or disheartened; see ท้อ p. 402; to lower (as a boat); to lessen, shorten, abridge or abbreviate: เดิน-ย่อๆ to walk stoopingly: โดยย่อๆ briefly: มิได้ย่อท้อต่ออันตราย to have undaunted courage in the face of danger: ย่อความ to abbreviate; to epitomize: ย่อท้อ to act in a cowardly manner, to be dismayed, or to yield unduely; see ขยั้น p. 142: ย่อตัว to stoop, kneel, bow or bend down: ย่อพล to congregate troops ready to resist the approaching enemy; to retreat in order to resist the attacking foe better (as in a skirmish): ย่อ-แย่ to be weakened, or tired; see ท้อแท้ p. 402: ย่อหย่อน reduced gradually in strength; weakened; dismayed; discouraged; disheartened: ย่อเหลี่ยม to reduce the acuteness of an angle or corner.

ยอก   yauk[3] *v.* to pierce; to sting; to have shooting pains (as in muscular rheumatism): *n.* a prick; a sting; a sharp lancinating pain; see แทง p. 427: คำยอกเสียด sharp, stinging words: ปวดยอกเสียด lancinating or shooting pains: หนามยอก to be pierced by a thorn.

ยอกย้อน   yauk[3]-yawn[5] *adj.* incoherent; in a round-about manner; zigzaging; circuitous: พูดยอกย้อน to talk in a round-about or evasive manner.

ยอง   yaung *n.* a roe; a deer; a stag: ยองคำ (กวางทอง) the golden deer or stag.

ย่อง   yaung[3] *v.* to walk stealthily; to creep up to a person or object (as when tracking game): *adv.* cautiously; gingerly; secretly; secretively: คนย่องเบา a filcher; a pilferer; a snatch-thief: เดินย่องแย่ง to walk staggeringly; to walk dragging the feet listlessly (as in forms of muscular paralysis): ย่อง-เข้าไป to approach secretly: ย่องมอง to peep at slyly: ย่องแย่ง crippled; decrepit; disabled; shaky; enfeebled: ย่องเหยียบ to tread softly or cautiously.

ย้อง   yaung[5] *adj.* pretty; see งาน p. 223.

ยอง ๆ   yaung-yaung *adj.* squatting; crouching (as in a sitting posture): นั่งยอง ๆ see นั่ง p. 448.

ย่องเหง็ด   see จ้องหน่อง p. 234.

ยอด   yaut[3] *n.* top; summit; peak; see ปลาย p. 512: พระยอด a boil or abscess (used only for royalty).: ยอดเงินคงจ่ายเกิน debit balance: ยอดเงินคงเหลือ credit balance: ยอดดี the best possible: ยอดสร้อย, ยอดรัก a favourite; one most beloved; a fiancée.

ยอน   yaun *v.* to insert, gently pulling back and forth (as a probe in a sinus); to pick out or clean (from a cavity); see ไช p. 304: ยอน, สังกะวาด (ปลา) *Laides hexanema (Schilbeidae)* (suvatti p. 82): ยอนจมูก to swab

out the nasal cavity: ยอนหู to pick wax from the ear: ศิลายอน flint, or a very hard rock.

ย้อน   yaun[5] *v.* to return; to retrace one's steps; see กลับ p. 60: ย้อนกล่าว to reiterate; to repeat or revert to what has been said: ย้อนคำ to retract one's words: ย้อน-ทวนต้น to review from the beginning (as some previous lesson): ย้อนรอย to return by the same way.

ยอบ   yaup[3] *v.* to be in a reduced state of (as to one's finances or physical condition); see บกพร่อง p. 465; to become crouched, stooped, or prostrated; see ฟุบ p. 609: ยอบแยบ to become wholly overcome (as with an adverse economic condition); to become insufficiently supplied (as with the necessaries of life); to become curtailed in the means of gaining a livelihood; to become poor or impoverished: *adj.* stranded; destitute; starved; poverty-stricken; penniless.

ยอม   yaum *v.* to allow, or permit (as to go or do); to agree, or consent (as in a controversy); to ratify, or become a partner in (as an agreement); to volunteer to go or do (as on a mission); to acquiesce, assent, comply, concede, endorse, or subscribe to: *adj.* willing-minded; favourably disposed: ยอม-ความ to come to a compromise in a legal case: ยอมตัว to give up one's liberty (by marrying or becoming a slave): ยอมตาม to be favourably disposed and act accordingly: ยอมตาย to die without reluctance or demur: ยอมปล่อยสิทธิอันหนึ่งอันใด to waive an issue gladly: ยอมรวมกันรับผิด willingly to become jointly liable: ยอมให้ to grant of one's own accord or with a good grace.

ย่อม   yaum[3] *adj.* mean; middle; small; middling; intermediate in size; moderate; low (in price): ย่อมเป็น, ย่อมมีมา habitually; according to custom: ย่อมว่า it is commonly said or reported: ย่อมเห็น generally seen; usually noticed: ราคาย่อมเยาว์ cheap or moderate in price.

ย้อม yaum[5] v. to dye; to colour; to tinge, stain, paint, or wash (in pigment): เครื่องย้อม pigment; colouring matter; dyes (chemical or vegetable): ช่างย้อม a professional dyer: ย้อมความ to falsify or misinterpret (as evidence, statements, or documents): ย้อมใจ *lit.* "to make a heart brighter," *i. e.* to encourage; to strengthen the mind (as in time of adversity); see บำรุง p. 482: ย้อมทอง to heighten the quality of gold: ย้อมแมวขาย to falsify goods for sale.

ย่อย yauy[3] v. to cause to break into fine particles; to digest (as food); to break up into fragments; to divide minutely; see บ่น p. 494: *adj.* trifling; unimportant: ซื้อย่อย to buy piecemeal: ย่อยยับ ruined; broken by some calamity.

ย้อย yoy[5] v. to hang down loosely; to droop; to trickle down; to run down or ooze out (as sap): ย้อยหยด to flow or come down in drops (as tears).

ยะ ya[6] a prefix for words beginning with "ย" having no meaning (only used to add another syllable to complete the rhythm or verse in poetry) as ย้าย, ยะย้าย; also used as an ending to questions, to beautify the sense, or render more polite as, ยะ yes.

ยะงันจะคับ ya[6]-ngun-chja[4]-kup[6] *Jav. adj.* taciturn; unable to speak; dumb.

ยะยอบ ya[6]-yaup[3] v. to kneel or bow down; to manifest respect to; see นอบ p. 446.

ยะยัด see ยัด p. 669.

ยะยัน ya[6]-yun v. to prop up; to use means of support: *adj.* vivid; flashing; lustrous; dazzling.

ยะยับ ya[6]-yup[6] *adj.* flashing; twinkling; sparkling; emitting rays; effulgent: งามยะยับยะยาบ beautifully resplendent with rays, [or colour.
ยะยั่ว see ยั่ว p. 670.

ยะยัว, ยั้วเยีย ya[6]-yoo-ah[5] v. to crawl over each other in a seething mass (as worms or snakes); to be in a disordered condition.

ยะยาน ya[6]-yarn *adj.* flapping; waving; oscillating; moving (as leaves in a breeze).

ยะย้าย ya[6]-yai[5] v. to move from one place to another; to move back and forth.

ยะย้าว ya[6]-yow[5] v. to be cheerful, pleased, happy or glad.

ยะยิ้ม ya[6]-yim[5] v. to smile laughingly or [blandly.
ยะยัด see ยัด p. 676.

ยะยน see ยน p. 677.

ยะยุ่ง ya[6]-yoong[3] v. to be in confusion; to be tangled, or in a conglomerate mass.

ยะแย่ง ya[6]-yaang[5] v. to snatch from; to take possession of by force.

ยะแย้ม ya[6]-yaam[5] v. to be on the verge of smiling; to be gay or light-hearted; to be about to bloom or blossom out (as a bud into a flower).
[thread.
ยะใย ya[6]-yai *n.* a filament, strand or

ยะหิทา (เย็บ) ya[6]-hi[4]-tah *Jav. v.* to sew.

ยัก yuk[6] v. to move, raise, lift, or tilt up (indicating successive motions); see กระดิก p. 28: ยักคิ้ว to raise the eyebrows (as for a signal of assent or flirting): ยักยอก, ยักแยก to conceal, put apart, filch, steal or appropriate another's property or funds; to misappropriate; to embezzle: ยักย้าย to change the place of, or take away from the proper place; to remove; to displace: ยักหน้า to make faces (as in disgust): ยักหน้ายักตา *colloq.* to signal by moving the face or eyes: ยักหล่ม the supra-clavicular fossa: ยักไหล่ to raise a shoulder (as a sign): ยักไปยักมา to wriggle or squirm about (as fish caught in [a net.
ยักข์ see ยักษ์ p. 669.

ยักขินี, ยักษิณี   yuk⁶-ki⁴-nee *P. S. n.* a female giant (chd. p. 595); a giantess.

ยักยัน   yuk⁶-yun *adj.* strong; permanent; stable; durable; see มั่นคง p. 646; แข็งแรง p. 169.

ยักยี่ยักยัน, ยักแย่ยักยัน   yuk⁶-yee³-yuk⁶-yun *adj.* clumsy; awkward; swaying to and fro (as when carrying anything very heavy); see เก้กัง p. 118.

ยักษ์, ยักข์   yuk⁶ *P. S. n.* a living supernatural being; a class of semi-divine beings; a demigod; an apparition; a ghost; a giant; a spirit (S. E. D. p. 838); superhuman creatures (Ala. p. 178): ยักษี a poetical term for female giants.

ยักษากร   yuk⁶-sah²-gkorn *n.* a group, or community of giants.

ยัง   yang *v.* to remain still; to have some still: *adv.* till; still; yet; eventually; until: *prep.* to; as far as: คำนับมายัง a polite form of address for personal letters: คืนยังรุ่ง all night; till dawn; from dark to daylight: ยังก่อน not just now; not yet; presently: ยังค่ำ all day long: ยังชั่ว *lit.* "still bad," *i. e.* to be getting better; to improve somewhat (used in reference to a patient): ยังมีอยู่ to have some left still: ยังไม่มา not yet having arrived: ยังแล้ว about to be completed; just finished shortly: ยังให้นอน to make to sleep: ยังอยู่แต่บิดา the father only is still living.

ยั่ง, ยะยั่ง   yung³ *v.* to exist, stand, last, or endure for a long time: ความยั่งยืน durability; stability; permanence: ยั่งยืน to be constant, permanent, durable, lasting; to live long.

ยั้ง   yung⁵ *v.* to stop; to defer or desist from; see งด p. 220: ยั้งคิด to stop and reflect or think: หยุดยั้งการ to defer the work.

ยัช   yut⁶ *S. v.* to worship, adore, honour, or consecrate; to present, grant, or bestow (S. E. D. p. 838).

ยัชน   yut⁶-cha⁶-na⁶ *P. S. n.* the act of sacrificing or worshipping (S. E. D. p. 838).

ยัชมาน   yut⁶-cha⁶-marn *S. n.* a worshipper; a sacrificer; any patron; a host; a rich man; the head of a family or tribe (S. E. D. p. 839).

ยัญญ   yun-ya⁶ *P. n.* (Brahminical) sacrifice (chd. p. 596).

ยัญญงค์   yun-yong *P. n.* the Glomerous fig-tree (chd. p. 596).

ยัฏฐิ, ยัษฏิ   yut⁶-ti⁴ *P. n.* a cane; a staff; a stick; a pole; a stem; a stalk; a measure of length equal to seven ratanas (chd. p. 599); a goad: ยัฏฐิมธุกา, ชะเอมเครือ liquorice (chd. p. 599).

ยัด, ยะยัด   yut⁶ *v.* to cram, or stuff (as cotton into a pillow); to tuck, or press down into (so as to fill the cavity): ยัดกิน to gorge, bolt, gulp down, or devour with voracity (as food): ยัดปืน to ram the load or charge into a gun: ยัดเบียด, เบียดยัด to be compressed, jammed, crushed, cramped, or crowded together (as steerage passengers); see เบียด p. 490: ยัดเบียดให้ to insist on giving; to make an unwelcome or unappreciated gift: ไม้ยัดปืน a ram-rod for guns.

ยัน   yun *v.* to prop, brace, support, sustain; see ค้ำจุน p. 201; to push against (so as to prevent falling); to abut on; to touch, meet or be contiguous (as two boards or pieces of land); to be adjoining: ไม้ยัน a prop, brace, or support: ยืนยัน to affirm with positiveness: ยันหมาก nauseated; sickened (as after chewing a quid of betel-nut): หน้ายัน descriptive of the strong or sickening species of the areca-nut when split open.

ยั่น, ยะยั่น   yun³ *v.* to fear; to be dismayed; to dread; see กลัว p. 60.

ยันต์, ยันตร์, ยนตร์   yun *P. n.* implement; appliance; machine; engine (chd. p. 596); a mystic drawing with magical letters placed in the spaces; automatic machinery: วิชา-ยันตรกรรม Mechanical Engineering: เลขยันต์ mystical drawings or characters placed on metal plates, or painted oʟ gable-ends of houses: เศกยันต์ to pronounce or consecrate by mystical forms or formulas.

ยันเย้า   yun-yow[5] *v.* to wrestle (for sport); see ปล้ำ p. 512.

ยับ ๑   yup[6] *v.* to be damaged, creased, bruised, ruined, totally injured, crushed, broken, torn: ใช้ยับเยิน harshly used or treated (as slaves were in former times): ด่ายับเยิน cursed to the limit: ยับย่อย, ยับเยิน totally damaged; irreparably broken or injured: หมากยับ areca-nuts kept till well-dried or seasoned.

ยับ ๒, ยิบ ๆ   yup[6] *adj.* twinkling; flashing; sparkling; dazzling; effulgent; emitting rays: ยับ ๆ flapping or waving in the wind; moving in quick succession (as short strokes of paddles): ยับยง beautifully brilliant: ยับยาน to shake, flap, wave or be agitated; to waver (in purpose or opinion).

ยับยั้ง   yup[6]-yung[5] *v.* to constrain; to stop; to defer going; to stay; to rest: · ยับยั้งอยู่ to stay, wait, or rest for awhile.

ยั่ว, ยะยั่ว   yoo-ah[3] *v.* to excite; to irritate; to delight: ยั่วกัน to excite or arouse each other's passions: ยั่วใจ to arouse desire; to inflame or stimulate the mind or feelings: ยั่วยวน to caress, fondle, tickle or act so as to excite sexual passions; to feel pleasure in voluptuousness: ยั่วเย้า to speak or act in a mocking, playful manner; to incite anger by mockery or jesting: ยุยั่ว to incite, excite, urge or arouse the feelings to action, anger or sexual pleasure; to mock or irritate vexatiously.

ยั่วรยาตร see ยุรยาตร p. 679.

ยา   yah *v.* to apply a remedy; to use means for the restoration to health; to plug, close, stop, cork, or occlude (as a leak or opening); to renovate, repair, mend, or patch (as in plumbing): *n.* a drug; medicines; remedies; a panacea; a syllable in the names of royalty to indicate the masculine gender as, ลูกยาเธอ, น้องยาเธอ, พี่ยาเธอ; see เธอ p. 437: พอเยี่ยวยาไปได้ to give temporary help (as in tiding over some stress of circumtances): ยาแก้ a specific remedy for or against: ยาแก้ปวด an opiate; an anodyne: ยาแก้ลงท้อง a remedy for diarrhoea: ยาแก้ไอ a cough-mixture, etc.: ยาขี้ผึ้ง medicinal ointments; cerates: ยาเขียว (ต้น) *Thunbergia laurifolia*; *T. grandiflora* (*Acanthaceae*), a big, rather soft but woody climber, which goes to the tops of considerable trees, and falls over their branches in dense masses covered with beautiful, dark lilac flowers. It kills the trees which it smothers. It was brought into European cultivation some seventy years ago from the Malay Peninsula. The Malays use it medicinally. The juice of the leaves may be swallowed for menorrhagia; and it may be put into the ear for deafness; cuts and boils may be poulticed with the leaves (MCM. pp. 127, 208: V. P. p. 225: Burk. p. 2158): ยาดำ extract of aloes; the dried sap of *Euphorbia antiquorum*, used as a purgative in combination with other ingredients (never alone) (V. P. p. 253): ยาแดง Chinese tobacco, imported and smoked chiefly by the Chinese: ยาถ่าย, ยาทุเลา, ยารุ various degrees of purgatives: ยาทา liniments; embrocations: ยานัตถุ์ snuff: ยาบำรุงธาตุ a tonic: ยาเบื่อ, ยาพิษ poisons: ยาผง remedies in powder form: ยาฝิ่น opium: ยาพอก poultices: ยาเม็ด pills: ยารม a remedy applied by fumigation: ยาเรือ to apply dammar pitch, or to caulk up a boat: ยาเบี่ย to cause to be cured or healed; to cause an amelioration or relief (as in a financial condition): ยาสวน a clyster: ยาสูบ smoking tobacco: ยาหม้อ

vegetable drugs boiled in a rice-pot : ยา-หยอดตา various collyriums for diseases of the eyes : รับประทานยา to take medicine or a remedy : วางยา to apply, or prescribe a remedy : วางยาเบื่อ to apply or give a dose of poison (as to rats or dogs) : สูบยา to smoke tobacco : สูบยาฝิ่น to smoke opium.

ย่า yah[3] *n.* a paternal grandmother : ปู่ย่า, ปู่ย่าตายาย ancestors : ย่าทวด a paternal great-grandmother : ย่านาง the guardian goddess of carts and boats.

ยาก yark[3] *v.* to be in difficulty, a dilemma, or straits ; to be sorely pressed ; to bear the brunt ; to swim against the stream : *n.* hardship ; embarrassment ; trouble ; difficulty ; paucity ; scantiness : *adj.* poor ; insufficient ; inadequate ; ill-provided : ข้าวยากหมากแพง famine : คนยาก, คนยากจน poor people ; paupers ; see เข็ญใจ p. 163 : ได้โดยยาก to acquire with difficulty or hardship : ตกยาก to be afflicted with poverty or distress : ยากแค้น distressed or harrassed by poverty : ยาก-ง่ายอะไร wherein lies the difference : ยาก-เต็มประดา distress, poverty or difficulty in the extreme : ยากเย็นเข็ญใจ miserable ; slavish, poor, or in the extreme of difficulty : ยากไร้ being in trouble through poverty or need ; see ขัดสน p. 150.

ยาค, ยัชน yah-ka[6] *P. S. n.* a sacrifice (chd. p. 594).

ยาคุ, ยากู, ยวาคุ yah-koo[6] *P. n.* rice-gruel (chd. p. 594) ; a glutinous, starchy drink extracted from immature grains of rice by pounding ; it is sweetened slightly and then boiled. This is commonly presented to Buddhist monks before the time of rice-harvest ; a soup made of young rice.

ยาง yang *n.* resin ; gum ; guttapercha ; latex : ยาง *Thai, Laos,* ยางขาว *Sriracha,* เยียง *Khmer, Surin,* ขะยาง *Chaobon, Korat,* ร่าลอย *Sui, Surin,* ล้อดยี่ *So, Nakawn Panom, Karen, Chiengmai* (ต้น) *Dipterocarpus alatus*

(*Dipterocarpaceae*), a tall tree found from the eastern edge of Bengal through Burma and Thailand, where it is common, to the northern parts of British Malaya and as far south as the Kinta district of Perak. The timber is exported from Burma and Thailand. It is reddish-brown and moderately hard, not durable when exposed to the weather, but under cover lasts well and is used for cheap planking. It has been suggested as useful for the interior parts of railway rolling-stock. The demand for it has increased, and it is carried as far as London. When treated, it may be used for sleepers if the chair for the rail is seated on a bearing plate. It is very curious that the first signs of decay should be said to be due to a fungus attacking the oleo-resin. The Burmese and Thai extract the oleo-resin ; but the industry is dying in Burma. The chief use is local and only for torches. The oleo-resin which it gives is one of the most limpid of those of the genus. It is used for plasters in Cambodia. A partial analysis states that 71.65 per cent of volatile oil was found with 28.35 per cent of resins, etc. The oil was tried for zinc paints in the place of linseed oil, and thought to be good. In Cambodia the bark enters into decoctions taken for liver complaints and into lotions used hot for rheumatism. The seeds contain no fixed oil, but resin (cb. p. 133 : Burk. p. 841) : ยาง (นก) the pond heron, *Ardeola grayi* ; the Indian pond heron (Gaird. J. S. S. IX, 1, p. 10) : ยางกรอก (นก) chestnut bittern, *Ardetta cinnamomea* (Gaird. J. S. S. IX, 1, p. 10) : ยางกี๊ก (นก) the black bittern, *Dupetor flavicollis* (Herb. N. H. J. S. S. VI, 4, p. 354) : ยางขาว (นก) cattle egret, *Bubulcus ibis coromandus* (Deig. N. H. J. S. S. VIII, 3, p. 173) : ยางดำ *Thai, Korat,* หมักบ้าลิ้มตำ *Thai, Sukotai,* มะบ้าแมง *Laos, Chiengmai,* แฮนเฮาห้อม *Laos, Loi,* สบ้า-ลิ้ง *Thai, Kanburi* (ต้น) *Mucuna collettii* (*Leguminosae*) (cb. p. 443) : ยางแดง *Thai, Korat to Krat,* ยางมันหมู *Thai, Pattani,* ยางยี้

Laos, Chiengmai, Malay, Pattani (ต้น) *Dip-terocarpus costatus* (*Dipterocarpaceae*), a tall tree found from the eastern borders of Bengal to the Malay Peninsula, where it extends along the hills to central Johore. It contains a rather large amount of wood-oil, and is a common source of it in Cambodia (BURK. p. 842); *D. turbinatus* (Cb. pp. 134, 139 : V. P. p. 228): ยางแดง (นก) chestnut bittern, *Ixobry-chus cinnamomeus* (Deig. N. H. J. S. S. VIII, 3, p. 173): ยางโทน (นก) the little egret, *Egretta garzetta* (Herb. N. H. J. S. S, VI, 4, p. 351): ยาง-น่อง (ต้น) *Antiaris toxicaria* (*Urticaceae*), sack-tree, upas-tree, a giant tree found in southern India, Ceylon, and from southern China to the eastern limits of Malaysia (MCM. pp. 383, 428, 429 : Burk. p. 174); see ยวน p. 664 : ยางลบ an eraser for pencil or ink : ยางสน turpentine : ยางเสวย (นก) cattle egret, *Bubulous coromandus* (Gaird. J. S. S. IX, 1, p. 10): ยางอินเดียรับเบอร์ (ต้น) *Ficus elastica* (*Urticaceae*), India-rubber fig, rambong, a big tree, very widely spreading, starting life as an epiphyte, found from the eastern Himlaya to Java. In the Malay Peninsula it occurs as a result of cultivation in many places, but appears to be truly wild in others, just as in Java. The Spaniards used it as a road-side tree in the Philippine Islands. It has undergone a long trial in experimental cultivation as a source of rubber, but has quite lost its place before *Hevea brasiliensis*, though a little rubber is still got from it in Assam and Burma. The chief reason why it has lost its place is that there is a resin—about 4 to 20 per cent. in the rubber, which hardening in the course of time, annuls the elasticity. The leaves contain slime, which is not elastic. Rubber from this fig appears to have been used in north-eastern India for lining receptacles long before Europeans knew anything about it, but when they did come to know of it they began extensive experimentation to ascertain its value. The tree is not cultivated for rubber now. Very young leaf tips, before the leaves expand, are eaten in Java in salads (MCM. pp. 99, 407 : V. P. p. 230 : BURK. p. 1007).

ย่าง yang[3] *v.* to take slow, short steps; to treat, cure, flavour or bake with smoke (as meat, ham, ducks, or fish); see ปิ้ง p. 526 : ย่องย่าง to creep cautiously, watching guardedly (as when approaching game) : ย่างเท้า to take slow, measured steps : ย่างเยื้อง to walk with a pompous attitude, with an exaggerated swinging of the arms; see กรีดกราย p. 53 : ย่างสามขุม to advance with cautious steps (as when boxing or fencing) : *n.* name of a special attitude taken while boxing or fencing.

ยาจก, ยาจนก yah-chjok[4] *P. n.* a beggar; one asking alms (chd. p. 593).

ยาจน, ยาจนา yah-chja[4]-na[6] *P. n.* the aet of asking, soliciting, begging or desiring (a gift or alms) (chd. p. 593).

ยาชก yah-cha[6]-gka[4] *n.* one who officiates at sacrifices; a priest; a Brahmin.

ยาตนา yah-dta[4]-nah *P. S. n.* torment; agony; pain (chd. p. 596).

ยาตร, ยาตรา yart[3]-dtra[4] *P. S. v.* to walk, march, go or travel : *n.* a march, procession or expedition; a moving of troops; livelihood (chd. p. 599): ยาตรฟ้า travelling skyward or heavenward : ยาตราเรือ travelling by boat.

ยาน ๑ yarn *P. S. n.* means of going or travelling; a conveyance, vehicle, carriage, car, boat, litter or palanquin (S. E. D. p. 849): ยานนาวา a boat or ship (as means of transportation) : วัดยานนาวา a temple in Ban Tawai District, Bangkok.

ยาน ๒ yarn *adj.* drooping; sagging; dangling; trailing; swinging; pendulous.

ย่าน yarn[3] *v.* to be fearful of; see กลัว p. 60 : *n.* region; side; location; district; extent : ย่านกว้าง, ย่านกลาง the length of, or extent of the middle section; the intervening portion (as of land): ข่านบ้าน extent of territory covered by a village.

ยานก yah-na⁶-gka⁴ *P. S. n.* a cart, carriage or car (implying one of small size) (chd. p. 595).

ยานมาศ, ยานุมาศ yah-na⁶-mart³ *n.* a royal palanquin or litter; a throne-shaped state palanquin.

ยานิก, ยานิก yah-nik⁶ *P. n.* anything which is used as a means of transportation: รถยานิก a carriage, car or cart (used as means of transportation): วิบัสสนายานิก spiritual insight (chd. p. 580), as a means of transportation: สมถยานิก tranquility (chd. p. 429), as a means of transportation.

ยาบ ๑ yarp³ *adj.* hemp; jute fibre; see ปอ p. 513.

ยาบ ๒, ยะยาบ yarp³ *adj.* ossilating, swaying or waving slowly; rising and falling slowly (as a flag, or wings beating the air, as a bird flying); see แกว่ง p. 130.

ยาปน yah-bpa⁴-na⁶ *P. S. n.* support; maintenance (chd. p. 596); livelihood: ยาปนมัตต์ food sufficient to support life (chd. p. 596): *adj.* just sufficient to sustain life; living from hand to mouth.

ยาม yarm *P. n.* a method to mark time; occasion; duration; period; space; span; spell; a period or watch of three hours; a night-watch (chd. p. 595): ปฐมยาม the first watch, *i. e.* 6 to 9 p.m.: มัชฌิมยาม the middle watch, *i. e.* 9 p. m. to midnight: บัจฉิมยาม from midnight to 3 a. m.: จับยาม to prognosticate by divination: ตียาม to announce the night-watches by striking a bell or gong: เฝ้ายาม to be on watch as watchman or sentinal: ยามกาลิก see กาล ๒ p. 100: ยามตุดชาย the afternoon: ยามใถ ploughing time: ยามทุกข์ยามสุข on occasions of adversity or happiness: ยามเทวบุตร name of the inhabitants of the third deva

world: ยามพวาน a monkey character in the Ramayana: ยามพาด morning: ยามโยค, ยามฤกษ์, ยามอุษาโยค the auspicious time or period of luck or fortune: ยามสามตา a diviner's chart consisting of a triangle divided into three spaces, by means of which he makes prognostications.

ย่าม yarm³ *v.* to become bolder, impudent, haughty or over-confident; see ทะยาน p. 406: *n.* a large-sized bag or minature sack with arm-loop (as carried by Buddhist priests); see ถุง p. 389: สะพายย่าม to carry the bag with the arm-loop strung on the shoulder.

ยามักการ yah-muk⁶-gkarn *n.* a diacritical mark silencing a letter, e. g. "ไ"

ยามิก yah-mik⁶ *P. S. n.* a guard; a watchman; a night-watcher (S. E. D. p. 850).

ยาย yai *n.* a maternal grandmother; a common personal pronoun for old women: แม่ยาย a mother-in-law: ยายแก่ a term of disrespect for old women: ยายชี a nun: ยายทวด a maternal great-grandmother: ยายท้าว an honourable appellation for old ladies of the palace.

ย้าย yai⁵ *v.* to be removed, displaced, shifted, or changed in place or position; to be transferred from one office or place to another; see เปลี่ยน p. 534; to sway, or swing; see แกว่ง p. 130: ย้ายไปย้ายมา to be nomadic, vagrant, or migratory (in abode or purpose).

ยายี yah-yee *v.* to annoy; to attack; to disturb; to molest; to trouble or torment (chd. p. 601).

ยาว ๑ yah-wa⁶ *P.. adv.* until; while; as long as; in order that (chd. p. 599): ยาวชีวิก things that are permissible (for Buddhist monks) to partake of irrespective of time (as water, or medicines).

ยาว ๒ yow *adj.* long; lengthy; extended; lengthened; protracted; prolonged; see นาน p. 451: คนลิ้นยาว a fluent talker *colloq.*:

คำยาว a long speech, discourse or harangue : เพลงยาว amorous songs ; love ballads ; ditties : ยาวรี long and tapering to a point (as a blade of grass or a rice stalk) : ยืดยาว lengthy ; prolonged.

ย้าว, เหย้า, ย้าวเรือน   yow⁵ *n.* a house.

ยาวัส   yah-wat⁶ *P. S. n.* pasture ; fodder (chd. p. 600) ; a quantity or heap of grass, fodder, or provisions (S. E. D. p. 852).

ยาหยี   yah-yee² *Jav. n.* a term of endearment, *e. g.* very dear sister, my dear, darling.

ยำ   yum *v.* to slice and mix together ; to fear ; to show respect for : *n.* a salad or relish consisting of vegetables, meat or fish mixed together : ยำเกรง, ยำแยง, ยำแยง to have abject fear of ; see คร้าม p. 181 : ยำเกรงอำนาจ to respect the authority of : *n.* respectful fear : ยำผัก to mince vegetables for a salad : ยำยี broken, shattered, or reduced to fragments : ระยำ cursed ; crushed or broken into pieces *vulgar.*

ย่ำ   yum³ *v.* to be trodden under foot ; to exert pressure on ; to trample or tread upon ; to be severe with ; to put on the screws ; to strike with repeated strokes (as a bell or gong) ; see จวน ๑ *adv.* p. 233 : ย่ำค่ำ six p. m. : ย่ำใจ to become braver gradually, step by step : ย่ำเทือก to tread, trample or loosen up well-soaked ground (as in the preparation of a field for planting rice) : ย่ำเท้า to mark time goose-step fashion *military* : ย่ำยาม to strike the watches of the night : ย่ำยี to rule with a rod of iron ; to oppress, override, overrule or tyrannize ; to force down the throat : ย่ำรุ่ง dawn ; 6 a. m. ; the act of beating a drum announcing dawn.

ย้ำ   yum⁵ *v.* to repeat, or lay stress on by reiterating what has been said ; to reaffirm (as some important part or points) ; see ซ้ำ p. 308 ; to flatten down smooth with the surface (as nail-heads or rivets) ; to make firm by repeated pounding : พูดย้ำ to emphasize by

repetition of one's words : สั่งย้ำ to repeat an order for emphasis or positiveness.

ย่ายาม   yum-yarm *v.* to praise, laud or extol.

ยิกๆ   yik⁶-yik⁶ *adj.* quick ; with quick movements ; in quick succession ; see ถี่ p. 388.

ยิง   ying *v.* to shoot, propel or project (as a bullet by means of a gun or cannon) : กิ้งยิง a sty : ยิงนก to shoot birds : ยิงปืน to fire a gun ; to shoot with a gun or cannon : ยิงลูกกระสุน to shoot dried mud-balls by means of a cross-bow.

ยิ่ง   ying³ *adj.* signifying the superlative degree ; excessive ; overmuch ; superabundant ; lavish ; profuse ; prodigal : *adv.* over and above ; too much ; over ; extremely ; exceedingly ; beyond all bounds ; see เกิน p. 126 : ยิ่งกว่า better than ; more than that : ยิ่งกว่านั้นอีก all the better for ; still better than ; still more than that : ยิ่งดีเสียอีก still better than that ; preferable : ยิ่งกินยิ่งผอม growing leaner in spite of all that is eaten : ยิ่งยง growing braver ; becoming more beautiful or superior to all others : ยิ่งยวด par excellence : ยิ่งวัน increasing hour by hour, or day by day : ยิ่งวันยิ่งจน growing poorer as the days advance : ยุ่งยิ่ง complicated ; entangled ; knotted ; involved ; disorderly ; without order ; unsystematic.

ยิงฟัน   ying-fun *v.* to show the teeth (by retracting the lips).

ยิฏฐะ   yit⁶-ta⁴ *P. v.* to sacrifice ; to make an offering (in a Hindu sense) ; to give alms (chd. p. 601).

ยิน ๑   yin *n.* audition : ความยินดี pleasure : ด้วยความยินดี joyfully ; gladly : ได้ยิน to hear *past tense* : ได้ยินกันมา according to tradition : ได้ยินเขาว่า it is generally reported that : ยินใจ to be content or satisfied with ; see พอใจ p. 263 : ยินดี, ยินมลาก to be glad ; to be pleased with ; to be joyful ; to rejoice : ยินยอม to consent ; to agree

with; to acquiesce in: ยินร้าย to be dissatisfied with; to hate; to be displeased, annoyed or angry with: เหล้ายิน gin; a liquor
made from juniper berries.

ยิน ๒   yin *n.* the beak (of a bird); the comb
(of a cock); a hooked goad used on elephants;
an image of the garuda carved in iron, sometimes with Vishnu seated on its back.

ยิบ   yip[6] *adj.* close-grained (as of structure);
finely woven (as fabrics in which fine threads
are woven closely): คันยิบๆ to itch severely;
see คัน p. 194.

ยิ้ม   yim[5] *v.* to smile: *n.* a smile: ยิ้ม-
แฉ่ง to smile broadly (as though overflowing
with happiness): ยิ้มย่อง to smile with a
heart full of joy or satisfaction: ยิ้มแต้ม
to smile with an open countenance, merrily
and gaily: ยิ้มละไม to smile most beautifully: ยิ้มหัว to smile and laugh at the
same time: *n.* a laughing smile.

ยิหวา   yi[6]-wah[2] *Jav. n.* life; heart.

ยี, ขยี   yee *v.* to apply pressure with rotating
force; to rub on; to anoint; to fondle; to
massage; to knead in order to loosen up the
mass: ยีเข้า, ยีหยอก to excite sexual passion
by touching, tickling or caressing.

ยี่   yee[3] *adj.* two: เดือนยี่ the second
lunar month.

ยี่ก่า   yee[3]-gkah[4] *n.* an aperture in an official's hat, for inserting a feather as an insignia of rank.

ยี่เก   yee[3]-gkay *n.* a burlesque theatrical
performance in which the actors are generally men, singing or speaking extemporaneously.

ยี่เข่ง *Thai* yee[3]-keng[4], คำฮ่อ *Laos, Chiengmai* (ต้น) *n. Lagerstroemia indica (Lythraceae)*, Indian lilac, a shrub with pretty pink,
white or lilac flowers falling in sprays. It
grows 6 to 8 feet high. It is said to be
a native of China, but it has long been cul-

tivated in south-eastern Asia. The Atlas
silk-worm moth, which has many food-plants,
will feed on it. Charcoal made from it is
used in Japan for thickening lacquer (cb.
p. 724: MCM. pp. 113, 208: Burk. p. 1299).

ยี่โถ (ต้น)   yee[3]-toh[2] *n. Nerium oleander
(Apocynaceae)*, oleander, a beautiful free-
flowering shrub 5 to 8 feet high, found wild
from Portugal to Persia. It has double bright
red flowers which grow in large clusters.
The plant is especially suited to a dry, sandy,
sunny locality (BURK. p. 1550: MCM. p. 114);
Nerium odorum is found from Persia to Japan; to the eye it ~~is rather~~ like the Mediterranean oleander but differs in having scented
flowers. Both are poisonous; both are cultivated in Malaysia for the sake of their
pretty flowers, which range in colour from
white to deep rose-pink (BURK. p. 1550: MCM.
pp. 226, 386); *N. oleander alba* has white
flowers and grows 5 to 8 feet high. There
are single and double varieties (MCM. p. 114):
ยี่โถฝรั่ง (ต้น) *Thevetia peruviana (neriifolia)
(Apocynaceae)*, a yellow-flowered shrub found
from Mexico and the West Indies to Brazil.
It was brought into cultivation in Europe in
1735, and from Europe was distributed to the
tropics in general, as a showy plant. It is
sometimes called the yellow oleander. After
reaching India it seems soon to have shown
signs of running wild. It was brought to
Thailand from Ceylon in 1843 or 1844, and
received a fancy name, 'rampoe' from a royal
princess. All parts of the plant are poisonous,
owing to the presence of a glucoside in the
latex. This glucoside is closely allied to that
of *Strophanthus* and acts as a heart-poison.
Another glucoside is present with it in the
seed; it gives a blue colour with hydrochloric
acid. Comparatively early, the American
Indian used the seed for criminal poisoning.
Modern writers report it as so used in India.
Fifteen to twenty grammes of green leaves
kill a horse, and an even less amount kills

cattle. In the West Indies half a leaf is administered as an emetic and purgative; a tincture of the bark has the same action; also the oil extracted from the seed. The latex sets to a resinous substance peculiarly rich in ash—47.9 per cent resins and 20.4 per cent ash. In Java Indian immigrants sometimes dry and smoke the leaves. Lucky beans are produced which are sometimes employed as charms or pendants (BURK. p. 2154: MCM. pp. 117, 462: V. P. p. 226).

ยฏู yee³-poo³ *n.* a mattress; a bed: พระ-ยฏู same for royalty.

ยียวน, ยียวน yee-yu-an *v.* to fondle; to caress; to arouse or excite sexual lust by caressing.

ยีสก (ปลา) yee³-sok⁴ *n. Probarbus jullieni,* a carp found in sandy-bottomed rivers of Rajaburi.

ยีสง see ถั่ว p. 384.

ยีสน (ปลา) yee³-son² *n.* a kind of salt-water fish belonging to the ray family.

ยีสาน, ยีส่าน yee³-sarn² *n.* a market; a place where goods are sold.

ยีสีบ yee³-sip⁴ *adj. lit.* "twice ten," *i. e.* twenty.

ยีสุ่น (ต้น) yee³-soon⁴ *n. Tagetes patula* (*Compositae*), the so-called African marigold of European gardens which has been in cultivation since 1596. There is a yellow dye—quercetagetin—in the flowers, and an oil in the seeds (BURK. p. 2120); *T. erecta,* an annual 2 to 3 feet high. The flowers are bright lemon-yellow, orange, etc. (MCM. pp. 135, 199: BURK. p. 2120).

ยีหร่า yee³-rah⁴ *Thai, Bangkok,* ผักชี, ผักชีฝรั่ง *Laos, Chiengmai,* ผักชี *Laos, Nakawn Panom* (ต้น) *n. Foeniculum vulgare* (*Umbelliferae*), fennel, an annual cultivated for its seed-like fruits, which are much used for flavouring in

confectionery, cookery and in the manufacture of a well known cordial. The young leaves of fennel serve as a flavouring raw, or more commonly cooked. The seeds also serve as a flavouring, and are distilled for their oil. They are officinal in all pharmacopoeias of all countries of Europe, and the oil is allowed to be used instead of seed in most of them. The seeds have a large place in the bazaars of the East and are imported. In oriental medicine fennel has been put on the market as anise; but typical fennel and typical aniseed have quite different odours (MCM. p. 344: Cb. p. 790: BURK. p. 1027).

ยีห้อ yee³-haw³ *Chin. n.* trade mark; guild; chop; company; group.

ยีหบ yee³-hoop⁴ *Laos, Chiengmai* (ต้น) *n. Talauma longifolia* (*Magnoliaceae*), a flowering shrub with large leaves and white flowers: *Thai, Bangkok, T. candellei* (*mutabilis*), a tree found from Moulmein, through western Malaysia; in the Peninsula wild in the mountains in the north, and cultivated in gardens on account of its aromatic flowers. The wood is too small and crooked to be useful (Cb. p. 25: BURK. p. 2120).

ยึด yurt⁶ *v.* to hold; to seize; to pull or hold back; to restrain; to take hold of and keep fast; to hold back by means of a cord: ผู้ยึดถือ a holder: ยึดตัวไว้ to hold in restraint: ยึดถือ to grasp, hold or keep (some important document, as a lease or license): ยึดทรัพย์ to attach (property): ยึดทรัพย์ของสัตรูในระหว่างสงคราม to capture the enemy's possessions in time of war: ยึดทรัพย์ที่จำนอง to foreclose.

ยึด, ยะยึด yurt³ *v.* to stretch out; to extend or expand; to be elastic: *adj.* extended: stretched out; long; prolonged; lasting; เดินให้เส้นยึด to stretch the muscles and blood vessels by walking: น้ำลายไหลยึด viscid, sticky, slimy, flowing saliva: ผ้ายึด elastic cloth: ยึดยาด, ยึดเยื้อ too long; almost endless; very long; longer than necessary; greatly prolonged: ยืดยาว prolonged: สายยืด an elastic cord.

ยืน, ยะยืน yurn v. to stand erect: adj. long; stable; lasting; continued: ยั่งยืน to be durable: คงยืนกระต่ายขาเดียว to make an irrevocable promise: ยืนกีด to stand in the way; to obstruct: ยืนเข่ง to stand on the toes; to tip-toe: ยืนตัวแข็ง to stand stolidly still: ยืนยง to be durable; to continue for a long time; to be permanent: ยืนยัน, ยืนคำ to attest or assert firmly (as an eye-witness); to insist emphatically or declare positively; to stand by one's word; to keep faith: ยืนยาม to stand on guard: อายุยืน having a long life.

ยื่น yurn[3] v. to stretch out; to project; to reach out too far; to put forward; to push out; to make an offer: ยื่นชื่อ to produce or hand in, in another's name (as in case of an absent witness): ยื่นบัญชี to render an account: ยื่นฟ้อง to institute a charge against; see ฟ้อง p. 605: ยื่นฟ้องต่อศาล to enter an action in court: ยื่นหมูยื่นแมว to make an interchange (of something) between two parties at the same time: ยื่นให้ to hand in, or to; to submit to.

ยืม yurm v. to borrow or lend; to take a loan; to loan legal: กู้ยืม to lend with interest: ขอยืม to ask to borrow; to ask as a loan: ของยืม borrowed or loaned property: ยืมใช้คงรูป to borrow and return unchanged: ยืมใช้สิ้นเปลือง to borrow and return in a transformed condition: ให้ยืมกัน to lend to each other: ให้ยืมเปล่า ๆ to lend (without interest).

ยื้อ yur[5] v. to take by force; to take possession of violently; to pull away from; to pull off; to seize in satisfaction of a debt: ยื้อแย่ง to take by force.

ยุ, ยุยง yoo[6] v. to incite or abet; to provoke to action; to lead into evil; to incite to mischief; to rouse or irritate; to encourage or

kindle (as anger); to sow (as discord); to excite dissatisfaction: ยุแหย่ to incite one against another.

ยุกกระบัตร, ยกกระบัตร yook[6]-gkra[4]-bat[4] n. the third governor of a town or province; the title of one acting in behalf of the defendent.

ยุกต์, ยุตต์ yook[6] P. S. adj. yoked; harnessed; joined; connected; attached; right; fitting; possessing; engaged in; devoted to; versed in (chd. p. 607).

ยุกติ, ยุตติ yook[6]-dti[4] P. S. n. use; application; aptness; fitness; propriety (chd. p. 607); connection; mixture; preparation; custom; trick; strategy; method.

ยุค yook[6] P. S. n. period of time; age; a pair; a couple; a generation; an age of the world (chd. p. 605); the yoke of a carriage or plough (chd. p. 606): ยุคเข็ญ a period or time of calamity (as famine, confusion, or war) (H. C. D. p. 331): ยุคศตวรรษปัจจุบัน the present century.

ยุคนธร, ยุคันธร, ยุคุนธร yoo[6]-kon-torn P. n. one of the seven vast concentric circles of rocks or mountains which surround Mount Meru, being the nearest to Meru (chd. p. 606).

ยุคล yoo[6]-kon P. S. n. twins; a pair: ยุคลบาท two feet; a pair of feet.

ยุคันต yoo[6]-kun-dta[4] P. n. the end of a yuga or age of the world (chd. p. 606); the end of a lifetime: ยุคันตวาต the great wind by which the destruction of the world is to be effected at the end of a yuga (chd. p. 606).

ยุง yoong n. mosquito: ปัดยุง to fan away the mosquitoes: ยุงก้นปล่อง the Anopheles mosquito: ยุงบัด (ต้น) Sida acuta (Malvaceae), a small shrub, up to 3 feet in height, found widely in the tropics; in the Malay Peninsula it occurs down both coasts. The leaves and roots may be boiled and used for poulticing the chest for coughs in the place of coriander in Malacca. The Chinese herbalists stock it in Malaya. It is medicinal generally in the East. Its fibre, like that of *S. rhombifolia*, is a possible substitute for jute (cb. p. 150: V. P. p. 230: BURK. p. 2024): ยุงรึ้น mosquitoes and gnats (in general).

ยุ่ง   yoong³ *adj.* entangled; entwined; confused; disordered; knotted: ผมยุ่งเหยิง unkempt or tangled hair: ยุ่งด้วย to be embroiled or complicated with: ยุ่งยาก complicated and difficult: ยุ่งย่าม meddlesome; interferring: ยุ่งยิ่ง intricate; confused; perplexing; complicated: ยุ่งเหยิง tangled; knotted; disordered: เรื่องยุ่งยิ่ง a complicated affair.

ยุ้ง   yoong⁵ *n.* granary; see ฉาง p. 268: คนท้องยุ้ง *slang* a great eater, or one with an insatiable thirst: ท้องยุ้งพุงกระสอบ *idiomatic* having an insatiable appetite as though the stomach were a granary and the belly a gunny bag.

ยุด   yoot⁶ *v.* to hold back; to detain; to cause to stop or stay; to jerk or pull; see ฉุด p. 270.

ยุต   yoo⁶-dta⁴ *P. S. adj.* being furnished or fitted with; yoked or harnessed together [(chd. p. 606).
ยุตต see ยุกต์ p. 677.

ยุตติ, ยุกติ   yoot⁶-dti⁴ *P. S. n.* use; application; aptness; fitness; propriety; rightness; truthfulness (chd. p. 607): *adj.* stopped; ceased; ended; done; disbanded; closed (as a discourse): ยุตติธรรม justice: อยุตติธรรม injustice: ยุตติธรรมธร one who upholds or regards justice and truthfulness.

ยุติ   yoo⁶-dti⁴ *S. n.* congregation; accumulation; union; a meeting-place; the act of meeting, uniting, joining, or coming together.

ยุทธ   yoot⁶-ta⁶ *P. n.* a war; a battle; a conflict; a fight: ยุทธกีฬา military sports; see กีฬา p. 109: ยุทธภูมิ, ยุทธรงค์ a battle field: ยุทธศาสตร์ the science of warfare or military tactics: ยุทธวิธี military tactics

or methods: ยุทธวินัย military ethics; principles or laws governing warfare.

ยุทธน   yoot⁶-ta⁶-na⁶ *n.* a war; warfare; a fight: ยุทธนาการ manner, methods, mode or style of waging a battle or war: ยุทธนา-ธิการ the War Department; the Ministry of Defence.

ยุบ   yoop⁶ *v.* to diminish in size (as a swelling); to be lowered or lessened; to subside; to give way or sink under a heavy weight; to beat out of normal shape; to cut down or off; to abolish or abandom (as a position); to give up; to melt down (as may be done with stolen jewelry): ยุบยอบ to lessen; to be diminished; to cause to subside: ยุบยับ to be broken, damaged, injured or ruined; to come to extreme poverty.

ยุบยิบ   yoop⁶-yip⁶ *adj.* minute; exceedingly small; very closely woven (as fabrics); too small to be easily seen (as objects seen through a microscope).

ยุบล   yoo⁶-bon *n.* news; incidents; events; a story; the contents of a letter, lecture or discourse: แจ้งยุบล to declare all of the events or incidents of an affair.

ยุพ, ยุว   *P.* yoo⁶-pa⁶ *n.* a young man; a lad: *adj.* young; adolescent (chd. p. 607): ยุพยง approaching maturity; youthful; young; beautiful (used in regard to girls or women): ยุพเยาว์ young (used in regard to girls): ยุพราช, ยุพราชา, ยุวราช, ยุวราชา *lit.* "the young king," *i. e.* a royal prince; a Crown Prince associated with the King in the government (chd. p. 607): ยุพเรศ a queen or young princess; also used in regard to girls in general.

ยุพดี, ยุวดี   yoop⁶-pa⁶-dee *n.* a young girl; a maiden; a lass.

ยุพา   yoo⁶-pah *adj.* young and handsome: ยุพาพาล, ยุพาพิน *lit.* "approaching puberty," *i. e.* an adolescent girl; a maiden.

ยุ่มย่าม　　yoom³-yarm³ *adv.* disorderly;
coarsely (in conduct); ungracefully; awkwardly; inelegantly: กินยุ่มย่าม to eat in an
impolite or unbecoming manner: เดินยุ่มย่าม
to walk rudely, or in a disorderly manner.

ยุ่ย　　yoo-ie³ *adj.* fragile; friable; crumbling
to pieces: ความยุ่ย quality or condition of
being fragile; fragility: คนยุ่ย a spendthrift: ยุ่ย (1) breakable; brittle; frangible; easily pulverized (as clay, soil, chalk or
soap-stone): (2) carious; rotten; friable (as
disintegrated tissue): (3) softened; made
pulpy, or tender by processes of digestion or
cooking (as food or meat), or by grinding
with mechanical means (as bamboo into paper
pulp): (4) deteriorated; frayed; worse for
wear (as silk): (5) fluffy; downy (as cotton
fibre or filaments): เปื่อยยุ่ย rotten into a
softened condition (as too ripe fruit): ผุจนยุ่ย
to become friable from dry-rot or from the
ravages of time.

ยุ้ย　　yoo-ie⁵ *adj.* bulging; puffed out; inflated; swelled out; protuberant: ท้องยุ้ย
pot-bellied; obese.

ยุรบาท,ยุรบาตร,ยะยุรบาท,ยุรบาท　　yoo⁶-
ra⁶-bart⁴ *v.* to travel on foot; to walk or go.

ยุรยาตร, ยุรยาตร, ยวรยาตร, ยั่วรยาตร
yoo⁶-ra⁶-yart³ *v.* to travel, go or walk in a
regal or pompous manner (as with a retinue).

ยุว see ยุพ p. 678: ยุวราช, ยุวราชา see ยุพราช
p. 678.

ยุวด, ยุพดี　　yoo⁶-wa⁶-dee *n.* a lass; a
maiden; a young girl.

ยุหบาตร see พยุหบาตร p. 563.

ยู, สายยู　　yoo *n.* a hasp; an iron ring;
rings passing from a staple and secured by a
padlock or wooden bolt; a common fastening
for doors or gates.

ยู่　　yoo³ *v.* to be made blunt, notched, or to
have the keen edge dulled by striking a hard

substance: *adj.* blunt; obtuse; blunted (as
with the edge smoothed off); see บิ่น p. 483:
ยู่ยี่ dinted; creased; distorted in shape;
bruised; battered: หน้ายู่ยี่ a distorted, half-
crying face.

ยูง (นก)　　yoong *n.* Burmese peafowl, *Pavo
muticus* (Gaird. J. S. S. IX, 1, p. 12): ยูง,
ยางยูง, ยางมันหมู *Thai, Pattani* (ต้น) *Dipterocarpus grandiflorus* (*Dipterocarpaceae*),
a big tree widely distributed; it occurs from
the Andaman Islands and Tenasserim to the
Philippine Islands. It is usually a tree of low
hills and ridges up to 2,000 feet above sea-
level. The timber is much cut in the Andaman Islands. It enters the lumber market in
the Philippine Islands as "apitong"; and, being the most abundant of its genus, probably
supplies the greatest part of that wood, which
is commonly used for ordinary construction
and medium grade furniture. There is oleo-
resin containing a more or less volatile oil
(Burk. p. 843); *D. duperreanus* (cb. p. 135: V. P.
p. 230).

ยูถะ　　yoo-ta⁴ *n.* a herd or flock of animals
(chd. p. 606); see ฝูง p. 556.

ยูถิกา, โยถิกา　　yoo-ti⁴-gkah *P. S. n.* a
species of jasmine (chd. p. 606); *Jasminum
auriculatum* (*Oleaceae*); *Randia siamensis*
(*Rubiaceae*) (V.P. p. 67); *Rauwolfia serpentina*
(*Apocynaceae*) (V. P. p. 54); *Desmodium cephalotoides* (*Leguminosae*) (V. P. p. 54).

ยูปะ　　yoo-bpa⁴ *P. S. n.* a pillar; a column;
a sacrificial post (chd. p. 606); a palace:
ชัยสตมภ์ a pillar or column erected as a memorial of some victory.

ยูษะ　　yoo-sa⁴ *S. n.* juice (chd. p. 606); vegetable soups.

เย้　　yay⁵ *adj.* leaning or inclined to one
side; near toppling over from decay; deviating from the perpendicular: เดินโย้เย้ to
walk reeling from side to side.

เย ๆ   yay-yay *onomat.* the long-drawn-out sound of crying of peevish children.

เยง, แยง   yeng *v.* to fear; to be afraid of; to respect; see กลัว p. 60.

เยซู (พระ)   yay-soo *Eng. n.* Jesus Christ.

เย็น   yen *n.* evening; dusk: *adj.* cool; cold; fresh (for weather): ขอให้อยู่เย็นเป็นสุข may joy and happiness attend you: ใจเย็น estranged; indifferent; cold towards another; having an absence of love for; see เฉย p. 271: ตะวันเย็น a setting sun: น้ำเย็น cold water: เย็นใจ to be refreshed; to be satisfied with; to have a sense of happiness, tranquility, and freedom from anxiety; to be light-hearted: ลมเย็น a cold or cool breeze.

เย็บ   yep⁶ *v.* to sew, stitch (as cloth), or string together (as flowers); to unite or fasten together by means of a needle and thread; to bind (as a book): ช่างเย็บรองเท้า a shoe-maker: ช่างเย็บเสื้อ a tailor; a seamstress.

เยภุยยะ   yay-poo-ie-ya⁶ *P. n.* abundance; preponderance (chd. p. 601): *adj.* abundant; เยภุยยนัย various methods, ways or means at hand: เยภุยยสิกา an incident which often occurs or takes place; a reoccurring incident, or occasion.

เย้ย   yur-ie⁵ *v.* to mock, ridicule or deride; to speak or act in a contemptuous manner.

เยอ   yur *v.* to praise, extol, laud or do honour to; see ชม p. 278.

เย่อ   yur³ *v.* to tug, jerk, pull at or drag by force; to tear off from; see ฉุด p. 270: เย่อลาก to drag away violently; to kidnap or abduct: เล่นชักกะเย่อ to play tug-of-war.

เยอว   yaa-oh *onomat.* from the sound made by the paddlers of long royal ceremonial boats, during the intervals in which their paddles are held up out of the water.

เย่อหยิ่ง   yur³-ying⁴ *adj.* proud; ostentatious; pretentious; puffed up; pompous; self-important.

เยอะ, เยอะแยะ   yur⁶ *adj.* much; abundant; very many; ample; in great abundance.

เยา   yow *adj.* low (in price); insignificant; little; unimportant; see น้อย • p. 446.

เย้า   yow⁵ *v.* to pat, stroke, caress or fondle; to vex; to tease or annoy; to jest or joke with in order to induce laughter: *n.* a mountain tribe of northern Thailand. According to the traditions of the Yao, they originally lived in Nanking, China, and, on the capture of Nanking, the inhabitants emigrated to Law Chang Chuan close to Canton (for further particulars see J.S.S. XIX, 3, p. 83): เย้า-หยอก to jest or joke with while caressing (as with little children).

เยาว   yow-wa⁶ *adj.* young; youthful (about 10 to 12 years of age); still a minor: ทรง-พระเยาว์ still a child or minor (used in reference to princes): เยาวพาณี a species of balsam used medicinally: เยาวภาค pertaining to the age of a minor or a young person; youthful: เยาวมาลย์ *lit.* "a budding or blooming flower," *i. e.* a lass; a young girl: เยาวยอด *lit.* "one reaching the limit in age of a minor," *i. e.* one coming of age: เยาวโยช one possessing youth; youthfulness: เยาว-เรศ corrupted form of ยุพเรศ p. 678: เยาว-ลักษณ์ having youthful features.

เยาวน   yow-wa⁶-na⁶ *S. n.* youthfulness; adolescence; puberty (S. E. D. p. 589).

เยาะ   yaw⁶ *v.* to deride; to jeer; to chide; to ridicule or laugh at: เยาะเย้ย to ridicule or make sport of contemptuously: เยาะเล่น to jest playfully; to joke or jeer; see เย้ย p. 680.

เยิง ๑   yerng *n.* a forest; woods; a thicket; a jungle.

เยิง ๒   yerng *Cam. pron.* we; us.

เยิน   yern *adj.* broken, dinted, chipped, nicked or damaged (at the edges): เยิน-จนยับเยิน flogged unmercifully: ยับเยิน completely damaged : ยู่เยิน blunted ; nicked : เยินยอ in a praising or laudatory manner.

เยิ่น yern[3] *adj.* long; extended; prolonged; protracted; lengthy : คนพูดเยิ่น a lengthy talker or speaker : เยิ่นเยื้อ very long; too long or extended; being far too protracted : สะพานเยิ่น a sagging bridge (from the excessive length and weight) : เยิ่นอ่อน flexible, because of the great length.

เยิบ yerp[3] *adv.* slowly; gently; regularly; in order (as paddlers of a boat).

เยิ้ม yerm[5] *adj.* oozing; flowing gradually (as sap from a tree); wet or moistened (with secretions); excessively wet or bathed with (as an ulcer with purulent secretions).

เยีย ye-ah *v.* to do or perform (in a mocking manner) : ไก่เยีย a cock which resembles a hen : เยียใด why? when? how? how to do? what can be done? เยียมั่ง to feign affluence : เยียใหญ่ to assume self-importance; to exhibit boastfulness; to pretend undue greatness.

เยี่ยง, เยื่อง yee-ang[3] *n.* a pattern; an example; manners; established usages : *adj.* like; as; such as : เยี่ยงอย่างโบราณ according to ancient customs or manners : เอาเยี่ยงอย่าง to imitate the example (of others).

เยี่ยงผา, เลียงผา yee-ang-pah[2] *n.* the goat-antelope or serow. In the districts of Petchaburi and Pran it is called โคร่า (p. 217).

เยียดยัด, ยัดเยียด yee-at[3]-yut[6] *v.* to be massed or crowded together; to be compactly or closely jammed together (as people in a crowd, or as steerage passengers) : เยียดยัดกันแน่น squeezed together to the fullest capacity.

เยียน yee-an *v.* to make a friendly visit; to call upon; to go to visit (as a friend).

เยียบ yee-ap[3] *adj.* damp and cool (as in a cave); sheltered and chilly : เยียบเย็น, เย็นเยียบ piercing, excessive cold : เยียบเย็นใจ a sense of loneliness, fear or terror (as in a solitary place).

เยี่ยม ๑ yee-am[3] *v.* to protrude the head or face (as from a window); to peep or look out; to appear, or come out in front of (as from a curtain on a stage); see ชะโงก p. 285 : ไปเยี่ยมเยียน to go calling; to call upon : เยี่ยมจากหน้าต่าง to look out from a window (as to a crowd below) : เยี่ยมเยียน, เยี่ยมเยือน to call upon in a friendly manner; to visit or call upon friends : เยี่ยม ๆ มอง ๆ to peep out; to look around from time to time or repeatedly (as though flirting) : เยี่ยมไข้ to make a professional visit or call.

เยี่ยม ๒, ยิ่ง yee-am[3] *adj.* the very best; beyond comparison; par excellence : *adv.* very.

เยียร์ yee-ah *adj.* pretty; beautiful; fine : ดูงามเยียร์ยง most beautiful or handsome to behold : เยียร์ยง very pretty; especially fine; most handsome.

เยียรบับ yee-ah-ra[6]-bup[4] *n.* a kind of figured cloth woven with golden threads.

เยี่ยว yee-oh *adj.* beautiful; handsome : *conj.* if; provided that; perchance : เยี่ยวยง most beautiful; exquisitely handsome.

เยี่ยว yee-oh[3] *v.* to pass water; to urinate : *n.* urine; see ปัสสาวะ p. 521 : กะเพาะเยี่ยว the bladder : กลิ่นเยี่ยว the odour of urine : เยี่ยวแตก involuntary passing of urine; incontinence : เยี่ยวไม่ออก inability to pass urine : เยี่ยวหยด to pass urine in drops.

เยี่ยวยา yee-oh-yah *v.* to cause to heal; to be cured; to support in time of need; to use means to prolong life or extend the usefulness of (as in patching up a boat).

เยื่อ yur-ah[3] *n.* a membrane; thin skin; a pellicle; a film; a fibrous sheath; a covering or lining (as of cavities) : เยื่อเคย shrimp paste : เยื่อไม้ไผ่, กระพี้ไม้ไผ่ the delicate inside film or pellicle of young bamboo : เยื่อใย *lit.* " inner fibrous membrane," *i.e.* bonds, feeling of love, attachment for, or anxiety towards : เยื่อร่างแห peritoneum *anatomy* : เยื่อหุ้มกระดูก periosteum.

เยือ yur-ah[5] *v.* to be stable, durable or permanent; to stand or last a long period of time; see คง p. 176.

เยือก yur-ak[3] *adj.* cold, clammy, moist (as the skin in a condition of collapse); swaying; shaking; vibrating or agitated (as leaves or coconut fronds by the wind) : เยือกเย็น a feeling of chilly coldness : เยือกเย็นใจ a cold feeling from fear or dread : ลมพัด-เยือกเย็น a cool refreshing breeze.

เยื่อง see เยื้อง p. 681.

เยื่อง, เยื้อง yur-ang[5] *v.* to go, or be diagonally across from; to deviate from the direct course or line (towards a point) : *adj.* deflected from the direct line; turning aside : พูดยักเยื้อง to seek a false excuse for concealment; to resort to subterfuges : เยื้องกัน ill-fitting; inconsistent : เยื้องกราย to walk with a swaying side to side motion and undue swinging of the arms : เยื้องยัก to change the place (of something) continually, back and forth.

เยือน yur-an *v.* to go to visit; to call upon in a friendly manner : ไปเยือน, ไปเยี่ยม to go for a visit. [p. 595.

เยือน yur-an[5] *v.* to say; to speak; see พูด

แย yaa *adj.* capricious; whimsical; quarrelsome : คนต่อแย a fickle, whimsical person : เด็กขี้แย a child given to crying.

แย่ yaa[3] *v.* to crouch by bending the knees : *adj.* exhausted or fatigued; being in a bad condition, or in great trouble; excessive fatigue : ใจย่อแย่ weary at heart : เดินย่อแย่ to walk in an exhausted manner : เต็มแย่ overburdened by a heavy load; being excessively weary with trouble or hardships : แบกเต็มแย่ to carry a full or excessive load on the shoulder.

แย้ yaa[5] *n.* an edible wood lizard; the ground lizard, *Liolepis belliana* (Gaird. J. S. S. I, 1, p. 40). These lizards are found in warm dry soils. The big ones seem to stay below ground during bad weather stopping up the entrance from beneath. They run very fast and have the habit of elevating the head and front part of the body to observe anything at a distance. They form an important article of food for peasants both in northern and southern Thailand.

แยก yaak[3] *v.* to separate, sever or disjoin; to choose, and put aside what is wanted; to separate into small parcels : แตกแยก to be divided, separated or dispersed : ทางแยก a fork in a road : ผัวเมียแยกกัน a family separation; a divorce : แยกกันไป to go separately (as in a hunting trip) : แยกเขี้ยว-ยิงฟัน to show the fangs and teeth (as a dog or tiger); a simile denoting revenge, retaliation or vengeance : แยกธาตุ to assay (as minerals); to analyse (as soils) : แยกย้าย to separate (from others) and go elsewhere : แยกยัก to put aside secretly : แยกแย้ง *lit.* "to sever by violence," *i. e.* disputing; opposing; contending; contentious : แยกแยะ to elucidate, explain or throw light upon (a condition or problem) : แยกหมู่แยกคณะ to break off or separate from a group, sect, or company.

แยง yaang *v.* to prod, poke or insert into; to excite or incite; to look or peek from a hiding-place : คนยุแยง a trouble-maker who incites others : ยุแยง to incite or stimulate to action : แยงยล to look at stealthily : แยงรู, แยงดู to prod or run a stick or probe into a hole or sinus : แยงหู to insert an instrument into the ear (as for cleaning) : วัดแยงมุม to measure the diagonal corners in order to make exactly square.

แย่ง yaang[3] *v.* to snatch, grab or take by force; to rob or plunder; to cause to scatter or disperse : ช้อแย่ง to snatch or grab away by force : แย่งกัน to scramble for (as beggars for pennies thrown to them); to dispute about the possession of (as heirs regarding an inheritance): แย่งเงิน to deprive of money by force: แย่งมรดก to take unlawful possession of an inheritance.

แย้ง   yaang[5] *v.* to contradict; to oppose; to speak in opposition to: การโต้แย้ง an altercation; a dispute: แย้งกัน to dispute a point: แย้งกันกับ *legal* inconsistent with: แย้งพินัยกรรม์ *legal* to dispute a will.

แยงแย่ (นั่ง)   yaang-yaa[3] *v.* to squat with the knees widely separated.

แยงแย้   yaang-yaa[5] *n.* a vegetable climber.

แยบ   yaap[3] *n.* artifice; wile; a secret art; a concealed plan; a trick: พูดแยบคาย to speak in an evasive manner: ยอบแยบ nearly all gone; poor; down to the last extremity: แยบคาย wisely; properly; suitably; appropriately; reasonably: แยบยนตร์ trick, wile, secret or sly procedure; artifice; a snare.

แย้ม   yaam[5] *v.* to begin to open (into a flower); to open slightly; to be on the verge of speaking or laughing: แย้มกลีบ the first opening petals of a flower: แย้มขึ้ม smiling; gay; cheerful (of expression): แย้มพระโอฐ to open the mouth prior to speaking (used for royalty).

แยแส   yaa-saa[2] *v.* to assume concern for; to pay attention to; to be interested in or keen for: ไม่แยแส to be indifferent; to pay no attention.

แยะ   yaa[6] *v.* to split or crack (as hard-baked ground); to open; to burst asunder; to break or tear off from (as a limb of a tree): *adj.* very many; much; ample; in great quantities; plenty: คนมากันแยะ a great crowd has gathered: ลูกไม้สุกแยะ great quantities of ripe fruit.

โย (พูด)   yoh *v.* to speak in an irritating, challenging or defiant manner as though to incite a fight: *adj.* fat; plump; bulging (as

the cheeks): โยเย poor; wretched; worthless; obnoxious (to others); see เกเร p. 121.

โย้   yoh[5] *v.* to lift, drag or move, by leverage, from one place to another: *adj.* leaning to one side; protruding or overlapping (as irregular teeth): โย้เย้ inclined to lean, stagger or sway from one side to the other (as in walking when under the influence of intoxicants).

โยก   yoke[3] *v.* to sway from side to side (as forest trees in a storm); to move or push from side to side so as to loosen (as a post): คนโยกเยก one unstable in principle: พื้นโยก loose teeth: โยกโคลง to sway or cause to rock (as a boat): โยกย้าย to change from place to place: โยกเยก tottering; loose in the foundation or socket: โยกโย้ to equivocate, evade or elude the point at issue irrelevantly, or to dispute about trifles (in order to kill time).

โยกตร์, โยตต์   yoke[3] *P. S. n.* any instrument for tying or fastening; a rope; a girdle; a halter; the thongs by which an animal is attached to the pole of a carriage (S. E. D. p. 854).

โยค   yoh-ka[6] *P. S. n.* yoga (from the root "yug" meaning to join); a union; a junction. It signifies the union of the body of the disciple with the visible world, and of his spirit with cosmic consciousness. Yoga has also the sense of a yoke, attachment, combination, contact with, relation or discipline which the student must undergo in order to reach happiness and heaven. The body of the yogi is the universe (The Lives of a Bengal Lancer, Yeates Brown, p. 291). A species of asceticism among the Hindus, which consists in a complete abstraction from all worldly objects, by which the votary expects to obtain union with the universal spirit, and to acquire superhuman faculties (web.); a mystical philosophical system (Ala. p. 33); a system of mental training that will lead the soul of the votary to unite with the Supreme Spirit; a method; a means; a plan; devotion; mental concentration; attachment (chd. p. 604); an omen; luck; fortune: โยคจักษุ mental vision by means of meditation: โยคนิทรา meditation-sleep; a state of half meditation and half sleep: โยคมายา magic; the magical power of abstract meditation: โยคยาตร the road or way to union with the Supreme Spirit; the way of profound meditation: โยคักเขม security; Nirvana (chd. p. 604): โย-คาพจร, โยคาพวจร an ascetic mendicant; a priest; one given to perseverance; one who practices mental concentration (implying a Buddhist priest): โยคลัทธิ practices and principles of yoga.

โยคเกณฑ์ yoke[3]-gken *n.* the calculation or divination of auspicious and inauspicious days of the month (according to the lunar asterisms).

โยคยะ yoke[3]-kah[6]-ya[6] *S. n.* conveyances; carriages (chd. p. 604); means of transportation: *adj.* worthy; suitable; proper; fitting; adapted to.

โยคยา yoke[3]-kah[6]-yah *P. n.* preparation; training; practice (chd. p. 604).

โยคินี yoh-ki[6]-nee *P. n.* a female ascetic.

โยคี yoh-kee *P. n.* an ascetic (chd. p. 604); a pilgrim or one wandering through the forest; one given to perseverance, or diligence in rightness; a certain sect of ascetic bonzes.

โยง yong *v.* to tow; to drag through the water with a rope; to tie or fasten together; to separate the grains of rice by stirring with a spoon or stick while cooking: เชือกระโยง shrouds; guy ropes for a mast or smoke-stack: ผูกโยง to tie or tether to a stake or post (as horses or elephants): เรือโยง a boat for towing purposes: เล่นอยู่โยง to play catcher having a fixed place as base: โยงมื่อ to

tie the hands (as to a post): โยงเรือ to tie boats together prior to towing: โยงเสา to make fast to a post.

โย่ง yong[3] *adj.* too tall or high; top-heavy: สูงโย่ง too high, or reaching too far up (suggesting danger of collapsing, falling or sinking).

โย่ง ๆ yong[3]-yong[3] *adj.* striding: เดิน-โย่ง ๆ to walk with strides.

โยงโย่, ยงโย่ yong-yoh[3] *v.* to touch the floor with the hands without lifting the feet off the floor; to stand on all-fours.

โยชก yoh-choke[6] *S. n.* one who yokes or harnesses animals; an arranger; a preparer (S. E. D. p. 858).

โยชน์ yote[3] *P. S. n.* a measure of length (chd. p. 604); a length or distance of 400 *sen*, or about 9.94 statute miles (S. E. D. p. 858).

โยชนา yoh-cha[6]-nah *P. n.* a Pali grammatical treatise.

โยตต์ see **โยกตร์** p. 683.

โยถิกา see **ยูถิกา** p. 679.

โยทะกา yoh-ta[6]-gkah *n.* a large hook; an anchor.

โยธ, โยธา ๑ yoh-ta[6] *P. S. n.* a warrior; soldiers; troops; a battle; a fight; war (S.E.D. p. 858): พลโยธา an army; troops: โยธา-ทัพ an army: โยธาหาญ an army; a squadron or battalion.

โยธา ๒ yoh-tah *n.* work performed by physical strength (as building or construction by coolie labour).

โยธิน yoh-tin *P. S. n.* warriors; fighters; soldiers, or conquerors (S. E. D. p. 858).

โยน yone *v.* to throw, pitch, cast or swing, and then let go (as a heavy weight): โยน-กลองให้คนอื่นตี *idiomatic* to shift responsibility to other shoulders: โยนขึ้น to toss up:

โยนเชือก to throw a rope: โยนน้ำ to throw into the water: โยนให้ to throw to or at (as coins to beggars).

โยน ๒, โยนก yone *P. n.* a foreigner; a barbarian; a Greek (chd. p. 605); the people of Bayap Circle of northern Thailand; mountain tribes.

โยนิโส yoh-ni[6]-soh[2] *P. adv.* adroitly; suitably; really; wisely (chd. p. 605): โยนิ-โสมนสิการ enlightened or philosophical attention or devotion of the mind; the act of investigating in a wise or appropriate manner.

โยนิ yoh-nee *P. n.* the female organ (H.C.D. p. 377); the vagina; source; origin; form of birth or existence; knowledge; wisdom (chd. p. 605); pudenda feminae.

โยพพนะ yope[3]-pa[6]-na[6] *P. n.* youth (chd. p. 604); adolescence: โยพพนมัท pride or arrogance of youth.

โยม yome *n.* parishioners; people attached to a temple or related to a priest; a parent (used as a personal pronoun by Buddhist priests): โยมวัด those serving the bonzes or performing necessary deeds in temple grounds: โยมสงฆ์ one, or those who serve or attend to the wants of a Buddhist priest: โยมอุปถาก one who has made up his mind to be attached as a servant to a priest: ศิษย์-โยม disciples of a Buddhist priest.

โยเย yoh-yay *v.* to be given to crying, whining or fretting: เด็กโยเย a child given to pouting, crying or being peevish.

โยเย yoh[5]-yay[5] *adj.* leaning; tilting; deflected from the perpendicular.

โยโส yoh-soh[2] *adj.* annoying (to others); roguish; vexatious; troublesome; boastful; haughty; arrogant.

ใย yai *n.* filaments; vegetable threads, fibre or down: *adj.* pretty; beautiful; good-looking; fair; clear and attractive (of complexion): เชื่อใย secret bonds of love; liasons: เหนียวเป็นใยเป็นยวง glutinous; sticky; adhesive; viscous (as the exudation from the bark of some trees, or as some kinds of fruit).

ใยยอง, ใยเชื่อ yai-yaung *n.* strands (as of a cobweb): *adj.* fine; soft; delicate; frail; fragile: ใยไฟ soot-covered cobwebs: ใย-แมงมุม cobwebs.

ไย yai *adv.* why; what (is the use of); wherefore? ไยจะต้องไป why need one go?

ไย่, ยะไย่, ยะไย้ yai[3] *adj.* blurred; indistinct; misty (used in regard to eyesight).

ไยดี yai-dee *v.* to be eager; to wish for; to hanker after; to want or desire; to take pleasure in.

ไยไพ yai-pai *v.* to ridicule; to mock; to jest or jeer; to find fault with; to blame: เย้ยไยไพ to ridicule severely; to laugh at.

ร

ร The thirty-fifth consonant of the Thai alphabet, a low class letter of which there are twenty-four, *viz.* ค, ฅ, ม, ง, ช, ซ, ฌ, ญ, ย, ฑ, ฒ, ฑ, ฌ, น, ณ, พ, ฟ, ภ, ม, ร, ล, ว, ฬ, ฮ. รอเรือ, รอรักษา are the designating names of this letter, equivalent to the English "r." It is used both as a prefix and a suffix in Thai, Pali, and Sanskrit words. When occurring double after a consonant, it is pronounced "un" as in กรรไตร: if singly is equal to "orn" as in กร.

รก rok[6] *n.* placenta; afterbirth: *adj.* scattered about in disorderly fashion; obstructing;

cluttered; strewn about (as sweepings or shavings): รก (ไม้) fibrous growth on branches, fronds, fruit, or palms and some other species of tree (as รกมะตัน, รกมะพร้าว): ที่รกหนาม a place over-grown with bramble bushes or thorns: บ้านรก a cluttered up compound or house: ป่ารก a jungle with dense undergrowth: รกใจ to have the mind cluttered with questions, worries, or problems: รกชัฏ intertwined confusedly; tangled; interlaced (as bushes, grass and vines in a dense forest): รกฟ้า *Thai, Kanburi, Korat* and *Krabin*, ฮกฟ้า *N. Laos*, เบ้ยก or เชื้อก *E. Laos*, สิพิแคล *Karen, Chiengmai*, จะลี *Khmer, Buriram*, คลี้ *Sui, Surin*, กอง *Thai, Utaradit* and *Sukotai* (ต้น) *Terminalia alata* (*Combretaceae*), the best species of a large genus of trees or woody sprawlers found throughout the tropics (BURK. p. 2134); *T. tomentosa* (cb. p. 600: V. P. p. 235): รกราก place of origin or birth; fatherland; home land: รกร้าง deserted and overgrown with jungle; desolate; ownerless; ruinous: รกเรี้ยว to be greatly overgrown (with grass or climbers); to be uncared for or unkempt: รกเรื้อรัง to be disorderly, desultory, or deserted for a long time: สนามรก an ill-kept or untidy lawn: หญ้าขึ้นรก to be overgrown with grass.

รง, รงทอง *Thai, Kaw Chang* (ต้น) rong *n. Garcinia hanburyi* (*Guttiferae*), the gamboge-tree which is the source of Thai and Cambodian gamboge. It is known to grow wild in Chantaburi. Cambodia and Lower Cochin-China also produce gamboge. A Chinese traveller of 1295-7 was the first to write about gamboge. He classified it with yellow substances used medicinally. In the East gamboge is only used as a pigment. It comes into market in various shapes, due to the moulds in which it is allowed to set, after running from the spiral tapping incisions made in the bark, or to being pressed into cakes when half set. It makes the golden yellow ink of Thailand, which is used for writing on locally made books of black paper. A little is used in Europe in water-colour painting, and more in making a golden spirit-varnish, or gold lacquer for coating metals, known as pear-ground lacquer, used in association with gold-dust. Gamboge paint is an emulsion in water. There is a gum (cb. p. 115 : V. P. p. 236 : MCM. p. 411 : BURK. p. 1050).

รงค์, รํงค์ rong *P. n.* colour; paint; dye; hue; a theatre; a stage; a play-house; sexual love; lust; a battle-field (chd. p. 401): รงคการก a painter; an artist: รงคจร actors or actresses: รงคเทวดา the goddess of amusements, gayeties, mirth, and pleasures: รงคพัสดุ any colouring substance; paint; dyes: รงคภูมิ a platform; a stage; a theatre; a battle-field; a lawn: รงคมณฑป a playhouse; a theatre: รงควารางคนา a ballet dancer: รงคศาลา a theatre; a ball-room or dancing pavilion (S. E. D. p. 862).

รงคาชีวะ, รงคาชีพ rong-kah-chee-wa[6] *S. n.* a professional actor (S. E. D. p. 862).

รงคุ์ rong *P. n.* a species of deer, or antelope (chd. p. 401).

รงรอง rong-raung *adj.* beautiful; pretty; handsome.

รจนา rote[6]-chja[4]-nah *P. n.* the act of composing, preparing, making, forming, or arranging (S. E. D. p. 860).

รจเรข, รจเลข rote[6]-chja[4]-rake[3] *n.* writing; composition: *adj.* beautiful.

รจิต ra[6]-chjit[4] *P. v.* to prepare; to compose; to arrange (chd. p. 397): *adj.* beautiful.

รช ra[6]-cha[6] *P. n.* dust; dirt; sediment: รโชหรณ์ *lit.* "carrier of sediment," *i. e.* water (chd. p. 400).

รชก, รํชก ra[6]-cha[6]-gka[4] *P. n.* washerman; a dyer of cloth (chd. p. 398).

รชต, รัชต, รัชฏ ra[6]-cha[6]-dta[4] *P. n.* silver (chd. p. 399): *adj.* made of silver; silvery.

รชนิ, รชนี ra⁶-cha⁶-ni⁶ *P. S. n.* night; tumeric; red lac; an epithet for Lady Uma, the consort of Siva (S. E. D. p. 863): รชนิกร *lit.* "one that denotes or indicates night-time," *i. e.* the moon: รชนิจร *lit.* "a night-rover," *i. e.* a thief; one wandering about during the night; a night-watcher; the moon: รชนิขล dew: รชนิบดี, รชนิมุข evening; dusk; sunset: รชนิรมณ์ the moon.

รชนีย ra⁶-cha⁶-nee-ya⁶ *P. n.* lust, or that which is wrong, bad, evil, obscure, unexplainable (chd. p. 399).

รณ ๑ ron *P. n.* noise; sound; voice (of singing or roaring) (S. E. D. p. 864).

รณ ๒ ron *P. S. v.* to fight; to wage war: *n.* a fight; an enemy; sin; turmoil; war; battle: *adj.* sinful; bad; wrong (S.E.D. p. 863): รณกรรม, รณการ the act of fighting; a battle; a conflict: รณเกษตร, รณภู, รณภูมิ, รณสถาน, รณรงค์ a battle-field or ground (S. E. D. p. 864): รณโคจร one, or those who are engaged in a fight, skirmish or war: รณจักรี์ a martial king: รณดุรย์ a battle drum; a drum used as a signal in war: รณธุรา, รณาเชียร, รณรงค์ the heavy burden of a war or battle: รณ-ปรีย์ a warlike person; a lover of war or contests: รณมุขย์, รณมุรต, รณเคียร the front line of troops; the battle front; the commander of a battalion or company of troops: รณรณก an anxious regret for some beloved object; anxiety (for loved ones on the battle-field): รณวาทย์ a war-song; a soldier's musical instrument; a marching tune or song; a war-time tune; a soldiers' band, or instruments of music: รณศึกษา the art or science of war; education in military tactics: รณสดมภ์ war or battle, regarded as a sacrifice: รณสหาย *lit.* "comrades in a war," *i. e.* those allied, confederated or leagued together in waging a war: รณสังกุล the confusion or noise of battle; a skirmish or tumultuous combat: รณสัชชา military accoutrements: รณางค์ implements of warfare for warriors (as swords,

spears, bayonets, etc.): รณางคน์ a battle-field or arena: รณางคร the front line of troops; the vanguard of an army in a battle.

รด rote⁶ *v.* to anoint; to pour on; to sprinkle (with water): เครื่องรดน้ำ sprinklers; pumps; watering appliances: รดน้ำ to solemnize by the pouring on of consecrated water (as in weddings, as a blessing): รดน้ำผัก to water a vegetable garden: รดน้ำศพ anointing the dead (as a token of respect): รดสวน to water the garden: ลายรดน้ำ a form of Thai art where the figure is traced in gold thread or gold wire on a lacquer base.

รต, รัต ra⁶-dta⁴ *P. S. v.* to enjoy oneself; to delight in (chd. p. 401); to be pleased with, or take pleasure in: *n.* happiness; pleasure; attachment; comfort (S. E. D. p. 867).

รตนะ, รัตน ra⁶-dta⁴-na⁶ *n.* a jewel; a precious or desirable article (chd. p. 402).

รติ, รดี, ฤดี ra⁶-dti⁴ *P.S. n.* pleasure; love; attachment; sexual passion (chd. p. 403; S.E.D. p. 867): รติกร causing pleasure or joy; being in love: รติกรรม sexual intercourse: รติคฤห์, รติภพน์, รติมนเทียร a place of amusement, satisfaction, pleasure or enjoyment; the female pudendum: รติดัสกร a paramour; a charmer; one exciting voluptuousness: รติทูติ, รติทูตี one carrying love-letters or messages; a match-maker: รติบดี, รติปรีย์, รติรมย์ the god of Love; Cupid: รติรส a taste of the pleasure of love; the spice of love: รติลักษ์ sexual intercourse; cohabitation.

รถ, รัถ rot⁶ *P. n.* a carriage; a calash, equipage, wagon or vehicle; a chariot (chd. p. 402); a champion; power; a warrior; a fighting king or monarch: รถการ a coach- or carriage-builder; a carpenter; a wheelwright (S. E. D. p. 865): รถเก๋ง a gharry; a low, four-wheeled, box-shaped conveyance drawn by one pony. These have fixed glass windows in front and back; on both sides are doors having adjustable glass windows which invariably rattle. The two or four occupants face each other; the driver, being on the outside, sits on a seat just behind the horse's tail. These vehicles of Indian origin were imported to Thailand from Singapore for hire, before carriages were in use: รถเกตุ a flag or banner attached to a vehicle, car, chariot or carriage: รถจรณะ, รถบาท the wheels of a carriage or vehicle; a wheel; รถจรรยา the travelling or going by a carriage: the course of a chariot: รถจักรยานยนต์ a motor-cycle: รถธุรับ a good warrior; a lion in warfare; an expert warrior (in a war-chariot): รถนอน a sleeping car: รถประทุน a victoria; a covered carriage: รถปุงควะ, รถปุงคพ a leader or chief of warriors: รถจักร์ (รถไฟ) a locomotive engine: รถพ่วง a trailer: รถพ่วงข้าง a side-car: รถไฟ(กระบวน) a railway train: รถม้าคู่ a carriage drawn by two horses: รถมุข the front part of a carriage; the hood of a motor-car; the fore-part of a locomotive: รถยนต์ motor-car: รถยาตรา a car procession; the festival of taking an image in a procession of cars: รถยุทธ์ a conflict or combat while the riding contestants are in cars or war-chariots: รถโยชก one who harnesses a team to a carriage: รถรับส่งคนบ่วย an ambulance: รถราง a tram-car: รถเรณุ the dust whirled up by a passing chariot: รถล้อเดียว a wheel-barrow: รถลาก, รถเจ๊ก a jinrikisha: รถวร a state chariot (chd. p. 402); the most valiant of warriors: รถวาหะ, รถพ่าห์ a carriage- or chariot-horse; a driver of the same; a charioteer: รถวิถี a carriage road: รถวิทยา, รถศาสตร์, รถศึกษา the technique, science or experience displayed in handling or steering cars, carriages or chariots: รถศักดิ์ the flagstaff of a war-chariot: รถศาลา a garage; a carriage shed; a royal chariot storehouse: รถานึก an array of war-chariots (chd. p. 402): รถเศ an owner of carriages or chariots; fighters using javelins from war-chariots: รถเสภ lit. "lord of charioteers," i.e. a king (chd. p. 402); a renowned warrior: สายรถไฟ a railway system.

รถยา see รัถยา p. 704.

รท, รทนะ rot[6] P. n. a tooth (chd. p. 397); a tusk: ทวิรท lit. "with two tusks," i.e. an elephant.

รน rone v. to manifest earnest desire or ardent effort for; to struggle, writhe or make violent efforts; to toss or roll in a restless or agitated manner; see ดิ้น p. 329: ใจร้อนรน in an impatient or ardent manner: ดิ้นรน to try, or strive to accomplish in an agitated manner: รนเล่น to be restless to get out to play: รนหา to seek with earnest effort: ร้อนรน ardent; impetuous; hot-headed: รุกรน to plunge or rush into heedlessly.

ร่น, รื้น ron[3] v. to cause to recede, retire, retreat, lessen, or reduce; to draw or peel back; to be forced to move backward; to move closer together (as when in a crowd); see ถอย p. 382: ร่นเข้า to lessen or reduce numerically; to diminish or curtail (as in the size of, or in the length of time for an undertaking or project): ร่นเข้าไป to invade or encroach gradually into (another's domain): ร่นหนัง to peel back the skin: ร่นออก to back out; to retrace one's steps backwards: ร่นปี, ร่นเดือน, ร่นวัน to antidate by a year, month or day, ex. a project is estimated to take three years to finish but by favourable circumstances the completion is accelerated by a year.

รบ, รบาล rop[6] v. to fight; to make war; see ต่อสู้ p. 347: การรบกัน a battle; a fight; a conflict: รบกวน to molest; to worry; to vex; to annoy; to trouble continually: รบกิน, เร้ากิน to tease or plead for something to eat: รบรา to fight or oppose each other (with weapons): รบราฆ่าฟัน a general fight or slaughter: รบเร้า to beg piteously and mournfully; to plead or beseech (for something) from time to time: รบรุก to fight while advancing to attack: เรือรบ a battle-ship: อย่ามารบกวนเลย do not continue to vex or annoy longer.

รบส, รบัส ra[6]-bot[4] S. v. to take care of; to nourish, nurse or support; to protect; see ป้องกัน p. 516: n. disease; a bodily defect; an injury; an infirmity (S. E. D. p. 867).

รพา ra[6]-pah P. n. noise (chd. p. 403); din; tumult; a roar; a yell; a cry; a howl (S. E. D. p. 868).

รม ๑ rom v. to fumigate; to smoke; to heat, bake or anneal (as in the process of welding pieces of sheet iron while hammering out Buddhist alms-bowls); to expose to vapour or heat (as a medicinal vapour bath or fumes); to cure by heat (as meat or fruit): รม- กระบอก to smoke or bake bamboo joints used in the collection of palm juice in order to prevent the adhering juice from turning sour: รมเด็ก to hold the face of a child over a smoking fire (as a form of punishment): รมยา to fumigate: อบรมเครื่องหอม to saturate with; to cause vaporous perfumes to penetrate.

รม ๒, รเมศ rom P. v. to enjoy oneself; to delight in; to give pleasure to (chd. p. 401).

ร่ม rom[3] v. to shade or protect from: n. a shade; a shelter; a shield; a covert or screen; an umbrella; a sunshade; a parasol: adj. shady; sheltered: กางร่ม to raise or open a sunshade: นั่งในร่ม to sit in the shade: ร่มแดด to be sheltered from the sun: ร่มธง under the protection of consular jurisdiction: ในร่มผ้า parts (of the body) covered by clothing.

รมณ rom-ma[6]-nee P. n. a woman (chd. p. 400); a beautiful young woman, wife or mistress (S. E. D. p. 868).

รมณีย rom-ma[6]-nee-ya[6] P. adj. delightful; beautiful (chd. p. 400): รมณียสถาน a delightful place.

รมดี rom-ma[6]-dee S. n. a place of enjoyment, happiness, bliss, or pleasure; paradise; heaven (S. E. D. p. 868).

รมย์, รมเยศ, รมัย, รัมย์ rom adj. abounding in charms, pleasure, and beauty: บุรี- รมย์ a town abounding in pleasures and delights.

รย, รัย ra[6]-ya[6] P. adj. speedy; urgent; quick (chd. p. 403).

รยา ra[6]-yah P. n. a pendant; that which is hanging or suspended (as clusters of flowers).

รว, รพ ra[6]-wa[6] P. S. v. to roar, growl, hum or buzz (as animals or insects) (chd. p. 403).

รวก (ไม้) ru-ak[3] n. Thrysostachys siamensis, a thornless bamboo with the light straight thornless culms about 1 to 1½ inches in diameter, forming compact vertical clumps 2-4 feet in diameter and 15-25 feet high (McM. p. 172: V. P. p. 236).

รวง roo-ang v. to dig, bore, puncture, or perforate; to make a hole with an auger; see เจาะ p. 258: n. ears of corn; heads of paddy; see พวง p. 575: รวงก้น to perforate holes in the bottom (as in making a pot for steaming rice): รวงเข้าไป to penetrate into: รวงปี่ to make perforations or holes along a fife or flute in order to produce various sounds or notes: รวงผึ้ง a honeycomb; a bee-hive: รวงไม้ to knock out the joints along the interior of bamboos: ออกรวง to form into ears or heads.

ร่วง roo-ang[3] v. to fall; to drop off (as fruit in great numbers): ใบไม้ร่วง the falling of leaves: ร่วงรุ้ง brilliant; sparkling; lustrous; bright and shining (as rays of light): ร่วงโรย to decline, decrease or gradually become less in quality, state or condition; to crumble into decay, disuse or ruin: adj. wilted; withered; faded; jaded (as from age or sickness): ร่วงออกจากพวกจากแถว to lag, stray, or straggle off (as from the main group or body): สมเด็จพระร่วงเจ้า otherwise called พระเจ้ารามกำแหงมหาราช.

รวด roo-at[3] n. one round (as in racing); a circle of wire, rope or string; a ring, loop or hoop: adv. lively; sprightly: รวดเดียว once around, or circling; one time around (as when tying rope or string): รวดเร็ว very quick; very speedy, spry or active: *adv.* very quickly; very speedily; nimbly: วิ่ง-รวดหนึ่ง one run around; running once around.

รวน   ru-an *v.* to roast; to fry (as chopped meat or fish); to sway; to be pushed here and there (as in a mob or crush or people); to lean to one side (as fence posts): *adj.* not standing straight; deviated; leaning; forced out of the normal direction: พื้นรวน teeth separated or irregular: รวนเร, เรรวน uncertain; wavering; undecided; doubtful (as actions or intentions).

ร่วน   ru-an[3] *adj.* crumbling; brittle; friable; softened by decay or dry-rot; see ชุย p. 310.

รวบ   ru-ap[3] *v.* to gather together; to heap up into a pile; to tie into a bundle or bunch: รวบรวม to gather or collect all the different parts, pieces, factions or members together: รวบรัด to summarize; to sum up or make an epitome (as of a lecture, story or evidence); to bind, include, or bundle everything up together: รวบยอด to add up the totals (as in figures); to bundle together (as heads of grain).

รวม   ru-am *v.* to collect or gather together; to total up; to compound; to mix; to add together: *n.* total; sum: รวมกำลัง concentration of strength or action: รวมเงิน to collect varying amounts of money together: รวมไว้เป็นแห่งเดียว all brought or collected into one place: รวมสำนวนความ *legal* consolidation of evidence: รวมหัวกันคิด to secure concerted action of heads or brains (as on the solution of a problem): รวมหัวรวมหางเรื่อง the accumulating or gathering together of various fragments or incidents and weaving them into a connected story.

ร่วม   ru-am[3] *v.* to live together; to be joined together or united; to be affiliated with: *adj.* lessening by degrees in quantity, time or distance: *adv.* nearly; almost; partially: ร่วมคิด to be united in thought, plans or schemes: ร่วมใจ to agree in; to be unanimous in opinion, decisions, habits or purposes: ร่วมท้องเดียวกัน born of the same mother: ร่วมบิดา, ร่วมพ่อ born of the same father: ร่วมประเวณี, ร่วมสังวาส to cohabit; to live as man and wife: ร่วมฟูก sleeping in the same bed: ร่วมมือ to cooperate or consolidate action: ร่วมรักกัน to be banded together in love or friendship: ร่วมรู้รส, ร่วมสนิทเสน่หา conjugal union: ร่วมหมอน sharing the same pillow: อยู่ร่วมธง to be under the same flag: อยู่ร่วมเรือนกัน living in the same house.

รวย ๑   ru-ie *v.* to be rich; to gain or acquire riches: *adj.* rich; lucky; fortunate; well-off; affluent: กลิ่นรวย an agreeable odour: รูปรวย pretty: หอมรวย odorous; odoriferous.

รวย ๒   ru-ie *adv.* mildly; weakly; softly; slightly; see แผ่ว p. 552: รวยริน gently; mildly; moderately; continuously; pleasantly (as a breeze): รวยรื่น agreeably; mildly; pleasantly: หายใจรวยๆ breathing lightly or slowly as one in a faint, or when nearing death.

รวิ, รวี, รพิ, รพี, รำไพ   ra[6]-wi[6] *P. S. n.* the sun; rays of the sun (chd. p. 403): รวิวงษ์ of the race of the Sun: รวิวาร Sunday (chd. p. 403).

รศนา   ra[6]-sa[4]-nah *S. n.* a rope; a cord; a rein; a girdle; a zone (S. E. D. p. 869); a woman's belt or girdle (chd. p. 401).

รส   rot[6] *P. n.* sap; juice; flavour; taste; essence; sweetness; the best part or extract of a thing (chd. p. 402): ชิมรส to taste: รสจืด, ไม่มีรส tasteless; insipid: รสสุคนธ์ เสวรส *Thai, Bangkok,* เถาอรคน *Thai,* ยานป๊อด and ปด *Thai, Peninsula* (ต้น) *Tetracera loureiri (Dilleniaceae),* a vine with white fragrant flowers in masses (cb. p. 20): รสอร่อย of pleasing taste; savoury: โอชารสดี very delicious.

รสก   ra[6]-sok[4] *P. n.* a cook (chd. p. 401),

รสนา　ra⁶-sa⁴-nah　*P. n.* the tongue (chd. p. 401):　รสนารท　a bird.

รสายนวิทยา　ra⁶-sah²-ya⁶-na⁶-wit⁶-ta⁶-yah　*S. n.* chemistry:　รสายนเวท　alchemy.

รสิก　ra⁶-sik⁴　*P. adj.* spirited; witty (chd. p. 401); tasty; delicious; well-flavoured (S.E.D. p. 871).

รหัท　ra⁶-hut⁴　*P. n.* a deep pool; a lake (chd. p. 397); a lagoon; a pond; the sea.

รหัส　ra⁶-hut⁴　*P. n.* a secret; a private matter; something mysterious; unknown or obscure facts (chd. p. 397).

รหัสย์　ra⁶-hut⁴　*S. adj.* secret; private; concealed (chd. p. 397); quiet; silent.

รหิต　ra⁶-hit⁴　*P. v.* to be deprived of; to be without; to cause to disappear:　*adj.* deprived of; robbed of (chd. p. 397).

รโห　ra⁶-hoh²　*P. n.* solitude; secrecy; privacy (chd. p. 397); seclusion; retirement: ความรโหฐาน the condition of secrecy, privacy, solitude or retirement:　รโหคต one who is alone or in retirement (chd. p. 397):　รโหฐาน a solitary, secret, silent or quiet place:　รโห-นิสัชช the act of sitting or being in a private or secret place.

รอ　raw *v.* to stop or suspend; to restrain; to delay; to wait for; to go slowly; see คอย p. 192:　*n.* a flood-gate; a sluice-way; a break-water or weir:　ปักรอ to drive in stakes; to bank up with posts in order to prevent the current washing the bank away: รอการพิจารณา to await investigation by the court:　รอการลงอาชญา punishment conditionally suspended:　รอใจ to exert self-control; to restrain the mind:　รอท่า to wait for in order to receive (as orders or a message):　รอรา, รอรั้ง to delay; to procrastinate or defer:　รอรับคำสั่ง to wait for orders:　รอเรือ to wait for a boat to come: รอหน้า to be directly in advance of; to wait ahead (for others):　รีๆรอๆ to loiter,

hesitate or dilly-dally:　ไม่ต้องรอกัน you do not need to wait for others.

ร่อ　raw³ *v.* to place adjoining, close by or contiguous to:　*adj.* near by; contiguous; adjoining:　ร่อหัว nearly touching the head (as an umbrella held low):　อยู่จ่อร่อ being in close proximity to.

ร่อแร่　raw³-raa³ *adj.* very weak; in a bad condition physically; near to a fatal end: หายใจร่อแร่ extremely weak respirations.

รอก　rauk³ *n.* a pulley:　ชักรอก to hoist by the use of pulleys:　รอก (ต้น) *Elaeocarpus sp.* (*Elaeocarpaceae*) near *E. robustus* (V. P. p. 236):　รอกแฝด a twin pulley; a double pulley.

รอง ๑　raung *v.* to place something under; to sustain; to support by means of a prop; to be in the second place; to underlay:　*adj.* next, or following in order or series:　กินพอ-รองท้อง to eat just a little to appease the appetite:　เป็นรอง to be inferior to; to be worse than; to be a runner-up (in a race or competition):　รองกงสุล a vice-consul: รองช้ำ a painful pustule forming under the thick skin of the palms of the hands or soles of the feet:　รองทรง a fashion of wearing the hair in a long tuft or bunch; a subsidary garment:　รองเท้า a shoe; slippers; footgear:　รองเงิน to borrow money with promise of future payment (as in making an urgent purchase):　รองนอน a cloth or mattress on which one lies:　รองน้ำ to catch water from a spout:　รองบ่อน animals kept for competitive gambling purposes:　รองพื้น (แผล) a painful ulcer or pustule on the arch of the foot:　รองพื้น (ไม้) a floor-supporting timber:　รองอำมาตย์ rank of Deputy Councillor:　รับรอง to endorse or guarantee another:　ลูกรองหัวปี the next to the oldest child.

รอง ๒, เรืองรอง　raung *adj.* pretty; beautiful.

ร่อง   raung[3] *n.* channel; trick; path; way; ditch; canal: ท้องร่อง an irrigation ditch or water-way for gardens and plantations: ร่องน้ำ a deep course or channel of a river, or bar: ร่องรอย a track, trace, or clue: ร่อง มด a white or black line or stripe running from the under surface of the chin, along the neck through the fork of the front legs to the hind quarters (of animals).

ร้อง   raung[5] *v.* to cry, scream, exclaim or cry out; to shout; to bawl; to screech: ฟ้อง ร้อง to lodge an accusation: ร้องขัดทรัพย์ *legal* to intervene: ร้องทุกข์ to make a complaint; to complain (as to ill-treatment or hardships):   ร้องเพลง to sing songs, hymns, or any melody: ร้องเรียก, ร้องหา to call; to cry out for; to shout, or yell after: ร้องเรียน to complain, or make accusation to a superior: ร้องไห้ to mourn, cry, or weep: ร้องไห้ร้องห่ม *colloq.* to weep; to cry for; to mourn, or sorrow for: ร้องอึงไปทำไม why cry, or scream so loudly, or tumultuously: แกะร้อง sheep bleat: ไก่ (ตัวผู้) ร้อง the cock crows: ไก่ (ตัวเมีย) ร้อง hens cackle; hens cluck: ช้าง ร้อง the elephants trumpet: ฟ้าร้อง there is a sound of thunder: แมวร้อง the cat mews; the cat purrs; cats caterwaul: วัวร้อง the cow lows; the cow moos: เสียงร้อง cries, screams, or sounds of clamourous voices: สุนัขเห่าร้อง the dog barks; the dog yelps; dogs bay; dogs yap; dogs growl, howl and yowl: ม้าร้อง horses neigh and whinny.

ร่องถุนอินทนู   raung[3]-toon[2]-in-ta[6]-noo *n.* ornamental ceiling or overhead covering cloth for royal, temporary pavilions during public ceremonies. On ordinary occasions, green or red cloth gathered into folds is used.

ร่องแร่ง   raung[3]-raang[3] *adv.* swaying or hanging (as though by a hair); ready to drop (as a nearly severed finger).

รอด   raut[3] *v.* to be rescued; to be saved; to escape from danger or calamity; to be freed, or rid of: *n.* floor girders or beams: รอดตัว to be rid or freed of some annoyance: รอดตาย to escape from death: รอดหาย to be relieved or cured successfully (as after an operation):   ไม่รู้รอดเลย is it never going to be finished?   ให้รู้รอด make it come to a finish: เอาตัวรอด to gain one's escape from; to accomplish one's own safety.

รอน   raun *v.* to cut into short lengths; to break off pieces; see บั้น p. 476:   ตัดรอน to sever relations of friendship with family, relations or society: ฟืนรอน firewood cut into suitable lengths.

ร่อน   raun[3] *v.* to sift (as with a sieve); to brandish (as swords); to fly hovering or circling around over an object (as hawks): นกบินร่อนเร่ the bird flies hovering around: ร่อนดาบ to brandish or swing swords: ร่อน ทอง to wash or separate gold (ore):   ร่อนรำ to winnow out the bran from grains of rice: ร่อนรับร่อนเร่ aimlessly; purposely; haphazard-ly (implying a condition of taking what comes while wandering or roaming about):   ร่อนเร่ to ramble or roam hither and thither; to wander about; to be a nomad.

ร้อน   raun[5] *adj.* hot; serious; pressing; urgent: การร้อน urgent or pressing business: ความร้อน heat: เดือดร้อน to suffer oppres-sion; to be in distress: เผ็ดร้อน peppery; pungent; highly spiced; hot to the taste: ร้อนใจ to be anxious, eager, troubled or un-easy (concerning some person or matter); see ใจร้อน p. 263:   ร้อนตัว to feel that danger is imminent or threatening; to be hard pushed (as in meeting financial obligations); to be anxious about the results (as fearing punish-ment):   ร้อนรน to be zealous, ardent, active, restless, fearful or anxious: แสบร้อน burn-ing pain (as after a scald).

ร้อน ๆ   raun-raun *adj.* declining; lessening; waning (as rays of the setting sun).

รอบ   raup[3] *n.* a circuit; a cycle; a trip, turn, or time around: *adj.* round about:

ดีรอบคอบ perfect in all respects; skillful in management; careful; clever; adroit: โดย-รอบคอบ circumference: รอบรู้ wise; intelligent; well-versed in: รอบเมือง to circle around the city (as during a procession): รอบองค์ around the body (court language): ล้อมรอบ to encircle (as with a cordon of soldiers, troops or police); to be endowed with skillful, careful judgements; to be perfect in all respects: สามรอบ thrice around; three turns around (as of wire or rope).

รอม raum *adj.* curved or bent so the ends will almost complete a circle (descriptive of the horns of cattle); see คลุ่ม p. 187.

รอมชอม raum-chaum *v.* to agree amicably, or by a give-and-take policy; see ปรองดอง p. 496.

รอมร่อ raum-ma⁶-raw³ *adv.* nearly; almost.

รอย roy *n.* a trace; a mark; a line; a track; a path; a vestige; a stain: ชะรอย it may be; perhaps; probably; at a guess: เดินตามรอย to follow in the path, track or principles (of another); to trace by means of the foot-prints: รอยแผล a scar; a cicatrix: รอยไถ furrows made by ploughing: รอยเท้า foot-prints: รอยเย็บ marks of stitches.

ร่อย roy³ *v.* to be blunted; to lose the sharp edge (descriptive of razors, knives or axes); see บิ่น p. 483: เงินร่อยหรอ decreased to almost the last stang; the money is almost all spent: ร่อยหรอ to get less gradually; to deteriorate; to be worn off by attrition; to be almost used up, or worn out.

ร้อย roy⁵ *v.* to string (as beads or flowers); to insert (as thread or wire through an opening): *adj.* one hundred: ไปกันเป็นร้อย to go by hundreds: ร้อยกรอง to compose in verse or rhyme: ร้อยแก้ว composition other than poetry or rhyme; plain, ordinary literature; prose: ร้อยลิ้น to equivocate; to lie; to falsify; to utter falsehoods.

ระ ra⁶ *v.* to strike, cut or slash first on one side and then on the other (as when clearing a path through dense jungle); to bend down upon and hit or brush (as branches on a roof); to touch, scrape or scratch one against another (as boats in transit); to hit one after the other (as running a stick along the palings of a fence); see กระทบ p. 33: ระทาง to obstruct a path, passage or canal (as do over-hanging, over-reaching limbs or weeds): เรือระกัน the boats clashed or scraped against each other.

ระกะ ra⁶-gka⁴ *v.* to be in disorder, confused or scattered about (in great quantities).

ระกา ra⁶-gkah *n.* the cock; the 10th year of the Thai animal cycle: ใบระกา an ornamental roof-edging for sacred buildings, formed in the shape of leaves.

ระกำ (ต้น) ra⁶-gkum, and sometimes สละ *n. Zalacca wallichiana (Palmae)*, a palm with a short, stout stem, found from Tenasserim and Thailand southward in Sumatra and the Malay Peninsula. There are two sorts, sweet and acid. The acid flesh inside the thorny skin is eaten raw, the flesh around the seeds is used in curries (V. P. p. 234: BURK. p. 2283): น้ำพริกระกำ eaten with vegetables: น้ำมันระกำ wintergreen oil; see p. 455: ระกำนา, ระกำป่า *Thai* (ต้น) *Pithecolobium malayanum (Leguminosae)* (cb. p. 560).

ระกำ ra⁶-gkum *n.* trouble; sorrow; grief; affliction; see ความทุกข์ p. 417: ความระกำใจ sadness; grief.

ระคน ra⁶-kon *v.* to mix; to stir together, or compound various ingredients: ระคนทอง *Laos, Chiengmai*, พวงทอง *Thai* (ต้น) *Tristellateia australasiae (Malpighiaceae)*, *T. australis*, a plant of the neighbourhood of the sea from China and Indo-China to the Pacific; in the Malay Peninsula it occurs round the coast. It makes a pretty garden climber and is in cultivation. It is an elegant and free bloomer, having yellow flowers in erect racemes (BURK. p. 2187 : cb. p. 201 : MCM. pp. 127, 208).

ระคาง ๑ ra[6]-kang *n.* small itching pimples on the skin of the legs, appearing after riding cattle, or walking through the grass.

ระคาง ๒ ra[6]-kang *v.* to doubt another's genuineness; to manifest resentment, chagrin, discord, or anger against (as a result of some insult); see เคือง p. 212.

ระคาย ra[6]-kai *v.* to be peeved, piqued, or angered; to be lacking in concord : *n.* spines; needles; prickles, or nettles (of grasses or weeds): *adj.* rasping; grating; irritating : คำระคาย harsh, irritating, aggravating words : คิดระคาย suspicious, questionable thoughts : ได้ยินข่าวที่ระคายหู to have heard exasperating, slanderous news, or rumours : ระคายหมาง, ระคายหมอง baneful; harmful; evil in effect.

ระเค็ดระคาย ra[6]-ket[6]-ra[6]-kai *n.* a clue; a hint, line or something that leads to the solution of a mystery; secret rumours.

ระแคะ, ระแคะระคาย ra[6]-kaa[6] *n.* strategy; artifice; a hint; an intimation (as to some mystery); see เค้า p. 209 : ฟังระแคะระคาย to eavesdrop; to listen secretly; to hear accidentally (what schemes others are concocting).

ระฆัง ra[6]-kung *n.* a bell : ตีระฆัง to ring a bell : ระฆังเพลง chimes : ลูกระฆัง a bell-clapper : หอระฆัง a belfry; a bell-tower; a steeple.

ระงม ra[6]-ngom *adj.* hot; warm; heated; smoking; fumigated by smoke, or sterilized by heat; see synonym เชิงแช่ p. 310.

ระงับ, ร่ำงับ ra[6]-ngup[6] *v.* to curb; to appease (as hunger); to lessen, or cause to become milder; to repress, or suppress; to cause to moderate; to mitigate: ระงับ or ไมยราบ *Thai,* กระทืบยอบ *Thai, Kaw Chang,* หญ้าบันยอด *N. Laos,* หญ้าจิยอบ *Laos, Chiengmai* (ต้น) *Mimosa pudica (Leguminosae)* the sensitive

plant, which grows low and thorny, bearing pink flowers (cb. p. 546); see กระทืบยอด p. 35 : ยาระงับพิษ an antiphlogistic remedy : ระงับ-สิ้นไป *legal* to be extinguished; to be completely suppressed.

ระงั่ง ra[6]-ngee[3] *adj.* noisy; loud; boisterous; tumultuous; see ดัง ๒ p. 322.

ระแง้ ra[6]-ngaa[5] *n.* rudimentary twigs growing out from the bunches, or clusters of the areca-nut tree.

ระรวย see ชวย p. 283, and ไชย p. 304.

ระดม ra[6]-dom *v.* to unite; to call up (as reserves of the army); to gather together (different units); to assemble, muster or collect (as the help, or workmen for a stipulated task): ยิงระดม to fire a volley; to fire a salvo; to discharge missiles simultaneously : รบประดม a fight with concerted action, or concentrated forces : ระดมกัน to unite all the help : ระดมคนงาน to assemble all the workmen on a job : ระดมพล to mobilize troops : เรียกเกณฑ์ที่ระดม a general order for corvée labour.

ระดะ, ระดา ra[6]-da[4] *adj.* much; abundant; ample; spread; strewn; scattered or covered with; disseminated : มีดอกไม้ระดาษระดา to have flowers scattered about.

ระดับ ra[6]-dup[4] *v.* to spread out or place perfectly level; see ปูลาด p. 530 : *n.* a level surface; a spirit-level (carpenter's tool): พื้น-ระดับทะเล sea level : ระดับเสียง the pitch of musical notes, or of the voice.

ระด่าว ra[6]-dow[4] *adj.* shivering; shaking; struggling; trembling (all over the body, as in cases of extreme anxiety or illness).

ระเด่น ra[6]-den[4] *Jav. n.* a princess : ระเด่น-มนตรี a prince; title of the sons of the Javanese kings.

ระเดียง ra[6]-dee-ang *n.* a clothes-line (used by Buddhist monks for drying their robes).

ระแด ra⁶-daa *n.* a group or clan of the Kha tribe of northern Thailand: ระแดดาร silent; swooned.

ระตู ra⁶-dtoo *Jav. n.* the governor of a province or town.

ระทก ra⁶-tok⁶ *adj.* cool; cold; clammy.

ระทด, รันทด, ระทาย ra⁶-tot⁶ *v.* to moan; to groan; to sigh; to be sad or sorry for; to be oppressed or afflicted: ระทดใจ of a broken heart; overcome by grief or sorrow: ระทดถอนใจใหญ่ to heave great sighs of sorrow or anguish.

ระทอด ra⁶-taut³ *v.* to discard; to cast off; to leave alone, or pay no attention to; see ทิ้ง p. 414.

ระทม ra⁶-tom *v.* to suffer from a condition of excessive anguish, agony, sorrow or anxiety: ระทมใจ anguish of heart; see ตรอม p. 341.

ระทวย, รันทวย ra⁶-tu-ey *adj.* oppressed; afflicted (with grief); languishing; tired; hungry; weak: ระทวยกาย physical weakness; languor; hunger: อ่อนระทวย becoming weak, frail or languishing (in consequence of sorrow).

ระทา ra⁶-tah *n.* a square, tapering tower bearing the face of Rahu, the dragon of the Eclipse, represented on each side. These towers are placed above archways, pavilions, or public buildings. The same, made for a pyrotechnic display.

ระทาย see ระทด p. 695.

ระทึก ra⁶-teuk⁶ *v.* to be extremely frightened, fearful, or excited (with the resulting quick, weak pulse); see ตกใจ p. 339.

ระแทะ, รันแทะ ra⁶-taa⁶ *n.* a small-sized bullock cart or wagon.

ระนด ra⁶-note⁶ *Cam. n.* a harrow or rake.

ระนาด ๑ ra⁶-nart³ *n.* a Thai musical instrument consisting of an oblong curved box in which are hung keys or strips made of sonorous wood or brass. These are set in a scale and emit a staccato note when struck with a wooden mallet; a xylophone; a bamboo harmonica: ระนาดแก้ว carillon: ระนาดทุ้ม basso xylophone: ระนาดทอง brass xylophone: ระนาดเอก alto xylophone: ระนาดเหล็ก iron xylophone: รางระนาด cradle or case for the above.

ระนาด ๒ ra⁶-nart³ *adj.* lying superimposed, disorderly, or on top of each other (as posts, scantlings, branches of trees piled up in heaps or lying about promiscuously).

ระนาบ ra⁶-narp³ *v.* to lie level, flat or smoothly (used in poetry or rhyme).

ระนาม, ระนัม ra⁶-narm *n.* entangled jungle; a dense jungle overgrown with underbrush.

ระนาว ra⁶-now *v.* to be levelled or flattened down (as stalks of grain by strong winds): *n.* a row; a line; a string; an array; a procession or queue: *adv.* in a row; in abundance: *adj.* arranged or lined up in a line or row.

ระเนน ra⁶-nen *adj.* lying superimposed in disorder on top of each other.

ระเนียด ra⁶-nee-at³ *n.* fence posts; stockade pillars; see ต้าย p. 364.

ระแนง ra⁶-naang *v.* to stand, place or be placed in a row, or in order: *n.* laths or battens supporting the tiles of a roof.

ระแนะ, และ ra⁶-naa⁶ *n.* means for supporting foundations of buildings and house-posts.

ระบบ ra⁶-bop⁴ *n.* custom; manner; usual procedure or order: เป็นระบบธรรมเนียม this is the customary procedure: ระบบใบไม้ leaves or grass strewn in layers.

ระบม ra⁶-bom *v.* to feel a condition of soreness; to be tired, contused or bruised; to experience a bruised feeling (of the body); to heat, bake or anneal (as is done in welding pieces of sheet iron in the process of making Buddhist alms-bowls). เจ็บระบม to suffer from soreness of the muscles (as in dengue): ตีจนระบม to be badly bruised by flogging or blows: ระบมใจ to be vexed, annoyed or broken-hearted (as over some affliction): ระมมบอบช้ำ *colloq.* a condition of being generally bruised, sore, wounded or contused (as after a fight): ระบมบาตร to heat Buddhist monks' alms-bowls to give them an iron-grey colour: ระบมผี localized inflammation around an abscess: ระบมหนอง pain caused by confined pus.

ระบอบ ra[6]-baup[4] *n.* custom; pattern; precedence: ระบอบความ to follow the text of the story.

ระบัด ra[6]-but[4] *v.* to shoot forth tender buds, leaves or sprouts; see ผลิ p. 541: *adj.* young, tender sprouts or newly formed leaves: ขนระบัด nascent feathers (as during moulting of fowls): ระบัดใบ to shoot forth new leaves or tender sprouts.

ระบับ ra[6]-bup[4] *n.* a pattern (original), manuscript or copy; see ฉบับ p. 267.

ระบาญ, รรรบาญ ra[6]-barn *v.* to wage a battle with; to fight.

ระบาน, ระบาน ra[6]-bah-nee *adv.* thus; in this or that way; very; extremely; actually; see นัก ๒ p. 447.

ระบาด ๑ ra[6]-bart[4] *Cam. n.* an insect; a horse-fly.

ระบาด ๒ ra[6]-bart[4] *v.* to be scattered in all directions; to extend or be spread far and wide: *adj.* separated; scattered; spreading; disseminated: โรคระบาด, โรคติดต่อ an epidemic disease.

ระบาย ra[6]-bai *v.* to paint with colours; to ornament with fringe or edging; to release (as flatus from the bowels); to exhale or inhale (as respirations): ประตูระบายน้ำ sluice

gates to regulate irrigation water: ยาระบาย a laxative remedy: ระบายช้าง to release a herd of elephants: ระบายหน้ามุ้ง fringe or edging along the front of a mosquito net: ระบายลมเข้าออก breathing; respiration: ลาย-ระบาย drawings or etchings in colour: ห้อย-ระบาย to hang as a border or edging.

ระบำ ra[6]-bum *v.* to dance solo style; to skip about (as girls in a stage performance): *n.* a solo dance: นางระบำ a ballet dancer: ระบำร้อง to dance and sing together.

ระบิ, ระบิล ra[6]-bi[4] *n.* a story; matter; a copy; a pattern; see ฉบับ p. 267.

ระบือ ra[6]-bur *adj.* rumoured; spread about; divulged; disseminated: ระบือลือลั่น to be widely noised about, or rumoured everywhere: ระบือลือเลื่อง *idiomatic* the sound of the affair has spread abroad.

ระบุ ra[6]-boo[4] *v.* to speak about (as of a person, problem or incident); to address (as an envelope) specifically or exclusively; to have all ripen at the same time (as fruit): ระบุแจ้ง to be explicit: ระบุชื่อ to speak about a person by name; to write a person's name in (as in a will or promissory note): ระบุให้-แจ่มแจ้ง to declare, or define specifically.

ระเบง ra[6]-beng *v.* to beat or pound (as drums); see ตี p. 368.

ระเบ็ง ra[6]-beng *n.* a form of solo dancing (similar to ระบำ).

ระเบิด ra[6]-bert[4] *v.* to explode; to blow up; to break out or burst forth; to apply explosives; to widen to a proper shape (as in the making of a dug-out boat): การระเบิด an explosion: ดินระเบิด gunpowder or explosives: ปืนระเบิด the gun exploded: ระเบิดหิน to use explosives in a stone quarry.

ระเบียง ra[6]-bee-ang *n.* a long, narrow, roofed gallery encircling a Buddhist sanctuary; a verandah; a portico. In house architecture among the Thai, this is a covered verandah built on the same or slightly lower level than the main floor but in front of the living rooms. Usually there is an additional enclosed un-roofed extension called ชาน used as a bath-room: *adj.* in a row; well-arranged; in good order.

ระเบียน see ทะเบียน p. 406: หอทะเบียนที่ดิน Land Registration Office.

ระเบียบ ra[6]-bee-ap[4] *n.* method; procedure: rule; order; form; programme: มีระเบียบเรียบร้อย well-behaved or acting according to recognized rule or form: ระเบียบการ order of procedure: ระเบียบวาระ programme for the day.

ระมัด ra[6]-mut[6] a prefix occurring with ระวัง; to be on one's guard, careful, attentive or watchful: ระมัดใจ to exercise restraint, self-control or repression (of one's desires): ระมัดระเมียด *colloq.* to be frugal, economical or [saving.

ระมา ra[6]-mah *Jav. n.* a horse-fly.

ระมาด (แรด) ra[6]-mart[3] *n.* a rhinoceros (one-horned).

ระย่อ ra[6]-yaw[3] *v.* to fear; to be discouraged; to lose heart, or be disheartened: มีใจระย่อ to be scared, fearful or timid.

ระย่อม (ต้น) ra[6]-yawm[3] sometime spelled ขยอมหลวง *n. Rauwolfia serpentia (Apocynaceae)*, a small shrub which is found in India from the Himalayas to Ceylon and to Thailand, and then again in Java. It is extensively medicinal (BURK. p. 1885: V. P. p. 234).

ระยัง ra[6]-yung *v.* to restrain; to remain; to cause to stop or stay.

ระยั้ง ra[6]-yung[5] *v.* to restrain; to cause to stop.

ระยัด ra[6]-yut[6] *v.* to press or jam down into (tightly); to force down into (so as to completely fill); see ยัด p. 669.

ระยับ, ระยาบ ra[6]-yup[6] *adj.* glittering; dazzling; brilliant (as rays of the sun, or glory); to flutter, wave or be agitated by the wind: ธงปลิวระยับ the flag flutters in the breeze.

ระยะ ra[6]-ya[6] *n.* a space, interval or separation (as in punctuation); a period (of time or age); *legal* a stage (of proceedings); interval of distance, or sections (of railroad or tramway); a bar, meter or measure (in music, rhyme or poetry): เดินเป็นระยะไป to travel by stages, or sections: ระยะกลาง an intermediate stage, state, period or space: ระยะทาง stages or distances of a journey: ระยะว่างเปล่า an unoccupied, or unobstructed section (of land): ให้ไว้ระยะ to leave a space, or make a separation in what is being written or printed.

ระย้า, รยา ra[6]-yah[5] *n.* a hanging ornament with several branches or tassels; a pendant; clusters drooping downward (as sprays of flowers): โคมระย้า a chandelier: ตุ้มหูระย้า pendent earrings: ห้อยเป็นระย้าลงมา hanging down or drooping loosely in tassels, bunches or clusters.

ระยาน (ยาน) ra[6]-yarn *adj.* hanging down; pendulous; too long.

ระยำ ra[6]-yum *adj.* accursed; detestable; mean; low; miserable; soiled or damaged (in reputation); wicked; unlucky (a term of contempt used as a curse); see ชั่ว p. 289.

ระโยง (สาย) ra[6]-yong *n.* stay or guy ropes for holding masts in position.

ระรวย ra[6]-ru-ey *v.* to emit fragrant odours; to send forth or waft perfume (on the breeze).

ระรอง ra[6]-raung *adj.* brilliant (in colour); beautifully yellow or orange.

ระร่อน ra[6]-rawn[3] *v.* to fly hovering, or circling around over an object (as do hawks).

ระรัว ra⁶-ru-ah v. to beat repeatedly with quick strokes; to slash or beat with quick repeated strokes: adj. trembling; shaking; shivering.

ระราน ra⁶-rarn v. to oppress; to trouble; to vex; to annoy; to tease or irritate (a weaker or younger person).

ระร่าย (ไต่) ra⁶-rai³ v. to climb along (as monkeys from branch to branch).

ระริก ra⁶-rik⁶ adj. shaking (with laughter); shuddering; trembling (with fear): สั่น- ระริกระรัว to shudder, shake, tremble or suffer from palpitation of the heart (from fear): เสียงระริกขิกขัก idiomatic the sound of giggling or laughter.

ระรี, เรื่อย ra⁶-ree³ adv. continually; steadily (as a breeze).

ระรึง ra⁶-reung v. to tie loosely or temporarily: มัดระรึง to fasten or tie insecurely and temporarily.

ระรื่น, ระรื่น ra⁶-reun³ adj. fragrant; pleasing; sweet; agreeable (odours): หอมระรื่น- ชื่นใจ sweet-scented odours; delicious perfumes, pleasing to the person.

ระเร ra⁶-ray v. to stray or wander aimlessly from place to place: adj. truant; loitering; idling; shirking.

ระเร่ง ra⁶-reng⁵ v. to hurry; to haste with extra energy.

ระเรื่ว ra⁶-re-oh v. to be dexterous, quick, or fast.

ระเริง ra⁶-rerng v. to be happy, joyous, gay, [or cheerful.
ระเรียง see เรียง p. 719.

ระเรียม see เรียม p. 719.

ระเรื่อย ra⁶-reu-ie³ adv. mildly; gently; agreeably; continually (used descriptive of breezes): ระเรื่อยเฉื่อยฉ่ำ a mild, invigorating, continuous breeze.

ระแร่ ra⁶-raa³ adj. going directly in; running, or rushing away.

ระแรง see แรง p. 721.

ระลง ra⁶-long v. to be afraid of; to fear; to be a coward (as after a scolding or words [of reproof).
ระลวง see ระลุง p. 698.

ระลวย ra⁶-lu-ey preferably ละลวย v. to delude; to mislead; to beguile or cause to go astray: adj. having much; getting much; soft; pliable; yielding.

ระลอก, ละลอก ra⁶-lauk³ n. small waves or ripples forming foam or froth (as along the bank or shore); small pustules (occurring on the skin).

ระลัด ra⁶-lut⁶ v. to flip; to fillip with finger or thumb; see ดีด p. 331: ระลัดได the act (or time) of flipping a finger.

ระลึก, รำลึก ra⁶-leuk⁶ v. to think of; to recollect; to remember; to recall; to bring back to mind: ระลึกคิดถึง to meditate on; to ponder over; to contemplate: ระลึกตรึกตรอง to deliberate over and try to recall to mind.

ระลุก ra⁶-look⁶ Cam. adj. fitting tightly, closely, or not being slack (as a bolt or ring).

ระลุง, ระลวง ra⁶-loong v. to beg, pray for or beseech: adj. pitiable; mournful; sad; lamentable.

ระเลิง ra⁶-lerng v. to cut down; to hew down or fell (as trees or underbrush); see โค่น p. 216.

ระวัง ra⁶-wang v. to be careful, watchful or diligent in guarding against: ระวังตัว self-preservation; watchfulness: ระวังไฟ to be on the look-out for fire: ระวังให้จงดี to be on extra careful watch.

ระวาง ra⁶-wang n. the hold of a vessel; a register; a list; a piece; a portion (as of garden land or paddy fields): adj. at a regular distance apart (as the feet of infantry while marching); spacing or intervals in poetical feet: *prep.* between: ขึ้นระวาง to enroll or register (as an elephant): ⁄ ค่าระวาง freight dues (in transit); a registration fee: นายระวาง a supercargo; the Civil Officer in charge of garden- or field-taxes: ใบระวาง shipping papers; a receipt; a registration receipt.

ระวาดระไว   ra[6]-wart[3]-ra[6]-wai *adv.* hurriedly; dexterously; hastily; precipitately.

ระวาม (ว่วาม)   ra[6]-warm *adv.* vigorously; rapidly; violently (as fire when fanned by a wind).

ระวิง   ra[6]-wing *n.* a reel or spool (for rope, yarn or silk): ระวิงเวียนวน to loiter about.

ระแวง   ra[6]-waang *v.* to suspect; to doubt; to mistrust; to distrust; to be inclined to an opposite side (in opinion or conduct); to lack unity: คิดระแวง to suspect: ระแวงแหนง to mistrust fidelity; to doubt the sincerity of: เสียงระแวง discordant sounds (as in music, pronunciation, or opinions).

ระแวดระวัง   ra[6]-waat[3]-ra[6]-wang *v.* to be on extra good guard; to take good care; to be watchful.

ระไว   ra[6]-wai *v.* to take care; to be watchful: ระวังระไว, ระแวดระไว to be on the alert; to watch diligently.

ระส่ำระสาย   ra[6]-sum[4]-ra[6]-sai[2] *v.* to be scattered or in disorder (as a routed army); to be separated, scattered, dismayed or agitated.

ระสี   ra[6]-see[2] *Cam. n.* the bamboo.

ระเส็ดระสัง   ra[6]-see-at[4]-ra[6]-sung[2] *adj.* driven, straying or wandering (hither and thither); reeling; staggering; swaggering along.

ระหกระเหิน   ra[6]-hok[4]-ra[6]-hern[2] *adj.* standing pain, distress, difficulty, misfortune or homelessness: ระหกระเหินเดินดง to travel with hazard, danger or risk through a forest.

ระหง   ra[6]-hong[2] *adj.* tall and straight; erect; handsome; towering (as trees): งาม-ระหง beautifully tall and sightly: ไพรระหง a forest of tall, stately trees.

ระหวย   see ระโหย   p. 700.

ระหว่าง   ra[6]-wang[4] *n.* middle; midway; intermediate: *adv.* between; intervening in space, time, position, or relation; during, or at intervals of: ที่เตียนระหว่าง an intervening clearing: ในระหว่างโทษ *legal* during the interval of punishment, or sentence: พื้นที่ในระหว่างภูเขา valleys.

ระห้องระแห้ง   ra[6]-haung[2]-ra[6]-haang[2] *v.* to harbour, or conceive any of the following conditions: *n.* a condition of jealousy, suspicion, estrangement, dislike, or ill-will (as between persons, or groups of people): *adj.* unsociable; lacking unamimity, or harmony.

ระหัด   ra[6]-hut[4] *n.* a Chinese irrigating pump, known in China as the "dragon bone pump" because of the imagined similarity to a dragon's back bone. It consists of a continuous chain of square wooden paddles operating in a square flume with a wheel at each end. It is worked by foot or hand power, or by engine; a cotton gin, or seeding machine: ถีบระหัด to work an irrigating pump by foot-power.

ระหาย, กระหาย   ra[6]-hai[2] *v.* to want, crave, or hanker after; to be hungry for; to be desirous of; to strive, or yearn eagerly after: *adj.* thirsty; hungry; longing; craving: ระ-หายระโหย to become exhausted by yearning for: ระหายหิว to be hungry and thirsty for.

ระเห็ด, ระเหิด (เหาะไป)   ra[6]-het[4] *v.* to ascend, or pass through the air by miraculous power; to fly; to go, or be carried rapidly through space (as by supernatural power, or mechanical means).

ระเหย   ra[6]-hur-ie[2] *v.* to evaporate (by being opened, or exposed); to cause to become dissipated, dispersed, attenuated, or lessened : กลิ่นระเหยไปหมด the odour has all been dissipated.

ระเหหน, ระเหระหน ra⁶-hay²-hon² *adj.* vagrant; strolling; wandering about; unsettled; nomadic.

ระเหหัน ra⁶-hay²-hun² *adj.* turning from one direction or purpose to another; wandering; deviating; rotating; circling about (as one going about aimlessly): ใจระเหหัน vacillating; wavering in mind or purpose.

ระแหง ra⁶-haang² *n.* chaps; cracks (as in the skin); crevices; gaps; splits or fissures (as ground becomes from long continued drought): ดินแตกแห้งเป็นระแหงมาก the dry ground is badly cracked.

ระโหย, ระหวย ra⁶-ho-ie² *v.* to be debilitated; to be weakened, tired, languid, or enfeebled (as by hunger or illness): ระโหยหวน to be weakened by mourning or grumbling plaintively (at one's fate or condition): ระโหยหิว weakened by hunger.

ระอา, ระอิดระอา ra⁶-ah *v.* to be wearied by being pestered or teased (by continual nagging); to be disheartened or discouraged: ระอาใจ to be disgusted, or sick at heart: ระอาระอม annoyed; vexed; provoked.

ระอึก, สะอึก ra⁶-euk⁴ *v.* to jump; to pounce upon; see กระโจน p. 23: *n.* hiccoughs.

ระอุ ra⁶-oo⁴ *adj.* warm; close; muggy; stuffy; heated (as in fever); being completely cooked (as meat in an oven), or ripened (as fruit by artificial heat).

รัก ruk⁶ *v.* to love; to cherish; to foster: รัก (ดอก) *Calotropis gigantea* (*Asclepiadeae*), a fleshy shrub, nearly a tree, with large, soft leaves. It occurs throughout India, reaching Ceylon, extending to China, and is found southward to Singapore, Borneo, Java, the lesser Sunda Islands, and Moluccas. The stems yield a hemp-like fibre used for fishing

lines. The lavender flowers are much used in set floral pieces used at cremations. A silky floss from the fruit is used for stuffing pillows. The Chinese in Java candy the central part of the flower to make a sweetmeat. The Malays believe that the latex kills the worm that causes toothache; and by an extension of the idea, in Perak, the leaves are placed in the runnels by which water enters rice-fields, that worms and other pests, carried along by the water, may be killed before they enter. The leaf is used for poulticing sores. It is burned, and the smoke inhaled, for ulceration of the nose. The leaves are rubbed over the skin of elephants which have certain diseases, and the roots are chopped fine with other substances as a tonic to make elephants grow fat (V.P. p. 235: McM. p. 429: Burk. p. 415): รัก, รักใหญ่ *Thai*, ฮัก, ฮักหลวง *Laos, Karen, Kanburi* (ต้น) *Melanorrhoea usitata* (*Anacardiaceae*), a tree which is the source of Burmese lacquer (Burk. p. 1435); *Semecarpus cassuvium* (*Anacardiaceae*), a tree found in the Moluccas, the resin of which is used to varnish shields, spear-handles, walking-sticks, *etc.* Its fruits are even sold in the markets of Amboina. They taste like apples. The fruit is oily; the kernel is edible (Burk. p. 1931); *M. usitatissima* (*Anacardiaceae*) (Cb. p. 351: V.P. p. 235: McM. p. 412): รักน้ำ (ต้น) *Gluta coarctata* (*Anacardiaceae*) (Cb. p. 346): รักเร่ (ต้น) *Dahlia sp.* (*Compositae*); *D. variabilis*, a perennial herb with beautiful flowers like zinnia (McM. p. 191: N. H. J. S. S. IX, 3, p. 272): รักหมู, รักขี้หมู *Thai*, ฮักขี้หมู *Laos, Chiengmai*, (ต้น) *Buchanania latifolia* (*Anacardiaceae*); *Semecarpus cochinchinensis* (Cb. pp. 348, 354): ความรัก love; charity; devotion; amity: ตัดรัก to sever; to cut off, or dismiss any feeling of love for: ที่รัก well-beloved; well-favoured: น่ารัก charming; graceful; handsome; adorable: น้ำรัก lacquer: ร่วมรัก unity; attachment; longing for: รักซ้อน (ดอก) *Calotropis gigantea* (*Asclepiadaceae*), a shrub producing double-petalled flowers (V. P. p. 235:

BURK. p. 415); see รัก (ดอก): รักซึ่งกันและกัน
to love one another: รักน้ำ (ต้น) *Gluta
coarctata* (*Anacardiaceae*), a tree of small to
fair size growing on the coasts of Thailand,
and along the western coast of the Malay
Peninsula, and the southern part of the eastern coast. It grows on the water's edge, but
too far up the rivers for the water to be
more than very slightly brackish. It gives
a beautiful red timber but is not much used
because of the very poisonous sap. This sap
is used by the Malays as a vindictive poison
(BURK. p. 1018: cb. p. 347): รักร้อย a conventional, ornamental design representing the
Calotropis gigantea flowers in rows, or series:
รักอาลัย *idiomatic* solicitious devotion: ร่ำรัก
to repeat, or continue amorous advances:
ลงรัก to apply black lacquer: หลงรัก infatuated; enamoured of; mad with love.

รักขสะ see รากษส p. 706.

รักขิต ruk[6]-kit[4] *P. adj.* having been cared
for, protected, or guarded (chd. p. 400).

รักด, รักต see รัตต p. 703.

รักดป ruk[6]-dop[4] *S. n.* a leech (chd. p. 403).
[(McM. p. 191).

รักเร่ (ต้น) ruk[6]-ray[3] *n. Dahlia compositae*
[illary space.

รักแร้ ruk[6]-raa[5] *n.* the armpits; the ax-

รักษ์, รักษา, รักข, รักขา ruk[6] *P. v.* to
keep; to save from; to take care of; to watch
over; to treat; to protect; to guard against;
to ward off; to preserve; to beware of (chd.
p. 400): พิทักษ์รักษา to be loyal in the care
of: รักษาพยาบาล to apply remedies and
nurse (the sick): รักษาศีล to observe the
commandments, or rites of a religion: รักษา-
ให้หาย to cure or heal: องค์รักษา a tutelary,
guardian spirit or genius: รักษาการ to be
on duty.

รัง rung *n.* a nest: รัง *Thai*, เปา *N. Laos*,
ฮัง *E. Laos*, เรียง *Khmer, Surin*, เหล่บ่อง or
ลักบ้าว *Karen, Lawa, Chiengmai* (ต้น) *Pen-*

tacme siamensis (*Dipterocarpaceae*), a tree,
usually of small size in Malaya, and branching low. Though it is common in Burma,
Thailand, and Indo-China, it is distinctly rare
in the Peninsula, being found only in a very
limited area towards the north-west where it
experiences a dry season. This area includes
peninsular Thailand. It occurs on sandy, or
rocky soil. The wood is very hard, very
heavy, strong, very durable and suitable for
heavy construction. Thailand enjoys a small
export. It is said to be more cross-grained
than *Shorea obtusa* and more difficult to plane,
but otherwise very similar. The cotyledons
are thick and contain fat; 9 per cent of tannin is present in the bark, and 6 per cent in
the wood. A lac-insect feeds on the tree
(BURK. p. 1690): รังกะต่าย *slang* in rags and
tatters: รังกะแท้ *Thai, Chantaburi*, ลุ่ย *An-
namite, Chantaburi* (ต้น) *Kandelia rheedei*
(*Rhizophoraceae*), a small tree, up to 20 feet
in height, found among other mangroves on
the coasts of south-eastern Asia and western
Malaysia. The timber is too small to have
any real value. The wood is soft, close-
grained, reddish-brown, and only used for
firewood (cb. p. 594: BURK. p. 1277): รังกะสา
หรือ รังนกกะสา, ฝอยทอง (ต้น) *Cassytha filiformis*
(*Lauraceae*), a parasitic plant, like *Cusanta
sp.* (*Anvulvulaceae*): รังกา a crow's nest:
รังดุม a button-hole: รังแตน *lit.* "wasps'
nests," *i. e.* a form of Thai art, being
hexagonal-shaped circles placed in rows:
รังนก the edible sea-swallow's nest found in
island caves along the southern sea coast of
Thailand. These remarkable nests consist
essentially of mucus which is secreted by the
salivary glands of the birds and which dries
and looks like isinglass. These are made
into a soup which is very highly esteemed,
especially by the Chinese: รังบวย the dried
tough fibers of the sponge-gourd, used in
place of straw as packing: รังผึ้ง a bee-
hive: รังพา the act of singing and asking
for donations (as for funds to defray the

expenses of one entering the Buddhist priest-hood): รังรวง nests (in general): แหวน-รังแตน a ring from which are suspended plates having small hexagonal perforations sugges-tive of wasps' nests.

รัง ๒   rung *v.* to adorn; to make; to create; to prepare; to build, or establish; see แต่ง p. 376: รังเกียจ to have an aversion for; to dislike, or object to (complying with a request); to feel unfavourable towards; to be dissatisfied with (as with a person, or proposition): รังรอง beautiful; pretty; decorated (in a pleasing manner): รังรักษ์ to be decorated; to be adorned, ornamented or embellished; to govern, create or produce: รังเรข to be beautifully adorned or embellished with decorations or artistic designs: รังแรก primary; first; original; beginning: รังสรรค์ *lit.* "the creator," *i. e.* an epithet for Siva and Vishnu: *v.* to create, fashion, establish or build; to give rank or honour; see แต่งตง p. 276: รังสรัง to set the face or purpose; to run or go; to begin to run: รังสฤษฏ์ to create; to establish; to build or found.

รัง ๓   rung *conj.* for; all for; only for or to: รังคนนินทา only for others to blame, slander or say evil about: รังเขาหัวเราะ for others to laugh at; only as a laughing stock: รังแช่ง, รังด่า evil, disreputable persons that are cursed for their evil deeds.

รัง   rung[5] *v.* to haul; to pull; to wait; to delay; to watch over, or care for; to control, or govern: ผู้รังการ a deputy or one acting on behalf of another; a superintendent: ผู้รัง-ตำแหน่งเจ้าเมือง one acting as lieutenant gov-ernor: รังรอ to delay; to prolong; to retard; to loiter.

รังแก   rung-gkaa *v.* to tease; to bully; to vex; to worry; to annoy; to torment; to provoke: *n.* the nest of the small-sized crow.

รังค์ see รงค์ p. 686.

รังควาน   rung-kwarn *v.* to vex; to annoy; to provoke or torment: มรานควาน, รังควาน *n.* spirits of those who have died by accident (as by drowning or falling from trees), and which return to haunt other human beings.

รังแค   rung-kaa *n.* dandruff, or fine parti-cles of scurf on the head.

รังวัด   rung-wat[6] *v.* to survey, or measure the area of a piece of land: เสียค่ารังวัด to pay the fee for surveying.

รังสิ, รังสี   rung-si[4] *P. n.* rays of light; a halo; glory; a rope; a rein; a bridle (chd. p. 402): ฉพรรณรังสี the six rays of glory of the Buddha.

รังสิมันต์, รังสิมา   rung-si[4]-mun *P. n. lit.* "that which has rays of light," *i. e.* the sun (chd. p. 401).

รัช   rut[6] *P. n.* fine dust; particles of pul-verized earth; sediment; the pollen of flowers (chd. p. 400); see ธุลี p. 436.

รัชช, รัช   rut[6]-cha[6] *P. n.* a sovereign; roy-alty; a monarch; a government; a kingdom; an empire; a country; a domain (chd. p. 399); royal treasure: รัชชกาล a reign: รัช-ทายาท a Crown Prince, or Crown Princess; the heir-apparent to the throne: รัชชุปการ *lit.* "additions to the government's treasury," *i. e.* capitation or poll-tax; taxes. [p. 400).

รัชชุ   rut[6]-choo[6] *P. n.* a rope; a string (chd.

รัชด, รัชต   rut[6]-chote[6] *n.* silver (ch. p. 399): *adj.* made of silver.

รัชดาภิเษก, รัชฏาภิเษก   rut[6]-cha[6]-dah-pi[6] sek[4] *n. lit.* "anointment (of kings or em-perors) on a heap, mass or pile of silver," *i. e.* a royal rite performed by kings of Thailand every twenty-five years of their reign. The Thai people preserve this ancient term for coronation, meaning literally anointment on a throne, which symbolizes the supreme moment (wales, siamese state ceremonies, p. 70).

รัชน rut⁶-cha⁶-na⁶ *P. n.* the act of colouring: *adj.* dyed (chd. p. 399).

รัชนี rut⁶-cha⁶-nee *P. S. n.* night (chd. p. 399): รัชนีกร the moon.

รัชส rut⁶-cha⁶-sa⁴ *S. adj.* impure; filthy; dirty; unclean; foul; soiled (S. E. D. p. 863).

รัญจวน, รำจวน run-chju-an *v.* to lament; to bemoan or be perturbed; to be agitated; to be disordered or confused (in mind); see ป่วน p. 513.

รัญช run-cha⁶ *P. v.* to colour or dye; to be glad or pleased with; to lust after or desire (chd. p. 403).

รัฏฐ, รัฐ rut⁶-ta⁴ *P. n.* territory; state; country; realm; kingdom; district (chd. p. 403); the people; the population of a state: นายกรัฐมนตรี the Premier: รัฐนิยม state code of conduct; Conventions of State: รัฐบาล a Government: รัฐบุรุษ a statesman: รัฐ-ประศาสน์ administration policies, or methods of government: รัฐประศาสนนัย, รัฐประศาส-โนบาย administrative policy; political science; politics: รัฐมนตรี a state councillor; a minister, or statesman: รัฐสภา the State Council; Parliament.

รัด rut⁶ *v.* to compress; to contract; to condense; to squeeze; to encircle or gird up: งูรัด the python: ผูกรัด to encircle and tie: รัดกุม dexterous; quick; adroit; skillful: รัดคอ to strangle or choke (as by compressing the throat): รัดจุก to gather the hair of the topknot together: รัดประคด the girdle of a priest's robe; a breast-girdle or cloth; a corset: รัดพัสตร์ a waist-band; a zone, or belt: รัดรวม to tie up many articles, points, or parts together (as summing up a discourse or evidence): รัดให้สั้นเข้า to shorten or abridge: รัดโอบ to enclose or gird in (as iron hoops around a box or bales of cotton): เร่งรัด to expedite, hasten, urge, or quicken the progress of: สายรัดอก a girdle for the breast: เอารัดเอาเปรียบ to take undue advantage of; to be too grasping; to be overly covetous.

รัดประคน, รัตคน rut⁶-bpra⁴-kon *n.* ornamental trappings for elephants.

รัต see รต p. 687.

รัตต, รักด, รักต rut⁶-dta⁴ *n.* night; *lit.* "a long night," *i. e.* a long period of time (chd. p. 403); blood: *adj.* coloured; dyed; red; agitated or inflamed by passion (chd. p. 403): being in love, fond of, affected by or attracted to by love, or interest in: รัตต-กัมพล a crimson blanket (chd. p. 403); a scarlet-dyed cloth: รัตตคาวี a red cow: รัตต-จันทน์ the red sandal-wood: รัตตมณี a ruby; red precious jewels or stones: รัตตโลหิต arterial blood.

รัตน์, รัตนะ rut⁶ *S. n.* a gem; a jewel; glass; crystal; a precious stone; a valuable, precious, or desirable thing. The seven treasures of the Emperor (จักรพรรดิ์) are จักรรัตนะ the wheel; หัตถิรัตนะ the elephant; อัสสรัตนะ the horse; มณิรัตนะ the gem; อิตถิรัตนะ the Empress; คหบดีรัตนะ the retinue of house-holders; ปริณายกรัตนะ the Crown Prince. The three gems (ไตรรัตน์) or treasures are the Buddha (พระพุทธ); Dhammo (พระธรรม) natural law, the Law or Truth; Sangho (พระสงฆ์), talapoins, the Church or clergy (chd. p. 402: S. E. D. p. 864): รัตนกนทล coral: รัตนกร *lit.* "the creator or producer of jewels or gems," *i. e.* Kuvera, son of Visravas the god of Wealth (H. C. D. p. 362): รัตนกรัณฑ์ a jewel box or case: รัตนโกสินทร์ "Indra's precious gem or jewel," applied by the Thai people to the Emerald Image of Buddha and as a name for Bangkok or the era commencing with the founding of Bangkok: รัตน-ครรภ *lit.* "one with a belly full of jewels," *i. e.* an epithet for Kuvera, the god of Wealth. He is represented as a gloomy, selfish being of disagreeable countenance, deformed in body, having three legs and only 8 teeth (Gods of India, p. 293): รัตนครรภา, รัตนประภา the earth: รัตนตรัย the triple gems, *e. g.* the Buddha, the Law or Truth, the Church or Clergy (chd. p. 402): รัตนนิธิ *lit.* "the crystal cradle," *i. e.* the ocean; mount Meru; an epithet for Vishnu: รัตนมาลา, รัตนวลี a diamond necklace; a necklace adorned with precious stones or brilliants: รัตนมุขย์ diamonds: รัตนราช, รัตนราค gems; rubies; precious crystal or stones: รัตนราศี a collection, pile or accumulation of crystals (as reflected light on the water); the ocean: รัตน-สาน a name for mount Meru: รัตนสุ, รัตนสุติ the earth: รัตนากร diamonds; jewels; gems; crystals; the sea or ocean: รัตนาภรณ์ ornaments or adornments made of precious stones; jewelery (of various designs or descriptions): รัตนาโลก the sparkle, gleam, glitter, flash or reflection of diamonds or brilliants.

รัตตัญญู rut⁶-dtun-yoo *P. n. lit.* "one who understands the night," *i. e.* one who is old; one learned, or experienced about incidents of the past (chd. p. 403).

รัตติ rut⁶-dti⁴ *P. n.* night (chd. p. 403): [รัตติกาล night-time.

รัถ see รถ p. 687.

รัถยา, รัถยา, รัจฉา rut⁶-yah *S. n.* a carriage road or street (chd. p. 397); a public highway; a boulevard; a number of carriages, chariots, carts or waggons (s. e. d. p. 866).

รัน run *v.* to beat; to thrash; to whip; to flog; to strike or smite; see ตี p. 368: รุกรัน to force an entrance by beating or thrashing: รันเข้าไป to enter or penetrate by force: ตีรัน-พื้นแทง *idiomatic* to strike by a sudden forward movement, piercing the opponent with a weapon; see ตีรันพื้นแทง p. 369.

รั้น run⁵ *v.* to move aback; to pull or cause to slip back: *adj.* obstinate; headstrong; undisciplined; stubborn: จมูกรั้น a short, stumpy or stubby nose.

รันแชง run-chaang *n.* a district or tract (of land); see แขวง p. 170.

รันทด see ระทด p. 695.

รันทวย see ระทวย p. 695.

รันทำ run-tum *v.* to oppress or afflict.

รันธ run-ta⁶ *P. n.* a hole; a cavity; a funnel or tube; a fault; neglect; a defect; a flaw or blemish (chd. p. 401).

รับ rup⁶ *v.* to receive; to accept; to agree to; to affirm: ผู้รับขนของ a carrier of goods: ผู้รับประโยชน์ a beneficiary: ผู้รับเวร to be the one to go on duty, or assume an obligation: ผู้รับโอน a transferee: ร้องรับ, รับร้อง to answer a call from a distance; to make responses (as in chanting or chorus singing): รับกัน to fit, suit or harmonize with: รับขน to agree to carry goods: รับขวัญ to invoke or invite the genii of Good Fortune to abide in a person (as at the time of cutting the topknot): รับของโจร, รับของร้าย the receiving of stolen goods: รับขาด to assume the entire responsibility for (as when the assistance of another has failed): รับแขก to welcome or receive guests or visitors: รับ-คนโดยสาร the carrying of passengers: รับค้าง to carry on something that has been left unfinished: รับคำ to accept the words of instruction or advice (as where children receive instruction); to agree, assent, consent or concur (to what has been said or proposed): รับจ้าง to engage as an hireling: รับใช้ to act according to instructions (as servants or messengers); to serve on an errand; to be at the services of another: รับตัว to act as security for: รับตำแหน่งผู้บังคับการทหาร to assume the command of troops: รับท้อง to acknowledge the paternity of: รับทุกข์ to assume or undergo punishment for: รับ-ประกัน to guarantee against loss or injury; to insure safe delivery; to go or stand bail: รับประทาน to take or receive (as when a gift is bestowed); to partake; to eat: รับปาก to make verbal acknowledgement of; to agree to verbally; to signify the acceptance (as of an agreement): รับเป็นสัตย์ to confess truthfully: รับผิด to acknowledge one's fault : รับผิดชอบ to be responsible for ; to be answerable or accountable for : รับแพ้ to acknowledge defeat : รับมรดก to inherit : รับมื่อ to fight, cope, combat or struggle with (as hand to hand) : รับรอง *lit.* "to assume the consequences," *i. e.* to answer for another ; to guarantee ; to entertain invited guests : รับรองประคองสู้ to entertain or care for (a guest) even though the entertainer is put to some inconvenience or difficulty : รับรองว่าถูกแล้ว to endorse the correctness of : รับราชการ to take up a post or position in the government : รับรู้ to be cognizant or aware of : รับเรือน to guarantee a bailer or guarantor : รับศีล to receive the sacrament of baptism : รับสั่ง an order of the king or of a prince : รับสารภาพ to confess, admit, concede or avow one's error ; *legal* to plead guilty : รับสินบน, ติดสินบน to receive bribes : รับสู้ to resist (with force) ; to prevent aggression ; to withstand assault (of an adversary) : รับหน้า to face or confront : รับเหมา to contract for by the job : รับไหว้ to acknowledge the salutation of "weying" ; to accept a gift from pupils, visitors or from the bride and groom when they call to pay their respects or visit, showing respect by "weying" : รับส่ง to say, speak, command, or give an order (for royalty).

รัมภา rum-pah *P. n.* an appellation for the Apsaras or celebrated nymphs of Indra's heaven (H. C. D. p. 19 : chd. p. 401) ; name of a species of banana.

รัมม์ rum *P. n.* joy ; delight ; pleasure ; gladness : *adj.* agreeable ; beautiful (chd. p. [401).

รัมมก rum-ma⁶-gka⁴ *P. n.* name of the month Citta (chd. p. 401) ; the fifth lunar month.

รัมย์ see รมย์ p. 689.

รัย see รย p. 689.

รัว ru-ah *v.* to vibrate, tremble, quiver or produce vocal tremors ; to beat a small drum

with quick, staccato strokes : *n.* tremble ; tremor ; quiver : *adj.* dim ; indistinct ; blurred : เพลงรัว Thai band music where the accompanying drums are struck with short quick strokes suggesting the tremulo : สั่นรัว an involuntary tremor, trembling or quivering.

รั่ว ru-ah³ *v.* to leak ; to divulge secrets ; to let be known to outsiders : *adj.* leaky : รั่วไหล to leak in streams (as water) : เรือรั่ว the boat leaks.

รั้ว ru-ah⁵ *n.* an hedge ; an enclosure ; a fence ; a barrier : ตัรั้ว, กั้นรั้ว to put up a fence ; to enclose with fencing.

รัศมิมัต, รัศมิมาน rut⁶-sa⁴-mi⁶-mut⁶ *S. adj. lit.* "radiant," *i. e.* having rays or beams ; radiant : *n.* the sun (chd. p. 401).

รัศมิ, รัสมิ rut⁶-sa⁴-mee² *P. S. n.* rays ; glory ; brightness ; brilliancy ; a rope ; a rein ; a bridle ; a ray of light or glory (chd. p. 402) : เปล่งรัศมิ to emit rays of light or glory.

รัษฎากร rut⁶-sa⁴-dah-gkorn *n. lit.* "the nation's wealth," *i.e.* national revenues ; public incomes, funds, profits, or wealth : หอรัษฎา-กร the royal treasury.

รัสสะ rut⁶-sa⁴ *P. adj.* short (chd. p. 402) : ที่นสระ long vowels *e. g.* อา, อี, etc. : รัสสระ short vowels *e. g.* อะ, อิ, etc.

รา rah *v.* to wait for ; to retard or slacken the speed ; to resist ; to scatter ; to pull or haul in : *n.* a person or individual ; a mould ; mustiness : *pron.* we ; us : *interj.* used in rhymes or poetry expressing fond thoughts of, or meditations on, or about : ขึ้นรา to become mouldy : ราปีก to slacken the speed when about to alight by reversing the wings ; to back wind by reversing the wings (as birds do) : ราไฟ to bank or check (as a fire) : ราเริด to be abandoned, discarded, deserted or allowed to fall into a state of decay : ราเรือน joists, or timbers to which the ceiling boards are attached : รานรม to be separated from ; to be deserted or forsaken ;

to wait over for the night; to spend a night: ราก้นไป to be dispersed gradually; to stop action: สองรา two persons.

ร่า rah[3] *adv.* openly; manifestly; distinctly; not clouded or obscure: เดินเร่ร่า to stroll aimlessly about (as though looking at the sights during some fair): แดดส่องร่า the sun shines brightly: ร่าเริง to be gay, gleeful, cheerful, merry, light-hearted or jolly; see ดีใจ p. 263: หัวเราะร่าๆ to laugh in a loud, cheerful, open-hearted manner.

ร้า rah[5] *v.* to be abandoned, discarded or allowed to fall into a state of decay; to be rotted: *n.* a species of bird of the heron family: ปลาร้า partly decomposed pickled fish.

ราก rark[3] *v.* to vomit, spew or belch forth: *n.* roots of trees or plants; foundation (as of buildings); origin or source; vomited matter: รากแก้ว a main root; a tap root: รากขวัญ the clavicular region of the thorax: รากเง่า source; origin; primary cause: รากดิน earthworm: รากฝอย small, minute roots; rootlets: รากฟัน fangs or roots of teeth: เหียนราก a nauseated, squeamish or qualmish feeling.

รากษส, รากโษส, รักขสะ rark[3]-sot[4] *S. n.* a demon; an ogre (chd. p. 400); goblins or evil spirits; fabulous giants (S. E. D. p. 860).

ราค rah-ka[6] *P. n.* one of the three daughters of King Mara, personifying "love." The other two are Aradi personifying "angry passion" and Tanha personifying "desire." These three maidens being beautifully bedecked and escorted by five hundred maidens danced before the Buddha. Raka tried to tempt him with concupiscence; Aradi tried to arouse his temper; Tanha tried to arouse his delight in voluptuous sensations. The Great Being drove them all away as they had no power over him (Ala. p. 222); concupiscence; lust; sexual desire or passions; sensuality (chd. p. 391).

ราคา rah-kah *n.* price; cost; purchase money; value: ของมีราคา valuables; precious articles: ขึ้นราคา to advance, or raise the price: ตีราคา, ตั้งราคา to set a price on, or for: ถนนราคา, มูลราคา values, or prices in general: ราคาขาดตัว, ราคาเด็ดขาด the net price: ราคาตลาด extrinsic value: ราคาที่ขาย sale price: ราคาที่ซื้อ cost price: ราคาที่จำนำ value in pledge: ราคาที่เป็นประกัน value in security: ราคาอยู่ที่เรียกเก็บ *legal* value in collection: ลงราคา to reduce, or lessen the price: ไม่ได้ราคา not to realize the outlay.

ราคิ, ราคิน rah-kee *P. S. n.* defect; stain; blotch; flaw; blemish; guilt: ติดราคี to be tainted with a fault or blemish (in the character): ราคีมลทิน *idiomatic* for the above.

รามพ rah-kop[6] *S. n.* a descendant from Raghu a king of the Solar race and an ancestor of Rama. A character in the Ramakean (H. C. D. p. 252: S. E. D. p. 872).

ราง rang *v.* to parch, roast or scorch in order to make brittle or crisp: *n.* groove; conduit; rail; gutter; trough: *adj.* dim; indistinct; dull; obscure; dusky: ราง *Sui, Surin,* ร้าง *E. Laos,* กร่าเซก *Khmer, Surin,* อะราง *Chaobon, Korat* (ต้น) *Peltophorum dasyrachis (Liguminosae)* (cb. p. 498): กบราง a groove-cutting plane; see กบ p. 6: เครื่องราง amulets; talismen; spirit charms: บ ราง, บ ได้ did not; can not: รางเก็บตัวหนังสือ a type-setter's composing stick: รางโค (กินน้ำ) a drinking trough for cattle: รางรองน้ำ eaves; troughs; gutters: รางปืน the stock or carriage of a gun or cannon: รางรถ rails for tram-cars: รางรถไฟ rails for steam-cars: รางหมู a swine- or pig-trough.

ร่าง rang[3] *v.* to sketch roughly; to draft in a rough form: *n.* figure; form; shape; sketch; plan or draft: เขียนเป็นร่างก่อน to write out roughly first (as in long hand): ร่างกฎหมาย to legislate or draft laws: ร่างกาย body; form; shape: ร่างงาม of beautiful form or appearance : ร่างน้อย small of figure or stature : ร่างบาง of small slender shape : ร่างผี a corpse : ร่างร้าน, นั่งร้าน a scaffold ; scaffolding : ร่างแห meshes of a net ; a species of fungus having poisonous or intoxicating properties : รูปร่าง stature ; physical shape ; form.

ร้าง rang⁵ *v.* to be abandoned, left, or deserted ; to be separated from : *adj.* abandoned ; deserted ; forsaken ; desolate ; in ruins ; dilapidated : ทิ้งร้าง to allow to become dilapidated : รกร้างว่างเปล่า, ร้างรัก to discontinue loving attentions : ร้างเมีย to be divorced from the wife : วัดร้าง a deserted or forsaken temple : หักร้างป่า to make a clearing in the jungle : อย่าร้าง, ร้างกัน to be divorced, or separated from (each other).

รางช้าง rarng-chang *v.* to be pretty, beautiful or attractive ; see งาม p. 223.

รางแดง, เถาวัลย์เหล็ก or แสงอาทิตย์ *Thai,* rang-daang, ก้องแกบ *Laos* (ต้น) *n. Ventilago calyculata* (*Rhamnaceae*) (cb. p. 294).

รางนาน, รังนาน a species of bird.

รางวัล rang-won *v.* to reward, or make remuneration for (services rendered) : *n.* reward ; recompense ; remuneration ; a prize : รางวัลของแม่สื่อ a marriage brokerage : รางวัล-ร้างวัล *an euphonic combination* : ให้ร้างวัล to distribute prizes.

ราช rart³ *P. n.* a king ; a prince ; a ruler ; a governor ; the Crown (chd. p. 397) : ข้า-ราชการ government officials : เทวราช king of the celestial hosts : นาคราช king of serpents : มหาราช the great king or ruler : ราชกร Crown revenues, taxes, tribute, duty or toll : ราชกรรม royal duties ; kingly responsibilities : ราชกันยา a princess ; a king's daughter : ราชการ government service ; Civil Service : ราชกิจ royal duties, work or obligations : ราชกุมาร a prince ; a prince of royal blood : ราชกุมารี a princess ; a royal princess : ราชกุล, ราชนิกุล a royal

family ; a member of a royal family ; a prince ; a kingly race or lineage ; a royal palace or household : ราชครู an adviser, or counsellor to the king ; a king's minister : ราชครูดำ *Thai, Pattani,* กายาะบรนนาะ *Malay, Pattani* (ต้น) *Goniothalamus macrophyllus* (*Annonaceae*), a bush or tree found in western Malaysia ; in the Peninsula it is common. The wood is aromatic. It is not known to be used in Malaya, and it is little used, if any, in Java. A decoction of the roots is used externally by the Jakuns for colds and by the Malays for steaming a patient suffering from fever, and for administering after childbirth (Burk. p. 1098 : Cb. p. 51) : ราชคฤห์ the name of the capital of Maghada. Its site is still traceable in the hills between Patna and Gaya (H. C. D. p. 253) ; a royal palace ; one of the sixteen celebrated towns of India : ราชทรัพย์, ราชสมบัติ Crown property ; royal treasures : ราชทฤศัท a grind-stone ; a mill-stone : ราช-ทวาร the king's gate ; the gate of a royal palace : ราชทัณฑ์ punishment by royal decree : ราชทินนาม a conferred title or rank : ราชทูต an envoy ; an ambassador ; a minister : ราชโทรหะ ill-treatment, oppression or maltreatment (by Crown officials) : ราชธรรม duties of a king ; obligations or responsibilities of a sovereign to his people ; laws of justice which the king might do well to observe : ราชธาน, ราชธานกะ, ราชธานิกา, ราชธานี a royal city ; a royal palace ; a capital city : ราชธามัน a royal palace : ราชธิดา a daughter of a king : ราชธุระ obligations, duties or responsibilities of the government ; the burden of governing : ราชนัดดา a cousin of the king ; the king's nephew : ราชนัย, ราชนีติ royal conduct or policy ; policies ; statesmanship : ราชนิพนธ์ compositions or literary productions of a king : ราชนีล *lit.* "royal jewel," *i. e.* the emerald : ราชบท the rank, position, office or state of being a sovereign ; kingship ; sovereignty : ราชบัณฑิตย์ sagacious men attached to the Crown : ราชบัณฑิตสภา National Bar Association : ราชบัณฑูร royal decrees : ราชบัลลังก์

royal throne : ราชบาตร a royal command : ราชบุตร a royal prince ; title of a northern vassal king : ราชบุตรี a royal princess : ราชบุร. ราชบุรี a city ; a provincial capital : ราชบุรุษ *lit.* "men, people, or followers of a king," *i. e.* government officials, or servants of the Crown ; guards of the king : ราชพี่ชิน, ราชวงศ์ of royal blood, or lineage : ราชภักดี a title for noblemen especially attached, or faithful to a king : ราชภูต a royal guard : ราชโภค the king's food : ราชโภต royal clowns and actors : ราชมนตรธร, ราชมนตรี Ministers of State : ราชมาลก a royal pavilion, or enclosure for State functions : ราชมุทรา the royal signet, or seal : ราชไมตรี a treaty, or agreement between two kings, or rulers : ราชยาน royal palanquins, cars, boats, barges, or other means of transportation for the king : ราชโยค the horoscope of those who are destined to become kings : ราชรงค์ money ; silver : ราชรถ a royal car : ราชรากษส a cruel, wicked king : ราชราช a universal emperor (wales, siamese state ceremonies p. 31) ; a supreme sovereign : ราชฤษิ, ราชรรษี an inspired poet, a sage, or saint of royal blood, or lineage : ราชลักษณ์ royal characteristics indicating that one is destined to become a king : ราชลักษมี, ราชศรี the good fortune and prosperity of a king : ราชเลข royal letters, writings, or compositions : ราชเลขานุการ the Royal Private Secretary : ราชวงศ์ the royal family, or lineage ; a title of northern vassal princes : ราชวโรงการ, ราชโองการ the king's command, decree, or instructions : ราชวสดี the royal palace, or the king's Court : ราชวัฏิ a lattice fence decorated at intervals with small, tiered, paper umbrellas. It is erected around the area in which ceremonies are performed when these take place in the open air, in order to exclude evil influences (wales, state ceremonies p. 122) : ราชวาห, ราชพาห, ราชพ่าห์ the royal charger or horse : ราชวาหยะ a royal elephant : ราชวิทยา, ราชศาสตร์ royal science ; state policy ; statesmanship : ราชวิถี a royal road ; a royal

boulevard : ราชวิหาร *lit.* "royal pleasure-seat," *i. e.* a royal monastery : ราชศฤงค์ the golden-handled umbrella ; an insignia of a royal ruler : ราชศาสน์ an autograph letter from a king to another government ; the credentials of an ambassador ; an ambassador sent by the king with the king's letter ; ราชสกนธ์ a horse : ราชสภา the king's Court ; a court constituted by a king : ราชสมบัติ kingdom : ราชสารส the royal crane ; a peacock : ราชสีห์ a king-lion ; an illustrious king : ราชสุยะ a ceremony held on the occasion of the king's accession to the throne, which all vassal monarchs must attend to offer their allegiance. In case of non-attendance, the vassal king is understood to have rebelled : ราชหัตถเลขา a letter of the king : ราชหัสดิน, ราชหัสดี elephant of the royal stable ; royal elephants : ราชโองการ, ราชวโรงการ, ราโองการ the king's decree, or command : ราชอุทยาน the king's pleasure grounds : ราชาคณะ a high Buddhist ecclesiastical official appointed by the king : ราชาธิการิน, ราชาธิการี, ราชาธิกฤต a civil service official ; a judge : ราชาธิราช, ราเชนทร์ a mighty king, emperor, or ruler (implying one ruling over vassal kings) : ราชาภิเษก a term restricted by the Thai people to coronation, meaning literally "royal anoint-ment," or ceremony for the consecration of an emperor ; the ceremony of sprinkling consecrated water upon the new king ; the coronation of the king : ราชาศัพท์ royal, or court language, *e. g.* เสวย to eat, บรรทม to sleep, etc : ราชาสนะ a throne (chd. p. 398) : ราชูปถัมภ์, ราโชปถัมภ์ royal patron, or benefactor : ราชูปโภค, ราโชปโภค royal personal utensils, implements, or vessels : ราโชปกรณ์ royal paraphernalia ; the royal standard, banner, or flag : ราโชวาท the commands, decrees, public utterances, instruction, or speeches made by the king.

ราชดัด rat[3]-cha[6]-dut[4] *Thai* see กะดัด p. 72 : การจับหลัก *Laos, Chiengmai* (ต้น) *n.* *Brucea amarissima (Simarubaceae)*, a small shrub, reaching 6 feet in height, found from

India to northern Australia; in the Peninsula it is common in open country, but is not able to spread into forest, and is therefore more or less dependent on man for its place. Considerable study has been made as to its utility and the Dutch did introduce it into their pharmacopoeia. The Malays and Javanese poultice with the leaves, pounded alone, or with a little coral-lime, for scurf, ringworm, boils, and centipede-bites. They use a poultice of it over enlarged spleens, in fever (cb. p. 241: BURK. p. 370).

ราชพฤกษ์ (ต้น) rat[3]-cha[6]-pruke[6] *n. Cassia fistula (Leguminosae)*, Indian laburnum, golden shower, a small upright tree, native to the forests of the dry region of India. From there it has been carried by man to all parts of the tropics; apparently it is also native of Java, Sumatra and Celebes. It is a beautiful object when in blossom, bearing masses of yellow flowers in pendulous racemes, suggesting the laburnum. The flowers are used as temple offerings, and the astringent bark for tanning and in native medicine. The black cylindrical pods grow to a length of from 20 to 30 inches; the pulp of these is a well known purgative. It is suited chiefly to a semi-dry region but with good drainage will thrive in moist districts up to 2,000 feet elevation. The timber is good. The heartwood is very hard, very heavy, grey to brick-red in colour, darkening on exposure, difficult to work, apt to split, but when finished may be given the appearance of old Cuban mahogany. It is said, in Java, to last longer in the ground than teak. It is used for posts, carts, agricultural implements, etc. The Thai use the heart-wood as a masticatory, and trade in it. The leaves are given to elephants medicinally. The plant has been tried as a green manure in southern India, and for this purpose was found moderately rich in phosphates (MCM. p. 85; BURK. p. 475).

ราชย์, ราชัย rart[3] *S. n.* sovereignty; royal-ty; monarchy; government; kingdom; empire; country (chd. p. 399): ราชยางค์ the requisite of regal administration (chd. p. 339); virtues of a king, or monarch.

ราชัน, ราชา rah-chun *P. n.* a king; a prince; a ruler; a governor (chd. p. 397).

ราชันย์ rah-chun *S. n.* a vassal sovereign, or prince; one of royal blood, or lineage.

ราชายตนะ see เกตกี(ต้น) p. 119.

ราชาวดี rah-chah-wa[6]-dee *n.* an enamel for gold or silver (as bases); a wash basin for the king's use.

ราชิ, ราชี rah-chi[6] *P. n.* a streak; a line; a row (chd. p. 399); the body: ราชีกา series; order.

ราชินี, ราชญี rah-chi[6]-nee *P. n.* a queen (chd. p. 399): ราชินีกุล, ราชินิกุล lineage of the queen; relatives of the queen.

ราชิล rah-chin *P. adj.* stupid; silly (chd. p. 399); see โง่ p. 227.

ราเชน rah-chain *n.* a scented substance; perfumes for the use of the king.

ราญ rarn, ราญรอน, รำราญ see รบ p. 688. *v.* to fight; to be in combat.

ราด rart[3] *v.* to spread or sprinkle about; to pour out; to pour down upon or over; to cause to splash against: เรี่ยราด scattered or strewn about in a disorderly manner.

ราต rart[3] *P. v.* to enjoy oneself; to delight in (chd. p. 401): ธรรมราต to delight in the observance of the Law.

ราตร, ราตรี rart[3] *P. n.* night (chd. p. 403): ในเวลาราตรี during the night: ราตรีกาล night-time: ราตรีภาค part of the night: เสื้อ-ราตรี evening dress.

ราตรี (ต้น) rah-dtree *n. Cestrum nocturnum (Solanaceae)*, lady of the night, *dama de nocke*, a large straggling shrub, 5 to 8 feet high, having long drooping branches which bear greenish white flowers which are strongly scented at night. These are very tiny, being only about 2½ cm. long (V. P. p. 234 : MCM. p. 109) : - ราตรีแดง (ต้น) *Beloperone plumbagi-nifolia.* Mom Rajota is said to have introduced this Brazilian flowering shrub to Bangkok about 30 years ago from Peninsular Thailand (winit, N. H. J. S. S. IX, 1, p. 90.

ราโท   rah-toh *n.* the sides, or edges of a boat; the gunwale of a boat, or vessel : บันทุก-จมราโท to load the boat over the water-line : ไม้ราโท a protecting, wooden edging attached to the sides of junks; a strake.

ราธา   rah-tah *S. n.* prosperity; success; accomplishment (S. E. D. p. 876).

ราน   rarn *v.* to break; to crack; to sever, or shatter; to cut, trim, or lop off (as branches); to rush in; to burst upon : *adj.* crackled; cracked; veined (as Sawankaloke pottery): รานรอน *idiomatic* to cut or trim (as timber into proper sizes): ร้าวราน to offend against : รุกราน to break in, or penetrate by force.

ร่าน   rarn[3] *v.* to want or desire; to be eager for; to hasten forward, or after : ร่านดู to be eager to look at : ร่านทำ eager to do : เร่งร่าน overly hasty; impetuous; exceedingly furious; rapid.

ร้าน   rarn[5] *n.* market shop or stall; a shop or compartment in the bazaar; a booth; a bamboo seat, bench, horse or platform, used as a day-bed, or as a place for displaying goods for sale : แตงร้าน see แตง p. 376 : เฝ้าร้าน to be in charge of the stall : ร้าน-ขายเครื่องหอม a perfumery shop : ร้านเฝียงขับนก a hut for shelter while driving away birds : ร้านชำ a grocer's store : ร้านผัก a vegetable stall; a scaffolding for vines : ร้านผ้า a stall for selling cloth or piece goods : ร้าน-ตลาด a stall in the market : ร้านเหล้า a public bar; a liquor shop : ออกร้าน to sell goods at a fair.

ราบ   rarp[3] *adj.* flat; level; even; smooth : ที่ราบ a level place or plain : บ้านเมืองราบคาบ

the country is in a quiet peaceful condition : ปราบราบ to have been completely subdued : ราบดังหน้ากลอง smooth and even as a drum head : ราบรื่น flat, smooth, level and pleasing to the eye (as a lawn): ราบเรียบ, ราบคาบ, ราบเสมอ *idiomatic* tranquil, peaceful, undisturbed.

ราพณ์   rarp[8] *P. n.* the giant Ravana; the demon king of Lanka or Ceylon (H. C. D. p. 264); giants in general; also, a name for Totsakan; see ทศกัณฐ์ under ทศ ๒ p. 401 : ราพณา-สูร Ravana, the demon king (used in poetical language).

ราม   rarm *P. n.* gold; Rama; a character in the Ramayana; name of three celebrated Indian kings and adopted by the kings of the Chakri (Bangkok) dynasty : *adj.* gay; joyous; delightful; agreeable; lovable; affording pleasure.

รามสูร   rarm-ma[6]-soon[2] *n.* a mythological giant, or demon armed with an ax; an altered form of รามปรศุ a fierce, or cruel Brahmin.

รามัญ, มอญ   rah-mun *n.* Pegu; Peguan; Mohn; see ตะเลง p. 357.

รามายณะ   rah-mah-ya[6]-na[6] *S. n.* the Ramayana, the oldest of the Sanskrit epic poems in which the adventures of Rama are recounted. This poem was written by the sage Valmiki. It is supposed to have been composed about five centuries B. C. and to have received its present form a century or two later. The Ramakean is the Thai version which contains some new episodes (H. C. D. p. 262).

ราย   rai *v.* to scatter, or be scattered; to stand, or be posted at intervals, or distances apart (as sentries along a road): *n.* a list, account, section, or item; a report, statement or declaration; a narrative or record : *adj.* a numerical designatory particle for lawsuits, litigations, robberies, letters, documents, and sums of money : กระจายเรียรายตามทาง strewn in disorderly fashion along the road : ความ-รายนี้ this matter, affair, event or litigation :

เงินรายนี้ this money account : เงินเรี่ยราย sub-scriptions or donations : จากรายหนึ่ง from one account, quarter or section : บาญชีรายรับ-รายจ่าย credit and debit account : รับจ้าง-เป็นรายวัน hired (to work) by the day : ราย-ขัดข้อง a case where default is made (as when one fails to appear in court after being summoned) : รายจ่าย a disbursement account : ทำรายงาน, ทำรายการ to make a report or submit particulars respecting some trans-action : รายงานการประชุม minutes of a meeting : รายงานการประชุมครั้งก่อน minutes of the previous meeting : รายชื่อ a roll ; a register ; a registry : รายชื่อสิ่งของ a catalogue, or inventory of goods : รายได้ที่ตั้งไว้สำหรับ-บุคคลหรือการกุศล endowments for individuals or for philanthropic purposes : (เงิน) อากรรายได้ income tax : รายทาง, ราย ๆ ป along the way, journey or tour ; little by little but often (as เสียรายทาง to spend by driblets along the way here and there a little) : รายรับ, รายได้ a credit account ; income ; receipts : รายวัน by the day, or day by day (as of workmen) : เรียงรายตามยศ placed according to order, rank or position : เรี่ยรายเงิน to take up a collec-tion ; to issue a subscription list (for money) : หลายราย several lists, items or accounts.

ร่าย rai[3] v. to read ; to recite incantations or formulas used in sorcery ; to go in a ser-pentine course or line ; to zigzag ; to walk here and there, this way and that way : n. a Thai comedy, or poetry : เที่ยวเร่ร่าย to wander here and there : ร่ายเจ้า to change from one master to another : ร่ายที่ to change from one place to another : ร่ายไม้ to climb or crawl along zigzag, clinging to fence posts or trees (set in a line) while seek-ing for a way to go along (as a squirrel) : ร่ายหนี fleeing in a side to side course, or in a crooked direction : ร่ายอาจารย์ to change from one teacher (or school) to another.

ร้าย rai[5] adj. cruel ; fierce ; evil ; bad ; harsh ; brutal ; violent : คิดร้าย, ปองร้าย to plot evil against ; to work or plan under-handedly : เคราะห์ร้าย misfortune : ดีร้าย

by chance ; but ; as if : ดุร้าย fierce ; vicious : ร้ายกาจ idiomatic ferociously savage (see กาจ p. 91) : ร้ายแรง superlative degree evil, brutal, or harsh in the extreme : สัตว์ร้าย fierce or ferocious animals.

ร่ายรัง rai[3]-rung adj. radiant ; brilliant.

ราว, ระราว row n. hand-rail ; balustrade ; row ; line ; edging, hedge or border (as around flower beds or compounds) ; a matter or in-cident : adv. about (in respect to quantity) ; approximately : ราวกะ, ราวกับ being about like that ; resembling, or analogous to : ราว-กะได a staircase rail : ราวดาบ a rack for swords : ราวตากผ้า a clothes-line or rail : ราวป่า edge of the forest ; forest line or boun-dary of the jungle : ราวพระแสง a rack for royal swords, canes or weapons : ราวเรื่อง a collection of papers or documents pertaining to some subject : รุ่นราว approximately of the age of puberty : วิ่งราว to snatch, or grab and run.

ร้าว row[5] v. to be cracked, splintered, split, cleaved or chipped : แตกร้าว, แตกราน to be-come estranged, alienated, or unfriendly ; to be enemies : รอยร้าว traces of a crack, or split : ร้าวฉาน to become antagonistic ; to break the bonds of friendship : ร้าวแตก idiomatic cracked, fractured, splintered, cleft.

ราว rah-wee v. to attack ; to harass ; to vex ; to annoy or molest : รบราว to besiege ; to wage a merciless, devastating war.

ราศี, ราสี rah-see[2] P. S. n. a heap ; a mass ; a pile ; a quantity ; a group ; a sign of the zodiac (chd. p. 401) ; 30 degrees of a circle, being the number of degrees in each sign of the zodiac ; beauty ; grandure ; splendour ; glory ; rays : ราศีเมษ the first sign of the zodiac, the Ram or Aries : ราศีพฤษก the second sign of the zodiac, the Bull or Taurus : ราศีมิถุน the third sign of the zodiac, the Twins or Gemini : ราศีกรกฎ the fourth sign of the zodiac, the Crab or Cancer : ราศีสิงห์ the fifth sign of the zodiac, the Lion or Leo :

ราศีกันย์ the sixth sign of the zodiac, the Virgin or Virgo : ราศีดุล the seventh sign of the zodiac, the Balance or Libra : ราศีพฤศจิก the seventh sign of the zodiac, the Scorpion or Scorpio : ราศีธนุ the ninth sign of the zodiac, the Archer or Sagitarius : ราศีมังกร the tenth sign of the zodiac, the Horn-goat or Capricornus : ราศีกุมภ์ the eleventh sign of the zodiac, the Water-bearer or Aquarius : ราศีมีน the twelfth sign of the zodiac, the Fish, or Pisces : สง่าราศี magnificent splendour : สิบสองราศี the twelve signs of the zodiac.

ราษฎร์, ราษฎร rart[3] n. territory ; country ; realm ; kingdom ; district (chd. p. 403) ; people ; multitude ; citizens ; population of a country ; a king's subjects : ผู้แทนราษฎร a representative of the people.

ราษตรี rart[3]-sa[4]-dtree n. night : ราษตรี- [มัธยม midnight.

ราส rart[3] adj. short.

ราหุ, ร่าหุ์, ราหู rah-hoo[4] P. S. n. "the seizer," i. e. name of a monster who is supposed to cause eclipses by taking the sun, or moon into his mouth (chd. p 397) ; a celestial monster which causes eclipses by eating the sun, or moon (Ala. p. 218) ; mythologically, Rahu is a Daitya, a race of demons and giants, who is supposed to seize the sun, or moon and swallow them, thus obscuring their rays and causing eclipses (H. C. D. p. 252).

ราหุล rah-hoon[2] P. n. name of Gotama Buddha's son, born before he retired from the world (chd. p. 397).

รำ rum v. to gesticulate, dance, or act in pantomimic fashion : n. bran of rice and other cereals ; a pantomime ; a solo dance : แกลบรำ chaff and bran ; เต้นรำ to dance (European fashion) : ฟ้อนรำ, ระบำ two similar forms of solo dancing which may be combined. These dances consist of undulating motions of the body, combined with a swaying movement, while the arms wave gracefully. The dancer keeps step to music. ฟ้อนรำ is considered more classical and is performed only

by people of high birth and rank, and on state occasions, as when a king is entering a provincial capital. ระบำ is the corresponding theatrical dance : รำกระบอง single-stick fencing, a marital exercise which appears to prevail throughout Indonesia. It was a great feature in Chinese monasteries from the sixteenth century onwards : รำกระบี่กระบอง to dance the ancient sword and club dance to military music : รำเขนง to dance the ceremonial Brahmin dance in honour of Siva in which the dancer carries a horn (เขนง) of consecrated water that he sprinkles all around over the assembly (probably typifying the cornucopia dance) : รำโคม to dance the lantern dance : รำช้อย to dance gracefully or attractively : รำดาบ sword dancing or brandishing : รำเท้า to dance with artistic gestures, movements or attitude of the feet ; to dance on the toes : รำผี to dance around a coffin (as practiced by some people) : รำเพลง to dance to music : รำแพน to strut about with tail-feathers spread (as a peacock) : รำแพนพ้อน to make gestures or turns waving peacock feathers (as an acrobat or tight-rope walker) : รำรงค์ lit. "to dance on the battlefield," i. e. to dance a war dance (as before going into war, or on the celebration of a victory) : รำร้อง to sing while dancing : รำละคร to act in a comedy or in a theatre : มอญรำ Peguan dancing.

ร่ำ rum[3] v. to recite, tell, complain, murmur or speak continually or incessantly ; to incorporate with scents or perfumes, as แป้งร่ำ scented powders : ร่ำผ้า to perfume clothes or cloth : บ่นร่ำไป to complain persistently : ร่ำบ่น to complain continually : ร่ำไป uninterruptedly ; continually ; often ; unbrokenly : ร่ำรวย to be rich : ร่ำรัก to pursue uninterruptedly with loving advances : ร่ำร่าไร dilatory ; tardy : ร่ำเรียน to study energetically or continuously ; ร่ำไร to be slow, sluggish, indolent, inactive or slothful ; to be given to truancy : ร่ำสั่ง to command continually : ร่ำให้, ร่ำร้อง to mourn or weep unceasingly.

รำคาญ   rum-karn v. to be vexed, teased or annoyed; to be tortured or tormented to the limit of endurance: ความรำคาญใจ annoyance; agony or anguish of mind: รำคาญตา annoying to the eyes; being an eyesore: รำคาญหู irritating to the ear.

รำงับ see ระงับ p. 694.

รำจวน see รัญจวน p. 703.

รำบาญ, รำราญ   rum-barn v. to be in combat; to fight; derived from ราญ see p. 709.

รำพัน   rum-pun v. to regret, repine or bewail (the absence of); to speak about; to bemoan the absence of (in a friendly or solicitous manner): พร่ำรำพัน to grieve or mourn for: ร่ำรำพัน to lament incessantly.

รำพาย, รำเพย   rum-pai v. to blow in gusts, or puffs (of wind); to flap (as wings); to fan; to cause the air to move in gusts; see กระพือ p. 41: รำพายพัด blowing in gusts, or squalls: รำพายหวนพัด a whirlwind: วายุรำพาย the wind blows.

รำพึง   rum-perng v. to think of; to meditate, or ponder about; to consider, or reflect: รำพึงคิด to contemplate; to deliberate; to ruminate: รำพึงถึง to contemplate, reflect, or consider: รำพึงในใจ to ponder; to think over ceaselessly.

รำเพย (ต้น)   rum-pur-ie n. Thevetia neriifolia (Apocynaceae), lucky-beans, lucky-seeds, a tree with long yellow blossoms. It is found from the West Indies to Brazil. It was brought into cultivation in Europe in 1735, and from Europe was distributed to the tropics in general, as a showy plant. It is sometimes called the yellow oleander. The stems are milky; the leaves are narrow and four, or five inches long (MCM. pp. 117, 462: BURK. p. 2154).

รำมะนา   rum-ma⁶-nah n. a small drum.

รำมะนาด   rum-ma⁶-nart³ n. pyorrhoea alveolaris, a purulent inflammation of the dental periosteum with progressive necrosis of the alveoli, and looseness of the teeth; a dental disease which causes swelling of the gum, giving severe pain to the victim.

รำมะร่อ   rum-ma⁶-raw³ adv. nearly; imminently; almost; see เกือบ p. 127; ใกล้ p. 135: จะสิ้นใจอยู่รำมะร่อ nearly dead; being at death's door.

รำย้อย   rum-yaw-ie⁵ v. to be hanging loosely; to be pendulous; to swing to and fro.

รำแย้   rum-yaa⁵ n. a kind of grain.

รำรา, ลำลำ see เกือบ p. 127; จวน p. 233.

รำไร   rum-rai adj. blurred; indistinct; smeared; small; waving.

รำลึก see ระลึก p. 698.

รำหัด   rum-hut⁴ v. to add to or sprinkle on afterwards (as an ingredient in compounding a remedy); to put into or insert (in among): adj. slight; weak; soft.

ริ   ri⁶ v. to consult; to resolve; to start or begin to think or plan for: ริขึ้น, ริทำ to be the first to originate: ริคิดอ่าน to initiate or originate plans: ริป้อง to plan for; to make a scheme for; to forecast, devise or design (for the future).

ริก ๆ   rik⁶-rik⁶ adj. trembling; struggling; shivering; shaking; shuddering (lightly or gently, but continuously).

ริดสีดวง   rit⁶-see²-du-ang n. a term applied to several chronic maladies: ริดสีดวงงอก hoemorrhoids, piles: ริดสีดวงปอด phthisis: ริดสีดวงพลวก sprue: ริดสีดวงมูก dysentery: ริดสีดวงแห้ง tuberculosis with progressive aenemia.

ริตติ, ริกติ   rit⁶ P. adj. emptied; void; bared; vacant (chd. p. 404).

ริน   rin v. to pour off slowly or carefully; to decant: adv. slowly; gently; continually (used regarding the flow of water): รินแต่ส่วนใส to decant off the clear portion: รินน้ำชา to pour the tea.

รื่น rin[5] *n.* a gnat; a sand-fly: รื่นร่าน gnats and insects.

ริบ rip[6] *v.* to seize in default of meeting an obligation; to confiscate: กวาดริบหมด to seize and carry off everything: โทษริบ judgement with confiscation (of goods): ริบ-เครื่องยศ to recall insignia of rank (as when an official has committed a crime): ริบ-ราชบาตร *lit.* "to confiscate according to the royal order," *i. e.* to seize property on behalf of the Crown.

ริบรี่, ริบหรี่ rip[6]-ree[3] *adj.* dimmed; dusky; darkish; obscure; almost extinguished (as a lamp).

ริปู, ริปู ri[6]-bpoo[4] *P. n.* an enemy (chd. p. 404); a foe; a crook; a rogue; a crafty person.

ริม rim *n.* rim; brim; edge; border; shore-line: *adj.* nearby; at the side of; contiguous to; beside: *adv.* nearly; almost: ริมน้ำ along the water's edge; by the brink of the water: ริมฝีปาก, ริมสีปาก lips.

รี่, รี่ ri[6]-ree *P. n.* brass (chd. p. 404).

ริ้ว riew[5] *n.* line; strip; slice; stripe; streak; welt or scratch marks (as caused by the claws of an animal): คนขี้ริ้ว mean, vulgar, abject, wretched persons; a vagrant; a vagabond; a loafer: ผ้าขี้ริ้ว rags; tatters: ปลาริ้ว fish cut into strips and dried: รอยเฆี่ยน-เป็นริ้วๆ streaks or welts on the skin from flogging: ริ้วแร่ง *idiomatic* inherent strength.

ริษยา rit[6]-sa[4]-yah[2] ฤษยา *incorrect n.* envy; jealousy; ill-will (chd. p. 160): คิดริษยา to have jealous thoughts: อิจฉาริษยา *idiomatic* envy and jealousy.

รี ree *v.* to wait for, delay, stop or hesitate; see คอย p. 192: *adj.* oblong; oval; tapering (to a rounded point): ยาวรี tapering in length.

รี่ ree[3] *v.* to move straight to the place; to approach or rush directly in: *adv.* rapidly; promptly; rather quickly; straight towards;

head on (as two goats when butting each other): รี่เข้าไปหา to approach recklessly, abruptly or rashly (as two dogs or two fight-ing fishes attacking each other): น้ำไหลรี่ๆ the water flows at a great rate.

รี้ ree[5] *v.* to remove from; to march forward: *n.* a force; an army; troops; soldiers: รี้กร to fawn upon; to allure; to entice a fascinat-ing, dangerous woman: รี้พล, รี้พลโยธา an army; a troop; a battalion; an array of sol-diers or forces.

รีด, รูด reet[3] *v.* to force out, or extract by circular pressure; to lengthen by squeezing, milling or pressing; to forge or beat out (as metals): รีดท้อง, รีดลูก to produce an abortion: รีดผ้า to iron clothes: รีดนม to draw milk from: รีดน้ำ to squeeze out the water: รีดเหล็ก to shape iron with a hammer or in a rolling mill: รีดออก to extract, or express (as juice).

รีต, จารีตร reet[3] *n.* ritual; rule; custom; religious rites of sects: เข้ารีต to become a member of a different sect; to be converted, or to embrace another religion: นอกรีต to be an apostate; to desert one's faith, religion, custom, or party.

รีบ, รีบเร่ง, รีบร้อน reep[3] *v.* to make haste; to push on; to hurry, press, urge on or accel-erate: *adv.* quickly; hastily; precipitately; see ด่วน p. 320.

รี้ริก ree[5]-rik[6] *onomat.* from the sound of a child's laughter: หัวเราะรี้ริก to laugh mer-rily or cheerfully.

รีรอ, รีๆรอๆ ree-raw *v.* to hesitate, waver or demur; to be undecided (as regarding [action).

รึกต์ see ฤตต์ p. 713.

รึง reung *v.* to bind or tie tightly together: *adj.* hot; warm; tepid: ผูกรึงตรึงตรา *idi-omatic* to tie up or nail down securely and seal; see ตรึง p. 345: เถ้ารึง coals that are still warm; see เถ้า p. 392: รึงรัด, มัดรึง to tie, unite or link together firmly.

รุ่ง　reung[5] _v._ to pull, drag, haul, tug or draw; see ดึง p. 331; ฉุด p. 270.

รื่น　rurn[3] _v._ to be delighted, pleased, charmed, gratified or joyful; see ชื่น p. 298: รื่นรื่น a delightful shade: รื่นชื่น _idiomatic_ joyous hilarity: รื่นเริง to be enchanted, captivated or amused (as by some entertainment); to feel a state of delight, pleasure or ecstasy; see เพลิน p. 597: หอมรื่น an agreeable fragrance.

รื้น, รก　rurn[5] _adj._ disordered; unkempt; confused; overgrown with weeds; cluttered with rubbish.

รื้อ　rur[5] _v._ to tear down; to undo; to destroy; to demolish; to dismantle; to raze, or pull to pieces: รื้อไข้ to convalesce from a sickness: รื้อฟื้น to reestablish, revive or renew (as an old acquaintance).

รุ　roo[6] _v._ to clean out; to clear off (as shopworn goods); to evacuate; to take a laxative or physic; to dismiss employees (as during retrenchment time): รุท้อง to effect a good purge: รุหลังคา to clean out the old roofing material: ยารุ a purgative.

รุก　rook[6] _v._ to move or push forward; to advance the pieces (as in playing chess); to penetrate by force; to invade (another's territory): บุกรุกหนาม to climb through thorny bushes: พูดรุกราน to use harsh, piercing, severe language: รุกกิน to capture: รุกจน to checkmate: รุกราฏ to check the king in order to capture another piece (in chess): รุกรบ, รุกราญ to charge or fight, advancing into the enemy's land: รุกรื้น to drive forward, thus causing the enemy to fall back: รุกราน to trespass into; to rush in forcibly or impetuously; to oppress: รุกเอา to try to get the truth out of a person by using wise, adroit, or threatening questions: หมากรุก the game of chess.

รุกข์, รุกษ　rook[6] _P. n._ a tree: _adj._ rough; cruel (chd. p. 405): รุกขชาติ the vegetable kingdom: รุกขเทวดา a tree fairy, genius or spirit: รุกขธิดา nymphs of the trees: รุกขพิมาน a tree spirit's heavenly abode: รุกขมูลิก one who lives at the foot of a tree (chd. p. 405); one of thirteen ascetic practices that lead Buddhist monks out of a condition of passion: รุกขาทนี _lit._ "that which eats trees," _i. e._ parasites; parasitical plants (chd. p. 405).

รุกขก　rook[6]-ka[4]-gka[4] _P. n._ a small tree [(chd. p. 405).

รุกรุย　rook[6]-ru-ie _adj._ tattered; scattered; dispersed; disordered; confused; strewn about; mean; worthless. [

รุกษ　see รุกข์ p. 715.

รุ่ง　roong[3] _n._ dawn: _adj._ shining; bright; radiant; luminous: ใกล้รุ่ง, ย่ำรุ่ง nearing dawn: รุ่งขึ้น, รุ่งพรุ่งนี้ on the morrow: รุ่งแจ้ง, รุ่งสว่าง clear daylight: รุ่งเช้า, รุ่งราตรี at dawn; at daybreak: รุ่งราง early break of dawn: รุ่งเรือง brilliant; magnificent; bright; shining; luminous; radiant: รุ่งโรจน์ glittering rays of light: รุ่งโรจน์ โชตนาการ dazzling light or rays: รุ่งแล้ว after daybreak: รุ่งสาง the passing of the dawn; the growing light of day: รุ่งแสง rays of the dawn.

รุ้ง (นก)　roong[5] _n._ the crested serpent eagle, _Spilornis chula_ (Gaird. J. S. S. IX, p. 9).

รุ้ง　roong[5] a rainbow; lustre; sparkle (of gems, etc.): _adj._ wide; broad: รุ้งกินน้ำ a rainbow resting on the sea: รุ้งเป็นคุ้งเข้าไป washed into the shape of a semicircle (as the bank of a river or canal): รุ้งพราย the iridescence of shells, mother of pearl, and gems: รุ้งแวง width and length: เส้นรุ้ง length or distance (as in measuring the area).

รุ่งรัง　roong-rung _adj._ tattered; ragged; having things strewn about without order; confused: ผมรุ่งรัง dishevelled hair: เรือนรุ่งรัง an unkempt, untidy, or disorderly house.

รุจ, รุจา　root[6] _P. S. adj._ bright; radiant; brilliant (S. E. D. p. 882).

รุจิ, รุจี, รุจิ　roo[6]-chji[4] _P. n._ light; splendour; ray; desire; inclination; pleasure;

preference (Chd. p. 404); beauty: *adj.* bright and shining; illuminated; glorious.

รุจิร roo⁶-chji⁴-ra⁶ *P. n.* brilliant; beautiful; agreeable (Chd. p. 404); see งาม p. 223; กระทัดรัด p. 24.

รุชา roo⁶-chah *P. n.* disease; pain; ruin; damage; destruction (Chd. p. 405): รุชาโรค a malcondition causing pain in the abdomen or stomach.

รุด, รีบรุด root⁶ *adv.* hastily; speedily; without delay; promptly: รีบรุด acceleration of action: รุดหนี to expedite the act of fleeing.

รุต root⁶ *P. n.* a cry; a noise (Chd. p. 406); a roar, bay or bleat.

รุทธิ์ root⁶ *P. n.* obstruction; hindrance; prevention; extinction (Chd. p. 404); see ปิด p. 526; ดับ p. 323.

รุทร root⁶ *S. adj.* furious; dreadful; terrific; horrible (S. E. D. p. 883).

รุธิร, รุเธียร roo⁶-ti⁶-ra⁶ *P. n.* blood; a red colour (Chd. p. 405).

รุน, ดุน roon *v.* to push; to urge on; see ดัน p. 323; to evacuate or clean out (as by a laxative): *n.* a bag-net for prawns and shrimps: รุนกุ้ง to catch prawns by means of a scoop-net: รุนแรง violently; excessively: รุนหลัง to push from the back: ยารุน a laxative or mild purgative remedy.

รุ่น roon³ *n.* time; period; age (of life): *adj.* growing up; young; youthful: รุ่นราวคราวกัน being of about the same youthful age: รุ่นสาว a young girl: รุ่นหนุ่ม adolescence.

รุบรู้ roop⁶-roo³ *adj.* indistinct; dim; murky; misty; faint (as early dawn or the phase of the waning of the moon).

รุม room *v.* to flock together; to be collected in crowds or herds; see ประดัง p. 499: กลุ้มรุม to gather in crowds, throngs, mobs or masses: รุมกันจับ to collect together in a throng in order to catch or capture: รุมกันตี to stick together in throngs or crowds in order to fight, or attack: รุมทำ to act in unison, or in concerted action: รุมร้อน to suffer from a continuous condition of heat or fever.

รุ่ม room³ *v.* to strike, hit or knock repeatedly with quick strokes: *adj.* peppery; heated; warm; tepid: รุ่มรัก a condition of lukewarm or fitful love or affection.

รุ่มร่าม room³-rarm³ *adj.* wearing shabby garments; badly dressed; having ill-fitting clothes; (dressed) in rags or tatters; without order or proper fit.

รุ่ย ru-ie³ *adj.* loose; fragile; brittle; loamy (as soil): รุ่ย (ต้น) see ถั่ว (ต้น) p. 384: รุ่ยร่วน brittle; easily pulverized: รุ่ยร่าย badly arranged; scattering; in disorder; helter skelter: ขาดรุ่ย ragged; rent; frayed.

รุ่ยโรม ru-ie-rome *Cam. n.* a domestic fly.

รุษฎ์ root⁶ *P. v.* to be enraged (Chd. p. 406); to be angry, irritated, vexed, or provoked at; see โกรธ p. 133.

รุหะ, รูหะ roo⁶-ha⁴ *S. adj.* growing; sprouting; shooting; rising (S. E. D. p. 885); see งอก [p. 221.

รู้ see ช่อง p. 283.

รู roo³ *v.* to rub, scrape or scratch against; to cause to grate or drag against; see ครูด p. 183: รูกระเบื้อง to scrape off the old roof tiles: รูด้าย to smooth out into a thread (as flax).

รู้ roo⁵ *v.* to have an understanding of; to be able to perceive; to comprehend the meaning; to have an acquired knowledge by study, mental exertion, or experience: ความรู้ practical wisdom; understanding: นักรู้ *slang* a cunning person; a crafty or sly person: ผู้รับรู้ accomplices: ผู้รู้ผู้เห็น eye-witnesses: ฟังไม่รู้เรื่อง to be unable to understand what is said: ไม่รู้ตาย immortal: ไม่รู้ปรวนแปร immutable; unchangeable: รู้กล to see through another's scheme or stratagem: รู้ความ, อายุรู้ความ rational; of age: รู้คิด to be courteous, wise or clever; to be unwilling to be outwitted, or a loser in a transaction; to be a careful, able, skillful thinker; to be a good schemer or planner: รู้คุณ to be grateful, thankful or indebted to: รู้คุณรู้บุญ to be grateful for; to manifest gratitude for: รู้จัก to be acquainted with; to remember or recognize on meeting: รู้จักชอบพอกัน to have just a passing acquaintance with: รู้จักโดยรูปพรรณ to be able to identify: รู้จักมักจี่ to be friendly towards; to become acquainted with (well enough to tickle): รู้ตัว to be conscious of one's fault or danger; to perceive or become aware of through intuitive faculties: รู้ที่ to become wise regarding a rival's or opponent's schemes or tricks: รู้มลาก to know much; to understand well: รู้มาก to know how to get the advantage (over another); to be sly, tricky, cunning or designing: รู้ไม่ได้ it is impossible to know: รู้รอบ, รู้จบ to be completely conversant with or about: รู้เล่น to be proficient in all games (as gambling): รู้สึก to experience; to feel or know (by the sense of touch); to be cognizant or aware of: รู้สึกผิด to be conscious of a fault: รู้สึกเสียใจ to be repentant; to feel sorry for: เรียนรู้ to learn: สอนให้รู้ to teach: แสนรู้ clever; adroit.

รูด, รีด root[3] *v.* to cause to glide, slide or slip smoothly and easily (as curtain rings along a wire); to grasp with one hand and pull with the other (as when separating leaves from the stems); to express or dislodge by a constricting downward motion (as in milking): รูดเข้า to strip off grains of rice from the stalk: รูดโคลน to scrape off mud (as from the limbs): รูดปลาไหล to clean off eels (as by scraping them with straw or leaves): รูดม่านออก to slide open the curtain; to pull the curtain open: รูดออก, รีดออก to express or expel by a constricting pressure.

รูป roop[3] *P. S. n.* form; materiality (Ala. p. 172); an image; a picture; a figure; a shape; representation; the body; *grammar* a verbal

or nominal form; beauty; natural state; characteristic (chd. p. 405): ถ่ายรูป, ถอดรูป, ชักรูป to take a photograph: ทองรูปพรรณ gold ornaments in general: พระพุทธรูป a statue of the Buddha: รูปแกะ carved images; sculpture: รูปเขียน a drawing; an etching: รูปความ *legal* nature of the case: รูปเครื่องหมาย emblem; รูปฉาก painted scenery on a screen or curtain: รูปถ่าย a photograph: รูปทรง a statue: รูปธรรม nature of form or appearance: รูปปั้น an image moulded in plaster, clay or wax: รูปประดิษฐ a device: รูปเปรียบ an effigy: รูปภาพ a picture, portrait or drawing: รูปภาพบ้านเมือง views of towns or cities: รูปพรรณ form, shape and appearance; wrought gold or silver ornaments; a descriptive form for identification (as for cattle or horses): รูปพระ, รูปเคารพ religious images: รูปร่าง appearance; features; figure; shape: รูปวาด a drawing or sketch: รูปหล่อ a statue of cast metal.

รูปิยะ roo-bpi[4]-ya[6] *P. n.* silver bullion; specie (chd. p. 406); a silver coin used during the time of the Buddha; wrought silver or gold (S. E. D. p. 886).

เร่ ray[3] *v.* to wander about; to go in a crooked or zigzag course: ใจเร่ร่อน inconstant, changeable or fickle in disposition: เที่ยวเร่ to wander about aimlessly, or homelessly: เร่ขอ to wander about asking alms: เร่รวน doubting; wavering; undecided: เร่หา to wander about seeking (as for strayed cattle): เร่ร่อน, เร่ร่าย to wander about at random.

เรข, เรขา ray-ka[4] *P. v.* to write; to draw; to paint: *n.* a line; a streak; a stroke; a scratch; a stripe (chd. p. 404): *adj.* handsome; as beautiful as a picture or drawing: เรขาคณิต geometry.

เร่ง reng *adj.* rapid; agile; swift; speedy; doing with quick short acts or strokes; see คี่ p. 388.

เร่ง, เร้ง   reng[3] *v.* to urge on, hasten or accelerate; to tighten (as the binding around a box): เร่งเงิน to request prompt payment; to reclaim or recover money due, by force: เร่งทำ, เร่งงาน to speed up the work or job: เร่งเท้า to accelerate the walking speed or gait: เร่งรัด, เร่งรีบ, รีบเร่ง *idiomatic* to haste, or act with alacrity: เร่งร่าย to go urgently, eagerly or expeditiously: เร่งลูกหนี้ to take steps to make the debtors pay.

เรณุ, เรณุ, เรณุก   ray-noo[6] *P. S. n.* dust; pollen; sand; fine particles (chd. p. 404): เรณุเกสรดอกไม้ pollen of flowers.

เร้น   ren[5] *v.* to hide; to conceal; to secrete; to evade; to avoid; see ซ่อน p. 306; บัง p. 474: ซ่อนเร้น *idiomatic* concealed, veiled, or wrapped in mystery: เที่ยวเร่เร้น to wander about hiding here and there: หนีเร้น fleeing here and there under cover.

เรไร   ray-rai *v.* to sing or make a noise like the cicada: *n.* a cicada that utters a plaintive note (also known as จั๊กจั่น); a kind of wind instrument played at Buddhist religious services; a kind of sweetmeat, or cake made of fine strands of vermicelli (eaten with sesame seeds and coconut milk).

เร็ว   ray-oh *adv.* quickly; hastily; hurriedly; speedily; rapidly; see ด่วน p. 320: คนใจเร็ว one quick "on the trigger," impetuous, or impulsive; one acting unguardedly: เร็ว ๆ very quickly; be quick; make haste; hurry.

เร่ว (ต้น)   ray-oh[3] *n.* cardamom; wild cardamom; *Amomum krervanh (Zingiberaceae)*, one of the first rank substitutes for cardamoms is probably the Thai กระวาน. A second Thai cardamom is the เร่ว which in Customs returns is called "bastard cardamoms." This plant comes chiefly from north-eastern Thailand, from a region lying west of the Mekong River, in the provinces of Nakawn Panom and Sakon Nakawn. The fruit of this species is soft and spiny. The เร่ว may be *A. xan-*

thioides (burk. p. 131); *A. villosum* (j. s. s. ii, 2, p. 38); *Alpinia sp. (Zingiberaceae)*.

เรวดี   ray-wa[6]-dee *n.* wife of Bala-rama, daughter of king Raivata (h. c. d. p. 226); a constellation of 32 stars, or the Pisces (ดาว-ปลาตะเพียน): เรวดีภพ (ดาว) the planet Saturn.

เรอ   rur *v.* to belch; to eruct (gas): หาว-เรอ to yawn and belch.

เร่อ   rur[3] *v.* to wander, or stray aimlessly: *adv.* continually; uninterruptedly; ceaselessly; carelessly: *adj.* stupid; awkard; silly: เดิน-เร่อร่า to strut in a silly manner: หัวเราะ-เร่อร่า to laugh in a foolish, senseless manner.

เรา   row *pron.* we; I; us; me: พวกเรา our crowd. class, society or company: เรา-ท่านทั้งหลาย all of you.

เร่า   row[3] *v.* to be mentally inflamed, anxious or uneasy; to squirm, wrench, or struggle vigorously; see เต่า p. 334: เร่าร้อนใจ restive; impatient; overwhelmed with distress; extremely anxious: เร่าร้อน to be mentally inflamed or agitated by anxiety, anger or love.

เร้า   row[5] *v.* to stimulate, urge, animate, or encourage (to greater efforts): เร้ารบ to incite to fight (with greater ardour); เร้าเร่ง to animate to a greater speed: *adj.* urgently; eagerly.

เราะ   raw[6] *v.* to chip or break off in small pieces by striking with light rapid strokes: *n.* bamboo strips stitched together for enclosing fish: เดินเราะรั้ว to walk or run back and forth along a fence seeking for an opening to pass through: เราะตะเข็บ to cut out a seam; to take out basting threads: เราะร้าย, เราะราย rudely; insolently; impudently; hatefully; harshly (descriptive of sarcastic language used to another).

เริง   rerng *adj.* cheerful; playful; joyful; glad; contented: ความมีเริง pleasures; entertainments: แมวไม่อยู่หนูก็เริง "when the cat is away the mice do play."

เริด rert[3] v. to leave off, to be interrupted, or stopped (as work or a task); to be parted from, abandoned or forsaken; to be turned upwards (as the face): ค้างเริด to be left half-finished; to abandon half-way: ปากเริด to have thick, upturned lips: เริดรามเรมโรย being abandoned a long time ago: วิ่งหน้าเริด *slang* to run excitedly with upturned face.

เริ่ม (โรค) rerm n. nettle-rash; nettles; hives; urticaria, a skin disease characterized by the sudden appearance of smooth, slightly elevated patches, attended by severe itching.

เริ่ม rerm[3] v. to begin; to start: *adj.* beginnings: *adv.* newly; just begun: แต่เริ่มการ at the inauguration of a work or project: แต่เริ่มแรก as from the very beginning: เริ่มก่อการบริษัท to promote a business.

เรีย reer[3] v. to be ashamed; to blush from chagrin or mortification; to let drop, let fall, or spill over: ใบเรี่ยไร a subscription list: เรี่ยราด to let drop, drip, spill, strew or dribble while in transit (as blood): เรี่ยราย scattered; strewn; disseminated; dissipated: *adv.* in all directions: เรี่ยไร to collect or subscribe money or gifts from the public or members of a community or assembly.

เรียก ree-ak[3] v. to call; to address; to demand; to exact: ร้องเรียก to call or shout for: เรียกเงิน to urge or call up a payment of money due (as in the purchase of company shares): เรียกเงินประกัน to demand money as security or bail: เรียกตะโกน to call with a loud yell: เรียกประชุม *legal* to convene or convoke a meeting: เรียกหา, เรียกมา to request the presence of.

เรียง, ระเรียง, รันเรียง, เรียงรัน ree-ang v. to arrange in consecutive order, in series or in sequence: n. a descriptive name for betel leaves arranged in the hand (ten leaves make a handful or packet): *adv.* successively: เรียงความ to compose a document, petition or letter: เรียงเคียง arranged or placed adjoining each other according to rank or series:

เรียงตัว in single file: เรียงพี่เรียงน้อง arranged in order of age (as children standing in a row): เรียงราย scattered though in line (as houses along the banks of rivers or canals): เรียงไสว placed in line or order and waving (as flags or lights moved by the wind).

เรียด ree-at[3] *adj.* level for the full length; approaching near to; almost touching, skimming or moving along over the surface of ground or water (as pieces of tiles thrown so as to skim over the surface); see เฉียด p. 272: เรียดน้ำไป to ricochet over the water: เรียดเสมอ *idiomatic* dead level.

เรียน ree-an v. to learn; to study; to practice (in order to become proficient); to inform (a superior): กราบเรียน a form of address to a superior: นักเรียน students; pupils; scholars; learners: ร่ำเรียน to learn by repetition: เรียนขึ้นใจ to memorize; to learn by heart: เรียนความรู้ to study occult or magical sciences: เรียนนาย to tell something to a superior: เรียนปฏิบัติ to consult with, or seek advice from; to discuss matters; to confer with: เรียนมายัง a form of address used on the envelopes of letters addressed to officials below the rank of Phya: เรียนโหร the studying of methods of predicting or prophesying events: เล่าเรียน to learn by reciting: หมั่นเรียน studious or diligent in studies.

เรียบ ree-ap[3] *adv.* in good order: *adj.* even; plain; smooth; level: เรียบร้อย wellordered; well-arranged: เรียบเรียง to compose, compile, or write (as a newspaper article or book); to arrange personal articles in good order.

เรียม, ระเรียม ree-am *pron.* I; me; we; older brother; commonly used in poetry or songs as a personal pronoun, considered to be derived from the Cambodian language.

เรี่ยม ree-am[3] *adj.* clean; spotless; unstained; unsoiled; *colloquial* beautiful; perfect; excellent; approved of in all respects.

เรียว๑ ree-oh *adj.* tapering straight to a point; conical or pyramidal (in shape): ไม่เรียว a whip: เรียวปลาย tapering to a sharp point: เรียวแหลม tapering to a sharp point: เหลาให้เรียว to sharpen to a fine tapering point.

เรียว๒ stay ropes for sails of Thai boats.

เรียว ree-oh[3] *n.* strength; force; power; see กำลัง p. 105: มีเรียวแรง robust; energetic; able-bodied; vigorous; strong (when used regarding a foundation or structure); firm; solid: หักเรียวหักแรง to overdo, or imperil one's strength.

เรือ rur-ah *n.* boat; ship; barque; barge: กองเรือรบ fleet; flotilla or squadron (of fighting ships): เรือกรรเชียง a sculling-boat: เรือกลจักร์ steamer; launch: เรือกัญญา barges used in state processions: เรือกิ่ง a magnificently carved and decorated state barge: เรือจ้าง a water-taxi; a ferry-boat: เรือช่วยผู้ตกน้ำเมื่อเรือแตก a life boat: เรือชะล่า a punting-boat: เรือดำน้ำ a submarine: เรือตัวร้าย an ill-fated boat, or one in which there is an evil spirit or joss: เรือธง a flagship: เรือนำ, เรือชัก a pair of barges going in advance of the royal barge in river processions: เรือนำร่อง a pilot's boat: เรือบิน, เรือเหาะ an airplane; an aeroplane; airships; aircraft: เรือใบ a sail-boat; a schooner: เรือพระที่นั่ง the royal yacht: เรือยนตร์ a motor boat or launch: เรือรบ a warship; a man-of-war: เรือรบมหิมา a dreadnought: เรือรบมีเกราะ a protected cruiser: เรือลาดตระเวน a cruiser: เรือสำปั้น a small paddle boat, or one rowed gondola style: เรือสำภา a junk: เรือสำหรับเที่ยว a pleasure yacht: เรือหมากรุก the castle or rook (in chess): เรือหมู a pork hawker's boat: เรือหงส์ a barge with the beautiful head of a swan as a figurehead: ลูกเรือ sailors; a ship's crew.

เรือ rur-ah[3] *adj.* dull; faded; dim; faint (as colour or light): ดำเรือๆ blackish; murky; dingy black: สีเรือๆ faintly or slightly discoloured; somewhat faded in colour.

เรือ rur-ah[5] *v.* to be in disorder; to be deserted, or neglected: เรื้อรัง chronic; lingering; slow in recovering (used regarding sicknesses).

เรือก rur-ak[3] *n.* a floor mat, made by sewing strips of bamboo with fine strands of rattan: เรือกสะพาน a bridge made of bamboo slats sewed with rattan: เรือกห่อผี a bamboo mat, so made, for enveloping a corpse.

เรือกสวน rur-ak[3]-su-an[2] *n.* an orchard; a plantation: เรือกสวนไร่นา fields and gardens (in general).

เรือง, เรืองรอง, เรื่อง rur-ang *adj.* shining; glowing; bright; glittering; resplendent: เรืองไร beautiful with gold (decorations): เรืองศรี, รุ่งเรือง glorious; magnificent; brilliant; lustrous; luminous; radiant.

เรื่อง rur-ang[3] *n.* a story; a naration; a tale; a chronicle; an account: การเล่าเรื่อง story-telling: ไม่ได้เรื่อง unsuccessful; unintelligible: ไม่เป็นเรื่อง of no value, nor sense: เรื่องขันๆ an amusing story or anecdote: เรื่องความ a charge; a legal document or report of a case: เรื่องนิทาน a fable: เรื่องราว a narrative; a report of an accusation or charge; a petition: เล่าเรื่อง to relate the incidents in a story or case.

เรือด (สัตว์) rur-at[3] *n.* bed bug.

เรือน rur-an *n.* house; home; family; dwelling-place; numerical designation for watches and clocks: เครื่องเรือน household effects; furniture: มีเรือนแล้ว one married: มีเหย้ามีเรือน married; domiciled: แม่เรือน a housekeeper; a home-maker: โรงง้าน-เหย้าเรือน *idiomatic* shacks, sheds, and houses: เรือนเกวียน a cart shed or shelter: เรือนเงิน an amount of money (as the sum paid for a slave, or horse): เรือนจำ jail; prison; goal: เรือนทอง, เรือนเงิน a gold or silver watch: เรือนเบ้ย a sum or amount of money: เรือน-

ผม the manner of cutting, arranging or wearing the hair: เรือนเพ็ชร์, เรือนแหวน the setting of a gem; the bezel: เรือนไฟ a kitchen: เรือนมุงกระเบื้อง a tile-roofed house: เรือนมุงจาก a house thatched with nipa palm leaves: เรือนโรงต่าง ๆ various buildings (as in a compound): เรือนหูก a weaver's house or shed.

เรือน (โรค)   rur-an[5] *n.* leprosy: เรือนน้ำเต้า white leprosy or macular leprosy.

เรื่อย   rur-ie[3] *adv.* continually; always; constantly; unceasingly; moderately or gently, but regularly: เดินเรื่อย ๆ a regular but moderate gait: ทำการเรื่อย ๆ to work constantly and uniformly.

แร   raa *v.* to draw (lines); to write; to paint; to sketch; to design or make an outline; see ขีด p. 160; เขียน p. 167: **แรดอก,** แรใบ to scratch lines or designs in colour on the petals of flowers, or on the leaves.

แร่   raa[3] *v.* to rush into, upon, or at: *n.* metallic ore; minerals: ถลุงแร่ to smelt ore: บ่อแร่, เหมือง a mine: แร่เข้าไป to go directly forward or for (as wild animals when attacking): แร่เงินแร่ทอง gold and silver ore: แร่ตะกั่ว lead ore: แร่เหล็ก iron ore.

แรก   raak[3] *n.* beginning; origin; start; principal: *adj.* first; original; primary: *adv.* at first; before: แต่แรกมา from the beginning down till now: แรกนา, แรกนาขวัญ festival of the commencement of sowing. The ceremony of the first ploughing is entirely Brahminical and it takes place outside the city in some Crown paddy field. The day is fixed by the royal Brahmin astrologers and is usually early in May. Officially it is called พระราชพิธีจรดพระนังคัล: แรกมา the first to come.

แรง, ระแรง   raang *n.* strength; power; force; might; dental caries causing decay of a tooth; a prefix for royal actions: *adj.* strong; powerful; able; capable; see กำลัง

p. 105: เต็มแรง with all one's strength: ไปพอแรง gone far in excess of: พอกับแรง in proportion to the strength: แม่แรง a vise or clamping device; a lifting jack: แรงบุญ the power or might of merit: แรงเทียน candle-power (for light measurements): แรงม้า horse-power (for power measurements): เสียแรงเปล่า wasted strength; done all in vain: หักเรี่ยวหักแรง to over-tax one's strength: ออกแรง to exert the strength: ขอแรง to solicit the assistance of.

แร้ง   raang[3] *n.* a sieve or strainer made of fine wire or horse-hair.

แร้ง (นก)   raang[5] *n.* the Indian white backed vulture, *Pseudogyps bengalensis* (Gaird. J. S. S. IX, 1, p. 9): แร้งเจ้าพระยา (นก) the black vulture, *Otogyps calvus* (Gaird. I. S. S. IX, 1, p, 9): แร้งหัวแดง (นก) the black, or king vulture, *Sarcogyps* or *Torgos calvus* (Herbert, N. H. J. S. S. VI, 4, p. 329): หัวแร้ง (เหล็ก) a soldering-iron.

แรด   raat[3] *n.* the rhinoceros: นอแรด the horns of the rhinoceros: แรด (ปลา) *Osphronemus goramy* (Osphronemidae) (Suvatti p. 103): แรดนอเดียว the one-horned rhinoceros, *Rhinoceros sondaicus* (Minutes of S. S. Regarding wild Game Preservation in Thailand): แรดสองนอ the two-horned rhinoceros, *Rhinoceros sumatrensis* (Minutes of S. S. Regarding wild Game Preservation in Thailand): แรดน้ำ a hippopotamus.

แร้นแค้น   raan[5]-kaan[5] *adj.* poor; needy; penniless; moneyless.

แรม   raam *v.* to remain, stop at, or lodge (as at a hotel); to be separated or absent from for a long time; to decrease, or wane (as the moon): ข้างแรม the latter fortnight of the moon: แรมคืน to spend the night in the course of a trip or journey: แรมทาง a stop-over (as while on a journey or trip): แรมรอน to stop for a period of rest: โรงแรม a hotel; a rest house: แรมร้าง, แรมรา to stop, defer, leave or abandon: แรมวัน

to remain over for a day (as work unfinished in one day is taken up on the following day).

แร้ว raa-oh[5] *n.* a spring trap, slip noose, net, gin or snare (for birds and animals): ติดบ่วงแร้ว to be caught in a trap or snare: แร้วดักไก่ a snare for trapping chickens: แร้วดักนก a trap for catching birds.

โร roh *adj.* enlarged; distended; swollen; protruding (used descriptive of the abdomen in conditions like dropsy, or worms in children): ผอมพุงโร lean and yet pot-bellied.

โร่, ทนโท่ roh[3] *adj.* distinct; not dim nor obscure; obvious; distinguishable: *adv.* distinctly; see ปรากฏ p. 506: แดงโร่ very red; scarlet red; distinctly red: โร่ไป, โร่มา going or coming in a conspicuous manner.

โรค roke[3] *Thai,* โรคา *P.S. n.* disease; infirmity; sickness; malady; ailment; illness (S. E. D. p. 888: คนมักโรค sickly; easily diseased: โรคกระดูกอ่อน rickets: โรคคางทูม mumps: กาฬี, กาฬโรคแห่งสัตว์ anthrax: โรคนิทาน an ancient medical treatise giving the seat or origin of various diseases: โรคบิด dysentery: โรคกลัวน้ำ (แห่งสุนัขขี้บ้า), โรคพิษสุนัขขี้บ้ากัด rabies; hydrophobia: โรคภัย pestilential diseases: โรคฤๅ *lit.* "the seat of disease," *i. e.* the body: โรคระบาด, โรคติดต่อ contagious or epidemic diseases: โรคราช pulmonary tuberculosis; consumption: โรคลักษณ์ characteristic symptoms or manifestations of diseases: โรคศานต์ the alleviation or cure of a disease: โรคศิลปะ the alleviation or healing of disease by whatever means necessary, whether surgical, medicinal, massaging, or nursing: โรคหร remedies; curative means: โรคหะ remedies; medicaments: โรคหัน, โรคหาริน, โรคหารี a physician, or one in charge of a case: โรคายตนะ the human body.

โรง rong *n.* a shed; a hall; a temporary shelter; an out-house (roughly built); a hut; an habitation: โรงกระสาปน์ the Royal Mint:

โรงโขน a pavilion or hall for masked plays: โรงคลังสินค้า a warehouse: โรงคัล an audience hall or throne room: โรงชาวนา a farmer's house: โรงทหาร a military barrack: โรงทาน an almonry; a place where alms are dispensed; a house where the king's alms are distributed: โรงธาร a throne hall; a drawing room or parlour where guests are received or entertained: โรงธารคำนัล a house provided for the reception of guests; provincial rest houses: โรงบ่อน, โรงโป a gambling house or den: โรงปูน a limekiln: โรงโปเก a second-hand shop for iron-ware: โรงพยาบาล a hospital: โรงพยาบาลคนวิกลจิต a lunatic asylum: โรงพิมพ์ a printing office: โรงภาษี a custom house: โรงมหรสพ an entertainment hall: โรงรับจำนำ a pawn shop: โรงเรียนกฎหมาย a law school: โรงเรียนดัดสันดาน a reformatory school: โรงเรียนนายร้อยทหารบก a military or cadet college: โรงเรียนประชาบาล a community private school: โรงเรียนประถม an elementary school: โรงเรียนฝึกหัดครู a normal school: โรงเรียนพาณิชย์การ commercial school: โรงเรียนราษฎร์ a self-supporting school but following the Government Educational Code: โรงเรียนวิสามัญ special schools: โรงเรียนสามัญ common schools: โรงเรียนอนุบาล a school under the patronage of some one: โรงเรียนอาชีวะ a vocational school: โรงแรม a hotel; an inn: โรงละคร a theatre: โรงวิเศษ the royal kitchen: โรงสีข้าว a rice mill: โรงสูบฝิ่น an opium den or shop for smoking opium: โรงแสง an arsenal: โรงหญิงนครโสเภณี a brothel: โรงหล่อ a foundry: โรงหีบ a cane mill: โรงกลั่นเหล้า a distillery: โหมโรง an overture at the beginning of a play or any program or entertainment.

โรจ rote[3] *adj.* resplendent: glowing; shining: รุ่งโรจน์ brilliant; luminous: เรืองโรจน์ sparkling; dazzling.

โรท roh-ta[6] *P. v.* to weep; to wail; to cry or mourn for (chd. p. 404).

โรธ   rote[3] *P. S.* see กั้น ๑ p. 85; ปิด p. 526; ทำลาย p. 414: *n.* acts, such as stopping, checking, suppressing, preventing, confining, besieging, blockading, or imprisoning; a bank; a shore; a dam (S. E. D. p. 884).

โรนัน (ปลา)   roh-nun *n. Rhynchobatus djiddensis (Rhinobatidae)* (suvatti p. 4).

โรปนะ   roh-bpa[4]-na[6] *S. n.* the act of planting, transplanting, sowing or setting out of plants (S. E. D. p. 889).

โรม ๑   roh-ma[6] *S. n.* the hair on the body of men and animals; feathers; bristles; wool; down; nap (S. E. D. p. 889).

โรม ๒, โรมรัน   rome *v.* to fight; to be in combat or battle; to fight in a skirmish; to rush at, or in upon; to quarrel noisily.

โรย   ro-ie *v.* to be withered, faded or jaded; to slacken, loosen or play out (as rope); to look sickly or jaded; to sprinkle on, spread, or scatter over: ร่วงโรยลง to be withered, dried up or drooping; to lack a flourishing condition: โรยเชือก to play out or slacken rope: โรยดอกไม้ to scatter flowers: โรยร่วง withered and falling off (as the petals of flowers):   โรยรา, โรยราน to grow less; to decrease gradually in sprightliness, strength or vigour: โรยแรง to become lessened in strength gradually: โรยหน้า to sprinkle on, or scatter over (as seasoning).

โรเร   roh-ray *adj.* enfeebled; weakened; debilitated; lessened in strength; tottering (as from sickness or old age).

โรษ   rote[3] *S. n.* anger; rage; wrath; fury (S. E. D. p. 885).

โรษก   roh-sok[4] *S. n.* one who is angry, furious, or enraged.

โรหิณี   roh-hi[4]-nee *P. n.* a red cow; the fourth lunar asterism or constellation; the daughter of Kasyapa and Surabhi, and mother of horned cattle, including Kama-dhenu, the cow which grants desires. She was produced at the time of the churning of the ocean (H. C. D. pp. 147, 269).

โรหิต   roh-hit[4] *P. n.* the colour red; a kind of deer (chd. p. 404); *lit.* "red," *i.e.* a red horse; a horse of the sun, or of fire (H. C. D. p. 269); *Thai* โลหิต blood.

ไร   rai *v.* to collect for charities; to collect money or articles for a purpose (as to give a feast): *n.* rim; edge; margin: *adj.* what; which; whatever: *adv.* indistinctly; dimly; faintly: ถอนไร to pull out the hairs (as around the topknot or at the nape of the neck): เป็นไร what is the matter? ไม่เป็นไร no matter; no difference; it matters nothing: เรี่ยไร to collect subscriptions of money or articles (as for some charity):   ไรเกษ hair lice: ไรไก่ chicken lice: ไรจุก, ไรผม marks of hairs pulled out (around the topknot):   ไรไม้ a plant louse: สิ่งไร what thing is that?

ไร่   rai[3] *n.* an upland field; a farm for other than lowland (padi) rice cultivation; a plantation on which *rai* cultivation of cotton, peppers, upland rice, etc. is followed. This involves the clearing of the forest, burning it in the dry season, then the seeds are planted without loosening the soil. After one to three crops have been obtained the land is allowed to revert to forest; a square surface measure equal to 4 *ngan*, or 400 square *wah*, or 1600 square metres.

ไร้   rai[5] *adj.* poor; needy; destitute; unfortunate: *prep.* without: คนไร้เมีย one without a wife; a bachelor: ตกไร้ได้ยาก to become destitute: ไร้ญาติ to be without relatives: ไร้ทรัพย์ to be without money; to be poor, or needy.

ฤ

ฤ A vowel (adopted from the Sanskrit) with three pronounciations, *e. g.* "ริ" as in ฤทธิ์ (ริด), "รื" as in พฤกษ์ (พรึก), and "เรอ" as in ฤกษ์ (เริก): *conj.* either; else; otherwise.

ฤกษ์๑ rerk[3] *n.* favourableness; auspiciousness; presentiment; a propitious, or lucky time, day, hour, or moment; supernatural omens. The fixing of such propitious days, or hours is the duty of the Brahmin astrologers and soothsayers; once considered to be of the greatest importance before any great enterprise could, or should be undertaken: ดาวฤกษ์ a star of omen; a planet: ตฤฤกษ์, เอายาม to calculate the auspicious moment, or hour: ได้ฤกษ์ to arrive at a favourable portent: ฤกษ์ชัย a prognosticated time for the advance of an army in order to assure victory: ฤกษ์เช้า the propitious time is during the morning: ฤกษ์ดี, ฤกษ์ยามดี a favourable harbinger: ฤกษ์พระ the sacred time, or period, is that nearing daylight.

ฤกษ์๒ rerk[3] *P. S. n.* a bear (chd. p. 158); a star, constellation, or lunar mansion; the particular star under which a person happens to be born (S. E. D. p. 224).

ฤกษณะ rurk[3]-sa[4]-na[6] *P. v.* to look; to see (chd. p. 158).

ฤกษระ rurk[6]-sa[4]-ra[6] *S. n.* a shower of rain (estimated, when enough falls to fill the bonze's kettle) (S. E. D. p. 224).

ฤกเษศ rurk[3]-set[4] *S. n. lit.* "lord of the stars," *i. e.* the moon (S. E. D. p. 224).

ฤกขะ rurk[6]-ka[4] *S. n.* property; wealth; possessions; effects; gold (S. E. D. p. 224).

ฤคเวท rur[6]-ka[6]-wet[3] *S. n.* "the Veda of Song," the most ancient sacred book of the Hindus in which the Vedic poets invoked prosperity on themselves and their flocks, and offered praises to deities they worshipped, such as Agni, Indra and Surya (H. C. D. p. 345; S. E. D. p. 225).

ฤจ rurt[6] *S. v.* to praise; to sing hymns, or chant prayers: *n.* praise; sacred text; a sacred verse recited in praise of a deity (S. E. D. p. 225).

ฤชา rur[6]-chah *n.* the fee, fine or tax paid by a litigant into the court: ฤชากร tax, or revenue stamp on court documents.

ฤณ rin *S. n.* an obligation, duty, debt, or anything due; a debt of money; money owed (S. E. D. p. 225).

ฤดิยา, ฤติยา rur[6]-dee-yah *S. n.* contempt; scorn; hatred; fear (S. E. D. p. 226).

ฤดู, ฤตุ ra[6]-doo *S. n.* a season; an epoch, period, fixed time, or time appointed for any action (S. E. D. p. 224): ฤดุกาล any settled, or suitable period of time; any fixed order, or rule: ฤดุผู้หญิง, โรคประจำเดือน, ถึงผ้า, มีเลือด, มีแดง ๆ the menses; menstruation; catamenia: ฤดุฝน the rainy season: ฤดุแล้ง the dry season.

ฤต rurt[6] *S. n.* law; rule; code of conduct; ethics; sacred or pious actions or customs (as applied to the Buddhist religion): *adj.* proper; right; fit; suitable; honest; true [(S. E. D. p. 223).

ฤตวิก see ประโรหิต p. 504.

ฤตุราช rur[6]-dtoo[4]-rart[3] *n.* springtime.

ฤตุสนาน rur[6]-dtoo[4]-sa[4]-narn[2] *S. n.* the purification bath of a woman taken on the fourth day after the menstruation (a custom not unknown in Thailand) (S. E. D. p. 224).

ฤทธ์ rit[6] *S. adj.* thriving; increasing; prosperous; abundant; wealthy (S. E. D. p. 226).

ฤทธิ์   rit[6] *S. n.* magical power; supeɪnatural power; potency; power; might; force; energy; prosperity; accomplishment (S. E. D. p. 226): ฤทธิ์กุศล power or virtues acquired from meritorious acts: ฤทธิ์ไกร of very great power: ฤทธิยา the potency of a drug or remedy: ฤทธิรณ, มีฤทธิ์อำนาจ endowed with very great power: ฤทธิรุทร possessing great magical powers; extremely potent in might, or energy.

ฤทัย, ฤๅทัย   rur[6]-tai *n.* mind; will; consciousness; mental faculties.

ฤษี, ฤๅษี   rur[6]-see[2] *S. n.* a saint; a sage; a holy man; an anchorite (chd. p. 160); a Raci, or hermit; a person living by himself in some lonely and solitary recess, far from the contagious atmosphere of impure society, devoting his time to meditation and contemplation. His diet is of the coarsest kind, supplied to him by the forest he lives in; the skins of wild animals afford him a sufficient dress. There is no doubt but that these devotees in the days of the Buddha were Brahmins. A Raci is any person who alone, or with others, invokes the deities in rhythmical speech or song of a sacred character. They were regarded by later generations as patriarchal sages, or saints, occupying the same position in Indian history as the heroes and patriarchs of other countries (S. E. D. p. 226): ฤษีกุล one in the lineage of the sages.

ฤษฎี   rurt[6]-sa[4]-dtee *S. n.* a sword; a lance or spear (S. E. D. p. 226).

ฤษภ   rur[6]-sop[4] *S. n.* a bull (chd. p. 537); any male animal (in general); the best or most excellent of any kind or race.

ฤษยา   rit[6]-sa[4]-yah[2] *n.* envy; jealousy; ill-will (chd. p. 160); ริษยา *preferable spelling is* อิจฉา.

ฤๅ

ฤๅ   A vowel (adopted from the Sanskrit), pronounced as "รือ." In the Thai language it is altered to "หรือ" a word denoting inquiry, equivalent to the interrogation mark "?" and is placed as a final word to all questions: *interrog.* what; who; which.

ฤๅ, ฤๅว่า   rur *adv.* or.

ฤๅชุ   rur[6]-choo[6] *S. adj.* straight; right; upright; correct; honest; sincere (S. E. D. p. 225): ฤๅชุตา a straight direction, or way; justice; faithfulness; truthfulness.

ฤๅดี   rur-dee *n.* pleasure; love; attachment; sexual desire; joy; delight; felicity.

ฤๅทัย see ฤทัย

ฤๅษี see ฤษี   ฤๅษีผะสมแล้ว (ต้น) *Coleus blumei* (*Labiateae*), an annual with beautifully marked, soft, velvety leaves. It is easily propagated by cuttings, but requires rich loamy soil, abundant manure and moisture (MCM. p. 202).

ฤๅสาย   rur-sai[2] a form of address showing veneration for great personages (as for a king): *adj.* respected; venerated; reverenced.

ล

ล The thirty-sixth consonant of the Thai alphabet, a low class letter of which there are twenty-four, *viz.* ค, ค, ฆ, ง, ช, ฌ, ซ, ญ, ฑ, ฑ, ฒ, ท, ฌ, น, ณ, พ, ฟ, ภ, ม, ร, ล, ว, ฬ, ฮ. ลอลิง, ลอวิลาส are the names of this letter. It is pronounced like the English "l." It occurs generally in Pali, Sanskrit and Thai words, both as a prefix and a suffix.

ลก lok⁶ *adj.* sixth: *n. ancient Thai*, the sixth son (the sixth daughter is called อก).

ลการ ๑ la⁶-gkarn *P. n.* another name for the character "ล" (chd. p. 217).

ลการ ๒ la⁶-gkarn *P. n.* a sail (chd. p. 217).

ลกุจ la⁶-gkoot⁴ *S. n.* similar to the bread-fruit tree, *Artocarpus lakoocha* (*Urticaceae*) (S. E. D. p. 891: BURK. p. 257); see ขนุนสำมะลอ p. 140.

ลคุฑ, ลคุฬ la⁶-koot⁶ *S. n.* a club; a mallet (chd. p. 217); a walking-stick; a staff, or cane (S. E. D. p. 893).

ลฆุ la⁶-koo⁶ *S. adj.* light; quick; swift; active; nimble (S. E. D. p. 393): ลฆุกรม, ลฆุคติ taking, or going by quick, or rapid steps: ลฆุจิตต์ light-minded; fickle: ลฆุโภชน์ a light repast; refreshments.

ลง long *v.* to descend (as from a mountain); to decrease (as the ebb-tide); to diminish (as a fever); to over-lay (as with lacquer); to write, or inscribe (as cabalistic letters, or designs); to alight (as from a ship, or motor car); to dismount (as from a horse): ปราบลง to pacify by force; see ปราบ p. 507: ลงขัน to deposit voluntary gifts of money in a bowl (as at the tonsorial ceremony to help defray the expenses): ลงแขก to ask the help of friends and neighbours for special work (as a bee held during the time of transplanting rice plants): ลงคอ suitably; fittingly; cooper-

atingly; friendly; undiffidently (as when there is no bashfulness, or restraint between comrades): ลงเงิน to subscribe money towards; to take shares in a business concern: ลงใจ, ลงด้วย, ลงรอย to endorse the opinion of, or to agree with another: ลงชาติ to become degraded, or degenerated; to bring dishonour on one's family, or ancestors: ลงชื่อ, ลงนาม to sign, or affix one's name: ลงแตง to suffer from excessive bloody flux, or severe dysentery: ลงตัว to be divisible without a remainder; to become thinner and thinner (till nothing but bones are left): ลงท้อง to suffer from diarrhoea, or looseness of the bowels: ลงท่า a royal ceremony of giving the king's son a bath in the river: ลงทุน to invest money in a business concern: ลงโทษ, ลงอาชญา to punish by flogging, imprisonment, or fining; to inflict chastisement: ลงนอน to assume a reclining posture: ลงนั่ง to assume a sitting position: ลงนา to begin ploughing and planting rice: ลงไป to go down into (as into the water, or a cave): ลงผี, ลงมด to invite the spirits of the departed to possess a medium in order to foretell the future, or to beg for prosperity; to be bewitched; to cause a person to become bewitched; to use methods of sorcery or witchcraft; to invite demoniacal possession (of a medium): ลงพุง to become pot-bellied: ลงมติ to decide by a vote: ลงมา to alight: ลงมีด *lit.* "down with the knife," *i. e.* to make the initial incision (as in surgery, or the cutting of logs, or felling of trees): ลงมือ *lit.* "down with the hands," *i. e.* to begin; to commence an undertaking: ลงยา to enamel; to cover with lacquer: ลงยาราชาวดี to over-lay with a coloured enamel: ลงรัก to paint over with a preparation of resin and dammer prior to gilding (as is done on the rough surface of idols): ลงราก diarrhoea

accompanied with vomiting; cholera: ลง
รากตึก to lay the foundation of a house:
ลงเรือ to go on board a boat; to embark:
ลงโรง to begin a play, theatre, or entertainment; to set up housekeeping, or begin living
together (as man and wife): ลงสรง a Thai
tune called สรงน้ำ, played by musicians on
the occasion of royalty taking a bath:
ลงอวน, ลงแห to cast, or let down fishing nets
(especially the bag nets): เอาลง to take
down; to remove, or displace.

ล่ง, โล่ง long[3] *adj.* void; vacant; opened;
unobstructed (as a view).

ลงกา, ลังกา (preferable spelling) long-gkah *n.*
Hindi Langka, the ancient name of Ceylon,
the city of the famous monkey king ทศกัณฐ์.

ลด lote[6] *v.* to lower; to let down; to reduce; to cause to diminish; to decrease:
ลดการ to lessen the work required: ลดเขื่อน
to put down a bunding to protect a water
front: ลดค่าจ้าง to lessen the wages of:
ลดเงิน to make a reduction (as in price, or
amount to be paid): ลดจากที่ to be de
moted, or removed from office, place, or rank:
ลดธง to dip the flag; to fly a flag at halfmast: ลดใบ to unfurl a sail; to lower a
sail (as when rolled up): ลดราคา to reduce
the price: ลดลง to abate, lower, or be
lowered: ลดลาวาศอก to be clement, lenient,
or generous towards (as in reduction of price,
fines, or penalties): ลดเลี้ยว to go in a
winding or circuitous route; to make a
detour; to take a tortuous course: ลดวัน
to reduce, or lessen by a day: ลดหลั่น to
be lowered; to be arranged by stages, in tiers,
or terraces: ลดให้ to give a reduction; to
offer a discount: สิบลด ten per cent: หัก
ลด to deduct (as for fines or fees).

ลดา, ลตา la[6]-dah *P. S. n.* a creeping plant;
a creeper; a branch (chd. p. 219); ivy; the
wild jasmine: ลดาวัลล์, ลัดาวัลล์ (ต้น) *Porana volubilis (Convolvulaceae)*, a large quickgrowing climber, taken from India into cul

tivation in Europe a century ago. From
there it was widely distributed to gardens in
other countries. It is commonly called the
bridal wreath or snow creeper owing to the
creamy-white flowers in long panicles. The
leaves may be eaten to remove a nasty taste
from the mouth; the juice enters into a tonic
(MCM. pp. 124, 126, 208: V. P. 241: BURK. p. 1800).

ลน lone *v.* to hold over, or expose to fire,
heat, or smoke; to run restlessly; to hasten
about: ลนไม้ to soften a bamboo rod or
stick by heat in order to straighten it out (as
in making a fishing rod or cane): ลนลาน
to run about hurriedly and excitedly.

ล่น (วิ่ง) lone[3] *v.* to run: to run quickly.

ล้น lone[5] *v.* to overflow (as water boiling
over); to flood, flow over, inundate, or overrun (as a river in spate): *adj.* excellent;
supreme; most precious: ล้นเกล้าล้นกระหม่อม
lit. "a benefactor whose kindnesses overwhelm
the head," *i. e.* a form of address for His
Majesty the King, indicating profound gratefulness for favours bestowed: ล้นจาน, ล้นชาม
full to overflowing (of dish or plate): ล้นพ้น
exceeding all others: ล้นเหลือ *expressing
a superlative degree of abundance,* as มีเงิน
ล้นเหลือ, งามล้นเหลือ, สูงล้นเหลือ: เลิศล้น powerful; mighty; lordly (in the superlative degree).

ลบ lop[6] *v.* to erase; to expunge; to efface;
to deface; to destroy; *arithmetic* to subtract
from: ยางลบ an eraser (see p. 672 under
ยาง): ลบคุณ to be ungrateful; to lack
gratitude: ลบล้าง to forgive (as by erasing,
or blotting out sins): ลบเลือน disfigured;
blurred; injured; partly defaced: ลบโลก
lit. "obliterating the world," *i. e.* surpassing,
exceeding, or superior to all others in the
world: ลบหลู่ to treat with scorn, contempt,
disregard, or disdain; to insult.

ลปก la[6]-bpoke[4] *P. n.* one who fawns or
intrigues (chd. p. 219).

ลปน la⁶-bpa⁴-na⁶ *P. n.* the act of speaking; the mouth : ลปนัช *lit.* "that which is born in the mouth," *i. e.* a tooth.

ลพ see ลวะ p. 730.

ลพบุรี lop⁶-boo⁴-ree *n.* Lopburi, an ancient and, from an archaeological standpoint, a very important city 133 km. by rail north of Bangkok. The ancient city of Lopburi, which was then called Lavo, was an important city as early as the seventh century. It was then a dependency of the Mon Kingdom whose princess founded the city of Lampoon in the North. From the tenth to the thirteenth century Lavo was the seat of a province belonging to the Khmer Empire, whose capital was at Angkor. In 1665, King Phra Narayana made Lopburi his summer residence as well as an alternate capital, to which the Court could retire should Ayudhya fall into the hand of the enemy. The building of the outer wall, the royal palace and the water pipes was carried out by French architects and engineers. After the fall of Ayudhya, Lopburi was abandoned until King Mongkut ascended the Throne, and in his turn established his residence there.

ลม ๑ lome *n.* air; a common prefix for the names of various maladies which were formerly attributed, through superstitious ignorance, to a disordered condition of the vital air of the body, as ลมขึ้น an increased action of the heart, indicating a condition of fever : ลมเข้าข้อ articular affections of uncertain origin; rheumatism; gout, etc. : ลมจับ, เป็นลม to be seized with a fainting fit, or spell of faintness : ลมจุก, ลมแดก a condition of extreme flatulency producing epigastric pain and impaired respiration : ลมชัก convulsions; spasms : ลมตะคิว cramps : ลมบ้าหมู epilepsy.

ลม ๒ *n.* air in motion; wind : ไปกินลม to take an airing by enjoying the breeze; *lit.* "to eat the wind" : ลมกินใบ the wind fills the sails : ลมตวันออก an eastern wind which blows usually during January and February : ลมปราณ breath; tidal respirations : ลมปาก language; speech; talk; prattle : ลมพายุ a storm : ลมล่อง a wind blowing down a river : ลมสลาตัน a southern wind (derived from the Malay word "salatan" meaning "south"). This wind blows during April and May : ลมสำเภา *lit.* "junk wind," *i. e.* the south-west monsoon, so termed because favourable for junks sailing up to China. It is taken advantage of for kite flying during the months of May and June : ลมหัวเขา the south-east wind (February-March) so called because of blowing from the mountains of the south-eastern coast of the gulf : ลมหายใจ respirations : ลมเหี่ยน, ลมหวน a circular blowing wind (as one blowing around a sky-scraper or mountain); a whirlwind : หน้าลม the season of wind : หัวลม the beginning of the south-west or north-east monsoon; the start of any wind or storm : ให้ใบกินลม to set the sails so as to catch the wind.

ลิงลม ling-lome *n.* slow lorris; angwantibo, *Arctocebus calabarensis*, a small lemuroid mammal having only a rudimentary tail (web.).

ล่ม lom³ *v.* to capsize; to turn turtle; to be inverted; to be overturned (as a boat); to be turned upside-down; to fail : เรือล่ม the boat has capsized : ล่มจม to lose all of one's possessions; to be totally ruined, or bankrupt; to keel over and sink : ล่มฟ้า *lit.* "to cause the sky to sink," *i. e.* to be superior to the powers of heaven : ล่มเรือ to sink a boat : ล่มล้ม to be unable to withstand (as fate), or to exist; to be swamped and sink (a metaphor for complete ruination in one's business undertaking).

ล้ม lom⁵ *v.* to topple over; to fall prostrate; to trip; to stumble; to tumble; to flop over : ต้นไม้ล้ม a tree topples over : ล้มคว่ำ to fall face down : ล้มต้นไม้ to chop down a tree: ล้มเนรมาท to fail completely; to fall with a great crashing sound: ล้มบ้า to make a clearing in the forest: ล้มละลาย to be in bankruptcy; a state of bankruptcy: ล้มลุก to fall and rise again; to be too weak to stand long; to fluctuate or waver (in opinion or action): ล้มหมอนนอนเสื่อ to lie sick in bed; to be bedridden: หกล้ม to stumble and fall or sprawl.

ลมเพลมพัด lom-pay-lom-pat[6] *n.* a disorder affecting women, causing them to manifest symptoms of mental derangement.

ลยะ see ลัย

ลลนา la[6]-la[6]-nah *P. S. n.* a woman (chd. p. 218); a wanton woman; any wanton wife (S. E. D. p. 897).

ลลาฏ la[6]-lah-dta[4] *P. S. n.* the brow; the forehead (chd. p. 218).

ลลิต la[6]-lit[6] *S. adj.* sporting; playing; wanton; amorous; volumptous; soft; gentle; charming (S. E. D. p. 897).

ลวก lu-ak[3] *v.* to scald; to parboil; to cook slightly; to cleanse in a hot liquid: น้ำร้อน- ลวก to be burnt or scalded by hot water: ลวกไข่ to soft-boil eggs: ทำโดยลวกๆ to do or make carelessly or roughly; to produce an unfinished or unattractive article: ลวก- น้ำร้อน to scald in hot water.

ลวง lu-ang *v.* to deceive; to dupe; to gull; to impose upon by craftiness or guile; to lure, entice or tempt into some snare or trap (for the purpose of defrauding): ลวงเล่น to deceive playfully; to mystify (as though for a joke).

ล่วง lu-ang[3] *v.* to pass by (as time); to go beyond or exceed; to go on further than is proper; to slip away (as days, months or years); to do violence to: ล่วงกฎหมาย to violate a law: ล่วงกำหนด past the appointed time: ล่วงเกิน to insult; to offend against (as by impoliteness); to advance rudely or rashly (as into a private room); to trespass encroach, intrude, or exceed: ล่วงเกินคำสั่ง to disobey instructions: ล่วงขื่อ the cross walls, or crosswise measurements of a house: ล่วงเขตต์ to trespass: ล่วงหน้า previously; prior; earlier; before; in anticipation; beforehand: ล่วงประเวณี to commit adultery: ล่วงแป the lengthwise walls, or lengthwise measurements of a house.

ล้วง lu-ang[5] *v.* to extricate, withdraw, or remove (as from a cavity or hole); to slip a finger, hand, or instrument in; to pull, tear, or get out (as though to remove): คนล้วง- กระเป๋า a pickpocket: ล้วงควัก to put the hand in and take out with force: ล้วงตับ- ล้วงไส้ to be completely deceived or cheated by a clever trick; to remove the entrails (as of animals): ล้วงถาม, ล้วงเอาความจริง to elicit the truth by tricky questioning: ล้วงมือ to pass the hand into (as into the abdominal cavity during an autopsy).

ลวงค์ la[6]-wong *P. S. n.* cloves (chd. p. 219).

ลวงเล้า (ปีระกา) lu-ang-low[5] *n.* the year of the cock; the tenth year in the animal cycle.

ลวณะ la[6]-wa[6]-na[6] *P. S. n.* brine; salt; saltiness (chd. p. 219).

ลวด lu-at[3] *n.* wire (metallic): ไต่ลวด to walk or dance on a wire rope: ลวดเงิน silver wire: ลวดดอกไม้ไหว wire attached to flowers in order to let them vibrate: ลวดหนัง fine strands or strips of hide; thongs; decorative designs resembling wire placed on woodwork.

ลวดลาย lu-at[3]-lai *n.* flutings; carvings; sculptural or architectural ornamentations; ornamental drawings, paintings or designs.

ล้วน lu-an[5] *adv.* absolutely; simply; genuinely; entirely; totally; unmixedly; purely: งามล้วน the only one that is beautiful: ล้วน- แต่, ล้วนแล้วแต่ nothing but; only for.

ลวนลาม see เกินเลย p. 126.

ลวนะ la⁶-wa⁶-na⁶ *P. S. n.* one who cuts ; a reaper (chd. p. 219).

ล่วม lu-am³ *n.* a cloth pouch ; a bag ; a woven bamboo receptacle for small articles (used by ancient Thai people for carrying tobacco, or betel-nut and other small necessary articles) : พระล่วม the same for royalty : ล่วมยา a medicine bag.

ลวะ, ลพ la⁶-wa⁶ *P. S. n.* the act of cutting or reaping (chd. p. 219) ; the part cut from the main body ; a chip ; a chunk ; a piece ; a fragment ; a spark ; the name of Ramacandra's second son.

ลวิตร la⁶-wit⁶ *S. n.* a sickle (chd. p. 219) ; an implement or tool for cutting ; a reaping hook.

ลหุ la⁶-hoo⁴ *P. adj.* light ; small ; short ; quick ; unimportant ; vain ; frivolous ; flighty ; trifling ; insignificant ; beautiful ; delightful (chd. p. 217) ; *gram.* short accented vowels ; syllables (occurring in poetry) : ลหุโทษ light punishment for petty or trifling crimes.

ลหุก la⁶-hoo⁴-gka⁴ *P. adj.* light ; trifling (chd. p. 217) ; petty ; trivial.

ล่อ law³ *v.* to cause, create, raise, excite or provoke desire ; to allure ; to tempt ; to ensnare ; to inveigle (as by the use of a decoy) ; to induce to appear (as by a bait offered to an animal) ; to encourage to walk (as a doll held before a child) : *n.* an animal similar to a mule : *adj.* being partly visible : ล่อด้วยแม่เหล็ก to use an electric magnet to attract : ล่อปลา to angle for fish : ล่อลวง to victimize by deceptive means ; to entice for the purpose of defrauding : ล่อแล่ weak ; feeble ; languid : ล่อหลอก to allure ; to coax in a deceptive manner : ล่อแหลม endangered by being very high (as a hut or house built on a crag or mountain side) ; being surrounded by dangers : ลับ ๆ ล่อ ๆ to appear and disappear ; to hide in a covert and peep out shyly (as in playing hide and seek) : สายล่อฟ้า a lightning rod ; a lightning conductor : หญิงล่อชาย a woman who tempts or seduces a man : หายใจล่อแล่ weakened or enfeebled respiration (as of one nearing death).

ล้อ law⁵ *v.* to ridicule ; to deride ; to twit ; to banter ; to joke ; to jeer ; to rag ; to chaff, or tease ; to poke fun at ; to mimic another in order to provoke laughter ; to roll, wheel, or cause to revolve : *n.* a wheel (as of cart or waggon) : ล้อกันเล่น to twit or banter playfully : ล้อเลียน to mimic with a teasing purpose : ล้อหลอกเล่น to tease or twit in a sporting, but deceiving manner.

ลอก lauk³ *v.* to flay ; to skin ; to peel (as a rind or skin) ; to detach or remove by pulling : ปอกลอก to peel off (as bark) : ถูกปอกลอก to be filched of one's possessions (by craft, guile or a confidence trick) : ลอกคราบ to shed the skin or scarf : ลอกท้องร่อง to clean out or deepen garden ditches (by digging up the loam or mud and placing it around the roots of trees) : ลอกเลน to dig up or remove mud from canals, or small waterways ; to clean out stagnant waterways or pools : ลอกหนังสือ to make a copy (of a manuscript) : ลอกกระดาษ to detach or remove paper in sheets or strips (as when it adheres).

ลอกแลก lauk³-laak³ *v.* to be restless or unable to remain quiet : *adv.* shakingly ; restlessly ; agitatedly.

ลอง laung *v.* to put to a test ; to try out ; to experiment with ; to practice with ; to try on (as a suit of clothes) : *n.* a base or foundation (as for inlaid or niello work) : ลองใจ to prove or test another's purpose, love, or goodwill : ลองดู, ทดลอง (p. 394) to put to a trial or test ; to give a trial : ลองดูก่อน to make an initial trial : ลองยิงปืน to make experiments with, or practice shooting a gun : ลองมือ to make a stab at doing ; to test out one's ability.

ลองเชิง laung-cherng v. to act excitedly as when jumping, skipping or leaping (used for young animals as colts, cats, pups, etc.).

ลองใน laung-nai n. a species of locust; cicada; see เรไร p. 718.

ล่อง laung³ v. to follow the current of a river downwards; to descend; to come down : n. a hole or space between floor boards into which refuse is swept or thrown : ล่องชาด to trace designs with vermilion on a gold base : ล่องชุง to raft logs down stream : ล่องตามลม to descend, following the wind (as on a river) : ล่องแพ to raft bamboos down stream : ล่องเรือ to float boats down stream : หนังสือเบิกล่อง a ship's clearance papers.

ล่องหน laung³-hon² v. to be possessed with the supernatural power of making oneself invisible.

ลอด laut³ v. to pass through (as under an archway, or through a tunnel); to evade; to be able to crawl through : ลอดบ่วง to escape from a trap : ลอดลัด to pass through a narrow passage in making a short cut : ลอดห่วง to pass through a hoop or loop : ลอดออกไปได้ to be able to wiggle out (as a chicken through the palings of a coop).

ลอดช่อง laut³-chaung³ n. a sweetmeat similar in shape to noodles (about one inch long), eaten with sweetened coconut milk.

ลอน laun n. a ridge; a part; a portion; a slice; a section (as the cavity between joints of a bamboo stalk, or the space between the knots on a rope) : adj. raised; elevated; uneven; unequal in height (compared with the surrounding surface) : เป็นลอนเป็นพร่อง undulating; being in ridges or elevations, with depressions between : ลอนทอง to slice gold.

ล่อน laun³ v. to shell (as peanuts); to be stripped bare, denuded or divested of meat, flesh, or pulp : adj. easily peeled or pitted (as the rind or stones of fruit) : ล่อนกระดูก to remove the bones : ล่อนจ้อน bare; naked; nude; empty; destitute.

ลอบ laup³ v. to be concealed, hidden, or secreted : n. a common form of basket-work fish-trap with a narrow neck, small opening, and a round long body : adv. furtively; slyly; secretly; stealthily : ลอบเข้าไป to enter by stealthy means : ลอบทำ to act in an underhanded manner, by stealth, or like a thief in the night : ลอบมองดู to peep from a hidden position : ลอบยิง to shoot from under a cover or ambush.

ลอม laum n. a summit; a peak; an apex (of a rounded contour); see จอม p 235.

ล้อม laum⁵ v. to surround (as with a fence); to enclose : ล้อมคอก to pen up; to enclose with a fence (as animals) : ล้อมจับ to surround and capture (as dacoits or robbers) : ล้อมเมือง to besiege a town or city : ล้อมรั้ว to fence in.

ลอมพอก laum-pauk³ n. a witch's hat; a dunce's cap; a clown's cap; an ancient ceremonial hat or head-gear used in comedies.

ลอย loy v. to float; to be buoyed up; to be wafted or carried in the wind (as smoke); to send, or let go adrift : adj. afloat; vagrant; alterable; plastic; fleeting; transient; wavering : โคมลอย a balloon; a hoax; a myth; an unreal or immaterial state or condition : ลอยกระทง, การลอยพระประทีป an annual festival or ceremony of Brahmin origin for the propitiation to the goddess of the River and water in general. It is held on two occasions, first during the nights of the fourteenth and fifteenth of the waxing, and the first of the waning moon of Asvina (October), and second a month later. It consists of setting adrift fancy minature ships, huge tissue paper lotus lilies, little rafts and baskets made of plantain stocks and leaves gaily decorated with paper flags, paper umbrellas, etc. In these are placed food, flowers incense sticks, lighted tapers, betel-nut, tobacco, sugar and sweetmeats. These are intended as thank-offerings and propitiary gifts to the goddess for her gracious care during the past year, as the donors have bathed in her flood, drunk of her sweet water and rowed their boats over her bosom. During the celebration of this festival fire-works of all descriptions are an important adjunct. With the multitudinous lights flashing here and there, brilliantly reflected in the water, the scene is entrancing. This ceremony has fallen into desuetude (The Directory for Bangkok and Siam 1909): ลอยแก้ว a preserve made of sour fruit steeped in syrup and a little salt : ลอยชาย *lit.* " the edges floating, or flapping about," *i. e.* to wear the loin cloth with unrolled edges and not fastened up at the back (a negligé attire for ruffians); to walk in a comfortable manner : ลอยนวล unmolested; happy; unfettered; unhampered; free to do, or go as one pleases : ลอยบาป to be freed from sin or guilt : ลอยไป-ในอากาศ to float off, or to be carried along by the air (as a toy balloon): ลอยแพ to be set adrift : to float majestically (as a swan): ลอยฟ้า, ลอยเมฆ floating high into the clouds; excellent; transcendent; distinguished : ลอย-ลงมา to descend, or float down gradually (by water or through the air): ลอยหน้า to sway the head from side to side with dramatic facial expressions (as actors).

ล่อแล่ (พูด) law³-laa³ *v.* to stutter or stammer incoherently : *adv.* indistinctly; without premeditation (as childish prattle, or the speech of a demented person).

ละ la⁶ *v.* to forsake; to abandon; to leave by oneself; to give up (as a job half finished): *adj.* each; every; one at a time : ที่ละคน one person at a time : ที่ละเล็กที่ละน้อย little by little; a little at a time : ปีละครั้ง once a year : ละทิ้ง to forsake; to relinquish all care of, or interest in : ละเมิน to cease caring for; to turn the affections away from : ละลด to exempt from (as dues, or fines that should be paid); to be lenient or forbearing : ละเลย to leave behind or alone; to pay no heed or attention to : ละไว้ to leave vacant

or unoccupied (as a house); to omit (as a line or space in typewriting); to be neglected (as an orphan): วันละ per day (as pay for services): อ่านที่ละคำ to read word by word.

ละกูมะนิส la⁶-gkoo-ma⁶-nit⁶ *Jav. n.* a lover; a fiancé or sweetheart.

ละขัดละขืน la⁶-kut⁴-la⁶-kurn² *v.* to resist, oppose, or strive against (used in poetical compositions); see ขัดขืน p. 150.

ละคร la⁶-korn *n.* a theatre; a staged play, show, or comedy; a pantomime : รำละคร to dance (as an actor in a comedy): ละครพูด a staged play consisting of dialogues with no accompanying music and but little acting.

ละคิ la⁶-ki⁶ *Cam. adj.* yet; still more; still existing, or still having; see ยัง p. 669.

ละคึก la⁶-kurk⁶ *v.* to hasten; to hurry; to push on; to accelerate.

ละงาด, ล้างงาด la⁶-ngart³ *Cam. n.* evening; eventide.

ละงิด la⁶-ngit⁶ *Jav. n.* the sky; the abode of celestial deities.

ละบม, ระบม la⁶-bom *v.* to heat, bake, or anneal (as is done in welding pieces of sheet iron in the process of making Buddhist almsbowls): *adj.* bruised; see ชอกช้ำ p. 294; ฟกช้ำ p. 605.

ละบอง ๑ *Cam.* see แต่ง p. 376; แบบ p. 490; ฉบับ p. 267.

ละบอง ๒, ลำบอง la⁶-baung *n.* small enlargements, pustules, or vesicles resulting from fever or inflammation; enlarged axillary glands resulting from vaccination : ละบอง-ไฟ blisters, vesicles, or heat rash appearing on the skin of women, resulting from the heat as they lie by the fire after childbirth.

ละบัด, ระบัด la⁶-but⁴ *v.* to shoot forth tender buds, leaves, or sprouts : *n.* leaves (young or tender); see ผลิ p. 541.

ละบอ, ระบอ, ลือ la⁶-beu *v.* to be spread about; to be rumoured; to be divulged or disseminated.

ละเบ็ง, ระเบ็ง la⁶-beng *adj.* noisy; clamorous; boisterous; see เซ็งแซ่ p. 310.

ละโบม la⁶-bome *v.* to mitigate; to appease; to caress; to console.

ละปะนัช, ละมา la⁶-bpa⁴-nut⁶ *Cam. n.* time; period; occasion; see กาล ๒ p. 99; คราว p. 181.

ละม่อม la⁶-maum³ *v.* to handle gently, tenderly, or with kindliness: *adj.* well governed; good tempered; well mannered; gentle; well behaved; soft; delicate (as flesh).

ละมั่ง, ละอง la⁶-mung³ *n.* the brow-antlered deer, *Cervus eldi* (Minutes of s. s. Regarding wild Game Preservation in Thailand).

ละมาด la⁶-mart³ *Cam. n.* gnats.

ละมาน la⁶-marn *n.* darnel; tares; a species of wild grain.

ละม้าย la⁶-mai⁵ *adj.* like; similar; allied; see คล้าย p. 186.

ละมุ (โป๊ะ) la⁶-moo⁶ *n.* a small-sized sea-fish trap with bamboo stakes as arms extended (used in shallow water, or on mud flats).

ละมุด la⁶-moot⁶, มะมุด (ต้น) *Thai, Peninsula n. Mangifera foetida (Anacardiaceae)*, a considerable tree, cultivated and encouraged in a semi-wild state throughout Malaysia. The fruits when immature are quite inedible, but are much eaten when ripe, in which state they are still green; their flavour is coarse, their smell objectionable, but the flesh is rather sweet. They are chiefly used in curries and are pickled by salting. Sometimes they are made into sweetmeats. The resinous sap in the stem has an irritant action on the human skin. Intestinal troubles result from an injudicious eating of the fruit. This same juice is used to deepen tattoo scars. The timber is yellowish, or pale grey in colour, with coarse fibre and not durable (cb. p. 344: Burk. p. 1402): ละมุดไทย (ต้น) *Mimusops kauki (Sapotaceae)*, a fair-sized tree, cultivated here and there throughout the East, and also in tropical America; and found wild, though rare, by the sea in the Dutch Indies. The fruits are eaten raw or cooked; they are sweet but rather flavourless. The timber is very durable. In the eastern parts of Malaysia it is used for uprights of houses. It is suitable for furniture. No other timber, it is said, can be compared with it as material for mills; it shows not the least tendency to crack, stands friction, and wears as if it were metal. The flowers and seeds are medicinal. There is saponin in the seeds. Another use for the tree is as a stock on which to graft the chiku —*Achras zapota*—which it dwarfs (v. p. p. 238: Burk. pp. 1475, 1421): ละมุดฝรั่ง (ต้น) *Achras zapota (Sapotaceae)*, the chiku tree, sapodilla, naseberry, a small, or medium-sized symmetrical tree, 20 to 30 feet high, with dark-green, shining, leathery leaves. It grows wild from southern Mexico southwards, possibly to Colombia and Venezuela, and is now in cultivation all round the world in the moister tropics. It was cultivated in the West Indies before the time of Columbus; and Oviedo, who was there from 1513 to 1525, wrote enthusiastically of it as the best of all fruits. The Spaniards carried the chiku to the Philippine Islands, taking with it the Aztec name 'chikl' which they corrupted, then or afterwards, to 'chiko.' They also formed the diminutive sapodilla from the Mexican zapota. The tree has but one use in Malaysia, namely as a fruit-tree; in tropical America it yields timber and is the chief source of chicle gum. The round, or ovoid, russet-brown, thin-skinned fruit contains, when fully ripe, a mass of pale brown, soft, luscious pulp, in which the large black shining seeds are embedded. It is not relished by every one, and unless perfectly ripe is unfit for eating owing to its gummy consistency.

The fruit of the chiku can be kept at temperatures between 40° and 50° F. for a month and ripened on release from cold. Acting on this, the Dutch have found it possible to ship the fruits to Holland. The seeds contain 23 per cent of oil and are diuretic. The timber is hard and heavy, fine-textured and durable. It is so durable that it has been found still in an excellent state of preservation in Yucatan, in ruins of the Mayas, whose civilization passed away before A. D. 1600 (мсм. p. 231: BURK. p. 29).

ละมุน, ละมุนละม่อม   la⁶-moon *adj.* soft; tender; smooth; pretty (descriptive of the skin); teachable; obliging; affable; gentle (descriptive of disposition).

ละเมอ, มะเมอ   la⁶-mur *v.* to speak or act while asleep, unconsciously (similar to nightmare), or while delirious.

ละเมาะ   la⁶-maw⁶ *n.* islets located around a large island or promontary: ป่าละเมาะ see ป่า p. 521.

ละเมิด   la⁶-mert³ *v.* to show disrespect, or abuse authority; to disobey orders: *n.* contumacy: ผู้ละเมิดอำนาจศาล a contemner, or one wilfully disregarding the authority of the court: ละเมิดอำนาจศาล to disregard the authority of the court.

ละเมียด   la⁶-mee-at³ *v.* to be well-behaved, well mannered: *adj.* similar; bearing a resemblance to; see คล้าย p. 186.

ละโมภ   la⁶-mope³ *adj.* greedy; gluttonous; covetous; desirous; lustful: ความละโมภ cupidity; greediness.

ละไม   la⁶-mai *adj.* tender; soft; sweet; pretty; agreeable (to the touch, or ear).

ละร์ (แล่นไป)   la⁶-ree *Jav. v.* to glide, or skim along (as a boat); to go, or run along smoothly.

ละลมละลาย   la⁶-lome-la⁶-lai *v.* to have lost all of one's possessions (as after a fire); to be totally ruined, or come to naught.

ละลวย, ระลวย   la⁶-luey *v.* to be deceived, deluded, beguiled, or misled; see งงงวย p. 220: *adj.* having plenty; getting much; soft.

ละลอก   la⁶-lauk³ *n.* ripples; wavelets; waves; foam (forming on the above); a skin disease characterized by pustules, or small boils (with severe burning pain): ผื่นละลอก small superficial boils; abscesses: ละลอกฉกฉาน the waves break violently.

ละลอบละเล้า   la⁶-laup³-la⁶-low⁵ *adj.* clever in avoiding, evading, or eluding danger.

ละลัง   la⁶-lung *adj.* quick; fast; speedy.

ละลัด   la⁶-lut⁶ *Cam. n.* the common house-fly.

ละล้า   la⁶-lah⁵ *v.* to be slow, tardy, late, dilatory; see ช้า p. 289: ละล้าใจ to become careless or incautious: ละล้าละลัง *lit.* "slowly" (alternating actions), *i. e.* hesitating; timid; cowardly; fluctuating; vacillating.

ละลาน   la⁶-larn *v. lit.* "to leave the threshing floor," *i. e.* to run about thoughtlessly, or act excitedly or hurridly; to be confused, bewildered, or mentally blurred (regarding purpose or actions): อย่าละลาน do not leave your job.

ละลาบละล้วง   la⁶-larp³-la⁶-lu-ang⁵ *v.* to trespass, encroach, intrude, or infringe upon.

ละลาย   la⁶-lai *v.* to cause to liquefy; to be fused together; to dissolve; to be dissolved; to melt (as lead): ละลายน้ำ to dissolve in water.

ละล้าว, สล้าง   la⁶-low⁵ *adj.* high; lofty; prominent: ไหวละล้าว waving or fluttering from a lofty position (as leaves or branches of trees).

ละล่ำละลัก   la⁶-lum³-la⁶-luck⁶ *adj.* erring; blundering; confused; impaired; reduced (in strength); see พลั้ง p. 573: พลาด p. 574: เดินละล่ำละลัก to walk with difficulty (as though burdened with a weight): พูดละล่ำละลัก to be unable to talk fluently, easily, or readily.

ละลิบ, ละลิ่ว la^6-lip^6 *adj.* high; distant; far away; nearly out of sight; floating a great distance off (as a kite or ship far in the distance): สูงละลิบ very high or distant (appearing only as a speck in the sky).

ละลุง la^6-loong *adj.* jumbled; thrown together; turbulent; riotous; agitated; see ชุลมุน p. 300.

ละเลง la^6-leng *v.* to mix or dissolve (by stirring); to smear, daub, or spread on roughly (as butter on bread, or paint on a wall): ละเลงขนมเบื้องด้วยปาก *lit.* "to mix the batter for pancakes with one's mouth," *i. e. proverb* to speak about doing a difficult task, as though it was very easy: ละเลงปูนขาว to stir up a portion of lime making white-wash.

ละเล้า, ละลุ่ม la^6-low^5 *v.* to caress, fondle, dandle, or cuddle; to cause to mix, mingle, or be blended together by kneading, rubbing, or stirring.

ละเลาะ la^6-law^6 *v. nautical* to move cautiously, carefully, heedfully (in order to avoid obstacles or dangers); see ค่อย p. 192.

ละเลาะละลอง la^6-law^6-la^6-laung *v.* to reach the shore, bank, or destination (safely).

ละเลิง la^6-lerng *v.* to be characterized by exuberance, excessiveness, or copiousness; to be uncontrollable, or mad with pride, desire, or joy: ละเลิงใจ to be possessed with an uncontrollable or unrestrained desire: ละเลิงมือ to allow the hands to act as though uncontrolled (as in playing tricks, or in making indecent gestures): ละเลิงหลง to be deceived by desire; to be heedless (of the consequences).

ละเลียบ la^6-li-ep^3 *v.* to skirt; to pass along the border, edge, or rim.

ละเลือก la^6-leu-ak^3 *adv.* hurriedly; excitedly; rashly; recklessly; see ลนลาน under ลน p. 727.

ละไล้ la^6-lai^5 *v.* to smear on or over; to caress, fondle, stroke or cuddle (in an affectionate manner).

ละวล la^6-worn *adj.* echoing; resounding; reverberating; see ก้อง p. 68.

ละว้อ, ละว้า la^6-waw^5 *n.* wild hill-tribes in north-western Thailand; one of two original races inhabiting Thailand (wood p. 40).

ละวาด la^6-wart^3 *adj.* resembling a drawing.

ละเวง la^6-weng *adj.* agreeable to the sense of hearing; melodious; harmonious; resounding; far reaching (sounds).

ละแวก ๑ la^6-waak^3 *n.* an ancient town of [Cambodia.

ละแวก ๒ la^6-waak^3 *n.* the fork in a road; a narrow path or lane entering a village.

ละโว้ la^6-woh^5 *n.* the ancient name for Lopburi: มะเขือละโว้ a species of egg-plant, *Solanum*; see มะเขือขาว p. 632; a kind of small wild apple.

ละหลัด la^6-lut^4 *adv.* rapidly; swiftly; hastily. [tily.

ละห้อย la^6-hoy^3 *v.* to moan or groan for; to sigh; to think of; to languish for (one being absent): *adj.* sorrowful; sad; downhearted.

ละหาน la^6-harn^2 *n.* a brook; a mountain stream; a waterway; a ditch: *adj.* hanging; suspended.

ละหุ่ง (ต้น) la^6-hoong^4 *n. Ricinus communis (Euphorbiaceae)*, the castor-oil plant, a tall, quick-growing perennial with large, handsome palmate-pelcate leaves. It is cultivated in all warm countries, more particularly in Thailand, India, Southern Europe, and United States, generally as an annual but sometimes as a perennial crop. The original home was Africa where it came into cultivation at a very early date, certainly in Egypt under the Pharaohs for seeds have been found in graves dating from 4000 B. C. The castor-oil plant and *Sesamum* were sources of oil there long before the olive. The well-known oil, of which good seed contains 30 to 40 per cent or more, is obtained from the seed by pressure and is valued at £60 or more per ton. Besides its use in a refined state in medicine, castor-oil is largely employed as a body for lubricating oils, also for dressing leather and in soap manufacture, etc. (MCM. pp 27, 388 : Burk. p. 1907) : ละหุ่งเคือ *Laos*, *Korat* (ต้น) *Buettneria andamanensis (Sterculiaceae)* (cb. p. 181) : น้ำมันละหุ่ง castoroil ; see น้ำ p. 455.

ละเหย see ระเหย p. 699.

ละเหี่ย la[6]-he-ah[4] *v.* to languish ; to feel weak, tired or spiritless : ละเหี่ยใจ to feel a sense of discouragement, dejection, or depression.

ละออ la[6]-aw *Cam. adj.* good-looking ; beautiful ; handsome ; pretty : นวลละออ soft, smooth, delicate, and beautiful (as skin or complexion).

ละออง la[6]-awng *n.* dust ; powder ; small particles : นวลละออง *idiomatic* a creamy white powder (used to describe skin) : ละอองฝน fine drops or mist of rain : ละอองธุลีพระบาท *lit.* "dust of your feet," *i. e.* a form of address to His Majesty the King.

ละอาย la[6]-ai *v.* to be ashamed of ; to be timid or shy.

ละเอียด la[6]-ee-at[4] *adj.* thin but of good quality (as of cloth) ; delicate (as a membrane or tissue) ; fine, or in minute particles (as powder) : คนละเอียด one attending to small details ; one who is careful, cautious, or watchful : ละเอียดเป็นแบ้ง finely pulverized (as flour) : ละเอียดละออ exacting ; precise ; strict ; methodical ; scrupulous ; careful about the smallest detail ; see ถี่ถ้วน under ถี่ p. 388.

ลัก luck[6] *v.* to steal ; to pilfer ; to thieve : *n.* larceny : ฉกลัก to defraud by stealth : ลักทรัพย์ theft or larceny : ลักยิ้ม a dimple : ลักลอม, ลอบลัก to steal furtively : ลักลั่น conglomerate ; heterogeneous ; incongruous ; differing from all others : ลักสร้อย to hide, conceal, or mask one's sorrow ; to cry in secret.

ลักขณะ luck[6]-ka[4]-na[4] *P. n.* a mark ; a sign ; a symptom ; a characteristic ; an attribute ; nature ; quality ; a definition ; auspicious marks ; the thirty-two special marks of a Buddha ; a personal characteristic from which good fortune may be predicted (chd. p. 217).

ลักข luck[6]-kee[2] *P. n.* prosperity ; splendour ; beauty ; power ; luck ; good fortune (chd. p. 218).

ลักจั่น luck[6]-gka[4]-chjun[4] *n.* a water flask used by ascetics, pilgrims or travellers.

ลักปิดลักเปิด (โรค) luck[6]-gka[4]-bpit[4]-luck[6]-gka[4]-bpert[4] *n.* an oral disease characterized by periodical bleeding (from the gums).

ลักเพศ luck[6]-gka[4]-pet[3] *v.* to disguise or mask in order to conceal one's identity or sex.

ลักษณะ luck[6]-sa[4]-na[4] *P. n.* a mark ; a sign ; a symbol ; a token ; a quality ; characteristic properties (chd. p. 217) : ไม่รู้ลักษณะ undiscerning ; silly ; ignorant : รู้ลักษณะ discerning ; prudent ; wise : ลักษณะทาษ laws on slavery : ลักษณะอาญา the criminal code.

ลักษมณ์ luck[6] *S. n.* Lakshama, name of the younger brother and companion of Rama during his travels and adventures ; one endowed with auspicious signs or marks (s. E. D. p. 892).

ลักษมี luck[6]-sa[4]-mee[2] *S. n.* name of the goddess of Fortune and Beauty ; Vishnu's consort ; prosperity ; success ; happiness ; wealth ; beauty ; loveliness ; grace ; charm (S.E.D. p. 892).

ลัค luck[6] *P. S. v.* to meet ; to come into contact with ; to adhere ; to cling ; to attach oneself to (S. E. D. p. 893) ; see ติด p. 367.

ลัคคะ luck[6]-ka[6] *P. adj.* attached ; tied to ; adhering (chd. p. 217).

ลัคน, ลัคนา, ลัคนกาล luck[6]-ka[6]-na[6] *S. n.* an auspicious moment or time fixed upon as lucky by astrologers for the beginning or performing of any work, project, or function :

adj. fixed on; intent on; attached; sticking to; remaining in (S. E. D. p. 893): ลัคนทิน an auspicious day.

ลั้ง   lung *n.* a shallow receptacle or basket made of bamboo or wood; a packing box; a crate: ลั้ง (ปลา) *Rastrelliger brachysomus (Scombridae)* (suvatti p. 111).

ลั้ง   lung[3] *adj.* egg-shaped; equal, or nearly equal in size at both ends; bulging or enlarged in the middle.

ลังกา, ลงกา   lung-gkah *n. Hindi* Ceylon.

ลังคิ, ลังคี   lung-ki[6] *P. n.* a bolt; a bar; a pin; a wedge (chd. p. 219).

ลังถึง   lung-turng[2] *Chin. n.* a tin cooking utensil with three perforated tiers (used for steaming cakes or food).

ลังลอง, รังรอง   lung-laung *adj.* beautiful.

ลังเล   lung-lay *v.* hesitating: doubtful; undecided; uncertain.

ลัชชา   lut[6]-chah *P. S. n.* shame; modesty; bashfulness; timidity (chd. p. 217); the sensitive plant; see กระทืบยอด p. 35.

ลัญจ์   lun *P. n.* a present; a douceur; a bribe; a wage (chd. p. 218).

ลัญฉ์, ลัญฉน์   lun *P. n.* a mark; an imprint; the seal upon a letter (chd. p. 218); the royal seal.

ลัฏฐิ, ลัฏฐิกา   lut[6]-ti[4] *P. n.* a staff; a walking-stick; a stick; the offshoot of a plant (chd. p. 219); a cane: *adj.* tender; young; soft.

ลัด   lut[6] *v.* to sprout; to put forth young leaves or tops (as grass or trees); to take or make a short cut; to flip (as with the finger); to assume a straight position after being bent (as the bow after shooting): ปากลัด the mouth, or entrance channel to a short cut: ลัดนิ้วมือ the time consumed in bending and extending a finger or fingers; a very short

space of time: ลัดเนื้อ to put on fat; to become fleshy.

ลัดา see ลดา p. 727.

ลัทธ์   lut[6] *P. adj.* taken; obtained; received (chd. p. 217); confiscated.

ลัทธิ   lut[6]-ti[6] *n.* religious beliefs; tenets; opinions; practices; faith: ถือลัทธิต่างกัน adhering to the tenets of a different religion; heresy.

ลัน   lun *n.* an eel trap made of bamboo slats.

ลั่น   lun[3] *n.* to explode; to burst; to detonate; to make a sudden loud noise or sound (as of a bomb or firecracker): *n.* a crack; a burst; a snap: กระดูกลั่น, ข้อลั่น the bones or joints crack (as when cracking the knuckles): ท้องลั่น the rumbling noise of gas in the intestines: ฟ้าลั่น thunder: ลั่นกุญแจ to turn the key in a lock (thereby making a noise): ลั่นไก, ลั่นนกปืน to pull the trigger; to cause an explosion by some mechanism: ลั่นฆ้อง to strike a gong or cymbals: ลั่นดาน to bolt, or to cause a bolt or bar to catch (as on doors or windows of Buddhist temple buildings): ลั่นปาก, ลั่นวาจา, ลั่นคำ to make a promise; to speak; to tell; to declare: ลั่นปืน to cause a gun to shoot: เสียงลั่น a far reaching or resounding sound (as the firing of cannon).

ลั่นเตา (ถั่ว)   lun-dtow *n.* a species of bean; the Holland bean.

ลั่นไต   lun-dtai *n.* a kind of mat made of wicker-work.

ลั่นทม (ต้น)   lun[3]-tom, จำปา *n. Plumeria acutifolia (Apocynaceae)*, frangipanni; temple-tree; pagoda-tree, a low, spreading, succulent tree or large shrub which the Spaniards took from Mexico to the Philippines at an early date. The date at which it reached India, and by what course it travelled, are unrecorded; but it was thoroughly established there during the eighteenth century; and as it had been brought to Europe long before this. it is not unlikely that it was taken to India in

more than one way. The Spaniards may
have taken it across the Pacific as an ornamental tree, but it is more probable that
they took it because it was medicinal. Her-
nandez had, for instance, written of it as used
by the Indians for skin complaints and inter-
mittant fevers, and for dispersing dropsies,
by purging caused when it is applied to the
abdomen. He tasted the milk and says that
he nearly killed himself thereby. At the
present day the bark is used as a diuretic in
the West Indies, and the latex for purging.
In the Philippines the bark is used as a purgative, emmenagogue, and febrifuge. In Java
and Madoera a decoction of the bark is given
for gonorrhoea, dropsy, and dysuria due to
venereal disease. Very rarely, the milk is
now used as a purgative. It is used as a
counter-irritant on the gums for tooth-ache,
and is sometimes dropped into sores. A
decoction of the leaves may be used as a
lotion for cracks and eruptions on the soles
of the feet, and a paste of the leaves for
poulticing swellings. No such uses are recorded in Malaya, but in India the bark is
used for diarrhoea and the plant for fever.
The flowers are much milder in action than
other parts of the plant. They are said to
be eaten in India with betel to cure ague.
These flowers grow in large heads, each separate flower being snowy white with a yellow
centre. Another and rarer variety has a pink
throat. They are highly fragrant and it has
been suggested they might be used in scent-
making. In Malaya the frangipanni has
been adopted as a graveyard tree; in Thailand, India and Ceylon it is sacred and is
found planted about temples, and is not popular in door yards. It seems strange that an
American tree should thus become a sacred
tree in the Far East (MCM. p. 91 : V. P. p. 237 :
BURK. p. 1777): ลั่นทมแดง (ต้น) *P. rubra*, a
tree similar to the former, bearing bright
crimson flowers in profusion, also a few fruits

occasionally. Also a native of Central America, it was first introduced into Ceylon in 1900
(MCM. p. 91 : BURK. p. 1776).

ลั่นทวย   lun-tu-ie *adj.* fatigued ; tired ; weak ;
exhausted ; see ระไหย p. 700 ; ระทวย p. 695.

ลั่นโทม   lun-tome *Cam. v.* to bow down ;
to stoop ; to crouch ; see ก้ม p 8.

ลับ   lup[6] *v.* to whet; to sharpen (as a knife
or edged tool): *adj.* hidden ; secret ; private ;
concealed ; unknown ; mysterious :   ความลับ
a mystery ; a secret ; *government* confidential :
ที่ลับ the private parts (of the body) ; a secret
spot ; an unseen or secluded place :   ทำลับล่อ
to do or act secretly :   นินทาลับหลัง to slander
the absent; to defame another behind his back:
ลับตา concealed ; unseen by the owner or guardian ; different to what would be done if seen :
ลับลึก hidden ; mysterious ; profound :   ลับแล
lit. "to hide the view," *i. e.* a screen (as a
light movable structure or trellis):   ลับล่อ,
ลับ ๆ ล่อ ๆ uncertain ; vague ; appearing and
disappearing (as a flash-light):   ลับหลัง behind one's back ; unseen ; unnoticed :   ลับหู
unheard.

ลัพธ์   lup[6] *S. adj.* taken ; seized ; caught ;
obtained ; found ; gotten (S. E. D. p. 896):   เลข-
ลัพธ์, ผลลัพธ์ *math.* the result in adding, or
subtracting.

ลัพธิ   lup[6]-ti[6] *S. n.* acquisition ; gain ; profit ; the quotient (S. E. D. p. 896).

ลัภ   lup[6] *P. S. v.* to take ; to seize ; to catch ;
to gain possession of ; to obtain or receive
(S. E. D. p. 896).

ลัย, ลยะ   lai *P. S. n.* dissolution ; disappearance ; absorption (Chd. p. 219):   ลัยกาล
time of destruction or dissolution :   ลัยคต
**gone into dissolution ; demolished ; dissolved ;
melted away ; vanished.**

ลำ ๑   lah *Cam. adj.* small ; diminutive ; tiny ;
stunted :   พุดลา, มะลิลา a small *Ervatamia*
(see พุด p. 593) ; also a *Jasminum* (see มะลิ
p. 639).

ลา ๒   lah *v.* to bid farewell; to take leave of; to say goodbye; to become straightened out; to lose the curved contour (as a weak fish hook): *n.* ass; donkey; a time; a turn; a numerical designatory particle for cheers, shouts, etc: *adj.* weak; feeble; languid: กราบลา to make an obeisance (before a superior) on leaving: ขอลา "kindly permit me to leave" (as a pupil asking to be excused): ลาตาย to be conscious of approaching death: ลาผนวช to leave the brotherhood; to be divested of the robes of the Buddhist priesthood: ลาพรรษา to leave a Buddhist temple at the end of lent: ลาไปก่อน I take leave of you: ลาโลก *lit.* "to take leave of the world," *i.e.* to pass on; to die: ลาออก to resign from a position.

ล่า   lah[3] *v.* to hunt; to pursue; to cause to flee; to retreat, or withdraw: *n.* bait; food; a snare: *adj.* delayed; retarded; hindered; lagging: ผู้ล่าสัตว์โดยไม่ได้รับอนุญาต a poacher: ล่าทัพ to retreat (as an army): ล่าเนื้อ to stalk game: ล่าสัตว์ to drive, chase, or hunt game: สุนัขขี่ล่าสัตว์ bloodhounds; hunting dogs.

ล้า, มล้า   lah[5] *v.* to be straightened or extended; the antithesis of coiled; to be run down (as a clock spring); to lose or lack energy or pep: *adj.* slow; tardy; late; fatigued; tired; weakened (by exertion): เมื่อยล้า debilitated by fatigue or disease: ล้าเต้ to be slow, tardy, dilatory, or deliberate (in walking): ล้าหลัง to loiter, linger, or be delayed behind others (from fatigue or while sight-seeing): เหตุไรจึงมาล้าไป why is it you have come so late?

ลาก   lark[3] *v.* to pull; to haul; to drag; to draw; see ฉุด p. 270: ลากข้าง *lit.* "tagged on to the side," *i.e. grammatical* name of " า", the third vowel.

ลากษา, ลาขา   lark[3]-sah[2] *P. S. n.* lac; an animal dye (chd. p. 217); the insect or animal which produces a red dye (S. E. D. p. 899).

ลาง ๑   larng *n.* a sign or omen of destiny, calamity or misfortune: ลางลิง *Pinanga,* a small or medium-sized ornamental palm (burk. p. 1729).

ลาง ๒   larng *adj.* some; a certain kind, sort, or class: ลางคน certain people or persons: ลางที sometimes; perhaps: ลางที่, ลางแห่ง certain places: ลางเนื้อชอบลางยา not every one prefers the same thing; one's meat is another's poison: ลางพวก some classes of people.

ล่าง   larng[3] *adj.* below; underneath; beneath; under; lower; see ต่ำ p. 365; ใต้ p. 378: ข้าง-ล่าง below; downstairs: ชั้นล่าง the lower storey (of a house); inferior grade or order (of rank): ลงไปข้างล่าง to go down below; to descend.

ล้าง   larng[5] *v.* to wash; to clean; to rinse; to bathe; to purify (with water): ล้างกฎหมาย to abolish a law: ล้างใจ, ชำระใจ to purify the heart: ล้างผลาญ to destroy, overturn, or upset; to execute, kill, cause to dissipate, scatter, or disperse (as one's fortune or substance): ล้างโลก to destroy the world (as by a flood).

ลางงิด   larng-ngit[6] *Jav. n.* sky; heaven.

ลางสาด (ต้น)   larng-sart[4] *n. Lansium domesticum (Meliaceae),* a small tree found wild in western Malaysia and also much cultivated. 'Langsat' denotes the wild tree and some of the cultivated races. The fruit is much esteemed and may be eaten, raw or preserved in syrup, by a short boiling, after the skin has been removed. The timber is light-coloured, and not very hard; fine grained. Derived from wild trees, it is used in Java for tool-handles and sometimes for house-posts; it is durable, tough, and elastic. It is used for rafters in Malacca. Wood-tar is used for blackening the teeth. The bark is astringent and is used in a decoction for dysentery in Java, Borneo, and Malaya. The crushed bitter seeds are used by the Sakai to cure fever. The seeds are anthelmintic. The leaves may enter into a decoction for dysentery, and their juice may be dropped into sore eyes. The bark may be used for poulticing scorpion stings. The bark and the fruit-skins contain a poisonous substance, lansium acid, which, if injected into a frog, arrests the beating of the heart. The juice is recorded as a Dyak arrow-poison. The fruit-shells, when burned, give an aromatic smell, and are used by the Javanese to drive away mosquitoes. These fruit-shells may be mixed with benzoin (MCM. p. 265: cb. p. 259: BURK.

[P. 1314).

ล้างาด see **ละงาด** p. 732.

ล้าเง็ด   lah[5]-nget[6] *Jav. n.* a prince; a commander-in-chief (of an army).

ลาชะ   lah-cha[6] *P. S. n.* dried or parched grain; popped rice or corn (S. E. D. p. 900).

ลาญ   larn *v.* to break; to be destroyed; to be broken; see **ประลัย** p. 504.

ลาด   lart[3] *v.* to spread down (as carpet); to pave; to go around (as on inspection); to cruise or scout about: *adj.* sloping; inclining slightly; deviating from the horizontal: ลาด, เสือ, เสือตอ (ปลา) *Datnioides microlepis* (*Lobotidae*) (Suvatti p. 126): เรือลาดตระเวน a cruiser: ลาดตระเวน to go on a cruise; to scout about (as on inspection).

ลาดเลา   lart[3]-lao *n.* clue; sign; trace; indication of some secret; see **เค้าเงื่อน** p. 209.

ล้าต้า   lah[5]-dtah[3] *n.* a captain; one in charge of a ship (while at sea).

ล้าเตียง   lah[5]-dti-ang *n.* a relish eaten with rice, prepared by making small croquets of fried minced pork and shrimps with proper seasoning. One is sufficient for a mouthful.

ลาน   larn *v.* to be dim, or undistinguishable against a dazzling light: *n.* a coiled spring; a level flat open space, lawn, or ground:

กลัวลาน to be extremely afraid; to tremble with fear: จานใบลาน to write on palm leaves with a metal stylus: ใบลาน dried and ironed palm leaves of the ต้นตาล (p. 364) used for writing purposes: พระลานหน้าวัง a lawn in front of a palace: ลนลาน zealous; active; hasty; ardent; eager; fervent: ลาน-ใจ to be excited, alarmed, frightened, or dismayed: ลานตา dim; indistinct; blurred (to the sight): ลานนวดข้าว a threshing floor (where buffaloes or bullocks tread out the grain): ลานนาฬิกา the spring of a watch or clock.

ล้าน   larn[5] *n.* (numerically) a million; (of the scalp) baldness; alopecia: *adj.* bald; hairless (from a diseased condition).

ลาบ   larp[3] *n.* a condiment made of raw meat or fish mixed with cooked chilli sauce and caviar (eaten with rice).

ลาป ๑   larp[3] *P. n.* a sort of quail, *perdix chinensis* (chd. p. 219); see **มูลไถ (นก)** p. 655.

ลาป ๒, ลาปนะ   lah-bpa[4] *P. S. n.* the act of speaking, talking, or producing vocal sounds; the mouth (S. E. D. p. 896).

ลาพุ   lah-poo[6] *P. S. n.* a pumpkin; a gourd (chd. p. 216); see **น้ำเต้า** p. 454.

ลาเพ, เล้าโลม   lah-pay *v.* to comfort; to console; to solace.

ลาภ   larp[3] *P. S. n.* the act of receiving, getting, obtaining, or gaining profits; acquisition of gain (S. E. D. p. 897).

ลาม   larm *v.* to advance; to extend along the surface; to encroach upon; to spread; to widen out: แผลลามออกไป the wound or sore continues to spread: ลามปาม spreading; expanding; over-spreading (as ringworm or sundry skin diseases); rude; impudent; audacious; insolent: ลามลวน to be playfully rude, harsh, or indecent: ล่วงลามลวน to over-reach the bounds of politeness (as in jesting, sport, or joking): ไฟลุกลามเข้ามา the fire spreads inward.

ล่าม　　larm[3] *v.* to tether; to tie up; to chain together: *n.* an interpreter: เป็นล่าม to act as an interpreter: ล่ามโซ่ to tether with chains; to put into irons.

ลามก　　lah-mok[6] *P. adj.* low; inferior; vile (chd. p. 218); mean; ill-behaved; dirty; immoral; immodest; indecent: ความลามก lewdness; lubricity: ชั่วช้าลามก wicked; perverse; lewd.

ลาย　　lai *n.* marks, lines, designs, or art ornamentions (as drawings or carvings): *adj.* streaked; striped; lineal: ผ้าลาย fabrics with lineal designs: ลวดลาย art designs; chased work, figures or patterns: หลังลาย a streaked back (as one marked by strokes of a stick, whip, or rattan): ลายแทง a treatise or chart indicating the position of buried treasures, or hidden valuables: ลายน้ำ-ในกระดาษ watermarks in paper: ลายพิมพ์-นิ้วมือ finger-prints: ลายมือ handwriting; signature; lines on the palms of the hands: ลวดลายแกะ carvings.

ล้าย　　lai[5] *v.* to daub, smear, or apply in a rough manner (as paint or white-wash); see บ้าย, ป้าย p. 481; ทา p. 410; see ไล้ p. 759.

ลายสอ (งู)　　lai-saw[2] *n. Tropidonotus piscator (Colubridae)*, a species of slightly poisonous snake with yellow and black stripes, found in paddy fields during the wet weather (Malcolm Smith N. H. J. S. S. I, 1, p. 14).

ลายสาบ　　lai-sarp[4] *n.* a species of snake with a red neck.

ลาฬนะ　　lah-la[6]-na[6] *S. n.* dalliance; fondling; coaxing; interchange of caresses; wanton play or sport (chd. p. 218).

ลาลส　　lah-lote[6] *P. S. n.* ardent desire (chd. p. 218); eager longing for; delight or absorption in (S. E. D. p. 900).

ลาลา (น้ำลาย)　　lah-lah *P. S. n.* saliva (chd. [p. 218); spittle.

ลาว　　lao *adj.* Lao; Laosian. " The original Lao are to be identified in the people styled Lua (ล้วะ), or Lawa (ลวา) who are still to be found among the forests and hills in almost all the provincial circles included in the old Lao domain, and who speak a distinct language of their own" (Prince Damrong J. S. S. XIII, 2, p. 2).

ลาวก　　lah-wok[6] *P. S. n.* a reaper (chd. p. 219); the act of reaping grain.

ลาวัณย์　　lah-wun *S. n.* beauty; loveliness; comeliness; amiability.

ลาสนะ　　lah-sa[4]-na[6] *P. n.* the act of dancing [(chd. p. 219); a dance.

ลำ ๑　　lum *Cam. adj.* resembling; similar; alike.

ลำ ๒　　lum *n.* the bed of a canal or waterway; song; rhyme; poetry; a designatory particle for long slender tapering objects, as boats, ships, bamboos and sugarcane stalks: ประทุกเต็มลำ to load to full capacity (as a boat, or freighter): ลำกะโดง a small waterway in plantations, or between fields (for irrigating purposes): ลำแข้ง the length of one's shin: ลำแขน the upper portion of the arm (from shoulder to the elbow): ลำคลอง a canal: ลำคอ the neck: ลำต้น the bole or trunk of a tree: ลำท่อ a conduit; a water-passage (as a sewer or viaduct): ลำ-ธาร a stream; a brook; a creek; a rivulet: ลำนำ the theme of a song, or metrical composition: ลำน้ำ a waterway: ลำผู้กัน pencil-shaped rays; a phenomenon of nature where a luminous streak or arch (as a white rainbow) appears in the sky. If this appears for several nights it is considered to be a prognostication of future events: ลำมาบ a creek, stream, or brook overgrown with grass or weeds: ลำเสา (ฝี) a name applied to extensively indurated abscesses occurring in the region of the leg (as a proas abscess): ลำห้วย a shallow mountain watercourse or stream (in the dry season); a swift torrential volume of water (during the rainy season): หากินด้วยลำแข้ง to be self-supporting.

ล่ำ lum[3] *adj.* fat; stout; sturdy; stalwart; muscular: โตล่ำ huge; monstrous (in physique): ล่ำสัน fat; very stout; corpulent; robust; strong; well-developed (physically).

ล้ำ lum[5] *v.* to trespass; to invade; to infringe; to protrude; to project: *adj.* superior; excellent; precious: งามล้ำ most beautiful: ล้ำเลิศ most excellent; the best; *the sign of the superlative degree.*

ลำเค็ญ lum-ken *adj.* poverty; adversity; misfortune; calamity; suffering; misery.

ลำเคือง lum-keung *adj.* wailing; grieving; bemoaning; sad.

ลำงาด lum-ngat[3] *Cam. adj.* cool.

ลำเจียก (ต้น) lum-chjie-ak[4] *n. Pandanus tectorius (Pandanaceae)*, a considerably branched screw-pine, which grows to the height of about 15 feet, with numerous aerial shoots, which descend and fix the plant in the sand. It is common on sea coasts from the Mascarene Islands to the Pacific. From the wild plant, which is var. *littoralis*, man, in cultivation, has selected various races. *P. tectorious* is very widely used for matting, sugar bags, etc., for which it is well suited. In Thailand mats are made from it, with Chantabun and Songkla as the chief centres. In the Philippine Islands it is considerably used for rough work hats and matting. In Guam, in addition to the above uses, cordage for securing thatch is made; it is cultivated for this purpose, but never fruits. It is possible, by beating out the end of one of the roots, to make a rough paint-brush; these are used in India. The scent of the male flower is very powerful. A century ago the inflorescences were sold in the market of Penang to Malay women who folded portions of it into their hair for the scent. In India the inflorescence is distilled to make an essence, which is medicinal. It is believed that some species of *Pandanus* can be used as antidote for poisoning (BURK. p. 1650 : V. P. pp. 238, 239 : MCM. pp. 208, 209); see เตย (ต้น) p. 373.

ลำดวน (ต้น) lum-du-an *n. Sphaerocoryne clavipes (Annonaceae)*, a tree bearing three-petaled, strongly scented blossoms producing no fruit. These blossoms are commonly given as offerings to Buddhist monks (cb. p. 48).

ลำดับ lum-dup[4] *v.* to set in order; to arrange in series, or order (either numerically or alphabetically): *n.* order; line; series; list: จัดให้เป็นลำดับ to arrange in order or sequence.

ลำตัด lum-dtut[4] *n.* an antiphon: *adj.* antiphonal singing or speaking.

ลำเนา lum-now *n.* place; rank; domain; gist; tenor; course; manner; way: ลำเนาความ course, gist, epitome, or essence of an affair (as of legal proceedings).

ลำบอง see ละบอง p. 732.

ลำบาก lum-bak[4] *adj.* difficult; arduous; laborious; painful; annoying; tormenting; see ยาก p. 671: ตกยากลำบาก to become poverty-stricken: ทนลำบากมาก undergoing great trouble or vexation: ลำบากใจ vexatious; annoying; irritating; harassing.

ลำบุ (ปืนใหญ่) lum-boo[4] *n.* a piece of field artillery; a cannon.

ลำพอง lum-paung *adj.* vain; haughty; restive: ม้าลำพอง an untamed or headstrong horse.

ลำพัง lum-pung *adv.* by one's own exertion; by oneself; alone; singly; solitarily; separately; individually: ตามลำพังใจ unrestrained; unrestricted; with full freedom: ทำแต่ลำพัง by one's own strength or exertion: ไปลำพังคนเดียว to go alone.

ลำพัน (ปลา), ปลาดุกลำพัน lum-pun *n.* a subdivisional species of the catfish family.

ลำพู (ต้น) see ปาด (ต้น) p. 523.

ลำเพ็ญ see ตรง p. 341.

ลำเพา   lum-pow *adj.* beautiful; handsome; young; plastic; smooth; delicate (descriptive of handsome youths or women); see งาม p. 223; นุ่ม p. 462.

[dagger.

ลำแพง   lum-paang *n.* a spear; a lance; a

ลำแพน   lum-paan *Thai, Surat* and *Songkla* (ต้น) *n. Duabanga sonneratioides* (*Lythraceae*), a tall tree of rather characteristic appearance, found from north-eastern India to the Malay Peninsula, but only as far south as Negri Sembilan. The timber is grey, with lighter yellowish streaks, easily worked, being moderately soft; it take a good finish and polish; it seasons well, but if the seasoning is done too quickly is liable to warp. It is not durable when placed in exposed positions, but lasts well under cover, or when in contact with water. Canoes are made of it, and it is used for tea-boxes, house-building, boat-building, etc., in India. Malays eat the very acid fruits (BURK. p. 869); *Sonneratia alba* (*Lythraceae*), a tree found in the mangrove forests from East Africa to the Pacific. There are three species in the Malay Peninsula. This tree grows up to 80 feet in height with a girth of 6 feet, but it is usually much smaller. It grows back of the mangrove belt at some distance from the water, and usually on a sandy soil on the coasts of India and Malaysia. The timber is used for firewood in Malaysia, but is not chosen when other trees are available. In Java the wood is not used at all, but in Celebes it is valued for house-building under the roof, for when protected it is imperishable. In the Philippine Islands it is used for clogs and firewood. The bark tans, but is not used commercially. The quite ripe fruits are eaten by the Malays in Java, and particularly in the Moluccas, as a flavouring with fish. The leaves are eaten both raw and cooked. The breathing roots are small—rather too small for use as corks (BURK. p. 2051); *S. griffithii*, a tree, up to 120

feet in height with a girth of 7 feet or more, found toward the sea-face of the mangrove swamps where the mud is soft. It occurs in the Andaman Islands and on the coast of Tenasserim, extending south to Singapore. In the Peninsula it is the commonest species of the genus. The timber serves as firewood, but not much. It is capable of better use, if well grown. It is very hard, moderately heavy to very heavy, pink to reddish-brown, but usually found in small sizes and short lengths. It is useful for piles and bridges, as it is resistant to teredo attack, but corrodes iron. Sleepers are made of it in the Dutch Indies. The fruits are very acid. The pounded root is rubbed on the skin as a treatment for ringworm (BURK. p. 2053: cb. pp. 730, 731, 732): เสื่อลำแพน large mats made of plaited bamboo or rattan.

ลำโพง (ต้น)   lum-poong *n. Datura bojeri* (*Solanaceae*) stramonium; *D. fastuosa* (BURK. p. 767): ลำโพงกาสลัก (ต้น) an annual two to three feet high. The leaves are large and angular : the trumpet-shaped flowers are purple or white. The roots are used for bites from mad dogs and are supposed to cure insanity. The whole plant is dried and smoked as tobacco for asthma. The round fruit, which is covered with prickles, is very poisonous. The poisonous property resides chiefly in the seeds which are oblong, kidney-shaped, laterally compressed, with convoluted edges, the free convex edge being definitely double-ridged. In size the seed is 1 mm. thick and 6.35 mm. long, light fawn-coloured when dry. There is no marked odour; the taste is slightly bitter. The use of the seeds for criminal purposes is well known in Thailand, Malaya and India. Usually the dose administered is only sufficient to produce a temporary mania and stupor during which the victim is robbed. It seems to produce an entire loss of memory during the period of its action, but the victim fully recovers, unless the dose has been a large one, when coma and death result. It is frequently administered ground, in tea, coffee or curry. The effect becomes manifest in about fifteen minutes but lasts about twenty-four hours. The seeds are frequently burnt to produce lethargy by means of the fumes (Gimlette : Malay Poisons and Charm Cures, p. 204 : McM. pp. 110, 141, 378, 385 : Burk. p. 768).

ลำไพ่ lum-pai[3] *n.* petty, private gains (money, profits, perquisites, earnings acquired by other means than as wages or salary) : ได้โดยลำไพ่ to acquire gain, riches, or wealth by special individual efforts.

ลำมาด lum-mart[3] *n.* shape; form; erect [figure.

ลำยอง lum-yaung *n.* carvings in the shape of leaves, placed as ornamentations along the edges of the roofs of Buddhist temple buildings; see ช่อฟ้า under ช่อ p. 283 : *adj.* pretty; beautiful.

ลำใย lum-yai *Thai* and *Laos* (ต้น) *n.* *Nephelium* (*Euphoria*) *longana* (*Sapindaceae*), a tree of relativelly small size, cultivated in southern China, in some parts of India, throughout Malaysia and Thailand to the northern limits of Malaya. It grows from seed, and can be grafted on the rambutan. But, like the litchi, it is exacting in the conditions which it requires for fruiting. The fruit is eaten, and is like an acid litchi. Like the litchi, the Chinese dry it but only the flesh which is used for making a tea; this tea is regarded as a tonic and has been long so used in Java. The Chinese now use the dried flowers medicinally, and import them into the Straits. The seeds contain saponin and are used in China for washing the hair. They contain a very little oil and much starch. The timber is red, hard, good for furniture and buildings, but even where the tree is at home is rarely available (McM. p. 267 : cb. p. 331 : V. P. pp. 216, 239 : Burk. p. 1547); see นิ่ม-นวล under นิ่ม p. 458.

ลำลอง lum-laung *adj.* gay; gaudy; showy; unrestricted; self-directing; independent; living according to one's fancy.

ลำลา lum[3]-lah *v.* to bid farewell; to take [leave of.

ลำลาบ lum-larp[3] *n.* a small waterway, or rivulet; a swamp; an eczematous eruption of the skin characterized by spreading, as the exudation extends over the surface.

ลำลำ lum-lum *adv.* nearly; almost; see เกือบ p. 127 : ลำลำจะพุ่ง a dancing attitude assumed by the mahouts on the first occasion of testing the strength of elephants.

ลำเลิก lum-lerk[3] *v.* to recount incidents of the past; to recall, or extol favours, benefactions, or meritorious deeds done to others in the past.

ลำเลียง lum-lee-ang *v.* to lighter by using transport boats; to transport in small quantities (as either to, or from a ship or large boat) : เรือลำเลียง a transport boat.

ลำเวียง lum-we-ang *n.* a camp enclosed by a line of posts or fencing; a stockade.

ลำเอียง lum-ee-ang *v.* to show partiality, or preference for; to be unfair, or unequitable : *adj.* inclined; crooked; bowed; bent : ตัดสิน-ด้วยความลำเอียง *legal* to pronounce judgement with partiality.

ลิ li[6] to be splintered, cracked, chipped, or nicked (as the edges of pottery or glass-ware); see บิ่น p. 483.

ลิกขา, ลิกษา lick[6]-kah[2] *P. S. n.* a nit; a young louse; the eggs of lice (S. E. D. p. 901).

ลิกุจ see ขนุน p. 140.

ลิเก, ยี่เก (p. 675) li[6]-gkay *n.* a burlesque theatrical performance in which the actors are generally men singing or speaking extemporaneously.

ลิขนะ lik[6]-ka[4]-na[6] *P. n.* the act of writing (chd. p. 220), inscribing, scratching, imprinting, or engraving.

ลิขิต li[6]-kit[4] *P. v.* to scratch; to scrape; to write, or to inscribe (chd. p. 220): *n.* writing; drawing; carving; letters (restricted in meaning to letters, or writings of Buddhist monks); a diplomatic note.

ลิง ling *n.* a monkey; an ape; a prefix to which the particular designating name is added: ทำเป็นลิง to make grimaces; to act like a monkey: มือลิง ribs of a boat; mischievous fingers: ลิงลม the slow loris; the wind monkey, *Nycticebus cinereus*, a small tailless nocturnal animal covered with a soft dense fur. It is sometimes carried on native sailing crafts because of the popular superstition that it has second sight, and exercises some influence over the wind: ลิงเสน the rufous, or stump-tailed monkey, *Macaca arctoides* and *rufescens* (Gaird. N. H. J. S. S. III, 2, p. 121): ลิงแสม the crab-eating monkey, *Macaca irus*.

ลิงค์, ลึงค์ ling *P. S. n.* a mark; a spot; a sign; a token; a badge; an emblem; a characteristic; the sign of gender or sex; the copulatory male organ; the linga (S.E.D. p. 901): ปลลิงค์ masculine gender: นปุงสกลิงค์ neuter gender: อลิงค์ common gender: อิตถีลิงค์, สตรีลิงค์ feminine gender.

ลิงโลด ling-lote[3] *v.* to jump joyfully; to be contented, pleased, or glad.

ลิด lit[6] *v.* to trim, prune, or cut off the rough part (as branches) with a knife or ax.

ลิตต์, ลิปต์ lip[6] *P. adj.* having been smeared, plastered, painted, or made dirty (chd. p. 221).

ลิตร lit[6] *n.* a liter; a metric measure of capacity equal to 1 cubic decimetre or 61.016 cubic inches, or 2.113 American pints (web.).

ลิ่น lin[3] *n.* pangolin; the scaly ant-eater, *Manis javanica* (Gaird. N.H.J.S.S. III, 2, p. 126).

ลิ้น lin[5] *n.* the tongue: คนลิ้นยาว a great talker; a babbler: คนลิ้นไม่มีกระดูก *proverb* one whose word cannot be relied on; a deceiver: ผิ่นลิ้นกระบือ raw opium made in the northern parts of Thailand: ลิ้นกระบือ a thin narrow strip or tongue of wood inserted in grooves between two floor-planks: ลิ้นไก่ *lit.* "a fowl's tongue," *i.e.* the uvula: ลิ้นงูเห่า *lit.* "the cobra's tongue," *i.e.* a vegetable plant with small poisonous leaves: ลิ้นชัก *lit.* "a tongue to be drawn," *i.e.* drawers (of a table or cupboard): ลิ้นตู้ the drawer (of cupboard or dresser): ลิ้นทอง a species of yellow bird about the size of a magpie: ลิ้นทะเล *lit.* "sea tongues," *i.e.* cuttle-fish bones; the internal calcarious plate of a cuttle-fish: ลิ้นปี่ tonguelets; reeds (of an organ or flute); the ensiform cartilage: ลิ้นมังกร, เบี๊ญจวรรณ *Thai, Bangkok* (ต้น) *Passiflora edulis* (*Passifloraceae*), a passion fruit of southern Brazil, which has been in cultivation in various parts of the tropics for well over a century. The climate of the low country of Malaya is *too* hot for it but it is cultivated on elevations from 1500 to 5000 feet. It bears in great abundance a smooth, ovoid fruit of the size of a hen's egg, purple when ripe, the rind afterwards shrinking and becoming much wrinkled. Two crops a year are sometimes produced, the principal season being from May to July. The fruit contains in its hollow centre a quantity of fragrant, sweet, juicy pulp, inseparable from which are the small seeds; this, when emptied out of the shell and beaten up with a pinch of bicarbonate of soda and sugar, makes a delicious drink (MCM. p. 279: Cb. p. 743: Burk. p. 1676): ลิ้นลม *lit.* "airy words"; "fairy's tongue," *i.e.* utterances; idiomatic or eloquent sayings: ลิ้นลาย *lit.* "a striped tongue," *i.e.* lying; falsifying; fibbing: ลิ้นเสือ *lit.* "a tiger's tongue," *i.e.* a climber, the coarse hairy leaves of which are used for polishing purposes (in place of sand-paper): ลิ้นเสือ (ปลา) *Pseudorhombus arsius* (*Paralichthyidae*) (suvatti p. 94): ลิ้นหมา (ปลา) *Cynoglossus borneensis*; *C. microlepis*; *C. monopus* (*Cynoglossidae*), (suvatti pp. 96, 97): ลิ้นหมาลาย (ปลา) *Synaptura zebra* (*Synapturidae*) (suvatti p. 96): ลิ้นทืบ the tray (of a trunk).

ลินจง, เลนจง   lin-chjong *n.* a species of *Nymphea*; a lotus; a water-lily.

ลิ้นจี่ (ต้น)   lin⁵-chjee⁴ *n. Nephelium litchi* (*Sapindaceae*), lichi, a very handsome ever-green tree of southern China, now cultivated in many parts of the subtropics, or the tropics, with a pronounced dry season. It blossoms usually in the dry season producing sprays of pale green flowers, and ripens fruit from August to September. The fruit, borne in large clusters, is of the size and form of a large plum, with a rough, thin, warty rind, which on ripening, assumes a beautiful pinkish-crimson tint, turning to a dull brown colour. The jelly-like aril which covers the seed is of a translucent whiteness and of an agreeable sweet-acid flavour. The litchi is cultivated for the abundant fleshy aril of its fruit, which has a taste, suggesting grapes; and the dried fruits which the Chinese pre-pare, suggesting raisins. Its cultivation has spread in Asia from China, through northern India, and into the hills elsewhere, and south-wards through Indo-China and Thailand. The climate of Malaya allows it to grow well, but prevents it from flowering and fruiting; magnificent trees exist which are quite sterile. It refuses to flower, also, in the Philippine Islands where now it is being grafted exper-imentally on the allied *Litchi philippinensis*, in the hope that a vigorous root may make fruiting possible. The Chinese use the seeds medicinally and the leaves for poultices. In Tonkin a tincture made from them is used for intestinal complaints. The flowers, bark, and roots are made into a gargle for throat complaints. The lac-insect feeds on this tree. The timber is said to be nearly indestructible (MCM. p. 247 : Cb. p. 331 : V.P. p. 241 : BURK. p. 1546).

ลินลากะทุ่ม   lin-lah-gka⁴-toom³ *n.* a Thai song tune.

ลินลากะบี่   [song tune.
lin-lah-gka⁴-bee⁴ *n.* a Thai

ลิบ, ลิ่ว   lip⁶ *adj.* far distant; highest pos-sible; a long way off; nearly out of sight; as far as the eye can see; very far away; very high up in the air : ไกลลิบ, ลิบลับ in the dim distance : เดินไปไกลลิบ to walk far off and nearly out of sight of others : ลิบตา as far as the eye can reach : สูงลิบ very high and almost out of sight.

ลิป, ลิปิกา   li⁶-bpi⁴ *P. n.* a letter of the alphabet; writing (chd. p. 221); drawings; tracings : ลิปิกร, ลิปิการ a clerk; a scribe; an engraver; a copyist.

ลิ่ม   lim³ *n.* a lump (of ore); a wedge; a bolt; a wooden pin, or peg (as for fastening the boards of native boats); a quadrat or space (used in printing) : เงินลิ่ม an ingot of silver : ลิ่มกลอน an additional wedge to hold a bolt in place.

ลิ้ม   lim⁵ *v.* to taste, or try out before eat-ing; see ชิม p. 297 : ลิ้มเลีย to taste by licking.

ลิมปิ   lim *P. v.* to smear; to daub; to plaster on; to stain (chd. p. 220); see ฉาบ p. 269.

ลิมปนะ   lim-bpa⁴-na⁶ *P. n.* the act of smearing or plastering (chd. p. 220).

ลิลิต   li⁶-lit⁶ *n.* stanzas composed of vary-ing types of poetic feet (as five, seven, or eleven syllables to a line).

ลิ่ว, ลิบ   liew³ *adj.* far distant; nearly out of sight : ลอยลิ่ว drifting far up in the wind, or floating far from the mooring : สูง-ลิ่ว very high.

ลิสเตอร์   lis-dter *n.* Joseph Lister. Lord Lister (1827-1912) was an English surgeon, the father of antiseptic surgery. At the age of 20 years he commenced the study of med-icine and in 1852 received the M. B. with exceptional honours including a scholarship in surgery. In 1853 he went to spend a month at Edinburgh with James Syme. Syme so impressed him that he stayed on and took consulting rooms opposite Syme's office occupying his spare time with attending lectures. In 1867 the "antiseptic system" commenced when Lister employed carbolic acid as a germicide in surgery, for he noted its powerful effect in deodorizing and cleansing the sewage. It was at first applied undiluted in compound fractures; this however was found too caustic for further applications, so tests were undertaken to combine it with inert substances. At one time Lister made use of a fine spray of watery solution of the acid to purify the air while operating. The results were even more promising, so he used carbolic solutions for cleansing his own hands (as he used no rubber gloves), the hands of all attendants, the patient's body, instruments, threads, dressings, and carbolized lint to wipe out the wound. Thus antiseptic surgery was inaugurated.

ลิ lee[5] *v.* to slip, or sneak away; to hide or secrete oneself; to abscond or bolt: *n.* a Chinese unit of measure for distances, equal to 2,000 lengths of the foot, or about one-third of an Englieh mile: ลิลับ to be utterly lost; to disappear or vanish from sight completely.

ลีบ leep[3] *adj.* dry; parched; atrophied; shrivelled; sterile; grainless; undeveloped (as ears of corn or grain): ไข่ลีบ undeveloped or unhatchable eggs; sterile eggs: ลีบชุบ a parched and crumbling condition (as undeveloped grains of rice or corn dried so that they can be easily mashed in the hand).

ลีลา, ลีลาศ lee-lah *v.* to walk, go or advance with pomp, vivacity, or with graceful stately attitude: *n.* amusements; games; recreations; attitudes or gestures that are graceful, pretty, or beautiful: ลีลากมล lotus flowers held or worn by women for pleasure: ลีลาเคหะ a place or house for amusements, games, or entertainments: ลีลา-ภรณ์ decorations or ornaments of a temporary

or valueless nature (as fresh flowers): ลีลาวดี a girl or woman beautifully adorned or attired: ลีลาวาปี a place for bathing or aquatic sports, or amusements; a lake.

ลีฬหา leen-hah[2] *P. n.* ease; grace; dignity; proficiency; skill; adroitness (chd. p. 220).

ลึก leuk[6] *adj.* deep; profound; obscure: คำลึก words of obscure or obstruse meaning: น้ำลึก deep water: ลึกซึ้ง, ลึกลับ secret; mysterious; hidden; concealed; see ซึ้ง p. 309.

ลึงค์ see ลิงค์ p. 745.

ลื่น lurn[3] *adj.* slippery; smooth; gliding; skidding: ล้มลื่นพลาด to slip and tumble down: ลื่นเมือก, ลื่นเลือก slippery and slimy from being soaked in water or mud: ลื่น-เลอะ slippery and muddy; slushy (as semi-melted snow on a pavement): ลื่นไหล smooth (as stones or pebbles in a water-course).

ลืน, มลืน lurn[5] *v.* to suffer pain; to be ashamed; to be distressed, sad, or sorry for: บวมลืน ๆ slightly swollen; odematous; puffy.

ลืบ lurp[3] *n.* a great, great grandchild, or a great grandnephew.

ลืม leum *v.* to forget; to open (used only for the eyes): ขี้ลืม to be forgetful: ลืม-คำพูด to forget what has been said: ลืมตน to become forgetful of oneself (as when sound asleep or semi-conscious): ลืมตัว to forget one's existence (as when being carried away by a spell of ecstasy, a trance, or rapture): ลืมตา to open the eyes: ลืมตาย to forget about death (thinking only of temporal matters): ลืมหลัง to forget from absent-mindedness.

ลือ leu *v.* to be carried (as a rumour); to be reported as true, or merely as hearsay: เขาลือกันว่า it is rumoured that: ชื่อเสียง-เลื่องลือ notoriety; renown; a celebrated reputation: ลือกันทั้งเมือง it is the talk of the town: ลือขจร to be famed far and wide:

ลือฉาว a rumour that has attained wide publicity: ลือชา to be known far and wide; to be published or divulged; to be far-famed; to be illustrious, renowned, or eminent: ลือชื่อ *lit.* "published name," *i. e.* to be far-famed, noted, or famous: ลือสาย, ฤๅสาย born of illustrious lineage, or of a renowned family line.

ลือ leu[3] *n.* a child, or children of a great grandchild, or of a grandnephew.

ลือ ๑ leu[5] *n.* a tribe of hill people, of Lao-Thai origin living in the north-eastern part of Thailand (Graham I, p. 111). They are to be found also to the east and north of the Mekong and in the eastern part of the Chieng Tung state, as well as in the Chieng Rung state of south-western Yunnan (J. S. S. XIX, 3, [p. 186).

ลือ ๒ leu[5] *Chin. pron.* you.

ลุ loo[6] *Cam. v.* to gain; to reach; to arrive at; to attain; to obtain; see ถึง p. 388: ไปลุแก่โทษ to go and make amends for a fault; to obtain pardon: ลุแก่โทษ to confess one's fault or guilt; to ask pardon: ลุยง beautiful (in the highest degree): ลุล่วง to overcome, reach, or arrive at (after some striving or hardship): ลุอำนาจ to disobey; to act contrary to rule, instructions, or authority.

ลุก look[6] *v.* to rise (as from a bed or chair); to stand up; to get up; to burst into flames; to blaze up, or burn with a flame: เป่าไฟให้ลุก to blow smoldering coals into a flame: ลุกขึ้นยืน to arise and stand: ลุกนั่ง to sit up from a recumbent position: ลุกเป็นไฟ *simile* angry; passionate; indignant; irritated to a heated condition (as by fire): ลุกล้ม to rise and fall again.

ลุกลน look[6]-lon *v.* to act hastily, hurridly, or excitedly: ทำโดยลุกลน to perform a deed unsatisfactorily.

ลุง loong *n.* an uncle; an older brother of either parent.

ลุ้ง loong[5] *n.* a hamper with compartments for food (made either of brass, or as a covered basket). [(chd. p. 223).

ลุทท์, ลุพธ์ loot[6] *P. adj.* cruel; murderous

ลุททก, ลุพธก loot[6]-ta[6]-gka[4] *n.* a huntsman; a sportsman (chd. p. 223).

ลุทธ์, โลภ loot[6] *P. adj.* greedy; covetous (chd. p. 223); lustful; desirous.

ลุ่น loon[3] *adj.* stunted; shortened; cut off; amputated; uncovered; bare (of hair, or feathers); branchless: ลุ่นโคง deprived of feathers (used regarding fowls that have had the tail feathers pulled): ลุ่นท้าย with curtailed stern piece: ลุ่นหัว with a rounded off or abbreviated head piece.

ลุ่ม loom[3] *adj.* low, depressed, sunken, marshy, boggy or swampy (ground): ที่ลุ่ม ๆ ดอน ๆ uneven ground; a plain with alternating swampy and high land: ที่ลุ่มมีน้ำ a depression (in the ground) containing water: ลุ่มตุ้ม without branches (used in regard to trees where the branches have all been lopped off): ลุ่มเนื้อ *lit.* "depressions in the meat," *i. e.* impressible; showing, or bearing dints, finger marks, or indentations (a characteristic of semi-decayed, rotten meat or fish).

ลุมป์ loom *P. v.* to rob; to plunder; to attack and destroy; to cause separations, dissensions, anger, or strife; see ปล้น p. 511.

ลุมพลี, ลมพินี loom-pa[6]-lee *P. n.* name of a princess; a grove named after her; the birth-place of the Buddha.

ลุ่มหลง loom[3]-long[2] *v.* to be infatuated, or intoxicated by; to be blinded by excessive greed or passion; to be deceived by vain promises or outward appearances.

ลุย luie *v.* to walk across, or walk through water; to wade (across); see บุก p. 483: ลุยน้ำ to wade in water: ลุยน้ำไม่ขุ่น a proverb applied to one who is slow, dilatory and sluggish because, if he should wade in water, it would not even become cloudy : ลุยไฟ the ordeal of walking through fire (as proof of one's innocence) : ลุยไล่ to wade (through water or mud) in pursuit of.

ลุย luie[3] v. to become disjoined, unfastened, loosed, or unattached (as clothing); see ร่วง p. 689 : ลุ่ยหลุด to become disconnected and falling off.

ลู loo[3] n. path; foot-way; a track or course that is smooth and level : adj. not stiff; soft; supple; flexible; pliant (used regarding hair or fur); pointing backwards (as ears of a horse when rushing at, or attacking some enemy) : ผมลู่ soft, pliant hair that stays down smoothly when brushed; see ทาง p. 411.

ลู loo[5] n. a kind of Laos fife.

ลูก (๑) look[3] n. a descriptive word for a mound, a knoll, a child, a marble, or bullet. When used as a suffix it functions as a verb, as เฆี่ยนลูก to whip one's child : แท้งลูก, ตกลูก to have a miscarriage, abortion, or premature birth : ยกบุตรี (ลูก)ให้เป็นภรรยา to give one's daughter in marriage : เลี้ยงลูก to tend, nourish, or care for a child : ออกลูก, คลอดบุตร to be delivered of a child·

ลูก (๒) When used as a prefix it functions as a noun. Nouns relative to the family, as ลูกกก, ลูกหัวปี the first-born, or eldest of a family : ลูกกรอก a foetus born prematurely, or one not fully developed : ลูกกำพร้า an orphan : ลูกเขย a son-in-law : ลูกครอก a child born in slavery : ลูกครึ่ง a half-breed : ลูกชู้ the child of a paramour; a bastard; an illegitimate child : ลูกแดง ๆ an infant; one newly born : ลูกตัว one's own child : ลูกต้าว children in general; progeny : ลูกแฝด twins : ลูกพี่ลูกน้อง cousins : ลูกเมีย a family : ลูกเลี้ยง, ลูกบุญธรรม a foster child; a step-child; an adopted child : ลูกสวาท a boy or man kept for purposes of sodomy, or unnatural vices : ลูกสะใภ้ a daughter-in-law : ลูกสาว, ธิดา a

daughter : ลูกสุดท้อง the youngest of a family : ลูกหลาน descendants; posterity : ลูกอ่อน a baby; a nursing child.

ลูก (๓) Nouns relating to persons, or people, ลูกขุน a jury-man, or a judge in a tribunal : ลูกความ litigants; clients in a legal case : ลูกค้า patrons; customers of a store : ลูกจ้าง an employé; an hireling : ลูกช่วง a sub-agent; a middle-man in a transaction : ลูกน้อง, ลูกแล่ง intimate associates : ลูกบท chorus singers : ลูกบ้าน villagers; rural inhabitants : ลูกมือ an apprentice; an assistant workman : ลูกเมือง citizens of a city : ลูกเรือ a sailor : ลูกไล่ the runner-up in a race, game, or competition : ลูกวัด members of the Buddhist clergy in a temple, other than the chief monk : ลูกศิษย์ a disciple; a pupil; a scholar : ลูกสมุน, ลูกกะโล่ go-betweens; cat's-paws; satelites; hangers-on of a retinue, party, crowd, or gang : ลูกหนี้ a debtor : ลูกเสือ boy-scouts : ลูกหมู่ young men of a family, group, or village liable for Crown service : ลูกห้าง an employé in a store or firm.

ลูก (๔) Nouns relating to the body, ลูกกระเดือก the thyroid cartilage : ลูกคอ a tremolo; a tremulous quavering, or trembling sound, or note produced by the voice, or by an instrument : ลูกสะบ้า the patella.

ลูก (๕) Nouns relating to circular, spherical and cylindrical objects, ลูกกระดุม a button : ลูกกระสุน dried mud-balls shot by the natives from bows : ลูกกลอน a bolus, or pill of pulverized drugs : ลูกกวาด candy; crystallized fruits; sweets : ลูกข่าง a toy top : ลูกปัดแก้ว glass beads (as strung on a string) : ลูกคลี a ball used for a lawn game (as croquet or golf) : ลูกคิด an abacus; see คิด p. 202 : ลูกฆ้อง the knocker or hammer for a gong : ลูกโดด a cartridge or rifle-ball; a projectile; a missile : ลูกตา the eyeball : ลูกแตก a bomb; an explosive : ลูกประคบ a badmington shuttlecock-shaped bag containing

medicinal agents used hot as a compress; see
ประคบ p. 497: ลูกประคำ rosary beads: ลูก-
ปราย bird-shot: ลูกบีทม์ beads: ลูกปืน
bullets; cannon-balls: ลูกไม้ (ถัก) fancy
crochet work: ลูกยาง rubber balls (as tennis): ลูกยางพิมพ์ดีด a typewriter platen:
ลูกโยน, ลูกปา balls used in pitching games (as
cricket): ลูกระฆัง the clapper of a bell:
ลูกรุ่ย decorative glass pendants (as are hung
from chandeliers): ลูกล้อ a wheel: ลูก-
โลก the terrestrial globe: ลูกหิน marbles:
ลูกเห็บ hail-stones; hail: ลูกอม a quid, wad,
or small article held in the mouth for protective purposes (as charms).

ลูก (๖) *Nouns relating to mechanical appliances,* ลูกกลิ้ง a lawn-roller: ลูกกุญแจ
a key; see กุญแจ p. 110: ลูกคลัก a trigger,
trip, or release lever in a trap; a stick placed
crosswise in the neck of a water-jar, with a
rope attached serving as a handle for carrying it: ลูกโซ่ the links of a chain: ลูกดิ่ง
a plummet, or plumb attached to the end of
a string: ลูกตุ้ม (นาฬิกา) the pendulum of
a clock: ลูกถ่วง counter weights; sinkers;
see ถ่วง p. 381: ลูกถ้วยกันไฟฟ้า porcelain insulators (for live wires): ลูกบิด (ก๊อกน้ำ)
the handle of a faucet; a spiggot; a turning
plug fitting into a faucet: ลูกบิด (เครื่องจักร์)
a key or wrench for engaging the knot of a
machine bolt: ลูกบิด (หัวปิดประตู) a door-
knob or handle: ลูกประสัก wooden pins or
wedges used in the construction of native
boats instead of iron bolts or nails: ลูกปืน
ball-bearings in machinery: ลูกหยั่ง a
marine sounding-lead: ลูกรอก a pulley
block: ลูกหมึก an ink-roller: ลูกหินบด
a round pillow-shaped grinding stone (about
eight inches long) operated back and forth
with the hands on the flat concave surface of
a counterpart stone (serving the purpose of
a mortar and pestle). These are used by
doctors of the old school for macerating
drugs; see บด p. 466: ลูกหีบ the rollers of a
sugar-cane mill; rollers of a calender or roller-

machine to press cloth or paper: ลูกแห
sinkers, or a lead chain attached around the
opening of cast-nets: ลูกสลัก, ลูกกลอน a
bolt for window or door.

ลูก (๗) *Nouns relating to fruit,* ลูกไม้เชื่อม
preserved fruit in syrup: ลูกไม้ดอง pickled
fruit: ลูกไม้สด fresh fruit: ลูกไม้แห้ง
dried fruit.

ลูก (๘) see ใบ p. 491; ผล p. 540: กล้วย-
ห้าใบ five bananas: ส้มสามลูก three oranges.

ลูก (๙) *Nouns relating to the young of
animals,* ลูกกบ a tadpole; a polliwog: ลูกแกะ
a lamb: ลูกไก่ a chick: ลูกไก่ตัวเมีย a
pullet: ลูกช้าง a calf: ลูกนก a fledgling:
ลูกเนื้อ a fawn: ลูกประสม an hybrid; the
results of cross-breeding (of animals): ลูกปละ
the young of ranch cattle, *i. e.* cattle allowed
to roam at will and served by the wild ox:
ลูกเป็ด a duckling: ลูกม้า a colt; a foal:
ลูกม้าตัวเมีย a filly: ลูกแมว a kitten: ลูกวัว-
ตัวผู้ a bullock; a steer: ลูกวัวตัวเมีย an heifer:
ลูกสิงห์โต a cub; a whelp: ลูกสุนักข์ a pup-
py; a pup: ลูกหงษ์ a swan; a cygnet:
ลูกหนู a mouse: ลูกหมี a cub: ลูกห่าน
a gosling: ลูกฬา the foal of an ass.

ลูก (๑๐) *Nouns relating to weapons,* ลูกดอก
feather-tipped darts blown through a reed:
ลูกศร, ลูกธนู an arrow: ลูกศร (หน้าไม้) a
cross-bow arrow.

ลูก (๑๑) *Nouns relating to fish,* ลูกปลา, ลูกทุ่ง
the fighting, or needle-fish resulting from
spawning in their normal habitat: ลูกไล่
small fishes kept as objects of chase by larger
ones, for the purpose of amusement.

ลูก (๑๒) *Unclassified nouns,* ลูกกรง bars
of a cage or cell: ลูกกัลปพฤกษ์ limes, each
containing a silver coin, thrown as alms to the
crowd (on the occasion of a cremation): ลูก-
แก้ว ornamental glass tips, tops, or caps placed
on balustrades, or over the ends of table legs:
ลูกข้าว rice stalks growing from the stumps
of reaped rice: ลูกคัน small-sized, or low

dikes marking paddy field boundaries : ลูกตั้ง a baluster ; one of a set of small pillars that supports a hand-rail ; fence palings : ลูก-นิมิตต์ round stones about the size of a Buddhist monk's alms bowl, buried as boundary marks around a Buddhist sanctuary : ลูกบวบ the rolled portion of the outer garment of a Buddhist monk's robe, which is wound around the left arm ; a bundle of 50 bamboos bound firmly together : ลูกบาศก์ a cube ; a dice : ลูกประหล่ำ charms or amulets worn on the wrists of children : ลูกปลา diamond-shaped pieces of paper pasted on kites, in order to strengthen certain parts or points : ลูกไฟ sparks ; firebrands ; incendary materials blown by a breeze : ลูกฟูก corrugations ; flutings ; alternating ridges and depressions : ลูกฟัก a panel, the edges of which are inserted into a groove in the framing timber : ลูกย่าง chains or manacles composed of long iron links : ลูกหม้อ the fighting or needle-fish spawned in captivity : ลูกหนู a variety of fireworks, which, when lighted, shoot along a stretched wire to which they are attached ; indurated superficial glands of the neck.

ลูข, ลูกษ์ loo-ka⁴ *adj.* rough ; unpleasant ; hard ; harsh (chd. p. 223) ; poor ; mean ; common ; see ไพร่ p. 604.

[p. 223).

ลูตา, ลูติกา loo-dtah *P. S. n.* a spider (chd.

ลูนะ loo-na⁶ *P. S. adj.* cut ; reaped ; gathered (chd. p. 223) ; severed ; clipped ; plucked ; pierced ; wounded (S. E. D. p. 905).

ลูบ loop³ *v.* to pat fondly ; to touch affectionately ; to stroke ; see คล้ำ p. 186 : ลูบคล้ำ to stroke, handle, or fumble (as with passion) : ลูบคล้ำเคล้น to pass or run the fingers over ; to rub ; to knead (with pressure) : ลูบผม to stroke the hair : ลูบไล้ a rubbing, kneading motion (as when applying an oil, perfume or powder to the face) : ลูบหน้าเช็ดเหงื่อ to wipe the perspiration from the face : ลูบหน้าลูบหลัง to stroke the face and pat the

back (as in caressing an infant) : ลูบตัว to rub oneself with the open palms (as during [a bath).

ลูพ see ลวนะ p. 730.

เลก see ไพร่ p. 604.

เล็ก lek⁶ *adj.* little ; small ; tiny ; wee ; diminutive ; see น้อย ๑ p. 446 ; นิด p. 457 : คนละเล็กละน้อย a little for each one : เล็กน้อย a little (in quantity).

เลข, เลขผา lek³ *n.* a writing ; a manuscript ; an inscription ; a letter ; an epistle ; a drawing ; delineations (chd. p. 219) ; figures ; numbers ; arithmetic diagrams ; those liable for corvée : เลขคูณ the multiplicand : เลข-ทาษ those liable for corvée service who sell themselves into slavery : เลขยันต์ cabalistic or mystic charms (inscribed on fragments of cloth which have been placed around to prevent the intrusion of malignant spirits who are believed to bring calamity, disease and death) : เลขลัพธ์ the product in either division or multiplication : เลขหาร the divisor : สักเลข to tattoo marks or figures on the forearm of clients, followers, or dependents (as a means of identification).

เลขกะ lay-ka⁴-gka⁴ *P. n.* a scribe ; a secretary (chd. p. 219) ; see เขียน p. 167.

เลขนะ lay-ka⁴-na⁶ *P. n.* the act of inscribing, writing or drawing lines, figures, or diagrams (chd. p. 219).

เลขา lay-kah² *P. n.* a line ; a streak ; a scratch (chd. p. 219) ; marks ; drawings ; writings ; inscriptions : เลขาธิการ a secretary : เลขานุการ a junior or assistant secretary : เลขานุการิณี an associate woman secretary.

เล็ง leng *v.* to aim (as with a gun) ; to look at ; to gaze at intently ; to stare at ; see เพ่ง p. 595.

เลททุ, เลณทุ, เลษฏ let³-doo⁴ *n.* a clod of earth (chd. p. 219) ; a chip ; a chunk ; a lump ; a seed.

เลณ, เลน   lay-na[6] *P. n.* a cave; a rock; a cavern; an asylum; a retreat; a place of refuge; Nirvana (chd. p. 220).

เล็ด   let[6] *n.* an abbreviated form for เมล็ด (seed); see p. 656; a stone; pits (of fruit); grains (of cereals): น้ำตาเล็ด the dropping, flowing, or trickling of tears: เล็ดลอด to escape by stealth; to pass through, in or out swiftly or adroitly.

เลน   len *n.* mud; loam; mire; see โคลน p. 217: เป็นตมเป็นเลน marshy; boggy; swampy; miry.

เล็น   len *n.* lice: เหาเล็น vermin.

เล่น   len[3] *v.* to play; to frolic; to toy; to frisk; to sport; to jest; to gambol; to be amused with a passing fancy or hobby (as the cultivation of caladiums): *adv.* playfully; jestingly: เล่นงาน to fight; to attack; to assault; to oppress; see ต่อสู้ p. 347: เล่นชู้ to be enamoured with a paramour: เล่นเพื่อน to indulge in sexual pleasures (between women): เล่นตัว to pretend or disguise one's feelings or actions in order to save one's face: เล่นตา to goggle: เล่นสวาท to practice sodomy; to keep a lad for unnatural carnal pleasure: เล่นผู้หญิง to have carnal intercourse: นี่ไม่ใช่-เป็นการเล่น this is not a trifling matter: พูด-เล่น to indulge in frivolous speech.

เลนจง   see ลินจง p. 746.

เล็บ   lep[6] *n.* nails (of the finger or toe); claws; talons: รอยเล็บ the marks of the finger-nails or claws: เล็บเท้า toe-nails: เล็บมือ finger-nails: ไว้เล็บ to allow the finger-nails to grow long.

เล็บครุฑ   lep[6]-kroot[6] *Thai* (ต้น) *n.* *Notho-panax fruticosum* (*Araliaceae*), a shrub, native of the Pacific, or eastern Malaysia, which was introduced into European horticulture about 1800, and is very plentifully found in gardens in Malaysia as an ornamental plant, largely on account of the great variability of its foliage. In Cambodia it is used for neuralgic and rheumatic pains. The very young leaves are eaten cooked as a flavouring (burk. p. 1563: cb. p. 795: mcm. p. 119: v. p. p. 242); *Aralia balfourii*; *Aralia filicifolia* (*Araliaceae*), a very showy shrub with large pinnate and pinnatifid leaves (mcm. p. 119).

เล็บควาย   lep[6]-kwai *Thai, Badang Besar* (ต้น) *n.* *Bauhinia elongata* (*Leguminosae*) (cb. p. 520).

เล็บมือนาง   lep[6]-meu-nang *Thai, Chumpawn* (ต้น) *n.* *Quisqualis densiflora* (*Combretaceae*), a woody climber found in southern Thailand and in the northern parts of the Malay Peninsula, and southwards to Malacca. The Malays use it medicinally. As a vermifuge, they take a decoction of the leaves, or, in the case of children, the juice pounded out of the roots (burk. p. 1860); *Q. indica*, Rangoon Creeper, a big woody climber found throughout south-eastern Asia and Malaysia, not wild perhaps in any part of India proper, but wild on the east side of the Bay of Bengal. It was brought into European cultivation rather more than a century ago. Its flowers are pleasantly scented. They are pale pink to deep crimson, in drooping clusters. The fruits are not a little used as a vermifuge. They should be picked half-ripe when they are bitter, pulped in water and the liquid drunk; alternatively, seeds from ripe fruits may be used, but the effect which 2 to 3 half-ripe seeds produce, requires about 5 ripe seeds. At ripeness they taste like a coconut. A large dose produces hiccough, and an overdose causes unconsciousness. The ovary-wall and seed-coats particularly cause hiccough. In Perak a decoction may be given to children to stop diarrhoea. The ripe seeds are sometimes used as food but only in moderation as some people are made ill by eating two or three; others can eat about twenty. They are soporific. The very young shoots are eaten in the Dutch East Indies, steamed or raw (burk. p. 1860: cb. p. 622: mcm. pp. 127, 130, 208).

เล็บเหยี่ยว   lep[6]-yiew[4] *Thai,* มะตันขอ *N. Laos* (ต้น) *n. Zizyphus oenoplia (Rhamnaceae),* a thorny, sprawling bush, widely spread from Africa, through India to Australia; in the Peninsula it is chiefly in the north, but not absent from the south. It has been suggested that the bark might be used direct in tanneries, but it would not pay to make extracts of it (BURK. p. 2307: cb. p. 298).

เลป, เลปนะ   lay-bpa[4] *P. S. n.* plaster; mortar; the act of smearing, daubing, plastering or anointing; anything smeared on (as ointment or a coat of paint); any grease or dirt sticking to vessels, or particles wiped off from the hands (S. E. D. p. 902): เลปกร a mason or bricklayer; a worker in mortar.

เลเพ   lay-pay *adj.* disarranged; misarranged; out of order; scattered; confused: เลเพลาดพลาด out of order; out of place; untidy; topsyturvy.

เล็ม   lem *v.* to hem the border or edge (as the edges of a garment); to nibble, browse, or gnaw (as cattle or goats foraging for food): เก็บเล็ม to procure a little here and a little there; to scrape up the fragments: เล็มล่า to nibble or browse a little here and a bit there: เล็มหน้าผ้า to sew by folding in the edge of a cloth (to prevent ravelling): เล็มแห่งละเล็กละน้อย to gather a little here and a little there.

เล่ม   lem[3] *n.* the numerical designatory particle for knives, scissors, books, needles, sickles, and oars: เกวียนหนึ่งเล่ม (or คัน) a bullock cart: เล่มเล็ก a small one (as a small pocket knife).

เลย   ler-ie *adv.* beyond; further; farther; more: เกินเลย too far; too much; in excess of what is required: จะไม่ทำอีกเลย will never do so again: ไปเลย to go indefinitely; to go beyond: ไปเลยเมือง to go beyond the city: ปล่อยเลย to relinquish, quit, or resign:

ไม่ให้อีกเลย will positively be given no more: ลืมเลย to forget completely: เลยไป to surpass, exceed, outdo, excel, or transcend: เลยเวลาแล้ว past the time (appointed); see พ้น p. 560: ว่าเกินเลย to use provoking, insulting, or abusive language.

เลว   liew *n.* a war, fight, battle, or conflict: *adj.* inferior; poor; low; ignorant; base; worthless; shameful; see ทราม p. 398: ของเลว an article of inferior quality: คนเลว a contemptible, disreputable person: ทำเลว of inferior workmanship.

เลวง   lah-weng *adj.* blown about, or floating in the breeze or air; see ปลิว p. 512.

เลศ, เลส   let[3] *P. S. n.* a trick or stratagem (chd. p. 220); see กล ● p. 57.

เลห, เล่ห์   lay-ha[4] *n.* fraud; artifice; a wile; cunning; a trick; a delusion: *adj.* like; similar to; such as; just as; as if: เจ้าเล่ห์เจ้ากล a deceiver or tricker: เล่ห์กะเท่ห์ a trick; a delusion; a deception: เล่ห์ลมคมสัน *idiomatic* deceptive; deluding; cheating; beguiling.

เลหยะ   lay-ha[4]-ya[6] *S. n.* nectar; any food that has to be licked, lapped up, sucked or sipped (as syrup or an electuary) (S. E. D. p. 903).

เลหลัง   lay-lung[2] *v.* to auction, vend, dispose of, or sell over the counter for the highest offer: การเลหลัง an auction: ขายเลหลัง to put up to auction; to be under the hammer.

เลหะ   lay-ha[4] *P. v.* to lick, lap, suck, or sip (chd. p. 219); see ชิม p. 297.

เลอ   lur *Cam.* above; over; on top of: *Thai adj.* highest; most excellent; best; supreme; superior: *prep.* above; over: เลอมาน over, superior to, or surpassing the mind.

เล่อล่า   lur[3]-lah[3] *adj.* scared into flight (as birds); awakened; excited by fright; alarmed; startled and rushing off through panic.

เลอะ lur[6] *adj.* smeared; blotched; dirty; foul; see เปื้อน p. 535: ทำเลอะเทอะ to do without thought or consideration; to make a mess of things (as one's business, or life): เปื้อนเลอะ spattered; dirty; soiled, or begrimed: พูดเลอะเทอะ to talk incoherently or confusedly (as though drunk or demented): เลอะเทอะ dirty; filthy; blotched; tainted; disordered; disarranged (as personal articles strewn about).

เละ la[6] *adj.* fluid; liquid; watery.

เลา low *n.* the numerical designation for musical wind-instruments (as fife or flute); a species of grass similar to the pampas grass having greyish white flowers; a brief, concise, curt, or short explanation, definition, or statement.

เลา ๆ low-low *adv.* approximately; roughly; abbreviatedly (as when making an estimate as to the cost); indistinctly; dimly; faintly; guessingly.

เล่า low[3] *v.* to relate; to describe; to tell; to recite: *conj.* then; therefore; for what reason; well then: *adv.* again; repeatedly: เขาทำอะไรเล่า what then is he doing? บอกเล่า to recount, narrate, or relate: บอกเล่าความลับ to divulge; to disclose; to expose a secret: พูดแล้วพูดเล่า to repeat again and again: เล่าเรียน to learn (by repetition): อะไรอีกเล่า well then, what is there still more?

เล้า low[5] *n.* an enclosure for confining animals; a pen; a sty.

เลากัย see โลกัย p. 758.

เล้าโลม low[5]-lome *v.* to console; to solace; see ประเล้าประโลม p. 504; see ปลอบ p. 511.

เลาะ law[6] *v.* to undo; to ravel; to remove (as basting threads); to rip out (a seam); to cut off (the small branches from a stalk of bamboo); to go along the side, or base of (as when circling a mountain, or walking along the brink of a precipice, or by the side of boats or barges in a procession).

เลิก lerk[3] *v.* to remove or raise the coverings of (as clothing or bedclothes); to adjourn (as an assembly meeting); to discontinue; to abrogate or cancel (as an order); see งด p. 220: เลิกล้าง to abolish; to wipe out completely: เป็นอันเลิกกัน the matter between us comes to an end.

เลิ้ง lerng[5] *adj.* great; big; large; corpulent.

เลิด lert[3] *adj.* excellent; best; supreme.

เลินเล่อ lern-lur[3] *v.* to be careless, negligent, rash, indifferent, regardless or imprudent: ความเลินเล่อ heedlessness.

เลีย lee-ah *v.* to lick; to lap (as a dog): ไฟเลีย to be licked up, or burnt by fire (as stubble on a harvested rice-field): เลียกิน to eat by lapping: เลียลาม to be licked up gradually by a spreading fire.

เลียง (แกง) lee-ang *Chin. n.* a mild vegetable curry: *adj.* cool; lukewarm; not peppery.

เลี่ยง lee-ang[3] *v.* to evade; to elude; to shun the presence of; escape or steal away from: เลี่ยงการ to dodge; to escape work by evasion.

เลี้ยง lee-ang[5] *v.* to keep; to feed; to nourish; to provide food and shelter for; see บำรุง p. 482: เบี้ยเลี้ยง a daily or monthly allowance; a stipend: พี่เลี้ยง a nurse or benefactor: เลี้ยงแขก to entertain one's friends by giving a banquet: เลี้ยงโต๊ะ a feed; a dinner; to spread food for.

เลียงผา, เยียงผา (p. 681) lee-ang-pah[2] *n.* the goat-antelope, or scrow, *nemorhaedus* (species) (Gaird. N. H. J. S. S. III, 2, 125). In the districts of Petchaburi and Pran it is called โครำ, see โค p. 217.

เลียน lee-an *v.* to mimic; to ape; to mock; to imitate: ล้อเลียน to jeer; to ridicule by mimicing in a comical way.

เลี่ยน   lee-an[3] *Thai* (ต้น) *n. Melia azedarach*
(*Meliaceae*), Persian lilac, a very pleasant tree,
nowhere indutiably wild, but said to be so at
the foot of the Himalayas, and in Baluchistan.
It is very widely cultivated throughout the
warmer parts of the world for the sake of
its scent and shade. It has been brought, in
cultivation, into the Malay Peninsula, and
occurs there in gardens; but it is apt to flower
at a very small size, and has not been known
to grow large. In some countries it is planted
as a shade-tree for coffee. It is medicinal
like the *M. indica*, but in a much less measure
and a different way. It is not used for
fevers, and in that lies the great difference.
The Arabs and Persians give the juice of the
leaves internally as a vermifuge, diuretic, and
emmenagogue. In the U.S.A. and Mexico,
a decoction of the root-bark is recognized for
use in the removal of round worms. The
plant is used as a fish-poison, stupefying them
by some substance soluble in water. This
substance is destroyed by boiling. An overdose of the extract produces symptoms like
those of poisoning with *Atropa belladonna*,
and after stupor death may follow. Poultices
of the leaves are used in India for nervous
headache. A poultice of the flowers is said
to kill lice. Pounded seeds may be applied
for rheumatism, and pounded bark for leprosy,
scrofula, and eruptive skin diseases. In Java
a paste of the leaves is used for itch. The
fruit is poisonous to man, though birds eat it,
and sheep seem unharmed by it. Six to eight
seeds are said to poison a man. Criminal
poisoning with it seems to have occurred in
Java. In China it is said to serve as a fish-
poison. A preparation of the fruits is used
in America as an insecticide or flea-powder.
The timber is useful, pretty and well spoken
of. It takes a good polish, and then is handsome. It is sometimes sold as cedarwood
(McM. pp. 184, 466: Burk. p. 1439).

เลี่ยน   lee-an[3] *adj.* cleared; level; see เตียน

p. 374; polished (so as to be slippery as a
dancing floor); oily (descriptive of the taste
of food when too much oil is mixed in): ผ้า-
เลี่ยน a greasy fabric.

เลียบ   lee-ap[3] *v.* to follow the edge or shore:
พูดเลียบเคียง to use paraphrases; to talk indirectly about another: เลียบฝั่ง to follow
the shore line: แห่เลียบเมือง to go in procession skirting a city, or following the city
wall; see ริม p. 714.

เลี่ยม   lee-am[3] *v.* to edge, garnish, decorate,
bind, or put on a rim, or mounting of metal,
silver, or gold (as on spoons, or buttons made
out of shells): เลี่ยมด้วยทอง to embellish
or beautify with an edging or strips of gold
(as canes, vases, or trays).

เลียว ๑   lee-ow *n.* Laos.

เลียว ๒   lee-ow *n.* stays or gaffs of a sail.

เลี้ยว   lee-ow[5] *v.* to make, or take a turn or
curve; to go in a circuitous, devious, or semicircular course: เลี้ยวลด to go in a tortuous,
spiral, or zigzaging course (as spiral stairs, or
snakish movements).

เลือก   leu-ak[3] *v.* to choose; to elect; to pick
out; to sort out; to select out those preferred
(as precious stones): *adj.* some; some one;
certain ones: เลือกคน selected persons:
เลือกวัน certain selected days.

เลือง, เรือง   leu-ang *adj.* luminous; bright;
shining; beautiful.

เลือง   leu-ang[3] *n.* a rumour; hearsay; fame;
news: เลืองลือ famed; famous; noted;
notorious; remarkable.

เลือด, โลหิต   leu-at[3] *n.* blood: ตกเลือด
to suffer from a flow of blood: เลือดนอง-
ทั้งตัว to be covered with blood: เลือดออก
to bleed.

เลือน   leu-an *adj.* illegible; effaced; defaced:
blotted out; forgotten; indistinct; unable to
be remembered; blurred: เปื้อนเลือน soiled;

blurred or effaced by deposits; dirty (as old stone monuments or writings): ลบเลือน to be so erased as to be indistinct; see มัว p. 646.

เลือน leu-an[3] v. to slide, slip, or skid; to move from one place to another; to be displaced or dislodged; to be changed in place or position: n. a sled; a sledge drawn by cattle in order to transport reaped rice: เลื่อนขึ้น to be promoted (in rank or class): เลื่อนตำแหน่ง to be changed in position or appointment: เลื่อนที่ to take another's place, employment, or title; to be moved from one place, position, or rank to another; to be transferred to another position: เลื่อน-บรรดาศักดิ์, เลื่อนยศ to receive promotion in rank or title: เลื่อนลง to be demoted, humilitated, or brought down to an inferior class, rank, or position: เลื่อนลอย unstable; unreliable; ambiguous; indefinite: ไส้เลื่อน [hernia.

เลื่อม leu-am[3] adj. clean; bright; glittering; shining; smooth; polished.

เลื่อมใส leu-am[3]-sai[2] v. to be devout in the observance of (as religious duties); to serve with a whole-hearted devotion; to give complete consent, or compliance to.

เลื่อย lu-ie[3] v. to saw: n. a saw: ขี้เลื่อย sawdust: ฟันเลื่อย saw-teeth: โรงเลื่อยไม้ a saw-mill.

เลื่อยล้า, เมื่อยล้า lu-ie[3]-lah[5] adj. fatigued; tired; weak; worn out; jaded; falling behind others (from exhaustion).

เลื้อย leu-ie[5] v. to creep (as vines); to crawl (as snakes and worms): adj. long: เลื้อย-เจื้อย long and tortuous, turning and twisting.

แล laa v. to look; to behold; to direct the eyes to; to lift up the eyes; to turn one's looks upon: conj. also; besides; likewise: interj. amen; so it is; so be it; a final expletive: ดูแล to superintend, oversee, or watch over; to care for: แลดู to look; to observe: แลเห็น to see; to perceive; to comprehend; to understand; to know full well.

แล่ laa[3] v. to carve or cut (as meat or fowls); to dissect; to dress (by removing the entrails (as fish or fowl); see ชำแหละ p. 295.

แล้ laa[5] adj. up to one's utmost strength; loaded to the fullest capacity; see เพียบ p. 599: conj. and; also; with.

แลก laak[3] v. to trade; to exchange; to barter: แลกข้าว to bargain and sell produce for rice: แลกเงิน to change money: แลกเปลี่ยน to swop; แลกแหวนกัน to exchange rings (as in betrothals): ค่าการแลกเปลี่ยน brokerage.

แลง laang, ศิลาแลง n. laterite; หินตัด, หินลัด are north-eastern Thai terms. Laterite is a ferruginous hardpan which is found in certain soils. A weathering product, it is soft enough to be easily excavated and dressed but hardens on exposure to the air. The art of quarrying and shaping large blocks of it for structural purposes was brought with the architecture and other culture from India. Being easier to work than stone, and often obtainable closer at hand than stronger materials, laterite was used extensively in building in ancient Thailand. As the arch was then still unknown here, sandstone posts and lintels were used in door and window openings. To receive surface decoration, sandstone slabs were used to cover walls and floors. There are notable ruins widely scattered in Thailand: Sawankalok, Sukotai, Lopburi, Petchaburi, Roi-et, Khukhan, Chantabun. A large proportion of the structures of Angkor are of laterite. In Chantabun laterite is still quarried and used, particularly for well-curbing. In regions where stone is hard to obtain for road-metal, laterite is used extensively for surfacing, even though it does not stand heavy traffic: ตลาดผี expanses where the laterite is naturally exposed on the surface: ลูกรัง the smaller separate iron concretions in the soil.

แล่ง   laang[3] *v.* to split; to divide; see ผ่า p. 546 : *n.* a box, bag, or wallet for sun-dried mud arrow-balls : แล่งตวงข้าว a unit of capacity for measuring rice, equal to one half of a tanan (used by Thai peasants) : แล่งศร a quiver or sheath for arrows : แล่ง (ลูกปืน) a cartridge case.

แล้ง   laang[5] *n.* dryness; drought; scarcity, or dearth of rain or moisture : *adj.* dry; arid; waterless; parched : ฝนแล้ง scarcity of rain : ฤดูแล้ง, หน้าแล้ง the dry season.

แล่น   laan[3] *v.* to move, glide, slide, or skim over (easily or rapidly) : เป่าแล่น to solder by means of a blow-pipe : แล่นใบ to use the sails : แล่นเร็ว to sweep along, sail, or glide over the surface quickly.

แลบ   laap[3] *v.* to project or protrude (slightly) : ฟ้าแลบ lightning : แลบลิ้น to project the tongue : แลบแสงสว่าง to emit; to give out, or send forth flashes of light or rays; see ประกาย p. 496 : แลบเหลื่อมกัน to extend, overlapping each other slightly.

แล้ว   laa-oh[5] *gram.* a sign of the past tense : *adj.* finished; complete in itself : *adv.* already; even now : เขามาแล้ว he has (already) come : ทำแล้ว it is done : ไปแล้ว gone : รู้แล้ว knew; known : แล้วก็ then; if in that case : สุดแล้วแต่ท่าน it depends on your discretion, opinion, or actions as final : แล้วกัน an exclamation of despair, surprise, or disheartenment (equal to "alas! nothing more can be done") : แล้วด้วย made or composed of; embellished with

และ ๑   laa[6] *v.* to flay, carve, cut, or dissect; see เชือด p. 302.

และ ๒   *conj.* and; a particle denoting addition, used as a connective : *adv.* with; withal; also; likewise : ไปกันทั้งคนมีและคนจน the rich, likewise the poor are to go.

และ ๓   a meaningless expletive, used for emphasis or euphony, as ลงกันที่นั่นและ here is the place where we get down; นั่นและ that is quite right.

และ   (4) *n.* beams or planks placed as a supporting foundation for posts, pillars, or columns.

และเล็ม   laa[6]-lem *v.* to nibble or browse here a little and there a little (as cattle or goats); see เก็บเล็กประสมน้อย under เก็บ p. 120.

และเลียม see ทาบทาม p. 412; พาดพิง p. 583.

โล่   loh[3] *n.* a kind of fine-textured Chinese silk.

โล้   loh[5] *v.* to move to and fro while suspended (as a swing); see ไกว p. 137 : *n.* a Chinese nautical term, descriptive of the pitching and rising motion of junks or ships when following or facing the wind and waves : โล้ชิงช้า to work up a swinging motion on a swing : เรือโล้ a Chinese water-taxi, in which the propelling oar or scull projects over the stern and is worked to and fro on a pivot.

โลก   loke[3] *P. S. n.* the earth; the world; the inhabitants of the world; mankind; a being; a creature (chd. p. 222); a tract of land; a region; a district; a country; a province; a free open space, room or place; the world of human beings (S. E. D. p. 906) : โลกคติ *lit.* "methods, or processes of the world," *i. e.* business; work; employment; manners of human beings : โลกจักษุ *lit.* "the world's eye," *i. e.* the sun : โลกชนนี *lit.* "the world's mother," *i. e.* Lady Lakshami, Vishnu's consort : โลกเชษฐ์ *lit.* "the one superior among men," *i. e.* the Buddha : โลกธรรม worldly conditions of which there are eight, *viz.* gain, loss, fame, dishonour, praise, blame, happiness, suffering (chd. p. 221) : โลกธาดา *lit.* "the world's creator,' *i. e.* Siva : โลกธาตุ elements composing the world or any astronomical body : โลกบท *lit.* "paths of the world," *i. e.* customs; manners; practices : โลกบาล the four (or eight) guardians or supporters of the world (chd. p. 222); the genii or deities who preside over the eight points of the compass, *viz.* the four cardinal and four intermediate points of the compass (H. C. D. p. 180): โลกบิดร *lit.* "the world's father," *i. e.* Kasyapa (พระกัศยป) who, according to the Ramayana, was the son of Marichi, the son of Brahma, and the father of Vivaswat, the father of Manu, thus the progenitor of mankind (H. C. D. p. 153): โลกประทีป *lit.* "the world's radiant rays," *i. e.* a title for the Buddha: โลกยาตรา the course of human events: โลกวัจน์ *lit.* "worldly speech," *i. e.* gossip; rumours; news; talk; prattle: โลกวินาศ the destruction of the world: โลกศัพท์ *lit.* "worldly voices," *i. e.* clamours; exclamations; outcries; noises; uproars, etc.: โลกสงเคราะห์ an encyclopedia; a directory; a book of universal knowledge: โลกอุดร, โลกกุตตร transcending the natural powers of the world; supernatural; spiritual (chd. p. 222); infinite; illimitable: โลกัตถจริยา useful deeds; good conduct or behaviour that will benefit (the people of) the world: โลกันต์ conclusion of the world: โลกาธิบดี *lit.* "a premier of the world," *i. e.* a universal emperor (H. C. D. p. 65): โลกานุวัตร the condition of adhering, or abiding by worldly tradition, fashions, or customs; proverbs of the world: โลกามิส worldly seductive means; snares; traps; foils; allurements or enticements.

โลกย, โลกัย loke³-ya⁶ *S. adj.* customary; ordinary; correct; right; actual; usual; the granting of a free sphere of action, or that which is conducive to the attainment of a better world (S. E. D. p. 907): โลกยโวหาร sayings, statements, or declarations of worldly origin (not words of a god).

โลกิย, โลกีย, เลากัย loh-gki⁴-ya⁶ *P. adj.* common; popular; worldly; earthly; temporal (chd. p. 222); temporary; transient: โลกียชน commoners; every day people; the unconverted (chd. p. 222); those engrossed, engulfed, or absorbed in worldly affairs or pursuits.

โลง long *n.* bier; coffin; hearse: โลงศิลา sarcophagus.

โล่ง, ล่ง long³ *adj.* open; empty; vacant; bare; unfurnished; unoccupied: ที่โล่งเตียน a place cleared of underbrush, or of all unsightly, unnecessary obstructions: โล่งเตียน-ตลอดไป cleared all the way through (as for a path or road); see โปร่ง p. 537.

โล้งโต้ง long⁵-dtong³ *adj.* spacious; roomy; extensive (but vacant); bare; naked.

โลจนะ loh-chja⁴-na⁶ *P. S. n.* the eye (chd. p. 221): *adj.* illuminating; brightening (S.E.D. p. 907).

โลณะ loh-na⁶ *P. S. n.* salt (chd. p. 223): [*adj.* saltish; brackish.

โลด lote³ *v.* to jump; to leap while skipping; to spring; to bound; to caper: โลดเต้น to jump around in a dancing manner: โลด-โผน to leap or spring upon; to rush violently or dangerously upon, or towards.

โลน lone *n.* body lice, *Pediculus corporis*; crab lice; a scamp, rogue, or babbler: คนปากโลน a shameless babbler about indecent or obscene matters.

โล้น lone⁵ *adj.* hairless; shaved; shaven; tonsured.

โลป lope³ *P. S. n.* the act of cutting off; elision (or striking out of a part of a word); apocope; deletion; cancellation; erasure, or omission (chd. p. 223); see ตัด p. 359.

โลภ lope³ *P. v.* to desire; to hanker after; to covet: *n.* covetousness; desire; avarice; cupidity; greed (chd. p. 221); lust (Ala. p. 213): โลภมากลากหาย fortune forsakes the greedy: โลภโลโภ cupidity; concupiscence.

โลม, โลมเล้า lome *v.* to flatter; to caress; to soothe; to make much of; to comfort; to console: โลมเล้าเอาใจ to seduce; to flatter in order to gain the affection of: โลมไล้ to stroke, rub, or anoint (with oil or perfumery).

โลมะ, โลมา ๑   loh-ma⁶ *P. n.* the hair of
the body (chd. p. 223): โลมะชาติ *lit.* "races
of hairs," *i. e.* (collectively) hairs of the body.

โลมา ๒   loh-mah *n.* a great sea-fish.

โลโล   loh-loh *n.* a tribe of people inhabiting northern Thailand.

โลลุป   loh-loop⁶ *P. adj.* desirous; covetous;
greedy; lustful (chd. p. 222); see กรรหาย p 17.

โลเล   loh-lay *adj.* unsteady; unstable; fluctuating; unreliable; variable (in disposition).

โล้เล้   lon⁵-lay⁵ *adj.* dilatory; slow; tardy;
late; procrastinating.

โล่ห์   loh³ *n.* a shield; a buckler; an aegis
or guard: โล่ห์แขน an arm-shield.

โลหะ   loh-ha⁴ *P. n.* iron; copper; brass;
any metal; gold (chd. p. 221): โลหกรรม
the act of mining; the occupation of mining:
โลหการ, โลหกรก a blacksmith (chd. p. 221); a
brass-smith; a goldsmith; a worker in metals:
โลหกิจ the work connected with mining, or
working with metals: โลหกุมภี an iron
cauldron; name of a lake in hell (chd. p. 221);
a copper or iron pot or vessel: โลหศาสตร์
minerology.
                                        [p. 221].

โลหัช   loh-hut⁴ *P. n.* brass; bronze (chd.

โลหิต   loh-hit⁴ *P. n.* the colour red; blood
(chd. p. 221): โลหิตปาณี murderous; hands
smeared with blood; blood-stained hands:
โลหิตุปบาท the crime of wounding a supreme
Buddha so as to draw blood (chd. p. 221).

โละ   loh⁶ *Chin. v.* to throw down; to put
down; to pour into.

ไล่   lai³ *v.* to chase; to pursue; to run after;
to put to flight, drive, or send away; to purify; to clarify or refine (by removing the
dross): *adj.* decreasing in consecutive, or
serial order; graded in size, shape, or height
(as students according to their standing in
class, or soldiers according to the height of
the body): การสอบไล่ classical examinations
(as at the close of a semester): ขับไล่ to
expel; to eject; to banish; to exile: ไล่ติดตาม
to chase; to pursue or follow the tracks of
(as while stalking game): ไล่เลี่ย similar
to; closely resembling another; almost alike:
ไล่เลียง to enquire minutely regarding; to question, interrogate, or cross-question: ไล่เสีย
to dismiss (as a servant); to order away (as
an intruder): ไล่ให้จน to corner a person
by cross-questioning.

ไล้   lai⁵ *v.* to cover; to overlay; to overspread;
to rub on or over; to coat; to paint; to cause
to become fluid, so as to run or flow (as solder
or wax); see ฉาบ p. 269.

ไลน์   lai *n. Cam. adj.* all; see ทั้งหมด p. 408.

ไลย   lai *n.* mucilaginous or glutinous food
(chd. p. 220): *adj.* delicious; savoury; worth
while tasting.

ไลลา   lai-lah *n.* an exaggerated swinging
motion (of the arms); an insolent, haughty,
swaggering throwing of the body (as in walking).

ไลไล้   lai-lai⁵ ลูบไลไล้บีบคลำ *v.* to caress; to
fondle; to pat; to dandle; to coddle (incessantly).

ภ, ภา

ภ, ภา   vowels adopted from the
Sanskrit and used as ลิ,
ลี.

ภาชา see ลือชา under ลือ p. 747.

ภาสาย see ลือสาย p. 748.

ว

ว The thirty-seventh letter of the Thai alphabet, a low class letter of which there are twenty-four, *viz.* ค, ฅ, ฆ, ง, ช, ซ, ฌ, ญ, ฑ, ฒ, ณ, ท, ธ, ฝ, น, ฌ, พ, ฟ, ภ, ม, ร, ล, ว, ฬ, ฮ. วอแหวน is the name of this letter which occurs in Pali, Sanskrit and Thai both as a prefix and suffix. In Thai "ว" is pronounced like "w"; in Pali and Sanskrit like "วะ". It is generally interchangeable with "พ," as เทวดา, เทพดา; วิจิตร, พิจิตร.

วก ๑ wa⁶-gka⁴ *n.* a wolf (chd. p. 546).

วก ๒ wok⁶ *v.* to turn, or deviate to one side; to bend; to be deflected: เดินวกกลับ to retrace one's steps; to return to the same place: วกเผือก a fish-trap made of woven bamboo in the shape of a tube or funnel some twenty *wah* long: วกเวียน to wander around and return to the starting point.

วกุล see พิกุล p. 585.

วง wong *n.* an arc of a circle; a curvature; a semicircle; a crescent; a numerical designatory particle for finger rings or circles: *adj.* curved; bowed; bent: ขอบวงกลม the circumference of a circle: คดเป็นวง to bend into an arc of a circle: ตีเป็นวง to arrange into a circle (as players in a game): ทำเป็น- วงกลม to draw a circle (as with a pair of compasses): นั่งเป็นวง to sit forming a circle or ring (as players in a game): ล้อมเป็นวง to surround, encompass, or encircle (as besiegers closing in on a city or palace): วงกลม a circle; a sphere; an orb; a circuit; วงเดือน, วงจันทร์ the orb of the moon: วงพาด a secondary semicircle added to a main circle (as a subsidiary enclosure added to an elephant kraal): วงเล็บ brackets, used to enclose any part of the text: วงเวียน an instrument for describing circles; a pair of compasses.

วงก์, วังก์ wong *P. n.* a fish-hook: *adj.* crooked; bent; cunning; dishonest (chd. p. 549); untrustworthy.

วงกต wong-gkot⁴ *P. n.* the name of a celebrated mountain mentioned in the account of Phra Vetra Sundorn (S. E. D. p. 911).

วงศ์, วงส์, วังศ์, วังส์ wong *S. n.* a bamboo cane; any cane; the upper timbers or beams of a house; lineage; race; family; stock; offspring; an assemblage; a multitude (S. E. D. p. 910): วงศกร the making or founding of a family; the propagating or perpetuating of a family or race; an ancestor: วงศ์กษัตริย์ of royal lineage, family, or race (used as an ending for many proper names): วงศจริต a family history; the history of a race or dynasty; geneology: วงศ์ญาติ relationships; relatives; kinsfolk: วงศนาถ the chief of a race; the head of a family: วงศโกษย์ perpetuating a family; hereditary: วงศสถิติ the state or condition of life of a family: วงศสมาจาร family usages.

วงส์, วังส์ wong *P. n.* a race; a family; lineage; dynasty; hereditary custom or tradition (chd. p. 548).

วจนะ, วัจน์ wa⁶-chja⁴-na⁶ *P.S. n.* a speaker; the act of speaking, mentioning, declaring or expressing (S. E. D. p. 912): วจนกร, วจนการ obedient; doing what one is commanded to do: วจนเคารพ deference to a command; having respect for an order: วจนรจนา skillful arrangement of speech; eloquence: วจนสหาย a companion to converse with; any one who is a sociable companion.

วจะ wa⁶-chja⁴ *P. n.* speech; words; sayings; advice; injunctions or orders (chd. p. 542): วจะวาที dialogues; conversations; discourses.

วจี wa⁶-chjee *P. n.* speech; words; a discourse; utterances (chd. p. 542).

วชะ   wa⁶-cha⁶ *P. n.* a cow-pen (chd. p. 546).

วชิร, วิเชียร, วัชระ   wa⁶-chi⁶-ra⁶ *P. n.* the Vajra, or thunderbolt of Indra (chd. p. 546). According to some, it is a circular weapon, with a hole in the centre, but others represent it as consisting of two transverse bars (H. C. D. p. 332): วชิรปาณี, วชิรหัตถ์ *lit.* "the one who holds the thunderbolt," *i. e.* Indra (chd. p. 546): วชิราวุธ *lit.* "one armed with the thunderbolt," *i. e.* Indra (chd. p. 546).

วฏากาน   wa⁶-dtah-gkarn *P. S. n.* a cord, string or rope (chd. p. 555).

วฏุมะ   wa⁶-dtoo⁴-ma⁶ *P. n.* a road, highway or path (chd. p. 560).

วฐระ   wa⁶-ta⁴-ra⁶ *P. adj.* bulky; gross; plump; fat; corpulent (chd. p. 560).

วณะ, วัณ   wa⁶-na⁶ *P. n.* a sore; a wound; an abscess; a break, gap or orifice (in tissues) (chd. p. 548).

วณิช   wa⁶-nit⁶-cha⁶ *S. n.* a trader; a merchant; a tradesman (chd. p. 549); see พาณิช p. 583.

วณิชชา   wa⁶-nit⁶-chah *P. n.* trade; traffic; commerce (chd. p. 549): วณิชชากร a trader; a merchant; a tradesman.

วณิชย์, วณิชยา   wa⁶-nit⁶ *S. n.* trade; com- [merce.

วณิต   wa⁶-nit⁶ *P. adj.* wounded; bruised; injured (chd. 549).

วดี, วติ, วัติ   wa⁶-nee *P. n.* a fence; a barrier; a wall (chd. p. 556).

วทนะ, วัทน์   wa⁶-ta⁶-na⁶ *P. S. n.* the mouth; the face; speech; utterance (chd. [p. 542).

วทัญญู, วทานิย   wa⁶-tun-yoo *P. adj. lit.* "heeding supplications," *i. e.* bountiful; charitable; merciful; compassionate; kind (chd. [p. 542).

วธ   wa⁶-ta⁶ *P. S. n.* one who kills; a slayer; a destroyer; a murderer; a deadly weapon;

the act of striking or killing; death; destruction (S. E. D. p. 916).

วธก   wa⁶-ta⁶-gka⁴ *P. S. n.* a murderer; an executioner (chd. p. 544).

วธุกา   wa⁶-too⁶-gkah *P. n.* a daughter-in-law (chd. p. 544).

วธู   wa⁶-too *P. S. n.* a bride; a young wife; a girl; a daughter-in-law (chd. p. 544).

วน ๑   won *v.* to whirl; to rotate; to twirl or spin around: น้ำวน an eddy (of water): วนเวียน to move in a circuitous, tortuous, or devious course: วนหา to go round and round seeking for something: เดินวนวก to wander in a crooked but circuitous manner (as one lost in a jungle).

วน ๒   won *P. S. n.* water (chd. p. 548): วนช, วนัช *lit.* "born in the water," *i. e.* a lotus plant or flower: วนท, วนัท *lit.* "a giver of water," *i. e.* a cloud: วนมุจ, วนมุก *lit.* "a releaser of water," *i. e.* clouds: วนภูต *lit.* "composed of water," *i. e.* clouds.

วน ๓   wa⁶-na⁶ *P. S. n.* woods; a grove; a forest; jungle; a thicket (chd. p. 548): วนกุสุม, วนบุษป์ wild flowers: วนคช a wild elephant: วนจร, วนจรก roaming in the wood; living in a forest: วนช, วนัช forest born; wild; a forester: วนชีวิกา forest life: วนทาห์ a forest fire; the burning of a forest or wood: วนเทวดา tree spirits; forest goddesses; nymphs: วนมฤค the wild deer: วนราช *lit.* "king of the jungle," *i. e.* a lion: วนสถิต situated or being in a forest: วนัปปติ, วนัสบดี trees of large size; mammoth or giant trees: วนาลัย, วนาวาส, วนาศรม forest-habitations; tents, pavilions or shacks in a forest or woods (as shelters for camping parties): วนาลี a row of trees; a road or path through the forest.

วนัส   wa⁶-nut⁶ *P. S. n.* forest; woods; jungle (S. E. D. p. 918).

วนิดา   wa⁶-ni⁶-dah *P. S. n.* a woman; a fiancée; a wife; a handsome woman.

วนิพพก, วณิพพก, วนปก, วันิพพก wa⁶-nip⁶-pok⁶ *P. n.* a beggar; a mendicant; a pauper (chd. p. 549); an asker of alms, using musical instruments (as an organ grinder); an indigent, poor, or needy person.

วปนะ wa⁶-bpa⁴-na⁶ *P. S. n.* seed sowing; planting; agricultural pursuits (S. E. D. p. 919).

วปา wa⁶-bpah *P. S. n.* the serous secretion, or fat that permeates through the tissues; marrow; fat; oil (chd. p. 550).

วปุ wa⁶-bpoo⁴ *P. S. n.* the body (chd. p. 550); see ตัว p. 360.

วมนะ wa⁶-ma⁶-na⁶ *P. S. n.* the act of vomiting (chd. p. 547); an emetic.

วยวัสถาน wa⁶-ya⁶-wat⁶-sa⁴-tarn² *S. n.* fixedness; stability; determination; see ตั้งใจ p. 358.

วยะ, วัย wa⁶-ya⁶ *S. n.* youth; the prime of life; adolescence; strength; health; vigour (S. E. D. p. 920).

วยัมหะ wa⁶-yum-ha⁴ *P. n.* paradise; heaven; the abodes of celestial beings.

วยัสย์ wa⁶-yut⁶ *S. n.* one being of the same age; a contemporary; an associate; a companion; a friend (S. E. D. p. 920).

วยาธ wa⁶-yart³ *P. n.* a murderer; a hunter who kills.

วยาธิ see พยาธิ p. 562.

วยาปาทะ see พยาบาท p. 562.

วยาพาธ see ข่มเหง p. 141.

วยาล wa⁶-yah-la⁶ *S. n.* animals that are cruel, fierce, furious or savage (as snakes, lions, tigers): *adj.* fierce; cruel; violent; wild; ferocious.

วร wa⁶-ra⁶ *P. S. n.* the condition of choosing, or of being a chooser; a boon; a blessing; a favour; one who solicits a girl in marriage; a suitor; a bridegroom; a husband (S. E. D. p. 922): วรคนุ a beautiful woman; one having a beautiful body: วรทาน the granting of a boon or request; the giving of a compensation or reward: วรนารี a most excellent woman: วรปักษ์ the party or friends of a bridegroom at a wedding: วรรูป having an excellent or graceful form: วรวรรณินี a woman with a beautiful spotless complexion.

วรงค์ wa⁶-rong *P. n. lit.* "an important or best member of the body," *i. e.* the head (chd. p. 550).

วรณะ wa⁶-ra⁶-na⁶ *P. S. n.* a surrounding wall; a rampart; a causeway; a bridge (chd. p. 550).

วรท wa⁶-rote⁶ *P. n. lit.* "the giver of a boon," *i. e.* the Buddha, as having shown men the way to Nirvana (chd. p. 550).

วรรค, วัคค์ wuk⁶ *n.* a paragraph; an expression; a sentence; a phrase; a passage; a section or a clause (in literature); *gram.* class of consonants.

วรรณ see พรรณ p. 564: วรรณคดี literature; poetical compositions: วรรณยุกต์, วรรณยุตต์ the four tone marks, *viz.* ˋ, ˊ, ˇ, ˆ, used with all three classes of consonants.

วรรณนา see พรรณนา p. 564: วรรณนาการ praises; eulogies.

วรรณึก won-neuk⁶ *S. n.* a writer; a composer; a secretary.

วรรษ, วรรษา see พรรษา p. 564.

วรากะ wa⁶-rah-gka⁴ *P. n.* a water-jar; a pot or brass basin: *adj.* poor; wretched; miserable; orphaned (chd. p. 550).

วรางคณา wa⁶-rarng-ka⁶-nah *P. n.* a noble or beautiful woman (chd. p. 550).

วราห์, วราหะ wa⁶-rah *P. S. n.* a boar; a wild hog; a wild pig; *suscristatus* (Gaird. N. H. J. S. S. III, 2, p. 126: chd. p. 550).

วราหร wa⁶-rah-horn² *P. n. lit.* "one bringing the boon (of Nirvana)," *i. e.* the Buddha (chd. p. 550).

วรุณ wa⁶-roon *S. n.* Varuna, "the universal encompasser, the all-embracer." He is one of the oldest of the Vedic deities, a personification of the all-investing sky, the maker and upholder of heaven and earth. As such he is king of the universe, king of gods and men, possessor of illimitable knowledge, the supreme deity to whom especial honour is due. In later times he was chief among the lower celestial deities called Aditya, and later still he became a sort of Neptune, a god of the seas and rivers, who rides upon the Makars. His emblem is a fish (H. C. D. p. 336); see พิรุณ p. 589.

วรูถ wa -roo-ta⁴ *S. n.* a means of protection; armour; coat of mail; see เกราะ p. 120.

วฤษภ see พฤษภ p. 571.

วฤษล see วสละ p. 763.

วลัญช์ wa⁶-lun *P. n.* a sign; a mark; a token; a symbol; an indication (chd. p. 547).

วลัญชน์ wa⁶-lun *P. n.* the act of using, resorting to, depending upon, or trusting in (chd. p. 547).

วลัย wa⁶-lai *P. S. n.* bracelets; rings; armlets; a girdle; a circle (S. E. D. p. 927).

วลาหก wa⁶-lah-hok⁴ *P. n.* clouds; rain (chd. p. 546); see เมฆ p. 655.

วลิ wa⁶-lee *P. S. n.* a fold of the skin; wrinkles; a line; a streak (as on the face) (chd. p. 547); *gram.* a phrase or a portion of a sentence.

วลิมุข wa⁶-lee-mook⁶ *P. S. n. lit.* "having a wrinkled face," *i. e.* a monkey.

วศ wa⁶-sa⁴ *S. n.* will; wish; desire; authority; power; dominion (S. E. D. p. 929).

วศค wa⁶-sok⁴ *S. n.* one being in the power of; one subject or obedient to, or dependent on; subjugation (S. E. D. p. 929).

วศา wa⁶-sah² *S. n.* a (sterile) cow; an ewe; a female elephant; any woman or wife; a barren woman (S. E. D. p. 929).

วศิน wa⁶-sin² *S. adj.* having authority, right, power or control; being master, ruler, or governor; having conquered one's carnal desires (S. E. D. p. 929).

วสนะ ๑, วัสน์ wa⁶-sa⁴-na⁶ *P. S. n.* a dwelling-place; a house; a home (S. E. D. p. 932).

วสนะ ๒ wa⁶-sa⁴-na⁶ *P. S. n.* cloth; clothes; dress; a garment; wearing apparel; attire (S. E. D. p. 932); see พสนะ p. 576.

วสภ wa⁶-sop⁴ *P. n.* a bull (chd. p. 551); see พสุ ๑ p. 576.

วสละ, วฤษล wa⁶-sa⁴-la⁶ *P. n.* a reprobate, or castaway; an outcast or low, wicked person (chd. p. 551); see ต่ำช้า p. 365.

วสลิ wa⁶-sa⁴-lee *P. n.* a vile woman; a prostitute (chd. p. 551).

วสวัตตี wa⁶-sa⁴-wat⁶-dtee *P. n. lit.* "bringing into subjection," *i. e.* a tamer or trainer of animals; another name for Mara (chd. p. 552).

วสะ wa⁶-sa⁴ *P. n.* control; influence; ownership; mastership (chd. p. 553).

วสันต์ wa⁶-sun² *P. S. n.* spring; a season of the year (some consider this to be from March to May): วสันตฤดู season of rain.

วสา wa⁶-sah² *P. S. n.* serum; marrow; fat; lard; oil (chd. p. 551)

วสี wa⁶-see² *P. n.* one who has conquered or controlled the senses, or all carnal desires; one who is master, ruler or all-powerful (chd. p. 552).

วสุ wa⁶-soo⁴ *P. S. n.* wealth; riches; goods; property; gold; a jewel, gem, or pearl; any valuable or precious object (S. E. D. p. 930); a class of eight deities chiefly known as atten-

dants upon Indra, and in Vedic times personification of natural phenomena (H. C. D. p. 342):
วสุเทพ name of the son of Sura, of the Yadava
branch of the Lunar race and father of Krishna (H. C. D. p. 342).

วสุธา   wa⁶-soo⁴-tah   *P. S. n. lit.* "birth-
place of wealth," *i. e.* the earth; a country;
the ground; the soil; a kingdom; a territory.

วสุนธรา   wa⁶-soon²-ta⁶-rah   *P. n.* the earth;
a country; territory (chd. p. 555).

วสุมดี   wa⁶-soo⁴-ma⁶-dee   *P. S. n.* the earth;
a wealthy woman (S. E. D. p. 931).

วหา   wa⁶-hah²   *S. n.* a river; streams in
general (chd. p. 545).

[p. 546].

วฬภิ, วฏภิ   wa⁶-la⁶-pi⁶   *P. n.* a roof (chd.

วฬวา, วฏวา   wa⁶-la⁶-wah   *P. n.* a mare
(chd. p. 547).

วอ   wau *n.* a roofed or canopied palanquin:
ทรงวอ to be carried in a palanquin: วอเจ้า
a palanquin for the use of princes: วอศพ
a palanquin used as a hearse: วอหลวง an
elaborately decorated palanquin for royalty.

วอก   wauk³ *n.* a monkey: ปีวอก the
ninth year of the Thai animal circle of years.

วอกแวก   wauk³-waak³ *adj.* unsettled; infirm; unstable; shaking; distracted; changeable; irresolute; variable: ใจวอกแวก of an
unstable mind or disposition: พูดวอกแวก
undependable words or language.

ว่อง   waung³ *v.* to be agile, quick, active, or
dextrous: ปัญญาว่องไว of quick mentality:
ว่องไว clever; energetic; vigorous; nimble:
adj. light, feathery, buoyant (as a boat riding
the water):   วิ่งว่อง light-footed or agile
in running.

วอด   waut³ *v.* to come to an end (as a supply of food); to be exhausted (as fruit at the
close of a season); to reach a condition of termination or conclusion: วอดวาย to die; to
be ruined; to be destroyed.

วอน   waun *v.* to pray for; to implore, supplicate or beseech: วอนขอ, วิงวอน to ask
for repeatedly, or with importunity: วอนไหว้,
ไหว้วอน to beg while the hands are placed in
a respectful attitude of worship.

ว่อน, วะว่อน   waun³ *adj.* in great swarms
(as birds hovering around overhead); in great
flocks, herds or droves.

วอแว see เซ้าซี้ p. 311; จอแจ p. 234.

วะ ๑, หวา, วา   wa⁶ a meaningless word used
by the rabble or between intimate friends to
close questions or short sentences instead of
ครับ, as เอาซิวะ, ไปไหนวะ, อะไรวะ; *explective* indicating dislike, disgust or astonishment.

วะ ๒   wa⁶ a permissable prefix to words
beginning with " ว " wherever needed (as in
poetry), as วะว่อน, วะวาว, วะวาบ.

วัก   wuk⁶ *v.* to scoop water up with the
palms of the hands: ปลูกผักวักถั่ว an idiomatic expression used by vegetable gardeners
indicating various kinds of garden produce
watered: วักน้ำ to dip up water with the
hands (as in bathing):   วักน้ำกิน to dip up
water with the hands to drink: วักน้ำสาด
to dash water held in the palm or palms of
the hands.

วักกะ ๑, วฤกก์   wuk⁶-gka⁴ *P. n.* the
kidney (chd. p. 546); see ไต p. 378.

วักกะ ๒   wuk⁶-gka⁴ *P. adj.* crooked; see
คด p. 175; โกง p. 131.

วัคค์ see วรรค p. 762.

วัคคิย, วัคคีย์   wuk⁶-ki⁶-ya⁶ *P. adj.* belonging to a class, clan, company or sect; arranged in a class or classes (chd. p. 545).

วัคคุ   wuk⁶-koo⁶ *P. adj.* beautiful; agreeable to the ears; melodious; tuneful; musical;
harmonious: วัคคุวาท spoken in a melodious,
clever or attractive manner.

วัง　wang *n.* a palace; the residence of a sovereign, or royalty: ในรั้วในวัง within the precincts of a palace: วังช้าง the name of a district north-east of Bangkok, so named because it is a rendezvous of elephants: วังนอก palaces other than that of the king: วังวน a large whirlpool; a deep lagoon; a crocodile pit or wallow: วังหน้า the Second King's palace: วังหลวง, พระราชวัง the Grand Palace: วังหลัง the site of the palace of the senior son of the Second King, located on the west bank of the Menam Chao-phya, opposite to that of his royal father.

วังชา　wang-chah *adj.* powerful; possessing great strength, force, or robustness: มีกำลังวังชา having great physical strength.

วังเวง see กังวาล p. 83: เพราะวังเวง harmonious melodies which rejoice the mind.

วังศ์ วังส์ see วงศ์ p. 760.
[(chd. p. 542).

วัจจะ　wat[6]-chja[4] *P. n.* excrement; feces

วัจฉ์ วัจฉก　wat[6] *P. n.* a calf (chd. p. 542).

วัจฉละ　wat[6]-cha[4]-la[6] *P. adj.* affectionate; merciful; charitable; loving (chd. p. 542).

วัจนะ see วจนะ p. 760.

วัช see วชะ p. 761.

วัชช์, ๑, วรรชย์　wat[6] *n.* that which should be avoided; fault; sin; punishments (chd. [p. 546).

วัชช์ ๒　wat[6] *P. n.* speech; a musical instrument (chd. p. 546); in the Rig-Veda, Vach appears to be the personification of speech by whom knowledge was communicated to man (H. C. D. p. 329): *adj.* worth while speaking, saying, or making mention of.

วัชณ์　wat[6] *P. v.* to be killed or destroyed; meriting death (chd. p. 546).

วัชระ see วชิร p. 761: วัชรชวาลา lightning; flashes or spark of electric light: วัชรมัย adamantine; adamant; like, or made of diamonds: วัชรโลหก a magnet; magnetic ore or iron: วัชรากร a diamond mine: วัชรี *lit.* "he who holds the thunderbolt," *i. e.* Indra.

วัญจก　wan-chjok[4] *P. S. n.* a deceiver; a deluder; a beguiler; a rogue; a cheat: *adj.* fraudulent; deceitful (chd. p. 548).

วัญจนะ　wan-cha[4]-na[6] *P. S. n.* illusion; deception; imitation; counterfeit; cheat; sham [(chd. p. 548).

วัฏฏูก see กระจาบ (นก) p. 21.

วัฏฏิ see ขอบ p. 148.

วัฑฒ, วัฑฒ　wat[6]-ta[6] *P. v.* to grow; to increase; to multiply; to prosper (chd. p. 543).

วัฑฒกี, วัฑฒกี　wat[6]-ta[6]-gkee *n.* an artisan; a carpenter; a mason (chd. p. 543).

วัฑฒน, วัฑฒน, วรรธนะ　wat[6]-ta[6]-na[6] *P. n.* increase; enlargement; expansion; growth; augmentation.

วัณ, วณะ　wan-na[6] *n.* a sore; a wound; an abscess; a break, gap, or orifice (in tissues): วัณโรค tuberculosis; consumption.

วัณณ　wan-na[6] *P. n.* appearance; form. figure; colour; complexion; beauty (chd; p. 549): วัณณทาสี *lit.* "a slave to beauty," *i. e.* "a prostitute.

วัณณนา　wan[6]-na[6]-nah *P. n.* description; narration; explanation; a comment; a commentary.

วัด　wat[6] *v.* to measure; to give a sudden violent upward jerk (as with a fishing-rod): ทำการรางวัด to make a survey and calculate the area: วัดที่วัดทาง to take the dimensions of (as of a piece of land): วัดวา equal to or even with another: วัดเหวี่ยง to hurl, throw, fling or scatter (as when sowing grain); to be like, or equal to another (in strength or ability).

วัด　*n.* a place sacred to prayer or worship; a church; a Buddhist temple or monastery; a tabernacle: จำวัด to remain in the Buddhist

temple (as during lenten season): วัดนางชี
a convent; a nunnery: วัดอาราม a cathe-
dral; an abbey: วัดสุเหร่า a mosque.
[p. 556].

วัตต์ wat⁶ *P. n.* the mouth; the face (chd.

วัตตนะ wat⁶-dta⁴-na⁶ *P. n.* existence; livelihood; subsistence; a condition of going on
or continuing (chd. p. 556).

วัตตนิ wat⁶-dta⁴-ni⁶ *P. n.* a road; a way;
a path (chd.p. 556).

วัตตา wat⁶-dtah *P. n.* a speaker; a talker;
a converser (chd. p. 556).

วัตถ์, วัสตร์ wat⁶ *P. n.* clothes; raiment;
garments (chd. p. 558).

วัตถุ wat⁶-too⁴ *P. n.* matter; substance;
personal goods or possessions; the plot or subject of a story; narrative (chd. p. 558): วัตถุ-
ประสงค์ purpose; aim; desire: วัตถุปัจจัย
substances or things (as money) that product
benefits in various ways.

วัตสดร wat⁶-sa⁶-dorn *S. n.* a young cow;
a young bull; a heifer (S. E. D. p. 915).

วัตสะ wat⁶-sa⁴ *S. n.* a calf; the young of
various animals (as pups, cubs, etc.); children
(S. E. D. p. 915).

วัน wan *n.* day; any day of the week: ทุกวัน
every day: ทุกวันนี้ during the present
time; at present: วันกำหนด the appointed
day: วันเกิด birthday: วันโกน see โกน
p. 132: วันดี an auspicious, lucky day:
วันตาย the day of death: วันถึงกำหนดที่ใช้เงิน
date of maturity (of payment): วันที่ day
of ......: วันหน้า, วันพรุ่ง tomorrow; on the
morrow: วันนี้ today; at the present time;
วันพระ Buddhist holy days, falling on the
eighth and fifteenth of the waxing and also
of the waning moon: วันเพ็ญ day of the
full moon (according to the lunar calculation);
วันร้าย, วันอุบาทว์ an unauspicious day: วันวาน
yesterday; gone; gone by; bygone; passed:
วันสงบศึก armistice day.

วันต์ wan *P. adj.* vomited; ejected; put
away; abandoned; forsaken (chd. p. 547).

วันท, ไหว้ wan-ta⁶ *P. S. v.* to salute; to
wey; to make obeisance; to pay homage to
(by raising the hands placed palm to palm up
to the face or head); to revere; to venerate
(chd. p. 549): ไหว้วันทา to salute; to make
obeisance to.

วันทน, วันทนา wan-ta⁶-na⁶ *P. n.* salutation; the paying of reverence, veneration, or
homage to: วันทนาการ the act of saluting
or adoring (by raising the hands placed palm
to palm up to the face or head).

วันทนีย์ wan-ta⁶-nee *P. S. adj.* deserving
homage, veneration, reverence, or salutations
of respect (chd. p. 548).

วันทย wan-ta⁶-ya⁶ *v.* to be praised, highly
regarded, or respected; to be saluted reveren-
tially (S. E. D. p. 919): วันทยหัตถ์ a military
command to salute with the hand: วันทยาวุธ
a military command to salute by presenting
arms.

วันที wan-ti⁶ *P. S. n.* a prisoner; a convict;
a captive; a slave (S. E. D. p. 919).

วันิพพก see วนิพพก p. 762.

วับ wup⁶ *adj.* intermittent flashing (of
light), sparkling, glittering or shining.

วัปปะ wup⁶-bpa⁴ *P. n.* the act of, or place
for sowing; the bank of a river (chd. p. 550).

วัมมิก wum-mik⁶ *P. n.* an ant-hill (chd.
[p. 547].

วัยะ see วยะ p. 762.

วัลก์ wan *n.* a covering; the bark of trees;
the scales of fishes.

วัลคุ wan-la⁶-koo⁶ *S. adj.* beautiful; pretty;
lovable; attractive (S E. D. p. 928).

วัลลิ wan-lee *P. S. n.* a creeper; a creeping
plant; creepers in general (chd. p. 547).

วัว woo-ah (งัว p. 222) *n.* a cow; cattle; a bull; an ox; a prefix to which the designating name is added: วัวกระทิง see กระทิง (วัว) p. 35: วัวแดง, วัวป่า the banteng, *Bos sondaicus* or *Bos banteng* (Minutes of s. s. Regarding wild Game Preservation In Siam): วัวถึก young strong cattle.

วัสตร์ see วัตถ์ p. 766.

วัสน์ see วสนะ ๑ p. 763.

วัสส wat⁶-sa⁴ *P. n.* a year; rain (chd. p. 554): วัสโสทก rain-water.

วัสสานะ wat⁶-sah²-na⁶ *P. n.* the rainy season (chd. p. 554).

วา wah *n.* a measure of length equal to two meters, or about 80 English inches: วาตารางเหลี่ยม a square wah, or two meters square.

ว่า wah³ *v.* to say; to speak; to declare; to announce: ผู้ว่าจ้าง an employer: ผู้ว่าราชการจังหวัด a provincial governor: ไม่ว่า it makes no difference whether that is so or not: ไม่ว่ากระไร there is nothing more to be said: ว่ากระไร what did you say? ว่ากล่าว to admonish, exhort, remonstrate, advise or criticize (in a constructive manner); see ติเตียน p. 366: ว่าการ to direct; to administer; to manage or oversee (as some business or project): ว่าขาน to discourse; to converse; to discuss; to confer together; tº reply to one's name when called: ว่าความ to litigate; to assume the duties of a lawyer, barrister or advocate in legal affairs: ว่าความที่ศาลหลวง to plead law cases in government courts: ว่าจ้าง to employ or engage (as an hireling): ว่าด้วย to treat of; to speak about, or concerning (as the caption of a chapter): ว่าที่, ว่าต่าง to act as, or in the capacity of; acting provisionally for another: ว่าที่นายสิบ a lance-sergeant or provisional sergeant: ว่าไป, ว่าอีก to continue saying or speaking: ว่าไป ว่ามา to argue back and forth: ว่าราชการ to administer public or civil affairs: เห็นว่า, คิดว่า to be of the opinion that.....

ว้า, ว้าเหว่ wah⁵ *v.* to be lonely, lonesome or afflicted with solitude, moroseness or sadness: ว้าว่อน swarming or flying in all directions (as bees, locusts, vultures and crows over carrion): ว้าเหว่ใจ a sense of solitude or dreariness.

วาก wah-gka⁴ *P. n.* the bark of a tree; hemp; jute (chd. p. 546): วากจิรพัสตร์ cloth woven from vegetable fibers (as from flax, pineapple, hemp or the bark of trees).

วากย wak³-gka⁴-ya⁶ *P. n.* speech; a sentence (chd. p. 546).

วากรา wak³-gka⁴-rah *P. n.* a noose; a net; a snare (chd. p. 546).

วาง wang *v.* to lay down; to deposit; to place on; to let go; to release: การวางเพลิง arson: วางการ to abandon, relinquish, or withdraw from a work or project: วางของ to lay down an article held in the hand: วางโครงการณ์ to propose or submit a plan: วางเงิน to make a monitary deposit (as when redeeming a slave): วางใจ, วางเนื้อวางใจ to rely on a person's integrity; to place confidence in a person: วางธุระ to entrust the care of some affair or business to another: วางเบ็ด to place line and hook for fishing: วางพื้น to lay down flooring: วางยา to administer or apply a remedy: วางยาเบื่อ to administer a poison: วางแร้ว to place traps (as for rabbits): วางวาย to die: วางเสนัด *lit.* "to let go a gun, *i. e.* to shoot a gun.

ว่าง waang³ *v.* to be at leisure or at liberty *adj.* unoccupied; empty; vacant; unobstructed, clear or open (space): ที่ว่างเตียน a clearing; a space free from trees or shrubbery: ไม่ว่างคน no vacancy (as in a business concern or office): ว่างการ being without work or occupation: ว่างคน free from people going or coming; there is a vacancy on the staff: ว่างใจ free from cares or worries: ว่างตา a clear, open and unobstructed view: ว่างเปล่า empty; void; vacant; unoccupied: ว่างมือ

having nothing to do; being at leisure: ว่าง-
เว้น uncultivated; unimproved (as districts of
land): เวลาว่าง free time; unengaged:
อยู่ว่าง free from duties or engagements.

ว่าง, ว้างเวิ้ง wang[5] *adj.* spacious; expansive; wide; extensive (as vast stretches of
plains, sea or ocean).

วาจก wah-chjok[4] *P. S. n.* a speaker; an
informer; *grammar* voice: กรรตุวาจก active voice: กรรมวาจก passive voice.

วาจน wah-chja[4]-na[6] *P. S. n.* recitation;
the act of reading, teaching, or declaring
(chd. p. 541).

วาจา, วจะ, วจี wah-chjah *P. n.* word;
speech; discourse; the act of talking, speaking, or saying; language; voice (chd. p. 541):
วาจาไวหาร eloquence; oratory; vivid expressions: เสียวาจา to default in one's word or
promises.

วาจาล wah-chjarn *P. S. adj.* talkative;
loquacious; chatty (chd. p. 541).

วาจิก wah-chji[4]-gka[4] *P. S. n.* news; tidings;
information; intelligence (chd. p. 542).

วาช wah-cha[6] *P. S. n.* feathers attached
to arrows (chd. p. 546); strength; energy;
food; the Soma, the juice of a milky climbing
plant, *asclepias acida*, extracted and fermented, forming a beverage offered in libations to
the deities and drunk by the Brahmins (H. C. D.
[p. 301].
วาช see พาช p. 582.

วาฏกะ wah-dta[4]-gka[4] *P. n.* an enclosure;
a circle (chd. p. 555).

วาณิช, วาณิชก see พาณิช p. 583.

วาณิชย์ see พาณิชย์ p. 583.

วาด wat[3] *v.* to design, outline, plan, sketch,
or draft by rough sketches; to represent by
outlining: วาดเขียน to complete the details
of a design or outline (as a portrait or mural
painting): วาดจำลอง to reproduce designs

or sketches from a pattern (as by the use of
carbon paper): วาดเรือ to steer a boat by
making the stern move to the left: วาดรูป
to outline or sketch a portrait or picture.

วาต wah-dta[4] *P. n.* wind; air; wind emitted
from the body; wind or air as one of the
humours of the body.

วาตตา wat[3]-dtah *P. n.* rumour; news
(chd. p. 556).

วาตปานะ wah-dta[4]-bpah-na[6] *P. n.* a window (chd. p. 556).

วาท wah-ta[6] *P. S. n.* assertion; speech;
utterance; discourse; controversy; dispute
(S. E. D. p. 939): วาทยุทธ์ discussion, disputa-
tion, or controversy (regarding some problem).

วาทก wah-ta[6]-gka[4] *P. S. n.* a musician;
an orchestra; a player, or performer on a
musical instrument.

วาทน wah-ta[6]-na[6] *P. S. n.* the act of playing on a musical instrument; music (chd.
p. 542).

วาทย์ wat[3] *S. v.* to be spoken, pronounced
or uttered; to be sounded or played (as musical
instruments) (S. E. D. p. 940).

วาทิต wah-tit[6] *P. S. adj.* meant to be uttered, sounded or played; instrumental music
(S. E. D. p. 940).

วาทิตต์ wah-tit[6] *n.* a fife; a flute; musical
instruments in general.

วาทิน, วาที wah-tin *P. S. adj.* speaking;
saying; asserting; declaring; disputing (chd.
p. 544).

วาน wan *v.* to ask gratuitous service; to
solicit the aid of another to serve as a favour
in some capacity; to make bold to ask another
to serve as a substitute; to request, beg or
pray another to do a deed, or run an errand
as a labour of love: ช่องวาน holes in the
convex side of boat ribs to facilitate free passage of bilge water: วานขอ to ask another

as a favour to make a request (as to a third person): วานใช้ to serve another as a favour (as in time of harvesting); วานชื่นนี้ day before yesterday: วานทำ to ask another to do something as a favour: วานนี้ yesterday: ไม้วาน intermediate ribs, or additional strips placed between the ribs of native boats.

ว่านกระสือ see ไพล p. 604.

ว่านกีบแรด

wan³-gkeep⁴-raat³ n. *Angiopteris evecta* (*Marattiaceae*), a big stemless fern, found in moist tropical Africa, Asia, and eastwards toward the Pacific. In Malaya a decoction of the roots is used to arrest the discharge of blood after a miscarriage; and the pounded plant is applied for coughs. Fresh fronds are used for poulticing. Apparently, at one time the Hawaiians used to put the leaves into coconut oil to impart their scent to it (BURK. p. 159): ว่านงู, ว่านลาย, ว่านหางเสือ *Sansevieria guineensis* (*Liliaceae*), bowstring hemp, a succulent herb widely used as a medicinal plant (BURK. p. 1948): ว่านงูเหลือม, ว่านเพ็ชร์หึ่ง, ว่านหางช้าง *Grammatophyllum speciosum* (*Orchidaceae*), a big orchid found from Tenasserim throughout Malaysia to the Solomon Isles. A love philtre is made from the seeds (BURK. p. 1109): ว่านตะกร้อ, ว่านพระอาทิตย์ *Haemanthus multiflorus*, blood lily (WINIT, N. H. J. S. S. IX, 3, p. 245): ว่านธรณีสาร *Phyllanthus pulcher* (*Euphorbiaceae*), an undershrub, found from Thailand to Java; in the Peninsula it is not uncommon in inhabited parts and along stream-banks. It is much used medicinally by the Malays. A decoction may be drunk for stomach-ache. The leaves may be applied to the gums for aching teeth. A decoction is used as an eye-wash, and poultices are applied to the nose for ulceration; to the skin for boils, carbuncles, abscesses, and itch; to the abdomen for fever, and to the abdomens of children for kidney trouble (BURK. p. 1719): ว่านน้ำ *Acorus calamus* (*Araceae*), sweet flag, a marsh plant with its original home in warm, temperate Asia,

including parts of India, and possibly the neighbourhood of the Black Sea and Caspian Sea; having a creeping rhizome, which runs in the mud and gives rise to tufts of narrow iris-like leaves. The rhizome is very fragrant, containing an aromatic volatile oil, with which is associated a bitter principle and trace of alkaloids; further, there is an abundance of starch and a little tannin. The rhizome is a drug of value. Extant writings prove the knowledge and use of *A. calamus* in India as early as A. D. 600. In China it also was early used and seems to have been introduced into Malaya from China rather than from the West, as the Chinese character of the Malay name would indicate. In the sixteenth century it was in cultivation in Vienna and soon after in both France and England. The medicinal uses throughout its vast present habitat are too numerous to mention here (BURK. p. 34): ว่านมีดยับ, อีเหนียว, ช้อยนางรำ *Desmodium gangeticum* (*Leguminosae*), a slightly woody plant found throughout the tropics of the Old World, and in the West Indies; in the Peninsula it occurs down the west coast, and here and there on the east coast. In India it has a considerable reputation as a febrifuge and for catarrh; though medicinal in Malaysia it is used in a different way. In Java it is one of a group of plants used against stones in the gall-bladder, kidneys or bladder, a decoction of the leaves being given. The Malays give a decoction of the root for diarrhoea, and as a sedative to fretful children. They apply the root to the gums for tooth-ache, and the leaves to the head for head-ache. In Java it has been tried as a green manure, but among tea was of no practical use, though in rubber it ultimately formed a mat which suppressed weeds. In the Philippine Islands the stems are used for making prawn-traps (BURK. p. 793: MCM. p. 451); *D. gyrans*; see ช้อยนางรำ p. 284: ว่านสามร้อยรู, หัวร้อยรู *Hydnophytum formicarium*

(*Rubiaceae*), a woody plant, with an ant-tenanted tuber, found from the Andamans, Tenasserim, and Cochin-China to the Philippine Islands; in the Peninsula, on the coasts and in the mountains. It is said that in the Dutch Indies the stem-tuber of a *Hydnophytum* is pounded and used for poulticing for head-aches (BURK. p. 1209).

ว่านเครือ see เชือ p. 302.

วานร see พานร p. 583.

วานรินทร์ see พานรินทร์ p. 583.

วาบ warp[3] *adv.* flashing; twinkling; blinking; sparkling; scintillating (as fire-flies): ใจวาบ to have a sudden sinking, or depressed sensation (as from emotion, fright or sudden rapid descent).

วาปิต wah-bpi[4]-dta[4] *P. S. adj.* caused to be sown (S. E. D. p. 941).

วาป see บ่อ p. 472; บึง p. 483.

วาม ๑ see งาม p. 223; น่ารัก p. 449.

วาม ๒ see พาม p. 583.

วาม ๓ warm *adj.* glittering; flashing; growing brighter; sparkling; glowing (intermittantly): วามแวม flickering; flashing (dimly).

วามน wah-mon *P. n.* a dwarf; the elephant at the southern point of the compass (CHD. p. 547); an epithet of Vishnu, called after the name of one of his incarnations (H. C. D. p. 37): *adj.* dwarfish; stunted; diminutive; low in stature.

วาย ๑, วาโย wah-ya[6] *P. n.* air; wind (CHD. p. 561): วาโยธาตุ one of the four great elements of air (as hydrogen and oxygen).

วาย ๒ wai *v.* to become less abundant (as fruit going out of season); to decrease in beauty, or fade (as flowers); to become scarce or ended by being out of season; to beat,

strike or smite: วายคน a lessening of the number of people in a crowd, or of sightseers (as after a fair): วายคิด to cease thinking or worrying about: วายทรวง to beat one's chest: วายทุกข์ to alleviate a condition of sorrow: วายปราณ, วายชีพ to become gradually without breath; to die; to grow less by degrees (as a supply of goods): วายวอด to come to an end; to be finished; to be all exhausted; to die (figuratively); to be ruined (financially).

ว่าย, วะว่าย wai[3] *v.* to glide, float or be wafted along through the air in the semblance of a swimmer: ว่ายน้ำ to swim in the water.

ว้าย wai[5] *onomat.* a sound uttered from fright or fear (generally by women).

วายส wah-ya[6]-sa[4] *P. S. n.* a crow; a hawk; a falcon (CHD. p. 560).

วายุ wah-yoo[6] *P. S. n.* air; wind (CHD. p. 561); breath; the wind god Eolus (H.C.D. p. 343): วายุกูล, ไวกุณฐ์ names for Indra; Vishnu, or Vishnu's abode; *lit.* "borne by the wind": วายุบถ course or currents of the wind or storm: วายุบุตร *lit.* "son of the wind," *i. e.* the monkey king, Hanuman.

วาร warn *S. n.* any cause, means or instrument of restraint, obstruction or hindrance; a cover; a doorway; a gate; a lid; limited time (S. E. D. p. 943): วารกันยกา, วารวนิตา, วารวารี a prostitute; women of the street.

วารณ wah-ra[6]-na[6] *P.S. n.* prohibition; resistance; opposition; restraint; an elephant (S. E. D. p. 944): วารณกร an elephant's trunk.

วารวารี see ชะบา (ดอก) p. 286.

วารี, วารี wah-ri[6] *P. S. n.* water; rain; fluid; fluidity (S. E. D. p. 943): วารีครรภ impregnated with water (as clouds): วารีจร aquatic animals, fishes, crabs, shrimps, etc.: วารีช, วารีช born in, or produced while in the water; a lotus; the conch-shell: วารีชาต the conch-shell: วารีท, วารีธร holding water;

a rain cloud : วาริธานี a reservoir or water receptacle : วาริธิ a huge water-holder ; the sea or ocean : วารีบถ water communications or traffic ; a voyage, cruise or trip by water : วาริพันธนี the impounding, banking up, or confining of water : วาริพินทุ fine particles of water, as mist, fog, or spray : วาริรถ water vehicles ; ships ; boats.

วาล ๑   warn *P. S. n.* hair of the head ; hair of animals ; the hairy tail of animals (chd. p. 547) ; bristles ; see ผม p. 539 : วาลกัมพล blankets made of the hair of animals or wool : วาลธิ tail-hairs : วาลวิชนี a fan or whisk made of the tail-hairs of animals : วาลเวธี an expert archer who can shoot hitting a hair : วาลหัตถี tail-hairs of animals.

วาล ๒   wah-la[6] *n.* water (chd. p. 546).

วาลิกา, วาลกา see พาลุก p. 584.

วาว, วาววาม   wah-oh *adj.* bright ; shining ; flashing : วาวแวว twinkling ; sparkling.

ว่าว   wah-oh[3] *n.* a kite : ลมว่าว the kite wind ; the south-west monsoon : ว่าวจุฬา a star-kite : ว่าวตุ้ยตุ่ย the Jew's-harp kite. This kite with numerous tails, is built upon one main bamboo rod, with an anterior bend at the upper end. Perpendicularly in the concavity of this bend or bow, strings are tensely strung, to which strips of paper have been pasted. These vibrate in the breeze as do the reeds of an organ, producing melodious sounds ; an onomatopoeia : ว่าวปักเป้า a small diamond-shaped kite with a single long tail : ว่าวแมงดา a king-crab-shaped kite with one tail : ว่าวอีลุ้ม a diamond-shaped kite with no tail : หางว่าว the waste cut off when pages of a book or magazine are trimmed ; narrow strips of paper resembling kite tails. These may be used for scribbling notes.

วาส ๑, พาส (p. 584) wah-sa[4] *P.S. n.* an abode ; an habitation ; a residence ; state ; situation ; condition : *adj.* staying ; remaining ; abiding (S. E. D. p. 947) : วาสเคหะ, วาสาคาร bedroom ; bedchamber.

วาส ๒   wah-sa[4] *P. S. n.* a garment ; a dress ; clothes (S. E. D. p. 947).

วาส ๓   wah-sa[4] *P. S. n.* perfumery, scents (chd. p. 553).

วาสน ๑   wah-sa[4]-na[6] *P. S. n.* the state of belonging to an abode ; being fit for a dwelling ; causing to abide or dwell (S. E. D. p. 947).

วาสน ๒   wah-sa[4]-na[6] *P. S. n.* an envelope ; a covering ; a box or casket.

วาสน ๓   wah-sa[4]-na[6] *P. S. n.* the act of perfuming, fumigating, infusing, or steeping (S. E. D. p. 947).

วาสนา, พาสนา (p. 584) wat[3]-sa[4]-nah[2] *P. S. n.* impressions remaining in the mind from past good or evil actions and producing pleasure or pain (chd. p. 551) ; the present consciousness of past perceptions ; knowledge derived from memory, fancy or imagination (S. E. D. p. 947) ; the faculty of forming mental images.

วาสิ   wah-si[4] *P. n.* the razor, a part of the equipment of a Buddhist priest, as he is obliged to keep his head shaven (chd. p. 552) ; see มีด p. 652 ; ขวาน p. 146.

วาสุกร, วาสุกี see พาสุกรี p. 584.

วาห see พาห p. 584.

วาหนะ see พาหนะ p. 584.

วาหิน, วาห์   wah-hin[2] *n.* a chariot ; a car a cart ; a carriage ; a waggon or van.

วาหินี   wah-hi[4]-nee *P. S. n.* an army ; a host or body of forces (as elephants, cars, horses and infantry) ; a river ; a channel (S. E. D. p. 949).

วาฬ   wah-la[6] *P. n.* a snake ; beasts of prey (as tigers or bears) ; a whale : *adj.* savage, fierce, wild ; see พาฬ p. 585 : วาฬมิค dangerous beasts, or creatures of prey.

วิ   wi[6] not ; used to express negation, incompleteness or opposition ; equivalent to "minus,". "un," "in," "dis"; see พฤ p. 570 : วิบุตร without children; childless : วิมรรค incorrect; erring; straying from the normal course : วิสม unbecoming; unmatched; unequal.

วิกขัมภ์ wik⁶-kum² *P. n.* the diameter.

วิกกัย (การขาย) wik⁶-gkai *P. n.* a sale of goods (chd. p. 572).

วิกจ wi⁶-gka⁴-chja⁴ *P. adj.* blossoming; blooming; budding (chd. p. 571).

วิกรม wi⁶-gkrom *S. n.* step; stride; gait; pace (S. E. D. p. 955).

วิกรัย wi⁶-gkrai *S. n.* a sale; selling; vending (S. E. D. p. 956).

วิกล wi⁶-gkon *adj.* maimed; crippled; impaired; imperfect; deficient in, or destitute of; deprived of a part, limb or member; agitated; confused; exhausted (S. E. D. p. 953); see พิกล p. 585 : วิกลจริต deprived of sanity; insane; mad; bereft of reason; deranged.

วิกฤต, วิกัต wi⁶-gkrit⁴ *S. n.* a condition of change of any kind, as of purpose, mind or form : *adj.* transformed; changed; altered; deformed; disfigured; unnatural (S.E.D. p. 954).

วิกฤติ wi⁶-gkrit⁴ *S. n.* change; alteration; modification; transformation (S. E. D. p. 954).

วิกสิต, พิกสิต wi⁶-gka⁴-sit⁴ *P. S. adj.* caused to expand; blooming; opened; blown; spreading (S. E. D. p. 954).

วิกัติ wi⁶-gkut⁴ *P. n.* sort; kind; altered form; product (chd. p. 572); article; implement; pattern; model; form; the act of making, arranging or preparing : ทันตวิกัติ ivory products; articles made of ivory : บุปผวิกัติ methods or manner of arranging or preparing flowers : วิกัติกรรม *gram.* substantives.

วิกัปปิต wi⁶-gkup⁴-bpi⁴-dta⁴ *P. v.* to apportion; to assign; to allot; to allocate (chd. p. 572) : วิกัปปิตจีวร robes entrusted to the care of another in accordance with the ethics of the Buddhist religion (as a monk is not allowed to have more than one set of three robes at one time. If perchance he acquires one or two pieces by way of a gift he is not permitted to retain them more than ten days, thus he must give them over to the care of another).

วิกัลป์ wi⁶-gkup⁴ *S. n.* error; ignorance; some questionable condition; doubt; mistake : วิกัลปสันธาน *gram.* a conjunction (or, either, otherwise, etc.).

วิการ see พิการ p. 585.

วิกาล wi⁶-gkarn *P. n.* time that is improper, wrong or forbidden; the afternoon; evening (chd. p. 571) : วิกาลโภชน์ the taking of food at a wrong time (said of a meal taken by a Buddhist priest at any but the appointed time, which is between sunrise and noon).

วิเกษป wik⁶-sep⁴ *S. n.* the act of scattering, throwing away or about; dispersion; moving about, or to and fro (S. E. D. p. 956).

วิคคหะ wik⁶-ka⁶-ha⁴ *P. n.* analysis; *gram.* the resolution or analyzing of a word into its component parts.

วิเคราะห์ see พิเคราะห์ p. 585.

วิฆน wik⁶-na⁶ *S. n.* a breaker; a destroyer; an obstacle, impediment, hindrance or opposition (S. E. D. p. 957); see พิฆน์ p. 585.

วิฆเนศ, วิฆเนศวร see พิฆเนศ p. 586.

วิฆาต wi⁶-kah-dta⁴ *P. S. v.* to cause the death of : *n.* a blow; a stroke; destruction; ruin; the act of killing or slaughtering (S. E. D. p. 957); see พิฆาต p. 586.

วิฆาส wi⁶-kah-sa⁴ *P. n.* remnants or fragments of food; scraps (chd. p. 569); see เดน p. 334.

วิ้ง wing *v.* to revolve; to whirl; to rotate; to gyrate : วิ้งเวียน giddy; dizzy; lightheaded.

วิ่ง   wing[3] *v.* to run; to speed: วิ่งตาม to follow after on a run; to run after: วิ่ง-เต้น to run or dance at the bidding of another; to assume the leadership in some scheme or project; to exert oneself on behalf of another: วิ่งเปี้ยว a relay race: วิ่งม้า to race horses: วิ่งราว to snatch and run: วิ่งเล่น, วิ่งระแบง to run and play (as children):   วิ่งไล่ to chase; to pursue; to run after: วิ่งวัว to race bullocks harnessed to light carts (two to a cart); to arrange racing matches between men or boys: วิ่งหนี to flee, escape or run away.

วิ่งวอน   wing-worn *v.* to implore; to entreat; to beseech; to supplicate; to pray or beg (with importunity).

วิจฉิก see พฤศจิก p. 571.

วิจรณ   wi[6]-chja[4]-ra[6]-na[6] *P. v.* to walk, wander, or go about (chd. p. 566); see เที่ยว p. 426.

วิจล, พิจล   wi[6]-chja[4]-la[6] *S. adj.* swaying; oscillating; swinging; shaking; unsteady; perplexed; purturbed (S. E. D. p. 958).

วิจักขณ์, วิจักษณ์   wi[6]-chja[4]-la[6] *P. S. adj.* knowing; wise; discerning; sensible; skillful (chd. p. 566).

วิจัย   wi[6]-chjai *P. S. n.* research; investigation; examination (chd. p. 566); see พิจย p 586.

วิจาร, วิจารณ์   wi[6]-chjan *P. S. n.* investigation; examination; consideration; reflection; research (chd. p. 566); see พิจาร p. 586.

วิจารก   wi[6]-chjah-rok[6] *P. n.* a judge; one who investigates, decides or adjudicates (in matters of law) (chd. p. 566).

วิจิกิจฉา   wi[6]-chji[4]-gkit[4]-chah[2] *P. n.* doubt; uncertainty; distrust (chd. p. 567).

วิจิต   wi[6]-chjit[4] *S. v.* to perceive; to discern; to understand (S. E. D. p. 959); see พิจิต p. 586.

วิจิตร see พิจิตร p. 586.

วิจิน   wi[6]-chjin *P. v.* to seek; to search; to investigate; to examine; to gather; to collect; to select (chd. p. 567).

วิชชา, วิชา (present spelling) wit[6]-chah *P. n.* knowledge; learning; scholarship; science; wisdom (chd. p. 571):   วิชชาธร an expert in occult science.

วิชชุ, วิชชุตา, วิชชุลลดา   wit[6]-choo[6] *P. n.* a flash of lightning; chain, zigzag or forked lightning (chd. p. 571).

วิชญ   wit[6]-ya[6] *S. n.* a sage; a philosopher; a scientist: *adj.* knowing; wise; clever; skillful (S. E. D. p. 961).

วิชน   wi[6]-cha[6]-na[6] *P. S. adj.* lonely; deserted; solitary; desolate (chd. p. 570).

วิชย, วิชัย   wi[6]-cha[6]-ya[6] *P. S. n.* victory; conquest; triumph (chd. p. 571):   วิชยฤกษ์ an auspicious hour or time for victory.

วิชิต   wi[6]-chit[6] *P. S. v.* to conquer; to master; to triumph over (chd. p. 571).

วิญญัตติ   win-yat[6]-dti[4] *P. n.* information; intimation of a want; the act of asking (chd. p. 579).

วิญญาณ   win-yarn *P. n.* intelligence; knowledge; conciousness; thought; mind; spirit (chd. p. 576).

วิญญู   win-yoo *P. n.* a sage; a philosophy: *adj.* intelligent; wise; learned; discreet (chd. p. 579):   วิญญูชน a sage; a wise, intelligent person; those attaining the age of normal understanding: วิญญูภาพ the condition of becoming of age, or attaining the state of normal understanding.

วิฑูรย์ see ไพฑูรย์ p. 603.

วิณหุ see วิษณุ p. 779.

วิด   wit[6] *v.* to dip; to shovel; to ladle, bale or draw off (as water by some appliance); see ตัก p. 358:   วิดให้แห้ง to empty by dipping [out.

วิดัสดี see วิทัตถิ p. 774.

วิตก   wi[6]-dtok[4] *n.* anxiety for; uneasiness regarding; reflection or thoughts of; solicitous consideration for (Ala. p. 195); see ตรึก p. 345; พิตรก p. 586: ทรงพระวิตก court language for วิตก: วิตกจริต being in the habit of, or given to anxious fears regarding.

วิตต์   wit[6] *P. S. adj.* known; understood; celebrated; notorious; famous (S. E. D. p. 963).

วิตถาร   wit[6]-tarn[2] *P. adj.* lengthy; extensive; extended; amplified; going too much into details.

วิถี   see พิถี p. 586: บาทวิถี a foot-path, or side-walk.

วิทธ   wit[6]-ta[6] *P. S. adj.* pierced; punctured; perforated; struck; hit; hurt; wounded (chd. p. 568: Ala. p. 571).

วิทธังส, วิธวงส์   wit[6]-tung-sa[4] *P. v.* to crush; to destroy; to overthrow; to scatter; to disperse: *n.* demolition (chd. p. 568).

วิทธังสนะ   wit[6]-tung-sa[4]-na[6] *P. n.* destruction; demolition; annihilation; a state of ruin (chd. p. 568).

วิทยา   wit[6]-ta[6]-yah *S. n.* knowledge; science; learning; philosophy (S. E. D. p. 963): วิทยา-กร a learned person; one who gives, or causes the dissemination of knowledge or science: วิทยาคาร a school; a place of learning: วิทยา-ทาน the instruction given in a school; the imparting of knowledge: วิทยาทายาท the inheritor of knowledge: วิทยาธรี a woman scientist: วิทยาผล the fruits, gain, or profits accruing from learning: วิทยาลาภ any acquirements or attainments resulting from learning: วิทยาลัย the abode or seat of learning; a school; a college: วิทยาศาสตร์ science.

วิทยุต   wit[6]-ta[6]-yoot[6] *S. n.* radio; a ray; a flash of lightning or spark of electricity (S.E.D. p. 966).

วิทยุโทรเลข   wit[6]-ta[6]-yoo[6]-toh-ra[6]-lek[3] *n.* wireless telegraph.

วิทวัส   wit[6]-ta[6]-wat[6] *S. n.* one who is learned, intelligent, wise, mindful of, familiar with, or skilled in (S. E. D. p. 964).

วิทัตถิ, วิดัสดี   wi[6]-tut[6]-ti[4] *P. n.* a unit of measurement equal to a span of twelve *angula* (chd. p. 568).

วิทารณ์   wi[6]-tarn *P. S. n.* the act of rending (chd. p. 567); breaking; splitting; tearing asunder; rupture; cutting (S. E. D. p. 966).

วิทิต   wi[6]-tit[6] *P. S. v.* to know; to ascertain (chd. p. 568): *n.* a learned or clever person; a philosopher: *adj.* given to learning, or liking knowledge.

วิทุร   wi[6]-too[6]-ra[6] *P. S. adj.* knowing; wise; intelligent; skilled (s. E. D. p. 963); see พิทูระ p. 587.

วิทู   wi[6]-too *P. adj.* knowing; skilled; wise [(chd. p. 568).

วิทูร   wi[6]-too-ra[6] *P. S. adj.* very remote or distant; far removed; not attainable (S. E. D. p. 699): วิทูรัช *lit.* "born in a distant place," *i. e.* a cat's-eye gem.

วิเทวย   wi[6]-ta[6]-wet[3] *S. adj.* hatred; dislike; enmity (S. E. D. p. 967).

วิเทศ   wi[6]-tet[3] *S. n.* a foreign country; another land from that of one's birth; a foreigner; an alien (S.E.D. p. 966): วิเทศคมน์ the going to a foreign country: วิเทศช being of, or coming from a foreign country (implying goods or merchandise): วิเทศวาส the condition of dwelling in a foreign country.

วิเทหะ   wi[6]-tay-ha[4] *P. S. n.* an ancient country of India of which the capital was Mithila, corresponding with the modern Tirhut or North Bihar; name of one of the sixteen famous towns of India: *adj.* bodiless; incorporeal; deceased (S. E. D. p. 966).

วิธ   wi[6]-ta[6] *P. n.* kind; sort; part; form (chd. p. 568): อเนกวิธ many kinds; different sorts; see ชะนิด p. 285.

                                 [p. 568).

วิธวา   wit[6]-ta[6]-wah *P. S. n.* a widow (chd.

วิธา wi[6]-tah *P. S. n.* division; part; sort; form; kind; portion; manner (S. E. D. p. 967).

วิธาน see พิธาน p. 587.

วิธี wi[6]-tee *n.* method; rule; formula; injunction; ordinance; statute; precept; law; ceremony (S. E. D. p. 968): วิธีจ่ายเงินเดือน-โดยรับสินค้าจากร้านของผู้จ้างแทนเงินสด the truckage system of making payments for salary due: วิธีพิจารณา the procedure in an investigation.

วิธุร wi[6]-too[6]-ra[6] *P. S. adj.* bereft; bereaved; alone; separated from, or destitute of; miserable; distressed; depressed; dejected (S. E. D. p. 968).

วิธู wi[6]-too *n.* the moon (chd. p. 568).

วิธูปนะ wi[6]-too-bpa[4]-na[6] *n.* a fan; the act of fanning (chd. p. 568).

วิ่น win[3] *v.* to become worn out, ragged and frayed; see ฉีก p. 270; ขาด p. 154.

วินัย, วินย wi[6]-nai *P. S. n.* the book of discipline (for monks); training; discipline; control; propriety of conduct; decency; modesty; the condition of putting away; avoidance; subduing (S.E.D. p. 971); see พินัย p. 587: พระวินัย name of the first portion of the Traipidok or Buddhist scriptures, consisting of a series of instructions for the ecclesiastical code or common law by which the Buddhist monks are governed (chd. p. 575): วินัยกรรม adhering to, or living by the code of ethics: วินัยธร one who upholds the ecclesiastical code of ethics, or laws of the Buddhist religion; one versed in these rules: วินัยธรรม taking the code of ethics as a means of attaining righteousness and truth.

วินาที wi[6]-nah-tee *n.* a second (of time).

วินายก wi[6]-nah-yok[6] *P. S. n.* a spiritual leader or teacher; the Buddha (chd. p. 575).

วินาศ wi[6]-nat[3] *S. n.* utter loss; annihilation; perdition; destruction; removal; decay; death (S. E. D. p. 969); see พินาศ p. 587.

วินิจ see พิจาร p. 586; พินิจ p. 587.

วินิจฉัย wi[6]-nit[6]-chai[2] *P. n.* investigation; examination; ascertainment; decision; judgement (chd. p. 576); see พินิศจัย p. 587: ศาลา-วินิจฉัย a courthouse or tribunal.

วินิต, วินีต see พินิต p. 587.

วินิบาต wi[6]-ni[6]-bat[4] *P. n.* the state of punishment or suffering; destruction; ruin; a state of trouble or misfortune (chd. p. 576).

วินีตวัตถุ wi[6]-nee-dta[4]-wat[6]-too[4] *n.* a leading, or introductory article; the preface.

วิเนต wi[6]-net[3] *P. v.* to instruct; to educate; to train (chd. p. 576); see พิเนต p. 587.

วิโนทก wi[6]-noh-tok[6] *P. n.* one who dispells, dissipates or causes to vanish (chd. p. 579); see บรรเทา p. 469.

วิบัติ wi[6]-bat[4] *n.* adversity; misfortune; disaster; ruin; destruction; end; agony; torment (S. E. D. p. 973): วิบัติจากอุปาสก the condition of calamity or ruin by forsaking or abandoning one's religious principles.

วิบาก wi[6]-bak[4] *P. S. n.* retribution; result; product; see พิบาก p. 587: ผลวิบาก retribution as a result of sins: มหาวิบาก great judgements or severe torments for evil deeds: วิบากกรรม torments resulting from sins: วิ-บากแก่เจ้า woe be to you (a curse).

วิบุล, วิบุลย์, วิบูลย์ wi[6]-boon *P. S. adj.* large; great; broad; extensive; numerous; important (S. E. D. p. 974); see พิบูล p. 588.

วิปปวาส wip[6]-bpa[4]-wat[3] *P. n.* absence, separation, or the act of withdrawing away from, or living in another place (chd. p. 581).

วิประการ wi[6]-bpra[4]-gkan *S. n.* treatment showing disrespect; revenge; retaliation (S.E.D. p. 975).

วิประติสาร wi[6]-bpra[4]-dti[4]-san[2] *S. n.* remorse; regret; repentance; a sense of guilt, sorrow, or grief (S. E. D. p. 975).

วิประโยค   wi[6]-bpra[4]-yoke[3] *S. n.* disjunction ; separation ; dissociation ; disagreement ; dispute (S. E. D. p. 975).

วิประลาป   wi[6]-bpra[4]-lap[3] *S. n.* an altercation ; the act of brawling, wrangling, arguing, bewailing, or complaining (chd. p. 580).

วิปริต see พิปริต p. 588 : วิปริตผิดเพศ a monstrous being ; a monstrosity.

วิปลาส   wi[6]-bpa[4]-lat[3] *adj.* abnormal ; exceptional ; irregular ; unnatural ; unusual ; extraordinary ; see พิปลาส p. 588 : เกิดการวิปลาส something extraordinary has occurred : สัญญาวิปลาส an abnormal mentality.

วิปักษ์   wi[6]-bpak[4] *S. n.* an opponent ; an adversary ; an enemy ; a disputant ; one on the opposing side ; *gram.* an exception.

วิบัสสนา, พิบัสสนา   wi[6]-bpat[4]-sa[4]-nah[2] *P. n.* spiritual insight ; seeing clearly ; thorough investigation (Ala. p. 323) ; contemplation on the results of good and evil : นั่งวิบัสสนา the sitting in contemplation.

วิพุธ   wi[6]-poot[6] *P. S. n.* a learned or wise man ; a deva ; a teacher : *adj.* wise ; learned ; educated.

วิภว, พิภพ   wi[6]-pa[6]-wa[6] *P. S. n.* power ; prosperity ; majesty ; splendour ; property (chd. p. 566).

วิภังค์   wi[6]-pang *P. n.* division ; distinction ; determination ; explanation (chd. p. 565).

วิภัช, วิภาช   wi[6]-pat[6] *P. S. v.* to divide ; to distribute ; to apportion ; to assign ; to separate, cut or parcel out.

วิภัตติ   wi[6]-pat[6]-dti[4] *P. n. gram.* declension of nouns ; inflection of verbs ; conjugation (chd. p. 565).

วิภา   wi[6]-pah *P. S. adj.* shining ; bright ; lustrous ; splendid ; beautiful (S. E. D. p. 977).

วิภาค   wi[6]-pak[3] *P. S. n.* distribution ; apportionment ; partition ; share ; portion ; sec-

tion ; a constituent part of anything (S. E. D. p. 977).

วิภาวรี   wi[6]-pah-wa[6]-ree *P. n.* night (chd. [p. 566).

วิภาษ   wi[6]-pat[3] *S. v.* to be able to speak in various languages ; to be a linguist (S. E. D. p. 977).

วิภาส   wi[6]-pat[3] *S. v.* to shine brightly or pleasingly (S. E. D. p. 978).

วิภู   wi[6]-poo *S. n.* a lord ; a ruler ; a sovereign ; a king ; a chief : *adj.* all-pervading ; far-extending ; omnipresent ; able, or capable of (S. E. D. p. 978).

วิภูษณะ, วิภูสนะ see พฤฒูษณ p. 570.

วิภูษิต see พฤฒูษิต p. 571.

วิมติ, วิมัติ   wi[6]-ma[6]-dtee *n.* a difference of opinion ; a disagreement about ; an aversion ; dislike ; doubt ; uncertainty (S. E. D. p. 979).

วิมน   wi[6]-mon *P. adj.* perplexed ; distressed (chd. p. 574).

วิมล   wi[6]-mon *P. S. adj.* untainted ; unsullied (chd. p. 979) ; see พิมล p. 588 : วิมลโฉม flawlessly beautiful.

วิมังสา   wi[6]-mang-sah[2] *P. n.* investigation ; examination ; trial (chd. p. 573).

วิมาน see พิมาน p. 589 : วิมานทอง a golden abode : วิมานสวรรค์ a heavenly abode or mansion in the skies.

วิมุข see พิมุข p. 589.

วิมุตต์   wi[6]-moot[6] *P. adj.* released ; emancipated ; freed ; saved (chd. p. 574).

วิมุตติ   wi[6]-moot[6]-dti[4] *P. n.* release, emancipation, freedom, liberation (from existence) ; Nirvana (chd. p. 574).

วิโมกข์ see พิโมกข์ p. 589.

วิเยน   wi[6]-yen *Jav. n.* an eunuch.

วิโยค see พิโยค p. 589.

วิร, วีร wi⁶-ra⁶ *n.* a person who is brave, strong, mighty or valiant; a hero; a warrior; heroism.

วิรต, วิรัต wi⁶-rot⁶ *P.S. v.* to abstain, refrain or desist (chd. p. 581): *adj.* stopped; ceased; ended (S. E. D. p. 982).

วิรมณะ wi⁶-rom-ma⁶-na⁶ *P.S. adj.* abstaining; desisting (chd. p. 581).

วิรช wi⁶-rat⁶ *P.S. adj.* free from corruption or human passion; pure; spotless; clean (chd. p. 581)

วิรัติ wi⁶-rat⁶ *P.S. n.* abstinence; temperance; self-denial (chd. p. 587).

วิราค wi⁶-rah-ka⁶ *P.S. n.* a state of neutrality or indifference; perfect equanimity (Ala. p. 168); absence of desire or human passion (S. E. D. p. 952).

วิริยะ, เวียร see พิริยะ p. 589.

วิรุธ see พิรุธ p. 589.

วิรุพห์ see พิรุพห์ p. 589.

วิรุพหก see พิรุพห์ p. 589.

วิรุฒ wi⁶-root³ *S. adj.* sprouted; budded; grown; formed; produced; born; arisen; ascended (S. E. D. p. 984).

วิรุพหิ wi⁶-roon-hi⁴ *P. n.* growth; increase; enlargement; expansion (chd. p. 582).

วิรูป wi-⁶roop³ *P.S. adj.* deformed; misshapen; ugly; monstrous; un-natural; altered; changed; different (S. E. D. p. 683).

วิรูบักข์, วิรูปากษ์ wi⁶-roo-bpak⁴ *P. n.* name of the regent of the West and chief of the Nagas (chd. p. 582).

วิเรก wi⁶-rake³ *P.S. n.* a cathartic; a purging evacuation of the bowels (chd. p. 582).

วิเรนทร์, พิเรนทร์ see พิร p. 589.

วิโรค wi⁶-roke³ *P. adj.* undiseased.

วิโรจ wi⁶-rote³ *P. S. v.* to shine; to be brilliant or splendid; to be eminent or conspicuous (chd. p. 582).

วิโรจน์ wi⁶-rote³ *P. S. adj.* illuminating; brightening; shedding, shining, or glowing with light.

วิโรธ, วิโรธน์ see พิโรธ p. 589.

วิลย, วิลัย wi⁶-la⁶-ya⁶ *P. S. n.* destruction; dissolution; termination; death (S. E. D. p. 985).

วิลาต (เหล็ก) wi⁶-lat³ *n.* thin tin sheets.

วิลาป see พิลาป p. 589.

วิลาวัณย์ wi⁶-lah-wan *adj.* beautiful; charming; extremely beautiful; seductive.

วิลาส wi⁶-late³ *P. S. n.* sport; play; pastime; diversion; charm; dalliance (S.E.D. p. 985).

วิลิปดา wi⁶-lip⁶-dah *n.* one second.

วิเลป wi⁶-lep³ *P. S. n.* ointments; unguents; mortar; plaster (S. E. D. p. 985).

วิเลปนะ wi⁶-lay-bpa⁴-na⁶ *P. S. n.* toilet perfumes; scented ointments (S. E. D. p. 895).

วิโลก wi⁶-loke³ *P. S. v.* to look at or upon; to regard, examine, study or test (S.E.D. p. 986).

วิโลกนะ wi⁶-loh-gka⁴-na⁶ *S. n.* the act of looking, seeing, regarding, contemplating, finding out, or perceiving (S. E. D. p. 986).

วิโลจนะ wi⁶-loh-chja⁴-na⁶ *S. n.* the eye; sight (chd. p. 573).

วิโลม wi⁶-lom *P. S. adj.* against the hair or grain; turned the wrong way; reversed contrary to the usual or proper course; inverted (S. E. D. p. 986).

วิไล see พิไล p. 590.

วิวร wi⁶-wa⁶-ra⁶ *P. S. n.* a fissure; a hole; a chasm; a gap; a slit; a cleft; a hollow; a breach; a fault; a flaw; a vulnerable or weak point (S. E. D. p. 988).

วิวรณ์   wi[6]-won *P. S. n.* the act of uncovering, spreading out, laying bare or opening; exposition; explanation; description; interpretation; translation (S. E. D. p. 988).

วิวัฏฏ์   wi[6]-wat[6] *P. n.* revolution; a condition of turning around, or beginning again (chd. p. 589).

วิวัฑฒน์, วิวัฒน์   wi[3]-wat[6] *P. n.* prosperity; progress; see เจริญ p. 257.

วิวาท   wi[6]-wat[3] *P. n.* a dispute; a quarrel; a contention; a litigation (chd. p. 588).

วิวาหะ   wi[6]-wah-ha[4] *P. n.* nuptials; a marriage; a wedding; a leading away of the bride from her father's house.

วิวิตต์   wi[6]-wit[6] *P. v.* to separate oneself; to retire from.

วิวิธ   wi[6]-wit[6]-ta[6] *P. S. adj.* of various sorts; multifold; multiform; divers (S. E. D. p. 988).

วิเวก   wi[6]-wake[3] *P. n.* separation; solitude; seclusion; quietness (chd. p. 589): วิเวกวังเวง retirement from anxiety; a condition of isolation or estrangement from the world.

วิศว   wit[6]-sa[4]-wa[6] *P. S. adj.* all; every; whole; total; entire; universal; all-pervading or all-containing; omnipresent (S. E. D. p. 992): วิศวกรรก the creator of the universe: วิศวจักษ์, วิศวจักษุ an eye for all things: วิศวจันทร์ all-radiant; all-brilliant: วิศวชน all men; all mankind: วิศวชิต all-subduing; all-conquering: วิศวธร preserving all things: วิศววิท knowing everything; universal knowledge: วิศวศุจิ all-enlightening: วิศวสมภพ one from whom all things arise.

วิศวกรรม   wit[6]-sa[4]-wa[6]-gkum *n.* the Omnificent. This name seems to have been originally an epithet of any powerful god, as of Indra and Surya, but in course of time it came to designate a personification of the creative power. In this character he was the great architect of the universe, general artificer of the gods and maker of their weapons (H. C. D. p. 363): *adj.* accomplishing everything; all-working (S. E. D. p. 994); see พิศวกรรม p. 590.

วิศวามิตร   wi[6]-sa[4]-wah-mit[6] *n. lit.* "a universal friend," *i. e.* a celebrated sage, who was born a Kshatriya, but by intense austerities raised himself to the Brahmin caste, and became one of the seven great Rishis (H. C. D. [p. 364].

วิศวาส   see พิศวาส p. 590.

วิศัลย์   wi[6]-san[2] *P. S. adj.* painless; free from thorns, darts, or any extraneous substance in the body (S. E. D. p. 989).

วิศาข, วิศาขา, วิสาข, วิสาขา   wi[6]-sah[2]-ka[4] *P. S. n.* name of the sixteenth lunar asterism; name of a celebrated female saint, a contemporary and disciple of the Buddha (chd. p. 583); the sixth month of the Thai lunar year: วิศาขบูชา, วิสาขบูชา the festival of offerings in commemoration of the Birth, Enlightenment and Death of the Buddha. It is the occasion of ceremonies which are kept up for three successive days, beginning on the day before the full moon of the sixth Thai lunation. The real day of observance is the fifteenth of the waxing or full moon day of the sixth Thai [lunation.

วิศาล   see พิศาล p. 590.

วิศิษฏ์   wi[6]-sit[4] *P. S. adj.* superior; excellent; chief; best (S. E. D. p. 990).

วิเศษ   see พิเศษ p. 590.

วิเศษณ์   wi[6]-set[4] *S. n. gram.* predicate: *adj.* specifying; qualifying; distinctive; discriminative (S. E. D. p. 991).

วิโศธน์   wi[6]-sote[4] *S. n.* the act of washing away, cleansing, purging, or purifying (S. E. D. p. 991).

วิษกัมภ์   wit[6]-sa[4]-gkam *P. S. n.* the diameter of a circle; the bolt or bar of a door; the supporting beam or pillar of a house (S. E. D. p. 998).

วิษณุ, วิณหุ see พิษณุ p. 590 : วิษณุโคล the equator (S. E. D. p. 999): วิษณุบท *lit.* "footmark of Vishnu," *i. e.* the sky; the zenith: วิษณุพาหนะ, วิษณุพาหยะ *lit.* "Vishnu's vehicle," *i. e.* the Garuda: วิษณุภักดี the worship of Vishnu: วิษณุมหิมา the glory or majesty of Vishnu: วิษณุรถ Vishnu's chariot: วิษณุวัลลภ *lit.* "one beloved by Vishnu," *i. e.* Lakshmi, the wife of Vishnu and mother of Kama, the goddess of Fortune (H. C. D. p. 176).

วิษธร wi⁶-sa⁴-taun *P. n.* a snake (chd. p. 582).

วีษาณ wi⁶-san² *P. S. n.* a horn; the horn of any animal; the tusk of an elephant (S. E. D. p. 997).

วิสม wi⁶-sa⁴-ma⁶ *P. S. adj.* unbecoming; unequal; irregular; unjust; lawless; wicked (chd. p. 583).

วิสมย, วิสมัย see พิสมัย p. 591.

วิสย, วิสัย, วิษัย wi⁶-sa⁴-ya⁶ *P. S. n.* district; region; country; realm; domain; sphere; scope; an object of the senses (as colour, form, odour and sound) (chd. p. 584); see พิษัย p. 591: รูปวิษัย qualities of the four senses.

วิสรรชนีย์ wi⁶-san²-cha⁶-nee *S. n.* a grammatical symbol indicating a short vowel, thus "ะ".

วิสฤต wit⁶-sa⁴-rit⁶ *adj.* strewn, covered, or furnished with; out-stretched; expanded; displayed; spread; diffused (S. E. D. p. 1001).

วิสวระ wit⁶-sa⁴-wa⁶-ra⁶ *adj.* discordant; pronounced with a wrong accent (S. E. D. p. 953).

วิสสาสะ wit⁶-sah²-sa⁴ *P. S. v.* to converse in a friendly, intimate way: *n.* intimacy; confidence; familiarity; sincerity (chd. p. 585).

วิสสุต, วิศรุต wit⁶-soot⁴ *P. n.* one who is famous (chd. p. 586): *adj.* renowned; illustrious; eminent; famous; celebrated.

วิสัชชนา wi⁶-sat⁴-cha⁶-nah *P. n.* an answer; a reply; an explanation; an interpreta-

tion; an elucidation (chd. p. 585): ปุจฉาวิสัชชนา questions and answers.

วิสัญญี see พิสัญญี p. 591: วิสัญญีภาพ the condition of being anaesthetized.

วิสัตติกา wi⁶-sat⁴-dti⁴-gkah *P. n.* desire; lust (chd. p. 583).

วิสาข, วิสาขา, วิสาขบูชา see วิศาข p. 778.

วิสารท wi⁶-sah²-ra⁶-ta⁶ *S. adj.* bold; confident; ready; self-possessed; wise; skilled (chd. p. 583).

วิสาล see พิศาล p. 590.

วิสุทธ์ see พิศุทธ์ p. 590.

วิหค, วิหงค์, เวหังค์ see พิหค p. 591.

วิหัปปติ see พฤหัศบดี p. 571.

วิหายสะ wi⁶-hah²-ya⁶-sa⁴ *n.* an open space; sky; air; atmosphere (S. E. D. p. 1003).

วิหาร wi⁶-han² *n.* a sanctuary; an abbey; a church edifice; a place for preaching, meditation, and prayer (S. E. D. p. 1003); see พิหาร p. 591.

วิหิงส, วิหิงสา, วิเหสา wi⁶-hing²-sa⁴ *P. adj.* hurting; injuring; cruel (chd. p. 570).

วิฬาร see พิฬาร p. 591.

วี๋ see โบก p. 491; แกว่ง p. 130.

วีจิ, วีจิ wee-chji⁴ *P. S. n.* a wave; billows; breakers (S. E. D. p. 958).

วีชนี, เพียชนี wee-cha⁶-nee *P. S. n.* a fan; the royal fan, an emblem of royalty (chd. p. 570); see พัชนี p. 580.

วีณา see พิณ p. 586.

วีต wee-dta⁴ *P. adj.* immune from; free from; devoid of (chd. p. 587): วีตโลภ exempt from covetousness.

วี๋วัน wee³-wan *n.* a day.

วี๋แวว wee³-waa-oh *n.* the condition of appearing or becoming manifest, and disappearing quickly (as an apparition or dream); an appearance that is quick, brief, sudden and transient.

วิส wee-sa[4] *P. adj.* twenty (chd. p. 583).

วุ้ง woong[5] *adj.* bent; curved; sinuous; winding; rounding; detouring; see คุ้ง p. 204 : ทางวุ้งเวิ้ง, เป็นคุ้งเวิ้ง a serpentine way or road : เป็นวุ้งเป็นคุ้ง in a tortuous winding manner (as a sinus or crooked canal).

วุฏฐิ woot[6]-ti[4] *P. n.* rain (chd. p. 591).

วุฑฒน์, วุฒ, วุทธ์ woot[6] *P. v.* to grow; to increase; to multiply; to prosper (chd. p. 543).

วุฑฒิ, วุฒิ, วุทธิ์ woot[6]-ti[4] *P. n.* increase; success; growth; prosperity; advantage; riches (chd. p. 590).

วุตต์ woot[6] *P. adj.* sown (as grain or seed-[ling rice).

วุตติ woot[6]-dti[4] *n.* conduct; behaviour; style; manner; business; profession; livelihood; *poetry* measure; rhythm; metre (chd. p. 591).

วุติ woo[6]-dti[4] *n.* an enclosure; a fence; a barrier; a hedge (chd. p. 591).

วุ่น woon[3] *v.* to be busily engaged or overburdened with various affairs; to be troubled, anxious or disturbed about : เกิดวุ่นวาย a disturbance has occurred or arisen : ความวุ่นวาย trouble; tumult; disturbance; trepidation : วุ่นไป to fuss, fidget and be in a stew about affairs : วุ่นวายใจ mentally perturbed : วุ่นวาย to be agitated, restless, or disturbed.

วุ้น woon[5] *n.* jelly (made of cooked lichens or seaweed) : วุ้นซอย boiled jelly that is allowed to cool and then sliced into thin pieces : วุ้นเส้น shredded jelly; vermicelli : วุ้นหวาน sweetened jelly : วุ้นแห้ง jelly, sweetened and allowed to cool; candied jelly.

วุบ woop[6] *v.* to flash, blaze forth, or appear for an instant (as a burst of gun-powder); to sparkle, flash or shine for a few seconds and then be extinguished : ใจวุบวาบ a mental condition characterized by sudden fits of anger or excitement, and followed by tranquility.

วุย woo-ie[5] *onomat.* from the sound of fright, pain or call for help.

วูส see พฤษ p. 571.

วูดวาด woot[3]-wat[3] *onomat.* the sound of a tempestuous wind blowing in gusts.

วูบ woop[3] *v.* to pass like a shot (as a hawk swooping down); to disappear instantly (as a puff of ignited powder) : ไฟลุกวูบวาบ, วูบวาบ flaming up in violent sheets of fire : หนาวร้อนวูบวาบ glowing in periods of heat and cold.

เวค way-ka[6] *P. S. n.* the impulse of the mind; impetus; speed; emotion; passion (chd. p. 562).

เว็จ, เว็จจ์ wet[6] *n.* excrement; refuse; feces; fecal matter : เว็จจกุฎี a lavatory; a water-closet; เว็จ an abbreviated form : เว็จจมรรค the anus.

เวชช์, ไวทย์ wet[3] *P. n.* a physician; a doctor; a surgeon : เวชกรรม the treatment of diseases : เวชภัณฑ์ medical supplies : เวชศาสตร์ the science of medicine; scientific books or treatises on the practice of medicine.

เวชยันต์ way-cha[6]-yan *P. n.* name of the banner, palace or chariot of Indra (chd. p. 563).

เวฏฐิ wet[3] *P. v.* to surround; to encircle; to encompass; to envelop, wrap up, or clothe (chd. p. 564); see โพก p. 601.

เวฏฐิน์ wet[3] *P. n.* a turban; a diadem; an enveloping wrap for the head (chd. p. 564).

เวณ way-na[6] *P. n.* a worker in bamboo or wicker-work (chd. p. 563).

เวณวิก way-na[6]-wik[6] *P. n.* a player on a [flute (chd. p. 563).

เวณ see เพณ p. 596.

เวณิก way-nik[6] *P. n.* a player on the lute or harp (chd. p. 563).

เวณุ way-noo[6] *S. n.* a bamboo reed; a cane; a flute; a fife or pipe (S. E. D. p. 1014): เวณุการ a flute-maker: เวณุรม, เวณุวาท a flute-player; a piper: เวณุวัน a bamboo grove; name of a monastery presented by King Bunbisara to Gautama Buddha.

เวตน์ wet[3] *P. S. n.* wages; hire; salary; livelihood; subsistence (S. E. D. p. 1014).

เวตร wet[3] *S. n.* a reed; a cane; the rod or mace of an officer; the staff of a door-keeper (S. E. D. p. 1015).

เวท wet[3] *P. S. n.* name of certain celebrated works which constitute the basis of the first period of the Hindu religion (S. E. D. p. 1015); see เพท p. 596: เวทกุศล proficiency in the Vedas: เวทู *lit.* "knowing the Vedas," *i. e.* Brahmins (chd. p. 561); *lit.* "one attaining the highest degree of knowledge (regarding the Vedas)," *i. e.* a saint or Arahat: เวทรัย the three Vedas: เวทนินทา denying, or defaming the Vedas; unbelief; heresy: เวท-พรต one who devotes himself to the study of the Vedas: เวทพันธุ์ one well-versed in the Vedas: เวทมนตร์ mantras, magical formulas, or incantations considered by the Hindus so powerful that they can "enchain the power of the gods in themselves." They are used for invocation, for evocation, or as means to induce spells: เวทวิทยา knowledge of the Vedas: เวทสาร the essence of the Vedas; name of Vishnu.

เวทนา wit[3]-ta[6]-nah *P. S. n.* feeling; sensation; perception; pain; suffering (chd. p. 561); see เพทนา p. 596: น่าเวทนา worthy of pity, compassion or commiseration.

เวทย์ wet[3] *P. S. adj.* famous; notorious; celebrated; far-famed; recognized or regarded as relating to the Vedas (S. E. D. p. 1017).

เวทัลล way-tan-la[6] *P. n.* name of one of the nine divisions of the Buddhist scriptures according to the subject matter (chd. p. 561).

เวทางค์ way-tang *S. n.* name of certain works, or classes of works, regarded as auxillary to, and even in some cases as part of the Veda. [the Veda.

เวที, เวที ๑ see ไพที p. 603.

เวที ๒ way-tee *P. n.* a wise man; a teacher; knowledge; science (S. E. D. p. 1017).

เวธ wet[3] *P. S. n.* a breach; a wound; penetration; perforation acts, as piercing, hitting, puncturing, wounding (S. E. D. p. 1018).

เวธี way-tee *P. n.* one who pierces, shoots, or causes perforations (chd. p. 563).

เวน wen *v.* to transfer, convey, assign, shift or relegate (to others); to substitute, supplant, supersede or replace: เวนของ to make a presentation (as a gift); see ถวาย p. 381: เวนคืน to return or restore (as to the proper owner): เวนตำแหน่งคืน to resign from, or surrender an office or position.

เว้น wen[5] *v.* to omit; to reject; to exclude; to except; to be exempt from; to be unmentioned, unnumbered, discarded, or eliminated: เว้นการ to be at leisure, free or exempt from labour: เว้นจาก to abstain, desist or refrain from: เว้นตาม to refrain from doing, in accordance with religious principles: เว้นแต่ except; unless; but; that; all but: เว้นไป to miss or let slip (as a stitch in sewing or knitting); to allow a portion to be eliminated (as while making a copy of some typing); to desist from working on a particular piece or section (as workmen on a job, or while doing sectional work along a railroad): เว้นว่าง, ว่างเว้น to allow an interval or interruption (as in a job or task): เว้นไว้ excepted, or exempted from: เว้นเสีย to be excluded from: เว้นให้ to allow an exemption (as in corvée or because of sickness).

เวนไตย way-na[6]-dtai *n.* the Garuda or Krut; see ครุฑ p. 183.

เวไนย์ see เพไนย p. 596.

เวม   way-ma[6] *P. n.* a loom (chd. p. 563).

เวมัตต์   way-mat[6] *P. n.* difference; distinction (chd. p. 563).

เวมัติก   way-mat[6]-dti[4]-gka[4] *P. adj.* wavering; variable; vacillating; inconsistent (chd. p. 563).

เวมาติก   way-mah-dtik[4] *P. n.* those born of different mothers: บุตรเวมาติก a step-child.

เว้ย   wur-ie[5] *onomat.* from the sound of warning, or a call of encouragement, or for concerted action, as มาเว้ย, ระวังตัวเว้ย.

เวยยากรณ์, ไวยากรณ์   wai-yah-gkaun *P. n.* an answer; an explanation; an exposition; an exegesis (chd. p. 564).

เวยยาวัจจ   wai-yah-wat[6]-chja[4] *P. n.* a service or duty performed by an inferior for a superior (chd. p. 565): เวยยาวัจจกร, ไวยาวัจจกร one, or those who minister to the wants of Buddhist priests.

เวร   wen *P. n.* wrath; anger; animosity; resentment; indignation; enmity; estrangement (chd. p. 563): ผูกเวร, จองเวร to harbour revenge: เวร *Thai adj.* in turns, or by shifts; in rotation or order; see ทำเวร under ทำ • p. 413.

เวรมณี   way-ra[6]-ma[6]-nee *P. n.* abstinence (chd. p. 563).

เวรี   way-ree *P. adj.* hating; hostile; revengeful (chd. p. 563).

เวลา   way-lah *P. S. n.* limit; end; boundary of sea and land; time of day; hour; period; season; occasion (S. E. D. p. 1018): จวนเวลาแล้ว the time is near at hand: ได้เวลา the proper time has come: ในเวลานั้น at that time; during such time as will come: ในเวลานี้ at this time; during the present period: มาพอดีเวลา to come or arrive just at the proper or favourable time: เวลาค่ำ night-time: เวลาเช้า morning: เวลาเที่ยง noon: เวลาบ่าย afternoon: เวลาสาย forenoon; late morning.

เววจนะ, ไวพจน์   way-wa[6]-chja[4]-na[6] *P. n.* a synonym (chd. p. 564).

เววัณณ์   way-wan *P. adj.* various; different (chd. p. 564).

เวศ   wet[3] *S. n.* a settler; a small farmer; a tenant; a dependent; a vassal; a tent; a house; a dwelling (S. E. D. p. 1019).

เวศม์   wet[3] *S. n.* a house; an abode; a residence; a dwelling; a mansion (S.E.D. p. 1019).

เวศย์   see แพศย์ p. 600.

เวศยา   see แพศยา p. 600.

เวสน์   wet[3] *P. n.* a residence; a house (chd. p. 564).

เวสส, เวสิยาน   wet[3]-sa[4] *P. n.* a man of the merchantile class; a tradesman (chd. p. 564): เวสสภู name of a Buddha (chd. p. 564): เวสสันดร Wetsandon, a prince who was a Bodhisatta in the last birth but one (chd. p. 564).

เวสสวัณ   see ไพศรพณ์ p. 604.

เวสม   way-sa[4]-ma[6] *P. n.* inequality; unevenness (chd. p. 564).

เวสสานร   wet[3]-sah[2]-na[6]-ra[6] *P. n.* fire (chd. p. 564).

เวสาข   way-sah[2]-ka[4] *P. n.* the month in which the moon is full near the southern scale or the constellation Visakha; the sixth lunar month April—May (chd. p. 564).

เวสารัชช์   way-sah[2]-rat[6] *P. n.* confidence [(chd. p. 564).

เวสาลี   see ไพศาลี p. 605.

เวสิ, เวสิยา   see แพศยา p. 600.

เวห, เวหา   way-ha[4] *n.* the air; the sky (chd. p. 562): อากาศเวหา upper strata of the atmosphere.

เวหน   way-hon[2] *P. n. poetical* the air; the [sky.

เวหปปติ   see พฤหัสบดี p. 571.

เวหาส   way-hat[4] *P. n.* the air; the sky; the heavens (chd. p. 562).

เวฬุ   way-loo[6] *P. n.* a bamboo; a reed; a flute (chd. p. 563): เวฬุการ a weaver of bamboo: เวฬุวัน a bamboo grove; name of a monastery presented by King Bimbisara to Gotama Buddha (chd. p. 563).

เวฬุริย   way-loo[6]-ri[6]-ya[6] *P. n.* a precious stone of a dark colour (perhaps lapis lazuli) (chd. p. 563).

เว้า   wow[5] *v.* to speak; to say; to talk: *adj.* concaved; excavated or scooped out in shape; torn; frayed; see วิ่น p. 775: เว้าวอก shrivelled, withered, or shrunken (as a face in old age): เว้าแหว่ง notched; jagged; indented; imperfect in circumference or contour.

เวิก   werk[3] *v.* to remove (as a protecting curtain or scarf); to open partly, uncover, or expose (as by removal of clothing); see เปิด p. 535: เวิกคลองนา to open or re-dig a small irrigating ditch.

เวิ้ง   werng[5] *adj.* a wide, open, empty clearing; a spacious, unobstructed stretch of land (as is seen along spacious valleys or between forests): เวิ้งว้าง wide, open, unsettled or unprotected (stretch of land).

เวิด (ปลา)   wert[3] *n. Lissochilus sumatranus (Cyprinidae)* (suvatti p. 55).

เวี่ย, เวี่ยว   wee-ah[3] *v.* to hang down or be suspended from (as a vine on a trellis, or a snake hanging on a limb by the tail).

เวียง   wee-ang *n.* a city; a palace; a walled city: เวียงไชย a city commemorating a victory: เวียงวัง a walled palace.

เวียน   wee-an *v.* to revolve; to whirl; to wheel; to swirl; to gyrate; to move in rotation; to encircle; to make a revolution or circumambulation: เวียน, จาด (ปลา) *Labeobarbus tambroides (Cyprinidae)* (suvatti p. 36): เวียนเกิด to be reborn in rotating stages: เวียน-

เข้า to rotate, circle or eddy around, gradually approaching the center: เวียนตาม to follow in succession (as a rotation of crops, or in office): เวียนเทียน the light-waving rite frequently performed in Thai ceremonies. The Brahmins and others pass from hand to hand tapers, fixed in lenticular holders, around the person or thing they desire to honour, and fan the smoke towards that person or thing. It is intended to ward off evil influences (siamese state ceremonies p. 102); circumambulating with candles around the "Bai Sees" (Ala. p. 298): เวียนไปเวียนมา to retrace one's steps back and forth; to haunt: เวียน-วง to occur or revolve in regular order or succession: เวียนวน to spin or whirl around a central point: เวียนศีรษะ, เวียนหัว to be giddy or dizzy; to feel a sensation of vertigo, swimming, or whirling of the head: เวียน-หมุน to turn on an axle or pivot while revolving (as a windmill).

เวียร   see วิริยะ p. 777.

เวี่ยว   see เวี่ย p. 783.

แว้   waa[5] *onomat.* from the cry of an infant.

แวง ๑   waang *Cam. adj.* long (length of one side) (used in measuring land): รุ้งแวง the length and breadth.

แวง ๒   see ดาบ p. 325.

แว้ง   waang[5] *v.* to hurl with a sidewise motion (as used in bowling); to shake to and fro; to throw, fling, shy, or toss with the motion of a knight's move (in chess); to turn the head to one side (as a snake when suspended by the tail): งูแว้งเอา, แว้งกัด the serpent makes a sideways position of the head and strikes from the side: แว้งขบ, แว้งงับ to bite sideways (as does a dog when teased): แว้งจับ to make a sharp sidelong lunge in order to catch another: แว้งวิดคันเบ็ด to jerk up a fishing rod sideways: แว้งหาง to make a sideways slash with the tail (as does an alligator).

แวด   waat[3] *v.* to approach cautiously and linger near (for purposes of spying): แวดขาย to hover casually around the outskirts for purposes of inspection and protection (as police at a public gathering): แวดล้อม, แวดวง to encircle or surround for purposes of protection (as with a fence).

แวตร   waat[3] *n.* a cane; a stick; a mace; see ตะพด p. 354.

แว่น (ส่องกระจก)   waan[3] *v.* to look at in a mirror or looking-glass: *n.* a sphere; a circle; a ring; a washer (mechanical); a slice (as of sausage); a piece of polished metal used by ancient Thai in place of the present-day mirror; lenticular taper-holders made of gold, silver, or brass (used in the light-waving ceremony); see ดวง p. 319:   แว่นแก้ว a disc of glass: แว่นแคว้น the boundary or limits of a country or territory: แว่นตา spectacles; eye-glasses.

แว่นฟ้า   waan[3]-fah[5] *n.* trays, platforms or altars in ornate superimposed graded tiers.

แว่นไว see คล่องแคล่ว under คล่อง p. 184.

แวบ, วะแวบ   waap[3] *adj.* scintillating; flashing; twinkling; sparkling; glittering: แวบ-วับ an euphonic combination with same meaning; see วาบ p. 770.

แวว, วะแวว   waa-ow *adj.* sheen; reflected light or images from a highly polished surface (as on the cornea of the eye); changing colour (as in some kinds of silk): มีแววตา to see reflected images on the field of vision: มีแววมีเค้า to have, or get a clue as to the source or cause of an affair or crime: แววขนนกยูง the iridescent colouring of the peacock's tail-feathers: แววาม, แววาว radiant; shining; flashing; bright.

แว่ว   waa-ow[3] *v.* to hear indistinctly, vaguely, uncertainly or indefinitely: ได้ยินแว่ว ๆ to hear imperfectly (as a rumour): แว่วลำเนียง to hear inarticulate or indistinct sounds or voices: แว่วหู indistinct or undistinguishable sounds that reach the ears: เสียงแว่ว ๆ indistinct, faint or confused sounds: เห็นแว่ว to see dimly or faintly.

แวะ   waa[6] *v.* to call in on the way (as a servant stops while going to market); to make a call, or touch intermediate points for passengers (as a ferry-boat); to make a temporary stop (as during a trip or journey); to make a small detour or move to one side (as when letting another motor car pass).

โว่   woh[3] *n.* a cavity or concavity; a depression; an indentation; a dent; an excavation: *adj.* concave; cavernous; spoon-shaped; hollow; scooped out; staved in; bell-shaped.

โวการ   woh-gkarn *P. n.* worthlessness; uselessness; nothing worth speaking of; a matter of indifference (chd. p. 589).

โว่ง   wong[3] *adj.* open; vacant; void; see โปร่ง p. 537.

โวทาน   woh-tan *P. n.* purification; lavation (chd. p. 589).

โวย, โว้ย   woh-ie *onomat.* the sound of reply to a call (as commoners to each other).

โวยวาย   woh-ie-wai *onomat.* a sound of tumult or outcry (as when screaming or shouting for help).

โว้เว้ (พูด)   woh[5]-way[5] *v.* to talk loudly, roughly, boisterously, or nonsensically; to do or act carelessly or in a bad manner: คนโว้เว้ a vagabond; a vulgar person.

โวสาน   woh-san[2] *P. n.* the end; the consummation; the finish; the conclusion; the termination (chd. p. 590).

โวหาร   woh-han[2] *P. n.* speech; vernacular; idiom; idiomatic use of the language; trade; business; custom (chd. p. 589): โดยโวหาร by speech, word, or from what has been said: มีโวหารดี eloquence; fluency of speech.

ไว wai *adj.* quick; dexterous; prompt; active; agile; nimble: *adv.* quickly; hastily; dexterously; promptly; see คล่อง p. 184: มือไว rapacity; given to thieving; light-fingered: เห็นไว quick to see; having an active presentiment.

ไว้ wai[5] *v.* to preserve; to conserve; to keep; to guard; to retain; to uphold; to protect; when used in combination with a verb, it means stability; permanency; fixedness; continuousness: เก็บไว้ to put in a place, for safe keeping: ตั้งไว้ to set down, place or establish: ประสมไว้ to lay up, or accumulate: ไว้การ to leave a position, work or duty for another to carry on: ไว้ของ to store, or put goods in a safe place: ไว้ใจ to have confidence in; to trust, rely upon, or hope for: ไว้ตัว, ไว้โต to act the dude; to be proud, haughty or imperious; to put on side: ไว้ทาง to set aside space for a path (as through a garden-plot): ไว้ยศ to uphold one's rank, or position: ไว้หน้า to exalt one's name or honour; to do for the sake of praise, or to be seen of men.

ไวฑูรย์ see ไพฑูรย์ p. 603.

ไวทย์ see เวชช์ p. 780.

ไวพจน์ see เววจนะ p. 782.

ไวยราพณ์ wai-ya[6]-rap[3] *n.* name of a giant appearing as a character in the Ramayana.

ไวยากรณ์ see เวยยากรณ์ p. 782.

ไวยาว๊จจกร see เวยยาว๊จจกร p. 782.

ศ

ศ The thirty-eighth consonant of the Thai alphabet, a high class letter of which there are eleven, *viz.* ข, ฃ, ฉ, ฐ, ถ, ผ, ฝ, ศ, ษ, ส, ห. ศอคอ is the name of this letter. It is equivalent to "s" in English, when used as an initial letter, and to "t" when occurring as a final. It occurs in words of Sanskrit origin, as โศก, ศักดิ์, ยศ, and a few Thai words, as ศอก, ศึก, เศร้า.

ศก ๑ sok[4] *Cam. n.* the hair of the head; a lock of hair; see ผม p. 539: ศกกันต์ the tonsure ceremony of princes. That of nobles and commoners is known as การโกนจุก.

ศก ๒ sok[4] *S. n.* a year, years, era or decade. Each year of a decade is distinguished by a Pali numeral in addition to the name it bears in the twelve-year animal cycle. The years of the decade are as follows,

1st. year of decade เอกศก;
2nd. „ „ „ โทศก;
3rd. „ „ „ ตรีศก;
4th. „ „ „ จัตวาศก;
5th. „ „ „ บัญจศก;
6th. „ „ „ ฉอศก;
7th. „ „ „ สัปตศก;
8th. „ „ „ อัฐศก;
9th. „ „ „ นพศก;
10th. „ „ „ สัมฤทธิศก.

ศก ๓ *S.* name of a particular white-skinned tribe or race of people (S. E. D. p. 1045). These people are supposed to be the Sakas and are probably to be identified with the Turk or Tatar tribes who over-ran south India before the coming of the Aryans (H. C. D. p. 273). Their celebrated king Salivahana (ศาลิวาหนะ) attained great power, and in order to prolong his glory, inaugurated the era มหาศักราช beginning with the date of his birth, 78 A. D. (B. E. 621) (H. C. D. p. 275). The name of the king was later dropped; so we have the มหาศักราช or ศักราช of the Thai and Cambodians. This nomenclature is also in general use in southern India.

ศกฏ sa⁴-gka⁴-dta⁴ *S. n.* a cart; a waggon; a sleigh; a measure of capacity; a cart-load (chd. p. 416); see เกวียน p. 123; name of a demon slain by Krishna.

ศกฏา sak⁴-gka⁴-tah *Bengali n.* a cart; a waggon; a carriage; a sleigh; a vehicle on wheels.

ศกล sa⁴-gkon *S. n.* a chip; a fragment; a piece; a bit; a half; a half-verse; the half of an egg-shell; skin; bark (S. E. D. p. 1046).

ศกุน sa⁴-gkoon *S. n.* a large bird which is considered to be a sign of good or bad omen (S. E. D. p. 1046).

ศกุนต์ sa⁴-gkoon *S. n.* a bird of prey, probably the Indian vulture (S. E. D. p. 1046).

ศกุนิ sa⁴-gkoo⁴-ni⁶ *S. n.* a large bird (S. E. D. p. 1046).

ศกุนี sa⁴-gkoo⁴-nee *S. n.* a female bird; a hen-sparrow; a thing or sign of good omen (S. E. D. p. 1046).

ศกุร sa⁴-gkoo⁴-ra⁶ *S. adj.* tame; quiet; still; silent (S. E. D. p. 1046); see เชื่อง p. 302; นิ่ง p. 456.

ศงกา see ศังกา p. 792.

ศจี sa⁴-chjee *S. n.* assistance; aid; kindness; favour; grace; skill; the rendering of powerful or mighty help (S. E. D. p. 1048); name of the wife of Indra, or Indrani, mother of Jayanta and Jayanti (H. C. D. p. 271).

ศฎา sa⁴-dah *S. n.* a tuft, tussock or toupee of plaited hair; an ascetic's knotted hair (S. E. D. p. 1048); see ชฎา p. 275.

ศฐู sa⁴-ta⁴ *S. n.* craftiness; treachery; fraud; a rogue; a crook; a crafty person; a lazy person: *adj.* deceitful; fraudulent; wicked; cheating; roguish (S. E. D. p. 1048).

ศตก see ศตก p. 786.

ศต, ศัต sa⁴-dta⁴ *S. n.* a hundred; any very large number (S. E. D. p. 1048): ศตขัณฑ์ *lit.* "having a hundred pieces," *i. e.* gold: ศตบถ an astronomical circular diagram having an hundred points for studying the positions of various objects of the starry firmament; see นักษัตร p. 447: ศตบัตร *lit.* "having one hundred petals," *i. e.* a species of lotus; a species of bird; the Indian crane (chd. p. 466): ศตบาท, ศตปที *lit.* "having a hundred feet" *i. e.* a centipede: ศตมูลี *Asparagus racemosus* (*Liliaceae*), a sprawler, with woody stems. It occurs across Africa, in India from Kashmir to Ceylon, and through Burma and Thailand just into the northern part of British Malaya, disappearing in Langkawi, to reappear in Java, from which island it extends to northern Australia. In Java the Chinese make a confection of its roots; in India a similar conserve is used for impotence. In India the root has yet other uses—as a stimulant, restorative, demulcent, diuretic, anti-dysenteric, etc. (BURK. p. 262): ศตรัศมี *lit.* "having a hundred rays," *i. e.* the sun (chd. p. 466): ศตวรรษ, ศตศารท a century; a period of one hundred years: ศตสังวัตสร์ lasting a hundred years: ศตสุข hundred-fold happiness; a state of endless delight: ศตรมย high-priced; valuable; expensive: ศตัชนี a weapon or missile to be thrown, hurled or pitched: ศตายุ one hundred years of age.

ศตก, ศตก sa⁴-dta⁴-gka⁴ *n.* a cycle or period of a hundred years (chd. p. 465); a century: *adj.* amounting to, or consisting of one hundred.

ศตี sa⁴-dtee *S. n. Rhizoma zedoary*; see ขมิ้นอ้อย p. 141.

ศนะ sa⁴-na⁶ *S. adj.* silent; quiet; smooth; calm; soft (S. E. D. p. 1051).

ศนิ sa⁴-ni⁶ *S. n.* Saturn (the planet), or its regent: ศนิวาร Saturday.

ศไนรภาพ sa⁴-nai-pap³ *S. n.* slowness; deliberateness; the act of changing, moving, progressing slowly or by degrees (S. E. D. p. 1051).

ศไนส์ sa⁴-nai *adv.* quietly; softly; gently; gradually; alternately (S. E. D. p. 1051).

ศบถ sa⁴-bot⁴ *S. n.* a curse; a profane word; an imprecation; a vow (that is malicious); an oath; an anathema.

ศปนะ, ศัปนะ sa⁴-bpa⁴-na⁶ *S. n.* an oath; an assertion by oath or ordeal (S. E. D. p. 1052).

ศผ sa⁴-pa⁴ *S. n.* the hoof of a horse; a claw; a wooden implement formed like a claw or hook (S. E. D. p. 1052).

ศพ, ศว sop⁴ *n.* a corpse; a dead body: การศพ funeral services; interment ceremonies: ทรากศพ a corpse; a lifeless body: เตาเผาศพ a crematorium: ปลงศพ, ฝังศพ to bury, or perform the funeral obsequies: เผาศพ to cremate a corpse: ศพกรรม a cremation: ศพทาห์ a cremation pyre: ศพมนเทียร a building specially erected for the cremation of a royal body; a Meru: ศพยาน, ศพรถ a funeral car or carriage: คพวาหะ, ศพวาหก pall-bearers: อาบน้ำศพ to perform the bathing ceremony of a corpse as the last token of respect.

[sequies.

ศพย์ sop⁴ *n.* a funeral; a cremation; ob-

ศพร sa⁴-pa⁶-ra⁶ *S. n.* a mountain tribe inhabiting the Deccan region (ทักษิฌาบถ); wild tribes in general: *adj.* varigated (colours or hues); striped; spotted: ศพรกันต์ potatoes; see มันเทศ p. 645.

ศพล sa⁴-pa⁶-la⁶ *S. adj.* variegated; brindled; dappled; mottled (colours); striped; tinted or spotted; piebald; disfigured (S. E. D. p. 1052): ศพลหฤทัย unhappy; miserable; wretched.

ศม sa⁴-ma⁶ *S. n.* calmness; tranquillity; equanimity; quietude; abstraction from ex-

ternal objects through intense meditation; absence of gloominess and sullenness (S. E. D. p. 1053): ศมสุข the joy or happiness of tranquillity.

ศมก sa⁴-ma⁶-gka⁴ *S. n.* a pacifier; a peacemaker; one who allays, sooths, or calms (S. E. D. p. 1054).

ศมถ sa⁴-ma⁶-ta⁴ *S. n.* tranquillity; calmness; quietude; cessation or freedom from perturbation, sin or guilt (S. E. D. p. 1054).

ศมน sa⁴-ma⁶-na⁶ *S. n.* the act of giving or causing calmness or tranquillity of mind; self-control against lust and desire (S. E. D. p. 1054).

ศมนี sa⁴-ma⁶-nee *S. n.* the calming time; night; night-time.

ศมนีย์ sa⁴-ma⁶-nee *S. adj.* giving, causing, or producing coolness and tranquillity of mind (S. E. D. p. 1054).

ศมพร som²-paun *S. n.* name of the Asura or supreme spirit (the same as the Ahura of the Zoroastrians). In the sense of "god," it was applied to several of the chief deities (as to Indra, Agni and Varuna). It afterwards acquired an entirely opposite meaning and came to signify enemy of the gods, fightings, treachery, trickery, or jugglery (S. E. D. p. 1055: H. C. D. p. 27).

ศมพล som²-pon *S. n.* provender or provisions for a journey.

ศมล sa⁴-ma⁶-la⁶ *S. n.* impurity; sin; blemish; fault; harm (S. E. D. p. 1054).

ศมยา som²-yah *S. n.* a stick; a staff; a wooden pin or peg; a wedge (S. E. D. p. 1054).

ศมศาน, ศัมศาน sa⁴-ma⁶-san² *S. n.* an elevated place for burning dead bodies; a cemetery or burial place for the bones of cremated corpses; a crematorium; an oblation offered to deceased ancestors (S. E. D. p. 1094).

ศมาหะ   sa⁴-mah-ha⁴ *S. n.* a place of quietness, tranquillity of mind, or one in which religious meditations can be carried on undisturbed; an hermitage (S. E. D. p. 1054).

ศย   sa⁴-ya⁶ *S. v.* to sleep; to be asleep, to dwell or stay; to rest or relax: *n.* sleep; a bed; a couch (S. E. D. p. 1055).

ศยนะ   sa⁴-ya⁶-na⁶ *S. n.* the act of lying, sleeping, resting or relaxing; a bed; a couch; a berth; a pillow; a mattress (S. E. D. p. 1055).

ศยาม   sa⁴-yam *S. adj.* black; dark-coloured; dark blue, brown or grey; having a dark or swarthy complexion (S. E. D. p. 1094): ศยาม-กัณฐ์ *lit.* "black-throated," *i. e.* a peacock or peahen.

ศยามล   sa⁴-yah-mon *S. n.* black colour, pigment or paint: *adj.* having a dark complexion, or a black skin (S. E. D. p. 1094).

ศยาล, สยาล   sa⁴-yan *S. n.* an older or younger brother of a wife.

ศร   saun² *S. n.* an arrow; an arrow-shaft; a hurt; a wound; an injury; pain; suffering; the reed *Saccharum sara,* used for arrows (S. E. D. p. 1056): ศรเกษป, ศรโคจร the range of an arrow-shot: ศรฆาต the shooting of an arrow with the intention of killing: ศรธิ a quiver; an arrow case: ศรผล the arrow-head, iron point or barb: ศรเภท the wound caused by an arrow-head: ศรายุธ *lit.* "a weapon having an issue," *i. e.* a bow and arrow; a cross-bow: ศราวร, ศราวรณ์ *lit.* "a warder off of arrows," *i. e.* a shield; a cover; a guard or buckler: ศราสน์ archery; the act of shooting arrows with a bow.

ศรณะ   sa⁴-ra⁶-na⁶ *S. n.* protection; preservation; a place of shelter, refuge, or rest; a hut; a house; a home; an habitation; an abode; a lair; an asylum.

ศรณิ, ศรณี   sa⁴-ra⁶-ni⁶ *S. n.* a road; a path; a way; a track; a street; see ถนน p. 379.

ศรนารายณ์ (ต้น)   sorn²-nah-rai *n. Sansevieria zeylanica (Liliaceae),* one of a genus of fifty more or less succulent herbs, found in tropical Africa and sparingly in tropical Asia. The species are difficult to discriminate. There are medicinal uses and it is thought of for fibre (Burk. p. 1948 : MCM. p. 418); see ว่านงู p. 769.

ศรภ   sa⁴-ra⁶-pa⁶ *S. n.* an elephant calf; a camel; a fabulous animal supposed to have eight legs (S. E. D. p. 1057).

ศรม   sa⁴-ra⁶-ma⁶ *S. n.* fatigue; weariness; toil; exhaustion; exertion; exercise; effort (either physical or mental); hard work of any kind (S. E. D. p. 1096): ศรมชล *lit.* "toil-water," *i. e.* sweat; perspiration: ศรมสถาน a place for work or exercise; a gymnasium; a drilling ground or hall: ศรมสิทธิ์ accomplished by exertion, effort or endeavour.

ศรมณะ   sa⁴-ra⁶-ma⁶-na⁶ *S. n.* one who performs acts of mortification or austerity; an ascetic; a monk; a devotee; a religious mendicant; a Buddhist monk (S. E. D. p. 1096).

ศรรกร   suk⁴-gkorn *S. n.* gravel; pebbles; small stones: *adj.* consisting of gravel or grit; gritty (S. E. D. p. 1058).

ศรรกรา   suk⁴-gka⁴-rah *S. n.* grit; pebbles; a spot abounding in stony fragments; sugar; candied sugar; rock-candy (S. E. D. p. 1058).

ศรรพร   sup⁴-pa⁶-ra⁶ *S. adj.* spotted; variegated (S. E. D. p. 1058).

ศรรพรี   sup⁴-pa⁶-ree *S. n.* evening; twilight (S. E. D. p. 1058).

ศรลก   sa⁴-ra⁶-lok⁶ *S. n.* water (S.E.D. p. 1057).

ศรวณะ ๑   sa⁴-ra⁶-wa⁶-na⁶ *S. n.* the act of hearing, listening, acquiring knowledge by hearing, learning or studying: ศรวณโคจร, ศรวณวิษัย the distance within reach of the hearing; ear-shot; reaching the range of hearing: ศรวณบถ auditory canal; the ear: ศรวณรุช diseases of the ear; ear-ache: ศรวณ-สุข, ศรวณสุภัค agreeable or pleasing to the ear.

ศรวณะ ๒   *S. n.* lameness; name of the lunar month Sravana (July and August), corresponding to the solar month Simha or Leo in the sign of the Zodiac (The Hindu Religious Year p. 18).

ศรวณย์   sa[4]-ra[6]-wa[6]-nee *S. n.* that which should be heard; that which is pleasing or agreeable to be listened to; an admirable or praiseworthy thing (S. E. D. p. 1097).

ศรวยะ   sa[4]-ra[6]-wa[6]-ya[6] *S. adj.* that which is to be heard, or should be listened to; that which is admirable (S. E. D. p. 1097).

ศรัณย์   sa[4]-ran *S. adj.* affording shelter; yielding help or protection; needing or seeking refuge, shelter, or protection (S. E. D. p. 1057).

ศรัณยุ   sa[4]-ran-yoo[6] *S. n.* a defender; a protector; a guardian; a cloud; wind; air (S. E. D. p. 1057).

ศรัถ   sa[4]-rat[6] *S. v.* to be liberated, loosened, or set free; to become loose or slack; to untie, or relax; to remit (punishment); to pardon (sins) (S. E. D. p. 1096); see ปล่อย p. 511.

ศรัถนะ   sa[4]-rat[6]-ta[4]-na[6] *S. n.* the act of untying, liberating, or releasing (S.E.D. p. 1096).

ศรัทธา   sat[4]-tah *S. n.* faith; trust; belief in; loyalty to; reverence towards; trustfulness; faithfulness; determination; confidence or purpose (S. E. D. p. 1096).

ศรัปนะ   sup[4]-bpa[4]-na[6] *S. n.* the act of cooking or boiling (as of food) (S. E. D. p. 1097).

ศรัย   sai[2] *S. n.* an asylum; a place of shelter or refuge; a residence; an abode; a shaded, cool place or retreat; a caravanserai or halting place for a caravan (S. E. D. p. 1096).

ศรัยนะ   sai[2]-ya[6]-na[6] *S. n.* the act of searching for, going to, approaching, or having recourse to an asylum as a place of refuge, protection, or shelter (S. E. D. p. 1096).

ศราทธ์   sart[4] *S. n.* the making of merit, or the saying of mass for the benefit of deceased relatives: *adj.* believing in; trusting; faithful; obedient to; having confidence in (S. E. D. p. 1096); see เชื่อถือ p. 302.

ศรานต์   san[2] *S. adj.* fatigued; exhausted; weakened; hungry; suffering; silent; calmed; tranquil (S. E. D. p. 1096); see เงียบ p. 226.

ศราพ ๑   sarp[4] *S. n:* a shallow cup; a dish; a platter; an earthen-ware vessel (S. E. D. p. 1057); see ชาม p. 293.

ศราพ ๒   sarp[4] *S. n.* the act of listening, or hearing (S. E. D. p. 1097).

ศราวก, ศราพก   sa[4]-rah-wok[6] *S. n.* a pupil; a follower or adherent; disciples of the Buddha, and originally understood to include only those who had received instruction direct from him, but at present the term is applied to Buddhist monks in general.

ศราวณะ ๑   sa[4]-rah-wa[6]-na[6] *S. adj.* audible; relating to, or perceived by the ear (S. E. D. p. 1097)

ศราวณะ ๒   *n.* the lunar month Sravana (July and August): *adj.* relating to, or occurring during this month.

ศราวัสดี   sa[4]-rah-wat[6]-sa[4]-dee *S. n.* a capital city in India, founded by King Sravasta, situated towards the north of the river Ganges in the territory of Kosala renowned for a monastery named Jettubon (เชตุพน) where the Buddha dwelt for a long time (S. E. D. p. 1098).

ศริต   sa[4]-rit[6] *S. adj.* stopping; sticking for, or adhering to; standing or lying; fixed or situated in or on (S. E. D. p. 1098).

ศรี   see[2] *S. n.* auspiciousness; splendour; beauty; glory; good fortune; prosperity; success; riches; loveliness (S. E. D. p. 1098): ศรีธร *lit.* "the bearer or possessor of fortune," *i.e.* Vishnu (H. C. D. p. 300); name for the lunar month Sravana (July and August): ศรีนาถ

lit. " the husband of Sri," *i. e.* name of Vishnu : ศรีบถ a public road, thoroughfare or highway : ศรีบรรณ *Premna spinosa,* or *longifolia* : ศรี- พระลักษมี name of the goddess of Good Fortune and Beauty ; consort of Vishnu ; see ลักษมี p. 736 : ศรีพระสรสวดี Saraswati the goddess of Speech and Learning ; consort of Brahma (H. C. D. p. 284) : ศรีมกุฎ gold : ศรียุกต์ happy ; fortunate ; famous ; illustrious ; re- nowned : ศรีวราหะ *lit.* " divine boar," *i. e.* Vishnu in his incarnation as a boar : ศรี- วัลลภ being Fortune's love or favourite ; name of various authors : ศรีวิศาล abounding in, or enriched by good fortune.

ศรีระ sa⁴-ree-ra⁶ *S. n.* the body ; the bodily frame ; solid parts of the body (S. E. D. p. 1057) : ศรีรจินดา hygienic care or preservative meas- ures for the body (as bathing) : ศรีรตุลย์ dear as one's own person ; equal to oneself (in value and preciousness) : ศรีรตยาค the abandonment of one's body ; renunciation of one's life : ศรีรบีฑา bodily pain or suffering ; ศรีรประภพ a father ; a begetter ; a progenitor ; ศรีรเภท the dissolution, or breaking up of the body ; death : ศรีรรักษา the defence of the body ; protection of the person : ศรีรสัมพันธ์ relationships formed by marriage ; bodily con- nections : ศรีรศาสตร์, ศรีรวิทยา physiology : ศรีรนยาส the neglect of one's body ; death.

ศรีรกะ sa⁴-ree-ra⁶-gka⁴ *S. n.* a pitious figure ; a diminutive body ; a form that is pitiable, wretched or miserable (S. E. D. p. 1068).

ศรีรี sa⁴-ree-ree *S. n.* animals ; creatures ; one who, or that which assumes a bodily shape ; man ; mankind : *adj.* physical ; cor- poreal ; fleshy ; being connected to, or combined with a body (S. E. D. p. 1058).

ศรุ sa⁴-roo⁶ *S. n.* an arrow ; a missile (to be thrown or projected from a gun or bow) ; anger.

ศรุต sa⁴-roo⁶-dta⁴ *S. adj.* heard ; listened to ; heard about or of ; taught ; mentioned orally ; transmitted or communicated from age to age ; known ; famous ; renowned ; cele- brated (S. E. D. p. 1101).

ศรุติ sa⁴-roo⁶-dti⁴ *S. n.* the ear ; the organ, or power of hearing ; that which is heard or perceived with the ear ; sound ; noise ; an ag- gregate of sounds ; report ; news ; intelligence ; hearsay (S. E. D. p. 1101) : ศรุติกฎุ disagree- able to the sense of hearing ; unpleasant to the ear : ศรุติโคจร preceptible by the ear ; permitted to be heard by— : ศรุติทุษก rough ; vulgar ; indecent ; offending the ear : ศรุติบถ the radius within which sounds can be heard ; ear-shot : ศรุติวิวร the auditory pas- sage : ศรุติสุข pleasing to the ear ; sonorous, harmonious, or edifying (sounds).

ศฤกาล, ศฤคาล sa⁴-ri⁶-gkan *S. n.* a kind of wolf ; a jackal (S. E. D. p. 1087).

ศฤงขละ sing²-ka⁴-la⁶ *S. n.* a chain ; fet- ters ; a belt ; manacles ; a measuring chain (S. E. D. p. 1087).

ศฤงขลก sing²-ka⁴-loke⁶ *n.* a shackle ; a young camel, or other young animal with wooden rings or clogs on its feet (S. E. D. p. 1087).

ศฤงค์ sing² *n.* horns or antlers of an animal ; the tusk of an elephant ; the top, peak, crag or summit of a mountain ; the summit, pinnacle or turret of a building ; the horn as a symbol of sovereignty, self-reliance, strength or haughtiness ; the rising of desire ; excess of love or passion (S. E. D. p. 1087) : ศฤงคช horn-produced ; made of, or from horn : ศฤงควัต being supplied with horns, spires or peaks ; name of a mythical mountain forming one of the boundaries of the earth : ศฤงค- วรรชิต a hornless quadruped : ศฤงควาทย์ a horn ; a bullock's or ram's horn, used for blowing.

ศฤงคาร sing²-kan *S. n.* love ; sexual pas- sion, desire, or enjoyment ; a dress suitable for amorous purposes ; an elegant dress ; *the Thai meaning is* possessions (S. E. D. p. 1087) :

ศฤงคารรรพ the pride of love: ศฤงคารเจษฎา love gestures; any outward action indicating love: ศฤงคารธารึน, ศฤงคารธารี decked out; adorned; ornamented; decorated (with dress, jewelry or finery): ศฤงคารภาษิต a love story; amorous, wooing, or seductive talk: ศฤงคารโยนิ *lit.* "love-source," *i. e.* Cupid; the goddess of Love; name of Kama-deva: ศฤงคารรส the erotic sentiment, passion or zeal: ศฤงคารศูร an expert or hero in love affairs.

ศฤงคาริน, ศฤงคารี sing²-kah-rin *S. adj.* relating to love; enamoured; erotic (S. E. D. p. 1088).

ศฤงคิน sing²-kin *S. adj.* horned (as a bull); crested; peaked (as a mountain); pointed; tusked (as an elephant) (S. E. D. p. .1088).

ศล sa⁴-la⁶ *S. n.* the quill of a porcupine; a dart; a spike, stake, lance or spear: *adj.* spear-like; dagger-like; like a porcupine's quill (S. E. D. p. 1058).

ศลภ sa⁴-la⁶-pa⁶ *S. n.* a grasshopper (S. E. D. p. 1058).

ศลักษณ์ sa⁶-lak⁶ *S. adj.* slippery; smooth; polished; even; soft; tender; gentle; bland; thin; slim; fine (S. E. D. p. 1103).

ศลถ sa⁴-lat⁶ *S. adj.* loosed; relaxed; flaccid; weak; feeble; lanquid; unfastened dishevelled (S. E. D. p. 1103); see ลุ่ย p. 749.

ศลาฆ sa⁴-lak⁴ *S. v.* to vaunt, boast or be proud of; to praise; to commend; to eulogize; to flatter; to brag of, or exalt (S. E. D. p. 1103).

ศลาฆนะ sa⁴-lah-ka⁶-na⁶ *S. n.* a boaster; boastfulness (S. E. D. p. 1103).

ศลาฆา sa⁴-lah-kah *S. n.* flattery; praise; commendation (S. E. D. p. 1104).

ศลิษ sa⁴-lit⁴ *S. v.* to adhere; to cling to; to clasp; to embrace; to be joined or connected; to be implied or intimated (S. E. D. p. 1104).

ศลิษฏ์ sa⁴-lit⁴ *S. adj.* clinging or adhering

to; fitting closely and tightly; united; connected; clasped; embraced (S. E. D. p. 1104).

ศลิษา sa⁴-li⁶-sah² *S. n.* an embrace; a hug; [a caress.

ศว ๑ see ศพ p. 787.

ศว ๒ sa⁴-wa⁶ *S. n.* a dog; a hound (S. E. D. p. 1105): ศวกรีฑ a breeder of sporting dogs; keeping dogs for pleasure: ศวชีวิกา a dog-like existence; servitude; bondage: ศวชีว a keeper and breeder of dogs: ศวบท wild animals: ศวป a keeper or possessor of dogs: ศวปจ one who cooks dogs; a person of low caste: ศวผล the coconut palm: ศวพยาฆร์ a beast of prey; a tiger or hunting leopard.

ศวกะ sa⁴-wa⁶-gka⁴ *S. n.* a wolf (S. E. D. p. 1105).

ศวภร sa⁴-wa⁶-pa⁶-ra⁶ *S. n.* a hole; a gap; a pit; a den; a chasm; hell (S. E. D. p. 1105).

ศวศุร sa⁴-wa⁶-soo⁴-ra⁶ *S. n.* a father-in-law; a father- or mother-in-law.

ศวศุรย sa⁴-wa⁶-soo⁴-ra⁶-ya⁶ *S. n.* a brother-in-law; a wife's or husband's brother (S. E. D. p. 1105).

ศวสาน sa⁴-wa⁶-san² *S. n.* a path; a traveller; a cemetery: *adj.* strong; powerful; mighty.

ศวัศรู sa⁴-wat⁴-sa⁴-roo *S. n.* mother-in-law; the mother of one's husband, wife or wives.

ศวัส ๑ sa⁴-wat⁶ *S. n.* power; might; superiority; bravery; prowess; heroism (S. E. D. p. 1059).

ศวัส ๒, โศว sa⁴-wat⁶ *S. v.* to blow; to hiss; to pant; to snort; to breathe; to sigh or groan; to cause to blow (S. E. D. p. 1105).

ศวัส ๓ sa⁴-wat⁶ *S. n.* tomorrow; on the following day (S. E. D. p. 1106): ศวัสกาล tomorrow; the next day: โศวภาพ the state or condition of affairs that may exist on a future day: โศวสวสีย prosperity, riches or affluence that may come on a future day.

ศวัสตน   sa⁴-wat⁶-sa⁴-dta⁴-na⁶ *n.* future :
adj. relating or belonging to the future or
subsequent time (S. E. D. p. 1106).

ศวัสถ   sa⁴-wat⁶-sa⁴-ta⁴ *S. n.* the act of
blowing; the act of breathing; the act of
sighing or hissing (S. E. D. p. 1105).

ศวา, ศวาน   sa⁴-wah *S. n.* a dog (S.E.D. p. 1105).

ศวาตร   sa⁴-wah-dtra⁴ *S. adj.* imparting
strength, or causing invigoration (as food or
stimulants).

ศวาวิต   sa⁴-wah-wit⁶ *S. n.* a porcupine.

ศวิต   sa⁴-wit⁶ *S. adj.* white (S. E. D. p. 1106).

ศวิตร   sa⁴-wit⁶ *S. n.* leprosy : *adj.* white ;
whitish ; having morbid whiteness of the
skin ; having white leprosy (S. E. D. p. 1106) ;
see เกลื้อน p. 123.

ศศะ, สศ, สศก   sa⁴-sa⁴ *S. n.* a hare ; a
rabbit, or antelope (the markings on the moon
are supposed to resemble a hare or rabbit)
(S. E. D. p. 1060) :   ศศธร *lit.* " bearer of hare-
marks," *i. e.* the moon :   ศศบท tracks of a
rabbit :   ศศปลุตก the marks of scratches
by finger-nails or claws :   ศศวิษาณ *lit.* "the
horns of a rabbit," *i. e.* a metaphor for anything visionary, unreal, impossible, or improbable :   ศศางค์, ศศพินทุ์, ศศลักษณ์ the moon.

ศศิ, ศศิน, ศศี, สสิ, สสี   sa⁴-si⁴ *S. n. lit.*
" containing the figure of a rabbit," *i. e.* the
moon (S. E. D. p. 1060) :   ศศิกร moonlight :
ศศิเคราะห์ a lunar eclipse :   ศศิบาท moon-
beams :   ศศิประภา moonlight ; moonshine :
ศศิมณฑล the circle or orb of the moon :   ศศิ-
วงศ์ the lunar race ; an extensive lineage or
race in India which claims descent from the
moon ; *otherwise known as* จันทรวงศ์.

ศอ see คอ p. 189.

ศอก   sauk⁴ *n.* the elbow ; an ancient unit
of measure equal to the distance from the tip
of the middle finger to the elbow joint ; two
spans length ; half a metre.

ศักราช see ศก ๓ p. 785.

ศักดิ์   suk⁴ *S. adj.* able ; competent ; capable ;
equal to (S. E. D. p. 1044).

ศักดิ   suk⁴ *S. n.* (1) power ; ability ; rank ;
honour ; regal power ; energy ; faculty ; skill ;
capability ; the energy or active power of a
deity (S. E. D. p. 1044) :   (2) a spear ; a lance ;
a sword ; a javelin :   ศักดิกร strength-giving :
ศักดิเคราะห์ a person who carries a lance or
spear :   ศักดิธร bearing spears or lances :
ศักดินา degrees of dignity or rank expressed
by numbers, giving the right to rule over
certain grants of land :   ศักดิปาณี holding
lances or javelins.

ศักตุ   suk⁴-dtoo⁴ *P. n.* flour ; cakes or food
made with barley meal (chd. p. 470) :   ข้าวตุ
Thai a sweetmeat made with sun-dried rice,
fried, ground to a powder, and mixed with
syrup.

ศักย   suk⁴-gka⁴-ya⁶ *S. adj.* able ; possible ;
capable ; practicable ; potential ; explicit ; direct ; literal (S. E. D. p. 1045).

ศักร   suk⁴-gkra⁴ *S. n.* a title for Indra
(H.C.D. p. 127) : *adj.* powerful ; mighty ; strong :
ศักรการมุก *lit.* " the bow of Indra," *i. e.* the
rainbow :   ศักรกาษฐา *lit.* " the domain of
Indra," *i. e.* the East :   ศักรเกตุ the banner
or standard of Indra :   ศักรชาต, ศักรัช *lit.*
" Indra born," *i. e.* a crow :   ศักรชาล the
science of magic ; witchcraft ; sorcery ; enchantments ; necromancy ; the black art ; voodooism :   ศักรภพน์, ศักรโลก *lit.* " the world
of Indra," *i. e.* the heavens :   ศักรวาหะ *lit.*
" the vehicles of Indra," *i. e.* the clouds :   ศักร-
สารถี *lit.* " the charioteer of Indra," *i. e.* Phra
Matali, or his bow (H. C. D. p. 127) :   ศักรินทร์,
ศักเรนทร์ Indra, the great and supreme.

ศักริ   suk⁴-gkri⁴ *S. n.* a cloud ; a thunderbolt ; an elephant ; a mountain.

ศังกา, ศงกา   sung²-gkah *S. n.* fear ; doubt ;
distrust ; alarm ; suspicion of ; uncertainty ;
hesitation ; apprehension (S. E. D. p. 1047).

ศังกิต sung²-gkit⁴ *S. adj.* distrustful; a-larmed; suspicious; afraid of; anxious about; doubtful; uncertain (S. E. D. p. 1047).

ศังกุ ๑ sung²-gkoo⁴ *S. n.* a peg; a nail; a spike; a stick; a stake; a post; a pillar; an arrow; a spear; a dart; the pin or gnomon of a dial (S. E. D. p. 1047): ศังกุจฉายา the shadow on a sun-dial: ศังกุมุข *lit.* "one having a pointed or sharp snout," *i.e.* a mouse, crocodile or pig.

[dread.
ศังกุ ๒ sung²-gkoo⁴ *S. n.* fear; terror;

ศังกุร sung²-gkoo⁴-ra⁶ *S. adj.* causing fear; formidable; frightful (S. E. D. p. 1047).

ศังข์, สังข sung² *n.* a shell; a conch-shell (as used for the pouring of lustral water); a conch-shell trumpet (chd. p. 456).

ศังขิน sung²-kin² *S. n.* the ocean: *adj. lit.* "possessing the conch-shell," *i.e.* Vishnu (H. C. D. p. 361).

ศังขินี sung²-ki⁴-nee *S. n.* mother-of-pearl; a form of semi-divine being, elf or fairy (S. E. D. p. 1048).

ศัณฑ์ sun² *S. n.* a childless man; an eunuch.

ศัต see ศต p. 786.

[p. 1051).
ศัตตริ sut⁴-dtri⁴ *S. n.* an elephant (S. E. D.

ศัตรุ, ศัตรู sut⁴-dtroo⁴ *S. n.* an enemy; a foe; an opponent; a competitor; an adversary; a rival (chd. p. 470: S. E. D. p. 1051): ศัตรุฆาต a killer or destroyer of his enemies: ศัตรุชน an enemy, foe, or antagonist: ศัตรุปักษ์ taking the side of the foe or enemy; being on the part of an enemy: ศัตรุวิเคราะห์ the trampling down or oppression of the enemy.

ศันนะ sun²-na⁶ *S. adj.* wasting; decaying; faded; withered; fallen.

ศันสนะ sun²-sa⁴-na⁶ *S. n.* reciting by rote; recitation; announcement; communication; report (S. E. D. p. 1044).

ศันสนีย. sun²-sa⁴-nee-ya⁶ *S. adj.* worthy of praise or admiration; praiseworthy (S. E. D. p. 1044).

ศัปต์ sup⁴ *S. adj.* cursed; adjured; conjured; reviled; taken as an oath, or sworn to (S. E. D. p. 1052).

ศัพท์ sup⁴ *S. n.* speech; word; language; voice; sound; correct expression; verbal communication or testimony; oral tradition (S E.D. p. 1052): กิติศัพท์ rumour: โทรศัพท์ telephone; see โทร p. 428: ราชาศัพท์ court language: ศัพทการ, ศัพทการี making a noise or sound; noisy; boisterous: ศัพทคติ *lit.* "rhythm of sounds," *i. e.* songs; hymns; music of bands or orchestras: ศัพทเคราะห์ *lit.* "the receiver of sounds," *i. e.* the ear: ศัพทโคจร *lit.* "the aim or object of speech," *i. e.* stories; rumours; discourses; words spoken to or about: ศัพทจาตุรย์ skill in words; cleverness of diction; proficiency in a language; eloquence: ศัพทโจร *lit.* "word-thief," *i. e.* a plagarist: ศัพทบดี a leader only in name: ศัพทวิทยา *lit.* "the science of sounds or words," *i.e.* grammar; philology: ศัพทศุทธิ purity of language: ศัพทเศลษ the use of puns; verbal quibbles: ศัพทอินทรีย์ *lit.* "sound organ," *i. e.* the ear; auditory nerves.

ศัพทน์ sup⁴ *S. adj.* sounding; uttering (sounds or words) (S. E. D. p. 1053).

ศัพทาละ sup⁴-tah-la⁶ *S. adj.* sonorous (S. E. D. p. 1053); see ดัง ๒ p. 322.

ศัมภุ, ศัมภู sum²-poo⁶ *S. n.* titles for Siva, Brahma, or Vishnu; a person of veneration: *adj.* benevolent; helpful; kind; beneficent; granting or causing happiness; existing for the welfare of others (S. E. D. p. 1055).

ศัมยุ sum²-yoo⁶ *adj.* benevolent; kind-hearted; generous; happy; fortunate (S. E. D. p. 1054).

ศัยยา sai²-yah *S. n.* a bed; a bedstead; a couch; a sofa (S. E. D. p. 1056): ศัยยากาล

bedtime : ศัยยาคต being in bed ; lying on a couch : ศัยยาคฤทะ a bedroom : ศัยยาทาน offering a couch, a refuge or a resting-place.

ศัลย, ศัลยา sun²-la⁶-ya⁶ *S. n.* a dart ; a javelin ; a lance ; a spear ; any iron-headed weapon ; anything causing pain or torment, such as extraneous substances lodged in the body (as thorns, splinters, or calculi in the bladder) (S. E. D. p. 1059) : ศัลยกรรม operative surgery : ศัลยโลม the quills or spines of a porcupine : ศัลยศาสตร์ surgery ; that branch of the healing art that relates to injuries, deformities and morbid conditions that require to be remedied by operations.

ศัลยก sun²-la⁶-ya⁶-gka⁴ *S. n.* an arrow ; a dart ; a spear ; a thorn ; an error ; difficulty ; a porcupine (S. E. D. p. 1059).

ศัลลกี sun²-la⁶-gkee *S. n.* the porcupine, *Boswellia thurifera* (S. E. D. p. 1059).

ศัศวัต sut⁴-sa⁴-wat⁶ *S. adv.* always ; continually ; forever ; perpetually ; repeatedly (S. E. D. p. 1060) ; see นิตย์ p. 457.

ศัส sut⁴ *S. v.* to cut down, kill, slaughter, or destroy (S. E. D. p. 1060) ; see ฆ่า p. 219.

ศัสตร ๑ sut⁴-sa⁴-dtra⁴ *S. n.* an invocation ; praise ; a recitation (S. E. D. p. 1044).

ศัสตร ๒, ศัสตรา, ศาสตรา, สาตรา sut⁴-sa⁴-stra⁴ *S. n.* a sword ; a knife ; a dagger ; a razor ; a spear ; any implement for cutting or wounding (S. E. D. p. 1060) : ศัสตรกรรม *lit.* " knife-operation," *i. e.* any surgical operation : ศัสตรการ a maker of arms or weapons ; an armorer : ศัสตรโกป war ; combat ; conflict ; a fight ; a battle : ศัสตรฆาต the fatal stroke of a sword : ศัสตรธร a warrior ; soldiers ; infantry : ศัสตรศาสตร์ the science of the use of arms ; military science.

ศัสตรี sut⁴-sa⁴-dtree *P. n.* a knife ; a sword ; a dagger ; a spear (chd. p. 469).

ศัสติ sut⁴-sa⁴-dti⁴ *S. n.* words of praise, admiration, blessing or benediction ; one who praises (S. E. D. p. 1044).

ศัสนะ sut⁴-sa⁴-na⁶ *S. n.* immolation ; the act of killing, slaughtering or causing destruction (as when offering an animal in sacrifice) (S. E. D. p. 1060).

ศัสย sut⁴-sa⁴-ya⁶ *S. n.* grain, cereals, corn, annual plants which are cut down or destroyed year by year (S. E. D. p. 1061).

ศาก ๑ sak⁴ *S. n.* power ; might ; help ; aid ; a helper or friend (S. E. D. p. 1061).

ศาก ๒ sak⁴ *S. n.* a pot herb (chd. p. 421) ; vegetables (in general) ; any vegetable food ; (ต้น) teak trees (S. E. D. p. 1061) : ศากบัตร the leaves of teak trees : ศากพรต the practice of abstaining from vegetable food : ศากพฤกษ์ teak trees : ศากภักษ์ a vegetarian : ศากวงค์ chillies ; peppers : ศากาหาร eating only vegetables, or living on vegetable food.

ศากย sa²-gka⁴-ya⁶ *S. n.* name of the princely family to which Gotama Buddha belonged (chd. p. 417) ; a name for Gotama Buddha : *adj.* pertaining or relative to the Indo-Scythians of the Ptolemies (H. C. D. p. 273) : ศากยเกตุ, ศากยพุทธ, ศากยมุนี names for Gotama Buddha : ศากยโพธิสัตว์ an epithet for Gotama Buddha before his attainment of enlightenment ; a Buddhist monk or mendicant : ศากยวงศ์ the princely family of Sakya to which Gotama Buddha belonged : ศากยศาสน์ the doctrines or teachings of Gotama Buddha.

ศากล sa²-gkon *S. n.* name of a city which, in the time of Gotama Buddha, was ruled over by the famous king Milindara.

ศากวร sa²-gka⁴-wa⁶-ra⁶ *S. n.* a bull : *adj.* mighty ; strong ; powerful ; vigorous (S. E. D. p. 1062).

ศากิน sa²-gki⁴-nee *S. n.* a vegetable garden or plot ; a kitchen garden (S. E. D. p. 1061).

ศากุน sa²-gkoon *S. adj.* relating or pertaining to birds ; indicating good luck ; being a sign of good fortune or auspiciousness ; ominous ; portentous (S. E. D. p. 1062).

ศางกร sang²-gkorn *S. n. lit.* "relating or belonging to Siva," *i. e.* a bull (S. E. D. p. 1063).

ศาฏก sah²-dok⁴ *P. n.* a strip of cloth; an outer garment; a tunic; a cloak; a frock (chd. p. 465).

ศาฐยะ sah²-ta⁴-ya⁶ *S. n.* wickedness; treachery; deceit; guile; fraud; roguery; dishonesty (S. E. D. p. 1063).

ศาณ ๑, ศาน sah²-na⁶ *S. n.* a grindstone; a whetstone; a touchstone (chd. p. 459); a saw.

ศาณ ๒ sah²-na⁶ *S. n.* linen cloth; canvas; sackcloth; a hempen garment (S. E. D. p. 1063).

ศาณี sah²-nee *S. n.* a curtain; a screen; a tent (chd. p. 451); a tattered, ragged or torn garment; a single breadth of cloth given to a student at his investiture (S. E. D. p. 1063).

ศาต ๑ sah²-dta⁴ *S. adj.* whetted; sharpened; thin; feeble; slender; emaciated (S. E. D. p. 1063).

ศาต ๒ sah²-dta⁴ *S. n.* the act of falling off, decaying, or dropping out (as hairs or teeth) (S. E. D. p. 1063).

ศาต ๓ sah²-dta⁴ *S. n.* pleasure (chd. p. 467); happiness; amusements; joy: *adj.* happy; amusing; joyous; joyful; gay; bright; pure; clear (as water) (S. E. D. p. 1064).

ศาตนะ sah²-dta⁴-na⁶ *S. n.* the act of whetting or sharpening; cleverness; sharpness; expertness (S. E. D. p. 1063).

ศานต์ san² *adj.* (1) appeased; tranquil; calm; free from passion: (2) gentle; mild; friendly; kind; soft; pliant: (3) come to an end; gone to rest; deceased; departed; dead (S. E. D. p. 1064): ศานตมนัส composed in mind; unannoyed; unconcerned: ศานตมล having all defilement removed: ศานตรส the sentiment of composure; calmness; tranquillity: ศานตวิวาท having disputes allayed; reconciled; appeased.

ศานติ san²-dti⁴ *S. n.* tranquillity; ease; peace; calmness of mind; absence of passion; indifference to objects of pleasure or pain; alleviation; cessation; abatement; extinction; any expiatory or propitiatory rite for averting evil or calamity; eternal rest; death (S. E. D. p. 1064): ศานติกร causing peace or prosperity: ศานติการี rendering or producing calmness or tranquillity (of mind): ศานติชล lustral water; water consecrated by a priest: ศานติบาตร a vessel or receptacle for propitiatory libations: ศานติยุกต์ connected with welfare or prosperity; auspicious: ศานติโหม a propitiatory oblation.

ศานติก san²-dtik⁴ *S. adj.* expiatory; propitiatory; averting evil; producing, or relating to ease or quiet (S. E. D. p. 1065).

ศาป sap⁴ *S. v.* to invoke evil upon; to abuse or curse: *n.* oath; curse; abuse; malediction; imprecation; ban (S. E. D. p. 1065): ศาปประทาน the utterance of a curse: ศาปมุกติ์ deliverance from a curse: ศาปานต์ the end, time limit, or the period of the effects of a curse.

ศาพ, ศาว, ศาพก see ศาวก p. 796.

ศาพท์ sap⁴ *S. adj.* sonorous; loud; noisy; boisterous; sounding; pertaining to sound or noise; verbal; oral (S. E. D. p. 1065).

ศาพร sah²-paun *S. n.* injury; harm; offence; hurt; maltreatment: *adj.* wicked; malicious (S. E. D. p. 1065).

ศามะ sah²-ma⁶ *S. adj.* lessening; appeasing; curing; using palliative or curative measures; promoting peaceful relations or mutual goodwill (S. E. D. p. 1065).

ศามีล sah²-meen *S. n.* cinders; ashes (S. E. D. p. 1065).

ศาย sah²-ya⁶ *S. adj.* lying; sleeping; staying; remaining; abiding (S. E. D. p. 1065).

ศายึน sah²-yin *S. adj.* reclining; resting; remaining; recreating (S. E. D. p. 1066).

ศาร sah²-ra⁶ *S. adj.* variegated in colour; motley; spotted; speckled (S. E. D. p. 1066).

ศารท sart⁴ *S. n.* an annual; a year; the harvest festival; the feasting ceremony; the half year (autumnal) festival; festival of first-fruits; a merit-making occasion taking place annually during the eleventh and twelfth lunar months (wales, state ceremonies p. 231): *adj.* new; mature; recent; autumnal (S. E. D. p. 1066).

ศารทูล sah²-ra⁶-toon *S. n.* a tiger; a leopard; a lion; any eminent person; one who is excellent, prominent, or famous.

ศาริกา (นก) sah²-ri⁶-gkah *n.* the mynah bird, *Gracula religiosa* (chd. p. 422); *Acrido theres tristis*, the common mynah (Aagaard p. 53).

ศารีระ sah²-ree-ra⁶ *S. adj.* corporeal; relating, or belonging to the body; being in, or connected with the body; pertaining to the science of the functions of the body and organs (S. E. D. p. 1066).

ศาล ๑ san² *S. n. Shorea robusta*, an important tree of India, esteemed for its timber (chd. p. 422); a rampart; a barrier; a wall; a fence.

ศาล ๒ san² *n.* a court of justice; a tribunal; a joss-house: ศาลแขวง a district court: ศาลจังหวัด, ศาลเมือง a provincial court: ศาลเจ้า a building erected by the Chinese for the worship of their guardian spirits: ศาลฎีกา the Supreme Court: ศาลต่างประเทศ the International Court: ศาลทหาร court martial: ศาลโปรีสภา a police court: ศาลพระราชอาญา a criminal court: ศาลแพ่ง a civil court: ศาลอุทธรณ์ an appeal court.

ศาลก sah²-lok⁶ *S. n.* a clown; a jester; a buffoon (S. E. D. p. 1067).

ศาลา sah²-lah *S. n.* a house; a hall; a room (chd. p. 421); an out of doors shed, workshop or building; a public rest-house (S. E. D. p. 1067): ศาลากรรม house construction: ศาลาบดี the owner of a house; the lord of a house: ศาลามุข the front of the house: ศาลามฤค *lit.* "a domesticated animal," *i. e.* a dog.

ศาลาร sah²-lan *S. n.* a bird-cage; a ladder; a flight of stairs; a staircase; a bracket; a shelf; hooks, pegs or hangers (for clothing) (S. E. D. p. 1067).

ศาลิ sah²-li⁶ *P. n.* rice-; wheat; *especially* hill paddy (chd. p. 421); cereals: ศาลิกัณ a grain of rice: ศาลิเกษตร, ศาลิกพน์, ศาลิก rice fields: ศาลิจุรณ rice flour; rice ground into flour: ศาลิวาหนะ (พระเจ้า) Salivahana, a celebrated king of the southern part of India, whose era, the Saka, dates from A. D. 78 (H. C. D. p. 275).

ศาวก, ศาว, ศาพก, ศาพ sah²-wa⁶-gka⁴ *S. n.* the young of any animal (S. E. D. p. 1068).

ศาส sart⁴ *S. n.* an order; a command; a commander; a director; a ruler; a chastiser (S. E. D. p. 1068).

ศาสดา sart⁴-sa⁴-dah *P. n.* a teacher; a preceptor; a master; a tutor (chd. p. 469); an epithet for Gotama Buddha.

ศาสตร์ sart⁴ *S. n.* an order; a command; a rule; precepts; instruction; direction; advice; any manual or compendium of rules; any religious or scientific treatise; any sacred book or composition of divine authority (S. E. D. p. 1069): ศาสตรจักษุ *lit.* "the eye of science," *i. e.* grammar; having authoritative words as eyes: ศาสตรมติ having a well-trained mind: ศาสตรวาท a precept, statement or maxim of any treatise or science: ศาสตราจารย์ a professor.

ศาสติ sah²-sa⁴-dti⁴ *S. n.* correction; command; government; punishment; administration; a sceptre or baton borne by kings as an emblem of authority or royal power.

ศาสนา, ศาสน์, สาสนะ, สาสนา sart⁴-sa⁴-nah² *S. n.* a rule; a book; a treatise (H. C. D.

p. 285); an order; a command; an edict; a message; instructions; an epistle; a contract or agreement (chd. p. 465); Buddhist religious scriptures; devotion to, or belief in the scriptures as means of governing the passions; an instructor; any written book or work of authority; scriptures (S. E. D. p. 1068): ศาสนบัตร *lit.* "edict-plate," *i. e.* a plaque of copper or of stone on which an edict, commandment, or grant is inscribed.

ศาสนูบ็ตถัมภก, ศาสนูปถัมภก sart⁴-sa⁴-noo-bput⁴-tum²-pok⁶ *n.* adherents of a religion.

ศาสโนวาท sart⁴-sa⁴-noh-wart³ *n.* teachings of a religion.

ศิกกุ sik⁴-gkoo⁻ *S. adj.* lazy; idle; indolent; unoccupied (S. E. D. p. 1069).

ศิกยะ sik⁴-gka⁴-ya⁶ *S. n.* a kind of loop or swing made of rope and suspended from either end of a pole or yoke to receive a load; see สาแหรก (S. E. D. p. 1069).

ศิกษ์ sik⁴ *S. v.* to endeavour; to strive; to struggle to learn sciences, or to acquire knowledge; to undergo practice or study (S. E. D. p. 1070).

ศิกษก sik⁴-sok⁴ *S. n.* a teacher; an instructor, preceptor or tutor; a trainer (S. E. D. p. 1070).

ศิกษณะ sik⁴-sa⁴-na⁶ *S. n.* study; training; drill; education; tutoring; teaching (chd. [p. 475).

ศิกษา see ศึกษา p. 799.

ศิขร, ศิงขร, ศีขร si⁴-kaun² *S. n.* a point; a peak; the top or summit; the end or point; a pinnacle, turret or spire (S. E. D. p. 1070).

ศิขัณฑ์ si⁴-kan² *S. n.* a topknot or tuft of hair, left on the crown or sides of the head at the time of tonsure (S. E. D. p. 1070).

ศิขา si⁴-kah² *S. n.* a tuft or lock of hair on the crown of the head; the topknot; a

crest; a plume; a pointed flame; a point; a spike; a peak; a summit; a pinnacle; the border of a garment (S. E. D. p. 1070).

ศิขิน si⁴-kin² *S. n.* one who has reached the summit of knowledge; an epithet for the Buddha; a religious mendicant; a Brahmin (S. E. D. p. 1071).

ศิถิล si⁴-tin² *S. adj.* loose; slack; relaxed; untied; flaccid; not rigid or compact; soft; pliant; supple (S. E. D. p. 1071).

ศิปิ si⁴-bpi⁴ *S. n.* a ray of light; rays; glory (S. E. D. p. 1072).

ศิพิระ si⁴-pi⁶-ra⁶ *S. n.* a royal camp or residence; a tent in a royal camp; any tent; an entrenchment for the protection of an army (S. E. D. p. 1072).

ศิระ, เศียร si⁴-ra⁶ *S. n.* the head; the skull; the acme; an elevation (chd. p. 478); a person of importance; a patron; a leader; a director (as of a company or group) (S. E. D. p. 1072): ศิรกบาล a religious mendicant who carries about a skull: ศิรกัมป์ the act of turning, tossing, shaking, or nodding of the head: ศิรบัฏฏ์ head-bands; cloth used as a head-band or covering; a turban: ศิร-บีฑา headache: ศิรประณาม the act of bowing or bending the head (as in the performance of a salutation): ศิรสรัช a garland of flowers worn as a head decoration: ศิโรฆาต the act of beating, knocking or striking the head: ศิโรช *lit.* "head-produced," *i. e.* hair of the head: ศิโรธร, ศิโรธิ *lit.* "the supporter of the head," *i. e.* the neck (chd. p. 478): ศิโรเมาลี *lit.* "crest-jewel," *i. e.* an eminent, noted, famous or distinguished person: ศิโร-รักษ์ *lit.* "those who protect the (royal) head," *i. e.* the royal body-guard: ศิโรรัตน์ crest-gem; jewels worn on the head: ศิโรรุหะ *lit.* "head-growing," "head-crowning," *i. e.* hair of the head.

ศิรา, สิลา si⁴-rah *n.* water; a stream; a canal; a water-pipe or conduit.

ศิริ si⁴-ri⁴ *n.* beauty; prosperity; glory: ศิริวิลาศ characterized by having soft skin and a clear complexion (as of a beautiful virgin): ศิริยศ high dignity; honour; glory.

ศิริณา si⁴-ri⁶-nah *S. n.* night (S. E. D. p. 1073)

ศิโร- si⁴-roh *a prefix used in certain words* เช่น, ศิโรมณี a precious stone which adorns the hair.

ศิลป sin²-la⁶-bpa⁴ *S. n.* any manual art or craft; any artistic, decorative, or ornamental work; any handicraft displaying skill, artfulness, ingenuity and dexterity; art of manufacturing articles of diversified appearance. Trades, according to the Hindus, are divided into 128 professions, as carpentry, architecture, dancing, literary composition, etc. (S. E. D. p. 1073): ศิลปกรรม, ศิลปกิจ manual decorative work: ศิลปการ a craftsman; an artisan; a mechanic or expert in any mechanical trade: ศิลปเคหะ a workshop; a work-room; a manufactory: ศิลปชีวิกา subsistence by art, or by handicraft work: ศิลปวิทยา, ศิลปศาสตร์ the science of arts or mechanics.

ศิลป์ sin²-la⁶-bpee *S. n.* an artisan; an artificer; a craftsman; an expert; an artist (S. E. D. p. 1074).

ศิลา si⁴-lah *S. n.* stone; rock (Chd. p. 475); a boulder; a crag; the lower millstone (S. E. D. p. 1073): ก้อนศิลา a rock or stone: แล้วด้วยศิลา made of, or decorated with stone: ศิลาคฤห์ *lit.* "rock-house," *i. e.* a cave; a grotto: ศิลาช *lit.* "produced in a rock or mountain," *i. e.* minerals; iron; petroleum, etc.; any fossil production: ศิลาดล a slab of stone; a surface or floor of stone or rock: ศิลาแดง sandstone; tufa: ศิลาธาตุ *lit.* "rock-mineral," *i. e.* chalk; a white fossil substance; an aluminous earth of a white or yellowish colour: ศิลาปราสาท a pretentious stone building: ศิลาลาย marble: ศิลาแลง see แลง p. 756: ศิลาสาร *lit.* "rock-essence," *i. e.* iron.

ศิวะ si⁴-wa⁶ *S. n.* Siva, the Hindu deity, a fair man with four faces and four arms. He is commonly represented seated in profound thought, with a third eye in the middle of his forehead, contained in, or surmounted by the moon's crescent; his matted locks are gathered up into a coil like a horn, which bears upon it a symbol of the river Ganges, which he caught as it fell from heaven; a a necklace of skulls (มุณฑมาลา munda-mala) hangs round his neck, and serpents entwine about his neck as a collar (นาคกุณฑล Naga-kundala); his neck is blue from drinking the deadly poison which would have destroyed the world, and in his hand he holds a trident (ตรีศูล Trisula) called Pinaka. His garment is the skin of a tiger, a deer, or an elephant, hence he is called Kritti-vasas (กฤติวาสัส); sometimes he is clothed in a skin and seated upon a tiger-skin, and he holds a deer in his hand. He is generally accompanied by his bull (นนทิ). He also carries the bow (อัชควะ Ajaga-va), a drum in the shape of an hour-glass, the Khatwanga or club with a skull at the end, or a cord (บาศ Pasa) for binding refractory offenders. His Pramathas, or attendants, are numerous, and are imps and demons of various kinds. His third eye has been very destructive. With it he reduced to ashes Kama (กาม) the god of Love for daring to inspire amorous thoughts of his consort Parvati while he was engaged in penance (H. C. D. p. 298). Siva is represented by the phallic emblem: *adj.* auspicious; propitious; gracious; benevolent (S. E. D. p. 1074).

ศิวิกา, ศิพิกา si⁴-wi⁶-gkah *S. n.* a palanquin; a stretcher; a vehicle; a litter; a bier (Chd. p. 479).

ศิศุ si⁴-soo⁴ *S. n.* an infant; a baby; a child; a boy under eight years of age; a lad (S. E. D. p. 1076): ศิศุกรันท์ the crying of an infant or child: ศิศุกรีฑา a child's play: ศิศุกาล the period of infancy; childhood: ศิศุชน children; young people: ศิศุภาพ the state of childhood; infancy.

ศิษฎิ sit[4]-di[4] *S. n.* education; instruction; teaching; advice; an order; a command (S. E. D. p. 1077).

ศิษฏ์ sit[4] *S. adj.* taught; directed; disciplined; cultured; educated; learned; wise; eminent (S. E. D. p. 1076).

ศิษย์ sit[4] *S. n.* a pupil; a scholar; a disciple; a student (chd. p. 479): ลูกศิษย์ a novice; an apprentice; a follower: สานุศิษย์ pupils; disciples.

ศึกร see[2]-gkaun *S. n.* fine or drizzling rain; spray (of rain); fog; mist; coolness (chd. p. 474).

ศีฆร see[2]-kra[6] *S. adj.* urgent; quick; hasty; swift; vigorous; dexterous (S. E. D. p. 1077).

ศีต see[2]-dta[4] *S. adj.* cool; cold; chill; frigid; dull; apathetic; sluggish; indolent (S. E. D. p. 1077): ศีตกาล winter; the cold season: ศีตกิรณะ, ศีตภานุ *lit.* "cool-rayed," *i.e.* the moon: ศีตคันธ์ *lit.* "having a cooling fragrance," *i. e.* white sandal-wood.

ศีตก · see[2]-dta[4]-gka[4] *S. adj.* sluggish; idle; lazy (S. E. D. p. 1078).

ศีตล see[2]-dta[4]-la[6] *S. adj.* cold; chilly; shivering from cold; frosty; free from passion; not exciting emotion (S. E, D. p. 1078).

ศีรษะ see[2]-sa[4] *S. n.* the head; the skull; the top; the upper part; the forepart; the front (S. E. D. p. 1078): ศีรษฆาดี an executioner: ศีรษตราณ *lit.* "a protection for the head," *i. e.* a hat; a helmet: ศีรษบัฎฎก a head-band; a turban: ศีรษเวทนา, ศีรษพยาธา an headache.

ศีล seen[2] *S. n.* a code of moral or sacred precepts; commandments; Christian sacraments. A system of moral rules laid down by the Lord Buddha as a preliminary drill binding on those who have professed to follow the path indicated by him, *viz.* integrity; morality; piety; virtue; practice; conduct; nature; disposition or character (S. E. D. p. 1079): จำศีล, ถือศีล to observe religious principles, doctrines or precepts; to observe times of fasting or lent: ผู้ทรงศีล one who is endued with virtue: ศีลขาด to interdict on account of sin; to exclude from religious privileges (referring to members of a religious sect): ศีลตยาค the condition of utter abandonment, or renouncement of virtuous practices, or good conduct: ศีลมหาสนิท the sacrament of the Eucharist, or Holy Communion: ศีลวัต, ศีลวา, ศีลวาน virtuous; being in good religious standing; having good behaviour; following religious precepts; practicing good morals: ศีลสมาทาน the abiding by the principles of morality; the observance of virtue: ศีลสิบ the decalogue; the ten commandments: ศีลห้า the code of five precepts as laid down by the Buddhist religion: ให้ศีลให้พร to pronounce a blessing on (as at a wedding); to say grace (as before a meal).

ศึก suk[4] *n.* troops; an army; a fight; a combat; a conflict: ข้าศึก an enemy; adversaries: ศึกเสื้อเหนือใต้ *colloquial* wars or defeats on all sides: ศึกหน้าเมีย brave undaunted (as though the wife were facing an enemy): ไส้ศึก a spy; a traitor; an instigator of war or rebellion; a malcontent.

ศึกษา, ศิกษา suk[4]-sah[2] *n.* an endeavour to accomplish or gain education by studying, training, and learning; skill; experience; instruction; practice; lesson: กรมศึกษาธิการ the Department of Public Instruction: การ-ศึกษา educational pursuits.

ศุก sook[4] *S. n.* a parrot (chd. p. 488).

ศุกร์ sook[4] *S. n.* name of Agni, the god of Fire; the planet Venus; the evening star; brightness; clearness; the pulp or inner part of fruit, grains, seeds: *adj.* white; bright; pure; good (chd. p. 488); clear; spotless (as jewels): วันศุกร์ the day of Venus; Friday: ศุกรวรรณ bright; clear; fresh in colour or appearance: ศุกรโสจิ bright-rayed.

ศุกล soo⁴-gkla⁴ *S. adj.* white; bright; pure; spotless (Chd. p. 488): ศุกลกรรม pure in action or conduct: ศุกลธาตุ *lit.* "a white mineral," *i. e.* chalk: ศุกลธยาน the act of meditating or considering the truth.

ศุกลก sook⁴-la⁶-gka⁴ *S. n.* whiteness; white (colour) (S. E. D. p. 1080).

ศุจ soot⁴ *S. n.* sorrow; sadness; grief (S. E. D. p. 1081).

ศุจิ soo⁴-chji⁴ *S. n.* purification; purity; honesty; virtue: *adj.* radiant; bright; gleaming; clear; clean; pure; undefiled; innocent; virtuous; honest (S. E. D. p. 1081): ศุจิกรรม loving purity: ศุจิกรันท์ one having a clear voice: ศุจิจริต honest, loyal, and faithful in conduct: ศุจิมนัส one pure in heart: ศุจิโรจิ *lit.* "white-rayed," *i. e.* the moon.

ศุจิต soo⁴-chjit⁴ *S. adj.* grieved; sad; lamenting (S. E. D. p. 1081).

ศุณฑ์ soon² *S. n.* the juice exuding from the temples of an elephant in rut; an elephant's trunk (S. E. D. p. 1081).

ศุณฑี soon²-tee *S. n.* a tavern; a saloon; a barman; a barmaid; a dispenser of intoxicants; a licensed house for the sale of liquors, with accommodations for travellers (S. E. D. p. 1081).

ศุทธ soot⁴-ta⁶ *S. adj.* cleansed; cleared; clean; white; free from error; acquitted; innocent; correct; accurate (S. E. D. p. 1082): ศุทธปักษ์ the waxing phase of the moon: ศุทธภาพ purity of mind; guilelessness: ศุทธพรรณ having a pure, clear colour or complexion; being of high caste: ศุทธหฤทัย one endowed with a pure heart: ศุทโธทน name of the royal father of Gotama Buddha.

ศุทธิ soot⁴-ti⁶ *S. n.* purity; purification; justification; exculpation; innocence; acquittal; freedom from defilement (S. E. D. p. 1082): ศุทธิบัตร a certificate or testimonial of good conduct; a certificate of purification by pen-

ance; an errata list; a sheet or paper of corrections.

[p. 489).

ศุน, ศุนัก, ศุนิ soo⁴-na⁶ *S. n.* a dog (chd.

ศุภ, ศุภางค์, สุภ soo⁴-pa⁶ *S. n.* that which is good, pure, honest, auspicious, fortunate, prosperous, bright, beautiful, virtuous (S. E. D. p. 1083): ศุภกร affording welfare, prosperity, or good fortune; propitious: ศุภกษณะ an auspicious or propitious day or moment: ศุภเคราะห์ an auspious planet; a lucky star: ศุภนิมิตต์ a dream foretelling fortune, good luck, or happiness; a favourable dream: ศุภผล results or consequences that are good and propitious: ศุภมงคล luck; fortune; destiny that is good: ศุภมาส an auspicious day, month, or year (when projects may be undertaken with favourable results): ศุภลักษณ์ endowed with auspicious characteristics or marks: ศุภลัคน์ the rising of an auspicious constellation; a lucky moment.

ศุลก soon²-la⁶-gka⁴ *S. n.* tax; fee; tribute; revenue; custom; duty; value; price (chd. p. 489); money or valuables presented by a groom to the bride's parents as an engagement gift; pledge money given by the parents of the bride and the groom to be used by them as capital with which to set up housekeeping; a dowry; a marriage settlement (S.E.D. p. 1084): ศุลกสถาน a toll-house; a custom house; a tax office: ศุลกากร tax; duty; royalty; dues collected from taxation.

ศุลพ์, ศุลว soon² *S. n.* thread; yarn; cord; string; rope (S. E. D. p. 1084).

ศุษ soo⁴-sa⁴ *S. v.* to become dry or withered; to fade; to languish; to make dry, or become parched; to injure, hurt or destroy (S. E. D. p. 1084).

ศุษก soo⁴-sa⁴-gka⁴ *S. adj.* dry; dried; arid; parched; withered; shrivelled; shrunken; useless; groundless; empty; unprofitable (S. E. D. p. 1084): ศุษกกัลหะ a groundless quarrel: ศุษกกาส a dry cough: ศุษกผล sun-dried fruit: ศุษกมางสะ meat or fish that has been dried: ศุษกวิเคราะห์ a useless contention.

ศุษ soo⁴-si⁴ *S. n.* the act of drying by gentle heat, or setting out in the sun to dry (S. E. D. p. 1084).

ศุษิล soo⁴-sin² *S. n.* air; wind (S.E.D. p. 1085).

ศูกร soo²-gka⁴-ra⁶ *S. n.* a hog; a boar; a pig or sow (chd. p. 487).

ศูทร soot⁴ *S. n.* the fourth or servile Hindu caste (H. C. D. p. 306).

ศูนย์ soon² *S. n.* a vacuum; emptiness: *adj.* empty; void; hollow; barren; desolate; deserted; vacant; having no use, object or aim; wholly alone or solitary; having no friends or companions (S. E. D. p. 1085): ศูนยภาพ a void; emptiness; vacantness: ศูนยวาท atheism; the Buddhist doctrine of non-existence.

ศูร soo²-ra⁶ *S. n.* heroism; intrepidity; a hero; a champion; one who acts heroically towards another, or with regard to anything: *adj.* strong; powerful; valiant; heroic; courageous (S. E. D. p. 1086).

ศูล soo²-la⁶ *S. n.* a sharp iron pin or stake; a spike; a spit; any sharp instrument or pointed dart; a lance; a pike; a spear; a trident (as is carried by Siva); any sharp or acute pain, grief or sorrow (S. E. D. p. 1086).

ศูลิน, ศูลี soo²-lin *S. n. lit.* "one who bears a lance or trident," *i. e.* Siva (chd. p. 488); one armed with a spear; a lancer; a spearman (S. E. D. p. 1087).

เศยน sa⁴-yen *S. n.* a hawk; a falcon; an eagle; any bird of prey (S. E. D. p. 1095).

เศรณ say²-nee *S. n.* a line; a row; a range; a series; succession; troop; flock; a swarm; a company of artisans following the same business; a guild or association of traders dealing in the same articles (S. E. D. p. 1102).

เศรยส say²-yot⁶ *S. n.* welfare; happiness; health; bliss (S. E. D. p. 1102).

เศรษฐ set⁴ *S. adj.* best; first; chief; distinguished; most auspicious or salutary (S. E. D. p. 1102); see ประเสริฐ p. 505: กระทรวงเศรษฐการ Ministry of Economics: เศรษฐวิทยา *occasionally used to imply* economics.

เศรษฐี set⁴-tee² *S. n.* a distinguished man; a person of affluence or authority; an eminent artisan; the president or foreman of a guild (S. E. D. p. 1102): มหาเศรษฐี a multi-millionaire: ลูกเศรษฐี the child of an opulent family.

เศร้า sow³ *v.* to be overcome with grief; to be sorrowful: เศร้าโศก sad; sullen; doleful; depressed or morose; grieved: เศร้าหมอง smirched; stained; tainted (in character from a cause, or as a result of corruption).

เศลษม์ sa⁴-let³ *S. n.* phlegm; rheum; the phlegmatic humour (chd. p. 472); mucus collecting in the throat, or passed in dysentery (S. E. D. p. 1104).

เศวต sa⁴-wet⁴ *S. n.* white (in colour); a a white horse; a small white shell; a cowry: *adj.* white-dressed, or decorated in white (S. E. D. p. 1106): เศวตกุญชร, เศวตคช *lit.* "the white elephant," *i. e.* Airavata, the elephant of Indra (H. C. D. p. 127); white elephants (in general): เศวตงค์, เศวตดงค์ having a white body: เศวตฉัตร a royal, nine-tiered, white umbrella; the white canopy of sovereignty; the white umbrella of kingship: เศวตฉัท *lit.* "one having white wings," *i. e.* a goose: เศวตธาตุ chalk; opal; chalcedony; a white mineral: เศวตดิก, เศวตดีภ, เศวตเตภ, เศวตดีภ a white elephant: เศวตพาชี *lit.* "having or riding a white horse," *i. e.* Indra: เศวตภานุ, เศวตโรจิ *lit.* "white-rayed; having white light," *i. e.* the moon.

[p. 1107].

เศวตร sa⁴-wet⁴ *S. n.* white leprosy (S. E. D.

เศษ set⁴ *S. n.* remainder (chd. p. 473); the part that remains; the balance left over; a fractional part; the leavings; the residue; the surplus: เดนเศษ remnants; fragments: เศษไม้ chips of wood: เศษส่วน fractions: เศษสตางค์ change: เหลือเศษ a fractional part that remains over.

เศาจ sow²-chja⁴ *S. n.* cleanliness; purity; purification (by ablution); purity of mind; integrity; honesty.

เศาจิก, เศาไจย sow²-chjik⁴ *S. n.* a washerman; a laundryman; a laundress; a cleaner; a cleanser (s. e. d. p. 1092).

เศาณฑร์ sow²-dtee *S. n.* pride; haughtiness; self-exaltation; arrogance: *adj.* proud; conceited; haughty (s. e. d. p. 1092).

เศารยะ sow²-ra⁶-ya⁶ *S. n.* heroism; valour; prowess; bravery (s. e. d. p. 1093).

เศิก serk⁴ *n.* an enemy; a foe; an adversary.

โศก, โสก soke⁴ *S. n.* sorrow; grief; mourning (chd. p. 482); affliction; anguish; pain; trouble (s. e. d. p. 1091).

โศก *Thai,* (ต้น) soke⁴ *n. Saraca indica* (*Leguminosae*), the asoka tree of India. It is sacred among the Hindus, and particularly sacred to the Buddhists as being the tree under which the Buddha was born. In India it is called the asoka tree; in Thailand this has been shortened to โศก. It is a small, spreading tree, bearing on the stems and branches, chiefly in the dry weather, large sessile clusters of scented flowers which change from yellow to orange and red. The young leaves are developed in long, drooping clusters, as in *Brownea* and *Amherstia*. It thrives in shady situations, especially near water, in the wet or semi-dry districts, up to 2,000 feet or higher (cb. p. 537: mcm. p. 93: burk. p. 1964); *S. zollingeriana* is a synonym of *Saraca indica*: โศกเขา *Thai, Pattani,* ตะบีกะ *Malay, Pattani* (ต้น) *Saraca triandra* (*Leguminosae*), a shrub or small tree found in Thailand, Sumatra, the Malay Peninsula, Borneo, and Java. The wood is very crooked and for the most part too small to be useful

(cb. p. 536: burk. p. 1965): โศกน้ำ *Thai, Pattani,* ตะโคลีเต๊าะ *Malay, Pattani* (ต้น) *Saraca bijuga* (*Leguminosae*), a small tree found in the peninsular part of Thailand, and in Malaya southwards toward Negri Sembilan. The flowers and young leaves are eaten by the Thai (burk. p. 1964); *S. pierreana* (cb. pp. 534, 536): โศกระย้า, โศกฝรั่ง (ต้น) *Amherstia nobilis* (*Leguminosae*), a small tree with flowers of great beauty. It was found first in 1826 as a tree planted near a monastery in the neighbourhood of Moulmein, and subsequently was found wild to the northwards. It is named after Lady Amherst, whose husband was Governor of Burma. Its large, graceful sprays of vermillion and yellow flowers, drooping from every branch and interspersed with the handsome foliage, present an appearance of astonishing elegance and loveliness. It is in blossom for the greater part of the year, except during long periods of rainy weather, the chief flowering season in Ceylon being from November to April. The tree grows to a height of 50 to 60 feet, is usually round-topped, with many slender branches and dark-green, pinnate leaves. A remarkable feature is the long, hanging, brownish-pink clusters in which the young leaves appear. This tree is very rare. Two specimens are known in Bangkok, one in Dang Toi Nursery and one in the old Insane Asylum (cb. p. 533: mcm. p. 83: burk. p. 131): โศกสะบัน, โศกฝรั่ง (ต้น) asoka spunge, *Brownea sp.*, a tree having a large bunch of flowers and leaves like a cluster of Amherstia white leaves: โศกใหญ่ *Thai, Pattani* (ต้น) *Saraca declinata* (*Leguminosae*), a small tree, found from Thailand to Java. It is said to be native of Sumatra, introduced into Ceylon in 1870. On the stems and older branches it produces very large heads of bright orange-yellow flowers, usually during February and March. It bears a few, flat, bright red pods. The wood is very crooked and is not durable (cb. p. 535: mcm. p. 93: burk. p. 1964).

โศกิน, โศกี soh²-gkin *S. n.* one who is sad.

โศกินี soh²-gki⁴-nee *n. feminine* a woman who is sad.

โศจนะ soh²-chja⁴-na⁶ *S. n.* the condition of mourning, wailing, sorrowing or lamenting; grief; sorrow (Chd. p. 481).

โศจิ soh²-chji⁴ *S. n.* a flame; glow; radiance; rays of light; splendour: *adj.* shining; luminous; brilliant.
[woody climber.

โศณ soh²-na⁶ *S. n. Bignonia indica*, a

โศถ soh²-ta⁴ *S. n.* a swelling; a tumour; a blister; a morbid intumescence, as a condition of dropsy (S. E. D. p. 1091).

โศพิต soh²-pit⁶ *S. n.* blood: *adj.* bright-red; scarlet; see โลหิต p. 759.

โศภา soh²-pah *S. n.* splendour; brilliance; radiance; lustre; beauty; grace (S.E.D. p. 1092).

โศภิต soh²-pit⁶ *S. adj.* splendid; beautiful; adorned or embellished (S. E. D. p. 1092).

โศภิษฐ์ soh²-pit⁶ *S. adj.* most brilliant or splendid.

โศรณ son² *S. adj.* lame; limping; crippled; crooked (S. E. D. p. 1102).

โศรณิ soh²-ni⁶ *S. n.* hip; waist; thigh; loins; buttocks (S. E. D. p. 1102).

โศรดา, โศรตฤ soh²-dah *S. n.* an audience; a listener; a hearer.

โศรตร sote⁴ *S. n.* the organ of hearing; the ear (Chd. p. 483); the auditory meatus; the auricle; the act of listening, hearing or giving ear (S. E. D. p. 1103).

โศรตรีย์ soh²-dtree *S. adj.* docile; modest; teachable; tractable; manageable; well-behaved (S. E. D. p. 1103).

โศลก sa⁴-loke⁶ *S. n.* a proverb; a maxim; a kind of common epic metre; a hymn of praise; a sound; a noise (S. E. D. p. 1104).

โศษ ๑ sote⁴ *S. n.* breath; vital energy (S. E. D. p. 1092).

โศษ ๒ sote⁴ *S. adj.* dry; dried; parched; scorched by the sun; desiccated.

ไศล sai²-la⁶ *S. n.* a rock; a crag; a hill; a mountain: *adj.* made of stone; stony; rocky; stone-like; rigid: ไศลกฎ the brow of a hill; the slope of a mountain: ไศลชน a person inhabiting mountains; a highlander; a mountaineer: ไศลวาส a mountain habitation: ไศลศฤงค์, ไศลสิขร a mountain peak: ไศลาฏ a forester; wild mountain tribes; hill-tribes.

ษ

ษ The thirty-ninth consonant of the Thai alphabet, a high class letter of which there are eleven, *viz.* ข, ฃ, ฉ, ฐ, ถ, ผ, ฝ, ศ, ษ, ส, ห. สอบอ and สอฤษี are the names of this letter. ษ is derived from Sanskrit and is used in words of Sanskrit origin, both as a prefix and suffix. Often it is pronounced like the English "sh," but more frequently like "s" or "ส".

ษฐีว sa⁴-tee²-wa⁶ *S. v.* to spit, expectorate, or eject from the mouth (S. E. D. p. 1111).

ษฐีวน sa⁴-tee²-won *S. n.* spittle; expectoration: *adj.* ejecting of saliva frequently; spitting; sputtering (S. E. D. p. 1111).

ษฑร sa⁴-ton *S. n.* a hexagon: *adj.* hexagonal (in shape).

ษฑังค์ sa⁴-dang *S. n.* the six principal parts of the body (comprising 2 arms, 2 legs, 1 head and the trunk); the six main divisions of the Vedas which are called เวทางค์ (H. C. D. p. 352); six auspicious things (S. E. D. p. 1108).

มณฑ์ son[2] *S. n.* a group; a company; a multitude; a flock; a pack; a community; a bull; a clump of trees, or bushes (S.E.D. p. 1107).

มณฑาลี son[2]-tah-lee *S. n.* a pond; a well; a pool; a playful woman or girl; a wanton woman (S. E. D. p. 1108).

มมา sa[4]-mah *S. n.* repression; suppression; restraint (as of anger or revenge); the act of begging pardon or forgiveness; see กมมา p. 64: มมาไทษ to ask forgiveness for wrongs or sins: มมายุมแปลง adornment (personal); offerings or presents borne when asking pardon or forgiveness (as to the parents of the girl after an elopement).

ษัฏ sat[4] *S. adj.* six; used also as a prefix in words beginning with any low class consonant (S. E. D. p. 1108): ษัฏกรรณ a kind of lute, fife, or flute: *adj.* being heard by six ears, or by three persons (as secrets or private affairs passed on from one to another): ษัฏกรรม the six-fold duties of all Brahmins: ษัฏกษณะ a period of time which equals twenty-four minutes: ษัฏจรณ, ษัฏบท *lit.* "six-footed," *i. e.* a bee; a locust: ษัฏบุรุษ a period of six generations of a house, family or lineage.

ษัฏกะ sat[4]-gka[4] *S. n.* the numeral six; an amount equal to six: *adj.* consisting of six; occurring for the sixth time; doing anything in six ways.

ษัฑ sat[4] *S. adj.* consisting of six parts (S. E. D. p. 1108): ษัฑธา six-fold; in six different ways: ษัฑธาร hexagonal (in shape); six-edged: ษัฑกุช six-armed; having six sides and six angles; hexagonal: ษัฑวิธ six-fold; six-tiered; of six sorts: ษัฑานน *lit.* "one having six mouths or six faces," *i. e.* Jayanta, son of Indra (H. C. D. pp. 126, 136).

ษัณ san[2] *S. adj.* sixth (S. E. D. p. 1109): ษัณณาภี having six navels: ษัณมาส a period of six months.

ษัณฑ์ san[2] *S. n.* an eunuch; the neuter gender (S. E. D. p. 1108).

ษัษ sat[4] *S. adj.* six; sixth; used interchangeably with ษัฏ, ษัฑ, ษัณ (S. E. D. p. 1108).

ษัษฏิ sat[4]-sa[4]-dtee *S. n.* the numeral sixty; sixty in number (S. E. D. p. 1109).

ษัษฐี sat[4]-sa[4]-tee[2] *S. n.* the sixth day of a lunar fortnight (S. E. D. p. 1110).

ษาฑพ sah[2]-top[6] *n.* confectionery; sweetmeats; delicacies; cakes; candy; fruit preserves (S. E. D. p. 1110).

โษฑาศ soh[2]-ta[6]-sa[4] *S. adj.* sixteenth (S. E. D. p. 1110).

โษฑาศัน soh[2]-ta[6]-san[2] *S. n.* sixteen.

ส

ส The fortieth consonant of the Thai alphabet, a high class letter of which there are eleven, *viz.* ข, ฃ, ฉ, ฐ, ฏ, ผ, ฝ, ส, ษ, ศ, ห. สอลอ and สอเสือ are the names of this letter, which is used both as a prefix and suffix generally, in Thai, Pali and Sanskrit; it is pronounced like an English "s".

ส ๒ sa[4] *P. S. n.* a prefix much used with adjectives and adverbs, generally conveying the idea of *possession* (chd. p. 406); an inseparable prefix expressing *junction, similarity, equality.* When compounded with nouns to form adjectives and adverbs it may be translated by *with, together or along with, accompanied by, added to, containing, having the same* (S. E. D. p. 1111): สเทวก attended by, or furnished with celestial beings: สธัมมิก possessing the united principles of righteousness, virtue and justice: สชาติ having the same birth-place or born of the same parents.

สก sa⁴-gka⁴ *P. n.* own; one's own advantage (chd. p. 421): สกวาที *lit.* "one who expresses the positive side in a discussion," *i. e.* the affirmer: ปรวาที *lit.* "one who expresses the opposing side in a discussion," *i. e.* the negator.

สกฏ sa⁴-gkot⁴ *P. n.* a cart; a waggon; a measure of capacity (chd. p. 416): สกฏภาร the load carried or transported by a cart or waggon; a cart-load; see ศกฏ p. 786.

สกนธ์ sa⁴-gkon *S. n.* the part of a plant from one joint to another; a branch or stalk; a section or chapter of a book; a part; a portion; a piece (chd. p. 182); a shoulder; the bole of a tree; a great number; a large quantity; see ขันธ์ ๑ p. 151.

สกปรก sok⁴-gka⁴-bprok⁴ *adj.* dirty; filthy; unclean; foul; squalid: คนพูดสกปรก a foul-mouthed person: ทำสกปรก to cause dirt or foulness: พูดสกปรก to use foul or indecent language.

สกรณีย์ sa⁴-gka⁴-ra⁶-nee *P. n.* one still having duties to perform (chd. p. 416).

สกรรจ์, ฉกรรจ์ sa⁴-gkan *adj.* in the prime or vigour of life; vigorous; powerful (say from 20 to 30 years of age); see ฉกรรจ์ p. 264: คนสกรรจ์ a man fit for military service: หนุ่มสกรรจ์ young and fit for service.

สกรรมกริยา sa⁴-gkum-ma⁶-gka⁴-ri⁶-yah *n. grammar* a transitive verb.

สกล ๑, สากล sa⁴-gkon *P. S. adj.* all (chd. p. 416); full; whole; complete; universal; entire: สกลกาย the entire body: สกลชมพู all of India: สกลโลก universal; the whole world; everybody.

สกล ๒ sa⁴-gkon *n.* a portion; a potsherd (chd. p. 416); a part; a quarter; a half.

สกาว sa⁴-gkow *Cam. adj.* white; clean; unstained; purified.

สกาศ sa⁴-gkart⁴ *S. n.* propinquity; vicinity; the act of being near: *adj.* near (chd. p. 416); close to, or in the presence of; visible.

สกุณ sa⁴-gkoon *P. n.* a bird (chd. p. 412); a flock of birds: สกุณไกรสร a mythical bird-monster; a bird-lion; the traditional colour, light yellow: สกุณจาป the young of birds: สกุณบท *lit.* "the path of birds," *i. e.* the sky; the atmosphere; the air: สกุณเหรา a mythical bird-monster; a crocodile-bird; the traditional colour, light yellow.

สกุณี sa⁴-gkoo⁴-nee *P. n.* female birds: สกุโณ male birds.

สกุนต์ sa⁴-gkoon *P. n.* a bird; the Indian vulture (chd. p. 421).

สกุล sa⁴-gkoon *n.* lineage; descendants: เชื้อสกุล of a noble lineage: มีสกุลสูง of a high or noble family: นามสกุล the family name: โรงเรียนสำหรับเด็กมีสกุล a school for the children of the nobility; a high grade school.

สข, สขา, สขิ sa⁴-ka⁴ *. P. S. n.* a male companion; a friend (chd. p. 416): สขี a female companion.

สง song² *v.* to lift up loosely in the fingers (so that water, dirt, or small useless particles can fall through); to lift out; to remove or lift up: *adj.* ripe; matured (as the arecanut): สงข้าว to take handsful of rice out of the washing water prior to cooking it; to take out the washed rice handful by handful: สงฟาง to draw or rake the threshed straw out from the threshing floor in order to leave only the grain: หมากสง the fully matured areca-nut.

ส่ง song⁴ *v.* to hand; to deliver; to conduct; to send; to escort to, or out (as a visitor or traveller): ส่งกลิ่น to emit a fragrance: ส่งขวัญข้าว to make a thank-offering (as to a doctor after effecting a cure): ส่งข่าว, บอกส่ง to make a report, or bring news from a distant place: ส่งคำสัตย์ to forward an affidavit (as to a court): ส่งดิน to load gun-powder or projectiles: ส่งตัว to conduct or escort (as the bride to the home of the groom): ส่งตัวไปศาล to conduct or deliver a person to a court or tribunal: ส่งทุกข์ to void or pass fecal matter: ส่งผู้ร้ายข้ามเขตรแดน *legal* to extradite a prisoner: ส่งมา to send to; to send by, or deliver to (as a gift): ส่งรัศมี to radiate rays: ส่งสิ่งของออกจากประเทศ to export: ส่งส่วย to make payment of taxes or assessments: ส่งเสริม to supplement; to support, or provide what is lacking: ส่งเสีย to supply; to support; to give to, or provide for the wants of another (as food or funds while in school): ส่งเลี้ยง to acclaim with a loud voice; to make a loud noise; to shout: ส่งหนังสือ, ส่งจดหมาย to send or deliver a letter: เหล็กส่ง a nail set (for sinking nail-heads).

สงกร ๑   song[2]-gkon *P. S. n.* confusion (chd. p. 452); the offspring of a mixed marriage: *adj.* mixing together; intermixture; commingling (S. E. D. p. 1126).

สงกร ๒   song[2]-gkon *P. adj.* pleased; glad; delighted; joyous.

สงกรานต์   song[2]-gkran *n.* passage; change of place; removal from one place to another; the passage of the sun into the zodical sign Aries; one of the three Thai New Year's Festivals which in 1889 were officially combined in one, making the official New Year falling on the 1st April. The New Year Festivals are lunar and astrological (old solar) and essentially religious, being connected with the old calendar adopted from India on the basis of the Saka reckoning. They are still used by the Brahmins in the arrangement of their ceremonial calendar and are also celebrated by the masses to whom they mean more than the civil New Year (modern solar). Songkran is one of these. It is the astrological (solar) New Year and falls on either the 12th or the 13th April, the date of the assumed entrance of the sun into Aries, according to the traditional local (Hindu-imported) reckoning. Formerly the year's serial number in the era was changed on the third day which was actually regarded as New Year's Day (solar). This has now been changed to 1st January as from the beginning of A. D. 1941 which became the beginning of B. E. 2484. For the people the Songkran is a season of much rejoicing and merit-making by washing the images in the temples, building hillocks of sand for covering the monastery courtyards, sprinkling the monks as an act of respect, and making offerings of candles and incense before the images (wales, state Ceremonies p. 299).

สงกา, สังกา   song[2]-gkah *P. n.* doubt; doubtfulness; uncertainty (chd. p. 452); distrust; suspicion.

สงโกจ see เขมัน p. 164.

สงค์ see สังค์

สงคร   song[2]-kon *S. n.* an agreement; a promise; war; conflict; calamity.

สงคราม   song[2]-kram *S. n.* combat; conflict; battle (chd. p. 447); war; warfare; hostile encounters (S. E. D. p. 1129): ทำสงคราม to wage war: ไปในการสงคราม to serve in war, or in battle: สงครามภูมิ a battle-field: สงครามมฤตยู casualties in war.

สงเคราะห์   song[2]-kraw[6] *v.* to oblige by coming to the aid of; to render the necessary support (as one would to a friend in need); to be the "Good Samaritan": *n.* help; aid; support; assistance.

สงฆ์, สังฆ์   song[2] *P. n.* a multitude; an assemblage; an assembly of Buddhist priests; the priesthood; the clergy; the church; a brotherhood of priests; a chapter of priests (chd. p. 449); *Thai* a Buddhist priest; a bonze or talapoin: สงฆ์สาวก a disciple of the Buddha.

สงบ   sa[4]-ngop[4] *v.* to become calmed, quieted, stilled or peaceful; to stop, cease, or become mild and more normal (used of a high fever, or of the wind, waves or sea): สงบคน solitariness; privacy; seclusion; retirement: ให้สงบลง to smooth over; to quiet, hush, quell, or pacify: ให้สงบสงคราม to stop or cease fighting: ให้สงบเสงี่ยม to be quiet; to be still; to be gentle and well-behaved; see เงียบ p. 226.

สงวน   sa⁴-ngu-an² v. to be careful of; to keep safely; to husband, retain, or reserve (with the strictest care): สงวนความงาม to preserve one's beauty: สงวนความรัก to husband one's love.

สงสัย   song²-sai² v. to doubt (chd. p. 440); to suspect; to mistrust; to distrust: ความ-สงสัย doubt; suspicion: เป็นที่สงสัย giving ground, or reason for doubt: สงสัยสนเท่ห์ *idiomatic* suspicious of fraud or guile; see มารยา p. 649: ให้สิ้นสงสัย to rid of all doubt or distrust.

สงสาร, สังสาร   song²-san² *Thai v.* to pity; to manifest compassion or sympathy: *P. S. n.* the act of passing through a succession of births; continued existence; transmigration (chd. p. 440); a state of continual transition; the act of going on; the passing along; the condition of changing; the transitoriness of life; passing through a succession of states or circuits of mundane existences; metempsychosis (S. E. D. p. 1119): น่าสงสาร worthy of pity: สงสารจักร transition of things worldly; the world compared to a wheel: สงสารทุกข์ pain or sorrow of the world: สงสารพันธน์ entanglements or fetters of the world; lust; desire; sin: สงสารภัย fear during the states of transmigration: สงสารโมกข์ the condition of disannulment of worldy temptations and allurements: สงสารวัฏฏี the uncertainties, transitions, rotations of life, or the condition of the world: สงสารสาร the condition of quietness, or essence of the world.

สงด, สงัด   sa⁴-ngote⁴ *adj.* solitary; hush-

ed; quiet; calm; tranquil; peaceful: ที่สงัด a place of solitude or seclusion: ที่สงัดคน a place of privacy or retirement; see วิเวก p. 778.

สง่า   sa⁴-ngah⁴ *adj.* majestic; grand; glorious; splendour with dignity; majesty and magnificence: มีสง่า dignified; pompous; magnificent (as a king dressed in state uniform): สง่างาม regal grandeur: สง่าโฉม beautiful; lovely; graceful: สง่าราศี glory; grandeur as of the rising sun.

สฐะ   sa⁴-ta⁴ *P. adj.* crafty; treacherous; fraudulent; wicked (chd. p. 466); crooked; deceitful; boastful; see ทุจจริต p. 418.

สณฑ์, สัณฑ์   son² *P. n.* a multitude (chd. p. 466); a group, company, or party (of people); an avenue, grove, clump, or thicket (of trees or bushes); see พวก p. 575.

สด   sot⁴ *adj.* green; fresh; new; recent; vivid (in colour): เงินสด ready money; cash: น้ำตาลสด the fresh juice of the toddy palm: สดชื่น fresh; merry; glad; joyful: สดใส flourishing (as a plant); fresh (as flowers): สดสว่าง fresh; vivid; brilliant in colour (as a flower): หน้าสดใสชื่นบาน *idiomatic* having a bright, clear, clean, cheerful expression.

สดับปกรณ์, สัตดับปกรณ์, สบัตประกรณ์, สบัตประกรณ์   sa⁴-dup⁴-bpa⁴-gkorn *n. lit.* "the time of meditation around a corpse," *i. e.* an occasion for reflection on the frailty of life and certainty of death. On such occasions a chapter of seven Buddhist monks chant prayers for the dead.

สดายุ   sa⁴-dah-yoo⁶ *n.* a fabulous bird, the son of Aruna, killed by Ravana.

สดี   see สติ

สดุดี   sa⁴-doo⁴-dee *P. n.* praise; thanks; commendation; an eulogy (chd. p. 505).

สดุตย์   sa⁴-doot⁴ *adj.* admirable; praiseworthy; worthy of eulogy.

สดูป see สถูป

สต ๑   sa⁴-dta⁴ *P. n.* an hundred (chd. p. 465).

สต ๒   sa⁴-dta⁴ *P. adj.* recollecting; mindful; attentive; thoughtful; conscious (chd. p. 467).

สตก, สดก   sa⁴-dta⁴-gka⁴ *P. n.* the numeral one hundred; a hundred (chd. p. 465).

สตน, สตัน, สดน, สดัน   sa⁴-dton *S. n.* the female breast; the teat; the nipple; the mamma (S. E. D. p. 1257): สตนป an infant still at the breast; a suckling child; a nursing baby: สตนบาน the act of suckling or feeding at the breast.

สตรี   sa⁴-dtree *S. n.* a woman; a female; a wife (S. E. D. p. 1260): สตรีกาม desirous of, or devoted to women: สตรีชน, สตรีชาติ womankind; the female sex; women in general: สตรีทวิษ one averse to women; one who shuns women's company: สตรีภาพ womanhood; wifehood: สตรีรัตน์ *lit.* "a jewel of a woman," *i. e.* a charming, excellent or attractive woman: สตรีลิงค์ *grammar* the feminine gender.

[p. 503].

สตันย์   sa⁴-dtun *S. n.* mother's milk (chd.

สตัพธ์   sa⁴-dtup⁴ *S. adj.* firm; hard; solid; dense; obstinate; stolid; stubborn (S. E. D. p. 1258).

สตัมภ์, สดมภ์   sa⁴-dtum *S. n.* a post; a pillar; a column; a stem; a support (S. E. D. p. 1258).

สตางค์   sa⁴-dtang *n.* a copper coin, worth one hundredth of a baht.

สติ   sa⁴-dti⁴ *P. n.* attention; attentiveness; thought; reflection; consciousness; an active state of the mind; fixing the mind firmly upon any subject (chd. p. 466): ตั้งสติ to compose one's mind; to calm oneself in the face of danger: สติปัญญา knowledge; prudence; intelligence: สติปัฏฐาน the four objects for earnest meditation, which are (1)

the (uncertainness of) the body (กาย), (2) the spirit, life, or soul (จิตต์), (3) sensation of pleasure or pain (เวทนา), (4) the law, rightness, truth, and the eternal principles followed by nature (ธรรม) (chd. p. 466): สติวินัย teachings based on the code of ethics followed by Buddhist monks: สติสัมปชัญญะ the condition of constant self-consciousness; carefulness; self-government: สติอารมณ์ a tranquil mind; placidity; serenity; calmness of the mind (used in cases of great perplexity): เสียสติ to become demented; to lose the power of mind and reason: สติฟั่นเฟือน of unsound mind; demented.

สตี, สดี   sa⁴-dtee *S. n.* a good, virtuous, faithful wife; a female ascetic (S. E. D. p. 1135).

สตูป see สถูป

สถน   sa⁴-ton² *n.* the female breast (chd. p. 503); the udder; the mamma.

สถบดี   sa⁴-ta⁴-bau-dee *S. n. lit.* "a place-lord," *i. e.* a king; a chief; a governor; an head official; an architect; a master builder (S. E. D. p. 1262).

สถล   sa⁴-ton² *S. n.* an eminence; a mound; a heap of artifically raised earth; a table-land; soil; ground; firm earth; a place; a spot; a site (S. E. D. p. 1261): สถลเทวดา a local or rural deity; a tutelary genie presiding over some particular spot: สถลบท, สถลมารค land routes, paths, courses, or ways: สถลวาณิช a trader by land (as by car or caravan): สถลวิเคราะห์ a land battle.

สถวิร   sa⁴-ta⁴-wi⁶-ra⁶ *S. n.* an old man; a Buddhist monk of a certain standing; a senior priest (chd. p. 504): *adj.* old; ancient; venerable; solid; strong; powerful (S. E. D. p. 1265).

สถาน   sa⁴-tarn² *S. n.* site; place; state; position; locality; a situation; the act of standing, or condition of being fixed or stationary; a station, rank, office or appointment; an abode, dwelling-place or room (S. E. D. p. 1263): เคหะสถาน houses; dwelling-places;

sheds: แปลได้สองสถาน there are two ways of translating it, or two meanings (the sentence in question): อยู่สถานใด where do you live?

สถานก sa⁴-tah²-nok⁶ S. n. the position, situation, or rank of an officer (S. E. D. p. 1263).

สถานี sa⁴-tah²-nee n. a station; a town of small size; a stopping place for trade, or caravans; a shipping office; a central office or headquarters: สถานีตำรวจ a police station: สถานีรถไฟ a railway station.

สถาปนะ, สถาปนา sa⁴-tah²-bpa⁴-na⁶ v. to construct; to establish; to maintain; to preserve (as some edifice); to build; to install (as in a position of rank or importance): n. construction; erection; establishment; the act of causing to stand firmly or fixedly.

สถาปนิก sa⁴-tah²-bpa⁴-nik⁶ S. n. one who embellishes, erects, or decorates; a master-builder or architect (S. E. D. p. 1263).

สถาปัตยกรรม sa⁴-tah²-bpit⁴-ya⁶-gkum n. architecture.

สถาพร, สถาวร sa⁴-tah²-paun S. adj. permanent; invariable; established; constant; immovable; firm; stable (S. E. D. p. 1264).

สถาล sa⁴-tarn² S. n. a plate; a cup; a bowl; a dish; a pot; a caldron; any culinary utensil (S. E. D. p. 1262); see ถ้วย p. 381.

สถาวิร sa⁴-tah²-wi⁶-ra⁶ S. n. age; the condition of being old, ancient, senile (S. E. D. p. 1265).

สถิต sa⁴-tit⁴ S. adj. immovable; steady; stable; domiciled; abiding, remaining, or staying permanently or continuously (S.E.D. p. 1264).

สถิติ sa⁴-ti⁴-dti⁴ Eng. statistics S. n. durability; stability; continuation; existence; life (chd. p. 504); continuance or steadfastness in the path of duty; virtuous conduct; rectitude; propriety; constancy; firm persuasion or opinion; custom (S. E. D. p. 1264).

สถิร see เสถียร

สถุล sa⁴-toon² P. adj. big; large; thick; clumsy (chd. p. 505); coarse; rude; fat; bulky: สถุลกาย corpulent; large (physically): สถุลธี stupid; silly; dull: สถุลบฏ tent-cloth; sail-cloth; a kind of coarse heavy cloth: สถุลบาท lit. "one having big feet," i. e. an elephant: สถุลภาพ bulkiness; corpulency; hugeness; immensity; crudeness.

สถูป, สดูป, สตูป sa⁴-toop⁴ n. a mound; a conical, or bell-shaped shrine containing a relic; a stupa; a dagoba; a cetiya; a tope (chd. p. 505).

สทุม sa⁴-toom P. n. a house; a dwelling-place; an abode (chd. p. 412).

สธน sa⁴-ta⁶-na⁶ P. S. adj. rich; wealthy; affluent (chd. p. 411).

สธุสะ, สาธุสะ sa⁴-too⁶-sa⁴ onomat. from the sound of assent or approval to what has been said, similar to "amen."

สน son² v. to fix (one's mind) upon; to pass (thread through the eye of a needle): สนใจ to have an interest in; to pay good attention to: สนตะพาย to pass a rope through the nostrils of an animal.

สน (ต้น) son² n. Pinus merkusii (Coniferae), a pine found throughout the relatively cool parts of the world, but not well suited to Malaysia. It occurs from Burma through Thailand to the mountains of northern Sumatra. It has grown to a height of 120 feet at Buitenzorg, Java, and attempts are being made to exploit the forests of it in Sumatra, for colophony and turpentine, as is done elsewhere, where this pine grows (burk. p. 1735); P. khasya a pine tree native of India (v. p. p. 261): สนฉัตร์ (ต้น) Araucaria cookii (Araucariaceae), a tree producing valuable timber, native of New Caledonia. It is a very tall, conical tree, with short, slender horizontal branches. The Norfolk

Island pine, *A. excelsa*, is another well known species. The wood is resinous, yellowish-white, straight-grained, and easily worked. It is almost identical with deal. Australia demands all it produces—for it is the best soft-wood of that continent—and there is no surplus for export. The supplies in New Caledonia are being destroyed very rapidly. In the face of the approaching scarcity of soft-woods, the *Araucarias*, of which there twelve species, have become very desirable trees for planting in places truly suited to them. In Singapore these trees have reached a height of 80 feet, though in their own homes they attain 200 feet. However the time has not been long enough to prove to what size they may grow in this part of the world. *Araucarias* are quite ornamental and are widely planted in subtropical regions of the world. The bark of some species contains tannin. The seeds are edible (MCM. p. 97: BURK. p. 213): สนทะเล (ต้น) *Casuarina equisetifolia* (*Casuarinaceae*), Queensland swamp oak, beefwood, ironwood, a sea-coast tree demanding sandy shores, and limited in a wild condition in Malaya by their restricted distribution; but planted extensively. It occurs from the shores at the head of the Bay of Bengal to the easternmost islands of the Pacific. The growth is rapid and it has been known to attain a height of 143 feet in lower Thailand. · The timber is very hard, reddish brown, and splits much. It is used for firewood extensively, and is well suited for the purpose. It may be used for poles and rafters, and is not liable to be attacked by white ants, but it is only moderately durable in the open air. The poles are sometimes used for masts and occasionally for yokes, felloes, and wheels of native carts. It is stronger than teak. It has been reported to be the best firewood in the world; it will burn when green. In Thailand it is made into charcoal. The bark tans; it also dyes fabrics a light reddish drab. It is used in Aram for toughening fishing-lines. The bark is used medicinally to arrest diarrhoea and dysentery. A lotion of it is used for beri-beri. A decoction of the twigs is used by the Malays as a lotion for swellings. A powder of the bark is prescribed for pimples on the face. The resin is used by persons demented by elephant-spirits (V. P. p. 261: BURK. p. 491): สนนา *Thai, Surat*, สนสร้อย *Thai, Nakawn Sritamarat* (ต้น) *Baeckea frutescens* (*Myrtaceae*), a shrub or small tree, found from Sumatra, the Malay Peninsula, and the coasts of southern China to Australia. In the Peninsula it is met with alike on mountain-tops and sandy coasts. A very refreshing tea, made from the leaves, is used for fevers and lassitude. It is at times of child-birth that the Malays make most use of this plant; then they prepare draughts into which it enters, and powders for rubbing on the body. In Sumatra, draughts containing it are used also for regulating the menses. The volatile oil is pale yellow. It smells of lavender and is said to be capable of use in perfumery. The timber is hard, dark brown, and very durable. In Tonkin the branches serve as brooms (cb. p. 624: BURK. p. 282): สนวน *Thai, Ratburi* (ต้น) *Dalbergia nigrescens* (*Leguminosae*) (cb. p. 482): สนหางสิงห์ (ต้น) *Thuja orientalis* (*Coniferae*), Chinese arbor vitae, a small, dense, bushy tree or shrub, of a conical shape, with laterally flattened branches, native of China and Japan. The Chinese use both seeds and leaves medicinally (MCM. p. 182: V. P. p. 261: BURK. p. 2157): สนหนาม (ต้น) *Araucaria bidwillii* (*Coniferae*), similar to สนฉัตร์ (MCM. p. 97: BURK. p. 213): สนอินเดีย (ต้น) *Grevillea robusta* (*Proteaceae*), silky oak, silver oak, a medium-sized tree, native of southern Australia, introduced into Ceylon in 1856, now extensively planted in Malaya and Ceylon amongst tea for shade, as well as for fuel, wind-breaks, and ornament. The pretty, fern-like leaves, which are silvery-white beneath, render the tree very ornamental. The tree does not thrive well under 1,000 feet. The wood is very prettily marked, and is much used for furniture in Australia (MCM. p. 181: Burk. p. 1111).

ส้น son[3] *n.* the heel: ส้นปืน the butt [of a gun.

สนเดก see **สันติก**

สนทนา son[2]-ta[6]-nah *P. v.* to converse; to discourse; to talk to, or with: *n.* conversation: สนทนาปราศรัย to carry on a courteous, genial, or friendly conversation; see ปราศรัย p. 508.

สนทรรศ son[2]-tat[6] *S. n.* a picture; a scene; a sight; a view; something that is visible (S. E. D. p. 1144).

สนทรรศน์ son[2]-tat[6] *S. n.* sight; vision; the act of looking steadfastly, gazing, viewing, beholding, seeing (S. E. D. p. 1144).

สนทิศ, สันทิส son[2]-tit[6] *S. v.* to appoint; to assign; to state, tell, direct or command; to give an order or message (S. E. D. p. 1143).

สนเทศ, สันเทส son[2]-tet[3] *P. n.* news; information; a message; a communication; an order; a command (chd. p. 445).

สนเทห์, สนเท่ห์, สันเทห์ son[2]-tay *P. S. n.* doubt; suspicion; uncertainty about; risk; danger (S. E. D. p. 1143); see บัตรสนเท่ห์ p. 476.

สนธยา son[2]-ta[6]-yah *S. n.* union; the junction of day and night, of morning and evening, of dawn or daylight and dusk or twilight: สนธยาค่ำ eventide; sunset: สนธยาราตรี nighttime; during the night.

สนธิ son[2]-ti[6] *S. n.* junction; connection; combination; union or intercourse; agreement; compact; league; negotiated alliances; *grammar* euphonic union of final and initial letters to form compound words: ปฏิสนธิ์ birth or conception; see p. 493: สนธิสัญญา a treaty.

สนม sa[4]-nom[2] *n.* ladies-in-waiting in a palace; a maid; a concubine; a place of custody for those of high rank; a royal funeral-

officer: สนมกรมวัง a department of palace officials acting as police or guardians, and also as undertakers for royalty.

สนอง sa[4]-naung[2] *v.* to do a favour; to give a gift in recompense (for some kindness shown); to repay a favour by some form of service: สนองไข to make a reply; to explain in response to some enquiry: สนองคุณ to recompense a kindness; to be grateful: สนองได a back-scratcher: สนองถ้อยคำ to answer (respectfully) the words or speech of another: สนองสาร to reply; to answer a letter from another: สนองโอษฐ์ *lit.* "a substitute for one's mouth," *i. e.* receiver of another's instructions, messages, or commands (used in connection with royalty).

สนอบ, สนะ sa[4]-naup[4] *v.* to sew; to bind; to darn; to tie; to bandage: *n.* a garment; a coat: ช่างสนะ a tailor.

สนัด see **ถนัด** (preferable) p. 379.

สนั่น sa[4]-nun[4] *adj.* loud; resounding; echoing (as thunder): ก้องสนั่น reverberations (of a sound, or of some political incident): สนั่นกึกก้อง re-echoing, resounding reverberations; see กึกก้อง p. 109: สนั่นหวั่นไหว to shake or tremble as a result of some tremendous noise (as an eruption of a volcano or earthquake).

สนับ sa[4]-nup[4] *v.* to cover or protect from injury; to cause to fit over: *n.* a coat; a shirt; a glove; a tight-fitting garment; see ทับ p. 409; an area covered by barnacles: ตกสนับ dry stems of grass that bend over, smothering the new sprouts or shoots: สนับแข้ง puttees (leather, canvas, or flannel): สนับนิ้วมือ a thimble: สนับเพลา tight-fitting undergarments; shorts or leggings (as worn by acrobats or actors): สนับมือ a hand-rest or book-rest (used while writing on palm leaves, painting, or drawing); short, padded gloves (as worn by base-ball catchers); metal-lined gloves (used in fist-fighting); padded gloves (used by boxers): สนับหนังสวมนิ้วมือ finger protectors or gloves.

สนับสนุน   sa⁴-nup⁴-sa⁴-noon² *v.* to support, back up, encourage, help, or render assistance; to speak a good word for (as in pleading some one's case); see ช่วย p. 283.

สนาดก   sa⁴-nah-dok⁴ *S. n.* one whose spiritual instruction is complete. This is a Brahminical term. It is applied to the young Brahmin who has returned from the house of his preceptor, his studies being completed. He is so called because previous to leaving his preceptor he goes through the ceremony of bathing (chd. p. 256); ablution; self-purification; the act of bathing; washing.

สนาน   sa⁴-narn² *S. n.* an ablution; a bath; the act of bathing, washing, or removal by washing; religious or ceremonial lustration; bathing in sacred waters (S. E. D. p. 1266): สนานคฤห์, สนานภู a bath-room; a swimming-pool; a place for ceremonial bathing.

สนาบก   sa⁴-nah-bok⁴ *S. n.* a bath attendant (chd. p. 255); a servant who brings the bath-water, or who applies it on his master in the bath-room (S. E. D. p. 1267).

สนาม   sa⁴-narm² *n.* the arena; a public playground; a stadium; open ground; a field for sports (as is seen in temple grounds, or in the outskirts of a town): ท้องสนาม a large lawn or plaza in the middle of a town: สนามชนไก่ a cockpit: สนามคลี a hockey field: สนามควาย an arena for bullfighting: สนามเพลาะ a war trench; an entrenchment, breastworks, or mounds for the protection of soldiers (in time or war): สนามเพลาะที่มีน้ำ waterlogged trenches: สนามเพลาะแนวที่หนึ่ง first line of trenches: สนามมวย a wrestling arena; a boxing stand: สนามม้า a race-course: สนามรบ a battle-field; an arena for military manoeuvres: สนามแข่งวัวเกวียน a run way for bullock-cart racing: สนามหญ้า a lawn; a yard; a grass plot.

สนายุ   sa⁴-nah-yoo⁶ *S. n.* muscle; tendon; fibrous connective tissue; sinews; ligaments (S. E. D. p. 1267).

สนิก   sa⁴-ni⁶-gka⁴ *P. adv.* slowly; softly (chd. p. 456); see ค่อย p. 192.

สนิท, สนิธ   sa⁴-nit⁴ *adj.* affectionate; amiable; lovable; united; closely joined: *adv.* closely; unitedly; intimately; snugly; familiarly; affectionately: คนสนิท, เพื่อนสนิท a close friend; an intimate: ติดสนิท to be well, or snugly joined together (as pieces of broken pottery fastened together): ทำสนิท to feign friendship: นอนสนิท to sleep soundly: เล่นกลสนิท skillfully played (as a sleight of hand trick): ศีลมหาสนิท the Eucharist; Holy Communion: สนิทกันเข้า to be placed or joined closely or snugly together: สนิทสนม well acquainted; perfect in all respects; perfect in union; well mixed or united: หวานสนิท faultlessly sweet (as fruit).

สนิม   sa⁴-nim² *n.* rust; the oxide of any metal: สนิมจับ, เป็นสนิม to become rusty or rust-covered: สนิมทองแดง verdigris.

สนุก   sa⁴-nook⁴ *adj.* amusing; interesting (as a play or fair); deriving pleasure from; jolly; cheery; cheerful; agreeable: คนพูดสนุก a jolly talker or, joking speaker: ไปเที่ยวกันสนุก had a pleasant jolly walk together: สนุกสบาย happy and well.

สนุข   sa⁴-nook⁴ *n.* bliss; happiness; delight; pleasure: *adj.* blest; pleasant; happy; delightful (chd. p. 487); see สุข.

สนุต   sa⁴-noot⁶ *S. adj.* flowing; trickling; oozing; dripping (S. E. D. p. 1267); see ย้อย p. 668.

สนุติ   sa⁴-noo⁶-dti⁴ *S. n.* the condition of flowing, trickling, oozing, or dripping (S.E.D. p. 1267).

สนุ่น, ตะไคร้บก (ต้น)   sa⁴-noon⁴ *n. Salix tetrasperma (Salicaceae)*, a tree of subtropical India and China. which has been brought southward—the male sex only—into the Malay Peninsula. It is found in every village in some of the northern parts of the Peninsula. Propagation is by cuttings. It is usually planted in the garden as a boundary fence. The Chinese are particularly fond of planting it on embankments of water tanks and mines. Sometimes it is planted and pollarded to make the fence itself. It is not employed as an osier. It is said to be used for fever. A decoction is used cold for ulceration of the nose (BURK. p. 1943 : V. P. p. 248).

สบ sop^4 v. to consummate or realize (as one's desires); to acquire, win, or procure; to meet; see เจอะ p. 257; to find; see ปะ p. 516; to come across (as meeting a friend accidentally); see พะ p. 578; พะพาน p. 579; to come into contact (as two billiard balls); see ถูก ๑ p. 390 : n. the mouth: Cam. adj. every: adv. always : สงฆ์สบสังวาส Buddhist priests of similar sects living together : สบใจ obtaining the desires of the heart; being pleased with, or agreeable to : สบตา meeting the eye; coming into sight : สบไถง Cam. every day; daily : สบเนื้อสบใจ fulfilling the desires of the senses : สบพระทัย concurring with the royal desires : สบประสงค์ achieving the desires : สบปาก assembled or united in the mouth, i. e. pleasing to the taste : สบสังวาส living together : สบเหมาะ finding luck; being lucky; see ประสพ p. 505.

สบง sa^4-bong Cam. n. cloth : Thai n. the loin-cloth, or sarong worn by Buddhist monks.

สบจ sa^4-bot^4 P. n. a pariah; an outcaste (chd. p. 461); a person of low, or menial caste.

สบถ sa^4-bot^4 P. v. to swear to; to take an oath : n. an oath (chd. p. 462); a promise; a curse; an imprecation : สบถให้ได้หรือ can you swear to the truth of your statement?

สบประมาท sop^4-bpra^4-mart^4 v. to be disrespectful; to offend by word or deed; see ดูหมิ่น p. 333.

สบเสีย sop^4-see-ah^2 v. to insult by con-

sidering, or saying that another is of no standing, or valueless to society; to be impolite to another; to take a dislike to; to be displeased with; see ดูถูก p. 333.

สบัน sa^4-bun P. n. an oath (chd. p. 462).

สบาย, สับปาย, สะเบย sa^4-bai v. to be well, happy, or contented : adj. being well, happy, at ease, or contented; desirable; advantageous; beneficial (chd. p. 462) : ท่าน-สบายดีหรือ a salutation are you well? how are you? ไปตามสบาย to go at your pleasure; to go along in leisurely fashion.

สภา sa^4-pah P. S. n. an assembly; a hall; a court; a mansion; a court of justice (chd. p. 407); a council; a society; an association : สภากาชาด the Red Cross Society : สภาคฤห์ a place of meeting; an assembly hall : สภา-จาร parliamentary rules; the constitution, or by-laws governing the proceedings of an assembly, association, club, or society : สภา-ชั้นต่ำ House of Commons : สภาชั้นสูง House of Lords : สภานายก, สภาบดี a president; a chairman; a presiding officer of an assembly or association : สภาผู้แทนราษฎร House of Representatives; The Assembly.

สภาค sa^4-park^3 P. adj. in common; shared by all; identical (chd. p. 408); all alike; shared equally by all.

สภาพ, สภาวะ sa^4-parp^3 P. n. the natural state; nature (chd. p. 408); condition; habit; behaviour; manner; situation in society; standing in life : สภาพธรรม laws governing nature, or the successive changes that life is heir to : สภาพแห่งหนี้ legal nature of the obligation.

สม ๑ som^2 adj. becoming; fitting; worthy of; suitable for; appropriate; united (in action); conforming (to rules of conduct); fit for each other (as bride and groom); well matched (as a pair of horses); of similar quality or qualifications : สมคบ, ร่วมคบคิดกัน to be an accomplice; to cooperate with (in some evil deed): สมคบโจร to cooperate, or act with thieves: สมควร worthy of; suitable for; becoming to; reasonable; proper; fitting: สมคะเน to be as was surmised, guessed, or conjectured: สมคำ correct as said; corresponding to what has been said: สมเงิน satisfactory for the price paid: สมจริง credible; trustworthy; truthful; according to the facts: สมได้สมเสีย to break even in an enterprise or undertaking: สมทบ to join (with another) in action; to act as an auxiliary, or accessory; to be a confederate, confrere, or helper (in some project); to join forces in a united action (as two armies): สมทบเชือก a rope having double strands: สมนาคุณ a thank-offering; a gift: สมน้ำหน้า just dues; "it serves you quite right;" used as a slang expression for some contemptible deed when punishment is meted out (as a result); to have gotten what one deserves: สมบุญ being a fitting reward for the merit made: สมประกอบ to be physically complete; to have all the natural functions (in good condition); to be appropriate, or well fitted for; to corroborate (as a secondary witness): สมประสงค์, สมความปรารถนา fully satisfying the wish or desire: สมปอง as one thinks, or as they had wished: สมพร may the blessing be as was wished, or be accomplished as was desired: สมยศ, สมวาสนา to be worthy of the rank conferred; possessing the requisite money, household goods and servants to fit the position: สมรส to marry; to know carnally; to cohabit: สมรัก, สมอารมณ์ corresponding to what a person has proposed, or desired to get or obtain: สมรู้ to be a participant; to partake in; to be an accomplice, consort, or witness: สมรู้เป็นใจ to be an accomplice or participant: สมลุ, สมนึก, สมคิด to be consummated as one thought; to correspond with what has been thought of; to accord with what has been surmised: สมศัก, เลกสมศัก lit. "fit to be tattooed (at the wrist)," i. e. an adult of eighteen years and above who is deemed capable of serving in the army or navy and so is tattooed on a wrist as a permanent designating mark: สมหน้า, สมตน, สมตัว well-fitting; appropriate; in accordance with rank and standing (as clothes or uniform): สมหวัง to be achieved as one wished: สมเหมือนคำเขาว่า exactly like what he has said; corresponding to the description given: สมอ้าง to be a willing witness, ready to swear, or to be cited (to substantiate any claim).

สม ๒ sa⁴-ma⁶ P. n. tranquillity (chd. p. 436); calmness; peacefulness; composure.

สม ๓ sa⁴-ma⁶ S. n. toil; fatigue; weariness (chd. p. 728).

สม ๔ sa⁴-ma⁶ P. adj. even; level; like; similar; same; equal; upright; just; impartial; unbiassed; full; complete; entire (chd. p. 436); a prefix implying completeness (Alab. p. 227).

ส้ม Thai and Laos (ต้น) som³ n. a generic term for all citrus fruits and almost invariably qualified by a term designating the variety meant (cb. p. 237: burk. p. 561): ส้มกุ้ง Thai, Chantaburi, ฟ้าแลบ Thai, Surat and Ranawng (ต้น) Rubus moluccanus (Rosaceae), a bramble found in western Malaysia and peninsular Thailánd. The Malays use it for dysentery and other internal complaints, and for a mild stroke of paralysis. In Java the young leaves are chewed for sprue and coughs, and in eastern Malaysia to prevent miscarriage. In Java they are applied to boils. The fruit is edible but not worth eating. It is as a medicinal plant that it has importance (cb. p. 573: burk. p. 1918); ส้มกุ้ง Laos, Nan (ต้น) Begonia inflata (Begoniaceae) (cb. p 774): ส้มเกลี้ยงหรือจีน (ต้น) Citrus aurantium (Rutaceae), sour orange, Seville orange, a small tree or shrub, 8 to 12 feet high, supposed to be indigenous to northern India. It reached the Mediterranean in the ninth or tenth century, and was well known in Europe long before the tardy arrival of the sweet orange. Then the early Europeans brought it back to the East, though there was little room for it in competition with the other sour *Citrus* fruits. Still, the Spaniards apparently established it in the southern part of the Philippine Islands. This orange is especially adapted to regions where the trees are subject to light wintering, or to a short period of rest. There is considerable cultivation of it in parts of Europe. It is the best orange for marmalade; the peel is sometimes candied. It is used in making patent medicines; *var. bigaradia* is a variety which is used as a source of Oil of Petit-grain. Orange flowers, preserved in salt, make a preparation in European medicine akin in nature to the pared rind. Neroli oil distilled from the fresh blossoms is used in perfumery, etc. The timber is extremely hard, and compares well with boxwood. It may be of great beauty, and is used in cabinet-making and turnery (McM. pp. 236, 399 : V.P. p. 263 : Burk. pp. 566, 574): ส้มเช้า see กะเร p. 78 : ส้มชื่น see เขยตาย p. 165 : ส้มป่อย *N. Laos* (ต้น) *Acacia concinna* (*Leguminosae*), a climber, the pods of which are important commercially. In India its pods are sold everywhere in the markets, and are used chiefly for washing the hair, but they are also medicinal as a mild cathartic and emetic (Burk. p. 13 : Cb. p. 548 : V.P. p. 264): ส้มป่อยหวาน see ชะเอมป่า p. 287 : ส้มบู่ see จำบู่ p. 248 : ส้มเปรี้ยว see แคงโค p. 213 : ส้มม่วง-ชหน่วย see ตำหยาว p. 866 : ส้มมะกรูด *Thai.* ส้มมั่วผี *Thai, Pattani* (ต้น) *Citrus hystrix* (*Rutaceae*), a small tree with a pear-shaped fruit, the skin intensely green, or ultimately yellowish, and wrinkled. The chief use of the fruit is for washing the hair and other parts of the body. The juice is used in ointments and with the Malays the peel enters into their universal tonic medicines; apparently its function is the driving away of evil spirits. The juice is very acid; but is sometimes used as a flavouring in sauces, but only in small quantities, as much of it upsets the

digestion. Before the fruit is ripe the juice becomes gummy, but with ripeness becomes thin and watery, though never abundant. The timber is a favourite material for tool-handles in some parts of the Dutch Indies (Cb. p. 237 : V.P. p. 264 : Burk. p. 567): ส้มสันดาน *Thai, Chonburi* (ต้น) *Cissus* (*Vitis*) *hastata* (*Ampelidaceae*), a rather succulent climber of moderate size, found widely in Malaysia, and by no means infrequent in the Malay Peninsula. The pounded leaves are not uncommonly used to poultice boils, or are boiled and put on the abdomen for ague (Cb. p. 307 : Burk. p. 2244): ส้มมะนาว see มะนาว p. 635 : ส้มโอ *Thai* and *Laos* (ต้น) *Citrus maxima* (*Rutaceae*), pomelo, shaddock, native of Indo-China, Thailand and Malaysia. Varieties with fruits too acid to be eaten are common in the north along the Mekhong. In Thailand, at the present time, there is grown a seedless pomelo superior to those of any other part of the East. The pomelo reached northern India from Java, and became known as the Batavia lemon. It reached the West Indies by the agency of a man named Shaddock, master of a trading vessel, and there took his name. The pomelo is a broad tree, and bears fruits near the ground. The fruits of some races are as big as a man's head; others are less than half as much in diameter. เขาแบน is the round, slightly flattened variety preferred in Thailand. เขาพวง is the pear shaped variety, which is not as good in flavour but is preferred in the Singapore market. The skin is always thick. The rind of different races vary but some contain sufficient oil to make them a good substitute for candied lemon peel. The oil of the seeds of an inferior race is extracted in Indo-China and used as oil for lighting opium pipes. A very fragrant perfume may be got from the flowers by enfleurage. The leaves are used medicinally in Malaya. They are boiled to make a lotion used hot on painful places and swellings. The Chinese make various medicaments from the fruit. The timber is white to yellowish, moderately heavy, hard and close-grained. It may be used for tool-handles (Burk. p. 570); *C. decumana*, (cb. p. 238 : v. p. p. 265 : MCM. p. 258): ส้มตำ a salad, or relish composed of sliced green papayas, guavas, dried shrimps, etc., flavoured with sugar, shrimp-sauce and chillies: ส้มมือ a fruit resembling the pomelo, growing on trees having serrated leaves: สารส้ม alum: น้ำส้ม vinegar; see p. 456.

สมจร som²-chjaun *S. v.* to perform an act in union, or jointly with another; to cover, or copulate (as in breeding): *n.* bestiality; incest.

สมจาร sa⁴-ma⁶-chjah-ree *P. n.* one who lives tranquilly (chd. p. 423).

สมญา, สมเญศ, สมัญญา som²-yah *n.* appellation; name; fame; renown (implying good).

สมณะ sa⁴-ma⁶-na⁶ *P. v.* to curb the passions: *n.* an ascetic; a Buddhist ascetic or monk; a Buddhist priest (chd. p. 427); one who does penance, as a monk or priest (Ala. p. 203); a religious mendicant; those who have separated themselves from their families and quieted their minds from all intruding thoughts, desire and lust.

สมเด็จ som²-det⁴ *Cam. n.* a great one; an abbot; a title of high rank for a Buddhist monk; a form of address, or title for royalty: *adj.* high; excellent; superior; eminent: สมเด็จเจ้าพระยา a title for the highest rank, or first order of civil service government officials.

สมถะ sa⁴-ma⁶-ta⁴ *P. n.* tranquillity; calmness; quietude; cessation of thought (chd. p. 429); meditation; concentration (of mind): สมถยานิก those who make tranquillity of mind and cessation of thought the vehicle for the attainment of Arhatship (chd. p. 429): สมถ-วิปัสสนา tranquillity, calmness and cessation of thought are frequently mentioned as attributes of the Arhat (chd. p. 429).

สมนะ sa⁴-ma⁶-na⁶ *P. n.* suppression; the act of stopping, checking, or repressing (as of thoughts, carnal desires and passions) (chd. p. 425).

สมนา som²-ma⁶-nah *v.* to do (something) in return, or as a thank-offering: สมนาคุณ to do with a sense of gratitude; to perform a deed, or give a present to a benefactor; to manifest gratitude (by a recipient); to return thanks.

สมบัติ, สมบัตติ som²-bat⁴ *P. n.* success; prosperity; happiness; glory; magnificence; beauty; attainment (chd. p. 439); possession: ครองสมบัติ to reign over the wealth of a country: ทรัพย์สมบัติ treasures; riches; fortunes; wealth (accumulated): ราชสมบัติ royal wealth or treasures: มอบสมบัติ to give, or make over to another person one's wealth or riches (as by a will).

สมบุกสมบัน som²-book⁴-som²-bun *v.* to accomplish through difficulties, or against great odds (as when travelling through a dense jungle); see ฝ่า p. 554.

สมบูรณ์, สัมปุณณ์ som²-boon *P. adj.* filled; full (chd. p. 439); accomplished (as a job, or task); superabundant; plentiful; ample; over-flowing; whole; entire; complete.

สมประดี som²-bpra⁴-dee *n.* the present time; immediateness; now; at this time; at once.

สมปัก som²-bpuk⁴ *n.* cloth richly embroidered and worn by officials on state occasions: สมปักปูม richly embroidered silk.

สมพงศ์ som²-pong *n.* the act of joining, uniting, mixing, or being mixed (as those of different families, or of two lineages uniting in marriage); the state of being man and wife.

สมพล som²-pon *n.* one voluntarily surrendering himself to serve the government.

สมพัตสร, สัมพัจฉร, สัมพัตสร som²-put⁶-sorn² *n.* a year; an annual tax collected on fruit trees and certain kinds of plants.

สมพาส see สังวาส

สมเพช see สังเวช

สมโพธน์ som²-pote³ *S. n.* speech; the act of calling, addressing, arousing, perceiving; *grammar* the vocative case (S. E. D. p. 1178).

สมโพธิ, สัมโพธิ som²-pote³ *P. n.* perfect knowledge or enlightenment; completeness; perception of the truth; attainment of Buddhaship; Buddhahood (Chd. p. 431); the completeness of the intelligence of a Buddha (Ala. p. 227): สมโพธิญาณ the perfect omniscience of a Buddha (Ala. p. 227).

สมภพ, สัมภวะ som²-pop⁶ *P. S. v.* to be born; to come into existence: *n.* production; birth; origin; source; union (Chd. p. 431); the being produced from a cause (S. E. D. p. 1179).

สมภาร, สัมภาร som²-parn *n.* the abbot, or chief monk of a Buddhist monastery; materials; constituent parts (Chd. p. 341); necessaries (of life); riches; property; abundance; an assemblage; a multitude.

สมโภค som²-poke³ *P. S. n.* sensual enjoyment; happiness; pleasure; delight; complete enjoyment (Chd. p. 431).

สมโภช som²-pote³ *P. S. n.* food; meals; a feast; the act of joining in, or serving meals; *Thai* a dedication or celebration; festivities solemnizing some occasion; a ceremony of joyfulness: วันสมโภช the date, or day of dedication, or of a solemnizing festivity.

สมมต, สมมุต som²-mot⁶ *P. S. v.* to take as an example; to suppose, consider or assume (as true for the sake of an illustration) (S. E. D. p. 1180): สมมุติ an hypothesis; a conjecture or supposition.

สมโมท ๑ som²-mote³ *P. S. n.* fragrance; smell; odour (S. E. D. p. 1180).

สมโมท ๒ som²-mote³ *P. v.* to agree with; to be in harmony with, or to be friendly to (Chd. p. 435); see ร่าเริง under ร่า p. 706.

สมยุค see สังยุค

สมโยค see สังโยค

สมร ๑ sa⁴-mawn² *P. S. n.* a battle (Chd. p. 429); a war; a conflict; a combat: สมรภูมิ a battle-field; the field of battle or conflict: สมรภูมิไชย the field of victory.

สมร ๒ sa⁴-mawn² *S. n.* a memory; a recollection; an amulet; a souvenir or memento (relating to sensuous subjects); love; Cupid; a beautiful, attractive, amiable girl or woman: มิ่งสมร a girl or beloved, cherished lady; amulets, talismans, or (love-inducing) charms strung on a string: สมรกถา words, proverbs, or sayings relating to love, Cupid, or sensuous matters: สมรกรรม manners, methods, behaviour, or deportment manifesting love or sexual attraction: สมรทศา the manners or physical attributes resulting from the passions and the desires of love, said to be ten, *viz.* dazzling, bewitching eyes; continual thinking or concentration of the mind upon the beloved; sleeplessness; unconcern about outside duties or affairs; shamelessness; *etc.*: สมรโมหะ being deluded or blinded by love and its allurements: สมรรุช lovesickness: สมรเลข love letters; amorous poems: สมรวดี a woman (desperately) in love: สมรศาสตร์ treatises; books relative to the subject of love and methods of lovemaking: สมรลัช *lit.* "friends of lovers," *i. e.* the rainy season; the moon; moonlight: สมราดุร restlessness, or confusion of mind resulting from passions and the desires of love.

สมรด *preferably* สำรด som²-rot⁶ *n.* the embroidered velvet border or edging of a long thin robe worn over other garments to signify rank; a velvet embroidered belt or band worn with this long thin robe.

สมรรถ, สมัตถ์, สามารถ sa⁴-mut⁶ *P. adj.* fit; able; adequate; competent; strong; efficient (Chd. p. 430); powerful; capable: สมรรถภาพ ability; power (Chd. p. 430); efficiency.

สมรรถนะ sa[4]-mut[6]-ta[4]-na[6] *S. n.* strength; power; ability; experience; capability; fitness.

สมฤดี, สมฤๅดี, สมประดี ๒, สมปฤดี som[2]-ma[6]-rur[6]-dee *S. n.* consciousness; reflection; recollection; an active state of mind (chd. p. 466); memory: *adj.* recovering or mastering (of one's senses) (s. e. d. p. 1122).

สมฤต sa[4]-ma[6]-rur[6]-dta[4] *S. adj.* remembered; recollected, or recalled (to memory); prescribed or enjoined (as traditions or customs) (s. e. d. p. 1122).

สมวัย sa[4]-ma[6]-wai *P. adj.* of the same age; born in the same year.

สมวาย sa[4]-ma[6]-wai *P. S. n.* combination; union; multitude (chd. p. 430); assemblage; collection (as of a crowd or company); concourse; congress (s. e. d. p. 1157).

สมเยป see สังเขป

สมอ sa[4]-maw[2] *n.* an anchor: คนทำสมอ an anchor-smith: เงี่ยงสมอ flukes of an anchor: ถอนสมอ to hoist an anchor: ทอดสมอ to cast an anchor: ที่ทอดสมอ anchorage: เรือทอดสมอ riding at anchor; at anchor: สมอดึง *Thai, Bangkok* and *Rachaburi*, สมอเหลี่ยม *Thai, Chumpawn*, สมอหมึก *Thai, Tungsong* (ต้น) *Terminalia citrina* (*Combretaceae*), a large tree found in India, and, as it grows there, scarcely separable from *T. chebula*, but apparently very distinct sometimes in the Malay Peninsula, when it grows as a sprawling woody plant. As a timber tree in Assam, it gives wood used for planking and building; one cannot expect timber from the sprawling form. The fruit is like that of the *T. chebula* but not so useful. The tannin may be between 30 and 40 per cent of the dry weight. The bark used for dyeing gives a dark blue colour (cb. p. 603: burk. p. 2140): สมอตีนเป็ด, สมอตีนนก, สมอหิน (ต้น) *Vitex pubescens* (*Verbenaceae*), Malayan teak, a tree of fair size, found throughout south-eastern Asia and Malaysia; in the Peninsula it is the com-monest species of the genus, both in open country and in secondary jungle. It often persists in lalang, and will grow in rather poor soil if it has full light. It has been mentioned as possibly useful for reclothing old tin workings. The tree often has a crooked trunk, so that it is not possible to get long timbers. The wood is hard, heavy, fine-grained with no distinction between sap-wood and heart-wood, yellow, greyish, or olive-coloured, very durable in contact with the ground. It is the most in demand of any wood for the manufacture of Malay ploughs and other agricultural implements. The wood from young trees is not durable, and trees should reach a girth of three feet before they are cut. The leaves and bark are medicinal. To the plant is assigned a protective power, and so it is used as a charm against convulsions (burk. p. 2239); *V. limonifolia* (v. p. p. 250): สมอไทย *Thai*, มะนะ *N. Laos*, มานแน่ *Karen, Chiengmai* (ต้น) *Terminalia chebula*, a deciduous tree of India, extending into Burma, sometimes large but often small, with a good timber, and valuable fruits which are converted into commercial myrobalans for use in tanning. The ovoid fruit is about an inch long, and is collected from the time it is just yellowish until it is quite yellow and dead ripe. It is sun dried and converted into the myrobalan of commerce. It must not be made wet by rain while drying. During drying it shrivels considerably, and becomes ridged. In a small percentage of fruits the interior, under the skin, powders; such fruits are not used for tanning, but are made into ink. The penetration of hides by this tan is very slow. The dye produced is black or yellow. The fruit has been a medicine of the Hindus from very ancient times, being used for treatment of fever, asthma, chronic diarrhoea, skin-diseases, etc. The wood is fairly durable, and is used in India for furniture, carts, agricultural implements and house-building. Indian foresters have proposed that it be marketed as myrobalan wood (Cb. p. 602 : V. P. p. 249 : MCM. pp. 380, 444 : Burk. p. 2139) : สมอเม๊ย *Laos, Nawngkai* (ต้น) *T. citrina* (Cb. p. 603 : Burk. p. 2140) ; see สมอดีๆ *above* : สมอภิเพก *Thai*, แหน *N. Laos* (ต้น) *T. belerica*, a tall tree found through the greater part of India and Burma, away from the arid regions, and extending to the centre of the Malay Peninsula. It reappears in Java. The timber is used for house-building, etc. in India, after steeping in water, which makes it more durable. It is little sought for and little used in Java. It is good for firewood. In Java leather is tanned with it, and dyed black with the aid of a little sulphate of iron. The unripe fruit is a purgative ; when ripe it is astringent, and is extensively used in India for dropsy, haemorrhoids, and diarrhoea. In Java a powder is made of the seeds which is placed on the navel of an infant when the navel string drops off. Native ink is made from the fruit in India and Java. The kernels of the fruit may be eaten but are dangerous, having a narcotic effect. There is a small quantity of oil in them which can be used medicinally. The tree gives a copious and insoluble gum, which is sold in the bazaars of India. Crystals of calcium carbonate occur in it, which have evidently been carried out of the bark. The wood is not durable, but finds a considerable number of uses in India, largely for articles not required to last, such as packing cases (Cb. p. 601 : MCM. pp. 105, 380, 444 : Burk. p. 2136).

สมอง　　sa^4-maung^2 *n.* brain ; thought ; astuteness : สมองดี cleverness.

สมัก　　sa^4-muk^4 *Cam. n.* a servant or attendant ; those in waiting on royalty.

สมัคร　　sa^4-muk^4 *P. v.* to volunteer ; to join willingly ; to consent to serving (as in the army) : *adj.* all ; entire ; harmonious ; unanimous (Chd. p. 425) : ใจสมัคร a consenting, willing, or volunteering disposition : สมัคร-เข้าพรรคพวก willing to join up, or to be counted as a member (as of a society) : สมัครงาน to volunteer service (as an employé) : สมัคร-เต็มใจ unreservedly ; completely ; wholeheartedly : สมัครสมา volunteering, or consenting to ask pardon (for an offense) : ผู้สมัคร a candidate.

สมังคี　　sa^4-mung-kee *P. adj.* possessing ; endowed with (Chd. p. 426).

สมัชช์, สมัชชา　　sa^4-mut^6 *P. n.* an assembly (Chd. p. 425) ; a meeting together ; an acquaintance ; a concourse of people (as at a fair, theatre or public celebration) ; an assembly (as of the League of Nations).

สมัญญา, สมญา　　sa^4-mun-yah *P. n.* name ; designation ; term (Chd. p. 426).

สมัตต์　　sa^4-mut^6 *P. v.* to conclude ; to be completed (Chd. p. 430) ; to be finished ; to be accomplished or achieved.

สมัตถ์ see สมรรถ

สมัน　　sa^4-mun^2 *n.* Schomburgk's deer, or saman, *Cervus Schomburgki* (Minutes of S. S. Regarding wild Game Preservation in Siam).

สมัย　　sa^4-mai^2 *P. S. n.* season ; time ; occasion ; age ; period (favourable) ; opportunity ; custom ; rule : ในสมัยครั้งหนึ่ง once upon a time ; on such an occasion.

สมา　　sa^4-mah *P. S. n.* a year (Chd. p. 423).

สมาคม　　sa^4-mah-kom *Thai v.* to frequent (a place) ; to reunite with ; to associate with ; to make friends ; to be friendly with : *P. n.* an assembly ; an union ; an encounter or meeting with ; a society ; an association (Chd. p. 425) : สมาคมกันแลกัน to fraternize : สมาคมการกุศล a charitable or benevolent society : สมาคม-การค้า a trade union : สมาคมทางศาสนา a religious society : สมาคมลับ a secret society : สมาคมสงเคราะห์สัตว์ the Society for the Prevention of Cruelty to Animals.

สมาจาร　　sa^4-mah-chjan *P. S. n.* conduct ; manners ; behaviour ; customs ; usage ; the accepted methods of procedure (Chd. p. 423).

สมาช   sa[4]-mart[3] *P. S. n.* an assembly (Chd. p. 425); an association; a society; a congregation; a conclave; a congress; a club.

สมาชิก   sa[4]-mah-chik[6] *P. S. n.* a member of an assembly, club, or society; deputies; proxies (Chd. p. 425).

สมาทาน   sa[4]-mah-tan *P. S. n.* the act of taking upon oneself fully or entirely; contracting; incurring; undertaking; determination; resolve (S. E. D. p. 1159).

สมาธิ   sa[4]-mah-ti[6] *P. S. n.* a trance induced by concentration of the mind; intense application, or fixing the mind on some particular object or idea; deep and devout meditation; a state of absolute indifference to all influences from within or without; tranquillity; the restraint of the senses; the controlling and confining of the mind to contemplation on the nature of the Universal Spirit; a sort of terrestrial Nirvana (S. E. D. p. 1159).

สมาน ๑   sa[4]-mah-na[6] *P. S. adj.* similar; equal; same (Chd. p. 428); uniform; identical; the same as; alike (S. E. D. p. 1160): สมานคติ the act of going together, or in unison; being of the same opinion: สมานคุณ having equal virtues: สมานโคตร the condition of being of the same family: สมานชน persons of the same rank, family or race; being of the same people: สมานชาติ being of the same kind: สมานทุกข์ *lit.* "having the same griefs," *i. e.* sympathetic: สมานสังวาส the condition of living together, being man and wife.

สมาน ๒   sa[4]-man[2] *v.* to join together; to make a contract; to unite; to combine; to astringe, connect, incorporate, or blend together: ยาสมาน an astringent drug, or remedy: สมานไมตรี to cement friendships.

สมาบัติ   sa[4]-mah-but[4] *P. n.* attainment; there are eight attainments or endowments, which are successive states induced by ecstatic meditation (Chd. p. 428); see ฌาณ p. 314; the

eight accomplishments, or perfections (Ala. p. 183).

สมารมภ์   sa[4]-mah-rom *P. S. n.* the condition of undertaking; the spirit of enterprise (Chd. p. 429).

สมาส   sa[4]-mat[4] *P. n.* a combination (Chd. p. 437); the act, or condition of adding to, or joining on (as a prefix, or suffix to words).

สมิง   sa[4]-ming[2] *n.* a tiger; a Peguan title of rank: สมิงพลาย a demon in the form of a wild beast: สมิงมิ่งชาง a man brave as a tiger; a man of the race of soldiers or warriors; a valiant, fearless man: สมิงพระราม a knight of Hongsavadi, Pegu.

สมิต   sa[4]-mit[6] *P. S. adj.* joined, united, or combined with; mixed; amalgamated; compounded (as gold, brass, or copper) (S. E. D. p. 1164).

สมิติ   sa[4]-mi[6]-dti[4] *P. S. n.* an union (of people); an assembly (Chd. p. 433); a council; a society; a flock; a herd (S. E. D. p. 1164).

สมิทธ์   sa[4]-mit[6] *P. adj.* successful; accomplished; reaching a condition of affluence or prosperity (Chd. p. 432).

สมิทธิ   sa[4]-mit[6]-ti[6] *P. n.* success; accomplishment (Chd. p. 432); affluence; prosperity.

สมี ๑   sa[4]-mee[2] *n.* the name given to a Buddhist priest guilty of a legal offense, or who has had a legal action brought against him.

สมี ๒ *Thai* (ต้น)   sa[4]-mee[2] *n. Sesbania aegyptiaca (Leguminosae)*, a plant which is believed to be one of the first garden plants grown in Egypt. It has spread eastwards in cultivation and is planted in India and beyond India to Thailand. It is not known to be in the Malay Peninsula, though it is in the Dutch Indies. It has all of the uses of *S. roxburghii* for which it is a good substitute. The Thai eat the leaves during the last four months of the year. The leaves and young branches are fed to cattle. In India the leaves are much used in poultices, and the seeds are a stimulant, emmenagogue and astringent. The very soft wood is made into toys, mats, etc. The plant grows 6 to 8 feet high, having bi-pennate leaves (Cb. p. 399 : V.P. p. 250 : MCM. p. 122 : Burk. p. 1997).

สมุร sa[4]-mee-ra[6] *P. S. n.* air; wind (Chd. p. 433); atmosphere.

สมุก sa[4]-mook[4] *n.* a mixture of pulverized charcoal and the juice of the *Melanorrhoea usitata*, or the varnish tree. It is used for painting or coating wooden surfaces (as doors of Buddhist sanctuaries prior to guilding).

สมุคค์ sa[4]-mook[4] *P. n.* a box; a basket (Chd. p. 441); a hamper; a woven bamboo box or basket with a lid; a basket made of plaited bamboo strips with a square bottom and rounded top, provided with a lid.

สมุจจัย sa[4]-moot[4]-chjai *P. S. n.* a collection; an accumulation (Chd. p. 440); a collection of words or sentences; an accretion.

สมุจเฉท sa[4]-moot[4]-chet[4] *P. S. n.* extirpation (Chd. p. 440); abandonment; banishment; extermination.

สมุฏฐาน, สมุตถาน sa[4]-moot[4]-tan[2] *P. n.* the site of rising; origination (Chd. p. 442); place of origin; the seat of (as the cause of some disease).

สมุด sa[4]-moot[4] *n.* a book; a volume; an exercise book: ลงสมุด to inscribe in a book; to make a record: สมุดบัญชีเงิน a ledger: สมุดเปล่า a blank book: สมุดหัดลายมือ a copy-book: ห้องสมุด a library; a reading room.

สมุทร sa[4]-moot[4] *n.* a sea; an ocean: *adj.* marine (Chd. p. 441): ท้องสมุทร the bosom of the ocean or sea: สมุทรก a seaman; a trader by sea: สมุทรกฎูก a boat; a ship: สมุทรกานดา *lit.* "sea-beloved," *i. e.* a river: สมุทรโจร pirates: สมุทรเดีียร the seashore; dwelling on the seashore: สมุทรปราการ

name of a city at the mouth of the Chao Phya river: สมุทรเมขลา *lit.* "sea girdled," *i. e.* the earth; the world: สมุทรยาตร a sea voyage: สมุทรยาน *lit.* "an ocean vehicle," *i. e.* a sea-going boat; an ocean liner or steamship: สมุทรเวลา a water-way; a stream; a current; waves of the sea or ocean; billows: สมุทรสาร *lit.* "quintessence of the sea," *i. e.* the pearl.

สมุทัย sa[4]-moot[4]-tai *P. S. n.* rise; origin; commencement; origination; accumulation; collection (Chd. p. 441).

สมุน (ลูกสมุน) sa[4]-moon[2] *n.* an attendant; an errand boy or servant; an apprentice; leaves stitched together and used as roofing, or for temporary shelter: หลบสมุน to use leaves sewn together as a roof.

สมุนไพร sa[4]-moon[2]-prai *n.* roots, bark or leaves in the crude form, indigenous to the country, and used medicinally.

สมุลแว้ง (ต้น) sa[4]-moon[2]-waang[5] *n.* a tree belonging to the genus *Cinnamomum silvestre* (*Lauraceae*), the wild cinnamon.

สมุห, สมุห์ sa[4]-moo[4]-ha[4] *P. n.* a multitude; an assemblage; an aggregation (Chd. p. 441); *Thai* the chief, or principal person in a company or group: สมุหบัญชี a chief bookkeeper; a chief accountant; a secretary.

สโมธาน sa[4]-moh-tan *P. n.* a combination (Chd. p. 47); an assembly; the condition of meeting, joining up to, or uniting with.

สโมสร sa[4]-moh-saun[2] *P. v.* to rejoice together; to come together; to congregate; to assemble: *n.* a society; a club; an association: สโมสรณ an union; a meeting together of people or members (Chd. p. 437); the condition of uniting, or being united into a club, or fraternity.

สย sa[4]-ya[6] *P. v.* to lie; to sleep (Chd. p. 734).

สยด, สยดสยอง, สยดแสยง sa[4]-yot[4] *v.* to be frightened, afraid of, scared, or dismayed (as in conditions that cause the hair to stand on end); to have the creeps at a repulsive sight (as blood in a surgical operation).

สยนะ, สัยน์   sa⁴-ya⁶-na⁶ *P. n.* a bed; a couch; the act of lying or sleeping (chd. p. 471).

สยบ   sa⁴-yop⁴ *v.* to bow, or bend the head down (as in sorrow or grief); to tremble, shudder, or be overcome with grief or fear; see ซบ p. 305.

สยมพร, สยุมพร, สยัมพร   sa⁴-yom²-paun *n.* the act of making an independent choice; the act of making a choice according to one's own liking or decision; an ancient Indian custom, in which a princess chooses her husband herself; a maiden choosing her own husband.

สยมภู, สวยม   sa⁴-yom²-poo *P. n.* one who is self-produced, self-created, self-existent, self-sufficient, independent; an epithet of a Buddha (chd. p. 471): สยมภูวญาณ possessing independent knowledge.

สยอง   sa⁴-yaung² *Cam. v.* to rise, or stand erect (as hairs of the body bristle when one is frightened, horrified, or afraid); see ครั้น p. 180: สยองเกล้า to have the hairs of the head stand on end.

สยอน   sa⁴-yaun² *Cam. v.* to feel a sense of horror, repulsion, or fear.

สยัมวรา   sa⁴-yum-wa⁶-rah *P. S. n.* a maiden who chooses her own husband (chd. p. 471); one who makes an independent choice or decision about matrimony.

สยาน   sa⁴-yan *P. n.* the act of lying down or sleeping (chd. p. 471).

สยาม   sa⁴-yam² *adj.* brown: *n.* a brown race. Siam (also spelled Syam, Siao, Sion, Sian, Ciama), all seemingly derived from Sayam, the Malay name of the country, and further modified for some unknown reason to Anseam and Siom (Introduction p. 17 and 64, English Intercourse with Siam, John Anderson): ชาวสยาม the Thai people: สยาม-

ประเทศ, สยามพิภพ the country, territory or kingdom of Thailand: สยามรัฐ Siam (chd. p. 492); the state, or kingdom of Thailand.

สยาย   sa⁴-yai² *v.* to unfold; to untie or release; see คลี่ p. 186; คลาย p. 186; ขยาย p. 142: ขยำสยาย to squeeze repeatedly, then expose (as clothes after being washed); see ขยำ p. 143: สยายเกษ to unroll; to untangle (the hair.)

สยิว   sa⁴-yiew³ *v.* to wrinkle the face; to frown (as in anger).

สยุ่น   sa⁴-yoon⁴ *n.* a curved chisel used in carving wood or stone.

สร ๑ see ศร p. 788.

สร ๒   sorn² *n.* motion; the condition of flowing or going (chd. p. 464).

สร ๓   sorn² *n.* sound; voice; musical sounds or tones; a vowel (chd. p. 464).

สรก   sa⁴-ra⁶-gka⁴ *n.* a vessel used for drinking (chd. p. 463); a cup; a chalice.

สรง   song² *Camb. v.* to bathe; to wash; to lave; to cleanse (with water): *n.* a bath; an ablution.

สรฏะ   sa⁴-ra⁶-dta⁴ *P. S. n.* a chameleon (chd. p. 464); a house lizard.

สรณะ ๑   sa⁴-ra⁶-na⁶ *P. n.* a place of refuge; protection; salvation; a protector; a house; a home (chd. p. 463): สรณคมน์ the quest for a place of refuge. This is accomplished by repetition of the Suttra or formula addressed to the Three Gems, *i. e.* to The Buddha, the Dharma, and the Church. It is equivalent to the Buddhist creed or profession of faith. By the repetition of this formula, a trust in the three places of refuge is cultivated. It is used on many solemn occasions: สรณตรัย the three places of refuge, or objects of faith are the Buddha, the Law and the Church (chd. p. 463).

สรณะ ๒   sa⁴-ra⁶-na⁶ *n.* memory; remembrance (chd. p. 463); recollection.

สรทะ   sa⁴-ra⁶-ta⁶ *P. n.* autumn; the two months succeeding the rains (chd. p. 463).

สรพ   sa⁴-ra⁶-pa⁶ *P. adj.* noisy (chd. p. 464); clamorous; tumultuous.

สรพัตร, สารพัตร   sa⁴-ra⁶-pat⁶ *P. adv.* everywhere (chd. p. 407); wherever; in general.

สรพัน, สารพัน   sa⁴-ra⁶-pan *adj.* all; every; whole; entire (chd. p. 407).

สรเพ็ชญ์   see   สรรเพ็ชญ์

สรภะ   sa⁴-ra⁶-pa⁶ *P. n.* a species of deer (chd. p. 462); a fabulous animal represented as having eight legs and as dwelling in the Himalayas; one of Rama's monkey allies (H. C. D. p. 282).

สรภัญญะ   sa⁴-ra⁶-pan-ya⁶ *P. n.* a particular mode of reciting, or intoning sacred compositions (chd. p. 462).

สรภู ๑   sa⁴-ra⁶-poo *P. n.* a lizard (chd. p. 462); a house lizard; the gecko.

สรภู ๒   sa⁴-ra⁶-poo *P. n.* the river Sarayu, Sarju, or Gogra of India (H. C. D. p. 285 : chd. p. 462).

สรม   som² *Cam. v.* to pray for; to beg; to ask for.

สรร   sun² *v.* to choose; to select; to elect; to prefer: *adj.* chosen; preferred; elected: ผู้เลือกสรร *idiomatic* the elect; selected persons: สรรแสร้ง to speak with premeditated enmity; to speak invidiously against another; to speak spitefully.

สรรค์   sun² *v.* to create; to originate; to erect; to construct; to adorn: *n.* creation (as of the world); source; origin; beginning.

สรรพ, สัพพ์   sup⁴ *adj.* all; every; whole; complete; entire; universal: นิยมสรรพนาม *a demonstrative pronoun* one; this; that; such: บุรุษสรรพนาม *a personal pronoun* I, he, she, they: ประพันธ์สรรพนาม *a relative or conjunctive pronoun* who, which, that:

ปฤจฉาสรรพนาม *an interrogative pronoun* who? which? what?   สรรพกร *lit.* "the creator of all things," *i. e.* Siva: สรรพกษัย the destruction of the world: สรรพคิด various thoughts: สรรพค *lit.* "the soul of the world," *i. e.* Brahma; Siva: *adj.* being found, or present everywhere: สรรพคราส an eclipse of the moon or sun, producing entire darkness: สรรพคุณ qualities; properties; characteristics; peculiarities: สรรพคุณยา physiological actions of a remedy or drug: สรรพนาม *grammar* a pronoun: สรรพประการ in all respects, particulars, states, conditions, or circumstances: สรรพบุณย์ complete, beautiful, graceful in all respects: สรรพภาวะ completeness of the natural state, or entirety of the physical being (full power of mind, and normal functioning of the organs):   สรรพยุทธ all kinds of weapons: สรรพรส, สับปะรด see ขนุนทอง p. 140:   สรรพโลก the entire world; all people, places, positions, or locations: สรรพเวทย์ all-knowing; well-read; informed; literary: สรรพศานต์ complete peacefulness; calmness; concord; amity; harmony: สรรพสมบัติ riches, property, wealth, or possessions: สรรพสัตว์ all of the animal creation: สรรพอุดม an abundance of everything.

สรรพางค์, สารพางค์   sun²-pang *n.* entireness: completeness; perfectness: สรรพางค์กาย the body as a whole.

สรรเพ็ชญ์, สรรพัชญ์, สรเพ็ชญ์, สัพพัญญู   sun²-pet⁶ *P. n. lit.* "an omniscient one," *i. e.* the Buddha, the only being who is omniscient (chd. p. 407); the all-knowing one.

สรรเพชุดา   sun²-pet⁶-choo⁶-dah *n.* omniscience (chd. p. 407):   สรรเพชุดาญาณ omniscient (implying that attribute of the Buddha); the all-knowing one; an attribute of the Christian God.

สรรเสริญ, สระเสริญ   sun²-ra⁶-sern² *v.* to praise; to laud; to commend; to glorify; to approve; to admire: คำสรรเสริญ words of admiration or approval : เป็นที่สรรเสริญ worthy of commendation or praise : เพลง- สรรเสริญพระบารมี the national anthem : สรร- เสริญและติเตียนโดยความเห็นสุจริต *legal* to make a fair comment.

สรวง, สระรวง, สันรวง su-ang[2] *v.* to sacrifice to angels, genii, household gods, or ancestrial spirits : *n.* sky ; heaven ; paradise ; celestial beings : *adj.* high ; above ; overhead : สรวงเส to worship by offering a sacrifice ; to appease the spirits by making a sacrifice.

สรวป see สรุป

สรวล, สรวลเส su-an[2] *v.* to laugh ; to smile ; to be merry, joyous, or happy (used in regard to royalty).

สร้อย soy[3] *n.* a collar ; a sash ; a neck- lace ; a neck chain : *Cam.* a piece ; a frag- ment ; a part or portion : คำสร้อย a word or syllable added for euphony : สร้อย- นกเขา, ลูกนุ่น, หลาวทอง (ปลา) *Dangila leptocheila (Cyprinidae); Crossocheilus reba (Cyprini- dae)* (suvatti pp. 34, 37) : สร้อยทอง (ต้น) *Solidago sp. (Compositae)*, golden rod. When Dr. H. M. Smith arrived in this country, in 1923, he stayed at the Hotel Royal, in the garden of which he noticed quantities of golden rod. He was informed that, a few years previously, an American lady who was staying at the hotel, feeling rather homesick for American flowers, had sent for seeds of this species and had sown them in the hotel garden (kerr. n. h. j. s. s. III, 3, p. 211 : Burk. p. 2049) : สร้อยนกเขา *Thai, Sriracha* (ต้น) *Mol- lugo pentaphylla (Ficoideae), (Aizoaceae)*, a slender herb found from India to New Cale- donia ; in the Malay Peninsula it is general in open sandy places. The Malays use it for poulticing sore legs. It is medicinal for sprue in Java. It is used in India as a mild aperient medicine, and is eaten as a pot-herb in Thailand and Java. A saponin and much saltpetre have been found in it (cb. p. 785) :

Burk. p. 1484) : สร้อยบัว (ปลา) *Labeo dyo- cheilus (Cyprinidae)* (suvatti p. 24) : สร้อย- หลอด (ปลา) *Labeo munensis (Cyprinidae)* (suvatti p. 24) : สร้อยอุก (ปลา) *Dangila siamensis (Cyprinidae)* (suvatti p. 38) : สร้อย- สังวาลย์ a chain (of gold) worn crosswise, across the breast and back.

สร้อยเศร้า soy[3]-sow[3] *n.* sorrow ; grief ; sadnes : *adj.* sad ; sorrowful ; melancholy.

สระ ๑ sa[4] *P. n.* a large body of impound- ed water ; a lake (chd. p. 464) ; a pond ; a pool of water : สระแก้ว a specially protected pond of water reserved for drinking ; a pond of crystal water : สระโบกขรณี a pond of *Victoria regia (Nymphaeaceae)* (mcm. p. 175).

สระ ๒ sa[4]-ra[4] *n.* a sound ; a voice ; a musi- cal note ; a tone ; a vowel (chd. p. 464) ; an accent mark.

สระ ๓ sa[4] *v.* to wash ; to cleanse ; to rinse ; to lave : สระผม to shampoo (the hair): สระสาง to shampoo and comb out the hair : สระสางบัญชี to audit ; to clean up ; to check over, or adjust accounts ; to discover the dis- crepencies in the accounts.

สระกอ see สะกอ

สระคราญ see สะคราญ [p 61.

สระดอ, สระดั้น see เกลื้อน p. 123; กลาด

สระท้อน, สะท้อน sa[4]-torn[5] *Cam. adj.* soft ; flexible ; bounding, or rebounding (as a rubber ball).

สระเนาะ, เสนาะ sa[4]-naw[4] *adj.* melodious ; agreeable to the ear.

สระนุก, สนุก sa[4]-nook[4] *adj.* funny ; amus- ing ; delightful ; interesting ; having an agree- able time (as at a fair or theatre).

สระบบ, สระบับ see สารบบ, สารบับ

สระรวง see สรวง

สระลน sa[4]-ra[6]-lon *adj.* high ; elevated ;

exalted; prominent; conspicuous; see เชิดชู

สระลอด (ต้น) see สลอด (ต้น)   [p. 302.

สระละ, สระหละ   sa⁴-la⁴ *v.* to leave; to abandon; to forsake; to desert; to withdraw from; see ทิ้ง p. 414.

สระล้าย   sa⁴-lai³ *v.* to be completely destroyed; to be cracked; to be broken; to be scattered, or strewn about.

สระลิด, สลิด (ต้น)   sa⁴-lit⁴ *n. Telosma minor (Asclepiadaceae)*, a small woody climber (V. P. p. 253).

สระเสริญ see สรรเสริญ

สระอาด see สะอาด

สระอื้น see สะอื้น

สรัสวดี   sa⁴-rut⁶-sa⁴-wa⁶-dee *n. lit.* "watery, elegant" *i. e.* the name of a river, Saraswati, a tributary of the Ganges, formerly important but now a feeble, inconsiderable stream but celebrated both as a river and a deity by the Hindus. As a river it was once a boundary of Brahmavarta, the home of the early Aryans, and was to them, in all likelihood, a sacred river, as the Ganges has long been to their descendants. As a river goddess, she is lauded for the fertilizing and purifying powers of her waters and as the bestower of fertility, fatness and wealth. She is represented as of a white colour, without any superfluity of limbs, and not infrequently of a graceful figure, wearing a slender crescent on her brow and sitting on a lotus. In later times she is the wife of Brahma, the goddess of Knowledge, Science, Speech and Learning and patroness of the Arts and Sciences (H.C.D. p. 284).

สร่าง   sang⁴ *v.* to subside; to abate, or decrease (as fever or other symptoms); see ทุเลา p. 420: ค่อยสร่าง to show slight symptoms of the malady abating, or of convalescence; สร่างเมา, สร่างเหล้า gradually to

become sober after a drunken spree: สร่าง-โศก to be consoled; to moderate, or relax in one's sorrow: สร่างแสง to fade (as colour); to moderate, or be reduced in brightness (as rays of the sun).

สร้าง (ทำ, ปลูก, ก่อ)   sang³ *v.* to make; to produce; to create; to build; to construct: *n.* an elevated stand, stage, or platform (as is prepared for Buddhist monks to sit on while reciting scripture portions at a royal cremation): สร้างกรรม to create self-punishment, or karma (in a future existence) by unmeritorious deeds in this life: สร้างบุญกุศล to create, or increase one's merit: สร้างเมือง to build the walls, gates and battlements on the founding of a city: สร้างโลก to create the world: สร้างวัด to build a Buddhist sanctuary, or any of the separate buildings: สร้างสม to lay up wealth; to hoard riches: สร้างหนังสือ to write books, publish tracts, or inscribe religious precepts (for the public).

สราญ see สำราญ

สร้าวเสียว (เตือนใจ)   sow³-see-oh² *v.* to urge on; to arouse to greater action, or to stimulate the mind (in order to accomplish one's purpose); see เร่ง p. 718.

สรี   sa⁴-ri⁶ *S. n.* a waterfall; a cascade (S. E. D. p. 1182).

สริต   sa⁴-rit⁶ *S. n.* a river; a stream; a brook (S. E. D. p. 1182).

สรีระ   sa⁴-ree-ra⁶ *P. n.* the body (chd. p. 464); a corpse; a skeleton: สรีรกิจ natural acts of the body (as urinating); funeral obsequies: สรีรธาตุ corporal relics (chd. p. 464); ashes of a meritorious person: สรีร-วรรณ complexion; colour of the skin: สรีร-สัณฐาน shape; figure; form; features; general appearance of the body.

สรีสฤป   sa⁴-ree-sa⁴-rip⁶ *S. n.* creeping or crawling animals (as snakes, lizards) (S. E. D. p. 1183).

สรุก   sa[4]-rook[6] *Cam. n.* a town; a city: สรุกเกรา peasants; country folk; farmers; citizens of the rural districts.

สรุง (อำนาจ)   soong[2] *n.* power; authority.

สรุโนก, สุโนก   sa[4]-roo[6]-noke[6] *n.* a bird.

สรุป, สรุป, สรวป   sa[4]-roop[4] *v.* to make a summary; to summarize briefly and concisely.

สรุสระ   sa[4]-roo[6]-sa[4]-ra[6] *adj.* rough; jagged; uneven; untrimmed; unplaned; unpolished; see ขรุขระ p. 143.

สโรช   sa[4]-rote[3] *S. n.* lotus flower; *lit.* "produced or found in lakes, or ponds," *i. e.* the lotus plant (S. E. D. p. 1183).

สฤช   sa[4]-ri[6]-cha[6] *S. v.* to release or set free; to let go or fly; to discharge, throw, cast, or hurl at; to emit, shed or cause to flow (S. E. D. p. 1245); see ปล่อย p. 511.

สฤษฏ   sa[4]-rit[6]-sa[4]-dee *S. n.* production; procreation; creation (S. E. D. p. 1245).

สล   sa[4]-la[6] *P. n.* a porcupine's quill (chd. p. 421).

สลด   sa[4]-lote[4] *v.* to be sad; to be sorrowful; to be disheartened, or afflicted with sorrow; to be faded, jaded, fagged, or exhausted (by continued grief); to be melancholy.

สลบ   sa[4]-lop[4] *v.* to become unconscious in a fainting or syncopal fit, swoon, or from taking an anaesthetic: สลบไสล to faint and remain lying unconscious.

สลวย   sa[4]-lu-ie[2] *adj.* in good order; well arranged; well made up (as in dress or hair); neat; pretty; beautiful: ผมสลวยสร่าง well-combed; well-kept (as hair).

สลอด, สระลอด (ต้น)   sa[4]-laut[4] *n. Croton tiglium (Euphorbiaceae)*, a bush or small tree found from the Himalayas and southern China, southwards through Malaysia to the Philippines and New Guinea. Arabs have carried it to east Africa. The seeds contain one of the most purgative substances known, which, if applied to the skin, produces pustular eruptions. This vesicant substance is a resin. It is associated in the seed with stearine, palmitine, oleine, and some other common fats, and when the oil is extracted it passes out with them; the result is that the oil is a purgative, and blisters the mouth and intestines if more than the minutest quantity is taken. The amount of the oil in the kernel is 53.56 per cent. Croton seeds were known in sanskritic times in India for their medicinal value. They were known in China at least as early as the third century. China seems to have communicated them to the Arabs, for their name for them means "seeds of Cathay." They did not enter European medicine until the Portuguese were well established in the Indian trade, and entrenched in Goa. The Dutch, at a later date, crushed the seed and administered the oil thus obtained in wine. British surgeons in India, from 1821 forward, used oil instead of the seeds. After this, croton oil became official in various pharmacopoeias. Its action is too violent, and it is now scarcely used in Europe. It has been maliciously used for poisoning in the Dutch Indies; and also, it is sometimes used in fishing to stupefy fish (MCM. pp. 372, 395: BURK. p. 690); see น้ำมันสระลอด p. 455: สลอดน้ำ (ต้น) *Ficus heterophylla (Urticaceae)* (V. P. p. 253).

สลอน, สระลอน   sa[4]-laun[2] *adj.* much; many; abundant; ample; many together; high; exalted; elevated; conspicuous: คนดูสลอน spectators in great numbers: นั่งสลอน many sitting around together (as in gambling games): ลืมตาสลอน to look with the eyes turned high up: สล้างสลอน standing high in great numbers, and conspicuous (as trees in a forest): หัวสลอน many heads reaching high up (as tall persons in a crowd).

สลอย   sa[4]-loy[2] *Cam. adj.* pretty; beautiful; fine looking (as a row of trees).

สละ sa⁴-la⁴ *v.* to renounce; to relinquish; to let go; to leave off; to quit; to abandon; to forsake: สละ, ระกำ (ต้น) *Zalacca wallichiana* (*Palmae*), a palm with a short stout stem, found from Tenasserim and Thailand southwards in Sumatra and the Malay Peninsula. The acid seeds are used in curries. It has medicinal uses in Malaya (V. P. p. 252: BURK. p. 2283): สละ (ปลา) *Scomberoides sancti-petri* (*Carangidae*) (suvatti p. 115): สละตน self-sacrifice: สละทิ้ง to cast off, or abandon; to get rid of, or reject: สละทิ้งกิริยาชั่ว to forsake one's depraved habits; to reform.

สละสลวย sa⁴-la⁴-sa⁴-lu-ie² *adv.* compact and nicely placed (in a case, as a manicure set); slender; slim (as the form of a girl blooming into womanhood); distinct; definite; clear; fluent (as the speech of an orator); beautiful; symmetrical (as the lines of a yacht, or sailing vessel).

สลัก sa⁴-lak⁴ *v.* to carve; to chisel out sculpture; to chase (by carving out, or indenting): *n.* a bolt, pin, peg, or wedge (of wood): ช่างสลัก a sculptor: สลักเสลา sculpture, or carvings in stone: สลักหลัง to endorse: สลักหน้าจดหมาย to address a letter: สลักหลังโดยฉะเภาะ to be endorsed by the addressee only: ใส่สลัก to fasten with a bolt: เหล็กสลัก a burin; an engraver's tool.

สลักเพ็ชร sa⁴-lak⁴-pet⁶ *n.* a bolt with a retaining pin; the hip; the hip joint; the thigh: สลักสำคัญ important; significant; momentous (matters).

สลัด (สะบัด) sa⁴-lat⁴ *v.* to shake (as a cloth); to toss away; to reject: *n.* pirates; salad oil or dressing: สลัดชัดขว้าง to chuck, to fling; to get rid of (as some obstacle): สลัดตีเรือ the pirates have attacked a boat or ship: สลัดทิ้ง to reject and throw away (as tea leaves after being soaked): สลัดผง to shake off the dust.

สลัดได (ต้น) sa⁴-lat⁴-dai *n. Euphorbia an-tiquorum* (*Euphorbiaceae*), Malayan Spurge tree, a cactus-like shrub or tree up to 25 feet in height, with stiff, 3 to 6 angled branches, carrying succulent tissue within, and a woody ring outside. The leaves are small and soon fall, leaving the spinous stipules. It occurs in the dry parts of south-eastern Asia, and is found on limestone cliffs in the north of the Malay Peninsula. It is also cultivated. The hard woody part of the stem gives a medicine of great repute. In Java the Chinese women take the young shoots, boil them, soak them in water for two hours, and then reboil them in sugar. The latex is poisonous and must be removed (MCM. pp. 73, 74, 385: BURK. p. 978); *E. trigona,* a shrub of India with stiff 3 to 5 angled branches, carrying succulent tissues within and a woody ring without; the leaves, up to 4 inches long, fall early on old plants, but persist for some time on smaller plants. It is much more frequently met with in Malaya than *E. Antiquorum.* The juice from heated leaves is squeezed into the ear for ear-ache exactly as that of *E. neri-ifolia.* Every villager seems to know of this treatment; but he takes the leaves of whichever of these two is near at hand. The leaves are made into a sweetmeat. They are punctured all over so that the poisonous latex may run out, and then they are boiled in syrup. This is much the same use as Chinese women are said to make of the young shoots of *E. antiquorum* in Java. This plant is much less poisonous than its close allies, and only stupefies fish after long contact (V. P. p. 253: BURK. p. 982).

สลับ sa⁴-lap⁴ *Cam. n.* a tier, or series (of things placed one above another); a gradation (upward or downward); a step; a degree; a grade: *adj.* alternating; every other one (of a series); following by turns; reciprocal: กระแสไฟสลับ alternating current (electric): สลับซ้อน to place in tiers alternatingly (as of a series): สลับไพ่ to shuffle cards; to disarrange the cards: สลับสลอน promiscuous;

assorted; various; miscellaneous: สลับสี to arrange colours in an alternating fashion.

สลัว sa⁴-loo-ah² *adj.* pale, faded or murky; not clear or bright (in colour); see มัว p. 646.

สลา sa⁴-lah² *Cam. n.* the areca-nut.

สลาก sa⁴-lak⁴ *P. n.* a label (as on a bottle of medicine); a ballot; a ticket; a lottery ticket; see ฉลาก p. 265: สลากภัตต์ *lit.* "food tickets," *i.e.* food belonging to a group of Buddhist priests in a monastery, distributed to the monks by tickets (chd. p. 421).

สลากา sa⁴-lah-gkah *P. n.* a peg; a slip; a bit of wood; a blade, or sprout (chd. p. 421).

สล้าง sa⁴-lang³ *adj.* lofty; straight; many together; numerous (as a clump of high trees): เรียงสล้าง in rows; a dense avenue of tall trees; see ละล้าว p. 734.

สลาด (ปลา) see ฉลาด (ปลา) p. 265.

สลาตัน sa⁴-lah²-dtun *n.* the south-west wind; see ลมสลาตัน under ลม ๒ p. 728.

สลาบ sa⁴-lap⁴ *Cam. n.* a wing; feathers; hair.

สลาย sa⁴-lai² *v.* to be split, cracked (as a diamond), fractured, or sprung (open): *adj.* high, lofty, and in rows; see ทิว ๑ p. 416: แตกสลาย to be broken, or chipped (as porce- [lain).

สลิด (ต้น) see ขจร (ต้น) p. 138.

สลิด (ปลา) sa⁴-lit⁴ *n. Trichopodus pectoralis (Osphronemidae); Kyphosus waigiensis (Kyphosidae)* (suvatti pp. 104, 134); also called แม่กระแชง p. 658: สลิดหิน (ปลา) *Abudefduf bengalensis (Pomacentridae)*, damsel fish (suvatti p. 147).

สลิล sa⁴-lin *P. S. n.* water (chd. p. 422); a [river.

สลึก sa⁴-leuk⁴ *Cam. n.* a leaf.

สลึง sa⁴-leung² *n.* an ancient silver coin equal to the fourth of a baht, or twenty-five stangs in the currency of the present time.

สว ๑ sa⁴-wa⁶ *P. n.* the act of flowing, dripping, or oozing (chd. p. 470).

สว ๒ sa⁴-wa⁶ *S. n.* own; one's own (S.E.D. p. 1275): สวกรรม one's own deed, business or occupation; one's private affair: สวกัมบน *lit.* "that which moves independently," *i.e.* the wind, breeze, air: สวการย์ personal duties or obligations: สวชน a man of one's own people; a kinsman; relatives: สวภาพ natural state or condition; native place; natural impulse; spontaneity: สวราชย์ independent dominion or sovereignty; one's own dominion or kingdom: สววินาศ suicide; self-destruction: สวสถิต free; independent; self-directing; self-governing.

สวก sa⁴-wok⁴ *n.* a small-sized dip-net.

ส้วง su-ang³ *n.* the anus.

สวด su-aat⁴ *v.* to perform devotional services: *n.* devotions; adoration; worship: นำสวด to conduct religious services: ไปสวด to attend a religious service: สวดบรรยาย to chant in a very lengthy manner: สวด-พระธรรม to recite portions from the Buddhist scriptures: สวดภาวนา to worship with reverence: สวดมนตร์ to chant, according to Buddhist religious rites: สวดหนังสือ to recite portions from a book.

สวธา sa⁴-wa⁶-tah *S. n.* inherent power; one's own state, condition or nature; one's own habitual custom, rule, comfort or pleasure (S. E. D. p. 1278).

สวน su-an² *v.* to inject into the anus (as an enema); to pass, thrust or introduce into the urethra (as a catheter); to pass, while going in opposite directions: *n.* a garden; a plantation; an orchard: กลับสวนมา to go a short distance and return again: ชาวสวน gardeners: ไต่สวนปากคำ to examine; to cross-question, or investigate (as in taking the testimony of witnesses): ยาสวน an enema; a clyster: เรือกสวนไร่นา gardens and fields (in general): สวนครัว a kitchen

garden: สวนดอกไม้ a flower garden: สวน-
มะพร้าว a coconut estate: สวนยา to administer an enema: สวนหลวง the royal garden:
สวนอุทยาน name of a royal garden or park:
สอบสวน to check up; to compare; to verify;
to test; to examine (as witnesses).

ส่วน su-an[4] n. a part; a portion; a share;
a divided portion: conj. for instance; thus;
to wit; as for: gram. a disjunctive or alternative particle: มีส่วนด้วย to have a share
with; to be counted into: ส่วนของเนื้อที่ดิน
a parcel of ground: ส่วนเขา as regarding
him or you: ส่วนเดียว one part only: ส่วน-
ตัว, ฝ่ายตน personal: private; one's own self:
ส่วนต่าง ๆ ของร่างกาย various parts, or members
of the body: ส่วนท่าน you, for instance:
ส่วนน้อย minority: ส่วนแบ่งปันเท่า ๆ กัน to
divide proportionately; to divide pro rata:
ส่วนมรดก part of an inheritance: ส่วนมาก
majority: ส่วนของแม่ in reference to the
mother's share: ส่วนเรา but as for me or
us: ส่วนสัด a true division, or in exact
proportion: ส่วนเติม a complement; an accessory; see ส่วนประกอบ under ประกอบ p. 496.

สวนะ ๑ sa[4]-wa[6]-na[6] P. n. the act of hearing; the ear (chd. p. 470): สวนาการ the
manner of hearing; pertaining to the organ,
or act of hearing.

สวนะ ๒ sa[4]-wa[6]-na[6] P. n. the act of
flowing (chd. p. 470).

สวนีย sa[4]-wa[6]-nee-ya[6] P. n. words that
are pleasing or agreeable to the ear (chd. p. 470).

สวบ su-ap[4] onomat. suggestive of the
sound produced by musicians beating time, or
a sound caused by treading on dry leaves, or
of breaking through a thicket.

สวม su-am[2] v. to put upon; to cover; to
clothe, or invest (as with something made to
fit); to put on (as a coat or garment); to put
on the head (as a hat); to cover and extinguish (as to snuff a candle): สวมที่ to
be replaced by another (as when one dies an-

other takes that place or office): สวมนิ้ว
to put on the finger (as a ring): สวมรองเท้า
to put on the shoes: สวมสอด, สวมกอด to
pass the arm around (as in hugging or embracing: สวมองค์ to invest (as with a robe,
crown, or garment indicating some rank); see
ครอบ p. 179.

สวม su-am[3] n. to encircle; see กอด p. 68:
n. a water-closet; a privy.

สวย, สะสวย su-ie[2] adj. well-dressed;
nice-appearing, elegant and presentable; beautiful; lovely; fashionable; graceful: ข้าวสวย
well-cooked rice, or rice cooked dry and fluffy.

ส่วย su-ie[4] n. poll-tax; tribute paid to the
Crown by male citizens: เงินส่วยปี a yearly
poll-tax: ส่วยเกลือ salt-tax collected in
kind: ส่วยข้าว rice-tax paid in kind (thus
through the whole list, as of pepper, areca-nut
and tin).

สวยม, สยมภู sa[4]-wa[6]-yom[2] S. adv. by
oneself; spontaneously; voluntarily; independently (S. E. D. p. 1278): สวยมชาต self-born
สวยมพร see สยมพร: สวยมฐาน lit. "voluntary advances" i. e. the forward marching, or
advancing of the front lines in making an
attack (military): สวยมมฤต dying from
natural causes: สวยมเวทน์ self-consciousness; self-perception (the condition of the
"prodigal son" when he came to himself):
สวยมสังโยค a marriage willingly and cheerfully entered into.

สวรร, สวรรค์, สัคค์ sa[4]-wan[2] n. heaven;
paradise (chd. p. 412); celestial regions; heaven
upon the summit of Mount Meru; a soul's
future abode with varying degrees of highness; the future world of happiness (S. E. D.
p. 1281): ชาวสวรรค์ saints; inhabitants of
heaven: เมืองสวรรค์ heavenly kingdoms:
วิมานสวรรค์ heavenly habitations: สวรรคต
to die; to enter paradise (used for royalty):
สวรรคคีรี lit. "the heavenly mountain," i. e.
Mount Meru: สวรรคชิต the attaining or

winning of heaven or paradise: สวรรคทวาร
the gate of heaven; the entrance into paradise:
สวรรคบดี *lit.* "the lord of heaven," *i. e.* the
god Indra: สวรรคพฤ heavenly nymphs, or
female occupants of Indra's heaven; the
Apsarases: สวรรคมรรค *lit.* "a path, track,
or way of the heavens," *i. e.* the Milky Way:
สวรรคราชย์ the kingdom of heaven: สวรรค-
โลก *lit.* "the celestial world," *i. e.* Sawankaloke, otherwise known as Sri Sajja Nalaya
(ศรีสัชนาลัย), or the "Twin City." This city
is especially known today by the famous
pottery made in its kilns by the artisans
brought from China by King Ramkamheng
in about 1300. From 1257 to 1350 Sukothai,
the other "Twin City," was the capital of the
Thai territory (Siam from Ancient to Present
Times p. 9). In 1340 King Ramkamheng's
son and successor, King Loethai (ลือไทย), was
crowned King of Sawankaloke. From this
it derives its claim to being one of the twin
capitals of the Sukothai Dynasty. During
the following reign, that of King Thamma-
raja Luthai (ธรรมราชลือไทย), a road was constructed connecting Sawankaloke and Sukothai: สวรรคสุข joy, bliss, or happiness of
heaven.

สวะ   sa⁴-wa⁴ *n.* a collection of floating
weeds; floating refuse or rubbish.

สวับน์   sa⁴-wup⁶ *S. n.* the condition of
sleeping; sleepiness; drowsiness (S.E.D. p. 1280).

สวัสดิ์, สวัสดี   sa⁴-wat⁴ *n.* a salutation;
a word of welcome, blessing, welfare, prosperity, fortune, good luck (chd. p. 492); *equivalent to* "good-day," "good-night," "goodbye": สวัสดิมงคล a salutation expressing
benediction for happiness and good fortune:
สวัสดิรักษา a prayer for the protecting power
of Fortune to bless one during the day (used
when taking the morning bath).

สวัสติก   sa⁴-wat⁴-sa⁴-dti⁴-gka⁴ *S. n.* the
swastika, mystical cross or mark made on
persons and things to denote good-luck (S.E.D.

p. 1283). The swastika is of very great antiquity dating back to the 35th to 30th century
B. C. Its persistence down through all the
years seems very wonderful. It has been
used as a symbolic motif in Buddhist symbol-
ism appearing on Buddha's footprint, on ancient Greek jewellery, on a Cretan seal of
the middle Minoan age (about 1800 B. C.), as a
symbolic motif among the North American
Indians, and as an emblem raised to the rank
of a solar system by the Empress Wu of China
about 684—704 A. D.

The swastika takes two forms—the dexter
(right-handed) and sinister (left-handed).
The dexter form is said to represent the sun's
path from east to west, symbolizing day, light,
life, glory, the hosts of heaven, and blessings.
The sinister represents the sun's path from
west to east symbolizing night, darkness,
death and the hordes of hell (Illustrated London News, 18th Nov. 1933).

สวา   sa⁴-wah *Cam n.* a monkey.

สวากย์ see ศากย p. 794.

สวาคต   sa⁴-wah-ka⁶-dta⁴ *P. S. n.* a welcome; a salutation (chd. p. 492) (as at the reception of guests): *adj.* received or wel-
comed with gladness (S. E. D. p. 1283).

สวาง, สาง   sa⁴-wang² *n.* ghosts; demons.

สว่าง   sa⁴-wang⁴ *adj.* bright; clear; glowing; luminous; shining: ความสว่าง light;
clearness; radiance; brightness: สว่างข้ำรุ่ง
daylight; early dawn: สว่างอกสว่างใจ to
have all doubts dispelled; to see or understand
clearly: ส่องสว่าง to shine; to gleam, to
glitter; to glisten or sparkle.

สวาด *Thai,* หวาด *N. Laos,* บ่าขี้แฮด *Laos,
Chiengmai,* มะกาเลง *Shan,Chiengmai,* ว้าด,
เวียด *Thai, Surat* (ต้น) sa⁴-wat⁴ *n. Caesalpinia crista, C. jayabo, C. bonduc, C. bon-
ducella (Leguminosae),* Brazil wood, a woody,
prickly climber found throughout the tropics;

in the Peninsula they are recorded as round the coasts and sparingly in the interior. The Malays encourage them near their homes so that they may be available when wanted. The roots, leaves, and seeds are medicinal in various ways all round the world. The plant has been used in the East possibly from remotest times. As the seeds contain the active substance equally with the leaves, and are convenient to keep in shops, they are more used outside the region where the plant freely grows than its other parts; but where the plant is readily available, it seems to be common to resort to the leaves. The active principle in the seeds and leaves is a bitter substance, bonducin, as yet only partially studied. As the roots are not bitter it would seem that any medicinal value they may have must be due to some other substance. In India the seeds, the testa having been removed, are ground in water, and the liquid is anthelmintic, and as a tonic is given in many complaints. In the Dutch Indies the seeds are used as a vermifuge, and chewed for coughs. In the Philippine Islands the seeds are eaten for all stomach troubles, the dose being 10–12 of them, and it may be repeated once, in an hour or two. An overdose is followed by vomiting. There are various other medicinal uses. There is 17 per cent of fat in the seeds, which is used in cosmetic preparations in India; it is said to soften the skin and to remove pimples. Malay boys use the hard seeds as marbles for games. In tropical Africa they are likewise used for games, and also for oracles, etc. These seeds are large, ash-grey, polished, very hard and either globular or ovoid (cb. p. 501: v. p. p. 254: mcm. p. 461: burk. p. 388).

สวาดิ   sa[4]-wat[4] *S. n.* the star Arcturus, the principal star in the constellation Bootes; the fifteenth lunar asterism and a star of omen (s. e. d. p. 1283).

สวาท   sa[4]-wat[4] *S. v.* to join in pleasure;

to cohabit; to be pleased, or rejoice with; to love: *n.* taste; flavour; nourishment; sweetness; charm; amiability; beauty (s.e.d. p. 1279).

สวาน   sa[4]-wan[2] *S. n.* noise; sound; boisterousness (ill-sounding) (s. e. d. p. 1280).

สว่าน   sa[4]-wan[4] *n.* a drill; a gimlet; a wimble: สว่านชัก a bow-drill: สว่านหมุน an auger.

สว้าน   sa[4]-wan[3] *v.* to have a gurgling in the throat, and a sense of fullness or regurgitation of the gas from the stomach (as one in a moribund state).

สวาบ   sa[4]-wap[4] *Cam. n.* the flank; that portion of the body between the last rib and the hips (used in reference to cattle or horses).

สวาปาม   sa[4]-wah[2]-bpam *v.* to eat greedily or gluttonously (a vulgar word used to manifest contempt).

สวามิ, สวามี   sa[4]-wah-mi[6] *S. n.* lord; owner; proprietor; master; husband (s. e. d. p. 1284): สวามินี a wife (chd. p. 432); feminine form of สวามิ: สวามิภักดิ์ fidelity; loyalty: *adj.* being faithful, willing, or true to a master or lord.

สวาย (ต้น) see ขุ (ต้น) p. 161.

สวาย (ปลา)   sa[4]-wai[2] *n. Pangasius fowleri* (*Pangasiidae*) (suvatti p. 85): สวายกล้วย (ปลา) *Pangasius pangasius* (*Pangasiidae*) (suvatti p. 86): สวายหนุ (ปลา) *Eutropiichthys vacha* (*Schilbeidae*) (suvatti p. 81).

สวายสอ   sa[4]-wai[2]-saw[2] *Cam. n.* a species of mango.

สวาหะ   sa[4]-wah-ha[4] *S. interj.* a closing exclamation of greeting; hail; hail to; well said; may a blessing rest on you (s. e. d. p. 1284).

สวิง   sa[4]-wing[2] *n.* a small-sized dip-net, or net to land fish (as trout).

สวิงสวาย   sa[4]-wing[2]-sa[4]-wai[2] *v.* to be agitated; to be troubled; to be anxious; to be restless; to be uneasy; to be purturbed (mentally).

สส, สสก see ศศะ p. 792.

สสงก์　sa⁴-song² *P. n.* the moon (chd. [p. 465].

สสิ, สสี see ศศิ p. 792.

สสุระ　sa⁴-soo⁴-ra⁶ *P. n.* a father-in-law (chd. p. 465).

สสุรี, สัสุรี　sa⁴-soo⁴-ree *P. n.* a mother-in-law (chd. p. 465).

สห　sa⁴-ha⁴ *P. adv.* with; together with (chd. p. 412): *adj.* united; joined; connected; incorporated; combined; *the prefix* "co": การสหกรณ์ co-operation: สหกรณ์ co-operative society: สหจร a fellow-traveller; a friend; a partner; a mate: สหชาต born at the same time (chd. p. 413); of the same age; twins: สหธรรม co-religionists; co-believers (in the same religion): สหบาน fellow-drinkers: สหปาลิรัฐ states with a united government (as The United States of America): สหภาพ an organization; see คณะ p. 174: สหวาส the condition of living together: สหศัยยา the condition of lying with, or sleeping together (chd. p. 412); co-habitation: สหัช combined gestation, or double birth (chd. p. 413); twins; the condition of being connate.

สหัส　sa⁴-hat⁴ *S. n.* strength; power; victory: *adj.* strong; powerful; victorious.

สหัสสะ　sa⁴-hat⁴-sa⁴ *n.* a thousand: *adj.* thousand (chd. p. 413): สหัสเนตร *lit.* "one with a thousand eyes," *i. e.* an epithet for Indra (used figuratively); vigilant; all-seeing; all-knowing: สหัสรังสี *lit.* "one who emits a thousand rays," *i. e.* the sun.

สหัสา　sa⁴-hat⁴-sah² *adv.* hastily; arbitrarily (chd. p. 413); suddenly; precipitately; immediately.

สหาย　sa⁴-hai² *P. S. n.* a companion; an ally; a friend (chd. p. 414); pals; comrades; a follower; a helper.

สอ ๑　saw² *Cam. n.* the neck: *adj.* white:

โกฏฐูสอ (ต้น) a tree resembling the rattan and having a fascicle of fruits, which are oval, oblong, smooth, sessile and fleshy inside. The fleshy part encloses the kernel which is an oblong nut and contains some red juice which dyes linen red. The natives of Pullu Jambu (แหลมย้ามุ) sometimes use this nut instead of the ordinary betel-nut (J.S.S. II, 2, p. 39 Gerini); see โกฏฐู p. 131): ปูนสอ (ดินสอ) lime writing; chalk; white mineral; see ดิน p. 329: ลายสอ white-lined.

สอ ๒　saw² *adj.* collected; massed; accumulated; crowded; huddled (together as in a great mob); connected or continuous: น้ำลายไหลสอ the accumulated saliva trickles out continuously.

ส่อ　saw⁴ *v.* to tell; to reveal; to impart; to hint, or intimate (as a clue to the solution of a mystery, or to a better understanding of a problem): ส่อให้เห็น to elucidate; to make easier of understanding.

สอง　saung² *adj.* two: ที่สอง second: สองคู่ two pairs; two couples: สองง่าม two prongs: สองใจ doubtful; undecided: สองตา a pair of eyes: สองปี two years: สองรา two persons (used in poetry and rhymes): สองเสียง two voices (as manifested by a ventriloquist): สององค์ two persons (of high rank): สิบสอง twelve.

ส่อง　saung⁴ *v.* to illuminate; to enlighten, or throw light upon: ส่อง (กระจกฉาย) to look in a mirror or reflector: ส่องกล้อง to look through (as a telescope, field- or opera-glasses): ส่องโคม to lighten the way with a lantern: ส่องญาณ to investigate with super-natural power or knowledge: ส่องได้ to use a torch to light the way: ส่องทิพย์จักษุ to fix the all-seeing eyes on: ส่องสว่าง to shine; to emit light: ส่องสอด to enquire into; to investigate.

ส้อง　saung³ *v.* to frequent; to congregate at, or in (such a place): *n.* a secret place of meeting; a den; a haunt; a resort; a retreat; a rendezvous, or concealed place (as for robbers, fugitives, or secret societies): ส้องโจร a criminals' haunt or rendezvous: ส้องสุม to assemble, congregate, or gather together (secretly or otherwise): ส้องเสพย์ *lit.* "to eat, drink, do, or live together secretly," *i. e.* to associate together; to meet together at clubs (as at some private card- or drinking-party): ส้องอั้งยี่ a Chinese secret society's meeting-place.

สอด saut[4] *v.* to insert; to place in (among or between); to string together (as beads): สอดเข็ม to thrust a needle into cloth: สอด-คล้อง being of the same opinion; agreeing with (the statements made): สอดแคล้ว doubtful; ambiguous (as in conversation having a possible double meaning): สอดดู, สอดมอง to peep, or peer attentively and inquiringly: สอดแนม to spy out, explore, investigate, or examine (secretly): สอดพูด to break in while another is talking; to be officious, or to interfere in a conversation (inconsiderately): สอดรู้ to be inquisitive, curious, or inquiring: สอดรู้สอดเห็น to manifest inquisitiveness: สอดว่า to speak, or talk in an interfering, or interrupting manner (without consideration to politeness): สอดส่อง to weigh (as evidence); to investigate; to examine, or enquire into minutely; to be inquisitive, prying into with curiosity (as into other people's business): สอดเห็น to see by sly peeping, or peering.

สอน saun[2] *v.* to teach; to instruct; to educate; to train; to impart knowledge: คำสอน doctrines; precepts; tenets: ผู้สอน a tutor; a preceptor; an instructor; an educator: สอนใจ to stimulate thoughts and meditations (as to what would be the best method of procedure): สอนตัว self-instruction: สอนลูก to instruct a child: สอน-สาสนา to give instruction relating to a religion: สั่งสอน to teach by words of command, or with authority: เสี้ยมสอน to

sharpen the intellect by instruction; to give advice secretly.

ส้อน saun[4] *adj.* slanting; showing only the white of the eyes; not placed normally (as regarding the eyes).

สอบ saup[4] *v.* to compare; to verify by comparison; to taper, or grow smaller at the mouth; to be cone-shaped and truncated (as a basket for holding fish): สอบซ้อม to test out; to re-examine by questioning (as to one's knowledge either in studies, or as to what has happened): สอบถาม to make inquiries; to gather information by re-examination; to verify by comparison (as the testimonies of witnesses): สอบทาน to re-examine, attest, or corroborate by a comparison with the original, or by re-reading (as a letter or proof-sheet): สอบบัญชี to audit the accounts: สอบปาก to compare verbal testimonies: สอบพยาน to cross-question a witness: สอบไล่ to examine (as students); to hold an examination: สอบไล่ตก to fail in an examination: สอบสวน to verify, attest, or corroborate; to authenticate: สอบทางง่าว to examine, or verify lengthy documents, or accounts (the length of the document is compared to the length of a kite's tail).

สอพลอ saw[2]-plaw *v.* to flatter; to cajole; to wheedle by insincere, apparently complimentary speech; to encourage by apparently plausible representations: คนสอพลอ one who resorts to any of the above methods; a courtier; one who intrigues: คำสอพลอ vain praises; insincere promises.

ส้อม saum[3] *n.* a fork (for domestic purposes); see ช้อม p. 306.

สอย soy[2] *v.* to hem (as cloth); to break off by means of the forked end of a pole (as fruit, or flowering tops of trees); to gather by means of a basket attached to the end of a pole (as mangoes): ใช้สอย to use; to employ: คนใช้สอย domestic servants: เครื่องใช้สอย domestic utensils: ไม้สอย a

forked pole (for breaking off flowers or fruit
from high branches).

ส่อเสียด saw⁴-see-at⁴ *v.* to incite, rouse,
provoke, or stir up anger, discord, or animosity
(by defamatory language): คำส่อเสียด slanderous defamation; calumny (language).

สะ sa⁴ *v.* to be satisfied with; see พอใจ
under พอ p. 576; to cover, surround or place
in layers; see พอก p. 577: สะสม to accumulate (as wealth); to collect, store, hoard,
amass or pile up: สะสาง to disentangle,
unravel, unfold, or explain (as a plot or mystery): สะหนาม to place thorns in layers
(as an obstruction or barrier).

สะกด sa⁴-gkot⁴ *v.* to curb, suppress, repress, keep back, restrain, check, or stop:
ตัวสะกด a final consonant that is used to complete a word: สะกดใจ to restrain one's
desires: สะกดตัณหา to curb one's passions:
สะกดตัว self-restraint or self-control: สะกด-
รอย to follow the tracks; to dog after (as
following along after a stolen horse): หมอ-
สะกด magicians; wizards; sorcerers; en-
chanters; see ระงับ p. 694.

สะกอ, สระกอ sa⁴-gkaw *Cam. n.* a company, party, crowd, or assembly of people:
Thai adj. adolescent; adult; young; youthful; vigorous; see ตะกอ p. 350.

สะกัด sa⁴-gkut⁴ *v.* to obstruct; to offer
opposition; to hinder; to interrupt; to oppose;
to bar (as an advance); to chisel out; to chip
or mortise (as wood or stone); see กั้น p. 85;
ขวาง p. 145: ก้าวสะกัด to take a short cut
in advance of, in order to oppose or intercept:
กั้นฝาสะกัดเรือน to put cross partitions in a
house: กั้นสะกัด to oppose or obstruct the
advance (as by placing some obstruction, or
by spreading out the arms): กำแพงต้านสะกัด
the transverse wall: ด้านสะกัด the width;
the breadth: ตัดด้านสะกัด to intersect; to cut
squarely across (as a board): วัดด้านสะกัด
to measure the transverse distance: สะกัด-
ทาง to intercept the way: สะกัดน้ำมัน to

express or extract oil, as from sesame seeds:
สะกัดหน้า to block, or oppose one's forward
movements: เหล็กสะกัด a chisel for cutting
cold iron.

สะกา sa⁴-gkah *n.* draughts; backgammon;
a popular indoor game of the class of chess,
checkers, draughts and backgammon. There
are 15 round flat pieces (like checker men)
for each player, which are moved according.
to the spots on two dice thrown. Along the
inside edge of the board are twelve half-
moon-shaped spaces into which the pieces are
moved according to the throw of the dice.

สะกาง sa⁴-gkang *v.* to hire; to bribe: สิน-
สะกาง wages.

สะการะตาหรา sa⁴-gkah-ra⁶-dtah-rah² *Jav.*
n. the flower of *Nyctanthes arbor-tristis*
(*Oleaceae*); see กรรณิการ์ under กณิการ p. 3.

สะกิด sa⁴-gkit⁴ *v.* to touch, nudge, scratch
(gently), gesture, nod, wink, or glance (as a
forewarning); to make aware, or call the attention to (by a slight scratch or touch of the
finger); to warn, caution, or draw the attention to (by a word, or a nudge): พูดให้-
สะกิดใจ to say something so as to forewarn,
apprise, admonish, or serve as food for
thought.

สะเก็ด sa⁴-gket⁴ *n.* fragments; chips;
pieces; chunks; scraps: ลอกสะเก็ด to remove, or peel off a scab: สะเก็ดแผล the
scab over a wound.

สะแก (ต้น) sa⁴-gkaa *n. Combretum quad-*
rangulare (*Combretaceae*), a small tree, the
seeds of which are commonly used in Thailand
as an anthelmintic. They are said to be efficacious with *taenia* and *ascaris*. Both these
affections are very common in this country.
These trees grow on padi dikes and other
elevated ground. They are an important
source of firewood for domestic use for
Bangkok (cb. p. 619: v. p. p. 247): สะแกเถา
(ต้น) *Combretum procursum* (*Combretaceae*),

a creeper (cb. p. 618): สะแกหน่วย *Thai,*
Chumpawn (ต้น) *Combretum squamosum*
(*Combretaceae*) (cb. p. 620): สะคร้อ (ต้น)
see ตะคร้อ (ต้น) p. 351.

สะคราญ, สระคราญ   sa[4]-kran *n.* a pretty
woman; one in the vigour of life: *adj.* pretty; beautiful; youthful: สั่งสะคราญจงใคร่ครวญ
think over the beautiful, charming things
of life.

สะค้าน, ตะค้าน (ต้น)   sa[4]-kan[5] *n. Piper,*
a species of wild pepper, used as an intestinal
tonic.

สะดม   sa[4]-dom *v.* to plunder, or rob with
violence, or by mass attack; to make an
assault (as a charge of troops).

สะดวก   sa[4]-du-ak[4] *adv.* freely; easily;
conveniently; comfortably; readily; safely:
adj. with facility and without accident or
hindrance: คล่องสะดวก to run easily, freely
and without a hitch (as machinery): ไปมา-
สะดวก a successful round-trip.

สะดัก, สังดัก   sa[4]-duk[4] *v.* to prevent, hinder, obstruct, or stop the advance of (as by
waiting in ambush): สะดักหน้า, สังดักหน้า
to block, or obstruct an advance (as in the
case of a runaway horse); see กั้น p. 85.

สะดำ (ขวา)   sa[4]-dum *Cam. adj.* right; the
right hand or side.

สะดิ้ง   sa[4]-ding[3] *see* ดีดดิ้น under ดีด p. 831;
ตัดจริต under ตัด p. 323.

สะดึง   sa[4]-deung *n.* a case or frame made
to enclose or surround a thing; a window-
frame; a frame for embroidery work: สะดึง-
เปล a frame for a square cradle: สะดึงจีงไหม
a comb or card for dressing flax or silk:
สะดึงหน้าต่าง the frame of a window.

สะดือ   sa[4]-deu *n.* the navel: สะดือทะเล
the centre, the midst, or middle portion of
the sea or ocean; a whirlpool supposed to
exist in the middle of the ocean.

สะดุ้ง   sa[4]-doong[3] *v.* to be startled, convulsed, shocked, or shaken suddenly (as by
fright, or a scare): นอนสะดุ้งทั้งตัว to be
startled or shudder in sleep: สะดุ้งตกใจ
to be frightened and convulsed with fear.

สะดุด   sa[4]-doot[4] *v.* to trip or stumble:
เป็นที่สะดุด a stumbling-block, or cause of
offence: สะดุดเท้า to trip over something
that comes into contact with the feet: สะ-
ดุดไม้ to hit the foot against a stick.

สะเด็ด   sa[4]-det[4] *v.* to be free from moisture
or water; to be dried; to be wrung dry:
บิดผ้าให้น้ำสะเด็ด to dry a cloth by wringing
out the water.

สะเดา   sa[4]-dow *Thai* and *E. Laos* (ต้น) *n.*
Melia indica (*Meliaceae*), nim, or neem-tree
(India), magosa (Portuguese), a tall tree of
Thailand, India, Ceylon, etc. In India it is
an important roodside tree. In Thailand the
flowers are eaten with น้ำปลาหวาน and sugar.
The strong-smelling, aromatic oil, obtained
from the fruit, is much valued in native
medicine, being a universal external application for rheumatism, etc., and is taken internally by women in pregnancy. It is also
antiseptic and commonly used for animals,
both internally and externally. It is a most
valuable tree to the peasants, all parts of it
being used for medicine, or domestic purposes.
Nim leaves are used in India to protect woollen
clothing packed away during the summer.
Green twigs are used as tooth brushes. The
leaves and fruit are vermifugal; the fruit
is purgative; oil (from seed) is taken for
rheumatism (MCM. pp. 206, 377, 394: Cb. p. 251:
V. P. p. 247: BURK. p. 1443). In Thailand it is
also known as ต้นควินิน: สะเดาหิน *Thai,* สะเดา-
ช้าง *Thai, Korat,* ช้ากะเดา *Thai, Peninsula,*
ยมหิน, ยมขาว *N. Laos,* โต๊ะโย้ง *Karen, Chieng-*
mai (ต้น) *Chukrasia velutina* (*Meliaceae*)
(cb. p. 266).

สะเดาะ   sa[4]-daw[4] *v.* to perform deeds by

the power of magic; to avert, release, lessen, dispel, dissipate, or scatter (by magical power): สะเดาะเคราะห์ to avert a catastrophe by the power of magic; to counteract, by magical means, evil results that threaten.

สะตอ   sa[4]-dtaw *Thai* (ต้น) *n. Parkia, speciosa (Leguminosae)*, a tree of 60 to 80 feet in height, native of Malaysia, and often cultivated by the Malays. In the Peninsula it seems to be cultivated, or cared for, in all the more inhabited parts, and is wild on the main range of mountains. The flowers are produced in globose heads, and after flowering the pods are extruded upon stalks in a characteristic way; at maturity the pods may be as much as 20 inches long, turning from green to black. It is for these pods that the tree is cultivated; yet, in spite of cultivation, it is everywhere rare. The pods contain 12 to 18 seeds, and round the seeds is a little pulp. The Malays eat the pods with food, as a flavouring, remotely suggesting garlic, which gives them great pleasure, despite an objectionable odour. When the pods have been eaten, this odour is exhaled by the eater. No one eats much at a time as a little suffices: moreover the price is high. The immature seeds, the young leaves, and the fleshy part of the flower-stalk can be eaten raw; but they are not used to any great extent. Sometimes half-ripe pods are pickled in salt. The action of the flavouring is diuretic and relaxing, and the system evidently endeavours to excrete the substance, whatever it is, by the skin, in the urine and faeces. The timber, which is very rarely available has an unpleasant odour. The wood is fairly heavy, not very hard, and of a pale reddish-fawn colour. As it is not durable, it is not much used except for boxes and such work (BURK. p. 1671); *P. roxburghii*, a remarkably handsome, quickgrowing, very large tree, attaining a height of 100 feet or more, with a clear smooth trunk, and beautiful, fine, feathery, large,

pinnate leaves, flowering in November to December, followed in February to March by large, hanging clusters of long, brown pods, which contain a quantity of white powdery substance (cb. p. 541: MCM. p. 102).

สะตาหมั่น   sa[4]-dtah-mun[2] *Jav. n.* a garden; an orchard; a plantation.

สะเตอ   sa[4]-dteu *Thai* (ต้น) *n. Crudia chrysantha (Leguminosae)* (cb. p. 537).

สะตุ   sa[4]-dtoo[4] *v.* to sublimate, refine, or purify by heat (as salt or camphor); to evaporate the water by gentle heat; to cause crystalization (as alum): สะตุข้าวสุก to dry cooked rice by steam.

สะโตง (ชื่อแม่น้ำ)   sa[4]-dtong *n.* the name of a river in the Mon kingdom mentioned in the annals during the period of King Naresuan; see ตะเลง p. 357.

สะทก   sa[4]-tok[6] *v.* to be frightened, stagestruck, dazed, abashed, confused, or disconcerted (as an amateur actor on the stage); see งกเงิ่น under งก p. 220: สะทกสะท้าน, สะทกสะเทิ้น to be abashed, ashamed, or disconcerted; to have a shaking, or trembling of the knees from fright: สะทกสะท้านใจ to have a feeling of collapse (from sudden fright, or impending disaster).

สะท้อน   sa[4]-taun[5] *v.* to rebound; to recoil; to be reflected: *n.* (ต้น) *Millettia buteoides (Leguminosae); Sandoricum indicum (Meliaceae)*, santol, a rather tall fruit-tree, found throughout Malaysia, rare in a wild state, but commonly cultivated, and extended in cultivation northward into Thailand, Cochin-China, and to Rangoon; and in the last century taken to Mauritius, the West Indies, etc. The fruit is a poor one. Within the capsule wall, and coating the three or four big seeds, is an edible, fleshy aril of sour taste, and vinous when quite ripe. It is said that an excellent jelly can be made from the fruit. In eastern Malaysia the fruits are candied. The tree

grows fast, and its best place is the road-side.
It makes quite a good shade-tree, as it causes
little litter and is not easily broken by the
wind. The timber is red, moderately hard,
close-grained, and takes a beautiful polish. It
is used for carts and boats in Burma; for
house-building in Java; for clogs in Malaya;
and for light framing, cabinet-work, house-
posts, etc. in the Philippine Islands. The
bark contains a bitter substance—sandoricum
acid. It is used by the Malays as a protective
medicine after childbirth, but it is the root
which is most used in Malay medicine, both
for this purpose and as a general tonic. The
water in which leaves have been pounded may
be drunk for remittent fever, or the leaves
may be boiled and the decoction taken. The
pounded bark may be applied for ringworm
(Burk. p. 1946); see กระท้อน p. 34; *syn.* กะท้อน,
สท้อน.

สะท้าน　　sa[4]-tarn[5] *v.* to be agitated; to be
convulsed; to tremble, shake, quiver, or quake;
see ก้อง p. 68.

สะทิ่น　　sa[4]-tin[3] *adv.* like; as; such; such
as; see ดัง p. 322.

สะทึง, สระทึง, ชระทึง　　sa[4]-teung *n.* a river.

สะเทิน ๑　　sa[4]-tern *adj.* half; mid; half-
way; see ครั้ง p. 182: *conj.* both: สะเทินน้ำ,
สะเทินบก both by land and water.

สะเทิน, สะเทิน ๒　　sa[4]-tern[5] *v.* to be abashed,
ashamed, or disturbed (mentally); see กระดาก
p. 27: สะเทินใจ to become estranged from
one another (as man and wife because of some
indiscretion).

สะเทือน, สะเทือน　　sa[4]-teurn *v.* to shake,
shiver, tremble, or shudder: สะเทือนทั้งเรือน
the whole house is shaking: สะเทือนหวั่นไหว
to be shaky, or easily shaken (as a flimsy
house which is shaken by one walking through
it): สะท้านสะเทือน a violent commotion,
agitation, or disturbance.

สะบะ　　sa[4]-ba[4] *Jav.* (*possibly Malay*) *n.* a
ball made of woven rattan (played with as a
foot-ball); see ตะกร้อ p. 349.

สะบัก　　sa[4]-buk[4] *n.* the scapula; the collar-
bone: ชายสะบัก the edge of the scapula:
สะบักจม to have the scapula displaced downward (as by a knock on the shoulder): สะบัก-
สะบอม completely knocked out, worn out, or
badly bruised (as after a boxing bout).

สะบัด　　sa[4]-but[4] *v.* to shake; to wave; to
flap; to flutter (as clothes, or a flag in the
wind); see ทะทัด p. 405: สะบัดแขน to
straighten out the arms with a sudden jerk
(as while exercising): สะบัดดีสะบัดร้าย conditions of saneness and insanity occurring
alternately: สะบัดตัวหนี to squirm, writhe,
struggle, or wriggle oneself in order to get
free and flee: สะบัดย่างเท้าไป to move the
feet in a lively manner, or to make run in a
dog-trot (as while speeding up the action of
cattle hitched to a cart): สะบัดร้อนสะบัดหนาว
to have alternate sensations of heat and cold
(as in malarial fever): สะบัดลุกสะบัดนั่ง to
rise and sit again; to be restless or agitated:
สะบัดสะบิ้ง to twist, writhe, squirm, or wriggle,
turning first one way and then another (as in
a temper); to swing; to sway the body and
arms listlessly: สะบัดสะบิ้งตัว to flaunt,
shuffle or shake (garments), or over-agitate
the body (as ladies of fashion while walking).

สะบั้น　　sa[4]-bun[3] *v.* to be broken off; to
have a break in the continuity: *adj.* in
pieces; in bits; in particles; in sections or
lengths: ขาดสะบั้น to be severed into pieces
or lengths: ฟันหักสะบั้น the tooth is broken
into fragments.

สะบ้า　　sa[4]-bah[3] *Thai* (ต้น) *n. Entada phaseo-
loides* (*scandens*) (*Leguminosae*), elephant-
creeper, St. Thomas's bean, a vine twisted
like a corkscrew, bearing large flat pods, 3½
to 4½ feet long and 3 to 4 inches broad, containing very large, hard, brown, flat seeds,

used for snuff boxes. The climber is found throughout tropical Asia, and out into the Pacific Islands, and, in a variety, in tropical Africa. If a length of the stem be cut from this great liane, a quantity of fresh water runs out, which can be drunk. When fresh, the liane is tough enough for making fish-traps, but it soon loses its strength. In the Dutch Indies the young leaves are eaten. Elephants eat the leaves. Saponin is present in the tissues. It is abundantly present in the seeds. In the seeds, accompanying this saponin, were found traces of an alkaloid and 18 per cent of a yellow tasteless oil. This oil is said to be extracted in the Sunda Islands for burning. The use of *Entada* oil as a fish-poison seems to be more common in the Philippine Islands than elsewhere. This use is also reported from Ceylon. The juice in the eye produces conjunctivitis. Owing to the presence of saponin, *Entada* is almost the universal hair-wash in Malaysia, and in South Africa the bark is used for soap. The pods are used for chest complaints. Javanese women, in child-bed, eat the roasted seeds, with the idea that they purify. The seeds are emetic and purging. Apparently there are similar uses in India. The seeds can be used as food but must be boiled a whole day; heat destroys the saponin. The big seeds are so smooth they can be used in polishing. Burmese potters burnish pottery with them; and Javanese country-made paper is smoothed by means them. They are used in Samoa in playing certain games. There is a game called สะบ้า which is sometimes played in Thailand in the time of merit-making (ตรุษสงกรานต์) (Cb. p. 542: MCM. pp. 132, 461, 462: V. P. p. 248: Burk. p. 925): สะบ้าหัวเข่า the patella; the knee-cap; the knee-pan.

สะบู่   sa⁴-boo⁴ *n.* soap: สะบู่ดำ (ต้น) *Jatropha curcas* (*Euphorbiaceae*), a well-known, quick-growing shrub, an American plant which the Portuguese brought into the East,

where it is now very abundant. It was established in Africa by the same agency. It is often used in rural Thai villages as a hedge plant along paths and cart tracks. There are two races in the Malay Peninsula, one with dark seeds, and one with pale seeds. The seeds yield a strongly purgative oil, used in medicine and for lighting, etc. The seed is albuminous and the albumen rich in oil. In the husk is one poison; in the kernel through the albumen is another, which is present in greatest quantity in the embryo. The chief poison is an albuminoid, called curcin of undetermined composition, but of the group of ricin from *Ricinus* and crotin from *Croton tiglium*. Owing particularly to this curin, the plant has been responsible for many cases of poisoning, curiosity leading to tasting, and the pleasant taste to eating. The action of the poison is very uncertain and varies in different people. A burning of the throat commences, followed by distension of the stomach, giddiness, vomiting, diarrhoea, drowsiness, collapse and death. The oil can be used as an illuminant, burning without smoke; and in soap boiling, giving a hard soap. It dries somewhat quickly and cannot replace castor oil as a lubricant. The medicinal use seems to be on the wane, and tends to disappear entirely, though at one time it was important. The bark will produce a blue dye (MCM. pp. 73, 396: Burk. p. 1268): สะบู่แดง (ต้น) *J. gossypiifolia*, an American plant, which seems to have reached the East at a later date than the *J. curcas*, and which has not attained so wide a distribution. It can be planted in hedges in the same way, but it makes a fence which is inferior. Medicinal uses are similar to those of *J. curcas*. The seeds give an oil which is said to be useful in treating leprosy (V. P. p. 248: Burk. p. 1270).

สะเบย see สบาย p. 813.

สะเบียง   sa⁴-bee-ang *n.* food; victuals; supplies; provisions prepared for a journey:

สะเบียงกรัง *lit.* "nest egg food," *i. e.* stored provisions, as canned, steamed, dried or preserved foods.

[epidermis.

สะแบก sa⁴-baak⁴ *Cam. n.* skin; the

สะไบ sa⁴-bai *Cam. n.* a cloth, scarf, or sash worn crossed over the left shoulder and under the right arm (a former style of upper garment for Thai women).

สะพรัก (พรักพร้อม) sa⁴-pruk⁶ *adj.* ready; prepared; provided for.

สะพรั่ง, สระพรั่ง sa⁴-prung³ *adj.* whole; complete; total; entire; all: สะพรั่งพร้อม in a state of complete preparedness; see ระคะ

[p. 694.

สะพรีบ see พร้อม p. 566.

สะพัก sa⁴-puk⁶ *v.* to cover with a scarf: *n.* a cloth, scarf or sash worn across the breast and suspended from the left shoulder.

สะพัด sa⁴-put⁶ *v.* to surround; to fence in on every side; to encircle completely; see กั้น. p. 85.

สะพั้น, ตะพั้น (p. 354) sa⁴-pun⁵ *n.* brass; copper; a disease of infants characterized by

[convulsions.

สะพาน see ตะพาน p. 355.

สะพาบ see พังพาบ p. 580: ล้มสะพาบ to fall flat on the face.

สะพาย see ตะพาย p. 355.

สะเพร่า sa⁴-prow³ *v.* to do things in a haphazard, half-finished way; to be careless; to be negligent; to be thoughtless; to be heedless or incautious.

สะเภา see ตะเภา p. 355.

สะใภ้ sa⁴-pai⁵ *n.* a female relative (by marriage): น้องสะใภ้ a younger brother's wife, or a cousin: น้าสะใภ้ the wife of the younger brother of the mother: บ๊าสะใภ้ the wife of the elder brother of the father or mother: พี่สะใภ้ an older brother's wife, or cousin: ลูกสะใภ้ a daughter-in-law; a

sister-in-law: หลานสะใภ้ the wife of a grandson or nephew: อาสะใภ้ the wife of a younger brother of the father.

สะระแหน่ (ต้น) sa⁴-ra⁶-naa⁴ *n. Menthae piperita (Labiatae),* mint, peppermint, or peppermint camphor, a dwarf, creeping herb with a strong aromatic odour. A volatile oil obtained from the plant is well known in medicine for its antiseptic, stimulant, and carminative properties; this yields the crystaline camphor-like substance known as "menthol," commonly used for neuralgia, etc. Menthol and peppermint oil are exported from Japan. *M. piperita* is thought by most botanists to be a hybrid of *M. viridis* and *M. arvensis.* This grows easily in the Malay Peninsula, but the mint of the Peninsula and Thailand is *M. arvensis* (MCM. p. 274: BURK. p. 1453); see น้ำมันสะระแหน่ under น้ำ p. 455.

สะวานนา sa⁴-wan-nah *n.* savanna or savannah; a tract of level land covered with low vegetation.

สะสวย see สวย p. 829.

[skins of animals.

สะแหก sa⁴-haak⁴ *Cam. n.* a hide; the

สะอาง sa⁴-ang *adj.* beautiful; clear complexioned; pretty; gay: เครื่องสะอาง cosmetics.

สะอาด, สระอาด sa⁴-art⁴ *adj.* clean; pure (as water); neat; tidy; spotless; unspotted; unsoiled; beautiful (as regards dress): แต่งตัวสะอาดสะอ้าน *colloquial* beautifully clean and becomingly dressed.

สะอ้าน sa⁴-an³ *adj.* comely; graceful; swanky; elegant; spruce; smart; neat.

สะอิ้ง, สะเอิ้ง sa⁴-ing³ *n.* a girdle; a belt; a gold or silver waist-chain; a waist-chain with a "fig-leaf" (as worn by young girls).

สะอิดสะเอียน sa⁴-it⁴-sa⁴-ee-an *v.* to have a feeling of repulsion, estrangement, or qualms because of anger, hate or disgust; see ขยะแขยง p. 142.

สะอึก   sa⁴-euk⁴ (see ระอึก *n.* p. 700): *n.* (ต้น) *Ipomoea obscura (Convolvulaceae)*, a woody climber: สะอึกสะอื้น to weep; to cry; to sob in a continuous manner; to have sighs with hiccoughs, while sobbing or crying.

สะเอว   sa⁴-ay-oh *n.* the hips, waist, or loins: สะเอวบางร่างน้อย *idiomatic* small-waisted and slender in figure.

สะเออะ   sa⁴-urh⁴ *v.* to speak, or otherwise interfere while others are conversing; to push oneself in, or meddle in another's affairs: สะเออะหน้า to break in abruptly and rudely, joining in the conversation; see ทะลึ่ง p. 407.

สะแอก   sa⁴-aak⁴ *Cam. n.* tomorrow; the day following.

สะโอดสะอง   sa⁴-oat⁴-sa⁴-aung *adj.* slim; slender; tall and spindling (as trees).

สัก   suk⁴ *v.* to bind, tie, or encircle with a string or thread (as charm-strings around the wrist); to puncture, prod, probe or pierce with a long, sharp-pointed iron (as while exploring bags of grain for hidden contraband goods); to tattoo; to decorate the skin in patterns or designs with indelible pigments. The method is to take either one at a time, or five needles fastened together on weighted handles, and by repeated rapid punctures press in till blood is drawn. Then black indelible colouring matter is rubbed into the punctures. If the design is a simple one it may be finished at one operation, but if extensive may take several, while female relatives drown the cries of the sufferer with songs and beating of drums. This practice is common among the Chinese, Japanese, Burmese and Thai. Remarkable examples of tattooing are to be found among the Laos who often completely cover the parts of the body usually covered by clothing with fantastic figures or designs of animals. In Japan it has become a highly specialized art; many artizens indicate their profession by tattooing designs of their oc-cupation. For example a fisherman has a fish or fishes, a fireman his hat or a coil of hose. A most elegant design is tattooing white chrysanthemums over the whole body. The purpose may be considered as purely orna-mental, or to attract the opposite sex, or to display courage, or to produce invulnerability to the person, or because of eccentricity (as is the case with soldiers or sailors): *adv.* as for; as to; at least; about; approximately: สัก (ต้น) *Tectona grandis (Verbenaceae)*, teak, one of the important timber trees of Thailand. The export trade has been considerable owing to the enduring qualities of the teak and its durability as decking over steel plates (BURK. p. 2127); *Vatica sp. (Dipterocarpaceae)* near *V. grandiflora* (V. P. p. 259: MCM. p. 219): สักกระบี่, สักดาบ to tie the sword-hilt to the wrist: สักข้อมือ to tattoo a mark on the wrist indicating a condition of corvée: สัก-ครู่หนึ่ง, สักประเดี๋ยว in a few minutes; in a moment or two: สักชะรา to tattoo a mark on the wrist, denoting over-age for corvée: สักดินหาของ to probe the ground in search of hidden treasure: สักแต่ว่า, สักว่า only this; simply that; solely; merely: สักเท่าไร about how much in price? สักนิดสักหน่อย a trifling bit: สักพิการ to tattoo a mark of exemp-tion because of some defect or infirmity: สักเล็กสักน้อย just a very little: สักว่าว to tie threads crosswise to the frame of a kite in order to support the paper: สักสองวัน in about two days: สักหน้า to tattoo a designating mark on the face, indicating some criminal offence has been committed against the government: เหล็กสัก a tattoo-ing needle; a sharp probing, or piercing iron.

สักก์ ๑   suk⁴ *P. n.* a disk; the chakra; a common name for the Brahminical Indra: *adj.* great; supreme (Chd. p. 419).

สักก์ ๒   suk⁴ *P. adj.* able; possible; cap-able; competent; specific (Chd. p. 419): สักก์-สิทธิ์ effectual: efficient; specific; producing immediate beneficial results (as a remedy).

สักกฏะ, สักกตะ ๑ suk⁴-gka⁴-dta⁴ *P. n.* the Sanskrit language (chd. p. 418); a language formed by perfect grammatical rules; the classical and sacred language of the Hindus.

สักกตะ ๒ suk⁴-gka⁴-dta⁴ *P. adj.* entertained; honoured (chd. p. 418); respected; venerated.

สักกัจจ์ suk⁴-gkut⁴ *P. adv.* respectfully; carefully; zealously; thoroughly (chd. p. 417).

สักกาย suk⁴-gkah-ya⁶ *P. n.* one's body or self (chd. p. 418); an individual; a personality: สักกายทิฏฐิ *lit.* "the heresy of individuality," *i. e.* one of the three bonds, causing bondage. Release from individuality is obtained by entrance into the first of the four paths leading to the highest degree of saintship or Srota-apatti (Ala. p. 170: chd. p. 418): สักกายนิโรธ the annihilation of self (chd. p. 418); the destruction, or abolition of one's personality and habits: สักกายสมุทัย the origination of the self (chd. p. 418), or personality; the beginning, or commencement of habits, temperament and disposition.

สักการ suk⁴-gkah-ra⁶ *P. n.* an offering or tribute manifesting reverence towards, or respect for (implying gifts or flowers): สักการบูชา to worship with offerings; to offer a sacrifice; to propitiate; to expiate; to atone or make amends for; to make payment of a vow: สักการศพ to present offerings at a cremation, or at a burial, manifesting respect to the dead.

สักขรา suk⁴-ka⁴-rah *P. n.* a piece; a fragment; a potsherd; gravel; rock-sugar; brown sugar (chd. p. 418).

สักขี, สากษิน, สากษี suk⁴-kee² *P. n.* a witness (chd. p. 418); see พะยาน p. 579.

สักยะ, สักกะ suk⁴-gka⁴-ya⁶ *P. n.* name of the princely family to which Gotama Buddha belonged (chd. 417).

สักวา suk⁴-gka⁴-wah *n.* a form of poetry; the initial word of a dialogue which is sung; *contracted form* สกวาท or สกวาที.

สักหลาด suk⁴-gka⁴-lart⁴ *n.* woollen cloth; flannel. This is said to have derived its Thai name from "scarlet" which was the colour of the early woollen cloth imported into Thailand.

สขยะ (มิตรภาพ) suk⁴-ka⁴-ya⁶ *S. n.* friendship; acquaintance; friendliness; association; companionship (S. E. D. p. 1198).

สัคค์ ๑ suk⁴ *P. n.* the act of making; creation (chd. p. 412).

สัคค์ ๒ (สวรรค์) suk⁴ *P. n.* heaven; paradise (chd. p. 412); the future world of happiness; a future abode of the soul with varying degrees of bliss.

สั่ง sung⁴ *v.* to command; to order; to charge; to enjoin; to direct; to bid; to dictate; to decree: คำสั่ง an order, command, or injunction: คำสั่งขาด an irrevocable order: รับสั่งว่า a royal command or order: สั่งขี้มูก to blow the nose: สั่งงานการ to instruct, or leave orders for work (to be continued): สั่งแล้ว the order has already been given: สั่งไว้ to leave word with another: สั่งสม, สะสม to amass, accumulate, collect, pile, or heap up (as riches): สั่งสอน to instruct; to reprimand; to admonish; to teach or advise: สั่งเสีย to adjure with explicit instructions: สั่งเสียลูกเมีย to give final instructions (as may be given to the family before death, or on departure to a foreign country): สั่งให้มา a summons to come (as into the presence of some one).

สังกร sung²-gkorn *P. S. n.* confusion; intermixture; the blending together of metaphors which ought to be kept distinct (S.E.D. p. 1126): สังกรประโยค *gram.* an involved or complex sentence; see ปน p. 494.

สังกะตัง sung²-gka⁴-dtung *adj.* badly tangled; intertwisted; matted (as hair); confused; not so well done (as a botched up job):

ผมสังกะตั้ง hair so matted as to be impossible to be combed out: ยางสังกะตั้ง tanglefoot, or stickfast gum (for catching birds or flies).

สังกะวาด sung²-gka⁴-wart³ สังกะวาดกล้วย, สังกะวาดขาว, สวาย, สวายกล้วย, อ้ายด้อง (ปลา) *n.* *Pangasius pangasius* (*Pangasiidae*); *P. cultratus* (suvatti pp. 84, 86): สังกะวาดท้องเหลือง (ปลา) *Pangasius siamensis* (*Pangasiidae*) (suvatti p. 87).

สังกะสี ๑ sung²-gka⁴-see² *n.* zinc; a name for fighting fishes having mixed breeding: สังกะสีลูกฟูก galvanized iron sheets; corrugated iron sheets.

สังกะสี ๒ (ต้น) *Mussaenda sp. Rubiaceae,* an erect shrub (Burk. p. 1518).

สังกัด sung²-gkut⁴ *r.* to be under the jurisdiction of, or in the service of, or subject to: *n.* limit; boundary; confines (of some circumscribed area): กินอยู่ในสังกัดของ to be dependent on (some one) for food and lodging: สังกัดขึ้นอยู่ to be subject to, or under the jurisdiction of.

สังกัปปะ sung²-gkup⁴-bpa⁴ *P. n.* thought; imagination; determination; resolve; wish [(Chd. p. 452).

สังกา see สงกา p. 806.

สังการ sung²-gkarn *P. n.* dust; sweepings; rubbish (Chd. p. 452).

สังกาศ sung²-gkart⁴ *P. adj.* resembling (Chd. p. 452); similar; analogous; see คล้าย p. 186.

สังกิเลส sung²-gki⁴-let⁴ *P. n.* personal impurities (Chd. p. 457); one's lower nature; innate wickedness.

สังเกตุ sung²-gket⁴ *Thai v.* to observe; to notice; to perceive; to distinguish; to recognize, or bear in mind: *P.S. n.* engagement; appointment; rendezvous (Chd. p. 452); intimation; allusion; hint (S.E.D. p. 1126): เคยสังเกตุ being familiar with, or having seen

often: ตามที่เคยสังเกตุมา according to what one has been accustomed to notice or perceive: ไม่ทันสังเกตุ failed to notice, or recognize (as one passing another rapidly on the street): สังเกตุตามรูป to recognize or distinguish by the form or shape: สังเกตุสังกาแห่งชีวา *idiomatic* to recognize the uncertainty of life.

สังข์, ศังข์ (p. 793) sung² *P. n.* a shell; a conch shell (as used for the pouring of lustral water); a conch shell trumpet (Chd. p. 456): สังขกร *lit.* "one holding a conch shell," *i.e.* an epithet for Vishnu.

สังขตะ sung²-ka⁴-dta⁴ *P. adj.* built; created; wrought; embellished (Chd. p. 455).

สังขยา ๑, สังขา sung²-ka⁴-yah² *P.S. n.* a high numeral; a word or figure used to denote a number; a calculation; the act of counting, summing up, or totalling (of figures) (S. E. D. p. 1128).

สังขยา ๒ sung²-ka⁴-yah² *n.* a sweetmeat, or custard made by steaming the yolks of eggs, coconut milk and sugar well-mixed together.

สังขลิก, สังขลิกา sung²-ka⁴-lik⁶ *P. n.* a chain (Chd. p. 453); fetters.

สังขาร, สังสการ sung²-karn² *P. n.* matter; construction (Chd. p. 453); adornments; embellishments; aggregation; component parts (as the various portions or members of the body); arrangement (Ala. p. 235); perfection; completion; preparation; life; soul; instability of life; thought; being one of five elements of corporal being (Ala. p. 172): สังขารทุกข์ troubles, afflictions, adversities, calamities of life: สังขารปธาน the condition of meditative introspection into the instability of corporal being: สังขารโลก *lit.* "the realm of matter," *i.e.* the world of corporal being; the course of nature as manifested in the component parts, or arrangements of the physical being: สังขารอุเบกขา, สังขารุเบกขา the condition of impartiality, indifference, or equanimity in respect to

the things, or circumstances of life : สังขาร-
ธรรม the principles of law and right ; good
and evil in the affairs of life.

สังเขป, สมเขป sung²-kep⁴ *P. n.* abridgement; an abstract (chd. p. 456); a compendium;
a summary ; an abbreviation ; a synopsis ; an
outline : ทำสังเขป to give the gist ; to make
an outline.

สังโขภ sung²-kop³ *P. n.* commotion (chd.
p. 457); disturbance ; agitation ; the condition
of overturning or overthrowing.

สังค์, สงค์ sung² *P. n.* attachment; bond;
tie (chd. p. 450); affiliation ; adhesion ; a condition of cleaving to, or holding fast.

สังคติ sung²-ka⁶-dit⁴ *P. n.* union; intercourse; familiarity ; intimacy (chd. p. 448).

สังคม sung²-kom *P. n.* an association ; a
meeting ; a concourse; communion (chd. p.
447); see วิสสาสะ p. 779.

สังคาตา sung²-kah-dtah *Jav. n.* father.

สังคาม see สงคราม p. 806.

สังคายนะ, สังคายนา sung²-kah-ya⁶-na⁶
P. n. clarification ; the act of rehearsing (chd.
p. 448); an occasion in which all great Buddhist
priests assemble and discuss the Tri-pitaka
(ไตรปิฎก) to eliminate all discrepancies.

สังคีติ sung²-kee-di⁴ *P. n.* the act of
chanting, singing, or the playing of a band in
unison ; a rehearsal ; the clarification of the
Buddhist scriptures (chd. p. 450).

สังเค็ด sung²-ket⁶ *n.* gifts (as tables, carpets, lamps) presented to Buddhist monks
officiating at cremations or funeral obsequies.

สังฆ, สงฆ์ (p. 806): สังฆกรรม, สังฆกิจ an act,
deed, duty, or ceremony performed by a
chapter of Buddhist monks assembled in
solemn conclave (chd. p. 448) ; some work done
by a group of four or more Buddhist monks :
สังฆการี *lit.* "those who control the affairs of
Buddhist monks," *i. e.* The Ecclesiastical De-

partment of the Ministry of Public Instruction : สังฆคต observing the rules of
etiquette governing the approach to Buddhist
monks; observing the rules governing the
initiation into the brotherhood : สังฆเถระ
the senior member of a fraternity, or assembly of Buddhist monks (chd. p. 450): สังฆ-
ทาน gifts, alms, or food presented to Buddhist
monks : สังฆนวก the most recently initiated, or junior member of a fraternity of
Buddhist monks : สังฆปาโมกข์ the chief,
head, or leader of any fraternity of Buddhist
monks : สังฆภัตต์ food that an individual
takes to the temple and presents to a Buddhist monk, which, after due permission is
granted, is distributed among other monks :
สังฆมามกะ *lit.* "one who for selfish purposes
considers the Buddhist brotherhood as a means
to an end," *i.e.* as a place of protection or preservation (so as to evade the law) : สังฆราช
a patriarch ; a pontiff (chd. p. 450) ; a bishop :
สังฆราชา a high dignitary of the Buddhist
brotherhood, but lower than a สังฆราช : สังฆ-
ราชี a disagreement, separation or division
(among Buddhist monks) : สังฆาณัติ a command or order of, or for Buddhist monks :
สังฆานุสสติ gratitude towards, or the thankful
meditation regarding the kindnesses received
from Buddhist monks : สังฆาราม a Buddhist
temple ; the living quarters of Buddhist
monks.

สังฆาฏิ sung²-kah-dti⁴ *P. n.* one of the
three robes of a Buddhist monk (chd. p. 449);
a Buddhist monk's cold-weather attire, consisting of a double or composite robe, reaching
from the shoulders to the knees and fastened
around the waist.

สังปะติเหงะ, สังปะลิเหงะ sung²-bpa⁴-dti⁴-
nga⁴ *Jav. n.* an inspired poet or sage (H. C. D.
p. 268); see ฤษี p. 725.

สังยุค, สมยุค (p. 817) sung²-yook⁶ *P. S. n.*
strife (chd. p. 444); war; battle; conflict;
combat.

สังโยค, สัญโญค, สมโยค   sung[2]-yoke[3] *P. S. n.* union; bond; link; connection; association; society; criminal intercourse: *gram.* contraction, or running together of letters in a word or sentence; a conjunctive consonant (chd. p. 444).

สังโยชน์, สัญโญชน์   sung[2]-yote[3] *P. n.* a bond; an attachment. In a religious sense, it is the bond of human passion which binds men to continued existence and the removal of which is obtained by entrance into the Paths (chd. p. 444).

สังวร, สำรวม   sung[2]-worn *P. v.* to restrain; to hold in; to suppress or check (as one's inclinations) (chd. p. 442): *n.* carefulness; self-restraint; constraint; subjugation (of one's senses and desires): สังวรวินัย rules governing one striving for self-subjugation: สังวร-ศีล observing the commandments regarding self-restraint and moderation.

สังวรณ์   sung[2]-worn *n.* the act of covering (chd. p. 442), sheltering, or guarding; protection; see ป้อง p. 516.

สังวรี   sung[2]-wa[6]-ree *P. n.* night (chd. p. 442).

สังวัจฉระ   sung[2]-wat[6]-cha[4]-ra[6] *P. n.* a year (chd. p. 442); the period, or revolution of a year.

สังวัธยาย, สัชฌายะ   sung[2]-wat[6]-ta[6]-yai *P. v.* to repeat; to rehearse; to read aloud (chd. p. 415); to memorize; to recite (as prayers); to recite the Vedas or scriptures with intonations.

สังวาล   sung[2]-warn *n.* a chain; chains of gold or silver worn from both shoulders across the breast, and fastened in front with a pin or brooch: สังวาลแฝด double chains worn as the above.

สังวาส, สมพาส (p. 817) sung[2]-wart[3] *P. n.* copulation; coition; cohabitation; the condition of living with, or having carnal knowledge:

สมสังวาส fit, or suited for the condition of being a wife: สมัครสังวาส a condition of free love, or unrestrained carnal knowledge.

สังเวคะ   sung[2]-way-ka[6] *P. n.* agitation; emotion; grief; sorrow (chd. p. 443).

สังเวช, สมเพช (p. 817) sung[2]-wet[3] *n.* pity; compassion; commiseration; sympathy: *adj.* deplorable; miserable; pitiable.

สังเวย   sung[2]-wur-ie *v.* to make propitiatory offerings (of food), or sacrifices to guardian spirits of the city, of trees, or mountains (wales, state ceremonies pp. 73, 194); see บนบาน p. 467.

สังเวียน   sung[2]-wee-an *n.* a pen; an enclosure; an arena, stadium, or boxing-ring; see คอก p. 190: สังเวียนชนไก่ a pit for cock-fighting.

สังสกฤต see สันสกฤต p. 850.

สังสการ see สังขาร p. 842.

สังสดมภ์   sung[2]-sa[4]-dom *S. n.* obstinacy; pertinacity; firmness in resistance (S. E. D. p. 1121).

สังสดร   sung[2]-sa[4]-dorn *S. n.* a bed; a couch; a mattress; a bed covering (S. E. D. p. 1121).

สังสถาน see สัณฐาน p. 846.

สังสรรค์   sung[2]-sun[2] *S. n.* coalition; amalgamation; union; commixture; conjunction; association (S. E. D. p. 1119); see ปน p. 494.

สังสฤช   sung[2]-sa[4]-rit[6] *S. n.* commingling; collision; the act of touching, hitting, or knocking together (S. E. D. p. 1120); see กระทบ p. 33.

สังสฤติ   sung[2]-sa[4]-rit[6] *S. n.* course; revolution; passage through successive states of existence; course of mundane existence; transmigration (S. E. D. p. 1119).

สังสาร see สงสาร p. 807.

สังสิทธ์   sung[2]-sit[4] *S. adj.* won; accomplished; achieved; attained; conquered (S.E.D. p. 1119).

สังสุทธ์   sung²-soot⁴ *S. adj.* completely purified or cleansed; pure; clean; expiated; acquitted (S. E. D. p. 1117).

สังหร   sung²-horn² *v.* to warn; to caution or restrain (by spiritual influence); to convince (of wrong doing); see คลใจ under คล ๓ p. 319.

สังหรณ์   sung²-horn² *n.* the act of suppressing or restraining; a means of dissuading (by mental influence); correction of evil conduct (by spiritual power).

สังหรรษ   sung²-hut⁴ *S. n.* joy; pleasure; a thrill of delight; a bristling or erection of the hair of the body; sexual excitement (S. E. D. p. 1123).

สังหาร   sung²-harn² *P. S. n.* a bringing together; contraction; an abridgement; a compendium; a manual; a contraction or drawing in; destruction; conclusion (S. E. D. p. 1123).

สังหาริมะ, สังหาริมทรัพย์   sung²-hah²-ri⁶-ma⁶ *P. n.* movable property (as boats and cattle): อสังหาริมะ immovable property (as land or houses).

สังหิต   sung²-hi⁴-dta⁴ *S. adj.* joined; put together; attached; fixed; composed of; placed together (S. E. D. p. 1123).

สังหิตา   sung²-hi⁴-dtah *S. n.* conjunction; connection; union; the combination of letters according to euphonic rules (S. E. D. p. 1123).

สัจ, สัจจ   sut⁴ *P. n.* truth; veracity; truthfulness: *adj.* true (Chd. p. 409); exact; precisely right: สัจจกิริยา *lit.* "made a truthful act," *i.e.* a solemn asseveration (Chd. p. 408): สัจจญาณ knowledge of the truth. According to the Buddhist religion, this is defined as "knowledge of the four pre-eminent truths, or the truths of the saints," which are, (1) that sorrow ever attends (transmigratory) existence, (2) that the cause of sorrow lies in the passions or desires, (3) that cessation of

sorrow can only be procured by the extinction of desire, (4) that desire can be extinguished by holiness (by entry into the Paths) (Ala. p. 197): สัจจวจน words of truthfulness and veracity; the truth of an asseveration: สัจจ-สัมมตา speech; sayings; proverbs.

สัชฌะ, สัชฌุ   sut⁴-cha⁶ *P. n.* silver (Chd. p. 415): สัชฌการ a silversmith.

สัชฌายะ see สังวัธยาย p. 844.

สัญจร   sun²-chjorn *P. S. v.* to be a vagrant; to go about; to wander around; to meet another; to unite (Chd. p. 445); to move, stray, or go about; to belong together while going about: *n.* passage; way; course; the act of passing; vagrancy: สัญจรไปไกล to wander a great distance away: สัญจรโรค *lit.* "a disease contracted while wandering about," *i. e.* syphilis; venereal disease.

สัญจาร   sun²-chjah-ra⁶ *P. S. n.* road; course; way; tract; progress or passage through difficulties (as in a defile or gorge) (S.E.D. p. 1131).

สัญชัย, สัญชัย   sun²-chai *S. adj.* completely victorious; triumphant; conquering; successfully subjugated (S. E. D. p. 1133).

สัญชาต   sun²-chart³ *P. adj.* self-sufficient; self-produced; self-generated; spontaneous; not having material causation outside of itself (Chd. p. 471): สัญชาตสระ an implied vowel.

สัญชาติ   sun²-chart³ *P. n.* place of birth; origin (Chd. p. 451); nationality; source: สัญ-ชาติญาณแห่งมนุษย์ human instinct: สัญชาติ-ญาณแห่งสัตว์ animal instinct: สัญชาติญาณ instinct.

สัญฌา   sun²-chah *P. n.* evening (Chd. p 452).

สัญญา   sun²-yah *P. S. v.* to promise, pledge or make an agreement: *n.* a promise; a covenant; a vow; an agreement; a pledge; a contract; an assurance; an engagement; perception (the sixth sense): ข้อสัญญา clauses of a contract: คำสัญญา a promise: สนธิ-สัญญา a treaty; see สนธิ: สัญญากลายหรือ-

สัญญาเทียบ a quasi-contract: สัญญาเช่า a contract of hire: สัญญาเช่าเรือ a charter contract for a boat: สัญญาซึ่งเกี่ยวด้วยการ-กระทำอนาจาร an immoral contract: สัญญา-ซึ่งขัดด้วยรัฐประศาสโนบาย a contract contrary to public policy: สัญญาซึ่งตัดการค้าขาย a contract in restraint of trade: สัญญาซึ่งบังคับ-ไม่ได้ an unenforceable contract: สัญญา-ซึ่งไม่มีสิ่นจ้างอะไรเลย a contract without consideration; a nude contract; a void pact: สัญญาด้วยวาจา a verbal contract: สัญญาโดย-กรมธรรม์ a contract under legal seal: สัญญา-โดยปริยาย an agreement made by recapitulation: สัญญาโดยสุจริตและมีข้อความบริสุทธิ์ที่สุด contract "uberrimae fidei": สัญญาที่ดิน covenant running with the land: สัญญาทุกชนิด-อันไม่โดยหนังสือกรมธรรม์ parol contract: สัญญา-บัตร a certificate of conferred rank signed by the king: สัญญาเป็นหนังสือ a written contract: สัญญาโรธ the condition of complete loss of memory or consciousness: สัญญา-วางประจำ an optional contract: สัญญาวิปลาส, สัญญาวิบัลลาส unreliable; changeable; having uncertain memory: สัญญาวิโมกข์ the state of being without the power of memory or recollection; state of loss of memory: สัญญา-วิรัต lit. "one who needs no power of memory," i.e. an Arahat, or "a perfect saint" in that he has acquired a habit of not sinning: สัญญาให้รางวัลแก่แม่สื่อ a marriage brokerage contract: สัญญาเอาเปรียบ the securing of a bargain, or contract under undue influence or pressure: หนังสือสัญญา a compact, covenant, or contract: อนุสัญญา convention.

สัญญ์   sun² -yee P. adj. conscious; perceiving; thinking; imagining (chd. p. 458); recollecting; remembering. Pali grammar a common noun, e. g. town.

สัญโญค see สังโยค p. 844.

สัญโญชน์ see สังโยชน์ p. 844.

สัญฐิ   sut⁴ -ti⁴ P. adj. sixty (chd. p. 469).

สัญฐาน, สังสถาน   sun² -tarn² P. n. form;

figure; shape; station; condition (in life); characteristics (chd. p. 640): รูปสัณฐาน physical appearance; see รูป p. 717.

สัณฑ์ see สณฑ์ p. 807.

สัณห์   sun² P. adj. smooth; soft; gentle; mild; delicate; subtle; abstruse (chd. p. 450).

สัด   sut⁴ v. to copulate (used for animals): n. a measure of capacity (for paddy or rice) equal to 20 litres.

สัดจอง   sut⁴ -chjaung n. a pontoon; a floating house; a raft; a small boat, or one in tow.

สัต, สัท   sut⁴ S. n. an animal (chd. p. 470); truthfulness; frankness; integrity; probity; trustworthiness: adj. upright; honest; truthful; true; veracious; sincere; candid; frank; open; straightforward; reliable; see จริง p. 232: สัตกฤติ virtue; goodness; elegance in manners: สัตกุล a family that is praiseworthy, of good standing, or possessed of respectable lineage: สัตเกียรติ famous; illustrious; praiseworthy: สัตบดี a master that is good, honest and trustworthy: สัตบถ the right way; a way leading to good results: สัตบุรุษ, สัปปุริส, สัปปุรุษ a good, faithful, just, or pious man (chd. p. 462); a man of integrity and justice: สัตสงค์, สัตสังสรรค์ trade or commercial dealings with good, trustworthy people: สัตสหาย friends that are sincere, honest and trustworthy.

สัตต ๑   sut⁴ -dta⁴ P. n. a being; a creature; an animal; a sentient being; man (chd. p. 468): สัตตโลก the animal kingdom.

สัตต ๒   sut⁴ -dta⁴ P. adj. seven (chd. p. 467): สัตตคุณ sevenfold (chd. p. 467); seven tiers or layers: สัตตภัณฑ์, สัตตปริภัณฑ์ the seven chains, or circles of mountains surrounding Mount Meru; see บริภัณฑ์ p. 471: สัตตวาร a week; seven days: สัตตาห seven days: สัตตาหกาลิก see กาลิก p. 100.

สัตตมะ   sut⁴ -dta⁴ -ma⁶ P. adj. seventh (chd. p. 468).

สัตติ ๑　sut⁴-dti⁴　*P. n.* ability; power; adroitness; expertness (Chd. p. 469).

สัตติ ๒　sut⁴-dti⁴　*P. n.* a knife; a sword; a dagger; a spear (Chd. p. 469).

สัตตุ　sut⁴-dtoo⁴　*P. n.* an enemy (Chd. p. 470); a foe; one who plans injury or harm.

สัตถ ๑　sut⁴-ta⁴　*P. n.* a treatise or book; a science or art (Chd. p. 469); an institute of religion; law books in general.

สัตถ ๒　sut⁴-ta⁴　*P. n.* a weapon; a sword; a knife; a spear; iron; steel (Chd. p. 469).

สัตถา　sut⁴-tah²　*P. n.* a teacher; a master (Chd. p. 469); a learned man; a teacher of holy science.

สัตถิ　sut⁴-ti⁴　*P. n.* the thigh (Chd. p. 469); the leg.

สัตถุ　sut⁴-too⁴　*n.* a teacher; a master; a learned man (Chd. p. 469): สัตถุปาวจนะ, สัตถุ-ศาสนา *lit.* "a learned man's sayings," *i. e.* the Buddhist scriptures.

สัตย์　sut⁴　*S. n.* truth; fact; reality; verity; veracity; genuineness: *adj.* true; real; valid; actual; certain; absolute; veritable; virtuous (S. E. D. p. 1135); see ซื่อ p. 309; จริง p. 232: ความซื่อสัตย์ loyalty; fidelity: คำให้การตามความสัตย์จริง a bonafide statement or report: สัตยกรรม sincerity in action; truthfulness: สัตย์จริง *idiomatic* truthfully; genuinely; authentic: สัตยชิต a victory: สัตย์ชื่อต่อนาย loyalty, fidelity, or integrity towards one's master: สัตยธรรม the law of truth or integrity; a never-ending condition of veracity: สัตยพรต the condition of adhering faithfully to, or abiding by one's word or solemn promise: สัตยโลก the uppermost of the seven worlds or Brahma-loka, which is the abode of Brahma, and translation to which world exempts beings from further rebirth (H. C. D. p. 179): สัตยวัต true; possessing truth; exact; faithful; see ซื่อ p. 309: สัตยวากย์ veracity; true and reliable speech:

สัตยสถ one who discharges his promises or oaths; one who abides by the truth: สัตย-สากษี a true and trustworthy witness: สัตยา-ธิษฐาน a prayer, vow or promise (such as is made in the case of sickness or adversity).

สัตว์　sut⁴　*n.* sentient beings; beasts; animal creation; dumb creatures; domain of beings having life, growth, strength, and sensation; see ดิรัจฉาน p. 329: โพธิสัตว์ the chief, superior, or best of all animals; human beings: สัตวกษัย a condition of exhaustion; complete loss of strength: สัตวคุณ goodness; properties or characteristics of purity: สัตว์-จัตุบาท quadrupeds: สัตว์ที่ให้ลูกกินนม mammals: สัตว์เดียรัจฉาน irrational creatures: สัตว์โต elephants: สัตว์ทวิบาท bipeds: สัตว์-น้ำ aquatic animals: สัตว์นิกร a herd of animals: สัตว์บก land animals: สัตว์บ้าน, สัตว์เลี้ยง domesticated animals: สัตว์ป่า wild animals: สัตว์พาหนะ beasts of burden: สัตว์ร้าย ferocious, vicious animals: สัตวราศี fundamental principles; the essence underlying bravery, power, or strength: สัตวโลก *lit.* "the animal kingdom," *i. e.* creatures of the world in general: สัตววิต possessing breath; living; brave; strong: สัตววิทยา zoology: สัตวสาร fundamental principles underlying the greatest degree of intrepidity (as astuteness, foresight, sagacity, etc.).

สัท see สัต: สัทคติ a prosperous state or condition of existence; good fortune: สัทคุณ integrity (as a quality or characteristic): สัทธรรม doctrine of the good; good laws; principles of integrity and justice that direct a pious man: สัทพัสดุ, สัทภิต goods, chattels, or possessions that are genuinely good: สัท-ภาพ the state or condition of veracity; truthfulness: สัทเวลา the time, occasion or opportunity that is good, proper or auspicious.

สัทท์, สัททา　sut⁴　*P. n.* sound; noise; voice; a word (Chd. p. 410); *gram.* a declinable word, as a noun or pronoun: สัททโกวิท an expert in grammar: สัททหนัย the foundation principles of grammar governing a language:

สัททนีติ, สัททนีติ *lit.* "a treatise regarding words," *i. e.* name of a Pali text-book on grammar : สัททาวิเศษ, สัททวิเศษ a treatise regarding speech, or language formation (used in conjunction with the Pali grammar).

สัทธา sut[4]-tah *P. n.* faith (chd. p. 409); belief; trust; religious piety; fidelity or allegiance : ความสัทธา piety or devotion (to a cause) : สัทธาจริต an easy or willing believer; one with a disposition to believe readily : สัทธาจริยา one whose deportment signifies a believer : สัทธินทรีย์ the condition of having a trusting heart : สัทธาเลื่อมใส sincere piety.

สัธนะ sut[4]-ta[6]-na[6] *P. n.* a rich man; a millionaire (chd. p. 411).

สัน sun[2] *n.* a ridge; the back side of something that has a sharp edge; a range (as mountains); see แนว p. 465 : กระดูกสันหลัง the backbone : ล่ำสัน stout; strong; robust (in figure) : สันคันนา a ridge dividing rice fields : สันเขา peaks or ridges in a range of mountains : สันดอน the bar at the mouth of a river : สันดาบ the dull edge of a sword : สันทัด well-versed in; proficient : สันมีด the dull edge of a knife : สันหลัง the ridge of the spine.

สั่น sun[4] *v.* to vibrate; to tremble; to shiver; to shake; to undulate; to quiver : *n.* shake; quiver; flutter : กลัวจนตัวสั่น to shake from fear : สั่นกระดิ่ง to ring a bell : สั่นงก ๆ an involuntary or persistent tremor of senility, or as in *paralysis agitans* : สั่นโตกเตก to move to and fro (as a stick moved by waves, or by a current of water) : สั่นเท้า to shake the foot (to rid it of water, as after a bath) : สั่นระรัว to shiver from the cold : สั่นหวั่นไหว to shake or undulate violently (as during an earthquake) : สั่นหัว ,สั่นศีร์ษะ to shake the head.

สั้น sun[3] *adj.* short; abbreviated; shortened; brief; cut off; see ย่อ p. 666 : ตัดให้สั้น

to shorten by cutting; to curtail : สั้นเต็มที่, สั้นนัก entirely too short.

สันดาน sun[2]-darn *P. S. n.* in-born traits; disposition; characteristics; habit; condition of expanding, extending, spreading, prolonging, or multiplying (as race, family or offspring); one of the five trees growing in the celestial regions (chd. p. 459) : คนสันดานร้อนเย็น one with a changeable, or irritable disposition : ลมสันดาน a chronic ailment characterized by severe colic, disordered digestion and constipation : สันดานสืบ ๆ กันมา an inherited disposition, or family trait.

สันดาป sun[2]-darp[4] *P. S. n.* fire; burning; torment; distress; suffering; anguish; remorse; pain; a division of hell (chd. p. 459).

สันดุษฎ์, สันตุฏฐ, สันดุษฎ์, สันตุฏฐ์ sun[2]-doot[4] *S. adj.* delighted or contented with; completely satisfied (S. E. D. p. 1142).

สันโดษ, สันดุษฎ์, สันตุฏฐ์ sun[2]-dot[4] *S. n.* contentedness; satisfaction; contentment (as with what one has) (S. E. D. p. 1142).

สันต sun[2]-dta[4] *P. adj.* (1) good; genuine; true; wise : (2) quiet; calm; secluded; solitary; cool; pure : (3) weary; weak; exhausted; fatigued (chd. p. 461).

สันตะปาปา sun[2]-dta[4]-bpah-bpah *n.* one supreme in the Roman Catholic Church; the Pope.

สันตะวา (ผัก) sun[2]-dta[4]-wah *n. Ottelia alismoides (Hydrocharitaceae),* a plant growing submerged in fresh water, with its flowers on the surface. It is found throughout the Old World tropics and is very common in the **more** inhabited parts of the Malay Peninsula. It grows in fish-ponds in Java, and aids in keeping the water sweet. It is used as a flavouring with rice in the Pattani circle of lower Thailand. The petioles and leaves are likewise eaten in the Philippine Islands. The plant is medicinal in the Philippines, where the leaves are applied in the treatment of haemorrhoids (v.p. p. 262 : Burk. p. 1614); *Alisma plantago* water plantain, an edible water plant, resembling the cabbage, having dark brown leaves.

สันติ　　sun^2-dti^4 *P. n.* calmness; blissfulness; tranquillity; felicity; peacefulness; Nirvana (chd. p. 460):　　สันติภาพ the condition of calmness, peacefulness, concord, amity and harmony.

สันติก, สนเดก　　sun^2-dtik^4 *P. n.* vicinity (chd. p. 460); a place near by; the area around, or adjoining (a certain point).

สันตุฏฐ see **สันดุษฎ์** p. 848.

สันถต, สันถัต　　sun^2-ta^4-dta^4 *P. v.* to have been spread down, opened out, or unfolded (as a rug or carpet); see ปู p. 530.

สันถนะ　　sun^2-ta^4-na^6 *P. n.* conciliation; reconciliation; appeasement (chd. p. 460).

สันถระ　　sun^2-ta^4-ra^6 *P. n.* a bed; a couch; a sleeping mat (chd. p. 460).

สันถวะ　　sun^2-ta^4-wa^6 *P. n.* an acquaintance; intimacy; friendship (chd. p. 460).

สันถัต　　sun^2-tut^4 *P. n.* a Buddhist monk's sleeping-mat, or cloth for sitting on while receiving guests, or for kneeling on while reciting prayers; see กราบพระ (ผ้า) under กราบ p. 51.

สันถาร　　sun^2-tarn^2 *P. n.* the act of spreading down, opening out, or unfolding (a cloth so as to cover the floor during the time of meditation).

สันทน　　sun^2-ton *n.* a war-chariot (chd. p. 445); a waggon; a cart.

สันทะ　　sun^2-ta^6 *P. adj.* thick; coarse (in texture) (chd. p. 446); see ทึบ p. 417.

สันทัด　　sun^2-tut^6 *adj.* (1) skilled; proficient; adept; expert: (2) *as regarding size* intermediate; medium; middle-sized; middle-aged: สาวสันทัด a medium-sized, half-grown girl.

สันทัสสนะ　　sun^2-tut^6-sa^4-na^6 *P. n.* exhibition; display; explanation; demonstration (chd. p. 445).

สันทาน　　sun^2-tarn *P. n.* a cord; a string; a rope; a bond (of union) (chd. p. 445).

สันทิฏฐ　　sun^2-tit^6 *P. n.* a friend at-first-sight; a friend; a companion; an associate (chd. p. 446); see เพื่อน p. 599.

สันทิส see **สนทิศ** p. 811.

สันเทส see **สนเทศ** p. 811.

สันเทห see **สนเท่ห์** p. 811.

สันธาน　　sun^2-tarn *P. n.* a coalition; a joining; the state of being united; the act of uniting; connection; bond (of union); *gram.* a conjunction (S. E. D. p. 1144).

สันธาร　　sun^2-tarn *P. v.* to reserve, withhold, or retain; to hold back, or repress (so as to keep for one's own use or pleasure) (chd. p. 445).

สันนิฏฐาน see **สันนิษฐาน** p. 849.

สันนิบาต　　sun^2-ni^6-bart^4 *P. n.* a congress; an assemblage; a congregation; an association; an assembly; a league (chd. p. 459): สันนิบาตชาติ the League of Nations.

สันนิวาส　　sun^2-ni^6-wart^3 *P. n.* the act of living or associating with (chd. p. 459); cohabitation.

สันนิเวส　　sun^2-ni^6-wet^3 *P. n.* construction; preparation; station; encampment (chd. p. 459).

สันนิษฐาน, สันนิฏฐาน　　sun^2-nit^6-tarn^2 *n.* ascertainment; grasp of intellect; discernment of differences (chd. p. 459): สันนิษฐานระหว่าง to discriminate between; to weigh between the pros and cons: สันนิษฐานระหว่างดีและชั่ว to discern between good and evil.

สันพร้านางแอ (ต้น)　　sun^2-prah^5-nang-aa *n. Carallia lancefolia (Legnotidaceae)*, a tree with medicinal properties.

สันพร้ามอญ (ต้น)   sun²-prah⁵-maun   n. Justicia gendarussa (Acanthaceae), a small bushy shrub, three to four feet high. The plant has medicinal properties (MCM. p. 73).

สันพร้าหอม (ต้น)   sun²-prah⁵-horm²   n. Justicia ventricosa (Acanthaceae), a tree with medicinal properties.

สันรวง see สรวง p. 824.

สันสกฤต preferable, สังสกฤต   sun²-sa⁴-gkrit⁴ S. n. Sanskrit; the classical and sacred language of the Hindus; a language formed by perfect grammatical rules; many words in the Thai language are derived from the San-skrit thus making it a valuable source for enlargement: adj. well or completely formed; perfected (S. E. D. p. 1120).

สับ   sup⁴ v. to hack, chop, hash, slash, or mince (by repeated strokes of a knife); to slice; see ซอย p. 306: ขอสับช้าง an iron hook attached to a stout staff (used as a means of control for elephants): สับกัน to interchange; to become interchanged: สับ-นกปืน to pull the trigger of a gun: สับบุก-สับบัน under great privations; to the limit of one's strength (as when travelling through a jungle): สับปะทุน ignorant: สับสน mixed; confused; disarranged; disordered (as a crowd of people): สับเสร็จ, สำเร็จ, เสร็จ-สับ accomplished; completed; finished; ful-filled: สับเสียร to cut, or hack only on the head.

สับปะรด, สรรพรส   sup⁴-bpa⁴-rot⁶ n. the pineapple; see ขนุนทอง (ต้น) p. 140.

สับปลับ, สับปลิ้   sup⁴-bplup⁴ adj. deceitful; untrue; false; unreliable; deceptive (used only for speech): คนสับปลิ้สับปลับ idiomatic a liar: พูดสับปลับ to tell falsehoods, un-truths, or unreliable stories.

สัปด์, สัปต   sup⁴ adj. seven (chd. p. 467): สัปดสตก in groups, or sets of seven hundred: สัปดประกรณ์ see สตับปกรณ์ p. 807: สัปดาห์,

สัปดาหะ a week (chd. p. 467).

สัปดน   sup⁴-bpa⁴-don adj. vulgar; obscene; indecent; immodest (in speech or actions): คนสัปดน one who uses obscene language, or commits immodest actions: หมอสัปดน an unskillful doctor; a quack.

สัปตศก   sup⁴-bpa⁴-dta⁴-sok⁴ n. the seventh year of a decade.·

สัปทน   sup⁴-bpa⁴-ton n. a silk, embroidered, long-handled umbrella (borne as an insignia of rank).

สัปป   sup⁴-bpa⁴ P. n. a snake (chd. p. 462); a serpent.

สัปปิ   sup⁴-bpi⁴ P. n. clarified butter; ghee (chd. p. 462).   [p. 846.

สัปปุริส, สัปปุรุษ see สัตบุรุษ under สัต

สัประคับ   sup⁴-bpra⁴-kup⁶ n. an howdah.

สัประยุทธ์   sup⁴-bpra⁴-yoot⁶ v. to fight; to engage in war or combat.

สัปหงก   sup⁴-bpa⁴-ngok⁴ adj. sleepy; in-clined to fall asleep; nodding (due to sleepi-ness); see ง่วง p. 221.

สัปเหร่อ   sup⁴-bpa⁴-rur⁴ n. an undertaker; a class of men living near Buddhist temples, who can be hired to perform the necessary duties for a corpse, either for entombment or cremation.

สัพพ์ see สรรพ p. 823.

สัพพัญญ see สรรเพ็ชญ์ p. 823.

สัพยอก   sup⁴-pa⁶-yauk³ v. to speak jest-ingly; to joke; to fool; to mimic; to make fun, or sport of: สัพยอกเข้าเล่น, สัพยอกหยอก-หยอน idiomatic to caress sportingly; to joke or jest with in a playful manner.

สัมปชัญญ   sum²-bpa⁴-chun-ya⁶ P. n. con-sciousness; intelligence; discrimination (chd. p. 437).

สัมปทา   sum[2]-bpa[4]-tah   *P. n.* prosperity; happiness; blessings; successful attainment; success in obtaining; attainments; possessions (chd. p. 437).

สัมปทาน   sum[2]-bpa[4]-tarn   *P. n.* gifts; donations; the act of giving; *gram.* the dative case (chd. p. 437).

สัมปยุตต์   sum[2]-bpa[4]-yoot[6]   *P. adj.* connected with, dependent on, or resulting from (chd. p. 439).

สัมปโยค   sum[2]-bpa[4]-yoke[6]   *P. n.* union; agreement (chd. p. 439); see ร่วม p. 690.

สัมประหาร   sum[2]-bpra[4]-harn[2]   *S. n.* the condition of mutual striking, wounding, or killing; war; strife; battle (S. E. D. p. 1177).

สัมบื้นน์   sum[2]-bpun   *P. n.* completeness; success; fullness; a state of abounding in; plenty; abundance (chd. p. 439).

สัมปุณณ์ see สมบูรณ์ p. 816.

สัมผัปปลาป   sum[2]-pup[4]-bpa[4]-larp[3]   *P. n.* frivolous, foolish, nonsensical speech or language (chd. p. 439); see เพ้อเจ้อ under เพ้อ p. 598.

สัมผัสส์, สัมผัส   sum[2]-pat[4]   *P. n.* the sense of touch, feeling, or contact (chd. p. 439): ความสัมผัสส์ general sensation: จักษุสัมผัสส์ sense of sight: สัมผัสส์นอก the rhyming of words in different verses (of poetry), or in separate paragraphs of prose: สัมผัสส์ใน the rhyming words in the same stanza of poetry, or in the same paragraph of prose: ล้มผัสส์อ่อน tender to the touch or feel.

สัมผุส, สมผุส   sum[2]-poot[4]   *P. n.* to come into contact with; to touch (chd. p. 439).

สัมพล, สมพล   sum[2]-pon   *P. n.* food or provisions for a journey (chd. p. 431).

สัมพัจฉร see สมพัตสร p. 816: สัมพัจฉรฉินท์ an annual ceremony of firing the guns, at the time of the Thai lunar New Year; see ตรุษ p. 345.

สัมพัทธ์   sum[2]-pat[6]   *P. adj.* tied; bound; attached; adherent to (chd. p. 431).

สัมพันธ์   sum[2]-pan   *P. v.* to bind; to join; to combine or couple together: *n.* connection; link; association; relationship; kinship (chd. p. 431); *gram.* a conjunction.

สัมพันธน์   sum[2]-pan   *P. n.* the act of binding (chd. p. 431) or linking together.

สัมพาธ   sum[2]-part[3]   *P. n.* the condition of crowding, thronging, squeezing, or pressing (as in a crowd); obstruction; difficulty; impediment (as in one's way) (chd. p. 430).

สัมพาหน์   sum[2]-pah   *P. n.* the act of rubbing the body; a shampoo; a massage (chd. p. 431).

สัมพาหะ   sum[2]-pah-ha[4]   *P. v.* to massage, rub, or shampoo (chd. p. 431).

สัมพุทธ   sum[2]-poot[6]   *P. n.* one who is thoroughly enlightened and has known, or discovered the Truth; a Buddha (chd. p. 431); The Enlightened One.

สัมโพธิ see สมโพธิ p. 817.

สัมภวะ see สมภพ p. 817.

สัมภัตตะ   sum[2]-put[6]-dta[4]   *P. n.* a friend; a loved one; a lover; one devoted, or faithfully attached to another (chd. p. 431).

สัมภาร, สมภาร (p. 817) sum[2]-pah-ra[6]   *P. S. n.* (1) the abbot, or chief monk of a Buddhist monastery: (2) preparation; accumulation; materials; constituent parts (chd. p. 431): (3) equipment; provision; a collection of things required for any purpose (S. E. D. p. 1179).

สัมภาษ   sum[2]-part[3]   *S. n.* a conversation (chd. p. 431); a dialogue; a discourse; a greeting; a salutation; a welcome; an agreement; a watchword (S. E. D. p. 1178).

สัมเภทะ   sum[2]-pay-ta[6]   *P. S. n.* the confluence of two rivers; the junction of a river with the sea; union; junction; mixture (S.E.D. p. 1178).

ส้มมา sum²-mah *P. adj.* thoroughly; accurately; rightly; properly; really; truly; fully (chd. p. 433); *used as a prefix as in the following words*: ส้มมาวายาโม true, right, or proper methods of life pursuits; right exertion (chd. p. 434); renouncing unjust methods in one's dealings: ส้มมากัมมันโต right occupations (chd. p. 433): ส้มมาทิฏฐิ right views or opinions; accurate understanding of the true doctrine; orthodoxy (chd. p. 433): ส้มมาวาจา right speech (chd. p. 434): ส้มมาสติ rightly or intently directed activities of the mind; attention; reflection; attentiveness (chd. p. 466): ส้มมาสมาธิ right abstraction of the mind (chd. p. 433): ส้มมาสังกัปโป right thought or wish (chd. p. 434): ส้มมา-ส้มพุทโธ one who is thoroughly enlightened; one who knows, or has discovered the Truth; a Buddha (chd. p. 431): ส้มมาส้มโพธิ perfect knowledge or enlightenment; perception of the Truth; attainment of Buddhaship (chd. p. 431): ส้มมาอาชีวะ, ส้มมาอาชีโว right methods of securing a livelihood (chd. p. 433).

ส้มฤทธิ์ sum²-rit⁶ *n.* desires; purposes; accomplishment; fulfillment: *Thai* an alloy: ทองส้มฤทธิ์ the product of mixing one of the baser metals with gold: ส้มฤทธิศก *lit.* "the completing year," *i. e.* the tenth year of a decade; see ศก ๒ p. 785.

ส้ลลาป sun²-larp³ *P. n.* conversation (chd. p. 422).

ส้ลเลข sun²-lek³ *P. n.* the act of blotting out, scratching out, or erasing. This word appears to be only used in a religious sense, with the meaning of eradication of sin (chd. p. 422).

ส้สดี, สุรัสวดี sut⁴-sa⁴-dee *n.* an official registrar; the one in charge of the roll-book, records and statistics of soldiers; an army or navy conscription registrar.

ส้สส sut⁴-sa⁴ *P. n.* corn in the field; a crop (chd. p. 465); corn; grain; see ข้าวกล้า under ข้าว p. 155.

ส้สสต sut⁴-sa⁴-dta⁴ *P. adj.* sure; permanent; stable; perpetual; eternal (chd. p. 465); incessant; ceaseless: ส้สสตทิฏฐิ the heretical doctrine that spirit and matter are eternal (chd. p. 465).

ส้สสุ, ส้สสู sut⁴-soo⁴ *P. n.* a mother-in-law; the mother of one's husband (chd. p. 465).

สา ๑ sah² *P. n.* a dog (chd. p. 406).

สา ๒ (สม) sah² *adj.* suitable; proper; fit for; befitting; adequate; becoming: ส่วย-สาอากร *idiomatic* taxes in general: สาแก่ใจ, สมแก่ใจ befitting one's feelings (as when angry, harsh words are said, or blows given which in substance say, "It serves you right," or "You get what you deserve").

ส่า sah⁴ *n.* yeast; ferment; the earliest manifestation of development or germination of fruit; *medical* a blister; a bleb; a lesion of the skin due to fever and marked by redness, prominence and burning pain: ส่าขนุน the inflorescence, or flower-cluster of the jack-fruit: ส่าไข้ the initial eruption of fever; fever-blisters: ส่าผี่ดาษ the initial eruption of small-pox: ส่าเห็ด the fungus from which mushrooms grow: ส่าเหล้า the yeast used in the fermentation of arrack.

สาก ๑ sark⁴ *n.* a pestle (of wood, stone or metal): *adj.* coarse; rough; bristly; jagged: สากกะเบือ, สากข้าวเบือ a pestle for pulverizing the uncooked rice which northern mountain tribes eat with curry; see ข้าวเบือ p. 156: สากกระเดื่อง a pestle attached to one end of a pole which is pivoted in the middle. A man or woman stepping on or off the opposite end makes the counter-weight. This is used for hulling paddy or polishing rice: สากกระเบื้อง-ถ้วย a burnt clay, or porcelain pestle: หัวสาก the gland of the membrum virile.

สาก ๒ (ผัก) sah²-gka⁴ *P. n.* vegetables; potherbs (chd. p. 421).

สากรรจ์ see ฉกรรจ์ p. 264.

สากล see สกล p. 805.

สากลย์, สากัลย์   sah²-gkon S. n. totality
(chd. p. 416); universality; completeness; entirety (S. E. D. p. 1197).

สากัจฉา   sah²-gkut⁴-chah² P. n. conversation (chd. p. 415); discussion; conference; con-
sultation; see ปรึกษา p. 510.

สากิยะ   sah²-gki⁴-ya⁶ P. n. the name of
the princely family or clan to which Gotama
Buddha belonged (chd. p. 417). The grandfather of the Lord Buddha was King Singhanu
of the ·noble race of Sakyas who ruled the
kingdom of Kapila. He had three sons (Ala.
p. 78). An interesting incident of the history
of the Sakya race is that its founder princes
who had been defrauded of their own birth-
rights, established a sovereignty for themselves in forests they found uninhabited; in the
absence of any other princesses of sufficiently
illustrious decent to be fit mates for them,
they took their sisters as their wives or
queens and were thence called " Sakya," or
" self·potential " (Ala. p. 173): สากิยา, สากิยานี
feminine forms of สากิยะ: สากิยบุตร lit.
" sons of Sakya," i. e. the disciples of the
Buddha: สากิยมุนี the Sakya sage or philosopher is given as an epithet of Gotama
Buddha (chd. p. 417).

สาเก (ต้น)   sah²-gkay n. Artocarpus communis (Urticaceae), the bread-fruit tree, an
important food tree of the Pacific: both flesh
and seeds are eaten. The timber is yellow,
and is said to resist white ants but is not
hard (MCM. p. 253: V. P. p. 255: BURK. p. 250).

สาเกต   sah²-gket⁴ P. n. an ancient city in
India, Ayodhya (chd. p. 416).

สาขา   sah²-kah² P. n. a branch (chd. p. 416);
a twig; a subdivision; a projecting part; see
กิ่ง p. 106.

สาคร ๑, สาคเรศ   sah²-kaun P. n. an ocean
(chd. p. 412); a sea; a lake; a river.

สาคร ๒   sah²-kaun n. a large basin having
two rings which serve as handles: ขันสาคร
a large basin raised on a pedestal (such as
are sometimes used for serving rice to Buddhist monks).

สาคละ, สาคลา   sah²-ka⁶-la⁶ P. n. name
of the capital of King Milinda's realm (chd.
p. 412); the capital of Videha or north Bihar,
which corresponds to the modern Tirhut and
Puraniya between the Gandaki and Kosi
rivers. It was the country of King Janaka
and the name of his capital was Janaka-pura
(H. C. D. p. 209).

สาคู (ต้น)   sah²-koo n. Metroxylon sagus
(Palmae), the sago palm with large pinnate
leaves and a creeping or erect stem, 12 to 15
feet high, usually occupying fresh water
swamps. The underground parts throw up
stems in succession, each stem in turn flowering, fruiting, and dying after a life of about
fifteen years. The sago of commerce is obtained from the mature stems. The yield of
sago from a palm-trunk ranges from 250 to
660 lbs., and it is said to reach 1200 lbs.
on rare occasions. Sago (สาคู) is also made
in great quantity from cassava (มันสำปะหรัง)
starch in southern Thailand. Sago is one of
the first substitutes for rice (MCM. p. 365: Burk.
p. 1460): สาคูกวน sago boiled in syrup and
commonly hawked along the streets as a
sweetmeat: สาคูเปียก boiled sago: สาคู-
วิลาด lit. " the English sago," i. e. the small-
grained sago: สาคูลาน the large-grained
sago made from the marrow of the sago palm,
which can be ground into a powder.

สาง (ผี)   sarng² n. ghosts; spirits, genii or
demons; see สวาง p. 830.

สาง   sarng² v. to find out the meaning
of; to decode; to interpret; to decipher;
to disentangle; to unravel; to appear but
dimly, indistinctly, faintly or vaguely: สาง-
บัญชี to unravel, straighten out, or clear up

accounts: สางผม to disentangle, comb out or loosen (as hair): เสือสาง a panther: เหม็นสาง an offensive odour; an intolerable stench (as that of a pile of refuse): รุ่งสาง early dawn; near the break of day.

สาฏ, สาฏก sah²-dta⁴ P. n. cloth; an outer garment; a tunic; a cloak (chd. p. 465); a bathing cloth for the talapoins.

สาฏิก sah²-dti⁴-gka⁴ P. n. an upper robe, mantle or cloak (chd. p. 466).

สาไฐย sah²-tai² n. craft; treachery (chd. p. 466); cleverness; cunning; shrewdness; deception.

สาณ sarn² P. n. hempen cloth; coarse cloth (chd. p. 444); canvas; sackcloth.

สาณี sah²-nee P. n. a curtain, screen or tent (chd. p. 451); hempen cloth; see ฉาก p. 268.

สาด sart⁴ v. to douse; to splash; to dash; to hurl water (on, or at another): n. a mat; matting: ฝนสาด the rain splashes or dashes in: สาดน้ำกัน to splash water on another (as while bathing in the sea): เสื่อสาด idiomatic mats; matting of varying kinds.

สาต sart⁴ P. adj. joyful; jubilant; blithe; gleeful (chd. p. 467).

สาตรา sart⁴-dtrah n. arms; weapons of warfare; see ศัสตร p. 794.

สาทร sah²-taun P. S. adj. reverential; affectionate (chd. p. 409); attentive; pleasing; agreeable; see นบนอบ under นบ p. 440.

สาทิส sah²-tit⁶ P. adj. like; alike; similar (chd. p. 411).

สาทิสส sah²-tit⁶-sa⁴ P. n. resemblance; similarity (chd. p. 412).

สาธก sah²-tok⁶ P. S. n. accomplishment; completion; achievement (chd. p. 411): Thai an example used as an explanation: สาธก-สัมปชัญญ the knowledge of discrimination of what is useful and what is not, so that one

may perform only those things that are useful.

สาธารณ sah²-tah-ra⁶-na⁶ P. S. adj. common; general; public; mutual; neutral; common to all; universal; unrestricted (chd. p. 411): สาธารณชน the public; people in general: สาธารณประโยชน์ for the benefit of the public; for the common good or unrestricted use: สาธารณสถาน a public place: สาธารณสุข public health.

สาธิต sah²-tit⁶ S. adj. accomplished; brought about; perfected; demonstrated (S.E.D. p. 1201).

สาธุ sah²-too⁶ P. S. v. to consent, accede or acquiesce; to agree or harmonize; to comply with: n. approval; approbation; consent; acquiescence: adv. yes; be it so; even so; well and good: interj. hail; all hail; honour be to you (S. E. D. p. 1201): สาธุการ an exclamation of approval, praise, agreement or congratulation (chd. p. 411); a meter in music; a xylophone orchestra: สาธุคต well-behaved; respectable; pious; virtuous; pure (in conduct); excellent (in works): สาธุชน persons of good, honest, trustworthy, reliable character: สาธุบทวี the path or way of the good: สาธุผล bearing good fruit, having good results or consequences: สาธุพาหะ a good, or well trained horse: สาธุภาพ good nature; kindness; compassion; mercy; tenderness: สาธุโมทนา a response of approval (as "amen"), or agreement (to what has been said). This expression is much used at the conclusion of Buddhist religious services (chd. p. 411).

สาน ๑ sarn² P. n. a dog (chd. p. 459).

สาน ๒ sarn² v. to weave (as strips of bamboo); to plait (as mats or baskets): โดยสาน-เรอ to take passage in a boat or ship: ผู้-โดยสาน passengers.

ส่าน sarn⁴ n. cloth; a shawl; an ancient coarse cloth made from the bark of trees: ส่านสุรัศ an inexpensive cloth made in Surat.

สานตวะ   sarn²-dta⁴-wa⁶ *S. n.* the act of speaking in a friendly manner; the act of appeasing; soothing, agreeable words or speech (S. E. D. p. 1203).

สานุ   sah²-noó⁶ *P. S. n.* a tableland (chd. p. 461); a level space along the top or ridge of a mountain (S. E. D. p. 1202).

สานุศิษย์   sah²-noo⁶-sit⁴ *n.* a disciple; a pupil; a follower; a supporter; an adherent; scholars; students (of all grades or degrees).

สาบ   sarp⁴ *n.* a pungent, musty, disagreeable odour (resembling that of a garment saturated with perspiration and allowed to dry); the odour of goats: แมลงสาบ cockroaches: สาบเสื้อ an extra inside strip of cloth sewed along the edge of a garment, to which buttons are attached, or in which button-holes are made.

สาบแร้งสาบกา (ต้น)   sarp⁴-raang⁵-sarp⁴-gkah *n.* a species of plant resembling the tobacco plant, the leaves of which are fuzzy and of a strong disagreeable odour (as the name implies).

สาบาน   sah²-barn *v.* to take an oath; to declare solemnly: *n.* an oath; a solemn attestation in support of a declaration or promise; a conjuration: สบถสาบาน to affirm or promise with an oath: สาบานตัว to swear or make a solemn promise to speak the truth (as is done in the common courts before an image of the Buddha).

สาป   sarp⁴ *P. v.* to curse: *n.* a curse; an imprecation; abuse; an oath (chd. p. 462); see แช่ง p. 303:   แช่งสาป to call down a judgement or calamity on some one (as that he be born an inferior animal in a future state, such as a snake or monkey):   สาปสูญ to disappear or vanish entirely; to melt or dissolve away, never to appear again.

สาม ๑   sah²-ma⁶ *P. n.* the colour black (chd. p. 437); a dark, or dark blue colour.

สาม ๒   sah²-ma⁶ *P. S. n.* a song; a hymn of praise or worship; the act of singing or chanting in prayer or worship: สามเวท the name of one of the three principal Vedas, the Sama Veda, or Veda of chants which is wholly metrical. It contains 1549 verses which have been arranged for the purpose of being chanted at the sacrifices of offerings of the Soma. Many of the invocations are addressed to Soma, some to Agni, and some to Indra (H. C. D. p. 349: chd. p. 425).

สาม ๓   sarm² *adj.* three: สามขา a tripod; a stool with three legs; a metal ring with three feet (used as a support for pots or kettles while standing over a fire):   สามแช่ a sweetmeat made of edible birds'-nests, minced dried persimmons, and slices of white gourd boiled in syrup: สามตา a method of fortune-telling; see ขามสามตา under ขาม p. 673:   สามหาบ a ceremony observed by the relatives on the occasion of gathering up the relics after a cremation. This consists of six persons each bearing two trays of food suspended from the ends of a decorated bamboo stick carried on the shoulder. Three of these persons have trays of sweetmeats and rice, three have trays of meat prepared in various ways (as curry). Food thus carried in procession is to be presented to the Buddhist monks officiating at the ceremony: สามเหลี่ยม (รูป) *lit.* "a triangle," *i. e. Bungarus fasciatus,* the banded krait, a species of poisonous snake having a triangular-shaped body with alternating black and yellow rings or bands (smith N. H. J. S. S. I, 3, p. 177).

สามเณร   sah²-ma⁶-nen *P. n.* a Buddhist monk in deacon's orders; a novice; a neophyte (chd. p. 426); these, whether male or female, have vowed to observe the ten commandments (สิกขาบท).

สามเณรี   sah²-ma⁶-nay-ree *n.* a nun; a girl novice; the feminine form of สามเณร.

สามล   sah²-mon *P. adj.* brown; dark; dark

blue or black; of a darkish brown colour (chd. p. 425).

สามสิบ (ต้น)   sam²-sip⁴ n. Maranta arundinacea (Marantaceae), arrowroot, an herb of the West Indies found in use there in the early days of European voyages across the Atlantic, for the treatment of wounds caused by poisoned arrows. From this use has arisen the name 'arrowroot,' which has travelled about the world with improved races, used for food. These improved races, which have been selected during the last two centuries, originated in the West Indies, and the improvement was chiefly effected in Jamaica. Arrowroot tubers can be eaten cooked, either by boiling or roasting; they may also be used rasped and made into a coarse meal containing starch. The Annamites mask its flavour with sugar. The chief use of the tubers is to make a very digestible starch, which has been adopted for invalids since its introduction more than a century ago. The arrowroot starch industry is chiefly centred in the West Indies and Bermuda, but Brazil, Sierra Leone, Natal, and India have shared in it. In the West Indies, besides poulticing with the roots for poisoned and other wounds, the root is used in treating cases when poisons have been swallowed (burk. p. 1423); Asparagus racemosus (Liliaceae), a sprawler with large leaves. In Java the Chinese make a confection of the roots, and in India a similar conserve is used for impotence. In India the root has other uses—as a stimulant, restorative, demulcent, diuretic, anti-dysenteric, etc. (mcm. p. 300: v. p. p. 265: burk. p. 262).

สามหาว   sam²-how² n. words that are vulgar, rude, rough, immodest or insolent.

สามหาว (ต้น) หรือ ผักตบ see ตบ p. 340.

สามัคคี   sah²-muk⁶-kee P. n. concord (chd. p. 425); unity; harmony; unanimity; agreement.

สามัญ ๑   sah²-mun n. the state of being an ascetic or Buddhist monk (chd. p. 426); lit. "one who tames the senses or has quieted the evil in him," i. e. a Buddha (Ala. p. 203).

สามัญ ๒   sah²-mun P. adj. general; common; universal (chd. p. 427); public; ordinary; everyday; mediocre; low; unimportant: สามัญชน ordinary people: ชาติสามัญ a mediocre race of people.

สามัตถิยะ   sah²-mut⁶-ti⁴-ya⁶ P. n. strength; ability; competence (chd. p. 430).

สามารถ   sah²-mart³ adj. talented; skillful; competent; capable; see สมรรถ.

สามิก   sah²-mik⁶ P. n. lord; master; husband (chd. p. 433).

สามิตต์   sah²-mit⁶ n. ownership; proprietorship: รัฐฐสามิตต์ income; revenue; receipts or taxes accruing to the King or Government from Crown lands on the basis of ownership.

สามินี   sah²-mi⁶-nee P. n. a wife (chd. p. 432); a woman who is the owner of property.

สามิภักดิ์   sah²-mi⁶-puk⁶ n. faithfulness towards a husband or one's lord: adj. faithful; loyal; sincere; truthful; see ซื่อตรง under ซื่อ p. 309.

สามี   sah²-mee P. n. lord; master; owner; husband (chd. p. 432).

สามีจิ   sah²-mee-chji⁴ P. n. correctness; propriety; proper or respectful acts or duties (chd. p. 432): สามีจิกรรม dutifulness; respectfulness; obligation: สามีจิปฏิบัติ deportment, practices, conduct, behaviour or actions that are proper and seemly.

สาย   sai² n. lateness; a numerical classifier for strings, ropes, road, etc.; lineage; descendants; issue: adj. late; slow; tardy; delayed: ตะวันสาย lateness of the day: สายใจ lit. "heart strings," i. e. a term of endearment: สายบัว edible stems of lotus plants: สายบันทัด a string either chalked or inked for making a line (to saw by, or to hew to, as in carpentering): สายเบ็ด a fishing-line: สายนาฬิกา a watch-chain: สายน้ำ the current of a watercourse (of a river): สายพาน belting (for transmitting power in machinery): สายฟ้า streaked lightning; flashes of lightning; สายดู a hasp of Chinese origin for fastening doors, windows, boxes or gates. It consists of two iron links (one about 4 inches long), and a short chain. The butt end has a long, tipped staple or loop which passes through one leaf of the door and the ends, which are separated on the inside, securely fasten it. The other end has a loop through which the padlock passes and engages another staple similarly fastened: สายชนต์ strings attached to marionette figures (as to the arms or legs in order to make them move); strings or ropes to produce apparent auto-motion: สายระยาง, สายระโยง stay-ropes for masts or sails (of ships, boats, or poles for fireworks): สายโลหิต blood relationship; lineage; issue: สายสมร one much beloved; one bound by the ties of love or marriage; a fiancée; a term of endearment for a lovely girl: สายสมอ an anchor-chain, rope or cable: สายสมอเอก the main anchor-chain: สายสร้อย (ทองคำ) (gold) chains worn on the person (as on neck or wrist): สายสวาท lit. "an article of endearment," i. e. an attractive, dashing, lovable girl, belle or woman: สายสะดึง the thread or string holding the cloth to be embroidered to the frame: สายสะดือ the umbilical cord: สายสะอิ้ง gold waist-chains (as worn by young girls): สายสิญจน์, สายสิญจนสตร a protective thread of spun but untwisted cotton which monks or people pass around anything that they wish to preserve from evil influences (such as the scenes of their rites, a building, or even the whole city) (wales, state ceremonies p. 73): สายหยุด, สาวหยุด Thai, Bangkok (ต้น) Desmos chinensis (Annonaceae), a fragrant, flowering climber, the fragrance of which ceases late in the

morning. This liane is found in southern China and southwards throughout Malaysia; in the Peninsula it is general. The root is used medicinally as a decoction which is given for dysentery, or after child-birth, and for vertigo. The fragrant flowers can be made to yield a volatile oil, which is very like that from flowers of Artabotrys odoratissimus; and there is also oil in the fruits (cb. p. 37: Burk. p. 796: V. P. p. 267); see เครือเขาแกบ (ต้น) p. 211: สายใช่ a chain: เส้นสายแห่งร่างกาย idiomatic various ligaments, tendons, nerves and blood-vessels of the body.

ส่าย sai[4] v. to move from left to right and back again while in a perpendicular position (descriptive of the motion of a kite while flying); to swish back and forth (as while washing the foot, a cloth or clothes in water); to run in a zigzag, or a dashing-hither-and-thither manner; to strike the notes on a xylophone or carillon with a quick-running motion back and forth: n. a hoop skirt: ส่ายแขน, กรายแขน to move the arms in a back-and-forth, or in a pendulous motion (as while washing them in water): ส่ายเสีย a command to swish a cloth or the foot in water (in order to cleanse it): ส่ายหัว, ส่ายหน้า to turn the head to face one way and then another: ส่ายศึก, ส่ายเศิก lit. "to cleanse or rid (a place) of the condition of war," i. e. to quell, crush or suppress enemies, or a condition of war and conflict simile: ส่ายออก to wander away casually for pleasure or sport (as while shooting game).

ส้าย sai[3] v. to oppose; to resist; to expel or get rid of (as enemies); see กำจัด p. 102.

สายชู sai[2]-choo n. the "mother," a stringy mucilaginous substance that causes fermentation of palm sugar, producing vinegar: น้ำส้มสายชู vinegar made from arrack; see p. 456.

สายัณห์, สายาห์ sah[2]-yun P. n. evening (chd. p. 471); the close of a day.

สาร ๑, สำนาร sarn[2] *P. n.* a letter, dis-patch, message or document (as one carried on official or royal business); the crux, core, pith, substance, essence, marrow, cream or essential part of anything; the real meaning; a synopsis, summary, epitome or compendium (as of books, or dispatches); a class of medic-inal, though poisonous, salts (as arsenic): *adj.* powerful; strong; valuable; potent; genuine (chd. p. 464: s. e. d. p. 1208): สารกรมธรรม์ a receipt given on payment of money for a slave. This paper gives full particulars as to sex, age, height, complexion, etc.; a bond: สารตรา a state document, addressed to a Lord Lieutenant or Provincial Governor bearing the Royal Signature and stamped with the Major Seal: สารบบ, สารบับ, สระบบ, สระบับ an index; a roll; a register; a table of contents or reference: สารบรรณ a file or register of important documents: สารบัญ, สารบาญ index; table of contents or reference: สารบาญชี an official register; see สัสดี p. 852.

สาร ๒ sarn[2] *n.* an elephant; a tusker: ข้าวสาร milled or hulled rice: ช้างสาร a strong elephant.

สาร ๓ sah[2]-ra[6] *prefix* entire; complete; all; every; various: สารทุกข์ various troubles, afflictions or hardships: สารทิศ in all directions; at all points of the compass.

สารถี sah[2]-ra[6]-tee[2] *P. S. n.* a charioteer, coachman or driver; a trainer of horses; any leader or guide (s. e. d. p. 1208).

สารท sart[4] *P. n.* autumn; the two months succeeding the rains (chd. p. 463); the "Feast-ing (or half-year autumnal) Ceremony," taking place annually from the last day of the tenth lunar month until the second day of the eleventh month. This ceremony is celebrated by making special food-cakes to be presented to the monks as an act of merit-making (wales, state ceremonies p. 231).

สารพัตร, สารพัน sah[2]-ra[6]-put[6] *adj.* en-tire; in all places; everywhere; in every way; all complete; throughout; see ทั้ง p. 408.

สารพางค์ see สรรพางค์ p. 823.

สารภาพ sah[2]-ra[6]-parp[3] *v.* to confess; to vow; to admit; to grant; to concede.

สารภี sah[2]-ra[6]-pee, สุรภี *Thai* and *Laos* (ต้น) *n. Ochrocarpus siamensis (Guttiferae)*, a sweet-scented, flowering tree of Burma and Cochin-China, whence it extends southwards to the Langkawi Islands. It is not uncom-monly planted near temples in Thailand. The timber is excellent, but the growth of the tree is slow. It is dark red, hard, close, and even grained (cb. p. 119: v. p. p. 255: burk. p. 1569).

สารวัตร sah[2]-ra[6]-wat[6] *n.* an assistant in-spector, supervisor or headman; a monitor (as of a school or a class of students): *adv.* in all places; in every way; everywhere; throughout; see ทั่วไป under ทั่ว p. 410: สารวัตรทหาร a provost marshal.

สารส้ม sarn[2]-som[3] *n.* sulphate of alu-minium and potassium; alum.

สารหนู sarn[2]-noo[2] *n.* arsenic: สารปากหนู another form of arsenic.

สาระโกก sah[2]-ra[6]-gkok[4] *adj.* rude; inso-lent; impudent; saucy; provoking or inciting trouble and lawlessness: คนสาระโกก a buffoon; a rude, low, coarse jester; one who provokes trouble by insolent words.

สาระพา, สาระพาเฮโล sah[2]-ra[6]-pah *n.* a working song of labourers (similar to the chantey of sailors).

สาระเลว sah[2]-ra[6]-lay-oh *adj.* all that is low, mean, bad or evil.

สาระวอน sah[2]-ra[6]-waun *adj.* flattering, cajoling, fawning (words or acts); solicitous; anxious; uneasy, or concerned for.

สารัทธ์ sah[2]-rut[6] *P. adj.* angered; dis-contented; provoked; irritated; furious; vio-lent (chd. p. 463).

สาราณียะ sah²-rah-nee-ya⁶ *P. n.* friendly; affable; courteous; agreeable (as on terms of friendship) (chd. p. 463): สาราณียกร an usher; a host or hostess; an entertainer; a landlord: สาราณียธรรม ex-changes of friendly greetings; service to one another in action, in word, in consideration of one another's interests, in sparing part of rightful gain, in respecting fraternal equity, and in seeking conciliation with one another.

สารี sah²-ree *P. n.* one who goes on foot: *adj.* going homeless (chd. p. 464).

สารีบุตร sah²-ree-boot⁴ *n.* a famous apostle and contemporary of Gotama Buddha (chd. p. 464).

สารีริก sah²-ree-rik⁶ *P. adj.* corporal (chd. p. 464); bodily; physical: สารีริกธาตุ relics of the Buddha.

สารูป sah²-roop³ *P. adj.* fit; proper; suitable; in conformity with, or to (chd. p. 465).

สาโรช sah²-rote³ *n.* water-plants; lotus plants; lotus flowers.

สาละวน, สลวน sah²-la⁶-won *v.* to be confused, perplexed, embarrassed, bewildered, or engrossed with; see กังวล p. 83.

สาลา, ศาลา (p. 796) sah²-lah *P. n.* a building erected by the piety of Buddhists for the purpose of affording shelter and a place of rest to devotees, travellers and strangers. These buildings are to be found at the entrances of towns, in villages, and often in the neighbourhood of pagodas (chd. p. 421): สาลา-ลูกขุน a jury tribunal.

สาลิ, สาลี sah²-li⁶ *P. n.* rice, especially hill-paddy; wheat (chd. p. 421); primitive wheat.

สาลิกา (นก) sah²-li⁶-gkah *P. n.* the common mynah, *Acridotheres tristis* (Will. N. H. J. S. S. I, 3, p. 205: chd. p. 422).

สาลี่ sah²-lee³ *n.* (ต้น) the Chinese pear, sand pear, *Pyrus serotina* (*Rosaceae*); a two-wheeled timber cart (either drawn by hand or pushed) for transporting heavy burdens (as logs or timber); an electric trolley.

สาโลหิต sah²-loh-hit⁴ *P. n.* descendents in a direct line; blood relations; kinship by direct descent (chd. p. 422).

สาว ๑ sow² *v.* to haul, draw or pull in (as a rope or a kite string): *n.* a girl; a young woman; a virgin; a tree bearing flowers or fruit for the first time: เจ้าสาว the bride: น้องสาว a younger sister: พี่สาว an elder sister: ยังเป็นสาว still unmarried: ลูกสาว a daughter: สาวกะทืบหอ a species of mango: สาวก้าว, สาวเท้า to take quick steps; to walk quickly, briskly, in lively manner or expeditiously: สาวแก่ an old maid: สาวใช้ a maid-in-waiting; a slave girl: สาวน้อย an unmarriageable girl: สาวพรหมจารีย์ a virgin of about fifteen or eighteen years of age: สาวรุ่น girls of about fifteen years of age, just entering womanhood: สาวสนม concubines of the King; service maids in the royal palace: สาวสวรรค์ celestial nymphs: สาว-หยุด see สาธหยุด p. 857: สาวใหญ่ virgins of about twenty to thirty years of age: หลาน-สาว a niece.

สาว ๒ sah²-wa⁶ *P. adj.* of a dark brown or bay colour (chd. p. 470).

สาวก sah²-wok⁶ *P. n.* a hearer; a listener; a pupil; a disciple (chd. p. 470); one who has the power of listening to and pondering on, or believing in what has been said; see ศิษย์ p. 799.

สาวะนะ sah²-wa⁶-na⁶ *P. n.* name of a month (chd. p. 470); the ninth lunar month (corresponding to August).

สาวัตถี sah²-wat⁶-tee² *P. n.* a celebrated city in India, the capital of Kosala (chd. p. 470).

สาวิตร sah²-wit⁶ *S. n.* the sun: *adj.* relating or belonging to, derived or descending from the sun or solar dynasty (S.E.D. p. 1211).

สาวิตรี sah²-wi⁶-dtree *S. n.* a Vedic poem of praise and prayer to the Sun (S.E.D. p. 1211).

สาสนะ, สาสนา see ศาสนา p. 796.

สาหร่าย (ต้น) sah²-rai⁴ *n.* water-weeds; aquatic plants (as cress): สาหร่ายทะเล wrack; marine vegetation; sea-cress.

สาหรี่ sah²-ree² *Jav. v.* to be very lovable, pretty or good; see น่ารัก under น่า p. 449.

สาหัตถ, สาหัตถิก sah²-hut⁴-ta⁴ *P. n.* a cruel act committed or inflicted by one's own hand (chd. p. 414).

สาหัส sah²-hut⁴ *P. S. n.* violence; cruelty; ferocity: *adj.* violent; cruel; ferocious (chd. p. 413); oppressive; cruel; harsh; brutal; severe; hard; unrelenting; savage; pitiless (S.E.D. p. 1193): เจ็บสาหัส brutally wounded, or in excruciating pain: ใจสาหัส of a cruel, pitiless disposition: สาหัสสาโหด *idiomatic* in an inhuman, barbarous, or cruel manner.

สาเหตุ sah²-het⁴ *n.* animosity; provocation; a grudge; bad feeling, or a cause of quarrelling: ก่อสาเหตุ to originate, create or produce some cause for ill-feeling: ผูกสาเหตุ to foster, bear or cherish some grudge (as a cause for animosity): มีสาเหตุ there is some cause or provocation (as for a fight).

สาแหรก, แสรก sah²-raak⁴ *n.* a rattan or wire carrying-frame for the baskets of market-women or hawkers of sweetmeats or garden produce; these are carried suspended from the two ends of a shoulder carrying-pole; a species of the rose-apple tree; see ชมพู่ (ต้น) p. 278: บ้านแตกสาแหรกขาด *idiomatic* a discordant family brings ruin.

สำ sum² *v.* to mix or be mixed; see ซับซ้อน p. 307; ปน p. 494: สำส่อน disordered; confused; mixed; disarranged; piled up irregularly; not choosing or preferring one to another (as of race or colour).

ส่ำ sum⁴ *n.* group; class; company; see พวก p. 575; ชะนิด p. 285: ผู้สำสม persons who

save, scrimp, stint, pinch or lay by little by little (as of money): พวกสำสาม people who are "thrice" wicked, low or degraded: คนสำเสือก a curse, implying a low, degraded, mean, abject, gambling or good-for-nothing person.

สำคัญ sum²-kun *v.* to estimate, surmise, suspect or imagine: *n.* token; sign; mark; note; symbol; signal; omen: *adj.* important; chief; essential; necessary; weighty; remarkable: ทำสำคัญไว้ to place, or make a distinguishing mark or sign (as placing a flag or stick in advance of a proposed road, or in the line of a survey): ที่สำคัญแห่งร่างกาย the vital or essential parts or places of the body: ให้เป็นสำคัญ in witness thereof (as in signing a document): สำคัญนัก being most important: สำคัญว่า to surmise, conjecture or imagine.

สำแดง ๑, แสดง sum²-daang *v.* to show, display, reveal or make manifest; to expound: สำแดงกาย to show the bodily form to the gaze of the world: สำแดงความ to explain, expound, tell, or reveal a fact or truth to others: สำแดงความรัก to show one's love or affection: สำแดงธรรม, แสดงธรรม to expound, preach, or explain the principles, dogmas, or doctrines of a religion: สำแดงพระกาย to show a divine body (as when Jesus Christ appeared to the disciples after His resurrection): สำแดงฤทธิ์ to manifest one's power; to reveal miraculous power (as Jesus Christ did when raising the dead): สำแดงเหตุ to explain, or show the cause (as a demonstration to a class of students): สำแดงอำนาจ to make evident one's power or authority.

สำแดง ๒ sum²-daang *pron.* you (used by a Buddhist monk of high standing to one of a lower rank), as when the Buddha spoke to Ananda, viz. ดูก่อนสำแดงอานนท์ listen, thou, Ananda.

สำทับ sum²-tup⁶ *v.* to intimidate, or threaten by repeated accusations, charges, or recriminations; see ขู่ p. 162; ซ้ำ p. 308.

สำนวน   sum[2]-noo-an   *n.* an idiom; idiomatic expressions; the act, means or result of evading; subterfuge; prevarication; deceit; artifice; sophistry: เจ้าสำนวน one given to using deceitful or evasive language: พูด-เป็นสำนวน using idiomatic expressions: พูด-สำนวนดี eloquent; fluent (in speech):   สำนวน-ความ *legal* the file of a case.

สำนอง, สนอง   (p. 811) sum[2]-naung   *v.* to return a favour by some form of service; to recompense some favour by a gift or service; to serve; to assist, help or minister to another from a sense of gratitude (for past kindnesses).

สำนัก   sum[2]-nak[6]   *n.* a house, lodging-place, rest-house, residence, or place of abode: ราชสำนัก a palace, or palatial dwelling (as of the king or some prince).

สำนาน   sum[2]-narn   *n.* the voice; a sound; the sound of talking or singing.

สำนาร   see สาร ๑ p. 858.

สำนึก   sum[2]-neuk[6]   *v.* to contemplate, meditate, reflect, ruminate, or call to mind; to become conscious of one's past sins, faults, or omissions: รู้สำนึกตัว to acknowledge one's fault; to repent (as of past misdeeds):   สำนึก-ตัวขึ้นได้ to regain one's presence of mind or consciousness; see รู้สึก under รู้ p. 716·

สำเนา   sum[2]-now   *n.* a rough copy; the first draft or copy of a document; a history, narrative, or account for filing purposes: คัด-สำเนา to take extracts; to summarize the points in any document: สำเนาความ *legal* the abstract of a case; a digest, brief statement, or outline of a case (as might be used in an investigation):   สำเนาที่รับรอง a certified copy: สำเนาบอก the rough draft, synopsis, or original of any document.

สำเนียง, เสียง   sum[2]-nee-ang   *n.* the voice; the sound of words, language, speech: สำ-เนียงแปล่ง brogue: สำเนียงร้อง the sound of the voice in singing; the chirping of birds.

สำบอก   sum[2]-bauk[4]   *Jav. n.* rind; bark; peelings.

สำบั่น (เรือ)   sum[2]-bpan   *Chin. n.* a sanpan; a small river-boat propelled by paddles.

สำบั๊น   sum[2]-bpan[3]   *n.* a river taxi-boat; a small river-boat of Chinese origin, built with three bottom boards and two gunwale strips, propelled by an oar at the stern. Generally it is used as a marketing- or ferry-boat.

สำเภา   sum[2]-pow   *n.* a Chinese junk.

สำมะงา (ต้น)   sum[2]-ma[6]-ngah   *n.* a tree having medicinal properties; *Clerodendron inerme (Verbenaceae)*, an untidy sea-shore shrub, with somewhat soft, greenish-brown or black fruit, found from Bombay to the Pacific; in the Peninsula it is found round the coasts. The Malays apparently make no use of it, but to the eastward it seems to be held medicinal in the Celebes, in the Philippine Islands, and in Guam. It has been considered beneficial when the stomach is upset by eating poisonous fish, crabs, etc., and is also eaten with rice to increase the appetite. The fruits are said to be good for dysentery, and the root as a febrifuge and general alternative, and the leaves for poultices. Both leaves and roots are used for poulticing in the Dutch Indies (BURK. p. 585).

สำมะโนครัว   sum[2]-ma[6]-noh-kroo-ah   *n.* a census; an enumeration of the population: ทำสำมะโนครัว to take a census.

สำมะลอ (ขนุน)   sum[2]-ma[6]-law   *n.* the wild bread-fruit, *Artocarpus lakoocha (Urticaceae)*, a noble tree characterized by large leathery, crinkled or wavy, undivided leaves. It is found from the Himalayas to Ceylon, and to the Malay Peninsula, where it is common. The fruit is cone-like, similar in texture to the bread-fruit proper. The round, white seeds of the form of large peas are edible.

The timber is good; it is used for house-posts, beams, and for boats, but is considered inferior to that of some of the other species of the genus. It seasons well, and takes a good polish. It is marketed in India, and is useful for cabinet-making, brush-backs, turnery, inlaying, and fancy-work generally. A yellow dye can be obtained from the wood. Its bark is chewed in Assam, as a substitute for betel-nut. A fibre can be extracted from it, and is used for cordage in India (BURK. p. 257); *Artocarpus nobilis* (MCM. p. 254).

สำมะเลเทเมา sum[2]-ma[6]-lay-tay-mow *v.* to keep company, be friendly, or carouse with bad characters; to associate promiscuously with drunkards, opium-smokers, or gamblers.

สำรด, สมรด (p. 817) sum[2]-rote[6] *n.* a tinsel-embroidered velvet border or edging of a long, thin robe worn over other garments to signify rank; a broad, velvet, tinsel-embroidered belt or band worn with the long robe.

สำรวจ sum[2]-roo-at[4] *v.* to examine (for the purpose of enumeration); to make an inventory of goods; to go around on an inspection tour over various districts (so as to check upon existing conditions); to survey (as soils); to chant; to recite or intone (as prayers for the dead).

สำรวม sum[2]-roo-am *v.* to regulate, curb, repress or control (as one's feelings or desires): สำรวมใจ to compose or moderate the emotions or passions: สำรวมอินทรีย์ to curb or control one's senses (so as not to see, hear or taste things that would be improper, or lead the mind astray); see สังวร p. 844.

สำรวย sum[2]-ru-ie *adj.* pretty; elegant; extravagant; neat; trim; tasteful (as to clothes); foppish; dudish; dandified (as to manner).

สำรวล sum[2]-roo-an *v.* to laugh; to giggle; to be merry (used by royalty); see หรรษา.

สำรอก sum[2]-rauk[3] *v.* to vomit; to puke;

to spew out; to eructate: เด็กสำรอกน้ำนม the child vomits the milk: สำรอกสี to wash out the colour from a cloth or garment: สำรอกอาหาร to regurgitate into the mouth from the first stomach (of a ruminant): อาหารที่สำรอกขึ้น the cud.

สำรอง sum[2]-raung *v.* to keep in reserve; to be prepared for the unexpected; to serve as an auxiliary, or in a subsidiary capacity: *adj.* reserved for use instead of; provided for in anticipation of; kept as a second choice.

สำรับ sum[2]-rup[6] *n.* set, suite, or succession of things forming a series; a sequence; a tray containing curry and assorted condiments or sweetmeats to be eaten with the rice: สำรับหนึ่ง one such tray so prepared: เสื้อสำรับหนึ่ง one suit of clothes.

สำราก sum[2]-rak[3] *v.* to reprimand or scold in a threatening, menancing or rude manner; to threaten in a loud, bullying, or harsh manner: *adj.* nauseous; nauseating; disgusting: พูดสำรากชั่งหาพเราะมิได้ *idiomatic* harsh and inelegant language.

สำราญ, สราญ sum[2]-ran *v.* to have a sense of happiness, satisfaction, contentment, tranquillity or peacefulness; to be happy and perfectly at ease: ความสำราญ contentment: ความสุขสำราญ peacefulness; calmness; perfect repose: สำราญใจ a feeling of composure, serenity, and assurance.

สำเร็จ sum[2]-ret[4] *v.* to be accomplished, finished, or completed; to have attained (as to a state or condition of salvation or enlightenment): *adj.* done; executed; achieved; effected: ความสำเร็จ accomplishment; one having completed, finished, attained or terminated (as of a course of training or study): ผู้สำเร็จราชการ one with authority to execute governmental affairs (as the chief of a province or department).

สำเรา sum[2]-row *v.* to abate; to moderate; to be reduced; to subside (as symptoms in a condition of fever or inflammation); see ทุเลา p. 420.

สำเริง sum[2]-rurng v. to be joyful, merry, happy, hilarious, or with exuberant spirits (as in gaining a victory or winning a cup in a contest, as in a football game): สำเริง-หฤหรรษ์ *idiomatic* to manifest a heart full of joy; see รื่นเริง under รื่น p. 715.

สำโรง (ต้น) sum[2]-rong *Thai* and *Khmer n. Sterculia foetida* (Sterculiaceae), a tall tree bearing offensive-smelling flowers. It is found from Africa to Australia. It would make an excellent avenue tree were it not for this stench of the flowers; they smell of skatol. The timber is greyish white, and soft, but harder than that of most of the species of the genus. The seeds have a pleasant taste, and are eaten as nuts by the Malays, and in other countries. An oil extracted from the seed is called fruit-oil. There are various medicinal uses. An infusion of the leaves is said to be refreshing in a fever: it is suggested that it acts as an aperient. Pounded leaves are used in applications on broken limbs and dislocated joints. Hydrocyanic acid has been found in the roots, stems and leaves (cb. p. 166: v. p. p. 258: MCM. p. 218: BURK. p. 2078): มันสำโรง (ต้น) a species of edible yam similar to cassava or *Manihot utilissma* (MCM. p. 299).

สำลัก sum[2]-luk[6] v. to choke or be choked (as by food going down the windpipe); to be strangled or suffocated: ต้น ข้าวสำลักน้ำ the rice plants are smothered by the water: สำลักน้ำ to be stifled, choked or drowned by being submerged under water.

สำลาน sum[2]-lan *adj.* light red; rosy-tinted.

สำลี sum[2]-lee *n.* cotton; surgical cotton.

สำแลง sum[2]-laang *adj.* harmful; hurtful; causing indigestion or sickness.

สำหรับ sum[2]-rup[4] *prep.* for; in order that;

so as; in behalf of; in favour of; destined for: เกิดมาสำหรับกันและกัน *idiomatic* predestined for each other: สำหรับตัว for one's own use.

สำหาอะไร sum[2]-hah[2]-ah[4]-rai *idiomatic* "what's the difference"; "why talk about it at all, being such a trifle."

สำเหนียก sum[2]-nee-ak[4] v. to listen; to observe or give ear to attentively; to pay careful attention to; to endeavour to remember; to discern (between good and evil): ความสำเหนียก discernment.

สำออย sum[2]-aw-ie v. to implore, beseech or entreat in a fawning, flattering or solicitous manner; to supplicate in a ceaseless manner.

สำอาง sum[2]-arng *n.* toilet articles: *adj.* clean; neat; well-dressed; stylish; fashionable: แต่งตัวงามสำอาง elegantly dressed: พระสำอาง perfumery or toilet articles of royalty: รูปร่างสำอาง of a beautiful shape.

สำอ้าง, สมอ้าง sum[2]-arng[3] v. to claim under false pretences or misrepresentation: รับสำอ้าง to falsify ownership (for self-aggrandizement), *ex.* a person offers a reward for a lost article. Tom found it but Henry took it from him, and brought it to the owner, saying he found it; to volunteer one's services for gain or favour (as offering to become a witness).

สิ si[4] *adv.* certainly; *a sign of the imperative; a word of emphasis to strengthen a statement; a command used in combination with verbs but never used to equals, as* ไปสิ, ทำสิ, ลินะ.

สึกขา, สึกข์ sik[4]-kah[2] *P. n.* the act of learning, studying, or training (chd. p. 475); discernment of rules, doctrines, dogmas or tenets (of the Buddhist religion): ไตรสึกขา the three ordained steps of mental practice towards a higher morality, *viz*, (1) the observance of the five and eight commandments of abstinence (Ala. p. 174); (2) continuance in a state of meditation or contemplation in which the mind is shut up in itself and insensible to that which is passing around it (Ala. p. 219); (3) the gaining of wisdom (chd. p. 475): สิกขาบท a code of ethics, precepts or tenets in Buddhist training.

สิขร   si⁴-korn² *P. n.* a peak; a top; the summit of a mountain; a cock's comb (chd. p. 475).

สิขรี   si⁴-ka⁴-ree *P. n.* a tree; a mountain (chd. p. 475).

สิขา   si⁴-kah² *P. n.* a flame; a peak; a point; the crest; a topknot (chd. p. 474); a tuft, or lock of hair on the crown of the head . สิขานล fire.

สิขี   si⁴-kee² *P. n.* fire; a peacock; the name of a Buddha (chd. p. 475).

สิง   sing² *Cam. v.* to be possessed (as by spirits); to enter in and inhabit : เข้าสิงอยู่ to be entered by genii, or under their power : ความโทโษสิงเป็นเจ้าเรือน anger sits as owner of the place : มีผีสิงอยู่ to be bewitched by evil spirits; to be malevolent.

สิ่ง   sing⁴ *n.* things; articles; objects : *adj. a designatory particle* (as of things or goods); สิ่งของ goods and chattels; articles of various kinds; possessions : สิ่งของที่เก็บได้แต่ไม่มีเจ้าของ articles found and unclaimed : สิ่งของที่จำเป็นแก่ชีวิตร necessities of life : สิ่งของทุกอย่างซึ่งได้เป็นทรัพย์ยมรดก *legal* inheritable property : สิ่งของหรือทรัพย์ things; goods; property : สิ่งใดๆหรือการกระทำใดๆซึ่งเป็นที่รำคาญแก่เพื่อนบ้านหรือมหาชน a nuisance : สิ่งใดสิ่งหนึ่ง any one among many : สิ่งใดสิ่งหนึ่งซึ่งทำให้ผู้ใด ผู้หนึ่งสมควรจะประกอบอาชีพหรือรับราชการได้ *legal* qualifications for a livelihood, or for government service : สิ่งที่น่าใคร่ทุกอย่าง all the treasures to be desired : สิ่งไร, สิ่งใด what thing? สิ่งเหล่านี้ these things : สิ่งเหล่านั้น those things : สิ่งอันทำเทียบ a facsimile; a replica : หาสิ่งใดมาเปรียบ what is it to be compared with?

สิงคลิ้ง   sing²-kling⁵ *adj.* lovely; admirable; adorable; handsome.

สิงคลี   sing²-klee *Cam. v.* to go away from one's abode or habitation; to secrete oneself and remain : *adj.* confused; disordered; sneaking; secreting.

สิงคาร   sing²-kan *P. n.* love; sexual passion (chd. p. 477); see ศฤงคาร p. 790.

สิงคาล, สิคาล   sing²-kan *n.* a jackal, fox or wolf (chd. p. 474); see จิ้งจอก p. 249.

สิงห์, สีห์, สีหะ   sing² *n.* a lion (chd. p. 474); the fifth sign of the Zodiac, Leo : จมูกสิงห์ a large, snubbed nose : ตราราชสีห์, ตราสิงห์ "the seal of the lion," formerly used to stamp official documents of the Ministry of the Interior : สิงห์กิเลน a mythical lion-shaped monster : สิงห์โต (จีน) *lit.* "the Chinese lion," *i.e.* the brilliantly coloured mask intended to resemble a mythical monster, which is carried around in procession with drums and gongs during the Chinese New Year celebrations : สิงห์โตหิน Chinese stone images of the lion : สิงหนาท the roar of a lion; a war-cry or shout of exultation; the voice of the king (chd. p. 474) : สิงหบัญชร *lit.* "the window of one impersonating a lion," *i.e.* a window of the royal residence where the king appears to receive the homage of his subjects : สิงหราช a king-lion (sometimes used in poetry); see ราชสีห์ p. 708 : สิงหาสน์ *lit.* "the seat of one impersonating a lion," *i.e.* the royal throne; a throne ornamented with lions; the royal palace.

สิงหล, สิงหพ, สีหล, สีหพ   sing²-hon² *n.* the country of the Singhalese (chd. p. 474): สิงหลภาคย์ the island of Ceylon : สิงหลภาษา the language of the Singhalese.

สิงหลก   sing²-ha⁴-lok⁶ *S. adj.* relating to Ceylon; the inhabitants of Ceylon (S. E. D. p. 1213).

สิงหาคม   sing²-hah²-kom *P. n. lit.* "the

entrance of the sun into the constellation Leo," *i. e.* August, approximately the fifth lunar month.

สิญจน์ sin[2] *P. n.* the pouring on of lustral or holy water; the applying of an unguent (as a sign of blessing): สายสิญจน์ a thread or rope of spun but untwisted cotton passed with due religious ceremonies around anything that is to be protected or preserved from evil influences (as a house, or wall of a city).

สิต ๑ si[4]-dta[4] *P. adj.* bound; tied (chd. p. 479).

สิต ๒ si[4]-dta[4] *P. adj.* white; clean; clear; pure (chd. p. 479): สิตวงกุ์ *lit.* "one with silvery rays," *i. e.* the moon.

สิต ๓ si[4]-dta[4] *P. n.* a smile (chd. p. 479): *adj.* smiling.

สิทธ, สิทธา sit[4] *P. S. n.* a sect or group of inspired poets or sages (H. C. D. p. 268); one who has attained his object, been endowed with knowledge, or has become perfect (chd. p 474): *adj.* accomplished; completed; fulfilled; successful; perfected (S. E. D. p. 1215): สิทธการิยะ a task, duty, work or undertaking that is finished or accomplished; one who has accomplished a task: สิทธชน a person or people who have behaved well or succeeded (as in some effort); the blest: สิทธธาตุ quicksilver; mercury; a metallic element (that moves like magic); the perfected mineral: สิทธนร a magician; a conjurer; a fortuneteller; a sorcerer: สิทธโยค amulets; charms; talismans; magical agencies: สิทธวิทยา the doctrines of purification: สิทธาจารย์ one versed in miraculous power; see ขลัง p. 144; a rasi or hermit; see ฤษี p. 725: สิทธานต์ religious beliefs, opinions, dogmas, or tenets; proverbs (chd. p. 474): สิทธารถ one who has accomplished his wish or purpose; an epithet for the Buddha.

สิทธิ sit[4] *P. S. n.* accomplishment; success;

prosperity (chd. p. 474); affluence; happiness; liberty; freedom; proof; final results; *Thai* right (by possession); right to; valid authority; power; privilege; franchise; immunity: ขาดสิทธิ to lose the right of; to become invalid: โดยสิทธิขาด irrevocably; positively: ถือเป็น-กรรมสิทธิ *legal* to hold the rights of (as an owner or author): เป็นสิทธิแก่ตน *legal* to hold the valid authority in one's own hands: สิทธิเกิดขึ้นก่อน *legal* priority of claim: สิทธิ-ของคนใดคนหนึ่งที่ยึดถือความปกครองเนื้อที่ดิน มาเป็น-เวลานาน *legal* squatter's rights: สิทธิเดินทาง-ข้ามที่ดินของผู้อื่น *legal* right of way: สิทธิ-ถือเอาและหน่วงเรือหรือสินค้าในเรือจนกว่าลูกหนี้จะชำระ หนี้เสร็จแล้ว *legal* maritime lien: สิทธิถือเอา-แลหน่วงทรัพย์จนกว่าลูกหนี้จะชำระหนี้เสร็จ *legal* a lien on the property of a debtor till he pays his debt: สิทธิระหว่างสามีภรรยาซึ่งมีต่อกัน *legal* matrimonial rights: สิทธิไล่เบี้ย *legal* right of recourse: สิทธิเดินทางข้ามแม่น้ำ *legal* right of passage across a river: สิทธิโดยความเป็นเจ้า-ของที่ดิน *legal* rightful title or tenure: สิทธิ-โดยความเป็นเจ้าของที่ดินโดยได้รับราชการทหาร *legal* military tenure of land: สิทธิโดย จะเภาะของ-ผู้ แต่งหนังสือให้ พิมพ์และ ทำการ โฆษณาขายหนังสือนั้น, ลิ้ขสิทธิ์ copyright: สิทธิโดยฉะเภาะซึ่งสามารถ-ให้ผู้นั้นเที่ยวค้าขายสินค้าต่าง ๆ แต่ผู้เดียว monopoly: สิทธิถ่ายคืนที่ดินโดยชอบธรรม (หมายความที่ดินที่ได้จำ-นอง) equity of redemption: สิทธิการ successful; resulting favourably: สิทธิการิยะ a prayer craving the success of some remedy, project, scheme or prophesy. In old treatises of medicine where prescriptions are given, or in prognostications of the horoscope, this word is placed first as a request for a successful issue: สิทธิโชค a time or opportunity of propitiousness or auspiciousness (as for the beginning of some major undertaking or ceremony): สิทธิมนตร์ mantras; magical incantations, charms, or amulets that are efficient or powerful in warding off evil influences: สิทธิโยค the use of charms, magical incantations, or amulets.

สิน sin[2] *v,* to cut (true to a square); to sever:

n. money; property; riches: สินไม้ to cut a timber, board or plank squarely across: ทรัพย์สินเงินทอง possessions; valuables: หนี้สิน debts: สินบริคณ the marriage settlement: ตัดสิน to make a decision; to pass judgement: ตัดสินขาด to give a final judgement or decision: เป็นหนี้เป็นสินท่วมตัว to be completely swamped by debts; to be "head over heels" in debt: สินค้า goods; merchandise: สินค้าขาออก exports: สินค้าขาเข้า imports: สินค้าที่หลีก-เลี่ยงภาษี contraband goods: สินค้าที่ผู้ส่งเลี่ย-ค่าระวาง "free on board merchandise"; F.O.B.: สินค้าที่ลอยอยู่ในทะเล flotsam; goods lost by shipwreck and floating on the sea: สินค้า-ที่จมลงในทะเลเวลาเรือแตก jetsam; goods which are cast into the sea and are washed ashore (as in case of a shipwreck): สินจ้าง pay, or consideration for services; wages; salary: สินจ้างโดยใจบุญ *legal* meritorious consideration: สินจ้างไม่พอ *legal* failure of consideration: สินจ้างที่คิดได้เป็นราคาเงินสินเดิม goods or valuables serving as a consideration: สินเดิม property of husband or wife acquired before marriage: สินเดิมของภรรยา a wife's property before marriage: สินไถ่ a ransom; money paid for the liberation of a slave: สินน้ำใจ bonus; reward; gift; premium; benefit: สินบน bribe; the informer's reward: แก้สินบน to pay the amount of the bribe; *lit.* "to release the bribe," *i.e.* to pay off the vow or the informer: สินบนสินบาน *idiomatic* bribes and money paid for service rendered: สินมฤดก inheritance; heritage; estate; patri-mony: สินระบาด valuables or property scattered about in various places: สินสมรส *legal* property of the husband and wife acquired after marriage: สินส่วนตัว *legal* separate property of the husband or wife: สินสอด money paid for a girl at the time of her marriage (to re-emburse the parents for her upraising): สินไหม fines (imposed by the court) for the gain of the injured party; a penalty: สินใช้ *legal* a fee or fine paid under protest.

สิ้น sin[3] *v.* to terminate, end, be finished,

concluded, or closed; see จบ p. 230: *n.* a skirt worn by Laos, Anamese and Thai women: ด้วยสิ้นสุดใจ *lit.* "from the remote parts of the heart," *i.e.* with all the heart or mind: ถึงที่สิ้นสุดแล้ว having reached the final end: ทั้งสิ้น all; everything: สิ้นกิเลส being puri-fied of all evil, passion and desire (as cupidity, anger, arrogance, doubt, etc.) (Ala. p. 212): having attained the highest degree of saint-ship and, according to the doctrines of Bud-dhism, able to pass into Nirvana without further re-birth (Ala. p. 271): สิ้นความ the matter has come to, or reached its final condition or conclusion: สิ้นคิด losing all power of thinking, or sense of shame; being devoted to a life of immorality; being stupe-fied by the allurements of the world: สิ้นใจ, สิ้นชนม์, สิ้นชีพ, สิ้นชีวิตร *v.* to die: *n.* death: สิ้นตัว, ruined, having lost all (by riotous living): สิ้นแต้ม, สิ้นท่า coming to the end of one's wits; completely cornered; baffled; foiled; frustrated: สิ้นทุกข์ to be relieved of all trouble or responsibility: สิ้นทุน having exhausted all the capital: สิ้นเนื้อประดาตัว being filched of all one's money or valuables; ruined (financially); penniless: สิ้นบุญ hav-ing lost all of one's merit or fortune (implying a state of misfortune or catastrophy): สิ้นสุด to come to the end; to reach the limit.

สินธพ sin[2]-top[6] *P. n. lit.* "belonging to the Sindhu or Indus river," *i.e.* a breed of much-prized Sindhu horses; horses (in general); rock-salt (chd. p. 477).

สินธุ sin[2]-too[6] *P. S. n.* the sea; the ocean (chd. p. 477); a river; a stream; the name of an important river in Malwa, India. From Sindhu came the "Hind" of the Arabs, the "Hindoi" or "Indoi" of the Greeks and the present "India" (H. C. D. p. 293).

สินธุระ sin[2]-too[6]-ra[6] *P. S. n.* an elephant (chd. p. 477).

[p. 477.

สินเธาว์ sin[2]-tow *n.* rock-salt; potash (chd.

สินะ, สีหนา si⁴-na⁶ *a sign of the imperative; a polite expletive to strengthen a command.* It is used to equals and to those of
inferior social standing, as ไปสินะ; see เถอะ
p. 391.

สินิทธ si⁴-nit⁶ *P. adj.* oily; greasy; smooth;
glossy; affectionate; amiable (chd. p. 477).

สิเนรุ si⁴-nen *P. n.* a name of Mount
Meru in India (chd. p. 477): สิเนรุราช king
of mountains.

สิเนห si⁴-nay *P. n.* friendship; affection;
love; lust; desire (chd. p. 477); oil; gum (exuding from trees).

สิเนหก si⁴-nay-hok⁴ *P. n.* an intimate
friend (chd. p. 477).

สิบ sip⁴ *adj.* ten; the numeral one followed
by one cypher: นายสิบตรี lance-corporal:
นายสิบโท corporal: นายสิบเอก sergeant:
สิบเอ็ด eleven: สิบลดหนึ่ง one tenth (1/10):
สิบองค์ ten persons of rank (as kings, Buddhist
monks, or princes): สิบแปดมงกุฎ *lit* "eighteen crowns," *i. e.* the eighteen chief monkey
warriors of Rama (characters appearing in
the Ramayana).

สิปปะ see ศิลป p. 798.

สิปปี see ศิลปี p. 798.

สิพพนะ sip⁴-pa⁶-na⁶ *P. n.* the act or art
of sewing (chd. p. 474).

สิมพลี sim²-pa⁶-lee *P. n.* the silk-cotton
tree, *Bombax heptaphyllum (Bombacaceae)*
(chd. p. 477); see งิ้ว (ต้น) under งิ้ว p. 224.

สิร si⁴-ra⁶ *P. n.* the head; the top of a
tree; the acme; an elevation; the van of an
army (chd. p. 478): สิโรตม์ the head.

สิริ ๑ si⁴-ri⁴ *P. v.* to mix; to totalize; to
add all together; to sum up.

สิริ ๒, สีริ si⁴-ri⁴ *P. n.* fortune; prosperity;
beauty; a name for Lakshmi (the goddess of
Beauty and Abundance); majesty; royalty;

magnificence; glory (chd. p. 478); a royal bedroom; an honorific prefix to the names of
gods, kings, heroes, men and books held in
high esteem (H. C. D. p. 304).

สิลา si⁴-lah *P. n.* a stone; a rock (chd. p. 475):
สิลาแลง laterite; see แลง p. 766.

สิเลส si⁴-let³ *P. n.* an embrace; union;
cohabitation; copulation (chd. p. 476).

สิว ๑ siew² *n.* a pimple; a pustule; a
papule: สิวช้าง a large pimple: สิวเสี้ยน
a small pimple (so called because it resembles
a splinter in the skin).

สิว ๒ si⁴-wa⁶ *P. n.* bliss; the Hindu deity
Siva; prosperity; happiness; auspiciousness
(chd. p. 479): สิวาลัย the celestial abode of
Siva (implying Nirvana).

สิ่ว siew⁴ *n.* a chisel: สิ่วแกะ a sculptor's
chisel; an engraver's burin: สิ่วตอกหมัน
a chisel for driving in caulking (as in the
seams of boats or ships): สิ่วปากกลาง a
medium-sized chisel: สิ่วเล็บมือ a curved
or finger-nail-shaped chisel.

สิวิกา, สิวิกา, ศิวิกา (p. 798) si⁴-wi⁶-gkah *P.
n.* a litter; a palanquin (chd. p. 479): สิวิกา-
มาศ a decorated palanquin (for royalty).

สิสส์ see ศิษย์ p. 799.

สี see² *v.* to rub; to grind; to abrade; to
grate; see ครู่ p. 183: *n.* colour; hue; tinge;
paint; a grist-mill; friction: ขัดสี to polish
the paint: สีผึ้งสีปาก lip-wax: ขูดสี to
scrape off the paint: ดีดสีตีเป่า a general
term for playing on various wind and percussion musical instruments: ทาสี to paint:
ย้อมสี to dye: โรงสีข้าว a rice-mill: โรงสีไฟ
a steam rice-mill: สีกา a woman (a word
used by Buddhist monks for women in
general): สีกากี khaki colour: สีกุก a
district west of Ayuthia where three canals
join. This was the location of a fortified camp
of the Burmese during the seige of Ayuthia

which fell in 1767 : สีขัด to polish (as for silverware) : สีข้าว to mill or husk paddy : สีเข้ม, สีสด bright or vivid colouring : สีเขียว green : สีเขียวมรกต jade green : สีคราม indigo blue ; prussion blue : สีซอฝรั่ง to play on the violin : สีทาเหล็ก enamel paint (for coating iron) : สีเทา grey : สีน้ำตาล brown : สีเผือด a pale colour : สีฝัด a winnowing machine, consisting of revolving fans for removing chaff, bran and other impurities from the grain : สีฟ้า sky blue : สีไฟ to kindle fire by friction : สีม่วงอ่อน, สีม่วงแก่ light or dark purple : สีลม a windmill : สีลาย striped in colour : สีสรร colour and outline (as of the physical body) : สีสรรพรรณงาม *idiomatic* fair of skin, and beautiful in shape and appearance : สีสวรรค์ an aniline dye : สีสุก (ไผ่) a species of tough bamboo, well fitted for splitting up and weaving, or for making into baskets ; *Bambusa arundinacea* (*Gramineae*), a bamboo which grows to a height of 100 feet (Burk. p. 292).

สี่ see[4] *Chin. adj.* four : ที่สี่ fourth place : สี่ข้อ four verses or paragraphs : สี่คน four persons : สี่คืน four nights : สี่คืนเดินมา หลังคามุงกระเบื้อง *riddle, answer* a turtle : สี่-ประการ four points of an indictment ; four sections or arguments (as in a sermon) : สี่ไม้สี่มือ *colloquial* four strokes of a stick or rattan (as in flogging) : สี่สิบ forty.

สี่ see[3] *n.* a black, pasty substance made by burning coconut shells, used to rub on the teeth to give them a black luster (once considered beautiful).

สีข้าง see[2]-kang[3] *n.* the ribs ; the sides of the thorax ; an animal's flank.

สีกุน, หางกิ่วหม้อ, หางแข็ง (ปลา) see[2]-gkoon *n. Caranx forsteri* (*Carangidae*) (suvatti p. 114) : สีกบ, หางกิ่ว (ปลา) *Caranx affinis* (*Carangidae*) (suvatti p. 113) : สีทอง, หางเหลี่ยมทอง (ปลา) *Selar malam* (*Carangidae*) (suvatti p. 117).

สีฆ see[2]-ka[6] *P. adj.* quick ; swift ; nimble

(chd. p. 474).

สีจัก see[2]-chjak[4] *n.* the whorl-shaped hair in the middle of the forehead (as seen on oxen or monkeys).

สีชมพู (นก) see[2]-chom-poo *n.* scarlet backed flower-pecker, *Dicaeum cruentatun* (Gaird. J. S. S. IX, 1, p. 3) : สีชมพูดง (นก) the small minivet, *Pericrocotus peregrinus* (will. N. H. J. S. S. I, 2, p. 90) : สีชมพูทะเล (นก) the Burmese small minivet, *Pericrocotus perigrinus vividus* (Herb. N. H. J. S. S. VI, 1, p. 108) : สีชมพูสวน (นก) the scarlet-backed flower-pecker, *Dicaeum cruentatum* (will. N. H. J. S. S. II, 3, p. 211).

สีด (สูด) seet[4] *v.* to inhale by forced effort ; to take a long nasal inspiration (as in the application of a remedy for the nasal passages).

สีดอ see[2]-daw *n.* a bull elephant with short tusks.

สีดา see[2]-dah *n.* a furrow or track of a ploughshare (chd. p. 479). In the Veda, Sita is the furrow, or husbandry personified, and is worshipped as a deity presiding over agriculture and fruits (H. C. D. p. 294). She is the wife of Rama : ละมุดสีดา see ละมุด p. 733.

สีดอไก่ฟ้า (นก) see[2]-daw-gkai[4]-fah[5] *n.* Grant's silver pheasant, *Gennaeus lineatus sharpei* (Herb. N. H. J. S. S. VI, 4, p. 336).

สีต, สีตล see[2]-dta[4] *P. adj.* cold ; cool (chd. p. 479) : สีตลหฤทัย cold ; indifferent ; disinterested ; unexcitable (disposition).

สีพลาย (นก) see[2]-plai *n.* Hume's flower-pecker, *Piprisoma modestum* (will. N. H. J. S. S. II, 3, p. 213).

สีมันต์ see[2]-mun *P. S. n.* a boundary or limit of a field ; a mode of parting or combing the hair (chd. p. 477).

สีมันตินี see[2]-mun-dti[4]-nee *P. n.* a woman (chd. p. 477).

สีมา see[2]-mah *P. n.* a boundary ; a limit

(chd. p. 477); the frontier of a kingdom; a wall; a district: ขอบขัณฑ์สีมา *idiomatic* the circumferential boundaries of a kingdom.

ส̂ระ see[2]-ra[6] *P. S. n.* a plough (chd. p. 478).

ส̂วถา see ส̂วิกา

ส̂สะ ๑ see[2]-sa[4] *P. n.* lead (chd. p. 478); *L. plumbum.*

ส̂สะ ๒, ศี̂รษะ (p. 799) see[2]-sa[4] *n.* the head; the front; the skull; the top (chd. p. 478).

ส̂เสียด (ต้น) see[2]-see-at[4] *n.* cutch and the following trees from which cutch is extracted, (1) *Pentace burmanica* (*Tiliaceae*), a very large tree of rapid growth, with a valued timber which is exported to Europe and is used locally in Thailand. It is used in Burma for making boats, boxes, etc., where lightness is of value. In appearance it resembles mahogany and is sold as Burma mahogany (BURK. p. 1688); (2) *Acacia catechu* (*Leguminosae*), the cutch-tree, khair-tree, a moderate-sized deciduous tree found throughout the greater part of India, except in the most humid regions, through Burma, with the same exception, and into Thailand. It has three important varieties, *viz.* var. *catechu*, var. *catechuoides*, and var. *sundra*. The chief importance of *A. catechu* is that it gives the valued tanning substance, cutch. Cutch was familiar to those who wrote Sanskrit and it would seem that the Indian conquerors introduced it elsewhere. Certainly it was imported into China from the earliest years of its sea-borne trade with India. Cutch is manufactured by boiling the tannin out of the chopped-up heart-wood of the tree, and continuing heat until the extract is concentrated enough to solidify. Cutch resembles gambier. Pure cutch is used for chewing; the dyeing industry takes a large part of the less pure cutch. Cutch, which is imported into Europe, is used for dyeing dark leathers, as it contains a dye of well-proved perma-

nence; and in dyeing cottons and silks a considerable quantity is required; but it is not clearly distinguished in trade from other tanning-extracts which are substitutes, e. g. mangrove extracts and extracts of *Areca catechu*. The substances forwarded through Singapore westward under the name *cutch* are indeed largely mangrove extract, and only very little *Acacia cutch* reaches Singapore. The timber of *Acacia catechu* is red or reddish, very durable and peculiarly suitable for making the handles of tools, cart-wheels, and in general where boxwood or beechwood might be used (BURK. p. 16: Cb. pp. 182, 547): ส̂เสียดเทส *Thai, Korat*, สำลีปุ *Karen, Chiengmai* (ต้น) *Poupartia axillaris* (*Anacardiaceae*); *Catechu gambir* (Cb. p. 357).

ส̂ห์, ส̂หะ, ส̂งห์ see[2] *P. n.* a lion (chd. p. [474].

ส̂หล, ส̂หพ see ส̂งหล p. 864.

ส̂ก seuk[4] *v.* to produce attrition; a grinding down; see กร่อน p. 18; to leave the Buddhist monkhood: *n.* attrition; reflection; recollection; consciousness; power of self-knowledge; sense of feeling: รู̂ส̂ก to be conscious of; to perceive or to be aware of (as by touch); to be cognizant of: ส̂กหรอ to be worn down; to be badly perforated by vermin or barnacles (as a submerged post).

ส̂กขี̂ see ส̂กขา p. 863.

ส̂บ seup[4] *v.* to interrogate; to catechize; to pump; to make enquiry after or for; to pass on to another (as taint of a disease): เที̂ยวส̂บไป to go around enquiring of different people: นักส̂บ a detective: ผู̂ส̂บสายโลหิต a successor; one, or those following on consectively; blood relationship; a blood relation: ส̂บข่าว to make secret investigations for news: ส̂บคน to search for a person: ส̂บความ to go around enquiring for particulars regarding some incident or crime: ส̂บชาติ to continue, or propagate the race: ส̂บด̂ายต่อ to continue weaving by joining new threads to the broken ends of the weft : สืบด้ายหูก to continue weaving by joining new threads to the warp : สืบได้ความว่า to produce proof of : สืบถาม to question ; to elicit information : สืบเฉียง *legal* to rebutt, disprove, or refute (another's evidence) : สืบผล to fructify ; to use for replanting or resowing ; to continue bearing fruit (as a tree) : สืบพยาน *legal* to examine or cross-question a witness : สืบพยานอีกที to re-examine a witness : สืบมาได้ to have found out by enquiry : สืบมาแต่โบราณ to come into possession from antiquity ; handed down from the ancestors ; hereditary : สืบเรื่อง to continue an interrupted narrative : สืบสวน to enquire into ; to investigate (getting information from all sources) : สืบสันดาน to re-produce ; to replace or fill the place of : สืบสาย to continue the lineage, line, family, or race : สืบสาวราวเรื่อง to continue inquiries that will lead to the unravelling and solution of an incident or tragedy : สืบ ๆ ไป to continue regularly in succession : สืบเสาะ, สืบแสวงหา. สืบหา to seek, search, and enquire after or for ; to enquire for, while searching ; see ค้น p. 176 : สืบให้ลูก to pass on, or down to the children (as taints of disease).

สื่อ seu[4] *v.* to act as a procurer or procuress ; to act as a medium or go-between for libidinous gratification : คนสื่อสาร a carrier, or the sender of secret messages : แม่สื่อ a panderer ; a go-between ; a match-maker ; a pimp ; a medium ; a seducer : สื่อสาร to be guilty of espionage ; to carry messages secretly (as from one city, or army to another).

สุ soo[4] *a particle used only as an inseparable prefix implying* excellence ; facility ; excess (chd. p. 484) *e. g.* สุวัฒนา.

สุก ๑ sook[4] *v.* to be ripe (as fruit) ; to be well cooked (as meat or rice) : ดวดสุก to complete a game with dice : สุกงอม to be over-ripe ; to be decrepit : สุกจ่ำบ่ม to be picked green and allowed to ripen in a warm place : สุกดิบ (วัน) *lit.* "the day between

the cooked and uncooked food," *i. e.* the day preceding the day of a feast or celebration, on which food is prepared in advance : สุก ๆ ดิบ ๆ *idiomatic* par-boiled ; half-ripened : สุกใส shining ; bright ; vivid ; transparent ; flawless (as jewels) : สุกอร่าม to be of a glistening, bright yellow, or golden colour (as of a gilded spire, or well-matured fruit).

สุก ๒ (นก) sook[4] *P. n.* a parrot (chd. p. 488).

สุกก์ sook[4] *P. n.* Friday ; day of Venus : *adj.* white ; bright ; pure ; good (chd. p. 488).

สุกข์ sook[4] *P. adj.* dry ; dried up (chd. p. 488).

สุกร soo[4]-gkaun *n.* a hog ; a boar ; a pig (chd. p. 487) : *adj.* clever with the hands ; having beautiful hands : เนื้อสุกร pork.

สุกรรม soo[4]-gkum *v.* to do well ; to arrange everything in proper order ; *Thai* to wrap up a corpse properly and seal the same.

สุข, สนุข sook[4] *n.* bliss ; happiness ; delight ; pleasure ; ease (chd. p. 487) ; health ; prosperity ; *when occurring alone in a sentence this word has a double meaning both physical joy and mental happiness* : *adj.* pleased ; joyful ; satisfied ; prosperous : โสมนัสส์สุข physical or carnal joy and delight : ความสุข peace ; happiness ; joyfulness ; tranquillity ; felicity : บรมสุข the highest state of peace, health, and happiness : ไม่อยู่สุข never still ; restless ; disquieted : สุขกิริยา acts done for the sake of happiness and pleasure : สุขคันธ์ sweet-scented ; odorous ; fragrant ; ambrosial : สุขจิตต์ a condition of mental happiness ; joy : สุขพันธน์ engrossed in worldly ease, pleasures, and attractions : สุขพุทธิ knowledge ; understanding ; a condition of ready or prompt comprehension : สุขภาค fortune ; riches ; good luck : สุขภาพ a state of health, happiness, ease, luxury, and prosperity : สุขภูมิ the source or origin of a condition of ease, happiness, and luxury : สุขวิทยา the science of health ;

hygiene: สุขสังโยค a state of continual happiness, ease, and luxury: สุขสำราญ happiness and perfect felicity; goodwill towards all: อยู่เย็นเป็นสุข to enjoy the peacefulness of life.

สุขาภิบาล sook⁴-kah²-pi⁶-barn *n.* the work or duty of promoting the public health and welfare; Public Health Department.

สุขิน, สุขี soo⁴-kin² *P. n.* a healthy or happy person: *adj.* happy; blest; healthy (chd. p. 487): สุขีภิรมย์ *idiomatic* felicity and joy.

สุขุม, สุกษม soo⁴-koom² *P. adj.* mild; soft; tender; delicate; intricate; small; minute; exquisite (as handiwork); subtil; shrewd; artful; underhanded (chd. p. 488): ความคิด-สุขุม profound in thought: ยาสุขุม a mild remedy; an anodyne: สุขุมลับลึก secret, hidden, subtle and crafty (as actions of a professional criminal or sharper).

สุขุมาล soo⁴-koo⁴-man *P. adj.* youthful; tender; delicate; soft; graceful (chd. p. 487).

สุโขทัย, ศรีสัชนาลัย soo⁴-khoh²-tai *n.* Sukhodaya; Sukkhothai; *lit.* "to promote peace and happiness to the Thai." Sukhothai had long been the northern capital of Cambodia but about 1257 A. D. under the leadership of King Sri Intharthitya (ศรีอินทราทิตย์), the first king of Thailand, it successfully broke away from Cambodian suzerainty and became an independent state. The third king of the dynasty, Ram Khamheng (รามกำแหง) is rightly the outstanding figure of the Sukhothai dynasty for under him the kingdom extended its borders and he originated the Thai written language. The Sukhothai period was brought to an early close in about 1350 when the king was forced to become vassal of the king of the rising kingdom of Ayuthia. His descendants continued to reign as vassal kings for 70 years or more (wood, History of siam p. 51).

สุคติ soo⁴-ka⁶-dti⁴ *P. n.* a state of happiness; a condition of peacefulness; heaven; a path to rightness, goodness, perfectness or completeness: สุคติภูมิ the land of happiness; heaven (chd. p. 486).

สุคนธ์, สุคันธ์, สุวคนธ์, เสาวคนธ์, สุวคันธ์, เสาวคันธ์ soo⁴-kon *P. n.* fragrance; perfume; scent; odour; scented powder (chd. p. 486): ทรงพระสุคนธ์ to sprinkle on perfume (used for royalty): สรงพระสุคนธ์ธารา *idiomatic* to bathe or lave with scented water (used for royalty).

สุครีพ soo⁴-kreep³ *S. n. lit.* "handsome necked, *i. e.* Sugriva, a monkey king who was dethroned by his brother Bali, but after the latter had been killed, Sugriva was reinstated by Rama as King at Kish Kindhya. He, with his adviser Hanuman and their army of monkeys, were allies of Rama in his war against Ravana, in which war he was mortally wounded. He is described as being grateful, active in aiding his friends, and able to change his form at will (H. C. D. p. 306).

สุงก์ soong² *P. n.* tax; tribute; revenue (chd. p. 489); toll; duty; customs: สุงกฆาต the act of avoiding the payment of taxes, duty or customs; smuggling.

สุงสิง, สูสี see จุกจิก p. 253; จู้จี้ p. 255.

สุจริต soot⁴-chja⁴-rit⁴ *P. S. adj.* faithful; truthful; trustworthy; virtuous; conducting oneself well; good; upright (in dealings with others) (chd. p. 485).

สุจหนี่ soot⁴-chja⁴-nee⁴ *n.* a bed-spread; a [sheet.

สุจิ soo⁴-chji⁴ *P. adj.* bright; clear; pure; clean; white (chd. p. 485); free from fault or error.

สุ, จิ, ปุ, ลิ *abbreviations* สุ=สุต to listen; จิ=จิต to think; ปุ=ปุจฉา to ask; ลิ=ลิขิต to write down. These four principles are deemed of vital importance towards the gaining of knowledge.

สุชน soo⁴-chon *P. S. n.* a good man; a man of good character (chd. p. 486).

สุชัมบดี soo⁴-chum-bau-dee *P. n.* name of Sakka (สักกะ), husband of Sujada (สุชาดา) (chd. p. 486).

สุชาต soo⁴-chart³ *P. adj.* well-born; of good or noble birth; well-grown; fine (chd. p. 486).

สุชาติ soo⁴-chart³ *P. adj.* of a high-standing family; of good pedigree (chd. p. 486).

สุญญ์ soon² *P. adj.* empty; void; deprived of (chd. p. 489); see เปล่า p. 533.

สุญญตา soon²-ya⁶-dtah *P. n.* emptiness; void; vacuum; nudeness; falseness (chd. p. 489).

สุณ soon² *P. n.* a dog (chd. p. 489).

สุณหา, สุณิสา soon²-hah² *P. n.* a daughter-in-law (chd. p. 489).

สุด soot⁴ *v.* to come to an end; to be finished, concluded, closed or terminated: *n.* end; close; conclusion; finality: ครั้งสุดท้าย the last time: มาถึงที่สุด to have reached the end or conclusion; to be terminated: ไม่รู้สิ้น-ไม่รู้สุด infinite; eternal: สุดกำลัง with all one's strength: สุดความสามารถ to the maximum of one's ability or power: สุดคิด coming to one's wits end; reaching no conclusion; unable to think a way out (of difficulties): สุดแค้น to be aggrieved or exasperated to the limit of one's endurance; to be tormented to the fullest extent; see แค้น p. 213: สุดจิตต์, สุดใจ with the supreme power of mind and soul: สุด-แดน to the utmost limit of a boundary: สุด-ท้อง the youngest of a family: สุดทาง to the end of a way, passage, or journey: สุดท้าย the last, hindmost, or concluding fact or person: สุดที่จะหาได้ to the limit of one's endeavour to find: สุดปลาย end; extremity; conclusion; finality: สุดมือ to be at the limit of one's wisdom and experience; to be beyond one's reach: สุดยอด the tiptop of

a spire or tree: สุดแล้ว to be finished, concluded, or at an end (as defecation): สุด-แล้วแต่ in accordance with your indulgence: สุดแล้วแต่ควร according to the exigency or necessity of the case; just what is right and proper: สุดแล้วแต่จะงาม in whichever way will be most beautiful or becoming (as in decorations): สุดแล้วแต่จะโปรด praying for your indulgence, or kind consideration (for help): สุดแล้วแต่ใจ just as you feel inclined; just follow your own inclinations; be it as you wish: สุดแล้วแต่ท่าน just as you wish; just suit yourself, sir; in compliance with your desires or purposes: สุดสวาท love in the superlative degree: สุดสายตา as far as eye can see; almost out of sight: สิ้นสุด, ที่สิ้นสุด finale; end; finish; completion: สิ้นสุดกำลัง with all the strength, might, or power.

สุด *adj.* terminal; conclusive; ultimate; ending: ดีที่สุด best; second to none; supreme: ที่สุด *a suffix forming the superlative degree*; see นัก ๒ p. 447: มากที่สุด most; the utmost limit or extent in quantity: สูงที่สุด the highest; greatest.

สุดา, สุตา soo⁴-dah *P. S. n.* a daughter (of youthful age); women in general: สุดาจันทร์ a girl whose countenance is likened to the moon: สุดาโฉม a beautiful girl; a handsome woman: สุดาดวงสมร *poetical* the girl of my love.

สุต ๑ soot⁴ *P. n.* a son; a child; offspring (chd. p. 491).

สุต ๒ soot⁴ *P. adj.* heard; heeded; understood (chd. p. 491).

สุต ๓ soot⁴ *P. adj.* flowing; dripping; moving; running; rolling on (chd. p. 491).

สุตต ๑ soot⁴-dta⁴ *P. n.* a string; a thread; a portion of the Buddhist scriptures; a rule or aphorism (chd. p. 491); precepts in morals or sciences; the first of the three Pitaka of the Buddha's precepts; a verse expressed in brief and technical language; a favourite form among the Hindus of embodying and transmitting rules (H. C. D. p. 312); a clause, chapter, or division of the Sutras: สุตตการ a spinner of cotton thread: สุตตกุล a ball of string; a spool of thread: สุตตมัย *lit.* "being made of strings," *i. e.* a net.

สุตต ๒ soot[4]-dta[4] *P. adj.* sewn; stitched; strung together (chd. p. 492).

สุตต ๓ soot[4]-dta[4] *P. adj.* asleep (chd. p. 492).

สุติ ๑ soo[4]-dti[4] *P. n.* the act of oozing; the the act of flowing, dripping or gliding (as the flight of an arrow) (chd. p. 491).

สุติ ๒ soo[4]-dti[4] *P. n.* the ear; the act of hearing; sound; report; rumour; tradition; intelligence; news (chd. p. 491).

สุทท์ soot[4] *P. n.* the sudra caste; persons of the fourth or servile caste, said to have sprung from the feet of Brahma; one belonging to the lowest (Hindu) caste; one of low birth; see ศูทร p. 801.

สุทธ์ see บริสุทธ์ p. 471: สุทธปีติ joy and gladness of a clean, unsullied nature: สุทธพุทธิ a clear understanding; a perfect comprehension: สุทธาชีวะ the condition of earning a livelihood by true, clean or just methods: สุทธาโภชน์ food or provisions that are clean and pure; a meal that is prepared with utmost cleanliness.

สุทธิ soot[4]-ti[6] *P. n.* purity (chd. p. 486): ใบสุทธิ a testimonial of good character.

สุทโธทน์ soot[4]-tote[3] *P. n.* name of a king of Kapilavatthu, the father of Gotama Buddha (chd. p. 486: H. C. D. p. 150).

สุทรรศ soo[4]-tut[6] *S. adj.* handsome; good-looking; easily seen; conspicious; obvious (chd. p. 485).

สุทรรศน์, สุทัศน์ soo[4]-tut[6] *S. n.* the condition of being prominent and easily seen; an agreeable sight; name for the city of Indra:

adj. handsome; beautiful (S. E. D. p. 1224).

สุเทพ see เจ้าชู้ under เจ้า p. 258.

สุธรรม soo[4]-tum *n.* justice; duty; obligation; laws that are good.

สุธา soo[4]-tah *P. S. n.* ambrosia; nectar (chd. p. 486); the beverage of the gods; honey of flowers; milk; fruit juices; water (S. E. D. p. 1225): สุธาการ a mason; a plasterer: สุธางค์ *lit.* "nectar-bodied," *i. e.* an epithet for Indra: สุธาภุช *lit.* "those who partake of ambrosial food," *i. e.* gods; angels: สุธาโภชน์ ambrosial food (chd. p. 486): สุธารส ambrosial water; milk; nectar: พระสุธารส *a court term* tea.

สุธาสี, สุธาสินี soo[4]-tah-see[2] *P. n. lit.* "those who partake of ambrosial food," *i. e.* gods; devas; angels (chd. p. 486): สุธาสินี the feminine gender of สุธาสี.

สุธี soo[4]-tee *P. n.* a learned man; an intelligent person; understanding; wisdom; acumen (chd. 486).

สุนทร soon[2]-taun *P. adj.* beautiful; good; handsome; eloquent; well-spoken; harmonious; agreeable to the sense of hearing (chd. p. 489): สุนทรวาจา eloquent language (as in public speaking): สุนทรโวหาร pertaining to, or displaying oratory,

สุนัข soo[4]-nuk[6] *P. n.* a dog (chd. p. 489): สุนัขจิ้งจอก *Canis aureus*, jackal (Gaird. N. H. J. S. S. III, p. 122): สุนัขป่า, สุนัขใน *Cuon rutilons* or *Javanicus*, Malay wild dog (Gaird. N. H. J. S. S. III, p. 122).

สุนันทา soo[4]-nun-tah *P. n.* name of a lake in the Davadungsa heaven in which Indra dwells, being located in the second tier above the earth (Ala. p. 201); name of the mother of Maya (Ala. pp. 85, 181).

สุนีติ soo[4]-nee-dti[4] *S. n.* politeness; the condition of being courteous, well-bred, polite, having good manners (S. E. D. p. 1226).

สุโนก　　soo⁴-noke³ *n.* a bird.

สุบดี　　soo⁴-bau-dee *S. n.* a husband who is good; an owner, master or proprietor who is good (S. E. D. p. 1227).

สุบิน　　soo⁴-bin *P. n.* sleep; a dream; nocturnal illusions (chd. p. 482): ทรงพระสุบิน to dream a dream (for royalty): ทายสุบิน to guess at the meaning of a dream: สุบิน-นิมิตร a vision during sleep.

สุประดิษฐ์　　soo⁴-bpra⁴-dit⁴ *S. n.* stableness; stability; permanence: *adj.* strong; stable; reliable; famous; far-famed (S. E. D. p. 1228).

สุปรีดิ์　　soo⁴-bpree *S. n.* gladness; joyfulness; cheerfulness of the greatest degree (S. E. D. p. 1229).

สุปาณิ　　soo⁴-bpah-nee *S. adj.* having good or beautiful hands; dexterous-handed (S. E. D. p. 1228).

สุพรรณ　　soo⁴-pun *n.* gold: *adj.* golden; bright; brilliant: สุพรรณบัฏ a gold plate, tablet or placque on which is inscribed the name of a king, prince, or high official (as on the occasion of raising the same to a higher rank): สุพรรณภาชน์ gilded or golden vases or trays: สุพรรณภิงคาร a gold goblet or drinking cup: สุพรรณรังษี rays of a golden colour: สุพรรณราช a large spittoon (for the use of royalty): สุพรรณศรี a small spittoon (for royalty).

สุพพัต　　soop⁴-put⁶ *P. n.* a man who practices good deeds, is of a strict pious nature, and a blessing to others: สุพพตา the feminine gender of สุพพัต (chd. p. 483).

สุภ　　see ศุภ p. 800.

สุภร　　soo⁴-paun *S. adj.* easily carried, handled or cared for (as a child); thoroughly trained; supple; flexible in disposition (resulting in frugality, stability; and strength of character) (S. E. D. p. 1229).

สุภัค　　soo⁴-puk⁶ *S. adj.* wealthy; fortunate; prosperous; rich; pretty; beloved (S. E. D. p. 1229).

สุภา　　soo⁴-pah *n.* a judge: สุภาตระลาการ, สภาตระลาการ the jury.

สุภาพ, เสาวภาพ　　soo⁴-parp³ *adj.* meek; gentle; humble; mild; affable; civil; well-bred: ความสุภาพ humility; humbleness (of spirit): สุภาพบุรุษ a gentleman: สุภาพราบเรียบ *idiomatic* screnely submissive: สุภาพเรียบร้อย of good decorum; polite: สุภาพอ่อนหวาน meek, affable and polite in behaviour.

สุภาษิต　　soo⁴-pah-sit⁴ *S. n.* a proverb; a wise or witty saying; an adage; aphorisms; maxims (S. E. D. p. 1229).

สุม ๑　　soo⁴-ma⁶ *P. n.* the moon (chd. p. 488).

สุม ๒　　soom² *v.* to allow to burn in a slow fire, or smoulder (as rubbish or dry leaves); to heap, or pile up prior to making a bonfire; see ก่อไฟ under กอ p. 67; กอง p. 67; พอก p. 577: สุมแกลบ to allow paddy husk to smoulder (a common method, among farmers, of protecting cattle from mosquitoes): สุมตอ, สุมฟอน to allow a log of wood or stump of a tree to smoulder (a common method of ridding fields of stumps): สุมแร่ to smelt ores or minerals: สุมหัว to apply a plaster or a cooling poultice to the head (as a remedial agent); a common method of treatment for diseases of children.

สุ่ม　　soom⁴ *n.* a cone-shaped trap having sharpened ribs, which is used for catching fish in shallow water. This is thrust down at random from place to place and when the fish swims against the side, the hand is run down through the hole in the trap and grabs the fated fish, or it is impaled on the sharp ribs, or held fast in the mud; a hemispherical coop made of bamboo strips woven in large meshes (used to confine fighting cocks or chickens)—commonly seen around farm houses; a large wicker or bamboo coop: สุ่มปลา the act of catching fish with a cone-shaped trap: สุ่มสี่สุ่มห้า to rush madly from one thing, or job to another ; to do or grab in an awkward, clumsy or thoughtless manner ; to meddle (as an unrestrained child).

สุมทุม   soom²-toom *n.* a shaded arbour or grove ; a pergola : สุมทุมพุ่มไม้ *idiomatic* a shaded grove composed of bushes.

สุมนา, สุมนะ   soo⁴-ma⁶-nah *P. n.* the great flowering jessamine or jasmine (chd. p. 488) ; see มะลิ p. 639.

สุมาลี   soo⁴-mah-lee *n.* a flower ; a collection of very pretty flowers : พวงสุมาลี a garland of very choice flowers ; *simile* a beautiful girl, handsome as a bouquet.

สุเมธ   soo⁴-met³ *P. S. n.* a wise man ; a sage ; an epithet of the Buddha ; a hermit : *adj.* wise ; intelligent ; clever (chd. p. 488).

สุเมรุ   soo⁴-men *n.* Mount Meru in India (chd. p. 488) ; the lofty mountain (actual or personified), supposed to stand in the middle of the universe, on the summit of which is the Dawadungsa heaven or abode of Indra (chd. p. 308).

สุร ๑   soo⁴-ra⁶ *P. n.* the sun ; a hero ; a valiant man (chd. p. 490) : *adj.* valiant ; heroic ; gallant ; fearless ; courageous (chd. p. 490) : สุรสาคร a tempestuous sea : สุรภาพ of a courageous nature : สุรโยธา a valiant army : สุรสีหนาท a roar (as that of a fierce lion) : สุรเสียง a strong, bold voice ; a voice resounding with power and authority.

สุร ๒   soo⁴-ra⁶ *P. S. n.* an idol ; the image of a god ; a deva, god or deity (chd. p. 490) ; see เทวดา p. 423 : สุรคต *lit.* " to depart and be reborn as a deity," *i. e.* to die (used for royalty) : สุรคิรี *lit.* " deity's mount," *i. e.* Mountain Meru : สุรชน the race of gods : สุรบดี *lit.* " the chief of the gods or deities," *i. e.* Indra (H. C. D. p. 127) : สุรบถ sky ; heaven ; the Milky Way : สุรภาพ the power of a god : สุรราชย์ dominion over the gods : สุรโลก the world or regions of

the gods ; heaven : สุรสตรี, สุรางคนา women of the celestial regions : สุรารักษ์ tutelary deities : สุราลัย the abode of the gods ; a spirit shrine : สุรเนทร์ chief of the gods, *i. e.* [Indra.

สุรภี see สารภี p. 858.

สุรชินี   soo⁴-rut⁶-cha⁶-nee *S. n.* night ; midnight (S. E. D. p. 1232).

สุรติ   soo⁴-rut⁶ *S. n.* a condition or occasion of great joy, delight or supreme happiness (S. E. D. p. 1232).

สุรัสวดี see สัสดี p. 852.

สุรา   soo⁴-rah *P. S. n.* wine ; spirituous liquors ; toddy ; every kind of intoxicating liquor (S. E. D. p. 1235) ; see เมรย p. 656 : สุราบาน the act of drinking intoxicating liquor ; an intoxicant : สุรามัตต์ drunk ; intoxicated ; made tipsy : สุรามัท drunkenness ; intoxication : สุราเมรัย various kinds of intoxicating liquors : สุราเถื่อน illicit spirits.

สุริย, สุริยน, สุริยัน, สุรย   soo⁴-ri⁶-ya⁶ *S. n.* the sun (chd. p. 490) ; the sun-god ; the Sun as a deity. He is one of the three chief deities in the Vedas and is the great source of light and warmth (H. C. D. p. 310) : สุริยกมล see ทานตะวัน p. 411 : สุริยกันต์, สุริยกานต์ *lit.* " the sun gem," *i. e.* a crystal supposed to be formed of condensed rays of the sun and, though cool to the touch, to give out heat in the sun's rays (H. C. D. p. 312) : สุริยการ, สุริยบาท the rays of the sun : สุริยกาล daytime ; daylight : สุริยคราส an eclipse of the sun (chd. p. 490) : สุริยเคราะห์ Rahu, who is supposed to devour the sun or moon during an eclipse ; see ราหุ p. 712 : สุริยมณฑล the ball or sphere of the sun : สุริยรังสี, สุริยรัศมี sunlight ; the sun's rays : สุริยวงศ์ the solar race. There are two dynasties of the solar race, the elder branch of which reigned at Ayodhya, the other dynasty reigning at Mithila (H. C. D. p. 312). Rama-Chandra belonged to the elder branch, and is considered as the seventh incarnation of Vishnu (H. C. D. p. 256) : สุริยวาร

day of the Sun; Sunday: สุริยโสภา sun-light; the brightness of the sun's rays; light.

สุริยงค์ soo[4]-ri[6]-yong *n.* the Sun as a personified deity.

สุริเยศ, สุริเยนทร์ soo[4]-ri[6]-yet[3] *n. lit.* "the one supreme in the firmament," *i. e.* the sun, *poetical.*

สุริโยทัย soo[4]-ri[6]-yoh-tai *n.* Queen Suri-yothai. One of the most stirring incidents in the history of Thailand is undoubtedly the heroic sacrifice by which Queen Suriyothai lost her life, reminding us more than any-thing else of some episode in the pages of ancient history. The following is a short account of the event, abridged from the an-nals of Ayuthia. In the winter season of A. D. 1544, Bureng Nong, the King of Pegu invaded Thailand for the second time—with an army of 300,000 footmen, 700 elephants and 3,000 horses,—to renew the attack on Ayuthia, in which he had not been successful on a former occasion. Phra Maha Chakra-phat, the King of Thailand, organized the defence to the best of his ability, stationing bodies of troops outside the city, and strength-ening its defences both internal and exter-nal. In the beginning of March the enemy arrived before the city and commenced the siege. A few days afterwards—on Sun-day the 6th day of the 4th month—King Chakraphat sallied out to attack the Peguans, and to try and break their lines in the plain of the Phu Klao Thong spire. His Queen, Suriyothai by name, followed him in the warlike attire of the Second King, mounted on a male elephant and followed by her two sons. The King deployed his troops to the right and left, and shortly became engaged in a sharp conflict with the enemy's advanced guard. With the intent to break the centre of the Peguan line, and cutting it in two parts, he gallantly pushed on his elephant against the elephants of the enemy. Un-fortunately, his animal became frightened

and turned face, and in spite of all the efforts of its driver, it could not be brought back to face the foe. At this juncture the King of Pre— a tributary and ally of the King of Pegu—urged his elephant in pursuit of King Chakraphat.

Queen Suriyothai, seeing the imminent danger to which her Royal Consort was ex-posed, advanced to contest the passage with the King of Pre. Her elephant became en-gaged with that of her antagonist—but was unable to make a stand and began to lose ground. The King of Pre, taking advantage of the opportunity, struck the Queen a heavy blow on the shoulder with the sharpened blade of his elephant hook, cleaving it right down to the breast. The unfortunate Queen dropped lifeless in the howdah, and would have fallen a prey to the enemy, but for the bravery of her two sons, who boldly advancing, succeeded in recovering her body and bringing it safely into Ayuthia. It was thus that the gallant Queen sacrificed her life to save her husband. This tragical event has been celebrated both in prose and verse. His Majesty King Chulalongkorn composed some verses on the subject These are inscribed on the frame of the picture in the Palace, which served as a copy for the embroidered representation by Lady Bhaska-rawongse.

สุลักษณะ soo[4]-lak[6]-sa[4]-na[6] *S. n.* one whose marks, condition, nature, or characteristics are auspicious.

สุวภาพ soo[4]-wa[6]-parp[3] *n.* politeness; gen-tleness; affability; humbleness; meekness; see สุภาพ.

สุวรรณ, สุพรรณ soo[4]-wan *S. n.* gold; money; wealth; property (S. E. D. p. 1236): สุวรรณภูมิ a part of Thailand known in ancient history as *lit.* "the land of gold," "the penin-sula of gold." Some authorities claim that this was Pegu while others claim it was southern Thailand. No gold has been found in Pegu but there are gold mines in southern Thailand. It was the capital of the state ruled over by King Rama Tibodi I before he founded Ayuthia in 1350 or 1351 (wood p. 43 *foot-note*).

สุวาน soo⁴-wan *P. n.* a dog (Chd. p. 492).

สุวิมล soo⁴-wi⁶-mon *S. adj.* very clear; pure; clean; unstained (S. E. D. p. 1233).

สุวินัย soo⁴-wi⁶-nai *P. S. adj.* teachable; obedient; compliant; easily trained or educated (S. E. D. p. 1233).

สุศานติ์ soo⁴-san² *S. n.* calmness; placidness; serenity; tranquillity (S. E. D. p. 1237).

สุสาน soo⁴-san² *P. n.* a cemetery; a charnel-house; an enclosed ground in which bodies are cremated (Chd. p. 490): มหาสุสาน a great cemetery.

สุหร่าย soo⁴-rai⁴ *n.* a sprinkler (for water); a shower-bath; a means for spraying water or perfume.

สุหัท, สุหฤท, โสหัท, เสาหฤท soo⁴-hut⁴ *P. n.* a friend; an ally (Chd. p. 486); a merciful person; see เพื่อน p. 599.

สุเหร่า soo⁴-row⁴ *n.* a mosque; a Mohammedan temple of worship.

สู soo² *pron.* thou; you. *A word of Laos origin*: สูจะไปไหน where are you going? สูทั้งหลาย all of you folks: สูรู้บ่นลำ to be boastful or arrogant (as to one's knowledge).

สู่ soo⁴ *v.* to get to; to come to; to arrive at or reach: *adv.* toward, or into (a place); together; conjointly: *prep.* by; for; in with: เข้าสู่ที่ to go, or put into place: ที่ไปมาหาสู่กัน a rendezvous: ไปมาหาสู่กัน to exchange visits; to call on each other frequently: ภรรยาที่สู่ขอ a wife that has been duly asked for in accordance with the customs of the country: มีผีสิงสู่อยู่ to have been taken possession of, or haunted by spirits (the implication is evil spirits): สมสู่, สู่สม to live

as man and wife; to be united: สิงสู่ to possess, or be possessed by: สู่กันกิน to share food, eatables, or refreshments with others: สู่กันทำ to divide the work or job, for the purpose of getting help at the expense of others: สู่ขอ *idiomatic* to go in person to ask for (as a daughter in marriage): สู่บ้าน, สู่สำนัก to arrive at, or enter the dwelling-place of another: สู่เมือง to come to, or enter the city: สู่รู้ to boast about one's knowledge; to assume knowledge of, and act without instructions; to be officious and interferring; to know conjointly (as secret plans or schemes): สู่เรือน to come to, or go into the house: สู่สภาพเดิม *legal* to reinstate or put in *statu quo ante*: สู่สวรรค์ to get to, or to reach heaven: สู่หา to seek an interview with; to call upon, or visit frequently (as a suitor on a young lady): อ่านสู่กันฟัง to read (aloud) for the benefit of others; to share with others what one is reading.

สู้ soo⁵ *v.* to oppose; to resist; to meet in combat; to withstand; to confront; to strive against; to endure; to undergo (as hardships); to meet in competition; to compete with (as in a game); to endure trouble or adversity meekly and patiently: *onomat.* derived from the sound of waves dashing against rocks, or heavy rain blown by a strong wind: มีใจสู้ to be ready or inclined to fight: ไม่สู้ to be unwilling to compete (as in a competition, or for a tender); to refuse to fight the opponent (as a fighting-fish): ไม่สู้ดี not overly good; ill-advised or misdirected: ไม่สู้เป็นอะไร of little importance; can be easily overlooked: ยาสู้โรคไม่ไหว the remedies have not successfully combatted the disease; an ineffectual remedy: สู้กันตัวต่อตัว in single combat: สู้ความ *legal* to put up a defence in a legal action: สู้จน to bear or endure poverty with fortitude: สู้จนตาย to resist unto death: สู้เดินดีกว่าขี่ช้าง it is better to confront the trials of walking, rather than to ride an elephant: สู้ได้ to be able to compete with (as for a tender, or against an opponent in a game): สู้ต้านทาน to resist successfully, or to be able to withstand the enemy (as in a skirmish): สู้ทน to undergo or bear with fortitude: สู้ไม่ได้ cannot, or does not excel, surpass, or conquer: สู้ไม่ไหว, สู้ไม่ได้ to be unable to resist or fight against the enemy: สู้รบ to resist (boldly) an attacking foe: สู้เลียชีวิตร, สู้ตาย to lay down one's life willingly (as for a good cause): สู้เสียสละ to undergo the sorrow or privations of giving up all that is dear to one's heart (as Abraham when called by God to sacrifice his son): สู้หาความ to incriminate maliciously; to pick a quarrel spitefully: สู้อดกลั้น to strive to suppress the feelings (as in a time of sorrow): แหวนของท่านสู้ของฉันไม่ได้ your ring does not surpass mine; my ring is superior to yours.

สูกษม see สุขุม p 871.

สูง soong[2] *adj.* high; tall; lofty; towering; advanced (as in age or rank): ไข้ขึ้นสูงมาก the fever runs a very high course: คำสูง court language or words; grandiloquent forms of speech: เครื่องสูง insignia of high rank (royal): ผีเท้าสูง a high-stepper (as a horse): ยอดสูงที่สุด the very highest pinnacle, or the summit: ระดับน้ำขึ้นสูง the level of the water is high: ราคาสูงไป the price is too high; the goods are very expensive: ร่างสูง of high stature: ศัพท์ที่สูง special words (as of Pali or Sanskrit origin): สูงขึ้น to rise to a loftier plane: สูงโดด towering singly (as the spire of Wat Aroon); standing stately and prominently alone (as a spire, tree or mountain peak): สูงตระกูล of royal or regal birth or lineage: สูงนัก entirely too high: สูงระหง tall; stately and majestic; gloriously high: สูงลิ่ว towering extremely high or lofty: สูงศักดิ์ of high official rank (as ministers of state): สูงส่ง of high civil dignity: stateliness; having majestic grandeur: สูงสุด the very highest point: สูง ๆ ต่ำ ๆ

undulating (as ground): เสียงสูง a high operatic voice: อายุสูง, สูงอายุ of advanced age; of mature age; having reached old age.

สูจก soo[2]-chja[4]-gka[4] *P. S. n.* an informer; a teacher; an instructor; a spy (S.E.D. p. 1241).

สูจน soo[2]-chja[4]-na[6] *P. S. n.* the act of indicating, exhibiting, or pointing out.

สูจิ soo[2]-chji[4] *P. S. n.* a needle or any sharp-pointed instrument; an index; an itemized account (S. E. D. p. 1241): สูจิบัตร a pro-
[gramme.

สูญ see ศูนย์ p. 801.

สูด soot[4] *v.* to inhale by forced effort; see สึด p. 868; to play a chessman across one or two squares in one move. In playing Thai chess, the pieces that can be so moved are the king, queen and bishop but only once in a game: สูดกลิ่น to inhale the fragrance (of flowers): สูดยานัด to take snuff.

สูต ๑ soot[4] *P. n.* a charioteer; the son of a prince or noble by a Brahmin woman and belonging to the warrior caste (chd. p. 491); a half-caste; an Eurasian; persons of mixed races.

สูต ๒ soot[4] *S. n.* birth: *adj.* born; coming into existence; see เกิด p. 125.

สูตร soot[4] *S. n.* a formula; a short sentence or aphoristic rule; thread, yarn, cord or wire; a string or series of portions of scriptural precepts or texts (S. E. D. p. 1241): สูตร-เลข the multiplication table.

สูติ soo[2]-dti[4] *S. n.* birth; progeny; nativity; offspring; child-birth (S. E. D. p. 1240): สูติกรรม the act of being delivered of a child: สูติแพทย์, แพทย์ผดุงครรภ์ an obstetrical surgeon: สูติศาสตร์ the science of midwifery.

สูท soot[4] *P. S. n.* a cook; a well; a pond, or pool of water (S. E. D. p. 1242): สูทศาสตร์ cookery; the art or science of cooking: สูท-กรรม a cook's work; cooking.

สูน   soon[2] *S. adj.* born; produced; blown; budded; bringing forth (as flowers or fruit) (S. E. D. p. 1240).

[p. 489].

สูนุ   soo[2]-noo[6] *P. S. n.* a son; a child (chd.

สูบ   soop[4] *v.* to pump; to draw in smoke (as when inhaling and exhaling the smoke of tobacco); to inflate (as tires of motor cars); to distend or expand (by forcing in gas or air); to inhale smoke: *n.* a pump for air or water; a bellows: แกนลูกสูบ a piston-rod: ชักสูบ to work a hand-bellows: เตาสูบ a forge: ธรณีสูบ *idiomatic* the earth absorbs, sucks up, or swallows down: ลิ้นลูกสูบ cylinder valves: แว่นลูกสูบ piston rings: ลูกสูบ cylinders (of an engine): สูบกล้อง to smoke a pipe: สูบกันชา to smoke the flowering tops of *Cannabis* or hemp: สูบตั้ง a cylinder placed vertically: สูบทอง to melt gold (in a crucible) by means of a hand-bellows: สูบนอน a cylinder placed horizontally: สูบน้ำ to pump water; to spout water (as a whale): สูบบุหรี่, สูบยา to smoke cigars, or tobacco in any form: สูบฝิ่น to smoke opium: สูบแฝด a double cylinder: สูบหอยโข่ง a centrifugal pump: สูบยาสูบ to smoke pipe tobacco.

สูร   soo[2]-ra[6] *P. n.* a hero; a valiant man; the sun: *adj.* valiant; heroic; brave; bold

[(chd. p. 490).

สูรย see สุริย p. 875.

สูร   soo[2]-ree *P. n.* a sage; a learned man.

สูล   soo[2]-la[6] *P. n.* any sharp-pointed instrument; a pike, lance or stake (chd. p. 488); an iron pin or spit; a stake for impaling criminals; an instrument used when inflicting the death penalty; a spear; a dart; a trident.

สูลี   soo[2]-lee *P. n. lit.* "one who holds a trident," *i. e.* Siva; a spearman (chd. p. 488).

สูส, สุงสิง   soo[2]-see[2] *v.* to associate or converse with in a questionable manner; to have secret dealings with (as with infamous characters).

เส   say[2] *adj.* loitering; lazy; playing truant; negligent; dilly-dallying (as when one is sent on an errand); dilatory; intentionally prolonging (as the consideration of some problem); see ไถล p. 394: เสความ to delay proceedings (as by needless discussions); to gain time by deviating from a direct line of argument; to procrastinate by evading the point at issue; see เชือน p. 302: เสแสร้ง to disguise cunningly, or to obscure the crux of a problem; to digress from a preconceived course, or predetermined purpose of action (as if one, going for a doctor, strays into, or stops at, some intermediate place): เสออก to be lazy, or loitering about while others are at work (as some in a gang of workmen): เสพูด a form of hypocritical speech whereby a speaker slanders some one in his absence, but on his appearance turns his remarks to words of praise, or to some general topic of conversation: เสไป a form of circumlocution much used by the Thai, whereby the speaker addresses uncomplimentary remarks, or even curses, to some inanimate object, with the expectation that the real object of his wrath will hear and understand what he longs to say to his face but dare not.

เสก   sek[4] *P. v.* to sprinkle (chd. p. 472), or pour water over; to pronounce incantations over; to pronounce magical or religious formulas; to produce spells or trances by exorcism; to employ enchantments, sorceries or philters as agents; to solemnize, or consecrate by sprinkling on water (as a blessing in marriage ceremonies): เสกสรร to make a choice, or speak from auto-suggestion; to act under the guidance of magical incantations: การเสกอาคม witchcraft; enchantments; sorcery; necromacy.

เสกข   sek[4]-ka[4] *P. adj.* having still to undergo training. This term is applied to those who have not yet attained the highest degree of perfection or saintship (according to the Buddhist religion). It implies that they still have a remainder of human passion to eradicate, still have duties to perform, still have a probationary stage to be passed through (chd. p. 472): เสกขบุคคล those who still have to undergo instruction and training or a probationary stage ere they attain the highest degree of saintship.

เส่ง see **ปอกะเจา** p. 514.

เส่งเครี่ง seng[2]-kreng *adj.* low; mean; bad (used in regard to persons); valueless; unimportant (used in regard to trees).

เส่งียม sa[4]-ngee-am[4] *adj.* modest; polite; reserved; unassuming; chaste: เส่งียมเจี่ยม-ตัว one whose manners are gentle, polite, modest and proper in all respects: เส่งียมใจ to exhibit humility, modesty or moderation in one's desires.

เสฏฐ see **เศรษฐี** p. 801.

เสฏฐี see **เศรษฐี** p. 801.

เสด็จ sa[4]-det[4] *v.* to go (for royalty): *n.* a personal pronoun for princes or royal personages: ตามเสด็จ to follow in the retinue of a king or prince: เฝ้าเสด็จ to enter into the presence of a prince; to pay one's respects to a prince or princess: ยังไม่เสด็จ the royal person has not yet come: เสด็จกลับ to return: เสด็จประพาส to go on a pleasure trip: เสด็จพระราชดำเนิน to go (used for a king); เสด็จมา to come: เสด็จมาประทับ to come (in state), and remain seated or in residence at some place.

เสดน, เสตน see **เถน** p. 390.

เสต say[4]-dta[4] *n.* the colour white; whiteness (chd. p. 473); see **เศวต** p. 801.

เสตุ say[4]-dtoo[4] *P. n.* a bridge; an embankment; a dike; a causeway (chd. p. 473).

เสถียร, สถิร sa[4]-tee-an[2] *P. adj.* firm; hard; solid; strong; immovable (chd. p. 504).

เสท, เสโท say[4]-ta[6] *P. n.* sweat; perspiration (chd. p. 472).

เสน ๑ sen[2] *n.* minium; a vivid red, opaque lead oxide (used chiefly as a pigment); cinnabar: เสน (ลิง) the rufous stump-tailed monkey, *Macaca arctoides* and *rufescens* (N. H. J. S. S. III, p. 121): เสนทอง a gold pigment-powder used for colouring purposes.

เสน ๒ sey[2]-na[6] *P. n.* a bed; a couch (chd. p. 471): เสนาสนะ a bed which is also used as a seat; a bed-like seat.

เสน ๓ say[2]-na[6] *P. n.* a hawk (chd. p. 472).

เส้น sen[3] *n.* filaments; see **ไย** p. 685; fibers (as thread-like structures of organic tissues); a stroke; a streak, stripe or narrow ridge; a line (as when drawn by pen or pencil); *a numerical designatory particle for* threads, rope, strings, hair; a unit of linear measurement equal to 40 metres, or 20 wah; 25 sen equal 1 kilometre; *a prefix followed by the designating name which is used for anatomical terms:* เส้นกลาง, สายกลาง the middle strand or core (as of a cable or electric main wire); an intermediate stretch of land (as paddy fields of one owner dividing those of another owner): เส้นชัก the contraction of a group of muscles (as in lock-jaw or tetanus): เส้นชีพจร the radial artery; the pulse: เส้นด้าย a thread: เส้น (หลอด) น้ำขาว (น้ำนม) lacteals: เส้น (หลอด) น้ำเหลือง lymphatics: เส้นบรรทัด a line drawn by pen or pencil: เส้นประสาท nerves; incorrect, see **วิถี** p. 774: เส้นป่าน the strands of a string; a string (as for kite-flying): เส้นโลหิต, หลอดโลหิต a blood-vessel: เส้นโลหิตแดง, หลอดโลหิตแดง an artery: เส้นศูนย์ (กาย) the *linia-alba* or "white line." The tendenous medial line down the front of the abdomen giving attachment to the tendons of the transverse abdominal muscles: เส้นสาย, เส้นเอ็น *idiomatic* tendons; sinews; fibrous cords: เส้นหนึ่ง one sen, being 40 metres, or 20 wah: เส้นอำมพฤกษ์ the pulsating line of the descending abdominal aorta, running parallel with the *linea-alba*.

เสนง, เสน่ง, แสนง see เขนง p. 163.

เสนห, เสน่ห์, เสนหา, เสน่หา sa⁴-nay-hah⁴ *S. n.* (1) friendship; affection; tenderness; lust; desire (chd. p. 477): (2) smoothness; greasiness; oiliness (S. E. D. p. 1267): (3) *Thai* love; love-potions; philters; a secret charm one is supposed to be able to exert on another (the inference is with evil design): คู่เสน่หา partners in love (as husband or wife): ถูกเสน่ห์ to be influenced or captivated by this secret power or magnetism: ทำเสน่ห์ to exert power by means of love-potions; to influence with guile or wiles in order to create love: มีความเสน่หาแก่กัน to reciprocate love: ลูก-เสน่หา child of one's love: สนิทในทางเสน่ห์ to be an adept or expert in exerting personal magnetism: สนิทเสน่หา to be well-acquainted with; to love each other; to be affectionate: สุดเสน่หา to the utmost limit of passionate love.

เสนอ sa⁴-nur² *v.* to submit respectfully, or to pass on to a superior (as to a higher officer); to mediate another's cause before a higher authority; to take the part of: ผู้-เสนอ an intermediary person, or advocate; an intercessor: สน้ำเสนอ *idiomatic* to plead for mercy: เสนอความ to propose, or make a motion for consideration (as in a meeting); to intercede for, or on behalf of another (as to a higher court or presiding officer): เสนอ-ลูกขุน to present to, or plead before a jury on behalf of a client.

เสนา, เสน say²-nah *P. S. n.* a missile; an army; armed forces; soldiers; troops (S. E. D. p. 1246): *when occurring as a suffix in a compound word, either of neutral or masculine gender the contraction to* เสน *is permissable*, as มหาเสน, ราชเสน one in command of a vast army; เสนาธิการ the chief officer of the army; duties pertaining to national defense: เสนาธิการทหารบก chief of the general staff: เสนาบดี a general, or the commander-in-chief (of military forces); a minister of state; the chief of a department: เสนาพยุห์, เสนาพยุห์

troops in marching formation (as out on parade, or in battle array): เสนามาตย์ a courtier; one who seeks favour by flattery.

เสน่า sa⁴-now⁴ *n.* a bow; a cross-bow; an arrow; a spear; a dart.

เสนางค์ say²-nang *P. n.* the four divisions of an army according to ancient methods of warfare, consisting of an elephant corps, cavalry, war chariots and infantry.

เสนาะ sa⁴-naw⁴ *adj.* melodious; harmonious; musical; concordant: เสนาะเพราะหู pleasing to the ear.

เสนีย say²-nee-ya² *P. n.* those composing an army; soldiers; officers (chd. p. 472).

เสนียด sa⁴-nee-at⁴ *n.* evil; misfortune; wickedness: *adj.* of ill-omen; defective; unpropitious; unauspicious: กันเสนียด to take steps, or to find means for averting evil consequences or ill-luck: ไม่มีเสนียด perfect; flawless: หวีเสนียด a comb with very fine teeth: หัวแหวนมีเสนียด the setting or stone of a ring has flaws or imperfections: เสนียด-จัญไร full of defects, flaws or blemishes (a curse word).

เสพ sep⁴ *v.* to eat or partake of (as food); to drink (as liquors); to associate with (as friends); to use or enjoy carnally (as a mistress); to practice, partake or perform (as forming a habit); to live or inhabit together (as with others in the same house); to serve (as a servant); to devote oneself to (as to a hobby or cause); to extol (as the greatness or goodness of); to indulge in (as eating of the forbidden fruit): ยาเสพติด habit-forming drugs.

เสเพล say²-play *adj.* ill-behaved; rude uncouth; vulgar; ill-mannered.

เสภา say²-pah *n.* solo singing with accompanying music; songs of an amatory nature, an example of which is ขุนช้าง, ขุนแผน a scurrilous story of the illicit affairs of noblemen

and their wives, ending in the assassination of
the king by the state sword at the hand of
the son of one of the noblemen.   These events
are supposed to have taken place as long ago as
A. D. 185 (wales, siam state ceremonies p. 84).

เสม็ด   sa⁴-met⁴ *Laos, Sakon Nakawn,* เม็ด-
ขุน *Thai, Peninsula,* ใต้เม็ด *Laos, Chiengmai*
(ต้น) *n. Eugenia grata (Myrtaceae),* a small
tree found from Tenasserim to Sumatra and
Johore, not uncommon near the coasts.   The
bark seems to be used in Penang for toughening fishing-nets by tanning them.   The wood
is weak, and not valued (cb. p. 646 : v. p. p. 251 :
burk. p. 968) :   เสม็ดขาว *Thai, Chantaburi,*
เม็ด *Thai, Pang-nga* and *Satul* (ต้น) *Melaleuca
leucadendron (Myrtaceae),* cajeput, a large
bush or a tree, very variable, found from
Tenasserim to the Moluccas, but not present in
the Philippine Islands ; in the Malay Peninsula
it occurs near both coasts.   The variability is
not only in stature, but in the amount of oil
in different parts.   The wood is so much in
demand in the Peninsula that the tree is
planted.   The tree grows in wet soil and even
in standing water.   In the Peninsula, there
are several small forests of it in low valleys
behind the coast, which are reserved for the
sake of the firewood they yield.   The tree
has been used as a road-side shade-tree on
roads in Malacca, in low-lying stretches where
they cross rice-plains, but it has not enough
spread to shade wide roads.   The timber is
reddish-brown, or violet-brown ; mottled or
veined ; cracks a little, and warps badly during
drying ; is rather like beech, hard, very durable in contact with wet ground and sea-water,
so that it is used for posts, piles, and ship-
building.   It burns well, and as it burns the
resin may be seen oozing out of the wood,
melted by the heat.   It is the chief firewood
of Malacca, and of some other places where
mangrove wood is not available.   Paper-pulp
made from it appears similar to pulp of poplar,
but is not necessarily a possible commercial
material for paper-making : indeed it is found

quite unsuited.   Sometimes in boat-building,
a layer of its papery bark is placed over the
edge of a timber before the next is fastened
overlapping it, and this, swelling when wet,
seals the seam.   With dammar, it is made
into torches ; and is used for caulking boats.
It is used as floats for fishing-nets.   Where
cajeput oil is made, it serves for packing the
bottles for transit ; it is also used for luting
the joints of distilling apparatus.   In eastern
Malaysia the softened bark, after mastication,
is used on suppurating wounds to draw out
pus.   In Sarawak the bark is used with
Hydrocotyle leaves on festering wounds,
evidently because of its absorbent power.   A
tea is made from the leaves in New Caledonia.
A green oil, carrying 50 to 65 per cent of
cineol is of commercial value but the trade
suffers much from adulteration.   Singapore is a
clearing-house for this trade.   In Malaysia the
oil is used for head-ache, tooth-ache, ear-ache,
rheumatism, cramps and fresh wounds.   In
European medicine the oil is sometimes administered as a sudorific.   It produces a
sensation of warmth, increases the beat of
the heart, and may cause excessive sweating.
The dried fruits are used in medicines (cb. p.
625 : burk. p. 1431) :   เสม็ดแดง *Thai, Chumpawn* (ต้น) *Eugenia zeylanica (Myrtaceae),*
a small, or medium-sized tree found from
southern India to Java ; in the Peninsula it is
not uncommon near the coasts.   The fruit is
sweet and aromatic, and is eaten.   The reddish
or brown wood serves in Malaya for fuel, and
perhaps for rafts.   In southern India it is
used for building purposes and agricultural
implements.   The leaves and roots may be
used to form a decoction used as a vermifuge.
The tree has stimulant and anti-rheumatic
properties.   It is said that the plant may be
rubbed over the chest of an elephant to make
it docile (cb. p. 666 : burk. p. 975) :   ไต้เสม็ด
torches made by soaking the rotten wood of
this tree in dammar, or more probably of the
bark of the cajeput tree and dammar.

เสมหะ   sem²-ha⁴ *P. n.* phlegm; mucus, especially that of the throat and nose. One of the four humours of the body according to obsolete humoral pathology; pituita (a glutinous mucus) (chd. p. 472): เสมหะตีขึ้น an expression used in moribund cases when mucus collects in the throat: เสมหะหางวัว stringy, tough, tenacious mucus; *simile* phlegm which comes out in long shreds like the tail of a kite: ไอเป็นเสมหะเจือโลหิต to cough up mucus streaked with blood.

เสมอ   sa⁴-mur² *v.* to act as a second, or in behalf of; to abet; to assist, back up, or support (as in a game, race or boxing-bout); to be uniform in all respects: *adv.* throughout; always: *adj.* equal to in length, size, quality and ability; continuous; level; flat; on a par with: ใจเสมอ unbiassed; unprejudiced; disinterested; impartial: ได้เสมอทั่ว ๆ กัน all receiving a uniform, or equal amount: ไปเสมอ to frequent; to attend regularly: เพลงเสมอ a tune played by a Thai xylophone band: ไม่มีใครเสมอ there is none to match, or be on a par: เรียบเสมอ smooth, level, or even throughout: เล่นม้าเสมอ to be a regular attendant at horse-races: เสมอกัน resulting evenly or uniformly: เสมอใจ *lit.* "uniformity of mind," *i. e.* conjointly; connectedly; intimately (as bosom friends or as "hearts that beat as one"): เสมอตัว neither to gain nor lose (as in some trading enterprise, or in playing games of chance): เสมอนอก *lit.* "betting outside (the ring or combine)" *i. e.* the condition of private betting or wagering without putting stakes into the pool, or playing through the totalizator: เสมอน้ำเสมอเนื้อ *lit.* "corresponding in water levels and tissues," *i. e.* being of equal status and social standing; equal in rank, wealth, and ability; suitable for each other in every respect; a well-matched couple (said of a bride and groom): เสมอภาค equal to in all respects; conforming to a uniform status and social standing: เสมอหนึ่ง for example; as if; as though; like the following: เสมอไหน which one of the two contestants are you backing or betting on? The reply would be on that one (with some designating mark). This is a common expression at cock-fights, boxing-bouts, or other contests: อุปมาเสมอหนึ่งว่า figuratively speaking.

เสมา (ต้น)   say²-mah *Thai, Chonburi n. Opuntia elatior (Cactaceae); O. vulgaris* (cb. p. 782): เสมา (อุโบสถ) eight boundary stones placed around the sanctuary in a Buddhist monastery. These indicate that the ground within has been deeded to the Order by the government. Thus it became consecrated to the religion and thereby has sufficient rank so that men may be ordained to the Buddhist brotherhood within its precincts: เสมา (คล้องคอ) a votive-tablet shaped plaque of gold, attached to a chain and worn as a neck pendant: เสมา (พระภูมิ) a terra-cotta or wooden votive-tablet, mounted on a base, and placed in a shrine dedicated to the tutelary gods of the place: เสมา (กำแพงป้อม) merlons of city walls, parapets, bastions or other parts of defence works. They are the solid part of the embattlement between the embrasures. In Thai architecture these are shaped like the leaf of the bodh tree.

เสมียน   sa⁴-mee-an² *n.* a clerk; a secretary; an amanuensis.

เสมือน, เสมือนหนึ่ง   sa⁴-meu-an² *adj.* being likened unto: *adv.* thus; as for example; virtually.

เสย   su-ie² *v.* to cause to rise or stand erect; to scoop up (as fish by a dip-net): เสยผม to comb up, or push back the hair in pompadour style.

เสร็จ, สำเร็จ, จบ   set⁴ *v.* to be completed; to come to an end; to be concluded, terminated or finished: ใบเสร็จ a receipt: เสร็จความ the matter has come to an end.

เสริด   sert⁴ *v.* to escape; to flee from; to

elude or pass unnoticed to a place of safety :
adv. quick ; alert ; rapid ; swift ; see รอด p. 692.

เสริม serm[2] *v.* to supplement ; to add to ;
to augment ; to insert, increase, or enlarge ;
see เติม p. 374 : เสริมซ้ำ to make several
additions : เสริมไม้ที่หัวเรือ to make additions
(with extra wood) at the prow of a boat ; to
lengthen by splicing (as timbers by overlapping at the ends).

เสรี say[2]-ree *P. adj.* independent ; self-
willed ; following one's own will or inclination ;
uncontrolled (chd. p. 473) : เสรีภาพ, อิสรภาพ
liberty ; freedom ; license ; franchise ; privilege ; independence (chd. p. 473) : เสรีภาพ-
ในการพูด freedom of speech.

เสล, เสลา say[2]-la[6] *P. n.* a rock ; a hill ;
a mountain ; a boulder ; a rocky place (chd. p.
472) : *adj.* rocky ; stony ; mountainous ; made
of, or decorated with stones : สลักเสลา
carvings in stone : เสลบรรพต a hill or
mountain abounding in rocks ; the Rocky
Mountains.

เสลา (ต้น) say[2]-lah *Thai, Saraburi* and
Rachaburi, เสลาเปลือกบาง *Thai, Kampengpet,*
เส้าเบาะ *Laos, Chiengmai* and *Lampang,* เปื้อย-
สะแอน *Laos, Nan,* ฉ่วงฟ้า *Karen, Kanburi n.*
Lagerstroemia tomentosa (Lythraceae), a tree
giving timber of economic importance in
India (cb. p. 727).

เสลี่ยง sa[4]-lee-ang[4] *n.* a litter ; a stretcher ;
a palanquin (for royalty) ; see เฉลี่ยง p. 272.

เสลือกสลน sa[4]-leu-ak[4]-sa[4]-lon[2] *adv.* excitedly ; animatedly ; agitatedly : hurridly.

เสโลห์, โล่ห์ say[2]-loh *n.* a shield.

เสวก say[2]-wok[6] *P. n.* a personal servant ;
a follower or attendant ; a retinue (chd. p.
473) : *Thai* a conferred rank in the Royal
Household, divided into three classes, *viz.*
รองเสวก, เสวก, มหาเสวก each of which are subdivided into three grades.

เสวย sa[4]-wur-ie[2] *v.* to eat ; to partake of ;
to enjoy ; to be in possession of ; to acquire
or receive (used for royalty) : เครื่องเสวย
royal food or utensils : เสวยทุกข์ for
royalty to be afflicted with trouble, distress,
sickness, or tormented by some calamity :
เสวยรมย์ for royalty to enjoy peace, happiness
and prosperity : เสวยราชสมบัติ to be proclaimed king, or sovereign ; to come into
possession of a kingdom : เสวยศุข for royalty to enjoy, or be in possession of happiness
and peace.

เสวียน sa[4]-we-an[2] *n.* rests for rice pots
and other kitchen utensils. These are made
of rattan woven into a circle, grass or
straw coiled and tied into shape, serving as
floor protectors against the soot. Rice pot
carriers are the rests, plus loops as handles.
Portable mats, made of closely plaited bamboo
strips and smeared with cow-dung are used
as temporary enclosures for storing grain.

เสส set[4] *P. n.* fragments ; pieces ; bits ;
scraps : *arithmetic* the remainder or fraction
carried forward (chd. p. 473) ; see เดน p. 334 ;
เศษ p. 801.

เสสรวล say[2]-su-an[2] *v.* to laugh boisterously and rudely.

เสา sow[2] *n.* a pillar ; a stake ; a post :
เสากระโดง a mast : เสากางมุ้ง mosquito-net
supports : เสาเกียด the pole in the centre
of a threshing-floor to which the cattle are
tied while treading out the grains of rice :
เสาเขื่อน the posts of a dike ; protection stakes
or posts around temple grounds, to prevent
the intrusion of molesting cattle : เสาคอก
the posts around a pen or enclosure for cattle
(used at night) : เสาค่าย posts or stakes
protecting a camp (as a stockade in time of
war) ; see ค่าย p. 199 : เสาโคม a lamp-post ;
เสาตั้ง the uprights supporting the ridge-pole :
เสาได่ a forked pole placed either in the bow
or stern of a boat, as a support for the canopy,
mast or punting poles : เสาตะพาน bridge

posts : เสาตะลุง tethering posts for elephants : เสาตำหนัก the posts of a pavillion
or building for royalty : เสาเตาม่อ the
posts supporting a kiln ; shores for a leaning
or tilting house : เสานั่งร้าน posts or supports
for a scaffolding : เสาธง a flagstaff : เสา-
นางเรียง posts or pillars placed around the base
of a pagoda : เสาประโคน, หลักประโคน landmarks or linestakes (as in the delimitation of
property) ; stakes indicating the junction of
two boundaries : เสาโพงพาง stakes in water-
courses to which bag-nets are fastened : เสา-
ไม้จริง a hardwood post : เสาไม้ไผ่ a bamboo
post or stake : เสาร้าน the posts of a shelter
or stall for selling goods by the wayside :
เสาเรือน the posts of a house : เสาหมอ two
small short supplementary posts put in at the
sides of a larger post. In case of needing to
pull the large one up, these can serve as ful-
crums for the levers. Usually the main post
does not go into the soil. This arrangement is
evidently a Chinese invention : เสาหิน stone
pillars (as boundary stakes) : เสาชี้ทาง a road
signpost : เสาเอก the first two posts or pillars
of a Thai house, considered to be the best and
usually decorated with small red flags.

เส้า   sow[3] n. a cane or walking-stick :
ก้อนเส้า a trivet ; a three-legged stand (as for
supporting cooking vessels) : ไม้กะทุ้งเส้า a
pile driver ; a pole decorated with fancy paper rings in decreasing size up to the tip.
This is held by the one in charge of the barge
during royal processions by water, and the
sound of the butt end striking a board marks
the time for the strokes of the paddlers :
สามเส้า a tripod : คอนเส้าต่อนก a long pole
for supporting a dove-trap up among the
branches of a tree.

เสาร์, เสาริ   sow[2] S. n. the seventh constellation, Saturn (S. E. D. p. 1254) : วันเสาร์
Saturday.

เสารภย์, เสาวรภย์   sow[2]-rop[6] S. n. fragrance ; perfume : adj. fragrant (S. E. D. p.

1255).

เสาว   sow[2]-wa[6] a prefix, substitute for สุ,
สว and โส, meaning agreeable, beautiful,
delicious, according to the root meaning of
the following words. The following substitutes are permissable, โสภา for เสาวภา, สวนีย
for เสาวนีย์, สุคนธ์ for เสาวคนธ์.

เสาวคนธ์, เสาวคันธ์   sow[2]-wa[6]-kon n. perfume ; scents ; a fragrant substance or mixture ; agreeable odours.

เสาวณิต   sow[2]-wa[6]-nit[6] adj. having been
heard ; having been received or acknowledged.

เสาวธาร   sow[2]-wa[6]-tan n. perfumery ; cologne ; scented lotions.

เสาวนีย์   sow[2]-wa[6]-nee P. n. a blessing
(chd. p. 470) ; Thai the words, orders or utterances of a queen or princess.

เสาวภา   sow[2]-wa[6]-pah P. n. splendour ;
radiance ; light ; beauty (chd. p. 481).

เสาวภาคย์   sow[2]-wa[6]-pak[3] n. auspiciousness ; fortune ; prosperity ; beauty ; handsomeness (chd. p. 481).

เสาวภาพ see สุภาพ p. 874.

เสาวรส   sow[2]-wa[6]-rot[6] adj. delicious ; luscious ; dainty ; tasty : เสาวรส Thai (ต้น)
Passiflora laurifolia (Passifloraceae), passion
fruit, bell apple, water lemon, a climber of
tropical America, the fruits of which contain
seeds in a thin mucilaginous juice. This is
eaten by some (see แตง p. 376 : Burk. p. 1677) ;
Tetracera loureiri (Dilleniaceae) (cb. pp. 20,
744).

เสาวลักษณ์   sow[2]-wa[6]-luk[6] S. n. one possessing good characteristics ; one endowed
with beautiful features : adj. well-shaped,
handsome and adorable.

เสาหฤท see สุหัท p. 877.

เสาะ, สืบ, แสวง, หา   saw[4] v. to pry into ;
to seek or strive to find ; to enquire after ; to

search diligently for; to investigate (as for the cause): ใจเสาะ fearful; timid; faint-hearted: ทำเสาะ to act a coward: นักสืบ-เสาะ detectives; spies; investigators: สืบ-เสาะสาวราวเรื่อง to investigate carefully in order to unravel a mystery (as C. I. D. men do): สืบเสาะแสวงหา to enquire diligently for; to search after (as Herod for the child Jesus): เสาะด้าย to untangle or wind off silk or cotton threads carefully (as from the skein): เสาะท้อง to exert a loosening effect on the bowels (as do some kinds of fruit); to act as a laxative: เสาะไปเสาะมา to make inquiries in the search back and forth for (as one hunting a doctor): เสาะหา, เที่ยวหา to search carefully in the effort to find (as the woman for the lost coin): เสาะออกไปไกล to extend the search far and wide: เสาะเอาตัว to strive to capture by searching diligently for.

เสาะแสะ   saw⁴-saa⁴ *adj.* weakened; fa-tigued; worn out or exhausted (as by long-continued sickness): ป่วยเสาะแสะ to be prone, or given to a recurrence of some ail-ment; to be sick often: เป็นบิดเสาะแสะ-มานานแล้ว to be troubled off and on with a chronic dysentery.

เสีย   see-ah² *v.* to be despoiled of (as by force or plunder); to be lost; to be spoiled or destroyed; to have to be abandoned, thrown away or discarded (a term implying imperativeness and expressing loss); separated or destroyed: *adj.* bad; rotten; *it is fre-quently used as a final particle but without meaning:* กรุงศรีอยุธยาเสียแก่พม่า Ayuthia was defeated by the Burmese: ความเสียหาย-เท่าไร what is the estimated loss? คิดเสียดาย to long after with regret: ได้ไม่เท่าเสีย the gain is not commensurate with the loss: ได้เสียเท่ากัน to break even in a venture; no loss, no profit: ทำเสีย to cause injury, damage, loss, or destruction: ไปเสียเดี๋ยวนี้ to go at once: น่าเสียดาย what a pity; how regret-able such a state of affairs exists (as incom-patibility between husband and wife): ลูกตี-

ฉันเสีย ๆ เมื่อเดือนก่อนนี้ my child died last month. *Usually it means* previous to *but idiomati-cally here it means* last: เสียกล· to be frus-trated in the carrying out of some deceptive plan or scheme: เสียการ to spend one's time, pains and efforts fruitlessly: เสียเกียรติยศ to lose honour, prestige, or rank: เสียเงินให้ to make payments on behalf of (as when re-deeming one from slavery): เสียเงินเป็นรายเดือน to make monthly payments: เสียจริต insane; mad; demented: เสียใจ distressed in be-half of; sorry for; with a heart full of despair for: เสียใจเหลือเกิน to be extremely grieved or saddened (by some calamity, as from the death of a child): เสียชื่อ to sacrifice one's good name and honour; to spoil one's good reputation by some mean trick or bad deed: เสียชาติ to become a degenerate; to bring disgrace and not honour to one's name, family or race: เสียชีวิต to perish; to lose one's life: เสียชีพดีกว่าเสียสัตย์ honesty at all costs, even to sacrificing one's life: เสียดาย to be regretted; to deplore the condition resulting from some accident or calamity: เสียตัว, เสียคน to sacrifice one's virginity; to be in a condition of dishonour and shame by being worthy of punishment: เสียตา to be defec-tive in the eyes; *idiomatic* to be duped: เสีย-ทัพ the condition of defeat of an army: เสียท่า, เสียที to miss a good opportunity; to make a misstep or move (as in playing chess); to regret the predicament resulting from what might have been avoided: เสียบน to make a sacrifice to the household deities in pay-ment of a vow; to pay off vows by pro-pitiating the spirits; to fail in receiving from the spirits what had been requested of them, thus considering them in default: เสียบ้านเสียเมือง the city has surrendered, or fallen a prey to the enemy: เสียปาก to advise or admonish deaf ears; to waste one's words on a heedless person: เสียเปรียบ to be prejudiced against; to lose a favorable circumstance; to lose by some inequality, handicap, encumbrance or accident; to lose in a transaction through some fault, flaw or defect : เสียเปล่าๆ to discard as useless : to spend without some return (as gambling away one's salary) : เสียผิว to mar or disfigure the surface (as chalk-marks or scratches on a beautiful wall) : เสียมาก เสียได้ เสียน้อยเสียตาย to be penny-wise and pound-foolish : เสียเมืองแก่ข้าศึก the city has surrendered to the enemy : เสียรอย *lit.* "to lose the blazed trail," *i. e.* to be misled or deluded by false information ; to lose the track, trace or scent of ; to let a clue, hint or intimation of some tragedy be lost : เสียรู้ to have been stung, duped, fooled, deceived or misled by credulity (as in a confidence-trick) ; to realize one's lack of discernment and foresight when pitted against another's : เสียแรงเปล่าๆ to spend one's strength and energies to no purpose : เสียศีล to transgress some commandment or religious principle : เสียสองต่อ to pay double money : เสียๆ แล้ว dead ; died ; เสียสูญ an irrecoverable loss : เสียหน้า, เสียความงาม to have the face disfigured (as by scars, flaws, or blemishes) ; see ขายหน้า under ขาย p. 155 : ความเสียหาย losses or deficits incurred (as in some trading venture) ; personal injuries through some fight or brawl.

เสียง   see-ang[2] *n.* sound ; noise ; tone ; strain ; intonation : เครื่องส่งเสียง a loud-speaker (as for a radio set) : ชื่อเสียง reputation ; fame ; renoun : ดักเสียง to intercept the sound (as of a wireless message) : ได้ยินเสียง to hear the sound of : พระสุรเสียง a loud voice from a divinity : มีชื่อมีเสียงเลื่องลือทั่วโลก a world-wide reputation : มีเสียงหรือออกคะแนน to vote : ไม่มีเสียง to have no voice in the matter under discussion : ไม่มีเสียงในที่ประชุม to have had no voice in the meeting : ไม่มีเสียงพูด the condition of one suffering from aphasia (loss or impairment of the voice) : เสียงกบ a croak : เสียงกา a caw ; a croak : เสียงแกะ a bleat : เสียงไก่ (ตัวผู้) a crow : เสียงไก่ (ตัวเมีย) a cackle ; a cluck : เสียงแข็ง a bold, fearless voice or speaker ; the persis-

tent language or arguing of one upholding his opinions in an assembly : เสียงฆ้อง the ringing of a metal gong : เสียงงู a hiss ; a blow : เสียงแจ่มใส a clear, cultivated voice with distinct pronunciation : เสียงช้าง, เสียงคชสาร the trumpeting of elephants : เสียงแตก a cracked voice : เสียงทำเป็น a voice or sound imitating something : เสียงนกเขา a coo : เสียงนกเค้าแมว a hoot ; a screech : เสียงประสาน voices in unison ; musical instruments properly tuned together : เสียงเป็ด a quack : เสียงเพราะ, เสียงไพเราะ melodious sounds : เสียงฟ้า thunder : เสียงร้องไห้ sounds of crying or weeping : เสียงราษฎร public opinion : เสียงฬา a bray : เสียงลือ a rumour ; an unverified report passing from person to person : เสียงวัว a moo ; a low : เสียงหมู a grunt ; a squeal : เสียงห่าน a hiss ; a cackle ; a gabble ; a gaggle : เสียงห่านป่า a honk : เสียงแห้ง, เสียงผากแผ่ว a dry parched voice (as of one suffering from continued fever) : เสียงอึกทึก noises of a disturbing and distracting nature (as of those quarreling, or of Chinese gongs) : เสียงฮึกฮัก the voice of one very excited and angry, mixed with abusive language.

เสียง   see-ang[4] *v.* to guess at ; to estimate or approximate ; to recite incantations in order to enquire of the witches or oracles before taking chances, or venturing on any risk : *n.* splinters ; fragments ; parts ; portions ; pieces ; see ทาง ๑ p. 412 ; เดา p. 334 ; คะเน p. 192 : ได้ตามที่เสี่ยงทาย to receive according to what was requested of the oracles : แตกเป็นเสี่ยง to be shattered into pieces : เสี่ยงเคราะห์ to pray to the spirits that ill-fortune may be averted, but if all is propitious, let come what will : เสี่ยงโชค to propitiate the spirits for luck or fortune ; see โชค p. 303 : เสี่ยงทาย to prognosticate by casting lots ; to consult the spirits (as to the auspiciousness or otherwise of an undertaking or act) ; to consult the priests, soothsayers and magicians (this is commonly resorted to before buying lottery tickets) :

เสี่ยงบุญเสี่ยงกรรม to recite incantations that the merit in past existences may bring prosperity in the present life : เสี่ยงวาสนา to recite incantations requesting the divinities to favour or facilitate the gaining of a title, position of honour, or rank : เสี่ยงศร to propitiate the spirits for the effectiveness of arrows : เสี่ยงสาว to propitiate the spirits for propitiousness of philters and conversations : เสี่ยงสัตย์ to recite magical formulas that the honest desires of one's heart may be attained (as in the effort to abstain from intoxicants).

เสียด   see-at[4] *v.* to rub or scratch against; to feel a griping pain, or stitch in the side : *n.* a piercing, lancinating pain ; a griping sensation in the stomach ; a stitch in the muscles of the side; see ขอก p. 667; จุก p. 235 : เบียดเสียดเข้าไป to squeeze, press or push one's way into, or through (as in a crowd of people) : พูดเสียดสี, ส่อเสียด, เสียดส่อ to provoke or excite by contemptuous comparisons : เสียดแซก to squeeze or press into very close quarters : เสียดท้อง to suffer with a lancinating, griping pain or colic in the abdomen : ปวดเสียดแทง to suffer from a piercing pain (as in pleurisy) : เสียดขอก a griping, piercing pain : พูดเสียดแทง to injure the feelings of another by sharp piercing words.

เสี้ยน   see-an[3] *n.* a thorn; a splinter (run into the flesh); a needle-like piece split off from a solid body (as cactus thorns) : คนนั้น-เป็นเสี้ยนหนาม that person is a menace (to law and order) : เป็นเสี้ยนหนามแก่รัฐบาล instigators of disorder; disturbers of the peace : เสี้ยนตาล tough wire-like fibers of the toddy-palm : เสี้ยนขอก to be run into by a splinter or cactus thorn : เสี้ยนศัตรู *simili* enemies in a camp; traitors to a cause : เสี้ยนแก่ศาสนา traitors in a religious sect or community : เสี้ยนหนาม *simile* foe; enemy; opponents; disturbers of the peace of a community : เสี้ยน-หนามแผ่นดิน traitors; rebels; insurgents; revolters; revolutionists : ผักเสี้ยน, ผักเสี้ยนผี

see ผัก p. 544.

เสียบ   see-ap[4] *v.* to thrust into; to pin on to, or fix at a point; to stick into or insert at some designated points (as when running a line through a forest, small flags are stuck on trees in the line); see แทง p. 427 : เสียบ-แทง to impale to the floor, or to a log by the thrust of a knife or sword : เสียบอก to thrust into the chest (letting the knife or javelin remain) : เสียบประจานนักโทษทั้งเป็น to fasten criminals to a stake publicly as a warning to others : เสียบปลายไม้ to pass through a loop and fasten on to the end of a pole (as a flag) : เสียบปลาปิ้ง to spit fish : เสียบหนู (ไม้) the vowel marks changing a short vowel to a long vowel as, อิ to อี or อี; sharpened, barbed bamboo staples. These are of quartered or split bamboo stalks about 24 inches long, serving an important part in the nipa thatch roofing of Thai houses. In the process of roofing, the attap strips are stitched, and, beginning at the eaves, are laid overlapping each other up to the ridge pole. There are two full lengths of split strips of bamboo, containing perforations about three feet apart made to match each other. These are placed, one on each side of, and parallel with the ridge pole. They are held in place by the staples which are thrust through the perforated strip on one side, passing under the ridge pole and out through the perforation on the opposite side, engaging all three and holding them together firmly : เอาดาบ-เสียบฝัก to thrust or insert the sword into the scabbard : เอาผู้ร้ายไปเสียบไม้ to impale a criminal with a stake.

เสียม ๑   see-am[2] *n.* a small hand-spade. This has a handle a metre long, and a small rounded blade like that of a garden trowel.

เสียม ๒   see-am[2] *Cam. n. obsolete form* Siam : เสียมราฐ, สยามราบ *obsolete* a Cambodian city.

เสี้ยม   see-am[3] *v.* to grind down, or whittle

to a point; to sharpen to a point: เสี้ยมปลายให้แหลม to whittle the end to a sharp point: เสี้ยมไม้, เสี้ยมเหล็ก to put a point on wood or iron: เสี้ยมสอน to sharpen another's wits; to instruct privately (as Herodias instructed her daughter); to be advised (secretly); to be put on one's guard by private information; to instil hatred or animosity in the heart of a person.

เสียว   see-oh[2] *v.* to produce neuralgic pain; to cause a darting pain (as when an exposed dental pulp is touched): เสียวฟัน a hyper-sensative condition of denuded teeth: เสียวสร้าน a state of general excitability: เสียวไส้ to have a sense of revulsion at the sight of something revolting: เสียวหวาด to have a giddy feeling at the sight of blood; to experience fear, fright, or pain; to shudder or tremble (as when looking down from a high building).

เสียว   see-oh[4] *v.* to switch, attack, strike, pierce or prick with horns or antlers; to swoop down upon, and seize suddenly (as a hawk on little chickens); see เฉี่ยว p. 272; ขวิด p. 146: กระบือเสียว the buffalo attacks with its horns.

เสียว   see-oh[3] *n.* a quarter; one-fourth part; *adj.* tapering to a point, being partly visible (as a quarter face in a photograph); being thinner or narrower at one end than at the other; bias (said of cloth when cut diagonally): ตัดไม้เสียว the wood is not cut true to the square on all sides.

เสือ   sur-ah[2] *n.* tiger; see ขาล p. 155: ข้อเสือ an angular lever; a crank shaft: ที่นั่นเสือชุม that place abounds in tigers: เสือกินวัว a game played on a checker board with sixteen squares and sixteen pieces, four being tigers and twelve being cows: เสือข้ามห้วย the game of *leap-frog*: เสือโคร่ง, เสือพยัคฆ์ *Felis tigris* (*Felidae*), the tiger (N. H. J. S. S. III. 2, p. 121: BURK. p. 998): เสือดำ the black tiger, a colour phase of *F. pardus*, especially common in Peninsular Thailand: เสือดาว, เสือลายตลับ the leopard, *Felis viverrina*; *Felis pardus*, the panther (BURK. p. 998): เสือตกถัง an automatic rat-trap. This rat-trap is so made that the bait is balanced on a platform at one end of a beam, which slides up and down in a box. When the rat gets on, the beam being over-balanced, disappears down into the cage below. The rat in trying to escape leaves the platform into an adjoining compartment. The platform, by the counter-weight, rises again into place ready for another rat to go through the same process: เสือปลา tiger cat; fishing cat, *Felis viverrina* (N. H. J. S. S. III, 2, p. 122): เสือป่า, ลูกเสือ the Wild Tiger Scout Organization—established during the reign of King Rama VI: เสือป่าแมวเซา, เสือแมวมอง an ancient organization of army scouts whose duty it was to wait in ambush and cut off or capture the provisions of the enemy: เสือไฟ the golden cat, *Felis temmincki* (N. H. J. S. S. III, 2, p. 122): เสือสิงห์ tigers and lions in general: เสือหมอบ a rank growing weed of roadsides and abandoned clearings, with small blue flowers. It is also known as หญ้าเมืองวาย *Eupatorium odoratum* (*Compositae*): หางเสือ (เรือ) a rudder; the helm.

เสื่อ, สาด   sur-ah[4] *n.* a mat; matting: เสื่อกก rush-mats; mats woven with the dried split stalks of *Cyperus tegetiformis* (*Cyperaceae*) which grows in Madagascar, China, India, and Japan, giving material for matting and string in Hong Kong and Indo-China. It does not extend farther south (BURK. p. 732): เสื่อกะจูด mats made of *Lepironia mucronata* (*Cyperaceae*) (BURK. p. 1331): เสื่อคล้า mats woven with *Maranta dichotoma* (*Marantaceae*): เสื่อเตย mats woven from the leaves of *Pandanus leram* (*Pandanaceae*): เสื่อหวาย mats woven from strips of rattan: เสื่ออ่อน a soft mat woven from the leaves of *Metroxylon sagus* (*Palmae*), the sago palm (BURK. p. 1460).

เสื้อ   sur-ah[3] *n.* a coat; a dress; a garment:

ผีเสื้อ butterflies : เสื้อกระบอก a mother hubbard dress : เสื้อกั๊ก a fitted jacket ; a vest : เสื้อกันหนาว an overcoat : เสื้อเกราะ coats of mail : เสื้อนอน night clothes ; pajamas : เสื้อผ้า clothing : เสื้อฝน rain-coats : เสื้อราตรีสโมสร evening clothes (for gentlemen) : เสื้อรัดเอว a corset.

เสือก seu-ak[4] v. to push, thrust at, or shove to or into (rudely) : adj. butting in on another's business ; rude ; impertinent ; officious (in what does not concern that person) ; see ทะลึ่ง p. 407 : เสือกกะโหลก, เสือกกระบาล lit. "to thrust one's skull into ill-chosen places," i. e. rude ; foolish ; officious ; saying what does not pertain to, or concern a person but only annoys or interrupts others (a rude phrase and used as a curse) : เสือกเรือลงน้ำ to push or shove a boat on dry land down into the water : เสือกสน to interfere while others are busy (by asking annoying questions) : เสือกให้ to shove something at another with an air of rudeness : เสือกไส to carry off secretly or entice away from one's residence (as in an elopement) ; to conceal the flight or escape of (as prisoners or outlaws) ; to facilitate an escape by obscure means.

เสื้อน้ำ sur-ah[3]-num[5] n. a water demon supposed to haunt deserted lakes.

เสื่อม seu-am[4] v. to deteriorate ; to degenerate ; to be depraved, corrupted, or vitiated (in character) ; to decrease in severity ; to decline or lessen in quantity, quality, number, or self-respect : คนเสื่อมชาติ a reprobate : เสื่อมจากผลดี to have the good results that might accrue lessened by evil conduct : เสื่อมลง to become corrupted or indifferent, in principle and practice (as religious practices) : เสื่อมสูญ gradually to decrease till the vanishing point is reached : เสื่อมสร่าง to have the effects of a drug or remedy gradually decrease till a normal condition exists ; to sleep off a spell (as of fever).

เสื้อเมือง sur-ah[3]-meu-ang n. a tutelary deity ; deities of a city.

แส saa[2] v. to settle (as boundaries) ; to adjust, rectify, or make harmonize (as accounts, difficulties or misunderstandings) ; " to lay all the cards on the table" ; see แฉ p. 273 ; ชำระ p. 295 : แสความ to make a full and free confession or explanation : แสแฉเบี้ย to expose to full view all the cowries (as in a form of gambling) : แสนา to measure the area of a field, farm, or plot of land ; to verify the boundaries of a land-holding : แสงอน coquettish ; pretended fondness.

แส่ saa[4] v. to instigate, incite, provoke animate, stir up or stimulate (as to some lawlessness) ; to push or shove rudely (as with the foot) ; to seek or enquire for (as an occasion or opportunity to stir up trouble) ; see ค้น p. 176 : แส่ความ to revive a matter or subject once hushed up ; to rekindle a quarrel : แส่หา to enquire for seekingly.

แส้ saa[3] n. a whip ; a switch ; a tassel ; a fan ; a mosquito wisp made of horse or yak hairs, having a handle : แส้จามรี a wisp or tassel made of yak hairs : แส้บั่น a ramrod ; a cleaning rod (for guns or cannon) : แส้ม้า a horse-hair wisp ; a horse-whip : แส้หวาย a rattan whip.

แสก saak[4] n. a space where the hair divides ; a dividing line ; a middle line of separation or demarcation : ผมตกแสก hair falling on either side of the parting line : แสกกระดูก the line of union or demarcation between bones : แสกผม a line of parting of the hair : แสกหน้า the median or dividing line of the face, forehead, and skull.

แสง saang[2] n. arms ; weapons ; swords ; munitions of war ; rays of light ; brightness radiating from a luminous source : ดาบฝังแสง a sword inlaid with brilliants : โรงช่างแสง an arsenal : แสงขรรค์, แสงพระขรรค์ the royal sceptre : แสงพระจันทร์ moonlight : แสงดาว starlight ; star brightness : แสงทอง, แสงเงิน the golden rays of dawn : แสงประกาย

flashing lights of burning sparks : แสง-
พระอาทิตย์, แสงแดด the sun's rays : แสงฟ้า
lightning : แสงไฟ, แสงเพลิง the brightness
of fire ; the reflected light of a conflagration
against the sky : แสงแวบ ๆ วาบ ๆ twinkling or flashing light (as of the fire-fly) :
แสงอาทิตย์ (งู) a venomous snake having a brilliant purple skin, *Xenopeltis unicolor* (smith,
N. H. J. S. S. I, 1, p. 12).

แสด (สี)   saat[4] *adj.* reddish yellow ; orange
yellow : คำแสด (ต้น) see จำปู้ (ต้น) p. 248.

แสดง ๑ see สำแดง ๒ p. 860.

แสดง ๒   sa[4]-daang *v.* to show, demonstrate, manifest, explain or point out to ; see
สำแดง ๑ p. 860 : แสดงความอาฆาต to utter
threats ; to threaten to inflict pain or injury
vindictively : แสดงน้ำใจดี to manifest goodwill towards others.

แสน   saan[2] *n.* a conferred rank among the
Laos ; a numeral followed by five cyphers ;
one hundred thousand : *adj.* endless ; boundless ; numberless ; limitless : เจ้าเล่ห์แสนกล
a beguiler ; a conjurer ; a deceiver : แสน-
คำนึงถึง to have unceasing thoughts of love
and devotion : แสนแค้น heart-aches by the
thousands ; limitless vexations ; sore aggra-
vations : แสนงอน uppish ; snobbish ; self-
assertive ; pretending ; feigning : แสนดี the
very best possible ; goodness (to the superlative degree) : แสนทวี increased a hundred
thousand times : แสนที่จะประจาน to be unceasingly talked about in public : แสนรัก,
แสนอาลัย love to a boundless degree : แสนรู้
knowledge to a limitless degree : แสนเล่ห์-
แสนกล expert in black art : แสนโศรก
in the very depths of sorrow and despair :
แสนสลดใจ, แสนสงสาร to have pity or compassion for, to a boundless degree ; to feel an
intense degree of compassion for (as Jesus
Christ did for the multitude when they were
without food) : แสนสาหัส, แสนเข็ญ to have
to undergo oppressions, afflictions and torments to the extreme limit of one's endurance
(as floggings and chains in a jail).

แสนง see แขนง p. 163.

แสนย์, แสนยา   saan[2] *n.* soldiers ; infantry ;
an army : แสนยากร an army ; troops :
แสนยานุภาพ the fighting strength or efficiency
of an army.

แสบ   saap[4] *v.* to smart ; to sting with pain :
adj. stinging ; biting ; piercing (pain). ปวด-
แสบปวดร้อน a burning stinging pain (as from
a burn or scald) ; the pain of erysipelas :
แสบตา a smarting of the eyes ; obnoxious to
the sight : แสบท้อง to feel the pangs of
hunger : แสบใบหู a stinging pain in the
ear ; *idiomatic* sharp, poignant, caustic remarks : แสบบ่า a smarting of the skin of
the shoulder (as from constant carrying of
loads suspended from a stick).

แสม   sa[4]-maa[2] *n. Aegiceras corniculatum*
(*Myrsinaceae*), a bush or small tree, abundant
on mud above tide-limit, used as firewood. It
grows in marshy, salty ground (BURK. p. 54) :
ปูแสม a species of small, edible crab salted
and sold : ลิงแสม a species of monkey living in seaside groves : แสมขาว (ต้น) *A. tomentosa,* a tree supplying a good firewood :
แสมดำ, แสมทะเล (ต้น) *A. officinalis,* a tree attaining 60 feet in height, sporadic on the
banks of rivers in their course through the
mangrove belt. It is found from Persia to
Hong Kong and New Guinea (V. P. p. 251 :
BURK. p. 275) : แสมสาร (ต้น) *Thai Cassia
garrettiana* (*Leguminosae*), a tree whose
heart-wood is used as pins in boat-making
(cb. p. 510 : V. P. p. 251) :

แสยง   sa[4]-yaang[2] *v.* to fear ; to be afraid
of, or dread ; to have the creeps (as of the
feeling of insects creeping on the flesh) at
the sight of a disgusting or revolting object ;
see กลัว p. 60 ; คร้าม p. 181 : แสยงขน to
have the hair stand on end (as from sudden
fear or fright).

แสยะ   sa[4]-yaa[4] *v.* to make a cross, wry
face while showing the teeth : *n.* an exaggerated grinning expression with the mouth

half open and the fangs showing in a most menacing manner, the sculptor's idea of a giant (as are seen standing as guardians at the gates of some temples): แสยะยิ้ม to wear a tiger-like grimace.

แสรก see **สาแหรก** p. 860.

แสร้ง saang[3] *v.* to pretend, feign or simulate; to do wilfully or purposely; see แกล้ง p. 129: แสร้งว่า to make mean remarks about another designedly.

แสลง sa[4]-laang[2] *adj.* harmful; hurtful, prejudicial to one's health; irritating to the mucus membrane (as along the intestinal tract); unwholesome; injurious: แสลงใจ (ต้น) see กะกลึ้ง p. 69: แสลงตา irritating to the eyes: งดการรับประทานของแสลง to abstain from injurious foods, or from what will retard recovery.

แสวง sa[4]-waang[2] *v.* to seek, search or look for; see ค้น p. 176: แสวงหา to search for carefully (as the woman for the lost coin); to go in search of.

โสก see **โศก** p. 802.

โสกโดก sok[4]-gka[4]-doke[4] *adj.* obscene; vulgar; shameless; immodest.

โสกันต์ soh[2]-gkun *v.* to perform the tonsorial ceremony: *n.* the ceremony of shaving off the topknot of royal children.

โสกินี soh[2]-gki[4]-nee *P. n.* a sorrowing, mourning woman; a woman wearing mourning.

โสกี soh[2]-gkee *P. n.* sadness; a man wearing mourning; a man in sorrow or grief (Chd. p. 482).

โสโครก soh[2]-kroke[3] *adj.* dirty; foul; squalid; filthy; nasty; unclean: พูดโสโครก to use obscene or immodest language: หิน-โสโครก submerged or uncharted rocks.

โสณ soh[2]-na[6] *P. n.* a dog (Chd. p. 482).

โสณห์ soh[2]-na[6] *P. n.* a ruffian; a drunkard; an intoxicated person; one fond of, or addicted to drink (Chd. p. 482).

โสณิ soh[2]-ni[6] *P. n.* the buttocks (Chd. p. p. 482); see ตะโพก p. 355.

โสต sote[4] *n.* a theme; a subject; a point; a clause (as in a charge or indictment); a celibate; celibacy: *adj.* single; unmarried; free; independent: ชายโสต a bachelor: หญิงโสต a spinster: หนึ่งโสต moreover; besides what has been said; another point is this—.

โสตก soh[2]-dok[4] *P. adj.* little; small; short; slight (Chd. p. 504).

โสตม soh[2]-dom *S. v.* to praise (Chd. p. 505); to admire, eulogize, applaud, extol, or commend.

โสดา ๑ soh[2]-dah *n.* a hearer; a listener (Chd. p. 483).

โสดา ๒ soh[2]-dah *P. n.* stream; flood; torrent (Chd. p. 483); a current or natural stream; a watercourse; *lit.* "the state of entering into the stream of wisdom," *i. e.* the first degree of sanctity or saintship (Ala. p. 170): โสดาบันน์ an enterer into the stream of wisdom, or one who has attained the first degree of saintship. The saint who has attained this step cannot still have more than seven births among men and angels before he enters Nirvana (Ala. p. 170): โสดาปัตติมรรค the first stage, step or degree in the attaining of the state of saving truth, or the highest degree of saintship (Ala. p. 171): โสดาปัตติผล the fruits or results accruing to one who has attained the first degree towards saintship.

โสต ๑ soh[2]-dta[4] *P. n.* the ear or organ of hearing; a hole; an opening; an aperture (Chd. 483): เงี่ยโสต to give heed to what is being said; to listen attentively: โสตประสาท the auditory nerve.

โสต ๒ soh²-dta⁴ *P. n.* stream; flood; torrent; current or course of water; rivulet; spring (chd. p. 483).

โสตถิ soh²-dta⁴-ti⁴ *P. n.* health; welfare; blessing; happiness (chd. p. 483); a farewell salutation; adieu.

โสตก soh²-tok⁶ *P. n.* a waterway; a canal: *adj.* containing (water) (chd. p. 481).

โสทร soh²-taun *P. n.* sons of the same mother (chd. p. 481).

โสทรี soh²-ta⁶-ree *n.* daughters of the [same mother.

โสธก soh²-tok⁶ *P. n.* one who cleanses; a washerman (chd. p. 481).

โสธนะ soh²-ta⁶-na⁶ *P. n.* the act of purifying; correcting mistakes: โสธนบัตร erratum.

โสน sa⁴-noh² *Thai* (ต้น) *Sesbania roxburghii* (*Leguminosae*), a tall, marsh plant found in south-eastern Asia and Malaysia; in the Peninsula it is not common, but occurs here and there down the west side. It is planted as garden fences in Bengal. The Thai eat the leaves during the last four months of the year. The leaves and young branches are fed to cattle. The edible flowers are yellow and slightly fragrant; the leaves resemble those of the tamarind. In India the leaves are much used in poultices and the seeds are a stimulant emmenagogue and astringent. The very soft wood is made into toys, mats, etc. (cb. p. 440: burk. p. 1998): โสนคางคก *Thai* (ต้น) *Aeschynomene aspera* (*Leguminosae*), the sola-plant, a marsh-plant, almost shrubby. It is found in Thailand, at least as far south as Bangkok, and in Java. The very light pith of the stem is used in India in the making of sun-helmets or sola-topis, and most efficiently protects the head from the sun. The manufacture is largely carried on in Calcutta, because the supply of pith from the neighbouring swamps is large. The pith undergoes no preparation except drying. It is also used for making models of temples, artificial flowers, etc. of temporary use. It is also used to make floats for nets. The Thai make charcoal from it with which they blacken the books of *Streblus* wood whereon they write with crayon (burk. p. 59); *A. indica*, a marsh-weed found up and down the Peninsula in open swamps. There seems to be no special economic use for it (cb. p. 401: burk. p. 59): โสนหางไก่ a small, aquatic plant with edible leaves.

โสนหวง sa⁴-noh²-hoo-ang² *Cam. n.* a valley.

โสภ, เสาวภา soh²-pa⁶ *P. v.* to shine; to be radiant or beautiful (chd. p. 481); to be handsomely or richly dressed; to be conspicuous in one's dress.

โสภา soh²-pah *P. n.* splendour; radiance; light; beauty (chd. p. 481).

โสภิณี soh²-pi⁶-nee *n.* a beautiful woman.

โสเภณี, นครโสเภณี, นครโสภิณี soh²-pay-nee *n.* prostitutes; women of the street.

โสม ๑ som² *Thai, Bangkok n. Talinum patens* (*Portulacaceae*), a small, handsome shrub with variegated foliage, native of tropical America. It is cultivated by the Thai for ornamental and medicinal uses, the swollen roots being employed (cb. p. 110: v. p. p. 266: burk. p. 2121): โสมคน (ต้น) *Aralia quinquefolia* (*Araliaceae*), ginseng, a well-known plant in the Far East which supplies a root much used in pharmacy. This root, which is largely dug in Manchuria, China and Japan, grows in fanciful shapes which has added to the esteem in which it is held. The real properties depend, apparently, on the presence of a saponin (mcm. p. 373: burk. p. 211).

โสม ๒ som² *S. n.* the juice of a milky climbing plant, *Asclepias acida*, extracted and fermented, forming a beverage offered in libations to the deities, and drunk by the Brahmins (chd. p. 301).

โสม ๓ som[2] *P. n.* the moon (chd. p. 482).

โสมนัส, โสมนัสส์ som[2]-ma[6]-nat[6] *P. n.* satisfaction; enjoyment; joyousness (chd. p. 482); rejoicings; exultations; see ปลาบปลื้มใจ under ปลาบ p. 512.

โสมม soh[2]-mom *adj.* besmeared; muddy; dirty; filthy; foul; slovenly.

โสร่ง sa[4]-rong[4] *Malay n.* a garment worn especially by Malays, both men and women. It is a cylindrical piece of cloth of sufficient length so that it is doubled over in front, and held in place by tying or by a belt. A pasin is similar but narrower; the sarong.

โสรจ sote[4] *v.* to bathe; to wash; to cleanse or purify (with water); see ชำระ p. 295: โสรจสรง to pour on, or apply water in the act of bathing (as in the ceremony of purification of royalty).

โสวรรณ soh[2]-wan *adj.* golden; pertaining to gold; abounding with gold.

โสหุ้ย soh[2]-hu-ie[3] *Chin. n.* expenses; disbursements.

โสฬส soh[2]-lot[6] *P. adj.* sixteenth (chd. p. 482); sixteen: *n.* an obsolete copper coin which, when in use, was worth half of an att: โสฬสมหาพรหม the sixteenth tier of heaven.

ใส sai[2] *adj.* clear; bright; pure; transparent; unclouded; translucent; limpid: ความ-ใสสอาด pure; undefiled in heart and character: ใจใสสอาด pure in heart: ด้วยน้ำใส-ใจจริง with a clear conscience; with a heart true and pure (as clear water): ผ่องใส untarnished (as character): เลื่อมใสศัทธา true fidelity and allegiance; with pure devotion: ใสสอาด perfectly clean and pure: หน้าแจ่มใส a clear open countenance.

ใส่ sai[4] *v.* to insert (as a pin or staple); to put into (as clothes into a wardrobe); to put on (as garments): ใส่ยา to apply a remedy: อย่าใส่ความเขา refrain from calumniating or slandering thy neighbour: เอาใจใส่ pay attention to; take heed of; take to heart; put your heart into the work or instructions being given: เอาน้ำใส่ถังให้เต็ม fill the bucket with water: เอาลูกปืนใส่ load the gun: ใส่ความ, ใส่ไคล้ to impute, charge or attribute: แกล้งใส่ความ to calumniate; to accuse or defame falsely; to impute undeservingly; see แกล้ง p. 129: ใส่ตรวน to put in irons: ใส่ใจ to bear in mind; to listen attentively; to remember faithfully to do; to engrave upon the tablets of one's heart.

ไส sai[2] *v.* to push forward or away from; to shove, thrust or press forward; see รุน p. 716: ไสกบ to plane; to push a handplane: ไสช้าง to move with a pushing, shoving, forward motion (as is done by the mahout while riding an elephant to make it go faster): ไสต่อ to urge, animate or incite to more aggressive actions or methods (as one going to law is urged forward by his friends): ไสไป to shove forward: ไสเสือก *idiomatic* to urge on by pushing: ไสหัว, ดุนหัว to shove or push the head (as of a child to make it go away, a harsh method of getting rid of a child).

ไส้ sai[3] *n.* bowels; the intestines; the wick of candles or lamps; the contents, or what is put in: คนไส้เดียวกัน those of the same mother: เบี้ยต่อไส้ to live a hand to mouth existence; to exist on each day's earnings: ยาขับไส้เดือน remedies for the expulsion of intestinal worms (as santonin): ไส้กรอก sausage: ไส้ด้ายดิบ wicks of unbleached thread: ไส้เดือน earthworms (used for baiting fish-hooks); intestinal worms (as pinworms, seatworms and tapeworms): ไส้ตัน (ปลา) a very small salt water fish, *Corica soborna (Clupeidae)* (suvatti p. 9): ไส้ตัน the appendix: ไส้ตันอักเสบ appendicitis: ไส้ตัวเองเป็นหนองเอ็ง one incriminating himself or his friends will come to naught: ไส้พุง *colloquial* the intestines (collectively); see พุง p. 592: ไส้เลื่อน hernia: ไส้ศึก a spy; a fire-brand (socially); a secret mutineer; a traitor (to party or country); one who secretly instigates a plot against his employer or superior (as by inciting others).

ไสถย, ไถย see เถยยะ p. 390.

ไสย sai² *n.* a treatise of great importance; books of special teachings; the tenets of Brahminical philosophers: ไสยเวท the science of magical art as taught by the Brahminical philosophers: ไสยศาสตร์ philosophies; beliefs; magical art; black art, as taught and practiced by the Brahmins.

ไสยา, เสยยา sai²-yah *v.* to lie down; to sleep: ไสยาสน์ a combined bed and seat; *Thai* a couch; a bed.

ไสร้ sai³ *adj.* true; real; certain; see จริง p. 232; เที่ยง p. 425.

ไสว sa⁴-wai² *adj.* much; abundant; ample; copious; plentiful; see ดั้น p. 331.

ไส้หมินปี่ sai³-min²-bpee⁴ *n.* a sweet, melodious voice; a voice pleasing in tone and volume.

ห

ห The forty-first letter of the Thai alphabet, a high class letter of which there are eleven, *viz.* ข, ข. ฉ, ถ, ฐ, ผ, ฝ, ศ, ษ, ส, ห. หอหีบ is the popular name. It corresponds to the English "h". In Thai it is used as an initial consonant followed by ง, ญ, ณ, น, ม, ย, ล, ว, ฬ in order that the word may be pronounced according to the rules governing high class consonants, *e. g.* หญ้า, หงอย.

หก hok⁴ *v.* to spill; to splash over (as tea from a cup); to cause to flow over the edge or rim; to lower or tilt one side: *n.* a species of parrot similar to the Malayan parrot. It gets its name from the position it assumes while sleeping, hanging its head downward; the numeral six: โกหก to prevaricate; to lie: ตะพานหก a tilting, or lifting bridge: ที่หก the sixth: นกหก *colloquial* for birds in general: หกกลับ to return or retrace one's steps: หกคว่ำ to tilt or lean till completely overturned; to capsize: หกกะเมน to turn a somersault; to make a revolution in the air, head first (as acrobats): หกที six times, or occasions: หกบ่า to spill or flow over from a dish (as curry from a falling or tilted dish): หกมา to tilt or cant to the near side: หกมาทางนี้

imperative slope or slant it this way: หกล้ม to slip or stumble, and fall: หกล้มหงาย to fall backwards: หกสิบ sixty: หกหลัง to turn back after going only a short distance: หกหัน to modulate tones: อย่าให้หกไป *imperative* do not tilt for fear the contents will spill over.

หงกๆ ngok⁴-ngok⁴ *adj.* embarrassed; puzzled; confused; dazed; bewildered (conditions resulting from too speedy action),

หงส์, หังส hong² *P. S. n.* a goose; a swan (chd. p. 151); *Thai* a swan: หงส์ทอง the golden mallard: หงสคติ resembling swans in actions: หงสบาท *lit.* "resembling the colour of a swan's foot," *i. e.* pink; reddish yellow: หงสโปดก goslings: หงสรถ *lit.* "having a swan as a means of transportation," *i. e.* the god Brahma: หงสราช king of the swans; the imperial swan.

หงสาวดี hong²-sah²-wa⁶-dee *n.* Pegu, the ancient capital city of the Peguans.

หงอก ngauk⁴ *adj.* grey or white (descriptive of the human hair): ผมหงอก white hair.

หง่องๆ ngaung⁴-ngaung⁴ *adv.* hurriedly; hastily; acceleratedly (descriptive of a person walking).

หงองแหงง   ngaung²-ngaang² *adj.* growing; snarling: *onomat.* from the sound of dogs fighting.

หงอด ๆ   ngaut⁴-ngaut⁴ *adj.* tardy; slow; delayed in recovery (descriptive of one with a chronic disease).

หงอน   ngaun² *n.* the comb of fowls: หงอนไก่ *Thai,* ตะลิงปลิงป่า *Thai, Ratburi,* หงอนไก่หน่วย *Thai, Chumpawn* (ต้น) *Cnestis palala (Connaraceae),* a small liane, found from the delta of the Irrawaddy to Sumatra and the Philippine Islands. The Malays use it medicinally. They boil the roots and drink the decoction for stomach-ache; they poultice the abdomen with the boiled roots; they give the same decoction to women after childbirth; for malaria they use a decoction of it with *Phyllanthus pulcher*; and they foment with it for sprains (BURK. p. 591: CB. p. 365); *Heritiera littoralis (Sterculiaceae),* cock's comb, a low-growing, much branched tree found on the warmer coasts of the Indian and Pacific oceans. The timber is dark brown, crooked, tough, and durable; trees sufficiently straight to be valuable are scarce. The tree grows slowly. It is valued for masts, when it can be got straight enough, and, in eastern Malaysia, for rudders. Other uses are for canoes, outriggers, firewood, house-posts, joists, presses, telegraph poles, wheel-hubs, and boat ribs. It is certainly one of the toughest of Malayan timbers. It is also moderately durable when buried in the soil. The peoples of Malaysia formerly valued it for stopping bullets. They built stockades of it and raised the gunwales of their pirate canoes with it. The bark contains tannin to the extent of 14 per cent of the dry matter, which is very little; but it is said to be used in the Philippine Islands for toughening fishing-nets. The tree is medicinal in the Moluccas, an extract of the seeds being used for diarrhoea and dysentery. The twigs are used for tooth-brushes; it may be that the

tannin in them is beneficial to the gums. The seeds are eaten with fish when seeds of *Parinarium glaberrimum,* which are preferred, are not available (BURK. p. 1140: CB. p. 170): หงอนไก่เล็ก *Thai, Chumpawn* (ต้น) *Santaloides villosum (Connaraceae)* (CB. p. 361): หงอนไก่เอื้อง (ต้น) *Dendrobium secundum (Orchidaceae)* (V. P. p. 74: BURK. p. 778).

หง่อม   ngaum⁴ *adj.* very old; decrepit; bent over with age; over-ripe (as fruit); badly battered by rough usage.

หงอย   ngoy² *adj.* uninteresting; dreary; lonesome; sad; sleepy; inactive; sluggish: หงอยก๋อย dejected; disheartened; depressed; lonesome; bored; descriptive of a person brooding (as Jonah under the gourd).

หง่อย   ngoy⁴ *adv,* slowly; deliberately; dilatorily; inactively; see ค่อย p. 192.

หงัก ๆ   nguk⁴-nguk⁴ *adv.* shaking; shivering; quivering; agitated (descriptive of the condition during the cold' spell in malarial fever, or convulsions).

หงับ   ngup⁴ *adv.* opening and closing rapidly (as the mouth of a fish when out of water); lowering and raising (as the jaws while eating), (descriptive of the motion of the mouth and jaw).

หง่าง   ngang⁴ *onomat.* from the sound of ringing or clanging of a bell, bells, or cymbals.

หงาย   ngai² *v.* to turn up; to lay or lie face up; to recover the position of being right side up (as righting a capsized boat): เดือนหงาย *lit.* "the moon's face is turned up," *i. e.* full moon; the period of moonlight: นอนหงาย to lie flat on the back: ปลานอนหงายท้อง the fish lie around with their bellies up; the fish float around dead: หงายถ้วย to drain the cup: หงายหน้าขึ้น to turn up the face, or bend back the head.

หง่าว   ngow⁴ *n.* a kind of kite made with tensely drawn strings that vibrate in the

currents of air, making sounds like this
word: *adv.* lonesomely ; solitarily ; drearily ;
see เงิน p. 259 : *onomat.* from the sound of
the mewing of a cat.

หงำ ngum[2] *adv.* excessively ; unreasonably ;
see จัด p. 238 : เมาหงำ very drunk ; dead
drunk : หงำเหงอะ doting ; doltish ; incapable ; incompetent ; unfitted ; irresponsible (as
from old age).

หงิก ngik[4] *adj.* curly ; wrinkled ; creased ;
fluted : นิ้วมือหงิก the fingers are bent and
stiff : ใบไม้หงิก convoluted leaves : ผมหงิก
curly hair.

หงิง ๆ nging[2]-nging[2] *onomat.* soft ; gentle
(descriptive of crying).

หงิม ngim[2] *v.* to be of a reserved, silent,
polite, courteous nature ; see เจียม p. 259.

หงิก ๆ nguk[4]-nguk[4] *adj.* winking or blinking (of the eyes) ; a raising of the eye-brows ;
a motioning or sign-making with the head ;
descriptive of a nervous twitching of some
facial muscle.

หงุงหงิง ngoong[2]-nging[2] *onomat.* descriptive of soft, gentle, tender speech.

หงุบ ngoop[4] *v.* to nod the head (as one
who goes to sleep while sitting) ; see ฟุบ
p. 609.

หงุ่ย see ขลุกขลุ่ย p. 144.

หญ้า yah[3] *n.* grass or low herb ; *a prefix to
which the particular designating name is
added* : สนามหญ้า lawn ; a grass plot : หญ้า-
เก็็ดหอย *Laos, Chiengmai, Drymaria cordata*
(*Caryophyllaceae*), a fodder plant of small size.
It grows so freely on estates in the hills of
Ceylon that it has come under observation as
a plant perhaps useful for covering the soil.
Though not its natural habitat, it is found in
the Malay Peninsula. The Bataks in Sumatra
regard the juice as a laxative, and in Java it
is given for fever (Burk. p. 861 : cb. p. 108) :

หญ้าเกล็ดหอย, หญ้าเกล็ดปลา *Thai, Bangkok,* หญ้า-
ตานทราย *Laos, Chiengmai, Desmodium triflorum* (*Leguminosae*), a small herb found
throughout the tropics ; in the Peninsula it
occurs as short grass on lawns, road-sides, and
other artificial places. It has been tried in
pure culture as a cover crop, but pests attack
it badly. In Ceylon it has been used on tea
estates ; but condemned. Cattle eat it, but it
does not yield much fodder. In Java it is
medicinal, being given in an infusion for
diarrhoea, and is used for dysentery. The
Malays drink a decoction of the roots for
stomach-ache. The plant is also used for
poulticing. In south India the fresh leaves
are applied to wounds and abscesses which do
not heal well (Burk. p. 795) ; *Hydrocotyle sib-
thorpioides* (*Umbelliferae*), an herb found
extensively in south-eastern Asia ; but rare in
the Malay Peninsula. In Malaya it may be
mixed with sugar-candy and cassia bark, and
given to children for coughs. The juice is
emetic. The leaves may be pounded with
alum for poulticing the scrotum if affected by
a skin disease. In Indo-China the root may
be chewed for liver complaints (Burk. p. 1212 :
cb. pp. 419, 787 : McM. p. 452) : หญ้าไก่นกคุ้ม
Elephantopus scaber (*Compositae*), an herb
found throughout the tropics. It has been
conjectured that it reached the Philippine
Islands from America across the Pacific by
Spanish agency. It has a basal rosette of
leaves in which the Malays see the pentacle
seal of Solomon, by which he confined the
jinns underground. It is found almost all
through the tropics in pasturage, as an undesirable weed ; for it occupies, by means of
its pentacle which lies flat on the ground,
more than its share of space ; but cattle will
eat it. As Solomon's seal, it is reputed to be
potent in all diseases. Thus it is used in a decoction of the leaves or roots as a preventative
medicine after child-birth, in tonics, to drive
out round worms, for coughs, for venereal
diseases, etc. Chinese herbalists, domiciled

in Malaya, stock it fresh in their shops; and seem to be accepting it as a drug to stock dry. The Malays consider that the smoke drives away ghosts, and protects new-born infants. If sprinkled on the head of a decoy elephant, it serves as a charm, to make the male come near (BURK. p. 939: V. P. p. 107: MCM. p. 474): หญ้าขัด *Laos, Chiengmai,* ขัดมอน *Thai, Bangkok, Sida rhombifolia (Malvaceae),* a small, slightly woody plant, found as a weed all around the world, and now plentiful in the Malay Peninsula in cleared places, such as road-sides. The Malays make great use of it in medicine, and attribute magic powers to it. As it has been seriously considered in Europe as a remedy in pulmonary tuberculosis and in rheumatism, they have some justification, but Europe did not accept it. The plant is much used for poulticing ulcers, boils, swellings, broken bones, herpes, styes on eyes, and for the skin in chicken-pox. It is applied to the abdomen for abdominal complaints, and is said to prevent boils from maturing, though it is possible it ripens them. The pulped leaves are applied to the head for head-ache, to gums for tooth-ache, and to the eyes for soreness. In the case of head-ache they are combined with *Blumea balsamifera.* As a plant of magic, the leaves may be carried for protection when elephant-hunting. A patient may be stroked with them in order that the mischief may be stroked out of him. As a fibre-plant, it has received considerable attention, and in various places it is actually used. If well prepared, the fibre obtains the same prices as jute, and is used for mixing with it. It has been reported that cattle eat it, but it is scarcely a fodder-plant. Its charcoal (wood tar) may be used for blackening teeth (BURK. p. 2025: cb. p. 151): หญ้าขัดใบป้อม *Laos, Raheng, Sida cordifolia (Malvaceae),* a small, slightly woody plant found throughout the tropics; in the Peninsula it occurs down both coasts. The leaves are used for poulticing aching heads. The fibre has a

value like that of jute (BURK. p. 2024: cb. p. 150): หญ้าขัดใบขาว *Laos, Chiengmai,* ยุงบิ๊ด *Thai; Sida acuta (Malvaceae),* a small shrub, up to 3 feet in height, found widely in the tropics; in the Peninsula it occurs down both coasts. The leaves and root boiled may be used for poulticing the chest for coughs in the place of coriander seed in Malacca. The Chinese herbalists stock it in the Peninsula. It is medicinal with, and for, *S. rhombifolia,* generally in the East. Its fibre, like *S. rhombifolia,* is a possible substitute for jute (BURK. p. 2024: cb. p. 150): หญ้าขัดหลวง,ขัดมอนหลวง *N. Laos; Sida corylifolia (Malvaceae)* (cb. p. 150): หญ้าคา *Imperata cylindrica var. koenigii* and other species (*Gramineae*), lalang, alang-alang, cogon, thatch-grass, a grass not often more than one meter high found throughout the tropics, but apparently more vigorous in Malaysia than elsewhere. It varies considerably, but the varieties so run into one another that they cannot be defined precisely. In Malaya it occurs throughout, its abundance directly proportionate to the careless destructiveness and indifferent cultivation of man. Its light seeds are carried by the wind to new situations, and the seedlings rapidly establish themselves on good, or moderately good soil, in a sunny spot, such as a plantation often affords. From the very commencement of growth, they spread by underground runners of intense vitality, little pieces of which are at all times ready to reproduce the whole plant. These runners extend about 3 inches under the surface. The leaves make a bad fodder for they are so harsh that cattle will not eat them; but if the plant is burnt down, they will eat the new leaves while very young. This plant will burn while still quite green. Intense grazing without firing keeps it under, so that close to villages, a sward of small grasses is established in its place; but such grazing is effective only over a few yards bordering the paths which the liberated animals take, in going out from the stalls to feed. Repeated slashing, as in regular cutting of a lawn, exhausts it in time. Graziers, who fire the grass to get a bite for their stock, do long-lasting damage for a short-lived gain, as the grass recovers while its competitors are killed, and the renewed growth is yet more dense and more useless than what went before. Another occasional incentive to firing the lalang is that it produces flowers more freely after firing, and the seeds so got are used by the Malays for stuffing pillows. If fire is withheld, trees soon begin to smother the lalang in ten years; but it is rare for any lalang waste to be allowed to go unfired for so long, and upwards of thirty years may be required in such parts of the country as Malacca, for its suppression. Considerable experimentation indicates that lalang may be used commercially to make paper. One of the important reasons why shifting (caingin, or *rai*) cultivation of uplands and hill slopes is so prevalant in most equatorial countries is that the farmers have no adequate tools or cultivation methods of controlling this cogon or lalang grass. The forest is cut, burned in the dry season, and the upland crop planted by dibbling the seed into the unploughed soil. After one or two crops the cogon and other grasses and weeds become abundant, so that the field is abandoned, and forest allowed to return as it will, though one tribe in upper Burma actually plants a wild peach thickly in the abandoned clearings, to help in reforesting. Thai farmers, as those in the Philippines, will not by choice re-clear forest land and plant until the last vestiges of the cogon have disappeared by the shading of the forest trees. If the density of the population demands more frequent clearing, and the soil is fertile, the cogon becomes well established, burns annually, and as stated, the forest may never return unless artificially assisted, as is being done on an extensive scale in the Philippines. The vast expanses of such grass, fortunately

not common in Thailand except between Chumporn and Prachuap Girikan, are really "grassy deserts," which the upland farmer, who never uses a plough, cannot, contend with at all. (All this and much more, about this, the most important and serious weed of the tropics, a weed which probably was an important factor in the downfall of the Maya and other civilizations, will be found in papers by Dr. R. L. Pendleton in the Thailand Research Society, Natural History Supplement). Various medicinal uses of runners, leaves and ashes are recorded (BURK. p. 1228); *Imperata arundinaceae* (V. P. p. 107: MCM. p. 472): หญ้างวงช้าง *Heliotropium indicum* (*Boragineae*), an herb, found throughout the tropics; in the Peninsula it is a weed of the more cultivated parts. The leaves dye an impermanent black. It is reported useless as an insecticide. There is hydrocyanic acid present in its leaves, bark, flowers, fruit and roots. It is widely used in India, China and by the Malays for poultices (BURK. p. 1136: V. P. p. 107); *Tournefortia roxburghii* (*Boraginaceae*) (V. P. p. 107): หญ้าจิยอบ *Laos, Chiengmai,* ระงับ, ไมยราบ *Thai,* กะทืบยอบ *Thai, Kaw Chang,* หญ้าปันยอด *N. Laos, Mimosa pudica* (*Leguminosae*), the sensitive plant, an American, slightly woody plant, which attracted interest in Europe, very soon after the discovery of America on account of the movement of its leaves, and it became common in the gardens of those curious in natural history. Then it was carried to all parts of the tropics, and is now abundantly established wherever the climate is warm and moist. It was so common in Malaya in 1836 that it was described as a weed which should be destroyed. Cattle can be got to eat it and thrive, but if they swallow the pods they are liable to intestinal inflammation; and as it grows old the thorns on the stems become very evident. The plant is too small for use as a green manure, and is also objectionable because of its thorns, and indeed is more of a curse than a blessing. In Java, and among the Malays, the idea prevails that the proximity of such a plant as this which 'goes to sleep' by folding its leaves, induces sleep, and bits of the plant are placed under the sleeping-mat of a fretful child. In Java twigs are sold for this purpose; the Malays bathe a fretful child in a decoction of it; also they pound the leaves to make a poultice for swellings. The plant has magic medicinal uses in connection with elephants (BURK. p. 1474: Cb. p. 545: MCM. p. 209); see กะทืบยอบ p. 251: หญ้าเจ้าชู้ *Chrysopogon aciculatus* (*Gramineae*), love grass, a perennial grass, with short horizontal stems and ascending flowering culms, which produce seeds that adhere to objects passing by. It is very common in south-eastern Asia and more or less throughout Malaysia. It occurs in the Mascarene Islands, and in west Africa as a recent introduction. So long as it is possible to mow it very frequently, it is a not un-suitable component of the herbage of lawns. Animals eat it, but avoid the fruiting spikes, so that it has a tendency to increase when grazed. The seeds get among the animals' hairs, and may even cause pain by pressing on the skin. It has been suggested that it could be employed in the brush industry, and it is reported that the haulms are woven into cigarette cases. The plant is used medi-cinally. In Ternate, a decoction is drunk by those who think they have swallowed poison, or it may be chewed with betel. The Perak Malays burn and swallow the ashes for rheumatism (BURK. p. 535: MCM. pp. 71, 452): หญ้าชุ่มตอ, ยาบขี้ไก่ *Laos, Lampun*; *Grewia wi-nitii* (*Tiliaceae*) (Cb. p. 188): หญ้าชุ่มกระต่าย *Saccharum munja* (*Gramineae*): หญ้า-ดอกขาว *Eupatorium odoratum* (*Compositae*), an herb of American origin spreading in Thailand (BURK. p. 976). The common name here is หญ้าเมืองวาย: หญ้าตืดแมว *Laos, Lam-pang, Desmodium zonatum* (*Leguminosae*) (Cb. p. 423): หญ้าใต้ใบ *Phyllantus niruri*

(*Euphorbiaceae*), an herb of small size, found very widely throughout the tropics; in the Peninsula it occurs near the coasts. It is used equally with *P. urinaria* as a medicine. Its action is diuretic; and this is largely due to the considerable amount of potash which the tissues contain. In addition, phyllanthin, a bitter substance, exists in it. This bitter substance is said to poison fish. All through the East the plant, particularly its thinner roots and young leaves, is used in cases where the juice, or an extract, taken internally, may do good by stimulating the kidneys. In India it is used in cases of jaundice, dysentery, dropsy, gonorrhoea, men-orrhagia, and mild fever. The Malays find similar uses for it. The pounded leaves and stems are used as poultices for skin com-plaints including caterpillar itch. In India they are used for sores. The leaves are used as a diuretic in the Philippine Islands, and the bark as an alternative. A decoction of the stem and leaves dyes cotton black (BURK. p. 1718): หญ้านกเขา *Thai, Chainat*, สร้อย-นกเขา *Thai, Sriracha, Mollugo pentaphylla* (*Ficoideae*), a slender herb found from India to New Caledonia; in the Peninsula it is general in open sandy places. The Malays use it for poulticing sore legs. It is medicinal for sprue in Java. It is used in India as a mild aperient medicine, and is eaten as a pot-herb (BURK. p. 1484: Cb. p. 785): หญ้าถบถาบ *Laos, Lampang, Desmodium kurzii* (*Legumi-nosae*) (Cb. p. 411): หญ้านกคุ่ม *Andropogon aciculatus* (V. P. p. 107). *This is the same plant as* หญ้าเจ้าชู้ *Chrysopogon aciculatus*: หญ้า-นางช้าง *Thai, Korat*, เกื้อหมักเหิบ *Laos, Udawn, Pachygone dasycarpa* (*Menispermaceae*) (Cb. p. 72): หญ้านิ้วมือผี *Laos, Chiengmai, Adenia pinnatisecta* (*Passifloraceae*) (Cb. p. 749): หญ้าปล้อง *Scirpus capsularis* (*Cyperaceae*); *Sorghum halepense* (*Gramineae*), Johnson grass, a perennial grass of the Mediterranean region with underground root-stocks. About 1830 a cotton planter from South Carolina, who had gone to Turkey to instruct cultivators there in cotton growing, brought this grass back with him when he returned to the United States. Another planter adopted it and grew it extensively; and from him it obtained the name Johnson grass. In the United States and in certain other countries, it proved to be a valuable fodder-grass; and it is useful possibly as an annual, even in places where the winter kills it. In Malaya it is not useful because it remains continually coarse and produces little foliage (BURK. p. 2056 : V. P. p. 107 : MCM. p. 477) : หญ้าปากควาย *Strychnos robrans (Loganiaceae)* : หญ้า-ผมยุง *Laos, Chiengmai,* ขัดรอก *Thai, Urena lobata (Malvaceae)*, a slightly woody plant, usually 2 to 3 feet high, found throughout the tropics. Like other plants of its natural alliance, it is mucilaginous; and it shares its names with some of them. It is used medicinally more freely by the Malays than by their neighbours. On the Karo highlands a decoction of the root in oil of *Aleurites* with raw rice, is taken for abdominal pain and fever, and the leaves are considered good for cuts and head wounds with the addition of a little gambier; while in Java they are held to be a styptic, and serve also to arrest bad diarrhoea. In Chota Nagpur the root is used externally for rheumatism. The Malays apply the leaves to wounds, and use the juice of the root in long-established fever; they also use it for dysentery. These uses seem to be very generally known. For dysentery they seem, in particular, to use it when the stage of passing blood has been reached. A lotion made from the plant is used for yaws, and on the head for head-ache. A decoction made from leaves and roots is drunk as a tea to relieve pains all over the body due to excessive exertion; the juice of the leaves is drunk, and the root chewed for gonorrhoea. In Kelantan it is associated with *Hibiscus rosasinensis* as an antidote for poison. It is inevitable that a plant with such a reputation among the Malays should be used in their spirit ceremonies. Animals eat the foliage. The bark is fibrous, and in consequence of the great quantity of the plant available, it has attracted attention, though the length of the fibre obtainable is small. It will sell alongside jute and usually get no more than the price of jute, though, if properly prepared, it is a trifle stronger. As the plant is so much smaller than jute, the return per acre is much less; but it has been cultivated for fibre in Brazil. Countries which cannot grow jute—Malaya is one—and use gunny-bags in trade, have naturally turned their attention to it, and in several countries encouragement to grow it has been given. It is said that very tough paper can be made from it. Its charcoal is used for blackening teeth (BURK. p. 2210 : cb. p. 154 : V. P. p. 108 : MCM. p. 432) : หญ้าแฝก *Saccharum spontaneum (Gramineae)* (V. P. p. 108) : หญ้าฝรั่น *Crocus sativus (Iridaceae)*, a bulbous herb found in the Mediterranean region yielding saffron. Saffron has been known from remotest times. The classic Greek and Latin writings often mention it. The Phoenicians dyed the marriage vests of women with it. It has a similar use in India, and may enter into the cosmetics used by bridal couples in Java. True saffron is no more than stigmas; second grade saffron contains anthers mixed with the stigmas. Saffron is always costly owing to the smallness of the yield and the labour involved. Saffron is used medicinally (BURK. p. 683 : MCM. p. 439) : หญ้าเพลองขน *Thai, Chumpawn,* อ้าน้อย *Laos, Chiengmai,* เอ็นอ้าน้อย *Laos, Ubon, Osbeckia chinensis (Melastomaceae)* (cb. p. 675) : หญ้า-เพ็ก *Milium efuseum* (a kind of millet grass) : หญ้าแพรก *Cynodon dactylon (Gramineae)*, Bermuda grass, dub-grass, a creeping grass of all parts of the tropics. In some parts of the tropics it is the most important of all fodder grasses; vast amounts of hay are made from it in Bengal; it is very important in Java. It is also a perfect lawn grass. When it grows well its herbage attains a depth of 12 to 13 inches, and a single plant may cover several square yards (BURK. p. 729: MCM. p. 448): หญ้าพั้นงูขาว, หญ้าพั้นงูแดง a small plant used medicinally: หญ้าเมืองวาย, หญ้าดอกขาว *Eupatorium odoratum* (*Compositae*), an herb which hinders forest-regeneration (BURK. p. 976: V. P. p. 108): หญ้าแมงหมี่ *Laos, Desmodium heterophyllum* (*Leguminosae*), a trailing herb found throughout south-eastern Asia and to the Philippine Islands; in the Peninsula it is very common. Its roots and leaves pounded together are applied to sores; the juice is dropped into the ear for ear-ache. In Singapore, a pulp in coconut milk is dabbed on discoloured skin; but it is not quite certain that this species is used. A decoction is taken for stomach-ache, and abdominal complaints. Cattle eat it readily but it yields little (BURK. p. 794: Cb. p. 409: MCM. p. 456): หญ้ายองไฟ soot clinging to cob webs over a fire-place, or in kitchens: หญ้ายอนหู *Cynodon dactylon* (*Gramineae*) (MCM. p. 448); see แพรก (ต้น) p. 600: หญ้ายุง *Pollinia monantha* (*Gramineae*) (V. P. p. 108): หญ้ารกช้าง see กระทกลก p. 33: หญ้าร้องไห้ a plant of the genus *Selaginella* (*Selaginellaceae*): หญ้ารักนา, หญ้าลักนาง see เทียนนา p. 426: หญ้าสี่เภา a creeping plant, *Lygodium salicifolium* (*Schizaeaceae*): หญ้าสามร้อยยอด *Lycopodium cernum* (*Lycopodiaeeae*), a prostrate plant, which because it preserves its appearance when it dries, is used for ornament at festivals (BURK. p. 1377: MCM. p. 106): หญ้าเสื้อหมอบ *Eupatorium odoratum* (*Compositae*) see หญ้าเมืองวาย: หญ้าหนวดแมว a species of grass used medicinally: หญ้าหอม *Cymbopogon Schoenanthus* (*Gramineae*), a fragrant grass resembling lemon grass (BURK. p. 728): หญ้าหัวนกเค้า *Laos, Chiengmai, Waltheria indica* (*Sterculiaceae*) (cb. p. 179: BURK. p. 2253); see ตามทราย p. 363: หญ้าหัวโต *Scripus grossus* (*Cyperaceae*), a tall sedge abundant throughout Malaysia and often used for making mats (BURK. p. 1981): หญ้าหัวนาค *Bar-*

leria polytricha (*Acanthaceae*) (V. P. p. 109): หญ้าหางเสือ *Laos, Chiengmai, Uraria macrostachya* (*Leguminosae*) (cb. p. 427): หญ้าหางอ้น *Laos, Lampun,* ขี้ตุ่น *Thai, Korat,* ขี้อ้น *Thai, Kanburi, Helicteres obtusa* (*Sterculiceae*); *Uraria latifolia* (*Leguminosae*) (cb. pp. 174; 426): หญ้าหิ่งแม่น *Laos, Chiengmai,* หิ่งหาย *Thai, Bangkok,* มะหิ่งดง *Laos, Lampun, Crotalaria bracteata* (*Leguminosae*) (cb. p. 368): หญ้าหุ่นไห้ see แก่นดง p. 129.

หญิง ying[2] *n.* a female; a woman; a lady; a matron: เพศหญิง of the feminine sex: หญิงชู้ an adulteress: หญิงซึ่งถูกหย่าร้าง, เมียร้าง a divorced woman: หญิงบริสุทธิ์, หญิงพรหมจารีย์ a virgin: หญิงผู้จัดการมรดก an executrix: หญิงแพศยา a prostitute: หญิงแม่หม้าย a widow: หญิงริงเรื่อ *idiomatic* women of the street; women of suspicious character: หญิงโสด a spinster.

หญิบ, ญิบ (p. 314) yip[4] *adj.* two.

หฏ ha[4]-dta[4] *P. adj.* seized; carried away; banished; disappeared; lost (chd. p. 153).

หฐ ha[4]-ta[4] *P. S. n.* violence; force; rapine (chd. p. 153); see ข่มเหง p. 141.

หด hot[4] *v.* to draw back; to draw in; to curl up; to shrink; to contract; to cause to become shorter or shrivelled: ผ้ายังไม่ได้หด the cloth has not yet been shrunk: หดห่อ, งอห่อ to shrink and become folded (as leaves bound together by ants in making their nests): หดหัว to withdraw the head (as from the window of a moving car): หดหู่ to curl up (as fresh leaves when held against a fire, or as a milleped when touched): หดเหี่ยว to become dried and shrivelled.

หต see หัต

หทย, หทัย ha[4]-ta[6]-ya[6] *P. n.* the heart; the mind; the breast; the soul (chd. p. 151: Ala. p. 237).

หน hon[2] *n.* time; times; turn; direction; way; see ครั้ง p. 180; ทาง p. 411: ล่องหน

to disappear : สามหน three times : หนทาง way ; path ; road : หนแรก the first time : หนหลัง the last time.

หนนะ ha⁴-na⁶-na⁶ *P. S. n.* the act of killing, deporting, expelling, destroying or removing (chd. p. 151).

หนวก nu-ak⁴ *adj.* deaf ; incapable of hearing : คนหูหนวก a deaf person : น้ำหนวก discharges from the ear : หนวกหู to be noisy ; to produce or cause a deafening or disturbing noise.

หน่วง nu-ang⁴ *v.* to hold back ; to hinder ; to cause delay ; to retard (progress) : หน่วง-เหนี่ยว to pull back ; to prevent from going forward ; to cause to wait or procrastinate.

หนวด nu-at⁴ *n.* the beard ; a moustache ; feelers, barbels or wattles of fishes or crabs : หนวดคาง a goatee : หนวดเครา whiskers : หนวดเต่าเขากระต่าย a thing, statement, story or rumour that is fabulous, mythical, absurd, incredible, false ; the impossible ; the certainly improbable : หนวดปลาดุก *Thai, Pattani* (ต้น) *Desmos crinitus (Anonaceae)* (cb. p. 38) : หนวดพรหมณ์ a species of tree ; stay ropes for a pole (used to raise or hold it in place) ; ropes used in raising heavy weights (as locomotives up out of the hold of a ship) ; a species of sea fish having numerous feelers : หนวดแมว an herb used medicinally, *Leucas sp. (Labiatae)* (burk. p. 1338).

หน่วย nu-ey⁴ *n.* a unit ; *the numeral* one ; the initial figure of a series ; a single digit ; a subdivision of an organization ; a numerical designation for fruits, eggs, etc. : หน่วยก้าน attitudes ; manners ; characteristics ; appearances : หน่วยทหาร a detachment of soldiers : หน่วยปืนใหญ่ a battery : หน่วยสุด *Thai, Ranawng,* มันแดง *Thai, Krabi,* ตีนต้าง *Laos, Chiengmai,* งวงสุ่ม *E. Laos,* เต้าดอกแตก *Thai,* สุด *Langsuan* and *Satul* (ต้น) *Calycopteris floribunda (Combretaceae)* (burk. p. 416 ; see ข้าวตอกแตก p. 156) ; *Combretum porianum (Combretaceae)* (cb. pp. 611, 618).

หนอ naw² *a sign of the interrogative* : งามหนอ how beautiful ? Oh ! is it not beautiful ? เลิกหนอ are you stopping, or leaving off ?

หน่อ naw⁴ *n.* **a sprout** ; a shoot ; a sapling ; offspring ; the young (human or animal) ; descendents ; children ; a form of yaws or frambesia occurring on the arch or sole of the foot : หน่อกล้วย suckers ; ratoons : หน่อช้าง the forehead of an elephant : หน่อไม้ bamboo shoots ; shoots or sprouts of plants : หน่อแรด the horn of a rhinoceros.

หนอก nauk⁴ *n.* the pubic and suprapubic regions ; the hump on the back of cattle : ผักหนอก see บัวบก p. 477.

หนอง naung² *n.* a marsh ; a swamp ; a bog ; a lagoon ; pus : หนองน้ำไปกขรณ์ a lake : หนองใน gonorrhoea : หนองมิ่งไจ่ see ข้อ่าย p. 160.

หนอน naun² *n.* worm ; maggot ; grub : หนอนกระทู้ a paddy cutting-worm, *Cirphis unipuncta* : หนอนตายหยาก *Thai, Chonburi,* ทำพะขาว *Laos, Chiengmai* (ต้น) *Clitoria macrophylla (Leguminosae)* (cb. p. 436) ; *Pouzolzia zeylanica, P. indica (Urticaceae),* an herb which grows as a weed from India and China to Australia ; in the Peninsula it occurs here and there. The leaves are occasionally eaten as a vegetable. They are insipid. It is thought that the eating of the leaves thus leads to the expulsion of worms. The plant is more widely employed as a medicine for external application. It contains an haematinic (burk. p. 1804) ; *Stemona collinsae (Roxburghiaceae)*. Several species of this genus occur in Thailand, and the tubers of all are used in much the same way. Paste made from them is commonly employed as an external application to sores that have become infected with maggots, as happens not infrequently in live-stock. Emulsions are also used as insecticides (burk. p. 2073) : หนอน-ไหม silk-worms.

หน่อย noie[4] *adj.* little; a trifle; a few; not very much; not very long: *onomat.* from the sound, tone or intonation of a gong or bell: คอยนิดหน่อย just wait a few moments: นิดหน่อย, นิดเดียว a little bit: เรื่องนิดหน่อย only a trifling matter.

หนอยแน่ noy[2]-naa[3] *onomat.* a sound expressing contempt or bravado (as in reckless bravery).

หนัก nak[4] *n.* excrement; fecal matter: *adj.* much; severe; hard; heavy; grave: เฆี่ยนหนักมือไป to whip with too heavy a hand: ทวารหนัก the rectum; the anus: เทหนักมือไป to pour too freely, or too much: ปิดหนัก an obstruction to the passing of fecal matter: บังคนหนัก fecal discharges (for royalty): หนักใจ, หนักอก to be anxious or worried about; to be heavy-hearted regarding; to be fearful (as to what the future results will be): หนักแน่น constant; stable; reliable; firm; untiring in efforts (as a friend in time of adversity): หนักไป to increase in severity; to be too heavy: หนักมือ too violent; too strong, hard or much: หนักหน่วง to be slow but sure; to be composed and self-possessed in actions and words; to stick fast to one's principles: หนักหนา too much; too many; too plentiful; entirely beyond what is deserved: หนักหน้า too much for; too burdensome; taxed beyond one's strength and power of endurance; too overpowering (as an opposing force).

หนัง nang[2] *n.* skin; hide; a cinematograph (from the early use of leather in making figures for shadow plays); a species of jackfruit, so called because when ripe the pulp is tougher, and more like leather than the other kinds: เนื้อหนัง skin, tissues, and fleshy parts of the body: เป็นหนังหน้าไฟ *simile* to take the brunt of blame or criticism: หนังกลางวัน a species of mango bearing long fruit; a daytime movie: หนังกำพร้า the epidermis: หนังตะลุง a shadow show: หนังตา eyelids:

หนังฟอก dressed skins; leather: หนังสือ a book; a document, written or printed; see สมุด p. 821: หนังสือกรมธรรม a deed of sale (as for slaves): หนังสือคู่มือสำหรับเบิกเงินที่ธนาคารโดยฉะเพาะเกาะตัว a letter of credit: หนังสือชักชวน a prospectus: หนังสือเดินทาง a passport: หนังสือตราสารหรือเอกสาร a written instrument: หนังสือนำตัว a letter of introduction: หนังสือริคณสนธิ a memorandum: หนังสือบัตรสนเท่ห์ see บัตรสนเท่ห์ under บัตร p. 476: หนังสือบอกกล่าวป่าวร้อง, หนังสือโฆษณาขายของ advertisement: หนังสือประกัน bail; bond; guarantee: หนังสือปลอม forgery: หนังสือแปลงชาติ naturalisation papers: หนังสือมอบฉันทะ power of attorney: หนังสือรูปพรรณ หรือใบสำคัญ แสดงรูปพรรณ identification papers: หนังสือรับรองสัญชาติ a certificate of nationality: หนังสือสัญญาเช่า a lease: หนังสือสัญญาเช่าเรือ a lease for a boat: หนังสือสัญญาทางพระราชไมตรี see สนธิสัญญา under สัญญา p. 845: หนังสือสัญญา a compact: หนังสือพิมพ์รายเดือน a monthly magazine: หนังสือพิมพ์รายวัน a daily newspaper: หนังสือคู่มือ a reference book: หนังสือส่งด่วน an express letter: หนังสือที่ส่งไม่ถึงผู้รับ a dead letter: หนังสือพินัยกรรม a will: หนังสือเรียน a text-book: หนังสืออ่านเล่น a novel; a periodical; a magazine: ตัวหนังสือ type; letters; characters.

หนุน nan[4] *v.* to brace; to support; to prop; to help; to uphold; see หนุน: *adj.* firm; durable; constant; see แน่น p. 464.

หนับ nup[4] *adj.* gluey; gummy; sticky: *onomat.* a word imitating the sound produced when the finger is raised or removed from a sticky surface.

หนา nah[2] *adj.* thick; dense; massive (as to structure); much; many; abundant (as to fruit or people): ความหนา thickness: คนเดินหนาแน่น a thick, dense crowd of people walking: ดีนักหนา worthy of great commendation: นักหนา very abundant; overly much: แน่นหนา exceedingly solid and firm: หนานัก too thick.

หน้า nah[3] *n.* face; front; facing; season; page; width (of boards): ขายหน้า *lit.* "to sell one's face," *i. e.* to be abashed; see under ขาย p. 155: ดูข้างหน้า to face the future; to look forward to future events: ได้หน้าได้ตา to gain the approbation, praise or favour of men (or of an employer): ต่อหน้า in front of; in the presence of: นำหน้า to precede; to lead, head or go before: ภายหน้า, ภาคหน้า the future: สมน้ำหน้า just desserts, or the deserving of all that is coming to one (as reward or punishment): หน้ากาก masks: หน้าแข้ง the ridge of the tibia; the shin bone: หน้าผง the supranasal region of the forehead: หน้าจืด to be crest-fallen: หน้าโฉนด the title deed for a piece of land: หน้าชืด paleness of the face: หน้าด้าน shameless; brazen-faced: หน้าแดง a blushing face; a flushed face: หน้าตั้ง crusted rice mixed with pork and shrimps, flavoured with spices and coconut milk: หน้าตา facial features; countenance: หน้าต่าง a window: หน้าถัง the front of shops, market stalls or sheds, consisting of removable boards placed in a perpendicular position and slid either in or out along upper and lower grooves. The last going in is locked to a main immovable timber; also, a shed so made as to be shut and opened by boards placed perpendicularily as described above: หน้าทับ the leader, or beater of time on a drum, in a Thai orchestra: หน้าท่า a water landing-place; a wharf: หน้าที่ post; duty; obligation or position in an office: หน้าที่ตามกฎหมาย official duty (legal duty): หน้าน้ำ flood season: น่านน้ำที่อยู่ในเขตต์ของ ประเทศ territorial waters: น่านน้ำที่ห่างจาก ทะเล สามไมล์ ซึ่งถือเป็นของประเทศนั้น the three mile limit from the coast line: หน้าเนื้อใจเสือ innocent in appearance but fierce at heart; wolves in sheep's clothing: หน้าบัน the gable-end of a house: หน้าบาง timid; bashful; fearful; cowardly; shrinking: หน้าบึ้ง surly; cross; ill-natured; crabbed: หน้าปัทม์ the dial or face of a watch or clock: หน้าเป็น an expressive face: หน้าฝน the rainy season:

หน้าม้า an assistant to one acting as a decoy; an allurer; an inveigler or seducer: หน้ามุข a balcony; an uncovered front veranda: หน้าไม้ the width of a board or plank; the flat surface of a board; a cross-bow: หน้าร้อน the hot season: หน้าแล้ง the dry season: หน้าวัว (ต้น) *Anthurium andraeanum* and other species (*Araceae*), a perennial ornamental herb with heart-shaped dark green leaves and a delicate red flower (MCM. p. 149): หน้าวัว (กระเบื้อง) kiln-burnt flooring tiles: หน้าวัว-เจ้า (ต้น) *Anthurium warocqueanum* (MCM. p. 149: N. H. J. S. S. IX, 1, p. 90): หน้าเว่น the front surface of a disk: หน้า-สิ่วหน้าขวาน a place exposed to perils or dangers of all kinds; a hazardous or risky place or condition: หน้าเสีย a look of guilt or shame; the look betraying a guilty conscience: หน้า-เสี้ยว a profile; a side view (as the human face seen from the side); a silhouette: หน้า-หนาว the cold season: หัวหน้า chief; leader; president: หน้าหมอน an ornamented or embroidered pillow top: หน้าเหี่ยวหน้าแห้ง a wrinkled, shriveled face: หน้าอัด full face; front face: เอาหน้าเอาตา *idiomatic* to be seen of men.

หน่าง nang[4] *n.* a snare; a net; a fence; a ditch; a stockade; see ข่าย p. 155; คู p. 206.

หนาดใหญ่, หนาดหลวง (ต้น) nart[4]-yai[4] *n. Blumea balsamifera* (*Compositae*), camphor-plant, a plant up to 12 feet high, subshrubby, the most woody of all *Blumeas*, found from the Himalaya of Kepal to the Philippines and Moluccas; in the Peninsula, throughout. The leaves when bruised smell strongly of camphor, and are used medicinally by the local inhabitants (V. P. p. 152: MCM. p. 414: BURK. p. 334): หนาดขม (ต้น) *Inula cappa* (*Compositae*), an herb (V. P. p. 151): หนาดคำ (ต้น) *Trifonostimon reidioides* (V. P. p. 152): หนาดดอย (ต้น) *Clerodendron vanprukii* (*Verbenaceae*); *C. lloydianum* (V. P. p. 152).

หนาน nan[2] *n.* one who has ceased to be a

Buddhist monk (used as a title before the name in northern Thailand).

หนาม nam[2] *n.* a thorn; prickles; jaggers: หนาม (ผัก) *Lasia heterophylla* (*Araceae*) (V. P. p. 156): หนามขี้แรด *Thai, Ratburi* and *Kanburi,* ฮาง *Thai, Surat,* หนามหัน *N. Laos* (ต้น) *Acacia pennata* (*Leguminosae*), a stout prickly climber, of the moister parts of India and tropical Africa, and found in rather open country throughout Thailand. The leaves are made into a poultice and applied to the head for headache, in Malacca. The leaves are used for fever in Batavia. The roots are boiled and applied as a poultice for rheumatism in Negri Sembilan, or rubbed over the body for small-pox. In Kelantan the root is used as a medicine for cough. The bark is used in Bombay for tanning fishing-nets (cb. p. 550: Burk. p. 22): หนามแดง *Thai, Bangkok,* หนามก้านจาง *Laos, Nakawn Panom* (ต้น) *Gymnosporia mekongensis* (*Celastraceae*) (cb. p. 285): หนามเสี้ยน foe; enemy; see เสี้ยนหนาม.

หน่าย nai[4] *v.* to be offended at or disgusted with; to be displeased or irritated by; to lose one's respect for; see เบื่อ p. 490; จืดจาง p. 252: เบื่อหน่าย to detest; to loathe; to hate or abhor; see เบื่อ p. 490: หน่ายหนี to flee from because of hatred or abhorrence: หน่ายเหนื่อย to withdraw from work because of weariness or disgust (as workmen from the ill-treatment they get from the foreman): หน่ายแหนง a feeling of revulsion (as from suspicion).

หนาว now[2] *adj.* cold; cool; being chilly; shivering: ความหนาว coldness: หนาวใจ fearful; apprehensive; fearsome; alarming; timid; frightened; see คร้าม p. 181: หนาวเย็น chilliness.

หนำ num[2] *v.* to be filled; to have enough (of food); to be satisfied and contented: ความอิ่มหนำใจ contentment; joy: อิ่มหนำสำราญ the appetite being fully assuaged, one rests in tranquillity of mind and body.

หนี nee[2] *v.* to flee; to escape; to shun; to hurry away; to leave hastily: วิ่งหนี to escape (by running): หนีหายไป to disappear mysteriously: หนีเอาตัวรอด to flee to a place of refuge: หลบหนี to make an escape secretly; to dodge being captured.

หนี้ nee[3] *n.* debt; obligation; liability; debit: เจ้าหนี้ a creditor: ใช้หนี้ to pay one's debts; to meet one's obligations; to pay off liabilities: เป็นหนี้เป็นสิน badly involved in debt: ผ่อนใช้หนี้ to pay off a debt by installments: ลูกหนี้ a debtor:

หนีบ neep[4] *v.* to seize; to nip; to squeeze; see คีบ p. 203; บีบ p. 483: ใช้คีมหนีบ to grasp with pliers or pincers: ประตูหนีบนิ้ว the door has pinched the fingers.

หนึก, หนืด neuk[4] *adj.* pliable and sticky (as putty); *a descriptive word for something with adhesive properties.*

หนึ่ง neung[4] *adj.* one: ครั้งหนึ่ง one time; once upon a time: ที่หนึ่ง first: ประหนึ่งว่า as if; just as; even as: อันหนึ่งอันเดียวกัน *idiomatic* one and the same.

หนุ ha[4]-noo[6] *P. S. n.* the jaw; the chin (chd. p: 152).

หนุน noon[2] *v.* to support; to sustain; to prop up or reinforce (by putting something under); to help; to aid; to assist: ทหารกองหนุน reserve forces: หนุนขึ้นให้สูง to raise up higher with props: ทัพหนุน reinforcements; to help those at the front line: หนุนหลัง to back up; to support the back: อุดหนุน to give a helping hand (as by giving financial aid): เอาหมอนหนุน to prop up by means of pillows (as an invalid); to insert supports (as under a boat).

หนุบ ๆ noop[4]-noop[4] *adj.* nibbling (as fish at a bait); sudden short repeated twitches; see ตุบ p. 371: เต้นหนุบ ๆ the pulsations of an artery; the throbbing of an abscess: ปวดหนุบหนิบ a pulsating, pricking pain.

หนุ่ม noom[4] *n.* juvenility; a youth; a young lad or boy: *adj.* young; juvenile; adolescent: หนุ่มเหน้า in the period of adolescence or minority.

หนุมาน ha[4]-noo[6]-man *P. S. n.* Hanuman, *lit.* "one who has a chin," *i. e.* a celebrated monkey chief. He was able to fly and is a conspicuous figure in the Ramayana (H. C. D. p. 116).

หนุย noo-ie[4] *adj.* swelling; protuberant; bulging; see โน p. 465.

หนู noo[2] *n.* (1) a rat; a mouse: (2) a pet name for children, meaning "small one": หนูตุ่น the small bamboo rat: หนูท้องขาว house rats; field rats; หนูผี pygmy shrews, *Pachyura*: หนูพุก guinea pigs: หนูตะเภา a large field rat: หนูอ้น the large bamboo rat, *Nyctocleptes cinereus.*

ห่ม hom[4] *v.* to cover; to clothe; to dress or drape with clothes, cloth or a blanket; to exert the body weight by jumping or springing on (serving the purpose of a hammer or pile-driver): เครื่องนุ่งห่ม clothing; clothes: ผ้าห่ม a shawl; a breast-cloth; a scarf: ผ้า-ห่มนอน a blanket or bed-spread: ห่มกิ่งไม้ to bend down the limb of a tree with the body weight: ห่มผ้า to cover with a cloth.

หมก mok[4] *v.* to hide; to bury; to cover up (as under the ground, or under sweepings of leaves or branches); see กลบ p. 57: หมก-ซ่อน to hide by a covering of rubbish or sweepings of leaves: หมกไฟ to bank up or damp the fire (as with ashes or cinders): หมกมุ่น to be engrossed or occupied with some duty; to devote one's time and energies exclusively to the execution of some task: หมกไว้ใต้ดิน to hide by being buried underground: หมกไหม้ to allow to smoulder or burn with a gentle fire (as in burning charcoal).

หมด mot[4] *v.* to be finished; to come to the end of; to be all used up; to have nothing

remaining: *adj.* all; entire; complete; the whole lot: คนหมดจด an innocent, virtuous or chaste person: ทั้งหมด entirely: หมดจด clean; pure; beautiful; spotless: หมดตัว to be stripped of all one's possessions; to have lost all (as in case one's house is burnt down): หมดทางหากิน unemployed: หมดมลทิน free from any defect; unstained; undefiled: หมด-แล้ว the supply is exhausted; the larder is empty; there is no more; all gone: หมดสิ้น nothing remains: หมดอายุความ *legal* the case is barred by limitations.

หม่น mon[4] *adj.* grey; dull; dark; blackish in colour; clouded; sad; melancholy in disposition or countenance: หน้าหม่นหมอง a sad countenance: หม่นไหม้ในใจ burning with resentment, anger, or vexation.

หมวก mu-ak[4] *n.* a hat; various headdresses; the wooden handle of edged-tools for chopping or hewing: หมวกกะบัง a cap with a vizor: หมวกแจว the cross-piece or handle on a Thai oar: หมวกฟาง straw hats: หมวกเหล็ก steel helmets.

หมวด mu-at[4] *n.* a chapter; a group; a division; a section; see พวก p. 575; กลุ่ม p. 62: แบ่งเป็นหมวด ๆ หมู่ ๆ divided into subdivisions or sections: นายหมวด chief or leader of a section (as of police or workmen): หมวดทหาร a company or sub-division of soldiers.

หมอ maw[2] *n.* a doctor; a physician; a medical man: เรียนเป็นหมอ to undergo study and training in order to become a doctor: หมอความ, หมอกฎหมาย a lawyer; a solicitor: หมอช้าง a doctor for elephants; an elephant driver: หมองู a snake-charmer: หมอดู a fortune-teller; a soothsayer: หมอที่ไม่มี-ภูมิรู้โดยไม่เคยเป็นนักเรียน a quack doctor: หมอ-นวด a masseur: หมอน้อย a leech: หมอน้อย *Thai* (ต้น) *Murraya koenigii (Rutaceae)*, the curry-leaf tree of India, the leaves being used as a flavouring in curries. It has a hard, useful wood. Its leaves, bark, and roots are medicinal, both externally and internally. It contains sabinene and pesquiterpenes oils but in too meagre quantities to be economically valuable (Ob. p. 230 : MCM. p. 346 : BURK. p. 1505): หมอผี a sorcerer ; a magician.

หมอ, หมอไทย (ปลา)   maw[2] *n. Anabas testudineus (Anabantidae)* (suvatti p. 106): หมอช้างเหยียบ, หมอทะเล, หมอน้ำ (ปลา) *Pristolepis fasciata (Nandidae)* (suvatti p. 139).

หม่อ, ลูกหม่อ   maw[4] *n.* young of cattle ; a calf.

หม้อ   maw[3] *n.* a general name for baked clay or enamelled pots, followed by the designating name :   ช่างหม้อ a potter :   ปั้น- หม้อ to mould clay pots :   ดินหม้อ, กระเหม่า (p. 48) soot on the bottoms of pots and pans : หม้อกรอง a filter :   หม้อกรัน, หม้อคะนน an ornamented, baked clay water-jar with cover : หม้อกลส a baked clay goblet-like vessel for consecrated water :   หม้อเกาเหลา a Chinese self-warming, lead or pewter soup tureen. This consists of a circular dish with a funnel-like part in the middle (like a cake form with a hollowed out centre). This holds the soup. Under this is another dish with some burning charcoal, the fumes of which rise through the funnel :   หม้อแกง a curry pot, similar in size to a rice pot but marked by diagonal lines around the outside :   หม้อข้าว a pot for boiling rice (formerly made of baked clay, with a lid, but now replaced by imported brass pots) :   หม้อตาล a sugar pot ; small baked clay pots into which the toddy palm sugar is poured and transported for sale :   หม้อตุ้งก่า a bamboo water-pipe for smoking Indian hemp ; see ตุ้งกา p. 371 :   หม้อตุ่น a double boiler, consisting of a large-mouthed baked clay pot containing water. On the mouth can be added another covered vessel, with perforated bottom, containing the food to be steamed :   หม้อน้ำ a water-pot or jug :   หม้อ-น้ำมีหู a pitcher :   หม้อน้ำเรือไฟ the boiler of a steamer :   หม้อมัสสาวะ, หม้อมูตร an urinal :

หม้อยา a pot for boiling medicinal decoctions : หม้อหนู a pot provided with a handle, used for boiling small quantities of water or medicinal ingredients in a hurry :   หม้ออุจจาระ a bed-pan.

หมอก   mauk[4] *n.* fog ; mist :   ตามัวเป็นหมอก eyesight that is dimmed or misty ; seeing indistinctly :   มัวหมอก obscured by mist or fog :   หมอกบังฟ้า a mist-covered sky.

หมอง   maung[2] *adj.* soiled ; dull ; tarnished ; impure ; disgraced ; clouded ; dirty ; stained ; tainted (in character) :   มัวหมอง darkened or obscured (as a room where the light has been cut off) :   วันที่ไม่มัวหมอง an unclouded day :   เศร้าหมอง sorrowful ; mournful ; grieved :   หม่นหมอง melancholy ; dismal ; sad : หมองใจ to be sullen ; to be ill-natured : to manifest anger or anxiety :   หมองหมาง estranged ; alienated ; made unfriendly or indifferent towards ; covered with shame.

หม่อง   maung[4] *n. a Burmese word used as a title meaning* Mister, Master or Nai : ยาหม่อง Burmese balm : *onomat.* from the sound made by striking gongs or cymbals.

หมอน   maun[2] *n.* a pillow ; a cushion ; a bolster ; a roller (any device that rolls so as to reduce friction) :   หมอนข้าง "a dutch-wife" or long pillow :   หมอนทอง a species of mango :   หมอนบุ้น the breech-end support for a cannon ; a wad to hold powder and shot in a gun barrel :   หมอนอิง a three-cornered pillow.

หม่อน (ต้น)   maun[4] *n. Morus* including *N. indica (Urticaceae)*, Indian mulberry, a small quick-growing tree. The fruit resembles a small, red pepper-corn, cylindrical in shape, rather deficient in flavour, and quite inferior to the European mulberry. It is a native of northern India. Its leaves afford food for the silk worm (V. P. p. 223 : MCM. p. 278 : BURK. p. 1497).

หมอบ   maup[4] *v.* to kneel :   **หมอบกราบ**

to crouch on "all fours" with the hands placed palm to palm touching the forehead and floor, a position of humble adoration (as before the king or an image of the Buddha): หมอบโดยยกลั้ว to cringe or crouch from fear.

หม่อม maum[4] *n.* a plebian wife of a prince: หม่อมเจ้า a child of a พระองค์เจ้า; a Serene Highness; a grandchild of a king: หม่อมฉัน I (used by a plebian in addressing royalty): หม่อมราชวงศ์ a title used by a great grandchild of a king: หม่อมหลวง a title used by a son of a หม่อมราชวงศ์: หม่อมแม่ a plebian mother of a prince or princess: หม่อมห้าม a king's plebian concubine.

หมอย moy[2] *n.* hair around the sexual parts; a sign of puberty.

หมัก mak[4] *v.* to leaven; to cause fermentation; to cause froth, foam or bubbles; to preserve by slow fermentation; to steep or soak with a yeast till fermentation takes place: หมักแป้ง to brew flour or meal: หมักหมม to allow refuse to accumulate in a pile; to be accumulated in a most disorderly manner (as dirty clothes ready for the wash).

หมัด mat[4] *n.* the fist; a flea; a pulex: กำหมัด to clinch the fist: หมัดคน (กัดคันมาก) *Pulex irritans*: หมัดหนู (ที่นำเชื้อกาฬโรคสู่บุคคล) *Xenopsylla cheopis*: หมัดสุนัขขี้ *ctenocephalus cemis.*

หมัน man[2] *n.* tow; caulking soaked in dammar for plugging the seams of boats: *adj.* barren; sterile; fruitless: ตอกหมัน to caulk up the seams or crevices with tow (as boats or ships): ก้านหมัน (ต้น) *Cordia myxa* (*Boraginaceae*), a bush resembling hemp. Its mucilaginous fruits are good for coughs (Burk. p. 660).

หมั่น man[4] *v.* to be diligent; to be industrious; to be persevering, attentive, assiduous; see ขยัน p. 142.

หมั่นไส้, มันไส้ man[4]-sai[3] *v.* to hate; to

be angry or disgusted with; to be provoked at, or detest for some misdeed (as a servant breaking some valuable piece of porcelain); see เกลียด p. 122; โกรธ p. 133.

หมับ, หมุบ mup[4] *adv.* suddenly; quickly; rapidly; swiftly; speedily (as a boxer giving a hit, or one giving a kick).

หมา mah[2] *n.* a dog; see สุนัข p. 873: หมาจิ้งจอก a jackal, *Canis aureus*: หมาจู a Japanese or Chinese poodle or spaniel: หมา (ตัวเมีย) a bitch: หมาใน, หมาป่า the Malay wild dog, *Cuon rutilons*: หมาบ้า a rabid dog: หมามุ้ย (ต้น) a creeping plant, the fruit of which, if touched, produces a rash: หมาไม้ a large black and yellow squirrel, *Ratufa* (species): หมาลิ่ง, หมูลิ่งหมูลิ่ง hog-badger, *Arctonyx collaris dictator* (Gaird. N. H. J. S. S. III, 11, p. 124): หมาไล่เนื้อ a greyhound: หมาหอน the howling or baying of a dog: หมาเห่า the barking of a dog.

หม่า mah[4] *v.* to pickle; to preserve in salt, vinegar or sugar; to keep by soaking in water; see แช่ p. 303.

หม้า mah[3] *adj.* most beautiful, becoming, or exceedingly pretty; see งาม p. 223.

หมาก see เต่าเกียด p. 374: ข้าวหมาก a sweetmeat made of fermented rice: เจียนหมาก to cut the betel fruit into sections and peel in preparation for chewing the same: ชานหมาก the insipid remains after masticating a pellet of betel: เชิญกินหมากกินพลู an invitation to chew a pellet of betel; a common invitation to a guest: ทะลายหมาก a bunch of the areca fruit: หมากเก็บ jackstones, a game played by children with five fruit pits, stones, or fragments of brick. These are laid down; one is tossed up and, while in the air, one of the other pieces is picked up, the one tossed up being caught in the hand. One pit is laid aside and the process repeated till all have been thus picked up. The aim is to see who can toss and pick the total number without a miss: หมากเขี่ย a nursery game played with small fruit pits. When a number are thrown down, one is flipped with the fingers aimed to hit another seed. When this is successful the two seeds are picked up and the player continues till a miss is made; then the other party plays; thus the players alternate till all of the seeds are picked up: หมากเขี่ยว (ต้น) *Ptychosperma macarthuri* (*Palmae*), an exceedingly graceful palm, introduced into European cultivation in 1870 from New Guinea. It is reported to be poisonous (BURK. p. 1837: N. H. J. S. S. IX, 1, p. 102); *Oncosperma filamentosa* (*Palmae*) or *O. tigillaria*, a tall, tufted palm growing in the dryer parts of the mangrove forest, found in Cochin-China, throughout Malaysia to the Philippine Islands. The wood is very hard and durable, and is so much used for various purposes that the supplies are greatly diminished. Split into four, it is used for flooring, and split into smaller parts, as rafters for roofing and walls. Its elasticity is great. It is used in deeply planted fishing stakes, and for the wash-strake of boats. Walking-sticks can be made from it, and weapons are commonly made from it. The pirates who formerly infested the Archipelago, employed lances made from it, which they threw in battle before coming to grips. The spines which stud the stems are used for blowpipe darts, and as the heads of javelins for spearing fish. The "cabbage" or terminal end is excellent, and even preferred to that of the coconut (MCM. p. 165: BURK. p. 1581). The flowers are said to be used for flavouring rice. The small, flat, pulpy fruits can be made into a preserve. They are also chewed as a substitute for betel. The sheaths of the flowers very commonly serve as buckets, and as containers for boiling water. In Annam baskets are made of the leaves: หมากคั้น areca-nut developed under pressure (pressed by the other nuts, or growing at the base of a bunch): หมากดิน areca fruit; the edible

fruit when still green and soft: หมากดิบ unripe: หมากดิบน้ำค้าง *Thai, Kaw Chang* (ต้น), *Salomonia cantoniensis* (*Polygalaceae*), a small annual herb found in India, China, and more or less throughout Thailand. In southern Sumatra it is medicinal, being a children's medicine against sprue; for which it is pulped and rubbed about the mouth (cb. p. 99: Burk. p. 1944): หมากแดง a small palm with red stalks and stems, *Pinanga* (MCM. p. 165): หมากทุย partially fertilized areca fruit. These are oblong in shape with a small seed or nut, and useless: หมากนอย see บวบงู p. 472: หมากบหงา a species of fragrant areca nut:. หมากผู้, หมากเมีย a species of palm: หมากมวน a species of peach tree growing in the province of Chiengmai. The fruit is edible: หมากมู้ *Laos, Lampang* (ต้น) *Gymnosporia stylosa* (*Celastraceae*) (cb. p. 285): หมากเม่า, หมากควาย (ต้น) *Antidesma ghaesembilla*, a shrub or small tree, rising to 40 feet, very widely distributed, and common throughout south-eastern Asia and Malaysia, to tropical Africa. The fruits are edible but rather acid. The leaves are also edible, and are used as an acid flavouring to food. They are used for poultices in various ways, viz. for headache, scurf, and abdominal swellings. They are infused and the water used for bathing in cases of fever. The timber is white and soft, with a very coarse grain; it splits in drying. It is used for light rafters in native houses (BURK. p. 186): หมากเมี่ยง a sweetmeat composed of fried, grated, coconut meat, minced shrimps, onions, and spices: หมากขั้น cured areca nuts. The fresh fruits are stored in small-sized water-jars till the husk has become dried and pulpy: หมากแยก a form of chess where the chess-men are moved in diverging directions, differing from the game where the pieces are moved in straight courses: หม่ากรุก the game of chess: หม่ากลิ้ง a species of dwarf areca palm: หมากสง the ripe areca-nut: หมากสุก yellow or orange-yellow (as the colour of the ripe areca-fruit): หมากหนาม a species of palm used medicinally: หมากหมก *Thai, Chumpawn* and *Surat,* ปากกา *Thai, Krabi* (ต้น) *Adenia augustisepala* (*Passifloraceae*) a slender climbing plant (cb. p. 745): หมากหอมควาย a species of palm used medicinally: หมาก-เหลือง (ต้น) *Chrysalidocarpus lutescens* (*Palmae*), an ornamental palm of the Mascarene Islands, which grows well in the Malay Peninsula. Some botanists reduce the genus to *Hyophorbe* (BURK. p. 532); *Areca tutescens* (*Palmae*), feather palm; cane palm. This graceful, handsome, bushy and decorative soboliferous feather-palm is a native of Bourbon and is said to have been introduced to Thailand by Phya Pradibhat Phubal about thirty years ago probably from Singapore (MCM. p. 164: N. H. J. S. S. IX, 1, p. 93).

หมาง   mang[2] *v.* to have an aversion to; to be embittered or resentful against; to be alienated, unfriendly, or estranged from; to endure with shame: หมางใจ to be displeased or aggrieved at, angered, or ready to quarrel with; to be spitefully inclined: ความหมาง-ใจ estrangement; alienation; embitterment: หมางหมอง to have an aversion to, or antipathy against on account if some disagreement: อามาตบาดหมาง revengeful; angered; spiteful; vindictive; retaliative.

หมาด (เหล็ก)   mart[4] *n.* an awl: *adj.* sticky (as half-dried paint); still soft and yielding (as freshly made pottery); plastic; pliable; half-dry.

หมามุ้ย, หมามุ่ย   mah[2]-moo-ie[5] *Thai,* บะ-เหยื่อง *Laos, Chiengmai,* โพล่ยู *Karen, Kanburi* (ต้น) *n. Mucuna pruriens* (*Leguminosae*), horse-eye bean, cowage or cowitch, a climber found in south-eastern Asia and Malaysia. Its boiled seeds have been used in India from sanskritic times as an aphrodisiac; and its roots as a tonic. It is medicinal in Indo-China. The plant was taken to the West Indies some centuries ago and occurs there alongside a very similar species, *M. urens, DC.* The stinging hairs from the surface of the pods are said to be used by the Negroes as a verminfuge, and were introduced into European medicine in 1640, and then suggested for India; but the treatment is dangerous, and strong doses of the hairs cause diseases of the bowels, and may bring about death. In some places the hairs are used criminally for poisoning. The large seeds are considered to resemble the eye of a horse and are believed to absorb the poison from a scorpion wound (cb. p. 445: MCM. pp. 379, 461: BURK. p. 1503).

หมาย   mai[2] *v.* to intend; to purpose; to fix or appoint (as to time); to imagine; to expect; to design: *n.* a warrant; a decree; a notice; an order: ขัดหมาย to refuse an order: คิดหมายไว้ในใจ to intend or resolve (as New Year's good resolutions): คาดหมายไว้ว่า to surmise, conjecture, suppose or presume: เครื่องหมาย a mark, sign, token, symbol or signal: ทำเครื่องหมายไว้เป็นสำคัญ to make a mark or sign in witness thereto (as one unable to write the name): แปลหมาย to give reasons for refusing to comply to a warrant or order: มาดหมาย intention: มุ่งหมาย to purpose or intend (as an ultimate object to be attained): หมายกำหนดการ a programme or schedule: หมายขังระหว่างพิจารณา a remand order: หมายจับ warrant of arrest: หมาย-จับของศาลเพื่อให้จับผู้ละเมิดอำนาจศาล bench warrant: หมายแจ้งโทษเด็ดขาด committal order: หมายบังคับ judgement order: หมายประกาศ notices, announcements, or appraisements, displayed in public places: หมายพยาน sub poena: หมายว่าจะไป proposing or intending to go: หมายศาล writ: หมายศาลเรียก court summons: หมายสั่งปล่อย order to discharge: หมายอนุญาตให้ตรวจ a search-warrant: หมาย-อายัดทรัพย์ *legal* an attachment of goods pending litigation: หมายเหตุ remarks; corrections; notes; opinions added to a document; a memorandum (as made out during a trip).

หมาร่ำ   mah[2]-rah[3] *n.* solitary wasps of the family *Vespidae.* They construct cells of mud along the walls of houses or in key holes. They are commonly called " mud daubers ".

หมิ่น   min[4] *v.* to insult; to despise or treat with contempt; to offer an affront or outrage; to disdain: *adv.* very near the edge; too close to the rim; on the verge or brink, in danger of falling off: *adj.* careless; heedless; incautious; unguarded: ตฤกดูหมิ่น *idiomatic* to disparage: หมิ่นในตนเอ็ง an inferiority complex: หมิ่นประมาท to defame or libel; to insult; to abuse, or act in a scornful, contemptuous, insolent, or insulting manner: หมิ่นประมาทโดยวาจา to slander.

หมี   mee[2] *n.* a bear: ดีหมี the gall of a bear (considered an efficient remedy by Thai doctors of the old school): มืดมิดหมี oppressively or dangerously dark: หมีขอ bear-cat, *Arctictis binturong* (Karen): หมีควาย Himalayan black bear, *Ursus torguatus* or *tibetanus* (Gaird. N. H. J. S. S. III, 2, p. 123): หมีเล็ก (ดาว) *Ursa minor, astron.* the Little Bear: หมีหมา, หมีหมู Malay bear, *Ursus malayanus*: หมีเหม็น (ต้น) *Litsaea semicarpifolia* (V. P. P. 220): หมีใหญ่ (ดาว) *Ursa major, astron.* the Great Bear.

หมี่   mee[4] *n.* vermicelli eaten with a sauce made of minced pork or chicken and various spices.

หมึก   meuk[4] *n.* a general word for ink, followed by the designating name: กระดอง-ปลาหมึก cuttle-bone: กระปุกหมึก an ink-stand: ปลาหมึก cuttle-fish or squids: ปลาหมึกยักษ์ octopus: ปากกาหมึกซึม a fountain pen: มอมแมมไปด้วยหมึก blotched with ink: หมึกจีน Chinese (stick) ink: หมึกแดง red ink: หมึกพิมพ์แท่น printing ink: หมึกไม่ตก indelible ink: ผ้าหมึกพิมพ์ดีด a typewriter ribbon.

หมึน   murn[2] *v.* to be covered with an eruption (as in small-pox).

หมื่น   murn[4] *n.* a numeral followed by four figures or cyphers: *adj.* ten thousand; much; ample; abundant: กรมหมื่น a title of royal princes: ขุนหมื่น a conferred rank or title next below กรมหมื่น.

หมุด   moot[4] *n.* a plug; pins (machinery): tacks; pegs; a strip of lint placed in a wound for the purpose of drainage: เข็มหมุด pins (household): หมุดควง a small-sized screw.

หมุน   moon[2] *v.* to revolve; to turn; to whirl; to cause to rotate on a pivot: หมุน-กลับ to turn in the reverse direction: หมุน-เครื่องกลึง to turn on a lathe: หมุนเงิน to get quick returns on investments; to turn money over frequently; to make short-time loans or investments: หมุนไปหมุนมา to revolve in alternating directions (first forward, then backward); see เวียน p. 783.

หมุบ   see หมับ p. 909.

หมุ่ย   moo-ie[4] *onomat.* from the sound produced when striking a big gong.

หมู   moo[2] *n.* a pig; a hog; a boar: แม่-หมู a sow: ลมบ้าหมู epilepsy: หมูจ่อม minced pork preserved in fermented rice: หมูแนม a relish composed of minced pork and ground fried rice: หมู (ปลา) *Acanthopsis choirorhynchus* (*Cobitidae*) (suvatti p. 57): หมูป่า wild pig; Indian pig, *Sus cristatus* (Gaird. N. H. J. S. S. III, 2, p. 126): หมูสี a dwarf coconut tree: หมูหยอง, (หมูปุ่น, หมูฝอย) a relish composed of shredded pork and spices: หมูย่างหั้น sliced roasted sucking-pig: หัวหมู a plough-share; the head of a pig cooked and decorated (often seen carried in Chinese processions).

หมู่, หมวด   moo[4] *n.* group; cluster; series; class; company; genus; crowd; collection; flock; herd; drove (of animals); race (of man); see กลุ่ม p. 62; พวก p. 575: จัดเป็น-หมู่ ๆ to arrange or classify into groups or classes: ลูกหมู่ those of the same group or company: หมู่ทหารลาดตระเวน skirmishers: หมู่นี้ at present; during this time.

หย, หัย ha[4]-ya[6] *P. S. n.* a horse (Chd. p. 154): หยรถ a horse-cart or carriage: หย- ศาสตร์ the act, condition, or art of training horses (as for a circus).

หยก yok[4] *n.* jade. Jade includes two kinds of hard stone known as the nephrite and jadeite. In the nephrite the green is said to deepen as the proportion of iron in its composition increases. A white jade is also greatly admired and is compared to mutton fat. Jadeite is described as being of a brighter and more vivid green than nephrite though it also appears in lavender. The word jade comes from Spanish, *Piedra de hijada* or "stone of loins." (A sketch of Chinese Arts and Crafts, Hilda Arthur Strong, page 201): *adv.* rapidly; quickly; hurriedly: หยก ๆ in a lively, animated, active, or sprightly manner (used in regard to running): เห็น- เขาเดินหยก ๆ ไป he was seen walking rapidly along (as though hastening to get out of sight).

หย่ง yong[4] *v.* to cause to raise slightly; to rise, puff, or swell up; to inflate with air; to loosen or break up the ground (as around the root of a plant): *adj.* fluffy; downy: เดิน- หย่งเท้า to walk on tip-toe or with an exaggerated raising of the feet: ผมหย่ง hair so combed as to stand puffed up: หย่งผมขึ้น to loosen or fluff the hair: หยิบหย่ง to pick up cautiously or gingerly, in a fastidious or affected manner; see ฟู p. 609.

หยด yot[4] *v.* to let fall drop by drop: *n.* a drop; a minim: น้ำหยดแปะ ๆ the water falls or leaks out drop by drop: น้ำหยดย้อย, หยดหยาด the water drops down or oozes out (as in the formation of stalactites).

หยวก yu-ak[4] *n.* the stalk or bole of the plantain or banana tree: ใบหยวก the soft inside or heart layers of the same: หยวก- มีเครือดกคอ the banana tree having a bunch of fruit attached: หยวกปลี the banana flower-stalk which issues from the centre of the crown of large leaves: หยวกผ้า the fresh rolled, or partly unrolled banana leaf (so called from its resemblance to cloth).

หยวบ yu-ap[4] *adj.* sagging; bending; waving (as branches from the antics of monkeys).

หยอก yauk[4] *v.* to joke; to jest; to make fun of; to sport with; to caress or play jokingly with: หยอกเย้า, หยอกขั้ว see เย้า p. 680: หยอกลูกอ่อน to fondle or dandle an infant: หยอกหยิก to pinch jokingly.

หยอง yaung[2] *v.* to stand erect or to bristle up (as hair or fur of a cat); see ชัน p. 288: *adj.* fearful; timid; frightened; see กลัว p. 60: เก็บทองหยองไปได้มาก they took away a great quantity of gold ornaments (as loot): ขนหยอง the standing erect (of hair). ทอง- หยอง *idiomatic* various ornaments of gold.

หย่อง yaung[4] *n.* a betel-nut tray fitted with all that is necessary for chewing; a carved pedestal support or base for trays of food, images or souvenirs: นั่งหย่อง, นั่งหย่อง ๆ to sit on the heels; see นั่ง p. 448: หย่อง- ใส่หมาก a brass or silver cup-shaped dish for areca fruit prepared for chewing; see เชี่ยน- หมาก p. 362.

หย่อง ๆ yaung[4]-yaung[4] *adv.* leisurely; slowly; at half speed; with mincing steps: วิ่งหย่อง ๆ to run along sluggishly.

หยอด yaut[4] *v.* to let fall drop by drop; to let (liquid) flow or pour into; to drop a drop of liquid into or upon: ยาหยอดตา a lotion for the eyes; an eye-wash; collyrium: หยอด- ข้าว to feed small quantities of rice gruel (as to a bed-ridden patient): หยอดคอ to let small quantities flow into the throat (as by a feeding cup). หยอดปาก to let small quantities flow into the mouth (as nourishment or medicines to a bed-ridden patient).

หยอน yaun[2] *v.* to dread; to fear; to respect; to regard with veneration: กลัวหยอน

a respectful fear: นึกหยอน thoughts of fear or dread (as of some future ordeal).

หย่อน yaun[4] v. to slacken; to loosen (as rope); to play out (more rope or string): ค่อย ๆ หย่อนลง gradually to slacken the rope and let down: ผูกหย่อนไป tied too loosely: ผูกหย่อน ๆ to fasten or tie loosely: หย่อน-คลาย to become less severe, or less painful: หย่อนใจ, หย่อนอารมณ์ to relax; to rest or take some recreation: หย่อนเชือก to slacken the rope: หยุดหย่อนใจ to take some time off for recreative pleasure, or diversion.

หย่อม yaum[4] n. a tapering top or pinnacle; isolated piles or heaps; nodes or patches on the skin; a small gathering or group (of people); clusters; clumps (of bushes or grass); a tuft (of hair): กองหญ้าเป็นหย่อม ๆ isolated piles of grass: ในเป็นหย่อม ๆ isolated nodes (over the body): บวมเป็นหย่อม ๆ swellings occurring at intervals of time or space: เรือนเป็นหย่อม ๆ groups of houses scattered along at intervals.

หยอย yoy[2] adv. quickly; nimbly; lively (descriptive of running or jumping): กระ-โดดหยอย ๆ to jump in a quick, nimble manner (as over hurdles).

หย่อย yoy[4] adj. often; a little at a time; in driblets; small sums paid at a time: ให้หย่อย ๆ to give out by piecemeal, or a little at a time.

หยัก yak[4] v. to indent; to cut notches, or make small incisions: adj. notched; barbed; jagged: หยักควั่น to girdle or groove the bark all around; see ควั่น p. 187: หยักเงี่ยง to put a barb on (as on a fish-hook): หยัก-เป็นฟันเลื่อย serrated or toothed (like a saw): หยักรั้ง being drawn up tightly or worn unduly high (descriptive of the manner of wearing the loin-cloth): หยักไว้ to notch; to slit; to incise, or mark by chopping.

หยักเหยา yak[4]-yow[2] v. to vex; to trouble; to annoy; to be overly particular about trifles:

พูดหยักเหยา to tease or annoy by mimicing or imitating the words spoken.

หยัง yang[2] adv. why; for what reason: adj. what; very surprising; see ทำไม p. 414.

หยั่ง yang[4] v. to fathom; to make soundings; to interpret; to explore; to investigate (like taking soundings at sea): หยั่งใจ to make a mental decision, resolve or determination: หยั่งรู้, หยั่งเห็น insight; foresight; acumen; discernment: ขาหยั่ง sheer-legs, see under ขา p. 152.

หยัง ๆ yang[2]-yang[2] Jav. adj. pretty; beautiful; fine-looking: รูปหยังจัง an exceedingly graceful or beautiful figure.

หยัด yat[4] v. to percolate (as through a filter); to trickle down gradually; to leak or fall in minute particles; to train the body so as to keep supple and limber; to bend a joint backwards, like the arm or fingers, so as to make them pliant (this is often done as a punishment): หยัดกาย to exercise, train, or drill so that the body will remain lithe and limber; to render the body supple, pliant, lithesome; see ดัดกาย under ดัด ๑ p. 323: หยัดฝน minute raindrops: หยัดหยาด to fall or percolate through in fine drops: หยัด-หยาดน้ำค้าง very fine particles of moisture, or dew drops.

หยัน yan[2] v. to mock; to jeer; to deride; to make fun of; see เยาะ p. 680: เย้ยหยัน to ridicule; to scoff, sneer or laugh at.

หยับ yap[4] adj. pliable; flexible; limber; pliant (descriptive of softness): adv. quickly; rapidly; swiftly; speedily (descriptive of a person running, or the motion of boats and canoes).

หยั่วเมือง see แม่ยั่วเมือง under แม่ ๒ p. 658.

หยากเยื่อ refuse; debris; useless fragments; see มูลฝอย under มูล ๒ p. 655.

หยาด yat[4] n. water or other liquids dis-

persed in fine particles; spray: หยาดน้ำ
fine particles of water: หยาดน้ำค้าง, นฤคหิต
the small circular vowel mark placed over
some vowels, as in น้ำ, คำ. This mark occurs in
words of Pali and Sanskrit origin: หยาดฟ้า
atmospheric dust; fine particles of water or
moisture (as dew or minute drops of rain);
an exceedingly beautiful person or thing (as
though having come from the celestial regions).

หยาบ yap[4] *adj.* rough; rude; ill-bred;
crude; impolite; obscene; see คาย ๑ p. 199:
ทำหยาบยุ่ง deeds or conduct that is wrong,
corrupt, pernicious, or wicked: ผ้าเนื้อหยาบ
coarse fabrics; tapestry: เนื้อหยาบ coarse-
grained (as wood or cloth): หยาบคาย, หยาบ-
ช้า mean; low; bad; uncivil; impudent; rude;
unpolished; impolite (in manners); coarse;
rough (to the touch); vulgar; indelicate; unrefined; gruff; inelegant (in speech or manners): หยาบหยาม insulting, abusive, derisive words or language; contemptuous, scornful, insulting, or insolent manners.

หยาม yam[2] *v.* to maltreat; to revile;
to deride or insult; see ดูหมิ่น under ดู p. 333:
หยามน้ำหน้า to look down upon; to show disrespect; "to hate the very looks of": หยาม-
หยาบ vulgar; arrogant; insulting.
[p. 269.

หยาว yow[2] *adj.* noised about; see ฉาว

หยำเป yam[2]-bpay *adv.* badly; terribly;
frightfully; *an expletive*; see เต็มที่ under เต็ม
p. 373: ทำหยำเป to do, or be done in an
awkward, clumsy, or crude manner (used
as a curse): เมาหยำเป indecently drunk;
ยุ่งหยำเป, ปนกันหยำเป terribly mixed, confused
or tangled.

หยิก yik[4] *v.* to pinch; to squeeze; to nip
(with the fingers): *adj.* curled; wavy (as
hair); fluted (as cloth): หยิกข่วน to pinch
and scratch the skin; a nipping scratch:
หยิกทึ้ง to pinch and pull folds of the skin; a
method of counter irritation used by Chinese

doctors; see ทึ้ง p. 417: หยุกหยิก disposed
to be quarrelsome; irritable; fretful; impatient; touchy.

หยิ่ง ying[4] *adj.* impudent; ostentatious;
proud; haughty; conceited; vain; arrogant;
see จองหอง p. 234: หยิ่งยศ to be conceited
or vain on account of rank or title: หยิ่งเย่อ
idiomatic cheeky and brazen-faced.

หยิบ yip[4] *v.* to take hold of; to grasp; to
clasp; to clutch; to hand something to another: *n.* a pinch; the quantity that can
be taken with two fingers and the thumb:
ที่หยิบได้ what can be reached; within one's
reach: ลืมตาหยิบหยี the eyelids can be
opened only a very little bit: หยิบเงิน to
hand some money to another: หยิบฉวย to
snatch, take, or pick up: หยิบผิด to find
fault with, or pick petty flaws in another;
to see only evil in others; to bring or hand
an article to another in error: หยิบฝ่ายมือ
a handful: หยิบมือหนึ่ง the quantity that can
be dipped up in one hand; a handful (as sand
or cooked rice): หยิบยืม to borrow or ask
the loan of (as small amounts of money now
and then): หยิบหนึ่ง a pinch, or what can
be held in three fingers: หยิบหย่ง dressy;
foppish; dandyish; dandified; arrayed in
ribbons, ruffles and frills: หยิบหยี infinites-
imal in quantity or size; very minute (as a
kite flying a great distance up in the air).

หยิม ๆ yim[2]-yim[2] *adv.* scanty; in small
quantities or drops; sparse; meager; *descriptive of rain falling.*

หยี, หรี yee[2] *adj.* drooping; hanging down;
almost closed; only slightly opened (descriptive of the eyelids): หยีน้ำ (ต้น) *Pongamia
glabra* (*Leguminosae*), Indian beech, a handsome tree with glossy-green pinnate leaves,
bearing racemes of creamy-white, scented
flowers. The timber is good; the foliage is
relished by cattle in time of drought. The
juice of the roots is used for sores, and also
for cleaning the teeth and strengthening the

gums (V. P. p. 226 : MCM. pp. 213, 215, 379 : Burk. p. 1797).

[p. 444.

หยุ yoo[4] *adj.* soft; impressionable; see น่วม

หยุกหยิก yook[4]-yik[4] *v.* to be quarrelsome, troublesome, annoying, restless, fidgety; see จุกจิก p. 253; ยุ่งยิ่ง under ยุ่ง p. 678: การ-หยุกหยิก various petty duties or affairs: ใจ-หยุกหยิก of a quarrelsome nature or disposition: ทำหยุกหยิก to do in an annoying, uneasy or irritating manner: ผมหยุกหยิก disordered hair.

หยุด yoot[4] *v.* to discontinue; to cease from; to stop; to pause or leave off doing; to give up (as a job); see ชะงัก p. 285: หยุดก่อน to leave off working before the others (as in a gang of workmen); an invitation to stay and rest (as at an inn or wayside house): หยุดการ to cease working: หยุดการเสีย a command to discontinue working: หยุดช้านาน to remain some time, or make a lengthy visit: หยุดนอน to stop and sleep; to take a siesta: หยุดนิ่ง to remain perfectly quiet: หยุดบ้าน to break the journey at a house, or stop at a certain village: หยุดพัก to pause for rest; to stop over (night), as on a trip: หยุดยั้ง to make a temporary stop; to break the journey: หยุดร่ม to stop or rest in the shade: หยุดแล้ว to cease flowing (as stopping a leak): หยุดหน่อย to discontinue working or walking for a short period: หยุดหายเหนื่อย to take a brief rest: หยุดให้-สบาย to take a comfortable rest.

หยุ่น yoon[4] *adj.* soft; yielding; flabby; flaccid; lax; elastic; see น่วน p. 444: คล้า-ของหยุ่น ๆ to touch or feel something flabby and yielding.

หยุบ ๆ yoop[4]-yoop[4] *adj.* rising and falling consecutively (as the skin over the apex heart-beat).

หยุมหยิม yoom[2]-yim[2] *adv.* peevish; capricious; whimsical; fickle: พูดหยุมหยิม to talk in an ill-natured, ill-tempered manner,

or about trifles; see จุกจิก p. 253.

หยูกยา yook[4]-yah *n. idiomatic* medicines; remedies in general.

หร ha[4]-ra[6] *P. S. n.* an epithet for Siva; one who takes, seizes, carries off, or conveys away: *adj.* carrying off; removing (S. E. D. p. 1289).

หรคุณ hau[2]-ra[6]-koon *n. lit.* "the counting or adding of days together," *i. e.* the total number of days, as from the beginning of any era: ชาตหรคุณ a vermilion pigment or colouring matter suitable for making paint.

หรดาล hau[2]-ra[6]-dan *n.* a yellow mineral which, when ground to powder, is used as a pigment or dye-stuff; *preferable spelling is* หรดาล p. 917.

หรบ ๆ, หรับ ๆ rop[4]-rop[4] *adv.* actively; energetically; vigorously (descriptive of struggling); see เด่า p. 334; see เร่า 718: เต้น-หรบ ๆ to jump, hop or leap actively (as colts or calves).

หรรษ, หรรษา han[2]-sa[4] *n.* laughter; mirth; joy; pleasure; happiness; love; contentment; lust, or desire (sexual): หรรษจล shaking or trembling from (supreme) joy or pleasure: หรรษทาน gifts or alms given gladly, willingly, and joyfully: หรรษนาท the sounds of joy and mirth at the time of making a gift; a merry shout; sounds of merriment: หรรษช resulting from, or being the consequence of pleasure, joy, contentment or desire.

หรอ raw[2] to be worn thin, or shorter; to become dull or dented by friction: *n.* a condition of attrition.

หร่อมแหร่ม raum[2]-raam[2] *adj.* sparse; scattered; diffused; not dense (descriptive of rain or undergrowth in a forest).

หรอย ๆ roy[2]-roy[2] see ต้อย p. 349.

หรา rah[2] *adv.* gaily; lively; sprightly; *a suffix,* as เต้นหรา; see ร่า p. 706.

หรี ha⁴-ri⁶ *P. S. n. lit.* "a deliverer from," *i. e.* an epithet for Vishnu; a horse; a lion: *adj.* green; yellow; brown; tawny (S. E. D. p. 1289): หรีคันธ์, หรีจันทน์ yellow sandal-wood; red sandal-wood (Chd. p. 152): หรีทาส, หรีภักดี worship or veneration of Vishnu: หรีบท the vernal equinox: หรีพาหนะ *lit.* "the vehicle of Vishnu," *i. e.* the Garuda.

หริ่ง (หนู) ring⁴ *n.* a species of small rat, *Crocidura murina* (Palig. p. 831).

หริ่ง ๆ ring⁴-ring⁴ *onomat.* from the rasping sound of crickets.

หริณะ ha⁴-ri⁶-na⁶ *P. S. n.* a deer or antelope; a fawn; a stag: *adj.* brown; tawny; yellow or light green (in colour) (S. E. D. p. 1291): หริณลักษก์, หริณังก์ *lit.* "deer-spotted," *i.e.* the moon: หริณหฤทัย *lit.* "deer-hearted," *i.e.* cowardly; timid; fearful; faint-hearted; chicken-hearted.

หรีดาล hau²-ri⁶-dan *P. S. n.* yellow orpiment; a sectile, flexible, pearly, lemon-yellow form of arsenic. It is ground into powder for use as a pigment and as a dye-stuff; a pigeon of a yellowish green colour, *Columba hurriyala* (S. E. D. p. 1291).

หรีตกิ, หรีตกี ha⁴-ri⁶-dta⁴-gkee *P. n.* yellow myrobalan; chebulic or black myrobalans; (Chd p. 152); ink-nuts; gall-nuts; *Terminalia chebula (Combretaceae)*, a deciduous tree of India, extending into Burma, sometimes large, but often small, with a good timber; and valuable fruits which, converted into commercial myrobalans, are used for tanning. The ovoid fruit is about one inch long, and is collected from the time when it is just yellowish until it is quite yellow and dead ripe. It is sun dried and converted into the myrobalan of commerce. It must not be made wet by rain during drying. In a small percentage of fruits the interior, under the skin, powders; fruits in which this has happened are not used for tanning, but are made into ink. The penetration of hides by this tan is very slow. The fruit has been a medicine of the Hindus from very ancient times. The fruits contain tannins, being the glucosides of gallic acid, ellagic acid and ellagotannic acid. Although so full of tannin, they are administered with aromatics, and perhaps disguised with honey. The fruits, with alum, dye yellow; and with iron, make ink. The branches produce galls which are used in the same way. The wood is fairly durable, and is used in India for furniture, carts, agricultural implements, and house-building (Burk. p. 2139); see สมอไทย under สมอ p. 818.

หรีภุญชัย ha⁴-ri⁶-poon-chai *n.* an ancient name of Lampoon.

หรี ree⁴ *v.* to lower; to render or make dim; to lessen the light (by turning down the wick or lessening the aperture where light might penetrate): *adj.* partly closed or half open; dimmed: หรีตา partially to open or close the eye-lids.

หรือ reu² *conj.* or; is that so; *a final interrogative particle*: จริงหรือ is that possible? is it true? จะไปหรือว่าจะให้คอย is it that you want me to go or to wait? นี่หรือว่าโน่น is it either this or that? แล้วหรือยัง is the (prescribed) job finished? หรือว่า or; else.

หรุบ ๆ (ร่วงหรุบ ๆ) roop⁴-roop⁴ *adj.* falling one after another (descriptive of fruit falling, as when the branches are shaken).

หรุบรู้ roop⁴-roo³ *adj.* dimmed; dim; obscured; dusky; imperfect (light); murky.

หรู, หรูหรา roo² *adj.* very beautiful; gay; gaudy; flashing; striking; showy; festive (descriptive of clothes worn during a festival).

หฤทัย, หฤทย ha⁴-rur⁶-tai *S. n.* the heart; the mind; the power of reasoning; the seat of thought and feeling (S.E.D. p. 1202): หฤทัยกลม *lit.* "weakness of the heart," *i. e.* one who is lenient, tender, forbearing, docile or

obedient: หฤทัยกัปน์, หฤทัยกัมป์ the pulsations or palpation of the heart: หฤทัยพันธน์
lit. "captivating the heart," *i. e.* enticing;
alluring; interesting; tempting; attractive;
see จับจิตต์ under จับ p. 241: หฤทัยโรค
disease of the heart: หฤทัยเลข *lit.* "heart-
impressions," *i. e.* knowledge; understanding;
discernment; discrimination; *lit.* "furrows of
the heart," *i. e.* anxiety: หฤทัยสถลี,หฤทัย-
สถาน *lit.* "heart-region," *i. e.* the thorax; the
breast; the bosom.

หฤษฏ์, หฤหรรษ์ ha⁴-rit⁶ *S. adj.* pleased;
delighted; merry; joyful; smiling; laughing;
thrilled; see ดีใจ under ดี p. 330.

หฤษฏ ha⁴-rit⁶-sa⁴-dee *S. n.* gladness; rapture; joy; delight; see ปลาบปลื้มใจ under
ปลาบ p. 512.

หฤโหด ha⁴-rur⁶-hote⁴ *adj.* vindictive; savage; brutal; cruel; see ใจร้าย under ใจ p. 263.

หล ha⁴-la⁶ *S. n.* the handle of a plough:
adj. see ควร p. 187.

หลง long² *v.* to forget; to become enamoured or fascinated with; to have an
inordinate desire for; to go astray or be lost
(as while travelling through a forest); to be
obsessed with: *adj.* forgotten; overlooked;
neglected: พิศวงหลงใหล to be forgetful
from embarrassment, astonishment or perplexity: ลุ่มหลง to be deceived or carried
away by appearances or hearsay: หลงกล,
หลงเล่ห์ to be deceived, beguiled, or entrapped
by some trickery: หลงกิน to eat by mistake, absent-mindedly, or greedily (as without due care): หลงเกินไป to go thoughtlessly
beyond the intended destination: หลง-
เข้ามา to trespass inadvertently or heedlessly:
หลงคอย to wait for another beyond the appointed time: หลงเงิน to be obsessed with
the idea of making money, or the acquiring of riches: หลงตา unnoticed; unseen;
slighted: หลงทาง to lose the way; to take
the wrong path or road: หลงไป to go by
a wrong path or road (as when forgetting

which fork of the road to take): หลงมา
to come to a place by mistake, or to take one
house for another (as one, who is going for
a doctor, enters the wrong house): หลงมาก
to be unduly fascinated with, or endeared
to (as a husband to his wife): หลงเมีย to be
unduly influenced by one's wife: หลงแม่
to stray away or be separated from one's
mother (as a child in a crowd of people):
หลงรัก to become overly fascinated with some
woman, girl or flapper: หลงละเลิง, หลงละลาน
a state of rapture, ecstacy or exultation:
หลงลาภ to be obsessed with a desire for good
fortune, luck or success (as when buying lottery tickets): หลงลิ้น to believe the words
of another readily, or to concur in his
opinions: หลงลืม, ขี้หลงขี้ลืม to be forgetful,
or to become absent-minded: หลงเลอะ
to be confused, embarrassed, or flustered by
forgetfulness: หลงโลภ inordinate desire
for; covetousness; avariciousness: หลงใหล
to be forgetful from feebleness of mind; to
be in one's dotage; see พั้นเพื่อน under พั้น ๒
p. 607: หลงเอา to be unduly avaricious or
grasping: หลงเอาไป to take away unthinkingly, or by mistake.

หลด (ปลา) lot⁴ *n. Mastacembelus circum-
cinctus (Mastacembelidae); Rhynchobdella
aculeata; Muraenesox cinereus (Muraenesocidae)* (suvatti pp. 20, 21, 22).

หลน lon² *v.* to boil to a jelly, or stew till
quite tender (as salted fish, dried shrimps or
prawns); see เคี่ยว p. 211: หลนปลาเจ่า, หลน
ปลาร้า to boil fish, which has been preserved
in brine, with coconut milk.

หล่น lon⁴ *v.* to fall or drop (singly as ripe
fruit from off a tree); see ร่วง p. 689: เก็บ-
ที่หล่น to pick up what has fallen: แก่-
หล่น to fall on account of being fully ripe:
ตกหล่นอยู่บ้าง some have been unavoidably left
behind, or fallen by the way: หล่นกลาดเกลื่อน
to fall in abundance: หล่นกลิ้ง to fall and
roll away: หล่นหรือร่วง *idiomatic* are they

falling singly (as fruit) or collectively (as leaves)?

หลบ, หลบหลีก lop[4] *v.* to shirk; to evade or elude; to avoid meeting or seeing; to hide or conceal oneself; to escape secretly, or slip away from; to shun the face of: ไข้หลบ concealed or latent manifestations of disease: หลบการ to shirk work: หลบการเรียน to be truant from school: หลบกะเบื้อง to roof a building with tiles: โรคหลบเข้าห้อง to develop on internal organs and not on external surfaces (as suppressed small-pox): หลบเจ้าหนี้ to avoid meeting the creditors: หลบตัว, หลบหน้า to escape from showing one's face; to hide: หลบฝาก to be kept secretly under the protection of another (as a mistress under her mother's care and in her home): หลบลี้ to hide oneself completely; successfully to avoid being found or seen: หลบหนี to make good one's escape: หลบหนีจากที่คุมขัง to escape from custody: หลบหลังคา to place a final covering over the ridge of a roof: หลบอยู่ being secreted in, or at a certain place.

หล่ม lom[4] *n.* mud; mire: ที่หล่ม marshy ground: เมืองหล่ม an ancient Laotian town: หล่ม (ในเนื้อ) a natural physical depression (as over the clavicle).

หลวง lu-ang[2] *n.* a title, being the second of a series of five conferred ranks for officials of the civil service. ขุน is the first or lowest rank of conferred nobility (the others are หลวง, พระ, พระยา, เจ้าพระยา); a title of respect shown to elderly relatives while in the Buddhist priesthood, as หลวงพี่, หลวงน้ำ: *adj.* great; royal; chief; superior; pertaining to the king: ของหลวง, ที่หลวง crown or state property: นายหลวง, ในหลวง the king: เมืองหลวง a capital: วังหลวง the Royal Palace.

หลวม lu-am[2] *adj.* loose; too large or big; fitting badly; moving freely or without friction (as in a prescribed space): เจาะรูหลวมไป to mortise, bore, or pierce a hole larger than is necessary: ฟันหลวม shaky teeth; a loose

dental plate: หลวมไป to make or become too loose: หลวมโพลกเพลก so loose as to cause a rattling sound: หลวมรู to be smaller than the hole made (as a screw in a hole too large): ข้าวหลวมหม้อ an insufficient quantity, or too small an amount of rice (in a rice-pot) to supply the family.

หลอ, เหลอ law[2] *v.* to have some left over; to keep a reserve supply on hand; not to have an empty larder: *adj.* indented; hollowed out; excavated by degrees; blunted: ดูให้มีข้าวหลอหม้อ see to it that some rice is left in the rice-pot: ไม่เหลือหลอ to have no reserve remaining: ไม่มีแรงเหลือหลอ to have no reserve strength.

หล่อ law[4] *v.* to cast molten metals in a form or mould (as images): ช่างหล่อ a smelter: โรงหล่อ a smeltery; a foundry: หล่อพระ to cast images as objects of worship: หล่อยัน to shape charms, amulets or talismans of metal: หล่อหลอม *idiomatic* to reduce (metals) to a liquid state.

หลอก, หลอน lauk[4] *v.* to deceive; to delude; to beguile; to scare; to terrify; to startle; to frighten (as by telling stories or by jesting); see ลวง p. 729: ผีหลอก the ghost will get you! (a common expression for intimidating children): หลอกนาย to deceive one's master; fraudulently to declare certain things to be true: หลอกล่อให้กิน to induce to eat or drink by deceptive means: หลอกเล่น to deceive jestingly; to allure by false pretenses: หลอกหลอนลวงกัน to deceive by incredible stories: ถูกหลอกเอา to be a victim of an imposture.

หลอด laut[4] *n.* a pipe; a tube with flanges; a bushing: ด้ายหลอด thread rolled on a reel, bobbin or spool: ไม้หลอด a weaver's bobbin or reel: หลอดแก้ว glass tubing: หลอดจังหัน a short bushing placed between the blades of a whirligig to prevent their interfering: หลอดชะนวนกระสุนแตก a powder chamber, or fuse tube for bombs: หลอด-

ชุด a tinder tube used with a flint and steel igniter; a tinder-box: หลอดต้าย a spool of thread: หลอดตะเกียง a lamp chimney: หลอดไฟฟ้า an electric light bulb: หลอดยานัตถุ์ a tube for taking snuff: หลอดลมสู่ปอด air passages (of the lungs): หลอดหูก a short cylinder for thread; a bobbin for a loom.

หล็อน laun[2] *adj.* too small in size, or too little in quantity (in contradistinction to what should be large or abundant).

หลอน laun[2] *v.* to intimidate by teasing; see ล้อ p. 730.

หล่อน laun[4] *pron.* you; she; her; a term of endearment used by men: เจ้าหล่อนว่า she said that.

หลอม laum[2] *v.* to smelt; to melt or fuse (as metals): หลอมตะกั่ว to melt lead: หลอมเหล็ก to liquefy iron by heat.

หละหลวม la[4]-lu-am[2] *adj.* careless; in too lax a manner; too free or reckless; incautious; heedless; inconsiderate.

หลัก lak[4] *n.* a stake; a picket; a paling; a basis; a post supporting groundwork; a place of refuge; a strong principle; a maxim; a rule; a doctrine; a tenet; an opinion; integrity: ปักหลัก, ลงหลัก to drive down or plant posts: ผู้หลักผู้ใหญ่ superiors; ancestors; the "old folks": ไม่มีหลัก groundless; false: หลักกฎหมายทั่วไป general principles of law: หลักคำ *lit.* "a golden wand," *i. e.* a Laotian rank for high religious dignitaries: หลักแจว see แจว p. 261: หลักฐาน wealth; property; stability; security; guaranty: หลักเมือง boundaries of a city or town; the zero milestone of a city: หลักลอย *lit.* "tossed on life's ocean," *i. e.* vagrant; unstable; groundless; without security (as a house built on sand): หลักโลก *simile* a person or some article held in national veneration; a national palladium: หลักสูตร curriculum; syllabus: หลักหลาย to have many supporting stakes or posts; to be firm, permanent, durable: หลักแหลม *n.* a post with a sharpened end; a spike: *adj.* skillful; bright; sharp; intelligent; expert: หลักแหล่ง permanent (abode); constant; secure (as a house built on a rock); a tethering post for cattle: หลักใหญ่ eminent; superior in rank.

หลัง lang[2] *n.* the back: *adv.* after; behind: *adj. a numerical designation for houses and buildings*; next; latter; posterior; reversed (side); afterwards: ข้างหลัง behind; in the rear of: ครั้งหลัง, ที่หลัง some future time; next time: ตามหลัง to follow on behind; to come after or afterwards: ที่หน้าที่หลัง *idiomatic* in the future: ภายหลัง afterwards; later: เรือนหลังหนึ่ง a house: หลังโกง, หลังกุ้ง hump-backed: หลังแข็ง perverse; stubborn; stiff-backed: หลังคา a roof; a canopy: หนังหลังตา the external surface of the eyelid: หลังเต่า a bar (as at the mouth of a river); the back of a turtle: หลังเท้า the dorsal surface of the foot: หลังบ้าน the back yard.

หลั่ง lang[4] *v.* to pour; to cause to flow down; to shed (as tears); see เท p. 421: น้ำตาหลั่งไหล to shed copious tears: หลั่งน้ำพระพุทธมนตร์ to pour lustral water as an act of consumation of some ceremony (as in the marriage ceremony).

หลัดๆ lat[4]-lat[4] *adv.* quickly; see เร็ว p. 718.

หลั่น lan[4] *n.* degrees; folds; order; series; tiers; layers; steps; grades; see ระเบียบ p. 697; ลำดับ p. 742: เป็นหลั่นๆ in degrees or gradations: หลั่นลาด descending in terraces, tiers or by degrees (as a succession of mountain peaks).

หลับ lap[4] *v.* to shut (as eyes); to be asleep: หลับนอน to take a nap; to sleep: หลับนิ่ง to be sleeping quietly: หลับพระเนตร, หลับตา to close the eyes: หลับไป to go off into a sleep: หลับเพ้อ to mumble, groan or be delirious while asleep: see เพ้อ p. 598: ที่หลับที่นอนเสื่อหมอน *idiomatic* bedding in general.

หลัว lu-ah[2] *n.* a large deep wicker basket for holding or carrying fish : *adj.* dull ; dusky (colour) ; dim ; faded ; pale ; obscure ; see สลัว p. 828.

หลา, เลหลา lah[2] *n.* a yard-stick ; a yard.

หล้า lah[3] *n.* world ; earth ; firmament : ใต้หล้า under the heavens : แหล่งหล้า terrestrial plains ; see แผ่นดิน under แผ่น p. 551.

หลาก lak[4] *adj.* wonderful ; unexpected ; surprising ; different ; strange ; various : น้ำไหลหลาก the water has flooded to a remarkable degree : หลากใจ to be astonished or surprised ; see แปลก p. 536 ; ท่วม p. 399.

หลาน lan[2] *n.* grandchildren ; nephews ; nieces : ลูกหลาน posterity : หลานเขย a grandson by marriage, or a nephew by marriage : หลานชาย grandsons : หลานผัว the husband's nephew or niece ; the husband's granddaughter or grandson : หลานเมีย the wife's nephew or niece ; the wife granddaughter or grandson : หลานสะใภ้ a niece by marriage or a granddaughter by marriage : หลานสาว granddaughters : หลานหัวปี a firstborn nephew or niece : หลานเหลน a greatgrandchild ; a great-nephew or great-niece.

หลาบ lap[4] *v.* to fear ; to dread ; to remember severe punishment or suffering ; to fear to repeat an offense ; to be afraid of (as after a reprimand or punishment) ; to cause to remember and to profit by some correction or discipline ; see เข็ด p. 163 : เข็ดหลาบ to be taught, or profit by experience : ไม่รู้เข็ดหลาบ to be incorrigible ; to be depraved beyond reform : ลงโทษให้เข็ดหลาบ to punish in order to instill a fear of repeating the offense : หลาบแล้ว to profit by reproof or punishment ; to reform or mend one's conduct.

หลาม lam[2] *v.* to cook, boil or roast in bamboo joints ; to come in great quantities (as an overflow of water) ; to gather around in great crowds (as excited people during some big fire) : *n.* a boa constrictor ; a python :

หลาม, เหลื่อม (ง) the reticulated python, *Python reticulatus* (smith, N. H. J. S. S. I, 1, p. 9) : ข้าวหลาม rice in coconut milk, roasted in bamboo joints. After the joints have been filled, the mouth is corked with banana leaves and set leaning in two rows against an iron rod over a brisk fire. The hard, charred outside of the bamboo joint is carefully peeled off so as to expose the rice which is eaten cold : หลามเข้ามา to approach in great crowds or flocks : หลามดูแห่ to throng around to witness a procession.

หลาย lai[2] *adj.* many ; several ; sundry ; divers ; various ; *sign of the plural* ; see มาก p. 647 : หลายก๊ก many cliques, clans, societies or fraternaties : หลายกล, หลายเล่ห์ many secret devices (as in sleight-of-hand tricks) : หลายคน several persons ; many people : หลายครั้ง, หลายหน many times, or on several occasions : หลายใจ of many opinions, or of varying dispositions : หลายเติบ in great quantities ; very many ; very much : หลายลิ้น various versions of the same story : หลายส่วน many pieces, divisions or sections : ทั้งหลาย all : หลายแหล่, มากหลาย in great abundance ; copious ; plenteous : หลายอย่าง a great variety ; in many ways.

หลาว low[2] *n.* a long, sharp-pointed, bamboo stick : หลาวทอก a wooden spear or dagger : หลาวแหลน an iron dagger with a long wooden handle.

หลิทท์ see ขมิ้น p. 141

หลิน lin[2] *Chin. n.* a kind of Chinese silk.

หลิม lim[2] *adj.* small ; tapering ; pyramidal ; conical ; see เรียว ๑ p. 720 : หัวหลิม a small undeveloped head ; see แกร็น p. 129.

หลิ่ว liew[4] *adj.* one ; single ; sole ; see เดียว p. 335 : นกเขาหลิ่ว a dove that coos with a single note : แลหลิ่ว to look with one eye shut ; to squint with one eye : หลิ่วตา to look with one eye only (as while aiming to shoot a gun).

หลี lee[2] *n.* a Chinese unit of weight equal to 37.5 milligrams (used by jewelers) (The Central Bureau of Weights and Measures, Ministry of Commerce); see หุน.

หลีก, หลบ leek[4] *v.* to avoid; to evade; to elude; to escape from; to get or keep out of the way, or away from; to turn or detour to one side (as when letting another pass); to absent oneself: ทางหลีก a switch (as along the tramway): หลีกการ to evade working: หลีกบาป to eschew evil: หลีกไปหน่อย to make way for another to pass; to get a little out of the way: หลีกลี้ to run away from and hide: หลีกหนี to make good one's escape.

หลิบ leep[4] *n.* a shrill-toned wind instrument; a soprano flute.

หลิบ leup[4] *n.* a mountain pass, hole, or aperture with terraced entrance (as into a cave): หลิบผา jutting rocks or boulders, forming tiers: หลิบเหว steps, or a series of gradations into an abyss.

หลุกหลิก look[4]-lik[4] *v.* to do in a hurry, restlessly, hastily, or impetuously; see ลุกลน p. 748; to be mischievous, rude or naughty (as children who are never still).

หลุด loot[4] *v.* to be detached from; to be untied or loosened; to be released from (as from jail); to fall off (as do buttons): จำนำหลุด to forfeit (the ownership of) pawned articles by default of payment: หลุดลุ่ย to be dishevelled (as hair); to be detached (as clothing); to be so badly disunited or torn asunder that there is no hope of joining together again (as a sail blown into shreds): แพ้หลุดลุ่ย to be badly beaten in a game, or out-distanced in a race; to be without hope of winning (as a contestant in some game).

หลุน ๆ loon[2]-loon[2] *onomat.* from the sound used to excite or stimulate cattle and buffaloes to fight: วิ่งหลุน ๆ to run in a reeling, lungiug manner; see เช p. 310.

หลุบ loop[4] *v.* to become flattened down (as the feathers of a cock after fighting); to be folded down over the edges (as the cloth covering of books): หลุบผม see ผมลุ่ under ลุ่ p. 749: หลุบลู่ veiled; hidden (as by hair or feathers); see ปก p. 492: หลุบหัว to hang down the head.

หลุม loom[2] *n.* a pit; a ditch; a hole; a cavity; see บ่อ p. 472: ตกหลุมพราง to be ensnared in a trap-hole: หลุมถ่านเพลิง a pit of burning coals (the implication is hell): หลุมถ่านหิน a coal-mine: หลุมฝังศพ a grave: หลุมพราง a pit; a hole dug as a trap for tigers or elephants; a trap; a snare or trick.

หลู่ loo[4] *v.* to scorn, slight or show disdain; to be unappreciative, ungrateful, scornful, disrespectful, or insulting; see ดูถูก under ดู p. 333: ลบหลู่ to treat with contempt or disdain: หลู่คุณ to be ungrateful or disregardful of favours: หลู่หลี bold; rude; saucy; impudent.

หวง hoo-ang[2] *v.* to hoard; to store; to reserve; to retain; to withhold or keep back; to be selfish; to be envious; to be jealous of, or zealous for: ผัวหวงเมีย a husband zealously guards his wife: สุนัขหวงลูก a mother dog zealously cares for her pups: หวงกิน to eat selfishly (as a dog): หวงเข้าของ to guard one's household possessions zealously: หวงเงิน to be "close fisted" with one's money: หวงหึง to be jealous of another's love or attentions: หวงแหน *idiomatic* to withhold or guard with ardent care; see สงวน p. 807.

ห่วง hoo-ang[4] *n.* a ring; a loop; links; worries; obstacles; entanglements; impediments: เข้าห่วง to be entrapped; to be tied or fastened: เป็นห่วง to be worried; to be anxious for, or interested in; to be solicitous about; to ask after another's welfare (as in case of sickness): เป็นห่วงด้วย to be anxious about: ห่วงกิน to be anxious about what one is going to get to eat: ห่วงคนไข้ to be worried about the condition of a sick person, or patient: ห่วง-

งาน to be engrossed in one's work: ห่วงโซ่
links of a chain: ห่วงใย to be engrossed
or absorbed about; see ผูกพัน under ผูก p. 549:
ห่วงรูด a slip-knot, running-knot, or noose:
ห่วงสงสาร to have feelings of pity for those
in distress.

ห้วง   hoo-ang³ *n.* a stage; a section; a part;
a portion or division (as of a journey); see
ตอน p. 348; a lake; a pool (as at the base of
a waterfall); a puddle of water: ห้วงน้ำ
an ocean; a sea; a wide expanse of water, or
the broad stretch of a river (as occurs at the
confluence of two branches of a river): ห้วง-
น้ำวน a whirlpool: ห้วงหนอง *idiomatic* a
marsh; a swamp.

หวด   hu-at⁴ *v.* to whip; to scourge; to
lash; to slash or strike; see ฟาด p. 608: *n.*
a perforated steaming-pot; an earthenware
steamer for cooking glutinous rice, consisting
of a lower vessel for the water, onto the
mouth of which fits another vessel with perforations in the bottom; this latter vessel
holds the rice: หวดกลั่น a retort for distillation: หวดหญ้า to cut grass with a
slashing motion of a knife (as along road-
sides).

หวน   hu-an² *v.* to reverse; to turn or return; to turn right-about face; to whirl or
revolve (as by the wind): ลมหวน the wind
changes in its course: หวนกลับ to turn
back or retrace one's steps (as when having
gone part way on a walk): หวนใจ to be
vacillating in mind or purpose; to be of a
wavering or inconstant disposition; see ย้อน
p. 667.

ห้วน   hu-an³ *adj.* short; shortened; curtailed; abbreviated; abridged; scant; see ลุ่น
p. 748; สั้น p. 848.

หวย   hu-ie² *n.* lottery; a system of gambling by betting on letters of the alphabet.
This is of Chinese origin and was introduced
into Thailand in 1835 A. D. The system, as

it originally existed in China, was to place
stakes on the names of pictures of thirty-four
important personages of the period; these
were intended to represent the thirty-four
letters of the lottery. When introduced into
Thailand, these were increased to thirty-six
and, to popularize the system to the Thai,
each was assigned a Thai consonant, each
letter to represent the personage and the
animal which was the former birth-state of
the said personage. On placing a bet, the
better received a ticket and, if successful, received twenty-nine times the amount of his
bet. The huey lottery was stopped on April
1st, 1916, having had an existence of eighty-
one years.

ห้วย   hu-ie³ *n.* a stream; a creek; a brook;
a rivulet; see ลำห้วย under ลำ ๒ p. 741:
ห้วยหนอง a small water-way by which water
discharges from a swamp or marsh: ห้วยเหว
a stream along the bottom of a chasm or
valley; see ลำธาร under ลำ ๒ p. 741.

หวอ   waw² *adj.* sunken; hollowed out;
concaved; excavated; see โบ๋ p. 491: บินหวอ
to fly off in a stately manner (as an air-ship
or bird); see โพรง p. 602.

หวอด   waut⁴ *n.* bubbles which help to
deposit eggs or roe that some species of fishes
produce (as the fighting fish).

หวะ   wa⁴ *adj.* opened; excavated; scooped
out; see เว้า p. 783; *descriptive of immensity
or extensiveness, as lacerated wounds or blow-
outs;* see โบ p. 491.

หวัง   wang² *v.* to hope for; to expect, or
long for (as something to be gained or accomplished); to purpose, or intend; see ปรารถนา
p. 507: หวังจะได้ to hope confidently for a
successful result: หวังจะเลือก expecting to
select (as when trying to decide which of two
persons to take as a guardian): หวังหมาย-
จะให้ intending to give; trusting to be able
to give: หวังอยู่ว่า one's purpose of mind:
หวังจะเอา expected or wished for.

หวัด   wat[4] *n.* a cold; a catarrhal disorder due to exposure to cold or wet: *adv.* carelessly; rapidly; heedlessly (descriptive of writing): เขียนหวัด to write with a fast, free, running hand (as when taking notes of a lecture); see สะเพร่า p. 839: ไข้หวัด a cold with fever: ไม่หวัดไม่ไหว to be utterly beyond one's strength; to be absolutely impossible: หนังสือสำหรับหวัด a book for scribbling notes.

หวั่น   wan[4] *v.* to shake; to quiver; to be agitated or convulsed by fear or emotion: ใจหวั่น to be moved by a feeling of fear or dread; see พรั่น p. 568: แผ่นดินหวั่นไหว the earth rocks and trembles (as in an earthquake): หวั่นหวาดไหว *idiomatic* to be exceedingly agitated: หวั่นหวาด to tremble with anxious fear (as in case of a fire coming near to one's house): หวั่นไหว to shake, tremble, rock or quake (violently).

หวา   wah[2] *onomat.* the sound or exclamation placed at the end of a sentence or phrase, as เอาเถิดหวา; see โวย p. 784.

หว่า   wah[4] *adj.* empty; vacant; bare; see เปล่า p. 533.

หว้า, หว้าบ่า   wah[3] *Thai,* มะห้า *Laos, Chiengmai* (ต้น) *n. Eugenia cumini (Myrtaceae),* jambolan, a fruit-tree of moderate size, wild in India and Malaysia, as well as in cultivation. Improved races may bear fruits as large as pigeons' eggs, and one exists in the Philippine Islands which may bear seedless but small fruits. The races differ considerably in the colour of the fruit. In India a vinegar is made from the juice of the unripe fruit, and in Goa a wine is made from the ripe fruit. The seed is medicinal in India. A powder of the seed is administered in diabetes, diarrhoea, dysentery; and as an antidote in poisoning from nux-vomica. It has been used also, in diabetes in Europe serving in some cases as the basis of patent medicines. Whatever the active substance may be, it is suggested that it has an influence upon the diastatic ferments found in the saliva and serum of the blood. In India the bark is medicinal, being used as an astringent for dysentery and as a gargle. There is tannin in the bark, but the really active substance has not been isolated. Leaves and flowers are said also to carry it. The timber is hard, and is sometimes used in the Dutch Indies for houses, but it is difficult to work. It is said to make good fuel (BURK. p. 965); *E. zimmermanii* (cb. pp. 637, 655, 667): หว้าขาว *Thai, Trang* (ต้น) *Eugenia kurzii (Myrtaceae)* (cb. p. 648); *E. operculata,* var. *obovata,* a tree of moderate size, found from the Himalayas and southern Burma to western Malaysia. It is useful in reclothing grassy blanks in the forests of *Shorea robusta,* and the mixed forests of northern India. The timber is only moderately good, but is used in India for building, and for agricultural implements. It it sometimes used for housebuilding. The fruit is sometimes eaten in Java and India. A substitute for tea is made from the leaves in Indo-China (BURK. p. 972): หว้าขึ้นก *Laos, Loi,* มะห้านก *Laos, Lampun* (ต้น) *Eugenia ripicola (Myrtaceae)* (cb. p. 660): หว้าขี้มูด *Thai, Krat,* แดงนา *Thai, Chumpawn,* มัก *Thai, Ranawng* and *Langsuan,* แพ *Thai, Surat, Nakawn Sritamarat* and *Pattani* (ต้น) *Eugenia polyantha (Myrtaceae),* a tall tree found in Burma and southwards throughout western Malaysia. The wood is fairly hard, but splits on drying. It is used for housebuilding and is durable. In the Dutch Indies the bark is considerably used for tanning fishing-nets; and for colouring mats. For this purpose it is pounded in water; after straining, the split bamboos used for the matting are repeatedly dipped in the infusion, over two days. Then they are immersed in mud to blacken. An extract of the bark is given in Java for diarrhoea; as also, alternatively, an infusion of the leaves. The bark, root, and leaves are used for poulticing for itch by the Malays. In the Dutch Indies the young leaves are commonly used with food. The fruit may be eaten. Other names for *E. polyantha* are แพ, มัก, แดงนา (cb. p. 656; burk. p. 973): หว้าป่า *Thai*, *Pattani* (ต้น) *Eugenia clarkeana* (*Myrtaceae*) (cb. p. 635).

หว้า (นก) wah[3] *n.* Argus pheasant (*Argusianus*) (minutes of s. s. Regarding wild Game Preservation in siam).

หวาก wak[4] *onomat.* from the loud crying of children.

หวาด wat[4] *v.* to be startled or frightened (as at the alarm of fire); to be roused suddenly or awakened (as by a sharp peal of thunder): ความหวาด apprehensive fear: หวาดหวั่นไหว to tremble with fright; see สะดุ้ง p. 835.

หวาด wat[4] *N. Laos*, สวาด *Thai*, บ่าขี้แฮด *Laos*, *Chiengmai*, มะกาแลง *Shan*, *Chiengmai* (ต้น) *n. Caesalpinia crista* (*Leguminosae*), also *C. jayabo*, two species of half-woody climbers found throughout the tropics. The Malays encourage them near their homes so that they may be available when wanted. The roots, leaves, and seeds are medicinal in various ways all around the world. The plant has long been used in the east, possibly from remotest times. As the seeds contain the active substance equally with the leaves, and are convenient to keep in shops, they are more used outside the region where the plant freely grows than its other parts; but where the plant is readily available, it seems to be common to use the leaves. A century ago the seeds became official as a tonic and antiperiodic, in the Indian Pharmacopoeia. The active principle in the seeds is a bitter substance, bonducin. The taste of the seeds is extremely bitter. In India the seeds, the testa having been removed, are ground in water, and the liquid drunk for colic; they may be roasted and then powdered, and the powder swallowed for hydrocele. The liquor

is anthelmintic, and as a tonic is given in many complaints. In the Dutch Indies the seeds are used as a vermifuge, and chewed for coughs. In the Philippine Islands they are eaten for all stomach troubles. The Malays use an infusion of the leaves for tapeworm, and for rheumatism. In Java an alcoholic extract is used for jaundice. There are many other medicinal uses. The Malay boys use the hard seeds as marbles for games. In tropical Africa they are likewise used for games, and also for oracles, etc. (cb. p. 501; burk. p. 388).

หวาดเสียว wat[4]-see-oh[2] *v.* to have a sinking, shrinking or flinching feeling from fear (as when looking down from a high building): หวาดหวั่น to shudder, shiver, or be startled from fear, or from some sudden noise; see กลัว p. 60.

หวาน wan[2] *adj.* sweet; honied; sugary; soft; melodious; harmonious: ของคาวหวาน courses of fish, meat and sweets: ของหวาน cakes; dainties; sweets (eaten as dessert): คนปากหวาน a pleasing talker: น้ำหวาน aeriated waters; various sweetened drinks: หวานสนิท unadulterated sweetness: หวานแสบคอ exceedingly sweet; overly sweet.

หวาน (ผัก) wan[2] *n. Melientha suavis* (*Opiliaceae*), a species of shrub grown abundantly in the dry forest; it sends up shoots in the hot season from January to March. The young leaves and shoots are eaten as a vegetable possessing a taste similar to that of spinach but the abnormal young ears and shoots, which are probably due to parasital larva, are poisonous. The symptoms of being poisoned by the consumption of this shoot is that the eater first feels nauseated and fainting, then collapse and death follow shortly thereafter (medical journal. XIV, 4, pp. 696, 700).

หว่าน wan[4] *v.* to sow, cast or scatter (grain); to distribute or disseminate (as discord or false doctrines); see โปรย p. 537):

หว่านกล้า, ตกกล้า to sow seedling paddy: หว่านนา to sow paddy (directly) in a field: หว่านล้อม to surround with pleasing, alluring, seductive, or consoling words: ผู้หว่าน a sower.

หวาม wam[2] *adj.* having a lonely, lonesome, or dreary feeling; see เปลี่ยว p. 534.

หวาย wai[2] *n. Calamus spp. (Palmae)*, rattan (V. P. p. 245 : BURK. p. 396): หวายขม a tough rattan-like vine growing some fifteen to eighteen feet in length: หวายตะค้า a species of large yellow rattan about the size of the thumb. It is imported into Thailand: หวายตะมอย *Dendrobium crumenatum*, pigeon orchid, a very common plant in the Malay Peninsula, also found in Ceylon, Burma, southern China, and eastwards to Amboina and the Philippines. It was brought into cultivation in Europe a century and a half ago, for its beautiful but short-lived flowers and delicious scent. The Malays commonly use the juice of the pseudo-bulbs of any similar orchids for treating ears; and this being the commonest orchid in the country, is most used. The pseudo-bulb is usually heated as a preliminary to squeezing the juice into the ear. The same treatment is used in Java. The Malays poultice boils and pimples with the pounded leaves (V. P. p. 245 : BURK. p. 779): หวายลิง *Flagellaria indica (Flagellariaceae)*, a half-woody, small-sized climber growing along the seashore from the Mascarene Islands to New Caledonia. In Malaya it is not uncommon in the interior. Its stems are tough enough to be used for basket-making, and are used for stitching ataps, nipa thatch, etc. in Thailand and eastern Malaysia. Its leaves and fruits are medicinal. The young leaves are used for making a hairwash (BURK. p. 1024).

หว่ำ wum[2] *adj.* depressed; hollowed out; excavated; pitted; see บุ๋ม p. 485: หวำเป็นรุ having pits, holes or perforations: หวำหวะ

pitted with wide gashes (as a tree with knife-marks).

หวีด wit[4] *adj.* passing near by; grazed; see เฉียด p. 272: หวุดหวีด a very narrow escape.

หวิว wiew[2] *adj.* weak; soft; faint; see เบา p. 489: ใจหวิว ๆ a feeling of faintness or giddiness from a gentle, flickering heart action: ลมพัดหวิว ๆ a light gentle breeze.

หวี wee[2] *v.* to draw a comb through; to disentangle or card: *n.* a comb (for the hair); a *hand* or *cluster* (of bananas): หวีเสนียด a fine-toothed comb.

หวี่ (แมลง) wee[4] *n.* gnats; a species of small fly: *onomat.* from the buzzing of insects.

หวีด weet[4] *onomat.* from a sound uttered in alarm or fear; a word imitating the shrill note of a whistle: เสียงหวีดหวาด a general cry in case of danger or alarm.

หวือ weu[2] *onomat.* from the sound of chips or splinters flying past the ear.

หวุดหวีด woot[4]-wit[4] *adj.* just grazing; passing near to; almost touching while passing; see เฉียด p. 272.

หวุ่ม woom[2] *adj.* depressed; pitted; see บุ๋ม p. 485; บ่ำ p. 482.

หวูด woot[4] *n.* a steam whistle; the sound of a ship's whistle: เป่าหวูด to blow the whistle.

หอ hau[2] *n.* a castle; a tower; the residence of a superior person or noble; a lofty room: เรือนหอ the rooms or home of the bride and groom: หอกลอง an observation tower of three stories, each storey having a drum which the watchman beats as an alarm in cases of fire, riot or the approach of an enemy: หอกลาง a hall or tower centrally located among other buildings or rooms: หอคอย a look-out tower; a watch-tower built along the city wall; a light-house: หอคำ a gilded tower, house or palace: หอเครื่อง a house or room where valuable personal effects (as kingly jewels) are kept or stored; a royal store-house: หอไตร, หอไตรปิฎก a monastic library where Buddhistic scriptures are kept; a pagoda library: หอทะเบียนที่ดิน a land registration office: หอโทน an isolated tower-like building: หอนก a small pavilion resembling a bird-house built for recreation at the side of a body of water, or on a lawn: หอแปลพระราชสาสน์ a building where royal commands or edicts were read out and explained to the public, as was the custom in ancient times: หอพระ small buildings where images of the Buddha are placed for public adoration and worship: หอรบ forts built along walls or at gates where cannons are placed; fighting tops (on a battle ship): หอระฆัง a bell-tower or belfry; a building seen in all Buddhist monasteries where a bell is struck at regular times (as at eleven a. m.).

ห่อ   hau[4] v. to wrap up or envelop: n. a parcel; a package; a bundle of medicinal powders; *a numerical designation for articles wrapped in paper or leaves*: ห่อหมก a relish composed of fish or meat, coconut milk, and spices wrapped in banana leaves and steamed.

ห้อ   hau[3] v. to gallop: n. black and blue marks from bruises or floggiug: ห้อม้า to gallop or race horses; see ควบ p. 187: ห้อเลือด hematoma; a tumour containing effused blood.

หอก   hauk[4] n. a lance; a spear (with wooden shaft): หอกข้างแคร่ a spear kept by the side of the warrior as he rides in a howdah, palanquin or litter: หอกคู่ a pair of javelins carried by two persons walking abreast (as in processions): หอกซัด a far-darting weapon for throwing or pitching: หอกปลายปืน a bayonet.

ห้อง   haung[3] n. a room; a chamber; a saloon; an apartment: ห้องขัง a place of confinement; a lock-up: ห้องครัว a kitchen: ห้องช่วม a lavatory; a toilet-room: ห้องแต่งตัว a dressing-room: ห้องทหารยาม a guard's room: ห้องนอก an ante-room or chamber: ห้องนอน a bedroom: ห้องนักเรียนนอน a dormitory: ห้องบรรทม the chamber of state; the royal bedchamber: ห้องรับแขก a reception room; a parlour: ห้องเรียน a class room; a study room: ห้องเวร an orderly's room: ห้องสูบบุหรี่ a smoking-room: ห้องหับ *idiomatic* rooms in general.

หอน   haun[2] v. to bay; to bark hoarsely (as of dogs baying or howling at the moon).

ห่อน   haun[4] *Laos adj.* accustomed to; habitual; *poetical* not; never; see เคย p. 27: ห่อนจะได้กลับ never to return.

หอบ   haup[4] v. to pant (from fatigue); to gasp or heave with short and laboured breath (as in asthma); to pick up, or make into a bundle; to carry anything folded or tied in both arms (as straw); to collect and carry away with both arms full (as clothing or bedding): ลมหอบหวน a swift-revolving wind causing waterspouts, sand-pillars, and dust-whirls: หอบครอบครัวหนี to flee with one's family and possessions carried in the arms: เหนื่อยหอบ tired and panting.

หอม   haum[2] n. fragrance: *adj.* fragrant; odorous; sweet-scented; aromatic: กล้วยหอม the fragrant banana: เครื่องหอม scented powders; perfumes: น้ำมันหอม scented oils: น้ำหอม cologne; sweet-scented waters: น้ำหอมกลั่น distilled essences: หอมจันทน์ a species of fragrant banana: หอมยับ to collect; to accumulate; to assemble; to gather together; see รวม p. 690: หมึกหอม odorous Chinese ink used for medicinal purposes: หัวหอม *Allium cepa* (*Liliaceae*), the onion, which took its origin in western Asia and reached Greece and Italy at an early date.

It spread to Egypt, and, at a very remote date, it had already become a plant of India. That it should have a sanskritic name in the Philippine Islands suggests that it reached Malaysia from India. Most of Malaysia is too moist for it, with the result that in wetter parts it cannot be raised beyond the state of a spring onion, i. e. half-grown. The Chinese in Malaya so raise it, and are very expert in producing small, round, white bulbs. In the mountains of Java and in the Philippine Islands, larger bulbs can be raised. Raised from seed, the crop is ready for use in five months in Malaya. Various races of European origin have been tested and found worth growing to this age. The onion is used in flavouring foods, and as a pickle in vinegar or brine. The onion, as well as garlic and even a white shallot, is used in many Malay medicines (MCM. p. 322: BURK. p. 100).

ห้อม   haum³ v. to surround; to accompany or attend on all sides: n. a line or boundary by which a space is enclosed: เฝ้าห้อมล้อม to surround or encompass with attentive care; to wait upon the pleasure or command of (as of the king or princes): ห้อมล้อม to escort; to convoy; to hover or float about near to; to protect with encircling care.

หอย   hoy² n. shells: หอยกะพง mussel, Modiola senhauseni (Mytilidae) (suvatti p. 53): หอยกาบ Nodularia scobinata (Cardi-tidae) (suvatti p. 57): หอยขม Vivipara doliaris (Viviparidae) (suvatti p. 16): หอย-โข่ง Pila ampullacea (Ampullariidae) (suvatti p. 18): หอยแครง an ark shell or cockle, Arca granosa (Arcidae) (suvatti p. 50): หอย-จุ๊บแจง Cerithidea obtusa (Cerithiidae) (suvatti p. 20): หอยตลับ sea clam, Mactra antiquata (Mactridae) (suvatti p. 62): หอยทาก, หอยโข่ง a creeping snail, Rhysota distincta (Limacidae) (suvatti p. 46): หอยนมสาว top shell, Tro-chus maculatus (Trochidae) (suvatti p. 3): หอยมือเสือ, หอยมือแมว Tridacna squamosa (Tridacnidae) (suvatti p. 68): หอยมุกข์

pearl oyster, Meleagrina (Aviculidae) (suvatti p. 53): หอยแมลงภู่ sea mussel, Mytilus smaragdinus (Mytilidae) (suvatti p. 52): หอยสังข์ conch-shell, Strombus canarium (Strombidae) (suvatti p. 23): หอยเสียบ Donax faba (Donacidae) (suvatti p. 61): หอยหนาม Murex tenuispina (Muricidae) (suvatti p. 30): หอยหลอด Vermetus sp. (Vermetidae) (suvatti p. 23): หอยนางรม oyster, Ostrea edulis (Ostreidae) (suvatti p. 54): เกล็ดหอย (ต้น) Cassia pumila (Lam) (Burk. p. 479).

ห้อย   hoy³ v. to hang down; to be suspended from, or attached to; to dangle or droop down from; see ย้อย p. 668: ผ้าห้อยบ่า an amice: ห้อยคอ to be dangling from the neck: ห้อยโหน to swing while being suspended (as a gibbon).

หะ   ha⁴ onomat. from a signal for work-men to exert united action (as when hauling logs or launching a boat): หะแรก at the beginning of; from the start of; at the insti-tution of; at the first sound or signal for united action.

หะห้าย, ฮะฮ้าย   ha⁴-hai³ onomat. from a sound uttered in derision or laughter, as ha! ha!

หะแห้น   ha⁴-haan³ onomat. from the sound of the trumpeting of elephants.

หัก   hak⁴ v. to break; to be broken off; to subtract; to deduct; to be reduced by a certain amount; to have a certain amount deducted; to reflect (as light): ทำหักสุกหักดิบ to break off or suspend proceedings before a satisfactory settlement has been attained; to render a judgement before the truth has been estab-lished (but yet requiring that the court fees be paid): หักใจ to practice self-restraint, or self-control; to act in moderation; to quell or quench one's feelings (as anger or revenge): หักดังเผาะ to break with a crack: หักเดาะ to half break, or to rend partly (as in bending a green stick): หักบัญชี to strike a balance (in accounts); to make a partial payment: หักมุก (กล้วย) a species of banana suitable for baking (for invalids), and for making into preserves: หักราคา to under-sell; to sell at a price less than the standard market price, or that of competitors: หักร้าง to clear land of jungle, grass, stumps or stubble prior to cultivation: หักร้างถางพง *idiomatic* to make a clearing in a virgin forest: หักลด to make a deduction (as if given for commission): หักหน้า to have a sense of chagrin when others are dressed better, or when one is beaten by another (as in competition); to be ashamed of being outwitted or outdone; to cut across close ahead (as when a car cuts across the track of another); see under ข้าม p. 155: หักหลัง to decline, fail or refuse to do as promised: หักหาญ to do with boldness, violence or impudence; to use force in oppressing: หักโหม to attack ruthlessly; to fight or kill without showing mercy; to be unmercifully severe.

หัด   hut[4] *v.* to train, practice, drill or exercise; to make proficient: *n.* measles; rubseola; a highly contagious skin disease: สมุดหัดเขียน a copy or exercise book: หัดเขียน to drill in penmanship, drawing or painting: หัดตัว physical exercises: หัดทหาร to drill soldiers: หัดมวย to drill in boxing: หัดวิชชา to acquire scientific knowledge; to learn methods of using incantations and witchcraft: หัดสวด to drill in reciting Buddhist chants, or responses in religious services: หัดจารหนังสือ to practice writing with a stylus (as on palm leaves); see จาร ๒ p. 245.

หัต, หต   hut[4] *P. S. adj.* killed; destroyed; injured; put an end to (chd. p. 153).

หัตถ์, หัสต์   hut[4] *P. n.* the hand; the trunk of an elephant; a cubit; a unit of linear measurement represented by the length from the elbow to the tip of the little finger; 50 centimeters; the thirteenth lunar asterism

(chd. p. 154): ลายพระราชหัตถ์ the royal signature or handwriting: หัตถกรรม, หัตถการ, หัตถกิจ manufacture; manual labour; handicraft; industrial arts: หัตถคต passed into one's hands; in his power or possession (chd. p. 153): หัตถตล the palm of the hand: หัตถบาส a linear measure equal to two and a half cubits, being the prescribed space in which two Buddhist monks may sit side by side while chanting: หัตถพันธ์, หัตถาภรณ์, หัตถาลังการ a bracelet.

หัตถินี   hut[4]-ti[4]-nee *P. n.* a female elephant.

หัตถี, หัตถา   hut[4]-tee[2] *P. n.* a male elephant (chd. p. 153): หัตถาจารย์ a trainer of elephants; a mahout: หัตถานึก the elephants of an army; an elephant host: หัตถาโรห one who rides on an elephant; an elephant driver; a mahout: หัตถิมารก *lit.* "those who kill elephants," *i. e.* elephant hunters.

หัน   hun[2] *v.* to turn; to revolve; to whirl: หันกลับ to reverse (as machinery); to turn back (as on a trip): หันรอบ to revolve around (as the earth around the sun); see เขจร under จร ๒ p. 230: หันหน้า to turn the face towards; to face: หันเห to turn away from (as a ferry-boat at a landing is swept off by the tide): หันอากาศ the vowel " ั "; other names are ไม้ผัด, หางกังหัน.

หั่น   hun[4] *v.* to slice: สับหั่น to chop into small pieces.

หั้น   see นั้น p. 448.

หันตรา   hun[2]-dtrah *n.* a sweetmeat made of beans, or the seeds of the jack-fruit, boiled in syrup, with custard or shredded boiled eggs as dressing.

หับ   hup[4] *v.* to shut, or close partly (as a door or window); to fold together (as a sectional screen); see ปิด p. 526; งับ p 222: หับเผย a hut; a hovel; a cabin; a jail (in ancient times).

หัมมิยะ   hum[2]-mee-ya[6] *P. n.* a house,

palace, mansion or any palatial dwelling (Chd.
[p. 151).

หับ see หย p. 913.

หัว ๑, หัวเราะ, หวัวเราะ, หวัวร่อ   hu-ah[2]
v. to laugh ; to giggle ; to titter ; to chuckle.

หัว ๒   hu-ah[2]   n. the head ; the fore-part ;
the front ; bulbs ; tubers ; corms ; the head or
crown side of a coin (as " heads I win, tails
you lose " in flipping coins), the reverse side
being called ก้อย ; the little circle occurring
in most of the Thai consonants ; *a designatory
particle for* books, pamphlets, bulbs and tubers
(as for onions and garlic) :   *adj.* chief ; principal ; best ; greatest ; conspicuous :   หัวกะทิ
the undiluted milk squeezed out of grated
coconut ; the best in a group or collection,
as prize-winners in an exhibition (commonly
used regarding fruit) :   หัวกะเท็น, หัวแก่น-
หัวมัน articles that are the largest or best in
a group or collection, as prize-winners in an
exhibition (commonly used regarding fruit) :
หัวแกละ wearing two tufts of hair on the
back of the head :   หัวขวง an area or plot
of land adjacent to the royal plaza ; at the
side of a palace :   หัวขวาน the metal portion
of an ax :   หัวขวาน (นก) the Thai scaly-
bellied green woodpecker, *Gecinus vittatus
eisenhoferi* (will. N. H. J. S. S. II, 3, p. 319) ; the
Thai rufous woodpecker, *Micropternus brachyurus williamsoni* (Herb. N. H. J. S. S. VI, 4, p.
323) :   หัวขวานเล็ก (นก) the spotted-breasted
pied woodpecker, *Dryobates pectoralis pectoralis* (Herb. N. H. J. S. S. VI, 4, p. 323) :   หัว-
ขวานแดง (นก) the Burmese golden-backed three-
toed woodpecker, *Tiya javanensis intermedia*
(Herb. N. H. J. S. S. VI, 4, p. 325) :   หัวข้อ the
beginning of a paragraph :   หัวขั้ว coun-
terfoils ; a stub or coupon (as of a cheque) :
หัวขาด the apex of an inflammatory process
prior to pus being formed :   หัวเข่า the knee :
หัวเข้า having the little circle occurring in Thai
consonants turned in (the antithesis of those
being turned out which are called หัวออก) :
หัวแข็ง stubborn ; wilful ; headstrong ; obdurate ;

perverse ; cantankerous ; not liable to sickness
(children) :   หัวโขน masks (as worn by come-
dians or in masked performances) :   หัวขะโมย
having a desire for plundering and robbing
as an important element in one's disposition ;
the chief of a gang of robbers :   หัวค่ำ
twilight ; dusk ; evening ; the cool of the day :
หัวคิด an active brain, filled with ideas,
thoughts and wisdom ; an instigator ; an
originator ; the brains behind a project :
หัวกั้ง the first portion in the bend of a river,
or the course of a canal :   หัวใคร่ a person
or article most beloved (synonomous with
หัวรัก) :   หัวงาน the start, or initial stage of
a job, project, function or entertainment :
หัวเงื่อน the free end of a piece of twine, or
ball of yarn or rope ; the free end of the
twine to be pulled in a slip-knot :   หัวจุก
having a tuft of hair or topknot on the head :
หัวโจก the leader of a gang of ruffians :
หัวใจ the heart (the organ that maintains the
circulation of the blood) ; the core ; the inner
part ; the essential part ; initials, or letters
credited with magic power, strung on a string
and hung around the neck of men and beasts
of burden :   หัวดาวหัวเดือน a skin disease
characterized by pustules and severe con-
stitutional symptoms :   หัวดึก the time
when the night begins to wane (as referring
to an entertainment which carries on until
very late) :   หัวดื้อ stubborn ; refractory ;
disobedient ; undutiful :   หัวเดียว singly ;
alone ; an individual :   หัวตลิ่ง the edge of
the bank of a river :   หัวต่อ an end to end
joining (as of boards) ; the condition of tying
or splicing (as of rope) ; a joint or articulation
(as of bones) ; the running of two sentences
into one ; the merging of two eras or periods
of time ; the junction of two timbers (as in a
building) :   หัวเตา the tax on stoves and
kilns (as lime kilns, pottery kilns, etc.) :
หัวตะคาก the head of the femur, *caput femoris* :
หัวตะปู the head of a nail :   หัวตา the inner
or nasal canthi (see หางตา) :   หัวถนน the
beginning of a road or street :   หัวแถว the

first or head of a line or row (as a student at the head of a class): หัวที the beginning; the inauguration; the start; the initiation: หัวนม the nipple: หัวนอน the head of the bed: หัวน้ำขึ้น the start of the flood-tide: หัวน้ำมัน the first drawing, or the unadulterated portion of any oil: หัวน้ำลง the start of the ebb-tide; หัวบัว a bulbous plant with medicinal properties; the nipple, teat or mammilla: หัวเบา easily influenced; tractable; manageable; docile; teachable; obedient: หัวเบี้ย the banker in a gambling game (using cowries): หัวประจบ flattering; cajoling: หัวปลวก, จอมปลวก a termite hill: หัวปลี the bud end of a flowering banana stalk (used as a vegetable): หัวปี the beginning of a year; the first-born: หัวฝน the setting in of the rainy season: หัวพลอย the one who butts in while others are conversing; an intruder: หัวพุงหัวมัน a choice titbit of a fish (as the roe and fat); the essentials of any scheme or proposition; the master-piece in any set or collection: หัวมือ rewards for services rendered (as when help is given to reap a field or gather fruit): หัวมุม a corner; an angle: หัวเม็ด an ornamental knob at the top of a post: หัวเมือง a provincial town or city; the chief city of a province: หัวแม่ตีน, หัวแม่เท้า the big toe: หัวแม่มือ the thumb: หัวแมลงวัน small mangoes just developed from the flowers: หัวไม้ stumps of trees; fragments of log ends; ruffians; rogues; lawless persons: หัวยา the essential ingredient in a compounded remedy: หัวรอ the beginning of a line of posts serving as a breakwater: หัวระแหง land that has been cracked by excessive drought and heat; crevices in parched ground: หัวรักหัวใคร่ a person or article most beloved: หัวรั้น disobedient; stubborn; pigheaded; disbelieving; doubting; distrusting: หัวเรือ the bow; the prow; the fore or front part of a boat: หัวแรง the directing power, or main mover in a gang of workmen: หัวแร้ง a soldering iron: หัวลม the direction from which the wind is blowing: หัวล้าน bald; hairless: หัวล้าน (ต้น) a species of flat berry having fuzzy vegetable fibers along each edge, leaving the sides clean (this berry resembles a bald head): หัวล้ำมะลอก pustules occurring on the skin, accompanied with severe inflammatory symptoms: หัวลิง a small fruit growing on a vine, having fuzzy vegetable fibers in rugas or folds (resembling the hair on the head of a monkey). This fruit is edible by human beings but is poisonous to animals: บิดหัวลูก dysentery resulting from pressure by the infant's head: หัวเลี้ยว the beginning or ending of a curve or turn in a path or road: หัวโล้น a clean-shaven head: หัวสะพาน the foot, base, or approach to a bridge: หัวเสีย being perturbed, agitated or angered: หัวหงอก a head of grey hair; grey-headed: หัวหน้า a chieftain; a chief; a leader; a headman of a gang of workmen: หัวหน้าโรงเรียน the principal of a school: หัวหน่าว the suprapubic region: หัวหมู a ploughshare; the dressed head of a pig (intended as a present): หัวหมอความ having the head, mind or disposition of a lawyer: หัวเห็ด incorrigible; very head-strong; intractable; see ดื้อ p. 331: ตะปูหัวเห็ด a large-headed nail: หัวเหล้า the yeast or fermenting agent in distilling intoxicants: หัวแหยม small, braided tufts of hair on the back of the head (as is often seen on the heads of Chinese children): หัวแหลม a promontory; a headland (jutting seaward): หัวไหล่ the tip of the shoulder; the acromion: หัวแหวน the setting of a ring: หัวแหวน Thai, Krat (ต้น) Decaspermum cambodianum (Myrtaceae) (cb. p. 630): หัวอก the breast; the bosom; a mental state or mood; a sense of propriety, or otherwise: หัวออก turning outward or away from a landing (as a boat); having the little circle occurring in Thai consonants turned out (the antithesis of those being turned in): หัวอ่อน obedient; docile; tractable; easy to teach or manage; submissive.

หัสต์ see หัตถ์ p. 929.

หัสดิน, หัสดี   hat⁴-sa⁴-din *S. adj.* belonging to an elephant (S. E. D. p. 1296).

หา   bah² *v.* to search for; to seek; to look for; to inquire for; to solicit or ask: *when followed by "ไม่" forms the negative,* as หามีไม่, หาเห็นไม่, หาใช่ไม่, หาเป็นเช่นนั้นไม่: จัดหาให้ to plan, or devise a means for getting (as of living accomodations): โจทย์หาว่า the prosecution claims that.......: เที่ยวหา to enquire around for; to make a thorough search for (as for a lost coin): บ่นหา to enquire repeatedly after (the condition of); to grieve or regret (the long absence of a friend): พ้องหาว่า to enter a complaint against; to lodge a legal charge against: หากิน to earn one's living; to seek means for securing a livelihood; to hunt for a bit to eat; to prowl around for prey: หาความ to charge with some fault or imperfection; to seek causes for another's dispute; to challenge another's word or actions (so as to pick a quarrel): หาความจริง to ferret out the truth (as during an investigation); to seek for the truth: หาเงิน to find means for raising money; to sell a child into slavery (as a means of getting money): หาเงินได้ to be able to earn money: หาโทษมิได้ to find no fault; to be pronounced innocent: หาม่มิได้, หามิได้ no, it is not so; it is not that way at all: หาไม่ not; no; the reverse, negative, or sign of refusal: หาไม่ก็ or if not; if not that, what else? หาไม่ก็แล้วกัน if not (getting what is desired) then the matter is ended: หารือ to consult; to counsel; to confer; to seek advice: หาเรื่อง to blame; to make charges against (which may be fictitious): หาสู่ to call on; to visit; to frequent the home of some friend: หาเหตุ to be on the alert; to pick flaws; to seek for causes for complaint (as to watch for errors or false steps in another).

ห่า   hah⁴ *n.* a group of evil spirits supposed to produce epidemics of disease; pestilential diseases; a numerical designation for gauging the rainfall. This is done by estimating how many times the water would fill a Buddhist monk's alms-bowl if it were placed in the rain: *adj.* coming, or occurring in great abundance (as rain or disease); in great flocks or droves: ผีห่า pestilential spirits or demons: ฝนห่าใหญ่ a copious fall of rain: โรคห่า an epidemic with high mortality: ห่ากิน, ตายห่า to die from some contageous disease: ห่าฝน a shower of rain: อ้ายห่า a swear word, implying having come from this group of pestilential spirits.

ห้า   hah³ *n.* the numeral five: ที่ห้า fifth: ห้าสิบ fifty: สิบห้า fifteen: ห้าแต้ม to be unconsciously guilty of some mortifying accident or incident in public (as having the tucked-in end of the panung slip down): *adj.* abashed; embarrassed; mortified; ashamed; humiliated.

หาก   hak⁴ *v.* to be fitting; shall or ought to do: *conj.* if; allowing that: *adj.* apart from; different; separated; removed from; some distance away from, as ต่างหาก: หากทำ capable of doing: หากรู้เอ็ง having capacity for self-knowledge (as children gradually growing older are capable of forming ideas and performing acts): หากว่า if perchance; supposing that; provided that such were the case; see พึ่ง p 592; ควร p. 187.

หาง   hang² *n.* the end (of a rope or string); the tail (of animals, birds, boats and fishes); the over-reaching end (of some Thai letters); the extremity (as the posterior tip of a bone); the end of a row or line (as of posts or persons); the foot (as of a class of students): ดาวหาง a comet; see ดาว pp. 326, 327: ถือหาง to take up the management of affairs for another; to back one up; to assist or urge another on (a term used in cock-fighting); to espouse the cause of another: มีคนถือหาง there is some one (secretly) defending or espousing the cause of another: หางกระ-

หมวด, หางขมวด having curled ends (as in ฬ, ฮ): หางกะเบน the rolled portion of the loin-cloth, the end of which is worn tucked into the belt behind: หางกะรอก the tail of a squirrel: หางกะลวย the tail of a cock which is longer than the tail of any other in the flock: หางกังหัน the vowel mark " ์ " otherwise called หันอากาศ, ไม้ผัด: หางกิ่ว, สีกุนกบ (ปลา) *Caranx affinis (Carangidae)*, a species of salt-water fish (suvatti p. 113): หางกิ่วหม้อ, สีกุน, หางแข็ง (ปลา) *Caranx forsteri (Carangidae)* (suvatti p. 114): หางแกละ two tufts of hair worn on the back of the head (of a child): หางไก่ (ปลา) *Coilia macrognathus (Engraulidae)* (suvatti p. 16): หางขอด having a tail with a kink in it (as some cats have): หางจระเข้ an alligator's tail; a species of gummy, medicinal plant with leaves resembling the shape of an alligator's tail; *Aloes sp.*: หางจิ้งเหลน a small braided tuft of hair worn by children on the occipital portion of the head; a small-sized queue: หางช้าง the tail of an elephant: หางช้าง (ต้น) *Belamcanda chinensis (Iridaceae)*, an herb found wild in China and Japan, whence it has been brought southwards in cultivation. It is medicinal, particularly among the Chinese, who cultivate it in their own country, where also it is wild. They use the very purgative dried rhizomes in complaints of chest and liver, and add it to tonics. The Chinese in Singapore import it. In the Dutch East Indies the plant is established in many places. In Sumatra, women newly confined chew it with betel. It would be dangerous to use more than a little. In Perak it is used in a medicinal bath after child-birth. In Batavia it is applied to the loins for lumbago (MCM. p. 136: BURK. p. 315): หางตา the outer or temporal canthi of the eye: หางนกยูง see ชมพอ p. 305: หางนกยูงฝรั่ง see ช้ำพอ p. 308: หางน้ำ the second or final time of infusion or brewing of tea or coffee: หางแพน (นก) the Java fantail flycatcher, *Rhipidura javanica* (WILL. N. H. J. S. S. I, 3, p. 210): หางปลา (พัด) a brand of fans in which thin

paper is pasted on the ribs so that the spread fan resembles the tail of a large fish: หางเปีย, หางหนู the queue (as formerly worn by the Chinese): หางแมงป่อง (เรือ) an ancient kind of long, shallow draft boat made out of a log. It has a long, curved tail, similar to the tail of a scorpion (used on rivers in the northern parts of Thailand): หางยาม the handle of a Thai plough: หางว่าว the tail of a kite; a catalogue, list or register of soldiers and those who are liable for corvée service. Formerly these were kept on long strips of paper resembling strips of paper used as kite tails: หางสิงห์ (ต้น) Chinese arbor vitae, *Thuja orientalis (Coniferae)*, an ornamental evergreen tree of northern China, Korea, and Manchuria, which is in cultivation widely in the world. It can only be grown in pots in Singapore. The Chinese use both seeds and leaves medicinally, and import them into the Straits (MCM. p. 182: BURK. p. 2157): หางเสือ the rudder of a boat; the helm of a ship: โจงกระเบนหางหงส์ a method ancient star actors had of wearing the loin-cloth. To accomplish the proper effect, the two ends of the loin-cloth were rolled together but half of the available distance, and then passed up and fastened in the belt behind, leaving the two sides free to be spread out in the shape of swan tails: หางไหล (ต้น) *Anamirta cocculus; Cocculus tudicus*, a species of wild tree poisonous to insects and used by fishermen to stupify fish: หางไหลแดง (ต้น) *Amarantus cruentus (Amaranthaceae)*, a genus of tree used medicinally (MCM. p. 196: BURK. p. 125): หางไหลเผือก see เคือป๊ป p. 212

ห้าง hang[4] *adj.* distanced; separated; far apart; disconnected; away from; see พ้น p. 560: แนวนั้นห่างไป that seam or joining is too far separated (as of boards or planks): ไปห่างไกล to go far away; to be greatly separated from: ห่างจากคลอง situated some distance from a canal: ห่างเหิน to drift asunder; to grow cold, estranged, or distant.

ห้าง   hang³ *n.* a store; a firm; a shop: นายห้าง the proprietor of a store: ห้างนา a temporary shed, shelter or sunshade erected in fields: ห้างสวน a shed erected among fruit trees, or in gardens (for watching): ห้างหอ a shooting platform or crow's nest built in tree tops (for shooting game): ห้างหุ้นส่วนจำกัด a limited liability partnership or company: ห้างฮ้วง the Laos pronunciation of the name of the city ห้างหลวง.

หาญ   han² *adj.* bold; brave; audacious; valiant; courageous: หาญเหี้ยม undaunted; intrepid; fearless.

หาด   hat⁴ *n.* a shoal; a sand-bank: เกยหาด to run aground on a shoal: หาดขวาง a shoal situated across the mouth of a river or body of water: หาดชายทะเล a seashore; a beach: หาดส่วย a beach on which a revenue station is located (as in localities where taxes on eggs of sea turtles are collected).

หาดก, หาตก   hah²-dok⁴ *P. S. n.* gold.

หาน   hah²-na⁶ *P. n.* deterioration; degeneration; relinquishment; abandonment; a condition of ruin (chd. p. 152).

ห่าน   han⁴ *n.* goose; swan.

หาบ   hap⁴ *n.* a picul, a unit of standard weight equal to 60 kg. or 100 catties (Table of Weights of Ministry of Commerce); see ชั่ง under กล่อม p. 59.

หาบ   hap⁴ *v.* to carry on the shoulder by means of a rod or pole, the weight being suspended from both ends: *n.* a measure of weight equal to one picul of 60 kilogrammes or 100 catties. (1940-41 Directory for Bangkok and Thailand p. 196): หาบคอน to carry on the shoulder by means of a stick, but with the weight on one end only: หาบหลวง a standard metric picul equal to 60 kg.

หาม   harm² *v.* to carry a weight or load directly on the shoulder (as a coolie carrying a trunk); to bear or transport a burden by means of two or more sticks on the shoulders of two or more persons (as coolies carrying a piano): หามรอก (ต้น) *Pterospermum sernisagittaturn (Sterculiaceae)*, a tree with medicinal properties; see กระนาน p. 37: หามรุ่งหามค่ำ carrying burdens all the day and night; *idiomatic* continuous service: หามโลง to carry a coffin by means of poles on the shoulders of two or four men: หามแล่น portable cannons used in ancient warfare.

หาม   harm⁴ *adj.* partly ripe; a little underripe (as fruit); half-witted; near to madness; a little off mentally (for persons).

ห้าม   harm³ *v.* to forbid; to prohibit; to disallow; to interdict; to hinder or prevent: ขอห้าม articles forbidden to be touched or taken: ต้องห้าม forbidden; prohibited: ตราคุ้มห้าม exemption papers; documents granting privileges: นางห้าม, หม่อมห้าม a general name for wives or concubines of kings, princes or noblemen: ห้ามการ to prohibit working: ห้ามกิน to forbid the eating of: ห้ามของแสลง to forbid what would be injurious to the sick (as certain kinds of food or fruit): ห้ามใจห้ามจิตต์ to exert self-control; to inhibit one's desires: ห้ามประตู to prevent the entrance or exit at a gate or door (as of a palace): ห้ามปราม to quell; to put down by forceful means; to calm; to mollify; to quiet: ห้ามเปลี่ยนมื้อ not negotiable: ห้ามเยี่ยม to forbid visitors; a notice "visitors not allowed": ห้ามล้อ a brake (as on a wheel): ห้ามแล้ว having already been forbidden once: ห้ามหวง to guard zealously and prohibit any intrusion (as to a reserve): ห้ามหู to turn a deaf ear; to desist from listening.

หาย   hai² *v.* to cease; to stop (as rain or a storm); to be lost; to disappear; to be cured; to become healed: ความฉิบหาย ruin; destruction; a condition of total loss: ค่าเสียหาย damages, or the amount paid as indemnity: หายกวน to cease troubling, or stop dunning (for a debt): หายกัน having paid all that is due; "we are even now"; to be appeased in all respects: หายขาด to be entirely healed or cured; to have no balance due (as on an account): หายที่ค้าง to have paid all due (as on an account): หายเจ็บหายไข้ to return to a normal condition of health after a sickness: หายฉิบ to have disappeared mysteriously: หายตัว to vanish from the sight of others; to make oneself invisible: หายสั่น, หายงก to cease shaking or shivering (as in the cold spell of malarial fever); to be cured of a condition of tremor or quivering of the hands or feet: หายเหนื่อย to become rested: หายเหือด to cause to diminish or moderate; to be appeased gradually, or mollified (as in a fit of anger or during some disagreement).

หายใจ hai²-chjai *v.* to breathe: การหายใจ respirations; breathings: ถอนหายใจ to exhale a long breath; to sigh.

หายนะ ๑ hah²-ya⁶-na⁶ *P. n.* a condition of diminution, decay, disaster, ruin, or destruction (chd. p. 154); see ลดลง under ลด p. 727.

หายนะ ๒ hah²-ya⁶-na⁶ *P. S. n.* a year [(S. E. D. p. 1297).

หาร han² *P. v.* to divide, distribute or apportion: *n. arithmetic* division; the act of taking away, claiming, demanding, or requiring (chd. p. 153): ผลที่หารได้ the quotient: เลขที่หาร the divisor.

หารี hah²-ri⁶ *P. adj.* handsome; pretty; beautiful; attractive (chd. p. 152).

หาริน, หารี hah²-rin *P. adj.* taking away; holding; robbing; captivating; *often used as a suffix* (chd. p. 152): อทินนหารี *lit.* "one taking things without permission," *i. e.* a robber, plunderer or thief.

หาว how² *v.* to yawn: *n.* an open space; the firmament; the sky: กลางหาว in the open air; openly: หาวนอน to be sleepy;

to be drowsy: หาวเรอ to yawn and belch up gas.

ห้าว how³ *adj.* over-ripe; hard and dried from being on the tree too long (used in regard to coconuts); strong; fierce; bold; impudent; insolent; audacious: ห้าวหาญ extremely bold and self-confident.

หาส hah²-sa⁴ *P. n.* laughter; mirth; joy; fun; a jest; a joke or raillery (chd. p. 153).

หาสก hah²-sok⁴ *P. S. n.* a clown; a buffoon; a maker of jokes and jests (s. e. d. p. [1294).

หำ, ไข่หำ hum² *n.* the testicles.

ห้ำ hum³ *v.* to pounce upon for the purpose of striking, hurting, cutting, or wounding; to bite; to claw; to maul (as do wild animals): ห้ำหัก to rush upon and break to pieces; to destroy utterly (as if in the power of an adversary): ห้ำหั่น to approach suddenly and cut, chop, mangle or hack (as bandits might do to a victim).

หิ้ง hing³ *n.* a shelf: หิ้งติดฝา shelves attached to the wall; a wall-bracket: หิ้งหวย a bulletin board in front of a lottery gambling house on which are fastened tickets, pending such time as the winning letter will be announced; an ancient method of placing bets [on the lottery.

หิงคุ see มหาหิงคุ์ p. 628.

หิงสา, หิงส, หิงสา hing²-sah² *P. S. n.* oppression; persecution; malevolence; the act of hurting or injuring (s. e. d. p. 1297).

หิงห้อย, หิ่งห้อย hing²-hoi³ *n.* fire-flies.

หิงหาย hing²-hai² *Thai, Bangkok,* หญ้าหิ่งเม่น *Laos, Chiengmai,* มะหิ่งดง *Laos, Lampun* (ต้น) *n. Crotalaria bracteata (Leguminosae); C. hossei; C. striata* sometimes classified *C. saltiana* (burk. p. 686); *C. laburnifolia,* an herbaceous shrub; see ติ่งหาย p. 367.

หิด hit⁴ *n.* scabies; the itch; a contagious skin disease due to the itch-mite, *sarcoptes* *scabiei*, which bores beneath the skin forming burrows : หิดด้าน the dry form of itch with small pustules : หิดเปื่อย, หิดตะมอย the moist form with large pustules.

หิต hi⁴-dta⁴ *P. S. n.* a friend ; a benefactor ; an ally ; a companion or confidant : *adj.* appropriate ; useful ; suitable ; advantageous ; beneficial (S. E. D. p. 1298) : หิตกร a benefactor ; one doing a service or furthering another's interests : หิตมิตร a friend in need ; a benevolent friend : หิตวจนะ, หิตพจน์ friendly advice ; good counsel.

หิน ๑ hin² *adj.* wretched ; forsaken ; abject ; defective ; worthless ; inferior ; deficient ; base ; wasted ; low (chd. p. 156) : หีนชาติ of a low caste ; degraded ; ill-born ; base ; of low extraction or ancestors : หีนยาน, หีนยาน Hinayana. By the beginning of the first century A. D. Buddhism had become separated by tenets and language into two main branches—the Mahayana (greater vehicle) (see มหายาน p. 628) and the Hinayana (หีนยาน), or Pali Hinayana (lesser vehicle). This second branch of Buddhism is much more conservative in character, from the fact that it considered Pali the sacred language, and held to a restricted or " lesser " way of release from the sufferings of the world. It made its way south and spread over Ceylon, Burma, Thailand and Cambodia. The Hinayana monks maintained that Nirvana (*Pali* Nibbana) alone gave surcease from the desires and impermanence of existence,—the impermanence found even in the various heavens, and that an individual could achieve Nibbana solely by means of his own efforts, by meritorious thought and deeds, and by cutting off desires of all kinds which caused him to cling to existence. The principal doctrines of this more conservative school seem to have been formulated by the time of King Asoka (270-230 B. C.), although the canon, carried in the form of oral tradition, was subjected to some variation until it was committed to writing in

Ceylon about 20 B. C. (Thai Buddhism, its Rites and Activities by Kenneth E. Wells, p. 6).

หิน ๒ hin² *n.* stone ; rock : หินลาย marble : หินเหล็กไฟ a flint rock striking fire : หินลับมีด a whetstone : หินปูน stone lime : หินปูน (ตามฟัน) tartar (incrustations that form on neglected teeth) : หินไม่แบ้ง millstones : หินอ่อน soap-stone.

หิม hi⁴-ma⁶ *P. S. n.* cold ; snow ; frost (chd. p. 155) : หิมกร *lit.* " causing coldness," *i. e.* the moon : หิมบาท the falling of snow ; cold rain : หิมภาน, หิมรัศมี *lit.* " having cold lustre," *i. e.* the moon : หิมวาส, หิมเวศ *lit.* " a cold place of residence," *i. e.* the snowy forests of the Himalayas ; snowy forests (in general) : หิมานต์ the close of the cold season : หิมาลัย *lit.* " the abiding place of snow," *i. e.* the northern regions of the Himalayas.

หิมพาน, หิมพ่านต์ him²-ma⁶-parn *n.* the title of the second division of Buddha's birth-stories, or Vesadorn Jataka.

หิมวัต him²-ma⁶-wat⁶ *S. n.* this word may occur in the following forms, *viz.* หิมวาต, หิมวาน, หิมพาน, หิมวันต์, หิมพานต์, หิมวา and is the personification of the Himalayan mountains ; the husband of Mena or Menaka and father of Uma and Ganga (H. C. D. p. 121) : *adj.* cold ; snowy ; covered with snow.

หิรัญ, หิรัญญ์, หิรัณย์ hi⁴-run *P. n.* gold ; bullion ; treasure (chd. p. 156) ; riches ; silver coins : แสงหิรัญ silver rays of dawn : หิรัญญการ, หิรัญยการ a goldsmith : หิรัญญบัฏ a plaque, plate or slab of silver inscribed with the name of the prince or nobleman newly raised in rank : หิรัญยเกศ having golden hair or locks : หิรัญยรัศมี being silvery white (descriptive of the white elephants).

หิริ hi⁴-ri⁶ *P. n.* shame ; modesty ; bashfulness (chd. p. 156) : หิริโอตะปะ the shame of sins committed ; the shame which deters a person from sinning.

หิว hiew[2] *v.* to be hungry; to desire eagerly; to thirst after; to wish for: หิวตาย to die from starvation: หิวหอบ hungry and panting (as from fatigue): หิวโหย hungry and exhausted; perishing.

หิว hiew[3] *v.* to hold or carry hanging from the hand (as a bucket of water).

หี hee[2] *n.* the pudendum: หีตา the opening of the lacrymal duct at the inner canthi of the eye: หีเต่า the hair ends over the back of the neck.

หีด heet[4] *adj.* small; diminutive; little; tiny; few; see นีด p. 457.

หีบ heep[4] *v.* to press and crush; to squeeze between two rollers (as sugar-cane): *n.* a box; a trunk; a casket; a packing case: โรงหีบอ้อย a sugar-cane mill: ลูกหีบ rollers or cylinders used in crushing cane or milling paper: หีบกระจก a box or manicure set provided with a mirror: หีบเงิน a money-box; a safe; an iron chest: หีบผ้าย a cotton gin: หีบเพลง an organ; a harmonium; a piano: หีบเพลงชัก an accordion: หีบเพลง-ลาน a mechanical musical box: หีบเพลง-หมุนด้วยมือ a hand-organ: หีบเสียง a gramophone: หีบหนัง a leather trunk, valise or bag.

หึ heu[4] *onomat.* from the sound of giggling or snickering.

หึง heung[2] *v.* to be jealous or envious through love; to have a feeling of malice or ill-will against: *adj.* long (time), *Laos* delayed: มีใจมักหึง of a jealous or suspicious disposition: หึงกัน to have a condition of jealousy arise between two parties: หึงหวง to restrain or keep back with zealous care and loving attention.

หึ่ง, หึ่งๆ heung[4] *onomat.* from the sound of the buzzing of bees, humming of insects, or a sounded gong.

หืด heurt[4] *n.* asthma: หืดจับ to be attacked with asthma: หืดหอบ laboured breathing in asthma.

หืน heurn[2] *adj.* rancid; of offensive, sour odour; musty (as the odour of drying copra): กลิ่นหืน a musty fetid odour.

หืน heurn[4] *v.* to be filled with lustful desires; to be desirous of; to be passionately inclined for; to hanker after (something evil); see ทะยาน p. 406: หืนหรรษ์ to be excited, elated, puffed up, or exhilarated (by success or passion); see ร่าเริง under ร่า p. 706.

หือ hur[2] *onomat.* what? "eh"? หือไม่ขึ้น to be undeniable; to be indisputable.

หือ ๑ hur[3] *v.* to give; to bestow; to grant; to present: *n.* a word of assent or approval equivalent to yes (used between friends); see จ๊ะ p. 235.

หือๆ ๒ hur[4]-hur[3] *onomat.* from the sound of snarling or growling of dogs.

หุง hoong[2] *v.* to cook; to boil (as rice): เครื่องหุงต้ม kitchen utensils: หุงข้าวหุงปลา *idiomatic* to prepare the food: หุงดิน the process of boiling the refuse of bats so as to extract saltpetre or niter: หุงต้ม to cook by boiling, without pouring off the water: หุงทอง to refine gold: หุงน้ำมัน to refine oils; หุงยา to purify a drug by boiling; see ต้ม p. 341.

หุต hoo[4]-dta[4] *P. S. n.* oblations (as to spirits); the act of making burnt offerings or sacrifices: *adj.* offered; sacrificed; burnt as an oblation (chd. p. 156); see บุชาชัญ under บุชา p. 487: หุตาค, หุตภุช, หุตาศ *lit.* "that which devours offerings," *i. e.* fire: หุตโภวิท those who are proficient or experienced in making offerings or in worshipping with fire: หุตวทะ *lit.* "the one that takes up the offerings made with fire," *i. e.* the god of Fire (H. C. D. p. 6): หุตาจารย์ a professional in the art and methods of worshipping or making oblations with fire.

หุน hoon[2] *n.* a Chinese unit of weight used by jewellers, equal to 375.0 milligrams or 0.375 grammes :

    5 *hoon* or one *fuang* (เฟ้อง) equals 1875.0 milligrams :

    10 *hoon* or one *salung* (สลึง) equals 3750 milligrams :

    40 *hoon* or four *salungs* equals one baht (บาท) or 15 gramms (The Bureau of weights and Measures, Ministry of commerce).

หุ่น   hoon[4] *n.* form ; mould ; model : หุ่น-กระบอก marionettes ; puppets moved by wires or strings : หุ่นโครง the skeleton or frame for *papier mâché* figures : หุ่นหล่อรูป wax models or moulds encased in clay. The wax is melted out and molten metal is poured in.

หุ้น   hoon[3] *Chin. n.* a share (in a company) ; capital invested in a joint stock business : เข้าหุ้นเข้าส่วน to become a partner in a business : ผู้ถือหุ้น a share-holder : หุ้นส่วน partnership : หุ้นบุริมสิทธิ preferred shares : หุ้นส่วนจดทะเบียน a registered partnership : หุ้นส่วนสามัญ an ordinary share.

หุนหัน   hoon[2]-hun[2] *adj.* quick-tempered ; rash ; hasty ; inconstant ; angry ; impetuous.

หุบ   hoop[4] *n.* to shut ; to fold together (as a fan) ; to enclose ; to cover : หุบขา to place the knees together : หุบเขา, หุบผา a valley ; a ravine ; a cavern ; a vale ; a mountain pass : หุบใบ to close up (as leaves) ; to furl a sail : หุบปาก to close the mouth : หุบร่ม to close an umbrella : หุบห้วย the ravine through which a mountain stream flows.

หุ้ม   hoom[3] *v.* to clothe ; to veil ; to cover (as binding a book) ; to gild (as with gold) : หุ้มกลอง the end walls of a house : หุ้มกล้อง to attach a beautifying band of gold or silver (as on a tobacco pipe) : หุ้มคลุม to envelop : หุ้มแพร a rank in the Royal Pages Department.

หุยหุย   hoo-ie[3]-hoo-ie[2] *adj.* passing close by another ; just grazing ; see เฉียด p. 272.

หุนนิงหงัน   hoo[4]-ning[2]-ngun[2] *Jav.* บานไม่รู้โรย *Thai* (ต้น) *n. Gomphrena globosa* (*Amar-*

antaceae), the bachelor's button, everlasting flower, a plant found chiefly in America but now spread throughout the tropics. It has a bright flower-head, and on this account it is cultivated (Burk. p. 1097) ; see บานไม่รู้โรย p. 481.

หู   hoo[2] *n.* the ear ; handles ; any loop or ring for attaching purposes (as of mosquito nets, frying pans, hand-bags or cups) : ตุ้มหู ear-rings : ใบหู the external portion of the ear : มูลหู, ขี้หู ear-wax ; cerumen : หูกวาง (ต้น) see ตาบั้ง (ต้น) p. 363 : หูกะต่าย a double bow-knot (so called because the two loops resemble the ears of a rabbit) : หูแจว the cotton twine or jute ring attaching an oar to the stanchion : หูช้าง a board cut to a right angle to fit into corners (as a shelf or bracket) : หูตึง hard of hearing : หูปลาช่อน (ต้น) *Capsella bursa pastoris*, an edible vegetable. It is also an ornamental herb or shrub : หูบึ้น the fuse chamber of a cannon : หูรูด the external rim of the sphincter muscle of the anus ; the loops of a bag through which a cord is run : หูเสือ (ต้น) *Asarum virginicum*, the Virginian snake-root : หูหนวก *n.* deafness : *adj.* deaf : หูหนาตาโต, หูหนาตาเล่อ leprosy : หูหนู (เห็ด) *Hineola polytrichi* (*Tremellinaceae*), [European form *H. auricula-judae* called Jew's ear], a brown or black fungus used as an ingredient in curries (so called because the growths are shaped like the ears of rats) : หูหิ้ว handles of all kinds (as for trunks, buckets, vases and kerosene tins) : หนวกหู disturbing, offensive noises : แก้วหู the ear-drum ; the tympanum.

หู้, ย่น   hoo[4] *v.* to become wrinkled, curled up, contracted or shrunken (as leaves or flowers from long drought) : หู่หด wrinkled and shrivelled (as leaves in autumn) : หู่ห่อ to become rolled up from dryness : หู่หี่ wrinkled ; creased ; crumpled ; puckered : หู่เหี่ยว curled and withered : หู่เหี่ยวหดไป *idiomatic* to become withered and shrunken.

หูก   hook[4] *n.* a loom.

หูด　hoot[4] *n.* a wart; verruca: ตัวหูด a small insect found in resin from trees: หูดข้าวสุก a form of flat verruca with finger-like excrescences found in rancid rice: หูดด้าน a callous form of wart.

หูติ　hoo[2]-dti[4] *P. n.* the act of calling or challenging (chd. p. 156); crying; yelling.

เห　hay[2] *v.* to turn to one side; to deviate from a straight course; to diverge from a normal direction; see เขว p. 165: ลมพัดเหไป the wind has veered to another quarter: เหไปเหมา to turn from one side to the other (as a boat without a rudder).

เห่　hay[4] *n.* a lullaby or cradle song; a song sung by the boatmen while paddling royal barges during river processions.

เหง่ง　ngeng[4] *onomat.* from the sound produced by ringing a bell.

เหงา　ngow[2] *adv.* lonely: *adj.* lonesome; dreary; uninteresting; of a sad countenance.

เหงื่อ, เหื่อ　ngeu-ah[4] *n.* sweat; perspiration: เหงื่อกาฬ the sweat of approaching death: เหงื่อแตก a profuse sweating spell (as from exhaustion): เหงื่อไหลไคลย้อย *lit.* "a dropping of perspiration and oozing of marrow," *i. e.* a condition of extreme strain, effort, or exertion *idiomatic.*

เหงือก　ngeu-ak[4] *n.* the gums (around the teeth); the gills (of fishes): เหงือกปลาหมอ, จะเกร็ง (ต้น) *Acanthus ilicifolius (Acanthaceae)*, sea-holly, a semi-aquatic plant with spiny stems and leaves, found along muddy banks of canals and rivers and in salt-marshes. This is a more conspicuous plant than the *A. ebracteatus* though both seem to have the same vernacular names. It has larger blue flowers, as well as other slight differences. A Malay would use these two plants interchangeably. On the coasts of India as well as towards the eastern parts of Malaysia *A. ilicifolius* is the common species, often to the complete exclusion of the other. It is the medical *Acanthus* of Java. Fomentations with the aid of the leaves as a treatment for rheumatism and neuralgia is practiced in Goa; otherwise there is nothing in India. In the Dutch Indies leaves are widely used for poultices for various pains as well as for wounds of poisoned arrows. The young leaves are boiled along with the bark of *Cinnamomum culitlawan*, to make a drink for flatulence. In default of anything better, the leaves are used as a masticatory in Tonkin. A slight quantity of tannin is in the leaves, but so little it is quite innocuous. In India they chop and bruise the plant to feed to cattle which begin to like it in a couple of days. Tried as a tan in Bengal, it was rejected (mcm. p. 139: burk. p. 27).

เห็จ, ระเห็จ (เหาะ)　het[4] *v.* to ascend, or travel independently through the air.

เห็ด　het[4] *v.* to do: *n.* a vegetable fungus of various species; a mushroom: เห็ดแก้ว a kind of agaric: เห็ดโคน the common Thai white mushroom: เห็ดปลวก mushrooms growing on termite hills: เห็ดยาง edible mushrooms growing under rubber trees.

เหตวาเนกัตถประโยค　het[4]-dta[4]-wah-nay-gkut[4]-ta[4]-bpra[4]-yoke[4] *n. gram.* a sentence including both cause and effect clauses.

เหติ　hay[2]-dti[4] *P. n.* a weapon (chd. p. 154).

เหตุ　het[4] *P. S. n.* cause; reason; motive; origin; the reason or middle term of an inference (s. e. d. p. 1303); event; accident; circumstance; principle; motive or reason for an action: เกิดเหตุ an incident has arisen; something has occurred: ต้นเหตุ a causal reason: ปฐมเหตุ the original cause: สาเหตุ an underlying cause or reason for vindictive action: เหตุก่อความรำคาญ disturbances: เหตุการณ์ circumstances: เหตุการณ์ไม่แน่นอน contingencies: เหตุการณ์อันเหลือความสามารถที่มนุษย์จะบังคับได้ an act of God: เหตุจำเป็นอันมิอาจ

หลีกเลี่ยงได้ an unavoidable necessity : เหตุฉะนี้ on this account ; for this reason : เหตุฉะนั้น therefore ; then ; because : เหตุฉุกเฉิน an emergency : เหตุใด, เหตุอันใด why? what for? เหตุที่ควรเชื่อได้ reasonable grounds for belief : เหตุที่มิทันคิดก่อน unforseen circumstances : เหตุบังเอิญ an accident : เหตุปรานี extenuating or mitigating circumstances : เหตุผล cause and effect ; the reason for, and the consequences that follow ; the beginning and the termination of an affair : เหตุผล-สันธาน *gram.* a conjunction joining clauses giving the cause and effect, as because, therefore : เหตุฟ้องอย่า cause of action for a divorce : เหตุร้ายแก่สาธารณชน public danger : เหตุไร, เหตุไฉน why ; wherefore : เหตุวิทยา, เหตุ-ศาสตร์ตรรกวิทยา logic ; the process of drawing conclusions from known or supposed facts : เหตุว่า because : เหตุอุกฉกรรจ์ หรือ เหตุฉกรรจ์ aggravating circumstances.

เห็น hen[2] *v.* to see ; to have vision ; to understand or perceive : ตามแต่จะเห็นควร in accordance with your kind consideration : รู้เห็น to be an eye-witness ; to know surely : เห็นกัน to see each other : เห็นแก่ to do for the sake of ; to do as a favour for ; to do on account of : เห็นแก่กัน for the sake of others : เห็นแก่หน้า to do for the sake of being seen of men ; to do for the sake of another's honour, face or name ; to perform a deed especially for the sake of another (as on the basis of friendship) : เห็นโกง to catch one red-handed while cheating : เห็นคุณ to appreciate any kindness bestowed : เห็นจริง to be thoroughly convinced of the truth : เห็นใจ to appreciate another's feelings : เห็นชอบด้วย to approve of ; to concur with ; to assent : เห็น-ตาม, เห็นพ้องด้วย to concur in another's opinion ; see พ้อง p. 578 : เห็นที่จะ apparently ; probably : เห็นผล to see the results (as an effective remedy) : เห็นแข้ง to dissent ; to be opposed to : เห็นว่า to think ; to be of the opinion that ; to find that : เห็นว่าจำเลย-ไม่มีความผิด *legal* to acquit the defendant.

เหน่ง neng[4] *adj.* pure ; clear ; bright ; shining ; glistening : *onomat.* from the sound produced when playing on a xylophone.

เหน็ดเหนื่อย net[4]-nur-ie[4] *v.* to be quite exhausted or fatigued (as after working hard) : ค่าเหน็ดเหนื่อย fee or recompense for strenuous efforts on behalf of another.

เหน็บ nep[4] *v.* to attach, insert or tuck into ; to fix or push the point into (as a knife into the trunk of a tree) ; to thrust in (as a sword into the scabbard) : *n.* numbness ; a sensation of tingling or "going to sleep" of a limb : มีดเหน็บ a knife carried in the belt ; a knife which hangs from the belt : เหน็บชายกะเบน to tuck the end of the rolled portion of the loin-cloth into the belt behind : เหน็บชา (โรค) an infective form of polyneuritis, resulting in anesthesia of the skin : เหน็บแนม insulting ; insolent ; contemptible ; mean ; vile (used in regard to words or language used to hurt another's feelings).

เหน่อ nur[4] *adj.* having a brogue ; imperfect ; incorrect ; poor (pronunciation) ; see แปร่ง p. 536.

เหน้า now[3] *adj.* young ; adolescent ; adult ; see รุ่น p. 716.

เหนาะ ๆ naw[4]-naw[4] *adj.* easily gained ; acquired without much effort (used in regard to answers to prayers accompanied by propitiatory offerings) : *onomat.* from the sound produced by beating, knocking or patting lightly on the bottom of an empty rice pot.

เหนี่ยง nee-ang[2] *n.* the small comb-like appendage hanging from below the beak of certain fowls : เหนี่ยงนกกะทุง a variety of mango.

เหนี่ยง (แมง) nee-ang[4] *n.* a whirligig ; a gyrinid water beetle, metallic in luster, found on the surface of smooth water. It has four eyes, two of which are under water and two above. It darts about constantly in intricate circles searching for prey. This beetle is considered to be the blackest of all insects, hence the expression ดำเหมือนเหนี่ยง.

เหนี่ยน nee-an[4] v. a relish eaten with other food.

เหนี่ยม nee-am[2] v. to be shy; to be backward; to be bashful; see กระดาก p. 27.

เหนี่ยว nee-ow[2] adj. viscous; sticky; gummy; glutinous; tough; stingy; avaricious: เหนี่ยวแน่น penurious; close-fisted; stingy.

เหนี่ยว nee-ow[4] v. to pull; to haul in (as rope); to hold steady in place; to drag; to tug together (as on loose string or rope); to retard; to cause delay; to hold back what is due another (as salary); see รั้ง p. 702.

เหนือ neu-ah[2] n. the north: adj. over; above; upper; on top: prep. upon: หญิง-เหนือผัว a woman who rules her husband: เหนือกฎหมาย not subject to law, or any other authority.

เหนื่อย, เหน็ดเหนื่อย neu-ie[4] v. to be tired; to be wearied; to be exhausted (as after continuous work); to be weakened (by disease).

เห็บ hep[4] n. dog or cattle ticks; crab-lice: ลูกเห็บ hail-stones.

เหม hem[2] P. n. gold; a certain sort of elephant (chd. p. 154); the spire of the canopy of a meru: adj. ending in a decorated tip, point or spire: เหมหงส์ the golden swan.

เหม่ may[4] onomat. from the sound indicating disdain, anger, surprise or a threat (used by Thai actors).

เหม่ง meng[4] adj. bright; polished; untarnished: onomat. from the sound of bells, gongs or cymbals, when struck.

เหม็น men[2] v. to stink; to detect a foul, offensive odour: n. a fetid, rancid, foul odour: adj. stinking; disagreeable; nauseating; disgusting (smells); bad-smelling: เหม็นของเน่า the odour of something rotten: เหม็นเขียว

the odour of crushed, green vegetables or leaves: เหม็นคาว the odour of fresh fish: เหม็นซาก the foul odour of a corpse: เหม็นอับ the musty odour of a closed room.

เหมวดี ๑ hay[2]-ma[6]-wa[6]-dee n. a very sweet substance, having medicinal properties; see ขัณฑสกร under ขัณฑ์ p. 150.

เหมวดี ๒ see หิมวัต p. 936.

เหม่อ mur[4] v. to be careless; to be inattentive; to be absent-minded.

เหมันต์ hay[2]-mun P. S. n. the cold season; winter (S. E. D. p. 1304).

เหมา mow[2] v. to do or cause to be done by the job; to be taken as a whole for a price agreed upon: การเหมา a piece of work done, or to be done as a whole: ขาย-เหมา to sell in a lot; to job lot the goods for sale: รับเหมา to undertake a job as a whole; to think, or conjecture that such was the case: เหมาแรง to bargain to pay only for the labour in a job.

เหมาะ, เหมาะเจาะ maw[4] adj. fitting; suitable; elegant; appropriate; proper for the occasion; see พอดี under พอ p. 577: มาพอ-เหมาะเจาะ to come just at the opportune time for the affair: เหมาะงาม quite becoming (as a dress); beautifully arranged (as a room): เหมาะแก่ตา pleasing to the sight.

เหมียว, เหมี่ยว mee-ow[2] onomat. from the sound of the mewing of a cat (used as a call for cats).

เหมือง meu-ang[2] n. a marsh; a quarry; a natural passageway for water to flow (as for irrigating or mining purposes); land that is low-lying and liable to be flooded; see บ่อ p. 472: เหมืองดีบุก a tin mine: เหมืองผ้าย a cooperatively built irrigating ditch (used in northern Thailand).

เหมือด meu-at[4] n. a salad made of green papaya and the banana flower, and eaten with vermicelli and curry sauce.

เหมือน   meu-an[2] *adj.* similar to; the same as; alike: ทำเหมือนกับแบบ being an exact copy of the pattern: เหมือนกัน all the same; equal to: เหมือนดังว่า as has been said: เหมือนหนึ่ง in like manner; as; see ดุจเหมือน under ดุจ p. 332: เหมือนกับ, เหมือน- ว่า just like; as though; such as; supposing that; in like manner; as was said; equal to.

เหมือย, เหมือย ๆ   meu-ie[4] *adv.* frequently; repeatedly; recurrently; often; see บ่อย p. 474.

เหย   yay[2] *adj.* pouting; deformed (face); cross-looking; unhealthy-looking; see เบ้ p. 487: หน้าเหย wry-faced; having distorted, unsightly facial features.

เหยง   yeng[2] *adv.* briskly; nimbly; quickly; lively; agilely (used in regard to running, jumping, or dancing).

เหยา   yow[2] *v.* to mimic; to ape; to laugh at; to chaff; to taunt; to jeer; to scoff (as when some slight mistake is made); see เยาะ p. 680.

เหย่า   yow[4] *adv.* slowly; deliberately (used in regard to walking or running); see หย่อง ๆ p. 913.

เหย้า, ย้าว, หย้าว   yow[3] *n.* a house; a home; an abode; a residence: มีเหย้ามีเรือน to be established in a house and home (as a bride and groom).

เหยาะ   yaw[4] *v.* to drop, drop by drop; to add gradually (as seasonings, salt or sugar): *adv.* gradually; carefully; deliberately.

เหยิง   yerng[2] *adj.* entangled; confused; mixed; intertwisted; intricate; see ยุ่ง p. 678.

เหยิบ ๆ   yerp[4]-yerp[4] *adv.* with slow, regular movements (as of fanning, or of the movement of the wings of birds in flight).

เหยียด   yee-at[4] *v.* to stretch out straight (as arms and legs); to extend to the full length; to lengthen (as when drawing gold or silver wire); to expand; to enlarge (as boundaries); to treat with contempt; to look down upon; to make invidious comparisons: เหยียดคนเป็นสัตว์ to treat human beings like animals *idiomatic.*

เหยียบ   yee-ap[4] *v.* to put one's foot upon; to trample under foot; to walk or tread upon: เหยียบขาให้เส้นอ่อน a method of massaging, by which a lad stands on the outstretched limbs, and gradually moves himself up and down the limbs: เหยียบขี้ไก่ไม่ฝ่อ a proverb applied in derision to one who is easily daunted by labour, or who detests work; one given to laziness, shiftlessness and indetermination, because when he treads on a pile of chicken dung, it is not even squashed: เหยียบที่ to pace off a plot of ground for the purpose of measuring it: เหยียบเมือง to walk the streets of a city (as tourists); to over-run a city (as a victorious army): เหยียบย่ำ to oppress; to crush; to persecute; to maltreat: ใบเหยียบย่ำ a certificate issued by the land officer giving squatters' rights to a plot of land.

เหยี่ยว   yee-ew[4] *n.* hawk; kite; *generic term for birds of prey*: เหยี่ยวคะไกร (นก) black-legged falconet, *Microhierax fringillarius* (Gaird. J. S. S. IX, 1, p. 9): เหยี่ยวขาว (นก) the black-winged kite, *Elanus caeruleus caeruleus* (Herb. N. H. J. S. S. VI, 4, p. 332): เหยี่ยวดำ (นก) the common pariah kite, *Milvus migrans govinda* (Herb. N. H. J. S. S. VI, 4, p. 331): เหยี่ยวแดง (นก) the brahminy kite, *Haliastur indus indus* (Herb. N. H. J. S. S. VI, 4, p. 330): เหยี่ยวนกเขา (นก) black-shouldered kite, *Elanus caeruleus* (Gaird. J. S. S. IX, 1, p. 9): เหยี่ยวอะยะวา (นก) kestrel, *Tinnunculus alaudarius* (Gaird. J. S. S. IX, 1, p. 9).

เหยื่อ   yeu-ah[4] *n.* bait; prey; allurements of all descriptions: ลูกเหยื่อ small fishes used as bait.

เหยือก   yeu-ak[4] *n.* a jug; a pitcher.

เหรัญญิก, ไหรัญญิก, ไหรัญฌิก   hay[2]-run-yik[6] *P. n.* a treasurer (chd. p. 154).

เหรา hay²-rah *n.* a fabulous marine creature; a dragon crocodile; the poisonous horseshoe crab, แมลงดาทะเล.

เหราะๆ raw⁴-raw⁴ *adv.* gradually; slowly;
deliberately (descriptive of one running).

เหรียญ ree-an² *n.* a coin; a medal: เหรียญ-
เงิน a silver dollar: เหรียญทอง a gold dollar.

เหล่ lay⁴ *adj.* awry; athwart; crossed:
ตาเหล่ squint-eyed; strabismus.

เหล็ก lek⁴ *n.* iron: ขี้เหล็ก (ต้น) see
under ขี้ p. 160: ตีเหล็ก to forge iron:
แม่เหล็ก a magnet: เหล็กกล้า steel: เหล็ก-
จาน a stylus for writing on palm-leaves:
เหล็กไช, เหล็กสว่าน a gimlet; an auger: เหล็กใน
the stinging apparatus of insects: เหล็กไฟ
flint used with steel for striking fire: เหล็ก-
วิลาต sheet tin; tin foil: เหล็กสกัด a cold-
chisel or shears for cutting iron: เหล็กหมาด
an awl: เหล็กไหล miraculous iron, characterized by its quality of becoming soft like
gum when exposed to heat, even that of a
candle (believed to render the owner invulnerable).

เหลน len² *n.* great-grandchild: จิ้งเหลน
the skink; see under จิ้ง p. 249.

เหลว lay-oh² *adj.* fluid; liquid; pliable;
melted: เหลวคว้าง melted into a state of complete fusion (as metals): เหลวแหลก broken
into splinters; smashed into fragments; ruined;
badly damaged; utterly destroyed: เหลว-
ไหล worthless; without foundation; unsuccessful: พูดเหลวไหล unreliable; nonsensical
(speech): คนเหลวไหล one not to be trusted;
one not obedient to instructions given; one
failing in trustworthiness.

เหลอ ler-ie² *adj.* stupid; abashed; shame-
faced; unkempt; dirty; besmeared (as a face).

เหลา ๑ hay²-lah *S. n.* disrespect; contempt;
frivolity; sport; pastime; amorous dalliances
(S. E. D. p. 1305).

เหลา ๒ low² *v.* to whittle (as with a
knife); to trim; to sharpen (to a point); to
smooth off branches or knots (as on bamboo):
เหลาหวาย to trim snarled fibers off rattan
strips.

เหล่า low⁴ *n.* race; group; class; order;
company; kind; species; caste; society; *sign
of the plural*; see พวก p. 575: เหล่ากอ race;
family; relatives: เหล่านั้น, เหล่าโน้น those;
all of those: เหล่านี้ these; all of these:
เหล่าพ่อ related to the father: เหล่าแม่ on
the mother's side of the family: อยู่เหล่าไหน
to which company or group do they belong?

เหล้า lao³ *n.* whiskey; distilled and intoxicating liquors of all kinds: หัวเหล้า the
first portion run off in the process of distilling
whiskey: เหล้าเถื่อน unlawfully distilled
liquor; moon-shine: เหล้าโรง arrack locally
distilled: เมาเหล้า drunk.

เหลาชะโอน (ต้น) lao²-cha⁶-own *n. Oncosperma tigillaria (Palmae)*, a tall, tufted
palm growing in the drier parts of the mangrove forest, found in Cochin-China, throughout Malaysia to the Philippine Islands; in the
Peninsula it is common all round the coasts.
The wood is very hard and durable, and is so
much used for various purposes that the
supplies are greatly diminished. Split into
four, it is used for flooring, and split into
smaller strips, as rafters for roofing and walls.
Its elasticity is great. It is used in deeply
planted fishing stakes, and for the wash-strake
of boats. Walking sticks can be made from
it, and weapons are commonly made from it.
The pirates who formerly infested the Archipelago, employed lances made from it, which
they threw in battle before coming to grips.
Sakai, when following an elephant, may catch
it by driving a sharpened piece of this wood
into the sole of its foot. The spines which stud
the stems are used for blow-pipe darts, and
as the heads of javelins for spearing fish.
The cabbage is excellent, and is even preferred

to that of the coconut. The flowers are said
to be used for flavouring rice. The small flat
pulpy fruits can be made into a preserve.
They are chewed as a substitute for betel.
The sheaths of the flowers very commonly
serve as buckets, and as containers for boiling
water. In Annam baskets are made of the
leaves (Burk. p. 1581); *O. horrida*, a palm
differing from the *O. tigillaria* in having
fewer stems in the tuft, and in growing inland.
It is found from the Malay Peninsula to the
Philippine Islands; in the Peninsula it is
distributed generally in dry forests. The
wood has uses similar to the *D. tigillaria*.
Some say it is harder, but others say it is not
durable. A decoction of the root, apparently
of this palm or perhaps of *O. tigillaria*, is
drunk for fever on the Pahang coast (Burk.
p. 1581).

เหลาหลก (ต้น)   lao²-lok⁴ *n.* a species of
areca-nut having soft rind.

เหลาะแหละ   lao⁴-laa⁴ *adj.* useless; trifling;
foolish; nonsensical; unreliable; untrue (used
in regard to conversation).

เหลิง   lerng² *adj.* going up too high (as a
kite); being too proud, haughty or puffed up;
disdainful; over-important; behaving as if
above one's social position; carrying oneself too
"high and mighty": น้ำเหลิง full tide;
high water; see เจิ่ง p. 259.

เหลียน   lee-an² *n.* a large, hooked knife,
fitted to a long pole (used for lopping off
branches of trees or bamboos that are out of
reach).

เหลี่ยม   lee-am⁴ *n.* a corner; an angle; an
edge; a side; see ด้าน p. 325; แง่ p. 226: บวบ-
เหลี่ยม see under บวบ p. 472: มีแปดเหลี่ยม
octagonal: มีเหลี่ยม angular in shape:
ย่อเหลี่ยม to round off the corners or edges:
รูปสามเหลี่ยม a triangle: รูปสี่เหลี่ยม a quadrilateral figure: รูปหกเหลี่ยม an hexagonal
figure: รูปห้าเหลี่ยม a pentagonal figure:

เหลี่ยมลูกบาศก์ a cube; *a numerical designation for calculating volume.*

เหลียว   lee-ew² *v.* to look sideways; to
look askance; to turn the face from side to
side: ไม่เหลียวแลบ้างเลย *idiomatic* to extend
no helping hand, nor pay attention to in time
of another's distress: เหลียวแล to look or
stare over the shoulder; to rubberneck; to care
for; to take an interest in: เหลียวหลัง to
look behind, or back: เหลียวหา to look for
something, or some person who is behind.

เหลือ   lur-ah² *v.* to have some still left or
remaining; to have more than enough: กิน-
อยู่เหลือเฟือ *idiomatic* to have all of life's
necessities: บุญล้นเหลือ *idiomatic* overflowing with kindness: เศษเหลือ remnants;
the remainder: เหลือเกิน beyond one's endurance; too severe; too excessive; more than
what is deserved (as flogging or punishment):
เหลือเข็ญ most laborious; troublesome; arduous;
involving great labour or hardship; beyond
one's strength to budge: เหลือใจ too taxing
on one's strength; incorrigible; intractable;
incapable of taking instruction (as a mother
would complain about her bad son): เหลือบ่า-
กว่าแรง *idiomatic* to be beyond one's strength
or ability; being unable to do: เหลือเฟือ
overflowing with; more than enough; more
than is required; super-abundant; super-
fluous: เหลือล้น, เหลือหลาย, เหลือแหล่ overflowing; over-abundant; overly sufficient:
เหลือวิสัย to have the unexpected, or the unforeseen happen; to be beyond one's power or
ability (to cope with); to be utterly impossible.

เหลือก   leu-ak⁴ *v.* to turn the eyes up; to
look upwards: *adv.* turned up (referring to
the eyes): ทำตาเหลือกตาพอง *idiomatic* to
open the eyes wide in an angry stare: ตา-
เหลือก a threatening look (as with widely
opened eyes).

เหลือง   leu-ang² *adj.* yellow: ไข้ตัวเหลือง
(โรค) jaundice: น้ำเหลือง serum (purulent),
as that exuding from septic wounds.

เหลือบ leu-ap[4] v. to glimpse; to glance upwards or sidewise: n. a horse-fly; a gad-fly; cattle-flies: adj. gleaming; glittering (in various colours of an indistinct yellow hue).

เหลือม (ง) leu-am[2] n. the reticulated python, *Python reticulatus* (smith, N. H. J. S. S. I, 1, p. 9); the boa-constrictor.

เหลื่อม leu-am[4] adj. overlapping; projecting; over-riding slightly at one end or side; not in line with the adjoining member (as boards or dislocated bones).

เหว hay-oh[2] n. an abyss; a gorge; a chasm; a pit; a valley: ซอกเหว niches or crevices of a chasm.

เหว่ way[4] adj. wild; solitary; lonely; deserted; unfrequented (by human beings); see เปลี่ยว p. 534: ว้าเหว่ใจ idiomatic sad because of loneliness; dejected; depressed in spirit (as by being in a strange or deserted place).

เหวง weng[2] adj. the lightest possible in weight, e. g. เบาเหวง feathery (in weight); *superlative for light in weight.*

เหวย, เว้ย, โว้ย wur-ie[2] onomat. from the sound denoting derision, contempt, or mockery; an exclamation calling attention for united action (as for all to come or go together, e. g. ไปกันเหวย); see โวย p. 784.

เหวี่ยง wee-ang[4] v. to dash to pieces (as a cup in a rage); to hurl (as a javelin); to thrust; to throw after making a whirling movement to secure momentum (as David threw a stone at Goliath); to brandish (as a cane): to chuck (as something thrown away in disgust).

เห่อ hur[4] adj. elated; haughty; lofty; arrogant; boastful; conceited (as the quick-rich); swollen; raised or spreading (as a rash or disease of the skin): เห่อเหิม having the disposition to long unduly for greatness or honour; having the "big head"; elated over

minor successes; lusting **after fame.**

เหะ hay[4] onomat. from the sound made by a crowd of rowdy, drunken men.

เหา how[2] n. a louse; an ancient Thai unit of weight, equal to the eighth part of a grain of rice: ไข่เหา the eighth part of the เหา: สายเหา crupper; the looped strap that passes under a horse's tail and keeps the saddle or harness from slipping forward.

เห่า how[4] v. to bark: เห่า (ง) the common Asiatic cobra, *Naja naja* (smith, N. H. J. S. S. VI, 1, p. 57): เห่าดง, งวงอาง (ง) the king cobra or hamadryad, *Naja hannah* (smith, N. H. J. S. S. VI, 1, p. 59): เห่าตลาน (ง) the common rat snake, *Zamenis mucosus; Zamensis korros* (smith, N. H. J. S. S. I, 2, pp. 93, 94): เห่าปื๊ดแก้ว (ง) *Simotes cyclurus* (smith, N. H. J. S. S. I, 2, p. 97): เห่าม่อง, เห่าดอกจันทน์ (ง) the cobra, *Naja tripudians* (smith, N. H. J. S. S. I, 3, p. 179).

เหาะ haw[4] v. to ascend; to travel overhead; to float through the air by mechanical means, or by super-natural power: เรือเหาะ aircraft; airplanes; dirigible balloons: เหาะได้ having the power of aerial motion or transportation.

เหิม herm[2] adj. inflated; elated; intensified; bold; insolent: เหิมหาญ puffed up or exhilarated by being bold, or accomplishing much through bravery: เหิมห้าว aggravated or emboldened by anger: เหิมฮึก highly elated through boldness, pride, or fearlessness

เหิ่ม herm[4] adj. excited; stirred up; inflamed; aroused.

เหิร hern[2] v. to fly; to float; to travel through the air; see บิน p. 483.

เหิย he-ah[3] n. the warran; the water monitor; the iguana.

เหียง hee-ang[2] *Thai, Chantabun,* กราด *Thai, Korat* and *Laos, Korat* to *Ubon,* สะแบง or ตะแบง *Laos, N. Ubon* to *Udown, Krabin,*

ตร๊าชต์ *Khmer* and *Sui* (ต้น) *n. Dipterocarpus intricatus* (*Dipterocarpaceae*; *D. obtusifolius* (cb. pp. 136, 137 : V. P. p. 270).

เหียน hee-an[2] *v.* to be nauseated : *adj.* nauseous : หันเหียน to whirl ; to revolve ; to rotate ; to shift or be shifted (as contents of the stomach prior to vomiting) : เหียนราก to be on the verge of vomiting ; to be sick at the stomach.

เหียน hee-an[3] *v.* to be ruined ; to be despoiled ; to be stripped of all ; to have spent or squandered all (of one's money as through gambling) ; to be worn thin by friction (as a table-knife or rope) ; see เตียน p. 374.

เหียม hee-am[3] *n.* cause ; reason : *adj.* cruel ; brutal ; fierce ; ferocious ; harsh : ใจ-เหี้ยม of a brutal, pitiless disposition : เหี้ยม-เกรียม unmerciful ; "nigger-hearted" ; cruel ; unrelenting : เหี้ยมนั้น therefore : เหี้ยมหาญ cruel ; merciless ; atrocious : เหี้ยมโหด excessively cruel, brutal and harsh ; acting without mercy or pity.

เหี่ยว hee-ew[4] *adj.* withered ; faded ; jaded ; drooping ; languishing ; wrinkled ; puckered : ใจเหี่ยว dejected ; disheartened ; discouraged : เหี่ยวแห้ง *idiomatic* parched and dried ; see แห้ง p. 136.

เหือด heu-at[4] *v.* to decrease ; to be diminished ; to abate ; to dry up ; to disappear : *n.* rubella ; German measles : เหือดหาย to decrease gradually and become dissipated.

แห haa[2] *n.* a cast-net (the edge being weighted with a lead chain) : *adj.* wild ; untamed ; shy ; far-away ; separated : ร่างแห meshes or spaces of the cast-net ; a net (as for playing tennis).

แห่ haa[4] *v.* to go in procession ; to accompany those forming the procession : *n.* a procession ; a parade : กระบวนแห่ sections or divisions of a parade : แห่นาค to go in procession, conducting the person with his outfit to the Buddhist temple where he is to take the vows of the brotherhood : แห่เรือ a procession of boats : แห่เลียบเมือง a procession around a city wall : แห่ล้อม to attend on all sides, while in procession (as attendants, guards of honour, or bearers of offerings).

แห้ ! haa[3] *onomat.* from the sound of the snarling of enraged dogs.

แหก haak[4] *v.* to open forcefully ; to break through (as the bars of a prison) ; to pull apart ; to force open : แหกจมูก to enlarge the nose (as for an examination) : แหกคอก *idiomatic* to break through the bars (of control) ; to become unruly ; to resist rule, law or dicipline.

แหง ngaa[2] *adj.* abashed ; confused ; nonplussed ; confounded (descriptive of facial expressions).

แหง่ ngaa[4] *adj.* small ; little ; young ; see เล็ก p. 751 : ลูกแหง่ a buffalo calf.

แห่ง haang[4] *n.* place ; spot ; location ; locality ; situation ; see ตำบล p. 365 : *prep.* of : ทุกแห่ง, ทุกตำบล every place ; everywhere : บางแห่ง some places : แห่งไน้น that place yonder : แห่งใด where ? แห่งไร, แห่งไหน which place ? แห่งอื่น some other place.

แห้ง haang[3] *adj.* dry ; parched ; faded ; withered ; without moisture : ใจแห้งเหี่ยว foiled ; defeated ; disappointed ; balked ; frustrated : ผอมแห้ง emaciated ; thin : แห้งแล้ง a dried and parched condition : แห้งหมาด ๆ partly dried (as fresh paint).

แหง่ง ! ngaang[4] *onomat.* from the sound produced when striking a bell.

แหงน ngaan[2] *v.* to turn the face upwards ; to look up ; see เงย p. 224 : แหงนหงาย an euphonic combination with the same meaning.

แหน ๑ naa[2] *n.* a vegetable scum growing on stagnant water.

แหน ๒ haan[2] *v.* to be solicitous for ; to

care for ardently; to wait upon; to guard on all sides; see ล้อม p. 731: เผ้าแหน to attend during public audiences of the king: หวง-แหน to protect jealously; to be fervent or zealous in one's care of; to keep for one's private use.

แห้น see **แทะ** p. 427.

แหนง naang[2] *v.* to suspect; to doubt the sincerity of; to distrust; to mistrust.

แหนบ naap[4] *v.* to pinch with the finger tips: *n.* clothes-pins; tongs; tweezers; nippers; pincers; springs (for cars or carriages); clasps (attached to the lapels of coats, or edges of pockets); a bundle of banana leaves rolled up for sale.

แหนม (หมู) naam[2] *n.* a condiment made from fermented pork.

แหบ haap[4] *adj.* hoarse; harsh; rasping; dry; grating (descriptive of the voice, or music); see เครือ p. 207.

แหม maa[2] *n.* a protecting sheath placed over the length of ancient guns or cannon (to prevent bursting): *onomat.* from the sound uttered in surprise, disapprobation or blame: ปืนสามแหม a gun with three metal rings or bands.

แหม่! maa[4] *onomat.* from the sound expressing a threat or anger (used to intimidate children).

แหม่ม maam[4] *n.* madam; a title adopted from India (used for married European ladies).

แหมะ maa[4] *v.* to slap on; to paste on while still pliable (as mortar or cement); to let drop and be spread over a surface (as frosting on a cake).

แหย yaa[2] *adj.* abashed; confused; confounded; silly (descriptive of facial expressions).

แหย่ yaa[4] *v.* to insert (as an instrument into a sinus); to annoy (by constantly poking fun at); to jeer; to probe; to poke; to push (with the end of rod or stick); see แยง p. 682.

แหยง see ขยาด p. 142.

แหยม yaam[2] *n.* a small tuft of hair (other than the topknot); scattered patches of hair or beard: *adj.* scanty; scattered; sparce; patchy; see ปอย p. 516: ผมหยอมแหยม *idiomatic* thin or scanty hair.

แหยะ yaa[4] *adv.* carelessly; unwillingly; forcelessly; negligently; indifferently (descriptive of eating tasteless food).

แหล่ laa[4] *n.* a chapter or section in the account of Buddha's transmigration previous to his last one. This word is derived from นั้นแล, being the closing expression pronounced by the preacher.

แหลก laak[4] *adj.* crushed; reduced to atoms; powdered; ground to pulp: ข้าวแหลก broken grains of rice: แหลกยับ completely dashed to pieces (as a ship on rocks): แหลก-เหลว triturated; powdered.

แหล่ง laang[4] *n.* location; place; domicile; place of abode; a rest; a support: หลักแหล่ง post; support; permanent place of abode or residence: แหล่งศร a rest for supporting an arrow when it is to be shot; a bag in which arrows are carried: แหล่งหล้า the terrestrial plain; see ที่ ๑ p. 416.

แหลน laan[2] *n.* a long, pointed, iron bar (used as a weapon in ancient warfare, also hurled in sport contests): แหลนแทงปลา an harpoon for spearing fish.

แหลม laam[2] *n.* a cape; a promontory; a peninsula: *adj.* tapering to a sharp point; pointed: ปัญญาหลักแหลม sharp-witted; bright; intelligent; artful; clever: แหลมหลัก *idiomatic* ingenious; subtle; witty; intelligent; dexterous.

แหละ laa[4] *n.* an exclamation indicating certainty and specificness: นั้นแหละ that's it; that's right.

แหว waa[2] *onomat.* from the sound uttered in anger (as of elephants or children).

แห้ว haa-oh[3] *n. Tuber cibarium; Scirpus tuberosus (Cyperaceae)*, the black truffle or Chinese truffle, a variety of fleshy underground fungus prized mainly as condiments (Web.): แห้วประดู่ *Thai* (ต้น) *Eriosema chinese (Leguminosae)* (cb. p. 468): แห้วระบาด *Thai, Prachuap,* กาเสดโคก *Laos, Udawn* (ต้น) *Neptunia triquetra (Leguminosae)* (cb. p. 545): แห้วหมู (ต้น) *Cyperus rotundus (Cyperaceae)*, nut grass, a low sedge with numerous underground, edible tubers. Decoctions of the tubers are given in fever, diarrhoea, dyspepsia and stomach complaints. It is a pestiferous weed of gardens and waste ground, extending by its short underground stolons, and persisting by hard black tubers, while it spreads by seeding abundantly; it is found in all warm parts of the world; in the Peninsula it is common in cultivated parts. In literature it has been confused with other tuberous sedges, such as *C. tuberosus, C. esculentus,* and *C. bulbosus.* The tubers of all four are edible; but those of *C. bulbosus* are so small that only when famine is severe in the dry countries where it grows, is it worth a man's while to dig them up. The larger tubers of the others are more used. Though the tubers of *C. rotundus* are edible, it is never cultivated for them. They are eaten from plants growing wild, and chiefly as a famine food. They seem to carry little oil and differ greatly as food. They are somewhat aromatic. It is their aroma which brings them into use, and, from the circumstance that two sanskritic names are applied to the plant in Malaysia, it is clear that the Hindu conquerors of Java used them, and brought the knowledge of these uses into Java at least. Its use is old in China, in India, and in the Levant, for it is named in the oldest writings, of each country. Heroditus states that the Scythians used it in embalming, but its chief use was as a diuretic and emmenagogue remedy, and as such it is still valued in various countries. In India the rhizomes are scraped and pounded, and administered internally as part of various mixtures in which they function as diuretics. They are said to be vermifugal, and because of their aroma they are used in compound medicaments (McM. pp. 378, 474: Burk. p. 735).

แหวก waak[4] *v.* to separate; to open; to part (as a curtain or screen); to push others aside (as when making a way through a crowd of people): แหวกผม to part the hair: แหวกมุ้ง to open the flaps of a mosquito net: แหวกน้ำว่าย to separate the water in the act of swimming.

แหว่ง waang[4] *adj.* nicked (as porcelain); chipped; partly broken; torn; imperfect; see วิ่น p. 775: ปากแหว่ง hare-lip: แหว่งกึ่งดวง to have half cut off (as during a partial eclipse of the sun or moon).

แหวด (เรือ) waat[4] *n.* a type of shallow-draft river boat with a long curving stern piece, propelled by long fore and aft oars.

แหวน waan[2] *n.* a ring; a circular band; a washer: แก้วแหวนเงินทอง *idiomatic* sundry riches, as rings and trinkets: หัวแหวน the bezel or setting of a ring: แหวนก้านพลู a clove-shaped ring: แหวนงู a dragon-shaped ring: แหวนแต่งงาน a wedding-ring: แหวนนพเก้า the ring of the nine gems: แหวนมั่น an engagement ring.

แหวะ waa[4] *v.* to enlarge by making an extra incision; to cut open roughly (as when making a post-mortem); to cut and pull the edges apart; to carve; to sever (as a butcher): แหวะฝา to break open a partition: แหวะพุง, แหวะท้อง to make an abdominal section; see ผ่า p. 546; แล่ง p. 757.

แหะ ! haa[4] *onomat.* from the sound of laughter.

โห่ hoh[4] *v.* to give a long undulating shout or cheer (as when marching in a procession, or on the occasion of some festival): *n.* a shout; a yell; cries (to others at a distance): ไห่ขึ้น to start a cheer and have others follow with a succeeding yell: ไห่สามลา to give three cheers: ไห่เอาชัย to shout or cheer for victory.

โหก   hok[4] *n.* a cleft; a crevice; a rift; a chasm; a gap; a breach; see ช่อง p. 283.

โหง   hong[2] *n.* a ghost; the devil; demons; plague-bringers: ตายโหง to die from some fearful disease; *used as an imprecation*: โหงพราย a class of demons, considered to be under the power of sorcerers; spirits of those dying from some dreaded disease.

โหฎ   hote[4] *S. n.* a boat; a raft.

โหด   hote[4] *adj.* ill-tempered; cruel; base; harsh-mannered; see ร้ายกาจ p. 711: โหดร้าย cruel to the extreme; pitiless; unmerciful.

โหน   hone[2] *v.* to swing, hanging by the hands; to hang; to dangle (as while the hands are holding on): โหนโตงเตง to sway while hanging (as a gibbon from a branch).

โหนก   noke[4] *n.* a swelling; a lump; hematoma or blood tumour (as after a blow on the head): *adj.* raised; protruding; bulging; see โน p. 465.

โหน่ง!   nong[4] *onomat.* from the sound made when striking a gong.

โหม   hoh[2]-ma[6] *v.* to fight; to urge on; to rush in upon, or attack violently; to have all join or unite in (as members of a chorus or orchestra); to increase the strength of (by enlisting the help of others): *P. S. n.* an oblation to the gods; a burnt offering; a sacrifice; the casting of clarified butter (ghee) into the sacrificial fire; a Brahminical ceremony (S. E. D. p. 1036): โหมกรรม a sacrificial act or rite: โหมกระโจมจับ *idiomatic* to rush in, pouncing upon in order to capture: โหมกาล the time of sacrifice: โหมกัณฑ์ the implements or paraphernalia used in making

sacrifices: โหมโรง an orchestral overture: โหมหัก to fight or advance bravely; to unite in a vigorous effort (as against a common enemy); to try to break in suddenly, or to overcome the enemies' position: อย่าโหมไฟ *idiomatic* do not urge on the fire (as by opening the draught); see เร่ง p. 718.

โหม ๒   hom[2] *n. a prefix for a group of many common vegetables to which the particular designating name is added:* โหมหิน *Thai, Bangkok and Chainat* (ผัก) *Trianthema portulacastrum (Ficoideae)* (cb. p. 784); *Boerhaavia diffusa (Nyctaginaceae)*, spreading hog-weed, an herb, usually prostrate, in fallows and waste places, very common in India, spreading southwards into the Malay Peninsula, occurring about the ports, and elsewhere only in Kedah; found to the east of the Peninsula in Java, and forwards through Malaysia and the Pacific. The Malays have not begun to use it medicinally, but the swollen roots are widely resorted to in India. The leaves are eaten by cattle, and in some parts of India, by man. The roots also may be eaten, and it is recorded that the Australian natives eat it and that Figians fall back on it in times of scarcity. As a drug the root seems to operate as a diuretic, acting through a slight influence on the heart, the beat of which it strengthens, so that the blood-pressure in the kidneys is heightened. In large doses the root is said to be emetic; but the action of the leaves is so mild that the plant is regarded, in Australia, not as an objectionable weed, but as a good forage for sheep and cattle (V. P. p. 54: MCM. p. 311: BURK. p. 343): โหมหนาม (ผัก) *Amaranthus spinosus (Amarantaceae)*, prickly-edged amarant or spiny tumble weed, a weed native of tropical America and now throughout the whole tropics. It tends to become the commonest amarant in any thickly populated tropical country, by selection, animals eating it less than the thornless species; and that is why it is the most abundant species in India, and why it is growing increasingly abundant in the Peninsula. It is collected for use as spinach. It is best of the *Amaranthus* available in Singapore, and is much used elsewhere. It is much resorted to in Indo-China, and even used by Europeans. It is also much used in east Africa. In Indo-China it is a cattle and pig food, and is claimed to increase the quantity of the milk as regards cows. It is given to cattle in India, boiled with pulse to increase the yield of milk. The plant, when taken internally, has a diuretic action, which may reside more strongly in the root, for the root is more used as an internal medicine than the leaves and stems. It is used in almost every part of the world where the weed has exhibited itself, sometimes in the form of a decoction, and sometimes the root itself is boiled until soft. Heat does not seem to reduce its efficacy. Among the complaints for which it is used, gonorrhoea is more frequently treated by it than others; and the value would seem to lie in its diuretic properties and probably resides almost wholly in the potash present. However it is also mentioned as useful for cholera, which is not a complaint requiring diuretic treatment. The plant is regarded as an emmenagogue and a lactagogue — in fact, in general promoting discharges. For external use, as an emollient, the above-ground parts are employed even more frequently than the root is internally, and in all countries where the plant occurs. This is an entirely different action, for now it is saponin which is active. The above-ground parts are applied to bruises and inflammations. Saltpetre is obtained from the ashes in Thailand (V. P. pp. 53, 178: MCM. p. 473: Burk. p. 127).

โหม่ see โด่ p. 337; โผล่ p. 552.

โหม่ง mong[4] *v.* to use the head in hitting a ball (as when playing foot-ball): *onomat.*

from the sound produced when beating a gong hung on a tripod.

โหมด mote[4] *n.* a pattern of embroidered silk where threads of gold or silver are woven in alternately.

โหย ho-ie[2] *v.* to moan or groan for; to lament; to deplore (the absence of); to make lamentation for; see กระโหย p. 49: โหยหา to make expression of loving thoughts for, or in regard to: โหยไห้ to grieve; to sigh; to cry; to lament (the deceased one).

โหยกเหยก yoke[4]-yake[4] *adj.* vagrant; being a scamp; troublesome; unstable like a vagabond; roguish; see เกเร p. 121.

โหยง yong[2] *adj.* nimble; quick; regular in action (as one jumping over hurdles): เต้นโหยงเหยง *idiomatic* to jump around in a lively manner.

โหร hone[2] *n.* a Brahmin astrologer; a fortune-teller; a soothsayer.

โหรง, โหรงเหรง rong[2] *adv.* sparcely; thinly; meagrely (as relating to the quantity of hair); slenderly.

โหรดาจารย์ see หุตาจารย์ under หุต p. 937.

โหระพา (ต้น) hoh[2]-ra[6]-pah *n. Ocimum basilicum (Labiatae)* sweet basil, an annual, about 2 feet high, cultivated for its highly fragrant and aromatic leaves which are used for flavouring soups, etc. It is found throughout the Old World tropics; in the Peninsula it is not uncommon in gardens in the more settled parts. It has several cultivated varieties; some are more aromatic than others. The aroma has a faint suggestion of cloves. The Malays, who classify by uses, recognize four varieties: (1) strong-flavoured dark-coloured, (2) strong-flavoured light-coloured, (3) mild-flavoured dark-coloured, (4) mild-flavoured light-coloured. The juice of the leaves is a common domestic remedy for coughs among them. It has a slightly narcotic effect, which allays irritation in the throat. This same narcotic effect is made use of in India, where the juice is used as a nasal douche. It is used elsewhere also. A decoction of the leaves may be administered after child-birth. For high fever, a decoction into which it may enter, is administered. This use extends to Cambodia and India, if not farther. For treating coughs in children, the flowers are used, being less aromatic than the leaves. Oil of *O. basilicum* is distilled in Europe from several varieties. It is a yellow liquid with an aromatic pleasant odour, containing about 55 per cent of methyl-chavicol, and also linalol. The oil is used to give the scent of mignonette (MCM. p. 344: BURK. p. 1571).

โหรา hoh[2]-rah *S. n.* an hour; the half of a zodiacal sign; the horoscope (S. E. D. p. 1306): โหราผักกูด *Diplazium esculentum* (*Polypodiaceae*), a common, somewhat tufted fern, generally about three feet high but sometimes higher than a man, found throughout moist tropical Asia, and throughout the Pacific; in the Peninsula, generally. The young fronds are eaten, either as a salad or cooked as a spinach, in almost every country of its distribution, and in many it is commonly offered in the markets. The nutritive value is small. The Malays make a little use of it medicinally, pounding the old plant in water and sprinkling a fever patient with it. A decoction may be given after child-birth (Medical Dictionary: BURK. p. 835): โหราบอน *Alocasia sp.* (*Araceae*), a genus of herbs with swollen stems, found in tropical Asia, Malaysia, and the Pacific. All seem to be irritant (MCM. pp. 149, 295: BURK. p. 105): โหราจารย์ an astrologer; a skilled observer of the stars; chief among the Brahminical astrologers: โหรา-ศาสตร์ the science of astrology (S. E. D. p. 1306).

โหล loh[2] *n.* a dozen; twelve things of a kind: *adj.* deeply or widely hollowed out; excavated; having gaps or holes; see โบ้ p.

491: ขวดโหล a wide-mouth glass-stoppered bottle: ฟันโหล to be devoid of teeth: โหล-เหล weakened; enfeebled; indisposed; unable to go on.

โหล่ loh[4] *adj.* last; least; hindmost; final; slowest (in a race).

โหลากา, โหลี hoh[2]-lah-gkah *S. n.* Holi; Holika, a popular Hindu festival held on the full moon of Phalguna (March) for the worship of Vishnu. This consists of singing of songs, beating of drums, blowing of horns, throwing coloured liquids and powder over one another and passers-by, and dancing by men and boys of the lower castes (Underhill, The Hindu Religious Year, pp. 44, 46).

โหว่, โหว, โหว้ woh[4] *adj.* hollowed out; perforated; pierced; decayed into holes by disease, or eaten by vermin; see โพรง p. 602: ฟันมีรูโหว่ the tooth has a large cavity.

โหวด wote[4] *n.* the sound produced by a steam whistle.

ให้ hai[3] *v.* to cause; to give; to offer to another; to allow; to permit; *an auxilliary verb of the imperative mood*: ให้การ to give evidence; to make a report; to make a statement in defence or explanation of: ให้คุณ beneficial; efficient (as a remedy combating disease): ให้คำมั่น to make a verbal promise; to urge or demand that a promise be made: ให้จับ to give permission to catch or capture (as an escaped convict); to occur (as chills in malarial fever): ให้จับจอง to be allowed to take possession of (as squatters' rights to a piece of land): ให้จำคุก must be imprisoned: ให้ชื่อผิดโดยหลง an accidental misnomer: ให้เช่า to be allowed to hire; to be for rent, or for lease (as vacant houses): ให้เช่าช่วง to be allowed to sub-let or sub lease: ให้ทั้งสองฝ่ายใช้ค่าฤชาธรรมเนียม *legal* both parties must pay their own costs: ให้ทราบว่า to be informed; should, or ought to be told: ให้-ทานแก่คนจน to give alms to the poor: ให้บรรับ

to be fined; to be penalized: ให้เป็นส่วนช่วย to contribute towards; to cooperate with: ให้ผล to bring results; to bear fruit: ให้พิจารณาใหม่ to make an order for a new trial: ให้มีโอกาศทำตามความพอใจ to have unconditional permission or authority; to have *carte blanche* authority: ให้ยืม to lend; to be permitted to loan; to be advanced (as money on good security): ให้ริบเสีย to be forfeited or confiscated (as a penalty for some default): ให้ราคาของในการขายทอดตลาด to make a bid at an auction sale: ให้รับประกัน *legal* to forfeit bail: ให้สินบน to bribe: ให้สืบพยานต่อไป to order further evidence to be heard: ให้หา to desire the presence of; to call: ให้อนุญาติผู้เป็นคนกลางพิจารณา to submit to arbitration: ให้อำนาจไว้, ให้มีอำนาจ to have power vested in.

ไห hai[2] *n. a prefix for small-mouthed, glazed, earthen jugs to which the particular designating name is added:* ไหกระเทียม garlic jugs: ไหปลาร้า (กระตุก) the collar-bone; the clavicle.

ไห่ hai[4] *n.* an aquatic vegetable with medicinal properties.

ไห้ hai[3] *v.* to cry; to sob; to weep; to mourn; to lament; see ร้องไห้ under ร้อง p. 692.

ไหน ๑ nai[2] *adj.* which? where? whither? คนไหน which person is it? ข้างไหน on which side? ที่ไหนจะทำได้ *idiomatic* how is the impossible to be accomplished? ที่ไหนได้ it is quite impossible: ที่ไหน ๆ ก็ได้ any where will do; where ever you please: ไปไหน where are you going? see สั่งไร under สั่ง p. 864.

ไหน ๒, พุทรา (p. 594) nai[2] *Chin. n.* Chinese date, *Zizyphus jujuba* (*Rhamnaceae*) or Indian jujube. It is a tree of small size, in cultivation in relatively dry parts of the world. It must have come into cultivation first in Asia, perhaps in India, but it exists in the greatest variety in China, where there are produced fruits shaped like cherries and of smaller size; and fruits shaped like olives, of every size from that of an olive to that of a hen's egg. An American explorer estimates the Chinese races at 300 to 400. Some of the fruits the Chinese eat fresh, some they dry, in which state they keep indefinitely, and some are preserved in syrup. Botanists look upon India as its home, for it exists in a wild state there, though there are fewer races in that country. In Java it grows wild throughout the whole of the low country, and is sometimes cultivated. In India, coming down from sanskritic times, the fruit is held to purify the blood, and to aid weak digestion. At the present time, the bark and seeds are given as a remedy for diarrhoea, and the root in the form of a decoction for fever. The powdered root and a poultice of the leaves are used on wounds. The timber is hard, and used for small objects. The bark will tan. The lac-insect feeds on the tree (BURK. p. 2305).

ไหม (ผ้า) mai[2] *n.* silk cloth or fabrics: *adj.* silky; made of silk; *gram. a final interrogative particle used instead of* หรือ (p. 917) *but not so acceptable:* ไหม (ตัว) the silk worm: กินไหม, กินหรือไม่ are you going to eat it or not? ปรับไหม, สินไหม a fine; a remuneration; an indemnity; to indemnify or reimburse (as in default of some payment or obligation): หมวกไหมสับปะรด hats made of pine-apple threads or silk: ไหม, หรือไม่ or not: ไหมทอง gold and silk threads (woven together).

ใหม่ mai[4] *adj.* new; fresh; novel; modern; recent: ทำใหม่ to do anew; to make over again; to repair; to re-commence: ใหม่ถอดด้าม unused; that which has just been unpacked (as a machine): ใหม่ ๆ quite new; never been used.

ไหม้ mai[3] *v.* to burn; to be on fire; to be consumed by fire: *adj.* scorched; burnt; parched; charred; shrivelled (by heat); brown (as by exposure to the sun).

ไหรญ, ไหรณย์　hai²-ron　n. silver; money; gold treasures: adj. golden; made of gold or silver.

ไหรญฎิก, ไหรญฌิก see เหรัญญิก p. 942.

ไหล　lie²　v. to flow (as liquids or molten metals): ไหล (ปลา) *Monopterus albus* (*Monopteridae*), a swamp eel which lives in ponds and swamps, burying itself in mud at times. It is caught in rice-fields, fish-ponds, etc. and is, as a rule, eaten only by the Chinese, who esteem its flesh (Burk. p. 1490); *Symbranchus bengalensis* (*Symbranchidae*); *Pisodonophis cancrivorus* (*Ophichthyidae*), a small edible eel (Suvatti pp. 19, 23: Burk. p. 1766): ไหลทะเล (ปลา) *Pisodonophis boro* (*Ophichthyidae*) (suvatti p. 22): ไหลอาบ to flow profusely: ไหลเชี่ยว to flow swiftly.

ไหล่　lai⁴　n. the scapular region of the back; the back of the shoulder: ไหล่รวบ

the position in which the edges of the two scapulas are approximated (as in extreme expansion of the chest, in callisthenic drills).

ไหว　wai²　v. to shake; to totter; to oscillate; to tremble; to quiver (as leaves or branches of trees); to be able to do; to be able to lift; to be capable of: adj. trembling; shaking; see สะเทือน p. 837: แผ่นดินหวั่นไหว idiomatic the earth trembles or quakes: ไหวหวาด to quake or tremble from fright or fear: ไหว-พริบ adroitness; cleverness; astuteness: ยก-ไม่ไหว to be unable to lift.

ไหว้ (วะไหว้)　wai³　v. to salute; to worship; to make obeisance to; to show respect to by placing the hands palm to palm and raising them to the face or forehead: กราบ-ไหว้ to prostrate. oneself on the floor while offering a salutation or worshipping: ไหว้-สามลา to perform the salutation three times.

ไหหลำ　hai²-lum²　Chin. n. Hainanese.

ฬ

ฬ　The forty-second letter of the Thai alphabet, a low class letter of which there are twenty-four, viz. ค, ต, ม, ง, ช, ฌ, ซ, ญ, ฑ, ฒ, ฐ, ฑ, ฒ, น, ณ, พ, ฟ, ภ, ม, ร, ล, ว, ฬ, ฮ. ฬอจุฬา is the name of this letter. It is pronounced like the English "l". It

does not occur generally in Pali, Sanskrit and Thai words. It is used in only a few words, as จุฬา see จุฑา p. 253; กีฬา see p. 109; เขฬะ see p. 165; วิรุฬห์ see พิรุฬห์ p. 589; เบียด-เบียฬ see p. 490; ฬา ass; donkey; see ลา ๒ p. 739; ฬ่อ see ล่อ p. 738; บาฬี see บาลี p. 482.

อ

อ　The forty-third consonant of the Thai alphabet, a middle class letter of which there are nine, viz. ก, จ, ฎ, ฏ, ด, ต, บ, ป, อ. It is equivalent to the English "au," or short "o." The designating name is ออ่าง. It can be used as an auxillary vowel, as in คือ, ถือ, เสือ, เรือ, เธอ; as an initial consonant, as in อา, อก, องค์, องุ่น, อนึ่ง; as a prefix it may

be a substitute for ห, which is not pronounced, as in the four following words only, อย่า, อย่าง, อยาก, อยู่.

อ ๒　P. S. a privative particle; a prefix indicating negation as a-; an-; un-; in, e.g. อศุภ not beautiful; อธรรม unrighteous. When occurring before a vowel, it is changed to

อน, as อนาจาร.　ออ, อ่อ, อ้อ are signs of the vocative; ออเจ้า is a word of address, Oh ! Sir.

อก ๑　　ok[4] *n.* the breast; the thorax; the bosom; the chest: ไม่เห็นอกเห็นใจ *idiomatic* to be unappreciative or unmindful (of another's trouble): อกไก่ the ridge of a roof (so called from its resemblance to the breast-bone of a fowl): อกตั้ง with extreme expansion of the chest; signifying utmost effort or exertion: อกเต่า a sand-bank or bar (as at the mouth of a river); the ridge along the back of a turtle: อกทะเล a postlude to certain kinds of Thai music: อกร่อง a species of mango (so called because of a longitudinal groove along one side): อกเลา an overlapping strip of wood attached to one leaf of a double door or hinged window, to keep out the weather: อกเลื่อย a fulcrum, bar, brace or strut for exerting tension on a buck-saw.

อก ๒　　ok[4] *Cam. n.* a group; a crowd; a flock; a company; a party.

อกตัญญุตา　　ah[4]-gka[4]-dtun-yoo[6]-dtah *P. n.* ingratitude; ungratefulness (chd. p. 23).

อกตัญญู　　ah[4]-gka[4]-dtun-yoo *P. adj.* ungrateful; perfidious; rebellious (chd p. 23): คนอกตัญญู an ungrateful person.

อกนิษฐ์　　ah[4]-gka[4]-nit[6] *n.* inhabitants of the highest regions of the Brahminical spiritual world, or the world of the superior deities (H. C. D. p. 179: chd. p. 22): *adj.* greatest; highest; superior to all others.　According to Brahminical mythology the spiritual realms are divided into three ascending spheres or tiers, and the inhabitants or deities in each have three forms of existence.　The lowest are those with form and perception.

อกรณีย์　　ah[4]-gka[4]-ra[6]-nee *P. n.* deeds that should not be performed, or should be abstained from (chd. p. 23).

อกรรมกริยา　　ah[4]-gkum-ma[6]-gka[4]-ri[6]-yah *n. gram.* an intransitive verb.

อกัปปิยะ　　ah[4]-gkup[4]-bpi[4]-ya[6] *P. adj.* that which should or ought not be done; unsuitable; improper; wrong (chd. p. 23):　อกัปปิย-วัตถุ prohibited food and forbidden articles (considered as impure): อกัปปิยโวหาร words and utterances which are unsuitable and should be left unsaid.

อกุศล, อกุสล　　ah[4]-gkoo[4]-son[2] *S. n.* demerit; sins meriting the severest of punishments: *adj.* sinful; evil; bad; unhealthful; unmeritorious: อกุศลกรรม sin and its punishments: อกุศลกรรมบถ the broad road to destruction; the paths of sin: อกุศลเจตนา the intentional committing of sin; evil thoughts; deliberate wrong acts: อกุศลธาตุ the elements, rudiments or first principles of sins of which there are three, *viz.* lust, malice, avarice or cupidity:　อกุศลมูล the origin, source or cause of sin, of which there are three, *viz.* desire or covetousness, anger or hatred, and ignorance.

อคติ　　ah[4]-ka[6]-dti[4] *P. n.* the condition of going in a wrong course; acts wrongly motivated, of which there are four, *viz.* partiality from love; prejudice from anger; prejudice from ignorance; prejudice from fear (chd. p. [16]).

อคเนสัน (ผี)　　ah[4]-ka[6]-nay-sun[2] *n.* the name of an abscess along the region of the back (almost invariably fatal).

อคาธ　　ah[4]-kart[3] *S. n.* a hole; an abyss; a bottomless pit: *adj.* bottomless; unfathomable (S. E. D. p. 4).

อคาร, อาคาร　　ah[4]-kah-ra[6] *P. S. n.* a house; a building; an apartment; a hall (chd. p. 16); a shed; a residence; a dwelling-place.

อฆ ๑　　ah[4]-ka[6] *P. S. n.* evil; sin; grief; suffering; passion; misfortune (chd. p. 18).

อฆ ๒　　ah[4]-ka[6] *P. n.* the sky; a void; darkness; a dark place (chd. p. 18).

อง   ong *Anam. n.* a title of official rank among the Anamese; a complimentary Anamite title for civilians, as คุณ and Mr.

องก์, อังก์   ong *P. S. n.* a curved line; a numerical figure; a seal, stamp or mark; an act of a drama (S. E. D. p. 7): อังกา the twelve pages of a palm leaf book, each page being numbered by one of twelve letters used in succession. Two of such series form a ผูก.

อังกนะ   ung-gka[4]-na[6] *S. n.* the act of marking, stamping, branding, writing or ciphering (S. E. D. p. 7).

องค์   ong *P. S. n.* the body, or any portion thereof; a limb; a member; an organ; a portion or division (of the body); a subordinate division or department; a quality; an attribute (chd. p. 33); *a designatory particle for royal or revered personages, images of the Buddha, a member of the Buddhist clergy; examples*: พระทนต์ ๏ องค์ a royal or sacred tooth: พระที่นั่ง ๏ องค์ a royal hall, throne or palace: พระศรี ๏ องค์ a portion of betel (as for chewing): พระองค์ a title of God; a personal pronoun for a king or prince: พระองค์เจ้า the birth-title of the king's son by a plebian: องค์มนตรี a privy councillor: องค์มนตรีสภา the Privy Council: องคมรรษ pain in the limbs; rheumatism: องคยัษฎิ a slender form; a fairy-like figure: องครักษ์ one of the royal body-guard: องควิการ physical deformities: องควิเกษป gesticulations; attitudes; movements; postures (of the body); a kind of dance: องควิทยา that branch of anthropology which treats of the physical characteristics of man; the science of prognostigation of a person's future from the appearances of his body (chd. p. 34): องคสัมผัสส์ the act of two objects touching, or coming into contact with each other.

องคต   ong-kot[6] *P. n.* bracelets; ornaments; gold chains for the body (chd. p. 32); see สังวาล p. 844; one of Rama's monkey warriors, being the son of Bali and Lady Mondho.

องคาพยพ   ong-kah-pa[6]-yop[6] *P. n.* all parts of the body, both great and small; the body as a whole.

องคุล   ong-koo[6]-la[6] *P. S. n.* a finger's breadth; an inch (chd. p. 34).

องคุลี   ong-koo[6]-lee *P. n.* a finger (chd. p. 34); a unit of measurement equal to the length of the phalanx of the middle finger; approximately one inch.

องค์   ong *S. n.* a piece; a share; a part; a portion; a division; *used as a suffix*, as ไตรองค์ three portions.

องศา   ong-sah[2] *n.* a degree; 1/360th part of a circle.

องอาจ   ong-art[4] *adj.* brave; audacious; bold; powerful; rash.

องุ่น (ต้น)   ah[4]-ngoon[4] *n. Vitis vinifera,* the grape (MCM. p. 250): น้ำองุ่น grape juice.

อจร   ah[4]-chja[4]-ra[6] *P. S. adj.* immovable; firmly fixed; firm; unchangeable; immutable (S. E. D. p. 8).

อจล   ah[4]-chja[4]-la[6] *P. S. n. lit.* "that which is unshakable," *i. e.* a mountain; a door or window bolt: *adj.* firm; steady; immoveable (chd. p. 8).

อจลา   ah[4]-chja[4]-lah *S. n. lit.* "that which is unshakable," *i. e.* the earth (S. E. D. p. 8).

อจิตติ   ah[4]-chjit[4]-dti[4] *S. n.* ignorance; lack of education or knowledge; mental stupor; lacking understanding.

อจินตา   ah[4]-chjin-dtah *S. n.* want of knowledge or reasoning power; thoughtlessness (S. E. D. p. 8).

อจินไตย์   ah[4]-chjin-dtai *P. adj.* beyond reach of thought or reason; inconceivable; incomprehensible; infinite (chd. p. 9).

อจิระ   ah[4]-chji[4]-ra[6] *P. S. adj.* short; brief; temporary; not of long duration: *adv.* soon; ere long; instantaneously (chd. p. 9).

อเจตน   ah[4]-chjay-dta[4]-na[6] *S. adj.* uncon-scious; insensible; senseless; inanimate (chd. p. 9).

อเจล, อเจลก   ah[4]-chjay-la[6] *P. n.* a naked ascetic; a nudist; a sect of Brahmins: *adj.* unclothed (chd. p. 9).

อช   ah[4]-cha[6] *S. n.* an he-goat; a ram (chd. p. 22); a driver; a chaser; a leader; an epithet for Indra.

อชา   ah[4]-chah *P. S. n.* a she-goat (chd. p. 20); a nanny goat.

อชิน   ah[4]-chin *P. S. n.* the hide of an ani-mal, especially of the black antelope (chd. p. 21); a hide used as a bed; a seat or covering used by an ascetic or religious student; the hide of a panther.

อชิร   ah[4]-chi[6]-ra[6] *P. S. n.* a court; a yard; a lawn (chd. p. 21); a field; a plain; a vacant place; a battle-field (S.E.D. p. 10): *adj.* agile; quick; active; rapid.

อฏ   ah[4]-dta[4] *S. v.* to go; to roam; to travel; to wander at random (S. E. D. p. 11).

อฏนะ   ah[4]-dta[4]-na[6] *S. n.* the act or habit of travelling, wandering or roaming (S.E.D. p. 11).

อฏวี   ah[4]-dta[4]-wee *P. S. n. lit.* "a place to roam in," *i. e.* a forest; woods (S. E. D. p 11).

อณิ   ah[4]-ni[6] *P. n.* the pin of a wheel-axle; a linch-pin; a peg or pin (chd. p. 34); the rim; the edge; the end; see ลิ่ม p. 746.

อณุ   ah[4]-noo[6] *P. S. n.* a molecule; a unit of measure equal to thirty-six atoms (chd. p. 40); see ปรมาณุ under ปรม p. 495: *adj.* small; minute; fine; subtil.

อโณทัย, อรุโณทัย   ah[4]-noh-tai *n.* the ris-ing sun.

อด, อำนด   ot[4] *v.* to abstain from (as from food); to refrain, or desist from (as from the use of drugs or liquor); to restrain; to control (as desires or feelings); to deny oneself: *n.*

want; poverty; lack, or absence of something; abstinence; privation; indigence: อดกลั้น to suppress; to restrain oneself: อดจิตต์, อดใจ to restrain; to repress the desires; to be patient, long-suffering and forbearing: อดได้ to be able to endure or bear: อดทน to bear; to suffer; to endure manfully; to undergo (as suffering); to be courageous under adversities: อดนอน to be deprived of sleep: อดน้ำ to be in want of water: อดเนื้อ to refrain from eating meat: อดพูด to refrain from speaking: อดเหล้า to ab-stain from liquors: อดออม to conserve; to economize; to desist from using lavishly for fear of future want: อดอาย to endure ignominy: อดอาหาร to fast; to abstain from food: อดสู shame; shamefacedness; em-barrassment; perplexity; abashment: อด-อยาก needy; poor; destitute; starving.

อดิ, อติ   ah[4]-di[4] *P. S. a prefix much used in composition meaning* special, much, ex-ceedingly, over, beyond, on the other side (chd. p. 63).

อดิถิ   ah[4]-di[4]-tee[2] *n.* a guest; a stranger (chd. p. 65); a visitor; see อติถิพลี under พลี [p. 575.

อดิเรก see อติเรก p. 957.

อดิศัย   ah[4]-di[4]-sai[2] *S. n.* pre-eminence; superiority in quality, quantity or number (S. E. D. p. 15): *P. adj.* excellent; glorious; magnificent (chd. p. 64).

อดีต   ah[4]-deet[4] *P. S. n. the tense that ex-presses absolute past time,* the preterite: *adj.* elapsed: อดีตกาล, อดีตสมัย the time that has elapsed: อดีตชาติ, อดีตภพ a life or exis-tence succeeding, or after the present one (S. E. D. p. 16: chd. p. 65).

อดุล   ah[4]-doon *P. S. adj.* incomparable; peerless; unequalled; beyond estimate; ad-mirable (chd. p. 70).

อติกรม   ah[4]-dti[4]-grom *S. n.* preterition; omission; the act of passing over, overstep-ping, overcoming; the condition of conquering or being victorious (S. E. D. p. 13).

อติจาร   ah⁴-dti⁴-chjah-ra⁶ *P. S. n.* transgression; adultery (chd. p. 63).

อติชาต   ah⁴-dti⁴-chart³ *S. adj.* surpassing others of the same family, race or lineage; superior to one's parents (S. E. D. p. 13).

อติมาน   ah⁴-dti⁴-marn *P. n.* vanity; pride; haughtiness; conceit; inordinate self-esteem (S. E. D. p. 15).

อติราช   ah⁴-dti⁴-rart³ *P. n.* a supreme king or ruler; an emperor (S. E. D. p. 15).

อติเรก, อดิเรก   ah⁴-dti⁴-rek³ *P. adj.* supreme; superior; excessive; exceeding; plentiful; abundant; ample (chd. p. 64): งาน-อติเรก an hobby; something in which one takes special interest: อติเรกจีวร an extra allowance; an extra robe presented to a bonze: อติเรกลาภ extraordinary good fortune; luck in an excessive measure; riches in abundance.

อติสาร   ah⁴-dti⁴-sarn² *S. n.* purging; dysentery (S. E. D. p. 16); the last stages of a disease where blood is mixed with the excrement; a morabund condition.

อถรรพ   ah⁴-tup⁴ *S. n.* the first priest who is said to have introduced the religious rite of worshipping fire and making an offerring of soma juice to the gods. He was the author of the treatise called อถรรพเวท (S. E. D. p. 17): อถรรพเวท, อาถรรพณ์, อาถรรพณะ the Atharva Veda, the fourth Veda. This consists of Mantras, incantations, and charms, their secrets and uses. The most prominent characteristic feature of the Atharva is the multitude of incantations which it contains; these are pronounced either by the person who is himself to be benefitted, or more often, by tbe sorcerer for him, and are directed to the procuring of the greatest variety of desirable ends; most frequently, perhaps, long life or recovery from grievous sickness is the object sought; then a talisman, such as a necklace, is sometimes given, or in very numer-

ous cases some plant endowed with marvellous virtues is to be the immediate external means of the cure; farther, the attainment of wealth or power is aimed at, the down-fall of enemies, success in love or in play, the removal of petty pests, and so on, even down to the growth of hair on a bald pate. The number of the hymns is about 760, and of the verses about 6000 (H. C. D. p. 350).

อท   ah⁴-ta⁶ *P. S. v.* to eat: *n.* the act of eating or feeding on (chd. p. 15); see กิน p. 107.

อทน   ah⁴-ta⁶-na⁶ *P. S. n.* food; a meal to be eaten; provisions (chd. p. 9).

อทิติ   ah⁴-ti⁶-dti⁴ *S. n. lit.* "free, not tied," *i. e.* boundless, unbroken, unimpaired freedom; name of one of the most ancient of the Indian goddesses (S. E. D. p. 18).

อทินน   ah⁴-tin-na⁶ *P. adj.* not given; denied the possession of (chd. p. 15): อทินน-หารี, อทินนาทายี *lit.* "one who takes without permission," *i. e.* a thief; a robber (chd. p. 15).

อทินนาทาน   ah⁴-tin-nah-tarn *P. n.* act of taking what is not given; a misappropriation; a theft; the robbing others of their possessions (chd. p. 15).

อธม, อธัม   ah⁴-ta⁶-ma⁶ *P. S. n.* an unblushing paramour: *adj.* low; lowest; inferior; vile; meanest: บุรุษาธม, บุริสาธัม a most contemptable person (chd. p. 11).

อธรรม   ah⁴-tum *S. n.* lawlessness; wrong; injustice; irreligiousness; impiety; unrighteousness; demerit; guilt (S. E. D. p, 20).

อธิ   ah⁴-ti⁶ *P. a prefix, meaning* eminent, above, over, superior to (chd. p. 11); see ยิ่ง p. 674: อธิกรรม a heinous sin: อธิคุณ a notable or conspicuous favour: อธิจิตต์ a spirit given to meritorious acts: อธิปัญญา with superior wisdom.

อธิก, อธึก   ah⁴-ti⁶-gka⁴ *P. S. adj.* exceeding; surpassing all others; more than; better than; superior to (chd. p. 12); additional;

subsequent; redundant (S. E. D. p. 20): อธิก-
มาส an inter-calendar month formerly added
to the ordinary Thai lunar calendar. When
it occurs it is placed between the eighth and
ninth months and is called the second eighth
month: อธิกวาร the additional day occasionally added to the seventh month of the
Thai lunar calendar, making it a thirty-day
month: อธิกสุรทิน the additional day occasionally added to the month corresponding
to February of the Thai lunar calendar making it a twenty-nine day month.

อธิกรณ์ ah[4]-ti[6]-gkaun *P. S. n.* relation;
location; question; subject; case; cause; suit;
trial; *gram.* the locative case, indicating place,
or relative position in a series (chd. p. 12).

อธิการ ah[4]-ti[6]-gkan *P. S. n.* authority;
rule; administration; office; jurisdiction; prerogative (S. E. D. p. 20); *Thai* the abbot of a
Buddhist monastery; the superior of a religious order.

อธิการ, อธิการิน ah[4]-ti[6]-gkah-ree *P. S. n.*
see ฤษ p. 725; a governor; a superintendent
(S. E. D. p. 20): อธิการิณี the feminine form
of อธิการ.

อธิคม ah[4]-ti[6]-kom *P. S. n.* the act of attaining; acquisition; acquirement; achievement; victory; the act of studying, or reading
(S. E. D. p. 20).

อธิฏฐาน, อธิษฐาน ah[4]-tit[6]-tarn[2] *P. v.*
to pray; to vow; to petition; to supplicate;
to implore; to fix the mind upon; to resolve
(chd. p. 13): *n.* a prayer; a vow; an entreaty;
a resolution; a determination, intention or
purpose (Ala. p. 184).

อธิบดี ah[4]-ti[6]-bau-dee *P. S. n.* a chief
official; a master; a lord; a ruler; a sovereign
(chd. p. 13); the director general of a governmental department.

อธิบาย ah[4]-ti[6]-bai *v.* to explain; to point
out the meaning of; to demonstrate; to enlarge upon; to elucidate: *n.* intention; wish;

meaning; thought (chd. p. 13); explanation;
demonstration; amplification: คำอธิบาย explanations: อธิบายว่า the meaning is as
follows.

อธิป, อธิบ ah[4]-tip[6] *P. n.* king; ruler;
master; lord (chd. p. 13); *commonly used as a
suffix,* e. g. นราธิป, ชนาธิป. It is also used as a
prefix but when followed by a word beginning
with a vowel, the อธิป is softened or changed
to อธิบ, *e. g.* นราธิเบศร์, นราธิเบนทร์.

อธิมาตร ah[4]-ti[6]-mart[3] *P. adj.* excessive;
countless; numberless; innumerable (chd p. 12).

อธิมุตติ ah[4]-ti[6]-moot[6]-dti[4] *P. n.* inclination; disposition; intention; resolution; faith
(chd. p. 13).

อธิราช ah[4]-ti[6]-rart[3] *S. n.* a supreme ruler;
a king; an emperor (S. E. D. p. 21).

อธิวาส ah[4]-ti[6]-wart[3] *P. S. n.* an abode; a
house; a dwelling; a residence; toleration;
forbearance (chd. p. 14).

อธิวาสนะ ah[4]-ti[6]-wah-sa[4]-na[6] *P. n.* assent; consent; acceptance (chd. p. 14).

อธิศีล ah[4]-ti[6]-seen[2] *n.* precepts of a superlative degree; commandments of the greatest
[importance.
อธิษฐาน see อธิฏฐาน p. 958.

อธิต ah[4]-tee-dta[4] *S. adj.* attained; learned; studied; well informed (S. E. D. p. 22).

อธิติ ah[4]-tee-dti[4] *S. n.* perusal; study
(S. E. D. p. 22).

อธิ ah[4]-tee *P. S. adj.* resting on or in;
depending on; subservient to (S. E. D. p. 22).

อธิก see อธิก p. 957.

อน ๑ ah[4]-na[6] *a prefix used in words beginning with a vowel, implying negation,* as
" in-" " un-" *e. g.* อาทร, อนาทร unattentive.

อน ๒ ah[4]-na[6] *S. v.* to breathe: *n.* inhaled air; inhalation; inspired breath (chd.
p. 31).

อ้น (ตัว)   own[3] *n.* the large bamboo-rat, *Nyctocleptes cinereus* (Gaird N. H. J. S. S. III, 2, p. 124): อ้นอั้นใจ oppressed in mind; perplexed; unable to make any plans; at one's wit's end.

อนงค์   ah[4]-nong *S. n.* an epithet for Kama, the Hindu god of Love, who had been reduced to ashes by the fiery eye of Siva; a beautiful woman: *adj.* formless; bodiless (S.E.D. p. 24): อนงคเลข, อนงคเลขา a love-letter; a love song or ballad.

อนงคณะ   ah[4]-nong-ka[6]-na[6] *P. adj.* free from impurities or lust; pure; clean; undefiled; unstained; guileless (S. E. D. p. 31).

อนนต์   ah[4]-non *n.* fabulous sea-monsters, superstitiously believed to support the world, and cause earthquakes.

อนยะ   ah[4]-na[6]-ya[6] *P. S. n.* fate; ill-luck; distress; sin; misfortune (chd. p. 33).

อนรรฆ, อำนรรฆ   ah[4]-nuk[6] *S. adj.* most valuable; priceless (S. E. D. p. 26).

อนรรถ, อนัตถ   ah[4]-nut[6] *S. n.* uselessness; fruitlessness; unproductiveness: *adj.* useless; fruitless; nonsensical; worthless (S. E. D. p. 26).

อนล   ah[4]-non *S. n.* fire (chd. p. 31); the god of Fire.

อนวัชช์   ah[4]-na[6]-wat[6] *P. adj.* blameless; sinless; harmless; without sin (chd. p. 32); unreproachable; spotless.

อนัญญ์   ah[4]-nun *P. adj.* without another; alone; sole; the only one; the same (chd. p. 31): อนัญญุคติ necessity; compulsion.

อนัตตา   ah[4]-nut[6]-dtah *P. n.* a soulless self; (chd. p. 32).

อนัตถ see อนรรถ

อนันต์   ah[4]-nun *P. S. adj.* endless; eternal; boundless; infinite (chd. p. 31); perpetual; everlasting.

อนันตะ   ah[4]-nun-dta[4] *n.* Ananda, a favourite disciple of Gotama Buddha (Ala. p. 77); name of a cousin and eminent apostle of the Buddha (chd. p. 44).

อนันตร   ah[4]-nun *P. S. adj.* continuous; uninterrupted; unbroken; adjoining; contiguous; next of kin (S. E. D. p. 25): อนันตริย-กรรม sins or crimes of which there are five that are followed immediately by punishment, *viz.* (1) patricide; (2) matricide; (3) the killing of an Arahat; (4) the causing of a falling out among Buddhist monks; (5) an injuring of the body of the Buddha (causing a congestion or hematoma).

อนัม, อานำ   ah[4]-num *Chin. n.* Anam; Anamese; see ญวน p. 314.

อนาคต   ah[4]-nah-kot[6] *P. S. n.* the future; the time to come; *grammar* the future tense: *adj.* future; not come; not having arrived yet (chd. p. 30): อนาคตกาล a future time or era: อนาคตกาลสมบูรณ์ *grammar* the future perfect tense.

อนาคติ   ah[4]-nah-ka[6]-dti[4] *S. n.* failure in accomplishing, attaining, acquiring, or reaching (S. E. D. p. 27).

อนาคามิ   ah[4]-nah-kah-mi[6] *P. n. lit.* "one who does not return," *i. e.* a technical term for one who has entered the third of the four paths to Nirvana. He is so called because he cannot be reborn into the world of men or of devas, but only in a Brahma world, from which he may attain Nirvana (chd. p. 30: Ala. p. 171): อนาคามิมรรค the path of one that does not return. This is the third of the four paths to Nirvana: อนาคามิผล fruition of the state of Anagami. This is the second or perfect stage of the path to the highest degree of saintship.

อนาจาร   ah[4]-nah-charn *P. S. n.* immorality; bad conduct; bad manners (chd. p. 30); improper behaviour, regardless of custom, propriety, or law (S. E. D. p. 27).

อนาถ, อำนาถ ah[4]-nart[4] *P. S. adj. lit.* "having no master or protector," *i.e.* helpless; widowed; forlorn; destitute (chd. p. 32); friendless; pitiable; wretched.

อนาถา ah[4]-nah-tah[2] *adj.* poor; needy; penniless; forsaken; orphaned; parentless; destitute: คนอนาถา a destitute or unfortunate person.

อนาทร ah[4]-nah-taun *P. S. n.* disrespect; disregard; neglect; slight; indifference; contempt; the act of turning one's back upon another: *adj.* regardless of; indifferent to; disrespectful; contemptuous; neglectful (S.E.D. p. 28): อนาทรร้อนใจ distress or anxiety from being slighted or disrespected.

อนามัย ah[4]-nah-mai *P. S. n.* freedom from sickness; health; vigour; soundness (of body) (chd. p. 31): สถานือนามัย Public Health Centre.

อนารย ah[4]-nah-ra[6]-ya[6] *S. adj.* despicable; shameful; ignoble; dishonourable; disgraceful; infamous; mean; contemptable; base; uncivilized (S. E. D. p. 28): อนารยชน savages; uncivilized, uncultivated people or tribes; aborigines: อนารยธรรม baseness; despicableness; degeneracy; depravity; dishonourableness.

อนาลัย ah[4]-nah-lai *P. n.* the condition of freedom from desire; freedom from entanglements, attachments, or affections; Nirvana (chd. p. 31).

อนิจจ ah[4]-nit[6]-chja[4] *P. adj.* impermanent; unstable; unenduring; brief; transitory; fleeting; perishable; ephemoral (chd. p. 34): ถึง-อนิจจกรรม used to signify the death of a nobleman of high rank.

อนิจจัง, อนิจจา ah[4]-nit[6]-chjung *adj.* unstable: *onomat.* an exclamation of sympathy, sorrow, or disappointment in the transitoriness of life, and perishableness of all things. "Alas! vanity of vanities."

อนิยต ah[4]-ni[6]-yot[6] *P. n. lit.* "uncertain; doubtful" (chd. p. 35). This refers to a class of sins or misdeeds that may be committed by Buddhist monks and which are considered offences calling for undetermined punishments ranging in degree from the infliction of a light punishment to excommunication. The matter must be decided according to the code of discipline.

อนิยม ah[4]-ni[6]-yom *P. S. adj.* transitory; uncertain, improper (conduct): doubtful; unusual; not conforming to rule, custom or precedent (S. E. D. p. 29): อนิยมคุณศัพท์ a substantive, *e. g.* which: อนิยมสรรพนาม an interrogative pronoun, *e. g.* who, what.

อนิรุทธ์ ah[4]-ni[6]-root[6] *S. n. lit.* "headstrong; ungovernable; unthwartable," *i. e.* a son of Pradyumna and grandson of Krishna, a famous character in Hindu literature (S. E. D. p. 30).

อนิล ah[4]-ni[6]-la[6] *P. S. n.* wind; air (chd. p. 34: S. E. D. p. 30): อนิลบถ currents of air or wind.

อนิวรรต ah[4]-ni[6]-wat[6] *adj.* undaunted; never being a slacker or shirker; always facing danger or duty.

อนิวรรตน์ ah[4]-ni[6]-wat[6] *S. adj.* dauntless; steadfast; intrepid; brave; valiant; heroic; never turning back (S. E. D. p. 30).

อนีก, อนีก ah[4]-nee-gka[4] *P. S. n.* an army; a host; military troops; the front ranks, line or row; the front (of soldiers in action) (chd. p. 34): อนีกัฏฐ cavalry; mounted troops; the royal body-guard; a life-guard: อนีก-ทรรศนะ, อนีกทัสสนะ the inspection, or reviewing of an army, soldiers, or military troops.

อนีจ ah[4]-nee-chja[4] *S. adj.* not low, mean, or inferior; good; respectable; honourable; beautiful; pretty (S. E. D. p. 30).

อนึ่ง ah[4]-neung[4] *prep.* besides; other than; in addition to; on the other hand: *adv.* furthermore; moreover.

อนุ ah[4]-noo[6] *P. S. adv.* and *prep.* after; under; less than; in like manner; according to; along; again; in consequence of (chd. p. 40); *a collective particle used as a prefix denoting* smallest, subordinate to, afterwards: อนุทิศ the less important direction (of the compass): อนุวรรตน์ in like manner: อนุมูล a radical: อนุสัญญา a convention.

อนุกร ah[4]-noo[6]-gkaun *S. n.* an assistant; an apprentice: *adj.* imitating; following the example of; acting according to (instruction) (S. E. D. p. 31).

อนุกรม ah[4]-noo[6]-gkrom *S. n.* succession; order; sequence; arrangement: *adj.* proceeding in order; following after according to rank (S. E. D. p. 31).

อนุกะเบียด ah[4]-noo[6]-gka[4]-bee-at[4] *n.* a unit of measure equal to one-eighth of a Thai inch.

อนุการ ah[4]-noo[6]-gkan *P. S. n.* imitation; duplication; resemblance (chd. p. 42); similarity; the act of aping, mocking, impersonating, simulating an act or work.

อนุกูล ah[4]-noo[6]-gkoon *Thai v.* to help; to succour; to relieve; to befriend: *S. n.* a favour; kindness; aid; support: *adj.* kind; obliging; benevolent; generous; bounteous; compassionate; merciful; friendly; well-disposed; agreeable (S. E. D. p. 31).

อนุคามิก ah[4]-noo[6]-kah-mik[6] *P. adj.* following; accompanying (chd. p. 41); continuing; connected with.

อนุคามี ah[4]-noo[6]-kah-mee *P. S. n.* an assistant; a follower; a friend (S. E. D. p. 31).

อนุเคราะห์, อนุคคหะ ah[4]-noo[6]-kraw[6] *S. v.* to render assistance; to be the "good Samaritan"; to relieve another's distress; to do another a good turn: *n.* favour; assistance; conferring benefits (S. E. D. p. 32).

อนุจร ah[4]-noo[6]-chjaun *P. S. v.* to follow; to obey; to be under the jurisdiction, direction or command of: *n.* a friend; an attendant; a companion; a servant (chd. p. 41): พระอนุจร, พระอันดับ the lesser members or attendants of a Buddhist brotherhood in a temple.

อนุจินตน์ ah[4]-noo[6]-chjin *P. S. n.* the act of thinking or reflecting about, or of meditating on; recalling or recollecting (S. E. D. p. 32).

อนุช, อนุชา ah[4]-noot[6] *P. S. n. lit.* "one born after," *i. e.* a younger brother; a junior; *poetical* younger sister or fiancée.

อนุชาต ah[4]-noo[6]-chart[3] *P. S. adj.* following in the ancestral line; being of one's kind, according to family, or of the same lineage; hereditary disposition (S. E. D. p. 32): อนุชาต-บุตร a child worthy of one's ancestry; offspring bearing the characteristics of the parents.

อนุญาต ah[4]-noo[6]-yart[3] *v.* to permit; to grant; to sanction; to allow; to consent; to give leave, license or permission: ใบอนุญาต a permit; a license: อนุญาโตตุลาการ an arbitrator; an umpire; see ชี้ขาด under ชี้ p. 297.

อนุตตร ah[4]-noot[6]-dta[4]-ra[6] *P. S. adj.* unrivalled; preeminent; incomparable; supreme; best; chief (chd. p. 45); see ยิ่ง p. 674.

อนุเถร ah[4]-noo[6]-tay[2]-ra[6] *P. n.* a novice of inferior rank or low standing in a Buddhist monastery; one who is in subordination to the Lord Abbot (chd. p. 45).

อนุบท ah[4]-noo[6]-bot[4] *P. S. n.* a minor refrain, strain or chorus, sung antiphonally with the main singer in operatic or theatrical performances (S. E. D. p. 34).

อนุบาล ah[4]-noo[6]-barn *P. v.* to take care of; to watch over continually; to foster; to nourish, rear, or aid.

อนุบุพพ์ ah[4]-noo[6]-boop[4] *P. adj.* according to order; consecutive; successive; regular; symmetrical (chd. p. 44).

อนุปสัมบัน ah⁴-noo⁶-bpa⁴-sum²-bun *P. n. lit.* "one in the Buddhist monkhood not yet ordained," *i. e.* a novice; a layman; one not belonging to the Buddhist clergy (chd. p. 43).

อนุบัสสนา ah⁴-noo⁶-bpat⁴-sa⁴-nah *P. n.* observation; contemplation; meditation; the act of looking or listening (chd. p. 43).

อนุพงศ์ see อนุวงศ์

อนุพนธ์, อนุพันธ์ ah⁴-noo⁶-paun *P. S. v.* to tie; to bind; to fasten; to connect or link together : *n.* the state of being connected, fastened, tied, or bound together; continuation; succession; sequence : *adj.* uninterrupted (succession) (S. E. D. p. 86).

อนุโพธ ah⁴-noo⁶-pote³ *P. S. n.* afterthought; knowledge; understanding; recollection (S.E.D. p. 36).

อนุภาพ ah⁴-noo⁶-parp³ *S. n.* ascertainment; clearness of understanding; familiarity; authority; influence; dignity; majesty (S. E. D. p. 36): อนุภาพที่เอาเปรียบโดยทุจริต undue influence.

อนุภาษ ah⁴-noo⁶-part³ *S. v.* to speak; to teach; to explain; to demonstrate (S.E.D. p. 36).

อนุมัติ ah⁴-noo⁶-mut⁶ *P. S. v.* to approve; to consent; to concur; to give permission; to adopt : *n.* consent; assent; sanction; approbation; permission (chd. p. 42).

อนุมาน ah⁴-noo⁶-marn *P. v.* to doubt; to suppose; to conjecture; to examine : *n.* doubt; supposition; guess; uncertainty; reference; inference; drawing a conclusion from given premises (chd. p. 42).

อนุโมทนา ah⁴-noo⁶-moh-ta⁶-nah *P. v.* to express satisfaction; to rejoice in, or for; to express gratitude for favours received; to return thanks : *n.* joyfulness; satisfaction; approval; thankfulness; sympathy (chd. p. 42).

อนุโยค ah⁴-noo⁶-yoke³ *P. v.* to question; to interrogate; to exert oneself : *n.* an interrogation; a question (chd. p. 46).

อนุรักติ ah⁴-noo⁶-ruk⁶-dti⁴ *S. n.* affection; love; devotion (S. E. D. p. 37).

อนุรักษ์ ah⁴-noo⁶-ruk⁶ *S. v.* to guard while following; to take care of (S. E. D. p. 37).

อนุราช ah⁴-noo⁶-rart³ *P. n.* a king or monarch reigning in direct succession; a successor (chd. p. 44).

อนุรูป ah⁴-noo⁶-roop³ *P. S. adj. lit.* "conforming to form," *i. e.* suitable; conformable; corresponding; like; proper (chd. p. 44).

อนุโลม ah⁴-noo⁶-lome *P. S. adj. lit.* "with the hair or grain," *i. e.* in a natural direction; in direct order or rule (S. E. D. p. 38).

อนุวงศ์, อนุพงศ์ ah⁴-noo⁶-wong *n.* the line or lineage that follows.

อนุวรรตน์ ah⁴-noo⁶-wat⁶ *P. n.* to imitate; to copy; to follow the example of others.

อนุวาต ๑ ah⁴-noo⁶-wart³ *P. n.* cloth that is joined, patched or mended; a seam; see ตะเข็บ p. 351; ตาม p. 325.

อนุวาต ๒ ah⁴-noo⁶-wart³ *P. S. adj.* in the direction of the wind (chd. p. 45); see วาต p. 768.

อนุวาท ah⁴-noo⁶-wart³ *P. S. n.* repetition; reiteration; blame; censure; admonition (chd. p. 45); see วาท p. 768.

อนุศาสก ah⁴-noo⁶-sah²-sok⁴ *S. v.* a tutor; a teacher; an instructor; a preceptor; a mentor (chd. p. 44); see ศึกษา p. 799.

อนุศาสน์, อนุสาสน์ ah⁴-noo⁶-sart⁴ *S. n.* instruction; direction; command; precept (S. E. D. p. 39).

อนุศาสนี, อนุสาสนี ah⁴-noo⁶-sah²-sa⁴-nee *S. n.* administration; government; punishment.

อนุศิษฏ์ ah⁴-noo⁶-sit⁴ *S. adj.* taught; revealed; adjudged (s. E. D. p 39).

อนุโศก, อนุโศจน์   ah[4]-noo[6]-soke[4] *S. n.*
sorrow ; repentance ; regret (S. E. D. p. 39).

อนุสนธิ   ah[4]-noo[6]-son[2]-ti[6] *P. n.* connection ;
application (chd. p. 44) ; continuation.

อนุสภากาชาด   ah[4]-noo[6]-sa[4]-pah-gkah-chart[3]
n. the Junior Red Cross Organization.

อนุสสติ   ah[4]-noot[6]-sa[4]-dti[4] *P. n.* recollection ; rememberance (chd. p. 45).

อนุสสร   ah[4]-noot[6]-saun[2] *P. v.* to call to
mind ; to think of ; to remember (chd. p. 45).

อนุสสาวรีย์   ah[4]-noot[6]-sah[2]-wa[6]-ree *n.* a
memorial ; a statue ; a building or monument.

อนุสัย   ah[4]-noo[6]-sai[2] *P. n.* regret ; repentance ; penitence ; inclination, desire or thought
towards reformation (chd. p. 45).

อนุสาวนา   ah[4]-noo[6]-sah[2]-wa[6]-nah *n.* the
discussion of a subject or problem placed before a meeting for its action.

อเนก   ah[4]-nake[4] *P. S. adj.* more than one ;
several ; many ; manifold ; various ; innumerable ; countless (chd. p. 33) :   อเนกบรรยาย a
lengthy discourse or explanation :   อเนกวิธ
of many kinds ; various ; diverse ; sundry.

อเนกคูณ   ah[4]-nake[4]-koon *n.* a tree or
remedy with multiple medicinal properties.

อโนชา (ต้น) see อังกาบ (ต้น)

อบ   ope[4] *v.* to perfume ; to saturate (as
with scents or powders) ; to become hot and
stuffy (as in a crowded room) :   ความอบอุ่น
warmth :   เครื่องอบ vaporous, fragrant substances or mixtures :   เตาอบ a closed oven
(as for baking enamel or porcelain) :   น้ำอบ
perfumery (in general) :   อบผ้าด้วยเกสร to
allow the fragrance of flowers to permeate
cloth or clothing (by confining them together
in a closed box) :   อบพุ้ง filled with perfumes or agreeable odours :   อบรม to afford
an opportunity for intensive study or instruction ; to take care of especially ; to coach,
tutor, train or drill :   อบห้อง to fumigate

a room :   อบอ้าว close and stuffy (as a
closed room) ; badly ventilated ; hot and
muggy :   อบอุ่น warm ; sunny ; genial.

อบเชย (ต้น)   op[4]-chur-ie *n. Cinnamonum
zeylanicum (Lauraceæ)*, cinnamon. True
cinnamon bark is obtained from this tree,
which is common in a wild condition down
the southern half of the western side of
India, where it ascends to 6,000 feet ; on the
moist western side of Ceylon, where it ascends
2,000 feet and probably higher ; and on the
western slopes of Tenasserim. The European
market is chiefly supplied from Ceylon which,
for some undiscovered reason, seems to produce the best grade of cinnamon. Java com-
petes some in this trade. The bark is stripped
from the trees when still small, the outer
layers scraped away, and the inner parts
allowed to roll inwards on themselves in
drying, so that they make the familiar quills.
Cinnamon oil is distilled from leaves, bark
and root. Fat from the seeds is made into
costly candles, such as are still used in
churches. Cinnamon enters into cordials.
When the Portuguese were in power in India,
they used to distil the half-dried bark and
send the liqueur to Europe. This was considered good for digestion, and was prescribed
to correct the effects of other drugs. As
cinnamon has mildly astringent properties
with its aromatic properties, it is used in
European medicine in powders and tinctures.
It is much more used in the East (BURK p.
556) ; *C. iners*, wild cinnamon, a tree of
moderate size found in western India and
Tenasserim to Sumatra and Java, and eastwards to the southern parts of the Philippine
Islands. The species is variable and perplexing as, in some places, the bark is utterly
devoid of aroma. The roots are used medicinally. They are boiled, and a decoction is
commonly given after child-birth ; and also
for fever. Frequently the root is used alone,
but sometimes it is mixed with other roots.

The leaves are medicinal. Sometimes they are used with the roots, as above. It is said that the juice of the leaves is a Sakai remedy for poisoning with *Antiaris*, being squeezed into the wound. They serve as a poultice for rheumatism. The timber is good, and would be valuable for export if obtainable in large quantities and cheap. It is pleasantly scented. Children eat the fruits in Malacca (MCM. p. 334 : V. P. p. 276 : BURK. p. 551); see น้ำมันอบเชย under น้ำ p. 453.

อบาย   ah[4]-bai *P. n. lit.* "places, states or conditions of suffering," *i. e.* punishment, loss, misfortune, destruction, ruin, hell (CHD. p. 49) : อบายภูมิ *lit.* "places or phases of punishment," *i. e.* rebirths where there is no hope of progress, growth upwards, nor of escape. Of such there are four, *viz.* นรก hell; ดิรัจฉาน inferior animals; เปรต insatiable demons; อสุร fallen angels (H. C. D. p. 28) : อบายมุข *lit.* "the portals of hell," *i. e.* all allurements and causes of misfortune, destruction, or ruin.

อป   ah[4]-bpa[4] *P. S. adv.* and *prep.* away from. *Used as a prefix in composition with verbs and their derivatives it implies the negative,* as in-, un-, not, without, wanting in, away from (CHD. p. 46).

อปกรณ์   ah[4]-bpa[4]-gkaun *S. n. lit.* "unwonted acts," *i. e.* wrong acts; ill-treatment; offence; injury (S. E. D. p 48).

อปการ   ah[4]-bpa[4]-gkarn *P. S. n. lit.* "an improper act," *i. e.* an offence; injury; an insult; hurt; disdain (S. E. D. p. 48).

อปจายน   ah[4]-bpa[4]-chjah-ya[6]-na[6] *P. n.* acts that manifest honour, respect, veneration, or reverence : อปจายนมัย merit gained by acting in an humble manner towards superiors, or by honouring the aged.

อปเทศ   ah[4]-bpa[4]-tet[3] *S. n.* deception; strategem (CHD. p. 47); a pretext; a pretense; an evasion; a disguise; contrivance (S.E.D. p. 49).

อปภาษ   ah[4]-bpa[4]-part[3] *S. v.* to revile; to blame; to censure; to accuse; to reprove; to reproach (S. E. D. p. 50).

อปมงคล   ah[4]-bpa[4]-mong-kon *P. S. adj.* unauspicious; unpropitious; unfavourable : unpromising; unlucky.

อปมาน   ah[4]-bpa[4]-man *S. n.* a disgrace; an insult; a contemptible or disrespectful act (S. E. D. p. 50).

อปยศ   ah[4]-bpa[4]-yot[6] *S. adj.* disgraceful; dishonourable; ignoble; discreditable; infamous; shameful (S. E. D. p. 50).

อปร   ah[4]-bpa[4]-ra[6] *P. S. adj.* other; various; subsequent; following (CHD. p. 48); succeeding; posterior (to); latter : อปรภาค *lit.* "other part; other time," *i. e.* opposite; opposing; contrary; antagonistic : อปรโลก *lit.* "another world," *i. e.* heaven; paradise.

อปรัณณ   ah[4]-bpa[4]-run-na[6] *P. n. lit* "other kinds of food," *i. e.* articles, other than rice (such as beans, peas, peanuts, sesame seeds, and vegetables) (CHD. p. 38).

อปราชัย   ah[4]-bpa[4]-rah-chai *P. n. lit.* "unvanquished; undefeated," *i.e.* victory; triumph.

อปราชิต   ah[4]-bpa[4]-rah-chit[6] *P. S. adj.* unconquered; victorious; triumphant; successful (S. E. D. p. 51).

อปราณห์   ah[4]-bpa[4]-rarn *S. n.* the afternoon or evening (CHD. p. 48).

อปราธ   ah[4]-bpa[4]-rah-ta[6] *P. S. n.* fault; offence; crime; guilt; transgression; sin (CHD. p. 48).

อปริมาณ   ah[4]-bpa[4]-ri[6]-man *P. S. adj.* beyond calculation; unlimited; immense; boundless; indefinite (CHD. p. 48).

อปรูป   ah[4]-bpa[4]-roop[3] *S. adj.* ugly; misshapen; deformed; ill-looking; odd-shaped.

อปโลกน์   ah[4]-bpa[4]-loke[3] *P. n.* the act of giving notice of an intention; the condition of obtaining leave (chd. p. 47).

อปวรรค ah[4]-bpa[4]-wuk[6] *S. n.* completion; end; finality (S. E. D. p. 52).

อปวาท ah[4]-bpa[4]-wart[3] *S. n.* censure, blame or abuse (chd. p. 49); contradiction; refutation.

อปหาร ah[4]-bpa[4]-harn[2] *S. n. lit.* " unlawful taking," *i. e.* theft; robbery; the act of stealing; plundering; pillaging; spending another's property (S. E. D. p. 53).

อปาจิ ah[4]-bpah-chjee *S. n.* the south (chd. [p. 46).

อปาจิน ah[4]-bpah-chjeen *P. S. adj.* turned back; behind; western (S. E. D. p. 54).

อพดงส์, อพดํงส์, อพตํงส์, อวตํงส, อวตํง-
สกะ ah[4]-pa[6]-dong *n.* an earring; a crest; an ornament (for the head) (chd. p. 72).

อพพะ ah[4]-pa[6]-pa[6] *P. n.* an exceedingly large number, as one followed by seventy-seven ciphers (chd. p. 1).

อพยพ ๑ op[4]-pa[6]-yop[6] *v.* to migrate; to remove from one country or region to another : อพยพเข้าเมือง to immigrate : อพยพทั้งครัวเรือน *idiomatic* the migration of whole families.

อพยพ ๒ see **อวยวะ** p. 974.

อพล ah[4]-pa[6]-la[6] *P. S. adj.* weak; feeble; fatigued; infirm (chd. p. 1).

อพลา ah[4]-pa[6]-lah *P. n. lit.* " the weaker sex," *i. e.* a woman (chd. p. 1).

อพุทธิ ah[4]-poot[6] *S. n.* ignorance; stupidity; illiteracy (S. E. D. p. 60).

อภว ah[4]-pa[6]-wa[6] *P. S. n.* non-existence; emptiness; desolation; decay; misfortune; decrease (chd. p. 3).

อภัพพ ah[4]-pup[6]-pa[6] *P. adj.* not liable; impossible; incapable; unable (chd. p. 3): อภัพพบุคคล an unqualified person.

อภัย ah[4]-pai *P. S. n.* protection; safety; security; deliverance from danger or punish-

ment : *adj.* harmless; fearless; safe (chd. p. 3): ขออภัยโทษ to ask for pardon.

อภิ ah[4]-pi[6] *P. a prefix meaning* to; towards; into; over; upon; above : in front of; facing (S. E. D. p. 61): อภิมุข the highest degree. อภิรม

อภิกรม ah[4]-pi[6]-gkrom *S. n.* the condition of advancing, approaching, overpowering; invading; assaulting (chd.. 4).

อภิคม ah[4]-pi[6]-kom *S. n.* the condition of meeting; approaching; visiting; sexual intercourse (S. E. D. p. 61).

อภิฆาต ah[4]-pi[6]-kart[3] *P. S. n.* torture; infliction of injury or damage; the act of striking, wounding, or causing concussion (chd. p. 4).

อภิจฉา ah[4]-pit[6]-chah[2] *P. n.* desire; longing; lust after; thirst for (chd. p. 3).

อภิชฌา ah[4]-pit[6]-chah *P. n.* covetousness; desire; coveting another's property (chd. p. 4).

อภิชน ah[4]-pi[6]-chon *P. S. n.* house; family; people; race; tribe (chd. p. 4).

อภิชัย ah[4]-pi[6]-chai *P. S. n.* complete victory; conquest; subjugation; see ปราบ p. 507).

อภิชาต ah[4]-pi[6]-chart[3] *P. S. adj.* noble; well-born; wise; learned; respectable; renowned (chd. p. 4): อภิชาตบุตร members of a noble family or lineage who excel all other members.

อภิชาติ ah[4]-pi[6]-chart[3] *P. S. n.* birth; origin; descent; race (chd. p. 4).

อภิชิต ah[4]-pi[6]-chit[6] *P. S. adj.* victorious; conquering; triumphant (S. E. D. p. 62).

อภิญญ์ ah[4]-pin *P. n.* higher knowledge; supernatural knowledge (chd. p. 5).

อภิญญาณ ah[4]-pin-yarn *P. adj.* having known; becoming cognizant of (chd. p. 5).

อภิณห ah[4]-pin-ha[4] *P. adv.* repeatedly; every day (chd. p. 5).

อภิธรรม   ah⁴-pi⁶-tum *n.* higher doctrine; transcendental doctrine; metaphysics (chd. p. 3).

อภิธา   ah⁴-pi⁶-tah *S. n.* a name; an appellation; the literal sense of a word; a sound; words (S. E. D. p. 63).

อภิธาน   ah⁴-pi⁶-tarn *P. S. n.* a name; a noun; an appellation; a word: a dictionary; a vocabulary (chd. p. 3).

อภิไธย   ah⁴-pi⁶-tai *P. n.* a name; an appellation; a significant word (chd. p. 3).

อภินันทน์   ah⁴-pi⁶-nun *P. S. v.* to delight in; to approve of; to rejoice at (chd. p. 5); ด้วยอภินันทนาการ with the compliments of: อภินันทนาการ the condition of praising; applauding (S. E. D. p. 63).

อภินัย   ah⁴-pi⁶-nai *P. S. n.* a dramatical representation; the portraying of feelings by the postures, gestures or attitudes of actors in a drama or comedy, as pain, sadness or fright (chd. p. 5).

อภินิกขมน   ah⁴-pi⁶-nik⁶-ka⁴-ma⁶-na⁶ *P. n.* the condition of going out, departing, or retiring from the world; giving up the world to devote oneself to an ascetic life (chd. p. 5).

อภินิหาร   ah⁴-pi⁶-ni⁶-harn² *P. n.* earnest wish or aspiration (chd. p. 5): *Thai* supernatural power; see บุญญานุภาพ under บุญ p. 484.

อภิบาล   ah⁴-pi⁶-barn *P. v.* to care for; to watch over; to protect; to nurse: *n.* a protector (S. E. D. p. 65).

อภิปราย   ah⁴-pi⁶-bprai *S. n.* intention; purpose; opinion; meaning (chd. p. 13): *Thai* interpolation; sense.

อภิมุข   ah⁴-pi⁶-mook⁶ *P.S. n.* leader; chief; director; conductor: *adj.* opposite; in front of; facing towards; in the presence of; ready for (chd. p. 4): เสนาภิมุข a commander of soldiers or troops.

อภิโยค   ah⁴-pi⁶-yoke³ *P.S. n.* perseverance; endeavour; exertion (S.E.D. p. 68); a challenge; a charge; an attack; an accusation (chd. p. 8).

อภิรม   ah⁴-pi⁶-rom *P. S. v.* to be pleased; to be delighted; to be gratified; to be enraptured (chd. p. 6).

อภิรักษ์   ah⁴-pi⁶-ruk⁶ *S. v.* to protect; to guard; to defend; to shelter (S. E. D. p. 68).

อภิรัฐมนตรี   ah⁴-pi⁶-rut⁶-mon-dtree *n.* a supreme councillor.

อภิราม   ah⁴-pi⁶-ram *P. S. adj.* delightful; agreeable; pleasing; beautiful (chd. p. 6).

อภิรุต   ah⁴-pi⁶-root⁶ *P. S. n.* a sound: *adj.* roaring; resounding with (chd. p. 6).

อภิรูป   ah⁴-pi⁶-roop³ *P. S. adj.* beautiful; handsome; attractive (chd. p. 6).

อภิลักขิต   ah⁴-pi⁶-luk⁶-kit⁴ *P. adj.* appointed; marked; characterized; designated; indicated (chd. p. 4): อภิลักขิตกาล, อภิลักขิตสมัย the time appointed or prescribed by custom or precedent for an annual ceremony (as the annual visitation to Buddhist monasteries).

อภิเลปน์   ah⁴-pi⁶-lep³ *P. n.* pollution; besmearment; filth; dirtiness; the act of smearing, daubing, blotching (chd. p. 4).

อภิวันท์   ah⁴-pi⁶-wan *S. v.* to make a reverential obeisance; to make a bow; to salute in a respectful manner (S. E. D. p. 69).

อภิวันทน์, อภิวาท, อภิวาทน์   ah⁴-pi⁶-wan *S. n.* a reverential salutation; an obeisance (S. E. D. p. 68).

อภิเษก   ah⁴-pi⁶-sak⁴ *S. n.* ablution (S. E. D. p. 71); (1) the ceremony of anointing, sprinkling or taking a purificatory bath; (2) the ceremony of solemnizing the ascension of a king to the highest rank as emperor, or his coronation by sprinkling on of water either from the four ponds of Subanaburi สุพรรณบุรี, or water which has been consecrated by the monks at various shrines in all the provinces of Thailand (wales, state ceremonies, page 70); (3) attainment; acquirement; the condition of achieving, arriving at, or reaching: อภิ-เษกมเหสี the ceremony of being raised to the rank of queen (solemnized by the sprinkling of water).

อภิสัมโพธิ, อภิสมโพธิ ah[4]-pi[6]-sum[2]-poh *P. n.* perfect understanding; infallible knowledge (chd. p. 6); self-procured knowledge to a superlative degree of wisdom. The implication is the enlightenment attained by the Buddha.

อภิสาร ah[4]-pi[6]-sarn[2] *S. n.* the condition of meeting, facing, attacking; assault; coming in contact, or into combat (S. E. D. p. 73).

อภิสิทธิ ah[4]-pi[6]-sit[4] *S. n.* the state of being effected or realized (S. E. D. p. 73).

อภูต ah[4]-poo-dta[4] *P. S. adj.* false; indicating that which has not been, or is not (chd. p. 8).

อม ๑ om *v.* to be confined in; to be kept or held in (as in the mouth); to be contained in (as pus in an abscess): อมเปรี้ยวอมหวาน *idiomatic* containing both sweet and sour flavour; intermingled sorrow and happiness: อมพะนำ being silent; keeping one's mouth shut; not talkative: อมมือ *lit.* "still sucking the finger," *i. e.* a minor: อมเลือดอมหนอง *lit.* "containing blood and pus," *i. e.* used in regard to an insufficiently drained wound, or an improperly opened abscess: อมหนอง containing pus: อมโรค a carrier of disease; appearing as though suffering from some disease: อมยา holding some medicine in the mouth (as a lozenge).

อม ๒ ah[4]-ma[6] *S. n.* violence; strength; fright; terror (S. E. D. p. 80).

อ้ม (ต้น) see **เนียม (ต้น)** p. 464.

อมต ๑, อมฤต ah[4]-ma[6]-dta[4] *P. n.* the elixir of life; nectar; food of the gods; drink

of the gods; the sweet dew, or ambrosia: *adj.* eternal; everlasting (chd. p. 28: H. C. D. p. 12): อมตบท the path that leads to Nirvana.

อมต ๒, อำมฤต ah[4]-ma[6]-dta[4] *S. n.* sickness; disease; death (S. E. D. p. 80).

อมนุษ ah[4]-ma[6]-noot[6] *S. n.* not a human being; demons; genie; Satan; evil spirits (chd. p. 28).

อมร, อำมร ah[4]-maun *P. S. n. lit.* "immortal," *i. e.* angels; devas; gods (chd. p. 28): *adj.* imperishable; undying: อมรประ the residence of the immortals; paradise: อมร-รัตน์ *lit.* "jewel of the gods," *i. e.* crystal: อมรราช *lit.* "king of the gods," *i. e.* Indra: อมรสตรี *lit.* "wives of the gods," *i. e.* apsaras or nymphs of heaven: อมราวดี the capital of Indra's heaven, renowned for its greatness and splendour. It is situated somewhere in the vicinity of mount Meru (chd. p. 88: H. C. D. p. 11).

อมฤต ah[4]-ma[6]-rit[6] *S.* an eternal draught; the elixir of life; food of the gods; drink of the gods; the sweet dew or ambrosia; immortal nectar (S. E. D. p. 82): อมฤตกร *lit.* "having celestial rays," *i. e.* Indra: อมฤตป, อมฤตป, อำมฤตป *lit.* "those who drink nectar, the elixir of life," *i. e.* devas; gods (chd. p. 28): อมฤตรส nectar. According to Buddhism this is the Truth, the Law, Nirvana: อมฤตโลก the world of the immortals.

อมฤตยุ ah[4]-ma[6]-rit[6]-dta[4]-yoo *S. n.* immortality.

อมัจจ ah[4]-mut[6]-chja[4] *P. n.* a companion or friend; a privy councillor; an advisor; a minister (of state) (chd. p. 27).

อมัตร ah[4]-mut[6] *S. n.* a vessel; an utensil; cups (for drinking).

อมาตย์, อำมาตย์ ah[4]-mart[4] *S. n.* councillor; minister (S. E. D. p. 81); courtier; a conferred rank for civil service officials of which there are the following degrees : มหาอำมาตย์นายก Principal Grand Councillor : มหาอำมาตย์เอก First Grand Councillor : มหาอำมาตย์โท Second Grand Councillor : มหาอำมาตย์ตรี Third Grand Councillor : อำมาตย์เอก First Councillor : อำมาตย์โท Second Councillor : อำมาตย์ตรี Third Councillor : รองอำมาตย์เอก First Deputy Councillor : รองอำมาตย์โท Second Deputy Councillor : รองอำมาตย์ตรี Third Deputy Councillor : เสนาอำมาตย์ a corresponding rank conferred on army officials : อำมาตย์ทั้งหลาย Ministers in general.

อมาวสึ, อมาวสุ, อามาวาสึ ah[4]-mah-wa[6]-see[2] _P. n._ the day of the new moon (chd. p. 28); the last day of the lunar month.

อมิตร ah[4]-mit[6] _S. n._ one (other than a friend); an enemy; a competitor; an opponent (chd. p. 29); an adversary.

อย, อยัส, อโย ah[4]-ya[6] _P. S. n._ iron (chd. p. 75); metal; an iron weapon : อยการ a worker in iron; a blacksmith.

อยน ah[4]-ya[6]-na[6] _P. S. n._ a road; a path; a way; a route; a course; motion (chd. p. 75)

อย่า yah[4] _v._ to forbid; to prohibit; to ask not to do; don't; do not do; _an auxilliary used to form the imperative mode :_ อย่ากล่าวเกินควร do not use too harsh, severe or disagreeable words : อย่ากั้น co-partners that agree not to take the stakes from the loser in a gambling game : อย่ากิน do not eat : อย่าแข็ง do not be too overbearing or cruel while playing; do not be stubborn (a word of censure for children) : อย่านม to wean (a child) : อย่าเพ่อทำ, อย่าเพ่อก่อน _idiomatic_ do not do yet; suspend operations; wait awhile : อย่าร้าง, อย่าเมีย to divorce; to separate (from each other) : อย่าเลย to forbid absolutely : อย่าโหดร้าย do not let the angry passions rise : อย่าว่าแต่เท่านั้น _idiomatic_ not only that much; not limited to that amount : อย่าอวดรู้ do not vaunt (your)

knowledge.

อยาก yark[4] _v._ to desire; to want; to crave; to hanker after; to wish for; to lust after; to be hungry for : อยากน้ำ to be thirsty : อยากอาหาร to be hungry for food.

อย่าง yang[4] _n._ manner; mode; fashion; kind; pattern : ขายอย่างไร at what price will you sell ? เขาเป็นอย่างไร how is he getting along (an inquiry about one who is sick) ? จะไปอย่างไร how are you going to go ? ตัวอย่าง pattern; sample; example : ตามอย่าง according to the precedence : อย่างดี of the best quality : อย่างเดียว only one kind : อย่างแบบ, อย่างเยี่ยง following the pattern : อย่างไร what kind ? whatever ; whatsoever ; how ; in what way or manner ? by what means ? however : อย่างไรก็ดี, อย่างไรก็ตาม nevertheless; howsoever; notwithstanding : อย่างไรจึงจะพอใจ by what means, or in what manner will it please you ? อย่างหนึ่งอย่างใด in any case; by all means : เอาเยี่ยงเอาอย่าง _idiomatic_ to imitate; to follow the example of; to mimic, ape or reflect another.

อยุทธ์, อยุทธย์ ah[4]-yoot[6] _S. adj._ unvanquished; unconquered; impregnable (S. E. D. p. 86) : เวลาอยุทธ์ time of peace; state of absence of war.

อยุธยา, กรุงเก่า ah[4]-yoot[6]-ta[6]-yah _n._ Phra Nakorn Sri Ayutia, Ayuthaya, Ayuthia, Ayutia, Ayutthaya, Juthia Udaya, Iudia, Sri Ayuthia, Ayodya, Ayudhya, the capital of Thailand from 1350 to 1767, a period of 417 years. During this period thirty-four kings reigned and the country suffered eight invasions, The first historical dynasty was that established at Sukhodaya in 1257 A. D. This kingdom lasted a little less than one century but during that period a national unity and strength was achieved which resulted in the Thai people freeing themselves from the Khmer suzerainty, and also in an extension of the borders to Ligor (Sritamaraj) and the Malay States. The Thai language was reduced to writing and arts were introduced and developed. But after a century of brilliance, that dynasty fell and the capital was moved to Ayuthya. The Ayuthian period was marked by the establishment of suzerainty over the neighbouring Thai principalities; by extension of territory, especially in the north; by great wars with powerful neighbours especially the Burmese; and by relations with foreign nations, including France. During the seventeenth century Thailand was a mighty nation, being a clearing-house for merchandise which found its way overland to Tenasserim from Japan and China for India and Europe. But the kingdom declined and in 1763 was invaded by the Burmese. After a four year contest, they captured Ayuthya which they rased to the ground, destroying priceless records and much treasure.

The following is a list of the kings of the Ayuthian period as furnished by King Mongkut's chief scribe. This is taken from the Bangkok Calendar of 1863, compiled by Dan B. Bradley, M. D.

First Dynasty

Began to reign A. D.

1. Somdet Pra Rama Tibawdee I 1351 (สมเด็จพระรามาธิบดี ที่ ๑)

2. Somdet Pra Rama-sooan (สมเด็จพระ- 1371 ราเมศวร), son of the 1st who abdicated for.—

3. Somdet Pra Bawroma-Racha-Tirat 1371 (สมเด็จพระบรมราชาธิราช)

4. Chow Oo-T'awng lan (เจ้าอู่ทองลาน) 1383 son of the 3rd.

5. Somdet Pra Rame-sooan (สมเด็จ- 1383 พระราเมศวร) assassinated the 4th. being the same person of the 2nd. reign.

6. Somdet Praya Pra-Ram (สมเด็จ- 1398 พระยาพระราม) son of the 5th.

7. Somdet Pra Nakawn In (สมเด็จ- 1402 พระนครอินทร์)

8. Somdet Pra Bawroma Racha Tirat 1419 II (สมเด็จพระบรมราชาธิราช) son of

the 7th.

9. Somdet Pra Bawroma Trei Loka- 1435 nat (สมเด็จพระบรมไตรโลกนารถ) son of the 8th.

10. Somdet Pra Inta-Racha (สมเด็จ- 1450 พระอินทราชา) son of the 9th.

11. Somdet Pra Rama-Tibawdee II 1489 (สมเด็จพระรามาธิบดี ที่ ๒)

12. Somdet Pra Bawroma-Racha Naw 1510 Poot Tang (สมเด็จพระบรมราชา- หน่อพุทธางกูร) son of the 11th.

13. Pra Ratsata Tirat (พระรัตสาทรธิราช) 1514 son of the 12th. 5 years old.

14. Somdet Pra Chei Racha Tirat 1514 (สมเด็จพระไชยราชาธิราช) son of the 12th. killed by the 13th.

15. Pra Yawt Fa (พระยอดฟ้า) son of 1528 the 14th. aged 11 years. The 15th. was slain by Koon Warawongsa Tirat who took the throne and reigned 5 months. Being a usurper, his name is not allowed to have a place among the names of Siamese kings. He was assassinated by Koon Pirenatep, who placed on the throne Pra Teean Racha who bore the name—

16. Somdet Pra Maha Chakra-Patdi- 1530 Racha Tirat (สมเด็จพระมหาจักร- พรรดิธิราช)

17. Pra Mahin Ta Racha Tirat (พระมหิน- 1556 ทราธิราช) son of the 16th. The Capital of the kingdom was taken in 918 (Little Era) by the king of Hongsawadee or Pegu.

18. Somdet Pra Maha Tama Racha 1557 Tirat (สมเด็จพระมหาธรรมราชาธิราช)

19. Somdet Pra Naresooan (สมเด็จ- 1579 พระนเรศวร) son of the 18th.

20. Somdet Pra Aka-Totsarot (สมเด็จ- 1584 พระเอกาทศรศ) a younger brother of the 19th.

21. Chow Fa Sri Sawara Pak (เจ้าฟ้า- 1603

ศรี เสาว ภาค) son of the 20th.
Here closes the dynasty of
Somdet Pra Rama Ti-Bawdee,
being 20 different kings, one
of them having reigned twice.

Second Dynasty

22. Pra Chow Song Tam (พระเจ้าทรง-
ธรรม) slew the 21st. and reigned. — 1603

23. Pra Cheta Tirat Otsarot (พระเชษฐ-
ธิราชโอรสสา) an elder brother
of the 22nd. The Prime Minister Chow Praya Kralahom Sri
Sooriwong assassinated the
23rd, and placed on the throne. — 1628

24. Pra Atitaya Wong (พระอาทิตยวงศ์)
a brother of the 23rd. 9 years
old. Here closes the Dynasty
of Pra Chow Song Tam. — 1631

Third Dynasty

The former king was driven
from the throne by the Siamese
Nobles and Lords, whose place
they filled by the Prime Minister above mentioned named

25. Pra Chow Prasat Tawng (พระเจ้า-
ปราสาททอง) — 1631

26. Chow Fa Chei (เจ้าฟ้าไชย) son of
the 25th. — 1656

27. Pra Sootama Racha (พระสุธรรม-
ราชา) killed the 26th. and reigned. — 1657

28. Somdet Pra Narai (สมเด็จพระนา-
รายน์) son of 25th. killed the
27th. — 1657

29. Pra Pet Racha (พระเพทราชา). He is
called a usurper, and is not
allowed an honourable place
among the kings. — 1683

30. Pra Poota Chow Sua (พระพุทธเจ้าเสือ)
son of the 27th. — 1698

31. Pra Chow Yoo-hooa Tei (พระเจ้า-
อยู่หัวไทย) son of the 30th. — 1708

32. Pra Chow Yoo-hooa Bawromakot
(พระเจ้าอยู่หัวบรมโกษ) brother of — 1733

the 31st.

33. Chow Fa Dawk-madua (เจ้าฟ้าดอก-
มะเดื่อ) son of the 32nd. and
then abdicated the throne for
his elder brother. — 1759

34. Pra Chow Tinang Sooriya-Marin-
tara (พระเจ้าที่นั่งสุริยามรินทรา). — 1759

The close of the Dynasty of Prasat Tawng,
being 9 kings in all, the usurper being excluded. The whole term in which the above
named 34 kings reigned is 417 years, averag-
ing 12.3 years each. (The Burmese sacked
the capital in the year 1767 and carried
away many captives. The chief of the Siamese army rallied the Siamese under him at
Tonta-Booree, which is now the site of H.R.H.
Kromalooang Wongsa-tirat-sanit's palace. He
built a walled city in this place and reigned
as king Praya Tak).

อยู่ yoo[4] v. to stay; to remain (with or
at); to live; to dwell; to reside; to inhabit;
to be still alive; still to be able to hold one's
own: กินอยู่ to board with; to be provided
with lodging and board: เขาอยู่บ้านหรือ is
he, or are they at home? ครั้นอยู่มา in due
time: อยู่กิน to live (as man and wife); to
abide; to reside; to dwell or sojourn: อยู่งาน
to serve; to minister to; to wait on; to attend
to the wants of (as fanning a king or prince):
อยู่ดีหรือ the salutation, "Are you well?":
อยู่นานมา to be in residence a long time:
อยู่บ้าน to be at home: อยู่ไปได้ permitted
to remain: อยู่พัก to remain temporarily:
อยู่เป็นเพื่อน to remain with as a companion or
comforter: อยู่ไฟ to remain by a fire after
parturition: อยู่มา it so happened: อยู่-
เย็นเป็นสุข to be enjoying peace and good
health: อยู่ยาม to be on duty (as a watchman); to be stationed as a guard or watcher:
อยู่เวร to take turns being on duty: อยู่ไหน
where are you? where is it? (as an article
searched for): อยู่คง to be invulnerable;
to be proof against all weapons; to be un-
breakable.

อร ๑ ah⁴-ra⁶ *P. S. n.* the spoke of a wheel; the radius of a circle (S. E. D. p. 86).

อร ๒ ah⁴-ra⁶ *n.* a girl; a virgin; a woman: *adj.* beautiful; handsome; elegant; excellent: อรกาย beautiful of body.

อรช ah⁴-ra⁶-cha⁶ *P. S. adj.* free from dust or blemish; spotless; clean; pure (S.E.D. p. 86).

อรชร, อ่อนชอน, อ่อนชอน ah⁴-ra⁶-chaun *adj.* fine; beautiful; fair; pretty; lovable; pleasing; sweet; small of form and slender-waisted.

อรชุน ah⁴-ra⁶-choon *n. lit.* "white," *i. e.* Arjuna, the third Pandu prince. All of the five brothers were of divine paternity. Arjuna's father was Indra. He was a brave warrior, high-minded, generous, upright and handsome, the most prominent and the most amiable and interesting of the five brothers (H. C. D. p. 21): *adj.* white; clear; unclouded.

อรณ ๑ ah⁴-ra⁶-na⁶ *P. S. adj.* distant; far beyond; passed on; gone over or beyond (S. E. D. p. 86).

อรณ ๒ ah⁴-ra⁶-na⁶ *P. S. n.* the condition of freedom from toil, struggle, endeavour, or labour, *i. e.* calmness; tranquillity; quietness.

อรดี, อรติ, อราดี, อราติ ah⁴-ra⁶-dee *P. S. n.* dislike; distaste; aversion; discontent; dissatisfaction; distress (S. E. D. p. 86).

อรทัย, อ่อนไท, อ่อนไท้ ah⁴-ra⁶-tai *n.* a maiden; a young girl; a beautiful woman.

อรนุช ah⁴-ra⁶-noot⁶ *n.* a younger sister; a fiancée.

อรรก see อักก์ p. 980.

อรรค see อัคร

[p. 17].

อรรฆ awk⁴ *S. n.* value; cost; price (chd.

อรรฆย์ awk⁴ *S. adj.* deserving a respectful reception; valuable; precious; praiseworthy; admirable (S. E. D. p. 89).

อรรจ aut⁴ *S. v.* to shine; to praise; to admire; to honour or treat with respect (S. E. D. p. 89).

อรรณพ, อัณณพ un-nop⁶ *n.* the sea; the ocean; a lake; a body of water (chd. p. 36).

อรรถ, อัฏฐ ๒, อัตถ์ ๒ aut⁴ *S. n.* purpose; aim; motive; reason; advantage; utility (S. E. D. p. 90): อรรถกร fruitful; useful; beneficial; advantageous (chd. p. 66): อรรถกาม wishing to be useful; desirous of riches and wealth: อรรถโกวิท an expert; one who is adroit, skillful, dexterous, proficient: อรรถคฤห a treasury; see คลัง p. 185: อรรถจินตา attention to, or consideration of affairs: อรรถโทษ a mistake with regard to the meaning: อรรถบดี lord of wealth; a rich man: อรรถประโยค the application of wealth (as to trade or usury): อรรถศาสตร์, อรรถวิทยา economics; the science of a practical life and government; ethics (chd. p. 68): อรรถสงเคราะห์ the accumulation of wealth.

อรรธ aut⁴ *S. n.* a part; a half (chd. p. 10: S. E. D. p. 91): อรรธกรรณ half of the diameter; a radius: อรรธคราส the condition of only half of an orb being observed; a crescent or half moon (as a partial eclipse): อรรธนิศา midnight: อรรธบท one half of the way: อรรธภาค a half: อรรธมาส a fortnight; half of a month: อรรธางค์ the center; the middle portion; the waist; the half of a body.

อรสุม, อุสุม ah⁴-ra⁶-soom² *P. n.* heat; vapour; passion; fury; anger; the hot season (chd. p. 538): อรสุมพล steam power.

อรหะ ah⁴-ra⁶-ha⁴ *P. S. adj.* proper; fit; worthwhile; being entitled to; deserving (chd. p. 54).

อรหัตต์ ah⁴-ra⁶-hut⁴ *P. n.* the state of being an Arhat; Arhatship; final sanctification (chd. p. 54); the venerables, who by their age, great proficiency in the knowledge of

the Law, and remarkable fervour in the assiduous practice of all its ordinances, occupy
deservedly the first rank amongst the disciples
of the Buddha: อรหัตตผล *lit.* "the fruition
of Arhatship," *i. e.* saintliness: อรหัตตมัคค์
lit. "the path of Arhatship," *i. e.* sanctification: อรหัตตวิโมกข์ the salvation of an
Arhat.

อรหันต์, อรหัง, อรหา   ah^4-ra^6-hun^2 *P. n.*
a holy man; a saint; one who has attained
the highest degree of religious aspiration;
one worthy of veneration; the highest degree
of saintship (Ala. p. 171); one who has attained
final sanctification (Chd. p. 53): *adj.* honourable; venerable; sanctified; holy; virtuous:
อรหันตฆาต the killing of an Arhat, being one
of the five major sins.

อร่อย   ah^4-roy^4 *adj.* delicious; luscious;
savoury; dainty; nutritious.

อรัญญ์, อรัณย์   ah^4-run *P. n.* a forest; a
wood (Chd. p. 56); a deserted or lonely place:
อรัญญวาส a temple or residence in the forest:
อรัญญวาสี *lit.* "those who live in the wood,"
i. e. an ancient sect of Buddhist priests who
reside in the forests (as ascetics or anchorites):
อรัญญประเทศ a wooded country or district;
Aranya Prades, a city on the eastern border
between Thailand and French Indo-China.

อราดี, อราติ see อรดี p. 971.

อร่าม   ah^4-ram^4 *adj.* bright; lustrous; glowing; shining; brilliant; glistening; see เถือก-
ถ่อง under เถือก p. 392: เหลืองอร่าม bright
yellow.

อริ   ah^4-ri^4 *P. S. n.* an enemy: *adj.* hateful; revengeful; retaliating; avenging (Chd.
p. 56): อริราช an enemy of the Crown or
kingdom: อรินทร์ *lit.* "chief over an enemy,"
i. e. a victorious or conquering king.

อริน   ah^4-rin *S. n. lit.* "having spokes," *i. e.*
a wheel; a discus (S. E. D. p. 86): อรินภัย
reverses; pestilence; misfortunes (that might

befall an enemy).

อริยกะ   ah^4-ri^6-ya^6-gka^4 *P. n.* the Aryan
race, being the ancestors of the ancient Hindus
(Chd. p. 56); the immigrating race from which
the Hindu originated (H. C. D. p. 24).

อริยะ, อารยะ   ah^4-ri^6-ya^6 *P. n.* one who
has "entered into the stream of wisdom," or
the Four Paths. The saint who has attained
this cannot have more than seven births
among men and angels before he enters
Nirvana (Ala. p. 170); one who has attained
final sanctification; a converted man (Chd. p.
57): *adj.* honourable; respectable; venerable;
noble; excellent; eminent; pious; sanctified
(Chd. p. 57): อริยธรรม, อารยะธรรม civilization; enlightenment; advancement: อริย-
บุคคล a saint; one who has attained the
highest degree of saintship; one who is in
one of the Four Paths or Four Fruitions
(Chd. p. 56): อริยมรรค *lit.* "the sublime
path," *i. e.* the Four Paths and Four Fruitions
by which saintship is attained, according to
the Buddhist religion (Chd. p. 56): อริยสัจจ์
lit. "the sublime truth," *i. e.* the four great
truths which are the foundation doctrines of
the Buddhist religion, *viz.* (1) that sorrow
ever attends (transmigratory) existence: (2)
that the cause of sorrow lies in the passions
or desires: (3) that cessation of sorrow can
be procured by the extinction of desire: (4)
that desire can be extinguished by holiness
(Ala. p. 197).

อรุ   ah^4-roo^6 *P. S. n.* a wound (Chd. p. 57).

อรุณ   ah^4-roon *P. S. n. lit.* "red; ruddy;
tawny," *i. e.* the dawn; the sun (Chd. p. 58):
รุ่งอรุณ the break of day: แสงอรุณ the
dawn rays of the sun: อรุณกร *lit.* "having
red rays," *i. e.* the sun.

อรุโณทัย see อโณทัย p. 956.

อรุ่ม   ah^4-room^4 *adj.* darkened; gloomy;
dusky; clouded; misty.

อรูป   ah[4]-roop[3] *P. S. adj.* without form ;
incorporeal ; immaterial (chd. p. 58) ; formless ; shapeless ; ugly (S. E. D. p. 88) : อรูปภพ
the world of spirits, or those without form.

อลงกต   ah[4]-long-gkot[4] *P. S. adj.* adorned ;
decorated ; embellished (chd. p. 26) ; ornamented ; beautiful ; magnificent.

อลงกรณ์   ah[4]-long-gkaun *P.S. n.* personal
decorations ; ornaments ; adornments ; embellishments (chd. p. 26).

อลงการ see อลังการ

อลวน   on-la[6]-won *adj.* mixed ; confused ;
disordered ; see วุ่นวาย under วุ่น p. 780.

อลเวง   on-la[6]-weng *adj.* musical ; agreeable
to the ears ; loud ; reverberating ; echoing.

อลหม่าน   on-la[6]-marn[4] *adj.* tumultuous ;
disturbing ; confusing ; disordered ; riotous ;
running here and there excitedly.

อลักเอลื่อ   ah[4]-luk[4]-ah[4]-leu-ah[4] *adj.* perplexed ; doubtful ; suspicious of ; suspecting ;
distrusting ; see ฉงน p. 264.

อลังการ, อลงการ   ah[4]-lung-gkarn *P.S. n.*
the act of decorating or ornamenting ; trinkets ; jewels ; rhetorical figures.

อลัชช   ah[4]-lut[6]-chee *P. adj.* brazen-faced ;
shameless ; lawless ; impudent ; bold ; unbecoming (chd. p. 26).

อล่างฉ่าง, อลั่งฉั่ง   ah[4]-lang[4]-chang[4] *adj.*
clear ; distinct ; open ; plain ; easily seen ;
pleasing to the eye.

อลิงค์, อลึงค์   ah[4]-ling *P. S. adj.* having
no designating mark as to gender or sex
(S. E. D. p. 95) : *grammar* neuter gender.

อโลหะ   ah[4]-loh-ha[4] *adj.* non-metalic.

อวก, อ้วก   oo-ak[3] *v.* to vomit ; to be sick
at the stomach ; to be nauseated : *onomat.*
from the sound made when belching gas ; see
ราก p. 706.

อวคม   ah[4]-wa[6]-kom *P.S. n.* understanding ; comprehension ; intelligence (S.E.D. p. 97).

อวเคราะห์   ah[4]-wa[6]-kraw[6] *S. n.* hindrance ;
obstacle ; impediment ; barrier : *grammar*
the separation of the component parts of a
compound word, or of the stem and certain
suffixes and terminations (S. E. D. p. 97).

อวจร   ah[4]-wa[6]-chjaun *P.S. n.* the dominion
or sphere of a realm (chd. p. 70).

อวชัย   ah[4]-wa[6]-chai *P. S. n.* the condition
of overcoming or winning by conquest (S.E.D.
p. 98).

อวชาต   ah[4]-wa[6]-chart[3] *P.S. adj.* degenerate ;
base-born ; mean ; corrupt ; used for a mother
lower in caste than her husband (chd. p. 71) :
อวชาตบุตร children who do not measure up
to their ancestors ; sons who are degenerate,
mean, base, and corrupt.

อวด   oo-at[4] *v.* to boast ; to vaunt ; to exult ;
to display ostentatiously ; to be proud of ; to
brag : อวดดี proud ; cheeky ; vain ; arrogant ;
haughty ; boastful :   อวดตัว to boast of one's
achievements or capabilities ; to praise oneself :   อวดเสียง to be proud of one's voice :
อวดอ้าง to allude boastfully to oneself ; to
praise or commend one's own, or another's
good qualities.

อวตังส, อวตังสกะ see อพฑงส์ p. 965.

อวตาร   ah[4]-wa[6]-dtarn *S. n.* an epithet
for a king, a pious or distinguished person,
or the incarnation of a deity, especially of
Vishnu (chd. p. 33) ; the descent of a deity
from heaven ; the earthly manifestation of a
divinity.

อวน   oo-an *n.* a long bag-net for catching
fish :   ลงอวน to drop a bag-net into place
(as between permanent stakes in a water-
course).

อ้วน   oo-an[3] *adj.* fat ; corpulent ; plump.

อวบ   oo-ap[4] *adj.* fully developed ; juicy or

luscious (regarding fruit); muscular; stalwart; strong; brawny; robust (regarding a person); full of sap; budding into flowers and fresh leaves; approaching puberty.

อวย oo-ie *v.* to give; to consent to; to bestow upon; to grant; to permit: คำอวยพร a benediction; a blessing: อวยชัย to invoke a blessing for victory: อวยทาน to give or bestow alms: อวยผล, อำนวยผล to reap the results of either good or evil action: อวยพร to invoke a blessing.

อวยวะ, อวัยวะ, อพยพ ๒ ah[4]-wa[6]-ya[6]-wa[6] *P. n.* a part; a portion; a limb; a member; an organ (of the body) (chd. p. 72).

อวรุทธ์, อวรุทธก ah[4]-wa[6]-root[6] *P. adj.* expelled; ejected; banished; exiled; being an outcast; driven from home.

อวล oo-an *v.* to be scattered about; to be disseminated (as smoke or odours); to be diffused; see ฟุ้ง p. 609: *adj. Cam.* full; tight; crowded; massed together.

อวสาน, โอสาน ah[4]-wa[6]-sarn[2] *P. S. n.* termination; conclusion; end; finality; cessation; boundary; limit (of life): *grammar* a disjunction of words, letters, or end of a phrase (s. e. d. p. 105).

อวหาร ah[4]-wa[6]-harn[2] *P. S. n.* the act of taking away, snatching, or stealing; a thief (chd. p. 71).

อวัตถา, อวัสตา, อวัสตา ah[4]-wat[6]-tah[2] *P. n.* state; condition; time; occasion (chd. p. 72).

อวันตี ah[4]-wan-dtee *S. n.* the modern Ujjain in the Malwa plateau, the southern capital of Gwalior State. It was the capital of Vikramaditya and one of the seven sacred cities. Hindu geographers calculate their longitude from it, making it their first meridian (h. c. d. p. 325: s. e. d. p. 100).

อวาจี ah[4]-wah-chjee *P. n.* the south.

อวีจิ, อวีจิ, อเวจิ ah[4]-wi[6]-chji[4] *P. n.* name of one of the eight hells; the hell of everlasting fire (chd. p. 73).

อวิชชา ah[4]-wit[6]-chah *P. n.* nascience; the condition of lacking knowledge; error (chd. p. 73); spiritual ignorance; Maya or personified illusion.

อวิญญาณ ah[4]-win-yarn *P. adj.* inanimate; lifeless; soulless; spiritless (chd. p. 74): อวิญญาณกทรัพย์ inanimate possessions (as landed property).

อวิญญู ah[4]-win-yoo *P. adj.* ignorant; foolish; stupid (chd. p. 74).

อศรพิษ, อาศิรพิษ ah[4]-saw[2]-ra[6]-pit[6] *adj.* poisonous; venomous: งูอศรพิษ a poisonous snake.

อโศก ah[4]-soke[4] *adj.* not causing sorrow, sadness or grief (s. e. d. p. 113): อโศก, พระเจ้าศรีธรรมาโศกราช King Sritumma Sokaraht (270-230 B.C.), a celebrated king of the Maurya dynasty of Magadha and grandson of its founder Chandragupta (see จันทรคุปต under จันทร์ p. 240). This king is the most celebrated of any in the annals of the Buddhists. In the commencement of his reign he followed the Brahminical faith, but became a convert to that of the Buddha and a zealous encourager of it. He is said to have maintained in his palace 64,000 Buddhist priests and to have erected 84,000 columns (or stupas) throughout India. He reigned forty years (h. c. d. p. 26); see มหายาน p. 628; หินยาน under หิน ๑ p. 936.

อสงไขย ah[4]-song[2]-kai[2] *P. n.* the highest of the numerals; a numeral followed by 140 ciphers (chd. p. 59): *adj.* incalculable; innumerable; countless.

อสนี, อสนี, อศนี ah[4]-sa[4]-nee *P. n.* the thunderbolt of Indra (chd. p. 59); a sharp-pointed weapon: อสนีบาต *lit.* "an ax falling from the sky," *i. e.* lightning.

อสังหาริมะ ah[4]-sung[2]-hah[2]-ri[6]-ma[6] *P. adj.* immovable; stable; steadfast: อสังหาริมทรัพย์

movable property: สังหาริมทรัพย์ immovable property.

อสัจ, อสัจจ์ see **อสัตย์**

อสัญญ์ ah[4]-sun[2] *P. adj.* unconscious; lacking in the power of perception, of feeling, or of knowledge: ถึงแก่อสัญญกรรม to die (used in reference to nobility of the highest rank): อสัญญกรรม *lit.* "in the state of unconsciousness," *i. e.* death.

อสัญญี ah[4]-sun[2]-yee *P. adj.* unconscious (chd. p. 59); insensible; feelingless; anesthetized: อสัญญีแพทย์ an anesthetist: อสัญญี-ภาพ, อสัญญีภาวะ unconsciousness; insensibility; a state of fainting; a swoon: อสัญญีสัตว์ a group of Brahminical deities who have forms but no perception; see อกนิษฐ์ p. 954.

อสัตย์, อสัจ, อสัจจ์, อาสัตย์ ah[4]-sut[4] *S. adj.* untrue; false (chd. p. 58); erroneous; untruthful; dishonest; faithless.

อสัมภินน์ ah[4]-sum[2]-pin *S. adj.* separate; not being in contact; unmixed; unadulterated (S. E. D. p. 119): อสัมภินนพงศ์, อสัมภินนวงศ์ an unmixed lineage; pure blood; descendants of one single race.

อสาธร, อสาธุ ah[4]-sah[2]-taun *P. S. adj.* bad; mean; low; wicked (chd. p. 58).

อสิ ah[4]-si[4] *P. S. n.* a sword; a knife; a simitar; a sabre having an extreme curve (chd. p. 60): อสิจรรยาการ the practicing of war-songs, fencing songs, lance dancing songs, or songs used while practicing with any other form of weapon: อสิธารา the sharp edge of a sword.

อสิต ah[4]-sit[4] *P. S. adj.* black; dark; dark blue (chd. p. 60).

อสีตยานุพยัญชนะ ah[4]-see[2]-dta[4]-yah-noo[6]-pa[6]-yun-cha[6]-na[6] *P. n.* the thirty-two major and forty-eight minor characteristics: พระ-มหาบุรุษลักษณะ one having the thirty-two characteristics or "major signs" of a great man, *viz.* (1) his head is crowned with a protuberance of the skull; (2) his curly hair is of a brilliant black, shining like the tail of a peacock, or sparkling collyrium (eye-salve), and each curl turns from left to right; (3) he has a broad and regular forehead; (4) between his eyebrows is a circle of down, brilliant as snow or silver; (5) his eyelids are like those of a heifer; (6) he has brilliant black eyes; (7, 8, 9) he has forty teeth, all equal, set closely together, and of the most perfect whiteness; (10) his voice is like that of Brahma; (11) he has an exquisite sense of taste; (12) his tongue is broad, thin, or according to the Thibetan version, "long and thread-like"; (13) he has the jaw of a lion; (14) his shoulders or arms are perfectly rounded; (15) he has seven parts of his body filled out, or with protuberances, *i. e.* soles of the feet, palms of the hands, shoulders, and back; (16) the space between his shoulders is covered; (17) his skin has the lustre or colour of gold; (18) his arms are so long that when he stands upright his hands reach to his knees; (19) his front is lion-like; (20) his body is perfectly straight, tall as a banyan tree, and round in proportion; (21) his hairs grow one by one; (22) and their ends are curled to the right; (23) the generative organs are concealed; (24, 25) he has perfectly round thighs, and his legs are like those of the king of the gazelles; (26) his toes and fingers are long; (27) the nails of the toes are well developed; (28) his instep is high; (29) his feet and hands are soft and delicate; (30) his toes and fingers are marked with lines forming a network; (31) under the soles of his feet are marked two beautiful, luminous, brilliant white wheels, with a thousand rays; (32) his feet are even and well placed.

อสีติ ah[4]-see[2]-dti[4] *P. adj.* eighty (chd. p. 60): อสีติมหาสาวก the eighty great disciples of the Buddha.

อสุ   ah[4]-soo[4] *P. S. n.* breath; life (chd. p. 62).

อสุจิ   ah[4]-soo[4]-chji[4] *P. adj.* impure; unclean (chd. p. 62).

อสุก, อสภ   ah[4]-soop[4] *P. adj.* bad; ugly; disagreeable; nasty; disgusting (chd. p. 62).

อสุร, อสุร   ah[4]-soo[4]-ra[6] *P. S. n.* an Asura, a Titan or fallen angel (chd. p. 62). In the oldest part of the Rigveda this term is used for the supreme spirit, and is the same as the Ahura of the Zoroastrians. In the sense of *god* it was applied to several of the chief deities, as to Indra, Agni and Varuna. It afterwards acquired an entirely opposite meaning and came to signify, as now, a demon or enemy of the gods; devils; fallen angels; fabulous giants (H. C. D. p. 27): อสุรี feminine form of อสุร: อสุรกย์น์ the state of destroying the demons or giants; the freeing of people (from their power): อสุรกัญญา *lit.* "a beautiful giantess," *i. e.* lady Suchada (สุชาดา), daughter of Viprachitti the king of giants, and consort of Indra: อสุรกาย spectres; ghosts; phantoms; apparitions; demons: อสุรภพ, อสุรโลก region; world or domain of the fabulous giants: อสุรวิมาน the palace of the giants: อสุรภักตร์ faces of the Asuras.

อสุรินทร์, อสุเรนทร์   ah[4]-soo[4]-rin *S. n. lit.* "chief of the fabulous Asuras," *i. e.* a name for Rahu (the dragon that is supposed to cause eclipses) and Viprachitti (chd. p. 62: H. C. D. p. 358).

อห   ah[4]-ha[4] *P. n.* a day (chd. p. 19): สัปดาห seven days; a week.

อหังการ   ah[4]-hung[2]-gkarn *P. S. n.* pride; arrogance; selfishness; haughtiness; egotism; boastfulness (chd. p. 19).

อหิ   ah[4]-hi[4] *P. S. n.* a snake (chd. p. 20): อหิวาตโรค, อหิวาตกโรค cholera.

อหิงสา, อหึงสา   ah[4]-hing[2]-sah[2] *P. S. n.* harmlessness; non-oppression; the condition

of not hurting or injurying humanity, *i. e.* kindness (chd. p. 20).

อเหตุกทิฏฐิ   ah[4]-hay[2]-dtoo[4]-gka[4]-tit[6]-ti[4] *P. n.* the belief of a non-Buddhist sect of ascetics that there is no cause or effect in the universe.

อโหสิกรรม   ah[4]-hoh[2]-si[4]-gkum *P. n. lit.* "non-existence of the consequences for sins," *i. e.* the condition of cancellation, blotting out, or crossing off of penalties for all sins.

ออ   aw *v.* to congregate in great numbers; to gather in crowds or groups (as the populace at a fair or festival, or as sheep or cattle standing still in a field): *n. an ancient prefix for names,* corresponding to Nai or Mr.

อ้อ   see นพ, นัท p. 445.

อ๋อ   aw[3] *onomat.* from the **words** indicative of understanding all that is said; "Oh, yes I quite understand".

อ้อ   aw[2] *n.* a word of Chinese origin used in gambling when the banker pays three times the stake placed by a player.

ออก   awk[4] *v.* to issue or put forth (as an edition of a book or newspaper); to exit or retire (as actors from a stage); to go out or away; to rise or appear (as the sun); to start or begin to move (as a caravan, or horses racing); to be hatched; to give birth to; to be apparent or visible (as the seams on the reverse side of a garment); to distribute or pay out (as funds); to give (as a receipt or bill); to open; to set up a shop or stall; to be liberated or freed (as out of a state of bondage or confinement); to produce fruit or flowers; to be inclined; to be disposed to (as to anger or wrath): *n. an ancient prefix to an official's name,* as ออกญา, ออกพระ, ออกหลวง; the condition of having issued forth or away (as from a place, state or relation); the act of going out: *adv.* out; outward bound; off (as a ship); apart; aside; asunder; by itself; in a high degree; in large measure; actually; really: ออก (นก) bar-tailed fishing eagle, *Polioaetus ichthyaetus*; the osprey, *Pandion haliaetus* (Gaird. J. S. S. IX, I. pp. 10, 16): เข้าออก to have free access in and out; to pass back and forth at will: เมื่อไรเรือจะออก when will the boat or ship leave? ออกกฎหมาย to legislate: ออกกำลัง, ออกแรง to exert; to strive; to strain with one's fullest power; to endeavour with one's utmost efforts to perform various exercises: ออกแขก to appear before guests; to welcome visitors; to appear before the public (as from a balcony): ออกขุนนาง to give a public audience (as to government officials): ออกโขน to act as a masked player or actor: ออกไข้หัว, ออกผัดาษ to develop any eruptive fever; to exhibit the symptoms of small-pox: ออกความเห็น to express an opinion: ออกความเห็นแข้ง to protest against: ออกงาน to begin one's task or duty; to stage a play or entertainment; to have the orchestra play the overture of a performance: ออกจะดี that promises to be a success; it will be successful: ออกจากราชการ to retire from government service: ออกจากเรือน to leave the house: ออกชื่อ to mention one by name; to speak directly of one, or of some object by name; to nominate a person: ออกดอก an exanthematous disease; a disease characterized by an eruption; to suffer from some one of the eruptive diseases: ออกดอกออกผล *idiomatic* to flourish; to bear or produce flowers and fruit; to bring results: ออกได้ to be released from prison or punishment: ออกตัว to assert, plead or avow one's innocence; to repudiate, disavow or disclaim any responsibility or connection with: ออกท่า. ออกทาง to assume various attitudes (as in dancing); to pose (as representing fear, anger or delight): ออกทุน to make an investment (as capital in a business concern); to provide the capital or funds for a business: ออกนอกออกในได้ *idiomatic* to be familiar or intimate with; to be unrestricted in going or coming: ออกเนื้อ to expand or enlarge the

capital by adding more assets; to make good the defalcation of another person: ออกปาก, ออกคำ to make a verbal promise; to express one's opinion; to speak; to ask (for aid, cooperation or support): ออกผัดาษ pox-marked (as over the face); to be suffering from small-pox: ออกไผ่ marked by pimples, papules, or pustules (as over the face); marked by pimples or comedones; to suffer from pimples and comedones: ออกพรรษา the last day of Buddhist lent, calculated to fall on the last day of the first fortnight of the eleventh lunar month (which is during October): ออกไฟ *lit.* "to cease lying by the fire," which is an ancient practice in parturition; to complete the puerperal state, condition or lying-in period; to rise from child-bed: ออกภาษา *lit.* "to exhibit (a foreign) language," *i. e.* to imitate the speech, attitudes or manners of foreigners in dramatic performances; to impersonate Chinese, Indians or Europeans in a play: ออกยาม to go off duty (as guards or watchmen): ออกรับ to represent a person in a quarrel; to render oneself a party in a quarrel, dispute or combat: ออกรับเบี้ยบำนาญ to retire on pension: ออกเรือ to set sail; to leave by boat: ออกร้าน to set up a stall for selling sundry articles (as at a fair): ออกโรง to stage a play or theatrical performance; to be the first appearance of actors or performers: ออกลูก to give birth to a child; to be delivered of a child; parturition: ออกเวร to complete a period of service performed by various persons in rotation (as the changing of the royal guards): ออกเสียง to express oneself with a loud voice; to read or sing with a loud, clear voice: ออกเสียงลงคะแนน to vote by ballot: ออกหน้า to precede; to head; to take the lead (as a horse in a race); to take the initiative in any matter; to act as a leader; to go before (as an advance guard): ออกหวย to announce the winning letter, ticket or number in a lottery; to write or issue tickets in the "letter lottery system": ออก-

หาก, ออกจากกัน to be separated from; to be disengaged; to retire from; to go away from; to let go of (as the dragon of eclipses withdraws from before the sun or moon).

อ่อง   aung⁴ *adj.* bright; clear; pure; see กระจ่าง p. 20:   อ่องขาว beautifully clear, sparkling, and spotless as cut glass: อ่อง-เอี่ยม spotless; bright; brand new.

อ่อง   aung² *Chin. n.* a king; a prince; a monarch; a sovereign; a tributary or vassal king.

อ้องแอ้ง   aung³ aang³ *adj.* feeble; weak; frail; thin; infirm (as pertaining to the physical condition of children); slouching, wabbling (as of gait); see แบบบาง under แบบ p. 490.

ออเซาะ   aw-saw⁶ *v.* to impose on (as by flattery); to cajole; to dupe; to wheedle (for the purpose of seduction); see ฉอเลาะ p. 266.

ออด   aut⁴ *adj.* whining; teasing; complaining; vexing; harassing with importunities: ออดๆ continually; repeatedly; endlessly: *onomat.* from the squeaking sound made by new shoes: ออดแอด feeble; weak; sickly; frail; debilitated; enervated (as one given to frequent spells of sickness).

อ๊อด, อ๊อดแอ๊ด   aut⁶ *onomat.* from the squeaking sound of machinery, or of a cartwheel.

อ่อน   aun⁴ *n.* a pretty maiden or woman: *adj.* soft; tender; feeble; flexible; pliable; gentle; humble; young; slight; not severe (as a sickness):   คำอ่อนหวานกำจัดโทษะ *idiomatic* a soft answer driveth away wrath: ลูกอ่อน a babe; an infant: สีอ่อน a soft or light colour: อ่อนเกล้า, น้อมเกล้า to bow the head in humility and reverential fear: อ่อนจิตต์, อ่อนใจ *idiomatic* to become discouraged; to get dispirited; to become dejected or depressed: อ่อนไท้ a queen; a woman of princely rank: อ่อนนวล (flesh) soft as down: อ่อนน้อม to yield to the dictates of another;

to consent; to accede; to submit to "the powers that be"; soft; yielding to the touch: อ่อนนุ่ม, อ่อนนิ่ม, อ่อนน่วม soft and yielding (as a pillow or mattress):   อ่อนปัญญา feeble-minded; reduced in wisdom or knowledge: อ่อนเปียก soft and wet (as a sponge, mud or clay):   อ่อนเพลีย to feel exhausted; to be enfeebled (as by disease or continuous labour); to become very tired: อ่อนโยน indulgent; polite; courteous; affable; obliging: อ่อน-ศักดิ์ a novice; one low in rank; one who has been degraded or removed from a position or rank: อ่อนหวาน soft and sweet; gentle and pleasing; agreeable (used in regard to words):   อ่อนหย่อน to be deficient; not to come up to the mark of high standing: อ่อนสวิงสวาย *idiomatic* weakened, debilitated, or exhausted (as from hunger or sickness).

อ้อน   aun³ *v.* to be given to shedding tears easily; to lack stability of mind; to cry; to scream; to bawl; to weep or sob on the least provocation (as do children):   เด็กมักอ้อน given to childish whining, crying or bawling: เสียอ้อนวอนไม่ได้ *idiomatic* to be unable to resist continual supplication: อ้อนวอน to supplicate humbly; to beg; to pray; to ask for with importunity; see อัฏฐฐาน p. 958.

ออนซอน, อ่อนซอน see อรชร p. 971.

อ้อนแอ้น   aun³-aan³ *adj.* frail; fragile; delicate; thin; breakable.

ออม   aum *v.* to save up; to husband; to collect together; to economize; to hoard or store away (as treasures); to allow to accumulate (as savings); see ประหยัด p. 505:   คลัง-ออมสิน a savings bank: ออมแรง to economize one's strength: ออมสิน to hoard or store away (as savings); to practice accumulating one's money: ออมอด to undergo deprivations of food for the purpose of economizing; to bear or endure hardships.

อ้อม   aum³ *v.* to go or travel in a circuitous, indirect or round-about course: *adj.* round-about: tortuous; winding: ทางอ้อม a detour; the long way round: ผ้าอ้อม a diaper: เดินอ้อมค้อม to take a devious, wandering, or indirect road: พูดอ้อมค้อม to converse in an indirect manner; to talk "around the bush": อ้อมค้อม in a round-about manner; in a circling or deviating course: อ้อมวก to go around in circles, but to come back again to the starting-point.

ออมซอม, ออมครอม aum-saum *adj.* clumsy; ill-fitting (as a garment); ill-shaped; awkward; uncouth.

อ้อมแอ้ม aum³-aam³ *adv.* indistinctly; not clearly; hesitatingly (in respect to conversational powers).

อ่อย oy⁴ *v.* to drop or scatter bait; to induce; to persuade: *n.* bait to lure fishes to congregate. For this purpose ants' nests, termite eggs or their young are thrown into the water. The fishes that are thus attracted are scooped up with hand-nets, or caught in a cast-net: *adv.* tardily; dilatorily; slowly; sluggishly; laggingly; lingeringly; lightly; gently: อ่อยกันมา to come straggling in, or together; to be tardy in arriving.

อ้อย (ต้น) oy³ *n. Saccharum officinarum* (*Gramineae*), sugar-cane, a tall grass or reed cultivated for the sake of the sugar obtained from the thick juicy stems. Sugar-cane has been known from remotest times but it is only during the Christian era that cultivation of it has developed until the present day commercial refining of sugar has produced an important new industry (BURK. p. 1925): น้ำอ้อย molasses made from the milled sugar-cane: หีบอ้อย to mill sugarcane stalks: อ้อยควั่น sugar-cane stems, peeled and cut into disks (usually hawked around for sale): อ้อยช้าง *Thai, Nakawn Sawan,* ตะคร้ำ *Thai, Kanburi* and *Ratburi,* กุ๊ก *N. Laos,* กอกกั่น *E. Laos,* เส้งลู่ไค้ *Karen, Chiengmai,* แม่อขูร้าย *Karen, Kanburi* (ต้น) *Odina wodier* (*Anacardiaceae*); *Heteropanax frag-*

rans (*Araliaceae*) (CB. pp. 352, 802): อ้อยแดง a species of red-stemed sugar-cane.

อ่อย oy² *adj.* vivid; bright; striking; *descriptive of a yellow colour,* as เหลืองอ่อย: *onomat.* from the sound of friction of a wheel on the axle of a cart.

อ้อยส้อย, อ้อยอิ่ง oy³-soy³ *adj.* dilatory; sluggish; lingering; indolent; slow; inactive.

ออระหัน aw-ra⁶-hun² *n.* a mythical monster having the body of a bird and the head of man.

อ้อแอ้ aw³-aa³ *adv.* indistinctly; imperfectly; inaccurately: *onomat.* from the indistinct sounds a child makes when trying to pronounce some words.

อะคร้าว see มาก p. 647; ยิ่ง p. 647.

อะเคอ see งาม p. 223; สวย p. 829.

อะดัก ah⁴-duk⁴ *adj.* perplexed; embarrassed; anxious; troublesome; troublous; worried; being in a "tight fix": อะดักอะแด่ *idiomatic* puzzled; confused; distracted (to the fullest degree or extent).

อะดุง ah⁴-doong *adj.* highest; most excellent; beyond comparison; *par excellence.*

อะนะ ah⁴-na⁶ *Jav. n.* a child; an infant; offspring; see บุตร p. 484.

อะนั้น a⁴-nun⁵ *the poetical form of* อันนั้น that; that one; that thing.

อะนี้ a⁴-nee⁵ *the poetical form of* อันนี้ this; this one; this thing.

อะร้าอร่าม a⁴-rah⁵-a⁴-ram⁴ *v.* to be anxious for; to be watchful on all sides; to be on the alert; to be wary as to what may happen on any front (as with an army).

อะไร a⁴-rai what? an interrogation: *adv.* in what respect; to what extent.

อะลุ้มอล่วย a⁴-loom⁵-a⁴-lu-ie⁴ *v.* to apply a give-and-take policy; to use conciliatory methods; to pacify; to quiet; to soothe; to appease by making concessions.

อะเอื้อย a⁴-eur-ie³ *adv.* clearly; slowly; freely; pleasingly (as the notes of birds chirping or warbelling).

อะหม a⁴-hom² *n.* the Assamese; a race of people inhabiting the north-eastern corner of India.

อะไหล่ a⁴-lai⁴ *n.* spare parts; parts held in reserve (as for machinery); parts intended for replacing those which are broken or lost.

อัก uk⁴ *n.* bobbins or spools for winding different sizes of cotton or silk threads, separately.

อั้ก, อั๊ก uk³ *onomat.* from the sound caused by a blow on the chest with the fist.

อักก์, อรรก uk⁴ *P. n.* the sun; the sun's rays or light (chd. p. 25).

อักโกธะ uk⁴-gkoh-ta⁶ *P. n. lit.* "the condition of freedom from wrath, *i. e.* mildness; conciliation (chd. p. 25).

อักข ๑ uk⁴ *P. n.* the axles of wheels, cars or waggons; the clavicle; the collar bone (chd. p. 25).

อักข ๒ uk⁴ *P. n.* die; quoits; dice (used in gambling games).

อักข ๓ uk⁴ *P. n.* the eyeball; the organ [of sight.

อักขณะ uk⁴-ka⁴-na⁶ *P. n.* an unpropitious, or unauspicious time; an unfavourable occasion; a time of ill-omen, or bad luck (chd. p. 24).

อักขระ uk⁴-ka⁴-ra⁴ *P. n.* a letter of the alphabet (chd. p. 24); consonants; written characters; words; sounds of letters: *adj.* unchangeable; unalterable; imperishable: อักขรวิธี a treatise dealing with the construction of words, rules for spelling, reading and writing: อักขรสมัย the (standard) rules for spelling, reading and writing.

อักขาน uk⁴-karn² *P. n.* the act of telling stories, tales or legends; a recitation of fables, myths, traditions (chd. p. 24).

อักโข uk⁴-koh² *adj.* very much; very many; in great abundance, as มีเงินอักโข.

อักโขภิณี, อักโขเภณี, อักเษาหิณี uk⁴-koh²-pi⁶-nee *P. n.* one of the high numerals; a figure followed by 42 ciphers; a host; an army in full fighting strength.

อักษร uk⁴-saun² *S. n.* a letter (of the alphabet); a word, sentence, sounds of words, vowels and consonants: *adj.* unchangeable; unalterable; imperishable (S. E. D. p. 3): อักษรบฏ lesson leaves; sheets; posters: อักษรประโยค abbreviations; contracted forms of words, as gr. Dr. lb. Mr.: อักษรลักษณ์ important documents, or letters (as Wills or Title Deeds): อักษรเลข a numerical code; figures used in place of letters: อักษรศาสตร์ literature; literary work; literary productions; publications; writings; the science that treats of composition: อักษรศาสน์ newspapers; travelogues; descriptive letters; accounts of travel or expeditions: อักษรสมัย a method or system of (proper) reading and writing: อักษรสังโยค orthography; a mode or system of spelling and composing.

อักเสบ uk⁴-sep⁴ *n.* inflammation; a morbid process in some part of the body, characterized by heat, redness, swelling and pain.

อักอ่วน (ใจ) uk⁴-oo-an⁴ *adj.* uncertain; undecided; perplexed; confused; bewildered.

อัคนิ, อัคนี, อัคคิ, อัคคี uk⁴-ni⁶ *P. S. n.* fire; the sacrifical fire; the god of Fire (S. E. D. p. 5): อัคคีภัย a pestilential fire: อัคนิคณะ the flames of a fire: อัคนิพ่าห์, อัคนิวาหะ the smoke of a fire: อัคนิพืช pure gold: อัคนิรุทร a most destructive conflagration; a violent blaze: อัคนิโหตร the ceremony of an oblation to the god of Fire (usually with milk and oil).

อัคร, อรรค, อัคค์   uk[4] *S. adj.* pre-eminent; foremost; chief; first in rank; principal (S. E. D. p. 6):   อัครชายา   *lit.* "the first in rank, or chief wife," *i. e.* a queen; an empress: อัครมหาเสนาบดี a prime minister; chief of the ministerial body: อัครมเหสี   a queen; a royal consort; an empress; an empress dowager: อัครราชทูต an ambassador; a minister plenipotentiary.

อัง   ung *v.* to place before, or to hold near a fire; to toast before a fire (as hands and feet); see ผิง p. 547; ลน p. 727:   อังไฟ to expose to the warmth of a fire (as while drying clothes); to stretch out before a fire: อังมือ to warm the hands before a fire.

อังกนะ   ung-gka[4]-na[6] *S. n.* the act of ciphering, writing, marking, stamping with figures, or branding (as the numbering of the pages of a book) (S. E. D. p. 7).

อังกฤษ   ung-gkrit[4] *n.* English: ทอง-อังกฤษ thin, glittering gold-foil or tinsel, used as material to make artificial ornaments (as rosettes, leaves or flowers for the decorations of cremation buildings or coffins).

อังกวด   ung-gku-at[4] *Jav. n.* a Javanese musical instrument resembling the jew's-harp; see จ้องหน่อง p. 234.

อังกะลุง   ung-gka[4]-loong *n.* angklung, the indigenous percussion musical instrument of western Java. Especially in the Preanger district of western Java the angklung is ubiquitous. Scholars hold that it is one of the most ancient musical instruments in Java and that it was known there long before the arrival of the first Hindu immigrants. This makes the fact all the more interesting that it should to this day have remained so highly esteemed. The angklung produces its music by being shaken. As a rule it consists of three bamboo tubes suspended vertically within a framework in such a manner that they move when the instrument is shaken.

At their upper ends these tubes are cut off at a slant, in the way one used to sharpen a quill. At the bottom end they are closed by one of the natural partitions that split up bamboo. At that end two short projections are found that slide back and forth in a narrow slit cut into the tube which forms the base of the framework. By shaking the instrument, vibrations are set up in the suspended bamboo tubes, the exact tone of which depends upon the shape, length and thickness of the tone-tubes. The strength of the tune is determined by shaking the frame with greater or less vigour.

Only the best quality bamboo must be used for the making of angklungs, and freshly cut reeds are useless. They must first be carefully dried and seasoned indoors before the expert can start on his work of turning them into musical instruments.

The angklung is essentially an instrument to be played in the open air. It is there that its enormous volume of sound can be fully developed, and that one can best enjoy its bell-like tones that will reverberate away into far distances (From the Nederland Mail, Vol. 6, No. 4, April 1939).

อังกา   see   องก์   p. 955.

อังกาบ, อโนชา (ต้น)   ung-gkarp[4] *n. Barleria cristata (Acanthaceae)*, a free flowering, dense shrub, having white, mauve or rose-pink flowers; *Barleria prionitis*, a small, stiff, prickly plant, up to five feet in height, found throughout tropical Africa and Asia; as it is often cultivated, it obtains an extension by man, but there is no reason for thinking it is not a native of both Africa and Asia. In the Malay Peninsula it spreads in from the north for a short distance, as a wild plant. When planted in hedges, as in India and Java, it strengthens and makes them more impenetrable by reason of its spines. In India the bitter juice of the leaves is given to children for catarrh; in Java the leaves are chewed for toothache; in Thailand a febrifuge is prepared from its roots. The juice of the leaves is applied externally to the feet to prevent cracking. A poultice of the leaves is used in Java for ringworm, rheumatism, etc. (MCM. pp. 72, 140: BURK. p. 303): อังกาบสี่ปุ่น (ต้น) *Crossandra undulae-folia,* a shrub of the Old World, having pinkish orange blossoms (MCM. p. 141: BURK. p. 684).

อังกุร, อังกูร ung-gkoo^4-ra^6 *P. S. n.* a sprout; a shoot; a blade; descendents of a family line (S. E. D. p. 7).

อังกุศ ung-gkoot^4 *S. n.* a hook with which to guide an elephant; a hooked goad; a mahout's hook (chd. p. 35).

อังคณะ ung-ka^6-na^6 *S. n.* a lawn; a yard; a court; an area (S. E. D. p. 8).

อังคณา ung-ka^6-nah *P. n.* a woman; a maiden (chd. p. 33).

อังคาด ung-kart^3 *v.* to give; to elevate and present, thereby showing respect; to supply (implying to Buddhist monks).

อังคาร ung-karn *P. S. n.* the planet Mars; live coals; embers; ashes; charcoal (S. E. D. p. 8): วันอังคาร Tuesday.

อังคีรส ung-kee-rot^6 *P. S. n.* a title for one of the Buddhas; a name for one of the rishi or hermits who composed lauditory hymns appearing in the Vedas (chd. p. 34: H. C. D. p. 16).

อังคุษฐ์ ung-koot^6 *S. n.* the thumb (chd. p. 34).

อังฆาต ung-kart^3 *v.* to foster silent revenge; to seek an opportunity to retaliate; to avenge oneself for some wrong or insult: *n.* rancour; malice; spitefulness.

อั้งยี่ ung^3-yee^3 *n.* a Chinese secret society or club composed of outlaws; the Chinese "underworld".

อั้งโล่ ung^3-loh^3 *n.* a charcoal brazier of Chinese origin, made of terra cotta, with a perforated grate.

อังวะ ung-wa^6 *n.* Ava; the ancient capital of Burma.

อังศ, องศ์ (p. 955) ung-sa^4·*S. n.* a part; a portion; a share; a piece; a fragment (chd. p. 29); a portion of an angle.

อังศุ ung-soo^4 *S. n.* a thread; a filament; a cord; a string; a ray; a gleam; a streak of light; a sunbeam (chd. p. 29): อังศุธร, อังศุ-มาลี the sun.

อังศุก ung-sook^4 *S. n.* cloth; fine cloth; thin muslin (chd. p. 29).

อังสนา ung-sa^4-nah *Jav. n.* flowers of *Pterocarpus cambodianus* (*Leguminosae*); see ประดู่ (ต้น) p. 499.

อังสะ, อังสา ung-sa^4 *n.* the shoulder (chd. p. 29); a broad band worn over the shoulder, by the Buddhist monks: อังสกุฏ the a-cromial process of the scapula; the hump on the back of Indian bulls: อังสภาระ a load to be carried on the shoulder.

อัจกลับ ut^4-chja^4-gklup^4 *n.* a brass lantern decorated with fancy pendants and tassels.

อัจจะ ut^4-chja^4 *P. v.* to worship; to adore; to venerate; to hold in reverence (as by making offerings).

อัจจิ ut^4-chji^4 *P. n.* a flame; rays of a light; the light of a fire; a sunbeam (chd. p. 9).

อัจจิมา ut^4-chji^4-mah *P. n.* fire (chd. p. 9): *adj.* radiant; shining; glowing; beaming.

อัจจุต ut^4-chjoot^4 *P. adj.* immovable; permanent; sure; everlasting; eternal (chd. p. 9).

อัจฉรา ๑ ut^4-cha^4-rah *P. n.* celestial nymphs; attendants on Indra (chd. p. 8).

อัจฉรา ๒ ut^4-cha^4-rah *n.* a second; an instant or moment of time; the time of snapping a finger, or of the winking of an eyelid (chd. p. 8).

อัจฉริย, อัจเฉระ ut[4]-cha[4]-ri[6]-ya[6] *adj.* wonderful; marvellous; extraordinary; astonishing (chd. p. 9); surprising; amazing: อัจฉริยบุคคล a marvellous or wonderful person (as the Buddha); a dictator; an emperor.

อัชฌัตติก ut[4]-chut[6]-dtik[4] *P. adj.* relating or belonging to the individual or self; personal; internal; subjective (chd. p. 22).

อัชฌา ut[4]-chah *n.* politeness; courteousness; affability; a conciliatory spirit.

อัชฌาจาร ut[4]-chah-chjarn *P. n.* impoliteness; transgression of the customs of the country; excesses; offences against propriety; misbehaviour (chd. p. 21).

อัชฌาสัย, อัธยาศัย ut[4]-chah-sai[2] *P. n.* purpose; intention; inclination; disposition (chd. p. 21).

อัญ, อัญขยม un *Cam. pron.* I; me.

อัญชนะ un-cha[6]-na[6] *P. n.* a medicated oil; an eye lotion; a collyrium applied to the eyelashes to darken them (chd. p. 35).

อัญชลี, อัญชุลี un-cha[6]-lee *P. S. n.* an appropriate salutation given by placing the hands palm to palm and raising them to the face or chest; a respectful salutation performed by raising the joined hands to the forehead (chd. p. 35); see ชุลี p. 300.

อัญชัน, อังชัน un-chun *Thai, Lomsak,* เอื้องงัน *Laos, Chiengmai* (ต้น) *n. Clitoria ternatea (Leguminosae)*, a climber with conspicuous blue flowers, probably South American, but now found throughout the tropics. It must have been carried to India very early, and from India it was sent to gardens in Europe about the end of the seventeenth century. It probably reached Malaysia from India. In Malaysia the flowers have long been used to colour rice, as the rice when boiled with them is turned blue. It has been said that, in various places, the dye of the flowers has been used to give a fleeting colour to white cloth. It is used on matting in the Rhio Archipelago. The colour can be used in the same way as litmus, as a reagent for detecting acid and alkaline liquids. Sheep and goats will eat the foliage. The seeds are aperient, and contain a toxic alkaloid; the roots are cathartic. The leaves are used as poultices in Java, and the juice of the flowers for inflamed eyes. In the Philippine Islands the seeds are used in poultices for swollen joints. The plant has been used as a green manure, but it climbs too much, though it is fair in some respects on land that is to be fallow for a short time (burk. p. 588); *Dalbergia duperreana (Leguminosae)* (cb. pp. 436, 477: mcm. pp. 124, 140).

อัญเชิญ un-chern *adj.* welcoming guests with respect; supplicating one to come to, or in.

อัญญะ un-ya[6] *P. adj.* other; other than; different from (chd. p. 36): อัญญดิตถี believers in religions other than Buddhism.

อัฏฏี ut[4] *P. n.* a legal case, action or lawsuit; a cause (chd. p. 70); see คดี p. 175.

อัฏฐ ๑, อัฐ ut[4] *P. adj.* eight (chd. p. 66): *n.* an att, an ancient copper coin, being one eighth of a fuang in value, or one sixty-fourth part of a baht: อัฏฐังค์ eight parts or divisions; eight tiers, steps or degrees (as of a ladder); eight qualities or attributes (chd. p. 67): อัฏฐังคิกะ composed of eight divisions; eight-fold (chd. p. 67): อัฏฐังคิกมรรค the eight-fold path, as pointed out by the Buddha, whereby one can escape from the miseries of existence (chd. p. 67): อัฏฐังสะ an octagonal figure.

อัฏฐ ๒ see อรรถ p. 971.

อัฏฐมะ ut[4]-ta[4]-ma[6] *P. n.* one eighth part: *adj.* eighth (chd. p. 67).

อัฏฐิ, อัฐิ ut[4]-ti[4] *P. n.* a bone; fragments of bone; the kernel, pit or stone of fruit; a seed; a burnt bone relic (chd. p. 68): อัฐิ-

มิญฺชะ marrow of bones (chd. p. 69): อัฏฐิ-
สัณฐาน a skeleton; the shape or configuration
of bones.

อัฑฒ์ ut⁴ *P. n.* a half; a part; a portion
(chd. p. 10); see ครึ่ง p. 182: อัฑฒจันทฺ์ an
amphitheatre; a crescent-shaped cupboard or
sideboard; crescent-shaped, semicircular, half-
moon-shaped articles: อัฑฒมณฑล a semicircle: อัฑฒมาส half of a month; a fortnight: อัฑฒรัตติ midnight.

อัณฑะ un-ta⁶ *P. S. n.* an egg; the testicles
(S. E. D. p. 134): อัณฑโกส an egg-shell:
อัณฑชะ *lit.* "born from eggs," *i. e.* a bird; a
fish (chd. p. 33): อัณฑาการ oval; ovoid;
ovoidal; elliptical.

อัด ut⁴ *v.* to compress; to crowd in together; to press; to squeeze; to condense:
adj. having a full front view (as a picture or
photograph); facing frontwise: อัดอั้น oppressed; crushed; weighed down; perplexed;
completely at a loss as to what to do next:
อัดแอ crowded; thronged; closely packed in
together: อัดควัน to hold inhaled smoke
(as from a cigarette).

อัตคัด ut⁴-dta⁴-kat⁶ *v.* to be in want; to
be hard-pressed (for the necessities of life):
adj. indigent; needy; starving; poor; penniless; destitute; in a straightened condition
(financially); hard up; see ขัดสน under ขัด
p. 150.

อัตต์ ut⁴ *P. n.* oneself; one's body; one's
own person; an individual life, mind, soul
(chd. p. 65): อัตตภาพ person; self; individual; one's personality (chd. p. 65); one's
natural temperament or disposition: อัตตวิ-
นิบาตกรรม suicide: อัตตหิต personal advantages, gain, benefits or profits: อัตตเหตุ
selfishness; self-interest; self-love.

อัตตโนมัติ ut⁴-dta⁴-noh-mut⁶ *P. n.* one's
private opinions or views; one's conclusions,
or convictions; see ลำพัง p. 742.

อัตถิ์ ut⁴ *P. n.* disappearance; wane (chd.
p. 67); the condition of vanishing, decreasing,
fading away (as the rays of a setting sun).

อัตรชะ ut⁴-dta⁴-ra⁶-cha⁶ *P. adj. lit.* "born
from one's self," *i. e.* offspring; a son; a
daughter; children (chd. p. 65).

อัตรา ut⁴-dtrah *n.* rate; limit; standard
(as prescribed by custom or law); scale of
proportion; assignment: อัตราเร่ง rate of
acceleration: อัตราแลกเปลี่ยนเงิน the rate of
money exchange.

อัทธ์, อัทธา, อัทธาน ut⁴ *P. n.* a road; a
way; a journey; the distance covered or traversed; stage; occasion (chd. p. 10): อัทธคต
one who has made a long (life's) journey;
one who has lived for a long time; an aged
person: อัทธคู a traveller; an adventurer;
a tourist; a globe-trotter: อัทธายุ a lifetime.

อัธยาตมวิทยา ut⁴-ta⁶-yart³-ma⁶-wit⁶-ta⁶-
yah *S. n.* psychology.

อัธยาศัย see อัชฌาสัย p. 983.

อัน un *n.* a turn; a round; a spell; a
change in some succession or rotation (as a
game of cards or a cock-fight); *a numerical
designation for various small things as
pieces of kindling wood; a relative pronoun
who, which, that:* เป็นอันขาด absolutely
nothing doing; entirely unpermitted: เป็น-
อันมาก in great abundance: สองอัน two of
such things: อันดี the good one: อันเดียว
only one: อันที่ดี that good one: อันนี้
this one: อันนั้น that one: อันโน้น that
thing yonder: อันเป็นขึ้น an unexpected
calamity, event or accident: อันว่า that is
to say; as for instance; now then; *an ancient
form for the beginning of an explanation,
speech or address:* อันหนึ่ง, อันเดียว one of
those things: อันไหน ๆ ก็ได้ any one will
do; just any thing: อันไหนอันใด which
one? what one?

อั้น   un[3] *v.* to misfire (as a bomb); to fail to explode (as a fire-cracker); to be smothered; to be suppressed; to be stifled; to become deadened or non-active: อั้นตัน oppressed; choked; silenced; obstructed; stifled; see กลั้น p. 60:   อั้นตู้ baffled with difficulties and perplexities; unable to think or devise (ways out of a critical situation):   อั้นอ้น silenced; speechless; balked; confused; foiled: อั้นลม, อั้นใจ to hold one's breath: อั้นตันใจ to be thwarted; to be baffled on all sides.

อั้น   un[2] *adj.* fat; corpulent; plump; sturdy.

อันดับ   un-dup[4] *n.* series; order; rank; file or sequence; Buddhist monks of junior standing or rank.

อันด๊าก   un-dark[6] *Peguan n.* the tongue.

อันโด๊ก   un-doke[6] *Peguan n.* tortoise; turtle.

อันต ๑   un-dta[4] *P. S. n.* boundary; limit; end (of a course); finality; a concluding act; destruction; death (chd. p. 39):   อันตก, อันตก *lit.* "one who causes the end to come," *i. e.* death; the god of Death; Yama (chd. p. 37): อันตกร *lit.* "one who performs (his duties) to the last," *i. e.* one who helps others to reach a state of bliss.   The inference is the Buddha: อันตกาล the time of death: อันตคู one who reaches the end; one who conquers sorrow, sufferings, and trouble: อันตชาติ one of low birth or caste.

อันต ๒   un-dta[4] *P. n.* the intestines; entrails; bowels (chd. p. 37):   อันตคุณ the small intestines; the coiled up intestines.

อันตร, อันดร   un-dta[4]-ra[6] *P. S. n.* a hole; a cavity; the interior; the midst; an undergarment; the space enclosed or included; opportunity: *adj.* inner; inside; middle: *adv.* within; among; in (chd. p. 37):   อันตร- การณ์ obstacle; hindrance; obstruction; barrier; impediment: อันตรวาสก an undergarment. being one of the three garments worn by

Buddhist monks (chd. p. 38).

อันตรธาน, ดรธาน   un-dta[4]-ra[6]-tarn *P. S. v.* to disappear; to vanish from sight; to become as vapour: *n.* disappearance; concealment; the condition of being invisible or vanishing from sight (S. E. D. p. 44):   อันตร- ธานสูญหาย to vanish completely out of sight.

อันตราย   un-dta[4]-rai *P. S. n.* obstacle; impediment; prevention; hindrance; danger; peril; calamity; misfortune (chd. p. 38): อันตรายิกธรรม *lit.* "impediments," "disqualifications," *i. e.* conditions or circumstances which disqualify a man for entering the Buddhist brotherhood (as debt, disease, etc.) (chd. p. 38).

อันติก   un-dti[4]-gka[4] *P.S. n.* vicinity; proximity; nearness: *adj.* near; near to; near by; in the neighborhood of (chd. p. 38).

อันเต, อันโต   un-dtay *adj.* inside; within; in among; inner; interior: อันเตบุระ, อันเต- ปุระ within the royal precincts; inside a royal palace or enclosure: อันเตบุริก, อันเตปุริก officials of the Royal Household: อันเตบุริกา, อันเตปุริกา ladies-in-waiting of the Royal Household; women acting as guards, watch-women or police; see สนม p. 811:   อันเตวาสิก *lit.* "one on the inside," *i. e.* a pupil; a student: อันโตชน *lit.* "one belonging to the inner precincts," *i. e.* a wife; children; servants.

อันทุ   un-too[6] *P. S. n.* a chain; manacles; shackles; fetters; ankle chains for elephants (chd. p. 33).

อันโทน   un-tone *Cam. v.* to wander about; to travel or tour from place to place.

อันธ, อนธ   un-ta[6] *P. S. adj.* blind (chd. p. 33); cloudy (as of sight); stupid; simple; senseless; dense; ignorant: อันธการ, อนธการ darkness; blindness; cloudiness; ignorance: อันธพาล a person bereft of reason, conducting himself as though blind; one densely ignorant, stupid or illiterate.

[night.
อันธิกา   un-ti[6]-gkah *S. n.* night-time; mid-

อันนะ   un-na[6] *P. S. n.* food; boiled rice (chd. p. 35); victuals; food in a mystical sense (S. E. D. p. 45).

อันย   un-ya[6] *S. adj.* other than; differing from; opposed to another; different (S. E. D. p. 45): อันยพรต *lit.* "alienated affection," *i. e.* untrue; unloyal to; inconstant; insincere: อันยรูป allotropic: อันยสังคม *lit.* "one mingling with others," *i. e.* a paramour; an adulterer or adulteress.

อันโยนย   un-yone-ya[6] *S. n.* mutual; one another; together (S. E. D. p. 46): อันโยนย-สรรพนาม *a relative pronoun* who, which, that.

อันวย, อันวัย   un-wa[6]-ya[6] *n.* connection; coordination; the condition of following or obeying established rules, customs, or precedents: *adj.* harmonizing: *adv.* according to; in accordance or agreement with; in conformity to: อันวยสันธาน *gram.* a coordinate conjunction.

อันวยาเนกัตถ, อเนกัตถประโยค   un-wa[6]-yah-nay-gkut[4]-ta[4] *n. gram.* a compound sentence.

อันเวส   un-wet[3] *P. n.* research; examination; exploration; investigation (chd. p. 46).

อับ   up[4] *n. (Chin.* อั้บ) a small toilet box of wood, ivory, or silver with a tight-fitting lid; see ตลับ p. 346: *adj.* (1) sour; fetid; stale; musty; unventillated; close; muggy; (2) deficient; deprived; wanting; lacking: ถึงที่อับจน to have reached the condition of misery, poverty and want: อับจน, อับเงิน extreme distress; reduced to the last extremity; impoverished (to the utmost degree): อับ-ปัญญา to be slow of intelligence; to be stupid, dull, and uncomprehensive: อับลง to decrease; to become damaged; to lose one's standing in society: อับสี to become faded or less decided in colour: อับแสง to become less bright; to be obscured, (as sun's rays): อับอาย shameful; disgraceful; degrading; infamous; ignominious.

อับเฉา   up[4]-chow[2] *n.* ballast; weights (to steady ships or boats).

อับปาง   up[4]-bpang *v.* to become wrecked or injured; to capsize; to sink; to reach a condition of being a total loss (as of ships).

อัป   up[4] *adv.* off; away; from: *adj.* free from; lacking in; wanting in; *used in composition with verbs and their derivities* (chd. p. 46).

อัปป ๑, อัลป   up[4]-bpa[4] *adj.* little; slight; unimportant; few; not much or many (chd. p. 52); trifling; small; minor; *used as a prefix*: อัปปทรัพย์, อัปปธน *lit.* "having but little money," *i. e.* poor; financially wrecked: อัปปพุทธิ with but little knowledge; foolish; stupid; dull of comprehension: อัปปวัย childish; young; still a junior; youthful; adolescent: อัปปวิชช์ uneducated; ignorant; with but little learning, training or experience.

อัปป ๒   up[4]-bpa[4] *a negative prefix* no, not, never; see ไม่ p. 660.

อัปปกะ, อัลปกะ   up[4]-bpa[4]-gka[4] *P. adj.* little; slight; few; trifling (chd. p. 51).

อัปปการ   up[4]-bpa[4]-gkarn *P. adj.* ugly; deformed; ill-made.

อัปปฏิฆะ   up[4]-bpa[4]-dti[4]-ka[6] *P. adj.* unopposed; unobstructed; unhindered (chd. p. 52).

อัปปฏิภาค   up[4]-bpa[4]-dti[4]-park[3] *P. adj.* incomparable; unparalleled.

อัปภาคย์   up[4]-bpa[4]-park[3] *S. adj.* unfortunate; lacking in luck or good fortune; see ภาคย์ p. 613.

อัปมงคล, อปมงคล   up[4]-bpa[4]-mong-kon *P. S. adj.* of bad augury; of bad omen; unauspicious; unpromising; unpropitious; unfavourable; unlucky; see มงคล p. 619.

อัปยศ, อปยศ   up[4]-bpa[4]-yot[6] *adj.* disgraceful; dishonourable; degraded; infamous.

อัประมาณ, อประมาณ, อัปปมาณ   up[4]-bpra[4]-

marn *S. adj.* incalculable; unlimited; boundless; infinite; innumerable (chd. p. 51); see ประมาณ p. 503.

อัประมาท, อประมาท, อัปปมาท up⁴-bpra⁴-mart⁴ *S. n.* vigilance; carefulness; thoughtfulness; earnestness; zeal; diligence (chd. p. 51); see ประมาท p. 503.

อัประไมย, อประไมย, อัปปไมย up⁴-bpra⁴-mai *adj.* unlimited; boundless; innumerable; abundant; ample.

อัปราชัย, อปราชัย up⁴-bpa⁴-rah-chai *P.S. adj. lit.* "lacking in defeat," *i. e.* victorious; undefeated; unvanquished.

อัปลักษ์, อปลักษ์ up⁴-bpa⁴-luk⁶ *adj. lit.* "deficient in goodness," *i. e.* low; wicked; bad; inferior.

อัปสร up⁴-saun² *S. n.* Apsarases; celestial nymphs. They are fairy-like beings, beautiful and voluptuous, the celebrated nymphs of Indra's heaven. The name, which signifies "moving in the water," has some analogy to that of Aphrodite, the Greek goddess of Love (H. C. D. p. 19); see นางฟ้า under นาง p. 450.

อัพพุท up⁴-poot⁶ *P. n.* a high numeral; a figure followed by fifty-six cyphers (chd. p. 2).

อัพภันดร, อัพภันตร up⁴-pun-daun *P. n.* the space inside; the middle; the part that is internal; a standard of measurement equal to about seven *wah* or fourteen meters (chd. p 2).

อัพภาน up⁴-parn *P. n.* the rehabilitation of a priest who has undergone penance for an expiable offence (chd. p. 2): สวดอัพภาน the prayers recited on such an occasion.

อัม um *S. n.* sickness; ill-health; disease; fear; pestilence (chd. p. 28): อัมพาต paralysis.

อัมพ um-pa⁶ *P. n.* the mango tree (chd. p. 28): อัมพวัน a grove of mango trees; a mango orchard.

อัมพร um-paun *P. S. n.* apparel; clothes; garments; sky; atmosphere (S. E. D. p. 83): ทิคัมพร *lit.* "wearing the air," *i. e.* nudity.

อัมพา um-pah *P. S. n.* a mother; a good woman; an epithet for the goddess Durga (S. E. D. p. 23).

อัมพิล um-pi⁶-la⁶ *P. adj.* sour; acetous; tart; acid (chd. p. 28).

อัมพุ um-poo⁶ *P. S. n.* water (chd. p. 28): อัมพุช *lit.* "water born," *i. e.* the lotus; fishes: อัมพุชินี a lotus-lake or pond: อัมพุท *lit.* "a giver of water," *i. e.* a cloud: อัมพุนาถ *lit.* "lord of waters," *i. e.* the ocean; the sea: อัมพุนิธิ *lit.* "a treasury of water," *i. e.* the ocean; the sea: อัมพุพ่าห์, อัมพุวาหะ *lit.* "conveyers of water," *i. e.* clouds.

อัยย ai-ya⁶ *n.* a master, chief or lord: กรมอัยยการ the Public Prosecutor's Department: อัยยการ a public prosecutor.

อัยยกา, อัยยกะ ai-ya⁶-gkah *n.* a grandfather.

อัยยก, อัยยิกา ai-ya⁶-gkee *n.* a grand- [mother.

อัลป see อัปป ๑ (p. 986): อัลปการย์ a matter of trifling importance.

อัลละ un-la⁶ *P. adj.* fresh; moist; damp [(chd. p. 27).

อัลละมังด์ un-la⁶-mung *n.* pewter vessels or utensils; an alloy, usually of tin and lead.

อัศว, อัสส ut⁴-sa⁴-wa⁶ *S. n.* a horse; a stallion (S. E. D. p. 114): อัศวโกวิท skilled with horses: อัศวทูต a messenger on horseback: อัศวบดี master of the horse; chief of the horsemen: อัศวปะ a groom; a hostler: อัศวภาร loads carried on horse-back: อัศวมุข, อัศวมุขี *lit.* "having the head of a horse," *i. e.* mythical beings with the form of a man and the head of a horse. They are celestial choristers and musicians dwelling in the paradise of Kuvera on Kailasa (H. C. D. p. 158): อัศวเมธ the horse sacrifice. This is a sacrifice which in Vedic times was performed by kings desirous of offspring (H. C. D. p. 28): อัศวราช *lit.* "lord-of-horses," *i. e.* master of the royal horse: กรมอัศวราช the Department of The Royal Horse.

อัศวานึก, อัสสานิก, อัสสานึก, อัสสานึก
ut⁴-sa⁴-wah-neuk⁶ *n.* cavalary; cavalarymen; horsemen.

อัศวิน ut⁴-sa⁴-win *n. lit.* "the horsemen," *i. e.* two Vedic deities, twin sons of the sun or the sky. They are ever young, handsome, bright, and of a golden brilliancy, agile, swift as falcons and possessed of many forms; and they ride in a golden car drawn by horses or birds as harbingers of the dawn (H. C. D. p. 29).

อัษฎ, อัษฎ ut⁴-sa⁴-da⁴ *S. n.* the numeral eight (S. E. D. p. 116): อัษฎมงคล, อัษฎมงคล eight propitious things, *viz.* a lion, a bull, an elephant, a water-jar, a fan, a flag, a trumpet, and a lamp: อัษฎางคิกมรรค the Eight-fold Path, *viz.* right views, right thoughts, right speech, right actions, right living, right exertions, right recollections, right meditations (Ala. p. 200).

[p. 117.]
อัษฎมะ ut⁴-dta⁴-ma⁶ *S. adj.* eighth (S. E. D.

อัสดง, อัสดม ut⁴-sa⁴-dong *adj.* obscured; eclipsed; darkened; disappeared; settled or gone down (as regarding the sun).

อัสสดร ut⁴-sa⁴-daun *n.* an excellent horse; a horse of good breeding: อัสสดรวิหค a mythical monster; a bird-horse: อัสสดรเหรา a mythical monster; a horned lion-horse.

อัสสาส ut⁴-sah²-sa⁴ *P. n.* inhaled air; expirations; the condition of unlaboured respiration, *i.e.*, comfort, refreshment (Chd. p. 61).

อัสสุ, อัสสุชล ut⁴-soo⁴ *n.* tears (Chd. p. 61): อัสสุธารา the condition of shedding tears.

อา, อาว ah *n.* a father's younger brother or sister; an aunt; an uncle: *onomat.* from

the sound expressive of surprise, satisfaction, admiration or approval: อาเขย the husband of the father's younger sister: อาสะใภ้ the wife of the father's younger brother.

อ่า ah⁴ *adv.* adorned; decked; stunning; beautified; graceful; freshened up; neatly dressed; see ผึ่งผาย under ผึ่ง p. 548: อ่าองค์ august; dignified; neat; tasteful; elegant (as princes or royalty in full-dress attire): อ่าโอ่, อ่าโฉม pompous; gorgeous; showy; elegant (as dress and bearing).

อ้า ah³ *v.* to open; to spread; to expand; to unclose; see เปิด p. 535: ถ่างขา, อ้าซ่า to spread the legs immodestly: อ้าก้าม to open the nippers (as do crabs or prawns): อ้าซ่า openly; impolitely; immodestly; indecently; unblushingly: อ้าปาก, อ้าโอษฐ์ to open the mouth: อ้ามือ, แบมือ to hold up the open hand in the attitude of begging.

อากร ah-gkaun *n.* revenue: *P.* a mine; a multitude; a rich source of anything (Chd. p. 23): ภาษีอากร taxes: นายอากร a farmer or holder of government monopolies (secured by being the highest bidder).

อากังขา ah-gkung-kah² *P. n.* a wish; a desire or purpose; a hope or intention (Chd. p. 22).

อากัมป, อากัมปนะ ah-gkum-bpa⁴ *S. n.* the condition of shaking, trembling, quivering, quaking, tottering (S. E. D. p. 126).

อาการ ah-gkarn *P. S. n.* a symptom; a token; a sign; indication; characteristics; condition; appearance; shape; mien; bearing; a constituent part of the body (Chd. p. 23): บอกอาการ to describe the symptoms; to report on the condition of affairs: อาการ-สามสิบสอง the thirty two integral members or organs of the body, as hair, teeth, skin, finger- and toe-nails, heart, lungs, stomach, brain, etc.: อาการแห่งหน้า *idiomatic* countenance; facial expression.

อากาศ ah-gkart[4] *S. n.* air; atmosphere; the free or open space; the sustainer of life and vehicle of sound (S. E. D. p. 126): วิมาน- ในอากาศ "air castles": อากาศธาตุ the chemical elements of the atmosphere; the etherous elements of the air: อากาศยาน air cars, craft, or planes.

อากุล, อากูล ah-gkoon *adj.* confused; troubled; perplexed; distressed (chd. p. 25).

อาขยา ah-ka[4]-yah *S. n.* a name; a title; an appellation (S. E. D. p. 129).

อาขยาต ah-ka[4]-yart[4] *P. S. n.* a Pali and Sanskrit treatise dealing with verbs: *adj.* told; said; declared; announced (S.E.D. p. 129).

อาขยาติ ah-ka[4]-yart[4] *P. S. n.* the act of telling, proclaiming, announcing, publishing (S. E. D. p. 129).

อาขยาน ah-ka[4]-yarn *S. n.* a tale; a story; a legend; the narration of a previous event (S. E. D. p. 129).

อาคเนย์ ah-ka[6]-nay *S. n. lit.* "the point of the compass guarded by the god of Fire," *i. e.* the south-east: *adj.* relating, belonging, or consecrated to fire or its deity (S.E.D. p. 130).

อาคม ah-kom *P. n.* the condition of coming to, or arriving at; advent; spells, charms, magical incantations, exorcisms, and enchantments such as are prescribed by custom (chd. p. 16).

อาคาร, อคาร ah-karn *P. S. n.* a house; a dwelling; an abode (chd. p. 16).

อาฆาต ah-kart[3] *P. S. n.* ill-will; revenge; malice; retaliation (chd. p. 18): คิดอาฆาต to harbour ill-will, anger or wrath; to seek an opportunity to repay, requite, or avenge oneself: อาฆาตคน a slaughter-house; a place of execution (chd. p. 18).

อ่าง arng[4] *n.* a large, burnt clay basin or shallow bowl (used inverted as covers for water-jars): พูดติดอ่าง to stammer; to stutter: อ่างแก้ว a glass bowl: อ่างเคลือบ a glazed basin or bowl: อ่างปลา a deep burnt clay basin used for keeping fish.

อ้าง arng[3] *v.* to refer to; to attribute to; to allude to one (as an associate or an accomplice); to designate or indicate another (as by name): คำอ้าง testimony; evidence; proof; affirmation: รับสำอ้าง under สำอ้าง p. 863: อ้างพยาน to cite as a witness: อ้างว่า to allege; to quote; to assert; to aver: อ้าง- อวด to cite boastfully what has been accomplished or said: อ้างอิง to allege; to maintain; to declare; to quote another's word as witness.

อางขนาง arng-ka[4]-nang[2] *v.* to be abashed; to be ashamed; to be shy, confused, or disconcerted; see ขวย p. 144.

อ้างว้าง arng[3]-wang[5] *adj.* alone; solitary; lonesome; having a feeling of helplessness (as when lost in a forest): อ้างว้างกลางป่า *idiomatic* to have a sense of sadness, lonesomeness, dreariness (as one lost in a jungle).

อาจ, อาจหาญ art[4] *adj.* daring; bold; brave; intrepid; courageous; fearless; valiant; undaunted; unweakened; rigid (used in regard to a bow for shooting mud-balls): อาจอง, องอาจ audacious; intrepid; dauntless; daring: อาจสามารถ capable; proficient; qualified; fitted: อาจเอื้อม, เอื้อมอาจ infringement; encroachment; invasion: *adj.* trespassing; reaching or wishing for the impossible (as the rabbit which wanted the moon); bold in trying to secure.

อาจม ah-chjom *n. lit.* "refuse that should be cleansed," *i. e.* excrement; feces; fecal matter.

อาจมน ah-chja[4]-ma[6]-na[6] *P. S. n.* purification; the act of washing, cleansing, rinsing (as the mouth) (chd. p. 8).

อาจาร ah-chjarn *P. S. n.* conduct, manners; practices; usages; customs or precepts that are worthy of commendation; rules for good conduct (S. E. D. p. 131): อาจารี those who have good manners; those who lead an exemplary life.

อาจารย์, อาจริย   ah-chjarn *S. n.* a teacher; a tutor: a preceptor; a professor (S. E. D. p. 131); see ครู p. 183.

อาจิณ, อาจิณณ์   ah-chjin *P.S. adj.* habitual; customary; accustomed to: *adv.* continually; permanently; constantly; continuously; habitually (chd. p. 9): เป็นอาจิณ to become a habit: อาจิณณสมาจาร manners that have become habitual.

อาเจียน   ah-chjee-an *v.* to vomit; to spew; [to puke.]

อาชชว   art⁴-cha⁶-wa⁶ *P.S. n.* rectitude; equity; justice; integrity; honesty (chd. p. 21).

อาชญัปต์, อาชญัปติ   art⁴-yup⁶ *P.S. n.* orders; commands; instructions (S.E.D. p. 133): อาชญัปติมาลา *gram.* the imperative mood (as used for command or entreaty).

อาชญา, อาญา   art⁴-yah *P.S. n.* power; command; decree; penalties; punishments of a major degree: *adj.* criminal; culpable; felonous (S.E.D. p. 133): ความอาชญา a criminal case; antithesis of ศาลแพ่ง p. 599: พระราชอาชญา punishments inflicted by the Crown: ศาลอาชญา the criminal court: อาชญาโทษ penalties for crimes, fixed by the law: อาชญาบท chapters, paragraphs, sections or clauses of (criminal) laws: อาชญาบัตร an edict granting special licenses: อาชญาบัตรขายสุรา a spirit license: อาชญาบัตรโค่นต้นสัก a license to fell teak trees: อาชญาบัตรจับปลา a fishing license: อาชญาศึก martial law: อาชญาสิทธิ์ absolute, unlimited, arbitary or despotic power: อาชญากรรม acts or conduct meriting punishment.

อาชา   ah-chah *n.* a horse.

อาชาน, อาชานิ   ah-chah-na⁶ *S. n.* birth; pedigree; lineage; birth-place (S. E. D. p. 132).

อาชาไนย   ah-chah-nai *n.* a blooded horse;

thoroughbred animals: *adj.* blooded (horses); high-spirited; having pure blood or good lineage: ช้างอาชาไนย elephants of good pedigree: ม้าอาชาไนย thoroughbred horses: โคอาชาไนย blooded cows.

อาชพ, อาชีวะ, อาชีวนะ   ah-cheep³ *P. S. n.* livelihood; sustenance; support; living; calling; trade; vocation; profession (S. E. D. p. 133).

อาชีวก   ah-chee-wok⁶ *P. n.* a sect of religious mendicants, non-conformists to the Buddhist doctrines, (during the early period of its foundation); one belonging to a Hindu sect of naked ascetics (chd. p. 21).

อาฏานาฏิยะ   ah-dtah-nah-dti⁴-ya⁶ *P. n.* the Sutra or stanzas chanted at intervals, by the Buddhist monks, at the celebration of the Krut or lunar New Year ceremonies, During these intervals cannons are fired for the general expulsion of evil (wales, state Ceremonies p. 299).

อาณัตติ, อาณัติ   ah-nut⁶ *P. n.* signal; sign; token; mandate; ordinance; injunction (chd. p. 32): ให้อาณัติดิสัญญา to signal with a pre-arranged code (as with flags): อาณัตติ-สัญญา a pre-arranged sign or signal.

อาณา   ah-nah *P. n.* authority; command; order (chd. p. 30): อาณาเกษตร, อาณาเขตต์ boundary; border; margin; frontier: อาณาจักร realm; domain; dominion; kingdom; jurisdiction; sovereignty: อาณาประชาราษฎร์ citizens of a tributary state or city; people of a realm or kingdom: อาณาประโยชน์ philanthropy; utility; utilitarianism; public good; the greatest happiness of the greatest number.

อาดูร, อาดูร, อาตุร   ah-doo⁴-ra⁶ *P.S. adj.* ill; diseased; sick; suffering (chd. p. 70).

อาตม, อาตมา, อาตมัน   art⁴-dta⁴-ma⁶ *n.* the soulless self; the individual; the principle of life; the supreme soul (H. C. D. p. 32): *pron.* used by Buddhist monks I; me; myself:

อาตมฆาต suicide : อาตมทรรศ *lit.* "something that shows the individual," *i. e.* a mirror ; a looking-glass : อาตมทาน self-sacrifice ; see พลีตน under พลี p. 574 : อาตมประศังสา self-laudation ; self-praise : อาตมภาพ I, me, myself (used only by Buddhist monks or novices to royalty or persons of importance) : อาตมวิทยา science pertaining to the soul (of the universe) : อาตมสังยมะ self-control ; self-command.

อาถรรพณ์, อาถรรพณะ see อถรรพเวท under อถรรพ p. 957.

อาทร ah-taun *P. S. n.* esteem ; regard ; respect ; devotion ; affection (chd. p. 9).

อาทาตา ah-tah-dtah *P. S. n.* a receiver ; a recipient ; one who takes (chd. p. 10).

อาทาน ah-tarn *P. S. n.* desire ; the state of taking, seizing, receiving or accepting ; appropriation (chd. p. 9).

อาทิ ah-ti[6] *P. S. n.* a start ; priority ; primacy ; a starting point : *adj.* first ; prior ; beginning with : *adv.* over ; over all ; above (S. E. D. p. 136 : chd. p. 14) : เป็นอาทิ primarily ; chiefly ; constantly.

อาทิตย์, สุริย ah-tit[6] *S. n.* the sun or its deity (H.C.D. p. 310). In the early Vedic times the Adityas were six, or more frequently seven, celestial deities of whom Varuna was chief ; consequently he was *the* Aditya (H. C. D. p. 3 : S. E. D. p. 137) : ขวบอาทิตย์ a week : วันอาทิตย์, อาทิตยวาร Sunday : อาทิตยคติ the course of the sun : อาทิตยพันธุ์, อาทิตยพงศ์, อาทิตยวงศ์ *lit.* "the sun's friends," *i. e.* the solar race of kings, prominent in the history of India. The race sprang from Ikshwaku (อิกษวากุ), grandson of the sun. There were two dynasties. The elder branch, which reigned at Ayodhya, descended from Ikshwaku through his eldest son. The other dynasty reigned at Mithila, descended from another of Ikshwaku's sons named Nimi (H. C. D. p. 312) : อาทิตยมณฑล the disk or orb of the sun.

อาทึก, อาทิก ah-teuk[6] *P. adj.* first ; beginning ; primary.

อาเทศ ah-tet[3] *S. n.* advice ; instruction ; precept ; rule ; command ; order (S. E. D. p. 137).

อาธรรม์, อาธรรม, อาธรรมิก, อาธรรมึก ah-tun *n.* unrighteousness ; injustice ; wickedness ; an unjust act ; unfairness ; wrong ; iniquity.

อาธาน ah-tarn *S. n.* the act of laying down, putting into, laying before, or using (S. E. D. p. 138).

อาธาร ah-tarn *n.* a prop ; a support ; aid ; patronage ; the power of sustaining, or the support given ; a reservoir ; a pond (S. E. D. p. 139).

อาน arn *v.* to sharpen ; to whet ; to polish ; to brighten : *n.* a saddle (for riding horseback) : อานดาบ to sharpen a sword : อานมีด to whet a knife : อานอาวุธ to polish weapons.

อ่าน arn[4] *v.* to read ; to recite : คิดอ่าน to devise, or deliberate regarding means for ; to consider ways and means : ช่วยคิดอ่าน to ask help in considering (as in the solution of a problem) : อ่านกฎหมาย to read the laws : อ่านตรวจ to read critically ; to examine carefully while reading : อ่านท้องสำนวน *legal* to read the evidence given by either side in a law case.

อานก, อานิก ah-nok[6] *Cam. v.* to love ; to be lovable.

อานน ah-non *S. n.* the mouth ; the face ; a door ; an entrance (S.E.D. p. 139) ; see ประตู p. 500.

อานนท์, อานันท์ ah-non *P. S. n.* joy ; happiness ; ecstasy ; rapture ; merriment ; Annonta, name of a prominent disciple and first cousin of the Buddha (S. E. D. p. 139).

อานันทนะ ah-nun-ta[6]-na[6] *P. S. n.* civility ; courteousness ; refined manners (as towards visitors); the giving of pleasure, delight, and entertainment (to guests) (S. E. D. p. 140).

อานิสงส์   ah-ni[6]-song[2] *P. S. n.* advantage; profit; blessing; reward; merit (chd. p. 34).

อานุภาพ, อานุภาวะ   ah-noo[6]-parp[3] *P. n.* majesty; power; authority; dignity; augustness; stateliness; efficency; supernatural power (chd. p. 40).

อาบ   arp[4] *v.* to immerse (as in a nickeling process); to wash; to bathe; to sprinkle (as with water):   อาบแดด to take sun baths: อาบทอง to gild or overlay with gold: อาบน้ำ to take a bath: อาบน้ำมนตร์ to be sprinkled with consecrated water: อาบไปด้วยโลหิต to be covered with blood: อาบรัก to overlay with a layer of lacquer prior to laying on the gold-leaf: อาบอบ to perfume (as in an enclosed place):   อาบเอิบ, เอิบอาบ to be saturated or soaked in some liquid; to cause a liquid to permeate throughout.

อาบัตติ์, อาบัติ   ah-but[4] *P. n.* sin; guilt; crime; a transgression; a violation; a contravention of rules (laid down in the Buddhist religion) (chd. p. 49).

อาป, อาโป   ah-bpa[4] *S. n.* water: อาโปกสิณ the using of water as a theme of consideration, meditation and introspection. The object contemplated is a bowl full of water. This is one of ten topics upon which mystic meditation may be induced. Some of the others are the world, fire, wind, blue, yellow, red and light (chd. p. 191). He who would exercise this method concentrates his mind on the instability of the object, coming to the final conclusion that all is "vanity of vanities"; see **กสิณ** p. 66:   อาโปธาตุ water, one the four principal elements. The other three are ปฐวีธาตุ earth; เตโชธาตุ fire; วาโยธาตุ air; wind.

อาปณะ   ah-bpa[4]-na[6] *P. S. n.* a market-place; a bazaar; commerce; trade; a shop; a stall (chd. p. 48):   อาปณก a merchant; a

trader in foods; a tradesman.

อาปาน   ah-bpah-na[6] *P. S. n.* the act of drinking; a banquet; a drinking party (S. E. D. p. 143):   อาปานภูมิ a tavern; a saloon; a beer-hall; a bar-room; a place for drinking in company: อาปานศาลา a liquor shop.

อาพัทธ์   ah-put[6] *P. S. adj.* connected; tied; joined; coupled or linked together (S. E. D. p. 144).

อาพันธ์   ah-pun *P. S. n.* implements or means for tying, joining or coupling; decorations; affection: *adj.* tied; united; bound: อาพันธนะ the act of binding on, or tying around.

อาพาธ   ah-part[3] *P. S. n.* sickness; illness; disease; a malady; an ailment; indisposition (used by Buddhist monks) (chd. p. 1):   อาพาธิก, อาพาธึก *adj.* unhealthy; diseased; sick; ailing; suffering with some malady.

อาพิล, อาวิล   ah-pin *P. S. adj.* dirty; confounded; embarrassed (S. E. D. p. 145).

อาเพียน   ah-pee-an[3] *Chin. n.* opium.

อาภรณ์   ah-paun *P. S. n.* investitures; ornaments; decorations; embellishments; adornments (as orders and medals given by the king) (chd. p. 3).

อาภัพพ์, อาภัพ   ah-pup[6] *adj.* unworthy; deplorable; disasterous; ruinous; miserable; deprived of everything.

อาภัสสระ   ah-put[6]-sa[4]-ra[6] *P. S. n.* one of the realms of the Brahma future world: *adj.* luminous; radiant; sparkling (chd. p. 3).

อาภา   ah-pah *P. S. n.* light; colour; beauty; splendour; radiancy (chd. p. 3):   อาภากร *ltt.* "the maker of light," *i. e.* the sun.

อาภาษ   ah-part[3] *S. n.* a preface; an introduction; a foreword (as a book); a speech; a talk; a discourse; a proverb (S. E. D. p. 145).

อาภาส   ah-part[3] *P. S. n.* light; glory; rays;

appearance; phantom (S. E. D. p. 145).

อามลก see **มะขามบ้อม** p. 632.

อามัย ah-mai *P. S. n.* sickness; disease; ailments (chd. p. 28).

อามิษ, อามิส ah-mit[6] *P. S. n.* allurements; baits; temptations; lust; desire; savoury foods; gifts (S. E. D. p. 147).

อาย ๑ ai *v.* to be ashamed; to be abashed; to be confused by consciousness of fault or impropriety: **อายแขก** bashful; timid; shy; diffident before strangers: **อายเหนียม** to be confused; to be embarrassed; to be humiliated or put to shame (as a girl wanting to hide her face and drop through the floor).

อาย ๒ ai *n.* profits; benefits; increments; the condition of funds or money coming into hand or being received (as taxes or fines paid in).

อ้าย ai[3] *n.* the elder brother; the oldest son: *adj.* first: **เดือนอ้าย** the first lunar month: **อ้ายป๊อก, ชะโด, แมลงพู่ (ปลา)** *Ophicephalus micropeltes (Ophicephalidae)* (suvatti p. 102): **อ้ายแรด, กะทุงเหวทะเล (ปลา)** *Tylosurus leiurus (Phallostethidae)* (suvatti p. 90): **อ้ายอ้าว, อ้าว (ปลา)** *Luciosoma setigerum (Cyprinidae)* (suvatti p. 40).

อายต ah-ya[6]-dta[4] *P. S. adj.* long; stretched out; extended; distended; lengthened; broadened; spread over (S. E. D. p. 148).

อายตนะ ah-ya[6]-dta[4]-na[6] *P. S. n.* means; mediums of communication, or objects that connect the mind of the individual with the outer world. According to the teachings of Buddhism these are divided into two groups. Internally are the senses of sight, smell, hearing, tasting, the intellect, the body (or physical being) and the sense of morality and energy. Externally are various forms, shapes, sounds, odours, flavours, sensations, house, home, family, altars, shrines, haunts, places of rendezvous (chd. p. 75).

อายัด ah-yut[6] *v.* to deliver to the **proper** authorities; to give information regarding (as to the police in case of a robbery); to make an attachment a declaration or statement.

อายัตต ah-yut[6]-dta[4] *P. S. adj.* industrious; diligent; persevering; exerting oneself; making efforts; being ready or prepared (S. E. D. p. 148).

อายน ah-yon *P. S. n.* the state of arriving, coming to, reaching or entering (S. E. D. p. 148).

อายัน ah-yun *Jav. n.* an ascetic; one belonging to a religious or clerical order.

อายาจนะ ah-yah-chja[4]-na[6] *P. n.* an invitation; an entreaty; a supplication; a petition; a request (chd. p. 74).

อายาน ah-yah-na[6] *P. S. n.* the condition of reaching, **arriving**, or coming to (S.E.D. p. 148).

อายุ, อายุร, อายุษ ah-yoo[6] *P. S. n.* age; life; lifetime; maturity; years of discretion; durability (chd. p. 76): **ขอให้มีอายุยืน** may your life be a long one: **ผู้มีอายุสูง** an old or aged person: **อายุกษัย** the end of life; death: **อายุขัย** the limit of life; "three score years and ten": **อายุรแพทย์, อายุรเวชช์** *lit.* "an extender of life," *i. e.* a doctor; a physician; one who cures diseases: **อายุยัง-เด็กอยู่** childhood; infancy: **อายุวัฒนะ** longevity; a great length of life: **อายุรเวท** the science of medicine; the science of public welfare.

อายุกต์ ah-yook[6] *S. n.* an official; an agent; a deputy; a representative; a commissioner: *adj.* having been appointed; having an official position; constituted as, or empowered with (S. E. D. p. 149).

อายุธ see **อาวุธ** p. 995.

อายุส ah-yoot[6] *S. n. poetical* age.

อารดี, อารติ ah-ra[6]-dee *S. n.* danger; disease; sickness; mischief; injury; pain (S. E. D. [p. 149).

อารมณ์　ah-rom　*P. n.* mental environment, state, mood, or attitude; concentration; fixedness of · mind; centralization of thoughts, ideas or purposes; the state of feeling at any one time: ตั้งสติอารมณ์ให้ดี to compose oneself (as in case of some calamity): อารมณ์ชั้นบาน *idiomatic* cheerfulness; exhilaration; animation; enlivenment.

อารยะ　ah-ra⁶-ya⁶　*P. S. n.* the Aryan race, the immigrant race from which all that is Hindu originated (H.C.D. p. 24); see อริยะ p. 972: อารยชน those who are noble, honourable, respectable, and leading an exemplary life: อารยชาติ an enlightened or civilized race or nation: อารยธรรม civilization; enlightenment; advancement.

อาระ　ah-ra⁶　*Jav. n.* arrack.

อารักขา　ah-ruk⁶-kah²　*P. S. n.* protection; supervision (chd. p. 54): คนซึ่งอยู่ในอารักขา persons under the protection of.

อารักษ์　ah-ruk⁶　*S. n.* protection; defence; preservation (S. E. D. p. 149).

อารัญ, อารัญญ์, อารัณย์　ah-ruk⁶　*P.S. adj.* living in the forest; occurring in the woods; being forest-born.

อารัมภ์　ah-rum　*P. S. n.* a beginning; the origin; incipience; inception; a preface; a prelude; a prologue; an exertion; an effort (S. E. D. p. 150): อารัมภกถา a foreword; a prologue; a preface; some introductory remarks.

อาราธนา, อาราธน์　ah-rat³-ta⁶-nah　*Thai. v.* to invite; to bid; to call; to entreat; to worship (used to Buddhist monks): *P. S. adj.* satisfying; accomplishing; propitiating (chd. p. 53).

อาราม ๑　ah-ram　*P. S. n.* a garden; a grove; a lawn; a place for pleasure and open air enjoyment; grounds of a Buddhist monastery; temple buildings and their enclosure (chd. p. 55): อารามิก a gardener; those living on Buddhist temple grounds; see โยมสงฆ์ under โยม p. 685.

อาราม ๒　ah-ram　*adv.* urgently; anxiously; impatiently; impetuously; fretfully, as อารามจะไป, อารามจะกิน.

อารี　ah-ree　*adj.* kind; compassionate; merciful; charitable; generous; benevolent; benign: มีใจอารีอารอบ good-natured toward all.

อาลป　ah-lop⁶　*P. S. v. imperative mood* to talk; to address; to discourse; to converse; to call to; to chat together: อาลปน์ conversation; the act of speaking to, addressing or calling (chd. p. 26): อาลปนบุรพบท the vocative case.

อาละวาด　ah-la⁶-wart³　*v.* to cause a quarrel or strife; to be at variance with; to pick a squabble; to dispute: *adj.* quarrelsome; contentious; disputing; given to disagreeing: มักอาละวาด *idiomatic* inclined to cause trouble, tumults or disagreements.

อาลักษณ์　ah-luk⁶　*S.-adj.* perceiving; beholding; observing (S. E. D. p. 153): *Thai n.* a scribe; a secretary; a proficient writer; one doing literary work.

อาลัย, อาลย　ah-lai　*P. S. n.* a house; a dwelling-place; a residence; a desire; an attachment; love; friendship; a condition of longing, craving or yearning (chd. p. 27); see ทอดอาลัย under ทอด ๑ p. 405: ด้วยความอาลัย prompted by a sense of love and affection.

อาลิ, อาลี　ah-li⁶　*P. S. n.* a scorpion; a bee; a line; a row; a range; a dike (as between paddy fields); an embankment (chd. p. 27).

อาโลก　ah-loke³　*P. S. v.* to look; to see; to notice; to know about; to investigate: *n.* light; sight; a look; vision: *adj.* looking; seeing; beholding (S. E. D. p. 154): อาโลกนะ the condition of looking at, seeing, considering, pondering, weighing, contemplating, or meditating about.

[or sister.

อาว, อา　ah　*n.* a father's younger brother

อ้าว   ow[4] *n.* bay; gulf.

อ้าว   ow[3] *adj.* hot; sultry; close; stuffy;
stifling; suffocating (as the weather); quick;
very much : *onomat.* used to intensify the
words that follow, e. g. อ้าว ! แล้วกัน ; *an introductory expletive,* e. g. อ้าว ! ทำอย่างนี้ไม่ถูก
why ! this is not right ! อ้าว ! จะไปไหนกัน hello !
where are you going ?   อ้าว, ชิวอ้าว, อ้ายอ้าว,
อีโอ (ปลา) *Luciosoma harmandi* (*Cyprinidae*);
Luciosoma setigerum (*Cyprinidae*) (suvatti
p. 40) : ร้อนอ้าว excessively hot and sultry :
แล่นอ้าว sailing "like the wind" : วิ่งอ้าว
to run like lightning : เสียงอ้าว exceedingly
loud and boisterous ; a deafening noise.

อาวรณ์   ah-waun *Thai v.* to have longings,
cravings, attachments or yearnings; to love,
desire or be enamoured : *P. n.* an obstruction;
an obstacle; hindrance; barrier; a wall;
restraint; impediments (chd. p. 71).

อาวาส   ah-wart[3] *P. S. n.* dwelling-places;
houses; a residence for Buddhist monks; a
hermitage; a monastery (chd. p. 72) : อาวาสิก
the director, manager or administrator of the
residence of Buddhist monks; the monks
themselves.

อาวาหะ   ah-wah-ha[4] *P. S. n.* a marriage;
a wedding; nuptials (chd. p. 71); see วิวาหะ
p. 778.

อาวุธ, อายุธ   ah-woot[6] *P. n.* arms; weapons
or warfare :   อาวุธหัตถ์ having or holding
weapons of defense, or for warfare.

อาวุโส   ah-woo[6]-soh[2] *P. n.* a word of address as " brother," " friend," used by a senior
Buddhist monk in speaking to an equal or
junior in standing (chd. p. 74).

อาเวศ   ah-wet[3] *S. n.* a path; a passage,
road or route; a door; an entrance; a portal;
a purpose; a determination; devotedness to a
purpose (S. E. D. p. 155).

อาศรพิษ see อศรพิษ p. 974.

อาศรม   ah-som[2] *S. n.* a hermitage; a cloister; a convent; the abode of sages, saints or
groups of religious students; a school or
college; woods or thickets (chd. p. 61 : S. E. D.
p. 158) :   อาศรมบท the site of a cloister or
convent; the enclosure of a hermitage.

อาศัย, อาศรัย, อาสัย   ah-sai[2] *S. v. lit.*
" the coming to a place of rest," *i. e.* to take
refuge in (as a storm-blown ship in the lee of
a point of land); to live; to dwell; to reside in
(S. E. D. p. 157) :   ที่อาศัย a place of refuge; a
shelter; a retreat or covert; a dwelling-place;
an asylum :   ผู้อาศัย a patron; a protector;
a tenant.

อาศิส, อาศิร   ah-sit[4] *S. n.* a prayer; a
benediction; the condition of bestowing a
blessing (chd. p. 60) :   อาศิรพจน์, อาศิรพาท, อา-
ศิรวจนะ, อาศิรวาท, อาเศียรพจน์, อาเศียรพาท, อาเศียร-
วจนะ, อาเศียรวาท blessings ; praise ; commendation :   อาศิรพิษ, อาศิรวิษ, อาศีรพิษ, อาศีรวิษ, อศรพิษ,
อาศรพิษ, อาศีพิษ, อาศีวิษ *n.* a snake : *adj.* poisonous; venomous.

อาศี   ah-see[2] *n.* a serpant's fangs (S.E.D. p. 157).

อาศุ   ah-soo[4] *S. adj.* quick; fast; swift;
fleet; rapid (S. E. D. p. 157).

อาสน   art[4] *P. S. n.* a seat; a stool; a chair;
a mat or carpet : *adj.* sitting; halting; en-
camping; abiding (S. E. D. p. 159).

อาสัญญ์   ah-sun[2] *n.* a state of unconsciousness; death; the termination of life (S. E. D.
p. 160).

อาสัตย์   ah-sut[4] *S. n.* unfaithfulness; dishonesty; perjury; a lie; untruthfulness : *adj.*
untrue; false; lying; dishonest.

อาสันนะ   ah-sun[2]-na[6] *P. S. adj.* approximate : *adv.* near; almost to; close to; adjacent; adjoining; contiguous (S. E. D. p. 160).

อาสา   ah-sah[2] *P. n.* a volunteer; a desire or
state of longing to tender asssistance : *adj.*
voluntary; purposed; intended; ready; wil-

ling: ทหารอาสา volunteers for the army: รับอาสา to be willing to render help (chd. p. 58).

อาสิญจ์ ah-sin[2] *P. v.* to sprinkle; to moisten; to anoint (chd. p. 60); to scatter; see โปรย p. 537.

อาสูร ah-soon[2] *Cam. v.* to pity; to deplore the condition of; see สงสาร p. 807.

อาหต ah-ha[4]-dta[4] *S. adj*: struck; pounded; beaten; thrashed; buffeted; frustrated (S. E. D. [p. 162).

อาหติ ah-ha[4]-dtee *S. n.* a blow; a hit.

อาหพ ๑ ah-hop[4] *S. n.* a sacrifice; an offering; propitiatory offerings (to the household spirits and deities) (S. E. D. p. 162).

อาหพ ๒ ah-hop[4] *P. S. n.* war; battle; conflict; a challenge provoking a combat (S. E. D. p. 163).

อาหร ah-ha[4]-ra[6] *P. S. n.* the act of bringing, fetching, seizing, accomplishing, holding (S. E. D. p. 162: chd. p. 20).

อาหลักอาเหลื่อ ah-luk[4]-ah-leu-ah[4] *adj.* stammering; impaired; reduced; enfeebled; weakened.

อาหาร ah-harn[2] *P. n.* food; nourishment; provisions; victuals (chd. p. 20); see สะเบียง p. 838: อดอาหาร to abstain from taking food; to fast: อาหารเช้า breakfast: อาหารเย็น dinner; the evening meal.

อาหุดี ๑ ah-hoo[4]-dee *S. n.* offerings; oblations; sacrifices (to the deities or spirits).

อาหุดี ๒ ah-hoo[4]-dee *n.* the act of calling or invoking (S. E. D. p. 163).

อาฬวี ah-la[6]-wee *P. S. n.* the name of a city in India (chd. p. 27).

อาฬหก arn-la[6]-hok[4] *P. n.* tethering posts or stakes for elephants; a Pali unit of capacity equal to 4 *nali* or 4 *tanans*. One standard *tanan* equals one *litre*.

อาฬาริก ah-lah-rik[6] *P. S. n.* a cook (chd. p. 26); a chef.

อำ um *v.* to cover up; to conceal; to hide; to secrete; to keep silent about: อำความ to keep silent regarding a matter (even though the person knows about it): อำพราง to equivocate (in a reply or statement); to dissimulate; to conceal by feigning not to know; to use ambiguous language with intent to deceive; to dissimulate.

อำ um[4] *n.* night; darkness: *adj.* dark; misty; cloudy; darkened; see มัว p. 646.

อำแดง um-daang *n.* an ancient title for women, equal to Madam, Mrs., Miss; see แม่ ๑ under แม่ p. 657.

อำนด see อด p. 956.

อำนรรฆ see อนรรฆ p. 959.

อำนวย um-nu-ey *v.* to give; to produce; to bestow: ผู้อำนวยการ a manager; a director (as of a business): อำนวยการ to superintend; to manage; to give orders; to direct; to administer the affairs of: อำนวยผล to produce results: อำนวยพร to bestow a blessing.

อำนาจ um-nart[3] *n.* power; authority; right; jurisdiction; ability; capability: มีอำนาจ to have the right to command; to be all-powerful, or able to do: ให้อำนาจ to give license to; to sanction the acts of: อยู่ในอำนาจ to be under the authority or control of: อำนาจที่บังคับให้เป็นไปตามกฎหมาย sanction of the law: อำนาจฟ้องร้องโดยชอบด้วยกฎหมาย right of action: อำนาจศาล jurisdiction of the court: อำนาจหรือคำสั่งกระทำการพิเศษ a special commission.

อำนิฏฐ์, อำนิษฏ์ see อิฏฐ, อิษฏ์ p. 997.

อำพน um-pon *adj.* much; many; plentiful; beautiful; adorned; ornate.

อำพะนำ um-pa[6]-num *v.* to be indifferent; to be disinterested; to refrain from speaking; to be non-committal.

อำพัน um-pun *n.* amber; a fossil resin occurring generally in small detached masses in alluvial deposits in different parts of the world: น้ำมันอำพัน see น้ำมัน p. 455: อำพัน-ขี้ปลา a kind of amber used medicinally: อำพันทอง yellow amber.

อำไพ um-pai *adj.* beautiful; clear; brilliant; handsome; shining.

อำเภอ um-pur *n.* a district; the portion of a territory or city especially set apart or defined for police jurisdiction, or for political, educational or other purposes; a local magistrate's office: ตามอำเภอใจ unrestrained; according to one's free will or discretion: นายอำเภอ the officer in charge of a district; อำเภอใจ freedom; liberty; independence; permission; franchise.

อำมร see อมร p. 967.

อำมฤคโชค um-ma⁶-rur⁶-ka⁶-choke³ *n.* success; propitiousness; favourable issue; auspiciousness; good augury.

อำมฤตป see อมฤตป under อมฤต p. 967.

อำมฤต see อมต ๒ p. 967.

อำมหิต um-ma⁶-hit⁴ *adj.* cruel; savage; ferocious; fierce; merciless; bloodthirsty; see [ทารุณ p. 413.

อำมาตย์ see อมาตย์ p. 967.

อำยวน um-yu-an *Cam. v.* to cover up; to conceal by feigning not to know: *adj.* secret; obscure; private.

อำรุง um-roong *v.* to support; to feed; to take care of; see บำรุง p. 482.

อำลา um-lah *v.* to take leave; to withdraw; to depart; to bid farewell or adieu.

อำอึง um³-eung³ *v.* to refrain from; to abstain from speaking; to repress one's words; to hesitate or equivocate in a confused manner.

อึกก์ ik⁴ *P. n.* a bear (chd. p. 58).

อิง ing *v.* to lean on; to rest against; see พิง p. 586: กระดานอิง a board back-rest: หมอนอิง a pillow or cushion to have at one's back: อ้างอิง to have another to corroborate a statement; to call another as a witness: อิงแอบ to be contiguous to; to be beside (another person); to embrace; to be touching (as a partner).

อิงกะ ing-ka⁶ *P. S. n.* a hint or sign; a gesture or indication of sentiment (as winking one eye in flirting) (S. E. D. p. 164).

อิงอร ing-aun *Cam. adj.* glad; see ดีใจ under ดี p. 330.

อิจฉา, อิสสา it⁴-chah² *P. S. n.* envy; malice; jealousy; enviousness; see ฤษยา p. 725.

อิชย์ it⁴ *S. adj.* worthy to be revered or honoured (as a teacher or deity) (S.E.D. p. 164).

อิชยา it⁴-cha⁶-yah *S. n.* a sacrifice; a gift; a donation; worship (S. E. D. p. 164).

อิฏฐี, อำนิฏฐี, อำนิษฏ์ it⁴ *P.S. adj.* worthy to be desired; captivating to the senses; should be wished for (chd. p. 163): อิฏฐผล results that come up to one's expectation; terminations that are satisfactory; benefits that are [gratifying.

อิฐ it⁴ *P. S. n.* a brick.

อิณ i⁴-na⁶ *P. S. n.* a debt; liability; obliga-[tion (chd. p. 158).

อิด it⁴ *v.* to become wearied, tired, fatigued or exhausted: อิดโรย to become jaded, worn out, or enfeebled; to become disheartened, depressed, dejected, or cast down: อิดหนา-ระอาใจ *idiomatic* to have an aversion for; to be disgusted with; to loathe: อิดออด to be disinclined or unwilling to do for, or serve; to be reticent or reserved in utterances (as a sick person is disinclined to talk): อิดเอื้อน to be afraid to express an opinion; to be timid in testifying, or making a declaration; to refrain from, or to withhold a reply.

อิตถี it⁴-tee² *P. S. n.* a woman; a female

(chd. p. 163): อิตถีกถา conversations relating to, or about women: อิตถีกุตต์ the charms of a woman; the (bewitching or captivating) conduct, behaviour, or deportment of women: อิตถีภาพ womanhood: อิตถีรูป a woman's shape, beauty, loveliness, grace and attractiveness: อิตถีลิงค์ *grammar* feminine gender.

อิทธิ it^4-ti^6 *P. S. n.* power; might; supernatural power; ability; competency (chd. p. 157): อิทธิบาท the effective means to attain miraculous power (Ala. p. 195): อิทธิ-พล influence; the ability to sway the will of another: อิทธิฤทธิ์ a miraculous faculty; a superhuman power (such as being able to perform miracles).

อิน (ต้น) in *n.* a species of tree of the red sandal-wood group, but with larger fruit.

อินทขีล in-ta^6-kee-la^6 *P. n.* a post; a pillar; a shaft; a stake (as for landmarks); a pillar, placed in front of a city's gate; a pillar, shrine or pagoda, marking the center of a city; a large slab of stone placed in the ground at the entrance of a house (chd. p. 158).

อินทนิล *Thai, Buriram* and *Prachinburi*, อินนะชิต *Thai, Krabin*, เสลา *Thai, Saraburi* and *Prachup*, ตะเกรียบ *Chawng, Chantaburi* (ต้น) in-ta^6-nin *n. Lagerstroemia loudonii* (*Lythraceae*); *L. flosreginae*; *L. ovalifolia*, a tree of fair size found in western Malaysia. It yields a valuable timber resembling walnut (cb. pp. 724, 725: Burk. p. 1299): อินทนิลบก *Thai* (ต้น) *Lagerstroemia macrocarpa* (*Lythraceae*), a tree of open country and river-banks, found from Burma to Selangor and Negri Sembilan in the Malay Peninsula. Its timber seems to be like that of *L. speciosa*. There is sufficient tannin in the leaves and fruit to warrant tannin-extract manufacture (cb. p. 725: Burk. p. 1299).

อินทผลัม (ต้น) in-ta^6-pa^4-lum *n.* the date-palm; *Phoenia dactylifera* (*Palmae*), the date-palm, a tree known from prehistoric times to have been cultivated in the dry belt from Senegal to the Indus. The Arabs depended so much on this fruit that they carried it with them wherever they went. In the time of the Tang dynasty (A. D. 618-907), the Chinese knew the fruit sufficiently well to call it the Persian jujube, but were so ignorant of the tree as to confuse it with *Cycas revoluta*. The tree grows to a height of 120 feet, keeping the bases of its petioles upon the trunk, which is made rough by them, and producing suckers at the base. The best flavoured dates are propagated by suckers, and there are innumerable named races (clones). They fall into two groups—dry and moist or soft, with intermediates, or semi-dry dates. Dry dates are sweeter than moist dates. In the great date countries, they are eaten slightly unripe as well as fully ripe. The juice of the fruit is used to sweeten food. The ancients made a fermented liquor by macerating the fruit, and from it they made vinegar. They tapped the trunk of the tree for toddy, and sometimes ate the cabbage. The leaves are nowadays made into matting, screens, and twisted ropes. The trunks are used for various purposes. As this palm is a dry country fruit, it is not important in Thailand (MCM. p. 248: N. H. J. S. S. IX, 3, p. 379: Burk. p. 1713).

อินทร์, อินท์, อินทรา, อินทุ in *P. S. n.* Indra. king of the minor deities of the Hindu pantheon and king of the lower Deva heaven (Ala. p. 171); also god of the firmament, the personified atmosphere. As deity of the atmosphere, he governs the weather and dispenses the rain; he sends forth his lightnings and thunder, and he is continually at war with the demons of drought and inclement weather, whom he overcomes with his thunderbolts, and whom he compels to pour down the rain. He is described as being of a ruddy or golden colour, and as having arms of enormous length; "but his forms are endless, and he can assume any shape at will." He rides in a bright golden car, drawn by two tawny or ruddy horses with flowing manes and tails. His weapon is the thunderbolt, which he carries in his right hand; he also uses arrows, a great hook, and a net, in which he is said to entangle his foes (H. C. D. p. 123 ; S. E. D. p. 166): อินทรชาลิก a juggler ; a performer of sleight-of-hand tricks : อินทรชิต see ทศกัณฐ์ under ทศ ๒ p. 401 : อินทรธนู shoulder straps ; epaulettes : อินทรวงศ์, อินทรวิเชียร forms of poetry adapted from the Sanskrit : อินทร-ศักดิ์. อินทราณี the consort of Indra and mother of Jayanta and Jayanti (H. C. D. p. 127): อินทราวุธ the weapons of Indra, viz. the rainbow, his bow, the lightning and thunderbolt which he hurls (H. C. D. p. 125).

อินทรี in-see *n.* an eagle : อินทรี (ปลา) *Cybium commersoni* (*Scombridea*); *C. guttatum*; *C. lineolatum* (suvatti p. 110).

อินทรีย์ in-see *P. S. n.* any one of the five senses, as sight, hearing, smell, taste and touch; faculties, functions, or organs of the body; moral quality or power; perception; the five moral powers (Ala. p. 241 : chd. p. 159): *adj.* organic : อินทรีย์โคจร capable of feeling; having the power of sensation : อินทรีย-ญาณ perceptibility; knowledge through the senses; apprehension : อินทรีย์สังวร restraint, subjugation, or suppression of the feelings or senses.

อินทัวร in-tee-waun *P. S. n.* the blue water-lily (chd. p. 159).

อินธน์ in *P. S. n.* firewood; fuel; the act of kindling or lighting a fire (S. E. D. p. 167).

อินัง i[4]-nung *v.* to take an interest in; see ดูแล under ดู p. 333.

อิ่ม im[4] *v.* to be fully satisfied (as after eating); to have the appetite assuaged; to be surfeited; to have finished eating or drinking : *adj.* delighted; rejoiced; gladdened; exhilarated; plump; chubby; fleshy (as regarding the face) : อิ่มใจ to be contented; to be satisfied with; to be pleased; to be gratified; to be delighted with, or proud of (as a teacher at the success of a pupil): อิ่ม-หน้า comfortably satisfied; refreshed; invigorated (as after a symptuous meal): อิ่ม-อาบ, อิ่มเอิบ happy; gratified; delighted; being fully requited, or repaid for all the efforts made : อิ่มตัว saturated.

อิรา i[4]-rah *S. n.* one of the voluptuous, celebrated numphs of Indra's heaven; the goddess of Speech; any drinkable fluid; a draught; refreshments (S. E. D. p. 168).

อิรม (หอย) i[4]-rom *n.* oysters.

อิริยา i[4]-ri[6]-yah *P. S. n.* movements; motions; actions; postures; attitudes; deportment; demeanour; behaviour (chd. p. 160): อิริยาบถ manners (of deportment); postures or attitudes (as standing, walking, sitting or lying).

อิร, อิรุพเพท see ฤคเวท p. 724.

อิศวร, อิศร, อีศวร i[4]-su-an[2] *S. n.* the god Siva; the supreme Ruler of the Universe. He is lauded as the lord of songs, the lord of sacrifices, who heals maladies, is brilliant as the sun, the best and most bountiful of gods, who grants prosperity and welfare to horses, sheep, men, women, and cows; the lord of nourishment, who drives away diseases, dispenses remedies, and removes sin (H.C.D. p. 296); see ศิวะ p. 798.

อิษฏ ๑ it[4] *S. adj.* wished; desired; regarded as good (S. E. D. p. 169).

อิษฏ ๒ it[4] *S. n.* sacrament : *adj.* sacrificed; worshipped with animal sacrifices (S. E. D. p. 169).

อิษฏิ ๑ it[4]-sa[4]-dtee *S. n.* a desire; a thirst for; a wish; a want (chd. p. 135); see ต้องการ under ต้อง p. 347.

อิษฏิ ๒ it[4]-sa[4]-dtee *S. n.* a sacrifice; propitiatory offerings to spirits or deities; the antithesis of animal sacrifices (S. E. D. p. 169).

อิส, อิสส์   it⁴ *P. n.* a bear (chd. p. 160).

อิสตรี, อิสัตรี   see สตรี p. 808.

อิสสระ   it⁴-sa⁴-ra⁴ *P. S. v.* to be independent; to be absolute; to be unconstrained : *n.* lord; chief; ruler; master; king; leader (chd. p. 160): อิสสรภาพ liberty; independence; freedom.

อิสสริยะ   it⁴-sa⁴-ri⁶-ya⁶ *P. S. n.* the state or right of being supreme; chief; ruler; king (chd. p. 160): อิสสริยยศ the rank of one holding the highest position of power; the supreme one; dominion; supremacy : อิส-สริยาภรณ์ investitures; decorations; medals or orders (as given by the king as marks of [favour].

อิสสา   see อิจฉา p. 997.

อิสิ   i⁴-si⁴ *P. S. n.* an inspired poet or sage; an anchorite; see ฤษี p. 725.

อิหร่าน   i⁴-rarn⁴ *n.* Persians.

อี   ee *pron. a prefix to the names of questionable women, for female slaves and for the females of cattle; a term denoting derision, corresponding to* ไอ้ *(for criminals).*

อี่   ee⁴ *n.* an ancient term for the second daughter : เอื้อย for the eldest daughter.

อี๊   ee³ *n.* a nasal sound; the sound indicating that something is abnormal in the nasal cavity (like the voice of one with a cleft palate).

อี   ee² *Chin. n.* a Chinese sweetmeat: *onomat.* from the sound of the cry or squeal when pain is produced.

อีก   eek⁴ *adj.* again; more; greater in amount, extent, or degree; see ซ้ำ p. 308: มีอีก there is still more to come, or still some left over : อีกที่ again; repeated; once more : อีกนิด just a little more (as for good measure).

[a sea bird.
อีก๋อย (นก)   ee-gkoy² *n.* the sandpiper,

อีเก้อีกุ้ง   ee-gkay³-ee-gkung *adj.* awkward; bungling; unskillful (descriptive of one who does not know how to row a boat).

อีเก้ง   ee-gkeng³ *n.* the barking deer, *Cervulus muntjac* (Minutes of s. s. Regarding wild Game Preservation in siam).

อีเกร๋ง, จะเกร๋ง, เหง๋อกปลาหมอ (ต้น)   ee-gkreng *n. Acanthus ilicifolius* (*Acanthaceae*), an ornamental plant bearing bright purple-blue flowers. It is very similar to *A ebracteatus*, sea holly, but the flowers are larger; there are other slight differences but, generally speaking, the two species are not differentiated but pass under the same vernacular names· In India there seems to be little use make of this genus medicinally, but in the Dutch Indies leaves are widely used for poultices for various pains, as well as for wounds of poisoned arrows; and the young leaves are boiled, along with the bark of *Cinnamomum culitlawan*, to make a drink for flatulence. In absence of something better, the leaves are used as a masticatory in Tonkin. There is a slight quantity of tannin, but so little it is quite innocuous. In India the plant is chopped and bruised and fed to cattle at the rate of twelve to fifteen pounds per day to each animal (v. p. p. 73 : mcm. p. 139 : burk. p. 27).

อีแก   ee-gkaa³ *n.* a calender machine; a large shell fastened to a weighted stationary upright pole, used to put a gloss and stiffness on starched cloth by rubbing (as on the panung).

อีโก้ง (นก)   ee-gkong³ *n.* Indian gallinule, *Porphyrio poliocephalus* (Gaird. j. s. s, IX, 1, p. 13).

อีคว่ำอีหงาย   ee-kwum³-ee-ngai² *n.* the game of "faces down or faces up," a game of chance for two, played on a board similar to a chess or checker board with 64 squares. Each player starts with 16 cowries. One player turns his cowries faces up; the other faces down. The moves are made in straight lines, a square at a time. Cowries may be captured, as in checkers, but not removed from the board. When a "face up" captures a "face down" the cowrie is turned "face up" in order to increase the number of the "faces up" side and can be moved as though on the same side. The "faces down" side abides by the same rule. The object is as in checkers, *i. e.* to reach the opposite side but with as many captured cowries as possible. If so decided, a fine is paid on each cowrie lost to the winner.

อจู ee-chjoo[3] *P.* an eel trap made of woven strips of bamboo.

อฉุยอแฉก see กระจัดกระจาย p. 20.

อชุก ee-chook[6] *n.* a species of fish found in the rivers of northern Thailand.

อี๊ด it[6] *onomat.* from the sound of the grunting of a pig.

อีดำอีแดง ee-dum-ee-daang *n.* measles (used by uneducated people); a temporary name for infants or new-born babes.

อีนุงตุงนัง ec-noong-dtoong-nung *adj.* badly tangled; in terrible disorder (as hair); interlocked; intertwisted.

อีโน ee-noh *adj.* broad; wide; large; big (as a large plate or wide-mouthed dish).

อีโนงโตงเนง ee-nong-dtong-neng *adj.* tattered; frayed; hanging in shreds and disorder; see รุ่งริ่ง p. 715.

อีเป็ด (เรือ) ee-bpet[6] *n.* a long, roofed cargo boat propelled by oars (used in transporting freight, as baled cotton, down from the northern districts of Thailand).

อีเบ้า ee-bpow[3] *n.* a diamond or rhomb-shaped kite with a long tail (flown in competition against the star-shaped kite).

อีแปะ ee-bpaa[4] *n.* Chinese cash made of copper, zinc or tin (formerly used as currency).

อีโปง (เรือ) ee-bpong *n.* a dug-out boat with long rounded bow and stern, used along the shallow rivers of the northern parts of Thailand; see ชะล่า p. 287.

อีเพา (นก) ee-pow *n.* the Thai white crested laughing thrush, *Garrulax diardi* (Gaird. J. S. S. IX, 1, p. 9).

อีรุ้ง (นก) ee-roong[5] *n.* the crested serpent eagle, *Spilornis cheela* (Gaird. J.S.S. IX, 1, p. 9).

อีล่อยบ่อยแอ ee-loy[3]-bpoy[4]-aa *adj.* delaying; prolonging; retarding; loitering; impeding.

อีลุ้ม (นก) ee-loom[5] *n.* the kora, or water cock, *Gallicrex cinerea* (Herb. N. H. J. S. S. VI, 4, p. 342): ว่าวอีลุ้ม, อีลุ้ม (ว่าว) a diamond or rhomb-shaped kite without a tail.

อีเลิ้ง ee-lerng[5] *n.* a large glazed water-jar.

อีแล่ง ee-laang[3] *n.* a large-sized pot for steeping yeast prior to the process of distillation (as for alcohol or liquors).

อิศ, อิศ, อิส eet[4] *P. S. n.* a lord, master, ruler, governor or king (S. E. D. p. 171).

อิศวร see อิศวร p. 999.

อีสา, อีษา ee-sah[2] *P. n.* the pole or shaft of a cart or plough: *adj.* curving upwards.

อีสาน, อีศาน ee-sarn[2] *P. n.* the north-eastern quarter of Thailand; Siva, the regent of the north-eastern quarter of the world.

อีสุกอีใส ee-sook[4]-ee-sai[2] *n.* varicella; chicken-pox.

อีหนองอีแหนง ee-naung[2]-ee-naang[2] *adj.* indistinct; muffled; thick (as of speech); see แปร่ง p. 536.

อีหลัดถัดทา ee-lut[4]-tut[4]-tah *n.* a marching tune played during festivals or public functions.

อีหลี ee-lee[2] *adj.* very good; excellent;

genuine; exquisite; worthy; choice, as ดีหลี.

อึหลุกขลุกขลัก ee-look[4]-klook[4]-kluk[4] *adj.*
idiomatic rattling; clattering (as a patched
up motor-car, or machinery out of order);
not running smoothly, easily, nor freely.

อึหลุกขลุกขลุ่ย ee-look[4]-klook[4]-klu-ey[4]
adj. idiomatic absorbed or engrossed in (as
with household duties): *adv.* earnestly; intently or assiduously engaged in; engulfed in
(as regarding one's hobby); see ง่วน p. 221.

อึหลุยฉุยแฉก ee-lu-ie[2]-chu-ie[2]-chaak[4] *adj.*
idiomatic lavish; wasteful; extravagant; excessive; unrestrained (in spending money):
adv. squanderingly; see พุ่มเพื่อย p. 609.

อีเห็น ee-hen[2] *n.* the palm civet, *Viverra
zibetha* (Caird. J. S. S. I, 1, p. 36).

อีโหน่อีเหน่ ee-noh[4]-ee-nay[4] *n. idiomatic*
story; incident; event; episode: ไม่รู้อีโหน่-
อีเหน่กับเขาเลย knowing nothing about the incident as others might.

อีแอ่น (นก) ee-aan[4] *n.* the eastern swallow, *Hirundo gutturalis* (Will. N. H. J. S. S. II,
3, p. 199): อีแอ่นพง (นก) the ashy swallow
shrike, *Artamus fuscus* (Herb. N. H. J. S. S. VI,
1, p. 109).

อึก, อึก euk[4] *n.* the sound produced when
thumping the chest with the fist: *onomat.*
from the sound produced by the glottis contracting in deglutition: อึกหนึ่ง one swallow; one draught.

อึกทึก euk[4]-gka[4]-tuk[6] *v.* to make a noise;
to be tumultuous; to be noisy: *adj.* noisy;
turbulent; boisterous; see โครมคราม p. 217.

อึกอัก euk[4]-uk[4] *adj.* being unable or unwilling to reply promptly (to a question);
refusing or declining to speak (as when dazed
or excited): *onomat.* from the sound of two
persons pounding each other (as in a hand-
to-hand fight).

อึง eung *adj.* noisy; boisterous; uproarious;
tumultuous: อึงคนึง shoutings; yellings;
noises; clattering; hubbub: อึงมี่ loud;
reverberating; echoing (as the sound of cannons being fired, or of thunder): อึงอล
turbulent; boisterous; clamourous; uproarious; riotous (as voices of people in a mob).

อง, องอ่าง eung[4] *n.* a bull-frog.

อึ้ง eung[3] *adj.* silent; hushed; stifled; quiet;
speechless: อึ้งความ to remain silent about,
or receive no reply regarding (as an un-
answered petition): อึ้งอ้า to preserve a
condition of silence; to be speechless.

อึด eut[4] *v.* to suppress; to restrain; to
check; to stop; to stifle: อึดใจ *v.* to hold
the breath; the period of time when the
breath is suppressed: อึดอัด suppressed
(as respirations); stifled; repressed; embarrassed: อึดอัดใจ to be nonplussed; to be
harassed: to be subdued or crushed (in one's
feelings); to be uncertain or perplexed (as to
what to do).

อึดตะบ๋อ eut[4]-dta[4]-bpeu *adj.* abundant;
plentiful; ample; copious; see ล้น p. 727.

อืดทืด eut[3]-teut[3] *adj.* swollen; inflated;
puffed up; distended (with gas, as a corpse
or carrion); see พอง p. 577.

อืด eut[4] *adj.* slow; delaying; dilatory;
careless; dilly-dallying: ท้องอืด a condition of distension of the abdomen (from
gas, or as in peritonitis): อืดอาด slowly;
moderatly; deliberately; inactively; tediously
(descriptive of one working under the pressure of an overseer); see เฉื่อยชา under เฉื่อย
p. 272.

อืน eurn[4] *adj.* other; opposite; contrary;
different: ใจเป็นอื่น an estranged condition
of the heart or affections (as a wife loving
another man): ที่อื่น in some other place;
elsewhere: เป็นอย่างอื่นไป being completely

changed: ผู้อื่น other people; another person; strangers: เวลาอื่น another time; some other occasion.

อืน　　eurn³ *v.* to speak; to tell; to relate; see พูด p. 595.

อือ　　eur *onomat.* from the sound indicating consent; a lazy person's "yes".

อื้อ　　eur³ *adj.* noisy; tumultuous; boisterous; loud: หูอื้อ a ringing in the ears; being hard of hearing; being a little deaf: อื้อฉาว dissipated; scattered; noised about (as cries or voices of complaints): อื้ออึง uproarious; violent disturbance and noise; turmoil and disturbance.

อุ　　oo⁴ *n.* a brand of intoxicant brewed by the Laos people from glutinous rice.

อุก　　ook⁴ *v.* to rush in boldly; to enter or trespass courageously or impudently: *adj.* audacious; rash; bold; brave: อุก, อุกเข็ม, อุกขาว, อุกแดง, กดโพธิ์ (ปลา) *Hemipimelodus borneensis (Tachysuridae)* (suvatti p. 66): อุกฉกรรจ์ violently cruel; savage; rash; pitiless; barbarous; ferocious; brutal; see ร้ายแรง under ร้าย p. 711: อุตอาจ to enter uncouthly; to be impolite; to offend the sense of decency; to be immodest in behaviour; see บุกรุก under บุก p. 483: อุกอาจหยาบหยาม *idiomatic* to be audaciously coarse and impudent.

อุกฤษฏ์, อุกกัฏฐ์, อุตกฤษฏ์　　ook⁴-gkrit⁴ *P.S. adj.* best; excellent; highest; supreme; greatest: โทษอุกฤษฏ์ the severest punishment.

อุกลา, อุกกา, อุกกา　　ook⁴-lah *P.S. n.* a torch; a fire-brand; a fire flame; a meteor; a falling star (chd. p. 521): อุกลาบาต falling stars; a meteor (of ill-omen); an aerolite.

อุกค์, อุกร์　　ook⁴ *P.S. adj.* cruel; fierce; savage; violent; (chd. p. 521): อุกร์อาจ savage; rough; brutal; murderous.

อุคคหะ　　ook⁴-ka⁶-ha⁴ *P. n.* the state of observing, studying, learning, acquiring and retaining (knowledge) (chd. p. 520): อุคคหนิมิตต์ *lit.* "a mental picture, impression or reproduction," *i. e.* a state produced in the mind of those undergoing concentrative meditation where the mind so firmly retains the image of what is meditated on that even when the eyes are averted or closed the impression of it still remains as a distinct reproduction. The deeper and longer the contemplation is continued, the more vivid and permanent the reflexion in the mind becomes.

อุคโฆส　　ook⁴-kote³ *S. v.* to publish; to proclaim; to relate; to advertise throughout (chd. p. 521); see ประกาศ p. 497: *adj. Thai* resounding; reverberating; re-echoing; ringing: เสียงอุคโฆส a far-reaching noise or loud voice.

อุคโฆสนา　　ook⁴-kote³-sa⁴-nah *P.S. n.* a proclamation; an announcement; a general declaration (as the broadcasting of news) (chd. p. 521); see ป่าวร้อง under ป่าว p. 525.

อุ้ง　　oong³ *n.* a concave cavity; an hollowed-out space: อุ้งมือ the hollow of the palm of the hand: อุ้งเท้า the plantar arch.

อุจจ์　　oot⁴ *P.S. adj.* high; tall; lofty; towering; elevated (S. E. D. p. 172).

อุจจาระ, อาจม　　oot⁴-chjah-ra⁶ *P.S. n.* feces; dung; excrement; filth; fecal matter (chd. p. 516): อุจจารมรรค *lit.* "the passage-way of fecal matter," *i. e.* the rectum; the anus; see ทวารหนัก under ทวาร p. 400.

อุจเฉท　　oot⁴-chet *P.S. n.* annihilation; excision; the act of cutting off, destroying, demolishing (chd. p. 516).

อุจาด　　oo⁴-chjart⁴ *adj.* immodest; shameless; obscene; indecent; lewd; foul; filthy; unchaste.

อุชุ　　oo⁴-choo⁶ *P. adj.* honest; straightforward; upright; just; honourable (chd. p. 521);

see ตรง p. 341 : *Thai* pretty ; beautiful ; hand-some ; elegant.

อุณณา oon-nah *P. n.* wool ; fleece ; hair between the eyebrows (chd. p. 524) : อุณณา-นาภี a spider : อุณณาโลม, อุณาโลม, โลมา *lit.* "hair of the body" *i. e.* a peculiarly curled tuft of hair appearing between the eyebrows like that adorning the breast of Vishnu (chd. p. 223) ; see วิษณุ p. 779. This symbol is con-sidered as sacred and mystic. Such a lock, curling towards the right, was, it is said, present on the forehead of the Buddha, and it constitutes one of the thirty-two charac-teristic marks of superior beings. In origin, it probably represented the conch shell. This symbol may be traced in odorous paste, turn-ing toward the right, on the forehead of a female, or turning toward the left, on the fore-head of a male (as is done in the tonsure cere-mony) (The Tonsure ceremony p. 80, Gerini).

อุณหะ oon-ha[4] *P. S. n.* heat ; warmth ; the hot season : *adj.* hot ; warm ; pungent ; sharp ; biting (chd. p. 523) ; see ฆน p. 720 : อุณหภูมิ temperature : อุณหรังสี heated rays ; heat radiating from rays of a hot sun.

อุณหิส oon-na[6]-hit[4] *P. S. n.* an ornament or decoration for the head ; a crown ; a turban ; a diadem ; a coronet ; a chaplet or wreath (chd. p. 523).

อุด oot[4] *v.* to close with a cork or plug ; to shut ; to block up (as an entrance by means of a barricade) ; to fill or close up (as a cavity in a tooth) : อุดปาก to gag a person with a cloth (as is the custom of thieves) : อุดปืน to cork the muzzle of a gun : อุดอู้ narrow ; small ; cramped ; re-stricted ; contracted ; stifling (as a small closed room) ; see คับแคบ under คับ p. 195.

อุดม oo[4]-dom *P. S. adj.* abundant ; copious ; fertile ; plentiful ; uppermost (as standard of education) ; best ; excellent (chd. p. 538) ; see บริบูรณ์ p. 470 : อุดมมัธยม the highest Mata-

yome Standard in school.

อุดร, อุตดร, อุตตร oo[4]-daun *P. S. adj.* higher ; upper ; superior ; northern ; situated on the left side (chd. p. 539).

อุดหนุน oot[4]-noon[2] *v.* to render assistance ; to support a cause ; to help ; to assist (in any way possible) ; see เกื้อ p. 127 : อุดหนุนให้ดำรงค์อยู่ to assist in maintaining the status [quo.

อุตกฤษฏ์ see อุกฤษฏ์ p. 1003.

อุตดม, อุตตมะ oot[4]-dom *P. S. n.* the state of being the highest ; the best ; the chief ; the greatest ; the most eminent, promi-nent or distinguished : อุตตมภาพ a posi-tion of eminence ; a good state or standing (in life) : อุตตมังค์ *lit.* "highest part of the body," *i. e.* the head : อุตตรกุรุ, อุตตรกุรุ a large continent, which according to ancient annals, was situated towards the north : อุตตรนิกาย the northern school or sect of the Buddhists, following Mahayana ; see มหายาน p. 628.

อุตตริ oot[4]-dta[4]-ri[4] *P. S. adv.* beyond ; fur-ther away or above ; besides ; other than (chd. p. 539) : *Thai* out of the ordinary ; unbecom-ing ; improper ; strange ; unusual.

อุตบล see อุบล p. 1006.

อุตพิด (ต้น) oot[4]-dta[4]-pit[6] *n. Typhonium trilobatum*, a plant with flowers having a strong offensive odour during the night.

อุตลุด oot[4]-dta[4]-loot[4] *n.* confusion ; tumult : see วุ่นวาย under วุ่น p. 780.

อุตสาห (preferable to all others), **อุตส่าห์, อุษาหะ, อุสสาหะ, อุสส่าห์** oot[4]-sah[2]-ha[4] *P. S. n.* diligence ; endeavour ; effort ; exertion ; perseverance ; persistance ; strenuous and con-tinuous exertion (S.E.D. p. 182) : มีความอุตส่าห์ to manifest diligence, or persistency : อุต-สาหกรรม commercialized industries.

อุตุ ๑   oo⁴-dtoo⁴ *adj.* comfortable; free from anxiety, worry or fear; see สบาย p. 813.

อุตุ ๒ see ฤดู p. 724.

อุตุนิยมวิทยา   oo⁴-dtoo⁴-ni⁶-yome-wit⁶-ta⁶-yah *n.* meteorology.

อุท ๑   oot⁴ *P. S. adv.* before; ahead; in front; beyond; *a form used in combination to elucidate the meaning of the root word.*

อุท ๒   oot⁴ *P. S. n.* water (S. E. D. p. 183): อุทัช born in the water: อุทบาตร a water-pot (chd. p. 517): อุทบาน a pond; a well of water: อุทพินทุ a drop of water (chd. p. 516); minute particles of water.

อุทก   oo⁴-tok⁶ *P. S. n.* water; *a form used in combination with some root word;* see น้ำ p. 453: อุทกธารา, อุทกธาร the state of flowing water; a current; a stream of water; a water conduit: อุทกภัย disaster or devastation by a flood; the calamity caused by a flood: อุทกศาสตร์ hydrology.

อุทโมษ see อุคโฆส p. 1003.

อุททาม   oot⁴-tarm *P. adj.* unrestrained; uncontrolled; uncurbed; free or at liberty to do what one pleases.

อุททิศ, อุทิศ   oot⁴-tit⁶ *S. v.* to allot; to assign; to make over to another person or cause; to give specifically to; to make, give or do on behalf of, or in the memory of, or for the merit of another person; a monument, a building, a pulpit, or the saying of mass in the name of the deceased (S. E. D. p. 188): อุทิศส่งไป to send with a particular person, with an object in view (as making merit for certain deceased relatives): อุทิศส่วนบุญ to signify that a portion of one's merit be for the benefit of another person: อุทิศแผ่กุศล to transfer the merit obtained by one's good deeds to others: อุทิศให้แก่ sacred to the memory of.

อุทเทศ   oot⁴-tet³ *P. S. n.* an explanation,

interpretation, elucidation, or illustration; the indicating of a thing by name (S. E. D. p. 188).

อุทยาน, อุยยาน   oot⁴-ta⁶-yarn *P. S. n.* a park; a pleasure ground; a flower garden; a royal garden (S. E. D. p. 191).

อุทร   oo⁴-taun *P. S. n.* the *supra pubic* portion of the abdomen; the womb; an internal cavity; the uterus (chd. p. 517): อุทรประเทศ the abdomen; the abdominal regions.

อุทริยะ   oot⁴-ta⁶-ri⁶-ya⁶ *P. n.* the stomach (chd. p. 517).

อุทธรณ์   oot⁴-taun *P. S. n.* the act of raising, lifting up, pulling up, appealing to a higher official (for decision) (S. E. D. p. 189); *according to Thai usage* the appeal of cases for a second hearing; entering an appeal from a lower to a higher court: ผู้อุทธรณ์ the appellant; the petitioner: ศาลอุทธรณ์ the Appeal Court.

อุทธัจจ์   oot⁴-tut⁶ *P. n.* pride; haughtiness; arrogance; vain-glory (chd. p. 518); see กำเริบ p. 105.

อุทลุม   oot⁴-ta⁶-loom *adj.* doing things out of the ordinary; wrong; incorrect; improper; immodest.

อุทัย   oo⁴-tai *P. S. n.* the condition of rising, beginning, appearing (the implied meaning is production, development, creation); the eastern mountain behind which the sun rises (chd. p. 517): *Thai* the rising sun (sheds glittering rays): แสงอุทัย rays of the appearing sun: อุทัยธานี a city in north-eastern Thailand.

อุทาน   oo⁴-tarn *P. n.* a canon of the Buddhist scriptures containing the exclamations of the Lord Buddha and of his disciples: *grammar* an interjection; an ejaculation; an exclamation (of fear or of joy).

อุทาร, เอาทาร   oo⁴-tarn *adj.* high; lofty; exalted; great; noble; generous; honest (S.E.D. p. 185); สูง p. 878.

อุทาหรณ์ oo⁴-tah-haun² *P. S. n.* an example; an illustration; an instance (as the case in point); one of five modes of logical reasoning (S. E. D. p. 185).

อุทิศ see อุททิศ p. 1005.

อุทุมพร see มะเดื่ออุทุมพร p. 634.

อุ่น oon⁴ *v.* to heat just a trifle; to warm over again: *adj.* warm; luke warm; comfortably warm and pleasant; moderately hot; tepid: ความอบอุ่น warmth; tepidness: อุ่นเกินไป too warm: อุ่นใจ free from anxiety or worry; having a feeling of security (as when accompanied by a friend); not feeling lonely, but at ease; อุ่นท้อง to eat a little, just enough to warm up the stomach: อุ่นมือ to warm the hands: อุ่นสบาย an agreeable warmth: อุ่นหนาฝาคั่ง *idiomatic* being at ease by having collateral securities; being comfortably supplied with the necessities of life: อุ่นอาหาร to warm over food.

อุบ oop⁴ *v.* to seize (with the mouth); to snatch; to clutch; to hide; to secrete; see ซ่อน p. 306: อุบ, อุย, ผีหลอก, บู่ทะเล, กบ (ปลา) *Batrachus grunniens (Brotulidae)* (suvatti p. 162): อุบอิบ whisperings; speech in low, soft, sibilant tones.

อุบรรธ oo⁴-but⁴-ta⁶ *S. n.* a part; a half; a fourth; a fraction; a three-quarter part (S. E. D. p. 214); see เสี้ยว p. 889.

อุบล, อุปบล, อุตบล oo⁴-bon *P. S. n.* a nymph; a water-lily; a lotus flower; see บัว p. 477.

อุบะ oo⁴-ba⁴ *n.* a bouquet (of flowers); flowers stitched together in the shape of tassels, tufts or flower-heads. These are used for decorative purposes and are often hung on garlands.

อุบ๊ะ oo⁴-ba⁶ *onomat.* from the sound indicating disgust, dissatisfaction, disappointment, disapproval.

อุบัติ oo⁴-but⁴ *P. S. n.* birth; origination; source; beginning: *adj.* born; produced (chd. p. 514); ancestry; parentage; lineage: *Thai v.* to be born; to come forth: อุบัติเหตุ an accident; a casual incident; an accidental event: *adj.* accidental; incidental; uncertain; unforeseen; unannounced.

อุบาทว์, อุบัททวะ, อุบัทรพ oo⁴-bart⁴ *P. S. n.* an unfortunate accident; a misfortune; a calamity; a disaster; adversity: คนอุบาทว์ a wicked, corrupted, demoralized person: วันอุบาทว์ a day of ill-omen: อุบาทว์จัญไร harm; misadventure; mishap; an unfortunate calamity with ominous forebodings *vulgar.*

อุบาย oo⁴-bai *P. S. n.* a trick; a means; an expedient; a device or stratagem to deceive; an artifice; a manoeuvre; trickery; a means of success against an enemy (S. E. D. p. 215): คิดอุบาย to devise ways and means to deceive or play tricks on others: อุบายหลอกลวง methods designed to deceive.

อุบาสก oo⁴-bah-sok⁴ *P. S. n. lit.* "one sitting near by," *i. e.* a worshipper; an attendant; one ready to render service; a servant; one waiting on, or keeping near in order to render aid; a layman observing the Buddhist religious precepts: อุบาสิกา the feminine form (S. E. D. p. 215).

อุเบกขา oo⁴-bek⁴-kah² *P. S. n.* "the doctrine of the golden mean," *i. e.* equanimity; the condition of following a neutral course in actions, passions and desires; a condition of indifference to the affairs of the world; impartiality; one of the four sublime moods, a state of leaving, abandoning, neglecting, or disdaining worldly attractions; stoicism (chd. p. 534).

อุโบสถ (วันพระ) oo⁴-boh-sot⁴ *P. S. n.* the Buddhist holy day or fast day, occurring on the days of the new and full moon. On these days the monastic ceremony of reading the 227 rules of the monks is held, and any monk who has offended against them is bound to declare his offence and request his superior to appoint a penance (Ala. p. 190). On these days the layman observes the eight commandments which are, *viz.* abstinence from taking life, from theft, from fornication, from lying, from intoxication, from taking food between midday and the next sunrise, and from feasting, theatrical spectacles, songs, and dances (Ala. p. 175); the building where this monastic ceremony is held; see โบสถ์ p. 491 (chd. p. 535): อุโบสถกรรม the holding of the monastic ceremony of reading the rules governing the monks.

อุป   oo⁴-bpa⁴ *P. S. a prefix conveying the meaning of* above, upon, over, upwards, beyond, further (chd. p. 531), *e. g.* อุปนายก, อุปถัมภ์.

อุปกรณ์   oop⁴-bpa⁴-gkaun *P. S. n.* a benefit; service; assistance; instrument; implement; accessories or spare parts (for machinery); furniture; apparatus; life-prolonging appliances (chd. p. 528); means of gaining a livelihood: อุปทูต Charge d'Affairs; Vice Minister: อุปนายก Vice President: อุปราช Viceroy.

อุปกรม   oop⁴-bpa⁴-gkrom *P. S. n.* a means; an expedient; stratagem; anything leading to a result (S. E. D. p. 196).

อุปการ   oop⁴-bpa⁴-gkan *P. n.* help; assistance; support; a favour; a benefit; a service (chd. p. 528): อุปการี, อุปการิณี a promoter; a helping hand; one rendering support or assistance; a benefactor.

อุปกิณณ   oop⁴-bpa⁴-gkin-na⁶ *P. adj.* covered; concealed; hidden; see ปกคลุม under ปก p. 492.

อุปกิเลส   oop⁴-bpa⁴-gki⁴-let⁴ *P. n.* impurities (in character); depravities; evils; distress; molestations (chd. p. 528).

อุปจักษุ   oop⁴-bpa⁴-chjuk⁴-soo⁴ *S. n. lit.* "celestial eyes," *i. e.* spectacles; eye-glasses;

a telescope.

อุปจาร   oop⁴-bpa⁴-chjarn *P. S. n.* approach; service; attendance; civility; attention (S. E. D. p. 197).

อุปถัมภ์   oop⁴-bpa⁴-tum² *P. v.* to uphold; to stand by in time of need; to sustain; to nourish; to maintain; to befriend: *n.* support; assistance; help; encouragement; see ค้ำจุน under ค้ำ p. 201: อุปถัมภ์ค้ำชู to support; to exert means for the uplift, or alleviation of; see ประมุข p. 503.

อุปถัมภก   oop⁴-bpa⁴-tum²-pok⁶ *P. n.* a benefactor; a patron; an advocate (of the cause); one who protects or fosters.

อุปเทศ, อุปเท่ห์   oop⁴-bpa⁴-tet³ *P. S. v.* to teach; to explain; to advise: *n.* instruction; advise; information (S. E. D. p. 199).

อุปธิ   oop⁴-bpa⁴-ti⁶ *P. n.* the body, state or condition of existence; immorality, impurity or depravity; entanglements of the world (Ala. p. 212).

อุปนิกขิตต์ see จารบุรุษ p. 245.

อุปนิษัท   oop⁴-bpa⁴-ni⁶-sut⁴ *S. n.* the condition of sitting at the feet of, or listening to the words of wisdom from a celebrated person (as St. Paul did at the feet of Gamaliel) (S. E. D. p. 201).

อุปนิสสัย   oop⁴-bpa⁴-nit⁶-sai² *S. n.* disposition; propensity; bent; tendency; inclination; potentiality; faculty (chd. p. 529).

อุปบล see อุบล p. 1006.

อุปพัทธ์   oop⁴-bpa⁴-put⁶ *P. v.* to connect; to join up or be tied to (S. E. D. p. 202); see เนื่อง p. 464.

อุปพันธ์   oop⁴-bpa⁴-pun *S. n.* a tie; a bond; union; unison; connection (S. E. D. p. 202).

อุปโภค   oop⁴-bpa⁴-poke³ *Thai v.* to eat; see เสพ p. 881; ใช้สอย under ใช้ p. 304: บริโภค p. 471: *P. n.* enjoyment; pleasure :*adj.* eating;

consuming; using (chd. p. 524): เครื่องอุปโภค chattels; various utensils or furniture for personal or household use.

อุปมา   oop⁴-bpa⁴-mah *P. S. n.* a simile; a comparison; an illustration; a figure (of speech); an allegory; an example for comparison: คำอุปมา a parable: อุปมาเหมือน- หนึ่ง as if; as for example; just to illustrate.

อุปมาน   oop⁴-bpa⁴-marn *P. S. n.* a statement of comparison; a resemblance to the object with which anything is compared (S. E. D. p. 203).

อุปไมย   oop⁴-bpa⁴-mai *P. n.* skill or ingenuity in selecting apt or appropriate comparisons; the subjects that are applicable for similes or metaphors.

อุปยุวราช   oop⁴-bpa⁴-yoo⁶-wa⁶-rart³ *P. n.* the honorary rank of the ruling prince of the capital of Lanchang, holding the power above the viceroy and next to the king.

อุปโยค   oop⁴-bpa⁴-yoke³ *P. S. n.* the art of using one's possessions properly or usefully, making them serve as assets (not as liabilities); employment; use; application; any act tending to achievement of a desired object (S. E. D. p. 204): อุปโยคบุรพบท *gram.* a preposition.

อุปราช   oop⁴-bpa⁴-rart⁴ *P. n.* the official rank or title of a viceroy (chd. p. 302): อุปราชย์ the official rank or title of the Second King (now abolished).

อุปริ   oop⁴-bpa⁴-ri⁶ *P. S. adv.* upwards; beyond; above; upon; over; in addition to (S. E. D. p. 205): อุปริจร moving or walking above, or in the air: อุปริพุทธิ of lofty intellect; raised above the ground: อุปริภาค the upper portion or side: อุปริภาพ the state of being higher, or above.

อุปริม   oo⁴-bpa⁴-ri⁶-ma⁶ *P. adj.* uppermost; highest; overhead (chd. p. 531): อุปริมปริยาย the gist, essence or substance (of a discourse)

that is of the highest value.

อุปสมบท   oop⁴-bpa⁴-som²-bot⁴ *n.* the ceremony of ordination, or taking the vows of the Buddhist brotherhood; the taking, obtaining, or acquiring of priestly orders (chd. p. 532).

อุปสรรค   oop⁴-bpa⁴-suk⁴ *P. S. n.* danger; trouble; misfortune; an obstruction; an impediment, hindrance or barrier (to the carrying out of one's plans or purposes) (chd. p. 531); a cause for changing one's plans or course of action; *used also as a prefix.*

อุปสัมปทา   oop⁴-bpa⁴-sum²-bpa⁴-tah *P. S. v.* to take the vows of priesthood: *n.* the ceremony of ordination, or entering the Buddhist brotherhood (S. E. D. p. 209): อุป- สัมปทาเปกข์, อุปสัมปทาเปกข์ *lit.* "one desiring to join the Buddhist brotherhood," *i. e.* a novice who is willing to take higher orders in the Buddhist brotherhood.

อุปฮาด, อุปราช   oop⁴-bpa⁴-hart³ *Laos n.* the official rank or title of a ruling prince of the northern Thai states.

อุปชฌาย์, อุปชฌายะ, อุปาธยาย   oo⁴-bput⁴- chah *P. S. n.* a spiritual teacher or preceptor; the officiating Buddhist monk who ordains or installs "his son" in the religious brotherhood (chd. p. 527): อุปัชฌายวัตต์ the rules of procedure that must be observed by the newly initiated towards his initiator in the installation ceremony.

อุปัฏฐาก   oo⁴-bput⁴-tark⁴ *P. n.* a servant; a servitor; a personal attendant: โยมอุปัฏฐาก the one who supports, maintains, provides for, or supplies with whatever is necessary (for a Buddhist monk) (chd. p. 533): อุปัฏฐา- ยิกา feminine form: อุปัฏฐานะ the condition of maintaining, providing for, supplying for, supporting, sustaining, or serving (understood to mean for Buddhist monks).

อุปาทาน   oo⁴-bpah-tarn *P. n.* the condition of holding firmly on to, seizing, or grasping; attachment; food; provisions.

อุปาหนา oo⁴-bpah-ha⁴-nah *P. n.* shoes; sandals (chd. p. 527).

อุภัย oo⁴-pai *P. S. adj.* both.

อุ้ม oom³ *v.* to hold; to carry (as to carry a child in the arms, or on the hip); to transfer (as clouds carry rain); to remove (as by the armsful): อุ้มครรภ์ to carry or bear (as when with child): อุ้มชู to coddle; to nurse carefully, caress, or fondle; to take the best care of; to support, cherish, nourish or maintain.

อุมงค์, อุโมงค์ oo⁴-mong *P. n.* an artificial underground passage, chamber, vault: คลองอุโมงค์ a mine-shaft, boring, or tunnel: อุโมงค์ฝังศพ a sepulchre; a tomb or rock vault.

อุมา oo⁴-mah *P. n. lit.* "light," *i. e.* Pravati, the consort of Siva. The earliest known mention of the name is in the Kena Upantishad, where she appears as a mediatrix between Brahma and the other gods (H. C. D. p. 325); see ศิวะ p. 798.

อุย (ปลา) oo-ie *n. Batrachus grunniens* (*Brotulidae*) (suvatti p. 162): ขนอุย soft, new hair of the body (as of an infant): เนื้ออุย soft, fatty flesh (as that of children).

อุ๊ย oo-ie⁶ *onomat.* from the exclamation of a person in slight pain (as when an abscess is lanced, or when one is being whipped); ouch.

อุยยาน see อุทยาน p. 1005.

อุยยาม oo-ie-yah-ma⁶ *P. S. n.* exertion; strenuous effort (chd. p. 540).

อุยโยค oo-ie-yoke³ *P. n.* departure; separation; severance; death (chd. p. 541).

อุ๊ยอ้าย oo-ie³-ai³ *adj.* clumsy; unwieldy; lumbering; awkward (descriptive of an obese person's movements).

อุร, อุรส, อุรัส oo⁴-ra⁶ *P. S. n.* the breast; the chest; the bosom (chd. p. 537); see ทรวง p. 397: ร้อนอุร anxiety; distress; disquietude;

alarm: อุรค *lit.* "nurtured at the breast," *i. e.* mammals: อุรเคนทร์, พญานาค the king of snakes; the cobra-capella; a mythical semidivine being, having a human face with the tail of a serpent and the expanded neck of the cobra (H. C. D. p. 213).

อุรณ oo⁴-ra⁶-na⁶ *P. S. n.* a ram (chd. p. 537).

อุรัจฉทะ, อุรัจฉัท oo⁴-rut⁶-cha⁴-ta⁶ *P. S. n.* armour; a coat of mail; a breast-plate; mail armour (chd. p. 537).

อุรา oo⁴-rah *n.* an ewe; female sheep.

อุรุ oo⁴-roo⁶ *P. S. n.* a surface which is flat, level, and plain: *adj.* wide; broad; extended; great; large; excessive; excellent (S.E.D. p. 217).

อุไร oo⁴-rai *n.* pure gold; a bright yellow but pliable gold.

อุลลป oon-lop⁶ *P. v.* to speak; to talk; to assert oneself as the owner (chd. p. 523).

อุลโลจ oon-lote³ *P. n.* a ceiling; a canopy; an awning; a protection (against the weather) (chd. p. 523).

อุลโลละ oon-loh-la⁶ *P. n.* a wave; breakers; billows; a surge; turmoil; agitation; confusion (chd. p. 523).

อุลามก oo⁴-lah-mok⁶ *adj.* indecent; obscene; immodest; lewd; foul; disgusting; shameless; see สกปรก p. 805.

อุลูก oo⁴-look³ *P. S. n.* an owl; a species of owl, *Tetranthera pilosa* (chd. p. 523).

อุโลก oo⁴-loke³ *n. Hymenodictyon excelsum*, a tree of which the white wood was formerly used in making coffins for common people (V. P. p. 274).

อุษ oo⁴-sa⁴ *S. n.* morning; dawn; break of day (S. E. D. p. 220).

อุษณ oo⁴-sa⁴-na⁶ *P. S. n.* heat; the hot season; hot or heated articles: *adj.* pungent; sharp; biting; penetrating; impetuous; passionate; ardent (S. E. D. p. 220): อุษณกร *lit.*

"hot rayed," *i. e.* the sun: อุษณกาล the hot season; summer time: อุษฌาการ heat; feverishness; excitement; passion; fervour.

อุษณิษ์ oo⁴-sa⁴-nee *S. n.* a crown; a decoration for the head; a diadem; a turban; anything wound round the head (S. E. D. p. 220).

อุษา oo⁴-sah² *S. n.* the aurora; dawn: daybreak; rays of the rising sun (S. E. D. p. 220): อุษาโยค the time nearing the break of day.

อุษาหะ see อุตสาห p. 1004.

อุสภ ๑, อุสุภ oo⁴-sop⁴ *P. S. n.* a bull; an ox; *conveying the meaning of* strength; vigour; powerfulness (chd. p. 537).

อุสภ ๒ oo⁴-sop⁴ *P. n.* a unit of surface measure equal to seventy meters (or 1 *sen* and 15 *wah*).

อุสสวะ oot⁴-sa⁴-wa⁶ *P.S. n.* a celebration; a festival; an occasion of merry-making; a holiday (chd. p. 538).

อุสุ oo⁴-soo⁴ *P.S. n.* an arrow; a cross-bow; a gun; an instrument for projecting a missile (chd. p. 538); see ธนุส p. 430: อุสุการ a maker of arrows.

อุสุม, อุษม, อุษมัน oo⁴-soom² *P. S. n.* vapour; steam; heat; the hot season; anger; passion (chd. p 537); the class of consonants that are pronounced like escaping steam, as ศ, ษ, ส.

อุหลบ oo⁴-lop⁴ *n.* menses; menstruation; see ฤดูผู้หญิง under ฤดู p. 724: พระอุหลบ (used by royalty).

อุเหม่ oo⁴-may⁴ *onomat.* from the sound of reproof, reprimand or censure (to children).

อุฬาร oo⁴-larn *P. S. adj.* great; lofty; noble; good; excellent; eminent (chd. p. 523).

อู (ไก่) oo *n.* a species of large, indigenous fowl, generally kept as fighting cocks; see ไก่อู under ไก่ p. 136.

อู้ oo⁴ *n.* a cradle; a place of nativity or birth; a small dock, ditch or blind water-way for docking boats, logs or rafts: อู่ทอง a gilded cradle for the children of royalty: พระเจ้าอู่ทอง "Prince of the Golden Cradle," *i. e.* King Uthong Rama Tibaudee or Somdetch Pra Rama Tibaudee I, who founded his capital at Ayuddha in the year B. E. 1893 (A. D. 1350 or 1351) and reigned 20 years (Thai History Prior to Founding of Ayuthia: Prince Damrong); see อยุธยา p. 969.

อู้ oo³ *n.* a two-stringed fiddle: *onomat.* from the sound of the roaring, howling, rustling or rushing of a violent wind: อู้อี้ *onomat.* from the sound of one talking through an obstructed nose or cleft palate.

อู้ oo² *Chin. v.* to have: *adj.* rich; affluent.

อูฐ, อุษฏร์ oot⁴ *n.* a camel: อูฐลาย *n.* a giraffe; *Camelopardalis giraffe*; an African ruminant related to the deers and antelopes, but placed in a family by itself. It is the tallest of animals, being sometimes twenty feet from the hoofs to the top of the head.

อูด oot⁴ *n.* the sound-producing mechanism at the head of a pentagonal-shaped kite, consisting of paper strung on a tensely drawn string that vibrates in the breeze; see ว่าว-ตุ๋ยตุ๋ย under ว่าว p. 771.

อูม oom *v.* to be distended; to be swollen (as swollen feet, or the cheek from an inflamed tooth): *n.* edema, due to effusion of watery fluid into the connective tissue.

อูรุ oo-roo⁶ *P. n.* the thigh (chd. p. 537).

อู้อี้ oo²-ee² *onomat.* from the sound of the squeaking of a fiddle or violin.

เอ, เอ้ ay *adj.* one; single; alone; solitary; see ลำพัง p. 742.

เอก ake⁴ *P. S. n.* one: *adj.* identical; alone; solitary; sole; only; single; chief; important; first; pre-eminent; incomparable;

unique; unsurpassed; supreme; without a peer (chd. p. 134 : S. E. D. p. 227) : ชั้นเอก (โรงเรียน) primary grade : ตัวเอก the primadonna or star in a performance or opera : ไม้เอก *grammar* the first of the accent marks, producing a depressed tone when used : เอกจักษุ *lit.* "one eyed," *i. e.* one having lost the sight of one eye : เอกจิตต์ fixedness of thought on one single object; intent upon; absorbed in; having the same mind; agreeing; concurring : เอกฉันท์ singleness of purpose, design or contemplation : เอกชน an individual; only one person; chief; leader; head-man of a community : เอกเทศ one spot or place; one and the same place; a part, portion or division of the whole : เอกบุคคล, เอกบุรุษ a unique or peerless person; one unexampled; an unequaled or unmatched person; one attaining the highest standards : เอกกริยา the chief wife; the wife recognized by law : เอกภักต์, เอกภักดิ์ loyalty; allegiance ; fidelity : *adj.* rendering allegiance or loyal service to : เอกมติ concentration of minds; u-nanimous : เอกมัย uniform; consisting of one : เอกรส the supreme pleasure; the only object of one's affection; relishing or finding pleasure in only one thing or person : เอกราช a monarch; the only king or ruler; independent; absolute; unrestricted : เอกลาภ a stroke of good fortune : เอกสาร important papers, documents, letters; files of value : เอกสารใด ๆ ที่แสดงกรรมสิทธิ์ *legal* documents of title : เอกพจน์ *grammar* the singular number : เอกัคคตา tranquillity of mind; the state of contemplation or abstraction (chd. p. 132).

เอ๊ก   ake[6] *onomat.* from the crowing of cocks.

เอกเขนก   ake[4]-ka[4]-nek[4] *adj.* being at ease; reclining comfortably; assuming a semi-recumbent position (as on pillows); being in negligé.

เอกา, เอ๊กา   ay-gkah *adj.* one; alone; single.

เอง   eng *adj.* alone; without cause; without company : เป็นเอง spontaneously; of one's or its own accord; voluntarily.

เอ๋ง   eng *pron. the second personal pronoun*; thou; you; thyself; *only permissable by superiors to inferiors.*

เอ๋ง   eng[2] *onomat.* from the yelping of a dog from pain.

เอ็ด ๑   et[4] *adj.* one : สิบเอ็ด eleven : ร้อย-เอ็ด one hundred one : เมืองร้อยเอ็ด a famous ancient confederacy of one hundred and one districts.

เอ็ด ๒   et[4] *adj.* loquacious; talking loudly or noisily; noisy; brawling (in moderation) : เอ็ดตะโร *idiomatic* the making of a great noise, hubbub or uproar.

เอน   en *v.* to lean (as a boat when sailing); to slant; to be off the perpendicular; to be biassed in opinion or actions : *adj.* see เท p. 421 : เอนกาย, เอนตัว, เอนองค์ to assume a recumbent position; to recline; to lie down : เอนหลัง to ease the back : เอนเอียง *idiomatic* unfair; partial; unjust; one-sided.

เอ็น   en *n.* tendon; a large sinew : ด้ายเอ็น surgical cat-gut : เอ็นร้อยหวาย Achilles' tendon; the tendon of the heel or ankle : เอ็นอ่อน a species of vine with medicinal properties.

เอ็นดู   en-doo *v.* to show mercy; to have compassion on or for; to be tender towards; to be humane : ความเอ็นดู mercy; compassion; sympathy; pity; tenderness; showing commiseration.

เอนทร์   en-ta[6]-ree *S. n.* the wife of Indra and mother of Jayanta and Jayanti. She is also called Sachi and Aindri (H. C. D. p. 127) : see อินทราณี under อินทร์ p. 999.

เอม   em *adj.* savoury; sweet to the taste; delicious : เอมอร captivating; attractive; tempting; alluring; beautiful; pleasing :

เอมโอช luscious; delicious; sweet tasting; savoury; tasty; palatable.

เอย ur-ie *adj.* *a meaningless terminal word* placed at the close of a verse of poetry, chapter, or discourse: ลงเอย this makes an end of what is to be said.

เอ่ย ur-ie⁴ *v.* to mention; to allude to; to refer to; to intimate; to hint; to raise the voice (as when beginning to cheer); to commence speaking or shouting: *onomat.* from the sound indicating a question; *equals a question mark when placed at the end of a sentence, e. g.* นกอะไรเอ่ย: เอ่ยขึ้น to allude to a matter; to suggest the circumstance (of a matter past and gone).

เอ๋ย ur-ie² *onomat.* from the sound denoting affection, endearment or politeness; *used following the name of a girl or woman*; *sign of the vocative.*

เอร็ดอร่อย ah⁴-ret⁴-ah⁴-roy⁴ *idiomatic adj.* delicious; luscious; tasty; toothsome; savoury.

เอราวดี ay-rah-wa⁶-dee *n.* the Irrawadi river, forming the boundary between Thailand and Burma, flowing into the Bay of Bengal. It's length is 1,060 miles.

เอราวัณ, ไอราวัณ, ไอราพต ay-rah-wan *P. S. n. lit.* "a fine elephant," *i. e.* the three-headed elephant of Indra (Ala. p. 171); an elephant produced at the churning of the ocean, and appropriated by the god Indra (H. C. D. p. 9); Indra's elephant (chd. p. 135).

เอลา see กระวาน p. 44.

เอว ay-oh *n.* the waist; the loins; the flanks: คาดเอว to gird up the loins: เอว-กลม a well-rounded waist: เอวบาง slender-waisted; see บั้นเอว under บั้น p. 476.

เอ๊ว ay-oh⁶ *onomat.* from the derisive sound of mocking, jeering, scoffing, bantering.

เอฬก ay-la⁶-gka⁴ *P. S. n.* a ram; a wild goat; sheep; goats (chd. p. 134).

เอฬา ay-lah *P. n.* saliva; spittle (chd. p. 134).

เออ ur *onomat.* from the sound used to introduce a wish or question, as "oh! where were you going yesterday;" *used also for* yes, just so, as you say: เออออย to agree with; to comply; to grant permission for; see เห็นตาม under เห็น p. 940; *an exclamation denoting assent, consent, acquiescence*: เออออ to listen; to pay attention to; to agree with; to believe in.

เอ่อ ur⁴ *adj.* motionless; still; slack; relaxed: น้ำเอ่อ the tide on the verge of turning; the period of slack water; see ท้อ p. 424.

เอ้อเร้อ ur³-rur³ *adj.* satisfied; satiated; gratified (as regarding the appetite).

เอ้อเฮอ ur³-hur *onomat.* from the sound denoting surprise, wonder, alarm, or amazement; see ประหลาดใจ under ประหลาด p. 506.

เอ๋แอ่น ay³-aan⁴ *adj.* loitering; delaying; procrastinating; loafing.

เอะอะ ay⁴-a⁴ *v.* to cause an uproar; to produce confused sounds of shouting or yelling (as of a mob).

เอ๊ะ ay⁶ *onomat.* from the sound denoting perplexity, bewilderment, embarrassment: เอ๊ะไม่ได้การ oh! this will never do.

เอา ow *v.* to want; to receive; to hold; to take; to consent; to agree to: ไม่เอา not to desire; to refuse; to be unwilling: ไม่เอาใจใส่ *idiomatic* to be negligent; to be careless; to be inattentive to instruction; to turn a deaf ear to orders given; to take no heed; to pay no attention to: เอาการ, เอาถ่าน capable; able; competent; efficient; skillful, fitted or suited for (as to become a good workman): เอางาน to manifest due respect before receiving a gift: เอาใจ, เอาอกเอาใจ *idiomatic* to be indulgent towards; to pamper; to humour; to favour; to yield willingly to requests: เอาใจช่วย *idiomatic* to support another's efforts fully; to cherish another's cause; to befriend another in time of adversity: เอาใจใส่ *idiomatic* to be attentive to one's duties; to be industrious; to be painstaking about one's work, or lessons: เอาชัย to gain a victory; to be victorious: เอาเถิด the game of run and catch, or of hide and seek. Those who are hiding or running give this as a signal when ready: เอาไทน to punish; to deem worthy of punishment: เอาบุญ to perform a deed for the sake of gaining merit: เอาเปรียบ to take advantage of: เอาไป to take away: เอามา to bring: เอาเยี่ยง to imitate; to copy; to ape: เอาไว้ to keep: เอาหน้า to do for the sake of popularity or favour; "to make face"; to "sound one's trumpet" regardless of whether the facts justify it or not: เอาออกไป to take out; to remove from.

เอาทาร see อุทาร p. 1005.

เอาทารย์ ow-tarn *S. n.* kindness; compassionateness; benevolence; graciousness; liberal-mindedness; magnanimity (S. E. D. p. [237].

เอารส see โอรส p. 1016.

เอาพาร see โอพาร p. 1017.

เอาพาริก, เอาพารึก see โอพาริก p. 1017.

เอิก, เอิกเกริก erk[4] *v.* to display grandure, show, or gorgeousness: *adj.* noisy; tumultuous; turbulent; boisterous (in a great degree); displaying great pomp, state, or splendour.

เอิน ern[3] *v.* to call; to shout words or questions to another (as at a distance); see เรียก p. 719.

เอิบ erp[4] *v.* to percolate or exude (as perspiration); to ooze out; to filter through: เอิบอาบ to be covered or bathed with perspiration (moisture that has oozed out).

เอียง ee-ang *v.* to be inclined; to slant; to be tilted; to lean to one side; to turn sidewise (as the head): เอียงตัว to lean the body to one side: เอียงเรือ to cause a boat to tilt: เอียงหัว to incline the head to one side: เอียงอาย to wear a face indicating shame: เอียงเอน *idiomatic* slanting; leaning; sloping; deflected; bent; tilted.

เอี้ยง (นก) ee-ang[3] *n.* the Thai mynah, *Acridotheres siamensis* (Gaird. J. S. S. IX, 1, p. 4): เอี้ยงโครงใหญ่ (นก) the Burmese pied mynah, *Sturnopastor superciliaris* (will. N. H. J. S. S. I, 3, p. 206): เอี้ยงโครงเล็ก (นก) the Burmese pied mynah, *Sturnopastor superciliaris* (will. N. H. J. S. S. I, 3, p. 206): เอี้ยงดำ (นก) the Thai mynah, *Aethiopsar grandis* (will. N. H. J. S. S. I, 3, p. 205): เอี้ยงแดง (นก) the common mynah, *Acridotheres tristis tristis* (Deig. N. H. J. S. S. VIII, 3, p. 151): เอี้ยงคำ (นก) Indian grackle, *Gracula religiosa intermedia* (Deig. N. H. J. S. S. VIII, 3, p. 151): เอี้ยงหัวล้าน (นก) black-necked mynah, *Gracupica nigricollis* (Deig. N. H. J. S. S. VIII, 3, p. 151).

เอียน (ปลา) ee-an *n.* an eel: *adj.* too sweet; nauciatingly sweet (descriptive of flavour); see เผื่อน p. 557.

เอี่ยม ee-am[4] *adj.* glossy; new; fresh; shining; glistening; see ผ่อง p. 542: เอี่ยมอ่อง clean; pure; unsoiled; unspotted.

เอี่ยม ee-am[5] *Chin. n.* an apron or garment tied behind (worn by Chinese children covering the chest and abdomen).

เอี่ยว ee-aw[4] *Chin. adj.* one; the first (card of a series played in a Chinese gambling game); one (spot on a dice).

เอี้ยว ee-ow[3] *v.* to flinch; to swerve; to wince (as from pain); to turn; to bend to one side; see บิดไปบิดมา under บิด p. 483: เอี้ยวตัว to turn the body partly around (as when looking backwards).

เอื้อ, เอื้อเพื่อ ee-ah[3] *v.* to support (by an act of kindness in time of want or adversity);

to manifest a charitable spirit; to extend a helping hand; see เจือจาน under เจือ p. 260: ใจเอื้อเพื่อเผื่อแผ่ *idiomatic* charitableness; generosity; liberality; benevolence.

เอื๋อง eur-ang[3] *n.* a species of orchid; the cud: *adv.* slowly; deliberately; repeatedly (as cattle chewing the cud): เคี้ยวเอื้อง to chew the cud; to ruminate.

เอือด see เกลือ p. 122.

เอือน eur-an *n.* a condition of incomplete development of copra in coconuts: มะพร้าว-เป็นเอือน coconuts where the copra is partially developed, dried, or full of holes (as though eaten by worms): เอือนกิน having a thin, dried, pitted layer, of copra (a misnomer in that it is thus on account of a worm or insect having penetrated).

เอื๋อน eur-an[3] *v.* to speak; to articulate; to enunciate; to utter words or sounds (as in singing); to drag, lag or draw out sounds or words in singing so as to fit the music: อิดเอื้อน hesitating; drawling in speech; slow in replying: เอื้อนความ being backward or reserved in speaking or narrating.

เอื๋อม eur-am *adj.* irksome; distasteful; repugnant; repulsive; see เบื่อ p. 490.

เอื๋อม eur-am[3] *v.* to reach or stretch out for something (as with the arm); to lust or long after; to wish for; to crave hopelessly (for some exalted object): เอื้อมอาจ overreaching; grasping or striving for (unduly).

เอื๋อย ur-ie[4] *adv.* slowly; moderately; dilatorily; tediously; inactively: เรือแล่นเอื้อยๆ *idiomatic* the boat sails or moves sluggishly; slowly (as with a gentle wind).

เอื๋อย ur-ie[3] *n.* the eldest child (of a family). In ancient literature the following may occur: พี่เอื้อย the eldest daughter: พี่อี่ the second eldest daughter: พี่อ้าย the eldest son: พี่ยี่ the second eldest son.

แอ aa *n.* the eleventh vowel: *adj.* young; feeble; small: *onomat.* from the sound of childish shrieks: ลูกแอ calves or young buffaloes: อัดแอ being closely packed or squeezed together: ใจอ่อนแอ timid; fearful; shrinking; diffident; faint-hearted.

แอ๋ aa[2] *adj.* descriptive of a drunken man's inarticulate speech; dead drunk.

แอก aak[4] *n.* the yoke of a plough: แก้วัวจากแอก to unyoke oxen: แอกเกวียน the yoke of a bullock cart: แอกคราด the yoke of a harrow: แอกน้อย a stick serving as a secondary yoke for pulling a plough.

แอ่ง aang[4] *n.* a small excavation (along the bank of a canal or river); a bay; a pool; a pond; a small swamp; a depression in the ground (where water may be confined); a natural concavity along the edge of a strip of land.

แอด aat[4] *onomat.* from the sound of the squeaking or creaking of a cart wheel.

แอ่น aan[4] *v.* to bend the body backward (as when looking up intently); to be bent; to be curved; to be in a position of extreme posterior flexure: อกแอ่น an expanded position of the chest; a pigeon-breasted posture: แอ่นกาย to bend the body into various postures (as an acrobat): แอ่นพง (นก) the ashy swallow-shrike, *Artamus fuscus* (Will. N. H. J. S. S. I, 2, p. 91): แอ่นลม (นก) the tropical house swallow, *Hypurolepis javanica* (Gaird. J. S. S. XI, 1, p. 3): แอ่นเล็ก (นก) the eastern palm-swift, *Tachornis batassiensis infumatus* (Herb. N. H. J. S. S. VI, 4, p. 325): แอ่นแวน (นก) the eastern palm-swift *Cypsiurus batassiensis infumatus* (Deig. N. H. J. S. S. VIII, 3, p. 163).

แอบ aap[4] *v.* to hide; see ซ่อน p. 306; ซุ่ม p. 310: *n.* a small toilet box of wood or bamboo for tobacco or cigars: แอบเข้ามา to approach stealthily: แอบตลิ่ง to come to, or travel alongside the shore: แอบแฝง to hide; to be concealed; to be hidden; to be secluded : แอบมอง to peep at : แอบขา a cigar-case or tobacco-pouch ; see อับ p. 986.

แอ่ว   aa-oh⁴ *n.* a method of singing where responses are made alternately by other partners : แอ่วลาว Laotian comedy singing with solo dancing.

แอหนัง   aa-nung² *Jav. n.* a nun ; a female religious devotee.

โอ   oh *n.* a cup ; a small basin or bowl made of fine bamboo strips, woven into shape, covered with dammar, varnished and decorated with various colours : *onomat.* from the sound expressing surprise or excitement, as "oh" : จันทน์โอ a species of nutmeg : see ส้มโอ under ส้ม p. 815 : สระโอ the fourteenth vowel.

โอ่   oh⁴ *v.* to boast ; to be boastful ; to brag ; to be ostentatious ; to be conceited : *n.* a small boat, similar to the *sampan* : โอ่โถง pompous ; splendid ; magnificent ; gorgeous ; grand (as a building) ; see ผึ่งผาย under ผึ่ง p. 548 : โอ่อ่า beautiful ; magnificent ; imposing ; superb ; splendid (used in regard to an assembly room).

โอ้, โอ้   oh³ *n.* signs of the vocative : *onomat.* from the sound indicating sympathy, pity or condolence in sorrow.

โอก ๑   oak⁴ *P. n.* water ; a place of shelter and safety ; a house ; a home ; a resting place ; an asylum (chd. p. 299).

โอก ๒   oak⁴ *v.* to eject ; to cause to come out.

โอ้ก   oak³ *onomat.* from the sound produced when vomiting.

โอ๊ก   oak⁶ *Eng. n.* the oak tree : *onomat.* from the sound of a cock crowing.

โอกาส   oh-gkart⁴ *P. S. n.* opportunity ; occasion ; chance ; place ; space ; room (chd. p. 299) ; see ช่อง p. 283 : มีโอกาส to find time or opportunity (to go or do) : ให้โอกาส to give permission for ; to give leave ; to afford

an opportunity for (as an interview).

โอฆ   oak⁴ *P. S. n.* a flood ; a torrent ; an inundation ; an overflow of a great quantity of water ; *metaphorically* the evils or passions which overwhelm humanity like a flood, of which there are four, *viz.* : กาโมฆะ the flood of sensual desires : ภโวฆะ the flood of renewed existence : ทิฎฐิโฆะ the flood of false doctrines : อวิชโชฆะ the flood of ignorance : โอฆชล the water in a deep lake, pool or sea : โอฆสงสาร *lit.* "to be a sojourner in a labyrinth of water," *i. e.* the condition of transmigration of the soul in this and future worlds (chd. p. 299).

โอง   ong *Cam. n.* speech ; utterances.

โอ่ง   ong⁴ *n.* a large-sized water-jar : โอ่งเคลือบ a glazed water-jar.

โองการ, โอมการ   oong-gkarn *P. S. n. lit.* "the mystic symbol 'OM'," *i. e.* a word of solemn invocation, affirmation, benediction, and consent, used at the commencement of prayers and religious ceremonies(H.C.D. p. 224). From the sanctity of the formula it has come to be used for utterances or pronouncements of His Majesty the King, as พระราชโองการ orders, edicts, proclamations or promulgations of the king.

โอช, โอชา   oh-cha⁶ *n. lit.* "invigorating substances," *i. e.* foods that are luscious, juicy, savoury, sweet, delicious to the taste (chd. p. 299) : *adj.* succulent ; savoury ; delicious ; vigour producing.

โอฏฐ์, โอฐ   see โอษฐ์ p. 1016.

โอด   ote⁴ *v.* to cry ; to weep ; to lament : *n.* a dirge ; a funeral chant or lament ; a threnody : โอดครวญ to wail ; to moan ; to sigh for ; to grieve ; to languish ; to lament (for the deceased).

โอตตัปปะ   ote⁴-dtup⁴-bpa⁴ *P. n.* decency in one's outward behaviour ; fear of sin ; con-

scientiousness; a conscience fearing or shrinking from sin (chd. p. 304).

โอทน   oh-ta⁶-na⁶ *P. n.* boiled rice (chd.
p. 298).

โอน   own *v.* to transfer into the possession
of another (as land); to bend over; to be inclined; to lean: ผู้โอน a transferer: โอน-
ไม่ได้ non-transferable; inalienable: โอนอ่อน
to be indulgent; to concede (to the wishes
of others); to have regard for: โอนเอน *v.*
to sway back and forth: *adj.* inconstant;
unstable; fickle; capricious; vacillating; unsteady; uncertain; untrustworthy.

โอบ   ope⁴ *v.* to encircle with the arms; to
embrace; to clasp; to manifest love and affection for by hugging: โอบอ้อมอารี to be kind
to; to be tender to; to manifest a humane
spirit towards: *adj.* compassionate; benevolent; liberal; charitable; generous: โอบอุ้ม
to support; to uphold; to render assistance;
to hug; to carry; to hold (as in the arms);
see ค้ำชู under ค้ำ p. 201: โอบเอื้อ to manifest charitableness, or liberality; to render
help or support; to surround with loving
arms.

โอภาปราศรัย   oh-pah-bprah-sai² *v.* to speak
to; to converse with, or enquire of in a kindly manner; to assume a glad attitude while
addressing another; to extend a cordial welcome.

โอภาส   oh-part³ *P. v.* to shed light, rays
or radiance: *n.* light; lustre; rays; radiant
brightness; refulgence.

โอม   ome *P. n.* the mystical symbol "OM,"
used in prefacing or closing all prayers and
most of the writings of the Hindus. Solemn
affirmation and respectful assent are expressed; it is translated by "yes" "so be it." It
represents the Hindu triad, or the union of
the three gods, Vishnu, Siva, Brahma; "the
three in one" (H. C. D. p. 224); according to
the Buddhist religion the symbols signify The

Buddha, The Law, The Brotherhood, or the
Triple Gems.

โอย   oh-ie *onomat.* from the sound indicating pain when being whipped (as "ouch").

โอร   oh-ra⁶ *P. adj.* below; less; posterior;
later (chd. p. 302).

โอรส, เอารส   oh-rot⁶ *P. S. n.* a son; a
legitimate child: *adj.* issuing from one's
self; proceeding from the breast (chd. p. 302):
ราชโอรส a royal son: โอรสธิราช a Crown
Prince.

โอละน้อ   oh-la⁶-naw⁵ *onomat.* from the
sound uttered as an interlude to draw attention to what is to be said or sung.

โอละพ่อ   oh-la⁶-paw³ *n.* a preliminary call
for singers, actors, or marchers to begin (as
peasantry forming processions for festivals):
adj. being the opposite; antithetical; reversed
(as turning head to tail): *onomat.* from the
sound of "Oh! fathers begin."

โอวาท   on-wart³ *P. S. n.* admonition; exhortation; advice; instruction (chd. p. 305)
utterances; discourses: กล่าวโอวาท to deliver a speech; to give a discourse, a rescript,
order, or advice: อยู่ในโอวาท under the
jurisdiction of.

โอษฐ์, โอฏฐ์, โอฐ   oat⁴ *P. S. n.* lips
(S. E. D. p. 236): *Thai* mouth: โอษฐชะ *lit.*
"produced by the lips," *i. e.* labial letters, *e. g.*
บ, ป, ว.

โอสถ, โอสธ, โอสธิ   oh-sot⁴ *P. S. n.* remedies; drugs; medicinal herbs or minerals
(chd. p. 302): เสวยโอสถ to take a dose of
medicine (used for royalty): โอสถกรรม
the use of medicines; the alleviation of sickness by medical means: โอสถคาร a dis-
pensary: พระโอสถมวน a cigar (used by
royalty): พระโอสถกล้อง a tobacco pipe
(used by royalty).

โอสาน see อวสาน p. 974.

โอหนอ oh-naw[2] *onomat.* from the sound indicating gladness, sadness, or despair.

โอหัง oh-hung[2] *adj.* proud; conceited; haughty; arrogant; boastful; vain: ใจโอหัง puffed up with pride.

โอฬาร, เอาฬาร oh-larn *P. adj.* large; magnificent; illustrious; beautiful; gorgeous; grand (as Angkor Wat); pompous.

โอฬาริก, โอฬาริก, เอาฬาริก oh-lah-rik[6] *P. S. adj.* broad; great; gross; coarse; rough; crude (chd. p. 300).

โอ้อวด oh[3]-oo-at[4] *v.* to boast; to brag; to vaunt; to exalt oneself; to flourish one's riches about.

โอ้เอ้ oh[3]-ay[3] *n.* a hymn or chant sung by a class of pupils on religious ceremonial occasions (as at the beginning, during the middle, or at the close of the Buddhist lental season): *adv.* slowly; protractedly; dilatorily; tediously; lingeringly.

ไอ ai *v.* to cough: *n.* vapour; emanations: ไอจาม to cough and sneeze: ไอหวัด a cough caused by a cold contracted by exposure to cold and wet: ไอแห้ง ๆ a dry cough.

ไอราพต ai-rah-pot[6] *P. S. n.* the three-headed elephant of Indra (S. E. D. p. 234).

ไอราวัณ see เอราวัณ p. 1012.

ไอศวรรย์, ไอศุริย, ไอศูรย์ ai-sa[4]-wan[2] *S. n.* the state of being a king; the state of having supreme authority, sway, rule, control; dominion; a kingdom; a domain (S. E. D. p. 234): ไอศุริยสมบัติ property or treasures of the state or government; resources accruing from the royal domains.

ฮ

ฮ The forty-fourth consonant of the Thai alphabet, a low class letter of which there are twenty-four, *viz.* ค, ค, ฆ, ง, ช, ฌ, ซ, ญ, ฑ, ฒ, ฐ, ท, ธ, น, ณ, พ, ฟ, ภ, ม, ร, ล, ว, ฬ, ฮ. ฮอนกฮูก is the designating name of this letter. It is pronounced as a strong "h," but is seldom used, and when used is only found as an initial consonant.

ฮด hot[6] *v.* to sprinkle; to splash over or upon (as water); to appoint; to promote; to advance; to elevate (as in rank or position); see รด p. 687; ยก ๑ p. 661. [p. 728].

ฮวง hoo-ang *Chin. n.* air; wind; see ลม ๒

ฮวน hoo-an *Chin. n.* non-Chinese people or persons; races of people other than Chinese.

ฮ้วน hoo-an[5] *Chin. v.* to fight; to be in combat; to battle; to strive with, or against; see รบ p. 688.

ฮ่อ (ห้อ p. 927) haw[3] *v.* to gallop: *n.* Yunnanese (Chinese) traders who run mule caravans from China into northern Thailand.

ฮ้อ haw[5] *Chin. adj.* good; excellent: *onomat.* from the sound indicating approval, as "it is all right," "that is excellent"; see ดี p. 350.

ฮอด haut[3] *v.* to attain; to succeed; to escape from (as from danger); see รอด p. 692.

ฮะ ha[6] *onomat.* from the sound given as a signal for all concerned to act or do in union (as the hauling of a log, a boat, or the lifting of a heavy weight); also from the sound given to startle a person, or to prevent cattle going in a wrong direction, or as a call to attract a person's attention: ฮะไฮ้, ฮะฮ้าย *onomat.* from the sound indicative of derision, mockery, ridicule; see เยาะ p. 680.

ฮัก ๆ   huk[6]-huk[6] *adj.* gasping; panting.

ฮั่น   hun[3] *Eng. n.* Hun, an obscure Asiatic (Turanian) nomadic and warlike race living between the Ural and the Volga rivers about the dawn of the Christain era. In the fourth century they overrun and desolated a large part of Europe and laid Rome under tribute.

ฮา   hah *onomat.* from the sound made by a quick expulsion of breath, as in laughter or joy (as of a crowd of people cheering " ha; ha!" "hear! hear!"); also used to call one's attention to something important, as at the end of a sentence or a stanza of poetry. When thus used the form is พ่อฮา, พี่ฮา: ฮาป่า the untimely or rude laughter, contempt or derision of a crowd.

ฮ้า   hah[5] *onomat.* from the sound indicating the wish to forbid, prohibit, hinder or disallow: ฮ้าไฮ้ *onomat.* from the sound indicating approval or encouragement (sung at intervals by the choir or partners during a form of extemporaneous folk repartee).

ฮื   hur[6] *onomat.* from the sound indicating displeasure, surprise, alarm.

ฮึก   heuk[6] *adj.* impetuous; boisterous; furious; violent; passionate (used in regard to animals); see คึก p. 203: ฮึกหาญ brave; bold; fearless; intrepid (used in regard to animals during the mating season): ฮึกห้าว amorous; erotic; excited by sexual desire (as animals during the mating season): ฮึกโหม to rush violently or fearlessly in or upon; to act haughtily, insolently, or boldly (as while in anger or passion): ฮึกฮัก discontented; dissatisfied; angered; provoked; infuriated; see ขัดใจ under ขัด p. 150.

ฮึดฮัด   heut[6]-hut[6] *adj.* raging (anger); wrathful; wrathy: *onomat.* from the ejaculations, sighs, groanings, or mumblings during the period of excessive anger; see โกรธ p. 133.

ฮึม   heum *adj.* resounding; echoing; reverberating: ฟ้าร้องฮึม ๆ the resounding, echoing or re-echoing of thunder: เสียงฮึมแห่งปืนใหญ่ *idiomatic.* the thundering reports of cannon.

ฮือ   heu *v.* to burn fiercely, furiously, violently; see ลุก p. 748: *onomat.* from the sound of groaning, moaning, lamenting audibly; also descriptive of the sound produced by a moving mass of people, a mob, or cattle: ไฟลุกฮือ ๆ the fire burns vehemently: เสียงครางฮือ ๆ the sound of grieving, groaning or lamentation.

ฮือ   heu[3] *onomat.* from the sound of the growling or gnarling of a dog: คำรามฮื้อ ๆ to growl in a threatening manner.

ฮือแซ   heu[3]-saa *Chin. n.* a Chinese relish composed of sliced fish, vegetables and vinegar.

ฮึดฮาด   heut[3]-hart[3] *onomat.* from the sound produced in asthmatic breathing, heaves, panting, or gasping.

ฮุบ   hoop[6] *v.* to seize, bite, catch, nab or snatch (as fish at a bait); see งับ p. 222: ปลาฮุบเหยื่อ *idiomatic* the fish makes a dart and splash for the bait.

ฮู้   (รู้ p. 716) hoo[5] *Laos. v.* to know about.

ฮูก (นก)   hook[3] *n.* the large horned owl.

ฮูม   hoom *onomat.* from the sound of the trumpeting of elephants, reports of cannon, or claps of thunder.

เฮ   hay *onomat.* from the sound expressing joy or approval (as from a crowd of people): เฮฮา *onomat.* from the sound of a crowd expressing glee, gaiety, mirth or merriment: เฮโล *onomat.* from the signal shouted by the leader of a gang of workmen for united efforts in hauling or dragging.

เฮกโตกรัม   hek[6]-dtoh-gkrum *n.* hectogram, a unit of weight, equal to one hundred grammes or 3.527 ounces avoirdupois.

เฮกโตเมตร   hek[6]-dtoh-met[6] *n.* hectometer,
a unit for measurements of length, equal
to one hundred meters or 328 feet 1 inch.

เฮกโตลิตร   hek[6]-dtoh-lit[6] *n.* hectoliter, a
unit for measurements of capacity, equal to
one hundred liters or two bushels and 3.35
pecks.

เฮย, แฮย   hur-ie *onomat.* from the sound
used to attract another's attention (as when
calling a person but being ignorant of the
name); *often used in poetry.*

เฮ้ย   hur-ie[5] *onomat.* from the sound used
when desiring to attract another's attention
vulgar.

เฮ้ว   he-ow[5] *onomat.* from the sound indicating contempt, derision, insolence, mockery, scoffing, or bantering.

เฮอ   hur *onomat.* from the sound of heav-
ing a sigh.

เฮือก   heu-ak[3] *adj.* shaking; tottering;
quaking; quivering; trembling: *onomat.*
from the thud of a heavy weight striking
upon, or sinking down into a comparatively
soft substance; see ทรุด p. 398.

เฮือน (เรือน p. 720) heu-an *Laos. n.* a house.

แฮ่   haa[3] *onomat.* from the sound of the
gnarling, or growling of an enraged tiger.

โฮ   hoh *onomat.* from the sound of a loud
cheer.

โฮก   hok[3] *v.* to pounce upon; to jump at;
to attack suddenly with claws (as does a
tiger): *onomat.* from the sound imitating
the actions and growl of a tiger or dog; the
sound of sucking up liquid foods (such as
soup or tea), or of inhaling air: โฮกอื้อ a
sour-flavoured curry: โฮกฮาก abruptly;
rudely; roughly; impolitely; insolently (used
in regard to speech or actions).

ไฮ้   hai[5] *onomat.* from the sound expressing
a command to prohibit, forbid, hinder, disallow or stop.

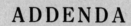

ADDENDA

ONE THOUSAND COMMON WORDS MOST USED.

To secure this list 167,546 words were tabulated from literature covering thirty sources.

ก	เกตา	กิน	แกะ	ข้า	ค
ก่	เกต้า	กิริยา	โกร่ง	ข้าง	คอ
กฎหมาย	กว่า	กิเลศ	โกรธ	ข้าพเจ้า	คอย
กร	กว้าง	ก๋	ใกล้	ข้าม	ค่อย
กรกฎาคม	กษัตริย์	กุมภาพันธุ์	ไก่	ข้าราชการ	คับ
กรม	กสิกรรม	กุมาร	ไกล	ข้าศึก	ค่า
กรรม	ก่อ	กู้		ขัง	ค้า
กรรมการ	ก่อน	เก็บ	ๆ	ขัด	คำ
กระจาย	ก้อน	เกรง	ขด	ขัน	ค่ำ
กระดาษ	กอบ	เกณฑ์	ขน	ขับ	คิด
กระด้าง	กะ	เกวียน	ขนาด	เขตต์	คน
กระดูก	กะดาน	เก่า	ขณะ	ขีด	คอ
กระทรวง	กัน	เก้า	ขยาย	ขี	คุณ
กระทำ	กันยายน	เกาอี	ขวาง	ขึ้น	คู
กระนั้น	กับ	เกิด	ขว้าง	เขา	คุณ
กระมัง	กำไร	เกิน	ขอ	เข้า	คด
กระไร	กำลัง	เกียรติยศ	ขอรับ	เขียน	คน
กรุง	กำหนด	เกียจคร้าน	ของ	เขียว	ค้น
กรุงเทพ ๆ	กา	เกียว	ขอบ	แขก	คณะ
กลม	กาง	เกียวของ	ข้อ	แข็ง	ครั้ง
กลับ	กาชาด	เกือบ	ขา	แข่ง	ครั้ง
กลาง	กาย	แก	ขาด	ไข	ครัน
กล่าว	การ	แก่	ขาย	ไข่	ครบ
กล้า	เกาะ	แก้	ขาว	ไข้	ครอบครัว
กลัว	กิจ	แก้ว	ข้าว		ครอง

คราว	จด	เจ้า	ชัด	ซ้าย	ดู
ครู	จดหมาย	เจาะ	ชั่ว	ซ้ำ	เด็ก
คลอง	จน	แจง	ชั่วโมง	ซี	เดิน
คลาย	จบ	แจ้ง	ชั้น	ซึก	เดิม
คลุม	จม	แจ่ม	ชาย	ซึ่ง	เดียว
ความ	จาก	ใจ	ชาว	ซื่อ	เดี่ยว
ควร	จ่าย	โจทย์	ชา	ซื้อ	เดียว
ควาย	จ้าง		ช้า		เดียวกัน
เคย	จะ	ฉ	ช่าง	ญ	เดือด
เคียง	จัก	ฉลาด	ช้าง	ญาติ	เดือน
เครื่อง	จักร์	ฉัน	ชาติ	ญี่ปุ่น	แดง
เคลื่อน	จง	ฉะนั้น	ชำนาญ		แดด
เคือง	จังหวัด	ฉะนั้น	ชิง	ด	แดน
โคม	จัด	ฉบับ	ชีวิต	ดง	โดย
ใคร	จันทร์	ฉะเพาะ	ชีพ	ดวง	ใด
ใคร่	จับ	ไฉน	ชี	ด้วย	ได้
	จำ		ชื่อ	ดอก	
ง	จำนวน	ช	ชม	ดัง	ต
งอก	จำเป็น	ชน	เช่น	ดับ	ตก
งาน	จำพวก	ชม ٭	เช้า	ดาว	ตน
งาม	จิตต์	ชอบ	เชิญ	ด้าน	ตรง
ง่าย	จริง	ชวน	เชื่อ	ด่า	ตรวจ
งู	จริต	ช่วย	เชื้อ	ดำเนิน	ตระกูล
เงิน	จีน	ช่อง	ใช่	ดำริ	ตรัส
โง่	จึง	ชะนวน	ใช้	ดิน	ตรา
	เจ็บ	ชะนะ		ดี	ตลอด
จ	เจริญ	ชะนิด	ซ	ดื่ม	ตลาด
จง	เจ็ด	ชัก	ซ่อน	ดุจ	ตวัน

ตอน	ตุลาคม	ทวี	ที่	ธาตุ	นิด
ต่อ	ตู้	ทวีป	ที่เดียว	ธุระ	นิทาน
ต้อง	โต	ทหาร	ที่	เธอ	นิยม
ต้อน	ใต้	ท่อ	ทุก		นว
ตอบ	ไต่	ทอง	ทุกข์	น	นี้
ตะเกียง		ท้อง	ทุง	นก	นี่
ต่ำ	ถ	ทอด	ทูต	นอก	นี้
ต่ำ	ถนน	ทะเล	ทูน	นอกจาก	นุ่ง
ต่ำบต	ถวาย	ทัน	เท	นอน	เนื่อง
ตำแหน่ง	ถอย	ทับ	เท็จ	น้อง	เนือ
ตัว	ถ้อย	ทัพ	เทวดา	น้อย	แนะนำ
ตัวอย่าง	ถั่ว	ทั่ว	เท่า	นัก	แน่
ตัด	ถ้า	ทั้ง	เทียง	นักปราชญ์	แน่น
ตัดสิน	ถาน	ทั้งปวง	เทียบ	นักเรียน	โน้น
ตั้ง	ถาม	ทั้งหลาย	เทียม	นั่ง	ใน
ตา	ถูก	ทา	เทียว	นั้น	
ตาน	เถิด	ทาง	แทน	นั้น	บ
ตาม	เถียง	ทาน	แทบ	นับ	บก
ตาย	แถว	ท่าน	แท้	นับถือ	บท
ติ	ไถ	ทาบ	โทษ	นา	บน
ติด		ทาย	ไทย	น่า	บรรณาธิการ
ตึก	ท	ท้าย		นาง	บรรดา
เต็ม	ทดลอง	ท้าว	ธ	นาน	บริบูรณ์
เตรียม	ทน	ทำ	ธง	นาม	บริษัท
เดือน	ทรง	ทำไม	ธันวาคม	นาฬิกา	บริสุทธิ์
แต่	ทราบ	ทำลาย	ธรรม	น่า	บอก
แตก	ทรัพย์	ทิศ	ธรรมดา	น้ำ	บ่อย
แต่ง	ทราย	ทั้ง	ธรรมเนียม	นิ่ง	บัง

บังเกิด	ปกครอง	บัญญา	ผูก	พระยา	พี่
บังคับ	ปฏิบัต	บัญหา	เผย	พราหมณ์	พง
บดัน	ปรกติ	บ่า	เผื่อ	พฤศจิกายน	พง
บัญชา	ประกอบ	ปาก	แผ่	พฤศภาคม	พืช
บัญญัติ	ประการ	บีด	แผน	พฤหัสบดี	พน
บาง	ประกาศ	บ	แผ่น	พต	พุทธ
บางที	ประจำ	เปน	แผ่นดิน	พตเมือง	พุธ
บ้าง	ประชุม	เบีด		พตอย	พูด
บาท	ประตู	เปรียบ	ฝ	พดิก	เพาะ
บาน	ประเทศ	เปล่า	ฝน	พวก	เพราะ
บ้าน	ประพฤติ	เปลี่ยน	ฝรั่ง	พอ	เพลิง
บ่าย	ประมาณ	เปลือก	ผัก	พ่อ	เพลิน
บำรุง	ประโยชน์	เปลื้อง	ผัง	พอก	เพียง
บิดา	ประสงค์	แปด	ฝา	พ้อง	เพียงไร
บุคคล	ประเสริฐ	แปดก	ฝาก	พะยาน	เพียน
บุตร	ประหลาด	แปดง	ผ่าย	พัก	เพิ่ม
บุตรี	ปรากฏ	โปรด	ผัก	พัน	เพ่อ
บุญ	ปรารถนา	ไป	ผักหัด	พันธ์	เพื่อน
บุรุษ	ปราบปราม	ไปรษณีย์		พา	แพง
บุหรี่	ปราศจาก		พ	พาณิชย์	แพ้
เบีย	ปรัตยุบัน	ผ	พงศาวดาร	พาย	
เบ้อง	ปดา	ผด	พ้น	พาด	ฟ
แบ่ง	ปดาย	ผะสม	พบ	พาหนะ	ฟ้อง
แบน	ปด่อย	ผ้า	พม่า	พิจารณา	ฟัก
โบราณ	ปฏูก	ผ่าน	พยายาม	พิธ	ฟัง
ใบ	ปวง	ผิด	พรวน	พิมพ์	ฟัน
	ป้องกัน	ผิว	พร้อม	พิษ	ฟ้า
ป	บัน	ผู้	พระ	พิเศษ	ไฟ

ภ	มาก	ยอด	รอง	ราว	ลง
ภรรยา	มากมาย	ยอม	ร้อง	ริม	ลด
ภัย	มารดา	ย่อม	ร้อน	รับ	ลบ
ภาค	ม้า	ยัง	รอบ	รุ่ง	ลม
ภาพ	มิตร	ยา	รอย	รู	ล้ม
ภาย	มิถุนายน	ยาก	ร้อย	รู้	ลวง
ภายนอก	มีนาคม	ยาม	ระงับ	รู้จัก	ล่วง
ภายใน	มิ่	ย้าย	ระเบียบ	รู้สึก	ล้วน
ภายหลัง	มิด	ยาว	ระดึก	รูป	ลอง
ภาษิต	มุ่งหมาย	ยุง	ระยะ	เรา	ลอย
ภาษี	เมฆ	ยุติธรรม	ระหว่าง	เริ่ม	ละ
ภูเขา	เมตตา	ยุโรป	รัก	เรียก	ละคร
ภูม	เม็ด	ยิง	รักษา	เรียง	ละลาย
	เมษายน	ยิ่ง	รัง	เรียน	ละออง
ม	เมา	ยิน	รัฐบาล	เรียบร้อย	ละเอียด
มกราคม	เมีย	ยินดี	รับ	เรือ	ลัก
มณฑล	เมื่อ	ยืน	รับประทาน	เรื่อง	ลักษณะ
มนตรี	เมือง	เย็น	ราก	เรือน	ลา
มนุษย์	แมลง	แยก	ราคา	แรก	ลาก
มอง	แม่	แย่ง	รางวัล	แรง	ล่าง
มอญ	แม่น้ำ	โยน	ราชการ	โรค	ล้าง
มอบ	แม้		ราชา	โรง	ล้าน
มัก	ไม่	ร	ราง	โรงเรียน	ลำดับ
มั่งมี	ไมตรี	รถ	ร่าง	ไร	ลำบาก
มัธยม		รบ	ร้าน	ไร่	ลำพัง
มัน	ย	ร่ม	ราษฎร	ไร้	ลน
มั่นคง	ยก	รวม	ราย		ลึก
มา	ยนต์	ร่วม	ร้าย	ล	ล่ม

ดุก	ว่า	สนุก	สั่ง	เส่นาบดี	หน้า
ดูก	ว่าง	สภา	สั่งเกตุ	เส้น	หน้าท
ดุง	วาจา	สม	สัญญา	เส่มอ	หนาว
เด็ก	วาน	สมควร	สัตว์	เสมี่ยน	หนี่
เด่น	วิ่ง	สมเด็จ	สั้น	เสร็จ	หนี
เด่ม	วิชชา	สมบัต	สัมมา	เสี่ย	หนิ่ง
เดว	วิทยา	สมมุติ	สาม	เสี่ยง	หนุ่ม
เด่า	วิธี	สมัย	สามารถ	เสื่อ	ห่ม
เดิก	เวทนา	สมาชิก	สาม่	เสื่ย	หมด
เดียง	เว้น	สมาคม	สาย	เสื่อม	หม้อ
เดียว	เวตา	สรรเสริญ	สาว	เส่าร์	หมอก
เดือก		สระ	สำนัก	แส่ง	หมา
เดือน	ศ	สร้าง	สำราญ	แสดง	หมาย
เดือม	ศุกร์	สตะ	สำเร็จ	แสวง	หมุน
แด	ศาสนา	สดิ่ง	สำหรับ	ใส่	หมู
แด้ง		สว่าง	สิงหาคม	ใส่	หมู่
แด่น	ส	สวน	สิ่ง	ไส่	หยด
แด้ว	ส่ง	สวม	สิน		หยาบ
แดะ	สงคราม	สวรรค์	สินค้า	ห	หยิม
โดก	สงสัย	สอง	สิบ	หก	หยุด
	สงสาร	ส่อง	สี่	หญ้า	หรือ
ว	สด	สอน	สี่	หญิง	หลวง
วงศ์	สตรี	สหาย	สืบ	หนทาง	หลัก
วัง	สตางค์	สะดวก	สุข	หน่อย	หลัง
วัด	สติ	สะบาย	สุง	หนัก	หลับ
วัน	สถาน	สะพาน	สู้	หนัง	หลาน
วัว	สถานี	สะอาด	สูง	หนังสื่อ	หลาย
วาง	สนาม	สัก	เส็ดจ	หนา	หลัก

หลุม	หาง	ไหด	ออก	อ้าง	อึก
หวัง	ห่าง	อ	อ่อน	อาจ	อื่น
หวาน	ห้าม	อก	ออม	อาณาเขตต์	อุ้ม
ห้อง	เหดน	อด	อะไร	อาณาจักร์	อุดสาหะ
หัก	แหดะ	อธิบาย	อักษร	อาทิตย์	เอก
หัด	ให้	อนุญาติ	อังกฤษ	อ่าน	เอง
หัดถ์	ใหญ่	อยาก	อังคาร	อาบน้ำ	เอา
หัน	ใหม่	อย่าง	อัตรา	อาศัย	เออเพอ
หัว	ไหน	อยู่	อัน	อาหาร	โอ
หา	ไหม	อริยะ	อันตราย	อ่านาจ	โอกาส
หาก	ไหม้	อวด	อากาศ	อำเภอ	โอรส

BIRDS

Acridotheres siamensis เอี้ยง p. 1013

Acridotheres tristis tristis สาลิกา, เอี้ยงแดง [pp. 859; 1013]

Aegithina tiphia tiphia กระจิบสีถั่ว, ขมิ้นเหลืองอ่อน [pp. 21; 141]

Aenopopelia tranquebarica humelis เปล้า p. 533

Aethiopsar fuscus grandis กิ้งโครงดำ p. 106

Aethiopsar grandis กิ้งโครง, เอี้ยงดำ pp. 106; 1013

Alauda gulgula sala ขี้ไก่, กระจาบฝน, กระจาบฝนเล็บยาว p. 158; 21

Alauda wattersi กระเต้าลม, นกแอ่นลม p. 29

Alcedo atthis bengalensis กระเต็นน้อย p. 31

Alsocumus puniceus นกเขาเปล้า, ลำภู p. 166

Amaurornis phoenicura chinensis ขวาก, แขวก [p. 145]

Amaurornis phoenicurus chinensis กวัก p. 63

Anastomus oscitans ปากห่าง p. 522

Anthracoceros albirostris เงือก p. 226

Anthrothreptes malaccensis กินปลีใหญ่ p. 107

Anthus richardi malayensis กระจาบฝนหางยาว

Anthus rufulus กระตืด p. 31 [p. 21]

Arachuechthra flammaxillaris กินปลี p. 107

Arborophila brunneopectus ข่อ p. 146

Ardea cinerea กระสา, กะสา p. 45

Ardeacinerea rectirostris ขวากตน p. 145.

Ardeola grayi กระยาง, กะยาง p. 43.

Ardetta cinnamomea ยางกรอก p. 43; 18

Argusianus หว้า p. 925

Artamus fuscus แอ่นพง p. 1014

Bubo orientalis ทึดทือ p. 417

Bubulcus ibis coromandus ยางขาว p. 671

Bubulous coromandus ยางเสวย, ยางขาว pp. 73; 672

Buchanga atra แชงแชว, ซังแชว p. 311

Cacatuinae กระตั้ว, กะตั้ว p. 30

Caloperdix oculea กระทาดง p. 34

Capella stenura ช้อม p. 306

Caprimulgus asiaticus กะบ้า p. 75

Caprimulgus macrourus bimaculatus ตาฟาง, กะบ้า pp. 75; 363

Carpophago aenea นกเขาเปล้า, ลำภู p. 166

Carpophaga griseicapilla มุม p. 654

Carponago paenea กระลุมพู้ไฟ p. 44

Centrococcyx intermedius ปูด, กะปูด p. 530

FISHES

FLORA

SHELLS

SNAKES